The IVP
Dictionary
of the
New Testament

A One-Volume Compendium of
Contemporary Biblical Scholarship

Editor: Daniel G. Reid

InterVarsity Press
Downers Grove, Illinois
Leicester, England

InterVarsity Press
P.O. Box 1400
Downers Grove, Illinois 60515-1426
World Wide Web: www.ivpress.com
E-mail: mail@ivpress.com

Inter-Varsity Press, England
38 De Montfort Street, Leicester LE1 7GP, England
World Wide Web: www.ivpbooks.com
E-mail: ivp@uccf.org.uk

InterVarsity Press®, U.S.A., is the book-publishing division of InterVarsity Christian Fellowship/USA®, a student movement active on campus at hundreds of universities, colleges and schools of nursing in the United States of America, and a member movement of the International Fellowship of Evangelical Students. For information about local and regional activities, write Public Relations Dept., InterVarsity Christian Fellowship/USA, 6400 Schroeder Rd., P.O. Box 7895, Madison, WI 53707-7895, or visit the IVCF website at <www.intervarsity.org>.

Inter-Varsity Press, England, is the book-publishing division of the Universities and Colleges Christian Fellowship (formerly the Inter-Varsity Fellowship), a student movement linking Christian Unions in universities and colleges throughout the United Kingdom and the Republic of Ireland, and a member movement of the International Fellowship of Evangelical Students. For information about local and national activities write to UCCF, 38 De Montfort Street, Leicester LE1 7GP.

All Scripture quotations, unless otherwise indicated, are taken from the Holy Bible, New International Version®. NIV®. *Copyright © 1973, 1978, 1984 by International Bible Society. Used by permission of Zondervan Publishing House. Distributed in the U.K. by permission of Hodder and Stoughton Ltd. All rights reserved. "NIV" is a registered trademark of International Bible Society. UK trademark number 1448790.*

Design: Cindy Kiple

Image: Lowe Art Museum/SuperStock

USA ISBN 0-8308-1787-5
UK ISBN 1-84474-028-5

Printed in the United States of America ∞

Library of Congress Cataloging-in-Publication Data

The IVP dictionary of the New Testament: a one-volume compendium of
contemporary biblical scholarship / editor, Daniel G. Reid.
    p. cm.
Includes bibliographical references and indexes.
 ISBN 0-8308-1787-5 (alk. paper)
 1. Bible. N.T.—Dictionaries. I. Reid, Daniel G., 1949-
BS2312.I89 2004
225.3—dc22

    2003025930

British Library Cataloguing in Publication Data

A catalogue record for this book is available from the British Library.

P	26	25	24	23	22	21	29	19	18	17	16	15	14	13	12	11	10	9	8	7	6	5	4	3	2	1
Y	25	24	23	22	21	20	19	18	17	16	15	14	13	12	11	10	09	08	07	06	05	04				

InterVarsity Press

Project Staff

Reference Book Editor
Daniel G. Reid

Copyeditor
Linda Triemstra

Editorial Assistants
Joice Gouw
David A. Zimmerman

Design
Cindy Kiple

Typesetters
Gail Munroe
Marjorie Sire
Maureen Tobey

Proofreaders
Todd Best
Bill Kerschbaum
Heather Mascarello
Allison Rieck
Lisa Rieck
Laura Tarro
Elaina Whittenhall

Technical Support
Mark Gates
Tricia Koning
Andy Shermer

InterVarsity Press

Publisher
Robert Fryling

Editorial Director
Andrew T. Le Peau

Associate Editorial Director
James Hoover

Production Manager
Anne Gerth

Contents

Preface

The *IVP Dictionary of the New Testament* is a one-volume compilation of essential articles found in a series of dictionaries published by InterVarsity Press: *Dictionary of Jesus and the Gospels, Dictionary of Paul and His Letters, Dictionary of the Later New Testament and Its Developments* and *Dictionary of New Testament Background*. Otherwise known in the trade as IVP's "Black Dictionary" series, from their black dust jackets, this series has proven its worth since the first volume was published in 1992. Each volume has won the Gold Medallion Book Award annually presented by the Evangelical Christian Publishers Association for biblical or theological reference books. At the time of this writing translations of individual volumes are completed or underway in several languages, including French, Russian, Spanish, Portuguese, Chinese and Korean. This series, in its own quiet way, is having a worldwide impact.

The selection of articles in this volume has been made with students and the classroom in mind, though it is expected that others who have not collected the series—including those engaged in ministry—will find it a valuable addition to their libraries. For the most part, the articles appear in the same form as in their dictionary of origin. It is important to note that this volume is *not* a condensation—a sort of *Reader's Digest* version—of the four-volume New Testament dictionary series. Such an approach would have done violence to most of the articles and defeated the original vision of the series, which was to provide encyclopedia-length articles that engage their topics with greater depth than a one-volume Bible dictionary can afford. As we approached the editing of each volume in the series, our rule of thumb was that if a one-volume Bible dictionary article would handle a topic sufficiently, there was probably no need to include that topic. We would stick with the major topics but offer "more"—more depth, more detail, more specialized scholarship, more bibliography, etc. In many cases the articles were written by scholars who are specialists in their topic(s) rather than by generalists. In some cases we were granted previews of important work in progress, and several articles have come to be regarded as authoritative epitomes (in the ancient Greek sense) of published research on their topic.

A few editorial changes are, however, worth noting. Where they are not integral to the text of an article, foreign language works have generally been deleted from bibliographies (it is assumed that most readers of this volume will not have access to these works anyway). On the other hand, important recent works have frequently been added to the bibliographies, particularly commentaries in those articles focusing on the individual New Testament documents. In their original form, topical articles taken from the *Dictionary of the Later New Testament and Its Developments* also cover the apostolic fathers. However, unless the postapostolic perspective is integral to the discussion, it has not been included in this volume.

Over the years of producing these volumes the editor has joined many others who have used these dictionaries as teaching tools in seminary and undergraduate classrooms. We have found students to be remarkably appreciative of the series. But there are many contexts where assigning the three or four volumes is out of the question, even in a curriculum in which more than one term is devoted to New Testament introduction. And in undergraduate contexts, a full-scale use of the series has been nearly prohibitive (though some have valiantly attempted). Over the years we have heard requests for a one-volume edition that would offer the most essential articles. We agreed that it was a good idea, one that would serve students as well as extend the vision of the series. We have tried to fill that need with this volume.

However, the task of deciding which articles are the most essential was not as easy as it first seemed. We began by envisioning a course in New Testament introduction. Obviously we would include the articles on the New Testament documents themselves. Then the most salient theological topics would be included—christology, God, Holy Spirit, baptism, Lord's Supper, death of Christ, resurrection, eschatology, etc. But where should we stop when already we were rapidly approaching our targeted length? We could not leave out articles on the literary genres of the New Testament and important areas of New Testament background. A long "wish list" was painfully whittled down with the help of others who have used the volumes in teaching. But ultimately the decisions rested with the editor to work out a compromise between the demands of the subject and the space limitations imposed on the project. And even at the eleventh editorial hour, there was a Last Judgment, with numerous articles being sent away with weeping and gnashing of teeth—on the part of the judge and his court! There is some consolation in knowing that no two editors would have come up with the same solution. So many excellent articles, including some personal favorites, had to be left out.

One feature may help offset this editorial tension and remorse. At the end of articles, and in addition to those "See also" references to articles within the volume, we have placed crossreferences to relevant articles that have not been included in this volume. These crossreferences are typically made only to the source volume of a given article (i.e., if an article came from the *Dictionary of Jesus and the Gospels*, the crossreferences will be to other relevant articles in the *DJG*). This feature is intended to provide a service to both curious students and their demanding professors. It also suggests the value of readers eventually graduating up to the full four-volume series.

Articles on the same topic from different dictionaries (e.g., kingdom of God in the Gospels, Paul and the later New Testament) are generally presented separately and in canonical order, with the main title followed by the numerals I, II and III, and a subtitle indicating the scope of literature covered. In a handful of cases such articles have been combined, but this approach was not practical or even desirable across the board. For one thing, the variety of contributors and viewpoints are sometimes in tension with—even critical of—each other. While these multiple points of view are an enriching feature of the series and of this volume, it seemed like editorial mischief to meld them into one article here.

For those who are new to the field of New Testament studies, a glossary of terms has been included at the end of the book, with definitions mostly derived from Arthur G. Patzia and Anthony J. Petrotta's *Pocket Dictionary of Biblical Studies* (IVP). This little "dictionary within the dictionary" will assist students who are newly immersing themselves in the strange world and vocabulary of New Testament studies.

Working through this material yet again has been a reminder of the extensive collaborative and sacrificial contribution of numerous scholars to this dictionary series as well as the long-suffering labors of the eight editors who steered each volume to its publication. These scholars have poured far more time and labor into their research and writing than most popular writers would venture to guess or care to endure. With high teaching and administrative loads, many scholars find writing and editing forced into the margins of their days and weeks and careers, and the monetary rewards of this labor are nothing to envy. And yet, like alpine guides leading their clients to the view from the summit, those who are called to teaching and research do find rich reward in introducing a wider audience to the fascinating world they are privileged professionally to inhabit—the text, the world and the message of the New Testament. And while this extended classroom does not usually allow teachers those moments of gratification when students' eyes brighten with curiosity and understanding, the reports uniformly affirm that it is happening day by day. With the hope and prayer that this quiet transaction will be extended and broadened, we send this repackaging of their work back into the world.

Daniel G. Reid
Senior Editor
InterVarsity Press

How to Use This Dictionary

Abbreviations

Comprehensive tables of abbreviations for general matters as well as for scholarly, biblical and ancient literature may be found on pages xiii-xxii.

Authorship of Articles

The authors of articles are indicated by their first initials and last name at the end of each article. Articles that are composites of previous articles have the author's names in brackets at the end of their material. A full list of contributors may be found on pages xxiv-xxvi, in alphabetical order of their last name. The contribution of each author is listed following their identification.

Bibliographies

A bibliography will be found at the end of each article. The bibliographies include works cited in the articles and other significant related works. Bibliographical entries are listed in alphabetical order by the author's name; where an author has more than one work cited, they are listed alphabetically by title. In articles focused on New Testament books, the bibliographies are divided into the categories "Commentaries" and "Studies."

Cross-References

This *Dictionary* has been extensively cross-referenced in order to aid readers in making the most of material appearing throughout this volume and in the source volumes of the articles. Five types of cross-referencing will be found:

1. One-line entries appearing in alphabetical order throughout the *Dictionary* direct readers to articles where a topic is discussed:

AFTERLIFE. *See* RESURRECTION.

2. An asterisk before a word in the body of an article indicates that an article by that title (or closely worded title) appears in the *Dictionary*. For example, "*Son of God" directs the reader to the articles entitled **SON OF GOD**. Asterisks typically are found only at the first occurrence of a word in an article.

3. A cross-reference appearing within parentheses in the body of an article directs the reader to an article by that title. For example, (*see* Christology).

4. Cross-references have been appended to the end of articles to direct readers to articles significantly related to the subject:

See also COVENANT, NEW COVENANT; CREATION, NEW CREATION; HOLY SPIRIT.

5. Cross-references to articles in the source volumes—*Dictionary of Jesus and the Gospels (DJG)*, *Dictionary of Paul and His Letters (DPL)*, *Dictionary of the Later New Testament and Its Developments (DLNTD)* and *Dictionary of New Testament Background (DNTB)*—are found at the end of articles, preceding the bibliography. In some cases cross-references to more than one volume are provided.

Indexes

A *Scripture Index* is provided to assist readers in gaining quick access to the numerous Scripture texts referred to throughout the *Dictionary*.

An *Articles Index* found at the end of the *Dictionary* allows readers quickly to review the breadth of topics covered and select the ones most apt to serve their interests or needs. For those who wish to identify the articles written by specific contributors, they are listed with the name of the contributor in the list of contributors.

Transliteration

Greek and Hebrew has been transliterated according to a system set out on page xxiii.

Abbreviations

General Abbreviations

κτλ	etc. (Greek)		MT	Masoretic Text (standard Hebrew text of the Old Testament)
2d ed.	second edition			
3d ed.	third edition		n.d.	no date
A	Codex Alexandrinus		n.s.	new series
B	Codex Vaticanus		NT	New Testament
C	Codex Ephraemi Syri		*Olim*	formerly
c.	circa, about (with dates); column		o.s.	old series
cent.	century		OT	Old Testament
cf.	compare		p. or pp.	page or pages
chap(s).	chapter(s)		*pace*	with due respect to, but differing from
D	Codex Bezae		par.	parallel passage in another/other Gospel(s)
DSS	Dead Sea Scrolls			
e.g.	*exempli gratia*, for example		passim	elsewhere
ed.	edition; editor(s); edited by		pl.	plural
esp.	especially		presc.	prescript
ET	English translation		Q	sayings source for Synoptic Gospels
EVV	English versions of the Bible		repr.	reprint
exp.	expanded (edition)		rev.	revised (edition)
Frag.	Fragment (of document)		Sy	Syriac
Gk	Greek		Symm.	Symmachus's Greek translation of the Old Testament
Heb	Hebrew			
i.e.	*id est*, that is		Tg.	Targum
km.	kilometer		v. or vv.	verse or verses
Lat	Latin		v.l.	*vario lectio* ("variant reading")
LXX	Septuagint (Greek translation of the Old Testament)		vol.	volume
			x	times (2x = two times, etc.)
mg.	margin		§ or §§	section or paragraph number(s) (usually indicating Loeb Classical Library numbering system for Josephus)
MS or MSS	manuscript or manuscripts			
			ℵ	Codex Sinaiticus

Translations of the Bible

ASV	American Standard Version (1901)		NEB	New English Bible
AV	Authorized Version (or KJV)		NIV	New International Version
JB	Jerusalem Bible		NRSV	New Revised Standard Version
KJV	King James Version (or AV)		REB	Revised English Bible
NASB	New American Standard Bible		RV	Revised Version (1881-1885)

Books of the Bible

Old Testament	1-2 Kings	Is	Mic	Mk	1-2 Thess
Gen	1-2 Chron	Jer	Nahum	Lk	1-2 Tim
Ex	Ezra	Lam	Hab	Jn	Tit
Lev	Neh	Ezek	Zeph	Acts	Philem
Num	Esther	Dan	Hag	Rom	Heb
Deut	Job	Hos	Zech	1-2 Cor	Jas
Josh	Ps	Joel	Mal	Gal	1-2 Pet
Judg	Prov	Amos		Eph	1-2-3 Jn
Ruth	Eccles	Obad	*New Testament*	Phil	Jude
1-2 Sam	Song	Jon	Mt	Col	Rev

The Apocrypha and Septuagint

1-2-3-4 Kgdms	1-2-3-4 Kingdoms	Jdt	Judith	Sir	Sirach (or Ecclesiasticus)
Add Esth	Additions to Esther	Ep Jer	Epistle of Jeremiah	Sus	Susanna
Bar	Baruch	1-2-3-4 Macc	1-2-3-4 Maccabees	Tob	Tobit
Bel	Bel and the Dragon	Pr Azar	Prayer of Azariah	Wis	Wisdom of Solomon
1-2 Esdr	1-2 Esdras	Pr Man	Prayer of Manasseh		

The Old Testament Pseudepigrapha

Adam and Eve	Life of Adam and Eve	Pss. Sol.	Psalms of Solomon
Ahiq.	Ahiqar	Pseud.-Phoc.	Pseudo-Phocylides
Apoc. Abr.	Apocalypse of Abraham	Sib. Or.	Sibylline Oracles
2-3 Apoc. Bar.	Syriac, Greek Apocalypse of Baruch	Testaments of the Twelve Patriarchs	
Apoc. Mos.	Apocalypse of Moses	T. Reub.	Testament of Reuben
Apoc. Elijah	Apocalypse of Elijah	T. Sim.	Testament of Simeon
Apoc. Zeph.	Apocalypse of Zephaniah	T. Levi	Testament of Levi
Apoc. Sed.	Apocalypse of Sedrach	T. Jud.	Testament of Judah
As. Mos.	Assumption of Moses (or Testament of Moses)	T. Iss.	Testament of Issachar
		T. Zeb.	Testament of Zebulon
Asc. Isa.	Ascension of Isaiah	T. Dan.	Testament of Dan
Bib. Ant.	Biblical Antiquities of Pseudo-Philo	T. Naph.	Testament of Naphthali
		T. Gad.	Testament of Gad
1-2-3 Enoch	Ethiopic, Slavonic, Hebrew Enoch	T. Asher	Testament of Asher
Ep. Arist.	Epistle of Aristeas	T. Jos.	Testament of Joseph
Jos. and As.	Joseph and Asenath	T. Benj	Testament of Benjamin
Jub.	Jubilees	T. Abr.	Testament of Abraham
Liv. Proph.	Lives of the Prophets (followed by prophet's name)	T. Job	Testament of Job
		T. Mos.	Testament of Moses
Mart. Isa.	Martyrdom of Isaiah		

Apostolic Fathers

Barn.	Epistle of Barnabas	Ign. Magn.	Ignatius Letter to the Magnesians
1 Clem.	1 Clement	Ign. Phld.	Ignatius Letter to the Philadelphians
2 Clem.	2 Clement	Ign. Pol.	Ignatius Letter to Polycarp
Did.	Didache	Ign. Rom.	Ignatius Letter to the Romans
Diogn.	Epistle to Diognetus	Ign. Smyrn.	Ignatius Letter to the Smyrneans
Herm. Man	Shepherd of Hermas, Mandate(s)	Ign. Trall.	Ignatius Letter to the Trallians
Herm. Sim.	Shepherd of Hermas, Similitude(s)	Mart. Pol.	Martyrdom of Polycarp
Herm. Vis.	Shepherd of Hermas, Vision(s)	Pol. Phil.	Polycarp Letter to the Philippians
Ign. Eph.	Ignatius Letter to the Ephesians		

Early Christian Literature

Acts		Apocalypses	
Acts Apoll.	Acts of Apollonius	Apoc. Paul	Apocalypse of Paul
Acts Pil.	Acts of Pilate	Apoc. Peter	Apocalypse of Peter
Acts Paul & Thec.	Acts of Paul and Thecla	Aristides	
Acts Thom.	Acts of Thomas	Apol.	Apologia
Ambrose		Athanasius	
Abr.	De Abrahamo	Ar.	Adversus Arianos
Exp. Ev. Luc.	Expositio Evangelii Secundum Lucam	Ep. Fest.	Festal Epistles
		Fug.	Apologia pro Fuga Sua
Ps.	In Psalmos	Athenagoras	
Virg.	De Virginibus	Leg.	Legatio pro Christianis
Ap. Jas.	Apocryphon of James	Suppl.	Supplicatio pro Christianis
Aphrahat (or Aphraates)			
Dem.	Demonstrations		

Augustine			Comm. Matt.	Commentary on Matthew
Civ. D.	De Civitate Dei		Comm. Mic.	Commentary on Micah
Conf.	Confessiones		Ep.	Epistulae
De Cons.	De Consensu Evangelistarum		Vir.	De Viris Illustribus
Doctr. Christ.	De Doctrina Christiana		Prol. in Matt.	Prologue to Matthew
Ep.	Epistulae		Praef. in Quat. Ev.	Preface to the Four Gospels
Haer.	De Haeresibus		Justin Martyr	
Hom.	Homilia		Apol. I, II	Apology I, II
Quaest. Evan.	Quaestiones Evangeliorum		Cohor. Graec.	Cohortatio ad Graecos
BG	Berlin Gnostic Codex		Dial. Tryph.	Dialogue with Trypho the Jew
CG	Nag Hammadi Gnostic Codices		Resurrec.	On the Resurrection
Chrysostom			Lactantius	
Hom. Gen.	Homilies on Genesis		Div. Inst.	Divinae Institutiones
Hom. Mt.	Homilies on Matthew		Mart. Justin	The Martyrdom of Justin and
Regno	De Regno			Companions
Clement of Alexandria			Mur. Frag.	Muratorian Fragment
Ecl. Proph.	Eclogae Propheticae		Odes Sol.	Odes of Solomon
Excerpta	Excerpta ex Theodoto		Origen	
Frag. Adum.	Fragmente in Adumbrationes		Comm. Joh.	Commentary on John
Frag. Ep. Jude	Fragmente in Epistle of Jude		Comm. Mt.	Commentary on Matthew
Paed.	Paedagogus		Cont. Cels.	Contra Celsum
Protr.	Protreptikos		De Princ.	De Principiis
Quis Div.	Quis Dives Salvetur		Exhort. Mart.	Exhortatio ad Martyrium
Strom.	Stromateis		Hom. Ez.	Homiliae in Ezechiel
Theod.	Letter to Theodore		Hom. Luc.	Homiliae in Lucam
Cyprian			Pass. Perp.	Fel. Passion of Perpetua and
Dom. Or.	De Dominica Oratione			Felicitas
Ep.	Epistulae		Peri Arch.	Peri Archon
Laps.	De Lapsis		Selec. Ps.	Selecta in Psalmos
Cyril of Jerusalem			Pap. Frag.	Fragments of Papias
Myst. Cat.	Mystagogical Catecheses		PBerol	Papyrus Berolinensis
Ep. Apos.	Epistola Apostolorum		Protev. Jas.	Protevangelium of James
Epiphanius			Pseudo-Clementines	
Haer.	Haereses		Hom.	Homilies
Eusebius			Recogn.	Recognitions
Eccl. Theol.	De Ecclesiastica Theologia		Rufinus	
Hist. Eccl.	Historia Ecclesiastica		Hist. Eccl.	Historia Ecclesiastica
Dem. Ev.	Demonstratio Evangelica		Tatian	
In Ps	Commentary on the Psalms		Or. Graec.	Oratio ad Graecos
Praep. Ev.	Praeparatio Evangelica		Tertullian	
Gospels			Adv. Jud.	Adversus Judaeos
Gos. Bar.	Gospel of Bartholomew		Ad Nat.	Ad Nationes
Gos. Eb.	Gospel of the Ebionites		Ad Ux.	Ad Uxorem
Gos. Eg.	Gospel of the Egyptians		Apol.	Apologeticus
Gos. Heb.	Gospel of the Hebrews		De Anim.	De Anima
Gos. Mary	Gospel of Mary		De Carn.	De Carne Christi
Gos. Naass.	Gospel of the Naassenes		De Praescr.	De Praescriptione Haereticorum
Gos. Phil.	Gospel of Philip		De Bapt.	De Baptismo
Gos. Pet.	Gospel of Peter		De Cor.	De Corona
Gos. Thom.	Gospel of Thomas		De Cult. Fem.	De Cultu Feminarum
Hilary of Poitiers			De Idol.	De Idololatria
Trin.	De trinitate		De. Jejun.	De Jejunio Adversus Psychicos
Hippolytus			De Orat.	De Oratione
Apos. Trad.	Apostolic Tradition		De Pud.	De Pudicitia
Dem. Chr.	Demonstratio de Christo et		De Resur.	De Resurrectione Carnis
	Antichristo		De Spect.	De Spectaculis
Haer.	De Haeresibus		Marc.	Adversus Marcionem
Refut.	Refutation of All Heresies, or		Pud.	De Pudicitia
	Philosophumena		Prax.	Adversus Praxeas
Irenaeus			Scorp.	Scorpiace
Haer.	Adversus Haereses		Theophilus of Antioch	
Jerome			Autol.	Ad Autolycum
Comm. Gal.	Commentary on Galatians			

Classical and Hellenistic Writers and Sources

Aelian
    De Nat. Anim.   *De Natura Animalum*
Aeschylus
    Pers.   *Persae*
    Sept. c. Theb.   *Septem contra Thebas*
    Suppl.   *Supplices*
Ammonius
    Adfin. Vocab. Diff.   *De Adfinium Vocabulorum Differentia*
Anacharsis
    Ep.   *Epistle to Tereus*
Antipater
    Anth. Pal.   *Anthologia Palatina*
Appian
    Mith. W.   *Mithridatic Wars*
    Civ. W.   *Civil Wars*
Apuleius
    Met.   *Metamorphoses*
Aratus
    Phaen.   *Phaenomena*
Aristophanes
    Thes.   *Thesmophorizousai*
    Acharn.   *Acharnenses*
Aristotle
    Cael.   *De Caelo*
    Eth. Nic.   *Ethica Nicomachea*
    Pol.   *Politica*
    Prob.   *Problemata*
Artemidorus
    Oneir.   *Oneirocriticon*
Aulus Gellius
    Noc. Att.   *Noctes Atticae*
Callimachus
    Epigr.   *Epigrammata*
Chariton
    Chaer.   *Chaereas and Callirhoe*
Cicero
    De Div.   *De Divinatione*
    De Leg.   *De Legibus*
    De Offic.   *De Officiis*
    De Orat.   *De Oratore*
    De Repub.   *De Republica*
    Phil.   *Orationes Philippicae*
    Rab. Perd.   *Rabirio Perduellionis*
    Tusc.   *Tusculanae Disputationes*
    Code Just.   *Code of Justinian*
    Corp. Herm.   *Corpus Hermeticum*
Demosthenes
    Ag. Conon   *Against Conon*
    Lacrit.   *Against Lacritus*
    Dig. Just.   *Digest of Justinian*
Dio Cassius
    Epit.   *Roman History*
    Hist.   *Roman History*
Dio Chrysostom
    De Homero   *De Homero et Socrate*
    Disc.   *Discourses*
    Or.   *Orationes*

Diodorus Siculus
    Bib. Hist.   *Bibliotheca Historica*
Diogenes Laertius
    Vit.   *Vitae*
Dion. Hal.   Dionysius of Halicarnassus
Epictetus
    Disc.   *Discourses*
    Diss.   *Dissertationes*
    Ench.   *Enchiridion*
Euripides
    Hipp.   *Hippolytus*
Galen
    De Placitis   *De Placitis Hippocratis et Platonis*
    Grk. Anth.   *Greek Anthology*
Hesiod
    Op.   *Opera et Dies*
Homer
    Il.   *Iliad*
    Odys.   *Odyssey*
Horace
    Sat.   *Satires*
Iamblichus
    De Myst.   *De Mysteriis*
    Inscr. Cos   *The Inscriptions of Cos, ed. W. R. Paton and E. L. Hicks (1891)*
Isocrates
    Dem.   *Demonicus*
    Panath.   *Panathenaicus*
    Paneg.   *Panegyricus*
Josephus
    Ant.   *Antiquities of the Jews*
    J.W.   *Jewish Wars*
    Life   *Life of Flavius Josephus*
    Ag. Ap.   *Against Apion*
Justinian
    Digest   *Digest of Roman Law*
Juvenal
    Sat.   *Satirae*
Livy
    Epit.   *Epitomae*
    Hist.   *History of Rome*
Lucian of Samosata
    Alex.   *Alexander the False Prophet*
    Herm.   *Hermotimus*
    Peregr.   *De Morte Peregrini*
    Philops.   *Philopseudes*
    Tox.   *Toxaris*
Marcus Aurelius
    Med.   *Meditations*
Martial
    Epigr.   *Epigrams*
Muson. Ruf.   Musonius Rufus
Nicolaus of Damascus
    Vit. Caes.   *Vita Caesaris*
Orosius
    Pag.   *Adversus Paganos*
Orph. Frag.   Orphic Fragments
Ovid
    Met.   *Metamorphoses*

P Cair. Zen.	Zenon Papyri, ed. C. C. Edgar, *Zenon Payri*, vols. 1-4 (Le Caire, 1925-1931; Catalogue générale des antiquités égyptiennes du Musée du Caire).	*Tim.*	*Timaeus*
		Pliny (the elder)	
		Nat. Hist.	*Naturalis Historia*
		Panegyr.	*Panegyricus*
		Pliny (the younger)	
Pausanius		*Ep.*	*Epistles*
Descr.	*Description of Greece*	Plutarch	
Petronius		*Mor.*	*Moralia*
Sat.	*Satyricon*	*Adulat.*	*De Adulatore et Amico*
PGM	*Papyri-Graecae Magicae*	*Colot.*	*Adversus Colotem*
Philo		*Con. Praec.*	*Coniugalia Praecepta*
Abr.	*De Abrahamo*	*Conv.*	*Quaestiones Convivales*
Aet. Mund.	*De Aeternitate Mundi*	*Def. Orac.*	*De Defectu Oraculorum*
Agric.	*De Agricultura*	*Fac. Lun.*	*De Facie in Orbe Lunae*
Cher.	*De Cherubim*	*Fort. Rom.*	*De Fortuna Romanorum*
Conf. Ling.	*De Confusione Linguarum*	*Gen. Socr.*	*De Genio Socratis*
Congr.	*De Congressu Eruditionis Gratia*	*Iside*	*De Iside et Osiride*
Decal.	*De Decalogo*	*Lib. Educ.*	*De Liberis Educandis*
Det. Pot. Ins.	*Quod Deterius Potiori Insidiari Soleat*	*Mul. Virt.*	*Mulierum Virtutes*
		Non Posse Suav.	*Non Posse Suaviter Vivi Secundum Epicurum*
Deus Imm.	*Quod Deus Sit Immutabilis*		
Ebr.	*De Ebrietate*	*Praec. Ger. Reipub.*	*Praecepta Gerendae Reipublicae*
Flacc.	*In Flaccum*	*Rom.*	*Quaestiones Romanae*
Fug.	*De Fuga et Inventione*	*Ser. Num. Vind.*	*De Sera Numinis Vindicta*
Gig.	*De Gigantibus*	*Vit.*	*Vitae*
Jos.	*De Josepho*	*Alex.*	*De Alexandro*
Leg. All.	*Legum Allegoriae*	*Anton.*	*De Antonio*
Leg. Gai.	*Legatio ad Gaium*	*Caesar*	*De Caesar*
Migr. Abr.	*De Migratione Abrahami*	*Pomp.*	*De Pompeio*
Mut. Nom.	*De Mutatione Nominum*	Polybius	
Omn. Prob.	*Lib. Quod Omnis Probus Liber Sit*	*Hist.*	*Histories*
		Proclus	
Op. Mund.	*De Opificio Mundi*	*In Tim.*	*In Platonis Timaeum Commentarius*
Plant.	*De Plantatione*	Quintilian	
Poster. C.	*De Posteritate Caini*	*Inst. Orat.*	*Institutio Oratoria*
Praem. Poen.	*De Praemiis et Poenis*	Seneca	
Prov.	*De Providentia*	*Ben.*	*De Beneficius*
Quaest. in Ex.	*Quaestiones in Exodum*	*Brev. Vit.*	*De Brevitate Vitae*
Quaest. in Gen.	*Quaestiones in Genesin*	*De Clem.*	*De Clementia*
Rer. Div. Her.	*Quis Rerum Divinarum Heres Sit.*	*Ep. Lucil.*	*Epistles to Lucilius*
Sacr.	*De Sacrificiis Abelis et Caini*	*Ep. Mor.*	*Epistulae Morales*
Som.	*De Somnis*	Sophocles	
Spec. Leg.	*De Specialibus Legibus*	*Elec.*	*Electra*
Virt.	*De Virtibus*	*Oed. Tyr.*	*Oedipus Tyrannus*
Vit. Cont.	*De Vita Contemplativa*	Stobaeus	
Vit. Mos.	*De Vita Mosis*	*Ecl.*	*Ecloge*
Philostratus		Strabo	
Vit. Ap.	*Vita Apollonii*	*Geog.*	*Geography*
Pindar		Suetonius	
Isth.	*Isthmia*	*Claudius*	from *The Twelve Caesars*
Plato		*Domitian*	*The Twelve Caesars*
Alc.	*Alcibiades*	*Galba*	*The Twelve Caesars*
Apol.	*Apologia*	*Julius*	*The Twelve Caesars*
Crat.	*Cratylus*	*Nero*	*The Twelve Caesars*
Gorg.	*Gorgias*	*Tiberius*	*The Twelve Caesars*
Leg.	*Leges*	*Titus*	*The Twelve Caesars*
Phaedr.	*Phaedrus*	*Vespasian*	*The Twelve Caesars*
Protag.	*Protagoras*	Tacitus	
Rep.	*Res Publica*	*Ann.*	*Annales ab Excessu Divi Augusti*
Soph.	*Sophista*		
Symp.	*Symposion*	*Hist.*	*Historiae*

Theon		*Memorabilium Libri*
Progymn.	*Progymnasmata*	Vegetius Renatus
Thucydides		*Epit. Rei Milit.* *Epitoma Rei Militaris*
Hist.	*History of the Peloponnesian War*	Xenophon
Valerius Maximus		*Hist. Gr.* *Historia Graeca*
Fact. ac Dict.	*Factorum ac Dictorum*	*Mem.* *Memorabilia Socratis*

Dead Sea Scrolls and Related Texts

CD	Cairo (Genizah text of the) *Damascus (Document/Rule)*
Q	Qumran
1Q, 3Q,	Numbered caves of Qumran, yielding written
4Q etc.	material; followed by abbreviation or number of document
1QapGen	*Genesis Apocryphon* (1Q20)
1QH	*Hodayot* or *Thanksgiving Hymns*
1QIsa^{a,b}	First and second copy of Isaiah
1QM	*Milhamah* or *War Scroll*
1QMyst	Mysteries (1Q27)
1QpHab	*Pesher on Habakkuk*
1QPsa^a	Fragmentary copy of Psalms (1Q10)
1QS	*Serek hayyaad* or *Rule of the Community, Manual of Discipline*
1QSa	Appendix A, *Messianic Rule*, to 1QS
1QSb	Appendix B, *Rule of the Blessings*, to 1QS
3QCopper Scroll	*Copper Scroll* from Qumran Cave 3 (3Q15)
4Q139	Ordinances or commentaries on biblical laws
4Q169	Pesher on Nahum
4Q171	Pesher on Psalms
4Q176	*Tanhumim* or *Consolations*
4Q186	(see 4QMess ar)
4Q246	(see 4QPs DanA^a)
4Q400-407	(see 4QShirShabb)
4Q504	*Words of the Luminaries*
4Q513-14	Ordinances or commentaries on biblical laws
4QDibHam^a	Words of the Luminaries^a (4Q504)
4QEnGiants	*1 Enoch* fragments from Book of Giants (4Q203)
4QEn^{a-g}	*1 Enoch* fragments (4Q201-212)
4QEnastr^{a-g}	*1 Enoch* fragments from Astronomical Book (4Q208-211)
4QFlor	*Florilegium* or *Eschatological Midrashim* (4Q174)
4QMess ar	Aramaic "Messianic" text (4Q534)
4QMMT	*Miqsat Ma_aseh Torah* (4Q394-399)
4QpNah	Nahum Pesher (4Q169)
4QPhyl	Phylacteries (4Q128-148)
4QPrNab	*Prayer of Nabonidus* (4Q242)
4QPsDanA^a	Pseudo-Danielic Writings (4Q246)
4QPssJosh	*Psalms of Joshua* (4Q379)
4QShirShabb	*Songs of Sabbath Sacrifice* or *Angelic Liturgy* (4Q400-407)
4QTestim	*Testimonia* (4Q175)
4QtgJob	*Targum of Job* (4Q157)
4QtgLev	*Targum of Leviticus* (4Q156)
5Q15	*New Jerusalem* (5Q15)
11QH	*Hymns* (11Q15-16)
11QMelch	*Melchizedek* (11Q13)
11QpaleoLev	Leviticus in paleo-Hebrew script (11Q1)
11QPs^a	*Psalms Scroll* (11Q5)
11QTemple	*Temple Scroll* (11Q19)
11QtgJob	*Targum of Job* (11Q10)

Targumic Material

Tg. Onq.	Targum Onqelos	Tg. Neof.	Targum Neofiti I
Tg. Neb.	Targum of the Prophets	Tg. Ps.-J.	Targum Pseudo-Jonathan
Tg. Ket.	Targum of the Writings	Tg. Yer. I	Targum YeruÜalmi I
Frg. Tg.	Fragmentary Targum	Tg. Yer. II	Targum YeruÜalmi II
Sam. Tg.	Samaritan Targum	Yem. Tg.	Yemenite Targum
Tg. Isa	Targum of Isaiah	Tg. Esth I, II	First or Second Targum of Esther

Order and Tractates in the Mishnah, Tosefta and Talmud

Same-named tractates in the Mishnah, Tosefta, Babylonian Talmud and Jerusalem Talmud are distinguished by *m.*, *t.*, *b.* and *y.* respectively.

ʾAbot	ʾAbot	Mak	Makkot	Qod.	Qodašin
ʿArak.	ʿArakin	Makš.	Makširin (=Mašqin)	Roš Haš.	Roš Haššana
ʿAbod. Zar.	ʿAboda Zara	Meg.	Megilla	Sanh.	Sanhedrin
B. Bat.	Baba Batra	Meʿil.	Meʿila	Šabb.	Šabbat
Bek.	Bekorot	Menaḥ.	Menaḥot	Šeb.	Šebiʿit
Ber.	Berakot	Mid.	Middot	Šebu.	Šebuʿot
Beṣa	Beṣa (= Yom Ṭob)	Miqw.	Miqwaʾot	Šeqal.	Šeqalim
Bik.	Bikkurim	Moʿed	Moʿed	Soṭa	Soṭa
B. Meṣ.	Baba Meṣiʿa	Moʿed Qaṭ	Moʿed Qaṭan	Sukk	Sukka
B. Qam.	Baba Qamma	Maʿaś. Šeni	Maʿaśer Šeni	Taʿan.	Taʿanit
Dem.	Demai	Našim	Našim	Tamid	Tamid
ʿErub.	ʿErubin	Nazir	Nazir	Tem.	Temura
ʿEd.	ʿEduyyot	Ned.	Nedarim	Ter.	Terumot
Giṭ.	Giṭṭin	Neg.	Negaʿim	Ṭohar.	Ṭoharot
Ḥag.	Ḥagiga	Nez.	Neziqin	Ṭ. Yom	Ṭebul Yom
Ḥal.	Ḥalla	Nid.	Niddah	ʿUq.	ʿUqṣin
Hor.	Horayot	Ohol.	Oholot	Yad.	Yadayim
Ḥul.	Ḥullin	ʿOr.	ʿOrla	Yebam.	Yebamot
Kelim	Kelim	Para	Para	Yoma	Yoma (= Kippurim)
Ker.	Keritot	Peʾa	Peʾa	Zabim	Zabim
Ketub.	Ketubot	Pesaḥ.	Pesaḥim	Zebaḥ.	Zebaḥim
Kil.	Kilʾayim	Qinnim	Qinnim	Zer.	Zeraʿim
Maʿaś.	Maʿaśerot	Qidd.	Qiddušin		

Other Rabbinic Works

ʾAbot R. Nat.	ʾAbot de Rabbi Nathan	Pesiq. Rab Kah.	Pesiqta de Rab Kahana
ʾAg. Ber.	ʾAggadat Berešit	Pirqe R. El.	Pirqe Rabbi Eliezer
Bab.	Babylonian	Rab.	Rabbah (following abbreviation
Bar.	Baraita		for biblical book: Gen. Rab. =
Der. Er. Rab.	Derek Ereṣ Rabba		Genesis Rabbah)
Der. Er. Zuṭ.	Derek Ereṣ Zuṭa	Ṣem.	Ṣemaḥot
Gem.	Gemara	Sipra	Sipra
Kalla	Kalla	Sipre	Sipre
Mek.	Mekilta	Sop.	Soperim
Midr.	Midraš (cited with abbreviation	S. ʿOlam Rab.	Seder ʿOlam Rabbah
	for biblical book)	Talm.	Talmud
Pal.	Palestinian	Yal.	Yalquṭ
Pesiq. R.	Pesiqta Rabbati		

Nag Hammadi Tractates

Acts Pet. 12 Apost.	The Acts of Peter and the	Allogenes	Allogenes
	Twelve Apostles	Ap. Jas.	The Apocryphon of James

Ap. John	The Apocryphon of John	Norea	The Thought of Norea
Apoc. Adam	The Apocalypse of Adam	On Anoint.	On the Anointing
1 Apoc. Jas.	The (First) Apocalypse of James	On Bapt. A	On Baptism A
2 Apoc. Jas.	The (Second) Apocalypse of James	On Bapt. B	On Baptism B
Apoc. Paul	The Apocalypse of Paul	On Bapt. C	On Baptism C
Apoc. Peter	Apocalypse of Peter	On Euch. A	On the Eucharist A
Asclepius	Asclepius 21-29	On Euch. B	On the Eucharist B
Auth. Teach.	Authoritative Teaching	Orig. World	On the Origin of the World
Dial. Sav.	The Dialogue of the Savior	Paraph. Shem	The Paraphrase of Shem
Disc. 8-9	The Discourse on the Eighth and Ninth	Pr. Paul	The Prayer of the Apostle Paul
		Pr. Thanks.	The Prayer of Thanksgiving
Ep. Pet. Phil.	The Letter of Peter to Philip	Sent. Sextus	The Sentences of Sextus
Eugnostos	Eugnostos the Blessed	Soph. Jes. Chr.	The Sophia of Jesus Christ
Exeg. Soul	The Exegesis on the Soul	Steles Seth	The Three Steles of Seth
Gos. Eg.	The Gospel of the Egyptians	Teach. Silv.	The Teachings of Silvanus
Gos. Phil.	The Gospel of Philip	Testim. Truth	The Testimony of Truth
Gos. Thom.	The Gospel of Thomas	Thom. Cont.	The Book of Thomas the Contender
Gos. Truth	The Gospel of Truth	Thund.	The Thunder: Perfect Mind
Great Pow.	The Concept of Our Great Power	Treat. Res.	The Treatise on the Resurrection
Hyp. Arch.	The Hypostasis of the Archons	Treat. Seth	The Second Treatise of the Great Seth
Hypsiph.	Hypsiphrone	Tri. Trac.	The Tripartite Tractate
Interp. Know.	The Interpretation of Knowledge	Trim. Prot.	Trimorphic Protennoia
Marsanes	Marsanes	Val. Exp.	A Valentinian Exposition
Melch.	Melchizedek	Zost.	Zostrianos

Periodicals, Reference Works and Serials

CGTC	Cambridge Greek Testament Commentary	FF	Foundations and Facet
ConBNT	Coniectanea biblica neotestamentica	FIRA	Fontes iuris romani antejustiniani
ConNT	Coniectanea neotestamentica	FJ	The Foundation of Judaism
CovQ	Covenant Quarterly	FRLANT	Forschungen zur Religion und Literature des
CRINT	Compendia rerum iudaicarum ad novum testamentum		Alten und Neuen Testaments
		GLS	Grove Liturgical Studies
CTJ	Calvin Theological Journal	GNS	Good News Studies
CTM	Concordia Theological Monthly	GTJ	Grace Theological Journal
CTR	Criswell Theological Review	HBT	Horizons in Biblical Theology
CV	Communio Viatorum	HDR	Harvard Dissertations in Religion
DHL	Dissertationes humanarum litterarum	Herm	Hermeneia
DJG	Dictionary of Jesus and the Gospels, ed. J. B. Green, S. McKnight and I. Howard Marshall	HNT	Handbuch zum Neuen Testament
		HNTC	Harper's New Testament Commentaries
		HR	History of Religions
DLNTD	Dictionary of the Later New Testament and Its Developments, ed. R. P. Martin and P. H. Davids.	HTKNT	Herders theologischer Kommentar zum Neuen Testament
		HTR	Harvard Theological Review
DNTB	Dictionary of New Testament Background, ed. C. A. Evans and S. E. Porter	HTS	Harvard Theological Studies
		HUCA	Hebrew Union College Annual
DPL	Dictionary of Paul and His Letters, ed. R. P. Martin, G. F. Hawthorne and D. G. Reid	HUT	Hermeneutische Untersuchungen zur Theologie
		HZ	Historische Zeitschrift
DRev	Downside Review	IBS	Irish Biblical Studies
DSB	Daily Study Bible	ICC	International Critical Commentary
EBC	The Expositor's Bible Commentary	IDB	Interpreter's Dictionary of the Bible
EC	Epworth Commentaries	IDBSup	Interpreter's Dictionary of the Bible, Supplementary Volume
EDNT	Exegetical Dictionary of the New Testament, ed. H. Balz and G. Schneider		
		IEJ	Israel Exploration Journal
ESW	Ecumenical Studies in Worship	ILS	Inscriptiones latinae selectae (Berlin, 1892)
ETS	Erfurter theologische Studien	Int	Interpretation
EvQ	Evangelical Quarterly	IntC	Interpretation Commentaries
EvT	Evangelische Theologie	IRT	Issues in Religion and Theology
ExpT	Expository Times	ISBE	International Standard Bible Encyclopedia (rev. ed.)
FB	Facet Books		
FBBS	Facet Books, Biblical Series	IVPNTC	InterVarsity Press New Testament Commentary

JAAR	Journal of the American Academy of Religion	NovT	Novum Testamentum
JBL	Journal of Biblical Literature	NovTSup	Supplement to Novum Testamentum
JCSR	Journal of Comparative Sociology and Religion	NSBT	New Studies in Biblical Theology
		NTAbh	Neutestamentliche Abhandlungen
JEH	Journal of Ecclesiastical History	NTC	TPI New Testament Commentaries
JES	Journal of Ecumenical Studies	NTCom	New Testament Commentary (Baker)
JETS	Journal of the Evangelical Theological Society	NTG	New Testament Guides
JJS	Journal of Jewish Studies	NTS	New Testament Studies
JPTSup	Journal of Pentecostal Theology Supplement Series	NTT	New Testament Theology
		OCD	Oxford Classical Dictionary
JQR	Jewish Quarterly Review	OGIS	Orientis graeci inscriptiones selectae, ed. W. Dittenberger
JR	Journal of Religion		
JRS	Journal of Roman Studies	OTP	The Old Testament Pseudepigrapha, ed. J. H. Charlesworth
JSJ	Journal for the Study of Judaism in the Persian, Hellenistic and Roman Period		
		PBSR	Papers of the British School at Rome
JSNT	Journal for the Study of the New Testament	PC	Proclamation Commentaries
JSNTSup	Journal for the Study of the New Testament Supplement Series	PG	Patrologiae Graeca, ed. J.-P. Migne. 162 vols.
		PGL	Patristic Greek Lexicon, ed. G. W. H. Lampe
JSOT	Journal for the Study of the Old Testament	PL	Patrologia Latina, ed. J.-P. Migne. 217 vols.
JSOTSup	Journal for the Study of the Old Testament Supplement Series	PNTC	Pillar New Testament Commentary
		PRS	Perspectives in Religious Studies
JSPSup	Journal for the Study of the Pseudepigrapha and Related Literature Supplement Series	PTMS	Pittsburgh Theological Monograph Series
		QD	Quaestiones disputatae
JTC	Journal for Theology and the Church	RAC	Reallexikon für Antike und Christentum
JTS	Journal of Theological Studies	RB	Revue biblique
JTS(n.s.)	Journal of Theological Studies (new series)	RevExp	Review and Expositor
JTSA	Journal of Theology for Southern Africa	RevQ	Revue de Qumran
LEC	Library of Early Christianity	RGG	Religion in Geschichte und Gegenwart
Louw-Nida	Greek-English Lexicon, ed. J. P. Louw and E. A. Nida	RGRW	Religions in the Graeco-Roman World
		RHE	Revue d'histoire ecclésiastique
LSJ	Liddell-Scott-Jones, Greek-English Lexicon	RHPR	Revue d'histoire et de philosophie religieuses
LW	Luther's Works, ed. J. Pelikan and H. T. Lehmann	RQ	Restoration Quarterly
		RSB	Religious Studies Bulletin
MAMA	Monumenta asiae minoris antiqua	RTR	Reformed Theological Review
MM	J. H. Moulton and G. Milligan, The Vocabulary of the Greek Testament, Illustrated from the Papyri and Other Non-Literary Sources (1930)	SacP	Sacra Pagina
		SAJ	Studies in Ancient Judaism
		SANT	Studien zum Alten und Neuen Testament
		SB	Sources bibliques
MNTC	Moffatt New Testament Commentary	SBEC	Studies in the Bible and Early Christianity
Mus	Le Muséon	SBL	Studies in Biblical Literature
NA²⁶	Nestle-Aland Novum Testamentum Graece 26th ed.	SBLASP	Society of Biblical Literature Abstracts and Seminar Papers
NABPRSS	National Association of Baptist Professors of Religion Special Studies	SBLDS	Society of Biblical Literature Dissertation Series
		SBLMS	Society of Biblical Literature Monograph Series
NAC	The New American Commentary	SBLSBS	Society of Biblical Literature Sources for Biblical Study
NCB	New Century Bible		
NClB	New Clarendon Bible	SBLSP	Society of Biblical Literature Seminar Papers
Neot	Neotestamentica	SBT	Studies in Biblical Theology
NewDocs	New Documents Illustrating Early Christianity, ed. G. H. R. Horsley	Schürer E.	
		Schürer	The History of the Jewish People in the Age of Jesus Chjrist (175 B.C.—A.D. 135), rev. and ed. G. Vermes et al. (3 vols.; Edinburgh: 1973-87)
NHC	Nag Hammadi Codices		
NHS	Nag Hammadi Studies		
NIBC	The New Interpreter's Bible Commentary		
NICNT	The New International Commentary on the New Testament	SCS	Septuagint and Cognate Studies
		SE	Studia evangelica
NIDNTT	New International Dictionary of New Testament Theology	SEÅ	Svensk exegetisk årsbok
		SEG	Supplementum epigraphicum graecum (Leiden, 1923-)
NIGTC	New International Greek Testament Commentary		
		SESJ	Suomen Ekseegeettisen Seuran Julkaisuja
NIVAC	New International Version Application Commentary	SFSHJ	South Florida Studies in the History of Judaism
		SHR	Studies in the History of Religions

SHT	Studies in Historical Theology	TLZ	Theologische Literaturzeitung
SJ	Studia judaica	TNTC	Tyndale New Testament Commentary
SJLA	Studies in Judaism in Late Antiquity	TOP	Theology Occasional Papers
SJT	Scottish Journal of Theology	TPINTC	Trinity Press International New Testament
SJTOP	Scottish Journal of Theology Occasional Papers		Commentaries
SNTW	Studies in the New Testament and Its World	TS	Theological Studies
SNTSMS	Society for New Testament Studies Monograph	TSFBul	TSF Bulletin
	Series	TToday	Theology Today
SNTSU	Studien zum Neuen Testament und seiner	TU	Texte und Untersuchungen
	Umwelt	TWOT	Theological Wordbook of the Old Testament
SPB	Studia post-biblica	TynB	Tyndale Bulletin
SR	Studies in Religion	TZ	Theologische Zeitschrift
ST	Studia theologica	USQR	Union Seminary Quarterly Review
STDJ	Studies on the Texts of the Desert of Judah	VC	Vigiliae christianae
Str-B	Strack and Billerbeck, Kommentar zum Neuen	VoxEv	Vox evangelica
	Testament	VTSup	Vetus Testamentum Supplements
StudLit	Studia liturgica	WBC	Word Biblical Commentary
SWJT	Southwestern Journal of Theology	WEC	Wycliffe Exegetical Commentary
TBC	Torch Bible Commentaries	WMANT	Wissenschaftliche Monographien zum Alten
TD	Theology Digest		und Neuen Testament
TDGR	Translated Documents of Greece and Rome, ed.	WTJ	Westminster Theological Journal
	R. K. Sherk	WUNT	Wissenschaftliche Untersuchungen zum Neuen
TDNT	Theological Dictionary of the New Testament,		Testament
	ed. G. Kittel and G. Friedrich	ZNW	Zeitschrift für die neutestamentliche
TEH	Theologische Existenz heute, (new series)		Wissenschaft
TheolRev	Theological Review (Beirut)	ZRG	Zeitschrift für Religions und Geistesgeschichte
TI	Theological Inquiries	ZS:NT	Zacchaeus Studies: New Testament
TJ (n.s.)	Trinity Journal (new series)	ZT	Zeitschrift für Theologie und Kirche

Transliteration of Hebrew and Greek

HEBREW

Consonants

א = ʾ
ב = b
ג = g
ד = d
ה = h
ו = w
ז = z
ח = ḥ
ט = ṭ
י = y
כ = k
ל = l
מ = m
נ = n
ס = s
ע = ʿ
פ = p
צ = ṣ
ק = q
ר = r
שׂ = ś
שׁ = š
ת = t

Long Vowels

(ה)ָ = â
יֵ = ê
יִ = î
ו = û
הָ = ā
ֵ = ē
בֹ = ō

Short Vowels

ַ = a
ֶ = e
ִ = i
ָ = o
ֻ = u

Very Short Vowels

ֲ = ᵃ
ֱ = ᵉ
ְ = ᵉ (if vocal)
ֳ = ᵒ

GREEK

A = A
α = a
B = B
β = b
Γ = G
γ = g
Δ = D
δ = d
E = E
ε = e
Z = Z
ζ = z
H = Ē
η = ē
Θ = Th
θ = th
I = I
ι = I
K = K
κ = k
Λ = L
λ = l
M = M
μ = m
N = N
ν = n
Ξ = X
ξ = x

O = O
o = o
Π = P
π = p
P = R
ρ = r
Σ = S
σ/ς = s
T = T
τ = t
Y = Y
υ = y
Φ = Ph
φ = ph
X = Ch
χ = ch
Ψ = Ps
ψ = ps
Ω = Ō
ω = ō
ʿP = Rh
ῥ = rh
ʿ = h
γξ = nx
γγ = ng
αυ = au
ευ = eu
ου = ou
υι = ui

Contributors

Allison, Dale C. Jr., PhD. Errett M. Grable Professor of New Testament Exegesis and Early Christianity, Pittsburgh Theological Seminary, Pittsburgh, Pennsylvania, USA: **Eschatology I.**

Arnold, Clinton E., PhD. Professor of New Testament Language and Literature, Talbot School of Theology, La Mirada, California, USA: **Ephesians, Letter to the.**

Aune, David E., PhD. Professor of New Testament and Christian Origins, University of Notre Dame, Notre Dame, Indiana, USA: **Apocalypticism.**

Barclay, John M. G., PhD. Professor of New Testament and Christian origins, University of Glasgow, Glasgow, Scotland: **Jesus and Paul.**

Barnett, Paul W., PhD. Retired Bishop of North Sydney, Anglican Church, Diocese of Sydney, Sydney, New South Wales, Australia: **Adversaries I; Apostle; Salvation III.**

Bartchy, S. Scott, PhD. Director, UCLA Center for the Study of Religion and Adjunct Professor of Christian Origins and History of Religions, Department of History, University of California, Los Angeles, Los Angeles, California, USA: **Table Fellowship.**

Bauckham, Richard J., PhD. Professor of New Testament Studies, St. Mary's College, University of St. Andrews, St. Andrews, UK: **Peter, Second Letter of.**

Bauer, David R., PhD. Professor of Biblical Studies, Asbury Theological Seminary, Wilmore, Kentucky, USA: **Son of David; Son of God I.**

Beale, Gregory K., PhD. Kenneth T. Wessner Chair of Biblical Studies, Professor of New Testament, Wheaton College Graduate School, Wheaton, Illinois, USA: **Eschatology III.**

Beasley-Murray, George R. Late Professor of New Testament, The Southern Baptist Theological Seminary, Louisville, Kentucky, USA: **Baptism II; Revelation, Book of.**

Blackburn, Barry L., PhD. Professor, Atlanta Christian College, East Point, Georgia, USA: **Miracles, Miracle Stories I.**

Blomberg, Craig L., PhD. Distinguished Professor of New Testament, Denver Seminary, Denver, Colorado, USA: **Gospels, Historical Reliability of.**

Bock, Darrell L., PhD. Research Professor for New Testament Studies, Dallas Theological Seminary, Dallas, Texas, USA: **Luke, Gospel of.**

Brauch, Manfred T., PhD. James A. Maxwell Professor of Biblical Theology, Eastern Baptist Theological Seminary, Wynnewood, Pennsylvania, USA: **Righteousness II.**

Bruce, F. F., DD. Late Rylands Professor of Biblical Criticism and Exegesis, University of Manchester, Manchester, UK: **Paul in Acts and Letters.**

Burge, Gary M., PhD. Professor of New Testament, Wheaton College, Wheaton, Illinois, USA: **John, Letters of.**

Calvert-Koyzis, Nancy, PhD. Instructor in Religion and Theology, Redeemer University College, Ancaster, Ontario, Canada: **Abraham.**

Campbell, William S., PhD. Reader in Religious and Theological Studies, Westhill College, University of Birmingham, Birmingham, UK: **Covenant, New Covenant; Israel II.**

Caragounis, Chrys C. ThD. Professor in New Testament Exegesis, Lund University, Lund, Sweden: **Kingdom of God I.**

Chilton, Bruce D., PhD. Bernard Iddings Bell Professor of Religion, Bard College, Annandale, New York, USA: **Judaism and the New Testament; Rabbinic Traditions and Literature.**

Corley, Bruce, ThD. Professor of New Testament, Southwestern Baptist Theological Seminary, Fort Worth, Texas, USA: **Trial of Jesus.**

Davids, Peter H., PhD. Scholar in Residence, The Vineyard Church, Stafford, Texas, USA: **Miracles, Miracle Stories II; Riches and Poverty I.**

deSilva, David A., PhD. Professor of New Testament and Greek, Ashland Theological Seminary, Ashland, Ohio, USA: **Apocrypha and Pseudepigrapha.**

Dillon, John M., PhD. Regius Professor of Greek, Trinity College, Dublin, Ireland: **Philosophy.**

Dockery, David, PhD. President and Professor of Christian Studies, Union University, Jackson, Tennessee, USA: **Baptism I.**

Drane, John W., DD. Director, Centre for the Study of Christianity and Contemporary Society, University of Stirling, Stirling, UK: **Son of God III.**

Dunn, James D. G., DD. Lightfoot Professor of Divinity, University of Durham, Durham, UK: **Romans, Letter to the.**

Edwards, Ruth B., PhD. Honorary Senior Lecturer in New Testament, Department of Divinity and Religious Studies, University of Aberdeen, Aberdeen, UK: **Rome.**

Elliott, Mark A., PhD. Adjunct Professor, University of Western Ontario and Conrad Grebel College, University of Waterloo; Pastor, Frank Street Baptist Church, Wiarton, Ontario, Canada: **Israel I.**

Ellis, E. Earl, PhD. Research Professor of Theology, Southwestern Baptist Theological Seminary, Fort Worth, Texas, USA: **Pastoral Letters.**

Erickson, Richard J., PhD. Associate Professor of New Testament, Fuller Theological Seminary Northwest, Seattle, Washington, USA: **Flesh.**

Evans, Craig A., PhD. Payzant Distinguished Professor of New Testament, Acadia Divinity College, Wolfville, Nova Scotia, Canada: **Apocalypticism.**

Farris, Stephen C., PhD. Professor of Preaching and Worship, Knox College, Toronto School of Theology, Toronto, Ontario, Canada: **Worship I.**

Ferguson, Everett, PhD. Professor Emeritus, Abilene Christian University, Abilene, Texas, USA: **Religions, Greco-Roman.**

France, Richard T., PhD. Retired, Principal, Wycliffe Hall, Oxford, UK: **Servant of Yahweh.**

Fung, Ronald Y. K., PhD. Retired, Resident Scholar and Lecturer, China Graduate School of Theology, Hong Kong: **Body of Christ.**

Geddert, Timothy J., PhD. Associate Professor of New Testament, Mennonite Brethren Biblical Seminary, Fresno, California, USA: **Apocalypticism.**

Giles, Kevin N., ThD. Vicar, St. Michaels Church, North Carlton, Australia: **Church III.**

Green, Joel B., PhD. Dean of Academic Affairs and School of Theology, and Professor of New Testament Interpretation, Asbury Theological Seminary, Wilmore, Kentucky, USA:

Acts of the Apostles; Death of Christ I; Death of Christ II.

Guelich, Robert A., DTheol. Late Professor of New Testament, Fuller Theological Seminary, Pasadena, California, USA: **Mark, Gospel of.**

Guthrie, Donald, PhD. Late Lecturer in New Testament Studies and Vice Principal, London Bible College, Northwood, England: **God II.**

Hafemann, Scott J., DTheol. Gerald F. Hawthorne Chair of New Testament Greek, Wheaton College, Wheaton, Illinois, USA: **Corinthians, Letters to the.**

Hansen, G. Walter, ThD. Director of the Global Research Institute and Associate Professor of New Testament , Fuller Theological Seminary, Pasadena, California, USA: **Galatians, Letter to the.**

Hawthorne, Gerald F., PhD. Emeritus Professor of Greek and New Testament Exegesis, Wheaton College, Wheaton, Illinois, USA: **Holy Spirit III; Philippians, Letter to the.**

Herzog, William R. II, PhD. Dean of Faculty and Professor of New Testament Interpretation, Colgate Rochester Divinity School/Bexley Hall/Crozer Theological Seminary, Rochester, New York, USA: **Temple Cleansing.**

Hurst, Lincoln D., PhD. Associate Professor of Religious Studies, University of California, Davis, California, USA: **Ethics I.**

Hurtado, Larry W., PhD. Professor of New Testament Language, Literature and Theology, The University of Edinburgh, Edinburgh, UK: **Christology II; God I; Gospel (Genre); Lord II; Son of God II.**

Keener, Craig S., PhD. Professor of New Testament, Eastern Baptist Theological Seminary, Wynnewood, Pennsylvania, USA: **Women II.**

Kim, Seyoon, PhD. Professor of New Testament, Fuller Theological Seminary, Pasadena, California, USA: **Kingdom of God III.**

Kreitzer, Larry J., PhD. Tutor of New Testament, Regent's Park College, University of Oxford, Oxford, UK: **Adam and Christ; Eschatology II; Kingdom of God II; Resurrection II.**

Kroeger, Catherine C., PhD. Adjunct Associate Professor of Classical and Ministry Studies, Gordon-Conwell Theological Seminary, South Hamilton, Massachusetts, USA: **Women III.**

Kruse, Colin G., PhD. Coordinator of Post-Graduate Research, Bible College of Victoria, Lilydale, Victoria, Australia: **Apostle.**

Lane, William L., ThD. Late Paul T. Walls Professor of Biblical Studies, Seattle Pacific University, Seattle, Washington, USA: **Hebrews, Letter to the.**

Levison, John R., PhD. Professor of New Testament, Seattle Pacific University, Seattle, Washington, USA: **Creation, New Creation.**

Marshall, I. Howard, DD. Emeritus Professor of New Testament Exegesis and Honorary Research Professor, University of Aberdeen, Aberdeen, UK: **Church I; Lord's Supper I; Salvation; Son of Man.**

Martin, Ralph P., PhD. Distinguished Scholar in Residence, Fuller Theological Seminary, Pasadena, California, USA: **God II; Worship II; Worship III.**

McGrath, Alister E., PhD. Principal, Wycliffe Hall, Professor of Historical Theology, Oxford University, Oxford, UK: **Justification.**

McKnight, Scot, PhD. Karl A. Olsson Professor of Religious Studies, North Park University, Chicago, Illinois, USA: **Matthew, Gospel; Righteousness I.**

Michaels, J. Ramsey, ThD. Professor Emeritus, Southwest Missouri State University, Springfield, Missouri, USA: **Peter, First Letter of.**

Moo, Douglas J., PhD. Blanchard Professor of New Testament,

Wheaton College Graduate School, Wheaton, Illinois, USA: **Law I.**

Morris, Leon, PhD. Retired, Melbourne, Victoria, Australia: **Salvation II; Sin I.**

Mott, Stephen C., PhD. Pastor, Cochesett United Methodist Church, West Bridgewater, Massachusetts, USA: **Ethics II.**

Newman, Carey C., PhD. Director, Baylor University Press, Waco, Texas, USA: **Covenant, New Covenant; God III; Righteousness III.**

O'Brien, Peter T., PhD. Senior Research Fellow, Moore Theological College, Newtown, New South Wales, Australia: **Church II; Colossians, Letter to the; Letters, Letter Forms I.**

Onesti, Karen L., PhD (Cand.) Pastor, Rancocas and Masonville United Methodist Churches, New Jersey, USA: **Righteousness II.**

Osborne, Grant R., PhD. Professor of New Testament, Trinity Evangelical Divinity School, Deerfield, Illinois, USA: **Resurrection I.**

Paige, Terence P., PhD. Associate Professor of New Testament, Houghton College, Houghton, New York, USA: **Holy Spirit II.**

Patzia, Arthur G., PhD. Professor of New Testament, Fuller Theological Seminary, Northern California, Menlo Park, California, USA: **Philemon, Letter to.**

Porter, Stanley E., PhD. President, Professor of New Testament, McMaster Divinity School, Hamilton, Ontario, Canada: **Sin II.**

Powers, Janet Everts, PhD. Associate Professor of Religion, Hope College, Holland, Michigan, USA: **Conversion and Call of Paul.**

Reasoner, Mark, PhD. Associate Professor of Biblical Studies, Bethel College, St. Paul, Minnesota, USA: **Rome.**

Schmidt, Thomas E., PhD. Santa Barbara, California, USA: **Riches and Poverty II; Riches and Poverty III.**

Scholer, David M., ThD. Professor of New Testament and Associate Dean of the Center for Advanced Theological Studies, Fuller Theological Seminary, Pasadena, California, USA: **Women I.**

Schreiner, Thomas R., PhD. Professor of New Testament, The Southern Baptist Theological Seminary, Louisville, Kentucky, USA: **Law III.**

Scott, James M., DTheol. Professor of Religious Studies, Trinity Western University, Langley, British Columbia, Canada: **Adoption, Sonship.**

Seifrid, Mark A., PhD. Associate Professor of New Testament, The Southern Baptist Theological Seminary, Louisville, Kentucky, USA: **Death of Christ III; In Christ; Judgment III.**

Simpson, John W. Jr., PhD. Editor, William B. Eerdmans, Grand Rapids, Michigan, USA: **Thessalonians, Letters to the.**

Snodgrass, Klyne R., PhD. Paul W. Brandel Professor of New Testament Studies, North Park Theological Seminary, Chicago, Illinois, USA: **Parables.**

Stamps, Dennis L., PhD. Principal of the West Midlands Ministerial Training Course, The Queens Foundation for Ecumenical Theological Education, Birmingham, UK: **Rhetoric.**

Stegner, W. Richard, PhD. Late Professor of New Testament, Garrett-Evangelical Theological Seminary, Evanston, Illinois, USA: **Jew, Paul the.**

Stein, Robert H., PhD. Mildred and Ernest Hogan Professor of New Testament, The Southern Baptist Theological Seminary, Louisville, Kentucky, USA: **Last Supper; Synoptic Problem.**

Sumney, Jerry L., PhD. Professor of Biblical Studies, Lexington Theological Seminary, Lexington, Kentucky, USA: **Adver-**

saries II.

Thielman, Frank S., PhD. Presbyterian Professor of Divinity, Beeson Divinity School, Birmingham, Alabama, USA: **Law II.**

Thompson, Marianne Meye, PhD. Professor of New Testament Interpretation, Fuller Theological Seminary, Pasadena, California, USA: **John, Gospel of.**

Travis, Stephen H., PhD. Vice-Principal, St. John's College, Nottingham, Nottingham, UK: **Judgment I; Judgment II; Resurrection III.**

Turner, Max M. B., PhD. Professor of New Testament Studies, London Bible College, Northwood, UK: **Holy Spirit I.**

Verhey, Allen D., PhD. Evert J. and Hattie E. Blekkink Professor of Religion, Hope College, Holland, Michigan, USA: **Ethics III.**

Wainwright, Geoffrey, DTheol., DD. Cushman Professor of Christian Theology, Duke University, Durham, North Carolina, USA: **Baptism III; Lord's Supper II.**

Wall, Robert W., ThD. Professor of Christian Scriptures, Seattle Pacific University, Seattle, Washington, USA: **James, Letter of.**

Watson, Duane F., PhD. Professor of New Testament, Malone College, Canton, Ohio, USA: **Letters, Letter Forms II.**

Webb, Robert L., PhD. Adjunct Associate Professor of New Testament, McMaster Divinity College, Hamilton, Ontario, Canada: **Jude, Letter of.**

Wilkins, Michael J., PhD. Professor of New Testament Language and Literature, Dean of the Faculty, Talbot School of Theology, La Mirada, California, USA: **Disciples; Sinners.**

Wise, Michael O., PhD. Professor of Bible and History, Scholar in Residence, Northwestern College, Saint Paul, Minnesota, USA: **Dead Sea Scrolls.**

Witherington, Ben III, PhD. Professor of New Testament, Asbury Theological Seminary, Wilmore, Kentucky, USA: **Birth of Jesus; Christ I; Christ II; Christ III; Christology I; John the Baptist; Lord I; Lord III.**

Yamauchi, Edwin M., PhD. Professor of History, Miami University, Oxford, Ohio, USA: **Gnosticism; Synagogue.**

ABBA. *See* ADOPTION, SONSHIP.

ABRAHAM: NEW TESTAMENT

A key figure in early Jewish literature, Abraham is mentioned in all four Gospels and plays a central part in Paul's letters to the Galatians and Romans. Later NT authors continue to employ Abraham in significant ways in Acts and Hebrews, and to a lesser degree in James and 1 Peter.

    1. Old Testament and Jewish Literature
    2. Synoptic Gospels
    3. Gospel According to John
    4. Acts of the Apostles
    5. Paul's Letters
    6. Hebrews
    7. James and 1 Peter

1. Old Testament and Jewish Literature.

The role played by the patriarchs became increasingly important to the Jewish people after they returned from exile in Babylon. Abraham was one of these important figures whose stature is reflected in extrabiblical Jewish literature and in the NT.

1.1. Abraham in the Old Testament. Later accounts of Abraham are based on the Genesis stories of the patriarch. The depiction of the life of Abraham is found in the first book of the Hebrew Bible, from his inclusion in the genealogy of his father, Terah (Gen 11:27), to his death and burial (Gen 25:7-10). The major events in Abraham's life are his leaving his father and birthplace (Gen 12:1), his sojourns in Egypt and Gerar (Gen 12:10-20; 20:1-18), his battle with the kings (Gen 14:1-16), his meeting with Melchizedek (Gen 14:17-20), God's covenant with him (Gen 15:7-21; 17:2, 4), his union with Hagar and the birth of Ishmael (Gen 16:1-15), God's commandment of circumcision for Abraham and his descendants (Gen 17:9-14), the promise of the birth of Isaac (Gen 17:15-21), the birth of Isaac (Gen 21:1-7), the proposed offering of Isaac (Gen 22:1-19) and the death and burial of Sarah (Gen 23:1-20).

Four primary themes are found in the Genesis account: the promises from God that Abraham would have many descendants (Gen 12:2; 13:16; 15:5; 17:2, 4; 22:17), the gift of a land (Gen 12:7; 13:14-15; 15:7), the obedience of Abraham (Gen 12:1-4; 17:1; 22:16-18) and the subsequent blessing of all nations through Abraham (Gen 12:3; 22:18).

Within the OT Abraham functions in three primary ways. First, he is the father of the Jewish people (Gen 25:19; 26:15, 24; 28:13; 32:9; 48:15-16; Ex 3:6; Deut 1:8; 6:10; 9:5; 30:20; Josh 24:3; 1 Chron 1:27-28, 34; 16:13; Ps 105:6; Is 41:8; Jer 33:26; Mic 7:20). Second, he is the original source of blessing for the Jewish people (Gen 26:24; 28:4; 35:12; 50:24; Ex 2:24; 6:3-8; 32:13; 33:1; Num 32:11; Deut 1:8; 6:10; 9:5, 27; 29:13; 30:20; 34:4; 2 Kings 13:23; 1 Chron 16:15-16; 2 Chron 20:7; Ps 105:7-11, 42; Is 51:2; Mic 7:20). Third, his name is used to identify the God of the Jewish people as "the God of Abraham" (Gen 28:13; 31:42, 53; 32:9; Ex 3:6, 15-16; 4:5; 1 Kings 18:36; 1 Chron 29:18; 2 Chron 30:6; Ps 47:9).

Abraham functions in three additional noteworthy ways. His obedience to God and his laws (Gen 26:4-5; see also Neh 9:7-8) was the basis for the blessing of his descendants. God's compassion toward the Jewish people is sometimes invoked on the basis of his covenant with Abraham (Deut 9:27; 2 Kings 13:23; Mic 7:18-20). Finally, God brings Abraham out of the midst of idolatry (Josh 24:2-3).

1.2. Abraham in Early Jewish Literature. The authors of Jewish literature from 200 B.C. to A.D. 200 used many of the same themes found in the OT accounts in accordance with their particular situations. Josephus and Philo portray Abraham as one who assimilates pagan, particularly Hellenistic, culture (e.g., Josephus *Ant.* 1.8.2 §§166-68; Philo *Abr.* 88). In other texts Abraham is one who isolates himself from Gentile influence (*Jub.* 22:16; Pseudo-Philo *Bib. Ant.* 6:4). The authors of these texts have apologetic and didactic motives. The Jews are instructed to live in their respective situations in the same way that Abraham is portrayed as living in the literature.

Four major themes are found in these texts. First, the stress on Abraham as a tenacious monotheist, often portrayed as the first of his kind, is prevalent in texts from Palestine and the Diaspora from 200 B.C. to A.D. 200 (*Jub.* 11:16-17; 12:1-5, 16-21; 20:6-9; Pseudo-Philo *Bib. Ant.* 6:4; Josephus *Ant.* 1.7.1 §§154-57; Philo *Abr.* 68-71, 88; *Apoc. Abr.* 1-8). Second, God establishes a covenant with Abraham through which his descendants are blessed (*Jub.* 15:9-10; Pseudo-Philo *Bib. Ant.* 7:4; 1QapGen 21:8-14) and are shown compassion (Pseudo-Philo *Bib. Ant.* 30:7; *Pss. Sol.* 9:8-11; *T. Levi* 15:4; *As. Mos.* 3:8-9). However, sometimes one must obey the stipulations of the covenant in order to remain within it (*Jub.* 15:26-27). Eventually other nations would be blessed as well (Sir 44:21). Third, Abraham's character is extolled. He is righteous (*T. Abr.* 1:1A), hospitable (*T. Abr.* 1:1-3A; Philo *Abr.* 107-110; Josephus *Ant.* 1.11.2 §196) and virtuous (Josephus *Ant.* 1.7.1 §154; Philo *Abr.* 68). He is faithful (Sir 44:20; 1 Macc 2:52; *Jub.* 17:17-18). He loves God (*Jub.* 17:18) and is even called the friend of God (CD 3:2-4). Josephus maintains that Abraham and his seed are rewarded because of the patriarch's virtue and piety (*Ant.* 1.13.4 §234). Fourth, Abraham lived according to the Mosaic law (*Jub.* 15:1-2; 16:20; Sir 44:20) or the natural/philosophical law (Philo *Abr.* 3-6). Abraham is alive (4 Macc 7:19; 16:25; *T. Levi* 18:14; *T. Jud.* 25:1; *T. Benj.* 10:6) and praises those who die for keeping the Law (4 Macc 13:13-18). Abraham established the covenant by being circumcised (Sir 44:20). Additionally, Abraham is noted for his powers of intercession (*T. Abr.* 18:10-11A) and his ascension to the heavens, where he receives revelation (Pseudo-Philo *Bib. Ant.* 18:5; *T. Abr.* 10-14; *Apoc. Abr.* 15:4-30).

2. Synoptic Gospels.

Abraham is mentioned in all of the Synoptic Gospels (Mt 1:1-2, 17; 3:9; 8:11; 22:32; Mk 12:26; Lk 1:55, 73; 3:8, 34; 13:16, 28; 16:22-30; 19:9; 20:37).

2.1. Abraham Traditions Common to All Three Synoptics. Abraham is mentioned only once in Mark (Mk 12:26), and then within the context of the Sadducees' question regarding the marital status in the resurrection of the woman who had married seven brothers consecutively (Mk 12:18-27; see also Mt 22:23-33; Lk 20:27-40). The Sadducees, who did not believe in the resurrection (Mk 12:18; Mt 22:23; Lk 20:27), present the idea as an absurdity within the context of present human relationships.

In Mark and Matthew, Jesus gives the Sadducees a twofold answer since they know neither the "Scriptures nor the power of God" (Mk 12:24; Mt 22:29). By the power of God, those who have risen from the dead are like angels and do not marry. Thus marriage is made obsolete. Second, Jesus uses God's identification of himself to Moses at the burning bush (Ex 3:6) as proof that God is the God of the living, not of the dead. God is faithful to his promises to the patriarchs to be their God (in the case of Abraham, see Gen 17:7) and, subsequently, to his covenant people as well. The account in Luke divides the modes of life into present and future ages (Lk 20:34-35), adding "for all live to him" (Lk 20:38). The author of 4 Maccabees similarly portrays the patriarchs as those who "do not die to God, but live in (or 'to') God" (4 Macc 7:19; 16:25).

2.2. Abraham Traditions Common to Matthew and Luke.

2.2.1. The Genealogies. Although Matthew and Luke include Abraham in their genealogies (Mt 1:1-2, 17; Lk 3:34), he is more significant in Matthew. The Evangelist introduces the Gospel with "the book of the genealogy of Jesus Christ, the son of David (*see* Son of David), the son of Abraham" (Mt 1:1). The transition to the genealogy is simple since it begins with Abraham "the father of Isaac" (Mt 1:2; see also 1 Chron 1:34). Abraham is mentioned a third time in Matthew 1:17, where the Evangelist outlines turning points in Israelite history as being fourteen generations from Abraham to David, fourteen generations from David to the Babylonian exile and fourteen generations from the exile to the Christ.

It is important that Jesus is the son of Abraham for three major reasons. (1) It means that Jesus is a Jew, a physical descendant of Abraham. (2) Although the title "son of Abraham" was not messianic (Davies and Allison, 158), in order for the Messiah to transmit the blessings begun with Abraham to his people, he had to be a descendant of Abraham. (3) Abraham was the originator of Israelite history while Jesus appears to be its culminator (Mt 1:17).

Although Luke's genealogy only mentions Abraham (Lk 3:34), it is still significant that Jesus is a "son of Abraham" since as such he is a Jew and a channel of blessing to the people of God. In Luke, Jesus' genealogy, traced back to Adam and God, may reflect the theme of extension of salvation to the Gentiles, since it envisages his relationship to all humankind as God's Son (*see* Son of God; Fitzmyer, 1:190).

2.2.2. Children of Abraham from Stone (Mt 3:9; Lk 3:8). Both Evangelists mention Abraham within the larger context of the ministry of John the Baptist at the Jordan River (Mt 3:1-17; Lk 3:1-9; see Jn 8:33, 39). John warns those coming to him for baptism (Pharisees and Sadducees in Mt 3:7; a "multitude" in Lk 3:7) that they can rely no longer on their ethnic privilege as descendants of Abraham to guarantee them protection from the wrath of God. God can raise up "children" (Mt 3:9; Lk 3:8) of Abraham from stone (see Is 51:1-2; Pseudo-Philo *Bib. Ant.* 23.4-5; Gen 17:17; 18:10-14). The genealogical tree of Abraham (Is 11:1; see Wallace-Hadrill) is even in danger of destruction. It is not Abrahamic descent that will save them from the wrath of God but conduct that is "consonant with an inner reform of life" (Fitzmyer, 1:468; see also Jn 8:39).

2.2.3. Abraham at the Eschatological Banquet (Mt 8:10-11; Lk 13:28-29). Matthew and Luke speak of the eschatological banquet (*see* Table Fellowship) at which Abraham, Isaac and Jacob will preside (Luke adds "all the prophets" in Lk 13:28). It is common in Jewish tradition that Abraham, Isaac and Jacob are found together with the righteous (*see* Righteousness; see Ward, 176; cf. 4 Macc 13:17; *T. Levi* 18:14; *T. Judah* 25:1; *T. Benj.* 10:6. See also Acts 3:13; 7:32 for occurrences of the threesome.). The Matthean account occurs at the conclusion of the story of the Gentile centurion (Mt 8:1-13; see Lk 7:1-10), whose faith is unrivaled even by the Jews (Mt 8:10). In Luke the eschatological banquet scene is inserted within the parable of the narrow door (Lk 13:22-30). Both contexts, however, depict the inclusion of the Gentiles at the eschatological banquet in the kingdom of God (Mt 8:11; Lk 13:29; see Ps 107:3; Is 49:12) and the exclusion of certain Jews (Mt 8:12; Lk 13:27-28). In these accounts Abraham is primarily an eschato-

logical figure, although in Matthew as well as in Luke the Evangelist is establishing a "connection and continuity between the history of Abraham and the events of which he himself is writing" (Dahl, 140). The portrayal of Abraham as a heavenly figure is certainly not unique, nor is his reputation for hospitality, even to Gentiles (see 1.2 above; *T. Ab Rec. A* 1:1-2).

2.3 References to Abraham Particular to Luke.

2.3.1. The Hymns. Luke is unique in his inclusion of hymns within his infancy narrative. Luke may have used outside source material in the composition of these hymns. However, to "admit such sources does not mean that Luke has not reworked them, in his own style" (Fitzmyer, 1:309). Two of these hymns refer to Abraham (Lk 1:46-55, 67-79). The Magnificat is the hymn of Mary as she rejoices in anticipation of the birth of Jesus (see also 1 Sam 2:1-10). The theme of the hymn is that God helps his people in the present as he helped them in the past. Historically, he has destroyed the powerful and rich (*see* Riches and Poverty); he has helped the oppressed and the poor (Ex 2:24). God continues to help the poor and oppressed in the present time (Lk 1:47-48). This assistance is based on God's faithfulness to the descendants (literally "seed"; see also Acts 3:25; 7:1-5) of Abraham because of his promises to him (see 1 above; Mic 7:20). Abraham was without land or descendants until he was blessed by God (Gen 17:7-8; 18:18; 22:17-18). Mary's experience "is not an isolated incident but rather part of the merciful remembrance of God who wants to fulfill his promises of salvation" (Zorrilla, 233). Successive generations will also experience the compassion of God (Lk 1:48).

The Benedictus is a prophecy given by Zechariah concerning his son, John. John will prepare the way before the Lord (Lk 1:76), who will bring salvation to his people (Lk 1:68-69). This salvation, the purpose of which is to enable persons to serve God without fear from enemies (Lk 1:71, 73), is based on the mercy promised to the Jewish ancestors for which the covenant (or oath, Gen 22:16-17; 26:3) sworn to Abraham (Lk 1:72-73; Ps 105:7-11) is the foundation. N. A. Dahl (146-47) sees the messianic redemption as described in terms "reminiscent of the deliverance from Egypt, and seen as the fulfillment of God's oath to Abraham" (Ps 106:10; Gen 15:13-14; Acts 7:2-8, 17).

2.3.2. A Daughter of Abraham. The "bent"

woman who is healed on the sabbath (Lk 13:10-17) is called a "daughter of Abraham" (Lk 13:16). This is the only use of the expression "daughter of Abraham" in the Greek Bible. In Luke only Jews are called children of Abraham (Dahl, 151). In the pericope the sabbath and the synagogue "segregate this needy woman from divine help" (Green, 649). Jesus recognizes that as a child of Abraham she is one to whom salvation was promised (Lk 1:46-55; see 2.3.1 above). God's faithfulness to the descendants of Abraham continues because of his promises to the patriarch. This is seen especially in the case of the excluded and the outcast. The daughter of Abraham who is excluded by the religious structure is healed (see 2.3.2 above). Zacchaeus, the outcast son of Abraham, has salvation extended to him. Luke's special concern for the oppressed is noticeable when the rich man, though he is a child of Abraham, is not allowed to join Lazarus in Abraham's bosom (see 2.3.3 below) because of his lack of compassion toward Lazarus while they both were alive. Thus those thought to be excluded from the chosen are included, while those thought to be chosen are excluded.

The healing of the bent woman is a sign of salvation happening as fulfilled by the ministry of Jesus, the "Lord of the Sabbath" (Lk 6:5). Notably, she is healed on the sabbath, a day commemorating the Israelites' liberation from bondage (Deut 5:15; see Lk 13:16), and it is on this day that the woman's bondage is removed. By rebuking the disease, Jesus is also rebuking Satan (Lk 13:16; see also Green, 653). She may be one of those who is included in the eschatological banquet presided over by Abraham and his descendants (Lk 13:28-30; see 2.2.3 above).

2.3.3. Abraham's Bosom. The heavenly Abraham (see 1.2 above) is included within this pericope, which condemns the rich man and exalts the poor man Lazarus. (For analyses of similar folk tales, see Fitzmyer, 2:1126). After his death Lazarus is carried by angels to "Abraham's bosom." "Abraham's bosom" is not a synonym for Paradise, although this passage reflects the tradition in which Abraham is thought to be in heaven (see 1.2 above). The poor man enjoys close fellowship with Abraham (Marshall, 636), perhaps reminiscent of the intimacy between Abraham and Jacob in *Jubilees* 23:1-3 (see also Lk 13:29). The rich man has died and resides in Hades, separated from Abraham by a great chasm (Lk 16:26; cf. *1 Enoch* 22). The rich man

cries out to Abraham, calling him "Father" (Lk 16:24, 27, 30) and demanding assistance from Lazarus. Abraham answers him, calling him "child" (Lk 16:25). The rich man's status as a child of Abraham does not bring him relief. Father Abraham refuses to assist him (Lk 16:25-26; for Abraham as judge, see *T. Ab.* 10:6-16A). Abraham will not even send Lazarus to the rich man's family to warn them because they already have the law of Moses (Lk 16:31). Luke is stressing that salvation involves a "reaction of faith" (Fitzmyer, 2:1129), which the rich man did not have. He was thus condemned, although he was a Jew. Abraham is also appropriate in this pericope because, unlike the rich man, he was often portrayed as having followed the Law (see 1.2 above), which was not burdensome (Philo *Abr.* 5; Deut 30:11-14).

2.3.4. Zacchaeus As Son of Abraham. Zacchaeus is a rich, chief tax collector for the Romans (Lk 19:2), and as such he is a sinner (Lk 6:24), especially in the eyes of the Jews (Lk 18:9-14; 19:7; see also Loewe, 321-23). Upon interacting with Jesus, Zacchaeus repents (Lk 19:8; see Lev 6:1-7; cf. the story of the rich ruler, Lk 18:18-25). Salvation is extended to Zacchaeus, the "son of Abraham" who once was lost, by Jesus who "came to seek and to save the lost" (Lk 19:10; Ezek 34:16). Zacchaeus is again a true son of Abraham who, like other outcast Jews, has received the fulfillment of the promises to Abraham in the ministry of Jesus (Gen 17:7; see 2.3.2 above; Dahl, 149-54).

3. Gospel According to John.

The name of Abraham, while occurring nowhere else in the Johannine writings, is found ten times in John 8:31-59. Throughout the account Jesus points out that although the questioning Jews are descendants of Abraham in a physical sense (Jn 8:37), they deny it by their actions (Brown, 357). First, they are not like Abraham because they strive to kill Jesus, a messenger of God (Jn 8:40, 42; Gen 18:1-15; perhaps Jn 8:35 refers to Eliezer and Isaac, the house slave and the son; see Gen 15:2; 17:19). Second, while Abraham was known for his exemplary character (see 1.2 above), Jesus' opponents are said to be children of the devil, whose desires they fulfill (Jn 8:44). Third, Jesus' opponents are unlike Abraham because they do not recognize that Jesus is God (Jn 8:58-59; for Abraham as the first monotheist, see 1.2 above). Other references to Abraham in the chapter concern the death of Abraham (Gen 25:8, which lacks a testament; see *T. Ab.*, which provides an explanation for this lack) and Abraham's rejoicing to see Jesus' day (Jn 8:56).

Just how Abraham saw Jesus' day goes unexplained. R. E. Brown refers to *Jubilees* 16:17-19: "Abraham was told that it was through Isaac that the holy people of God would be descendant, and that both Abraham and Sarah rejoiced at the news" (Brown, 360; see Gen 17:17; 21:6). Perhaps the Evangelist is referring to the Genesis account in the knowledge that Jesus would come from this holy people. Another explanation might be that Abraham was given a revelation of the future like the one in *Apocalypse of Abraham* 31:1, which mentions God's "chosen one." Abraham had special knowledge of God (see 1.2 above, especially so in the works of Philo; see Jn 8:32), which, in terms of contemporary Jewish thought, meant that he escaped idolatry (*Apoc. Abr.* 6-8; *Jub.* 12) and the consequent slavery to sin (*Jub.* 20:6-10). This portrayal of Abraham fits the theme of freedom (Jn 8:32) and slavery (Jn 8:34-35) in John 8.

4. Acts of the Apostles.

In Acts, Abraham does not play an exemplary role for Christians to be emulated as he is in the Pauline epistles, but he remains the father of the Jews. Using Abraham exclusively in his sermons, Luke establishes a connection and continuity between Abraham and the events about which he is writing (Dahl, 140).

4.1. Acts 3. Peter uses the figure of Abraham during his speech in Solomon's portico to identify the God of Abraham, Isaac and Jacob (Acts 3:13, 25; cf. Acts 7:32; Ex 3:6) as the God whose "servant" Jesus was and through whose name Peter had just healed the lame beggar (Acts 3:6, 16). The usage of the uncommon and early title *servant* (cf. Acts 3:26) for Jesus here may indicate that an allusion is being made to the Suffering Servant of Isaiah (Is 52:13—53:12). By using this appellation Peter clearly implicates the Jews as those who killed Jesus, the chosen servant of their God (Acts 3:15).

Yet in Acts 3:25 Peter invokes the blessing to Abraham that through his seed all the families of the earth would be blessed (Gen 22:18; cf. Gen 12:3; 18:18; Gal 3:8). The Septuagint has "nations" *(ethnē)*, which could be interpreted to mean Gentiles. Peter instead uses the ambiguous "families" *(patria)*, which probably refers

first to Jews (cf. Acts 3:26) and implicitly to Gentiles. Thus Peter tells his listeners that they are the descendants of the prophets and the covenant that foretold the Messiah, Jesus (Acts 3:22-23), who was the fulfillment of the covenant with Abraham through whom the Jews and other families may be blessed.

4.2. Acts 7. Stephen's speech provides the framework for several allusions to Abraham (Acts 7:2-8, 16-17, 32) in which he appears as the recipient of promises by which his descendants later benefit.

Luke's affinity with Hellenistic Judaism is seen most clearly in Acts 7:2-8 (Dahl, 142). In Acts 7:2 Stephen places God's call to Abraham in Ur rather than in Haran (Gen 12:1). Luke's tradition could be drawn from OT texts (Gen 15:7; Neh 9:7) that suggest the call from Ur. Philo assumes that a divine call came to Abraham in both places (Philo *Abr.* 62, 85), while Josephus sees the two migrations as a single exodus (Josephus *Ant.* 1.7.1 §154). Luke further remarks (Acts 7:4) that Abraham left the country of the "Chaldeans," a term that often referred to astrologers and the interpreters of dreams (*Jub.* 11:8; Philo *Abr.* 69, 71), traditions connected with Abraham before his call (*Jub.* 12:16; Philo *Abr.* 70; Josephus *Ant.* 1.7.1 §156; *Apoc. Abr.* 7:9; cf. Josh 24:2).

In a free rendering of Genesis 17:7 Stephen remains true to the Genesis account in which Abraham possessed no land but received only a promise of land (Acts 7:5; cf. Gen 12:7; 13:15; 48:4) for himself and his offspring. Abraham followed God, although he neither took ownership of any part of the land (cf. Deut 2:5) nor yet had his descendants who would eventually inherit the land. While authors sometimes magnify Abraham's taking ownership of the land (1QapGen 21:15-19), Stephen instead magnifies Abraham's trust in God (cf. Rom 4:16-22).

By including references to the prophecy to Abraham about his descendants' four-hundred-year (Acts 7:6; cf. Ex 12:40; Gal 3:17) bondage in Egypt (Gen 15:13-14; cf. Ex 2:22), Luke emphasizes God's faithfulness to his people in the midst of crisis. In an expansion of Exodus 3:12 (Acts 7:7) Luke modifies the term *mountain (oros)* used for Sinai in the Septuagint, using instead "place" *(topos)*, referring to Jerusalem or the temple itself (cf. Acts 6:13-14). God's faithfulness to his promise to Abraham is demonstrated in that Stephen and his Jewish contemporaries in Jerusalem could worship God in that very "place."

Stephen then refers to the "covenant of circumcision" (*diathēkē peritomēs*, Acts 7:8) established with Abraham (Gen 17:10, 12), a covenant that confirmed God's promise to grant him descendants (Gen 21:1-4), who include his listeners.

Stephen returns to Abraham when he suggests that Jacob, Joseph and his relatives were buried at the cave Abraham bought near Shechem (Acts 7:16). In Genesis, Abraham bought the cave of Machpelah near Hebron (Gen 23), not Shechem. Jacob is reportedly buried in the cave Abraham bought near Hebron (Gen 49:29-32; 50:13), while Joseph was buried at Shechem (Josh 24:32) in land that Jacob had bought (Gen 33:18-20). Stephen may have telescoped the two accounts of purchases of land in Canaan as he telescoped earlier events (see Acts 7:2, 7) and has attributed the purchase of the grave in Shechem to Abraham.

4.3. Acts 13. During his speech in the synagogue of Antioch of Pisidia on his first missionary journey, Paul refers to his Jewish listeners as "Abraham's family," to whom the message of salvation was sent (Acts 13:26). Paul calls upon them to be different from the residents of Jerusalem who rejected the Messiah, Jesus, and fulfilled the message of the prophets (e.g., Is 52:13—53:12) by condemning him to death (Acts 13:27-29). It was through David's people, those chosen in Abraham, that their Messiah had come (Acts 13:22-25). The Jews tragically would later reject the message of salvation (Acts 13:45).

5. Paul's Letters.
5.1. Galatians.
5.1.1. The Situation in Galatia. From the letter it is evident that Gentile Christians were part of the community at Galatia (Gal 4:8) and that some persons came among them who contradicted Paul's gospel and confused these recent converts (Gal 1:7-9; 5:8-10). These persons persuaded Gentile converts to obey stipulations of Mosaic law (Gal 3:1-2; 4:8-10), especially circumcision (Gal 5:2-3; 6:12-13). In view of the evidence in the letter, it seems most likely that Paul's opponents were Jewish Christians (Gal 4:30; Paul refers to them as preaching "another gospel" in Gal 1:6-9).

Many scholars have noted that Abraham must have played a central role in the argu-ments of Paul's opponents. For example, J. C. Beker maintains Paul's opponents were those who thought that the Gentiles' turning to Christ was not enough. In order to be sure that God's blessing was upon them and that they were true children of Abraham, they had to participate fully in the Torah (Beker, 42-44).

5.1.2. The Text of Galatians.
5.1.2.1. Galatians 3:1-14. Paul's angry tone is evident from the beginning of his letter to the Galatians, omitting as it does the thanksgiving section usually found in his letters. He calls them "foolish" (Gal 3:1, 3) for having been "bewitched" (Gal 3:1) into obeying the requirements of the Law (Gal 3:2, 3, 5). His scathing questions in Galatians 3:1-5 serve to pinpoint his themes in his discussion that follows.

In his barbed questions, Paul sets up an antithesis between "works of the Law" *(ergōn nomou)* and "hearing with faith" *(akoēs pisteōs)*. Did God work miracles among them by their doing "works of the Law" or by their "hearing with faith" (Gal 3:5)? Paul's major concern here is to alert his readers to the contrast between "hearing with faith" and "works of the Law" and for them to consider the gross error into which they have fallen.

Paul's argument from Scripture, which is his answer to his previous rhetorical questions (Betz, 130), revolves around Abraham: "just as Abraham believed God, and it was reckoned to him as righteousness" (Gal 3:6). Byrne points out that the use of *kathōs* ("just as") implies that what follows corresponds to what has just been described (Byrne, 148). Abraham becomes the one who believed in God and, by God's action, was reckoned righteous. This corresponds to the Spirit supplied by God because of the faith of the Galatian believers. The receipt of the Spirit by the Galatian believers is parallel to Abraham's receipt of righteousness (Barclay, 80; *see* Holy Spirit).

In using Abraham to discuss the contrast of faith versus works, Paul is using Abraham in a new way. Previously, Judaism had viewed Abraham's faith and his works together. For example, in *Jubilees* Abraham is not only the first to separate from his family and worship the one Creator God (*Jub.* 11:16-17; 12:16-21), but also he observes stipulations of the Mosaic law such as the Feast of Tabernacles (*Jub.* 16:20; cf. 22:1-2). In Philo's works Abraham is portrayed as following the natural law (Philo *Abr.* 275-76). To Philo, the law of nature and the law of Moses are identical. Only law that was revealed by God, the creator of nature, can really be in accordance with natural law. By following the natural law Abraham becomes an example of obedience to the Law for his descendants (Philo *Abr.* 6).

Philo is the only one who tells us that Genesis 15:6 was interpreted to mean that Abraham believed in the one Creator God in contrast to other gods or philosophies. Genesis 15:6 states "and Abraham believed God, and it was reckoned to him as righteousness." Philo describes Abraham by saying "he is spoken of as the first person to believe in God, since he first grasped a firm and unswerving conception of the truth that there is one Cause above all and that it provides for the world and all that there is therein" (Philo *Virt.* 216). Abraham is the first one to be spoken of in the LXX and the Hebrew Bible as believing in God. Most often those who spoke of the faith of Abraham spoke of it as faith in the one God (Josephus *Ant.* 1.7.1 §§155-56; *Apoc. Abr.* 7:10; Pseudo-Philo *Bib. Ant.* 6:4; 23:5) in contrast to idolatry. The law, whether Mosaic or natural, was a necessary corollary to his belief in God. Because Abraham was believed to have embodied these characteristics, he functioned as an ideal representative of the Jewish people.

In Galatians 3:7 Paul commands the Galatian believers to recognize from his proof in Galatians 3:6 (cf. Gen 15:6; Betz, 141) that "it is the people of faith who are the sons of Abraham." Anyone among them who was at all familiar with the traditions of Abraham as the first monotheist and anti-idolater would realize that the Jewish people had interpreted Abraham as the man of faith all along. This statement of Paul's would ring true. To them the descendants of Abraham—the Jews—would be the people of faith in God.

Paul again uses Scripture to back up his claim that the children of Abraham are those who have faith in God. In Galatians 3:8-9 he states, "And the Scriptures, seeing that God would justify the Gentiles by faith, declared the gospel beforehand to Abraham saying that 'All the Gentiles will be blessed in you.' " Paul personifies the Scripture, saying that it saw in advance that God would justify the Gentiles by faith and declared the gospel beforehand to Abraham that all the Gentiles would be blessed in him (Gal 3:8; Gen 12:3). Paul understands the promise to Abraham that he would be a blessing to

the nations (Gentiles) as the anticipatory preaching of the gospel to Abraham. Because the message of the gospel was that justification comes by faith, and thus Gentiles were included in justification, the announcement that God would bless the Gentiles through Abraham anticipated the gospel.

In the meantime Paul picks up the other thread of his argument, the "works of the Law" (Gal 3:10). Using Deuteronomy 27:26, Habakkuk 2:4 and Leviticus 18:5, Paul argues that obedience to the *Law does not bring righteousness. He uses Deuteronomy 21:23 to show that the era of faith has now arrived through Christ's becoming a curse and providing redemption from the curse of the Law (Gal 3:13; Byrne, 156). It is probable that Paul is dealing here with the very passages that his opponents used in their message in support of the Law (Longenecker, 116-21, 124).

In Galatians 3:14 Paul includes two purpose clauses. Christ became a curse and provided redemption from the curse of the Law in order that in Christ Jesus the blessing of Abraham might come upon the Gentiles (cf. Gal 3:8). The second purpose clause is parallel to the first: "In order that we might receive the promise of the Spirit through faith" (Gal 3:14). The Spirit becomes the blessing of Abraham, which has come upon the Gentiles (Betz, 143). This blessing is by faith (Gal 3:1-5) in Christ (Gal 3:14). Formerly the promise to Abraham referred to land and descendants. But now the promise refers to the Spirit, which is a foretaste of the inheritance of the world to come (Byrne, 156-57). And if the Gentiles in Galatia have the Spirit, which is the blessing promised to Abraham in Christ, they have the sign that they are members of the descendants of Abraham.

What is noteworthy in the letter thus far is that Paul alludes to two aspects of Judaism that are also related to the major traditions about Abraham found in Jewish texts mentioned above: faith and law. Paul has argued forcefully against the Law. The Gentiles have received the blessing of Abraham, the Spirit, solely according to their faith. If the opponents are using Abraham in their arguments to convince the Gentiles that they must be obedient to the Mosaic law, especially with regard to circumcision, it would seem that they are aware of the tradition of Abraham's obedience to the Law and are making use of that tradition (see also Hansen, 172).

5.1.2.2. Galatians 3:15-18. Paul begins this section by referring to an everyday example, namely, a person's testament or will, which is neither annulled nor added to once it has been ratified. Paul uses this example to discuss Abraham by showing that the promises, originally made to Abraham and his seed (Gal 3:16), were made not to many but to one, which actually refers to Christ (Gen 12:7; 22:17-18). Paul plays upon the word *seed,* which, in Hebrew and Greek (Heb *zera*ʿ; Gk *sperma*), is a collective singular (Ellis, 73). The one descendant, Christ, represents not only the fulfillment of the promises to Abraham (Gal 3:8, 14) but also the head of the spiritual race and, subsequently, the solidarity of believers. Gentiles, who were formerly considered to be outside of the descendants of Abraham, are now included within the realm of his descendants by virtue of their faith in Christ.

Paul next argues from a chronological standpoint. The Law came 430 years after the covenant that God ratified with Abraham (Gal 3:17); in fact the Law was "added" (Gal 3:19). God's promise to Abraham is foundational and unchanging (Gal 3:16, 18). Those who are children of Abraham "in Christ" benefit from the promise and inheritance he received before the coming of the Law.

If the opponents of Paul in Galatia are using the popular tradition that Abraham obeyed the Law (see above), the opponents must also have argued that Abraham was obedient to the Law before it was given by Moses. If this was the example of Abraham that the opponents were giving to the believers in Galatia, Paul must argue forcefully that the Mosaic law came after the promise had been made to Abraham. If the Mosaic law arrived centuries after the promise to Abraham, then Abraham could not have been obedient to that law. This new chronology (overturning the principle of eternal law as found, for example, in Jubilees) establishes the priority of Paul's gospel of justification by faith over the opponents' insistence of obedience to the Law.

5.1.2.3. Galatians 3:19-22. In this section Paul addresses the reasons why law was necessary (Gal 3:19). It was added because of transgressions until the offspring (Christ) should come to whom the promises had been made (Gal 3:19; cf. Gal 3:16). According to Paul, God gave Abraham this inheritance directly through promise: "For if the inheritance is based on Law, it does not come from the promise; but God granted it to Abraham through the promise" (Gal 3:18). Paul states that the Law, however, was "ordained through angels by means of a mediator" (Gal 3:19). The giving of the Law by angels was a common Jewish tradition (LXX Deut 33:2; LXX Ps 67:18; *Jub.* 2:2; *1 Enoch* 60:1; also NT, Acts 7:38, 53; Heb 2:2). Paul deviates from the tradition in that he argues that the giving of the Law by angels is taken as a point against the Law, which becomes clear in the next verse.

In Galatians 3:20 Paul makes a statement that has long puzzled interpreters of Galatians: "but the mediator is not one, but God is one." The plurality associated with the "mediator" has been understood in several ways (Longenecker, 141-42). Interpreters have searched for Paul's exact referent in his allusion to the plurality of angels who served as mediators involved in giving the Law (cf. Wright for the view that Moses is the mediator). But this is to miss Paul's overall point. The most important item to glean from Paul's statement is that somehow the Law coming through angels via the agency of a mediator implies more than one intermediary in contrast to God, who gave the promise to Abraham and who is one. In reference to Jewish monotheism of the day, this kind of statement, which contrasts the oneness of God who gave the promise to Abraham with the plurality of intermediaries through whom the Law was given, clearly demonstrates again the superiority of the promise to Abraham over the Law (*see* God).

It was noted above that popular traditions of Abraham found in Jewish literature included the notion that Abraham was the first monotheist and that he obeyed the Law before it was given. If these traditions were also held by Paul's opponents, their appeal to the example of Abraham probably had something to do with his monotheism and obedience to law. In Galatians 3:20, using the opponents' contentions and the popular traditions that linked Abraham to monotheism and law, Paul demonstrates that the Law is second-rate when compared with God's promises to Abraham. Consequently, if the promises are superior to the Law, and if it is through the promises to Abraham that the inheritance comes to those united in Christ (the "one" seed, Gal 3:16), the Law becomes superfluous. Not only does being a descendant of Abraham no longer mean that one has to follow Jewish law, but also obedience to the Law, which is based upon a plurality, is now a contradiction of the oneness of God.

5.1.2.4. Galatians 3:23-29. In this section Paul uses the example of the *paidagōgos* (NRSV "disciplinarian") to explain the function of the Law. The use of a *paidagōgos* was a prevalent custom in Paul's day. It entailed placing one's child or children under the care or oversight of a trusted slave until the child reached late adolescence. Just what Paul had in mind when he related the *paidagōgos* to the Law has been much debated. Rather than viewing the *paidagōgos* in terms of severity, as had previously been the case (Betz, 177-78), more recently scholars have concentrated upon positive aspects of the *paidagōgos*. For example, the guardianship of the *paidagōgos* protected the charge from outside immoral influences (Young, Gordon). In Galatians 3:24 Paul associates the Law with the *paidagōgos*, which functioned "until Christ came, in order that we might be justified by faith" (Gal 3:24). Once faith came, the *paidagōgos* was no longer necessary (Gal 3:25).

Jewish literature testifies that one of the primary functions of the Law was that it served to separate and protect Israel from its Gentile neighbors (*Jub.* 20:6-10; 21:21-24; 22:16-19; Josephus *Ant.* 1.10.5 §192). The Law also functioned to identify the Jews (*Quaest. in Gen.* 3.49; cf. *Jub.* 15:26). In the context of Paul's letter to the Galatians he speaks primarily of those aspects of the Law that were especially known to identify the Jewish people (circumcision, food laws, and the observation of the sabbath and festival days). One way that the Law functioned as a *paidagōgos* was to guard the Jewish people from outside influences of idolatry and immorality. Paul says that now that faith has come, the Law is no longer necessary. The Law as a protective device in a community like the one at Galatia, where Gentile and Jewish Christians exist side by side, is obsolete because they all have faith and belong to the same community "in Christ" (Gal 3:26). Separation by means of the Law is now unnecessary. Additionally, the identifying symbol of circumcision is no longer necessary. All the believers in Galatia were now one in Christ Jesus (Gal 3:28). Because the believers in Galatia are one by virtue of their faith in Christ, they are Abraham's descendants and heirs of the promise made to him (Gal 3:29; cf. Gal 3:8).

5.1.2.5. Galatians 4:1-11. In Galatians 4:1-2 Paul uses the imagery of an heir who, as a child, is under "guardians and trustees" until the date set by his father. Paul is probably referring to practices in Roman law in which guardians were appointed over a minor by the father either in a will or in a court of law (Belleville, 63). The father could also stipulate the age at which the child would no longer be under such guardians. Paul asserts the temporary nature of the Law, and it is apparent that the heir is not in control of his own affairs. In this sense the heir is no better than a slave.

It is the minors, probably Jews (cf. Gal 3:23, 25; 4:1-2; Longenecker, 165), who were enslaved to the "elements of the world" *(stoicheia tou kosmou).* However, now that the "fullness of time has come" (Gal 4:4; cf. Gal 4:2) Gentiles and Jews are heirs, the Spirit being proof that they are no longer slaves (Gal 4:6-7).

In Galatians 4:8 Paul addresses the Gentiles alone. In the previous age they neither knew God nor were they recognized by God. They were enslaved by things that by nature "were not gods." The phrase "were not gods" is a familiar one in Septuagintal literature where it refers to idols (2 Chron 13:9-10; Is 37:18-19; Jer 2:11-28). Paul accuses them of returning to their former idolatry (Gal 4:9).

In the context of the situation in Galatia, these Gentile believers are being persuaded to obey different aspects of Jewish law (Gal 5:2-3; 6:12-13; 4:10). Paul compares their obedience to the Law with their former idolatry (Gal 4:8-9) and their enslavement under the "elements of the world." Obedience to the Law and idolatry are forms of enslavement under these "elements of the world." Obedience to the Law has become tantamount to idolatry.

It was noted above that in Jewish traditions about Abraham he was portrayed as believing in the one Creator God in contrast to other gods or philosophies. Most often Jews who spoke of the faith of Abraham thought of it as faith in the one God in contrast to idolatry (*Jub.* 11:16-17; 12:2-8, 16-24; Pseudo-Philo *Bib. Ant.* 6:4; 23:5; Philo *Abr.* 68-71; *Apoc. Abr.* 1-8). For Paul, Jewish and Gentile believers are now true children of Abraham (Gal 3:29; 4:6-7). As such they are no longer to be enslaved to the elements of the world, which formerly functioned as Gentile paganism and Jewish law. In equating the observance of the Law with idolatry, Paul makes the Law the ultimate taboo for a true child of Abraham. Like Abraham, who rejected idolatry, these children of Abraham are to avoid idolatry. In Galatians 4:1-10, however, now that these children of Abraham have a new identity "in Christ," the idolatry to be avoided is obedience to the Law.

5.1.2.6. Galatians 4:21—5:1. Paul's final discourse on Abrahamic descendants is found in his allegory of Sarah and Hagar (Gal 4:21—5:1). Paul's apparently arbitrary exegesis in this allegory may indicate that this was not his choice of text (Gen 16:15; 21:2-12) but that it was being used by his opponents to their advantage (Lincoln, 12; Barclay, 91). Paul constructs the allegory around the literal sons of Abraham, Isaac and Ishmael. Hagar is interpreted to represent the covenant of slavery, the Law (Gal 4:24-25). Sarah is interpreted to represent the covenant of freedom (Gal 4:24, 26). Anyone (even those at Jerusalem, Gal 4:25) who is in bondage to the Law (Gal 4:24) is enslaved and will not inherit with the true children. The children of promise, who are born of Isaac (Gal 4:28), are members of the heavenly Jerusalem (Gal 4:26) and are more numerous than those in bondage (Gal 4:27).

Paul concludes the allegory in Galatians 4:28—5:1. He identifies the Galatians as being like Isaac, the children of promise (Gal 4:28). At the present time the persecution they are experiencing is like that which Isaac experienced at the hand of Ishmael (Gen 21:9; Gal 4:29; see also Betz, 249-50). Paul uses Genesis 21:10 as instruction for the present: the Galatians who are being persecuted for not being obedient to the Law are to "cast out" those who are persecuting them (Gal 4:30; Lincoln, 22-29). They are children of the free woman; Christ has set them free from the Law. They are commanded not to submit again to the Law, the "yoke of slavery" (Gal 5:1; see also Gal 4:3, 9).

5.2. Romans. Most of the discussion of Abraham is found in Romans 4, where Paul uses the patriarch to show how Gentiles as well as Jews can now be righteous before God by virtue of their faith in Jesus Christ. In Romans 9—11 Paul again refers to Abraham in order to show how God's promises to his chosen people have not failed (Rom 9:6).

5.2.1. The Situation in Rome. Paul's purpose in writing Romans has been a matter of debate (Donfried). It is likely that the house churches (Rom 16:5, 10-11, 14-15) to which Paul writes were influenced to some degree by the Jewish community (Dunn, xlvi-xlvii; Calvert 1993) and struggled over the relationship Gentile Christians now had with God (Rom 4:2, 11-12), especially in light of practices related to Jewish law (Rom 14:2, 5, 6, 21; Wedderburn, 33-34).

5.2.2. The Text in Light of Abrahamic Traditions.

5.2.2.1. Romans 1:1—3:26. After his section of thanksgiving and travel plans (Rom 1:8-15), Paul announces his thesis statement, proclaiming that the gospel is the "power of God for salvation to everyone who has faith," both Jew and Greek (Rom 1:16), and that through faith in this gospel the righteousness of God is revealed (Rom 1:17; Ziesler, 186-87). In Romans 1:1—3:20 Paul shows that idolatrous and immoral Gentiles (Rom 1:18-32; cf. *Jub.* 22:11-23; *1 Enoch* 91:7-10; although Jews may be idolaters implicitly, see Hays, 93-94), and Jews who boast in their relationship to God and the Law (Rom 2:1-29, esp. Rom 2:17), are condemned before God (Rom 3:9-20).

In Romans 3:21-26 Paul shows how God has continued to be righteous, but now apart from the Law (Rom 3:21; cf. Rom 1:17). Participation in the realm of the righteousness of God (Ziesler, 186-87) is now to be found through faith in Jesus Christ for Jew and Gentile (Rom 3:22): there is no distinction.

5.2.2.2. Romans 3:27—4:25. Romans 3:27—4:25 functions as a clarification of what Paul has already discussed and as an introduction to the example of faith provided by Abraham. Paul uses the principle of Jewish monotheism against a common contention of Jewish particularism. Because God is one, he is the God of Jews and Gentiles (Rom 3:29). And because God is one, he justifies Jews and Gentiles on the basis of the same criterion—faith (Rom 3:30). Jews and Gentiles then have equal access to salvation. "This is, in effect, an argument against the law as being in any way necessary for salvation" (Sanders 1977, 489). Through his example of Abraham, Paul will show how his interpretation upholds the Law (Rom 3:31).

Paul first identifies Abraham in a strictly Jewish sense as "our forefather according to the flesh" (Rom 4:1) and asks what it was that Abraham "found" (the verb is *heuriskō*). Several traditions of Abraham depicted him finding the one God (see above; especially Philo *Abr.* 68-71 and Josephus *Ant.* 1.7.1 §§154-57, where he discerns God's existence from the creation). It is generally held that Paul in Romans 1:18-32 is indebted to the Hellenistic Jewish thought that lies behind Wisdom 12—15, if not to that text itself (Dunn, 56-57; Calvert 1993). Wisdom 13:6-9 speaks of people seeking to find *(heuriskō)* God. Additional texts that refer to people "finding" God through intellectual discovery are also present in the LXX (Is 55:6; 65:1), the works of Philo *(Spec. Leg.* 1.36; *Leg. All.* 3.47) and the NT (Acts 17:26-27; Rom 10:20). In Romans 4:17 Paul also refers to Abraham as believing in God the Creator. This belief in the one God as the Creator was foundational to Jewish monotheism. Only if the God of the Jews was the Creator was he the one true God (cf. *Sib. Or.* Fr. 1.7). In the context of idolatry in Romans 1, in his use of "one God" in proving that Jew and Gentile are justified by faith (Rom 3:29-30) and in his introduction of the example of Abraham, it might be assumed that he expects his readers to assume he will speak of Abraham, who "found" the one true Creator God. But Paul has a different topic in mind, which he will reveal in his subsequent discussion.

Someone who was familiar with the traditions of Abraham might also be familiar with the tradition of his obedience to the law before it was given to Moses. Paul foresees this interpretation in his statement in Romans 4:2: "For if Abraham was justified by works, he has something to boast about, but not before God." Paul already used the term for boasting to describe the boasting by the Jews in reference to their perceived privileged status (Rom 2:17, 23; 3:27). Abraham, who was understood to have been obedient to the Law before it was given and who represented the ideal Jew, could indeed boast—but not before God (Rom 4:2).

Paul proves why it is that Abraham cannot boast in his works before God by citing Genesis 15:6, "Abraham believed God and it was reckoned to him as righteousness." Abraham becomes a paradigmatic type of how it is that God makes human beings righteous (Sanders 1983, 33). In clarifying what he means by "reckoned" Paul uses the analogy of one who works and to whom wages are paid, not as a gift but as what is due (Rom 4:4), in contrast to one who believes in him who justifies the ungodly (Rom 4:5). All of this is given in order that Paul may answer his first question about what Abraham found. Through his faith Abraham found grace (Rom 4:4; cf. Gen 18:3; 30:27; 32:5; 33:8, 10, 15; 34:11; 39:4; 47:25, 29; 50:4).

In Romans 4:9-12 Paul shows how Abraham is the father of the Jews (circumcised) and the Gentiles (uncircumcised). The figure of Abraham was connected with circumcision in the Jewish world because Abraham was the first to participate in the covenant of circumcision (Gen 17:9-14; Sir 44:20). Referring to the "blessed" whose sins are forgiven (Rom 4:7-8; cf. Ps 32:1-2), Paul asks whether this blessedness is "pronounced on the circumcised alone, or also upon the uncircumcised?" (Rom 4:9). In order to answer the question Paul begins by paraphrasing Genesis 15:6: It was Abraham's faith that resulted in God's forgiveness because Abraham as a result of his faith was reckoned righteous. Through further rhetorical questions in Romans 4:10-12 Paul proves that Abraham was reckoned righteous while he was uncircumcised (Rom 4:10; cf. Gen 15:6, Gen 17). For Paul, circumcision was a seal of the righteousness Abraham had by faith while he was yet uncircumcised (Rom 4:11). Thus Abraham is the father of all those who believe who are not circumcised and who are reckoned righteous (Gentiles; Rom 4:11), and of those who are not only circumcised but who also follow the example of the faith of Abraham while he was still uncircumcised (Jews; Rom 4:12). Whereas circumcision once marked one as a descendant of Abraham (Gen 17:9-14), Paul has shown that by virtue of their common faith in Christ, Gentiles and Jews have Abraham as their father.

Paul's concern in Romans 4:13-17 is the promise to Abraham and his seed. He states that the promise did not come through the Law but through the "righteousness of faith" (Rom 4:13). What Abraham was to inherit here, as in other Jewish literature, was not just the land of promise but the world (Rom 4:14; Sir 44:21; *Jub.* 17:3; 22:14; 32:19; Philo *Som.* 1.175; Dunn, 213). The necessity of the Law for the Jewish people was a major part of their identity. Paul is refuting the idea that in order to be an heir of the promise of Abraham, one has to be Jewish in terms of obedience to the Mosaic Law. Paul further states that if "those of the Law" *(hoi ek nomou)* are the heirs, then "faith is empty and the promise is nullified" (Rom 4:14). According to Dunn the phrase should be taken to mean those who saw their continuing existence as Jews arising out of the Law, which determined all that was characteristic and distinctive in all that they were and did as God's people (Dunn, 213-14). If those who identify themselves as the people of God by their obedience to the Law are heirs, then faith is empty because it is not the basis for the inheritance. Additionally, the Law brings wrath and reveals transgression (Rom 4:15).

Most Jews would have seen the function of the Law in a positive light as that which identified them and separated them from other nations. Instead, Paul here points out negative functions of the Law. Paul gives a further reason why the promise must be according to faith: the promise must be according to grace so that it may be guaranteed to all the descendants of Abraham. It is not only for those Christians who identify themselves as the people of God by virtue of their obedience to the Law (Rom 4:16) but also for those Christians who share the faith of Abraham who is the "father of many nations" (Rom 4:17; 12:3). Abraham is not merely the father of the chosen nation Israel.

Abraham's faith is described by two familiar phrases from Jewish literature (Rom 4:17). Abraham's faith was in God's creative ability to call into being that which existed from that which did not exist (2 Apoc. Bar. 21:4; 48:8; Philo Rer. Div. Her. 36; Spec. Leg. 4.187; 2 Macc 7:28). And Abraham had faith in the God "who gives life to the dead" (Rom 4:17). This description of God was also popular in Judaism, as is attested by its use to describe the conversion of Gentiles (Jos. and As. 27:10). However, in Romans 4:18-22 Paul explains Abraham's faith in the God who gave life to the dead by referring to the Genesis narrative. Abraham's faith in God's promise that he would become the father of many nations (Rom 4:18; Gen 15:5) did not weaken even when he considered his own body which was already "as good as dead" (impotent; Rom 4:19) or when he considered that Sarah's womb was "dead." Paul is describing Abraham's faith in God (Rom 4:21) and his promise of offspring (Rom 4:20) in spite of the physical incapability on the part of the marriage partners, himself and Sarah. Therefore it was written that Abraham's faith was "reckoned to him as righteousness" (Rom 4:21; cf. Gen 15:6), not for the sake of Abraham alone but for the sake of Paul and his readers as well (Rom 4:23-24). Faith will be reckoned as righteousness to those who believe in him who raised Jesus Christ from the dead, who was handed over to death for their trespasses and raised for their justification (Rom 4:25).

The monotheistic faith of Abraham that was so central in Jewish tradition has been transformed by Paul. The faith of believers who follow after the faith of Abraham is now in the one creator God who raised Jesus Christ from the dead so that they too could be made righteous.

5.2.2.3. Romans 9—11. In Romans 9—11 Paul proceeds generally to show how it is that God's word to Israel has not failed (Rom 9:6). The foundational patriarch Paul uses in his discussion is Abraham (Rom 9:3-9; 11:1). Paul's first point in his argument is that God's word has not failed because "not all of Abraham's children are his true descendants" (Rom 9:7). For proof he cites Genesis 21:12: "through Isaac descendants will be named for you." Paul further clarifies in Romans 9:8 that the children of the flesh (all ethnic Jews) are not the children of God, but the children of promise are reckoned as the descendants of Abraham (see Israel).

By using Genesis 21:12 Paul is making the point that the Jewish Christians at Rome already know that ethnic descent from Abraham is not the same as being his true descendant. It was through Isaac that Abraham's true descendants were named (cf. Rom 9:10, 13). Neither Ishmael nor the sons of Keturah (Gen 25:1-4) were counted as the true descendants of Abraham. According to Paul's proof, this is because Isaac was the descendant of the promise of God. To further support his argument Paul includes the promise from the angel to Abraham, "About this time I will return and Sarah will have a son" (Rom 9:9; Gen 18:10). Neither Hagar nor Keturah was the woman through whom the promise was actualized. Only Sarah, whose childbearing years were long over (Rom 4:19), was the woman through whom God fulfilled his promise of a descendant to Abraham.

Paul's final use of Abraham in Romans occurs in Romans 11:1, where he calls himself "an Israelite, a descendant of Abraham." In view of Paul's previous discussion about the definition of a true descendant of Abraham (Rom 4:13-18; 9:7-8), it is reasonable to assume that here Paul is not simply referring to his ethnic Jewish heritage. Paul continues to argue that God's word has not failed (Rom 9:6) by showing that the stumbling of Israel has brought salvation to the Gentiles (Rom 11:11-13), who have been grafted into the people of God because of their faith (Rom 11:20). In Paul's argument, "hardening" has come upon a part of Israel, and in their present unbelief (Rom 11:29) ethnic Jews have been broken off (Rom 11:20). The Jews, however, can be grafted back into the olive tree (Rom 11:24). This leads Paul to state that with respect to the gospel, ethnic Jews are enemies, but with respect to their election they are beloved "for the sake of their fathers" (Rom 11:28). In this case Paul gives evidence of knowing the tradition of Abraham's ethnic descendants receiving special consideration (*Bib. Ant.* 30:7; 35:3). God's original word has not failed (Rom 9:6). Ethnic Jews will also be among the true descendants of Abraham once again, not by virtue of their identity found in obedience to the Law but by reason of their faith. This faith will be after the example of Abraham's faith (Rom 4:17-25), a faith that has been deepened from its starting point in Jewish monotheism to incorporate faith in Jesus Christ (*see* God).

5.3. 2 Corinthians. In 2 Corinthians 11:22 Paul, in response to the boasts of his opponents in Corinth, calls himself a descendant of Abraham. Most scholars agree that by designating himself a "descendant of Abraham" Paul has more in mind than ethnic derivation. For example, R. P. Martin suggests that Paul is using the term for himself "as a badge of honor to mark out his Christian self-identity over against his rivals" (Martin, 375).

6. Hebrews.
Abraham functions in the letter to the Hebrews as the prototype of faithful endurance that the believing readers are to emulate.

6.1. Hebrews 2:14-16. In the context of showing how the Son of God has solidarity with the human family by virtue of having become one of them (Heb 2:14), the author of Hebrews first uses the figure of Abraham to identify those whom Jesus Christ came to liberate (Heb 2:15-16). Those who are now called descendants of Abraham are those who are of the faithful remnant (cf. Is 41:8-10), oppressed men and women of whom Jesus takes hold to deliver from the bondage to Satan and to bring them under the authority of the exalted Son.

6.2. Hebrews 6:13-20. In this passage God's promise of descendants to Abraham (Heb 6:13-15; Gen 12:2-3; 15:5; 17:5) is brought to the fore. The author repeats a phrase from the sacrifice of Isaac concerning an oath God swore "by himself" (Heb 6:13; Gen 22:16) because there was no one greater by whom God could swear (Heb 6:16-17) in order to guarantee the promise. The

author reminds the readers of the popular tradition of the binding of Isaac, reinforcing the portrayal of Abraham as the prototype of faithful endurance (Heb 6:15) who in obedience was willing to sacrifice his only son, thereby receiving God's promises. The exposition provides an example for the addressees to emulate in the expectation that they will receive what God has promised them because their high priest, Jesus Christ, has already obtained the promises and is a forerunner on their behalf (Heb 6:19-20).

6.3. Hebrews 7:1-10. Within his broader goal of proving that Jesus' priestly office is greater than the levitical priesthood, the writer interprets the account of Abraham and Melchizedek (Gen 14:17-20; cf. Ps 110:4) in order to show how Melchizedek is greater than Abraham and the levitical priests (Heb 7:7). His proof lies in the account of Abraham the exalted patriarch (Heb 7:4) giving Melchizedek a tenth of the spoils of war (Gen 14:20). Because the levitical priests received tithes (cf. Lev 18:21; Num 18:26-28; Neh 10:38-39; Josephus *Ant.* 20.9.8 §181; 20.9.2 §206-7; Josephus *Life* 15 §80) and because Abraham represented the Levites as the progenitor of Israel, this fact signifies that Levi was tithing to Melchizedek (Acts 7:5-6, 8-10), who is thereby even greater than Israel's progenitor. It is not clear in Genesis who gave tithes to whom, but the author of Hebrews reflects the tradition that Abraham was the one who tithed (cf. 1QapGen 22:17; Josephus *Ant.* 1.10.2 §181). The author further provides a contrast between Abraham, who received promises (Acts 7:6), and the Levites, who received their office according to the law (Acts 7:5). For the author, promise connotes something effective and certain (see Acts 6:13), while the Law implied that which was ineffective. Thus the contrast between Melchizedek and the Levitical priests heightens Melchizedek's priesthood because the levitical priests collected tithes according to law while Melchizedek received tithes from and blessed the one to whom God had made promises (Acts 7:6) and to whom he is superior (Acts 7:7).

6.4. Hebrews 11:8-12, 17-19. In this chapter the author employs Abraham more than any other figure as an example of faith. Abraham first exemplifies his faith by his obedience to God's call (Heb 11:8; Gen 12:1-2; cf. Gen 15:7; Neh 9:7; Acts 7:2-8; Philo *Abr.* 60, 62, 85, 88).

Abraham's sojourn as an alien indicates his unsettled status as a foreigner, without native and civil rights, "living in tents" (Heb 11:9; Gen 12:8; 13:3; 18:1) as a nomad. His obedience brought not immediate settlement in the promised land but a life of sojourning for himself and his descendants (Heb 11:9) as he looked toward the ultimate goal. For the author of Hebrews that goal was not Canaan but the firmly established city of God (Heb 11:10; cf. Heb 11:1; Ps 48:8; 87:1-3; Is 14:32). Jewish apocalyptic tradition affirms that Abraham saw the heavenly city (*2 Apoc. Bar.* 4:2-5; cf. *4 Ezra* 3:13-14).

Abraham further exemplifies faith through his trust that God would give him a son, even though he and his wife had never produced children and were no longer physically capable of doing so (Heb 11:11-12; cf. Rom 4:19-21; Gen 15:1-6; 17:15-22; 18:9-15). The reliability of God is heightened in the contrast between the singular Abraham and the multitude of his descendants (Heb 11:12; cf. Heb 11:11) in accordance with the promise (Gen 15:5; 22:17; cf. Heb 6:13-15).

Finally, Abraham exemplifies faith through his willingness to sacrifice his only son and fulfillment of promise, Isaac (Heb 11:17-19). This event of Abraham's testing (Sir 44:20; 1 Macc 2:52; see 3.2 above) became central to the Jewish exegetical imagination in postbiblical Judaism (Jub. 17:15-18:19; Philo Abr. 167-297; 4 Macc 7:11-14; 13:12; 16:18-20; Josephus Ant. 1.13.1-4 §222-36; Pseudo-Philo Bib. Ant. 18.5; 23.8; 32.1-4; 40.2-3). Abraham's action was celebrated as a model of faithfulness and obedience to God in the literary tradition of Jewish models of faith (Sir 44:20; Jdt 8:25-26; 1 Macc 2:52; 4 Macc 16:20; cf. Jas 2:21-24; 1 Clem. 10.7). Details in the presentation in Hebrews suggest that the author was influenced by this tradition.

The tense and sacrificial nuance of the verb *offered* (*prospherō*, Heb 11:17) suggests that in some sense the sacrifice was an accomplished event because of Abraham's intention (Philo *Abr.* 177; Pseudo-Philo *Bib. Ant.* 32.4; Swetnam, 122). The second use of the verb (Heb 11:17, the second part of the verse) indicates that Abraham did not make the sacrifice but was interrupted by God's intervention. Jewish tradition refers to blood that was shed during the sacrifice; because of this God chose Abraham and his family (Pseudo-Philo *Bib. Ant.* 18.5-6), perhaps implying that the blood had some kind of atoning value.

The author's reference to Genesis 21:12 (Heb 11:18) and subsequent reference to God

raising "someone from the dead" (Heb 11:19; cf. *Pirqe R. El.* 31) simultaneously refers to Hebrews 11:12, where Abraham is said to be as "good as dead" in reference to procreation. The implication is that Abraham had faith that God was able to raise someone from the dead—namely, Isaac—through procreation and his salvation from sacrifice. The Christian readers would also see the sacrifice of Isaac as a foreshadowing of God's raising Jesus from the dead. From this they could derive faith in the God who is faithful to his promises (Swetnam, 122-23, 128).

6.5. Hebrews 13:1-2. The author reminds his readers that they are to have the attitude of welcoming fellow Christians who are strangers. Hospitality was a mark not only of one who was cultured but also of Christians, who met in the homes of others. Hospitality was necessary especially in regard to itinerant preachers. In the Christian community the guest/host relationship attained an almost sacramental quality as they expected that God would play a significant role in the exchange between guests and hosts (Lane, 512). Abraham, who was known for his hospitality (*1 Clem.* 31; *T. Abr.* 1:1-3A; Philo *Abr.* 107-10; Josephus *Ant.* 1.11.2 §196), is alluded to in reference to his meeting with the three visitors to his tent at Mamre, when he and his wife received the promise of the birth of their son, Isaac (Heb 13:1-2; Gen 18:1-21; 1 Clem. 10.7).

7. James and 1 Peter.

7.1. James 2:21-24. Abraham, known for his exemplary faith (see 3.4 above), was also revered for his obedience to God for his willingness to sacrifice Isaac (see 3.2 above), which was a story popular in Jewish circles (see 3.4 above). James 2:21-24 brings these two traditions together; Abraham becomes the example of one who completes his faith by his works.

Because James 2:21 implies that Abraham was justified (*dikaioō*) by works and that sounds as if it contradicts statements by Paul about justification (cf. Gal 2:15-16; Rom 3:22) by faith alone, a few observations must be made. First, the sense in which *dikaioō* is used in James is in reference to Abraham's demonstrated faithfulness, perhaps in reference to the theme of testings (Jas 1:2, 12). Thus God declares Abraham "righteous" or "faithful." The sense in which Paul uses *dikaioō* refers to the eschatological act in which God declares sinners rightly related to himself. Paul then can say that Abraham was made righteous by faith (Gal 3:6-9; Rom 4:22). Furthermore, the sense of "works" in the two letters is different. In James it refers to acts of obedience and compassion that should arise out of faith in Christ (Jas 2:14-17), which complete faith. The works (as in "works of the law") against which Paul builds his polemic of Abraham's becoming righteous by faith alone are those markers (e.g. circumcision) that formerly identified the people of God and that are still being used by some to identify the people of God in Christ. Paul uses Abraham as an example of righteousness by faith because he is contending with those who would undermine the foundation of his gospel.

7.2. 1 Peter 3:4-5. Within the context of a household code the focus is on Sarah, whose example the readers are to emulate. It is surprising that the author did not reflect the situation of the OT account, in which Sarah laughs at the promise of a son, saying that her "lord" is too old (Gen 18:12).

Many of the *women reading the letter would have had unbelieving husbands. It is through their demeanor that they are to bring their husbands to the gospel (1 Pet 3:1-2). The principle is that one influences a spouse by modest behavior worthy of respect. In the culture of the time this meant that wives were to defer to the authority of their husbands.

See also GALATIANS, LETTER TO THE; JUDAISM AND THE NEW TESTAMENT; ROMANS, LETTER TO THE.

DPL: CIRCUMCISION; FAITH; GENTILES; JUDAIZERS; OLD TESTAMENT IN PAUL; WORKS OF THE LAW. *DLNTD:* ANCESTORS; MOSES; PROMISE.

BIBLIOGRAPHY. H. W. Attridge, *Hebrews* (Herm; Philadelphia: Fortress, 1989); W. Baird, "Abraham in the New Testament: Tradition and the New Identity," *Int* 42 (1988) 367-79; J. Barclay, *Obeying the Truth: A Study of Paul's Ethics in Galatians* (Edinburgh: T & T Clark, 1988); J. C. Beker, *Paul the Apostle: The Triumph of God in Life and Thought* (Philadelphia: Fortress, 1980); L. L. Belleville, " 'Under Law': Structural Analysis and the Pauline Concept of Law in Galatians 3:21—4:11," *JSNT* 26 (1986) 53-78; H. D. Betz, *Galatians: A Commentary on Paul's Letter to the Churches in Galatia* (Philadelphia: Fortress, 1979); R. E. Brown, *The Gospel According to John (I-XII)* (AB 29A; Garden City, NY: Doubleday, 1985); B. Byrne, *Son of God, Seed of Abraham: A Study of the Idea of the Sonship of God of All Christians in Paul Against the Jewish Background* (Rome: Biblical Institute, 1979); N. L. Calvert, "Abraham and Idolatry: Paul's Comparison of Obedience to the Law to Idolatry in Galatians 4:1-10," in *Paul and the Scriptures of Israel,* ed. C. A. Evans and J. A. Sanders (JSNTSup 83; Sheffield: JSOT, 1992); idem, *Paul, Monotheism and the People of God: The Significance of Abraham for Early Jewish and Christian Identity* (T&T International, forthcoming); idem, "Traditions of Abraham in Middle Jewish Literature: Implications for the Interpretation of Paul's Epistles to the Galatians and to the Romans" (Ph.D. diss., University of Sheffield, 1993); N. A. Dahl, "The Story of Abraham in Luke-Acts," in *Studies in Luke-Acts: Essays Presented in Honor of Paul Schubert,* ed. L. E. Keck and J. L. Martyn (Nashville: Abingdon, 1966) 139-58; W. D. Davies and D. C. Allison Jr., *The Gospel According to Saint Matthew* (ICC; Edinburgh: T & T Clark, 1988) vol. 1; K. P. Donfried, ed., *The Romans Debate* (rev. ed.; Peabody, MA: Hendrickson, 1991); J. D. G. Dunn, *Romans 1—8* (WBC 38A; Dallas: Word, 1988); W. E. E. Ellis, *Paul's Use of the Old Testament* (Edinburgh: Oliver & Boyd, 1957); J. A. Fitzmyer, *The Gospel According to Luke* (AB 28A, 28B; Garden City, NY: Doubleday, 1981, 1985); J. B. Green, "Jesus and a Daughter of Abraham (Luke 13:10-17): Test Case for a Lucan Perspective on Jesus' Miracles," *CBQ* 51 (1989) 643-54; T. D. Gordon, "A Note on PAIDAGOGOS in Galatians 3:24-25," *NTS* 35 (1989) 150-54; G. W. Hansen, *Abraham in Galatians: Epistolary and Rhetorical Contexts* (Sheffield: JSOT, 1989); R. B. Hays, *Echoes of Scripture in the Letters of Paul* (New Haven, CT: Yale University Press, 1989); W. L. Lane, *Hebrews* (2 vols.; WBC; Dallas: Word, 1991); A. T. Lincoln, "Abraham Goes to Rome: Paul's Treatment of Abraham in Romans 4," in *Worship, Theology and Ministry in the Early Church,* ed. M. J. Wilkins and T. Paige (JSNTSup 87; Sheffield: JSOT, 1992); W. P. Loewe, "Towards an Interpretation of Luke 19:1-10," *CBQ* 36 (1974) 321-31; R. N. Longenecker, *Galatians* (WBC 41; Dallas: Word, 1990); I. H. Marshall, *Commentary on Luke* (NIGTC; Grand Rapids: Eerdmans, 1978); R. P. Martin, *2 Corinthians* (WBC 40; Waco, TX: Word, 1986); E. P. Sanders, *Paul and Palestinian Judaism* (Philadelphia: Fortress, 1977); idem, *Paul, the Law, and the Jewish People* (Philadelphia: Fortress, 1983); J. Swetnam, *Jesus and Isaac: A Study of the Epistle to the Hebrews in Light of the Aqedah* (Rome: Biblical Institute Press, 1981); D. S. Wallace-Hadrill, "A

Suggested Exegesis of Matthew 3:9, 10 (= Luke 3:8, 9)," *ExpT* 62 (1950-51) 349; R. B. Ward, "Abraham Traditions in Early Christianity," in *Studies on the Testament of Abraham*, ed. G. W. E. Nickelsburg Jr. (SCS 6; Missoula, MT: Scholars Press, 1976) 173-84; A. J. M. Wedderburn, *The Reasons for Romans* (Minneapolis: Fortress, 1991); N. T. Wright, "The Seed and the Mediator: Galatians 3:15-20," in *The Climax of the Covenant* (Minneapolis: Fortress, 1991) 157-74; N. H. Young, "*Paidagōgos*: The Social Setting of a Pauline Metaphor," *NovT* 29.2 (1987) 150-76; J. A. Ziesler, *Paul's Letter to the Romans* (London: SCM, 1989); C. H. Zorrilla, "The Magnificat: Song of Justice," in *Conflict and Context: Hermeneutics in the Americas*, ed. M. L. Branson and C. R. Padilla (Grand Rapids: Eerdmans, 1986) 220-37.   N. Calvert-Koyzis

ACTS OF THE APOSTLES

The Acts of the Apostles is the fifth book in the NT canon, located between collections of Gospels and letters. Although it is not the first Christian or NT document to have incorporated an interest in narrative history, together with the Gospel of *Luke it is the earliest example of Christian historiography.

    1. Genre of Acts
    2. Text of Acts
    3. Speeches in Acts
    4. Narrative Unity of Luke-Acts
    5. Theology and Purpose of Acts

1. Genre of Acts

Particularly because of the content of Acts as well as the nature of the prefaces to Luke-Acts (Lk 1:1-4; Acts 1:1-3; cf. Josephus *Ag. Ap.* 1.1 §§1-5; 2.1 §§1-2), Acts has long been understood as the first example of Christian historiography. Following the influential work of H. J. Cadbury early in the twentieth century, study of Acts has until recently identified the work within the genre of ancient historiography. Questions about the historical veracity of the narrative of Acts, combined with ongoing reassessments of Acts within the context of the literature of Jewish and Greco-Roman antiquity, have opened to a lively discussion the problem of the genre of Acts. Consequently Acts has been located within each of the three primary genres of the Roman world—historiography, the novel and biography.

1.1. Acts: Novel? Biography? Scientific Treatise? Ancient Historiography? Those scholars with doubts about the classification of Acts as historiography have tended to maximize the formal discrepancies between the Lukan prefaces and those of Hellenistic historiography, contended that the preface to the Third Gospel does not intend the narrative of Acts and/or argued that because Acts is not reliable as a historical account it should not be seen as an example of the genre of ancient historiography.

R. I. Pervo, for example, maintains that Acts is an ancient historical novel written with the purpose of entertaining and edifying its readers. In making his case Pervo caricatures some of the more radical studies of Acts (e.g., Haenchen) as demonstrating that Luke was a "bumbling and incompetent" historian but a "brilliant and creative" writer. The problem with this characterization of Luke, according to Pervo, is that it wrongly assumes that Acts is intended as history. If one recognizes Acts as historical fiction, he observes, then the impasse is breached and Acts can be read for what it is rather than what it fails to achieve. Pervo correctly acknowledges the humor and wit of Acts but is unable to squeeze all of Acts into the mold demanded by aesthetic delight. Even those formal features that Acts shares with the novel are not peculiar to ancient novels; in his second-century treatise *How to Write History*, Lucian advised historians to give their audiences "what will interest and instruct them" (§53).

Potentially more useful is the identification of (Luke-)Acts as "biography," since ancient biographers, like historians, dealt with people who lived and events that took place. However, the narrative of Acts is manifestly not focused on the performance of one person, so it can hardly be pressed into the biographical genre. C. H. Talbert has tried to overcome this obstacle in his proposal that Luke-Acts is a biographical "succession narrative," analogous to Diogenes Laertius's *Lives of the Philosophers* (mid-third century A.D.). These biographies, he proposes, more or less conform to a threefold format: the life of the founder, a description of the community of his followers and a précis of the teachings of the community in its contemporary form. Accordingly, Luke's first volume, the Third Gospel, highlights the life of Jesus (founder), with Acts concentrating on the deeds and teachings of his followers (*see* Luke, Gospel of). D. E. Aune has criticized this approach, questioning the existence of any such genre and noting the significant discrepancies between the respective functions of Laertius's *Lives* and Acts (Aune, 78-79). Moreover, Luke signals his interest not so much in particular people as in "events" (Lk 1:1-4); and the two parts of Luke's work are held together more basically by the overarching redemptive purpose of God than by the life of one or more individuals, as would be expected in a biography. That Luke has been influenced in his writing by features of the genre of biography is clear even if Acts cannot simply be identified as a specimen of the ancient biographical genre.

A different approach has been followed by L. C. A. Alexander, who draws attention to the formal differences between Luke's preface (Lk 1:1-4) and those of the Greek historiographers. Luke's preface seems too brief, consisting of only one sentence, as compared with the more elaborate openings of Greek historians. The transition from Luke's preface to the narrative is surprisingly abrupt; unlike others, Luke does not engage in explicit criticism of his predecessors. Luke's preface exhibits such a personal style, with its first-person pronouns and dedication, that it has seemed inappropriate for inclusion in the genre of "dispassionate and timeless historiography." And Luke's opening offers no general moral reflections, common among Greek historians. Such problems led Alexander to a reassessment of the literary map of Greek preface writing, with the result that she finds the closest analogues to Luke 1:1-4 and Acts 1:1 in the "scientific tradition"—that is, technical and professional writing on medicine, mathematics, engineering and the like. Alexander proposes that Luke's narrative presentation of Jesus and the early Christian movement is scientific in the sense that it is concerned to pass on the tradition of accumulated teaching on this subject.

The affinities between Luke and the scientific tradition do not negate the identification of Luke 1:1-4 and Luke-Acts with historiography, however. First, that Luke-Acts does not match in every instance the formal features of Greco-Roman historiography presents no immediate problem, for the genre was easily manipulated. What is more, Luke has been influenced as well by OT and Jewish historiography, especially with respect to the use of historical sequences to shape a narrative theology; and Luke's predecessors in Israelite and Jewish historiography did not reflect on their aims and procedures within the context of the writing itself. More-

over, in describing his work as *diēgēsis* ("narrative," Lk 1:1), Luke identifies his project as a long narrative account of many events, for which the chief prototypes were the early Greek histories of Herodotus and Thucydides (cf. Hermogenes *Progymnasmata* 2; Lucian *How to Write History* §55). Further, numerous components of Luke's work—symposia, travel narratives, letters, speeches—support a positive comparison of Luke's work with Greco-Roman historiography.

A number of recent studies have strengthened the earlier consensus that Acts is an example of the genre of ancient historiography. For example, viewing Acts in the context of descriptions of Hellenistic, Israelite and Hellenistic Jewish historiography, Aune concludes that "Luke was an eclectic Hellenistic Christian who narrated the early history of Christianity from its origins in Judaism with Jesus of Nazareth through its emergence as a relatively independent religious movement open to all ethnic groups" (Aune, 138-39); this qualifies Luke-Acts as belonging to the genre of "general history." G. L. Sterling, however, argues that Acts belongs to a type of history whose narratives "relate the story of a particular people by deliberately hellenizing their native traditions" (Sterling, 374). Other subgenres (e.g., historical monograph and political history) have also been proposed. Critical work in historiography has begun to underscore the apologetic role of all historiography (see 1.2 below), and this is the case with Acts, written to defend the unfolding of the divine purpose, from Israel to the life and ministry of Jesus to the early church with its inclusion of Gentile believers as full participants, and thus to legitimate the Christian movement of which Luke was a part.

1.2. Historiography and Historicism. In what sense, though, is it appropriate to refer to the narrative of Acts as history? What are we to make of the denial of Acts as historiography on the basis of its alleged duplicity in historical matters? Two points merit reflection. First, an attempt to present material in the generic framework of historiography is no guarantee of historical veracity; choice of genre and quality of performance are separate issues. Hence, even if more radical critics are correct in their indictments of Acts as poor history, this would not be tantamount to excluding a generic identification of Acts as historiography.

At the same time it must be admitted that

17

such indictments against Luke as a historian are not so firmly based as is sometimes claimed. (1) Although study of Acts as history continues to be plagued by a relative dearth of corroborative evidence, whether literary or physical, recent examination of that evidence by C. J. Hemer has encouraged a much more positive assessment of the historical reliability of Acts (see also Hengel). (2) The sometimes spectacular accounts of healing in Acts (e.g., Acts 5:15-16; 19:11-12) have given some scholars pause in accepting the whole as a historically faithful account. However, in the wake of postmodern epistemology and in light of increasing criticism of the biomedical paradigm for making sense of non-Western accounts of healing, such miraculous phenomena—previously understood as expressions of duplicity, mental pathology, superstition, fantasy and/or a prescientific worldview—are not so easily dismissed and have begun to be reexamined for their sociohistorical significance.

Second, Acts has too often been and continues in some quarters to be evaluated as historiography on the basis of modernist, positivistic canons—that is, on the basis of criteria that have themselves been made problematic and are anachronistic with reference to Luke as historiographer (see, e.g., Green 1996). The central problem on which the debate on Luke the historian has typically turned has had much less to do with the nature of Luke-Acts than with modern, problematic conceptions of the historian's enterprise and with the concomitant, absurd divorce of event from interpretation. The view of the last two centuries, that historical inquiry is interested in establishing that certain events took place and in objectively reporting those facts, is being eclipsed by a conception of the historiographical project in which Luke would have found himself more at home. The primary question is not How can the past be accurately captured? or What methods will allow the recovery of what actually happened? for it is increasingly recognized that historiography is always teleological. It imposes significance on the past by its choice of events to record and to order as well as by its inherent efforts to postulate for those events an end and/or origin. The emphasis thus shifts from validation to signification, so the issue is How is the past being represented? Luke's concern with truth or certainty (see Lk 1:4) resides in his narrative interpretation of the past.

Identification of Acts as ancient historiography adds to the expectations we may bring to the narrative. Alongside those raised by Luke's professed intentions (Lk 1:1-4), we may anticipate a narrative in which recent history is given prominence, issues of causation and teleology are accorded privilege and determined research is placed in the service of persuasive and engaging instruction.

2. Text of Acts.

Textual criticism of Acts presents a special quandary because of the existence of two primary and disparate textual types, the Alexandrian (A B C 81) and the Western (esp. Codex Bezae Cantabrigiensis [D]). The book of Acts in the Western tradition is almost 10 percent longer than the Alexandrian, and the character of each of these two textual types is distinctive. The essential question is Whence the Western text? Is it the product of a studied recension of Acts? If so, can this effort be assigned a particular provenance? Or does the Western text bear witness to an ongoing process of emendation? Is the Western text thoroughly secondary to the Alexandrian textual type? Can it be traced back to the hand of the Third Evangelist himself? Or does it display an amalgam of more or less original and secondary readings that must be considered (according to the eclectic method of textual criticism) on a case-by-case basis? In the history of research on the text of Acts, several related proposals have continued to surface (see the surveys in Strange, 1-34; Barrett, 2-29).

As early as the late seventeenth century it was suggested that Luke was responsible for two recensions of Acts and that this explains the existence of the two major text types. This view has gained new momentum since the onset of redaction criticism in the twentieth century as a result of the detection of alleged Lukanisms in the Western versions. It is represented today by M.-É. Boismard and A. Lamouille, who postulate two authentically Lukan versions of Acts, of which Codex Bezae (D) and Codex Vaticanus (B) are the best, though not unsullied, representatives; in their view the Western text type stems from the first edition of Acts while the Alexandrian reflects Luke's later, revised perspective. With this view one may compare the work of W. A. Strange; he believes that Acts was published posthumously by editors who left two versions of Acts now represented by the two manuscript types.

In spite of theories of this nature, most scholars continue to contend that the witnesses of the so-called Western tradition do not contain something approximating the original text of Acts and to deny that with the Western tradition we have access to a revision, primary or secondary, from the hand of the Third Evangelist. Agreeing with such earlier work as that of M. Dibelius (84-92), they assume that while the Western text has no claim to originality, it may contain superior readings at some points.

Although there remains little agreement on the nature of the original text of Acts, it remains true that most study of Acts continues to proceed on the basis of the relative superiority of the Alexandrian text type. In some cases the Western text type is neglected, on the supposition that it represents a deliberate and sustained revision of the book of Acts; in others Western-type readings are considered on a case-by-case basis. Given this unsettled state of affairs, we may hope that calls for the production of a critical edition of the text of Acts will be heeded.

3. Speeches in Acts.

Among the narrative elements that abound in Acts, the speeches are especially conspicuous, in the narrative as well as on the landscape of the past century of scholarly work on Acts. Many of these are missionary speeches, delivered to Jewish and Gentile audiences. These would include such important sermons as those delivered by Peter at Pentecost (Acts 2:14-40) and by Paul at Pisidian Antioch (Acts 13:16-41); these speeches play programmatic roles within their narrative contexts. This category of speeches, the missionary sermons, has been at the center of scholarly debate: How accurately has Luke reproduced early Christian missionary discourse? Other speeches have important roles within the narrative, however, including Stephen's defense speech to the Jerusalem council (Acts 7:2-53), Paul's farewell address to the Ephesian elders (Acts 20:18-35), Paul's forensic addresses before Roman officials (e.g., Acts 24:10-21; 26:2-23), addresses by Peter and James at the Jerusalem council (Acts 15:7-11, 13-21), and so on. Of approximately 1,000 verses in Acts, 365 are found in major and minor speeches and dialogues (Soards, 1), with direct address responsible for more than half of the book.

3.1. The Debate over Sources and Tradition. The agenda for the modern study of the speeches in Acts was set by the work of Dibelius, first published in 1949 (ET 1956). He sought to locate the speeches of Acts within the matrix of ancient historiography, where, he insisted, the speech was "the natural complement of the deed" (Dibelius, 139). Accordingly, the chief question was not the transcription of a particular address but the aim of a speech in the hands of the historiographer—that is, within the historical writing as a whole. A speech might impart to the reader insight into the total situation of the narrative, interpretive insight into the historical moment, insight into the character of a speaker and/or insight into general ideas that might explain the situation. Additionally, a speech might advance the action of the account (Dibelius, 139-40). But the inclusion of speeches in historical writing would not constitute any claim for the historicity of the address. In his examination of the speeches in Acts, Dibelius was concerned with its function in the book as a whole.

With the hegemony of diachronic approaches to NT study in general, subsequent study of the speeches of Acts remembered Dibelius mostly for his view that the speeches were Lukan compositions (see esp. Haenchen). Even though practically no one would claim that the addresses in Acts are verbatim representations of what was said, it is with reference to just such categories that the debate on their historicity has typically been framed. On the basis of what have now been shown to be largely specious arguments, scholars have referred to consistency of language and style from speech to speech and from indirect to direct discourse, and consistency of content from speech to speech, in order to deny their historicity.

Viewed primarily as a traditiohistorical problem, the speeches of Acts have been studied for their historicity. With few exceptions (e.g., Bruce 1942), such examinations have led to largely negative conclusions, even if on matters of detail the handprint of apostolic tradition might be discerned here and there (e.g., Acts 13:38-39; 20:28, where Pauline-type categories are found). Most scholars have concluded that the speeches in Acts are Lukan in composition, typically with little if any traditional basis, and that they serve primarily as instruments of discourse from the author of Acts to his audience.

Until recently, scholarship has not taken as seriously as it might that by "composition" Dibelius pointed not only to "Lukan invention" but also and fundamentally to Lukan artistry. With the rise of interest in narrative and rhetorical criticisms, however, some interpreters have begun largely to disregard questions of tradition and history and to examine how the setting and elements of each speech are deployed so as to portend the importance of each speech as an action in the unfolding narrative (see Neyrey 1984, Tannehill 1991, Soards).

An important reexamination of speech writing in ancient historiography by C. H. Gempf has surfaced via a media that moves beyond the impasse of these conflicting paradigms of study. Gempf insists that the principal question relevant to ancient historiography is not, Is it accurate or inaccurate in its representation of this speech? thus producing a false either-or choice or a continuum concerned primarily with faithfulness to an alleged source. Instead, ancient writers sought to achieve a twofold balance between artistic and historical appropriateness. This is because speeches are included in narrative representations of history not to provide a transcript of what was spoken on a given occasion but to document the speech event. Historiographers (like Luke) would be concerned, therefore, with composing speeches that would cohere with the work as a whole in terms of language, style and content (the literary dimension) and that would not be regarded as anachronistic or out of character with what was known of the person to whom the speech was attributed (the sociohistorical dimension).

In other words, contra the modern consensus in the discussion on tradition and sources in the speeches of Acts, literary aspirations do not preclude historical value, and the presence of Lukan style and theology in the speeches of Acts does not lead necessarily to the inference that these speeches are Lukan in origin. With respect to historical appropriateness the issue is not narrowly defined in terms of accuracy; instead, the writer would compose a speech in keeping with what could be known of the historical data available to him.

3.2. The Role of the Speeches.

3.2.1. A Unified Worldview. As has often been demonstrated, one can discern a pattern in the missionary speeches of Acts: appeal for hearing, including a connection between the situation and the speech; christological kerygma supported with scriptural proof; the offer of salvation;

and often the interruption of the sermon by the audience or by the narrator himself. Taken as a whole, the speeches in Acts by followers of Jesus evidence a kerygma that is overwhelmingly christocentric but that also features a medley of reoccurring motifs, including the centrality of Jesus' exaltation (i.e., resurrection and/or ascension), together with its salvific effect; repentance and/or forgiveness of sins; the universal offer of salvation; the Holy Spirit; and, frequently through scriptural interpretation, the assurance that the message of this salvation is the manifestation of the divine will.

As we would expect, each of these motifs is integral to Luke's theology (see 5 below), but this does not render the speeches in Acts as simply a collective deposit of Lukan thought. Where comparative material is available, close examination will indicate how the speeches of Acts have struggled to hold in tension the sometimes competing aims of speech writing in historiography, literary and sociohistorical faithfulness. These instances of repetition within the narrative of Acts demonstrate more particularly Luke's concern to advance through these speeches a distinct (though not at all points distinctive) view of God's purpose. This perspective is then propagated by each of the major figures who serve as witnesses to redemption in Acts.

3.2.2. Performative Utterances. It would not be appropriate in every case to catalog these addresses as commentary, even if, as deliberate pauses in the action, they possess an interpretive function. Instead, the speeches often have performative roles; they advance the action of the narrative as they provide the logic and impetus for further developments in the realization of the narrative aim of Luke-Acts. The speeches of Stephen and Peter in Acts 7:2-53 and Acts 10:34-43 (and Acts 11:5-17), for example, appear at crucial junctures, pushing the narrative beyond Jerusalem and Judea to Samaria and to "the end of the earth" (Acts 1:8).

3.2.3. "Revealed History." Paul's sermon at Pisidian Antioch (Acts 13:16-41) exemplifies a common concern of the speeches in Acts to locate historical events in an interpretive web by splicing together in one narrative thread the past, present and future of God's salvific activity. In this perspective the meaning of historical data is not self-evident but must be interpreted, and legitimate interpretation is a product of divine revelation. Paul's speech moves deliberately and naturally from divine activity in the OT to the work of John and Jesus to the need for present response, thus providing christological interpretations of the Scriptures and of history.

3.2.4. Acts as Witness. The sheer amount of the narrative given over to speeches when compared with other exemplars of ancient historiography (or biography or novel) is suggestive of another narrative role for the speeches in Acts. Combined with the fact that in Acts speeches are typically given by witnesses, or for or against the witness, this suggests that via the speeches Luke himself is giving witness, relating "all that God had done with them" (Acts 14:27). "In Luke-Acts, speeches are an essential feature of the action itself, which is the spread of the word of God" (Aune, 125).

4. Narrative Unity of Luke-Acts.

4.1. Luke-Acts, or Luke and Acts. Since H. J. Cadbury fixed the hyphen between Luke and Acts early in the twentieth century, the relationship between these two books has been more assumed than explored. The canonical separation of the two notwithstanding, until recently most scholars have assumed that the Third Gospel and Acts shared the same author, genre and a common theological perspective and that the narrative of Acts was written as the calculated continuation of the narrative of the Gospel. Such assumptions have been called into question by M. C. Parsons and R. I. Pervo, among others. Although they agree that Luke and Acts share authorship, they question whether these two books belong to the same genre, are theologically harmonious and together embody one continuous narrative.

The issues raised by Parsons and Pervo are important if only because their central observation is correct: the unity of Luke-Acts has been more assumed than justified and explored. But their arguments are difficult to sustain.

Because scholarship has not reached a consensus on the generic identification of Luke and Acts, Parsons and Pervo conclude that Luke and Acts do not share unity at the level of genre. This discussion begs important questions: Given the fluidity of generic forms in antiquity, why must one work for the high level of precision on which this rejection of generic unity depends? With respect to the Third Gospel, why must we assume Luke worked with constraints related to an evolving Gospel genre? Could Luke not be

setting out to do something for which previous models or forms proved inadequate? And the possible analogues for serial volumes using multiple genres posed by the authors (e.g., 1-4 Kingdoms and 1-2 Maccabees) are hardly material, given our understanding of the composition and unity of those books.

Further, Parsons and Pervo deny narrative unity by positing the potential identification of two different (textually constructed) narrators, one for Luke, the other for Acts—this in spite of the fact that the application of narratology to even one of these books surfaces multiple narrators and levels of narration (Kurz). Nor do the authors deal constructively with the possible claim of the narrator of Luke 1:1-4 to have been of the circle of those ("us") among whom (some of) these events "have been fulfilled" (cf. the "we" passages in Acts, 4.5 below). Nor do they raise the possibility that Luke and Acts share a single narrative purpose and that in this lies their essential narrative unity.

Along more constructive lines it is important to note that the division of Luke-Acts into two volumes does not signify that one account had ended and a new one begun or that volume 2 would turn to a different subject matter. Rather, as a matter of physical expediency ancient authors divided their lengthy works into books, each of which fit on one papyrus roll. The maximum length of a papyrus roll extended to thirty-five feet, and Luke's two volumes, the two longest books in the NT, would have each required a full papyrus roll.

Moreover, in size the two are roughly equivalent—the Gospel with about 19,400 words, Acts with approximately 18,400 words—so that they would have required papyrus rolls of about the same length. Thus the division between Luke and Acts conformed to the desire of contemporary writers to keep the size of their books symmetrical (cf. Diodorus 1.29.6; 1.41.10; Josephus *Ag. Ap.* 1.35 §320). In other ways too the plan of Luke and Acts suggests a purposeful proportionality. Both narratives begin in Jerusalem. The Gospel ends and Acts begins with commission narratives associated with reports of Jesus' ascension. The time span covered by each volume is approximately thirty years. Luke's narration of Jesus' last days in Jerusalem (Lk 19:28—24:53) and of Paul's arrest, trials and arrival in Rome (Acts 21:27—28:31) each occupy 25 percent of their respective books. And Luke has regularly developed parallels between Jesus in the Gospel of Luke and his disciples in the Acts of the Apostles.

Further, though Parsons and Pervo do not consider this question in their 1993 work, Luke 1:1-4 serves as a prologue for the whole of Luke's work, two volumes, Luke-Acts. This is suggested by the parallel between the primary and recapitulatory prefaces in Luke-Acts and Josephus's *Against Apion*. In addition, Acts 1:1 not only refers to a "first book" but also denotes as the subject of that first book "all that Jesus began to do and to teach." This is a transparent summary of the Third Gospel, which continues the characteristic Lukan emphasis on the inseparable connection of word and deed. With the term *began*, this summary suggests a continuation of the mission of Jesus, an expectation that is not disappointed, for Jesus' followers "call on his name" (e.g., Acts 2:21; 9:21; 15:17; 18:15; 22:16)—a name that signifies the continuing presence of Jesus to bring wholeness of life (e.g., Acts 3:6, 16; 4:7, 10, 12, 17, 30; 8:12; 9:15, 34; 10:43; 16:18). The Gospel of Luke and the Acts of the Apostles narrate one continuous story (see Augustine *De Cons.* 4.8), therefore, and the phrase "the events that have been fulfilled among us" (Lk 1:1-4) refers both to the story of Jesus and to the activity of the early church.

The Gospel of Luke thus anticipates the Acts of the Apostles, and it also authorizes the narrative of Acts, with Acts continuing the narrative of God's mighty acts of salvation begun with the births of John and Jesus (Lk 1—2) and at the same time showing how the significance of the Jesus story might be worked out and articulated for changing times. Acts thus builds on the foundation established in Luke, demonstrating the ongoing relation of the church to the Jesus event by interpreting the significance of Jesus for a new day.

The narrative unity of Luke-Acts has important implications for our reading of Luke's work. Most significantly, it requires that our understanding of Luke's purpose in writing and thus our understanding of the need(s) and audience he addressed account for all the evidence, both the Gospel and Acts. Similarly, it is critical that we understand that incidents in the Gospel anticipate aspects of the story narrated only (finally) in Acts. Notably, in Luke 2:25-35 Simeon realizes that in this child Jesus a salvation has come that will be experienced as "a light for revelation to the Gentiles" (Lk 2:32), but during his ministry as recorded in the Gospel of Luke, Jesus interacts only rarely with non-Jews. One must wait for Acts to see how the Gentile mission is begun, legitimated and takes firm shape at the behest of God and as guided and empowered by the Holy Spirit. The last chapter of the Gospel closes off significant aspects of the story's plot, but there is a more overarching intent at work, the redemptive purpose of God for all people. Seen against this purpose, the Gospel of Luke is incomplete in itself, for it opens up possibilities in the narrative cycle that go unrealized in the Gospel but materialize in the Acts of the Apostles.

4.2. Luke, Acts and the New Testament Canon. The unity of Luke-Acts—two volumes, one story—easily escapes the modern reader in large part due to the canonical placement of these two books in the NT. Although the Gospel and Acts may have been completed and made available to the wider public separately, in the second century A.D. the Gospel of Luke came to be located with the other Gospels so as to form the fourfold Gospel. Not surprisingly, then, Luke's first volume has come to be thought of primarily as a Gospel. It is worth reflecting on the probability that in Luke's day no such literary form existed, however, so that we would be amiss to think either that Luke set out to write a Gospel or that his readership would have understood his work within this category. Luke refers to his predecessors as "narratives," not as "Gospels," and there is no a priori reason to imagine that Luke's purpose was to write a story of Jesus to which he later appended an account of the early church. Rather, the narrative he wished to relate developed naturally and purposefully from the story of Jesus' earthly ministry to that of the continuation of Jesus' mission through the early church.

Nevertheless, according to the logic of the canonical placement of Acts, Luke's second volume rests in an interpretive relationship with the Pauline letters. In fact, early lists of NT books usually situated Acts sometimes before, sometimes after the Pauline corpus. Presumably as a bridge from the story of Jesus to the ministry of Paul, Acts was eventually located in its present position between the Gospels and the letters. The consequence of its location in the canon is that Acts came to provide a sequential, biographical and missionary framework within which to fit the Pauline letters—a framework that is presumed in most biblical study even though critical scholarship has surfaced important tensions between the portraits of Paul and his mission available to us in Acts and in his letters.

4.3. Luke-Acts: One Narrative Aim. A conclusion for the unity of Luke-Acts has as its immediate consequence the rejection of any proposed purpose for Luke's writing that does not account for the evidence of both volumes. Although the primary purpose of Acts may have as its corollary, for example, a defense of Paul (as has been argued), this formulation does not grapple fully with the whole of Luke-Acts. A conclusion for the narrative unity of Luke-Acts would presuppose that the whole could be examined as the unfolding of one continuous narrative cycle moving from anticipation to narrative possibilities to probabilities to actualities to consequences and serving one primary narrative aim.

If we view Luke-Acts on the large canvas of narrative analysis, it is possible to see in its entirety one narrative aim unfolding in a simple narrative cycle. In it we see the working out of one aim: God's purpose to bring salvation in all of its fullness to all (Green 1994, 62-63). This aim is anticipated by the angelic and prophetic voices that speak on God's behalf (Lk 1:5—2:52). It is made possible by the birth and growth of John and Jesus in households that honor God. According to the Lukan birth narrative, though, this is not an aim that will be reached easily or without opposition. Not all will respond favorably to God's agent of salvation, Jesus, resulting in antagonism, division and conflict. The realization of God's aim is made probable through the preparatory mission of John and the life, death and exaltation of Jesus, with its concomitant commissioning and promised empowering of Jesus' followers to extend the message to all people (Lk 3—Acts 1). Jesus himself prepares the way for this universal mission by systematically dissolving the barriers that predetermine and have as their consequence division between ethnic groups, men and women, adults and children, rich and poor, righteous and sinner, and so on. In his ministry, even conflict is understood within the bounds of God's salvific purpose, Jesus' death as a divine necessity, his exaltation a vindication of his ministry and powerful act of God making possible the extension of salvation to Jew and Gentile alike.

The subsequent story in Acts consists of a narration of the realization of God's purpose, particularly in Acts 2—15, as the Christian mission is directed by God to take the necessary steps to achieve a community of God's people composed of Jews, Samaritans and Gentiles. The results of this narrative aim (Acts 16—28) highlight more and more Jewish antagonism to the Christian movement, and the church appears more and more to be Gentile in makeup. This too is God's purpose, according to the narrator, speaking above all through his spokesperson Paul (and through Paul, the Scriptures), even if efforts among the Jewish people at interpreting Moses and the prophets as showing the Messiah is Jesus should continue.

4.4. Acts 1:8 and the Outline of the Book of Acts. The story related in Acts begins in Jerusalem and ends in Rome, with the plan of the book thus giving form to the centrifugal shape of the mission it recounts. It would not be unusual for a Hellenistic writer of sequential books to provide in a second or subsequent book a preface that includes a summary of the former and outline of the present book. Many readers of Acts have found in Jesus' words in Acts 1:8—"Rather, you will receive power when the Holy Spirit comes upon you, and you will be my witnesses in Jerusalem, in all Judea and Samaria, and to the end of the earth"—a summary outline of Acts. Many who see an outline of the book in Acts 1:8 further identify "the end of the earth" as Rome. Although Jesus' words may be taken as the outline of Acts, albeit in a superficial sense, this identification of Rome as "the end of the earth" is almost certainly mistaken.

Acts 1:8 relates Jesus' response to the disciples' question about the restoration of the kingdom to Israel. Jesus does not replace a parochial, nationalistic hope for the restoration of Israel's dominion with a universal mission as much as he sets the future of Israel within the now more widely defined plan of God. Jesus' references to a mission in Jerusalem, Judea (i.e., "the land of the Jews"—cf. Lk 4:44; Acts 10:37) and Samaria represent significant progress in this direction and portend the development of the mission in Acts 2—8.

Beyond Samaria the Spirit-endowed mission was to continue to "the end of the earth." Various options have been championed for making sense of the phrase *heōs eschatou tēs gēs* Some regard it as a geographical location: Ethiopia, Spain, Rome, or even the "Land [of Israel]."

23

Others find in it a more symbolic reference to a universal mission including the Gentiles—that is, a mission to the whole world.

That Luke must have had in view in Acts 1:8 a purely geographical connotation (as is often emphasized) can hardly be sustained, for space is never measured in purely geographical terms but is always imbued with symbolic power. Geography—and especially such geographical markers as "Judea" and "Samaria"—is not a "naively given container" but rather a social production that reflects and configures being in the world. Note, for example, the identification of Jerusalem as the location of the temple and abode of God in Jewish and Lukan perspective and the religious sensibilities that would have been transgressed by this juxtaposition of "Judea" (land of the Jews) and "Samaria" (land of the Samaritans; cf. Lk 10:30-37; 17:11-19). Nor is it necessary to restrict the referent of this phrase to a location within the narrative of Acts; other possibilities generated within the narrative are left unfulfilled at its close (other examples of external prolepsis include Paul's execution and Jesus' parousia).

Nor does Luke ever identify Rome as the mission's final point; Rome may serve as nothing more than a new point of departure for the mission, like Jerusalem and Antioch earlier in the story. Moreover, even in Acts "witnesses" precede Paul to Rome, so that Acts 27—28 brings Paul, not the gospel, to Rome.

Although in the literature of Greco-Roman antiquity the meaning of the phrase "the end of the earth" was used to refer to Spain, Ethiopia, and so on, one must inquire into how this phrase functions in this context. At this juncture in Acts, the meaning of "the end of the earth" is polysemous—that is, we have been given almost nothing by way of interpretive guidelines for identifying the referent of this phrase. As a result, one may read through the narrative inquiring at multiple points, Is this "the end"? (And if so, will God's dominion now be realized?) Greek usage elsewhere allows for such open-endedness (cf. Strabo *Geog.*). But these various interpretive possibilities are narrowed considerably upon reading Acts 13:47, with its citation of Isaiah 49:6, where the phrase "the end of the earth" is again found but with the sense more transparent: "everywhere," "among all peoples," "across all boundaries." Luke's evident dependence on the Isaianic eschatological vision elsewhere provides corroborative evidence for the conclusion that the narrative encourages an identification of "the end of the earth" with a mission to all peoples, Jew and Gentile. This underscores the redemptive-historical continuity between this text and its Isaianic pretext (also Is 8:9; 45:22; 48:20; 62:11; cf. Deut 28:49; Ps 135:6-7; Jer 10:12; 16:19; 1 Macc 3:9).

In only a very limited sense might one take Acts 1:8 as an outline of Acts. Much more significant is the way it identifies God's aim within the narrative and, one may presume, for the story as it extends beyond the narrative of Acts. As it clarifies God's purpose, it also gives us a measure by which to ascertain what persons within the narrative have oriented themselves fully around serving God's design. That is, those who obey the missionary program of Acts 1:8 are shown to be operating under the guidance and power of the Spirit and thus following God's plan; they are shown to be authentic witnesses.

The importance of Acts 1:8 is not diminished if it is not regarded as framing the outline of Acts, for its statement of God's aim within the narrative has left its imprint on the form of the narrative. One can easily follow the centrifugal shape of the mission, though sometimes the progression of the mission is less geographical and more theological, as when Jesus' witnesses return to Jerusalem in order to work out further the theological rationale for a mission that includes those "at the end of the earth" (Acts 11:1-18; 15; 21:1—26:32). Moreover, our identification of "the end of the earth" as a reference to the universal scope and not the geographical goal of the mission suggests that the story of Acts does not end with the close of the narrative in Acts 28:31. Rather, the challenge to mission reaches beyond the narrative to Luke's subsequent readers.

4.5. The Author and the Narrator of Acts. Examining Acts as a narrative raises the question of the voice through whom the story is told—that is, the identity of the narrator. An author might choose to adopt some voice other than his or her own, and in narrative theory narrators differ in how much they choose to tell, the degree of their reliability and how willing they are to intrude into the narrative itself. Narrative critics agree that the narrators of the Gospels and Acts are knowledgeable and are willing to alert their audiences to realities other than those on the surface of recounted events—the motivations of characters within the story (e.g., Acts 24:27;

25:3); that they are so reliable that their points of view are consistent with those expressed by God and God's agents within the narratives; and that they are generally unobtrusive in telling their stories. At the same time, the narrator of Acts might on occasion provide an explanatory comment to his reader (e.g., Acts 9:36 [Tabitha's name in Greek is Dorcas]; Acts 12:9 [Peter's inner thoughts]), and in Acts 16:10-17; 20:5-15; 21:1-18; 27:1-28:16 (i.e., in the "we" passages) he steps into the story as a character. Today, when many scholars speak of "Luke" with reference to the hand behind Luke-Acts, they have reference to Luke as narrator, often without any necessary inference regarding the identification of the actual author of this work.

Luke-Acts, like the Gospels of Matthew, Mark and John, are anonymous documents (though see John 21:24-25), and the "we" passages do nothing at a literary level to alter this state of affairs. That is, even when involved in first-person narration, the narrator of Acts identifies himself not as an individual with a name but as one of a group. He is present, sometimes as a participant, other times as an observer, at some events, but his focus is not his individual identity; rather, the "we" of his narration contributes to the vividness of his account and invites his audience into active participation in the narrative. That first-person narration happens in only selected portions of the account underscores that the narrator makes no claim to being a constant companion of Paul and his circle. It also suggests, however, that first-person narration is more than a literary device calculated to enliven the narrative.

Long before the onset of narrative criticism, this last set of observations led readers of Acts to an identification of the author of Acts as Luke, Paul's fellow worker (Philem 24) and sometime companion, a physician (Col 4:11, 14; 2 Tim 4:11). Eusebius, for example, identifies the author of Acts as Luke, an Antiochene, a physician and frequent companion of Paul (Eusebius *Hist. Eccl.* 3.4.1), as do Jerome (*Vir.* 7) and many others (see Barrett, 30-48; Fitzmyer, 1-26).

In the second century, Irenaeus identified Luke, the companion of Paul, as the author of Acts, though he also goes further, to speak of the relationship between Luke and Paul as "inseparable" (Irenaeus *Haer.* 3.1.1, 4). This latter inference lies behind critical rejection of Luke as the author of Acts since, it is alleged, the author of Acts has distorted the message of Paul and so could not have been his regular companion. But the inseparability of Luke and Paul is not a necessary inference from Acts; indeed, it is contradicted by Acts, wherein we are informed repeatedly that the narrator was part of a company whose traveling agenda overlapped with that of Paul but that did not join Paul's entourage regularly, permanently or even for lengthy periods of time.

When it is further remembered that the portrait of Paul available to us via his letters is itself tendentious, shaped by sometimes tension-filled relations with his audiences; that discussions of the incongruity between the Paul of Acts and the Paul of the Pauline correspondence have sometimes suffered from critical hyperbole; that in any case the narrator of Acts is more concerned with telling the story of the realization of God's salvific aim than with developing personalities; and that characters within Acts are more important for what they add to that story than with reference to their own stories, then the critical concerns that have led to the denial of the identity of Luke as the author of Acts dissipate considerably.

Nevertheless, it is worth inquiring into what is at stake in the identification of the real author of Acts. That, for example, C. K. Barrett can engage in a critical reading of Acts without first deciding the issue of authorship is surely suggestive. This is all the more true when it is recalled that Luke makes no apparent attempt to assert himself into the narrative in order to serve concerns of historical veracity. Final resolution of the question of authorship would not table questions of historical accuracy, and, as we know almost nothing of the background of the historical Luke, our insisting that he is responsible for Acts adds almost nothing to our understanding of his narrative. As with the canonical Gospels, then, so with Acts: our reading proceeds best on the basis of what we are able to discern about its narrator from within the narrative.

5. Theology and Purpose of Acts.
Numerous proposals for the purpose of Acts have been defended in recent scholarship, including the following.

1. Acts is a defense of the Christian church to Rome.

2. Acts is a defense of Rome to the Christian church.

3. Acts is an apology for Paul against Judaizers who have sided with non-Christian Jews against Paul's notion that Christianity is the true successor to Judaism.

4. Acts is a work of edification designed to provide an eschatological corrective for a church in crisis.

5. Acts was written to reassure believers struggling with the reliability of the kerygma—either with regard to its truth and relevance or with respect to its firm foundation in the story of God's people.

6. Acts was intended to assist the Christian movement in its attempts to legitimate itself over against Judaism.

7. Acts was written to encourage among Christians a fundamental allegiance to Jesus that called for a basic social and political stance within the empire.

In light of our earlier comments on the narrative unity of Luke-Acts, some of these can be excluded from the outset—namely, those centering on aims particular to Acts and/or Paul (i.e., Acts 1—3)—since these do not account for the whole of the Lukan narrative. This is not immediately to deny that Luke may have had such concerns, however, for the Evangelist may have been motivated by multiple aims that might not lay a claim on the narrative as a whole.

Our understanding of the aim of (Luke-)Acts flows from our understanding of its genre and narrative aim. We have seen that the genre of Acts suggests Luke's concern with legitimation and apologetic. Our discussion of the narrative aim of Acts highlighted the centrality of God's purpose to bring salvation to all. In the conflicted world of the first-century Mediterranean, not least within the larger Jewish world, it is not difficult to see how this understanding of God's purpose and its embodiment in the Christian movement would have been the source of controversy and uncertainty. We may then propose that the purpose of Luke-Acts would have been to strengthen the Christian movement in the face of opposition by ensuring them in their interpretation and experience of the redemptive purpose of God and by calling them to continued faithfulness and witness in God's salvific project. The purpose of Luke-Acts would thus be primarily ecclesiological, centered on the invitation to participate in God's project.

Our understanding of the aim of (Luke-)Acts must also account for its primary theological emphases. Recent scholarship has repeatedly identified salvation as the primary theme of Luke-Acts, theme being understood as that which unifies other textual elements within the narrative. In order to make sense of the theme of salvation and to show the degree to which it is integrated into the overall purpose of strengthening the church (as we have just described), we must develop it within what can only be an outline of key theological motifs.

5.1. God's Purpose. The purpose or plan of God is of signal importance for Acts, and its presence behind and in the narrative is paraded in a variety of ways. This motif is present especially through a constellation of terms expressive of God's design (e.g., *boulē/boulomai* ["purpose/to purpose"—Acts 2:23; 4:28; 13:36; 20:27], *dei* ["it is necessary"—Acts 1:16, 21; 3:21; 4:12; 5:29; 9:16; 14:22; 16:30; 17:3; 19:21; 20:35; 23:11; 27:24, 26], *horizō* ["to determine"—Acts 2:23; 10:42; 17:26, 31]); through angels, visions and prophecies; through instances of divine choreography of events; through the employment of the Scriptures of Israel; and through the activity of the Holy Spirit.

This pronounced emphasis on the divine will is present in Acts to certify that the direction of the Christian mission is legitimate but not to eclipse human decision making and involvement in the mission. Indeed, the dramatic quality of the narrative is noticeably enhanced by the conflict engendered as some people choose to oppose the divine aim. God does not coerce people into serving his will, but neither will God's plan ultimately be derailed by opposition to it. The communication of his purpose comes as an invitation for people to align themselves with that purpose; some may refuse to do so, but others (and the invitation is to all) will embrace his will, receive the gift of salvation and join in his redemptive activity (see further Squires; Green, 1995, 22-49).

5.1.1. The Divine Purpose. Although God never enters the narrative of Acts as a character, his presence is everywhere apparent through the activity of the Holy Spirit (see 5.1.3 below) and angels and through visions and prophecies. Through these agents and agencies, God choreographs human encounters and events and verifies that the mission to the Gentiles is consonant with his will.

Two case studies in divine choreography (Philip and the Ethiopian eunuch, Peter and

Cornelius) accompany the narration of the beginnings of the mission to the Gentiles. There is no sociohistorical or narratological reason to suspect that the Ethiopian eunuch is anything but a Gentile (Acts 8:26-40). Philip's encounter with him on the road to Gaza comes at the intersection of (1) the Ethiopian's having made pilgrimage, like many Gentiles in the ancient Mediterranean, to worship in Jerusalem; (2) his reading of a text (Is 53:7-8) that highlights the humility of the Isaianic servant and so declares the solidarity of Yahweh's servant with the eunuch in his own humble status (even though he went to worship in Jerusalem, as a eunuch he would have been excluded from the Lord's assembly; cf. Deut 23:1; Is 56:3-5); (3) Philip's being directed by an angel of the Lord to travel on the same road, then instructed by the Spirit to join the entourage of the Ethiopian court official; (5) his being able to serve as interpreter of the Scriptures. Following the eunuch's baptism, Philip is snatched away by the Spirit of the Lord; this divine encounter has reached its conclusion.

Philip's appointment with the eunuch may have initiated the Gentile mission, but this innovation is unknown to anyone within the narrative. Philip does not report what has happened to Jerusalem, and presumably the eunuch journeys home. Hence the encounter between Peter and Cornelius (Acts 10:1—11:18) initiates the Gentile mission in its own way, particularly since in this case the believers in Jerusalem are included in the account. As with Philip, so with Peter, this novelty comes at God's behest, through the careful staging of visionary and angelic messages to communicate the divine purpose (Acts 10:1-16).

In both cases, but more explicitly in the latter, the importance of human volition is not diminished. Cornelius and Peter have separate divine directives, neither of which is complete in itself. According to this choreography, both persons must obey what disclosure they have received in order to understand more fully what God is working to accomplish in their encounter. As if to underscore again that the Gentile mission is God's doing, when they do follow through on God's purpose, the Holy Spirit breaks into their gathering, falling upon "all who heard the word" (Acts 10:44). This work of the autonomous Spirit is taken as the proof that the Gentile mission, together with full fellowship between Jewish and Gentile believers, was God's purpose (Acts 11:17-18).

Angels are active elsewhere too (cf. Acts 5:19, 21; 12:7-11, 23; 27:23-24), indicating the ongoing direction and providential care of God, as do visions (Acts 10:10-16; 16:6-10; 18:9-20; 22:17-21).

5.1.2. The Scriptures of Israel. By the Scriptures of Israel, we mean the Septuagint, and especially Deuteronomy, the Psalms and Isaiah, for these are the authoritative texts that appear most in Acts. Two factors characterize the use of the Scriptures by God's spokespersons in Acts. First, characters within Acts are concerned to show that what has happened with Jesus and what is happening with the movement of those who name him as Lord are continuous with the Scriptures. Second and inseparably related, however, is an important proviso—namely, it is not the Scriptures per se that speak authoritatively but the Scriptures as they bear witness to God's purpose, an interpretation accessible only in light of the mission, death and exaltation of Jesus of Nazareth. Hence, even if it is vital that the actions of the Christian community be grounded in Scripture, that their christological formulations be shaped in dialogue with Scripture, and that they understand the rejection of the message by some Jews and the mission to the Gentiles via scriptural precedent, the Scriptures speak authoritatively only when they are legitimately interpreted.

This suggests that the primary significance of the Scriptures in Acts is ecclesiological and hermeneutical, as the Christian community struggles with its own identity, not least over against those who also read the Scriptures but who refuse faith in Christ. In Luke's view it is through the Scriptures that Jesus' followers should be able to confirm their status as the heirs of the Scriptures, God's people serving God's mission. The struggle with the Jewish people and with Jewish institutions in Acts is essentially hermeneutical: Who interprets the Scriptures faithfully? Or, to put it more starkly, Whose interpretation has the divine imprimatur? Whose receives divine legitimation? In Acts the answer is simple: Jesus has been accredited by God (Acts 2:22) and vindicated in his resurrection and ascension (e.g., Acts 2:23-36; 3:13-26). Those whose form of life is like his serve as his witnesses, and their charismatic preaching includes authorized scriptural interpretation (e.g., Acts 4:8-13). The validity of their message is further validated by the signs and wonders God does through them (Acts 14:3).

5.1.3. The Holy Spirit. If God does not explicitly appear within the narrative of Acts, his virtual stand-in is the *Holy Spirit, and it is by means of the activity of the Spirit that God's purpose is known, the mission is directed and the universality of the gospel is legitimated. This is not because the Holy Spirit is for Luke the immanence of God, as is often suggested, but because the Spirit highlights God's transcendence, his freedom of purpose. Throughout Acts, the Lord's witnesses never control or possess the Spirit but attempt to catch up with the Spirit's work whose activity is often serendipitous.

Just as the Spirit had been active in and through the whole of Jesus' ministry (cf. Lk 3:21-22; 4:1, 14-15, 18-19 et al.), so the Spirit would empower the mission of the Lord's witnesses in Acts (esp. Acts 1:8). The Spirit directs the mission (e.g., Acts 13:1-4; 16:6-7) and empowers witness in word and deed. Within Acts, signs and wonders certify the presence of God in the ministry of his witnesses, legitimating the universal reach of salvation as they authenticate the message among the Gentiles (Acts 14:3; 15:12; cf. Acts 2:19, 22, 43; 4:30; 5:12; 6:8; 7:36; 8:6, 13).

One of the primary purposes of Luke's portrayal of the Spirit's activity is legitimation for the breaching of barriers that separate Jew and Gentile. The gift of the Spirit is one of the primary ways in which Luke articulates the content of salvation (see 5.2.2 below), and in Luke's economy of salvation those on whom the Spirit has been poured out are believers. The Spirit thus clarifies the status of believers, especially Gentiles (Acts 10:45-47; 11:15-18; 15:8).

This authorizing role of the Spirit reaches further, however. It is through the Spirit that prophets prophesy in Acts, and this verifies that their messages are grounded in the divine will. The plot of the narrative, behind and through which the Spirit is active, is thereby shown to be a faithful interpretation of the early Christian mission. Moreover, because Luke's presentation of the Spirit is in its essence continuous with the understanding of the Spirit in Second Temple Judaism, he portrays the Christian mission, which proceeds with the direction and empowerment of the Spirit, as the fulfillment of Israel. This is true even if in the Lukan conception the activity of the Spirit has been recast along christological lines: Spirit-empowered witness focuses on Christ, and it is through the agency of the exalted Messiah that the Spirit is poured out (Acts 2:33). As a consequence Luke's pneumatology can be viewed as providing an apologetic for God; the Spirit substantiates the direction God's purpose takes in Acts: from Israel to the life and ministry of Jesus to the early church with its inclusion of Gentile believers as full participants.

5.2. Salvation. *Salvation is the principal theme of Acts, its narrative centrally concerned with the realization of God's purpose to bring salvation in all of its fullness to all people. Conflict within the narrative arises as a consequence of the division between those who embrace and serve that aim, who join the community of God's people who bear witness to God's salvific work, and those who refuse to do so (cf. Lk 2:34; on 5.2 see Green 1997).

5.2.1. God as Savior, Jesus as Savior. For Luke, salvation is first and always from God. God initiates salvation, and even in the salvific activity of Jesus, God is the often silent but nonetheless primary actor. Jesus' powerful deeds are repeatedly attributed to God (Acts 2:22; 10:38). God appointed him Lord and Messiah; God glorified him, sent him raised him and so on. Luke's soteriology is christocentric, but above all it is theocentric. (Given the strength of this emphasis, it is not surprising [contra those who find in Acts a "divine man" portrayal of the apostles and Paul] that those who align themselves with God's salvific aim in Acts are never credited with possessing the power to minister salvation. The signs and wonders that partially constitute their missionary activity are effected by God, granted by the Lord [cf., e.g., Acts 3:12, 16; 4:10, 29-30; 5:12, 38-39; 8:18-24; 14:3, 14-15 et al.].)

Nevertheless, Jesus is God's agent of salvation, the Savior (Lk 2:11; Acts 5:30-31); as Lord, Jesus is the one on whom people call for salvation. How did Jesus achieve this status? For Luke, a corollary of Jesus' being raised up is that he now administers the promise of the Father (cf. Lk 11:13; 24:49; Acts 1:4), the gift of the Spirit—that is, salvation (Acts 2:29-36). Similarly in Acts 5:30-31 we find a straightforward affirmation that Jesus' confirmation as Savior, as the one who "gives" repentance and forgiveness, is grounded in his resurrection and ascension. As the enthroned one (Messiah), as the Benefactor of the people (Lord), the exalted Jesus now reigns as Savior, pouring out the blessings of salvation, including the Spirit with whom he was anointed at the outset of his ministry, to all.

What then of the crucifixion of Jesus? The sheer frequency of times that we read in Acts of the divine necessity *(dei)* of the suffering of Jesus is warning enough that salvation has not come in spite of the crucifixion of Jesus. What is more, the specifically covenantal language employed in Acts 20:28 (*peripoieomai,*, "to acquire"; cf. Ex 19:5; Is 43:21) and Acts 20:32; 26:18 (*hagiazō*, "to sanctify"; cf. Deut 33:3) reminds us of Luke's record of Jesus' last meal with his disciples, wherein he grounds the "new covenant" in his own death (Lk 22:19-20). Although sparsely mentioned, the salvific effect of the cross is not absent from Luke, even if it is not woven fully into the fabric of Luke's theology of the cross (*see* Death of Christ).

Luke's broader perspective on the suffering of the Messiah can be outlined along three interrelated lines.

First, the rejection of Jesus by the Jewish leaders in Jerusalem leads to the widening of the mission to embrace all peoples, Jew and Gentile. Indeed, suffering and rejection foster the propagation of the word (cf. Lk 21:13-19; Acts 13:44-49; 14:1-18; 18:2-6; 28:17-29). As Luke is fond of narrating, struggle and opposition do not impede but seem to promote the progress of the gospel: "It is through many persecutions that we must enter the kingdom of God" (Acts 14:22; cf., e.g., Acts 6:1, 7; 8:1-3, 4).

Second, the passion of Jesus is paradigmatic for all of those who follow Jesus (cf. Lk 9:23; Acts 9:16). For Luke the *theologia crucis* is rooted not so much in a theory of the atonement but in a narrative portrayal of the life of faithful discipleship as the way of the cross.

Third, in describing Jesus' crucifixion, Acts echoes the words of Deuteronomy 21:22-23: Jesus was "hung on a tree" (Acts 5:30; 10:39; 13:29). The narrative thus signals the disgrace of Jesus' execution while at the same time it locates Jesus' death firmly in the necessity of God's purpose. The ultimate disgrace, the curse from God, is antecedent to exaltation. Thus in his suffering and resurrection Jesus embodied the fullness of salvation interpreted as status reversal; his death was the center point of the divine-human struggle over how life is to be lived, in humility or self-glorification. Though anointed by God, though righteous before God, though innocent, he is put to death. Rejected by people, he is raised up by God—and with him the least, the

lost, the left out are also raised. In his death, and in consequence of his resurrection by God, the way of salvation is exemplified and made accessible to all those who will follow.

5.2.2. The Message of Salvation. Luke develops the content of salvation along five related lines.

First, salvation entails incorporation and participation in the christocentric community of God's people. These are people whose unity is emphatic in the narrative (e.g., Acts 1:14-15, 24; 14:1; cf. Acts 2:44-45; 4:32—5:11; Plato *Rep.* 5.46.2c; Cicero *De Offic.* 1.16.51; Aristotle *Eth. Nic.* 9.8.1168b; Josephus *J.W.* 2.8.3 §§122-23), who together "call on the name of the Lord [Jesus]" and are baptized in his name (Acts 2:21-22, 38; 8:16; 9:14, 21; 10:48; 19:5; 22:16); who heal (Acts 3:6, 16; 4:10, 30; 19:13) and preach (Acts 4:12; 5:28, 40) in his name; and who suffer for his name (Acts 5:41; 9:16; 21:13).

What may be surprising is the identification of those who belong to this community. The invitation is for everyone, for "you, your children and all who are far off" (Acts 2:39; cf. Is 57:19; Acts 1:8; 2:5, 9-11, 17, 21; 10:1-11:18; et al.). By pouring upon them the blessing of forgiveness and the gift of the Spirit, God testifies to the authenticity of the membership of Gentiles in the number of God's people and confirms that "he has made no distinction between them and us" (Acts 15:7-8; cf. 11:15-18). Jesus is Lord of all (Acts 10:43). Also "saved" are those set apart from normal social discourse by sickness and demon possession (e.g., Acts 3:1-4:12; 5:12-16; 8:7; 14:8-10). This reminds us that the Lukan soteriology knows no distinction between the physical, spiritual and social; that in the larger Greco-Roman world "salvation" would be recognized in the healing of physical disorders; and that physical restoration had as one of its ramifications restoration to social intercourse.

Second, salvation entails "rescue from our enemies" (cf. Lk 1:68-79). Salvation as divine rescue does not appear to be prominent in Acts, but there are important hints in this direction. For example, the use of Joel 2:28-32 in Acts 2 brings onto the stage apocalyptic connotations reminding us that the coming of God signifies the downfall of those who oppose God's purpose, and elsewhere Luke employs exodus typology to characterize salvation (Acts 3:17-26; 7:25). Salvation as rescue from peril takes on concrete form elsewhere when the language of salvation is used to signify safe travel in spite of the threat of ambush (Acts 23:16-24) or storms at sea (Acts 27:31, 43-28:6) or escape from prison and mob action (cf. Acts 5:17-21; 12:1-19; 16:19-40; 19:23-41).

What of salvation from foreign domination (as anticipated in Zechariah's song)? First, although Luke does not report the dismantling of Roman overlordship, he does narrate the relativizing of the sovereignty Rome wielded, as R. J. Cassidy has suggested. More importantly for Luke, the real enemy from which deliverance is needed is not Rome but the cosmic power of evil resident and active behind all forms of opposition to God and God's people. This form of salvation—from the power of darkness, of Satan—is prominent in Acts (e.g., Acts 26:17-18; 5:16; 13:4-12; 16:16-18; 19:8-20).

Third, salvation is forgiveness of sins. In Acts, Luke continues an emphasis on forgiveness firmly rooted in Jesus' mission according to the Third Gospel (see Acts 2:38; 3:19; 5:31; 10:43; 13:38; 15:9; 22:16; 26:18). This signals a renewed or new relationship with God but also with God's people: as sin is the means by which persons exclude themselves or are excluded from the community of God's people, so forgiveness marks their restoration to the community.

Fourth, salvation is the reception of the Holy Spirit. Peter also promises those who respond to the message that they will receive "the gift of the Holy Spirit" (Acts 2:38), an emphasis that will resurface repeatedly (Acts 9:17; 10:43-44; 11:15-17; 15:8). The gift of the Spirit marks persons, whether Gentile or Jew, as members of the community of God's people and thus clarifies the status of those, especially Gentiles, who believe.

Finally, the offer of salvation calls for response. The necessity of response is set forth programmatically in the narration of the Pentecost address, where Peter is interrupted by his audience: "What shall we do?" (Acts 2:37; cf. 16:30-34). What is the appropriate response to the good news of salvation? Luke addresses this question with an arsenal of possibilities—calls to believe (Acts 2:44; 3:16; 11:17; 13:39; 14:9; 15:7; 16:30-31; 18:8), to be baptized (Acts 2:41; 8:12, 36; 9:18; 10:47-48; 16:15) and to turn to God or to repent (Acts 2:38; 3:19; 5:31; 11:18; 17:30; 20:21; 26:20); and other potential responses, including some that employ metaphors of illumination (e.g., Acts 26:17-18)—but singles out no particular pattern of response as paradigmatic. God has acted graciously in Christ to bring salvation to all humanity. All humanity is called to welcome the good news, to respond with receptivity and thus to share in that salvation not only as recipients but also as those who serve God's redemptive aim.

5.2.3. Eschatology. Students of Acts have long noticed that eschatological hope has not been developed within the narrative (*see* Eschatology). Although the future of salvation is not missing (e.g., Acts 3:21; 10:42; 17:31), the focus has moved from the eschaton to the present. In Acts 1:6-8 Jesus reorients concerns about the restoration of the *kingdom to Israel, an eschatological concern, to the importance of faithful witness in the present. This should not be taken as an attempt on Luke's part to diminish the importance of the parousia (as Conzelmann argued); in counseling agnosticism about "the times and seasons" established by the Father (Acts 1:7), Jesus emphasizes the unpredictability of the parousia. "Luke sought to reinforce living eschatological faith, all the while summoning his readers to vigilant, faithful service" (Carroll, 166). That is, Luke employs eschatology as a motivation for mission.

5.2.4. Judaism. The question of Luke's relationship to Jewish institutions and Jewish people is one of the most debated in Lukan studies, with some scholars arguing that Luke's theology is irretrievably anti-Jewish, others insisting that Lukan thought derives from a lively Jewish Christian church and many viewpoints falling between these poles. How does the Lukan treatment of people and things Jewish point toward Luke's overall purpose? Without engaging fully this larger debate, two observations are possible.

First, the centrality of the temple and the *synagogue, the continuous use of Israel's Scriptures, the primacy of the mission to the Jewish people—these and related phenomena within the narrative of Acts suggest the degree to which the story of the Christian community is continuous with the ancient story of God's people.

Second, however, the critical perspective on the temple and the synagogue, for example, and the contested nature of the relationship between the Christian movement and Jewish structures suggests the degree to which the *Judaism with which Luke is interested is an interpreted Judaism. That is, "the religion of Israel—its institutions, practices, and so on—is to be embraced fully when understood *vis-à-vis* the redemptive purpose of God. But in order to be understood thus, Israel's religion must cohere with the purpose of God as articulated by God's own authorized interpretive agent, God's Son, Jesus of Nazareth" and in Acts by the Lord's witnesses who thus serve as interpretive agents (Green 1995, 75). This perspective on the question of Judaism within Acts underscores the nature of the fundamental struggle between the Christian movement and its representatives on the one hand, and Judaism on the other, just as it also provides a rationale for the opposition faced by that movement.

5.3. Discipleship. The interdependence of the Gospel of Luke and Acts is perhaps nowhere more evident than in the Lukan perspective on discipleship. Especially when compared with the other Synoptic Gospels, the Third Gospel is noteworthy for how little it has the disciples participating in Jesus' ministry. This is easily explained, since the Third Gospel can provide instruction and models for discipleship while allowing Acts to document more fully how the disciples came to serve actively in the missionary work of Jesus. Among the motifs that might be developed, two are of particular importance: economic koinonia, and witness and allegiance.

5.3.1. Economic Koinonia. Throughout the Third Gospel, Jesus' message has returned again and again to undercut the determination of social relations on the basis of widespread canons of status and to affirm the redefinition of economic relations within the community of his followers. These two points address the same set of issues, since economic exchange is a function and representation of social relations. Patrons, for example, have higher status than their clients, and in their acts of benefaction they obligate others to supply them with loyalty, recognition and venerated status. Among friends and within kinship groups, however, giving and receiving need not have stipulations carried over from the patronal ethic that pervaded the empire. In these cases giving is a function not of obligations and debt but of mutuality, generosity, solidarity and need. Economic koinonia would thus grow out of, as well as symbolize, kinship.

What Jesus had called for in his Sermon on the Plain (Lk 6:27-38, esp. Lk 6:35; see Sermon on the Mount)—dispositions of kinship giving rise to practices of material generosity—the early church is reported to practice (Acts 2:44-45; 4:32—5:11; see also Acts 6:1-6; 11:27-30). What Luke describes in the summary statements of

Acts 2:44-45 and Acts 4:32-35, however, is not communitarianism, either as a requisite for belonging to the people of God or as an ideal. Instead he outlines a disposition of kinship and generosity, an orientation toward the needs of others and toward the generosity of God that characterizes the Christian community outside the normal constraints of reciprocity and the gift-obligation cycle. Accordingly, Barnabas is introduced as an exemplary figure who embodied the ideal of kinship that was to characterize the whole community (Acts 4:32, 36-37). Similarly, Ananias and Sapphira demonstrate by their falsehood and their choice of private ownership that they have not refused the way of patronage and status-seeking of the larger empire and so that they are not members of this new community of God's people (Acts 5:1-11).

5.3.2. Witness and Allegiance. One of the hallmarks of Luke's narrative is the consistency with which faithful witnesses attract opposition and with which opposition leads to the spread of the gospel. Exemplars include Jesus, Peter and John (e.g., Acts 4:23-31; 5:41-42), Stephen (Acts 8:1-4), and Paul (e.g., Acts 13:45-49). The conflict surrounding these key characters, whose faithfulness is underscored repeatedly by the narrator (e.g., Acts 3:14-15; 5:38-39; 6:8-10; 7:55; 25:25; 26:32; 28:17-22), portends the opposition that faithful witnesses outside the narrative, including those among Luke's audience, may also encounter in the course of the mission.

That is, opposition in the course of the church's mission should not necessarily be interpreted as a sign of misapprehension of the divine purpose. Faithfulness calls for a fundamental allegiance to Jesus as Lord, which calls for a basic social and political stance within the empire (Cassidy), and this may well generate opposition. Peter, John, Stephen and Paul may thus serve as models for Christians who in the course of the church's mission face similar struggles.

See also LUKE, GOSPEL OF; PAUL IN ACTS AND LETTERS.

DLNTD: CORNELIUS; EVANGELISM IN THE EARLY CHURCH; GENTILES, GENTILE MISSION; HELLENISTS; MISSION, EARLY NON-PAULINE; NARRATIVE CRITICISM; OLD TESTAMENT IN ACTS; PAUL AND PAULINISMS IN ACTS; PENTECOST; PHILIP THE EVANGELIST; SAMARIA; SIGNS AND WONDERS; STEPHEN; TONGUES.

BIBLIOGRAPHY. **Commentaries:** C. K. Barrett, *The Acts of the Apostles* (2 vols.; ICC; Edinburgh:

T & T Clark, 1994); F. F. Bruce, *The Acts of the Apostles: The Greek Text with Introduction and Commentary* (3d ed.; Leicester: Inter-Varsity [Apollos]/Grand Rapids: Eerdmans, 1990); idem, *The Book of the Acts* (NICNT; rev. ed.; Grand Rapids: Eerdmans, 1988); H. Conzelmann, *The Acts of the Apostles: A Commentary on the Acts of the Apostles* (Herm; Philadelphia: Fortress, 1987); E. Haenchen, *The Acts of the Apostles: A Commentary* (Oxford: Blackwell; Philadelphia: Westminster, 1971); L. T. Johnson, *The Acts of the Apostles* (SacP 5; Collegeville, MN: Liturgical Press, 1992); I. H. Marshall, *The Acts of the Apostles: An Introduction and Commentary* (TNTC; Leicester: Inter-Varsity; Grand Rapids: Eerdmans, 1980); J. B. Polhill, *Acts* (NAC; Nashville: Broadman, 1992); R. C. Tannehill, *The Narrative Unity of Luke-Acts: A Literary Interpretation, 2: The Acts of the Apostles* (Minneapolis: Fortress, 1990); B. Witherington III, *The Acts of the Apostles: A Socio-Rhetorical Commentary* (Grand Rapids: Eerdmans, 1977). **Studies:** L. C. A. Alexander, *The Preface to Luke's Gospel: Literary Convention and Social Context in Luke 1:1-4 and Acts 1:1* (SNTSMS 78; Cambridge: Cambridge University Press, 1993); D. E. Aune, *The New Testament in Its Literary Environment* (LEC 8; Philadelphia: Westminster, 1987) esp. 77-157; M.-É. Boismard and A. Lamouille, *Le Texte Occidental des Actes des Apôtres: Reconstitution et Réhabitaliation* (2 vols.; Paris: Recherche sur les Civilisations, 1984); F. F. Bruce, *The Speeches in the Acts of the Apostles* (London: Tyndale, 1942); H. J. Cadbury, "Commentary on the Preface of Luke," in *The Beginnings of Christianity*, pt. 1: *The Acts of the Apostles*, ed. F. J. Foakes Jackson and K. Lake (5 vols.; London: Macmillan, 1922; repr. Grand Rapids: Baker, 1979) 2:489-510; idem, *The Making of Luke-Acts* (2d ed.; London: SPCK, 1958); J. T. Carroll, *Response to the End of History: Eschatology and Situation in Luke-Acts* (SBLDS 92; Atlanta: Scholars Press, 1988); R. J. Cassidy, *Society and Politics in the Acts of the Apostles* (Maryknoll, NY: Orbis, 1987); M. Dibelius, *Studies in the Acts of the Apostles* (London: SCM; New York: Scribner's, 1956); P. F. Esler, *Community and Gospel in Luke-Acts: The Social and Political Motivations of Lukan Theology* (SNTSMS 57; Cambridge: Cambridge University Press, 1987); J. A. Fitzmyer, *Luke the Theologian: Aspects of His Teaching* (Mahwah, NJ: Paulist, 1989); C. H. Gempf, "Public Speaking and Published Accounts," in *The Book of Acts in Its Ancient Literary Setting*, ed. B. W. Winter and A. D. Clarke (BAFCS 1; Grand Rapids: Eerdmans, 1993) 259-303; J. B. Green, "Internal Repetition in Luke-Acts: Contemporary Narratology and Lukan Historiography," in *History, Literature and Society in the Book of Acts*, ed. Ben Witherington III (Cambridge: Cambridge University Press, 1996) 283-99; idem, "The Problem of a Beginning: Israel's Scriptures in Luke 1—2," *BBR* 4 (1994) 61-85; idem, "'Salvation to the End of the Earth' (Acts 13:47): God as Savior in the Acts of the Apostles," in *The Book of Acts and Its Theology*, ed. I. H. Marshall and D. Peterson (BAFCS 6; Grand Rapids: Eerdmans, 1997) 83-106; idem, *The Theology of the Gospel of Luke* (NTT; Cambridge: Cambridge University Press, 1995); C. J. Hemer, *The Book of Acts in the Setting of Hellenistic History*, ed. C. H. Gempf (WUNT 49; Tübingen: Mohr Siebeck, 1989); M. Hengel, *Acts and the History of Earliest Christianity* (London: SCM; Philadelphia: Fortress, 1979); F. J. Foakes Jackson and K. Lake, eds., *The Beginnings of Christianity*, pt. 1: *The Acts of the Apostles* (5 vols.; London: Macmillan, 1920-33; repr. Grand Rapids: Baker, 1979); J. Jervell, *The Theology of the Acts of the Apostles* (NTT; Cambridge: Cambridge University Press, 1996); W. S. Kurz, *Reading Luke-Acts: Dynamics of Biblical Narrative* (Louisville, KY: Westminster/John Knox, 1993); R. Maddox, *The Purpose of Luke-Acts* (FRLANT 126; Göttingen: Vandenhoeck & Ruprecht, 1982); I. H. Marshall, *The Acts of the Apostles* (NTG; Sheffield: JSOT, 1992); J. H. Neyrey, "The Forensic Defense Speech and Paul's Trial Speeches in Acts 22—26: Form and Function," in *Luke-Acts: New Perspectives from the Society of Biblical Literature Seminar*, ed. C. H. Talbert (New York: Crossroad, 1984) 210-24; idem, ed., *The Social World of Luke-Acts: Models for Interpretation* (Peabody, MA: Hendrickson, 1991); M. C. Parsons and R. I. Pervo, *Rethinking the Unity of Luke and Acts* (Minneapolis: Fortress, 1993); R. I. Pervo, *Profit with Delight: The Literary Genre of the Acts of the Apostles* (Philadelphia: Fortress, 1987); M. A. Powell, *What Are They Saying About Acts?* (Mahwah, NJ: Paulist, 1991); M. L. Soards, *The Speeches in Acts: Their Content, Context, and Concerns* (Louisville, KY: Westminster/John Knox, 1994); J. T. Squires, *The Plan of God in Luke-Acts* (SNTSMS 76; Cambridge: Cambridge University Press, 1993); G. L. Sterling, *Historiography and Self-Definition: Josephus, Luke-Acts and Apologetic Historiography* (NovTSup 64; Leiden: E. J. Brill, 1992); W. A. Strange, *The Problem of the Text of Acts* (SNTSMS 71; Cambridge: Cambridge University Press,

1992); C. H. Talbert, *Literary Patterns, Theological Themes and the Genre of Luke-Acts* (SBLMS 20; Missoula, MT: Scholars Press, 1974); R. C. Tannehill, "The Functions of Peter's Mission Speeches in the Narrative of Acts," *NTS* 37 (1991) 400-14; M. Turner, *Power from on High: The Spirit in Israel's Restoration and Witness in Luke-Acts* (JPTSup 9; Sheffield: Sheffield Academic Press, 1996); J. B. Tyson, ed., *Luke-Acts and the Jewish People: Eight Critical Perspectives* (Minneapolis: Augsburg, 1988); W. C. van Unnik, *Sparsa Collecta: The Collected Essays of W. C. van Unnik*, pt. 1: *Evangelia—Paulina—Acta* (NovTSup 29; Leiden: E. J. Brill, 1973) esp. 6-15, 340-73; R. W. Wall, "The Acts of the Apostles in Canonical Context," *BTB* 18 (1988) 16-24; B. W. Winter, ed., *The Book of Acts in Its First-Century Setting* (6 vols.; Grand Rapids: Eerdmans, 1993-97); B. Witherington III, ed., *History, Literature and Society in the Book of Acts* (Cambridge: Cambridge University Press, 1996).

J. B. Green

ADAM AND CHRIST: PAUL

Although references to the OT figure of Adam in Paul's letters are by no means extensive, its use is highly significant in that Adam serves as a vehicle to communicate tremendous theological truths about marriage, sin, death, human nature and eschatological hope. Most importantly, "Adam" stands as a theological counterpart within Paul's christological teaching, with Adam and Christ as the two halves of an analogy explicitly formulated in both Romans 5 and 1 Corinthians 15.

This analogy presents Adam and *Christ as corporate heads of two contrasting orders of existence and may be taken as one of the most revealing ways in which the apostle's theological thought is expressed: Adam embodies fallen humanity and Christ embodies redeemed humanity. Thus, within these two chapters we see the intersection of several key theological concerns, namely anthropology, *christology, soteriology and ecclesiology. It is because of the fact that so many central Pauline themes come together in connection with the Adam-Christ analogy that it could be said to lie close to the heart of Paul's thought. It is precisely because of its central significance that the Adam-Christ analogy has remained an important focus of NT interpretation over the years.

1. Adam: The Generic Sense of the Term
2. Adam: The Historical Figure
3. Adam: The Typological Figure
4. Adam and the Image of God
5. Adam and the Body of Christ

1. Adam: The Generic Sense of the Term.

The name *Adam* occurs within the Pauline corpus only seven times (Rom 5:14 [twice]; 1 Cor 15:22, 45 [twice]; 1 Tim 2:13, 14), although some scholars would see a few of the more generalized discussions about "man" *(anthrōpos)* as also having an Adamic background in Paul's thought. This is due to the fact that the Hebrew term *'ādām* can refer to not only "Adam" the individual but to the generic "humankind" as well. It is entirely proper to view Paul's use of Adam as closely connected to a number of other anthropological images and expressions he uses to communicate the Christian experience, the new life found in Jesus Christ. Included among these are old man/new man (Rom 6:6; Col 3:9-10; Eph 2:15; 4:22-24); outer man/inner man (2 Cor 4:16; Rom 7:22; Eph 3:15); physical man/spiritual man (2 Cor 2:14-16). Related to this larger anthropological sense of Adam are those passages where Paul uses the pronoun "I" in such a way as to suggest that he has in mind Adamic humankind, or humankind outside of the new experience which for believers is found in Christ (*see* In Christ). A good example of this is found in Romans 7:7-25, where the apostle appears to use the "I" in a corporate sense which demonstrates some overlap with the generic sense of the more explicit Adam motif.

It is virtually certain that the narrative of Genesis 2—3 underlies the use of "Adam" within the Pauline letters and provides the background for it. The same fascination for the figure of Adam can also be seen in a number of first-century Jewish and Christian documents, including *4 Ezra*, *2 Baruch* and the *Apocalypse of Moses*, as J. R. Levison has duly noted. Speculation about Adam is also well documented within the Qumran materials and in the writings of Paul's contemporary, Philo of Alexandria. In light of the fact that Adam figures regularly in Gnostic materials, such as the Nag Hammadi texts, some scholars have attempted to see a link between the Adamic motif and Gnostic ideas of "a second man." Generally, this has not been well received, the evidence probably representing precisely the reverse flow of influence (it is more likely that the biblical theme is taken up by the later Gnostic writers; *see* Gnosticism).

All of these relevant background documents help us understand the interest that the tradition of Adam, the first created human being, generated among ancient writers and how they came to rely on it and express it in their writing. When this is recognized the Pauline discussion of the theme is seen to be wholly consistent with other documents of its day, although the specifically christological use to which it is connected distinguishes Paul's treatment. Paul seems to be the first to describe Jesus Christ as "the last (or second) Adam" (1 Cor 15:45, 47), a description that points unambiguously to the eschatological character of the apostle's thought.

2. Adam: The Historical Figure.

Clearly the figure Adam was understood by many first-century people to be the first historical person; this explains why Jude 14 (quoting *1 Enoch* 1:9) describes Enoch as "the seventh generation from Adam" (NRSV). Luke offers similar assessment when he includes Adam within the genealogy of Jesus (Lk 3:38). The historicity of Adam as the first created person appears to have been taken for granted by the apostle Paul, although such historicity is not the primary focal point of the two key Pauline texts that discuss the Adam/Christ motif.

2.1. Adam (and Eve) As Ethical Example(s). The historicity of Adam (and Eve) does, however, seem to underlie teaching within the Pauline letters concerning the man-woman relationship and, by extension, the relationship that exists between Christ and his church. Similarly, the figures of Adam and Eve are used sparingly within the Pauline letters to make a point about authority within the divine order of creation. In both of these ways the role(s) of Adam (and Eve) as ethical example(s) is preeminent, although the historicity of the first man (and woman) seems to be assumed as part of the ethical argument. The use of Adam (and Eve) as ethical model(s) anticipates the more typological use of Adam within the Adam/Christ analogy in Romans 5 and 1 Corinthians 15.

2.1.1. Adam (and Eve): Marriage and Sexual Roles. Paul alludes to the story of Adam and Eve in 1 Corinthians 6:16 via his quotation of Genesis 2:24. Although the names of the first couple are not used here, it is clear that they stand as key ethical models for how proper sexual relationships between man and woman should function in the life of the church. Paul here em-

phasizes the importance and sanctity of the sexual union of a man and a woman as a means to exhort the Corinthian believers to a more worthy lifestyle and impress upon them the fact that they belong to the body of Christ (*see* Body of Christ). The story of Adam and Eve also underlies the advice offered on the union of the marriage relationship in Ephesians 5:22-33. Here, once again, Ephesians builds on the OT imagery of Adam and Eve and an understanding of their union with that "mystery" which exists between Christ and the church (especially seen in Eph 5:32).

2.1.2. Adam (and Eve): Sin and the Order of Creation. First Timothy 2:13-14 also clearly demonstrates reliance upon the Adam and Eve story of Genesis 2—3. In a section given over to ethical teaching (1 Tim 2:9-15), the argument turns to the story of Adam and Eve in Genesis for scriptural support of an understanding of the authority structure, the order of creation, that exists between men and women. The emphasis is on the priority of Adam's creation (1 Tim 2:13) and the priority of Eve's deception (1 Tim 2:14) in the Garden of Eden. Adam and Eve are called into service as normative examples of how men and women should interrelate and what can happen if the proper authority structure is adhered to by subsequent peoples. In short, the point is that 1 Timothy presents Adam and Eve in a specific way, as a means of regulating conduct within the life of the church, particularly in its worship practices. They are put forward as ethical examples from the past both to follow (as in the case of Eve's proper submission to Adam based upon her creational dependence upon him), and as models of behavior to guard against (as in the case of Eve's deception and its aftermath). Again, the historicity of the Genesis account seems to be taken for granted within this ethical explication of the story.

3. Adam: The Typological Figure.

When we turn to consider the relevant passages in Romans 5 and 1 Corinthians 15, we find a much more complicated and extended use of "Adam" by Paul. Here the focus shifts from Adam as a mere historical figure to Adam as a typological or figurative character set over against Jesus Christ (in Rom 5:14 the actual term *typos,* "type," is used of Adam). Commenting on the significance of Adam in the apostle's thought, C. K. Barrett remarks that "Paul sees history gathering at nodal points, and crystallizing upon outstanding figures—men who are notable in themselves as individual persons, but even more notable as representative figures" (Barrett, 5). Thus we see that in Romans 5 and 1 Corinthians 15 Paul juxtaposes Adam and Christ and uses several key features of OT background to communicate christological truths about Jesus Christ, who encompasses humanity in himself. We could even summarize Paul's understanding of Christian redemption as the transition from being "in Adam" to being "in Christ" as the saving movement from one sphere of life, one realm of existence, to another. Given the fact that Paul's theology arises out of an eschatological mindset (*see* Eschatology), with its emphasis on the new creation having supplanted the old (*see* Creation, New Creation), it is proper to see the Adam/Christ motif as expressing his teaching concerning what R. Scroggs has described as "eschatological humanity."

3.1. Adam and Eschatological Humanity. First Corinthians 15 is a self-contained discussion of the *resurrection of the dead, the primary purpose of which is not so much to assert the truth of the resurrection of Jesus (since this is assumed) as to explain its significance for the life of the faithful. Thus the chapter deals with the reality of the resurrection of Christ and its implications in the lives of the Christian believers. Within this discussion the Adam/Christ analogy is explicitly used at two points, in 1 Corinthians 15:20-22 and in 1 Corinthians 15:44-49. Christ's resurrection is the event that inaugurates and constitutes his being the "first fruits" of those who have died (1 Cor 15:20, 23); it is in connection with this idea that the Adam/Christ analogy is initially introduced. It has been suggested by M. Thrall that the christological debate that develops in Corinth arises out of Paul's previous introduction of the Adamic motif and the Corinthian church's misunderstanding of it. Such an idea is far from certain and assumes a vacillation in Paul's thought that is much more deliberate than this suggests.

3.1.1. Christ as Last Adam: The First Fruits. The first use of the Adam/Christ analogy is introduced by a statement (1 Cor 15:20), built upon the declaration of Christ's resurrection stated in 1 Corinthians 15:3-5. In the second half of 1 Corinthians 15:20 the meaning of Christ's resurrection is amplified—Christ is also the "first fruits of those who are asleep." In this way a new

point is injected into the discussion of Christ's resurrection, namely, the unity of the risen Lord with those who believe in him. The resurrection bodies of the redeemed (it is important to note that the focus of the discussion is on this "somatic" point) are to correspond to and flow from Christ's in the same way that the harvest corresponds to and flows from the first fruits.

It is to amplify further and explain the relationship between Christ and his believers that the Adam/Christ analogy is used by Paul. The Adam/Christ typology becomes an argument for the certainty of the resurrection of the believing community and, in J. Lambrecht's words, sets us a "temporal, as well as a causal," relationship between the Lord and those who believe in him. In 1 Corinthians 15:21-22 Paul sets forth a double parallelism showing this relationship:

21a   For since by a man came death,
21b   so also by a man came the resurrection of the dead,
22a   For as in Adam all die,
22b   so also in Christ shall all be made alive.

The two verses should be taken together, as the second serves to clarify the meaning of the first. The essentially eschatological outlook of the analogy is demonstrated by the use of the future passive verb in 1 Corinthians 15:22b.

Some debate arises as to the universal salvation implied in 1 Corinthians 15:22. How much weight should be given to the two uses of "all" in 1 Corinthians 15:22? Is Paul teaching the ultimate salvation of all humankind in Christ in the same way that he asserts the universal death of all humankind in Adam? Most commentators agree that such an idea is incompatible with the rest of Paul's teaching; throughout this letter Paul has spoken of those who perish (1 Cor 1:18; 3:17; 5:13; 6:9; 9:27). In light of this it seems that we are left to limit both (or at least the second) "all" clauses of 1 Corinthians 15:22 and have them act as modifiers of "in Adam" and "in Christ." Thus we can take the meaning of the verse to be "all who are in Adam die, while all who are in Christ shall be made alive."

3.1.2. Christ as Last Adam: The Life-Giving Spirit. First Corinthians 15:45-49 is a quotation of the midrashic commentary on Genesis 2:7. The section is founded on Paul's statement in 1 Corinthians 15:44b: "If there is a physical body, there is also a spiritual body" (NRSV). This statement in 1 Corinthians 15:44 is a summary of the preceding paragraph, beginning in 1 Corinthians 15:35, which contains a discussion about the nature of the resurrection body. Paul speaks here of a *sōma psychikon* ("physical body") and a *sōma pneumatikon* ("spiritual body"), effectively outflanking his Corinthian opponents (Dunn 1973). The exact identification of these opponents has remained a matter of considerable scholarly debate over the years. B. Pearson, however, has identified their use of *pneumatikos-psychikos* terminology as forming one of the points of friction with Paul. It is in attempting to explain the relationship that exists between these two *sōmata* ("bodies," both *pneumatikos* and *psychikos*) that Paul turns once again to the Adam/Christ analogy in 1 Corinthians 15:45-49.

Paul quotes Genesis 2:7 from the LXX, adding the words "first" and "Adam" to the OT text in order to set up the typological contrast with Christ which follows in 1 Corinthians 15:45b: "the last Adam became a life-giving spirit" (NRSV). In setting up the contrast in the way he has, Paul is addressing the question of the "bodies" of physical and spiritual existence as can readily be seen in the use of the neuter definite articles in 1 Corinthians 15:46 (the antecedent being "body") instead of masculine ones (which would refer to "man"). The point is that Adam, in having a "physical body" (NRSV), also became a "living being" (NRSV); Christ, in becoming a "spiritual body" (NRSV), also became a "life-giving spirit" (NRSV). Paul is not merely making an anthropological claim about Christ as "Last Adam" here; his meaning goes beyond that. He is also making a christological statement about the risen Lord who has manifested himself as the regenerating Spirit within the church. The passage in Genesis lent itself toward that purpose, although, as N. T. Wright notes, the connection of this christological point with the primary discussion about the "spiritual body" is not immediately obvious.

In a sense, therefore, Paul's use of the Adam/Christ analogy is not entirely consistent. In calling Christ the "life-giving spirit" Paul is making a statement about the work of Christ within the church that has no parallel on the Adamic side of the analogy. The motivating factor in Paul's use of the analogy was his desire to show that a relationship exists between Adam and the rest of humankind. But the wonder of what God had done for humankind through Christ was so great that the Adam/Christ analogy broke down. It was employed by the apostle insofar as it was useful in demonstrating the solidarity of the two Adams with their respective followers, but when it could no longer communicate or contain the message of Christ's life-transforming power in the life of the believer, it was laid aside.

It is significant that both structured references to the Adam/Christ analogy in 1 Corinthians 15 (1 Cor 15:21 and 1 Cor 15:45) are followed by passages that speak of Jesus Christ in very exalted terms and are sometimes taken to express a Pauline understanding of preexistence. Thus in 1 Corinthians 15:25-28 there is the christological use of Psalm 8:6 and Psalm 110:1, while in 1 Corinthians 15:47-49 there is repeated reference to the "heavenly man." The question then becomes: Is there any relationship between Paul's calling Jesus Christ the "last Adam" and the exaltation/heavenly man language ascribed to him in 1 Corinthians 15:25-28 and 1 Corinthians 15:47-49? If there is such a relationship, a link might be discovered between Paul's Adamic theology and his belief in the preexistence of Christ, or even a vestigial "Son of man" figure. Many (like Dunn) feel that this is purely speculative and that it presses the evidence too far; we must proceed with caution. In any event, we should not allow the fascinating question of an overlap between preexistence ideas and exaltation/heavenly man language to distract us from the essentially eschatological character of the Christ/Adam analogy as it is found in this letter.

3.2. Adam and the Origin of Sin. Largely because of the narrative of Genesis 3, the figure of Adam has been one of the focal points for discussions about human sinfulness in both Judaism and Christianity (*see* Sin). Romans 5:12-21 contains the fullest treatment of this theme within the Pauline letters. These verses have exerted an enormous influence upon Christian theology over the centuries as various interpreters have sought to plumb the depths of the apostle's teaching about the origin of sin. Clearly Paul associates the entry of sin and death into the world with the transgression of Adam. Although in Romans 5 he is (presumably) thinking historically of the fall, it is readily apparent that he had far more in mind than a historical assessment of Adam and his rebellious act. In effect, Paul's use of Adam in Romans 5:12-21 is protological (pointing back to the beginning) in its emphasis; Adam serves as a means to describe the entry of sin and death into the world and (by extension) the condition of humankind following that first transgression. There is a shift from a focus on Adam and Christ as corporate persons in 1 Corinthians to their respective acts in Romans 5.

This is not to say that the whole perspective of Romans 5 is simply a retrospective (backward-looking) one, for there is at the same time a real sense in which all that has happened in Adam is transcended by what happens in Jesus Christ, the Last Adam. As Paul says in Romans 5:14, Adam is "a type of the one who was to come" (NRSV). Adam's act of disobedience is contrasted with Christ's act of obedience, which carries with it a promise of future life within the new creation. Indeed, in Romans 5:15-21, within a highly structured section of his argument, Paul goes to great lengths to make it clear that Jesus Christ has met the negative effects of Adam's transgression in every way: transgression is met by obedience, condemnation by justification, death by life. The argument *a minori ad maius* ("from the lesser to the greater") is employed throughout, and the tremendous truth concerning the surpassing of sin and its effects by God's grace in Christ is emphasized. However, the protological dimension of the Adam/Christ analogy does come to the fore here in a way that it does not in 1 Corinthians 15.

The fact that Romans 5:12 is an unfinished sentence in Greek has led to a variety of attempts to interpret the direction in which Paul's argument was heading. As F. W. Danker has noted, part of the dilemma is the difficulty in deciding what the antecedent for the dative relative pronoun *ho* is (sin, death, Adam or neither, but with the preposition *epi [eph']*, an idiom meaning "for which reason," "because"). In addition, the Augustinian rendering of Romans 5:12 as "in whom (Adam) all sinned" (Latin *in quo omnes peccaverunt*) has ever since, for better or worse, governed the church's theological interpretation of the Adam declaration. C. E. B. Cranfield lists six major possibilities for interpreting Romans 5:12d alone and notes that support for each can be found within church history. G. Bonner laments that Augustine did not "concentrate more upon the rich and profound conception of the antithesis between the two Adams, rather than on the macabre theory of the participation of unbegotten humanity in the first Adam's primal sin" (Bonner, 247).

It is important to note that while Paul does turn to Adam as the means whereby sin enters the world, he does not tell us the means whereby that sin is transmitted from one generation to another. The mechanics are left unexplained, beyond the simple declaration that "all humankind sinned" (a more correct rendering of Rom 5:12). Adam's responsibility for the origin of sin's introduction into the world is affirmed by Paul alongside an affirmation of the individual's responsibility for the presence of sin in his or her life. For Paul, both elements (personal guilt and responsibility as well as universal guilt and sin in Adam) are active. This paradox becomes clear by the way in which Paul's thought flows quite freely from the intensely personal statement in Romans 5:12 ("because all men sinned" [NRSV], to the more deterministic statement of Romans 5:19 ("by the one man's disobedience the many were made sinners" [NRSV]. Paul's teaching is echoed in *2 Baruch* 54:15, 19: "For although Adam sinned first and has brought death upon all who were not in his own time, yet each of them who has been born from him has prepared for himself the coming torment. . . . Adam is, therefore, not the cause, except only for himself, but each of us has become our own Adam" (Charlesworth edition).

4. Adam and the Image of God.

Adamic theology has also had an important role to play in several other key passages within the Pauline letters, notably those, such as the hymnic materials in Philippians 2:6-11 and Colossians 1:15-20 and the declaration in 2 Corinthians 4:4, which speak of Jesus Christ in terms of his being "the image of God." Here the OT background of Adam is one who is created "in the image of God" (*morphē* is used in Phil 2:6 and *eikōn* in Col 1:15 and 2 Cor 4:4). The description of the "glory of God (or man)" also figures in the discussion at this point. This confluence of imagery and description has recently led some scholars to see the preponderance of "image of God" language found throughout the Pauline letters as another expression of Adamic theology. J. D. G. Dunn (1980), for instance, argues strongly for such an Adamic understanding of the Philippian hymn; M. D. Hooker sees an Adamic motif underlying Romans 1:18-32, where the apostle describes humankind's predicament in terms of Adam's fall.

A. J. M. Wedderburn offers some clarifications to Hooker's suggestion. In addition, there is some justification for seeing the fall of Adam as underlying the declaration made by Paul in Romans 3:23.

4.1. Image of God: Nature and Existence in Romans 5. Closely related to this matter is the consideration of how being made "in the image of God" stands as a description of human nature and existence. This is a matter that has long occupied the attention of Christian commentators, many of whom, like J. Calvin (as R. Prins notes), have concentrated on Paul's letters in addressing the issue. It is interesting to note that the whole of Romans 5, particularly the Adam/Christ analogy in Romans 5:12-21, becomes critical in this regard.

The interpretations of Romans 5 offered by K. Barth and R. Bultmann are helpful comparisons on this point, standing as interpretations concentrating on the christological and anthropological halves of the analogy respectively. Thus Barth focuses on the christological element within the analogy and sees the passage as essentially one expressing humankind's nature. Bultmann focuses on the anthropological element within the analogy and sees the passage as essentially expressing humankind's existence. In short, the crucial question concerns how we understand humankind (Adam) to be made "in the image of God." Is it in Adam or Christ that we truly see "the image of God"? Do we begin with Christ and move to interpret humankind as the image of Christ (Barth's position)? Or do we begin with humankind and move to interpret Christ as the true expression of what the image of God means (Bultmann's position)?

These two interpretative approaches are dependent, in part, on the way in which the two halves of Romans 5 (Rom 5:1-11 and Rom 5:12-21) are seen to fit together. Thus Barth effectively places Romans 5:12-21, with its description of Adamic humankind, within the boundaries of Romans 5:1-11, which states the real condition of humankind in Christ. Bultmann grounds Romans 5:12-21 in the lifestyle motivated by Christ's example of faith and stresses that Romans 5:1-11 concerns the paradoxical existence of believers in hope. In other words, Romans 5:12-21 is taken to express this life of the believer more fully, and it is only at that point that the christological component, as it were, is introduced into the scheme.

4.2. Image of God: Stages of Salvation History. Another way to express this essential difference of interpreting the meaning of humankind (whether it is Adamic humankind or the new humankind in Christ) as being made "in the image of God" is via an illustration of successive stages which are negotiated in salvation history. The eschatological framework that underlies the whole of Paul's thought sees the old age, in the light of the Christ event, as having given way to a new age, as texts such as 2 Corinthians 5:17 demonstrate.

J. A. Ziesler sets this out in terms of a possible three-stage scheme in which "original state—fall—restored state" serves as a description of this development. Such a three-stage scheme would tend toward the kind of interpretation offered by Bultmann. However, Ziesler argues that Paul's view of man is so overwhelmingly directed toward the eschatological vision of the Last Adam that such a three-stage scheme becomes irrelevant to any discussion of Paul. He notes that nowhere does Paul talk of Adam in terms of his being "in the image of God" and on that basis suggests that a two-stage scheme is closer to Paul's central teaching. This would trace the steps in salvation history as a simpler movement (fall—restored state) and would tend toward the kind of interpretation offered by Barth.

Is such a radical break between Adam and Christ as the image of God justified? Ziesler's ideas need to be modified somewhat by a more rigorous consideration of 1 Corinthians 11:3-9, where Paul employs the creation story of Genesis as a basis for proper ethical behavior among men and women with respect to covering one's head during worship. The crucial verse is 1 Corinthians 11:7: "For a man ought not to have his head veiled, since he is the image and reflection of God; but woman is the reflection of man" (NRSV). The point here is that Paul shows some flexibility in his usage of "image of God" and is willing to apply the concept broadly if it suits his purposes, even if it is true that the passage does, as Ziesler notes, occur in a nonsoteriological context. Nevertheless, we should not overlook the Adamic undertone of this verse—Paul means to say that man, that is, every human being, bears in some way the image and glory (or "reflection" as in the NRSV) of God just as the first Adam did.

This is not to deny that, according to Paul, there is a strong sense in which humankind's glory as the image of God finds its fulfillment in Christ. In Philippians 3:20-21 we find this clearly expressed in terms of the believer's transformation from a "body of humility" into "the body of his (Christ's) glory," and in Romans 8:29 the believer is described as one who is "conformed to the image of his (God's) Son."

4.3. Image of God: Christophany. Is it possible to determine the origin of Paul's understanding of Jesus Christ in terms of the Last Adam and its connection with an "image of God" motif? There appears to be a close relationship between image-christophany and descriptions of the risen Lord Jesus Christ that build upon the OT tradition of theophany and are properly described as christophany. This means that those passages where Paul describes or alludes to his own conversion experience and his vision of Christ can be taken as supplementing an Adamic christology. This brings passages such as 1 Corinthians 9:1; 15:8-10; 2 Corinthians 3:4—4:6; Galatians 1:13-17 and Philippians 3:4-11 into the discussion and sees within them an underlying Adamic theme. S. Kim argues that this brings together two different bases of christological thought in Paul, a wisdom christology and an image christology, both of which converge in the person of Jesus Christ, the Second Adam within Paul's thought.

5. Adam and the Body of Christ.

In that Paul viewed humankind as embodied in both Adam and Christ, unredeemed and redeemed respectively, he demonstrated or contributes to a conceptual overlap between an Adamic theology and the idea of the body of Christ (*see* Body of Christ). In other words, this body of Christ is made up of believers who are all joined together so as to form a united humanity, that of the last Adam. Although explicit reference to Adam is not made within the key texts under discussion here, it is clear that fallen Adamic humankind is spiritually reconstituted (Eph 1:10) in Christ in such a way that Adamic language and body of Christ imagery merge. We see this particular emphasis at various points in the Pauline letters, including Colossians 3:12-17 and Ephesians 2:13-18.

In the modern era W. D. Davies has spearheaded investigation into this matter by pointing out the Jewish rabbinic background to such an understanding of Adam and its relevance to a study of Paul's teaching about a corporate Christ. Central to this issue is the recognition that discussion about Adam in these terms is not primarily about humankind per se, so much as about the nation of Israel viewed from an eschatological perspective, as N. T. Wright argues. The contribution brought by a sense of the corporate, whether it be seen in terms of an Adamic humankind or in terms of the body of Christ, to an analysis of the Pauline letters should not be underestimated. Such a reinterpretation of the OT promises to the nation of Israel in terms of the new creation in Christ seems implied in Galatians 6:15-16, and it is certainly made unambiguous within some of the writings of later Christian leaders, such as Justin Martyr, who declared that the Christian church is "the true spiritual Israel" (Justin *Dial. Tryph.* 11.5). However, who constitutes "Israel" is a difficult matter to decide throughout Paul's letters, and a one-for-one exchange between the nation and the church cannot be easily sustained, especially in light of difficult verses such as Romans 11:26.

See also CHRISTOLOGY; ESCHATOLOGY; IN CHRIST.

DPL: IMAGE, IMAGE OF GOD; NEW NATURE AND OLD NATURE.

BIBLIOGRAPHY. C. K. Barrett, *From First Adam to Last* (London: A & C Black, 1962); K. Barth, *Christ and Adam: Man and Humanity in Romans 5* (SJTOP 5; Edinburgh: Oliver & Boyd, 1956); G. Bonner, "Augustine on Romans 5:12," in *Studia Evangelica* 5, ed. F. L. Cross (Berlin: Akademie Verlag, 1968) 242-47; R. Bultmann, "Adam and Christ According to Romans 5," in *Current Issues in New Testament Interpretation: Essays in Honor of O. A. Piper*, ed. W. Klassen and G. F. Snyder (London: SCM, 1962) 143-65; C. E. B. Cranfield, *The Epistle to the Romans* (2 vols.; Edinburgh: T & T Clark, 1975); F. W. Danker, "Romans 5:12: Sin Under Law," *NTS* 14 (1967-68) 424-39; W. D. Davies, *Paul and Rabbinic Judaism* (4th ed.; Philadelphia: Fortress, 1980); J. D. G. Dunn, *Christology in the Making* (Philadelphia: Westminster, 1980) xviii-xix, 98-128; idem, "1 Corinthians 15.45—Last Adam, Life-Giving Spirit," in *Christ and Spirit in the New Testament: Studies in Honor of C. F. D. Moule*, ed. B. Lindars and S. Smalley (Cambridge: Cambridge University Press, 1973) 127-41; M. D. Hooker, *From Adam to Christ: Essays on Paul* (Cambridge: Cambridge University Press, 1990); S. Kim, *The Origin of Paul's Gospel* (Grand Rapids: Eerdmans, 1982); L. J. Kreitzer, "Christ as Second Adam in Paul,"

CV 32 (1989) 55-101; J. Lambrecht, "Paul's Christological Use of Scripture in 1 Corinthians 15.20-28," *NTS* 28 (1982) 502-27; J. R. Levison, *Portraits of Adam in Early Judaism* (JSPSup 1; Sheffield: Academic Press, 1988); B. Pearson, *The Pneumatikos-Psychikos Terminology in 1 Corinthians* (Missoula, MT: Scholars Press, 1973); R. Prins, "The Image of God in Adam and the Restoration of Man in Jesus Christ," *SJT* 25 (1972) 32-44; R. Scroggs, *The Last Adam* (Oxford: Basil Blackwell, 1966); M. Thrall, "Christ Crucified or Second Adam? A Christological Debate Between Paul and the Corinthians," in *Christ and Spirit in the New Testament: Studies in Honor of C. F. D. Moule,* ed. B. Lindars and S. Smalley (Cambridge: Cambridge University Press, 1973) 143-56; A. J. M. Wedderburn, "Adam in Paul's Letter to the Romans," in *Studia Biblica* 1978: 3. *Papers on Paul and Other New Testament Authors,* ed. E. A. Livingstone (JSNTSup 3: Sheffield: Academic Press, 1980) 413-30; N. T. Wright, "Adam, Israel and the Messiah," in *The Climax of the Covenant* (Minneapolis: Fortress, 1991) 18-40; J. A. Ziesler, "Anthropology of Hope," *ExpT* 90 (1978-79) 104-9.   L. J. Kreitzer

ADOPTION, SONSHIP: PAUL

In the Pauline letters the Greek word *huiothesia* is used either of the Israelites (Rom 9:4) or of believers (Gal 4:5; Rom 8:15, 23; Eph 1:5) as sons of God. There is, however, some disagreement as to how to translate the term, whether as "adoption" or, more generally, as "sonship." This problem must be resolved before the specific background of the term can be discussed.

    1. The Meaning of *Huiothesia* in Paul
    2. The Background of Divine "Adoption as Sons" in Paul
    3. The Sonship of Believers in Paul

1. The Meaning of *Huiothesia* in Paul.

The fact that Paul uses *huiothesia* in the sense of "adoption" has sometimes been denied in favor of the translation "sonship" (e.g., Byrne), but the overwhelming lexical evidence hardly supports this contention (see Scott 1992). In Paul, as in contemporary extrabiblical sources, *huiothesia* always denotes either the process or the state of being adopted as son(s). This is substantiated not only by the univocal and widespread usage of the term in literary and nonliterary sources but also by ancient Greek lexicographers dating to the time of the NT. Paul's use of *huiothesia* ob-

viously appropriates this normal usage of the term, because the construction in Galatians 4:5 is closely paralleled in Hellenistic literature (cf. Nicolaus of Damascus *Vit. Caes.* 130.55). Hence any attempt to translate the term more generally as "sonship" sets the study of the background off on the wrong foot from the start.

2. The Background of Divine "Adoption as Sons" in Paul.

Among those authors who agree that *huiothesia* denotes "adoption," there is diversity of opinion as to the background of the term. This is due in part to the fact that Paul seems to be the first to use the term in a theological context (let alone of divine adoption) and yet he never explains what he means by the term. The apostle evidently assumes that his readers would know what was meant by *the* adoption as sons of God.

    2.1. Adoption as a Theological Abstraction. Some scholars treat Paul's concept of adoption simply as an abstraction that is linked with another Pauline concept. In this way the question of background is obviated altogether. For example, H. Hübner takes adoption as a synonym of "freedom" (*eleutheria*) in the sense of freedom from the law. R. Bultmann and others following him treat adoption as a forensic-eschatological term parallel to "righteousness" *(dikaiosynē)*. S. Kim considers Paul's concept of *huiothesia* a secondary deduction of the Damascus Road christophany, in which Paul perceived the risen Lord as the image of God or the *Son of God.

    2.2. Adoption Against a Greco-Roman Background. When, as is more commonly done, Paul's concept of divine adoption is considered against a Greco-Roman background, it is usually compared either with a particular case of divine adoption in Greco-Roman mythology or with the actual practice of adoption in Greco-Roman jurisprudence.

    2.2.1. Divine Adoption in Greco-Roman Mythology. Divine adoption plays very little role in Greco-Roman sources. Outside of Paul, *huiothesia* is not used of such adoptions in the period under consideration. The few unequivocal examples of divine adoption that can be adduced from Greco-Roman sources using other terms of adoption do not provide a background for Paul's concept (cf. the adoption of Heracles by Hera [Diodorus Siculus 4.39.2], that of Alexander the Great by Amon-Zeus [Plutarch *Alex.* 50.6], that of Solon by Fortune [Plutarch *Mor.* 318C] and that of the Lybian goddess "Athena" by Ammon-Zeus [Herodotus 4.180]). The mystery religions have sometimes been suggested as a possible background (cf. Betz), but there is no evidence for divine adoption in the mysteries (*see* Religion, Greco-Roman).

2.2.2. Adoption as a Legal Metaphor. Many scholars have suggested that Paul's concept of adoption is a legal metaphor that Paul constructed ad hoc from his Greco-Roman background. Among them, a few have considered it a metaphor drawn from Hellenistic law, because there adoption is an institution connected especially with inheritance, and Galatians 4:5 speaks of the adoption that makes believers heirs (cf. Wenger). More often, however, proponents of this kind of approach (e.g., Lyall, Bruce) have seen Paul's concept of adoption in light of the elaborate Roman ceremony in which the minor to be adopted was emancipated from the authority of his natural father and placed under the new authority of his adoptive father, often for the purpose of social and/or political maneuvering. Galatians 4:5 does indeed put redemption and adoption in parallel, but the notion that the witness of the Spirit (*see* Holy Spirit) in Romans 8:16 reflects the witnesses in the Roman ceremony hardly deserves serious consideration. Circumstantial evidence such as Paul's Roman citizenship and the prevalence of Roman adoptions in Paul's day also fails to establish the case for a legal metaphor.

2.3. Adoption Against an Old Testament/Jewish Background. The term *huiothesia* occurs in the NT only in Paul and never in the Septuagint or other Jewish sources. Despite frequent claims to the contrary, however, the concept of adoption—even divine adoption—was known to the OT and Judaism, regardless of whether it was ever practiced (see Scott 1992, Malul). Therefore it is not impossible that the roots of Paul's concept could be found here.

2.3.1. Galatians 4:5. The context of the earliest occurrence of the term, in Galatians 4:5, does in fact give a decisive clue to understanding *huiothesia* against an OT/Jewish background. For when Galatians 4:1-2 is properly understood not as an illustration from Greco-Roman law but as an allusion to the OT (see Scott 1992), it is clear that Galatians 4:5 is set within a context framed by Exodus typology (Gal 4:1-7). Just as Israel, as heir to the Abrahamic promise (*see* Abraham), was redeemed as

son of God from slavery in Egypt at the time appointed by the Father (Gal 4:1-2; cf. Hos 11:1; Gen 15:13), so also believers were redeemed to adoption as sons of God from slavery under the "elements of the world" at the fullness of time and thereby became heirs to the Abrahamic promise (Gal 4:3-7).

The fact that "the" *huiothesia* is to be seen here against a particular OT/Jewish background is further substantiated by Romans 9:4, where the articular term occurs in a list of Israel's historical privileges (cf. Ex 4:22; Hos 11:1), and more specifically, by the broader context of Galatians 3—4, which makes it clear that believers are sons and heirs as they participate by baptism (Gal 3:27) in the Son of God who was sent to redeem them (Gal 4:4-5; cf. Gal 3:13-14). For, strictly speaking, Christ is the seed of Abraham (Gal 3:16) and the messianic Son of God promised in 2 Samuel 7:12 and 14, respectively. Seen in context, therefore, "the adoption" in Galatians 4:5 must refer to the Jewish eschatological expectation based on 2 Samuel 7:14.

It can be shown that 2 Samuel 7:14 ("I will be to him [the Davidide] a Father, and he will be to me a son") contains an adoption formula (cf. Ex 2:10; Esther 2:7; Gen 48:5), which subsequent Judaism applied not only to the Davidic Messiah but, under influence of New *Covenant theology (cf. Hos 2:1, cited in Rom 9:26), also to the eschatological people of God. In accordance with the Deuteronomic framework of sin-exile-restoration, this 2 Samuel 7:14 tradition expects that at the advent of the Messiah, God would redeem his people from exile in a second exodus; he would restore them to a covenantal relationship; and he would adopt them, with the Messiah, as his sons (cf. *Jub.* 1:24; *T. Judah* 24:3; 4QFlor 1:11). In fact 2 Corinthians 6:18 cites the adoption formula of 2 Samuel 7:14 (+Is 43:6), and that in the context of the same exodus typology, the same New Covenant theology and in the same generalized form as in the Jewish tradition. As in the 2 Samuel 7:14 tradition, furthermore, Galatians 4:4-6 connects divine adoption with the reception of the Spirit (of the New Covenant) in the heart. Hence, while the context of *huiothesia* in Galatians 4:5 gives no reason to suspect a Greco-Roman background for the term, the whole line of argumentation in Galatians 3—4, together with Pauline parallels, leads unambiguously to an OT/Jewish background for the term (cf. Rom 9:4) and particularly to the

2 Samuel 7:14 tradition (cf. 2 Cor 6:18). In other words, believers who are thus baptized (*see* Baptism) into the messianic Son of God and take up his very cry of "Abba!" to the Father (Gal 4:6; Rom 8:15; cf. Mk 14:36) participate with him in the Davidic promise of divine adoption and in the Abrahamic promise of universal sovereignty (cf. Gal 4:1).

2.3.2. Romans 8:15, 23. This interpretation of *huiothesia* in Galatians 4:5 applies equally to the use of the term in the closely parallel passage of Romans 8. For here, too, participation by adoption in the messianic Son of God who is sent (Rom 8:3; cf. Gal 4:4) is so integrally connected with the reception of the indwelling Spirit that the Spirit can now be called the "Spirit of adoption" (Rom 8:15), the Spirit by which also the righteous requirement of the law is fulfilled (Rom 8:4). Like Galatians 4:5, furthermore, the context of *huiothesia* in Romans 8 contains elements of exodus typology, and divine adoptive sonship implies heirship with Christ in the Abrahamic promise (Rom 8:17). Unlike Galatians 4:5, however, Romans 8 develops the point that participation in the messianic Son of God by adoption extends not only to the present (Romans 8:15) but, by means of the Spirit, to the future as well (Romans 8:23). For just as Jesus once received the Spirit at his baptism and was pronounced the Son of God (cf. Mk 1:11 pars.), so also believers presently receive the Spirit of adoption at their baptism, the Spirit by which, again, believers share in the Son's cry of "Abba!" to the Father (Rom 8:15). Likewise, just as Jesus as the seed of David was set as messianic Son of God in power by the Holy Spirit at the proleptic resurrection of the dead (Rom 1:3-4; cf. 2 Sam 7:12, 14), so also believers, who have the Spirit as the means of resurrection (Rom 8:11), eagerly await their revelation (Rom 8:19), their predestined resurrection/adoption into the glorified image of the resurrected Son (Rom 8:23, 29; cf. Eph 1:5), when the Son will be the firstborn among many brothers and sisters (Rom 8:29; cf. Ps 89:27). At that time the sons of God will share in the Abrahamic promise of universal sovereignty as fellow heirs with Christ the Messiah (Rom 8:17; cf. Rom 4:13; 8:32; Gal 4:1). Hence the present and future aspects of *huiothesia* in Romans 8 reflect successive stages of participation in the Son by the Spirit and, as such, constitute ways that believers share with the Son in the Davidic promise.

2.3.3. Conclusion: The Place of Adoption in Pauline Theology. In sum, there is a coherent and specific OT/Jewish background of "adoption as sons" *(huiothesia)* in the Pauline letters: the word occurs four times in the sense of adoption expected by the 2 Samuel 7:14 tradition (cf. 2 Cor 6:18), and that in either a present (Gal 4:5; Rom 8:15) or future aspect (Rom 8:23; Eph 1:5), depending on the christological and salvation-historical moment stressed in each context. Once the word occurs in the sense of the exodus type that underlies this *huiothesia* of messianic salvation in the other four occurrences (Rom 9:4; cf. Gal 4:1-2). The whole concept must be seen in light of Paul's restoration theology (cf. Sanders, who, although failing to discuss the full Deuteronomic framework, does unwittingly present a major Jewish alternative to business-as-usual "covenantal nomism" [cf. Scott 1993]).

3. The Sonship of Believers in Paul.

The foregoing interpretation of *huiothesia* against the background of the 2 Samuel 7:14 tradition provides the logical and necessary starting point for interpreting Paul's more general references to the sonship of believers; for adoption as sons of God provides the means of entry into divine sonship. Hence the Pauline passages that attribute adoption to believers also call them "son(s)" (cf. Gal 3:26; 4:6, 7; Rom 8:14, 19; 9:26) or, without specifying gender, "children" *(tekna;* cf. Rom 8:16, 17, 21) of God. Second Corinthians 6:18, under the influence of Isaiah 43:6, explicitly broadens the concept of adoption to "daughters." Hence males and females are included in Paul's concept of divine "sonship." In Philippians 2:14-15, Paul instructs his readers to "do everything without grumbling and dispute, in order that you may be faultless and pure, blameless children of God in the midst of a crooked and perverse generation." The reference here to the "children" of God being "blameless" *(amōma)* alludes to Deuteronomy 32:5 where, because they had sinned, the Israelites are characterized as "blameful" *(mōmēta)* and as "not his children" in the context of the Song of Moses, which predicts sin-exile-restoration. In this way Paul contrasts the situation that led up to the punishment of the Israelites as sons of God with the way in which believers as sons of God should now behave (cf. 2 Cor 6:14—7:1; Rom 8:4, 12-14).

See also HOLY SPIRIT; SON OF GOD.

BIBLIOGRAPHY. H. D. Betz, *Galatians: A Commentary on Paul's Letter to the Churches in Galatia* (Herm; Philadelphia: Fortress, 1979); F. F. Bruce, *The Epistle to the Galatians: A Commentary on the Greek Text* (NIGTC; Grand Rapids: Eerdmans, 1982); R. Bultmann, *Theology of the New Testament* (2 vols.; New York: Scribner's, 1951, 1955); B. Byrne, *"Sons of God"—"Seed of Abraham": A Study of the Idea of the Sonship of God of All Christians Against the Jewish Background* (AnBib 83; Rome: Biblical Institute, 1979); M. Hengel, *The Son of God: The Origin of Christology and the History of Jewish-Hellenistic Religion* (Philadelphia: Fortress, 1976); H. Hübner, *Law in Paul's Thought* (Edinburgh: T & T Clark, 1984); S. Kim, *The Origin of Paul's Gospel* (Grand Rapids: Eerdmans, 1981); F. Lyall, *Slaves, Citizens, Sons: Legal Metaphors in the Epistles* (Grand Rapids: Zondervan, 1984); M. Malul, "Foundlings and Their Adoption in the Bible and in Mesopotamian Documents: A Study of Several Legal Metaphors in Ezek 16:1-7," *JSOT* 46 (1990) 97-126; E. P. Sanders, *Jesus and Judaism* (Philadelphia: Fortress, 1985); J. M. Scott, *Adoption as Sons of God: An Exegetical Investigation into the Background of ΥΙΟΘΕΣΙΑ in the Corpus Paulinum* (WUNT 2.48; Tübingen: Mohr Siebeck, 1992); idem, " 'For as Many as Are of Works of the Law Are Under a Curse' (Gal 3:10)," in *Paul and the Scriptures of Israel,* ed. C. A. Evans and J. A. Sanders (JSNTSup 83; Sheffield: Sheffield Academic Press, 1993) 187-221; L. Wenger, "Adoption," *RAC* 1.100.

J. M. Scott

ADVERSARIES I: PAUL

Adversaries are often presupposed in Paul's letters, which are not theoretical treatises but reasoned replies to living situations in the churches. Paul's epistolary responses are often in rebuttal of opposition, whether to his person or to his teachings. Sometimes these are general and merely imply the existence of local resistance to Paul's doctrines, in which case they are deemed to lie outside the scope of this article. At other times, however, Paul refers to adversaries from outside who have infiltrated the churches established by him with a view to overturning his doctrines and influence. In what follows we will limit our discussion to outsiders who have penetrated the Pauline assemblies.

Scholars have devoted considerable effort in identifying such opponents. So important is the question of the identity of the opponents in 2 Corinthians that C. K. Barrett declared it to be "one of the crucial questions for the understanding of the New Testament and the origins of Christianity," a view with which we concur.

Second Corinthians, where opposition to Paul comes into clearest focus, has been submitted to intense investigation and has proved to be the most appropriate point at which to begin.

1. Survey of Opinion
2. Paul's Adversaries at Corinth: "Servants of Righteousness"
3. Paul and the Jerusalem Apostles
4. Adversaries in the Galatian Churches
5. Paul's Adversaries: A Profile
6. The Judaizers, James and Paul
7. Opposition at Colossae: Jewish Gnosticism
8. Opposition at Philippi: Judaizers
9. Opposition in the Pastoral Letters.

1. Survey of Opinion.

The range of opinion on the identity of Paul's adversaries is usefully summarized by E. E. Ellis and J. J. Gunther. Broadly speaking, the identity of the opponents in 2 Corinthians has been classified in three ways.

1.1. Judaizers. This view has been classically expressed by F. C. Baur and repeated with refinements by Barrett, M. E. Thrall and R. P. Martin. It argues that the newcomers to Corinth were Palestinian Jews bent on bringing the Gentile Corinthians within the framework of Judaism. There is much to be said for this hypothesis.

However, based on 1 Corinthians 1:12, Baur also argued that the opponents were emissaries of Peter who came to Corinth claiming to be "of Christ" (2 Cor 10:7). Moreover, Baur drew a distinction between the false apostles (*pseudapostoloi,* 2 Cor 11:13-15) and the exalted apostles (*hyperlian apostoloi,* 2 Cor 11:5; 12:11) from whom the false apostles came, namely the Jerusalem apostles (*see* Apostle).

Against this it should be noted, first, that neither Peter nor James is mentioned within 2 Corinthians, although Paul does not hesitate to refer to them by name—and sometimes in negative terms—on other occasions (Gal 1:18-19; 2:9, 11-14; 1 Cor 1:12; 9:5).

Moreover, the differentiation of *hyperlian apostoloi* from *pseudapostoloi* appears to be arbitrary. R. Bultmann argued that the transition from *pseudapostoloi* (2 Cor 11:1-4) to the *hyperlian apostoloi* (2 Cor 11:5) is far too abrupt to make sense. The distinction is perhaps necessitated by Baur's thesis. Baur would not go so far as to suggest that Paul would call Peter and James "false apostles . . . disguising themselves as apostles of Christ . . . servants [of Satan]" (2 Cor 11:13, 15 RSV). The less sinister sounding *hyperlian apostoloi* is more of a tribute paid to the Jerusalem leaders.

Furthermore, the one explicit reference to *pseudapostoloi* is sandwiched between the two references to *hyperlian apostoloi* in a part of the letter (2 Cor 10—12) where Paul utilizes the idea of *hyper* ("better") ironically. Paul uses words prefixed with *hyper* to attack the *pseudapostoloi* for their missionary imperialism (overextending themselves, *hyperektenein*, 2 Cor 10:14) into lands beyond (*ta hyperekeina*, 2 Cor 10:16), for their boast of abundance of revelations, (*tē hyperbolē tōn apokalyseōn*, 2 Cor 12:7) and the resulting superelation (*hyperairesthai* 2 Cor 12:7). To expose their boastfulness Paul boasts ironically of being a "better" *(hyper)* servant of *Christ in terms of the sufferings that he catalog (2 Cor 11:23-33). The close association of *hyper* words with *pseudapostoloi* makes it likely that the *hyperlian apostoloi* and the *pseudapostoloi* are the same people.

1.2. Gnostics. Diametrically opposed to the Baur thesis is the opinion that the opponents were "gnostic pneumatics" who minimized the earthly Jesus in favor of a heavenly *Lord and who pushed Paul's doctrines of grace to antinomian extremes. This theory holds that since the opponents preached "another spirit" (2 Cor 11:4) they must have been antinomian, since *Law and Spirit (*see* Holy Spirit) are mutually exclusive. 2 Corinthians 6:14—7:1 is held to be Paul's reaction against their antinomianism. They despise Paul's inferior *gnōsis* (2 Cor 11:6) and self-confessed weakness (2 Cor 10:10) and present themselves as offering a higher *gnōsis* supported by miraculous and visionary "signs." This hypothesis regards the opposition to Paul in 2 Corinthians as an extension of the gnosticizing tendencies evident in 1 Corinthians.

An early advocate of this theory was W. Lütgert (see Gunther) who saw the adversaries' background in liberal diaspora Judaism. Lütgert in turn influenced the more recent expositions of Bultmann and W. Schmithals. This view is undermined by the strongly Hebraic/Israelite character of those who oppose Paul (2 Cor 11:22) and by their message, which appears to have focused on Moses and therefore the Law (2 Cor 3:4-16). Furthermore, it is far from certain that *Gnosticism was as clearly defined during Paul's time as this hypothesis would require.

1.3. Divine Men. More recently D. Georgi has developed the hypothesis that Paul's opponents claimed—on the basis of their gifts and signs— to be "divine men" in succession to Jesus and Moses, who both were charismatic, wonder-working figures. These were itinerant Hellenistic Jewish missionaries whose methods and beliefs arose from a Hellenistic milieu. Their confident claims and strong demands made on the Corinthians were part of their legitimacy as *theioi andres* which they insisted upon over against the manifest weaknesses of Paul.

A variation of this theory may be found in that of G. Friedrich, who holds that the models to which the newcomers pointed were not drawn from the Hellenistic world but from early Christianity. According to Friedrich, Stephen and Philip, the miracle-working Hellenist leaders of Acts 6, gathered supporters who have now come with similar powers to Corinth to present Jesus as a triumphant second Moses, as opposed to the suffering figure preached by Paul.

Georgi's theory suffers from the problem that the *theioi andres* are not the clearly defined type he presupposes, and reference to them generally comes from texts later than the NT (see Blackburn). His argument for their claim to "being sufficient," "sufficiency" (*hikanos, hikanotēs*, 2 Cor 2:16; cf. 2 Cor 3:5) does not necessitate self-presentation as "divine men"; mere superiority over Paul would suffice.

Friedrich's hypothesis, while helpfully suggestive, does not reckon on the many points at which Stephen's theology may have anticipated and indeed been the source of Paul's doctrines rather than being antipathetic to them.

While the growing knowledge of the world of the NT will doubtless stimulate further theories of their identity and intentions, given that we only meet Paul's adversaries in his passing rebuttal of them, it is unlikely that a scholarly consensus will be reached. The evidence from Paul's letters is too unsystematic and indeed polemical to permit ultimately secure historical decisions.

2. Paul's Adversaries at Corinth: "Servants of Righteousness."

2.1. Evidence from 2 Corinthians. The key to the identity of Paul's opponents in Corinth is to be found in his statement, "For such men are false apostles, deceitful workmen, disguising themselves as apostles of Christ . . . [Satan's] servants also disguise themselves as servants of righteousness" (2 Cor 11:13-15).

In terms of their self-presentation the adversaries came as "apostles of Christ," "workmen" and "servants," that is, on the same terms as Paul (2 Cor 11:12), having a vocabulary of ministry identical with Paul's. Their "deceit," their "disguise" was that they purported to be "servants of righteousness" (diakonoi dikaiosynēs).

Earlier Paul had contrasted two ministries (diakoniai)—of Moses and of Christ (2 Cor 3:4-18). The former, a "written code" which "kills," the latter—"a *new covenant"—"[written] in the Spirit," "gives life" (2 Cor 3:6). The former is a "ministry (diakonia) of condemnation," the latter "a ministry (diakonia) of righteousness" (dikaiosynēs, 2 Cor 3:9).

How does "this ministry," which Paul says he "has" (2 Cor 4:1), mediate "life" and "righteousness"? It is by Christ's death, Paul declares, that "God made him to be *sin . . . that in him we might become the righteousness (dikaiosynē) of God" (2 Cor 5:21). This is "the ministry (diakonia) of reconciliation . . . the message of reconciliation" that God has entrusted to Paul (2 Cor 5:18-19; cf. 2 Cor 6:3).

Paul, therefore, is a diakonos in the "diakonia of righteousness" through the cross of Christ, while the opponents are diakonoi of Moses' diakonia of righteousness through "the written code" which, however, brings not "righteousness" but "condemnation" (2 Cor 3:7). The adversaries' "deceit" lies in their "message" to the Corinthians that *God imputes righteousness by the "written code" rather than through the cross. In proposing to the Corinthians an alternative to the death of Christ as the means of "the righteousness of God," Paul declares these men to be "servants of Satan" (2 Cor 11:15).

The phrase "servants of righteousness," therefore, is critical in the identification of Paul's opponents in Corinth. Since theirs was "the ministry . . . of the written code," that is, of "Moses" (2 Cor 3:6-7), we take it that these men were indeed Judaizers and that their version of the "righteousness of God" by means of the "written code" lay at the heart of their message and was their chief point of difference from the apostle to the Gentiles.

Unfortunately, we may only speculate about their precise message. Once more, however, the word *righteousness may come to our assistance. Righteousness occurs not at all in the Thessalonian letters and only once in 1 Corinthians. The single appearance of "righteousness" to this point, in a letter written to a Greek church, suggests that the issues associated with righteousness had not been raised in Macedonia or Achaia until the writing of 2 Corinthians in about A.D. 56.

2.2. Evidence from Romans. By general agreement, Romans was written in Corinth around A.D. 56 or 57, not long after the writing of 2 Corinthians from Macedonia. There we find "righteousness" occurring forty-nine times with numerous occurrences of the closely related words justify (dikaioō) and righteous (dikaios; see Justification). Since the "righteousness" family of words lies at the heart of the argument of Romans (see the key text, Rom 1:17), it is likely that Paul is there addressing the same issues and the same (kind of) opponents as in 2 Corinthians. Although Paul makes no mention of circumcision in 2 Corinthians, it is quite possible that circumcision was part of the dispute at Corinth. It was certainly prominent in both Romans and Galatians.

The Romans letter may well be Paul's more measured response to the issue of righteousness so painfully raised in Corinth and passionately but unevenly addressed in 2 Corinthians. Certainly polemical echoes may still be heard in Romans that may relate to the same opponents as in 2 Corinthians. There are those who "slanderously charge" Paul with saying "why not do evil that good may come?" (Rom 3:8; cf. Rom 6:1; Gal 2:17). His defensive comments about the Jews (Rom 3:1, 9; 4:1; 9:3-5; 11:1) are consistent with accusations that might arise from a Judaizing apostolate whose message focused on righteousness through the keeping of the works of the law (cf. Rom 3:21—4:3, 16; 10:3-4). Possibly, "those who create dissensions and difficulties in opposition to the doctrines you have been taught" (Rom 16:17) represents Paul's general warning to Roman Christians about the Judaizing message arising out of problems recently encountered in Corinth.

2.3. Newcomers at Corinth. It is evident from 2 Corinthians that Paul's adversaries in Corinth were a group ("many," 2 Cor 2:17) of persons (hoi kapēleuntes, "hucksters" or "peddlers," 2 Cor 2:17) who had "come" to Corinth (2 Cor 11:4-5) from outside (their "letters of commendation," 2 Cor 3:1) where they and their message had been "received" (2 Cor 11:4, 20).

It emerges from 2 Corinthians that these newcomers legitimated their *diakonia* in Corinth by "boasting" (*kauchasthai*, 2 Cor 10—12 passim) of their achievements, "contrasting" (*synkrinein*, 2 Cor 10:12) their strengths with Paul's weaknesses. In their missionary journey to Corinth they have come a greater, Paul a lesser, distance (2 Cor 10:13-14). They have "letters of commendation" (from Jerusalem?); Paul has none (2 Cor 3:1-3). They are "sufficient," triumphant figures; Paul is inadequate, a sorry figure as he limps from place to place in defeat (2 Cor 2:14—3:5; 4:1, 16). Extrapolating from remarks Paul makes about himself, some scholars affirm that these experiences were being claimed by his adversaries. They are men of divine power ("beside" themselves, 2 Cor 5:13), "caught up . . . out of the body . . . into paradise," where they see "visions" and hear "revelations" of what "cannot be told" (2 Cor 12:1-5), whereas Paul is mundane, a minister without power, worldly and weak (2 Cor 10:3-6; 12:1-10; cf. 2 Cor 5:12-13). Possibly they performed "the signs of an apostle" (2 Cor 12:12) whereas, they allege, Paul did not. They are powerful in speech (2 Cor 11:5-6) and in wisdom whereas he is in speech "unskilled" and in general "a fool" (2 Cor 11:1—12:13). In all things he is "inferior" (cf. 2 Cor 11:5), whereas they are superior, "better" (*hyper*, 2 Cor 11:23).

Herein lies the difficulty of identifying these adversaries as Judaizing "Hebrews" bent on imposing "Moses" (the law) on the Corinthians (2 Cor 11:22; 3:4-16). Corinth was a Greco-Roman metropolis. How can we account for "Hebrews" having sufficient style to find acceptance with such an audience and, moreover, displaying proficiency in the rhetorical arts of "boasting" and "comparison"? These "Hebrews" would appear to be behaving like Greeks.

The two main theories about the opponents—that they must have been Judaizers *or* Gnostics—are perfectly understandable given the apparent contradiction implicit in the evidence about them in 2 Corinthians.

New information is available, however, which changes our whole idea of life in first-century Judea. On the basis of funerary inscriptions, M. Hengel has argued that there may have been as many as 16,000 Greek-speaking Jews in Jerusalem out of an estimated population of 100,000 (Hengel, 10). He reasons that many of these must have enjoyed a high level of classical education. It is quite conceivable, therefore, that the "Hebrews" who came to Corinth spoke polished Greek and possessed skills in *rhetoric. Saul/Paul was not altogether without abilities in these areas, to say nothing of his coworker Silas/Silvanus, the Jewish-Christian prophet of Jerusalem to whom is attributed the stylishly written 1 Peter (Acts 15:32; 2 Cor 1:19; 1 Pet 5:12).

What then of the paranormal ecstasy, visions, revelations and miracles on which Paul's opponents depended, in part at least, for their acceptance in Corinth? Study of the history of Judea in the period A.D. 44-66 reveals a milieu of political disintegration, revolutionary activism and apocalyptic fervor that was expressed in prophetic inspiration and miraculous signs (see, e.g., Josephus *J.W.* 2.13.4 §§258-59). It is quite possible that Judea at the time represented the kind of religious milieu from which the *pseudapostoloi* could have come. It is unnecessary, therefore, to require a gnostic provenance for these newcomers.

3. Paul and the Jerusalem Apostles.

If the newcomers in Corinth, as reflected in 2 Corinthians, were Judaizers, were they emissaries of the Jerusalem apostles, as Baur suggested? Paul's relationship with the Jerusalem church and its apostles is set out most clearly in Galatians, particularly in Galatians 1—2. Contrary to Baur's thesis, it emerges from these chapters that while tension existed between Paul and the Jerusalem apostles, they are distinct from his adversaries, in Jerusalem and Antioch.

Paul outlines his relationship with the Jerusalem apostles by referring to four critical occasions in his own ministry. He writes autobiographically but so as to establish with the Galatians the delicate nature of relationship with "those who were apostles before" him in Jerusalem (Gal 1:17).

First, he refers to his "call" on the way to Damascus (Gal 1:15-17; *see* Conversion and Call of Paul). It was God, not the Jerusalem apostles, who "called" Paul and "revealed his Son" to him that he "might preach him among the Gentiles" (Gal 1:16). Not even after his call did Paul "confer with (literally, "seek corroboration from") flesh and blood," that is, the apostles in Jerusalem. He went away to Arabia and then to Damascus. Paul's knowledge of the risen Christ has been mediated directly to Paul by God.

The second occasion was in Jerusalem (Gal 1:18-21). Only "after three years" from his "call" did Paul go up to Jerusalem "to visit Cephas," with whom he remained fifteen days (Gal 1:18). Paul's word *visit* (Gk *historēsai*), whose meaning is much debated, could be interpreted "meet" or perhaps "inquire of," suggesting some indebtedness to Cephas for information about the historical, as opposed to the heavenly, Christ (*see* Jesus and Paul). Paul underlines his apostolic autonomy by commenting in passing, "I saw none of the other apostles except James the Lord's brother," suggesting no more than a courtesy call. His carefully chosen words are highlighted by his solemn assurance, "In what I am writing to you, before God, I do not lie" (Gal 1:20; but cf. Acts 9:26-30). "Still not known by sight to the churches of Judea" (i.e., in and around Jerusalem) he went to Syria and Cilicia (Gal 1:21-22; cf. Acts 9:30).

The third occasion, also in Jerusalem, occurred "after fourteen years" (Gal 2:1-10), that is fourteen years from his great watershed "call" en route to Damascus. Concerned to know of the acceptability to James, Cephas and John "of the gospel which [he] preach[ed] among the Gentiles," a gospel that did not require circumcision of Gentiles, Paul brought with him as a test case the uncircumcised Titus. While Paul's apostolic authority was independent of Jerusalem, it was important that his circumcision-free Gentile converts were accepted, along with believing Jews, as spiritual heirs of *Abraham.

Despite the attempts of "false brethren" (Gk *pseudadelphoi*, Gal 2:4) to have Titus circumcised, the "pillar apostles"—James, Cephas and John— made no such demands on Paul's Gentile companion (Gal 2:6). Rather, the three Jerusalem apostles formally recognized that Paul had been "entrusted [i.e., by God] with the gospel to the uncircumcised," whereupon they joined hands with Paul and Barnabas in a gospel "fellowship" whereby Paul and Barnabas should "go to the Gentiles" and the Jerusalem triumvirate should "[go] to the circumcised" (Gal 2:7-9).

In other words, the Jerusalem apostles recognized two apostolates, one to Jews led by Peter, the other to Gentiles led by the Antioch delegates Paul and Barnabas. Despite the decision to approve two racially distinct apostolates, there was overarching agreement in the fundamentals of the gospel based on the death and resurrection of Christ (see 1 Cor 15:3-5, 11).

The fourth occasion was at Antioch in Syria, a church of mixed Jew-Gentile membership (Gal 2:11-14). Cephas had come (from Jerusalem) to Antioch, where he had shared table fellowship with Gentile members (including the *Lord's Supper?), something he had presumably been prepared to do following the conversion of Cornelius (Gal 2:14; cf. Acts 10:28). Though a Jew, Peter now "lived like a Gentile" (Gal 2:14), that is, he had eaten with Gentiles, which meant eating what they ate.

But a serious division along racial-religious lines developed within the church in Antioch with the dramatic arrival of "certain men . . . from James" (in Jerusalem, Acts 15:23-24; cf. Acts 15:1), whom Paul calls "the circumcision party." Cephas "drew back and separated himself" [from eating with the Gentile members of the church]. The rest of the Jewish members, including even Barnabas, acted "insincerely" (literally "hypocritically"). Paul "opposed [Cephas] to the face because he stood condemned" for withdrawing into an exclusively Jewish table fellowship. It was hypocritical for Peter to "live like a Gentile" but now by this action "compel the Gentiles to live like Jews" (Gal 2:14).

At stake at Antioch was "the truth of the gospel" (Gal 2:14), which was raised by the demand that the Jewish Christians must eat separately from Gentile believers, which had the effect of demanding that Gentiles adopt Jewish eating practices. Paul used the telling phrase "the truth of the gospel" in the previous incident in Jerusalem when he opposed the necessity of the circumcision of the Gentile Titus (Gal 2:5). In other words, "the truth of the gospel" is preserved when circumcision and Jewish food laws are regarded as extraneous to the gospel and nonmandatory for Gentiles.

This long autobiographical passage (Gal 1:15–2:14), covering a decade and a half of Paul's life, is invaluable for identifying the degrees of difference between Paul and various persons within the Jerusalem church. We are able to distinguish between "those who were apostles before him" in Jerusalem—with whom certain tensions may be recognized—and others with whom there is outright opposition. Thus Paul insists that his "call" to be an apostle to the Gentiles was mediated directly by God and after some years formally recognized by the "pillar" apostles of Jerusalem. He expresses deference to Cephas in one situation but fierce opposition in another. In regard to James there is a certain ambivalence. At his first visit to Jerusalem he merely "saw" James. He acknowledges by his order of names the primacy of James at the second meeting in Jerusalem, while implying criticism of James because the trouble in Antioch was caused by "men who came from James."

Nonetheless, Cephas and James are not adversaries. No qualifying remarks are used in regard to the "false brethren secretly brought in who slipped in to spy out our freedom . . . that they might bring us under bondage" (Gal 2:4). They may be associated with or more probably identified with the "men who came from James" to Antioch and who had such a dramatic effect on the eating practices of Cephas, Barnabas and the Jewish believers (Gal 2:12-13).

The same distinction is to be found in the *Acts of the Apostles. On one hand there are the "apostles and elders" of the Jerusalem church (Acts 15:2, 6, 22, 23), among whom are named Peter (Acts 15:7) and James (Acts 15:13), while on the other are "believers who belonged to the party of the Pharisees" who said, "It is necessary to circumcise [Gentiles] and to charge them to keep the Law of Moses" (Acts 15:5; cf. Acts 15:1). Whether or not we identify the meeting of the Antioch delegates and the "pillar" apostles (Gal 2) with the so-called Jerusalem Council (Acts 15), it is probable that the "false brethren" of Galatians 2:4 are to be equated with the "believers of the party of the Pharisees" of Acts 15:5.

Acts 15:5, therefore, supplies the precious clue, which is found nowhere else, and which goes a long way toward solving the mystery of the identity of Paul's opponents in Jerusalem. These "false brethren" of Jerusalem, these "men who came from James [from Jerusalem to Antioch] . . . the circumcision party" (Gal 2:4, 12) were "believers who belonged to the party of the Pharisees."

What, then, was the relationship between the pillar apostles of the Jerusalem church—James, Cephas and John—and these men?

4. Adversaries in the Galatian Churches.
Scholars are divided over the dating of the letter to the Galatians. Some place it in the late forties, following hard on the dispute in Antioch (Gal 2:11-14) on the eve of the Jerusalem Council. Others date the letter at about the same time as

2 Corinthians and Romans, that is, around the mid-fifties. Certainly the "righteousness" vocabulary is very prominent in the letter, suggesting that the same issues were at stake as in 2 Corinthians and Romans. But this does not necessarily demand that Galatians was written in the mid-fifties. Paul may have used the "righteousness" vocabulary whenever the Judaizing question was raised.

Unlike Antioch and Corinth, there is no mention of anyone from outside coming to the Galatian churches (2 Cor 11:4; Gal 2:12). The churches were being troubled by a group of Jews led by an unidentified individual (Gal 5:10, 12; 3:1; 1:7, 9) who said that circumcision was a prerequisite for membership in the *Israel of God (Gal 3:6-14; 6:16). These "agitators" and their leader were putting pressure on other Jewish believers to compel the Gentile members to be circumcised (Gal 6:12). They claimed that Paul owed his authority to the Jerusalem apostles (Gal 1:15–2:9) and that Paul "preached circumcision" (Gal 5:11).

Were these agitators and their leader indigenous to the Galatian region or had they in fact come there from somewhere else? The letter of the Jerusalem Council to the "brethren in Antioch, Syria and Cilicia" acknowledges that "some persons from us have troubled you" (Acts 15:23). If such agitators had come from Jerusalem to Cilicia, it would have been no great surprise had they traveled on to southern Galatia. Since the focus of Galatians is on circumcision related to Christian freedom (see, e.g., Gal 5:1-2), a theme that is also prominent in the autobiographical section where "false brethren" in Jerusalem "spy out our freedom . . . that they might bring us into bondage" by having Titus circumcised (Gal 2:3-5), it is reasonable to argue that those who came to the Galatian churches were in fact the "false brethren" of Jerusalem, the "believers who belonged to the party of the Pharisees" (Acts 15:5).

5. Paul's Adversaries: A Profile.
A pattern emerges from the study of 2 Corinthians, Romans and Galatians that enables us to define more closely Paul's adversaries in Corinth as reflected in 2 Corinthians. The supersession of the "written code" associated with Moses by means of "a new covenant" (see Covenant, New Covenant), "a *diakonia* of righteousness," along with Paul's rejection of the opponents in Corinth as "servants of righteous-

ness," suggests that the newcomers had come on a Judaizing mission to bring the Gentile Corinthians under obligation to the written Mosaic code. The proliferation of "righteousness" and related words in Romans and Galatians, concerned as they are to rebut righteousness arising from the works of the Jewish law, add confirmation to the profile of the opponents in Corinth as Judaizers.

Galatians assists us to see that while significant tensions existed between himself and the Jerusalem apostles, it is important to differentiate these from persons Paul calls "false brethren . . . the circumcision party" whom we have been able to more closely identify as "believers from the party of the Pharisees."

The "false brethren" who are also "false apostles" are one and the same group as the "superlative apostles" (*hyperlian apostoloi*, 2 Cor 11:5; 12:11). It emerges from 2 Corinthians that their claim to superiority is based, in part, on their boast that they have traveled as far as they have, possibly that they have traveled farther than Paul (2 Cor 10:13-18). Paul rejects this claim in the terms of the missionary agreement made in Jerusalem in the late forties by the pillar apostles with Paul and Barnabas (Gal 2:7-9). In their coming to Corinth the "superlative apostles" have crossed the line of demarcation and entered Paul's sphere of agreed missionary labor: ministry to the Gentiles. They have "overextend[ed] themselves . . . [not kept] to the limits God has apportioned . . . boasted of work already done in another's field."

From 2 Corinthians there emerges a fascinating profile of these men, their mission and their means of legitimating their mission. Driven in all probability by a heightened religious zeal arising from the rapid deterioration of Roman-Jewish relationships in Judea under Felix's notorious regime, these "superlative apostles" have apparently armed themselves with an array of paranormal abilities calculated to impress the Gentiles in Corinth so as to supplant Paul as their apostle. Their determination to overturn Paul is perhaps also indicative of their awareness of his success in establishing messianic assemblies among the Greeks. But, so far as they were concerned, such assemblies, though connected to the Messiah Jesus, were schisms from Israel, because they gave no real place for Moses and the law (Acts 15:1, 5).

In their countermission, Paul's adversaries have, by any measure, shown zeal comparable with his own. They have opposed him in Jerusalem and traveled from there to churches in Antioch, Syria-Cilicia and Galatia, and now they have come all the way to the city of Corinth in Achaia. This is a remarkable historical phenomenon. They claimed, he says, to be "servants of Christ" (2 Cor 11:23) yet, from his viewpoint, so misguided as to the ministry of "righteousness" that he calls them "[Satan's] servants" (2 Cor 11:14). Their mission and activities have constituted a major threat to the survival of Paul's churches and have provoked him to write letters that are among his most powerful. It is fair to say that lack of appreciation of their identity and zealous program by modern readers significantly hinders our grasp of Paul's argument in those letters where he is responding to their doctrines.

6. The Judaizers, James and Paul.

It is clear from the above argument that we may not too closely associate the name of Peter with Paul's opponents. The incident at Antioch (Gal 2:11-14) shows that Peter was susceptible to their influence, but not the source of it. But what of James, the brother of the Lord, an "apostle before" Paul, who by the late forties had emerged as the preeminent pillar apostle of the Jerusalem church? Was James the source of the opposition that flowed from Jerusalem to the churches of the Gentiles?

James had been a member of the Jerusalem church from its beginning until his death in A.D. 62, a period of about thirty years. At first the leader was Peter, supported by John Zebedee. By the late forties, however, James, not Peter, was the leader (Gal 2:9; Acts 15:13-22). At that time there were apostles and elders at Jerusalem (Acts 15:2, 4, 6, 22, 23). However, when Paul came for the last time to Jerusalem in about A.D. 57, there was no reference to "apostles"; only the Jerusalem elders remained, with James the clear leader.

Over this thirty-year period the Jerusalem church became more conservatively Jewish, doubtless reflecting the rise of Jewish religious nationalism in the face of worsening Roman-Jewish relationships in Judea (Josephus *J.W.* 2.12.1–13.7 §§223-271 passim). First, the Hellenists emigrated in the thirties, and by the late forties they were followed by Peter (and John?) and possibly the other apostles. The final glimpse of the Jerusalem church given by Acts at the time of Paul's final visit is of a thoroughly Jewish enclave.

Despite the good face Acts gives to the meeting, it is clear enough that the Jerusalem elders expressed profound unhappiness with Paul. No speech of gratitude for the collection from the Gentile churches is mentioned, though Luke knew of the collection's existence (Acts 24:17). Rather, the elders pointedly remark on the size and thorough Jewishness of the believing community in Jerusalem, whose widely held conviction it is that Paul has betrayed the cause of Judaism in the Diaspora. It is their understanding that Paul has taught Jews to abandon Moses and not to circumcise their children (Acts 21:21), and he has not required Gentiles to uphold the decisions of the Jerusalem Council over ritual and moral matters (Acts 21:25).

These accusations are instructive since they clearly reflect the views of the Jerusalem elders. Yet these opinions are continuous with and closely resemble the commitment to Moses of the men from Judea who a decade and a half earlier went from Jerusalem to the Gentiles in Antioch insisting on circumcision as a prerequisite to salvation and who, we have argued, were "believers who . . . belonged to the party of the Pharisees" (Acts 15:1, 5).

It is not suggested they were necessarily the same men. Rather, that there was from at least the forties a strongly held theological viewpoint within the messianic community in Jerusalem, which, influenced by Pharisaism, promoted a nationalistic and therefore a Mosaic version of the faith and which therefore regarded Paul's mission to the Gentiles with profound unease. The rising tide of religious nationalism during the crises in Judea of the forties and fifties, together with the decreased influence of more liberal leaders like Stephen, Philip, John and Peter, and the emergence of James as the undisputed leader—the brother of the Lord no less—created an environment in which there arose a mission to counter Paul's influence in the Diaspora. But these persons are never named, either by Paul or in Acts. They remain "certain men" (*tines*, Acts 15:1, 5; Gal 2:12) who on account of their assault on the doctrines of Christ, Paul will portray as "false brothers," "false apostles" and even "[Satan's] servants."

James must have been a significant figure in Jerusalem by the late fifties since he presided over such a large religious community (Acts 21:18-20). In his account of James's death in A.D. 62, Josephus corroborates this impression. The high priest Ananus II seized the opportunity presented by the unexpected death of the procurator Festus to have James stoned. Clearly, James must have been important to pose a threat to the high priest. But his death provoked a protest by those Jerusalemites who were "considered the most fair-minded and who were strict in their observance of the Law" (Josephus *Ant.* 20.9.1 §201), which can only mean citizens of Pharisaic sympathy.

Thus James appears to have enjoyed significant respect within the wider community of Jerusalem. From his viewpoint, as a leader of a messianic community in Jerusalem, Paul's mission to Gentiles in the Diaspora must have raised acute difficulties for relationships between the messianic Jewish community and the wider Jewish community at a time of rapidly increasing religious nationalism.

From Paul's perspective there may have been a degree of nervousness about the Lord's brother since his opponents appear to have come from James's community. It is true that Paul refuses to allow that his apostleship is derived from James (Gal 1:19; cf. Gal 1:17) and to a degree he deprecates the authority of the Jerusalem apostles (Gal 2:6-9), and indeed he voices an angry complaint about "the men who came from James" creating division in Antioch (Gal 2:12). Nonetheless, Paul acknowledges James's apostleship and indeed his primacy as a Jerusalem apostle (Gal 1:19; 2:9). There is no good reason to believe that the "letters of recommendation" brought by the newcomers to Corinth (2 Cor 2:17—3:1) bore the name of James. Paul is hardly likely to have persevered with the collection for the Jerusalem church if James was the wellspring for the opposition that flowed out from Jerusalem to the Pauline churches. Indeed, one of Paul's motives for the collection may have been to maintain a gospel fellowship between his apostolate to the Gentiles and that other apostolate, which was directed to Jews and which was based at Jerusalem, where James was the undisputed leader.

A comparable impression of James may be discerned in Luke's account of the council in Jerusalem. James does not demand circumcision of the Gentiles, and he denies that those who have gone from Jerusalem "unsettling" the Gentiles in Antioch, Syria and Cilicia did so on his authority (Acts 15:19, 23-24). At Paul's final and tense visit to Jerusalem, the complaints about the apostle to the Gentiles come from the mouths of the elders, not from James (Acts 21:18-25).

7. Opposition at Colossae: Jewish Gnosticism.

Mindful of the major theories that Paul's opponents were either Judaizers or Gnostics, a neat solution would be to identify Paul's adversaries, particularly those in Corinth, where so much is said about them, as Jewish Gnostics. The existence of such people is made probable by Paul's rebuttal of what is generally regarded as some species of Jewish *Gnosticism within the Colossian church (*see* Colossians, Letter to the). Unquestionably, there was a version of Christianity at Colossae that was characterized by circumcision, asceticism, Jewish calendrical observance, mysticism and worship of angels (Col 2:8-23).

These elements are largely missing from Paul's rejection of the teaching of his opponents in Corinth. Paul's presentation of Christ's person and work to the Corinthians—in terms of his fulfillment of the promise and righteousness of the law (2 Cor 1:19-20; 3:4-9; 5:18-21)—has a very different emphasis from the cosmic Christ of the Colossians letter (Col 1:15-20; 2:9-10, 19; 3:1-3).

There is no hint in Colossians about the origin of this Jewish Gnosticism, whether it was indigenous or imported. It is, however, well known that Judaism flourished even in remote regions of Anatolia such as the Lycus Valley. The most probable explanation is that a local version of Jewish Gnosticism had found its way into the life of the Christian church at Colossae. In any case, Paul had not visited this region. The more typical Judaizers seem to have been attracted to churches directly established by the apostle.

8. Opposition at Philippi: Judaizers.

According to many scholars, Paul wrote his letter to the Philippians from Rome in the early sixties. Once again opposition to Paul from Jewish believers is evident. But the nature of the opposition to Paul at Philippi is debated (*see* Philippians, Letter to the). Paul's imprisonment has encouraged the "brethren" in Rome to "speak the word of God" (Phil 1:14). Some of these, however, do so "from envy and rivalry . . . out of partisanship, not sincerely, but thinking to afflict me in my imprisonment" (Phil 1:15, 17).

In all probability these are "those who mutilate the *flesh" (Phil 3:2), the circumcisers of Gentile believers, "whose god is the belly" (Phil 3:19), that is they observe Jewish food regulations.

As with other letters—Galatians and Romans—where the imposition of circumcision on Gentiles is being promoted, we notice the apostle's use of "righteousness . . . the righteousness of God which is through faith in Christ" (see Phil 3:6, 9 *bis*).

From the time of the arrival of believers in the world capital there had been problems within the large Jewish community. It was forced to withdraw from Rome in A.D. 49 "on account of Chrestus" (Suetonius *Claudius* 25.4; cf. Acts 18:1), a probable misspelling of *Christus*. It is likely that the conversion of Jews to Jesus the Christ had created such turmoil within the Jewish community that Claudius expelled all the Jews. The accession of Nero in A.D. 54 meant that Jews could return to the city, doubtless fearful that further disturbances might mean more reprisals from the authorities. Known to be a storm center wherever he went, it is possible that Paul's Jewish-Christian opponents in Rome even resorted to preaching Christ—their version, of course—to precipitate unrest within the Jewish community and so prejudice the impending hearing of Paul's case.

There is no hint that these persons had come from Jerusalem to Rome to harass Paul. Possibly the Judaizing movement, like Paul's mission, had by then developed its own momentum so that it had no direct connection with the mother city, Jerusalem. This may support the argument that the Judaizing program is not directly associated with James, who would have been dead by the time Paul wrote to the Philippians.

9. Opposition in the Pastoral Letters.

We have limited our discussion to opponents from outside who penetrated the churches established by Paul. In our opinion the false teachers and other opponents referred to in the *Pastoral Letters were indigenous to the churches. In this we follow E. E. Ellis: "Unlike the earlier letters, the opponents appear to include a considerable number of former co-workers whose apostasy creates an especially bitter situation" (Ellis, 214).

See also APOSTLE; GNOSTICISM; LAW.
DPL: JUDAIZERS.
BIBLIOGRAPHY. F. A. Agnew, "Paul's Theolog-

ical Adversary in the Doctrine of Justification by Faith: A Contribution to Jewish Christian Dialogue," *JES* 25 (1988) 538-54; P. Barnett, "Opposition in Corinth," *JSNT* 22 (1984) 3-17; C. K. Barrett, "Paul's Opponents in 2 Corinthians," *NTS* 17 (1971) 233-54; B. Blackburn, "Miracle Working *Theioi Andres* in Hellenism (and Hellenistic Judaism)," in *Gospel Perspectives 6: The Miracles of Jesus,* ed. D. Wenham and C. Blomberg (Sheffield: JSOT, 1986) 185-218; J. D. G. Dunn, "The Relationship between Paul and Jerusalem According to Galatians 1 and 2," *NTS* 28 (1982) 461-78 [= *Jesus, Paul and the Law: Studies in Mark and Galatians* (Louisville, KY: Westminster/John Knox, 1990) 108-26]; E. E. Ellis, "Paul and His Opponents," in *Christianity, Judaism and Other Greco-Roman Cults,* ed. J. Neusner (Leiden: E. J. Brill, 1975) 264-98; C. Forbes, "Paul's Opponents in Corinth," *Buried History* 19 (1983) 19-23; D. Georgi, *The Opponents of Paul in Second Corinthians* (Philadelphia: Fortress, 1986); J. J. Gunther, *St. Paul's Opponents and Their Background* (NovTSup 35; Leiden: E. J. Brill, 1973); M. Hengel, *The "Hellenization" of Judaea in the First Century after Christ* (Philadelphia: Trinity Press International, 1989); D. Kee, "Who Were the 'Super-Apostles' of 2 Corinthians 10—13?" *RQ* 23 (1980) 65-76; C. G. Kruse, "The Offender and the Offense in 2 Corinthians 2:5 and 7:12," *EvQ* 60 (1988) 129-39; idem, "The Relationship Between the Opposition to Paul Reflected in 2 Corinthians 1–7 and 10–13," *EvQ* 61 (1989) 195-202; R. P. Martin, "The Opponents of Paul in 2 Corinthians: An Old Issue Revisited," in *Tradition and Interpretation in the New Testament,* ed. G. F. Hawthorne with O. Betz, (Grand Rapids: Eerdmans, 1987) 279-89; S. E. McClelland, " 'Super-Apostles, Servants of Christ, Servants of Satan': a Response," *JSNT* 14 (1982) 82-87; J. Murphy-O'Connor, "*Pneumatikoi* and Judaizers in 2 Cor 2:14–4:6," *ABR* 34 (1986) 42-58; D. W. Oostendorp, *Another Jesus: A Gospel of Jewish Christian Superiority in 2 Corinthians* (Kampen: Kok, 1967); E. P. Sanders, "Paul on the Law, His Opponents, and the Jewish People in Philippians 3 and 2 Corinthians 11," in *Anti-Judaism in Early Christianity* 1, ed. P. Richardson and D. Granskou (Waterloo, ON: Wilfred Laurier University, 1986) 75-90; J. Sumney, *Identifying Paul's Opponents* (JSNTSup 40; Sheffield: JSOT, 1990); idem, "The Role of Historical Reconstructions of Early Christianity in Identifying Paul's Opponents," *PRS* 16 (1989) 45-53; M. E. Thrall, "Super-Apos-

tles, Servants of Christ, and Servants of Satan," *JSNT* 6 (1980) 42-57.   P. W. Barnett

ADVERSARIES II: GENERAL EPISTLES, PASTORALS, REVELATION

Several later NT writings combat what their authors view as unacceptable beliefs and practices. As they do, they are setting limits to the diversity of earliest Christianity. Interpreters have usually identified the adversaries of most of these writings as Gnostics of some description. This identification was based on a reconstruction of the late first and early second century that envisioned Gnosticism as the primary heresy Christians faced. Thus it was simply assumed that since these writings come from that period, their adversaries were probably Gnostic and could be identified as such with very little evidence. More recent scholarship has recognized diversity among those rejected by the developing orthodoxy of this period and so less often simply assumes a particular type of adversary for these writings.

1. Defining Adversaries
2. Revelation
3. Johannine Epistles
4. Jude
5. 2 Peter
6. Pastoral Epistles

1. Defining Adversaries.

Adversaries, understood as those who identify themselves as Christians (hinted at in Paul's farewell discourse in Acts 20:29-30) but who are rejected and opposed by a particular author, are not part of the occasion of all late NT writings. *First Peter, for example, addresses Christians troubled by persecution and offers encouragement to help them interpret and endure persecution but has no Christian adversaries in view. Other writings mention unacceptable views while not having the defeat of those who hold these views as their primary goal. For example, the central purpose of *James is to pass on ethical instructions, but it alludes to some use of Pauline teaching that it rejects (2:18-26). This view is opposed in passing, but opposing its proponents is not central to the purpose of James.

It is also necessary to distinguish between correcting dangerous or unacceptable tendencies or views and opposing adversaries. Not every person who held views our authors thought needed correction was viewed as an adversary. *Hebrews opposes some attraction to cultic practices associated with the Jerusalem temple or its replacement. Those with such inclinations are not, however, treated as heretics or adversaries, but rather as Christians in need of instruction.

When the primary goal is the defeat of adversaries, later NT writings often take up a polemical tone, which means that many of their accusations and charges cannot be straightforwardly attributed to their adversaries. In early Christian and earlier non-Christian writings, polemics often involved stock charges of immorality applied to whatever opposition one encountered. Often this was done in the belief that deviation from the acceptable inevitably led to such behavior. Thus we must be cautious when such charges appear.

2. Revelation.
*Revelation is a special case. Its primary purpose is to encourage those enduring persecution, but the opening section (Rev 1—3) treats some within the communities addressed as adversaries. The seven letters to the churches are often thought to address a single type of adversary. But some interpreters resist this assumption and examine them individually before making connections. The adversaries repudiated in Revelation 1—3 have been identified as Gnostic libertines or libertines with gnostic tendencies. A few interpreters find a dispute between moderate and conservative Jewish Christians, with John taking the more conservative position. Many interpreters identify these adversaries as Christians willing to accommodate themselves to the culture by participating in trade guild meetings, which were held in temples and included a meal in which sacrificed food was eaten.

Only the letters to Ephesus, Pergamum and Thyatira deal with adversaries within the church. The Nicolaitans are mentioned in the messages to Ephesus and Pergamum. John commends the Ephesians for hating the Nicolaitans and for rejecting some who claim to be apostles. If, as seems probable, these apostles were Nicolaitans, this brand of teaching was brought to Ephesus by teachers claiming some authority. But it seems they were unsuccessful there. There is no hint of the content of their teaching. John rebukes the church at Pergamum for having within its congregation Nicolaitans and those who hold the teachings of Balaam. While it initially appears that these are separate groups, the name Balaam is probably used metaphorically for the Nicolaitans, because the two names have similar meanings. Again, no teachings are ascribed to the Nicolaitans. The Balaamites are accused of eating food sacrificed to idols and of fornication. The charge of fornication is probably figurative, standing for religious infidelity. This is its usual meaning in Revelation. Additionally, fornication had long been associated with idolatry (see Num 25:1-2, which immediately follows the Balaam story, and the apostolic decree in Acts 15:23-29). Since this accusation is a polemically charged metaphor, these Balaamites are not libertines. The only other charge leveled against them is that they eat idol meat. Such conduct was viewed as an unacceptable accommodation to the surrounding culture.

John condemns the Thyatirans for tolerating Jezebel, who is accused of teaching and practicing fornication and eating sacrificed meat. This Jezebel, who claimed to be a prophet, must have been an influential member of this church. The charge of fornication is again metaphorical. So the only practice Jezebel is condemned for is eating idol meat, the same accusation made against the Nicolaitans/Balaamites. However, the Seer adds that those who follow Jezebel call their teaching "the deep things of Satan." It is doubtful that the followers of Jezebel attribute their teachings to Satan, but they must claim some insight that reconciles their eating of idol meat and Christian conduct.

In the end, all the adversaries mentioned are accused only of eating idol meat, and thus of being unfaithful. So John's opposition to them is based on their accommodation to the surrounding culture and whatever reasons they give for allowing it. There is no evidence that allows us to associate any tendency of these adversaries, whether taken individually or as a group, with any other known group.

3. Johannine Epistles.
The adversaries of 1 and 2 John (*see* John, Letters of) are usually discussed together, and 3 John is often included within the same broad situation as well. The adversaries in 1 and 2 John are recognized as former members of the Johannine community who have split off from that group. Nearly all interpreters understand the debate to be over the proper interpre-

tation of the traditions now found in John. Throughout the first half of the twentieth century most interpreters identified these separatists as docetic, libertine Gnostics. However, many recent interpreters deny that these adversaries were Gnostic, libertine or fully docetic. Several (e.g., Brown) argue that these opponents deny only the salvific significance of Jesus' earthly life, not the reality of his material existence. Some interpreters also find 1 John opposing an adoptionist *christology and argue that the separatists see the life of Jesus as one phase of the work of the "divine word." Similarly, Painter identifies them as pneumatics who see Jesus as merely an example of the spiritual person's life.

3.1. 1 John. First John yields clear evidence that its adversaries have seceded from the addressed community and are now viewed as enemies; they are even identified as antichrists (1 Jn 2:18-19). Two issues dominate 1 John: keeping the commandments, particularly the love commandment, and christology.

First John frames the christological debate so that denying that Jesus is the Christ is equivalent to denying "the Son" (1 Jn 2:22-23), and these are further synonymous with denying "Jesus" and not confessing that "Jesus Christ is come in flesh" (1 Jn 4:2-3). These carefully worded statements indicate that the adversaries separate the earthly Jesus from the Son in some way unacceptable to 1 John, perhaps denying that the heavenly Christ is to be fully identified with the human Jesus. First John's prologue (1 Jn 1:1-4) supports the notion that these adversaries have a docetic tendency, as does 1 John 4:3, where the issue is cast as denying Jesus. If they are docetists, they are not necessarily Gnostics. One needs only the common Hellenistic devaluing of the material world to find docetism attractive. However, the question may not be whether Jesus had a material body, but rather whether Jesus is to be fully identified with the *Son of God, or for how long such an identification is envisioned. The opponents may have an adoptionist christology that has the Son come upon Jesus at his baptism. This could be based in part on their interpretation of the first chapter of the Gospel of John.

But this part of the adversaries' christology may not be at issue; the dispute may concern when or whether the Son separated himself from Jesus. Most interpreters see the reference to blood in 1 John 5:5-6 as an allusion to the cru-

cifixion. The antithetical structure of these verses suggests that this mention of blood opposes some teaching advocated by the separatists. If it does, they seem to deny that the Son (or the Christ) was crucified and only allow that Jesus was. This—in 1 John's view—premature departure of the Son was unacceptable because it at least implicitly denied the importance of that death for the forgiveness of sins, a function 1 John affirms as central (1 Jn 1:7; 2:1-2, 12; 4:9-10). This understanding of 1 John 5:5-6 also fits if the separatists are docetists.

Thus the most we can say with relative certainty is that these separatists advocated a christology that does not affirm a sufficient identification of Jesus with the Son of God. That insufficiency may involve some form of docetism, or alternatively an adoptionist christology that does not identify Jesus completely enough with the Son and has the Son leave Jesus before the crucifixion. Neither of these positions requires a gnostic theology, but only a descending/ascending redeemer schema, a schema that the Johannine community affirmed.

Beyond the broad indictment that they do not keep the commandments, the sole recurring accusation about the adversaries' ethics is that they lack love for fellow Christians. This charge probably stems from their separation from the Johannine community. Their lack of love is demonstrated by their absence from the assembly of the remaining community. So this accusation reveals little about the separatists' ethical conduct and certainly does not indicate that they were libertines.

It appears from 1 John 1:8, 10 that the secessionists claim to be sinless. Based on the presence of the perfect tense in 1 John 1:8 ("we have not sinned"), some interpreters discern a perfectionism, based on gnostic beliefs, which claims either that material existence is so unimportant that sin does not affect them or that their spiritual nature has made them "intrinsically sinless" (Bogart, 33). However, these statements are probably 1 John's interpretation of the adversaries' views, not quotations of their claims. Still, they must advocate a type of perfectionism that the author of 1 John rejects, even as he embraces a perfectionism of another type in 1 John 3:4-9.

The rejected perfectionism may be a correlate of the separatists' denial of the expiatory function of the crucifixion: if they claimed never to have sinned, atonement would be superfluous (*see* Death of Christ). But their position on Jesus' death may be based on a different understanding of the means of salvation rather than a gnostic-like anthropology. They may argue that the vital element is that the Son brought down eternal life from God, an act that has nothing to do with Jesus' death (cf. Brown 1979). Since 1 John rejects their assertions of sinlessness in 1 John 1:8, 10 with comments on the atoning function of Jesus' death in 1 John 1:7, 9; 2:1-2, these two points are either related in the adversaries' teachings or inseparable from 1 John's perspective. While these adversaries seem to claim an advanced spiritual status that includes sinlessness, there is insufficient evidence to tie this claim to any system of thought (e.g., Gnosticism or a realized *eschatology). Perhaps 1 John denies them this status because of their christology and their secession from his community—after all, he expects sinlessness from those "born of God" (1 Jn 3:9).

Our understanding of these separatists must remain vague. We can establish that they refuse to identify the Son of God with Jesus as completely as 1 John demands and that they deny the expiatory significance of the death of Jesus. Furthermore, they claim a spiritual status that probably includes the assertion that they are beyond sin. There is no good evidence that they are libertines or Gnostics or that they belong to any other known group.

3.2. 2 John. The adversaries of 2 John are described in essentially identical ways to those of 1 John. Again in 2 John these adversaries are perceived as secessionists (2 Jn 7) who have not remained "in the teaching of Christ" (2 Jn 9). The Elder warns his readers to beware of the antichrist who does not confess that "Jesus Christ is come in flesh" (2 Jn 7-8). This shorthand for the adversaries' teaching gives more weight to the view that they are docetists, but in light of its use in 1 John, this phrase remains too ambiguous to be decisive. This letter may represent a later stage in the dispute than 1 John because now there are "many" deceivers (2 Jn 7). Unfortunately, even though we can see that 1 John and 2 John address the same adversaries, 2 John does not appreciably clarify our understanding of them.

3.3. 3 John. Third John identifies the adversary by name, Diotrephes. The Elder writes that Diotrephes is fond of holding a position of leadership, does not acknowledge the Elder's authority, makes false charges against the Elder and does not welcome itinerant preachers associated with the Elder's community. Some interpreters find here a further disintegration of the Johannine community at the hands of the adversaries of 1 John and 2 John. On this reading, the adversaries can now claim an adherent from among those with institutional authority. Others identify Diotrephes as one of the first monarchical bishops and locate the dispute between him and the Elder in issues of ecclesial structure. E. Käsemann argues that Diotrephes legitimately holds the office that was soon to develop into the monarchical episcopacy. Occupying this position, Diotrephes has, Käsemann asserts, excommunicated the Presbyter for being an enthusiast who valued the immediate encounter of the presence of Christ above the tradition.

Third John serves a dual purpose: it is a commendation for Gaius and a letter of recommendation for Demetrius as he travels to the area where Gaius and Diotrephes are church leaders, probably the leading members of separate house churches in the same immediate area. The main issue of 3 John is Diotrephes' refusal of hospitality for itinerant preachers sent by the Elder. The Elder interprets this action as an affront to his honor, a primary value in Greco-Roman culture, and thus as a personal matter and a matter that affects his standing in the broader Christian community in that area.

While this action by Diotrephes may have been due to doctrinal disputes, any such dispute remains veiled. If the false charges brought against the Elder involve some doctrinal issue, the text gives no indication that this is the case. There is no evidence to support Käsemann's claim that the Presbyter has been excommunicated as a heretic. The Elder approaches this problem as he does (i.e., he seems to be on the defensive according to Käsemann) because of Diotrephes' position in the church, not because he has been excommunicated. The dispute could involve ecclesial structure, but again there is no evidence to support this view; it could equally concern Diotrephes' exercise of a recognized office. Thus while we can identify this single adversary by name, we cannot identify or assume the presence of any doctrinal, ecclesial or ethical issues beyond inhospitality for itinerants as the root of this struggle for control of a segment of the Johannine community.

4. Jude.

The adversaries of Jude and 2 Peter have often been identified together and assumed to be the same because 2 Peter borrows so heavily from Jude. But methodologically this is a mistake. Even though 2 Peter uses much of Jude's polemic, he may well apply this stereotyped material to a different group. Thus, as with all NT writings, adversaries must be identified solely on the basis of the text under consideration.

Most interpreters find some sort of Gnostics or proto-Gnostics as the target of Jude's attack. But this identification can be supported only by reading far more into Jude than his statements reasonably permit. Most interpreters also fail to take the thoroughly polemical nature of Jude into account and so accept at face value his often exaggerated charges and accusations. Consequently they identify his adversaries as libertines. F. Wisse has shown that such charges were typical of polemics in both Christian antiheretical writings and the broader Hellenistic milieu.

Jude's adversaries were traveling, perhaps charismatic, teachers (Jude 4, 8) who participated in the churches' worship services (Jude 12). Their presence and teaching were causing divisions, as some accepted their teaching and others did not (Jude 18-19). This much is clear. Even though Jude constantly charges these adversaries with being immoral, the level of polemic makes it doubtful that we should see them as libertines. Such charges probably do indicate that Jude and these teachers disagree about some aspect of Christian behavior. But it is difficult to imagine that Jude's rather broad audience (basically all Christians, Jude 1) needed special instructions to reject the kind of sexually profligate teachers many interpreters find opposed. Charges of "defiling the flesh" (Jude 8) or even of being licentious (Jude 4) do not necessarily indicate that these adversaries were without any moral code. At most, such charges show only that they allowed something(s) the author does not.

Given that Jude is totally immersed in Jewish traditions, it seems likely that the author and audience were Christian Jews. It seems most likely that Jude represents a more law-observant perspective than that advocated by the itinerant teachers. If the "glories" of Jude 8 are the angels involved with giving the law (as many interpreters assert), the "insult" of the adversaries is that they do not keep part of the law. They need not be devoid of morality to insult the law and its mediators; they need only to ignore one aspect of it. In addition, if the traditional archenemies of God's people cited in Jude 11-12 are intended to portray Jude's adversaries in any specific way, the inclusion of Korah may be significant. In Jewish tradition he is known not only for rebellion but also for not keeping the law properly—though with no hint of antinomianism. We are left with almost no clues about the aspect of the law the teachers fail to keep. Jude's characterization of them as problematic at fellowship meals (Jude 12) may indicate that their nonobservance involves food laws or some other purity regulation that complicated association at table, but this is far from certain.

So Jude's adversaries are itinerant teachers whose primary offense involves their understanding of the responsibilities of Christians with respect to the law. They may cite visionary experiences as evidence of their authority. Taking a more law-observant stance, Jude rejects them as the false teachers of the last days and characterizes them as ungodly, lawless and haughty. They undoubtedly had a different picture of themselves.

5. 2 Peter.

Many interpreters also identify the adversaries of 2 Peter as Gnostics or proto-Gnostics, in large part because they deny the parousia. But this is insufficient evidence to make a connection with Gnosticism, for no beliefs central to Gnosticism are combated in 2 Peter. Rejecting a gnostic connection, J. H. Neyrey identifies these adversaries as teachers who draw on Epicurean ideas that had filtered out into the broader culture. Specifically, their denial of the parousia is a manifestation of popular doubts about the reality of divine judgment. R. J. Bauckham (1983) also finds eschatological skepticism to be their central tenet but does not connect their teaching with Epicurean beliefs. Based on their denial of the judgment, Bauckham argues that they advocate antinomianism.

Like Jude, 2 Peter is a thoroughly polemical document. Once again, such direct and fierce polemic must be read carefully, taking into account that stock accusations served to discredit, not accurately describe, adversaries. All of 2 Peter 1:16—3:13 is intended to refute, accuse and denounce the adversaries, not objectively describe them.

The clearest point about these adversaries, who were formerly part of the communities 2 Peter addresses (2 Pet 2:1, 15), is that they deny the parousia (2 Pet 3:3-4). They base their rejection of it on two things: the passing of the first-generation Christians who thought the parousia would occur in their lifetime (2 Pet 3:8-10) and the absence of God's action against evil in the world (2 Pet 3:4-6). References to the reality of the parousia at the beginning and end of the polemical section (2 Pet 1:16—3:13) show that this is the central issue. In 2 Peter 1:16 the author asserts that the parousia is not a myth and interprets the denial of the parousia as a rejection of the apostolic testimony. While it is possible that the adversaries explicitly rejected apostolic teaching, it seems unlikely. Even though 2 Peter interprets their view in this way, it is difficult to see how they could have gained influence (2 Pet 2:2) in a community that reveres apostles (as the attribution of this letter to Peter indicates) if they rejected apostolic testimony. Instead they probably argued that the apostles had been misunderstood. 2 Peter 1:16-19 intends to make this claim untenable.

It seems that these adversaries expect no future judgment, but this may only be 2 Peter's interpretation of what it means to deny the parousia. Some interpreters combine the adversaries' rejection of the judgment with 2 Peter's accusations about their licentiousness to argue that they are libertines. However, this section's sharp polemic prohibits us from reading such charges literally. These denunciations were intended to damage the adversaries' ethos, not accurately describe them. The writer of 2 Peter has no doubt that the adversaries' beliefs lead to moral corruptness, but these polemical denunciations are insufficient evidence that they, for example, "revel in the daytime" (2 Pet 2:13)—a stock polemical accusation.

Second Peter also says that these adversaries revile "glories" (2 Pet 2:10). This expression is taken from Jude but given new meaning here. Second Peter 2:11 indicates that these "glories" are spiritual beings subject to God's judgment. The charge of reviling may be 2 Peter's interpretation of the adversaries' rejection of the parousia and its attending judgment. If these "glories" are involved with the judgment, as Neyrey contends, they may be beings who accuse humans before God at judgment. Thus the adversaries' reviling consists in their disbelief that such judging and accusing takes place.

These teachers also "promise freedom" to those who accept their views. Although 2 Peter gives no clear indication of what this freedom involves, many see it as freedom from moral constraint, perhaps because it is juxtaposed to the charge that the adversaries are "slaves of corruption." But again, such polemical accusations are primarily denunciation. If the "glories" of 2 Peter 2:10 are accusers at the judgment, the freedom of 2 Peter 2:19 may be freedom from fear of such beings. This fits well with the adversaries' denial of the parousia, but no interpretation of this freedom is certain. Second Peter also accuses these adversaries of despising authority or lordship. This is a polemical implication the author draws from their denial of the parousia.

These adversaries are further accused of "twisting" the Scriptures (2 Pet 3:15-16; cf. 1:20-21). Second Peter mentions Paul as an authority who agrees that the delay of the parousia is a sign of God's patience (2 Pet 3:15), but then adds that some misuse Paul's writings and other Scriptures. This is no basis for identifying these teachers as hyper-Paulinists or for asserting that they claim him as their primary authority. He may be simply one apostle they call on. However important Paul is, the reference to him shows that the adversaries do not reject apostolic testimony. Their "twisting" of the prophets shows that particular interpretations of Scripture contribute significantly to their arguments for their teaching.

Second Peter, then, opposes teachers who previously held the same beliefs about the parousia as the author but now deny its reality and use Scripture to support their position. They do not reject apostolic authority, but 2 Peter interprets their denial of the parousia as implying such a rejection. Their denial of the parousia may include a rejection of a final divine judgment; at least 2 Peter presents the two as necessarily related. Denial of a final judgment need not entail the removal of all moral constraints (consider the Sadducees), but the writer of 2 Peter is certain it will lead to licentiousness. Their beliefs about the parousia and judgment seem to allow them to claim freedom from the fear of certain spirit beings, perhaps accusers at judgment. Clearly, the primary issue for the writer of 2 Peter is the adversaries' rejection of the parousia, which he sees as a rejection of Scripture, apostolic authority and morality. So all questions and accusations stem from this one central concern.

6. Pastoral Epistles.

Although the authorship and dating of the Pastorals are debated (*see* Pastoral Letters), the majority opinion of scholarship is that the Pastorals are pseudepigraphic and date from the post-Pauline era. However, those who maintain the Pauline authorship of the Pastorals frequently date these letters in the mid-sixties, at the close of Paul's life and ministry, and regard them as reflective of a changing situation. Whether Pauline or post-Pauline, the identity of the adversaries depicted in the Pastorals has long been an issue in reconstructions of early Christianity and the study of the texts under review in this volume.

Most scholars have assumed that the three Pastoral Epistles address a single type of adversary. This single front is usually identified as a type of Jewish Gnosticism or proto-Gnosticism. A few interpreters, however, identify these adversaries as Judaizing Christians with an ascetic regime and a realized eschatology, or alternatively as Jewish Christians who engage in rabbinic exegesis and emphasize keeping the Torah and ascetic practices. Others identify them as Hellenistic-Jewish legalists, and still others see the main problem to be that these teachers are perceived as a threat by those in authority. Barrett comments that the Pastorals seem to mention every heresy that comes to the author's mind and so are directed at no single, specific adversary. Fiore finds these adversaries to be largely indefinite and described in ways contemporary paraenetic writings typically describe rejected teachers.

6.1. 1 Timothy. A growing number of scholars identify the adversaries of these letters individually. Among types of opponents interpreters have proposed for 1 Timothy we find proto-Gnostics, libertines, elitists from within, some who hold a fully realized eschatology, Jewish Christians who keep the food laws of Judaism, and a circle of Torah-observing Jewish Christians who included the author of Revelation in their number. Interpreters have identified the opponents of 2 Timothy as Gnostics, proto-Gnostics and enthusiastic Paulinists with a realized eschatology. For Titus scholars have found proto-Gnostics, Judaizers and perhaps Marcionites, rival Jewish missionaries, and the same two types of law-observant Jewish Christians proposed for 1 Timothy.

First Timothy, like the other Pastorals, yields little specific information about its adversaries. Its primary concern is not to describe and oppose some false teaching but to encourage a particular type of behavior by placing it in antithesis with a different type. Consistent with this purpose, its polemic is rather stylized, drawing on stock accusations and denunciations. Still, some things are discernible about these adversaries. First, the author's assertion in 1 Timothy 1:6-7 that they want to be teachers of the law implies that they require more Torah observance than 1 Timothy does. This may be corroborated by 1 Timothy 4:3, where we find that they demand abstinence from certain unspecified foods. This food prohibition is usually taken to signify that these adversaries have an ascetic tendency, especially since it is combined with a proscription against marriage. But the marriage prohibition could be also associated with an expectation that the parousia was near (see Paul's comments in 1 Cor 7) or any number of rationales, including some relationship between prophecy and celibacy or the emancipation of women. Still, they may have had some ascetic tendency. Even if they did, their food regulations probably originated with the food laws of Judaism, since other passages allude to questions about the law. One of these is 1 Timothy 1:8-11, where 1 Timothy distinguishes between proper and improper uses of the law. First Timothy 2:5-7 may include a passing defense of Paul's mission to Gentiles and so intimate that observance of the law is an issue.

First Timothy also accuses the adversaries of propagating myths, genealogies and old wives' tales (1 Tim 1:3-4; 4:7-8). Modern interpreters have often used these characterizations to identify these adversaries as Gnostics. But such accusations were commonly employed as a polemical device designed to disparage one's adversaries, no matter what their teaching was. That seems to be their function here. Even if these statements have specific teachings in view, there is no clear information about their content. Not even the reference to their teaching as *gnōsis* (knowledge) in 1 Timothy 6:20 is sufficient to attribute gnostic tendencies to these adversaries, for many groups used this language to designate their teachings in this period.

There is, then, insufficient evidence to connect the teachings of these adversaries with Gnostic or proto-Gnostic beliefs. They do advocate adherence to more of the law than the author of 1 Timothy allows. Their urging of food and marriage prohibitions may indicate that they have some ascetic tendencies. 1 Timothy's comments about these adversaries give us no further information about them.

6.2. 2 Timothy. The adversaries of 2 Timothy are identified by name and by problematic teaching in 2 Timothy 2:17-18; they are Hymenaeus and Philetus, and they claim that the resurrection has already taken place. Second Timothy 2:17-18 is probably a polemical recasting of their teaching which makes it as unacceptable as possible to the readers. But it still shows that they advocate an eschatology which asserts that Christians now participate (or at least can participate) in blessings that the author believes are reserved for the parousia. Their teaching surely excludes a future bodily resurrection but may not deny every sort of afterlife with God. Though some interpreters use this more fully realized eschatology to identify these adversaries as Gnostics, this is not sufficient evidence of such a tendency. Not only are there other bases for a more fully realized eschatology, but no other Gnostic teachings are opposed in this letter.

These opponents are also identified as the predicted eschatological false teachers (2 Tim 3:1-9). The licentiousness attributed to them in this role is again part of the stock polemic against one's adversaries and so is not to be taken at face value without corroborating evidence. The function of this characterization is twofold in 2 Timothy: it makes them odious to the readers, and it is a foil against which to describe and recommend the proper manner of life (e.g., 2 Tim 3:10-15). The remaining references to adversaries in 2 Timothy charge them only with engaging in worthless and harmful disputations (2 Tim 2:14-17, 23-26), an accusation that fits nearly any adversary.

Second Timothy 1:15 may indicate that these teachers who advocated a more fully realized eschatology were fairly successful, because it says that everyone in Asia had deserted Paul. Some interpreters use this as evidence that 2 Timothy represents a later stage in the battle with the same adversaries found in 1 Timothy. However, 2 Timothy 2:24-26 not only encourages Timothy to correct these adversaries gently but also grants the possibility that they may repent. That hardly sounds like a later stage of the controversy that provoked the accusations in 1 Timothy.

More important, nothing in 2 Timothy links its adversaries with those of 1 Timothy beyond the broad and stock rejection of their teaching as worthless disputing. Thus the adversaries of 1 and 2 Timothy do not seem to be related.

6.3. Titus. Titus identifies its adversaries as "the circumcision," a group actively propagating a message that included "Jewish myths and commands of those who turn away from the truth" (Tit 1:10-14). This same passage also indicates that they are native Cretans. The mention of "myths" here is, again, an insufficient basis on which to support the idea that they are Gnostics. These adversaries are Jewish Christians who have begun to demand observance of parts of the law beyond those this author allows. Confirmation that the adversaries' commands involve the law comes from Titus 3:9-11, where Titus is exhorted not to engage in arguments about the law and to exclude from the community anyone who presses such discussions. Further confirmation of this origin of their commands and perhaps more specification of them is found in Titus 1:15. Immediately following the condemnatory description of the adversaries' commands in Titus 1:14, the author turns to the question of what is "clean" and "unclean" for Christians. Thus the adversaries probably urged some purity laws of the Torah. In addition to holding these views, the accusation that these adversaries teach for "dishonorable profit" (Tit 1:11) indicates that they are active teachers who accept pay from their followers.

While these adversaries do seem intent on spreading their message, there is no sign that they are part of a traveling band of missionaries. While they may possibly belong to such a group, any such group must be composed of native Cretans. This makes a direct connection between these adversaries and those of 1 Timothy unlikely, even though the two groups have similar tendencies.

When examined individually, the evidence shows that the Pastorals do not all address the same adversaries. First Timothy and Titus do address adversaries with similar tendencies, but we have no evidence that they are part of the same larger Jewish-Christian, law-observant movement. The discussion about the law, particularly among Jewish Christians, continued well into the fourth century and beyond. Any Jews who joined the Christian fellowship would be confronted by questions about their (and Christian Gentiles') observance of the law and could arrive at a more law-observant view than 1 Timothy and Titus deemed acceptable. Thus the adversaries of these two letters need not be part of a large or organized movement. Unlike those of 1 Timothy and Titus, the adversaries of 2 Timothy do not seem interested in Torah observance. Rather, the primary charge against them is that they hold a faulty and harmful eschatology, a more fully realized eschatology than 2 Timothy can accept. Our finding that these letters address significantly different types of adversaries requires future study of these letters to begin by treating them individually rather than simply viewing them as part of the Pastoral Epistles.

See also CHRISTOLOGY; ESCHATOLOGY; GNOSTICISM.

DPL: CIRCUMCISION; FAITH; GENTILES; JUDAIZERS; OLD TESTAMENT IN PAUL; WORKS OF THE LAW. *DLNTD:* ANCESTORS; ANTICHRIST; DOCETISM; EBIONITES; FALSE PROPHETS; GNOSIS, GNOSTICISM; JEWISH CHRISTIANITY; MOSES; PROMISE; PROPHECY, PROPHETS.

BIBLIOGRAPHY. C. K. Barrett, "Pauline Controversies in the Post-Pauline Period," *NTS* 20 (1973-74) 229-45; R. J. Bauckham, *Jude and the Relatives of Jesus in the Early Church* (Edinburgh: T & T Clark, 1990); idem, *Jude, 2 Peter* (WBC; Waco, TX: Word, 1983); J. Bogart, *Orthodox and Heretical Perfectionism in the Johannine Community as Evident in the First Epistle of John* (SBLDS 33; Missoula, MT: Scholars Press, 1973); R. E. Brown, *The Community of the Beloved Disciple* (New York: Paulist, 1979); idem, *The Epistles of John* (AB; Garden City, NY: Doubleday, 1982); R. Bultmann, *The Johannine Epistles* (Herm; Philadelphia: Fortress, 1973); H. C. C. Cavallin, "The False Teachers of 2 Peter as Pseudo-Prophets," *NovT* 21 (1979) 263-70; B. Fiore, *The Function of Personal Example in the Socratic and Pastoral Epistles* (AnBib 105; Rome: Biblical Institute Press, 1986); T. Fornberg, *An Early Church in a Pluralistic Society: A Study of 2 Peter* (ConBNT 9; Lund: C. W. K. Gleerup, 1977); R. M. Grant, *Heresy and Criticism: The Search for Authority in Early Christian Literature* (Louisville, KY: Westminster/John Knox, 1993); R. J. Hoffmann, *Marcion: On the Restitution of Christianity* (AARAS 46; Chico, CA: Scholars Press, 1984); L. T. Johnson, "2 Timothy and the Polemic Against False Teachers: A Reexamination," *JRS* 6-7 (1978-79) 1-26; R. J. Karris, "The Background and Significance of the Polemic of the Pastoral Epistles," *JBL* 92 (1973) 549-64; E. Käsemann, "Ketzer und Zeuge: Zum johanneischen Verfasserproblem," *ZTK* 48 (1951) 292-311; A. F. J. Klijn and G. J. Reinink, *Patristic Evidence for Jewish-Christian Sects* (NovTSup 36; Leiden: E. J. Brill, 1973); G. W. Knight III, *The Pastoral Epistles: A Commentary on the Greek Text* (NIGTC; Grand Rapids: Eerdmans, 1992); J. Lieu, *The Second and Third Epistles of John: History and Background*, ed. J. Riches (Edinburgh: T & T Clark, 1986); A. J. Malherbe, *Social Aspects of Early Christianity* (2d ed.; Philadelphia: Fortress, 1983); I. H. Marshall, *The Epistles of John* (NICNT; Grand Rapids: Eerdmans, 1978); J. Murphy-O'Connor, "2 Timothy Contrasted with 1 Timothy and Titus," *RB* 98 (1991) 403-18; J. H. Neyrey, *2 Peter, Jude* (AB; Garden City, NY: Doubleday, 1993); J. Painter, "The 'Opponents' of 1 John," *NTS* 32 (1986) 48-71; A. F. Segal, "Jewish Christianity," in *Eusebius, Christianity and Judaism*, ed. H. W. Attridge and G. Hata (SPB 42; Leiden: E. J. Brill, 1992) 326-51; T. V. Smith, *Petrine Controversies in Early Christianity: Attitudes Toward Peter in Christian Writings of the First Two Centuries* (WUNT 15; Tübingen: Mohr Siebeck, 1985); J. L. Sumney, 'Servants of Satan', 'False Brothers' and Other Opponents of Paul (JSNTSup 188; Sheffield: Sheffield Academic Press, 1999); C. H. Talbert, "2 Peter and the Delay of the Parousia," *VC* 20 (1966) 137-45; D. C. Verner, *The Household of God: The Social World of the Pastoral Epistles* (SBLDS 71; Chico, CA: Scholars Press, 1983); D. F. Watson, "Amplification Techniques in 1 John: The Interaction of Rhetorical Style and Invention," *JSNT* 51 (1993) 99-123; idem, *Invention, Arrangement and Style: Rhetorical Criticism of Jude and 2 Peter* (SBLDS; Atlanta: Scholars Press, 1986); R. A. Whitacre, *Johannine Polemic: The Role of Tradition and Theology* (SBLDS 104; Chico, CA: Scholars Press, 1980); F. Wisse, "The Epistle of Jude in the History of Heresiology," in *Essays on the Nag Hammadi Texts in Honor of Alexander Böhlig*, ed. M. Krause (NHS 3; Leiden: E. J. Brill, 1972) 133-43.   J. L. Sumney

AFTERLIFE. *See* RESURRECTION.

ALLEGORY. *See* GALATIANS, LETTER TO THE.

AMORAIM. *See* RABBINIC TRADITIONS AND WRITINGS.

ANNAS. *See* TRIAL OF JESUS.

ANTICHRIST. *See* REVELATION, BOOK OF.

ANTITHESES. *See* LAW I.

APOCALYPSE, THE. *See* REVELATION, BOOK OF.

APOCALYPTIC LITERATURE. *See* APOCALYPTICISM; APOCRYPHA AND PSEUDEPIGRAPHA.

APOCALYPTICISM: NEW TESTAMENT

The term *apocalypticism* is a transliterated form of the Greek term *apokalypsis*, which means "disclosure" or "revelation." The author of the NT Apocalypse, or Revelation of John, was the first Jewish or Christian author to use the term *apokalypsis* in describing the content of his book. The book is essentially a narrative of a series of revelatory visions that disclose the events surrounding the imminent end of the present age: "[This is] the revelation *[apokalyspsis]* of John, which *God gave to him, to show to his servants what must soon take place" (Rev 1:1). Following Revelation 1:1, the term *apocalypse* has been used since the early nineteenth century, when it was popularized by the German NT scholar F. Luecke (1791-1854), as a generic term to describe documents with a content and structure similar to the Revelation of John.

1. Defining Apocalypticism
2. The Origins of Apocalypticism
3. Characteristics of Apocalypticism
4. Jesus and Apocalypticism
5. Paul and Apocalypticism
6. Later New Testament Writings and Apocalypticism

1. Defining Apocalypticism.

The term *apocalypticism* is a modern designation widely used to refer to a worldview that characterized segments of early Judaism from about 200 B.C. to A.D. 200. This view centered on the expectation of God's imminent intervention into human history in a decisive manner to save his people and punish their enemies by destroying the existing fallen cosmic order and by restoring or recreating the cosmos in its original, pristine perfection. Knowledge of cosmic secrets (one of the contributions of the wisdom tradition to apocalypticism) and the imminent eschatological plans of God were revealed to apocalyptists through dreams and visions, and the apocalypses they wrote were primarily narratives of the visions they had received and which were explained to them by an interpreting angel. All extant Jewish apocalypses are believed to be pseudonymous, that is, written under the names of prominent ancient Israelite or Jewish figures such as Adam, Enoch, Moses, Daniel, Ezra and Baruch. Only the earliest Christian apocalypses, the Revelation of John and the *Shepherd of Hermas,* were written under the names of the actual authors. The most likely reason for the phenomenon of apocalyptic pseudonymity is that it was a strategy to provide credentials and thereby assure the acceptance of these revelatory writings at a point in Israelite history when the reputation of prophets had sunk to an extremely low point. *Apocalypticism* is therefore a term used to describe the particular type of eschatological expectation characteristic of early Jewish and early Christian apocalypses. The Jewish religious compositions that are generally regarded as apocalypses include Daniel 7—12 (the only OT apocalypse), the five documents that make up *1 Enoch* (1–36, the Book of Watchers; 37–71, the Similitudes of Enoch; 72–82, the Book of Heavenly Luminaries; 83–90, the Animal Apocalypse; 92–104, the Epistle of Enoch), *2 Enoch,* *4 Ezra, 2 Baruch, 3 Baruch* and the *Apocalypse of Abraham.* Early Christian apocalypses include the Revelation of John (the only NT apocalypse) and the *Shepherd of Hermas.*

Four aspects of apocalypticism need to be distinguished.

Apocalyptic eschatology is a type of *eschatology that is found in apocalypses or is similar to the eschatology of apocalypses, characterized by the tendency to view reality from the perspective of divine sovereignty (e.g., the eschatologies of the Qumran community, Jesus and Paul).

Apocalypticism or *millennialism* is a form of collective behavior based on those beliefs (e.g., the movement led by *John the Baptist, and the revolts of Theudas reported in Acts 5:36 and Josephus *Ant.* 20.5.1 §§97-98, and the unnamed Egyptian reported in Acts 21:38; Josephus *Ant.* 20.8.6 §§169-72; *J. W.* 2.13.5 §§261-63).

Apocalypse is a type of literature in which those beliefs occur in their most basic and complete form and which centers on the revelation of cosmic lore and the end of the age.

Apocalyptic imagery is the various constituent themes and motifs of apocalyptic eschatology used in various ways in early Jewish and early

Christian literature.

The focus in this article will be on Jewish apocalyptic eschatology and the ways in which Jesus and NT authors adapted some of the basic themes and structures of apocalyptic eschatology into their theological thought.

2. The Origins of Apocalypticism.

A number of proposals have been made regarding the origins of apocalypticism, and these proposals have often reflected the positive or negative attitude that scholars have had toward the phenomenon of apocalypticism. Following the lead of F. Luecke in the mid-nineteenth century, many scholars have viewed apocalypticism favorably as a development of OT prophecy, perhaps as a result of the disillusionment of the postexilic period, which included subjection to foreign nations and tension within the Jewish community. Other scholars who discerned a sharp break between OT prophecy and later apocalypticism proposed that many of the basic features of apocalypticism originated in ancient Iran and had penetrated Jewish thought during the Hellenistic period (c. 400-200 B.C.) or more generally from the syncretistic tendencies during the Hellenistic period, when there was a blending of religious ideas from West and East.

2.1. The Setting of Apocalypticism. The fact that most apocalypses are pseudonymous has made it difficult to reconstruct the social situations within which they were written and to which they responded. There is nevertheless wide agreement that Jewish apocalypses were written or revised during times of social or political crisis, though such crises may run the spectrum from real to perceived. Focusing his attention on the period 400-200 B.C., O. Ploeger discerned a split in the postexilic Jewish community into two sharp divisions, the theocratic party (the ruling priestly aristocrats), which interpreted prophetic eschatology in terms of the Jewish state, and the eschatological party (forerunners of the apocalyptists), which awaited the fulfillment of the eschatological predictions of the prophets. More recently, P. D. Hanson has argued that apocalypticism is a natural development of Israelite prophecy originating in the intramural struggle between visionary prophets and hierocratic (Zadokite) priests which took place from the sixth through the fourth centuries B.C.

2.2. Eschatology and Apocalypticism. A distinction has generally been made between eschatol-

ogy and apocalypticism. *Eschatology* is a term that began to be used in the nineteenth century as a label for that aspect of systematic theology that dealt with topics relating to the future of the individual (death, *resurrection, *judgment, eternal life, heaven and hell) and topics relating to corporate or national eschatology, that is, the future of the Christian church or the Jewish people (e.g., the coming of the Messiah, the great tribulation, resurrection, judgment, the second coming of Christ, the temporary messianic kingdom, the re-creation of the universe). A distinction has often been made between prophetic eschatology and apocalyptic eschatology, which serves the useful function of emphasizing the continuities as well as the changes in Israelite-Jewish eschatological expectation. Following this model, prophetic eschatology was an optimistic perspective that anticipated that God would eventually restore the originally idyllic and pristine conditions by acting through historical processes. The Israelite prophet proclaimed God's plans for *Israel to king and people in terms of actual historical and political events and processes. Prophecy sees the future as arising out of the present, while apocalyptic eschatology regards the future as breaking into the present; the former is essentially optimistic, while the latter is pessimistic.

2.3. Prophecy and Apocalypticism. The problem of the relationship between prophecy and apocalypticism is one aspect of the problem of the degree of continuity or discontinuity thought to exist between Jewish apocalypticism and earlier Israelite religious and political traditions. It is important to recognize that prophecy and apocalypticism exhibit both elements of continuity and discontinuity. The sharp contrasts often thought to exist between prophecy and apocalypticism are somewhat mitigated by the recognition that prophecy underwent many changes and that there are numerous striking similarities between late prophecy and early apocalyptic (Hanson). Late prophetic books that exhibit tendencies that were later to emerge more fully developed in Jewish apocalyptic literature include the visions of Zechariah 1—6 (with the presence of an angelic interpreter), Isaiah 24—27, 56—66, Joel and Zechariah 9—14.

2.4. Wisdom and Apocalypticism. Many scholars have argued that there was a fundamental break between prophecy and apocalypticism. G. von Rad, for example, rejected the view that the primary roots of apocalypticism were to be found in Israelite prophecy. Von Rad described apocalypticism as consisting in a clear-cut dualism, radical transcendence, esotericism and *Gnosticism, and he proposed that apocalypticism arose out of the wisdom literature of the OT. Themes common to wisdom and apocalyptic literature, and which suggest the connection between the two types of literature, include the following: (1) both sages and apocalyptists are referred to as "the wise," and preserved their teaching in written form, often emphasizing their special "knowledge" and its antiquity; (2) both exhibit individualistic and universalistic tendencies; (3) both are concerned with the mysteries of nature from a celestial perspective; and (4) both reflect a deterministic view of history.

The proposal that Israelite wisdom, not Israelite prophecy, was the mother of Jewish apocalypticism has found little scholarly support in the form in which it was proposed by von Rad. Yet there are undeniably links between wisdom and apocalyptic (Wis 7:27; Sir 24:33), both of which are scribal phenomena. The wisdom tradition in Israel was certainly one of the many influences upon the development of Jewish apocalypticism. Nevertheless, it is important to distinguish between two types of wisdom: proverbial wisdom and mantic wisdom. The latter type is related to the role of the "wise" in interpreting dreams as reflected in the biblical traditions concerning Joseph and Daniel, both of whom were able to explain the meaning of ambiguous revelatory dreams through divine wisdom (Gen 40:8; 41:25, 39; Dan 2:19-23, 30, 45; 5:11-12). The figure of the *angelus interpres* ("interpreting angel") occurs frequently in Jewish apocalypses where he plays the analogous role of a supernatural revealer who is able to reveal the deeper significance of the dreams and visions experienced by the apocalyptist (Dan 7—12; Zech 1—6; 4 Ezra).

2.5. Pharisaism and Apocalypticism. The monumental three-volume work on Judaism by G. F. Moore was based on the assumption that "normative" Judaism of the first few centuries of the Christian era, "the age of the Tannaim," did not include Jewish apocalypticism. Similarly, A. Schweitzer sharply distinguished the teaching of the apocalyptists (and therefore Jesus) from the teaching of the rabbis. However, the pharisaic emphases on the resurrection, the age to come and the Messiah make it difficult to distinguish

sharply the religious and political concerns of apocalyptists from the Pharisees, even though Pharisees appear to have become disenchanted with many aspects of apocalypticism in the aftermath of the disastrous first revolt against Rome (A.D. 66-73). W. D. Davies has argued that there are several links between apocalypticism and Pharisaism: (1) both share a similar piety and attitude toward the Torah; (2) both share similar views on such eschatological topics as the travail of the messianic era, the gathering of exiles, the days of the Messiah, the New Jerusalem, the judgment and Gehenna; (3) both have populist and scholastic tendencies.

3. Characteristics of Apocalypticism.

3.1. Major Aspects of Apocalypticism. There are a number of features of apocalyptic eschatology upon which there is some scholarly agreement:

the temporal dualism of the two ages

the radical discontinuity between this age and the next coupled with pessimism regarding the existing order and otherworldly hope directed toward the future order

the division of history into segments (four, seven, twelve) reflecting a predetermined plan of history

the expectation of the imminent arrival of the reign of God as an act of God and spelling the doom of existing earthly conditions

a cosmic perspective in which the primary location of an individual is no longer within a collective entity such as Israel or the people of God, and the impending crisis is not local but cosmic in scope

the cataclysmic intervention of God will result in salvation for the righteous, conceived as the regaining of Edenic conditions

the introduction of angels and demons to explain historical and eschatological events

the introduction of a new mediator with royal functions

These characteristics are not exhaustive, but they serve the useful purpose of focusing on some of the distinctive features of the apocalyptic worldview.

3.2. The Apocalyptic Scenarios. Since narratives that describe the events attending the close of the present era and the inauguration of the future era are essentially a type of folklore, there are many divergent descriptions of expected future events with little consistency between them. In producing a synthesis of the great variety of apocalyptic scenarios found in apocalyptic literature, therefore, the emphasis must be on the more typical features found in such descriptions. Apocalypticism or apocalyptic eschatology centers on the belief that the present world order, which is evil and oppressive, is under the temporary control of Satan and his human accomplices. This present evil world order will shortly be destroyed by God and replaced with a new and perfect order corresponding to Eden. During the present evil age, the people of God are an oppressed minority who fervently await the intervention of God or his specially chosen agent, the Messiah. The transition between the old and the new ages, the end of the old age and the beginning of the new, will be introduced by a final series of battles fought by the people of God against the human allies of Satan. The outcome is never in question, however, for the enemies of God are predestined to be defeated and destroyed. The inauguration of the new age will begin with the arrival of God or his accredited agent to judge the wicked and reward the righteous and will be concluded by the re-creation or transformation of the universe.

3.3. Limited Dualism. One of the basic features of apocalypticism is the conviction that the cosmos is divided under two opposing supernatural forces, God and Satan, who represent the moral qualities of good and evil (cosmological dualism). However, the Jewish conviction that God is absolutely sovereign implies that he is the originator of evil and that the resultant dualism of good and evil is neither eternal nor absolute (like the dualism of ancient Iranian religion), but limited. This essentially limited cosmological dualism was understood in various different but related types of dualistic thought in early Jewish apocalypticism: (1) *Temporal or eschatological dualism* makes a sharp distinction between the present age and the age to come. (2) *Ethical dualism* is based on a moral distinction between good and evil and sees humanity divided into two groups, the righteous and the wicked, in a

way that corresponds to good and evil supernatural powers. (3) *Psychological* or *microcosmic dualism* is the internalization of the two-age schema that sees the forces of good and evil struggling for supremacy within each individual.

3.3.1. Temporal or Eschatological Dualism. The belief in two successive ages, or worlds, developed only gradually in Judaism. The earliest occurrence of the rabbinic phrase "the world to come" is found in *1 Enoch* 71:15 (c. 200 B.C.). The doctrine of two ages is fully developed by about A.D. 90, for according to 4 Ezra 7:50, "The Most High has not made one Age but two" (see 4 Ezra 8:1). The day of judgment is considered the dividing point between the two ages (4 Ezra 7:113): the "day of judgment will be the end of this age and beginning of the immortal age to come."

3.3.2. Ethical Dualism. Daniel 12:10 distinguishes between the "wicked" and the "wise"; *Jubilees* distinguishes between Israelites who are "the righteous nation" (*Jub.* 24:29), "a righteous generation" (*Jub.* 25:3) and the Gentiles who are sinners (*Jub.* 23:24; 24:28); the Qumran *War Scroll* similarly distinguishes between the people of God and the Kittim (1QM 1:6; 18:2-3); and the *Testament of Asher* contrasts "good and single-faced people" (*T. Asher* 4:1) with "people of two faces" (*T. Asher* 3:1).

3.3.3. Psychological or Microcosmic Dualism. In this type of dualism the antithetical supernatural cosmic powers, conceived of in the moral categories of good and evil, have an analogous correspondence to the struggle between good and evil experienced by individuals. In some strands of Jewish apocalyptic thought, notably the Qumran community and the circles that produced the *Testaments of the Twelve Patriarchs*, it was believed that God created two spirits, the spirit of truth and the spirit of error (i.e., the evil spirit called Belial, 1QS 1:18-24; *T. Jud.* 20:1-5; see Jn 14:17; 15:26; 16:13; 1 Jn 4:6), and humans may live in accordance with one or the other. The Prince of Lights controls the lives of the children of righteousness, while the Angel of Darkness has dominion over the children of falsehood (1QS 3:17—4:1; 4:2-11; 1QM 13:9-12). However, even the sins of the children of righteousness are ultimately caused by the spirit of error, for both spirits strive for supremacy within the heart of the individual (1QS 4:23-26; *T. Asher* 1:3-5). The dominion of the spirit of error is temporally limited, however, for God will ultimately destroy it (1QS 4:18-19). The doctrine that the spirit of truth and the spirit of error strive for supremacy in the heart of each person is similar to the rabbinic doctrine of the good and evil impulses.

3.4. Messianic Expectation. Messianism was not an invariable feature of all the various eschatological schemes that made up Jewish apocalypticism. During the Second Temple period there were at least two main types of Jewish messianism, restorative and utopian messianism. Restorative messianism anticipated the restoration of the Davidic monarchy and centered on an expectation of the improvement and perfection of the present world through natural development (*Pss. Sol.* 17) and modeled on an idealized historical period; the memory of the past is projected into the future. Utopian messianism anticipated a future era that would surpass everything previously known. Jewish messianism tended to focus not on the restoration of a dynasty but on a single messianic king sent by God to restore the fortunes of Israel. However, as a theocratic symbol, the Messiah is dispensable, since a Messiah is not invariably part of all Jewish eschatological expectation. No such figure, for example, plays a role in the eschatological scenarios of Joel, Isaiah 24—27, Daniel, Sirach, *Jubilees,* the *Testament of Moses,* Tobit, 1 and 2 Maccabees, Wisdom, *1 Enoch* 1—36 (the Book of Watchers), 90—104 (the Epistle of Enoch) and *2 Enoch.*

3.5. The Temporary Messianic Kingdom. There is little consistency in Jewish apocalyptic regarding the arrival of the kingdom of God. It was conceptualized by some as the arrival of an eternal kingdom but by others as a temporary messianic kingdom that would be succeeded by an eternal kingdom (see 1 Cor 15:24). The conception of a temporary messianic kingdom that would function as a transition between the present evil age and the age to come, between monarchy and theocracy, solved the problem of how the transition from the Messiah to the eternal reign of God (where such a conception is present) might be conceived. In Jewish apocalyptic thought generally, the kingdom of God is more centrally important than the figure of a Messiah. A messianic interregnum, therefore, functions as an anticipation of the perfect and eternal theocratic state that will exist when primordial conditions are reinstated forever. This interim kingdom was expected to be transitional

since it is depicted as combining some of the characteristics of this age with those of the age to come. In Christian apocalypticism this anticipation of a temporary messianic kingdom is clearly reflected in Revelation 20:4-6, and according to some scholars is also reflected in 1 Corinthians 15:20-28. The expectation of a future temporary messianic kingdom is found in only three early Jewish apocalypses, the Apocalypse of Weeks, or *1 Enoch* 91:12-17, 93:1-10; (written between 175 and 167 B.C.), 4 Ezra 7:26-44; 12:31-34 (written c. A.D. 90), and *2 Baruch* 29:3—30:1; 40:1-4; 72:2—74:3 (written c. A.D. 110). Though some have claimed that the conception of a temporary messianic kingdom is found in *2 Enoch* 32:2—33:1 and *Jubilees* 1:27-29; 23:26-31, the evidence is not compelling.

3.5.1. Apocalypse of Weeks. In *1 Enoch* 91:12-17 and 93:1-10, an earlier apocalypse inserted into the Epistle of Enoch (*1 Enoch* 91–104), history is divided into ten weeks (i.e., ten ages), with a nonmessianic temporary kingdom appearing in the eighth week and an eternal kingdom arriving in the tenth week (*1 Enoch* 91:12-17).

3.5.2. Fourth Ezra. According to 4 Ezra 7:26-30, the Messiah will appear in the last days and live with the righteous for four hundred years. The Messiah, together with all other people on earth, will then die and the world will return to seven days of primeval silence. After this the resurrection will occur (4 Ezra 7:32), and the Most High will take his place on the seat of judgment and will execute judgment on all nations (4 Ezra 7:36-43). In 4 Ezra 12:31-34, on the other hand, the Davidic Messiah will sit on the seat of judgment and, after reproving the ungodly and the wicked, will destroy them (4 Ezra 12:32). This judgment exercised by the Messiah is preliminary to the final judgment, which will be exercised by God after the arrival of the end (4 Ezra 12:34). Nowhere in 4 Ezra, however, does the Messiah play a role in the eternal theocratic kingdom that is inaugurated with the resurrection.

3.5.3. Second Baruch. After twelve periods of tribulation (*2 Bar.* 27:1-5), the messianic kingdom is depicted as a period of phenomenal abundance inaugurated by the appearance of the Messiah (*2 Bar.* 29:3) and concluded by his return to glory (*2 Bar.* 30:1). The elect who lived during the messianic kingdom will then be joined by the resurrected righteous, but the souls of the wicked will fear judgment (*2 Bar.* 30:1-5). The author assumes rather than clearly states the fact that those who lived during the messianic kingdom will experience a transformation into a resurrection mode of existence like the resurrected righteous. In *2 Baruch* 39—40 the predicted fall of the fourth kingdom (Rome) will be followed by the revelation of the Messiah (*2 Bar.* 39:7), who will destroy the armies of the final wicked ruler, who will be brought bound to Zion, where he will be judged and executed by the Messiah (*2 Bar.* 40:1-2). The kingdom of the Messiah will last "forever," that is, until the world of corruption has ended, which means that this kingdom is temporary but of unspecified duration. Finally, in *2 Baruch* 72:2—74:3 the warrior Messiah will summon all nations together, sparing some and executing others (*2 Bar.* 72:2-6). Following this period of judgment will be an era in which Edenic conditions will be restored to the earth (*2 Bar.* 73:1-7). As in 4 Ezra, the Messiah plays no role in the eternal kingdom that is inaugurated after he is taken up into heaven.

3.6. The Eschatological Antagonist. In Jewish apocalyptic literature there are two traditions of a wicked eschatological figure who functions as an agent of Satan, or Beliar, in leading astray, opposing and persecuting the people of God; both traditions represent historicizations of the ancient combat myth. One tradition focuses on a godless tyrannical ruler who will arise in the last generation to become the primary adversary of God or the Messiah. This satanic agent was expected to lead the forces of evil in the final battle between the forces of evil and the people of God (1QM 18:1; 1QS 4:18-19; *T. Dan* 5:10-11; *T. Mos.* 8).

The historicization of the combat myth is already found in the OT where the chaos monsters Rahab and Leviathan are sometimes used to symbolize foreign oppressors like Egypt (Ps 74:14; 87:4; Is 30:7; Ezek 29:3; 32:2-4). Several OT traditions provided the basis for the later apocalyptic conception of the eschatological antagonist, including the figure of Gog, the ruler of Magog in the Gog and Magog oracle in Ezekiel 38–39 (see Rev 20:8; *3 Enoch* 45:5), the references to a vague "enemy from the north" found in several OT prophecies (Ezek 38:6, 15; 39:2; Jer 1:13-15; 3:18; 4:6; 6:1, 22), and the depicting of Antiochus IV Epiphanes, the "little horn" in Daniel 7–8 as the oppressor of the people of God. The career of the Greco-Syrian king Antiochus IV Epiphanes (175-164 B.C.), whose actions against the Jewish people are described in 1 Maccabees 1:20-61 and 2 Maccabees 5:11—

6:11, is presented as a mythologized apocalyptic figure in Daniel 11:36-39, claiming to be God or to be equal with God (Dan 11:36-37; *Sib. Or.* 5:33-34; *Asc. Isa.* 4:6; *2 Enoch* [Rec. J] 29:4).

Later, the characteristics of the eschatological adversary were augmented and embellished by traditions about the Roman emperors Caligula and Nero, both of whom had divine pretensions that their Roman contemporaries considered tacky and that outraged the Jews. The other tradition concerns the false prophet who performs signs and wonders to legitimate his false teaching (cf. Deut 13:2-6). Occasionally, Satan and the eschatological antagonist are identified as the same person, as in *Sibylline Oracles* 3:63-74 and *Ascension of Isaiah* 7:1-7, where Nero (= the eschatological antagonist) is regarded as Beliar (= Satan) incarnate.

3.7. The Re-creation or Transformation of the Cosmos. In Isaiah 65:17 and Isaiah 66:22 the creation of a new heavens and a new earth is predicted. The theme of the re-creation or renewal of creation was taken up into apocalyptic literature as the final eschatological act. Essentially, the expectation of a new creation or a renewed creation is a particular application of the two-age schema in which the first creation is identified with the present evil age (or world) and the new or renewed creation is identified with the age (or world) to come. While there are many references to the new creation in Jewish apocalyptic literature, it is not always clear whether the present order of creation is reduced to chaos before the act of re-creation (*1 Enoch* 72:1; 91:16; *Sib. Or.* 5:212; *Jub.* 1:29; 4:26; *Bib. Ant.* 3:10; *Apoc. Elijah* 5:38; 2 Pet 3:13; Rev 21:1, 5; see 2 Cor 5:17; Gal 6:15), or whether the renewal or transformation of the existing world is in view (*1Enoch* 45:4-5; *2 Bar.* 32:6; 44:12; 49:3; 57:2; *Bib. Ant.* 32:17; 4Ezra 7:30-31, 75; see Rom 8:21). In many of these passages the pattern for the new or transformed creation is based on the Edenic conditions thought to have existed on the earth before the fall of Adam and Eve.

[D. E. Aune]

4. Jesus and Apocalypticism.

During the nineteenth century, biblical scholars attempted to defend Jesus against the charge that he was an apocalyptic dreamer who wrongly predicted an early and cataclysmic end to the existing world order. Some defended Jesus by claiming that Jesus did not intend to predict literal future events for the world but was speaking spiritually. The apocalyptic predictions, it was argued, all had been spiritually fulfilled.

Others defended Jesus by charging the early church and the Gospel writers with error. One view is that chapters like Mark 13 did not derive from anything Jesus really said. Rather, an early Jewish apocalypse was taken up by the Gospel writers and erroneously credited to Jesus. This "little apocalypse" theory, first advanced by T. Colani, has been defended by an array of scholars ever since.

Many nineteenth-century scholars portrayed Jesus as a gentle teacher who taught the nearness of God. Unfortunately, they lamented, Jesus has been misrepresented in the Gospels as a fanatical preacher of coming judgment.

At the turn of the century J. Weiss and A. Schweitzer overturned that consensus by reconstructing a historical Jesus who was thoroughly apocalyptic in outlook, indeed more so than those who had preserved the traditions about him. Under this new reckoning, Jesus believed that the expected divine intervention that would inaugurate the new age would occur at some time during his ministry. His expectations were disappointed more than once, and he finally went to his death imagining that by so doing he would surely spur God to act. The early church was left with the challenge of giving Jesus a more respectable image, covering up his errors and presenting his teaching in a way that served the needs of a community that knew the end (and the *kingdom of God) had not come as predicted but that still believed it would come soon.

This view in its various forms, generally known as "consistent eschatology," has been influential during the twentieth century. Some, like R. Bultmann, have been unconcerned with defending Jesus' apocalyptic perspective or even attempting to reconstruct a portrait of the historical Jesus. Bultmann's famous program of demythologizing the NT did not attempt to strip Jesus of his mythological trappings (as did many nineteenth-century interpreters) but to reinterpret those mythical elements in terms of their existential meaning. Understood from this perspective, the mythology inherent in Jesus' apocalyptic teaching was a means of addressing men and women with the need to be open to God's future—a future near at hand for each individual. Others scholars, such as R. H. Hiers,

do not find it troubling to think of Jesus as someone who had mistaken expectations and made inaccurate predictions.

Not all twentieth-century interpreters have been persuaded that Jesus was an apocalyptic preacher who predicted an imminent end to the world. C. H. Dodd and others have insisted on a realized eschatology, maintaining that Jesus fulfilled OT prophetic hopes and preached a kingdom that was inaugurated in his own ministry. Those passages that suggested a future fulfillment were either intended to be interpreted in this light or were the creation of the early church.

Both consistent and realized eschatology seem problematic. Many conservative scholars such as G. E. Ladd, E. E. Ellis and I. H. Marshall have adopted a compromise position first defended by W. G. Kümmel. The kingdom is paradoxically "present" and "still to come." Jesus' mission was to inaugurate the kingdom, but he taught that it would be consummated at a future coming.

The Gospel writers faithfully preserve this paradoxical position. They use apocalyptic imagery to report and interpret events in Jesus' earthly life (e.g., Mt 27:51-53; 28:2-4), and they also use apocalyptic imagery to refer to events predicted for the future (God's final act of judgment and salvation at the coming of the Son of man; cf. Mt 25:31-46; Mk 13:24-27).

This already/not yet approach may be open to the charge that it is very convenient (unfalsifiable and therefore indefensible, some would say), but unless some such paradoxical interpretation is adopted, neither Jesus' view nor any of the Gospel writers' views can be understood adequately. [T. J. Geddert]

5. Paul and Apocalypticism.

5.1. Sources and Problems. Critical scholarship regards the seven generally acknowledged Pauline letters as providing a firm basis for analyzing Pauline theology. These letters include Romans, 1 and 2 Corinthians, Galatians, Philippians, 1 Thessalonians and Philemon. Letters whose authenticity remains in some doubt (2 Thessalonians; Colossians) or whose Pauline authorship is generally rejected (Ephesians; 1 and 2 Timothy; Titus) are used only to supplement data found in the basic corpus of seven letters. The book of Acts is another important source for our knowledge of Paul's life, but this work too must be used only as a supplement to the core of genuine letters.

One of the major problems in the study of Paul's life and thought is that of determining the extent to which it is appropriate to label Pauline thought as "apocalyptic." There is widespread agreement that Paul was influenced by apocalyptic eschatology, but the extent to which he modified apocalypticism in light of his faith in *Christ remains a central problem. J. Baumgarten holds that Paul demythologizes apocalyptic traditions by consistently applying them to the present life of the community.

Another problem centers on the issue of the origin of Paul's apocalyptic thought. Baumgarten (43-53) has suggested that apocalyptic traditions came to Paul through the Hellenists at Antioch.

5.2. The Center or Structure of Pauline Thought.
The complexity of Paul's theological thought is exacerbated by the fact that the primary evidence for his views is found in occasional letters written in a variety of specific contexts for the purpose of addressing particular problems and issues; they are historically contingent pastoral communications. Further, the basic seven-letter corpus can hardly be regarded as a representative sample of Pauline thought. Despite the difficulties, many attempts have been made to understand the coherence of Paul's thought and on that basis to identify the core or center of his thought. Some scholars have doubted whether Paul thought in terms of such a "core" or whether the evidence from seven occasional letters is adequate for such a task. Some of the more important suggestions for identifying the central message of Paul's thought include: (1) the gospel, (2) *christology, (3) the death and resurrection of Jesus, (4) the theme *"in Christ" (participatory categories), (5) ecclesiology, (6) justification by faith (the traditional Lutheran view) and (7) anthropology (Baur; Bultmann). It is evident, however, that many of these topics are closely related to others, so that the choice of a core for Pauline thought becomes a matter of nuance. It is clear, for example, that Paul's polemical doctrine of *justification by faith is an aspect of his christology and that the topics of anthropology and ecclesiology are two ways of looking at individual Christians who at the same time hold membership in the people of God.

Other scholars have proposed that it is more important to identify the structure of Paul's thought. Two of the most important proposals include: (1) salvation history, that is, God, who is the central actor in history, has had an ultimate salvific goal for humanity from the beginning, which originally centered on Israel and ultimately on all who believe in Christ, a structure particularly evident in Romans 9—11; and (2) apocalyptic eschatology. However, salvation history and apocalyptic eschatology must not be considered antithetical, since the latter is simply a more specific and particular version of the former. Further, it is a matter of continuing debate whether these suggestions constitute the horizon or kernel of Paul's thought.

5.3. Paul as a Visionary and Mystic.
The authors of apocalypses, though they usually concealed their true identities behind pseudonyms, received divine revelations through visions and for that reason they structured the apocalypses they wrote as narratives of the visions they had actually received or pretended to receive. There was a close relationship between Jewish *merkabah* mysticism (based on Ezek 1) and apocalypticism (Gruenwald), though out-of-body visions were more common in the former and bodily ascensions to heaven more common in the latter. While there is no evidence that Paul wrote an apocalypse, he claims to have been the recipient of revelatory visions or ecstatic experiences (Gal 1:11-17; 1 Cor 9:1; 15:8; see Acts 9:1-9; 16:9; 18:9-10; 22:6-11, 17-21; 26:12-18; 27:23-24). In Galatians 1:12 he speaks of his Damascus Road experience as an *apokalypsis* ("revelation") from Jesus Christ, and in 2 Corinthians 12:1 he speaks of "visions and revelations [*apokalypseis*] of the * Lord," which are presumably descriptions of his own experience. It is likely that Paul is the man of whom he speaks, who experienced a journey to the third heaven, where he heard unspeakable things (2 Cor 12:1-10).

5.4. Apocalyptic Scenarios.
There are four relatively extensive apocalyptic scenarios in the Pauline letters, three of which center on the parousia of Jesus (1 Thess 4:13-18; 2 Thess 1:5-12; 1 Cor 15:51-57), and the so-called Pauline apocalypse, which centers on the coming of the eschatological antagonist (2 Thess 2:1-12). There are also a number of shorter scenarios that appear to be formulaic in character and therefore of pre-Pauline or extra-Pauline origin (1 Thess 1:9-10; 3:13; 5:23).

5.5. Limited Dualism.
The Pauline view of the sovereignty of God (Rom 9—11) makes it apparent that he shares the basic dualistic convictions

of Jewish apocalypticism during the late Second Temple period.

5.5.1. Temporal or Eschatological Dualism. In continuity with the temporal dualistic thought of Jewish apocalypticism, Paul also contrasted the present evil age with the coming age of *salvation (Gal 1:4; Rom 8:18; 1 Cor 1:26; see Eph 5:16) and believed that he was living at the end of the ages (1 Cor 10:11). Yet Paul considerably modified the sharp distinction usually made in apocalyptic thought between these two ages. Paul understood the death and resurrection of Jesus in the past as cosmic eschatological events that separated "this age" (Rom 12:2; 1 Cor 1:20; 2:6), or "this present evil age" (Gal 1:4), from "the age to come." This present age is dominated by rulers, demonic powers who are doomed to pass away (1 Cor 2:6-7).

Paul's belief in the resurrection of Jesus the Messiah convinced him that eschatological events had begun to take place within history and that the resurrection of Jesus was part of the traditional Jewish expectation of the resurrection of the righteous (1 Cor 15:20-23). For Paul the present is a temporary period between the death and resurrection of Christ and his return in glory in which those who believe in the gospel share in the salvific benefits of the age to come (Gal 1:4; 2 Cor 5:17). This temporary period is characterized by the eschatological gift of the Spirit of God, who is experienced as present within the Christian community in general as well as within particular believers who are members of the Christian community (Rom 8:9-11; 1 Cor 6:19; 12:4-11; 1 Thess 4:8). While Paul did not explicitly use the phrase "the age to come" in 2 Corinthians 5:17 and Galatians 6:15, he uses the phrase "new creation," a phrase with apocalyptic associations (Is 65:17; 66:22; Rev 21:1). Though the final consummation still lay in the future, for Christians the new age was present because the Messiah had come.

The basic salvation-history framework of Paul's thought incorporates within it the apocalyptic notion of the two successive ages. This is evident in Romans 5:12-21, where Paul schematizes history in terms of the two realms of Adam and Christ, which are both made part of present experience. Paul therefore made an "already"/ "not yet" distinction indicated by his use of the indicative and imperative in passages such as Galatians 5:25: "If we live [indicative] in the Spirit, let us also walk [imperative] in the Spirit." While

the flesh has been crucified with Christ (Gal 2:20; 3:24; 6:14; Rom 6:2, 6-7, 22; 8:13), the desires of the flesh still pose temptations for Christians (Gal 5:16-18; Rom 6:12-14; 8:5-8). The daily obedience of the Christian provides the continual and necessary authentication of the original act of believing in Christ until the future redemption of creation and the freedom of the children of God becomes a reality (Rom 8:19-20).

5.5.2. Spatial Dualism. Ancient Israelite cosmology conceived of a cosmos in three levels: heaven, earth and Sheol. This same conception of the universe was transmitted to early Judaism, though the emphasis on the transcendence of God that characterized late Second Temple Judaism presupposed a sharper distinction between the heavenly world and the earthly world. This spatial dualism (heaven as the dwelling place of God and his angels; earth as the dwelling place of humanity) coincided with temporal or eschatological dualism in the sense that the kingdom of God, or the age to come, was a heavenly reality that would eventually displace the earthly reality of the present evil age. For Paul, "the things that are seen are transient, but the things that are not seen are eternal" (2 Cor 4:18; see Phil 3:20; 2 Cor 5:1-5). There are therefore three cosmic realms: heaven, earth and the region below the earth (Phil 2:10), though the normal focus is on the two primary cosmic realms: heaven and earth (1 Cor 8:5; 15:47-50; see Col 1:16, 20; Eph 1:10; 3:15). Heaven is where God and his angels dwell (Rom 1:18; 10:6; Gal 1:8; see Eph 6:9) and is the place where Christ is now seated at the right hand of God, a tradition based on the pre-Pauline Christian interpretation of Psalm 110:1 (Rom 8:34; Col 3:1). Heaven is the place from which Jesus will return in the near future as savior and judge (1 Thess 1:10; 4:16; Phil 3:20; see 2 Thess 1:7).

5.5.3. Ethical Dualism. For Paul the two antithetical cosmic powers were God and Satan, who respectively represent the moral qualities of good and evil. God is the ultimate source of love (Rom 5:5; 8:39; 2 Cor 13:14). It is God who has expressed love toward humanity by sending his Son to die an atoning death for them (Rom 5:8). The influence of the Spirit of God, that is, God's active presence in the world, is reflected in such ethical virtues as love, patience, kindness and self-control (Gal 5:22-23). There is an essential similarity between the lists in 1QS 4:2-6, 9-11, in which the virtues encouraged by the spirit of truth are contrasted with the vices promoted by the spirit of error, and the lists in Galatians 5:16-24, where vices are the products of the flesh, while virtues are the products of the Spirit. Satan is frequently mentioned as the supernatural opponent of God and Christians and as the source of evil in the world (Rom 16:20; 1 Cor 7:5; 2 Cor 2:11; 11:14; 12:7; 1 Thess 2:18).

5.5.4. Psychological or Microcosmic Dualism. Assuming that the structure of Paul's theology is in part the product of his adaptation of Jewish apocalypticism as the framework for understanding the significance of the death and resurrection of Jesus the Messiah, that same apocalyptic framework had a profound effect on the way in which he understood the effects of salvation on individual Christians. The basic structure of Jewish apocalypticism consisted of a temporal or eschatological dualism consisting of two ages, the present era (a period of oppression by the wicked), which will be succeeded by a blissful future era. While Jewish apocalypticism had a largely future orientation, Paul's recognition of the fact that Jesus was the Messiah who was a figure of the past, as well as the present and future, led him to introduce some significant modifications. The most significant modification is the softening of the distinction between this age and the age to come with his emphasis on the hidden presence of the age to come within the present age.

Paul exhibits a tendency to conceptualize human nature and existence as a microcosmic version of a Christianized form of apocalyptic eschatology. In other words, the apocalyptic structure of history was considered paradigmatic for understanding human nature. In effect the Christian person is situated at the center of history in the sense that in him or her the opposing powers that dominate the cosmos are engaged in a struggle. Just as Paul's Christian form of apocalyptic thought is characterized by a historical or eschatological dualism consisting in the juxtaposition of the old and new ages, so his view of human nature reflected a similarly homologous dualistic structure. This is evident in 2 Corinthians 5:17 (NRSV): "So if anyone is in Christ, there is a new creation: everything old has passed away; see, everything has become new!" Here Paul uses the basic apocalyptic expectation of the renewal of creation (i.e., the inauguration of the age to come) following the destruction of the present evil age as a paradigm

for the transformation experienced by the individual Christian who has moved from unbelief to belief. Thus the apocalyptic expectation of an impending cosmic change from the present evil age to the future age of salvation has become paradigmatic for the transformation of the individual believer.

Since this apocalyptic transformation affects only those "in Christ," the external world and its inhabitants remain under the sway of the old age. The new age is thus concealed in the old age. The phrase "new creation" refers to the renewal or re-creation of heaven and earth following the destruction of the old cosmos (Is 65:17; 66:22; *1 Enoch* 91:16; 72:1; *2 Bar.* 32:6; 44:12; 49:3; 57:2; *Bib. Ant.* 3:10; 2 Pet 3:11-13; Rev 21:1). Bultmann's existentialist understanding of Pauline anthropological terms (i.e., the human person as a free agent responsible for his or her own decisions), and E. Käsemann's apocalyptic or cosmological understanding of Paul's anthropology (i.e., the human person is a victim of supernatural cosmic forces) are not mutually exclusive categories. Paul also conceives of the struggle within each Christian as the conflict between the Spirit and the *flesh, as in Galatians 5:16: "Walk in the Spirit and you will not fulfill the desires of the flesh."

5.6. Jesus the Messiah. One of the major obstacles impeding Jewish belief in Jesus as the Messiah of Jewish expectation was the fact of the crucifixion (1 Cor 1:18-25; Gal 5:11; see Heb 12:2). One of the unsolved problems in the investigation of early Christianity is the reason why early Christians recognized the messianic status of Jesus despite the fact that he fulfilled none of the central functions that the Jewish people expected of the figure of the Davidic Messiah, including his role as an eschatological high priest, a paradigmatic benevolent and all-powerful king, a judge and destroyer of the wicked, and a deliverer of the people of God (*Pss. Sol.* 17; 4 Ezra 12; *2 Bar.* 40).

In the seven undisputed letters of Paul, the term *Christos,* meaning "Anointed One," "Christ" or "Messiah," occurs 266 times, usually as a proper name for Jesus (e.g., "Jesus Christ"), often with some residual titular quality (evident in the name "Christ Jesus"), and occasionally as a name for a specific Messiah, Jesus (Rom 9:5), but never as a general term for an eschatological deliverer within Judaism. In the seven core Pauline letters, *Christos* is never used as a predicate (e.g., "Jesus is the Christ"), *Christos* is never given a definite article following the name "Jesus" (e.g., "Jesus the Christ"), and *Christos* is never accompanied by a noun in the genitive (e.g., "the Christ of God"). It is safe to conclude that the messianic status of Jesus was not a matter of dispute or concern to Paul. Paul assumes but does not argue that Jesus is the Messiah.

5.7. The Parousia and Judgment. The later OT prophets frequently referred to the day of the Lord as the occasion when God would judge the world (Amos 5:18-20; Zeph 1:14-16; Joel 2:2). In Jewish apocalyptic literature the inauguration of the eschaton occurs with the coming of God or of an accredited agent of God, the Messiah, to bring salvation and judgment. While Paul can speak of "the day of the Lord" (1 Thess 5:2) and God's role as eschatological judge (Rom 3:6), the center of his eschatological hope has shifted from God to Christ, so that he can speak of the impending day of the Lord (1 Thess 5:2) but claim that on that day God will judge the secrets of humans by Christ Jesus (Rom 2:16; see 2 Tim 4:1). The parousia is referred to by Paul both as "the revelation *[apokalypsis]* of our Lord Jesus Christ" (1 Cor 1:6) and (on the analogy of the OT expression "the day of the Lord") as "the day of Jesus Christ" (1 Cor 1:8; Phil 1:6; 3:12-21; Rom 14:7-12, 17-18; 2 Cor 5:10; 1 Thess 4:13-18; 1 Cor 15:20-28, 50-58).

5.8. The Resurrection. For Paul the resurrection of Jesus was not an isolated miraculous event but rather the first stage of the general resurrection of the righteous dead (1 Cor 15:20-23). As an eschatological event, Paul expects that the resurrection of the righteous will occur when Christ returns (Phil 3:20; 1 Thess 4:13-18; 1 Cor 15:51-53). Those who are raised from the dead will be transformed into a new mode of existence (1 Cor 15:51-53; Phil 3:20-21). A similar expectation occurs in Jewish apocalyptic literature (Dan 12:3; *1 Enoch* 39:4-5; 62:15; *2 Enoch* 65:10; *2Bar.* 49:3). But the resurrection of Jesus, which guarantees the resurrection of believers, is not simply a past event with future consequences. Nor is the death of Jesus simply a historical fact. For Christians, *baptism represents a real identification with Christ in his death and resurrection, signaling death to the old life and resurrection to the new (Rom 6:1-14; 8:10-11; see Col 3:1-3; Eph 2:1-10).

5.9. The Eschatological Antagonist. The Christian doctrine of the incarnation of Christ made it all but inevitable that a satanic counterpart to Christ would be incorporated into early Christian apocalyptic expectation. In the Synoptic apocalypse the appearance of false messiahs and false prophets at the end of the age is predicted (Mk 13:21-22; Mt 24:23-24). This figure is called the antichrist in Johannine literature (1Jn 2:18, 22; 4:3; 2 Jn 7). In Revelation the two major antichrist traditions, the godless, tyrannical ruler and the false, seductive prophet, are kept separate. The evil ruler is called the Beast from the Sea (Rev 13:1-10; 16:13; 19:20), while the false prophet is called the Beast from the Land, or the False Prophet (Rev 13:11-18; 16:13; 19:20). There is a single extended discussion of the coming of the eschatological antagonist in the Pauline letters (2 Thess 2:1-12), though strangely there are no allusions to this figure elsewhere in the Pauline letters. There Paul combines into a single figure the two major eschatological antagonist traditions, that of the godless, tyrannical ruler and that of the false, seductive prophet. This person is called the "man of lawlessness" and the "son of perdition" (2 Thess 2:3; see Dan 11:36-37; *Sib. Or.* 5:33-34; *Asc. Isa.* 4:6; *2 Enoch* [Rec. J] 29:4), who will install himself in the temple of God, proclaim himself to be God (2 Thess 2:4) and perform miracles to legitimate his claims (2 Thess 2:9; see Mk 13:22; Mt 24:24; Rev 13:13-14). This eschatological antagonist has not yet appeared because someone or something is restraining him or it (2 Thess 2:7), though there is no agreement regarding whether this restraining force is Satan, the Roman Empire, the Roman emperor or perhaps some supernatural force. This eschatological antagonist will be slain by the Lord Jesus when he returns in judgment (2 Thess 2:8).

5.10. The Problem of a Temporary Messianic Kingdom. The relevance of 1 Corinthians 15:20-28 to the early Jewish and early Christian view of a temporary intermediate messianic kingdom is disputed, though the general view is that there is no clean and convincing evidence that Paul, like the author of Revelation (Rev 20:1-6), expected a messianic interregnum.

Schweitzer summarizes Paul's apocalyptic beliefs in this way: (1) the sudden and unexpected return of Jesus (1 Thess 5:1-4); (2) the resurrection of deceased believers and the transformation of living believers, all of whom meet the returning Jesus in midair (1 Thess 4:16-17); (3) the messianic judgment presided over either by

Christ (2 Cor 5:10) or God (Rom 14:10); (4) the inauguration of the messianic kingdom (not described by Paul but hinted at in 1 Cor 15:25; Gal 4:26); (5) the transformation of all nature from mortality to immortality during the messianic kingdom (Rom 8:19-22) and the struggle with angelic powers (Rom 16:20) until death is conquered (1 Cor 15:23-28); (6) the conclusion of the messianic kingdom (Paul does not mention its duration); (7) the general resurrection at the conclusion of the messianic kingdom (1 Cor 6:3); (8) the judgment on all humanity and defeated angels. According to Schweitzer, Paul introduced two resurrections, although Jewish eschatology before him knew only a single resurrection, either at the beginning or the end of the messianic kingdom. This modification was motivated by Paul's belief in the death and resurrection of Jesus the Messiah. The first resurrection enables believers who have died as well as living Christians to participate in the messianic kingdom, all enjoying a resurrection mode of existence.

Schweitzer's reconstruction of Pauline eschatology is subject to several criticisms. (1) There is no evidence in 1 Thessalonians 4:13-18 or 1 Corinthians 15:20-28 that Paul expected an intermediate messianic kingdom (Wilcke). (2) There is no evidence to indicate that Paul expected a general resurrection of the righteous and the wicked dead.

There are a number of reasons for thinking that it is more probable that 1 Corinthians 15:20-28 indicates that the parousia will shortly be followed by the resurrection and judgment, which together will usher in the final consummation of history (Davies 1970, 295-97). (1) For Paul the kingdom of God is an unending kingdom (1 Thess 2:12; Gal 5:21; 1 Cor 6:9-10; 15:50; see 2 Thess 1:4-5; Col 4:11). (2) The only text that mentions the "kingdom of Christ" (Col 1:12-13) understands it as a present fact. (3) Paul connects the parousia with the judgment of the world (1 Cor 1:7-8; 2 Cor 1:14; Phil 1:6, 10; 2:16). It is probable that Paul has essentially historicized the apocalyptic conception of a temporary messianic kingdom in terms of a temporary period between the crucifixion and resurrection of Jesus and his Parousia. [D. E. Aune]

6. Later New Testament Writings and Apocalypticism.

In later NT writings the expectation of the parousia is enriched by anticipations of a renewed heaven and earth, including a renewed Jerusalem. Second Peter 3:10-14 speaks of cosmic transformation, wherein the "the day of the Lord will come like a thief, and then the heavens will pass away with a loud noise, and the elements will be dissolved with fire, and the earth and the works that are upon it will be burned up" (2 Pet 3:10 RSV). Hebrews 12:18-24 and 13:14 speak of a new Jerusalem, a theme envisioned in several scrolls from Qumran (e.g., 1Q32, 2Q24, 4Q554-555, 5Q15, 11Q18) and ultimately inspired by the visions of Ezekiel. This theme is treated in the NT in the greatest detail in Revelation 21–22. According to the seer: "Then I saw a new heaven and a new earth; for the first heaven and the first earth had passed away, and the sea was no more. And I saw the holy city, new Jerusalem, coming down out of heaven from God, prepared as a bride adorned for her husband; and I heard a loud voice from the throne saying, 'Behold, the dwelling of God is with men. He will dwell with them, and they shall be his people, and God himself will be with them; he will wipe away every tear from their eyes, and death shall be no more, neither shall there be mourning nor crying nor pain any more, for the former things have passed away' " (Rev 21:1-4 RSV). The description of this new Jerusalem, which emphasizes the number twelve, blends together Jewish apocalyptic with Christian emphasis on Jesus, God's "lamb," whose return is eagerly awaited.

[C. A. Evans]

See also APOCRYPHA AND PSEUDEPIGRAPHA, OLD TESTAMENT; ESCHATOLOGY.

DNTB: APOCALYPSE OF ABRAHAM; APOCALYPSE OF ZEPHANIAH; APOCALYPTIC LITERATURE; BARUCH, BOOKS OF; ENOCH, BOOKS OF; ESCHATOLOGIES OF LATE ANTIQUITY; ESDRAS, BOOKS OF; HEAVENLY ASCENT IN JEWISH AND PAGAN TRADITIONS; MESSIANISM; MYSTICISM; NEW JERUSALEM TEXTS; SIBYLLINE ORACLES; TESTAMENT OF MOSES; TESTAMENTS OF THE TWELVE PATRIARCHS; WAR SCROLL (11QM) AND RELATED TEXTS.

BIBLIOGRAPHY. D. C. Allison, *The End of the Ages Has Come* (Philadelphia: Fortress, 1985); J. Baumgarten, *Paulus und die Apokalyptik* (Neukirchen-Vluyn: Neukirchener Verlag, 1975); G. R. Beasley-Murray, *Jesus and the Future* (London: Macmillan, 1954); idem, *Jesus and the Kingdom of God* (Grand Rapids: Eerdmans, 1986); J. Becker,

"Erwägungen zur apokalyptischen Tradition in der paulinischen Theologie," *EvT* 30 (1970) 593-609; J. C. Beker, *Paul the Apostle* (Philadelphia: Fortress, 1980); idem, *Paul's Apocalyptic Gospel: The Coming Triumph of God* (Philadelphia: Fortress, 1982); H. D. Betz, "On the Problem of the Religio-Historical Understanding of Apocalypticism," *JTC* 6 (1969) 134-56; V. P. Branick, "Apocalyptic Paul?" *CBQ* 47 (1985) 664-75; J. J. Collins, ed., *Apocalypse: The Morphology of a Genre* (Semeia 14; Missoula, MT: Scholars Press, 1979); idem, *Apocalypticism in the Dead Sea Scrolls* (London: Routledge, 1997); W. D. Davies, "Apocalyptic and Pharisaism," in *Christian Origins and Judaism* (Philadelphia: Westminster, 1962) 19-30; idem, *Paul and Rabbinic Judaism* (3d ed.; London: SPCK, 1970); I. Gruenwald, *Apocalyptic and Merkavah Mysticism* (Leiden: E. J. Brill, 1980); P. D. Hanson, *The Dawn of Apocalyptic* (Philadelphia: Fortress, 1975); R. H. Hiers, *Jesus and the Future* (Atlanta: John Knox, 1981); E. Käsemann, "On the Subject of Primitive Christian Apocalyptic," in *New Testament Questions of Today* (Philadelphia: Fortress, 1969) 108-37; K. Koch, *The Rediscovery of Apocalyptic* (SBT 2.22; Naperville, IL: Allenson, 1970); L. J. Kreitzer, *Jesus and God in Paul's Eschatology* (Sheffield: JSOT, 1987); H. P. Mueller, "Mantische Weisheit und Apokalyptik," in *Congress Volume* (VTSup 22; Leiden: E. J. Brill, 1972) 268-93; O. Ploeger, *Theocracy and Eschatology* (Richmond: John Knox, 1959); G. von Rad, *Old Testament Theology* (2 vols.; New York: Harper & Row, 1962-65); C. C. Rowland, *The Open Heaven: A Study of Apocalyptic in Judaism and Early Christianity* (New York: Crossroad, 1982); D. S. Russell, *The Method and Message of Jewish Apocalyptic* (Philadelphia: Fortress, 1964); A. Schweitzer, *The Mysticism of Paul the Apostle* (New York: Holt, 1931); M. Smith, "On the History of *Apokalypto* and *Apokalypsis*," in *Apocalypticism in the Mediterranean World and the Near East*, ed. D. Hellholm (Tübingen: Mohr Siebeck, 1983) 9-20; H.-A. Wilcke, *Das Problem eines messianischen Zwischenreichs bei Paulus* (ATANT 51; Zurich: Zwingli, 1967).

D. E. Aune, T. J. Geddert and C. A. Evans

APOCRYPHA AND PSEUDEPIGRAPHA

The term *Apocrypha* is applied by Protestant Christians to the books included in the OT by the Roman Catholic, Coptic and Eastern Orthodox churches but which are not found in the Jewish or Protestant canon. The term *Pseudepigrapha* refers to a much larger body of texts, most of which share the literary device of being written under the pseudonym of a great or an ancient figure in Israel's heritage (Roman Catholic and Orthodox writers usually refer to this body as Apocrypha). These collections preserve important voices that witness to the thought, piety and conversations within the Judaisms of the Second Temple period and that provide essential background for the theology, cosmology, ethics, history and culture of the authors of the NT and shapers of the early church, many of whom knew, valued and drew upon the traditions preserved in these texts.

1. Definitions of Terms
2. Contents and Leading Ideas
3. Significance

1. Definitions of Terms.

1.1. Apocrypha. The word *apocrypha* (Gk "hidden things") was originally an honorable title for books containing a special, esoteric wisdom that was "too sacred or profound to be disclosed to any save the initiated" (Charles). Some scholars locate the origin of this term in 4 Ezra 14:44-47 (= 2 Esdr 14:44-47), which speaks of "hidden books" containing divine wisdom for the "wise among the people" and which are distinct from the canonical collection that contains divine wisdom for the unworthy and the wise alike (Rowley; Fritsch). In the wake of controversies in the early church and again in the aftermath of the Reformation, the term took on negative connotations, signifying books that were withheld on account of their "secondary or questionable" value (Charles) and that were potentially "false, spurious, or heretical" (Charles; Rowley).

The term is now used in Protestant circles to designate thirteen to eighteen texts included as part of the OT that include historical works (1 and 2 Maccabees, 1 Esdras), tales (Tobit, Judith, 3 Maccabees, an expanded Esther, additional tales about Daniel), wisdom literature (Wisdom of Solomon, Wisdom of Ben Sira), pseudepigraphical prophetic literature (Baruch, Letter of Jeremiah), liturgical texts (Prayer of Manasseh, Psalm 150, Prayer of Azariah and the Song of the Three Young Men), an apocalypse (2 Esdras) and a philosophical encomium (4 Maccabees). 4 Ezra and Prayer of Manasseh, in numerous manuscripts of the Septuagint and were clearly prized by the early church and read as Scripture. Recent discoveries at Qumran show that such works were not only preserved among Christian circles—Ben Sira, Tobit and Letter of Jeremiah were all found among the Dead Sea Scrolls, together with numerous pseudepigrapha (*1 Enoch, Jubilees* and other pseudepigraphic works not previously known; Stone).

The lack of consensus concerning what books belong in the Apocrypha bears witness to the variety in OT canon among Christian churches. All of these books are considered by some Christian communions as canonical. J. H. Charlesworth calls for a uniform and exclusive delineation of Apocrypha, following the lists of the majority of LXX manuscripts rather than the Vulgate. He would exclude 3 and 4 Maccabees, Prayer of Manasseh and 2 Esdras (2 Esdras 3—14 = 4 Ezra) from the Apocrypha and include them among the Pseudepigrapha. The more recent study Bibles (Meeks; Metzger and Murphy) opt for a more inclusive collection of Apocrypha (all eighteen). In LXX manuscripts, 3 Maccabees and 4 Maccabees have in their favor a strong presence, commanding great respect in the Greek Orthodox church. C. A. Evans rightly notes that the line between Apocrypha and Pseudepigrapha is not clearly drawn and is blurred even further as one considers the relationship between Jude and *1 Enoch* and *Assumption of Moses* (Evans, 22; Russell 1993). We may never arrive at the consensus for which Charlesworth calls.

The books contained in the Apocrypha have had a spotted history of reception in the church, and not all eighteen (or thirteen) have fared equally well in that history (see Fritsch for a fuller discussion). Paul clearly knew and used Wisdom of Solomon, and echoes of Ben Sira appear in the sayings of Jesus. The apostolic fathers (Polycarp, Clement, Pseudo-Barnabas) quote from or allude to Wisdom of Solomon, Tobit and Ben Sira as authoritative writings, and numerous allusions to other Apocrypha appear as well. Some leading figures in the church, like Jerome and Origen, recognized the difference between the collection of OT Scriptures used by the church and the Hebrew canon, and Jerome especially calls for a practical distinction to be made between the "canonical" texts and "ecclesiastical" texts, which are useful and edifying but not of the same order. Other figures, such as Clement of Alexandria and Augustine, embrace the larger collection as of uniform inspiration and value.

Only the Protestant Reformation forced a decision. Martin Luther decisively separated the books or parts of books (e.g., the Additions to Esther and Daniel) that were not included in the Hebrew canon from his OT as "books which cannot be reckoned with the canonical books and yet are useful and good for reading" (quoted by Rowley). The rest of the Protestant Reformers followed his practice. The apocryphal books continued to be printed and recommended as edifying material, but they were not to be used as a basis for doctrine or ethics apart from the canonical books. The Roman Catholic church responded at the Council of Trent (1546) by declaring these books (excluding 1 and 2 Esdras, Prayer of Manasseh and 3 and 4 Maccabees) to be fully canonical.

The opinion of many Protestants concerning the Apocrypha has fallen considerably from Luther's estimation. Emphasis on "Scripture alone" and the "sufficiency of Scripture," fueled by centuries of tension between Catholic and Protestant churches, has rendered the Apocrypha more suspected than respected, and lack of acquaintance with the texts among most Protestants has reinforced this aversion. Nevertheless, the collection of texts included in the Apocrypha merits careful attention not only on the basis of its testimony to the currents and developments within Judaism during the intertestamental period but also on the basis of the influence these texts exercised on the church during its formative centuries.

1.2. Pseudepigrapha. The term *pseudepigrapha* (Gk, "things bearing a false ascription") highlights primarily a literary characteristic of many writings from the Hellenistic and Greco-Roman periods, that is, writing under the assumed name of a great figure from the distant past. The term does not in itself distinguish the body of texts to which it refers from canonical writings, as numerous scholars have maintained that pseudepigrapha are present within the canon (e.g., Daniel, Song of Songs, Deutero-Isaiah, numerous psalms). Study of the larger phenomenon of pseudepigraphy among Jewish and Greco-Roman writings of the period might, however, help students assess the implications of canonical pseudepigraphy (Evans).

This term, like *apocrypha,* has acquired negative connotations. Charlesworth's survey of several dictionary articles shows that in common parlance the term denotes "spurious works" that are "not considered canonical or inspired." These dictionaries, Charlesworth correctly avers, perpetuate a misleading equation of pseudepigraphy with illegitimacy. Moreover, he rightly asks for clarification concerning the question of canonicity and inspiration. A number of these books are cited as authentic and authoritative texts. We must beware, then, of attaching modern value judgments on an ancient literary practice.

The term is used by scholars to refer to the "rest of the 'outside books'" (Rowley) or to "literature similar to the Apocrypha which is not in the Apocrypha" (Stone 1984). The turn of the twentieth century witnessed the publication of two important collections of pseudepigrapha (Kautzsch and Charles), although these were "reductional" collections of only a dozen or so texts (Charlesworth). Charlesworth and his team sought a broader delineation of this body of literature, including sixty-three texts that matched the general description proposed for the corpus. These texts (1) were almost exclusively Jewish or Christian; (2) were often attributed to ideal figures in Israel's past; (3) customarily claimed to contain God's word or message; (4) built on narratives or ideas in the OT; (5) were written between 200 B.C. and A.D. 200 (or, if they were written later, appeared to preserve substantially earlier traditions). Charlesworth asserts that these criteria are meant to describe a collection, not present hard-and-fast criteria for what constitute Pseudepigrapha.

Major bodies of texts are not grouped among the Pseudepigrapha. Philo and Josephus have left voluminous materials, but, as the authorial attestation is not pseudepigraphic, their works stand outside of this category. The Dead Sea Scrolls contain many pseudepigraphic texts, but, since the "channel of transmission" (Stone) is so well defined, these are treated as a separate corpus. Finally, there are the targums (*see* Rabbinic Traditions and Writings) and other rewritings of biblical texts that share much in common with books like *Jubilees* but are not included in the Pseudepigrapha.

The phenomenon of pseudepigraphy is complex. R. H. Charles sought the origin of the practice in the rise of a monolithic Jewish orthodoxy based on a closed canon of Law and Prophets, which would not permit authors to claim inspiration in their own name. The image of a normative Judaism before A.D. 70 has largely been refuted. Perhaps more useful is S. Cohen's suggestion that Jews in the Second Temple period perceived themselves as living in a postclassical age: this awareness led authors to connect their work with some figure from the classical (preexilic or exilic) period. In the case of apocalypses, the phenomenon may be even more complex, with authors identifying, in some ecstatic experience, with the figure of the past and giving new voice to the ancient worthy. The choice of pseudonym may indicate a conscious attempt to link one's own work with the "received tradition of teaching" related to that name (Stone). Evans echoes this view with approval, extending it into the period after the apostolic age, during which authority was mediated only through the classical figures of the church's first generation and pseudepigraphy again became a common phenomenon.

Scholars have noted the limitations of both terms. First, *apocrypha* and *pseudepigrapha* are not equal terms. One derives from canonical debates and usage; the other from a peculiar literary characteristic. *Apocrypha* is an especially problematic term for the historical study of these documents, since decisions about canon are much later than the period in which the texts were produced and often come only centuries after a document has been in use and exercising an important influence (cf. Charlesworth; Nickelsburg). By using *pseudepigrapha* to refer to a body of texts outside the Protestant canon and the Apocrypha, we obscure the pseudepigraphic nature of many texts within these bodies of literature (Nickelsburg; Russell). C. T. Fritsch adds rightly that some pseudepigrapha are anonymous rather than pseudonymous (e.g., 3 and 4 Macc), and that, even where the label is correct, it "unduly emphasizes a feature of minor importance."

Problems with both terms lead many scholars to treat Jewish literature not by these often value-laden or anachronistic categories but by genre, geographic derivation or period (Newsome, Nickelsburg, Schürer, Kraft and Nickelsburg, Stone). Apocrypha and Pseudepigrapha appear side by side under the categories of wisdom literature, historical writings, liturgical pieces and the like. Fritsch and D. S. Russell advocate using the term *apocrypha* to cover all Protestant noncanonical texts, following the usage of the modern synagogue ("exterior books"), although this suggestion, too, betrays a certain canonical bias.

Despite these difficulties, there is some value in retaining the terms (Charlesworth). The consideration of the Apocrypha as a collection bears witness to the early church's selection of certain Jewish writings that, although they did not belong to the Hebrew canon, were nevertheless held to be of special value and inspiration and exercised an important influence on the church from its inception. As long as one recognizes that these categories could remain somewhat fluid (witnessed by Jude's use of *1 Enoch* and *As. Mos.* and the inclusion of 3 and 4 Macc in many LXX codices), the terms remain valuable as a prioritizing of the vast wealth of Jewish literature that has come down to us.

2. Contents and Leading Ideas.
Although there is significant overlap between the two collections, this article will survey them separately for the sake of clarity and definition.

2.1. Apocrypha. The two historical books, 1 and 2 Maccabees, provide essential information about a series of events that shaped Jewish consciousness during the later Second Temple period. The forced hellenization program of the high priests Jason and Menelaus (175-164 B.C.), the rise of the Hasmonean family as the saviors of Israel and the combining of the high priesthood and kingship under that one dynasty had long-lasting ramifications for the period. The ethos of the later Zealot movement, the notion of a military messiah and the aversion toward lowering the boundaries between Jew and Gentile (e.g., Jewish resistance to Paul's mission) all have strong roots in this period. It was also during this period that the major sects within Judaism took shape—frequently in reaction against (e.g., Qumran Essenes, Pharisees) or in support of (Sadducees) the Hasmonean administration of the temple. Second Maccabees also provides an important early witness to the belief in the resurrection of the righteous and to a growing angelology.

The Wisdom of Ben Sira, written in Jerusalem in about 180 B.C., supports commitment to Torah as the only path to honor and as the way of true wisdom. It contains instruction on a wide array of topics, but its teachings on prayer, forgiveness, almsgiving and the right use of wealth have left an indelible impression on later Jewish ethical instructions and on the early church. Wisdom of Solomon, a product of Egyptian Judaism from the turn of the era, also promotes the Jewish way of life, emphasizing the eternal importance of God's verdict on one's life, the rewards and nature of wisdom and the actions of God on behalf of God's people, Israel. The author takes the personification of Wisdom to its highest level, and this became very influential for the early church's reflection on the divinity and preexistence of Jesus. Wisdom of Solomon helps Jews remain dedicated to Torah also through a demonstration of the folly of Gentile religion, much of which is paralleled in Paul's attacks on Gentile depravity and on idolatry. Here we might mention also the Letter of Jeremiah, which reinforces Jews' conviction that idols are nothing and that Gentiles are alienated from true religion.

Although it is not properly a wisdom book, 4 Maccabees also promotes adherence to Judaism, assuring Jewish readers through a philosophical demonstration that strict obedience to Torah trains one in all the cardinal virtues so highly prized and regarded by the Greco-Roman culture. Indeed, Jews trained by Torah surpass all others in the exercise of virtue, as the courage and endurance of the martyrs of the hellenization crisis (the subjects of the author's praise) show. Particularly those commandments that separate Jews from people of other races—those laws that frequently occasion the contempt of non-Jews—are shown to lead to virtue and honor.

The Apocrypha also contains numerous edifying tales that provide useful windows into the piety of the period. Hebrew Esther was expanded to bring direct references to God and expressions of piety (prayer, dietary purity) into the story. Tobit, a story from the Diaspora and perhaps the oldest book in the Apocrypha, tells a tale of God's providence, the activity of angels and demons, the efficacy of prayer, and exorcism. The story promotes almsgiving and acts of charity within the Jewish community, as well as the value of kinship and endogamy. Judith, possibly a Palestinian work from the Maccabean period, tells of a heroine who used her charm to trap and kill a Gentile oppressor. The story affirms the importance of prayer, dietary purity, the virtue of chastity and God's care for God's people in times of adversity.

Third Maccabees may also be classified as an edifying legend that provides a saga for Diaspora Judaism that parallels the story of 2 Maccabees. It affirms God's special care and closeness to Jews living in the Diaspora and separated from the Promised Land, and it attests to the tensions between faithful Jews, apostate Jews and the dominant Gentile culture. First Esdras may be counted among this group, although it is more a rewriting of biblical books (2 Chron 35:1—36:23; Ezra; Neh 7:38—8:12). The only original portion of this book is a courtly tale about the wisdom of Zerubbabel (1 Esdr 3:1—5:6). Two tales featuring the hero Daniel (originally independent tales) appear in the expanded, Greek version of that book. The first, Susanna, like 1 Esdras 3:1—5:6, celebrates the wisdom of a Jewish leader. The second, Bel and the Dragon, demonstrates the folly of idolatry in Daniel's undermining of the credibility of an image of Bel and a living serpent as gods.

A number of liturgical texts are included among the Apocrypha. Psalm 150 recalls God's choice of David and David's triumph over the Philistine giant—surely a potent image for the place of Israel among the giant Gentile kingdoms that held sway over Israel throughout this period, save for the time of the Hasmonean dynasty. Jewish poets were watchful for points in the biblical story that called for a prayer or a psalm but did not record them. Two additions to Daniel and the Prayer of Manasseh supply what the narratives lack: a prayer of repentance and call for help in the fiery furnace (Prayer of Azariah), a psalm of deliverance (Song of the Three Young Men) and another penitential prayer (Prayer of Manasseh) that affirms that no sinner is beyond God's mercy and power to forgive. Although essentially a pseudepigraphic prophetic book, Baruch also contains much liturgical material. The opening chapters (Bar 1:1—3:8) present penitential prayers affirming God's justice in bringing upon Israel and Judah the curses of Deuteronomy but also open the door to the hope of return as God is remembered and obeyed afresh in the land of exile. There follows a wisdom psalm, identifying wisdom wholly and exclusively with the Torah of Moses in a manner reminiscent of Ben Sira (Bar 3:9—4:4). The final sections take on a more prophetic cast, introducing oracles promising the gathering of the Diaspora Jews, the judgment of the cities that oppressed the Jews and the exaltation of Zion.

Finally, the collection includes an apocalypse, 2 Esdras (also called 4 Ezra). The author writes in response to the destruction of Jerusalem in A.D. 70, and even more directly in response to God's slowness in punishing Rome, the instrument of destruction. In its negation of hope for this age, its hope for reward in the age to come, its visions of the many-headed eagle and the man from the sea, this text provides an important window into Jewish apocalypticism that offers instructive parallels for NT apocalyptic material.

Throughout this corpus, one notices the prominence of the covenant theology of Deuteronomy—the conviction, rooted in the blessings and curses of Deuteronomy 28—32, that the nation and the individuals who follow Torah will be rewarded, and the nation or individual who departs from Torah will be punished. During this tumultuous period, this view was frequently altered to seek that reward or punishment in the afterlife (whether by resurrection, as in 2 Macc, or in the immortality of the soul, as in Wis), but it was never abandoned. Much of the literature is vitally concerned with God's care for God's people, what it means to live as a faithful and obedient people and how to respond to the pressures that threaten that loyalty.

2.2. Pseudepigrapha. Among the Pseudepigrapha are found samples of a wide variety of genres: apocalypses, testaments, expansions of biblical narratives, wisdom literature, philosophical literature, liturgical texts, historical works, poetry and drama all have their representatives.

Many of the Pseudepigrapha fall into the genre of apocalypse. Of these the most important and accessible may be *1 Enoch* and *2 Baruch.* The oldest strata of *1 Enoch,* which is a composite work, may date from the third century B.C. This work presents a journey to the places prepared for the punishment of the wicked and reward of the righteous, an advanced angelology based on the story of the "Watchers" (cf. Gen 6:1-4) and a scheme of history placing the recipients near the time of God's breaking into the fabric of history to execute judgment. The Similitudes (*1 Enoch* 37—71), composed perhaps during the first century A.D., bear witness to developments of the figure of the Son of man and thus provide relevant material for the study of that title in the Gospels. The work as a whole left its mark on Jude (which quotes *1 Enoch* 1:9) and especially Revelation. Like 4 Ezra, *2 Baruch* is an apocalyptic response to the destruction of Jerusalem. It also counsels renewed commitment to Torah as the path to God's vindication of the chastised nation, assuring readers of the nearness of God's deliverance and the certainty of the chastisement of Rome. Other apocalypses of note include *2 Enoch,* the *Sibylline Oracles,* the *Apocryphon of Ezekiel,* the *Apocalypse of Abraham* and the *Treatise of Shem.*

Closely related to apocalypses are the texts that fall within the genre of testament. These are typically deathbed speeches by great figures of Israel's past, and they present a narrative review of the figure's life (often as a model for virtuous living), ethical exhortations and frequently eschatological predictions, closing with the death and burial of the hero. The most important of these are the *Testaments of the Twelve Patriarchs,* which preserve important examples of developments in angelology, demonology, the priestly and regal functions of the Messiah and ethics. The *Testament of Job* highlights once again the folly of idolatry but also provides important material for the development of the figure of Satan. The *Testament of Moses,* essentially an expansion of Deuteronomy 31-34, attests to the regard shown Moses as prophet, mediator and perpetual intercessor, thus providing useful background for NT reflections on Moses. The stance of nonviolent resistance advocated by this book stands in stark contrast to more militaristic ideologies of the period, and the idea of a day of repentance that precedes the coming of God's kingdom parallels Jesus' summons to repentance as a preparation for God's coming (cf. Mk 1:14-15).

Of the expansions of biblical narratives, the most important are *Jubilees* and *Martyrdom of Isaiah.* Dating from the late second century B.C., *Jubilees* rewrites the stories of Genesis and Exodus and is of great value for its witness to the development of a theology of Torah. The law revealed to Moses is presented as an eternal law, written on heavenly tablets and obeyed even by archangels. The patriarchal narratives are retold to emphasize their obedience to the Torah, particularly ritual and liturgical observances. The book also reinforces strong boundaries between Jew and Gentile (especially Idumeans) and locates the origin of evil in the activity of Satan and his angels rather than in Adam's weakness. The author looks forward to an imminent renewal of obedience to Torah that will result in a return to primeval longevity. *Martyrdom of Isaiah* tells of the apostasy of Manasseh and the arrest and execution of Isaiah (he was sawn in two; cf. Heb 11:37) at the instigation of a false

prophet, Belkira, a demon working to lead Jerusalem astray. In its present form, the *Martyrdom* has been thoroughly Christianized, presenting Isaiah as an explicit witness to Jesus and the history of the early church (*Mart. Isa.* 3:13-31).

Within this category we might also consider the *Letter of Aristeas,* written in Greek near the end of the second century B.C. This work is not directly based on a biblical narrative or character but is more of an edifying tale in defense of the Septuagint, the Greek translation of the Hebrew Scriptures and the rational character of a life lived according to Torah. It tells of the wisdom of the Jewish scholars who translated the Torah into Greek and the compatibility of obedience to Torah with the best traditions of Greek ethical philosophy, and it upholds the reliability of the LXX. Other notable expansions of biblical narratives include *Joseph and Asenath, Life of Adam and Eve* and the *Liber Antiquitatum Biblicarum,* otherwise known as Pseudo-Philo.

Among the Pseudepigrapha are also found liturgical texts. The collection of the eighteen *Psalms of Solomon* reflects upon the corruption of the Hasmonean house in its final decades, the intervention of Pompey the Great (who besieged Jerusalem at the request of a claimant for the Hasmonean throne and entered the holy place of the temple) and the death of Pompey in Egypt. All these events are seen as demonstrating the principle of Deuteronomy that departure from the law brings punishment, but also that the Gentile instrument of punishment will not go free. The psalms speak of God's generous provision for all creation, promote the way of life of the righteous person, critique hypocrisy and pride, affirm the value of God's correction and depict the advent of the messianic age under the leadership of a Son of David, the Lord Messiah. Of special interest also are the Hellenistic Synagogal Prayers, which show the blending of Jewish and Christian piety in the early church and which, stripped of their Christian additions, provide a unique view into the piety of the synagogue. Among these poetical texts may also be found several additional psalms of David and the *Odes of Solomon,* a Christian collection with close affinities to the Fourth Gospel.

A number of wisdom texts, often showing the degree to which Jews could adapt and use Greek philosophy, maxims and ethics, are also included in the collection, as well as literary works (poetry and drama), which again frequently show conscious imitation of Greek forms. Finally, the collection includes fragments of historians, which probe the early history of the Jews in a manner reminiscent of Josephus's *Antiquities*.

3. Significance.

The period between the Testaments is not a silent age. The texts contained in the Apocrypha and Pseudepigrapha introduce the modern reader to many important and influential voices from the Hellenistic and Roman periods. Without these texts our picture of the Judaism within which the church was born would be most incomplete. These voices demonstrate the diversity within Judaism during the Second Temple period, a view that has replaced early twentieth-century views about a "normative" (legalistic) Judaism before A.D. 70 (Charlesworth vs. Charles). It was a dynamic period of "ferment" within Judaism (Russell 1993), of wrestling with Jewish identity and covenant loyalty amid great social pressures and political upheavals.

The study of these texts leads to a deeper understanding of the Judaism and range of Jewish traditions that shape the proclamation of Jesus and the early church, and this is not the Judaism of the Hebrew Scriptures alone. The intertestamental voices highlight parts of the OT tradition that remained especially important but also attest to new developments, emphases and lines of interpretation that were not original to, but rather were assumed by, the early church. The cosmology, angelology, *eschatology, *christology and ethics of the early church owe much to the developments of this vibrant period. Some of these texts shed light on the ideology of those who opposed the Jesus movement or the Pauline mission. Many others were the conversation partners of founding figures within the church, and our full appreciation of the work of the latter depends on our acquaintance with the former.

See also JUDAISM AND THE NEW TESTAMENT; RABBINIC TRADITIONS AND WRITINGS.

DNTB: JEWISH LITERATURE: HISTORIANS AND POETS; PSEUDONYMITY AND PSEUDEPIGRAPHY; RABBINIC LITERATURE; REWRITTEN BIBLE IN PSEUDEPIGRAPHA AND QUMRAN.

BIBLIOGRAPHY. R. H. Charles, ed., *The Apocrypha and Pseudepigrapha of the Old Testament in English* (2 vols.; Oxford: Clarendon Press, 1913); J. H. Charlesworth, *The Pseudepigrapha and Modern Research, with a Supplement* (SCS 7; Chico, CA: Scholars Press, 1981); idem, "The Renaissance of Pseudepigrapha Studies: The SBL Pseudepigrapha Project," *JSJ* 2 (1971) 107-14; J. H. Charlesworth, ed., *The Old Testament Pseudepigrapha* (2 vols.; Garden City, NY: Doubleday, 1985); S. Cohen, *From the Maccabees to the Mishnah* (Philadelphia: Westminster, 1987); D. A. deSilva, *Introducing the Apocrypha: Message, Context, and Significance* (Grand Rapids: Baker, 2002); C. A. Evans, *Noncanonical Writings and New Testament Interpretation* (Peabody, MA: Hendrickson, 1992); C. T. Fritsch, "Apocrypha," *IDB* 1:161-66; idem, "Pseudepigrapha," *IDB* 3:960-64; L. R. Helyer, *Exploring Jewish Literature of the Second Temple Period: A Guide for New Testament Students* (Downers Grove, IL: InterVarsity Press, 2002); E. Kautzsch, ed., *Die Apokryphen und Pseudepigraphen des Alten Testaments* (2 vols.; Hildesheim: Georg Olms, 1962 [1900]); R. A. Kraft and G. W. E. Nickelsburg, eds., *Early Judaism and Its Modern Interpreters* (Philadelphia: Fortress; Atlanta: Scholars Press, 1986); W. A. Meeks, ed., *The HarperCollins Study Bible* (New York: HarperCollins, 1993); B. M. Metzger, *An Introduction to the Apocrypha* (Oxford: Oxford University Press, 1957); B. M. Metzger and R. E. Murphy, *The New Oxford Annotated Bible with the Apocrypha* (New York: Oxford University Press, 1991); J. D. Newsome, *Greeks, Romans, Jews* (Philadelphia: Trinity Press International, 1992); G. W. E. Nickelsburg, *Jewish Literature Between the Bible and the Mishnah* (Philadelphia: Fortress, 1981); H. H. Rowley, *The Relevance of Apocalyptic* (London: Athlone, 1944); D. S. Russell, *Between the Testaments* (London: SCM, 1960); idem, "Pseudepigrapha," in *The Oxford Companion to the Bible*, ed. B. M. Metzger and M. D. Coogan (Oxford: Oxford University Press, 1993) 629-31; E. Schürer, *The History of the Jewish People in the Age of Jesus Christ (175 B.C.-A.D. 135)*, rev. and ed. G. Vermes, F. Millar and M. Goodman (3 vols., Edinburgh: T & T Clark, 1986) 3.1; M. E. Stone, "The Dead Sea Scrolls and the Pseudepigrapha," *Dead Sea Discoveries* 3 (1996) 270-95; idem, "Pseudepigrapha," *IDBSup* 710-12; M. E. Stone, ed., *Jewish Writings of the Second Temple Period* (CRINT 2.2; Assen: Van Gorcum; Philadelphia: Fortress, 1984).			D. A. deSilva

APOSTLE: NEW TESTAMENT

The term *apostle (apostolos)* is used in the Gospels to designate the twelve disciples called and sent out by Jesus to preach the gospel of the *kingdom and demonstrate its presence by performing signs and wonders. The term is not applied to Jesus in the Gospels. Nevertheless there is good reason to believe that he thought of himself as the apostle of God, sent into the world to proclaim and inaugurate the kingdom of God. There is also good reason to believe that the origin of the Christian apostolate is to be traced back to Jesus, in particular to his sending of the Twelve on their Galilean mission, and that the notion of apostleship betrays certain affinities with the Jewish institution of the *šālîaḥ* ("envoy"). This in turn enables us to understand better the nature of the Christian apostolate, which we find developed in Acts as it continues the story of Jesus' *disciples.

The office of apostle, by which Paul pointedly referred to himself, is of singular importance in the appreciation of his life and ministry. There has been considerable debate over the criteria for apostleship and the nature of the authority that Paul claimed over the Gentile churches and that others questioned or rejected.

    1. "Apostle" in the Gospels
    2. "Apostle" in Paul's Letters
    3. "Apostle" in Acts, Hebrews, General Epistles and Revelation

1. "Apostle" in the Gospels.

1.1. Terminology. In addition to the word *apostolos,* two other terms are significant for our understanding of apostleship in the Gospels. First there is the cognate verb *apostellō* ("to send"), which is used in all four Gospels. The second is the verb *pempō* ("to send"), used synonymously in John's Gospel. The use of these terms in nonbiblical sources has been documented often (see, e.g., Rengstorf) and need only be noted here in the broadest outline.

1.1.1. Apostolos. In classical Greek *apostolos* was used in an impersonal way, for example, in reference to the dispatch of a fleet or an army and then in reference to the fleet or army itself. There are a couple of isolated places where *apostolos* is used personally; however, it is noteworthy that in these cases the idea of being an authorized agent is secondary; the quality of having been sent is primary. *Apostolos* is found only once in the LXX (3 Kings 14:6 par. 1 Kings 14:6 ET), which is quite surprising because the OT contains many references to messengers sent from God. In the papyri the term is used in an impersonal way (e.g., to designate an invoice accompanying a shipment of corn). Josephus

uses *apostolos* twice, and in one of these cases it refers to Jewish emissaries who came to Rome to petition Caesar for the liberty to live according to their own laws. This comes closer to the use of *apostolos* in the Gospels but clearly still falls somewhat short of it. The use of *apostolos* in the Gospels, and indeed its primary usage throughout the NT to designate someone who is sent (by Christ) to convey a message from God, is unique in ancient literature.

1.1.2. Apostellō and Pempō. In secular Greek the verbs *apostellō* and *pempō* are used of the sending of persons and things. There is, however, a discernible difference in the usage of the two terms. *Pempō* is used where mere sending is involved, whereas *apostellō* is used to denote sending of persons with a commission and in some cases to denote a divine sending and authorization.

In the LXX the verb *apostellō* is used more than 709 times, almost always as a translation equivalent for the Hebrew verb *šālaḥ* ("to send"). *Šālaḥ* denotes for the most part the idea of being sent with a commission, either by another human agent or by God. *Pempō* is used much less, and only five times to translate *šālaḥ*. Josephus uses both terms, sometimes as synonyms (where a mere sending is involved), but he chooses *apostellō* when he wants to convey the idea of being sent with a commission.

In the NT (with the exception of John's Gospel), it may be said that *pempō* is used where the simple idea of sending is conveyed and *apostellō* when something of a commission is involved. In John's Gospel, however, the two terms are used interchangeably.

1.2. The Origin of the Idea of Apostleship. The term *apostolos* occurs infrequently outside the NT, and this stands in marked contrast to the frequency of its use within the NT. It is found, for example, only once in the LXX, whereas it occurs seventy-nine times in the NT. How can we account for this? Where did this Christian use of *apostolos* originate?

1.2.1. The Traditional View. Mark 3:14 and Luke 6:13 affirm that Jesus chose twelve *disciples "whom he also named apostles," thus tracing the naming of the Twelve as apostles back to Jesus. This might seem to settle the issue for many. Those who trace the idea of the Christian apostolate back to Jesus recognize that Jesus probably did not use the Greek term *apostolos*. He would have used, most likely, either the Aramaic (šĕlîḥāʾ) or the Hebrew (šālîaḥ) equivalent. Those espousing this view argue that *apostolos* in our Gospels must be understood in terms of the Jewish institution of the šālîaḥ ("envoy"), an idea with which Jesus would have been well acquainted and had applied to his understanding of his relationship with his disciples.

The institution of the šālîaḥ is well documented in rabbinic writings (cf. e.g., *m. Ber.* 5:5), where it refers to someone who has been authorized to carry out certain functions on behalf of another. The adage "a man's envoy is as himself" occurs frequently in the rabbinic literature, and it underlines the representative character of the šālîaḥ and that he carries the full authority of his principal. It is suggested, then, that it was in terms of this institution that Jesus understood his relationship to his disciples and that it is his use of this idea that lies behind the use of *apostolos* in the Gospels.

1.2.2. Difficulties with the Traditional View. The traditional view is not as strong as it first seems, for two reasons. First, better manuscripts omit the words "whom he also named apostles" from Mark 3:14. That leaves Luke 6:13 as the lone testimony to the naming of the Twelve as apostles by Jesus. Luke's text may be based on a weakly attested variant of Mark, and the inclusion of this clause in Mark in some manuscripts may be due to a scribal gloss.

If we set Mark 3:14 and Luke 6:13 to one side, then all we are left with in the Gospels are a number of texts where the Twelve are spoken of by the Evangelists as apostles (Mt 10:2; Mk 6:30; Lk 9:10; 17:5; 22:14; 24:10); one saying of Jesus in Luke 11:49 ("Therefore also the Wisdom of God said, 'I will send to them prophets and apostles, and they will kill and persecute some of them' "), which does include a reference to apostles but is omitted in the parallel saying of Jesus in Matthew 23:34; and one Johannine saying of Jesus ("Truly, truly, I say to you, a servant is not greater than his master; nor is one sent [*apostolos*] greater than the one who sent him" [Jn 13:16]), which is clearly not a statement related primarily to the Christian apostolate.

Second, while the institution of the šālîaḥ ("envoy") is well documented in rabbinic literature, its documentation cannot be dated earlier than the second century A.D. There is no known use of the nominal form šālîaḥ before that time. It is very difficult to sustain the view that the use of the word *apostolos* in the Gospels demonstrates either that the origin of the Christian apostolate can be traced back to Jesus or that Jesus understood it in terms of the Jewish institution of the šālîaḥ. This has prompted some scholars to seek alternative ways to explain the origin of the Christian apostolate.

1.2.3. Alternative Views. One factor that seems to point to a possible alternative explanation for the origin of the apostolate is the rather uneven distribution of the word *apostolos* within the NT as a whole. Of the seventy-nine occurrences in the NT, sixty-eight are found in Luke-Acts and the Pauline corpus—documents that are particularly related to the early Christian mission. This has prompted a number of scholars (e.g., Schmithals) to argue that the idea of the Christian apostolate originated not in the time of Jesus' mission but in the early period of the church's post-Easter mission.

This view needs to be taken seriously. The major Pauline letters are among the earliest NT documents and were almost certainly written before any of the Gospels. Therefore the emergence of the Christian idea of apostle, at a literary level at least, must be traced to these. It is, therefore, theoretically possible that the idea of the Christian apostolate originated in the early period of the Christian mission, then found literary expression in the major Pauline letters, and later on was used by the Evangelists when they wrote their accounts of Jesus' calling and commissioning of his disciples.

Another view is that the concept originated in a Jewish or a Jewish-Christian Gnosticism native in Syria. As Antioch (in Syria) is thought to be the homeland of the church's mission, it is argued that the concept could have been easily borrowed and appropriated into the thinking of the early Christian mission there. However, this last suggestion has not generally commended itself to scholars, not least because the documents to which appeal is made in support of the existence of pre-Christian Gnosticism do not date from the pre-Christian period. Many scholars, therefore, favor the view that the concept of the apostolate arose from within the church's missionary experience.

1.2.4. Return to a Modified Traditional View. In more recent times a growing number of scholars have been willing to trace the origin of the Christian apostolate back to the period of Jesus. However, those who do so are reluctant to tie it too closely to the institution of šālîaḥ ("envoy") documented in rabbinic writings, as did the earlier proponents of this view. Attention is now focussed instead on the *šālaḥ/apostellō* sending terminology occurring in the OT and the NT.

The more recent approach begins appropriately with the earliest literary references to the Christian apostolate, that is, those in the letters of Paul. In these letters Paul speaks of himself frequently as an apostle (*apostolos*) of Jesus Christ, and of Christ's having sent (*apostellō*) him with a commission to proclaim the gospel to the Gentiles. *Apostolos/apostellō* in Paul's letters, then, bears the same basic meaning as the *šālaḥ/apostellō* terminology in the OT, that of a person being sent with a commission.

Turning to the Gospels, we find that while the use of the noun *apostolos* is meager, that of the verb *apostellō* (and in the case of John's Gospel the use of the verb *pempō* as well) is quite substantial. Each of the four Gospels uses *apostellō* many times, including what we might call technical uses in which the idea of being sent with a commission is involved. In each of the Gospels these technical uses occur in narrative statements made by the Evangelist and in sayings of Jesus that the Evangelist includes in his narrative. These technical uses, like those found in the Pauline letters, correspond with the use of the *šālaḥ/apostellō* sending terminology in the OT to denote the sending of a person with a commission (see 1.2. above). Thus it seems clear that the Christian notion of the apostolate has definite links with the OT notion of sending with a commission, and this in turn corresponds with the role of the Jewish *šālîaḥ* as it is documented in the rabbinic literature.

However, the question remains: Can we trace the forging of this link back to Jesus, and was he therefore the one who provided the church with its understanding of the apostolate? Theoretically this link could have been forged in the period of the early Christian mission, and once forged the resulting notion of the apostolate could have been used anachronistically by the Evangelists in their Gospel accounts of Jesus' ministry. Is there any way to reach a responsible decision as to which of these alternatives is to be preferred?

1.2.5. Jesus and the Christian Apostolate. The case for tracing the idea of the Christian apostolate back to Jesus would gain cogency if it could be shown that there are authentic sayings of Jesus in the Gospels (especially in the Synoptics) in which the technical use of *apostellō* mentioned above may be found. In fact there are a number of such sayings whose authenticity can be argued quite strongly on critical grounds. They include sayings in which Jesus speaks of his having been sent by the Father and sayings in which he speaks about his own sending of the Twelve/Seventy.

Examples of sayings relating to Jesus include Matthew 15:24, in which he says to the Canaanite woman, "I was sent only to the lost sheep of the house of Israel," and Luke 4:18, where Jesus cites Isaiah 61:1 saying, "The Spirit of the Lord is upon me, because he has anointed me to preach the gospel to the poor. He has sent me to proclaim release to the captives."

One example of the sayings that relate to Jesus' disciples having been sent by him is Luke 22:35, where Jesus asks them, "When I sent you out without purse or bag or sandals, did you lack anything?" In addition there is a series of sayings in which Jesus comments that those who receive his disciples receive him, and those who receive him receive the One who sent him (Mt 10:40/Lk 10:16; Mk 9:37/Lk 9:48/Mt 18:5).

It can be argued strongly on critical grounds that all these sayings rest on authentic Jesus tradition. For example, Matthew's retention of Matthew 15:24 with its exclusivist note ("only to the lost sheep of the house of Israel"), despite the embarrassment it may have caused in a church already involved in Gentile mission in the pre-Pauline era (cf. Acts 10:1-48; 11:20-24), strongly supports its dominical character. The reliability of the tradition behind Luke 4:18, with its citation from Isaiah 61:1, is underlined by the fact that allusion is made to Isaiah 61:1 in other sayings of Jesus (Lk 6:20/Mt 5:3-6 and Mt 11:2-6/Lk 7:18-23) that bear the hallmarks of authenticity. In the case of Luke 22:35 it can be argued that the whole pericope in which it is found (Lk 22:35-38), with its advice to take up the sword, is not the sort of saying the church would want to put on the lips of Jesus while at the same time trying to keep the remembrance of him free from any association with the Zealots. (For a fuller discussion of the case for the authenticity of the tradition underlying these sayings and others mentioned above, see Kruse, 13-29.)

Because there are strong arguments in favor of the authenticity of these sayings, there is also a strong case for claiming that the idea of the Christian apostolate originated with Jesus and that he understood it in a way similar to that reflected in the use of *šalah/apostellō* terminology in the OT. This in turn means that Jesus' understanding of the apostolate has close affinities with that of the function of the *šāliah* reflected in the rabbinic writings.

We can now turn our attention from arguments that the idea of the Christian apostolate originated with Jesus and seek to understand what, according to the Gospels, that apostolate entailed. We begin with a discussion of Jesus' own apostolic consciousness.

1.3. Jesus, Apostle of God. The term *apostolos* is only once applied to Jesus in the NT (Heb 3:1), it being nowhere used of him in the Gospels. However, there are a number of sayings of Jesus in the Synoptic Gospels in which he betrays a consciousness of having been sent by God (Mt 15:24; Lk 4:18; Mt 10:40; Mk 9:37; Lk 9:48; 10:16). The Gospel of John attributes to Jesus thirty-nine statements to the effect that he has been sent by God, including statements using both *apostellō* and *pempō* (e.g., Jn 5:30, 36, 38; 6:29, 57; 7:16, 29; 8:16, 42; 10:36).

1.3.1. The Source of Jesus' Apostolic Consciousness. It appears from the Gospels that the primary aspect of Jesus' consciousness was that of his filial relationship with the Father (e.g., the boy Jesus' reply to his parents in Lk 2:49: "Did you not know that I must be in my Father's house?"), and that he had been sent by the Father to carry out his mission (Lk 4:43: "I must preach the kingdom of God to the other cities also; for I was sent for this purpose"). This consciousness of having been sent by God is stressed heavily by the Fourth Evangelist. A secondary aspect of Jesus' apostolic consciousness is that of having been endowed with the Spirit (*see* Holy Spirit) to carry out the commission that the Father had given him. Each of the Gospels tells how Jesus was endowed with the Spirit at his baptism. On a number of occasions Jesus appeals to this endowment as evidence that he is the one sent by God to bring in the time of fulfillment spoken of in the OT. For example, in Luke 4:16-21 Jesus cites the prophecy of Isaiah 61:1-2, claiming that this prophecy has now been fulfilled. In Matthew 12:28 he replies to those who assert that he exorcises by the power of Beelzebul by saying, "If by the Spirit of God I cast out demons, then the kingdom of God has come upon you."

It seems, then, that Jesus' apostolic consciousness was rooted in his sense of unique filial relationship with the Father and of having

been commissioned by him to inaugurate the time of fulfillment. The activity of the Spirit in his ministry was something to which he called the attention of others so that they might come to recognize that he was sent by God, rather than being the evidence by which he himself was convinced of his calling.

1.3.2. The Scope of Jesus' Apostolate. One feature of Jesus' apostleship that is rather striking is its limited scope. According to Matthew 15:24 ("I was sent only to the lost sheep of the house of Israel"), Jesus understood his mission to be limited to the Jewish people, and this is reflected in the fact that the Synoptic Gospels never depict him deliberately setting out to evangelize non-Jews. He was sent to announce the coming of the kingdom of God among the Jewish towns of Galilee and Judea (Mk 1:35-39/Lk 4:42-43). Even the remarkable ministry in Samaria, recounted in John 4, is not presented as something that Jesus set out deliberately to undertake, as was the case with the ministry in Jewish towns.

1.3.3. A Prophetic and Prophecy-Fulfilling Apostolate. Jesus' mission was prophetic insofar as he, like other great prophets before him, proclaimed the coming of the kingdom of God (Mk 1:14-15/Mt 4:17). However, it went beyond anything that the prophets did in that he was sent not only to proclaim the kingdom but to inaugurate it as well. Accordingly, Luke tells us that Jesus understood the great prophecy of Isaiah 61:1-2 as being fulfilled in his mission (Lk 4:16-21; cf. Lk 6:20/Mt 5:3-6; Mt 11:2-6/Lk 7:18-23).

1.3.4. Jesus' Apostolate and the Kingdom. What did it mean in practice for Jesus to inaugurate the kingdom? Jesus' statement "the kingdom of God is drawing near" really means that *God himself is drawing near.* And what did God do when he drew near in the person and mission of Jesus? He began his work of bringing in a new era. He called a nation to repentance, he sat at table with tax collectors, sinners, Pharisees and others; he lifted the heavy burden of religious tradition from the shoulders of the people of the land and liberated those who suffered from disease and demonic oppression. But above all he drew near to forgive the sins of all who heeded the call to repentance, and to enter into a restored relationship with them.

But there was also a dark and mysterious side to what God was doing when he drew near in the person and mission of Jesus. The kingdom had not only to be proclaimed and inaugurated. A way had to be opened whereby sinful men and women could participate in it. The crucial part of Jesus' mission was the giving of his life as a ransom for many (Mk 10:45), the pouring out of his blood for the remission of sins (Mt 26:28; Mk 14:23-24; Lk 22:20). It was to achieve this, above all, that Jesus was sent as apostle of God.

1.4. The Apostleship of Jesus' Disciples. Each of the Synoptic Gospels recounts how Jesus called the Twelve and sent them out on a Galilean mission. Some doubts have been raised about the historicity of such a mission, but there are compelling reasons to reject such objections. Not least among these is the existence of a reference to that mission in the saying of Jesus in Luke 22:35: "When I sent you out without purse or bag or sandals, did you lack anything?" Leaving aside, then, the question of historicity, we may explore the mission traditions of the Gospels to discover what they reveal of the nature of the apostleship of the Twelve.

1.4.1. The Mission of the Twelve. Mark 3:13-14 reads: "And he went up on the mountain, and called to him those whom he wished; and they came to him. And he appointed Twelve, whom he also named apostles, so that they might be with him, and so that he might send them to preach." Mark emphasizes that the mission and apostolate of the Twelve originates in the call of Jesus. The purpose for which they were called is clearly spelled out: "so that they might be with him, and so that he might send them to preach." There are two parts to the call, and the second was intimately related to the first.

The first part (to be with him) involved traveling up and down the country with him, sharing food and accommodation with him, experiencing the same acceptance and rejection that he encountered, and observing and sometimes participating in the ministry that he was carrying out. The second part (being sent out to preach) was dependent on the first (being with him) for, as we shall see, their preaching ministry was essentially an extension of his. Mark 6:7-13, Matthew 10:1-42 and Luke 9:1-6 present Jesus' charge to the Twelve.

There are a number of significant points of comparison between their mission and the mission of Jesus. First, Jesus, who said that he had not been sent except to the lost sheep of the house of Israel (Mt 15:24), insisted that the same limitations apply to the mission of the Twelve:

"Do not go into the way of the Gentiles, and do not enter a Samaritan town, but go rather to the lost sheep of the house of Israel" (Mt 10:5-6). Second, the thrust of their mission was to be the same. They were to proclaim that the kingdom of heaven was at hand, and its presence was to be demonstrated by mighty works (Mt 10:7-8). Third, and possibly most important of all, Jesus maintained that the reception his disciples were accorded by the people would be regarded as the reception the people wished to accord to himself and to the Father who had sent him (Mt 10:40).

All of this has important significance for our understanding of the mission of the Twelve and of the nature of apostleship. That the limitations applying to their mission, its essential thrust and the significance of the people's response to it all closely parallel the essential features of Jesus' mission suggest strongly that their mission was in fact an extension of his. This in turn suggests that the *apostellō* sending terminology, which, as we have seen, is used by Jesus in the Synoptic Gospels (and John), reflects an understanding of the relationship existing between himself and his disciples in terms of the institution of the *šālîaḥ*. His disciples were commissioned to act as his representatives, under his authority, proclaiming his message and exercising his power. In the case of Jesus' disciples, then, the words of the rabbinic adage "a man's envoy is as himself" truly apply.

1.4.2. The Mission of the Seventy. Each of the Synoptic Gospels recounts a Galilean mission of the Twelve, but Luke alone recounts a mission of the Seventy. There are problems surrounding the latter. First, there is the question of whether the text of Luke 10:1 (and Lk 10:17) should read "seventy" or "seventy-two." Both readings are found in the manuscripts, and the witnesses seem evenly divided. Other considerations, such as the symbolism of the Seventy(-two), have produced no scholarly consensus about the original reading.

Second, material found in the Markan (Mk 6:7-13) and Matthean (Mt 10:1-42) charges to the Twelve appears in part in the Lukan charge to the Twelve (Lk 9:1-6) and in part in the Lukan charge to the Seventy (Lk 10:1-16). Assuming, as most scholars still do, that Mark was written first and that Matthew and Luke made use of some form of Mark as well as a sayings source (Q) in the composition of their Gospels, it seems that

Matthew used his Markan material plus the Q mission sayings when composing his charge to the Twelve, while Luke used the same sources to compose two charges—that to the Twelve and that to the Seventy.

Third, when Luke depicts Jesus referring to the mission of the Twelve (Lk 22:35), reference is made to material included in the charge to the Seventy. From this it may be inferred that Luke was not trying to reproduce verbatim different charges to different people but rather providing an account of the sort of thing that Jesus would have said to two different groups.

In light of all this, the question is asked whether the mission of the Seventy has any basis in history or if it should be regarded as a literary creation of the Evangelist. It has been suggested, for instance, that Luke invented the story to prefigure the wider mission of the church to the Gentiles. Thus, it is urged, just as the mission of the Twelve speaks of a mission to the tribes of Israel, so the mission of the Seventy speaks of the mission to the nations of the world. (Genesis 10 contains a list of nations comprising seventy names in the MT, and seventy-two in the LXX.) Another suggestion is that Luke invented the mission of the Seventy to deal with the tension between the church's tradition concerning the mission of the Twelve and its recognition of the mission of a far wider group of witnesses.

However, there are other ways of explaining the phenomena. First, it is theoretically possible that Luke regarded the existence of mission material in his two sources (Mark and Q) as evidence for two different missions, and he used those sources to compose two mission charges. Second, and more likely, Luke was the recipient of reliable tradition about the two historic missions, and in composing his Gospel he used the mission material from his two sources to provide an account of the sort of thing Jesus would have said in sending out the two groups.

1.4.3. Post-Easter Mission of Jesus' Disciples. While the mission accounts of the Synoptic Gospels (there is none in John) relate to activity in the pre-Easter period, there appear to be allusions in the charges to a later and wider mission of the disciples in the post-Easter period. For example, the saying "Behold, I am sending you out as sheep/lambs in the midst of wolves" (Mt 10:16/Lk 10:3) does not in some ways fit well with the disciples' Galilean mission experience

(e.g., Lk 10:17-20). They appear to have been halcyon days. This has led some to suggest that this saying and others that foreshadow great difficulties and persecution for the missionary band is a tradition that emanated from the post-Easter period when the church was experiencing persecution. However, it is not necessary to draw that conclusion. Jesus would have been well aware of the mounting tension created by his mission and would have been able to foresee the opposition that he would increasingly experience and that would culminate in his death in Jerusalem. It would have required no great insight or prophetic foreknowledge on Jesus' part to see that his followers would experience similar persecution at a later time.

All this suggests that the material now found together in the mission charges may include not only the sayings that related directly to the pre-Easter Galilean mission but also sayings of Jesus foreshadowing the post-Easter mission of his followers. Then they would encounter the same hostile opposition that he encountered toward the end of his ministry. This in turn lends support to the view that the apostolic role of the Twelve in the post-Easter period was at least anticipated by the historical Jesus.

Such a post-Easter mission is assumed in the postresurrection commission sayings that are found in one form or another in each of the four Gospels (but in Mark in the longer ending only) and Acts. In Matthew and Luke, Jesus (re)commissions the Twelve (less Judas Iscariot), this time to make disciples of all nations (Mt 28:18-20) and to proclaim repentance and remission of sins in his name to all nations (Lk 24:44-49). This reflects the Evangelists' belief that the Jesus who called and commissioned the Twelve for the limited Galilean mission recommissioned the same men (less Judas) to be apostles of the worldwide mission. It also shows that the early church understood that the restrictions applying to Jesus' mission, and which were also applied by him to the Galilean mission of the Twelve, were now deliberately lifted, and a mission to Samaritans and Gentiles, as well as Jews, was enjoined.

1.5. Nuances in the Evangelists' Understanding of the Apostolate. Each of the four Evangelists portrays the apostolate in his own way. Some things are common to all or most of the Evangelists, but others receive distinctive emphasis in one or other of the Evangelists alone.

1.5.1. Common Elements. Common to all the Evangelists is the firm belief that membership in the apostolate is a matter of choice on the part of Christ; there are no volunteers. Each of the Synoptic Gospels makes this plain by showing how Jesus took the initiative in specifically calling certain people to follow him (Mt 4:18-22; 9:9; Mk 1:16-20; 2:14; Lk 5:1-11, 27-28). And when it came to the appointment of the Twelve, again Jesus called those whom he desired (Mt 10:1-4; Mk 3:13-19; Lk 6:12-16). While the Gospel of John does not include an account of the appointment of the Twelve, it refers to them as such several times (Jn 6:67, 70-71; 20:24) and also stresses that membership in the apostolate is a matter of Christ's choice (Jn 6:70; 13:18; 15:16, 19).

All the Synoptic Evangelists indicate that the appointment of the Twelve was (initially at least) for a Galilean mission in which they would carry on in Jesus' name the same sort of activity in which he was involved (Mt 10:5-8; Mk 6:7-13; Lk 9:1-6).

1.5.2. Different Elements. While all four Gospels and Acts contain a postresurrection commission by Christ, these reveal different aspects and/or understandings of the apostolate.

1.5.2.1. Matthew. In Matthew, Jesus says to the Eleven, "All authority in heaven and on earth has been given to me. Therefore go and make disciples of all nations, baptizing them in the name of the Father and of the Son and of the Holy Spirit, teaching them to observe all that I have commanded you; and behold, I am with you always (lit. all the days), to the close of the age" (Mt 28:18-20). The fourfold use of the word *all* is our clue to Matthew's emphasis on the nature of the apostolic task: It rests on the authority of the risen Christ ("all authority . . . has been given to me. Go therefore"), its scope is to encompass "all the nations," its content is teaching "all that I have commanded you" and its promise is "Behold, I am with you always, to the close of the age."

1.5.2.2. Mark. In Mark the commission saying is found only in the longer ending, and there is considerable doubt whether this should be regarded as an authentic part of the Gospel (*see* Mark, Gospel of). The saying runs, "Go into all the world and preach the Gospel to the whole creation. He who believes and is baptized will be saved but he who does not believe will be condemned" (Mk 16:15-16). The stress here is on the universal nature of the apostolic commission and on the serious implications of people's response to the apostolic message.

1.5.2.3. Luke. In Luke's Gospel the commission saying reads, "Thus it is written, that the Christ should suffer and rise from the dead on the third day, and that repentance and forgiveness of sins should be preached in his name to all nations, beginning from Jerusalem. You are witnesses of these things. And behold, I send the promise of my Father upon you; but stay in the city, until you are clothed with power from on high" (Lk 24:46-49). Once again the universal scope of the apostolic commission is stressed ("to all nations"). In addition, Luke stresses that the role of the apostolate is to bear witness to the death and resurrection of Jesus Christ and to call for repentance and offer forgiveness in his name.

This notion of the apostolic task as witness is developed further in Acts, where the apostles are told they are to be Christ's "witnesses in Jerusalem and in all Judea and Samaria and to the end of the earth" (Acts 1:8). What this witness involves is spelled out in the account of Matthias's appointment to succeed Judas Iscariot: "So one of the men who have accompanied us all the time that the Lord Jesus went in and out among us, beginning from the baptism of John until the day when he was taken up from us—one of these men must become with us a witness to his resurrection" (Acts 1:21-22).

Finally, there is in the Lukan commission saying an emphasis on the empowering by the Spirit that the apostles were to receive to carry out their task (this also is further developed in Acts).

1.5.2.4. John. In John's Gospel, Jesus appears to his disciples after his resurrection and says to them, "Peace be with you. As the Father has sent me, even so I send you" (Jn 20:21). The wording of the commission here implies that the apostolic task involved an extension of the ministry of Jesus. In the verses that follow (Jn 20:22-23) Jesus breathed on his disciples and said, "Receive the Holy Spirit. If you forgive the sins of any, they are forgiven them; if you retain the sins of any, they are retained." This elucidates how their mission can be said to be an extension of his (because of the Holy Spirit bestowed) and something of what that means (the forgiving and retaining of sins—presumably by preaching the Gospel and informing people of the consequences of receiving or rejecting it, just as Jesus had done). [C. G. Kruse]

2. "Apostle" in Paul's Letters.

One of the major questions relating to Paul's apostleship is its character and authority. The traditional view that Christ's call (*see* Conversion and Call of Paul) on the road to Damascus conferred on Paul the Lord's authority over the Gentile churches, which carries over into the canonical status of his letters for churches today, has been challenged by broader definitions of apostleship. In effect these redefinitions make Paul's apostolic authority in the churches relative and conditional. R. Schnackenburg, for example, argues that Paul found no uniform definition of apostle when he became a Christian and provided no systematic criteria for apostleship, regarding apostles only as "preachers and missionaries of Christ" (Schnackenburg, 302). J. A. Kirk states that "for Paul apostleship is proved, not by any exclusive claim, but by the fruits of those who exercise it" (Kirk, 261), and "the same apostolic ministry, in differing historical circumstances, exists to this day" (Kirk, 264).

2.1. The Evidence from Paul's Letters. Since Paul's letters are the earliest writings of the NT, and since he uses *apostolos* more than any other NT author, all historical investigations of the origin, meaning and significance of the word properly begin with his letters.

However, lest it be thought that the concept of apostle originated with Paul, it should be noted that he writes of "those who were apostles before me" (Gk *tous pro emou apostolous*). These apostles were located in Jerusalem (Gal 1:17). The creedal tradition that he repeats to the Corinthians and that he "received" many years before, mentions that the risen Lord appeared [in Palestine] "to all the apostles" before he appeared to Paul (1 Cor 15:7, 8), suggesting that there were "apostles" at or close to the time of Jesus' resurrection.

This creedal tradition (1 Cor 15:5-9) is helpful in a second respect, namely, that it distinguishes between the Twelve and "all the apostles":

> [Christ] appeared
> to Cephas,
> then to the twelve . . .
> Then he appeared
> to James,
> then to all the apostles.
> Last of all he appeared
> also to me . . .

the least of the apostles.

There is a symmetry here regarding the appearances of the risen Lord in Palestine. Cephas is placed with the Twelve, and James with all the apostles. Since Cephas is elsewhere referred to as an apostle (Gal 1:18-19; 2:8; cf. 1 Pet 1:1; 2 Pet 1:1), we take it that the Twelve were called apostles but that there were more apostles than twelve, and that among them were James and Paul, as he claimed (1 Cor 15:9).

The most logical explanation of this differentiation between the Twelve and the apostles is that the Twelve had been a term applied to the twelve disciples of Jesus from the time of the Galilean mission and that apostles were these and others, who at the first Easter were among those who were commissioned by the risen Lord (see 1.2.5 above).

We are able to say, then, that the apostle—so common in Paul's letters—predates those letters and goes back to the first Easter in Palestine, and indeed earlier. The same is true of the notion of the Twelve.

2.2. Apostles in Paul's Letters. Broadly speaking, Paul uses the term *apostle* in two ways: in the nontechnical and in the solemn sense.

2.2.1. Apostle: Nontechnical. There are two references in Paul's writings to *apostle* in the nontechnical sense. In the first of these, Paul was writing from Macedonia to prepare the Corinthians for the coming of two men, about whom he writes a brief commendation (2 Cor 8:16-24). The purpose of their visit was to hasten the Corinthians' completion of the collection for the saints in Jerusalem. Paul wrote, "[With Titus] we are sending (*synepempsamen*) the brother who is famous among all the churches for his preaching of the gospel" and one whom Paul calls "our brother whom we have often tested and found earnest in many matters." Paul declared that these two "brothers" are "messengers [*apostoloi*] of the [Macedonian] churches" to the church in Corinth (2 Cor 8:23), sent for a practical and financial mission. This use of *apostolos* appears to resemble the *šālîaḥ* of later rabbinic writings who might be sent on a mission from Jerusalem to synagogues of the Diaspora.

In the second instance, Paul wrote from prison (possibly in Rome) to the church in Philippi explaining that due to illness Epaphroditus was returning to them. Epaphroditus was the Philippian church's "messenger [*apostolos*] and minister to [Paul's] need" (Phil 2:25). This apostle's role was practical and not directly religious. Once again the similarity between the *šālîaḥ* concept and the role of Epaphroditus, the apostle of the church of Philippi, seems too close to be coincidental.

These two references support the notion that "messengers *(apostoloi)* of the churches" were well established in the Pauline churches by the middle fifties of the first century. The most probable explanation for the origin of these apostles is that Paul borrowed the idea from Jewish practice and applied it to his churches.

2.2.2. Apostle: Solemn. By this we mean "apostles of Christ" (as, e.g., 1 Thess 2:6). These apostles are not sent by ordinary people on a mundane mission. The sender is Christ, the Messiah of God. The overwhelming number of Paul's references to *apostle* belong to this category, which, however, may be further divided into other apostles and Paul himself.

2.2.2.1. Other Apostles. There are "apostles before" Paul (Gal 1:17) located in Jerusalem. It is clear from Paul's reflection on his apostolic call en route to Damascus, which we may date in the mid thirties, that there were apostles from earliest times in the primitive church, indeed from the time of the first Easter ("Christ . . . appeared . . . to all the apostles," 1 Cor 15:8).

Were there apostles after Paul? Is there a historical point after which, according to Paul, there were no apostles?

First Corinthians 15:5-11 bears on these important questions. Paul's words "[Christ] appeared to Cephas, *then* to the twelve . . . *then* to more than five hundred brothers . . . *then* . . . to James . . . *then* to all the apostles. *Last of all* . . . he appeared also to me" seems to demarcate a span of resurrection appearances beginning with Cephas and ending with Paul. Paul does not say, "Then he appeared to me" but "Last of all he appeared to me," suggesting a finality of appearances. Paul is able to go on to say "I am the least of the apostles . . . by the grace of God I am [an apostle]" because the apostles are a group limited in number. He can say that he is the "least of the apostles" since he is, in reality, the "last" apostle to whom the Lord "appeared." The first and most basic test of apostolicity is that the claimant has "seen the Lord" (1 Cor 9:1).

The nature of Christ's appearance to Paul was atypical. He did not see the risen Lord in the context of the first Easter in Palestine as the other apostles before him did, but as the glorified heavenly Lord a year or two later. The unusual and much debated phrase, "As one untimely born" *(tō ektrōmati,* 1 Cor 15:8), whatever it means, reflects Paul's defense of his genuine apostleship despite the isolated and late appearance of the Lord to him. From Paul's standpoint the unusual nature of Christ's resurrection appearance to him serves to mark him out as the end point of such appearances and therefore the end point of apostolic appointment.

The apostles must have been numerous since the creed refers to "*all* the apostles" (1 Cor 15:7) and Paul can refer to "the rest of the apostles" (1 Cor 9:5). We do not know the exact number except that there were more than twelve who were the core group. The Twelve may have functioned as the symbolic foundation for the new community of the resurrected Christ. The apostles took their character from their name: they were sent by Christ to go to others. At the missionary meeting in Jerusalem there were two "apostolates" *(apostolai),* which involved two sendings: one to the circumcised, the other to the Gentiles (Gal 2:7-9).

We know the names of some but not all the apostles. James is linked with "all the apostles" (1 Cor 15:7; cf. Gal 1:19), suggesting that, while James was not counted among the Twelve, he was the most honored among the apostles. It is probable that James's relationship as "the brother of the Lord" gave him his special place (cf. Gal 1:19). The "brothers of the Lord," who are unnamed but among whom James would be included, are probably also to be thought of as apostles (see context of 1 Cor 9:5). Clearly John is to be thought of as an apostle (Gal 2:7-9). The link between Barnabas and Paul also suggests that Barnabas is to be regarded as an apostle (1 Cor 9:6; cf. Acts 14:4). The only others named as apostles in the writings of Paul are his relatives "Andronicus and Junia(s) . . . persons of note among the apostles" (Rom 16:7). If to the Twelve we add James, Barnabas, Andronicus, Junia(s) and Paul (last and least), we know the names of seventeen apostles; but the number was greater.

Paul has a high view of apostles. As founders of churches apostles are preeminent persons in early Christianity. Paul declares, "God has appointed apostles first in the church" (1 Cor 12:28; cf. Eph 2:20; 4:11). Moreover, theirs was a prophetic, revelatory ministry, illuminating the meaning of Christ and the gospel. Paul claims that he and the other apostles enjoyed the revelation of God through the Spirit (*see* Holy Spirit) to understand the mysteries of the gospel (Eph 3:1-9; cf. 1 Cor 2:6-16). Apostles made known this revelation of God orally and in their writings (Rom 16:25-26; 1 Cor 2:13; Eph 3:3-4).

2.2.2.2. Paul the Apostle. Paul refers to himself many times as an "apostle." He frequently introduces himself to his readers as "apostle of Jesus Christ" or by similar ascription (1 Cor 1:1; 2 Cor 1:1; Eph 1:1; Col 1:1; 1 Tim 1:1; 2 Tim 1:1; Tit 1:1). It is "through Jesus Christ" that Paul has "received apostleship (*apostolē*, Rom 1:5; cf. Gal 1:1) because Jesus has "called" Paul to be an apostle and "separated" him for the gospel of God (Rom 1:1; 1 Cor 1:1) to bring about the obedience of faith among the Gentiles (Rom 1:5; 11:13). All of this is due to the risen Christ appearing to Paul "last of all," as the persecutor was travelling to Damascus.

According to S. Kim, Paul alludes frequently to his Damascus Road encounter with Christ. In addition to more readily recognized passages such as 1 Corinthians 9:1; 15:8-10; Galatians 1:13-17; Philippians 3:4-11, there are others (e.g., Rom 10:2-4; 1 Cor 9:16-17; 2 Cor 3:4—4:6; 5:16; Eph 3:1-13; Col 1:23-29). Kim argues that to a remarkable degree the Damascus christophany has colored and shaped Paul's vocabulary and thought.

2.3. Paul's Apostleship Disputed. There is no hint in his letters to the Thessalonians that Paul's apostleship was in dispute in the Greek churches at the time of writing (c. A.D. 50-52). Paul feels free to bracket Silvanus and Timothy with himself on equal terms and to include them with him as "apostles of Christ" (1 Thess 2:6; cf. 1 Thess 1:1). But from that time, doubtless due to mounting criticism, Paul became explicit about his status as an apostle (Gal 1:1; 1 Cor 1:1; 2 Cor 1:1; Rom 1:1), and was careful to distance himself as an apostle from various coworkers (1 Cor 1:1; 2 Cor 1:1; Col 1:1; cf. Phil 1:1).

By about A.D. 55 Paul acknowledged that his apostleship was in dispute: "If to others I am not an apostle" (1 Cor 9:1). These "others" are probably the Judaizers whose views he may have been echoing in Galatians, when he wrote that he was not an "apostle" only "from and through men" (Gal 1:1). In other words (they said), Paul was nothing more than a *šālîaḥ* on an errand from the Jerusalem church, a surrogate of others.

Their further criticisms may be detected from Paul's comments in 1 Corinthians 15:8-9 where

he affirms his apostleship, even though he was not present when the risen Lord appeared to the apostles before him. Christ's appearance to Paul (they said) was later in time, of a different kind and to him alone. A true resurrection appearance did not occur in his case. He should not be counted among the apostles.

Paul, however, insisted that he was an apostle, notwithstanding his "untimely birth," and that he had seen the Lord in a manner different from others. If he was the "least of the apostles," it was only because he had been a persecutor. But for that he made amends by working "harder than them all." If they preached Christ crucified and risen, so too did he (1 Cor 15:3-5, 11).

2.3.1. 1 Corinthians: Paul's Apostleship Questioned. Similar defensive tones may be heard earlier in the letter reflecting local questioning of his apostleship: "Am I not an apostle? Have I not seen Jesus our Lord?" (1 Cor 9:1).

Here the question does not relate to the historical basis of Paul's claim to be an apostle but to his ministry lifestyle which some found unacceptable in the Greco-Roman environment of Corinth, namely, that he did not accept remuneration. From his "defense to those who would examine me" (1 Cor 9:3) that follows (1 Cor 9:4-18), it appears that according to some Corinthians his refusal to accept patronage was his tacit recognition that he was not in any true sense an apostle. A genuine apostle would accept full payment.

Nonetheless, this was a factional, unrepresentative complaint. Paul felt able to say "At least I am [an apostle] to you [Corinthians]" (1 Cor 9:3).

2.3.2. 2 Corinthians: Paul's Apostleship Opposed. Within no more than one or two years, however, questioning of Paul's apostleship by some of the Corinthians had hardened into widespread opposition. This dramatic development is attributable to the recent arrival of a number of self-professed "ministers" or "apostles" (2 Cor 11:13, 23), who had launched a counter mission against Paul and his version of Christianity (2 Cor 2:17-3:1; 11:4, 12; *see* Adversaries). The vocabulary of their ministry emerges from 2 Corinthians and includes such terms as "the word of God," "gospel," "Jesus," "Spirit" and "righteousness" (2 Cor 2:17; 4:1; 11:4, 15).

This was now a far-reaching assault on Paul's apostleship by newly arrived persons who sought to oust Paul from his place at Corinth.

They were superior, Paul inferior (2 Cor 11:5, 23), whom Paul mocks as "superlative apostles" (2 Cor 11:5; 12:11). If he has come to them, they have come further (2 Cor 10:12-14—Jerusalem compared with Antioch?). If he is an apostle, where are his "signs, wonders and mighty works" (2 Cor 12:12)? If he claimed to have "seen" the "Lord" (1 Cor 9:1; 15:8), they boast of an abundance of "visions and revelations of the Lord" (2 Cor 12:1, 7), the evidence of which is their ecstatic speech (2 Cor 5:12-13; cf. 2 Cor 12:2-4). Their credentials as "Hebrews . . . Israelites . . . the seed of Abraham" are impeccable, making them superior in every way.

For his part Paul is denigrated as inadequate, powerless, worldly and a "fool" to be "tolerated" (2 Cor 2:17; 3:5; 10:1-6). Paul is a "crafty" (2 Cor 4:2-3; 12:16), sorry figure as he limps from defeat to defeat (2 Cor 2:14-16; 4:1, 7-8, 16; 6:3-10; 11:23—12:10). What is the proof that "Christ is speaking through" this man (2 Cor 13:3; 10:7; cf. 1 Cor 2:13; 14:36)?

How did Paul answer this devastating attack on his apostleship? Significantly he did not reiterate the Lord's appearances to him (cf. 1 Cor 9:1; 15:8; Gal 1:15-16). His adversaries' "visions and revelations of the Lord" (2 Cor 12:1) had stolen that ground from him, at least in the eyes of the Corinthians.

Paul defends his apostleship in 2 Corinthians along the following lines. First, the Damascus Road call by the risen Lord is implicit throughout 2 Corinthians. He was an apostle "by the will of God" (2 Cor 1:1) who used the "authority *(exousia)* the Lord gave [him] for building up" the Gentile churches (2 Cor 10:8; 13:10; cf. 11:17; 12:19). He exercised "this ministry (of the new covenant, 3:6) by the mercy of God" (i.e., as a result of the Damascus call 2 Cor 4:1; cf. 1 Cor 15:9; Gal 1:15; 1 Tim 1:16). He spoke "from and before God" *(ek theou katenanti theou,* 2 Cor 2:17; cf. 2 Cor 12:10) and his "competence" to be a "minister of a new covenant" (*see* Covenant, New Covenant) is from God (*hikanotēs . . . ek tou theou,* 2 Cor 3:5-6).

If the Damascus call was the basis of Paul's apostleship, its legitimacy is demonstrated by the quality of his ministry, especially when seen in contrast to the new ministers in Corinth. He "refuse[s] to tamper with God's word" (2 Cor 4:2), unlike those who "peddle God's word" (2 Cor 2:17). Whereas they promote a view of the "righteousness of God" (based on circumcision or other works of the law? 2 Cor 11:15), Paul is true to the message entrusted to him by God, that God's *righteousness is to be found in Christ who became sin for us (2 Cor 5:19-21; cf. 2 Cor 3:9). Despite their claims for themselves and their assault on him, they are "false apostles . . . [servants of] Satan" (2 Cor 11:13-15). Through Paul's ministry, however, there is a church at Corinth, a living "letter from Christ" as proof of Paul's genuineness (2 Cor 3:2-3; 10:7) as an apostle who effectively "persuades" people to become Christians (2 Cor 5:11-13). Christ indeed speaks powerfully through Paul (2 Cor 13:4) and through Paul brings resistant people captive to obey the gospel (2 Cor 10:4-6).

Second, Paul accepted the observation about his weakness, indeed he expanded upon it, even boasting of his sufferings in three important passages (2 Cor 4:7-8; 6:3-10; 11:23—12:10; cf. 1 Cor 4:9-13; 15:30, 32). Paul proclaimed the one who had become sin, and that he had experienced in his life, in some measure, the sufferings of the Jesus whom he preached. Implicit in these catalogs of tribulation is the claim that the sufferings of Christ are reproduced in an apostle who is true to him (2 Cor 1:5). Unsaid but perhaps implied is that the powerful triumphalism of the "superlative apostles" arises from their crossless gospel and serves only to disqualify them (2 Cor 2:13; 5:16; 11:4). The "falsity" of these apostles lies in their "other" Jesus, their "different" gospel.

2.4. Summary. The use of the word *apostolos* is almost completely confined to the NT writings. Since Paul makes more use of the word than other NT writers and his writings are chronologically the earliest, it is clear that a historical study of this word must begin with Paul's letters.

It is evident from Paul's writings, however, that there were "apostles before [Paul]," going back at least to the resurrection appearances of Jesus in Jerusalem and elsewhere in Palestine. The appearance of the *apostle* vocabulary in the Gospel of Mark makes it likely that the notion of the apostle must be taken back into the Gospel story.

Jesus, followed by Paul and other early church leaders, appear to have been influenced in their use of the word *apostle* by the Jewish notion of the *šālîaḥ* who in late Judaism represented persons and institutions to others. While it is clear that nontechnical use of "apostle" by Paul resembles the secular *šāliaḥ* of later Jewish writings, the technical, or "solemn," use of this word takes on a special character from the unique circumstances associated with the rise of early Christianity.

Galatians, Romans and the two Corinthian letters reflect the rise of opposition to the recognition of Paul as an apostle of Christ. While some of this opposition arose at a local level over personal criticism of Paul, by far the greatest rejection of his apostleship arose from the Judaizers, who at best sought to classify him as a humble *šāliaḥ* of the Jerusalem church.

Paul himself sought to establish the limited extent of the numbers of apostles. His careful words that Christ "appeared to me last of all" (1 Cor 15:8) serve to show that while there were apostles before him, there were no apostles after him. According to Paul he is "the least" and "the last" of the apostles.

Questioning or outright rejection of Paul's authority as an "apostle of Christ" is by no means confined to Paul's day. Some modern scholars have attempted to broaden the definition of "apostle" in such a way (e.g., as "missionary" or "church planter") that Paul's distinctive authority is dissipated. Paul strenuously resisted attempts to downgrade him in this way. If Paul's apostleship meant and means no more than that, then he had and continues to have little real authority in the churches.

There should be no doubt that Paul based his claim to be an apostle on having seen the risen Lord and having been commissioned by him to go to the Gentiles (1 Cor 9:1; 15:8; Gal 1:11-17). To be sure, he pointed to his effectiveness in establishing churches, his own sufferings as a continuation in history of the sufferings of Christ and to his own integrity, but these served only to legitimize a ministry that had its basis in Christ's confronting him on the road to Damascus.

[P. W. Barnett]

3. "Apostle" in Acts, Hebrews, General Epistles and Revelation.

3.1. The Acts of the Apostles.

3.1.1. The Twelve Apostles. The primary use of the word *apostle* in Acts is to denote the Twelve. In this respect Acts follows the Gospel of Luke, where *apostle* nearly always refers to the twelve disciples whom Jesus called (Lk 6:13, cf. 9:1, 10; 22:14, 30), but following the defection of Judas it

is used of the eleven (Lk 24:9-10).

It was to the Eleven that Christ gave instructions following his resurrection (Acts 1:2). It was to their number that another person was added following Christ's ascension to replace Judas and so reconstitute the Twelve (Acts 1:15-22). Only those who had accompanied the Eleven during the whole time the Lord Jesus was among them (from his baptism to his ascension) were eligible for selection (Acts 1:21-22). The final choice was left to the Lord, to whom prayer was offered; then lots were cast, resulting in the selection of Matthias (Acts 1:24-26). It is to this reconstituted group of Twelve that the majority of references to apostles apply (Acts 1:26; 2:37, 42, 43; 4:33, 35, 36, 37; 5:2, 12, 18, 29, 40; 6:6; 8:1, 14, 18; 9:27; 11:1). The importance of completing again the full number of the Twelve is probably best understood in the light of Jesus' promise that the Twelve would sit on thrones judging the twelve tribes of Israel (Lk 22:30). K. H. Rengstorf says that "the re-establishment of the apostolate of the Twelve proves that the risen Lord, like the historical Jesus, has not given up his claim to incorporate the twelve tribes of Israel into his kingdom" (Rengstorf 1962, 192).

The ministry of the Twelve consisted essentially of preaching and bearing witness to the resurrection of Christ (Acts 1:22; 4:33), teaching (Acts 2:42) and prayer (Acts 6:2-4). Their preaching was often accompanied by signs and wonders (Acts 2:43; 5:12). They felt a special responsibility to continue preaching in Jerusalem, so they remained there even when many of the believers fled the city because of the persecution (Acts 8:1). They felt a responsibility also for new groups of believers that sprang up as the message of Christ was carried abroad by those who were scattered (Acts 8:4-17; 11:19-26). It was through the laying on of the apostles' hands that the Samaritan believers received the *Holy Spirit (Acts 8:14-17). In Acts 15 the apostles, together with the elders, form the group with whom Paul and Barnabas, being sent by the Antioch church, discussed the need or otherwise for Gentile believers to submit to circumcision.

The Twelve provide an important link between the ministry of Jesus in Luke's Gospel and the ministry of the early church in Acts. When Acts 1:2 speaks of the apostles whom Jesus chose (*exelexato*), it recalls Luke 6:13, which relates how Jesus called his disciples and chose (*ek lexamenos)* twelve of them. The Twelve provided the foundational testimony to the resurrection of Christ (Acts 2:14; 4:33; 5:29-32) and legitimized the Samaritan and Gentile missions (Acts 8:14; 11:1-18). Having accomplished these purposes, they fade from view in Acts. It is noteworthy that no attempt was made to reconstitute the group of twelve by choosing another replacement when the apostle James was put to death by Herod (Acts 12:1-2). When the Twelve as a group fade from view, the focus of attention in Acts shifts to the parts played by Peter, James (the brother of the Lord, who was not one of the Twelve) and most of all Paul.

3.1.2. The Apostleship of Peter. The activities of Peter dominate the first twelve chapters of Acts as the activities of Paul dominate the last sixteen. Peter takes the leading role in the church in Jerusalem in the earliest years. He takes the initiative in seeking a replacement for Judas Iscariot (Acts 1:15-26). Peter is the main spokesperson. He speaks on behalf of the Twelve on the day of Pentecost (Acts 2:14-40), addresses the crowd following the healing of the lame beggar (Acts 3:11-26), replies on behalf of himself and John when called to account by the Jewish leaders (Acts 4:5-22), and replies on behalf of the Twelve when they are interrogated by the Sanhedrin (Acts 5:27-32). He deals with the deception of Ananias and Sapphira (Acts 5:1-10) and the wickedness of Simon the sorcerer (Acts 8:18-24). Peter features in nearly all the healing stories of the first twelve chapters (Acts 3:1-10; 5:15; 9:32-43). He is involved in the expansion of the church into Samaria (Acts 8:14-25) and the conversion of the Gentile God-fearer Cornelius (Acts 10:1-48). Peter also defends the inclusion of Gentiles among the people of God without circumcision in respect of Cornelius (Acts 11:1-18) and those converted through Paul's missionary work (Acts 15:7-11).

One thing that emerges from all this is that Peter's apostolate was no more restricted solely to Jews than Paul's was to Gentiles. While Peter's main area of responsibility was to the circumcision (cf. Gal 2:7-9), he was also involved to a certain extent in the Gentile mission. This is consistent with what we find in 1 Peter (see 2.2 below) and with hints about Peter's ministry among Gentiles found in Paul's letters (cf. 1 Cor 1:12; 3:22; 9:5; Gal 2:11, 14).

3.1.3. The Joint Ministry of Barnabas and Paul. Paul and Barnabas were not included among the Twelve, nor were they eligible to be included, not having accompanied the Eleven from the time of Jesus' baptism to his ascension. The first hint of some special ministry for Barnabas is found in Acts 11:22, where he is sent by the Jerusalem apostles to Antioch in response to news of a great turning to the Lord among Greeks there. Barnabas and Paul were later sent as emissaries of the church in Antioch bearing gifts to the saints in Jerusalem (Acts 11:27-30).

In Acts 13:1-3 the prophets and teachers in the church at Antioch were directed by the Holy Spirit to set apart Barnabas and Paul for the work to which he had called them. The prophets and teachers released them for this ministry (Acts 13:3), and being sent out by the Holy Spirit, Barnabas and Paul made their way to Cyprus (Acts 13:4-12). In Acts it is only after being set apart for missionary work that Barnabas and Paul are referred to as apostles (Acts 14:4, 14).

It is worth noting that the sending agent in this context is not the church, as is often assumed, but the Holy Spirit. He directs the prophets and teachers to set apart *(aphorisate)* Barnabas and Paul to the work to which he had called them (Acts 13:2). The prophets and teachers lay their hands on Barnabas and Paul, pray for them and then release *(apelysan)* them (Acts 13:3). Being sent out *(ekpemphthentes)* by the Holy Spirit, Barnabas and Paul then make their way to Cyprus (13:4). It was the Holy Spirit who called Barnabas and Paul, it was the Holy Spirit who directed the prophets and teachers to set them apart, and it was the Holy Spirit who sent them out. The role of the prophets and teachers was to pray for them and to release them.

The mission that Barnabas and Paul carried out was initially one of proclaiming the word of God among Jews in the synagogues of Cyprus (Acts 13:4-5). It was widened to include Gentiles when Barnabas and Paul were sent for by the proconsul in Paphos, who also wanted to hear the word of God (Acts 13:6-12). However, when their message was later rejected by many of the Jews in Pisidian Antioch, they deliberately turned to the Gentiles, believing they had been commanded by God to do so (Acts 13:46-47). This decision was confirmed by God when he enabled them to perform signs and wonders (Acts 13:8-12; 14:1-3, 8-10).

3.1.4. The Apostleship of Paul. In Acts 13:2 the Holy Spirit directs the prophets and teachers to set aside Barnabas and Paul for the work to which he had called them. Paul's calling predates this and may be traced back to his encounter with the risen Christ on the Damascus Road (Acts 9:3-6; 22:6-11; 26:12-18). It was on this occasion, and through Ananias, that Paul was initially given details of his commission (Acts 9:10-19; 22:12-16). He was to make known what he had seen and heard to all peoples—to the Gentiles and their kings and to the people of Israel—so that they might repent and turn to God (Acts 9:15; 22:14-15, 21; 26:16-20). The comprehensive nature of this commission (involving preaching to both Gentiles and the people of Israel) is reflected in the accounts of Paul's missionary work in Acts. In town after town he preached first in the Jewish synagogue and afterward to the Gentiles. Acts indicates that it was Paul's practice to appoint elders in the churches that he founded (Acts 14:23, cf. 20:17).

Sometimes this presentation of Paul's missionary work is rejected as an invention of the writer of Acts. It is rejected because of Paul's own statements in Galatians 2:6-9 (that he was commissioned as the apostle to Gentiles and Peter as the apostle to the Jews). While this certainly represents the broad distinction between the apostolic ministries of Paul and Peter, it should not be read in such a way as to mean that Peter had no ministry to Gentiles or that Paul had none to Jews. That Paul ministered among Jews as well as Gentiles is confirmed by his own account of his persecutions at the hands of the Jews (2 Cor 11:24, 26), which were occasioned in part by his refusal to preach circumcision (Gal 5:11).

3.1.5. Apostles and the Spirit in Acts. Probably the most outstanding feature of apostleship as it is portrayed in Acts is the involvement of the Holy Spirit in apostolic ministry. The risen Jesus promised the apostles that they would receive power and be his witnesses when the Holy Spirit came upon them (Acts 1:5, 8). Having been filled with the Spirit on the day of Pentecost, they proceeded to give their witness to the resurrection (Acts 2:4; 4:8; 5:32). It was through the laying on of the apostles' hands that Samaritan believers received the Holy Spirit (Acts 8:14-17). When Paul was called and commissioned to be an apostle, he too was filled with the Holy Spirit (Acts 9:17). It was the Holy Spirit who prepared Peter to preach the gospel to the Gentile God-fearer Cornelius, and it was through Peter's ministry that Cornelius's household received the Spirit (Acts 10:19, 44-48; 11:12-17).

Barnabas, who along with Paul is described as an apostle in Acts 14:4, 14, is described as a good man who was full of the Holy Spirit (Acts 11:24). It was the Holy Spirit who told the prophets and teachers at Antioch to set apart Paul and Barnabas for the missionary work to which he had called them, and who sent them out on what was to be Paul's first missionary journey (Acts 13:1-4). On Paul's second missionary journey, the Holy Spirit prevented him and his companions from undertaking work in the regions of Asia and Bithynia (Acts 16:6-7), so that they would cross over into Macedonia following Paul's vision in Troas (Acts 16:8-10). The Spirit came upon the Ephesian believers when Paul laid his hands on them (Acts 19:6). Finally, it was the compulsion of the Holy Spirit that led Paul to continue on his way to Jerusalem, despite dire warnings of what awaited him there (Acts 20:22-23).

In Acts it is the Holy Spirit who impels the apostles into ever-widening circles of ministry and who provides authentication for the Gentile mission. The promise and bestowal of the Holy Spirit by Christ constitutes an important link between the ministry of the historical Jesus and that of the apostles.

3.2. Hebrews, General Epistles and Revelation.
3.2.1. Hebrews. There is in Hebrews only one reference to apostleship, and this is related to the commission given by God to Christ. The readers are urged to consider Jesus, the apostle and high priest of their confession, who was faithful to the One who appointed him (Heb 3:1-6). This forms the basis for an exhortation to the readers to be faithful as Jesus was and not to repeat the faithlessness of the exodus generation (Heb 3:7—4:11). In the context of Hebrews, Jesus' role, which reflects the nature of his apostleship, includes proclaiming the word of God and enduring suffering and death so that he might become high priest on behalf of God's people and the atoning sacrifice for their sins, in order that through his ministry God's children might be brought to glory.

3.2.2. 1 Peter. In 1 Peter the author introduces himself as an apostle of Jesus Christ and addresses his readers as exiles of the Dispersion in Pontus, Galatia, Cappadocia, Asia and Bithynia (1 Pet 1:1). On first reading this would appear to be in line with the view that Peter restricted himself to a ministry among Jews, in this case his ministry among Jews of the Diaspora. We have already seen that Acts depicts Peter working among Gentiles as well as Jews, and a close reading of 1 Peter discloses the same thing. In fact, 1 Peter is written to Gentiles. The preconversion period of the lives of the readers is described as a time when they did "what the Gentiles like to do, living in licentiousness, passions, drunkenness, revels, carousing, and lawless idolatry" (1 Pet 4:3-4). The readers were clearly Gentiles, and therefore Peter's address to them as "exiles of the Dispersion" is metaphorical. It refers to their status as Christian aliens and exiles in a hostile world.

3.2.3. 2 Peter and Jude. In 2 Peter the author introduces himself as an apostle of Jesus Christ (2 Pet 1:1). He exhorts his readers to remember the command of the Lord and Savior spoken in advance through the holy prophets and "your" apostles (2 Pet 3:2) and warns them about those who twist the teaching of Paul's letters to their own destruction, as they do other Scriptures (2 Pet 3:15-16). In the epistle of Jude the readers are exhorted to remember the words spoken beforehand (about the last days) by the apostles of the Lord Jesus Christ (Jude 17). In these two epistles, then, the function of the apostles that is stressed is teaching, and in particular handing on the teaching of Jesus. The mention of "your" apostles in 2 Peter 3:2 would seem to refer not to the Twelve but to those missionaries through whom the readers first heard the gospel, presumably including the apostle Paul (cf. 2 Pet 3:15-16).

3.2.4. 1-3 John. In 3 John the Elder commends Gaius for providing hospitality for itinerant preachers who were traveling about "for the sake of the name" and urges him to continue doing so (3 Jn 5-8). He criticizes a certain Diotrephes, apparently a leading figure in the Christian community in the town where Gaius lived, because he refused to provide them with hospitality (3 Jn 9-10). In 2 John the Elder warns the "Elect Lady" concerning certain deceivers who have gone out into the world—people who deny that Jesus Christ has come in the flesh. He urges the "Elect Lady" not to provide such itinerants with hospitality, for that would be to participate in their evil deeds (2 Jn 7-11). In 1 John the author warns his readers about certain people who had seceded from his community and were traveling about propagating false teaching concerning the person of Christ, and so leading people astray (1 Jn 2:18-19, 22-23, 26).

While the letters of 1-3 John do not use the word *apostle,* they do reflect the fact that toward the end of the first century itinerant preachers, some orthodox and some heretical, were moving around among the churches, at least in the area in which these letters were written. These people could not command the recognition enjoyed by either the Twelve or Paul, and congregations had to exercise discernment before providing them with hospitality and so supporting their work. (A similar situation is reflected in the *Didache.*) First John provides ethical and doctrinal criteria by which the readers should test the claims of itinerant preachers (*see* John, Letters of).

3.2.5. Revelation. The book of Revelation makes reference to those who claim to be apostles but are not (Rev 2:2), and to true apostles who are urged to join with saints and prophets in rejoicing over the downfall of "Babylon" (Rev 18:2). It also speaks of the names of the twelve apostles being written on the twelve foundations of the wall of the heavenly Jerusalem, a symbol of the church (Rev 21:9-14). From this last reference it may be inferred that the author of Revelation believed that the ministry of the twelve apostles was fundamental to the building of the church. Their preaching of the gospel laid the church's foundation.

[C. G. Kruse]

See also CONVERSION AND CALL OF PAUL; DISCIPLES.

DPL: AFFLICTIONS, TRIALS, HARDSHIPS; AUTHORITY; COWORKERS, PAUL AND HIS; MINISTRY; PASTORAL THEOLOGY; SIGNS, WONDERS, MIRACLES. *DLNTD:* APOSTOLIC FATHERS; AUTHORITY; CHURCH ORDER, GOVERNMENT; MISSION, EARLY NON-PAULINE.

BIBLIOGRAPHY. F. Agnew, "On the Origin of the Term *Apostolos*," *CBQ* 38 (1976) 49-53; idem, "The Origin of the NT Apostle-Concept: A Review of Research," *JBL* 105 (1986) 75-96; C. K. Barrett, *The Signs of an Apostle* (London: Epworth, 1970); S. Brown, "Apostleship in the New Testament as an Historical and Theological Problem," *NTS* 30 (1984) 474-80; A. C. Clark, "Apostleship: Evidence from the New Testament and Early Christian Literature," *VoxEv* 19 (1989) 49-82; idem, "The Role of the Apostles," in *Witness to the Gospels: The Theology of Acts,* ed. I. H. Marshall and D. Peterson (Grand Rapids: Eerdmans, 1998) 169-90; A. Ehrhardt, *The Apostolic Ministry* (SJT Occasional Papers 7; Edinburgh:

Oliver & Boyd, 1958); idem, *The Apostolic Succession in the First Two Centuries of the Church* (London: Lutterworth, 1953); B. Gerhardsson, *The Origins of the Gospel Traditions* (London: SCM, 1977); K. Giles, "Apostles Before and After Paul," *Churchman* 99 (1985) 241-56; idem, *Patterns of Ministry Among the First Christians* (Melbourne: Collins Dove, 1989); R. W. Herron, "The Origin of the New Testament Apostolate," *WTJ* 45 (1983) 101-31; J. Jeremias, *Jesus' Promise to the Nations* (Philadelphia: Fortress, 1982); S. Kim, *The Origins of Paul's Gospel* (Grand Rapids: Eerdmans, 1981); J. A. Kirk, "Apostleship Since Rengstorf: Towards a Synthesis," *NTS* 21 (1975) 249-64; C. G. Kruse, *New Testament Foundations for Ministry* (London: Marshall, Morgan & Scott, 1983); idem, *New Testament Models for Ministry: Jesus and Paul* (Nashville: Nelson, 1984); J. B. Lightfoot, "The Name and Office of an Apostle," in *Saint Paul's Epistle to the Galatians* (repr.; Grand Rapids: Zondervan, 1953) 92-101; H. Mosbech, "*Apostolos* in the New Testament," *ST* 2 (1948) 166-200; J. Munck, "Paul, the Apostles and the Twelve," *ST* 3 (1950-51) 96-110; V. C. Pfitzner, " 'Pneumatic' Apostleship? Apostle and Spirit in the Acts of the Apostles," in *Wort in der Zeit: Neutestamentliche Studien*, Festschrift for K. H. Rengstorf, ed. W. Haubeck and M. Bachmann (Leiden: E. J. Brill, 1980) 210-35; K. H. Rengstorf, "*Apostolos*," *TDNT* 1:407-47; idem, "The Election of Matthias: Acts 1.15 ff.," in *Current Issues in New Testament Interpretation: Essays in Honor of Otto A. Piper,* ed. W. Klassen and G. F. Snyder (London: SCM, 1962) 178-92; W. Schmithals, *The Office of Apostle in the Early Church* (Nashville: Abingdon, 1969); R. Schnackenburg, "Apostles Before and During Paul's Time," in *Apostolic History and the Gospel,* eds. W. W. Gasque and R. P. Martin (Grand Rapids: Eerdmans, 1970) 287-303.

C. G. Kruse and P. W. Barnett

ARISTOTLE, ARISTOTELIANISM. *See* PHILOSOPHY.

ARREST OF JESUS. *See* TRIAL OF JESUS.

ASCENSION. *See* ACTS OF THE APOSTLES; LUKE, GOSPEL OF.

ASTROLOGY. *See* RELIGIONS, GRECO-ROMAN.

ATONEMENT. *See* DEATH OF CHRIST.

AUTOBIOGRAPHY OF PAUL. *See* JEW, PAUL THE.

B

BABYLONIAN TALMUD. *See* RABBINIC TRADITIONS AND WRITINGS.

BAPTISM I: GOSPELS

Baptism is associated with a general group of practices related to washing. In addition to the common terms for baptism *(baptō, baptizō, baptisma, baptismos, baptistēs)*, one must also be aware of terms associated with the act of complete or partial washings *(louō, niptō)*. Here we will survey the common terminology associated with baptism, the background and context of NT baptism and the practice of baptism associated with the ministries of *John the Baptist and Jesus.

1. Terminology
2. Background and Context
3. The Baptism of John
4. The Baptism of Jesus

1. Terminology.

Of the five different words found in the NT that are built on the root *bap-*, two are verbs and three are nouns. The basic form is the Greek verb *baptō*, occurring three times (Lk 16:24; Jn 13:26; Rev 19:13) with the literal meaning "to dip" or "to dye." On the other hand the intensive form, *baptizō*, which occurs seventy-seven times, is used always or almost always in the cultic sense of Jewish washings (e.g., Mk 7:4), the baptism of John (e.g., Mk 1:4), the baptism that Jesus and/or his disciples performed during his public ministry (e.g., Jn 3:22, 26) and baptism with/in the Holy Spirit and fire (e.g., Mt 3:11, 14). In the latter usage the term takes on a metaphorical meaning that may be understood in terms of Judaism's eschatological imagery of a stream, deluge or flood of fire that would purge the righteous and destroy the wicked (*see* Holy Spirit).

The noun form, *baptisma*, is not found outside the NT and is found only in the singular. The term implies not only the external act of baptism but also denotes the inner meaning and force of the act. Baptism may then be appropriately employed for Spirit baptism as well as water baptism.

2. Background and Context.

2.1. World Religions. Baptism is not a distinctive or uniquely Christian idea. The practice of baptism is widespread. Examples include the Hindu rituals in the Ganges River, the purification ritual in the Babylonian cult of Enki, and the Egyptian practices of purifying newborn children and the symbolic revivification rites performed on the dead. *Baptizō* and related terms were used to define ritual practices in early Cretan religion, Thracian religion, Eleusinian mystery religions and in several gnostic groups and cults.

Common elements are associated with these widespread baptismal practices. Except when used metaphorically, baptism is always associated with water. Baptism is performed in connection with the removal of guilt, cleansing and the granting of a new start. Christian baptism shares these common traits and contexts; it also has specific historical contexts and theological significance that give it a distinctive Christian meaning. The context for John's baptism and Christian baptism is informed by the OT, Judaism and the practices of the Qumran community (*see* Dead Sea Scrolls).

2.2. Jewish Practices. Followers of John or Jesus who participated in the baptismal rite, whether Jew or Gentile, would not have found this practice totally unfamiliar. Water is the element naturally used for cleansing the body, and its symbolic use entered into almost every religious practice, and none more completely than Jewish practices. The purification rituals of Judaism stressed cleanliness and worthiness to serve the Lord (Lev 13—17; Num 19). The ritual of washing was similar to baptism in its purifying implications (Mk 7:4; Heb 9:20). In Psalm 51:2, 7 the psalmist asks for divine cleansing. Especially significant is Isaiah 4:4, which calls for a washing away of sins by the "spirit of burning," an adumbration of the theme taken up by John in his baptism.

In addition to these OT examples, Jews had a counterpart of the Christian practice in their proselyte rituals. It is not certain when Jewish proselyte baptism began, some scholars arguing that it began at the same time as the Christian rite (McKnight) and others that it preceded the Christian rite (Beasley-Murray). The account of Naaman the leper (2 Kings 5), which is possibly a purification washing, is similar to later proselyte baptism. Much later (by the third century A.D.), it became accepted that male Jewish proselytes were to be baptized in the presence of witnesses seven days after circumcision. In later traditions Judaism required three things of converts to Judaism: circumcision, baptism or ritual bath, and the offering of sacrifice. These rituals of circumcision and washing were most likely preceded by catechetical instruction. The Talmud refers to a baptized proselyte as a newborn child (b. Yebam. 22a). Yet for Judaism the decisive turn from heathenism took place in circumcision (see McKnight). The baptism or ritual bath prepared the newly made Jew to offer a sacrifice as the initial act of worship.

Conversion from heathenism to Judaism was viewed as an entry into life from the dead, and this was the source for the Christian doctrine of the new life of a convert to Christ. It should be noted, however, that in Judaism the concept is only secondarily associated with proselyte baptism, and it shows up only in later traditions. The distinctive Christian understanding of baptism in terms of dying and rising is based on the convert's relationship to Christ who died and rose from the dead (Beasley-Murray and Beckwith, 144-45).

3. The Baptism of John.

Just as John was the forerunner of Jesus, so his baptism was the forerunner of Christian baptism. Yet the background of John's baptism remains fiercely debated. The cultural and religious context at the time of Jesus requires that a number of factors be considered.

3.1. Jewish Proselyte Baptism as Antecedent to John's Baptism. It is natural to seek a prototype for John's baptism within Judaism of the first century. But determining the relationship between Jewish practices and understandings of baptism or lustration and those of John or the early church is fraught with difficulties.

In its most-developed form Jewish proselyte baptism was an initiatory rite performed only once upon the Gentile convert, as was John's baptism and Christian baptism. In line with OT lustrations, Jewish proselyte baptism served to cleanse the convert from moral and cultic impurity. John's baptism for the remission of sins reflects a similar concept. J. Jeremias has argued that *Testament of Levi* 14:6 supports a pre-Christian Jewish proselyte baptism. The passage, which he dates in the late second century B.C., reads "with harlots and adulteresses you shall be joined, and the daughters of the Gentiles you shall take as wives, purifying them with unlawful purifications" (*katharizontes autos katharismō paranomō*). He contends that the terminology, theology, catechetical instruction and performance of the rite by Christians resemble the Jewish performance of the rite (see Jeremias, 29-40; Daube, 106-8).

There is, however, no clear evidence prior to A.D. 70 that proselytes underwent baptism as a requirement of conversion (see McKnight). This has been argued forcefully, in spite of the continued citation of texts like *Sibylline Oracles* (4.165) and Epictetus (*Diss.* 2.9.19). In addition, the following arguments can be made against the idea that Jewish proselyte baptism served as the primary antecedent for John's baptism or Christian baptism. There is no mention of proselyte baptism in the OT, Philo or Josephus. Passages such as *Testament of Levi* 14:6 remain ambiguous or inconclusive at best. It is therefore doubtful that proselyte baptism existed, at least as a clearly analogous rite, in John's time.

A. Oepke points out that Jewish baptism was political and ritualistic, whereas John's baptism was ethical and eschatological (similar to Ps 51:7; Is 1:15-16; 4:4; Jer 2:22; 4:14; Ezek 36:25; Zech 13:1). Grammatically there is an important distinction to be observed. The NT uses active and passive (primarily) forms of *baptō* and *baptizō*, while texts referring to Jewish proselyte baptism primarily employ middle or reflexive forms (Oepke, 530-35). Thus what was self-administered in Judaism was seen more as an act of God and surrender to him in early Christianity.

It is especially significant that John's baptism was received by Jews rather than Gentiles. John demanded moral repentance and cleansing for the Pharisees. Jewish proselyte baptism, of course, served as an initiation rite for Gentiles, but Jews, since they were already the people of God, did not need the rite. If John's baptism was developed from Jewish proselyte practices, he transformed it significantly.

3.2. Qumran Washings As Antecedents of John's Baptism. A better alternative for the background of John's baptism can be found in the lustrations practiced by the Qumran community (*see* Dead Sea Scrolls). Numerous studies have been made of the relationship between the baptism of John and the lustrations spoken of in the *Manual of Discipline* (1QS 3:4-9; 6:14-23; see Badia). Such a relationship can be maintained without accepting suggestions such as John's full-fledged membership in an Essene community located in the area surrounding the Jordan River.

The Qumran community operated outside the temple cult and viewed the priests as evil and impure. Thus its only available rituals were the baths and lustrations described in the OT. John's practice of baptism, integrated with his call to repentance and renewal, complements this situation nicely. The Qumran community maintained a strong orientation toward eschatological fulfillment (*see* Eschatology), seeing itself, in light of Isaiah 40:3, as preparers of the way. John's message was dually focused around the call to repentance and eschatological expectation and preparation (Mt 3:2; Mk 1:4, 7-8; Jn 1:23).

Similarly, the Qumran community recognized the inability of the washings to cleanse a person apart from true repentance. John's preaching and baptism also created this tension (Mt 3:7-9). Like the sectarians of Qumran, John did not envision the water purifying apart from repentance (Mt 3:11; Lk 3:7). John's baptismal practices align themselves better with lustrations of Qumran than with Jewish proselyte baptism. However, we must not lose sight of the major distinction between John and Qumran: whereas the Qumran community's rite was self-administered and practiced daily (or frequently) and is thus best classified as "ritual lustrations," John's baptism was a one-time initiation rite.

3.3. The Significance of John's Baptism. We must not necessarily conclude that John was seeking to convert people into a messianic community. Rather, John was concerned with bringing about a messianic consciousness within the parameters of genuine repentance. John's call for a one-time baptism for those who had been born as Jews was unprecedented. He insisted that one's ancestry was not adequate to guarantee one's relationship with God. That new commitment was solemnized in baptism. There is no evidence that John permitted those who became followers of Jesus to be rebaptized.

The Gospel writers emphasize the points of linkage between Jesus' inauguration of his messianic rule and John's preaching and baptism. It would be mistaken to understand John's baptism as completely analogous to early Christian baptism, though the Gospel writers do not care to distinguish between John's baptism and early Christian baptism. Early Christian baptism was an obvious initiatory rite into the church, though it retained an emphasis on moral purity and cleansing (Acts 2:38). John operated within the perspective of OT expectations for *righteousness and, apparently, with a framework analogous to that of Qumran, where baptism was regarded as a means of accomplishing the necessary cleansing and as a sign of repentance. Though there are obvious connections between John and the early church, we must cautiously suggest a dependent relationship. In fact, though baptism was not a part of Jesus' ministry, Jesus initially allowed his disciples to continue the practice (Jn 3:22), though he later seems to have discontinued the rite (Jn 4:1-3). John's ministry looked forward, expecting the coming kingdom (*see* Kingdom of God), while Jesus' ministry celebrates the kingdom's inauguration in the present.

4. The Baptism of Jesus.

4.1. Jesus' Baptism by John. The baptism of Jesus at the hands of John the Baptist is explained in some detail in Matthew 3:13-17, briefly recounted in Mark 1:9-11, mentioned in Luke 3:21-22 and implied in John 1:29-34. All four accounts directly link with baptism the anointing of Jesus with the Spirit and the declaration of his sonship (*see* Son of God). It is this anointing that inaugurates the ministry of Jesus which will be characterized by the power of the Spirit of the new age (Mt 12:18; 28; Lk 4:18; 11:20; Acts 10:38).

What was the relevance of John's baptism to Jesus? Did Jesus need to repent? Matthew alone tells us that John tried to deter Jesus from being baptized, ostensibly because baptism implies that a person has sin of which they must repent. John seems to recognize his own sinfulness in comparison with Jesus and notes that their roles should be reversed—Jesus should be baptizing John. Jesus' reply seems to acknowledge the logic of John's argument, but he nevertheless requests baptism for a different reason.

Theologically, the baptism of Jesus identifies Jesus as the messianic servant who stands in solidarity with his people. As their representative he came "to fulfill all righteousness" (Mt 3:15). *Righteousness* in Matthew's Gospel refers to those who are upright and law-abiding, obedient and faithful to God's commandments (see Przybylski). Matthew has portrayed Jesus fulfilling specific prophecies as well as more general biblical themes. Now he fulfills the moral demands of God's will. In so doing, Jesus identifies and sanctions John's ministry as divinely ordained and his message as one to be heeded.

Jesus began his ministry with the same demand for repentance, affirming John's baptizing work. Yet one important difference must be observed. Jesus was to baptize with fire and the Spirit (Mt 3:11; Lk 3:16). The relationship between water baptism and Spirit baptism came to have greater significance in the Epistles and Acts, but its importance in the Gospel account conclusively shows that Jesus never thought of baptism as merely a mechanical act.

4.2. The Baptism with Which Jesus Is Baptized. When the sons of Zebedee asked Jesus to sit at his side, one on the left and the other on the right (Mk 10:35-37), a question apparently stemming from their mother (cf. Mt 20:20-21), Jesus referred them to his drinking of a bitter cup and his baptism, each of which alludes to some kind of physical distress. Jesus states that the sons of Zebedee would experience such—but he still had no right to assign seats in the kingdom. The meaning of this metaphorical use of *baptism* appears to be "painful destiny," in this case death or martyrdom. According to the grammar, while Mark 10:38 implies that the brothers cannot share in the same fate as Jesus (since the death of Jesus is a unique moment of God's judgment), Mark 10:39 backs up and concedes that they too may die for their association with Jesus (cf. Mk 8:34-38). At the same time, the Lukan form of the saying (Lk 12:50) suggests that the "baptism" also includes the persecution that led up to the death of Jesus and interprets it as an eschatological tribulation.

4.3. Jesus' Command to Baptize. Matthew 28:19 clearly joins baptism with teaching as partners in the process of making disciples. "Make disciples" is the mandate of the risen Christ (*see* Resurrection). "Baptizing and teaching" are the two procedures associated with the accomplishment of that mandate. Thus Matthew's commission, not unlike baptism in the Fourth Gospel (Jn 3:22-24), joins baptism with discipleship.

But the resurrection command has a fuller meaning. It is a commitment to ("in the name" is literally "into the name," implying entrance into an allegiance) the Father, the Son and the Holy Spirit, all three of whom were involved in the event of Jesus' baptism (Mt 3:16-17). Matthew wants his readers to know that Jesus has taken his place along with the Father and the Spirit as the object of the disciples' worship and commitment. Matthew's unique use of the trinitarian formula summarizes in the more formal language of the community the essence of what Jesus had taught his disciples about God, instruction that had implied a unique relationship between Jesus and the Spirit with the Father.

See also LORD'S SUPPER; WORSHIP.

DJG: GENTILES; REPENTANCE.

BIBLIOGRAPHY. L. F. Badia, *The Qumran Baptism and John the Baptist's Baptism* (Lanham, MD: University Press of America, 1980); G. R. Beasley-Murray, *Baptism in the New Testament* (Grand Rapids: Eerdmans, 1962); G. R. Beasley-Murray and R. T. Beckwith, "Baptism," *NIDNTT* 1:143-61; D. Daube, *The New Testament and Rabbinic Judaism* (London: Athlone, 1956); J. D. G. Dunn, *Baptism in the Holy Spirit* (Philadelphia: Westminster, 1970); J. Jeremias, *Infant Baptism in the First Four Centuries* (Philadelphia: Westminster, 1962); S. McKnight, *A Light Among the Gentiles* (Minneapolis: Fortress, 1991); A. Oepke, "βάπτω κτλ," *TDNT* 1:529-46; B. Przybylski, *Righteousness in Matthew and His World of Thought* (SNTSMS 41; Cambridge: Cambridge University Press, 1980).

D. S. Dockery

BAPTISM II: PAUL

From references to baptism in Paul's letters it is apparent that he assumes that all believers in Christ have been baptized. A single example will suffice to show this. Paul's exposition of baptism in Romans 6 commences by citing an objection to his teaching of justification by faith apart from the works of the law: "On that basis," says the objector, "why not sin more to give more room for God's justifying grace?" Paul answers by appealing to the meaning of baptism: "How can people like us who died to sin go on living in it?" He continues, "All of us who were baptized to Christ Jesus were baptized to his death," and he concludes, "so you also must consider yourselves dead to sin and alive to God in Christ Jesus." Self-evidently, "people like us who died to sin," "all of us who were baptized to Christ Jesus" and "you also must consider yourselves dead to sin" include Paul and all his readers; otherwise his argument against the allegedly antinomian effect of the doctrine of justification by faith falls to the ground. Similar examples of the assumption that all Christians are baptized are to be seen in Galatians 3:26-28, Colossians 2:12, 1 Corinthians 12:13 and the exposition of baptismal ethics in Colossians 2:20—3:15.

Since Paul had received baptism and had reason to believe that all other Christians were baptized, it is clear that the rite existed prior to his *conversion. (The conversion of Paul is commonly dated four years after the death of Jesus.) Since baptism existed prior to Paul's conversion, it is reasonable to view it as coexistent with the inception of the church. That conclusion concurs with the NT evidence as to the baptizing ministry of *John the Baptist (Mk 1:4-8), of Jesus (see Jn 3:25-26, 4:1-3), and of the apostles from the day of Pentecost on (Acts 2:37-41), and the missionary commission of the risen Lord, recorded in Matthew 28:19.

1. The Language and Actions of Baptism
2. Baptism and Christ
3. Baptism and the Spirit
4. Baptism and the Church
5. Baptism and Christian Ethics
6. Baptism and the Kingdom of God

1. The Language and Actions of Baptism.

1.1. Baptism "in the Name of Jesus." In Paul's letters, as in the book of Acts, baptism is typically represented as baptism "in the name" of Jesus. This is reflected in a significant manner in Paul's handling of the divisions in the Corinthian church. He cites its members as saying, "I belong to Paul," "I belong to Apollos," "I belong to Cephas (= Peter)," "I belong to Christ" (1 Cor 1:12). Paul, with some indignation, asks, "Has Christ been apportioned to any single group among you? Was Paul crucified for you? Or were you baptized in the name of Paul?" This final question echoes the language of baptism in the name of Jesus; its use in the context suggests that its normal usage is to make a person a follower of Jesus, even to belong to him, and somehow to be involved in his crucifixion and enjoy a special relation to him.

There has been much discussion as to whether the phrase "in the name of" reflects a Greek or Hebrew (and Aramaic) idiom, for it is found in all three languages. W. Heitmüller showed that while the expression *eis to onoma* ("in the name") did not appear in Greek classical literature, it was very common in everyday documents with the meaning of "to the account of," alike in banking and commercial sales. He cited with approval A. Deissmann's definition of "in the name of [someone]" as denoting "the setting up of the relation of belonging." Heitmüller added, "Our word 'for,' generally speaking, would rightly reproduce the meaning" (Heitmüller, 105). In using this expression, the name of the person to whom the possession is "made over" naturally follows. According to Heitmüller, then, baptism in the name of Jesus signifies the setting up of the relation of belonging to Jesus.

This explanation, however, is denied by some scholars in favor of a Hebrew origin of the phrase. In Jewish literature, including the OT, an equivalent of the Greek expression is frequently met, namely, *lĕšēm* (*lĕ* = "to," *šēm* = "name"). The term has a very elastic sense. Basically it means "with respect to," but the context determines its precise connotation. P. Billerbeck gave three illustrations of its use in his discussion of baptism in Matthew 28:19. (1) When pagans were bought by Jews as slaves they were baptized "in the name of slavery," that is, with a view to becoming slaves; when they were set free they were baptized "in the name of freedom," that is, for freedom. (2) An offering is slaughtered in the name of five things: in the name of the offering (i.e., with respect to its intention, whether it be a burnt or sin or peace offering, etc); in the name of God (for his sake and glory); in the name of the altar fires (that they be properly kindled); in the name of the sweet savor (for the delight it gives to God); and in the name of the good pleasure of God (in obedience to his will). (3) An Israelite can circumcise a Samaritan, but not a Samaritan an Israelite, because the Samaritans circumcise "in the name of Mount Gerizim," that is, with the obligation of worshiping the God of the Samaritans who is worshiped there (Strack-Billerbeck, 1054-55). In light of such evidence Billerbeck affirmed, "Baptism grounds a relation between the triune God and the baptized, which the latter has to affirm and express through his confession to the God in whose name he is baptized."

It is evident, therefore, that the Greek and Hebrew usages of "in the name" are remarkably similar in meaning, especially when applied to baptism, and they would be similarly interpreted in Greek-speaking and Hebrew-speaking circles, despite the greater elasticity of meaning in the Hebrew language.

Sometimes one finds in Paul a shorter expression, baptism *eis Christon,* which can be rendered either as "into Christ" or "to Christ" and is possibly a conscious abbreviation of the full phrase "in the name of Christ" (see Rom 6:3-4; Gal 3:27). Significantly, both the Greek preposition *eis* and the Hebrew prefix *lĕ* can have the meaning "with respect to," and also a final sense or dative of interest, "for" (BAGD, 229; BDB, 514-15). In such cases the context will help to determine its intention.

An important element of interpretation arises in connection with this formula. We have noted A. Deissmann's affirmation that "in the name" "sets up a relation of belonging." So also Billerbeck affirmed that baptism in the name of the triune God "grounds a relation between God and the baptized." Who is viewed as the prime mover in establishing this relationship? In the application to baptism God and humans are involved. The baptizer invokes the name of Jesus over the baptized, and the baptized calls on the name of the Lord as he or she is baptized (for the former see Jas 2:7; for the latter see Acts 22:16). It is likely that Paul has both aspects in mind in Romans 10:9. It is universally acknowledged that "Jesus is Lord" is the primitive confession of faith in Christ that was made at baptism; from it all later creeds of the church were developed (*see* Worship). But the salvation granted on confession of faith is in virtue of God's once-for-all action in Christ's death and resurrection and his action in the lives of those who believe. The priority of God's action applies in the reconciliation of the world in Christ and in the reconciliation of each believer who accepts it (2 Cor 5:18-21). In baptism, therefore, the Lord appropriates the baptized for his own, and the baptized owns Jesus as Lord and submits to his lordship.

1.2. Symbolism and Reality. It is important to observe that Paul never refers to baptism as a purely external rite, whether as a "mere symbol" for confessing faith in Christ or as a rite that effects what it symbolizes. Admittedly for Paul, as for the whole early church, the symbolic nature of baptism is plain. Most obviously it symbolizes cleansing from sin (cf. Acts 22:16). And this meaning seems clear in a pericope that is best understood as reflecting early Christian baptismal practice and its significance for the congregation (Eph 5:25-27: see commentaries, esp. Lincoln *ad loc.*). The actions of stripping off clothes for baptism and putting on clothes after baptism affords a symbol of "putting off" the old life without Christ and "putting on" the new life in Christ, and even putting on Christ (Gal 3:27; Col 3:9, 12). The sinking of the baptized beneath water and rising out of it vividly symbolizes sharing in Christ's burial and resurrection (Rom 6:3-4; the baptismal actions lie in the background of Eph 5:14, often regarded by interpreters as a baptismal chant addressed to the newly initiated believers: see commentaries). None of these spiritual realities, however, can be said to happen by the mere performance of appropriate symbolic actions; they depend on God's once-for-all acts in Christ, according to the gospel, and on God's action in believers as they respond to God's call in the gospel. For that reason Paul's use of baptismal language (in 1 Cor 10:1-12) speaks to a situation where the readers imagined that sacramental action carried its effective and operative power irrespective of moral choices. Paul insists, on the contrary, that the OT "sacraments" led to judgment on an idolatrous and immoral generation.

With these considerations in mind we turn to examine Paul's statements in his letters relating to the significance of baptism.

2. Baptism and Christ.

Baptism "in the name of Jesus" is distinguished from all other religious ablutions by virtue of its relation to Christ. Believers are united with Christ in his redemptive actions of death and resurrection, and so pass from the life of the old age to the life of the new.

2.1. Putting on Christ. The relationship between baptism and union with Christ is indicated not only through its administration "in the name of Jesus" but also in Paul's foundational baptismal utterance, Galatians 3:26-27: "You are all children of God in Christ Jesus through faith, for all you who were baptized to Christ clothed yourself with Christ." The statement is shaped by the discussion in the context as to who the children of Abraham are, for the promise of God that he should inherit the world to come was made to him and his descendants (Rom 4:16). To Jews the answer was plain: they are Abraham's descendants, and any who would be included with them must receive the sign of the covenant (circumcision) and live in obedience to the law of Moses. Paul, on the contrary, maintained that the "offspring" of Abraham, for whom the promise was intended, is Christ and all in union with him. Hence the pertinence of Galatians 3:26: "In Christ Jesus you are all God's children through faith." They are children not merely of Abraham but of God. For they are "in Christ," the unique Son of God. This has come about "through faith" (Gal 3:26), "for all you who were baptized to Christ clothed yourself with Christ" (Gal 3:27).

We have already noticed the symbolism used in this passage. The imagery of stripping off clothes and putting on fresh ones to indicate a transformation of character is frequent in the OT (cf., e.g., Is 52:1; 61:10; Zech 1:1-5). The symbolism was peculiarly apt for Christian baptism in apostolic times, since it normally took place by immersion, and apparently often in nakedness. (That was insisted on in Jewish proselyte baptism; when women were baptized the rabbis turned their backs on them while the women entered the water to their neck, and the latter were questioned and gave answers; they had to have their hair loose, to ensure that no part of their bodies was untouched by water. This feature reappears in Hippolytus, *The Apostolic Tradition* (c. A.D. 215). Cyril of Jerusalem later remarked on the fitness of being baptized in nakedness, as Jesus died on the cross in such a state.

More important than the symbolism is the reality expressed through it: the baptized "took off" their old life and "put on" Christ, thereby becoming one with him, and so qualified to participate in life in the kingdom of God. The two statements in Galatians 3:26-27 are complementary: Galatians 3:26 declares that believers are God's children "through faith," and Galatians 3:27 associates entry into God's family upon union with Christ and Christ sharing his sonship with the baptized. It is an example of Paul's linking faith and baptism in such a way that the

theological understanding of faith that turns to the Lord for salvation, and of baptism wherein faith is declared, is one and the same.

2.2. Union with Christ in Death and Resurrection. Because baptism signifies union with Christ, Paul saw it as extending to union with Christ in his redemptive actions, for the Christ who saves is forever the once crucified and now risen redeemer. Such is the message in Paul's exposition of baptism in Romans 6:1-11 (for a survey of interpretation, see Wedderburn).

First, it should be observed that in this passage Paul was not primarily giving a theological explanation of the nature of baptism but expounding its meaning for life. He was concerned to rebut the charge that the doctrine of justification by faith logically encourages sin. Accordingly he urged that "people like us who died to sin" could not still live in sin, for "death to sin" is the meaning of our baptism. When we were "baptized to Christ Jesus" we were "baptized to his death" (Rom 6:3, echoing Gal 3:27). That is the consequence of becoming one with the Lord, who died and rose for the conquest of sin and death. Moreover, "we were buried with him by baptism to death." Note that Paul did not write, "we were buried like him" but "buried with him." That is, we were laid with him in his grave in Jerusalem! So too the death he died on the cross was our death also. This entails a different way of looking at Christ's death for the world from what may be expected.

When we read in Romans 5 that Christ died for us while we were still sinners, we think of Christ as our substitute. Here, however, Paul speaks of Christ as our representative. If he died on the cross as our representative, and that death was accepted, then it was accepted as our death, so that when he died, we died (*see* Death of Christ). He was an effective representative! Taking that a step further, united with him in his death for sin, we rise in him to live the resurrection life. Through the faith expressed in baptism, what was done outside of us (*extra nos*) becomes effective faith within us. In Christ we are the reconciled children of God.

But a further element is involved in this exposition of baptism. The last two sentences echo Paul's statement of the gospel in 2 Corinthians 5:14-15: "We are convinced that one died for all, therefore all died. And he died for all that those who live might live . . . for him who died and was raised for them." "Those who live" are those who, having learned that Christ died as their representative, thankfully trust him, confess their faith in baptism, share his resurrection life and in gratitude have begun life in Christ to his glory.

This aspect of baptism—the end of life without God and the beginning of life with God—is explicitly stated in Colossians 2:11-12. Like the passage in Galatians, this passage rebuts an attempt to persuade Christians to submit to circumcision. However, Colossians 2:11-12 adopts a different approach by emphasizing the needlessness of the rite of Israel, for in Christ they have suffered a more drastic circumcision: "In him [Christ] you were circumcised with a spiritual circumcision, by putting off the body of flesh in the circumcision of Christ." Apparently Paul depicts Christ's death as a circumcision; cutting off the foreskin of the male sex organ is replaced by the tearing of Christ's whole fleshly body, hence his death. In him that happened to us; it happened in baptism understood as our turning to God in faith. "When you were buried with him in baptism, you were also raised with him." This is not so much an advance on Paul's teaching in Romans 6 as a clarification of what he wrote there. The person who hears the gospel, heeds it, believes it and confesses it in baptism, ends the old life apart from God, and begins life in the risen Christ. Colossians 2:12 makes the point: "buried with him in baptism . . . you were raised with him through faith in the power of God who raised him from the dead." Any effectiveness in baptism is due to the power of God operative "through faith." Clearly Paul is talking about conversion-baptism, a baptism that embodies the gospel and the convert's response to it. Some scholars find Paul's use of "sealing" (in 2 Cor 1:21) to include the latter element, as God certifies his acceptance of the human response.

Yet a third feature is inherent in baptism as Paul expounds it in Romans 6. The baptism which sets forth believers' identification with Christ in his death and resurrection, and the end of life apart from God for life in Christ, calls for renunciation of life unfit for the new age. Romans 6:4, when stripped of its parenthetical clause in the middle, reads, "We were buried with him by baptism for death . . . that we might walk in newness of life." Paul thereby gives the reason the Christian can never willfully "sin that grace may abound." In Christ's death believers died to sin, in Christ's resurrection they rose, henceforth to live for God who redeemed them in Christ (so 2 Cor 5:15).

3. Baptism and the Spirit.

A major consequence of the rise of modern Pentecostalism and the charismatic movement is to provoke the question of the relation of the rite of baptism to baptism in the Spirit (*see* Holy Spirit). Most members of those groups view the baptism of the Spirit as radically distinct from baptism in water, and it is the former on which emphasis is laid. The viewpoint is characteristic of the two groups, though for different reasons (see Dunn for discussion in detail); the question is whether Paul made such a distinction.

W. H. Griffith Thomas voiced a doubt commonly heard today: "How can that which is physical effect that which is spiritual?" From that standpoint some interpreters hold that passages such as Romans 6:1-11, Galatians 3:26-27, Colossians 2:11-12, Ephesians 5:26 and Titus 3:5-7, which all conjoin baptism with "spiritual effects," refer to Spirit baptism, not water baptism, thereby eliminating most of Paul's references to baptism. But such questioning of the relationship between the physical and the spiritual logically draws into question the Pauline emphasis on the incarnation (e.g., Rom 8:3) and the physical death of Christ which results in "the redemption of the body" (Rom 8:23). The corollary of this argument for baptism as solely the work of the Spirit without baptism in water is to make Pauline Christians too ethereal and unrelated to early Christian practices (cf., e.g., Acts 18:8; 1 Pet 3:21).

Galatians 3:26-27 associates baptism with union with Christ. Now Paul makes it clear that people can be "in Christ" only through the Holy Spirit. That is plainly stated in Romans 8:9-11 and is assumed in 2 Corinthians 3:17-18. Clearly Paul associates baptism and unity with Christ and all that follows from it on the basis that for him baptism in water and baptism in the Spirit are ideally one, just as conversion and baptism are part of one process. Accordingly, the sole reference in Paul's letters to baptism in the Spirit (1 Cor 12:13) must surely relate to baptism in the sense that Paul elsewhere uses it: "In one Spirit we were all baptized to one body," and in that body all racial and social barriers are done away. Precisely that is stated in Galatians 3:26-28 in relation to baptism.

The latter half of 1 Corinthians 12:13 is generally rendered, "We were all made to drink of one Spirit" (see Cuming for a reference to baptism in this text). In all likelihood that has in mind the outpouring of the Spirit in the last times (Is 32:15; Joel 2:28-29) and could be paraphrased, "we all received the floodtide of the Spirit" (i.e., we were saturated with the Spirit). That this experience belongs to the beginning of the Christian life hints at an important consideration: conversion is not only the result of human decision but is enabled by the Spirit. He is not only the fruit of conversion-baptism; he is the real baptizer, the agent who makes baptism what it was meant to be: entry upon life in Christ.

A similar line of understanding is in Titus 3:5, which the NRSV renders "He saved us, not because of any works of righteousness that we had done, but according to his mercy, through the water of rebirth and renewal by the Holy Spirit." The last clause may be rendered, "He saved us . . . through the washing characterized by the new beginning and renewal which the Holy Spirit effects." The text continues, "This Spirit he poured out on us richly," which is an echo of Joel 2:28.

4. Baptism and the Church.

From the beginning, baptism in the NT communities was understood as a corporate as well as an individual rite. We have already seen that for Paul this understanding of baptism was axiomatic, and at Corinth it is appealed to as a protest against individualism taken to the extreme. To be baptized to Christ was to be baptized to the body of Christ (1 Cor 12:13; see Body of Christ). In Galatians 3:26-27 Paul's thought immediately passes from that of "putting on" Christ in baptism to that of the body in which all distinctions among human beings lose their power. The same connection is apparent in the appeal for behavior worthy of baptism in Colossians 3:5-15, in which the baptismal imagery found in Galatians 3:27 is extensively applied: "You stripped off the old nature and put on the new, which is being renewed . . . according to the image of its creator [i.e., Christ as the perfect image of God], where there is no longer Greek or Jew, circumcised or uncircumcised, barbarian, Scythian, slave and free, but Christ is all and in all."

The question not infrequently has been raised, "To which church does baptism give entry: to the local or universal church, to the visible or the invisible church?" The question is essentially modern. It would have been inconceivable to Paul. The *church is the visible manifestation of the people of God, whose life is "hidden with Christ in God" (Col 3:3). Baptism is a visible act with a spiritual meaning; it is therefore well adapted to be the means of entry into a visible community of God's people and the body which transcends any one place or time. How to give satisfactory expression to the outward and inward elements, alike of baptism and of the church, is a perpetual pastoral problem; that dilemma, however, challenges believers to reform themselves according to the Word of God rather than to accept laxity of doctrine and practice.

5. Baptism and Christian Ethics.

It is surely significant that the longest exposition of baptism in Paul's letters is given for an ethical purpose. Romans 6:1-14 is filled with appeals for life consonant with participation in the redemption of Christ that lies at the heart of baptism: "How can we who died to sin go on living in it? . . . We were buried with him by baptism to death . . . that we might walk in newness of life. . . . Our old self was crucified with him that we might no longer be enslaved to sin. . . . You also must consider yourselves dead to sin and alive to God in Christ Jesus."

This appeal is most extensively developed in Colossians 2:20—3:13. Therein the fact that the believer died and rose in Christ is not only a motive for Christlike living but also a basis to work out the baptismal pattern of dying to sin and rising to righteousness: "Put to death what is earthly in you. . . . Put off all such things . . . seeing that you stripped off the old nature with its practices and put on the new nature. . . . Put on therefore compassion. . . . Above all put on love."

This led G. Bornkamm to affirm that in Paul's writings, "baptism is the appropriation of the new life, and the new life is the appropriation of baptism" (Bornkamm 1958, 50). To give substance to this principle the primitive church construed a system of ethics which is reflected in the practical sections of many of the NT letters, not least in Paul's writings. To this tradition Paul refers at times, notably in Romans 6:17: "Thanks be to God that although you once were slaves of sin, you became obedient from the heart to the pattern of teaching to which you were entrusted." From this it is clear that the believers addressed were instructed in the elements of Christian living that follow from baptism (see further 1 Thess 4:1-7; 2 Thess 3:6, 11-13).

6. Baptism and the Kingdom of God.

The baptism of John the Baptist was essentially an eschatological rite, anticipating the coming of the Messiah, the day of the Lord and the *kingdom of God. The baptism of Jesus at his hands saw the inauguration of that kingdom: the heavens were opened, the Spirit descended on Jesus, the voice of God came to him, affirming him as the messianic Servant of the Lord (with Mk 1:11; cf. Ps 2:7; Is 42:1), and his service for the kingdom reached its climax in his death and resurrection. Paul understood Christian baptism as participation in that inauguration of the kingdom of God through Jesus. The baptized shares in the death and resurrection of the Lord that initiated the new age; hence the believer lives in it now. The same truth is expressed by Paul in terms of new creation; when Jesus rose from death the new creation came into existence in him, hence Paul could say, "If anyone is in Christ there is a new creation: everything old has passed away; see, everything has become new!" (2 Cor 5:17). Christian existence is nothing less than life in the new creation.

Because this is so, the Christian life is a pilgrimage to the consummated kingdom, into which the believer enters by ultimate resurrection. So Paul states in Romans 6:5: "If we have been united with the form of his death, we shall be united with the form of his resurrection"— logically now, and finally in the day of his coming in this kingdom. That is expounded more fully in 1 Corinthians 15, the heart of which is in 1 Corinthians 15:20-28. Interestingly, this means that baptism, like the *Lord's Supper, sets the believer between the two poles of redemption— the death and resurrection of Jesus and the future coming of Jesus; standing in between them the Christian looks back to salvation accomplished, forward to salvation to be consummated, and to the risen Lord in the present for grace to persist to the goal and live worthily of such infinite love.

See also DEATH OF CHRIST; ESCHATOLOGY; HOLY SPIRIT; IN CHRIST; LORD'S SUPPER; RESURRECTION; WORSHIP.

DPL: CIRCUMCISION; DYING AND RISING WITH CHRIST; LIFE AND DEATH; NEW NATURE AND OLD NATURE.

BIBLIOGRAPHY. M. Barth, *Die Taufe ein Sakrament?* (Zollikon-Zürich: Evangelischer Verlag, 1951); G. R. Beasley-Murray, *Baptism in the New Testament* (London: Macmillan, 1962); W. Bieder, "βαπτίζω κτλ," *EDNT* 1:192-96; G. Bornkamm, *Das Ende Des Gesetzes, Paulusstudien, Gesammelte Aufsätzen I* (Munich: Kaiser, 1958); idem, *Early Christian Experience* (London: SCM, 1969); R. Burnish, *The Meaning of Baptism* (London: SPCK, 1985); R. P. Carlson, "The Role of Baptism in Paul's Thought," *Int* 47 (1993) 255-66; P. Carrington, *The Primitive Christian Catechism: A Study in the Epistles* (Cambridge: Cambridge University Press, 1940); N. Clark, *An Approach to the Theology of the Sacraments* (London: SCM, 1956); J. H. Crehan, *Early Christian Baptism and the Creeds* (London: Burns, Oates & Washburn, 1950); O. Cullmann, *Baptism in the New Testament* (Chicago: Regnery, 1950); G. J. Cuming, "*Epotisthēmen* 1 Corinthians 12.13," *NTS* 27 (1981) 283-85; J. D. G. Dunn, *Baptism in the Holy Spirit* (London: SCM, 1970); W. F. Flemington, *The New Testament Doctrine of Baptism* (London: SPCK, 1948); P. T. Forsyth, *The Church and the Sacraments* (London: Independent, 1953); A. Gilmore, ed., *Christian Baptism: A Fresh Attempt to Understand the Rite in Terms of Scripture, History and Theology* (London: Lutterworth, 1959); W. Heitmüller, *Im Namen Jesu, Eine Sprach-und religionsgeschichtliche Untersuchung zum Neuen Testament, speziell zur altchristliche Taufe* (FRLANT 1.2; Göttingen: Vandenhoeck & Ruprecht, 1903); G. Lampe, *The Seal of the Spirit: A Study in the Doctrine of Baptism and Confirmation in the New Testament and the Fathers* (London & New York: Longmans Green, 1951); A. T. Lincoln, *Ephesians* (WBC 42; Dallas: Word, 1990); J. Murray, *Christian Baptism* (Philadelphia: Commission on Christian Education [The Orthodox Presbyterian Church], 1952); R. Schnackenburg, *Baptism in the Thought of St. Paul: A Study in Pauline Theology* (Oxford: Blackwell, 1964); G. Wagner, *Pauline Baptism and the Pagan Mysteries: The Problem of the Pauline Doctrine of Baptism in Romans 6:1-11 in the Light of Its Religious-Historical Parallels* (Edinburgh: Oliver & Boyd, 1967); A. J. M. Wedderburn, *Baptism and Resurrection: Studies in Pauline Theology against Its Graeco-Roman Background* (WUNT 1/44; Tübingen: Mohr Siebeck, 1987); idem, "The Soteriology of the Mysteries and Pauline Baptismal Theology," *NovT* 29 (1987) 53-72; R. E. O. White, *The Biblical Doctrine of Initiation* (London: Hodder & Stoughton, 1960); World Council of Churches, *Baptism, Eucharist, Ministry* (Geneva: WCC, 1982); idem, *One Lord, One Baptism* (London: SCM, 1960); J. Ysebaert, *Greek Baptismal Terminology: Its Origins and Early Development* (Nijmegen: Dekker & Van de Vegt, 1962).

G. R. Beasley-Murray

BAPTISM III: ACTS, HEBREWS, GENERAL EPISTLES, REVELATION

The apostle Paul could presuppose that the addressees of his letters had received baptism. In Romans 6 he showed the absurdity of their continuing in sin since it contradicted their having died to sin when they had been baptized into Christ's death. In 1 Corinthians 12:12-13 it was their baptism by the one Spirit into the one *body of Christ that meant that the various gifts of the Corinthians were to serve the common good. In Galatians 3:27-28 baptism into Christ is seen as effecting a unity that overrides differences between Jew and Greek, slave and free, male and female (*see* Baptism II). Matthew records the command of the risen Lord to "make disciples of all nations, baptizing them in the name of the Father and of the Son and of the Holy Spirit" (Mt 28:19; *see* Baptism I). Here, then, are indications from the Epistles and the Gospels that baptism was from a very early date the universal rite of admission to the church.

The Acts of the Apostles relates that practice episodically in narrative form. Elsewhere in the later writings of the NT there are a few clear references to baptism and several more possible allusions to it. The detection of the latter can be controversial among scholars, since it involves hints toward rites surrounding the water bath that find their first direct attestation only in the second or third centuries.

The early postscriptural writings add some details to our knowledge about baptismal understanding and practice in their day, but it is not until Justin Martyr, in the middle of the second century, that we find a relatively full ritual description of baptismal practice. It is not until the late second century that we find sustained theological reflection in Tertullian's treatise *De Baptismo*. The early patristic evidence concerning Christian initiation is completed by the ancient church order that most twentieth-century scholarship identified with *The Apostolic Tradition* of Hippolytus. Tertullian and Hippolytus also provide the first uncontested evidence of the baptism of young children.

Confronted with the fragmentary and allusive material in the NT concerning baptism (in the Gospels and in the Pauline letters as well as in other writings), the historian and exegete has to make decisions concerning its relation to understandings and practices attested only in (say) Justin, Tertullian and Hippolytus. Do these latter illuminate directly what was believed, said and done concerning baptism in NT times? Or do the patristic texts rather represent additions or alterations to the apostolic rites and doctrines? Or is it possible (in something like a middle way) that the second century witnessed liturgical developments that elaborated what was embryonically present in the first century, or brought to concrete expression what existed at the level of theological statement in the apostolic writings? Any serious treatment of baptism according to the NT has to remain aware of such issues.

1. Water and the Spirit in the Acts of the Apostles
2. The Non-Pauline Epistles and Revelation
3. The Early Postapostolic Period
4. The Later Second Century
5. The Baptism of Young Children

1. Water and the Spirit in the Acts of the Apostles.

1.1. The Day of Pentecost. According to Acts 1:4-5, the risen Lord ordered his apostles to wait in Jerusalem for "the promise of the Father" (cf. Lk 24:49; Jn 14:26; 15:26), the fulfillment of Jesus' word that "John baptized with water, but before many days you shall be baptized with [the] Holy Spirit" (cf. Acts 11:16; also Mt 3:11; Mk 1:8; Lk 3:16). Acts 2 then relates the story of the first Christian Pentecost. With a sound like the rush of a mighty wind and the appearance as of tongues of fire resting on each recipient, the *Holy Spirit came from heaven and filled the apostles and their associates, so that they "began to speak in other tongues, as the Spirit gave them utterance" (Acts 2:4). To the crowd that gathers, Peter interprets this event in terms of Joel's prophecy: "And in the last days it shall be, God declares, that I will pour out my Spirit upon all flesh . . . and it shall be that whoever calls on the name of the Lord shall be saved" (Acts 2:17-21; cf. Joel 2:28-32 [LXX 3:1-5]). The apostle then rehearses to the "men of Israel" the life, death and resurrection of Jesus, whom "you crucified and killed by the hands of lawless men, but God raised him up" (Acts 2:23-24). Having now been "exalted to the right hand of God" (Acts 2:33) as "Lord and Christ" (Acts 2:36), and "having received from the Father the promise of the Holy Spirit," Jesus "has poured out this which you see and hear" (Acts 2:33). Cut to the heart, the hearers ask what they should do, and Peter replies, "Repent, and be baptized every one of you in the name of Jesus Christ for the forgiveness of your sins, and you shall receive the gift of the Holy Spirit" (Acts 2:38). The result was striking: "Those who received his word were baptized, and there were added that day about three thousand souls" (Acts 2:41).

Several points need to be noted from that narrative which are of significance for the practice and understanding of baptism in the church. First, Peter's listeners are summoned to repentance for their part in the death of Jesus, with the promise that their sins will be forgiven. Christian baptism will be understood as the seal of human repentance and divine forgiveness in reference to the weight of all that Jesus redemptively bore on the cross as the suffering servant (cf. Lk 3:22; 24:25-27; Acts 3:12-21; 10:43; 13:38-39).

Second, baptism takes place precisely "in the name of Jesus Christ." Much ink has been spilled on the phrase (cf. Acts 8:16; 10:48; 19:5). It seems sufficient to take "in the name of" as indicating Jesus as "the fundamental reference of the rite": L. Hartman suggests it was an application of a familiar Semitic phrase by the Palestinian church (*lĕšem* in Hebrew, or *lĕšûm* in Aramaic), with Luke letting Peter express himself in prepositional forms familiar in the biblical style of the LXX at Acts 2:38 *(epi tō nomati)* and Acts 10:48 *(en tō onomati)*, while the narrative at Acts 8:16 and 19:5 uses *eis to onoma* as the form that Luke himself had learned, with *eis* being the preposition that Paul employs in connection with baptism (Rom 6:3; 1 Cor 1:13, 15; Gal 3:27). It has been suggested that the beginnings of Christian baptism go hand in hand with the recognition of Jesus' resurrection and of his status as Christ and Lord (Pokorný). We do not know whether the phrase "in the name of [the Lord] Jesus [Christ]" was ritually pronounced by the minister at baptisms in the earliest times (cf. Jas 2:7 for a possible allusion). Third- and fourth-century evidence suggests that the earliest "form" by which the divine name was invoked at baptism was that

of a question or questions to the candidate, "Do you believe in . . . ?" (Whitaker 1965). In the NT "Jesus is Lord" may have been a confession of faith on the part of the candidate at baptism (cf. Rom 10:9, 13; 1 Cor 12:3).

Third, there is no indication that the apostles themselves had been baptized with water (perhaps they had received John's baptism) when they received the Holy Spirit, but the immediate message of Peter calls others to baptism "in the name of Jesus Christ" with the promise that they too will "receive the Holy Spirit." From this passage the expected post-Pentecostal sequence appears to be water baptism resulting in the reception of the Spirit: the Spirit, like the forgiveness of sins, remains God's to give; water baptism will be the occasion, or the means, of God's giving the Spirit.

In fact, however, the narrative episodes in Acts are complicated, as we shall see; and the varying sequence of events in them makes it difficult to draw theological conclusions regarding the relation between water baptism and the giving of the Spirit. In light of the various episodes in Acts, J. D. G. Dunn, for instance, will allow no more than that water baptism is for Luke a "vehicle of faith," a means whereby believers "reach out to God" (Dunn, 90-102). By contrast, a sacramental reading takes Acts 2:38 to establish water baptism as a divinely provided rite whereby God will regularly bestow the Holy Spirit when it is approached with right disposition. Somewhat mediatingly, G. Barth sees Acts 2:38 as stating a "normal" connection between water baptism and the reception of the Spirit, even though the narrative episodes in Acts show the Spirit to be free also to come before or after water baptism (Barth, 60-72).

Fourth, the baptized are thereby "added" to the company of those who "devoted themselves to the apostles' teaching and fellowship, to the breaking of bread and the prayers" (Acts 2:41-42). Baptism brings entry into the church, which is marked by a common faith, common worship and a common life (*see* Lord's Supper). Speaking "in other tongues" (cf. Acts 2:4) is not mentioned again of the Spirit-filled apostolic community, but boldness in witness is (Acts 4:23-33).

1.2. Samaria. The next baptismal episode occurs in Acts 8:1-25 with the spread of the gospel throughout Judea and Samaria (cf. Acts 1:8). Philip in particular went to a city in Samaria and preached the "good news about the kingdom of

God and the name of Jesus Christ" (Acts 8:12; cf. Acts 8:4-5). Many "believed" and "were baptized, both men and women" (Acts 8:12), including Simon "who had previously practiced magic in the city and amazed the nation of Samaria" (Acts 8:9, 12). This new stage in the mission apparently called for supervision from Jerusalem, for the apostles sent Peter and John down to Samaria (Acts 8:14). Peter and John "prayed" for the Samaritan believers "that they might receive the Holy Spirit, for it had not yet fallen on any of them, but they had only been baptized in the name of the Lord Jesus" (Acts 8:15-16): "Then they laid their hands on them and they received the Holy Spirit" (Acts 8:17).

This passage raises a number of issues. How could the Samaritans have come to believe the gospel and be baptized in the name of Christ without receiving the Holy Spirit? The impression which the result of the action by Peter and John made on Simon the magician suggests that what had been lacking was a spectacular manifestation of the Holy Spirit: "Now when Simon saw that the Spirit was given through the laying on of the apostles' hands, he offered them money, saying, 'Give me also this power, that any one on whom I lay my hands may receive the Holy Spirit' " (Acts 8:18-19). At another level, the passage has traditionally been invoked as an apostolic basis for "confirmation," or the imposition of episcopal hands, in ritual completion of water baptism.

1.3. The Ethiopian Eunuch. The gospel continues its spread to "all nations" (Lk 24:47; cf. Mt 28:19; Acts 1:8) in the story of the baptism of the Ethiopian eunuch (Acts 8:26-39). On the basis of a passage from Isaiah 53 concerning the Suffering Servant, Philip proclaims to the African courtier the gospel of Jesus and instructs him in the faith. His hearer's response is rapid: "See, here is water! What is to prevent my being baptized?" (Acts 8:36). The Western text at Acts 8:37 then continues the dialogue between the evangelist and the eunuch: "Philip said, 'If you believe with all your heart, you may.' And he replied, 'I believe that Jesus Christ is the Son of God.' " Philip and the eunuch "went down into the water," and "he baptized him" (Acts 8:38). The eunuch "went on his way rejoicing" (Acts 8:39): "joy" is a characteristic of the primitive Christian community, where it is associated with their common meals (Acts 2:46; cf. 16:34; Rom 14:17).

1.4. Paul. The next baptism, in Acts 9:18, is that of Paul, apostle to the Gentiles. In this first account, Ananias lays hands on Saul/Paul, so that he may "regain his sight" (Acts 9:12, 17-18) after the blinding vision on the road to Damascus. Then Paul rose "and was baptized, and took food and was strengthened" (Acts 9:18-19). It is not specified by which action Paul was "filled with the Holy Spirit" (Acts 9:17), although he immediately began preaching Jesus (Acts 9:20). As Paul recounts the events in his speech before the crowd in Jerusalem at Acts 22:16, Ananias after healing him had said: "Rise and be baptized, and wash away your sins, calling on his name." The imperatives, *baptisai* and *apolousai,* are in the middle voice ("Get yourself baptized, and get your sins washed away") but need not imply that the baptism was self-administered; unlike Jewish proselyte baptism (*see* Baptism I), Christian baptism appears always to have been administered by another (the story of the martyr Thecla is the exception that proves the rule). It is, however, Paul himself who is to call on the Lord's name (cf. Acts 4:12; Rom 10:9, 13). Paul's sins clearly include having persecuted Jesus in his followers (Acts 9:4-5; 22:7-8).

The final account of Paul's conversion comes in his speech before King Agrippa (Acts 26:2-23). This speech contains baptismal allusions. Paul's mission as an apostle is "to open their eyes, that they may turn from darkness to light and from the power of Satan to God, that they may receive forgiveness of sins and a place among those who are sanctified by faith in me [i.e., the Lord Jesus]" (Acts 26:18). Apart from the themes of belief in Christ and the forgiveness of sins, already encountered in connection with baptism, the turn from darkness to light, from the power of Satan to God, will find expression in the patristically attested rites of renunciation of the devil and profession of faith, and most dramatically in the Eastern ceremonies of the *apotaxis* and *syntaxis,* where the candidate faces west, the place of darkness, to renounce Satan (and even to spit on him in some rites!), and then is turned east, toward the rising sun, to enlist with Christ and the Holy Trinity. Being "sanctified" (*hēgiasmenois*) is mentioned in connection with baptism also at 1 Corinthians 6:11 ("You were washed, you were sanctified, you were justified in the name of the Lord Jesus Christ and in the Spirit of our God"). Finally, in Acts 26:23 Paul refers to the now fulfilled prophecies "that the Christ must suffer, and that, by being the first to rise from the dead, he would proclaim light both to the people and to the Gentiles." Death and resurrection are baptismal themes in the Pauline writings (especially Rom 6:1-23), and "enlightenment," or "illumination," was from at least the second century onward, as we shall see, a term for baptism (cf. already perhaps in Eph 5:14).

1.5. Cornelius. The next incident (Acts 10:1—11:17) is the case of the God-fearing centurion of the Italian Cohort, Cornelius, and thereby marks an important stage in the spread of the gospel to the Gentiles (Acts 10:44; 11:1, 18) and toward Rome. When Peter recounts in Cornelius's house the story of Jesus Christ, the apostle concludes with the promise that "every one who believes in him receives forgiveness of sins through his name" (Acts 10:43), which can also be described as the gift of "repentance unto life" (Acts 11:18). Immediately "the Holy Spirit fell on all who heard the word" (Acts 10:44), and they began "speaking in tongues and extolling God" (Acts 10:46). Peter's conclusion is that "these people have received the Holy Spirit just as we have" (Acts 10:47), "God gave the same gift to them as he gave to us when we believed in the Lord Jesus Christ" (Acts 11:17). Peter could not "withstand God" (Acts 11:17), so no one should "forbid water" (Acts 10:47). Therefore, Peter "commanded them to be baptized in the name of Jesus Christ" (Acts 10:48). Baptized with Cornelius, apparently, were "his relatives and close friends" (Acts 10:24).

The primary significance of the episode clearly resides, in Luke's historiography, in the extension of the mission—in God's footsteps, as it were—to the Gentiles. While the story undoubtedly shows God's freedom of action in giving the Spirit, and even the manifestation of the gift in glossolalia, it is debatable how far the manner of the Spirit's gift in this case may properly be claimed as a regular part of a more general doctrine of (say) "prevenient grace." It is to be noted that Cornelius and "his household" were already God-fearers (Acts 10:2) and in some way knew the story of Jesus (Acts 10:36). It was Peter's preaching that provoked their faith in Christ (as Acts 10:43 and 11:17 imply), and their baptism thus sealed their faith in Christ and God's forgiveness of their sin (Acts 10:43, 48) and, in their case, the gift of the Holy Spirit already (just) received.

1.6. The Philippian Jailer. When a nocturnal earthquake opened the doors of the prison at Philippi in which Paul and Silas were being kept, the terrified jailer asked them, "Men, what must I do to be saved?" (Acts 16:30). Taking their cue from the ambiguity of the verb *sōzō* ("to save"), the evangelists replied: "Believe in the Lord Jesus, and you will be saved, you and your household" (Acts 16:24). They then unfolded "the word of the Lord" to those present, by which the narrator means (as we know from similar cases) "the gospel of Jesus Christ." The preaching was successful, and the jailer "was baptized at once, with all his family" (Acts 16:33). He "set a table for them," and "he rejoiced with all his household that he had believed in God" (Acts 16:34). The table and the rejoicing suggest the common meal of Christians (*see* Lord's Supper). Certainly it was later the practice, as Justin Martyr testifies, for the newly baptized to share at once in the Holy Communion.

1.7. Ephesus. The most puzzling feature in Acts 19:1-7 is why those dozen whom Paul encountered at Ephesus are said from the start to be "disciples" who "believed" (Acts 19:1-2). It seems that they were disciples of John the Baptist. They had been baptized "into John's baptism" (Acts 19:3). They had never so much as heard "that there is a Holy Spirit," let alone "received the Holy Spirit" (Acts 19:2-3). Thus they appear to have caught only part of John's message (perhaps the "baptism of repentance"), to which Paul has to add that John told the people "to believe in the one who was to come after him, that is, Jesus" (Acts 19:4). Immediately on hearing this, "they were baptized in the name of the Lord Jesus" (Acts 19:5). Such was clearly not a repetition of Christian baptism. Paul next "laid his hands upon them," and the result was that "the Holy Spirit came upon them, and they spoke with tongues and prophesied" (Acts 19:6). That sequence of water baptism and imposition of apostolic hands has traditionally been invoked in favor of episcopal "confirmation" after baptism; more recently, the story has been used among Pentecostals and others in support of "Spirit baptism," even marked by glossolalia, as a second stage after water baptism in the making of Christians.

1.8. Conclusions. It is hard to put together from Acts a systematic understanding of baptism or a consistent ritual of Christian initiation.

There are differences in the circumstances of the episodes recounted and in the sequences of events within each story, and Luke is in any case chiefly concerned with the larger picture of the gospel's first spread. It is probably sufficient and wise to limit ourselves to noticing a cluster of recurrent themes that will appear in various configurations in the later theological and liturgical history: proclamation of the gospel, repentance, faith, the name of the Lord Jesus Christ, washing in water, the forgiveness of sin, imposition of hands, the reception of the Holy Spirit, glossolalia, life and salvation, entrance into the Christian community.

2. The Non-Pauline Epistles and Revelation.

2.1. Hebrews. This epistle (*see* Hebrews, Letter to the) contains two passages that demand consideration: Hebrews 5:11—6:6 and Hebrews 10:19-25. The first passage recalls to the addressees certain features from their first admission to Christianity that should not need repeating and perhaps cannot be repeated: learning "the first principles of God's word," "the elementary doctrine of Christ," which are likened to the milk that is succeeded by solid food; a "foundation of repentance from dead works and of faith toward God"; "instruction about ablutions *(baptismoi),* the laying on of hands, the resurrection of the dead and eternal judgment." So far the reference appears to be to the evangelism that elicits repentance and faith, and to the catechesis that instructs the recipients in basic Christian beliefs and in the significance of the rites of baptism in water and the imposition of hands which seal their entrance into the Christian community. The plural *baptismoi* may be due to the need for baptizands to be taught the difference between Christian baptism and other religious ablutions current at the time.

Then the text proceeds to mention in the aorist tense certain events, or a complex of events, that took place only once for each participant: they have "been enlightened," have "tasted the heavenly gift," have "become partakers of the Holy Spirit" and have "tasted the goodness of the word of God and the powers of the age to come." These could describe different facets of the entry into the realm of salvation and/or the corresponding parts of a complex ritual process of initiation. "Enlightenment" became a synonym for baptism; the gift of the Holy Spirit was associated with water and the imposition of hands; "tasting the goodness of the Lord," in the phrase borrowed from Psalm 34:8, was applied by the early church to receiving the Holy Communion. In the context of Hebrews, all this is part of an exhortation to press on and a warning against backsliding, for it is "impossible to restore again to repentance" any who should go so far as to "commit apostasy." Gradually the church would later develop a system of penance for the readmission of grave sinners, but a second baptism has always been excluded. Such would be tantamount to crucifying Christ afresh, said John of Damascus in an application of Hebrews 6:6 (see John of Damascus *On the Orthodox Faith* 4.9).

In the other passage (Heb 10:19-25), against a background of levitical ritual (Lev 8 and Lev 16), the writer appears to recall to the already baptized the meaning and effect of their baptism: it is an assurance of current access to God through Christ and a stimulus to mutual encouragement and love within the Christian community. The summons to present action is based in the enduring reality, spoken of by perfect participles, of having "our hearts sprinkled clean from an evil conscience and our bodies washed with pure water" (Heb 10:22). That phrase, which does not set up an antithesis between the internal and the external but rather in a positive "rhetorical parallelism" joins the inner and the outer in "one indivisible reality" (Beasley-Murray), suggests a view of baptism as "an outward and visible sign of an inward and spiritual grace" (to speak with the traditional Anglican Catechism). The rite enacts a meeting between the faithful God of promise and the believers who confess their hope (Heb 10:23; the noun *homologia,* "confession," became a technical term for the baptismal confession, and the Byzantine exegete Theophylact echoed the eschatological orientation of the baptismal creed when he wrote, "We confessed, when we made the covenants of faith, to believe in the resurrection of the dead and in the life eternal"). The original ground of baptism is "the blood of Jesus" (Heb 10:19), and its ultimate outlook is "the Day drawing near" (Heb 10:25). The verbs of "sprinkling" and "washing" have been invoked in favor of aspersion and affusion as modes of baptism.

2.2. 1 Peter. Baptism is directly mentioned at 1 Peter 3:20, where it is said that "baptism now saves you, not as a removal of dirt from the body but as an appeal to God for [or: a pledge to God from] a clear conscience, through the resurrection of Jesus Christ." Baptism's power derives from the resurrection of Christ, which is made available to believers for the sake of a life of righteousness in Christ (cf. 1 Pet 3:8-18; 4:1-19). The outward act of baptism has an inner significance: the saving gift of God is there met by the resolve of faith. The term *eperōtēma*, variously translated "appeal" or "pledge," appears to be contractual language and may refer to the baptizand's ethical commitment (Justin *Apology* I.61: the candidates "undertake to live accordingly") or the *responsio* ("response") to the questions put in baptism (Tertullian *De Resur.* 48; *De Cor.* 3). The passage sees Christian baptism as having been prefigured by God's saving of Noah and his family in the days of the flood, a theme which along with other OT "types" (such as the exodus through the Red Sea; cf. 1 Cor 10:1-2) will be sounded in later baptismal prayers and commentaries.

The entire epistle of 1 Peter has according to much recent scholarship a baptismal cast (*see* Worship). Within an epistolary framework, some have seen the bulk of it structured on the pattern of an entire rite of initiation, with the frequently repeated "now" constituting a trace of actual performance. The German Protestant H. Preisker found in the epistle the "deposit" (*Niederschlag*) of a baptismal service composed of hymns, sermons and prayers: a prayer psalm (*Gebetspsalm*) as introit (1 Pet 1:3-12); an instructional address (*belehrende Rede*) echoing confessional and liturgical formulae (1 Pet 1:13-21); the baptism (between 1 Pet 1:21 and 1:22), followed by a brief charge to the baptized, who have now "purified [their] souls" and "been born anew" (1 Pet 1:22-25); a festal hymn in three verses from a Spirit-inspired individual (1 Pet 2:1-10); an exhortation (*Paränese*) from another preacher (1 Pet 2:11—3:12), interrupted by a traditional Christ-hymn (*Christuslied*) from the congregation (1 Pet 2:21-24); an eschatological discourse (*Offenbarungsrede*) from an apocalypticist seer (1 Pet 3:13—4:7a); a concluding prayer (*Schlussgebet*) and sung doxology, bringing the baptismal service proper to an end (1 Pet 4:7b-11); a closing service for the whole church (*Schlussgottesdienst der Gesamtgemeinde*), consisting of an eschatological revelation (1 Pet 4:12-19), an exhortation (*Mahnrede*) to the presbyters, younger church members and the entire company (1 Pet 5:1-9), a blessing (*Segenspruch*) uttered by a presbyter (1 Pet 5:10) and a doxology by the entire congregation (1 Pet 5:11).

The Anglo-Catholic F. L. Cross saw even more precisely in 1 Peter the celebrant's part in the baptismal liturgy of a paschal vigil. The bishop's script ran as follows: solemn opening prayer (1 Pet 1:3-12); charge to the candidates, based on the exodus theme as a "type" of baptism (1 Pet 1:13-21); [baptism, followed by] welcome of the newly baptized into the redeemed community (1 Pet 1:22-25); address on the fundamentals of the sacramental life (i.e., baptism, Eucharist, sanctification, priesthood of God's people; 1 Pet 2:1-10); [eucharistic consecration and communion, followed by] address on the duties of Christian discipleship, comprising the moral responsibilities of Christians in their several callings (1 Pet 2:11—3:12) and the Christian's vocation to the "paschal life" (i.e., the life of mystical suffering in Christ; 1 Pet 3:13—4:6); final admonitions and doxology (1 Pet 4:7-11). The epistle's twelvefold use of *paschō* for "to suffer" encouraged Cross to locate the presumed liturgy in the Easter vigil, for such early patristic homilists as Melito of Sardis and Hippolytus of Rome make a (fanciful) linguistic connection between that verb and *ta pascha* ("Passover"), and we know from Tertullian (*De Bapt.* 19) that the Christian version of that feast was the favored time for the administration of baptism at least by the late second century (and so the likely season of the baptismal liturgy described in the ancient church order that much twentieth-century scholarship has identified with the otherwise lost *Apostolic Tradition* of Hippolytus).

Most exegetes have considered that Preisker and Cross were too ambitious in their respective reconstructions of a baptismal liturgy in 1 Peter, but there is widespread agreement that the language of the epistle does bear many baptismal associations. Whether or not such terms allude to existing rites of initiation, they certainly helped to establish the thematic repertoire of Christian baptism and thus also presage what may only later have found detailed ritual embodiment. Within the repeatedly recalled context of the preaching of the gospel and the response of faith, the following items deserve particular attention in connection with the understanding and practice of baptism: God's regenerative activity manifested in the resurrection of Christ (1 Pet 1:3) and the preached word (1 Pet 1:23), with the recipients being addressed as "newborn babes" (1 Pet 2:2), remembering that John 3:3-7 speaks of being born again of water and the Spirit and Titus 3:5-7 refers to baptism as "the washing of regeneration and renewal in the Holy Spirit"; the outline recital of Christ's saving work (1 Pet 3:18, 22) that echoes the apostolic kerygma of Paul and Acts and anticipates the confession of faith in baptismal creeds; the move from darkness into God's "marvelous light" (1 Pet 2:9), noting that "enlightenment" is found in Justin Martyr (c.150) as a term for baptism; the mention of "spiritual milk" and "tasting the goodness of the Lord" in 1 Peter 2:2-3, which may suggest the practice of joining a cup of milk and honey to the eucharistic communion of neophytes as alluded to by Tertullian (*De Cor.* 3) and described in *The Apostolic Tradition* of Hippolytus.

2.3. 1 John. Two passages in this letter (*see* John, Letters of) come into consideration. 1 John 5:6-8 speaks of Jesus Christ as having come "with the water and the blood," and of "three witnesses: the Spirit, the water and the blood." The primary reference may be to the baptism of Christ ("the water") and to his death ("the blood"), the Spirit having rested on him throughout his ministry (Jn 1:32-34). Or the reference may be to the "blood and water" that sprang from the pierced side of the crucified Christ (Jn 19:34) and in which patristic writers such as Ambrose (*De Virg.* 3.5.22) and Chrysostom (e.g., *Homily 85 on John* 3) found an origin of baptism and the Eucharist, and to the Spirit which became available to believers once Jesus was "glorified" on the cross (Jn 7:37-39). In either case, there will then be a secondary reference to the rites of Christian initiation, which bear a derivative witness to Christ dependent on the primary events of his life, death and resurrection.

It has been suggested (G. Dix) that this passage in the epistle matches an early Syrian pattern of Christian initiation in the sequence of the gift of the Spirit (which Dix equated with "confirmation" but which may have been either "pentecostal" or exorcistic), water baptism (which in Syrian understanding was chiefly associated with the filial adoption of the Christian) and first communion (Whitaker 1970, 12-23). While it may be dangerous to find such detailed correspondences between theological statements in the Scriptures and ritual practices that are securely attested only later, there can be no doubt that the Scriptures nourished subsequent

liturgical understanding even if not all the liturgical elements were present in scriptural times. Similar considerations apply in the case of the other passage in 1 John: twice in quick succession the epistle speaks of Christians having received an "anointing" by the Holy One (1 Jn 2:20, 27), which brings truth and life. Did an unction with oil, as in the chrismation found in patristic liturgies of initiation (attested from Tertullian on), already in the apostolic period convey the sealing by the Spirit (cf. 2 Cor 1:21-22; Eph 1:13-14; 4:30)?

2.4. Revelation. M. H. Shepherd proposed that the structure of the Apocalypse (*see* Revelation, Book of) reflects an already existing paschal liturgy, although admitting that elements in the scriptural book may rather have served as "a source of inspiration and suggestion for embellishments of the Church's liturgy that were developed in later times." (In the latter case, the charge could be made against Shepherd's thesis that "a paschal liturgy of a later age has been read into the Apocalypse, not read out of it.") The seven letters of Revelation 1—3 would correspond to the "scrutinies" or final screening of the candidates before baptism. Revelation 4—6 places the assembly before God in vigil. The "pause" of Revelation 7 houses "the initiation ceremony of washing and sealing." Revelation 8—19 matches the eucharistic synaxis, with prayers, readings from the Law, the Prophets and the Gospels, and the singing of the Hallel psalms (cf. Rev 19:1-8). The "marriage supper of the Lamb" (Rev 19:9) refers to the Eucharist, "a participation in and anticipation of the worship of heaven," "the earnest of the final consummation of the age to come" (Rev 20—22). What is certain is that the vision of the martyrs in Revelation 7 contains features that sooner or later were associated with baptism. Those features are the "washing" in the blood of the Lamb, or immersion in the saving death of Christ; the "sealing" of the foreheads, whether with a cross as a sign of belonging to the crucified Lord (cf. Tertullian *Marc.* 3.22) or with the name of God (cf. Rev 14:1) that was invoked over the initiands at several points in the baptismal process; the "clothing in white robes," whether as having "put on Christ" (cf. Gal 3:27; Col 3:9-10) or the "garment of righteousness" (as in the Byzantine rite); the allusions in Revelation 7:15-17 to Psalm 23 and Psalm 42, whose imagery of shepherd, waters and deer occurs in ancient baptist-ries. If martyrdom as viewed by the biblical Seer reflected or inspired the rites of baptism, conversely baptism supplied a category for describing martyrdom—the "baptism of blood" (as when *The Apostolic Tradition* speaks of a martyred catechumen's salvation being made secure through "baptism in his own blood").

3. The Early Postapostolic Period.

3.1. The Didache. This document, which may encode Syrian practice around the turn of the first century, presents in its first six chapters what looks like catechetical material as it expounds the "Two Ways" of "life" and "death." Then in *Didache* 7 the document prescribes: "Baptize in the name of the Father and of the Son and of the Holy Spirit, in running water." No more than in Matthew 28:19 is it specified how the threefold divine name was invoked: it may have been covered by the exchange of questions and answers between minister and candidate concerning the latter's faith (as in *The Apostolic Tradition* of Hippolytus), for we have no evidence before the fourth century of a declaratory pronouncement "I baptize you in the name of. . . ." "Running water" is literally "living water" *(hydōr zōn),* which has biblical associations with divine grace (e.g., Jer 2:13; 17:13). While running water is preferred, it is not indispensable: "If you do not have running water, baptize in other water; and if you cannot in cold, then in warm." Some form of immersion is envisaged, although affusion is allowed if running or standing water is lacking: "If you do not have either, pour water three times on the head." Both the minister and the candidate should come to the event fasting, together with "such others as are able"; the candidate's fast should be of one or two days. *Didache* 9.5 stipulates that none but those baptized in the name of the Lord may eat or drink at the community's thanksgiving meals, in accordance with the Lord's injunction not to give what is holy to the dogs (*see* Lord's Supper).

3.2. Ignatius of Antioch. Early in the second century Ignatius states that "without the bishop it is not lawful either to baptize or to hold a lovefeast" (Ign. *Smyrn.* 8.2). Later history will show the chief pastor's oversight of admission to the community maintained in various ways when the water rite is performed by other ministers. The Western churches will characteristically reserve to the bishop a postbaptismal imposition of hand and/or anointing signifying the gift of the Holy Spirit (eventually called "confirmation"); the Eastern churches will allow presbyters to baptize and to "chrismate," but always with the use of episcopally consecrated *mȳron* (lit., "ointment").

4. The Later Second Century.

4.1. Justin Martyr. In his *First Apology* written in Rome around the middle of the second century and addressed to the emperor Antoninus Pius, Justin Martyr offers the earliest direct and deliberate description of the process of Christian initiation, which he calls "the manner in which we dedicated ourselves to God when we were made new through Christ." *Apology* I.61 relates:

> As many as are persuaded and believe that these things which we teach and describe are true, and undertake to live accordingly, are taught to pray and ask God, while fasting, for the forgiveness of their sins: and we pray and fast with them. Then they are led by us to a place where there is water, and they are reborn after the manner of rebirth by which we also were reborn: for they are then washed in the water in the name of the Father and Lord God of all things, and of our Savior Jesus Christ, and of the Holy Spirit. . . . Over him that now chooses to be reborn and repents of his sins is named the Father and Lord God of all things. . . . This washing is called enlightenment, because those that are experiencing these things have their minds enlightened. And he that is being enlightened is washed in the name of Jesus Christ who was crucified under Pontius Pilate, and in the name of the Holy Spirit, which through the prophets foretold all things concerning Jesus.

Apology I.65 continues:

> After we have thus washed him that is persuaded and declares his assent, we lead him to those who are called brethren, where they are assembled, and make common prayer for ourselves, for him that has been enlightened, and for all people everywhere, that, embracing the truth, we may be found in our lives good and obedient citizens, and also attain to everlasting salvation. When we have ended the prayers we greet one another with a kiss.

A brief account of the Eucharist follows, in which the newly baptized will have participated for the first time ("for no one may partake of it unless he is convinced of the truth of our teaching, and has been cleansed with the washing for forgiveness of sins and regeneration, and lives as Christ handed down").

The following features of a process of Christian initiation are stated or clearly implied by Justin. Those who respond to the church's message are put through an unspecified time of learning (the technical term will be "catechumenate"), which includes doctrinal and moral instruction as well as prayer and fasting. They must express their repentance, faith and commitment. Their baptism takes place away from the congregation. Forgiveness of sins and rebirth are associated with baptism in the threefold name, and this baptism appears to play an instrumental role in the conveying of these divine gifts. Baptism is also termed a washing and an enlightenment. The newly baptized are brought into the liturgical assembly, where prayer is made for them (some scholars have seen this as the location of some kind of "confirmation," which is otherwise lacking). Then they join for the first time in the kiss of peace and the eucharistic communion.

4.2. Tertullian. Another, slightly later, description of the rites of initiation, together with fuller theological reflection on their meaning and effect, can be pieced together from the writings of the North African, Tertullian. His treatise "On Baptism" *(De Baptismo)* may be supplemented from passages in several other writings. The immediate preparation for the rite is thus: "Those who are at the point of entering upon baptism ought to pray, with frequent prayers, fastings, bendings of the knee, and all-night vigils, along with the confession of all their sins, so as to make a copy of the baptism of John [i.e., in its aspect of repentance]" *(De Bapt.* 20). The baptismal water is blessed in a prayer of invocation, technically called an epiclesis: "All waters, when God is invoked, acquire the sacred significance of conveying sanctity: for at once the Spirit comes down from heaven and stays upon the waters, sanctifying them from within himself, and when thus sanctified they absorb the power of sanctifying" *(De Bapt.* 4). At the edge of the water, the candidates make a renunciation of the devil. Once in the water they "make profession of the Christian faith in the words of its rule" *(De Spect.* 4): "When on the point of coming to the water, we then and there as somewhat earlier in church under the bishop's hand af-firm that we renounce the devil and his pomp and his angels. After this we are thrice immersed, while we answer interrogations rather more extensive than our Lord has prescribed in the gospel" *(De Cor.* 3). As *De Baptismo* 13 reveals, the reference is to the command to baptize in the threefold name of Matthew 28:19, and *Adversus Praxean* 26 makes explicit that "not once only, but thrice are we dipped *[tinguimur]*, into each of the three persons at each of the several names." Tertullian's phraseology is consonant with the practice in *The Apostolic Tradition* of Hippolytus, where the minister of baptism put questions to the baptizands in the form of a threefold "interrogatory creed" and "baptized" them at each affirmative reply.

Then "we come up from the washing and are anointed with the blessed unction," which is linked with Moses' anointing of Aaron to the priesthood and with Christ's anointing by the Father with the Spirit *(De Bapt.* 7). "Next follows the imposition of the hand in benediction, inviting and welcoming the Holy Spirit," and here the OT type is Jacob's blessing of Ephraim and Manasseh with "crossed hands" (cf. Gen 48:12-14) in prefiguration of "the blessing that was to be in Christ" *(De Bapt.* 8). Welcomed into the whole assembly, the neophytes receive at communion also from a cup of milk and honey *(De Cor.* 3; cf. *Marc.* 1.14).

As to the minister of baptism: "The supreme right of giving it belongs to the high priest, which is the bishop; after him, to the presbyters and deacons, yet not without commission from the bishop, on account of the church's dignity; for when this is safe, peace is safe. Except for that, even laymen have the right" *(De Bapt.* 17). As to the time of baptism: "The Passover [i.e., Easter] provides the day of most solemnity for baptism, for then was accomplished our Lord's passion, and into it we are baptized. . . . After that, [the fifty days of] Pentecost is a most auspicious period for arranging baptisms, for during it our Lord's resurrection was several times made known among the disciples, and the grace of the Holy Spirit first given. . . . For all that, every day is a Lord's day; any hour, any season, is suitable for baptism. If there is a difference of solemnity, it makes no difference to the grace" *(De Bapt.* 19). The special appropriateness of Passover and Pentecost for baptism matches the Pauline themes of baptism as participation in the death and resurrection of Christ (Rom 6) and of baptism by the one Spirit into the one body of Christ (1 Cor 12:12-13).

As to the significance and effect of baptism, God's powerful work is accomplished by incredibly simple means: "A person is sent down into the water, is washed to the accompaniment of very few words, and comes up little or no cleaner than he was"—and yet he has been "granted eternity" (*De Bapt.* 2). Tertullian describes the sacramental operation thus: "The spirit is in those waters corporally washed, while the flesh is in those same waters spiritually cleansed" (*De Bapt.* 4). Or, with a distribution of effect among the various elements in the rite, and bringing out Tertullian's belief that "the flesh (*caro*) is the hinge (*cardo*) of salvation": "The flesh is washed that the soul may be made spotless; the flesh is anointed that the soul may be consecrated; the flesh is signed [with the cross] that the soul too may be protected; the flesh is overshadowed by the imposition of the hand that the soul also may be illumined by the Spirit; the flesh feeds on the body and blood of Christ so that the soul as well may be replete with God" (*De Resur.* 8).

4.3. The Apostolic Tradition. If the ancient church order that twentieth-century scholarship has pieced together is correctly identified with the otherwise lost *Apostolic Tradition* of Hippolytus, then it bears witness to the practice of Christian initiation in the church of Rome around the turn of the second century into the third. This testimony is of vital importance for the two-way reading between the evidence of the NT and the early patristic writings.

According to Hippolytus, inquirers are to be examined by the church's teachers as to their motives for wanting to "hear the word," and their admittance to instruction depends on their readiness to forsake evil ways and forbidden occupations. The catechumenate normally lasts three years, but the time may be shortened "if a person be earnest and persevere, because it is not the time that is judged but the conduct." Teaching is accompanied by prayer. When the catechumens are "chosen" to receive baptism (they will be called "*electi*" in the Roman tradition for the weeks of their proximate preparation before a baptism that typically takes place at Easter), their lives are examined for good works. Then they may "hear the gospel"; this probably refers to a ceremony more fully described later, whereby the ears of the candidates were opened to all four Gospels. Thenceforth they are exor-

cised daily, and at last by the bishop. On the final Thursday they bathe, and on the Friday and Saturday they fast. On the Saturday (typically Easter Eve), the bishop assembles the candidates and gives them a definitive exorcism. The night is spent in vigil, with Scripture reading and instruction.

At cockcrow, a prayer is said over the water, which is to be "pure and flowing." The candidates divest, ready for baptism. First it is the children's turn, "and if they can answer for themselves, let them answer; but if they cannot, let their parents answer or someone from their family." Then come the adult males, and finally the women, "who shall have loosed their hair and laid aside their gold ornaments." A presbyter bids the candidates say, "I renounce thee, Satan, and all thy service and all thy works," anointing them with "the oil of exorcism" already prepared by the bishop. Then another presbyter takes over, assisted by a deacon. In the water the baptizer lays hand on the baptizand and asks, "Do you believe in God the Father Almighty?" On the response, "I believe," the candidate is "baptized (*baptizatur*)" by the minister once. And similarly twice more, after creedal questions concerning "Christ Jesus, the Son of God" and "the Holy Spirit in the Holy Church, and the resurrection of the flesh." On coming up from the water, the baptized is anointed with "the oil of thanksgiving" already blessed by the bishop, the presbyter saying, "I anoint you with holy oil in the name of Jesus Christ."

The newly baptized dry themselves and dress. Then they enter the main assembly. There the bishop lays hands on them, praying, "O Lord God, who didst grant these the forgiveness of sins by the bath of regeneration of the Holy Spirit, send upon them thy grace, that they may serve thee according to thy will" (Latin version) or "O Lord God, who didst grant these the forgiveness of sins by the bath of regeneration, fill them now with thy Holy Spirit and send upon them thy grace" (Oriental versions). (The different versions have been deemed significant in debates over "confirmation" and the moment of the Spirit's gift.) Then the bishop pours consecrated oil on each head and, resting his hand there, says, "I anoint you with holy oil in God the Father Almighty and Christ Jesus and the Holy Spirit." (The double postbaptismal anointing, by presbyter and by bishop, is a peculiarity of the Roman rite.) The bishop "seals" each forehead with the sign of the cross, kissing the neophyte and saying, "The Lord be with you" and getting the response, "And with your spirit."

Then for the first time the newly baptized pray with the whole congregation and exchange the kiss of peace. The Eucharist ensues, at which the neophytes not only receive the bread ("the antitype of the body of Christ," delivered with the words "The bread of heaven in Christ Jesus") but also taste of three cups: of water ("to signify the washing, that the inner man also, which is the soul, may receive the same things as the body"), of milk and honey ("in fulfillment of the promise made to the fathers," and now in Christ giving believers nourishment "like little children, making the bitterness of the heart sweet by the gentleness of his word"), and of mixed wine ("the antitype of the blood which was shed for all who have believed in him").

5. The Baptism of Young Children.

From the earliest documents certain facts about baptism emerge. On the divine side, baptism is an occasion or even a means, but certainly a testimony, of God's saving activity toward a person on the basis of the redemptive work of Christ. But nowhere is faith in Christ dispensed with on the human side. In the most clearly attested cases in the apostolic period and the early centuries, baptism is administered upon a confession of faith on the part of the recipient. The question, however, arises whether baptism was also given to some—particularly children—who were in a way "covered" by the faith of others or could at least be "spoken for" by them, as we see ritually encoded for the first time in *The Apostolic Tradition* of Hippolytus ("If [the children] cannot [answer for themselves], let their parents answer, or someone from their family"). Historians and exegetes often have a heavy ecclesial and ecclesiological investment here, for the answer affects, even if it does not finally settle, the contested issue of the impropriety, legitimacy or necessity of infant baptism.

Third- and fourth-century writers speak of the baptism of infants as an apostolic custom. The only piece of potentially hard evidence extant from apostolic times is the reference to the baptism of "households" in Acts (up to four cases) and in Paul (once). According to Acts 10:2, Cornelius feared God "with all his household [syn panti tō oikō autou]," and Peter was sent to declare to him "a message by which you will be saved, you and all your household [kai pas ho oikos sou]" (Acts 11:14). For Peter's visit, Cornelius called together "his relatives and close friends" (Acts 10:24), and when "the Holy Spirit fell on all who heard the word" spoken by Peter (Acts 10:44), the apostle commanded them to be baptized (Acts 10:48). According to Acts 16:14-15, Lydia, whose heart the Lord had opened to Paul's message, "was baptized, and her household [kai ho oikos autēs]." According to Acts 16:31-32, Paul and Silas told the Philippian jailor, "Believe in the Lord Jesus, and you will be saved, you and your household [sou kai ho oikos sou]." They "spoke the word of the Lord to him and to all that were in his house [pasin tois en tē oikia autou]"; at once the jailor "was baptized, and all those belonging to him [kai hoi autou hapantes]" (Acts 16:33), and "he rejoiced with all his household [panoikei] that he had believed in God" (Acts 16:34). According to Acts 18:8, "Crispus, the ruler of the synagogue, believed in the Lord, together with all his household [syn holō tō oikō autou]; and many of the Corinthians hearing Paul believed and were baptized." In 1 Corinthians 1:16 Paul writes that he "baptized the household of Stephen [ton Stephana oikon]," "the firstfruits of Achaia," who "have devoted themselves to the service of the saints" (1 Cor 16:15). As the story is told in some of these cases, it may be possible to equate the baptized with those who heard the word and believed, but in others the "household" that was "saved" may have been more extensive. In particular, those looking for apostolic evidence of infant baptism argue that the "households" that were "saved" and "baptized" will have included infants. In the estimation of those opposed to infant baptism, infants can hardly be said to have heard the word and believed and so will not have been baptized.

The classic modern debate on the early history of infant baptism is that between J. Jeremias and K. Aland. While Jeremias, against an OT background, holds that a quasi-ritual "*oikos*-formula" includes children, and even especially so, Aland considers that the reference of the common word *household* in any given case depends on the context and notes that small children are nowhere mentioned in the relevant NT passages. Aland is equally unimpressed by Jeremias's appeal to indirect literary evidence from the early or middle second century (such as the martyr Polycarp's confession of Christ, "Eighty-six years

I have been his slave") or the data of funerary inscriptions, which in any case belong to the third century. Aland finds the clue to the beginnings of infant baptism in Tertullian's treatise *On Baptism*. There Tertullian opposes what sounds to Aland like a new practice of bringing young children to baptism. Granting that the Lord said "Forbid them not to come to me," Tertullian draws the conclusion: "So let them come when they are growing up, when they are learning, when they are being taught what they are coming to; let them be made Christians when they have become competent to know Christ" (*De Bapt.* 18). For Tertullian, childhood remains an age of innocence *(innocens aetas)*: "Why should innocent infancy come with haste to the remission of sins?" Infant baptism will have arisen, according to Aland, with the shift toward the view of original sin finally represented in Cyprian: a newborn child "has not sinned, except that, being born after the flesh according to Adam, he has contracted the contagion of the ancient death at its earliest birth; yet on this very account he approaches more easily to the reception of the forgiveness of sins, because it is not his own sins that are forgiven him but the sins of another" (Cyprian *Epistle* 64; Aland adduces similar passages from Origen). Later, Augustine of Hippo would appeal to the church's practice of baptizing infants—when baptism is "for the remission of sins"—as liturgical proof of the doctrine of original sin (e.g., Augustine *Sermon* 174, Migne PL 38.944-45; *Epistle* 194, Migne PL 33.889-91).

On the theological plane, proponents of infant baptism offer various accounts, severally or in combination, of the relation between faith and such baptism. A child may have faith (like, in Luther's example, the embryonic John, who leaped in Elizabeth's womb when confronted by the Word in Mary's womb); a child may be given faith through baptism; sponsors may stand in for the faith of the child; the community of faith may "supply" the faith of one being aggregated to it; the child may be baptized with a view to its future faith. Moreover, the practice of infant baptism is considered warranted, or even necessitated, by its congruity with a variety of themes in biblical soteriology and anthropology: fallen humanity's need for redemption; the unity of God's covenant (with baptism as the Christian circumcision); the prevenience of grace; the universality of the gospel offer; unmerited justi-fication; the intercessory power of others; the solidarity of the family. Those who reject the baptism of infants in favor of baptism solely upon profession of faith by the candidate argue that faith includes a measure of understanding and is personally unsubstitutable. Moreover, the "new" covenant requires circumcision "of the heart"; the prevenience of grace and the universality of the gospel are properly and sufficiently embodied in the preaching of the Word to all; original sin does not imply personal guilt in each human being from birth; justification may be "by faith alone," but it does not occur "without faith"; parents, guardians and the church properly exercise their responsibilities and privileges toward children by prayer and teaching, as toward catechumens in preparation for baptism; even then, there is the prospect, according to the Lord's teaching in the Gospels, that the eschatological crisis will divide families (see Wainwright 1980, 139-42).

See also LORD'S SUPPER; WORSHIP.

DLNTD: LITURGICAL ELEMENTS; PENTECOST; TONGUES.

BIBLIOGRAPHY. K. Aland, *Did the Early Church Baptize Infants?* (London: SCM, 1963); idem, *Die Stellung der Kinder in den frühen christlichen Gemeinden—und ihre Taufe* (TEH 138; Munich: Kaiser, 1967); G. Barth, *Die Taufe in frühchristlicher Zeit* (BTS 4; Neukirchen-Vluyn: Neukirchener Verlag, 1981); G. R. Beasley-Murray, *Baptism in the New Testament* (London: Macmillan, 1962); P. F. Bradshaw, *The Search for the Origins of Christian Worship: Sources and Methods for the Study of Early Liturgy* (New York: Oxford University Press, 1992); F. L. Cross, *1 Peter: A Paschal Liturgy* (London: Mowbray, 1954); O. Cullmann, *Baptism in the New Testament* (SBT 1; London: SCM, 1950); G. J. Cuming, *Hippolytus: A Text for Students* (GLS 8; Bramcote, Notts: Grove Books, 1976); G. Dix, *Confirmation or Laying on of Hands?* (TOP 5; London: SPCK, 1936); J. D. G. Dunn, *Baptism in the Holy Spirit: A Reexamination of the New Testament Teaching on the Gift of the Spirit in Relation to Pentecostalism Today* (SBT 2d ser. 15; London: SCM, 1970); E. Evans, ed. and trans., *Tertullian's Homily on Baptism* (London: SPCK, 1964); W. F. Flemington, *The New Testament Doctrine of Baptism* (London: SPCK, 1948); L. Hartman, "Into the Name of Jesus," *NTS* 20 (1973-74) 432-40; J. Jeremias, *Infant Baptism in the First Four Centuries* (London: SCM, 1960); idem, *The Origins of Infant Baptism: A Further*

Study in Reply to Kurt Aland (SHT 1; London: SCM, 1963); G. W. H. Lampe, *The Seal of the Spirit: A Study in the Doctrine of Baptism and Confirmation in the New Testament and the Fathers* (2d ed.; London: SPCK, 1967); P. Pokorný, "Christologie et baptême à l'époque du christianisme primitif," *NTS* 27 (1980-81) 368-80; H. Preisker, *Die Katholischen Briefe* (HNT 15; 3d rev. ed. of H. Windisch's work; Tübingen: Mohr Siebeck, 1951); M. H. Shepherd, *The Paschal Liturgy and the Apocalypse* (ESW 6; London: Lutterworth, 1960); G. Wainwright, *Doxology: The Praise of God in Worship, Doctrine, and Life* (New York: Oxford University Press, 1980); idem, "The Rites and Ceremonies of Christian Initiation: Developments in the Past," *StudLit* 10 (1974) 2-24; E. C. Whitaker, *Documents of the Baptismal Liturgy* (2d ed.; London: SPCK, 1970); idem, "The History of the Baptismal Formula," *JEH* 16 (1965) 1-12.

G. Wainwright

BAPTISM, JEWISH PROSELYTE. *See* BAPTISM I; JOHN THE BAPTIST.

BAPTISM OF CHILDREN. *See* BAPTISM III.

BAPTISM OF JOHN. *See* BAPTISM I; JOHN THE BAPTIST.

BARABBAS. *See* TRIAL OF JESUS.

BARNABAS. *See* APOSTLE.

BARUCH, SECOND. *See* APOCRYPHA AND PSEUDE-PIGRAPHA.

BIOGRAPHY, GOSPELS AS. *See* GOSPEL (GENRE).

BIRTH NARRATIVES. *See* BIRTH OF JESUS; MIRACLES, MIRACLE STORIES I.

BIRTH OF JESUS

The examination of the birth of Jesus requires an extensive study of various aspects of the birth Narratives found in Matthew 1—2 and Luke 1—2.

1. Genre and Sources of the Birth Narratives
2. Theological and Redactional Emphases in Matthew 1—2 and Luke 1—2
3. Use of Old Testament Prophecy in the Birth Narratives
4. Genealogies in Matthew and Luke
5. The Date of Jesus' Birth
6. The Location of Jesus' Birth
7. The Virginal Conception
8. The Magi and the Shepherds
9. Canonical Information about Jesus' Childhood

1. Genre and Sources of the Birth Narratives.
The question of the genre of the birth narratives is still being debated, and opinions vary as to whether these stories are more like pagan birth legends or like Jewish infancy narratives, with most scholars now persuaded that they are closer to the latter than the former.

1.1. The Issue of Midrash. The attempt to see the birth narratives in light of Jewish literary practices has been taken a step further by those who view these stories as being essentially midrashic in character (Gundry 1982; Brown 1977). Midrash, or midrash pesher, by definition is an imaginative interpretation or expansion based on some OT text, usually in an attempt to show how particular OT material has contemporary relevance (Laurentin). Given this definition it is easy to see how Matthew's treatment of the OT in his formulaic quotations might be cited as examples of midrashic exegesis. But what the First Evangelist does with his OT quotes and how he handles his narrative material are not one and the same thing.

Midrash is a hermeneutical technique, not in itself a literary genre. It could also be argued that we have examples of imaginative haggadah in the birth narratives (cf. Hendrickx, who calls Mt 1—2 a "haggadic midrash," though it might be better to say midrashic haggadah). A haggadic tale, like a legend, generally develops over a much longer period of time than the few decades that exist between the time of Jesus and the final form of the Gospels. Even as late as the 80-90s there were still some eyewitnesses to the Gospel events, and Luke claims to have relied at least in part on their testimony. It is agreed by most scholars that no extrabiblical materials provide such precise parallels with the birth narrative material that they can definitely be affirmed as the source(s) of the Gospel material and that Matthew and Luke used sources for their birth narratives.

1.2. The Issue of Historical Tradition. To a great degree, how one evaluates the birth narratives is determined by one's presuppositions about the proper starting place for evaluating this material. For instance, if one assumes that Matthew and Luke received a historical tradition or traditions about the circumstances surrounding Jesus' birth and then took that source material, wrote it in their own manner so as to highlight the theological points they wanted to make, and especially in the case of Matthew wrote it so as to draw out potential links with the OT, it is possible to come to a plausible explanation of the character of this material. On this explanation real historical substance is posited for the birth narratives, with the Evangelists engaging in some creative editing and rewording of these historical sources according to their respective purposes and according to the conventions of ancient history writing.

In light of Luke's prologue (Lk 1:1-4) one would naturally expect that this Evangelist was not only using sources, but sources he felt were historically credible to which he contributed his editing, expansions and corrections. However, it is possible to assume that at most the authors only present us with some historical fragments in the midst of a largely fictional account and that the point of the narratives is primarily theological rather than historical. Thus, it has been argued, the authors should not be faulted for not presenting straightforward history. If one starts with this assumption it is possible to come to the conclusions found in works such as R. H. Gundry's commentary on Matthew or R. E. Brown's impressive study *The Birth of the Messiah*.

No approach is free from problems, but special difficulties attend those who begin with the assumption of the essential non-historicity of the birth narrative material. First, it means that one must treat the birth narrative material as substantially different in character from the rest of the Gospel tradition, a great deal of which can be plausibly argued to have a basis in historical events in Jesus' life (*see* Gospels, Historical Reliability of). In short, it requires that we see the birth stories as some sort of separate entities, perhaps even of a different genre from the rest of the Gospel material. There are, however, various indications that the birth narratives should not be separated from the rest of their respective Gospels. For instance, the thematic and theological unity of Luke 1—2 with the rest of Luke's Gospel has been demonstrated (Minear). Various of Luke's major themes are given their first airing in the birth narratives.

Second, the problem of supernatural phenomena is not unique to the birth narrative material, and unless one objects to the possibility of *miracles a priori, the supernatural occurrences recorded in the birth narratives present no greater obstacles to the case for historicity than do the supernatural events recorded elsewhere in the Gospels. Indeed, one may say that especially in the case of Luke 1—2 the birth narratives are in some ways less miraculous in character than some of the miracle narratives having to do with the ministry of Jesus.

Third, there is evidence in Matthew 1—2 and Luke 1—2 that we are not dealing with free compositions. The fact that Luke 1—2 abounds in Hebraisms in contrast to the classical Greek prologue in Luke 1:1-4 speaks for the use of a Semitic narrative source(s) of considerable proportions at least up to Luke 2:40 (Farris). Further, the way Matthew sometimes awkwardly works his formula citations into his narrative suggests he was working with one or several narrative sources to which he has added OT quotations.

Fourth, there are various details in these narratives that are theologically irrelevant and suggest a historical source (e.g., the name of Anna's father). In other cases they go against the grain of the Evangelist's purpose (e.g., Luke tries to cast John the Baptist and his parents in the shadow of Jesus and Mary to a certain extent, yet he has Mary visit Elizabeth, who is the first to utter Spirit-inspired words). This is more true of Luke 1—2 than Matthew 1—2, but even in the latter birth narrative we find some anomalies that suggest something other than free creation (e.g., Mt 1:23 says Jesus will be called Immanuel, but no one does so).

All of this suggests that to assume we must choose between either theology or history in this material is to accept a false dichotomy. What we likely have is material of historical substance that has been theologically interpreted so as to bring out its greater significance. Theological history writing, not historicized theology, might well describe what we find here and throughout the Gospels. Both historical material and theological redaction can be found throughout the Gospels.

It is true that the stories surrounding the birth of Jesus record some events in which only one or two people were involved. In such cases this would mean that ultimately if these traditions have historical kernels, they must finally go back to either Mary or Joseph (Laurentin).

The assumption of a testimony of the Holy Family, widely held in the church until the twentieth century, can be neither proved nor disproved by the historical critical study of the text. If there was such a testimony or testimonies that circulated not as a whole but in parts, perhaps grouped according to source, it would explain how the Gospel writers had access to such essentially private data as Mary's or Joseph's testimony of their encounters with or dreams about the supernatural. This might also explain why Matthew's Gospel seems to present Joseph's side of the story, while Luke's Gospel presents Mary's. It might suggest that Matthew and Luke had access to only one part of the birth traditions (Feuillet, McHugh).

2. Theological and Redactional Emphases in Matthew 1—2 and Luke 1—2.

Since the major theological and redactional thrusts of the birth narratives have been amply presented by Brown, we will highlight only some of the more prominent motifs. It is true that in terms of *dramatis personae*, the birth narratives do not focus on Jesus but on those who have contact with the child or his parent(s). Thus an examination of how the Evangelists portray some of the major figures in these birth stories should tell us a great deal about the authors' emphases and tendencies.

2.1. Matthew. Though the First Evangelist does mention Mary in the genealogy, it is Joseph and his dreams that link together the various narratives in Matthew 1—2 (cf. Mt 1:18-25; 2:13, 19-23). By contrast, Mary is the linking figure in Luke 1—2 (cf. Lk 1:26-38, 39-56; 2:5-7, 19, 34, 39, 48, 51).

The First Evangelist focuses on Joseph's reaction to the divine intervention in Mary's life, and in particular he shows how Joseph is repeatedly led by dreams to do God's will. It is no accident that, apart from Jesus, only Joseph is called "son of David" in these stories. He is seen as the typical patriarch who will guide and protect Mary and Jesus as God directs. It is Joseph who is presented to the Evangelist's audience as a model disciple and son of Israel. He is obedient to the heavenly dreams, but he is also called a *righteous man (Mt 1:19), that is, one who upholds the law. Thus in Matthew 1:18-19 he is depicted as caught between the holy law of God and his love for Mary (McHugh). The intention of the Evangelist is to paint a picture of a devout

Jewish man who is willing to give up what was often perceived to be a Jewish father's greatest privilege—siring his firstborn son—in order to obey God's will (Mt 1:24).

It is possible that this special attention given Joseph is due either to the concern of the author to demonstrate how Jesus became legally a son of David and/or is part of the attempt to show the respectability of Jesus' origins. In this presentation Mary is not only submissive to Joseph's leading but also completely silent. Thus it may be that the author reaffirms the traditional Jewish roles of male headship and female subordination, perhaps because he had a Jewish-Christian audience.

The interlude involving the magi and King Herod presents two contrasts: between the spiritually obtuse and those searching; and between the vulnerable babe born King of the Jews who is protected by God, and Herod the oriental tyrant who is protective of his throne but in the end is unable to keep it (Mt 2:19). The way these stories are interwoven is by a theological or christological structuring of the material. Thus Matthew 1 will answer the questions of who and how (Jesus' identity as son of David and how he came by it), while the second chapter will focus on locales—the where of Jesus' birth and the "whence" of his destiny (Stendahl, Brown). He is born in Bethlehem, but he is called out of the land of bondage and sent to Israel to begin to call it back to its true destiny. There is more focus on christology proper (who Jesus is) than on how he became such.

2.2. Luke. The Lukan birth narratives are more complex for several reasons. There is more narrative material and significant characters in the narration. There is also considerably more interest in presenting a connected narrative reflecting on the human drama, in particular the joys and anxieties wrapped up in childbearing. There are two major paeans of praise and also the shorter *Nunc Dimittis* (Lk 2:29-32), which help to structure this material. Note that there is no genealogy in the birth or infancy narratives proper.

Luke's birth narratives are in many respects the feminine counterpart to those found in Matthew 1—2, which is not surprising since a full one-third of the uniquely Lukan material in this Gospel is about women (Witherington 1988). In Luke 1—2 it is Elizabeth and Mary, not Zechariah and Joseph, who are the first to hear of

Christ's coming. It is these women who are praised and blessed, and they first sing and prophesy about the Christ child (*see* Women).

It is especially in the speech material that we hear one of Luke's major themes: Jesus' coming means God's liberation for the poor and oppressed among Israel (Lk 1:54, 68-69; *see* Riches and Poverty) but also light for the Gentiles (Lk 2:32). These songs have been characterized as a reflection of the piety of Jewish *ʿănāwîm,* or "poor." But to a large extent this is also how various of the key figures in Luke 1—2 are portrayed—Elizabeth, Mary, Simeon, Anna. All these characters are seen as devout but poor Jews longing for the salvation God had long since promised them. It appears, however, that Mary is portrayed as more than just a devout Jew, for she is open to God's new action through her and her son to a degree not true of the others—she alone is said to ponder the implications of all these events. As such, she may be seen as a model disciple. More certainly, Mary is seen as the type of an OT prophet (cf. Lk 1:46-55), and she represents Israel who willingly obeys God's bidding despite the personal cost. She is God's servant.

The theme of male-female role reversal comes into play in the presentation of Elizabeth and Zechariah. Elizabeth, not Zechariah, is seen as the person of true and full faith, and she gives her child the name the angel indicates (Lk 1:60). It is precisely at the point when Zechariah agrees with the action of Elizabeth that he is freed from his dumbness and is able to praise God.

In a sense we also see this reversal in the story of Anna and Simeon. Simeon is content to die, having seen the arrival of the Coming One, but Anna is invigorated to new roles—going forth to testify that redemption and liberation have come in this child (Lk 2:36-38). While Anna and Simeon are both old and both representatives of the old order of Jewish piety and of the yearnings of Israel for Messiah (*see* Christ), their contrasting reactions to seeing Jesus are striking. Note also how Luke frames his infancy narrative with a man and a woman who are connected with the temple (Lk 1:5-25; 2:22-40). Hence Luke indicates how Jesus affects the very heart of Israel—Jerusalem and the temple—a theme he will return to near the end of the story.

Luke stresses that it is the women especially who react with exuberance at the coming of

their liberator. Recent feminist analysis of Matthew 1—2 and Luke 1—2 has stressed, however, that the new roles of women or new portrayal of women in these stories is nonetheless contained in an essentially patriarchal package that highlights and even celebrates women's distinctively feminine role of childbearing (Anderson). By contrast, a recent feminist interpretation of Luke 2:41-52 argues that the stress on the fatherhood of God undermines male dominance by devaluing patriarchal institutions and human fatherhood (Fiorenza). This conclusion may be doubted and certainly could not be argued on the basis of Matthew 1—2. There it is essential to the author's argument that Joseph be established as legally Jesus' father so he may be counted as a son of David, a theme not absent in Luke (cf. Lk 1:69; 2:11; 3:31).

More play is given to the matter of the virginal conception in Luke 1—2 than in Matthew 1—2, but in both cases it is the fact of the coming of Messiah, not the how, that is stressed. One must not underestimate either the Jewish flavor of both birth narratives or the skill with which the Evangelists have integrated their source material into moving and meaningful presentations about the good news that is and has come in Jesus. The shape of their presentations strikingly differs—even when they use many of the same elements. This in itself demonstrates that the First and Third Evangelists were not rigid editors of their sources but creative shapers of their material who used their sources to highlight their own theological emphases, and successfully integrated this material into the larger schemas of their respective Gospels (cf. Minear).

3. Use of Old Testament Prophecy in the Birth Narratives.

No other section of the Gospels is so clearly linked to Old Testament prophecy as is Matthew 1—2. This is true not merely because these two chapters bear so many quotations or allusions to the OT, but also because their author uses scriptural language in his narrative and discourses. The very structure of the five pericopes in Matthew 1—2 seems to be determined largely by five formula quotations, which are frequently the focus of scholarly attention (France). Nevertheless it is the incidents in the story that have led to the collection and structuring of these quotations in their present forms.

Nowhere is it more evident that the story has

led the author to an appropriate scriptural prophecy to relate to it (rather than the Scripture engendering the story) than at the close of the birth narrative, where we find the problematic but ostensible OT quote "He will be called a Nazarene" (Mt 2:23). The way the author uses these quotes may reflect the midrash pesher technique, but this is a very different matter from the suggestion that the author's very narrative is an exercise in creative midrash on the OT (Gundry 1982). Matthew's text for the story is not primarily the OT but a collection of traditions about Jesus' birth that he has reshaped and retold in the light of OT prophecy. The effect of concluding narrative sections by recalling prophecies is that the prophecies seem almost like afterthoughts brought in to confirm information already given in the narrative. In fact, the function of the quotes is to confirm that some rather unusual twists in the story were all along part of God's plan for the coming Messiah.

Notice too that Matthew's narrative action turns on responses to dreams or visions, or to external sources of guidance such as the star. History is shown to reflect a divine schema, or at least God's repeated intervention by various means (words or actions) corrects the course of historical actions or prevents them from going awry. The reshaping of tradition must not be underestimated, but at the same time neither should the author's use of historical sources. R. T. France is right to query what fulfillment of the OT might mean to the First Evangelist if in fact he knew that his story was created out of the OT text.

Of course the argument could be pushed back one step further, and it could be maintained that the sources the Evangelist received were ahistorical to begin with, a fact he did not comprehend. Two important factors argue against this suggestion. First, various key ideas in these stories are shared in common by Luke and Matthew, such as the betrothed couple Mary and Joseph, the virginal conception, the Davidic descent of Joseph, the birth in Bethlehem during Herod the Great's reign, the angelic revelation of the name Jesus and Jesus' upbringing in Nazareth. These ideas are shared in common even though there is even more material in Matthew 1—2/Luke 1—2 that is not shared in common, and this shows that our authors are not likely to have borrowed from each other. Second, the character

of the narrative (not the quotations) in Matthew 1—2 and also in Luke 1—2 is not dramatically different from that of the narratives in the rest of these two Gospels, and few people would doubt that there are historical sources that lie behind at least some of the ministry material.

One must also recognize, however, that traditions about the birth of Moses, and particularly those found in the Palestinian Targums, may have affected the way Matthew words his narrative and presents Jesus (Bourke), just as it is likely that various sorts of OT prophetic material have affected the presentation in the Lukan birth narratives (cf. Mal 3:1-3; Dan 9).

Apart from the songs in Luke 1—2, the influence of the OT is less immediately apparent in the Lukan birth narratives than is the case with Matthew 1—2. Nevertheless, it may be reflected in the Septuagintalisms in Luke 1—2 (i.e., use of the language of the Greek OT, especially in the annunciation to Mary); the focus on women and the importance to them of the birth of a son to whom divine promises are attached (cf. the OT stories about Sarah, Hannah and others); the importance of the naming of the child and the significance of the name given; and the stress on the miraculous means by which conception was announced and then took place, thus emphasizing fulfillment of the divine word.

The first of the Matthean formula quotations and the most important for our purposes is the citation of Isaiah 7:14 at Matthew 1:23. The following observations are crucial.

First, the pre-Christian interpretation of Isaiah 7:14 seems to have seen its fulfillment in Hezekiah, the son and successor of Ahaz. Apparently there is no evidence that any early Jew saw this as a prophecy about Messiah, much less a prophecy about a virginal conception. The Targums do tend to interpret Isaiah 9:5-6 messianically, but it is not clear that they view Isaiah 7:14 in a similar light.

Second, the Hebrew term ʿalmâ, which is used in Isaiah 7:14 (MT) refers to a young woman of marriageable age. Though the idea of virginity is probably implicit in the term, this is not a technical term for *virgo intacta*. The Hebrew bĕtûlâ comes nearer to being such a term (Wenham).

Third, the term ʿalmâ is never used in the OT of a married woman but does refer to a sexually mature woman. There are no texts in the OT where ʿalmâ clearly means one who is sexually active, but it is possible that Song of Solomon 6:8 (cf. Prov 30:19) implies this. It would appear then that ʿalmâ normally, if not always, implies a virgin, though the term does not focus on that attribute.

Fourth, several of the Greek translations of the OT (i.e., Aq, Sym, Theod) translate ʿalmâ with *neanis;* however, the LXX clearly translates it with *parthenos.* It is probably correct to say that if ʿalmâ did not normally have overtones of virginity, it is difficult if not impossible to see why the translators of the LXX used *parthenos* as the Greek equivalent.

Fifth, the Hebrew texts speak of "the young woman," so the prophet has some particular person in view.

Sixth, the Greek term *parthenos* seems to mean or strongly imply one who is a virgin, but this may not always be the case. In the LXX of Genesis 34:3, Dinah is called a *parthenos* even though the story is about her being seduced by Shechem. It should be noted, however, that after the rape Dinah is called a *paidiskē* (Gen 34:4). This text then may imply that *parthenos* sometimes has a meaning broader than "virgin" (cf. Gen 24:16, 43, 57 MT and LXX), and it is clear that it can be virtually equivalent to ʿalmâ on occasion (Gen 24:43). It may be debated whether in some rare cases *parthenos* may even mean something other than a virgin (cf. Dodd, Carmignac). One must conclude that Matthew did not deduce the idea of a virginal conception from the Isaianic prophecy, though given a prior belief in such an idea, this text became an appropriate vehicle to express the idea in prophetic language.

Space does not allow a further treatment of all the formula quotations in Matthew 1—2 (cf. Gundry), but mention should be made of the citation of Micah 5:2 in Matthew 2:6. It is a curious fact that while it is Matthew who cites this text, he never refers to the shepherd tradition that Luke records, nor does he make anything of Jesus being a shepherd figure like David.

The Third Evangelist offers us no formula quotations comparable to what we find in Matthew, and when he does cite the OT in Luke 1—2, it is brief and enigmatic (cf. 2:23-24 citing Ex 13:2, 12, 15; Lev 12:8). Yet various of the speeches/songs in Luke 1—2 are redolent with OT language and are written in the spirit of OT prophecy (cf. Lk 1:46-55, 67-79; 2:29-32). In general, however, Luke's narrative is not structured on the basis of OT citations or allusions, nor does it stress the issue of fulfilled prophecy in the manner of Matthew 1—2.

4. Genealogies in Matthew and Luke.

Over the past twenty years scholars have spent a great deal of energy trying to unravel the mysteries of Jesus' two very different genealogies. Since at least the time of Annius of Viterbo in A.D. 1490 it has been traditional to assume that Matthew's genealogy traces Jesus' lineage through Joseph (his legal genealogy), whereas Luke's genealogy traces his lineage through Mary (his natural genealogy).

This conjecture finds some support from the fact that the Matthean birth narrative focuses more on the role of Joseph than of Mary, while Luke's narrative makes Mary the more central figure in the drama. It also comports with the ancient conjecture that Joseph is ultimately the source of much of the Matthean birth narratives, while Mary is the source for most of Luke's material. The theory that Luke presents Jesus' lineage through Mary requires not only that one take the phrase "as was supposed of Joseph" (*hōs enomizeto,* Lk 3:23) as a parenthetical remark, but even more awkwardly it requires that the author use the word *son* (*huios,* Lk 3:23) to mean both son and grandson in the same breath and leave out any mention of Mary's name!

Another theory that has gained some currency in recent debate is the view that Matthew presents the royal or legal genealogy, whereas Luke presents David's actual physical descendants. In view of the fact that there were ancient king lists that would trace only the line of succession, and selectively at that, this conjecture is not impossible, but unfortunately there is no way either to prove or disprove this theory. R. P. Nettlehorst has revived the theory that we have two genealogies from Joseph's side of the family, but he reverses one part of the usual conjecture and maintains that Luke traces the line through Joseph's father while Matthew traces the line through Joseph's maternal grandfather. None of these theories are free of difficulties. Since we do not have enough information to settle the issue, we can only show which conjectures are more or less probable.

4.1. Comparisons and Contrasts. One cannot help but be impressed with the notable differences in the two genealogies, differences that suggest they were deliberately schematized to serve rather different purposes in their respective Gospels. If so, then it may be counterproductive to treat them in the same manner as one would modern genealogies or try to reconcile the one genealogy with the other.

Some noteworthy differences may be listed. In Matthew the genealogy introduces the Gospel, in particular the birth narratives, and traces the line down from Abraham through Joseph to Jesus, using the term *begot (egennēsen)*. There is an artificial division of the names into three groups of fourteen. There is a notable insertion of several women and possibly some brothers; there is omission of various names. There is an awkward circumlocution at the end of the genealogy reflecting the author's belief in a virginal conception.

By contrast Luke's genealogy follows the baptism and introduces the ministry of Jesus and thus, properly speaking, is not part of the birth narratives. Luke repeatedly uses the phrase "the son of" without any verbs and traces the line from Jesus up to Adam and God. This genealogy begins with a circumlocution indicating the author's knowledge that Jesus was not really Joseph's son, and in fact omits the article before Joseph's name, which might place Joseph's name outside the actual list. Luke inserts a *Rhēsa* and an extra *Kainan* into the genealogical list (cf. Gen 10:24; 11:12; 1 Chron 1:24).

On the surface it would appear that Matthew's genealogy is trying to show Jesus as a true Israelite, and in particular of Davidic descent, while Luke is trying to show that Jesus is truly a human being. This might account for some of the differences in form and content between the genealogies we encounter. In both genealogies, however, the primary point is to say or explain something to the audience about Jesus and his character, not so much about his ancestors (Witherington 1988).

4.2. Theological Purposes. Several features of the Matthean genealogy call for special attention. The Matthean genealogy should be seen in light of the pericope that follows (Mt 1:18-25). Taken together this material focuses on Jesus as *son of David and *son of God, themes that are developed elsewhere. Matthew 1:18-25 is probably meant to explain the genealogy and in particular how Jesus could be born of Mary, but not of Joseph, and yet still be in the Davidic line (Stendahl). This means that the genealogy and

the pericope that follows it assume, and to some extent attempt to explain, the virginal conception. There seems to be recognition of the difficulties involved in the nature of Jesus' irregular origins, and thus this material may be seen as an attempt at apologetics in light of Matthew's acceptance of the virginal conception. This in part explains the anomaly of including several women in the genealogy, for it was unusual to list women in a genealogy unless the father was unknown, or when sons from one patriarch came from his union with different wives, or if the women were related to or were famous figures (as here).

Matthew's genealogy mentions not only Mary but four other women as well. Various theories have been advanced to explain the presence of women—in particular Tamar, Rahab, Ruth and Bathsheba—in the genealogy of Jesus.

First, it has been conjectured that the author is trying to identify Jesus with Gentiles and sinners, but it is not clear that all these women fit into one or both of these categories.

Second, possibly these women were subjects of controversy in the Jewish debate about Messiah. This is difficult, if not impossible, to prove for all four of these women; and in any case some of the data used to make such a case is later than the NT period.

Third, maybe the author mentions these four women because he wants to show how not only Jesus but other Davidic kings had irregularities in their past and yet were God's anointed ones. The problem with this conjecture is that it would seem not to illuminate and exonerate the Christian stories about Jesus' origins but cast them and the stories about Jesus' ancestors under the same cloud of suspicion.

Finally, it has been urged that the point of these four women being mentioned is that they were vehicles of God's messianic plan despite their irregular unions. This view is perhaps the least inadequate (Johnson). Thus it appears our author wishes by this genealogy to call attention to Mary as an instrument of God's messianic plan (and the source of Jesus' humanity) and to show Jesus' indebtedness to women as well as men for his Davidic ancestry.

By contrast, Luke's genealogy attempts to place Jesus in the broader context of humanity in general rather than Judaism in particular. This is only natural since Luke is writing for a Gentile audience and wishes to show that Jesus is for them as well. It is worth noting, however, that Jesus is presented as the ideal human who not only is one with all humanity but also grows in wisdom and stature and is to be seen as the model of how a person should relate to God, others, temptation and other aspects of discipleship. It is possible that Jesus is being portrayed by Luke as the new Adam, the initiator of a new race of human beings, the difference being that this Adam—unlike the first—is an obedient son of God. Perhaps more importantly, Luke probably added the words "son of God" at the end of a Jewish list he acquired, for it was not Jewish practice to call someone son of God in a genealogy. There is then stress not only on Jesus' full humanity (a son of Adam) but also on his origins ultimately being from God (a son of God).

It will be seen that in Matthew and Luke these genealogies serve primarily theological and christological purposes and only secondarily historical ones. Our authors were not concerned to present detailed or exhaustive lists of Jesus' actual ancestors but only to highlight some aspects of his heritage that would best illuminate for their respective audiences Jesus' significance and nature.

5. The Date of Jesus' Birth.

The reckoning of time in antiquity went through a variety of changes until Julius Caesar, on the basis of the Egyptian solar calendar, standardized a 365-day year with an extra day inserted on leap years. The church and the Western world followed this method of reckoning time until the reforms of Pope Gregory XIII promulgated on February 24, 1582. Since that time the Gregorian calendar has been followed.

In A.D. 525, when Pope John I asked a Scythian monk named Dionysius to prepare a standard calendar for the Western church that would be reckoned from the birthdate of Christ, Dionysius relied on the Julian calendar and on available information about the date of the founding of the city of Rome to compute the birthdate of Christ. In Dionysius's calendar, A.D. 1 was set at 754 A.U.C. (*anno urbis conditae*, i.e., from the founding of the city of Rome), with Jesus' birthday being set as December 25, 753 A.U.C. Unfortunately, Dionysius miscalculated the birth of Jesus, for the Gospels state that Jesus was born during the reign of Herod the Great, who died before the turn of the era (estimates range from about 4 to 1 B.C.). Thus, historically,

we come up with the anomaly of Jesus being born several years B.C.

Several key factors in the Gospels provide help in determining more precisely the birthdate of Jesus: (1) the date of Herod's death; (2) possibly the date of the census of Quirinius, which Luke uses as a synchronism (Lk 2:1-2); (3) possibly the date Luke assigns to the beginning of the Baptist's ministry (Lk 3:1) coupled with the reference to Jesus' approximate age (Lk 3:23); and (4) possibly the astral phenomenon the magi are said to have seen, *if* that phenomenon was the result of a natural occurrence (e.g., a conjunction of planets).

5.1. Herod's Death. In order to reckon the date of Herod the Great's death, evidence that is primarily literary and numismatic must be considered. Josephus tells us that Herod the Great was proclaimed king of Judea by the Romans when Calvinus and Pollio were proconsuls, or in late 40 B.C. (Josephus *Ant.* 14.381-85; *J.W.* 1.282-85; Tacitus *Hist.* 5.9). He then adds that Herod reigned for thirty-seven years from the time of that proclamation (Josephus *Ant.* 17.191; *J.W.* 1.665.). There is considerable debate as to whether Josephus was reckoning according to solar years or following the accession-year chronology (Herod did not gain possession of his domain until 37 B.C.). There is also the question of whether or not he was counting inclusively, that is, reckoning partial years as whole years.

Most scholars are still persuaded by the work of E. Schürer (cf. Bernegger, Hoehner) that Josephus is correct about the time of Herod's accession and the length of his reign. This would place the death of Herod at about 3 B.C. However, Josephus also tells us that an eclipse of the moon occurred shortly before Herod's death (*Ant.* 17.167), and in view of the fact that this is the only time Josephus mentions this sort of phenomenon, it is improbable that he fabricated this piece of information. There were no such eclipses in 3 B.C., but there was one on March 12/13, 4 B.C. He also informs us that Passover was celebrated shortly after Herod's death (Josephus *Ant.* 17.213; *J.W.* 2.10). In 4 B.C. the first day of Passover would have been April 11. Thus it is likely Herod died between March 12 and April 11, 4 B.C., and presumably the discrepancy of one year is accounted for by inclusive reckoning of regnal years. This means that Jesus was born some time before March of 4 B.C.

The numismatic evidence is complex, but we

do know that Herod's first coin was dated "Year 3." This coin was minted perhaps shortly after his final capture of Jerusalem in 37 B.C., thus backdating his reign to the time in 40 B.C., when the Romans proclaimed him to be ruler of Judea (cf. Edmonds). This evidence also places Herod's death at about 3 B.C., but here again the question of inclusive reckoning of years arises, which would seem to allow the possibility of 4 B.C.

5.2. Census Under Quirinius. For those who believe that the Gospels are accurate historical records of Jesus' life, one of the most difficult problems in the NT is the census Luke presents in Luke 2:1-2. First, there is no evidence for an empire-wide census being taken during the time of Augustus, and we might expect that such a mammoth undertaking would have been mentioned by one or another of the ancient historians who recorded the period.

Second, Quirinius was sent by Augustus to be governor of Syria and Judea in A.D. 6 (not 6 B.C.) and thereafter did take a notable census for the empire. Josephus tells us he visited Judea in A.D. 6-7 to assess the property of the Jews in preparation for the registering and taxing of that property (Josephus *Ant.* 18.1.1-2.). There is no evidence that he was governor of the region twice or that he undertook a census of the region twice. It has been suggested that Luke may have confused Quirinius with P. Quintilius Varus, who was legate of Syria during the period 6-3 B.C. Against this is the fact that Luke was apparently knowledgeable about Latin names and would have known a *cognomen* (Quirinius) from a mere *nomen* (Quintilius).

Third, a Roman census would not have required Jews to travel to their ancestral home for registration. In any case, is it probable that the Romans would undertake such a census in a client state that already had its own ruler (Herod)?

In response to these problems various answers have been given. In the first place, if there was a census that affected Judea during the reign of Herod the Great, it would probably proceed along the lines of a Jewish census, not a Roman one. In that case it is plausible that Jews would return to their ancestral homes and that both adults would go (especially if Mary was also of Davidic descent). Second, elsewhere Luke manifests knowledge of the later census by Quirinius, which prompted the revolt of Judas the Galilean in A.D. 6-7 (Acts 5:37). Is it likely that he would have confused this census, which

he knew to be a later one, with one during the reign of Herod?

Third, it is not certain that Luke in Luke 2:1 means that Augustus took one enormous census of the whole empire. The language is general and may mean no more than that the various parts of the empire were subject to various censuses during the time of Augustus. What the Greek in fact says is that Caesar decreed that "all of the Roman world be enrolled" (Thorley). Both the present tense of *apographō* ("to enroll") and the use of *pas* ("all") suggest that Luke means that Caesar decreed that the enrollment, which had previously been going on in some parts of the empire, should now be extended to all parts, including client states. The historian A. N. Sherwin-White states, "A census or taxation assessment of the whole provincial empire . . . was certainly accomplished for the first time in history under Augustus" (Sherwin-White, 168-69).

Fourth, there is some evidence of a census of Judea under Saturninus between 9-6 B.C. (cf. Tertullian *Adv. Marc.* 4.19). We also know that Quirinius undertook more than one census during his governorship and that he did not scruple to enroll a basically autonomous group such as the Apameans.

Fifth, Luke's precise wording in Luke 2:2 is curious, and could mean either that he is referring to the first or former census that was taken under Quirinius's rule of Syria, which would perhaps imply that this was an earlier census than the one mentioned in Acts 5:37. Or it is grammatically possible that *protē* means something like "prior to" or "before." In this case Luke is speaking of a census undertaken by someone else prior to the more famous or infamous census under Quirinius that led to Jewish revolt. Such a comparative use of *protē* is not unprecedented, but grammatically there are problems with such a view.

Thus it is more probable that Luke is referring to a census under Quirinius that took place prior to the famous one in A.D. 6-7. If so, we have no clear record outside Luke of such an action by Quirinius, though it is not impossible that it took place. Herod's power was on the wane at the time of Jesus' birth, and a census in preparation for the change of power could well have been forced on Herod since he had fallen into some disfavor with Augustus near the end of his life. We know also that Quirinius had been made consul in 12 B.C., and a person of his rank serving in the East frequently had far-reaching authority and duties. It is thus not improbable that, acting as Caesar's agent, he had Herod take a census. It is also possible he was governor more than once in Syria, though the possibility also remains that Luke may be identifying him by his later and, to his audience, more familiar office. It is less likely that Luke means that Quirinius started a census in 6 B.C. and finished it in A.D. 6-7, for he says that this was the first census the governor took (distinguishing it from some later one). The upshot of all this is that Luke's reference to the census does not suggest a different date for Jesus' birth than does the Matthean evidence.

5.3. John the Baptist. Luke also tells us that John the Baptist began his ministry during the fifteenth year of Tiberius's reign. Since Augustus died in the summer of A.D. 14 and Tiberius assumed the throne later that year, this would place John's ministry about A.D. 29, though possibly it might be reckoned as early as A.D. 27 (Hoehner). It is uncertain how long it was after John began his ministry that Jesus began his, but the Lukan narrative (Lk 3) as well as Mark 1:14 suggest that John's ministry came first. Luke then tells us that Jesus was about thirty years old when he began his ministry. The Greek word *hōsei* indicates an approximation or round number, which would allow for a few years on either side.

If Jesus did begin his ministry by working with or at the same time as the Baptist, as the Johannine tradition suggests (cf. Jn 3:22-30), and if rabbinic tradition is correct in saying that Jesus was age 33 or 34 when he began his ministry (*b. Sanh.* 106b), Jesus' ministry may have begun as early as A.D. 29, if not shortly before then. This would mean that Jesus was born about 4 B.C. or perhaps a bit earlier. Both Luke 1 and independently Matthew 2 are in agreement in placing the birth of Jesus during the reign of Herod, and Luke informs us that John was also born under that reign.

5.4. Astral Phenomenon. Those scholars who have insisted that the astral phenomenon should be primary in determining the date of Jesus' birth have had to deal with a multitude of problems. First of all, it is not clear that the First Evangelist intends some sort of purely natural phenomenon. In Matthew 2 it says that the magi saw the star at its rising, which presumably is what led them to Jerusalem (whether from the east or west is not clear), and then at Matthew 2:9 we are told that when they left Jerusalem "the star . . . went ahead of them until it stopped over the place where the child was." The text seems to suggest that the star led them not merely to Bethlehem (and why would they need such leading just for the six-mile trek from Jerusalem to Bethlehem?) but to the precise location of Jesus. This hardly sounds like a normal astral phenomenon, and certainly not one that could be identified with either a conjunction of planets or a comet.

Kepler long ago rejected the theory that it was a conjunction of planets, though there was a notable conjunction of Jupiter and Saturn in 7 B.C. in the constellation Pisces, and it is also true that the Berlin Star Table and the Sippar Star Almanac indicate great interest and close study of planetary movements during 7 B.C. and afterward (Brown). Modern astronomers have stressed that the conjunction of Jupiter and Saturn in question was not close enough to appear to be a single star (Boa and Proctor). E. L. Martin's careful and detailed study argues for the year of Herod's death as 1 B.C. and the star being the conjunction of Venus and Jupiter seen from August 12, 3 B.C. onward. He further urges that the magi did not come to honor Jesus until fifteen months after his birth (on December 25, 2 B.C.) and that at that time Jupiter had stopped over Bethlehem in the meridian position in the constellation of the Virgin. There are, however, many assumptions made in these calculations, and most scholars would reject such a late date for Herod's death (but cf. Thorley). Another theory appeals to the appearance of Halley's comet, which took place in the region in 12 B.C.—a date too early to be correlated with Jesus' birth.

Kepler's theory that the magi witnessed a supernova or the birth of a new star is possible, especially since Chinese astronomers did record such a nova for 5/4 B.C. (France). It is interesting that some early Christians thought that only a supernatural explanation of the star would suffice, for in the Arabic Infancy Gospel 7 the star is identified with an angel.

In short, it is doubtful that natural astral phenomena can help us pinpoint the time of Jesus' birth. There are various imponderables about the story of the magi that make calculations almost impossible (e.g., how long after Jesus' birth did the magi come and honor him?). Most scholars who consider the story of the magi historically possible would stress that there seems to have been an interval, perhaps over a year, between the time of the birth and the coming of the magi. Taking all the evidence together it appears that Jesus was born in or before 4 B.C.

In regard to the day of Jesus' birth, as early as Hippolytus (A.D. 165-235) it was said to be December 25, a date also set by John Chrysostom (A.D. 345-407), whose arguments prevailed in the Eastern church. There is nothing improbable about a midwinter birth. Luke 2:8 tells us that the shepherds' flocks were kept outside when Jesus was born. This detail might favor a date between March and November, when such animals would normally be outside. But the Mishnah (*m. Šeqal.* 7.4) suggests that sheep around Bethlehem might also be outside during the winter months (Hoehner). Therefore, though there is no certainty, it appears that Jesus was born somewhere between 4-6 B.C., perhaps in midwinter. Both the traditional Western date for Christmas (December 25) and the date observed by the Armenian church (January 6) are equally possible. The biblical and extrabiblical historical evidence is simply not specific enough to point decisively to either traditional date. The celebration of the nativity is attested in Rome as early as A.D. 336 and this celebration also involved recognizing January 6 as Epiphany, the day the magi visited Jesus.

6. The Location of Jesus' Birth.

Both the First and Third Gospels, probably based on independent sources, inform us that Jesus was born in Bethlehem, the city of David. While it is possible that this location was chosen by the Evangelists because of the prophecy found in Micah 5:2, only the First Evangelist makes anything of this connection, and it is only he that makes very much of Jesus being *a* or *the* son of David in his Gospel. It is likely that the reference to Bethlehem, at least in the case of Luke's Gospel, is historical in character. It is also worth pointing out that even in the First Gospel, it appears that the quotations, such as that found in Matthew 2:6, have been worked by the Evangelist into his source material. In this case it is likely on the basis of Matthew 2:1 that the reference to Bethlehem existed in the source used by the First Evangelist (France). In short, the source material led the Evangelist to use the quotation from Micah, not vice versa.

The question of the specific location of Jesus' birth is an intriguing one. Matthew 2:11 mentions

that the magi found Jesus in a house *(oikos)*, but this may have transpired some time after the birth and in a different location. Later Christian tradition unfortunately has tended to amalgamate the visit of the shepherds and the magi, locating both at the site of Jesus' birth. In reality, Matthew says nothing about shepherds and Luke nothing about magi, and only the former are connected with a scene involving a manger.

Luke 2:7 should be seen in light of the larger context of Luke 2:4-7, which does not suggest that Mary went into labor immediately or even shortly after she and Joseph arrived in Bethlehem. To the contrary, we are told that "while they were there" (not upon arrival) the days were fulfilled and Mary went into labor. This implies that they had been in Bethlehem for some unspecified amount of time prior to Mary going into labor. Thus the familiar image of Mary and Joseph arriving in Bethlehem and being unable to find a place to stay on the night of arrival probably has no basis in the text (Bailey).

A second crucial point is how one translates *pandocheion* in Luke 2:7. The word can mean guest room, house or inn. It can be doubted whether there would have been an inn in Bethlehem in Jesus' day, since Bethlehem was not on any major road, and inns normally were to be found only on major roads, especially the Roman ones (but cf. Jer 41:17, which does not refer to a place in Bethlehem). Furthermore, when Luke wants to speak of a commercial inn he uses *pandochein:* Luke 10:34 refers to an establishment found on the major road between Jerusalem and Jericho. Also, when Luke uses the word *katalyma* in his Gospel (Lk 22:11 and par.; cf. 1 Kings 1:18), it clearly does not mean an inn but a guest room. It is also worth pointing out that the Arabic and Syriac versions of the NT have never translated *katalyma* as inn.

It becomes more likely that by *katalyma* Luke means either house or guest room, and the latter translation must have the edge precisely because in the vast majority of ancient Near Eastern peasant homes for which we have archaeological and literary evidence, the manger was within the home, not in a separate barn. The animals as well as the family slept within one large, enclosed space that was divided so that usually the animals would be on a lower level and the family would sleep on a raised dais (Bailey). In this particular case, we should probably envision Mary and Joseph staying in the home of relatives or friends, a home that was crowded due to the census being taken, a home where Luke tells us there was no longer any room in "*the* guest room" (noting the definite article before the noun). Consequently Mary gave birth to her child perhaps in the family room and placed the baby in the stone manger. This means that a good deal of the popular conception of this scene has no basis in the text. In particular, the idea of Mary and Joseph being cast out from civilized accommodations and taking up temporary residence in a barn is probably based on a misunderstanding of the text.

There is also a tradition cited in the second century A.D. by Justin Martyr that Joseph and Mary, being unable to find accommodations in Bethlehem, took up quarters in a cave near the village (Justin Martyr *Dial. Tryph.* 79). This is a plausible conjecture, and in fact various peasants did make their homes in caves during the time of Jesus. But Luke suggests neither that the Holy Family took up residence outside the city nor that they were in a cave. Luke would hardly have spoken of a cave with a guest room.

7. The Virginal Conception.

Even in the twentieth century the virginal conception is still the subject of a debate that shows no signs of abating (Cranfield, Bostock, Benson). What is at issue is a virginal conception, not a virgin birth, and so the technically correct term will be used in this section (Brown 1973).

In our discussion of the genre of the birth narratives we noted that any comparison of Matthew 1—2 and Luke 1—2 with pagan divine birth stories leads to the conclusion that the Gospel stories cannot be explained simply on the basis of such comparisons. This is particularly the case in regard to the matter of the virginal conception, for what we find in Matthew and Luke is not the story of some sort of sacred marriage or a divine being descending to earth and, in the guise of a man, mating with a human woman, but rather the story of a miraculous conception without aid of any man, divine or otherwise. The Gospel story is rather about how Mary conceived without any form of intercourse through the agency of the Holy Spirit. As such this story is without precedent either in Jewish or pagan literature, even including the OT (Machen).

It is doubtful that the idea of a virginal conception was part of Jewish messianic expecta-

tions in or before the era when the Gospels were written (McHugh). While it may be that Jewish infancy narratives influenced the Evangelists in some respects, they did not derive the idea of the virginal conception from those sources.

7.1. The Issue of Historicity. There are also serious problems for those who maintain that the virginal conception is a theological idea without basis in historical fact. It is difficult if not impossible to explain why Christians would create so many problems for themselves and invite the charge of Jesus' illegitimate birth by promulgating such an idea if it had no historical basis. The reality of the charge of illegitimacy was well known in the time of Origen, but it may have existed even in the time the Gospels were written (cf. Jn 8:41; Mk 6:3). It is also evident that Luke and the First Evangelist felt under some constraint to refer to the virginal conception, even to the point of awkwardly alluding to the concept in their genealogies.

One must also explain why this idea was accepted so widely by Christians in the early second century. Ignatius of Antioch is very matter of fact about the idea (Ign. *Smyrn.* 1:1). While it might be argued that at least in the case of Matthew he derived the idea from Isaiah 7:14, even this is unlikely. As we have already pointed out, neither the Hebrew *ʿalmâ* nor the Greek *parthenos* are simply technical terms for a *virgo intacta*, though certainly the terms may imply or even point to virginity in some cases. The point is that even in the LXX version of Isaiah 7:14 the text would not lead one to come up with such an idea, for it would normally be understood to mean that a young woman of marriageable age, who had previously never had a child, would conceive and give birth.

Furthermore, it is not certain that the virginal conception is known only to the First and Third Evangelists. Even if that were true, we would have two likely independent witnesses to the idea. That Paul uses *ginomai* rather than *gennaō* in Romans 1:3 may reflect knowledge of the virginal conception, as may several other Pauline texts (Gal 4:4; Phil 2:7; cf. Cranfield). It is also possible that John 1:13 and John 6:41-42 reflect knowledge of this idea. Perhaps more plausible is the conjecture that Mark 6:3 reflects a knowledge that Jesus was not physically the son of Joseph. Although calling a person a son of his mother is not without some precedent in the Bible (cf. 1 Chron 2:16), it is quite unusual and in a patriarchal culture may well have had a pejorative thrust (Russell). Whether or not this material outside the First and Third Gospels reflects knowledge of the virginal conception, few would dispute that we do have such an idea in Matthew and Luke (but cf. Bostock).

7.1.1. Matthew. Matthew 1:18-25 may be seen in part as an explanation of Matthew's genealogical statement about Jesus' birth through Mary in Matthew 1:16. But Matthew 1:18 immediately confronts us with an exegetical difficulty. In the phrase *prin ē syneithein* we find an expression of a limitation. The question is, does the phrase, which literally says "before they came together," mean "before they had marital union," or "before they married and cohabited"? The former would imply that Mary and Joseph consummated their marriage after the birth of Jesus; the latter translation does not necessarily connote sexual sharing.

Under normal circumstances in a Jewish setting it is difficult to imagine a Jew or Jewish Christian separating the idea of marriage and its physical consummation, but many scholars, mostly Catholic, will contend that we are not dealing with a normal state of affairs (Laurentin). The point of this verse, however, is to make clear that Joseph could in no way have been responsible for siring Jesus. Jesus is the result of God's creative act in Mary alone. It is interesting that the First Evangelist is interested in Joseph's conduct only until the birth, so that it may be seen that Jesus was born of a virgin as prophecy foretold.

More crucial for our purposes is Matthew 1:25. The textual problem at this point is not major. Only Codex Bobiensis and the Sinaitic Syriac omit the key clause *ouk eginōsken autēn heōs ou,* probably because certain scribes thought this clause might imply that Mary had other children by Joseph, or at least had sexual relations with him after the birth of Jesus. The verb "to know" is in the imperfect and thus implies the duration of time Joseph did not have sexual relations with Mary. The stress is on what was the case prior to the birth of Jesus, but the phrase "he used not to" or "he was not knowing her until" at least implies that the previously abstained from action later took place. Neither the grammatical nor lexical evidence supports the attempts to take *heōs* to mean something like "while" or "without" in the case of Matthew 1:25,

when it precedes an aorist indicative verb and follows an imperfect. The translation "while" is only possible with a verb in the subjunctive. The meaning of *heōs* without *ou* is not relevant here. Thus Mary's virginity *ante partum* is affirmed here, but her virginity *post partum* is likely ruled out.

The mention of Jesus' brothers and sisters (e.g., Mk 6:3), who are never called by the Greek word for cousins, would also militate against the possibility of a perpetual virginity. But this idea must in no way be confused with the concept of the virginal conception. Nor should the later Catholic idea of the immaculate conception of Mary by her mother, of which the Gospels know nothing, be confused with the virginal conception by Mary. The First Evangelist simply affirms the virginal conception as a result of the action of the Holy Spirit in Mary but does not go into any detail about the nature of this miracle in the same way Luke does.

7.1.2. Luke. The crux of the Lukan story is found in Luke 1:34-35, but it must be kept in mind that Luke has already told us at Luke 1:27 that Mary was a virgin. Scholars have generally distinguished Mary's "how" question from the "how" question of Zechariah in Luke 1:18. The latter seems to reflect doubt on Zechariah's part, while the former seems to be a request by Mary for explanation as to how the promised event will transpire. It is also true that "how" questions are characteristic of biblical annunciation stories and there is no doubt that our author has shaped this story in light of OT precedents. It is rarely disputed that *ginoskō* has a sexual connotation here, but the question is how to interpret the present tense—whether as "I have not known before now," "I do not know at present" or "I do not intend to know" (eternal present).

The problems with the theory that Mary here takes a vow to virginity are as follows. (1) Luke portrays Mary as reflecting the normal Jewish mindset concerning marriage and children (Lk 1:48). (2) Mary has already entered the process of Jewish marriage. (3) Jewish views of virginity in the relevant period do not support the idea that Jewish women who were engaged might take a vow to virginity. (4) Luke's audience could hardly have understood our text to mean this without additional information.

One should probably understand Mary's words to mean that she wondered how this conception would transpire in the immediate present or near future since she was still in the betrothal period and had not yet had sexual relations with Joseph. The response of the angel explains that Mary will conceive through the agency of the Holy Spirit. The second verb in Luke 1:35—*episkiazō*—likely has the meaning of "to overshadow" in the sense of protecting, especially if there is an allusion here to the Shekinah glory cloud of God's divine presence (Lk 9:34). This latter verb is not likely a reference to divine impregnation but rather divine protection during the encounter with the Holy Spirit that results in conception. It may be that Luke intends for us to see here the beginning of the eschatological reversal of the curse on Eve (Gen 3:16). In any case, one or both of these verbs refer to the virginal conception.

There is nothing in the narrative that follows Luke 1:34-35 to suggest that Mary had anything other than a normal pregnancy and delivery. Indeed, the story in Luke 2:22-40 about the trip to the temple so that Mary could perform the ceremony of purification in fulfillment of the law (Lev 12:8) suggests that Luke thought Mary had a normal delivery and required ritual cleansing. Luke tells us a bit more than Matthew about the process that resulted in the virginal conception, but both writers maintain a discreet silence about the details. They affirm the virginal conception and alter their respective genealogies accordingly (Lk 1:23; Mt 1:16), but they are mainly concerned with the fact that Messiah has come and the significance of the event. Only secondarily do they show interest in how his coming was made possible. Furthermore, neither Evangelist ever directly refers to the matter again once the story of the ministry begins. When all is said and done, it is easier to explain the Gospel evidence on the assumption that the virginal conception was a historical event that the Gospel writers tried to explain, rather than to assume it was a theologoumenon.

7.2. The Meaning of the Event. The significance of this event should not be minimized. It indicates not merely that Jesus was God's Son through the Holy Spirit (Brown 1973), but that Jesus was a unique person who was the product of both the divine and the human in a manner unlike any others before or since. To be sure, our two authors do not try to address the relationship of a virginal conception to the doctrine of the incarnation of a preexistent Son, but it may be that the author of John 1 later saw that the two concepts were connected (cf. Jn 1:13).

In terms of its theological significance, the virginal conception explains how the incarnation transpired, though Matthew and Luke do not speak of the event in terms of the incarnation of a preexistent being (Fuller). Later theological reflection was also to see in the virginal conception the explanation of how Jesus could be born with a human nature not tainted with original sin. The doctrine of the virginal conception also stresses that Jesus was fully human, participating in the whole human life cycle from womb to tomb.

But perhaps most significantly of all, this concept conveys the fact that Jesus is a miraculous gift to humanity, not initially the product of any normal human activity or process. He is a gift that comes ultimately from God, but he comes through Mary in a way that allows one to say that Jesus' origins are both human and divine. It is clear that if Jesus had indeed been illegitimate, it would hardly have been possible for Luke with any personal integrity to present Jesus' conception as a greater miracle than that of John the Baptist's (contra Hellwig), or for Matthew to see in Jesus' conception something so holy that a righteous man like Joseph could be persuaded to accept it and accept Jesus as his legal son and thus as a son of David.

Both narratives collapse without the assumption of a virginal conception. Furthermore, the arguments of both Evangelists about the theological significance of Jesus' origins are predicated on the assumption by both writers of the historical reality of the virginal conception. Otherwise there would be no need for the sort of apologetics and adjustments of genealogies that we find in these narratives.

8. The Magi and the Shepherds.

Though Christian tradition and art have frequently depicted both shepherds and magi visiting the newborn Jesus simultaneously, they are never associated or mentioned in the same breath within the Gospels. Luke betrays no hint of knowing about the magi, nor does the First Evangelist ever mention shepherds. We may deduce from this that the stories about these different participants came from separate sources.

8.1. The Magi. The traditions about the magi as we find them in Matthew do not refer to kings but rather to astrologers and/or wise men, and the text says nothing about there being three of them, nor are they named. The term *magi* comes to us by way of the Latin but ultimately goes back to the Greek *magos* and refers to a magician, sorcerer or one wise in interpreting the stars and/or dreams (hence the translation "wise men"). In ancient Media and Persia these magi were often associated with the priestly caste, and it has often been assumed in Christian tradition that these men came from Persia to find the Christ.

Other conjectures about the magi's origins have included various parts of Arabia, and it has even been speculated that they might have come from Asia Minor. This conjecture is based on the phrase "we saw his star in the east" (Mt 2:2); magi in Persia would presumably have seen his star in the west. Against the conjecture that the wise men came from Asia Minor it seems probable that *en tē anatolē* (Mt 2:2) means "at its rising," not "in the east," and Matthew 2:1 says specifically these magi are from the east.

The historicity of the magi has been frequently challenged, and it has been said that their story was composed out of such OT texts as Psalm 72:10-11, Isaiah 60:1-11 and the visit of the Queen of Sheba bearing gifts from Arabia for Solomon. It has even been suggested that the whole story is a midrash on 1 Kings 10. These conjectures in most cases originated because it has been thought that the story in itself was highly improbable. What Persian wise man would come to honor the birth of a Jewish peasant?

But these objections overlook the well-documented intense interest by ancient astrologers in Persia and elsewhere in the connection between astral phenomena and political events and the fact that in A.D. 66 the eastern astrologer Tiridates and other magi visited Rome (cf. Dio Cassius 63.7; Suetonius *Nero* 13). It was also widely believed during this era that stars heralded the birth of human beings destined for greatness (Brown 1977), and in fact Suetonius and Tacitus tell us that at the turn of the era there was an expectation of a world ruler who would come from Judea (Suetonius *Vesp.* 4; Tacitus *Ann.* 5.13). Furthermore, the gifts brought by the magi are regularly mentioned in ancient sources as valuable products of Arabia and other eastern countries. There is nothing inherently improbable about the story, though doubtless the First Evangelist has shaped his source material to bring out the points he wishes to stress.

Finally, the view that the story is a midrash

on various OT texts fails to explain certain salient features in the text. Psalm 72:10-11 and Isaiah 60:1-11 are about kings, not magi, even if later Christian tradition wrongly identified the magi as kings, and 1 Kings 10 is about a singular queen, not about stargazers. As we noted in our discussion of genre, midrash is not a very apt description of Matthew's narrative material even after he has edited his sources, but it may be useful to describe how he handles his scriptural quotations and fits them into his source material (France).

The point of including the story about the wise men in Matthew's Gospel is probably to show how wise men, even Gentile wise men, sought Jesus out, while a Jewish king who should have known the OT prophecies neither personally sought out nor properly honored the new son of David. Indeed, this story may be part of Matthew's larger agenda of showing how Jesus' people largely rejected him.

8.2. The Shepherds. Due to their trade, the shepherds would have been viewed as unclean peasants in various Jewish circles. They present fewer historical difficulties to the interpreter than do the magi. In Luke's schema they represent the sort of simple and marginalized people for whom the birth of a liberating Messiah would be good news indeed (Lk 1:52; 4:18). Historically there is nothing improbable about finding shepherds in the vicinity of Bethlehem. Though it could be argued that Luke has created this scene out of such OT texts as 1 Samuel 16—17, this seems unlikely because there is no attempt here to portray Jesus as some sort of Davidic shepherd. He is seen rather as the world savior whom even the humble poor recognize. The suggestion that Luke created this scene bearing in mind the tower of the flock (mentioned in Gen 35:21 and Mic 4:8) and later traditions associating the coming of Messiah with that tower is also unlikely.

9. Canonical Information About Jesus' Childhood.

Though later apocryphal documents like the *Infancy Gospel of Thomas* have a good deal to say about the so-called hidden years of Jesus, these documents amount to little more than pious fiction and are generally recognized to be of little or no historical worth. In the Gospels themselves there is only one story about what Jesus was like between infancy and adulthood—Luke 2:41-52.

This story has historical value not least because it appears to reflect badly on Jesus' parents, that is, they do not adequately understand him (Lk 2:50). In view of the increasingly reverential portrait Christians painted of the Holy Family, it is unlikely that Luke invented this material. In particular, Mary, who is portrayed as a potential disciple in Luke 1—2, is shown to lack full understanding of Jesus and his actions (Lk 1:29, 34; 2:33), though like a good disciple she is reflecting on what she does not understand (Lk 2:50-51). Neither here nor earlier does Luke paint an idealized picture of Mary; he shows both her faith and her lack of understanding. These and other factors lead one to doubt that this story should be viewed as essentially legendary in character.

In terms of literary form, this is a pronouncement story (McHugh), and given that it has a less Semitic style and in fact has thirteen Lukanisms, it appears to have come from a different source than Luke's other birth narrative material. It may be that Luke composed this story himself on the basis of oral material. The story has no miraculous content that might raise historical difficulties, and a trip to the temple by a young man shortly before he came of age was customary as part of a Jewish father's obligation to acquaint his son with his religious duties. Nor is there anything improbable about Jesus' family traveling some distance from Jerusalem and expecting Jesus to be among the other pilgrims, some of whom would likely have been relatives or fellow residents from Nazareth or the surrounding area. It was customary for Galileans to go up to Jerusalem in rather large parties during the high feast days, not least because of concerns about safety along the roads (Lk 10:30). The story in itself has marks of authenticity since it is about Jesus beginning to disengage from parental authority and following the will of his heavenly Father alone, a motif we find in other authentic Gospel material (Witherington 1984). It may even be that in Luke 2:19 and Luke 2:51 Luke is indicating his source for this information (Brown 1977).

Here as elsewhere in Luke 1—2, Mary is in the foreground and Joseph in the background. Luke 2:41-52 is in some respects rather like John 2:1-12 because the story ends by Jesus doing what Mary wants, without verbally indicating that he would do so. The tensions between the claims of physical and spiritual allegiance are evident when Mary speaks of Jesus' father (Joseph) and Jesus replies in terms of his actual Father (God).

Jesus is portrayed as a sort of child prodigy here, but Luke also wishes to indicate that Jesus grew and matured like other children (Lk 2:52). He grew intellectually (wisdom), physically (stature) and spiritually (the grace of God). From this singular story we may gather that Jesus' childhood was in many respects like that of other children of devout parents—it was a period of growth, development and learning. In particular, it was a period of learning about one's faith, and as a youth a time for sorting out God's will from his parents' wishes. Absent in this story are any traces of Jesus the child miracle worker, which the authors of the apocryphal Gospels liked to stress. Instead, the one truly remarkable aspect about Jesus in this story is what he knows of God, of his Word and of his will—a knowledge that astounded teachers and parents.

See also CHRISTOLOGY; GOSPELS, HISTORICAL RELIABILITY OF; LUKE, GOSPEL OF; MATTHEW, GOSPEL OF.

DJG: GENEALOGY; MARY'S SONG; SIMEON'S SONG; ZECHARIAH'S SONG.

BIBLIOGRAPHY. J. C. Anderson, "Mary's Difference: Gender and Patriarchy in the Birth Narratives," *JR* 67 (1987) 183-202; K. E. Bailey, "The Manger and the Inn: The Cultural Background of Luke 2:7," *TheolRev* 2 (2, 1979) 33-44; G. P. Benson, "Virgin Birth, Virgin Conception," *ExpT* 98 (1987) 139-40; P. M. Bernegger, "Affirmation of Herod's Death in 4 B.C.," *JTS* n.s. 34 (1983) 526-31; K. Boa and W. Proctor, *The Return of the Star of Bethlehem* (Garden City, NY: Doubleday, 1980); G. Bostock, "Divine Birth, Human Conception," *ExpT* 98 (1987) 331-33; idem, "Virgin Birth or Human Conception?" *ExpT* 97 (1986) 260-63; M. M. Bourke, "The Literary Genus of Matthew 1—2," *CBQ* 22 (1960) 160-75; R. E. Brown, *The Birth of the Messiah* (New York: Doubleday, 1993); idem, "Gospel Infancy Narrative Research from 1976 to 1986: Part 1 (Matthew)," *CBQ* 48 (1986) 468-83, and "Part 2 (Luke)," *CBQ* 48 (1986) 660-73; idem, *The Virginal Conception and Bodily Resurrection of Jesus* (New York: Paulist, 1973); R. E. Brown et al., eds., *Mary in the New Testament* (Philadelphia: Fortress, 1978); J. Carmignac, "The Meaning of *Parthenos* in Luke 1.24: A Reply to C. H. Dodd," *BT* 28 (3, 1977) 324-30; C. E. B. Cranfield, "Some Reflections on the Subject of the Virgin Birth," *SJT* 41 (1988) 177-89; C. H. Dodd, "New Testament Translation Problems 1," *BT* 27 (1976) 301-11; O. Edmonds, "Herodian Chronology," *PEQ* (1982) 29-42; S. C. Farris, "On Discerning Semitic Sources in Luke 1—2," in *Gospel Perspectives 2: Studies of History and Tradition in the Four Gospels,* ed. R. T. France and D. Wenham (Sheffield: JSOT, 1981) 201-37; A. Feuillet, *Jesus and His Mother According to the Lukan Infancy Narratives* (Still River, MA: St. Bede's, 1984); E. S. Fiorenza, "Luke 2:41-52," *Int* 36 (1982) 399-403; R. T. France, "Scripture, Tradition and History in the Infancy Narratives of Matthew," in *Gospel Perspectives, 2: Studies of History and Tradition in the Four Gospels,* ed. R. T. France and D. Wenham (Sheffield: JSOT, 1981) 201-37; R. H. Gundry, *Matthew: A Commentary on His Literary and Theological Art* (Grand Rapids: Eerdmans, 1982); idem, *The Use of the Old Testament in St. Matthew's Gospel* (NovTSup 18; Leiden: E. J. Brill, 1967); M. K. Helwig, "The Dogmatic Implications of the Birth of the Messiah," *Emmanuel* 84 (1978) 21-4; H. Hendrickx, *The Infancy Narratives* (London: Geoffrey Chapman, 1984); H. W. Hoehner, *Chronological Aspects of the Life of Christ* (Grand Rapids: Zondervan, 1977); M. D. Johnson, *The Purpose of the Biblical Genealogies, with Special Reference to the Setting of the Genealogies of Jesus* (SNTSMS 8; Cambridge: Cambridge University Press, 1969); R. Laurentin, *The Truth of Christmas Beyond the Myths* (Petersham, MA: St. Bede's, 1986); J. G. Machen, *The Virgin Birth of Christ* (Grand Rapids: Baker, 1930); E. L. Martin, *The Birth of Christ Recalculated* (2d ed.; Pasadena, CA: Foundation for Biblical Research, 1980); J. McHugh, *The Mother of Jesus in the New Testament* (London: Darton, Longman & Todd, 1975); J. P. Meier, *A Marginal Jew: Rethinking the Historical Jesus,* vol. 1 (New York: Doubleday, 1991) 205-52; P. Minear, "Luke's Use of the Birth Stories," in *Studies in Luke-Acts,* ed. L. E. Keck and J. L. Martyn (London: SPCK, 1968) 111-30; R. P. Nettlehorst, "The Genealogy of Jesus," *JETS* 31 (1988) 169-72; J. K. Russell, " 'The Son of Mary' (Mark 6:3)," *ExpT* 60 (1948-49) 195; J. Schaberg, *The Illegitimacy of Jesus* (San Francisco: Harper and Row, 1985); A. N. Sherwin-White, *Roman Society and Roman Law in the New Testament* (Grand Rapids: Baker, repr. 1978); K. Stendahl, *"Quis et Unde? An Analysis of Mt 1—2,"* in *Judentum Urchris tentum Kirche, Festschrift fur Joachim Jeremias,* ed. W. Eltester (ZNW Beihefte 26; Berlin: Alfred Topelmann, 1960) 94-105; J. Thorley, "When Was Jesus Born?" *Greece and Rome* n.s. 28 (1981) 81-9; G. J. Wenham, "Betulah, 'A Girl of Marriageable Age,' " *VT* 22 (1972) 326-48; B. Witherington, *Women in the Earliest Churches* (SNTSMS 59; Cambridge: Cambridge University Press, 1988); idem, *Women in the Ministry of Jesus* (SNTSMS 51; Cambridge: Cambridge University Press, 1984).

B. Witherington III

BLASPHEMY. *See* TRIAL OF JESUS.

BODY OF CHRIST: PAUL

The Pauline writings use the exact phrase "the body of Christ" only four times (*to sōma tou Christou,* Rom 7:4; 1 Cor 10:16; Eph 4:12; *sōma Christou,* 1 Cor 12:27). Equivalent expressions include "the body of the Lord" (1 Cor 11:27), "his body of flesh" (Col 1:22), "his glorious body" (Phil 3:21), "his body" (Eph 1:23; 5:30; Col 1:24) and "my body" (1 Cor 11:24). Closely related to the above are the terms "the body" (1 Cor 11:29; Eph 5:23; Col 1:18; 2:19) and "one body" (Rom 12:5; 1 Cor 10:17; 12:13; Eph 2:16; 4:4; Col 3:15). These twenty-one phrases may be classified into the three uses set out in the following outline; significantly, however, they all relate to either the physical body (crucified or resurrected) of Christ or the metaphorical body of Christ, the church.

1. The Physical Body of Christ
2. The Body of Christ in Eucharistic Contexts
3. The Body of Christ as a Designation of the Church

1. The Physical Body of Christ.
In Romans 7:4 "the body of Christ," which is the instrument through which believers were rendered dead to and hence free from the law, refers to Christ's physical body in which he suffered death on the cross. Similarly, "his body of flesh" in Colossians 1:22 is a Hebraism (with Qumran parallels) denoting Christ's physical body, which in death became the means by which God reconciled sinners to himself: the addition "of flesh" insists, against the *Colossian heresy, on the true humanity of the incarnate Jesus. In Philippians 3:21 "his glorious body" stands in antithetical parallelism to "our lowly body" and refers to the resurrection body with which and in which the Lord Jesus is expected to return from heaven (cf. Phil 3:20).

2. The Body of Christ in Eucharistic Contexts.

Several times in 1 Corinthians the body concept appears in close conjunction with the Eucharist, or *Lord's Supper; the texts reveal a close relationship between the physical body of Christ that was crucified and the church as the body of the risen Christ.

Thus partaking of the cup and the bread in the Eucharist means participation in the blood and the body of Christ (1 Cor 10:16), that is, in the benefits of his death and in fellowship with him. The strict parallelism between "the body of Christ" and "the blood of Christ" shows that the former refers to the body of Jesus surrendered in death (cf. 1 Cor 11:24) just as the latter refers to his blood shed as atoning blood (cf. 1 Cor 11:25; see Jeremias). Just as there is only one loaf at the Eucharist, so those who participate jointly in the single loaf constitute a single body (1 Cor 10:17). The context, with its exhortation to shun the worship of idols (1 Cor 10:14), suggests that Paul's point in making use of the body analogy in 1 Corinthians 10:16-17 is not so much the unity of the body made up of Christians as their solidarity as one body in union with Christ which forbids a similar union with demons (cf. 1 Cor 10:21). This, in turn, implies that the "one body" of 1 Corinthians 10:17 refers to the body of Christ, the church.

A similar shift of meaning from the crucified body of Christ to the church as the body of Christ occurs in 1 Corinthians 11:23-32. The bread at the institution of the Lord's Supper signifies or represents Christ's actual body about to be offered up on the cross (1 Cor 11:24). It follows that to eat the bread in an unworthy manner is to be guilty of "the body . . . of the Lord" (1 Cor 11:27); that this phrase refers to the crucified body of Jesus is rendered certain by its linkage (cf. 1 Cor 10:16) with "the blood [of the Lord]." But in 1 Corinthians 11:29 the expression "not discerning the body" is probably a reference not to failure to discern in the bread of the Eucharist the body of the Lord surrendered on the cross (cf. 1 Cor 11:24, 27) but the failure to recognize in the group of believers gathered at the Lord's Supper the metaphorical body of Christ (cf. 1 Cor 10:17). This failure resulted in the shameful abuses described in 1 Corinthians 11:17-22 (Bornkamm, 190-95).

3. The Body of Christ as a Designation of the Church.

This particular use of the body concept, of which two instances have already been referred to (1 Cor 10:17; 11:29), is unique to Paul in the NT writings. The issues of the origin and nature of the concept will be addressed before examining its usage in the remaining Pauline texts.

3.1. The Origin of the Concept. There have been many suggestions regarding the possible sources of Paul's "body of Christ" idea. (1) The previously fashionable attempt to trace it to the Gnostic concept of the primal person, whose body was conceived of as cosmic (e.g., Bultmann, Käsemann), is generally discarded today because of the lateness (third century A.D.) of the evidence. (2) That the temple of Asclepius in Corinth, with its votive offerings in the form of clay representations of dismembered parts of the body that have been healed, provided the catalyst for the formation of the Pauline image (Hill) is surely farfetched. (3) That Paul's phrase "body of Christ" was constructed on the analogy of the phrase "body of Adam" allegedly implicit in rabbinic usage (see Davies), or at least was probably influenced by the Jewish "body of Adam" idea (Jewett) appears doubtful, since no examples of the phrase "body of Adam" in rabbinical literature are forthcoming, and it is admitted that "the Jewish body of Adam idea does not provide us with an exact parallel to Paul's *sōma Christou* [body of Christ] concept" (Jewett, 245). (4) The view (Rawlinson, Conzelmann) that Paul derived his expression "body of Christ" from the eucharistic tradition—the sacramentally acquired share in the body of Christ in the Eucharist makes the participants the body of Christ—faces the simple objection that "*eating* the body is not *being* the body" (Moule, 87). (5) The suggestion that Paul, from the concept of Israel as the bride of God (Jer 2:2) and through new-covenant theology (*see* Covenant, New Covenant), developed the concept of "the body of Christ" as its parallel for the new Israel, the church (Bass, 530-31), is not very likely, since the more logical line of development is from Israel as the bride of Yahweh to the church as the bride of Christ. (6) The statement that Genesis 2:24—"a man leaves his father and his mother and clings to his wife, and they become one flesh" (quoted in Eph 5:31)—"appears to provide the biblical rationale and the conceptual foundation for the Apostle's understanding, throughout his letters, of the church as the body of Christ" (Ellis, 42) calls to mind C. Chavasse's attempt to locate the origin of the Pauline phrase in the nuptial union of bridegroom and bride in the "one flesh." But F. F. Bruce thinks that "both the eucharistic . . . and the nuptial . . . applications of Paul's thought on this subject are derived from his conception of the church as the body of Christ rather than *vice versa*" (Bruce 1984, 69 n.141).

Rather than being attributable to a single source, the body of Christ concept is more likely the result of the interplay of several influences.

(1) The comparison of the state *(polis)* or world-state *(cosmopolis)* to a body consisting of interdependent members is a Stoic commonplace, and, as C. F. D. Moule (84-85) points out, close parallels to the Pauline use of the analogy are provided, for instance, by Seneca, who addresses Nero as "the soul of the republic [which] is your body" (Seneca *De Clem.* 1.5.1). He also speaks of Nero as the head, on whom the good health of the body, the empire, depends (Seneca *De Clem.* 2.2.1), and says, "We are limbs of a great body" (Seneca *Ep. Mor.* 95.52). Philo, with a change of context, says that the high priest's purpose in offering sacrifice for the nation is "that every age[-group] and all the parts of the nation may be welded into one and the same family as though it were a single body" (Philo *Spec. Leg.* 3.131).

(2) Paul was familiar with the Hebrew concept of "corporate personality," with its oscillation between the individual and the corporate and its notion of the inclusion of the many in the one: a figure standing at the head (e.g., *Adam, *Abraham, Noah, Moses) can be regarded as incorporating in his person those represented by him. It is this idea of solidarity between the one and the many, of the union between believers and Christ, that Paul emphasizes in his presentation of the church as the body of Christ. The analogy between all men and women by natural birth being "in Adam" and all believers by new birth being *"in Christ" (Rom 5:12-21; 1 Cor 15:22, 45) is an important datum of Pauline theology.

(3) The idea of solidarity between Christ and his people finds expression in the teaching of Jesus (Mk 9:37 and par.; cf. Mt 18:5; 25:40), and is clearly implied in the risen Lord's identification of himself with his persecuted people (Acts 9:4). While it is probably impossible to be certain about the precise origin(s) of the Pauline expression, it may be that it was Paul's coinage, based on the common image of the body in pop-

ular philosophy and the Hebrew concept of corporate personality, with the words of the risen Jesus to Paul on the Damascus Road providing the germ of the conception in his mind or the catalyst for the formation of the unique Pauline expression (see Kim, 252-56).

3.2. The Nature of the Concept. The body of Christ concept is plainly not used allegorically: in 1 Corinthians 12, for instance, different parts of the body do not represent different individuals or sections of the Corinthian church. It has been said that the phrase "the body of Christ" (meaning the church) "is used realistically, ontologically, and *therefore* metaphorically or symbolically or analogically" (Richardson, 256-57 n.1), but it is more usual to describe its use as either realistic/ontological or analogical/metaphorical. The realistic understanding of the expression, espoused by such scholars as A. Schweitzer, who thought of the elect as coming into corporeal union with the risen Christ, and J. A. T. Robinson, for whom the church is identified as literally the resurrected body of Christ, violates the clear indication of a comparison given in Romans 12:4-5 and 1 Corinthians 12:12 ("just as . . . so") and, besides, ignores Paul's careful distinction between Christ's resurrection in the past and believers' (yet awaited) resurrection in the future. We may, therefore, with most recent Protestant interpreters, understand the body concept metaphorically, not literally and biologically or mystically.

3.3. The Concept in Paul's Usage. Two stages may be distinguished in Paul's use of the body concept in reference to the *church: it is used largely as a simile in 1 Corinthians and Romans (the church is like a body), and as a metaphor in Colossians and Ephesians (the church is the body of which Christ is the head). "The advance from the language of simile in 1 Corinthians and Romans to the real interpersonal involvement expressed in the language of Colossians and Ephesians may have been stimulated by Paul's consideration of the issues involved in the Colossian heresy" (Bruce 1977, 421).

3.3.1. Earlier Letters: 1 Corinthians and Romans. In 1 Corinthians 6:15 the bodies of believers are said to be "members of Christ"; the word *members (melē)* means "bodily parts" and thus implies that believers are members of the "body" of Christ. However, Paul immediately goes on to speak of his own body as "members [plural] of Christ," which he will not turn into "members [plural] of a prostitute." This shows that here his concern is with the individual believer's relationship with the Lord, and there is no reference to believers as a corporate body.

Later in the letter Paul says to the local congregation at Corinth: "You are the body of Christ" (1 Cor 12:27; the Greek phrase has no article before either "body" or "Christ," but it means the same as if both nouns had the article—this is an instance of the grammatical rule known as "Apollonius's canon"). This metaphor comes as the summary and climax of the preceding fifteen verses (1 Cor 12:12-26), in which the character of the body concept as simile is plainly indicated by the opening statement: "For just as [kathaper] the body is one and has many members, . . . so [houtōs] also is Christ" (1 Cor 12:12; cf. NEB, "For Christ is *like* a single body" [italics added]). Since Paul does not say "so also is the church" or even "the body of Christ" but simply "(the) Christ," some interpreters have derived from this a view of Christ as the whole, of which the various members are parts; but in view of 1 Corinthians 12:27-28 it seems better to regard Paul here as using the figure of metonymy ("Christ" for "the body of Christ") or as having omitted the intermediate logical step: Christ himself may be described as a body with many members since the church is the body of Christ.

Into this one body believers—here the "we all" *(hēmeis pantes)* seems to refer to a wider group than the "you" *(hymeis)* of verse 27 and could include all Christians—are baptized in the one Spirit (1 Cor 12:13; the baptizer being, presumably, Christ: cf. Mt 3:11; Lk 3:16; *see* Holy Spirit). Within this one body there is, by God's design (1 Cor 12:18), a multiplicity of members and functions (1 Cor 12:14-16) that is necessary not only for the body as a whole (1 Cor 12:17, 19-20) but also for the members (1 Cor 12:21), all of whom are involved in a solidarity of experience or unity of destiny (1 Cor 12:26). Hence, resentment born of a sense of inferiority (1 Cor 12:15-16) and arrogance arising from a sense of superiority (1 Cor 12:21) are alike out of place. Indeed, the so-called weaker members of the human body are actually indispensable (1 Cor 12:22), and there is at work in the human body, again by God's design (1 Cor 12:24), a certain principle of compensation or complementarity that, Paul implies, provides a pattern for Christian conduct (1 Cor 12:23-25).

The same correlatives as are used in 1 Corin-

thians 12:12 appear also in Romans 12:4-5: "For as [kathaper] in one body we have many members, . . . so [houtōs] we, though many, are one body in Christ" (RSV). As in 1 Corinthians 12:27, the body simile is applied to the local Christian congregation, with a change in terminology from "the body of Christ" to "one body . . . in Christ"; the latter expression brings out the thought that the organic unity of Christians as a body is grounded in their common incorporation in Christ, but since these two verses in Romans 12 may reasonably be regarded as a summary of the fuller treatment of 1 Corinthians 12:12-26, "one body . . . in Christ" refers to the same reality as "the body of Christ."

In 1 Corinthians 12 and Romans 12, the theme of the body imagery is that of "one body, many members," of "diversity within unity" of the church as the body of Christ. So far, the body imagery emphasizes primarily the mutual relationships and obligations of believers one to another and secondarily their union with Christ, but the imagery leaves undefined the exact relation of the church as the body of Christ to Christ: the "head" of the body is in 1 Corinthians 12:21 apparently some self-important member of the local church.

3.3.2. Later Letters: Colossians and Ephesians. Despite appearances, the final words of Colossians 2:17 in the Greek *(to de sōma tou Christou)* is not a reference to "the body of Christ," but means "the *substance* [in contrast to the shadow] belongs to Christ." In Colossians 3:15 the believers in Colossae are described as having been called "in one body": they are thus members of a single organism. If, possibly by implication, this organism is identified with the body of Christ, then the same emphasis on the unity of the body of Christ is found here as in the two earlier letters. In Colossians 1:24 the body of Christ is definitely identified as the church, clearly in an "ecumenical" sense, for whose sake the apostle suffers. Colossians 1:18 calls Christ "the head of the body, the church."

The majority view believes (1) that Colossians 1:15-20 is a pre-Pauline hymn that has been inserted into the letter's train of thought, (2) that in it the "body" whose "head" is Christ is originally the universe or cosmos, and (3) that the words "the church" in Colossians 1:18 are a gloss added by either Paul or the final redactor of the letter so as to reinterpret the original cosmological reference along ecclesiological lines (e.g., Schweizer, 1074-77). This view has, however, been challenged (see, e.g., O'Brien 1982, 48-49), and the verse (Col 1:18) may be understood simply as it stands, with the result that the church as the body of Christ is now definitely related to Christ as its head. Although a few scholars (most notably Ridderbos, 379-83) have argued that "head" and "body" in this and other Pauline texts do not make up a composite metaphor but are to be kept distinct as two independent images, the more natural reading of the present text seems clearly to teach an organic relationship in which Christ as the head exercises control and direction over his body, the church.

In Colossians 2:19 the metaphor brings out the new element of growth: Christ as the head of the body is here the source of the body's growth (*ex hou*, "from whom [Christ]," rather than *ex hēs*, "from which [head]," is probably an instance of construction according to sense). The idea which follows of the whole body being knit together and growing together is appropriate in view of the fact that headship involves direction and control. W. A. Grudem has adduced several texts from Philo and Plutarch as well as Plato that explicitly say that the head is the ruling or governing part of the body.

Thus in Colossians the use of the body metaphor differs from that in the earlier letters in that the explicit application to the believers' mutual relationship is dropped—although the notion of their harmonious union and functioning is implied in the description of Colossians 2:19—and in its place are introduced the headship of Christ and the growth of the church as a living organism.

Whereas in the three letters already dealt with the term *body* is used in other ways as well, in Ephesians it is employed exclusively in connection with the church. Here the metaphor is even more fully developed than in Colossians, or at least its implications are more explicitly drawn out. In Ephesians 1:22-23 the church is designated the body of Christ, and Christ its "supreme head" (NEB). The text introduces the entirely new element of Christ's filling his body just as he fills the universe. (We take the noun *plērōma*, "fullness," passively and the participle *plēroumenou* as middle, "filling," rather than passive, "being filled"; cf. Eph 4:10.) In Ephesians 2:16 the "one body" within which both the reconciliation of Jew (*see* Israel) and Gentile to God and the reconciliation of Jews and Gentiles to

one another take place is a reference to the church (same as the "one new person" of Eph 2:15) rather than the crucified body of Christ. In favor of this conclusion are the use of "one body" and not "his body," and the order of the words *[the] both in one body (tous amphoterous en heni sōmati)*. The reference here to the unity of the body, not in terms of individuals, but in terms of the two great divisions of humankind (cf. Eph 3:6, which uses a cognate adjective, *syssōmos*, "concorporate, sharing in the same body"), again presents a new aspect to the use of the body metaphor, but the "one body" is not specifically called the body "of Christ." Similarly, in Ephesians 4:4 the "one body" vitalized by the "one Spirit" (who in Eph 2:18 creates the unity of the "one body" of Jewish and Gentile believers), is separate from the "one Lord" of Ephesians 4:5 and is simply a description of the Christian community as a unity. This unity of the body supplies the motivation for keeping the unity of the Spirit (Eph 4:3).

In Ephesians 4:12-16, where the church is again (cf. Eph 1:22-23) designated the body of Christ (Eph 1:22), the unity of the church is again (as already in Eph 4:4, and in Rom 12 and 1 Cor 12) described in terms of individual members, and their mutual dependence is seen to be necessary for the growth of the body, which is said to be both from Christ (Eph 4:16: *ex hou*, "from whom," as in Col 2:19) and to Christ (Eph 4:15: *eis auton*, "unto him"). The meaning appears to be that the growth of the body, which aims at conformity to Christ (cf. Eph 4:13), takes place as (1) the body is rightly related to the head, holding fast to him (cf. Col 2:19) and receiving nourishment from him (cf. Eph 1:23); and as (2) its members are rightly related to one another, each making its own contribution, according to the measure of its gift and function, to the upbuilding of the whole in love. An alternative view, which regards the participles, rendered in the RSV as "joined and knit together," in Ephesians 4:16 as indicating not the mutual relationship among believers but the relationship between believers on the one hand and Christ on the other, is less probable. Nor is it likely that the "joints" of Ephesians 4:16 refer to the ministers of Ephesians 4:11, the thought being that they are the ligaments which bind the church to Christ (as argued for by Lincoln, ad loc.).

In Ephesians 4:25 the fact that believers are "members one of another" (cf. Rom 12:5), meaning "fellow members in the one body which is the body of Christ," provides the motivation for honest dealings one with another. In Ephesians 5:23 the actual wording of the Greek describes Christ as "head of the church" and "the Savior of the body" (NEB) and not exactly as "the head of his body, the church" or even "the head of the church, his body" (RSV, NIV), so that it might be argued that here, at least, "head" and "body" do not make up one composite imagery. However, the fact that in Ephesians 5:30 believers are said to be "members of his body" suggests that in Ephesians 5:23 as well, the description of Christ as "the head of the church" involves the correlative figure of the church as his body (cf. Eph 1:22-23; 4:15-16), even though there is no corresponding correlative in the husband-wife relationship.

Thus the body metaphor in Ephesians combines the earlier expressions of the concept in the other three letters and advances beyond them in presenting the church as filled by Christ and as embracing Jew and Gentile in its unity. Another especially noteworthy feature of the use of the body metaphor in Ephesians is its fusion with other metaphors of the church. The building of the temple grows (Eph 2:21) while, conversely, the body is built up (Eph 4:16, cf. 4:12). In Ephesians 5:22-33, with the concept of bodily union providing the link (Gen 2:24; Eph 5:31), the figure of the church as the bride of Christ is supplemented by that of the body. The twin aspects of Christ's lordship over the church and his union with it, which are connected with the body concept, are made to serve the interests of illustrating and emphasizing (1) the church's obligation to Christ (the wife [cf. the church as the body] is to be subject to the husband [cf. Christ as the head]) and (2) Christ's love for the church (the husband is to love the wife as his own body, as Christ [the head] loved the church [his body]).

3.3.3. Summary and Conclusion. By way of summary and conclusion the following statements may be derived from Paul's use of the concept of the body of Christ as a designation of the church.

(1) The figure of the body of Christ is applied by Paul to a local congregation (1 Cor 12:27), to Christians who were not necessarily members of the same congregation (Rom 12:4-5; cf. 16:3-15), as well as to a wider group possibly inclusive of all believers in Christ (1 Cor 12:12-13). That Christ, the head of the body, is the exalted,

heavenly Lord is beyond doubt (Eph 1:20-21), but to argue that in Colossians and Ephesians "the 'body' image is used to denote *a heavenly entity,*" since his body the church is also where he is, in heaven (O'Brien 1987, 112, 110; but *see* Church), is to forget the nature of the body of Christ concept as metaphor. When believers are said to be raised and seated in the heavenlies with Christ (Col 3:1; Eph 2:6), this is not done in conjunction with the body image.

(2) The church as the body of Christ is a living organic unity composed of a multiplicity of members (i.e., individual believers, not individual congregations), each necessary to the other and to the growth of the whole (1 Cor 10:16-17; 12:12-27; Rom 12:4-5; Col 1:24; 3:15; Eph 4:16). The unity, from another angle, is a unity between diverse races of the world (Eph 2:16-18).

(3) This horizontal dimension of unity is based on the vertical unity between the church as the body of Christ and Christ as the head of the church. The church, in terms of its members, enters into union with Christ by baptism in the one Spirit (1 Cor 12:13; cf. Eph 2:18) and maintains it by participation in the Eucharist (1 Cor 10:16-17), so that the source of the church's unity is Christ and the Spirit (cf. Eph 4:4, 5).

(4) Christ as the head is not only united with the church, his body, as the source of its life, but also stands over it as its absolute ruler (Col 1:18; Eph 1:22-23; 4:15; 5:23) and fills it with all the resources of his power and grace (Eph 1:23).

(5) The church grows as its members are properly related to Christ the head and to one another as members of the same body (Col 2:19; Eph 4:16).

(6) The mingling of metaphors may indicate that no one metaphor is sufficient by itself to convey the total message concerning the nature and function of the church. Nevertheless, there can be little reasonable doubt that the picture of the body of Christ, more than any other, represents Paul's most mature reflections on the subject. As it has been maintained elsewhere, it is with this particular conception of the church that Paul's charisma (*see* Gifts of the Spirit) concept is in perfect correspondence, and it is in terms of this particular conception that the Pauline doctrine of the ministry is largely to be understood (see Fung, esp. 15-20).

(7) The image of the church as the body of Christ looks inward (to the mutual relationship of believers as members of the body) and up-

ward (to the relationship between the body and its head) but not outward (to the relationship between the church and the world). The view that Paul regarded the church as an extension of the incarnation in the world is surely excluded by the very fact that the body metaphor maintains a clear distinction between Christ as head and the church as body; such a view also ignores the fundamental difference between Christ as sinless and the church as not yet perfect.

(8) The body of Christ is usually the locus of the Christian ministry. The gift of evangelism, indeed, is orientated toward outsiders, and the work of "showing mercy" (Rom 12:8) is a service that reaches beyond the confines of the Christian fellowship. But there can be no denying that Paul's emphasis in speaking of the ministry rests on how the ministry should serve the church and not on how it should serve the world, and that the stated purpose of the church's being equipped by the ministry is not that it may serve the world but that it may upbuild itself (Eph 4:12, 16). By and large it may be said that for Paul, "ministry is of the body, for the body, and by the body" (Ellis, 14).

See also ADAM AND CHRIST; CHURCH; IN CHRIST.

DPL: BODY; FULLNESS; GIFTS OF THE SPIRIT.

BIBLIOGRAPHY. C. B. Bass, "Body," *ISBE* 1:528-31; E. Best, *One Body in Christ* (London: SPCK, 1955); G. Bornkamm, *The Epistles to the Colossians, to Philemon and to the Ephesians* (NICNT; Grand Rapids: Eerdmans, 1984); idem, *Paul* (New York: Harper & Row, 1971); F. F. Bruce, *Paul: Apostle of the Heart Set Free* (Grand Rapids: Eerdmans, 1977); R. Bultmann, *New Testament Theology* (2 vols.; New York: Charles Scribner's, 1951, 1955) 2:151-52; C. Chavasse, *The Bride of Christ* (London: Faber, 1940); H. Conzelmann, *1 Corinthians* (Herm; Philadelphia: Fortress, 1975); W. D. Davies, *Paul and Rabbinic Judaism* (4th ed.; Philadelphia: Fortress, 1980) 56-57; J. D. G. Dunn, " 'The Body of Christ' in Paul," in *Worship, Theology and Ministry in the Early Church,* ed. M. J. Wilkins and T. Paige (JSNT-Sup 87; Sheffield: JSOT, 1992) 146-62; E. E. Ellis, *Pauline Theology: Ministry and Society* (Grand Rapids: Eerdmans, 1989); R. Y. K. Fung, "Ministry, Community and Spiritual Gifts," *EvQ* 56 (1984) 3-20; W. A. Grudem, "The Meaning of *Kephalē* ('Head'): A Response to Recent Studies," *TJ* 11 NS (1990) 3-72; R. H. Gundry, *Sōma in Biblical Theology* (SNTSMS 29; Cambridge: Cambridge University Press, 1976); A. E. Hill, "The Temple of Asclepius: An Alternative Source for Paul's Body Theology," *JBL* 99 (1980) 437-39; J. Jeremias, *The Eucharistic Words of Jesus* (New York: Charles Scribner's, 1966); R. Jewett, *Paul's Anthropological Terms* (AGJU 10; Leiden: E. J. Brill, 1971); E. Käsemann, "The Theological Problem Presented by the Motif of the Body of Christ," in *Perspectives on Paul* (Philadelphia: Fortress, 1971) 102-21; S. Kim, *The Origin of Paul's Gospel* (Grand Rapids: Eerdmans, 1981); A. T. Lincoln, *Ephesians* (WBC 42; Dallas: Word, 1990); C. F. D. Moule, *The Origin of Christology* (Cambridge: Cambridge University Press, 1978) 47-96; P. T. O'Brien, *Colossians, Philemon* (WBC 44; Waco, TX: Word, 1982); idem, "The Church as a Heavenly and Eschatological Entity," in *The Church in the Bible and the World,* ed. D. A. Carson (Grand Rapids: Baker, 1987) 88-119; A. Perriman, " 'His Body, Which Is the Church . . . ' Coming to Terms with Metaphor," *EvQ* 62 (1990) 123-42; A. E. J. Rawlinson, "Corpus Christi," in *Mysterium Christi,* ed. G. K. A. Bell and A. Deissmann (London: Longmans, 1930) 225-46; A. Richardson, *An Introduction to the Theology of the New Testament* (New York: Harper, 1958); H. Ridderbos, *Paul: An Outline of His Theology* (Grand Rapids: Eerdmans, 1975) 362-95; J. A. T. Robinson, *The Body: A Study in Pauline Theology* (SBT 5; London: SCM, 1952); A. Schweitzer, *The Mysticism of Paul the Apostle* (London: Black, 1931); E. Schweizer, "σῶμα κτλ," *TDNT* 7:1024-94; A. J. M. Wedderburn, "The Body of Christ and Related Concepts in 1 Corinthians," *SJT* 24 (1971) 74-96.
R. Y. K. Fung

BOOK OF GLORY. *See* JOHN, GOSPEL OF.

BOOK OF SIGNS. *See* JOHN, GOSPEL OF; MIRACLES, MIRACLE STORIES.

C

CAIAPHAS. *See* TRIAL OF JESUS.

CERINTHUS. *See* JOHN, LETTERS OF.

CHARISMATA. *See* HOLY SPIRIT II.

CHRIST I: GOSPELS

The Greek word translated "christ" (*christos*) appears 531 times in the NT (Nestle-Aland, 26th ed.), and "Christ" is one of the most familiar terms by which Jesus is known in the NT and in subsequent Christian tradition. All the canonical Gospels apply the term to Jesus, but each has its own interesting variation in the way Jesus is presented as "Christ." The use of "Christ" in the Gospels reflects the Jewish origins (*see* Judaism and the New Testament) of Christianity and the distinctive modifications of Jewish tradition that characterize early Christian faith. For all the Evangelists Jesus is "the Christ," the Messiah of Israel's hope. But they also reflect the conviction that Jesus is also the Son of God and bears a significance that suggests divinity or is at least divine-like. Moreover, Jesus' crucifixion is pre-sented as a decisive aspect of his messianic work, although there seems to have been no Jewish precedent for seeing Messiah's work as involving his violent death (*see* Death of Christ).

In order to deal with the use of the term in the canonical Gospels, we must address related questions as well, especially the background of the term and the associated eschatological expectations of ancient Judaism, as well as the use of the term *Christ* in early Christianity prior to the Gospels.

1. Derivation, Meaning and Background
2. New Testament Usage Outside the Gospels
3. "Christ" in the Four Gospels
4. Conclusion

1. Derivation, Meaning and Background.

The term *christ* is an anglicized form of the Greek word *christos,* originally an adjective meaning "anointed (with ointment or oil)" from the verb *chriō* ("to anoint or smear with oil or ointment"). *Christos* had no special religious significance in Greek culture prior to the influence of ancient Jewish and Christian usage (on the history of the term, see Grundmann et al.). In ancient Greek-speaking Jewish and Christian circles *christos* translates the Hebrew term *māšîaḥ* about forty-five times in the LXX), which likewise means "anointed (with oil)" but carries a special significance owing to the Israelite practice of anointing with oil a person installed in a special office, such as king or priest (e.g., 1 Sam 9:15-16; 10:1, Saul; 1 Sam 16:3, 12-13, David; Ex 28:41, Aaron and his sons; 1 Chron 29:22, Zadok and Solomon). In such settings the anointing signified that the person was commissioned and approved (by God and the people) for the special office or task. The term *māšîaḥ* is especially significant in some OT passages in connection with the Israelite king (e.g., 1 Sam 24:6; 2 Sam 1:14; cf. Ps 2:2), where the term seems to be a royal title ("the Lord's anointed," etc.) and it appears that the religious connotation is emphasized.

In postexilic OT texts one finds the hope for a renewed (Davidic) monarchy, often pictured with grandiose dimensions and qualities (e.g., Hag 2:20-23; Zech 9:9-10; 12:7—13:1). Out of this hope, but probably not until sometime in the Hellenistic period (after 331 B.C.), Jews came to use *māšîaḥ* (and the Greek equivalent, *christos*) as a designation for a future agent ("messiah") to be sent by God, usually to restore Israel's independence and righteousness. Recent research suggests, however, that ancient Jewish eschatological expectations of deliverance and sanctification of the elect did not always include the explicit or prominent anticipation of a "messiah," and there seems to have been some variation in the ways "messiah" figures were pictured (e.g., Neusner, Green, Frerichs; de Jonge).

In the Qumran texts, for example (150 B.C.-A.D. 70; *see* Dead Sea Scrolls), we find what appears to be an expectation of two "anointed" figures (e.g., 1QS 9:10-11; CD 12:22-23) who would preside over the elect in the future: a "messiah of Israel" (probably a royal figure) and a "messiah of Aaron" (a priestly figure). For the Qumran community, the latter figure was apparently seen as outranking the royal "messiah" (see S. Talmon in Neusner, Green, Frerichs). In the *Psalms of Solomon* (late first century B.C.), however, hope for the restoration of Israel is tied to God's raising up a descendant of David as "the Lord's anointed one" (*christos kyriou, Pss. Sol.* 17:32; 18:7), and the messianism here is of a purely royal variety. *1 Enoch* conveys still another image, in which the messianic figure ("the elect one," "the son of man") is pictured in quite exalted terms in heavenly glory and seems to be identified as Enoch (cf. Gen 5:21-24). It is not clear whether this is another type of messianism or if royal/messianic imagery has been appropriated here to describe another type of exalted figure connected with hopes for eschatological salvation.

We cannot discuss further here the details of pre-Christian Jewish eschatological hopes and the diversity of messianic expectations. It must be emphasized, however, that in the Jewish texts the expectations and speculations about messiah(s) are tied to and overshadowed by other aspirations, such as freedom of the Jewish people from Gentile domination, and/or the triumph of a particular religious vision of the divine will (e.g., at Qumran), and/or a more general longing for God's kingdom or triumph over unrighteousness and injustice. That is, Jewish hope for messiah(s) was never the center of religious concern for its own sake but functioned as part of the attempt to project God's eschatological triumph and the realization of aspirations connected with God's triumph. This contrasts with the way the person of Jesus quickly became central and vital in early Christian devotion.

In the NT something like the royal messianism of the *Psalms of Solomon* seems to be the Jewish messianic expectation most often alluded to and presupposed in relating Jesus to the Jewish religious background. This suggests that the idea of a divinely appointed royal agent who would deliver and purify the nation may have been reasonably well known in Jewish circles (e.g., Acts 2:30-36), though it is not so clear how widely embraced such a hope was.

2. New Testament Usage Outside the Gospels.

It is worth noting the distribution of the term *christos* in the NT. Of the 531 occurrences of the term, 383 are in the Pauline corpus, and 270 of these are in the seven letters whose authorship is virtually undisputed today (Rom, 1 Cor, 2 Cor, Gal, Phil, 1 Thess, Philem). In some other NT writings, likewise, use of *christos* is quite frequent for their size: 1 Peter (22); 1 John (8); Jude (6). But in some larger writings the term is not comparatively frequent: Heb (12); Rev (7). Given their size, the Gospels (especially the Synoptics) do not use *christos* very frequently: Matthew (16); Mark (7); Luke (12, plus 25 occurrences in Acts); John (19).

This quick glimpse of the distribution of *christos* in the NT shows three things. First, the variation in the frequency of the term may indicate differences in the importance attached to it by the different NT authors. However, the differing subject matter and purposes of the individual authors may also have accounted for the frequency variation. Second, the heavy concentration of occurrences of *christos* in Paul's letters (the earliest NT writings) suggests that the term very early became an important part of the vocabulary of Christian faith. Third, the strikingly small share of the total NT occurrences of *christos* in the Gospels, and the variation among the Gospels in the number of uses of *christos* make it appropriate to question the meaning and role of the term in these specific writings. Before we discuss in detail the Gospels' use of *christos*, however, it will be helpful to comment further on the Christian use of *christos* prior to the Gospels.

2.1. Pre-Gospel Use. The Gospels are commonly dated approximately A.D. 65-100, several decades after the beginning of the Christian movement. For tracing the use of *christos* in the earlier decades, our most important evidence is found in the undisputed letters of Paul, which are generally dated approximately A.D. 50-60 and constitute the earliest surviving Christian writings. It is necessary here only to review some matters relevant to the use of *christos* in the Gospels.

First, we may compare Paul's use of *christos* with his use of other key christological titles in these writings. Occurrences of *christos* in the seven undisputed letters constitute 51 percent of the total NT occurrences of the term (72 percent of occurrences are in the writings attributed to Paul in the NT). Two things relevant to *christos* are evident: *christos* is by far Paul's favorite of early Christian titles for Jesus; on the basis of the early date of Paul's letters, we may conclude that in the earliest years of the Christian movement *christos* quickly became a prominent Christian title for Jesus.

Close examination of *christos* in Paul's letters, however, shows that he uses the term almost as a name, or as part of the name for Jesus, and not characteristically as a title. Thus, for example, in Paul *christos* usually appears in the following formulae: "Christ Jesus," "Jesus Christ," "the Lord Jesus Christ" and sometimes simply "Christ." This has led some to ask whether or how well Paul connected the term *christos* to an understanding of Jesus as "Messiah," and to what degree *christos* was for Paul, like a name, simply a way of referring to Jesus. In answering this question, several factors are important.

First, it is clear that *christos* was not immediately meaningful as a religious term to ancient Gentiles unfamiliar with Jewish messianic expectations. For example, evidence indicates that *christos* was often understood by pagans to be the name *chrestos* ("useful"), a common Greek name, especially for slaves (e.g., Suetonius *Claudius* 25.4).

Second, however, it is likely that Paul, as a Jew familiar with his ancestral tradition (Gal 1:13-14), knew the significance of *christos* in connection with Jewish messianic expectations. In all likelihood, the term *christos* began to be used with reference to Jesus among Jewish Christians even before Paul's apostolic mission. *Christos* must have been appropriated by Jewish Christians from Greek-speaking Jewish circles, where it functioned as the translation for *māšîaḥ*. Otherwise, it is impossible to account for the emergence of *christos* as a title for Jesus. Paul's frequent and easy use of the term reflects a well-established Christian usage and is strong evidence that *christos* was a part of the religious vocabulary of Christian groups within the first few years (A.D. 30-50).

Third, although in Paul's letters *christos* functions syntactically more characteristically as a

quasi-name for Jesus than a title (as in "the Christ"), it appears that the term retains in Paul something of its messianic connotation. This is so not only in explicit passages such as Romans 9:5, with its reference to Jesus as "the Christ" *(ho christos)* but also in the wider pattern of Paul's usage. As W. Kramer has shown, Paul characteristically uses *christos* (either alone or in connection with "Jesus") in passages that refer to Jesus' death and resurrection (e.g., 1 Cor 15; Rom 3:23; 5:6-7; Gal 3:13), and it is likely that these passages reflect Paul's familiarity with and emphasis on the early Christian conviction that Jesus' crucifixion was part of his mission as the "Messiah." (F. Hahn's view, 161-62, that the earliest Christian affirmation of Jesus as Messiah was exclusively in connection with the hope of his eschatological return does not do justice to this close connection between the term *christos* and Jesus' death and resurrection in Paul, the earliest evidence of Christian usage we possess.)

Thus, although Paul's letters do not seem to emphasize or make explicit the messianic connotation of the term *Christ,* they provide evidence that the term derived from circles of Jewish Christians where this connotation was emphasized and that the proclamation of Jesus as Messiah was a part of the earliest faith of Christianity. Paul's use of *christos* almost as a name for Jesus has been taken by some scholars as suggesting that among his Gentile converts the term's association with Jewish messianic expectations was not emphasized. But, as the Gospels demonstrate, the claim that Jesus is the Messiah remained a part of early Christian faith well after the Christian movement grew beyond its initial stage as a sect of ancient Judaism. As will be shown in the next sections, although early Christians modified the connotation of the term *christos* in light of Jesus' death and their experience of his resurrected glory, the term retained something of its sense as designating Jesus as the "Messiah," the divinely designated agent of salvation.

2.2. Use of "Christos" in Other New Testament Writings. In the many occurrences of *christos* in the writings in the Pauline corpus whose authorship is disputed or widely doubted among scholars (often called deutero-Pauline letters: Eph, Col, 2 Thess, 1 Tim, 2 Tim, Titus), the usage is basically like that found in the undisputed Pauline letters. However, the use of the term in NT writings outside the Pauline corpus and the

Gospels is relevant to understanding the background for the use of *christos* in the Gospels. For example, 1 Peter uses the term twenty-two times, often in connection with the theme of suffering—of Christ and/or of Christians: the OT prophets predicted Christ's sufferings (1 Pet 1:11); Christ's redemptive suffering is mentioned several times (e.g., 1 Pet 2:21; 3:18; 4:1; 5:1); and Christians share in Christ's sufferings (1 Pet 4:13). This connection between the term *christos* and suffering probably reflects the early Christian emphasis mentioned earlier—Jesus' crucifixion was a messianic event. It also shows how the idea of Jesus the suffering Messiah was used to inspire Christians to endure sufferings in his name.

In Revelation, along with more formulaic uses of *christos* ("Jesus Christ," e.g., Rev 1:1-2, 5), there are interesting passages where the term is used as a title, "messiah" (e.g., Rev 11:15, "our Lord and his Christ"; Rev 12:10, "the authority of his Christ"). These passages portray the eschatological triumph of God in terms drawn from Jewish messianic expectation and thus confirm the continuing awareness in Christian circles of the late first century A.D. that "Christ" is a messianic designation.

Likewise, in 1 John 2:22 and 1 John 5:1, the confession that Jesus is "the Christ" reflects the messianic claim. But this same document shows the emergence of distinctively Christian doctrinal disputes about the reality or importance of Jesus' human nature (e.g., 1 Jn 4:2, "Jesus Christ has come in the flesh"), and the author coins the term *antichrist* to describe those whose christology he finds seriously inadequate (1 Jn 2:22). In 1 John we see again how *christos* can function both to designate Jesus in messianic terms and also almost as a name for Jesus.

This brief survey of uses of *christos* in NT writings other than the Gospels gives us a general understanding of the first-century Christian background of the term that is presupposed as familiar to the readers of the Gospels. With this background in mind, we are now able to discuss in comparatively greater detail how the individual Evangelists use the term in their stories of Jesus.

3. "Christ" in the Four Gospels.

As we have indicated already, each Evangelist applies *christos* to Jesus but does so with particular nuances and emphases. We shall therefore discuss their usage individually; and, accepting commonly held scholarly opinion, we shall deal with the Evangelists in their probable chronological order.

Modern scholarly investigation of NT christology has expended a great deal of effort in analyzing the use of christological titles in the Gospels and in the other NT writings (e.g., Hahn). In spite of this, certain disagreements remain in contemporary discussions, making a survey such as this a difficult enterprise. To some degree conclusions about one particular title such as *christos* are connected with conclusions about the Evangelists' use of the other titles, and this will be reflected in the following discussion.

3.1. Mark. The earliest of the canonical Gospels, Mark, shows the complexity of applying the term *christos* to Jesus (*see* Mark, Gospel of). In varying ways this complexity characterizes all four Evangelists.

From the opening words in Mark 1:1, the author indicates familiarity and acceptance of the term as applied to Jesus ("the gospel of Jesus Christ"), and at various other points the author uses the term as a way of referring to Jesus. For example, in Mark 9:41 a reward is promised to anyone who gives a cup of water to Jesus' disciples "because you are Christ's" (cf. Mt 10:42).

The warning in Mark 13:21-22 about the coming times of crisis when some will say, "Look, here is the Christ!" and the caution about "false Christs" implicitly show that for Mark the title belongs properly to Jesus alone, whose coming with glory will need no such announcement (Mk 13:26-27). *Christos* is used as a title here, and this passage insists that the only genuine fulfillment of the messianic hopes—falsely appropriated by deceivers—will be Jesus' appearance as "the Son of Man coming in clouds with great glory." The warning about deceivers probably reflects a conflict between early Christian claims about Jesus as Messiah and other messianic hopes circulating among Jewish groups. (Cf. Mk 13:6, which refers to deceivers who claim "I am he!" The variation in some manuscripts, "I am the Christ," is probably a scribal harmonization with the form of the saying in Mt 24:5. Scholars debate whether the significance of "I am he" is a messianic claim or a claim to divinity alluding to God's self-description; see the discussion of Mk 14:61-62 below.)

In several other passages, however, *christos* is used with a certain reserve or subtlety that has generated scholarly debate over Mark's intent. Perhaps the most familiar of these is Mark 8:29-30, where Peter acclaims Jesus as "the Christ" *(ho christos)* and is immediately ordered by Jesus "to tell no one about him" (cf. Mt 16:16-20; Lk 9:20-21). Believing that Jesus did not see himself as the Messiah, some scholars have suggested that Jesus' original response to Peter's acclamation was the rebuke "Get behind me, Satan!" in Mark 8:33, and that Jesus rejected the messianic appellation. In this view, Mark recast the incident, introducing the command to secrecy (Mk 8:30) and making Jesus' rebuke apply to Peter's rejection of Jesus' sufferings (Mk 8:31-33). There are, then, two issues: Jesus' attitude toward the appellation "messiah" and Mark's treatment of the messiah/*christos* term here. The latter question is the primary concern before us, but a few comments about the authenticity of the Markan scene are relevant as well.

The speculative attempt to reconstruct the original dialogue between Peter and Jesus as described above is probably ill conceived. There is little basis for regarding Jesus' command to silence in Mark 8:30 as Markan invention while holding Jesus' rebuke of Peter in Mark 8:33 as authentically from Jesus. On the one hand, both function quite well as redactional elements in the scene, and both can be explained as deriving from Mark's editorial purpose (Lk 9:20-22 does not include Jesus' rebuke of Peter). On the other hand, both statements can equally well be attributed to Jesus. If Jesus did predict his rejection and death (not so unlikely in view of the ancient Jewish tradition of Israel's rejection of prophets and the martyrdom of *John the Baptist, with whom Jesus associated himself), Peter's negative response is thoroughly understandable, as is Jesus' rebuke of Peter in Mark 8:33. And the notion that Jesus could not possibly have seen himself in messianic terms rests to some degree on the assumption that "messiah" carried a single meaning, having to do with a Davidic, royal figure with military intentions. With such a figure, it is widely thought, Jesus cannot be compared, and he could not have thought of himself in this fashion. But the diversity evident in ancient Jewish messianic speculations (e.g., Smith; Neusner, Green, Frerichs; de Jonge) suggests that Jesus may have rejected this or that form of messianic speculation while understanding his mission in the light of his own definition of messiahship. Therefore Jesus

could have ordered silence about the use of the Messiah/Christ title among his disciples because the term did not itself communicate clearly his vision of his task and was subject to what he considered severe misunderstandings. In light of this, the command to silence in Mark 8:30 can be as plausibly authentic a saying as Jesus' rebuke of Peter in Mark 8:33.

Debates about what Jesus himself may or may not have felt about the term *messiah* are thus more complicated than even some scholars recognize. Determining Mark's intention is comparatively easier, though still not without problems. In view of Mark's use of *christos* in the passages examined already, we must conclude that Mark intends Peter's acclamation of Jesus as "Christ" to be taken at least in some sense positively. Jesus' command in Mark 8:30 is to say nothing about him to others; it is not a rejection of the term *christos* outright. Yet Mark 8:30-33 indicates a reserve about the term, and the reason seems to be that none of the pre-Christian definitions of *christos* prepare one to understand Jesus' mission, as is shown by Peter's reaction to Jesus' prediction of his suffering. Thus Mark 8:29-33 hints that the term *christos* achieves its proper meaning as a title for Jesus in light of his divinely mandated sufferings (the divine necessity indicated by the "must suffer" of Mk 8:31). That is, this passage suggests that Jesus is the Christ but cannot be so identified apart from an appreciation of his crucifixion as central to his messianic task.

The appearance of the title *Christ* in Mark 8:27-30 must also be seen in the light of the overall narrative of Mark. At various points earlier in Mark others have asked about Jesus (Mk 1:27; 2:7; 4:41; 6:2-3) or have offered identifications of him (Mk 1:24; 3:22; 5:7; 6:14-16). In Mark 8:27-30, however, Jesus poses the question of his identity and demands a response from the Twelve, which has the effect of making explicit the simmering question of his true significance. Consequently, Mark 8:27-30 is a turning point in Mark. Jesus' question is to be dealt with in light of the preceding narratives of his ministry and gathers up all that has gone before it in Mark. Structurally his question also anticipates the question of the priest in Mark 14:61, which is the climax of the Jewish trial and rejection of Jesus (*see* Trial of Jesus). In the latter episode Jesus is asked about his identity, and the messianic acclamation of Peter is affirmed by Jesus.

In Mark 14:61-62 the chief priest asks Jesus, "Are you the Christ, the son of the Blessed One?" Jesus responds affirmatively, "I am" (*egō eimi*), and then predicts his vindication at God's "right hand." The Markan form of Jesus' reply is more emphatic than the parallels (cf. Mt 26:64; Lk 22:70; the variants in some Markan manuscripts are probably scribal harmonizations with these parallels). The "I am," a possible allusion to the self-descriptive language of God in the OT (e.g., Is 43:10, 13), may also have been intended by Mark to hint at Jesus' transcendent significance.

This is made even more likely by the allusion here to the glorification of the "son of man" in Daniel 7:13-14. Jesus' full reply to the priest's question asserts that, though he does not seem to fit some messianic expectations (such as the royal-Davidic model mentioned in Mk 12:35), he is rightfully *christos*, and his status will be vindicated directly in glorious dimensions. Contrary to the views of some earlier scholars, the phrase "the son of man" (Mk 14:62) is not a title for a well-known figure in Jewish eschatological speculation (see, e.g., Casey) and was not intended by Mark as a preferred title in place of *christos* (see esp. Kingsbury 1983). For Mark, Jesus is the Christ (Messiah), the *Son of God, and the allusion to the Danielic scene of divine triumph serves to make it clear that "the son of man," rejected by the Jewish leaders, will in fact be vindicated as *christos* and divine Son in heavenly glory (*see* Son of Man).

Another much-discussed passage is Mark 12:35-37 (cf. Mt 22:41-45; Lk 20:41-44). Jesus' question about how the Christ can be the Son of David is not a theoretical question. The reader is expected to understand that the question really albeit somewhat obliquely has to do with Jesus' true identity and significance. And the point of Mark 12:35-37 is to indicate the inadequacy of "Son of David" as the category for understanding who the Christ is, for David calls him "Lord" (Gk *kyrios;* Heb *ădōnāy*), suggesting that the Christ is far superior to David. That is, David is not an adequate model for the work or person of the Christ. Here again, *christos* is implicitly accepted as a title for Jesus, but one popular understanding of the term (attributed to "the scribes," Mk 12:35) is found inadequate. In light of the places where God addresses Jesus as the divine Son (Mk 1:11; 9:7), as well as other indications of Jesus' divine-like significance in Mark

(e.g., stilling the storm in Mk 4:35-41, esp. the disciples' awe-filled question in Mk 4:41), the reader is expected to see that Jesus "the Christ" is far greater than the commonly accepted notions of the Messiah.

The final occurrence of *christos* in Mark is in Mark 15:32, where observers of Jesus' crucifixion mockingly address him as "the Christ, the king of Israel." This is one of many examples of Markan irony (especially frequent in the passion account), and is one of several places where the question of whether Jesus is the king of Israel or king of the Jews appears in the narrative of the trial and crucifixion (cf. Mk 15:2, 9, 12, 18-20, 26; see Juel). The Markan irony in the mockery of Jesus as "the Christ" in Mark 15:32 is that, contrary to the mockers, Jesus is "the Christ, the king of Israel," though his ultimate vindication lies by way of his crucifixion and apparent failure. The pagan form of the mockery, in the title attached to the cross ("The King of the Jews"), gives the charge for which Jesus was executed but is also an ironic truth: Jesus really is the rightful "king," rejected by pagan and Jewish leaders.

It is interesting to note the distribution of uses of *christos* in Mark. The occurrences of *christos* are concentrated in the second half of the book, where the shadow of Jesus' coming death looms over the narrative. After the opening words in Mark 1:1, *christos* does not appear in Mark until Mark 8:29-30, in a complex of material that combines Jesus' explicit question about his significance with the first prediction of his sufferings (the variants in Mk 1:34 are probably scribal harmonizations with Lk 4:41). Thereafter, aside from Mark 9:41, *christos* appears in the material describing Jesus' final confrontation with Jewish authorities in Jerusalem, which culminates in his execution. The true stature of "the Christ" is the one teasing question Jesus asks in a list of questions debated in Mark 11:27—12:40. Jesus' discourse about the future (Mk 13:5-37) includes the prominent reference to "false Christs," who are to be distinguished from the true Christ, Jesus. In the Jewish trial the question whether Jesus is the Christ culminates the interrogation. And in the crucifixion account the mocking acclamation of Jesus as "the Christ" is the final ironic indignity heaped on Jesus by his tormentors. Mark uses *christos* sparingly, but every occurrence is significant.

Thus, although Mark affirms other christological titles for Jesus (especially important is "Son of God" and its variations in Mk 1:1, 11, 24, 34; 3:11-12; 5:7; 9:7; 15:39; see, e.g., Kingsbury 1983), *christos* too is an important term in Mark's acclamation of Jesus. The cluster of uses of *christos* in the accounts of Jesus' final conflict with the Jewish religious establishment, their rejection of him and his execution at the hands of the Roman ruler reflects two things: the close link in early Christian proclamation and in Mark between the term *christos* and Jesus' death, and the recognition that the Christian identification of Jesus as *christos* involves a claim with special reference to Jewish religious hopes and beliefs.

Mark insists that *christos* receives its true meaning as a title for Jesus only in light of Jesus himself, his divinely ordained suffering and his transcendent significance as "Son of God." And Mark shows that the identification of Jesus as *christos* involves a claim that challenged the Jewish religious leadership, for its handling of Jesus in his ministry and for its continued negative response to the early Christian proclamation about Jesus.

The clustering of uses of *christos* in the final chapters of the story of Jesus is found also in Matthew and Luke, as we shall see. Thus Mark was either influential in this matter and/or with the other Synoptics reflected the association of *christos* with references to Jesus' death. But unlike the other Evangelists, Mark's use of *christos* is almost entirely confined to the passion material, making the association of the term with the death of Jesus more emphatic.

3.2. Matthew. With some 90 percent of Mark appearing also in Matthew, it is not surprising that a considerable number of the Markan uses of *christos* reappear in Matthew. But there are also noteworthy distinctives in Matthew's use of the term, including his pattern of usage (*see* Matthew, Gospel of).

First, there is a cluster of occurrences of *christos* early in the book. The opening words of Matthew (Mt 1:1) refer to "Jesus Christ, the son of David, the son of Abraham." This illustrates the Judaic flavor of Matthew's account and prefigures the way Matthew will connect Jesus to the history and religious hopes of Israel in the material that follows. The Judaic quality of Matthew's presentation of Jesus is evident also in Matthew 1:16, which concludes Jesus' genealogy by referring to him simply as "the Christ." The

connection between Jesus and Israel is illustrated in Matthew 1:17, which portrays Israel's history in three stages, culminating with "the Christ."

Matthew's emphasis on the royal connotations of the term *Christ* is indicated in Matthew 2:1-4, where the magi ask about the birth of the "king of the Jews" and Herod responds by inquiring about OT prophecies of the birthplace of "the Christ."

But following this cluster of occurrences, *christos* does not appear in Matthew until Matthew 11:2, where the imprisoned Baptist hears of "the deeds of the Christ," the works of Jesus (cf. Lk 7:18). This phrase may refer retrospectively to the entire preceding narrative of Jesus' ministry (Mt 1—10). If so, it gives an explicitly messianic coloring to the whole.

Matthew's affirmation of the *christos* title is also evident in the next occurrence of the term in Matthew 16:16, where Peter acclaims Jesus as "the Christ, the Son of the living God." This forms Matthew's parallel to Mark 8:29. The second part of the acclamation expands Mark's simpler form and makes each of the two titles interpret the other. That is, "Son of the living God" underscores Jesus' exalted status, and "the Christ" emphasizes that this divine Son fulfills all messianic hopes. Matthew 16:20 retains from Mark 8:30 Jesus' command to secrecy, but the order to silence concerning the *christos* title is more explicit in Matthew than in Mark. As in Mark, there is a cluster of occurrences of *christos* in the chapters concerning Jesus' final days in Jerusalem. Matthew 22:41-45 presents the question about the Christ as Son of David (discussed above), and like Mark makes the question the climax of a series of debates between Jesus and his critics. But in a saying unique to Matthew (Mt 23:10), the disciples are told that their true "master" *(kathēgētēs)* is "the Christ." This reflects Matthew's emphasis that "the Christ" is the authoritative teacher of the community, a theme most evident in the large blocks of teaching material in this Gospel (Mt 5—7, 10, 13, 18, 23—25).

The remaining occurrences in Matthew appear in passages paralleled in Mark. But the Matthean form of the passages generally make more explicit the theme of Jesus' messianic status. In Matthew 24:5 the deceivers' false claim, which conflicts with Jesus' rightful status, is directly messianic; "I am the Christ" (cf. Mt 24:23;

Mk 13:6, "I am"). In Matthew 26:63-64 the priest's question as to whether Jesus claims to be "the Christ, the Son of God" is introduced with a solemn adjuration; and though Jesus' response appears less direct ("You have said so"), it is to be taken as a positive reply. This is confirmed in Matthew 26:68 by the distinctively Matthean form of the taunt by Jesus' tormentors, "Prophesy to us, you Christ!" (cf. Mk 14:65; Lk 22:64). And finally, in a uniquely Matthean wording, Pilate twice asks what the Jews wish him to do with "Jesus who is called Christ" (Mt 7:17, 23), making the question of Jesus' messiahship quite explicit.

It is clear that *christos* is a major christological title for Matthew. In comparison with Mark, the title seems more prominent and important an item of religious vocabulary in Matthew. "Christ" appears in Matthew more than twice as many times as in Mark and in passages where the term is lacking in the Markan parallel. Further, there is a more explicit connection between *christos* and Israel in Matthew, a feature particularly evident in the nativity account. Like Mark, however, Matthew has a cluster of occurrences in the material describing Jesus' final conflict with the Jewish leaders and his execution. And like Mark, for Matthew it is Jesus who defines the term *Christ/Messiah* rather than it being defined by others. Jewish expectations about Messiah are not adequate for considering Jesus' messianic claims. Thus Jesus the Christ is "Son of the living God," and his rejection and crucifixion form an important part of his messianic mission, both of these claims constituting significant modifications of pre-Christian messianic speculation.

3.3. Luke-Acts. In considering the use of *christos* in Luke, we must also take account of the second volume of the author's work, the Acts of the Apostles, which we shall briefly examine first (see also Fitzmyer, 197-200; *see* Luke, Gospel of; Acts of the Apostles).

3.3.1. Usage in Acts. A little over half (thirteen) of the twenty-five occurrences of *christos* in Acts are in formulaic references to Jesus: "Jesus Christ" (Acts 2:38; 3:6; 4:10; 8:12; 9:34; 10:36, 48; 16:18), "Christ Jesus" (Acts 18:5; 24:24), "the Lord Jesus Christ" (Acts 11:17; 15:26; 28:31). Aside from Acts 4:26, where *christos* appears in a quotation from Psalm 2:2, the other eleven occurrences are in descriptions of Christians attempting to persuade Jews that Jesus is "the Christ," that is, they attempt to present Jesus as the fulfillment of messianic hopes. In these cases, the term is used as a title and obviously derives its meaning from the context of Jewish expectations of a messiah. Some of the Acts passages reflect the attempt to deal with Jesus' sufferings as the fulfillment of OT texts interpreted as messianic prophecies (Acts 2:31; 3:18; 17:3; 26:23). Other passages describe a more general claim that Jesus is the Messiah (Acts 2:36; 3:20; 5:42; 8:5; 9:22; 18:28).

Acts claims to present the preaching of the earliest decades of Christianity. This, plus the peculiar wording of some passages in Acts, has led some scholars to argue that from this book we can reconstruct early forms of Christian faith in the book that are distinguishable from more mature forms in other NT writings. Sometimes these suggestions focus on Acts 2:36, where God is said to have "made him [Jesus] both Lord and Christ," or on Acts 3:20, which describes Jesus as "the Christ appointed for you [Israel]." In the former passage, it is suggested, we may have a remnant of an early adoptionist type of christology in which Jesus is seen as being appointed Messiah at his resurrection. In the latter passage some have found a remnant of the view of Jesus as a kind of Messiah-designate who will exercise his office only in the future when he is sent to preside in the eschatological restoration of Israel. Scholars proposing these suggestions believe that we may be able to see traces of the development and change in the earliest Christian understanding of Jesus as Messiah.

The author of Acts did not embrace either of the forms of christology just described. Luke's birth narrative (Lk 1—2), for example, shows that the author regarded Jesus as Messiah from the time of his miraculous conception onward (*see* Birth of Jesus). And it is questionable that he would have incorporated christological views in tension with his own in his account of early Christianity without indicating that they were deficient. This does not settle fully the question of the original meaning of the statements, but it suggests that the author of Acts did not understand the statements the way some modern scholars have.

In fact, nothing in either passage conveys the christological views some attribute to them. The titles "Lord and Christ" (*kyrios and christos*) in Acts 2:36 represent quite an exalted view of Jesus, and the passage asserts that Jesus holds such an exalted status by God's will. Nothing demands the conclusion that Jesus was made Messiah only at his baptism or resurrection. It is anachronistic to read an adoptionist christology into this passage. Similarly, Acts 3:20 urges that, in spite of its rejection of Jesus, Israel may yet partake in the fulfillment of messianic hopes by recognizing in Jesus its only true Messiah. We have here a reflection of the eschatological orientation of early Christian faith, which included the conviction that Jesus the Messiah would be vindicated on a grand scale in a future triumph of God's purposes. But, again, nothing in Acts 3:20 requires the conclusion that it preserves traces of a purely futurist understanding of Jesus' messiahship. The passages can be read as reflecting some sort of adoptionist or purely futurist messianism only by first presuming what must first be demonstrated—that such views must have characterized the earliest Christian circles. But our constructions of early christologies must surely rest on more than presumptions.

In sum, the use of *christos* in Acts reflects three characteristics. (1) "Christ" is part of the common namelike designation of Jesus in early Christian circles. (2) The term was also used as a title when the author wished to make explicit the claim that Jesus was the fulfillment of Israel's hopes for God's redemption. (3) The author shows special concern to insist that Jesus' crucifixion was predicted in the OT and does not disqualify Jesus from being Messiah (*see* Death of Jesus).

3.3.2. Usage in the Gospel. The frequent use of *christos* as a title in Acts is to be set alongside the consistent use of the term in this way in all twelve occurrences in Luke's Gospel. The one possible exception is Luke 2:11, where the angel announces the birth of "a Savior, who is Christ the Lord" *[christos kyrios]*. But even here it is probable that the author uses the term as a title, "the Christ, the Lord" (cf. Acts 2:36; assuming that the variant attested in some versions, "the Lord's Christ" *[christos kyriou]*, is not the original reading).

Certainly in all other occurrences of *christos* in Luke the term is used as a title (Messiah) and Jesus is explicitly connected with ancient Jewish messianic hopes. This connection is evident in Luke 2:26, where we are introduced to Simeon, who awaited the "consolation of Israel" and had been promised by God that he would live to see "the Lord's Christ." Likewise, in Luke 3:15 the Baptist is asked if he is "the Christ" and replies

by contrasting himself with the "mightier" one coming after him. In Luke 4:41 the demons' knowledge of Jesus has to do explicitly with his messianic status: "they knew that he [Jesus] was the Christ" (cf. Mk 1:34). Thereafter, *christos* does not appear until Luke 9:20, in Peter's acclamation of Jesus as "The Christ of God," a more Judaic-sounding acclamation than the versions in Matthew 16:16 and Mark 8:29. (Note also the Jewish mockery of Jesus in Luke 23:35.)

As with the other Synoptics, Luke also presents a clustering of occurrences of *christos* in the material describing Jesus' final days of conflict in Jerusalem. There is Jesus' question about Messiah being thought of as David's son (Lk 20:41), an issue we have dealt with earlier in our discussion of Mark. Unlike Matthew and Mark, in Luke 21:8 Jesus' prediction of deceivers does not explicitly mention false messiahs but refers only to those who will say, "I am he!" In the Jewish trial, however, the priest demands whether Jesus claims to be "the Christ" (Lk 22:67), and the following question, "Are you the Son of God, then?" (Lk 22:70) should also be taken as an inquiry about Jesus' messianic claim. Jesus' response, "You say that I am," seems less direct than the Markan version (Mk 14:62) but is no doubt to be taken as an affirmation. As we have seen, Luke clearly presents Jesus as Messiah. This emphasis is further borne out in the Lukan version of the charges against Jesus before Pilate in Luke 23:2, which includes the statement that Jesus claimed to be "Christ, a king." Luke thereby links the Jewish and Roman trials as considerations of Jesus' messiahship. For, in spite of Pilate's statement that he found Jesus innocent of any of the charges against him (Lk 23:13-16, 22), the mockery by Jews and Romans (Lk 23:35-37) and the inscription on the cross (Lk 23:38) make Jesus' execution a rejection of his messianic claim.

The final Lukan affirmations of Jesus' messiahship appear in Luke 24:26-27 and Luke 24:44-47, where the risen Jesus identifies himself as "the Christ," whose sufferings and subsequent glory are predicted in the OT. At the same time, these passages also show that Jesus' messianic status involves a significant departure from more familiar Jewish messianic expectations, especially in light of his crucifixion. Even Jesus' disciples are pictured as ill prepared for his execution ("O foolish men, and slow of heart to believe," Lk 24:25), and the risen Jesus must "open their minds" to read the OT so as to see that all was predicted (Lk 24:27, 45).

Thus, as with the other Synoptics, in Luke the claim that Jesus is "Christ" is not simply an identification of him with Jewish expectations but is a redefinition of the meaning of messiahship. And this redefinition is based almost entirely on the story of Jesus, producing a distinctively Christian notion of "the Christ." Luke emphasizes the sufferings of "the Christ" as the divinely predicted completion and core of his earthly work, issuing in the proclamation of forgiveness to Israel and the world (Lk 24:47) recounted in Acts (e.g., Acts 1:8).

Like Matthew, Luke emphatically links Jesus with the OT and Israel. This is reflected in the pattern of occurrences of *christos* in both Gospels. Matthew and Luke have important occurrences in their nativity narratives as well as the cluster of occurrences in their final chapters, and both nativity accounts make Jesus' birth the fulfillment of Israelite hopes. To be sure, Matthew and Luke also make Jesus' messiahship a crisis for Israel and portray the Jewish rejection of Jesus as a failure to embrace Israel's true king. Modern scholarship has given much attention to the critique of the Jews in these Gospels. In light of the way Christian societies have treated Jews over the centuries, this critique has an uncomfortable ring to it. But the strongly negative portrayal of Jewish opponents of Jesus in the Gospels did not arise from simple maliciousness. It reflects how deeply important to early Christians was the conviction that Jesus was "the Christ," the Messiah understood to have been promised by God in the OT and pictured in various ways (inaccurately, in the eyes of early Christians) in ancient Jewish tradition. For the Christians whose faith is reflected in the Gospels, Jesus was much more than the Messiah of any Jewish expectation, but they never surrendered the claim that Jesus was also the true Messiah.

3.4. John. The profound redefinition of messiahship in early Christianity and the tension with Jewish messianic traditions is nowhere more evident than in John. Of the nineteen occurrences of *christos* in John, only two are formulaic ("Jesus Christ," Jn 1:17; 17:3). In all other occurrences *christos* is used as a title and Jewish messianic expectations are either mentioned or alluded to. Although there is much more to the christology of John than the claim that Jesus is the Messiah, the comparatively greater frequency of *christos* in John and the emphatic way the term functions in the narrative make it clear that Jesus' messiahship is a major feature of the author's faith (*see* John, Gospel of).

Perhaps most important for assessing the significance of *christos* in John is 20:31, where the author explicitly gives his purpose as seeking to promote belief that "Jesus is the Christ, the Son of God." On the one hand, the acclamation of Jesus as "the Christ" forms a central part of the author's own summary of Christian faith, one of the two titles the author chooses here to portray Jesus. On the other hand, "the Christ" is also "the Son of God," and John regards Jesus' divine sonship as the key christological category, involving the understanding of Jesus as preexistent and sharing richly in divine glory (e.g., Jn 17:1-5). Thus John 20:31 reflects the claims that Jesus is the Messiah and that this Messiah is much more exalted than Jewish messianic speculations characteristically allowed. Though these claims are also reflected in varying ways in the other canonical Gospels, in John they are asserted with particular force.

Much more than the other Evangelists, John uses Jewish messianic speculations as a foil for the presentation of Jesus. In John 1:19-28 he introduces us to Jewish speculations, where Jewish authorities interrogate the Baptist as to whether he claims to be "the Christ," Elijah or "the prophet"—and to each he answers negatively. The Baptist acclaims Jesus as "the Lamb of God" (Jn 1:29, 35) and "the Son of God" (Jn 1:34), but these titles must be read in connection with John 3:25-30, where the Baptist again denies that he is "the Christ" and applies the title to Jesus. The author presents the Baptist as a true witness to Jesus, and the Baptist's acclamations refer to Jesus' divine sonship and his messianic status.

The implied messianism in the Baptist's acclamation of Jesus is confirmed in the narratives reporting the responses to Jesus by, among others, the followers of the Baptist. In John 1:41 Andrew refers to Jesus as "the Messiah" (*messias*), and this transliterated Aramaic term is translated by the author as *christos*. In John 1:45 Philip describes Jesus as the one predicted in "the law and also the prophets." That the Messiah is in mind is confirmed shortly in the guileless Nathaniel's acclamation of Jesus as "the Son of God . . . the King of Israel" (Jn 1:49). As Jesus' response to Nathaniel suggests (Jn 1:50-51), these disciples do not realize the fullness of Jesus' person and status, but John intends us to see that their acclamations of Jesus in messianic categories are correct as far as they go.

In John 7:25-44 Jewish messianic speculations are played off against the messianic identity of Jesus. The crowd wonders if the authorities secretly think that Jesus is "the Christ" (Jn 7:26), but some find difficulty reconciling this interpretation of Jesus with a tradition that "when the Christ appears, no one will know where he comes from" (Jn 7:27, a messianic tradition not otherwise clearly attested). In John 7:31 there is an allusion to the Messiah as one who performs signs, and Jesus' signs are taken by some as suggesting Jesus' messiahship. A little later we read (Jn 7:40-44) that while some conclude that Jesus is "the Christ," others have difficulty reconciling Jesus' Galilean background with traditions that Messiah will come from Bethlehem and be a descendant of David.

Again, in John 12:34 the crowd refers to a tradition that "the Christ remains forever" and questions how this can be reconciled with Jesus' prediction that he will be "lifted up." And the Samaritan woman alludes to a tradition that Messiah "will show us all things" (Jn 4:25), finding in Jesus' uncanny knowledge of her life a suggestion that he may be "the Christ" (Jn 4:29).

The accuracy of John's references to Jewish messianic traditions is an interesting question that cannot detain us here. Some of these traditions are not otherwise clearly attested, but recent research suggests that John includes some material of Palestinian provenance and these references to Jewish messianic traditions may be more valuable than some have recognized (see, e.g., de Jonge, 1972/73).

More germane to the present discussion is the question of what the author's point is in these passages. In brief, it seems that John is utilizing irony in the passages where the Jews cannot reconcile Jesus and their messianic traditions. The Jews unwittingly show that they do not properly understand their own traditions and/or do not really know enough about Jesus whom they think they know and can dismiss so easily. Thus, in light of passages such as John 1:1-18 and John 6:41-45, the reader sees that the Jews do not really know where Jesus comes from (heaven) and that Jesus does fulfill the tradition about Messiah's origin being unknown. Similarly, in John 12:34 the Son of Man who is to be "lifted up" does also "remain forever," for he has come down from heaven and ascends back to heavenly glory with God, thus fulfilling the messianic tradition invoked here. We are probably to take John 7:40-42 as ironic also—John expects his readers to know the Christian tradition that Jesus was born in Bethlehem and so fulfills what "the Scripture said" about the birthplace of the Messiah.

The interplay between Jewish messianism and the early Christian redefinition is also evidenced in John 10:22-39. Here "the Jews" ask Jesus directly if he claims to be "the Christ" (Jn 10:34), and Jesus' response is an indirect affirmation (Jn 10:25-39). But Jesus also quickly employs the Father/Son language to describe his status, and its offensiveness to the Jews (Jn 10:33, 39) shows that it is intended to connote much more than a simple identification of Jesus as the Messiah of Jewish expectation. In this incident the Jews' problem is not their difficulty fitting what they know of Jesus into some specific messianic tradition but an inability to accept the claim that Jesus the Messiah is the Son of God who shares in divinity with the Father (Jn 10:37-38).

Other passages confirm that *christos* is an important christological title in John and that the author wishes to present Jesus as the true Messiah. In John 9:22 it is the confession of Jesus as "the Christ" that leads to synagogue expulsion, a passage commonly thought today to reflect the christological controversies between the Johannine Christians and the Jewish authorities of their day. In a manner unique among the Gospel writers, John twice links the term *christos* explicitly with the Semitic term Messiah (*messias*, Jn 1:41; 4:25). The Fourth Evangelist considers Jewish definitions of the Messiah inadequate, but he does not surrender the basic category in portraying Jesus.

Within the episode about Lazarus, structurally important as the seventh and climactic "sign" in John, Martha's acclamation of Jesus as "the Christ, the Son of God" (Jn 11:27) affirms Jesus' preceding self-description as "the resurrection and the life" and corresponds to the Evangelist's description of the proper Christian confession in John 20:31.

The tension between Jewish messianic traditions and the Johannine understanding of Jesus has led some scholars to suggest that *christos* was not such a major christological title for John (e.g., Maloney). The Johannine view of Jesus as "the Son (of God)" is the key to the author's christology and the controlling motif in his presentation of Jesus. It is as "the Son" that Jesus' true transcendent significance is best disclosed. But John does not consider *christos* an inadequate title. Rather, he considers Jewish messianic speculations inadequate for a proper understanding of who Messiah is, and he regards the Jewish authorities as incapable of accepting the proper definition of Messiah and the divine Son. John does not reject *christos* as a christological title in favor of others, such as "Son of Man" or "Son of God." He demands the recognition that Jesus, the divine Son and the Son of Man, is "the Christ." He reflects a redefinition of "the Christ" category in light of Jesus' divine significance and prefers the combination of "Christ" and "Son of God" as the way of confessing Jesus properly.

For John, Jesus is more than the messianic king of Israel, but he is the messianic king, albeit of such a transcendent stature as not imagined by "the Jews." This view of Jesus as Messiah is precisely why the author so sharply criticizes the Jewish authorities for rejecting Jesus. Jesus flees the crowd's attempt to make him king "by force" (Jn 6:15) after the miracle of the bread, but this should not be taken as a total rejection of the royal-messianic office, for other passages show that John affirms Jesus as the true king. For example, at Jesus' last entry into Jerusalem, the crowd greets Jesus as "the King of Israel" (Jn 12:13). In this event John sees the fulfillment of Zechariah 9:9, with its prediction of Zion's king coming to the city (Jn 12:14-16). Thus, however shallow the crowd's understanding as they acclaim Jesus king, the Evangelist sees the royal title as proper to Jesus.

The intertwining of the author's views of Jesus as royal Messiah and as transcendent Son of God appears also in the passion narrative. In John 18:33-38 Pilate asks Jesus if he claims to be "king of the Jews," the Roman interpretation of the messianic claim. Jesus' response comprises a rejection of ordinary earthly kingship but an affirmation of his higher kingship and a consequent mission to "bear witness to the truth" of God. Subsequently the author continues to weave together the theme of Jesus' kingship and his divine sonship. Several times Jesus is referred to contemptuously by the Romans as "king" (Jn 18:39; 19:3, 14-15), and in John 19:19-22 the kingship theme is emphasized in the uniquely Johan-

nine account of Pilate's refusal to remove the title on the cross. The charges against Jesus in John are a combination of the messianic and transcendent aspects of his christology. In John 19:12 "the Jews" accuse Jesus of making himself a king against Caesar, but in John 19:7 Jesus is accused of blasphemy for making himself "the Son of God." Though the Jewish and Roman opponents of Jesus are ignorant of the ironic truth of their mockeries and charges, the reader of John is to see the greater truth of Jesus' divine sonship and royal status.

Unlike the Synoptic Gospels, where *christos* is almost entirely confined to the passion and nativity accounts (Matthew and Luke), in John *christos* appears throughout the whole book, suggesting the title's importance for the Fourth Gospel. Uniquely, John makes it clear that the Baptist is not Messiah and has the Baptist endorse Jesus as Messiah. John is also unique in having Jesus' first disciples acclaim him in a variety of messianic terms. Jesus is recognized as Messiah by the Samaritan woman, and at several points John portrays the inability of "the Jews" to recognize Jesus' messiahship. All these data make it evident that the author believes Jesus to be the true Messiah and considers Jesus' messianic significance an important feature of Christian faith.

John does not play off one christological title against another. He uses an abundance of honorific titles—many more than the other Evangelists—to describe Jesus (e.g., the several "I am" formulas). "Son of Man" is not a preferred alternative to "Christ" (contra Maloney). The Son of Man, who has come down from heaven, is "the Christ, the Son of God"—this is the heart of John's faith.

4. Conclusion.

Modern scholarship has been criticized justly for depending too heavily on studies of the NT christological titles in its attempt to determine the nature of NT christology. No treatment of any or all the titles can disclose fully the christological faith of the NT writers. But titles such as "Christ" are significant indications of the faith of authors such as the four Evangelists. In all four Gospels, "Christ" is an important way of referring to Jesus. One can say that "Christ" is for the Evangelists an essential christological term. But they all show an awareness that early Christian faith involved an appropriation and a major adaptation of the significance of the term as applied to Jesus.

In varying ways two major modifications of the Messiah category are reflected in the Gospels. (1) The crucifixion of Jesus was a major obstacle to Jewish acceptance of Jesus as Messiah, requiring justification from the OT, and the event that demanded of the early Christian circles a reformulation of the nature of the Messiah and his work. (2) The early Christian conviction about the transcendent significance or nature of Jesus makes the Messiah much more exalted in nature and more centrally important for religious life than Jewish tradition was characteristically prepared to grant. (It would be anachronistic to read back into the Gospels the details of the two-nature christology of later centuries. But only a shallow reading of the Gospels can fail to note the exalted, even transcendent, role and qualities attributed to Jesus in differing ways by each of the Evangelists.)

In the modifications of the Messiah category and the dogged insistence on retaining "Christ" as a title for Jesus in the four Gospels, we see something of the essence of early Christian faith, a religious movement that emerged initially as a distinctive development of the pre-Christian biblical tradition. In this development Jesus became "the Christ" for all nations and not just for Israel. But the Gospels show that early Christians tied their confession of Jesus as "the Christ" to the biblical heritage and to Israel's hopes for a redeemer. However much "Christ" became part of the name formula for referring to Jesus, for the Evangelists the term retained a connection with ancient visions of God's decisive eschatological intervention on behalf of his people. For the Evangelists the Jewish rejection of Jesus was their rejection of Israel's Messiah.

As perhaps no other christological title, the Evangelists' use of "Christ" shows the Jewish roots of Christian faith and the innovation this faith represented.

See also CHRISTOLOGY; LORD; SON OF GOD; SON OF MAN.

BIBLIOGRAPHY. M. Casey, *Son of Man* (London: SPCK, 1979); O. Cullmann, *The Christology of the New Testament* (rev. ed.; Philadelphia: Westminster, 1963); N. Dahl, *The Crucified Messiah and Other Essays* (Minneapolis: Augsburg, 1974) 37-47; M. de Jonge, *Christology in Context* (Philadelphia: Westminster, 1988); idem, "Jewish Expectations About the 'Messiah' According to the Fourth Gospel," *NTS* 19 (1972/73) 246-70; idem, "The Use of *ho christos* in the Passion Narratives," in *Jesus aux origines de la christologie*, ed. J. Dupont (Leuven: Leuven University, 1975) 169-92; idem, "The Use of the Word 'Anointed' in the Time of Jesus," *NovT* 8 (1966) 132-48; J. Fitzmyer, *The Gospel According to Luke I-IX* (AB; Garden City: Doubleday, 1981) 192-219; W. Grundmann et al., "χρίω κτλ," *TDNT* 9:493-580; F. Hahn, *The Titles of Jesus in Christology* (New York: World, 1969); M. Hengel, *Between Jesus and Paul* (London: SCM, 1983) 65-77; D. Jones, "The Title *christos* in Luke-Acts," *CBQ* 32 (1970) 69-76; D. Juel, *Messiah and Temple* (SBLDS 31; Missoula, MT: Scholars Press, 1977); J. D. Kingsbury, *The Christology of Mark's Gospel* (Philadelphia: Fortress, 1983); idem, *Matthew: Structure, Christology, Kingdom* (Philadelphia: Fortress, 1975); W. Kramer, *Christ, Lord, Son of God* (SBT 50; London: SCM, 1966); F. Maloney, "The Fourth Gospel's Presentation of Jesus as 'the Christ' and J. A. T. Robinson's Redating," *Downside Review* 95 (1977) 239-53; C. F. D. Moule, "The Christology of Acts," in *Studies in Luke-Acts*, ed. L. E. Keck and J. L. Martyn (New York: Abingdon, 1966) 159-85; J. Neusner, W. S. Green and E. Frerichs, *Judaisms and Their Messiahs at the Turn of the Christian Era* (Cambridge: Cambridge University Press, 1987); K. Rengstorf, "χρίστος," *NIDNTT* 2:334-43; S. S. Smalley, "The Christology of Acts Again," in *Christ and Spirit in the New Testament*, ed. B. Lindars and S. S. Smalley (Cambridge: Cambridge University Press, 1973) 79-94; M. Smith, "What Is Implied by the Variety of Messianic Figures?" *JBL* 78 (1959) 66-72.   L. W. Hurtado

CHRIST II: PAUL

Paul's extraordinarily frequent use of the term *Christos* calls for explanation. Paul often used the term as a virtual second name for Jesus or as a way of distinguishing this particular Jesus from others. Various texts also show that Paul was well aware of the larger significance of the term *Christos/māšiaḥ*. It is also notable that there are certain ways Paul refrained from using the term *Christos;* for instance, we never find the phrase "Jesus the Christ." Careful study of the Jewish and Greek background does not explain the frequency and manner in which Paul used the term *Christos*. His usage is best explained by the fact that Paul received a tradition associating the term *Christ* with the core of the early Christian message: the death and resurrection of Jesus (cf.

1 Cor 15:3-4). This received tradition, coupled with the singular experience Paul had of Christ on the Damascus Road (*see* Conversion and Call of Paul), go far in explaining the distinctive ideas the apostle associated with Jesus being the Christ. There is, however, no clear explanation or rationale for the particular permutations and combinations that we find in Paul's letters where he juxtaposes Christ with various other names and titles. *Christos* most often seems to appear where Christ's death, resurrection and return are under discussion. The *en Christō* formula in many ways best encapsulates Paul's view of the condition and position of Christians—they are *"in Christ." The use of the term *Christos* in the disputed Pauline letters differs little from what we find in those letters generally regarded as authentic, except that there is more emphasis on what may be called cosmic christology.

1. Jewish Background
2. Greek Usage
3. Origin of the Christian *Christos* Usage
4. Pauline Usage
5. The *En Christō* Formula
6. *Christos* in the Contested Pauline Letters

1. Jewish Background.
The Greek verbal adjective *christos* (which came to be used as a noun) and its Hebrew analog *māšiah* are terms that were used in early Judaism and Christianity to refer to an anointed person set apart for a special task and, in particular, to a royal and/or messianic figure. In the political realm the term was used of Davidic kings (Ps 18:50; 89:20; 132:10-17). In this regard 2 Samuel 7:8-16 is especially crucial as it expresses the hope that God would provide the ideal Davidic ruler. It should be noted, however, that none of the later OT prophetic books use the term *christos* for the future royal one like unto David (cf., e.g., Zech 9:9-10; 12:7—13:1). Indeed, in Isaiah 45:1 the term refers to Cyrus, and in Habakkuk 3:13 it appears to refer to a presently reigning king. Furthermore, in early Jewish literature the term is found infrequently (cf. *Pss. Sol.* 18:5; 4QPBless 3; CD 12:23-24; 14:19; 19:10-11; *1 Enoch* 48:10; 52:4) and does not seem to have been "an essential designation for any future redeemer" (de Jonge 1966, 147).

There were various forms of messianic expectation in early Judaism, but it does not appear that the terms translated into English as "Messiah" were used with any frequency, and they probably were not technical terms for a future redeemer figure. The messianic hope of early Judaism could incorporate the idea of one or more messianic figures, as in the royal and priestly anointed figures at Qumran (e.g., 1QS 9:10-11; CD 12:22-23), or none at all when it was believed that Yahweh would finally rescue his people (e.g., 1QM 11-12).

2. Greek Usage.
It is surprising that the term *Christos* is used so frequently by Paul (270 out of a total of 531 uses in the NT) and that it seems to be used as a name for Jesus rather than as a title or descriptive term. This is especially remarkable since in the main Paul was writing to Gentiles who may or may not have been familiar with the Jewish background for this term. In secular Greek usage the term *christos* simply means an ointment or cosmetic, but apparently it never referred to the one anointed (cf. Euripides *Hipp.* 516; Moule, 32). A fragment from a manuscript written by Diodorus Siculus (1b; 38-39, 4) shortly before the time of Jesus uses the term *neochristos* to refer to a building "newly plastered." Thus the prolific Pauline use of the term *Christos* almost as a name for Jesus requires an explanation. This is especially so since there was a perfectly good Greek word available for speaking of an anointed person, *ēleimmenos* (from the verb *aleiphō*, "anoint"). And in fact Aquila used this term to render the Hebrew *māšiah* in his Greek translation of the OT citation.

The suggestion that the term *Christos* as a surname for Jesus arose in Gentile Christianity, where its original royal or messianic Jewish connotations were no longer understood, fails to explain why Paul, a Jew, is the chief employer of this term among NT writers (Hengel). Paul's understanding of the meaning of the term is clear from 2 Corinthians 1:21, where we find the play on words "God establishes us in Christ *(eis Christon)* and has anointed us *(chrisas)*." Yet, strikingly, Paul rarely speaks of *the Christ*, but rather *Iēsous Christos* (Jesus Christ) or sometimes *Christos Iēsous* (Christ Jesus) or even *ho Kyrios Iēsous Christos* (the Lord Jesus Christ). This usage strongly suggests that before Paul wrote his letters the term *Christos* was used widely in early Christianity as part of the name of Jesus. Were this not the case, we would expect Paul somewhere to explain to his audience(s) what the term meant. We must consider briefly the evidence that points to a pre-Pauline use of the term *Christos* for Jesus.

3. The Origin of the Christian *Christos* Usage.

In one of Paul's earliest letters, 1 Thessalonians, probably written in the 50s if not earlier, a variety of uses of *Christos* appear. For example, Paul speaks of the "Lord Jesus Christ" (1 Thess 1:1; cf. 1 Thess 5:23, 28), "Christ" (1 Thess 2:6), "in Christ Jesus" (1 Thess 2:14) and, what was to become one of Paul's favorite phrases, "in Christ" (1 Thess 4:16). This suggests that in the early 50s, and even earlier, the term *Christos* had already become a virtual name for Jesus and would be recognized as such by Paul's audience in Macedonia. A similar variety of usage and assumptions can be observed in 1 Corinthians. There, for instance, we find not only the phrase "Christ Jesus" (1 Cor 1:1-4) but also "Christ" (1 Cor 1:6) as well as "our Lord Jesus Christ" and "Jesus Christ our Lord" (1 Cor 1:2, 7-10). There is no obvious significance to this variation; all these terms and phrases refer to the same person in his relationship to his people. Detailed studies about Paul's use of the term *Christ* have made clear that Paul uses the term in a variety of ways and combinations with other names and titles, and only rarely is it possible to explain these permutations. It would appear that there is no theological rationale for Paul sometimes using the phrase "Christ Jesus" rather than "Jesus Christ," or sometimes preferring the phrase "the Lord Jesus Christ" as opposed to "Christ."

It can be shown that Paul uses the term *Christos* and its variants especially in contexts where he is drawing upon pre-Pauline tradition or is reflecting on the eschatological significance of Christ's death, resurrection and parousia (*see* Eschatology). These epochal events are the primary reason Paul is willing to call Jesus *Christos* (cf. Hengel, 146-48). A summary of Paul's theology of Christ can be found in 2 Corinthians 5:14-21. Christ is the one who died—once for all—and was raised so that those whom he has redeemed might live for him. These events bear witness to the self-sacrificial love that Christ expressed for his people and which they in turn are to emulate. Christ then is the great reconciler of humans to God (2 Cor 5:19) and of humans to each other (Gal 3:28). It is the climactic salvific events at the close of Jesus' life that especially cause Paul to call Jesus the *Christ*. The significance of these events for defining the Christ is also made

clear by Paul's virtual silence regarding Jesus' miracles. Furthermore, though Paul does draw on the tradition of Jesus' sayings in 1 Corinthians 7 and elsewhere, he does not cite such sayings as of the essence of his gospel or kerygma or as the heart of the early Christian confession of faith about Christ.

It is important to note that when Paul rehearses the *paradosis*, the sacred "tradition" of early Christians that he and others handed on, he indicates that it included the confession that "*Christos* died for our sins" (1 Cor 15:3). This extraordinary formula, having no known precedent in early Judaism, is regarded as the heart of Christian faith by Paul, who had learned of it from those who were "in Christ" before him. This means that in the period between A.D. 30 and the point at which Paul received this tradition (surely prior to his missionary journeys) the term *Christos* was not only being used by Christians as a term having exclusive reference to Jesus, but already it was being closely linked to Jesus' death as the means of eschatological salvation.

It is possible, as N. A. Dahl concludes, that this development can be traced back to the fact that Jesus was crucified as a messianic pretender. There is room for doubt about this, however, since the title on the cross may well have read (in Greek, Hebrew and Latin) *Basileus*, *Melek* and *Rex* rather than *Christos*, *Māšîaḥ* and *Christus*. It is perhaps more probable that the early and even pre-Pauline use of the word *Christos*, virtually as a name for Jesus, is explained by the fact that Jesus during his ministry in some way identified himself as God's final agent *(Māšîaḥ)* and also spoke of his death in terms something like those we find in Mark 10:45 (cf. Witherington 1990, 251-56). Perhaps also the early Hellenistic-Jewish Christians knew that the average Greek speaker might easily take the word *Christos* like the more familiar term *Christus* (cf. Suetonius *Claudius* 25, where evidently *Christus* is read as *Chrestus*) to be a name, distinguishing this Jesus from others by that name. Furthermore, it is possible that the double name *Jesus Christ* in part became common because early Christians wished to suggest the royal dignity of their Savior and thus gave him a double name like other notable figures of the era, such as Caesar Augustus.

4. Pauline Usage.

Paul, wherever he may have first heard of Jesus

being called *Christos* as a virtual second name, did not lose sight of the fact that *Christos* was originally likely to have been a title. This is shown by several pieces of evidence. First, Paul never juxtaposes *Kyrios* with *Christos* alone, for this would amount to awkwardly combining two titles (Grundmann, 542-43). The one possible exception to this rule is found in Colossians 3:24, where we find *tō kyriō Christō douleuete* ("you serve/are slaves to the Lord Christ"), but there *kyrios* may well carry its secular meaning of "master," not divine Lord (cf. Col 3:22-23). Second, Paul never adds a genitive to the term *Christos* (as may be observed in early Judaism, e.g., "the Anointed of the Lord"). In fact, he does not use the term in any sort of possessive expression, such as "God's Christ" (but cf. 1 Cor 3:23). Neither is *Christos* ever used as a simple predicate in the Pauline letters. Nor is the expression "Jesus the Christ" ever found (Dahl, 37). In fact, Paul never feels it necessary to state the formula "Jesus *is* the Christ," nor does he argue for the idea. However, he among others utilized what is commonly regarded as the earliest of Christian confessions, "Jesus is Lord" (Rom 10:9). This evidence strongly suggests that the messiahship of Jesus was not under debate in the Pauline communities and that Paul took it as a presupposition for all other confessions. In his letters he did not, for example, try to demonstrate by prooftexts the messiahship of Jesus. J. D. G. Dunn puts it this way: Paul "makes no attempt to prove that Jesus really is 'the Christ' despite his suffering and death. 'Christ' is no longer a title whose fitness in its application to Jesus has to be demonstrated. The belief in Jesus as the Christ has become so firmly established in his mind and message that he simply takes it for granted, and 'Christ' functions simply as a way of speaking of Jesus, as a proper name for Jesus (so even in 1 Cor. 15.3)" (Dunn, 43).

One of the most important ways Paul uses the term *Christos* is in a daring phrase meant to characterize his preaching: *Christos estaurōmenos* ("Christ crucified," 1 Cor 1:23). The phrase must have had some shock value for Jewish listeners since there is no conclusive evidence that early Jews expected a crucified Messiah. Crucifixion was a punishment reserved for the worst criminals and revolutionaries. Jews, on the basis of a certain reading of Deuteronomy 21:23 (cf. Gal 3:13), seem to have understood crucifixion to be a sign that the crucified person was cursed by

God. There is no conclusive evidence that Isaiah 53 was ever applied to the Messiah before Jesus' day (the significance of the evidence from *Tg. Isa* 53 is debatable).

Careful scrutiny of Paul's usage of the term *Christ* suggests that in the main Paul's meaning was not derived from early Jewish ideas about God's anointed but rather from traditions about the conclusion of Jesus' life and its sequel, coupled with Paul's Damascus Road experience. These events forced Paul to rethink what it meant for someone to be the Davidic Messiah (Kim). The fact that Paul and other early Christians used the term *Christos* to refer to someone who had died on the cross and had risen from the dead indicates the extent to which the meaning of the term was transformed. *Christos* brought redemption to his people by dying, rising and being exalted to authority and power at the right hand of God over all the principalities. He did not bring redemption by throwing off the yoke of Roman rule during his earthly ministry. In short, Paul has something rather different in mind from what is found in such texts as *Psalms of Solomon* 17—18, where Messiah is seen as a conquering hero throwing off the yoke of a foreign rule.

Yet it would not be quite true to say, as W. Grundmann does, that "the understanding of the Messiah loses its national, political, and religious significance and the significance of the Messiah in human history is attested and expounded. This is the distinctive theological achievement of Paul" (Grundmann, 555). In Romans 15:8 Paul very clearly recounts the fact that Christ became a servant to the circumcision, and he holds out the hope of the salvation of many Jews at the eschaton (Rom 11:25-26). Christ is only now a Savior to the Gentiles through his ministers and apostles like Paul (cf. Rom 15:16-18), but in Paul's mind this does not nullify the significance of Christ's prior mission and service to Jews. Indeed, Paul wishes to insist to his largely Gentile audience that salvation is from and for the Jew first and also the Gentile (Rom 1:16; *see* Israel).

Paul was well aware of early Jewish ideas about Messiah being a Jew born under the law (cf. Gal 4:4) and of Davidic ancestry (cf. Rom 1:3), and he is happy to affirm these things of Jesus. There are also various places where Paul refers to the fully human character of this *Christos* (Rom 5:17-19; Phil 2:7; Rom 8:3). He was also aware that early Jews by and large did not think of Messiah as some sort of superhuman figure but rather as an exemplary human being especially anointed with God's Spirit (Grundmann, 526; but cf. the parables of *1 Enoch*, which suggest a more-than-human figure, and possibly the Son of Man of Dan 7). Yet here too Paul appears to have gone far beyond the majority of his Jewish contemporaries in his understanding of the Davidic Messiah, for the most natural way to read the grammatically difficult phrase in Romans 9:5 is as follows: "comes the Christ who is over all God blessed forever" (Metzger). This suggests that Paul saw the Christ as not only assuming divine functions in heaven but in some sense properly being called God. This comports with Philippians 2:11, where Jesus *Christos* is called by the divine name used in the LXX, *kyrios* ("Lord"), as well as with Colossians 1:19 ("for in him all the fullness [*plērōma*] was pleased to dwell"). It should be noted that in Romans 9:5 Paul very clearly speaks of "the Christ," which once more indicates his understanding of the larger significance of the term.

Paul's use of *Christos* in the salutations of his letters also points to an exalted view of Jesus. Thus, for instance, in Philippians 1:2 grace and peace are said to come not only from God the Father but also from the Lord Jesus Christ. As C. F. D. Moule puts it, "The position here occupied by Jesus in relation to God, as well as in many other opening formulae of the New Testament letters, is nothing short of astounding—especially when one considers that they are written by monotheistic Jews with reference to a figure of recently past history" (Moule, 150). In these instances Jesus Christ is seen as one who dispenses what only God can truly give—shalom.

Romans 1:16 provides a possible clue indicating why Paul so persistently used the term *Christos* and occasionally gave hints that it was originally a title, rather than using a term such as *Sōtēr* ("Savior") to refer to Jesus. Though Paul was the apostle to the Gentiles, he wished to continue to affirm to his audience, and perhaps on occasion even stress, that salvation is from the Jews and for the Jews before it is for others. One way of doing this was to continue to juxtapose the two terms *Iēsous Christos*. Paul, as a Jew, wished it never to be forgotten that Jesus, who is Savior of the world, is such only as the Jewish Messiah. Thus it may be that Paul's use of the term *Christos* as a virtual name for Jesus, as well as the manner in which he refrained from

using the term, was not just a matter of habit. It was an attempt by Paul to remind an increasingly Gentile church of the Jewish origin and character of the Savior and his salvation.

The term *Christos*, if studied in the context of its varied uses in the Pauline corpus, reveals how the apostle drew on, amplified, transformed and transcended some early Jewish ideas about the Messiah. For Paul the content of the term *Christos* was mainly derived from the Christ event and his experience of that event. This led to three elements in his preaching about Christ that were without known precedent in early Judaism: (1) Messiah is called God; (2) Messiah is said to have been crucified, and his death is seen as redemptive; (3) Messiah is expected to come to earth again. Non-Christian Jews did not speak of a crucified Messiah, much less of a second coming of Messiah. Nor do we have any evidence that early Jews were willing to call the Messiah "God," or one in whom the fullness of deity dwells.

5. The *En Christō* Formula.

It was probably due to careful reflection on some of the three elements listed above that Paul came to use the phrase *en Christō* ("in Christ") as he did (*see* In Christ). *En Christō* was unquestionably one of Paul's favorite phrases, appearing 164 times in the chief Pauline letters and another half dozen in the form *en Christō Iēsou* ("in Christ Jesus") in the Pastorals. This total is especially remarkable in view of the fact that other NT writers hardly ever used the phrase (but cf., e.g., 1 Pet 3:16; 5:10, 14). Paul never used the term *Christianos* ("Christian"); rather *en Christō* seems to be his substitute for this adjective (cf. 1 Cor 3:1). At other points the phrase *en Christō* seems to have a more pregnant sense, indicating the environment or atmosphere in which Christians live; that is, they are "in Christ." A. Deissmann, in his pioneering study *Die Neutestamentliche Formel "in Christo Jesu"* (1892), argued that this formula had both a local and mystical meaning in which Christ, as a sort of universal Spirit, is the very atmosphere in which believers lived.

A good example of this usage is found in 2 Corinthians 5:17: "If anyone is in Christ, that person (or 'there') is a new creation" (cf. Phil 3:8-9; *see* Creation, New Creation). In fact, whole congregations could be said to be "in Christ" in the same way they were said to be "in God" (cf. Gal

1:22 and Phil 1:1 with 1 Thess 1:1). There are a variety of other passages that seem to have a locative sense (1 Thess 4:16; Gal 2:17; 1 Cor 1:2; 15:18). A. Schweitzer in *The Mysticism of Paul the Apostle* (1931), rejecting much of Deissmann's reasoning, argued that the solidarity that Paul envisioned Christians having with Christ and with each other is a corporate one of a quasi-physical nature that occurs through the material rite of water baptism and not through some subjective experience brought about through faith. This surely goes beyond the evidence and contradicts such texts as Galatians 2:16 and Romans 5:2. Schweitzer's view seems to have been more indebted to his own understanding of early Jewish eschatology than to Paul.

Paul does speak of Christ being in the believer (Gal 2:20; Rom 8:10), but this is not nearly so characteristic of the apostle as the phrase *en Christō*. It does not seem possible either to argue that Paul is simply using the language of transfer from one dominion to another or to eliminate completely the locative sense of *en Christō* in various instances. Nor can these texts simply be explained as another way of saying one belongs to Christ or that things are accomplished for the believer through Christ. Rather, for Paul both logically and theologically the concept of being *en Christō* is central. One cannot do something for or with Christ unless one is first *en Christō*. One cannot approach the Father through the Son (*see* Son of God) unless one is *en Christō*. If one is *en Christō*, then one is in his body—the *ekklēsia* (*see* Church). The effects of being in Christ are varied: human spiritual transformation by means of death to sin, possession of the Spirit (*see* Holy Spirit), being made a new creation or creature, having one's inner person and mind renewed, being given hope and assurance of a bodily resurrection like unto Christ's, and being united spiritually with a great host of other believers in a living entity Paul likens to a body.

The christological implications of this use of *en Christō* have been ably summed up by Moule: "if it is really true that Paul thought of himself and other Christians as 'included' or 'located' in Christ; . . . it indicates a more than individualistic conception of the person of Christ . . . a plurality of persons can find themselves 'in Christ', as limbs are in the body" (Moule, 62, 65).

This means that Paul conceives of the exalted Christ as a divine being in whom Christians

everywhere can dwell. Put another way, Paul's views on incorporation into Christ and its result, being in Christ, suggest a view of Christ as a divine being "in" whom all believers can dwell and at the same time a divine being who can be "in" all believers, through the presence of the Spirit.

6. *Christos* in the Contested Pauline Letters.

In Colossians and Ephesians we find a further development of Paul's christology focusing on what is called "the mystery of Christ." This mystery is that God in Christ has provided salvation and reconciliation for all peoples, Jews and Gentiles, and even for the whole cosmos. The cosmic scope of Christ's role becomes particularly evident in these two letters. It is thus not surprising that these letters place more emphasis on the ongoing role of the exalted Christ than do most of Paul's earlier letters, though reference to Christ's death and resurrection is not absent. In these two letters Christ is seen not only as a personal savior for individuals but also as a cosmic ruler. In Christ is found the storehouse of God's wisdom and knowledge (Col 2:2-10), although the mystery is not esoteric since it has to do with Christ's public work on the cross and in both letters the mystery is carefully related to the community of faith. According to Ephesians 1:22 Christ rules over the cosmos for the church, and in Ephesians 5:32 the mystery has to do with the relationship of Christ to his church. Furthermore, the relationship between Christ's headship over the cosmos and the church becomes evident in the Christ hymn of Colossians 1:15-20, where the two are mentioned in the same breath.

Among the "faithful sayings" that characterize the Pastoral Epistles (*see* Pastoral Letters), only two add anything new to the concept of Christ revealed in Paul's earlier letters. In 1 Timothy 6:13 Christ's witness is made before Pilate, thus tracing moments of christological significance back to an event prior to Christ's death. Earlier, in 1 Timothy 1:15 we read that Christ "came into the world" for the specific purpose of saving sinners. This theme presses the moments of christological significance even further back into the story of Christ, at least to the inception of Jesus' human life, and possibly alludes to Christ's preexistence (*see* Christology). The latter idea is expressed elsewhere in Paul, most clearly in the Christ hymns of Philippians 2:6-11 and Colossians 1:15-20. In 1 Timothy 2:5 the stress is on the humanity of Jesus as the mediator between God and humanity. Finally, it should be noted that the Pastorals reflect a certain predilection for the phrase "Christ Jesus" or occasionally "Christ Jesus" combined with "our Lord."

The study of Paul's use of the term *Christos* provides a window on the character of Paul's christological thought, but it must be supplemented with detailed study of other important christological ideas such as Lord, last Adam and Son of God.

See also CHRISTOLOGY; IN CHRIST.

DNTB: MESSIANISM

BIBLIOGRAPHY: O. Cullmann, *The Christology of the New Testament* (rev. ed.; Philadelphia: Westminster, 1963); N. A. Dahl, "The Messiahship of Jesus in Paul," in *The Crucified Messiah and Other Essays* (Minneapolis: Augsburg, 1974) 37-47; M. de Jonge, *Christology in Context* (Philadelphia: Westminster, 1988); idem, "The Earliest Christian use of χριστός: Some Suggestions," *NTS* 32 (1986) 321-43; idem, "The Use of the Word 'Anointed' in the Time of Jesus," *NovT* 8 (1966) 132-48; J. D. G. Dunn, *Unity and Diversity in the New Testament: An Inquiry into the Character of Earliest Christianity* (Philadelphia: Westminster, 1977); W. Grundmann, "Χριστός," *TDNT* 9:540-62; M. Hengel, " 'Christos' in Paul," in *Between Jesus and Paul* (Philadelphia: Fortress, 1983) 65-77; S. Kim, *The Origin of Paul's Gospel* (Grand Rapids: Eerdmans, 1982); W. Kramer, *Christ, Lord, Son of God* (SBT 50; London: SCM, 1966); I. H. Marshall, *The Origins of New Testament Christology* (Downers Grove, IL: InterVarsity, 1990 [1976]); B. M. Metzger, "The Punctuation of Romans 9:5," in *Christ and Spirit in the New Testament: Studies in Honor of C. F. D. Moule,* ed. B. Lindars and S. S. Smalley (Cambridge: Cambridge University Press, 1973) 95-112; C. F. D. Moule, *The Origin of Christology* (Cambridge: Cambridge University Press, 1977); J. Neusner, W. S. Green, E. Frerichs, *Judaisms and Their Messiahs at the Turn of the Christian Era* (Cambridge: Cambridge University Press, 1987); K. H. Rengstorf, "χριστός," *NIDNTT* 2.334-43; B. Witherington, *The Christology of Jesus* (Minneapolis: Fortress, 1990).

B. Witherington III

CHRIST III: ACTS, HEBREWS, GENERAL EPISTLES, REVELATION

The term *Christos,* transliterated as "Christ" in English, is used in Jewish and Christian contexts as the equivalent of the Hebrew term *māšîaḥ.* When they are used as nouns, the Hebrew and the Greek terms refer to an anointed person (*see* Christ I), though originally *Christos* was an adjective. Jews sometimes used the term *māšîaḥ* to refer to an individual anointed by God, a king (Ps 18:50; 89:20) or a priest (CD 12.23-24; 14.19), and sometimes they saw this person as one who would come to restore or renew Israel. The evidence that *māšîaḥ,* much less *Christos,* was a technical term for "messiah" before NT times is slim (de Jonge 1986).

Nevertheless the use of the term *Christos* in early Christian literature presupposes and draws on Jewish hopes for an anointed one, especially one in the line of David (*see* Judaism and the New Testament). We find in the Gospels and in Paul the use of *Christos* as a title or a term referring to this longed-for figure, but we also find it used as a second name for Jesus. For example, Mark's Gospel begins with the heading that he will relate good news about Jesus Christ, not Jesus "the Christ," though clearly Mark knows that the term began as a title (Mk 13:21-22). This duality is also found in Paul's writings, where most often the term is used as a name for Jesus, especially at the beginning of letters (e.g., Rom 1:1; 1 Cor 1:1). Equally clearly Paul knows the Jewish background of the term. For example, he does not juxtapose the term *Christ* with the term *Lord,* for that would be putting two titles together, and it appears his usage is primarily indebted to his reflection on the narrative about the end of Jesus' life (1 Cor 1:23).

The use of the term *Christos* outside the Gospels and the Pauline corpus also falls into certain definite patterns, some of which support the notion that "Christ" was frequently used as another name for Jesus of Nazareth and sometimes also was used to describe a role, function or position he assumed at some point in his career. The fact that on various occasions the same document, such as Acts or 1 Peter, can reflect both the titular and nominal use of *Christos* shows the flexibility with which the term could be used.

1. Acts
2. Hebrews
3. James and Jude
4. 1 and 2 Peter
5. Johannine Letters and Revelation
6. Conclusions

1. Acts.

The twenty-six references to *Christos* in Acts refer to Jesus. The term occurs only rarely in conjunction with an OT citation, no doubt because it is rather rare in the Greek OT. Nevertheless, Acts 4:26 does contain a citation of some form of Psalm 2:2, in which God as Lord is distinguished from "his anointed one" (in Acts, *tou Christou autou*). Texts such as this one and others where the qualifier *his* occurs (cf. Acts 3:18) make clear that the author knows the root meaning of the word *Christos* and understands its relational character. If one is the Christ, one must be anointed by someone else, in this case the Father. Hence when we find the phrase "our Lord, Jesus Christ" in Acts (Acts 15:26; 20:21) we see the two relationships that are implied—Jesus is the anointed one of God and the believer's Lord.

The author of Acts makes explicit that essential to being a Christian is confessing Jesus to be "the Christ" (*ho Christos,* Acts 9:22; 17:22). In the witness to Jews in the synagogue this issue is pressed; precisely this point had to be demonstrated from the Scriptures if Jews were to be followers of Jesus. In Acts it appears that "Christ" functions mainly as a name when the audience is Gentile but can serve as a functional description or title when the audience is Jewish. The phrase "in/by the name of Jesus Christ" or a variant (Acts 2:38; 4:10; 8:12; 10:48; 15:26; 16:18) shows, however, not only that *Christos* could be used as part of a name even in a Jewish context (Acts 4:18, noting the Jewish authorities leave out "Christ") but also that it was believed that confessing, invoking, proclaiming, praying or exorcising in this name produced miraculous events (*see* Miracles, Miracle Stories), including conversions and healings. *Baptism "in the name of Jesus Christ" is seen as the characteristic entrance rite into the Christian community for Jews and Gentiles (Acts 2:38; 10:48; see Jones).

Luke stresses the necessity of Jesus' sufferings and resurrection (Lk 24:26-27), and in this context he asserts that it was God's plan revealed in Scripture for "the Christ" to suffer (Acts 17:2-3) and to be raised (Acts 2:31, citing Ps 16:10; see Moessner). The fulfillment of Scripture in these matters is stressed in the context of the synagogue or where the audience is Jewish. When the audience is solely or almost solely Gentiles who are not synagogue adherents or connected with Jews the term *Christ* as a title or description does not arise. In various cases it does not arise

even as a name in such contexts (see Paul's speech to the Lystrans in Acts 14:15-17 and to the Athenians in Acts 17:22-31). For a Jewish audience it was critical to confess that Jesus is the Christ (Acts 5:22; 17:3), while for a Gentile audience it was paramount to confess that the person called Jesus Christ is Lord (cf. Acts 15:23 with Acts 15:26). The community of Christian Jews and Gentiles shared the confession of Jesus as "our Lord" (Acts 15:26; 20:21). One was to have faith in him (Acts 24:24; 20:21).

One should probably not make too much of Acts 2:36, for while this text does speak of God "making" Jesus the Messiah (presumably after his crucifixion; *see* Death of Christ) elsewhere he is spoken of as suffering as Messiah (Acts 17:3). At most, Acts 2:36 suggested to the author that Jesus entered a new stage of his messianic roles and duties after his death. What we find notably lacking in Acts is the Pauline idea of being *"in Christ" or being participants in his body (*see* Body of Christ) or the notion of Christ's preexistence. The author's christology has sometimes been dubbed "absentee christology," since Luke stresses that Christ ascended and rules from heaven (cf. Acts 3:11-26; Robinson; Moule).

2. Hebrews.

By contrast with Acts the references to Christ in Hebrews appear much closer to Pauline usage (see Witherington 1991) not only in the frequency with which Christ seems to be a name rather than a description or title but also in the use of the idea of sharing in or being partners of Christ (Heb 3:14). Again and again, however, "Christ" seems to be a name (Heb 5:5; 6:1; 9:11, 24, 28) for a human being who is flesh and blood (Heb 9:14; 10:10) yet is also much more than that, since "Jesus Christ is the same yesterday and today and forever" (Heb 13:8) and is one for whom Moses could suffer in advance (Heb 11:26).

One of the distinctive notes in Hebrews is relating the idea of sonship to the term *Christ* (cf. Hurst; *see* Son of God). At Hebrews 3:6 we hear of Christ being faithful over God's house as a son, and at Hebrews 5:5 it is Christ who is glorified and royally appointed by God, who said to him, "You are my Son, today I have begotten you" (using the language of Ps 2:7, part of a coronation ode). Notably missing in all the rich christological discussion in Hebrews is any discussion or explanation about Jesus being the Christ, the anointed one, unless we count the sonship language as a surrogate for such. The author is much more interested in the role of Jesus as both sacrifice and sacrificer—the heavenly high priest. The Pauline influence on this document makes unlikely the suggestion of J. D. G. Dunn that in Hebrews 1—2 the author is talking about the preexistence of an idea rather than the personal preexistence of the Son/Christ (cf. Dunn 1980 with Craddock and Schweizer).

3. James and Jude.

Little needs to be said about the use of *Christos* in James, since it appears twice (Jas 1:1; 2:1). In both cases it appears in one long appellation, "the [our] Lord Jesus Christ," with "Christ" used as a name. There are six references to Christ in Jude, all of the same variety as we find in James (Jude 4, 17, 21, 25) or even briefer ("Jesus Christ," Jude 1 [twice]). James, Jude and Hebrews show little reflection on Jesus as the Christ even though they appear to be directed to an audience that includes a goodly number of Jews or Jewish Christians. Perhaps the explanation lies in the fact that these documents are not apologetic or evangelistic documents but are meant for those who are already convinced Jesus is the Christ. By contrast, Luke-Acts, which is often thought to be the only document in the NT clearly written by a Gentile, shows considerable interest in this subject.

4. 1 and 2 Peter.

First Peter and 2 Peter reflect a variety of uses of the term *Christ,* and since the two letters manifest distinct tendencies they deserve to be treated separately. For example, in 1 Peter we find the formula *en Christō* (1 Pet 3:16; 5:14), while in 2 Peter we find the phrase "our Lord and Savior Jesus Christ" (2 Pet 1:11; 2:20; 3:18) (Richard, 380-96).

In 1 Peter there is a major stress on the suffering and resurrection of Christ (1 Pet 1:2, 3, 11, 19; 2:21; 3:18, 21; 4:1; 5:1). The author also emphasizes in Pauline fashion that the believer may share in these sufferings or ones of a similar nature (1 Pet 4:13; cf. Phil 3:10). The author of 1 Peter is also not reluctant to refer to Christ's return, in this case called "the revelation of Christ" (1 Pet 1:7, *en apokalypsei Iēsou Christou;* 1 Pet 1:13). There is also the reference in 1 Peter 1:11 to the spirit of Christ who inspired and illuminated the OT prophets. The author appears

to subscribe to Christ's preexistence, but he does not discourse on the matter (cf. 1 Pet 1:20; 2:4; Hanson; Craddock; contrast Dunn 1980). He also uses the phrase "the name of Christ," which one may be reviled for bearing or bearing witness to (1 Pet 4:14), and one is to hallow Christ in one's heart as Lord (1 Pet 3:15). The author seems to understand the relational character of the term *Christ,* for he refers to "the Father of ... Jesus Christ" (1 Pet 1:3).

In 2 Peter the usage is less varied with the most intriguing passage being the reference to "our God and Savior, Jesus Christ" (2 Pet 1:1). This appears to be a clear example of Jesus being called God in the NT (cf. Harris 1992). This letter stresses the connection of the term *Christ* with the term *Savior (sōtēr)*. Of the eight references to Christ in this letter, half of them (2 Pet 1:1, 11; 2:20; 3:18) connect these two terms. There is a special stress on the knowledge of Jesus Christ (2 Pet 1:16; 2:20; 3:18). The author clearly uses the term *Christ* as part of a name (e.g., 2 Pet 1:1) throughout, as is the case in 1 Peter. In 2 Peter, Jesus Christ is not seen as merely a hero of antiquity, for in 2 Peter 1:14 he reveals to the author in the present that his time of death is near. It is possible that there is a Petrine source in 2 Peter 1:16—2:4, as this section shares much vocabulary and ideas with 1 Peter, including the manner of the use of the term *Christ* in this subsection (cf. 1 Pet 3:1 with 2 Pet 1:16; see Witherington 1985).

5. Johannine Letters and Revelation.

Like the author of Hebrews, the writer of the Johannine epistles (*see* John, Letters of) has a penchant for combining ideas about sonship with the name Jesus Christ. We hear repeatedly of "his Son, Jesus Christ" (1 Jn 1:3; 3:23; 5:20; 2 Jn 3). There is also a special emphasis on the need for the true believer to confess "Jesus Christ has come in the flesh" (1 Jn 4:2; 2 Jn 7), probably reflecting the need to combat Docetic or protognostic (*see* Gnosticism) teachings offered by some false teachers who had frequented the Johannine community (*see* Adversaries). First John 2:22 shows that confessing Jesus to be the Christ is also seen as critical for his community.

The special concern with confession in these letters should not be overlooked, and the incarnational character of what is to be confessed is striking. Deceivers and antichrists are those who do not confess that the Christ has come in the flesh, in the person of Jesus (2 Jn 7). In view of the content of the confession, the crucial text (1 Jn 5:6) refers not to the sacraments but to the birth (water) and death (blood) of Jesus Christ— the two means by which he comes to the believer (see Witherington 1989). The author of these letters also knows of the idea of *koinōnia* in and with Jesus Christ (1 Jn 1:3) and in 1 John 5:20 refers to the believer being not only in the truth but also "in his Son Jesus Christ." Abiding in Christ involves abiding in the teaching of Christ (2 Jn 9), which likely means the teaching about Christ referred to in the confessional statements. Jesus Christ is seen as so closely associated with the Father that the divine blessings of grace, mercy and peace come to the believer from them both (2 Jn 3).

The term *Christos* does not appear in 3 John.

Despite the plethora of images of Christ in Revelation (*see* Revelation, Book of), the term *Christ* appears there only eight times, and half of these are in the opening and closing verses of the document. The seer John receives a revelation from or about Jesus Christ (Rev 1:1; probably the former is being emphasized), which is also a testimony *(martyrian)* about Jesus Christ (Rev 1:2) that encompasses all that follows in the Apocalypse. Jesus Christ is the faithful witness who reveals and testifies to all these things.

The author knows that *Christos* is more than a name, as is clear from the allusion to OT ideas referring to God as Lord and to God's Christ (Rev 11:15, drawing on a host of texts, including Ps 10:16; 22:28; Dan 7:14; Zech 14:9). It is also clear from Revelation 12:10, which speaks of the power or authority of God's Messiah. The martyrs in Revelation 20:4 are seen as those who will rise and reign with the Christ for one thousand years, indicating that the roles of Christ were not completed by what Jesus accomplished during his earthly ministry. These martyrs are said to be priests not only of God but also of Christ (Rev 20:6). The author has no difficulty distinguishing God from Christ, but he also clearly defines Christ in divine terms, roles and functions (Rev 19:16). Christ is the one who dispenses grace from heaven to God's people (Rev 22:21). Thus both the titular sense and "Christ" as a name are evident in this work, though the use as a name is notable only at the beginning of the document. Perhaps the intent is to orient the hearer or reader, who is about to be introduced to a multitude of apocalyptic images (cf.

Grundmann). Revelation shows that the original messianic meaning of *Christos* was still known in the last decade of the first century (cf. de Jonge 1992).

6. Conclusions.

We have endeavored to show the rich and varied use of the term *Christos* in the non-Pauline letters and Revelation. The following conclusions seem to be warranted.

There do not seem to be any clear distinctions to be made between Hellenistic and Jewish Christian handling of the "Christ" concept. Some of the more Jewish documents use "Christ" as a simple name, and some of those documents assumed to be less Jewish reflect knowledge of the Jewish background of the concept.

The term *Christ* is sometimes used indiscriminately of any and all phases of the career of Christ, including apparently his preincarnate and postincarnate existence. There is little or no evidence of adoptionist tendencies.

"Christ" is frequently used as a name and sometimes as a title but also as a description of a relationship. Jesus is God's anointed but the believer's Lord.

The general avoidance of juxtaposing the two titles "Lord Christ" is notable and suggests that the early Christian writers knew the background of the term *Christ* and knew it was not merely a name, even when they do not make this explicit by calling Jesus "the Christ."

Notably absent in all this material is any attempt to explain the term *Christ* by using the phrase "the *Son of Man."

The royal or messianic background of the term *Christos* is not emphasized in most of the sources we have considered, but it can be argued to be determinative of how the term is used in most cases (cf. Hahn).

As some have argued, the parting of the ways between Judaism and early Christianity in the late first century accelerated the process whereby Jesus was called God openly and frequently, and this may be so, but it is notable that some early Jews did use exalted language to speak of various agents, both supernatural (angelic) and human, between God and humankind (cf. Hurtado). We would suggest that the high christological language used by early Christians ultimately goes back to some of the sapiential language Jesus and early Jewish Christians used to portray the man from Nazareth as God's Wisdom come in the flesh (Witherington, *Sage* 1994). Jesus and his self-presentation stand as the middle term between the particularization of Wisdom as residing on earth in Torah (Sir) and the hypostasization of Wisdom (Wis) and the use of the term *theos* of Christ (in the NT and in Pliny).

See also CHRISTOLOGY.

DLNTD: DOCETISM; LAMB; PREEXISTENCE; SHEPHERD, FLOCK; STONE, CORNERSTONE.

BIBLIOGRAPHY: F. B. Craddock, *The Preexistence of Christ in the New Testament* (Nashville: Abingdon, 1968); O. Cullmann, *The Christology of the New Testament* (Philadelphia: Westminster, 1963); N. A. Dahl, *Jesus the Christ: The Historical Origins of Christological Doctrine* (Minneapolis: Augsburg, 1991); J. D. G. Dunn, *Christology in the Making* (Philadelphia: Westminster, 1980) 51-56; idem, "Christology (NT)," *ABD* 1:979-91; W. Grundmann, "Χρίω, Χριστός κτλ," *TDNT* 9:527-80; F. Hahn, "Χριστός," *EDNT* 3:478-86; A. T. Hanson, *Jesus Christ in the Old Testament* (London: SPCK, 1965); M. J. Harris, *Jesus as God: The New Testament Use of* Theos *in Reference to Jesus* (Grand Rapids: Baker, 1992); M. Hengel, *Between Jesus and Paul* (Philadelphia: Fortress, 1983); A. J. B. Higgins, "The Priestly Messiah," *NTS* 13 (1967) 211-39; P. E. Hughes, "The Christology of Hebrews," *SWJT* 28 (1985) 19-27; L. D. Hurst, "The Christology of Hebrews 1 and 2" in *The Glory of Christ in the New Testament*, ed. L. D. Hurst and N. T. Wright (Oxford: Oxford University Press, 1987) 151-64; L. Hurtado, *One God, One Lord* (Philadelphia: Fortress, 1988); D. Jones, "The Title Christos in Luke-Acts," *CBQ* 32 (1970) 69-76; M. de Jonge, "Christ," *ABD* (1992) 1:914-21; idem, "The Earliest Christian Use of *Christos*," *NTS* 32 (1986) 321-43; idem, "The Use of the Expression *ho Christos* in the Apocalypse of John" in *L'Apocalypse johannique et l'apocalyptique dan le Nouveau Testament*, ed. J. Lambrecht (BETL 53; Gembloux: Duculot; Louvain: Leuven University, 1980); D. Moessner, "The Script of the Scriptures: Suffering and the Cross in Acts," in *History, Literature and Society in the Book of Acts*, ed. B. Witherington III (Cambridge: Cambridge University Press, 1996); C. F. D. Moule, "The Christology of Acts," in *Studies in Luke-Acts*, ed. L. E. Keck and J. L. Martyn (Nashville: Abingdon, 1966) 159-85; T. E. Pollard, *Johannine Christology and the Early Church* (Cambridge: Cambridge University Press, 1970); E. Richard, "The Functional Christology of First Peter," in *Perspectives on First Peter*, ed. C. H. Talbert (Macon, GA: Mercer University Press, 1986) 121-39; idem, *Jesus One and Many: The Christological Concept of New Testament Authors* (Wilmington, DE: Michael Glazier, 1988); J. A. T. Robinson, "The Most Primitive Christology of All?" in *Twelve New Testament Studies* (London: SCM, 1962) 139-52; E. Schweizer, "Paul's Christology and Gnosticism," in *Paul and Paulinism: Essays in Honor of C. K. Barrett*, ed. M. D. Hooker and S. G. Wilson (London: SPCK, 1982) 115-23; S. S. Smalley, "The Christology of Acts Again," in *Christ and Spirit in the New Testament*, ed. B. Lindars and S. S. Smalley (Cambridge: Cambridge University Press, 1973) 79-94; B. Witherington III, "The Influence of Galatians on Hebrews," *NTS* 37 (1991) 146-52; idem, *Jesus the Sage: the Pilgrimage of Wisdom* (Minneapolis: Fortress, 1994); idem, *Paul's Narrative Thought World: The Tapestry of Tragedy and Triumph* (Louisville, KY: Westminster/John Knox, 1994); idem, "A Petrine Source in 2nd Peter?" *SBLSP* (1985) 187-92; idem, "The Waters of Birth—John 3:5 and 1 John 5:6-8," *NTS* 35 (1989) 155-60.

B. Witherington III

CHRISTOLOGY I: PAUL

Pauline christology has frequently been discussed under the headings of the prominent titles Paul employed—Christ, Lord, Son of God, Savior—and prominent analogies such as Adam and Wisdom. Important as this christological nomenclature may be, however, it does not engage the full picture of Pauline christology. In an attempt to enlarge on the perspective gained through an account of the individual facets of Paul's christology, this article will focus on the origins of Paul's christology, its narrative framework, its dual focus on the divinity and humanity of Christ, the significance of Paul's christology for the early church and its distinctive contribution in comparison and contrast with other canonical christologies. (For the christology of the individual Gospels, readers should consult the articles on each of the Gospels.)

1. The Origins of Paul's Christology
2. The Narrative Framework of Paul's Christology
3. The Divinity and Humanity of Jesus Christ in Paul's Christology
4. The Impact and Influence of Paul's Christology
5. The Distinctiveness and Commonality of Paul's Christology

1. The Origins of Paul's Christology.

There are various possible starting points for discussing the sources or origins of Paul's christology.

1.1. Judaism. One approach is to attempt to extrapolate from the NT documents and extra-canonical sources Paul the Pharisee's (*see* Jew, Paul the) beliefs about the coming Messiah. How much of a debt did Paul's christology owe to his pre-Christian messianic beliefs? This enterprise, however, involves a tremendous amount of conjecture not only about messianic faith in pre-A.D. 70 Pharisaism but also about Paul's unique appropriation of his heritage (for the complexity of the evidence representing the Judaisms of Paul's day, see Neusner et al.). Unfortunately, apart from a few references here and there, Paul says little about his pre-Christian beliefs about Messiah. The most one can assume, judging from a text such as Romans 9:5, is that he must have believed in a coming human and Davidic Messiah. While Paul's debt to Jewish messianism, and particularly Pharisaic messianism, was surely greater than this, the evidence for discovering the degree or character of this debt is not available (but see Hengel 1991).

1.2. Hellenism. Another method of ferreting out the origins of Paul's christological thinking has been the *religionsgeschichtliche* (history of religions) approach. Perhaps the paramount and most influential example of this approach is W. Bousset's classic work *Kyrios Christos* (1913). There the christology of Paul and the early church is compared with ideas from the Greco-Roman world, particularly those found in its various forms of pagan religious thought. For example, it was assumed that Paul appropriated the title *kyrios* ("Lord") from pagan usage and so reflected the Hellenizing influence on early Christian thought. An underlying premise of this approach, however, assumes a radical distinction between Hellenism and Palestinian Judaism, an assumption that has been severely discredited by the work of M. Hengel and others (Hengel 1974). Research has shown, for example, that documents such as Sirach and the Maccabean corpus attest to the influence of Hellenism on Palestinian Jewish thinking about God and other religious matters well before the Christian era.

But apart from these more general considerations, there is evidence that the title *kyrios* arose from an early chapter in the emergence of the church and was not a product of the later Hellenization of Christianity. The Aramaic cry *Marana tha*, "Our Lord, come" (1 Cor 16:22), which surely goes back to Aramaic-speaking Palestinian or bilingual Antiochean Jewish Christians, shows that prior to the writing of Paul's extant letters, Jesus was being invoked and beckoned as a divine Lord who would return to his people. Had early Christians believed Jesus was simply a deceased Palestinian Jewish teacher, this sort of address would never have arisen (cf. Moule; Longenecker). And its preservation in Aramaic, transliterated into Greek, attests to its revered place in early Christian devotion to Christ (*see* Worship).

1.3. Paul's Conversion/Call and Early Christian Tradition. For reasons such as we have just given, modern research into the origins of Paul's christology has found a more promising approach in examining early christological confessions embedded in Paul's letters and in exploring Paul's statements about his call/conversion (*see* Conversion and Call of Paul). From this evidence conclusions may be drawn about how that experience and his encounter with early Christian confessions may have shaped his christology.

Galatians 1:11-23 provides the clearest and probably the earliest statement from Paul about his conversion and its immediate consequences. Here Paul is adamant in stating that he did not receive his gospel through human beings, nor was it human in origin or the result of some human instruction he received. To the contrary, Paul claims to have received his gospel by revelation directly from God. It must be stressed that in this passage Paul is primarily defending the source and substance of his gospel, not his conversion to Christ, and this goes a long way toward explaining the differences that have been noted between this narrative and the accounts in Acts, particularly those of Acts 9 and Acts 22. Let us assume, for the sake of argument, that Acts does provide us with some reliable data on the matter of Paul's call/conversion. In Paul's letters and in the third account in Acts of his conversion/call (Acts 26), it is clear that Paul did not see his commission, mission and essential message as deriving from a human source. We read of no Christian instruction delivered to Saul prior to his Damascus Road experience, and, as Acts 26 makes clear, Ananias was not the ultimate source of Paul's commission and mission. All three elements are traced to his encounter with the exalted Lord. This point is equally clear in Acts 9:15 and to a lesser but significant degree in Acts 22:14.

1.3.1. "The Gospel of Christ." The real issue for Paul in Galatians is not to establish that he is an authentic Christian, or that he received a missionary commission or even to identify the source of the Pauline *gospel; the issue is the content of his gospel. In Galatians 1:7 Paul identifies his gospel with "the gospel of Christ," a gospel that his opponents in Galatia were seeking to pervert. This phrase "the gospel of Christ" could be understood as "the gospel that comes from Christ" or "the gospel of which Christ is the content." The difference is significant, and a clue to Paul's meaning is found within the immediate context when Paul says that "God . . . was pleased to reveal his Son to me" (Gal 1:15-16). Paul appeals to a revelation, the content of which was the "Son of God." This is likely the meaning of "gospel of Christ" in Galatians 1:7 as well. If this is so, then it is germane to this argument that in the accounts of Acts 9 and Acts 22 Ananias does not teach Saul about Jesus Christ. Rather, in Acts 9 he tells him to arise, receive his sight and be baptized, while in Acts 22 Ananias expounds the meaning of Paul's commission. In any event, in light of the word of the Lord that comes to Ananias in Acts 9:15-16, we are probably to understand Ananias as speaking a prophetic word to Paul, not offering mere human instruction or counsel.

Furthermore, whatever Paul may have meant by "the gospel of Christ," he was well aware that subsequent to his conversion he had received traditions about Jesus and his teachings from other Christians, probably including Peter when Paul first visited Jerusalem (Gal 1:18). And we can scarcely believe that when Paul went up to Jerusalem again "after fourteen years," Peter, James and John only listened quietly as Paul laid before them the gospel he had been proclaiming among the Gentiles (Gal 2:1-10). It is reasonably certain that while Paul can say "those leaders contributed nothing to me," their words with Paul amounted to more than simply an endorsement of his commission. Paul's point in Galatians 2 is that his "gospel of Christ," the distinctive and essential insights he received directly from Christ either during or as a result of reflecting on the Damascus Road experience,

was left undisturbed. What were the elements that he may have learned from this firsthand encounter on the Damascus Road?

1.3.2. The Risen and Exalted Christ. First, the apostle learned that Jesus was still alive—though in a form transcending mere flesh and blood. Since Paul was a Pharisee and believed in resurrection, he probably came to the immediate conclusion that the Christian claims about Jesus having risen must have been true. We know from his statement in 1 Corinthians 9:1, "Have I not seen the risen Lord?" (cf. 1 Cor 15:8), that Paul did draw such a conclusion, whether at his conversion/call or later. In Paul's mind certain things necessarily would have followed from this conclusion. If Jesus after his death had been exalted in heaven, then this surely meant Jesus' claims, or at least the claims made about Jesus, had been vindicated. Thus Paul in Romans 1:4 says that Jesus was vindicated as or designated to be the Son of God in power by his resurrection from the dead (*see* Resurrection). Inasmuch as Jesus did not reject the claim to be Messiah, Paul could have concluded that if Jesus was alive in heaven, then he must be God's anointed one. Why else would God vindicate someone who had died a death by crucifixion, a death that, in light of early Jewish understanding of Deuteronomy 21:22, meant the crucified was accursed? As Galatians 3:13 makes clear, Paul came to believe that Christ had become a curse for believers in order to redeem them from the curse of the law (cf. 1 Cor 12:3). In short, Paul's experience of a risen and exalted Jesus occasioned a reversal of his estimate of Jesus and his crucifixion.

Paul had once regarded Jesus from a purely human point of view (2 Cor 5:16)—a failure, perhaps a fool and certainly not the Jewish Messiah—but after the Damascus Road experience he did so no longer. He now viewed Jesus as the Son of God. This does not mean Paul had no use for apostolic traditions about Jesus or for the actual sayings of Jesus.

1.3.3. The Corporate Christ. The second thing Paul is likely to have deduced from his Damascus Road encounter was that Jesus closely identified himself with the Christians Paul had been persecuting. As Acts attests, the risen Lord asked Saul, "Why are you persecuting me? . . . I am Jesus whom you are persecuting" (Acts 9:4-5; cf. Acts 22:7-8; 26:14-15). This would have suggested to him that the Christians must be God's people. If God's special Son was so closely identifying himself with those whom Saul was persecuting, Saul needed to reevaluate his understanding of the people of God. Far from doing God's will in persecuting Christians, he found himself to be opposing God's Christ and thus opposing God. It is possible that Paul's later theology of the body of Christ (*see* Body of Christ) owed something to his Damascus Road experience, where he learned that the afflictions of Christians were also the afflictions of Christ (cf. Robinson, 58; Kim, 252-56).

1.3.4. The Savior Christ. Third, Paul may have learned that he had been saved or converted on the road to Damascus quite apart from his own actions and deserts. Indeed, Christ had laid claim on him in spite of Paul's actions. This could only lead to the conclusion that salvation in its forgiving and transforming power was a gift of grace (see Dunn 1977, 190).

This experience of grace in turn meant that Paul had to assume a new attitude toward the law. Whereas previously the law had been the center point of his religious life before God, Christ and the experience of Christ was now the integrating factor in his life. All of life had to be seen through the eyes of Christ, not through the lens of the law. For Paul, Christ was the terminus of the law, insofar as the law might be understood as a means of salvation. Salvation by works, or even salvation by responding to the initial work and grace of God by obedience to the Mosaic law (covenantal nomism; *see* Law), was no longer—if it ever had been—possible. Life before God could no longer be a matter of "do this and you shall live." Rather, it became a matter of a righteousness received by grace through faith, which enabled one to obey the law of Christ (a different matter from Moses' law) out of gratitude.

Nevertheless, none of this meant that Paul saw no value in the Mosaic law. Indeed he saw it as holy, just and good, and some of its instruction was seen as a valuable moral guide for Christian living, particularly the narrative portions that could be used in a typological manner (cf. 1 Cor 10). The law's problem was that while it could often inform a person about what was evil and what was good, it could not enable one to shun the evil or do the good. It could not provide the life and power that was available from Christ through the Spirit (*see* Holy Spirit), which made possible a lifestyle pleasing to God. In addition

the law, though splendid, had but a partial and fading splendor that was eclipsed by Christ—the fuller and final revelation of God's good and perfect will and character (cf. 2 Cor 3:4-18).

It is not surprising that Paul concentrated on preaching Christ crucified and risen, for in his mind these were the decisive events that had changed the human situation before God. One who formerly had stood under the law and its condemnation could now in Christ stand under grace and its justification. If salvation was by grace through faith in the Lord Jesus who was crucified and risen, nothing stood in the way of anyone, Gentiles included, being saved apart from the Mosaic law. For Paul the removal of the Mosaic law as a means of right standing with God, as a way of being saved or working out one's salvation, had broken down the barrier between Jew and Gentile (cf. Eph. 2:14-15). If faith in the risen Lord was the way of salvation, then it could be offered to all without prior religious commitment to the Jewish requirements of circumcision, food laws and keeping the whole of Torah.

Paul, according to Galatians 1:16, saw the purpose of his conversion to be his call as a missionary to the Gentiles. This call complemented his experience of God's grace. If one's standing before God was all of grace, there was no reason why grace could not be offered to all without the preconditions of the Mosaic law. Thus it is quite possible that Paul deduced the heart of his gospel from his conversion experience. When Paul spoke of the revelation (*apokalypsis*) of Christ (Gal 1:12, 16), or of Christ as the glory of God (2 Cor 4:6), he may have been reflecting the experience recorded in Acts of a blinding light that accompanied the revelation of the risen Lord. In Paul's mind the revelation of Jesus in glory on the Damascus Road probably signaled the arrival of the eschatological age (*see* Eschatology) in which old things were passing and would pass away and new things were coming into existence (Kim, 71-74; cf. also Burton, 42-43). The arrival of the new age initiated for Paul a new christocentric view of the law and ethics in general. This was but a part of his larger enterprise of revisioning the story of Israel in light of the story of Christ.

2. The Narrative Framework of Paul's Christology.

The universe of Paul's thought revolved around

the Son of God, Jesus Christ. Paul's christology illumined his thought in its entirety, sometimes shedding its light on aspects of his thought that one might have expected would have gone relatively untouched by christology. For instance, who would have expected Paul, in midrashic fashion, to tell his Corinthian listeners that the rock that gave forth water to the Israelites during their period of wilderness wanderings was Christ (1 Cor 10:4)? Here he draws on sapiential ideas about the role of personified Wisdom in Israel (cf. Wis 11:2-4, "They journeyed through the uninhabited wilderness. . . . When they were thirsty, they called upon [Wisdom], and water was given them out of flinty rock"). Paul's view of Christ was so broad that he could conceive of him as being involved in God's dealings with his people long before he was born and began his earthly ministry. This is apparently because he saw Christ as Wisdom come in the flesh (cf. 1 Cor 1:24), and therefore whatever had been said of Wisdom in early Jewish thought, including its existence in heaven before creation (cf. Prov 8; Sir 24; Wis 7), was now predicated of Christ (cf. Witherington 1994, chaps. 7-8).

2.1. Christology and Theology. Two opposite dangers must be avoided in the study of Pauline christology. First is the danger of underestimating the significance and weight of Pauline christology for Paul's thought world. Paul's christology should be seen as a subspecies of his theology. For Paul "Jesus is Lord" is not merely a functional description of Jesus' work since his resurrection. Many, though not all, of the names, titles, roles and functions of God were predicated of Christ precisely because Paul believed that he was dealing with God in Christ, and God as Christ, though in neither respect did Paul define this with the precision of the later church councils. Christ was one way God had manifested himself to the world. Christ could be an object of confession and worship for Paul and other early Jewish Christians precisely because Christ was seen as divine. Paul was not advocating a violation of Jewish monotheism (*see* God) by advocating the worship of Christ, because he believed that Christ was divine. L. W. Hurtado has demonstrated that early Jewish monotheism could include the idea of divine agency, which on occasion involved seeing a human figure of the distant past, such as an Enoch or a patriarch, as a divine agent of God (cf. Hurtado, 17-92). In such a context seeing the Messi-

ah as a divine agent of God, or as Wisdom in person, was not such a radical departure from Jewish orthodoxy as has sometimes been thought (see also Bauckham 1999).

Paul's letters do not present a developed doctrine of the Trinity or a lengthy explanation of the interrelationships in the Godhead, but in predicating divinity of Father, Son and Spirit, Paul provided the raw data for later Christian trinitarianism. Christology was a form of theology for Paul, though by no means the only form. When Paul spoke of Christ handing over the kingdom to the Father "so that God may be all in all" (1 Cor 15:28) he was not dissolving christology into theology (cf. Beker, 200, 344).

Likewise, Paul was not christomonistic, a perspective that regards christology as the exclusive or near-exclusive form of theology. While Paul reenvisioned the world and even God from a christocentric point of view, he maintained a significant place in his theology for the Father and the Spirit. For Paul it was the Father alone who had sent the Son, the Son alone who had died on the cross and the Spirit alone by whom believers were baptized into the one body of Christ. Paul distinguished these three not only by their functions but also by their nature—inasmuch as they might be compared with Christ's human nature (i.e., the Father and the Spirit do not have a human nature). Casting Paul's theology as a christomonism fails to appreciate the apostle's differentiation among the distinctive roles, functions and characteristics of Father, Son and Spirit.

Too often discussions of Paul's christology, while recognizing it to be a subspecies of his theology, have approached the subject piecemeal, analyzing christological titles in isolation from one another. The frequent outcome is a display of ideas torn from the fabric of Paul's thought with little accounting for the coherent core of Paul's christology as it was expressed in the contingencies of the situations he addressed. J. C. Beker rightly points to both the coherency of Paul's thought through time and its contingency as it addresses particular situations and concerns. The study of christological titles can be helpful, but it can also be reductionistic, treating elements of Paul's thought as permutations in the history of theological ideas. This approach overlooks the fact that Paul's theological thought is woven together with his ethical and practical thinking as well as with his social concerns. Isolating christology at the cost of neglecting the rest of his thought world often results in an imbalanced picture. The whole of Paul's christology is much greater than the sum of its parts.

2.2. The Fourfold Narrative. A more adequate approach to Paul's christology recognizes its narrative shape (cf. Hays). That is to say, Paul's christology implies a story in which four aspects may be identified: the story of Christ, the story of Israel, the story of the world and the story of God.

2.2.1. The Story of Christ. The narrative structure follows the course of one who was in the very form of God (Phil 2:6) but set aside his divine prerogatives and status in order to take the status of a slave and die a slave's death; for this reason God exalted him. Paul may have derived this much of the story from reflecting on already existing christological hymns that were part of early Christian worship (cf. Phil 2:6-11; Col 1:15-20; Heb 1:2-4; and also Jn 1:1-14). These hymns ascribed to Christ traits that early Judaism had ascribed to personified Wisdom (cf. Witherington 1994, chap. 7). Paul, however, continues the story in relating Christ's ongoing role in heaven and his future return to earth as divine judge and triumphant Lord. Thus Paul's story of Christ transcends the more familiar pattern of *Endzeit = Urzeit* (endtime = primal time). Christ's exalted state does not simply recapitulate his preexistent state. A few examples will illustrate some of these points.

First, the christological hymn in Philippians 2:6-11 indicates that the career of Christ determines how he should be confessed. Jesus was given a throne name of "Lord" precisely because God highly exalted him as a result of his finished work on earth, which included death on a cross. The *dio kai* of Philippians 2:9 is crucial and should be translated "and therefore" or "and that is why." Ever since his death, and precisely because of his earthly life and death as a servant, Jesus has been highly exalted to a place of divine honor and power, and so he is now functioning as Lord. This is why in the present age he may be properly confessed using the divine throne name "Lord."

Second, the title *Christ* became, among early Christians, another name for Jesus. But Jesus was a human being, just as various early Jews seem to have expected Messiah to be. *Christ*, on the rare occasions when it functions as a title in Paul, refers primarily to the role of Jesus during

his earthly career, climaxing in the cross. For this reason Paul can resolve to know nothing among the Corinthians but "Christ crucified" (cf. 1 Cor 1:23). It can also on occasion be used to refer to Christ's roles after his death and resurrection and even in his preexistence (cf. 1 Cor 10:4). Thus it is critical to understand the christological titles within the narrative framework of Paul's story of Christ.

2.2.2. The Story of Israel. A larger story, the story of Israel, also informed Paul's christology. Jesus was born of woman and born under the law (Gal 4:4). For Paul this meant a sending of God's Son to be the human Jesus. Moreover, this Son was sent to redeem those under the law, Israel, a fact that clearly presupposes the lostness of Israel. More importantly, this story of Israel influenced how Paul viewed the name and the roles of the Christ. He is God's royal and even preexistent Son, sent to redeem God's people. For it was to Israel that the promise of a Messiah had been made and from Israel the Messiah was to come (Rom 9:4-5). For Paul the sonship of Jesus was another way of speaking of Jesus as a Jewish royal or messianic figure who came to set his people free. For this reason Paul can speak of the gospel as for the Jew first (Rom 1:16).

2.2.3. The Story of the World. The story of Christ and of Israel is a part of yet a larger story, the story of the world. For Paul the world is fallen (cf. Rom 1) and living on borrowed time; the present form of this world is passing away (1 Cor 7:31; cf. Gal 1:4). On the one hand, this fact relativizes relationships and other social realities that may have seemed of paramount importance in the past. On the other hand, the fact of the world's gradual demise makes decisions about the critical issues in life all the more crucial. The world is bent on self-destruction yet longs for liberation, and this is true not just of the human world but of the whole material creation (Rom 8:20-22). In addition, Paul can speak of malevolent supernatural powers, including Satan and demons, who are part of the present age (cf. 1 Cor 10:20-21; 2 Cor 2:11; 4:4).

It is against this dark backdrop and in the midst of this world that the drama of Israel and its Messiah and the Christian community is played out (cf. Wright, chap. 2).

2.2.4. The Story of God. Transcending the story of the world is the story of the Son as part of the ongoing life of God. This is a story of the interrelationship of Father, Son and Spirit, and it too informs Paul's christology. The story of God is intertwined with the story of the world. The christological hymn of Colossians 1:15-20 (cf. 2 Cor 4:4) indicates that the Son played a role in the creation of all things, including humankind. Thus the role of Christ as redeemer is part of the divine initiative to reconcile all things to God. And the incarnation is part of the story of God. Moreover, the subduing and reconciling of the powers and principalities is also part of the larger story of God, though this cosmic mission is also intertwined with the story of Christ as redeemer of humankind (1 Cor 15:24). The place of this cosmic christology in Paul's thought is well founded, for whatever one may conclude about the authorship or contingent circumstances being addressed in Colossians, the elements of this christology were already evident in Paul's christology as it was expressed in 1 Corinthians 15:24-26. Moreover, this is an eschatological story, for in relating God's final action toward his creation, the story is eschatological in both framework and substance (see Eschatology).

3. The Divinity and Humanity of Jesus Christ in Paul's Christology.

3.1. Christ's Divinity. We have already seen that Paul, in appropriating the language of the christological hymns, subscribed to the christological notion that Christ existed prior to taking on human flesh. Paul spoke of Jesus as the wisdom of God, his agent in creation (1 Cor 1:24, 30; 8:6; Col 1:15-17; see Bruce, 195), and as the one who accompanied Israel as the "rock" in the wilderness (1 Cor 10:4). In view of the role Christ plays in 1 Corinthians 10:4, Paul is not founding the story of Christ on the archetypal story of Israel but rather on the story of divine Wisdom, which helped Israel in the wilderness.

3.1.1. "Christ . . . the Wisdom of God." Furthermore, it seems likely that the sapiential ideas we find in 1 Corinthians 1:24, 30 and 1 Corinthians 8:6 blossomed into Paul's concept of the cosmic Christ—not only Lord over land and universe but also involved in its creation. The full flower of this christological wisdom thinking comes to expression in the hymn in Colossians 1:15-20, where Christ is said to be the "image of the invisible God," the "firstborn" of creation, and the means and goal of creation. Here the qualities that Judaism could attribute to Wisdom are transferred to Christ, as illustrated by a text such as Wisdom of Solomon 7:25-26: "For she is

the breath of the power of God, and a pure emanation of the glory of the Almighty; therefore nothing defiled gains entrance into her. For she is a reflection of eternal light, a spotless mirror of the working of God, and an image of his goodness" (NRSV). While Paul adopted and adapted this understanding of Wisdom to his ends, the implications of its use are important—the apostle ascribed divine attributes to Jesus Christ.

Did Paul think of Jesus as being divine? Two difficult texts call for investigation: Romans 9:5 and Philippians 2:6-7.

3.1.2. "Messiah . . . God Blessed" (Rom 9:5). This verse comes at the outset of Paul's discussion of the advantages of the nation Israel, but it poses an exegetical problem in the form of punctuation. F. C. Burkitt once said, with some exaggeration, that the punctuation of Romans 9:5 has probably been more discussed than that of any other sentence in literature. Since there is little or no punctuation in the earliest Greek manuscripts, it must be supplied by the reader or exegete. In the case of Romans 9:5 this has resulted in the text being read in various ways (see Metzger). The argument turns on whether Romans 9:5b should be read with the NRSV's "Messiah, who is over all, God blessed forever," or with the NRSV margin's "Messiah, who is God over all, blessed forever" or with the NEB "Messiah. May God supreme over all be blessed for ever." In the latter case, Romans 9:5b becomes a separate sentence from Romans 9:5a, or at least a separate clause. The JB, NIV and NKJV support the reading "who is over all, God blessed for ever," as qualifying Christ. It appears that both the context and the grammar favor the reading of the NRSV or the NRSV margin.

Romans 9:5a has the phrase *ho Christos to kata sarka*. As B. Metzger points out, in the instance of Romans 1:3-4 and elsewhere it is normal to expect a contrast when we come to the phrase *kata sarka* ("according to the flesh"). So in Romans 1:3-4 the contrast is *kata sarka* ("according to the flesh") and *kata pneuma* ("according to spirit"). *Kata sarka* in Romans 9:5a is unnatural in its present form if the speaker does not go on to say what Christ is according to something else besides the flesh.

Secondly, the phrase "who is" (*ho ōn*) is normally taken as introducing a relative clause, and 2 Corinthians 11:31 ("who is blessed forever," *ho ōn eulogētos eis tous aiōnas*) provides a good parallel to Romans 9:5. As N. Turner (15) puts it, "The text of the NEB simply closes the sentence at 'Messiah' and begins anew with an exclamation 'May God, supreme above all, be blessed for ever!' So it avoids assigning the quality of godhead to Jesus Christ, but it introduces asyndeton and there is no grammatical reason why a participle agreeing with 'Messiah' should first be divorced from it and then be given the force of a wish, receiving a different person as its subject. It would in fact be unnatural to divorce it from its antecedent." It is better to follow the NRSV margin and read, "sprang the Messiah, who is God over all, blessed forever."

Metzger also notes that Pauline doxologies elsewhere are always attached to some previous antecedent; they are not asyndetic (i.e., lacking a conjunction). Furthermore, it is almost a universal pattern for doxologies in the Hebrew and LXX to be "blessed be God," not "God blessed," as we have here if one translation is followed. So the likelihood is that "God blessed" does not express a wish that God be blessed forever but that the Messiah, who is God, is by nature blessed forever (but cf. Dunn 1988, 528-29, 535-36). The early versions also favor the reading represented in the NRSV or the reading listed in the NRSV margin. If it is asked why Paul nowhere else so explicitly calls Christ "God," Metzger's response is a good one: "The reason why there are so few statements in Paul's epistles bearing on the essential nature of Christ . . . is doubtless connected with a feature often noticed by others, namely that the apostle, for purposes of instruction bearing on Christian nurture, usually prefers to speak of the functional rather than the ontological relationships of Christ" (Metzger, 111-12).

We conclude that in Romans 9:5 Paul calls Christ God, thus demonstrating the extent to which Paul's experience of the risen Lord had caused him to qualify or transform his Jewish monotheism (cf. Wright, 237). This means that Paul had a high christology even before he used the Christ hymn in Philippians 2 (assuming Philippians is later than Romans and that Paul did not already know the Christ hymn before he wrote Romans).

3.1.3. "Who Being in the Form of God" (Phil 2:6-7). A portion of the christological hymn of Philippians 2 must now be explored more fully. The argument turns on several key terms and phrases: (1) *morphē* ("form"), found in the NT only here and in Philippians 2:7 (except in Mk 16:12, which is part of a later addition to Mark); (2) *to einai isa theou* ("to be equal with God"); and (3) *harpagmos* ("a snatching, grasping"; "a desire to acquire").

It is entirely likely that *morphē* ("form") carries the same general meaning in Philippians 2:7 as it does in Philippians 2:6. In addition, the *alla* ("but") at the beginning of Philippians 2:7 suggests a contrast is being drawn between the before and after of Jesus becoming human. *Morphē* has been translated as "form," "appearance," "condition," "status," "image" or "mode of being." If one translates *morphē* as "status," "condition" or "appearance," it would seem to indicate Jesus' outward form, status, appearance or function, not what he was in his being. It is unlikely that Paul in Philippians 2:7 is saying that Jesus in his earthly ministry merely "looked like" or "appeared to be" or "functioned" as a servant. Rather, he became this—he was a servant. The parallel between the two states is not exact since the text says that he was in the form of God but then also took on the form of a servant. Elsewhere Paul clearly states that Jesus became "poor" and generously gave himself to his people (cf. 2 Cor 8:9). For Paul this was part and parcel of the meaning of Christ's taking on the condition and status of humanity.

Second, we note that Paul does not say Jesus was the form of God but that he was in the form of God. Thus the translation "likeness" in itself seems lexically improbable (unless one imports a Last Adam idea into this text, cf. Rom 5:18-19; 1 Cor 15:45-47). Paul is not calling Jesus the "image" or "likeness" of God. Rather, as G. F. Hawthorne has pointed out,

> from earliest Greek texts μορφή was at least used to express the way in which a thing, being what it is in itself, appears to our sense. "Μορφή always signifies a form which truly and fully expresses the being which underlies it" (MM 417). Thus, when this word is applied to God, his μορφή must refer to his deepest being, to what he is in himself, to that "which cannot be reached by our understanding or sight, precisely because God is ἀόρατο: in fact the word has meaning here only as referring to the reality of God's being" (Cerfaux, *Christ*, 305). Μορφὴ θεοῦ, then, may be correctly understood as "the essential nature and character of God" (Hawthorne, 83-84).

We thus translate Philippians 2:6a and Philippians 2:7b, "being in the form (i.e., character, nature) of God . . . he went on to take on the character, nature of a servant."

Third, *to einai isa theou* (Phil 2:6c) has a definite article with it: "*the* being equal with God." This probably indicates that this second phrase is closely connected to the first, pointing to what Christ already is. But Paul is going to move on to state what that meant for Jesus in view of his later actions.

Fourth, the word *harpagmos* has been taken to mean either groping for something one doesn't have, perhaps snatching at something, or clutching on to something one already has. More likely than either of these two views is that of R. W. Hoover, who demonstrates that it means "taking advantage of something that is already rightfully yours." The Christ hymn portrays Jesus in his self-giving. He did not consider being equal with God a matter of taking full advantage of his rights or glory but rather *(alla)* of giving them up and taking on the form of a servant.

We conclude that Philippians 2:6-7 indicates Paul saw Jesus as having preexistence and equality with God (against Dunn 1980), but that in his preexistence he did not take advantage of all the prerogatives of deity.

Fifth, one more matter needs to be dealt with at this juncture—what does it mean to say Christ *heauten ekenōsen,* usually translated "he emptied himself"? Philippians 2:7 begins with the word *alla* ("but"), probably suggesting a contrast followed by a verb and its object. This may be interpreted to mean either he "stripped himself" or "emptied himself." One may ask, emptied himself of what? Although Hawthorne argues that one cannot determine from this statement alone what Christ emptied himself of (Paul does not say), the context may give some clues. So-called kenotic christology, based chiefly on this text, suggests that Jesus emptied himself of certain divine attributes—omniscience, omnipotence and omnipresence—when he became a human being. The text must surely be referring to what Christ did at the point of taking on a human nature, not at his death (cf. Martin 1976, 97). The kenotic view might be thought to derive some support from a text like Mark 13:32, "no one knows . . . not even the Son." Mark 13:32, however, can just as easily be taken to suggest that Jesus limited himself, and to say that Christ limited himself is not the same as saying he emp-

tied himself of various divine attributes. It is also important to remember that Mark 13:32 does not attempt to answer the christological question addressed in Philippians 2.

Thus it seems likely that Paul in Philippians 2 means one of two things: (1) Jesus emptied himself of the prerogatives and glory of being divine, or of the right to claim such prerogatives (which Phil 2:6 seems to suggest if we are right about *harpagmos*). These prerogatives would entail glory and lordship, which belonged to Christ by virtue of his being equal with God. (2) Hawthorne suggests it simply means Jesus totally gave himself, poured himself out, rather than telling us what he gave up. The former seems more likely.

3.1.4. "In Christ." A third category of texts speak of Christ as a sort of omnipresent being in whom believers are included. The evidence cannot be rehearsed here (*see* Christ; Moule 1977, 62-65), but the essence is that when Paul speaks of believers being "in Christ" he often suggests that Christ has attributes that only a divine being could properly be said to have.

3.1.5. Christ and the Spirit. Finally, our understanding of Paul's view of the divinity of Christ is enhanced by comparing what Paul says about Christ with what he says about God's Holy Spirit. It has been noted often how closely Paul identifies Christ and the Spirit (*see* Holy Spirit) in his letters—indeed, at points they seem to be identical. Paul can speak of the Spirit coming to believers only because Christ is risen and ascended. For instance, in discussing Jesus' resurrection Paul speaks of Jesus, the last Adam, as a "life-giving spirit" (1 Cor 15:45). He is the one who sends the Spirit, and without his resurrection and exaltation the Spirit would not have come. Romans 1:3-4 indicates that it was through the power of the Spirit that Jesus was enabled to be Son of God in power. The Spirit empowered him, and he sends that power to believers. It is Christ who makes the eschatological age possible, and that age focuses on him.

Frequently in Pauline thought the functions of Jesus and the Spirit are identified, so much so that being in Christ is simply another way of speaking about being in the Spirit (*pace* Smalley). Consider the following:

Believers are righteous in Christ (Phil 3:8, 9) but also in the Spirit (Rom 14:17).

Believers have life in Christ (Col 3:4) but also in the Holy Spirit (Rom 8:11).

Believers have hope in Christ for life to come (1 Cor 15:19) and in the power of the Spirit to give them eternal life (Gal 6:8).

Believers rejoice and have joy in the Holy Spirit (Rom 14:17) but also in the Lord (Phil 4:4).

Believers have truth in Christ (Rom 9:1), and truth is also spoken in the Spirit (1 Cor 12:3-6).

Believers have fellowship in Christ (1 Cor 1:9) but also fellowship of Spirit (2 Cor 13:13).

Believers are consecrated and sanctified in Christ (1 Cor 1:2) but also in the Spirit (Rom 15:16).

Believers are sealed in Christ (Eph 1:13) and in the Spirit (Eph 4:30).

This identification between Christ and Spirit is taken even further when Paul ascribes to Christ various features characterizing the Spirit in the OT. Thus, for instance, Psalm 104:29 states that it is the Spirit that gives life (cf. Ezek 31), but in 1 Corinthians 15:45 it is Christ who gives life. This means that at his resurrection and exaltation Jesus assumed the functions previously ascribed to the Spirit. This characteristic of Paul has led some to ask whether he held to a binitarian rather than trinitarian view of God. Is the Lord the Spirit for Paul?

This is in fact what Paul seems to be saying in 2 Corinthians 3:17: "The Lord is the Spirit, for where the Spirit of the Lord is, there is freedom." It is sometimes pointed out that Paul in 2 Corinthians 3:14 identifies Christ with God. This is not quite correct, for Paul in fact says that in Christ the veil is lifted, not by Christ. Throughout this text Paul has in mind the OT context of Exodus 34:34-35. In 2 Corinthians 3:16 it does appear that on the surface Paul is referring to Christ, who is being identified with Yahweh in his role in Exodus. C. K. Barrett notes a subtle distinction: while "the Lord" in 2 Corinthians 3:11 is Christ, the one to whom people turn, the function of removing the veil from over a person's heart is for Paul preeminently the work of the Spirit, as Christ's agent. Christ in 2 Corinthians 3:11 is identified with his agent but only in his activity, and so it is not proper to speak of Paul having a Spirit christology. Rejecting a binitarianism on the part of Paul, Barrett concludes: "It is certainly true that for Paul Christ the Lord, and the Spirit, were two very closely related terms, each of which was un-

thinkable apart from the other, since the objective status of being in Christ carried with it the subjective accompaniment of receiving the Spirit, who was manifested in particular gifts . . . ; he was however capable of distinguishing them, as for example in the phrase 'Spirit of Christ' (Rom. viii.9). It is in the realm of action . . . rather than of person . . . that the terms Lord and Spirit are identified" (Barrett 1973, 123).

What Paul is saying, according to Barrett, is that the Spirit is Lord in such situations, illuminating believers and giving them freedom. Another way of looking at this, however, is to assume that Paul is commenting on Exodus 34 in a manner we may paraphrase as follows: "now the 'Lord' in this text is the 'Spirit,' and where the Spirit of the Lord is."

In any case, Paul speaks of "the Spirit of the Lord," which seems to imply a distinction between "Spirit" and "Lord." More clearly in Romans 8:9 the two seem to be distinguished in the phrase "the Spirit of Christ." Thus for Paul the "Spirit of Christ" = "Spirit of God" (cf. Rom 8:8) = "Spirit of the Lord." We must conclude then that the Spirit is Christ's agent, and he functions for Christ, one might almost say, as Christ, here on earth during the church age. This identity in function and effect surely implies the deity of Christ, for from the perspective of the OT it is only God who can send or be a life-giving Spirit.

Nevertheless, so far as their being is concerned, Christ and the Spirit are not to be equated and may even be distinguished in some of their activities. It was Christ, not the Spirit, who died and was raised. It is Christ, not the Spirit, who will return and judge (1 Cor 4:5). It was Christ, not the Spirit, who came in the flesh. In one sense the Spirit is the bridge between believers and Christ on this earth. But it is also interesting how Paul attributes tasks to Christ that in the OT were attributed to the Spirit. In Psalm 33:6 the world is said to have been created by the Spirit, but in Colossians 1:16 we read "by him [Christ] all things are created." In the OT it often appears that the Spirit is simply God on the move in creation and history. What was said of the Spirit is now predicated of the exalted Christ who is on the move and active in his church and in history.

To summarize: in the church age Christ and Spirit are not one but two in identity, but they are one in function because the Spirit is Christ's agent on earth (recalling the rabbinic adage, "a person's agent *[šālıah]* is as their self"). This also implies that receiving Christ and receiving the Spirit are simultaneous events. Paul knows no doctrine of a second baptism, for by the Spirit one enters Christ's body, and that is the only occasion that Paul speaks of as being baptized by the Spirit (cf. 1 Cor 12:13; *see* Baptism).

3.2. The Humanity of the Christ.

3.2.1. Christ as Son. As a preface to examining what Paul meant when he called Jesus Son of David, last Adam or a human being, it is helpful to summarize what Paul meant by the term **Son of God.*

M. Hengel has provided the valuable insight that for Paul " 'Son of God,' with its more complicated language, was kept for exceptional usage, at the climax of certain theological statements" (Hengel 1976, 14). By this title Paul signified the unique relationship between the exalted Christ and God. Its further significance for Paul is summed up by I. H. Marshall:

> It is the Son who is the theme of the gospel (Rom. 1:3, 9), and it is by means of this title that Paul emphasizes the supreme value of the death of the One who stood closest to God as the means of reconciling men with God (Rom. 5:10; 8:32; Gal. 2:20; Col. 1:13 f.). . . . For Paul Jesus was God's Son during his earthly life, and . . . it was as God's Son that he died. Consequently, he did not cease to be divine in his earthly existence, and his self-emptying cannot mean that he gave up his divine nature to assume human nature. (Marshall, 644-45)

Romans 1:3-4 is an important christological statement that speaks of the Son in two aspects, his earthly descent and his resurrection glory. Here we focus on Romans 1:3: in the sphere of the flesh *(kata sarka)*, Jesus is said to have been "born of the seed of David" (a phrase we find again at the end of the Pauline corpus in 2 Tim 2:8). This phrase in itself not only indicates Jesus' Jewishness and humanity but also focuses on the pedigree warranting his title Messiah/ Christ. This surely implies some stress on his royalty. The only other place where Paul highlights this fact is Romans 15:12 ("the shoot of Jesse shall come forth"), where he quotes from Isaiah 11:10 (LXX). Romans 1:3-4 indicates two stages of Jesus' career epitomized in what seems to be a primitive christological formula that Paul adopted and endorsed. Jesus' Davidic descent is well attested in various strands of NT material

(Mt 1:1; Acts 2:30; Rev 5:5). Paul introduces this christological formulation by appealing to God's promises through the prophets in Holy Scripture (Rom 1:2). Jesus Christ is the promised and prophesied Messiah.

For most Jews it appears that *messiah* was a term referring to a human being, not divine even if he was given certain divine gifts or authority (though cf. the picture of the "Elect One" in *1 Enoch* 55—69; *see* Neusner et al.). It is thus appropriate, in a context where messiahship is mentioned, to stress Jesus' humanity born of David's seed. Indeed, it is telling that Paul uses the term *Christ* of Jesus more than he does any other, suggesting that salvation comes to believers only through one who was human like them, who lived and died for them. The term *Christ*, coupled with a stress on his crucifixion, characterized Paul's preaching to a significant degree (cf. 1 Cor 1:23). In order to speak of salvation, Paul had to stress Jesus' humanity in various ways (cf. Dunn 1977, 43). The story of Jesus (i.e., his death) brought about a redefinition of Paul's understanding of the Davidic Messiah, a process that appears to have taken place prior to the writing of Paul's extant letters (*see* Christ).

If Paul had no difficulty identifying Jesus as Christ, and Jesus as a human who had died, how did he view Jesus' humanity in general? What little he had to say about this can be summed up in a few short phrases. There is enough to suggest that Paul understood Jesus to have been fully human, but not enough to spell out in any detail how he defined that humanity. This may be because the facts of Jesus and his ministry were assumed knowledge on the part of Paul and his readers. It may also reflect Paul's chosen emphasis in his letters on Jesus' death and resurrection and issues of life in the Spirit and in the church. Paul was not a Gospel writer or historian; he was a pastoral theologian called upon to deal with matters of theological weight and direct bearing on the issues which arose in the churches (*see* Jesus and Paul).

The christological events of first importance for Paul seem to have been Christ's taking on true human nature and humbling himself to the status of a servant, his death on the cross, and his resurrection. The significant events of Jesus' earthly career between his incarnation and death are scarcely mentioned (cf. 2 Cor 8:9, though this may also refer to the circumstances into which Jesus was born).

3.2.2. Born of a Woman. Paul could affirm that Jesus was born of woman (Gal 4:4). His appearance in this world was as a normal human being, who came forth from his mother's womb into this world. As F. F. Bruce points out (Bruce, 195), Paul's word choice *(genomenon)* is applicable to anyone born of a woman. The text implies nothing peculiar about Jesus' manner of birth. Nor does Paul mention the virginal conception, though we cannot be sure that he did not know of it.

Paul also states in Galatians 4:4 that Jesus was born under the law. His mother was a Jew, and so was he. And when Paul says Jesus was born under the law "to redeem those who were under the Law" (Gal 4:5), he seems to imply that Jesus' earthly ministry was essentially directed toward Israel. Paul's apostleship to the Gentiles may go some distance in explaining why he said so little about Jesus' earthly ministry, which was directed to the lost sheep that made up Israel. When Israel did not respond, a new door was opened to take the gospel to the Gentiles (cf. Rom 9—11). If Christ's death and resurrection was the decisive event for the mission to the Gentiles, it is not surprising that Paul focuses on those events in the story of Jesus that affected and involved the Gentiles.

3.2.3. Born in Human Likeness. In Philippians 2:7 we are told that Christ was born in human likeness (cf. Phil 2:8). In other words, Jesus took on human flesh, becoming a man who was subject to human frailty, even death. Romans 8:3 also comments on this point in similar and carefully worded terms. Jesus condemned sin in the flesh, taking on human flesh to do so. Thus any sort of docetism is ruled out. Jesus was real flesh and blood. But Romans 8:3 is probably worded as it is to indicate that Jesus did not participate in the sinfulness of *flesh. Barrett stresses: "One possible suggestion is that Paul distinguished between flesh as it was created by God, and 'flesh of sin,' that is, flesh which had fallen under the dominion of sin. Christ (on this view) had perfect, unfallen flesh, which nevertheless was indistinguishable in appearance from 'flesh of sin'; he came in flesh, so that the incarnation was perfectly real, but only in the likeness of 'flesh of sin,' so that he remained sinless" (Barrett 1957, 156).

It seems plausible that the very reason the word *likeness (homoiōma)* is used in Romans 8:3 is intentionally to avoid saying he came in sinful flesh (cf. Cranfield 1979, 381). This is compatible with Paul's emphasis in Romans and elsewhere that Jesus was a new Adam, starting a new creation and race. As such he did not participate in the fallen nature of the old Adam.

Paul may have spoken of Christ as being in the "likeness of sinful flesh" not to deny Jesus' sinlessness (2 Cor 5:21) or to deny his sinless human nature but to affirm that he took on human flesh and was like all humans in this respect. Perhaps part of the reason Paul worded Romans 8:3 as he did was because he thought of Jesus as the Paschal lamb, metaphorically speaking (cf. 1 Cor 5:7). An atoning sacrifice must be unblemished and spotless. Like Adam, Jesus was born with an unfallen nature that had the capacity to sin; unlike Adam, Jesus remained sinless and so in due course became an unblemished sacrifice.

Paul's letters yield little else about the earthly Jesus except for what is implied in his recital of the Last Supper tradition (1 Cor 11:23-26; *see* Lord's Supper). There he indicates Jesus was a person who broke bread, who poured wine, who gave thanks and thus was human, thanking the heavenly Father for such earthly gifts. Paul does not say Jesus ate at the Last Supper, but it is implied. Apart from the references to Jesus' death and burial, indicating he truly died and was resurrected, there is little else that needs mentioning (cf. 1 Cor 15:4).

3.2.4. Last Adam. We turn now to Paul's theme of Christ as the last Adam (*see* Adam and Christ). It has often been noted that Paul does not call Jesus the Son of man (none of the authors of the NT letters do). This may be due to the Jewish background and meaning of the title. To Gentile ears it may have been too easily assumed to mean simply that Jesus was a real human being, or as a title it may have been considered too obscure or too simple for the Gentile mission and the expanding church (cf. Moule 1977). However, Paul uses the Adam typology of Jesus and in 1 Corinthians 15:45 calls Jesus the last Adam. Perhaps in Paul's case reflection on Jesus as truly human led to a comparison between Jesus and the first and archetypal human being. In preparation for examining Paul's typology involving Adam and the man Christ, we must first examine certain references to Jesus as the human being.

For instance, in Romans 5:15, in the midst of developing the Adam-Christ typology, Paul writes that just as death came by "the one,"

Adam, so God's grace and the gift that accompanied it (righteousness, Rom 5:17) came by "the one," Jesus. Again, in 1 Corinthians 15:21 death comes through a human being *(anthrōpos)*, Adam, and the resurrection of the dead comes through a human being *(anthrōpos)*, Jesus. In the later and disputed Paulines, 1 Timothy 2:5 shows a further development along these lines when it speaks of Christ as mediator between God and humans, and he is said to be the human being Christ Jesus. What is Paul's point in saying that grace comes to us, as do resurrection and reconciliation, by a human being? Sin was a human problem that could be resolved for humanity only by a human being. Some may think the efficacy of salvation for humankind was due to Jesus being divine, but Paul wishes to emphasize the opposite. If Jesus had not been human, humanity would not have received grace, resurrection or, as Colossians and Ephesians stress, reconciliation. The extraordinary thing is that the human Jesus died and rose again. God—apart from the mystery of the Incarnation—is not subject to death.

First Timothy 2:5 goes beyond this in stressing Christ's mediatorial role. Jesus, this text seems to imply, had to be fully God and fully human in order to properly represent God to humans and humans to God. He had to stand on both sides of the fence in order to experience and fully know the God who grieves over sin and the sinner who causes God grief. In short, for salvation to reach humans, and to redeem humans, it had to be mediated through one who shared in humanity.

The "last" or "eschatological" Adam motif in 1 Corinthians 15:21-23, 44-49 calls for comment in some detail. This passage is quite unlike the other references to Adam we find in Paul. Here we have the responsibility for sin and its consequences placed squarely on Adam's shoulders, while Eve is not mentioned. To J. Jeremias we owe the insight that Paul may have avoided using the term "Son of Man" because he addressed a Gentile audience (Jeremias, 141-42). But he goes on to stress how Paul appears to know of the "Son of Man" tradition because in 1 Corinthians 15:27 Paul makes a messianic application of Psalm 8:6 to Jesus, "for he has made all things subject under his feet." This psalm is well known for the line that shortly precedes the part Paul is quoting—"or the son of man that you care for him" (Ps 8:4).

There are similarities and differences between Adam the type and Christ the antitype. Both were truly human, both are representative heads of a race, and both had a dramatic effect on their physical/spiritual progeny. However, in some ways the differences outweigh the similarities. The powerful effect of Adam's action on all humanity was death (1 Cor 15:21), but the powerful effect of Christ's action was life (in the specific form of the resurrection of the dead). Now the question may be raised, "Is the parallelism in 1 Corinthians 15:22 a perfect one?" In Adam all die. Does the *all* in 1 Corinthians 15:22b mean that all humans will one day be made alive in Christ? First Thessalonians 4:16 makes it clear that elsewhere when Paul spoke of human resurrection he meant the resurrection of the dead in Christ. This may also be true of 1 Corinthians 15:22. In fact, 1 Corinthians 15:23 lends strength to this interpretation when it speaks of the resurrection of those "who belong to him." Thus the parallelism of 1 Corinthians 15:22a and 1 Corinthians 15:22b is not perfect. Jeremias provides us with the following chart of the pertinent elements in 1 Corinthians 15:44-49 (Jeremias, 142).

15:45	the first adam	the last adam
	a living being	a life-giving spirit
15:47	the first human being	the second human being
15:47-48	from the dust of the earth	from heaven

In order to understand Paul's Adam-Christ typology, several things must be borne in mind. First is the idea of collective personality, or at least representative headship. In some sense all persons were in Adam—he was humankind and sinned for humanity. The human race died in him. This may suggest the idea of collective personality, that is, in some sense the whole race was present (seminally?) in Adam. Perhaps a better way to view this matter, however, would be to say that as the head and progenitor of the race Adam sinned for all, and thus all human beings felt the effects of this act. By analogy, it is like when a king in an absolute monarchy declares war on a nation. All the king's subjects are then at war with that nation, quite apart from their individual choices or predilections. The idea in Paul is perhaps of a corporate head who acts for all (cf. Rom 5:12 *eph' hō* with Col 1:14 *en hō*).

Second, salvation only comes "in Christ." A person must be in Christ to receive the benefits of Christ's work. Believers have died and risen in Christ (Rom 6:3-4). The idea of representative headship, when applied to the last Adam, means that Christ as head of a new race performed deeds that subsequently shaped that race. He died in the believer's place as his or her corporate head, just as Adam sinned in humanity's place and for humankind.

It will be seen from the chart above that Jesus is called the last Adam, which does not mean the last human being. Rather, it is an eschatological claim. Christ, as the first fruits of the dead, is the beginning of a new creation (*see* Creation, New Creation). But in another sense he is the end and goal of the human race. He is bringing in the last age, the new creation, the end of God's plan.

Further, Jesus is the "second" human being, in the corporate sense. He is the start of a second human race, but with a significant difference. Adam, from one perspective, was strictly an earth creature—he came from the earth, he returned to the earth, and his body and life was natural and physical. Insofar as humanity descends from him, humankind is earthly, physical, contingent and has a natural life in the body. Christ, by contrast, was from heaven and of heaven. He was not of earth. In what sense? He was also a life-giving Spirit.

Several points may be drawn from this: (1) Christ is not merely living, like Adam; he is gives life, whereas Adam gave us death. (2) When Paul calls Christ a life-giving spirit he does not mean to imply Jesus had or has no body but that he lived in a form of life characterized by the Spirit. (3) First Corinthians 15:45 ("The first man Adam became a living being") is a quote from Genesis 2:7, except that Paul has added the word "first" and the word "Adam." When Genesis speaks of Adam as a "living being" (Heb *nepeš ḥayāh*), it does not mean Adam gained a soul but that God animated his body and he became a living body, a living being. It is unlikely that the Greek *psychē* in 1 Corinthians 15:45 means "soul." Rather, here as in elsewhere in the NT (as with the Heb *nepeš*), it means "being"—Adam was a living being. (4) When Paul uses the term "spiritual body" *(sōma pneumatikon)* he does not mean a body consisting of nonmaterial substance but a body empowered by the Spirit. Notice that Jesus did not become a life-giving Spirit until after he rose from the dead, and the life he gave was everlasting life, unlike the life Adam gave. Moreover, it was given to believers by the Spirit—in part now, in full later.

It could be that Paul derived the raw material for these ideas from Jewish speculation about Adam and the coming Messiah. The Jewish philosopher Philo understood the created humanity of Genesis 1 as an ideal being, a Platonic type, whereas he interpreted the Adam of Genesis 2 in the same way as Paul. In 1 Corinthians 15, however, it is not the first founder of the human race who is the ideal or true model, but the last one. Moreover, never in rabbinic literature is the redeemer described as a last Adam. It would seem that Paul, reflecting on the Christian gospel and the ministry, death and resurrection of Jesus—all in the light of his own revelation of the ascended Lord—modified any previous ideas he may have held.

In closing, we turn to Romans 5:12-18. In Romans 5:12 we are told that not only sin, but also death, entered the world through Adam. Death came through or because of sin. Paul apparently accepted Genesis 1—3 as a straightforward account of historical events, but here he is concerned with its theological significance. He wishes to add that whatever believers may have inherited from Adam, and whatever effect his sin may have had on humanity, there is a real sense in which human beings dig their own graves. God has not unjustly punished any with death. Nonetheless it is also true in the primary sense that none of the human race would be dying if Adam had not sinned in the first place. So Paul can add in Romans 5:15, "many died by the trespasses of the one man." Through Adam's transgression death reigned (Rom 5:17), but Paul wishes to make clear that God's antidote is not merely an equal and opposite reaction. The gift is not like the trespass (Rom 5:17); salvation is not just paradise regained, as if the negativity of sin were counteracted by an equally positive force. If one trespass could effect so much and affect so many, how much more effective was the overflowing grace and gift of righteousness for believers (Rom 5:15)? The death penalty followed just one sin, but God's grace came after many sins and, quite apart from what humans deserved, it brought about their right standing with God.

Romans 5:17 implies clearly that the life believers have in Christ is not merely more powerful than the death Adam bequeathed to the human race. It is of a wholly different order. As 1 Corinthians 15 makes clear, it comes from the Spirit and heaven, and as such it transcends natural life and triumphs over natural death. Romans 5:10 goes on to point out that Christ's obedience even unto death (his righteous conduct and sinlessness) made possible the undoing of all that was brought about by the first Adam's disobedience (cf. Cranfield 1975, 290; Barrett 1957, 117).

4. The Impact and Influence of Paul's Christology.

4.1. Paul's Christology in His Thought World.
We have earlier spoken of how christology, as an aspect of Paul's thought, was the greatest shaping force on the rest of Paul's thought world. This can be shown in a number of ways.

4.1.1. Eschatology. Paul's eschatological outlook was surely transformed once he became a follower of Jesus. There is no evidence that early Jews were expecting *two* comings of Messiah; yet that is what Paul believed, and it dictated how he viewed the future and the life of believers. The future course of history had for Paul taken on an eschatological character. There was a sense in which the age to come had already arrived, the redemptive effect of God's reign had already broken into space and time in the coming of Christ, but redemption had not yet been completed. The form of this world was passing away (1 Cor 7:31), but it was not yet gone. Powers and principalities could no longer separate the believer from the love of God in Christ (Rom 8:38) because Christ's death had disarmed the supernatural forces of evil (Col 2:15). Likewise, the inner life of the believer was caught up in the tension between the already and not yet. The believer was already a new creature in Christ (2 Cor 5:17) but had not yet experienced physical resurrection, the full redemption of the body (Rom 8:21-22).

There is likewise no evidence of an early Jewish expectation of an isolated resurrection, much less an isolated resurrection of Messiah prior to the resurrection of believers. Yet on the basis of the story of Jesus' earthly career, that is what Paul proclaimed. This enabled Paul to explain the connection between Christ's resurrection and believers' resurrection (1 Cor 15).

4.1.2. Soteriology. Paul's christology changed the shape of his soteriology. Unless new finds from the Qumran scrolls change matters, there is no conclusive evidence that early Jews were expecting a crucified Messiah. It was the story of the death and resurrection of Jesus that caused Paul to rethink how salvation would be accomplished. This message was a scandal to Jews and folly to Gentiles because it ran in the face of expectations (1 Cor 1:23). Even in the case of the Suffering Servant of Yahweh referred to in Isaiah 53, there is no firm evidence that anyone in early Judaism prior to the ministry of Jesus had applied that text to the coming Messiah (though cf. *Tg. Isa.* 53). Furthermore, in light of Deuteronomy 21:23 ("anyone who is hung on a tree is under God's curse," NIV), even if the text had been thought to refer to a suffering Messiah, it is highly unlikely that it was understood to speak of a crucified Messiah.

Salvation also was an already/not yet matter. Already large numbers of Gentiles were being saved, but God had not yet completed his plan of salvation for the Jews (Rom 9—11). Already the believer had right standing and peace with God (Rom 5:1), but that same believer was not yet fully sanctified or glorified, as is clear from the ongoing tension between flesh and spirit in the believer's life (Gal 5:16-26).

4.1.3. People of God. Paul's thinking about the people of God was changed, especially regarding the basis of one's inclusion in that group. If God's people consisted of Jews and Gentiles united in Christ (Gal 3:28), and if that group could be called the "Israel of God" (Gal 6:16; *see* Israel), then neither heredity nor obedience to Torah could any longer be the basis for securing or maintaining a place in true Israel (cf. Rom 3:23—4:8). In Christ the law, at least as a means of obtaining or keeping right standing with God, was at an end (Rom 10:4). Paul clearly stated that it was no longer necessary to follow the dietary laws since no food was unclean (Rom 14:14). Thereby for Paul the very basis of fellowship with and marks of identity among God's people were changed.

If the three great pillars of early Judaism—Torah, temple and territory—are evaluated in light of Paul's theology, we discover how radically Paul had reconceptualized the people of God. We have already spoken of Paul's view of the law, but what does he say about temple and sacrifice? On the one hand, it is Jew and Gentile united in Christ that make up the temple of God's Spirit (1 Cor 6:19; on the individual believer as temple cf. 1 Cor 3:16-17). On the other hand, Christ is the once-for-all sacrificial lamb who made all other literal sacrifices no longer necessary (cf. 1 Cor 5:7). Finally, it is not clear that Paul reaffirmed the territorial doctrine, though it is possible that he made room for such an idea once the full number of Gentiles are saved and then all physical Israel is saved (cf. Rom 11:23-25). It is striking, however, that in his list of what God promised Israel according to the flesh, land is not mentioned (Rom 9:4-5, unless it is included under "the promises"; cf. Davies). Colossians 1:12 ("inheritance") may reflect Paul's appropriation of the territorial idea, but there it is apparently transferred to a non-material realm—heaven.

4.1.4. God. Earlier in this article it was pointed out how Paul's vision of God changed as a result of affirming Jesus as the divine and human Christ. Not only were the functions of God as Lord now assumed and exercised by Christ (cf. 1 Cor 15:24-27), but it was Christ who would return to judge the world and even believers (cf. 2 Cor 5:10; 1 Thess 5:4-10). In addition, Paul understood Christ and the Spirit as sharing many of the same functions, their earthly work and effect being seen as virtually interchangeable. Though Paul did not elaborate a trinitarian theology, the raw elements of such a theology were already evident in his letters, especially in his doxologies and benedictions (cf. e.g., 2 Cor 13:14). Paul only invoked blessing in God's name, but now God had three names by which he could be called (see Wright, 120-36).

4.2. The Wider Impact of Paul's Christology. Paul's christology also seems to have had an impact on early Christianity outside his own writings. Hebrews especially seems to know and draw on Pauline modes of thought about Christ and other matters. It appears that the author of Hebrews had a special indebtedness to elements of Paul's thought as it is known to us in Galatians and perhaps also 1 Corinthians and Romans (cf. e.g., 1 Cor 15:24-28, 45-49 with Heb 2:6-13; Witherington 1991).

It is worth pondering the possible impact of Paul's christology on the Fourth Evangelist (*see* John, Gospel of). Not only does the Gospel of John begin with a christological hymn displaying motifs similar to Paul's, but the Gospel also presents a "Pauline" notion of believers being incorporated into Christ (though under a different image, that of the vine and branches of John 15). There we also find an exalted view of Christ's sacrificial death, associated with the slaughter of the Passover lamb (cf. e.g., Jn 1:29; Jn 19:28-31). The pneumatology of the Fourth Gospel is also related to the death and resurrection of Christ (cf. Jn 14:18-21) in a way that finds its only full NT parallel in Paul.

Possible Pauline influence, particularly christological, may be present elsewhere in the NT. For instance, in 1 Peter the presence of the "in Christ" formula, and the use of the phrases "Lord Jesus Christ" or "revelation of Jesus Christ" (1 Peter 1:3, 13; 5:10, 14) may indicate Pauline influence (*see* Christ). The speech of Paul in Acts 20:18-32 is noteworthy for its Pauline themes, a fact that may be accounted for by the author epitomizing Paul's gospel as it was known from his letters or, if Luke was a first-hand witness to the speech, by recording what he spoke on the occasion (see Hemer). In any event, the author of 2 Peter (3:15-16) testifies to the impact of Paul's letters among the "Petrine" churches of the first century, though he confesses that Paul is difficult to comprehend.

5. The Distinctiveness and Commonality of Paul's Christology.

In discussing the distinctiveness of Paul's christology we need to be reminded that we are not exploring its uniqueness among NT christologies. To pursue its uniqueness would entail discussing what it is that completely sets Paul's christology apart from other NT christologies. Rather, we wish to discuss what characterizes Paul's christology. It can hardly be claimed that there is anything in Paul's christology that is unique, totally without analogy elsewhere in the NT. The preexistence, divinity and humanity of Christ can all be found outside of Paul. The emphasis on Christ crucified is found in the Gospels, as well as in Acts, Hebrews, 1 Peter and elsewhere in the NT. The stress on Jesus' Jewishness, or on his resurrection, also finds analogies. Finally, the idea of Christ as the embodiment of God's Wisdom can be found in Matthew and possibly in the Gospel source Q, though with differing emphases (cf. Witherington 1994).

We have pointed to the absence of any reference to Jesus as *Son of Man in Paul's christology. In this sense Paul is distinct from the Gospels. But it can also be argued that the most distinct aspect of Paul's christology is his last Adam typology. This christological theme was not simply an attempt to transpose the Son of man christology into a new key for Gentiles. For one thing, the sources are different; Paul's last Adam christology draws on Genesis, while the Son of man material in the Gospels draws on Daniel 7 (and less possibly on Ezekiel and the Parables of *1 Enoch*). Moreover, the Son of man christology has nothing to do with the founder of a new race of human beings; it is more specifically focused on a representative of and for Israel who comes before the presence of the Almighty and is given dominion. In short, the last Adam christology is more universal than the Son of man in scope. By comparing and contrasting Christ with the progenitor of the whole human race, Paul forged a concept in which Jews and Gentiles had a stake simply because they were human.

Paul's use of the *"in Christ" formula to speak of the spiritual union between Christ and Christians is also remarkable. The Pauline idea transcends the use found in 1 Peter or the parallel ideas found in the Fourth Gospel in depth and breadth of implication. This formula more than any other explains how Paul viewed the condition of believers—they were "in Christ." This goes well beyond the claim that Christians by God's grace have been conformed to the pattern of Christ's death and resurrection (Rom 6:3-11). Their burial with Christ was a one-time event that occurred in the past at their conversion, whereas their union and communion with Christ is an ongoing reality. Indeed, it was such a profound reality in the apostle's mind that it was incompatible with other forms of union that were spiritually antithetical to it (cf. 1 Cor 6:15-17). The person united to Christ through Christ's body (made up of believers) was one spirit with Christ. This union "in Christ" was also the very basis of Paul's imperatives to imitate the sacred story or character of Christ (cf. e.g., Phil 2:5; 1 Cor 11:1). "In Christ" is a concept developed by Paul in a way and degree without parallel in the NT canon.

Paul's christology has continued to have an impact on the church through the ages, a fact that plays a part in our evaluating it. For Protestants who draw their charter of foundation directly or indirectly from Martin Luther, John Calvin or John Wesley, Paul's christology continues to be central, sometimes even eclipsing the variety of other canonical NT christologies. But that fact is also testimony to the compelling force of Paul's christological vision. It is a christology that cannot be neatly summarized under the headings of the titles Paul employs. The whole of Paul's christology is much greater than the sum of its parts. It is grounded in the sacred story of the Christ, which in turn is grounded in the story of Israel and, by way of the last Adam christology, rooted in the story of the whole human race.

It is this sacred story of a Jesus who was born of woman, who took on human nature, who died on the cross and who arose from the dead—for the salvation of all human beings—which Paul held in common with the other NT theologians. This shared story, more than any influence of one NT writer upon another, best explains the similarities between the christologies of Paul and the Fourth Gospel or Hebrews or Peter. They all shared this story and, from the evidence of christological hymns and hymn fragments in these works, it appears that they all sang this story in one form or another as they worshiped Christ. Christ crucified and risen, human and divine, was the core of the gospel these early missionaries proclaimed and taught throughout the first-century Mediterranean world.

See also ADAM AND CHRIST; CHRIST; GOD; HOLY SPIRIT; IN CHRIST; LORD; SON OF GOD.

DPL: FIRSTBORN; IMAGE OF GOD; PREEXISTENCE; SAVIOR; WISDOM.

BIBLIOGRAPHY. C. K. Barrett, *A Commentary on the Epistle to the Romans* (New York: Harper & Row, 1957); idem, *A Commentary on the First Epistle to the Corinthians* (New York: Harper & Row, 1968); idem, *A Commentary on the Second Epistle to the Corinthians* (New York: Harper & Row, 1973); R. J. Bauckham, *God Crucified: Monotheism and Christology in the New Testament* (Grand Rapids: Eerdmans, 1999); J. C. Beker, *Paul the Apostle: The Triumph of God in Life and Thought* (Philadelphia: Fortress, 1980); W. Bousset, *Kyrios Christos* (Nashville: Abingdon, 1970); R. E. Brown, *The Virginal Conception and Bodily Resurrection of Jesus* (New York: Paulist, 1973); F. F. Bruce, *The Epistle to the Galatians* (NIGNT; Grand Rapids: Eerdmans, 1982); E. D. W. Burton, *A Critical and Exegetical Commentary on the Epistle to the Galatians* (ICC; Edinburgh: T & T Clark, 1920); M. Casey,

"Chronology and the Development of Pauline Christology," in *Paul and Paulinism: Essays in Honor of C. K. Barrett*, ed. M. D. Hooker and S. G. Wilson (London: SPCK, 1982) 124-34; L. Cerfaux, *Christ in the Theology of St. Paul* (New York: Herder & Herder, 1959); C. E. B. Cranfield, *A Critical and Exegetical Commentary on the Epistle to the Romans* (ICC; 2 vols.; Edinburgh: T & T Clark, 1975, 1979); O. Cullmann, *Christ and Time* (rev. ed.; Philadelphia: Westminster, 1975); idem, *The Christology of the New Testament* (Philadelphia: Westminster, 1959); W. D. Davies, *The Gospel and the Land: Early Christianity and Jewish Territorial Doctrine* (Berkeley: University of California, 1974); J. D. G. Dunn, *Christology in the Making* (Philadelphia: Westminster, 1980); idem, *Romans* (WBC 38; Dallas: Word, 1988); idem, *Unity and Diversity in the New Testament* (Philadelphia: Westminster, 1977); P. Fredriksen, *From Jesus to Christ: The Origins of the New Testament Images of Jesus* (New Haven, CT: Yale University Press, 1988); G. F. Hawthorne, *Philippians* (WBC 43; Waco, TX: Word, 1983); R. B. Hays, *Echoes of Scripture in the Letters of Paul* (New Haven, CT: Yale University Press, 1989); C. J. Hemer, *The Book of Acts in the Setting of Hellenistic History* (Winona Lake, IN: Eisebrauns, 1989); M. Hengel, *Judaism and Hellenism* (2 vols.; Philadelphia: Fortress, 1974); idem, *The Pre-Christian Paul* (Philadelphia: Trinity Press International, 1991); idem, *The Son of God* (Philadelphia: Fortress, 1976); R. W. Hoover, "The *Harpagmos* Enigma: A Philological Solution," *HTR* 64 (1971) 95-119; L. W. Hurtado, *Lord Jesus Christ: Devotion to Jesus in Earliest Christianity* (Grand Rapids: Eerdmans, 2003); idem, *One God, One Lord: Early Christian Devotion and Ancient Jewish Monotheism* (Philadelphia: Fortress, 1988); J. Jeremias, "ἀδάμ," *TDNT* 1:141-43; M. de Jonge, *Christology in Context: The Earliest Christian Responses to Jesus* (Philadelphia: Westminster, 1988); S. Kim, *The Origin of Paul's Gospel* (Grand Rapids: Eerdmans, 1982); J. B. Lightfoot, *St. Paul's Epistle to the Philippians* (London: Macmillan, 1894); R. N. Longenecker, *The Christology of Early Jewish Christianity* (SBT 2d series 17; London: SCM, 1970); J. G. Machen, *The Virgin Birth of Christ* (New York: Harper & Row, 1930); I. H. Marshall, "Son of God," *NIDNTT* 3:644-45; R. P. Martin, *Carmen Christi: Philippians 2:5-11 in Recent Interpretation and in the Setting of Early Christian Worship* (rev. ed.; Grand Rapids: Eerdmans, 1983); idem, *Philippians* (NCB; Grand Rapids: Eerdmans, 1976); B. M. Metzger, "Punc-

tuation of Romans 9:5," in *Christ and the Spirit in the New Testament*, ed. B. Lindars and S. S. Smalley (Cambridge: Cambridge University Press, 1973) 95-112; C. F. D. Moule, "Further Reflexions on Philippians 2.5-11," in *Apostolic History and the Gospel*, ed. W. W. Gasque and R. P. Martin (Grand Rapids: Eerdmans, 1970) 264-76; idem, "The Manhood of Jesus in the NT," in *Christ, Faith and History*, ed. S. W. Sykes and J. P. Clayton (Cambridge: Cambridge University Press, 1972) 95-110; idem, *The Origin of Christology* (Cambridge: Cambridge University Press, 1977); J. Neusner et al., eds., *Judaisms and Their Messiahs* (Cambridge: Cambridge University Press, 1987); J. A. T. Robinson, *The Body: A Study in Pauline Theology* (Philadelphia: Westminster, 1977); S. S. Smalley, "The Christ-Christian Relationship in Paul and John," in *Pauline Studies*, ed. D. A. Hagner and M. J. Harris (Grand Rapids: Eerdmans, 1980) 95-105; M. M. Thompson, *The Promise of the Father: Jesus and God in the New Testament* (Grand Rapids: Eerdmans, 2000); N. Turner, *Grammatical Insights into the New Testament* (Edinburgh: T & T Clark, 1966); B. Witherington III, *The Christology of Jesus* (Minneapolis: Fortress, 1990); idem, "The Influence of Galatians on Hebrews," *NTS* 37 (1991) 146-52; idem, *Jesus, Paul and the End of the World* (Downers Grove, IL: InterVarsity Press, 1992); idem, *Jesus the Sage and the Pilgrimage of Wisdom* (Minneapolis: Fortress, 1994); N. T. Wright, *The Climax of the Covenant* (Minneapolis: Fortress, 1992).

B. Witherington III

CHRISTOLOGY II: ACTS, HEBREWS, GENERAL EPISTLES, REVELATION

A great deal of scholarly effort has been devoted to analyzing the christological statements of early Christian texts as to how they reflect Jewish Christian or Hellenistic influences. The effort reflects an understanding of the formation of earliest christology as a historical process that was conditioned by the cultural, linguistic and religious environment of nascent Christianity. This standpoint can be accepted, whatever one's belief about the transcendent causes and significance behind the historical process.

The complexity of the issues and the diversity of the evidence make this investigation demanding. However, this work has also been hindered by such problems as a lack of agreement among scholars as to what the terms "Jewish Christian" and *Hellenistic* signify, overly simplified notions of the interaction between Jewish and non-Jewish culture in the Greco-Roman period and, sometimes, insufficiently examined assumptions and personal agendas of the scholars participating in the investigation. In this section our aims are to clarify the issues and categories involved in the modern discussion, survey the relevant texts as to their christological emphases, and offer some basic conclusions about the christological developments and diversification evident in NT writings: Acts and Hebrews through Revelation. (For the christology of the individual Gospels, readers should consult the articles on each of the Gospels.)

1. Terminology
2. Acts 1—11
3. Hebrews
4. James
5. First Peter
6. Second Peter and Jude
7. Johannine Epistles
8. Revelation
9. Summary

1. Terminology.

In one sense the christological expressions of all NT documents and of many early extra-canonical Christian writings are Jewish in that they reflect terms, concepts and values that are indebted to the OT and to Jewish tradition. But all earliest Christian literature is also Hellenistic, reflecting the impact of Hellenistic culture in the language (Koine Greek), rhetorical and literary conventions, and some of the conceptual categories and themes they exhibit. Also, the Jewish tradition, which served as the immediate matrix of earliest Christianity, had been in direct interaction with Hellenistic culture for more than three hundred years (since the time of Alexander the Great), variously reacting against and absorbing this or that feature of the larger cultural environment in the Diaspora and in Palestine. Consequently, distinguishing between Jewish and Hellenistic factors or elements in earliest christology, though not impossible, is more difficult than some have supposed.

It further complicates matters, however, that the labels *Jewish Christian* and *Hellenistic* have been used by scholars in varying ways. In some cases it appears that Jewish Christian christology is limited to beliefs that reflect what a given

scholar imagines Christian Jews would have found congenial as belief, usually a low christology in which Jesus is seen as a human Messiah or teacher and is not given divine honor. But such an approach is apt to tell us more about the assumptions of the scholar than about the actual beliefs of ancient Christian Jews.

In other cases the label *Jewish Christian* is restricted to Christian Jews who rejected Gentile Christians and their beliefs (e.g., the Ebionites). But, given that the ancient sources indicate a variety of Christian Jewish groups and beliefs, restricting Jewish Christian to one type is misleading.

At the other extreme the term "Jewish Christian" has sometimes been used for all forms of early Christianity that used any language, symbols and categories drawn from the Jewish tradition. But this definition applies to a wide spectrum of early Christianity, and used this way "Jewish Christian" merely functions to emphasize the Jewish religious and intellectual roots of the early Christian movement.

In this article, therefore, we shall classify as Jewish Christian the christological beliefs and practices of Christian Jews who understood themselves and articulated their faith and piety in terms and categories drawn from their Jewish religious tradition. Their faith, however, was usually not simply Judaism but was redefined in some major ways by the figure of Jesus and the consequences and implications of acknowledging him as uniquely authoritative divine agent. We shall also have to reckon with texts that may not have Jewish Christian authors but that show interest in and respect for Jewish Christian figures, beliefs and traditions, thereby giving us some further though perhaps indirect access to these beliefs and traditions.

It also has to be acknowledged that the question of what was Jewish and what was Hellenistic in early Christianity has often been dealt with in the service of agendas larger than historical inquiry. Alleging much Hellenistic syncretistic influence upon early Christian beliefs was often a useful way of downplaying the continuing validity of these beliefs for those engaged in an avowedly liberalizing and revisionist agenda for modern Christianity. Countering this agenda but accepting the notions of Hellenistic influences as indicative of corruption of early Christianity, conservative scholars often emphasized the Jewish roots of early Christianity and its beliefs, especially in the NT. In both camps, however, historical analysis has often been skewed under the influence of theological polemics.

Few can credibly claim to be disinterested in the question of the continuing validity of early christology. But it is important to try to prevent exegetical and historical judgments from being determined by theological agendas, whether of a revisionist or a traditionalist leaning. Also, it would be facile either to portray the development of christology as religious syncretism or to deny that early Christians interacted with and were shaped by the larger Greco-Roman religious and cultural environment. Moreover, the religious validity of a christological expression does not depend upon whether it appropriates Jewish or non-Jewish terms, concepts and cultural background. Consequently, we shall attempt to characterize the christology of the texts considered so far as possible with a view to accurate historical knowledge of developments and diversification in early Christian beliefs.

2. Acts 1—11.

The early chapters of Acts give us narratives describing the Jerusalem church, which was composed of Jews. These narratives include speeches and prayers as well as the author's summaries of the preaching and activities of these Christian Jews. Although scholars debate the source(s) and historical reliability of specific events in the narratives, Acts 1—11 contains a good deal of christological material that looks to be early and of Jewish Christian derivation.

In these materials Jesus' death (see Death of Christ) is presented as a misguided act of the Jewish leaders (Acts 3:14, 17; 4:10; 5:30; 7:52) and as a fulfillment of the divine redemptive plan (Acts 2:23-31; 3:18; 4:28; 10:39-43). There is no explanation of how Jesus' death is redemptive (no theory of atonement), only the firm proclamation that his death was essential and foreordained. There is a strong emphasis on Jesus' resurrection: the key event to which the apostles are to bear witness (Acts 1:22; 2:32; 4:33; 5:32) and the act of God by which Jesus is designated a unique position of salvific importance as "Lord and Christ" (Acts 2:36), "Leader and Savior" (Acts 5:31) and eschatological judge through whom forgiveness is given (Acts 10:42-43). This idea of Jesus being installed by God in a uniquely lofty position as a consequence of his resurrection (esp. Acts 2:36; 3:20) seems particu-

larly reflective of early, Jewish Christian christological conceptions (cf. Rom 1:3-4, also often thought to reflect Jewish Christian tradition). Jesus is the exclusive medium of salvation for all (Acts 4:10-12) and is now "Lord of all" (Acts 10:36). But by linking Jesus' exalted status to the act of God the traditional Jewish/biblical monotheistic concern seems reflected, so that Jesus' uniquely lofty role does not reduce God's status or importance.

The frequent references to Jesus as God's Messiah appear particularly in passages mentioning proclamation to Jews (Christos, Acts 2:36; 3:18-21; 5:42; 9:22; and in Acts 8:5 to Samaritans). "Son of God" in Acts 9:20 seems to be intended as a synonymous (royal) messianic title. Other honorific terms applied to Jesus reflect the Jewish tradition: a prophet like Moses (Acts 3:22), "the Righteous One" (Acts 7:52) and "servant" (pais, Acts 3:13, 26; 4:27, 30). This last term (applied also to David, Acts 4:25) is used as a (royal?) christological title only here in the NT and outside the NT only in texts showing strong Jewish Christian influence and a traditional (liturgical) flavor (e.g., 1 Clem. 59.2-4; Did. 9.3; 10.2-3; Mart. Pol. 14.1, 3). The emphasis upon the name (of Jesus, Acts 4:10-12, 18; 5:28, 40-41; 8:12) may also reflect ancient Jewish culture with its high reverence for the name of God.

3. Hebrews.

Several of the specific historical questions about the epistle to the Hebrews remain without satisfactory answers: author, date, destination (see Hebrews, Letter to the). Though we cannot be sure that the original recipients were Hebrews (i.e., Christian Jews), it is widely agreed that the document shows an elaborate effort to articulate Christ's significance in terms and categories drawn from Jewish tradition. In this sense Hebrews reflects Jewish Christian christological expression. In Hebrews 1, after appropriating Jewish *wisdom tradition to describe Christ's glorious relationship to God (Heb 1:1-4; cf. Wis 7:22—8:1), the author goes into a more lengthy statement of Christ's superiority to God's angels, using a seven-link catena of OT quotations to make his points (Heb 1:5-14). This contrast continues in Hebrews 2, with additional OT passages used as evidence, here emphasizing Christ's superiority to angels as Redeemer on account of his participation in human nature. The rhetorical force of this contrast with angels depends upon a sympathetic familiarity with OT material and with ancient Jewish reverence for angels. Although "sons of God" is one of the ancient terms for angels (e.g., Job 1:6; 2:1; 38:7), the author here draws upon royal Davidic references to God's son to make a strong contrast between the status of angels as servants (esp. Heb 1:7, 14) and Christ's status as unique Son (*see* Son of God).

Next the author asserts Christ's superiority to Moses (Heb 3:1—4:13), again emphasizing Jesus' sonship in comparison with Moses as faithful servant (esp. Heb 3:1-6). By reference to the rebellious generation of Israelites the author warns readers against disobedience to or abandonment of the Christian profession (Heb 3:7—4:13). As with the discussion of Christ and the angels, the force of this contrast of Christ with Moses depends upon an acquaintance with Jewish tradition, in this case the revered place it gives to Moses.

The author continues to argue for Christ's exalted significance by portraying his superiority as high priest over the Aaronic priesthood of the OT (Heb 4:14—7:28). The divine sonship of Christ resurfaces as an important christological category (Heb 5:5-10; 7:28); the superiority of Christ's high priesthood is connected with his being divine Son. In addition the author introduces the theme of Christ's priesthood "according to the order of Melchizedek" (Heb 5:6). The extended discussion of Christ's high priesthood by reference to this figure in Hebrews 7:1-28 is a unique christological emphasis of Hebrews (although there are brief references to Christ as heavenly intercessor in Rom 8:34; 1 Jn 2:1), and it too suggests an author and readers appreciative of Jewish traditions. Unlike the Aaronic priests, Christ is personally "a priest forever" (Heb 5:6; 7:15-17, 21), because he now "always lives" and is able "for all time to save those who approach God through him" (Heb 7:23-28, esp. Heb 7:25).

In the following chapters of Hebrews, Christ is shown to be the mediator of a new covenant better than that represented by the OT law (Heb 8:1-13); Christ's death establishes this new covenant (Heb 9:15-22) by providing for it the superior and permanently effective sacrifice (Heb 9:23—10:18). The author returns to this theme in Hebrews 12:18-29, where he contrasts phenomena of the revelation at Sinai (Heb 12:18-21) with the blessings of this new covenant (Heb 12:22-24), the climactic position of Jesus and his "sprinkled blood" indicating his importance.

In Hebrews 12:1-4 Jesus is referred to as the "pioneer and perfector of our faith" whose patient endurance of his sufferings can provide the encouraging precedent for Christians in their trials (Heb 12:5-13). The exemplary significance of Christ's sufferings is easily combined with reference to their redemptive effect in Hebrews 13:10-15.

Throughout the book the author is primarily concerned to emphasize two christological themes: Jesus' salvific death in imagery and language drawn from OT cultic traditions and Jesus' exalted status in imagery drawn from OT royal tradition. From the reference in Hebrews 1:3 to Christ having made "purification for sins" (priestly image) and having "sat down at the right hand" of God (royal image), through to the benediction in Hebrews 13:20-21 with its reference to Jesus as the resurrected "great shepherd" (a common royal image in the OT and the ancient Near East generally) and his "blood of the eternal covenant" (cultic imagery), this author focuses on Christ's death, resurrection and exaltation.

Also striking is the author's dual emphasis upon Christ as exalted divine Son and as full partaker in the human nature of those he redeems to God. This dialectic is particularly profound in Hebrews 1—2. After having affirmed Christ's vast superiority to the angels, the author then makes Christ's participation in human nature ("for a little while . . . lower than the angels," Heb 2:9) both evidence that humans are the object of God's redemptive purposes and precisely the strategic step that enables Christ to carry out that redemptive purpose effectively (Heb 2:14-18). In Hebrews 5:7-10 the author makes much of Jesus' humanity, Jesus being pictured as having "learned obedience through what he suffered."

The author of Hebrews produced one of the most developed treatments of Christ in the NT. He illustrates the early Christian appropriation and adaptation of Jewish categories in the effort to understand and communicate the significance of Christ.

4. James.

The Epistle of James is mainly concerned with exhortation about right behavior; its christology is implicit and largely a reflection of what the author and first readers held as traditional. Whatever one's view of the question of authorship, the attribution of the document to James the brother of Jesus (*see* James, Letter of), the description of the addressees as "the twelve tribes in the Dispersion" (Jas 1:1) and other factors, including the strongly eschatological outlook (e.g., Jas 5:1-9), combine to give the document a Jewish Christian flavor. It is therefore interesting to note what the author and readers, who either were Jewish Christians or revered Jewish Christian traditions, must have regarded as traditional and uncontroversial christology.

Jesus bears the titles *Christ* and *Lord (kyrios)* in formulaic expressions (Jas 1:1; 2:1). Indeed, in James 2:1 we have mention of "our glorious Lord Jesus Christ" *(tou kyriou hēmōn Iēsou Christou tēs doxēs)*, giving a particularly sonorous and honorific expression. In several other cases Jesus is probably intended in references to "the Lord." This holds for James 4:15, for example, where the will of "the Lord" is to govern Christian decisions. In James 5:7-11 it is also probable that Jesus is the "Lord" whose coming is awaited (Jas 5:7-8) and the judge standing at the door (Jas 5:9), in whose name the OT prophets spoke (Jas 5:10) and whose mercy and compassion are applauded (Jas 5:11). In all these cases it is noteworthy that Jesus is referred to in roles associated with God in the OT.

Jesus is likewise probably the "Lord" in whose name the sick are to be anointed and who will raise the sick and forgive their sins (Jas 5:13-15). There is probably a reference to Jesus' name in James 2:7 as "invoked [in baptism?] over you" and blasphemed by opponents. This emphasis upon the sacred significance of Jesus' name accords with references in Acts 1—11 and other evidence of Jewish Christian attitudes.

In addition, many commentators have noted that this epistle is full of allusions to sayings of Jesus preserved in the Synoptic Gospels. This indicates a familiarity with the Jesus tradition and a practical acceptance of Jesus' authority as Lord of Christian behavior. We may say that James emphasizes the practical and ethical consequences of the christological convictions shared by the author and intended readers.

5. 1 Peter.

Scholars remain divided as to whether 1 Peter stems from the apostle Peter or is a pseudonymous attempt to address the intended readers in his voice (*see* 1 Peter, Letter of). Whatever one's view of this issue, 1 Peter is an important window on Christian beliefs and concerns from sometime in the latter part of the first century and is particularly rich in christological material. As is James, 1 Peter is addressed to readers described in Judaic terms, "the exiles of the Dispersion" (1 Pet 1:1), which along with other data suggests Christians who revere Jewish Christian traditions.

The high status of Christ is set within God the Father's supremacy. For example, Christians have been "chosen and destined by God the Father" for obedience to Jesus Christ (1 Pet 1:2). "The God and Father of our Lord Jesus Christ" has given new birth through Christ's resurrection (1 Pet 1:3), which is explicitly an act of God (1 Pet 1:21). Readers are to come to Christ because he is "precious in God's sight" and the one through whom acceptable "spiritual sacrifices" are now offered to God (1 Pet 2:4-5). It is God's will that Christians are to heed (1 Pet 2:15; 4:19). First Peter 1:20 places Christ's redemptive work within the context of God's precosmic plan ("destined before the foundation of the world"; cf. 1 Pet 1:11, where "sufferings destined for Christ" are predicted by OT prophets). The liturgical-sounding benediction and doxologies are all directed to God the Father (1 Pet 1:3; 5:11; even 1 Pet 4:11, though slightly ambiguous, is probably directed to God, who is glorified "through Jesus Christ").

There can be no question, however, as to the author's high and richly textured view of Christ. One of the dominant emphases is the redemptive effect of Christ's death, expressed in sacrificial terms. Christians are "sprinkled with his blood" (1 Pet 1:2), alluding to the OT practice of sprinkling the blood of animal victims for dedication and ritual cleansing of people and cultic items (e.g., Ex 29:19-21; Lev 4:3-6, 13-17; 14:5-7). In 1 Peter 1:18-21 Christians are ransomed *(lytroō)* with the "precious blood of Christ, like that of a lamb without defect or blemish," likely alluding to the Passover lamb of Exodus 12:5 (cf. 1 Cor 5:7 for another echo of Passover imagery for Christ's death). First Peter 2:21-25 lifts wording from Isaiah 53:4-12 to reveal the significance of Christ's sufferings, emphasizing his exemplary behavior (1 Pet 2:21-23) and the vicarious nature of his death ("he himself bore our sins in his body") on the "tree" (*xylon*, 1 Pet 2:24, a probable allusion to

Deut 27:6, which seems early to have become a key OT text used to interpret the significance of Christ's crucifixion). In 1 Peter 3:18 the author refers to Christ's undeserved sufferings as exemplary for Christian behavior and vicariously redemptive ("the righteous for the unrighteous . . . to bring you to God").

The author's reference to "the Spirit of Christ within them" as the inspiring power of OT prophets (1 Pet 1:11) reflects a remarkably exalted view of Christ, perhaps implying some kind of preexistence conviction and certainly associating Christ with the divine Spirit (*see* Holy Spirit). The exhortation in 1 Peter 3:14-15 alludes directly to Isaiah 8:12-13 (LXX), and the command to "sanctify Christ as Lord" thus applies and extends to Christ an imperative there concerned with reverence to Yahweh, another direct and striking association of Christ with God. First Peter 3:22 explicitly proclaims Christ's unique exaltation above all heavenly ranks, using OT royal imagery in placing Christ "at the right hand of God" (cf. Ps 110:1). The references to Christ as shepherd and "chief shepherd" (1 Pet 2:25; 5:4) also probably draw upon OT royal imagery.

The exalted position of Christ in the author's beliefs is matched by the crucial place of Christ in practical living. As the chosen stone, Christ becomes the basis of the redeemed community (1 Pet 2:4-10), to which a variety of OT images are applied (temple and priesthood [1 Pet 2:5], chosen race and holy nation [1 Pet 2:9], God's people [1 Pet 2:10]). "For the Lord's sake" (i.e., out of reverence for Christ) Christians are to show respect for legitimate earthly authorities (1 Pet 2:13-17). Christians are to face unjust abuse looking to Christ's example and following "in his steps" (1 Pet 2:21). If they are persecuted on account of their Christian faith, they are to take inspiration from Christ's sufferings and subsequent exaltation (1 Pet 3:13-22). They are to take joy in "sharing Christ's sufferings," in being "reviled for the name of Christ," suffering "as a Christian" and glorifying God "because you bear this name" (1 Pet 4:12-16).

6. 2 Peter and Jude.

Scholars commonly see a direct literary relationship linking Jude and 2 Peter, 2 Peter probably being dependent upon Jude. The authorship of these texts is disputed (*see* 2 Peter, Letter of; Jude, Letter of). But whatever one's view of this question, both documents are attributed to figures associated with Jewish Christian groups, especially Jude, which is attributed to the "brother of James" (Jude 1:1), making him also a brother of Jesus. Both documents evidence an exalted view of Christ and share specific christological terms and convictions. But there are also variations.

In addition to more familiar formulaic expressions ("our Lord Jesus Christ" and variations: Jude 17, 21, 25; 2 Pet 1:8, 14, 16), in Jude 4 there is reference to those who "deny our only Master *[despotēs]* and Lord *[kyrios]*, Jesus Christ." This formula is echoed in 2 Peter 2:1, which condemns heretics who "deny the Master *[despotēs]* who bought them." "Master" and "Lord" are applied to God in other NT writings (e.g., in prayer to God: Lk 2:29; Acts 4:24; Rev 6:10) and in Jude and 2 Peter are to be taken as titles connoting divine honor extended to Christ. In 2 Peter we repeatedly find the distinctive expression "our Lord *[kyrios]* and Savior *[sōtēr]* Jesus Christ" (2 Pet 1:11; 2:20; 3:2, 18). The only occurrence of "Savior" in Jude, however, is with reference to God ("the only God our Savior," Jude 25). In the NT as a whole *sōtēr* refers to God in eight of its twenty-four uses and is otherwise applied to Christ (e.g., Phil 3:20; Lk 2:11; Jn 4:42).

This tendency to attribute divine titles to Christ occasionally results in some ambiguous passages in which it is difficult to tell whether God or Christ is intended. In Jude 5-16 there are references to "the Lord" who saved Israel from Egypt (Jude 5), Michael's invocation of "the Lord" against Satan (Jude 9) and Enoch's prophecy of the coming of "the Lord" with thousands of angels (Jude 14-15). Given that the author otherwise consistently uses "Lord" as a title for Christ and that he appears to expect Christ to come bringing eschatological judgment and mercy (Jude 17-21), it is probable that Jude 14-15 refers to Christ. But it is difficult to be sure who the "Lord" is in Jude 5 and Jude 9 (the textual variants, Jude 5 *[kyrios /Iēsous /christos /theos]* and Jude 9 *[kyrios /theos]*, indicate that ancient readers and scribes shared our difficulty). It seems likely that Christ is the "Lord" in this whole passage in Jude, indicating a rather far-reaching association of Christ with the God of the OT. In 2 Peter 3:8-10 it is also likely that Christ is the "Lord" whose promised coming is delayed but sure.

But 2 Peter 1:1 presents a particularly difficult case. The more likely Greek reading (*tou theou hēmōn kai sōtēros Iēsou Christou*) could easily be taken as "our God and Savior Jesus Christ," although it is possible that the phrase refers to God and Christ (cf. 2 Pet 1:2, where the best reading is probably "knowledge of God and of Jesus our Lord"). The textual variation here, substituting "Lord" for "God,", shows ancient scribes saw the ambiguity as well.

In addition to the honorific terms and divine roles applied to Christ, there is also evidence of cultic devotion offered to Christ. The elaborate doxology in Jude 24-25 is directed to God "through Jesus Christ our Lord," and the phrase "before all time and now and forever" implicitly seems to extend to Christ the eternal qualities of God. The concluding doxology in 2 Peter 3:18 is directed to Christ, extending to him liturgical expressions connoting divine status and probably reflecting liturgical practices of the readers.

In both documents there is a strong eschatological tone to the christology. In Jude, Christians are being "kept safe for/by Jesus Christ" (Jude 1), and Christians are told "keep [themselves] in the love of God" while they await the eschatological mercy of Christ that "leads to eternal life" (Jude 21). In 2 Peter 1:11 readers are offered the hope of "entry into the eternal kingdom of our Lord and Savior Jesus Christ." Against the scoffing of some, 2 Peter 3:1-18 is devoted to asserting the reality of the eschatological coming of Christ and the present ethical consequences of this hope. In 2 Peter 1:16-19 the author refers to the transfiguration story (Mk 9:2-8) as indicating that Christ "received honor and glory from God the Father" and urges readers to take encouragement from this to live in the light of Christ's "power and coming" until his eschatological appearance as "the morning star."

7. Johannine Epistles.

Although the Johannine epistles are thought to derive from the same early Christian group from which the Gospel of John came, it is widely recognized that there are differences in christological emphases (*see* John, Letters of). The Gospel of John asserts Jesus' divine significance over against Jewish refusal to recognize him as Christ and Son of God. In 1 John (the other Johannine epistles contain little christological material and nothing not found in 1 John), however, the author asserts his christology over against other Christians whose beliefs he regards as heretical.

Because of this doctrinal conflict, 1 John is particularly rich in christological material. It is also commonly accepted that the Johannine community was originally a Jewish Christian group that suffered a severe rupture in relations with the larger Jewish community and at some point included Gentile converts. First John seems to reflect this later stage of the Johannine community but still shows the influence of the Jewish Christian heritage of the group.

The major christological emphasis is that the corporal, historical figure Jesus is "the Son" of God. It appears that the opponents in some way distinguished between Jesus and the divine Son, perhaps holding a docetic (*dokēsis*, "appearance") christology in which the divine Christ only seemed to be a human. A few decades later Ignatius of Antioch attacked the same or similar views. In 1 John 2:18-27 the opponents are referred to directly as schismatics (1 Jn 2:19) who have left the Johannine group and appear to have sought to win other Johannine Christians over to their views, for which they claimed the authority of a superior enlightenment (1 Jn 2:26-27).

The opening statements of 1 John (1 Jn 1:1-4) emphasize the tangible, historical nature of the revelation witnessed to in the foundational ("from the beginning") gospel message and explicitly link fellowship with God and with "his Son Jesus Christ." The heretical alternative to "confessing the Son" (1 Jn 2:23) is described as denying that Jesus is the Christ (1 Jn 2:22), denying "the Son" and thus "the Father" (1 Jn 2:23). The heresy is described more specifically perhaps in 1 John 4:1-3, where in contrast to the genuine divine Spirit who "confesses that Jesus Christ has come in the flesh," the ungodly spirit "does not confess Jesus is from God" (1 Jn 4:3; this is probably the best reading among the textual variants). The implication is that the heretics hesitate to identify the man Jesus with the divine Son.

Repeatedly the author emphasizes this confessional link: the historical manifestation of the Son is affirmed (1 Jn 3:5, 8); the required confession is "Jesus is the Son of God" (1 Jn 4:15); the one born of God believes in Jesus as the Christ (1 Jn 5:1); in 1 John 3:23 God's command is to believe in the name of his Son Jesus Christ (probably alluding to the ritual use of Jesus' name in confession, healing and baptism), which makes precise the historical identification of the divine Son. Such a faith in the true, divine Son acknowledges thereby the Father also and brings eternal life (e.g., 1 Jn 5:11-12).

Unlike some later, Gentile Christian writers, this author does not try to define Jesus' sonship in metaphysical or philosophical terms; his main concern is to insist upon the direct identification of Jesus as divine Son. Nevertheless, the reference to Jesus as "the eternal life that was with the Father and was revealed/manifested to us" (1 Jn 1:2) at least suggests some notion of an "incarnation" of the divine in Jesus, all the more likely given the familiar prologue to John (Jn 1:1-18), which stems from the same community. In light of this it is difficult to be sure whether the referent in 1 John 5:20, "This [houtos] is the true God and eternal life," is Jesus (the immediate antecedent) or God the Father. In light of the close link between the Son and the Father in this document, it may be that the author did not intend a mutually exclusive choice, for in his view one cannot be in right relation to God the Father without reverencing the Son.

The author also repeatedly affirms the soteriological significance of Christ. The efficaciousness of Jesus' death is described in sacrificial terms: the blood of Jesus "cleanses us from all sin" (1 Jn 1:7); Jesus is the "atoning sacrifice" for our sins (1 Jn 2:2; 4:10). He is now "advocate" (paraklētos) for Christians "with the Father" (1 Jn 2:1). Jesus "was revealed to take away sins" (1 Jn 3:5) and "to destroy the works of the devil" (1 Jn 3:8). Christians hope to be made like Jesus when he appears again in future glory (1 Jn 3:2) and in the present time identify themselves with him as their model (1 Jn 4:17).

8. Revelation.

The Jewish elements in Revelation (see Revelation, Book of) are so plentiful that some scholars have offered the unlikely suggestion that the book is a Christian revision of an originally Jewish apocalypse, and some theologians (e.g., Luther, Bultmann) have erroneously regarded the book as deficient in the Christian beliefs reflected in it. Revelation presents a highly exalted view of Christ, perhaps unsurpassed in the NT. It is thus noteworthy that the author was in all likelihood a Christian Jew (e.g., John, apparently the author's actual name, is Jewish, only much later taken over as a Christian given name). Moreover, he seems to have had decidedly conservative attitudes (e.g., his condemnations of various Christian innovations, the Nicolaitans [Rev 2:6, 14-16] and the teachings of "Jezebel" [Rev 2:20-25]). Consequently, his christological views and practices are unlikely to be innovative and probably reflect much earlier Jewish Christian circles. The prophet John sought to respond to what he saw as immediate pressing concerns, both internal problems and the looming pressure from the larger society. In his references to the emperor cult (worship of the "beast") he was interacting with pagan religious phenomena and practices (see Religions, Greco-Roman), and these must be considered in understanding the book. But John responds to these influences negatively. Although he shows some acquaintance with pagan myth (e.g., the dragon and Leto analogy to Rev 12), his christology seems mainly expressed in terms from his biblical and Jewish tradition.

As with the Johannine Gospel and epistles, so in Revelation we see a dialectical combination of concern for the supremacy of the one God together with a high christology. The most direct manifestation of this is with regard to worship, which is a major theme of the book. The revelation claimed by the author is set on "the Lord's day" (the special weekly occasion of early Christian gathered worship). The vision of heavenly worship in Revelation 4—5 seems intended to overshadow the remainder of the book, in which there are repeated calls and references to worship of God (e.g., Rev 7:11-12, 15; 11:16-17) and repeated warnings against worshiping any other (e.g., Rev 9:20-21; 13:4; 14:9-11). In Revelation 19:10 and Revelation 22:9 the angel interpreter sent from God twice forbids John to worship him, insisting that worship may be directed to God alone. The author clearly pictures the exalted Christ receiving worship with God (Rev 5:8-14; 7:10), which must indicate for this author the highest imaginable status for Christ. If later Christian thinkers speak of Christ and God sharing a common substance, John seems to offer something like a functional approximation in portraying idealized heavenly worship as directed jointly to God and Christ.

The scenes of ideal worship must have been intended to reflect and inspire worship patterns among Christians. In Revelation 22:20 we probably have a fragment of early liturgical practice in which the Lord Jesus is invoked in the gathered worship setting (cf. 1 Cor 16:22, "maranatha," which suggests that this practice derived from very early Aramaic-speaking circles of Jewish Christians).

This close association of Christ with God is reflected in other ways too. The eschatological kingdom belongs jointly to "our Lord [or God] and his Christ" (Rev 11:15; 12:10). Christians hold to the word of God and the testimony of Jesus (Rev 1:2, 9; cf. Rev 12:17). The august self-designation "Alpha and the Omega" appears in the mouth of God in Revelation 1:8, but in Revelation 22:12-13 it seems likely that we are to take the voice as Christ's, designating himself with the same title. The opening greeting (Rev 1:4-5) comes jointly from God, the "seven spirits" and Jesus Christ, "the faithful witness [role model for the readers], the firstborn of the dead [assurance of resurrection of believers] and the ruler of the kings of the earth [against the blasphemous claims of the Roman emperor]."

Although there is a subordination of Christ to God (e.g., Rev 1:1, where God gives Jesus the revelation to be shown to his servants), the opening vision, which functions like the OT call visions, is a christophany (Rev 1:10-20) in which the glorious Christ is described with features taken from OT theophanies and angelophanies (e.g., Dan 7:9-10, 13-14; 10:5-6; Ezek 1:24-28). Moreover, in Revelation 2—3 it is Christ's assessment of the seven churches that is to be written to them, Christ's words voiced by the Spirit in prophecy through John (e.g., Rev 2:7, 11), and Christ who determines future reward or judgment (e.g., Rev 2:7, 10, 17, 22-23, 26-28). Also, the divine plan of redemption and judgment cannot proceed until the Lamb has conquered and is then alone qualified to open the heavenly book and execute its contents (Rev 5:1-5). Yet at the same time this exalted Christ positions his role under the supremacy of God (e.g., Rev 2:28; 3:4, 12, 21).

The image of Christ as the Lamb reflects another christological belief important to this author—the redemptive significance of Jesus' death. The initial doxology (Rev 1:5-6; again probably reflecting the binitarian liturgical patterns of his readers) is directed to Christ, "who loves us and freed us from our sins by his blood," thereby constituting believers as "a kingdom, priests to his God and Father." In the initial, christophanic vision Christ's self-identification includes the crucial reference to his death (Rev 1:18), as a result of which he now has "the keys of Death and Hades." The Lamb's conquest is accomplished through being slaughtered (Rev 1:9-10), and through his "blood" he has "ransomed" *(agorazō)* saints of all nations. References to Jesus' "blood" (sacrificial imagery) appear also in Revelation 7:14 (the elect have "washed their robes and made them white in the blood of the Lamb," a riveting image) and in Revelation 12:11 (believers conquer the great dragon "by the blood of the Lamb and by the word of their testimony," linking Jesus' death and the faithfulness of the saints). In the context of a highly symbolic passage the author drops this sacrificial imagery and makes direct reference to the crucifixion of the "Lord" in Revelation 11:8, making Jesus' death and its consequences the model for the witnesses who are killed and rise again (Rev 11:11).

9. Summary.

The NT documents considered were all written either by Christian Jews or by Christians with a good acquaintance with Jewish Christian traditions who sought to express their faith in Christ in categories and terms adapted from the biblical and Jewish tradition. The dominant mode of christological reflection and expression in the first century seems to have been constituted out of Jewish tradition, mediated through Jewish Christian circles and adapted under the impact of Jesus' ministry and subsequent early Christian experience. The Jewish matrix, from which basic terms and categories were derived and adapted, was Jewish tradition of the Greco-Roman period, a robust religious tradition that for several centuries had confidently interacted with the larger cultural environment, appropriating whatever seemed useful and compatible with its fundamental convictions. Thus it should occasion no surprise to find terms or concepts that may have originated much earlier in Greek tradition. Such interaction is the sign of a healthy cultural and religious tradition, not an indication of something negative, certainly not a betrayal or uncritical assimilation of pagan influences.

There can be little question, however, that the christological affirmations and the pattern of binitarian religious devotion reflected in these NT documents exceed in degree and kind the reverence characteristically shown toward divine agents in Jewish evidence relevant to the first century. In ancient Jewish sources amazingly honorific language can be applied to principal angels and also to revered human figures (esp. Moses or Enoch). Speculations about divine Wisdom or divine Logos make for interesting comparison with and may have contributed to Christian attempts to define plurality in God, leading to the doctrine of the Trinity in the centuries after the NT. But the exalted status of Christ reflected in the documents surveyed seems to represent a distinctive development in comparison with the pre-Christian Jewish tradition. This is especially so when we take account of the accommodation of the glorified Christ alongside God in the worship setting and practices of first-century Christians.

In the older history-of-religions school (e.g., Bousset), the distinctively exalted status of Christ was often portrayed as the unconscious and deliberate assimilation of a supposedly original and low christology (nondivine Jesus) to pagan-influenced beliefs in demigods, divine sons and lords. More recent research (e.g., Hurtado) indicates that the mutation or innovation represented in early Christian Christ-devotion had its decisive beginnings among Jewish Christian circles within the earliest years of the Christian movement. Moreover, the development in question was almost explosively rapid in the first few years, and elaborate theories of identifiable stages of christological development leading up to a divine status accorded to Christ are refuted by the evidence.

Not only in the texts surveyed but even in earliest NT writings (Paul's letters) Christ is associated with God in astonishing ways, is accorded divine titles (esp. "Lord," informed by OT passages referring to Yahweh), functions in divine roles (e.g., as eschatological judge and as the divine source of prophetic oracles) and is formally reverenced in specific ways otherwise reserved for God. Such Christ-devotion is not readily compatible with the Judaism familiar to us and was apparently an exception in Jewish practice as reflected in ancient Jewish sources. At least in the second century it appears that there were Jewish Christian groups whose reverence of Christ was significantly more modest (the so-called Ebionites, about whom, however, far too many overconfident claims have been made by scholars). But it is also clear that at least some Jewish Christian groups affirmed the sorts of exalted christological claims and binitarian devotional patterns surveyed.

The main features of Jewish Christian christology apparent to us in the NT and earliest Christian sources are the following. Jesus is proclaimed as the Messiah (Christ) promised by God in the OT, royal Davidic OT texts in particular interpreted as messianic predictions. One of the terms applied to Jesus in Greek-speaking circles of Jewish Christians is *pais* ("child" or "servant"), which appears to have carried royal Davidic connotations. It is likewise probably earliest Jewish Christian circles who felt required and empowered to interpret Jesus' death so as to see God acting through it in fulfillment of previously unrecognized prophecies of Messiah's sufferings. References to Jesus' death in terms taken from Jewish Passover and from OT sacrificial vocabulary (e.g., "blood," "lamb") probably began among Jewish Christian circles as well.

Jesus was also likely presented as the eschatological prophet like Moses, with consequent authority over the believing community to define obedience to God (reflected, e.g., in Matthew). Early Jewish Christian circles may therefore have begun early to organize and transmit in writing teachings or sayings of Jesus (as reflected in sayings collections thought to lie behind the Synoptics and James).

From Aramaic-speaking Jewish Christian circles of the earliest years of the Christian movement, the exalted Jesus was referred to as the "Lord" *(Marê)* of the community, a practice carried over into Greek-speaking circles in the common use of *Kyrios* for Jesus. Already by Paul's time this had generated a collection of Christian terms: Lord's day, Lord's Supper (1 Cor 11:20), Lord's brothers (1 Cor 9:5), which are used as terms familiar in Christian circles. Even more importantly, the exalted Jesus was invoked in corporate worship as "Lord" and, in other ways as well, functioned with God as the object of devotion.

Particulary noteworthy is the ritual use of Jesus' name, for example, in the initiatory rite of baptism ("into the name of Jesus"), indicating the exalted Jesus as the one through whom exclusively the elect community is constituted. Especially in the context of the larger Jewish community, sharply conflicting judgments about Jesus appear to have been formulated and expressed: "Jesus is Lord," versus "Jesus is Anathema" (1 Cor 12:3, "cursed," a use of the term suggesting Jewish provenance).

It is also particularly to Jewish Christian circles that we can trace the concern to avoid making the exalted Jesus a second god in any way, diminishing the supremacy of the Creator God of the OT. Thus, especially in texts showing Jewish Christian influence, we have Jesus' resurrection more characteristically portrayed as God raising Jesus, Jesus' exalted status as conferred or declared by God and Jesus' redemptive work as bringing the elect into relationship with God the Father. As we move farther from the influence of Jewish Christian christology, this concern to maintain a kind of functional subordination of Christ to God the Father is not always maintained, particularly in the apocryphal Christian writings from Gentile Christian circles of the late second century and thereafter.

See also CHRIST; GOD; HOLY SPIRIT; LORD; SON OF GOD.

DLNTD: DOCETISM; LAMB; LOGOS CHRISTOLOGY; PREEXISTENCE; SHEPHERD, FLOCK; STONE, CORNERSTONE.

BIBLIOGRAPHY. R. J. Bauckham, *God Crucified: Monotheism and Christology in the New Testament* (Grand Rapids: Eerdmans, 1999); idem, *The Theology of the Book of Revelation* (Cambridge: Cambridge University Press, 1993); idem, "The Worship of Jesus," in *The Climax of Prophecy* (Edinburgh: T & T Clark, 1993); W. Bousset, *Kyrios Christos* (Nashville: Abingdon, 1970); O. Cullmann, *Christ and Time* (rev. ed.; Philadelphia: Westminster, 1975); idem, *The Christology of the New Testament* (Philadelphia: Westminster, 1959); L. W. Hurtado, *Lord Jesus Christ: Devotion to Jesus in Earliest Christianity* (Grand Rapids: Eerdmans, 2003); idem, *One God, One Lord: Early Christian Devotion and Ancient Jewish Monotheism* (Philadelphia: Fortress, 1988); B. Lindars, *The Theology of the Letter to the Hebrews* (Cambridge: Cambridge University Press, 1991); R. N. Longenecker, *The Christology of Early Jewish Christianity* (SBT 2d series 17; London: SCM, 1970); G. N. Stanton, "Aspects of Early Christian-Jewish Polemic and Apologetics," *NTS* 31 (1985) 377-92.

L. W. Hurtado

CHRONOLOGY OF PAUL. *See* PAUL IN ACTS AND LETTERS.

CHURCH I: GOSPELS

The mission of Jesus was concerned with the creation of a community that formed the basis of the church that developed after Easter and Pentecost.

1. The Problem
2. The Kingdom of God and Community
3. The *ekklēsia* Sayings
4. Jesus and the Structures of the Church
5. Continuity Between the Church and Jesus

1. The Problem.

The four Gospels were produced in Christian communities by persons who believed that the existence of these groups was the proper consequence of the coming of Jesus. Inevitably they reflect to some extent the nature, life and interests of the churches in which they were produced. The actual word "church" (Gk *ekklēsia*) is found in Matthew 16:18 and Matthew 18:17. The latter passage describes a procedure to be followed if a person's "brother" sins against him; if the matter cannot be settled privately or by a small group, it is to be brought before "the church, and we may presume that this practice was followed in communities known to Matthew. In the former passage Jesus promises that he will build his church on this "rock" [Gk *petra*], having previously said to Peter: "You are Peter" [Gk *petros*, "rock"]. These, however, are the only two uses of the term in all four Gospels, and this infrequency of usage, combined with a suspicion that the texts may indeed represent primarily the theology and practice of groups known to Matthew, has caused doubts whether these sayings attributed to Jesus truly represent his words or even his mind.

Some scholars would go even further and deny that Jesus intended the church. They are not suggesting that Jesus thought purely in individualistic terms. Rather, their position is determined by an understanding of his teaching that holds that his mind was dominated by the imminent end of the world and the coming of the kingdom of God—a "thorough-going" eschatology that affected the entirety of his thinking and, in particular, left no time for the development of an organized community. Thus C. K. Barrett suggests that "beyond the time of suffering he envisaged no period of continuing history, in which a Church organized in this world might find a place, but an apocalyptic act of vindication" (Barrett, 87; *see* Apocalypticism). To be sure, events proved Jesus to be wrong: "Jesus foretold the kingdom, and it was the Church that came" (A. Loisy, quoted by Barrett, 68) sums up crisply what happened, according to this view. Such a denial that Jesus expected the church does not rest merely on a critical examination of two texts but on a total interpretation of the eschatology of Jesus.

A less radical view is presented by E. Schweizer, who allows that Jesus called disciples but claims that he did nothing to create a group distinguishable from the rest of the world. Schweizer here takes a remarkably existentialist view of the mission of Jesus, a view that seems to be shaped by his genuine concern to warn against thinking that belonging to a particular group can insulate a person from a real meeting with Jesus.

2. The Kingdom of God and Community.

Two factors may lead us to see things differently. The first is that a different interpretation of the eschatology of Jesus is possible and indeed preferable and is widely held. Jesus, it can be claimed, saw the fulfillment of the hope of the coming of the kingdom of God happening during his ministry and looked forward to its future consummation at an unspecified point in the future. If this point is granted, then a different understanding becomes possible. The second factor is that the original question may have been wrongly put or at least wrongly focused. It is more appropriate to ask what intention Jesus may have had with respect to community.

2.1. Community. The concept of the kingdom of God implies a community. While it has been emphasized almost ad nauseam that the primary concept is that of the sovereignty or kingship or actual rule of God and not of a territory ruled by a king, it must be also emphasized that kingship cannot be exercised in the abstract but only over a people. The concept of the kingship of God implies the existence of a group of people who own him as king and the establishment of a realm of people within which his gracious power is manifested. Past scholarship rightly reacted against the tendency to identify the kingdom of God with the empirical, visible church and above all to identify the rule of God with the exercise of authority by church leaders. But this reaction has obscured the fact that there is a community of people who own God as king, however imperfectly they may obey him, and in whom his gracious power is at work.

2.2. Israel. Jesus' message was directed toward Israel and was concerned with the renewal of Israel, that is, of the people of God. The goal was the renewal of the people as a community and not simply the repentance of individuals, al-

though the path to the former lay through the latter. This point has been emphasized by B. F. Meyer. Jesus used imagery that spoke of Israel as a vineyard which needed new tenants to care for it. He prophesied doom in collective terms for those who did not respond to his message. He expressed concern for the lost sheep of the house of Israel and might almost have been suspected of a concern for Israel to the exclusion of the Gentiles. His concern is expressed for people in that they are "daughters of Abraham" or "sons of Abraham" (Lk 13:16; 19:9; *see* Abraham).

An important text (Mt 19:28/Lk 22:29-30) promises that the Twelve will sit on thrones judging the twelve tribes of Israel (*see* Judgment). This text, which seems particularly time-bound to modern readers, probably refers to the Twelve sharing in judgment on the unbelieving people of Israel in association with Jesus rather than to some kind of rule over a reconstituted ethnic Israel. The language is symbolical, but the symbolism points to some kind of community that corresponds to the twelve tribes of Israel. Jesus is saying in the strongest way possible that the old Israel is coming under judgment and that the judgment will be in the hands of those who have been called by him as his close disciples. The implication is that there will be what we may call a new Israel.

2.3. Discipleship. Jesus called people to be his disciples. Here we have to make a distinction between the group of the Twelve who were specially called to be associated with him in his mission (and who came to be known as apostles) and the much wider group who did not in every case travel from place to place with him. Some of the sayings about discipleship may be particularly directed to the former group, but nevertheless the concept of "following Jesus" is part of the message addressed to all who sought eternal life or a place in the kingdom of God.

2.4. Communal Images. It is then not surprising that various communal images are found in the teaching of Jesus. The disciples form the "little flock" (Lk 12:32). They are likened to a "city" (Mt 5:14), to a planted field (Mt 13:24; 15:13) or to a group of wedding guests (Mk 2:19). In an important saying, Jesus speaks of his disciples as members of his family (Mk 3:34-35) and he regards their relationship to him as somehow replacing his normal kinship relationships and requires them to have a love for him greater than for their kin (Mk 10:29-30). Within this grouping the disciples are to regard themselves as brothers (Mt 23:8).

3. The *Ekklēsia* Sayings.

In the light of this argument it becomes credible that Jesus did speak of the disciples as constituting an *ekklēsia*. This term could be the translation equivalent of more than one Hebrew or Aramaic word. It can refer to a local group of pious people, equivalent to a "synagogue" (a synagogue is first of all a group of people and only secondarily the place where they meet).

3.1. Matthew 18:17. The saying in Matthew 18:17 can be taken in this way. It could admittedly make sense in the lifetime of Jesus as an isolated saying regarding discipline within a Jewish community (notice how Jesus assumes that his hearers offer sacrifices at the temple, Mt 5:23-24). In this setting it would not be surprising for pious Jews to regard recalcitrant brothers "like a Gentile or tax-collector."

However, Matthew certainly thought that Jesus was addressing disciples, for the pericope goes on to assume the hearers meet together "in my name" (Mt 18:20), which is precisely what "church" signifies. The saying presupposes that the disciples constitute such a group, which implies some kind of organization and to which there is no other reference in the teaching of Jesus. Nothing anywhere else indicates that he organized his disciples, whether the Twelve or a wider group, in this kind of way.

Further, this is an extraordinary statement on the lips of Jesus in view of his positive attitude to tax collectors (cf. Mk 2:15-17). It is not surprising that many commentators would regard this pericope as a creation of the early church and as reflecting a narrowly Jewish-Christian church with an exclusive attitude toward Gentiles and tax collectors.

One difficulty with this view is that elsewhere Matthew shows the same positive attitude to tax collectors as we find in the other Gospels (Mt 9:10-11; 11:19; 21:31-32). Clearly the saying refers to some kind of breaking off of relations with the unrepentant offender, and the problem is simply whether Jesus or his followers, who knew his attitude to tax collectors and sinners, could have used this form of expression to make the point. The solution may be that Jesus is deliberately using shocking language: so dreadful is it that within the community of disciples a person should persist in sin that his fellow disciples should treat him just as the Jews treated tax collectors and sinners. This interpretation frees Matthew from an almost unbelievable inconsistency. Jesus' language is startling and liable to misinterpretation—as it often has been.

The reference to the *ekklēsia* still remains strange. However, if Jesus expected persecution for his followers, he may well have foreseen their exclusion from the synagogues and their consequent organization into their own groups. Matthew's readers would have had no difficulty with the saying since they would assume that Jesus was speaking prophetically of the local church and they would read it in the light of the previous use of the term in Matthew 16.

3.2. Matthew 16:18. This passage creates less difficulty. It has been shown that the language used here corresponds to that used at Qumran, where God appointed the Teacher of Righteousness to build for himself a congregation (*'ēda*) (4QpPs37.III:16; *see* Dead Sea Scrolls). Several factors are significant for understanding this passage.

First, Jesus creates a (new) "congregation" that is evidently a special group within Judaism. This fits in with the self-consciousness of the Qumran community, who saw themselves in the same way. Second, whereas at Qumran God creates a congregation for himself, Jesus speaks of building "my congregation," thus apparently himself taking the place of God. More precisely, Jesus speaks as the Messiah (*see* Christ) and "my congregation" means "the congregation of me, the Messiah." Such a community may be seen in the concept of the "remnant" in the Old Testament and especially in the "saints of the Most High" who are represented by the Son of man as their leader.

Third, the congregation is built on "this rock," which is generally taken to refer to Peter, who has just been mentioned. The fact that the saying uses the feminine form *petra* is attributed to the fact that the masculine form *petros* signifies a "[lump of] stone" rather than a large expanse of rock that might serve as a foundation for a building. On this view it is Peter—as the one to whom God has revealed that Jesus is the Messiah and who confesses him as such—upon whom the congregation is built. However, it has been argued by C. Caragounis that the two Greek words do not necessarily refer to the same entity, that the Aramaic word underlying *petra* is not necessarily that which underlies *petros* and that the focus of the passage suggests that the foundation of the church is the content of Peter's confession that Jesus is the Messiah.

Finally, that Jesus is speaking on a cosmic scale is apparent from the references to the opposition from the "gates of Hades" and to the keys of the kingdom of God. This is the divinely instituted community of the end time against which the full force of evil is pitted.

All this material shows that Jesus proclaimed the rule of God and urged people to return to God in repentance and obedience, that he called them to be his own disciples and to constitute the *ekklēsia* of the Messiah, that he saw them as the children of God called to live together as brothers and sisters. It may surely be affirmed that here we have the essence of the church.

4. Jesus and the Structures of the Church.

The argument so far is based on the classical presentation by R. N. Flew. He detected five elements in the mission of Jesus that encapsulate the idea of the church: (1) the disciples as the nucleus of the new Israel; (2) the ethical teaching given to them and the power of the Spirit; (3) the conception of messiahship and the consequent allegiance; (4) the message as constitutive of a community; (5) the mission of the new community.

Each of these elements can be traced as part of the constitution of the church after Easter and leave no doubt that we are justified in thinking of the church as part of the purpose of Jesus. But to what extent did Jesus prepare for or anticipate other features of the church as it later developed?

The Twelve appear primarily as Jesus' companions and colleagues in his mission. Some kind of authority is given to them in Matthew 16 and Matthew 18. The promises made to Peter are repeated to all of the disciples in Matthew 18. They will make decisions that will be ratified by God. They will be able to act in concert in prayer and see their prayers answered. In this situation some kind of leadership is envisaged. But the horizon is limited to their lifetime, and nothing is said about leadership in the future except in the eschatological symbolism of Matthew 19:28 (par. Lk 22:29-30).

The question of baptism as an initiation rite does not arise in the Synoptic Gospels. When it is discussed in John it is as an expression of repentance and a type of Spirit baptism rather than as entry to a community, although the latter need not be excluded. According to John, the disciples practiced baptism during the lifetime of Jesus.

The Lord's Supper is established by Jesus as a memorial to him that is to be continued by his followers, but no instructions are given regarding the details of how it is to be conducted or by whom (*see* Last Supper).

5. Continuity Between the Church and Jesus.

According to Luke, soon after the resurrection the disciples met together and engaged in teaching by the apostles, fellowship, breaking of bread and prayers (Acts 2:42-47). All four of these items have their roots in the lifetime of Jesus.

First, the position of the apostles is that of those who teach on Jesus' behalf. The accounts of the calling and mission of the Twelve and the seventy(-two) indicate that Jesus taught them and prepared them for mission. The Gospels generally indicate that Jesus gave special teaching to the disciples over against his general teaching to the crowds. Second, the concept and practice of fellowship may reflect the common life of the inner group of disciples of Jesus. The concept of brotherhood within the community is reflected in Matthew 23:8. Third, the practice of the breaking of bread is linked to the common meals of the disciples with Jesus and to the Last Supper. Fourth, the prayers of the postresurrection community reflect the example and instruction of Jesus to them.

To these items we may add a fifth, the ongoing mission that continues the public teaching of Jesus with its challenge to Israel to repent. Thus there is significant continuity between Jesus and the church.

See also KINGDOM OF GOD.

BIBLIOGRAPHY. C. K. Barrett, *Jesus and the Gospel Tradition* (London: SPCK, 1967); M. Bockmuehl and M. B. Thompson, ed., *A Vision for the Church: Studies in Early Christian Ecclesiology* (Edinburgh: T & T Clark, 1997); C. C. Caragounis, *Peter and the Rock* (Berlin: Walter de Gruyter, 1990); E. Ferguson, *The Church of Christ: A Biblical Ecclesiology for Today* (Grand Rapids: Eerdmans, 1996); R. N. Flew, *Jesus and His Church* (2d ed.; London: Epworth, 1943); K. N. Giles, *What on Earth Is the Church? A Biblical and Theological Enquiry* (London: SPCK, 1995); L. Goppelt, *Theology of the New Testament* (Grand Rapids: Eerdmans, 1981) vol. 1; D. Guthrie, *New Testament Theology* (Downers Grove, IL: InterVarsity Press, 1981); J. Jeremias, *New Testament Theology* (New York: Scribners, 1971); R. N. Longenecker, ed., *Community Formation in the Early Church and in the Church Today* (Peabody, MA: Hendrickson, 2002); I. H. Marshall, "New Wine in Old Wine-Skins: V. The Biblical Use of the Word 'Ekklēsia,'" *ExpT* 84 (1972-73) 359-64; B. F. Meyer, *The Aims of Jesus* (London: SCM, 1979); A. G. Patzia, *The Emergence of the Church: Context, Growth, Leadership & Worship* (Downers Grove, IL: InterVarsity Press, 2001); E. Schweizer, *Church Order in the New Testament* (London: SCM, 1961).   I. H. Marshall

CHURCH II: PAUL

More than one hundred different terms, metaphors and images are used in the NT to describe God's people with whom he has entered into a saving relationship in Christ. In addition to these descriptions, several activities are said to characterize Christian believers. Integral to Paul's teaching about the people of God is his use of the important word *ekklēsia*, a term meaning "congregation," "church," "gathering" or "assembly."

    1. *Ekklēsia* Outside the Bible
    2. *Ekklēsia* in Paul
    3. The Origin of the Church
    4. Some Images of the Church
    5. The Purpose of the Church's Gathering
    6. Authority in the Church

1. *Ekklēsia* Outside the Bible.

1.1. Ekklēsia *in the Greek City-State.* The term *ekklēsia* ("assembly"), derived from *ek-kaleō* ("call out," a verb used for the summons to an army to assemble), is attested from the time of Euripides and Herodotus onward (fifth century B.C.) and denoted the popular assembly of the full citizens of the *polis* or Greek city state. During this period it met at regular intervals, though in cases of emergency the term could describe an extraordinary gathering. Every citizen had the right to speak and to propose matters for discussion. Centuries before the translation of the OT and the time of the NT, the term *ekklēsia* was clearly characterized as a political phenomenon. It was the assembly of full citizens, functionally rooted in the Greek democracy, an assembly in which fundamentally political and judicial decisions were taken (cf. Acts 19:39;

where at Acts 19:32 and 41 even an unconstitutional assembly is called an *ekklēsia*). It was regarded as existing only when it actually assembled (as such it was distinct from the *demos*, "people," "crowd," "populace").

1.2. Ekklēsia *in the LXX, Josephus and Philo.* In the LXX *ekklēsia* frequently was a translation of the Hebrew *qāhāl*, a term that could describe assemblies of a less specifically religious or nonreligious kind, such as the gathering of an army in preparation for war (1 Sam 17:47; 2 Chron 28:14) or the "coming together" of an unruly and potentially dangerous crowd (Ps 26 [LXX 25]:5). (*Ekklēsia* never renders *ʿēdāh*, "congregation," which represented the people as a national unit.) Of particular significance are those instances of *ekklēsia* (rendering *qāhāl*) that denote the congregation of Israel when it assembled to hear the Word of God on Mount Sinai, or later on Mount Zion, where all Israel was required to assemble three times a year. Sometimes the whole nation appears to be involved, as when Moses addresses the people prior to their entry into the Promised Land. Deuteronomy 4:10 describes "the day when you stood before the Lord your God, in Horeb, when he said to me, 'Assemble the people before me to hear my words' " (the LXX uses the term *ekklēsia* and its cognate verb *ekklēsiazō;* note also Deut 9:10; 18:16; 31:30; Judg 20:2; etc.). At other times it is only the chief representatives that seem to be present, as with the congregation of tribal leaders, or patriarchal chiefs, at Solomon's dedication of the temple of Jerusalem (1 Kings 8:14, 22, 55, etc.).

Josephus also used the word frequently (some forty-eight times, of which eighteen are LXX quotations), always of a gathering. These vary in character, for example, religious, political and spontaneous assemblies are mentioned (Josephus *Ant.* 4.8.45 §309; *Life* §268; *J.W.* 1.33.4 §654; 1.33.8 §666). Philo employs the term some thirty times, all but five of which are in quotations from the LXX. These five appear in a classical Greek sense.

So in the Greek and Jewish worlds prior to and contemporaneous with the NT, *ekklēsia* meant an assembly or gathering of people. It did not designate an "organization" or "society." Although it had no intrinsically religious meaning and could refer to meetings that were secular in character, of special significance are those occurrences of *ekklēsia* in the LXX that refer to the congregation of Israel when it assembled to hear the Word of God.

2. Ekklēsia in Paul.

The word *ekklēsia* appears 114 times in the NT, with 62 instances in Paul (3 instances are in Matthew, 23 in Acts, 20 in Revelation and in the non-Pauline letters 6 occurrences). Since Paul's uses all predate the other instances in the NT it is important to determine the meaning he attaches to it in various contexts.

2.1. A Local Assembly or Congregation of Christians.
Chronologically, the first use occurs at 1 Thessalonians 1:1 (cf. 2 Thess 1:1) in the greeting to the Christians at Thessalonica: "Paul, Silas and Timothy. To the church *(ekklēsia)* of the Thessalonians in God the Father and the Lord Jesus Christ." The term is employed in the same way as in Greek and Jewish circles, that is, like other assemblies *(ekklēsiai)* in the city, it is described as "a gathering of the Thessalonians." But it is distinguished from the regular political councils by the addition of the words "in God the Father," and from the regular synagogue meetings by the use of the term *ekklēsia* and the additional phrase "in the Lord Jesus Christ" (Banks). From the closing remarks of the letter it is clear that Paul has in mind an actual gathering of the Thessalonian Christians. So he requests that his letter "be read to all the brothers and sisters" and that they "greet them all with a holy kiss" (1 Thess 5:26-27).

Other instances of *ekklēsia* (singular) and *ekklēsiai* (plural) in Paul's letters also denote a local assembly or gathering of Christians in a particular place: it is thus not a metaphor, but a term descriptive of an identifiable object. In the two Thessalonian letters reference is made to "the churches of God" (2 Thess 1:4) and "the churches of God in Judea" (2 Thess 2:14). Other letters such as Galatians (Gal 1:2), the two letters to the Corinthians (1 Cor 7:17; 11:16; 14:33, 34; 2 Cor 8:19, 23, 24; 11:8, 28; 12:13) and Romans (Rom 16:4, 16) also employ the plural when more than one church is in view. (The only exceptions are the distributive expression "every church" [1 Cor 4:17] and the phrase "the church of God" [1 Cor 10:32] in a generic or possibly localized sense.) So reference is made to "the churches in Galatia" (Gal 1:2; 1 Cor 16:1), "the churches of Asia" (1 Cor 16:19), "the churches in Macedonia" (2 Cor 8:1) and "the churches of Judea" (Gal 1:22). This suggests that the term

was applied only to an actual gathering of people or to a group that gathers when viewed as a regularly constituted meeting (Banks). Although we often speak of a group of congregations collectively as "the church" (i.e., of a denomination), it is doubtful whether Paul or the rest of the NT uses *ekklēsia* in this collective way. Also, the notion of a unified provincial or national church appears to have been foreign to Paul's thinking. An *ekklēsia* was a meeting or an assembly. This primary sense of "gathering" comes out clearly in 1 Corinthians 11—14, where expressions are used, such as "when you assemble in church" (1 Cor 11:18) and "to speak in church" (1 Cor 14:35; cf. 1 Cor 14:4, 5, 12, 19, 28).

In one or two NT instances *ekklēsia* is found as an extension of the literal, descriptive use of "an assembly" to designate the persons who compose that gathering, whether they are assembled or not. This is a natural extension or linguistic development of group words (note our use of the word *team*) and may explain references such as Acts 8:3; 9:31; 20:17. However, two significant observations need to be made: first, the primary use of the word *ekklēsia* as gathering predominates overwhelmingly in the NT—and indeed through the Apostolic Fathers to the Apologists. Second, no theological constructs are made on the basis of these very few extended uses.

It is of particular significance that at the beginning of the two Corinthian letters (1 Cor 1:1; 2 Cor 1:1; cf. 1 Cor 10:32; 11:22; Rom 16:16) the church is described as belonging to the one who brought it into existence, that is, God, or the one through whom this has taken place, namely, Christ. Such an *ekklēsia* was not simply a human association or a religious club but a divinely created entity. As in the case of ancient Israel, the gatherings referred to by our term were in order to hear the word of God and to worship. Paul's reference in Galatians (Gal 1:13; cf. 1 Cor 15:9; Phil 3:6) to his original persecution of "the church of God" does not necessarily contradict this suggestion, since the expression may point to the church at Jerusalem before it was distributed into a smaller number of assemblies in various parts of Judea. Or it might be that as the believers met together, the arrests were made—their gathering provided evidence of their Christian associations (cf. Banks).

2.2. A House Church.
In a second group of ref-

erences, *ekklēsia* is again used as a descriptive term of an identifiable object—as distinct from a metaphor—this time of a gathering that met in a particular home, a house church. On occasion, a whole congregation in one city might be small enough to meet in the home of one of its members, and it must be remembered that it was not until about the middle of the third century that early Christianity owned property for purposes of worship. In other places, house churches appear to have been smaller circles of fellowship within the larger group. In addition to Nympha's house in Laodicea (Col 4:15), we know that in Colossae, Philemon's house was used as a meeting place (Philem 2). At Philippi, Lydia's home seems to have been used in this way (Acts 16:15, 40), while at Corinth, Gaius is described as "host . . . to the whole church" (Rom 16:23; the qualification *whole* would be unnecessary if the Christians at Corinth met only as a single group, and the word implies smaller groups also existed in the city; cf. 1 Cor 14:23; note also 1 Cor 16:19; Rom 16:5).

2.3. A Heavenly Gathering. Of particular significance for our study of the church are those instances in Paul's later letters where *ekklēsia* has a wider reference than either a local congregation or a house church and describes a heavenly and eschatological entity. We begin with Colossians 1:18, where it is stated that Christ is "the head of the body, that is the church." At Colossians 1:24 a similar expression is employed in the context of Paul's sufferings ("on behalf of his body, which is the church"). Most commentators interpret these references in Colossians (and the similar instances in Eph 1:22; 3:10, 21; 5:23-24, 27, 29, 32) of "the church universal, to which all believers belong" (Bauer) and which is scattered throughout the world. But there are two serious criticisms that may be leveled against this view. (1) The term *ekklēsia* can no longer have its usual meaning of "gathering" or "assembly," since it is difficult to envisage how the worldwide church could assemble, and so the word must be translated in some other way to denote an organization or society. (2) The context of Colossians 1:15-20, which is moving on a heavenly plane, suggests it is not an earthly phenomenon that is being spoken of in Colossians 1:18 but a supernatural and heavenly one.

This is not to suggest that believers have no relationships with one another if they do not gather together in church. As members of the body of Christ or of God's people, they are not only related to Christ but also to one another even when separated by time and distance. But the point being made here is that *ekklēsia* is not the term used in the NT of those wider, universal links. Earlier in the letter to the Colossians it had been mentioned that the readers have been fitted for a share in the inheritance of the saints in the kingdom of light and have been transferred from a tyranny of darkness to a kingdom in which God's beloved Son holds sway (Col 1:12-14). On the one hand, the Colossians are obviously members of an earthly realm (note the exhortations of Col 3:4—4:6, which show they have important earthly responsibilities), and the apostle looks forward to their being presented as "holy, irreproachable, and blameless" before God on the last day (Col 1:22). On the other hand, they are described as presently existing in a heavenly realm. Since they have been raised with Christ, they are to seek the things that are above, where Christ is, seated at God's right hand (Col 3:1). Because they live with Christ in this heavenly dimension (note that Christ who is their life is already in heaven, Col 3:1, 3), they are assured that when he appears they will also appear with him in glory (Col 3:4).

Later references in Ephesians are thought to point in this same direction of a heavenly gathering: it is expressly mentioned that God "made us alive with Christ . . . raised us up with him and seated us in the heavenly realms in Christ Jesus" (Eph 2:5-6). The same readers of this circular letter have been "blessed . . . in the heavenly realms with every spiritual blessing in Christ" (Eph 1:3). Again, reference is made to Christ's headship over the "church" *(ekklēsia),* which is his body (Eph 1:22-23). If the term *ekklēsia* is to be understood here as "church" or a gathering taking place in heaven, then this would mean that Christians participate in it as they go about their ordinary daily tasks. They are already gathered around Christ, and this is another way of saying that they now enjoy fellowship with him. Further references in Ephesians (Eph 3:10, 21; 5:23, 25, 27, 29, 32), though usually taken by interpreters to refer to the church universal, could also be understood as designating that heavenly gathering around Christ (see also below).

An important passage outside the Pauline letters where *ekklēsia* refers to a "gathering" that is heavenly and eschatological is Hebrews 12:23, where the unusual expression "the assembly of the firstborn" appears. Although the heavenly city is still the goal of the Christian's pilgrimage (Heb 13:14), Christians in their conversion have already come to that heavenly assembly.

2.4. The Relationship of Paul's Uses of Ekklēsia. The NT does not discuss the relationship between the local church and the heavenly gathering. The link is nowhere specifically spelled out. Certainly the local congregation was neither a part of the church of God nor a church of God. This is made plain in several places, including 1 Corinthians 1:2, where the apostle writes "to the church of God which is at Corinth." But we may suggest that local congregations, as well as house groups that met in the homes of Nympha and Lydia, for example, were concrete, visible expressions of that new relationship that believers have with the Lord Jesus. Local gatherings, whether in a congregation or a house church, were earthly manifestations of that heavenly gathering around the risen Christ.

If this heavenly meeting with Christ is a figurative or metaphorical way of speaking about believers' ongoing fellowship with him, then it was appropriate that this new relationship with the ascended Lord should find concrete expression in their regular coming together, that is, "in church." Apparently, the responsibility of meeting together in this way was not immediately obvious to some of the early Christians, since they still needed to be exhorted not to forsake "the assembling of . . . [themselves] together" (Heb 10:25). The context of Ephesians 3:10, where the manifold wisdom of God is being made known to the spiritual authorities *through the church*, suggests that "the church" refers not only to a heavenly gathering that is assembled around Christ, but also a local congregation of Christians, in which Jews and Gentiles are fellow members of the body of Christ. The local congregation is a concrete expression of this heavenly entity. Other references in Ephesians (e.g. 1:22; 3:21, etc.) appear to have this same two-fold referent.

Men and women were called into membership of this one church of Christ, the heavenly assembly, through the preaching of the gospel. They were brought into fellowship with God's Son (cf. 1 Cor 1:9), and to speak of their membership of this heavenly gathering assembled around Christ is another way of referring to this new relationship with him. They and other Christians were to assemble in local congregations here on earth, for this was an important

way in which their fellowship with Christ was expressed. Further, as they came together with others who were in fellowship with him, so they not only met with each other—they also met with Christ, who indwelt them corporately and individually.

3. The Origin of the Church.

3.1. "The Church of God." It has been claimed that whenever *ekklēsia* appears by itself it is to be understood as an abbreviation of the original term *hē ekklēsia tou theou* ("the church of God": 1 Cor 1:2; 10:32; 11:22; 15:9; 2 Cor 1:1; Gal 1:13; plural in 1 Cor 11:16, 22; 1 Thess 2:14; 2 Thess 1:4). Accordingly, the genitive *of God* is not merely an addition that defines more precisely the preceding word *church* but was part of an original fixed formulation. "The church of God" was the self-designation of the early Jerusalem church (1 Cor 15:9; cf. Gal 1:13; Phil 3:6), which understood itself to be the eschatological community of salvation. The full expression "the church of God" came to be applied to other congregations as well (1 Thess 2:14), including those in the Gentile mission ("the church of God which is at Corinth," 1 Cor 1:2; cf. 2 Thess 1:4). The genitive *of God* indicates that he is the source or origin of the church's life and existence. He summons men and women to himself through the preaching of Christ crucified and forms them into his *ekklēsia*.

3.2. Christ and the Church. On occasion, Paul mentions Christ in connection with the term *ekklēsia*: for example, "the churches of Christ greet you" (Rom 16:16). First Thessalonians 2:14 ("you became imitators of the churches of God in Christ which are in Judea") shows that Christ has not replaced God as the source of the church's life. God's act of founding the *ekklēsia* is mediated through Jesus Christ and his gospel. This was true of the *ekklēsia* in Thessalonica, no less than the churches in Judea. So, the churches of the NT are the congregations of God in Christ, the churches in Jesus Christ (1 Thess 2:14; Gal 1:22) or the churches of Jesus Christ (Rom 16:16).

4. Some Images of the Church.

In addition to his use of the important term *ekklēsia* ("church, congregation"), Paul employs many significant images and metaphors of God's people in Christ. These images are not always synonymous or coterminous with *ekklēsia*.

For example, the body metaphor can refer to Christians generally in their relationships in Christ, without suggesting that they are members of the same *ekklēsia*. But often in his letters the apostle applies these images to the same entity as the *ekklēsia*—for example, the congregation at Corinth. These metaphors have different or nuanced connotations, and therefore it is important to ask what point is being conveyed or taught through the image. More than a hundred are used in the NT generally. We shall confine our remarks to a limited number that throw special light on Paul's understanding of the church.

4.1. The Temple. The figure of the temple is used metaphorically in the NT to denote God's people. The apostle, in particular, develops this picture of the church as the community of the redeemed which, through the sanctifying activity of the Holy Spirit, is constituted as the dwelling place of God: this idea appears in 1 Corinthians 3:16-17; 2 Corinthians 6:16-18 and Ephesians 2:20-22 (cf. 1 Cor 6:19).

4.1.1. 1 Corinthians 3:16-17. In a context where he seeks to combat party strife in the church at Corinth (1:10-17; 3:5-9), Paul uses *naos theou* ("the temple of God") specifically of the local congregation. By means of the temple imagery he makes plain, first, that the congregation at Corinth is the temple of God because his Spirit dwells among God's assembled people (1 Cor 10:16). Second, the church is itself the dwelling place of God. His tabernacling on earth is not apart from his people; instead, it is an indwelling within them (1 Cor 10:16-17). Third, Paul stresses the unity and holiness of God's temple. All the Corinthians together constitute God's dwelling place, and as such it is holy. To defile it by internal schism, divisions or party spirit is to destroy it, and any attempt to do this will incur divine judgment.

4.1.2. 2 Corinthians 6:16-18. In one of the clearest statements in his letters about the idea of believers as God's temple, Paul, referring primarily to the members of the congregation at Corinth, states, "We are the temple of the living God." He quotes OT texts that speak of God's presence with his people (Lev 26:12; Ezek 37:27; etc.); however, it may be implied that for the apostle, God's dwelling in his people goes beyond OT notions of his "presence with or among" them; now it is an actual "dwelling in" them. Although it is not explicitly stated that this temple is holy, it is clearly implied from the admonition where the Corinthians are exhorted to separate from all that is unclean (2 Cor 6:17, quoting Is 52:11).

4.1.3. Ephesians 2:20-22. The third major temple reference in Paul's letters occurs in a passage where the apostle reminds his Gentile converts that through Christ's death they have been made heirs of God's promises. Here the church is set forth as the heavenly temple—teaching that is akin to the heavenly dimension we have already observed in relation to *ekklēsia*. According to OT prophecy, the temple at Jerusalem was to be the place where all nations at the end time would come to worship and pray (Is 66:18-20; cf. Is 2:1-5; Mic 4:1-5). The temple imagery here is to be understood in fulfillment of these promises. Through Christ, Gentiles have been brought near to God and along with Jews have become the new temple, the place where God's presence dwells. Christ's preeminent place in the temple is stressed: he is the "cornerstone," either the stone at the foot of the building, set in the corner to determine the line of the walls and so of the building as a whole, or the final stone set over the gate that holds the building together. "A holy temple in the Lord" and "a dwelling place of God in the Spirit" (Eph 2:21, 22) are parallel descriptions. The temple is God's heavenly abode, the place of his dwelling. Yet that temple is his people in whom he lives by his Spirit. Believers on earth, recipients of this circular letter, are linked with the heavenly realm in and through the Spirit of the risen Lord. Finally, the metaphor of the body is combined with that of the building to draw attention to the element of growth (Eph 2:21a, 22). Viewed as the temple, the church is a dwelling inhabited by God; but from the point of its being a building it is still under construction.

4.2. The Body. The metaphor of the body of Christ (*see* Body of Christ), employed by Paul to describe the church, is a highly significant one and is applied to a number of entities and with a range of connotations. It is used by the apostle in his earlier letters of a local congregation (at Corinth), of Christians (at Rome) in their relationships with one another—Christians who were not necessarily members of the same congregation (Rom 12:4-5)—and of a wider group, possibly including all Christians (1 Cor 12:13), that is, all who have been united to the Lord Jesus Christ. In Colossians and Ephesians, the body image denotes a heavenly entity, that is, all

Christians united to him. He is their life and is seated in heaven at God's right hand while believers themselves have not only been raised with Christ but also have been made to sit with him in the heavenly places. We shall treat only those references that throw light on Paul's use of *ekklēsia*.

4.2.1. The Earlier Letters. At 1 Corinthians 12:12-27, where the apostle is concerned to impress on the Corinthian Christians that they have mutual duties and common interests that they must not neglect, he asserts, "You are the body of Christ and severally members of it" (1 Cor 12:27). Within the body which is one, there is true diversity—a multiplicity of functions that are necessary to its being a real body (1 Cor 12:17-20). Each member with his or her gifts is necessary to the other members for the good of the body as a whole (1 Cor 12:17-21). The Spirit's activity is specifically mentioned: it is through baptism in or by the Spirit (*en heni pneumati*, 1 Cor 12:13) that members are added to the body of Christ. The Spirit then refreshes them just as he graciously gives them gifts for the common good (cf. 1 Cor 12:7, 11). The explicit reference to "you" *(hymeis)* at the conclusion of the paragraph (1 Cor 12:27) makes it plain that this metaphor of "the body of Christ" is predicated of the local congregation *(ekklēsia)* at Corinth. This church is neither a part of the body of Christ nor "a body of Christ." Such a description is similar to that in the opening words of the letter where the congregation is called "the church *[ekklēsia]* of God which is at Corinth" (1 Cor 1:2)—it is neither a part of the church of God nor a church of God in Corinth. Yet the statement in 1 Corinthians 12:13 about "we" being baptized into one body suggests that the image of the body of Christ can be used of Christians generally or at least a wider group than the believers at Corinth. There are thus two entities being referred to by the one expression—the local congregation at Corinth, which is specifically in mind at 1 Corinthians 12:27, and a wider group including Paul and possibly others (the "we" of 1 Cor 12:13). The phrase "the body of Christ" can be used comprehensively of all who are united in him and of a particular manifestation of that body, in this case the local congregation. This notion fits exactly with our interpretation of *ekklēsia* (and the temple motif) where the term can describe a local manifestation (in either a specific congregation or a house

church) and a heavenly entity.

At Romans 12:4-5 the body metaphor has reference to believers generally in their relationships with one another (perhaps scattered throughout the capital in Rome), rather than describing them as a single congregation.

4.2.2. The Later Letters. In Colossians and Ephesians there is an advance in Paul's thought, involving the setting forth of the relationship that the church, as the body of Christ, bears to Christ as head of the body (note the household code of Eph 5:22-33, which is an occasion for instruction about the relationship between Christ and the church). The church as the body of Christ occupies a highly significant role in the purposes of God. This is brought out particularly in Ephesians 1:23, where it is asserted that Christ's rule over all things is for, or on behalf of, the church, and at Ephesians 3:10, where it is stated that through the *ekklēsia* the wisdom of God is made known even to the cosmic powers (Eph 3:10; *see* Principalities and Powers). Christ's headship over the church is presented in terms of an organic relationship in which he exercises control over his people as the head of a body exercises control over its various parts. The living relationship between the members is kept in view, while the dependence of the members on Christ for life and power, as well as his supremacy, is reiterated. The element of the body's growth is made plain in Colossians 2:19 and even more so in Ephesians. Its upbuilding is mentioned in the context of unity in diversity; such a growth derives from Christ and leads to Christ as members are rightly related to him as the head and to one another (Eph 4:1-16). The church as the body of Christ is described as Christ's fullness (Eph 1:23). In one sense it is complete, for it is already a body just as there is already a Lord (Eph 4:4-6). Yet it grows and will be completed on the final day. The body thus partakes of the tension regularly seen in the NT between the already and the not yet, between what it is and what it will be. The body is a present reality, and yet it is an eschatological, that is, future, entity.

4.3. The Household. Throughout the NT God's people are regularly spoken of as a family, and a cluster of terms, drawn from family life, is used in discussions of the church and early Christian communities. God is "Father" (Rom 8:15; Gal 4:9), and those who are redeemed by Jesus Christ are God's children (Gal 4:1-7), with Jesus

Christ being the firstborn of the family (Rom 8:29). Paul speaks in warm terms when he addresses fellow Christians as "brothers" (note, for example, Phil 4:1, which includes "brothers and sisters"). The theme of family relationships is particularly prominent in 1 Timothy, where the church *(ekklēsia)* is described as "the household *(oikos)* of God, and the pillar and bulwark of the truth" (1 Tim 3:15; cf. Heb 3:1-6). The purpose of this letter as a whole is to indicate "how one ought to behave in God's household." The order of the church is analogous to that of a human household. Members are to treat one another as they would the members of their family (1 Tim 5:1-2). They are to care for one another in need (1 Tim 5:5, 16), while overseers are to be skillful at managing the household of God, as demonstrated by their skill with, and care for, their immediate families (1 Tim 3:1-7).

5. The Purpose of the Church's Gathering.

We have seen that coming together is an essential element of the *ekklēsia*. In many languages today the equivalent word for "church" is still used in relation to the act of gathering together: so expressions such as "it is time for church," "before [or after] church" or "in church" are used. The sense is always that of Christians congregating for a given reason. What, then, is the purpose of believers gathering together?

5.1. Edification. Although it is almost universally claimed that Christians meet together in church "to worship God," Paul's revolutionary teaching is that they are meant to worship him in every sphere of life (Rom 12:1). Worship terminology is transformed by the apostle and applied to the work of Christ (Rom 3:24-25; cf. Eph 5:2), the preaching of the gospel (Rom 1:9; 15:16; Phil 2:17) and the new lifestyle of believers (Rom 6:13, 16; 12:1; Phil 2:17; 1 Thess 1:9-10). It cannot be worship alone, therefore, that brings believers to church (cf. 1 Cor 14:25). Instead of the language of worship, Paul regularly uses the terminology of upbuilding, or edification, to indicate the purpose and function of Christian gatherings (1 Cor 14:3-5, 12, 17, 26; 1 Thess 5:11; Eph 4:11-16). "Edification" *(oikodomē)*, which refers to the growth and progress of believers, is not to be interpreted individualistically. There is a corporate as well as a personal dimension in the apostle's teaching on edification. According to Ephesians 4:7, the Messiah builds his church (cf. the OT promises of God

preparing a people for himself: Jer 24:6; 31:4; 33:7) through the people he gives as apostles, prophets, evangelists, pastors and teachers. The focus of attention here is on the ministries of the word (cf. Eph 2:20-22) that are to "equip the saints for works of service for building up the body of Christ" (Eph 4:12). The ultimate goal of this ministry, and therefore the purpose of the gathering, is to prepare believers for full maturity when they meet their Lord (Eph 4:13). Edification occurs through prophecy (1 Cor 14:3) and other verbal ministries of exhortation, comfort and admonition by congregational members (Eph 4:26; cf. 1 Thess 4:18; 5:11, 14; Eph 4:15). Of primary importance in the process of building up God's people is the regular and systematic exposition of Scripture, together with the teaching of "sound doctrine" by those equipped and appointed for the task (cf. 1 Tim 4:6, 11, 13; 5:17; 2 Tim 2:1-2, 14-15; 4:1-5; Tit 1:9). "When Christians gather together to minister to one another the truth of God in love, the church is manifested, maintained and advanced in God's way" (Peterson, 214). The well-being and strengthening of the congregation is a fundamental aim of the members gathering together.

In 1 Corinthians 11:17-34, although the terminology of edification is not used in Paul's discussion of the Lord's Supper at Corinth, the issue of upbuilding is clearly prominent. The apostle appears to be speaking about different aspects of the same meetings throughout the chapter (see 1 Cor 11:18, 22). The Christian congregation is not an ordinary association or club in which members have the same interests; rather, it is a gathering that arises out of a sharing together in the benefits of Christ's saving work. When the members met together, divisions of a social kind occurred. As long as individuals were preoccupied with consuming their own private meals, they were not holding a meal in honor of the Lord Jesus. By disregarding one another they were negating the very point of Christ's sacrifice for them. He had made it possible for them to share in the life of the age to come, but by their self-centered behavior they had failed to understand their partnership in the body of Christ. Rather than building up or edifying their fellow believers they were showing "contempt for the church of God" (1 Cor 11:22). Thus, by not caring for their fellow believers, they were not worshiping God or serving him acceptably.

5.2. Meeting with Christ. When NT believers

met with one another and shared a whole range of ministries of the word in the congregation, so that the body of Christ was edified, they met with Christ. As the members sang psalms, hymns and spiritual songs with gratitude in their hearts and thus fulfilled the apostolic injunction to let the word of Christ dwell among them richly (Col 3:16; cf. Eph 5:19-20), so Christ was present in their midst. "Any gospel-based ministry of encouragement or admonition will be a means by which Christ engages with his people" (Peterson, 198). This would take place when the Scriptures were formally expounded and taught, or when believers informally exhorted one another in the congregation to live out their obedience to the gospel. The model of the NT assembly was the congregation of Israel gathered at Mount Sinai to hear the word of the Lord. Now, however, under the new covenant there is a significant difference. The Lord meets with his people wherever they gather in his name and under his authority.

The assembling of believers "in church" was an appropriate and natural outworking of their relationship with Christ; meeting together in the congregation was obviously an important way in which this relationship with their Lord was expressed.

At the same time, their coming together was a foretaste and anticipation of the life of heaven. Reference has already been made to believers' membership in the heavenly gathering assembled around Christ. The end will bring the assembling of God's children to meet him (2 Thess 2:1), the moment when Christ is glorified in his saints (1 Thess 4:17; cf. 2 Thess 1:12) and when they obtain the glory of our Lord Jesus Christ (2 Thess 2:14). God's ultimate intention for them is the joy of fellowship, the restoration and enrichment of the relationships so rudely shattered in Eden. In this sense, fellowship with God and his Son, the Lord Jesus Christ, was not a means to an end but the end itself. Every authentic Christian gathering is not simply an expression of the heavenly church as it presently gathers round Christ in heaven; it is also an anticipation of that blessed consummation.

The OT hope for the nations was that they too might be united with Israel and with one another in serving God (Is 56:6-7; Rev 7). This hope should be anticipated in the gathering of God's people on earth in the here and now, and fulfilled on the final day. Accordingly, the

ekklēsia as it gathered was to keep looking "upward" or "forward," rather than simply "inward" at itself, or even "outward" at the world and its needs.

5.3. Worshiping God? If the worship terminology of the OT has been transformed by the NT writers, especially Paul, so that Christians are urged to worship the living God in every sphere of life (Rom 12:1), is it appropriate to speak of their gathering together in church for "the worship of God"? Also, how are we to understand the prayers, praises and thanksgivings that believers offer when they meet together in Christ's name? Should not these responses be viewed as significant elements in the corporate worship of God? If the emphasis is placed upon believers gathering together for the purpose of edification, how did Paul view the relationship between the horizontal and the vertical dimension of worship?

Central to Christian gatherings was the concern to proclaim and apply the truths of the gospel so as to stimulate and maintain saving faith. Prayers and praises were clearly part of the worship of God as faith responses to the gospel. Yet even these were to be expressed in church in a way that would build up the congregation. Prayers and thanksgivings were not to be purely private, God-directed activities when others were present. Whether inspired or not, they were to be intelligible, for otherwise they would fall short of the fundamental goal of building up other members of the assembly (1 Cor 14:16-17).

It seems "best to speak of congregational worship as a particular expression of the total life-response that is the worship of the New Covenant" (Peterson, 220). As the word of Christ was ministered and received in the congregation, so the body of Christ was built up. Christ himself was encountered in and through the "edification" *(oikodomē)*. And it was in building up the congregation that God was worshiped and glorified. A wedge should not be driven, therefore, between Paul's understanding of the vertical and horizontal dimensions of what took place in worship. Edification and worship, for example, were different sides of the same coin. Participating in the upbuilding of the church was an important expression of the believing community's devotion and service to God. It was, as D. G. Peterson puts it, an element of believers "engaging with God" (Peterson, 220). Therefore, one part of the meeting could not have been viewed as "worship time" (e.g., prayer and praise) and another part as "edification time," since the apostle's teaching encourages us to view the same activities from both points of view.

6. Authority in the Church.

6.1. Christ's Authority and the Apostolic Word.

From Paul's letters it is plain that the churches in his care stood under the authority of the Lord Jesus Christ. The church is Christ's body. He is its head, not only in the sense of being the source of its life and power but also as the one who exercises authority over it. The church of God in a particular place has been brought into existence through the proclamation of the apostolic gospel (cf. 1 Cor 1:4-9); its members have come into a living relationship with God's Son through his word. Christ continues to rule their lives by that same word. It is through the gospel that believers stand firm and by which they will be saved (1 Cor 15:1-2).

In the first instance that authority was exercised by Christ's apostles—initially through their preaching and later through their apostolic writings. They were his witnesses, emissaries and representatives (2 Cor 5:20), whose tasks were to found, build up and regulate the churches (2 Cor 10:8; 13:10; Gal 2:7-9). They appointed "men of good standing," or deacons (Acts 6:3, 6) and elders (Acts 14:23; cf. Tit 1:5-9). Their teaching was presented as Christ's truth, which was Spirit-given in its content and form of expression (1 Cor 2:9-13; cf. 1 Thess 2:13) and was a norm of faith (2 Thess 2:15; cf. Gal 1:8) and behavior (2 Thess 3:4, 6, 14). The church at Corinth, for example, was to realize that what the apostle wrote to them was a command of the Lord (1 Cor 14:37), while the Thessalonians were bound under oath to read and obey Paul's letters since they came with the authority of Christ (1 Thess 5:27; 2 Thess 2:15; 3:14).

6.2. The Authority of the Congregation.

The authority of an apostle, however, was not without limit. It came from the risen Lord Jesus Christ and was to be exercised within the sphere of the apostolic commission, while an apostle was to preach and teach what was consistent with the gospel (1 Cor 15:1-11; Gal 1:6-17).

Congregations, too, had a derived authority. Their elders and leaders were to rule over the church, teaching the members and urging them to follow the apostolic gospel and traditions (1 Thess 5:12-13; 1 Tim 3:5; 5:17; cf. 1 Cor 16:15-16). At 1 Corinthians 5, in the context of a serious pastoral problem involving immorality, Paul expects the congregation to make an important decision in relation to the offending Christian. The apostle gives his advice in no uncertain terms: "you are to hand this man over to Satan for the destruction of the flesh" (1 Cor 5:5). But the congregation is to make the decision. The Corinthians are to assemble, conscious that the guidance and power of the Lord Jesus will be with them as they pronounce a disciplining judgment in his name on their disobedient member (1 Cor 5:4-5).

Concerning the problem of discipline at the Lord's Supper in Corinth (1 Cor 10:14-22; 11:23-32), the apostle Paul lays down a number of principles that he expects the Corinthians to follow. But the actual details, the form of service, the way in which their errors were to be corrected, lay with the congregation. The apostle's instructions were addressed to the whole congregation, not to any particular leader or presiding elder within it.

See also BODY OF CHRIST; IN CHRIST; ISRAEL; WORSHIP.

DPL: CHURCH ORDER AND GOVERNMENT; FELLOWSHIP, COMMUNION, SHARING; GENTILES; HEAD, CHRIST AS; HOUSEHOLDS AND HOUSEHOLD CODES; PASTOR, PAUL AS; SOCIAL SETTING OF MISSION CHURCHES; TEMPLE.

BIBLIOGRAPHY. R. Banks, *Paul's Idea of Community: The Early House Churches in Their Historical Setting* (Grand Rapids: Eerdmans, 1980); L. Cerfaux, *The Church in the Theology of St. Paul* (New York: Herder, 1959); L. Coenen, "Church," *NIDNTT* 1:291-307; R. Y. K. Fung, "Some Pauline Pictures of the Church," *EvQ* 53 (1981) 89-107; H. Küng, *The Church* (London: Burns & Oates, 1968); A. T. Lincoln, *Paradise Now and Not Yet* (SNTSMS 43; Cambridge: Cambridge University Press, 1981); I. H. Marshall, "How Far Did the Early Christians *Worship* God?" *Churchman* 99 (1985) 216-29; idem, "New Wine in Old Wine Skins: V. The Biblical Use of the Word '*Ekklēsia*,' " *ExpT* 84 (1972-73) 359-64; P. T. O'Brien, "The Church as a Heavenly and Eschatological Entity," in *The Church in the Bible and the World*, ed. D. A. Carson (Grand Rapids: Baker, 1987) 88-119, 307-11; idem, *The Letter to the Ephesians* (Grand Rapids: Eerdmans; Leicester: Apollos, 1999); D. G. Peterson, *Engaging with God: A Biblical Theology of Worship* (Grand Rapids: Eerdmans, 1993); J. Roloff, "ἐκκλησία," *EDNT* 1:410-

15; K. L. Schmidt, "ἐκκλησία," *TDNT* 3:501-36; B. W. Winter, "The Problem with 'Church' for the Early Church," in *In the Fullness of Time: Biblical Studies in Honor of Archbishop Donald Robinson,* ed. D. Peterson and J. Pryor (Homebush West, NSW: Lancer, 1992) 203-17.

P. T. O'Brien

CHURCH III: ACTS, HEBREWS, GENERAL EPISTLES, REVELATION

The book of Acts ends with Paul in Rome. By this time the church is well established in Palestine, Syria, Asia Minor, Greece and Italy. By the middle of the second century the Christian church had spread around the Mediterranean basin and beyond. With this geographical dispersion the early localized Christian communities could have easily thought of themselves as self-contained groups, but their profound consciousness that they belonged to the one Christian community, the church dispersed throughout the world, did not allow this. In this period we see a widening gulf between Christians and Jews as each comes to recognize the separate identity of the other.

1. Presuppositions
2. Acts
3. Hebrews
4. James
5. 1 Peter
6. The Johannine Epistles
7. The Book of Revelation

1. Presuppositions.

In seeking to discover how early Christian writers understood the church, a number of basic presuppositions must be spelled out. In this article the idea that a doctrine of the church can be achieved solely by focusing on and determining a fixed meaning of the Greek word *ekklēsia* ("church") is rejected. Words are used with different meanings in different contexts and usually represent a concept that can be denoted by other words, metaphors or expressions. In what follows the focus is on the church concept, defined as the eschatological Christian community. One word used frequently to designate this concept is *ekklēsia,* but as we will see, many virtual synonyms, descriptive phrases and metaphors are also used. Furthermore, the concept can be in mind even when this one word is not present.

The church is to be thought of as "the eschatological Christian community" because the early Christians were one in understanding that while men and women individually came to faith in Christ, this involved by definition becoming part of the family of God open to all people everywhere. The goal of the Christian mission was not to save individuals, though it involved this, but to call out a people for God's name. All the apostolic and postapostolic writers see this new community emerging out of historic Israel. It is therefore, like Israel, a corporate entity. The local gathering of Christians was important because this was where communal life in Christ was most personally realized; but for the early Christians, belonging to the one community established by Christ was the primary reality. The modern Western individualistic spectacles through which we read the early Christian writings all too often blind us to seeing the profound communalism of early Christianity.

How each author understood the relationship between this community and the one from which it had emerged, namely, Israel, is one of the key issues to be worked out in any study of ecclesiology. As this was a difficult matter for the early Christians to resolve and as it was conditioned historically by an ever-widening breach between Jews and Christians, we would anticipate finding differing answers. The two stark alternatives were restoration or replacement. The church was a purified and renewed Israel into which Gentiles were welcomed, or the church was a breakaway from Israel, a new work of God. In the first case, continuity is to the fore; in the second, discontinuity.

In seeking to conceptualize the form of the church in this early period, we recognize that Christians normally met in relatively small groups in a home. The largest home would hold no more than fifty people. Most homes would have accommodated fewer than this number. Thus our modern experience of church must be put to one side as we try to visualize church life in the first and second centuries.

2. Acts.

Lukan ecclesiology has a number of distinctive features.

2.1. Spirit and Church. In Acts, Luke has the new Christian community coming into existence on the day of Pentecost, when the *Holy Spirit is poured out on those who confess Jesus as Lord and Christ. In Luke's thinking the Holy Spirit institutes and empowers the church. He sees the coming of the Holy Spirit as the fulfillment of the words of the prophet Joel, who along with other OT prophets had predicted a universal outpouring of the Holy Spirit on God's people in the age of final redemption (Joel 2:28-32; cf. Ezek 36:27; 37:14; Is 32:15; Zech 12:10). In quoting Joel's prophecy, Luke adds as an introduction the words "in the last days" (Acts 2:17) to show he understood that this mighty giving of the Spirit indicated that the eschatological age had dawned. In pouring out the Spirit, God was restoring Israel and inaugurating the new covenant (cf. Ezek 36:27 and Jer 31:33). The word *ekklēsia* does not appear in Acts until Acts 5:11. Immediately after the giving of the Holy Spirit, Luke is content to use a number of descriptive designations of the newly created, Spirit-filled community: "those who received the word" (Acts 2:41), "those who believed" (Acts 2:44), those who are being saved (Acts 2:47) and "the community" (*epi to auto*, Acts 2:47; see Giles 1995, 261 n. 9). Nevertheless, we can correctly speak of this event as the birth of the church. In Luke's mind this is when the post-Easter Christian community came into existence.

Having made the Holy Spirit foundational to the establishment of the new community, Luke has an abiding preoccupation with the Holy Spirit. Some seventy times the word *pneuma* ("Spirit") appears in Acts. R. E. Brown concludes, "The distinguishing feature of Lucan ecclesiology is the overshadowing presence of the Holy Spirit" (Brown, 65).

2.2. Church and Israel. A protracted debate has taken place as to how Luke views the relationship between historic Israel and the new Christian community. What seems to be the case is that Luke's distinctive ecclesiology depicts those Jews who recognize Jesus as the long-awaited Messiah and are empowered by the Holy Spirit as restored Israel. Gentiles who believe are included in this restored Israel, as the prophets had predicted (Acts 15:12-18). Jews who reject Christ are "rooted out" and lose their status as the people of God (Acts 3:23). In telling his story in historical sequence, Luke allows that the realization only gradually dawned on the first believers that historic Israel as such had ceased to be the people of God (for a different perspective on Israel's status *see* Covenant and New Covenant).

This new community, Luke insists, is like historic Israel, very much on earth. A heavenly church would have been a contradiction in terms for him. Christ has ascended into heaven to rule in power and glory (Acts 1:6-11; 2:33), and the church is on earth "passing through many tribulations" before "entering the (future) kingdom of God" (Acts 14:22).

2.3. Names for the Church. Luke gives a large number of names to the one reality we call the church. H. J. Cadbury lists and discusses nineteen collective titles. A few of these are doubtful, but even leaving two or three aside, a large number remain.

2.3.1. "Those Who . . . " Some titles are descriptive and may have been developed by Luke or taken over from common usage. The designations "those who believe" (several participial forms are used; see Acts 2:44; 4:32; 15:5; 16:34; 18:27); "those who call on the name" (Acts 9:14, 21; 22:16); "those who received the word" (Acts 2:41) and "those who are being saved" (Acts 2:47; cf. Lk 13:23) fall into this category.

2.3.2. Early Titles Preserved. Another group of titles seem to be almost historical fossils. They reflect very early Palestinian terminology. "Galileans" (Acts 1:11; 2:7) is one possible example. Others include "the Nazarenes" (Acts 24:5) and "the Way" (Acts 9:2; 19:9, 23; 24:14, 22), to which we can add Acts 22:4 ("this way"). In the OT and at Qumran the word *way* is often used figuratively of living in a manner pleasing or not pleasing to God (Ps 101:2; 119:1-3; Is 53:6; 57:17). Besides using the word absolutely, Luke also speaks of "the way of the Lord" (Acts 18:25), "the way of God" (Acts 18:26) and "the way of salvation" (Acts 16:17). Possibly the absolute usage is but an abbreviation. Both titles, "the Nazarenes" and "the Way," can designate what Jewish opponents call a "sect" or "party" *(hairesis)*. This word is not yet another title for Christians but a Jewish way of viewing the early believers as a sect within Israel. Luke uses this word of the Pharisees (Acts 15:15) and of the Sadducees (Acts 5:17), but he does not think it is appropriate to use it of the disciples of Christ. They are more than this. In the three instances (Acts 24:5, 14; 28:22) where this term is used of believers, it is on the tongue of opponents.

Another very early title used first by the enemies of the new community, this time from a Gentile setting, is "the Christians." The Greek transliteration of a Latin ending *(-ianos)* means "belonging to." In Acts 11:26 Luke says, "At Antioch the disciples were first called Christians."

Here and in the second usage (Acts 26:28) Luke has others calling Christians by this name. It was at this stage not a self-designation, and this is still the case when the title appears in 1 Peter 4:16. On a number of occasions Luke also calls Christians collectively *to plēthos*. He can use this word of any group of people ("a crowd"; Acts 14:1; 17:4; 21:22), but sometimes he allows it to have an almost technical meaning so that it can be translated "the [Christian] community" (Acts 6:2, 5; 15:12, 30; possibly Acts 21:22). Twice in the Septuagint *plēthosis* is used to render into Greek the Hebrew word *qāhāl* ("assembly/the Jewish covenant community"), which is usually translated by the word *ekklēsia* (Ex 12:6; 2 Chron 31:18).

2.3.3. Saints. The collective titles "the saints" *(hoi hagioi)* and "the people [of God]" *(ho laos)* may be grouped together. These two terms are given weighty theological content by their use in the Septuagint to designate Israel. Four times Luke calls Christians collectively "the saints" (Acts 9:13, 32, 41; 26:10), and twice he speaks of them as being "sanctified," using the participial form of the word (Acts 20:32; 26:18). In establishing the covenant with Israel God sets them apart as a holy nation (Ex 19:6; Lev 11:44-45). It is on this basis that the Jews became God's holy people, the saints (Num 16:13; Deut 33:3; Ps 16:3; 34:9; 89:5; Is 4:3). In calling Christians "the saints," Luke identifies them with restored Israel. Similarly, by twice designating Christians *ho laos,* "the people of God" (Acts 15:14; 18:10; cf. Acts 3:23), Luke makes the same point. In the Septuagint this term is a distinctive and theologically weighted designation of Israel.

2.3.4. Disciples and Brethren. It is, however, the titles "the disciples," "the brethren" and "the church" that Luke uses most commonly. The title "the brethren" *(hoi adelphoi),* a gender-inclusive term, is interesting because Luke uses it for Jews and Christians, which suggests the relationship between these two groups was still relatively fluid. Even as late as Acts 28:21 Luke can speak of fellow Jews as brethren. Nevertheless, without any apology he calls Christians "the brethren" twenty-five times (Acts 9:30; 10:23; 11:1; 12:17). This term underlines the familial nature of being a believer. The title "the disciples" *(hoi mathētai)* is almost as common, being used twenty-three times of Christians (Acts 6:7; 9:26; 11:26; 15:10). In this case this title is a reminder that believers are followers of Christ.

2.3.5. Church. Finally we come to the word *ekklēsia,* which Luke uses nineteen times of Christians (Acts 5:11; 8:1; 9:31; 11:26), three times of an unruly assembly of citizens in the theater at Ephesus (Acts 19:32, 39, 41) and once of the Jews assembled at Mount Sinai to receive the law (Acts 7:38). In classical Greek this word referred to people actually assembled, and Luke uses the word in this sense to denote the crowd at Ephesus. To argue on this basis that this is the meaning of the term in all the other uses in Acts is absurd. It would be like arguing that because Luke uses the verb "to save" of the rescue of Paul and the ship's crew (in Acts 27:20, 31) he believed salvation is only a this-worldly rescue. Elsewhere (excepting Acts 7:38) Luke uses the word *ekklēsia* in a specifically Christian sense to speak of Christians as a theologically defined community, restored Israel. In this sense it carries the content of the more developed meaning of this word in the Septuagint (see Giles 1995, 230-40).

Luke uses the one word to designate a local community of Christians (Acts 5:11; 8:1; 11:26; 13:1) and the Christian community in its entirety (Acts 20:28). The addition of the genitive "of God" in this last reference adds nothing. In the Gospels "the kingdom of God" means the same as "the kingdom" (*see* Kingdom of God). When Luke wishes to speak of local Christian communities in more than one place he uses the plural (Acts 15:41; 16:5). Acts 9:31 is problematic, as the word *ekklēsia* and the verbs and participles that follow are found in the singular and the plural in different manuscripts. Luke makes it clear that the church in Jerusalem, numbering many thousands, met in homes (Acts 2:46; 5:42; 10:2; 11:14; 12:12-17), but he never uses the word *ekklēsia* for a house church. For him the Christians in one geographical spot are "the" local church.

2.3.6. Synonymity of Titles. What is important to note is that while each of these collective titles has its own nuance, they are virtual synonyms that can be used interchangeably. Acts 9 is instructive, as Luke uses five collective titles for stylistic variation in this chapter. In Acts 9:1 he speaks of "the disciples" and repeats this term in Acts 9:25, 26 and 38. Next comes the title "[those] who belong to the way" (Acts 9:2). In Acts 9:30 he uses the title "the brethren"; in Acts 9:13 and 32, "the saints"; in Acts 9:14 and Acts 9:21, "those who call on the name." Elsewhere in Acts the most common titles—"the disciples," "the brethren" and "the church"—are frequently interchanged. For example, Luke speaks of the disciples of a city or of the church of a city (Acts 8:1; cf. Acts 9:19). He can speak of Paul strengthening the churches or the disciples (Acts 14:22; 15:41; 18:23). The overlapping but not identical meaning of each of these collective titles can be diagrammatically illustrated by using a selection of the terms.

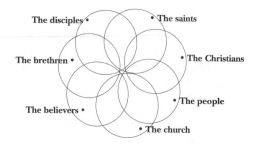

One reality, the Christian community, designated by different terms

3. Hebrews.

On reading *Hebrews one is immediately struck by the distinctive language, christology and use of the OT. It is not surprising, therefore, to discover that this epistle also has a distinctive ecclesiology. Although Hebrews appeals primarily to the OT to make its case, it envisages a radical breach with Israel. The old covenant has been replaced by the new (Heb 8:6-13); the Jewish priesthood and the office and work of the high priest have come to an end (Heb 7:11-14, 23-28); and Jesus in offering himself has made obsolete the old sacrificial system (Heb 9:25-28; 10:11-15). As a consequence, the author views the Christian community as new Israel in all but name. The Christians have taken the place of the historic people of God, assuming their distinctive titles and privileges. Thus in Hebrews 3—4 the author can typologically identify the Christian family with Israel. How God dealt with Israel and what he said to them in the past now, one for one, applies to the Christian community.

The author of Hebrews uses a number of terms to designate this new community. They are "the people of God" (*ho laos,* Heb 2:17; 4:9; 8:10; 10:30; 11:25; 13:12); "the children of God" (Heb 2:10; 12:5, 6, 7); "the saints" (Heb 6:10; 13:24) and "God's house" (Heb 3:6). All these titles were originally the prerogative of historic Is-

rael. By implication Christians are also understood to be the new covenant community (Heb 8:8-12; 10:16-17).

The word *ekklēsia* is used only twice. It appears first in Hebrews 2:12 in a quote from Psalm 22:22, in which God's people are depicted as a worshiping community (*see* Worship). This same thought appears in the second example (Heb 12:23), where again historic Israel and the Christian community are related typologically but this time by way of contrast. In Hebrews 12:18-24 the author speaks of the two communities, with different mediators, "drawing near" (*proserchesthai*) either to the earthly Mount Sinai or to the heavenly Jerusalem, identified as Mount Zion, the former group in terror, the latter with rejoicing. Those with whom these Christians are said to draw near is unclear. Possibly the three groups are angels (Heb 12:22), Christian believers who have died ("the *ekklēsia* / assembly of the firstborn") and whose names are enrolled in heaven (Heb 12:23), and OT believers described as "just men made perfect" (Heb 12:23).

If we ask, How did the author envisage the Christian community on earth drawing near in Hebrews 12:22, the best answer is, in worship. In Hebrews 2:12 the church is described as a worshiping community, and the key verb *proserchesthai* ("to draw near") is a cultic term drawn from the OT alluding to what takes place in worship (see Giles 1995, 155-56). At this point we should also add that the argument does not stand that because the word *ekklēsia* in Hebrews 12:23 is used of a heavenly assembly, all universal uses of the word *ekklēsia* in the NT refer exclusively to a heavenly gathering. The language and thought of the epistle to the Hebrews is distinctive, and all the writer seems to be suggesting is that in worship Christians come near to God along with a great heavenly company.

4. James.

The epistle of *James is a pastoral epistle, not a theological treatise. Most commentators think James is addressing Jewish Christians when he calls them "the twelve tribes of the dispersion" (Jas 1:1). This title is strongly communal and bears witness to a belief that the Christian community is dispersed throughout the world, but it is probably not a claim that Christians are the new Israel. In James 2:2 the writer calls a Christian gathering a synagogue (cf. Heb 10:25; Ign.

Pol. 5.2; *Herm. Man.* 11.9; Justin *Dial. Tryph.* 63.5). In James 5:14 he speaks of "the elders of the church" *(ekklēsia)*. This suggests that the Christian community addressed, called an *ekklēsia,* was a structured one with appointed office bearers. This means then that the two terms are used differently. In James 2:2 the Greek word *synagogue* refers to an assembly, to people as they are gathered; the word *ekklēsia* in James 5:14 refers to a community of Christians with an ongoing existence and an ordered life.

5. 1 Peter.

First Peter is important, for although it does not use the word *ekklēsia,* it is more interested in theologically defining the Christian community, the church, than is any other NT writing. It seems certain that the epistle is addressed to predominantly Gentile Christians living in northern Asia Minor, who are suffering for their faith.

In the opening address these Christians are explicitly identified as Israel. They are the "exiles of the dispersion," "chosen and destined by God," "sanctified by the Spirit and . . . sprinkled with his blood" (1 Pet 1:1-2). Three times elsewhere Peter speaks of the Christian community as being "chosen," or elect (1 Pet 2:4, 6, 9), a way of designating Israel (1 Chron 16:13; Ps 105:6; Is 65:9). The mention of them being sprinkled with blood marks them out as the new covenant community, for these words reflect the enactment of the Sinai covenant, which constituted Israel as God's elect and destined people (Ex 24:3-8; cf. 1 Pet 1:18-21).

But the most theologically pregnant comment about the Christian community is found in 1 Peter 2:4-10. The author begins by exhorting individual Christians to come to Jesus, the "living stone" (cf. Is 8:4; 28:16; Ps 118:22). He then moves to corporate imagery by speaking of a building process that creates a "spiritual house" (1 Pet 2:5), a community, which may be understood because of the associated cultic language to be the new temple of Jewish apocalyptic hope (cf. 1 Cor 3:16; Eph 2:19-22). It is "spiritual" in the sense that it is not a literal house or temple, being constituted by the Spirit, built up as believers are added. Collectively they are "a holy priesthood" *(hierateuma)*. This designation reflects Exodus 19:6, where it is applied to the whole people of Israel.

Finally in 1 Peter 2:9 an overlapping series of theologically weighted collective titles are given to the Christian community, Peter declares: "But you [plural] are a chosen race, a royal priesthood, a holy nation, a people *(laos)* belonging to God." The four titles are drawn from Exodus 19:6 and Isaiah 43:20-21, where they denote Israel as the covenant people of God. In applying them to the Christian community, Peter is emphatically saying the church is now Israel. The corporate identity of those belonging to the church is so profound that Peter calls them a chosen "race" *(genos)*. On this basis, later Christian writers would speak of the Christian community as "a third race," neither Jew nor Gentile *(Preaching of Peter;* Tertullian *Ad Nat.* 1.8).

Another characteristic of the ecclesiology of 1 Peter is a very strong sense of the separation between the believing community and the society in which the church finds itself. Believers are described as "exiles" (1 Pet 1:1, 17) and "aliens and exiles" (1 Pet 2:11); they are exhorted to be holy (1 Pet 1:15-16) and morally distinct (1 Pet 1:17-18; 3:1-2, 11-12, 18-22; 3:1-7, 8-17; 4:1-6, 12-19). They are to expect to suffer as Christ suffered (1 Pet 1:6-7; 2:19-25; 3:13-22; 4:1-6, 12-19; 5:9-10).

Peter, like most other NT writers, recognizes that the Christian community has both a localized and a universal expression. He designates the whole Christian community as God's "flock" (1 Pet 5:2), who have returned to their "shepherd and guardian" (1 Pet 2:25). The elders, however, as local leaders are exhorted to "tend the flock of God in your charge" (1 Pet 5:2); that is, the Christians whom they lead in one place. This same contrast appears in the concluding words of the epistle, in which the author distinguishes between those to whom he writes, a localized group of Christians, and "your brothers and sisters in all the world" (1 Pet 5:9).

6. The Johannine Epistles.

One of the special characteristics of the three epistles of John *(see* John, Letters of) is their concern to differentiate the "true church" from those who have broken away (1 Jn 2:19), whom the author thinks are the enemies of Christ (1 Jn 2:18-19; 4:3; 2 Jn 7). This means his main ecclesiological concern is the boundaries of the Christian community (what are the marks of the true church), not the church's relationship with Israel, a matter not alluded to in these epistles.

The true Christian community is made up of

believers who are in fellowship "with us," those representing the views of John the apostle. These believers confess that Jesus is the Christ (1 Jn 5:1), the Son of God (1 Jn 1:3, 7; 3:8, 23) who came in the flesh (1 Jn 4:2; 2 Jn 7). They love others who are in this restricted company (1 Jn 2:10; 3:11). Those who have broken with "us" are to be shown no welcome: they are to be turned away if they seek contact (2 Jn 10-11). The true church is to be separate from the wider society in which it finds itself. Members are "not to love the world" (1 Jn 2:15), for the "the whole world lies under the power of the evil one" (1 Jn 5:19). In return, the world hates them (1 Jn 3:13). This restricted understanding of love and hostility to unbelievers is less than the Christian ideal and must be explained as part of the damage control of a church under extreme pressure from schism and external threat.

In 3 John the word *ekklēsia* is used three times (3 Jn 6, 9, 10) of a circumscribed local group of believers, but otherwise these epistles do not use this word or other theologically significant communal terms such as "the saints" or "the people of God." Instead, the author addresses his readers as "beloved," "children" or "brothers." Some scholars have suggested on this basis and other evidence that we see here an individualistic view of the Christian life, but nothing could be further from the truth. The author underlines the distinctiveness and separation from the world of these believers as a community. They owe their communal identity to the fact that they have been "born of God" (1 Jn 2:29; 5:1); they are God's children (1 Jn 3:1, 10) in whom God abides and they in him (1 Jn 2:24, 27; 3:9).

Very little is said in these epistles about congregational life, and what can be deduced comes mainly from 2 John and 3 John. These epistles seem to reflect a situation in which Christians are meeting in a number of house churches. If this is so, then 2 John is a letter from one house church leader to another house church leader in the near vicinity. He calls those to whom he writes "the elect lady and her children" (2 Jn 1). His advice is that anyone who does not make the true confession of Christ should not be "received into the house or welcomed" (2 Jn 10), which almost certainly means not into "your" house church. In 3 John such house churches are three times designated by the word *ekklēsia* (3 Jn 6, 9, 10).

7. The Book of Revelation.

The final book of the Bible is addressed to "the seven churches" (Rev 1:4, 11) in Asia Minor. As the number seven is always the number of completeness for this author, the implication is that the whole church is being addressed, of which these seven churches are representative. This is made clear in the refrain at the end of each individual letter, "Let anyone who has an ear listen to what the Spirit is saying to the churches." This means "Listen well, for these words have a message for every believer, the universal church."

In Revelation (*see* Revelation, Book of) the universal church on earth is true Israel. The author makes this transfer of identity even more emphatically than does the author of the epistle to the Hebrews or 1 Peter. The Jewish people are allied with the forces of the beast and doomed to destruction (Rev 2:9; 3:9; 13:1, 5, 6; 17:3). Conversely, the Christian community is true Israel who inherit all the promises once made to the Jewish people. Twice the author applies the foundational OT covenant passage, Exodus 19:6, to Christians, declaring that they have been made "a kingdom of priests to God" (Rev 1:6; 5:10; cf. Rev 20:6). This is the text applied to Christians collectively in 1 Peter 2:9 ("you are a royal priesthood"). But whereas in 1 Peter the collective term *hierateuma* ("priesthood") is used, in Revelation the individual title *hiereus* ("priest") is found. Every believer is a priest in his or her own right, but collectively they are a kingdom. Christ is the king (Rev 9:11; 15:3; 17:4; 19:16), and the people over whom he rules are a kingdom of priests (Rev 1:6, 9; 5:10; 11:15; 12:10). Revelation also depicts the Christian community as a temple (*naos*, Rev 3:12; 11:1-2) and as a city (*polis*, Rev 3:12; 11:3; 20:9; 21:2, 22; 22:19)—a city that is opposed by another city, the embodiment of evil (Rev 11:8; 14:8; 16:19).

As in Hebrews, the author of Revelation identifies the Christian community typologically with historic Israel. It is the Christian community who is taking part in the second exodus, who has been redeemed from slavery by the death of the Lamb and is now enjoying the blessings of the new covenant; and it is the enemies of this community who fall under the judgment of God as he sends plagues on them (Rev 12:1—14:20). In Revelation 7 the Christian community is equated symbolically with historic Israel, having assumed its identity. In the first vision (Rev 7:1—

8) the 144,000, identified as "the servants of our God" (Rev 7:3), are God's new covenant people, the suffering church of the first century. In the second vision (Rev 7:9-17) the "great multitude that no one could number" is the same group at the climax of world history.

Particularly important for determining the ecclesiology of John the Seer is the final vision given in Revelation 21:1—22:21. This speaks amid a confusing number of visual images of the future that is promised to the church. It is described as the new creation (Rev 21:1), the new Jerusalem (Rev 21:2), the new temple (Rev 21:3a), the new covenant community (Rev 21:3b) and the new Israel (Rev 21:4). This vision proclaims that what is true now will be perfected and revealed for all to see when the Lamb returns in victory. At present, the church is the believing community on earth, which has a triumphant counterpart in heaven made up of angels and those who have been martyred (Rev 8:3-4). The final vision speaks of the merging into one of these two worshiping communities.

Viewing the church as a worshiping community is another special characteristic of the ecclesiology of Revelation. The term "worship" *(proskyneō)* is used twenty-four times; word pictures of worship in heaven are common and vivid (cf. Rev 4), and liturgical refrains appear frequently (Rev 4:11; 5:9-13; 7:9-17; 11:15-18; 12:10-12; 15:3-4; 16:5-7; 19:1-8). On earth there are two options. One can either "worship" the beast (Rev 9:20; 13:4, 8, 12, 15; 16:2; 19:20) or worship God and the Lamb (Rev 11:1; 14:7; 15:4).

See also ISRAEL; WORSHIP.

DLNTD: CHURCH AS ISRAEL, PEOPLE OF GOD; CHURCH ORDER, GOVERNMENT.

BIBLIOGRAPHY. B. Blue, "Acts and the House Church," in *The Book of Acts in Its First-Century Setting,* 2: *Greco-Roman Setting,* ed. D. W. J. Gill and C. Gempf (Grand Rapids: Eerdmans, 1994) 119-89; R. E. Brown, *The Churches the Apostles Left Behind* (London: Chapman, 1984); H. J. Cadbury, "Names for Christianity and Christians in Acts," in *The Beginnings of Christianity,* ed. F. J. Foakes-Jackson and K. Lake (5 vols.; London: Macmillan, 1927) 5:375-92; K. N. Giles, *Patterns of Ministry Among the First Christians* (Australia: Collins-Dove, 1989); idem, *What on Earth Is the Church? A Biblical and Theological Inquiry* (Melbourne: Harper-Collins; London: SPCK; Downers Grove, IL: InterVarsity Press, 1995); A. von Harnack, "The Names of Christian Believers,"

in *The Mission and Expansion of Christianity* (Gloucester, MA: Peter Smith, 1972 repr.) 399-418; E. G. Jay, *The Church: Its Changing Image Through Twenty Centuries,* 1: *The First Seventeen Centuries* (London: SPCK, 1977); H. C. Kee, *Who Are the People of God? Early Christian Models of Community* (New Haven, CT: Yale University Press, 1995); D. Ravens, *Luke and the Restoration of Israel* (Sheffield: Sheffield Academic Press, 1995); M. Turner, *Power from on High: The Spirit of Prophecy in Luke-Acts* (JPTSup 9; Sheffield: Sheffield Academic Press, 1996).

K. N. Giles

CIVIC CULTS. *See* RELIGION, GRECO-ROMAN.

CLEAN AND UNCLEAN. *See* LAW I.

CLEANSING OF THE TEMPLE. *See* TEMPLE CLEANSING.

COLLECTION FOR THE SAINTS. *See* CORINTHIANS, LETTERS TO THE; PAUL IN ACTS AND LETTERS.

COLOSSAE. *See* COLOSSIANS, LETTER TO THE.

COLOSSIANS, LETTER TO THE

Colossians, one of Paul's shortest letters, was written to the infant church at Colossae in the Lycus valley of the province of Asia. This Christian community had not been founded by Paul but came into existence during his Ephesian ministry (c. A.D. 52-55) through the efforts of Epaphras, one of his colleagues. Although it is not a theological treatise, Colossians has much to say about the importance of the *gospel; the person and work of the Lord Jesus Christ, especially as Lord in creation and author of reconciliation (Col 1:15-20); the people of God; eschatology; freedom from legalism; and the Christian life.

1. Colossae and Its Citizens
2. The Church at Colossae
3. The Occasion of the Letter
4. The Threat to Faith and the Colossian Heresy
5. Paul's Handling of the Colossian Philosophy
6. Some Critical Questions

1. Colossae and Its Citizens.

1.1. The City. The ancient city of Colossae

was situated 100 miles east of Ephesus in Phrygia on the southern bank of the river Lycus (in modern Turkey), and its fertile valley produced large crops of figs and olives. Colossae lay on the main road from Ephesus and Sardis to the Euphrates. In the fifth and fourth centuries B.C. it was described as populous, large and wealthy, its commercial significance being due to its wool industry. Later, the city declined in importance so that in Roman times it had become a "small town" (Strabo *Geog.* 12.8.13, though the text is debatable) and had been surpassed by Laodicea and Hierapolis, which were also in the Lycus valley. By the time Paul wrote to the Christians living at Colossae the commercial and social importance of the town was already on the wane, though coins and inscriptions attest to the civic life of the town in the second and third centuries A.D.

1.2. Its People. Laodicea, Hierapolis and Colossae belonged to the proconsular province of Asia. Colossae's population consisted mainly of indigenous Phrygian and Greek settlers, but in the early part of the second century B.C. two thousand Jewish families from Babylon and Mesopotamia were settled in Lydia and Phrygia by Antiochus III (Josephus *Ant.* 12.3.4 §§147-53). According to grave inscriptions in the area Jews had become part of the Asian culture by the first century B.C. So the Colossae of Paul's day seems to have been a cosmopolitan place in which differing cultural and religious elements mingled.

2. The Church at Colossae.

The believers at Colossae, who are addressed as faithful brothers and sisters in Christ (Col 1:2), were not converted through the ministry of Paul himself. This Christian community had come into existence during a period of vigorous missionary and evangelistic activity associated with Paul's Ephesian ministry (c. A.D. 52-55) recorded in Acts 19. But the apostle during his missionary work in Asia Minor had not reached Colossae in the upper valley of the Lycus (cf. Col 2:1). His daily evangelistic "dialogues" held in the hall of Tyrannus in Ephesus were so effective that Luke can claim "all the residents of Asia heard the word of the Lord, both Jews and Greeks" (Acts 19:10). While the work was directed by Paul, he was assisted by several coworkers through whom a number of churches were planted in the province of Asia. Among these were the congregations of Colossae, Laodicea and Hierapolis, which, we infer, were the fruit of Epaphras's evangelistic efforts (Col 1:7; 4:12, 13). Epaphras, a native of Colossae (Col 4:12), who may have become a Christian during a visit to Ephesus, was "a faithful minister of Christ," and as Paul's representative (Col 1:7) he had taught the Colossians the truth of the gospel.

The many allusions to the non-Christian past of the readers suggest that most of them were Gentile converts. They had once been utterly out of harmony with God, enmeshed in idolatry and slavery to sin, being hostile to God in mind and godless in their actions (Col 1:21; cf. Col 1:12, 27). They had been spiritually dead because of their sins and "the uncircumcision of . . . [their] flesh"—a statement that indicates they were heathen and godless (Col 2:13).

But God had effected a mighty change in their lives: he had reconciled them to himself in an earth-shattering event, namely, Christ's physical death on the cross (Col 1:22). He had delivered them from a tyranny of darkness and transferred them into a kingdom in which his beloved Son ruled (Col 1:13). They now possessed redemption and the forgiveness of sins (Col 1:14; 2:13; 3:13).

Because the congregation had received Christ Jesus the Lord as their tradition (*paradosis*, Col 2:6) when they accepted the gospel at the hands of Epaphras, they are admonished to conduct their lives as those who have been united to Christ in his *death and *resurrection. Since Christ Jesus is a more than adequate safeguard against empty human traditions, they are urged to see to it that their way of life and thought conform continually to Christ's teaching (Col 2:6-8).

The picture is therefore drawn of a Christian congregation obedient to the apostolic gospel and for which the apostle can give heartfelt thanks to God (Col 1:4-6). He knows of their love "in the Spirit" (Col 1:8) and was delighted to learn of their orderly Christian lives and the stability of their faith in Christ (Col 2:5).

3. The Occasion of the Letter.

Epaphras had paid Paul a visit in Rome (see 6.2 below) and informed him of the progress of the gospel in the Lycus valley. While much of the report was encouraging (cf. Col 1:8; 2:5), one disquieting feature was the attractive but false teaching that had recently been introduced into the congregation and that, if it went unchecked, would subvert the gospel and bring the Colossians into spiritual bondage. Paul's letter is written as a response to this urgent need. Perhaps Epaphras found it difficult to cope with the specious arguments and the feigned humility of those spreading this teaching, and so needed the greater wisdom of the apostle.

4. The Threat to Faith and the Colossian Heresy.

4.1. Was There a Colossian Heresy? Nowhere in the letter does the apostle give a formal exposition of the heresy; its chief features can be detected only by piecing together and interpreting his positive counterarguments (*see* Adversaries [Paul]). Several recent scholars have questioned whether these counterarguments point to the existence of a Colossian heresy at all. They prefer to speak in terms of tendencies rather than a clear-cut system with definite points and suggest that the young converts were under external pressure to conform to the beliefs and practices of their Jewish and pagan neighbors (Hooker). This view rightly stresses Paul's positive statements about the life and stability of the congregation (Col 1:3-8; 2:5) and warns against the danger of arguing in a circle when reconstructing the situation behind Paul's writings. However, in the light of Colossians 2:8-23, with its references to "fullness," specific ascetic injunctions (Col 2:21), regulations about food and holy days, unusual phrases that seem to be catchwords of Paul's opponents and the strong emphasis on what Christ has already achieved by his death and resurrection, it seems appropriate to speak of a heresy that had just begun to make some inroads into the congregation.

4.2. Some Distinguishing Marks of the Heresy. The teaching was set forth as "philosophy" (Col 2:8), based on "tradition" (*paradosis* denotes its antiquity, dignity and revelational character), that was supposed to impart true knowledge (Col 2:18, 23). Paul seems to be quoting catchwords of the opponents in his attack on their teaching: "all the fullness" (Col 2:9); "delighting in humility and the worship of angels," "things which he has seen upon entering" (perhaps "entering into visions"; Col 2:18); "Don't handle, don't taste, don't even touch!" (Col 2:21); and "voluntary worship," "humility" and "severe treatment of the body" (Col 2:23). Further, the keeping of these taboos in the "philosophy" was related to obedient submission to "the elemental spirits of the world" (Col 2:20).

4.3. Interpreting These Distinguishing Marks. No complete agreement has been achieved among scholars as to the nature of the teaching. The heresy seems to have been Jewish, because of the references to food regulations, the sabbath and other prescriptions of the Jewish calendar. Circumcision is mentioned (Col 2:11) but did not appear as one of the legal requirements. (Wright argues for an exclusively Jewish background to the heresy.)

But what kind of *Judaism? Apparently it was not the more straightforward kind against which the Galatian churches had to be warned, but it was one in which asceticism and mysticism were featured and where angels and principalities played a prominent role in creation and the giving of the law. They were regarded as controlling the communication between God and humankind, and so needed to be placated by keeping strict legal observances.

A number of important suggestions has been made as to the nature of the Colossian philosophy, ranging from a pagan mystery cult (Dibelius) and a syncretism of gnosticized Judaism and pagan elements (Bornkamm)—the "worship of angels" (Col 2:18) was regarded as a pagan element in the false teaching but should be understood as "the angelic worship [of God]"—to Essene Judaism of a gnostic kind (Lightfoot) and Judaizing syncretism (Lyonnet).

Many recent scholars, however, consider that the false teaching, which advanced beyond Epaphras's elementary gospel, is to be read against the background of ascetic and mystical forms of Jewish piety as evidenced, for example, at Qumran (*see* Dead Sea Scrolls). It was for a spiritual elite who were being urged to press on in wisdom and knowledge so as to attain true "fullness." "Self-abasement" (Col 2:18, 23) was a term used by opponents to denote ascetic practices that were effective for receiving visions of heavenly mysteries and participating in mystical experiences. The "mature" were thus able to gain entrance into heaven and join in the "angelic worship of God" as part of their present experience (Col 2:18).

5. Paul's Handling of the Colossian Philosophy.

Although there is a buildup in Paul's presentation in Colossians 1, it is not until Colossians 2:4 ("I am saying this in order that no one may deceive you with persuasive language") that the apostle expressly points to the dangers facing the congregation. He is aware of the methods of the false teachers and issues a strong warning to the Colossians to be on their guard lest they be carried off as spoil (Col 2:8, *sylagōgeo*, "kidnap, carry off as booty," is a rare and vivid word, showing how seriously Paul regarded the evil designs of those seeking to influence the congregation). These spiritual charlatans were trying to ensnare the Colossians by their "philosophy and empty deceit" (Col 2:8). Although they set forth their teaching as "tradition," Paul rejects any suggestion of divine origin. It was a human fabrication ("according to human tradition") that stood over against the tradition of Christ—the tradition that stems from the teaching of Christ, which also finds its embodiment in him (Col 2:6).

In a magnificent passage of praise exalting Christ as the Lord in creation and reconciliation (Col 1:15-20), Paul asserts that Christ is the one through whom all things were created, including the *principalities and powers that figured so prominently in the Colossian heresy. All things have been made in him as the sphere, through him as the agent and for him as the ultimate goal of all creation (Col 1:16).

Those who have been incorporated into Christ have come to fullness of life in the one who is master over every principality and power (Col 2:10). They need not seek perfection anywhere else but in him. It is in him, the one in whose death, burial and resurrection they have been united (Col 2:11-12), that the totality of wisdom and knowledge is concentrated and made available to all his people—not just an elite group.

Christ Jesus is the sole mediator between God and humankind. The Colossians are not to be misled by the false teachers into thinking it was necessary to obey the angelic powers who were said to control the communication between God and humankind. That way was now controlled by Christ, who by his death is revealed as conqueror of the principalities and powers (Col 2:13-15).

The apostle's criticisms of the advocates of the Colossian philosophy, with their false notions and aberrant behavior, are devastating (Col 2:16-23). Because of their legalism, the false teachers failed to recognize God's good gifts and his purpose in giving them, namely, that all of them should be enjoyed and consumed through their proper use (Col 2:22). The things covered by the taboos were perishable objects of the material world, destined to pass away when used. The taboos themselves, which belonged to a transitory order (Col 2:17), were merely human inventions that laid no claim to absoluteness but stood over against the revelation of the will of God (cf. Col 2:22). To place oneself under rules and regulations like those of Colossians 2:21 is to go back into slavery again—under the personal forces overthrown by Christ (Col 2:20). By his death he had freed the Colossians from bondage to the principalities and powers. They must not turn their backs on that life-changing event. Although the prohibitions (cf. Col 2:21) carried a reputation for wisdom in the spheres of voluntary worship, humility and severe treatment of the body, these practices were in fact spiritually and morally bankrupt. Such energetic endeavors could not hold the flesh in check. Instead, these self-made regulations actually pandered to the flesh (Col 2:23).

In his reply to the false teaching, Paul expounds the doctrine of the cosmic Christ more fully than in his earlier letters (*see* Christology). Hints had previously appeared in Romans 8:19-22 and 1 Corinthians 1:24, 1 Corinthians 2:6-10 and 1 Corinthians 8:6, but a more detailed exposition is given in Colossians 1:15-20 and Colossians 2:13-15. Against the false teachers who boasted in their exalted spiritual experiences, their fresh revelations and their participation in the divine fullness, the apostle's criticisms are trenchant: they are arrogant and in danger of being separated from Christ (Col 2:18-19).

In his handling of the Colossian false teaching Paul places his emphasis on realized eschatology (see esp. Col 2:12; 3:1-4). Within the already/not yet tension the stress is upon the former, called forth by the circumstances of the letter. The Colossians have a hope laid up for them in heaven (Col 1:5; cf. 3:1-4). They have been fitted for a share in the inheritance of the saints in light (Col 1:12), having already been delivered from a tyranny of darkness and transferred into the kingdom of God's beloved Son (Col 1:13). Not only did they die with Christ; they were also raised with him (Col 2:12; 3:1; cf. Col 3:3). Although the "not yet" of salvation does feature in the letter (esp. Col 3:4), the "already" needed to be asserted again and again over against those who were interested in "fullness" and the heavenly realm but who had false notions about them, believing they could be reached by legalistic observances, a special knowledge, visionary experiences and the like. Christ has done all that was necessary for the Colossians' salvation. They had died with Christ, been raised with him and given new life with him. Let them now zealously seek the things above (Col 3:1-2), that new order centered on the exalted Christ, and let them as a consequence show true heavenly-mindedness (cf. Col 3:5, 8, 12 and 3:18—4:1).

6. Some Critical Questions.

6.1. Authorship. The letter makes clear that the apostle Paul is the writer, not only in the opening greeting (Col 1:1) but also in the body of the letter (Col 1:23) and at its conclusion (Col 4:18). The character of Paul, as we know it from other letters, shines throughout this letter. There was no dispute over the authenticity of Colossians in the early period of the church, and the letter was included in Marcion's canonical list as well as in the Muratorian canon. However, the Pauline authorship has been challenged on a number of occasions in the last 150 years. The grounds presented concern the language and style of the letter and the supposed differences between Colossians and the theology of the main Pauline epistles.

6.1.1. Language and Style. Many of the formal features of Colossians show similarities with the other Pauline letters, including its structure (the introduction, Col 1:1-2; conclusion, Col 4:18; and thanksgiving prayer, Col 1:3-8), connecting words and phrases (Col 2:1, 6, 16; 3:1, 5), as well as the list of messages and greetings (cf. Col 4:8, 10, 12, 15).

Many expressions are Pauline in style: for example, the superfluous use of "and" after "therefore" (Col 1:9; cf. 1 Thess 2:13; 3:5), phrases like "his saints" (Col 1:26; cf. 1 Thess 3:13) and "in regard to" (Col 2:16; cf. 2 Cor 3:10; 9:3), as well as verbs such as *charizomai*, with the meaning "to forgive" (Col 2:13; 3:13; cf. 2 Cor 2:7, 10). The similarities extend to the theological terminology such as "in Christ" (Col 1:2, 4, 28), "in the Lord" (Col 3:18, 20, etc.), expressions about being united with Christ in baptism (Col 2:11, 12), about being freed from the power of the regulations (Col 2:14, 20, 21), the contrast between the old and the new person (Col 3:5-17), and the relation between the indicative and the imperative in exhortations (Col 3:5-17).

Yet there are linguistic differences between Colossians and the other Pauline letters: thirty-four words appear in Colossians but nowhere else in the NT, twenty-eight words do not occur in the other Pauline letters, and ten words Colossians has in common only with *Ephesians. But in assessing these statistics it ought to be borne in mind that many of these words appear in the hymnic paragraph of Colossians 1:15-20 or in interaction with the false teaching, either as catchwords of the Colossian philosophy or as part of the author's polemic. Further, *hapax legomena* and unusual expressions turn up in considerable numbers in the other Pauline letters; the absence of a word or concept may be due to the different subject matter being discussed.

Characteristic features of style, as distinct from vocabulary, include liturgical material with long clauses introduced by relative pronouns, inserted causal and participial phrases, combined and synonymous expressions ("strengthened with all power," Col 1:11; "praying and asking," Col 1:9), a series of dependent genitives ("the word of truth, of the gospel," Col 1:5) and loosely joined infinitival constructions ("to walk worthily of the Lord," Col 1:10).

These stylistic peculiarities have been understood as evidence of an author who, for all his dependence on Paul, argues differently from the apostle. But such a judgment appears to be unduly negative and presupposes an almost infallible understanding of what Paul could or could not have written. Further, it does not explain the close similarities between Colossians and the generally accepted Pauline letters. Rather, the stylistic peculiarities would seem to have their basis in the letter's content, which is clearly connected with the particular situation which necessitated the letter.

6.1.2. Teaching. For scholars such as E. Lohse, the supposed theological differences between Colossians and the generally accepted Pauline letters are decisive against the apostolic authorship of Colossians, even if the grounds of language and style are not. Some interpreters have argued that the post-Pauline author's christology belonged to a later period of church history when classical Gnostic influences had begun to assert themselves. But it is unnecessary to resort to full-blown Gnostic influences of the second century as a possible background. If a Jewish background of an ascetic mystical kind is likely, then there is no need to look beyond the apostolic age, and certainly Pauline authorship is not ruled out on this account.

The objections to Paul's authorship on the grounds of theology are as follows.

6.1.2.1. Christology. It has been claimed that Colossians develops its *christology on the basis of Colossians 1:15-20 and goes beyond Paul's statements in 1 Corinthians 8:6 and Romans 8:31-39 in its teaching that in Christ the entire fullness of deity dwells "bodily" (Col 2:9) and that he is the "head of every principality and power" (Col 2:10). But this latter statement spells out the implications of Colossians 1:15-20, which is central to the letter, while Colossians 2:9 applies the words of the hymn to the Colossian situation, making clear how the entire fullness of deity dwells in Christ, that is, in bodily form by his becoming incarnate. The cosmic dimension of Christ's rule is a fuller and more systematic exposition of the theme of Christ's universal lordship than is found in Paul's earlier letters (1 Cor 8:6; cf. Col 1:24; 2:6-10), and it is spelled out in relation to and as a correction of the false teaching at Colossae. There is no need to look for an author other than Paul as the source of such ideas.

6.1.2.2. Ecclesiology. The notion of Christ as the "head of the body, the church" is said to reflect a post-Pauline development. In 1 Corinthians 12:12-27 and Romans 12:4-5 Paul uses the terminology of the body (*see* Body of Christ) and its constituent parts to refer to the mutual relations and obligations of Christians. In these references the head of the body has no special position or honor; it is counted as an ordinary member (cf. 1 Cor 12:21). In Colossians and Ephesians there is an advance in the line of thought, from the language of simile (as in 1 Cor and Rom) to that of a real and interpersonal involvement. This advance has probably been stimulated by Paul's reflection on the issues involved in the Colossian heresy and is entirely appropriate. Further, the term *church* (Col 1:18), while usually taken to refer to the people of God all over the world, the universal or worldwide church where Christ here and now exercises his cosmic lordship, is best understood of a heavenly assembly gathered around the risen and exalted Christ (cf. Col 3:1-4; Eph 2:6). This heavenly gathering with Christ at its center is manifested here and now on earth. The same word *church* can be used of a local congregation at Colossae or even of a small house community (Col 4:15-16). The congregation in heaven finds its manifestation and becomes visible as the domain of Christ's rule where saints and faithful brothers and sisters in Christ gather (Col 1:2).

6.1.2.3. Eschatology. Future *eschatology has receded in Colossians, it is argued, with Colossians 3:4 the only explicit reference to this future event. Instead, spatial concepts are said to dominate, while none of the typically Pauline ideas—parousia, resurrection of the dead and judgment of the world—is encountered in the letter. Further, unlike the genuine Pauline letters, Colossians states that believers have already been raised with Christ (Col 2:12-13; 3:1), and this serves as the basis of the ethical imperative.

There is indeed an emphasis on realized eschatology in Colossians, but this has been called forth by the particular circumstances. Also, there is future eschatology not only at Colossians 3:4, 6, 24, but at Colossians 1:22, 28 (cf. Col 4:11) as well. Spatial concepts are used in the service of eschatology, while the antithesis between eschatological and transcendent perspectives is found together in the undisputed Paulines and at Colossians 3:1-4. There is an eschatological motivation in Colossians; it may not be dominant but is present nevertheless (Col 3:5 is based on Col 3:1-4 with its eschatological emphasis). At the same time there are other grounds for exhortation than eschatology in the generally accepted Pauline letters.

6.1.2.4. Tradition. The alleged differences in the above-mentioned areas are thought to derive from a "Pauline school tradition" probably based in Ephesus. The post-Pauline author took over the hymn now found in Colossians 1:15-20 and other traditional materials in order to combat heresy in the subapostolic age (Käsemann). Epaphras's name is especially emphasized in the list of greetings in Colossians. This document, which is a kind of pastoral letter, was to provide an apostolic authorization for Epaphras, whose teaching represents the mind of Paul. According to M. Kiley, the author of Colossians used Paul's two prison letters (Philippians and Philemon) as models for writing a letter of recommendation for Epaphras. The letter, which bears the marks of the "early catholicism" of the subapostolic age, was intended to show that "Paul's teaching is not strictly limited to the exigencies of time and place" (Kiley, 107). The "author of Colossians affirms to the communities the message of the Apostle in a powerful new formulation" (Lohse, 183).

But in Colossians 1:23—2:5 the gospel gives

validity to Paul's ministry; the paragraph does not legitimate the gospel through the apostolic office of Paul and then assert (Col 1:7; 4:7-13) the legitimation of Epaphras because of his relationship to the apostle. Both serve the gospel as coworkers and ministers of that word. No attempt is made in these passages to give an apostolic authorization to Epaphras or anyone else because he stands in an apostolic succession and his teaching represents the mind of Paul.

The so-called differences between Colossians and the generally accepted Pauline letters do not constitute sufficient grounds for rejecting the apostolic authorship of this letter. Differences of emphasis there are, but these are best interpreted as being called forth by the circumstances at Colossae.

6.2. Place and Date of Origin. The traditional view that Paul wrote Colossians during his imprisonment in Rome is more likely than that he penned the letter in Ephesus or Caesarea. No other imprisonment recorded in Acts seems a real alternative (there are difficulties regarding the Caesarean imprisonment of Acts 24:27; but *see* Philippians, Letter to the). The greetings from colleagues in Colossians 4 suggest they had direct access to him, and this is consistent with the Roman imprisonment of Acts 28:30. The reference to Onesimus, which brings into account the letter to Philemon, could be understood in the context of the imperial capital even though some have argued that the distance between Colossae and Rome is an obstacle to its Roman origin. It is precarious to place any weight on the progression in Pauline thought as a criterion for dating Colossians.

If the Roman hypothesis is accepted, then the most likely date is fairly early in Paul's first Roman imprisonment, that is, about A.D. 60-61. Those advocating an Ephesian alternative place the letter around A.D. 54-57, or even earlier, A.D. 52-55.

6.3. The Hymn in Praise of Christ. Colossians 1:15-20 is a magnificent passage of praise exalting Christ as the Lord in creation (Col 1:15-17) and author of reconciliation (Col 1:18-20). As to the structure of the hymn, no scholarly consensus has been reached about the number and content of the stanzas. It is better to speak of certain parallels (cf. Col 1:15 and 18), with relative clauses being followed by causal clauses (Col 1:16, 19), the frequent use of "all," and the formal chiasmus in Colossians 1:16c and Colossians 1:20 (note also Col 1:17, 18).

Although the backgrounds in pre-Christian *Gnosticism and rabbinic Judaism have been suggested as the source of the hymn's ideas, a general *Wisdom milieu in the OT and Hellenistic Judaism (Schweizer) is probably correct. But how the predicates and activities ascribed to Wisdom came to be applied to Jesus of Nazareth, recently crucified and risen from the dead, cannot be explained by the background.

This hymnic paragraph is not a christological digression or excursus but is clearly central to the context in which it stands. Paul's lengthy prayer (Col 1:9-14) leads up to the hymn, and themes from it are taken up and applied throughout the rest of the letter (cf. Col 1:19 with Col 2:9; Col 1:20 with Col 1:21-23 and Col 2:15). Although the passage praises Christ, surprisingly the names "Jesus," "Christ" and "Lord" do not appear with it. The stanza simply begins, "He is . . . " However, it is clear that the words of praise can apply to no one else.

The Pauline authorship of the hymn has been challenged on linguistic and structural grounds. The arguments for and against Paul's authorship are not decisive either way, so we should accept the passage as authentic. Thus, there has been considerable debate whether the apostle here incorporated an existing hymn into his letter. This is possible, but if so he has woven the rest of the letter around it, and the focus on the supremacy of Christ is intended to strengthen the readers and correct the erroneous views of the false teachers. Whether pre-Pauline or not, the passage perfectly suited the apostle's purposes in writing to the Colossians.

See also CHRISTOLOGY; CHURCH; EPHESIANS, LETTER TO THE; GNOSTICISM.

DPL: FULLNESS; MYSTICISM; PRINCIPALITIES AND POWERS; TRIUMPH.

BIBLIOGRAPHY. **Commentaries:** T. K. Abbott, *The Epistles to the Ephesians and to the Colossians* (ICC; Edinburgh: T & T Clark, 1897); F. F. Bruce, *The Epistles to the Colossians, to Philemon, and to the Ephesians* (NICNT; Grand Rapids: Eerdmans, 1984); G. B. Caird, *Paul's Letters from Prison* (Oxford: Oxford University Press, 1976); J. D. G. Dunn, *The Epistles to the Colossians and to Philemon* (NIGTC; Grand Rapids: Eerdmans, 1996); J. L. Houlden, *Paul's Letters from Prison* (Philadelphia: Westminster, 1970); J. B. Lightfoot, *Saint Paul's Epistles to the Colossians and to Philemon* (London: Macmillan, 1890); E. Lohse, *Colossians* *and Philemon* (Herm; Philadelphia: Fortress, 1971); R. P. Martin, *Colossians and Philemon* (NCB; Grand Rapids: Eerdmans, 1981); idem, *Ephesians, Colossians, and Philemon* (IntC; Louisville, KY: John Knox, 1991); C. F. D. Moule, *The Epistles of Paul the Apostle to the Colossians and to Philemon* (CGTC; Cambridge: Cambridge University Press, 1957); P. T. O'Brien, *Colossians, Philemon* (WBC 44; Waco, TX: Word, 1982); A. G. Patzia, *Colossians, Philemon, Ephesians* (San Francisco: Harper & Row, 1984); E. Schweizer, *The Letter to the Colossians: A Commentary* (Minneapolis: Augsburg, 1982); N. T. Wright, *The Epistles of Paul to the Colossians and to Philemon* (TNTC; Grand Rapids: Eerdmans, 1986). **Studies:** G. Bornkamm, "The Heresy of Colossians," in *Conflict at Colossae*, ed. F. O. Francis and W. A. Meeks (2d ed.; SBLSBS 4; Missoula, MT: Scholars Press, 1975) 123-45; G. E. Cannon, *The Use of Traditional Materials in Colossians* (Macon, GA: Mercer University Press, 1983); M. Dibelius, "The Isis Initiation in Apuleius and Related Initiatory Rites," in *Conflict at Colossae*, ed. F. O. Francis and W. A. Meeks (SBLSBS 4; 2d ed.; Missoula, MT: Scholars Press, 1975) 61-121; F. O. Francis and W. Meeks, eds., *Conflict at Colossae* (SBLSBS 4; Missoula, MT: Scholars Press, 1975); M. D. Hooker, "Were There False Teachers in Colossae?" in *Christ and Spirit in the New Testament: Studies in Honor of Charles Francis Digby Moule,* ed. B. Lindars and S. S. Smalley (Cambridge: Cambridge University Press, 1973) 315-31; E. Käsemann, "A Primitive Christian Baptismal Liturgy," in *Essays on New Testament Themes* (SBT; Naperville, IL: Allenson, 1964) 149-68; M. Kiley, *Colossians as Pseudepigraphy* (Sheffield: JSOT, 1986); A. T. Lincoln, *Paradise Now and Not Yet* (SNTSMS 41; Cambridge: Cambridge University Press, 1981); S. Lyonnet, "Paul's Adversaries in Colossae," in *Conflict at Colossae*, ed. F. O. Francis and W. A. Meeks (2d ed.; SBLSBS 4; Missoula, MT: Scholars Press, 1975) 147-61; J. T. Sanders, *The New Testament Christological Hymns* (SNTSMS 15; Cambridge: Cambridge University Press, 1971); T. J. Sappington, *Revelation and Redemption at Colossae* (Sheffield: Sheffield Academic Press, 1991); R. C. Tannehill, *Dying and Rising with Christ* (BZNW 32; Berlin: Töpelmann, 1967); N. T. Wright, "Poetry and Theology in Col. 1:15-20," *NTS* 36 (1990) 444-68.

P. T. O'Brien

COMMANDMENTS. *See* LAW.

CONVERSION AND CALL OF PAUL

One of the best-known narratives in the NT is the story of Paul's conversion and call to be the apostle to the Gentiles. Scholars have often disagreed about whether this experience of Paul is best understood as a conversion or a call to a specific mission as apostle to the Gentiles. References to Paul's conversion/call experience are found in Galatians 1, Philippians 3, Acts 9, Acts 22 and Acts 26.

1. History of the Interpretation of Paul's Conversion/Call
2. Accounts of Paul's Conversion/Call
3. Some Critical Questions

1. History of the Interpretation of Paul's Conversion/Call.

Several decades ago many biblical scholars would have agreed that Paul's remarkable experience on the road to Damascus was a paradigmatic instance of Christian conversion. Today many biblical scholars would describe the same experience as Paul's unique call to be apostle to the Gentiles. This shift in understanding has set the agenda for many recent studies of Paul's conversion/call.

The traditional way of understanding Paul's Damascus Road experience as a conversion has a long history in Western thought, going back to Augustine and his understanding of his own conversion. William James's psychological study of conversion was heavily dependent on this traditional view. James defined conversion as the process by which a person who struggles with a sense of guilt and inferiority becomes a person with a conscious sense of being right and unified as a consequence of achieving a firmer hold of religious realities. From this traditional perspective, Paul's Damascus Road experience is seen as a prime example of conversion. A Pharisaic Jew who is very conscious of his failure to keep the law experiences a profound inner change when it is revealed to him that he can be justified by faith in Jesus Christ. The Jewish persecutor becomes the Christian convert who preaches the message of justification by faith in Christ Jesus. Until quite recently, this understanding of Paul's conversion dominated biblical scholarship (see Nock, Stewart).

But in the past few decades this view of Paul's conversion has come under profound suspicion. The biblical scholar who is largely responsible for raising questions about the traditional way of understanding Paul's conversion is K. Stendahl in *Paul Among Jews and Gentiles* (1976). Stendahl claims that the Western understanding of Paul owes more to the introspective readings of Augustine and Luther than it does to the NT documents. Paul's experience on the Damascus Road was not the inner experience of conversion that Western theology has taken for granted, nor was it a conversion from the works righteousness of Judaism. In fact, Paul's experience on the road to Damascus was not a conversion at all, according to traditional definitions of conversion. Paul did not change religions, nor did he suffer from an inner experience of guilt or despair. Stendahl suggests that Paul's experience is better understood as a call to be the apostle to the Gentiles. Because of this call he begins to ask questions about what happens to the law now that the Messiah (*see* Christ) has come and what the Messiah's coming means for relationships between Jews and Gentiles. Paul arrives at a new view of the law as he answers these questions, not as he struggles with the meaning of the law in his life. Paul's Damascus Road experience is part of his unique apostolic call and is not meant to be an example of a Christian conversion.

Stendahl's understanding of Paul's Damascus Road experience as a call and his challenge to traditional understandings of Paul's conversion have created a whole new set of questions for biblical scholars who study Paul's conversion/call: How are we to define conversion and how are modern definitions applied to Paul? Did Paul remain a Jew, or did he change religions? Is his experience best understood as a call or a conversion? Is Paul's experience meant to be an example for Christians? How did Paul's conversion/call experience influence his theology? But even more importantly, Stendahl's challenge forced biblical scholars to return to the NT texts about Paul's conversion/call to answer these questions.

2. Accounts of Paul's Conversion/Call.

Accounts of Paul's conversion/call are found in two different places in the NT—Paul's letters and the book of Acts. Galatians 1:11-17 and Philippians 3:4-17 are two passages in which Paul writes about his conversion/call experience. In addition, 1 Timothy 1:12-17 and Romans 7 are sometimes considered autobiographical descriptions of this experience. Acts contains three different accounts of Paul's Damascus Road experience: Acts 9:1-20, Acts 22:1-21 and Acts 26:2-23. One of the issues involved in studying Paul's conversion/call is how to use the NT evidence. Historical research values the letters, which are Paul's accounts of his experience, over Acts, which is a later interpretation of Paul from a particular perspective. So methodologically it seems best to start with the accounts in Paul's letters and then examine the material in Acts. It is also important to ask how the accounts in the letters and Acts are related to each other.

2.1. Galatians 1:11-17. The autobiographical references in Galatians 1:11-17 are part of Paul's defense of his gospel. Many scholars see Paul's opponents as Judaizers, those who believed that Gentile Christians should keep the law and be circumcised. In Galatians, Paul argues against these Judaizers and claims that, in Christ, Gentiles should not keep the law or be circumcised. Paul makes his experience a part of his argument in order to emphasize the revelatory nature of the law-free gospel he preaches among the Gentiles.

The divine origin of the gospel Paul preaches (Gal 1:11-12) is also seen in the divine source of Paul's call (Gal 1:15-17). Paul's discussion of the revelation he received (Gal 1:15) is couched in the language of OT prophetic calls (cf. Jer 1:5). Such language emphasizes Paul's role as one called to proclaim the word of God and points to the divine origin of the word that is proclaimed. The object of this divine revelation is Jesus Christ; this is the word of God that Paul is called to proclaim among the Gentiles (Gal 1:16). Although Paul relates almost nothing of the events surrounding this revelation, he does report that subsequent to this experience he was not influenced by any human agency (Gal 1:16-17). Paul uses the experience of his conversion/call to show that his gospel to the Gentiles is rooted in divine revelation and divine calling.

It is in this context that Paul's mention of his earlier life in *Judaism (Gal 1:14-15) needs to be understood. There is no human explanation for his experience; nothing prepared him for the revelation he received. The Jew who was so zealous for the traditions of his ancestors that he persecuted those who believed in Christ is now the champion of a law-free gospel for the Gentiles. The contrast between Paul's former life as a Jew and his new life as apostle to the Gentiles is seen as evidence for the divine origin of the gospel Paul preaches as apostle to the Gentiles.

2.2. *Philippians 3:3-17.* The occasion that calls forth Paul's autobiographical statements in Philippians 3:3-17 is not as clear as that of Galatians 1:1-17. But it is probable that Paul is again arguing against Judaizing tendencies in the church. This is suggested by the reference to those who mutilate the flesh (Phil 3:2) and Paul's claim to be the true circumcision (Phil 3:3). Although Judaizing tendencies do not appear to be a major problem at Philippi, Paul uses his life as an example of what it means to be the true circumcision. Paul sees his experience as a paradigmatic expression of the great contrast between life under the law and the transforming grace of the new life in Christ.

Paul is willing to compare himself with those who think they have reason for confidence in the flesh, for he has even better reasons for such confidence (Phil 3:4-6). Three of Paul's reasons for having confidence in the flesh are based on hereditary factors: he was born a Jew; circumcised according to the law; and raised as a culturally pure, Hebrew-speaking Jew (*see* Jew, Paul the). Paul's personal convictions while a Jew also gave him reason to boast: his attitude toward the law was that of the strict sect of the Pharisees, he was a zealous persecutor of the church and was blameless in his observance of the law. Paul's background establishes him as one who is fully competent to judge any issue involving the law.

But coming to know Christ Jesus brought about a reversal in Paul's life. His judgment on all these former advantages, everything that he considered gain, is that he now considers it loss (Phil 3:7-8). The result of the conversion/call experience in which Paul came to know Christ is a complete transformation. Being found in Christ means that Paul is no longer found in the law (Phil 3:9). Now Paul's whole life is shaped by his sharing in Christ's death and resurrection (Phil 3:10-11). This process of being transformed in Christ is a continuing process in Paul's life as he responds to the call of God in Christ Jesus (Phil 3:12-14).

Because Paul's experience of conversion/call has resulted in a total transformation of his life, Paul sees his relation to his readers as that of a type to be imitated (Phil 3:15-17). This idea of himself as an example of the life in Christ is the underlying purpose of Paul's account of his experience in Philippians 3:3-17.

2.3. *Other Pauline Accounts?* Two other passages in the Pauline letters are often considered autobiographical accounts of Paul's conversion: 1 Timothy 1:12-16 and Romans 7:7-25.

First Timothy 1:12-16 is clearly an account of Paul's conversion. But many scholars do not think Paul wrote 1 Timothy, and so its value as an autobiographical statement is questioned (*see* Pastoral Letters). In this passage, the contrast between Paul's former life and his life in Christ (*see* In Christ) is again strongly emphasized. But two aspects of this contrast are different from the passages in Philippians and Galatians 1. The first is that there is no mention of Judaism. The second difference is that Paul identifies himself as the foremost of sinners, a judgment Paul does not make in either of the other passages. However, just as it is in Philippians 3, the transformation in Paul's life is held up as an example to believers. Whether or not it is Pauline, this passage represents the Pauline tradition and is useful as evidence of the way Paul's conversion/call experience was understood in the Gentile churches Paul founded.

The autobiographical character of Romans 7:7-25 is not just disputed; it is the center of a major controversy in Pauline studies. The central issue is how the "I" of Romans 7:7-25 is to be understood. (For a historical summary of the various ways this "I" has been interpreted, see Cranfield, 342-47.) Is Paul speaking of his personal experience, either as a Jew or a Christian? Is he speaking in a general way about Jewish, Christian or general human experience? Or is he using the "I" as a way of talking about the law in a more general sense?

The traditional view of Paul's conversion/call usually understands this passage as Paul's autobiographical account of his pre-Christian experience as a Jew. Romans 7:7-25 is seen as evidence of Paul's feelings of guilt and inferiority as a Jew because he is unable to keep the law perfectly. But this reading of Romans 7:7-25 is directly contradictory to Paul's statements in Galatians 1 and Philippians 3 about his life as a Jew. So most historical scholars now reject this possibility. Instead they usually understand this passage as Paul examining the law from a Christian perspective in a general sense; the "I" represents his deep personal involvement in the issue of the law. A. F. Segal offers a different and compelling interpretation of Romans 7:7-25. He suggests that Paul is describing Jewish-Christian experience with the law after conversion. Paul uses "I" because he speaks as a Jewish Christian for Jewish Christians. The struggle with the law is a struggle no Christian can win as long as observance of the law is a serious option in the Christian community. A law-free gospel is the only solution. Thus Romans 7:7-25 is a description of the personal struggle experienced by any Jewish Christian who tries to keep the law as a Christian.

Given the multiplicity of readings of Romans 7:7-25 and the lack of direct biographical information in the text, it seems best not to consider this passage as an account that refers to Paul's conversion/call.

2.4. The Acts Accounts. Paul's letters give us little information about the actual conversion/call event. Instead, the Pauline accounts reflect the radical change in Paul's values and commitments when he received a revelation of Christ. But the three accounts in Acts focus on the events surrounding the conversion/call. The fact that the conversion/call account occurs three times suggests that this event has major significance for Luke's narrative. The first account, in Acts 9:1-20, is told as part of the historical narrative; the other accounts, in Acts 22:1-21 and Acts 26:2-23, are contained in Paul's speeches before the Jews and King Agrippa. There has been a tendency in NT scholarship to isolate these conversion/call narratives from the rest of Acts and then to compare them with Paul's accounts. However, it is important to see these passages in their context in Acts. Luke uses them to show the progress of the church from a Jewish to a Gentile community and to justify the Pauline mission to the Gentiles. Because of Luke's definite apologetic stance, some scholars question the historical reliability of the accounts in Acts. It is true that Luke does not have firsthand knowledge of the conversion/call event. But he does have the advantage of a historical perspective and may be able to see the importance of Paul's conversion/call in ways that Paul could not.

The events of Acts 9:1-19 mark a major turning point in the narrative of Acts. Here Luke takes a piece of historical storytelling and describes an event of crucial importance for the Christian mission. The story of Paul's dramatic conversion/call is placed just before the story of Cornelius and introduces the beginning of the mission to the Gentiles. At the beginning of Acts

9 Paul is presented as the persecutor of the church, who completely opposes the disciples of the Lord. But as he pursues the disciples to Damascus, his journey is interrupted. Jesus appears to Paul in a vision. The blinding light, the double vocative ("Saul, Saul"), Saul's falling to the ground and the questions he asks clearly mark this extraordinary event as a theophany, similar to the theophanies of prophetic calls. Paul emerges from this experience a different person, but he has not yet received his call. That call comes through a disciple at Damascus, one of the people Paul had been persecuting. The fact that the call comes in a separate vision gives it greater emphasis, but it is still part of the same event. The new description of Saul, given through Ananias, indicates that Saul is a "chosen vessel" and has been picked for a particular role. The very name he has persecuted he will now bear before the Gentiles, kings and the people of Israel and will suffer for its sake. This call is far more than a call that belongs to any believer; it is an apostolic commissioning. Although Acts 9:1-19 presents Paul as a person who has experienced a dramatic reversal in his life, it emphasizes his call to be apostle to the Gentiles more than the change in his life.

Acts 22:1-21 and Acts 26:2-23 tell the same basic story but have a different emphasis and seem to be serving a different purpose in the narrative. Both speeches draw attention to Paul's relationship to Judaism and may reflect controversy between Jews and Christians about the validity of the Gentile mission. This emphasis on Paul's relationship to Judaism is especially evident in Acts 22:1-21, where Paul is presented as a pious and loyal Jew. In fact, most of the differences between Acts 9 and Acts 22 can be accounted for by the emphasis on Paul as a devout Jew. This is particularly clear in Paul's report of his commissioning. Here Ananias is also presented as a devout Jew and the call is couched in language acceptable to Jewish sensibilities. The call to go to the Gentiles is not given by Ananias but by Jesus in another vision during a time when Paul is praying in the temple. Here there is no doubt that it is the mission to the Gentiles that is the problem for Jewish/Christian relations. When Paul claims that the call to go to the Gentiles came in the temple, his Jewish listeners create an uproar.

Acts 26:2-23 has an only slightly different emphasis. Here Paul emphasizes his obedience to his call. It is in this passage that the expression "It hurts you to kick against the goads" appears. Even though many interpreters have seen this as a reference to Paul's inner struggle before his conversion, it more probably refers to his future task and the cost of obeying the call he is about to receive. This phrase indicates that the call of Christ will constrain Paul and conform his whole life to the goal of making Christ known among the Gentiles.

Luke has one tradition about Paul's conversion/call that he uses in different ways to further his purposes in Acts. Paul is the driving force behind Christianity's Gentile mission, and Luke uses Paul's conversion/call experience to justify that mission and the Gentile Christianity it produced.

2.5. Paul's Conversion/Call in the New Testament. Comparing the Acts account of Paul's conversion/call with Paul's accounts is not as straightforward a task as it might appear. Paul is making comments about his life as he writes letters to various churches. Luke is telling a story with an overarching narrative purpose. Even though historical research values the letters over Acts, the material in Acts is essential to understanding the events surrounding Paul's conversion/call experience. What are the major similarities and differences between the material in Acts and Paul's accounts?

It is important to note that all five accounts of Paul's conversion/call occur in contexts where the relationship between Judaism and Christianity is an issue. In Acts the validity of the Gentile mission is at stake; in Galatians 1, and probably Philippians 3 as well, the validity of Paul's law-free gospel is the issue. In these contexts the revelatory nature of Paul's conversion/call is stressed.

Paul's former life as a zealous Jew and persecutor of the church and his transformation into a follower of Christ is an important part of all five passages. This theme of the contrast between Paul's former and present life is especially prominent in the autobiographical passages in Galatians 1 and Philippians 3. This strong sense of contrast is one of the arguments for seeing 1 Timothy 1 and Romans 7 also as autobiographical.

All three passages in Acts and Galatians 1 describe a call to proclaim Christ to the Gentiles as part of the revelatory experience. But it is noteworthy that Philippians 3 does not even hint at a special apostolic call. Instead, Paul speaks of a general "heavenly call of God in Christ Jesus." Why is a perspective that is so prominent in the other accounts entirely absent from Philippians 3? Perhaps since Paul's Gentile mission and his gospel to the Gentiles are not being immediately threatened, he does not need to stress the divine origin of his gospel. Another possible explanation is that since Paul is stressing his role as an example to be imitated, he doesn't mention a part of his experience that is so obviously unique to him. If 1 Timothy 1 is taken as genuinely Pauline, another possibility emerges. As the Gentile mission became established and Paul needed to justify his gospel less frequently, Paul saw the transformation of his life as the most important part of his experience and understood being an example of the transforming grace of Christ as an integral part of his apostolic role.

The differences between Luke's and Paul's accounts of the conversion/call are rooted in their different purposes. Luke wants to show the progress of the church from the Jewish to the Gentile community; Paul is concerned with his relationship as apostle to the Gentile communities he has founded. But Paul and Luke ultimately understood Paul's conversion/call in similar ways. Both are concerned with the relationship between Jew and Gentile and see Paul's call as apostle to the Gentiles as an important factor in that relationship. Both see Paul's conversion/call as a revelatory and transforming event in Paul's life and the life of the church. And both Paul and Luke see Paul's experience as a model of the transforming grace of God for the church. These similarities make it possible to speak of the NT understanding of Paul's conversion/call experience.

3. Some Critical Questions.

The questions that biblical scholarship addresses to the NT text often challenge traditional assumptions about the text. This is especially true of the questions scholars ask about Paul's conversion/call experience. Not only has Stendahl challenged traditional Western understandings of Paul's experience, but also other scholars have challenged Stendahl's interpretation. These challenges have resulted in several critical questions that need to be addressed in any study of Paul's conversion/call experience. The answers to these several questions are all related to the major issue. Is Paul's experience better understood as a conversion or a call?

3.1. Defining "Conversion". If the term *conversion* is to be useful in understanding Paul, it needs to be defined. As Stendahl points out, Western definitions of conversion have been strongly influenced by Augustine's and Luther's views of Paul's conversion. These views of conversion dominated early psychological research, which tended to focus on dramatic conversion and understood conversion as a solution to unbearable sin and guilt. Social scientists as well as biblical scholars have questioned this definition of conversion and have tried to offer models that are more useful to those who seek to understand conversion from either a theological or social-scientific perspective.

Most recent studies of conversion have taken a sociological approach and defined conversion as a person transferring from one community to another. Such studies also point out that the main characteristic of converts is a predisposition to reinterpret their past from the perspective of their new communities. Conversion represents a conscious choice to socialize to a new group and accept the reality structure of that group (see Berger and Luckmann, 144-50). The analogies between this sociological definition of conversion and Paul's experience are striking. Paul came from a Pharisaic community and entered a community that included Gentiles. This new community helped him understand his revelatory experience and reinterpret his past. This reinterpretation of his past as a Pharisee is evident in Paul's autobiographical accounts in Galatians 1 and Philippians 3; Paul's statements about his past are greatly influenced by his present commitments.

Helpful as these modern sociological definitions are, we need to be careful in applying them to Paul's experience. We do not have enough historical data on Paul for an adequate psychological or sociological analysis. We need to be careful not to reduce Paul's unique experience to a formula or let modern studies define his experience. But we can use modern categories to illuminate certain aspects of his experience for us.

3.2. Did Paul Change Religions? Did Paul remain a Jew even after he changed communities? According to a sociological definition of conversion, this would be entirely possible and would answer one of Stendahl's objections to calling Paul's experience a conversion. Stendahl asserts that Paul did not really change religions. He had a new calling but still served the same God; as a Jew, he was to bring God's message to the Gentiles. His experience led not to a new religion but to a new understanding of the law in relation to the Gentiles. When Paul was transformed by his experience, Christianity was not yet defined as a different religion from Judaism, so it might be best to say that Paul changed communities within Judaism.

But this reading of Paul fails to take into account the radical nature of Paul's reinterpretation of Judaism. His claim that Gentiles did not have to be circumcised to enter the Christian community was more than a minor reinterpretation of the law. In addition, he claimed that he received this new understanding of the law in a revelatory event that changed his life. These claims got him into trouble even within the Christian community. Comparing Paul with the Pharisaic Christians of Acts 15 and Galatians 2, who wanted Gentile Christians to be circumcised, shows how radical his reinterpretation of Judaism was. Paul left the Pharisaic community and was rejected by that community. Paul's claim in Philippians 3:7-8 that he regards his Jewish reasons for confidence as "rubbish" indicates a complete break with his Jewish past. Although the Acts accounts of Paul's experience present him as a devout Jew, they also indicate that Paul's life and values were radically changed by his Damascus Road experience and that he was uncompromising in his insistence that Gentiles need not be circumcised. If Paul's entering the Christian community involved such a radical reorientation of his life and his religious values, it seems misleading to assert that Paul remained a Jew with a new calling. Paul may indeed have thought of himself as a Jew throughout his entire life. But he also insisted on a reinterpretation of Torah so radical that it eventually created a new pattern of religion.

3.3. Conversion or Call? In many ways the question of whether Paul's Damascus Road experience was a call or a conversion is an artificial one. The question seems to impose modern categories on ancient descriptions of a complex religious event. But asking the question also allows us to realize that Paul's experience is far too rich to fit neatly into any of our categories. It is both call and conversion. So when we ask if

Paul's experience is a call or a conversion, we are not only asking which term best describes Paul's experience, we are also asking whether any single term can do justice to that event.

Paul's call to be the apostle to the Gentiles is central to the accounts in Acts and Galatians 1. But it seems much more important in the accounts in Acts, which are seeking to justify the mission to the Gentiles, than it does in Paul's accounts. Paul mentions it in defense of his gospel in Galatians 1, but there is no mention of an apostolic call in Philippians 3. This would suggest that Paul did not understand his revelatory experience primarily as a call, even though his call to be apostle to the Gentiles was part of that experience. Those who see Paul's experience primarily as a call are probably being more influenced by Luke and his purposes than by Paul's interpretation of his experience.

The central theme of the autobiographical passages in Galatians 1 and Philippians 3 is the contrast between Paul's former life in Judaism and his present life in Christ. In Philippians 3 Paul claims that this contrast is due to the transforming character of his experience of knowing Christ. This same contrast is also found in all three accounts in Acts. Does this evidence of a profound change in Paul's life mean that the Damascus Road experience is best understood as a conversion? The answer to this question depends on how *conversion* is defined.

The traditional Western understanding of conversion, when imposed on the NT texts, leads to a distorted understanding of Paul's experience. This view of conversion sees Paul as a Jew who struggles with guilt over his failure to keep the law. Paul says that he was "as to righteousness under the law, blameless" (Phil 3:6). It also sees Paul's conversion as an experience of being justified by faith rather than an experience of knowing Christ and being called to proclaim him to the Gentiles. Although this is not a serious distortion of the NT texts, it is still an example of trying to fit Paul into traditional Protestant categories rather than trying to understand the complexities of Paul's experience.

Sociological definitions of conversion seem to be more consistent with the NT descriptions of Paul's experience. If conversion results in a change of communities and a reinterpretation of one's past life, Paul's experience certainly qualifies as a conversion. Even though sociological definitions of conversion do not distort Paul's experience, they do not really do justice to it either. Paul's experience had a powerful revelatory dimension to it, and Paul claims that his experience and the gospel he received were of divine origin. The event that caused him to change communities was a call to be apostle to the Gentiles and the event that caused him to reevaluate his life was a direct revelation of Christ. Social-scientific definitions of conversion cannot describe these revelatory elements in Paul's conversion experience.

No single term seems to be able to describe the complexities of Paul's Damascus Road experience. Because strong contrasts are part of every account of Paul's experience, it certainly qualifies as some sort of conversion experience. But it is also important to include the revelatory dimensions of Paul's experience and recognize it as an experience of call. In other words, Paul's call to be apostle to the Gentiles is part of a profound and transforming conversion experience. Call and conversion are both aspects of a divine revelation of Christ to Paul. The changes in Paul's life and his mission to the Gentiles are the results of this profound experience of knowing Christ.

3.4. Paul's Experience as a Model for Christians. To what extent is Paul's Damascus Road experience meant to be a model for Christians? In Philippians 3:17 Paul urges his readers to "join in imitating me, and observe those who live according to the example you have in us." What aspects of his experience is Paul urging his readers to imitate? In answering this question it is important to maintain a distinction between the call and conversion aspects of Paul's experience.

It is interesting that the only passage referring to Paul's Damascus Road experience in which Paul urges his readers to follow his example is the passage in which no mention of his apostolic call is made. There is no indication that Paul ever suggested that anyone imitate him in his role as apostle to the Gentiles. In fact, there is every indication in Galatians 1—2 that Paul saw his call as unique and that he zealously defended his unique mission and perspective. The accounts in Acts also present him as *the* apostle to the Gentiles and give him credit for the early church's Gentile mission. This is why scholars like Stendahl, who see Paul's experience primarily as a call, are suspicious of attempts to make Paul's experience normative for the church.

So what does Paul mean when he urges his readers to "join in imitating me"? In Philippians 3 Paul is reflecting on his personal experience of knowing Christ. Paul discusses knowing Christ in such a way that it can only be something gained in the process of being transformed. All Christians must be part of the community of those being transformed by Christ if they are truly to know Christ. In Philippians 3:14 Paul says that this transformation continues as he follows the "call of God in Christ Jesus." Here Paul is not talking about his apostolic call but about the call to be transformed—one that is addressed to all believers. Being transformed involves "forgetting what lies behind" and "straining forward to what lies ahead" (3:13). So the dynamic of this transformation is very similar to the dynamic of conversion, in which one completely rethinks the past in the light of present commitments. Paul shares with the Philippian community the "call of God in Christ Jesus" (3:14) and the experience of being transformed by that call. All Christians must be part of the community of those being transformed by Christ if they are to truly know Christ. When Paul urges the Philippians to imitate him, he is urging them to join him in responding to that call and allowing Christ to transform their lives. Knowing Christ has led to a total transformation of Paul's life and values. It is this experience of being transformed by Christ that Paul urges his readers to imitate.

3.5. Paul's Experience and His Theology. Most scholars either ignore the issue of Paul's experience and dismiss it as irrelevant or see it as the key to understanding Paul's theology. But those who think Paul's conversion/call affects his theology are not in agreement on exactly what influence the experience might have had. A great deal of this lack of agreement stems from the different ways Paul's experience is understood. Those who see it as a call think it has a very different influence on his theology from those who see it as a conversion.

The traditional view of Paul's conversion, which sees it as an experience of being justified by faith, also views the center of Paul's theology as the doctrine of *justification by faith. Paul arrives at his view of the law because of his struggle with the law as a Jew and his subsequent experience of being freed by Christ from this struggle. He rejects the works righteousness of Judaism in favor of the Christian way of justifica-

tion by faith. Although most biblical scholars no longer define Paul's conversion in the traditional way, this view of the relationship between Paul's experience and his theology is still presented in modified forms (see Theissen, 177-265).

Those who see Paul's experience as a call have a very different view of the relationship of this experience to Paul's theology. For these scholars, the center of Paul's theology lies in his call as apostle to the Gentiles (so, partly, Sanders). This call created questions about the law for Paul: If Gentiles are now included in the people of God, do they have to keep the law? What happens to the law now that the Messiah has come? What does this mean for Jew-Gentile relations and the place of Gentiles in the church? Paul arrived at his view of the law from answering these questions, not from his experience of the law before or after his call (see Stendahl, Munck, Dunn).

In recent years, scholars who understand Paul's experience as a conversion have linked it to his theology in ways that are quite different from the traditional model of justification by faith. These scholars think that all of Paul's theology, not just his doctrine of justification by faith, is derived from his Damascus Road experience.

S. Kim takes seriously Paul's claim to have received his gospel "through a revelation of Jesus Christ" (Gal 1:12) and argues that Paul's conversion experience on the Damascus road was the source for his apostolic call and his theological understanding of the gospel. Paul's christology comes from his recognition that the glory of God was revealed in the face of Christ (2 Cor 4:6). This revelation leads to Paul's proclamation of salvation as a present reality that will be consummated at the eschaton (*see* Eschatology), when the glory of Christ will be fully visible (see Newman). This Christ is the embodiment of God's plan of salvation that includes Jews and Gentiles; Christ is the end of the law. This is why Paul surrendered his righteousness based on the law to receive God's righteousness, which is based on faith in Christ. This experience of the reconciling grace of God allowed Paul to develop his distinctive doctrine of the atoning death of Christ as God reconciling the world to himself through Christ. Seeing this glorified Christ as the image of God who has restored the divine image and glory lost by Adam led directly to

Paul's conception of believers being conformed to the image of Christ and becoming a new creation. In other words, Paul really did receive his gospel as part of his conversion experience, and all of his theology is derived directly from that experience.

Segal makes a very strong case for the close connection between Paul's conversion experience, understood from a sociological perspective as a change of communities, and his theology. Paul's understanding of the law comes from his conversion experience and his subsequent experience in the Gentile church. Paul's legal principle in Romans 7:4, that those who have died with Christ are dead to the law, is a metaphor for his conversion. His experience of radical change led to a radical new evaluation of the law. Much of his theology of the law-free gospel was formed in battles with Jewish Christians about the role of the law in Gentile Christian communities. Paul's understanding of transformation, which is the result of his conversion experience, plays a crucial role in his understanding of Christian community. All Christians must be part of an evolving, transformed, redeemed community and all who are members of that community are equally members of Christ. All of Paul's theology can ultimately be traced to his experience of conversion: "Having begun with his own personal experience, Paul thereafter expands his theory not simply to involve his own salvation, and the salvation of the Gentiles, but also the entire history of humanity, from Adam to the eschaton" (Segal, 183). Since Paul's life, as well as much of his writings, embodied the solution to the issues facing the earliest church, Christianity received the influence of his personality and was seen as a community of converts. Paul's conversion not only influenced his theology; it defined Christianity.

See also JEW, PAUL THE; LAW; PAUL IN ACTS AND LETTERS.

DPL: CALL, CALLING; MYSTICISM; PROPHET, PAUL AS; VISIONS, ECSTATIC EXPERIENCE.

BIBLIOGRAPHY. P. Berger and T. Luckmann, *The Social Construction of Reality: A Treatise on the Sociology of Knowledge* (Garden City, NY: Doubleday, 1966); H. D. Betz, *Galatians: A Commentary on Paul's Letter to the Churches in Galatia* (Herm; Philadelphia: Fortress, 1979); M. Bouttier, *Christianity According to Paul* (Naperville, IL: Alec R. Allenson, 1966); C. E. D. Cranfield, *Romans: 1—8* (ICC; Edinburgh: T & T Clark, 1975); J. D. G. Dunn, " 'A Light to the Gentiles': The Significance of the Damascus Road Christophany for Paul," in *Jesus, Paul and the Law: Studies in Mark and Galatians* (Louisville, KY: Westminster/John Knox, 1990); B. R. Gaventa, *From Darkness to Light: Aspects of Paul's Conversion in the New Testament* (Philadelphia: Fortress, 1986); E. Haenchen, *The Acts of the Apostles: A Commentary* (Oxford: Blackwell, 1971); W. James, *The Varieties of Religious Experience* (New York: Collier Macmillan, 1961); S. Kim, *The Origin of Paul's Gospel* (Grand Rapids: Eerdmans, 1982); G. Lohfink, *The Conversion of St. Paul: Narrative and History in Acts* (Chicago: Franciscan Herald, 1976); R. N. Longenecker, ed., *The Road from Damascus: The Impact of Paul's Conversion on His Life, Thought, and Ministry* (Grand Rapids: Eerdmans, 1997); R. P. Martin, *The Epistle of Paul to the Philippians* (TNTC; Grand Rapids: Eerdmans, 1959); J. Munck, *Paul and the Salvation of Mankind* (Atlanta: John Knox, 1977); C. Newman, *Paul's Glory-Christology: Tradition and Rhetoric* (NovTSup 69; Leiden: E. J. Brill, 1992); A. D. Nock, *Conversion: The Old and New in Religion from Alexander the Great to Augustine of Hippo* (Oxford: Oxford University Press, 1933); E. P. Sanders, *Paul and Palestinian Judaism* (Philadelphia: Fortress, 1977); A. F. Segal, *Paul the Convert: The Apostolate and Apostasy of Saul the Pharisee* (New Haven, CT: Yale University Press, 1990); K. Stendahl, *Paul Among Jews and Gentiles* (Philadelphia: Fortress, 1976); J. S. Stewart, *A Man in Christ: The Vital Elements of St. Paul's Religion* (New York: Harper & Brothers, 1935); G. Theissen, *Psychological Aspects of Pauline Theology* (Philadelphia: Fortress, 1987).
J. E. Powers

CORINTH. *See* CORINTHIANS, LETTERS TO THE.

CORINTHIANS, LETTERS TO THE
The letters to the Corinthians represent at least two of the four or more letters that Paul wrote to his church in Corinth together with the churches in the region of Achaia, which surrounded this important Roman city (1 Cor 1:2; 2 Cor 1:1; cf. Rom 16:1). As its founder (1 Cor 4:14-15; 2 Cor 10:13-14), Paul knew well the church's history, character and problems. First Corinthians provides the most detailed example within the Pauline corpus of the way in which Paul applied his theological convictions, especially his *christology and *eschatology, to the

practical issues facing the church. In contrast, due to the circumstances that later developed in Corinth with the arrival of Paul's opponents, 2 Corinthians contains Paul's most sustained apologetic for his apostolic authority of any of the Pauline letters. In addition, both letters deal with the collection for the saints in Jerusalem, which was so important to Paul (1 Cor 16:1-9; 2 Cor 8—9).

1. Contents of 1 Corinthians
2. Contents of 2 Corinthians
3. Corinth and Its Citizens
4. The Church and Its Apostle
5. Some Critical Questions
6. Theological Themes of 1 and 2 Corinthians

1. Contents of 1 Corinthians.

1.1. The Salutation. Paul's salutation in 1 Corinthians 1:1-3 is typical of ancient *letters in that it first identifies the sender and then the recipients, after which a greeting is extended. Paul's salutation in 1 Corinthians is distinct, however, in that he expands the identification of the sender (Paul and Sosthenes) and the recipients (to the church in Corinth, "together with all those who are calling upon the name of our Lord Jesus Christ in every place," 1 Cor 1:2). On the one hand, joint authorship of an ancient letter is rare. We are not sure who Sosthenes was (cf. the same name in Acts 18:17 for the ruler of the synagogue in Corinth) or what contribution he made in writing the letter, for as 1 Corinthians unfolds it becomes clear that Paul alone is speaking. Moreover, Paul's position as "an apostle of Christ Jesus" is clearly distinguished from that of Sosthenes, who is identified merely as "our brother" (1 Cor 1:1). On the other hand, this is the most extensive elaboration of the recipients found among Paul's letters. In it Paul indicates that he views the church in Corinth to be the center of a cluster of house churches in the surrounding area.

But what is most striking in the salutation are the two supporting clauses that give the general reason for Paul's writing (i.e., because he has been called by the will of God to be an apostle of Christ Jesus) and for his writing to the Corinthians (i.e., because they too have been called to be "saints" as those "set apart" or "sanctified in Christ Jesus"). In both cases the focus on Christ in the salutation points forward to the christological foundation of Paul's arguments in 1 Cor-

inthians. The prayer/wish in 1 Corinthians 1:3, "grace (*charis*) . . . to you," is a Christianized form and expansion of the typical greeting used in ancient letters: "greetings (*chairein*) to you."

1.2. The Opening Thanksgiving. Again according to his normal custom, Paul follows his salutation with a thanksgiving for his church in 1 Corinthians 1:4-9. More than merely a spontaneous expression of personal praise, the thanksgiving introduces the central theme of the letter as a whole. Despite the Corinthians' current problems, Paul begins by expressing his gratitude to God for the sufficiency of their spiritual gifts (i.e., the concrete expression of the grace of God given to them), since Paul is thereby assured that God has irrevocably called the Corinthians and will therefore sustain them faithfully until judgment day. Hence, the problem in Corinth is not their spiritual gifts per se but their attitude toward and use of them (see 1 Cor 12—14). As will become clear, the Corinthians are boasting in the very calling and gifts (= grace) for which God alone is to be thanked (1 Cor 1:26-31; 4:7).

1.3. Responses to Reports About Corinth. First Corinthians 1:10 begins the body of Paul's letter and introduces the first major section (1 Cor 1:10—6:20). This section contains Paul's responses to the issues that he has heard about from "Chloe's people" (1 Cor 1:11, i.e., a certain group, most likely from Ephesus, in contact with the Corinthian situation) and from other oral reports (1 Cor 5:1; cf. 1 Cor 16:15-18). In this first major section Paul also attempts to clear up the Corinthians' misunderstanding of his earlier correspondence (1 Cor 5:9, 11).

In the first unit within this section (1 Cor 1:10—6:20), Paul deals with the causes of and the solution to the dissension and rivalry that has developed between some of the Corinthians based on their loyalty to various Christian leaders, including Paul. (To posit actual divisions or "parties" within the church is too strong a reading of 1 Corinthians 1:10-12.) The many attempts to ascertain the origin and distinctive theological perspective of those who claimed to belong to Paul, Apollos, Cephas and, more generally, to Christ (1 Cor 1:12) have not been successful. The attempt to read this text as evidence for a pervasive conflict within the early church between Peter, representing the Jewish Christians, and Paul, representing the Gentiles, as first championed by F. C. Baur, has also failed.

What can be said with confidence is that the

root of the problem was the Corinthian addiction to the power, prestige and pride represented in the Hellenistic rhetorical tradition, with its emphasis on the glory of human wisdom and attainment and its corresponding flagrant and flamboyant lifestyle. It is this Hellenistic "wisdom of the word" (1 Cor 1:17, 20, 26; 2:1; 3:19) that Paul combats by calling attention to the contrary "wisdom" and "power" of God as manifested first in the cross of Christ (1 Cor 1:18-25), then in the calling of the Corinthians (1 Cor 1:26-31), and finally in the intentional nature of Paul's ministry and apostolic way of life (1 Cor 2:1-5; 4:1-13).

Yet since "the word of the cross is foolishness to those who are perishing" (1 Cor 1:18; cf. 1 Cor 2:14), only those whose hearts have been transformed by the work of the Spirit will be able to accept the true wisdom and power of God as revealed in the gospel (1 Cor 1:20-24; 2:6-16). Paul therefore warns the Corinthians that their boasting in themselves and in their various spiritual leaders is a dangerous sign that the Spirit is not prevailing in their lives, since they are acting like those who are still "natural" or "unspiritual" (1 Cor 2:14—3:4). Should such an attitude and its behavior continue, they too will thus find themselves under the judgment of God, who will destroy the wisdom of this world and all those who work to destroy the church as the temple of the Spirit, built on the foundation of the cross of Christ (1 Cor 1:19-20; 3:10-23). The Corinthians must consequently repent of their boasting, recognize that everything they have is a gift, and follow in the pattern of their apostle, whose life of weakness and suffering manifests the power of the kingdom of God and the reality of the cross (1 Cor 1:31; 2:3-5; 4:6-13, 14-21).

The same arrogance and spiritual competition based on one's spiritual gifts and leaders, which some Corinthians had wed to a boasting in the achievements of Hellenistic wisdom (1 Cor 1:10—4:21), had also manifested itself in flagrant immorality within the church and in lawsuits between fellow believers (1 Cor 5:2, 6; 6:9). In 1 Corinthians 5:1—6:20 Paul now addresses these problems and their underlying causes.

In the first case, Paul responds by exercising his authority. With the cooperation and consent of the Corinthian church, he disciplines the man who is living with his father's wife with excommunication for the sake of his ultimate restoration (1 Cor 5:3-5). Paul then proceeds to make it clear that one's new position in and worship of Christ demand a corresponding purity and separation, not from the world but within the world (1 Cor 5:6-13), since "the unrighteous will not inherit the kingdom of God" (1 Cor 6:9). The Corinthians' present status of having been justified and sanctified in Christ must work itself out in a corresponding life of growing obedience to the demands of God, for they are the temple of God's Spirit (1 Cor 6:11, 12-20). Though all things are "lawful" for the believer, the Spirit does not free one from the call to holiness in this age; it frees one for it (1 Cor 6:12).

In the midst of this discussion, Paul addresses the fact that the Corinthians are taking their disputes to the secular courts for arbitration. Here too the Corinthians' spirituality ought to equip them to express God's wisdom rather than allowing them to capitulate to the world, especially when they are being equipped as God's people to share in God's ultimate judgment of the world (1 Cor 6:1-6). And in the event that no settlement can be reached, those who are spiritual ought to be willing and able to suffer wrong unjustly for the sake of Christ (1 Cor 6:7-8). As 1 Corinthians 8:1—11:1 and 1 Corinthians 13 will make clear, this is the true way of Christlike love and the true expression of one's spiritual power, maturity and giftedness.

1.4. Responses to the Letter from Corinth. Beginning with 1 Corinthians 7:1, Paul turns his attention to the issues concerning which the Corinthians have recently written to Paul for clarification of his views and their implications. Paul's treatment of these matters constitutes the second major section of the letter, which extends to 1 Corinthians 16:12 (cf. the repeated use of the "concerning" formula in 1 Cor 7:1; 8:1; 12:1; 16:1; 16:12).

In 1 Corinthians 7:1-40 Paul discusses marriage and celibacy. Here he is mindful of the tensions and anxieties caused by living in an evil age between the first and second comings of Christ (1 Cor 7:25-35), and of the God-given physical and emotional needs and desires of his people (1 Cor 7:1-5, 36-38). The basis of Paul's instruction is once again the determinative role that the calling and gifting of God play in one's life (cf. 1 Cor 7:15, 17-24 with 1 Cor 1:26-31). Here again, though Paul prefers being single as the way of life most suited to serving God (1 Cor 7:8, 32-34, 38), the goal is to live, whether married, widowed or single, in the kind of devotion to the Lord that corresponds to God's work in one's life and reflects God's character (1 Cor 7:19-20, 35).

In 1 Corinthians 8:1—11:1 Paul confronts the problems that have arisen due to the fact that the more knowledgeable within the church are eating food that has been sacrificed in a pagan temple. These individuals have come to understand that idols do not exist (1 Cor 8:4-6). But their behavior has become a stumbling block for those who do not yet share this understanding, defiling their weaker consciences and destroying their faith (1 Cor 8:7, 9, 11-12). Paul considers such disregard for the disposition of others, based on one's own rights and knowledge, to be a sin not only against them but also against Christ. Those who truly know God and are known by him will employ their freedom and knowledge for the sake of building up others in their faith, even when this entails denying one's own legitimate rights as a believer (1 Cor 8:1-3; 13). This is the "love that builds up," rather than knowledge alone, which merely "makes one arrogant" (1 Cor 8:1).

To support his point, Paul illustrates this principle of love by pointing to his decision to support himself financially while in Corinth (1 Cor 9:1-27). Although the Corinthians accepted Paul as an apostle (1 Cor 9:1-2), others criticized him for not exercising his legitimate apostolic right to financial support (1 Cor 9:3-14) even when this meant much undue hardship and suffering on Paul's part (1 Cor 4:11-13). Paul's answer is that he has given up his rights as an apostle for the sake of the progress of the gospel and for the reward God has promised for such acts of love (1 Cor 9:15-18). Paul thus makes himself "a slave to all, that [he] might win the more" (1 Cor 9:19) even though he is free to do as it is appropriate in Christ. This is the training in love that all must engage in, who, like Paul, are called to persevere in self-control in order to pursue the prize of the gospel (1 Cor 9:23-27).

In 1 Corinthians 10 Paul goes on to warn the Corinthians of what will happen if they too fail to persevere in love and misuse their knowledge and experience as an excuse for continual immorality and evil (1 Cor 10:11-12). Like Israel in the wilderness, they will be destroyed (1 Cor 10:1-10). Indeed, God has provided a way of escape from overwhelming temptation, so that there is no excuse for not enduring in the love

that is produced by genuine faith (1 Cor 10:13). As an example of this, Paul gives theological parameters and practical advice for dealing with the temptation to partake of food offered to idols. This temptation was common among the Corinthians in general, for whom it was a common social practice to eat in the precincts of a pagan temple. But Paul warns of the inherent spiritual dangers, arguing that even if an idol is "nothing," those who partake of food offered to idols are partaking of the table of demons (1 Cor 10:14-30). Finally, Paul returns once again to his own apostolic lifestyle of not seeking his own advantage but living to please others for Christ's sake (1 Cor 10:31-32). Here too this is an example for the Corinthians, calling them once more to be "imitators" of him, as he is of Christ (1 Cor 11:1; cf. 1 Cor 4:16).

In 1 Corinthians 11:2-34 and 1 Corinthians 12—14 Paul turns his attention to three matters concerning Christ-like behavior in worship: (1) the relationship between men and women in worship as expressed in the cultural practice of women wearing veils (1 Cor 11:2-16; unlike his response to the following two problems, Paul here praises the Corinthians and merely writes to give them a theological grounding for their practice); (2) the setting up of class distinctions during the celebration of the *Lord's Supper as an abuse of its meaning (1 Cor 11:17-34); and (3) the proper use of prophecy and tongues in worship (1 Cor 14:1-40) against the backdrop of the significance of spiritual gifts in general (1 Cor 12:1-31).

In view of Paul's arguments thus far in 1 Corinthians it is not surprising that in each of these cases Paul's approach is to make it clear that true spirituality and giftedness are not compatible with arrogant boasting and competition based on one's place in the *body of Christ or in society, or with parading one's gifts before others (cf. 1 Cor 11:18-22; 12:14-26; 14:6-12). Genuine spirituality manifests itself in mutual interdependence and complementarity, among men and women in view of their distinct roles and among those within the church due to the variety of their spiritual gifts. The same principles are to be manifest in dealing with their cultural diversity and economic distinctions (cf. 1 Cor 11:11, 33-34; 12:4-31; 14:26-40). And in each case this practical spirituality is grounded in theology, whether that is the creative work of God (1 Cor 11:2-16), the redemptive work of Christ (1 Cor

11:17-34) or the gifting of the Spirit (1 Cor 12—14).

Finally, as "the more excellent way" outlined in 1 Corinthians 13 makes evident, the criterion for establishing the appropriate application of this theology is that of love, the character of which is outlined in 1 Corinthians 13:4-7 (cf. its application in 1 Cor 12:4-11; 14:6-19). Hence, apart from faith in Christ working itself out in love for the body of Christ, participation in the Lord's Supper and apparent possession of spiritual gifts do not ensure one's right standing before God. In fact, they bring one under the judgment of God (cf. 1 Cor 11:16, 27-32; 14:37-38), since only love, as the outward expression of faith and hope, remains forever (1 Cor 13:1-3, 8-13). Paul can thus admonish the Corinthians, who pride themselves on their spiritual gifts and experiences, that "since you are eager for spiritual things and experiences, strive that you may abound in building up the church" (1 Cor 14:12).

Having begun by grounding his opening section in the cross of Christ (1 Cor 1:18-25), Paul concludes his application of theological truths to practical problems by dealing in 1 Corinthians 15:1-58 with the surety and nature of the future resurrection in view of the resurrection of Christ. Paul first calls attention in 1 Corinthians 15:1-5 to the death and resurrection of Christ as the center point of the gospel, which Paul had received as the common tradition of the church and then passed on to the Corinthians as the basis of their salvation. This is the earliest account we have of the contours of the early Christian message and its historical evidence. Paul then supplements this evidence with the recital of Christ's further resurrection appearances. He concludes with his own experience of the resurrected Christ and its consequences for his life as the "least of the apostles" (1 Cor 15:9-11).

In turning his attention to the Corinthians, Paul draws out a threefold significance from the fact of Christ's *resurrection. First, no one can conclude that there is no resurrection from the dead (1 Cor 15:12-19, 29-34). Second, Christ's resurrection is the "firstfruits" of what will happen to all "in Christ" at his second coming when God's "final enemy," death, is destroyed and all authorities are put back under subjection to the reign of God. Hence, contrary to the Corinthians' belief that they were already experiencing the fullness of the resurrection age to come

in their current life of the Spirit (i.e., their over-realized eschatology), the final resurrection is by no means merely an experience of spiritual power and gifting in the present (1 Cor 15:20-28). Rather, it is a qualitatively different bodily existence that can be gained only through the granting of a new, resurrected and spiritual body (1 Cor 15:35-56). Third, believers now live between the two resurrections, Christ's and their own. They live in the midst of an age that is still evil but that can be endured and overcome by the sure confidence that Christ's resurrection experience and victory over death as the "last Adam" will be shared by them because they are "in Christ" (1 Cor 15:42-54). The practical implication of this hope is that the believer is encouraged to "be steadfast, immovable, always abounding in the work of the Lord, knowing that in the Lord your labor is not in vain" (1 Cor 15:58).

As the last of the matters raised by the Corinthians' letter, Paul ends his responses by outlining his instructions concerning the management of the collection being taken for the poor believers in Jerusalem, noting his future travel plans, providing a recommendation for Timothy and then giving a brief explanation of Apollos's reason for not visiting Corinth (1 Cor 16:1-12).

1.5. Concluding Remarks. The letter ends with a final series of admonitions and greetings from Paul and those with Paul in Asia (1 Cor 16:13-24). As a fitting capstone to the letter as a whole, these admonitions center on the need for perseverance in one's faith as it works itself out in love (1 Cor 16:13-14) and the corresponding pronouncement of God's judgment on those who "have no love for the Lord," with Paul longing for the return of Christ (1 Cor 16:22).

2. Contents of 2 Corinthians.

2.1. The Salutation. The salutation in 2 Corinthians 1:1-2 follows the same pattern as 1 Corinthians 1:1-3, though in comparison the identification of the sender and of the recipients are abbreviated. Paul's apostolic identity by means of the will of God is again expressed, with Timothy now noted as the letter's co-sender. But as in the case of Sosthenes, here too Timothy is identified merely as a "brother," once again clearly highlighting Paul's apostolic office. Though there has been considerable discussion concerning whether the first person plurals in 2 Corinthians 1—7 refer to a wider circle of apostles or coworkers (cf., e.g., 2 Cor 1:19; 8:16-23), the internal evidence of the letter suggests that Paul alone remains the subject and object of the discussion throughout 2 Corinthians, apart from those texts where it is explicitly indicated otherwise (e.g., 2 Cor 3:18; the focus on the Corinthians in 2 Cor 6:14—7:1; 8—9). The recipients of the letter remain the house churches in Corinth and those believers scattered in small groups around this center. The greeting is also the same as in 1 Corinthians.

2.2. Opening Thanksgiving. But unlike the situation he faced in 1 Corinthians, Paul now finds himself in a new polemical situation in which his legitimacy as an apostle had been severely called into question at Corinth and still is being doubted by a significant minority within the church (see 4.2 below). This polemical situation and the corresponding apologetic tone that characterizes much of 2 Corinthians are evident from the beginning of the letter. In contrast to Paul's opening thanksgiving in 1 Corinthians 1:4-9, Paul begins 2 Corinthians not by thanking God for God's work of grace among the Corinthians but by praising God for his work of comfort and deliverance from adversity in his life (2 Cor 1:3-11). In doing so, Paul uses a formula in 2 Corinthians 1:3 that is typical of Jewish worship ("blessed be God") and that calls attention to blessings in which he has participated. These thanksgivings function in Paul's letters to introduce the main themes of his writing, to express his perspective on them, and to introduce an implicit appeal to his readers in response.

Second Corinthians 1:1-11 thus establishes the apologetic tone and central theme of what is to follow: rather than calling his apostleship into question, Paul's *suffering validates his call. God has called Paul to suffer in order that through the merciful comfort of God's sustaining power and ultimate deliverance, which Paul experiences in his affliction, he will be able to make God's power and comfort known to others (2 Cor 1:6-7, 10). Paul can thus interpret his suffering (= "death") in terms of the death of Christ and his deliverance from this suffering as a type of the resurrection (2 Cor 1:9). As such, these too become a means by which the church is encouraged in its faithfulness in the midst of adversity (2 Cor 1:7). Paul's suffering, being the vehicle through which the comfort God provides is made manifest, is therefore the mark of his genuine apostolic calling. Paul consequently concludes this section by calling the Corinthians to join him in thanking God for his suffering and deliverance, the very thing his opponents claimed disqualified him as an apostle (2 Cor 1:11).

2.3. Paul's Defense of the Change in His Travel Plans. In the first major section of Paul's letter, 2 Corinthians 1:12—2:13, Paul explains the theological rationale for the recent unexpected change in his travel plans (2 Cor 1:15-16). Paul's purpose is to demonstrate that his behavior has been an expression of the sincerity of motives that only God can discern (2 Cor 1:12). Conversely, Paul's actions have not been the result of "fleshly wisdom" (2 Cor 1:12) and the vacillations of one who makes his plans "according to the flesh." This may reflect an allegation, apparently made by his opponents, that Paul was guilty of an elaborate scheme to defraud the Corinthians in connection with the collection for Jerusalem and his practice of preaching for free (2 Cor 1:17; cf. 2 Cor 2:17; 7:2; 8:20-21; 11:7-11; 12:13-18).

Paul's point in 2 Corinthians 1:15—2:4 is that his earlier decision not to visit Corinth on his way to Jerusalem from Macedonia (cf. 1 Cor 16:5-9) but to come directly to Corinth first (2 Cor 1:15), as well as his later decision not to return to Corinth a second time (2 Cor 1:23), were all the actions of one who is "sealed by the Spirit" and is therefore acting in a Christlike manner. As the full realization of the promises of God (2 Cor 1:19-20), Christ makes it clear that God's purpose in acting toward his people is to establish mercy before judgment. In the same way, Paul's changes in travel plans were all motivated by his desire to extend mercy to the Corinthians in order to effect their restoration rather than to come in judgment (2 Cor 1:23-24). Paul changed his travel plans in order to give the Corinthians the chance for repentance (2 Cor 7:8-13), deciding not to come back to Corinth after his "painful visit" but writing the "sorrowful letter" instead (2 Cor 2:1-5). Far from being an expression of fleshly behavior, Paul's changes in plans were thus an extension of God's action in Christ.

In 2 Corinthians 2:5-11 Paul turns his attention back to those Corinthians who have already repented of their disloyalty to Paul in response to his previous "sorrowful letter" (cf. 2 Cor 2:5, 8-9; 7:7-16). Paul admonishes them to follow in his footsteps. Just as Paul acted to extend mercy to the Corinthians, they too should extend mercy to the repentant offender who caused Paul so much pain. They must welcome this one back, lest he be "overwhelmed by excessive sorrow" (2 Cor 2:7). Moreover, just as Paul's actions toward the Corinthians demonstrate his genuine apostolic standing, their willingness to extend mercy to this person takes on the character of a test of their faith (2 Cor 2:9). Those who have experienced God's mercy have no choice but to extend mercy to those who have sinned against them but have now repented. Paul therefore ends this section by reminding the Corinthians of the ultimate purpose of his admonitions: to prevent Satan from using this situation against the church (2 Cor 2:11).

Finally, Paul provides the transition to the next major section of his letter by calling attention to his most recent change in plans. When Titus failed to arrive as prearranged, Paul could not use opportunities for ministry in Troas but went to meet with Titus in Macedonia (cf. 2 Cor 7:5-7) because of his overwhelming concern for Titus and his earnest desire to hear the news Titus was to bring from Corinth (2 Cor 2:12-13). In view of 2 Corinthians 11:28 this anxiety over his "brother" and the Corinthians was yet another expression of Paul's greatest suffering as an apostle. This apparently insignificant transition thus calls us back to the central theme of the letter.

2.4. Paul's Direct Defense of His Apostolic Authority. Rather than calling the legitimacy of his apostleship into question, Paul's suffering as related in 2 Corinthians 2:12-13 leads him once again to praise God in 2 Corinthians 2:14, just as it did in 2 Corinthians 1:3-11. Moreover, here too Paul employs a typical Jewish thanksgiving formula in 2 Corinthians 2:14 ("thanks be to God") in order to signal the introduction of the central theme of the next section (2 Cor 2:14—7:16): "Thanks be to God who always leads us in a triumphal procession (*thriambeuō*) unto death in Christ, and in so doing manifests the fragrance of the knowledge of him through us in every place" (see Hafemann for a defense of this translation).

Just as in 1 Corinthians 4:9 Paul could picture himself as sentenced to death by God as a spectacle in the Roman arena, and in 2 Corinthians 1:9 as having been given the "sentence of death," Paul now portrays his suffering as an apostle in terms of the Roman triumphal procession in which those taken captive by the victor (like Paul by Christ!) are led like slaves to their death (2 Cor 2:14). Paul thus views his suffering as the divinely orchestrated means by which the knowledge of God is revealed in the world. With this as its introduction, this section sets forth Paul's most detailed defense of his apostolic ministry. Here his defense is aimed at those who called Paul's apostleship into question on account of his suffering (cf. 2 Cor 4:7-15; 6:3-10; 11:23-33), his weak personal appearance (cf. 2 Cor 10:10; 1 Cor 2:1-5) and his commitment to preach the gospel at his own expense. His opponents took these things to be signs of his inferiority as an apostle, of the worthlessness of his message and as part of his scheme to defraud the Corinthians (2 Cor 2:17; 11:7-15; 12:13-19).

At the heart of Paul's self-defense is the two-fold argument in 2 Corinthians 2:14—3:6 for his sufficiency and boldness as an apostle. On the one hand, Paul argues that he is sufficient for the apostolic calling (2 Cor 2:16) precisely because his apostolic life of suffering, as the means of revealing the knowledge of God, brings about the same dual effect in the world that Paul attributed to the word of the cross in 1 Corinthians 1:18-25 (2 Cor 2:15-16). Moreover, unlike his opponents, Paul has willingly taken up this suffering by preaching the gospel free of charge as evidence of his sincerity and divine call (2 Cor 2:17). On the other hand, Paul can point to the Corinthians as additional concrete evidence for his sufficiency, since their conversion and life in the Spirit, brought about through Paul, testify to the genuine nature of Paul's ministry among them (2 Cor 3:2-3). Paul's ministry of suffering and the Spirit thus combine to support his assertion that his sufficiency is from God and that God has made him a minister of the "new covenant" of the Spirit in fulfillment of Ezekiel 36 and Jeremiah 31 (2 Cor 3:4-6).

In 2 Corinthians 3:7-18, one of the most complex passages in the Pauline corpus, Paul proceeds to compare his role as an apostle of the "new covenant" established by Christ with that of Moses' role as mediator of the "old covenant" established at Sinai. Such a comparison is necessitated by the fact that in 2 Corinthians 2:16 and 2 Corinthians 3:5 Paul's sufficiency as an apostle is based on his call according to the pattern of the call of Moses as portrayed in Exodus 4:10 (LXX, *ouk hikanos eimi*). If Paul has been called like Moses, how then is his ministry different from that of Moses?

Paul answers this question by contrasting the events of Exodus 32—34 and their significance for understanding the nature and purpose of the old covenant to the new covenant in Christ. Paul's main point is that from the beginning the law functioned to "kill" Israel by condemning it for its sinfulness. This was not because the law was deficient but because the vast majority of Israel was left in a hardened condition so that it was unable to keep the covenant (cf. Ex 32:1-10; 33:3, 5; 34:9). As a result, Israel could not endure the glory of God without being destroyed (Ex 33:3, 5). Moses had to veil himself, therefore, not because the glory was fading but so that the effects of God's glory against a stiff-necked people might be brought to an end (*katargeō*; 2 Cor 3:7, 11-12, in view of Ex 34:29-35). This would make it possible for God's presence to continue in Israel's midst in spite of Israel's hardened nature. The veil of Moses thus becomes a metonymy for the hardness of Israel's hearts under the old *covenant (2 Cor 3:14-15).

The "letter" (*gramma*) of 2 Corinthians 3:6 is therefore the law apart from the power of the Spirit, which by itself can only declare God's will and pronounce judgment for not doing it but cannot empower one to keep it. Only God's Spirit, which is now being poured out in the new covenant as a result of the work of Christ, can "make one alive" (2 Cor 3:6) and bring about this righteousness (2 Cor 3:8-9). Hence, believers may now encounter in the Spirit the same glory of God that Moses encountered "with unveiled faces" (2 Cor 3:16-17). As a result, rather than being judged and destroyed by the presence of God, they are transformed by it into the image of God (2 Cor 3:18). Whereas Moses had to veil himself (2 Cor 3:12-13), as an apostle of the new covenant Paul can be bold in his declaration of the gospel because he is confident that he has been called to a ministry of the Spirit (2 Cor 3:8). Inasmuch as Paul's ministry thus mediates the glory of God to those whose hearts have been changed and thus need not fear their destruction, his ministry "outshines" that of the old covenant (2 Cor 3:10-11).

In 2 Corinthians 4:1-6 Paul draws the necessary conclusion from his preceding argument. On the one hand Paul's apostleship is legitimate in that it functions, through his preaching and his way of life, to make known the "light of the gospel of the glory of Christ, who is the image of God" (2 Cor 4:4). This was the purpose of Paul's call, pictured in 2 Corinthians 4:6 in terms of a new creation in which God "shone in our hearts to give the light of the knowledge of the glory of God in the face of Christ" (*see* Conversion and Call of Paul). On the other hand, this can only mean that those who reject Paul and his message do so because their minds have been hardened by Satan, the "god of this age" (2 Cor 4:3-4).

In 2 Corinthians 4:7—6:13 Paul returns once again to the theme of his suffering, this time by introducing and concluding this unit of thought with the second and third of his "catalogues of suffering" (2 Cor 4:7-15 and 2 Cor 6:3-13 respectively; cf. 1 Cor 4:11-13). Having argued for the legitimacy and function of his suffering thus far, Paul now addresses the question of the necessity for his suffering, which he says in 2 Corinthians 4:7 is to demonstrate that the power and glory that is revealed in him is clearly God's and not his own. The way in which this is accomplished is through Paul's repeated experience of suffering (i.e., "carrying around in our body the death of Jesus," 2 Cor 4:10; "being handed over to death for Jesus' sake," 2 Cor 4:11; and having "death at work in us," 2 Cor 4:12) in order that God's power to sustain him might be seen (i.e., "that the life of Jesus might also be manifested in our [mortal] body," 2 Cor 4:10, 11) and experienced by others (2 Cor 4:12). Paul thus follows in the footsteps of the suffering righteous of the OT (cf. the quote from Ps 115:1 LXX in 2 Cor 4:13) and of the suffering Righteous One, Jesus, in enduring suffering for the sake of others (cf. 2 Cor 4:15) and in his confidence in God's righteous vindication and reward in the future (2 Cor 4:14, 16-18).

Paul's confidence in his future vindication, when he will be "at home with the Lord" (2 Cor 5:8), is based on the guarantee of his present possession of the Holy Spirit (2 Cor 5:5). This confidence causes him not only to long with courage for its reality (2 Cor 5:2-4) but also to endeavor to be pleasing to God, knowing that all must appear before the judgment seat of Christ to be recompensed for their deeds (2 Cor 5:9-10). This healthy fear of God also motivates Paul in his ministry and in his defense of his apostleship (2 Cor 5:11), not for his sake but in order that the Corinthians might have just cause to be proud of Paul (2 Cor 5:12-15) and to affirm the truth of his gospel of reconciliation (2 Cor 5:14, 16-21).

The consequence of Paul's ministry is then made clear. Those who have been reconciled to God in Christ are a "new creation" (2 Cor 5:17; see Creation, New Creation), which in the context entails not only a new relationship with God but also a new, righteous way of life in which one takes on the character of God in Christ by living one's life for the sake of others (2 Cor 3:18; 4:5, 14-15; 5:21). Rather than rejecting Christ because of his suffering, as Paul formerly did when he regarded Christ from the nonspiritual point of view (i.e., "according to the flesh"), those who have been created anew see Christ and others in the light of God's purpose of reconciliation (2 Cor 5:16, 19, 21).

Paul concludes this section and at the same time introduces the next by calling those within the Corinthian church who are still rejecting Paul and his message to be reconciled to God and not to presume upon God's grace and mercy. By doing so they will demonstrate that their prior acceptance of God's grace has not been in vain (2 Cor 5:20; 6:1). For as an ambassador for Christ (2 Cor 5:20), Paul, like the servant in Isaiah 49:8, is called to bring the people back to their God (2 Cor 6:2). The catalog of suffering in 2 Corinthians 6:3-13 functions to support this appeal further by demonstrating again that rather than calling his legitimacy into question, his opponents should observe that Paul's endurance in the midst of adversity commends him as an apostle. The section therefore ends with yet another appeal to those Corinthians still under the influence of Paul's opponents to be reconciled to Paul (2 Cor 6:11-13).

In view of the fact that the Corinthian church stands divided over the legitimacy of Paul's apostleship and his understanding of Jesus and the Spirit (cf. 2 Cor 11:4), 2 Corinthians 6:14—7:2 addresses the question of the relationship between believers and unbelievers, the latter of which are now implicitly identified as those who will not repent and be reconciled to Paul as an apostle of the gospel of God. Paul's admonition is straightforward. Based on his understanding of the church as the temple of God (2 Cor 6:16) and the biblical injunction for God's people to separate themselves from idolatry in order to be God's "sons and daughters" (2 Cor 6:17), Paul calls the faithful Corinthians to separate themselves from those among them who

continue to reject Paul and his gospel (2 Cor 6:14-15; 7:1).

In 2 Corinthians 7:2-16 Paul resumes his account of the recent events in Corinth, focusing on the good news he received when he finally did meet Titus. Although Paul initially regretted having sent them such a severe reprimand, Paul is relieved by the fact that his letter of rebuke (2 Cor 7:5-8) brought about among the majority of Corinthian believers the kind of godly sorrow that leads to repentance rather than the "worldly grief" that merely brings death (2 Cor 7:9-13). Paul's defense of his apostleship in 2 Corinthians 2:14—7:16 consequently ends with a great expression of joy, comfort and confidence in the Corinthians as a whole, since their positive response to Paul's previous warnings and to Titus's mission was a sure sign of the genuine nature of their faith and of the bond between Paul and his church (2 Cor 7:2-5, 11-16).

2.5. The Collection. In 2 Corinthians 8:1—9:15 the subject matter changes. Paul takes up the theological foundation and practical administration of the collection for the believers in Jerusalem that he had initiated in Corinth but that, due to the problems in the church, had not been completed as anticipated (2 Cor 8:6-7, 10-11; 9:2; cf. 1 Cor 16:1-4). The necessity for the collection is based not only on the needs of the church in Jerusalem and the ability of the Corinthians to give (2 Cor 8:14-15) but also on the implications of Christ's self-giving for those under his lordship (2 Cor 8:8-9). Giving to the needs of others therefore becomes a test of the genuineness of one's faith (2 Cor 8:8, 24; 9:13), with Titus providing an example of just such a genuine faith and the love it produces (2 Cor 8:16-17). Two unnamed but well-known and respected brothers will be sent by Paul with Titus to ensure the completion and credibility of the collection to the glory of God (2 Cor 8:18-23; 9:1-5).

In 2 Corinthians 9:6-15 Paul then concludes his discussion of the collection by returning to its theological foundation. The collection is necessary because it expresses the church's trust in God to meet their needs to such a degree that they are willing and able to give cheerfully to others (2 Cor 9:6-9). God is faithful, and he will respond to such acts of faith by working to supply the needs of those who give and then by rewarding those who use their resources for the benefit of others (2 Cor 9:8, 10-12). In going forward with the collection the Corinthians will therefore glorify God by affirming with their actions the gospel of Christ (2 Cor 9:13) and causing others to join them in glorifying God (2 Cor 9:12). The collection will also create a unity of prayer and appreciation between the Corinthians and the church in Jerusalem (2 Cor 9:14), which leads Paul in response to close this section by praising God for his "inexpressible gift" (2 Cor 9:15).

2.6. Paul's Final Defense and Attack on His Opponents. In the last major section of 2 Corinthians (2 Cor 10:1—13:10), the tone, style and subject matter again change dramatically from the pastoral admonitions of 2 Corinthians 7:2-15 and 2 Corinthians 8—9. Here is an aggressive apologetic and counterattack against those within the church who still oppose Paul (2 Cor 13:5-10) and against his opponents from outside Corinth who stand in the shadows behind them (2 Cor 10:10; 11:4, 12-15, 21-23; *see* Adversaries I). The issues are still Paul's personal weakness and suffering (2 Cor 10:1, 10; 11:23-33), his voluntary self-support (2 Cor 11:7-15; 12:13-17) and his apparent lack of charismatic power (2 Cor 12:12; 13:3). Paul's upcoming visit consequently dominates this section in the hope that it will be a constructive time of healing rather than a time of judgment for the church (cf. 2 Cor 10:2; 12:14, 20-21; 13:1-4).

Second Corinthians 10:1-6 is Paul's final appeal to the church for reconciliation in order that he might not have to "show boldness" in punishing disobedience when he arrives—although he is ready to do so (2 Cor 10:2, 6). In 2 Corinthians 10:7-11 Paul supports this appeal by reaffirming his legitimacy as a Christian and as an apostle on the basis of the appropriate nature of his recent conduct, including his forceful boasting in his authority over the Corinthians. The appropriateness of Paul's conduct becomes evident once the right criterion for apostolic legitimacy is applied, namely, the concrete evidence of God's work through him as seen in Paul's apostolic activity of founding the church in Corinth (2 Cor 10:12-18). When Paul lays claim to his authority, he is thus not commending himself (2 Cor 10:12) but boasting "of the Lord," of what God has accomplished through Paul as evidence of the fact that he is the one whom the Lord "commends" (2 Cor 10:17-18).

Since God has already commended Paul through his apostolic work, the need to boast in one's own behavior or accomplishments is

"foolish" (cf. 2 Cor 11:1, 16-21; 12:11). Yet in 2 Corinthians 11:1—12:10 Paul feels forced to do just that in order to counter the claims of his opponents and to win back those who have fallen under their sway. At the heart of the issue is the opponents' claim that they, not Paul, represent and are equal to the "eminent apostles" in Jerusalem. In this section Paul endeavors to show that he is the one who is a genuine apostle, on a par with the leaders of the mother church (2 Cor 11:5; 12:11), while his opponents, claiming some connection with the Jerusalem leaders, are in fact "false apostles" and "deceitful workers" who disguise themselves as "servants of righteousness" (2 Cor 11:12-15). Thus in 2 Corinthians 11:5 and 2 Corinthians 12:11 Paul compares himself positively with the "eminent apostles," while in 2 Corinthians 11:12-15 he draws the sharpest possible distinction between himself and his opponents.

In this section Paul therefore "boasts" first in his decision to preach the gospel free of charge in Corinth (2 Cor 11:7-12) and then in his other sufferings (2 Cor 11:23-33) as the true marks of his legitimacy as an apostle, only to boast finally in his spiritual experiences. In this last case, however, Paul is exceedingly hesitant, knowing that this is the epitome of foolishness and the very thing concerning which God has given him a "thorn in the flesh" to keep him from doing (2 Cor 12:6-10). Furthermore, Paul asserts that the real reason his opponents have criticized him for his preaching free of charge, for his suffering and for his refusal to boast in his spiritual experiences is that his lifestyle and practice call their legitimacy as apostles into question, based as it is on a demand for payment and their tales of spiritual experiences (2 Cor 11:12). Paul's point is that neither human distinctives nor religious pedigree make one a servant of Christ (cf. 2 Cor 11:21-23), but weakness, since God has declared that his "power is made perfect in weakness" (2 Cor 12:9).

In 2 Corinthians 12:11—13:10 Paul brings the section to a close by reminding the Corinthians for the last time of his sincerity and apostolic legitimacy, as evidenced in his ministry of the Spirit and his suffering as a result of refusing to burden the Corinthians (2 Cor 12:11-18). Those who are still rejecting Paul must therefore repent in anticipation of his final visit (2 Cor 12:19—13:10). Not to do so will bring them under the judgment of God, since Paul has identified his person and message with the glory of God in Christ and the true gospel (2 Cor 11:4; 12:21; 13:1-4). The ultimate test of the genuine nature of their faith is thus whether or not they will be reconciled with Paul (2 Cor 13:5-9). Hence, Paul's elaborate self-defense has not been for his sake but for the good of the Corinthians (2 Cor 12:19), since Paul is writing "these things while being absent in order that when [he is] present [he] might not have to use his authority severely, which the Lord gave [him] for building up and not tearing down" (2 Cor 13:10).

2.7. Final Greetings. In 2 Corinthians 13:11-13 (14) Paul ends his letter by calling his church to mend its ways, heal its rivalries and live in unity and peace with one another. This closing appeal is based on the promise that in doing so "the God of love and peace" will be with them.

3. Corinth and Its Citizens.

More than perhaps any other of the Pauline letters, the sociological characteristics of Corinth, together with the religious and philosophical milieu of the region, influence one's interpretation of 1 and 2 Corinthians. Corinth was located at the foot of the 1,886-foot-high Acrocorinth, on the southern side of the 4.5-mile isthmus that connected the Peloponnese with the rest of Greece and separated the Saronic and Corinthian gulfs. Its location was strategic militarily and commercially. Corinth controlled the overland movement between Italy and Asia, as well as the traffic between the two ports of Lechaeum, 1.5 miles to the north, and Cenchreae, 5.1 miles to the east. A portage between these two ports, which ran through Corinth, made it possible to avoid sailing the treacherous waters around the Peloponnesus. This portage was facilitated by a paved road across the isthmus, which was built in the sixth century B.C. Corinth was thus known as a wealthy city due to its tariffs and commerce and as a crossroads for the ideas and traffic of the world (see Strabo *Geog.* 8.6.20-23). In terms of manufacturing, it was especially known for its highly treasured bronze ware, one use of which was as "resonance enhancers" in the theater (cf. 1 Cor 13:1; Murphy-O'Connor, 50, 76).

The history of ancient Corinth is the history of two cities. As a political entity, Corinth's history reaches back to the eighth century B.C., and until the mid-second century B.C. it flourished as a Greek city-state. But its status as the leader of the Achaean League led to Corinth's destruction by Rome in 146 B.C. Corinth then lay in ruins until 44 B.C., when it was refounded by Julius Caesar as a Roman colony, after which it quickly rose to prominence once again (Appian *Rom. Hist.* 8.136). By the first century, Corinth had become the foremost commercial center in southern Greece. Beginning in 27 B.C. it was the seat of the region's proconsul and the capital of the senatorial province of Achaia until A.D. 15, when it became an imperial province. It also became famous for its control of the Isthmian games, a biennial athletic competition second only to the Olympian games in importance. This background is reflected in 1 Corinthians 9:24-27 in Paul's use of the athletic metaphor and his emphasis on the imperishable crown reserved for believers. This, for the Corinthians, would be recognized as a contrast with the crowns given in the Isthmian games, which were made out of withered celery plants (cf. Murphy-O'Connor, 17).

As a wealthy hub for commerce and seafarers, Greek Corinth was evidently renowned for its vice, especially its sexual corruption, and for its many religious temples and rites. Aristophanes (c. 450-385 B.C.) even coined the term *korinthiazesthai* ("to act like a Corinthian," i.e., "to commit fornication") in view of the city's reputation. Plato used the term "Corinthian girl" as a euphemism for a prostitute (Murphy-O'Connor, 56). And although its historical accuracy is disputed, Strabo's account of one thousand prostitutes in the temple of Aphrodite does reflect the city's image, in which the many temples played their own role in the immoral tenor of its life (see Strabo *Geog.* 8.6.20, first written in 7 B.C. and revised slightly in A.D. 18).

After Corinth was reestablished in 44 B.C. as a Roman city, it received a rapid influx of people. It soon became the third city of the empire after Rome and Alexandria. In addition to the veterans and the many from the lower classes who moved to Corinth, the city was settled largely by freedmen from Rome, whose status as manumitted servants was just above that of a slave. The repopulation of Corinth provided Rome a way to ease its overcrowding and the freedmen a chance to take advantage of the socioeconomic opportunity offered by this new city. Moreover, Corinth also boasted a significant community of Jews, who exercised the right to govern their internal affairs (cf. Acts 18:8, 17). It is listed by Philo as one of the cities of the Jewish Diaspora (Philo *Leg. Gai.* 281-82), and a lintel inscribed with the words "synagogue of the Hebrews" has been found, though its date cannot be determined with certainty (cf. Murphy-O'Connor, 79). By Paul's day Corinth had thus become a pluralistic melting pot of cultures, philosophies, lifestyles and religions, and had the feel of an economic boomtown.

Paul's categories of people within the church, listed in 1 Corinthians 12:13 as Jew, Greek, slave and free, thus reflect the make-up of the city, as do the various Jewish, Roman and Greek names mentioned in the letters (the Jews Aquila, Priscilla, Crispus; the Romans Fortunatus, Quartus, Justus, etc.; the Greeks Stephanus, Achaicus, Erastus). We know from 1 Corinthians 7:20-24 that some of the believers in Corinth were slaves. Furthermore, since no landed aristocracy now existed in Roman Corinth, an "aristocracy of money" soon developed, accompanied by a fiercely independent spirit (so Fee, 2). This class distinction based on wealth is reflected in the tensions and factions that existed during the celebration of the Lord's Supper (1 Cor 11:17-34), since most of the church was apparently from the lower or middle socioeconomic class, with only a few wealthy families represented (cf. 1 Cor 1:26-27).

Roman law, culture and religion were dominant in Corinth, and Latin was the city's official language, but the Greek traditions and philosophies of the area and the mystery cults from Egypt and Asia were also strongly represented (cf. 1 Cor 1:20-22). Diogenes, the founder of the Cynics, was associated with Corinth and Craneum, a residential area near it. Indeed, it is judged that Corinth was the "most thoroughly Hellenistic city in the NT" (Fee, 4 n.12). The Corinthian theater at the time of Paul held fourteen thousand people (Murphy-O'Connor, 36) and is reflected in the image behind 1 Corinthians 4:9 and 1 Corinthians 9:24-25. Moreover, although the accounts that we have of the widespread sexual immorality in Corinth are of Greek Corinth and should not be taken to apply to the Corinth of Paul's day, it is the case that such a problem also came to be prevalent in the new, Roman city due to its character as a crossroads and seaport. First Corinthians 5:1-2 and 1 Corinthians 6:9-20 reflect just such an atmosphere. Finally, in Paul's day Corinth was filled

with pagan religious sites (cf. 1 Cor 8:4-6; 10:14, 20-30). Pausanias (d. c. A.D. 180), who gives us our earliest guidebook to Corinth in his *Description of Greece,* book 2, describes at least twenty-six sacred places for the Greco-Roman pantheon and mystery cults. But it must be kept in mind that much of Corinth was destroyed in an earthquake in A.D. 77, after which there was an extensive rebuilding of the city. For the time of Paul, archaeology has thus far attested a temple of Fortune and temples or shrines to Neptune, Apollo, Aphrodite (on the Acrocorinth), Venus, Octavia, Asclepius, Demeter, Core and Poseidon (cf. Murphy-O'Connor).

4. The Church and Its Apostle.

The church in Corinth was largely, though not exclusively, Gentile, as reflected in their former background in pagan idolatry (1 Cor 6:9-11; 8:7; 12:2) and in the issue of partaking in temple feasts (1 Cor 8:1—11:1). It was also normal for Greeks and Romans to go to secular law courts with their disputes, whereas Jews were forbidden to do so, which helps explain this practice in Corinth (cf. 1 Cor 6:1-6). The acceptance of prostitution discussed in 1 Corinthians 6:12-20 and the attitudes toward marriage reflected in 1 Corinthians 7 are also more in keeping with a Gentile background.

The church in Corinth met in various houses, since there was no possibility for a public meeting place, such as a synagogue, for a newly constituted religious movement that still lacked government recognition (cf. Rom 16:23). Based on the excavation of the four houses in Corinth from the Roman period (one from Paul's time) and the listing of the fourteen male members of the church in 1 and 2 Corinthians, J. Murphy-O'Connor estimates the base figure of the Corinthian church to be fifty members (Murphy-O'Connor, 158). But such a gathering of the "whole church" was unusual, since the church usually met in smaller groups in various members' homes (cf. 1 Cor 16:19; Rom 16:5; Col 4:15; Philem 2).

4.1. The Problems Behind 1 Corinthians. G. D. Fee's commentary on 1 Corinthians represents the most thoroughgoing presentation of the apologetic view of the problems behind 1 Corinthians. In this view the historical situation behind 1 Corinthians is fundamentally one of conflict between Paul and the church as a whole, in which the Corinthians' rejection of

Paul's authority as the founder of the church is perceived to be at the heart of their troubles. For Fee, therefore, the most serious division in the church is between the majority of the community and Paul (Fee, 8). Paul's language throughout the letter is taken to be combative, and his references to his apostleship are read to be apologetic (cf. esp. 1 Cor 4:1-21; 9:1-27; 15:8-11).

But Paul's purpose in writing 1 Corinthians is best seen not to be primarily apologetic but didactic. Nowhere in the letter does Paul argue for his authority as an apostle per se, since he continues to bank on the fact that the Corinthians recognize him as their founder (1 Cor 4:15) and as a legitimate apostle, even though others outside the church might not (1 Cor 9:1-2). Rather, Paul writes to "remind" the Corinthians of "his ways in Christ" (1 Cor 4:17) and to call their attention to the fact that as their "father" (1 Cor 4:15) it is his "way," the way of the cross, that is to be imitated (1 Cor 4:16; 11:1). The appropriateness of Paul's suffering is therefore nowhere defended in 1 Corinthians. Instead, it functions as the foundational premise for Paul's arguments (cf. esp. 1 Cor 1:10—4:21; 8:1—11:1; 13; 14:18-19), which in turn are based on his parental authority over the Corinthians in Christ (1 Cor 4:14-21). The fact that Paul can enlist his practice of preaching free of charge to support his hortatory purpose in 1 Corinthians 8—10 indicates that Paul's apostolic lifestyle and authority were still being held in high esteem. If not, Paul's larger argument in 1 Corinthians 8—10, climaxing in his call to imitate him in 1 Corinthians 11:1, would have collapsed. Throughout 1 Corinthians the focus of Paul's arguments is thus on the Corinthians and their behavior, and the mode of Paul's address is not apologetic but directive. Paul's ability to pronounce authoritative judgments on the Corinthians' behavior throughout the letter is based on his assumption that his apostolic authority is still in place in Corinth. The problems that 1 Corinthians addresses are essentially within the church, and not tensions between the church and its apostle.

4.2. The Problems Behind 2 Corinthians. By the time Paul wrote 2 Corinthians everything had changed. For a while, between the writing of 1 and 2 Corinthians, the church as a whole was in open rebellion against Paul and his gospel due to the influence of Paul's opponents who had recently arrived (cf. 2 Cor 11:4). Since then, a significant segment of the church had repent-

ed and returned to Paul's side. But Paul's apostolic authority is no longer common ground between Paul and his entire church. There is still a sizeable opposition to Paul among the Corinthians, with Paul's opponents lurking behind them. As a result, the church now stands divided over Paul and his legitimacy as an apostle. This current condition is reflected in the absence of the call to imitate Paul in 2 Corinthians, in the consistent focus on Paul's authority as an apostle throughout most of 2 Corinthians, and most clearly in the different ways in which Paul's suffering functions in the two letters. In 1 Corinthians 4:8-13 and 1 Corinthians 9:1-27 Paul's suffering can be used to support his argument on behalf of the Corinthians, whereas throughout 2 Corinthians Paul must argue for the legitimacy of his suffering (cf. 2 Cor 2:17; 11:7-15; 12:13-18). Hence, whereas the problems in 1 Corinthians were within the church, the central problem to be solved in 2 Corinthians is the authority and legitimacy of Paul as an apostle.

4.3. The Source of the Problems in Corinth and Paul's Response. The source of the problems in Corinth, whether in 1 or 2 Corinthians, can be traced back to the Hellenistic culture that so influenced the Corinthians. The key issue was what it meant to be "spiritual" (cf. Paul's use of *pneumatikos* fourteen times in 1 Corinthians alone, over against only four times in the other undisputed Pauline letters). Even as believers, the Corinthians held on to that part of the Hellenistic body/soul or material/immaterial dualism that disdained the physical world for the "higher" knowledge and wisdom of spiritual existence. Although it is anachronistic to speak of gnostics or gnosticism in Corinth, one may thus speak of an "incipient gnosticism" in the theology of the Corinthians (so Martin, following Bruce; *see* Gnosticism). Under its influence the Corinthians were prone to intellectual pride, placing a high value on their "knowledge" and spiritual experiences (cf. 1 Cor 1:5; 8:1, 7, 10, 11; 12:8; 13:2; etc.). The result was an attitude of boasting and competition within the church, which was further fed by their cultural arrogance and admiration of the public power, style and polish of the Sophistic rhetorical tradition. Such a disdain for this world could also lead them to consider participation in its law courts and immorality as of no consequence on the one hand (cf. 1 Cor 5:1—6:20) and to the practice of an undue asceticism on the other (cf. 1 Cor 7:1-5).

But equally important, this dualism also provided the conceptual support that made the Corinthians so susceptible to an overrealized eschatology that spiritualized the future resurrection as already having taken place in their experience (cf. 1 Cor 4:8; 15). One's present life was therefore viewed as already participating in the fullness of the heavenly reality of the world to come. Such an overrealized eschatology further inflated the Corinthians' estimation of their spiritual knowledge, gifts and religious experiences, especially that of tongues, which they saw as indicating that they too shared the spiritual existence of the angels (cf. 1 Cor 13:1; 14:37). This in turn led to more boasting and disunity in the church, as well as to the eventual rejection of Paul's legitimacy as an apostle and of his gospel.

Paul's response in 1 Corinthians was decidedly based on the twofold foundation of the OT and christology (cf. his OT response to the problem of boasting in wisdom in 1 Cor 1:18—3:23, with direct quotes of the OT in 1 Cor 1:19; 1:31; 2:9; 2:16; 3:19-20). Both make it clear that the power and wisdom of God have now been revealed in Christ and his cross. At the same time, Paul's message of the cross (1 Cor 1:17-19) and his apostolic experience of suffering (1 Cor 4:8-13) demonstrate that the kingdom of God, though here in power, is not yet present in all of its fullness. Hence, if suffering and weakness are the essential characteristics of the apostolic ministry upon which the Corinthians' lives are based, then as children of their spiritual father the lives of the Corinthians also ought to be characterized by the power of the cross and not by boasting in their spiritual attainments or leaders. Paul's most basic advice, therefore, was to "imitate me" (1 Cor 4:16; 11:1).

By the time of 2 Corinthians, however, Paul's opponents had arrived from outside Corinth and had capitalized on the Corinthians' overrealized eschatology, preaching a view of Christ and of the Spirit that the Corinthians were open to receiving (2 Cor 11:4). Instead of calling the Corinthians to endure faithfully in the midst of adversity in hope of their future resurrection and vindication, Paul's opponents promised the Corinthians a life in the Spirit that was characterized by deliverance from suffering and by a steady diet of miraculous experience. They supported their claims to be apostles with letters of recommendation from other churches (cf. 2 Cor

3:1), by their ethnic distinctives as Jews (2 Cor 3:4-18; 11:21-22), and by boasting in their spiritual attainments and supernatural signs, together with their rhetorical abilities (2 Cor 10:10, 12; 11:12, 18; 12:12). Paul's apologetic in 2 Corinthians 3 leads one to posit that they also tied their ministry in some way to the ministry of Moses and the law, although unlike Galatians the issues of ritual purity and circumcision are not mentioned in 2 Corinthians. Moreover, Paul's opponents sealed their claims by demanding money from the Corinthians as a sign of the value and legitimacy of their message (2 Cor 2:17). But in order to make these claims and demand this payment they had to attack Paul and his apostolic legitimacy, which called their gospel and their lifestyle into question.

In response, Paul had to defend his legitimacy as an apostle in order to establish the veracity of his gospel. Once again he does so by returning to the OT and to christology to demonstrate the necessity and purpose of his suffering in relationship to his ministry of the Spirit under the new covenant.

5. Some Critical Questions.

5.1. Authorship. Both 1 and 2 Corinthians are attributed to Paul in their salutations and show every historical and literary evidence of Pauline authorship. Indeed, the Pauline authorship of 1 Corinthians has never been disputed, and the letter is already attested in the 90s by Clement of Rome (cf. *1 Clem.* 37.5; 47.1-3; 49.5) and in the first decade of the second century by Ignatius (cf. Ignatius *Eph.* 16.1; 18.1; *Rom.* 5.1, etc.). Although 2 Corinthians is not clearly documented until Marcion's canon (A.D. 140), it is undisputed from that point on as part of the Pauline corpus. Even the most critical modern scholarship has consistently accepted these letters as genuine, apart from 1 Corinthians 1:2b and 1 Corinthians 14:34b-35, which some scholars have argued are non-Pauline interpolations. But the evidence for removing these texts has not convinced the majority of scholars, since no manuscript tradition has ever omitted these verses and both texts can be seen to fit within Paul's flow of thought. Other scholars have argued that the distinct vocabulary and subject matter of 2 Corinthians 6:14—7:1 indicate that Paul adopted this passage from a previous Pauline writing, from a non-Pauline Jewish source (often associated with the Essene movement or *Dead Sea Scrolls) or from a Jewish-Christian tradition. But even if this hypothesis stands against the views of those who maintain that its distinct character is due to the OT texts that Paul quotes in this section, the passage has been fully integrated by Paul into his train of thought in 2 Corinthians.

5.2. Unity and Occasion of 1 and 2 Corinthians. Paul's founding of the church at Corinth, recorded in Acts 18, took place in the years A.D. 49-51 as part of Paul's second missionary journey. When Paul left Corinth after eighteen months, the new church was flourishing. Sometime later Paul wrote a letter to the Corinthians from Ephesus, a document that is no longer extant, in order to deal with some specific ethical issues being faced by the new believers. But the Corinthians had difficulty understanding Paul's admonitions and misapplied them to their context (cf. 1 Cor 5:9-13). The church then sent a letter to Paul by the hands of the messengers listed in 1 Corinthians 16:15-17 in order to receive further clarification. In response to this letter Paul wrote canonical 1 Corinthians. Paul's aim was to clarify his positions and to respond to the other reports he had heard about the serious problems that had arisen in Corinth (1 Cor 1:11; 5:1; cf. 1 Cor 16:15-18; see 4.2 above). The somewhat disjointed and topical nature of 1 Corinthians is due to the fact that Paul is responding in turn to the variety of issues and questions brought to him by the church's letter and to the reports he has heard.

At the time he wrote 1 Corinthians, Paul intended to return to Corinth after staying in Ephesus until Pentecost and then visiting Macedonia (see 1 Cor 16:5-8). In the meantime he sent Timothy to visit the Corinthians on his behalf (1 Cor 16:10-11; Acts 19:22). Timothy found the tension between Paul and the Christians at Corinth to have escalated, due most probably to the arrival of opponents of Paul from outside Corinth. In response, Paul set out for Corinth immediately for what became a "painful visit," during which Paul's authority and gospel were severely called into question by the church. Paul was opposed and offended by one of its leaders (cf. 2 Cor 2:1, 5-8; 7:8-13; 11:4).

Paul left Corinth under attack, determined not to make another such "painful visit" to the Corinthians (2 Cor 2:1-2). Instead he sent Titus to them with a "tearful letter" of rebuke and a warning as an attempt to win them back (cf. 2 Cor 2:3-9; 7:8-12). The fact that Titus was also

to organize the collection (2 Cor 8:6) indicates, however, that Paul still held out hope for the Corinthians and did not consider them beyond repentance. This "tearful letter" is now lost, though some scholars have attempted to identify it with canonical 1 Corinthians or the four chapters of 2 Corinthians 10—13. But 1 Corinthians is neither severe nor painful enough to qualify, nor does its subject matter fit the nature of the description in 2 Corinthians 2:1-4, since in 1 Corinthians there is no consistent treatment of the theme of the Corinthians' rejection of Paul, the influence of Paul's opponents within Corinth or the offender of 2 Corinthians 2:5-11.

As Paul waited for Titus to return with his report concerning the impact of this letter, his mind could not rest due to his anxiety over the Corinthian situation (2 Cor 2:12-13). So Paul left Troas to find Titus, and when he did, Titus gave Paul the good news that his "tearful letter" had indeed won back the majority of the Corinthians (2 Cor 7:6-13). Moreover, because the church had responded so positively, Paul could now plan to visit them once again (cf. 2 Cor 2:3; 9:5; 12:20—13:1).

In anticipation of this third visit, Paul wrote canonical 2 Corinthians, or at least 2 Corinthians 1—9 as we now have it. The fact that the majority of the church had repented and returned to Paul, while a significant segment still resisted his authority and gospel, explains the mixed nature of this section. In it Paul comforts and encourages the majority of the church, while at the same time defending his apostleship in order to strengthen those who have repented and to win back the recalcitrant minority. Moreover, behind the Corinthians lurk Paul's opponents, whom Paul does not address directly but who are the most direct source of the problem. Paul's goal in writing, therefore, is to prepare for his next visit to the Corinthians in which he will have to judge those who persist in their rejection of him and his gospel. Paul did return to Corinth (cf. Acts 20:2), where less than a year later he wrote his letter to the Romans.

In view of this scenario the question of the literary unity of 2 Corinthians has been answered in various ways because of the seemingly abrupt transitions and change of subject matter within the letter. The key issues are the apparent breaks in thought between 2 Corinthians 2:13 and 2 Corinthians 2:14, 2 Corinthians 7:4 and 5, 2 Corinthians 6:13 and 14, and 2 Corinthians 7:1

and 2; the seemingly separate treatments of the collection in 2 Corinthians 8—9; and the distinct unit of 2 Corinthians 10:1—13:14. If each of these transitions marks out a separate document, 2 Corinthians becomes a composite of the following six major fragments, which were then later unified into a single letter: 2 Corinthians 1:1—2:13 and 2 Corinthians 7:5-16; 2 Corinthians 2:14—6:13; 2 Corinthians 6:14—7:1; 2 Corinthians 8; 2 Corinthians 9; 2 Corinthians 10—13.

A minority of scholars still maintain, however, the literary unity of the entire letter. Those who hold this position attempt to explain the integrity of the transitions within the letter at each point. In addition, they view the changes in subject matter throughout 2 Corinthians as the result of the mixed nature of the Corinthian community. Second Corinthians 10—13 is Paul's last direct defense and attack against his opponents, after primarily addressing the reconciled majority of the church in 2 Corinthians 1—9, and perhaps after some lapse in time or the arrival of new, menacing information. This is the approach taken in the overview of 2 Corinthians above.

At the other extreme, a few scholars have sought to isolate each of these sections as originally part of a separate writing and to assign them to the history of Paul's interaction with the Corinthians outlined above. In this scenario, as we noted, some view 2 Corinthians 10—13 to be part of the "tearful letter;" 2 Corinthians 2:14—6:13 to be part of a lost letter of defense; 2 Corinthians 1:1—2:13 and 2 Corinthians 7:5-16 to be Paul's letter of reconciliation after Titus's report; 2 Corinthians 6:14—7:1 to be part of yet another lost Pauline or non-Pauline writing, part of the "tearful letter," or even part of the "previous letter" of 1 Corinthians 5:9. The growing consensus is that 2 Corinthians 1—9 is a unified composition written after Paul's encounter with Titus (cf. 2 Cor 7:5-13). Second Corinthians 10—13 is then taken as a subsequent work that was written after a fresh outbreak of trouble in Corinth and appended to the previous section at some time early on in the history of these traditions, since there is no textual-critical evidence that 2 Corinthians 10—13 ever circulated independently of 2 Corinthians 1—9 (see, e.g., the commentaries by Martin and Furnish).

5.3. Place and Date. First Corinthians was written from Ephesus between the time Paul left Corinth in A.D. 51-52 and three years later, in the autumn of A.D. 52 to the spring of 55, depending on the following factors: the dating of the edict of Claudius and the term of office of Gallio (cf. Acts 18:2, 12); the time of Paul's departure from Corinth (Acts 18:18); and the subsequent length of his later stay in Ephesus. Second Corinthians (taken as a whole, or at least 2 Cor 1—9) was completed in the next year or so after 1 Corinthians and was written from Macedonia.

5.4. Paul's Opponents. The key passages for identifying Paul's opposition in Corinth have traditionally been 1 Corinthians 1:12; 3:22; 9:2-5; 2 Corinthians 3:1-18; 11:4; 11:22-23. From these texts it is clear that Paul's opponents were Jews who were familiar with the Hellenistic world and espoused Sophist values and rhetorical techniques on the one hand and relied on their spiritual heritage as Jews on the other (see 4.3 above). Beyond this bare sketch, the more exact identity and theology of the opponents must remain a matter of scholarly reconstruction, since 1 and 2 Corinthians are our only available evidence, though material from Philippians (when dated in Paul's Ephesian period) has been introduced by some scholars (see commentaries).

Since the seventeenth century, scholars have offered three basic theories concerning the identity of Paul's opponents in 2 Corinthians. These hypotheses have been constructed predominantly by reading Paul's arguments as a direct contrast to the positions of his opponents (the so-called mirror technique). The proposals are as follows: (1) gnostics; (2) legalistic Judaizers on a par with those Paul fought elsewhere; or (3) a mixture of legalistic and gnostic and/or enthusiastic or pneumatic elements of various persuasions. These basic positions have repeatedly been refined and combined in various ways, so that one scholar has listed no fewer than eleven different positions on 2 Corinthians between 1908 and 1940. Since then, these three basic positions have again been forcefully argued by R. Bultmann and W. Schmithals (the gnostic hypothesis), C. K. Barrett (the Judaizer hypothesis), and D. Georgi (Hellenistic Jewish pneumatics and missionaries of Palestinian origin with a "divine man" [*theios anēr*] theology centered on Moses).

The only major study of Paul's opponents in general to appear after these studies, J. J.

Gunther's *St. Paul's Opponents and Their Background*, offered neither a new methodology nor a clear way out of this scholarly impasse. Gunther's thesis is that the backdrop for Paul's opponents is to be found in the Qumran and Jewish apocryphal writings, so that Paul's opponents were from a mystic, apocalyptic, ascetic, nonconformist, syncretistic Judaism, more like Essenism than any other group (Gunther, 315). But in his attempt to forge a consensus among the thirteen different views he catalogued, Gunther cast his net so wide that his description becomes nondescript.

Hence, J. L. Sumney's recent proposal of a methodology based upon a "minimalist approach" for identifying Paul's opponents is to be welcomed. Sumney's proposal includes (1) an emphasis on the priority of exegesis in a "text-focused method"; (2) an insistence upon a sound evaluation of proper sources; (3) a "stringently" limited application of the "mirror technique" (i.e., the practice of reading Paul's statements as a direct reflection of his opponents' contrary views); and (4) a rejection of the attempt to approach the text with a previously determined, externally based reconstruction. But in view of the history of research it is significant that when Sumney applies his method to 2 Corinthians, he offers no new insights into the identity of Paul's opponents. Sumney ends up agreeing with the previous proposal of E. Käsemann that the opponents behind 2 Corinthians 10—13 were pneumatics rather than Judaizers, gnostics or Georgi's "divine men," and that the short time span between the letter fragments of 2 Corinthians 1—9 and 2 Corinthians 10—13 leads one to "reasonably conclude" that the opponents in both cases are part of the same group (Sumney, 183).

Today, the gnostic hypothesis has died due to a lack of evidence for gnosticism in the pre-Christian or NT era. And Georgi's proposal has met with serious criticism concerning his reconstruction of early Jewish missionaries and of their understanding of Moses as a "divine man." The way out of the remaining impasse will be to realize that the Judaizers' concern with the law was motivated not only by their desire to uphold their tradition but also by a desire to gain access to a deeper experience of the Spirit (*see* Holy Spirit). The artificial divorce between the law and the Spirit, which leads scholars to posit two distinct types of opponents, must therefore be overcome. The question raised by Paul's opponents, based on their Jewish heritage, was essentially the same one being raised by the Corinthians, based on their Hellenistic worldview: how does one participate fully in the power of the Spirit? The opponents' answer was based on a theology of overrealized glory, in which participation in their gospel, with its tie to the old covenant, was said to guarantee freedom from sin and suffering in this world. At the center of the debate was the relationship between the old and new covenants as this came to expression in the question of the authority and role of Moses and the law in regard to Paul's role as an apostle of Christ and mediator of the Spirit (cf. 2 Cor 2:16; 3:4-18).

6. Theological Themes of 1 and 2 Corinthians.

It is striking that most of the commands throughout 1 Corinthians center on some aspect of church unity (cf. 1 Cor 1:10; 3:1-3; 4:14, 16; 5:4, 5, 7, 8; 6:1, 4, 6-7, 18, 20; 8:9, 13; 10:14; 11:33-34; 12:14, etc.). Clearly Paul's primary concern is with the true nature and life of the church, making ecclesiology the most important theme of 1 Corinthians. As the "church of God" (1 Cor 1:2), the Corinthians are "the temple of God," due to their reception of the Holy Spirit (1 Cor 3:16-17; 14:24-25), and the "body of Christ," due to their submission to the lordship of Christ (1 Cor 6:17; 10:17; 11:29; 12:12-16, 27). But in focusing his attention on the Corinthians as the people of God, the eschatological framework of Paul's theology also stands out in this letter. Throughout 1 Corinthians Paul strives to make it clear that although the kingdom of God has already dawned, as evidenced by the resurrection power of Christ and the pouring out of the Spirit in the lives of the Corinthians (cf. 1 Cor 4:20), it is nevertheless not yet here in all of its fullness, a proviso seen clearly in Paul's suffering and the qualitatively different nature of the future bodily resurrection and the end of the age. At the same time, Paul must also make it clear to the Corinthians that although the kingdom of God is not yet present in all its fullness, one's ethical life as a follower of Christ is still to be controlled by the dawning reality of the age to come in which the power of the Spirit enables one to keep God's commandments (cf. 1 Cor 5:7-8; 6:1-6; 7:29-31; 10:11; etc.). Paul's insistence throughout 1 Corinthians on the inextricable link between faith and obedience is therefore framed theologically by the cross (cf. 1 Cor 1:10—4:21) and the resurrection of Christ (1 Cor 15). In the end, therefore, 1 Corinthians demonstrates that ecclesiology and eschatology are rooted in one's understanding of Christ "according to the Scriptures" (cf. 1 Cor 15:3-5).

In 2 Corinthians the central theological theme becomes the relationship between suffering and glory as this is determined and illustrated in Paul's apostolic experience. Here too Paul's arguments are grounded throughout in his eschatology and christology, both of which are developed within an OT framework and consistently applied to his life as an apostle. Paul's point is as simple as it is profound. Rather than calling his legitimacy as an apostle into question, Paul's suffering is the vehicle that God has ordained to validate his apostleship and to make known the knowledge of his power and glory, now revealed in the gospel of Christ. Paul's ministry of suffering and of the Spirit does not represent an unresolved tension that calls into question his sufficiency as a true apostle. Indeed, both the cross and the resurrection power of God are being revealed through Paul's life of divinely ordained suffering. And although in neither 1 or 2 Corinthians is there any call for all Christians to suffer or any sign of a martyrdom theology, Paul affirms that whenever God's people are brought into the same kinds of sufferings to which he was called as an apostle, they too will become vehicles for the manifestation of the power of God in the midst of their adversity (2 Cor 1:7). In support of this main point and his corresponding apologetic for his apostolic authority, Paul outlines the nature of the new covenant in relationship to the covenant at Sinai (2 Cor 3:6-18), the nature of the new creation in the midst of the old (2 Cor 4:6—5:21) and the christological foundation for living for the sake of others because one now lives for the sake of Christ (2 Cor 5:15; 8:1—9:14).

See also ADVERSARIES; APOSTLE; BODY OF CHRIST; ESCHATOLOGY; HOLY SPIRIT; LAW; RESURRECTION.

DPL: AUTHORITY; COLLECTION FOR THE SAINTS; CROSS, THEOLOGY OF THE; GIFTS OF THE SPIRIT; GLORY, GLORIFICATION; MOSES; POWER; SUFFERING; WISDOM.

BIBLIOGRAPHY. **Commentaries:** C. K. Barrett, *The First Epistle to the Corinthians* (HNTC; New York: Harper & Row, 1968); idem, *The Second Epistle to the Corinthians* (HNTC; New York: Harper & Row, 1973); L. L. Belleville, *2 Corinthians* (IVPNTC; Downers Grove, IL: InterVarsity Press, 1996); C. Blomberg, *1 Corinthians* (NIVAC; Grand Rapids: Zondervan, 1995); F. F. Bruce, *1 and 2 Corinthians* (NCB; Grand Rapids: Eerdmans, 1971); R. Bultmann, *The Second Letter to the Corinthians* (Minneapolis: Augsburg, 1985); H. Conzelmann, *1 Corinthians* (Herm; Philadelphia: Fortress, 1975); G. D. Fee, *The First Epistle to the Corinthians* (NICNT; Grand Rapids: Eerdmans, 1987); V. P. Furnish, *II Corinthians* (AB 32; Garden City, NY: Doubleday, 1984); S. J. Hafemann, *2 Corinthians* (NIVAC; Grand Rapids: Zondervan, 2000); R. B. Hays, *First Corinthians* (IntC; Louisville: Westminster John Knox, 1997); P. E. Hughes, *Paul's Second Epistle to the Corinthians* (NICNT; Grand Rapids: Eerdmans, 1962); R. P. Martin, *2 Corinthians* (WBC 40; Waco, TX: Word, 1986); A. Plummer, *Second Epistle of St. Paul to the Corinthians* (ICC; Edinburgh: T & T Clark, 1925); C. H. Talbert, *Reading Corinthians: A Literary and Theological Commentary on 1 and 2 Corinthians* (New York: Crossroad, 1987); A. C. Thiselton, *The First Epistle to the Corinthians* (NIGTC; Grand Rapids: Eerdmans, 2000); M. E. Thrall, *A Critical and Exegetical Commentary on the Second Epistle to the Corinthians* (ICC; Edinburgh: T & T Clark, 1994); B. Witherington III, *Conflict and Community in Corinth: A Socio-Rhetorical Commentary on 1 and 2 Corinthians* (Grand Rapids: Eerdmans, 1995). **Studies:** L. L. Belleville, *Reflections of Glory: Paul's Polemical Use of the Moses-Doxa Tradition in 2 Corinthians 3:12-18* (Sheffield: Sheffield Academic Press, 1991); D. A. Carson, *Showing the Spirit: A Theological Exposition of 1 Corinthians 12—14* (Grand Rapids: Baker, 1987); N. A. Dahl, "Paul and the Church at Corinth According to 1 Corinthians 1:10—4:21," in *Christian History and Interpretation: Studies Presented to John Knox,* ed. W. R. Farmer et al. (Cambridge: Cambridge University Press, 1976) 313-35; D. Georgi, *The Opponents of Paul in Second Corinthians* (Philadelphia: Fortress, 1986); J. J. Gunther, *St. Paul's Opponents and Their Background: A Study of Apocalyptic and Jewish Sectarian Teachings* (NovTSup 30; Leiden: E. J. Brill, 1973); S. J. Hafemann, " 'Self-Commendation' and Apostolic Legitimacy in 2 Corinthians: A Pauline Dialectic?" *NTS* 36 (1990) 66-88; idem, *Suffering and Ministry in the Spirit: Paul's Defense of His Ministry in II Corinthians 2:14—3:3* (Grand Rapids: Eerdmans, 1990); P. Marshall, *Enmity in*

Corinth: Social Conventions in Paul's Relations with the Corinthians (WUNT 2/23; Tübingen: Mohr Siebeck, 1987); W. A. Meeks, *The First Urban Christians: The Social World of the Apostle Paul* (New Haven, CT: Yale University Press, 1983); J. Murphy-O'Connor, *St. Paul's Corinth: Texts and Archaeology* (GNS 6; Wilmington, DE: Michael Glazier, 1983); idem, *The Theology of the Second Letter to the Corinthians* (NTT; Cambridge: Cambridge University Press, 1991); C. Newman, *Paul's Glory-Christology: Tradition and Rhetoric* (NovTSup 69; Leiden: E. J. Brill, 1992); C. K. Stockhausen, *Moses' Veil and the Glory of the New Covenant: The Exegetical Substructure of II Cor. 3:1—4:6* (Rome: Pontificio Instituto Biblico, 1989); J. L. Sumney, *Identifying Paul's Opponents: The Question of Method in 2 Corinthians* (JSNTSup 40, Sheffield; Sheffield Academic Press, 1990); G. Theissen, *The Social Setting of Pauline Christianity: Essays on Corinth* (Philadelphia: Fortress, 1982); B. W. Winter, *After Paul Left Corinth: The Influence of Secular Ethics and Social Change* (Grand Rapids: Eerdmans, 2001); F. Young and D. F. Ford, *Meaning and Truth in 2 Corinthians* (Grand Rapids: Eerdmans, 1987).   S. J. Hafemann

CORNELIUS. *See* BAPTISM III.

COVENANT, NEW COVENANT: PAUL, ACTS, HEBREWS

Covenant implies relationship, promise and expectation. Within the biblical tradition the covenant points to the unique relationship Yahweh established with the world through Israel, Yahweh's immutable and sacred pledge of faithfulness to this special relationship and Yahweh's legitimate expectation for his people to respond appropriately (i.e., to live as covenant people). The covenant thus plays a central, if not controlling, role in understanding Israel's identity, history and place within God's purposes.

Early Christianity also understood its relationship to God in covenantal terms. In and through the sacrificial death of Jesus (*see* Death of Christ), God had once and for all demonstrated his covenant faithfulness. For Christians to commemorate ritually Jesus' death as the beginning of a "new covenant" (1 Cor 11:25; cf. Mt 26:28; Mk 14:24; Lk 22:20) raises many questions about the historical and theological relationship between Judaism and Christianity.

1. Paul
2. Acts and Hebrews

1. Paul.

In the letters generally accepted as Pauline there are eight occurrences of covenant (*diathēkē*): Romans 9:4; 11:27; 1 Corinthians 11:25; 2 Corinthians 3:6, 14; Galatians 3:15, 17; 4:24 (cf. also Eph 2:12). Of special note among these are Galatians 4:24 (two covenants), 2 Corinthians 3:6 (the only use in Paul of new covenant, *kainē diathēkē*, apart from the eucharistic passage in 1 Cor 11:25) and 2 Corinthians 3:14, where we find the only reference to old covenant, *palaia diathēkē*.

The above references may indicate that covenant was not a dominant theme in Paul's theology, but there is little agreement on this issue. It may be argued that what is generally presumed need not always be explicitly stated. This would apply to covenant theology in the case of someone like Paul, who had been brought up in a Pharisaic tradition (*see* Jew, Paul the). Again, there may have been good reasons why Paul did not use the term more frequently, such as the possibility that his opponents used it and interpreted it differently.

In view of this and being conscious of how basic to NT interpretation are the themes "old and new covenant," we will proceed cautiously by looking at the instances of the term *covenant* in each of Paul's letters, as far as possible allowing the text to stand by itself without reading too much into it from other parts of the NT.

1.1. Galatians. Covenant theology is essentially a way of describing God's relationship with his people. Such a relationship does not exist in a vacuum but in time and place. Thus a question arises concerning the understanding of divine revelation and activity in history and, more specifically, in relation to the history of Israel. Paul's letter to the Galatians, though the story of Abraham is very much part of the discussion, does not give great significance to the history of Israel as such, at least not in the way that Romans does.

In Galatians 3:15-17 Paul, by means of a human example of covenant ratification, seeks to argue for the priority and inviolability of the Abrahamic covenant. Inasmuch as human wills cannot be added to or modified except by the testator, God's covenant with Abraham (*see* Abraham) into which Christians are incorporated in Christ, Abraham's "seed," is neither nullified nor added to by the later Sinai covenant, which is subsidiary to it.

Galatians 4:21-31 is a midrashic passage in which Paul may be taking up the arguments and the scriptural citations of his opponents. Hence some of the content may not be characteristically Pauline, though he doubtless shared elements of belief with other Jewish Christians and Jews. Although Paul speaks here of two covenants (*dyo diathēkē*), he explicitly describes his use of these two covenants as "allegory." Moreover, the impression one receives is not of one covenant being superseded by another, but rather of two parallel covenant options that possibly allegorically refer to two concurrent missions to Gentiles: (1) a law-observant one led by Paul's opponents and in opposition to (2) that of his own Gentile mission. The likelihood is that Paul intends the Sarah covenant to signify not Christianity (over against the Hagar covenant, i.e., Judaism) but rather the law-free Gentile mission. The entire discussion may be seen as two processes of begetting "children of God" (*see* Adoption, Sonship). In and through the Pauline mission the Galatians received the Spirit "by the hearing of faith"; no counter mission advocating circumcision or law observance for Gentiles could add to, or improve on, the standing of those in Christ by faith. They are exhorted to stand in the freedom of Christ (Gal 5:1). A law-observant mission for Gentiles is now treated as an anachronism.

This understanding of the passage releases us from any interpretation that sees Paul as referring to two sequential covenants, the first with Judaism succeeded by the second with Christianity. The problem with the passage, of course, is its midrashic content and Paul's use of allegory. Nevertheless, the important point Paul wishes to stress is that in the begetting of children, the type or quality of the children is dependent on the lineage of their parents. This is in keeping with the general meaning of covenant, which necessarily has at its heart some kind of continuity, even if it may not be an earthly continuity but only the theological continuity of those begotten by the word of God.

1.2. 1 and 2 Corinthians. First Corinthians 11:25 gives the rendering of Jesus' word at the Last Supper as "this cup is the new covenant [*kainē diathēkē*] in my blood." Luke also includes the adjective *new,* but there is a strong scholarly tradition that regards the Markan form of the words of institution as being the oldest (Jeremias). What is important for our study is whether something substantially different is intended by the addition of the word *new.* Maybe it is rather a drawing out of something already implicit in the death of Christ (*see* Lord's Supper).

In 2 Corinthians 3:6, in a section of the letter that has spawned numerous divergent interpretations, we find the only other reference to "new covenant" in Paul. In 2 Corinthians 3:14 we meet the sole reference in Paul to "old covenant" (*palaia diathēkē*). The unique occurrence in Paul of the adjectives *old* and *new* in relation to covenant within the Corinthian correspondence probably points to some factor at Corinth that gave particular significance to these designations. For instance, D. Georgi considers that Paul's opponents introduced the term *new covenant.* Christian theology has tended, in the past, to see in 2 Corinthians 3 a contrast between the new dispensation and the old. However warranted such a contrast may be, it is not clear that such a contrast was the immediate focus of Paul's thought when the letter was sent to the Corinthians. Commentators agree that Paul three times uses an a fortiori ("how much more") argument to contrast the amount of glory that attaches to two different ministries. Exodus 34 is clearly under discussion here, and it may also be true that midrashic interpretations of the passage lie behind Paul's comments. The introduction of Moses into the discussion has led some interpreters to find here a simple and explicit contrast between the old and new dispensations.

The context, however, indicates that Paul is grieved that the Corinthians are impressed by letters of commendation from rival missionaries. Paul does not wish to commend himself, nor does he need, like some, such letters of commendation. Paul's "letter" is the Corinthians, and the author of this letter is Christ; the apostle's letter is written with the Spirit of the living God, not with ink on papyrus (*see* Holy Spirit).

Paul has in mind Ezekiel 11:19 rather than Jeremiah 38:31 (LXX). S. J. Hafemann insists that the heart motif is drawn from the passage in Ezekiel, which includes the motif of the Spirit, missing entirely from the text in Jeremiah. He also notes that when we take as our starting point the actual passages Paul has in mind, we do not need to posit stark contrasts between ink and spirit, or stone and heart, or even to develop these into a full-blown antithesis between the dispensation of *law and the new dispensation of gospel. For Ezekiel the hope of the future work of God in the heart was not seen to alter the validity of the law. The comparison intended here is that Paul understood his ministry to his converts to be the eschatological counterpart to the giving of the law. Paul sees himself in the ministry of the gospel to be the Spirit-giver just as Moses was the lawgiver.

The relationship between the activity of God in Moses the lawgiver and in his new activity in Paul the Spirit-giver is best expressed in the *qal wahomer* ("how much more") type of argument. The movement is from something glorious to something even more glorious. In any case, when Paul says in 2 Corinthians 3:13 that Moses put a veil over his face so that the Israelites might not see *to telos tou katargoumenou* ("the end of the transitory [splendor?]"), he cannot possibly have been referring to the covenant as transitory, since *diathēkē* is a feminine noun, and the transitory splendor is indicated by a neuter participle.

The immediate issue in 2 Corinthians 3—4 is two concepts of Christian ministry. Paul is not addressing the Israelites at Sinai but the Corinthian Christians and his opponents. It is the latter whose thoughts have been dulled and over whose hearts lies a veil. We conclude therefore that despite a unique instance of "old covenant" in this passage, we are not warranted in reading into it the stark contrast of two antithetical ways of salvation, typical of some later Christian theology.

1.3. Romans. Covenantal relationship may be implied in Paul's addressing the Romans as *agapētoi theou* ("beloved [of God]") and *klētoi hagioi* ("called [to be] saints"). There are only two explicit references to covenant in the letter, Romans 9:4 and Romans 11:27. In Romans 9:4-5 Paul lists the covenant as one of the privileges belonging to Israel, along with sonship (*see* Adoption, Sonship), glory, the giving of the law, worship, the promises and the patriarchs. Whether or not we follow the singular reading of "covenant" in P[46] or the plural "covenants" as supported by the majority of manuscripts, it appears that here Paul has primarily in view the Abrahamic covenant. The focus is on the call and election of Abraham who in Romans 4 was depicted as a paradigm of the believer.

In Romans 11:27 Paul amalgamates two citations from Isaiah 59:12 and Isaiah 27:9 to produce a promise of future redemption for Israel despite its present refusal of the gospel: "this will be my covenant with them, when I take away their sins." The argument concerning the olive tree, and the theme of Romans 11 generally, is that despite the present enmity as regards the gospel, the election of Israel still stands. "God has not cast off Israel" (Rom 11:1, 7). The covenant is secure and Israel's election is not in doubt, for "the gifts and the call of God are irrevocable" (Rom 11:29).

Though we cannot insist that Paul's theology was covenantal in the sense that he explicitly used covenantal terminology, it may be that there existed at Rome a misunderstanding of the covenant with Israel arising from the success of Paul's Gentile mission (see Campbell). In view of this, Paul focused his thinking in Romans upon the theme of the covenant. Whereas in Galatians Christ is "the seed," in Romans the people of faith are "the seed," and there is continuity "from faith to faith," with the covenant being opened up to include Gentiles also.

1.4. Conclusion. R. D. Kaylor argues that the role of covenant functions at two levels in Paul's theology—at the levels of idea and of conviction. Though Paul may not always have had this distinction in mind, Kaylor holds, nevertheless, that the covenant as a conviction functions as a persistent presence and a dominant reality in Paul's life, work and thought.

Had Romans been written prior to Galatians, we might have argued that covenantal or *heilsgeschichtlich* (salvation historical) thinking is a relic of Paul's Jewish past, eventually to be cast aside. But the issue is very complicated. It centers upon the problem of what "descent from Abraham" means. In the case of Sarah—where discontinuity and covenant failure seemed inevitable, God miraculously intervened to provide an heir (cf. Is 54:1). This could be seen to indicate God's maintenance of earthly continuity (cf. Rom 4:19), but it may also be interpreted as the opposite—as the divine activity of the new creation. We should note, however, that in Sarah's case, it is divine creativity in relation to a people of promise. Only later in history did this creativity extend beyond Israel to Gentiles, and even then it will be through Jesus Christ—"of the seed of David."

The covenant concept indicates continuity in the divine purpose in history. It primarily depends on the faithfulness of God (e.g., Rom 3:21-26). But how can one give an adequate explanation of an earthly continuity in faith—Abraham—Isaac—Jesus? In Romans 9:21 Paul argues that it is not those of physical descent alone who are Abraham's children, it is those of physical descent who also share the faith of their father Abraham. Only in Romans 9:22-24 does Paul mention the inclusion of Gentiles. The Gentiles are included not in and of themselves but in and with the faithful in Israel (cf. Eph 2:11-22).

E. Käsemann rightly insists that right relationship and righteousness can only be ours insofar as God gives them to us anew every day (i.e., in faith). But does this mean that God's revelation comes to people only in a punctiliar manner, as "a bolt from the blue"? Or does revelation tend to occur in the context of a believing family or of a wider community of faith? The problem with the latter view is that history is not simply the record of divine achievement but also of human sinfulness. It was Jeremiah's despair at the latter that led him to posit a "new covenant."

Christians have tended to regard Jeremiah's new covenant as the clear basis for the fully developed Christian concept of a new dispensation. This is then frequently read back into Paul's writings via Hebrews. It is, however, by no means clear that "new covenant" was a term widely used in earliest Christianity. It is certainly reasonably correct to hold that "old covenant" was a rare concept up to the time of the death of Paul.

For various reasons, it seems, Paul did not frequently use explicit covenant terminology. Yet it does occur at important points in some of his writings. The frequency of "calling," "election" and related terms in 1 Corinthians, for example, may indicate it was significant in Paul's thought. But whatever we conclude from the above, it is clear that when Paul used the terms *old covenant* or *new covenant*, he did not include many of the associated ideas of a later, more developed Christianity. As W. D. Davies has reminded us, Jeremiah did not look forward to a new law but to "my law," and that the adjective *ḥādāš* in Jeremiah 31:31 can be applied to the new moon, which is simply the old moon in a new light.

[W. S. Campbell]

2. Acts and Hebrews.

2.1. Lexical Observations. The word *covenant* (*diathēkē*) appears only a handful of times in the later NT writings—twice in Acts (Acts 3:25; 7:8), seventeen times in Hebrews (Heb 7:22; 8:6, 9 [2x], 10; 9:4 [2x], 15 [2x], 16, 17, 20; 10:16, 29; 12:24; 13:20) and once in Revelation (Rev 11:19; *see* Revelation, Book of). The phrase "new covenant" (*kainē diathēkē*) appears even less frequently—three times in Hebrews (Heb 8:8 [quoting Jer 38:31 LXX; Jer 31:31 MT]; 9:15; 12:24). The numbers hardly swell when the constructions that bear the same semantic weight are added—"better covenant" (*kreittōn diathēkē*, Heb 7:22; 8:6), "eternal covenant" (*diathēke aiōniou*, Heb 13:20) and the reference to the "first covenant" (*prōtē [diathēkē]*, Heb 9:15; cf. Heb 9:1: *hē prōtē [diakaiomata]*), which implies a second or new covenant.

This relative lack of usage may come as a surprise, especially since the Christian Bible is divided into two "testaments" (Lat *testamentum*, "covenant") and since covenant is the "root metaphor" for Judaism (Segal, 4). However, the absence of extensive and explicit covenant language in early Christian writings could be due to several factors. (1) The identity and deeds of Jesus as a mediator eclipsed that which he mediated, the new covenant. The resultant contrast was not between an old Jewish covenant and a new Christian one but between the first covenant and Jesus. For earliest Christianity, christology thus became a way of speaking about the new covenant. (2) The identification of Jesus with the new covenant could have operated at such a deep level of shared Christian conviction that it rarely needed and consequently did not receive far-reaching elaboration in Christian writings. (3) At the same time that Christians attempted to show the theological inadequacy of their Jewish contemporaries, they also sought to ground their identity within the Jewish Scriptures. The drive to demonstrate historical and theological continuity with Jewish predecessors may well have tempered the Christian appropriation of new covenant language. Given these factors, what may surprise us most is that Christianity employed covenant language at all.

2.2. Old Testament Background. The Hebrew word *bĕrît* is most often translated as "covenant," although *bĕrît* possesses a much wider semantic range (see Barr). Of particular importance is the use of *bĕrît* to describe Yahweh's special relationship with his people.

Four covenants in particular take on a special

importance for the OT and Jewish tradition: God's unconditional covenant with the world through Noah (Gen 6:18; 9:8-16); the promise of land and posterity to Abraham (Gen 12:1-3; 15:18-19; 17:1-4), which was repeated to the ancestors Isaac, Jacob and Joseph (Gen 26:1-5; 28:13-15; 48-50 passim); the royal and eventually messianic covenant with David and his descendants (2 Sam 7:1-17; Ps 89; Is 9:2-7; *Pss. Sol.* 18—19); and the conditional covenant formed between God and Israel at Sinai (Ex 19—24; 34; Deut 5—28). Despite the multiplicity of covenants and any tension that may have existed between them, the Mosaic covenant is the one by which and through which all others should be understood (Childs, 419).

At the heart of the Mosaic covenant is Yahweh's choice of Israel to be his people and his promise to be Israel's God. For their part, Israel was to respond through obedience to the *law. Election and law thus gave shape to Jewish religious practice. Jews believed that they were elected by grace, that they were to respond to the historical expressions of Yahweh's mercy through obedience to the law, that Yahweh's blessing would follow obedience, that his judgment would follow their disobedience, and that forgiveness for their transgressions could be found through repentance and sacrifice. As E. P. Sanders has shown, this "pattern of religion" (what he terms "covenantal nomism") was a unifying feature of various Jewish groups from Deuteronomy onward.

The covenant is also a common thread running through the OT. Much of the Pentateuch seeks to elaborate and detail the covenant established through Moses. The historical books explain Israel's persistent difficulties as disobedience to the covenant. The prophets too see Israel's covenantal indiscretions as the chief reason for the punishment of exile. The prophets also describe the future in covenantal terms. God is going to reestablish the Mosaic covenant, variously depicted as a covenant of love (Hos 2:16-20) or peace (Ezek 34:25; 37:26) or as "everlasting" (Is 61:8; Jer 32:40; 50:5). The prophet Jeremiah even speaks of a "new covenant" that entails unprecedented forgiveness, reconciliation and re-creation (Jer 31:31-33). The prophets also universalize the particular covenant given to Israel: the future covenant includes the whole world (Is 42:6; 49:6-8). This eschatological and universal covenantal vision—a vision that

authentically reflects the covenants God forged with David, Israel, Abraham and Noah—provides the conceptual framework for understanding new covenant language in the NT.

2.3. Covenant in Acts. On several occasions Acts appeals to Israel's covenant history to identify the followers of the risen Jesus as the genuine heirs of the covenant. Acts accomplishes this without extensive reference to the word *diathēke* (which appears only twice: Acts 3:25; 7:8), using instead the word *promise* to show how Christianity identified itself as God's covenant people (Acts 1:4; 2:33, 39; 7:17; 13:23, 37; 23:21; 26:6).

Peter's sermons in Acts 2—3 illustrate this identification. Peter proclaims that the resurrection of Jesus fulfills the "oath" God swore to David (that one of David's descendants would inherit the throne, Acts 2:30; cf. Ps 132:11) and the promise made to Moses (that God would raise a prophet like him, Acts 3:22; cf. Deut 18:15-16). Further, repentance, baptism, forgiveness and the reception of the Holy Spirit confirm God's "promise" (Acts 2:39) and make believers "children of the prophets and of the covenant" (Acts 3:22-26).

Stephen's sermon points to how God's covenant with Abraham (Acts 7:2-8) epitomizes the history of Israel and thus of Christianity. God's covenant with Abraham is seen as a beginning in which partial realizations are interconnected with new beginnings; stories containing new promises are embedded within older, foundational narratives (Dahl). For example, Moses' prediction of a new prophet lies within the story of Abraham (Acts 7:37). Jesus, as the prophet like Moses, is thus placed squarely in Abrahamic covenant. The rhetorical force of this narrative suturing reaches a climax in the final appeal. Stephen derides his Jewish audience for being "stiff-necked" and "uncircumcised in the heart," a people who "always resist the Holy Spirit" (Acts 7:51). He does this precisely because they have failed to see the connection between Jesus and their own covenant history (Acts 7:52-53). The programmatic appeal to Abraham within the sermon thus locates those who follow Jesus as true Israel.

Paul's sermon at Pisidian Antioch explicitly links the message about Jesus with the covenant history of Israel. Israel's covenant history includes election, exodus, wilderness wanderings, conquest, the promise of land, the judges, the prophets and the office of the king (Acts 13:17-

21). This covenant now includes another, for out of David's posterity "God has brought to Israel a Savior, Jesus, as he promised" (Acts 13:24; cf. Acts 26:6). Indeed, Paul's gospel is that all of God's covenantal promises find their fulfillment in Jesus (Acts 13:33). Paul's sermon thus echoes the themes already heard in Peter's and Stephen's, namely, Christianity is the true heir of the Jewish covenant promises.

If Israel's covenant history could show that Jewish followers of Jesus were the genuine heirs, then an appeal to the covenant could also show that Gentiles, people traditionally thought to be outside the covenant, are (and always were?) also a part of it. This is best seen in the accounts of Cornelius's conversion (Acts 10:1—11:18) and the apostolic council (Acts 15:1-29). It took a heavenly vision and a thrice-repeated heavenly command to convince Peter too that it was not a covenantal breach to "associate or to visit with any one of another nation" (Acts 10:28). The dramatic coming of the Spirit (Acts 10:44-48), not unlike that at Pentecost, confirmed to him and the Jerusalem church that God's promise of forgiveness and salvation through Jesus was for everyone (Acts 11:17-18). The apostolic council (Acts 15) not only officially sanctioned Gentile inclusion but also clarified the role of circumcision and the law of Moses in salvation. Peter argued that God makes no distinction: all are saved "through the grace of the Lord Jesus" (Acts 15:11). James links Gentile inclusion with the covenant by citing a string of prophetic texts (Amos 9:11-12; Jer 12:15; Is 45:21). Not only are Christians the true covenant people, but also the covenant is seen now to include Gentiles.

In Acts the covenant promises given to Israel are never withdrawn. Israel is not rejected (Acts 13:46; 28:25-28 notwithstanding). It is better to speak of a separation within Israel, with the church (described within Acts as "believers," "brethren," "saints" or "disciples"; but see Church for a different reading of Luke's ecclesiology) as carrying on the unbroken line stemming from Abraham. There is no "new" Israel. The church is true Israel, the true covenant people of God. Acts does not emphasize the inadequacy of the Mosaic covenant (but cf. Acts 13:39; 15:10) but only the disobedience of the people. Indeed, Acts underscores the prophetic character of the covenant: its narrative and promissory linkages with the message and movement surrounding Jesus. Acts consistently portrays the community and the message as the intended destiny of Israel.

2.4. New Covenant in Hebrews. No NT document so extensively reflects upon the new covenant as does Hebrews. Although the book is full of covenantal imagery and terminology, it is the central section (Heb 4:14—10:15) that highlights the relationship between the old and new covenants.

The central section of Hebrews can be broken into two halves: the first half argues that Jesus was appointed a superior, eternal high priest after the order of Melchizedek (Heb 5:1-10; 7:1-28), while the second half (Heb 8:1—10:16) examines the character of Jesus' high-priestly ministry (Heb 8:1-6), the nature of the new covenant that he mediates (Heb 8:7-13) and the new covenant offering that his ministry includes (Heb 9:1—10:16). The author begins and ends this second section by quoting the new covenant prophecy of Jeremiah 31 (Heb 8:8-12; 10:16-17). Thus, against the backdrop of the OT priestly sacrificial system and within the horizon of hope generated by biblical prophecy, Hebrews presents a sustained, expositional argument that identifies Jesus as the superior, heavenly and sinless high priest, the mediator of a new and better covenant.

Numerous contrasts can be detected within the second half of this central section. The old covenant was earthly; the new covenant is heavenly (Heb 8:1; 9:1). The old covenant ministry was a copy and shadow (Heb 8:5; 9:23; 10:1); the new covenant is real (Heb 9:24) and true (Heb 8:2; 10:1). The old covenant featured human priests who were destined to die; the new covenant possesses a high priest who lives forever (Heb 9:28). The administration of a priest under the old covenant occurred according to the dictates of the law (Heb 8:4); the new covenant is directly and divinely administered (Heb 8:1-2). A priest under the old covenant had to offer sacrifice for his own sins (Heb 9:7); Jesus' sinlessness means that he did not offer sacrifice for himself (Heb 9:7). Under the old covenant, multiple priests had to enter repeatedly the sanctuary to offer numerous sacrifices (Heb 9:6-7, 25; 10:11); under the new covenant a single high priest, Jesus, enters the heavenly sanctuary once (through his death and resurrection) and offers a singular sacrifice once and for all time (Heb 9:12, 26; 10:10, 12). The old covenant contained the sacrificial blood of animals (Heb 9:18-22); under the new covenant, Jesus offers his own blood (Heb 9:12, 26). The efficacy of the old covenant offerings was limited (Heb 10:1-2); the efficacy of the new covenant sacrifice was definitive—there are no more offerings for sins. Under the old covenant the worshiper could not be perfected (Heb 9:9); under the new covenant a process of moral transformation has been enacted that will completely purify (Heb 9:14; 10:14).

S. G. Wilson reads these and other contrasts in Hebrews as a pointed effort to "denigrate" the old covenant and thus Judaism—an inference not necessarily demanded by the evidence. Wilson points to the pejorative connotation of such language as "weak and ineffectual," "shadow," "abolished," and "annulled" (see Wilson, 117-21). While the comparative character of much of Hebrews, especially of Hebrews 8:1—10:16, should not be denied, neither should the positive role of the first covenant be ignored. After all, the new covenant Jesus established was "concerned with the descendants of Abraham" (Heb 2:16).

Hebrews's valuation of the new covenant over the old was not a calculated anti-Jewish polemic, as Wilson would have us believe, but a natural consequence of the new covenant's eschatological character. The old covenant, tied to this "present age" (Heb 9:9), was seen as "growing old" and "passing away" (Heb 8:13); the new covenant excels because it is founded on "better promises" (Heb 8:6), those of resurrection life. The resulting contrast is not between something evil (old covenant/Judaism) and something good (new covenant/Christianity), but between something good (old covenant) and something better (new covenant). This is a very Jewish way of reasoning known as *qal wahomer,* the argument from the lesser to the greater: if the old covenant was good, then how much better will the new be? The argument of Hebrews about the relationship between the old and new covenants at this point is thus very similar to Paul's argument (2 Cor 3) about the two covenants.

The author of Hebrews uses spatial and temporal imagery to demonstrate the comparable yet provisionary character of the Sinai covenant. The elaborate analogies between the earthly and heavenly elements of the old and new covenants work to show similarity, while the strategic citations of Jeremiah 31 demonstrate that a new

day in salvation history has dawned.

2.5. Summary. Acts and Hebrews agree that God has demonstrated covenantal faithfulness in the death of his Son. However, each takes a different position on this new covenant's relationship to the old. Acts consistently presents those who follow Jesus as the true Israel, the genuine covenant people of God, a covenant newly shaped by the death and resurrection of Jesus. Working with a proof from prophecy/proclamation hermeneutic, Acts emphasizes continuity. Hebrews recognizes the legitimacy and efficacy of the first covenant; however, Hebrews argues that the "old" or "first" covenant pales in comparison with eschatological power of the new covenant.

[C. C. Newman]

See also ABRAHAM; HEBREWS, LETTER TO THE; ISRAEL; JEW, PAUL THE; LAW.

DPL: CIRCUMCISION; GENTILES; JUDAIZERS; MOSES; OLD TESTAMENT IN PAUL; OLIVE TREE; RESTORATION OF ISRAEL; WORKS OF THE LAW.

BIBLIOGRAPHY. J. B. Agus, "The Covenant Concept—Particularistic, Pluralistic or Futuristic," *JES* 18 (1981) 217-30; J. Barr, "Some Semantic Notes on the Covenant," in *Beiträge zur Alttestamentlichen Theologie: Festschrift für Walther Zimmerli,* ed. H. Donner (Göttingen: Vandenhoeck & Ruprecht, 1977) 23-38; C. K. Barrett, "The Allegory of Abraham, Sarah and Hagar in the Argument of Galatians," in *Essays on Paul* (London: SPCK, 1982) 154-69; R. T. Beckwith, "The Unity and Diversity of God's Covenants," *TynB* 38 (1987) 93-118; F. F. Bruce, "The People of God," in *New Testament Development of Old Testament Themes* (Grand Rapids: Eerdmans, 1968) 51-67; W. S. Campbell, *Paul's Gospel in an Intercultural Context: Jew and Gentile in the Letter to the Romans* (Frankfurt: Peter Lang, 1991); B. S. Childs, *Biblical Theology of the Old and New Testaments: Theological Reflection on the Christian Bible* (Philadelphia: Fortress, 1993); J. Cott, "The Biblical Problem of Election," *JES* 21 (1984) 199-228; N. A. Dahl, "The Story of Abraham in Luke-Acts," in *Studies in Luke-Acts,* ed. L. E. Keck and J. L. Martyn (London: SPCK, 1966) 139-58; W. D. Davies, "Paul and the People of Israel," *NTS* 24 (1978) 4-39; J. D. G. Dunn, *The Partings of the Ways: Between Christianity and Judaism and Their Significance for the Character of Christianity* (London: SCM; Philadelphia: Trinity Press International, 1991); idem, "The Theology of Galatians," in *Pauline Theology*, vol. 1, ed. J. M. Bassler (Minneapolis: Fortress, 1991) 160-79; L. Gaston, *Paul and the Torah* (Vancouver: University of British Columbia, 1987); D. Georgi, *The Opponents of Paul in Second Corinthians* (Philadelphia: Fortress, 1986); S. J. Hafemann, *Suffering and the Spirit* (WUNT 2.19; Tübingen: Mohr Siebeck, 1986); G. W. Hansen, *Abraham in Galatians: Epistolary and Rhetorical Contexts* (JSNTSup 29; Sheffield: JSOT, 1989); R. B. Hays, *Echoes of Scripture in the Letters of Paul* (New Haven, CT: Yale University Press, 1989); M. D. Hooker, "Paul and Covenantal Nomism," in *Paul and Paulinism: Essays in Honor of C. K. Barrett*, ed. M. D. Hooker and S. G. Wilson (London: SPCK, 1982) 47-56; J. J. Hughes, "Hebrews 9:15ff. and Galatians 3:15ff.: A Study in Covenant Practice and Procedure," *NovT* (1979) 27-96; J. Jeremias, *The Eucharistic Words of Jesus* (Philadelphia: Fortress, 1977); R. D. Kaylor, *Paul's Covenant Community: Jew and Gentile in Romans* (Atlanta: John Knox, 1988); S. Lehne, *The New Covenant in Hebrews* (JSNTSup 44; Sheffield: JSOT, 1990); R. P. Martin, *2 Corinthians* (WBC 40; Dallas: Word, 1986); J. L. Martyn, "The Covenants of Hagar and Sarah," in *Faith and History: Essays in Honor of Paul W. Meyer*, ed. J. T. Carroll et al. (Atlanta: Scholars Press, 1991) 160-92; idem, "Events in Galatia: Modified Covenantal Nomism Versus God's Invasion of the Cosmos in the Singular Gospel," in *Pauline Theology*, vol 1., ed. J. M. Bassler (Minneapolis: Fortress, 1991) 160-79; idem, "A Law Observant Mission to Gentiles: The Background of Galatians," *SJT* 38 (1985) 307-24; E. P. Sanders, *Paul* (Oxford: Oxford University Press, 1991); idem, *Paul and Palestinian Judaism: A Comparison of Patterns of Religions* (Philadelphia: Fortress, 1977); A. F. Segal, *Rebecca's Children: Judaism and Christianity in the Roman World* (Cambridge, MA: Harvard University Press, 1986); S. G. Wilson, *Related Strangers: Jews and Christians 70-170 CE* (Minneapolis: Fortress, 1995); N. T. Wright, *The Climax of the Covenant: Christ and the Law in Pauline Theology* (Edinburgh: T & T Clark, 1991).   W. S. Campbell and C. C. Newman

COVENANTAL NOMISM. *See* JUSTIFICATION; LAW II.

CREATION, NEW CREATION: PAUL

"New creation," *kainē ktisis*, is an expression Paul uses in 2 Corinthians 5:17 and Galatians 6:15. It is closely related to the expression "new human[ity]," *kainos anthrōpos*, in Ephesians 2:15, 4:23-24 and Colossians 3:9-10. This expression is not unique to Paul. It, and ideas associated with it, occur in several literary texts and traditions of Second Temple Judaism.

1. Need for a New Creation
2. Scope of the New Creation
3. Characteristics of the New Creation

1. Need for a New Creation.

Many early Jewish interpreters believed that God had created a good world through the mediation of Wisdom (Prov 8:22-31; Sir 24; Wis 7:22—8:1). Paul identified this Wisdom with Jesus Christ (1 Cor 1:17-25; Col 1:15-20). Paul also recognized that sin damages this good creation by subjecting humankind to death (Rom 5:12-14; 1 Cor 15:21-22; see *4 Ezra* 7:116-31; *2 Apoc. Bar.* 54:13-19) and the natural world to decay (Rom 8:19-22; see *4 Ezra* 7:11-14; *2 Apoc. Bar.* 56:6-10). Disillusionment with the present state of affairs led many early Jewish interpreters to expect a new creation in a new age to come when the entire creation would be liberated from futility and transformed into its original goodness (e.g., *4 Ezra* 7:75; *2 Apoc. Bar.* 73-74). For Paul, this age would accompany the parousia, or future appearance, of Jesus (Rom 8:18; Eph 1:9-10; Col 3:1-4; *see* Eschatology).

2. Scope of the New Creation.

In 2 Corinthians 5:17 Paul suggests that this future reality is already present. There are three options for explaining precisely how the new creation is to be understood: through individual converts, through the community of faith or through the cosmos as a whole. Each option reflects a different opinion about which particular early Jewish texts and traditions were foremost in Paul's mind when he referred to the new creation.

2.1. Converts. In *Genesis Rabbah* 39.4, a Gentile convert to Judaism is regarded as a new creation: "Whoever brings a heathen near to God and converts him [or her] is as though he had created him [or her]." Similarly, in the Jewish tale of Joseph and Asenath, a heavenly man says to Asenath, upon her conversion to Judaism, "you will be renewed and formed anew" (*Jos. and As.* 15:4). It is possible that Paul, like his Jewish counterparts, believed the convert to Christ to be a new creation.

2.2. Community of Faith. In Isaiah 65:17-19 the

author parallels a cosmic re-creation with the re-creation of Jerusalem and its inhabitants: "For I am about to create new heavens and a new earth . . . for I am about to create Jerusalem as a joy, and its people as a delight." In Isaiah 66:22-23 the author develops this thought further when he predicts that within this new creation, Israel will experience the influx of Gentiles to worship God.

Both of these elements—the re-creation of a new community of believers and the influx of Gentiles—underlie two of the Pauline passages that contain references to the new creation or new humanity. In both passages the new creation or new humanity is a communal reality. In Galatians 6:15-16 Paul even parallels the new creation with a specific community, "the Israel of God." In Ephesians 2:14-16 the new humanity is composed of communities rather than individuals: "in his flesh he has made both groups into one . . . that he might create in himself one new humanity in place of the two."

Concomitantly, in both passages Gentiles are the community included alongside Jews. In Galatians 6:15 the new creation is a community in which "neither circumcision nor uncircumcision is anything." In Ephesians 2:11-22 (and Col 3:11) the new humanity is composed of Jews as well as Gentiles "who once were far off" (see Is 57:19). The church, therefore, is a new Israel where Jews and Gentiles are united in peace.

2.3. Cosmos. Many apocalyptic Jewish interpreters developed in detail the anticipation of the new heavens and new earth introduced by Isaiah 56—66. The emphases of their developments varied, including: the restoration of Israel (*Jub.* 4:26; *1 Enoch* 45:4-5), the transformation of the righteous in a final resurrection (*2 Apoc. Bar.* 51:1-16), the liberation of the natural world (*1 Enoch* 51:4-5) and the return of the creation to its original state of goodness (*2 Apoc. Bar.* 73-74). The persistent conviction of the apocalyptic perspective is that the new age to come will be decidedly different from—and qualitatively better than—the present evil age.

Paul reflects this apocalyptic context when, in 2 Corinthians 5:17-18, he depicts a radical disjuncture between "old things" *(ta archaia)* and "new things" *(kaina).* Such words suggest much more than individual transformation. Indeed, Paul argues that God reconciled "all things" *(ta panta)* through Christ, including presumably the entire natural world. If 2 Corinthians 5:16-17

provides a glimpse of the beginning of the new creation, other passages presage the completion of the new creation. According to Romans 8:18-25, "the creation itself will be set free from its bondage to decay" (Rom 8:21), while, according to Ephesians 1:10, "all things . . . things in heaven and things on earth" will be gathered up in Christ (see 1 Cor 15:24-28).

It is not possible to choose definitively between these options. Nor is it necessary, for all three mutually illuminate each other. The convert, as part of a community of faith, enters the cosmic drama of re-creation that God inaugurated at the resurrection of Jesus Christ and will bring to completion at the parousia (*see* Eschatology).

3. Characteristics of the New Creation.
A study of the Pauline contexts of the expressions *new creation* and *new humanity* reveals the two quintessential values that characterize the community of faith. By embodying these values, this community anticipates the final cosmic restoration of creation's goodness.

3.1. Reconciliation. The key concept that accompanies Paul's references to the new creation or new humanity is reconciliation. The dominant theme of 2 Corinthians 5:17-21 is that believers, who have been reconciled to God, must continue by the apostolic ministry of proclamation and witness to bear testimony to the reconciliation of the world to God, which God inaugurated through Jesus. The thrust of Galatians 6:15, Ephesians 2:11-22 and Colossians 3:10-11 is that the new creation and new humanity come about only when peoples once divided are seen to be reconciled in Christ.

3.2. Rejection of Worldly Standards. Reconciliation can occur only when believers cease living and judging others according to worldly standards. The presence of a new creation means that new standards of unity and peace replace old standards of judgment and divisiveness. The racial division of Jew and Gentile, in particular, is based upon an obsolete criterion: "For neither circumcision nor uncircumcision is anything; but a new creation is everything!" (Gal 6:15; cf. Eph 2:11-22). Similarly, individual rivalry has no place in the new creation. Paul's reference to "new creation" in 2 Corinthians 5:17 is polemical; with it he confronts the faulty standards of his opponents at Corinth, who judge him according to worldly standards such as rhetorical ability and physical strength (e.g., 2 Cor 10:1-11). In the new creation, contends Paul, no one is judged "from a human point of view," for even Christ is no longer judged by human standards (2 Cor 5:16). These new standards apply not only to ethnic groups or to church leaders but also to every believer who participates in the new humanity. He or she must put away conduct that characterizes the "old humanity," such as greed, slander and abuse (Col 3:5-9; Eph 4:25-30), and put on the new humanity, "which is being renewed in knowledge according to the image of its creator," that is, which is being restored to its original goodness (Col 3:10; see Gen 1:26). This new humanity is characterized by compassion, patience, truthfulness (Col 3:12-17; Eph 4:23-24, 32) and, once again, by reconciliation of peoples once hostile to one another (Col 3:11).

See also ADAM AND CHRIST; ESCHATOLOGY.

DPL: CENTER OF PAUL'S THEOLOGY; NEW NATURE AND OLD NATURE; PEACE, RECONCILIATION; RESTORATION OF ISRAEL; WORLD, COSMOLOGY.

BIBLIOGRAPHY. N. A. Dahl, "Christ, Creation, and the Church," in *The Background of the New Testament and Its Eschatology,* ed. W. D. Davies and D. Daube (Cambridge: Cambridge University Press, 1956) 422-43; W. D. Davies, *Paul and Rabbinic Judaism* (4th ed.; Philadelphia: Fortress, 1980) 36-57, 119-31; J. D. M. Derrett, "New Creation: Qumran, Paul, the Church, and Jesus," *RevQ* 13 (1988) 597-608; V. P. Furnish, *2 Corinthians* (AB 32A; Garden City, NY: Doubleday, 1984) 309-16, 329-33; G. W. H. Lampe, "The New Testament Doctrine of *Ktisis,*" *SJT* 17 (1964) 449-62; M. Parsons, "The New Creation," *ExpT* 99 (1987) 3-4; L. M. Russell, "Partnership in New Creation," *ABQ* 3 (1984) 161-71; L. H. Taylor, *The New Creation: A Study of the Pauline Doctrines of Creation, Innocence, Sin and Redemption* (New York: Pageant, 1958). J. R. Levison

CREEDS. *See* WORSHIP.

CRUCIFIXION. *See* DEATH OF CHRIST I; TRIAL OF JESUS.

D

DAMASCUS ROAD EXPERIENCE. *See* Conversion and Call of Paul.

DAVID'S SON. *See* Son of David.

DAVIDIC KING. *See* Christ; Son of David.

DAY OF THE LORD. *See* Eschatology II; Judgment.

DEAD SEA SCROLLS

In late 1946 or early 1947 a Bedouin shepherd, Muhammed edh-Dhib, followed a stray into a cave along the shores of the Dead Sea and so chanced upon the first of a group of ancient manuscripts that have since revolutionized biblical studies and the study of ancient Judaism. Seven substantial scrolls emerged from that cave, copies of biblical and extrabiblical writings alike. They were only the beginning. Following the initial discovery, Bedouins and scholars competed to explore the caves of the region in hopes of new manuscript finds. After a search of hundreds of caves, eleven eventually yielded literary texts, now known as the Dead Sea Scrolls (DSS). Approximately 875 generally fragmentary manuscripts came to light in the course of these explorations. The nearby site of Qumran, hitherto regarded as an ancient fortress, was also excavated during five campaigns between 1952 and 1956, for scholars suspected that the site was connected to the caves and the scrolls.

Publication of the discoveries was comparatively rapid at first. Six of the seven major scrolls from the site of the first discovery, now known as cave 1, were completely published within seven years. The seventh, the *Genesis Apocryphon,* appeared in a partial edition in 1956, and much more of the work has since been deciphered and published in preliminary form. The great bulk of the discoveries were early consigned to an international editorial team of seven scholars from Europe and the United States. This team succeeded in sorting most of the fragments and published some of the DSS in a series of volumes, *Discoveries in the Judaean Desert* (DJD; "*of Jordan*" appears on some volumes). Five volumes of DJD appeared in the decade spanning the late 1950s to the late 1960s. In the decades that followed, however, even with occasional preliminary editions, the rate of publication slowed to a crawl. Volume 6 of the series appeared in 1977, nine years after volume 5; volume 7 had to wait another five years, and volume 8 seven more, only appearing in 1989. By 1991, estimates of the percentage of material that remained unpublished ranged between 40 and 60 percent. The reasons for failure to publish so much vital material after forty years were various, some legitimate (the fragmentary condition of the scrolls; deaths of original team members; the demands of academic responsibilities), but others suggesting scandalous scholarly conduct. The late 1980s, in particular, were marred by growing scholarly wrangling over the slow pace of publication and rights of access to the unpublished materials.

In December 1991, pressured by bootleg editions of the scrolls that had begun to appear and the Huntington Library's decision to open its virtually complete collection of photographs of the unpublished texts to all qualified scholars, the Israel Antiquities Authority (IAA) decided to lift restrictions. Henceforth it would allow people to study the unpublished manuscripts and, within certain limits, publish the results of their research. At about the same time, the IAA and the new editor-in-chief of the publication project, E. Tov, moved to expand the number of scholars working on the texts for official publication in the DJD series. Over sixty scholars were now assigned texts. The augmented team soon began to publish the scrolls at a pace much faster than ever before in the history of the project. Some twenty additional volumes of DJD appeared between 1994 and early 2000. As a result of these changes, what had been a stagnant field of research from 1968 to 1990 became a swirl of scholarly activity.

1. Description of Contents
2. Interpretation of the Finds
3. The Dead Sea Scrolls and the New Testament

1. Description of Contents.

1.1. Biblical Materials. The biblical scrolls recovered from the caves number about 225. They include copies of every book of the Hebrew Bible, with the exception of the book of Esther. The most frequently attested books are Genesis, Exodus, Deuteronomy, Isaiah and Psalms—this last book numbering some thirty-five copies.

The biblical scrolls from Qumran have had a tremendous impact on the study of the Hebrew Bible with regard to textual criticism and with regard to what was once known as higher criticism. Their importance for textual criticism is obvious when one considers that prior to their discovery the oldest complete manuscripts of the Hebrew Bible dated from the tenth century A.D. The DSS lifted the curtain to a period over a millennium earlier in the formation of the text.

With regard to matters of higher criticism, perhaps a discussion of the manuscript known as 11QPs^a can serve as a typical example of the rich applications the scrolls make possible. It contains forty-one of the biblical psalms as well as apocryphal Psalms 150, 154 and 155. 11QPs^a also embraces three hitherto unknown psalms, a portion of Ecclesiasticus 51, and a ten-line prose supplement enumerating the total of David's writings (given as 3,600). The date of composition for the three unknown psalms is disputed by scholars, but is probably the late Persian or early Hellenistic period. The scroll's text of Ecclesiasticus 51 differs markedly from the form previously familiar from the Septuagint and other early versions. Its presence in a collection attributed entirely to David is instructive, serving as a premier example of the tendency in Second Temple Judaism to ascribe poetic writings of unknown authorship to David. Concomitantly, its inclusion in 11QPs^a appears to confirm the long-held suspicion that Jesus ben Sirach did not write the fifty-first chapter of Ecclesiasticus.

But this manuscript of the book of Psalms raises much broader issues. The order of the psalms in 11QPs^a differs significantly from the order in the traditional or Masoretic Text. At least once (Ps 145), the Qumran scroll evidences a different form of a canonical psalm. Certain groupings of psalms, such as the Songs of Ascent and the Passover Hallel—viewed as units by the Masoretic Text—appear scattered throughout the Qumran text. And 11QPs^a is not an isolated example. Half a dozen other non-Masoretic psalters are included among the DSS. These facts suggest that the Psalter as we know it was only one variant in use among the Jews at the time of Jesus. Taken together with other similar evidence, 11QPs^a tends to suggest that the third division of the canon, the Writings, was still in flux at the time. Indeed, the Qumran biblical scrolls have reopened study of the formative process of the entire canon. Variant literary editions of Exodus, Numbers, Jeremiah, Psalms and numerous other books seem to show that the writings we consider canonical grew and assumed new forms for a considerable period after the traditional time of their composition. Other writings that did not become part of the canon for later Judaism or Christianity quite likely were such for some groups of Second Temple Jews.

1.2. Nonbiblical Materials. The vast majority of manuscripts from the caves near Qumran are nonbiblical texts. Many of these writings were unknown prior to the discoveries. Others were familiar to scholars only by name or through short quotations in ancient literature. Since the diversity of the scrolls does not lend itself to a single classificatory scheme, what follows is organized according to these broad categories: major (i.e., lengthy) texts, interpretive texts, apocryphal and pseudepigraphic texts, liturgical texts, legal texts, and "magical" and calendrical texts.

1.2.1. Major Texts.

Damascus Document (CD). This work, once known as the Zadokite Fragments, first came to light long before the discovery of the Qumran texts. At the end of the nineteenth century, S. Schechter discovered two fragmentary exemplars deposited in the genizah of a Karaite synagogue in Fustat, the old city of Cairo. To these medieval manuscripts the DSS have added extensive fragments of eight copies of the *Damascus Document* from Qumran cave 4 (4Q266-273) and tiny fragments of two other copies of the work from caves 5 and 6.

Taken as a whole, the twelve copies represent two versions, or recensions, conventionally designated A and B. Recension A is by far the better attested. When dealing with either recension, scholars usually subdivide the work into two approximate halves according to content: the Admonition and the Laws. The term *admonition* is something of a misnomer, for one can isolate at least four separate addresses or "sermons" within this section. The Admonition encompasses stylized historical summaries that prefer ciphers to actual names when designating the actors in the drama. So one finds mention of a "Teacher of Righteousness," a "Spouter of Lies" and an "Interpreter of the Law." An enemy group, the "Seekers After Smooth Things," is also prominent. The thrust of the Admonition is to compare two periods of God's wrath: the first at the time of Nebuchadnezzar (586 B.C.) and the second at the time of the Roman invasion of Palestine (63 B.C.). The point of the comparison is to proclaim a typological parallel: just as apostasy in the first instance led to destruction and exile for Israel, so too in the Roman period, disaster of an even greater magnitude lies ahead—unless the people repent and embrace the text's legal perspectives.

These perspectives, the laws, constitute halakic regulations for a communal life lived out in "camps," but their contents differ somewhat from manuscript to manuscript. No single "canonical" form of the *Damascus Document* ever developed. Rather, different leaders of the movement evidently modified a central core to fit their own needs. Most telling in this regard is the substantial overlap between the legal portions of the *Damascus Document* and the *Rule of the Community*. In some instances manuscripts of these two works contain identical laws, suggesting that one and the same sectarian group used both. This inference gains additional support from the fact that other Qumran writings also overlap similarly (e.g., *Halakha A* [4Q251], *Serekh-Damascus* [4Q265] and *4QMMT* [4Q394-399] all overlap one another). The oft-repeated hypothesis that a stricter branch of the sect lived at Qumran and followed the *Rule of the Community*, while a less disciplined, broader movement living throughout Palestine was regulated by the *Damascus Document,* no longer seems viable.

The Rule of the Community (1QS). Among the initial discoveries from cave 1 was a virtually complete copy of the writing variously termed the *Rule of the Community, Discipline Scroll* or *Manual of Discipline.* The *Rule of the Community* (its actual, ancient Hebrew designation, found inscribed on a scroll tab) describes sundry regulations for the communal life of a group calling itself the *Yahad.* They are to share all meals, pool their property and follow a very strict regimen of ritual purity. Scholars early recognized that this is a work whose form, as with the *Damascus Document,* is the result of a process of editing and redaction. Recent publication of the fragments of eleven copies of the *Rule of the Community* from cave 4 (4Q255-264a) have confirmed this understanding and afford insight into the redactional process by which the work grew. In turn, recognition of the literary growth pattern carries historical implications. It now appears that the movement behind the text was organized at first in semidemocratic fashion. "The Many" (*hārabbi'm*), or general membership, had much of the power to make decisions about policy and finances. At a certain juncture a group called the Sons of Zadok (presumably related, whether actually or mythically, to the Zadokite priesthood) usurped this power. The Many was thereafter governed by a priestly oligarchy. Why and when this change took place is unknown. The cave 4 copies also show that, as with the *Damascus Document,* no canonical version of the *Rule of the Community* ever displaced all rivals. Instead, earlier versions continued to be recopied even after more developed ones had come on the scene. Presumably, the unavailability of developed forms at the time a copy was needed explains the scribal decision to recopy older ones. Such scarcity was common in book cultures of Greco-Roman times.

In addition to the principal text, the cave 1 manuscript included two so-called appendices. The first, known as the *Rule of the Congregation* or *Serekh ha-edah* (1QSa/1Q28a), is two columns long and deals with the "last days." The work's actual connection with the principal text is unclear, for although it originally belonged to the same scroll, it was written by another scribe and differs in concept and terminology. The *Rule of the Congregation* legislates for the education of children raised in the community, the stages of progression within the movement according to age and ability, and procedures for the communal meal presided over by priests and a so-called messiah of Israel. Recently, five additional copies of the *Rule of the Congregation* have been identified, written in a cryptic script on papyrus (4Q249a-249e). The second appendix, the *Rule of Benediction* (1QSb/1Q28b), is very poorly preserved. Several blessings pronounced by the "wise leader" over the community, the priests and the prince make up its content. As with the *Rule of the Congregation*, this second appendix has a very pronounced eschatological setting.

The War Scroll (1QM). This scroll consists of nineteen badly deteriorated columns. It was originally somewhat longer, but how much is now impossible to determine. The work is ostensibly a manual to guide the self-styled "Sons of Light" in a final eschatological war, in which they are to face, and eventually vanquish, the "Sons of Darkness." Nevertheless, the text is essentially a theological, not a military, composition.

Among the topics the *War Scroll* treats are: preliminary preparations for the war; rules for the sounding and inscription of trumpets used to guide the course of the battle; the dimensions and inscriptions of shields and standards used; the battle array, including who may and may not participate in the conflict; the role of the priests and Levites; and the ebb and flow of the final battle against the *Kittîm* (probably the Romans).

Most scholars agree that the weapons and tactics that the scroll describes suggest Roman rather than Greek military strategy. If so, these descriptions enable the dating of the text in the form we have it to be narrowed to the later decades of the first century B.C. But literary analysis further suggests that the text as we now have it is considerably expanded and reworked from an earlier version or versions, perhaps utilizing as its kernel a work based on Daniel 11:40—12:3. This literary hypothesis finds some support in fragments of six exemplars of the *War Scroll* discovered in cave 4. Some of these fragments reveal a much shorter version of the work and otherwise differ markedly from the cave 1 manuscript.

A work intimately related to the *War Scroll*, even perhaps part of one recension of it, is *Sefer ha-Milhamah*. Two copies have survived, 4Q285 and 11Q14. One fragment of this writing has been interpreted to say that a messianic figure

known from several of the DSS, the "Prince of the Congregation," will be put to death by his enemies. He would then be a sort of dying messiah. A more probable interpretation of the ambiguous Hebrew phrase in question is that the Prince of the Congregation puts an enemy king to death.

The Hymns (1QH^a). The composition known as the *Hymns*, or 1QHodayot, comprises in the *editio princeps* eighteen partial columns and sixty-six numbered fragments. Subsequent to that original edition, scholars identified two additional fragments. Because none of the columns is complete, students of the text have proposed differing divisions and, consequently, competing reckonings as to the number of hymns 1QH^a contains. Six manuscripts from cave 4 further complicate the situation. While these copies fill in lacunae in the manuscript from cave 1, they also prove that the order of hymns was somewhat variable. Indeed, the cave 4 copies tend to support literary analysis arguing that more than one version of the work existed. At the core, and originally circulating as a self-contained book, were some eight columns of hymns authored by the Teacher of Righteousness. These were the so-called *Teacher Hymns*. Subsequent leaders of the movement added hymns fore and aft, sometimes deriving these added hymns from sources that have also come down to us separately. The added hymns are conventionally known as *Community Hymns*.

Most of the hymns begin either "I thank thee, Lord," or "Blessed art thou, O Lord." Many scholars have tried to fit them into a model known to biblical form critics as "psalms of individual thanksgiving." Deviations from the biblical patterns, however, are sufficient to make the genre of these compositions a moot point. Many of the hymns have nothing to do with thanksgiving, or even lament, but are more like a discourse. Also debated is the question of what function(s) the writings served within the movement(s) that produced or employed them. Another important aspect of the hymns is their midway position between the psalmic literature of the Hebrew Bible and that of later Judaism, including the NT.

One of the hymns added to the core of the *Teacher Hymns* (at 1QH^a 25:35—26:10) survived only in fragmentary form but has recently been the subject of considerable research. The cave 4 materials make it possible to reconstruct about half of the hymn. The writer portrays a remarkable figure who asks, "Who is like me among the angels?" (Heb 'ēlîm, lit. "gods"), echoing in daring fashion the biblical question addressed to God, "Who is like you among the angels?" He also asks, "Who is like me for lack of evil? Does any compare to me?" and (alluding to the Servant Songs of Isaiah) "Who has been contemptuously despised like me?" Though much research remains to be done on this "Hymn of the Exalted One," it bears obvious comparison to NT statements about Jesus and to the NT use of divine language from the OT to describe him. Moreover, the figure is, like the Jesus of Hebrews, seated on a throne at the right hand of God.

The Temple Scroll. Known in three copies from cave 11 and one or two from cave 4, the principal copy of the *Temple Scroll* (11QTemple; also 11QTorah) is the longest of the surviving DSS. Unwound, this copy of the scroll is twenty-eight feet from beginning to end. The *Temple Scroll* is a melange of biblical and extrabiblical ordinances and descriptions concerned with a temple, its services and its festivals. The first well-preserved columns describe the temple building with its key installations. From there the text proceeds to detail various festivals, sacrifices and procedures, the temple courtyards and laws of impurity, finishing with extracts from the Deuteronomic Code (Deut 12—26). Among the most striking literary features of the scroll is the change of all biblical quotations attributed to Moses from third to first person. This well-calculated change has the effect of making Moses seem at once the author and addressee of the text, thus imbuing its contents with Mosaic authority.

The New Jerusalem Text. Although not well enough preserved to be considered major, a text that is related to the *Temple Scroll* may conveniently be brought into the discussion here. This is the Aramaic writing designated the *New Jerusalem,* which is attested by copies from caves 1, 2, 4, 5 and 11. The author presents the work as a vision in which he ("Ezekiel"?) is led about a future Jerusalem by an angel and shown various buildings, streets and gates; in each case measurements in cubits and reeds are provided. The description is very schematic, and many measurements are unrealistically large. Evidently inspired by Ezekiel 48:16-17, the city described is approximately 18 by 13 miles in size. Numerous measurements for features of the city and its

temple are identical to those of the *Temple Scroll,* suggesting that the *New Jerusalem* was a source for that work.

The Copper Scroll (3Q15). Perhaps no DSS has occasioned greater difficulties in its reading and interpretation than the *Copper Scroll.* This is the only work inscribed on copper, and unlike all but a few it was composed in early Mishnaic Hebrew rather than in archaizing Late Biblical Hebrew. The twelve columns consist of a series of sixty-four or sixty-five topographic descriptions, or toponymns, often followed by the instruction to dig a given depth. Then follows a specified weight of bullion or amount of money, precious vessels or the like. The *Copper Scroll,* in other words, is a list of treasure trove and a guide to the hiding places. At first glance the amounts of treasure seem incredible; estimates in terms of modern value exceed one hundred million dollars.

Interpretations of this document include the original editor Milik's theses that it represents either a "folkloristic treasure trove" or the work of a madman, in either case having no connection to the Qumran movement. For Milik the *Copper Scroll* was only coincidentally found along with the group's materials in cave 3, being removed somewhat from the other deposits of that cave. His approach requires two independent deposits. The first deposit in cave 3 occurred about A.D. 70, when all the other DSS were hidden in the caves. The *Copper Scroll* belonged to a putative second deposit made around A.D. 100. Although popular in the 1950s and 1960s, Milik's views can claim no significant support today. Most scholars now believe that the scroll was placed in the cave at the same time as all the others. They further deny that the scroll is a work of imagination; its genre is documentary, that of "list," a common genre in Greco-Roman times. The contents described in the scroll are therefore of an actual treasure, probably associated with the Jerusalem temple. Only the connection with a major institution of Jewish society can explain the vast sum of treasure. Some argue that the treasure was taken from Herod's temple, others that it was intended for Herod's temple. Accordingly, the *Copper Scroll* occupies a central position in arguments about who wrote the Dead Sea Scrolls.

1.2.2. Interpretive Texts.

Pesharim. Among the most fascinating of the Hebrew texts discovered in the caves are those known as the pesharim (*pĕšārîm,* pl. of *pešer,* meaning "solution" or "interpretation"). These are usually grouped into two categories—thematic and continuous. Thematic pesharim consist of selected portions of the Bible with interpretive comments and are organized around a central theme or idea. In contrast, continuous pesharim comment *seriatim* on a portion of the Bible, usually the prophets, but sometimes so-called prophetic psalms. At least fifteen, perhaps eighteen, texts belonging to this latter category have been identified.

The pesharim purport to be mysterious explications of divine truth from Scripture, a truth revealed only to the author and his group. None of these commentaries is concerned with the literal sense of the text; instead, they use metaphor, paronomasia and development of key words or phrases to unmask the hidden significance of a given biblical portion. The most complete of the pesharim is the commentary on Habakkuk. This pesher preserves thirteen almost complete columns, providing the text of Habakkuk along with commentary. The form of the book of Habakkuk to which it witnesses is often different from that of the Masoretic Text.

Also relatively complete is the pesher designated 4Q171, which preserves the text of Psalms 37:7-40; Psalm 45:1-2 and possibly Psalm 60:8-9. Psalm 37 is a psalm of personal tribulation, offering the righteous hope in spite of the evident prosperity of the wicked. It thus fits perfectly the literary requirements for the author of the pesher, who interprets the tribulation in terms of his community's troubles, enemies and approaching eschatological justification.

From a historical vantagepoint, the pesher on Nahum (4Q169) is the most important of the pesharim. Eschewing ciphers at certain junctures, this author mentions a "Demetrius, King of Greece," and refers to a Jewish ruler who crucified great numbers of his opponents. Apparent references to these same persons and events appear in the writings of Josephus, leading most scholars to identify Demetrius as Demetrius III Eucaerus (95-87 B.C.) and the Jewish ruler as Alexander Janneus (103-76 B.C.). The crucifixion mentioned equates, most think, with Janneus's known execution of eight hundred of his opponents in the wake of a failed *coup d'état*. That event occurred in 88 B.C.

Of the thematic pesharim, none has aroused more profound interest than 11QMelchizedek. Fourteen fragments preserve the remains of three columns of this manuscript. The author comments on isolated OT texts (in particular Lev 25:9, 10, 13; Deut 15:2; Is 61:1), but Daniel 9:24-27 structures his commentary. The events connected with these biblical texts are portrayed as taking place in "the end of days," which is further identified as the "tenth Jubilee" and the "Day of Atonement." Melchizedek will free those who belong to his "inheritance" and (if suggested restorations are followed) "atone for their iniquities." He will further exact God's vengeance upon Belial and those of his "lot." The text presents a conception of Melchizedek that is approximately contemporary with and comparable to that of Hebrews 7: connecting him with divine judgment, a Day of Atonement and a primary role among God's angels. A second figure in the pesher, the "Herald," may be identified with the Teacher of Righteousness, but this point remains controversial.

Three additional thematic pesharim are important. The first of these is known as 4QOrdinances, which exists in three copies (4Q159, 513-514). This halakic pesher interprets Exodus 30:11-16 (the scriptural basis for the temple tax traditionally required of all male Jews annually) as referring not to annual taxes but instead to a one-time payment. Leviticus 25:39-46, which prohibits the purchase of fellow Israelites as slaves, is here understood to ban also the sale of a Jew to Gentiles.

The second thematic pesher is 4QFlorilegium. Here four large fragments have been joined to form two columns, leaving twenty-three extra, unjoined sections. The author combines quotations from 2 Samuel 7:10-14, Exodus 15:17-18, Amos 9:11, Psalm 1:1, Isaiah 8:11, Ezekiel 37:23 (uncertain) and Psalm 2:1 with interpretive comments. All of these verses are related to the "end of days," when God will order that a new "temple of Adam" be built. Therein people will perform sacrifices and the "deeds of the Torah," free from outside harassment or impurity. Prominent in the text are references to the "Shoot of David" and the "Interpreter of the Law," eschatological figures familiar from other Qumran texts.

The third thematic pesher, 4QTestimonia, has perhaps falsely furnished many scholars with the basic substance of Qumran messianic expectation. The text is a catena of quotations from Deuteronomy 5:28-29, Deuteronomy 18:18-19, Numbers 24:15-17, Deuteronomy 33:8-11,

Joshua 6:26 and an extrabiblical work also found among the scrolls, 4QPsalms of Joshua. The body of the text arranges these quotations into four groups, each group set off by a scribal device and so, inferentially, concerning separate topics. One reason this text is important is because it furnishes explicit evidence for the existence, long posited, of *testimonia,* or *florilegia* (collections of proof-texts), in pre-Christian Judaism.

Targumim. Three Aramaic targumim (*targûmîm,* plural of *targûm,* meaning "translation" or "interpretation" of the Hebrew Bible) number among the DSS. Much the longest and most complete of these is the Job targum from cave 11. This text represents the only incontestably pre-Christian targum of any appreciable length. Surviving portions include Job 17—42, with the last six chapters the least damaged. On the whole, despite slight additions, subtractions and dislocations, the Hebrew text behind the Aramaic translation seems to have been essentially the Masoretic Text. Even the supposedly disordered third cycle of debates (Job 22:1—31:40) and the Hymn to Wisdom (Job 28:1—28:28, often regarded as an interpolation) are here and in the same problematic order as in the Masoretic Text.

The other two targumim are extremely fragmentary. The first (4Q156) contains an Aramaic rendering of Leviticus 16:12-15, 18-21, but whether these fragments were part of a targum is uncertain. Equally conceivable is that they come from a liturgical work that quoted these verses. If, nevertheless, they do represent portions of a targum, then we have for the first time a pre-Christian targum to a book of the Pentateuch. The translation of the Hebrew is literal (unexpanded). Finally, 4Q157 preserves portions of Job 3:5-9 and Job 4:16—5:4, reflecting a text virtually identical to the Masoretic Text.

1.2.3. Apocryphal and Pseudepigraphic Texts. Included among the DSS are manuscripts of nonbiblical books that were known in some form even before the discoveries at the caves. Apocryphal writings attested include Tobit (in Hebrew and Aramaic) and Ecclesiasticus, also known as Sirach. Pseudepigraphic works include the *Testament of Levi* (in Aramaic), a portion of the *Testament of Naphtali* (in Hebrew), *Enoch* and *Jubilees.* *Jubilees* was especially popular, to judge by the fourteen or fifteen manuscripts thus far identified from caves 2, 3, 4 and 11. Not surprisingly,

previously unknown texts that can now be classified as pseudepigraphic were also unearthed. Among these are testaments of Jacob, Judah, Joseph and Kohath, the *Psalms of Joshua* mentioned above, and a Daniel cycle.

1 Enoch. In 1976, Milik published his long-awaited book on the fragments of *Enoch* discovered in cave 4. Milik's book contains most but not all of the Qumran *Enoch* manuscripts, all in Aramaic, and attests parts of every subdivision of *1 Enoch* except for one. Thus it includes seven fragmentary manuscripts (4QEn^{a-g}) that together preserve some of the Book of Watchers, the Book of Dreams and the Epistle of Enoch. Also included in the book are four other manuscripts (4QEnastr^{a-d}) that point to a much longer recension of what is known in *1 Enoch* as the Astronomical Book. Additionally, portions of a literature clearly related to *1 Enoch,* but previously unknown, are included under the title Book of Giants (4QEnGiants^{a-e}). Significant by its absence from the Qumran fragments is the so-called Book of Parables, which uses the term "son of man," an important self-designation of Jesus. Scholars are divided on the reason for this absence. Milik thought that the Book of Parables must be a Christian writing, but most scholars today reject that view. The Book of Parables was probably, at least in an early form, pre-Christian, but was not included among the Qumran deposits either fortuitously or because some of its ideas were unacceptable.

Genesis Apocryphon. One of the pseudepigraphic texts that surfaced among the DSS was the otherwise unknown *Genesis Apocryphon* (1QapGen). Dated around the turn of the eras, this Aramaic writing presents the patriarchs of Genesis telling their stories. In so doing it adheres closely to the biblical stories but with frequent expansions derived from unknown midrashic sources, including, it seems, a Testament of Noah. Columns 1 through 5 mostly concern the birth of Noah; 6 through 17 deal with the flood and the postdiluvian division of the earth among Noah's sons; 18 through 22 (where the text breaks off) concern Abram according to Genesis 11—15.

Most scholars, while recognizing features more akin to the known targumim, regard the *Genesis Apocryphon* as a midrashic composition. It is thus related to intertestamental works such as *Jubilees,* which are often called Rewritten Bible. Perhaps the primary importance of the text lies in its language. Because it is one of the longest Aramaic texts from Qumran, the *Genesis Apocryphon* is of special significance in the effort to recover the varieties of Palestinian Aramaic used by the Jews at the time of Jesus. In general its language is of a form transitional between the book of Daniel and the targumim, antedating as well the materials from the Wadi Murabbaʿat, Wadi Seiyal and Wadi Habra.

Prayer of Nabonidus. Fragments of an Aramaic pseudepigraphon known as the *Prayer of Nabonidus* were found in cave 4. The fragments make up two incomplete columns, including the beginning of column 1. As the name suggests, the text is ostensibly a prayer delivered by the last king of Babylon, Nabonidus, telling the story of the king's seven-year period of illness—a time when he prayed to "the gods of silver and gold" for a cure. At length, a Jewish "exorcist" delivered him, and in gratitude the king wrote this prayer. The parallels with the fourth chapter of Daniel and the story of Nebuchadnezzar's madness are patent, leading many scholars to conclude that in this text we have remnants of the popular traditions from which the Aramaic portions of Daniel derived.

The Daniel Cycle. The prayer of Nabonidus is just one part of a "Daniel cycle" that apparently included at least five additional works. Three of these (4QpsDan^a-c [4Q243-245]) contain one or more apocalyptic overviews of Jewish history narrated by or involving Daniel. The fourth writing (4Q552-553) recounts a dream in which four trees (or their "angels") speak to the author. Each tree represents a kingdom (cf. Dan 2; 7), the first of which is identified as Babylon and the second as Persia. This work has a bearing on the interpretation or history of interpretation of the fourth kingdom mentioned in Daniel 2 and Daniel 7. Another text from this Daniel cycle is known as 4QpsDanA^a. This fragmentary but striking work preserves the phrases "son of God" and "son of the Most High" as well as phraseology reminiscent of Luke 1:32 and Luke 1:35. One additional writing, 4Q248, the *Acts of a King,* is related to the contents of Daniel but of disputed interpretation. According to one view, it relates events from the time of Ptolemy I Soter, about 300 B.C.; according to the other, it records episodes of the reign of Antiochus IV Epiphanes, about 170 B.C.

Words of Moses. The *Words of Moses* (1Q22) is a sort of apocryphon to Deuteronomy. God speaks to Moses, who in turn relays the commands to the people, evidently via Eleazar and Joshua. At one point the text requires the appointment of officials (perhaps priests), "to clarify . . . all these words of the Torah." Another example of interpretive explanation occurs in the third column (3:8-10), where the date of the Day of Atonement is explained by reason that "your fathers were wandering in the desert until the tenth day of the month."

Book of Mysteries. Another tantalizing pseudepigraphon is the *Book of Mysteries,* known in three or four copies (1Q27, 4Q299-300; 4Q301 is disputed). The work derives its name from the recurrent and prominent term *raz,* "mystery, secret." Some of the work is cast as poetic oracles, while the eloquent prose that follows each poetic section provides signs by which the truth of the oracles is to be proved. The most extensive run of continuous text, in 1Q27 column 1, delivers an indictment against those who neither meditate upon the "former things" nor recognize the significance of the "mystery of existence" (*raz nihyeh,* [4Q412-413, 415-421]). Of particular interest is the appearance in 1Q27 of the phrase *razê pešaʿ.* This phrase is probably the Hebrew equivalent of the Greek *mystērion tēs anomias* of 2 Thessalonians 2:7.

Other Pseudepigraphic Writings. The cave 4 materials include a wealth of material that is difficult to classify using the scholarly categories familiar from the past. For many of these works the term now being used is *parabiblical.* They relate to the biblical corpus and to the authors of the Hebrew Bible in varied or even uncertain ways, yet the relation is incontestable. Such works include *Reworked Pentateuch* (4Q158, 364-367), a running commentary on the Pentateuch with exegetical additions and omissions. Some of the additions are of significant size. Other parabiblical writings new to scholarship include 4Q369, the *Prayer of Enosh;* 4Q382, *Parakings* (or *Paraphrase of Kings*); and 4Q422, a paraphrase of Genesis and Exodus. *Commentaries on Genesis* (or *Genesis Pesher*), including both straightforward and sectarian exegesis of the biblical text, are found in 4Q252-254a. Also parabiblical is 4Q473, *The Two Ways,* a work related to Deuteronomy but also bearing comparison with early Christian writings using this motif, such as *Didache* 1—6. Numerous additional, very fragmentary parabiblical works, most having no evident sectarian characteristics, have also come to light.

Among these are 4Q559, *Biblical Chronology*, an Aramaic chronograph whose surviving portions treat the length of the Egyptian sojourn, the time of Israel's wandering in the wilderness and the period of the early judges.

1.2.4. Liturgical Texts. Among the texts from Qumran, many are either clearly liturgical or plausibly so construed. Of these writings perhaps the most interesting is the *Angelic Liturgy*, or *Songs of the Sabbath Sacrifice*. The composition is partially preserved in eight manuscripts from cave 4 (4Q400-407), as well as in fragments from cave 11 (11Q17) and Masada (Mas1k). The author portrays heaven as a complicated temple consisting of seven sanctuaries attended by seven chief prince-priests, their deputies and seven angelic priesthoods. Also detailed are the praise offerings that the angels offer up on the sabbath. Altogether the work contains thirteen separate compositions, one for each of the first thirteen sabbaths of the year. The *Songs of the Sabbath Sacrifice* is important for the study of angelology, Second Temple liturgical song and early Jewish mysticism. A striking phrase in the first hymn avers that the angelic priests, by their heavenly cultus, "atone for those who turn from sin." One may understand this statement to mean that the earthly temple cultus is not essential. Here, then, is an important witness to a conception of Judaism that is not temple-centered, at least in a physical sense. Such ideas were starting points for Christianity and for rabbinic Judaism.

A second noteworthy liturgical opus is the *Words of the Luminaries* (4Q504-506). Fragmentary remaining headings show that the compositions contained in this manuscript were meant to be recited on given days of the week. With one exception, the mood of these compositions is penitential; hence, they may appropriately be classed as *taḥĕnûnîm*, confessional prayers reflecting such biblical passages as Daniel 9:4-19. The instructions evidence that these *taḥĕnûnîm* were used liturgically, as in later Judaism. The single evident exception to the somber tone of the *Words of the Luminaries* is a composition for the sabbath. This prayer is full of praise rather than contrition, reflecting the traditional Jewish understanding of the sabbath as a time of joy.

Among many that might be singled out, two further liturgically oriented works can be mentioned here. One is 4QApocryphal Lamentations A (4Q179). The text is made up of five fragments, the order of which is still uncertain. As the name implies, it is a lament or series of laments over the city of Jerusalem, whose imagery is achieved chiefly by allusion to Lamentations, Isaiah and Jeremiah. Possibly the work was occasioned by a destruction of Jerusalem at the time of Antiochus IV Epiphanes (cf. 1 Macc 1:29-32), or by another destruction at Roman hands in 63 B.C. Alternatively, 4Q179 may be no more than a poetic reminiscence of the famous razing by the forces of Nebuchadnezzar in 586 B.C.

The second text contains vocabulary strikingly similar to that of the *Rule of the Community* and the *Rule of Benediction*, and is known as *Berachot* (4Q286-290 [4Q280, 286-290]). The writing depicts a covenant ceremony incorporating numerous blessings and curses. The blessings are recited by all heavenly and earthly creatures faithful to the laws of creation and by the members of the movement who are faithful to the Law. The curses descend upon Belial and the evil angels who are his lot.

Another group of manuscripts from Qumran that are broadly related to liturgy and worship are the phylacteries, or *tĕpillîn*. A number have surfaced from caves 1, 4, 5, 8 and an unidentified cave, cave X. They are instructive regarding the content and order of the portions of Scripture they contain and also witness to noteworthy textual variants. Four *tĕpillîn* were discovered in their capsules, enabling scholars to investigate technical points that are treated extensively in rabbinic literature—such matters as the shape of the capsule, the nature of the leather for scriptural portions and the type of thread with which the capsules are tied.

Moreover, the order of the scriptural portions in the *tĕpillîn* has been a matter of heated controversy in the history of Judaism. The most famous controversy on this subject occurred in the early medieval period between Rashi and Rabbenu Tam. As a whole, the Qumran *tĕpillîn* are not strictly in the order for which either man argued. The fact that some from cave 8 are arranged according to Rashi's system, while others from the approximately contemporary finds at Murabba'at accord with the position of Rabbenu Tam, suggests that first-century Jews used both systems concurrently. The contents of the *tĕpillîn* published so far often add verses to the classical portion of Scripture, but the verses added differ among the various examples. No clear rationale has been adduced to explain this fact.

Notably, 1Q13, 4Qa (4Q128) and XQPhyl. 3 all contain the Decalogue (Deut 5:1-21), which is never included in rabbinic phylacteries. Thus the phylacteries from Qumran raise many questions about the laws governing their production and do not seem to fall into a single "sectarian" categorization.

1.2.5. Legal Texts. Many of the writings already discussed have a significant legal component, especially the *Rule of the Community,* the *Rule of the Congregation, Damascus Document, Temple Scroll* and 4QOrdinances. Another writing of great importance for understanding the types and functions of religious law in Second Temple Judaism is 4QMMT, short for *Miqṣat Maʿasey ha-Torah,* "some rulings concerning the Law." Published in the DJD series in 1994, 4QMMT includes a list of twenty-three legal controversies concerning which the authors find fault with current practice in the Jerusalem temple. The work appears to be addressed to someone in position to change those practices, presumably the reigning high priest, although some scholars have argued that the work is intrasectarian. In at least two instances, the laws of 4QMMT are identical to those of opponents to the Pharisees in rabbinic writings, making clear once again (for there are many other indicators) that the Qumran movement was in its essence antipharisaic. The laws of 4QMMT also demonstrate, if further demonstration were needed, the priestly character of the movement: the laws favor the priests when compared with rabbinic legislation. Such is true of the entire Qumran legal corpus. 4QMMT seems to prove that the Qumran movement split with greater Judaism primarily over legal issues, not matters of philosophy or the legitimacy of the high priest, as often suggested. Indeed, the publication of this writing has spurred—and coincided with—a much greater attention to the importance of religious law for an understanding not only of the culture but also of the history of the NT period. Different movements in Second Temple Judaism, including Christianity, were different in large part because of different ideas about the law.

A variety of other legal works among the scrolls have added impetus to this research. These writings include *Halakhah A* (4Q251), which tabulates a variety of laws on subjects such as the sabbath, firstfruits, the selling of ancestral lands and the slaughter of pregnant animals. *Torohot A* (4Q274) legislates for the type of impurity produced by leprosy. *Torohot B^b* and *Torohot B^c* (4Q276-277) deal with the ritual preparation of the red heifer—the only means for purification from impurity of the dead—as stipulated by Numbers 19. 4QLeqet (4Q284a) provides laws to regulate gleaning; unlike the Bible, it requires gleaners to be ritually pure. The work entitled *Rebukes by the Overseer* (4Q477) lists by name several members of the Qumran movement whom the Overseer has publicly rebuked for breach of the group's laws. The movement required the overseer to record all such rebukes in writing. Several of the legal causes for rebuke are unknown from other Qumran writings. *Serekh Damascus* (4Q265) regulates the paschal sacrifice, procedures for the novitiate, group life (with a penal code largely but not entirely identical to that known from the *Damascus Document* and the *Rule of the Community*), and the parturient.

1.2.6. "Magical" and Calendrical Texts. Calendar and "magic" were not entirely separate concerns in the ancient world, for magic often—and the calendar always—involved study of the heavenly bodies. Thus one magical work from Qumran combines a peculiar calendar (see below), the earliest known Jewish naming of the signs of the zodiac and divination by thunder (4Q318). 4QHoroscope (4Q186) is an encoded series of horoscopes whose scribe mixes the ordinary Jewish script with the alphabets of Paleo-Hebrew, Greek and Cryptic Script A (one of three secret alphabets found among the scrolls); he further inscribes his text, *à la* Leonardo da Vinci's notebooks, in mirror writing. The surviving fragments describe three people in reference to their astrological birth signs, deriving therefrom each person's physical and spiritual qualities. 4QHoroscope possesses notable terminological parallels with the *Rule of the Community.* These writings show that astrological ideas had been assimilated deeply by the Jews, in spite of the apparent biblical condemnations (e.g., Is 47:13-14; Jer 10:1-3). Interest in such matters may be related to the story of the magi in Matthew's Gospel. An Aramaic work similar in method to 4QHoroscope, but lacking the sectarian terminology, is 4Q561.

Another scroll, known as the *Elect of God* (4Q534), has been termed a "messianic horoscope." This very poorly preserved Aramaic text contains the phrase *bḥyr ʾlhʾ,* the equivalent of the Greek *ho eklektos tou theou* ("the elect of God") witnessed by some manuscripts of John

1:34. It is uncertain, however, that the Aramaic phrase carries a messianic connotation. The words occur as part of the description of an unborn child who will possess wisdom and precocious intellect. He is to have a long life, and the success of his plans is assured by his position as the "elect of God." Since the text lacks astrological terminology, it might better be considered an example of physiognomic literature rather than as a horoscope. Moreover, as some scholars maintain, the *Elect of God* may describe the birth of Noah, not a messiah (cf. *1 Enoch* 106).

A work hesitantly identified by the original team as a collection of proverbs, 4Q560, has now been shown to be an apotropaic incantation or exorcism, the earliest ever known from Palestine. The preserved portions of the formula adjure various spirits by name, evidently employing the sacred name of Yahweh. The concerns are those of similar texts elsewhere in the ancient Near East: childbirth, diseases, sleep or dreams, and (perhaps) safety of possessions. One of the demons, the Fever-demon, may illuminate the Synoptic story of Peter's sick mother-in-law. Matthew 8:15 and Mark 1:31 report the event as a simple healing by Jesus, but Luke 4:39 can be translated, "Then he stood over her and rebuked the Fever-demon, and it left her."

Perhaps the one element that more than any other binds the DSS into an ideological unity is the type of calendar they insist upon. Unlike the 354-day lunisolar calendar of the Pharisees and rabbinic Judaism (which is essentially the modern Jewish calendar), the calendar of the scrolls is a solar device. Each year has 364 days, and each quarter of the year has 91 days; months are either 30 or 31 days long. The regularity of this system is such that all festivals occur on the same day from year to year, and never on the sabbath. Avoiding having a festival fall on the sabbath solved all sorts of halakic problems. This Qumran calendar was actually a very old priestly mechanism antedating the rise of the Qumran movement. Forms of this calendar date to at least the third century B.C. Evidence of its use is clear from the Septuagint—even, some scholars believe, from the Hebrew Bible. And its later advocacy was not limited to Qumran circles. The texts found at Masada include at least two writings embracing, or probably embracing, the solar calendar (Mas1j, 1k), and Josephus's narrative describing the *sicarii* at Masada (Josephus *J.W.* 4.7.2 §§402-5) further suggests that this priestly group followed a calendar different from their contemporaries at En Gedi. In fact, for at least three centuries a kind of calendar war raged among the Jews of Palestine, finally being settled only by the destruction of one party to the dispute in the first revolt against Rome (A.D. 66-73/74). The DSS are a strong witness to the views of the losing priestly party.

The 364-day calendar underlies or is explicit in all of the major Qumran writings: the *Rule of the Community,* the *Damascus Document,* the *War Scroll,* the *Temple Scroll,* the *Hymns,* the pesharim, 4QMMT. Likewise, it underlies or is explicit in many of the lesser works. Hundreds of the DSS attest to this calendar. (Not a single Qumran writing favors the pharisaic version.) A significant number of calendrical works—that is, writings whose sole purpose is to explain certain details of the calendar—have also emerged from the caves. Such works include 4Q320-321a, synchronistic calendars that tabulate a form of the lunisolar calendar over against the 364-day instrument. Other calendar writings explain the timing of priestly service in the temple by sabbaths, months and seasons, according to a six-year cycle: 4Q325, 4Q326, 4Q328, 4Q329, 4Q329a and 4Q334. An especially interesting calendrical writing, sometimes called the *Annalistic Calendar,* is extant in six fragmentary copies (4Q322-324c). Similar to certain modern calendars that mention Presidents' Day or Independence Day on the appropriate day of the year, the *Annalistic Calendar* refers to historical events on given days and uses actual names of the Hasmonean period. The names of John Hyrcanus I, John Hyrcanus II, Aristobulus II and Shelamzion or Alexandra all appear in the work. These were rulers of the Jews between 134-63 B.C. The name Aemilius also appears, doubtless a reference to M. Aemilius Scaurus, one of Pompey's leading generals when the Romans invaded Palestine and ended Jewish independence in 63 B.C. This writing, in particular, is very important in the attempt to discover who wrote the scrolls and when.

2. Interpretation of the Finds.

The majority of scholars identify the DSS as the products of the ancient Jewish sect known as the Essenes. For this identification scholars rely on a combination of external and internal evidence.

The external evidence combines a passage

from Pliny the Elder with the archaeology of the site of Qumran. In the course of a late first-century travelogue, Pliny describes the Essenes as living along the shores of the Dead Sea, with En Gedi "below" or "south" of them (the Latin preposition *infra* is ambiguous; "below" means topometrically lower, as the bottom of a hill is below the top). This description could fit Qumran. Archaeology further indicates that the site was in use during the time Pliny describes. Structures found at Qumran have been identified as functional for such a community and include what have been understood as a potter's shop and a communal dining hall. Three inkwells and other materials construed as evidence of scribal activity suggest to some scholars that the scrolls found in the nearby caves were written on the site. Recent analysis of the graveyard near Qumran by J. Zias indicates that only men were buried there in ancient times; the few graves of women seem to be much later, early-modern Bedouin intrusions. If so, then the graveyard suggests a celibate male community, just what Pliny describes for the Essenes.

Internal evidence consists of a comparison between passages describing the Essenes in Philo and Josephus with the contents of texts such as 1QS and CD. All these sources agree in describing or presupposing a communal organization. Similarities include novitiate periods, communal regulations, strict observance of the sabbath vis-à-vis rabbinic law and certain legal positions such as the transmission of ritual impurity by oil.

Neither the external nor the internal evidence is without problems. N. Golb in postulating his "Jerusalem hypothesis" has pointed out many of them. As the name suggests, Golb argues that the DSS derive from Jerusalem and various libraries there. To date, however, Golb and his fellow advocates remain a minority in scholarship on the scrolls. One point on which he has persuaded many scholars is that of provenance. While most would reject his view that the DSS are not, as a whole, Essene products, the modified notion that many of the scrolls were produced by Essenes elsewhere than at the site, perhaps in Jerusalem, has proved attractive.

If such a view were correct, then the potential significance of the scrolls for an understanding of Judaism at the time of Jesus is substantially greater than the 1950s view of provenance would imply. For on this interpretation, the DSS represent the product of a wider portion of society than the hypothesis of their production at Qumran stipulates. The ancillary question of how much wider remains to be addressed by further research.

3. The Dead Sea Scrolls and the New Testament. On the whole, NT scholarship in relation to the DSS is best described as outdated. For example, no book is more often quoted in this regard than the volume edited by K. Stendahl in 1957, *The Scrolls and the New Testament*. It is paradigmatic that rather than produce a new series of essays on relations between Qumran studies and the NT, the book simply continues to be reprinted. Similarly, the excellent two-volume work by H. Braun, *Qumran und das Neue Testament*, is now outdated. Both of these works still contain useful material, but because so much has happened in DSS studies since they were written, one must use them very cautiously.

An illustration of the potential for new understandings may be found in the work alluded to above, 4QMMT. As noted, this text lists over twenty legal topics upon which the text's authors and the temple authorities disagree. In this fact alone its significance for NT studies is enormous, for previously we had no factual statement about what was going on in the temple just before Jesus' day. Josephus's descriptions of the temple cultus are difficult to use with confidence, because he often describes things the way they ought to have been (that is, as he understood the relevant OT texts) rather than the way they were. This fact becomes apparent when comparing the theoretical descriptions of his *Antiquities* with the historical narratives of his *War* and *Vita*; not infrequently they disagree. The tannaitic legal discussions are likewise often idealizing (*see* Rabbinic Traditions and Writings). With 4QMMT, we can discover what was really happening, at least with regard to the topics upon which it touches. For example, the authors oppose allowing Gentiles to make offerings on the grounds that such promotes idolatry. The assumption was that regardless of outward procedures, in their hearts Gentiles would be honoring their gods, not the God of Israel. It will be recalled that the first revolt with Rome was partly fueled by just such sentiments, as Eleazar bar Ananias seized control of the temple and refused to allow any more sacrifices on behalf of Gentiles.

Another insight from 4QMMT consists in the manner of its halakic argument. Repeatedly its authors precede their legal positions with the phrases *ʾănaḥnû ḥôšbîm ʾănaḥnû ʾômrîm*, "we believe, we say." The formal identity with Matthew's depiction of Jesus' legal arguments in the Sermon on the Mount ("You have heard . . . but I say") is patent. Presumably, therefore, Matthew has preserved a common first-century rhetorical structure heretofore unparalleled in early Jewish materials.

Moving to more general considerations, perhaps the most interesting relationship between the DSS and the NT concerns their principal personages. The NT focuses, of course, on Jesus of Nazareth; correspondingly, a group of the DSS focus on the enigmatic figure of the Teacher of Righteousness *(môrēh haṣṣedeq)*. One can examine the Teacher's writings, the *Teacher Hymns,* to extract his ideas about himself. To do so fully, one must in every case compare what he writes with the hundreds of OT portions that he cites or to which he alludes. Understanding the original literary context of his quotations is essential. Also, the Hebrew words his hymns do not actually quote, but that surround those quotes in the original OT context, are assumed to be in the minds of his audience. Analyzing the implied ideas these portions might communicate is very important too. By this method of "deep reading" one can reconstruct aspects of the Teacher's theology or ideology and then compare other DSS to round out the picture. It emerges that, like Jesus, the Teacher considered himself a prophet, and more than a prophet. Like Jesus, the Teacher proclaimed a completed law of Moses, perfected by his own direct revelation from God. Like Jesus, the Teacher spoke of charity, the poor and love of one's fellows; forbade divorce; and proclaimed the imminent coming of the kingdom of God. And, like Jesus, the Teacher was received as a messiah by his followers and founded an apocalyptic Jewish movement that within a century numbered in the thousands. Many other parallels exist, inviting much further research, just as is true of the DSS and the NT generally.

It has been said that Christianity is an apocalyptic Judaism that survived. The DSS are in many regards our best analogy, for this movement, too, was an apocalyptic Judaism. It did not survive, but thanks to the discovery of many of its writings in the Judean Desert, it lives again.

See also APOCRYPHA AND PSEUDEPIGRAPHA, OLD TESTAMENT; JUDAISM AND THE NEW TESTAMENT.

DNTB: QUMRAN: PLACE AND HISTORY; (ALSO NUMEROUS ARTICLES ON THE SCROLLS).

BIBLIOGRAPHY. **Texts and Translations:** M. Abegg Jr., P. Flint and E. Ulrich, *The Dead Sea Scrolls Bible* (San Francisco: HarperSanFrancisco, 1999); R. Eisenman and M. O. Wise, *The Dead Sea Scrolls Uncovered* (Shaftesbury, Dorset: Element, 1992); F. García Martínez, *The Dead Sea Scrolls Translated: The Qumran Texts in English* (2d ed.; Leiden: E. J. Brill/Grand Rapids: Eerdmans, 1996); G. Vermes, *The Complete Dead Sea Scrolls in English* (New York: Penguin, 1998); M. O. Wise, M. Abegg Jr. and E. Cook, *The Dead Sea Scrolls: A New Translation* (San Francisco: HarperSanFrancisco, 1996). **Studies:** E. Cook, *Solving the Mysteries of the Dead Sea Scrolls* (Grand Rapids: Zondervan, 1994); F. M. Cross, *The Ancient Library of Qumran and Modern Biblical Studies* (rev. ed.; New York: Doubleday, 1961); P. Flint, *Dead Sea Psalms Scrolls and the Book of Psalms* (STDJ 17; Leiden: E. J. Brill, 1997); N. Golb, *Who Wrote the Dead Sea Scrolls? The Search for the Secret of Qumran* (New York: Scribners, 1994); L. H. Schiffman, *Reclaiming the Dead Sea Scrolls* (New York: Jewish Publication Society of America, 1994); L. H. Schiffman and J. C. VanderKam, eds., *Encyclopedia of the Dead Sea Scrolls* (2 vols.; New York: Oxford University Press, 2000); E. Ulrich, *The Dead Sea Scrolls and the Origins of the Bible* (Grand Rapids: Eerdmans, 1999); J. C. VanderKam, *Calendars in the Dead Sea Scrolls: Measuring Time* (New York: Routledge, 1998); idem, *The Dead Sea Scrolls Today* (Grand Rapids: Eerdmans, 1994); M. O. Wise, *The First Messiah: Investigating the Savior Before Christ* (San Francisco: HarperSanFrancisco, 1999); idem, "*Mylob ynwmk ym*: A Study of 4Q491c, 4Q471b, 4Q427 7 and 1QHa 25:35—26:10," *DSD* 7 (2000); idem, "*Primo Annales Fuere:* An Annalistic Calendar from Qumran," *Thunder in Gemini* (JSPSup 15; Sheffield: JSOT, 1994) 186-221; idem, "Thunder in Gemini: An Aramaic Brontologion (4Q318) from Qumran," *Thunder in Gemini* (JSPSup 15; Sheffield: JSOT Press, 1994) 1-50. M. O. Wise

DEATH OF CHRIST I: GOSPELS

The crucifixion of Jesus under Pontius Pilate is among the most historically certain and theologically pregnant events of Jesus' life.

1. Crucifixion in the Ancient World.

In spite of its cruelty as a form of punishment, crucifixion was practiced throughout the ancient world. It was employed as a method of execution or, in some cases, impalement after death among the Persians, Indians, Assyrians and others, and later among the Greeks and Romans. Some evidence suggests crucifixion was used as a mode of execution by Jews before the time of Herod the Great (Josephus *J.W.* 1.4.6 §§97-98; *Ant.* 13.14.2 §§379-83; 11QTemple 64:6-13).

1.1. Crucifixion: A Cruel Practice.
Among the torturous penalties noted in the literature of antiquity, crucifixion was particularly heinous. The act damaged no vital organs, nor did it result in excessive bleeding. Hence, death came slowly, sometimes after several days, through shock or a painful process of asphyxiation as the muscles used in breathing suffered increasing fatigue. Often, as a further disgrace, the person was denied burial and the body was left on the cross to serve as carrion for the birds or to rot.

Crucifixion was quintessentially a public affair. Naked and affixed to a stake, cross or tree, the victim was subjected to savage ridicule by frequent passers-by, while the general populace was given a grim reminder of the fate of those who assert themselves against the authority of the state.

Descriptions of the act of crucifixion are rare in the extant literature of antiquity. This is not due to the infrequency of the practice, but rather to literary-aesthetic considerations. Members of the cultured literary elite were hesitant to dwell on this horrific, brutal act. Indeed, even the passion narratives of our Gospels, which M. Hengel regards as the most detailed descriptions of their kind (Hengel 1977, 25), are remarkably brief in their recounting of the actual act of crucifixion. Eschewing all details, they simply report, "They crucified him" (Mt 27:35; Mk 15:25; Lk 23:33; Jn 19:18).

Even where we find descriptions it is obvious that no standard form of crucifixion was uniformly practiced. In fact, the accounts are not always clear even on whether the crucifixion took place before or after the victim's death. Nor is it evident in each case whether the victim was bound or nailed to the stake, or whether a crossbeam was always used. In the Roman world, however, the form of crucifixion was apparently more uniform: it included a flogging beforehand, and victims often carried the crossbeam to the place of crucifixion, where they were nailed or bound to the cross with arms extended, raised up, and perhaps seated on a sedicula, or small wooden peg (Hengel 1977, 22-32).

Even in the Roman world the procedure was subject to variation, depending on the whims of the executioners. For example, in his eyewitness account of the Roman siege of Jerusalem, Josephus observes how hundreds of Jewish prisoners were "scourged and subjected to torture of every description . . . , and then crucified opposite the city walls." Hoping that the gruesome sight might induce the Jews to surrender the city, Titus, the Roman commander, gave his soldiers freedom to continue the crucifixions as they pleased. "The soldiers out of rage and hatred amused themselves by nailing their prisoners in different positions" (Josephus *J.W.* 5.11.1 §§449-51).

Archeological evidence related to the practice of crucifixion in first-century Palestine is even more sparse. In 1968 an ossuary was discovered in a buried cave at Giv'at ha-Mivtar in northern Jerusalem. It contained the bones of an adult male who had died by crucifixion during the period between the onset of the first century A.D. and the mid-60s. Initial study of the skeletal remains indicated that a nail had been driven through each of his forearms, and his heel bones had been pierced by a single iron nail. The latter nail was found still embedded in what investigators took to be the heel bones of both feet. Wood fragments found at both ends of the nail indicated that the nail first passed through a small wooden plaque, then through the victim's feet, and then into a vertical, olive-wood beam. Apparently as a coup de grâce, his shins had been broken intentionally.

J. Zias and E. Sekeles recently reevaluated the skeletal remains of the ossuary, together with related photographs, casts and radiographs. On this basis they proposed a number of amendments to earlier findings. Most importantly, they determined that the still-intact iron nail had passed from the right side to the left of the right heel bone (calcaneum) only. A different picture of the crucified man results, for on this reconstruction the feet were not anchored with one nail, but the victim apparently straddled the upright beam. Moreover, finding no clear evidence of traumatic injury to the bones of the forearm or hands, they propose the victim was tied to the crossbeam, not nailed. Finally, they questioned whether the bones of the lower limbs had been broken prior to death.

Although this discovery adds archeological evidence to literary descriptions of crucifixion, it is nevertheless clear that the paucity of direct anthropological evidence of this nature restricts the certainty one might attach to its interpretation.

1.2. Crucifixion: A Military and Political Punishment. As a rule, Roman citizens were spared from this form of execution, though in extreme occasions (e.g., high treason) death by crucifixion might be imposed. More generally among the Romans, crucifixion was a penalty reserved for those of lower status—namely, dangerous criminals, slaves and the populace of foreign provinces. Among these people, crucifixion served as a means of asserting Roman authority and maintaining law and order. Thus, in the province of Judea, it proved to be a generally effective weapon against resistance to Roman occupation.

1.3. Crucifixion: Interpretive Stigma. In his important survey of the treatment of crucifixion in ancient literature, Hengel queries whether, outside early Christianity, death by crucifixion was ever interpreted in a positive manner. Within the Gentile world, he finds in Stoicism the use of crucifixion as a metaphor "for the suffering from which the wise man can free himself only by death, which delivers the soul from the body to which it is tied" (Hengel 1977, 88; cf. 64-68). However, beyond this the cruelty of the cross seems to have forbidden any positive interpretation or metaphorical use of death by crucifixion.

If this was true for the Gentile world, it was even more so for the Jewish. Inasmuch as the use of crucifixion by the Romans as a deterrent against Jewish nationalism was widespread, we might have anticipated that the cross would come to serve as a symbol for martyrdom. However, in addition to the humiliation and brutality associated with this form of execution, for Jews an additional, profoundly religious, obstacle existed.

Already by the time of the first century A.D.,

the victim of crucifixion was understood in terms of Deuteronomy 21:22-23—specifically, "anyone who is hung on a tree is under the curse of God." In its context, this passage refers to the public display of the corpse of an executed criminal. But the NT gives evidence that this meaning was expanded considerably within the early church to include persons who had been crucified. This is seen in the verbal allusions to Deuteronomy 21:22-23 (e.g., Acts 5:30; 13:29; 1 Pet 2:24) and Paul's explicit citation of Deuteronomy 21:23 in Galatians 3:13. Apart from and prior to Christianity, evidence from the Qumran literature (4QpNah 3—4.1.7-8; 11QTemple 64:6-13) as well as from the writings of the first-century Alexandrian Jew Philo (*Spec. Leg.* 3.152; *Post C.* 61; *Somn.* 2.213) attests that victims of crucifixion could be understood this way within Judaism. Thus the cross could not be interpreted positively as a symbol of the Jewish resistance.

2. The Crucifixion of Jesus.

The crucifixion of Jesus of Nazareth under Pontius Pilate is well attested in Christian and non-Christian sources. It is reported in the four canonical Gospels in the midst of remarkably full passion accounts and referred to as a historical event throughout the NT, especially in Paul. The Latin historian Tacitus mentions Jesus' death in The Annals: "Christus . . . had undergone the death penalty in the reign of Tiberius, by sentence of the procurator Pontius Pilate" (15.44). In a text whose authenticity is under suspicion, Josephus recalls that Pilate condemned Jesus to be crucified (Josephus *Ant.* 18.3.3 §§63-64). For these and other reasons, the historicity of the death of Jesus on the cross is beyond doubt (Green 1988, 1). However, numerous problems revolve around our ability to date the crucifixion, the historicity of some details recorded in the crucifixion accounts and the interpretation of Jesus' death by Jesus and his first followers.

2.1. The Date of Jesus' Crucifixion. All four Gospels narrate the execution of Jesus on a Friday—that is, on the day before the sabbath (Mt 27:57, 62; Mk 15:42; Lk 23:54; Jn 19:31, 42). The major chronological issue, therefore, revolves around the relation of this Friday to Passover. Assuming the Jewish reckoning of the day from sunset to sunset, the Passover feast would have been eaten on the evening of 15 Nisan. The Synoptic Gospels (e.g., Mk 14:12-16) recount the Last Supper as a Passover meal on Thursday evening, 15 Nisan. Hence, in their reckoning, the day of Jesus' arrest, trial and death was 15 Nisan, the day of Passover. John's Gospel, however, dates the death of Jesus on 14 Nisan, the day of preparation for Passover (13:1-4; 18:28; 19:14, 31).

If we take these conclusions to the relevant astronomical data and assume Jesus was crucified around A.D. 30, we come up with the following options: According to the Johannine reckoning, Jesus was executed on April 3, A.D. 33 or April 7, A.D. 30; according to the Synoptic reckoning, A.D. 27 and 34 would be the probable years. Should we adopt the Johannine reckoning or the Synoptic?

Three avenues for solving this dilemma have been proposed. Some scholars argue that the Synoptics have preserved the correct chronology and that John has revised the tradition in order to portray Jesus more fully as the Passover Lamb. It is true that John has a theological concern of this nature (cf. Jn 1:29, 36; 18:28; 19:14, 31, 36-37); however, recent redaction-critical study has determined the high probability that the Johannine chronology came to him in his passion tradition (Dauer, 133-36, 140-42). Others have argued that the Synoptic account is tendentious, resulting from Mark's creative attempt to portray the Last Supper as a Passover meal. This argument fails to consider the tightly integrated character of the Passover elements in the Synoptic tradition, as well as the degree to which even John's narrative of the Last Supper is paschal in character (Green 1988, 113-16).

Third, many interpreters have attempted to harmonize the Synoptic and Johannine chronologies. Two of these theories are particularly noteworthy. First, some have championed the view that Galileans (like Jesus and his disciples) and Pharisees reckoned the day from sunrise to sunrise, unlike the Judeans and Sadducees, who reckoned the day from sunset to sunset. Hence, the Passover meal (Last Supper) was celebrated on Thursday evening 14 Nisan by Jesus, his disciples and other Galileans. The Judeans shared the Passover meal on Friday evening 15 Nisan. Others have found more plausible the theory that the Passover was celebrated on two different days in the year of the crucifixion, due to the disparity between the Pharisaic and Sadducean calendars. Both views require two consecutive days of Passover sacrifices, a possibility for which we have no clear evidence. At the same time, we can imagine this being allowed in order to maintain peace among the different groups within first-century Judaism (see the review in Marshall, 57-75, 184-85).

In the end, we are left with the conclusion that Jesus was crucified on 14 Nisan—that is, April 7, A.D. 30 or April 3, A.D. 33. The later date is corroborated by Pilate's need to appease the Jews in order to be "Caesar's friend" (Jn 19:12) and his new friendship with Herod (cf. Lk 23:12)—both of which are best understood in connection with Pilate's changing policies toward the Jews after A.D. 32 (Hoehner, 71-114). However, a date in A.D. 33 raises other problems inasmuch as it compresses the available time for the subsequent Christian movement and the Pauline mission.

2.2. The Crucifixion Accounts. Like the rest of the passion story, the crucifixion of Jesus is not recounted merely to chronicle what happened. This event, Jesus' execution on a cross, was of such a scandalous nature that it cried out for interpretation and legitimization. The result is a tightly woven tapestry combining both elements—event and interpretation—with the latter largely dependent on references to the OT. Thus Jesus' garments are divided (Ps 22:18). He is crucified with two criminals (Is 53:12). He is mocked (Ps 22:7; 70:3) and taunted (Ps 42:10). He is offered wine (Ps 69:21; Prov 31:6). He cries out from the cross (Ps 22:1; 31:5). He is acclaimed as God's Son (cf. Wis 2, 4-5) or as the Righteous One (Is 53:11) and is thus vindicated after maltreatment (Is 52:13-15; 53:10-12). The crucifixion narratives demonstrate in story form that Christ died "according to the Scriptures."

Some scholars continue the now outdated practice of trying to peel back the layers of theological interpretation in order to arrive at the story's historical kernel. Reported events, however, by virtue of their being reported, are always interpreted events. Hence, although the task of determining the historical plausibility of these narrated events remains an important one, attempts to sunder theology from history are misguided.

2.2.1. Crucifixion Traditions. Most scholars assume that Matthew's only narrative source for the crucifixion was Mark. In all likelihood, the Fourth Evangelist used his own, non-Markan source (Dauer; Green 1988, 105-34). In the past commentators largely worked with the hypothesis that Luke's account was for the most part also independent of the Markan narrative (e.g., Taylor). More recently, however, greater emphasis has been placed on Luke's creative shaping of the Markan story (e.g., Matera, 150-220; Neyrey).

Several lines of evidence point to Luke's use of early, non-Markan tradition for his account of Jesus' crucifixion, however, though scholars disagree on the nature of that traditional material (Green 1988, 86-101). First, Luke includes significant material not found in Mark which, under close literary analysis, does not appear to have come from Luke's creative pen. This material includes Jesus' warning to Jerusalem in Luke 23:27-31, Jesus' intercessory prayer from the cross in Luke 23:34, Jesus' interaction with the crucified criminals in Luke 23:39-43 and Luke's description of the repentance of the multitudes in Luke 23:48.

Second, in some cases Luke narrates actions also reported in Mark, but in ways sufficiently different so as to suggest his use of alternative traditional material. One example of this phenomenon appears in the use of Psalm 22:7 in the record of the mockery of Jesus by the passers-by. Interestingly, Mark 15:29-30 betrays the influence of the latter half of Psalm 22:7 ("shaking their heads"), while Luke 23:35 has been influenced by the first half of Psalm 22:7 ("seeing . . . they mocked"). This suggests the significance of Psalm 22:7 in the early passion tradition and indicates that this tradition came to Mark and Luke independently. Other noteworthy examples include the reports of Jesus' last words from the cross (see below) and the confession of the centurion.

Third, some aspects of the Lukan narrative that depart from Mark are paralleled in other sources. Thus, for example, the reaction of the crowds in Luke 23:48 is similar to that found in Gospel of Peter 7:25 ("Then the Jews and the elders and the priests, perceiving what great evil they had done to themselves, began to lament and to say, 'Woe on our sins, the judgment and the end of Israel is drawn nigh.' "). Finally, the linguistic and syntactic deviations from Mark's account in Luke are not easily explained on the basis of Luke's creativity alone.

Evidence of this character has suggested to some scholars that Luke knew a second, connected passion narrative; to others, that he was familiar with a series of disparate non-Markan traditions, whether oral or written. It is plausible that three roughly parallel early crucifixion accounts are represented in our canonical Gospels. This speaks in favor of the antiquity of the tradition, which may have been a part of a larger, early passion narrative.

2.2.2. History and Interpretation in the Crucifixion. Turning to the accounts, we see that they all agree in having Jesus led away to the place of crucifixion. The mention of the name of Simon of Cyrene serves no theological purpose, though his being drafted to carry the cross is reminiscent of Jesus' words about discipleship ("taking up the cross," Mk 8:34). Simon is missing from the Johannine narrative, probably as a result of John's overall attempt to indicate how, even in his passion, Jesus is master of his own fate. Others, however, see in Jesus' carrying "his own cross" (Jn 19:17) a reference to the Akedah—that is, the attempt by John to develop a parallel between Jesus' passion and the binding of Isaac (see Gen 22:6, where the wood was placed on Isaac by his father).

A number of other aspects of Jesus' crucifixion deserve brief discussion.

The Location of Golgotha. All of the Gospels mention that Golgotha was the place of Jesus' execution. Matthew, Mark and John translate the Aramaic *gûlgaltâ* (Heb *gulgôlāt*) as "Place of the Skull." Luke, who avoids Aramaic place names, has "Skull," a more accurate translation. Many attempts have been made to explain the meaning of this place reference: a hill in the shape of a skull? a rocky mound on which no vegetation could grow?

The precise location of Golgotha is disputed, though our knowledge of crucifixion in the Roman world and the Gospel accounts suggest its location outside the walls of Jerusalem (Jn 19:20; cf. Heb 13:12) in a public place, perhaps near a busy road (e.g., Mk 15:29, 40). According to John 19:41, the site of Jesus' crucifixion was in proximity to his borrowed tomb.

Strong circumstantial evidence supports the location of Golgotha in the area on which now stands the Church of the Holy Sepulchre, located within the Old City of Jerusalem. According to archeological findings in the 1960s, interpreted in tandem with Josephus's description of the city's fortifications, this site would have been well outside the city walls. Before the expansion of the city it was a quarry into which a number of tombs had been cut.

Before modern investigators realized the more narrow perimeter of the city walls as it was in the first third of the first century A.D., they focused their searches on the area to the north of the Old City. There they located a rocky hill whose stony face appeared to resemble a skull. K. M. Kenyon notes that the present shape of the hill is due largely to subsequent quarrying, however.

Jesus' Prayer. Only Luke records that following his crucifixion, Jesus prayed on behalf of those responsible for his death (Lk 23:34). This prayer is missing from a number of important manuscripts, presumably because some later copyists were uncomfortable with this portrait of Jesus extending mercy to his Jewish opponents. The major themes of the prayer—forgiveness and ignorance—are important in Luke-Acts (cf. Lk 1:77; 7:47-50; Acts 2:38; 3:17; 5:31; 10:43; 13:27, 38; 14:16); furthermore, its presence is important to the structure of the passion story, which narrates a saying of Jesus in each major section. Some scholars regard the prayer as having been created by Luke on the basis of the similar request of Stephen in Acts 7:60. But why should Stephen provide the model for Jesus, and not vice versa? Moreover, Jesus' request for the exoneration of his persecutors accords well with what we otherwise know of Jesus' teaching on one's attitude to hostility (e.g., Mt 5:44; see Lohse, 129-30).

The Division of Jesus' Clothing. The Evangelists agree in their narration of the division of Jesus' clothing among the soldiers. Some evidence suggests this distribution of the victim's clothing happened as a matter of course in antiquity, but the language of Psalm 22:18 has clearly influenced the way this event has been reported.

The Inscription on the Cross. The inscription on the cross is reported by all the Gospels with remarkable consistency, each noting that it was as "The King of the Jews" that Jesus was executed. Historically, this notice would have marked Jesus as a messianic pretender to the throne. No doubt Jesus' first followers saw in this charge an ironic proclamation of the true identity of Jesus, and this has been further emphasized in the Johannine elaboration of this report (Jn 19:19-22).

In the past it was common to assert that an inscription of this kind was normally affixed to the cross in a Roman crucifixion. Recent reexamination of the available evidence reveals the opposite. Prior to their execution, condemned persons might be required to display publicly the charge under which they had been sentenced to death, but the inscription reported by the Gospels is without parallel. For this reason the historical veracity of this measure should not be questioned. As A. E. Harvey has observed, "The first historians of Jesus' death can therefore have been under no compulsion to invent [such a notice]" (Harvey, 13).

The Mocking. Mark, Matthew and Luke agree that the Jewish leaders mocked Jesus on the cross, though Luke goes on to add that the soldiers joined in the derision (cf. Mk 15:16-20). In short, they insist, if Jesus were who he said he was, he would not be in this shameful, awful predicament. The historicity of the general contours of this account is almost certain for three reasons. First, it is consistent with what we know of Roman custom, which locates the act of crucifixion in the public arena precisely in order to foster this sort of derision. Second, it dovetails well with what we know of attitudes toward death in late Judaism, as suggested by a text like Psalm 22:7-8 or Wisdom 2:18, 20. Those who have a special relationship with God will not undergo shameful death. Third, the content of the mockery parodies the charges leading to Jesus' execution.

Jesus' Last Words. A more difficult issue is raised by Jesus' last words on the cross, reported variously as follows:

> Mark 15:34, citing Psalm 22:1: "My God, my God, why have you forsaken me?"
> Luke 23:46, citing Psalm 31:5: "Father, into your hands I commit my spirit."
> John 19:30: "It is finished."

The case for the historicity of the Markan version (followed by Mt 27:46) is strongest, though a number of modern interpreters argue that the quotation of Psalm 22:1 in Mark 15:34 is Mark's way of providing the content of the wordless shout in Mark 15:37. Aside from the fact that this would require Mark's narration of only one cry instead of two, the most prominent obstacle to this thesis is the offensiveness of Psalm 22:1 on the lips of Jesus. This is also the strongest argument favoring its authenticity. Assuming Luke had Mark's Gospel as a source for Jesus' passion, he clearly bypassed this cry of dereliction in his account. Also, in some manuscripts of Mark 15:34, "forsaken" has been replaced by "reproached," with the result that the force of the psalmic citation has been weakened dramatically. These provide literary evidence for the offensiveness of this citation in the early church.

Some interpreters have suggested that the use of Psalm 22:1 here was intended to call to mind the vindication of the Righteous One, promised in the psalm when read as a whole. In first-century Judaism, was the citation of the opening of a psalm designed to recall the psalm in its entirety? Evidence for this phenomenon is very late. We are left with the starkness of Jesus' cry from the cross, a starkness that speaks pointedly for its historicity. Who would invent for Jesus so scandalous an outburst?

What, then, of the quotation of Psalm 31:5 in the Lukan account? Has Luke simply substituted one psalmic citation for another? Three lines of evidence converge to suggest that Luke is not independently responsible for the use of Psalm 31:5 in this context (Green 1988, 97-98). First, we see an interesting coincidence of language when moving from Luke 23:46 to the way in which Matthew and John report Jesus' death. Luke, in the words of the psalm, reports that Jesus "commits his spirit," while Matthew 27:50 records that Jesus "yielded up his spirit" and John 19:30 has it that Jesus "delivered up his spirit." Luke is the only writer who cites Psalm 31:5 here, but these parallels suggest the common use of a very old tradition rooted in the psalm.

Second, even though Luke elsewhere consistently employs the Greek Old Testament (LXX), here his citation is drawn from the Hebrew text (MT). Luke, who gives no indication that he knew Hebrew, seems to have borrowed this material from a source that had already translated the Hebrew text into Greek.

Finally, some scholars have suggested that the allusions to Psalm 31:5 in Acts 7:59 and 1 Peter 4:19 indicate the general use of the psalm in dangerous settings. It may even have been used as an evening benediction in late Judaism. This speaks to the appropriateness of Psalm 31:5 in the final moments of Jesus' passion and leaves open the possibility of the saying's authenticity.

2.3. Jesus' Crucifixion as Interpretive Problem. "The chief priests and our rulers delivered him up to the death sentence. They crucified him, but we had hoped he was about to redeem Israel" (Lk 24:20-21). By not explicitly identifying the "they" responsible for the crucifixion in this text, Luke continues his strategy of exonerating the Roman authorities while inculpating the Jewish leadership. The dashed hopes of Jesus' followers are the real point at issue here, howev-

er. With these words, Cleopas and his friend voice their shock and discouragement over Jesus' death. They also strike at the root of the interpretive problem raised by a crucified Messiah (*see* Christ I: Gospels).

It is true that Christian apologetic found in Isaiah 52:13—53:12 is a prophecy of the suffering Messiah (e.g., Acts 3:13-18; 1 Pet 2:21-24; see later, Athanasius, "On the Incarnation"). But first-century Jewish messianic expectation focused preeminently on a royal, glorious Son of David. The Isaianic passage never mentions the Messiah, and late Judaism did not turn to this passage to fill in its portrait of the expected deliverer.

If the notion of a suffering Messiah runs counter to what we know of messianic speculation in the first century, how much more an oxymoron a crucified Messiah must have seemed. After all, according to current interpretation of Deuteronomy 21:22-23, a victim of crucifixion was cursed of God. Yet, the "Messiah" is literally "God's Anointed." Clearly the cross of Christ presented a conspicuous enigma—it cried out for reinterpretation.

Some interpreters regard the resurrection of Jesus as the crucial key to overturning the ignominy of the cross. Its role in authenticating Jesus' mission in spite of the cross should not be downplayed. At the same time, we would be gravely mistaken were we to assume the cross of Christ carried no significance apart from the resurrection. In fact, one might better say that the resurrection authenticated the mission and message of Jesus, including the message of his death on a cross. As we shall see, the Gospels present the cross as the culmination of his mission (cf., e.g., Mk 10:45; Lk 24:25-27; Jn 12:23-28). At this point, it will be worthwhile to reflect briefly on two closely related questions—namely, how Jesus understood his death and how it was interpreted by the earliest churches.

Combining his creative reflection on the development of atonement theology in earliest Christianity with his synthesis of traditional scholarship on the subject, Hengel has argued that the interpretation of Jesus' death as a vicarious, atoning sacrifice stems from Jesus' understanding of his death. His point of departure is the Pauline material and pre-Pauline traditions that ensure that the interpretation of Jesus' death as saving event can be traced back at least as far back as the earliest Greek-speaking Christian communities (e.g., Rom 4:25; 1 Cor 15:3-5; Gal 2:20-21).

Pushing further, Hengel insists that in order to understand the crucifixion of Jesus as the execution of the Messiah, Jewish Christians would have had to attribute to that death overwhelmingly positive significance. The interpretive categories offered by major currents of modern scholarship, Jesus as "righteous sufferer" and "prophet-martyr," are rejected by Hengel as inadequate for this purpose. The only satisfactory answer is that the first disciples, too, understood Jesus' death as an atoning sacrifice.

Pushing still further, Hengel traces this interpretation back to the ransom saying and Jesus' words at the Last Supper (Mk 10:45; 14:24). Thus Jesus anticipated his death and understood himself in his death as fulfilling the role of the Suffering Servant of the Lord (Is 52:13—53:12). Hengel concludes, "It was not primarily their own theological reflections, but above all the interpretive sayings of Jesus at the Last Supper which showed them how to understand his death properly" (Hengel 1981, 73; cf. Lohse).

Against this reconstruction, some scholars will take issue with Hengel's acceptance of the authenticity of the ransom sayings attributed to Jesus in Mark 10:45 and Mark 14:24. At the same time, it is worth noting that a growing number of scholars are admitting the probability that Jesus anticipated his execution by Roman authorities. He could scarcely have done otherwise given the content of his message (see below). To admit this, however, is to admit its corollary—namely, the probability that Jesus reflected on the relation of his mission and his death. For example, why did Jesus inquire of his disciples, "Who do you say that I am" (Mt 16:13-26; Mk 8:27-38; Lk 9:18-26)? Did his interest lie solely in soliciting from them a confession of his identity? Understood in its context, Jesus' inquiry and subsequent teaching on the suffering of the Son of man can be taken only as his attempt to relate in the most intimate way his execution and mission. Jesus thus regarded his imminent death as somehow integral to his mission, to bring redemption to Israel and the nations (see Meyer, 216-19).

A more pressing concern to be raised against Hengel's study is its claim to have recovered the one, earliest interpretation of Jesus' death. He is not alone in this pitfall, however. In spite of the rich variety of imagery employed in the NT for coming to terms with Jesus' death, the history of reflection on the cross is littered with attempts to discern its significance in narrow terms. In reality, just as the crucifixion of Jesus is the most historically certain of the events of Jesus' life, it is also the most widely interpreted.

Another perspective on Jesus' death with a claim to having been rooted in Jesus' understanding has been outlined by D. C. Allison. He undertakes an interesting survey of the expectation of a final, great tribulation in Jewish literature. From this he is able to show that the notion of a great tribulation was often associated with the coming of the eschatological era of salvation, but not according to any fixed model. Working backward from the passion accounts of our Gospels, he discovers that Jesus' death marked the beginning of the fulfillment of eschatological expectation, that the death of Jesus belongs to the messianic woes that mark the birth of the new era.

This crisis-oriented interpretation is suggested by several events of the passion—including darkness at noon (Mk 15:33), the rending of the temple curtain (Mk 15:38) and the resurrection of the holy ones (Mt 27:51-53). Allison also sifts through the Gospels to discover evidence that Jesus understood his ministry in terms of the eschatological distress (e.g., Mt 11:12-13; Lk 12:49-53). Accordingly, "Jesus foresaw for himself suffering, death, and vindication in the eschatological drama, which he took to be already unfolding" (Allison, 142). In short, Jesus' death and resurrection marked the dawning of the great Day of the Lord (see Eschatology I).

These are only two more focused interpretations of Jesus' execution that lay good claim to having arisen out of Jesus' understanding of his mission and death. Even more fundamental than these is the overarching reality that Jesus' suffering and death were recognized and proclaimed for their centrality to God's redemptive plan. The enigma of a crucified Messiah begged for interpretation. Taking their cues from Jesus' understanding, those first disciples saw in the cross the fulfillment of God's purpose.

3. Why Was Jesus Crucified?

For the most recent chapter in the quest of the historical Jesus a central question is, Why was Jesus crucified? On one level this query is answered easily enough. Historical data outside the Gospels points clearly to the reality that in a Roman province like Judea, an execution of this kind could be carried out only under the orders of the Roman procurator. Moreover, as we have seen, crucifixion was used in the Roman provinces above all as a deterrent against sedition. By inference, then, we might conclude that Jesus was crucified under Pontius Pilate as an insurrectionist. This inference is supported by the Gospels, for there the issue put before Pilate is clearly one of sedition.

In the only explicit record of the charges brought against Jesus, Luke 23:2, 5 reads, "We have found this man subverting our nation, opposing the payment of taxes to Caesar, and saying of himself that he is the Christ. . . . He stirs up the people throughout Judea by his teaching." Pilate's question to Jesus, reported in all four Gospels, is equally unambiguous in its political edge: "Are you the king of the Jews?" (Mt 27:11; Mk 15:2; Lk 23:3; Jn 18:33). Finally, Jesus is executed alongside two insurrectionists, and the inscription on the cross declares this to have been his crime as well.

Jesus, then, was executed for sedition. But rather than answering our initial question, this conclusion only sharpens it. We are left puzzled by the possible nexus between what we know of Jesus' life and the rationale for this death sentence. "The portrait of Jesus, as it is presented to us not only in the gospels but throughout the New Testament, is utterly irreconcilable with this explanation of his death" (Harvey, 14; see 11-35; Sanders, 294-318).

Indeed, at his arrest Jesus protests that he is not leading a rebellion against the state (Mt 26:55; Mk 14:48; Lk 22:52). Moreover, Jesus' followers were not rounded up and summarily executed, as one would have expected had Jesus been leading an insurrectionist movement (cf., e.g., Josephus *Ant.* 20.5.1—20.8.10 §§97-188; *J.W.* §§2.12.3—2.14.1 §§232-72). Furthermore, after Jesus' death his disciples were allowed to form a community in Jerusalem, an unthinkable development had they been known as a seditious party. Finally, had Jesus taught political resistance against Rome, we might imagine that his followers would have involved themselves in aggressive opposition against the state subsequent to his death. We are left, therefore, with a most enigmatic set of circumstances.

One scholar who has taken this problem seriously is E. P. Sanders. He tries to solve this puzzle with special reference to Jesus' physical demonstration against the temple (Mt 21:12-13; Mk 11:15-17; Lk 19:45-46). This act, Sanders insists, was not intended as a cleansing of the temple but as a portent of its destruction (*see* Temple Cleansing). This, he argues, was Jesus' last public act, after which was put in motion the decisive plot against his life. Set within the context of Jesus' proclamation of the kingdom of God and his capacity to excite the hopes of the people, this act against the temple was sufficient to bring Jesus to the attention of the Romans as a political threat. He was executed, then, at the behest of the Jewish leadership as a dangerous man but not as an actual leader of an insurgent party.

Although plausible in its way, Sanders's reconstruction of the rationale for Jesus' execution overlooks important aspects of the Gospel accounts. He is unable to come to terms with the role of the Jewish leaders in the process of Jesus' passion. In fact, his hypothesis leaves little room for the contribution of the Jews to this action, since, in his mind, the Jesus-Jewish (Pharisaic) conflict recorded in the Gospels is anachronistic. Moreover, his attempt to discount the material recorded in the Gospels that intervenes between the temple action and the onset of the passion story fails to convince. Although we can believe the temple action was a significant causal factor in Jesus' arrest and condemnation, it seems unlikely that it was the immediate cause.

Harvey, by contrast, argues that the Jewish leaders did hand Jesus over to Roman authority, but only after their failure to cope effectively with this Jew whom they regarded as a threat to general peace and security. In this regard, Harvey is drawn to the Lukan account, according to which Jesus was not found guilty or condemned as deserving death by the Jewish leaders (Lk 22:66-71; Acts 13:27-28; cf. Jn 18:19-23). Harvey therefore concludes that the Sanhedrin held an informal hearing, the purpose of which was to decide whether, and on what grounds, to hand Jesus over to Pilate. What is lacking from Harvey's account is any discussion of why the Sanhedrin might have regarded Jesus as a threat.

A hint in this direction is provided by John 11:45-53. Here the Sanhedrin, meeting informally, initiates a plot against Jesus because they fear reprisals from Rome: "If we allow Jesus to go on like this, everyone will believe in him and the Romans will come and destroy both our Temple and our nation" (Jn 11:48). In fact, in the decades before the Jewish war, Palestine was the scene of repeated liberation movements, and Rome's repeated response was to kill the leaders of such movements and their followers.

At this point, Sanders is correct: Jesus would have posed no immediate threat had it not been for his following. At the same time, we need not follow Sanders in aborting completely the record of Jesus-Jewish hostility recorded in the Gospels. First-century Judaism was marked by conflict—internally among the various forms of Judaism existing at the time and externally with Rome. Jesus' mission, construed in broad terms as the restoration of Israel in the context of the coming of God's universal rule, must have posed a threat within the social and power matrix of first-century Judaism. No less, of course, Jesus' proclamation of the eschatological kingdom would have posed a political threat to those most supportive of the present order, including the Roman authorities. Even though Jesus presented no threat of a violent, military takeover, his message of liberation and his growing popularity nevertheless made him a dangerous political risk. This threat, heightened by Jesus' activity subsequent to his arrival in Jerusalem for Passover, led to his execution.

4. The Death of Jesus in the Gospel of Matthew.
Any treatment of Jesus' death in the First Gospel must move beyond the boundaries of Matthew's passion narrative. Regardless of the tradition history of the passion story, it is now carefully integrated into the Gospel as a whole. We will discuss Matthew's portrayal of Jesus' death under four headings: the rejection of Jesus and the gospel, the death of Jesus and Matthew's christology, the way of the cross, and the death of Jesus and the new era of salvation.

4.1. The Rejection of Jesus and the Gospel. Matthew's tragic account of Israel's rejection of God's Messiah provides the central drama of his Gospel. This theme reaches its climax in Matthew 27:25, where the Jews accept full responsibility for Jesus' execution: "His blood be on us and our children!" Its roots lie deep in Matthew's narrative of Jesus' life and ministry, and can be traced back to the story of Herod and the magi from the East (*see* Birth of Jesus).

Matthew 2:1-12 is framed in such a way as to spotlight the character of the various responses to the birth of Jesus. The importance of this story and the reactions it describes lies in its posi-tion as the first story wherein the birth of Jesus is made public and in the reader's awareness of Jesus' identity as "Immanuel," the one who would save his people from their sins (Mt 1:21-23). How would Herod, king of the Jews, respond to the news of the birth of this king of the Jews?

Having discovered the place of Messiah's birth, the magi go to Bethlehem to worship him. Herod, however, and with him the chief priests and teachers of the Law, knew the town of the Messiah's birth but did not go to welcome him or pay him homage. Quite the contrary, Herod's troubled spirit gives way to malice, and he orders the deaths of the male children in the area of Bethlehem. Against Herod's plans for Jesus' premature death, God repeatedly intervenes to protect the child (Mt 2:12-13, 22). But the die is cast; Jesus' rejection and violent death are clearly foreshadowed.

Although with the onset of Jesus' mission the crowds respond favorably to his message (e.g., Mt 7:28-29), contained in that message are portents of the coming crisis: "Blessed are those who are persecuted for the sake of righteousness" (Mt 5:10; cf. Mt 5:44). No doubt for Matthew, Jesus, who was committed to the way of righteousness, was the ultimate exemplar of these words. Jesus did not seek death, but he recognized that a life of righteousness was a life lived contrary to the conventions of his world. Only persecution could result.

The seemingly inevitable change in attitude toward Jesus is prefigured by the introduction of John the Baptist in Matthew 11:1-19. Jesus compares his fate with that of the imprisoned John: just as they rejected John, so will they reject Jesus. This motif is consummated in Matthew 14:1-12, where Matthew narrates the decapitation of John. The parallels between the executions of John and Jesus are striking. In each story, the plot against the protagonist is forestalled by his popularity (Mt 14:3-5; 21:45-46; 26:3-5). Both indicate that the Roman ruler in each case is reluctant to carry out the execution but gives in to external pressure (Mt 14:9-10; 27:11-26). After his death, disciples of John come, take his body and bury it (Mt 14:12); likewise, after Jesus' death a disciple of Jesus comes, takes his body and buries it (Mt 27:57-60). These verbal and conceptual similarities mark the execution of John as an anticipatory allusion to the similar fate of Jesus.

Between the introduction of John in Matthew 11:1 and his reappearance in Matthew 14:1 lie additional portraitures of hostility and rejection. In Matthew 12:1-13 a conflict arises between Jesus and the Pharisees over appropriate behavior on the sabbath. This leads to the first mention of a Jewish plot against Jesus in Matthew 12:14. Additional records of conflict follow: in Matthew 12:24-32, where Jesus is accused by the Pharisees of casting out demons by Beelzebub; in Matthew 12:38-42, where the Pharisees and teachers of the Law, compared to an evil and adulterous generation, ask for a miraculous sign; and in Matthew 13:53-58, where Jesus is rejected even by his townspeople.

In the midst of this section marked by hostility and the anticipation of Israel's final rejection of Jesus, Matthew introduces a counterpoint: Jesus is the Spirit-anointed Servant chosen by God (Mt 12:17-21, citing Is 42:1-4). If he is rejected by Israel, it is as a result of his obedience to his divine mission. During Jesus' public ministry the Pharisees and teachers of the Law appear routinely as his opponents. With the opening of the passion narrative in Matthew 26:1-5, the chief priests and the elders assume this role. They in turn enter into a contract with one of Jesus' disciples (Mt 26:14-16), then incite the crowds against Jesus. Finally, this progressive circle of hostility reaches its climax: they "all" *(pas)* call for his death (Mt 27:25).

Thus the cross casts its shadow across the entirety of Matthew's Gospel. Its cruel reality is present by way of anticipation and threat in the motifs of hostility and rejection. Jesus' death is Israel's ultimate rejection of God's Messiah.

4.2. The Death of Jesus and Matthew's Christology. Matthew's christological interests are manifest already in his introduction of Jesus as Messiah, Son of David and Son of Abraham (*see* Abraham) in Matthew 1:1. The subsequent record of Jesus' genealogy (Mt 1:2-18) accentuates his identity as the Messiah.

Also evident early on, and of central importance to Matthew's christology, is his portrayal of Jesus' solidarity with God's people and God's purpose. As the genealogical record shows, Jesus' coming is rooted deeply in the history of God's dealings with Israel (Mt 1:1-18). The story of Jesus' birth, with its parallels to Israel's past, adds to this theme. He is born in the midst of hostility, forced into exile and brought out of Egypt into the land of Israel (Mt 2:1-23). Mat-

thew's employment of OT quotations to signify Jesus as the consummation of OT promise (e.g., Mt 1:22-23; 2:15-18) also fits into this scheme, rooting Jesus solidly in the history of Israel and divine promise. Jesus' mission thus reveals God's will and is inexorably intertwined with the pain and hope of Israel.

Jesus was crucified as a messianic pretender, but this would not have kept Matthew's readers from perceiving a deeper significance in the repeated recital of this charge (Mt 26:63; 27:11, 17, 22, 27-31, 37). Unwittingly and ironically, the high priest, Pilate and the soldiers all proclaim the true identity of Jesus. Yet, for this interpretive twist to occur, titles like "Messiah" and "king of the Jews" must have been filled with new content, for somehow, in this context, they must be correlated with the death of Jesus.

Not surprisingly, then, "Christ" is interpreted alongside other christological images in the passion story. Chief among these are "Son of God" and "Servant." The association of Christ and Son of God in the passion account is clearest in the request of the high priest, "Tell us if you are the Christ, the Son of God" (Mt 26:63). Also pertinent is the mockery of Jesus on the cross, where "Son of God" and "King of the Jews" are set in apposition (Mt 27:40, 42-43). The crucial question, then, concerns what significance we should attach to this usage. For the first clue to this riddle, we turn to the Gethsemane episode, for here Jesus addresses God in prayer as "my Father" (Mt 26:39, 42). This prayer is above all an act of submission to God. As Son of God, Jesus responds to the will of God with complete, unreserved obedience.

Likewise, in the arrest scene, Jesus makes reference to "my Father" (Mt 26:53). In this context Jesus' authority as God's Son occupies center stage, but he does not exercise this power as a means of escape. To have done so would have been to depart from his own teaching (Mt 5:44) and from God's will (Mt 26:54, 56).

A similar motif appears in the Son of God reference in Matthew 27:40. In their mockery of Jesus, the passers-by say, "Come down from the cross, if you are the Son of God," and in doing so model the form of the temptations presented Jesus by the devil in Matthew 4:3, 6: "If you are the Son of God." The inference in each case is that, as the Son of God, Jesus could do what his tempters request of him. To do so, however, would be to deny the character of obedience to

God inherent in his sonship (*see* Temptation of Jesus).

In short, to refer to Jesus as Son of God is to speak pointedly of his fidelity to his mission, of his total obedience to God. This motif is also highlighted by Matthew's portrayal of Jesus as Servant in the passion account. The repeated references to Jesus' silence (Mt 26:63; 27:14) and innocence (Mt 27:4, 18-19, 23-24) indicate Jesus' passion is the fulfillment of his role as God's Servant in ways that underscore his faithfulness to the divine mission (cf. Is 53:7, 11).

With the Servant motif, Matthew expands the theological field of his portrayal of the passion. This is evident in Jesus' interpretive words at the Last Supper, where terminology such as "on behalf of" and "poured out for many" are reminiscent of the work of the Servant in Isaiah 52:13—53:12. These sayings interpret Jesus' death as efficacious, thus showing how Jesus would "save his people from their sins" (Mt 1:21). And this helps us appreciate the significance of the taunt in Matthew 27:42: "He saved others, but he cannot save himself!" Jesus' mission is salvific, but he can open the way of salvation only by the sacrifice of his life (cf. Mt 16:25).

Commentators have often noted the heightened christology of Matthew's passion account when compared with Mark's. At the outset, Jesus announces his imminent execution (Mt 26:1-2). He declares the arrival of the appointed time (Mt 26:18). He prophesies his betrayal and identifies his betrayer (Mt 26:21, 25). He opens the way for Judas to perform his act of betrayal (Mt 26:50). He declares his capacity to escape his fate miraculously (Mt 26:53). Jesus is presented as one who has power and is in control of the events of his passion. And this is where Matthew's christological portrait comes into focus. Jesus does not exercise his power as Messiah, Son of God, to escape from death, but not because he lacks royal status or authority. Rather, Jesus exercises that power in unexpected ways: in obedience to God and in pouring out his life for others.

The story of Jesus' death in Matthew is thus the story of his fidelity to God, his faithfulness to his mission and his willing solidarity with the pain and hope of his people.

4.3. The Way of the Cross. The degree to which the cross is understood by Matthew as the ultimate expression of Jesus' mission is nowhere better seen than in the series of passion predictions in Matthew 16:21-27, Matthew 17:22-23 and Matthew 20:17-28. In these Jesus characterizes his mission as a journey to Jerusalem and thus to Golgotha.

The first is framed by Peter's confession of Jesus as "the Christ, the Son of the Living God" (Mt 16:16) and Peter's rebuke of Jesus following his announcement of imminent suffering. Clearly, Jesus' self-understanding, embracing the "divine must" *(dei)* of his passion, departs from more common messianic expectations, even among his disciples. Jesus, however, is convinced that suffering lies at the heart of his mission as Christ, Son of God, and even extends this definition to his view of discipleship. Like him, Jesus' disciples are faced with the challenge to lose their lives.

Even though Jesus' disciples have "little faith" (e.g., Mt 14:31; 17:20), they are unable to comprehend the way of the cross. After the second passion prediction they are "filled with grief" (Mt 17:23). And in the context of the third they seem to miss Jesus' whole point by concerning themselves with positions of eminence and authority. In the passion story their failure is sealed by their fearful abandonment of Jesus at his arrest (Mt 26:56). Their faithless behavior is accentuated by the actions of less well-known characters. The woman who anoints Jesus at Bethany (Mt 26:6-13), Joseph of Arimathea (Mt 27:57-60) and the faithful women at the cross and tomb (Mt 27:55-56, 61)—these are examples of persons in the passion narrative who are set in bold relief by their authentic responses to the good news (*see* Gospel [Genre]).

For apprehending the way of the cross, the importance of the final passion prediction cannot be overestimated. Here Jesus' ministry of service and redemption is cast in the language of sacrificial death: "the Son of Man did not come to be served but to serve and to give his life a ransom for many" (Mt 20:28). With this terminology, building on Matthew's earlier presentation of Jesus as the Suffering Servant (cf. Mt 8:17; 12:17-21), the cross is set squarely at the center of Jesus' life and work.

4.4. The Death of Jesus and the New Era of Salvation. Israel's rejection of Jesus and his message does not signify the end of the story for Matthew. Even in his predictions of suffering and death, Jesus' eyes focus also on resurrection (Mt 16:21; 17:23; 20:19). Likewise, his interpretive words at the Last Supper, so centered on his passion, anticipate his future in the kingdom of God (Mt 26:29). And in Matthew 26:32 he predicts his resurrection and future role in reconstituting the scattered band of disciples. Even without turning to the resurrection narrative itself, in the tearing of the temple curtain, the earthquake and the confession by the centurion, we have testimony of Jesus' vindication in spite of his rejection by Israel (Mt 27:51-54).

With mention of the centurion's confession, we open a further arena of discussion. In both subtle and transparent ways, Matthew proclaims the passing of the kingdom of God from Israel to "a people who will produce its fruit" (Mt 21:43). In his mind this reorientation of the kingdom is related directly to the crisis of rejection, Israel's delivering the Messiah over to be crucified. For example, we may observe the shift in Jesus' role as Savior. In Matthew 1:21, "he will save his people from their sins," but in Matthew 26:28 his blood "is poured out for many [i.e., "all"] for the forgiveness of sins." The time of Israel's ultimate rejection of Jesus is a time of death, but death leads to life, a new era of salvation for "the nations" (Mt 28:18-20).

The newness of this era is marked in a different way by the interpretive sayings of Jesus at the Last Supper. By his use of the words "covenant" and "forgiveness of sins" in the same breath (Mt 26:28), Jesus interprets his mission against the backdrop of Jeremiah 31:31-34. "The time is coming," Jeremiah proclaims, when the Lord will make a "new covenant." That time has come, according to Jesus. In his death he inaugurates the new order of salvation.

Here again is evidence that for Jesus, death was no unexpected event unrelated to his life and work. In his death Jesus' obedience to God is manifest, and in this the cross is comprehended as the heart of his mission to open the way of salvation to all.

5. The Death of Jesus in the Gospel of Mark.

The oft-cited judgment of a century ago that Mark's Gospel is a passion narrative with an extended introduction highlights the prominence of Jesus' death for Mark. It fails, however, to come to terms with the theological and literary nexus between Jesus' life and death. In fact, Mark represents Jesus' ministry as a relentless progression of events whose climax is Golgotha. In the cross Jesus is revealed as the Son of God who obtains salvation for the new community of

faith—a community called to follow him in sacrificial discipleship.

5.1. The Death of Jesus and Mark's Christology. Who is Jesus? This query constitutes an important leitmotif for the Second Gospel. Although we are informed at the outset that Jesus is Messiah and Son of God (Mk 1:1-15), the characters of Mark's account do not share this insight (e.g., Mk 5:41), and in any case we are well into the narrative before it becomes clear what these christological titles mean. Mark wants to instruct his audience about the true nature of Jesus, and he does so by means of a narrative oriented around the cross.

Anticipatory allusions to Jesus' passion dot the landscape of the Gospel of Mark, demonstrating the intimate relation between Jesus' identity and his suffering. Already in Mark 2:19-20 Jesus intimates his sudden, unexpected, puzzling death. Elsewhere, religious and political authorities plot his death (Mk 3:6; 11:18; 12:12), and Jesus prophetically announces his rejection and death (Mk 8:31; 9:12, 31; 10:32-34, 38-39, 45). As in Matthew's parallel (see 4.1 above), so in Mark 6:14-29 the story of John's passion prefigures Jesus' suffering and death.

The link between Jesus' death and his identity is nowhere better seen than in the crucifixion account, for Mark understands the moment of Jesus' death as the moment of divine revelation. Only in his death can Jesus be fully appreciated. This is the significance of the confession of the centurion, the only human throughout the Gospel to recognize Jesus as God's Son (Mk 15:39). In the crucifixion story Mark expressly notes that it is only as the centurion sees Jesus' dying breath that he makes his confession. That is, in the cross Jesus is recognized rightly as the Son of God. In the body of the Gospel, God acclaims Jesus as God's Son at the inauguration of his mission at his baptism (Mk 1:9-11) and in the brief revelation of Jesus' glory at the transfiguration (Mk 9:2-8). The relationship between these three events in Jesus' career emphasizes the centrality of Jesus' death to the mission for which he was ordained by God.

This understanding, focused on Jesus' status as Son of God, is paralleled in Mark's portrait of Jesus, Son of man. Indeed, it is precisely as Son of man that Jesus will suffer rejection and death (e.g., Mk 8:31; 14:21). As Son of man, Jesus' divine mission is consummated as he gives his life in service to humanity as a ransom for many

(Mk 10:45). As Son of man, he also anticipates his vindication and glory (e.g., Mk 8:38; 14:62).

What is the significance of the crucified Son of God for Mark? Of the aforementioned anticipatory references, the most consequential for interpreting the meaning of Jesus' death are the three passion predictions (Mk 8:31; 9:31; 10:32-34) and the ransom saying (Mk 10:45). These underscore the centrality of the cross to God's redemptive plan, Jesus' obedience in taking up the cross (cf. Mk 14:32-49) and so place Jesus' crucifixion at the heart of his divine mission. This interpretation is manifest not only in the "divine must" theme of the predictions (dei), but also in the later, repeated association of passion events with OT promise. The cross of Christ brings to consummation God's revealed will, as in Mark 14:21 where we should probably not think of any one text or set of texts but of OT promise as a whole. Yet, specific OT texts are fulfilled in Jesus' passion (e.g., Zech 13:7, cited in Mk 14:27). More prominent are the numerous ways in which Jesus is presented typologically as the Suffering Servant and Suffering Righteous One.

How Jesus' death functions as the center of God's redemptive plan comes to light in two Markan texts: Mark 10:45 and Mark 14:24. The significance of the former is indicated by its position at the close of the central section of Mark's Gospel, Mark 8:22—10:52, just before the triumphal entry. In this section, which boldly outlines the correlation between the way of the Christ and that of his disciples, the ransom saying is hardly ancillary to Mark's message, as some scholars have argued. The latter text serves as the climax of the Last Supper scene. In both cases Jesus' death is interpreted as salvific. In this ultimate act of service, Jesus lays down his life as an atoning sacrifice for the salvation of humanity. The irony of the scene of mockery at the cross may be understood along these lines: It is by refusing to save himself that he is able to save others (Mk 15:31; cf. Mk 8:35).

The irony of Mark's passion story is even more pervasive, extending through the appearance of Jesus before the Sanhedrin (e.g., even as Jesus is being mocked as a false prophet, his prophecy concerning Peter's denial is fulfilled [Mk 14:65-72]) and on to the crucifixion account. Paramount in this regard is the sixfold use of "king" with reference to Jesus (Mk 15:2, 9, 12, 18, 26, 32) combined with the threefold mockery of Jesus on the cross (Mk 15:29-32). Condemned as a pretender to the throne, Jesus ironically does have royal status, but not as one might have anticipated. His obedience to the divine mission expressed preeminently in the cross—this is a portent of his royal status that will be evident to all following his vindication and coming as the glorious Son of man.

5.2. The Way of the Cross. Golgotha is not only the ultimate expression of the Christ's mission for Mark. For disciples, too, there is a via dolorosa, a way of the cross.

5.2.1. "Take up the Cross." Mark 8:22—10:52 renders transparent the meeting of christology and discipleship around the cross. This section is framed by two healing miracles. The first (Mk 8:22-26) serves as a parable: The disciples understand Jesus only vaguely; they need a fuller, sharper vision of Christ's identity. Heretofore they have become cognizant of his power, his victory over evil forces of all kinds. Though Peter confesses him as Christ, he is unprepared for subsequent talk of suffering and death (Mk 8:27-33). Yet for Jesus, messiahship can be understood fully only within the matrix of the suffering Son of man. What is more, according to Jesus, if the way of the Christ is the way of suffering, so is the way of discipleship (Mk 8:34).

Prior to the second healing story (Mk 10:46-52), Jesus for the third time (Mk 10:32-45) announces his upcoming passion: Jesus and his disciples are on the way (hodos) to Jerusalem, the place of betrayal and death. Apparently still believing that "Christ" signifies "glorious king," James and John express their desire for seats of honor in the coming kingdom. Jesus redirects their thoughts to suffering and calamity, intimating that they would share his fate. Discipleship signifies a service best exemplified in the death of Jesus. Interestingly, like the healing account in Mark 8:22-26, the subsequent story of Bartimaeus can be read as a parable. Faithful, persistent Bartimaeus, first found sitting by the way (hodos), having been healed by Jesus, now sees clearly and follows Jesus on the way (hodos). The invitation to follow Jesus is an invitation to take the way of the cross.

5.2.2. The Suffering of the Community. This motif is continued and deepened in the relationship Mark draws between the suffering of the community (Mk 13) and the suffering of the Messiah (Mk 14—15). The signs of tribulation are paralleled in Jesus' passion as follows:

13:2	destruction of the temple	14:58; 15:38
13:9, 11-12	"delivered up"	14:10-11, 18, passim
13:12-13	Betrayal	14:10, 21, 43
13:24	Darkness	15:33
13:26	Son of man: tribulation, parousia	14:62
13:32-33	The "Hour"	14:32-42
13:5, 9, 23, 33, 35, 37	Eschatological watching	14:34, 37-38
13:25	provides the chronology for	14:17—15:1
13:36	"Come," "find," "sleep"	14:37, 40

On a literary level, these parallels tie together the fate of Jesus and his disciples; they are of profound theological importance too. On the one hand, they signify that the suffering of the disciples is a participation in the suffering of the Christ. On the other, they indicate the cosmic ramifications of this suffering. The cross of Christ is the turning point in history, the birthing of a new age, the coming of the kingdom of God into the world. This gives added gravity to the sufferings of Jesus' disciples. Like him, they will suffer rejection. Indeed, Mark's intended audience seems already to have found itself in a situation of persecution. This juxtaposition of images in Mark 13—15 affirms that their suffering, too, is a part of the divine plan; that their pain is a part of the process by which the kingdom of God is breaking into the world.

5.2.3. Discipleship Failure and the New Community. Mark's Gospel repeatedly intimates the failure of the hardhearted disciples (Mk 6:52) to understand the significance of Jesus' mission. Their failure reaches its acme in Mark 14:50-52 where they abandon Jesus to the arresting party in Gethsemane. It is true that Jesus anticipates their rehabilitation (Mk 14:27-28), but the intervening narrative provides unexpected tableaus of faithfulness. In a deliberate contrast with the actions of the Jewish leaders and Judas ("one of the Twelve"), the anonymous woman anoints Jesus for burial (Mk 14:1-11). Simon of Cyrene becomes a model disciple who "takes up the cross" (Mk 15:21; cf. Mk 8:34), and a group of women disciples stand by faithfully at Jesus' death (Mk 15:40-41).

Even more important for their role in Mark's theology of Jesus' passion are the rending of the temple veil (Mk 15:38) and the confession of the centurion. Together, these narrated events reveal Jesus' identity, as we have seen, but they also speak to the theme of discipleship. The first, drawing on the temple material found earlier in the Second Gospel, demonstrates that Jesus is the Messiah who destroys the temple and reconstitutes it as the community of the faithful. The importance of the latter in this context lies in the fact that it is precisely a Gentile centurion who makes the confession of Jesus as Son of God. A more emphatic word about the universal implications of Jesus' death could hardly be found.

6. The Death of Jesus in the Gospel of Luke.

The Third Evangelist leaves his readers in no doubt as to the centrality of Jesus' death for his Gospel. He sets the stage for Jesus' passion above all by highlighting his narrative of Jesus' life as a tale of conflict. In addition, throughout Luke-Acts he sounds the cadence: "the Christ must suffer!" What is less transparent is the meaning of Jesus' death for Luke.

6.1. The Rejection of the Messiah. Luke characterizes Jesus' life as a story of conflict and rejection—ominously predicted by Simeon (Lk 2:34-35), paradigmatically represented by Jesus' opposition at Nazareth (Lk 4:16-30), tragically fulfilled in Pilate's handing Jesus over to the will of the chief priests and Jewish public (Lk 23:25). On one level this portrait is nothing more than what one would have expected. For Luke, Jesus is a prophet (cf. e.g., Lk 4:24; 7:16, 39; 24:19; Acts 3:17-26; 7:37), and rejection and death are the lot of all the prophets (cf. Neh 9:26; Lk 4:24; 6:23; 11:47-51; 13:33-34; Acts 7:52). In Luke, Jesus the prophet attracted opposition especially by his concern for a brand of justice at odds with that practiced by the religious leadership and by his concomitant openness to outcasts through table fellowship (Karris). In the Gospel of Luke, Jesus' primary opponents appear to be the religious leadership in Jerusalem, and among them the chief priests are singled out for special development. Contrasting with their malevolence is the relatively benign political leadership. In each of the canonical Gospels we find that the major share of blame for the death of Jesus is attributed to the Jews, especially the Jewish leaders, rather than to the Romans. This is especially clear in Luke's Gospel, where Jesus' innocence is declared by Pilate three times and confirmed by Herod (Lk 23:4, 14-15, 22).

The Lukan motif of conflict is not limited to Jesus' interaction with the human characters of the Gospel, however. The divine anointing of Jesus for his mission is set within the immediate context of temptation by the devil (Lk 3:21—4:13), and the subsequent narrative demonstrates the continual cosmic dimensions of opposition against Jesus (e.g., Lk 13:10-17). With the onset of the passion story, supernatural conflict moves again to center court: Satan enters Judas (Lk 22:3; cf. 22:31), and Jesus' struggle on the Mount of Olives as throughout his mission is colored in eschatological, cosmic hues (Lk 22:53; cf. *peirasmos*, "struggle," in Lk 4:13; 8:13; 22:28, 40, 46).

Against this backdrop it is surely significant that Luke does not set the disciples over against Jesus as they are in the other Synoptics. Although Judas does betray Jesus, he does so under the power of Satan (Lk 22:3). Likewise, Peter's denial is related to Satan's influence (Lk 22:31-34). In recounting Jesus' arrest, Luke is conspicuously silent about the disciples, with the result that their fate is left open; they do not abandon Jesus, as in Matthew and Mark. Indeed, the disciples are "with" Jesus in a way not paralleled in the other Synoptic Gospels (Lk 22:28). This has important repercussions for our reading of the link between Jesus' crucifixion and discipleship, a theme to which we will return shortly.

6.2. "The Christ Must Suffer!" It is true that Luke inherited from Mark an emphasis on the necessity of Jesus' passion (e.g., Mk 8:31). But in Luke, Jesus evinces a purposefulness about the cross that is without parallel in the Synoptic Gospels. Not only does he "set his face to go up to Jerusalem" (Lk 9:51), the place of rejection and death (Lk 18:31-32), but also, with the onset of his passion, he exercises a surprising prescience regarding the details of his betrayal, arrest and death. More so than in the other Synoptics, here Jesus is in control of the events of his passion.

When Jesus foretells his suffering and rejection, he notes their necessity in salvation-historical terms *(dei)*. This characterization is continued even after the passion account by means of showing how the crucified Jesus could be the Messiah of God. "Was it not necessary for the Christ to suffer these things and to enter into his glory?" (Lk 24:25-27). Phrases of this kind appear again and again in Luke-Acts.

Students of Luke-Acts have long been aware of the gravity of Jesus' death for Luke. Noting that the weight of Luke's theological interest falls on Jesus' resurrection and exaltation, however, they have puzzled over the meaning of the cross. In what way is the death of Jesus crucial to God's redemptive purpose? On this theological problem Luke has seemed less than clear. Indeed, according to many interpreters, to the question Why did Jesus have to die? Luke seems only to answer, Because God willed it!

6.2.1. The Death of Jesus and Lukan Soteriology. In the past, many commentators have assumed Luke attributed to Jesus' death the salvific meaning found elsewhere in the NT. Thus Luke, like the other NT writers, affirmed that "Jesus died for our sins." More recent scholarship has reacted against this reading, insisting that Luke must be read on his own terms and not within the theological categories of the Pauline theology of the cross. Accordingly, students of Luke have pointed out that Luke neglects to recount the ransom logion in his parallel to Mark 10:41-45 (Lk 22:24-27); the sermons in Acts do not draw a direct line between the cross and forgiveness of sins; and material in Luke-Acts borrowed from Isaiah 52:13—53:12 fails to mention the vicarious, atoning significance of the Servant's death (e.g., Lk 22:37; Acts 8:32-33).

Of course, the eucharistic words of Jesus (Lk 22:19-20) do root human salvation in the death of Jesus (see Last Supper). However, noting their absence in some textual witnesses, a number of scholars have postulated that they were missing from Luke's original text (cf. RSV [some editions], NEB). Others, who accept their originality to the Lukan narrative, are nevertheless impressed with how non-Lukan these verses appear linguistically. As in Acts 20:28 (the only other passage in the Lukan corpus that clearly bases human salvation in the death of Jesus), Luke appears to be repeating ancient terminology without making its theology his own.

A conclusion of this sort is confirmed by those passages in which Luke makes transparent his understanding of the means of salvation. In Acts 2:33, Acts 5:30-31 and Acts 10:43 we discern Luke's concern to show that the means of salvation is the exaltation of Jesus. Of these three passages, Acts 5:30-31 is of particular interest for two reasons. First, it is here that the logic is most clear: as a result of his exaltation Jesus is enthroned as Prince and Savior and in these capacities is able to offer salvation. Second, this text underscores again the necessity of Jesus' death for salvation history.

Clearly the death of Jesus has positive significance for Luke, but just as clearly that significance is not centered on an interpretation of the cross as a vicarious sacrifice. How then might this significance be understood?

6.2.2. The Death of Jesus: A Martyrdom? The interpretation of Jesus' death as a martyrdom has enjoyed widespread support in this century (see Beck). This view exploits the connections between the Lukan passion and the literature of martyrdom in late Judaism. Common themes include the presence of supernatural conflict and divine help, the innocence and endurance of the victim and the portrait of the martyr's death as exemplary for the faithful.

Although this interpretation attributes positive significance to the death of Jesus in Luke and makes good on a number of important aspects of the Lukan portrayal, it has come under serious scrutiny in recent years. First, it has been questioned how far Luke anticipated Jesus' disciples would be asked to follow in Jesus' steps. Thus, the call to take up the cross (Mk 8:34) has become in Luke a call to a lifestyle marked by the cross ("day by day," Lk 9:23), not a reference to impending persecution. Second, a number of details integral to martyr tales are missing from Luke, most notably the horrific detail in descriptions of the means of death. Moreover, in Luke, Jesus, unlike the martyrs of Jewish literature, appears as one who struggles with the prospect of death (Lk 22:39-46). Third, as has become clear from continued study of the religious background of the first century, the themes of the martyrological literature are not in every case unique to that corpus. Thus one might postulate that Luke and the literature of martyrdom drew from a common world of thought. Finally, it has become evident that the notion of Jesus as martyr fails to do justice to the richness of Luke's mural of Jesus' passion. Although it may be one among other Lukan concerns, by itself it falls short as a summary of Luke's theology of Jesus' death.

6.3. From the Suffering Righteous One to the Suffering Servant. Other students of Luke have noted the repeated evidences of Jesus' innocence in Luke 23 and the many parallels between Jesus and the suffering Righteous One in the Psalms and book of Wisdom. On this basis they have postulated for Luke an interpretation of Jesus' passion as the suffering and death of God's Righteous Sufferer who goes to his death in spite of his innocence but is subsequently vindicated by God. This view makes sense of the innocence motif in the passion story, dovetails well with the "contrast formulae" in the speeches in Acts (e.g., "you put Jesus to death, but God raised him from the dead," Acts 2:23-24) and demonstrates in Jesus' life how God overturns injustice—an important theme in Luke-Acts.

At the same time, it is clear that even this interpretation is insufficient to grasp the heart of Luke's understanding of Jesus' death, for it fails to explain the divine necessity of the cross in salvation-historical terms. A more successful interpretive model focuses on the Suffering Servant of Isaiah, which is a clearer embodiment of the OT Righteous Sufferer (Green 1990).

That Luke is interested more pointedly in the Suffering Servant is manifest in the passion story and elsewhere in his two-part work. In the passion story, Jesus cites Isaiah 53:12 as a general allusion to his suffering and death, thus communicating that in his passion he fulfills the role of the Suffering Servant. Jesus is repeatedly declared innocent and acclaimed by the centurion as a "righteous man," an allusion to Isaiah 53:11 (cf. the conjunction of *dikaios* ["righteous"] and Jesus' suffering in Acts 3:13-14, where Jesus' passion is described in words borrowed from Is 52:13—53:12). Jesus refuses to speak in his own defense (Lk 23:9; Is 53:7). And in his mockery, Jesus is called "the Chosen One," a designation for God's Servant (Lk 23:35; Is 42:1). Outside the passion story, numerous references to Jesus' role as the Servant appear, the most explicit in the citation of Isaiah 53:7-8 in Acts 8:32-33 and the prophetic reference to Jesus' mission by Simeon in words borrowed from Isaiah 49:6 (Lk 2:32).

The significance of the identification of Jesus' passion as that of the Suffering Servant for Luke is threefold. First, it indicates how Luke can emphasize the salvation-historical necessity of the cross and spotlight Jesus' exaltation or vindication as the salvific event. The Isaianic portrayal of the Suffering Servant holds together these twin motifs, particularly in Isaiah 53:11, where, following his suffering, God's Righteous One will justify many. In other words, Luke's characterization of Jesus as the Servant indicates the necessity of his death and the salvific import of his vindication.

Second, Luke's emphasis on the Servant provides a framework for drawing out the universal implications of Jesus' mission. That Jesus would be "a light for revelation to the Gentiles" was predicted by Simeon (Lk 2:32; Is 49:6), so it is noteworthy that at Jesus' death he was acclaimed as the Righteous One by a Gentile. However, the importance of Jesus' death is not only for the Gentile but also for the Jew (e.g., Lk 23:34, 48) and the criminal (Lk 23:43). That is, in Jesus' death one finds the culmination of a life lived for others, including outsiders.

Third, by portraying Jesus' career, and especially his death and exaltation, as that of the Suffering Servant, Luke demonstrates in the ultimate manner his understanding of the way of salvation. Already in the lives of Elizabeth and Zechariah, Luke shows that God's salvation comes through a pattern of reversal, (Lk 1). For Luke the inbreaking of the kingdom of God marks a transposition of roles as the God who is faithful vindicates the faithful. The career of Jesus illustrates this theme of reversal, for he is the innocent Servant who suffers unto death but is raised up and designated Prince and Savior. By putting aside thoughts of self-glorification and obediently adopting the role of the servant (cf. Lk 12:37; 22:25-27), Jesus embodies the righteousness, humiliation and lowliness of the Servant. The cross is the consequence, but God overturned this humiliation, vindicating his Servant, exalting him and in so doing opened the way of repentance and forgiveness. For Luke this is the way of salvation, and this is the way of discipleship.

7. The Death of Jesus in the Gospel of John.

Until relatively recent years, students of the Fourth Gospel downplayed the importance of the passion for John's presentation of Jesus. Some interpreters even posited a theological chasm between John 17 and John 18, suggesting that Jesus' trial and execution had no place in the portrayal of the glorious Jesus found elsewhere in the Fourth Gospel. This view has begun to fall into disfavor among Johannine scholars, as studies have recognized the numerous allusions to the passion in the earlier sections of the Gospel (cf. Jn 2:12-22; 3:14) and the fact that eight chapters of the Gospel are related to the passion (Jn 12—19), and begun to demonstrate anew the integration of the cross into the totality of John's christology. We will discuss the meaning of Jesus' death for John first by mentioning two subsidiary themes—the sovereignty

of Jesus in the passion account and Jesus' death as sacrifice—then by noting how the cross relates to the journey of the Son of God from incarnation to exaltation.

7.1. Jesus, Sovereign King. When turning from the Synoptic versions to the Johannine account of Jesus' suffering and death, one is immediately struck with the majesty of Jesus in John. He has long known his betrayer (Jn 6:70) and sets in motion the act of betrayal (Jn 13:27). In the arrest scene it is neither Judas nor the arresting party that is in charge, but Jesus, revealing himself as the "I Am" *(egō eimi)* and negotiating the release of his disciples (Jn 18:1-11). In his hearing before Pilate he is presented as king and even takes the role of judge (Jn 18:28—19:16). Requiring no assistance, he bears his own cross (Jn 19:17). He cares for his mother from the cross (Jn 19:25-27), and before the soldiers can perform the coup de grâce, breaking his legs to speed his death, he dies of his own accord (Jn 19:20-33).

In this manner John demonstrates the truth of Jesus' words, "No one takes my life from me, but I lay it down of my own volition" (Jn 10:18). Clearly John is concerned to relate Jesus' passion to his larger representation of Jesus' glorious sojourn on earth (cf. Jn 1:14b) as a self-giving act.

7.2. Jesus' Death: Life for the World. Though it is not the linchpin for John's understanding of the death of Jesus, the sacrificial significance of the cross is nevertheless important to his Gospel. This motif initially appears in John 1:29, 36, where the forgiveness of sins is related to the appellation "Lamb of God." Though Lamb of God is capable of other nuances as well, it is at least associated with the theological world of the Passover lamb. This is suggested not only by the atonement theology resident in John 1:29, but also by John's clear attempts to portray Jesus' death as a Passover sacrifice in the passion story. In this regard the following details may be noted: the time of Jesus' death coincided with the time of the paschal sacrifice (Jn 19:14; cf. 18:28); the hyssop and basin are present at the cross (Jn 19:29; Ex 12:22); seeing the blood flow from the side of Jesus is emphasized (Jn 19:35; Ex 12:13); and the soldiers do not break Jesus' legs (Jn 19:31-37; Ex 12:46). This emphasis on Passover is probably related to the extended discourse on Jesus as the bread of life (Jn 6:25-59): Whoever partakes of Jesus' flesh and blood will have life.

Similarly, John 3:16 links the incarnation of God's Son to the offer of life. The language of atonement found more pervasively in Paul also has a place in the Johannine narrative. Thus *hyper* ("on behalf of") is used in John to underscore the redemptive nature of the cross in John 6:51; John 10:11, 15; John 11:50-52; and John 18:14. Finally, John understands the foot washing at Jesus' final meal with his disciples not only as a demonstration of exemplary behavior but also as a symbol of Jesus' salvific death (Jn 13:8-11).

7.3. Crucifixion and Exaltation. In terms of the integration of Jesus' death with the Johannine christology as a whole, the most pervasive motif is that of "raising up" or "exaltation." This, we are repeatedly informed, is the fate of Jesus the Son of Man (Jn 3:14-15; 8:28; 12:32-33). Clearly this "being lifted up" (*hypsoō*, Jn 3:14; 8:28; 12:32) has a double meaning. On the one hand, it is associated in John's schema with the terminology of glorification. On the other, in John 8:28 we read that the Jews will be the agents of Jesus' "lifting up," and in John 12:32-33 John notes that "lifting up" is a metaphor for the way Jesus will be put to death (cf. Jn 18:32).

John therefore sees some intimate connection between Jesus' crucifixion and his exaltation, and this suggests that Jesus' death must be set within the larger Johannine portrait of Jesus' earthly career. For the Fourth Evangelist, the life of the Son of God is best understood as a journey: He comes from his preexistent state in heaven, dwells among women and men, then returns to heaven. He who descended from glory must ascend to glory (e.g., Jn 3:13, 31; 6:38; 8:23; 13:1-3).

How is his passion related to this christological movement? It is the means by which he returns to the Father. That is, John overcomes the scandal of the cross by interpreting it in terms of Jesus' exaltation. This reading is encouraged by the fact that in those places where the reference to the "lifting up" of Jesus is clearest—John 3:14, John 8:28 and John 12:32-34—John has developed the larger theme of the Son's journey from and return to God. In this way the cross is interpreted by the journey motif as the means by which the Son of man left the world below to return to the world above (Nicholson).

What is more, Jesus' death, understood as a lifting up (Jn 3:14), appears as the ultimate expression of love, the gift of God (Jn 3:16). Indeed, Jesus' love for his followers reaches its acme in his sacrificial service and death (Jn 13:1; 15:13).

See also LAST SUPPER; RESURRECTION; SERVANT OF YAHWEH; TRIAL OF JESUS.

DJG: BURIAL OF JESUS; GETHSEMANE; PASSION NARRATIVE; PREDICTIONS OF JESUS' PASSION AND RESURRECTION; RANSOM SAYING.

BIBLIOGRAPHY. D. C. Allison Jr., *The End of the Ages Has Come: An Early Interpretation of the Passion and Resurrection of Jesus* (Philadelphia: Fortress, 1985); B. E. Beck, " 'Imitatio Christi' and the Lucan Passion Narrative," in *Suffering and Martyrdom in the New Testament: Studies Presented to G. M. Styler by the Cambridge New Testament Seminar,* ed. W. Horbury and B. McNeil (Cambridge: Cambridge University Press, 1981) 28-47; A. Dauer, *Die Passionsgeschichte im Johannesevangelium: Eine traditionsgeschichtliche und theologische Untersuchung zu John 18:1—19:30* (Munich: Kösel, 1972); J. B. Green, "The Death of Jesus, God's Servant," in *Reimaging the Death of the Lukan Jesus,* ed. D. Sylva (BBB 73; Frankfurt: Anton Hain, 1990) 1-28, 170-73; idem, *The Death of Jesus: Tradition and Interpretation in the Passion Narrative* (WUNT 2:33; Tübingen: Mohr Siebeck, 1988); A. E. Harvey, *Jesus and the Constraints of History* (Philadelphia: Westminster, 1982); M. Hengel, *The Atonement: The Origins of the Doctrine in the New Testament* (Philadelphia: Fortress, 1981); idem, *Crucifixion in the Ancient World and the Folly of the Message of the Cross* (London: SCM, 1977); H. W. Hoehner, *Chronological Aspects of the Life of Christ* (Grand Rapids: Zondervan, 1977); D. Juel, *Messiah and Temple: The Trial of Jesus in the Gospel of Mark* (SBLDS 31; Missoula, MT: Scholars Press, 1977); R. J. Karris, O.F.M., *Luke: Artist and Theologian: Luke's Passion Narrative as Literature* (TI; New York: Paulist, 1985); K. M. Kenyon, *The Bible and Recent Archaeology,* rev. ed. by P. R. S. Moorey (Atlanta: John Knox, 1987); J. Kodell, O.S.B., "Luke's Theology of the Death of Jesus," in *Sin, Salvation, and the Spirit,* ed. D. Durken, O.S.B. (Collegeville, MN: Liturgical Press, 1979) 221-30; B. Lindars, "The Passion in the Fourth Gospel," in *God's Christ and His People: Studies in Honor of Nils Alstrup Dahl,* ed. J. Jervell and W. A. Meeks (Oslo: Universitetsforlaget, 1977) 71-86; E. Lohse, *Märtyrer und Gottesknecht: Untersuchungen zur urchristlichen Verkündigung vom Sühntod Jesu Christi* (2d ed.; Göttingen: Vandenhoek & Ruprecht, 1963); I. H. Marshall, *Last Supper and Lord's Supper*

(Grand Rapids: Eerdmans, 1980); F. J. Matera, *Passion Narratives and Gospel Theologies: Interpreting the Synoptics Through Their Passion Stories* (TI; New York/Mahwah, NJ: Paulist, 1986); B. F. Meyer, *The Aims of Jesus* (London: SCM, 1979); J. Neyrey, S.J., *The Passion According to Luke: A Redaction Study of Luke's Soteriology* (TI; New York/Mahwah, NJ: Paulist, 1986); G. C. Nicholson, *Death as Departure: The Johannine Descent-Ascent Schema* (SBLDS 63; Chico, CA: Scholars Press, 1983); E. P. Sanders, *Jesus and Judaism* (London: SCM, 1985); D. Senior, *The Passion Narrative According to Matthew: A Redactional Study* (Leuven: Leuven University, 1975); idem, *The Passion of Jesus in the Gospel of Luke* (Wilmington, DE: Michael Glazier, 1989); idem, *The Passion of Jesus in the Gospel of Mark* (Wilmington, DE: Michael Glazier, 1984); idem, *The Passion of Jesus in the Gospel of Matthew* (Wilmington, DE: Michael Glazier, 1985); V. Taylor, *The Passion Narrative of St. Luke: A Critical and Historical Investigation* (SNTSMS 19; Cambridge: Cambridge University Press, 1982); J. B. Tyson, *The Death of Jesus in Luke-Acts* (Columbia: University of South Carolina, 1986); H.-R. Weber, *The Cross: Tradition and Interpretation* (London: SPCK, 1979); J. Zias and E. Sekeles, "The Crucified Man from Giv'at ha-Mivtar: A Reappraisal," IEJ 35 (1985) 22-27.

J. B. Green

DEATH OF CHRIST II: PAUL

The death of Christ, often mentioned in tandem with his *resurrection, occupies the central position in Paul's representation of the gospel. Paul is aware of, employs and develops its redemptive significance through creedal formulae and hymnic traditions; he probably has some familiarity with and reminds his readers of the story of Jesus' suffering and death; and he develops the importance of Christ's passion in contexts related to all aspects of his apostolic message—especially his soteriology and *christology, *eschatology and *ethics. This article is concerned not exclusively but especially with Paul's attribution of atoning significance to the suffering and death of Christ.

1. The Centrality of Christ's Death
2. The Significance of the Cross: A Plurality of Images
3. The Death of Christ and the Purpose of God
4. The Death of Christ and the Human Condition
5. The Crucified Messiah and the Christian Life

1. The Centrality of Christ's Death.

For Paul the cross of Christ was critical for Christian reflection and life, especially as the means by which God has provided for salvation and as the instrument and measure of new life in Christ.

It is of great consequence that the letters of Paul, themselves the earliest extant literary productions of Christianity, already document the central importance of the cross of Christ. This is true for our understanding of very early Christianity, for it evidences how quickly the followers of Jesus were compelled to grapple with the theological problem of his crucifixion. It is also true for our understanding of Paul, for it reveals the degree to which Paul struggled with and valued the cross of Christ and the degree to which his thought was at home in Christian reflection understood more broadly in the dawning years of the Jesus movement.

Leaving aside for the moment the variety of traditional materials concerned with Jesus' death that Paul incorporated into his correspondence, one can point to the example of 1 Corinthians. Some twenty-five years after Jesus' crucifixion Paul writes of the pivotal scandal and folly of the cross (1 Cor 1:18, 23), suggesting the harsh realities encountered in early missionary activity. Historically, Jesus' execution on a cross encouraged an understanding of his death as that of a common criminal, humiliated among his people—indeed, even cursed by God (cf. Deut 21:22-23). How could this Jesus also be the "Anointed One" (i.e., Messiah)? Despite this problem, Paul asserts that, while among the Corinthians, he had "resolved to know nothing . . . other than Jesus Christ and him crucified" (1 Cor 2:2). It is not too much to say that the early church had to come to terms with the cross of Christ precisely because it was this crucified-and-dead Jesus who was being proclaimed as Messiah (Green, 157-74). As a theologian of the cross, Paul played a key role in the exploration of the meaning of the crucified *Christ.

It is evident that Paul borrowed from preexisting Christian tradition regarding Jesus' passion and that such traditional materials are incorporated into his correspondence (cf., e.g., the language of the traditioning process in 1 Cor 11:23-25; 15:3-5; cf. Kertelge, 116-24). It is equally transparent that he exercised his own creativity in shaping the tradition. This is not surprising, since one of the primary motivations for his spirited opposition to the Christian movement prior to his encounter with the risen Lord must have been the contradiction offered by the Christian kerygma as it featured the divine exaltation of the "cursed one." Paul's embracing "the gospel of Christ" (Gal 1:6-17) entailed a theological conversion that enabled him to move beyond his initial negative interpretation of the cross; it also suggests one of the influences behind his subsequent reflection on the cross. It is noteworthy that Paul was able to come to terms with the seeming contradiction of a crucified Christ not by denying its perplexing character but by showing how God vindicated his Christ and filled his apparently ignominious demise with unexpected, positive significance.

By contrast, Paul's apostolic experience underscored the degree to which *suffering and powerlessness were integral to the Christian life, this in spite of Jesus' resurrection. In the Pauline perspective, apostolic weakness found its significance in light of the suffering of Christ. Thus, having reminded the Corinthians that among them he had sought only to present Christ and him crucified, Paul goes on to call to their attention his manner of life while with them: "I came to you in weakness, fear and much trembling" (1 Cor 2:2-3; cf. Col 1:24). Consequently, we see that a further inspiration for Paul's ongoing translation of the meaning of the cross was his and the church's life in Christ—life that was no stranger to weakness, opposition and suffering. The importance of the cross for Paul is thus grounded in his encounter with the risen Lord and in the demands of his apostolic ministry.

1.1. The Cross and Kerygma. How is the centrality of the cross manifest for Paul? It is implied by the phrases he uses to denote the kerygma. Thus in 1 Corinthians 1:18 "the message of the cross" is virtually a synonym for *"gospel." In 2 Corinthians 5:19 "the message of reconciliation" is employed similarly, in a context wherein the salvific event is presented in the parallelism "And he died for all, so that those who live might live no longer for themselves, but for him who on their behalf died and was raised" (cf. Phil 2:16: "word of life"; Acts 13:26: "word of salvation"; Kertelge, 124-27).

1.2. Formulaic Expressions. A close reading of the Pauline letters also reveals two stereotypical

expressions for the atoning significance of the cross (Hengel, 34-39). The first presents the "giving up" of Jesus for the salvation of humankind—either as a divine act (e.g., Rom 4:25: "who was given up on account of our trespasses"; Rom 8:32: "who did not spare his own son, but gave him up on behalf of us all") or as a self-giving (e.g., Gal 1:4: "who gave himself up for our sins"; Gal 2:20: "gave himself up for me"). The second expression, the "dying formula," is found repeatedly—for example, in the celebrated tradition represented in 1 Corinthians 15:3: "Christ died for our sins" (see further Rom 5:6, 8; 14:9; 1 Cor 8:11; 2 Cor 5:14, 15; Gal 2:21; 1 Thess 5:10). Paul's phrase "Christ died for us," according to M. Hengel, "is the most frequent and most important confessional statement in the Pauline epistles and at the same time in the primitive Christian tradition in the Greek language which underlies them" (Hengel, 37).

This traditional basis is important for showing the degree to which Paul aligns himself with the common faith of the early church. That is, his letters draw on the common vocabulary of the Christian communities; his innovations in theological expression build on the foundation of the shared faith. More particularly, in the face of such antagonism as Paul faced at Corinth and Galatia, his repetition of traditional materials related to the cross serves to indicate how Paul legitimized his authority in the face of opposition (*see* Adversaries).

1.3. The Story of Jesus. This is not to suggest that Paul was indebted only to the formulaic tradition he shared with early Christianity. There are also hints that he was aware of the story of Jesus' suffering and death, which would also have been handed down to him. Such a reference may lie behind Galatians 3:1, where Paul's language ("Before your eyes Jesus Christ was publicly portrayed as crucified") suggests the graphic quality of his proclamation, opening the possibility that his missionary preaching made use of a passion story. Similarly, his introduction to the tradition of the Last Supper, "in the night when he was delivered up" (1 Cor 11:23-25), presumes a shared knowledge of a narrative context for the eucharistic tradition (*see* Last Supper). Also suggestive are the themes with which Paul describes his own suffering in 2 Corinthians; for example, in 2 Corinthians 6:3-10 he lists the sufferings, grace and paradoxical aspects of his service in a way that echoes the story of the passion of Christ. Not unlike what one finds in the Gospel of Mark, then, Paul has his own understanding of the "way of the cross," the way of suffering through which one identifies with the manner of Christ's suffering. Finally, while Pauline only in the broad sense, 1 Timothy 6:13 alludes to Jesus' *trial before Pontius Pilate in a way that presupposes at least rudimentary knowledge of the passion story. In these and other texts, we recognize that Paul's theology has about it a narrative quality—that is, that he understands Christian experience within the larger mural of God's activity ranging from the formation of God's people to the parousia, and within this greater narrative and as its centerpiece is the narrative of Jesus' crucifixion. Even though Paul shows little interest in the historical details of Jesus' passion as historical data, it appears that he was aware of them and was concerned with their significance for Christian faith and life (see Jesus and Paul).

1.4. The Pattern of Christ. This again points to the degree to which Paul is ready to posit the cross of Christ as the basis of Christian faith and life. Indeed, Paul's reference to the Last Supper tradition is set contextually within his discussion of the community meal in order to attack the problem of divisions at Corinth (1 Cor 11:17-34; cf. 1 Cor 1:10-17); here a reminder of Jesus' sacrificial self-giving is the basis for Paul's call for a life modeled on the way of Jesus' passion, diaconal in orientation, cruciform in shape (see Lord's Supper).

At Corinth, as at Colossae, Paul reflects on the meaning of the crucified Christ in large part so as to counter competing ideas. In the case of his correspondence with the Corinthians, the word of the cross opposes wrong-headed thinking about the nature of present existence, as though this were the time for triumphalism following the consummation of the new age. Against the "wisdom of the world" and the status-seeking orientation of his Greco-Roman audience at Corinth, Paul posits the scandalous cross of Christ as the "power of God" "to us who are being saved." Social, philosophical, even soteriological norms are uprooted as Paul brings to the foreground "what is weak in the world," "what is low and despised in the world"—that is, "Christ crucified" and the community oriented around the crucified Christ (1 Cor 1:18-31).

For the Colossians Paul grounds his presentation of the cosmic Christ—who reconciled the whole cosmos, including the astral powers, to God—in the flesh-and-blood life and death of Christ: "through him God was pleased to reconcile to himself all things . . . by making peace through the blood of his cross" (Col 1:20; cf. Col 1:14; 2:13-14; 3:13). Thus Paul counters a lifestyle oriented around appeasing astral powers as though they were the means of human access to God and, against a quasi-gnostic spiritualizing of the way of discipleship, affirms in an impassioned way the importance of ethical behavior in this material world.

Elsewhere Paul presents Jesus' death as the culmination of his life. In Philippians 2:6-11 Paul has apparently added to an early hymn to Christ the words "even death on a cross." Here, Jesus' life as God's obedient Son is at center stage, and this obedience is seen most profoundly in his willingness to embrace rejection, human suffering and a heinous death by crucifixion. In this way, Paul contends that Christ's death "is the fullest expression of [his] life and establishes [for us] the pattern of a life of love and obedience" (Tambasco, 72). In these and many other ways, Paul shows how Christian thought and life build on the foundational event of the cross of Christ.

2. The Significance of the Cross: A Plurality of Images.

Just as Jesus' death lies at the foundation of Pauline theology, so Paul seems never to tire of adding new images to his interpretive vocabulary by way of explicating its significance.

It is true that Paul is much more concerned with laying out the significance of the death of Christ than with its historical circumstances, and he communicates this significance above all in terms of its benefits for humankind. In subsequent theological reflection, these benefits have been developed under the nomenclature of "atonement," and this presents the modern interpreter with two problems.

First, the word *atonement* is open to diverse definition. On the one hand, today many trace the meaning of the term back to its roots in Middle English—"at-one-ment"—and so understand the term above all as a synonym for *reconciliation* (e.g., Fitzmyer). As a consequence, a cleavage is drawn between atonement and notions of expiation, propitiation and other ideas related to doctrines of substitution or satisfaction; more to the point, the atoning significance of Jesus' death is thus divorced from any consideration on Paul's part regarding the means by which this at-one-ment or reconciliation is achieved.

After centuries of debate it is now difficult to read Paul without the overlay of one or more of the so-called classical theories of the atonement (see Driver, 37-67)—especially the "dramatic theory," which portrays the saving work of Christ as a cosmic drama of conflict and victory; the "satisfaction theory," which presents the cross of Christ as the means by which the barrier between God and humanity is removed, so that through Christ's death "satisfaction" is rendered to God; or the "moral influence theory," which concentrates on the cross as a demonstration to humanity of God's boundless love that is to be emulated. The ascendancy of the "satisfaction theory," with its often-held corollary, penal or forensic satisfaction (i.e., since human beings have been found guilty before God the judge, they must be punished, but Christ is made to suffer the penalty) as the way to understand Paul's theology of the cross has proven especially problematic in contemporary theological discussion. For some, Paul seems to portray God as a sadist who inflicts punishment and Jesus as the masochist who willingly endures it. Any attempt to sunder the interests and activity of God and Christ—as though the cross is the manifestation of God's wrath but of Christ's mercy—would be problematic on Pauline grounds (see below). And, in fact, it seems highly unlikely that those who formulated the substitutionary interpretation of the death of Christ would recognize this contemporary characterization of their view. This is true even if this classical theory of the atonement has subsequently proven itself susceptible to this problematic reading in some hymnody and popular interpretation (see the helpful discussion in Houts; Beker, 208-11).

The bulk of this article is given over to an examination of Paul's theology of atonement. First, however, it is important that we come to terms with the more fundamental reality that Paul has no one way of explicating the meaning of the cross. Although the crucified Christ lies at the center of his theology, this central truth is capable of multiple interpretations. In fact, Paul seems capable of tailoring his representation of the significance of the death of Jesus to the needs of his audience in particular, contextualized circumstances (see Driver; Boff, 78-84;

Cousar, 82-87). This fact has serious ramifications for the ongoing crosscultural mission of the church, for it suggests that interpreters, in drawing out the significance of Jesus' crucifixion, must continuously seek out metaphors that speak specifically to culture and/or circumstance. In their openness to shaping context-specific ways to communicate the meaning of the death of Christ, contemporary interpreters who would be faithful to Paul will be guided by apostolic testimony to the cross, grounded in the Scriptures and cognizant of the way Paul draws on them in his own hermeneutical enterprise, fully sensitive to the contemporary images and metaphors that carry redemptive meaning, and vitally concerned with the interplay between these three (see Green and Baker).

Of the several dozen metaphors Paul employs to lay bare the benefits of the death of Christ, only a handful can be mentioned here. These are conveniently brought together in two Pauline texts—2 Corinthians 5:14—6:2 and Galatians 3:10-14.

An examination of the presentation of the effects of Jesus' death in 2 Corinthians 5:14—6:2 underscores the degree to which the manifold categories by which Paul drew out the significance of the cross overlap with one another. Even though reconciliation stands at the center of this passage (2 Cor 5:18, 19, 20), other categories are in the foreground: vicarious substitution ("for us," 2 Cor 5:14, 15), representation (2 Cor 5:14, 21) or interchange (Hooker's term [1974, 1978]), sacrifice (2 Cor 5:21; cf. Dunn, 42-43), *justification (implicitly, 2 Cor 5:19, 21), forgiveness (2 Cor 5:19) and new creation (2 Cor 5:16-17; see Creation, New Creation). Moreover, the cross and resurrection of Christ appear in tandem as salvific events (2 Cor 5:15).

Reconciliation as a term is not found very often in the Pauline corpus. Apart from this passage it appears in Romans 5:10-11 with reference to the reconciliation of humanity to God; Colossians 1:20 with reference to the reconciliation of the cosmos to God; and in Ephesians 2:16 with reference to the reconciliation of Jew and Gentile to God and one another. Whether Ephesians is judged to be Pauline or not, its message at this juncture is clearly Pauline, for this notion of restored relationship in Paul consistently embraces the dynamic presence of divine love active to restore the divine-human relationship and extending a call for and an enablement of persons to exhibit toward one another this same social restoration. Moreover, especially in 2 Corinthians and Colossians, the work of reconciliation is extended to the entire creation.

In 2 Corinthians 5 Paul's choice of terminology and logic of argumentation is tailored to its context, for here Paul not only needs to counter the triumphalistic boasting of his opponents at Corinth but also to overcome the disharmony between himself and his "children" at Corinth. Rooting the message of reconciliation fundamentally in the sacrificial death of Jesus and asserting that reconciliation entails living no longer for oneself but for Christ and thus for others, he addresses his first aim. His impassioned appeal to the Corinthians to be reconciled to God (2 Cor 5:20; 6:1-2), followed by an affirmation of his own open-heartedness to the Corinthians (2 Cor 6:11-13; 7:2) will, he hopes, accomplish the second goal of restoring his relationship with the Corinthians.

Similarly, Galatians 3:10-14 consists of a convergence of images or theological categories by which Paul expounds the salvific character of the cross of Christ. The larger unit, Galatians 3:1-14, contends that the experience of the Galatians of receiving the Spirit by faith signified the fulfillment of God's promise to bless the Gentiles through Abraham and that this fulfillment was made possible through the death of Christ. The benefits of the death of Christ are presented in Galatians 3:10-14 through a combination of images: Christ as the *representative* of Israel in whose death the *covenant* reaches its climax (Wright, 137-56; cf. the notion of interchange [Hooker]); *justification* (Gal 3:11); *redemption* (Gal 3:13), evoking exodus and exilic themes (cf. the corollary of *adoption* in Gal 3:26-29); *substitution* ("for us," Gal 3:13); *sacrifice* (implicitly, Gal 3:13; cf. Wright, 153); the *promise of the Spirit* (Gal 3:14); and the *triumph over the powers.*

This last motif emerges in a similar way in Ephesians 2:14-15, where the law appears as a barrier separating Jew and Gentile; there the death of Christ abolishes this "dividing wall." In Galatians, however, the law is characterized more as a force, like the elemental spirits of this world, holding the Jewish people captive (Gal 4:1, 3). In a context-specific way, then, Paul insists that the death of Christ has triumphed not by denying the law but by demonstrating its validity and executing the blessing of the covenant.

Taken together, the message of the cross in 2 Corinthians and Galatians (but also elsewhere in the Pauline corpus) raises two issues requiring more explicit elucidation. On the one hand, attention must be drawn to the apocalyptic significance of the cross: set within apocalyptic horizons, the cross has cosmic repercussions. This is the importance of the use of such language as "new creation" in 2 Corinthians 5:17 and Galatians 6:15, for these texts must be understood not as in some modern translations as individual-focused (e.g., NIV, NASB), but as signifying the role of Jesus' death in the termination of the old epoch and the presentation of the new. The death of Christ marks the end of the rule of the apocalyptic powers (cf. Beker, 189-92; Col 2:15) and deliverance "from the present evil age" (Gal 1:4; *see* Eschatology). This intrusion of the new world into contemporary life has for Paul far-reaching consequences for those who would follow the crucified Christ and embody in their lives together the new creation revealed in the cross. Old ways of relating to one another (e.g., boasting in a continuous game of one-upmanship in the service of status seeking) and of drawing lines between Jew and Gentile, slave and free, male and female, are shown to be just that—old, out of date, and judged as such (cf., e.g., Gal 3:26-29; Philem).

On the other hand, we see in Paul's understanding of the cross his ongoing reflection on *Israel, and particularly his inclusion of believing Gentiles in the "Israel of God" (Gal 6:10). For Paul, believers, because of their inclusion in the salvific work of Christ, share in the benefits of the new creation and thus in their identity as the people of God. As Paul acknowledges, "I have been crucified with Christ. It is no longer I who live, but Christ who lives in me" (Gal 2:19-20). Even if the question of the eschatological role of Israel in Pauline thought is not thus settled, it is nonetheless apparent that the death of Christ marks the new aeon in which Gentiles may be embraced, in Christ, as children of Abraham.

Many other interpretive categories or images might be mentioned from within the Pauline letters, for he makes use of a rich variety of metaphors by way of comprehending the cross and encouraging both understanding and response among his varied audiences. This multiplicity raises a caution against moving too quickly to posit for Paul a single (or any one as the central) theory of the atonement. For him the depths of the significance of the death of Christ can scarcely be plumbed.

3. The Death of Christ and the Purpose of God.
For Paul the question of the meaning of the cross is first a question about God—theology—and only then a question about anthropology and soteriology. His theology of the cross is rooted in his understanding of the divine purpose, and of God as the primary actor in the drama of salvation. Although he affirms that Christ "gave himself for our sins in order to set us free from the present evil age," he goes on to affirm that Christ did so "according to the will of our God and Father" (Gal 1:4). That is, Christ's self-giving signifies his identification and solidarity with God's salvific aim. By this affirmation, any attribution to Paul of a view of the atonement that segregates the activity of God from that of God's Son is disallowed. Nevertheless, at center stage stands God's initiative (e.g.): "God was in Christ reconciling the world to himself" (2 Cor 5:19); "God . . . sent his own Son" (Rom 8:3). Paul's atonement theology is thus rooted in his understanding of *God, and especially of God's righteousness, wrath and love.

3.1. The Righteousness of God. The precedence Paul gives to the question about God in his atonement theology is perhaps underscored best in the central but tightly packed passage, Romans 3:21-26. Two questions related to the character of God are raised in the verses preceding this passage (see Cousar, 37-41). (1) What are we to make of God's faithfulness vis-à-vis his covenant promises to the Jewish people? If, as Paul has earlier argued, Jew and Gentile stand side by side before God as implicated in sin, what are we to make of God's covenantal history with Israel? "Will their faithlessness nullify the faithfulness of God?" (Rom 3:3). (2) If salvation is available outside the law, should we not engage in evil so that God's goodness may abound all the more (Rom 3:8)? Or, to raise the question in a way more oriented around the character of God, if God's goodness is available to sinners, how can God judge the world? The first is a question about the reliability of God, the second about the moral integrity of God.

These questions place the *righteousness of God in the dock, for in the OT the righteousness of God is a central affirmation, affirming God's faithful orientation toward the covenant

and setting the pattern for the character of Israel's comportment and behavior before God. Paul is not unaware of this. First, he grounds his treatment of these two questions in the prior disclosure of the righteousness of God ("attested by the law and the Prophets," Rom 3:21). Then he develops his present perspective on God's faithfulness, with clear echoes of occasions of covenant making and covenant keeping in Israel's past (cf. *redemption,* Rom 3:24; *sacrifice of atonement,* Rom 3:25 NRSV). Moreover, he does so via a traditional Jewish-Christian formula, demonstrating even more the rootedness of this representation of God's character in the history of God's interaction with the community of God's people.

In this context, Christ's salvific death, as it were, proves the reliability and integrity of God. To put it differently, the righteousness of God is manifest in his intervention to bring salvation to a humanity mired in sin. And it is manifest precisely in the revelation of God in the cross as one who keeps his promises. God does not wink at sin but, through the faithful obedience and sacrificial death of Jesus Christ, redeems all who believe, whether Jew or Gentile; and thus does not introduce a way of salvation that nullifies the law but upholds it (cf. Rom 3:31). Consequently, Paul affirms that the righteousness of God is revealed in Christ not merely as a description of God in his role as judge but also and more so as the activity of God oriented around covenant making and covenant keeping. In the death of Christ the righteousness of God is exhibited in God's delivering people from sin.

3.2. The Wrath of God. In some ways God's wrath stands as a corollary to God's righteousness: "since God's fidelity to covenant demands human response and responsibility, wrath is what one experiences when one rejects God's offer of justice" (Tambasco, 33; cf. Travis). It is imperative to recognize, however, that for Paul divine wrath is not a divine property, or essential attribute, but the active presence of God's *judgment toward "all ungodliness and wickedness" (Rom 1:18). The wrath of God is not vindictive indignation or the anger of divine retribution but the divine response to human unfaithfulness. For Paul God's wrath is future, *eschatological (Rom 2:5, 8; 1 Thess 1:10; 5:9; Col 3:6). It is also already present, for God is now handing people over to experience the consequences of the sin they choose (Rom 1:18, 24, 26, 28; cf. Wis 11:15-16; 12:23).

In any attempt to come to terms with Paul's theology of atonement, then, it is vital to keep in mind Paul's understanding of divine wrath. Paul does not portray an angry God requiring mollification. For him divine wrath is a means of underscoring how seriously God takes sin, but it is not an affective quality or feeling on God's part. The righteousness of God is effective in the present to save, but as men and women resist it they experience God's righteousness as condemnation.

3.3. The Love of God. According to Romans 5:6-8, the death of Christ is the ultimate expression of the boundless love of God: "But God demonstrates his love for us in that while we were still sinners Christ died for us" (Rom 5:8). This affirmation follows on the heels of the claim that the human experience of divine love guarantees that suffering will lead to a hope that will not disappoint (Rom 5:3-5). Three declarations are critical here. First, the love of God for humanity cannot be measured, for there are no anthropomorphic analogues on which to base such a measurement; even though someone might dare to die on behalf of a righteous person (Rom 5:7), Christ died for "the ungodly" (Rom 5:6), for "sinners" (Rom 5:8), for "enemies" of God (Rom 5:10).

Second, Paul's audience can be certain that their suffering has significance because the suffering of Christ has proven to be so meaningful. Through his death "we have been *justified*," "*saved* from the wrath of God," "*reconciled* to God" (Rom 5:9-11). In the midst of our impotence, Christ took on the measure of our powerlessness and died in our place; as a result of his death, we share in his life, and we find that our suffering has significance.

Third, in an unusual turn of phrase (Rom 5:8), we are told that God demonstrates his love by means of what Christ did. We might have anticipated that God's love would be manifest best in God's deed. This way of putting things certifies that "Christ's death does not merely express his own sentiment, . . . but God's; or to put it another way, God's stance toward the world is quintessentially demonstrated in the action of Christ" (Cousar, 45). Once more, then, we find in Paul the unrelenting affirmation of the oneness of purpose and activity of God and God's Son in the cross.

4. The Death of Christ and the Human Condition.

To affirm that Paul's understanding of the death of Christ is profoundly theocentric is not to downplay his interest in the need for atonement from the human side of the equation. Quite the contrary, it is to introduce the sharp contrast Paul sees between God and humanity—that is, between the faithfulness of God and human unfaithfulness (see, e.g., the wordplay in Rom 1:17-18: God's righteousness [*dikaiosynē*] versus human unrighteousness [*adikia*]). Paul's portrait of humanity "before Christ" is that of persons, collectively and individually, ensnared in sin, enslaved to powers from which they are impotent to escape. As with atonement, so with sin Paul is able to draw from a full linguistic arsenal to fill out his description of humankind apart from God.

Of special interest in this brief review of Paul's anthropology is Romans 1:18-32. Here *sin* (in the broad sense; the language Paul uses in Rom 1:18 is *ungodliness* and *unrighteousness*) is identified not with individual acts of wickedness but with a general disposition to refuse to honor God as God and to render him thanks, to substitute things created for the Creator—that is, to turn away from authentic human existence by turning away from God.

Four aspects of Paul's reflections in this passage are of particular significance here. First, Paul is not giving the autobiography of individual persons; he is not bent on outlining how each person in his or her own experience comes to be implicated in sin. Instead, his is a universalistic presentation, a diagnosis of the condition of the human family taken as a whole (cf. Rom 3:9).

Second, the acts of wickedness that Paul goes on to enumerate by way of illustration are not themselves the problem. Lust, gossip, envy, deceit, homosexual activity, rebelliousness toward parents and the rest—these are expressions of sin.

Third, within the fabric of Paul's argument, these activities are themselves expressions of the wrath of God. They evidence the moral integrity of a God who takes sin seriously. It is this, God's moral character, that Paul is defending here, and he does so by showing the progression from the human refusal to honor God with its consequent denial of the human vocation to live in relation to God; to God's giving humanity over to its own desires—giving humanity, as it were, the life apart from him it sought; and from this to human acts of wickedness—which then do not arouse the wrath of God but are themselves already the consequences of its active presence.

Finally, it is remarkable that for Paul, sin marks a rupture in the divine-human relationship but also manifests itself in human relations and in relations between humanity and the material creation. Sin, in this broad sense, then, can never be understood as something private or individualistic, for it always manifests itself in relation to others and to the cosmos (see Rom 1:26-32). What is more, Paul recognizes that *ungodliness* and *unrighteousness* have as their object their own self-legitimation: humanity embraces a lie (Rom 1:25) and receives a corrupt mind (Rom 1:28), with the consequence that it defines its unjust ways as just.

As a result, it is no wonder that Paul's preaching of and identification with the cross would excite opposition and misunderstanding. A humanity that has turned against itself as it turned against God will not easily sanction so revolutionary a re-ordering of the world as would be required by this accentuation of the crucified Christ. This would call for an apparently topsy-turvy way of understanding what it means to be human, for an inversion of the social system. Power rooted in powerlessness? This emphasizes the profound role the word of the cross would have in Paul's conception and experience of the Christian life (see 5 below), but also the severity of the predicament to which God's saving activity would have to address itself.

5. The Crucified Messiah and the Christian Life. We come finally to explore more directly the question How is the death of Christ efficacious? It is clear that for Paul the cross is the means by which God has provided salvation and that it is the instrument and measure of the new life in Christ. How is the cross operative in this way? Paul provides no single answer to this question, though we can ascertain in the Pauline letters certain parameters for this discussion.

5.1. The Atoning Death of Christ. For Paul, Jesus' death is not interpreted by metaphors drawn from the law court but from within the history of God's covenant with Israel. Thus Paul does not think of Christ's having been punished by execution on the cross so as to satisfy the justice of God (Travis; Tambasco). The cross of Christ can be understood as substitutionary, but within the matrix of the OT conception of sacrifice.

Although the rationale for the sacrificial system is not worked out fully in the OT, J. D. G. Dunn believes that the notion of "identification" or "representation" is basic to our understanding of it. That is, the sin offering in some way came to represent the sinners in their sin. Thus, by laying hands on the beast's head in the ritual of sacrifice, sinners identified themselves with the beast, indicating that the beast now represented the sinner in his or her sin (i.e., *qua* sinner). As a consequence, the sinner's sin was identified with the beast, and its life became forfeit—"just as Christ, taking the initiative from the other side, identified himself with [human beings] in their fallenness (Rom 8:3), and was made sin (2 Cor. 5:21)" (Dunn, 44).

This logic introduces Christ's dual role in his death—his substitution for humanity before God and in the face of God's justice, but also his substitution for God in the face of human sin.

This use of the language of representation to assist our understanding of substitution is not designed to deny the sense of Christ's having achieved something objective in his death. Indeed, according to Paul, Christ gave himself up for us so that we might live in him (cf. 1 Thess 5:9-10; Rom 8:3-4; 14:9; 2 Cor 5:15, 21; Travis). As significant as the theme of participation in Christ's death and resurrection is for Paul (cf., e.g., Phil 3:10), the possibility of such participation is grounded in his first dying "for us."

From where does Paul obtain this mode of interpretation? Attempts have been made in recent decades to find a Greco-Roman background for Paul's thought on the atoning death of Christ—either quite apart from the OT and Second Temple Judaism (Seeley) or mediated through Hellenistic Judaism (Williams). It is not clear, however, why one must draw such strict boundaries between OT influence and Greco-Roman philosophy, particularly given the degree to which Hellenism and Judaism had coalesced by the beginning of the first century A.D.

It is more probable that the redemptive interpretations of death in Hellenistic Judaism and in Paul are drawn from the common quarry of Israel's Scriptures and sacrificial practices. The sacrificial system of the OT provides a ready source for speculation concerning the relation of innocent death and forgiveness of sins, particularly since during the Second Temple period sacrifices in general were interpreted along redemptive lines. Of course, this is not to suggest that Paul would have been unaware of such martyrological interpretations of death as one finds in texts such as 2 Maccabees 7:37-38 and 4 Maccabees 6:28-29. But these texts themselves develop OT sacrificial and Servant themes, particularly making use of Isaianic material concerning the Suffering Servant of the Lord (Is 52:13—53:12)—just as did the early church and Paul (*see* Servant of Yahweh). Moreover, the degree to which Paul might have been directly indebted to Hellenistic Judaism via the martyr tales of the Maccabean literature is modulated by the strong influence of retributive ideas in those texts. Paul places a more profound stress on God's initiative in providing the sacrifice, and his evident concern is to establish the universality of Christ's atoning benefits, which are not limited to Israelite cultic and memorial rites needing repetition and reenactment (Hengel, 51). In addition to the sacrificial system of the OT, with its concern for maintaining the relationship between God and his covenant people, the Isaianic Suffering Servant and Jewish martyrology, scholars have also found reflections of the Jewish notion of the binding of Isaac in the background of Paul's thought (cf. Tambasco, Dunn, Hengel, Brown, et al.).

As Hengel has argued, it is not enough to peruse the OT and later Jewish texts for precursors to Paul's salvific interpretation of Jesus' death. An influence of significant proportions lies much closer to hand—namely, the interpretation of the cross of Christ mediated through the repetition of the Last Supper in the early Christian communities. Paul knows and repeats the eucharistic words of Jesus (1 Cor 11:23-25), words that interpret Jesus' self-giving as redemptive.

5.2. The Death of Christ and Following Christ. According to Paul, the death and resurrection of Christ mark the beginning of a new epoch that reaches forward to the time of Christ's parousia (cf. Hanson). This fundamentally changes the way one understands life in the present. First, awareness that Christ's death and resurrection has instituted a new epoch allows one to envision new life in contrast to old ways of living and to embrace the power of God requisite for new life. Moreover, considering the present in light of the past motivates believers to act in gratitude for deliverance from slavery to sin. Fi-

nally, recognition of this new time encourages believers' further recognition that life in the present is determined by the cross. This means that one effect of the cross is the possibility of restored humanity, restored in its relationships to God, to itself and to all creation. It also means that the definition of existence put forward by sinful humanity has been radically altered, so that those who follow Christ must look to Christ for the expression of restored humanity. "The church whose theology is shaped by the message of the cross must itself take on a cruciform life if its theology is to carry credibility" (Cousar, 186).

What this means practically is related above all to believers taking on themselves the form of obedience to God represented in Christ's life, expressed ultimately in his death. This thought lies behind Paul's use of the hymn to Christ in Philippians 2:6-11. It also lies behind his defense of his apostolic ministry, his sense that in his weakness and suffering he is engaged in the imitation of Christ and participating in the suffering of the Messiah (cf. Pobee, Hanson, Bloomquist).

5.3. The Death of Christ and the Life of God's People. The cross of Christ has as its effect the restoration of humanity in another sense too. The cross is understood by Paul as a boundary-shattering event (cf. Driver, esp. chap. 13). Thus Paul can assert in 1 Corinthians that those who follow the example of Christ in his selfless death will not nurture their status-based divisions within the Christian community but will gain a fuller understanding and appreciation of the body of Christ (1 Cor 11:17—12:31; *see* Body of Christ). This, after all, is a manifestation of the new covenant in Christ's blood (1 Cor 11:25). But Paul can also assert that faithful identification with Christ in his salvific work opposes even more fundamental ethnic, social and sexual boundaries, "for in Christ Jesus you are all children of God through faith" (Gal 3:26; cf. 3:27-29; Eph 2:11-22). In this way too, then, the cross not only enables new life, it also points beyond itself to disclose the norms of that life, and thus it inaugurates the new era wherein the salvific will of God will be realized.

Clearly the death of Christ occupies center stage in Paul's theology. He draws on an abundance of images by which he explicates its meaning, both by way of excavating the rich resources available to him in Israel's Scriptures and in the common faith of the early church, and by way of relating the message of the cross more directly to his audiences in their diverse backgrounds and with their diverse circumstances. The cross of Christ lies at the intersection of the major avenues of his theology and of his understanding of faithful living before Christ returns. For Paul, believers here and now manifest their obedience to Christ by proclaiming his death until he comes.

See also CHRISTOLOGY; ESCHATOLOGY; JUSTIFICATION; LORD'S SUPPER; RESURRECTION; SALVATION; SERVANT OF YAHWEH.

DPL: CENTER OF PAUL'S THEOLOGY; CROSS, THEOLOGY OF THE; CRUCIFIXION; CURSE, ACCURSED, ANATHEMA; DYING AND RISING WITH CHRIST; EXPIATION, PROPITIATION, MERCY SEAT; FORGIVENESS; PEACE, RECONCILIATION; REDEMPTION; SACRIFICE, OFFERING; TRIUMPH.

BIBLIOGRAPHY. J. C. Beker, *Paul the Apostle: The Triumph of God in Life and Thought* (Philadelphia: Fortress, 1980); L. G. Bloomquist, *The Function of Suffering in Philippians* (JSNTSup 78; Sheffield: Academic, 1993); L. Boff, *Passion of Christ, Passion of the World: The Facts, Their Interpretation and Their Meaning Yesterday and Today* (Maryknoll, NY: Orbis, 1987); C. A. Brown, "The Peace-Offerings (שלמים) and Pauline Soteriology," in *The New Testament and Christian-Jewish Dialogue: Studies in Honor of David Flusser, Immanuel* 24-25 (1990) 59-76; J. T. Carroll and J. B. Green, *The Death of Jesus in Early Christianity* (Peabody, MA: Hendrickson, 1995); C. B. Cousar, *A Theology of the Cross: The Death of Jesus in the Pauline Letters* (OBT; Minneapolis: Fortress, 1990); J. Driver, *Understanding the Atonement for the Mission of the Church* (Scottdale, PA: Herald, 1986); J. D. G. Dunn, "Paul's Understanding of the Death of Jesus as Sacrifice," in *Sacrifice and Redemption: Durham Essays in Theology,* ed. S. W. Sykes (Cambridge: Cambridge University Press, 1991) 35-56; J. A. Fitzmyer, "Reconciliation in Pauline Theology," in *To Advance the Gospel: New Testament Studies* (New York: Crossroad, 1981) 162-85; J. B. Green, *The Death of Jesus: Tradition and Interpretation in the Passion Narrative* (WUNT 2.33; Tübingen: J. C. B. Mohr, 1988); J. B. Green and M. D. Baker, *Recovering the Scandal of the Cross* (Downers Grove, IL: InterVarsity Press, 2000); A. T. Hanson, *The Paradox of the Cross in the Thought of St. Paul* (JSNTSup 17; Sheffield: JSOT, 1987); M. Hengel, *The Atonement: The Origins of the Doctrine in the New Testament* (Philadel-

phia: Fortress, 1981); M. D. Hooker, "Interchange and Atonement," *BJRL* 60 (1978) 462-81; idem, "Interchange in Christ," *JTS* 22 (1974) 349-61; M. Houts, "Classical Atonement Imagery: Feminist and Evangelical Challenges," *Catalyst* 19 (1993) 1, 5-6; K. Kertelge, "Das Verständnis des Todes Jesu bei Paulus," in *Der Tod Jesu: Deutungen im Neuen Testament,* ed. K. Kertelge (QD 74; 2d ed.; Freiburg: Herder, 1976) 114-36; J. S. Pobee, *Persecution and Martyrdom in the Theology of Paul* (JSNTSup 6; Sheffield: JSOT, 1985); D. Seeley, *The Noble Death: Greco-Roman Martyrology and Paul's Concept of Salvation* (JSNTSup 28; Sheffield: JSOT, 1990); S. H. Travis, "Christ as Bearer of Divine Judgment in Paul's Thought about the Atonement," in *Jesus of Nazareth: Lord and Christ. Essays on the Historical Jesus and New Testament Christology,* ed. J. B. Green and M. Turner (Grand Rapids: Eerdmans, 1994) 332-45; A. J. Tambasco, *A Theology of Atonement and Paul's Vision of Christianity* (ZS: NT; Collegeville, MN: Liturgical Press, 1991); S. K. Williams, *Jesus' Death as Saving Event: The Background and Origin of a Concept* (HDR 2; Missoula, MT: Scholars Press, 1975); N. T. Wright, *The Climax of the Covenant: Christ and the Law in Pauline Theology* (Minneapolis: Fortress, 1991). J. B. Green

DEATH OF CHRIST III: ACTS, HEBREWS, GENERAL EPISTLES, REVELATION

The writings of the NT under consideration here (Acts, Hebrews, 1 Peter, 1 John and Revelation) interpret the death of *Christ fundamentally in sacrificial terms. This is not to say that this understanding of the cross or the death of Christ itself always receives emphasis. Yet in the writings where it does appear, *salvation (in its various dimensions) is presented as having been accomplished in the forgiveness secured by the death of Christ on behalf of sinners. This category of thought clearly does not exclude others. The cross is also viewed as a divine victory, a deliverance of humanity from sin and evil, a revelation of *God and his love and a pattern of obedience. No one form of description is exhaustive. The innermost aspects of God's working in the cross necessarily lie beyond human language, as the metaphorical language of the NT and the multiplicity of its images indicate.

Yet it is obviously not the case that nothing can be known or said about the saving effects of Christ's death. Characteristically the NT writers place objective guilt and radical, eschatological forgiveness at the center of the structure of salvation, deriving all other aspects of the cross from it. The victory at the cross is victory because it secures the forgiveness of sins. Deliverance from sin's power issues from the release from objective guilt. The cross reveals God's love in that God gave his Son for our sins. This conception of salvation as full forgiveness distinguishes the NT writings from those of the postapostolic period. The various images of salvation and the OT texts used to derive them are taken up in early Christianity of the second century. But the framework of thought shifts, so that salvation is conceived as the attainment of incorruption and becomes contingent upon the obedience of the believer.

1. Acts
2. Hebrews
3. 1 Peter
4. 1 John
5. Revelation

1. Acts.

The understanding of the death of Christ in Luke-Acts has been a center of scholarly interest in recent years. Early redaction-critical studies, particularly those by P. Vielhauer, H. Conzelmann and E. Haenchen, regarded the author of Luke-Acts as lacking any interest in Jesus' death as an atonement and concomitantly charged him with embracing a theology of glory that measured divine favor by the outward success of the *church. Newer studies have moved in various directions. A number have called for an appreciation for a distinctively Lukan understanding of the death of Christ primarily as a pattern for Christian obedience (e.g., Green, Carroll, Garrett). A few have argued that the understanding of Jesus' death as an atonement holds a larger place in Lukan thought than is generally recognized (Moessner), and still·others have reasserted the claim that Luke rejects such an understanding of Jesus' death (Ehrman).

When all the evidence has been taken into account, it becomes clear that Luke does understand Jesus' death as a vicarious atonement and that this understanding is foundational to the message of Luke-Acts. Luke obviously emphasizes the salvific nature of Jesus' *resurrection, yet in doing so he undergirds rather than diminishes the atoning significance of Jesus' death. Jesus' death is also paradigmatic and exemplary for

Luke. Yet despite its current attractiveness as a category for understanding the death of Jesus in Luke-Acts, it is no more prominent than Luke's interpretation of the cross as an atonement. Finally, the Lukan emphasis on the divine purpose behind Jesus' death does not reduce the human responsibility for it.

1.1. Jesus' Death as an Atonement.

1.1.1. Text-Critical Considerations in Luke 22:19-20. Although twentieth-century textual criticism increasingly inclined to regard the longer version of the words of institution in Luke as original, B. D. Ehrman (198-209) has argued forcefully in favor of the judgment of Westcott and Hort that the shorter version is more likely authentic. The shorter text, one of Westcott and Hort's so-called Western noninterpolations, is preserved in Codex Bezae and various Old Latin manuscripts and omits the italicized material: "And taking bread, having given thanks he broke it and gave it to them, saying, 'This is my body *which is given for you. Do this in memory of me. And the cup likewise, after they had eaten, saying, "This cup is the new covenant in my blood, which is poured out for you.'"* But the hand of my betrayer is on the table."

Ehrman argues as follows: The external evidence for both readings runs back to the second century and cannot resolve the question. In cases such as this, in which the Western witness is shorter, it must be taken seriously. The usual explanations for an omission are inadequate (viz., that scribes were motivated by the desire either to harmonize Luke's account with Matthew and Mark or to keep the eucharistic words a secret). The vocabulary and more importantly the theology of the additional material are contrary to Lukan usage and thought.

Despite Ehrman's appeal to the significance of the shorter Western reading, its restriction to some Western witnesses at the very least raises some question about its originality, even if it does not decide the matter. And while Ehrman has rightly pointed out the inadequacy of the usual explanations for a scribal abbreviation of the text, an additional, persuasive possibility suggests itself. Although Luke undoubtedly intends the reader to understand Jesus to say that after this supper he will no longer eat and drink with his disciples, the tradition represented in Codex Bezae seems to have taken Jesus' words to mean that he would not participate in that very Passover. The Greek column of Bezae at Luke 22:15

divides *touto* to read *epethymēsa [tou to] to pascha phagein;* the genitive and accusative articles thereby created suggesting that Jesus' desire to eat the Passover with the apostles remained unfulfilled (cf. the genitive following *epithymeō* in 1 Tim 3:1; Ex 34:24 LXX; Prov 23:3, 6 LXX; Sir 16:1). Moreover, Bezae at Luke 22:16 reads: "I certainly will no longer eat *(ouketi mē phagomai; iam non manducabo)* of it until it is eaten *(brōthē; edatur)* new in the *kingdom of God." The scribal omission of Luke 22:19-20 removes the troublesome reference to Jesus' eating (Lk 22:20) and the words of institution. Given the parallels in the other Synoptics and Paul, these words of institution nearly require the subsequent mention of the second cup, which in Luke is necessarily distinguished from the first by the reference to Jesus' having eaten. Once emended in this way, the passage also harmonizes nicely with the Matthean and Markan wording concerning the bread, breaking off precisely where they do and leaving Luke with one cup, even if it is out of the usual order (see, however, *Did.* 9.1-5). The only problem that the emendation failed to overcome is the adversative *plēn* that begins Luke 22:21. In the shorter version the statement "the hand of my betrayer on the table" stands in contrast to Jesus' words "this is my body," an impossible juxtaposition, since the hand of the betrayer is not opposed to but is precisely the means of Jesus' death (i.e., his "body"). It appears then that the shorter version in Bezae and probably in the Western tradition in general represents an attempt to smooth out a perceived difficulty in the Lukan text and to remove Jesus' participation in the Passover.

The intrinsic probabilities of vocabulary do not weaken and may strengthen this judgment. Words otherwise absent in Luke-Acts appear in the longer text, in particular the references to the "remembrance" of Jesus and the new covenant. Yet this phenomenon is not different from the speeches of Acts, each of which contains distinctive vocabulary. Moreover, a number of vocabulary items link the longer text to the surrounding material. The second person language ("on behalf of you" [twice]) corresponds to the Lukan context quite closely, including Jesus' desire to eat the Passover "with you" and his instruction regarding the first cup: to "take this and divide it among yourselves" (Lk 22:17-18). "Blood poured out on behalf of you" (Lk 22:20) varies from the Markan and Matthean

"poured out on behalf of many" and corresponds to references to martyrdom elsewhere in Luke-Acts (Lk 11:50; Acts 22:20). Furthermore, like Mark, Luke indicates that Jesus gave the bread to his disciples (Lk 22:19; Mk 14:22). And in distinction to the Pauline version (1 Cor 11:24), Jesus indicates (Lk 22:19) that his body is "given for you." It is conceivable that a copyist artistically interwove the Markan ("giving") and Pauline ("for you"), but it is more likely that it is a Lukan composition, linking Luke 22:19 with its context (see also Green 1988, 28-42).

Intrinsic theological probabilities, because of the room they allow for subjective judgments, must be accorded the least weight in assessing the authenticity of any reading. The validity of Ehrman's claim that Luke nowhere else in the Gospel or Acts portrays Jesus' death as an atonement depends on three considerations: the interpretation of Acts 20:28, to which we will turn shortly; the absence of explicit development of the theme of Jesus' death as an atonement for *sin, despite numerous allusions to the Isaianic Servant that suggest such an understanding (see 1.1.4.1 below); Luke's decision not to include the ransom saying from Mark 10:45. The last two observations provide only arguments from silence, which are fragile, particularly in this case.

It is of considerable importance that Luke transposes the disciples' dispute over greatness from the Markan position immediately following the third passion prediction (Mk 10:41-45) to its place in his Gospel following the *Last Supper (Lk 22:24-27). The distinctively Lukan material in the longer version of the words of institution ("given for you," "new covenant in my blood") may serve as Luke's replacement for the saying he chose to omit. Luke's shifting of the material (or use of an alternative tradition; Green 1988, 44-46) adds considerable pathos and irony to the narrative. As Jesus speaks of his affection and self-giving, the disciples are caught up in self-seeking and quarrels. While in Mark greatness is described in terms of doing, in Luke it consists in what one is. The greatest is to be as the youngest and as one who serves, just as Jesus is one who serves. This emphasis corresponds to Luke's presentation of Jesus as the obedient Servant of God (see 1.1.3.1 below) and may therefore explain why Luke left out the ransom saying. He prefers to focus on Jesus' humility and submission to the divine will rather than on Jesus' own intent. The story line of Jesus' self-giving is inextricably linked to the story line of God's sending him (see *1.1.4.3.* below).

1.1.2. Summary of Luke 22:19-20. We may safely say that the weight of external and internal evidence favors the originality of Luke 22:19-20 (for further discussion see Green 1988, 35-42). In this case, Luke clearly attaches atoning significance to Jesus' death, especially in his allusion to Jeremiah 31:31-34. Jesus' body is given and his blood is poured out "on behalf of you," securing the new *covenant in which sins and transgressions are forgiven. This passage is pivotal to Luke-Acts, supplying for the reader the reason John's *baptism of repentance for forgiveness is inadequate and faith in Jesus is necessary (cf. Lk 3:3; 24:47; Acts 19:4). Luke does not want the reader to forget these words and intends the entire subsequent narrative of Acts to be read in light of them, as Acts 20:28 makes clear.

1.1.3. Acts 20:28. The second explicit reference to Christ's death as an atoning sacrifice appears in Acts 20:28, where text-critical and interpretive issues are again intertwined. Although the external evidence is evenly balanced, it is probable that the original text referred to "the church of God" rather than the variant "the church of the Lord." The latter reading most likely represents a scribal amelioration of the difficult wording, "the church of God that he acquired with his own blood," which suggests patripassianism (i.e., the Father is said to suffer) to modern ears, as it probably did to scribes of the third century and onward. As is the case with the NRSV, most commentators opt for reading the passage as speaking of "the church of God, which he obtained with the blood of his own [Son]," for which the word *Son* is supplied. This is grammatically possible but unlikely. Luke frequently places adjectival modifiers in the form in question. Had he intended to speak of "God's own Son," he most likely would have included the final noun (cf. Rom 8:32). We are left with his striking language to describe the death of Christ. But how are we to understand it?

Ehrman's claim (202-3) that Luke regards Jesus' blood not as an atonement but as saving because it brings a recognition of guilt is unconvincing. The charge of guilt for Jesus' death is present only within the Jerusalem speeches and disappears after Acts 7. Moreover, in Acts it is not Jesus' death but the proclamation of his resurrection that brings repentance.

Statements that speak of the "suffering of God," "the crucified God" or even "the blood of God" are common in Christian writers until the end of the second century, when (monarchialist) conceptions of God existing in sequential modes forced further definition to avoid connotations of patripassianism (e.g., Ign. *Eph.* 1.1; see Ehrman, 87-88). We therefore should not be surprised to find such forms of expression in NT writers. The antecedent reference to Jesus' blood (Lk 22:19-20) makes it clear that when Luke uses the expression "God's own blood," he is thinking of Christ's blood and that as with the Christian writers of the second century, this statement represents a bold ascription of deity to Christ. The directness of Luke's statement is not unanticipated, since elsewhere he stresses that Jesus is *Lord with overtones of deity (e.g., Acts 2:21). And Paul, in whose mouth these words appear, is quite capable of making such a statement (Rom 9:5; 1 Cor 8:6).

We should not overlook the biblical allusions conveyed by Luke's language. The word that the NRSV renders "obtained" (*peripoieō;* cf. *peripoiēsis*) carries salvific overtones and might better be rendered "spared for himself" or "delivered for himself" (see Lk 17:33; Mal 3:17 LXX; Num 22:33 LXX; Ps 78:11 LXX; Jdt 11:9). Yet the word also conveys the sense of possession and therefore recalls the exodus in which God savingly acquired a people for himself. They are his "special possession" (*sĕgullâ;* LXX *periousias;* Ex 19:5; Deut 7:6; 14:2; 26:18; cf. 1 Pet 2:9; Ps 73:2 LXX). Likewise, the description of the people of God as a flock has its basis in the exodus (Ps 78:52; cf. Num 27:15-17). The reference to "God's own blood" therefore likely recalls the Passover and suggests a typology in which Christ transcends the original Passover. The striking Lukan wording then signals a contrast between the original Passover and the cross. If this reading of the text is correct, we have in Paul's speech at Miletus a powerful recollection of the words of institution in Luke 22:19-20, where Luke reports Jesus' interpretation of his death (precisely, his blood) as a new covenant. Notions of fulfillment are present in both passages. And the striking ascription of deity to Christ marks Acts 20:28 as a pivotal text.

In narrative, as opposed to direct theological discourse, the character of the speaker and the placement of speech count a great deal. The frequency of appearance of a thought or an expression is far less important than who says it and when it is said. It therefore must not escape our notice that this single explicit reference in Acts to the death of Jesus as an atonement appears at a crucial point, in the mouth of the one whom Luke presents as Christ's chosen vessel, the apostolic witness in whom the promise of Acts 1:8 is fulfilled. Without diminishing the continuing witness of Paul, Luke presents his speech at Miletus as the closure of his ministry to the churches. That is apparent everywhere in the discourse, from Paul's prediction that he would not see the Ephesian elders again (Acts 20:25) to the potent *christology that we have noticed. The elders are in a sense responsible not merely for the Ephesian church but also for the "church of God." Therefore when Paul says that God has "delivered the church for himself with his own blood," Luke is indicating that Jesus' atoning death stands behind all that he has worked among Jews and Gentiles since the cross (Lk 22:19-20). Rather than serving an insignificant role, the two explicit references to Jesus' atoning death bracket and inform the entire intervening narrative.

1.1.4. Allusions to Jesus' Death as an Atonement. How is it that Luke employs numerous biblical allusions to Jesus' death as a substitutionary atonement yet does not develop them? The answer lies partly in his emphasis on Jesus' resurrection and partly in the bracketing we have just observed. The words of institution and the subsequent statement of Paul provide the interpretation of Jesus' death as an atonement, which Luke reinforces by repeated allusions to the Isaianic Servant, the breaking of bread and the divine necessity of Jesus' death.

1.1.4.1. Jesus as the Isaianic Servant. The most prominent of these allusions is the section of Isaiah 53 that Philip finds the Ethiopian eunuch reading (Acts 8:32-33; Is 53:7-8). Luke focuses on the unjust death of the Servant of God, yet notions of atonement lie tantalizingly close (Is 53:6) and come to mind for anyone who knows Jesus' words at the Last Supper and the larger Isaianic context.

This citation of Isaiah 53:7-8 does not stand alone in Luke-Acts. References to Jesus' identity as the Isaianic Servant extend back to Jesus' definition of his ministry (Lk 4:18-19; Is 61:1-2) and into his passion (Lk 22:37; Is 53:12). As J. B. Green observes, the latter is the only instance of the Servant material found on Jesus' lips in the NT (Green 1990, 22). And only in Luke's account of Jesus' death is there a suggestion that the watching centurion unwittingly acknowledges Jesus as the "Righteous One," the Servant (Lk 23:47; Is 53:11, see Karris). Indeed, Luke regards the Servant passages of Isaiah as reflecting a larger biblical understanding of the role of the Messiah (Lk 24:25-27, 44-49), including his mission to the Gentiles (Acts 13:47).

Jesus' role as the Servant clearly informs the speeches of Acts, where the running theme of reversal draws upon the biblical motif of the vindication of the suffering righteous, which is central to the Servant passage of Isaiah 52:13—53:12. When Peter proclaims that God has "glorified his servant *(pais)*, Jesus" and that the people rejected the "holy and righteous one," he uses the language of Isaiah 52:13 and Isaiah 53:11. The distinctive element of the Servant image that distinguishes it from the larger category of the righteous sufferer is the idea that forgiveness is given through him (Is 53:4-6, 10-11). This theme characterizes Luke's narrative. The offer of salvation to the thief on the cross and the omission of the words of derelection tilt the Lukan passion narrative away from the Markan presentation of Jesus as a righteous sufferer and toward the Isaianic background (cf. Green 1990, 23). Likewise, the offer of forgiveness is central to the proclamation of the Christ in Acts (Acts 2:38-39; 3:18-20; 10:43; 13:38-39).

Luke therefore does not regard Jesus' death as that of a martyr or a hero, or even that of a biblical, righteous sufferer, but as that of the suffering Servant-Messiah through whom God offers the forgiveness of sins. This conception of Jesus and the Isaianic background that serves as its source reinforce the two Lukan references to Jesus' atoning death, and these references inform the entire presentation. Given Luke's abundant allusions to the Isaianic Servant, it is overwhelmingly likely that he intends his readers to draw this connection.

1.1.4.2. The Breaking of Bread. Luke also intends his readers to understand the believing community's "breaking bread" as an expression of faith and obedience to Jesus' injunction to "do this in remembrance of me" (Lk 22:19). As D. P. Moessner (182) observes, the misunderstanding and disappointment of the disciples on the way to Emmaus is reversed not simply by instruction from the unrecognized Jesus but in Jesus' breaking of the bread, suggesting that Jesus' words at the Last Supper represent the culmination of the biblical witness and the focal point of revelation (Lk 24:30-32). Moreover, as is the case with Luke's references to Jesus' atoning death, his references to the communal "breaking bread" bracket his presentation of the spread of the gospel. He includes it in his sketch of the piety of the infant church (Acts 2:42, 46) and mentions it again in Paul's closing meeting with the church at Troas (Acts 20:7, 11). Believers "break bread" along with instruction, fellowship and prayer (Acts 2:42) and gather together for it on the first day of the week (Acts 20:7). Given their placement in the narrative, these descriptions are intended to show that the practices were typical of the churches. Luke thus indicates that the first disciples have followed Jesus' command to remember his atoning death. He expects his readers to do so as well.

1.1.4.3. Jesus' Death as a Divine Necessity. As with Matthew, Mark and John, in Luke-Acts Jesus' death is not simply the result of human ignorance and wrongdoing that God subsequently corrects by the resurrection. Rather, the suffering of the Messiah is the will and plan of God, which must come to fulfillment. This theme appears not only in the passion predictions (Lk 9:22, 43; 18:31) and in the prediction of betrayal (Lk 22:21) but also in Jesus' reference to his role as the Isaianic Servant (Lk 22:37; Is 53:12). The divine necessity of Jesus' death consists in that which is written about him (Lk 24:26-27, 44-47; Acts 3:18; 10:43; 13:27; 17:3; 26:23). As the Messiah, Jesus is destined to fulfill the role prescribed for him as the Suffering Servant. This recurring motif subtly underscores Jesus' interpretation of his death as an atonement (Lk 22:19-20), since in it we have the one point in Luke-Acts at which the divine purpose for the cross is disclosed. Luke does not merely assert that the Messiah died because God willed it but supplies Jesus' interpretation of that death.

Yet the theme of the necessity of the suffering of the Messiah also serves a larger, apologetic end in Acts. Far from disqualifying Jesus as the promised Messiah, his unjust death fulfills the words of the prophets (e.g., Acts 13:27). This apology for the cross and Luke's interpretation of Jesus' death as an atonement are bound up with one another, as is his emphasis on the resurrection.

1.1.5. Jesus' Atoning Death and His Saving Resurrection. Luke presents the resurrection of Jesus as the central saving event in Acts in order to undergird the exclusive claims of the gospel. The resurrection not only confirms Jesus as the Servant Messiah but also elevates him into the role of risen Lord. The saving promises of God for Israel and the nations have now been fulfilled in him. Having poured out the Spirit (*see* Holy Spirit), he is now at work in the world sending the message of salvation to the ends of the earth (*see* Creation, New Creation). He therefore is the sole mediator of salvation for humanity. He is not only the prophet like Moses, whom all *Israel must obey (Acts 3:22-26), but also the one who will judge the living and the dead and to whom all the world is accountable (Acts 10:42; 17:31). Salvation is given in his name alone (Acts 4:12).

As the fulfillment of promise, the resurrection also serves as an apology for the cross, vindicating Jesus as Messiah and Lord. This concern is especially apparent in Luke's references to Jesus' death "on the tree" (Acts 5:30; 10:39-40; 13:28-30), which reflect an early Jewish interpretation of Deuteronomy 21:22-23 as speaking of crucifixion as a punishment to be inflicted on those guilty of serious offenses (Wilcox; cf. 11QTemple 64:7-9). Questions of guilt and innocence are present in all three occurrences of this description of Jesus' death. In each case the speaker points to the resurrection as the exculpation of Jesus and confirmation of the divine favor resting on him. Luke's emphasis upon God's action suggests that he is aware of the divine curse that Deuteronomy 21:22-23 was regarded as pronouncing on the guilty, yet he does not develop the idea of Jesus' bearing a curse for others (cf. Gal 3:13). His focus is fixed on removing any doubts about God's vindication of Jesus.

Here we are brought back to one of the most pressing current questions about Luke's understanding of salvation. The tendency has been to suppose that since Luke leaves the theme of Jesus' death as an atonement undeveloped and places his main emphasis on the resurrection, he lacks such an understanding of Jesus' death (Vielhauer, Conzelmann) or rejects it, or, although he is aware of it, he has not appropriated it himself (see Marshall 1970, 169-75).

But these judgments overlook the character of Acts as a narrative and the function of Luke's emphasis on the resurrection. As we noted, the infrequency of reference to Jesus' death as an atonement is not important. In narrative the character of the speaker and the occasion of the utterance counts far more. Moreover, Luke wishes to provide assurance to a circle of readers who already have received basic Christian instruction (Lk 1:1-4), assurance that necessarily entails a confirmation of the events on which such instruction was based. In focusing on Jesus' resurrection and exaltation, Luke provides an apology for the claims of the gospel, supporting rather than diminishing the understanding of Jesus' death as a vicarious atonement. Furthermore, the central role of Jesus' exaltation in Acts is indicative of a salvation-historical perspective that is essential for understanding Jesus' death as an atonement. From Luke's point of view, unless the crucified Jesus was raised from the dead it makes no sense to speak of his death in this way. And unless there is a judgment to come, it makes no sense to speak of the forgiveness of sins. Luke does not confront a diminution of the atoning work of the cross, as do Paul and the author of Hebrews, but he does defend it in his circumstances by providing at length the framework and basis for its acceptance.

Two final observations help to confirm this conclusion. First, while it is true that the resurrection receives primary attention in Acts and that Luke does not directly connect forgiveness to the death of Jesus, it is nevertheless also true that Jesus' exaltation and the forgiveness of sins are not independent of the cross. The resurrection and exaltation are not viewed in the abstract but as God's act upon the crucified Servant of God (e.g., Acts 2:33; 5:30-31). Forgiveness is not proclaimed apart from Jesus' death (Acts 2:38; 3:18-21; 5:30-31; 10:40-43; 13:38-39; 26:18, 23). Second, and more importantly, NT writers characteristically attach saving significance to both the cross and the resurrection without suggesting that the significance of one eclipses the other (e.g., Rom 4:25). Both are essential elements of the saving work of God in Christ. If that is true elsewhere, we should not be surprised to find it in Luke-Acts.

1.2. Jesus' Suffering as a Pattern for Believers. Luke also provides indications that he regards Jesus' suffering and death as a paradigm for those who believe in him. The call to discipleship in Luke's Gospel includes a general appli-

cation. Those who follow Jesus must take up their cross "daily" (Lk 9:23). The one who does not bear a cross cannot be Jesus' disciple (Lk 14:27). Moreover, the apostles are those who have stood with Jesus in his trials and on whom he confers a kingdom just as the Father has on him (Lk 22:28-30; *see* Kingdom of God). Something more than following Jesus' example is operative. Just as it is necessary for the Messiah to suffer, it is necessary for those who believe in him to "enter the kingdom through many tribulations" (Acts 14:22). This instruction by Paul to the churches of Lystra, Iconium and Pisidian Antioch amounts to the only explicit statement of the matter in Acts. Yet Luke signals his expectation of suffering to his readers through his description of the experiences of the early church (Acts 8:1-3) and its leaders (Acts 5:41), the first martyr, Stephen (Acts 6—7), and Paul, "the chosen vessel" of the Lord, to whom Jesus promises to reveal "all that he must suffer on account of my name" (Acts 9:16).

The parallelism to Luke's treatment of Jesus' death as an atonement is striking. Again we have numerous allusions alongside a single clarifying pronouncement, which is to be understood as typical. And in this case Luke provides even less information as to the workings of this experience. He obviously regards the people of God as identified with the Messiah. That is clear from the dying Stephen's vision of the Son of man standing at the right hand of God (Acts 7:55) and from the words of the risen Jesus to the thunderstruck Saul ("Why are you persecuting me?" Acts 9:4 et al.). And just as Christ is identified with them, Luke implies that they are identified with him. The will of God was accomplished in the case of his Servant *(pais),* and his servants *(douloi)* pray that it will be worked out in them as well (Acts 4:23-31). Yet Luke does not spell out the nature and basis of this relation. From one perspective the persecution of believers is due to the witness they bear to the name of Jesus (Acts 5:41; 9:16; 15:17; 26:9). Luke also gently hints at the Messiah's role as a second Adam (Acts 26:13). Whatever its basis in Luke-Acts, this theme of conformation to Christ's death, which is quite different from the idea of imitation, reappears in the Pauline letters, Hebrews, 1 Peter, 1 John and Revelation (*see* Revelation, Book of) alongside the interpretation of Jesus' death as an atonement for sin.

1.3. Human Responsibility for Jesus' Death. Despite Luke's considerable emphasis on the divine purpose behind the death of the Messiah, he does not diminish human responsibility for Jesus' crucifixion. Indeed, here the biblical tension between divine sovereignty and human responsibility reaches its peak. The cross is not a tragedy from which God somehow retrieves some good but is part of his plan foretold by the prophets. Yet those who perpetrated the deed are not relieved of responsibility but are called to repent.

Unlike Christian writers of the second century, Luke also finely differentiates the guilt for Jesus' death. He regards as responsible for Jesus' death all who participated in his trials and execution: Herod and Pilate, the Gentiles and the people of Israel (Acts 4:23-28; cf. 7:51-53). Yet the Jews of Jerusalem especially are charged with guilt, since Luke understands Pilate to have decided to release Jesus, only to be opposed by the crowd (Lk 23:13-25; Acts 2:23; 3:13; 10:39; 13:27-28). Within Jerusalem the leaders are singled out as being especially culpable (Lk 22:66—23:5; Acts 3:17; 5:30-31).

Nevertheless, this guilt does not exclude any from salvation. Leaders and people acted in ignorance and are called to repent, believe and be baptized, so that they may receive the promises God made to Israel (Acts 2:38-39; 3:17-21; 5:31). Luke regards the door to salvation as remaining open to Israel. Paul's concluding words in the book of Acts do not indicate otherwise (Acts 28:25-28). The hardening of Israel's heart does not mean that no Jews have believed or yet will do so but that the time at which the whole nation will turn to the Messiah is still to come (Acts 3:19-21).

2. Hebrews.

Coupled with his exaltation, the death of Christ is the focal point and basis of the sermonic exhortation of Hebrews. The author derives his framework for interpreting the cross primarily from the OT cult, in particular from the high-priestly service on the Day of Atonement (Lev 16). Christ's death works purification from sin and enables approach to a gracious God (Heb 4:14-16). The levitical priesthood, the wilderness tabernacle and its sacrifices anticipated the saving significance of Christ's death, providing an earthly pattern or type of the heavenly benefits that Christ secured (Heb 8:5; 9:23). Christ's sacrifice is superior to those enjoined by the *Law,

since they are mere copies and shadows of the eternal realities achieved in the cross (Heb 8:5; 9:23; 10:1). While the OT cult has been superseded, its conceptual world is firmly retained as the basis for understanding the death of Christ (contra Tuckett, 1:521). This is evident in the concise, introductory description of the saving work of the Son as his "making purification for sins" (Heb 1:3), which interprets the cross in sacrificial terms and anticipates the subsequent theme of forgiveness as the surpassing effect of the cross. Other ways of interpreting Christ's death supplement and expand this idea. By death Christ divested the devil of the power of death. Moreover, he blazed a trail to the divine presence for all the children of God (Heb 2:10, 14-16).

2.1. The Great High Priest. The author introduces the motif of Christ as high priest as a summary of the purpose of the incarnation, a theme that figures prominently in the first part of the material (Heb 2:1-18; 4:14—5:10). Jesus had to share in "flesh and blood," including the suffering of death, so that he might become "a merciful and faithful high priest." This thought recurs and reaches a dramatic closure in Hebrews 5:7-9, where the author, recalling early Christian tradition of the prayer in Gethsemane, describes Jesus' fully human experience in facing the ordeal of the cross: "He offered up supplications and petitions with loud crying and tears to the one able to save him from death." Even the Son learned obedience in suffering and was "perfected" in his role as high priest. This attribute sets him apart from the earthly priesthood and qualifies him for an eternal one (Heb 4:15; 5:2-3; 7:26-28; Peterson, 104-25). His suffering enables him to have compassion toward our moral weakness (*astheneia;* cf. Heb 5:2; 7:28) and to help us (Heb 4:16). The Son became not only a merciful and faithful high priest (Heb 2:17) but also the great high priest who has passed through the heavens (Heb 4:14). This becomes the dominating theme of Hebrews 7 — 10, where the author presents Christ's superiority in both the effectual character of the sacrifice he made "once for all" and in his eternal status as high priest, a juxtaposition that raises the question as to what Christ's eternal ministry might be.

2.2. The Sacrifice.

2.2.1. Blood. Central to the author's argument is his claim that Christ's blood provides cleansing from sin (Heb 9:14, 22-23; 10:22). In such contexts "blood" signifies a sacrificial death and not, as has sometimes been argued, the life of the victim (see especially Heb 9:15-22; cf. Heb 10:5, 10, where the parallel term *body* appears). The author does not make use of every aspect of the atoning ritual in explicating Christ's work and in particular makes no mention of a presentation of blood in the heavenly sanctuary (cf. Lev 16:15-19). Christ enters into heaven not with his blood but through his blood; that is, through his death on the cross (Heb 9:12). Moreover, the finality of Christ's offering distinguishes his ministry from that of earthly priests (Heb 7:26-28). Christ's entrance into heaven, which is associated with his cross (Heb 9:12), is followed by his session at the right hand of God, as the author stresses (Heb 1:3; 8:1; 10:11-13). These considerations weigh heavily against interpreting Christ's ministry in Hebrews as including an application of his blood in the heavenly sanctuary subsequent to his death. Rather, the whole of Christ's work is accomplished at the cross, once for all (Heb 7:27; 9:28; 10:10). His ministry as high priest entails not a perpetual offering but his presence before God on our behalf (Heb 4:14-16; 6:19-20; 7:26-28; 9:23-28).

This heavenly ministry has two interrelated aspects. First, Christ serves as mediator, eternally interceding for those drawing near to God through him, providing grace and mercy (Heb 2:18; 4:16; 7:25). Second, his entrance into the presence of God for *us* is an entrance before us. By his struggles, suffering and death, he has established the pilgrimage of his brothers and sisters into the presence of God (Heb 6:19-20). In Jesus' humanity, humanity has been "perfected," having passed obediently through suffering and into heaven. By virtue of God's saving purpose for the human race (and not some material conception as in Ignatius or Irenaeus), the high-priestly language flows over into the imagery of progress and conquest. Christ is the "clan-leader" (*archēgos*; cf. Ex 6:14; Num 10:4; Deut 33:21) of salvation (Heb 2:10; 12:2) and its perfecter (Heb 12:2). He has entered into the presence of God as a forerunner for us (Heb 6:20). Yet Christ's unique high-priestly role is not set aside by these additional conceptions. He alone is the sinless mediator who deals mercifully with sinners (Heb 2:17; 7:26-28). The way into God's presence has its basis in the forgiveness secured at the cross, not in a divinization of humanity. And the forgiveness once and for all secured

has its application in the essential help it provides to "the children" on the difficult path to glory.

2.2.2. Offering. In expounding the relation between the sacrifices of the old covenant and the death of Christ, the author generally employs the familiar language of "offering." Significantly, however, at the outset and the conclusion of the main argument, interpretive theological terms appear.

The author introduces Jesus' high-priestly role by describing its purpose as "making propitiation with respect to the sins of the people" (*eis to hilaskesthai tas hamartias tou laou*, Heb 2:17). There has been extensive discussion as to whether the biblical usage of the Greek verb *hilaskesthai* signifies the propitiation of divine wrath, as in secular Greek, or the expiation of sin. Yet once it is acknowledged that the removal of sin averts divine wrath, as is the case here (see *2.2.2.* below), one arrives at the idea of "propitiation." To exclude the idea of aversion of punitive divine action is to remove biblical sacrifice from its covenantal context, where the means of atonement are gracious gifts of God (e.g., Lev 17:11). In the biblical writings the personal, covenantal understanding of the divine-human relation remains decisive—no matter how significant the cultic "space" and implements might be—as is evidenced by the close association between sacrifice and forgiveness (e.g., Ex 30:30-32; Lev 4:20, 26, 31, 35; and especially, 16:15-22).

In the passage at hand it is clear that the author understands Jesus' death to avert the wrath of God. It is of the greatest significance that he shifts without discussion from speaking of the forgiveness of the sins to the removal of sin and back again, all in the context of sacrificial language (Heb 9:22, 26; 10:4, 18). If covenantal provisions are rejected, divine wrath will be directed against the disobedient and unbelieving (Heb 2:1-4; 3:7-19; 4:7-8; 12:25-29). The syntax of this clause is paralleled in the Septuagint by only a few passages in Sirach, where atonement is closely connected to the avoidance of God's anger (see especially Sir 3:30; 28:5). Moreover, the author stresses that the capacity for mercy is a central duty of a high priest (Heb 2:17: 5:2), implying that strict judgment is the alternative to mediation.

The second passage in which the author interprets the language of "offering" corroborates this reading of Hebrews 2:17. As the author brings to a close his presentation of the death of Christ as a superior sacrifice, he describes the cross as Christ's "being offered up in order to bear the sins of many" (Heb 9:28). Here he obviously recalls the substitutionary suffering of the Isaianic Servant (Is 53:4-12). Bearing the sins "of many," the Christ bore their punishment. It is not simply that at the cross he represented them but that the punishment that was theirs became his, so that they now await salvation rather than condemning judgment (contra Hooker). As he does with the entire sacrificial structure, the author here assumes the reality and validity of this substitutionary act (on this topic see Hill, Morris 1965).

2.2.3. Atonement. As is the case with other NT contexts in which Christ's death is interpreted as an atonement, God is not only the object of Christ's sacrifice (Heb 2:17) but also its subject (Heb 9:28), as is apparent from the covenantal framework of Hebrews (e.g., Heb 8:6-13). It is God who ordains all high-priestly ministry and who chose Christ as an eternal high priest (Heb 5:1-6). He offered Christ up to bear sin (Heb 9:28), and by God's will Christ offered up his body for the sanctification of the people of God (Heb 10:10). God not only required a death for the forgiveness of sins but also provided it in the Son.

2.3. The Effect of Christ's Death. Like the sacrifices of the Law, Christ's death "atones," "cleanses" and "sanctifies," as do the sacrifices of the Law. Yet the cross alone, not the former sacrifices, secures forgiveness (Heb 10:4, 11). And once sins have been removed and forgiven, no need for sacrifice remains (Heb 8:12; 9:26; 10:18). Likewise, Christ's sacrifice and priesthood bring "perfection," in distinction from the sacrifices of the Law.

2.3.1. Forgiveness. "To sanctify," in Hebrews, generally signifies not the effecting of progressive moral improvement but forgiveness (Heb 2:11; 9:13; 10:10, 29; cf., however, Heb 12:14). Those who believe have been sanctified "once for all" through the offering of the body of Jesus Christ (Heb 10:10). This sanctification is nothing other than the forgiveness of sins (see Heb 10:2, 18). As James Denney (126) comments, "In the Epistle to the Hebrews, the word ἁγιάζειν, corresponds as nearly as possible to the Pauline δικαιοῦν. The sanctification of the one writer is the justification of the other; and

the προσαγωγή or access to God, which Paul emphasizes as the primary blessing of *justification, appears everywhere in Hebrews as the primary religious act of 'drawing near' to God through the great High Priest."

2.3.2. Perfection. The "perfection" of believers signifies their participation in the saving blessings of the age to come through the forgiveness won at the cross. "Perfection" could not be achieved through the levitical priesthood, since the law made nothing "perfect" and was not able "to perfect" those who offered sacrifices (Heb 7:11, 19; 10:1). In contrast, with one sacrifice Christ "perfected forever" those being sanctified (Heb 10:14). The provisions of the law were temporary and had only outward effects, cleansing "the flesh" and the copies of the heavenly things. Christ by his death, in contrast, achieved redemption and cleanses the conscience. Now exalted, he appears before God "for us" (Heb 9:1-15, 23-28).

As an eschatological term, "perfection" involves a fundamental distinction between material and spiritual orders but not an unconditioned dualism. It is misleading, therefore, to interpret Hebrews on the basis of Platonism or *Gnosticism, as was once common, despite its obvious coloring with Hellenistic religious terminology. The "vertical" opposition is not absolute, but appears as an element, albeit a pivotal one, in a salvation-historical framework.

In Hebrews, hope is not fixed on a disembodied eternity but on a transformation of the creation that has been subverted by sin and death into an eternal dwelling place for God and his people. The author speaks of the tent through which Christ entered as high priest as being not of this creation (Heb 9:11), implying that Christ entered into a new creation. Heavenly realities, then, are eschatological realities. Similarly, in a striking figure, he symbolically equates Jesus' material flesh with the veil before the holy place, making it plain that the "undecayed" *(prosphatos)* and "living way" into the divine presence is none other than the once crucified and now resurrected Jesus (Heb 9:11; cf. Heb 6:19-20). The world to come is a physical one, as is evidenced by the hope for a "better" resurrection of the dead (Heb 11:35). God will "yet once shake" the structure of the present creation, heaven and earth (Heb 12:26). Created things will then be subjected not to "removal" (wrongly NRSV, NIV) but to a radical "transposition" (*metathesis,* Heb 7:12; 11:5, cf. Heb 1:10-12). Salvation in Hebrews therefore does not involve a journey from the material into the immaterial but from the present world into the age to come.

Correspondingly, although it is varied in nuance, the language of "perfection" bears an eschatological thrust. The contrast between the earthly tent and the "more perfect" heavenly tent through which Christ entered in offering his sacrifice is strictly eschatological (Heb 9:11). The author's language of perfection therefore is essentially salvation-historical, underscoring the completion of the divine saving purposes. By virtue of the plan of God, eternal and complete salvation comes only in these last days through the Son (Heb 11:40; Heb 1:2; cf. Heb 9:10).

The perfection of believers is won at the expense of the perfection of the Son through suffering (Heb 2:10; 5:9; 7:28). Here too the eschatological sense is primary. Christ's sinlessness is never in question in Hebrews and in fact receives emphasis (Heb 4:15; 7:26-28; 9:14). His "perfection" represents his progress into his full role as mediator of salvation (Heb 7:26-28). In being perfected, the Son reaches his eschatological station and awaits the subjection of all things under his feet (Heb 1:13; 10:13).

Above all else, the perfection of believers signifies their access to God and participation in the heavenly Jerusalem (Heb 7:19; 12:22-24). Perfection also takes a cognitive sense in Hebrews 5:11—6:3, where maturity involves the capacity to comprehend "the word of *righteousness." Yet this perfection of the mind and heart is also obviously bound up with *eschatology, since it represents, among other things, "tasting" the heavenly gift and the powers of the age to come (Heb 6:4-8).

As with the language of sanctification in Hebrews, the "perfection" of believers that Christ wrought by his sacrifice entails in the first place the remission of sins (Heb 7:11, 19; 9:9; 11:40; and especially Heb 10:14-18). This corresponds to our earlier observation that the author's fundamental category for interpreting Christ's death lies in its effecting forgiveness. The "perfection" of believers implies the surpassing eschatological cleansing accomplished at the cross (Heb 10:14). In this way the difference between the perfection of the Son and the perfection of believers becomes understandable. He was perfected through suffering; they are perfected by his suffering. They are not thereby spared the

difficult path to glory (Heb 2:10; 12:1-13), but through Jesus they participate in their destination already. He is the perfecter of faith, since his arrival at his eschatological station ensures their arrival as well (Heb 12:2).

2.3.3. Human Transformation. This eternal redemption effected by Christ is reflected in the experience of the believer. In contrast to the sacrifices offered under the Law, Christ's death cleanses the conscience and not merely the "flesh" from sin and guilt (Heb 9:9, 14; 10:2, 22). There is to be a subjective appreciation of the objective and external reality. The sense of forgiveness does not come about automatically, however. The access to God that Christ's death has achieved must be grasped and held by faith. Indeed, the path of testing on which believers walk requires that they avail themselves of divine assistance. Unbelief, not faith, is passive and sluggish. The primary exhortation of the letter is the call to maintain confidence in the forgiveness that the cross has won (Heb 3:6; 4:16; 10:35).

In a pattern similar to Paul's letters, in Hebrews the forgiveness of sins is not an isolated gift but issues in service to God. The indicative of forgiveness forms the basis of the imperative. This is apparent in the author's understanding of suffering. Believers endure adversity not in order to become "sons" but because they are "sons" already. If they do not receive "discipline," they are not "sons." As a loving father, God works righteousness within them, which will bear peaceful fruit (Heb 12:4-11). Likewise, believers are pilgrims and wanderers because they have their true home already in the heavenly city (Heb 3:6; 12:18-24). Their progress is assured by virtue of Christ alone, who as a great high priest supplies the gracious help that they need (Heb 2:16-18; 4:16; 7:25).

In Hebrews, then, the transformation of the human heart has its basis in the forgiveness of sins. This is especially apparent in the repeated references to the promise of a new covenant from the book of Jeremiah (Jer 31:31-34). In Hebrews 8:7-12 the author cites the passage in order to establish the inadequacy of the Law, "the first, antiquated covenant." The inscription of the Law of God on the heart is summarized in Jeremiah as "knowing God," and this knowledge of God in turn is based on the forgiveness of sins (Jer 31:34; Heb 8:12). In his second recollection of the Jeremianic text (Heb 10:15-18) the author underscores the finality of Christ's sacrifice, which, by providing forgiveness of sins, sets aside the provisions of the Law. The author's inclusion in his citation of God's promise to implant his laws in the hearts of his people serves as a reminder of the inability of the Law to do so and implicitly presents inward renewal as the result of the forgiveness of sins.

It is important to observe, too, that for Hebrews the church, "the communion of the saints," derives from the forgiveness that each person individually has received, since forgiveness means common access to the throne of grace, participation in the heavenly city and a common sojourn (Heb 3:12-14; 10:24-25; 12:22-23).

2.3.4. Deliverance. Just as Christ's high-priestly role overflows into that of champion, the author portrays his work on the cross as deliverance from the devil, who held the power of death (Heb 2:14-15). Although he leaves the source of the devil's power unexplained, he no doubt assumes a biblical background, in which the devil incites human beings to sin (Gen 3; 1 Chron 21:1) and accuses them before God (Zech 3:1-5). The immediate context suggests that the devil's power derives from his accusations too, since the help that Christ extends to his brothers and sisters consists in his making propitiation for their sins (Heb 2:17-18; cf. Rev 12:9-10). It is likewise highly probable that the author assumes an inner connection between a guilty conscience and the fear of death, which subjected human beings all their lives to slavery (Heb 2:14-15). The "fear of death" in Hebrews has in view the judgment of God that follows (Heb 9:27; 10:27, 31; cf. Heb 12:21). Christ's sacrifice cleanses the conscience from "dead works," that is, from "works that bring the *judgment of death," so that believers may serve the living God (Heb 9:14). Just as forgiveness, as an objective reality and subjectively grasped, brings the freedom to serve, guilt in both respects makes one a slave.

2.3.5. Covenant Ratification. J. J. Hughes (27-66) has persuasively argued that in Hebrews 9:16-17 *diathēkē* retains the usual biblical sense of "covenant" (rather than the usual rendering as "testament") and that the proper background for the imagery is the sacrificial covenant ritual reflected in the OT (e.g., Gen 15:9-21). The verses then would be rendered: "For where there is a covenant, it is necessary for the death of the one who ratifies it to be attested [or represent-

ed], for a covenant is confirmed over dead animals, since it is not valid while the ratifier still lives [i.e., has not undergone representative death]." Christ's death provides the ratifying sacrifice prerequisite to the establishment of the new, eternal covenant (Heb 9:15-22), as well as redeeming from the transgressions committed under the "first covenant," the law.

But why would the author characterize Christ's death in this way? The ritual splitting of the carcasses of animals signified the fate that awaited the ratifying party should he or she violate the terms of the covenant. Therefore the mention of Christ's blood as a ratification almost certainly anticipates the warnings of the terrifying judgment that will come upon those who knowingly reject the new covenant, to which the author turns in Hebrews 10 (cf. Jer 34:18). In doing so he takes up the formula for covenant ratification he has used in Hebrews 9:20—the one who regards "the blood of the covenant by which he was cleansed as will receive the severest of punishments" (Heb 10:26-30). There is therefore an implicit reference to divine wrath in Hebrews 9:16-17, which corresponds to the author's usual method of presentation: he introduces an idea prior to developing it (cf. the description of Jesus as high priest in Heb 2:17-18, which is then followed by his exposition beginning Heb 5).

3. 1 Peter.

Viewed from the perspective of its supreme moral beauty and inestimable value, the death of Christ, or in the language of the letter, Christ's "suffering," serves as the leitmotif of 1 Peter. Elsewhere Christ's death is often described as his suffering (particularly in the Gospels, Acts and Hebrews; see Ign. *Eph.* 7.2; Ign. *Trall.* presc.; Ign. *Phld.* 9.2; *2 Clem.* 1.2), but 1 Peter does so exclusively, even altering traditional formulas (see 1 Pet 2:21; 3:18, where variant readings attest scribal tendencies to "correct" the wording).

Peter develops the theme of the excellence of Christ's innocence and humility in three ways. In language suggestive of a common confession, he reminds his readers of the undeserved favor that has come to them by Christ's suffering on their behalf. The sinless Christ accomplished redemption through his meek endurance of injustice, a redemption that therefore is worthy of highest esteem. A second prominent theme is regularly attached to this idea: in his suffering and death Christ freed believers from their empty past for conduct like his, thereby pleasing God. Finally, Peter points to the eschatological "glories" that follow the cross. Christ, although rejected by the disobedient, is precious to God who has now raised him from the dead and exalted him. Believers wait in faith and hope for the revelation of Christ's glory in which they shall be delivered and vindicated. The letter therefore serves as an encouragement to Gentile Christians under pressure and the threat of persecution to persevere in faith and in excellence of conduct.

These three themes characterize each of the three confessions of Christ's cross that appear in the letter (1 Pet 1:18-21; 2:21-25; 3:18). The cross is simultaneously the source of forgiveness, the basis for conduct and the ground of eschatological hope. Moreover, in the course of the letter a certain progression unfolds. In 1 Peter 1:18-21 emphasis falls on the contrast between the vanity of the past conduct of the readers and the exceeding value of Christ's redeeming death. In 1 Peter 2:21-25, while the same elements are retained, the focus shifts to the pattern of life that Christ's meekness set for believers to follow. And in the third passage (1 Pet 3:18 and its context) Peter stresses Christ's vindicating resurrection and the eschatological salvation of those who believe in him.

These passages may represent hymns or confessions of which the author made use (see Worship). Nevertheless, in each case the phrasing bears the distinct vocabulary of the author, reflects his particular interests and (as we are arguing) contains material integral to his argument in the letter, so that while the passages reflect early Christian traditions, they do not lend themselves to the reconstruction of underlying strata of thought. They are confessional in nature and form as they stand in the letter and may well have been constructed with catechesis in mind.

It is necessary to mention briefly the debate as to whether 1 Peter 3:18-22 includes a description of a postmortem or postresurrection descent of Christ to the dead. Despite its current disfavor, some form of the Augustinian interpretation of the passage is the most satisfactory interpretation (Feinberg, Grudem, cf. Dalton), since it best accounts for the particularity of reference to Noah and the evangelization of the

dead in 1 Peter 4:6. This interpretation also receives considerable support from the mention of the presence of the Spirit of Christ in the prophets (1 Pet 1:11), which among the NT writings is unique. In this reading Christ did not descend into hell or the underworld but was present by the Spirit in the preaching of Noah. The "spirits in prison" are those of persons who were then disobedient (1 Pet 3:20; cf. Heb 12:23).

3.1. The Suffering of Christ as an Atonement. In contrast to Hebrews, the theme of forgiveness remains undeveloped in 1 Peter. Yet it is clearly foundational, an essential element of the confession of Christ that Peter and his readers share and upon which he builds. This significance of the cross as a means of forgiveness is apparent in the opening greeting, which describes the ultimate saving aim of God for his people as "obedience and sprinkling with the blood of Jesus Christ."

The first element of the divine aim, "obedience," serves as a pregnant description of faith (see 1 Pet 1:22), which is thereby represented as the primary act of obedience (1 Pet 1:7-9; contra Garlington), with the underlying suggestion that faith is to issue in holy conduct (1 Pet 1:14). This language may represent Pauline influence, since the term *obedience* is infrequent apart from his letters. And the usage of "obedience" in the sense of "faith" is unmistakably Paul's. At the outset of the letter a pattern appears, which is prominent in letters of Paul and common to the NT generally. The forgiveness given by the cross is not an isolated gift but is joined to the new obedience. The focus of the letter is upon the new obedience, but its basis lies in the forgiveness worked by Christ's death.

The second phrase, which bears overtones of the covenantal ceremony described in Exodus 24 (cf. Heb 9:13; 10:22; 12:24), conveys assurance to the Gentile readers that they have now become the people of God and that they are so on the basis of the death of Christ. Notions of cleansing and forgiveness are also implicit (cf. *Barn.* 5.1), since the sprinkling of blood recalls the Day of Atonement as well (Lev 16; see too the red heifer ceremony, Num 19).

In the first christological confession (1 Pet 1:18-21) the reference to the blood of Christ as that of a "lamb unblemished and spotless" (1 Pet 1:19) recalls the sacrificial system (e.g., Lev 9:3), and in its personal and moral aspect it bears associations with the Suffering Servant of Isaiah 53. The understanding of Christ's death as a substitutionary atonement lies just under the surface in the biblical imagery that the passage evokes. The focal point of the confession is found in the contrast between the worthless conduct of the pagan world and the "precious blood of Christ."

The soteriology is profound. As L. Goppelt (117) observes, the "ancestral inheritance of empty conduct" (1 Pet 1:18) describes sociologically what the Adam-Christ typology (Rom 5:12-21) says theologically. There is something more here than a bad example that might be either followed or disregarded. Humanity is entrapped in an empty and reprehensible pattern of life. Yet God's redeeming work in Christ has overcome the fallen human condition. Before the foundation of the world, Christ and his saving work were determined (proginōskein), and this inestimable sacrifice was made for those whose deeds were worthless. Since God's impartial judgment yet stands before Christians, they are to conduct themselves in reverential fear, knowing the incalculable cost of redemption and the efficacy which that cost implies. The imperative springs from the indicative here in the same paradoxical manner that it does for Paul. The exhortation has faith, not mere gratitude, as its sustaining force (1 Pet 1:21), just as faith, which rightly treasures and loves Christ, is introduced in the letter as the prime virtue of Christians (1 Pet 1:5-9).

The theme of Christ's death as a substitutionary atonement appears again, explicitly, in the second, lengthier confession (1 Pet 2:21-25). "Christ suffered on behalf of you," the readers are told (1 Pet 2:21), a thought that is then expanded in the following confession. This confession is built around Isaiah 53 and represents the most extensive use of that passage in the NT. Thematically it is similar to the citation of Isaiah 53:7-8 in Acts 8:32-33 but goes beyond it precisely in its reference to the substitutionary nature of Christ's death and its saving benefits: "[Christ] who bore our sins in his body on the tree" (1 Pet 2:24; Is 53:12). The phrase "on the tree" reflects the biblical terminology used by early Christians for the shame associated with the cross, reflecting in particular the curse of Deuteronomy 21:23 (see Acts 5:30; 10:39; Gal 3:13; cf. Josh 8:29 LXX, Esther 7:9 LXX).

The underlying thought of 1 Peter 1:2 and 1 Peter 1:19 now becomes explicit. Christ, the sinless Servant of Isaiah 53, has borne the sins of believers upon the cross. Even more than in the earlier confession, attention is concentrated on the new pattern of conduct that Christ's cross has secured for his people. Yet, as before, the substitutionary and unique character of Christ's death provides the basis for exhortation, so that Christ's suffering is not merely exemplary. The indicative of forgiveness that appears in 1 Peter 2:21, 24 is extended to transformed life and gathered up together with the imperative in the summary statements. He bore our sins, that "having [by death] departed from sin, we might live to righteousness" (1 Pet 2:24). With remarkable similarity to Paul, Peter understands Christ's death for sin to include the death of believers to sin, which issues in a new life. In the words of N. Dahl, this is not imitation but conformation. Goppelt's claim (206-7) that the interpretation of Christ's death in terms of mere *imitatio* does not emerge until the second century is substantiated here.

A third succinct description of Christ's death as a vicarious atonement appears in the brief confession found in 1 Peter 3:18. The phrasing "Christ suffered concerning sins [peri hamartiōn]" again reflects sacrificial language (e.g., Lev 16:3, 5, 9 LXX). The following reference to "the righteous one on behalf of the unrighteous" (cf. Is 53:11) completes the substitutionary idea. As in the previous confessions, Peter interprets the cross in sacrificial terms, as an atoning act that brings grace and forgiveness. The stark moral contrast between Christ and those he redeemed reinforces the continuing theme of the virtue of Christ's suffering.

3.2. The Suffering of Christ as a Pattern for Christian Conduct. We have already observed that in 1 Peter Christ's death is interpreted as an atonement for sin in connection with and as the basis for the new obedience of believers and that the interest of the letter lies primarily in exhortation, as is indicated by the frequency of reference to "conduct" (the noun and verb appear seven times).

In the first confession this idea appears in a straightforward but undeveloped way. Christ's death has provided redemption (1 Pet 1:18) and release from slavery, which in context recalls not only contemporary practices of securing manumission but more particularly the exodus from

Egypt. Associations not only of the sacrificial system (and the Suffering Servant of Is 53) but also of the Passover lamb (Ex 12) are present. Bondage is bondage to sinful conduct, from which the "blood" of Christ secures release.

As we have noted, in the progression of emphases the second confession (1 Pet 2:21-25) makes the pattern of Christ's suffering its primary theme. With perhaps a backward glance to the corrupt ancestral inheritance (1 Pet 1:18), Peter indicates that in his patient suffering Christ left behind a model that believers are to follow, tracing his steps (1 Pet 2:21). The following description of Christ's meekness in the face of suffering makes it clear that discipleship consists in conformity to Christ's character. Peter does not suppose that all Christians will suffer crucifixion or even that they all will face persecution (1 Pet 1:6; 3:14; 4:14-16). He expects them to avoid it if possible and does not encourage them to seek abuse or martyrdom as, for example, Ignatius did. He assumes, however, that they cannot escape all suffering, and what they are called to endure they are called to face in the same manner as Christ did. The extensive reference to the Suffering Servant in Isaiah 53 has its basis here and is expanded with Christ's refusing verbal retaliation: "being railed at, he did not rail in return; while suffering, he did not threaten." Instead he entrusted himself to God the righteous judge (1 Pet 2:23).

In this extraordinary virtue Christ provided an example for believers (cf. 1 Pet 3:9-10; 4:19). Yet, as we observed, Peter does not call for mere imitation. Rather, salvation is understood as conformation to Christ's character: "the wounding of Christ has brought our healing" (1 Pet 2:24). Christ remains active in guarding and guiding his people, "for as wandering sheep you have now returned to your Shepherd and Guardian" (1 Pet 2:25). Christ by his cross has secured the wholeness of his people, and that wholeness consists in conformity to his character as righteous (see 1 Pet 2:20).

3.3. The Suffering of Christ and Eschatological Glory. In a manner reminiscent of Luke-Acts, (see, e.g., Lk 24:26, 46) Peter describes the interest of the prophets in the "sufferings of Christ and the subsequent glories" (1 Pet 1:11). Christ's rejection by human beings was overruled by God's delight in him and his virtue (1 Pet 2:4, 19; 3:4, 12). Although put to death in the flesh, he was made alive by the Spirit (1 Pet 3:18) and ex-

alted to the right hand of God (1 Pet 3:22). Christians who share in his sufferings therefore are to rejoice, since such hardship portends eschatological blessing for them at the revelation of Christ's glory (1 Pet 4:13; 1:7). Just as Christ's moral excellence was met with divine reward, so too those who share in his suffering will share in his glory.

4. 1 John.

The death of Christ in its sacrificial, atoning significance is again basic to the message of this letter. The author writes to a confused and battered believing community, which has been fractured by some form of docetism. The claims of the wayward group and the status of the remaining community are to be tested against the apostolic witness to the incarnation and atoning death of the Christ. The cross constitutes the eschatological revelation of God's love, which is to determine the confession and the conduct of those who belong to him. Faith and obedience are inherently bound up with one another, not merely by an ethic of obligation to Jesus' pattern of behavior but more fundamentally in the divine "begetting" of believers and the gift of the Spirit (1 Jn 2:29; 3:24). The world and the works of the devil have been overcome in the cross of Jesus (1 Jn 3:8; 5:4).

4.1. The Death of Christ as a Propitiatory Sacrifice. The opponents deny that "the Christ is Jesus" (1 Jn 2:22; 5:1, 5) and that "Jesus Christ has come in the flesh" (1 Jn 4:2). This implicit denial of the need for the cross is coupled with the errant group's claim that they were without guilt or sin (1 Jn 1:8-10). The author in response insists not only on the confession that Jesus is the Christ but also on the fundamental role Christ's death plays in securing salvation. Particularly the initial and final references to the cross in 1 John address this error, specifying the "blood" of Jesus the Christ as essential to the Christian confession (1 Jn 1:7; 5:6, 8). This language includes a certain stress upon the physical reality of the death of Christ and highlights its saving effect by presenting it in terms of an atoning sacrifice.

The placement of the first of these references to Christ's atoning death at the beginning of the letter (in 1 Jn 1:7—2:2) signals the importance of this topic to the whole discourse. Cultic language appears immediately, which carries associations of the violent death of Christ. "The blood of Jesus cleanses us from all sin" (cf. Lev 8:15; 16:30). Here the author has in view restoration of our persons, affected by the forgiveness of sins, as is suggested in his elaboration of the thought in 1 John 1:9, and the further development of the understanding that the work of Christ frees us from sin (1 John 2:1-2; 3:1-10).

The sacrificial interpretation of Christ's death concludes by the description of it as a *hilasmos* for sin, around which there has been considerable debate (as with the related term *hilaskesthai* in Heb 2:17, see 2.2.2 above). Does the expression merely convey the idea of expiation of sin or also that of propitiation of divine wrath? Although notions of wrath remain in the background, in this letter death is not an impersonal effect but the result of divine judgment (1 Jn 2:28; 4:17-18), the consequence of disobedience and unbelief (1 Jn 2:17; 3:14). Christ is our advocate *(paraklētos)* with the Father (1 Jn 2:1), and this advocacy implicitly derives from his being the *hilasmos* for sin (1 Jn 2:2). Consequently, it is best to understand the term as including the sense of propitiation along with the idea of cleansing, which is obviously present (1 Jn 1:7, 9).

Again, as with all other NT writings, God is both subject and object of Christ's atoning death. He is faithful and righteous to forgive our sins and cleanse us, even as Christ is our advocate before him (1 Jn 1:9; 2:1). He sent his Son as a propitiation *(hilasmos)* for our sins (1 Jn 4:10).

The concluding reference to Christ's death again uses the term *blood*, recalling the initial interpretation of his death as an atoning sacrifice and thus carrying salvific associations. These implicitly reinforce the author's assertion that Jesus Christ came not "through water only but through water and blood" (1 Jn 5:6), which here and in 1 John 5:8 most likely refer to Jesus' baptism and death on the cross (see Smalley). Jesus was attested as the Christ not only at his baptism but also in his crucifixion. His death, far from disqualifying him as the Christ, is essential to the divine witness to him.

Christ's death is an atoning sacrifice not only for believers but also for "the world." The "world" is not a neutral usage but has in view the hostility of fallen humanity to God and his purposes (e.g., 1 Jn 2:15-17; 3:1, 13; 4:4). The scope of the atonement stands in contrast to the apparent exclusiveness of the group that had de-

parted from the church. Yet 1 John is decidedly exclusive in its insistence on faith in Jesus and the belief that the entire world lies in the power of the evil one (1 Jn 5:19). Coupled with this belief are clear statements of divine ultimacy in salvation (e.g., 1 Jn 3:9; 4:4). The author shows no embarrassment at this juxtaposition. The God revealed in the offer of forgiveness in the cross is nevertheless the God who freely and sovereignly gives new birth.

4.2. The Death of Christ as Eschatological Revelation. The cross is centrally and predominantly interpreted as a revelation in 1 John, as is apparent from the emphasis of the prescript (1 Jn 1:1-4) and the running themes of truth, knowledge and revelation. This perspective does not diminish its status as an atoning event. As a sacrifice for sins, Jesus' death on the cross is the decisive revelatory event, the eschatological manifestation of God and his love and of eternal life.

A historical dimension is attached to this interpretation of the cross as revelation. The author is distinct from the audience. He has seen the "eternal life" (1 Jn 1:2-3), but they have not. They have only heard from him (1 Jn 1:5). Even his vision is only proleptic. He has seen neither God nor Christ "as he is" in his eschatological glory (1 Jn 3:2; 4:12). Yet he has seen and has borne witness that the Father sent the Son as Savior of the world (1 Jn 4:14). And in sending his only Son that "the world" might live, God has manifested his love (1 Jn 4:9). Revelation in 1 John, therefore, is objective in character rather than a matter of inner illumination. "Seeing" comes about only insofar as the testimony is heard, believed and obeyed (1 Jn 2:7-11, 24; 4:6; 5:5-12). The reception of this revelation is not ultimately a matter of human capacities but a divine work: a being begotten of God (1 Jn 5:1), anointed by him (1 Jn 2:20, 27), given the Spirit (1 Jn 4:13).

The cross is the revelation of the love of God and of love itself. And it reveals this love specifically as a death in our place, for our sins. We know love only through Christ's yielding his life for us on the cross (1 Jn 3:16; cf. Mk 10:45; Is 53:10). God manifest his love in sending his only *(monogenēs)* Son as a propitiation sacrifice *(hilasmos)* for our sins (1 Jn 4:9-10). The radical nature of this claim derives on the one hand from the author's view that "the world" is filled with hatred (1 Jn 3:11-12) and on the other that Christ gave his life for that world, which hates him (1 Jn 2:2). Love as a reality among believers derives not from our love for God but his love for us manifest in Christ's atoning death for our sins (1 Jn 4:10). Apart from the cross, love of this nature would remain unknown. Through the cross, it has dawned on the world as an eschatological reality (1 Jn 2:8-11).

The love of God revealed in the cross places believers under a moral obligation. "If God so loved us, we ought to love one another" (1 Jn 4:11). Yet the ethic of 1 John derives ultimately from the eschatological realities that the cross has introduced. Conduct reveals whether one knows God, whether one is "in him." God is active in the revelation of his love, so that love has its perfection in the re-creation of the human being (1 Jn 2:5; 4:17-18).

The eschatological character of the cross is apparent in other references (1 Jn 3:14; 5:4) and provides the essential structure for the seemingly conflicting statements regarding the relation of believers to sin. As we have seen, the opening declaration of the letter makes continuing confession of sins the mark of true spirituality (1 Jn 1:9-10). Yet the author claims that it is not possible for believers to sin (1 Jn 3:6, 9) and derives this assertion in part from the cross: "That one appeared that he might take away sins, and 'in him' there is no sin" (1 Jn 3:5). The following reference to "abiding in him" (1 Jn 3:6) suggests that the expression "in him there is no sin" refers to the eschatological state that Christ has brought.

"Taking away" sins most likely signifies both forgiveness and restorative, re-creation of life (especially 1 John 3:5). With the forgiveness won at the cross the eschatological state has arrived, in which the power of sin has been abolished by the forgiveness that has been granted. This corresponds to 1 John 3:8, where the purpose of the incarnation is said to be the "destruction of the works of the devil." Believers are now said to have the seed of God abiding within them (1 Jn 3:9), just as they abide in him (1 Jn 3:6). From the eschatological perspective, the perspective of the effects of the cross, the "inability to sin" has been granted. Yet this state of affairs is clearly proleptic. Believers live between the times. They therefore must continue to confess their sins. But they also must live in the light of the eschaton and purify themselves, as Christ is pure (1 Jn 3:3). As the reference to the divine seed implies, eschatological realities have entered the

present and indelibly mark the conduct of the believer.

As an eschatological reality, the death of Christ represents a triumph over the devil and destruction of his works (1 Jn 3:8), a triumph in which believers share (1 Jn 2:12, 14; 4:5). Moreover, victory consists in the confession of Jesus as the Son of God, including his "coming through water and blood," so that the forgiveness worked through the cross stands behind the triumph, a connection that is suggested by the parallel between 1 John 3:5 and 1 John 3:8 as well.

5. Revelation.

Paradoxically in the Revelation to John, the cross of Christ is the path to his lordship and the reign of those who belong to him. Moreover, as we have seen in the other NT writings, it is as an atoning sacrifice that the death of Christ achieves the divine triumph. Not only death and life, apparent defeat and overwhelming victory are juxtaposed in the letter, but also the deity and humanity of Christ. The paradox therefore is deeper than a mere reversal of fortune. Christ died as both God and human.

5.1. Christ's Death as the Death of God. Although Christ's deity and his death are not paired elsewhere in Revelation, the appearance of this juxtaposition in the opening vision and in the message to the church in Smyrna (Rev 2:8) significantly informs the unfolding drama, particularly the adoration of the Lamb (Rev 5:8-14). The worthiness of the Lamb to receive worship derives not only from his redeeming death but also, subtly and implicitly, from his very being. Christ is "the first and the last" (Rev 1:17; 2:8; 22:13), an ascription of divine self-sufficiency and uniqueness (cf. Is 43:10; 44:6; 48:12). He is "the Living One," the expression used to describe the one sitting on the throne (Rev 4:9-10; cf. Rev 10:6; Sir 18:1). Nevertheless, this very one died and lived again (Rev 1:18; 2:8) and now lives forever with authority over death (Rev 1:18), with which he grants encouragement to the suffering church (Rev 2:9-11). The paradoxical relation focuses attention on his death, which is explicable only as a redemptive act.

5.2. Christ's Death as Redemption and Triumph. Most often in Revelation, Christ's death is presented in its saving significance and in sacrificial language. As elsewhere, Christ's death is his "blood" that redeems from sin (Rev 1:5; 7:14) and purchases a people for God (Rev 5:9; cf. Rev 14:3, 4). This language of purchase, drawn from the field of slavery, expresses God's claim on the redeemed. The cross frees them for their divinely appointed role as rulers and as priests (Rev 1:6; 5:10). The image of Christ as "the Lamb who was slain" further links the language of redemption and purchase with the Passover and exodus (Ex 12—13; cf. 1 Cor 5:7) and with the Suffering Servant of Isaiah (Is 53:7; cf. Acts 8:32; 1 Pet 1:19; Jn 1:29).

The frequent depiction of Christ as the Lamb underscores the centrality of his saving death in Revelation (Rev 5:6; passim). In an ironic juxtaposition, this Lamb is first introduced as the conquering Lion of the tribe of Judah (Rev 5:5). God has achieved victory not through force but through weakness in the death of Christ. The violence and oppression of the world and the devil have only caused his purposes to succeed.

These purposes consist in the working of the forgiveness of sins. This idea is inherent to the sacrificial language of Revelation and appears strikingly in the proleptic announcement of triumph in Revelation 12:10-12. The kingdom of God has come, because the "accuser of the brothers and sisters" has been thrown down from heaven (Rev 12:10; cf. Job 1:9-11). The devil, who opposes the divine saving purpose by bringing charges against the people of God for their sins, has been overcome by "the blood of the Lamb" and by faithful testimony to this Lamb. Those who do not believe will be subject to the wrath of God and of the Lamb (Rev 6:16-17; 14:9-11).

The Lamb is supremely worthy of praise because of his sacrificial death (Rev 5:9-12). The moral excellence of his act distinguishes it from the beast's cheap imitation of it in a mortal wound (Rev 13:3, 12).

5.3. Christ's Death as the Destiny of Believers. A stark division between belief and unbelief emerges in Revelation. One is either a follower of the beast (Rev 13:3-4) or a follower of the Lamb (Rev 14:4), subject to the hostility he faced (Rev 12:17). The churches stand in the relation to the risen Lord that he stood to the Father in his earthly ministry (Rev 2:26-28; 3:21-22). They are martyred for their witness (Rev 6:9-11; 12:10), just as he was for his (Rev 1:5). And they likewise share in his triumph (Rev 7:17; 15:3-5; 19:1—20:15).

See also JUSTIFICATION; LORD'S SUPPER; RES-

URRECTION; SERVANT OF YAHWEH.

BIBLIOGRAPHY. G. Aulén, *Christus Victor: A Historical Study of the Three Main Types of the Idea of Atonement* (New York: Macmillan, 1969); D. P. Bailey, "Concepts of Stellvertretung in the Interpretation of Isaiah 53," in *Jesus and the Suffering Servant: Isaiah 53 and Christian Origins*, ed. W. R. Farmer (Harrisburg, PA: Trinity Press International, 1988) 223-51; R. E. Brown, *The Epistles of John* (AB; Garden City, NY: Doubleday, 1982); J. T. Carroll and J. B. Green, *The Death of Jesus in Early Christianity* (Peabody, MA: Hendrickson, 1995); H. Conzelmann, *The Theology of Luke* (New York: Harper & Row, 1961); O. Cullmann, *The Christology of the New Testament* (rev. ed.; Philadelphia: Westminster, 1959); W. J. Dalton, *Christ's Proclamation to the Spirits: A Study of 1 Peter 3:18—4:6* (2d ed.; AnBib 23; Rome: Pontifical Biblical Institute, 1989); P. H. Davids, *The First Epistle of Peter* (NICNT; Grand Rapids: Eerdmans, 1990); J. Denney, *The Death of Christ*, ed. R. V. G. Tasker (London: Tyndale, 1951); B. D. Ehrman, *The Orthodox Corruption of Scripture: The Effects of Early Christological Controversies on the Text of the New Testament* (Oxford: Oxford University Press, 1993); J. S. Feinberg, "1 Peter 3:18-20, Ancient Mythology and the Intermediate State," *WTJ* 48 (1986) 303-36; D. Garlington, *The Obedience of Faith* (WUNT 38; Tübingen: Mohr Siebeck, 1991); S. R. Garrett, "The Meaning of Jesus' Death in Luke," *Word & World* (1992) 11-16; H. Gese, *Essays on Biblical Theology*, trans. K. Crim (Minneapolis: Augsburg, 1981); L. Goppelt, *A Commentary on I Peter*, ed. F. Hahn (Grand Rapids: Eerdmans, 1993); K. Grayston, *Dying, We Live: A New Enquiry into the Death of Christ in the New Testament* (New York: Oxford University Press, 1990); J. B. Green, *The Death of Jesus* (WUNT 33; Tübingen: Mohr Siebeck, 1988); idem, "The Death of Jesus, God's Servant," in *Reimaging the Death of the Lukan Jesus*, ed. D. D. Sylva (Athenum Monographien/Theologie: BBB 73; Frankfurt: Hain, 1990) 1-28; J. B. Green and Mark D. Baker, *Recovering the Scandal of the Cross: Atonement in New Testament & Contemporary Contexts* (Downers Grove, IL: InterVarsity Press, 2000); W. Grudem, "Christ Preaching Through Noah: 1 Peter 3:19-20 in the Light of Dominant Themes in Jewish Literature," *TJ* 7 (1986) 3-31; E. Haen-chen, *The Acts of the Apostles: A Commentary* (Philadelphia: Westminster, 1971); D. Hill, *Greek Words and Hebrew Meanings: Studies in the Semantics of Soteriological Terms* (SNTSMS 5; London: Cambridge University Press, 1967); M. D. Hooker, *Not Ashamed of the Gospel: New Testament Interpretations of the Death of Christ* (Grand Rapids: Eerdmans, 1995); J. J. Hughes, "Hebrews 9:15ff. and Galatians 3:15ff.: A Study in Covenant Practice and Procedure," *NovT* 21 (1979) 27-96; B. Janowski, *Sühne als Heilsgeschehen: Studien zur Sühnetheologie der Priesterschrift und zur Wurzel KPR im alten Orient und im Alten Testament.* (WMANT 55; Neukirchen: Neukirchener, 1982); R. J. Karris, "Luke 23:47 and the Lukan View of Jesus' Death," in *Reimaging the Death of the Lukan Jesus,* ed. D. D. Sylva (Athenum Monographien/Theologie: BBB 73; Frankfurt: Hain, 1990) 68-78; J. Kodell, "Luke's Theology of the Death of Jesus," in *Sin, Salvation and the Spirit,* ed. D. Durken (Collegeville, MN: Liturgical Press, 1979) 221-30; I. H. Marshall, *The Epistles of John* (NICNT; Grand Rapids: Eerdmans, 1978); idem, *Luke: Historian and Theologian* (Exeter: Paternoster, 1970); D. P. Moessner, " 'The Christ Must Suffer,' The Church Must Suffer: Rethinking the Theology of the Cross in Luke-Acts," *SBLSP* 29 (1990) 165-95; L. L. Morris, *The Apostolic Preaching of the Cross* (Grand Rapids: Eerdmans, 1965); idem, *The Atonement: Its Meaning and Significance* (Downers Grove, IL: InterVarsity Press, 1983); J. H. Neyrey, *The Passion According to Luke* (New York: Paulist, 1985); D. Peterson, *Hebrews and Perfection: An Examination of the Concept of Perfection in the "Epistle to the Hebrews"* (SNTSMS 47; Cambridge: Cambridge University Press, 1982); S. S. Smalley, *1, 2, 3 John* (WBC; Waco, TX: Word, 1984); J. R. W. Stott, *The Cross of Christ* (Downers Grove, IL: InterVarsity Press, 1986); V. Taylor, *The Atonement in the New Testament Teaching* (London: Epworth, 1958); C. M. Tuckett, "Atonement in the NT," *ABD* 1.518-22; J. B. Tyson, *The Death of Jesus in Luke-Acts* (Columbia: University of South Carolina Press, 1986); P. Vielhauer, "On the 'Paulinism' of Acts," in *Studies in Luke-Acts,* ed. L. E. Keck and J. L. Martyn (Nashville: Abingdon, 1966) 33-50; R. S. Wallace, *The Atoning Death of Christ* (Westchester, IL: Crossway, 1981); M. Wilcox, " 'Upon the Tree'—Deut 21:22-23 in the New Testament," *JBL* 96 (1977) 85-99.   M. A. Seifrid

DEITY OF CHRIST. *See* CHRISTOLOGY II.

DELIVERANCE. *See* SALVATION.

DESTRUCTION OF THE TEMPLE. *See* JUDA-ISM AND THE NEW TESTAMENT; TEMPLE CLEANSING.

DIATRIBE. *See* ROMANS, LETTER TO THE.

DISCIPLES: GOSPELS

The first-century Greco-Roman world displayed a variety of religious, philosophical and political leaders, each of whom had followers committed to their cause, teaching and beliefs. While several different terms designated these followers, *disciple* was one of the most commonly used. It also became the most commonly used term to designate the followers of Jesus, to the extent that in Jesus' so-called Great Commission the objective of the worldwide mission was to "make disciples" of all nations (Mt 28:19).

    1. Terminology and Concept.
    2. Disciples of Jesus
    3. The Twelve
    4. The Early Church

1. Terminology and Concept.
The English word *disciple* normally designates a "follower," "adherent" or "student" of a great master, religious leader or teacher. "Disciple" is the word used most commonly to translate the Greek word *mathētēs* and the Hebrew words *talmid* and *limmûd.*

    1.1. OT Background. Disciple terminology is strikingly scarce in the OT, but other evidence points to master-disciple relationships within the national life of Israel. The single occurrence of *talmîd* in the OT (*mathētēs* does not occur in the LXX) indicates a student or apprentice in musical instruction (1 Chron 25:8). The prophet Isaiah refers to the group gathered around him as "my disciples" (Is 8:16; *limmûday*), and their relationship is characterized by an educational process accentuating speaking and listening (Is 50:4; *limmûd im*). The term *limmûd im* was used to specify the "disciples" of Yahweh (Is 54:13), indicating that *limmûd im* could be disciples of both Yahweh and a human master.

    In spite of the relative absence of disciple terminology and explicit teaching on discipleship, the nature of the prophetic ministry (the prophets associated with Samuel, 1 Sam 19:20-24; the sons of the prophets associated with Elisha, 2 Kings 4:1, 38; 9:1), the writing prophets (Jeremiah and Baruch, Jer 36:32), the scribes (Ezra, Ezra 7:6, 11) and the wisdom tradition (Prov 22:17; 25:1; wise counselors, Jer 18:18) provide compelling evidence for the existence of master-disciple relationships within the social structure of Israel. Each of these institutions was involved in the process of communicating the revelation of Yahweh (prophecy, law, wisdom) and the suggested intimacy of the relationship indicates mutual support in the task of revealing the word of the Lord to the nation.

1.2. Greek-Speaking World. In the earliest classical Greek literature, *mathētēs* was used in three ways: in a general sense (in morphological relation to the verb *manthanein,* "to learn") of "learner" (Isocrates *Panath.*16.7); with a technical sense of "adherent" to a great teacher, teaching or master (Xenophon *Mem.* 1.6.3.4); and with a more restricted sense of an "institutional pupil" of the Sophists (Demosthenes *Lacrit.* 35.41.7). Socrates and those opposed to the Sophists resisted using *mathētēs* for his followers in order to avoid Sophistic misassociations (Plato *Soph.* 233.B.6-C.6), but he used the term freely to refer to "learners" (Plato *Crat.* 428.B.4) and "adherents" (Plato *Symp.* 197.B.1) where there was no danger of misunderstanding. In the Hellenistic period at the time of Jesus, *mathētēs* continued to be used with general connotations of a "learner" (Diodorus *Bib. Hist.* 23.2.1.13, 26), but it was used more regularly to refer to an "adherent" (Dio Chrysostom *Regno* 1.38.6). The type of adherence was determined by the master, ranging from being the follower of a great thinker and master of the past like Socrates (Dio Chrysostom *De Homero.* 1.2), to being the pupil of a philosopher like Pythagoras (Diodorus *Bib. Hist.* 12.20.1.3), to being the devotee of a religious master like Epicurus (Plutarch *Non Posse Suav.* 1100.A.6).

1.3. Judaism at the Time of Jesus. Within Judaism of the first century, several different types of individuals were called "disciples," using the essentially equivalent terms *mathētēs* and *talmid.* The terms designated adherents or followers who were committed to a recognized leader, teacher or movement; relationships running the spectrum from philosophical (Philo *Sacr.* 7.4; 64.10; 79.10) to technical (rabbinical scribes; *m.* '*Abot* 1:1; *b.* Šabb. 31a) to sectarian (Pharisees in Josephus *Ant.* 13.289; 15.3, 370) to revolutionary (Zealot-like nationalists in *Midr Šir Haširim Zûta*). Apart from the disciples of Jesus, the Gospels present us with "disciples of the Pharisees" (Mt 22:15-16; Mk 2:18) who possibly belonged to one of the academic institutions;

"disciples of John the Baptist" (Mk 2:18), the courageous men and women who had left the status quo of Jewish society to follow the eschatological prophet John the Baptist; and the "disciples of Moses" (Jn 9:24-29), who were Jews focused on their privileged position as those to whom God had revealed himself through Moses.

2. Disciples of Jesus.

2.1. First Followers. From the beginning of his public ministry, Jesus had followers. His first followers, according to the Johannine tradition, were originally disciples of John the Baptist. Since the Baptist's ministry prepared the way for Jesus, it is natural that some of John's disciples would make the transition to following Jesus. The first followers were Andrew and another unnamed disciple (likely the apostle John). Andrew, convinced that Jesus was the Messiah (*see* Christ I), brought his brother, Simon Peter, to Jesus. Philip, another person from the same hometown as Andrew and Peter, was next called by Jesus, and he in turn brought Nathanael to Jesus (cf. Jn 1:35-49). These first followers were likely the "disciples" (Jn 2:2) who next traveled with Jesus to the wedding celebration at Cana, experienced the first miraculous sign and believed in Jesus.

This early movement to follow Jesus gained momentum as the news of Jesus traveled through social relationships in a relatively localized area. Since Jesus focused his ministry in the Galilee region, the early disciples were drawn from an existing network of relatives (e.g., the brothers: Andrew and Simon Peter; John and James), business partners (e.g., Peter and Andrew were partners in the fishing industry with James and John, Lk 5:10), neighbors and acquaintances (most of the twelve disciples were from Capernaum and Bethsaida).

The Jesus movement accelerated rapidly. In the early stages of his ministry a great company of disciples attached themselves to Jesus (Lk 6:17; 10:1; Jn 6:60). Jesus appealed to the multitude of people, and a groundswell of followers came after him to become his disciples. But the early company of disciples was apparently a mixed sort. In John's Gospel there is a unique record of disciples who had followed Jesus for some period of time, but after a discourse by Jesus which they found particularly hard to accept (see Jn 6:60), John writes, "As a result of this many of his disciples were going away to the things they left behind, and were no longer walking with him" (Jn 6:66). The expressions "going away to the things left behind" and "no longer walking with him" mark the return of these disciples to their old lives before they had begun to follow Jesus. In John's usage the expressions indicate that these disciples were following Jesus because he was an exciting new miracle worker and teacher (cf. Jn 2:23-25). They had made some kind of a commitment to Jesus, but when his teaching did not conform to their expectations, they left him. They were only loosely attached to the movement.

2.2. The Disciples and the Crowds. Two groups were in attendance for much of Jesus' ministry: the disciples and the "crowds," or "multitudes" *(hoi ochloi).* The disciples were those who obeyed Jesus' call to follow him. The crowds were those to whom Jesus continued to offer a call. The crowds were a neutral though curious group who were not attached in any serious way to Jesus. Although they followed Jesus (Mt 4:25), the crowds did not exhibit the twin prerequisites of discipleship: paying the cost and committing themselves to the cause. They followed only in a physical sense, never in the truest sense of devoting themselves to following Jesus. They were the people of Israel of Jesus' day who were the object of Jesus' evangelistic ministry. They flocked to him for healing (Mt 15:29-31) and teaching (Mt 5:28-29) but could not understand (Mt 13:10-17) because they were not true believers. At different times they were either positively or negatively oriented toward him. They were amazed at his teaching (Mt 7:28; 21:9-10) and shouted "Hosanna!" at his entry into Jerusalem, but at other times they laughed at him (Mt 9:23-25), came to arrest him (Mt 26:47), were led astray by the chief priests and elders (Mt 27:20) and in the end accepted responsibility for his death (Mt 27:24; *see* Death of Christ I).

The objective of Jesus' ministry among the crowd was to make them disciples. As he taught and preached to them, individuals were moved to faith and began to serve Jesus as Lord (Mt 8:18-21; 17:14-15; 19:16-22). Out of this neutral group referred to as the "crowd" came both disciples and opponents of Jesus. Making disciples from among the crowd was the object of Jesus' ministry in Israel (Mt 9:35-38), and the worldwide commission he gave to his disciples before he ascended was for them to make disciples of the nations (Mt 28:18).

2.3. The Twelve Disciples and Other Disciples. The four Evangelists witness that in the midst of the ebb and flow of the popularity of the Jesus movement, a core of twelve disciples were called by Jesus. Modern scholarship is widely agreed that Matthew and Mark (at least from Mk 3:13 par. Mt 10:1) generally identify the terms *disciple* and *the Twelve* with one another (e.g., Meye, Luz), though not to the extent of implying that the term "disciple" should be limited to the Twelve. Mark gives evidence of disciples outside the circle of the Twelve (Hengel), and Matthew specifically speaks of them (Mt 8:19, 21) and alludes to a wider circle of disciples (Mt 10:24-25, 42), even acknowledging through the verb *mathēteuō* the discipleship of Joseph of Arimathea (Mt 27:57; Przybylski, 109). Matthew and Mark have literary and theological purposes for generally identifying the disciples and the Twelve, but they are in agreement with Luke and John, who more clearly speak of other disciples of Jesus. Luke seems to indicate that Jesus chose the Twelve from among a much larger number of disciples (cf. Lk 6:13, 17).

"Following Jesus" is a technical expression for going after him as his disciple. Some disciples physically followed Jesus in his itinerant ministry (e.g., the Twelve), while a wider group of disciples followed Jesus in a more figurative sense (e.g., Joseph of Arimathea, Jn 19:38). Following Jesus meant togetherness with him while traveling on the Way, but that following could be manifested in either a physical or figurative sense. The difference between the Twelve and the broader group of disciples is the role to which they were called. The Twelve were called to be coworkers with Jesus, and leaving all to follow Jesus was a necessary sacrifice in order to join with him in the proclamation of the kingdom (cf. Mt 10:1-15) and to train for their future role in the church (cf. Mt 19:23-30).

2.4. The Women Who Followed Jesus. The Gospels and Acts give prominent place to various women who were disciples of Jesus. These women were part of the wider group of disciples around Jesus, but some of them physically accompanied Jesus during his itinerancy. Luke tells of a preaching tour through Galilee during which Jesus and the Twelve "with him" were accompanied by several women who had been healed by Jesus and were now contributing to the support of Jesus and the Twelve (Lk 8:1-3). While parallels can be found for women supporting rabbis and their disciples out of their own money, property or foodstuffs, the wording in Luke 8 indicates that these women were themselves disciples of Jesus (e.g., "with him" *[syn autō]* expresses discipleship in Luke's Gospel and seems in this case to apply to the women; cf. Lk 8:38; 9:18; 22:56). A great master with female disciples was an unusual occurrence in Palestine of the first century, as even the early disciples' reaction to Jesus' interaction with the Samaritan woman reveals (Jn 4:27), yet these women exhibited the twin characteristics of Jesus' disciples—they had paid the cost and were committed to him. This same group of women followed Jesus up to Jerusalem, attended the crucifixion and were the first ones to arrive at the empty tomb (Lk 23:49, 55; 24:9; *see* Resurrection I).

Later, in the book of Acts, we find many women who had significant roles in the early church. Luke uses the feminine form of the word for "disciple" (*mathētria*, Acts 9:36) in a casual way, so indicating that women believers were commonly called "disciples."

3. The Twelve.

The four Gospels unanimously testify to the core of Twelve who were called by Jesus into a special relationship with him. Although the Twelve are disciples, examples of what it means to be a believer in Jesus, they also are designated as "apostles." In the introduction to the list of the Twelve, Luke states that Jesus "called his disciples to him, and chose twelve of them, whom he also named apostles" (Lk 6:13). This is a clue to the role of the Twelve: not only are they Jesus' disciples (committed followers), but they are also in training to be his apostles (commissioned representatives). Although Acts and the Pauline letters evidence more specific uses of the term *apostle,* both "apostle" and "disciple" are applied to the Twelve in the Gospels. As "disciples" the Twelve are set aside as the examples of what Jesus accomplishes in his followers; as apostles the Twelve are set aside as the leaders within the new movement to come, the church. The chart below lists the Twelve as they are found in the Synoptic Gospels and Acts.

The Twelve displayed a remarkable diversity in background, including businessmen (Peter, Andrew, James and John), a tax collector (Matthew) and a zealous revolutionary (Simon the Zealot).

Within the Twelve is a recognizable division of groups of four. The first name of each of the groups remains the same in all of the lists (the first, fifth and ninth place is occupied, respectively, by Peter, Philip and James of Alphaeus).

The order of the names within the groups varies, except for the first name. The sequence of the groups is the same in each list. This grouping suggests that the Twelve were organized into smaller units, each with a leader.

The first group is composed of those two pairs of brothers who were the first called—Peter, Andrew, James and John (Mt 4:18-22 par.), commonly called the "inner circle." This inner circle accompanied Jesus on special occasions

Matthew 10:2-4	Mark 3:16-19	Luke 6:13-16	Acts 1:13
Simon, called Peter, first	*Simon, named Peter*	*Simon, named Peter*	*Peter*
Andrew, brother of Peter	James son of Zebedee	Andrew, brother of Peter	John
James son of Zebedee	John, brother of James	James	James
John, brother of James	Andrew	John	Andrew
Philip	*Philip*	*Philip*	*Philip*
Bartholomew	Bartholomew	Bartholomew	Thomas
Thomas	Matthew	Matthew	Bartholomew
Matthew the tax collector	Thomas	Thomas	Matthew
James son of Alphaeus	*James son of Alphaeus*	*James son of Alphaeus*	*James son of Alphaeus*
Thaddaeus (or Lebbaeus)	Thaddaeus	Simon, called the Zealot	Simon the Zealot
Simon the Cananean	Simon the Cananean	Judas son of James	Judas son of James
Judas Iscariot the betrayer	Judas Iscariot the betrayer	Judas Iscariot the betrayer	

The Twelve as they are found in the Synoptic Gospels and Acts

such as the healing of Jairus' daughter (Mk 5:37 par.) and the transfiguration (Mk 9:2 par.); they were the audience of the Olivet Discourse (Mk 13:3) and were with Jesus during his agony in the Garden of Gethsemane (Mt 26:37 par.).

The Twelve are normally mentioned as a group, with only occasional focus on individuals. Peter is the most familiar of the apostles to NT readers, with his name mentioned 210 times in the NT. The name of Paul is mentioned 162 times. The combined appearances of the names of all the other apostles totals only 142 times. Not much is known about the individual lives of the Twelve except what can be gathered from the scant biblical data and from some statements of the early church fathers.

3.1. Simon Peter. Simon, later called Peter, was a native of Galilee, where he grew up making his living as a fisherman along with his father and his brother, Andrew. After being called to follow Jesus, Peter soon became the most prominent of the disciples. Peter occurs first in all of the lists, indicating his place of leadership within the Twelve. In the Gospels he regularly functions as the spokesman for the Twelve (e.g., Mt 14:28; 15:15; 18:21; 26:35, 40; Mk 8:29; 9:5; 10:28; Jn 6:68), and during the days of the early church Peter fulfilled Jesus' prediction that he would play a foundational role as the rock of the church and holder of the keys of the kingdom of heaven (Mt 16:17-19; cf. Acts 1:8; 2:14-41; 8:14-25; 10:34-48). Peter is called "first" (e.g., Mt 10:2) in the sense that he was first among equals *(primus inter pares)* as the leader of the Twelve.

3.2. Andrew. Andrew is best known as the brother of Simon Peter. Originally a disciple of John the Baptist, Andrew is the first follower of Jesus to be identified by name. He immediately went to tell his brother Peter about Jesus (cf. Jn 1:35-42). Later he and Peter left their fishing business to follow Jesus in his earthly ministry, and he became part of the inner circle around Jesus (Mk 1:16 and par.; 1:29; 13:3). It was Andrew who brought to Jesus the boy with the loaves and fishes in John's account of the feeding of the five thousand (Jn 6:8: *see* Miracles, Miracle Stories I), and, again in John, Andrew with Philip brought the inquisitive Greeks to Jesus (Jn 12:22).

3.3. James and John (Sons of Zebedee). James and John, the sons of Zebedee, were also from Bethsaida. They were from a family of some wealth and influence, probably derived from a profitable fishing trade (cf. Mk 1:20; Lk 5:10; Jn 18:15). They were called "the sons of thunder" (Mk 3:17), quite likely because of their fiery temperament (Mk 9:38-41; Lk 9:51-54), which may explain their aggressive ambition (Mk 10:35-45; as well as their mother's, Mt 20:20-21). James and John, along with Peter and Andrew (all fishing partners, cf. Lk 5:10), were called to follow Jesus in his earthly ministry (Mk 1:19-20 par.) and became part of the inner circle around Jesus. James is distinguished as the first apostolic martyr, a victim of the sword during the persecution undertaken by Herod Agrippa I (Acts 12:2).

An unnamed disciple of Jesus, known as "one of the disciples, whom Jesus loved," is referred to only in John's Gospel (Jn 13:23; 19:26-27; 20:2; 21:7, 20; 21:4 [possibly Jn 1:40; 18:15; 19:35]), and is also said to be connected with the authorship of the Fourth Gospel (Jn 21:20-24). Proposals for the identity of the beloved disciple include: he was not a real person but a symbolic figure; Lazarus; John Mark; an unknown Jerusalem disciple of Jesus connected with the high priest; the apostle John, the son of Zebedee; disciples of the apostle John; and an unnamed woman disciple of Jesus. Notwithstanding vigorous scholarly support for the competing proposals, the internal evidence from the Fourth Gospel, particularly those disciples close to Jesus in the scenes in which he appears, plus the external evidence from early church fathers such as Irenaeus (*Haer.* 3.1.1) and Polycrates (cited in Eusebius *Hist. Eccl.* 3.31.3; also 5.24.2-3) weigh most heavily in favor of the apostle John, the son of Zebedee, as being the "beloved disciple."

"The Beloved Disciple" is the only one of the Twelve recorded to have witnessed the crucifixion, along with several women disciples. After the crucifixion he took Jesus' mother into his own home (Jn 19:25-27). He was the first of the Twelve to see the empty tomb and was one of the early leaders of the church, one of those recognized by Paul as a "pillar of the church" (Gal 2:9).

3.4. Philip. Philip was also from Bethsaida. He appears to have been a disciple of John the Baptist before Jesus called him (Jn 1:43-44). Philip and Andrew often occur together in the listings of the Twelve (Mk 3:18; Acts 1:13—the only two Greek names) and in the rare incidents in which they are mentioned by name (Jn 6:8; 12:22). In John he is depicted as having a clear understanding of OT expectations concerning Messiah as well as a missionary heart (Jn 1:43-46; 12:21-22), yet he also exhibited defective spiritual insight (Jn 6:5-7; 14:7-9).

3.5. Bartholomew. Bartholomew appears in all four lists of the twelve disciples, but he is otherwise unmentioned in the NT. From the ninth century onward Bartholomew has been frequently identified with Nathanael. This is based on the conjecture that Nathanael's surname was Bartholomew, so that his full name would have been Nathanael Bar-Tholami. Since the Synoptic Gospels never mention Nathanael, while John never mentions Bartholomew, the juxtaposition of the names Philip and Bartholomew in the Synoptic lists of the Twelve (not in the list in Acts) suggests the close relationship between Philip and Nathanael depicted in John 1:43-51. All of Nathanael's companions are apostles (Jn 1:35-51), he appears as a member of a group of apostles (Jn 21:1-2), and Christ's promise to him suggests an apostolic function (Jn 1:50-51).

If the identification of Bartholomew with Nathanael is correct, Philip brought Bartholomew (Nathanael), a native of Cana of Galilee (Jn 21:2), to acknowledge Jesus as the Messiah (Jn 1:45-46). A true Israelite, without guile, Nathanael gave a profound declaration of the messianic identity of Jesus. Jesus in turn stated that Nathanael would see even greater demonstrations of messianism (Jn 1:47-51).

If the identification of Bartholomew with Nathanael is incorrect, then we have no other NT information about Bartholomew other than the four lists.

3.6. Thomas. Thomas the "twin" (*didymus,* Jn 11:16; 20:24; 21:2), known popularly as "doubting Thomas" because of his misgivings concerning Jesus' resurrection (Jn 20:24) and his imperception of Jesus' destiny (Jn 14:5), is otherwise portrayed in the Gospels as a strong figure. His courage stands out when he urges the other disciples to travel with Jesus to Judea so that they might die with him (Jn 11:16). His faithfulness is revealed when he gathers with some of the other disciples in Galilee after the resurrection (Jn 21:2), and his spiritual insight is demonstrated in his confession of Jesus as Lord and God (Jn 20:28), one of the most profound declarations of Jesus' deity in the NT.

3.7. Matthew. Matthew, while employed as a tax collector, was called to follow Jesus (Mt 9:9). When recounting the call, Mark and Luke refer to him as Levi, suggesting that this tax collector had two names, Matthew Levi, originating either from birth or from the time of his conversion. His tax collector's booth was probably located on one of the main trade highways near Capernaum, where he collected tolls for Herod Antipas from the commercial traffic traveling through this area. After his call, Matthew immediately followed Jesus and arranged a banquet for him at his home (*see* Table Fellowship), to which were invited a large crowd of tax collectors and sinners (Lk 5:29-30). Little else is known of Matthew Levi, except for the widely attested tradition from the second century on that he was the author of the Gospel according to Matthew (*see* Matthew, Gospel of).

3.8. James (Son of Alphaeus). Apart from his name appearing in the four NT lists, James the son of Alphaeus is otherwise unmentioned. He is usually identified with "James the younger," the son of Mary and the brother of Joses (Mk 15:40; cf. Mt 27:56). If so, the designation "younger or less" (Gk *ho mikros*) distinguishes him from James the brother of Jesus and James the son of Zebedee, referring to his younger age, smaller stature or lesser renown. His mother, Mary, was in attendance at the crucifixion and the discovery of the empty tomb (Mt 27:56; Mk 15:40; 16:1; Lk 24:10).

3.9. Thaddaeus/Judas of James. Thaddaeus (some texts have Lebbaeus, or conflations) is mentioned in the third group of disciples by Matthew (Mt 10:3) and Mark (Mk 3:18), while Luke refers to "Judas the son of James" (lit. Judas of James) in his two lists (Lk 6:16; Acts 1:13). The uniformity of the rest of the names from list to list assures us that these names refer to the same person. Judas is probably the given name and Thaddaeus is a nickname or place name. The NT records only one incident about this person: his question to Jesus during the message to the disciples after the Last Supper (Jn 14:22).

3.10. Simon the Zealot. In addition to Simon Peter there was a disciple known as Simon the Cananaean (Mt 10:4; Mk 3:18; a Greek transliteration of the Aramaic word for "zeal" or "zealot" [*qan'ānā'*]) or Simon the Zealot (Lk 6:15; Acts 1:13). The expression indicates that this Simon was a zealous nationalist prior to his call to follow Jesus, and may indicate some of his ongoing temperament. Later, the term *zealot* was used to designate the religiously motivated Jewish revolutionaries who were active in guerilla-type warfare in the period leading up to A.D. 70 and the destruction of Jerusalem.

3.11. Judas Iscariot. "Iscariot" most likely identifies this Judas's place of origin, especially since his father is described as "Simon Iscariot" (Jn 6:71; 13:2, 26). Judas Iscariot was the treasurer for the apostolic band (Jn 12:4-6; 13:29). Since this office was not usually given to one known to be greedy and irresponsible, we may assume that he displayed positive characteristics recognizable by the others. However, John tells us that during his time as treasurer Judas had become a thief, pilfering from the treasury funds (Jn 12:6).

The event for which Judas is best known is his betrayal of Jesus. Luke and John portray him as under the direction of Satan (Lk 22:3; Jn 13:2). His greed, which prompted him to steal (Jn 12:4-6), may have motivated him to betray Jesus for the paltry amount of thirty pieces of silver, possibly only a partial payment of the agreed-on sum (Mt 26:14-16; Mk 14:10-11; Lk 22:3-6). The treacherous act, which took place at the Last Supper, apparently came as a surprise to all except Jesus (Mt 26:20-25; Mk 14:17-21). Securing a band of soldiers from the chief priests and Pharisees (Jn 18:3), Judas led them to where Jesus was alone with the disciples in the Garden of Gethsemane, away from the crowds, and kissed Jesus to identify him for the soldiers (Mt 26:47-56; Mk 14:43-52; Lk 22:47-53; Jn 18:2-12).

When Jesus was officially condemned to death, Judas was filled with remorse and returned the pieces of silver to the priests, who used the blood money to purchase a burial plot for strangers. Then Judas went and committed suicide (cf. Mt 27:3-10; Acts 1:18-19). After Jesus' ascension Judas was replaced in the circle of the Twelve by Matthias, about whom nothing else is known (Acts 1:26).

4. The Early Church.

The term *mathētēs* is used regularly in Luke-Acts to designate the person who has placed his faith in Jesus Christ. In Luke 6:13, 17 reference is made to a great multitude of disciples. These disciples of Jesus were convinced believers in Jesus' messiahship and are set in contrast with the "great throng of people" (Lk 6:17) who could be termed "the curious." This can be compared with Luke's usage of *mathētēs* in Acts, where he speaks of the multitude of believers (Acts 4:32) and the multitude of "disciples" (Acts 6:2). In Luke's writings the expressions "those who believe" and "the disciples" signify the same group of people (cf. Acts 6:7; 9:26; 11:26; 14:21-22). As Acts records, by the time of the early church the term *disciple* had become synonymous with the true believer—all those who confessed Jesus as Messiah—or, as they were first called at Antioch, "Christians" (Acts 11:26).

See also APOSTLE.

DJG: DISCIPLESHIP; JUDAS ISCARIOT.

BIBLIOGRAPHY. E. Best, *Disciples and Discipleship: Studies in the Gospel According to Mark* (Edinburgh: T & T Clark, 1986); M. Hengel, *The Charismatic Leader and His Followers* (New York: Crossroad, 1981); U. Luz, "The Disciples in the Gospel, according to Matthew," in *The Interpretation of Matthew* (IRT 3; Philadelphia: Fortress, 1983); R. Meye, *Jesus and the Twelve: Discipleship and Revelation in Mark's Gospel* (Grand Rapids: Eerdmans, 1968); B. Przybylski, *Righteousness in Matthew and His World of Thought* (SNTSMS 41; Cambridge: Cambridge University Press, 1980); K. H. Rengstorf, "μαθητής," *TDNT* 4:415-61; E. P. Sanders, *Jesus and Judaism* (Philadelphia: Fortress, 1985); F. Segovia, ed., *Discipleship in the New Testament* (Philadelphia: Fortress, 1985); G. Theissen, *Sociology of Early Palestinian Christianity* (Philadelphia: Fortress, 1978); J. J. Vincent, *Disciple and Lord: The Historical and Theological Significance of Discipleship in the Synoptic Gospels* (Sheffield: Academy, 1976); M. J. Wilkins, *The Concept of Disciple in Matthew's Gospel: As Reflected in the Use of the Term Μαθητής* " (NovTSup 59; Leiden: E. J. Brill, 1988); M. J. Wilkins, *Following the Master: A Biblical Theology of Discipleship* (Grand Rapids: Zondervan, 1992); B. Witherington, *Women in the Ministry of Jesus: A Study of Jesus' Attitude Toward Women and Their Roles as Reflected in His Earthly Ministry* (SNTSMS 51; Cambridge: Cambridge University Press, 1984).

M. J. Wilkins

DIVINE MAN. *See* MIRACLES, MIRACLE STORIES.

DIVORCE COMMANDMENT. *See* ETHICS I; LAW I.

DOCETISM. *See* JOHN, LETTERS OF.

DUALISM. *See* APOCALYPTICISM.

DYING AND RISING WITH CHRIST. *See* BAPTISM II.

E

ECCLESIASTICUS. *See* APOCRYPHA AND PSEUDE-PIGRAPHA.

ELECT LADY. *See* JOHN, LETTERS OF.

EMPEROR CULT/WORSHIP. *See* RELIGIONS, GRECO-ROMAN; REVELATION, BOOK OF; ROME.

EMPERORS. *See* ROME.

ENOCH, FIRST. See APOCRYPHA AND PSEUDE-PIGRAPHA.

EPHESIANS, LETTER TO THE

The letter to the Ephesians is unique among the letters attributed to Paul. Its language of worship and prayer, the depth and scope of its theology, and the many practical admonitions have led many Christians, including John Calvin, to cherish it as their favorite NT book. The letter's emphasis on the nature of the church and the present dynamic relationship of the exalted Christ to the church makes it an important and practical book for the church today.

    1. Style and Composition
    2. Authorship
    3. Relationship to Colossians
    4. The History of Religions Question
    5. Destination
    6. Life Setting and Purpose
    7. Themes in the Letter

1. Style and Composition.

The author's method of composition is characterized by an elevated style that reveals his affection for the subject he is discussing. He also identifies with the beliefs of the early church through his use of traditional material: hymns, creeds, liturgical material and household codes. Yet the writer is not content merely to reaffirm what the church is already confessing; he is a fresh thinker and advances his readers' understanding of Christ, the church and eschatology.

    The first half of Ephesians is well known for its lofty and exalted style. Here the author makes use of the language of worship, prayer and doxology. The letter begins with an elegantly composed eulogy (*berakah*) praising God for the election and redemption of his people (Eph 1:3-14). Consisting of one long sentence, the section abounds with participles, prepositional phrases and relative clauses and is punctuated with the refrain-like phrase "to the praise of his glory." In true poetic form, the passage also uses a variety of synonyms to repeat the key thoughts, such as the knowledge, power and will of God. Because of these poetic traits, some scholars have regarded this section as an early Christian hymn (see Lincoln, 10-19, for discussion). The majority of scholars, however, prefer to describe it as the author's "unified ad hoc composition, a hymnic passage in artistic, rhythmical prose" (Schlier, as cited in Schnackenburg, 46). The style is distinctively Jewish and has much in common with the hymns found among the *Dead Sea Scrolls. The switch from the first person plural ("we") to the second person plural ("you") in Ephesians 1:13 has occasioned much discussion, with some interpreters contending for an intentional contrast between Jewish Christians ("we") and Gentile Christians ("you") (e.g., Martin, Bruce, Robinson, Barth). Since the discussion of the relationship between Jews and Gentiles does not surface as a major theme until Ephesians 2:11, it is better to take "we" as a reference to all believers and "you" as referring to the readers in particular (e.g., Schnackenburg, Lincoln).

    The letter also contains two prayers (Eph 1:15-23; 3:14-21). The first consists of an introductory thanksgiving, an intercessory prayer report and a digression extolling the power of God that raised Jesus from the dead. The poetic language used in this praise of God's *resurrection power (Eph 1:20-23) has led some interpreters to regard it as a hymnic quotation, but it more likely reflects the author's poetic style with possible dependence on early creedal formulations (Lincoln, Schnackenburg). The second prayer properly begins in Ephesians 3:1 but is interrupted by an excursus on Paul's apostleship to the Gentiles (Eph 3:2-13), a topic extremely relevant to the predominantly Gentile readership. The prayer report consists of one long sentence but is structured around two requests and a summarizing request. The prayer reiterates and develops some of the themes of the first prayer (e.g., power, spirit). The exalted language of the prayer leads immediately into a doxology (Eph 3:20-21) praising God for his power effective in the lives of believers.

The first half of the letter is far from a dispassionate theological treatise. It exudes emotion in the praise and *worship of the almighty God who loves and responds to his people. The author writes with intense feeling and wants to elicit the same response—praise, worship and prayer—in the lives of his readers.

The letter's most explicit citation of an early Christian hymn appears in Ephesians 5:14, where it is introduced by a technical formula normally used for the introduction to an OT citation (*dio legei*; cf. Eph 4:8, where it is used to introduce an OT quotation). The original setting of this hymn is thought by most scholars to be the occasion of *baptism (e.g., Lincoln, Martin), but this is rather speculative. Another possible hymnic fragment appears in Ephesians 2:14-18, although this identification is disputed by P. Stuhlmacher, who regards it as a Christian midrash on Isaiah 57:19. The formal characteristics of the passage—the unique words, the use of participles, the intensely christological content, the parallelism of the lines, the "we" style that interrupts the "you" style—lead most scholars to conclude that it is indeed hymnic (Lincoln, Martin, Barth). Therefore, the author's admonition to "speak to one another in psalms and hymns and spiritual songs" (Eph 5:19) appears to be modeled by his own use of hymnic material in this letter. At the beginning of his call to unity in the second half of the letter, the author roots his appeal partly in a confession of the early church: "there is one body and one Spirit . . .

one Lord, one faith, one baptism, one God and father of all" (Eph 4:4-6). It appears that he wants to remind these believers of their common confession as the beginning step to increasing the unity of the churches.

In his composition of the letter, the author also makes use of a literary form commonly identified by scholars as a household code (Eph 5:21—6:9). This form was his vehicle for addressing the relationships within the household: husband-wife, parent-child and master-slave. This passage and Colossians 3:18—4:1 appear to be the first adaptations of this form from Hellenistic Judaism to describe the relationships in a Christian household. The use of the form here varies considerably from Colossians, particularly in the expanded discussion of the husband-wife relationship modeled on the relationship between Christ and the church.

Although the OT quotations in Ephesians are not numerous (there are only four explicit quotations), there are many allusions evidenced by the author's dependence on OT phraseology, terminology and concepts. In one quotation of the OT (Eph 4:8), the author uses Psalm 68:18 as an introduction to his discussion of the risen Christ endowing the church with gifted people. The citation appears to follow a rabbinic tradition preserved in a later targum that the victorious king "gave" gifts to people rather than "received" them (so the LXX and MT; see Bruce, 340-43). It also shows the writer's knowledge of rabbinic methods of exegesis as he then (in Eph 4:9-10) explains the meaning of the text in terms of a midrash pesher technique. A section of moral exhortation such as Ephesians 5:15-18 reveals the author's indebtedness to the OT wisdom tradition. References to such items as temple, redemption, God's choosing, hope, mercy, promise, wisdom, the Father, sons of men, helmet of salvation and many more show how deeply steeped the author was in the OT and how the language of the OT influenced his own composition.

The application of rhetorical criticism to NT documents is still in its infancy stage, so very little has yet been written on Ephesians from this perspective. A noteworthy beginning is A. T. Lincoln's commentary on Ephesians, which attempts to observe the rhetorical purpose of the flow of thought throughout the letter. He concludes that the writer combines the epideictic and the deliberative rhetorical genres (Lincoln, xli-xlii).

With its variety of literary forms, traditions and

sources, Ephesians is far from the straightforward prose of a typical letter of antiquity (*see* Letter, Letter Forms). What, then, is the best way to describe Ephesians? Is it even accurate to call it a letter?

E. Käsemann *(RGG)* described it as a "theological tract" merely dressed up like a letter. H. Schlier called it a "wisdom discourse" focusing on the role of Christ as personified wisdom (Schlier, 21; so also Bruce, 246, but who also sees it as a letter). J. Gnilka (33) refers to it as a "liturgical homily" clothed in the form of a letter. Similarly, and most recently, Lincoln characterizes it as "the written equivalent of a sermon or homily" (Lincoln, xxxix). Nevertheless, he still regards it as a letter adapted from the Pauline letter form.

Because Ephesians retains many conventions of the Pauline letter form, it is probably best explained as a letter. The language, literary and rhetorical forms and the traditions employed primarily grant us insight into the concerns of the author in communicating to his readers. The precise nature of the content and composition needs to be explained by the background and purpose of the author as well as his perceived understanding of the needs of the readers.

2. Authorship.
Scholarly opinion regarding the Pauline authorship of Ephesians is divided, with perhaps a majority of scholars today holding that the letter was not written by Paul. This situation is rather ironic in that a good number of scholars have esteemed Ephesians as "the crown" of Paul's thought (e.g., Dodd, Robinson). By contrast, W. G. Kümmel can assert, "The theology of Eph makes the Pauline composition of the letter completely impossible" (Kümmel, 360).

The Pauline authorship of Ephesians was not challenged until the late eighteenth century and early nineteenth century. It was the outspoken denial of authenticity by F. C. Baur and his followers, however, that had the greatest influence on the subsequent course of scholarship. Prior to that time, Ephesians was universally recognized as Pauline. As early as Ignatius (early second century) the letter was quoted as being from the hand of the apostle.

Until recently, British and American evangelical scholars unanimously affirmed Pauline authorship. Now, some evangelicals are convinced that the evidence of the letter is inconsistent with Pauline authorship. Lincoln, for instance, concludes, "Everything points instead to a later fol-lower of Paul who used Colossians as the basis for his own reinterpretation of the Pauline gospel" (Lincoln, lxvii). Similarly, R. P. Martin contends that the author was "a well-known disciple and companion of Paul who published this letter under the apostle's aegis either during the apostle's final imprisonment or (more probably) after his death" (Martin, 4). In an earlier writing, Martin identified this person as Luke. The arguments against Pauline authorship have been threefold.

2.1. Language and Style. The number of words in Ephesians that are not found in the other Pauline letters is proportionally insignificant. This fact is a point in favor of Pauline authorship. The criticism lies more in the observation that many of these unique terms are used in the apostolic fathers, thus giving the letter more of a postapostolic atmosphere. Since most scholars, however, acknowledge that early church fathers such as Clement knew and used Ephesians, the possibility that the vocabulary of Ephesians influenced these writers needs to be considered more seriously.

The style of writing exhibited in Ephesians has been the greater stumbling block to authenticity. It is often characterized as "pleonastic," that is, a fullness of style seen in the repeated use of prepositional phrases, abundant participles, numerous relative clauses, genitive upon genitive and lengthy sentences. R. Schnackenburg says that "there is scarcely anything comparable in Paul" (Schnackenburg, 26). What is not often observed, however, is that this unique style predominates in the first half of the letter. It is here where the author intentionally employs a lofty style of eulogy, praise, prayer and doxology. He also appears to be relying on the use of traditional material. This half of the letter does not consist of the straightforward prose, argument or admonition that usually characterizes the Pauline letters. Nevertheless, passages such as Romans 8:38-39 and Romans 11:33-36 demonstrate that Paul was capable of writing in an elevated style similar to what we find in the Qumran hymns. One should not underestimate Paul's resourcefulness in expressing himself.

2.2. Theology. Many scholars have contended that there are significant theological divergences in Ephesians compared with the eight recognized letters. Discussion has normally focused on the cosmic *christology, the realized *eschatology and the apparently advanced ecclesiology of the letter. Those denying Pauline authorship contend that there is not merely a development in

Paul's thought but an entirely changed perspective revealing a later stage of theological reflection (see Schnackenburg, 26-28; Lincoln, lxii-lxv).

There is no doubt about the development in Ephesians of the cosmic aspect of christology and the heightened emphasis on a realized eschatology. But this emphasis may have been prompted by the writer's concern to build up the readers in light of their ongoing struggle with the principalities and powers (Arnold, 124-29, 145-58, 171; *see* Principalities and Powers). The teaching of the letter on both of these topics does not represent a break with the apostle's teaching but the logical extension of his thought. Lincoln has done much to demonstrate that Ephesians is not devoid of a futurist eschatology as was once often charged (see Lincoln, lxxxix-xc).

Many aspects of the ecclesiology are thought to be discontinuous with Paul and to reflect a later temporal setting: the use of *"church" (*ekklēsia*) in a nonlocal sense, Christ now seen as "head" of the church, mention of the apostles and prophets as "holy" and as the foundation of the church, and so on. Some interpreters think that the author of the letter is looking back to the founding years of the church, emphasizing Paul as the guarantor of apostolic tradition, and building on his eschatology (see Schnackenburg, 28).

Each of these objections, however, can be met with a plausible explanation grounded in the lifetime of the apostle. (1) If the letter circulated among a network of churches, as is likely, it would be natural for the writer to use "church" in a more universal sense. (2) Christ as "head" of the church is a clear development over Paul's earlier presentation of the metaphor of the body of Christ, but it is not impossible that Paul's thinking developed in this direction. The needs of the Colossian church initially prompted this development, and Paul may have reflected on it further for the benefit of the readers of Ephesians. (3) The description of the apostles and prophets as "holy" (*hagios*, Eph 3:5) does not necessarily point to a time when they were receiving increasing veneration. "Saints" (*hagioi*) was the typical Pauline designation for believers. It was used of anyone or anything set apart for a sacred purpose (see Abbott, 82). (4) Although the apostles and the prophets form the foundation of the church through their foundational witness to the life, death and resurrection of Jesus Christ, they are not presented as dead, gone and off the scene. The resurrected Christ continues to give

them to the church (Eph 4:11-12). They are foundational in a dynamic continuing fashion.

In general, more consideration needs to be given to uncovering the plausible life setting of the letter in Asia Minor in the early 60s before recourse is made to the more extreme assumption of a different temporal and life setting toward the end of the first century. Furthermore, it is not irrational to assume that Paul could bring further development to his own ideas, especially as his circumstances and the circumstances of his readers would prompt him. D. A. Carson, D. Moo and L. Morris have recently observed, "What appears to some as impossible for one mind is for others quite a possibility for such a wide-ranging and inventive mind as Paul's" (Carson, Moo and Morris, 307).

2.3. The Use of Colossians. Scholars on both sides of the issue have recognized the close similarity in vocabulary, phraseology and thought between Ephesians and *Colossians. Many scholars now contend that there is a formal relationship between the two letters in terms of a one-way literary borrowing. The precise nature of the borrowing and the alleged alteration of the thought of Colossians are considered by some to point decisively away from Pauline authorship. The nature of this relationship will be explored in more detail below.

Since each of these objections to the authenticity of Ephesians can be met with a reasonable explanation, the scales are tipped in favor of the letter being precisely what it claims to be—a letter of Paul—when two other factors are taken into consideration.

2.3.1. Tradition. W. G. Kümmel observes and must concede that "Eph[esians] is extraordinarily well attested in the early church" (Kümmel, 357). It appears to have been used as a Pauline letter by many of the apostolic fathers, including Clement of Rome, Ignatius, Hermas and Polycarp. It was listed as a Pauline letter in the earliest canons, namely, Marcion's (c. A.D. 140) and the Muratorian Canon (c. A.D. 180). Many of the Gnostic writers quoted it as Paul's own words. A new line of evidence that has not entered the debate thus far is that Ephesians is quoted as Pauline in some of the Nag Hammadi documents (as early as the second century). For instance, Ephesians 6:12 is quoted in the *Hypostasis of the Archons* as from "the great apostle" (2.86.20-25). The same verse is cited in the *Exegesis on the Soul* (2.6.131) as the words of Paul.

2.3.2. Autobiographical Information. In addition to the address of the letter, which claims Paul as the author (Eph 1:1), Ephesians contains a substantial amount of material presented as a first-person address on the part of the apostle to the readers. The most significant is the reflection on his stewardship of the mystery (Eph 3:2-6) and the nature of his apostolic ministry (Eph 3:7-13). The first-person material also extends to the prayers, for example, "I, Paul, the servant of Christ Jesus [pray] for you Gentiles" (Eph 3:1; see also Eph 1:16; 3:14), and in his call to unity ("I, the prisoner of the Lord" [Eph 4:1]). Paul also asks specifically that the readers would pray for him (Eph 6:19-20) and then concludes the letter with comments on the role of Tychicus when he comes to them with words that in places exactly parallel the text of Colossians (Eph 6:21-22).

Those who argue in favor of pseudonymity have variously explained the autobiographical material. D. G. Meade has argued that the literary device of pseudonymity was not only acceptable to early Christians but also widely used. He contends that the author of Ephesians, an admirer of Paul, wrote in Paul's name as an attempt to secure the heritage of Paul in the Asia Minor churches after the death of the great apostle. According to Meade, by writing in Paul's name the author was able "to actualize the apostolic doctrine and lifestyle" (Meade, 139-61). Pseudonymity, he argues, "is primarily an assertion of authoritative tradition, not of literary origins" (161). Lincoln accepts Meade's thesis and attempts to provide additional exegetical support for it. According to Lincoln, "Instead of simply saying that he is passing on Pauline traditions, he [the author of Ephesians] makes it more personal, direct, and forceful by adopting the device of Paul himself appealing to the churches" (Lincoln, lxxxvii).

This thesis makes too strong a dichotomy between authoritative tradition and literary origins without corroborating it with convincing support. Meade's approach has also been criticized for presenting a facile and homogenous picture of ancient Jewish literature that blurs the distinctions of literary genre among the varied documents. With regard to Ephesians, however, the thesis is difficult to sustain in a passage like Ephesians 6:19-20, where Paul asks his readers to pray that he would be emboldened to proclaim the gospel in his prison situation. It is not enough to say that the writer is soliciting the readers' prayers for the progress of the apostolic gospel that is summed up by the image of Paul. The autobiographical information is much more naturally explained by the assumption of authenticity.

3. Relationship to Colossians.

Most scholars who see Ephesians as pseudonymous contend that it depends heavily on Colossians as its primary literary source (e.g., Lincoln, Schnackenburg, Mitton et al.). Some argue that the dependence is based on the author's memory of Colossians (so Schnackenburg, 32), but others contend that the author must have possessed a copy of Colossians, which he redacted according to his own interests (so Lincoln, lv; Mitton, 230).

The most extensive point of contact is the commendation of Tychicus (Col 4:7-8; Eph 6:21-22), where there is verbatim correspondence between twenty-nine consecutive words (although *kai syndoulos* is omitted in Ephesians). Beyond this there are only three additional places where seven words are exactly paralleled and two places where there are five words. This appears to be very slim evidence for the postulation of literary dependence. It seems especially odd that the longest passage reproduced in Ephesians is not from the theological argumentation or paraenesis of Colossians but about the sending of Tychicus. This passage is even more difficult under the assumption that the Ephesian author is reproducing the text of Colossians from memory.

Proponents of literary dependence put more stock in the similar overall structure and sequence of the letters with much of the same thematic material (e.g., Lincoln, xlvii) and the apparent dependence on certain key terms and concepts expressed in Colossians. Nevertheless, it is argued, the author of Ephesians had distinct interests: quite apart from being slavishly dependent, he rearranged and gave fresh expression to his source material to suit his theological purposes.

One example of this reworking is the digression in Ephesians 3:1-13 on Paul's apostolic ministry, which is said to depend on Colossians 1:23-29. The Ephesian passage sequences many of the same themes as the Colossian text and uses a number of the same or similar terms and expressions. Lincoln therefore concludes that the passage "derives from the author's distinctive reworking of the Colossians passage" (Lincoln, 170). In response, it must be said that the conclusion of literary dependence is not demanded by this passage, although it could fit the hypothesis. If the author were using Colossians as source material it is surprising that he did not reproduce more of his source in his writing; he was going far beyond the work of a redactor in his complete refashioning of the material and creative elaboration on it. This passage more likely reflects the same author giving a fresh exposition of a similar theme (with different emphases) a short time later for a different audience.

Many scholars, however, find the theology of Colossians at variance with that of Ephesians. Thus, some suggest that even assuming the authenticity of Colossians (which itself is disputed), it is highly doubtful that Paul could have written Ephesians. This conclusion is based on the way the author of Ephesians alters the theology of Colossians on certain points. For example, in Colossians 1:27 and Colossians 2:2 the content of the "mystery" appears to be Christ, whereas in Ephesians it is the fact that the Gentiles have been made fellow members, with the Jews, of the *body of Christ (Eph 3:6). But one must ask if this is truly a discrepancy or whether it could possibly be a matter of emphasis in the use of a term that expresses a multifaceted concept.

In a monograph on the Pauline concept of "mystery," M. Bockmuehl has argued that this use of the term reflects an emphasis on one aspect of the more comprehensive use of "mystery." In other words, it is more a matter of continuity and emphasis rather than discontinuity and a variant theology (Bockmuehl, 202; cf. Caragounis, 143: "they are not different *mysteria* but wider or narrower aspects of one and the same *mysterion*—God's *mysterion* in Christ"). On the relationship of the two letters as a whole, F. F. Bruce comments that the change of perspective from Christ (Colossians) to the church (Ephesians) may go far to account for the different nuances of terms held in common by the two letters (Bruce, 231).

Some significant problems with the postulation of literary dependence still remain. (1) The influential study by H. J. Holtzmann in 1872 concluded that the evidence of some of the parallels pointed more in the direction of the dependence of Colossians on Ephesians. Others, especially C. L. Mitton and now Lincoln, have argued that all the parallels point to a one-way dependence of Ephesians on Colossians. A. van

Roon, however, has once again brought this hypothesis into question. In his comparison of the two letters he found no indication of literary priority on the part of either letter, but what evidence there was pointed toward the priority of Ephesians (van Roon, 426). Although van Roon's postulation of a third document upon which both were dependent is highly questionable, he does demonstrate the difficulty of proving any literary dependence on the available evidence. (2) If the author of Ephesians did use Colossians as his literary source, it is difficult to explain why he neglected the hymn and omits any use of the polemic against the "heretics" in Colossians 2. (3) The theory does not give sufficient credit to Paul's ability and versatility as a writer and theologian. It is not unreasonable to think of Paul re-expressing, developing and modifying his own thoughts for a different readership facing a different set of circumstances. It seems that one must first prove that Paul was incapable of this versatility.

The traditional view, recently given fresh expression by Carson, Moo and Morris, still seems to have the most evidence in its favor: "The best explanation to many seems to be that the same man wrote Colossians and Ephesians a little later, with many of the same thoughts running through his head and with a more general application of the ideas he had so recently expressed" (Carson, Moo and Morris, 308). The precise nature, however, of the relationship between Ephesians and Colossians continues to stand in need of careful research from a literary, linguistic and theological perspective.

4. The History of Religions Question.
In the mid-nineteenth century, F. C. Baur argued that Ephesians must belong to the second century because of its dependence on Gnostic thought. Since then the affirmation of Gnostic influence on Ephesians has been widely promulgated by such writers as R. Bultmann, H. Schlier and Käsemann. They have found *Gnosticism evident in such terminology and concepts as the head-body imagery, mystery, *plērōma* ("fullness"), *aiōn* ("age"), *archōn* ("ruler"), the once-now schema and the so-called spatial eschatology. More conservative scholars argued rather for the influence of Gnosticism on the readers of the letter than on the author.

In recent years a dramatic shift away from the history of religions school's assumption of a pre-Christian Gnostic redeemer myth has taken place in NT scholarship in general, and in the study of Ephesians in particular. In light of new evidence about the origins of Gnosticism, it is now accurate to conclude that the reputed existence of any relatively coherent Gnostic system that would have been capable of influencing either the author of Ephesians or the communities to which the letter was addressed rests on a very weak foundation (Arnold, 12). Scholars are now using phrases such as "proto-Gnosticism" and "incipient Gnosticism" to describe the phenomena in the first century A.D.

The most productive approach is to examine the local religious traditions that were known to be active and influential at the time the letter was written. For western Asia Minor this would include the phenomena commonly referred to as magic, the Anatolian religions (such as the cults of Artemis and Cybele), astrological practices and astral religion, and the various other local cults (see Arnold, 5-40; *see* Religion, Greco-Roman). A deeper understanding of these traditions provides a firmer basis for interpreting the readers and assessing how Paul may have contextualized his theology to address their needs.

5. Destination.
In 1855 C. L. Ellicott wrote, "That the Epistle was addressed to the Christians of the important city of Ephesus seems scarcely open to serious doubt" (Ellicott, 1). Precisely the opposite sentiment is shared by the majority of scholars today.

The letter is traditionally understood to have been written to believers in Ephesus because the city is mentioned in the superscript "To the Ephesians" and the prescript "to the saints who are in Ephesus" (Eph 1:1). The words "in Ephesus," however, are not present in certain manuscripts generally regarded as the most reliable, viz. Sinaiticus (ℵ), Vaticanus (B) and a second-century papyrus (P^{46})—all published after Ellicott wrote his commentary. Further doubt is cast on the authenticity of the words "in Ephesus" because of the impersonal tone of the letter and the general nature of the contents. "Ephesians" does not look like an occasional letter written to one church that Paul had come to know well through his three years of ministry in Ephesus. Thus most interpreters see Ephesians as some form of a circular letter.

Various attempts have been made to explain the sense of Ephesians 1:1 without the addition of a geographical location. Some take the text as it stands in ℵ and B as original and translate it, "to the saints and to those who are faithful in Christ Jesus" (e.g., Schnackenburg, 41). But this leaves us with a very awkward participial expression *(tois ousin)* that always has a place name following it in prescripts of other Pauline letters (see Rom 1:7; 1 Cor 1:2; 2 Cor 1:1; Phil 1:1; Col 1:2).

Others resort to some form of conjectural emendation. For example, E. Best supposes that the original text may have been *tois hagiois kai pistois en Christō Iēsou* ("to the saints and faithful ones in Christ Jesus"). He argues that the address given on the outside of the papyrus roll originally read "to the saints" and was later modified to "to the saints who are in Ephesus (*tois ousin en Ephesō*)." According to Best, this occurred when the Pauline collection of letters was made (late first century) and the collectors realized that this letter did not conform to the rest because it had no geographical location. The phrase was then later carried into the body of the letter (Best, 3251). Against this view, one can say that it does not seem likely that such a process could have happened over the time required without at least a trace in some remaining manuscript evidence.

It is likely that there was some indication of place in the prescript of Ephesians 1:1. The participle *ousin* expects the subsequent naming of a place. Bruce, persuaded that "in Ephesus" was not original and that the letter has the appearance of a circular letter, conjectures that a space was left after *ousin* for Tychicus to insert the appropriate geographical name for each of the places to which he delivered a copy of the letter (Bruce, 240; so also Martin, 3-5). Bruce admits that such a practice is difficult to attest for the first century but nevertheless still finds this argument the most convincing. It is problematic to this view that Ephesus was preserved as the only geographical place name when the letter was presumably written to many other cities along the west coast of Asia Minor (although Tertullian reports that Marcion thought the letter was written to Laodicea—probably Marcion's conjecture based on Col 4:16).

Van Roon, followed by Lincoln, suggested that there were originally two place names—Hierapolis and Laodicea. These writers claim that this has the advantage of explaining the awkward *kai* (commonly translated "also") that connects "saints" with "faithful" (van Roon, 80-85; Lincoln, 3-4). Apart from the difficulty of no textual evidence to support these locations, this view cannot explain why a scribe—often concerned with smoothing the text—would have let the *kai* stand in the text (cf. Best, 3250).

We are left with no satisfactory explanation of the original text of Ephesians 1:1 if we assume the reliability of P^{46}, $\aleph$ and B on this reading. This is one point where it may be best to part company with these manuscripts and affirm the accuracy of the widely attested alternative tradition, that is, "in Ephesus" was the original reading. This view is finding an increasing number of supporters.

The following arguments support this conclusion. (1) There is still strong manuscript support for the inclusion. The entire Western and Byzantine traditions stand behind it as well as important Alexandrian witnesses, including Alexandrinus. (2) An Ephesian destination was the unanimous tradition of the early church (for references, see Ellicott, 1) and is the only reading known in all the extant versions. (3) There is a reasonable explanation to account for the omission of "in Ephesus." At a very early date, churches in a different location, perhaps Egypt, universalized the address in the prescript by omitting the prescript in copies that were made for their catechetical or liturgical purposes (Gnilka, 7). The contents of Ephesians, as also the book of Romans, were especially well suited to a broad readership. For the same reason, several witnesses omit "in Rome" (Rom 1:7) in the prescript to the book of Romans. On this passage B. Metzger notes that the words were eliminated "as a deliberate excision, made in order to show that the letter is of general, not local, application" (Metzger, *Textual Commentary*, 505). (4) When Paul says in Ephesians 1:15 that he had "heard" of their faith and love, it does not necessarily mean that he does not know them. It could just as easily refer to the progress they had made in the five or so years he had been absent from them. There is probably also a reference here to the many converts that had joined the church since he had been with them. (5) One cannot place too much emphasis on the fact that no greetings are attached since Paul sends no extended greetings to other churches he knew well (see 1 and 2 Corinthians, Galatians and Philippians).

Was the letter therefore written exclusively to the one church at Ephesus? Although many interpreters assume that there was one big church present in Ephesus when the letter was written, it is far more likely that there was a network of house churches scattered throughout the city and perhaps also in the nearby villages (e.g., Metropolis, Hypaipa, Diashieron, Neikaia). Many of these could have been started after Paul left Ephesus. One must not forget that population estimates for first-century Ephesus begin at one-quarter million. Furthermore, Paul may have envisioned and even encouraged the reading of the letter to a broader circle of churches throughout the west coast of Asia Minor (e.g., Pergamum, Laodicea, Colossae and Hierapolis).

The letter was probably a circular letter in the sense that it was intended primarily to circulate among the house churches of Ephesus, its environs and perhaps even more broadly in western Asia Minor (e.g., to the Lycus valley).

6. Life Setting and Purpose.

Of all the Pauline letters, Ephesians is the least situational. This does not mean that the letter fails to address real needs and problems faced by its readers; Ephesians simply does not have the same sense of urgency and response to crisis as do the apostle's other letters. Consequently, a vast array of opinions have been expressed regarding why the letter was written.

Of course, one's view on the authenticity of the letter has a significant impact on how this question is answered. Among those denying the Pauline authorship, a few have seen it as something other than a letter—such as a theological tract, a wisdom discourse or a liturgical homily—as was noted above. N. A. Dahl has stressed a baptismal setting for the document. He thinks the pseudonymous letter was addressed to some recently founded congregations to remind the young Gentile Christians of the implications of their faith and baptism and to exhort them to live up to their calling (Dahl, 38). Martin has described Ephesians as "an exalted prose-poem on the theme 'Christ-in-his-church' " (Martin, 5-6). He explains that the document was written in response to the needs of the predominantly Gentile readership to admonish them to appreciate the Jewish background of their faith and thus also their fellow Jewish Christians. He also sees a type of "gnosticizing" teaching that has led the readers into a libertine lifestyle and a fear of astrological fate.

Schnackenburg, however, describes Ephesians as a genuine letter. More specifically, he sees it as "a theologically based, pastorally-oriented" pseudonymous letter written to a circle of churches in Asia Minor around A.D. 90 addressing two pragmatic concerns: the internal unity of the congregations and the need for a distinctively Christian lifestyle in a pagan environment (Schnackenburg, 22-35). Lincoln stresses the temporal setting of the letter in the period after the death of the apostle Paul (Lincoln, lxxxv-lxxxvii). He concurs with Meade that many of the problems seen in Ephesians stem from the loss of Paul as a unifying source of authority. He sees the readers as consequently lacking a sense of cohesion and communal identity once the coordinating activity of the great apostle was gone.

Moving in an entirely different direction, E. J. Goodspeed, later supported by J. Knox and Mitton, argued that Ephesians was a general letter written toward the end of the first century as an introduction to the collected letters of Paul. Mitton concedes that Ephesians may not properly have served as an "introduction" to the letters but that it sprang from a relationship to the corpus and was used to present the message of the recently assembled Pauline letters comprehensively to a new generation (Mitton, 29). He believes that the writer was well aware of the context of the readers and thus wrote against the current Gnostic threat and the danger of the largely Gentile readership disowning their Jewish heritage (Mitton, 30-31).

There has also been a diversity of opinions offered by those affirming Pauline authorship. Ellicott said the letter was not prompted by any special circumstances, but was written to set forth the origin and development of the church for believers in Ephesus. He contended that Paul wrote the letter in a general way because he intended it for circulation among all the churches coterminous to or dependent on that city (Ellicott, xv-xvi). H. A. W. Meyer described the letter simply as a written discourse by Paul to the predominantly Gentile church in Ephesus to advance their understanding of the glory of their redemption and encourage them to proper conduct in keeping with their faith. He also thought that Paul had in the back of his mind as he wrote the dangers of the possible approach of Gnosticism (Meyer, 307-8).

J. A. Robinson envisioned Paul taking advantage of his tranquil circumstances (under house arrest in Rome, but with time to think) to write a positive exposition of the heart of his theology—"the doctrine of the unity of mankind in Christ and of the purpose of God for the world through the church" (Robinson, 10-11). Robinson thought the letter was written as an encyclical that would go first to Ephesus and then to the many churches in Asia Minor. E. F. Scott termed the letter "a private meditation," but composed as a letter for the church at Laodicea. Although a positive exposition, the letter addressed a problem of Jew-Gentile disunity in the church and the splintering effect of the heresies that were beginning to surface (Scott, 123-24). These heresies were also promoting a moral laxity and libertinism.

More recently, M. Barth has suggested that Ephesians was written by Paul to Christians in Ephesus, but only those of Gentile origin, "people whom he did not know personally and who had been converted and baptized after his final departure from that city" (Barth, 1.3-4). Bruce regarded it as a circular letter (with a blank space in Eph 1:1) written as a meditation on the divine "wisdom in a mystery" (so also Schlier, 21-22). Through this Paul also encouraged the Gentile Christians to appreciate the dignity of their calling (Bruce, 245-46).

Among all the viewpoints expressed, a few points of commonality emerge: Gentile believers are strongly in view; there is no specific crisis or problem the letter addresses; the letter gives a positive presentation of the Pauline gospel; and there is a need for the readers to receive teaching and admonishment on unity and a distinctively Christian lifestyle.

Based on the foregoing discussion and conclusions, the life setting and purpose of the letter could be described in the following way: In the period of time since Paul's ministry in Ephesus, the churches of the area had engaged in extensive evangelism among the Gentiles. These new believers lacked a personal acquaintance with Paul but respected his role as apostle. Being converts from a Hellenistic religious environment—mystery religions, magic, astrology—these people needed a positive grounding in the Pauline gospel from the apostle. Their fear of evil spirits and cosmic powers was also a great concern, especially the question of where Christ stands in relation to these forces. Because of their pagan past, they also needed help and admonishment in cultivating a lifestyle consistent with their salvation in Christ, a lifestyle free from drunkenness, sexual immorality, stealing and bitterness. Although there were many Jewish Christians and former God-fearers in the churches of the region, the flood of new Gentile converts created some significant tensions. Their lack of appreciation for the Jewish heritage of their faith prompted some serious Jewish-Gentile tensions in the churches.

Ephesians is therefore a genuine letter, without a specific crisis but addressed in a pastoral way to a multiplicity of needs shared by the readership. It was written by the apostle Paul to a network of churches in Ephesus but also intended for a broader readership among the churches of that region.

It has traditionally been regarded as written during Paul's first Roman imprisonment (see also Robinson, Barth, Bruce et al.), but a strong case has also been made for his prior imprisonment in Caesarea (Meyer). It is least likely to have been written during a possible Ephesian imprisonment. A date of A.D. 60-62 is probable.

7. Themes in the Letter.

The main themes of Ephesians could be summarized in the following way (not ordered according to importance).

7.1. The Greatness of God. The letter begins with an exclamation of praise to *God. He is eulogized as the Father of the Lord Jesus Christ and is magnified for all that he has done for his people in and through Christ (Eph 1:3). Most notably, he has chosen for himself a people and has provided them with redemption from bondage and forgiveness of sin. With a rich variety of terminology, Paul stresses that God is fulfilling a grand plan—his "will"—that encompasses the entire sweep of human history. One of the most awe-inspiring characteristics about God is his great love, which prompts him to act on behalf of his people (Eph 1:4; 2:4). His divine power is also brought into bold relief by his act of raising Jesus from the dead (Eph 1:19-20).

7.2. The Exalted Christ. Ephesians is often described as presenting a "cosmic christology." This stems from Paul's stress on the exaltation of Christ over all his enemies, especially the principalities and powers (Eph 1:21-22) and Christ's role in bringing all of history to completion (Eph 1:10). Nevertheless, the letter speaks of the suffering of Christ; it was through his blood that redemption was secured (Eph 1:7)

and by the cross that reconciliation was achieved (Eph 2:16). This letter builds on Paul's previous thought about the relationship of Christ to his church by depicting him as the "head" of his body (Eph 1:23; 4:15-16) and a bridegroom that nourishes and cares for his bride (Eph 5:29).

7.3. Salvation in Its Present Dimension. Ephesians is also often characterized as having a strongly "realized" eschatology. Although the future aspect of eschatology is not absent (see Eph 1:10, 14; 4:30; 5:6, 27), there is a significant stress on salvation as present. This is clearly expressed in Ephesians 2:5, 8 by the perfect tense of *sōzō* with the emphasis of the perfect on the present state of affairs: "you have been saved and are saved." It is also accented by the declaration that believers have been raised and exalted with Christ (Eph 2:6). This represents a distinctive Pauline development on ideas already present in Romans 6:1-13 (cf. Col 3:1).

Although *justification terminology does not appear in Ephesians, perhaps because there is no Judaizing controversy in the background (*see* Adversaries [Paul]), the Pauline emphasis on faith alone apart from works for salvation is clearly expressed (Eph 2:8-9). Christ's work of reconciliation is stressed (Eph 2:16) with the implication that believers now have access to God, their Father (Eph 2:18; 3:12).

7.4. The Status of Believers. Through use of the expression *"in Christ"—which occurs thirty-four times in Ephesians—Paul describes the corporate solidarity of believers with their resurrected and exalted Lord. The *syn* ("with") compounds also help express this notion, especially in Ephesians 2:5: he made us alive with Christ, he raised us with him, and he seated us with him. As people who are united with Christ, believers have redemption, forgiveness of sins, a heavenly existence, access to the Father, knowledge of the truth and the gift of the *Holy Spirit (Eph 1:13-14). They possess a new existence created by God and characterized by righteousness (Eph 4:24).

7.5. The Unity of Jew and Gentile. One of the central messages of the letter is that Christ has effected a reconciliation of Jew and Gentile by incorporating them into one body through his work on the cross (Eph 2:16; 3:6). Christ has removed all of the obstacles that separated the two groups and resulted in their hostility to one another (Eph 2:12-18). What matters now is the unity of the body of Christ, the church, composed of Jews and Gentiles who have equal access to the Father.

7.6. The Struggle with the Powers.
Believers within the young Christian communities in and around Ephesus lived in a culture where magical practices flourished. These practices were reinforced by the renowned Artemis cult. Artemis was worshiped as a goddess of the underworld with cosmic supremacy; she bore the six magical *Ephesia Grammata* on her cultic image. The people of the region had an extraordinary fear of the hostile spiritual powers. Through magical practices and cultic rituals, people sought relief and deliverance from the dreaded realm of the powers. This fear was not immediately allayed, however, when people became Christians. Demonstrating his sincere pastoral concern, Paul addressed their fear of this realm. More than any other Pauline letter, Ephesians stresses the hostile role of the principalities and powers against the church (see Arnold, 167-68).

In contrast to the power of the hostile supernatural realm, Paul emphasizes the superiority of the power of God and the supremacy of Christ (Eph 1:19-23; 4:8-10). He demonstrates that believers have access to this power by virtue of their union with Christ, thereby enabling them to resist the vicious attacks of the hostile powers (Eph 6:10-20). He regards all these spiritual powers as evil and under the leadership of a being he calls "the devil."

7.7. The Ethical Obligation of Believers.
The latter half of the letter is replete with specific ethical guidance for these believers. Paul wants them to rid their lives of vices that characterized their pre-Christian conduct and appropriate the virtues of Christ. He admonishes them to desist from such practices as lying, stealing, sexual immorality, dirty talk, excessive anger, bitterness, greed and many more. He instructs them on appropriate relationships within the Christian household.

He affirms that behavioral change is not only possible; it is part of their divine calling and God's purpose for them (Eph 1:4; 2:10; 4:1). They have access to God's power, which will enable them to resist temptation (Eph 6:10-18). They are enabled by the risen Christ, who has endowed the church with gifted people who depend on him for leadership and provision (Eph 4:11-16). Finally, they have an example in Christ, who modeled self-sacrificial love and service (Eph 5:2).

7.8. Apostle to the Gentiles.
In a lengthy digression Paul speaks about his apostolic ministry (Eph 3:1-13). He stresses that he has been given the special responsibility of administering God's grace (his saving favor) to the Gentiles (Eph 3:2, 7, 8). God revealed to Paul, as he did to all the apostles, his formerly secret plan to extend his favor to the Gentiles through the work of Jesus, the Messiah. On this basis, Paul claims special insight into "the mystery," the saving plan of God disclosed in Christ. He does not want his readers to be discouraged by his recent imprisonment or see it as the result of some crime; he wants them to know that it was for his service to Christ and his ministry to them as Gentiles (cf. Acts 21:17-36; Rom 15:14-32).

7.9. The Church.
Ephesians has a strong ecclesiological focus. Paul's teaching in this letter conceptualizes the many churches as a collective whole (*see* Church). In fact, the term *ekklēsia* is never used of one local church but in a universal sense (Eph 1:22; 3:10, 21; 5:23-25, 27, 29, 32). This may be due in part to the fact that a network of churches was addressed (if Ephesians was a circular letter), but more likely Paul is reflecting on the church as a universal, unified organism.

Some interpreters have argued that the ecclesiology of Ephesians reflects early catholicism (e.g., Käsemann 1971), but this is to misconstrue the teaching of the letter. The church is still viewed as an organism (thus, the head/body imagery and the teaching on the Spirit) and not as an institution. There is no interchurch organization and no established priesthood to mediate the means of grace (see Bruce, 238-39). All members are involved in the work of the ministry (Eph 4:12, 16).

In this letter Paul depicts the church as a building, the "household of God" (Eph 2:19-22), a growing body in connection to its head, which gives leadership and provision (Eph 1:23; 4:16; 5:23), and a bride in relationship to her loving and caring bridegroom (Eph 5:25-32). Each of these images shows continuity with but also advancement on Paul's prior teaching on the church.

See also BODY OF CHRIST; CHRISTOLOGY; CHURCH; COLOSSIANS, LETTER TO THE; WORSHIP.

DPL: EARLY CATHOLICISM; EPHESUS; EXALTATION AND ENTHRONEMENT; HEAVEN, HEAVENLIES, PARADISE; MAGIC; MYSTERY; POWER;

PRINCIPALITIES AND POWERS.

BIBLIOGRAPHY. **Commentaries:** T. K. Abbott, *A Critical and Exegetical Commentary on the Epistles to the Ephesians and to the Colossians* (ICC; Edinburgh: T & T Clark, 1897); M. Barth, *Ephesians* (AB 34; 2 vols.; New York: Doubleday, 1974); E. Best, *A Critical and Exegetical Commentary on the Epistle to the Ephesians* (ICC; Edinburgh: T & T Clark, 1997); F. F. Bruce, *The Epistles to the Colossians, to Philemon, and to the Ephesians* (NICNT; Grand Rapids: Eerdmans, 1984); G. B. Caird, *Paul's Letters from Prison* (NClB; Oxford: Oxford University Press, 1976); C. H. Dodd, "Ephesians," *The Abingdon Bible Commentary*, ed. F. C. Eiselen et al. (New York: Abingdon, 1928) 1224-25; C. J. Ellicott, *A Critical and Grammatical Commentary on St. Paul's Epistle to the Ephesians* (2d ed.; London: Parker & Son, 1859); J Gnilka, *Der Epheserbrief* (HTKNT X/2; Freiburg: Herder, 1971); H. W. Hoehner, *Ephesians* (Grand Rapids: Baker, 2003); A. T. Lincoln, *Ephesians* (WBC 42; Dallas: Word, 1990); R. P. Martin, *Ephesians, Colossians, and Philemon* (IntC; Louisville, KY: Westminster John Knox, 1992); H. A. W. Meyer, *Critical and Exegetical Hand-Book to the Epistle to the Ephesians* (4th ed.; New York: Funk & Wagnalls, 1884); C. L. Mitton, *Ephesians* (NCB; Grand Rapids: Eerdmans, 1973); P. T. O'Brien, *The Letter to the Ephesians* (PNTC; Grand Rapids: Eerdmans, 1999); J. A. Robinson, *St. Paul's Epistle to the Ephesians* (2d ed.; London: Macmillan, 1907); H. Schlier, *Der Brief an die Epheser* (Dusseldorf: Patmos, 1957); R. Schnackenburg, *The Epistle to the Ephesians* (Edinburgh: T & T Clark, 1991); E. F. Scott, *The Epistles of Paul to the Colossians, to Philemon and to the Ephesians* (MNTC; London: Hodder & Stoughton, 1930); K. Snodgrass, *Ephesians* (NIVAC; Grand Rapids: Zondervan, 1996). **Studies:** C. E. Arnold, *Ephesians: Power and Magic* (SNTSMS 63; Cambridge: Cambridge University Press, 1989); E. Best, *Essays on Ephesians* (Edinburgh: T & T Clark, 1997); idem, "Recipients and Title of the Letter to the Ephesians: Why and When the Designation 'Ephesians'?" *ANRW* 2.25.4 (1987) 3247-79; M. N. A. Bockmuehl, *Revelation and Mystery in Ancient Judaism and Pauline Christianity* (WUNT 2/36; Tübingen: Mohr Siebeck, 1990); R. Bultmann, *Theology of the New Testament* (2 vols.; New York: Scribners, 1951, 1955) 2:151-53; C. C. Caragounis, *The Ephesian Mysterion* (ConBNT 8; Lund: Gleerup, 1977); D. A. Carson, D. Moo and L. Morris, *An Introduction to the New Testament* (Grand Rapids: Zondervan, 1992); N. A. Dahl, "Gentiles, Christians, and Israelites in the Epistle to the Ephesians," *HTR* 79 (1986) 31-39; E. J. Goodspeed, *The Meaning of Ephesians* (Chicago: University of Chicago, 1933); E. Käsemann, "Epheserbrief," *RGG* 2.517-20; idem, "The Theological Problem Presented by the Motif of the Body of Christ," in *Perspectives on Paul* (Philadelphia: Fortress, 1971) 102-21; J. Knox, *Philemon Among the Letters of Paul* (Nashville: Abingdon, 1959); W. G. Kümmel, *Introduction to the New Testament* (rev. ed.; Nashville: Abingdon, 1975); D. G. Meade, *Pseudonymity and Canon* (WUNT 39; Tübingen: Mohr Siebeck, 1986; Grand Rapids: Eerdmans, 1987); C. L. Mitton, *The Epistle to the Ephesians* (Oxford: Clarendon Press, 1951); A. van Roon, *The Authenticity of Ephesians* (NovTSup 39; Leiden: E. J. Brill, 1974); P. Stuhlmacher, " 'He Is Our Peace' (Eph. 2:14). On the Exegesis and Significance of Ephesians 2:14-18," in *Reconciliation, Law and Righteousness: Essays in Biblical Theology* (Philadelphia: Fortress, 1986) 182-200.   C. E. Arnold

EPHESUS. *See* EPHESIANS, LETTER TO THE.

EPICUREANS, EPICUREANISM. *See* PHILOSOPHY.

EPISTLES. *See* LETTERS, LETTER FORMS.

ESCHATOLOGY I: GOSPELS

The word *eschatology* refers to teaching about the last things, specifically to history's consummation and the events directly associated with it. Characteristic of the Gospels is the note of eschatological fulfillment and the focus of eschatological hope in the person of Jesus. Perhaps the preeminent contribution of modern NT scholarship has been the demonstration that eschatology lies at the heart of Jesus' message and at the heart of all the NT.

1. The Message of Jesus
2. The Gospel Writers
3. Contemporary Interpretation

1. The Message of Jesus.

Against the once popular view of the kingdom of God as an evolving society, J. Weiss and A. Schweitzer argued around the turn of the twentieth century that Jesus expected history's near end. On their view, Jesus was a preacher of repentance in the face of impending judgment. Largely in response to this picture of Jesus as a mistaken apocalyptic visionary, C. H. Dodd developed his theory of "realized eschatology." According to Dodd, Jesus believed that the prophecies of the OT had already met fulfillment, that the "day of the Lord" had arrived. Most contemporary scholars now think of Weiss and Schweitzer on the one hand and of Dodd on the other as representing two extremes, between which a third position commends itself. Jesus did believe that the kingdom of God had, in some sense, already come. At the same time he spoke of eschatological events still to occur. The phrase "already and not yet" is now a commonplace of scholarship (*see* Kingdom of God).

1.1. The Future. Jesus' future expectations were drawn first from the well of OT and Jewish tradition. He anticipated the resurrection of the dead (Mk 12:18-27) and a great judgment (Lk 10:13-15; 11:31-32). He thought in terms of rewards for the righteous (Lk 6:20-23) and recompense for the wicked (Lk 6:46-49). He expected the end to be heralded by trouble for the saints (Lk 12:49-53) and, perhaps, by upheavals in nature (Mk 13:24-25). Exactly how Jesus imagined the coming aeon—whether as an earthly, millennial kingdom, or as an old world made new, or as a new world—is unclear.

Jesus' major contribution to eschatology was christological. He made response to himself a criterion for judgment (Lk 12:8-9). He also probably identified his fate with that of the Son of man in Daniel 7 and conceived of himself as the messianic Son of David. The fact that he chose twelve disciples—a symbol of the restoration of the twelve tribes of Israel—and stood above that group as its leader implies that he thought of himself as Israel's king.

1.2. The Present. Jesus did not relegate God's reign to the future. He explicitly announced its presence (Lk 11:20) and indirectly indicated its arrival by speaking of the defeat of Satan (Lk 10:18; 11:22), a secret presence (Mk 4:11-12, 26-29), new wine (Mk 2:22) and as joy opposed to fasting (Mk 2:18-20). Although controversial, it is probable that Luke 17:20-21, in which the kingdom is "in your midst," refers to Jesus. His presence meant the presence of the kingdom.

1.3. The Relationship Between Present and Future. Traditionally Christians have thought that the OT prophesies two messianic advents and that Jesus fulfilled certain OT prophecies at his first coming and will fulfill others at his second

coming. But the distinction between two advents cannot be found in the OT and is foreign to Jewish eschatology. It is not likely that Jesus thought in terms of or spoke about two messianic advents. More probably the end time was for him constituted by a sequence of events, some of which had already occurred. The formulation "eschatology in the process of realization" (Jeremias, 230) is apt. The Messiah (*see* Christ I) had appeared. Many prophecies had been fulfilled (Lk 17:18-23). But there had not been fulfillment without remainder. Much was left to unfold, particularly the Son of man's eschatological suffering and vindication (Mk 9:31).

1.4. When? According to the modern consensus, Jesus thought the eschatological judgment to be near. Recent attempts to deny this do not persuade. It must nonetheless be emphasized that Jesus rejected the type of chronological speculation found in some of the apocalypses (Lk 17:20-21) and plainly confessed his ignorance of the end's date (Mk 13:32). Further, Mark 13:20 (possibly dominical) and Luke 13:6-9 (probably dominical) assume that the day or hour of the consummation is not set in concrete, that its arrival is partly contingent upon divine grace and human response. In addition, Luke 10:13-15 and other texts reflect bitter disappointment over Jewish failure. How such disappointment affected Jesus' eschatological convictions we do not know; but the general failure of Israel to welcome the Messiah (something unforeseen by the tradition) cannot but have made for second thoughts about what the future held. Jesus' expectations were probably more contingent and indeterminate than many have supposed.

2. The Gospel Writers.

All four Gospels reflect the "already and not yet" pattern, but Matthew's eschatology is more realized than Mark's, and John's even more so. Luke's views are much harder to characterize.

2.1. Mark. The author of Mark, like Jesus before him, thought of eschatology as in the process of realization. For him, however, Jesus had suffered, died and risen, and this meant that the eschatological tribulation and the general resurrection had already commenced.

2.1.1. The Future. What Mark expected is found primarily in Mark 13. Here we have a Christian version of what is found so often in Jewish pictures of the end (*see* Apocalyptic). There will be a time of trial and difficulty. False prophets will arise (Mk 13:5-6). There will be wars, earthquakes and famines (Mk 13:7-8). The faithful will suffer (Mk 13:9-13). Palestine will be afflicted with dangers (Mk 13:14-23). The heavens will show great signs (Mk 13:24-25). And then God's eschatological agent (Jesus) will appear (Mk 13:26-27).

2.1.2. The Past. Jesus inaugurated the time of eschatological fulfillment (Mk 1:14-15). Especially noteworthy are the significant correlations between Mark 13 (about the end of the age) and Mark 14—15 (about the end of Jesus). Compare Mark 15:33 (darkness at the crucifixion) with Mark 13:24 (darkness at the end); Mark 15:38 (the temple veil torn) with Mark 13:2 (the temple will be destroyed); Mark 14:34, 37 (Jesus tells his disciples to "watch," then comes *[erchetai]* and finds *[heuriskei]* them sleeping *[katheudontas]*) with Mark 13:35-36 ("watch lest the master come *[elthōn]* and find *[heurē]* you sleeping" *[katheudontas]*); Mark 14:10, 18, 21, 41 (Jesus is "delivered up") with Mark 13:9 (the disciples will be "delivered up"); Mark 14:53-65 (Jesus appears before a council of Jewish elders) with Mark 13:9 (the disciples will appear before Jewish councils); Mark 14:65 (Jesus is beaten) with Mark 13:9 (the disciples will be beaten); Mark 15:1-15 (Jesus before Pilate) with Mark 13:9 (the disciples will stand before governors and kings). The meaning of these and other parallels, as well as of those between Mark 13 and Zechariah 9—14 (a little apocalypse) is plain: Jesus' end belongs to the eschatological drama (*see* Death of Christ I).

2.1.3. The Present. If the end began with the end of Jesus, then the period between the crucifixion and the parousia must be eschatological time. The present (characterized by Mk 13:5-13) is conceptualized as the tribulation attendant upon the new age. That is, the sufferings of Jesus and of his church together constitute the labor pains, after which the new world comes.

2.1.4. When? Mark 9:1 ("some standing here will not taste death before they see that the kingdom of God has come with power") may be taken to imply that Mark expected things to wind up shortly. But many scholars refer Mark 9:1 to the transfiguration or the resurrection or (less plausibly) to the destruction of Jerusalem in A.D. 70. Apart from Mark 9:1 it seems probable that, given his view of the present, Mark did not reckon with history going on for any great period of

time (cf. Mk 13:30). Yet Mark 13:32 means that no certainty surrounded the issue.

2.2. Matthew. Matthew's views on eschatology are very close to Mark's.

2.2.1. The Future. Almost everything that can be said about Mark's expectations holds equally for Matthew, if one does not follow the few interpreters who have thought Matthew 24 to be a realized apocalypse fulfilled in A.D. 70. The one outstanding difference is a concentration on Jesus' role as the Son of man in the final judgment (Mt 13:41; 16:28; 25:31; etc.). Also, if *krinontes* in Matthew 19:28 means "ruling," the verse implies the eschatological salvation of Israel, an idea not clearly present in Mark.

2.2.2. The Past. The emphasis on realized eschatology can be seen from two facts in particular. First, Matthew sprinkled his narrative with so-called formula quotations (Mt 1:23; 2:15, 18; etc.). These constantly remind readers that Jesus fulfilled the eschatological hopes and messianic expectations of Judaism. Second, Matthew 27:51b-53 (unique to Matthew) recounts that Jesus was not the only one to rise from the dead: so did many saints. Thus the Messiah's vindication cannot be viewed in isolation. Rather, Jesus' resurrection inaugurated the general resurrection. Compare the pre-Pauline confession in Romans 3:3-4, which literally proclaims that Jesus was designated Son of God by "(the) resurrection of the dead" (the Greek is the technical term for the general resurrection).

2.2.3. The Present. In Matthew, as in Mark, the present is eschatological time. Note especially that certain end-time prophecies of Mark 13 have been transferred to Matthew 10, with the result that the Christian mission draws to itself the language of eschatological tribulation. Also indicative of Matthew's outlook is the key promise of the Messiah's perpetual supporting presence (Mt 1:23; 18:20; 28:20). This brings to realization a Jewish eschatological expectation: God would be "with" his people especially in the latter days (Zech 8:23; *Jub.* 1:17, 26; etc.). So the present is simultaneously the age of tribulation and the age of the kingdom's presence—precisely the view of Jesus.

2.2.4. When? There is no indication that Matthew held the consummation to be imminent. But his constant dwelling on eschatology and his conception of the present imply that he expected the end to come sooner rather than later.

2.3. Luke. Luke's convictions—which must be

reconstructed with the help of Luke and Acts—are not easily determined. One fact, however, has seemed clear to many: Luke was especially conscious of the expanding interval of time between the first and second advents.

2.3.1. The Future. Luke believed that Jesus would return in the same way that he left (Acts 1:11), and that this event would open that day on which God judges the world by Jesus Christ (Acts 17:31). The Third Evangelist also believed in the general resurrection (Lk 20:27-40; Acts 24:15), but exactly how he envisaged the coming "times of refreshing" and "the restitution of all things" (Acts 3:19-21) is disputed.

2.3.2. The Past. Luke did not carry forward the connection between Jesus' end and the eschaton. Perhaps he shied away from some aspects of realized eschatology because it also characterized groups he perceived as heretical (proto-Gnostics?). Alternatively, many have urged that his perspective was due to a conception of salvation-history. H. Conzelmann claimed that in Luke-Acts, history is divided into three stages: the period of Israel, the period of Jesus and the period of the church. On this scheme the Jesus event, despite its fulfillment of OT prophecies, belongs to the past and is not properly eschatological. Several recent studies, however, have questioned Conzelmann and denied that Luke drove a wedge between history and eschatology. The issue demands further investigation.

2.3.3. The Present. "Eschatology in the process of realization" does not so obviously characterize Luke, and according to Conzelmann the time of the church is the time before the end, not part of the end. Present and future have been compartmentalized (cf. the "before all this" of Lk 21:12). It is just possible, however, that Luke recognized the eschatological content of such texts as Luke 1:32-33, Luke 2:38 and Acts 2:17-21 and equated the church age with the inaugurated messianic kingdom (cf. 1 Cor 15:20-28).

2.3.4. When? Some scholars have thought Luke held no near expectation, others that he thought the end very near. The disagreement is created by the existence in Luke-Acts of two different groups of texts. In one the end appears at hand (e.g., Lk 3:9; 18:7-8; 21:31-32), in the other there is an awareness of the delay of the parousia (e.g., Lk 12:45; 19:11). Rather than dismissing one group in favor of the other, it seems best to take

Acts 1:7 ("It is not for you to know times or seasons") seriously and surmise that Luke thought the time of the end an open question.

2.4. John. One of the distinctive features of the Fourth Gospel is its great emphasis on realized eschatology.

2.4.1. The Future. Very little is said about the eschatological future. There is a yet outstanding "last day" (Jn 6:39), which will feature the resurrection (Jn 5:28-29; 6:39-40); but other specifics are lacking. Also, there is no hint as to when the last day will arrive.

2.4.2. The Past. John, like Mark and Matthew, associated the end of Jesus with end-time themes. In his gospel the death of Jesus is "the judgment of this world" (Jn 12:31). The crucifixion brings about the casting out of the devil (Jn 16:11) and is associated with the destruction of "the son of perdition" (Jn 17:12; cf. 2 Thess 2:3). Moreover, in John the Son of man already has authority (Jn 5:27; cf. Dan 7:13-14), already judges (Jn 9:35-39; 12:30-34) and is already lifted up and exalted (Jn 3:14). One is tempted to say that in John, Jesus is the eschaton, its real content. When Jesus came, the end came.

2.4.3. The Present. In Johannine thought, eternal life (Jn 6:47), living water (Jn 4:14), bread from heaven (Jn 6:25-34), divine sonship (Jn 1:12) and even the resurrection (Jn 5:25)—all things traditionally associated with the eschaton—may be experienced now. Although there is in all this more continuity with the other Gospels than often assumed, the constant emphasis on the realization of eschatological hopes dominates the Fourth Gospel. Dodd exaggerated only a little when he wrote of John: "All that the church hoped for in the second coming of Christ is already given in its present experience of Christ through the Spirit" (Dodd, 121).

3. Contemporary Interpretation.

The theological problems posed by eschatology are numerous and complex. Was Jesus wrong in his imminent expectation? Should eschatological language be translated into existentialist categories? Can Christians, after two thousand years, still look forward to the parousia? Adequate answers must take into account at least four considerations. First, the Gospel prophecies were never intended to be understood with unimaginative literalness. Just as it is misguided to mine Genesis for scientific data about the physical universe, so too is it wrong to turn the similes and metaphors of NT eschatology into information about future cosmological states.

Second, if it is the end that determines the meaning of what has gone before, then those preoccupied with the meaning of history and human existence must be preoccupied with history's conclusion and its relationship to the present. This explains the focus of the Gospels. To grasp the significance of the here and now requires that vision be pulled from the present and cast toward the future. Third, salvation history is not a predetermined scheme. It is rather a dynamic relationship between God and his people. The Lord of the Gospels can shorten the interim period (Mk 13:20) or lengthen it (Lk 13:6-9). His grace means that history is open and that there can be no eschatological timetable. True prophecy, accordingly, does not so much depict the future as isolate one possible course of events, one which can be communicated either as a warning which may or may not be heeded, or as a promise whose conditions may or may not be met.

Finally, the heart of eschatology is not when or what but who, not a schedule or a plan but a person. The Gospels move us to contemplate the future not by giving us a blueprint but by relating all to Jesus, Messiah and Son of Man.

See also APOCALYPTICISM; JUDGMENT; KINGDOM OF GOD; RESURRECTION.

DJG: APOCALYPTIC TEACHING.

BIBLIOGRAPHY. D. C. Allison Jr., *The End of the Ages Has Come* (Philadelphia: Fortress, 1985); idem, *Jesus of Nazareth: Millenarian Prophet* (Minneapolis: Fortress, 1998); G. R. Beasley-Murray, *Jesus and the Kingdom of God* (Grand Rapids: Eerdmans, 1986); H. Conzelmann, *The Theology of St. Luke* (London: Faber and Faber, 1960); C. H. Dodd, *The Apostolic Preaching and Its Developments* (New York: Willett, Clark, 1937); E. E. Ellis, *Eschatology in Luke* (FBBS 30; Philadelphia: Fortress, 1972); J. Jeremias, *The Parables of Jesus* (2d rev. ed.; New York: Charles Scribner's Sons, 1972); A. J. Mattill Jr., *Luke and the Last Things* (Dillsboro, NC: Western North Carolina University Press, 1979); N. Perrin, *Jesus and the Language of the Kingdom* (Philadelphia: Fortress, 1976); J. A. T. Robinson, *Jesus and His Coming* (2d ed.; Philadelphia: Westminster, 1979); W. Willis, ed., *The Kingdom of God in Twentieth-Century Interpretation* (Peabody, MA: Hendrickson, 1987); N. T. Wright, *Jesus and the Victory of God* (Minneapolis: Fortress, 1996). D. C. Allison Jr.

ESCHATOLOGY II: PAUL

Eschatology has traditionally been understood as that branch of theology which is concerned with final things. Topics such as the future of the world, the parousia of Jesus Christ, the coming kingdom of God, the last judgment of humankind, the resurrection from the dead, heaven and hell, and the transformation of the cosmos are all generally considered under its heading. The term *eschatology* is often used interchangeably with *apocalyptic*, although in recent years the latter has been more correctly defined in terms of a distinctive literary genre that may or may not be concerned with temporal "last things," as J. J. Collins and C. C. Rowland demonstrate. The relationship between chronological history and eschatology has been a major source of scholarly discussion in recent years. G. B. Caird has offered an important linguistic assessment of eschatological language that focuses on the metaphorical sense as primary to its meaning. The result of such an approach is similar to genre investigations, namely, that a straightforward equation between temporal last things and eschatological literature, particularly apocalyptic texts, is qualified, if not challenged altogether.

Strictly speaking, a distinction should be maintained between the two terms *apocalyptic* and *eschatology,* despite the fact that much earlier scholarly endeavor uses *apocalyptic* without knowledge of the genre clarification, inadvertently providing the basis for some modern confusion when these older materials are consulted (see Sturm for an overview; cf. Marshall, Barker). L. Keck has tried to address this problem when he suggests that we take *apocalyptic* as an adjective "which characterizes *a type of theology,* not merely a type of eschatology" (Keck, 233). According to Keck, Paul's apocalyptic theology is to be distinguished from his wisdom theology since it arises from a different theological base. This is true, although it is possible to see both types of theology overlapping within the Pauline letters, often within key passages (such as 1 Cor 2—3; Phil 2:5-11; Col 1:13-20).

Paul's place within the area of eschatological theology is central, not least because his writings are among the earliest Christian documents preserved, thus reflecting foundational perspectives on eschatological matters. Most of the standard introductions on Paul have a section dealing with eschatology (Ridderbos, Whiteley, Bornkamm, Bruce). In addition, many of the classic interpretative studies of Paul in previous generations were dependent on critical analyses of his eschatological thought (e.g., Schweitzer, Vos, Käsemann, Munck, Schoeps, Davies). In the past decade or so, several important studies of Pauline eschatology have been produced, most notably that of J. C. Beker (1980). These have served to revitalize interest in the topic and have highlighted how central eschatology is to Pauline studies as a whole.

Paul's eschatology provides the background for many other important topics that constitute the substance of Pauline theology; christology, pneumatology, ecclesiology, soteriology and anthropology are all built upon the eschatological foundation of Paul's thought. This foundation is all pervading in Pauline studies, for it is possible to see eschatological concerns or presuppositions surfacing in virtually every letter within the Pauline corpus, although Galatians and Philemon have been suggested as possible exceptions since they do not contain explicit references to the future day of the Lord. Eschatological material occurs in a wide variety of contexts within the Pauline letters: creedal, polemical, pastoral, ethical, paraenetic and personal pericopae all contain such teaching. The importance of Pauline eschatology is evident no matter what one's opinion about the question of the authenticity of some of the letters, namely, 2 Thessalonians, Colossians and Ephesians, or the Pastorals. Even if some of these letters within the Pauline corpus are taken to be the work of Paul's followers in a subsequent generation, it is clear that Paul's eschatological viewpoint helps condition the teaching contained within them.

1. The Context of Pauline Eschatology: Jewish Apocalyptic Literature
2. The Contingency of the Pauline Letters
3. The Content of Pauline Eschatology: Some Central Tenets
4. Pauline Eschatology and Christology
5. Pauline Eschatology and Ethics
6. Pauline Eschatology and Jewish Mysticism
7. Social Dynamics in Paul's Eschatological Teaching

1. The Context of Pauline Eschatology: Jewish Apocalyptic Literature.

Recognition of the importance of the eschatological milieu of the NT materials is one of the most important results of twentieth-century investigations by biblical scholars. It needs to be recognized that the production of apocalypses was by no means restricted to Jewish or Christian writers; there are examples from many parts of the ancient Near East. However, it is the apocalypses of the first-century Jewish-Christian world, such as *1 Enoch*, 4 Ezra and *2 Baruch*, that are the most important parallels to Paul since these materials are closest to him in terms of date and geographical setting. They therefore afford us the best opportunity of appreciating the eschatological content of Paul's thinking.

In the memorable words of E. Käsemann, "apocalyptic was the mother of all Christian theology" (Käsemann 1969 "Beginnings," 102). Indeed, apocalyptic has been viewed as one of the keys for unlocking the meaning of the NT as a whole. It is for this reason that Beker has described the apocalyptic worldview as the "coherent center" of Paul's thought and "rejects those construals of Paul's thought that suppress, delimit, or compromise its apocalyptic texture" (Beker 1980, 135). Beker is here following the lead of Käsemann in defining apocalyptic eschatology in terms of a belief in the future, imminent consummation of the world, an event that is triggered by and at times even equated with the future parousia of Jesus Christ. At the same time Beker takes the argument a step further than Käsemann did, asserting that Paul's apocalyptic framework is not only the starting point for Paul's thought but also constitutes "the indispensable framework for his interpretation of the Christ-event" (Beker 1980, 19). This stands in contrast to Käsemann, who argues that Paul later departs from such an apocalyptically conditioned perspective. Beker serves as the advocate for many who would see the long-standing debate about the center and periphery of Paul's thought as resolved in favor of the centrality of the apocalyptic-eschatological element of his teaching. The focus of theological discussion is thereby shifted away from earlier arguments about justification by faith (e.g., Käsemann) and Christ mysticism (e.g., Schweitzer) as being the focal point(s) of Paul's theology. As an alternative, Beker asserts that "the triumph of God [is] the center of Paul's thought" (Beker 1980, 355), a suggestion that arises directly out of an apocalyptic framework of Paul's thought. Beker summarizes this approach as one that recognizes Paul's thought as an interaction between "contingency" and "coherency."

Some scholars have criticized the extent of Beker's approach, however, pointing out that in certain instances he imposed the apocalyptic scheme upon Paul's letters without due consideration to its appropriateness. J. L. Martyn, for example, has argued that Beker's interpretation of Galatians is misdirected and fails to take into account the role that the cross has in the letter (the letter is not easily fitted into an apocalyptic framework since eschatological material is notably absent within it). Nevertheless, according to Martyn, Galatians forms, as it were, an "apocalypse of the cross," which initiates a cosmic battle between the flesh and the spirit (as in Gal 5:16-25; see Beker's response in his preface to 2d ed., *Paul the Apostle*). A modification of the basic thesis is in order, as Beker (1991) now acknowledges.

Such attempts at interpreting Paul's theology from the standpoint of its eschatological foundation could legitimately be seen as a reaction to the overly realized approach of some interpreters such as C. H. Dodd or R. Bultmann, who build upon the presumed loss of an eschatological perspective as the Christian faith spread into the Hellenistic world. However, this is not to suggest that Paul's viewpoint is completely apocalyptic in substance, merely that it lies within an eschatological framework. Clearly there is, at the same time, a dimension of realized eschatology in Paul's thought that tempers his obviously futuristic teaching, as V. P. Branick argues. Any attempt to contrast what is present with what is eschatological in Paul's thought misrepresents his position—the two are dynamically interconnected. Recognition of Paul's two-dimensional eschatology (present/future; immanent/transcendent) is particularly important when it comes to determining how the message of Pauline eschatology is applicable to us today. The two dimensions of Paul's thought are sometimes usefully described as the vertical and horizontal (or the spatial and temporal) planes of his eschatology. The perceived relationship between the spatial and temporal dimensions of Paul's eschatological thought has proven to be one of the great divides among interpreters of Paul. Those who emphasize the vertical dimension tend to see the conflict implied by a two-age dualism in cosmological terms (earthly versus heavenly), while those who emphasize the horizontal dimension tend to see the conflict arising out of straightforward chronological consider-

ations (present versus future). A full examination of Paul's letters reveals that he uses the language of time and space within his eschatological teaching (see Lincoln). The latter should not be neglected nor the former overemphasized; both help constitute Paul's eschatological thought. Even such a passage as Colossians 3:1-6, dominated by spatial language, has a wider eschatological vision behind it which hints at its horizontal counterpart (see Levison for a discussion).

Over the years considerable discussion has been given over to determining the background sources for Paul's eschatological viewpoint: does it ultimately derive from his Jewish heritage or from the wider Hellenistic world of which he was a part? Most scholars now accept that Paul's Jewish heritage and background, including its twofold division of temporal history into two aeons, the "now" and the "not-yet," is determinative for his eschatological worldview. M. C. de Boer (1989) further subdivides Jewish apocalyptic eschatology by suggesting two tracks: a cosmological-apocalyptic eschatology and a forensic-apocalyptic eschatology. De Boer argues that these correspond respectively to Käsemann's cosmological understanding of apocalyptic and Bultmann's anthropological understanding of it. Be that as it may, for Paul Jewish apocalyptic is a worldview that has had to undergo significant adaptation in light of the crucial event of Jesus' resurrection from the dead. The resurrection of Jesus Christ conditions and determines Paul's eschatological teaching, for it is in the resurrection that the inauguration of the eschaton has truly taken place, the new order begun. While the resurrection is central to it, Pauline eschatology is by no means monolithic in its conceptualization, nor is it uniform in its expression. A great deal of variety characterizes the letters on this score. As W. Baird puts it, "Paul does not have a clear and simple apocalyptic picture of the end. His language is drawn from external sources and is not used consistently" (Baird, 325). Before we turn to consider some of the specifics of Paul's eschatological teaching there is one additional matter of significance that must first be addressed.

2. The Contingency of the Pauline Letters.
One of the most important contributions in recent Pauline studies has been the increased understanding of the contingent nature of the

letters that form the Pauline corpus. Even if, as we suggested above, Beker argues that apocalyptic be recognized as the "coherent center" of Paul's thought, he rightly notes that it must be translated into "the contingent particularities of the human situation" (Beker 1980, ix). More than ever before, scholarship has come to appreciate how the circumstances surrounding the production of a letter help to contribute to our understanding of its contents. In short, the greater our knowledge of precisely how and why the apostle Paul (or, perhaps one of his followers, in the case of the so-called Deutero-Pauline letters) came to write a given letter, the better our chances of understanding not only its original message but also of interpreting the meaning for us today.

An informed study of the relationship that Paul or his successors might have had with the intended congregation better enables us to expound the text as a whole. Unfortunately, the contingent nature of many of the letters is such that we are often left with many key questions unanswered. We do not know enough about what occasioned the apostle to write to the congregations or they to him, and we are often forced to hypothesize so as to fill in the gaps of our knowledge; we do not even have the complete Pauline corpus to work with, as 1 Corinthians 5:9 demonstrates. Hypothetical reconstructions of the correspondence between Paul and the various congregations are needed to overcome this problem, as J. C. Hurd's seminal "backward extrapolation" theory about the Corinthian correspondence illustrates. These problems affect virtually all of the letters in the Pauline corpus and involve many theological themes but become particularly acute in the area of eschatological teaching within several of the undisputed letters. Is Paul responding to questions arising from the congregations concerned? Have they misunderstood or misrepresented him? How much of what he writes in reply is dependent upon a common eschatological understanding that he shares with them or perhaps even was responsible for imparting to them? How much of what he writes is designed as conscious corrective? Two examples are worth citing at this point.

2.1. 1 Thessalonians 4:13—5:11: The Premature Death of Christian Believers? The Thessalonian letters both appear to have been written in response to serious questions raised by the con-gregation about the death of believers prior to the expected parousia of the Lord (1 Cor 11:30 and 1 Cor 15:18 may hint at the same issue being debated in Corinth). Paul's answer in 1 Thessalonians 4:13—5:11 attempts to deal with this concern and asserts that the dead suffer no disadvantage and will be joined with Christ at his coming. The difficulty here is that it is not clear what eschatological beliefs were held by the church at Thessalonica, nor why they were thrown into such theological turmoil by the death of some of the members of the congregation. Did they misunderstand what Paul (presumably) had taught them about the future when he helped found the congregation? Or could it be that Paul had altered his views about the resurrection in the interim and that he is correcting his earlier teaching within the letter? Part of the problem lies, no doubt, in the imprecise nature of eschatological material; K. J. F. Klijn notes that the question of the status of the deceased was a problem common to apocalyptic literature. However, because we do not know the earlier exchange between Paul and the Thessalonians, it is not possible to be sure about the accuracy of any interpretation; it is like trying to listen to one end of a telephone conversation and deduce the matter being discussed.

2.2. 1 Corinthians 7: The Institution of Marriage and Human Sexuality in the Face of the Parousia. In this chapter Paul responds to some questions raised by the Corinthians about sex and marriage in the lives of Christian believers. It appears that the Corinthians had adopted an ascetic attitude toward sexuality in light of their belief that full salvation in Christ had already arrived (in 1 Cor 7:1 Paul cites one of their slogans to this effect). Paul writes to correct this attitude, emphasizing in 1 Corinthians 7:2-6 the mutual obligations and responsibilities of sexual relationships between husbands and wives. This section presents little difficulty as far as eschatological matters are concerned. However, in 1 Corinthians 7:7-40 Paul continues with advice that seems much more conditioned by his views of the imminent parousia of Christ; this is particularly true in 1 Corinthians 7:25-35. There he advises those who are single for whatever reason to remain so in light of the "present distress" (1 Cor 7:26) and the "shortening of the time" (1 Cor 7:29). The chapter is an exegetical mine-field, but most scholars agree that to some degree Paul's eschatological perspective is coloring his ethical advice to those contemplating marriage. Whatever interpretation is eventually adopted, one must give due consideration to the eschatological backdrop of Paul's thought (see Moiser for an overview).

3. The Content of Pauline Eschatology: Some Central Tenets.

Clearly an eschatological viewpoint underlies the whole of Pauline theology. The extent to which the perspective is determinative and the variety of form and expression that it employs makes it difficult to assess the matter simply. However, the main points may be summarized under the following eight headings.

3.1. The Messiahship of Jesus of Nazareth. For Paul, Jesus of Nazareth is without doubt the Messiah, the Christ promised of old. So much is this so that the title *Christ* functions almost as if it is the surname of Jesus. Several other messianic titles and designations are accorded to Jesus within the Pauline corpus, including Son (of God) (sixteen times in Rom 1:4, 9; 5:10; 8:3, 29, 32; 1 Cor 1:9; 15:28; 2 Cor 1:19; Gal 1:16; 2:20; 4:4, 6; Eph 4:13; Col 1:13; 1 Thess 1:10), Son of David (two times in Rom 1:3; 2 Tim 2:8) and Lord (around 275 times, including such important christological passages as 1 Cor 8:6; Phil 2:11). Yet it cannot be forgotten that the appearance of the Messiah was regarded within many writings of first-century Judaism above all as an eschatological event, an indisputable sign that the age to come had arrived. In a sense it is true to say that the linchpin of Paul's eschatology is the proclamation of Jesus of Nazareth as the Messiah. At the same time it also needs to be said that the key event that guarantees or authenticates that messiahship is the raising of Jesus from the dead, for it is that act of resurrection that demonstrates how the eschatological age has impinged upon the present.

3.2. The Presence of the Eschatological Age. One of the standard features of Jewish apocalyptic literature is the division of time into two aeons (4 Ezra 7:50, "The Most High made not one age but two," is a classic statement of this). Perhaps the most demonstrable way that Paul shows his acceptance of this sort of an eschatological dualism of two aeons is in his use of the phrase "this age" (Rom 12:2; 1 Cor 1:20; 2:6-8; 3:18; 2 Cor 4:4). The corresponding phrase "the age to come," although implied at several points in the Pauline corpus, is never used in the undisputed

letters (it does appear in Eph 1:21). The present age is occasionally described as evil (*ponēros,* Gal 1:4; Eph 5:16; 6:13), and the inhabitants of the world are a "wicked and perverse generation" (Phil 2:15). And yet it becomes clear that Paul believes that the eschatological hope of the future has in some way impinged upon the present. As the apostle declares in 2 Corinthians 5:17, "the old has passed away, behold the new has come." In 1 Corinthians 10:11 he asserts that "the end of the ages has come" (with a deliberate use of the perfect verb *katēntēken*), and in 1 Corinthians 7:31 he states that "the form of this world is passing away." He describes this eschatological age as a "new creation" (*kainē ktisis,* 2 Cor 5:17; Gal 6:15). More than this, Paul associates the arrival of the eschatological age with the revelation of Jesus Christ as God's Messiah. Thus he declares in Galatians 4:4 that "when the time had fully come, God sent forth his own Son." All of this is to suggest that Paul's teaching about the presence of the eschatological age must be set against the backdrop of a temporal dualism.

Several related images are used to express this idea of two aeons, including the Adam/Christ analogy of Romans 5 and 1 Corinthians 15 (*see* Adam and Christ) and an extended anthropological image involving a contrast between the old self and the new self (Rom 6:6; Col 3:9-10; Eph 2:15; 4:22-24); outer self/inner self (Rom 7:22; 2 Cor 4:16; Eph 3:15); physical person/spiritual person (2 Cor 2:14-16). A spatial image involving the use of "heaven" (*ouranos*) and its related terms also offers an important means whereby eschatological truth is communicated in the Pauline letters, as A. T. Lincoln demonstrates.

The assurance of the present reality of the new age gave rise to an overly realized understanding of Christian existence within some congregations. So certain were they about the reality of eschatological existence now that there seemed little need for any resurrection in the future—the resurrection life was presently being lived (most scholars accept that 1 Cor 4:8; 15:12 and 2 Tim 2:18 can all be exegetically linked as expressive of this overrealized perspective, but see Wedderburn for a dissenting opinion). In the case of Corinth this overrealized enthusiasm seems to have manifested itself in an unhealthy preoccupation with spiritual gifts, demonstrating how closely allied eschatology and pneumatology were in Paul's time (as Thistleton argues; *see* Holy Spirit). Surely R. P. Martin is correct at this point in suggesting that 1 Corinthians 15 must not be separated from 1 Corinthians 12—14, particularly within an exegetical framework. It is not difficult to demonstrate that the same dynamic interplay between eschatology and pneumatology persists throughout church history and holds true even today, with appeal to the Pauline letters being made by all sides over the years. Paul counters the enthusiasm of the Corinthians in two major ways: first, by the use of sarcastic rebuke (as in 1 Cor 4:8); second, by forcefully reemphasizing the futuristic dimensions of their common faith (as in 1 Cor 15). Similar overly realized understandings of Christian existence are reflected and challenged in 2 Timothy 2:16-18, 2 Thessalonians 2:2 and possibly 1 Thessalonians 4:13. There exists in Paul a dialectic between the present and the future, particularly as it is connected to the concept of salvation.

However, despite the assurance of a present dimension of eschatological hope, it should not be overlooked that for Paul the final revelation of the eschatological age still lies in the future. The ultimate transformation of the world order, the final redemption of the believer (the granting of the resurrection body) and the final judgment are all events that are yet to be awaited. The present is conditioned by the past (death and resurrection of Jesus Christ) and the future (the awaited parousia at the end of time).

3.2.1. The Kingdom of God/Christ. Although the idea of the kingdom of God/Christ is a standard feature of the Jewish eschatological perspective that Paul shares and is something that clearly underlies much of his ethical teaching, the phrase is not a prominent one within the Pauline letters (*see* Kingdom of God). Apparently Paul does clearly assume the life and ministry of Jesus Christ to have been in some way the inauguration of the kingdom of God on earth, despite the fact that this is never explicitly stated anywhere within his letters.

Paul tends to talk of the kingdom of God/ Christ as if it is something awaited in the future, although occasionally he hints at the present reality of the kingdom in the life of the Christian (as in Rom 14:17 and 1 Cor 4:20). One of his most common statements about the kingdom is that it is something that the believer inherits (as in 1 Cor 6:9-10; 15:50; Gal 5:21) as a result of faith-

fulness; again, clearly it is a future inheritance that is in view. More central within Paul's teaching on the kingdom of God/Christ is the place that the resurrection of Jesus Christ has in bringing the kingdom to bear within human history.

3.3. The Resurrection of Jesus Christ from the Dead. For Paul the resurrection of Jesus is primarily an eschatological event affirming the fact that the new age has arrived. At the same time it is understandably seen as the vindication of Jesus' death on the cross and is closely associated with Christ's accession to power at the right hand of God (Rom 8:34), providing the basis for his intercession on behalf of the saints. Despite the fact that the resurrection is for Paul an eschatological act of God, it is never simply a spiritual event loosed from the moorings of history or distanced from some sort of physicality. For Paul the resurrection of Jesus clearly involves the risen Lord in some sort of somatic existence, although admittedly it is an existence of a different order.

3.3.1. Romans 1:3-4: Son of God and Resurrection. Most scholars agree that within these two verses we have the apostle alluding to a traditional creedal affirmation about Jesus Christ. Several features of the passage hint at an earlier setting of the declaration, perhaps arising from the Palestinian church. Notable among these are the unusual phrase "according to the Spirit of holiness" and the juxtaposition of Jesus' earthly credentials ("descended from David according to the flesh") with his heavenly status ("designated Son of God in power"). In short, we have here a dual affirmation of Jesus' sonship: he is Son of David and Son of God. What is significant in terms of Paul's eschatology is the fact that Jesus' credentials as Son of God are closely linked to his resurrection from the dead. It is no wonder that this passage is sometimes described as reflecting one of the earliest stages of theological reflection among the first Christians, where the resurrection is the act that accords Jesus his status as God's Son. When this consideration is held alongside the fact that the participial form in Romans 1:4 (translated as "designated" in the RSV, "declared" in the NRSV) is very difficult to interpret precisely, it is easy to understand how those who advocated adoptionism found the text a key one for their position.

3.3.2. 1 Corinthians 15: An Excursus on Resurrection. In 1 Corinthians 15 we have a semi-independent excursus on the resurrection and its implications for the believer. This is the most detailed discussion of the resurrection within the Pauline corpus. The focus of discussion within the chapter is not whether or not Jesus Christ has been raised from the dead, as is often assumed in popular apologetics, but what the implications of Christ's resurrection are for the believer. Thus 1 Corinthians 15:12 provides an important clue for the discussion as a whole: "Now if Christ is preached as raised from the dead, how can some of you say that there is no resurrection of the dead?" Important insight is here gained about the nature of the controversy at Corinth and the identity of the so-called Corinthian heresy. Paul is here confronting an overrealized eschatology within the Corinthian congregation, one that suggests that the Corinthians, or at least some of them, believed there was no need for their future resurrection since they had been baptized and were living the resurrection life already. Paul's initial defense of a futuristic eschatology involves his reminding the Corinthians of his earlier teaching on the matter, one built on traditional creedal declarations about the resurrection of Jesus Christ (1 Cor 15:3-7) and his appearance to witnesses. In other words, the Corinthians share Paul's acceptance of the resurrection of Jesus Christ as foundational to their Christian faith but differ as to their understanding of its significance for Christian hope.

3.3.2.1. The First Fruits (1 Cor 15:20, 23). Paul uses an illustration drawn from agriculture to demonstrate the connection between the resurrection of Jesus Christ and the resurrection of the believer. In 1 Corinthians 15:20 and 1 Corinthians 15:23 he describes the risen Lord Jesus Christ as the first fruits *(aparchē)*, implying that the believer will share in the resurrection life in the same way that the full harvest is related to the initial crop. The important qualifier interjected by means of this agricultural image is that the resurrection existence of the believer is still future and yet to be awaited. The whole image is dependent upon an understanding of a dynamic unity existing between Christ and the believers; whatever happens to the risen Lord Jesus Christ is automatically transferred to the Christian community, albeit within an eschatological context. As M. J. Harris (114) puts it, the first fruits image demonstrates that Christ is "both the pledge and the paradigm of the somatic resurrection of believers."

Paul also applies the *aparchē* images to his eschatological teaching about the gift of the Holy Spirit in Romans 8:23, as well as to Jewish/Gentile relationships within the plan of God in Romans 11:16; the image may also be present in 2 Thessalonians 2:13, depending on the textual variants adopted. A related image, describing the risen Christ as the "firstborn of the dead" *(prōtotokos ek tōn nekrōn)*, is contained in the pre-Pauline hymn of Colossians 1:15-20.

3.3.2.2. The Adam/Christ Analogy (1 Cor 15:20-21, 44b-45). Paul's use of the Adam/Christ analogy is one of the most important features of his eschatological teaching in the chapter. Beginning in 1 Corinthians 15:20 the apostle sets up a deliberate contrast between Adam and Jesus Christ as representative figures of humanity. The analogy is further extended in 1 Corinthians 15:44b-45, where Paul once again appears to correct an overrealized understanding of resurrection existence among the Corinthians. In 1 Corinthians 15:46 he reverses the order in which the physical body and the resurrection body are to appear (the Corinthians may be exhibiting dependence upon the kind of teaching about Adamic humankind found in Philo of Alexandria at this point). The result of this is that Christ is portrayed as embodying what R. Scroggs has described as "eschatological humanity."

3.3.2.3. Death: The Last Enemy (1 Cor 15:26). Within the Pauline letters death is portrayed in physical and spiritual terms. Thus, it is the cessation of mortal life (Phil 1:21) and the state of spiritual separation from God (Rom 7:9-14; Eph 2:1-3; Col 1:21). The destructive power of death is never downplayed in Paul (note the use of *katalyō* in 2 Cor 5:1), although it is occasionally presented as the doorway of departure to another existence (2 Cor 5:8; Phil 1:23; 2 Tim 4:6). In the midst of his extended discussion on the implications of Jesus Christ's resurrection, Paul uses an unusual phrase in describing physical death, referring to it as "the last enemy to be destroyed." De Boer argues that this defeat of death is central to 1 Corinthians 15:20-28, the heart of Paul's eschatological teaching in the chapter. This is a highly evocative image, emphasizing the importance of the cross for Paul's thought as it hints at a confrontation between Jesus Christ and Death, as if the latter is a personified figure who must be engaged in combat on this cross of Calvary. The figure of Death as an enemy is clearly drawn from Paul's eschatological worldview; similar instances of precisely this sort of personification of death can be found in other Jewish and Christian apocalypses such as 4 Ezra 8:53, Revelation 6:8 and Revelation 20:13-14 (see de Boer, 90-91, for further details).

At the same time the image sets up something of a tension within Paul's teaching on physical death, a tension that can perhaps best be highlighted by considering when it is that Paul views this enemy to be destroyed. Has it already been accomplished by Christ's death on the cross, as the use of the aorist *katargēsantos* in 2 Timothy 1:10 suggests? Or is it something that is still to occur in the indefinite future, at the awaited parousia of Christ? Clearly the immediate context of 1 Corinthians 15:20-28 would suggest the latter, although how this is then to be applied to believers and what its implications are for their present ethical conduct are matters that are far from certain. To put it another way, if death and sin are interconnected, as Paul forcefully asserts in Romans 5:12, how is it that the Christian is exhorted to live a life in the present that is freed from the power and effect of sin and yet be expected to await the deliverance from death as something in the future? Sin, which is personified (Rom 5:14, 17, 21; 7:8-11, 13-25), is already conquered—yes; but not the physical death that is so intimately associated with it—that must await the future consummation. At the very least we must admit a theological tension being expressed here, although we need not go so far as to suggest that Paul is involved in a damaging self-contradiction at this point.

3.4. The Awaited Day of the Lord and Final Judgment. The day of the Lord *(yôm YHWH)* is a standard feature in OT prophetic literature, one that Paul takes over and expands within his letters. As far as can be adduced it was originally conceived as a day of future joy, when God would intervene on behalf of his people and save them from calamity, righting injustice and defeating Israel's enemies. However, many of the prophets, such as Amos, Ezekiel, Isaiah, Zechariah, Zephaniah, Malachi and Joel, in an effort to call the people back to true obedience, shifted the focus within their message, proclaiming the day of the Lord to be not only a time of deliverance but a time of judgment for the nation of Israel as well (see Everson). The idea of an eschatological day of the Lord can also be found in Jewish pseudepigraphal documents (such as *1 Enoch*, 4 Ezra and *2 Baruch*) and in select Qumran documents (such as 1QM and 1QS). In the Gospels it is most closely associated with Jesus' statements about the coming Son of Man, but it can be identified within all Gospel strata. Paul takes over the Jewish concept of the day of the Lord, including the twin themes of eschatological salvation and future judgment, within his teaching on the theme. However, he creatively integrates this OT hope with his developing christology, effectively transforming the "day of the Lord (Yahweh)" into the "day of the Lord Jesus Christ." This creativity stands as one of the most important contributions within Pauline eschatology (see 4 below).

3.4.1. The Day of the Lord and the Parousia of Jesus Christ. A variety of expressions are used within the Pauline letters for the eschatological day of the Lord, particularly as it is used with reference to Jesus Christ. The simple phrase "day of the Lord" occurs in 1 Thessalonians 5:2 and 2 Thessalonians 2:2; the phrase "day of the Lord Jesus Christ" in 1 Corinthians 5:5; "day of the Lord Jesus" in 1 Corinthians 1:8 and 2 Corinthians 1:14; "day of Christ Jesus" in Philippians 1:6; "day of Christ" in Philippians 1:10 and Philippians 2:16; "the day" in 1 Thessalonians 5:4 and 1 Corinthians 3:13; "that day" in 2 Timothy 1:12, 18; 4:8. In addition, Paul is the major NT source for the use of the term *parousia* of the future coming of Jesus Christ (1 Cor 15:23; 1 Thess 2:19; 3:13; 4:15; 5:23; 2 Thess 2:1, 8-9). The noun *apokalypsis* ("revelation") is used in a similar way in 1 Corinthians 1:7 and 2 Thessalonians 1:7. In the Pastorals a significant change in vocabulary appears; the term *epiphaneia* is used with reference to the appearance of the Lord Jesus Christ in 1 Timothy 6:1, 2 Timothy 1:10, 2 Timothy 4:1, 8 and Titus 2:13, while the verb *epiphainō* ("appear") is used in Titus 2:11 and Titus 3:4 (the noun *epiphaneia* ["appearance"] also is used in 2 Thess 2:8). In all three Pastoral letters the immediate context of these verses suggests a future manifestation of the glory of the Lord Jesus Christ, although the present dimension is also clearly in evidence, especially in 2 Timothy 2:10. Several related verb forms are also used within the Pauline corpus to denote this future eschatological event: forms of *erchomai* ("come") appear in 1 Corinthians 4:5, 1 Corinthians 11:26 and 2 Thessalonians 2:10; *apoka-*

lyptō ("reveal") in 2 Thessalonians 1:7; and *phaneroō* ("make manifest") in Colossians 3:4. The phrase "the day of redemption" appears in Ephesians 4:30; while *to telos* ("the end") occurs in 1 Corinthians 1:8, 1 Corinthians 15:24 and 2 Corinthians 1:13; and *ta telē* in 1 Corinthians 10:11. The future parousia of Jesus Christ is often popularly described as "the second coming" or "the second advent," although it is worth noting that neither phrase is found within the Pauline letters, or anywhere in the NT for that matter. The first attested distinction between a "First Advent" and a "Second Advent" is found in the writings of Justin Martyr (c. A.D. 110), although a close approximation is found in Hebrews 9:28.

At several points in the Pauline letters it appears that traditional declarations of the coming of the Messiah from heaven are cited. Generally these statements are filled with apocalyptic language and imagery, much of it drawn from OT prophetic literature (as in 1 Thess 1:9-10; 4:13—5:11). One of the most interesting is the Greek transliteration of the Aramaic phrase *maranatha* found in 1 Corinthians 16:22. The linguistic evidence deriving from a bilingual setting makes this potentially the earliest recorded acknowledgement of the lordship of Jesus Christ. Some dispute remains about how *maranatha* should be divided and separated and whether it should be understood as an invocation for the Lord to come (*marana tha*, "Come, our Lord!") or as a straightforward declaration that he has already come (*maran atha*, "The Lord has come!"). In any event, the context of the passage is presumably the Lord's Supper (as in the interesting parallel in *Did.* 10:6), and it seems reasonable to take the Aramaic phrase to contain at least an element of future fulfillment within it. In short, the ejaculation *maranatha* is a prayer, uttered within a liturgical context, that may call for the future parousia of the Lord. The parallel in Revelation 22:20 would support such an interpretation.

3.4.2. The Delay of the Parousia. One prominent school of thought within NT scholarship has held that the nonarrival of the parousia of Jesus Christ created a crisis early within the life of the Christian church. This delay of the parousia is sometimes portrayed as triggering the need for a de-eschatologization of the Christian hope, a movement away from Jewish apocalyptic ideas that see the fulfillment of God's promises as taking place in the not-too-distant return of

Christ to earth. Such a belief is replaced by a more Hellenistic understanding of Christ's presence as taking place within the life of the believer. Under the impact of the delayed parousia, so the argument goes, eschatology is necessarily dehistoricized, and the meaning of the future hope was spiritualized and transposed into a more mystical union between Christ and the church. The Pauline materials figure prominently within such theories about the crisis presented by the delay of the parousia, although there is an increasing swell of voices objecting to the assumption that the parousia presented such a theological crisis among the early Christians that is so often supposed (see Aune, Bauckham). Many scholars have concluded that the later Pauline letters (such as 2 Cor 10—13 and Phil) reflect precisely this sort of shift in perspective, a suggestion that raises the question of development within Paul's eschatological thought.

3.4.3. The Question of Development in Pauline Eschatology. Two basic ways of approaching this question have been employed by Pauline scholars. The first is to note the differences (even inconsistencies) between sections of Paul's letters with regard to eschatological matters and suggest that the apostle has changed his mind or developed in his understanding of the issues, or that his follower(s) responsible for the Deutero-Pauline letters have done so (see Achtemeier; Beker 1991). Generally such an approach involves a detailed study of Pauline chronology and careful attention to the polemical contexts in which the letters are written. Indeed, J. W. Drane argues that the diversity of eschatological expression is directly related to the diversity of opponents against whom Paul is writing, although he rejects some of the more radical results of advocates of such an approach. In any event, the dating and circumstances surrounding the production of a letter are crucial in determining whether development of thought is detectable. In the main, the letters of the Pauline corpus are divided by scholars adopting this explanation of development into three groups, representing an increasingly Hellenistic and individualistic understanding of eschatology that occurs over time: Paul's early letters (1 Thess, 2 Thess); Paul's major letters (Rom, 1 Cor, 2 Cor, Gal); Paul's later letters (Phil, Col, Eph, Philem). Diversity of opinion about the categorization of some letters is common.

The second approach is to allow the differences to stand and to explain them as inevitable given the nature of the subject matter; to accept them as the apostle trying to explain the inexplicable and, not surprisingly, creating some real theological tensions within his writing. In the words of C. F. D. Moule, such tensions are "best explained as the result, simply, of the unmanageable dimensions of the Christian verities" (Moule, 4).

In summary, the question of development in Paul's eschatology inevitably involves one in scholarly investigation on at least three separate but interconnected fronts: controversy about the integrity of the Corinthian letters (two, three or four letters?), the chronological order of the letters (notably Phil) and debates about Pauline authorship of some of the disputed letters (namely, 2 Thess, Col and Eph). However, even within the undisputed letters the controversy about development of Paul's eschatological thought arises.

The eschatological teaching contained in 1 Corinthians 15 and 2 Corinthians 5:1-10 has long been one of the major areas of discussion (Gillmann offers a survey of interpretation). Many interpreters feel that in 1 Corinthians 15 we have Paul giving his clearest expression of the future hope for the believer, associating the granting of the resurrection body with the parousia of Christ, which is expected very soon, during Paul's lifetime. However, in 2 Corinthians 5:1-10 it appears that Paul provides an alternative perspective, one in which the Christian believer is somehow united with Christ at the point of death, and the granting of the resurrection body postponed indefinitely, presumably until the parousia. Many scholars have attempted to explain this shift in perspective between the two letters. Dodd, for example, explains the shift to have come about because of Paul's brush with death, something which, Dodd suggests, took place between the writing of the letters we know as 1 Corinthians and 2 Corinthians (this trauma is perhaps hinted at in 2 Cor 1:8-11). Many scholars, including F. F. Bruce and E. E. Ellis, would dispute this suggestion, arguing that it is highly improbable that Paul would have changed his mind on so central an issue within the span of a few short weeks or months (the supposed time lag between the writing of the two Corinthian letters). For them the essential teaching contained in 1 Corinthians 15 and 2 Corinthians 5:1-10 is compatible. Some scholars have attempted to explain the difference between the teaching contained within the two letters by arguing that 1 Corinthians 15 is concerned primarily with a collective eschatology and 2 Corinthians 5:1-10 is concerned primarily with an individualistic eschatology. The fact that so much attention and variety of interpretation is given to the problem raised by the eschatology of the Corinthian letters is some indication of its importance within Pauline studies.

Others have sought to identify a development in Paul's eschatological thought even within his earlier letters, namely, 1 and 2 Thessalonians. C. L. Mearns, for example, suggests that Paul's earliest eschatological teaching was radically realized and that the death of Christian believers within the Thessalonian congregation forced a radical shift in his understanding of such matters. This sort of approach assumes that the death of believers would have come as something unexpected and theologically worrying to Paul, resulting in him "re-conceptualizing the Parousia in the form of a 'Second Coming'" (Mearns, 139). While the death of some of the members of the congregation is certainly an issue within the church at Thessalonica (as in 1 Thess 4:13-18), there is little to suggest that this was a result of Paul's teaching to them. Indeed, it is difficult to imagine that in the approximately twenty years of missionary activity prior to his writing 1 Thessalonians, Paul had not yet been faced with the death of Christians or worked out the matter theologically.

3.4.4. The Judgment Seat of God/Christ. Paul takes over the standard Jewish expectation that all men and women will be held accountable before God for their lives (see Travis). There is within Paul's letters a close association between the parousia of the Lord Jesus Christ and the execution of final judgment. A classic example of this is found in 1 Thessalonians 3:13, where declaration of the parousia is placed within a judgment context "before God" *(emprosthen tou theou)*. In 1 Corinthians 3:12-15 Paul offers an extended passage about the final judgment, using an image of building materials being tested by the purifying fires of "the day" (1 Cor 3:13). Similar imagery of giving account before God is used in Romans 2:1-11 and Romans 14:10-12 and (with reference to Paul himself) in Philippians 2:16. In Romans 2:16 God is said to judge the secrets of humankind by Christ Jesus *(dia Christou Iēsou)*.

In connection with the final judgment at the

consummation of this age, Paul speaks explicitly of the judgment seat *(bēma)* twice within his letters (Rom 14:10; 2 Cor 5:10), building upon the image found in Isaiah 45. The curious thing about this motif is that the judgment seat is described as belonging to God in the first reference and as belonging to Christ in the second. There is some precedent for this fluctuation between God and messianic agent within Jewish pseudepigraphal texts (such as *1 Enoch* 37—71; *T. Abr.* 13:1-2); the same is carried on in Christian writings after Paul, probably under the apostle's influence (e.g., Polycarp *Phil.* 6.2). By extension, the right of judgment is extended to the Christian church acting as Christ's agents. Thus Paul feels able to pass judgment on unethical behavior (1 Cor 5:3-5) and exhorts the church to do the same (1 Cor 5:11-13). He even hints that the saints will execute eschatological judgment over the world and the angels (1 Cor 6:2-3).

3.4.5. The Judgment of Satan and His Angels. Satan is mentioned frequently in the Pauline letters, always as a power hostile to God and malevolent to the saints (Rom 16:20; 1 Cor 5:5; 7:5; 2 Cor 2:11; 11:14; 12:7; 1 Thess 2:18). The terms *Tempter (ho peirazōn)* and *devil (diabolos)* are also used (in 1 Thess 3:5 and Eph 6:11 respectively). This is perfectly in keeping with the eschatological dualism of other Jewish apocalyptic texts that characteristically describe the present age as one in which Satan's power and authority are in evidence. Indeed, Satan is called "the god of this age" in 2 Corinthians 4:4 and "the prince of the power of the air" in Ephesians 2:2. Also in keeping with these apocalyptic texts is a developed angelology, with Satan being supported by a host of figures; in the main, Paul conforms to this Jewish usage (see Carr). We find angels (sometimes friendly, but generally hostile) mentioned in passing throughout the Pauline letters (Rom 8:38; 1 Cor 4:9; 6:3; 11:10; 13:1; 2 Cor 11:14; 12:7; Gal 1:8; 3:19; 4:14; Col 2:18; 1 Thess 4:16). Related to this are the references to the "rulers of this age" (1 Cor 2:6-9); the "principalities and powers" (Rom 8:38; 1 Cor 15:24; Eph 6:12; Col 2:15); "world rulers of this present darkness and spiritual hosts of wickedness in high places" (Eph 6:13); and "the elemental spirits of the universe" (Gal 4:3; Col 2:8, 20). Yet the ultimate judgment and defeat of Satan, together with his angelic minions, is portrayed as a certainty in several key passages, notably Romans 16:20. Thus Paul balances the present and future dimensions of this judgment of Satan, with the cross of Christ being the fulcrum of the scales of justice.

There is considerable fluidity of referents within the language of angelic powers in the Pauline corpus. At times (such as Rom 8:38-39; Col 2:15; Eph 2:2; 3:10; 6:12) the referent is apparently a spiritual force, while at other times (such as Rom 13:1-7; 1 Cor 2:6-8) it is clearly a political power that is in view (see Carr, Wink). The relationship between the two basic categories (spiritual and political forces) inevitably involves one in discussions about Pauline chronology and the authorship of Colossians and Ephesians.

3.4.6. The Judgment of the Man of Lawlessness (2 Thess 2). There has been considerable debate about the identification of the "man of lawlessness (or sin)" mentioned in 2 Thessalonians 2:1-12. The fact that it is found in a letter that is disputed by some as genuinely Pauline has also contributed to the debate. The passage presents significant exegetical dilemmas in its own right, not least the difficulty in determining who the "man of lawlessness" (2 Thess 2:3) is supposed to represent. Is he a symbol of Satan, or one of his agents? Is he a figure in the tradition of the wicked Antiochus Epiphanes from the days of Daniel, associated with the "abomination of desolation" and the Roman emperor Caligula (Mk 13:14)? Should we identify this figure with the political leadership of Rome, a representative of civil authority or perhaps even with the emperor as the one who brings political upheaval *(apostasia)*? It seems clear that the underlying imagery for this ungodly figure is found in Ezekiel's passage about the king of Tyre (Ezek 28:1-19), but recognition of this does not necessarily aid in determining who is intended. Association with the antichrist figure in Revelation is understandable given the overall tone of the passage (see Mounce).

Similarly, who or what is "the restraining influence" (2 Thess 2:6-7)? Is it Paul, as Cullmann and J. Munck suggest? Or is it the need for the gospel message to be proclaimed throughout the world, as R. D. Aus argues? Again, one of the reasons why it is difficult to determine precisely what the author has in mind arises from an exegetical oddity, an unusual phrasing in the Greek text that provides a neuter expression *(to katechon,* 2 Thess 2:6) and a masculine one *(ho katechōn,* 2 Thess 2:7) in successive verses.

In any event, the main thrust of the passage is to place the rise of the "man of lawlessness" within a temporal framework (as in 2 Thess 2:3), while at the same time assert his ultimate defeat by the Lord Jesus at the future parousia.

3.4.7. The Wrath to Come. The coming wrath *(orgē)* is mentioned over twenty times within the Pauline letters, the noun appearing with the definite article and without it. Several other terms and phrases, mostly drawn from the verb *krinō* ("judge") and its cognates, are also used to express the just execution of judgment by God or his designated agent at the end of the age (see Kreitzer, 99-100, for details). The fact that Paul tends not to associate God directly with the execution of this wrath has prompted some scholars, notably Dodd, to suggest that he depersonalizes wrath. There is some validity to the suggestion, although the phrase "the wrath of God" *(hē orgē tou theou)* does appear three times (Rom 1:18; Eph 5:6; Col 3:6).

3.5. The Gentile Mission and the Fate of the Jewish Nation. According to his own testimony, Paul's calling as an apostle is intimately related to his encunter with the risen Lord Jesus (Gal 1:11-17). While the focus of Paul's Damascus Road" experience is often placed upon it being his conversion experience, it is important to note that it might be more properly described as his calling to participate in the fulfillment of God's promises to bring all nations to him in the fullness of time (as in Is 49; *see* Conversion and Call of Paul). This means that Paul sees the whole of his subsequent ministry among the nations as taking place within the context of an eschatological act, the resurrection of Jesus from the dead. Paul's commissioning as the "apostle to the Gentiles" (Gal 2:8) is alluded to throughout Paul's letters (see Kim, 1-31, for details). Clearly Paul sees his apostolic ministry as part of God's eschatological activity, and an essential component of that activity is the salvation of a people called to be his own, as N. T. Wright notes. But how does this affect his understanding of the fate of the Jewish nation (*see* Israel)? Several key texts deal with precisely this question.

3.5.1. Romans 9—11. Dodd long ago recognized the special nature of Romans 9—11, suggesting that it was an independent source, possibly a sermon that was inserted by Paul into the letter. The fact that it is possible to read from Romans 8:38 to Romans 12:1 without a discern-

ible break in thought lends weight to this suggestion. However, many Pauline interpreters feel that Romans 9—11 is an integral part of the overall argument of the letter and do not feel the interpolation approach is warranted. The problem of the fate of the Jewish nation lies at the heart of this section of the letter, but this is anticipated earlier in the letter (as in Rom 3:1-8 and the image of Abraham in Rom 4:1-25; *see* Abraham). Insofar as the section is concerned with the future fate of the Jewish nation, in light of their rejection of Jesus Christ as Messiah, it deals with eschatological matters.

What does Paul feel will ultimately happen to the Jewish nation, his people? In Romans 11:26 ("all Israel will be saved") he appears to come close to what might be described as a national universalism. How literally should we take the "all Israel" *(pas Israēl)* in Romans 11:26 to be? It is difficult to reconcile such teaching with the theme of justification by faith so strongly emphasized elsewhere in his writing. One way to understand Romans 9—11 is that it reflects an unresolved tension within Paul's thought, one that cannot quite seem to abandon faith in God's promises to historical Israel, yet one that is challenged by the redefinition of Israel into spiritual terms demanded by the Christ event. Traditionally Israel was seen as the instrument of God's salvation of the Gentile nations (as in Is 40—66); Paul's dilemma is how to maintain belief in this strand of prophetic proclamation in light of Israel's rejection of Jesus Christ. A volcanic eruption has taken place within Paul's thought, and the place of Israel within the revised eschatological scheme is like lava that has not yet cooled; it is not yet hardened or fixed, remaining somewhat resilient.

3.5.2. 1 Thessalonians 2:13-16. Since the days of F. C. Baur, scholars have often claimed that this pericope breaks the flow of Paul's argument in the letter and have suggested that it is an interpolation, perhaps inserted by a later editor after the fall of Jerusalem in A.D. 70. At the heart of such an interpretation is the assumption that the pericope is incompatible with Paul's eschatological teaching elsewhere concerning the fate of the Jewish nation. Competent cases have been made for both possibilities (the section is genuinely Pauline; alternatively, it is a non-Pauline interpolation). To a large degree the argument hinges on whether a historical setting can be determined to fit the judgment on the

Jewish nation implied, such as the Jewish Passover riot of A.D. 49.

3.6. The Eschatological Gift of the Spirit. Jewish eschatology traditionally associated the dawn of the age to come with the bestowal of the Spirit of God (*see* Holy Spirit). Paul carries through this idea, knitting together his doctrine of the risen Lord Jesus Christ as experienced by the indwelling presence of the Spirit of God in the life of the believer. In 1 Corinthians 15:45 the risen Christ, the last Adam, is even described as the "life-giving Spirit" *(pneuma zōopoioun)*. Several images are used to express the role that the Spirit has in the life of the believer. Similar declarations about the impartation of life by the Spirit are recorded in Romans 8:2, 10 and 2 Corinthians 3:6.

3.6.1. The Spirit as First Fruits. Paul explicitly describes the Spirit as the first fruits *(aparchē)* in Romans 8:23, paralleling what is said about the risen Christ in 1 Corinthians 15:20. This agricultural image is used extensively in the OT (as in Lev 23:10-14).

3.6.2. The Spirit as Guarantee. At several places within the Pauline letters the gift of the Holy Spirit is described as the guarantee *(arrabōn)* of God (2 Cor 1:22; 5:5; Eph 1:14). This unusual term is a Semitic loan word and was well established in Greek as a financial term. It denoted the promise to pay a full balance based on the handing over of an initial down payment. The financial metaphor lent itself readily to Paul's doctrine of the indwelling Spirit and is clearly eschatologically conditioned. The essential point is that the believer is assured of his or her ultimate redemption based on the present possession of the Holy Spirit.

3.6.3. The Spirit and Inheritance. The language of inheritance also figures within Paul's pneumatology (1 Cor 6:9-10; 15:50; Gal 5:21), where it is closely connected to his understanding of covenental blessing and the fulfillment of the promise of God to his people in Abraham. The idea of the Christian's possession of the Spirit as the basis for the adoption *(huiothesia)* as the children of God is declared at several places within the Pauline letters (Rom 8:15; 9:4; Gal 4:5; Eph 1:5). The use of the Greek transliteration of the Aramaic term *Abba* is linked to this (Rom 8:15; Gal 4:6). By virtue of the fact that the Christian by definition has the Spirit, the status of adoption exists as a present reality. Yet it is not difficult to detect a future dimension to this adoption within the passages, a feature that is consistent with the rest of Paul's eschatological teaching.

3.6.4. The Spirit and Christian Ethical Life. Paul's eschatological perspective informs his ethical teaching, often helping to frame the way in which he describes the Christian as one who is to live his or her life with an eye to the future. In effect, this means that Paul's ethical dualism is eschatological in nature, not anthropological, as many advocating a clash with Gnosticism have suggested in the past. For Paul, soteriology and eschatology are intertwined, finding the basis of expression through his christology. For example, in Galatians 1:4 the sacrificial death of Christ is described as the means of believers' deliverance "from the present evil age." Similarly, in Romans 8:4 he defines Christian existence in terms of a "life in the flesh" that has been surrendered for a "life in the Spirit." The Spirit is also spoken of as the power of resurrection existence made operative in the Christian's ethical life (as in Rom 8:11; 1 Cor 2:4-5).

3.7. The Transformation of the Cosmos. One of the standard features of apocalyptic eschatology is the transformation of the created order under the effects of the emerging age to come. This cosmic redemption is also reflected at several key points within the Pauline letters, demonstrating a close connection between the ideas of creation and redemption (see Gibbs). Cosmic redemption is also intimately connected to anthropological redemption within the Pauline letters. The destiny of the created order and the human race are determined by Christ's resurrection from the dead, and both find their fulfillment in his lordship. Thus Paul concludes his short excursus on creation in Romans 8:19-22 with the proclamation that this redemption includes the adoption of his children via the activity of the Spirit (Rom 8:23).

3.7.1. Romans 8:19-23. In the midst of an extended discussion of the effects of Jesus Christ's redeeming action for the Christian, we have a short section that describes its cosmic dimensions. Paul here employs the language of Jewish apocalyptic, anthropomorphizing the created order *(hē ktisis)* and mixing in the image of birth pangs *(synōdinei)*. As D. C. Allison demonstrates, "birth pangs" is something of a technical term within apocalyptic texts, often associated with the tribulations surrounding the advent of the Messiah. Interestingly, Paul also includes the image within the passage on the parousia in

1 Thessalonians 5:3, a section built very much on the traditional OT expectations of the day of the Lord. It is a common image within apocalyptic sections of the OT (Is 26:16-19; 66:7-14) and of the Synoptics (Mk 13:8; Mt 24:8), and it occurs within other apocalypses (4 Ezra 5:1-13, 50-55; 6:21-24; 9:3). Yet the paragraph from Romans is not intended as a detailed teaching about creation as such, but it is made to serve as a supporting illustration of Paul's main concern, the "adoption, the redemption of our body" (Rom 8:23 NRSV; see 7.2 below).

3.7.2. Philippians 3:21. In Philippians 3:20-21 we have another example of Paul's concern with the transformation of the believer's physical body into a glorious body by the power of the resurrection. Yet at the conclusion of this couplet Paul includes a phrase that breaks out of the boundaries of the anthropological imagery and interjects a cosmic note. The resurrection is said to be the power "which enables him even to subject all things to himself." This is similar to the declaration made in 1 Corinthians 15:27 and is built on Psalm 8:7. Once again the transformation of humankind and the subjection of the cosmos are interconnected ideas.

3.7.3. Colossians 1:15-20. The idea of Christ's role as creator is prominent within the pre-Pauline hymn of Colossians 1:15-20. This creator motif is also balanced within the hymn by the proclamation of Christ as the agent of redemption (*di' autou apokatallatai,* Col 1:20). The cosmic dimension of the redemptive action of Christ on the cross is brought out by the inclusion of *ta panta* ("all things") and *eite ta epi tēs gēs eite ta en tois ouranois* ("whether things on earth or in the heavenlies") in Colossians 1:20.

3.7.4. Ephesians 1:10. In Ephesians 1:9-10 the mystery of God's plan of salvation is described as preplanned in Christ and revealed in the fullness of time. The author of Ephesians then includes an unusual verb (*anakephalaiōsasthai*) to denote the ultimate goal of this plan as it is fulfilled in Christ. This verb carries with it a strongly eschatological note, as well as a cosmological one (it is *ta panta,* "all things," which is said to be "summed up" in Christ).

3.8. To Telos and To Teleios. The *telos* word group is used quite extensively within the Pauline letters, often with an eschatological meaning that is perhaps best interpreted in straightforward temporal terms. J. M. Court contends that this is part of the technical language

of apocalyptic that Paul adopts. Almost certainly a temporal sense of *to telos,* "finally," is intended in 1 Corinthians 15:24, where the noun is used to describe the conclusion of a sequence of eschatological events, including the Son's handing over of the kingdom to the Father (although some interpreters take *to telos* here as a noun). A related occurrence, again bearing a temporal sense, is 1 Corinthians 10:11, where Paul describes his Corinthian audience as those "upon whom the ends of the ages *(ta telē tōn aiōnōn)* have come." The noun *(to telos)* is also used in Romans 6:21-22 to denote the contrasting end results of sin (death) and grace (eternal life). *To telos* is used by Paul to communicate the time of ultimate judgment, as in Philippians 3:9, where the enemies of the cross of Christ are declared in Philippians 3:19 to have their end *(to telos)* in destruction. Similarly, in 2 Corinthians 11:15 the servants of Satan are also said to be heading for an appropriate end *(hōn to telos estai kata ta erga autōn);* and in 1 Thessalonians 2:16 the Judaizers are condemned as under judgment of the wrath of God which will come upon them "in the end" *(eis telos).* The term can also be used to denote the time of ultimate redemption, as in 1 Corinthians 1:8, where the Lord Jesus Christ is said to sustain the believing Christians "until the end" *(heōs telous).*

To telos can also carry the sense of "goal" or "destination," although it is difficult to separate this completely from the temporal sense just discussed. The most celebrated instance of this meaning is Romans 10:4, where the noun is used to describe the effect of Christ's coming upon the Jewish Law: "For Christ is the end *(telos)* of the Law, that every one who has faith may be justified." It may be that Paul is here reflecting the saying of Jesus recorded in Matthew 5:17, associating the end *(to telos)* with the idea of fulfillment of the Law *(plērōsas).* A similar use of *to telos* is found in 1 Timothy 1:5.

The neuter form *(to teleion)* of the adjective *teleios* is used as an abstract noun in 1 Corinthians 13:10, denoting "that which is perfect or completed" and thus sets up a contrast with the future eschatological age and the present imperfect world. The adjective *teleios* can also take the sense of "mature" or "adult" and is so used in 1 Corinthians 2:6; 14:20; Philippians 3:15. In Ephesians 4:13 and Colossians 1:28 the same term is applied anthropologically to the church and the believer respectively.

4. Pauline Eschatology and Christology.

The interface between Paul's eschatology and his christology is extensive, particularly as it concerns the role that Jesus Christ has as the executor of God's final judgment. Although Paul does not choose to use the title "Son of Man" (the most prevalent language in the Synoptic Gospels) to express this, he does nevertheless use equivalent ideas and images. Within the Pauline letters, OT theophanic traditions about the day of the Lord become invested with new meaning and are applied to the risen Lord Jesus Christ. This reemphasis generally builds upon a referential shift of "Lord" from God to Jesus Christ, or on the reapplication of "day of the Lord" passages to the messianic agent (see Kreitzer, 112-28, for a discussion of eleven key texts where this occurs).

The central feature of Paul's eschatology, the resurrection of Jesus Christ from the dead, is indisputably a theological declaration, as can be evidenced by the ways in which God is said to be active in Christ's resurrection. At several points within the Pauline letters, God the Father is explicitly said to be responsible for Jesus' resurrection (Rom 4:24; 10:9; 1 Cor 6:14; 15:15; 2 Cor 4:14; Gal 1:1; Eph 1:20; Col 2:12; 1 Thess 1:9-10). Once it is the God through his Spirit who accomplishes this (Rom 8:11); once it is the "Spirit of holiness" (Rom 1:4); and once it is the "glory of the Father" that raises Jesus (Rom 6:4). Other passages use an impersonal verb to denote the resurrection, generally taken to be a divine passive (Rom 4:25; 7:4; 1 Cor 15:4, 12, 20; 2 Cor 5:15; 2 Tim 2:8).

Yet Paul maintains a strong note of subordination of Jesus Christ to God the Father even in the midst of the most exalted christological passages. The two most important examples are 1 Corinthians 15:28c and Philippians 2:11c, lines that round off passages containing eschatological material.

One of the most intriguing features of Paul's eschatology (which anticipates the rise of the doctrine of the Trinity in the church) is the relationship between the risen Lord Jesus and the Holy Spirit. The Holy Spirit is described as "Christ's Spirit" (Rom 8:9; Phil 1:19) and the "Spirit of (God's) Son" (Gal 4:6). At the same time, in other passages the Holy Spirit is clearly "God's Spirit" (1 Cor 3:16; Phil 3:3; 1 Thess 4:8). The overlap between God and Christ (with reference to "the Spirit") is highlighted in 2 Corin-thians 3:17, a *crux interpretum* that it is possible to take in either direction.

5. Pauline Eschatology and Ethics.

It is sometimes suggested that an overemphasis on eschatological matters undermines the need for a strong ethical code for living in the present. Contrary to many popular assumptions about the detachment alleged to be inherent within eschatological teaching, Paul's letters demonstrate a close connection between eschatology and ethical exhortation. This is evident within the earliest of his letters, those written to the church at Thessalonica, where Paul confronts a misguided understanding about work that is based upon an erroneous view of the imminent return of Christ (see Kaye). Similarly, the ethical exhortations contained in Romans 12—13 are wholly conditioned by an eschatological perspective; the passage begins with an appeal that the believer not be "conformed to this world but be transformed by the renewal of your mind" (Rom 12:2) and concludes with an extended paragraph warning of the approaching day of Christ (Rom 13:11-14). The same observation can be made about 2 Corinthians 5:1-10, where the eschatological teaching about the implications of a Christian's death are interwoven with the exhortation to gain Christ's approval (1 Cor 5:9).

Indeed, it is possible to see the whole of Paul's ethical teaching as providing instruction about how the Christian is to live in the interval between the death and resurrection of Jesus Christ and his future parousia. In the evocative phrase of J. P. Sampey, Paul's moral teaching involves teaching the Christian about walking "between the times."

6. Pauline Eschatology and Jewish Mysticism.

We have already mentioned the horizontal (or spatial) dimension of eschatology (see 1 above). This feature of Paul's eschatological thought has received special treatment in recent years, particularly as it relates to the mystical traditions of Judaism. The so-called merkabah mysticism, influential within certain Jewish circles during the NT period, was built upon the opening vision of Ezekiel in which the prophet sees the throne chariot (*merkāba*) of God in heaven (Ezek 1:26-27). This mystical tradition is widespread within Judaism and has produced a separate subsection of literature that offers a comparative reference point for NT studies. The critical point with reference to Paul's letters comes in the supposed relationship between the apostle's apocalyptic eschatology and his mysticism, which manifested itself in ecstatic experiences. Some scholars have argued that the distinction between the two (apocalypticism and mysticism) is exceedingly fine, if not altogether artificial. A. F. Segal, for example, has recently argued that Jewish apocalypticism was mysticism in the way it was experienced and that it is proper to speak of Paul as an apocalyptic mystagogue. Crucial to Segal's argument is the contention that in terms of religious experience there is no distinction between apocalypticism and mysticism, despite the fact that the two are clearly distinct literary genres. Several key passages from the undisputed letters are appealed to in support of such an interpretation of Paul.

6.1. 2 Corinthians 12:1-10. Most scholars rightly feel that this curious passage is reflective of Paul's experience, although not necessarily his conversion/call on the Damascus Road (Acts 9:1-19; 22:1-21; 26:12-23). It is noted that he combines apocalyptic language with a denial of the validity of boasting (1 Cor 12:5-6) and a brief description of the tribulations he must suffer in fulfilling his role as the missionary to the Gentiles (1 Cor 12:7-10). He does begin this section by describing his experience as a revelation *(apokalypsis)* from the Lord (1 Cor 12:1).

6.2. 1 Corinthians 9:1. Paul bases a defense of his apostleship *(see* Apostle) on the fact that he has seen *(heoraka)* the Lord. The verb is usually taken to mean physical sight, but it is possible to interpret it as ecstatic insight given by means of revelation (similar descriptions of "seeing" the risen Lord occur in 2 Cor 4:4-6).

6.3. Galatians 1:11-17. Here, too, Paul employs the language of apocalyptic literature, choosing to describe his commissioning as an apostle coming to him via a revelation *(en emoi,* Gal 1:12) of Jesus Christ. Yet this revelation is not so much a revelation to Paul but a revelation in him (Gal 1:16) suggesting almost an incarnational understanding of the encounter with the risen Christ (cf. Gal 2:20; 6:4). Such highly personalized language could be taken as expressing the mystical and ecstatic experience of the visionary mind, as Segal suggests. However, it is doubtful if that is the way Paul perceived his encounter with Jesus Christ; he associates his sight of the risen Lord alongside the postresurrection

appearances found in early Christian tradition (1 Cor 15:5-7), firmly basing them in objective history and not subjective imagination. His use of the aorist passive verb *ōphthē* supports this (1 Cor 15:5, 6, 7, 8; cf. 1 Tim 3:16).

6.4 Apocalypticism, Mysticism and Christology. That apocalypticism and mysticism share the common ground of religious experience seems evident; there is much insight that can be gained into one aspect of Paul's eschatological thought as a result of a comparison of the two. However, too much can be made in straightforwardly equating them, not least the seeming evacuation of Paul's eschatology of any future significance. It is not only the way that the encounter of the risen Lord Jesus is communicated to Paul that is important to him; this is merely the form of the experience. Of at least equal importance is the content of that experience; who is revealed (not only how) is of crucial concern for Paul. As a result, perhaps the most helpful contribution that the Jewish mystical tradition has to offer to a study of Paul's eschatology is the fact that it helps provide a context in which Pauline christology can develop. There is much to suggest that the most enduring feature arising from the overlap between apocalypticism and mysticism is the importance of the theme of revealed "glory" (Heb *kābôd*) inherent within them (see Newman for a recent study of this and a critique of Segal's thesis). When applied to christological considerations, this allows the shift from a theocentric to an anthropocentric fulfillment to take place. In other words, the common ground of apocalyptic and mysticism within Judaism allows Paul and others to see the risen Lord Jesus Christ as the agent of the fulfillment of God's eschatological purposes. The future revelation of Jesus Christ is, in Paul's words, closely connected with the manifestation of the glory of God (1 Cor 3:18; 4:4, 6).

7. Social Dynamics in Paul's Eschatological Teaching.

Considerable understanding into Paul's letters has been gained in recent years by applying the insights gained through sociological approaches to the documents. This has also held true with respect to his eschatological teaching, especially when it is used to assess what W. A. Meeks has described as the "millenarian beliefs" of the congregations to which Paul responds. D. W. Kuck has carried the investigation a step further, examining the place that the judgment theme has within Paul's Corinthian correspondence and making some important observations about how such a futuristic eschatology functioned socially within the congregation.

Much work is yet to be done on this issue, particularly as it will help explain how eschatological ideas influenced and perhaps even determined the beliefs and practices of the congregations. Recognition of the social dimension of eschatological beliefs also enables us to discover the enduring relevance of Paul's teaching and begin to apply it to our own contemporary problems, as M. E. Glasswell points out. This is nowhere more acute for the contemporary situation than in the areas of human sexuality (matters involving sexual identity and role) and creation (matters involving ecology and the created order). In both instances eschatological perspectives can dictate the interpretations accepted for these passages and the practices adopted by the Christian church in expressing them.

7.1. Galatians 3:27-28. In recent years this has become one of the most debated passages within the whole of the Pauline corpus, largely because of the implications it has for social conventions. The pericope opens with a declaration about the believing community as having been "baptized into Christ" and having "clothed yourselves with Christ," two images that are powerful symbols of a resurrection theology in Paul. In Galatians 3:28 Paul goes on to assert that unity in Christ transcends various human barriers: ethnic (Jew/Greek), economic (slave/free) and sexual (male/female).

Many interpreters would argue that the focus of the passage is on the means of entry into the community of faith and that there is no difference between male and female on that point. But what does the passage imply about Paul's eschatological understanding of male-female relationships? Is Paul giving a programmatic statement about how human relationships should be conducted in the present, a manifesto for social activism? Or is he caught up in the enthusiasm of the moment and providing us with a visionary's glimpse of what the future ultimately will be like when Christ comes at the parousia to bring everything to its accomplishment? If so, what impact might this have on the way that women are often assigned lower places of value and service in modern societies? Does not Paul

challenge us with, in the enticing phrase of Scroggs, "the eschatological woman," whose place in society must be reassessed if we are to remain true to Paul's eschatological vision?

The visionary interpretation has been pursued by many interpreters, particularly as it does not necessarily demand that equality of role between men and women in the present order is what Paul intends. On the other hand, it is difficult to restrict the force of Galatians 3:27-28 to the future and not recognize its relevance for the present. The social implications (e.g., the role and ordination of women) are wide-ranging. No doubt Galatians 3:27-28 will continue to be a major focal point for contemporary theology (see MacDonald).

7.2. Romans 8:19-23. In these few short verses we have the most extensive discussion within the Pauline corpus about the future of the created order. As we mentioned above (see 3.7 above), the primary focus of the passage is to illustrate God's ultimate redemption of his children (Rom 8:23). Nevertheless, there clearly is an indication of God's concern for the created order (*see* Creation, New Creation), despite the fact that it has been tainted and suffers under the effects of Adam's disobedience (Gen 3 underlies the whole passage). God's concern that creation is worthy of being transformed and set free should inform our attitudes toward it. Thus it is possible to integrate fully a protectionist stance toward creation and the environment within Paul's eschatological perspective. Indeed, it could be argued that to do so is to demonstrate our continuing revelation as the children of God (Rom 8:19).

In conclusion, it is clear that Paul's thought is thoroughly conditioned by an eschatological perspective in which Jesus Christ's death and resurrection are seen in some way to inaugurate the long-awaited age to come. Virtually every letter within the Pauline corpus reflects, to a greater or lesser degree, this eschatological viewpoint. Many of the key areas of Pauline teaching, such as ethics, christology and ecclesiology, share as common ground this eschatological perspective. All of this helps to make Pauline eschatology one of the main arenas of modern scholarly debate.

See also ADAM AND CHRIST; APOCALYPTICISM; COVENANT, NEW COVENANT; CREATION, NEW CREATION; DEATH OF CHRIST; JUDGMENT; JUSTIFICATION; KINGDOM OF GOD; RESURRECTION.

DPL: DYING AND RISING WITH CHRIST; ETHICS; EXALTATION AND ENTHRONEMENT; FIRSTFRUITS, DOWN PAYMENT; GLORY, GLORIFICATION; HEAVEN, HEAVENLIES, PARADISE; HOPE; IMMORTALITY; INTERMEDIATE STATE; LIFE AND DEATH; MAN OF LAWLESSNESS AND RESTRAINING POWER; MYSTERY; MYSTICISM; PEACE, RECONCILIATION; RESTORATION OF ISRAEL; REWARDS; SALVATION; TRIUMPH; UNIVERSALISM; WRATH, DESTRUCTION.

BIBLIOGRAPHY. P. J. Achtemeier, "An Apocalyptic Shift in Early Christian Tradition: Reflections on Some Canonical Evidence," *CBQ* 45 (1983) 231-48; D. C. Allison, *The End of the Ages Has Come* (Philadelphia: Fortress, 1987); D. E. Aune, "(Early Christian) Eschatology," *ABD* 2:594-609; idem, "The Significance of the Delay of the Parousia for Early Christianity," in *Current Issues in Biblical and Patristic Interpretation*, ed. G. F. Hawthorne (Grand Rapids: Eerdmans, 1975) 87-109; R. D. Aus, "God's Plan and God's Power: Isaiah 66 and the Restraining Factors of 2 Thess 2:6-7," *JBL* 96 (1977) 537-53; W. Baird, "Pauline Eschatology in Hermeneutical Perspective," *NTS* 17 (1970-71) 314-27; M. Barker, "Slippery Words: Apocalyptic," *ExpT* 89 (1977-1978) 324-29; R. J. Bauckham, "The Delay of the Parousia," *TynB* 31 (1980) 3-36; J. C. Beker, *Heirs of Paul: Paul's Legacy in the New Testament and in the Church Today* (Minneapolis: Fortress, 1991); idem, *Paul the Apostle: The Triumph of God in Life and Thought* (Philadelphia: Fortress, 1980, 2d ed. 1984); idem, *Paul's Apocalyptic Gospel: The Coming Triumph of God* (Philadelphia: Fortress, 1982); idem, "Recasting Pauline Theology: The Coherence-Contingency Scheme as Interpretative Model," in *Pauline Theology*, vol. 1, *Thessalonians, Philippians, Galatians, Philemon*, ed. J. M. Bassler (Minneapolis: Fortress, 1991) 15-24; idem, *The Triumph of God: The Essence of Paul's Thought* (Minneapolis: Fortress, 1990); M. C. de Boer, *The Defeat of Death* (JSNTSup 22; Sheffield: Academic, 1988); idem, "Paul and Jewish Apocalyptic Eschatology," in *Apocalyptic and the New Testament: Essays in Honor of J. Louis Martyn*, ed. J. Marcus and M. L. Soards (JSNTSup 24; Sheffield: Academic, 1989) 169-90; G. Bornkamm, *Paul* (New York: Harper & Row, 1969); V. P. Branick, "Apocalyptic Paul?" *CBQ* 47 (1985) 664-75; F. F. Bruce, *Paul: Apostle of the Heart Set Free* (Grand Rapids: Eerdmans, 1977) 300-13; G. B. Caird, *The Language and Imagery of the Bible* (Philadelphia: Westminster, 1980) 201-71; W. Carr, *Angels and Principalities* (SNTSMS 42; Cambridge: Cambridge University Press, 1981); J. J. Collins, ed., *Apocalypse: The Morphology of a Genre*, Semeia 14 (Missoula, MT: Scholars Press, 1979); J. M. Court, "Paul and the Apocalyptic Pattern," in *Paul and Paulinism: Essays in Honor of C. K. Barrett*, ed. M. D. Hooker and S. G. Wilson (London: SPCK, 1982) 57-66; O. Cullmann, "Le caractère eschatologique du devoir missionnaire et de la conscience apostolique de saint Paul. Étude sur le katevcon (-wn) de 2 Thess. 2:6-7," *RHPR* 16 (1936) 210-45; W. D. Davies, *Paul and Rabbinic Judaism* (4th ed.; Philadelphia: Fortress, 1980); J. W. Drane, "Theological Diversity in the Letters of St. Paul," *TynB* 27 (1976) 3-26; E. E. Ellis, "2 Corinthians 5:1-10 in Pauline Eschatology," *NTS* 6 (1959-60) 211-24; A. J. Everson, "Day of the Lord," *IDBSup* 209-10; J. G. Gibbs, *Creation and Redemption: A Study in Paul's Theology* (NovTSup 26; Leiden: E. J. Brill, 1971); J. Gillmann, "A Thematic Comparison: 1 Cor 15:50-57 and 2 Cor 5:1-5," *JBL* 107 (1988) 439-54; M. E. Glasswell, "Some Issues of Church and Society in the Light of Paul's Eschatology," in *Paul and Paulinism: Essays in Honor of C. K. Barrett*, ed. M. D. Hooker and S. G. Wilson (London: SPCK, 1982) 310-19; M. J. Harris, *Raised Immortal: The Relation Between Resurrection and Immortality in New Testament Teaching* (Grand Rapids: Eerdmans, 1983); J. C. Hurd, *The Origin of 1 Corinthians* (2d ed.; Macon, GA: Mercer University Press, 1983); E. Käsemann, "The Beginnings of Christian Theology," in *New Testament Questions of Today* (Philadelphia: Fortress, 1969) 82-107; idem, "On the Subject of Primitive Christian Apocalyptic," in *New Testament Questions of Today* (Philadelphia: Fortress, 1969) 108-37; B. N. Kaye, "Eschatology and Ethics in 1 and 2 Thessalonians," *NovT* 17 (1975) 47-57; L. Keck, "Paul and Apocalyptic Theology," *Int* 38 (1984) 229-41; S. Kim, *The Origin of Paul's Gospel* (Grand Rapids: Eerdmans, 1982); B. Klappert, "King, Kingdom," *NIDNTT* 2:372-90; A. J. F. Klijn, "1 Thessalonians 4.13-18 and Its Background in Apocalyptic Literature," in *Paul and Paulinism: Essays in Honor of C. K. Barrett*, ed. M. D. Hooker and S. G. Wilson (London: SPCK, 1982) 67-73; L. J. Kreitzer, *Jesus and God in Paul's Eschatology* (JSNTS 19; Sheffield: JSOT, 1987); D. W. Kuck, *Judgment and Community Conflict: Paul's Use of Apocalyptic Judgment Language in 1 Corinthians 3:5—4:5* (NovTSup 66; Leiden: E. J. Brill, 1992); J. R. Levison, "2 Apoc. Bar. 48:42—52:7 and the Apocalyptic Dimension of Colossians 3:1-6," *JBL* 108 (1989) 93-108; A. T. Lincoln, *Paradise Now and Not Yet* (SNTSMS 43; Cambridge: Cambridge University Press, 1981); D. R. MacDonald, *There Is No Male and Female* (HDR 20; Philadelphia: Fortress, 1987); I. H. Marshall, "Is Apocalyptic the Mother of Christian Theology?" in *Tradition and Interpretation in the New Testament,* ed. G. F. Hawthorne with O. Betz (Tübingen: Mohr Siebeck; Grand Rapids: Eerdmans, 1987) 33-42; idem, "Slippery Words: Eschatology," *ExpT* 89 (1977-78) 264-69; R. P. Martin, *The Spirit and the Congregation* (Grand Rapids: Eerdmans, 1984); J. L. Martyn, "Apocalyptic Antinomies in the Letter to the Galatians," *NTS* 31 (1985) 410-24; C. L. Mearns, "Early Eschatological Development in Paul: The Evidence of 1 and 2 Thessalonians," *NTS* 27 (1981) 137-57; W. A. Meeks, "Social Functions of Apocalyptic Language in Pauline Christianity," in *Apocalypticism in the Mediterranean World and the Near East,* ed. D. Hellholm (Tübingen: Mohr Siebeck, 1983) 687-705; J. Moiser, "A Reassessment of Paul's View of Marriage with Reference to 1 Cor. 7," *JSNT* 18 (1983) 103-22; C. F. D. Moule, "The Influence of Circumstances on the Use of Eschatological Terms," *JTS* 15 (1964) 1-15; R. H. Mounce, "Pauline Eschatology and the Apocalypse," *EvQ* 46 (1974) 164-66; J. Munck, *Paul and the Salvation of Mankind* (Atlanta: John Knox, 1977); C. C. Newman, *Paul's Glory-Christology: Tradition and Rhetoric* (NovT-Sup 69; Leiden: E. J. Brill, 1992); idem, "Transforming Images of Paul: A Review Essay of Alan Segal, *Paul the Convert,*" *EvQ* 64 (1992) 61-74; H. Ridderbos, *Paul: An Outline of His Theology* (Grand Rapids: Eerdmans, 1975); C. C. Rowland, *The Open Heaven: A Study of Apocalyptic in Judaism and Early Christianity* (New York: Crossroad, 1982); J. P. Sampey, *Walking Between the Times* (Philadelphia: Fortress, 1991); R. Schippers, "Goal, Last, End, Near, Complete," *NIDNTT* 2:52-66; H. J. Schoeps, *Paul: The Theology of the Apostle in the Light of Jewish Religious History* (Philadelphia: Westminster, 1961); A. Schweitzer, *The Mysticism of Paul the Apostle* (London: Adam & Charles Black, 1931); R. Scroggs, *The Last Adam* (Oxford: Basil Blackwell, 1966); idem, "Paul and the Eschatological Woman," *JAAR* 40 (1972) 283-303; A. F. Segal, *Paul the Convert* (New Haven, CT: Yale University Press, 1990); R. E. Sturm, "Defining the Word 'Apocalyptic': A Problem in Biblical Criticism," in *Apocalyptic and the New Testament: Essays in Honor of J. Louis Martyn,* ed.

J. Marcus and M. L. Soards (JSNTS 19; Sheffield: Academic, 1989) 17-48; A. C. Thistleton, "Realized Eschatology at Corinth," *NTS* 24 (1978) 510-24; S. H. Travis, *Christ and the Judgment of God* (Grand Rapids: Zondervan, 1987) 31-124; G. Vos, *The Pauline Eschatology* (Princeton, NJ: Princeton University Press, 1930); A. J. M. Wedderburn, "The Problem of the Denial of Resurrection in 1 Corinthians 15," *NovT* 23 (1981) 229-41; D. E. H. Whiteley, *The Theology of St. Paul* (Philadelphia: Fortress, 1966); W. Wink, *Naming the Powers* (Philadelphia: Fortress, 1984); idem, *Unmasking the Powers* (Philadelphia: Fortress, 1986); B. Witherington III, *Jesus, Paul and the End of the World* (Downers Grove, IL: InterVarsity Press, 1992); N. T. Wright, "Putting Paul Together Again," in *Pauline Theology,* vol. 1, *Thessalonians, Philippians, Galatians, Philemon,* ed. J. M. Bassler (Minneapolis: Fortress, 1991) 183-211.   L. J. Kreitzer

ESCHATOLOGY III: ACTS, HEBREWS, GENERAL EPISTLES, REVELATION

In order to understand NT theology it is necessary to grasp how the NT authors viewed eschatology, or the "end times" (see Marshall 1978 "Slippery Words"). For them the end times were not a period coming only at the final phase of history. This can be illustrated by the phrase "latter days" or similar expressions, which occur numerous times in the NT and do not often refer exclusively to the end of history as we think of it. The expression "latter days" typically describes the end times as beginning in the events associated with the life, death and resurrection of Jesus Christ (*see* Death of Christ).

    1. Background
    2. Eschatology of Acts, Hebrews, the General Epistles and Revelation
    3. Special Problems of Eschatology in Revelation

1. Background.

1.1. Eschatology of the Old Testament. NT phrases such as "latter days" allude to or echo phrases in the OT, where this wording appears in prophetic contexts referring to a future series of events. (1) Israel will undergo tribulation consisting of exile (Jer 23:20; cf. Jer 30:24), subsequent oppression (Ezek 38:14-17), persecution (Dan 10:14; 11:27—12:10), false teaching, deception and apostasy (Dan 10:14ff.; 11:27-35). (2) After the tribulation Israel will seek the Lord (Hos 3:4-5) and will be delivered (Ezek 38:14-16; Dan 10:14; 12:1-13) while their enemies will be judged (Ezek 38:14-16; Dan 10:14; 11:40-45; 12:2). (3) This deliverance and judgment will occur because a leader (Messiah) from Israel will finally conquer all of its Gentile enemies (Gen 49:1, 8-12; Num 24:14-19; Is 2:2-4; Mic 4:1-3; Dan 2:28-45; 10:14—12:10). (4) The saints of Israel will be raised from the dead (Dan 12:2). (5) God will establish a new covenant with Israel (cf. Jer 31:31-34 with Jer 30:24). (6) God will establish a kingdom on the earth and rule over it (Is 2:2-4; Dan 2:28-45; Mic 4:1-3) together with a Davidic king (Hos 3:4-5). (7) Some of Israel's Gentile enemies will experience deliverance during these eschatological days (Jer 47—48; 49:39; cf. Is 19:19-25).

The OT does not always employ the technical terminology of "latter days" when it addresses eschatological themes. For example, Isaiah's prophecy of the new creation is overtly eschatological, but no eschatological formula introduces the prophecy (cf. Is 65:17; 66:22). Joel's prophecy of the Holy Spirit is introduced by "after this" (for further discussion of OT eschatology, see Pryor, Gowan).

1.2. Eschatology of Judaism. The writings of intertestamental Judaism express a hope in and an expectation of God's bringing history to consummation through a final, great tribulation (on which see Allison, 5-25), followed by judgment of the wicked and salvation of the faithful. Jewish apocalyptic literature usually views the end as imminent, though there are examples of something approaching an "inaugurated eschatology" (see Lincoln 1981, 177-78). The notion that the latter days have begun to be fulfilled on earth is found in the Dead Sea Scrolls of Qumran (see Carmignac; for further discussion of eschatology in postbiblical Jewish literature, see Howard).

1.3. Eschatology of the Gospels and Paul. The NT repeatedly uses the phrase "latter days" precisely as it is found in the OT prophecies. The meaning of the phrase is identical to that of the OT except that in the NT the end days are seen as beginning their fulfillment in Christ's first coming. All that the OT spoke of occurring in the end times has begun in the first century and continues until the final coming of Christ. The OT expectations of the great tribulation, God's domination of the Gentiles, deliverance of Israel from oppressors, Israel's resurrection, the new covenant, the new creation and the establishment of God's kingdom (*see* Kingdom of God) have been set in motion by Christ's death and resurrection and in the emergence of the Christian church. Christ's first coming marked the beginning of his messianic reign, which was underscored by the presence of the Holy Spirit in his ministry (e.g., at his baptism [Mt 3:13-17] and in the casting out of demons [Mt 12:22-32]). The resurrection marked a heightened level of Jesus' inaugurated reign. Persecution of Jesus and his followers indicated the beginning of the final tribulation. What the OT did not foresee so clearly was that the kingdom and the tribulation could coexist simultaneously (e.g., Rev 1:6-9). Thus for the NT the latter days do not take place only at a point in the future but occur throughout the church age.

Paul says that the OT was written to instruct Christians about how to live in the end times, since upon them "the ends of the ages have come" (1 Cor 10:11). He refers to Jesus' birth as occurring "when the fullness of the time came" in fulfillment of the messianic prophecies (Gal 4:4). Likewise, "the fullness of the times" alludes to when believers were delivered from Satan and sin through Christ's death and resurrection (Eph 1:7-10; 1:20—2:6), which commenced his rule over the created order (Eph 1:19-23). Christ's death and resurrection launched the beginning of the latter-day new creation prophesied by Isaiah (cf. 2 Cor 5:17 with Is 43; 65-66). The end-time prophecies of Israel's restoration from exile begin to find fulfillment in Christ's, the true Israel's, resurrection and in believers who identify by faith with him (e.g., 2 Cor 6:16-18; see Beale 1989). Tribulation in the form of false teaching is also one of the signs that the latter days had arrived (1 Tim 4; 2 Tim 3:1-9). Since 1 Timothy and 2 Timothy speak of the Ephesian church as already experiencing this tribulation of deceptive teaching and apostasy (see 1 Tim 1:3-4, 6, 7, 19-20; 4:7; 5:13-15; 6:20-21; 2 Tim 1:15; 2:16-19; 2:25-26; 3:2-9), it is evident that a distant, future time is not in view.

Other NT texts speak of the future consummation of the latter days. Many eschatological events will not be fulfilled until Christ returns, including the bodily resurrection of all people, the destruction of the present cosmos, the creation of a new heaven and earth, and the final judgment.

Until this consummation, Christ's followers

experience only a part of the eschatological blessings that will be fulfilled in the new heaven and earth. This is the already/not yet dimension of NT eschatology. O. Cullmann has described this tension by using the World War II analogy of D-day and V-Day. Jesus' first coming (the "already") is D-Day, since it marks the battle in which Satan is decisively defeated. The second coming of Christ is V-Day, when Jesus' enemies will surrender and bow down to him. (See Moule 1964; Lincoln 1981, 181-84, on how NT authors developed aspects of eschatological thought in response to a variety of situations. For further discussion of already/not yet, *see* Eschatology I and II. See also Allison; Caird 1980, 241-71; Hoekema; Ladd; Pate; Vos.)

2. Eschatology of Acts, Hebrews, the General Epistles and Revelation.

The eschatological pattern found in the Gospels and Paul is also found in the rest of the NT literature. The discussion of eschatology in this literature may be organized under the headings of "past and present" (the already) and "future" (the not yet).

2.1. Acts.

2.1.1. Past and Present. In Acts 2:17, the first place the words "last days" appear in the canonically ordered NT literature, Peter understands that the tongues being spoken at Pentecost begin to fulfill Joel's prophecy that a day would come when God's Spirit would gift not merely prophets, priests and kings but all of God's people (Acts 2:15-17; cf. Joel 2:28). The resurrection marked the beginning of Jesus' messianic reign, and the giving of the Holy Spirit signaled the inauguration of his rule through the church (Acts 1:6-8; 2:1-43). Subsequent outpourings of the Spirit mark significant transitional points in Acts, where the gospel is extended to new regions or ethnic groups. These later outpourings demonstrate Christ's exalted reign, and that Gentiles as well as Jews are included by their faith as subjects in the Messiah's new kingdom. This is implied in Acts 2, where we read that Jews representing all parts of the known Gentile world were present at Pentecost. The clearest example of a subsequent outpouring of the Spirit modeled on Pentecost is Acts 10:34-47, where the Roman soldier Cornelius and his Gentile associates believed in Christ.

Some scholars have identified in Acts a de-eschatologizing perspective in which a history

of the church is substituted for a near expectation of the end (see, e.g., Sabourin). But Luke sees the outpouring of the Spirit as a further stage of eschatological fulfillment, which makes the time of the church an eschatological era (for both sides of the debate see Gaventa).

In the OT (see 1.1 above) and Judaism, as well as elsewhere in the NT (e.g., Rom 1:3-4, 1 Tim 3:16), the Spirit was linked with the hope of resurrection life. As a consequence of Jesus' resurrection, the eschatological center of gravity had shifted from Jesus' ministry on earth to his reign in heaven. The notion that Jesus had been raised from the dead was charged with eschatological significance, with roots in the OT (Is 25:7-8; 26:18-19; Ezek 37:1-14; Dan 12:1-2) and postbiblical Judaism (e.g., 2 Macc 7:9, 14; 1QH 11.12; *1 Enoch* 51:1; *2 Apoc. Bar.* 30:1-3; 50:1-4; *T. Judah* 25:1; *Adam and Eve* [Apoc.] 41:3). In Acts other references to Jesus' resurrection, though they are not formally linked with eschatological terminology (as in Acts 2), are still eschatological in nature, especially since they are often associated with OT hopes and promises (see Acts 1:3-11, 22; 3:15, 26; 4:2, 10, 33; 5:30-31; 7:55-56; 9:3-6; 10:40-41; 13:30-37; 17:31-32; 22:6-11; 25:19; 26:6-18, 22-23). Likewise, the resurrection of some Christians was probably viewed as the corollary of Jesus' eschatological resurrection (Acts 9:37-41; 20:9-12; cf. Mt 27:52-53).

The fulfillment of other latter-day OT prophecies was an indication that the last times had begun (Acts 3:18, 22-26; 4:25-28; 13:27-29, 46-48; 15:14-18; 26:22-23). Possibly even the mention of entering the kingdom of God after enduring tribulation is an allusion not merely to an event at the end of history but also to the inaugurated messianic, heavenly realm that one enters at death (Acts 14:22; cf. Stephen's vision, just prior to his death, of Christ as the presently reigning "Son of Man" [Acts 7:55-56]).

The idea of a new creation is arguably the best encompassing term for the eschatology of Acts and the NT as a whole, for it ties together all the various thematic strands linked to NT eschatology. For example, the resurrection is an act of new creation (the creation of new life) that is brought about by the life-giving agency of the Spirit. Even the healings in Acts (Acts 3:1-16; 5:16; 9:33-34; 14:8-11; 19:11-12) and in the Gospels are best understood within the larger redemptive framework of new creation wherein the curses of the fallen creation begin to be reversed.

2.1.2. Future. In Acts 1:6 the disciples ask the resurrected Jesus if it is "at this time that you are restoring the kingdom to Israel." Jesus replies that "it is not for you to know times or epochs which the Father has fixed by his own authority" (Acts 1:7). He then promises (Acts 1:8) that the Spirit will come upon them and will empower them to witness. Some commentators understand Acts 1:7-8 to mean that there will be an indefinite delay of the coming of Israel's restored kingdom in its consummated form but that during the interim period the Spirit will maintain the witness of Jesus' followers (see Buzzard). Accordingly, the restoration of the kingdom is equated with the time of Jesus' second coming to conclude history (Acts 1:11). From this point of view, Acts 3:19-21 continues the theme of the future kingdom, with the "times of refreshing" and the "times of restoration of all things" occurring when Jesus returns to conclude history, apparently in the same way as he left at the ascension (Acts 1:11).

Another interpretation of Acts 1:6-8 is plausible, if not more probable. In Acts 1:7-8 Jesus responds to three misunderstandings inherent in the apostles' question (Acts 1:6). First, Acts 1:7 is a response to their mistaken assumption that it was proper for them to know the precise time (cf. 1 Thess 5:1-3) when the kingdom would be restored to Israel. Such knowledge is reserved for the Father alone.

Second, Acts 1:8 appears to be a response to an implicit assumption that future stages of the kingdom would be exclusively physical in expression. Although some interpreters understand Acts 1:8 to refer to a parenthetical period characterized by the Spirit, rather than a part of the messianic kingdom, it is more likely that the verse asserts that a future form of the kingdom is to be "spiritual" in nature ("you will receive power [of the kingdom] when the Holy *Spirit* has come"). This promise begins its fulfillment at Pentecost, which Peter understands to be an escalation of the "latter days" inaugurated when Jesus received the Spirit at his baptism. In the OT and Judaism "the latter days" was the time of the expected outpouring of God's Spirit; the OT inextricably links the "latter days" with the prophesied kingdom, so that Peter's reference to the "latter days" in Acts 2:17 alludes to the fulfillment of the foreseen kingdom (e.g., see the OT references in 1.1 above).

Third, Acts 1:8 appears to be a reply to an apparent ethnocentric presupposition expressed by the disciples: that the nature of the kingdom would be Israelite. Jesus' reply is that the kingdom would encompass subjects who lived even "unto to the end of the earth" (in partial allusion to Is 49:6; cf. Acts 13:47, which refers to the conclusion of Acts 1:8 and where the OT reference is explicit). Hence Acts 1:8 affirms an ongoing, progressive and nonconsummative fulfillment of the prophecy of the OT kingdom, which had already begun to be established in Jesus' earthly ministry (see Hill, though he denies that Luke has an inaugurated eschatological perspective; see Bruce for a balanced view of Acts 1:6-8 and of eschatology in Acts).

Acts 3:20-21 refers to a future consummation when Christ comes and achieves "the restoration of all things." Acts 3:19, however, may include an already and not yet notion, especially because of its placement directly following an assertion that God had already fulfilled the OT prophecy of Christ's suffering: "Repent therefore and return, that your sins may be wiped away, in order that times of refreshing may come from the presence of the Lord" (which may be parallel to Acts 2:38: "Repent, and . . . be baptized . . . for the forgiveness of your sins, and you will receive the gift of the Holy Spirit"). Likewise, Acts 3:22-26 refers to beginning fulfillments of OT messianic prophecy (for further argument in support of this analysis, see Kurz and sources cited; see also Bayer). Even the reference "until the times of restoration of all things" in Acts 3:21 has an already and not yet element, since the restoration had likely begun with Jesus' coming, resurrection and giving of the Spirit (Bayer).

An incontestably future reference to judgment is found in Acts 17:30-31, where Paul affirms that people should repent in the present because God has determined a specific day at the end of history when "he will judge the world in righteousness" through Jesus Christ (also Acts 24:25).

Paul also affirms a "hope of the promise" of the final resurrection for the nation Israel in Acts 26:6-7. Yet even this has been inaugurated when Christ, the true Israel, was resurrected from the dead, as is clear from Acts 13:32-33; 23:6-7; 26:22-24. (On futurist aspects of eschatology in Acts, see Nielsen; on the already and not yet, see Cadbury; Carroll, 121-67; Giles; Francis; Franklin; Gaventa; Smith; cf. also Mattill.)

2.2. Hebrews.

2.2.1. Past and Present.
In the opening sentence of Hebrews we read that God "in these last days has spoken to us in his son, whom he appointed heir of all things" (Heb 1:2). As with the Gospels, Acts and Paul, Christ's first coming commences the beginning of the end times. In this vein Hebrews 1:5-13 cites OT texts primarily concerning the messianic son's kingship which have begun their fulfillment in Jesus' first advent (see also Heb 5:5; 8:1; 10:12-13; 12:2). Likewise, the ideal Adam's reign as "the Son of man" portrayed in Psalm 8, never completely realized in the OT period, is applied to Christ as the one who has started to fill the shoes of this exemplary human figure (Heb 2:6-9). Christ has done what the first Adam and Israel, the corporate Adam, failed to achieve (for the notion of Israel as a corporate Adam, see Wright, 21-26). In this sense of Christ's "fulfillment" of end-time prophecy, he is a "son" who was "made [eschatologically] complete" (teleioō) and who has begun to lead and will finish leading his people to their eschatologically completed salvation (see also Heb 2:10; 5:8-9, 14; 6:1; 7:11, 19, 28; 9:9; 10:1, 14; 11:40; 12:2; see, e.g., Silva).

The work of Christ is viewed as eschatological fulfillment. Christ has decisively defeated the power of the devil and of death (Heb 2:14), a reality not expected to occur until the eschatological new creation. And Christ's mission "to put away sin by the sacrifice of himself" is an event taking place at the "consummation of the ages" (Heb 9:26; cf. Heb 10:10, 12, 14). Thus Jeremiah's prophecy of a new covenant is beginning to be fulfilled, a point underscored as Hebrews quotes Jeremiah 31:31-34 with the concluding words, "I will be merciful to their iniquities, and their sin I will remember no more" (Heb 8:8-12; cf. Heb 10:16-17). The eschatological tone of Hebrews 9:26 is true to the setting of Jeremiah's prophecy of a new covenant, which was inextricably linked to latter-day events (cf. Jer. 30:24; 31:31, 33). Finally, the author of Hebrews mentions another hallmark of the arrival of the last age, the resurrection of Christ (Heb 13:20).

Jesus' followers have also "tasted the powers of the age to come" (Heb 6:5), among which is "the heavenly gift . . . of the Holy Spirit" (Heb 6:4; cf. Ellingworth, 320). This is the closest the NT comes to formally identifying the Holy Spirit as a mark of the inbreaking eschatological age (though cf. Rom 8:23; Eph 1:13-14). The Chris-

tians' hope of a future, consummated salvation is rooted in Christ's having already begun to realize that hope (Heb 6:17-20; see Robinson). Christians have already "come to Mount Zion and to the city of the living God, the heavenly city" (the new Jerusalem; cf. Heb 12:22); the latter-day city of God has invisibly invaded the present age so that saints might participate in its life. In a related image, Hebrews speaks of Christ's priestly work of sacrificing himself as inaugurating the eschatological temple (Heb 9:8, 23; see Hurst). Those who spurn Christ's "once for all" sacrifice at the "consummation of the ages" (Heb 9:26) are not able to be "renewed to repentance," since no other sacrifice will be offered other than the one they have despised (Heb 6:4-6; 10:26-29; see Carlston).

The two-dimensional nature of Hebrews's eschatology, though it is found elsewhere in the NT (e.g., Ephesians), is striking: a vertical, or spatial, dimension is developed in addition to a horizontal, or temporal, dimension. The preceding discussion has focused on the temporal aspect. Yet from a spatial perspective, the end-time temple, for example, is viewed as a reality in present time and as having a spatial dimension other than that of the material, earthly dimension (Heb 9:1—10:26).

2.2. Future.
In Hebrews 3—4 there are repeated references to a "rest" that believers may "enter." Interpreters debate whether this "rest" has been inaugurated with Christ's first coming (so Barrett, 366-73; Lincoln 1982) or will transpire at the final consummation (Gaffin). Both views are supported by viable arguments, though the futuristic view is perhaps more likely. The emphasis throughout Hebrews 3—4, as well as the entire epistle, is upon persevering until the end when the final reward is to be received (Heb 3:6, 14). Furthermore, the "rest" is referred to as "a promise" that "remains," one that has not yet been fulfilled (Heb 4:1, 6, 9). While it is true that the "rest" is spoken of as being present (Heb 4:3) and even past (Heb 4:10), these expressions are best understood as being spoken from a future vantage point (e.g., Heb 4:10 can be understood in the sense of a Hebrew prophetic perfect, referring to the certainty of a future event by speaking of it as if it had already happened). The dominant theme of Hebrews 3—4 is that, in contrast with Israel's failure to enter the "rest" of the promised land after its wilderness sojourn, the Hebrew Christians are exhorted to persevere in

their earthly sojourn so that they will enter the "rest" of the "heavenly country" (Heb 11:16), which the land of Canaan typologically foreshadowed. Only then will the intended sabbath rest of the new creation be enjoyed.

The coming judgment of unbelievers and apostates at the end of the age is a repeated theme in Hebrews (Heb 6:2; 9:27), especially as a warning and an encouragement to persevere (Heb 10:27-31, 36-38; 12:25-29; 13:4; cf. Toussaint). Those who heed the warnings of judgment and the exhortations to persevere will receive at the consummation of history full salvation (Heb 9:28), their reward (Heb 10:35; 11:26) and the complete inheritance that was promised (Heb 6:11-12, 17-18; 9:15; 10:23, 34-35; 11:39). The inheritance of the promised land of the new earth is the author's irreducible summary of what true believers will receive at the eschaton (Heb 11:9-16; 13:14). God will raise them from the dead in order that they might participate in the inheritance (Heb 11:35; cf. Heb 6:20). This final inheritance will be indestructible (Heb 12:27-28) and eternal. There God's presence can be more fully experienced (cf. Heb 12:14). The readers should not be lax about these exhortations, because the final "day" is "near" (Heb 10:25; for further discussion see Barrett, MacRae, Woods).

2.3. General Epistles.

2.3.1. Past and Present. James 1:18 speaks of the incipient emergence of the new creation. Later, James alludes to the true nature of the time in which his audience is living as he chastises people for living in ungodly ways and not redeeming opportunities for doing righteousness: "It is in the last days that you have stored up your treasure" (Jas 5:3). Because it is already the last period of history, the final "coming of the Lord" and the time of judgment for the unrighteous is imminent (cf. Jas 5:7-9).

First Peter commences by mentioning that the latter-day new creation of believers has taken place: God has "caused us to be born again, unto a living hope, by means of the resurrection of Jesus Christ from the dead." The new birth and consequent "living hope" are linked to Christ's resurrection. This notion is developed further in 1 Peter 1:20-21, where Christ's resurrection is portrayed as part of "the end of the times." Through the resurrected Christ the readers have become believers possessing hope. Through this same resurrection, Jesus has been exalted to

God's right hand to begin ruling (1 Pet 3:18-19, 21-22). The latter-day Spirit is the agent who brings about the resurrection of Christ (1 Pet 3:18) as well as the resurrection life of his followers (1 Pet 4:6) and their ongoing conduct in that life (1 Pet 1:2). Like the author of Hebrews, Peter speaks of Christ's death for sins as "once for all" (1 Pet 3:18), an expression that evokes the turning of the ages. Not only this, but the final judgment has been set in motion with the divinely ordained sufferings that serve to test the faith of the Christian community (1 Pet 4:12-19).

Second Peter makes the most far-reaching reference to Christ's kingship by observing that it commenced at the beginning of his earthly ministry, when he was baptized (2 Pet 1:16-17). Christ and the apostles prophesied that false teachers would infiltrate the church in "the last days" (2 Pet 3:3; Jude has "last time"). Both 2 Peter and Jude contend that this expected latter-day tribulation of apostate teaching has come to expression through the appearance of false teachers who are attempting to pervert the truth in the Christian community (cf. 2 Pet 3:2-3 with 2 Pet 2:1-22; 3:16-17; cf. Jude 17-18 with Jude 4, 8, 10-13).

The Johannine epistles (*see* John, Letters of) reveal an acute awareness that the eschaton has already broken into history. The most notable expression of this is the repeated references to the Antichrist, especially in 1 John 2:18. There are false teachers, little antichrists, from within the community, who have departed but still threaten to deceive Christians about the nature of Christ's person and his commandments (cf. 1 Jn 2:22-23, 26; 4:1-6; 2 Jn 7-11). These deceivers are the corporate embodiment of the beginning fulfillment of the prophecy of Daniel 7—12 that an eschatological opponent of God's people would deceive and arouse covenant disloyalty within the community of faith (see also Mk 13; Mt 24; Lk 21; 2 Thess 2). First John 3:4 even labels these false teachers with the covenantal "lawlessness" that Daniel prophesied would characterize the deceivers who would arise from within the ranks of the faithful (cf. Dan 12:10 [esp. cf. LXX with Theod.]): "Everyone who does the sin also does the lawlessness, and the sin is the lawlessness" (see Marshall 1978 *John*, 176-77; Smalley, 155; R. E. Brown, 399-400). In this respect, the notion of lawlessness is to be identified with the end-time sin of the "lawless one" of 2 Thessalonians 2:3-12.

The readers of 1 John are made aware that they are living in the midst of the "great tribulation," which they are experiencing in the form of false teachers. They must not be taken off guard and deceived. In fact, "the sin to death" in 1 John 5:16 is best understood in light of this latter-day context of apostasy within the covenant community. Those who deceive others or allow themselves to be deceived by the false teachers are regarded as never having belonged truly to the community of faith and experiencing spiritual death (cf. 1 Jn 2:19; see Scholer, who argues that "the sin to death" is committed only by pseudo-believers).

From another perspective, Christ's life and death have such a cosmic impact that it can be said that the old, fallen world of darkness "is passing away" (cf. 1 Jn 2:2, 8, 12-14, 17). Christ's redemptive work has dealt a mortal blow to the evil ruler of the old age (1 Jn 3:8), and those who identify with Christ's redemptive work also participate in his victory over the devil (1 Jn 2:13-14).

Although the old world has begun to disintegrate spiritually, Christ's death and resurrection have also set in motion a new creation. There is an overlap of the old with the new: "the darkness is passing away and the true light is already shining" (1 Jn 2:8). The resurrection life of the eternal age to come has begun in Jesus' resurrection and in the spiritual resurrection of his followers who identify with his death and resurrection (1 Jn 1:2; 2:17, 25; 3:14; 4:9; 5:11-13, 20, especially in the light of Jn 5:21-29). The Spirit, prophesied to be poured out in the eschatological age (see 2.1.1 above), gives assurance to believers that they have entered into the divine presence characterizing the new age (1 Jn 3:24; 4:13).

2.3.2. Future. Judgment is also a significant theme in James (Jas 2:13; 3:1). People will be judged because of their selfishness, greed and persecution of the righteous (Jas 5:1-9). The day of the final judgment is near (Jas 5:7-9). However, those who demonstrate true faith through good works will receive a reward at the last day (Jas 1:12; 5:7-9).

First Peter affirms that a day will come when God will impartially judge everyone by their works, whether or not they have lived lives of godly obedience (1 Pet 1:17; cf. 1 Pet 4:17-18). Even now God "is ready to judge the living and the dead" (1 Pet 4:5), since "the end of all things has come near" (1 Pet 4:7). In view of such an imminent judgment, believers are advised to live circumspectly. Those who are able to persevere in faithfulness will receive definitive "salvation ready to be revealed in the last time" (1 Pet 1:5; cf. 1 Pet 1:9) when Christ returns again (1 Pet 1:13) and his followers can fully rejoice in the greater manifestation of his glory (1 Pet 4:13; cf. 1 Pet 5:1). At this "proper time" (1 Pet 5:6) believers "will receive the unfading crown of glory" (1 Pet 5:4), and God will "perfect, confirm, strengthen and establish" for all time those who have persevered (1 Pet 5:10; cf. 1 Pet 5:6). Another image of this final reward is that of receiving an "inheritance" that "will not fade away" (1 Pet 1:4; cf. 1 Pet 3:9). The believers' "hope" is focused on this goal (1 Pet 3:15). When the final day comes, God's "dominion" will be decisively manifested as being "forever and ever" (1 Pet 5:11; cf. 1 Pet 4:11). Both the already and the not yet aspects of the latter days provide a theological framework in which 1 Peter's readers might better understand their ethical obligations (see Russell; Selwyn).

The notion of the coming final judgment is developed in 2 Peter (2 Pet 2:3, 9; 3:7; see Michaels 1967) and Jude (Jude 6, 14-15). At the time of this judgment, "the earth and its works will be burned up" (2 Pet 3:7-13). This is likely a literal expectation on the part of the author, though some commentators interpret it figuratively as a picture of an ethical purification of the earth.

A figurative view of the fiery judgment is affirmed by some who favor the textual reading in 2 Peter 3:10 of "the earth and its works will be found [or, discovered]." If this is the original reading, it probably does not refer to the earth and what people have done as literally surviving a judgment but to the works of the wicked which will be laid bare, so that the ungodly will not be able to escape judgment (cf. Bauckham 1983, 301, 316-21; cf. Wenham).

The purpose of reflecting on the cosmic conflagration is pastoral and ethical: to encourage saints to be holy in order that they should "be found" faithful when the expected judgment day occurs (cf. 2 Pet 3:11-12, 14). In contrast to the ungodly, they will find mercy on this dreadful day (Jude 21). The old creation, which is to be destroyed, will be replaced by "a new heavens and a new earth" (2 Pet 3:13; see Rev 21:1; both passages are based on the prophecy of Is 65:17; 66:22). The kingdom that was inaugurated at

Jesus' first coming will be established in its completeness (2 Pet 1:11), and God's people will stand in the immediate presence of his glory (Jude 24).

First John 2:28 and 1 John 4:17 speak of the possibility of Christ's final parousia occurring at any time. Readers should therefore persevere in their faith, so that they will obtain salvation and not be ashamed as ones who deserve wrath on the day of judgment. Such perseverance until Christ's coming will result in their becoming fully conformed to his likeness, for the faithful will finally be able "to see him just as he is" (1 Jn 3:2). Those who maintain this hope will be motivated in the present to begin to resemble his holy image (1 Jn 3:3; similarly 1 Jn 4:17).

2.4. Revelation.

2.4.1. Past and Present. The technical vocabulary for the eschatological period is not to be found in John's Apocalypse. Nevertheless, other kinds of terminology are used, and the concepts of inaugurated and consummated eschatology are part of the fabric of the book.

The book opens with mention that Christ's resurrection has inaugurated the fulfillment of the prophesied resurrection of the saints (Rev 1:5, "Jesus Christ . . . the firstborn from among the dead"). This resurrection places Christ in the position of "ruler of the kings of the earth" (Rev 1:5) and as the one who now possesses the "keys of death and Hades" (Rev 1:18). The resurrection described in Revelation 1:5 is later explained to be none other than "the beginning of the [new] creation of God" (Rev 3:14; see Beale 1996). By virtue of his resurrection Christ has also continued to fulfill Daniel's prophecy of the eschatological, worldwide reign of the Son of Man (cf. Dan 7:13-14 with Rev 1:13) as well as the Son of God's rule predicted in Psalm 2 (cf. Rev 2:26-27; 12:5). Through the resurrection Christ likewise has been declared openly as God (e.g., "I am the first and the last" [Rev 1:17; 2:8; 22:13], based on the self-attribution of Yahweh in Is 41:4, 44:6; 48:12).

Christ's followers are also identified with him in the present age as subjects in his newly established messianic kingdom and as those who rule with him (Rev 1:6, 9; 5:10; see Beale 1994; Bandstra 1992). The predominantly Gentile church has also begun to fulfill the prophecies of Israel's latter-day restoration (cf. OT allusions of Rev 3:9 with Is 43:4; 45:14; 49:23; 60:14; as well as the LXX of Is 41:8; 44:2; etc.).

2.4.2. Future. Revelation expects the final coming of Christ to occur in the near future (e.g., Rev 16:15; 22:7, 12, 17, 20). The visions of the book also express parabolically an expectation of his coming, especially to judge the ungodly (e.g., Rev 6:12-17; 11:15-19; 14:14-20; 17:14; 19:11-21; or where either Christ or God is the agent of judgment [Rev 6:10-11; 11:11-13; 14:8-11; 16:17-21; 20:9-15; 21:8]). Nevertheless, Christ will come also to reward and finally bless his people (Rev 11:18; 19:7-9; 21:1—22:5, 12, 14; possibly Rev 7:9-17). He then will establish his kingdom in its final, complete and eternal form (Rev 11:15-17; 19:1; 22:5; possibly Rev 7:9-17). A tribulation of deception and persecution for God's people will directly precede the last judgment and the full coming of the kingdom (e.g., Rev 11:7-10; 16:12-14; 20:7-9; possibly Rev 3:10; 6:11; 7:14; 13:5-18), as well as a final period of torment for their persecutors (e.g., Rev 16:21; 17:16-17; cf. Rev 3:10).

3. Special Problems of Eschatology in Revelation.

A variety of exegetical problems in Revelation pertain to whether passages speak of inaugurated eschatological realities or eschatological fulfillment at the end of the present age (for discussion of the problem in general, see Bandstra 1970).

3.1. Christ's Comings in Revelation 1—3 and Revelation 22. Some of the references to Christ's "coming" in the letters to the churches (Rev 1—3) appear to refer to a conditional coming of Christ in judgment. If there is no repentance in response to the present warning, then Christ will come in a pre-parousia judgment on that particular church (so Rev 2:5, 16; 3:3; cf. Rev 3:20, referring to a conditional blessing). Some interpreters, however, argue that Christ's judgment or reward at the end of history, rather than his coming, is conditional on the response of the churches (cf. Bauckham 1977, 173-74; Krodel, 109; Thomas 1992, 143-47, 154). Although this interpretation is possible, it rests on a grammatical exception. In NT usages outside of Revelation of the conditional *ei de mē* ("if not"), the whole of what follows is always conditional. Thus in Revelation 2:5, without contextual indications that would suggest the contrary, Christ's activity of "removing" and "coming" are probably conditional (with the same principle holding for Rev 2:16; 3:3; 3:20; see, e.g., Caird

1966, 27-28; Roloff, 45). The references to Christ's coming in Revelation 2:25 and Revelation 3:11 could well refer to the final parousia, but they are not in the form of conditional statements.

Furthermore, in Revelation 2:5 the removal of the lampstand "from its place" indicates the removal of the church as a light of witness to the world. Since the witness of the churches is an activity that takes place prior to the final advent of Christ, the removal of the lampstand must take place prior to Christ's final coming, not afterward (cf. Thomas 1992, 146-47). Part of the "witness" of the churches is to the promise that Christ will return to judge and to redeem (Rev 19:7-21; 22:7-20; see Bauckham 1993, 166-67). This also suits the visionary context of Christ walking in the midst of the lampstands as their priestly custodian who repairs or removes them according to their function.

It is probably best to see the conditional and nonconditional comings as not precisely identical but to view the conditional comings as local interventions during the church age and the nonconditional ones as referring to the final parousia. There may be an intended ambiguity in these sayings as they express the tension between the already and not yet.

Other interpreters have proposed that the dual theme of promise and judgment is woven throughout the letters and that in part the imagery is drawn from a eucharistic background (cf. most prominently Rev 2:17, 20). In the Eucharist believers repeatedly anticipate the present judicial and salvific effects of Christ's final coming (see Moule 1956). The identification of the Spirit with Christ in the conclusion of each letter suggests that Christ's salvific presence with the churches is through the Spirit, and his threatened judgment will occur also through the Spirit's visitation.

The repeated affirmations of Christ's "comings" leads us to consider Revelation 1:7, which some interpreters understand as introducing the main idea of the book: "Behold, he is coming with the clouds, and every eye will see him, even those who pierced him, and all the tribes of the earth will mourn over him." The verse is composed of two OT citations, Daniel 7:13 and Zechariah 12:10. In its OT context Daniel 7:13 speaks of the enthronement of the Son of Man over all the nations following God's judgment of the evil empires (Dan 7:9-12, 14). Applied to

Jesus, it indicates the fulfillment of his eschatological kingship (Rev 1:5). In its original context Zechariah 12:10 pertains to God's eschatological defeat of the enemy nations surrounding Israel and his redemption of Israel after the nation has repented of sinfully rejecting God and his messenger (i.e., "the one they have pierced"; cf. Mt 24:30; *Midr. Wayosa'*; Justin Martyr Dial. Tryph. 14.8).

In Revelation 1:7 the text from Zechariah has been altered in two significant ways. The phrases *pas ophthalmos* ("every eye") and *tēs gēs* ("of the earth") have been added to universalize its original meaning, which was specific to Israel. Repentant Gentiles are viewed as fulfilling the prophecy at the second coming of Christ. However, the reference from Daniel 7 ("Behold he is coming with the clouds") may include the whole course of the church age during which Christ guides the events of history in judgment and blessing. (Note how the Son of Man allusion in Rev 1:13 is given a present application; see also Rev 1:5-6, 14-20; but cf. Rev 14:14.) Precedent may be found in the use of Daniel 7:13 in Mark 13:26 and Mark 14:62, both of which may refer not to the second coming but to the Son of man's coming in judgment of Jerusalem in A.D. 70 (cf. Mt 24:30; see France, 140-42, 227-39).

Christ's coming in the letters to the churches appears to refer to his conditional visitation in judgment of the churches, though an allusion to his second coming is not excluded. Therefore Christ's coming in Revelation 1:7 and elsewhere in the Apocalypse is understood better as a process occurring throughout history so that his second coming concludes the whole process.

3.2. The Promises and the "Overcomers" in the Letters of Revelation. Each of the letters to the churches concludes with a reference to "the one who overcomes" or "conquers" *(nikaō).* This is then followed by a promise. In the letters to Smyrna and Philadelphia, persecution is to be overcome. In the letters to the other five churches, particular sins are to be overcome. But it is clear that overcoming these problematic sins that compromise the witness of the churches will lead to persecution. The church that perseveres in its witnessing faith will win a victory on earth prior to the consummation of history, even though it suffers earthly defeat.

The use of *nikaō* (Rev 12:11; 15:2; Rom 8:35-37) confirms that "overcoming" is best understood individually, ironically and as an inaugurated event, not merely as a future reality on a corporate level. The ironic, or paradoxical, meaning of *nikaō* is modeled after that of Christ's eschatological "conquest" (Rev 3:21). In Revelation 5:5-6 and John 16:33 Christ's conquering is understood as his death on the cross (cf. also Rom 8:36-37 with Rev 5:5-6). Elsewhere in Revelation we find that the beast "overcomes" the saints (Rev 11:7; 13:7), and in turn Christ and the saints "overcome" the beast by maintaining their faithful testimony in the midst of suffering (Rev 5:5-6; 12:11; 15:2; 17:14). The origin of this ironic application of *nikaō* to the beast and to Christ and his saints may lie in Daniel 7:21, which speaks of the eschatological opponent overcoming the saints. John quotes this contextually in Revelation 11:7, Revelation 12:7 and Revelation 13:7 but then ironically applies it to Jesus and the saints in Revelation 17:14 and to the angels in Revelation 12:7-8 (see Beale 1997, 1998). But the image of conquering may also owe something to the Jewish interpretation of martyrs who were said to have "conquered the tyrant" (4 Macc 1:11; 6:10; 7:3; 9:6, 30; 11:20-21; 16:14; 17:12-18) because they maintained their faith and obedience to God's law.

The eschatological promises to the overcomers are intended not only for those who suffer martyrdom (e.g., Charles 1:54; Caird 1960, 27-28, 33-34, 58; Kiddle, 61-65) but also for all true believers (Beale 1998, excursus on Rev 2:28). Overcoming refers to the victory of one's whole life of faith. A parallel may be observed in 1 John (1 Jn 5:4-5; cf. 1 Jn 2:13-14), where *nikaō* always refers to not succumbing to false teaching from within the community, a theme underscored in the letters to Pergamum and Thyatira.

The eschatological promises to overcomers in Revelation pertain to the salvific blessing of communion with God and are focused on the essentials of life. All of these promises are described in the final vision of the book (Rev 21:1—22:5) and generally refer to participation in the eternal kingdom of God. They include protection from judgment (Rev 2:10; 3:5), an inheritance in the city of God (Rev 3:12), participation in Christ's reign (Rev 2:26-28; 3:21) and eternal life (Rev 2:7; 3:5). Those who overcome are promised that they will begin to partake of the blessings of the age to come prior to the final consummation.

3.3. Temporal References in Revelation 1:19 and Revelation 4:1. Many commentators see Revelation 1:19 ("Write what you have seen, the things which are and the things about to take place after these things") as denoting a straightforward, threefold, chronological division of Revelation and of the history of the church in relation to the world (e.g., Thomas 1967). In this view, the three clauses of Revelation 1:19 describe consecutive, mutually exclusive periods of the entire history of the church age; they do not overlap:

(1) "What you have seen" refers to the previous vision of Revelation 1, which concerns the events of the first century;

(2) "The things which are" relates to Revelation 2—3 and describes the condition of the churches in Asia Minor and the world during the church age, the time extending from the first century until the commencement of the "great tribulation";

(3) "The things about to take place after these things" applies exclusively to Revelation 4:1—22:5 and narrates the final tribulation, which will begin directly before the end of history and will continue for a brief period until Christ's final coming to conclude history.

Though the chronological perspective is a popular understanding of Revelation 1:19, making Revelation 4—22 come alive with tantalizing insight into future events, there are weighty objections to this interpretation. In general it interprets Revelation without sufficient sensitivity to its literary form, giving a straightforward, literal reading of the book rather than using a figurative approach that is more appropriate to its symbolic genre.

The principal argument against the chronological understanding of Revelation 1:19 is that since Revelation 2—3 and Revelation 4—22 contain repeated references both to the past (cf. Rev 2—3; 12:1-5) and future, neither Revelation 2—3 nor Revelation 4—22 can be understood as strictly chronological. Since these chapters are described in some sense by Revelation 1:19, if Revelation 2—3 and Revelation 4—22 are not strictly chronological, neither is Revelation 1:19 likely to be chronological.

Not only does Revelation 4—22 describe events of past, present and future, but also its subsections recapitulate the same events in different ways (see Beale 1998). There is no reason to assume that the past and future references are tangential allusions to past or future events. Too often it seems that an a priori assumption that the events of Revelation must be understood as a chronological ordering of the future impedes interpreters from seeing their recapitulatory nature.

The concluding phrase of Revelation 1:19 ("what must take place after these things") is probably a conscious allusion to Daniel 2:28-29, 45, which in the original context refers to the eschatological scope of the vision of God's kingdom being established throughout the earth. In Daniel 2:28, 45 the phrase "latter days" is used synonymously with "after these things." If "after these things" refers to the general eschatological age, then Revelation 1:19 cannot express such a tidy chronological formula. It would refer to the eschatological period that includes inauguration in the past, present and future (see Beale 1992).

The initial phrase of Revelation 1:19 ("what things you have seen") probably refers to the entire vision of the book. The section in which it stands, Revelation 1:9-20, is best viewed as a commissioning narrative, with Revelation 1:19 as a repetition of the initial command in Revelation 1:11 to record all of the visions of the book. The second phrase ("what things are") probably does not refer to the present time only of Revelation 2—3 but the present-time segments scattered throughout the book. Alternatively, it may not be a temporal reference but rather an allusion to the figurative nature of the book, which needs to be interpreted accordingly (i.e., Rev 1:19 could be rendered "what they mean"; Stuart, 54; Alford, 559; Johnson, 429; Gundry, 66; Michaels 1991).

W. C. van Unnik maintains that the entire formula of Revelation 1:19 refers to all of Revelation and explains that John is commissioned to prophesy about the totality and meaning of history, whose truths apply not only within history but transcend any one historical period. He is able to adduce numerous examples of comparable threefold prophetic formulae in pagan religious contexts, ranging from the time of Homer to the fourth century A.D. (van Unnik 1962-63, 1980; Sweet, 73).

Whereas the majority of these views understand the three clauses of Revelation 1:19 as in some way temporal designations of past, present and future, an alternative view is that they are primarily statements about the genre of the book. The threefold structure describes the literary nature of the visions, not when they will take place. Revelation 1:19 is thus an elaboration of the threefold hermeneutical nature or genre of the entire Apocalypse: (1) because the vision is apocalyptic (visionary), (2) the whole book is to be interpreted figuratively (cf. Rev 1:12-18 with Rev 1:20) and (3) eschatologically (Rev 1:19; Dan 2:28-29, 45). The phrases "what you have seen" and "the things which are" are not to be limited to the vision of Revelation 1:12-20 but include the whole book (see Beale 1992).

Revelation 4:1 ("I will show you what must come to pass after these things"), which repeats most of the last clause of Revelation 1:19, is likely to be understood in the same way, and not as a reference to visions pertaining exclusively to the future great tribulation, as some futuristically oriented commentators argue.

3.4. The Temporal Scope of the Sevenfold Series of Seals, Trumpets and Bowls, and the Unnumbered Visions of Revelation 12—14. Are the discernible sections within Revelation 4—16 related to one another chronologically, thematically or both? The main lines of debate revolve around whether Revelation 4—16 represents a forecast of events to happen sequentially or whether some segments overlap temporally and thematically. Typically the former interpretation views Revelation 4—16 as a panorama of events to happen only in the period immediately preceding and culminating with the final coming of Christ. The latter interpretation sees a threefold temporal reference to events associated with (1) the redemptive work of Christ's first coming, (2) the course of the inaugurated latter-day church age and (3) the second coming of Christ and consummation of cosmic history. An exception to this is G. R. Beasley-Murray, who is both a futurist and a recapitulationist, understanding the parallel sections to cover exclusively different aspects of the eschatological future (*see* Revelation, Book of).

See also APOCALYPTICISM; COVENANT, NEW COVENANT; CREATION, NEW CREATION; JUDGMENT; KINGDOM OF GOD; RESURRECTION.

DLNTD: ANTICHRIST; CREATION, COSMOLOGY; DAY OF THE LORD; GLORY; HEAVEN, NEW HEAVEN; HOPE; MILLENNIUM; MORTALITY AND IMMORTALITY; MYSTERY; PAROUSIA; REWARDS; TRIBULATION, MESSIANIC WOES; UNIVERSALISM; WRATH, DESTRUCTION.

BIBLIOGRAPHY. H. Alford, *The Greek Testament* (Cambridge: Deighton, Bell & Co., 1866) vol. 4; D. C. Allison, *The End of the Ages Has Come* (Philadelphia: Fortress, 1985); A. J. Bandstra, "History and Eschatology in the Apocalypse," *CTJ* 5 (1970) 180-83; idem, " 'A Kingship and Priests': Inaugurated Eschatology in the Apocalypse," *CTJ* 27 (1992) 10-25; C. K. Barrett, "The Eschatology of the Epistle to the Hebrews," in *The Background of the New Testament and Its Eschatology: Studies in Honor of C. H. Dodd,* ed. W. D. Davies and D. Daube (Cambridge: Cambridge University Press, 1956) 363-93; R. J. Bauckham, *The Climax of Prophecy: Studies in the Book of Revelation* (Edinburgh: T & T Clark, 1993); idem, *Jude, 2 Peter* (WBC; Waco, TX: Word, 1983); idem, "Synoptic Parousia Parables and the Apocalypse," *NTS* 23 (1977) 162-76; H. F. Bayer, "Christ-Centered Eschatology in Acts 3:17-26," in *Jesus of Nazareth: Lord and Christ,* ed. J. B. Green and M. Turner (Grand Rapids: Eerdmans, 1994) 236-50; G. K. Beale, *The Book of Revelation* (NIGTC; Grand Rapids: Eerdmans, 1998); idem, "The Formula 'He Who Has Ears Let Him Hear What the Spirit Says to the Churches' in Rev. 2—3," in *A Vision for the Church: Essays in Honor of J. P. M. Sweet,* ed. M. Bockmuehl and M. Thompson (Edinburgh: T & T Clark, 1997); idem, "The Interpretative Problem of Rev. 1:19," *NovT* 34 (1992) 360-87; idem, "The Old Testament Background of Reconciliation in 2 Corinthians 5—7 and Its Bearing on the Literary Problem of 2 Corinthians 6:14-18, " *NTS* (1989) 550-81; idem, "The Old Testament Background of Rev. 3:14," *NTS* 42 (1996) 133-52; idem, "Review Article: J. W. Mealy, *After the Thousand Years,*" *EvQ* 66 (1994) 242-45; idem, "The Use of the Old Testament in Revelation," in *It Is Written: Scripture Citing Scripture: Essays in Honor of B. Lindars,* ed. D. A. Carson and H. G. M. Williamson (Cambridge: Cambridge University Press, 1988) 318-36; C. Brown, "The Parousia and Eschatology in the New Testament," *NIDNTT* 2:901-35; R. E. Brown, *The Epistles of John* (AB; Garden City, NY: Doubleday, 1982); F. F. Bruce, "Eschatology in Acts," in *Eschatology and the New Testament: Essays in Honor of G. R. Beasley-Murray,* ed. W. H. Gloer (Peabody, MA: Hendrickson, 1988) 51-63; A. Buzzard, "Acts 1:6 and the Eclipse of the Biblical Kingdom," *EvQ* 66 (1994) 197-215; H. J. Cadbury, "Acts and Eschatology," in *The Background of the New Testament and Its Eschatology: Studies in Honor of C. H. Dodd,* ed. W. D. Davies and D. Daube (Cambridge: Cambridge University Press, 1956) 300-21; G. B. Caird, *A Commentary on the Revelation of St. John the Divine* (London: A & C Black; New York: Harper & Row, 1966); idem, *The Language and Imagery of the Bible* (Philadelphia: Westminster, 1980); C. E. Carlston, "Eschatology and Repentance in the Epistle to the Hebrews," *JBL* 78 (1959) 296-302; J. Carmignac, "La notion d'eschatologie dans la Bible et 'a Qumran," *RevQ* 7 (1969) 17-31; J. T. Carroll, *Response to the End of History: Eschatology and Situation in Luke-Acts* (Atlanta: Scholars Press, 1988); R. H. Charles, *A Critical and Exegetical Commentary on the Revelation of St. John* (2 vols.; ICC; Edinburgh: T & T Clark, 1920); O. Cullmann, *Christ and Time* (Philadelphia: Westminster, 1964); W. J. Dumbrell, *The Search for Order: Biblical Eschatology in Focus* (Grand Rapids: Baker, 1994); P. Ellingworth, *The Epistle to the Hebrews* (NIGTC; Grand Rapids: Eerdmans, 1993); E. E. Ellis, "Present and Future Eschatology in Luke," *NTS* 12 (1965) 27-41; A. Farrer, *The Revelation of St. John the Divine* (Oxford: Clarendon, 1964); R. T. France, *Jesus and the Old Testament* (London: Tyndale, 1971); F. O. Francis, "Eschatology and History in Luke-Acts," *JAAR* 37 (1969) 49-63; E. Franklin, "The Ascension and the Eschatology of Luke-Acts," *SJT* 23 (1970) 191-200; R. B. Gaffin, "A Sabbath Rest Still Awaits the People of God," in *Pressing Toward the Mark,* ed. C. G. Dennison and R. C. Gamble (Philadelphia: The Committee for the Historian of the Orthodox Presbyterian Church, 1986) 33-51; B. R. Gaventa, "The Eschatology of Luke-Acts Revisited," *Encounter* 43 (1982) 27-42; K. Giles, "Present-Future Eschatology in the Book of Acts (I)," *RTR* 40 (1981) 65-71; idem, "Present-Future Eschatology in the Book of Acts (II)," *RTR* 41 (1982) 11-18; D. E. Gowan, *Eschatology in the Old Testament* (Philadelphia: Fortress, 1986); R. H. Gundry, *The Church and the Tribulation* (Grand Rapids: Zondervan, 1973); D. Hill, "The Spirit and the Church's Witness: Observations on Acts 1:6-8, " *IBS* 6 (1984) 16-26; A. A. Hoekema, *The Bible and the Future* (Grand Rapids: Eerdmans, 1979); G. Howard, "Eschatology in the Period Between the Testaments," in *The Last Things: Essays Presented to W. B. West Jr.,* ed. J. P. Lewis (Austin, TX: Sweet, 1972) 60-73; L. D. Hurst, "Eschatology and 'Platonism' in the Epistle to the Hebrews," *SBLSP* (1984) 41-74; A. Johnson, *Revelation* (EBC; Grand Rapids: Zondervan, 1981) 397-603; M. Kiddle, *The Revelation of St. John* (MNTC; New York: Harper, 1940); G. A. Krodel, *Revelation* (ACNT; Minneapolis: Augsburg, 1989); W. S. Kurz, "Acts 3:19-26 as a Test of the Role of Eschatology in Lukan

Christology," *SBLSP* (1977) 309-23; G. E. Ladd, "Eschatology and the Unity of New Testament Theology," *ExpT* 68 (1957) 268-78; idem, *The Presence of the Future* (Grand Rapids: Eerdmans, 1974); A. T. Lincoln, *Paradise Now and Not Yet* (SNTSMS 43; Cambridge: Cambridge University Press, 1981); idem, "Sabbath, Rest and Eschatology in the New Testament," in *From Sabbath to Lord's Day*, ed. D. A. Carson (Grand Rapids: Zondervan, 1982), 197-220; G. W. MacRae, "Heavenly Temple and Eschatology in the Letter to the Hebrews," *Semeia* 12 (1978) 179-99; I. H. Marshall, *The Epistles of John* (NICNT; Grand Rapids: Eerdmans, 1978); idem, "Slippery Words," *ExpT* 89 (1978) 264-69; A. J. Mattill, *Luke and the Last Things* (Dillsboro, NC: Western North Carolina University Press, 1979); J. W. Mealy, *After the Thousand Years* (JSNTSup 70; Sheffield: JSOT, 1992); J. R. Michaels, "Eschatology in 1 Peter 3:17," *NTS* 13 (1967) 394-401; idem, "Revelation 1:19 and The Narrative Voices of the Apocalypse," *NTS* 37 (1991) 604-20; P. S. Minear, *I Saw a New Earth: An Introduction to the Visions of the Apocalypse* (Washington, DC: Corpus, 1969); C. F. D. Moule, "Influence of Circumstances on the Use of Escha-tological Terms," *JTS* 15 (1964) 1-15; idem, "The Judgment Theme in the Sacraments," in *The Background of the New Testament and Its Eschatology: Studies in Honor of C. H. Dodd*, ed. W. D. Davies and D. Daube (Cambridge: Cambridge University Press, 1956) 464-81; A. E. Nielsen, "The Purpose of the Lukan Writings with Particular Reference to Eschatology," in *Luke-Acts*, ed. P. Luomanen (Helsinki: The Finnish Exegetical Society, 1991) 76-93; C. M. Pate, *The End of the Ages Has Come: The Theology of Paul* (Grand Rapids: Zondervan, 1995); N. Pryor, "Eschatological Expectations in the Old Testament Prophets," in *The Last Things: Essays Presented to W. B. West Jr.*, ed. J. P. Lewis (Austin, TX: Sweet, 1972), 32-59; W. C. Robinson, "Eschatology of the Epistle to the Hebrews: A Study in the Christian Doctrine of Hope," *Encounter* 22 (1961) 37-51; J. Roloff, *Revelation* (Minneapolis: Fortress, 1993); R. Russell, "Eschatology and Ethics in 1 Peter," *EvQ* 47 (1975) 78-84; L. Sabourin, "The Eschatology of Luke," *BTB* 12 (1982) 73-76; D. M. Scholer, "Sins Within and Sins Without: An Interpretation of 1 John 5:16-17," in *Current Issues in Biblical and Patristic Interpretation*, ed. G. F. Hawthorne (Grand Rapids: Eerdmans, 1975) 230-46; E. F. Scott, *The Book of Revelation* (London: SCM, 1939); E. G. Selwyn,

"Eschatology in 1 Peter," in *The Background of the New Testament and Its Eschatology: Studies in Honor of C. H. Dodd*, ed. W. D. Davies and D. Daube (Cambridge: Cambridge University Press, 1956) 394-401; M. Silva, "Perfection and Eschatology in Hebrews," *WTJ* 39 (1976) 60-71; S. S. Smalley, *1, 2, 3 John* (WBC; Waco, TX: Word, 1984); R. H. Smith, "The Eschatology of Acts and Contemporary Exegesis," *CTM* 29 (1958) 641-63; idem, "History and Eschatology in Luke-Acts," *CTM* 29 (1958) 881-901; M. Stuart, *Commentary on the Apocalypse* (New York: M. H. Newman, 1845) vol. 2; J. P. M. Sweet, *Revelation* (SCM Pelican Series; London: SCM, 1979); R. L. Thomas, "The Chronological Interpretation of Revelation 2—3," *BSac* 124 (1967) 321-31; idem, *Revelation 1—7: An Exegetical Commentary* (Chicago: Moody, 1992); S. D. Toussaint, "The Eschatology of the Warning Passages in the Book of Hebrews," *GTJ* 3 (1982) 67-80; W. C. van Unnik, "A Formula Describing Prophecy," *NTS* 9 (1962-63) 86-94; idem, *Sparsa Collecta* 2 (NovTSup 30; Leiden: E. J. Brill, 1980) 183-93; G. Vos, *The Pauline Eschatology* (Grand Rapids: Baker, 1979); D. Wenham, "Being 'Found' on the Last Day: New Light on 2 Peter 3:10 and 2 Corinthians 5.3," *NTS* 33 (1987) 477-79; C. Woods, "Eschatological Motifs in the Epistle to the Hebrews," in *The Last Things: Essays Presented to W. B. West Jr.*, ed. J. P. Lewis (Austin, TX: Sweet, 1972) 140-51; N. T. Wright, *The Climax of the Covenant* (Minneapolis: Fortress, 1991).

G. K. Beale

ESDRAS, SECOND (4 EZRA). *See* APOCRYPHA AND PSEUDEPIGRAPHA.

ESSENES. *See* DEAD SEA SCROLLS; JUDAISM AND THE NEW TESTAMENT.

ETERNAL LIFE. *See* JOHN, GOSPEL OF.

ETHICS I: GOSPELS

Biblical thought may generally be divided into two categories: theology and ethics. Theology is the attempt to understand *God and his dealings with this world, while ethics is the human conduct which flows from that understanding. In Judaism, ethics was originally identified with the law, which was a gracious guide to the nation whose heart was to be in harmony with the God who was both its Father and King. In time, however, ethics degenerated for many into a preoccupation with outward acts, with no necessary corresponding inner loyalty to God. In Jesus' teaching we see a return to the radical belief in God as Father and King, a belief which for him pervades all areas of human life—social, intellectual, spiritual and moral. Other topics, such as eschatology, rewards, punishments and the law itself, must be understood in the light of that central conviction.

1. Ethics, Eschatology and the Kingdom
2. Ethics and the Presence of the Kingdom
3. Ethics and Rewards
4. Ethics and the Law
5. Conclusion

1. Ethics, Eschatology and the Kingdom.

The relationship of ethics to the topics of eschatology and the *kingdom of God is one of the most convoluted and confusing chapters in modern *Gospel study. Much discussion has centered on the meaning and role of the so-called eschatological sections of the Gospels (see Eschatology) and their relationship to Jesus' proclamation of the kingdom. The modern discussion, unfortunately, has been bogged down almost from the beginning as the result of three critical misunderstandings.

The first misunderstanding has been to go back to the usage of the OT or of the first-century Aramaic language, and from these backgrounds to try to fix limits on what the phrase "the kingdom of God" could have meant for Jesus. But Jesus spent a great deal of time explaining what he meant by the kingdom, and if so, it follows that he did not mean what his contemporaries meant by it.

The second misunderstanding, closely related to the first, is to attempt to make, as G. Dalman has done, a subtle distinction between the kingdom as "reign" rather than "realm." That it could not be both is hardly evident from Jesus' teaching. Even in English the word *kingdom* does service for both, and certainly few kings have ever exercised kingship without also having a realm over which to exercise it. We shall find ourselves in some difficulty if, when we hear Jesus talk of entering the kingdom of God, there is no realm into which his followers can enter. Few would believe that Jesus invited men and women to enter into the kingship of God— to share his sovereignty with him. What he invited was entry into that sphere of territory where God's kingly rule would be operating over them (see Church).

The third misunderstanding has been to ask whether the kingdom is present or future. Again, Jesus' teaching does not yield to such reductive reasoning. For him the kingdom is past, present and future.

The modern debate concerning the interrelationship of ethics, eschatology and the kingdom began in 1906 with A. Schweitzer's epochal work *The Quest of the Historical Jesus.* Schweitzer, having effectively dismissed all previous attempts to reconstruct the life of Jesus, then produced his own attempt, which was even more implausible than the ones he had rejected. Showing a complete disregard for critical method, Schweitzer declared that Jesus expected the coming of a *"Son of Man," other than himself, during his own ministry or during the mission of the Twelve, and that when that hope failed to materialize, he changed course and brought about his own crucifixion in order to force God's hand.

While this reconstruction was to win few enthusiasts, it had an unfortunate aftermath. What Schweitzer had erected was a colossal blunder— the "end-of-the-world Jesus"—which has, despite the arguments of critics from C. H. Dodd onward, weighed heavy on the ground of NT study. And perhaps what is most disturbing is that all that was needed to bring down the structure was the wrecking ball of accurate description.

But lack of exegetical accuracy was not the only difficulty with Schweitzer's theory. Another was its failure to accommodate ethical teaching to the question of eschatology. Having insisted with J. Weiss that eschatology was the indispensable framework for the interpretation of NT teaching, he was then faced with the ethical teaching of the Gospels, which he declared to be an "interim ethic" (*Interimsethik*)—an ethic of impractical idealism which could never have been designed for a long period. It was possible for Jesus to talk in this way only because he believed that the interval between his preaching and the end of the world was so short that he could afford to be impractical. That view of the ethics of Jesus was soon met not only with blanket incredulity but substantial arguments to the contrary. In the ethical teaching of Jesus (as in the ethics of the whole NT), the sanctions for the teaching are only in very rare cases the expectation of a future crisis. The reasons are nearly always based on what God has done, on the character of God himself, on the character of Jesus or on the nature of the Christian revelation. They are certainly *not* based on any final crisis.

Another writer to deal extensively with the question of the kingdom and eschatology was R. Bultmann. Reacting to Schweitzer, Bultmann observed that a teacher who believed that the end of the world was close would hardly have devoted so much of his time to arguments about the Jewish law and how one should live in this world. Bultmann's answer was to understand both eschatology and ethics existentially; while it cannot be denied that Jesus had an apocalyptic belief in the near end of the world, modern men and women who reject such primitive thinking can still see in the eschatological announcement and ethical demand the critical moment when they confront God. Bultmann's approach has been heavily criticized, even by his own pupils. In addition to replacing a first-century Jewish framework with a modern philosophical one, his position was fatally stricken by an uncritical acceptance of the notion that first-century people accepted with naive literalness their images of God and the universe. It is now recognized that figures such as Jesus and Paul were as aware of the metaphorical nature of their language as are sophisticated moderns like Bultmann.

Yet another major contributor to the debate was C. H. Dodd. According to Dodd's influential *The Parables of the Kingdom* (1941), Jesus proclaimed that the kingdom had arrived fully in his preaching, and that all future elements were realized in the present (hence, "realized eschatology"). Statements about the future were actually symbols for the present. Dodd's denuding of the kingdom of all futurity prompted a quick reaction, with some critics accusing him of being a Platonist. Dodd subsequently revised his views so as to account for future kingdom references in Jesus' teaching.

Other writers have proposed varying solutions to the problem of how present and future cohere in the teaching of Jesus. W. G. Kümmel suggested that Jesus understood the kingdom as the ultimate end of history, but that it was present in a proleptic manner in his own life and work. J. Jeremias produced a view almost indistinguishable from Dodd's, while G. E. Ladd tried to maintain an equal balance between present and future. On the whole, most recent writers have viewed Jesus' eschatology as

lying somewhere between thoroughgoing (e.g., Schweitzer) and realized (e.g., Dodd), with each element variously weighted.

2. Ethics and the Presence of the Kingdom.

As noted above, any attempt to limit the kingdom in Jesus' teaching to either present or future is to be rejected. Both elements are present in the Gospels—although, as we shall see, the present aspects far outweigh the future as the backdrop for Jesus' ethical pronouncements.

Those passages which indicate that the kingdom of God is in some sense still to come are, of course, not difficult to trace. Mark occasionally uses "the kingdom of God" to refer to that eternal life beyond the grave, which is the goal of the process (Mk 9:47; 14:25). In another sense Jesus is a king who has not yet entered his royal status (Mk 10:37), whose coronation occurs only when the places on his right and his left are occupied by those to whom they have been assigned (Mk 15:17, 27). Luke's version of the Lord's Prayer contains the phrase "your kingdom come" (Lk 11:2)—although Matthew adds the gloss, "your will be done on earth, as it is in heaven" (Mt 6:10), which shows that for him God's reign is active on earth so long as there are human agents to do his will. In Mark 14:25 (par. Mt 26:29 and Lk 22:18) Jesus says, "I will no more drink of the fruit of the vine until I drink it new in the kingdom of God," while Matthew 7:21-22 and 25:34 depict the kingdom as the final reward of the righteous (for other future references, cf., e.g., Mt 16:28; Mk 10:30; Lk 18:30).

But by far the overall tenor of Jesus' teaching supports Dodd's contention that for Jesus the kingdom was already substantially present. There are in fact eight possible ways to understand the kingdom in the ministry of Jesus, all of which, in various ways, illuminate Dodd's emphasis on the presence of the kingdom.

2.1. The Kingdom Is Present as the Fulfillment of Prophecy.
Here the primary text is Mark 1:15: "The time has come, the kingdom of God has drawn near (*ēngiken*), repent and believe the Gospel." What is most significant in this passage is that the first two verbs are in the perfect (i.e., past) tense. Mark could well have used the present "the time *is* coming, the kingdom *is* drawing near." Something appears *to have happened* for Jesus to speak in this way. The verb *ēngiken* furthermore, while it is related to the adjective *engus*, "near," must in Mark 1:15 mean

"has arrived." For the Hebrews the expressions "draw near" or "bring near" were simply idiomatic expressions for "arrive" or "put." The former usage is well known from Lamentations 4:18 (LXX): there *ēngiken ho kairos hēmōn, eplērōthēsan hai hēmerai hēmōn, parestin ho kairos hēmōn* means "our end *drew near*, our days were numbered, for our end *had come.*" "Draw near" *(ēngiken)* and "have come" *(parestin)* are synonymous expressions (cf. also Ezek 7:3-12 LXX). The latter usage appears also in (e.g.) Leviticus 2:8, where to bring a sacrifice "near" to the altar means to place it on the altar—not to drop it halfway between the altar and the Tabernacle entrance.

Two other points in regard to Mark 1:15 need to be noted. First, "The time has fully come." What time? Clearly, the time proclaimed in OT prophecy. Second, "Repent and believe the gospel." But what is the gospel? Clearly it is an announcement. The word *euangelion* is often translated as "good news"; but regularly in the LXX it means, simply, "news" (Heb *beśōrâ*). And any Jew who believed that at the end of time God would bring in an eschatological kingdom would have found little "news" in being told that this was still true and that nothing had subsequently altered the picture. If Jesus is proclaiming news, it is because he has something *new* to say.

The one context in the OT where we find the term *euangelion* frequently in use is in the prophecies of Isaiah 40—66. To the prophet "the good news" is the proclamation "Behold your God." And when we come to Isaiah 52:7— "How lovely on the mountain are the feet of the herald who comes to proclaim the prosperity and bring good news"—we find a news of deliverance which calls to Zion, "Your God reigns" (Is 52:8). In Isaiah 40—66 the good news is that God has arrived; he has come upon the scene of history to make his presence felt. Above all, *he has come to assert his kingly power:* "Your God has taken up the power of government and is reigning over his world." And if we can accept this as the character of the Isaian prophecy, it would be perverse to argue that Jesus was echoing the prophecy in his declaration without also insisting that he was proclaiming, "Your God is here; your God reigns."

But what could such kingly power mean in the time of Jesus? It is seldom considered that this question might equally have been asked in

545 B.C. At that time outward appearances hardly justified the idea that God's primal reign of justice had already begun. Jerusalem was in ruins, its leaders were in exile, and most were reluctant to return to Palestine to rebuild a ruined city. The prophet was idealizing, proclaiming that the sovereign reign of God is a reality even in these depressing circumstances, inviting *Israel to respond and be ready to receive their God. And if a prophet can do that five-and-a-half centuries before Jesus, there is no reason why Jesus should not have proclaimed also that in this hostile, unrepentant and beleaguered world, the kingdom of God has become a present reality.

2.2. The Kingdom Is Present as a Divine Power Breaking in on the Kingdom of Satan and Overthrowing the Power of Satan in the World. This point is made with special clarity in Jesus' response to the claim that he drives out demons by the authority of Beelzebul: "If I by the finger of God cast out demons, the kingdom of God has come upon you" (Lk 11:20; Mt 12:28). What is most interesting about this inbreaking is that it is not conditional on belief. In Luke's version of the proclamation of the missionaries to the cities of Galilee, the message is "the kingdom of God has arrived . . ." *(ēngiken hē basileia tou theou,* Lk 10:9). Elsewhere (Lk 16:16), the kingdom is being proclaimed *(euangelizetai,* present tense) and people are taking it by force *(biazetai,* present tense). We are clearly dealing with an explosion of activity which cannot be easily defined or categorized, but which is impacting the current state of affairs.

2.3. The Kingdom Is Present as a Small Beginning with Great Potential. In the three parables of growth (the mustard seed, the seed growing secretly, and the leaven, Mk 4:26-32; Mt 13:33; Lk 17:31), the kingdom has arrived, but in small, unexpected ways. It is like the mustard seed: One may not think much of it at the moment, but it has immense potential. It is like a little leaven which is put into the loaf and causes it to expand. It is like a seed that is put into the soil and produces its fruit. The kingdom is here. Do you find it hard to believe? Wait for the results. Do not be downhearted, nor take much notice of circumstances that appear to belie this gospel announcement. What is small now will have considerable results later. Under this heading we might also add (although with some tentativeness) the mysterious saying of Mark 9:1:

"There are some standing by who will not taste death until they see the kingdom having come with power."

The *parables of growth entitle us to draw distinctions between the coming of the kingdom, the kingdom arriving as a present reality and its future coming with power. It is, of course, extremely difficult to determine what Jesus intended by the "kingdom coming with power"—and what Mark thought he intended. But one meaning which may be ruled out in both instances is the Parousia. Our concern here, however, is the contrast between the coming of the kingdom incognito and its open coming with power in the future.

2.4. The Kingdom Is Present as an Opportunity Requiring Resolute Action. Here the parables of the pearl and of the treasure in the field (Mt 13:44-46) are especially noteworthy. In the second, as is so often the case in the parables of Jesus, we are not to ask niggling questions about the morality of the transaction. As with the parable of the unjust steward (Lk 16:1-9), the point of comparison is the need for resolute and determined action in the face of a crisis. Here is an opportunity that will not occur again; it is an opportunity to be grasped, even at the sacrifice of all else.

2.5. The Kingdom Is Present as a Call to Responsibility and Labor. In the parable of the two sons (Mt 21:28-31) a man says to one son, "Go, work in the vineyard," to which the son responds yes—but does not go. The other son is asked the same thing, and says no—but goes. "Which did the will of his father?" The appended comment from Jesus is, "Yes, and prostitutes and tax collectors are going into the kingdom ahead of you Pharisees." Here, the willing but disobedient son of the parable is applicable to the Pharisees. Unlike them, prostitutes and tax collectors are already entering the kingdom.

2.6. The Kingdom Is Present as a Way of Life Which Demands Total Obedience to God and Complete Self-Sacrifice. This theme appears in Matthew 5:26-33; Mark 8:34-37 and Mark 10:17-23. In the latter passage the hearer fails to follow Jesus and Jesus' response is, "How hard it is for the rich to enter the kingdom of God!" Following Jesus and entering the kingdom are equated. In Luke 9:57-62 (par. Mt 8:18-22) the three claimants to discipleship each want to be included among Jesus' disciples. Again, when Jesus says that the last one is not fit for the kingdom,

the natural implication is that being a disciple of Jesus and entering the kingdom are different ways of describing the same thing. One could possibly hold that the kingdom is the transcendent, everlasting kingdom for which one qualifies by being a disciple here on earth. But this would not be the natural way of taking the words. Those who become disciples of Jesus enter the service of the kingdom, and only those who are prepared to undergo drastic sacrifice are fit for the kingdom.

Luke 12:31-32 is the end of a passage which in very similar words is recorded by Matthew in the Sermon on the Mount (Mt 6:34). Luke's version, "But seek his kingdom and these things shall be added to you," is especially intriguing. What does he mean by "seeking his kingdom"? Is this a lifelong quest that ends only at death or at the Parousia? Or is it following Jesus in such a way that the present claims of the kingdom are put above all others? This passage raises the same question as the previous one. There are proper things that ought to be done, but in any ethical scheme there must also be a hierarchy of values, with following Jesus/entering the kingdom taking priority over all other claims.

2.7. The Kingdom Is Present as a Call to New Life and Service. In Jesus' teaching, the *paidion* ("child") sayings (Mk 10:13-16 par. Mt 19:13-15 and Lk 18:15-17; Matt 18:3), which stress the necessity of being like a child, must be taken in tandem with the servant sayings (Lk 22:26; Mk 10:43 par. Mt 20:26; see Chilton and McDonald)—the most obvious point of contact being the Greek root *pais*, which may mean either "child" or "servant." Yet the comparison moves beyond mere lexical likeness. Children embody a lack of self-consciousness and a newness of life, with their only point of reference being trust in the parent. Servants are likewise single-minded; they are concerned solely with serving the master. For Jesus the call of the kingdom is a call to newness and a job to be done, not a summons to spiritual self-awareness or an introverted search for salvation.

2.8. The Kingdom Is Present Not Only as a Challenge to Individuals but as a Challenge to the Nation. In Luke 12:32 we read, "Fear not, little flock; it is your Father's good pleasure to give you the kingdom." We will miss the national character of this saying (as well as that of the complementary passage in Mk 6:34 where Jesus observes that "the people were like sheep without a shepherd") if we are unfamiliar with the OT picture of the nation as a flock and the king as the shepherd. The classic text is Ezekiel 34, where the shepherds of Israel (the national leaders) are abandoning the flock. God answers, "I will be shepherd of my flock, I will make them lie down, I will seek the lost, I will bring back the strayed . . . and I will set up over them one shepherd, my servant David" (Ezek 34:15-27). It is the anointed king who is the shepherd of the flock. When Jesus addresses his disciples in this manner his language cannot but carry messianic and national overtones.

That much of Jesus' teaching is a political challenge to the nation of Israel is central to an accurate appreciation of his ethical teaching (Caird, Borg). In this regard the common distinction between "personal" and "social" in the ethics of Jesus is somewhat misleading. Israel had always been intended to be a community of "the one and the many," in which what affects the smallest member affects the whole—and vice versa. Social and personal dimensions could never ultimately be separated, and it is only a divorce of Jesus from his Jewish context that enables such a distinction to continue to flourish.

Recent opinion which stresses the role of politics in Jesus' disputes with the Pharisees points out that both sides of the debate were asking the same question: "What does it mean for Israel to be the holy nation of God?" For centuries the Jews had been preoccupied with questions concerning their national destiny as the chosen people, and especially with their undeserved suffering at the hands of the Gentile empires. But when God would bring his kingdom of justice and peace to earth, the tables would be turned, and Israel would reign over all.

Jesus does not challenge the close connection between Israel's destiny and its election, but for him God's sovereignty is the primary consideration. If God were truly their king they would know that they had been chosen not as vessels of vengeance but as a beacon light, pointing the way of *salvation for all. Suffering and service, not nationalism and pride, was to constitute their corporate life, a role Jesus acted out in his own experience and which he encouraged in his friends. In his understanding, even paying taxes to Caesar (Mk 12:17; Mt 22:21; Lk 20:25) was not incompatible with giving full and uncompromising obedience to God.

Herein has lain yet another mistake in interpreting the ethical teaching of Jesus. His comment regarding paying taxes to Caesar has been used by some (e.g., Martin Luther) to establish a complex theory that God has set up two realms, the divine and the secular, each with its own clearly defined aegis. Jesus' point was not intended to be put to this use. Far from establishing any elaborate theology, Jesus was answering a simple question of ethics. How far must I go in this world in trying to live with my enemies? The implications of his teaching can, of course, be drawn out and applied to a later age, but this should not be allowed to replace its original and sublimely simple meaning: insofar as it does not conflict with your duty to God, do all you can to live at peace with your adversaries (cf. also Mt 5:41, where "the extra mile" probably refers to the right of a Roman soldier to impress a Jewish native to carry his pack for a limited distance).

Ultimately, then, Jesus is confronting the Jews with a challenge: first let them learn what it means for God to rule over them; then perhaps they will know what place they will have in God's ultimate plan for the earth.

3. Ethics and Rewards.

In the light of what we have said above, the presence of the kingdom in Jesus' teaching may now be regarded as a datum from which other features of that teaching may be construed. And one of the most frequently discussed issues arising from Jesus' statements about the kingdom concerns the role of rewards and punishments. Both themes are well attested in the teaching of Jesus (for rewards cf., e.g., Mt 6:4, 6, 18; 16:27; for punishment cf., e.g., Mt 5:22, 29, 30; 7:19; 10:28; 13:49-50; 18:6; 25:30). To students of ethics both elements have always appeared as a difficulty; to do things out of a fear of punishment or hope of reward is not regarded as the highest of ethical motivations.

To this it must be admitted that there is an element of pragmatism in the ethical teaching of Jesus: "By their fruits you shall know them" (Mt 7:20 par. Lk 6:44). He judges by results, which was very different from the religion of most Pharisees. They obeyed the law not because it was sensible or reasonable or leads to desirable consequences, but simply because *it was commanded*. It was sheer, naked obedience. The rabbis could then take the view that all of the commandments are equal, since each gives equal opportunity to obey the will of God.

Jesus, on the other hand, distinguished between the *law's weightier and lesser matters. Sometimes it has been charged that his teaching on reward has the effect of making ethics prudential—it is nothing more than enlightened self-interest. To do good for the sake of gain is mercenary, even if that gain is spiritual.

What significance, then, do the elements of *judgment and reward have in the teaching of Jesus? This question may be treated under seven heads:

3.1. Jesus Distinguished Between Two Types of Reward. "Do not announce your good deeds with a flourish of trumpets. Those who do already have their reward" (apechousin ton misthon, Mt 6:2). The Greek verb apechō was the word ordinarily used on a receipt, meaning "paid in full." Hence for Jesus outward acts do, of themselves, carry a certain recompense (here, worldly recognition). But there is a deeper, more satisfying type of reward that Jesus advocates, and this reflects his pervasive distinction between that which is arbitrary and that which is proper. Arbitrary rewards have nothing to do with the nature of the activity being rewarded (e.g., "practice the piano two hours a day and you will get a new bicycle"); proper rewards are intrinsic to the activity itself (e.g., "practice the piano two hours a day and one day you will be able to play Mozart"). For Jesus the joys of the kingdom are the result of being a certain kind of person.

3.2. Jesus Encouraged Disinterested Goodness. Some deeds are to be done out of the uncalculating goodness of the heart. "If one in authority makes you go one mile, go with him two" (Mt 5:41). "When you are having guests for lunch or supper, do not invite your friends, your brothers or other relations, or your rich neighbors; they will only ask you back again, and so you will be repaid. But when you give a party, ask the poor, the crippled, the lame and the blind. That is the way to find happiness, because they have no means of repaying you" (Lk 14:12-14 REB). Disinterested goodness does not expect to be repaid. It is true that Luke has Jesus add, "You will be repaid on that day when the good rise from the dead" (Lk 14:14 REB), but there are no grounds for understanding this to mean anything extrinsic to the activity. We might paraphrase Jesus as saying: "If you do good out of the uncalculating goodness of your heart, then in the *resurrec-tion you will have the reward of being confirmed as the sort of person who enjoys doing good out of the uncalculating goodness of your heart."

3.3. Acts Are the Fruit of Character. This is more radical than anything we have yet encountered. Those who have a legal religion are told what to do; and the Pharisees on the whole believed that ethics consisted mainly in taking the law and doing what it says. According to Jesus, if you are the wrong sort of person you cannot do what you are told. First make the tree good, then the acts will follow (Mt 7:16-20). Good is the fruit which grows spontaneously on the tree of good character, an emphasis that profoundly deepens the quality of human ethics by insisting that it has to do not with acts but with what one is.

What one is determines what one does—a theory opposed not only to Pharisaism but also to classical Greek ethics, especially those of Aristotle. According to Aristotle, habit is the product of constantly doing the right thing; if one does it long enough, it becomes habitual, and one ends up being good. Aristotle and the Pharisees could agree that goodness is achieved by doing right until it becomes a habit. Jesus declares this to be impossible; only a good tree can produce good fruit (a point to be elaborated later by Paul in Rom 7:4-6 and Gal 5:22-23). Jesus looked for people who would not merely do good but be good, who enjoy goodness and for whom goodness is its own reward. This ethical point has a profound theological element within it, as appears in the parable of the sheep and the goats (Mt 25:32-34). The reward for good conduct is the invitation "enter into the joy of your *Lord." The ultimate reward is being the kind of person who can enjoy God. The true end of human beings is to glorify God and enjoy him forever, an idea which would then raise for Jesus' hearers a question: are they the sort of people who would enjoy God?

3.4. Good Acts Issuing from Good Character Is the Kind of Ethic Contained in the Beatitudes. Jesus' repeated words "Blessed are those . . ." suggest that the proper end of men and women is bliss. The Beatitudes (Mt 5:3-12; Lk 6:20-26) describe in a variety of ways how eternal bliss can be anticipated here and now by living the life of the kingdom. "Blessed are the poor in spirit" (Mt 5:3; cf. Lk 6:20, "Blessed are you poor"). Some of the verb tenses are future, but it is clear that this bliss is to be anticipated in the present.

With that Aristotle certainly would have agreed. In the tenth book of *Ethics* he sums up ethical obligation with the phrase "as far as possible here and now to live the life of heaven." But in the Beatitudes Jesus has turned normal human ethics upside down. The whole of Aristotle's ten books of *Ethics* is concerned with the nature of happiness; the true end of men and women is to be happy. As we have just seen, Jesus does not disagree with this. But of what does true happiness consist? "Wealth, joy, satisfaction and popularity" are the usual worldly answers. Jesus, however, addresses those for whom such temporal prizes have failed to satisfy. Wealth? "Blessed are you poor." Joy? "Blessed are you who mourn." Satisfaction? "Blessed are you who are hungry." Popularity? "Blessed are you when people hate you" (Lk 6:20-22). And if Jesus pronounces his benediction on these antitheses of worldly goals, it is because it is precisely the poor, the mourning, the hungry and the persecuted who are most open to receive the better gifts of God.

The above point is most easily grasped in the beatitude about the hungry (Lk 6:21; Mt 5:6). When is it blessed to be hungry? Just before dinner. Why is it blessed to be hungry? Because Jesus comes to announce the messianic banquet (*see* Table Fellowship). It is ready, and blessed are those who are hungry for it, who come to it with the most need for its unimaginable bounty. Undeterred by the bogus satisfactions of the present age, they are those who hunger for the banquet which only God has to offer.

3.5. Jesus Repudiated Any Idea of Moral Contract. Here the principal witness is Matthew's parable of the laborers in the vineyard (Mt 20:1-16). Some work the full day, others work only one hour. And when the owner pays them all the same day's wage, he meets the expected complaint by saying, "You contracted with me for one denarius, and I paid you the contract money; so what are you grumbling about?" The modern answer, of course, would be "differential." But the point of the parable is that God does not operate according to contracts. He pays men and women what they need, not what they have earned. So also the parable of Luke 17:7-10: Is the master grateful to the servant for carrying out orders? If one reckons in terms of duty done, then duty to God is unlimited; no matter how far one goes, enough has never been done. But the intention of this is not to load the human psyche with an impossible task, only to explode the notion that God deals with people in such a way. There is no such thing as a moral contract.

It follows that the Sermon on the Mount, and the Beatitudes in particular, must not be regarded as new law but as descriptive of life in the kingdom. So also in Mark 10:17-27, the story of the rich man who wanted to enter the kingdom of God. "What must I do to inherit eternal life?" he asks. The first thing he learns is that this is not the right question. If it is a matter of doing, it will mean unlimited demands. The disciples wonder, "Who then can be saved?" If the privileged cannot, what hope have the underprivileged? Jesus does not respond, "Oh, how easy it is for the underprivileged!" Rather, he says that with humans it is impossible, but not with God. With God all things are possible. Jesus thus undermines the whole contract system under which the man was operating.

The rewards that Jesus offers are open precisely to those who recognize that they cannot earn them, a point made most forcibly by the parable of the Pharisee and the publican (Lk 18:9-14). If obedience is possible, it is only because it is God's gift. Jesus requires unlimited obedience, but he also says, "Fear not, little flock, it is your Father's good pleasure to give you the kingdom" (Lk 12:32). It is for this reason that Jesus constantly emphasizes the calling of the downtrodden. They are the ones to whom he offers the free gift of God. For Jesus the ethical requirements of the Gospel are possible not because men and women are capable of doing them. They are possible because with God all things are possible.

3.6. For Jesus, God Is the Ultimate Reward. In Luke 10 we find a number of judgments pronounced on the cities of Galilee, and while these statements probably refer to imminent historical crises (Caird, Borg), they carry an implication for the theme in general. The last judgment means confronting God. Jesus' ethical principles are determined by his extraordinary affirmation that life, here and hereafter, is to be lived in the presence of God. It is from that central claim that all the statements about reward issue; God himself is the ultimate reward. For those who disregard the gospel of the kingdom, whose selfish horizons are bounded completely by this world, the presence of God would be far more terrifying than anything to be found in the lake of fire. But for those who practice the presence of God in this life, the vision of God in the next (Mt 5:8) is the final and fitting conclusion to their journey.

3.7. The Law of the Kingdom Is the Law of Love, and Those Who Love Reap the Reward of Being Like the Father of Love. The great commandment, "You shall love your neighbor as yourself" (Lev 19:18), is repeated by Jesus as the sum total of the law (Mk 12:28-31 par. Mt 22:34-40 and Lk 10:25-29; cf. Rom 13:10), but he weds it to Deuteronomy 6:4 ("You shall love the Lord your God with all your heart and all your soul and all your mind," Mt 22:37; Mk 12:30). This double command stands at the head of Jesus' ethical teaching as its quintessence. The uniting of the two commandments prevents love in Jesus' teaching from being misunderstood as a simple humanistic desire directed blindly at others, or a narcissistic preoccupation with oneself. For Jesus, love of others and of oneself is possible only if one first loves the God of Israel with all one's being.

The so-called Golden Rule (Mt 7:12; Lk 6:31) is found in other religions and philosophies, albeit in a negative form. The Rabbi Hillel, for example, said, "What you do not wish done to you, do not to others; this is the law, and all the rest is commentary." Inaction, on the other hand, is regarded by most ethicists as an unacceptable standard. It is hardly comparable with an ethic of unlimited concern and action on behalf of others. G. B. Caird has put it as follows: "The Pharisees, in their passionate devotion to the law, attempted to make it applicable to every vicissitude of daily life; and their method was to spell out in detail the exact reference of its terms, so as to define the precise limits of their liability. The question 'who is my neighbor?' is a request for definition; and the answer of Jesus frustrates the lawyer's desire to define his liability (Lk 10:29). . . . The righteousness which exceeds that of the Pharisees demands a positive commitment to the well-being of others; it is an ethic of unlimited liability" (Caird 1985, 24).

Luke's version, "You must be merciful" (Lk 6:36), is amplified by Matthew into the form "You must be perfect" (Mt 5:48). A great deal of commentary has been expended on Matthew's interpretation, which is often portrayed as an impossible ideal. In the OT, however, to be perfect is a human virtue indicating total loyalty (compare the "purity of heart" of Mt 5:8, which S. Kierkegaard once defined as "to will one thing"). Mercy, on the other hand, is the very nature of the God of Israel.

The law of non-retaliation (Mt 5:38-42) appears to be a reversal of the *lex talionis* of Exodus 21:24 ("an eye for an eye, a tooth for a tooth"), Leviticus 24:20 and Deuteronomy 19:21, and thus has implications for Jesus' view of the law (see 4 below). Some commentators, furthermore, have pointed out that to refuse to resist evil, even to encourage it (implied by turning the other cheek, inviting another blow), has often seemed unrealistic, if not outright immoral (cf. Dungen). On this two things may be said:

First, "love" in Jesus' command does not mean that Christians should have the same feeling for a Nero or a Hitler that they have for their family or friends. What Jesus requires is the unnatural act of putting others first, an act which will not be frustrated even by the abuse and hatred of an antagonist. This is the very nature of God. He does not return evil for evil (Mt 5:43-45; Lk 6:27-31); he expects no compensation (Mt 5:46-48; Lk 6:32-36); he does not prematurely condemn (Mt 7:1-5; Lk 6:37-38; cf. 1 Cor 13:4-7). Those, on the other hand, who harbor hatred in their hearts are guilty in God's eyes of murder (Mt 5:21-26), a precept the world cannot accept. While those who retaliate think that they have heroically resisted aggression, in fact they have made a complete surrender to evil. "Where before there was one under the control of evil, now there are two. Evil propagates by contagion. It can be contained and defeated only when hatred, insult and injury are absorbed and neutralized by love" (Caird 1968, 104).

Second, "turn the other cheek" is almost certainly an aphorism. Aphorisms are a common feature of human speech, and at times they are mutually contradictory (e.g., "Penny wise, pound foolish"; "look after the pennies, and the pounds will take care of themselves"). Such sayings are true of a certain person or situation. Elsewhere, Jesus implies that it is legitimate to resist evil. Rather than accepting the teaching of the Pharisees, for instance, he repudiates them for the wrongs they have committed against the people of the land (Lk 11; Mt 23). When struck on the cheek at his trial (Jn 18:22-23; *see* Trial of Jesus), Jesus is not seen to accept the affront quietly or to encourage another blow, but protests against its injustice. In Matthew 18:15-17 wrongs committed within the church are to be confronted and resolved, with the possible punishment of excommunication. It would seem that there are some instances in the Gospels where it is right and proper to remonstrate with an evildoer rather than let evil go unchecked.

4. Ethics and the Law.

Granted that this is the tone of Jesus' ethical teaching, what then becomes of the law? It is sometimes said that Jesus intended to found a new Torah, or at least that Matthew held this view of Jesus' teaching. In fact both impressions are false. The evidence that for Matthew Jesus is a new lawgiver is limited mainly to the arrangement of his teaching in five lengthy discourses, the first of which is given on a mountain, and the six so-called antitheses of Matthew 5:21-48. But over against these must be set other passages, particularly Matthew 5:17-20, which few will question enshrines *Matthew's view of the law and ethics.

The debate concerns whether, and to what extent, Matthew 5:17-20 represents Jesus' view. Much depends on the interpretation of almost every word of every sentence. What is meant, for instance, by "fulfilling" the law or by possessing a *"righteousness beyond that of the Scribes and Pharisees," or by keeping "the least of these commandments"? Such things could, of course, mean "to obey," to keep the law in its entirety. But this would make Jesus a martinet, a legalist par excellence. This reading is ruled out entirely both by the overall impression of Jesus' life and by Matthew's intention in his succeeding chapters to depict Jesus as setting aside parts of the law (at least the ritual parts concerning cleanness and uncleanness), and introducing drastic modifications of other parts. Or, on the other hand, "fulfilling the law" could indicate a penetration into the depths of the intention of the law, fulfilling its spirit rather than the details of its outward acts (see 4.7 below).

The great objection to the latter interpretation remains the "jot" (iota) and "tittle" (keraia) of verse 18. On the surface this appears to indicate a meticulous and literalistic legalism. But such an idea contradicts the manner in which Jesus behaves in the rest of the Gospels. There he is often attacked by the Pharisees precisely because he is *not* a legalist. One way out of the dilemma is to claim that Matthew 5:17-20 is Matthew's teaching, not that of Jesus. But this is unlikely insofar as we find the same tension preserved in Luke. In Luke 16:16-18 are three

verses wedged between two Lukan parables commonly attributed to the Q source (see Synoptic Problem), but which make an odd sequence. But it does not take long to see the connecting link: all three concern the law. The first (v. 16) affirms that the law has passed away, the second (v. 17) that the law can never pass away, while the third (v. 18) demands a radical obedience which even the Pharisees did not require. Thus by most canons of Gospel criticism these Lukan verses provide some justification for thinking that Matthew 5:17-20 is not peculiarly Matthean. The only sense in which they can be seen as such is that Matthew may have found them isolated in his source and put them together in his own interesting juxtaposition. But there is no longer any reason to doubt that Matthew could here be representing the viewpoint of Jesus.

Another passage which undermines the conception that Matthew represents Jesus as a new lawgiver is Matthew 23:2-3. Here the denunciation of the Pharisees opens with a sanction of Moses' teaching. "The Scribes and Pharisees sit upon the seat of Moses. Everything they tell you to do, do and observe. But do not do according to their works, for they say and do not do." But considering once again that in the Gospels Jesus spends much of his time engaging in debate with the Pharisees precisely over their respective interpretations of the law, this instruction seems odd at the very least.

We are therefore faced all the way through with a mystery, a paradoxical nature of Jesus' teaching. Part of the explanation may lie in the nature of the Jewish law. In addition to being the religious charter of the nation, the Torah was the civil and criminal code, and the Pharisees were its lawyers. In this case Matthew 5:20; 23:2-3 and Luke 16:17 probably raise the same questions as does Paul's advice in Romans 13:1-4: The civil powers are ordained by God; therefore, accept their authority.

If, then, there are indications that Jesus was in fact not a new lawgiver, what could he have been doing? The easiest way to understand his approach is to recognize that he is drawing a number of subtle distinctions. We may begin with his treatment of the sabbath.

4.1. The Sabbath. There is little doubt that the breaking of the sabbath by Jesus was one of the principal sources of friction with the Pharisees. In justice, however, it is important to realize what the sabbath meant to them. The sabbath was the outward symbol of the covenant with Israel (Ex 31:12-17). In the Diaspora the sabbath was the primary bulwark against the assimilation of the Jews into the culture and religion of pagan society, and any threat to the sabbath was a threat to the very existence of Israel. The Pharisees therefore had a legitimate cause for which they were fighting.

In light of this it comes as a surprise that in the Gospels Jesus is seen to break the sabbath deliberately, an act which undermines both Pharisaic and Mishnaic concerns. The Pharisees in particular were zealous to obey all 613 commandments in their everyday life, and, unlike the backward-looking and conservative Sadducees, they were progressive in their earnest desire to understand what the law means.

This desire is especially seen in the Pharisaic concern with defining "work." In the Mishnah, for example, work is broken down into thirty-nine different activities (see Rabbinic Traditions and Writings). This in turn gave rise to some very important disputes, such as whether a doctor may work on the sabbath. Doctors, it was decided, could work on the sabbath if death were imminent, but in other cases they must desist (cf. Mk 1:32, where the people waited until the end of the sabbath at sunset before presenting the sick to Jesus for healing).

Jesus apparently had no such reservations. The Gospels relate four accounts in which he invited the wrath of the Pharisees by healing on the sabbath, and in none of the four cases can the sick person be said to be in any immediate danger. One had a withered hand (Mk 3:1-6); two were paralytics, one for eighteen years (Lk 13:10-17), the other for thirty-eight (Jn 5:2-18); and one had dropsy (Lk 14:1-6). The Pharisees' claim that in each case the cure could have been delayed one more day seems justified. And yet in all four cases Jesus goes on the offensive, choosing the sabbath as the right day for such merciful interventions.

The gravamen of the Pharisees' complaint was that Jesus was setting himself above the sabbath, and therefore changing the law of Moses. Jesus' answer to this charge is found in his comment after he healed the woman who had been paralyzed: "Was it not necessary that this woman, a daughter of *Abraham whom Satan has bound for eighteen years, be loosed from this bond on the sabbath day?" (Lk 13:16). In Mark's three passion predictions (Mk 8:31; 9:31; 10:32-

34) the important word dei, "it is necessary," is used to denote a divine necessity for Jesus' death laid down for him in Scripture. There was also a divine necessity for healing on the sabbath, insofar as the sabbath was divinely ordained to be for Israel a foretaste of the kingdom of God. By healing those bound by the kingdom of Satan, Jesus had enabled the kingdom of God to break in on human life (Lk 11:20; Mk 3:27). Thus, since the sabbath was a foretaste of the kingdom, there was no better day for him to perform his acts of mercy. Since the kingdom had arrived, the *Son of Man was Lord of the sabbath (Mk 2:28).

When Jesus' disciples pluck ears of grain on the sabbath (Mk 2:23-28), it therefore comes as no surprise that Jesus should appeal to David's example in 1 Samuel 21:1-6, with the added comment that "the sabbath was made for humankind, not humankind for the sabbath" (Mk 2:27). This indicates something that for Jesus the Pharisees had missed—the humanitarian purpose of the sabbath in Deuteronomy. To interpret it in an antihumanitarian fashion is to misinterpret it. Matthew 12:5-7 makes the same case. If the kingdom has arrived, all this activity is justified. The Pharisees, of course, do not accept that the kingdom has arrived. Here it would appear that the author of Hebrews has faithfully represented Jesus' teaching by seeing the sabbath as a shadow of that rest which remains for the people of God when they enter the kingdom (cf. Heb 4). The followers of Jesus live in a constant sabbath rest insofar as they live in the kingdom. They are the weary and heavy-laden who have found rest (Mt 11:28).

4.2. Divorce. Another example of Jesus' approach to the law was his treatment of divorce. But any discussion of this issue will be complicated if one compares Mark and Matthew on the subject. We cannot here elaborate the problem, except to say that there are good grounds for assuming that Mark is right to say that Jesus did not allow divorce among his followers on any pretext, and that something has gone wrong in our extant version of Matthew, in which mē epi porneia indicates an exception (Mt 19:9; cf. Mk 10:2-12; see Banks, Guelich, Mohrlang).

The occasion of Jesus' teaching was a question about the interpretation of the Mosaic law found in Deuteronomy 24:1-2, where a man is allowed to divorce his wife if some "unseemly thing" (Heb erwaṭ dābār) is found in her. On the basis of this law the conservative followers of Rabbi Shammai permitted divorce only for proven adultery, the liberal followers of Rabbi Hillel allowed it if the husband disliked his wife's cooking, and Rabbi Akiba allowed it even if a man would see a woman more beautiful than his wife.

Jesus' response to all of this is that divorce was allowed by Moses—but only because of the hardness of the human heart. It was never the will of God, only permitted. Rather than abolishing the law, Jesus moves to another passage, Genesis 2—a weightier passage than Deuteronomy. Genesis 2 was Torah as much as Deuteronomy 24. But it reveals God's intention not merely as lawgiver but as Creator. There is a law of God built into creation—lifelong fidelity—to which Deuteronomy is but an afterthought. If Jesus goes on to say that remarriage after divorce is adultery, it would not represent for him new legislation. Where there is hardness of heart, divorce is inevitable and lawful. But where the kingdom has been preached, where men and women have accepted the invitation to enter the kingdom, putting themselves under God's kingly reign, it now becomes possible to deal with hardness of heart; it is now possible to attain to the purposes of the Creator. In the kingdom, divorce is not so much forbidden as it is unnecessary. There is now another way of dealing with it.

4.3. Tithing Mint and Herb. Jesus' concentration on "the weightier matters" of the law is also seen in one of his "woes" to the Pharisees recorded in Matthew 23:23 (par. Lk 11:42). The Pharisees "pay tithes on mint and dill and herb, but have no care for the weightier matters of the law, justice and the love of God. These you should have done, without neglecting the others." For the Jews who paid agricultural tithes, some produce fell into the category of the uncertain. Should one tithe on garden vegetables such as lettuce? Maybe. Parsley and mint? Probably not, but pay the tithe anyhow; you might be inadvertently breaking the law. Herein is illustrated the Pharisaic principle of "putting a hedge around the law"—not to protect it, but to provide a margin of safety. Whatever one thinks is right to do, go a little bit further. Any commandment is an opportunity to show one's obedience. The more trivial the commandment, the more disinterested and altruistic the obedience. For Jesus this kind of scrupulous observance of pettifogging possibilities will only lead in the end to a neglect of the cardinal principles. It is psychologically inevitable that such concerns concentrate on the manageable—the visual, perceptible things—to the neglect of "the weightier matters."

4.4. Other Legal Matters: Oaths, Murder. So far we have seen no evidence of Jesus rescinding the law. In Matthew and Luke it is clear that a superficial obedience to the Decalogue is in view, and that this is not radical obedience to the purposes of God. Such radical obedience is the *righteousness which exceeds that of the Scribes and Pharisees (Mt 5:20). How extreme Jesus is on this point is further seen from a study of the other antitheses. The one which best illustrates the change he is introducing is the third, on perjury (Mt 5:33-37).

Here all swearing is forbidden with the stunning conclusion, "Let your speech be Yes, Yes, No, No; anything more than this comes from the evil one" (Mt 5:37). If this seems more than a little inhibiting, it is because we miss the point. What Jesus meant is clearly seen in the only parallel to this logion in the NT, James 5:12. There the form is "let your Yes be Yes, and your No, No." A yes must always mean yes; a no must always mean no. The reason an oath is said to come from the devil is the implication which lies behind it. If one is not on oath, he or she is free to tell lies. Jesus therefore demands an honesty so radical, so universal, that one's word is always true, whether on oath or not.

The taking of oaths then becomes not merely irrelevant but dangerous; it undermines the demand for radical honesty. That kind of going behind the letter to the intention appears to form the gravamen of Jesus' complaint. Rather than going too far, the Pharisees *did not go far enough.* The same point is made in the commandment against murder (Mt 5:21-26). Such a law is to be kept by a fundamental attitude of the heart which would make it impossible even to *think* of murdering. Behind overt action lies character and motive. One can pass a law against murder and then enforce it. But one cannot pass a law against being a murderous person. Law by its very nature can deal only with activities. It can, of course, take account of intention. Today some countries have a law against "loitering with intent." But first one must at least loiter. Jesus has in fact moved out of the realm of law to ethics proper. Ethics has a debt beyond the reach of law.

This is hardly to claim that Jesus was not interested in actions. There are a number of recorded sayings, particularly the one with which the Sermon on the Mount ends (Mt 7:24-27)—the saying of the two houses—in which doing is important. As much as any Pharisee, Jesus requires that ethical principles of character should find their way into action. But at the same time, for him actions are not enough.

We are now in a position to summarize Jesus' teaching about the law in four propositions: (1) There are weightier matters to the law; (2) one needs to penetrate behind the law's letter to its original divine intention; (3) one needs to penetrate behind action to character; and (4) it is possible to take this view of the law because the kingdom has arrived.

4.5. The Role of the Heart. In Mark 10:43-44 (par. Mt 20:25-27) Jesus says, "Among you, whoever wants to be great must be your servant, and whoever wants to be first must be the slave of all" (REB). This text can be generalized as one of the major headings of the ethical teaching of Jesus. Among whom? Among you who have entered the kingdom. The ethical teaching of Jesus is the way of the kingdom. His teaching is not to be interpreted prescriptively as commandments to be obeyed as the Jews obeyed the Decalogue. For Jesus, ethics are primarily *descriptive;* they illustrate how men and *women will behave in the kingdom. "If you enter the kingdom, this is what you will be taking on—a higher standard of ethical observance than can ever be enforced by law." The reference to the heart (Mk 7:18-23 par. Mt 15:17-20) is especially noteworthy: "It is not what goes in that defiles . . . it is what comes out; for from within, from the heart, comes evil thoughts, fornications, thefts, murders, adulteries and so forth." Mark adds, in effect, that by saying this Jesus abrogated the whole Levitical law regarding cleanness and uncleanness (Mk 7:19; cf. Acts 10:10-16). Whatever else Jesus may complete and confirm, he does not keep that part of the law. It is the heart which is the source of evil, and it is the heart which must be changed, with behavior following spontaneously.

And where for Jesus does the law and his own example fit into all of this? The tree is known by its fruit (Mt 7:17-20; Lk 6:43-45). Behavior flows from the heart, and if the heart is changed, then with the law of the OT and the example of Jesus as a guide, men and women can find their way to the practical application of their obedience to the law of love and to the radical demands of the God who is king.

4.6. The Final Split with the Pharisees. Such an interpretation of the law was bound to bring Jesus and the Pharisees to a final parting of the ways. Here it is wiser to follow Luke's version of the vitriolic "woes" (Lk 11:37-52), which have undergone less editing than Matthew's (Mt 23:13-36). For Jesus the Pharisees concentrate on minutiae to the neglect of the weightier matters (Lk 11:42). They are like unmarked graves which men and women walk over without being aware of the contamination they incur (Lk 11:44 par. Mt 23:27)—a comment showing Jesus' deep sense of irony.

The Pharisees attacked Jesus for not avoiding the company of contaminating people; Jesus turns the Pharisees on their heads by telling the crowds, "Beware of the leaven of the Pharisees" (Mk 11:15). Leaven here is a symbol for silent, pervasive, spreading evil. For Jesus the Pharisees were superficial environmentalists: concerned with all kinds of outward pollution, they contain a deeper, more insidious, more virulent form of contamination—that contamination which comes from contact with those who think they know everything about God and his will but do not understand him in the slightest. Self-regarding and apprehensive, the Pharisees fear that the holiness of Israel will be contaminated by what it touches. To Jesus the holiness of God is capable of looking after itself; it is an outgoing power, reaching all who need help. It is incapable of being contaminated, except by selfishness.

But if the Pharisees and Jesus could not close ranks on this crucial point, it was also because they had vastly different conceptions of God. To the Pharisees, God was a lawgiver who approves of and rewards those who keep his law. To Jesus he was the heavenly Father who loves even his erring children and whose sovereign grace is a dynamic, redemptive force let loose into the world to restore and redeem. Those who took the Pharisaic view of God were relatively few, because in order to please such a deity one would have to be a professional; obeying 613 commandments is a full-time job. How is the layperson to carry such a weight? The Pharisees "load them with intolerable burdens and will not lift a finger to ease the load" (Lk 11:46). For Jesus the law is the gift of a gracious God, and to interpret it as an intolerable burden is wholly to misunderstand the God from whom it comes. If ordinary men and women break down under the strain of obedience to the law, then there must be something seriously wrong with that reading of the will of God.

4.7. Fulfilling the Law. If what we have said above constitutes Jesus' approach to the law, how then can it be said that Jesus fulfills it? Returning to Matthew 5:17, it is probable that the word *fulfill* here "includes not only an element of discontinuity (that which has now been realized *transcends* the law) but an element of continuity as well (that which transcends the law is nevertheless something to which the law itself *points forward*" [Banks]). Putting it another way, to say that the teaching of Jesus fulfills the law is to say that his teaching "fills the law full"—with new meaning.

5. Conclusion.

The ethical teaching of Jesus may now be summarized under five points.

5.1. The Presence of the Kingdom. On the question of Jesus' expectation of the future, Schweitzer was radically mistaken. But modified forms of his thesis are still with us. Too much attention continues to be paid to the notion that for Jesus the kingdom was focused primarily on some event or events subsequent to the initial proclamation recorded in Mark 1:15. Those who hold this view, of course, will always find deep embarrassment in fitting ethics into their scheme; but that has not stopped them from futurizing the kingdom, even at the expense of robbing Jesus' ethics of their ultimate basis. Jesus, on the other hand, taught that entry into the kingdom was synonymous with entering the life of discipleship—of submitting to the demands of the God who is king. His ethics are dominated by the central burning conviction that God's rule is now actively present in the affairs of individuals, kings and nations.

5.2. The Priority of Character. For Jesus, ethics are to some extent realistic and pragmatic. Those who freely receive God's gifts must (1) show them in outward acts, and (2) pass them on to others, lest they become stagnant and die. But ethics are also the fruit of character, a claim that many of the Pharisees, with their exclusive emphasis on outward acts, could not accept. The rewards that Jesus promises are not extrinsic to human character, but point to the building up of a personality which would ultimately be at home in the presence of God.

5.3. The Rediscovered Spirit of the Law. The law of Israel was understood by Jesus as a gracious provision, given not only by a sovereign king but by a loving Father. To obey his law meant to be in conformity with the purposes that are built into creation. Jesus, like Paul after him, understood that a rigid obedience to the law, because of corrupting influences (selfishness, nationalism, pride), had failed to achieve God's primal purposes. Therefore, those who would obey God's will and respond to his love must go behind the letter, back to the law's original intention.

5.4. The Redefined People of God. What we call the gospel of Jesus was not in the first instance a new religion. It was a call to the nation of Israel, asking it to believe that God's power is always breathtakingly fresh, always ready to break into their history, always an outgoing and transforming power reaching into the lives of those who need help. But in order to receive that power they must also accept a radically different interpretation of what it meant for them to be the chosen people. Going back to the prophecies of Isaiah 40—66, he reminded them of God's kingly reign. Rather than privilege, they had been chosen for responsibility; rather than authority and glory, they had been chosen for service and suffering; that through them God's kingly power might reach out into the world, overthrowing the forces of evil.

It is in this context that some of Jesus' most powerful ethical statements are to be understood, particularly those which concern love. Rather than hating their national enemies and exulting in their ruin, the Jews were to love them and ask God for their well-being. Instead of avoiding their corrupting contamination, they were to become their friends. And, in perhaps the most uncomfortable statement of all, they were to content themselves with the benevolent administration of Rome. To make friends with Caesar did not mean that they could not also give to God a full and uncompromising obedience.

5.5. The Personal and Communal Dynamic. Finally, too much distinction has been made between the personal and the social in the ethics of Jesus. For him ethics were surely personal, insofar as they flow from each individual's relationship to God. But ethics must also be incorporated into the community of God. If the majority of God's people had not responded to the challenge, Jesus would work through a remnant, as God had done so often in Israel's history. Through Jesus—and subsequently through his followers, whether Jew or Gentile—God's promise to the nations would be fulfilled. The community Jesus founded may be understood truly as a "church," but only if that term is seen as a community of men and women in whom Jesus is personally present, who put one another before themselves and through whom God's redemptive power can reach out into the world, driving out evil and drawing all into a body of individuals who are willing to put themselves under his kingly sovereignty and fatherly love.

See also JUDGMENT; KINGDOM OF GOD; LAW; RICHES AND POVERTY.

DJG: COMMANDMENT; DISCIPLESHIP; DIVORCE; FAMILY; FASTING; FORGIVENESS OF SINS; HYPOCRITE; MERCY; OATHS AND SWEARING; PEACE; SERMON ON THE MOUNT/PLAIN; SWEARING; SABBATH; TAXES.

BIBLIOGRAPHY. N. Anderson, *The Teaching of Jesus* (Downers Grove, IL: InterVarsity Press, 1983) 79-148; R. Banks, *Jesus and the Law in the Synoptic Tradition* (SNTSMS 28; Cambridge: Cambridge University Press, 1975); M. J. Borg, *Conflict, Holiness and Politics in the Teachings of Jesus* (New York: Edwin Mellen, 1984); idem, "An Orthodoxy Reconsidered: The 'End-of-the-World Jesus,' " in *The Glory of Christ in the New Testament: Studies in Christology in Memory of George Bradford Caird,* ed. L. D. Hurst and N. T. Wright (Oxford: Clarendon, 1987) 207-17; G. B. Caird, *The Gospel of St. Luke* (London: A & C Black, 1968); idem, *Jesus and the Jewish Nation* (The University of London: Athlone, 1965); idem, *New Testament Theology,* ed. and completed by L. D. Hurst (Oxford: Clarendon, 1992; an abbreviated and revised treatment of this dictionary article by L. D. Hurst is found in chap. 9 of this work); idem, "Perfection and Grace," in *Duty and Delight: Routley Remembered,* ed. C. R. Young et al. (Carol Stream, IL: Litton, 1985); B. D. Chilton and J. I. H. McDonald, *Jesus and the Ethics of the Kingdom* (London: SPCK, 1987); B. D. Chilton, *God in Strength: Jesus' Announcement of the Kingdom* (Sheffield: JSOT, 1987); idem, ed., *The Kingdom of God in the Teaching of Jesus* (IRT 5; Philadelphia: Fortress, 1984); G. Dalman, *The Words of Jesus* (Edinburgh: T & T Clark, 1902); C. H. Dodd, *The Parables of the Kingdom* (London, Nisbet, 1941); D. L. Dungen, "Jesus and Violence," in *Jesus, the Gospels, and the Church: Essays in Honor of William A. Farmer,* ed. E. P. Sanders (Macon, GA: Mercer University, 1987) 135-62; R. H. Fuller, ed., *Essays on the Love Commandment* (Philadelphia: Fortress, 1978); V. P. Furnish, *The Love Command in the New Testament* (Nashville: Abingdon, 1972); R. Guelich, *The Sermon on the Mount: A Foundation for Understanding* (Waco, TX: Word, 1982); D. Guthrie, *New Testament Theology* (Downers Grove, IL: InterVarsity Press, 1981) 896-910; A. E. Harvey, *Strenuous Commands: The Ethic of Jesus* (Philadelphia: Trinity, 1990); R. B. Hays, *The Moral Vision of the New Testament* (San Francisco: HarperSanFrancisco, 1996; R. Hiers, *Jesus and Ethics: Four Interpretations* (Philadelphia: Westminster, 1968); J. L. Houlden, *Ethics and the New Testament* (Baltimore: Penguin, 1973); J. Jeremias, *The Parables of Jesus* (3d ed.; New York: Scribner's, 1972); W. G. Kümmel, *Promise and Fulfilment* (London: SCM, 1961); G. E. Ladd, *The Presence of the Future* (Grand Rapids: Eerdmans, 1974); G. Lohfink, *Jesus and Community: The Social Dimension of Christian Faith* (Philadelphia: Fortress, 1984); T. W. Manson, *Ethics and the Gospel* (London: SCM, 1960); idem, *The Servant Messiah* (Cambridge: University Press, 1953); idem, *The Teaching of Jesus* (Cambridge: Cambridge University Press, 1935); R. Mohrlang, *Matthew and Paul on Ethics* (SNTSMS 48; Cambridge: Cambridge University Press, 1983); E. P. Sanders, *Jesus and Judaism* (Philadelphia: Fortress, 1985); W. Schrage, *The Ethics of the New Testament* (Philadelphia: Fortress, 1988); G. H. Stassen and D. P. Gushee, *Kingdom Ethics: Following Jesus in Contemporary Context* (Downers Grove, IL: InterVarsity Press, 2003); A. N. Wilder, *Eschatology and Ethics in the Teaching of Jesus* (New York: Harper, 1950).

L. D. Hurst

ETHICS II: PAUL

Paul demonstrated the personal character integral to the new life created by faith in Jesus *Christ as well as the obligations for personal, family, *church and social relationships. The radical implications of this new *creation soon to be fully manifest at the parousia were related to the realities of the continuing present age. The ethical struggle had become universal. The contexts for such teachings were particular situations in his churches, but the "ways in Christ Jesus" apply to all the churches (1 Cor 4:17) and general topics are introduced. Not all admonitions have the same weight, nor does Paul attempt to be comprehensive.

1. The Basis of Ethics in Grace
2. An Ethic of Love
3. The Actor and Thinker
4. The Eschatological Challenge
5. The Tension between the New and the Old
6. Universalizing the Moral Conflict

1. The Basis of Ethics in Grace.

1.1. A New Reality. God's saving act in Christ's death and *resurrection is the ground of ethical appeal for Paul. "The old yeast" of vice must be cleaned out "in order that you may be a fresh batch just as you are, without fermentation, because Christ our Paschal Lamb was sacrificed" (1 Cor 5:7). Ethical behavior is to correspond to what God has enabled them to be through Christ's sacrifice. This ethical appeal has been called the "indicative and imperative" (Bultmann; cf. Gal 5:1, 25), that is, "become in your character and conduct what God's action in Christ has made you to be."

The imperative is not a secondary application of the *gospel designed for the spiritually immature. Betz suggests that in Paul's early letters, as in 1 Thessalonians, ethics was a means of preserving the present state of holiness up to the day of *judgment (cf. 1 Thess 5:23). Certainly by the time of Paul's writing Romans the connection of the imperative to the indicative clearly had become implicit. God's claims upon our obedience is "a constitutive part of God's gift" (Furnish). In Romans 6 union with Christ (Rom 6:2-11) compels behavior which is consistent with it (Rom 6:12-23). Even in the section of instruction the indicative breaks through (Rom 6:13). In Philippians, where Paul is confronting rancor by an appeal to Christ's humility and exaltation (Phil 2:6-11), he does not urge a self-conscious imitation of Christ, representing a moral ideal. He invokes participation in the ethos of the drama of salvation which is at the basis of their being as believers (Phil 2:5 may be so understood, but this is the occasion of recent debate).

God's power and sovereignty accordingly dominate ethics. *Righteousness does not make its appearance as the consequence of a life lived for *God, except marginally, as in Galatians 5:5. It is the presupposition, as a gift in *salvation.

God's grace empowers the new being created in salvation. "Grace reigns through righteousness for eternal life" (Rom 5:21). God works through the will and actions of believers for God's own purpose (Phil 2:12-13). God's gift creates the integral response of a whole person, whose conduct (Gal 6:4) and fruit (Gal 5:22) are described in the singular.

1.2. Grace Corresponding to Grace. God's grace is a power within the believers reproducing its own character. The letter to the Ephesians admonishes them to be imitators of God and "gracious to each other just as God in Christ was gracious" to them (Eph 4:32). Their conduct is to be loving because its foundation is the love expressed in Christ's sacrifice (Eph 4:32–5:2). Paul expresses the relationship organically: since the indicative is union with Christ in *baptism, they are bidden to live the life of the risen Christ himself (Rom 6:5-12).

The immeasurable inequality between the recipients of Christ's gift and Christ, who sacrificially gave himself for them, should make the believers gracious to those who are poor. In motivating the church of Corinth to give to the poor Christians in Jerusalem, Paul reminds them that Christ in grace became poor for them although he was rich (2 Cor 8:9). A genuine love will be demonstrated in care for the poor (2 Cor 8:8). 2 Corinthians 8—9 is filled with such correspondence between God's grace and the believers' generosity in contributing to the poor (*see* Riches and Poverty). God is the actor. Giving to the poor is prompted by God's grace (2 Cor 8:6-7), which enables believers to give even beyond their ability (2 Cor 8:1-4). God's abundant grace provides ample means for every good action; the poor will thank God for the surpassing grace in the givers (2 Cor 9:8, 13-14). The distribution to the poor is a harvest of the seed provided by God; God's grace flowing through them is manifested in the form of justice (2 Cor 9:9-10).

The arrangement which Paul seeks among the Christians in response to God's grace is one of equality (*isotēs*, 2 Cor 8:13-14). In Hellenistic Judaism the ideal government would distribute for "the necessary needs" of life so that there would be no "excess for luxury" nor lack (Philo *Jos.* 243; cf. 2 Cor 8:15). That the recipients are the poor and that this standard of justice is applied reveals elements of a social ethic. These two chapters, however, have frequently been neglected in treatments of Paul's ethics. One factor is the interpretation that Paul's concern is missionary diplomacy, validating his mission by an offering from the Gentiles to the Judean church. The logic within these chapters, however, is the social requirements of grace. This applies also to the view that "the poor" (Rom 15:26; Gal 2:10) was a title of the Jerusalem Christians, denoting their piety, not their economic need. Evidence is lacking, however, for such a technical use of the term by Christians at the date of Paul's writing.

1.3. Social Ethic as well as Community Ethic. A further reason for the neglect of 2 Corinthians 8—9 is the view that not only here, but also in general, Paul's social concern is limited to the church; thus his ethic of sharing is a community ethic, not a social ethic. The collection was directed to the poor of the *saints* (2 Cor 8:4; Rom 15:26). The givers indeed will be praised for "their liberality of sharing to them *and to all*" (2 Cor 9:13; cf. Gal 6:10). Does this broader designation denote needy people in general, or only the needy among all Christians (not merely those in Judea)?

Indication of a more universal reference is found in other texts which apply to non-believers. In Galatians 6:10 (in a passage which may also relate to the collection for Jerusalem [cf. Gal 6:6; Rom 15:27; but in contrast 1 Cor 9:10-11]), Paul concludes his discussion of giving with the admonition, "Do good to all people *[pros pantas]*, but especially to the household of faith." "Doing good" *(ergazesthai to agathon)* is terminology for kindly, concrete acts of helping others. The first part of the phrase is the general principle, followed by the specific application to the church. Some have argued, however, that *malista de* ("but especially") should be translated with the rare rendering, "that is." The few examples of this usage that have been discovered are ambiguous, however, and differ significantly in form and context (also cf. 2 Cor 1:12).

Loving service to needy non-believers is also evident in Romans 12:13-14. Paul enjoins hospitality in its literal sense of love for or care of strangers *(philoxenia)*, here meaning nonbelievers since it contrasts the immediately preceding injunction of sharing with fellow Christians ("saints") and the following stipulation of love to one's enemies. (The last connection is reinforced by the repetition of the verb *diōkō: pursue [diōkontes]* hospitality and bless *persecutors [diōkontas]*). Eusebius describes Polycarp as showing hospitality to his persecutors (Eusebius *Hist. Eccl.* 4.15.14). Since Paul does enjoin lov-

ing care to non-believers, the more ambiguous references of doing concrete acts of good "for each other and for all" (1 Thess 3:12; 5:15 [v. 15a would strengthen universality]; cf. 2 Cor 9:13) can be understood as pointing beyond and outside the church (cf. Phil 4:5; 2 Tim 2:24; Tit 3:2, 8).

2. An Ethic of Love.

Love is the specific pattern of life by which grace forms the new reality of the believer. The supernatural infusion of love through the *Holy Spirit produces the character upon which eschatological hope about the final *judgment of God is built (Rom 5:3-5). Love is the first fruit of the Holy Spirit (Gal 5:22).

The most significant question in current scholarship pertinent to Pauline ethics is the place of the law. In Galatians 3—5 Paul presents the law as a slave in sharp contrast to faith as a free woman. The law also was a slave attendant when we were schoolchildren, having custody over us until we came to maturity with faith. Now we are set free. Love gives full expression to the law (Gal 5:14) as we bear each other's burdens and thus fulfill the *law of Christ (Gal 6:2; cf. "law of faith" in Rom 3:27). Some would suggest that the law is no longer pertinent as a moral authority. The believer has been freed to consider all kinds of ethical traditions, sifting them by the law of faith and love.

Others have argued effectively, however, that what is at stake in Paul's negative treatment of the law is not the question of the source of moral authority, but that of the grounds of membership in God's community. The parallelism in Galatians 3:24-25 indicates that not being under the slave attendant (the law) is equivalent to being justified by faith (cf. Rom 6:14). Those who feel compelled to be circumcised in order to enter community membership are attempting to be justified by the law (Gal 5:4; cf. 2:16, 21; 3:11), which is what being "under the law" means. The question of the remaining moral authority of the law is left open.

When love is actualized, the other demands of God are fulfilled. Freedom in Christ is not an opportunity for selfishness, but compels us to be slaves to one another in love (Gal 5:13-14; 1 Cor 9:19). The fulfillment of the law then is not its termination but the full expression of its principles, purpose and motivation. Good and evil are determinate realities established and revealed by God, rather than, in terms of content, subjectively grounded in the relationship to God by faith. Loving one's neighbor as oneself (Lev 19:18) fulfills the second half of the Decalogue and "any other commandment" (Rom 13:8-10).

Love thus is not a replacement of the law, but a new motivation, understanding and power for meeting and surpassing its moral demands. The combination is crucial. Obedient deeds of great justice and self-sacrifice which lack the motivation and attitude of love are empty (1 Cor 13:3; cf. Ps 112:9 LXX). The law was good but weak in the face of the power of sin (Rom 7:11-17; 2 Cor 3). The Spirit of God sets us free from condemnation, which comes from the weakness of the law as the result of *sin. God's purpose at the same time is that the just requirement of the law might be fulfilled by those empowered and guided by the Spirit (Rom 8:2-4, 9). The just requirement of the law, which is in tune with love, remains as a standard of righteous living (cf. also 2 Tim 3:16). It provides a pattern, warning, instruction and exhortation, including matters as specific as sexual immorality and remuneration of leaders (1 Cor 9:10; 10:6-11). The law of Christ is the criterion of love which fulfills the law as it makes that obedience possible. For example, the obligation in the law of responsibility to the poor is carried out through the grace of God flowing through the believer (2 Cor 9:9-10).

3. The Actor and Thinker.

For Paul the human being is created as a member of the material world and as a member of society. Paul uses "body" *(sōma)* to refer to the person in relationship with his or her environment. As part of the body, one is part of the world and communicates with the world. "Flesh" *(sarx),* when used neutrally, describes human beings in relationship and solidarity with others (e.g., Philem 16). Negatively, flesh represents the sphere of worldliness in which the individuals share and from which they draw their values and goals (e.g., Rom 7:5). It does not refer to an inferior, material part of the individual. The promise that God "will give life also to your mortal bodies" *(thnēta sōmata,* Rom 8:11; cf. 1 Cor 15:42-44, 53-54) reflects the value placed by Paul on the body. He thus reinforces the continuity of existence before and after redemption, as well as the individual's relationship to the surrounding world.

In salvation, people are called into a new community, which is a new realm of social existence which God is calling forth, a believing and obedient human community founded in God's love and grace (*see* Church). Community needs are given priority even when they conflict with personal rights and privileges (1 Cor 10:23-24). Love toward those whose conscience remains uninformed restricts freedom in dietary and ceremonial matters that are ethically *adiaphora* (i.e., "matters of relative indifference"; Rom 14; 1 Cor 8, 10). In such matters Paul gives individuals considerable leeway, and in the pursuit of the good of others, seeking one's own good is not excluded (Phil 2:4 [note *kai,* "also," though the word is textually uncertain]).

For Paul the renewed mind has a critical role in discerning good (Rom 12:2; Phil 1:9-10; 1 Thess 5:21) in conjunction with the instruction of Scripture and common moral traditions. Christ and Paul (who himself emulates Christ) provide patterns for this way of life (1 Cor 11:1; cf. Rom 15:5).

Considerable attention has been given recently to the Pauline use of precepts from Hellenistic moral *philosophy, such as the lists of virtues and vices. In Titus 2:12 the state to which people are brought in conversion is described by the Greek cardinal virtues. Vices define outer boundaries of behavior which are beyond dispute. Some would suggest that the Pauline ethic is distinct only in its christological motivation and empowerment.

Paul's attitude toward non-Christians provides support for that usage even if much of it was through the mediation of Hellenistic Judaism. As illustrated in Romans 1, Paul indeed is highly critical of Gentile morality. His relating morality to nature (*physis,* Rom 1:26; 2:14; *ta kathēkonta,* "what is fitting," the Stoic term for what nature teaches, Rom 1:28), however, illustrates his agreement with Hellenistic Judaism that there is an affinity between the morality in God's revealed law and that disclosed in the created order, which God's people share with the Gentiles. Even in Romans 1 the moral problem for Paul is rooted not in the error of judgment but in a refusal of obedience.

Correspondingly, Paul recognizes knowledge of genuine values by secular people. His followers are to take into consideration "that which is morally good in the judgment of all people" (Rom 12:17; cf. 2 Cor 8:21). They are to conduct themselves becomingly *(euschēmonōs)* with outsiders (1 Thess 4:12; Rom 13:13). The term implies a common standard of what is decent, and traditional elements of morality are cited in both passages. Paul also conducted himself in a way which would commend him to every human conscience (2 Cor 4:2; cf. Tit 2:5, 8-10).

4. The Eschatological Challenge.

Christ is King. God has exalted him. Not every knee, however, has yet bowed to him (Phil 2:9-11). The present time for Paul is situated between the initial triumph of Christ over the powers hostile to God and Christ's securing from them full and final obedience and submission. At the parousia every power in opposition to the will of God will be destroyed (1 Cor 15:24-26). Even the last of these, death, is already in process of being destroyed (*katargeitai*, present indicative, 1 Cor 15:26; though some commentators would maintain that the present tense refers to what takes place at the eschaton, v. 24). At present, life is a battlefield of the divine and the demonic.

There is a divine purpose in history: "that God may be everything in everything" (1 Cor 15:28), the total sovereignty of God over all things (cf. Col 1:20; Eph 1:10). In the end the whole created world with its people, supernatural powers, natural forces and institutions will be conformed to the will of God. The purpose of the life in faith is the glorification of God (Rom 15:5-6).

In this ultimate purpose we have solidarity with the rest of the material world. The fallen creation retains within it a redemptive purpose. It will be set free from corruption at the time when believers' mortal bodies are redeemed from their temporality and weakness (Rom 8:18-23). The material world thus gains significance. A privatized sphere of salvation is not partitioned off from the rest of creation. In Ephesians and Colossians the church as the body of Christ contributes to the cosmic reconciliation of all things to God (Eph 1:22-23). Within it the hostility between Jew and Gentile is overcome (Eph 2:11-22). The church exposes the works of darkness through the word of God and deeds of goodness, justice and truth (Eph 2:10; 5:8-11; 6:10-17; cf. Col 1:6, 10).

Paul's ethics are strongly influenced by the tension implicit in the belief that the coming new age is present already (Rom 13:11-12), yet only partially. The expectation creates moral se-

riousness (Rom 13:13-14). The eschatological teaching of 1 Thessalonians 4:13—5:11 is placed in the middle of the ethical sections of the letter so that 1 Thessalonians 5:12 smoothly resumes the thought of 1 Thessalonians 4:12. The eschatological reserve means that while voicing a powerful expression of Christian freedom (1 Cor 3:21-22), Paul also warns that the eschatological time is not yet: Judge not before the final judgment (1 Cor 4:5).

5. The Tension between the New and the Old.

A tension occurs in Paul's teaching. On the one hand, he opens up radically new social relationships. In the new Christian existence there is neither male nor female, bond nor free. On the other hand, Paul upholds responsibilities for the social institutions that continue. The household codes enjoin subordination. The overall evaluation of Paul's teaching must keep both elements together.

5.1. The New Reality. The coming of the Spirit in conversion has conspicuous ethical and social consequences in the love, joy, kindness and self-control that it imparts (Gal 5:22-23). Colossians presents the abolishing of false distinctions among human beings as a renewal of the situation at the creation (*see* Creation, New Creation). This new nature "is being renewed in knowledge according to the image of its Creator" (Col 3:10). Redemption in Christ restores human relationships to creation as God intended it (*see* Adam and Christ).

When a person joins Christ in conversion, "there is a new creation" (2 Cor 5:17; Gal 6:15). One then no longer views other people according to worldly standards but as those for whom Christ has died (2 Cor 5:15-16). The old external distinctions of superior status related to nationality or slavery cease to exist (Col 3:9-11; cf. Eph 2:14-16). By thus "putting on Christ," "there is neither Jew nor Greek; there is neither slave nor free; there is neither male nor female" (Gal 3:27-28). For Paul this equality is based on the direct access every individual has to God (Rom 10:11-12) and the need of all for redemption (Rom 3:22-24). Each believer is distinctly marked, possessing gifts that differ in function. The gifts are equal in dignity, however, because they derive from the common Spirit (1 Cor 12:4-13).

Some have argued that the canceling of status distinctions relates only to the religious situation of grounds for *justification before God. This concern provides the context of Galatians 3:28, for example. Colossians, however, draws direct consequences for human relationships from the abolishing of status distinctions (Col 3:11). "Therefore . . . put on a merciful heart, kindness, humility, patience, bearing with one another and forgiving each other . . . and in addition to all of these put on love, which is the bond of completeness" (Col 3:12-16).

Paul does radically challenge religious privilege. Through faith in Christ all have access to God, are heirs of *Abraham and are therefore one (Gal 3:26-29). In Ephesians the terminology of the foreigner is used to describe the negative status that is overcome in the new unity in Christ of Jew and Gentile (Eph 2:11-22). The challenge of religious status is socially significant, however. Religion had been the central status distinction in the social system so that when this distinction falls, other distinctions follow.

5.2. Responsible Conduct While the Old Remains.
Paul also enjoins conduct that is much less challenging of the present. He recognizes the continuation of institutional relationships which are less than ideal but which serve to keep a check on sin. Daube argues that Paul's qualification, "I say this as a concession, not as a command" (1 Cor 7:6), is technical language known from concessions to sinfulness in the Jewish background. Thus a more accommodating ethic controls behavior in areas not yet transformed by the higher command. Some suggest that the primary motivation is to protect the reputation and thus the mission of the church (cf. 1 Cor 9:19-23; 1 Tim 2:1-7; 6:1).

In what has been called a "Christian patriarchism," the ongoing unequal relationships of life are not directly challenged. The "Christian" qualification, however, denotes that these instructions are framed by the lordship of Christ (e.g., Col 3:17). This stipulation poses opportunity for the application of love, which modifies the tradition significantly. Superiors themselves are required to reciprocate with a care for those who for the time being are in a subordinate position. These subordinate persons have already been told to obey their superiors lovingly. Husbands now are admonished, not to rule their wives, but to love them with a selfless love (Eph 5:25; cf. 5:21). The rights of the husbands are not mentioned; instead the husbands have special obligations (see Women).

Elements of Paul's own message of freedom were exploited by his opponents. In 1 Corinthians spiritual enthusiasts claimed to possess already full eschatological privileges. Even now they reigned as kings (1 Cor 4:8). Claiming mystical powers in a spiritual resurrection from the dead (1 Cor 15:12), they were convinced of their freedom and power in the Spirit. Their spiritual achievement could allow either antinomianism (1 Cor 5:1) or asceticism. Urging celibacy, they counseled the married to refrain from sexual intercourse (1 Cor 7:3) or to separate (1 Cor 7:10), especially from a non-Christian spouse (1 Cor 7:12), and the unmarried to remain so (1 Cor 7:8). In view of the end time, Paul does not fully disagree with the avoidance of marriage, yet he counsels responsibility to the mutual obligations of marriage and the claims of sexual ethics.

To slaves, who are prompted by these opponents to achieve a higher spiritual status through manumission, Paul's response is that neither slavery nor manumission gives superior spiritual status. Slavery is not a disadvantage in relationship before God (1 Cor 7:21-24). The governing principle instead is to live according to the will of God in one's various relationships (Bartchy).

In the household code of Ephesians 5:21—6:9, the mutuality demanded of the masters is grounded in both master and slave having the same Master in heaven (Eph 6:9). The masters are to carry out "the same things" for the slaves that the slaves had been told to do (Eph 6:9): obedience (Eph 6:5) and service (Eph 6:7). (In the household code of Colossians 3:18—4:1 they are to "grant the slaves what is required by justice and equality [isotēs]," Col 4:1.) Slavery similarly is ultimately undercut in Philemon, where Paul requests that Onesimus be received back, not only as a brother in Christ, but as a brother in social relationships (sarx, "flesh") and as a partner (Philem 16-17).

In 2 Thessalonians, social responsibility means supporting oneself by working (2 Thess 3:10). Some interpret the teaching as common morality used to address a typical situation of human frailty. The passage is opened up more fully, however, by seeing eschatological enthusiasm as the motivation leading some Thessalonians to eschew labor; scholars differ, however, as to whether the excitement is over the imminence of Christ's coming or a realized *eschatology (see Thessalonians, Letters to the). The result in either case is abandoning labor as no longer necessary or required. There may be a link with a radical interpretation of Jesus' teaching about anxiety about material necessities (such as may have been associated with the so-called Q source of Synoptic criticism). In this teaching they found the restoration of the Edenic situation of dependence on God's sustenance apart from labor.

The Pauline response is to describe this group as acting "in a manner which shirks responsibility" (*ataktōs*, 2 Thess 3:6, 11). Paul's injunction of labor shows that eschatological newness must be qualified by the concession of ongoing organizational principles required by necessities of the created world. The reply to the enthusiasts' rejection of civil authority had also been a call to order (*hypotassō*, Rom 13:1, 5; cf. 1 Pet 2:13).

This concession, however, is not a retreat to a bourgeois ethic, which Dibelius saw developed not only here but particularly in the Pastoral letters. Instead, a higher level of fulfillment of the new order is achieved by the concession. Concerns for mission (2 Thess 3:7-9; cf. 1 Thess 2:9; 4:11-12) and mutual love prevail. Love provides the context in which the Thessalonian believers are to work with their own hands (1 Thess 4:9, 11; 2 Thess 3:12).

In the Pauline church mutual love in labor is to be expressed not only in providing for one's own needs, but also in working in order to share with those with basic needs (Eph 4:28). Acts 20:34-35 ties these elements together. The standard for possessions is to be sufficiency (1 Tim 6:8). Riches are not owed to the rich and are futile (1 Tim 6:7). They also are a danger to faith itself (1 Tim 6:9-10). Paul desired that his followers have a devotion to Christ freed from anxiety, which came from being tied more than necessary to the fallen social order, which is passing away (1 Cor 7:32-35). Economic relationships with the social order cannot be avoided, but they should not be overused. Purchases will have to be made but without retaining more than is needed (1 Cor 7:30-31).

6. Universalizing the Moral Conflict.

Evil exists in the order of society (*kosmos*, "world") and exerts an influence on the individual (Eph 2:1; cf. Rom 12:2, with *aiōn*). This evil order is comprehensive in society, including necessary economic relationships (1 Cor 7:31),

social stratification (1 Cor 1:27-28), status distinctions based on religion (Gal 6:14-15) and its own wisdom (1 Cor 1:20).

The universal dimensions of evil are even clearer in view of the fallen angelic powers which, particularly in the later Pauline letters, are perceived to control the social order. Individual sins are patterned not only by the social order but also by "the ruler of the domain of the air" (Eph 2:2). "Our battle is not with flesh and blood, but with the rulers, the authorities, the rulers of this [world's] order of darkness" (Eph 6:12). The background for these supernatural "principalities and powers" (cf. *1 Enoch* 61:10; *2 Enoch* 20:1) is to be found in the universal care of angels over the creation (Deut 32:8; *2 Enoch* 19:2-5; *Jub.* 4:15) who are now fallen. Understanding the powers as angels in Pauline thought (cf. Rom 8:38-39; cf. 1 Pet 3:22) is more satisfactory than the position that Paul has demythologized them as dominating principles of existence.

The Pauline understanding of structural evil gives a societal, cosmic and universal dimension to evil. Oppressive forces are not confined to particular communities. They belong to the structure of human community as a whole. The struggle against evil, grounded in Christ's conquest of these powers (Col 2:15; cf. 1:13-16), then deals with factors in the very fiber of social existence. Despite this conquest, for Paul the victory will not be completed by Christ until the end of history (1 Cor 15:24). In Ephesians the church is pivotal in the struggle against the powers of evil (Eph 3:10; 5:11).

The fallen aspect of the social order, and the control of the fallen angelic lieutenants, is not total, however. Earthly authorities are appointed by God and serve God, and this perception still guides normative behavior (Rom 13:1, 4).

Despite the influence of Hellenistic moral philosophy, Paul's view of the cosmos and history give a different cast to his ethical perspective. On one hand, for Paul evil deeply penetrates the created order; on the other hand, he anticipates final victory based on the present redemptive work of Christ.

At the very basis of Christian faith lies a disruptive claim which throws into disarray the sentiments on which institutions of social and political life are founded. Not only is the righteousness of God announced as separate from a standing based on performance of the law; the resurrection of the crucified Jesus vindicates and exalts as *Lord one who was cursed according to the law (Rom 1:4; Gal 3:13). The ruler of the world joins company with those in rebellion against that very ruler (Rom 5:6-8; see Georgi).

See also ESCHATOLOGY; LAW; RICHES AND POVERTY; RIGHTEOUSNESS.

DPL: CIVIL AUTHORITY; CONSCIENCE; FREEDOM; HOMOSEXUALITY; HOUSEHOLDS, HOUSEHOLD CODES; IMITATION OF PAUL/OF CHRIST; LAW OF CHRIST; LOVE; MARRIAGE AND DIVORCE; SEXUALITY, SEXUAL ETHICS; STRONG AND WEAK; VIRTUES AND VICES.

BIBLIOGRAPHY. J. M. G. Barclay, Obeying the Truth: Paul's Ethics in Galatians (Minneapolis: Fortress, 1988); S. Bartchy, Mallon Chrēsai: First Century Slavery and the Interpretation of 1 Corinthians 7:21 (SBLDS 11; Missoula, MT: Scholars, 1973); M. Barth, "Jews and Gentiles," JES 5 (1968) 241-67; H. D. Betz, "The Foundations of Christian Ethics According to Romans 12:1-2," in Witness and Existence, ed. P. Devenish and G. Goodwin (Chicago: University of Chicago Press, 1989) 55-72; R. Bultmann, "The Problem of Ethics in the Writings of Paul," in The Old and New Man (Richmond: John Knox, 1967 [1924]) 7-32; D. Daube, "Concessions to Sinfulness in Jewish Law," JJS 10 (1959) 1-13; V. P. Furnish, Theology and Ethics in Paul (Nashville: Abingdon, 1968); D. Georgi, Theocracy in Paul's Praxis and Theology (Minneapolis: Fortress, 1991); R. B. Hays, The Moral Vision of the New Testament (San Francisco: HarperSanFrancisco, 1996); L. Keck, "Justification of the Ungodly and Ethics," in Rechtfertigung, ed. J. Friedrich et al. (Tübingen: J. C. B. Mohr, 1976) 199-209; J. Kilner, "A Pauline Approach to Ethical Decision-Making," Int 43 (1989) 366-79; E. Lohse, Theological Ethics of the New Testament (Minneapolis: Fortress, 1991); R. N. Longenecker, New Testament Social Ethics for Today (Grand Rapids: Eerdmans, 1984); S. Rostagno, "The Bible: Is an Interclass Reading Legitimate?" in The Bible and Liberation, ed. N. Gottwald (2d ed.; Maryknoll: Orbis, 1983) 61-73; J. P. Sampley, Walking Between the Times (Minneapolis: Fortress, 1991); W. Schrage, The Ethics of the New Testament (Philadelphia: Fortress, 1988); B. M. Styler, "The Basis of Obligation in Paul's Christology and Ethics," in Christ and Spirit in the New Testament, ed. B. Lindars and S. Smalley (Cambridge: Cambridge University Press, 1973) 175-87; P. Towner, The Goal of Our Instruction: The Structure of Theology and Ethics in the Pastoral Epistles (JSNTSup 34; Sheffield: JSOT, 1989).

S. C. Mott

ETHICS III: HEBREWS, GENERAL EPISTLES, REVELATION

The equivalent of the term *ethics* is not found in the later NT writings—or in the Gospels or in the Pauline epistles—but there is ethics. There is reflection and instruction concerning the character and conduct worthy of the gospel, rich reflection and inspired instruction, but the ethical teaching of the later NT resists any simple summary.

The voices in the later NT are "many and various," to use the words of Hebrews 1:1 concerning the prophets. To be sure, the voices all proclaim that "in these last days" God has "spoken to us by a Son," the final and definitive revelation, the One from whom and unto whom are "all things" (Heb 1:2); and to be sure, the story of God's Son is the foundation for reflection and instruction concerning fitting human deeds and dispositions not only in Hebrews but also in all these writings of the later NT. Even so, there are distinct voices in this literature, using different genres and addressing diverse communities in disparate circumstances.

1. Life in Light of the End: Revelation
2. Life in Accord with the Tradition: 1 Peter, Hebrews, Jude, 2 Peter
3. Life with Wisdom from Above: James
4. Life in Mutual Love: The Epistles of John

1. Life in Light of the End: Revelation.

The later NT writings see the moral life in the light of the end. The proclamation of Jesus and the earliest proclamation about Jesus, of course, had announced the end. The final *judgment and the good future of God were "at hand." The end of the whole cosmic story had been anticipated in Jesus' works and words and in the gift of the *Holy Spirit. Moreover, the end had been already established when God raised the crucified Jesus of Nazareth from the dead (see Resurrection). When the later NT writings appropriated the Christian tradition, they appropriated certain convictions about the end. They knew the end of the story, and when they thought about the conduct and character appropriate to Christians, they thought about conduct and character in the light of the end.

Nowhere is the link between ethics and eschatology more obvious than in the *Revelation.

As apocalyptic literature, Revelation is an unveiling of the secrets of the end. It and other such literature was not, however, written for the sake of divining the future. Revelation was written to console and to encourage the churches of Asia Minor suffering the emperor's oppression. It called for patience, not computation; for courage, not calculation.

Instruction in the moral life did not here take the shape of traditional admonitions and sage advice; rather, the author constructed a symbolic universe that made intelligible both the readers' faith that Christ is *Lord and their daily experience of injustice and suffering at the hands of Caesar. The rock on which that universe was built and on which the author would have his readers build their lives was the confidence that God has acted, is acting and will act eschatologically in Jesus Christ (Rev 1:3-8). There are sovereignties in conflict; on the one side are *God, the *Christ of God and those who *worship them; on the other are Satan, his viceregents, the beasts and "the kings of the earth," and those who prostrate themselves before them. The victory has been won by Christ, the final triumph is assured, but Satan and his minions still battle and threaten Christ's people on earth. That conflict is the background of intelligibility for their suffering and for their obligations.

The seer, exiled on Patmos, was keen to be a part of the battle and anxious about the churches on the mainland where some tried to avoid the conflict, accommodating Caesar and the standards of this age. "On the Lord's day" (Rev 1:10), taken to be the day the victory of Christ was celebrated, he saw and communicated his apocalyptic visions of the end and called the churches to share "in Jesus the tribulation and the kingdom and the patient endurance" (Rev 1:9; see Kingdom of God).

Life in the light of the end was here first of all "patient endurance." In the letters to the churches (Rev 2:1–3:22) the patient endurance John commended and called for took the shape of faithfulness in spite of the persecution by the emperor (Rev 2:3, 10, 13; 3:10), the harassment by the *synagogues that had cast them out (Rev 2:9; 3:9) and the accommodation urged and practiced by the false teachers (Rev 2:2, 6, 14, 15, 20). Patient endurance required fidelity in their devotion to God (Rev 2:4, 3:15, 16) and in their love of and service to one another (Rev 2:19) and resistance to the temptations to immorality (Rev 2:14, 20; 3:4) and the seductions of ease (Rev 2:9; 3:17).

The vision of the enthronement of the Lamb that was slain (Rev 4:1—5:14) is at once political and liturgical. The churches already participated in hymnic acclaim given the Lamb in their worship. They were heralds of God's reign and a token of its realization; they were the voice in their time of the whole creation, of all that was abused and oppressed by the false sovereign, of all that will be liberated by the Lamb that was slain. They were in Domitian's empire a counter-empire. The promise that they shall reign (Rev 5:10) stood under the standard of the Lamb that was slain, not of Domitian's pomp and privilege; their reign might thus, like that of the Lamb, be found through death but at least through "patient endurance."

The subsequent visions unveil both God's *judgment against aspects of imperial culture and God's good future, and that good future includes the vindication of the counter-empire and the renewal of the creation. In the four horsemen the empire of Domitian rides on the earth with military expansionism, civil strife and war, the inflation that robs the poor of sustenance, and death (Rev 6:1-8), but the victory of God answers the plea of the martyrs (Rev 6:10) and brings in its train not strife and hunger and death but complete well-being (Rev 7:15-17). The beasts use political power (Rev 13:5-7) and economic power (Rev 13:16-17) to persecute and oppress, but the victory of God brings the fall of Babylon/Rome and the unveiling of a new Jerusalem.

The vision of Babylon and its fall (Rev 17:1—19:10) portrays the great splendor of Rome, but its wealth and power cannot hide the immorality, idolatry, oppression and murder that prompt God's judgment (Rev 18:2-8, 21-24). The fall of Babylon/Rome is lamented by those who are powerful and wealthy according to its standards and with its aid ("the kings of the earth," "the merchants" and "the shipmasters" [Rev 18:9-19]), but their dirge is overwhelmed by the rejoicing of those who heed the call for a spiritual exodus (Rev 18:4) and by the heavenly "hallelujah" (Rev 19:1, 3, 6). Such a spiritual exodus from the demonic values of Rome, the pride of power (Rev 18:3, 9-10) and the greed (Rev 18:3, 11-19) that marked Rome's life and justified its doom can be and must be undertaken in the light of the end, the victory of the "King of kings and Lord of lords" (Rev 19:16) and the gift of a new world and a new city where God dwells and reigns and blesses, and where God's people and God's creation flourish (Rev 21:1-5).

Watchfulness is hardly calculation. "Patient endurance" is not passivity. To be sure, the Christian communities in Asia Minor were not called to take up arms to achieve power; this counter-empire was not to plot a coup to seize economic and political control. But they were called to be a resistance movement, to defend God's claim to a world corrupted and abused by the spiritual and political powers. They were called to live courageously and faithfully, resisting the pollutions of the cult of the emperor, including its murder, sorcery, idolatry and the lie that Caesar is Lord (see the vice lists in Rev 9:20-21; 21:8; 22:15).

The exhortation to ethics in light of the end is found not only in Revelation but also in "many and various" ways throughout this literature. 1 Peter, for example, saw the moral life in the light of the "living hope" and "inheritance" secured by the *resurrection (1 Pet 1:3-5), reminding readers that "the end of all things is near" (1 Pet 4:7), warning them of the judgment (1 Pet 1:17; 4:17) and urging them to attend to Christ's glory (1 Pet 4:13; 5:1). Life in the light of the end is in 1 Peter, no less than in Revelation, patient endurance of suffering, "sharing Christ's suffering" (1 Pet 4:13) and his glory (1 Pet 5:1).

2. Life in Accord with the Tradition: 1 Peter, Hebrews, Jude, 2 Peter.

First Peter, however, is not an example of apocalyptic literature, though it reflects a church setting in a hostile world. It is a "baptismal anamnesis," to use the phrase of N. A. Dahl. Readers of 1 Peter are reminded of their *baptism, of their initiation into the death and resurrection of Christ (see Death of Christ) and into the Christian community—and of the moral instruction that was part of that initiation. Life in the light of the end was to be lived with fidelity to the identity given in baptism and in accord with the moral instruction that traditionally accompanied it. The use of these traditions is common in the later NT writings and in the apostolic fathers, but 1 Peter is a particularly rich account of the moral life as life in accord with the tradition.

The traditional elements utilized in 1 Peter include what E. G. Selwyn called an early Christian "holiness code," the instruction to "put off" vices and to "put on" virtues (here "rid yourselves" and "arm yourselves," 1 Pet 2:1; 4:1), the tradition concerning joy in suffering (1 Pet 1:6-7; 4:13; cf. Jas 1:2-4), the tradition of nonretaliation (1 Pet 3:9-12; cf. 1 Thess 5:12-22; Rom 12:3-20) and a *Haustafel* (1 Pet 2:13—3:8).

The holiness code instructed Gentile converts to "abstain" from pagan immorality (1 Pet 2:11; see also Acts 15:20, 29; 21:25; 1 Thess 4:3; 5:22; Pol. *Phil.* 2.2; 5.3) and called them to "be holy" (1 Pet 1:15-16; cf. 1 Thess 4:3, 7; *see* Holy) and to love one another (1 Pet 1:22; 1 Thess 4:9). It evidently related the Christian life to the end, to the revelation of Christ as judge and avenger (1 Pet 1:13, 17, 20; 1 Thess 4:6), and it construed the Christian life as testimony to those still in ignorance (1 Pet 2:12; 1 Thess 4:12).

The *Haustafeln*, or tables of rules for the household, instruct Christians to "be subject" (1 Pet 2:13-3:8; cf. Col 3:18—4:1; Eph 5:21—6:9; 1 Tim 2:1-15; Tit 2:4-10; *Did.* 4; *Barn.* 19; *1 Clem.* 21; Ign. *Pol.* 4-5; Pol. *Phil.* 4-5; 10, which called for mutual subjection). The *Haustafeln* take up conventional role responsibilities; it is God's will that while Christians wait for the end they should live lives beyond any reasonable reproach. Such lives will silence their detractors and serve the mission of the church (1 Pet 2:12, 15; 3:1-2, 16).

The redaction of this tradition in 1 Peter puts submission to government first. One may contrast this with Revelation, but 1 Peter knows that Christians are not merely subjects but "aliens" and "exiles" (1 Pet 2:11). Their submission is a free submission, not a constrained one, and it is balanced by the recognition of God's greater authority and finally set in context of a series of other obligations, obligations that may override duties to the emperor (1 Pet 2:17). The exhortation to slaves to be submissive (1 Pet 2:18-25) is not based on requirements of the role but on the example of Christ (1 Pet 2:21-23), and just as Christ's suffering led to his vindication and glory, so slaves may, like Jesus, trust the One who "judges justly." The admonition that wives be submissive (1 Pet 3:1-6) is given a missionary motive and is balanced by a reciprocal admonition that husbands "likewise" treat their wives with consideration and honor, recognizing "the weaker sex" as "joint heirs" (1 Pet 3:7) of life. "Finally" the duty of submission is the duty of all (1 Pet 3:8; 5:5). First Peter and the early Christian tradition of *Haustafeln* generally did not disown civic and domestic role responsibilities; however, by placing them in the context of the Christian identity and community and in the light of the end, it subtly relativized and qualified them.

Hebrews describes itself as a "word of exhortation" (Heb 13:22). There is little concrete moral instruction in Hebrews. The concern is not that the church does not know what it ought to do; it is that the church does not do what it knows it ought to. The Christian moral tradition has already informed the consciences of these people; the task the author undertakes is to exhort them against inattention to what they know (Heb 2:1), against disobedience (Heb 4:11), against becoming dull of hearing (Heb 5:11), against being "sluggish" (Heb 6:12), against weariness in their "struggle against sin" (Heb 12:4).

The theological basis for this "word of exhortation" is the covenant, more explicitly, the "second" (Heb 8:7), "new" (Heb 8:8, 13; 9:15: 12:24) and "better" (Heb 7:22; 8:6) *covenant, the covenant that cannot be reduced to a written code (Heb 8:10; 10:16). Keeping this *covenant is not a matter of obedience to the law of Moses; it is a matter of living in accord with the Christian tradition, in accord with the set of precepts that are exemplified rather than codified in the list in Hebrews 13: mutual love, hospitality, care for prisoners, respect for marriage. "Do not neglect to do good and to share what you have, for such sacrifices are pleasing to God" (Heb 13:16).

The failure to keep covenant evokes judgment no less in the new covenant than in the old. Hebrews warns against apostasy and deliberate sin with rigorous severity (Heb 6:4-6; cf. Heb 10:26-31; 12:16-17), and some early commentators took the letter to be introducing a system of penitential discipline in which there is no possibility of a second repentance (cf. Herm. *Man.* 4.3). The author, however, provides not a ruling in canon law but a warning, a "word of exhortation," lest the church become "sluggish" (Heb 6:12).

The letters of Jude and 2 Peter defend a life in accord with the tradition against the heretics who "promise freedom" (2 Pet 2:19) but "pervert the gospel of God into licentiousness" (Jude 4; cf. 2 Pet 2:2). Against those who "scoff" at the promise of Christ's return (Jude 18; 2 Pet 3:3-4), they remind their readers to live "lives of holiness and godliness" while they wait for the end

(2 Pet 3:11). Here 2 Peter adds a new note: such lives in accord with the tradition can "hasten" the end (2 Pet 3:12).

2 Peter also adds a carefully wrought catalog of virtues (2 Pet 1:5-8), noteworthy for the prominence of Hellenistic vocabulary in it and for its concern for moral development and progress.

3. Life with Wisdom from Above: James.

The letter of James is really a paraenesis, a didactic text that gathers moral instruction from a variety of sources, including Jewish and Greek, as well as Christian, traditions. As such it surely represents the moral life as living in accord with tradition, but it tests tradition and behavior by "the wisdom from above" (Jas 3:17). This wisdom is not simply based on experience; it is wisdom in light of the end. In the light of "the coming of the Lord," readers are advised to "be patient" (Jas 5:7-8). Such patience entails both the endurance of hardship (Jas 1:2-4; utilizing the tradition of joy in suffering [cf. 1 Pet 1:6-7; Rom 5:3-5]) and withstanding temptation (Jas 1:12-16, in the form of a beatitude, a wisdom form). Moreover, in the light of the coming great reversal (Jas 2:5; 4:6-10; 5:1), the rich are urged to repent. Such repentance entails rejecting the conventional reliance on wealth that passes for wisdom (Jas 1:9-11; 4:13—5:3), and it requires hospitality to the poor (Jas 2:2-6), justice (Jas 5:4) and tangible charity (Jas 1:27; 2:15-17; *see* Riches and Poverty).

The "wisdom from above" is not a human achievement but a gift "from above" (cf. Jas 1:5, 17-18). It is not an esoteric knowledge or Gnostic enlightenment; it results in virtue, in community-forming and community-preserving traits of character (Jas 3:17), so that Christians become "firstfruits of his creatures" (Jas 1:18), firstfruits of "a harvest of righteousness" (Jas 3:18; *see* Righteousness).

This wisdom must govern all things and not least for James that recalcitrant bit of human flesh, the tongue (Jas 1:19, 26; 3:1-12; 4:11; 5:9, 12). The tongue can be used to bless or to curse, to speak evil or to make peace, to deceive or to speak the truth in love; every time we open our mouths and let loose our tongues there is a struggle between the rule of wisdom and the reign of evil.

The "law" was obviously important to James (Jas 1:25; 2:8-12; 4:11), but it cannot be identified with the 613 commandments of the Torah or simply with the love commandment (Jas 2:10). It is the whole of morality as morality is known through Scripture and tradition and tested by the "wisdom from above" in the light of the end.

James's famous polemic against "*justification by faith alone" (Jas 2:14-26) was hardly interested in defending an alternative theology of justification or a new concept of faith. It was not Pauline theology that was opposed so much as the use of a Pauline slogan to justify libertine conduct (cf. 2 Pet 3:14-17). For Paul a faith that does not issue in good dispositions and deeds was incomprehensible; for James it was reprehensible. Both writers wanted a faith that acts (Jas 2:22; cf. Gal 5:6).

4. Life in Mutual Love: The Epistles of John.

The epistles of John (*see* John, Letters of) concentrate the Christian life into the duty of mutual love. Life in the light of the end in this "last hour" (1 Jn 2:18) is marked by mutual love, for it is love that marks the (already but awaited) good future of God: "We know we have passed out of death into life, because we love the brethren" (1 Jn 3:14). Life in accord with the tradition is marked by keeping "the commandments" of God (1 Jn 2:3, 4), but John never identifies "the commandments," except to say, "This is his commandment, that we should believe in the name of his Son Jesus Christ and love one another" (1 Jn 3:23; cf. 4:21; 2 Jn 6).

This "new commandment" (1 Jn 2:8) is not novel; it is really an "old" commandment (1 Jn 2:7; 2 Jn 5). It stands in continuity not only with the beginning of Christian preaching and with Jesus' proclamation (1 Jn 2:7, 24; 2 Jn 5, 6) but also with God's intention from the beginning, so that the devil's sin (1 Jn 3:8) and Cain's were precisely their violation of the unity and love that mark the heavenly reign of God. Love is the primal will of God, who "is love" (1 Jn 4:8, 16), the original and fundamental commandment, now "perfected" in Christ and in his community. To believe in this Christ is to stand under the obligation to love; his death on the cross is the way in which "we know love" (1 Jn 3:16; cf. 1 Jn 4:1-21). The faith that God sent Jesus in the flesh, that Jesus died on the cross and that the Spirit has been given expresses itself in love.

John's epistles, like his Gospel, focus on the community as the place love must be put into practice, but this focus should not be understood as a limit or a restriction. If we know love from the death of Christ, and if Christ's death is not only for us but also for the whole world (1 Jn 2:1, 2), then it would be quite unreasonable for the author to restrict love to members of the community.

See also JAMES, LETTER OF; LAW; RICHES AND POVERTY.

DLNTD: CIVIL AUTHORITY; COMMANDMENTS; CONSCIENCE; FAITH AND WORKS; FREEDOM, LIBERTY; HOSPITALITY; HOUSEHOLD CODES; IMITATION; MARRIAGE, DIVORCE, ADULTERY; OBEDIENCE, LAWLESSNESS; PASTORAL THEOLOGY; REPENTANCE, SECOND REPENTANCE; REWARDS; SEXUALITY, SEXUAL ETHICS; VIRTUES AND VICES.

BIBLIOGRAPHY. W. R. Baker, *Personal Speech-Ethics in the Epistle of James* (WUNT 2.65; Tübingen: J. C. B. Mohr, 1995); N. A. Dahl, "Anamnesis: Memory and Commemoration in Early Christianity," in *Jesus in the Memory of the Early Church* (Minneapolis: Augsburg, 1964) 11-29; R. B. Hays, *The Moral Vision of the New Testament* (San Francisco: HarperSanFrancisco, 1996); J. B. Lightfoot, ed., *The Apostolic Fathers* (Grand Rapids: Baker, 1965 [1891]); W. A. Meeks, *The Origins of Christian Morality: The First Two Centuries* (New Haven, CT: Yale University Press, 1993); F. X. Murphy, *Moral Teaching in the Primitive Church* (Glen Rock, NJ: Paulist, 1968); W. Schrage, *The Ethics of the New Testament* (Philadelphia: Fortress, 1988); E. G. Selwyn, *The First Epistle of St. Peter* (London: Macmillan, 1947); A. Verhey, *The Great Reversal: Ethics and the New Testament* (Grand Rapids: Eerdmans, 1984).

A. Verhey

ETHIOPIAN EUNUCH. *See* BAPTISM III.

EUCHARIST. *See* LORD'S SUPPER; WORSHIP.

EVIL. *See* SIN.

EXALTATION OF CHRIST. *See* RESURRECTION.

EXILE. *See* LAW II.

F

FALSE APOSTLES. *See* ADVERSARIES.

FATE. *See* RELIGIONS, GRECO-ROMAN; WORSHIP III.

FATHER, GOD AS. *See* GOD I.

FINAL JUDGMENT. *See* JUDGMENT.

FIRST FRUITS. *See* ESCHATOLOGY II.

FLESH: PAUL

Interpreters have long recognized a complexity in Paul's usage of the Greek word *sarx*, frequently translated "flesh" in English, and modern linguistics has shed more light on the nature of that complexity. Nevertheless, interpreters of Paul are still prone to speak of "Paul's view of the flesh." But to do so is to beg the question of whether by "flesh" we mean (1) the various notions to which that term refers in English usage; (2) the notions referred to by Paul in his use of the term *sarx;* or (3) one of Paul's more characteristic usages.

Option 1 is to be rejected, since it would imply that Paul wrote as a speaker of twenty-first-century English. In any event, there can be no consistent correlation between the various applications of the English term *flesh* and those of the Greek *sarx* as Paul used it. Option 3 is a better choice since it recognizes that even within a single language a word may have numerous meanings, some mutually unrelated. To speak of Paul's view of the flesh would entail selecting one meaning, or semantic field, from the array to which *sarx* belongs. This, however, raises the question: Which one? Such a selection would necessitate a different title for this article (e.g., "humanity" or "human rebellion") and would involve the study of the other terms belonging to

the chosen field (e.g., world, body, human, sin, spirit, promise). Option 2, then, is best here; it provides access to all the fields to which the Pauline term *sarx* belongs. One wonders, however, whether there are other concepts for which Paul might have employed *sarx* in his letters but for some reason did not.

1. The Represented Semantic Fields
2. Striking Formal Contextual Features
3. Comparison with Other Jewish and Christian Writers
4. Theological Issues

1. The Represented Semantic Fields.

Paul uses *sarx* in at least six different applications.

1.1. Physical Matter. Paul uses *sarx* to refer to the physical matter that makes up the living bodies of humans and animals. The most obvious instance of this application is 1 Corinthians 15:39, where Paul speaks of the various fleshly materials of animals (always living flesh, as opposed to meat). In this context Paul uses *sōma*, "body," in a manner parallel with *sarx* (1 Cor 15:38-39; cf. Col 1:22). Elsewhere, in Paul's metaphor "thorn in the flesh" (2 Cor 12:7) and in the synecdoche "flesh and blood" (1 Cor 15:50; Gal 1:16; reversed as "blood and flesh" in Eph 6:12; cf. literal use in Wis 12:5), *sarx* refers to physical matter. This point is not always noticed, since the entire expression in each case indicates "trouble" or "humanity," respectively. Similarly, in Paul's expression "fleshly hearts" (*kardiais sarkinais,* 2 Cor 3:3) *sarx* is part of an extended metaphor for the lives of the believers. Romans 2:28 (*en sarki peritomē*, "circumcision in the flesh") perhaps also belongs in this category, used here as a euphemism, though it could be included under the next category (see 1.2 below; note the qualifier *en tō phanerō*, "externally").

1.2. Human Body. By synecdoche, *sarx* in 1 Corinthians 6:16 envisions the entire body ("Do you not know that whoever is united to a prostitute becomes one body *[sōma]* with her? For it is said, 'The two shall be one flesh *[sarx]'* " NRSV, quoting Gen 2:24; cf. Eph 5:29-30; Col 2:1; 1:22?; 2:11?; Sir 25:26). Here *sarx* is placed parallel with *sōma*, and perhaps also with *melos*, "member" (1 Cor 6:15), and is contrasted with *pneuma*, "spirit" (1 Cor 6:17). In this way, *sōma* pulls *sarx* into its realm (contrast 1 Cor 15:38-39 in 1.1 above).

Under this category we should also include 2 Corinthians 7:1, where Paul can contrast flesh and spirit as a person's defilable outer and inner aspects respectively (cf. Col 2:5, and with *dianoiai*, Eph 2:3).

Sarx as human body is also subject to physiological states and religious rites. Paul first preached in Galatia owing to some bodily ailment (*di' astheneian tēs sarkos*, Gal 4:13-14), and his opponents there wished to circumcise the believers so as to boast in the condition of their bodies (*hina en tē hymetera sarki kauchēsōntai*, Gal 6:13, that condition contrasted with the cross of Christ in Gal 6:14). Paul's usage in 2 Corinthians 7:5, "our *sarx* had no rest," may be better classed in 1.3 (see the parallel in 2 Cor 2:13-14 where Paul's inner anxieties are the point; cf. Psalm 62:2 LXX [63:1]).

1.3. Human Person, Human Race. In imitation of LXX usage, *pasa sarx* ("all flesh") in Galatians 2:16 and 1 Corinthians 1:29 (both of which parallel the expression with a human being), and in Romans 3:20, refers to the whole of humanity or perhaps to an individual (cf. Mt 24:22). More ambiguous is Romans 8:3b ("God sent his son in the likeness of sinful *sarx*"), which can be read as "in the likeness of sinful humanity." Paul's reference to the entire Jewish nation as "my flesh" (Rom 11:14) arises possibly from certain usages listed under 1.4 (*see* Israel).

1.4. Morally Neutral Sphere. Forming a group under this rubric are those passages referring to human relationships based on natural birth processes. All of these passages are concerned in some way with Israel, its traditions and its descendants (1 Cor 10:18; Rom 1:3; 4:1; 9:3, 5, 8). Of these references, the contrast between *sarx* and *pneuma* in Romans 1:3 is between Christ's natural human existence "from the seed of David," on the one hand, and his divine dignity on the other (cf. 1 Tim 3:16; Phil 2:9-11). In this case a negative shadow is not cast on *sarx* as is the case elsewhere (see 1.6 below: rebellious human nature).

The occurrences in Galatians 4:23, 29 are more ambiguous however. Paul contrasts Ishmael, the son of the "slave woman" who was born "according to the flesh" *(kata sarka),* and Isaac, the son of the "free woman" who was born "through the promise." If Paul views Abraham's first son, Ishmael, as born through his father's rebellious unbelief, *sarx* would carry a sense more in line with the usage described in section 1.6 ("rebellious human nature"). The subsequent contrast in Galatians 4:29 between the one born *kata sarka* and the one born *kata pneuma* (= Holy Spirit?) tends to confirm this.

To this category also belong references to the natural course and conduct of human affairs: Galatians 2:20, Philippians 1:22, 24, and probably 1 Corinthians 7:28, where a parallel is drawn with *kosmos* ("world" 1 Cor 7:31). In Philemon 16 Onesimus's relationship to Philemon is said to have a social dimension (*en sarki,* "in the flesh") in contrast to a specifically Christian dimension (*en kyriō,* "in the Lord"). "Our mortal flesh" *(tē thnētē sarki hēmōn),* in which Christ's life is manifested (2 Cor 4:11; cf Col 1:24), may refer to the human body (see 1.2 above; cf. the parallel with *sōma,* 2 Cor 4:10), but more likely it is a reference to Paul's natural earthly life. Paul's usage in Romans 6:19 ("I am speaking in human terms because of the weakness of your flesh," *astheneian tēs sarkos;* contrast Gal 4:13 in 1.2 above) concerns more than bodily weakness (cf. NRSV, "natural limitations"). In 1 Corinthians 9:11 and Romans 15:27 Paul claims that those who impart "spiritual" blessings have a right to fiscal support.

1.5. Morally Negative Sphere. Here we refer to Paul's use of *sarx* as applied to the "world," humanity's value systems as they stand in opposition to God's. In Philippians 3:3-4, which prefaces a fine description of a Jewish culture-based value system, and Galatians 6:12, which presupposes it, Paul characterizes the whole as *en sarki* (*see* Jew, Paul the). Another value system, based in Hellenistic culture but perverse like the first, is at issue in 1 Corinthians 1:26. Here Paul can characterize the "wise" (*sophoi*) as *kata sarka*, which he sets in parallel with "world" in 1 Corinthians 1:27 (cf. 2 Cor 1:12). Paul is accused of making decisions and living his life by these values (2 Cor 1:17; 10:2). This he denies; one can live in the midst of such a system without patterning one's methods on it (2 Cor 10:3-4). People, even Christ, can be evaluated from this false perspective (2 Cor 5:16); and hollow boasting is its natural consequence (2 Cor 11:18).

1.6. Rebellious Human Nature. Paul's most characteristic use of *sarx,* and his most frequent, is his application of *sarx* to sinful human nature (*see* Sin). Well over half of these instances occur in Romans, mostly in Romans 8. All others but one (1 Cor 5:5; cf also 1 Cor 3:3) appear in Galatians. Correspondingly, in over two-thirds of the many contrasts between *sarx* and *pneuma, sarx* refers to fallen human nature. Most of these are found in Galatians 5—6 and Romans 8; of the others (Gal 3:3, Rom 7:5, 1 Cor 5:5), Galatians 3:3 is almost programmatic for the whole group (see 4 below).

First Corinthians 5:5 ("hand this man over to Satan for the destruction of the flesh *[sarx],* so that his spirit *[pneuma]* may be saved on the day of the Lord," NRSV) is distinct in that it employs *pneuma* for the human spirit; nevertheless, *sarx* there does not refer to the body. Depending on how one dates Galatians and the Thessalonian letters, this application is likely a later development for Paul. He is not here recommending sickness or death but the destruction of rebelliousness, an effect synonymous with the crucifixion of the flesh, the Spirit's goal in struggling against it (Gal 5:24, 17).

For Paul the unacceptable alternative for believers is to make opportunity for this rebellion to indulge its desires (Gal 5:13, 16, 19-21; 6:8; Rom 13:14). One lives in the rebellious nature, there is nothing good about it, and through it one serves the law of sin (cf. Rom 7:5, contrasting with Law and written code; Rom 7:18, in parallel with the ego of Paul; Rom 7:25, contrasting with *nous,* "mind"). As mentioned earlier (see 1.4 above), in Galatians 4:23, 29 the contrast is between the one born either by his father's rebellious impatience or by the normal process of human reproduction, on the one hand, and the one who was born by the Spirit's intervention in that process, on the other. The contrast in Galatians 4:23 between *sarx* and *epangelia* ("promise") suggests rebelliousness on Abraham's part. Romans 8:1-14 is the classical passage on this subject, where rebellious *sarx* and the life grounded in it are contrasted with life in the Spirit (see 4 below).

Paul's use of *sarkinos* in 1 Corinthians 3:1 reads like an *ad hominem* criticism of gnosticizing believers at Corinth and probably means "immature" rather than "rebellious."

2. Striking Formal Contextual Features.
Several correlations between formal grammatical structure and semantic field assignment are notable:

(1) When Paul uses *kata sarka* ("according to the flesh") + VERB (e.g., 2 Cor 1:17; 5:16), the semantic field is that of moral negativity (see 1.5 above). When he uses *kata sarka* + NOUN (e.g., Rom 4:1; 9:3), the semantic field is that of moral neutrality (see 1.4 above). This was noticed by R. Bultmann (236-37) and is confirmed here (cf. *kata anthrōpon,* "in an ordinary fashion," 1 Cor 3:3).

(2) Every occurrence of *sarx* as morally negative (see 1.5 above) lacks the article. This is probably due to the stereotyped prepositional phrases Paul employs. All formal contexts have either the shape *kata sarka* ("according to the flesh") + VERB (e.g., 2 Cor 10:2, 3) or the shape *en sarki* ("in the flesh") + VERB (e.g., Phil 3:3, 4; Gal 6:12).

(3) All uses of *sarx* in the broad sense of "humanity" (see 1.3 above), except one, are modeled on LXX style: *pasa sarx* ("all flesh").

(4) Those uses of *sarx* that refer to human rebelliousness (see 1.6 above) almost invariably appear with the article. To this category also belongs nearly every instance where *sarx* is construed as the subject or direct object of a verb (the verb usually being in the form of an abstract noun), unless it is qualified by a possessive personal pronoun, in which case it refers to the human body.

3. Comparison with Other Jewish and Christian Writers.
In the LXX the term seems never to be used either in a morally negative sense (see 1.5 above) or as a designation for human rebelliousness toward God (see 1.6 above). This contrasts with Paul, for whom these two senses account for half of his usage of *sarx.* The closest parallel to Paul's use of *sarx* in these senses is 4 Maccabees 7:18. But while that document is contemporary with Paul, the usage in that passage is more in line with the Hellenizing ethical dualism of Philo than with Paul's use.

However, "flesh" (Gk *sarx* or Heb *bāśār*) is used in the Qumran scrolls (e.g., 1QS 11:7[?],

9[?], 12; 1QM 4:3) and Jewish apocalyptic (e.g., *T. Judah* 19:4; *T. Zeb.* 9:7) to refer to fallen humanity or a cosmic evil sphere. Oddly, the apostolic fathers are nearly in line with the LXX here. Even the rest of the NT does not alter this picture by much: it is used once (?) for moral negativity (Jn 8:15) and five times for rebelliousness (mostly in 2 Pet and Jude; cf. 1 Jn 2:16). The employment of *sarx,* then, to indicate fallen humanity and the evil worldly system of values is a decidedly Pauline phenomenon, with its roots in Jewish apocalyptic literature. It is imitated perhaps, but not wholeheartedly adopted by any of the other early Christian writers.

4. Theological Issues.

For theological implications of these data, fields 1.1-1.4 and 1.5-1.6 form two distinct groups: the first indicating a natural aspect of creation and the latter an opposition toward God.

4.1. The Flesh as a Natural Aspect of Creation. The employment of the term *sarx* in 1.1-1.4 (i.e., physical matter, human body, human person/race, morally neutral sphere), especially as the natural sphere in which earthly life is conducted (cf. Rom 1:3), implies that Paul continued to share the Jewish heritage of a high regard for creation. The ontological dualism of Hellenistic thinkers is ruled out in Paul's view, since while the fleshly body and humanity generally are weak and open to defilement, they are nonetheless redeemable and subject to resurrection. Paul's suggestion that both the flesh and the (human) spirit can be defiled (2 Cor 7:1) probably means that he entertained no ethical dualism between higher and lower natures coexistent in and natural to a person. The seemingly negative attitude expressed in 2 Corinthians 5:1-10 toward the body of earthly existence is not to be taken to imply such a dualistic view.

4.2. Flesh as Opposition to God. R. Jewett has shown how the development of Paul's various conflicts sets the scene for, and explains the inconsistencies in, his use of the term in 1.5 and 1.6 (i.e., morally negative sphere and rebellious human nature).

The following remarks can be made. Galatians 3:2-3 neatly sets forth the dualism that does characterize Paul's peculiar use of *sarx.* It is a dualism between flesh and spirit in the sense of flesh as an independent reliance on one's accomplishments over against a spirit of dependence on God and submission to his rule (see esp. Rom 8). In the controversy with nomists in Galatians 3:2-3, this translates into a contrast between "works of the Law" and "hearing with faith." Dependence upon human value systems and institutions for securing power and position, as well as libertinistic self-indulgence as a means of attaining "life" (Jewett), are likewise manifestations of a rebellious independence from God's promised provision of life and personal worth through faith in Christ. Ironically, then, by trusting in the "flesh" one attains not life but death.

This in fact is an apocalyptic dualism that proleptically views the regenerate Christian as already "in the Spirit" and under the rule of God by faith while still living a "fleshly" existence in this present age. The solution to the tension thus created is the continual putting to death of the flesh and its works. But the "death of the flesh" is abhorrent to a person and can be endured only by virtue of God's promise to have already endowed humanity with resurrection life in Christ (cf. Rom 5:12-21). To die this death, and to "put on" Christ, is to place oneself again, as once in Eden, under the protection and provision of God, to become dependent and trusting. It issues furthermore in a love toward other people that arises out of the assurance of one's security in Christ (cf. Gal 5:22-26).

See also SINNERS, SIN, GUILT.

DPL: BODY; PSYCHOLOGY; WEAKNESS; WORLD, COSMOLOGY.

BIBLIOGRAPHY. F. F. Bruce, *Paul: Apostle of the Heart Set Free* (Grand Rapids: Eerdmans, 1977); R. Bultmann, *Theology of the New Testament* (2 vols.; New York: Scribners, 1951, 1955) 1:232-46; E. R. Goodenough, *By Light, Light: The Mystic Gospel of Hellenistic Judaism* (New Haven, CT: Yale University Press, 1935); R. H. Gundry, *Soma in Biblical Theology: With Emphasis on Pauline Anthropology* (Cambridge Cambridge University Press, 1976); D. Guthrie, *New Testament Theology* (Downers Grove, IL: InterVarsity Press, 1981); R. Jewett, *Paul's Anthropological Terms: A Study of Their Use in Conflict Settings* (Leiden: E. J. Brill, 1971); K. G. Kuhn, "New Light on Temptation, Sin and Flesh in the New Testament," in *The Scrolls and the New Testament,* ed. K. Stendahl (New York: Harper, 1957) 94-113; G. E. Ladd, *A Theology of the New Testament* (Grand Rapids: Eerdmans, 1974); E. Schweizer, R. Meyer, F. Baumgärtel, "σάρξ κτλ,"

TDNT 7:98-151; H. Seebass and A. C. Thiselton, "Flesh," *NIDNTT* 1:671-82; W. D. Stacey, *The Pauline View of Man in Relation to Its Judaic and Hellenistic Background* (London: Macmillan, 1956); A. C. Thiselton, "The Meaning of Σάρξ in 1 Corinthians 5:5: A Fresh Approach in the Light of Logical and Semantic Factors," *SJT* 26 (1973) 204-28.

R. J. Erickson

FOUR-DOCUMENT HYPOTHESIS. *See* SYNOPTIC PROBLEM.

G

GALATIA. *See* GALATIANS, LETTER TO THE.

GALATIANS, LETTER TO THE

Freedom and unity in Christ are central themes of Paul's letter to the Galatians. His letter addresses Christians whose preoccupation with keeping the *law was splitting their churches along racial lines, separating Jews from Gentiles. Such splits could not be tolerated because "there is neither Jew nor Greek, slave nor free, male nor female; for you are all one in Christ Jesus" (Gal 3:28). This new unity that transcends all racial, social and sexual barriers is based upon the "truth of the gospel" (Gal 2:5): Christ was crucified to set us free from the curse of the law so that we might receive his Spirit (Gal 3:13-14; *see* Holy Spirit). It is the Spirit, not the law, who gives us our identity as children of God (Gal 4:6; *see* Adoption, Sonship). Believers must protect their freedom from slavery to the law (Gal 5:1) and yet use their freedom to fulfill the law by serving one another through love (Gal 5:13-14). We are no longer under the law that divides us; we are led by the Spirit who unites us. Paul undergirds these central concepts of freedom through the cross of Christ and unity by his Spirit with other complementary themes: an account of his call to evangelize the Gentiles (Gal 1:13-16), a record of his loyalty to the gospel for the Gentiles in his relationships with the other apostles (Gal 1:17—2:21), an explanation of justification by faith, not by works of the law (Gal 2:16; 3:6-12), an exposition of OT texts on the Abrahamic promise and the Mosaic law in the context of salvation history (Gal 3:6-25; 4:21-31), and a definition of Christian ethics in terms of the flesh and the Spirit (Gal 5:13—6:10).

The significance of these central themes in Galatians gives this letter a predominant place in any consideration of Pauline chronology and theology. The letter has had a profound impact on Christian thought and action throughout the history of the church. Luther called it "my own epistle, to which I have plighted my troth; my Katie von Bora."

1. Galatia
2. Historical Context
3. Literary Forms
4. Contents

1. Galatia.

Paul's letter "to the churches in Galatia" (Gal 1:2) rebuked the recipients for being "foolish Galatians" (Gal 3:1). His letter to the Corinthian church instructed that church to do what he had told "the churches of Galatia" to do concerning the collection (1 Cor 16:1). In a letter to Timothy he informed Timothy that "Crescens has gone to Galatia" (2 Tim 4:10). The geographical location of the churches in Galatia and the ethnic origin of the Galatians referred to by Paul is still a topic much debated by NT scholars. Some (notably, J. B. Lightfoot and H. D. Betz), following the majority of patristic, medieval and Reformation commentators, have argued that Galatians was written to Christians of Celtic (Gaulish) descent who were living in or around Ancyra, Pessinus and Tavium, three cities in northern Asia Minor. Others (notably, E. deW. Burton, F. F. Bruce and R. N. Longenecker) argue that the "churches in Galatia" were planted by Paul, as recorded in Acts 13—14, in Pisidian Antioch, Iconium, Lystra and Derbe in southern Asia Minor and consisted of Gentiles from diverse ethnic origins (Phrygians, Pisidians and Lyconians). The references in Acts 16:6 ("the region of Phrygia and Galatia") and Acts 18:23 ("the region of Galatia and Phrygia") have been claimed as support by both sides in this debate. To understand the background for this debate, it is necessary to review three stages in the history of Galatia: the Celtic invasion, Hellenistic Galatia and Roman Galatia.

1.1. The Celtic Invasion. When an army of Celts, also called Gauls or Galatians by Greek and Latin authors, invaded and subsequently settled in north-central Asia Minor (modern Turkey), they gave their new homeland their name, Galatia. Those Celts (or Galatians, as they were usually called in Asia Minor), who were of the same ethnic origin as the Celts of France and Britain, had migrated from central Europe to Greece. According to the Roman historian Livy (A.D. 23-79), they became "inflamed with desire" to cross into the rich land of Asia. Their opportunity came when they were invited by Nicomedes I, king of Bithynia, who needed mercenaries in his campaign to recapture the greater part of Bithynia. In 278 B.C. some twenty thousand Galatians waged war on behalf of Nicomedes until all of Bithynia acknowledged his sovereignty. Livy describes those fierce Galatian warriors, who inspired such terror "that the most distant and nearest alike obeyed their orders: . . . tall bodies, long reddish hair, huge shields, very long swords; in addition, songs as they go into battle and yells and leapings and the dreadful din of arms as they clash shields according to some ancestral customs—all these are deliberately used to terrify their foes" (Livy *Hist.* 38.18.3-9).

Livy's real purpose in giving this description was to demonstrate the might of Rome in defeating such awesome foes ("how far Roman valor surpasses Gallic madness"). But there must be some truth in his account because other ancient sources describe the way they ravaged western and north-central Asia Minor and were paid tribute by even the Seleucid kingdom until Attalus I, king of Pergamum, was finally able to defeat them and confine them within fixed boundaries after 232 B.C. Their territory was more than two hundred miles from southwest to northeast, bounded by Lyconia and Pamphylia to the south, by Bithynia, Paphlagonia and Pontus to the north, by Cappadocia to the east and by Phrygia to the west.

The Galatian people inhabiting this territory consisted of three tribes: the most powerful, the Trocmi, settled in the east around Tavium; to the Tectosages belonged the fortress Ancyra (modern Ankara); the Tolistobogii lived in the area around Pessinus in the western part of the Gala-

tian territory. Each tribe was subdivided into four tetrarchies, each tetrarchy having its own tetrarch, judge, military commander and two subordinate commanders. Representatives from the twelve tetrarchies formed one council, which assembled at Drynemetum. The Galatian nobility ruled over the native population. Although the Galatians maintained their Celtic language, to some extent they adopted the religion of the country. Thus a Celtic invasion from the west was the origin of Galatia in Asia Minor.

1.2. Hellenistic Galatia. Writing in the first century A.D. from a Roman perspective, Livy described the Hellenization of the Galatians: "those forefathers of ours had to do with true Gauls, born in their own land; these are now degenerates, of mixed race, and really Gallogrecians, as they are named" (Livy *Hist.* 28.17.9). Although the Galatians became known as the Gallogrecians, Greek-speaking Galatians, they are depicted by the ancient Greek and Latin historians as barbaric warriors, invading and ransacking neighboring countries. They were more influenced by local Phrygian culture and religion than by Hellenization. In Pessinus they participated in the famous ancient temple of the Phrygian goddess, the mother of gods, called Agdistis. The sanctuary with its porticoes of white marble was an object of great veneration. The priests were called potentates because of the immense power they exercised in their society.

The Galatian form of government became more totalitarian: by 63 B.C. the tribes were no longer ruled by a council and tetrarchs, but by three tribal kings; by 42 B.C. Deiotarus gained control of all Galatia after a civil war. In a series of battles the Galatians fought against the power of Rome. In 190 B.C. they sided with the Seleucid king, Antiochus III, against Rome, but they were defeated at Magnesia in 189 B.C. by Consul Manlius Vulso.

The Galatians began to see the benefits of supporting the Roman cause. So when the Roman general, Pompey, marched against Mithradates V, the Galatians were on Pompey's side. In 64 B.C. Pompey rewarded their support by designating Galatia as a client kingdom and expanding its borders to include regions to the south and east. When in 36 B.C. Galatia was passed to Amyntas, the secretary and general of Deiotarus, the territory included portions of Pisidia and Phrygia. Later Amyntas acquired a large part of

Lyconia and was given a section of Cilicia, called Cilicia Tracheia, and also much of Pisidia and Isauria by Augustus as a reward for his aid in the battle of Actium. As a result the territory of Galatia included a large area in the southern part of Asia Minor that had never been ethnically Galatian. When Amyntas, the last king of Galatia, was killed in battle against the Homanadenses in 25 B.C., Augustus did not entrust the Galatian kingdom to the sons of Amyntas but instead reorganized it as a Roman province under the author-ity of a Roman governor. Thus the Galatian kingdom became the Roman province of Galatia.

1.3. Roman Galatia. As a Roman province, Galatia included the original territory (the area from Pessinus in the west to Tavium in the east) with major additions from other regions: Phrygia, Isauria and Pisidia. Such cities and villages as Antioch of Pisidia, Iconium, Lystra and Derbe were now within the boundaries of the Galatian province. Portions of Pamphylia formerly belonging to Amyntas were restored by Augustus to Pamphylia, and parts of eastern Lyconia and Cilicia Tracheia were transferred to his ally Archelaus, king of Cappadocia. But in 5 B.C. the Galatian province was again enlarged by new annexations: a large section of Paphlagonia to the north was added, and about three years later part of Pontus was added and then designated as Pontus Galatica, to distinguish it from the rest of Pontus, which did not belong to Galatia.

By analogy with this official Roman designation of Pontus Galatica, it has been inferred that the references in Acts 16:6 and Acts 18:23 should be taken as proper designations for Phrygia Galatica, that part of Phrygia that is included within the province of Galatia, to distinguish it from that part of Phrygia that lay within proconsular Asia (Phrygia Asiana). On this basis, Acts 13:14—14:23 is viewed as an account of the planting of churches in the region of Phrygia Galatica, and Acts 16:6 and Acts 18:23 are taken as references to Paul's subsequent visits in the same region. The alternative view that these references in Acts 16:6 and Acts 18:23 describe a visit of Paul in the northern, original territory of Galatia fails to recognize the grammatical construction of these phrases in Acts ("the region of Galatia and Phrygia" indicates one region, not two) and the historical construction of the Roman province of Galatia. It seems that Acts follows the typical Greek practice of describing a

Roman province by listing the regions within that province.

Thus in the time of Paul the Roman province of Galatia extended from Pontus on the Black Sea to Pamphylia on the Mediterranean. "The churches of Galatia" addressed by Paul might have been in the northern ethnic territory of the Galatian tribes in the vicinity of the chief cities, Pessinus, Ancyra and Tavium, or they might have been in the southern region of the expanded Roman province of Galatia, where, according to the account in Acts 13—14, Paul visited Antioch of Pisidia, Iconium, Lystra and Derbe. Either a north Galatia or a south Galatia address is theoretically possible as a result of the greatly expanded boundaries of the Roman province of Galatia in the first century A.D.

The Greek geographer Strabo describes the population of the province as a mixed one and distinguishes Galatians, Paphlagonians, Phrygians, Pisidians, Lyconians and Isaurians. Most of these ethnic groups maintained their own languages. But whatever their mother tongues or ethnic backgrounds may have been, all inhabitants of the Roman province of Galatia were considered Galatians. Inscriptions bearing the names of slaves refer to them as Galatians even though none of them has a Celtic name. An inscription (first century A.D.) of Pednelissus, on the southern edge of Pisidia, designates that city as "the city of the Galatians." Another inscription of Apollonia in the Phrygian region of the province called the residents of that city Galatians. In such places as Athens and Rhodes there are numerous inscriptions on tombstones that designate resident aliens as Galatians even though the names are almost uniformly Greek, though some show a Phrygian background.

It seems that the name of Galatians was widely used as a designation for persons of Phrygian as well as Celtic origin. Although this fact is well attested (see esp. Hemer, 299-305), it is disputed by such reputable authorities as W. Bauer's *Greek-English Lexicon* and the *IDB* article on Galatia. The latter insists that "the name of Galatians would hardly be an appropriate designation for all the inhabitants of the Roman province, but rather would evoke special memories of the history of the tribe" (Mellink, 338). But if Galatians were only a designation for pure-blooded Celts, it could have been applied to only a very small number of the Celtic aristocracy. S. Mitchell provides ample evidence to show that "although the nobility seems to have kept distinct from the subject population, the lower class probably intermarried freely and by the second century B.C. has become at least partly amalgamated with it. It is significant that the peasant population at this date was referred to not as Phrygian but as Galatian, although it is quite clear that most of it was of Anatolian origin" (Mitchell, 1058).

Even where Celtic names are found, they are usually in association with Greek, Roman or Phrygian family name types. So the pure-blooded Celt must have been very rare indeed. The entry in BAGD bases its case on Memmon's frequent use of the name of Galatians for "the people with a well-defined individuality, who came to Asia Minor from Europe." On this basis it is claimed that Memmon "would certainly never address Lycaonians as Galatians" (BAGD, 150). Presumably we are to infer that Paul would follow the same practice as Memmon, a questionable inference in itself. Memmon, a contemporary of Paul, wrote a lengthy history of his own city, Heraclea Pontica. The purpose of his references to the Galatians was to show how the Celtic invasion in the third century B.C. weakened his city and reduced its territory. So his references do not establish the proper designation for the residents of the Roman province of Galatia in the first century A.D.

The evidence indicates that the name of the Celtic invaders became the name of honor for many diverse peoples of Asia Minor within the expanded borders of the Roman province of Galatia in the first century A.D. So members of churches anywhere in the Roman province of Galatia would have been regarded as Galatians in Paul's time. The question of their location in North or South Galatia cannot be decided one way or the other simply on a geographical basis and must await further treatment in the discussion of Paul's letter to the Galatians.

Near the end of the first century (c. A.D. 74), Vespasian detached most of Pisidia from the Galatian province. In the second century (c. A.D. 137) the Lyconian portion of the province was transferred to Cilicia and Isauria to form an enlarged province of Cilicia. Then, near the end of the third century (c. A.D. 297), the remainder of the southern regions of Galatia were transferred to a new province of Pisidia, with Pisidian Antioch as its capital and Iconium as its second city. The province of Galatia was thus reduced to approximately its ancient ethnological dimensions, the original northern territory of the Celtic invaders. It is not surprising, therefore, that patristic commentators, followed by medieval and Reformation commentators, assumed that Paul addressed his letter to churches in north Galatia, since that was the only Galatia there was in patristic times.

1.4. Culture and Religion of Roman Galatia. Galatia was a rural province. The few major cities, notably Ancyra and Pisidian Antioch, and small villages were separated by vast tracts of countryside. The province was normally able to supply its own needs for food by the production of grain, the basic staple of life. Wool was the product that brought wealth to the province. Much of the central and southern area of the country was a huge sheep farm. Strabo informs us that many people made their fortunes from sheep, especially Amyntas, who had three hundred flocks. Many of the decorated tombstones of Galatia depict the same objects: a yoke of oxen with plow and sickles to portray the planting and harvesting of grain, a distaff and bobbin to indicate the care of sheep and weaving of wool, and a vine or bunch of grapes to show that for many the production of wine was important.

The vast areas of farmland and grazing land were crisscrossed by Roman roads that tied the cities and villages together in a remarkably efficient communications system. The Phrygian cult of the mother of gods was widespread, as were temples to Zeus (see Acts 14:13). When Ancyra became the capital of the Roman province of Galatia, the imperial cult was established there. The remains of the temple of Augustus and Roma can still be seen in Ancyra (now Ankara, the capital of modern Turkey).

2. Historical Context.

To understand the central themes of the letter we must consider the historical context: the authorship, addressees and date of the letter.

2.1. Authorship. Paul introduces himself in the first line as "Paul, an apostle" (Gal 1:1) and underlines the authority of his decision regarding the problem in the Galatian churches with the words, "Behold, I, Paul, say to you" (Gal 5:2). His authorship is accepted by all except a few radical critics. Almost all scholars view Galatians as the standard example of Paul's style and theology.

2.2. Addressees. Paul addresses the recipients as his children (Gal 4:19). To sharpen our focus on these believers we need to consider their location, Paul's relationship with them and the crisis they faced in their churches.

2.2.1. Location of the Churches. Paul addressed his letter to the "churches in Galatia " (Gal 1:2). Scholars are divided regarding the geographical location of these churches (see discussion above). The weight of evidence seems to be in favor of a south Galatian location. In Paul's time Galatia was the name for the entire Roman province, stretching from Pontus in the north to Pamphylia in the south. All the residents of this entire province were properly called Galatians, whatever their ethnic origin. Paul normally classified the churches that he founded according to provinces: "churches of Asia" (1 Cor 16:19); "churches of Macedonia" (2 Cor 8:1) or "Achaia" (2 Cor 9:2). So it would be natural for Paul to refer to churches in Antioch of Pisidia, Iconium, Lystra and Derbe (all cities within the Roman province of Galatia) as churches in Galatia and to refer to the members of those churches as Galatians. Indeed, there would be no other single name that would be appropriate for them. Since there is no clear evidence that Paul founded churches in north Galatia, it seems best to take the account of Acts 13—14 as a record of the founding of the churches in Galatia that are addressed in Paul's letter to the Galatians. Acts 16:6 and Acts 18:23 refer to subsequent visits by Paul to strengthen those same churches in Galatia.

2.2.2. Paul's Relation to the Churches in Galatia. Paul's description of his first visit to Galatia indicates that he went there because of some repulsive physical illness. Nevertheless, when he preached the gospel there his converts received him as if he were an angel of God, as if he were Christ. Their response to Paul was extremely generous. Paul says that if it were possible, they would have given him their own eyes (Gal 4:12-15). When Paul portrayed Christ crucified, they believed and received the Holy Spirit (Gal 3:1-2).

2.2.3. The Crisis in the Galatian Churches. Soon after Paul planted the churches in Galatia, they were infiltrated by "troublemakers" who preached a gospel different from Paul's (Gal 1:6-9). The identity of these troublemakers has been the subject of extensive discussion.

It is most likely that these troublemakers were Jewish Christians who insisted that it was necessary to belong to the Jewish nation in order to receive the blessing of God. Therefore, they required the badges of identity peculiar to the Jewish people: circumcision, sabbath observance and keeping the Mosaic *law. No doubt they appealed to the example of *Abraham's circumcision in their campaign to persuade the Galatian believers that without circumcision it was impossible to participate in the covenantal blessings promised to Abraham. Probably the intruders had preempted Paul's authority by claiming support from the higher authority of the original apostles in the Jerusalem church.

The troublemakers were winning the Galatian converts over to their side. Evidently their message met a need in the Galatian churches. They may well have felt a loss of identity since their faith in Christ excluded them from their pagan temples and from the Jewish synagogues. So they sought identification with the Jewish people to gain a sense of belonging to God's people. It also appears that they wanted to come under the discipline of the Mosaic law because they believed that the law would give them clear guidance in their moral struggle. In any case, they were mesmerized by the message of the intruders and had become negative toward Paul.

2.3. Date. Paul provides an autobiographical sketch of his life from the time of his conversion to the time of writing this letter. A comparison of this autobiography with his other letters and Acts has led to a number of conflicting hypotheses regarding the place of this letter in the chronology of Paul's life (*see* Paul in Acts and Letters). These hypotheses can be evaluated on the basis of a consideration of three lines of evidence: the Jerusalem visits; the meaning of "former" in Galatians 4:13; and the location of the churches in north or south Galatia.

2.3.1. The Jerusalem Visits and the Date. The basic point of dispute in the discussion of the Jerusalem visits revolves around the matching of Paul's visits to Jerusalem described in this letter and his visits to Jerusalem described in Acts. Only two visits are mentioned in Galatians: Galatians 1:18, first postconversion visit; and Galatians 2:1-10, conference visit. Five of Paul's visits to Jerusalem are recorded in Acts: Acts 9:26-30, first postconversion visit; Acts 11:30, famine relief visit; Acts 15:1-30, conference visit; Acts 18:22, quick visit; and Acts 21:15-17, arrest visit. Of the many attempts to relate the visits described in Galatians to those of Acts, two merit special attention: Galatians 2:1-10 = Acts 15:1-30; and Galatians 2:1-10 = Acts 11:30.

2.3.1.1. Galatians 2:1-10 = Acts 15:1-30. If we

match the Galatians 1:18 (first postconversion) visit with the Acts 9:26-30 (first postconversion) visit and the Galatians 2:1-10 conference visit with the Acts 15:1-30 conference visit, then Paul's letter to the Galatians would be placed after the Jerusalem conference described in Acts 15:1-30 (= Gal 2:1-10). Such an equation seems reasonable, since both accounts of the conference visit refer to the same issue (the obligation of Gentile converts to keep the Jewish law), the same participants (Paul and Barnabas go to Jerusalem to confer with Peter and James and others) and the same decision (the requirement of circumcision is not imposed upon Gentile converts).

Two major objections raised against this equation are Paul's omissions under oath in Galatians 1:20 of any reference to the famine relief visit (Acts 11:27-30) or any reference to the apostolic decrees of the conference (Acts 15:20, 29). Some scholars assert that to hold to the equation of Galatians 2:1-10 and Acts 15:1-20 in the light of these two omissions necessarily involves an attack on the truthfulness of Paul's account or the account in Acts or both. Yet such scholars as Lightfoot and J. G. Machen, who certainly uphold the reliability of both accounts, argue that these two omissions on Paul's part can be explained on the basis that they are not relevant to his discussion in Galatians and therefore Paul was not obliged to record them. Since the point of Paul's autobiography was to record his relationship with the original apostles in Jerusalem, not his visits to Jerusalem, it was not necessary for him to refer to the famine-relief visit (Acts 11:27-30) since he did not meet with the apostles then. At least the account in Acts of that visit makes no mention of such a meeting. And it makes sense that Paul would not refer to the apostolic decrees, since they are not viewed in the Acts account as a negation of the major decision not to require circumcision. Therefore Paul's claim that "those who seemed to be important . . . added nothing to my message" (Gal 2:6) fits with the record in Acts. Since the Galatian Christians were all too eager to come under whatever decrees came from the Jerusalem church, Paul may have decided that any mention of the apostolic decrees would have been ill advised, unless absolutely necessary. Since he never appealed to the apostolic decrees in any of his letters, we may conclude that he did not feel obligated to do so, though some interpreters have suggested

that he may have been out of sympathy with the decrees. After all, his authority was not based on decrees from Jerusalem but on "revelation from Jesus Christ" (Gal 1:12).

Another criticism of the Galatians 2:1-10 = Acts 15:1-20 equation is that this equation makes it difficult to explain the withdrawal of Peter and "even Barnabas" from table fellowship with Gentile Christians in Antioch (Gal 2:11-14) after guidelines for such fellowship were established at the conference according to the Acts account. But even if the conflict in Antioch occurred before the Acts 15 conference, as some scholars suggest, it still is difficult to explain Peter's behavior. We still have to ask why he would withdraw from table fellowship with Gentile Christians in Antioch after the Jerusalem conference described by Paul in Galatians 2:1-10. From Paul's perspective, Peter's conduct is indefensible because it violates the truth of the gospel that had been defended in the Jerusalem conference.

2.3.1.2. Galatians 2:1-10 = Acts 11:27-30. The criticisms of the Galatians 2:1-10 = Acts 15:1-20 equation have led some scholars to suggest another equation: Galatians 2:1-10 = Acts 11:27-30. The benefit of this equation is that it avoids any suspicion that Paul has failed to report all of his visits to Jerusalem after his conversion since in this equation the first two visits in Acts equal the two visits listed in Galatians. And Paul did not refer to the apostolic decrees for the simple reason that this letter was written before the Acts 15 conference when those decrees were set forth. This equation also takes at face value the statement in Galatians 1:21, "Later I went to Syria and Cilicia." If Galatians 2:1-20 refers to the Jerusalem conference that came after Paul's mission in Galatia, then Galatia must be read into the statement in Galatians 1:21. But if Galatians 2:1-10 refers to a conference that occurred during the Acts 11:27-30 visit, then the natural reading of the text stands: Paul was only in Syria and Cilicia between the two Jerusalem visits of Galatians 1:18 and Galatians 2:1-10.

It is also easy to see similarities between Paul's account of the conflict in Antioch in Galatians 2:11-14 and the conflict in Antioch before the Jerusalem conference described in Acts 15:1-2. Both refer to a conflict over the application of the Jewish law to Gentile converts, and both indicate that the conflict was caused by a delegation from Jerusalem. If these accounts refer to the same event, then it would be reasonable to conclude that Paul wrote Galatians on the eve of the Jerusalem conference of Acts 15:1-20. And if so, then we can identify the conference visit of Galatians 2:1-10 with the famine-relief visit of Acts 11:27-30.

But this identification also faces problems. There is no record of a conference visit in Acts 11:27-30 or even any indication that Paul and Barnabas met with the apostles. Of course, Acts is a selective account, but there is very little evidence in the text for matching the Galatians 2:1-10 visit with the Acts 11:27-30 visit. Even though there are minor differences between Galatians 2:1-10 and Acts 15:1-20, at least both passages seem to describe a conference in Jerusalem. Furthermore, if Galatians 2:1-10 = Acts 11:27-30, then there were two conferences in Jerusalem. Many scholars have thought that it is highly unlikely that there were two conferences where the same people debated the same issue with the same outcome. This duplication of conferences is unnecessary if the Galatians 2:1-10 = Acts 15:1-20 equation stands.

2.3.2. The "First" Visit and the Date (Gal 4:13). Paul's reference to the time when he "first preached the gospel" in Galatia (Gal 4:13) has been taken as a clue for the date of the letter. Unfortunately, all sides of the debate claim this clue as support. Even if the term *first* should be taken as a true comparative (the "former" of two), it is by no means clear which visit it designates. It could either refer to the Acts 16:6 visit as the one before the second visit of Acts 18:23, or it could refer to the visit of Acts 13:14—14:23 as the one before the second visit of Acts 16:6, or it could refer to the Acts 13:14—14:21a visit as the one before the return journey of Acts 14:21b-23. So this term does not provide much help in dating the letter to the Galatians.

2.3.3. The Destination and the Date. The question of the date of the letter is related to the question of destination. But it must be admitted that a determination of the destination does not necessarily decide the date. If the framework of Acts is accepted, then a destination of north Galatia means that the letter was written after the so-called second missionary journey (after Acts 18:22), sometime between A.D. 53 and 57. If south Galatia was the destination, as seems more likely in light of the discussion above, the letter could have been written immediately after the first missionary journey and before the Jeru-

salem conference in A.D. 49. But if the equation of Galatians 2:1-10 = Acts 15:1-20 is slightly favored by the evidence as argued above, then the letter was written to south Galatia sometime after the Jerusalem conference, anytime between A.D. 50 and 57.

It has often been noted that a comparison of Galatians with 2 Corinthians and Romans shows a similarity of tone and themes, especially related to the controversy over the role of the Jewish law in Gentile churches. This similarity may indicate that these three letters were written during the same time, a time when Paul faced a fierce struggle for the freedom of his Gentile churches from pressure to succumb to bondage to the Jewish way of life. But attempts to date the letter on the basis of such theological comparisons with other letters have been used to support early (Longenecker) and late (Lightfoot) dates. The subjective approach of such comparisons and the occasional nature of Paul's letters (each letter responds to a specific occasion) render these attempts at best only secondary lines of support for theories in search of firmer ground.

The dating of Galatians is a notorious and for some a fascinating historical puzzle. But the outcome of the protracted debate about the date has little if any effect on the interpretation of the major themes of the letter.

3. Literary Forms.

Considerable attention has been given in recent years to the literary form of Galatians.

3.1. The Form of the Letter. A detailed comparison of Galatians to Hellenistic letters (*see* Letter, Letter Forms) of the same period indicates that Paul used a standard form of letter called the "rebuke-request" form (see Hansen and Longenecker). Unlike his custom in all the rest of his letters, in Galatians Paul does not follow his salutation (Gal 1:1-5) with any form of thanksgiving. Instead, he expresses astonishment and rebuke: "I am astonished that you have so quickly departed from the one who called you by grace" (Gal 1:6).

The expression "I am astonished" was often used in letters of that time as a rebuke for not meeting the expectations of the writer. The expression of rebuke was usually followed by reasons for the rebuke. Paul scolds his readers for their disloyalty to the gospel (Gal 1:6-10) and undergirds that rebuke with an autobiographical account of his loyalty to the truth of the gospel (Gal 1:11—2:21). Then he rebukes them for their foolishness regarding the gospel (Gal 3:1-5) and undergirds that rebuke by explaining the meaning of the gospel in the light of his exposition of the Scriptures (Gal 3:6—4:11). Letters of rebuke contained requests to set things right. Paul begins his request in Galatians 4:12 with the personal appeal to imitate him in his stand for the freedom of the gospel. This appeal is strengthened by an autobiographical account of his relationship with the Galatian believers (Gal 4:12-20) and an allegorical treatment of the story of Abraham (Gal 4:21-31). The request to stand fast for freedom is then spelled out in a series of specific ethical instructions (Gal 5:1—6:10). Paul underlines the main themes of the letter in his hand-written subscription (Gal 6:11-18).

3.2. The Structure of the Argument. Recent rhetorical analyses have attempted to explain the methods and structures of Paul's argumentation in Galatians. They point to many similarities between the structure of Paul's argument in Galatians and the guidelines for rhetoric in the classical rhetorical handbooks. Betz classifies Paul's argument as an example of forensic rhetoric since he is viewed as adopting the tactics of persuasion used in the law court to address the judge or jury in order to defend or accuse someone regarding past actions. Paul defends himself against accusations (Gal 1:10); at the same time he accuses his opponents of perverting the gospel (Gal 1:7; *see* Adversaries [Paul]). Using the categories of classical forensic rhetoric, Betz outlines Galatians as follows:

I. Epistolary Prescript (Gal 1:1-5)
II. *Exordium* ("introduction," Gal 1:6-11)
III. *Narratio* ("narration," Gal 1:12—2:14)
IV. *Propositio* ("proposition," Gal 2:15-21)
V. *Probatio* ("confirmation," 3:1—4:31)
VI. *Exhortatio* ("exhortation," Gal 5:1—6:10)
VII. Epistolary Postscript—*Peroratio* ("conclusion," Gal 6:11-18)

But Betz has to admit that he is not able to cite parallels to the exhortation section (Gal 5:1—6:10) from the classical rhetorical handbooks. For this reason G. Kennedy argues that Galatians is best viewed as deliberative rhetoric, since it aims to exhort or dissuade the audience regarding future actions by demonstrating that those actions are expedient or harmful. Paul seeks to dissuade the Galatian believers from following the false teachers by pointing to the

harmful effects: severance from Christ and grace (Gal 5:4), exclusion from the kingdom of God (Gal 5:21) and a reaping of corruption (Gal 6:8). He underscores the expediency of the course of action that he has exhorted them to follow by giving them the promise of the harvest of eternal life (Gal 6:8) and granting them the benediction upon all those who walk according to "this canon" (Gal 6:16).

It seems best to classify Paul's argument in Galatians as a mixture of forensic and deliberative rhetoric. The rebuke section of the letter (Gal 1:6—4:11) has the characteristics of forensic rhetoric, but at Galatians 4:12 a major rhetorical shift to deliberative rhetoric occurs. Paul is no longer so much concerned to accuse or defend as he is to persuade the Galatian believers to adopt a certain course of action. He begins his appeal to this new course of action in Galatians 4:12: "Become as I am." That exhortation is then supported by the command from the story of Abraham to "cast out the slave and her son" (Gal 4:30), clarified by authoritative instructions to stand in freedom (Gal 5:1-12) and defined in specific terms in the ethical exhortation to walk in the Spirit (Gal 5:13—6:10). The following pattern thus emerges:

Salutation (Gal 1:1-5)
  Rebuke (Gal 1:6—4:11)
    Autobiography (Gal 1:13—2:21)
    Argument from Scripture (3:6-29)
  Request (Gal 4:12—6:10)
    Autobiography (Gal 4:12-20)
    Allegory from Scripture (Gal 4:21-31)
    Ethical instruction (Gal 5:1—6:10)
Subscription (Gal 6:11-18)

4. Contents.

4.1. Salutation (Gal 1:1-5). Beyond the standard elements of sender, addressees and greetings, present in all his salutations, this opening paragraph contains two significant theological statements that anticipate central themes of the letter. First, in Galatians 1:1 Paul's designation of himself as an apostle goes beyond his references to his apostolic position in his other letters. His double denial of any dependence on human agency or authority for the legitimacy of his apostleship and his claim to a divine commission place an emphasis on apostolic authority that will be an important feature in his letter. Second, Paul's declaration that the cross of Christ is the way to freedom from the present evil age (Gal 1:4) sets the cross in the center of his theology, where it stays through to the end of the letter (Gal 2:19, 21; 3:1, 13; 4:5; 5:11, 24; 6:12, 14). Paul's central argument is that the cross alone is the way of salvation and therefore all attempts to supplement the work of the cross with works of the law must be totally rejected.

4.2. Rebuke (Gal 1:6—4:11). Immediately after the opening paragraph Paul expresses his rebuke for the Galatians' desertion to a perverted gospel (Gal 1:6) and places anyone who distorts the gospel of Christ under a double curse (Gal 1:7-9). In this way Paul establishes at the outset the ultimate measure of genuine authority: adherence to the one gospel. Paul's recognition that he will be judged by the standard of the gospel as a servant of Christ keeps him from seeking human approval (Gal 1:10). The standard of the gospel was not derived from human tradition; it was given by "the revelation of Jesus Christ" (Gal 1:11-12): Jesus Christ is the source and the subject of the gospel.

4.2.1. Autobiography (Gal 1:13—2:21). Paul's autobiography is essentially a portrayal of his faithfulness to the one true gospel: he was called by God to preach the gospel (Gal 1:16); he defended the gospel in the Jerusalem conference (Gal 2:1-10) and in the conflict with Peter (Gal 2:11-14); and he embodied the essence of the gospel (Gal 2:15-21). His record as a loyal representative of the gospel stands as the basis of his authority as an apostle and as a sharp rebuke to the Galatian believers' disloyalty to the gospel.

The primary point of Paul's story of his call (Gal 1:13-21) is to stress that he was called by God, not by the church, to preach the gospel. Before God's gracious call stopped Paul in his tracks, he was engaged in a campaign to destroy the church of God because of his zealous devotion to the traditions of Judaism (Gal 1:13-14). God's call was not an afterthought; like the prophets of old (see Jer 1:5 and Is 49:1), Paul had been set aside from his mother's womb (Gal 1:15). Paul heard the call when God revealed his Son to him so that he would preach Christ to the Gentiles (Gal 1:16). When Paul heard the call, he did not confer with "flesh and blood" or go up to Jerusalem to those who were apostles before him; instead he went into Arabia and then returned to Damascus (Gal 1:16-17). It was only three years later that he first had a short visit with Peter in Jerusalem. Except for James, Peter was the only apostle that Paul saw at that time

(Gal 1:18-19). And after that visit he was in the regions of Syria and Cilicia, unknown by face to the church in Judea; they only heard that he was now preaching the faith he had previously tried to destroy (Gal 1:21-24). This part of the story defends Paul's independence from the original apostles. God directly commissioned him to be an apostle to the Gentiles.

But Paul did not work independently. As the next episode in his autobiography shows, he had the full support of those considered most important as leaders in Jerusalem (Gal 2:1-10). As a result of the council in Jerusalem, Paul and Barnabas were given the right hand of fellowship by the leaders of the mother church in support of their mission to the Gentiles. The leaders in Jerusalem did not add anything to Paul's message (Gal 2:6-9). But even though Paul worked to establish a consensus with these leaders, he was not willing to allow archconservative Jewish "Christians" (counterfeit Christians, in Paul's eyes) to destroy his mission to the Gentiles. When there was pressure to get his Gentile companion, Titus, circumcised, Paul refused to give in; he stood for "the truth of the gospel," as he hopes the Galatian believers will also do when they are pressured to be circumcised.

In the next episode of his autobiography, Paul describes how he confronted Peter in order to defend the truth of the gospel (Gal 2:11-14). When Peter visited the church in Antioch, he followed the custom in the integrated congregation of Christian Jews and Gentiles of eating with Gentile Christians. Undoubtedly his presence at table fellowship with Gentiles was taken as an official stamp of approval on the union and equality of Jews and Gentiles in the church. But when some representatives who were sent by James from the church in Jerusalem came to Antioch, they persuaded Peter to stop the practice of Jews eating with Gentiles in the church. According to Paul, Peter gave in to their demand because he feared those who were circumcised, namely, the Jews. This probably means that he became concerned about the detrimental effect that his table fellowship with the Gentiles would have on the mission of the church in Jerusalem to the Jews. If non-Christian Jews in Jerusalem heard that Peter was eating with Gentiles, they might not only turn away from the witness of the church but also become actively hostile to the church for tolerating such a practice.

Peter's withdrawal from table fellowship with

the Gentiles split the church into Jewish and Gentile factions and by action if not by word compelled the Gentiles to think that they would have to become Jews if they wanted to enjoy table fellowship with the apostles and the mother church. From Paul's perspective, Peter's action was not a legitimate accommodation for the sake of the gospel; it was a compromise of the essential truth of the gospel. Peter was charged with hypocrisy, not heresy. Peter and Paul did not disagree about the truth of the gospel, but Peter's action was inconsistent with his belief in the gospel. By going along with Jewish adherence to the law, which required the separation of Jews and Gentiles and implied that incorporation into the Jewish nation was necessary for salvation, Peter had denied the essence of the gospel, which proclaimed that salvation for Jews and Gentiles was by way of the cross and incorporation into Christ. The conflict in Antioch was a mirror image of the crisis faced by the Galatian believers, since the issue of compelling Gentiles to live like Jews was precisely the central issue for the churches in Galatia.

Paul wraps up his autobiography with a statement that is intensely personal and at the same time serves as a paradigm for all Christians (Gal 2:15-21). In his experience as a Jew by birth (Gal 2:15; *see* Jew, Paul the), he knew that he was justified by faith in Christ, not by works of the law (Gal 2:16). By implication it must be clear that those who are Gentile sinners (Gal 2:15) could be justified only by faith in Christ and not by works of the law. Paul sought *justification only in Christ, but he was found to be a sinner on the basis of the law (Gal 2:17) because he was eating with Gentiles. Since his table fellowship with Gentiles was on the basis of common faith in Christ, Christ was blamed for being the agent who caused Paul to break the law by eating with Gentiles (Gal 2:17). But Paul adamantly rejects any notion that Christ is an agent of sin. For it is only if the law that separates Jews and Gentiles were to be rebuilt that then Paul would be proved to be a sinner on the basis of the law (Gal 2:18). But in fact he has died to the law, so the law can no longer be used to condemn table fellowship with Gentiles. His death to law was accomplished by union with Christ in his death—"I am crucified with Christ" (Gal 2:19).

Death to the law did not mean moral license but the means for achieving the highest goal—"that I might live to God" (Gal 2:19). This life to

God is empowered by Christ ("Christ lives in me"); it is lived by faith in Christ ("I live by faith in the Son of God"); it is motivated by the sacrificial love of Christ ("who loved me and gave himself for me"). Paul's experience sets forth an either-or choice: either attempt to attain righteousness "through the Law" and so negate the value of Christ's death (Gal 2:21); or die to the law by participation in the death of Christ and so live to God by the indwelling life of Christ (Gal 2:19-20; *see* Death of Christ). Paul sets forth his experience in Galatians 2:15-21 to prove that participation in the events of the gospel, not adherence to the law, is the source of life and righteousness. In the next chapter he uses the story of Abraham to prove the same thesis.

4.2.2. Argument from Scripture (Gal 3:6-29). The *Abraham argument is introduced by five barbed questions (Gal 3:1-5) that rebuke the Galatians for their foolishness. Implied in these questions is the charge that the Galatians have failed to understand the significance of the message of Christ crucified (Gal 3:1) and have not realized the implications of their experience of the Spirit (Gal 3:2-5). Their past (Gal 3:2, 3) and present (Gal 3:5) experience of the Spirit is indisputable evidence that they are already experiencing the full blessing of God. Paul's questions are posed as sharp antitheses so that the Galatians will be compelled by their own experience of the Spirit to choose the right answer: "Not by observing the Law, but by believing what we heard about Christ crucified!"

The Galatians' expected answer is confirmed by the exposition of Scripture. Paul quotes Genesis 15:6 to redefine the basis of Abrahamic sonship. The sign of the covenant—the true sign of Abrahamic sonship—is faith, not circumcision. His second quote from the story of Abraham (Gen 12:3 and 18:18) is interpreted as a prophecy of the present experience of Gentile believers. Because Scripture foresaw that it would be by faith that God would justify the Gentiles, it preached the gospel beforehand to Abraham: Gentiles would be included in the blessing promised to Abraham.

The Galatian believers had been lured into thinking that they could be included in the promised blessing of Abraham by keeping the law of Moses. But in fact those who are of faith are already in the circle of blessing (Gal 3:9), while those who rely on the works of the law are under a curse (Gal 3:10) because Scripture (Deut

27:26) puts all who do not keep all the things written in the book of the law under a curse. If the law keepers are under a curse since even they have not kept all the law, then the risk of incurring a curse is even greater for Gentile believers who accept only certain items of the law in order to identify with Israel. Habakkuk 2:4 proves that righteousness by faith is the way to life (Gal 3:11).

But the law is not of faith because it demands doing works of the law as the way to life, as the quotation of Leviticus 18:5 proves (Gal 3:13). The law demands perfect obedience (Gal 3:10) and offers life on the basis of this perfect obedience (Gal 3:12), but the law is incapable of engendering life or righteousness before God (Gal 3:21). The way to blessing is not through the law but through the cross of Christ. Christ redeemed us from the curse of the law by becoming a curse in our place (Gal 3:13-14). The Galatian believers had already received the blessing of Abraham when they received the Spirit by believing in the message of the cross (Gal 3:1-2, 14).

Following this contrast of law and faith, Paul turns to a contrast of law and promise by sketching out the flow of salvation history. Since the promise of blessing had been given to Abraham and his seed 430 years before the giving of law, it could not be modified or annulled by the giving of the law. This argument from history is designed to destroy the synthesis of the Abrahamic promise and Mosaic law that had led the Galatians to turn to the law as the way to experience the promised blessing. And Paul's messianic definition of seed (Gal 3:16) removes Jewish national boundaries as the limits of the inheritance of the Abrahamic blessing. The link Paul makes between Abraham and Christ bypasses the Mosaic law and the Jewish nation as channels for the reception of the promises to Abraham, with the result that Christ alone is the channel of the promised blessing.

Two rhetorical questions in Galatians 3:19-21 disclose Paul's awareness that his argument so far would lead his readers to question whether he has denied any purpose to the law ("Why then the Law? . . . Is the Law therefore opposed to the promises of God?"). Paul's description of the negative purpose, temporary function and mediated origin of the law leaves the Galatian converts without any sound reason for turning to the law (Gal 3:19-25). The focus of Galatians 3:26-29 is the union of the Gentile believers with

Christ. The equal status of all believers as "children of God," "Abraham's seed" and "heirs" in Christ renders any attempt to gain superior status by circumcision or law observance of no value whatsoever. At the beginning and end of his argument from the Abraham story, Paul's main point is that the inclusion of Gentile believers in the people of God is based solely upon their identification with Christ. Identification by race, class or sex no longer has any significance because of identification with Christ.

Paul closes the rebuke section of his letter with a dramatic before-and-after picture (Gal 4:1-11) to contrast the slavery before and the freedom after Christ was sent by the Father and accepted by the Galatian believers. Now that they have experienced the Spirit who gives them assurance that they are children of God, it is absurd for them to turn back to live as slaves under the law. Formerly they were slaves to the gods of this world, now they are children of God. Paul's rebuke ends with an expression of fear that his efforts for them may be in vain (Gal 4:11).

4.3. Request Section (Gal 4:12—6:10). Paul turns from rebuke to request. The initial request of Galatians 4:12 ("Become as I am!") amounts to a call for loyalty to the truth of the gospel and decisive resistance against the troublemakers. Paul developed his autobiography to illustrate how at Jerusalem (Gal 2:3, 5) and at Antioch (Gal 2:11-14) he had remained loyal to the gospel and decisively resisted pressures from Jewish Christians similar to those faced by the Galatian churches. Now he turns to autobiography again to strengthen this initial request by reminding the Galatians of the close relationship that they and Paul enjoyed prior to their departure from the gospel.

4.3.1. Autobiography (Gal 4:12-20). Paul's account of the Galatians' previous welcome (as if he were Christ Jesus), even when he was suffering from repulsive illness and their willingness to give him their own eyes, adds great force to his request for renewed identification and imitation. His request that they imitate him is also intensified by contrasting the evil intentions of the intruders with his concern for his "children" as a mother in labor with unborn children, laboring for them until Christ is completely formed within them.

4.3.2. Allegory from Scripture (Gal 4:21-31). Paul's initial request of Galatians 4:12 is now spelled out by quoting an imperative from the law. If the Galatians are so eager to be under the law, then let them follow the law. The punch line of the allegory is to command the Galatians through the law to "cast out the bondwoman and her son" (Gal 4:30; Gen 21:10). Paul interprets Genesis 21 within the framework already established in Galatians 3. Within that framework Paul sees a real correspondence between the historical situation of the two sons of Abraham and the two sorts of descendants of Abraham in his day, those born according to the *flesh and those born according to the Spirit.

But Paul moves from typological interpretation built on historical correspondence to allegorical definitions. Here again, however, the key is the theological framework of Galatians 3. For in that argument Gentile converts were identified as true children and heirs of Abraham in the same sense as Isaac on the basis of the promise given to Abraham and their experience of the Spirit. And in that argument there is a contrast between the Abrahamic covenant and the Sinaitic covenant, which leads to slavery (see Covenant, New Covenant). Thus when Paul redefines the terms in his allegorical treatment of Genesis 21, Sarah (and her counterpart, the Jerusalem above, the true mother Zion) is identified as the mother of the Galatian believers in Christ.

Paul's Hagar = Sinai and Sinai = present Jerusalem equations are problematic. The major difficulty with them is their apparent lack of validity in the face of the fundamental Jewish conviction that the Mosaic law had been given to the descendants of Isaac at Mount Sinai and had nothing to do with Hagar. The most satisfactory explanation of Paul's allegorical equations is simply stated in Galatians 4:25: "for she is in slavery with her children." Slavery is the common feature that links Hagar (the slave woman), the covenant given at Mount Sinai and the present Jerusalem. Paul had already attributed this feature of slavery to the Mosaic law (Gal 3:22-24; 4:1-10) and to a certain faction at Jerusalem (Gal 2:4). His allegorization must be seen as a counterattack upon that Jewish-Christian faction within the church at Jerusalem that tried to rob Gentile believers of their freedom by requiring them to be circumcised (Gal 2:3-6) and that was now attempting to do the same thing at Galatia. It was this experience of "troublemakers" in the church that gave rise to Paul's allegorical treatment of the text and is the key to its interpretation.

While the Hagar-Sarah allegory serves primarily as the basis for Paul's biblical appeal to resist the influence of the intruders, it also sets up a conceptual foundation for the ethical instructions of the rest of the letter. The freedom-slavery and spirit-flesh antitheses presented in the allegory set the stage for the ethical appeal to stand for freedom against slavery under the law and to walk by the Spirit and so overcome the desires of the flesh.

4.3.3. Ethical Instructions (Gal 5:1—6:10). The new identity of the Galatian believers leads to a new behavior (see Barclay). By grace they are true children of the free woman (Gal 4:31), born by the power of the Spirit (Gal 4:29). Now they must learn to express their new identity in new behavior. Paul gives instructions about their behavior. But he constantly bases his imperatives on the indicatives of grace: "For freedom Christ has set you free (indicative). Stand firm" (Gal 5:1)! "You were called to freedom (indicative). Serve one another" (Gal 5:13)! "We live by the Spirit (indicative). Keep in step with the Spirit" (Gal 5:24)!

After the emphatic declaration in Galatians 5:2-12 that faith and Christ, on the one hand, and circumcision and law, on the other, are exclusive alternatives, Paul's imperative of Galatians 5:13 echoes the command of Galatians 5:1. In Galatians 5:1 and Galatians 5:13 there is first an indicative statement regarding freedom in Christ, which is then followed by an imperative and a warning. In Galatians 5:1 Paul commands the Galatians to stand fast; in Galatians 5:13 he exhorts them to serve one another in love. The warning of Galatians 5:1 is against a return to slavery under the law; in Galatians 5:13 it is against giving opportunity to the flesh.

The fact that in Galatians 5:13 Paul warns that the flesh is the danger to freedom in Christ, instead of slavery to the law, has led many to suppose that Paul begins to attack libertinism and lawlessness in Galatians 5:13. The description of the warfare between the flesh and the Spirit in the verses that follow is understood to confirm this supposition. But in the allegory that precedes this section, Paul identified slavery with the Sinaitic covenant and the flesh. Those who are according to the flesh, like Ishmael, are identified with those who are proponents of the Sinaitic covenant. And in the subscription that follows this section those who campaign for circumcision boast in the flesh. So it seems best to interpret Galatians 5:13—6:10 in context. Paul has not changed fronts to fight against libertinism in this section. His attack against the works of the flesh is a continuation of his attack against the works of the law.

The intruders' campaign for circumcision and the law evidently led to social disorder and a lack of love in the Galatian community. In Paul's list of the works of the flesh these social sins receive the major emphasis. Paul's description of the opposition of the flesh and the Spirit is developed as a way of explaining the Christian's relationship to the law. The law is still a central factor in Paul's thinking (Gal 5:14, 18, 23, 6:2). His statement that one who is led by the Spirit is not under law (Gal 5:18) implies that a life under the law is a life subject to the desires of the flesh. The works of the flesh, then, are to be seen as the result of living under the law rather than under the guidance of the Spirit. The result of living under the guidance of the Spirit results in the fruit of the Spirit, against which there is no law (Gal 5:23). For love fulfills the law (Gal 5:14), the "Law of Christ" (Gal 6:2). It is the Spirit, not the law, which has the power to liberate one from the desires of the flesh.

4.4. Subscription (Gal 6:11-18). In common Hellenistic letters, the author would close the letter by writing a summary of the contents of the letter in his own hand. Paul does that in this letter. The denunciation of the intruders (Gal 6:12-13), the autobiographical statement of personal loyalty to the cross of Christ (Gal 6:14), with the mention of the marks of Christ as evidence of that loyalty (Gal 6:17), and the reminder that circumcision means nothing whereas the new creation means everything (Gal 6:15) all repeat and underscore the main themes of the letter. The first benediction on those who follow his rule, even on the Israel of God (Gal 6:16), his second benediction (Gal 6:18), the appellation "brothers and sisters" (*adelphoi*) and the final "Amen" all express Paul's confidence that his request to "stand firm" for freedom in Christ by "keeping in step with the Spirit" will be followed by his Christian readers.

See also ABRAHAM; ADVERSARIES; CONVERSION AND CALL OF PAUL; GOSPEL; HOLY SPIRIT; JUSTIFICATION; LAW.

DPL: ANTIOCH ON THE ORONTES; CHRONOLOGY OF PAUL; CIRCUMCISION; CROSS, THEOLOGY OF THE; CURSE, ACCURSED, ANATHEMA; FAITH; FRUIT OF THE SPIRIT; GENTILES; JERUSALEM; JU-DAIZERS; LAW OF CHRIST; OLD TESTAMENT IN PAUL; PETER; RHETORIC, RHETORICAL CRITICISM; WORKS OF THE LAW.

BIBLIOGRAPHY. **Commentaries:** W. Barclay, *The Letters to the Galatians and Ephesians* (DSB; rev. ed.; Edinburgh: St. Andrews, 1976); H. D. Betz, *Galatians: A Commentary on Paul's Letter to the Churches in Galatia* (Herm; Philadelphia: Fortress, 1979); F. F. Bruce, *The Epistle to the Galatians* (NIGTC; Grand Rapids: Eerdmans, 1982); E. deW. Burton, *A Critical and Exegetical Commentary on the Epistle to the Galatians* (ICC; Edinburgh: T & T Clark, 1921); R. A. Cole, *The Epistle of Paul to the Galatians* (TNTC; rev. ed.; Grand Rapids: Eerdmans, 1989); C. B. Cousar, *Galatians* (IntC; Atlanta: John Knox, 1982); J. D. G. Dunn, *The Epistle to the Galatians* (BNTC; Peabody, MA: Hendrickson, 1993); G. Ebeling, *The Truth of the Gospel: An Exposition of Galatians* (Philadelphia: Fortress, 1985); R. Y. K. Fung, *The Epistle to the Galatians* (NICNT; Grand Rapids: Eerdmans, 1988); D. Guthrie, *Galatians* (NCB; London: Marshall, Morgan & Scott, 1973); G. W. Hansen, *Galatians* (IVPNTC; Downers Grove, IL: InterVarsity Press, 1994); J. B. Lightfoot, *Saint Paul's Epistle to the Galatians* (1st ed. 1865; repr., Grand Rapids: Zondervan, 1957); R. N. Longenecker, *Galatians* (WBC 41; Dallas: Word, 1990); M. Luther, *A Commentary on St. Paul's Epistle to the Galatians* (repr., Grand Rapids: Baker, 1979); J. G. Machen, *Machen's Notes on Galatians*, ed. J. H. Skilton (Nutley, NJ: P&R,1977); J. L. Martyn, *Galatians* (AB; New York: Doubleday, 1997); S. McKnight, *Galatians* (NIVAC; Grand Rapids: Zondervan, 1995); W. M. Ramsay, *A Historical Commentary on St. Paul's Epistle to the Galatians* (2d ed.; London: Hodder & Stoughton, 1900); H. N. Ridderbos, *The Epistle of Paul to the Churches of Galatia* (NICNT; Grand Rapids: Eerdmans, 1953); J. R. W. Stott, *The Message of Galatians* (Downers Grove, IL: InterVarsity Press, 1968); B. Witherington, *Grace in Galatia: A Commentary on St. Paul's Letter to the Galatians* (Grand Rapids: Eerdmans, 1998); J. Ziesler, *Galatians* (Valley Forge, PA: Trinity Press International, 1993). **Studies:** J. M. G. Barclay, *Obeying the Truth: A Study of Paul's Ethics in Galatians* (Edinburgh: T & T Clark, 1988); B. H. Brinsmead, *Galatians as Dialogical Response to Opponents* (SBLDS 65; Chico, CA: Scholars Press, 1982); C. H. Buck, "The Date of Galatians," *JBL* 70 (1951) 113-22; J. W. Drane, *Paul, Libertine or Legalist? A Study in the Theology of the*

Major Pauline Epistles (London: SPCK, 1975); J. D. G. Dunn, *Jesus, Paul and the Law: Studies in Mark and Galatians* (Louisville, KY: Westminster/John Knox, 1990); idem, *The Theology of Paul's Letter to the Galatians* (Cambridge: Cambridge University Press, 1993); G. W. Hansen, *Abraham in Galatians: Epistolary and Rhetorical Contexts* (JSNTSup 29; Sheffield: Sheffield Academic Press, 1989); R. B. Hays, *The Faith of Jesus Christ: An Investigation of the Narrative Substructure of Galatians 3:1—4:11* (SBLDS 56; Chico, CA: Scholars Press, 1983); C. J. Hemer, *The Book of Acts in the Setting of Hellenistic History*, ed. C. Gempf (Winona Lake, IN: Eisenbrauns, 1990); G. Howard, *Paul: Crisis in Galatia: A Study in Early Christian Theology* (SNTSMS 35; Cambridge: Cambridge University Press, 1979); D. Lull, *The Spirit in Galatia: Paul's Interpretation of Pneuma as Divine Power* (SBLDS 49; Chico, CA: Scholars Press, 1980); M. J. Mellink, "Galatia," *IDB* 2.336-38; S. Mitchell, "Population and Land in Roman Galatia," *ANRW* II.7.2.1053-81; W. Ramsay, *The Cities of St. Paul* (London: Hodder & Stoughton, 1907); idem, *St. Paul The Traveler and the Roman Citizen* (London: Hodder & Stoughton, 1896); R. K. Sherk, "Roman Galatia," *ANRW* II.7.2.954-1052; S. Westerholm, *Israel's Law and the Church's Faith: Paul and His Recent Interpreters* (Grand Rapids: Eerdmans, 1988). W. G. Hansen

GENERAL RESURRECTION. *See* RESURRECTION II.

GETHSEMANE. *See* TRIAL OF JESUS.

GIFTS OF THE SPIRIT. *See* HOLY SPIRIT II.

GLORIFICATION. *See* RESURRECTION II.

GLORY OF GOD. *See* GOD I.

GLOSSOLALIA. *See* HOLY SPIRIT.

GNOSTICISM

Gnosticism is a term that designates a variety of religious movements that stressed salvation through *gnōsis*, or "knowledge," that is, of one's origins. Most scholars would identify as an essential of Gnosticism the element of cosmological dualism—an opposition between the spiritual world and the evil, material world.

1. Varieties of Gnosticism
2. Sources
3. Gnostic Doctrines
4. Gnostic Ethics
5. Gnostic Communities
6. Scholarship on Gnosticism

1. Varieties of Gnosticism.
Because of the variegated nature of Gnosticism, it is difficult to fit every gnostic teacher into a common framework. Marcion, who advocated the concept of two gods, the god of the OT and the god of the NT, has many affinities with the Gnostics, yet he lacked their mythology and emphasized faith rather than saving *gnōsis*. A major branch of Gnosticism, which followed the teachings of Valentinus, was heavily influenced by Platonism. Scholars have recognized another branch of Gnosticism, which has been termed Sethianism, a more mythological system that exalted the OT figure Seth as a key revealer (see Layton).

It should be noted that the ancient sources of these movements and their Christian critics do not use the term *Gnosticism* and rarely used the term *Gnostics*. M. A. Williams has therefore called upon scholars to abandon the term. But it is not likely that his proposed substitution, "biblical demiurgical traditions," will be adopted. But his reminder that Gnosticism is a scholarly construct should always be borne in mind.

2. Sources.
Texts that are unambiguously gnostic date from the second century A.D. Those who maintain a pre-Christian Gnosticism assume the early existence of Gnosticism and interpret the NT texts in the light of this assumption. Some of the Nag Hammadi treatises, though late in composition, have been adduced by some scholars as evidence of a pre-Christian Gnosticism.

2.1. Patristic Sources. Until recently scholars were entirely dependent upon the descriptions of the Gnostics found in the church fathers. In some cases the patristic sources preserved extracts of the gnostic writings. Our most important sources include Justin Martyr of Samaria (d. 165), Irenaeus of Lyons (d. c. 225), Clement of Alexandria (d. c. 215), Tertullian of Carthage (d. c. 225), Hippolytus of Rome (d. c. 236), Origen of Alexandria and Caesarea (d. 254) and Epiphanius of Salamis in Cyprus (d. 403) (see Grant).

Especially valuable is Irenaeus's account, which has been preserved in a Latin translation,

Adversus Haereses. He refers to an *Apocryphon of John,* copies of which were found at Nag Hammadi. The *Philosophoumena* of Hippolytus was identified in 1842. Clement and Origen were in some ways sympathetic to the gnostic emphasis of a spiritual elite. Tertullian railed against Marcion and Valentinus. Though Epiphanius had some firsthand contact with Gnostics in Egypt, his *Panarion,* while comprehensive, is not very reliable.

As one would expect, the earlier sources are the most reliable and the later sources less so. Needless to say, these accounts were highly polemical. Nothing in the recently recovered gnostic sources from Nag Hammadi supports the patristic description of licentious Gnosticism.

2.2. Gnostic Teachers. The church fathers, including the historian Eusebius (fourth century), provide a list of prominent Gnostics and their teachings.

The church fathers were unanimous in regarding Simon of Samaria as the arch-Gnostic, though our earliest source, Acts 8, describes him only as someone who practiced magic. According to the patristic sources Simon claimed to be divine and taught that his companion, a former prostitute, was the reincarnated Helen of Troy. Those who accept the patristic view of Simon believe that Acts has not given us an accurate portrayal of Simon. Most scholars, however, believe that the church fathers were mistaken (see Filoramo, 148).

According to the church fathers, Simon was followed by a fellow Samaritan, Menander, who taught at Antioch in Syria toward the end of the first century. He claimed that those who believed in him would not die.

Also teaching in Antioch at the beginning of the second century was Saturninus, who held that the "incorporeal" Christ was the redeemer. That is, he held a docetic view of Christ that denied the incarnation (cf. 1 Jn 4:3). He also taught that marriage and procreation were from Satan.

Teaching in Asia Minor in the early second century was Cerinthus, who held that Jesus was but a man upon whom Christ descended as a dove at his baptism. As Christ could not suffer, he withdrew from Jesus before the crucifixion.

Another early gnostic teacher was Basilides, to whom we have attributed both a dualistic system by Irenaeus and a monistic system by Hippolytus. Basilides regarded the god of the Jews as an oppressive angel. He held that Christ did not suffer but that Simon of Cyrene was crucified in his place, while the invisible Christ stood by laughing. Similar docetic concepts are now attested in two Nag Hammadi tractates, the *Second Treatise of the Great Seth* (CG VII,2) and the *Apocalypse of Peter* (CG VII,3).

An important though atypical Gnostic was Marcion of Pontus (northern Turkey), who taught at Rome from 137 to 144. He contrasted the god of the OT with the god of the NT. Marcion drew up the first canon or closed list of NT books, including a truncated Gospel of Luke. Jesus simply appeared; his body was a "phantom." Marcion's followers spread to Egypt, Mesopotamia and Armenia. His docetic teachings were sharply rebuked by Tertullian. A. Harnack hailed Marcion as the church's first great theologian and characterized Gnosticism as the acute Hellenization of Christianity (see Helleman).

The most famous gnostic teacher was Valentinus, who came from Alexandria to Rome in 140. He taught that there was a series of divine eons or emanations. He divided humankind into three classes: *hylics,* or unbelievers immersed in nature and the flesh; *psychics,* or common Christians who lived by faith; and *pneumatics* or spiritual Gnostics. The later Valentinians divided into an Italian and an Oriental school over the question of whether Jesus had a psychic or pneumatic body. The many outstanding Valentinian teachers included Ptolemaeus, Theodotus and Marcus. The earliest known commentary on a NT book is Heracleon's on the Gospel of John, passages of which are preserved by Origen in his commentary.

A number of the Nag Hammadi tractates such as *The Gospel of Truth* (CG I,3 and XII,2), *The Treatise on the Resurrection* (CG I,4), *The Tripartite Tractate* (CG I,5), *The Gospel of Philip* (CG II,3) and *A Valentinian Exposition* (CG XI,2) have been identified as Valentinian. Contrary to the earlier impression that the Valentinians were only concerned with the pneumatics, who would be saved by the *gnōsis* of their nature, a study by M. R. Desjardins indicates that they were also concerned about the psychics, who would have to lead sinless lives to be saved.

2.3. Mandaic Sources. The Mandean communities in southern Iraq and southwestern Iran are today the sole surviving remnants of Gnosticism. Their texts, though known only through late (seventeenth- or eighteenth-century) manuscripts, were used by the history-of-religions scholars to reconstruct an alleged pre-Christian Gnosticism. In addition to the manuscripts, there are earlier magic bowl texts (A.D. 600) and some magical lead amulets, which may date to as early as the third century A.D. There is no firm evidence to date the origins of Mandeanism earlier than the second century A.D. (see Yamauchi 1970).

2.4. Coptic Sources. Coptic is a late form of Egyptian written mainly in Greek letters. In the nineteenth century two Coptic gnostic codices were published: the Codex Askewianus containing the *Pistis Sophia,* and the Codex Brucianus containing the *Books of Jeu*—both relatively late gnostic compositions. A third work, the Codex Berolinensis (BG 8502), though acquired in the nineteenth century, was not published until 1955. It contains a *Gospel of Mary* (Magdalene), a *Sophia of Jesus, Acts of Peter* and an *Apocryphon of John*—the work mentioned by Irenaeus.

2.5. The Nag Hammadi Library. In 1945 a cache of eleven Coptic codices and fragments of two others were found by peasants near Nag Hammadi in Upper Egypt, 370 miles south of Cairo, where the Nile bends from west to east. The first translation of a tractate, that of *The Gospel of Truth,* appeared in 1956. Through the efforts of J. M. Robinson and his collaborators, an English translation of the fifty-one treatises was produced in 1977.

The Nag Hammadi Library, as the collection is now called, contains a variety of texts: non-gnostic, non-Christian gnostic and Christian gnostic. The most famous tractate is *The Gospel of Thomas,* which contains 114 purported sayings of Jesus. In 1897 and in 1904 B. P. Grenfell and A. S. Hunt had discovered at Oxyrhynchus in Egypt noncanonical sayings or the so-called logia of Jesus. We now know that these papyri came from the Greek text that had been translated as the Coptic *Gospel of Thomas.*

2.6. Hermetic Sources. The *Hermetica* are writings ascribed to Hermes Trismegistos ("thrice-great"), the Greek title for Thoth, the Egyptian god of wisdom. Composed in the second to third century A.D. in Greek in Egypt, they were highly esteemed in medieval times. The Greek *Corpus Hermeticum* was influenced by dualistic Platonism and pantheistic Stoicism. Hermetic tractates have also been found in the Nag Hammadi Codex VI. Though there are affinities with Gnosticism, the *Hermetica* lack its radical dualism.

2.7. Syriac Sources. Some Syriac texts such as the *Odes of Solomon* and the *Hymn of the Pearl* from the *Acts of Thomas* have been cited by some scholars such as K. Rudolph as early gnostic sources. Other scholars, however, doubt their gnostic character.

2.8. Manichaean Sources. Mani (A.D. 216—276) established a remarkably successful gnostic movement, which spread from Mesopotamia to the West, where Augustine became an adherent for nine years, and to the East, where it reached China along the Silk Road. Manicheanism was a highly syncretistic religion that combined materials taken from Judaism, Christianity, Zoroastrianism and Buddhism. The publication of a tiny Greek manuscript in 1970, the Cologne Codex, confirmed that Mani had emerged from a baptistic sect known as the Elchasaites. Manichean texts were written in many languages, including Coptic, Syriac, Persian, Uighur (a Turkish dialect) and Chinese (see Klimkeit).

3. Gnostic Doctrines.

Because there was no central authority or canon of scriptures, the Gnostics taught a bewildering variety of views. Fundamental to clearly gnostic systems was a dualism that opposed the transcendent God and an ignorant demiurge, often a caricature of the OT Jehovah. In some systems the creation of the world resulted from the presumption of Sophia (Wisdom). The material creation, including the body, was regarded as inherently evil. Sparks of divinity, however, had been encapsuled in the bodies of certain pneumatic or spiritual individuals, who were ignorant of their celestial origins. The transcendent God sent down a redeemer, who brought them salvation in the form of secret *gnōsis*. Gnostics hoped to escape from the prison of their bodies at death and to traverse the planetary spheres of hostile demons to be reunited with God. There was for them, of course, no reason to believe in the resurrection of the body.

4. Gnostic Ethics.

According to the church fathers, Carpocrates urged his followers to participate in all sins, while his son Epiphanes taught that promiscuity was God's law. The Valentinians held a positive view of marriage, not so much for the sake of procreation but as a symbol of the archetypal unity of the sexes. Most Gnostics took a radically ascetic attitude toward sex and marriage, deeming the creation of woman the source of evil and the procreation of children but the multiplication of souls in bondage to the powers of darkness.

5. Gnostic Communities.

We know very little about the cult and the community of the Gnostics. As a general rule the Gnostics interpreted rites such as baptism and the Eucharist as spiritual symbols of *gnōsis*. Several of the Nag Hammadi tractates contain violent polemic against water baptism. E. Pagels has argued that gnostic groups gave women a greater position in leadership than the orthodox church fathers such as Irenaeus and Tertullian. But D. Hoffman has shown that women were exploited by Gnostics.

6. Scholarship on Gnosticism.

Prior to the twentieth century scholars had uncritically accepted the patristic description of Gnosticism as a failed Christian heresy. Though S. Pétrement has attempted to defend this traditional view, most scholars now believe that Gnosticism is best understood as an independent religion. Whether it existed prior to the birth of Christianity or was roughly contemporary with its development is still a disputed issue.

The concept of a pre-Christian Gnosticism was first proposed by W. Anz in 1897 and then forcefully promoted by the *religionsgeschichtliche Schule,* or history-of-religions school, most notably by W. Bousset (d. 1920) and R. Reitzenstein (d. 1931).

Inspired by the history-of-religions scholars as well as by publication of Mandaic texts, in 1925 R. Bultmann outlined a classic model of the pre-Christian gnostic redeemer myth. Bultmann and his influential students interpreted much of the NT on the assumption of a pre-Christian Gnosticism. An extreme application of this viewpoint has been promoted by W. Schmithals, who has interpreted all of Paul's opponents, even those in Galatia, as Gnostics.

With the discovery of the Nag Hammadi corpus, a renewed attempt has been made by J. M. Robinson and others to establish a case for a pre-Christian Gnosticism on the basis of a number of Nag Hammadi tractates.

One clear example of the appropriation of a gnostic text by a Christian editor is the recasting of the non-Christian *Eugnostos* (CG III,3 and V,1) by *The Sophia of Jesus Christ* (CG III,4 and BG 8502). But the alleged non-Christian nature of *Eugnostos* has been disputed as well as its Gnostic character.

Several scholars have contended that *The Apocalypse of Adam* (CG V,5) is a non-Christian work that provides evidence of a pre-Christian redeemer myth. One passage relates thirteen numbered kingdoms that are faulty explanations of the Illuminator. But the alleged non-Christian character of this tractate has been challenged because of a reference to the punishment of the flesh of the Illuminator upon whom the Holy Spirit came.

The Paraphrase of Shem (CG VII,1) has also been claimed to be evidence of a pre-Christian Gnosticism by F. Wisse, who first published studies on it. But more recent studies have concluded that its sharp polemic against water baptism is best understood as a sectarian protest against the dominant church.

G. (Schenke) Robinson has interpreted the *Trimorphic Protennoia* (CG XIII,1) as containing evidence of a pre-Christian gnostic Logos hymn underlying the prologue of the Gospel of John. Verbal parallels to the prologue, however, convince others that this Coptic text bears evidence of a dependence upon John's prologue.

W. Bauer's seminal work, *Rechtgläubigkeit und Ketzerei im ältesten Christentum,* first published in 1934, was belatedly translated into English as *Orthodoxy and Heresy in Earliest Christianity* in 1971. His provocative thesis was that contrary to the triumphalistic history of Eusebius, earliest Christianity was quite pluralistic. In fact, in Syria, Asia Minor and Egypt the earliest Christians and the most numerous Christians were gnostic rather than orthodox. Orthodoxy was established only much later through the influence of the Roman church. Scholars such as T. A. Robinson have pointed out that many of Bauer's propositions were based on arguments from silence. The evidence of the papyri in Egypt and other texts speak against his revisionist view of early Christian history.

See also ADVERSARIES; RELIGION, GRECO-ROMAN.

DLNTD: DOCETISM; GNOSIS, GNOSTICISM; MARCION; SYNCRETISM; THOMAS, GOSPEL OF.

BIBLIOGRAPHY. W. Bauer, *Orthodoxy and Heresy in Earliest Christianity,* ed. R. Kraft and G. Krodel (Philadelphia: Fortress, 1971); M. R. Desjardins, *Sin in Valentinianism* (Atlanta: Scholars Press, 1990); G. Filoramo, *A History of*

Gnosticism (Oxford: Blackwell, 1992); R. M. Grant, ed., *Gnosticism: A Sourcebook of Heretical Writings from the Early Christian Period* (New York: Harper & Brothers, 1961); W. E. Helleman, ed., *Hellenization Revisited* (Lanham, MD: University Press of America, 1994); D. Hoffman, *The Status of Women and Gnosticism in Irenaeus and Tertullian* (Lewiston, NY: Edwin Mellen Press, 1995); H.-J. Klimkeit, *Gnosis on the Silk Road* (New York: HarperCollins, 1993); B. Layton, ed., *The Rediscovery of Gnosticism* (2 vols.; Leiden: E. J. Brill, 1980-81); E. Pagels, *The Gnostic Gospels* (New York: Random House, 1979); B. A. Pearson, *Gnosticism, Judaism and Egyptian Christianity* (Minneapolis: Fortress, 1990); P. Perkins, *Gnosticism and the New Testament* (Minneapolis: Fortress, 1998); S. Pétrement, *A Separate God: The Christian Origins of Gnosticism* (San Francisco: HarperCollins, 1990); J. M. Robinson, ed., *The Nag Hammadi Library in English* (3d ed.; San Francisco: HarperCollins, 1990); T. A. Robinson, *The Bauer Thesis Examined* (Lewiston, NY: Edwin Mellen Press, 1988); K. Rudolph, *Gnosis* (San Francisco: HarperCollins, 1987); W. Schmithals, *Neues Testament und Gnosis* (Darmstadt: Wissenschaftliche Buchgesellschaft, 1984); J. D. Turner and A. McGuire, eds., *The Nag Hammadi Library After Fifty Years* (Leiden: E. J. Brill, 1997); M. A. Williams, *Rethinking "Gnosticism": An Argument for Dismantling a Dubious Category* (Princeton, NJ: Princeton University Press, 1996); E. M. Yamauchi, *Gnostic Ethics and Mandean Origins* (Cambridge, MA: Harvard University Press, 1970); idem, *Pre-Christian Gnosticism* (2d ed.; Grand Rapids: Baker, 1983).

E. M. Yamauchi

GOD I: GOSPELS

In the canonical Gospels, "God" *(theos)* is the traditional deity of ancient Israel referred to in the OT; and, as everywhere in the NT, the exclusivist monotheism of ancient Jewish piety, which involves a rejection of all other deities, is the religious orientation adapted to early Christian devotion to Jesus. In the Gospels God is the ultimate authority and the ultimate good. The Gospels are narratives about Jesus, but his whole significance rests on the claim that God is the source of Jesus' authority, the one whose kingdom (*see* Kingdom of God) he truly proclaims. That is, though the Gospels are undeniably christological narratives, they are also deeply God-centered. Their whole thrust is that the one whose story they narrate represents God's new overture of revelation, fulfillment and salvation. In this they agree, but there are also interesting differences in emphasis among the Evangelists in the ways they refer to God, which reflect their varying purposes, situations and destinations and may also indicate theological development across the decades that separate them from one another. Also, the Gospels allow us with some confidence to describe important features of Jesus' experience of and teaching about God. Jesus' special sense of God as his Father, to whom he was called to respond as God's obedient Son, probably formed a central feature of Jesus' mission and is reflected in the Gospels.

1. God in the Gospels: General Matters
2. God in the Individual Gospels
3. God in Jesus' Experience and Ministry

1. God in the Gospels: General Matters.
Understandably, scholarly study of the Gospels has tended to focus on their presentation of Jesus. But though the Gospels are narratives of Jesus' ministry and are explicitly concerned with presenting his significance (*see* Gospel [Genre]), they are on a deeper level dominated by God, whom Jesus proclaims and represents as *Son and Christ. The Gospels affirm as valid the OT witness to the unique God of Israel. Thus, for example, God is the Creator who instituted marriage (Mt 19:4-6) and gave divine commandments through Moses (Mk 7:5-13). But the Evangelists also proffer new information about God's purposes, which are now advanced significantly and definitively in Jesus; and so the Gospels are theological narratives.

1.1. Terminology. Exact figures for the frequency of the following terms dealt with may vary, depending upon decisions about textual variants and in some cases on the interpretation of particular passages; but the basic patterns of comparative frequencies are not affected. In addition to the actual term "God" *(theos)*, which is used frequently in each Gospel (48 times in Mark, 51 in Matthew, 122 in Luke, 73 in John), the term *Lord (kyrios)* is used with reference to God numerous times as well (9 times in Mark, 18 in Matthew, 37 in Luke, 5 in John; the term is also used frequently with reference to Jesus, e.g., Mt 7:21; 8:2; 15:22; Mk 11:3). Many of the uses of *kyrios* for God are in citations of the OT and in expressions derived from the OT (e.g., "angel of the Lord"), and in these passages the term functions as the Greek translation of the Hebrew OT name for God, Yahweh. For example, twenty-five of the uses of *kyrios* for God in Luke are in the first two chapters, where the phrasing is so heavily influenced by the OT.

The third frequently used term for God is "Father" *(patēr),* doubtless the most familiar term for God in Christian tradition and also perhaps the most theologically significant title for God in the NT. Unlike the other terms for God already mentioned—without exception in the Synoptics, and with only a few exceptions in John—"Father" as a title for God appears only in the sayings attributed to Jesus (the Johannine exceptions are in editorial remarks by the Evangelist in Jn 1:14, 18, a saying of Philip in Jn 14:8 and the crowd's claim in Jn 8:41).

But it must be noted that this usage is very unevenly distributed in the Gospels: 4 instances in Mark, 44 in Matthew, 15 in Luke and 109 in John. An even more remarkable variation appears if one considers only the occurrences of the absolute form "the Father": 1 time in Mark, 2 times in Matthew, 3 times in Luke and 73 times in John. J. Jeremias (1967, 29-35) pointed to such figures as indications of "a growing tendency to introduce the title 'Father' for God into the sayings of Jesus" in the early church (e.g., cf. Mk 3:35 par. Mt 12:50; Mk 14:25 par. Mt 26:29; Mk 10:40 par. Mt 20:23). He cogently argued that the Gospel of John was particularly reflective of and influential in the title "*the* Father" becoming "the name of God in Christendom."

In addition to John's considerably more frequent use of the absolute form "the Father," we should observe another interesting distinguishing feature in John's use of "Father" for God. In the Synoptics the divine title *Father* is restricted to Jesus' prayers and his sayings addressed to followers and to audiences made up of followers and the crowds. When speaking to others (e.g., Jewish religious leaders, Satan), Jesus uses *theos* or *kyrios.* In John, however, Jesus refers to God as "Father" in sayings addressed to an assortment of characters: among them the Samaritan woman (Jn 4:21-23) and hostile critics (e.g., Jn 5:17-47; 6:25-58; 8:12-30, 34-38). Indeed, in John, Jesus' reference to God as his Father often functions as the occasion for offense to be taken by critics. That is, "Father," which in the Synoptics denotes the situation of Jesus and his disciples

("your Father") before God, takes on a sharpened christological function in John as a sometimes polemical term intended primarily to express the exalted status of Jesus. In keeping with this, in the Johannine writings only Jesus is "son" *(huios)* of God; Jesus' followers are called God's "children" *(tekna),* a term lacking the connotation of special rights and status implied by "son."

In addition to "God," "Lord" and "Father," there are also indirect forms of speech used to refer to God. There is Jesus' demand of the Jerusalem priests whether the baptism ministry of John was "from Heaven" (Mk 11:30 par. Mt 21:25 and Lk 20:4), the high priest's reference to God as "the Blessed" in the interrogation of Jesus (Mk 14:61; cf. Mt 26:63) and Jesus' reference to God as "the Power" in his reply (Mk 14:62 par. Mt 26:64; cf. Lk 22:69). The several uses of "Most High" in Luke (Lk 1:32, 35, 76; 6:35) are to be included as well, though this particular expression is directly indebted to OT usage (e.g., Dan 4:17, 24-25). All these reverential circumlocutions reflect the profound reverence for God characteristic of the Jewish background of Jesus and the early Christian movement.

Moreover, in those passages where certain events "must" *(dei)* take place to advance or fulfill the redemptive plan, God is to be understood as the one whose purposes make the events necessary (e.g., Mk 8:31; 9:11; 13:7, 10). There are also a number of occurrences of what has been called the divine passive, where actions are described in passive verb forms with no subject explicitly mentioned but where God is to be understood as the subject of the verbs (e.g., Mk 3:28, "all sins will be forgiven [by God]"; Mt 7:1-2, 7). Still another type of indirect reference to God is found in all three Synoptic accounts of Jesus' baptism, where the divine acclamation of Jesus is attributed simply to "a voice from heaven" (Mk 1:11 par. Mt 3:17 and Lk 3:22). Likewise, the transfiguration accounts attribute the divine acknowledgment of Jesus to "a voice from the cloud" (Mk 9:7 par. Mt 17:5; Lk 9:35). In both scenes the context requires God to be understood as the one who speaks.

1.2. God's Role. In all the Gospels God is the enveloping presence, the overarching character in the narratives, who, though often referred to by others and only occasionally named as acting directly within the stories, gives the accounts, the characters and actions their whole significance.

The entire Gospel narratives consist in the portrayal of God's purpose, and all characters and events in the narratives receive their evaluation and meaning in the light of their relationship to this divine purpose.

Several major examples of Gospel characters will suffice to illustrate this. *John the Baptist is the forerunner of Jesus the Christ, but this in turn depends on the claim that the Baptist was sent by God (e.g., Jn 1:6; Mk 11:27-33). The crowds acclaim Jesus because they see in him some manifestation of what they believe to be God's saving purposes (e.g., Mk 2:12; 11:8-10). It is those who do the will of God who are Jesus' true family, his followers (Mk 3:35 par. Mt 12:50; Lk 8:21). The Sadducees (*see* Judaism and the New Testament) oppose Jesus because they are blind to God's power and purposes (Mk 12:24 par. Mt 22:29). Indeed, the ultimate theological irony of the Gospel stories is that the rejection of Jesus by the Jewish religious leaders constitutes the rejection of God's Son, the divinely appointed Christ. They accuse Jesus of blasphemy (Mk 14:64 par. Mt 26:65; Lk 22:71) but are themselves guilty of opposing God in the name of God.

Even the significance of Jesus, the explicitly central character in the Gospels, wholly has to do with his relationship to God. Jesus' message announces and interprets the kingdom of God (e.g., Mk 1:14-15, and the parables in Mk 4 par. Mt 13). The demons acclaim Jesus in various expressions that all denote his status before God (e.g., "the Holy One of God," Mk 1:24 par. Lk 4:34; "Son of God," Mk 3:11 par. Lk 4:41; Mk 5:7 par. Mt 8:29; Lk 8:28). Jesus surely claims authority, but either implicitly (e.g., Mk 2:10) or explicitly (e.g., Jn 3:35; 5:19-23; 12:49) indicates that this authority is from God and is intended to promote God's purpose and glory. In all the Gospels Jesus is the Messiah (*Christ) and is often referred to in royal terms (e.g., Mt 21:1-11). But this must be set in the context of Jesus' proclamation of the kingdom of God, which makes God as "king" one of the most pervasive, though often implicit, images in the Gospels. Thus God is the high king whom Jesus the Messiah represents in a unique way as a kind of vice-gerent.

Even in John, where we have the most explicitly exalted view of Christ's person presented, everything rests on the claim that Jesus has come from God (e.g., Jn 5:43; 6:57; 8:18; 9:33), Jesus' glorification depends upon God's act (e.g., Jn 17:1). Jesus' exaltation is completed by ascending to God (Jn 13:1-3; 14:28), and the claim that Jesus is "the way, the truth, and the life" has to do with the special access he provides to God (Jn 14:6).

God is not often directly mentioned as actor in Gospel scenes, but those where God is the actor are of major significance for the larger narratives. The Synoptic scenes of Jesus' baptism and transfiguration are crucial and function to confirm authoritatively for the readers Jesus' significance as God's Son. In both these scenes, uniquely in the Synoptics, God's voice sounds clearly above the din of conflicting views about Jesus that come from other characters in the narratives. God functions as the ultimate authority, and his acclamations of Jesus are in literary-critical terms the reliable voice in the narratives by which all other voices are to be judged. Likewise, in the crucifixion scenes (*see* Death of Christ) God's rending of the temple veil (an important example of the divine passive verb form mentioned earlier, Mk 15:38 par. Mt 27:51; Lk 23:45) functions as divine confirmation of Jesus' significance and of the negative view to be taken of the temple leaders who have rejected Jesus.

In John there are no baptismal and transfiguration acclamations by God. The only time God's voice sounds is in John 12:28, giving assurance to Jesus and the readers that God will "glorify [God's] name" through Jesus. John emphasizes, however, that Jesus' "works," including the "signs" that figure so prominently, are to be seen as acts of God that confirm Jesus' significance (Jn 5:36; cf. Jn 3:2). For example, in the climactic sign, the raising of Lazarus, Jesus' prayer in John 11:41-42 explicitly makes the miracle a divine answer to Jesus' appeal. Through these deeds and through the Scriptures, "the Father has borne witness" to Jesus, making Jesus' status hang entirely on God.

2. God in the Individual Gospels.

The individual Evangelists employ terminology and references to God in varying ways that reflect some thing of their individual literary purposes and style and that may also reflect their respective situations in the history of first-century Christianity.

2.1. Mark. In light of the commonly accepted view that Mark is the earliest Gospel, the references to God in this narrative are especially important historically (see Donahue). Of particular interest are the four references to God as "Father" (always in sayings of Jesus: Mk 8:38; 11:25; 13:32; 14:36). In Mark 8:38 Jesus warns that "the *Son of man" will be manifested "in the glory of his Father," stating implicitly Mark's christological affirmation that permeates the whole of his Gospel: Jesus, the Son of man of present lowly circumstance, is the Son of God.

The expression "your Father . . . who is in heaven" in Mark 11:25 may give a glimpse of the background to Matthew's familiar way of referring to God, unless one accepts H. F. D. Sparks's proposal that Mark 11:25 is not an original part of Mark.

In Mark 13:32 two things should be noted. First, Jesus, "the Son," does not know the time of the end; only God, "the Father," knows, reflecting a subordination of Jesus to God that Luke appears to have softened by omitting the statement from his form of the eschatological discourse in Luke 21. Second, this statement gives us the earliest Gospel use of the absolute forms "the Father" and "the Son," found elsewhere in the Synoptics only in Jesus' much-studied exclamation in Matthew 11:25-27 and its parallel in Luke 10:21-22, but frequent in John.

Finally, Mark 14:36 is unique in the Gospels in attributing to Jesus use of the term *abba*, used elsewhere in the NT only by Paul in references to early Christian prayer (Rom 8:15; Gal 4:6). It is remarkable that Mark, like Paul, in addressing Greek-speaking and largely Gentile readers, used this Aramaic expression alongside the Greek term for "father" (*patēr*). Writing for Christians acquainted with *abba* as a loan word associated with prayer, as Paul's references indicate, Mark probably intended his readers to see in Jesus' Gethsemane prayer a precedent for their submission to God and a reminder that the basis of their filial relationship to God lay in Jesus' own.

The role of God in the Synoptics as the ultimate reliable voice who confirms Jesus' status as Son of God is especially important in Mark, as J. D. Kingsbury has shown. In Mark the question of Jesus' transcendent identity is an important matter about which the human characters are obtuse, and various voices (e.g., disciples, crowds, Herod, religious leaders, demons) all make conflicting and inadequate attempts to label Jesus. In an expression unique in the Gospels, Mark 1:14 has Jesus preaching "the gospel of God" (a phrase found elsewhere in the NT only in Paul; e.g., Rom 1:1; 15:16), which reflects

a theocentric emphasis in Mark's presentation of Jesus' message. And J. R. Donahue's examination of Jesus' replies to questions in Mark 12 shows that Jesus' teaching here is "theistic rather than explicitly christological" (Donahue, 581). The teaching presents God as the one to whom true allegiance belongs (above what Caesar may claim, Mk 12:13-17), the life-giving deity who will raise the dead and vindicate those who trust in him (Mk 12:18-27), and the one God to be loved wholly, whose service is the basis for all other duty (Mk 12:28-34). This theistic emphasis is also implicit in Jesus' reply to the demand that he identify his authority (Mk 11:27-33), for the readers know that heaven sent the Baptist to prepare the way for Jesus and that Jesus' authority comes from God also.

2.2. Matthew. Among the Synoptics Matthew uses "Father" for God by far the most frequently (forty-four times), and is the only Synoptic "which refers to God as *patēr* nearly as often as it uses *theos*" (Mowery, 24). As the term appears only on the lips of Jesus, it is not found in Matthew until Jesus begins his teaching ministry in Matthew 5. The majority of instances of the divine title "Father" (mainly in the forms "your/our heavenly Father," e.g., Mt 5:16, 45; 6:1, 9) in Matthew are in passages where Jesus gives directions and assurances about various duties and situations of discipleship (e.g., seventeen instances in the Sermon on the Mount). Matthew sometimes replaced *theos* in Markan material with references to God as "Father" (Mt 12:50 par. Mk 3:35; Mt 26:29 par. Mk 14:25). And in the Q material comparison of Matthew's version of sayings with Luke's suggests that Matthew (or his tradition?) has a special fondness for the paternal image of God (cf. e.g., Mt 5:45 par. Lk 6:35; Mt 6:26 par. Lk 12:24; Mt 10:29-32 par. Lk 12:6-8).

Matthew is noted for the large amount of Jesus' teachings about God it contains, in which Jesus memorably emphasizes God's all-seeing, all-knowing faithfulness. Some of this material is unique to Matthew, such as Matthew 6:1-8 ("your Father" will reward genuine piety, will hear modest prayer "in secret" and "knows what you need before you ask him"). Other teaching material is paralleled in Luke (Q material), such as Matthew 6:25-34 and its parallel Luke 12:22-32 (God who feeds the birds and "clothes the grass of the field" will provide all you need), and Matthew 7:7-11 and its parallel Luke 11:9-13 (approach "your heavenly Father" confidently, for God is much more ready to give "good things" to his own than are earthly fathers). As Donahue observes, Matthew presents a very " 'human' and immediate picture of God" (Donahue, 567).

Both Matthew and Luke are structurally distinguished from Mark by a nativity account (*see* Birth of Jesus) in which God is directly active. In both cases God's actions are described in language influenced by the OT narratives of his works. In Matthew, Mary is "with child of the Holy Spirit" (of God), and an "angel of the Lord" directs Joseph at each major turning point.

2.3. Luke. In Luke there is not the same emphasis on God as "Father" characteristic of Matthew. Far and away, Luke prefers the term *theos* (122 times, not counting Acts). Four additional features of Luke's treatment of God are prominent. First, as shown by Luke's unique two-volume literary structure, which involves an account of the early church attached to his story of Jesus, Luke emphasizes that the events he narrates form the divine plan and purpose. That is, Luke particularly portrays God as the architect of the redemptive plan whose unfolding Luke narrates. Luke's interest in divine purpose is reflected in his more frequent use of the term *dei* as an expression of divine necessity (about 27 times in Luke-Acts, 14 times in Luke; cf. 4 times in Matthew, 5 times in Mark, 9 times in John). Luke's notion of divine necessity, however, is not the same as determinism, but dynamically incorporates human volitional cooperation, such as in Luke 4:43, where Jesus declares that he "must" proclaim God's kingdom in the other cities of Galilee (see also Lk 2:49; 13:33; 22:37; and Cosgrove, esp. 180-82).

Second, Luke is noted for the strong emphasis he places on God's miraculous works throughout Luke-Acts. From the nativity account onward, God acts powerfully to advance his purposes (see, e.g., the poetic exclamations in Lk 1:46-55, 68-79). Some interpreters have anachronistically characterized Luke's interest in miracles as reflecting a theology of glory rather than the cross, but this judgment of Luke through the categories of Protestant polemics of the sixteenth century hardly constitutes proper historical-critical method. Luke's purposes in narrating God's mighty works were to assure readers that God is genuinely in charge of the world and to provide examples of divine attestation of the

Christian message, rather than to provide a theology of the Christian life and much less to satisfy later critics of particular dogmatic orientations.

A third major feature of Luke's treatment of God is Luke's strong doxological interest. More emphatically than in the other Gospels, in Luke, "God is the one who is to be praised and glorified" (Donahue, 568). Some dozen times in the Gospel, Luke has people giving glory to God (e.g., Lk 2:14, 20; 5:25-26; 7:16; 13:13; 17:15; 18:43). In Mark 15:39 the centurion speaks of Jesus, but the Luke 23:47 parallel has him glorify God, and the Gospel ends with the disciples praising God (Lk 24:53).

Fourth, as reflected, for example, in the uniquely Lukan parables in Luke 15, the God of Luke's Gospel is emphatically merciful and eager to forgive and redeem. The songs of the birth narratives celebrate the sending of the Christ as God's mercy upon those who wait for his redemption (e.g., Lk 1:50, 54, 68-72). The God who orders all things, therefore, does so to accomplish his merciful intentions. In Luke divine providence orders all things in the service of divine mercy.

2.4. John. We have already noted John's considerably more frequent use of *patēr* as a title for God (109 times, more than twice the number for any other Evangelist) and have observed that in John the title plays a polemical role not associated with the term in the other Gospels. This polemical connotation is particularly clear in John 5:18, where Jesus' reference to God as "his own Father" is one of the reasons "the Jews" seek to kill Jesus. In John, more emphatically than in any other Gospel, one cannot honor God without honoring "the Son" (e.g., Jn 3:35-36; 5:22-23; 6:28-29).

This is because John emphasizes the transcendence of God more than the other Evangelists (e.g., Jn 1:18; 6:46). For John the invisible God can now be understood and approached only through the one whom God has sent to declare him, Jesus "the Son" (e.g., Jn 1:18; 14:6-9). This emphasis on God's invisible and transcendent nature makes John resemble other Greco-Roman-era Jewish writers, such as Philo of Alexandria (see, e.g., Hagner). But unlike Philo and other ancient Jewish writers who emphasize God's transcendence to criticize pagan religious traditions and to avoid crude anthropomorphism, John underscores God's transcendence and invisibility to undercut competing claims to know the true God from Jews who reject Christ.

When John refers to God's works, it is most often to associate Christ with them. Like God, the *Logos* was "in the beginning" (Jn 1:1-2), and God's creation was through the *Logos* (Jn 1:3). God, the judge of all who will reward the *righteous with resurrection life, has now given to the Son to share in the judgment and to "give life to whom he will" (Jn 5:21-22, 26-29).

Yet this strikingly exalted view of Christ is combined with an equally definite subordination of "the Son" to "the Father." The Son's prominence arises from the Father having given "all things" into the Son's hands (Jn 3:35). Believers can come to Christ only as God grants them the ability to respond (Jn 6:65). Repeatedly the exalted Son expresses his subordination and service to the Father, credits the Son's message as given to him by the Father, makes the Son's aim the glory of God and leaves it to God to bring the Son glory (e.g., Jn 5:19; 6:37-40; 8:28-29, 38, 42, 49-50, 54; 10:25, 29-30, 37-38).

Alleging a fundamental incompatibility between them, A. C. Sundberg claims that John combined an older subordinationist christology with a body of "disjunctive" material expressing a newer view, a "binitarian theology rather than christology" in which "the Son is a god like the Father is God" (Sundberg, 37). But one suspects that such comments reflect more an inability to grasp Johannine christological sophistication than any actual conflict in the christology of John. There is no indication whatsoever that the Fourth Evangelist noticed any tension between the subordinationist theme and his exalted view of Christ as one with the Father; the author repeatedly and effortlessly expresses both notions within the same or closely adjacent statements (e.g., Jn 10:29-30).

The two passages in which Jewish offense is taken at Christ associating himself improperly with God, which Sundberg offers as evidence of a new Johannine christology (Jn 5:18; 10:30-33), are not an entirely new feature in the Gospels; there are earlier echoes of the charge of blasphemous christology in Mark (Mk 14:64) and Matthew (Mt 26:65). Even more importantly, in John the two accusations of what amounts to di-theism are put on the lips of the Jewish opponents of Jesus and of the Johannine community, who are consistently portrayed by John as failing to understand the truth and as distorting the divine revelation. To be sure, Thomas's excla-

mation to the risen Christ, "My Lord and my God!" (Jn 20:28), represents an escalation of christological rhetoric distinctive in the Gospels, an escalation that probably resulted from, as much as it may have contributed to, Jewish rejection of Christian devotion to Christ. But the veneration of Christ in divine categories reflected in Thomas's exclamation can be traced back far earlier than the Gospel of John to the earliest levels of Christian tradition in the NT (see, e.g., Hurtado).

There is in John no clumsy introduction of a new di-theism, in which Christ is a second god. The accusations in John 5:19 and John 10:30 that portray Jesus as a second god are the complaints of hostile Jewish outsiders who distort the sophisticated monotheism of the Johannine community. John portrays a remarkable balancing of the convictions that Christ is uniquely associated with God and is also the obedient Son who is glorified by the one transcendent God precisely because the Son contentedly subordinates himself to God and seeks God's glory.

3. God in Jesus' Experience and Ministry.

The Gospels reflect and exemplify adaptations of the Jesus tradition to the needs and circumstances of various first-century churches, and one cannot use the Gospels simplistically to describe Jesus' teachings (*see* Gospels, Historical Reliability of). Still less do the Gospels provide us an unmediated access to Jesus' religious experience. Nevertheless, there is good reason for confidence in making certain basic claims about Jesus' references to God and perhaps even about Jesus' religious life. Two major features strongly attested in the Jesus tradition are especially worth noting: (1) Jesus refers to God as his Father, particularly in prayer, and (2) Jesus encourages his followers to use similar language and to relate to God as their Father as well.

Although details of his discussion have been challenged effectively (see, e.g., Barr), Jeremias's investigations into the tradition of Jesus' references to God as Father have proven generally persuasive about several main matters (1967; 1971, 61-67; see also Bauckham, Dunn, Fitzmyer). First, Jesus referred to God in a highly personal way (e.g., "my Father") and, especially in prayer, characteristically used the Aramaic term *abba* to address God. Second, *abba* constituted an unusual (perhaps unique) form of direct address to God for Jesus' day. Third, Jesus' use of this unusual and rather intimate form for addressing God in prayer suggests strongly that Jesus' religious life was characterized by relating to God in a very intense and personalized way that is not fully paralleled even in other examples of very devout spirituality in the ancient Jewish setting. "Jesus seems to have thought of himself as God's son in a distinctive sense" (Dunn, 38).

This special sense of sonship to God likely provided the experiential impetus of Jesus' mission. The Synoptic baptismal narratives (Mk 1:9-11 par. Mt 3:13-17; Lk 3:21-22), though stylized and adapted to the didactic needs of first-century churches, are intended to reflect an authentic feature of Jesus' religious experience: the divine acclamation of Jesus as "son" in a special sense, which also entailed the corollary of a special (and representative?) responsibility and mission. The dominant category in Jesus' religious life was probably not messiahship but sonship to God, and from this "his other basic convictions about himself and his mission arose" (Dunn, 39).

If Jesus did believe he had a special relationship with God that was a major part of the basis for his own mission, it is all the more striking that the early Christian tradition so strongly indicates that Jesus also encouraged his followers to relate to God as Father in quite an intimate manner. The earliest evidence for this is technically indirect but quite early and strong. In addition to the Gospel tradition about Jesus teaching his disciples to address God as Father, even earlier and more striking are Paul's references in Galatians 4:6 and Romans 8:15 to Greek-speaking Christian use of *abba* (along with the normal Greek term for "father," *patēr*) to address God in prayer, probably in corporate worship settings. These latter passages show that the practice was sufficiently well established already before the time of these letters (A.D. 50-60) as to need no introduction. And these remarkable references indicate that *abba* was taken over as a loan word from Aramaic-speaking churches and used in Greek-speaking (heavily Gentile) Christian churches, doubtless on account of the term's strong religious and sentimental connotations. Given that *abba* was a highly unusual form for addressing God in prayer in first-century Aramaic, some powerful influence must be posited for the practice becoming sufficiently regularized to have been influential even beyond Aramaic-speaking Christian groups. The only cogent suggestion is that Jesus' use of *abba* in prayer and his encouragement to his followers to do the same constitute the powerful originating influence required.

This makes Jesus' understanding of his relationship with God all the more remarkable. The God of Jesus' religious experience was Father in an unusually intense manner that involved a powerful sense of personal and special mission. And the mission to which God called Jesus apparently included extending an unusually intimate relationship to God as Father among those who accepted Jesus' proclamation of God's kingdom. Whatever the partial analogies offered (e.g., by Vermes) for Jesus' intimacy with God among ancient Jewish holy men, there is no parallel for Jesus' sense that God called him to become the pioneer and catalyst for a special filial relationship to God to be enjoyed by his disciples.

See also CHRISTOLOGY; HOLY SPIRIT; KINGDOM OF GOD; LOGOS; LORD; SON OF GOD; WORSHIP.

BIBLIOGRAPHY. J. Barr, "*Abba* Isn't Daddy," *JTS* 39 (1988) 28-47; C. K. Barrett, " 'The Father Is Greater Than I' (Jn 14:28): Subordinationist Christology in the New Testament" in *Neues Testament und Kirche,* ed. J. Gnilka (Freiburg: Herder, 1974) 144-59; R. Bauckham, "The Sonship of the Historical Jesus in Christology," *SJT* 31 (1978) 245-60; idem, *God Crucified: Monotheism and Christology in the New Testament* (Grand Rapids: Eerdmans, 1998); C. H. Cosgrove, "The Divine *Dei* in Luke-Acts," *NovT* 26 (1984) 168-90; J. R. Donahue, "A Neglected Factor in the Theology of Mark," *JBL* 101 (1982) 563-94; J. D. G. Dunn, *Jesus and the Spirit* (Philadelphia: Westminster, 1975); J. A. Fitzmyer, "Abba and Jesus' Relation to God" in *À cause de l'Évangile: Mélanges offerts aû Dom Jacques Dupont,* ed. R. Gantoy (Paris: Cerf, 1985) 16-38; D. A. Hagner, "The Vision of God in Philo and John: A Comparative Study," *JETS* 14 (1971) 81-94; L. W. Hurtado, *One God, One Lord: Early Christian Devotion and Ancient Jewish Monotheism* (Philadelphia: Fortress, 1988); J. Jeremias, *The Prayers of Jesus* (SBT 6; London: SCM, 1967); idem, *New Testament Theology: The Proclamation of Jesus* (New York: Scribner's, 1971); J. D. Kingsbury, *The Christology of Mark's Gospel* (Philadelphia: Fortress, 1983); R. L. Mowery, "God, Lord and Father: The Theology of the Gospel of Matthew," *BibRes* 33 (1988) 24-36; H. F. D. Sparks,

"The Doctrine of the Divine Fatherhood in the Gospels" in *Studies in the Gospels,* ed. D. E. Nineham (Oxford: Blackwell, 1967) 241-62; A. C. Sundberg, "Christology in the Fourth Gospel," *BibRes* 21 (1976) 29-37; M. M. Thompson, *The God of the Gospel of John* (Grand Rapids: Eerdmans, 2001); idem, *The Promise of the Father: Jesus and God in the New Testament* (Louisville, KY: Westminster John Knox, 2000); G. Vermes, *Jesus the Jew* (London: Collins, 1973).

L W. Hurtado

GOD II: PAUL

To try to capture in succinct and synthetic form Paul's understanding of God is an almost impossible task. There are several reasons why this enterprise is risky, even if necessary. For one thing, Paul's thought is never systematic, never speculative. Rather like the composition of his letters, his mind moves to express his teaching in response to the needs of his congregations. This makes his doctrine of God less part of his reasoned theology and more implicit in his pastoral and pragmatic handling of human situations. Yet he claims at all times to be reflecting "the mind of Christ" (1 Cor 2:16) as he expects the same disposition among his people (Phil 2:5). At the same time God is never far from his mind. He uses the word *God* so frequently that his use has forty percent of all the NT references (so Morris 1986).

Then, Paul's letters have in view the congregations gathered for worship where they are to be read out (1 Thess 5:27; Col 4:16; and implied in Philem 2). That means the doxological note is sounded throughout his correspondence. Often he will punctuate his writing with outbursts of praise to God and celebration of his grace and goodness (e.g., Rom 11:33-36; 2 Cor 9:15; Gal 1:5; Phil 4:20; 2 Thess 2:16). Paul's truest teaching on God is mirrored in these liturgical jubilations, notably in his use of creeds, hymns, poetic snatches and prayer speech.

Also, much of what Paul held dearest in his faith was shared with his ancestral beliefs in Judaism and underlay his whole viewpoint and outlook rather than coming to written, explicit expression. Hence a brief study of the OT Jewish background is given in what follows.

1. Some Basic Assumptions
2. God as Creator, Father and King
3. The Attributes of God
4. Summary

1. Some Basic Assumptions.

Paul, like the other NT writers, makes no attempt to prove the existence of God. He assumes, based on his Jewish ancestral beliefs and upbringing in a pious home of the Diaspora (Phil 3:5; 2 Cor 11:22; Gal 1:14; *see* Jew, Paul the), that God exists, that he created humankind and continues to maintain interest in his creation (1 Cor 11:7-8). Whatever the value of attempting to prove philosophically the existence of God, Paul offers no direct guidance. According to his reported responses and sermons in Acts 14:15-17 and Acts 17:22-31, he did argue his case for God's providential care from the evidence in his creation and its preservation. This line of reasoning—that God is known, at least in part, by his created works and his provision for human need—is amplified in Romans 1:19-23. Yet the revelation is only of limited value, since it is met by the human tendency to idolatry and perversion. Natural theology, for Paul, has the effect of increasing and giving focus to human sinfulness (see Hendry).

Paul, like the other writers of the NT, shares the view of God as maker of all, which is seen in the OT. The creation story concentrates on God's creative initiative, and this view of God as originator of the created world is basic to OT thought. Moreover, it is assumed that the Creator is also sustainer of his creation. The heavens and earth are the work of his hands, and he is seen to possess supreme power within the order of nature. In the intertestamental period the Jews firmly believed in the same basic creative relationship between God and his world, adding to it the conviction that Torah (Law) or Wisdom had served as an intermediary through which God created, a view that came close to personifying the Torah and Wisdom.

In Paul's hands this role of an intermediary is taken over by the preexistent Christ, notably in his redactional use of the christological hymn in Colossians 1:15-20 (see the commentaries). Yet it remains the case that Paul's monotheism, which retains God's creative act as the sole originator of creation, is firm (1 Cor 8:6; 2 Cor 4:4-6), even if it is enlarged to accord a cosmological role to the preincarnate Christ. Such christological monotheism has been regarded as Paul's unique contribution to NT thought about God and the cosmos (Wright, *Climax,* 120-36). It probably arose out of Paul's response to incipient gnosticism at Corinth, which placed a vast distance between the high God and the world. Later, at Colossae the Hellenistic idea of a set of intermediaries separating God and the universe had to be opposed by Paul's insistence that the entire fullness of deity resided in the person of Jesus Christ (Col 2:9), both transcendent and incarnate.

In this way, while Paul starts from the OT view of God as transcendent over his creation, as the holy one, he is able to relate God immanently to the world through the divine presence now located in the figure of the earthly Jesus, supremely in Jesus' death and resurrection. This was necessary because of the prevalent transcendental view of God during the intertestamental period. The Most High was removed so far from his own creation that he needed some intermediary to maintain contact with the world (but cf. Abelson, 46-54; Sanders, 44, 212-15; Dunn, 198-99). There is nothing of this remoteness in the NT approach. The NT view of God is linked with the OT revelation, not with current Jewish speculations.

Nevertheless, the transcendence of God finds some support in the majesty and particularly in the holiness of God, which is so characteristic of OT writings, especially of the Prophets. The statement in Isaiah 57:15 illustrates the essential difference between the OT view and much Jewish transcendental theology—"For thus says the high and lofty one who inhabits eternity, whose name is Holy: I dwell in the high and holy place, and also with those who are contrite and humble in spirit" (NRSV). This combination of loftiness and tenderness is an essential feature of the NT and makes the NT view of God intelligible. This high moral view was in strong contrast to the contemporary multifarious and often immoral deities worshiped by non-Jewish people at the time when the NT came into being. It is impossible to appreciate the NT revelation apart from maintaining its close connection with the OT view of God. Those movements, among which Marcionism was the earliest, which have created a cleavage between OT and NT, begin their approach to NT thought with a serious disadvantage for they have no clue to the understanding of the basic NT view of God. The latter did not arise *ex nihilo;* it was the result of a long period of revelation of which the NT was the consummation.

Paul equally builds on the inherited Jewish conviction of God's covenant love for Israel

which is undefeatable and sure (this assurance underlies the tenor of the argument in Rom 9—11; *see* Israel). Once more however, the OT Judaic confidence—that God is one, that he has revealed himself in Torah and that he has entered into covenant relations with his people Israel—received a christological modification by Paul. Yet it is not by denying these fundamental tenets in his ancestral faith that Paul argues for the finality of his new relationship (see Hays). Indeed he maintains his monotheism (Gal 3:20; 1 Cor 8:4, 6; cf. 1 Tim 2:5) and grants to the giving of Torah a glory that accompanied that event (2 Cor 3:7, 9). Israel is still an elect nation, beloved by God for the Jewish fathers' sake (Rom 11:28). On the other side, God's unity is understood in a way that makes room for the place of Jesus Christ as the "form" (Phil 2:6), "image" (2 Cor 4:4-6; Col 1:15) or "Son" (Col 1:13; Rom 8:29, 31) of God. Torah's glory was limited at its inception and is now passing away in the face of the greater glory that came in the new age of Messiah's appearing (2 Cor 3:7-11: see Belleville, Newman). And Israel in rejecting Paul's gospel stands under divine judgment at the present and in danger of being rejected as branches broken off (Rom 11:19-20).

The final word, however, is with God's unchanging love and purpose (Rom 11:29, 32) in grace, seen to be displayed and made effectual in Christ the elect one and the embodiment of divine love (Rom 8:29-38). Yahweh's love for Israel, itself uncaused (Deut 7:7-8) and persistent (Hosea), is but a foretaste of God's universal love for the world in its reconciliation (2 Cor 5:18-21) and the church in its destiny (Eph 1:1-10).

2. God as Creator, Father and King.

So basic to all parts of the Pauline corpus is the doctrine of God that much of the evidence consists of assumptions rather than specific statements. Nevertheless there are many statements that are highly significant. We shall discuss the following aspects—God as Creator, the providence of God, God as Father, God as King and Judge, various other titles for God, and then in summary form the attributes of God.

2.1. God as Creator. There is no doubt that the Christians assumed without discussion that God is the originator of the universe. They took this over from the OT and also from the teaching of Jesus. In his speech to the Athenians, Paul boldly announced the kind of God whom he worshiped as "the God who made the world and everything in it, being Lord of heaven and earth" (Acts 17:24). His creative power is also seen in the statement that mortals are his offspring (Acts 17:29), reflecting Paul's bid to establish a common ground with his audience, some of whom as Stoics cherished the notion that humans were the family of God (see Cleanthes' Hymn to Zeus). In his speech at Lystra, Paul makes a similar assertion about God's creative power (Acts 14:15).

In his letters Paul sets a distance between Creator and creatures as in Romans 1:25. Moreover, creation is said to reflect the work of the Creator (Rom 1:20). Indeed, it shows something of the character of God: his eternal power and deity. It can do this only because it is the direct work of his hands. There are specific assertions that all things were made by God (Rom 11:36; 1 Cor 8:6; 11:12; cf. Eph 3:9). Those who prohibit what God created for human good (1 Tim 4:3) on the mistaken assumption that God has no direct dealing with matter held to be evil per se—a gnostic trait—are refuted. This is why earlier Paul had appealed to Psalm 24:1 to maintain his teaching that all God's gifts of food and drink are good, provided we receive them with acknowledgment of him as giver (1 Cor 10:26-31; cf. 1 Tim 4:5). Alien teaching that places such activities as eating and drinking, along with marital sexual relations under a taboo (Col 2:21) is as firmly resisted (Col 2:23). Relations between spouses are honorable and necessary in normal circumstances (1 Cor 7:1-7).

Yet Paul reflects the same conviction that the OT shows, that the creation is not coeternal with the Creator, nor is creation the product of an inferior deity, as in later Gnosticism. God is the author of all that exists, though Paul's interest is chiefly in God's premundane election of his people. In Ephesians 1:4 the phrase "before the foundation of the world" is used of the choice of God and indicates that the Creator existed apart from the material existence of his creation.

Paul does not discuss the method of creation. He uses a common OT Jewish imagery (as in Heb 11:3, based on Ps 33:6, 9; cf. Gen 1:3) of a powerful word giving birth to created orders (2 Cor 4:6, based also on Ps 33). More important than the method is the agent. Whereas in Genesis the agency of the Spirit is mentioned (Gen 1:2), creation is said to have been effected through Christ. This has great significance for

christology. But for our present purpose it serves to put the Pauline view of creation in a somewhat different context from the OT view. The emphasis on the creative activity of Christ in no way lessens the creative activity of God. Indeed, the creative act is seen as a unity. As we have noted, the theme comes in Colossians 1:16— "for in him (i.e., Christ) all things were created, in heaven and on earth . . . all things were created through him and for him." First Corinthians 8:5-6 provides a similar statement, based on a creedal confession, in turn going back to the OT Jewish *Shema* (Deut 6:4; see Wright "One God").

These passages clearly teach not only that God created through *(dia)* Christ but also for *(eis)* Christ, which give some indication of the divine purpose for the created order. The infinite wisdom of the Creator is seen in his making the creation christocentric rather than anthropocentric. The NT does not support the view that the world belongs to humanity, except in the sense fulfilled in Jesus Christ (1 Cor 15:27, based on Ps 8). Paul does hint in one place (1 Cor 3:22) that believers are called to see the world as theirs, even if it is transitory (1 Cor 7:31), and they await the gift of their eternal homeland (Phil 3:20-21) at the parousia. Creation is bound up with the human condition, as Paul clearly recognized in speaking of the groaning of creation for deliverance (Rom 8:19-25). Modern concerns over misuse of creation have brought this into focus and have shown the extraordinary relevance of Paul's concept. The whole ecological issue of not wasting nature's resources and avoiding pollution of earth's environment as though it were an end, however laudable and necessary, in itself hardly tallies with the view of creation as made for Christ.

It is as important to consider Paul's teaching of God's providential dealing with his creation, as to note his basic assumptions about God's creative work. Paul provides an answer to the question of God's continued activity within the created order. No support is given for the view that, having created the world, God left it to its own devices. A very different picture lies behind the apostolic approach. Providence is based on the character of God, who is thought as constantly at work and vitally interested in the well-being of his handiwork. As we noted earlier, Paul's reported speech at Lystra (Acts 14:17) stresses God's control of the seasons and his harvest provision. In Paul's Areopagus address (Acts 17:25) he affirms that God gives to all people and creatures life and breath.

God's providence is attested in Paul's life as a missionary in Acts, especially in the hazards to which he was exposed and the way God is said to have brought him through (see Acts 27:24-26). The same conviction of a divine superintendence of events, in spite of obvious setbacks and dangers, runs through Paul's recital of a "litany of affliction" (*peristaseis-katalog* is the technical term current in studies on Paul's trials; 2 Cor 4:7-15; 6:4-10; 11:21-29; 1 Cor 15:30-32; Phil 2:17).

Although it is the case that providence embraces all peoples, God's special care is offered to his people in their experience of trial (Rom 5:1-10). His benign regard for all facets of life is celebrated in Romans 8:28, which is most likely to be rendered with modern translations as "in all things God works for good to those who love God and are chosen," even if they are called on to suffer for his sake. This leads on to the teaching on the fatherhood of God.

2.2. God as Father. It is the idea of God as Father that is most characteristic of NT teaching in general and especially of the teaching of Jesus. Whereas the contemporary pagan world held its gods in fear or uncertainty (*see* Worship), the Christian view of God's parenthood brings an unparalleled element of intimacy into human relationship with God. Nevertheless, while there are striking aspects in Jesus' concept of God as Father carried forward into the letters, the idea is not absent from the OT or from Jewish usage. God is conceived of as Father of his people. The Israelite king could be conceived of as an individual son of God (Ps 2; *see* Adoption, Sonship). Israel could be called "my son" (Hos 11:1). But this tended to be a nationalistic idea rather than an individual relationship, though there is a development in the direction of a personal relationship with God as parent in Sirach 4:10, *Psalms of Solomon* 17:30 and *Jubilees* 1:24-25 (*see* Son of God). At the same time, bearing in mind the Hebrew concept of solidarity, it should be noted that this corporate fatherhood did not exclude the idea of individual relationship. Indeed, it prepared the idea for its full development in the NT.

Some of the psalms, which are expressions of individual piety, come close to the more intimate character of God as seen in the NT, but the father-son relationship is not specifically formulated. The idea of God as shepherd (as in Ps 23; Is 40; Ezek 34), while introducing an amazingly tender view of God, falls short of the full acceptance of God as Father. With the advent of Christ these adumbrations of fatherhood emerge into a view of God that shows that the most intimate form of human relationships (parent-children) is but a reflection of the essential characteristic of God (see comment on Eph 3:14, 15 below).

In the Pauline literature the parenthood of God is seen in three ways. He is Father of Jesus, he is Father of the Christians, and he is Father of all creation. It is important to note that the father-child relationship in reference to God is almost wholly reserved for those who are believers. The relationship is the result of the redemptive activity of God. The creative relationship has already been discussed under the providence of God. Our concern here will be the special relationship with believers.

In the opening salutation in all the letters under Paul's name, God is described as Father. It forms a basic assumption behind all that the apostle writes in these letters. Moreover, it is frequently reflected in the course of the discussions, whether doctrinal or practical. No one concept of God dominates the theology of Paul more than this. Yet the maternal aspects of the divine-human relationship are not overlooked, even if they are only implicit in the way Paul describes his pastoral role (Gal 4:19; 1 Thess 2:7) as reflecting God's care.

The title *Father* is sometimes qualified to give added richness to the concept. God is many times described as the Father of Jesus Christ, but he is also Father of glory (Eph 1:17), that is, the one whose presence is surrounded by an aura of majesty and might, a numen that both attracts and is mysterious. He is described as "Father of mercies" (2 Cor 1:3), that is, he is known for his compassion, to which Paul appeals, by this use of a phrase drawn from the synagogue liturgy (see Martin 1986, 6-12), to enforce his exhortation to steadfastness under trial (2 Cor 1:4-7). All human fatherhood is said to derive from the fatherhood of God (Eph 3:14-15), which shows that God is not called Father on the basis of a human analogy, as if human fatherhood was the nearest approximation to the relationship between God and humanity. Fatherhood is seen rather to be inherent in the nature of God and in determining all that is highest and holiest in the human relationship of parenthood. Yet this interpretation of Ephesians 3:14-15, while it has support in some ancient authorities like Athanasius and among modern writers such as F. F. Bruce (see the discussion in Lincoln 1990, 201-4), has not gone uncontested; the text may simply mean that God is the Father of all family groupings in heaven and on earth.

But we need to inquire what fatherhood means when applied to God. As far as believers are concerned it means that God is the source of their spiritual life and pours his love upon them. God is concerned with their welfare (Rom 8:28) and with their growth in likeness to his holy, loving character (Eph 5:1; Col 1:12; 1 Thess 2:12; 4:7, 9). For Paul, then, this characterization of God is the criterion and norm of all that we are to understand by the name *God*. Supremely God is the Father of Jesus, the Son who is loved (Col 1:13; *see* Son of God). It is the divine purpose to replicate in the lives of Christ's people the image of his Son so that by the Spirit's ministry (2 Cor 3:18) the likeness of his Son is being made increasingly more apparent until at length, at the consummation of their salvation, they become "conformed to the image" of Christ (Rom 8:29). It may be that in the process they will be called on to experience suffering for Christ (Phil 3:10) in anticipation of the resurrection of the dead (Phil 3:11).

A further observation that is of great importance in any assessment of the Pauline view of God and that distinguishes the NT from any Jewish antecedents is the use of the form *Abba* by Christians in Paul's congregations (Rom 8:15; Gal 4:6), undoubtedly based on Jesus' use of the term in addressing God (Mk 14:36). This Aramaic form of address to a father was originally a term used by young children as part of nursery speech (though this is debated; see Barr), but it had acquired an extended meaning in familiar usage, roughly equivalent to "my father" or "dear father" (i.e., a caritative form of address). It is a unique form, for it finds no certain parallels either in the OT or in Judaism as an address to God. Its use by Jesus shows how completely his view of God as Father is divorced from any formal approach. The *Abba* form conveys a sense of intimacy and familiarity that introduced an entirely new factor into an approach to God. And the fact that Paul is able to cite it in its Semitic formulation, which is then rendered loosely into Greek, seems to indicate a liturgical

origin for the appellation. It is in converse with God in spoken prayer and in a congregational setting that the term is found (note the corresponding verb is *krazein*, "to cry," in both texts in Paul), and in the two instances given the work and witness of the Holy Spirit are invoked. The Spirit is the agency by which believers come to this recognition and acclamation of God as one known and approached intimately. It is the mark of the "spirit of sonship/adoption" that the Spirit places the seal of his witness on believers as sons/children of God, delivering them from nomistic religion with its uncertainty of God and the pagan fearfulness that is, for Paul, akin to slavery (Rom 8:15-16; Gal 4:5-7). Thus the cry *Abba* becomes for Paul's congregations a point of entry into the experience of a familial relationship to God that is their privilege and inheritance under the new covenant of grace (Byrne, J. M. Scott; *see* Adoption, Sonship).

2.3. God as King and Judge. Throughout the NT are traces of the idea of God as king. It comes into focus especially in the phrase kingdom of God or kingdom of heaven (*see* Kingdom of God). But clearly the idea of kingdom implies a king who exercises his rule over his subjects. There are many OT passages in which God is seen as king, and this furnishes a solid basis for the NT usage. In the contemporary world of NT times, most kings were tyrants, but this idea is nowhere suggested in the NT as applicable to God. Kingship implies sovereignty, which in its proper function carries with it responsibility. This is not to say that the idea of sovereignty is necessarily the major idea of the kingdom. The kingdom stands also for the entire blessings of salvation. Yet the two ideas are closely linked, since for believers the sovereignty of God has no meaning apart from the salvation that he has effected. The subjects of the kingdom are those who have committed themselves wholly to carrying out the will of the king.

This idea of kingship springs from the creatorship of God. When the early Christians prayed they acknowledged this fact, addressing God as "Sovereign Lord, who made the heaven and the earth and the sea and everything in them" (Acts 4:24). He who creates has a right to direct. The creature has no right to question the decisions of the Creator. Paul recognized this when he used the potter illustration in Romans 9:19-26 (ideas drawn from Isaiah and Jeremiah as understood in *Wisdom of Solomon*). Sovereignty is therefore seen to be an inherent part of the creative activity of God.

In harmony with idea of kingship is the use of the title *Lord* as applied to God, a lexical feature found often in Paul. This is another title that is prevalent in the OT and assumed in the NT. Lordship and sovereignty demand such rigorous standards of allegiance that the announcement of these themes is sufficiently attested in Paul (e.g., Phil 2:9-11; Rom 14:11-12). God's sole right to worship and homage is not open to question (announced in Is 45:23, which the two Pauline passages just referred to cite). For humans to act in any other way would result in their falling into temptation and consequently dishonoring God. This is the thrust in Paul's argument in Romans 3:1-6 in answer to those who in a diatribe-like debate reasoned that God is accountable to human reason (see Moxnes).

In the record of Paul's public preaching in the book of Acts and in the letters, the idea of the kingdom is less frequent, and consequently the concept of God as king is not as prominent. Yet the attestation is there in Acts 28:31, even if it is true that Paul is said chiefly to have preached Christ (Acts 17:18; cf. 1 Cor 1:23; 15:12; 2 Cor 1:19; Phil 1:15-18). For the early Christians, Jesus was seen to be the embodiment of the kingdom. This led to less emphasis on the kingdom but in no sense lessened the conviction that the reign of God had been inaugurated. His kingly function was everywhere assumed rather than expressed.

In Paul's letters there are many indirect indications that the apostle thought of God in terms of sovereignty, that is, under God Christ's kingdom is a present reality (1 Cor 15:25; Col 1:13; Eph 5:5). God is more powerful than the rulers of this age (1 Cor 2:6-8: *see* Principalities and Powers). All the powers of evil—the principalities and powers—are incapable of interfering with God's purposes in Christ (Rom 8:37-39). They have already been conquered (Col 2:15). The earlier notice in Colossians 1:16 that such cosmic powers were created in and by Christ poses a problem, which is most likely resolved by supposing that in the hands of the Colossian philosophers they were venerated in rivalry to Christ (Col 2:8, 18, 20) and so needed to be overcome and "reconciled." Paul sees the final act of history as God subduing his enemies "under his feet" (Rom 16:20; 1 Cor 15:23-28). In the apostle's thought there is little real distinction between the kingdom of God and the kingdom of Christ, although Christ at the parousia will deliver his kingdom to God (1 Cor 15:24) thereby transforming the *Regnum Christi* to the *Regnum Dei*. What is central to Paul's thinking in this context is the supreme sovereignty of God over everything (see Martin 1984, 107-25; Kreitzer). The Pastoral Letters contain one statement that clearly brings this aspect to the fore when God is described as "the blessed and only Sovereign, the King of kings and Lord of lords" (1 Tim 6:15).

The concept of king is closely allied to that of judge. For Paul the idea of God as judge was an integral part of his gospel (cf. Rom 2:16). Indeed, there was no doubt in his mind that God would judge the world (Rom 3:6). He speaks positively about "the judgment seat of God" (Rom 14:10; alternately this phrase appears as the judgment seat of Christ in 2 Cor 5:10 with no significant change of meaning; see Roetzel) and uses it as a basis for his verdict on Christians who were judging their fellows. What is not regarded as a legitimate prerogative for human beings—for the reason given in 1 Corinthians 4:3-5—is nevertheless of the essence of the divine nature (see Kuck). It is assumed as right and proper in Paul that the divine king should exercise his prerogative of judgment. There is admittedly a certain element of severity about this aspect of God (Rom 3:5-6, though with the concession made that Paul is speaking in human terms). Paul, who admits the severe side of God, is nevertheless careful to link it with the kindness of God (Rom 11:22). For that reason it is important to see the judgments of God as refracted through the prism of Paul's christology. God will judge the world in righteousness, as a facet of his righteous character. Yet, according to the speech in Acts 17:31, it is a universal judgment made by the standard set in Christ: "by the man whom he [God] has appointed." The effect of this clause is to recall how Paul's entire theology, his doctrine of God, is shaped by the revelation of God's nature and action that came into focus by the coming of Christ.

2.4. Other Titles for God.

2.4.1. Spirit. The entire NT presents the nature and character of God in a number of different titles that express various facets not found in a formal way but nonetheless significant. As part of the indictment he levels at the propensity to idolatry once the knowledge of God is perverted by human sinfulness (Rom 1:21-23), Paul takes it for granted that God is not a human creation or invention. His attitude toward idols is not easy to systematize. In 1 Corinthians 8:4 he joins with his Corinthian readers to affirm that "there is no God but one"; hence "an idol has no real existence" (RSV; this is placed in quotation marks to signify it is cited from the Corinthians). The idols are then dubbed "so-called" (1 Cor 8:5), since Paul cannot deny that idol worship does exist. Yet in 1 Corinthians 10:14-22 his tone is more serious, since he grants that there is a malignant demonic influence that can infect "food offered to idols," and Christians may be exposed to evil forces (otherwise the warnings in 2 Cor 6:4-7:1 would have no meaning). These powers are to be resisted (1 Cor 10:14) since they are rivals to the true God and yet are powerless to thwart his purpose, however much they seek to try by seducing believers (2 Cor 2:11). The "spiritual" essence of Paul's religion is something he assumes without much argumentation (e.g., Phil 3:3 and his teaching on the church as the dwelling place in God in the Spirit in 1 Cor 3:16; cf. Eph 2:18-21).

2.4.2. Savior. Although the title *Savior* is occasionally applied to Jesus Christ in the Pauline tradition, it is also used of God and in this respect tallies with a dominant activity of God the Savior in the OT. The main occurrences of the title are in the Pastorals (1 Tim 2:3; Tit 2:10, 13; 3:4). Although the title is relatively rare in Paul, the activity implicit in the title permeates the whole of Paul's soteriology. Indeed, Christian theology centers in the theme of God saving his people, and for Paul the power of God is displayed in the saving work initiated by God and executed in Christ (e.g., Gal 4:4-5). One notable treatise (by C. A. A. Scott; see too Morris 1986, 172-75) has placed the essential meaning of Pauline Christianity under the rubric of salvation.

2.4.3. Almighty/Most High. This is a title of supreme dignity that expresses the superiority of God over all other gods. It is used by the slave girl with an oracular spirit in Acts 16:17. Paul and his party at Philippi see this invocation as idolatrous, however, and the demon in the girl is expelled in the name of Jesus Christ. This vignette is an illustration of the way Paul opposed the deities of contemporary religion and superstition by asserting the lordship of Christ, an office and authority given him by God, the only Lord (see Acts 16:31). "Jesus is Lord" is the

Christian confession that is made in the light of the resurrection (Rom 10:9), which in turn in is, for Paul, the signal proof of the power of God and his approving of his Son's right to rule human lives and cosmic destiny (Phil 2:9-11; Rom 14:9; Eph 1:20-23). The similar title *pantokratōr* in 2 Corinthians 6:18 moves in the same circle of ideas (see the commentaries).

2.4.4. Sovereign. It is similarly the case with this appellation (found in 1 Tim 6:15), with the addition "the King of [all] kings," that is, world ruler and all-powerful emperor. Probably this fulsome description is designed to counter the claims of the emerging emperor cult in the Roman Empire, where the emperor was assuming divine honors and sanctioning the erecting of temples in his name.

3. The Attributes of God.

Anyone who seeks an answer to the question "What is the God of Paul's theology like?" will find no formal statements but a mass of incidental indications that nevertheless are invaluable in throwing light on many facets of the character of God. There is nothing to suggest that there were differences of opinion in the Pauline circles about the being of God, even when Paul had occasion to defend his gospel (Phil 1:8, 16) and to offer a counterattack on those whom he reproved as teachers who perverted his teaching (Gal 1:6-7; *see* Adversaries) and introduced an "alien gospel" (2 Cor 11:13-15). The closest Paul comes to meet head-on a rival theology is in Colossians, which opposes a bid to reduce his message to a species of Hellenistic philosophy (Col 2:8; see the commentaries). Whereas some parts of Paul's theologizing bring certain facets into focus more than other parts, there is no doubt that a unified picture is presented. While it is impossible to arrange the evidence in a systematic form, it will be helpful to group the main ideas under the following considerations—the glory of God, the wisdom of God, the holiness of God, the righteousness of God, the love and grace of God, the goodness of God, the uniqueness of God and the unity of God. Some of the ground has already been covered, but it will be convenient to set the evidence together in this way.

3.1. The Glory of God. There is a strong OT background to the frequent references in Paul to the glory of God. Whereas the Hebrew word for "glory" *(kābôd)* was used of anything that possessed splendor, honor or conspicuousness, it soon came to have a special significance when applied to God. It came to stand for the revelation of God, as when the psalmist maintained that the heavens declare the glory of God (Ps 19:1). OT history is seen as a record of God's revelation of his glory in his activities on behalf of his people. A more developed sense of the same idea is the use of "glory" to denote the presence of God in a theophany, which was later to become known in Jewish theology as the Shekinah (*šĕkînâ*). But it is the translation of the Hebrew *kābôd* by the Greek *doxa* that provides the key for understanding the Pauline ideas of the glory of God (see Newman). We shall note that in the texts there are two senses in which *doxa* is used, as visible glory (in the sense of seeing the glory of God) and as uttered praise (in the sense of ascribing glory to God).

It is astonishing how frequently the NT writers in general mention the glory and majesty of God. Moreover, men and women are prompted to glorify God. To ascribe glory to God in face of the mysterious working of his power is often spontaneous, yet in Pauline theology the theme is more implicit than fully spelled out. The pattern for measuring human shortcomings is "the glory of God" (Rom 3:23), which implies that sin has made it impossible for humans to be reflectors of God's glory as they should have been, as the way God designed them as part of his image and glory (1 Cor 11:7; see Scroggs). Nevertheless, through the process of justification and renewal Paul sees the possibility of men and women again sharing in God's glory (Rom 5:2; Col 3:10; see the commentaries). When describing the glory of Christ, he equates it with the glory shared by Christians (2 Cor 3:18). On one occasion he describes God as the "Father of glory" (Eph 1:17). He includes several doxologies that ascribe glory to God (Rom 16:27; Phil 4:20; 2 Tim 4:18). All that Christians do must be done to God's glory (cf. Rom 15:7; 2 Cor 4:15; Phil 1:11; 2:11). Moreover, eternal destruction is seen as exclusion from the presence of God and the glory of his might (2 Thess 1:9), which shows that any obscuring of God's glory is the worst possible happening in human experience.

Enough has been said to demonstrate the great importance in Paul's thought of the theme of God's glory as a basic assumption about the nature and character of God. Now we must consider how it bears upon other aspects of God. A vision of his glory cannot fail to promote a reaction of awe. It provides a ready preparation for the view of God's power, which is everywhere assumed in Paul. So glorious a being could never be impotent (cf. Rom 4:21; 11:23; 1 Cor 2:5; 2 Cor 9:8). The description "the power of God," when used absolutely, aptly indicates this dynamic aspect of God's character (cf. 2 Cor 6:7; 13:4; 2 Tim 1:8; see Powell).

With so exalted a view of the glory and power of God, it is not surprising that Paul at times alludes to the mysteries of God (see Caragounis; Harvey). The apostle speaks of "the depths of God" (1 Cor 2:10), which are known only to the Spirit of God. Some have interpreted this reference to the "depths" of God in a gnostic sense (so Wilckens, cited by but not supported by Conzelmann, 66). U. Wilckens supposes that "depths" are to be identified with the revealer, but H. Conzelmann finds this explanation of Paul's words incomprehensible. He contends that Paul is combating this view that humans could plumb the depths of God's being (see also Fee). There is a whole area of knowledge of God that is beyond the finite grasp. God is in a sense incomprehensible, although the Spirit's revelations of him are sufficient for our understanding of his redemptive purposes. There is no question of humans being able to set their own limits on God's nature and attributes. What we know is at most no more than a glimpse of the whole reality. A massive area of mystery must remain (as in the poetic passage 1 Cor 13:12). Paul can speak of God's servants as "stewards of the mysteries of God" (1 Cor 4:1), which shows that an element of mystery will always attend the proclamation of the gospel. The sense of awe is well brought out by the apostle at the conclusion of Romans 11, where he speaks of the unsearchable character of God's judgments and the inscrutable nature of his ways (Rom 11:33). No one has known the mind of God, as Isaiah 40:13-14, which Paul quotes, so patently implies. The identical thought lies behind the strange report of Paul's mystical experience in 2 Corinthians 12:1-10, especially in the "journey to heaven" motif (paralleled in rabbinic literature as well as esoteric Judaism) where Paul heard auditions "which cannot be told" (2 Cor 12:3; see the commentaries and Lincoln 1979; 1981).

3.2. The Wisdom and Knowledge of God. The Jewish wisdom writers often speak of wisdom, but not so much as an attribute of God as an emanation from God (Wis 7:25). She is described as the brightness of his everlasting light (Wis 7:26). She is created, but created before all things (Sir 1:4, 7-9; 24:14) and is the principle of creation (Sir 24:10-34; 42:21; Wis 7:21; 9:2; see Schnabel). This concept is more relevant to the NT understanding of Christ (*see* Christology); nevertheless, there is the strong implication that this personification of wisdom proceeds from God and therefore witnesses to an essential attribute of God.

The concept of the wisdom of God is especially prominent in Paul. He contrasts the wisdom of God with human wisdom (1 Cor 1:20) and shows its superiority. Human wisdom is turned to foolishness in the light of God's wisdom. This implies that the latter is the standard by which all other wisdom is gauged. In the same letter Paul speaks of the secret and hidden wisdom of God (1 Cor 2:7), which can nevertheless be imparted. It is clear that Paul identifies the wisdom that can be communicated with what the apostles proclaimed. Since in the same passage he identifies Christ as "our wisdom" (1 Cor 1:30), he is evidently thinking of the wise acts of God in the salvation of the church or, more specifically, of Christ as the embodiment of divine wisdom in human form. This is regarded in NT thought as the supreme manifestation of wisdom. (On the various ways "wisdom," good and bad, is used in 1 Corinthians see Barrett, 6-14; cf. Ellis 1978.) It is through the church that "the manifold wisdom of God" is made known even to spiritual powers (Eph 3:10). What is important for our present purpose is that God's work for his people is seen to spring from his wisdom. It is no wonder that Paul marvels at the depth of the "wisdom and knowledge of God" (Rom 11:33).

Some distinction has to be drawn between wisdom and knowledge in relation to humans, but this distinction is not so appropriate when applied to God. If wisdom is the right use of knowledge, perfect wisdom presupposes perfect knowledge. The NT writers like Paul never doubt the perfect knowledge of God. This unerring knowledge on the part of God is extended in some statements to include foreknowledge. The extension is a logical development. Paul insists that in the perfect planning of God to provide a people conformed to the image of God, he knew beforehand those who were to share that image (Rom 8:29). Paul's statement has provoked endless debate because it appears to limit human

free will. But here it may simply be noted that Paul does not discuss systematically the foreknowledge of God; he takes it for granted. He does not doubt that if God knows the present, he must also know the future as he has known the past. This seems to be an essential part of his total picture of God (cf. Eph 1:5), and seems to have its contextual setting not in speculative theology but in a pastoral concern to answer the needs of people in first-century society who felt threatened by a sense of purposelessness and powerlessness in the face of astrological determination and the role of impersonal fate (Martin 1991, 14-15).

There are certain deductions from this conviction that God is all-wise and all-knowing. Such perfect understanding means that when God wills, his plans and purposes are all-knowing and can never be in error. Although there are few specific statements in support of this in NT, it does not seem to be questioned. What God says must be true. He never lies (Rom 3:4; Tit 1:2). The absolute truth of God guarantees the consistency of his wisdom and knowledge. There is no suggestion that he ever modifies his plans in the light of his own progressive experience. This aspect of God, which will be expounded more fully in the discussion on the uniqueness of God (see 3.7 below), is essential if his acts in history are to have continuing validity.

Paul, like the NT writers generally, is conscious of the controlling character and obligatory nature of the will of God. This acceptance of the ruling character of God's will is frequently found in the letters. Paul begins several letters with the declaration of his apostleship "by the will of God" (1 Cor 1:1; 2 Cor 1:1; Eph 1:1; Col 1:1; 2 Tim 1:1). Moreover, his and other people's movements are controlled by God's will (Rom 1:10; 15:32; 1 Cor 16:12, which shows how human decision making is not ruled out; see Fee, 824). Even in his approach to those who challenged his change of plans and policies, Paul asserts that God's nature as trustworthy sets the stage for his own dealings with the Corinthians to be treated as reliable (2 Cor 1:15-22, with a word play on God's fixed nature as the faithful God [with *pistos*, "faithful," reflecting the Heb root *'mn*, as in "Amen," used of God in Deut 7:9 and Is 49:7] and the apostles' declaration of "yes" [Gk *nai* = Heb *'āmēn*] to God's promises validated in Christ whom he proclaimed and certified in the congregational Amen ["it is certain"] at worship; see Martin 1986, 26-27).

Paul also, at a later point in 2 Corinthians, reverts to this theme and justifies his ministry at Corinth by recalling how he always operated within the limits God imposed on him according to his good will (2 Cor 10:12-18: on this difficult section see Martin 1986, 314-26).

Life for the Christian is life according to God's will even in suffering. The ever-present problems involved in God's permitting suffering for his people are nowhere discussed. Does this mean that the NT writers like Paul were unaware of the problem? Yet it is hard to think this personal issue ever eluded Paul's notice or that of his congregations (it underlies much of Philippians). It must be assumed, therefore, that the Christians were convinced about the all-inclusive character of God's wisdom and the perfection of his will. This is bound up with the conviction of God's providential care for his people. If suffering comes, God must have a purpose in it.

Much confusion arises from the fact that it is generally assumed that all suffering should be avoided. The notion that God can use suffering does not come naturally. But the biblical approach to suffering constantly takes it into the sphere of God's purpose. Although it is true that suffering is nowhere explained, there is enough evidence to show what the Christian attitude toward it should be. There is no suggestion that God is less than wise or good because suffering exists. Since the supreme example of suffering lies at the heart of God's redemptive activity in Christ, it cannot be maintained that suffering is alien to the purpose of God. It will always remain a mystery why God chose to redeem humankind the way he did, but this fact must be taken into account in considering the Pauline view of God.

Arising from the necessity for Christ to suffer comes the problem of suffering for Christians. It is not surprising that in a hostile world Christians will meet with opposition on account of their faith. This is the least problematic aspect of suffering. Paul, in recounting his experiences in 2 Corinthians 4:7—5:10, in no way criticizes God for the hardships he has endured. He sees these hardships as tools in the hand of God. The present momentary affliction is regarded as "slight" (2 Cor 4:17) compared with the weight of glory to follow. Later in the same letter the apostle gives details of his "slight" affliction (cf. 2 Cor 6:4; 11:23-12:10), which consists of a harrowing list of calamities that have been seldom equaled or surpassed, and yet he has arrived at a triumphant attitude toward them. There is no hint anywhere in this letter that he resents or questions the wisdom of God in allowing suffering.

The one place where he does tackle the theodicy question (Why does God allow suffering, when undeserved?) provides Paul the opportunity to bring out the gracious character of God as seen paradoxically in the face of human trials. This appears in Philippians 1:19-30. The implicit questions relate to Paul's imprisonments and prospect of imminent martyrdom, and the Philippians share in his trials (Phil 1:7). To those who doubted Paul's authentic apostleship because he was a suffering leader (and in 2 Cor 12:1-10, a failed charismatic who could not heal himself) and to the Philippians, who took their suffering as a test of faith, Paul responds with a stirring assertion of God's overruling power in weakness and uses affliction as a mark of favor (Phil 1:29; see Bloomquist). This leads to Romans 5:3, where Paul actually rejoices in suffering because it develops the quality of endurance. In this same context he speaks of God's love being poured out in our hearts. The two things were clearly not incompatible in his mind.

It cannot be said that the writings of Paul answer all the intellectual problems that arise from God's permitting human suffering, but they do enable Christians to face suffering without losing confidence in the perfection of God's wisdom and his loving design to guide and support his people's lives in their times of testing (Rom 8:28-39).

3.3. The Holiness of God. One of the most characteristic qualities of God in the OT is his holiness. Although people and things and places are described as holy, this is in the sense of being set apart for God. Holiness is essentially an attribute of God. It marks him out as being utterly pure in thought and attitude. In the prophecy of Isaiah "the Holy One" is a characteristic name for God (cf. Is 6). It is this quality of holiness that creates at once a barrier in our approach to God, since we become conscious of our lack of holiness in the presence of God. It is because Israel had a holy God that demands were made upon its people to become a holy people, which they failed to fulfill.

Undoubtedly this conviction that God is holy forms an important element in the Pauline account of salvation. It underlies his argument in 1 Thessalonians 4:3-8 that his readers should steer clear of immoral practices and respond to God's call to "live a holy life" (1 Thess 4:7 NIV). Yet this for Paul is only possible and practicable if we have recourse to God's provision in the gift of the Holy Spirit (1 Thess 4:8), who is the sanctifying agent in redemption (cf. 2 Thess 2:13). Equally, in 1 Corinthians 6:12-20 the insistence of Paul's stringent advice to "flee from sexual immorality" (1 Cor 6:18) is governed and supported by his reminder that the holy Lord will have a holy people whose bodies are the temple of the Holy Spirit.

3.4. The Righteousness and Justice of God. So far the only moral characteristic of God that has been mentioned is his absolute truthfulness and his holiness. But more needs to be said about the righteousness of God, for this is basic to the Pauline plan of salvation. In the OT righteousness in God means more than that God always acts in a morally right way. It includes also the fact that God acts on behalf of his people when they are unjustly oppressed. In the NT the apostle Paul is the great exponent of this important characteristic of God. He does not question that God is righteous. He begins his exposition in the letter to the Romans with the assertion that God's righteousness has been revealed (Rom 1:17). This is reiterated in Romans 3:21-22.

Exegetes debate whether "the righteousness of God" in these contexts concentrates on what can be imparted rather than what is inherent to God. Is the expression intended to refer to a quality in God or not? The genitive may be taken in three ways: (1) as an objective genitive, in which case the righteousness is that which God grants (so Luther); (2) as a subjective genitive, in which case it refers to that which belongs to God; (3) as a genitive of origin, in which case it is God's righteousness but proceeds from God to humans. There is a notable reluctance among many recent writers to regard righteousness solely as an attribute of God. Whatever the conclusion, the association of God and righteousness is clear enough. True righteousness comes from God (cf. Rom 10:3; Phil 3:9). In 2 Corinthians 5:21 Paul even states that Christ was made sin "so that in him we might become the righteousness of God"—an unusual expression, which may indicate a taking over by Paul of an earlier statement (see the commentaries). Yet we may concede that 2 Corinthians 5:21 makes sense only if God is essentially righteous. Paul describes the Christian's new nature as "created after the likeness of God in true righteousness and holiness" (Eph 4:24), showing righteousness as an essential constituent in God's image, restored to his people in Christ by the Spirit (2 Cor 3:18).

The concept of God's judging in righteousness involves the idea of God's impartiality. It was difficult for Jews to accept this idea, for they were convinced that Israel was a favored nation, which made it superior to the Gentile peoples in the sight of God. It threatened to cause real problems when Jews and Gentiles had to mix in the early Christian communities.

Paul had already made a *volte-face* when he became a Christian. More than any other he wrestled with the problem of God's special concern for the Jewish people, but as a Christian he never doubted that God was impartial and that Jew and Gentile must be included in the plan of salvation on an equal footing. On two occasions he asserted as axiomatic that God shows no partiality (Rom 2:11; Gal 2:6), the second of which deals with the apostolic office. The idea definitely excluded any notion of favoritism with God, which would not be in keeping with absolute justice.

An important side to the righteousness and justice of God is his wrath. There are sufficient instances of emphasis on God's wrath and judgment in the NT and in Paul in particular to make it important to define its meaning. The precise meaning has been subject to debate (see Morris 1960). Of all the aspects of God in the NT this is perhaps the most questioned. Some interpreters reduce wrath *(orgē)* to the effect of human sin, thus getting rid of all notion of anger in God because this is considered to be irrational (Dodd, but see the reply in Tasker). But this is an unsatisfactory way of dealing with the NT evidence. In Romans 1:18 the expression "the wrath of God" occurs (cf. Rom 5:9; 12:19; 14:5; see also Rom 9:22), and it is impossible in this case to empty the phrase of any relevance to the attributes of God. Paul speaks of a wrath of God that is being revealed *(apokalyptetai)* in precisely the same way as he had just previously stated that God's righteousness is being revealed (Rom 1:17-18). It is inescapable that Paul intended a connection between the two concepts. It seems most reasonable to suppose that wrath is the negative aspect of God's righteousness. It does not express anger in the sense in which it is applied to humans, an uncontrolled outburst of passion, but it must express the revulsion of absolute holiness toward all that is unholy. This is in harmony with the context where "wrath" is explicitly said to be against *(epi)* ungodliness and wickedness. The same may be said of Romans 5:9, where salvation is said to be from "the wrath," which may well denote the wrath of God as an expression of God's rejection of all that is sinful.

It is not sufficient to define wrath as the principle of retribution in a moral universe without connecting the principle to its source, the nature of God. Unless we find some place for the moral displeasure of God we shall make light of his judgment, which finds no small place in NT thought. When Paul says in Colossians 3:6 that the wrath of God is coming, he must mean more than that a principle of retribution is approaching. The eschatological aspect is again present in this context and is more explicit than in Romans 1:18 (Martin 1972, 110). E. Lohse has denied that wrath in Colossians 3:6 indicates an emotion of God, but is God's judgment of wrath (Lohse, 139). Yet God's judgment cannot be wholly detached from his continual reaction against sin. Wrath cannot, in short, be received as a term that describes only God's final act of judgment. The expression has more force if the condemnation of the evils mentioned in the previous verse is based on the active opposition of God against them (see also Eph 5:6). It should be noted that when the apostle assures the Thessalonians that God has not destined them for wrath (1 Thess 5:9), he is writing to Christians, and his words cannot cancel out the statements about God's wrath elsewhere.

3.5. The Love and Grace of God. That God is a God of love is another assumption Paul makes, though he does not make it lightly, writing (Rom 5:8) that God's love is proved to believers by the death of his Son. The inference is that what was required is a demonstration of what we would not have imagined possible or conceivable without prior revelation of God, namely, that God loves undeserving and guilty sinners. It has a firm basis in the OT and Jewish literature but takes on a sharper focus and a more dominant role in the NT generally.

Hence the apostle Paul pursued this line of thought. In the letter that most emphasizes the righteousness of God, he can speak with equal certainty about the love of God. God's love has been poured into believers' hearts through the Spirit (Rom 5:5), a vivid way of speaking of the communicating of God's love to humankind. That love is most seen in God's saving work for sinners (Rom 5:8). The consequence for believers is that they will never be separated from that love (Rom 8:39). Love makes them more than conquerors (Rom 8:37). The love of God is a familiar part of such benedictions as 2 Corinthians 13:13 (14) (see also 2 Cor 13:11) and Ephesians 6:23. It comes in Paul's prayers for the Thessalonians (2 Thess 2:16; 3:5). In the latter prayer the love of God is regarded as the aim to which Christians' minds should be directed ("may the Lord direct your hearts to the love of God").

There are two other aspects of God that are so closely linked to love that they may properly be considered in conjunction with it. First there is the understanding that God is a God of grace. The whole concept of grace lies at the heart of Paul's soteriology, and in that connection we note that "the grace of God" denotes an essential feature of God's love. When applied to God, the word *grace* denotes the favor of God toward those who do not deserve his favor and therefore came to be used particularly of God's saving work in Christ. It has become a basic assumption, so much so that it frequently occurs in the opening salutations and in the concluding benedictions of the Pauline letters. God is seen as one who bestows unmerited favor on the objects of his love. God's grace is more than his gracious acts, although it includes these. It involves his nature. His love is of such a quality that it gives unstintingly. Grace is another name for the outgoing character of his love, especially to sinners and to his elect people. Sometimes God's grace becomes almost objectified in the results that it achieves, as when Paul can say that the Macedonians' response to the challenge to Christian giving is a sign of God's grace in human lives (2 Cor 8:1; cf. 2 Cor 8:7 as a summons to the Corinthians to excel in this "grace" of generosity also).

The apostle Paul was deeply convinced of his personal indebtedness to God's grace. He saw his calling as an act of grace (Gal 1:15). He had no doubt that Christians are saved by God's grace (Rom 3:24; 5:15; cf. Eph 2:5, 7; Tit 2:11). He sees it as a subject for praise (Eph 1:6). He views it as in some way a communicable gift (e.g., 1 Cor 1:4; 3:10; 15:10; 2 Tim 1:9). Living by grace is diametrically opposed to any religious claim depending on human effort (Gal 2:21; Rom 11:6). Grace also provided Paul with the assurance that God would work in his apostolic life (1 Cor 15:10-11); the term becomes almost indistinguishable from "strength" needed to fulfill his missionary task (2 Cor 12:9). In spite of the limitations Paul faced he was able to embrace a way of relying more fully on God's power-in-weakness (2 Cor 12:10; 13:4).

The second aspect of God closely allied to love is the mercy of God. The root meaning of "mercy" is compassion, hence its close link with love. It is essentially outgoing love marked by persistence and commitment (as in the Heb *ḥesed*). Mercy is also inseparably linked with grace but is more specifically connected with righteousness. It is when the righteous judgments of God are considered that his mercy becomes a vivid reality. If he must condemn what is unrighteous because he is righteous, he extends mercy to those who would otherwise be condemned because mercy is as much a part of his nature as righteousness. This idea of God's mercy is not unique to the NT. It finds its roots in the OT.

The apostle Paul was deeply aware of the mercy of God (Rom 9:15-16, 18) as part of God's gracious prerogative. He several times speaks, often autobiographically when reflecting on his apostolic calling and mission, of obtaining mercy, which means receiving the results of God's merciful acts (Rom 11:30-32; 1 Cor 7:25; 2 Cor 4:1; 1 Tim 1:16). There is no suggestion that the quality of mercy is alien to God or that it conflicts with his essential righteousness. It is part of the apostle's understanding of the total nature of God. Paul uses the striking expression "Father of mercies" of God in 2 Corinthians 1:3, which draws attention to his compassionate nature. It echoes Exodus 36:6, Psalm 86:15 and Psalm 145:8, which speak of God as merciful and gracious and is integral to the synagogue's liturgy in its acclamation of God as kind to Israel, especially in forgiving sins and restoring relations. (See Colossians 2:13-15, which suggestively finds its Jewish background in the New Year prayer of supplication for God's mercy to his people.)

Paul sometimes uses another word—"kindness" *(chrēstotēs)*—when describing the gracious attitude of God. He once links it with the quality of severity (Rom 11:22). It may seem difficult to see how these two facets of God's character can exist in one person, but Paul is not apparently embarrassed by this difficulty. To him kindness and severity are essential characteristics. He sees God's kindness as intended to lead people to repentance (Rom 2:4), although he recognizes that his Jewish contemporaries have incurred the righteous judgment of God (Rom 2:5). The close connection between God's grace and his kindness is clearly seen in Ephesians 2:7, where God's immeasurable riches of grace are equated with his kindness toward us in Christ. Kindness is therefore practically synonymous with grace. Kindness is further linked with the goodness of God in Titus 3:4, where both are stated to have "appeared" (i.e., in the provisions of salvation by the incarnate presence of Christ).

3.6. The Goodness and Faithfulness of God. There are a few significant statements in the Pauline library that focus on the goodness of God and that deserve separate consideration. The concept of goodness is difficult to define but is nevertheless generally recognized to be closely linked with the moral holiness of God. The Gospels' statement, "Only one is good, God," makes clear that the character of God is such that it is the standard that should determine all human notions of goodness. Whatever goodness anyone else possesses is derived from him. This is supported by such an OT statement as Psalm 53:1, which is cited by Paul in Romans 3:12, and affirms that no one is good. Paul uses it to demonstrate human need, but he does not bring out so specifically as Jesus had done the unique goodness of God (Mt 19:17; Mk 10:17; cf. Lk 18:18-19).

Although the faithfulness of God is a different kind of attribute from goodness, it may be linked with the sense that, were God faithless to his word, he could not be good. Paul was deeply impressed with the faithfulness of God. He is faithful in calling people into fellowship with his Son (1 Cor 1:9) and in guarding them against excessive testing of their faith (1 Cor 10:13) or from the attacks of the evil one (2 Thess 3:3). The faithfulness of God is even cited by Paul as a guarantee of the dependability of his own word (2 Cor 1:18). Moreover, God remains faithful even when others are faithless (2 Tim 2:13). There is a rock-like quality to the apostle's conviction of God's reliability.

We may perhaps include in this section a note about the expression "the God of peace," which is particularly familiar through the concluding salutation in Romans 15:33 and in 1 Thessalonians 5:23. The more widely used form of the idea "peace from *(apo)* God" occurs in the opening greetings in all Paul's letters. It appears that the quality that God can impart has become an ascription to him. The form "God of peace" is suggestive because it points to the absence of conflict in God and his solicitude for his people's welfare *(šālôm)*. First Corinthians 14:33 brings this out explicitly—"God is not a God of confusion, but of peace." Peace therefore describes an attitude of God as well as a quality that he imparts. Peace cannot be bestowed from God unless it is an integral part of his nature. Humankind in its fallen state is in a perpetual state of enmity and tension until reconciled to God (Rom 5:1-10; cf. Eph 2:1-3, 12). But such a state of tension does not exist in God. There is no suggestion anywhere in NT teaching that God is ever uncertain as to his actions or frustrated in his plans. His mind is always in a state of equilibrium. It is no wonder that Paul, in desiring to allay anxiety among Christians, not only exhorts them to commit themselves to God but also assures them that the peace of God will garrison *(phroureō,* i.e., act as a sentry or patrol, to guard the city gates against invading attack; see Hawthorne, 184) their hearts and minds (Phil 4:7). In the same passage he assures his readers of the continued presence of the God of peace (Phil 4:9).

3.7. The Uniqueness of God. Included here will be Paul's hints of teaching concerning the invisibility of God. The mystery conveyed in the expression "no one has ever seen God" is fully in accord with the OT conceptions. This invisibility is one of the ways to find a counterpoint in the revelatory character of the mission of Jesus. Paul makes clear that God the Creator has made himself known in his works (Rom 1:19), but in saying this he implies that there are also aspects of God that cannot be known. In 1 Timothy 1:17 is included in the somewhat formalized ascription to God his invisibility, which is specifically mentioned only here in the NT.

Closely linked and occurring in the same statement in 1 Timothy 1:17 is the idea of the immortality of God, which occurs also in Romans 1:23. The concept may be indebted more to Hellenistic than Jewish thought. A God who is changeless must be a God who is immortal. Such a God can rightly be described as "eternal" (Rom 16:26).

3.8. The Unity of God. Our purpose here will be to bring together the main NT evidence for the Trinity and then to assess its significance. It must be remembered that although the intertestamental Jews were strongly monotheistic, there are indications in the OT that God was not regarded as one in the mathematical sense of being unitary. (Recent studies have shown how Jewish theology in early Judaism could entertain notions of separate hypostases or personifications within the strict monotheism it cherished and defended; see Segal, Hurtado, Rainbow; more cautiously Dunn, 183-206.) Such an expression as "the Lord of hosts" at least implies that God is not alone (cf. 1 Kings 22:19-23; Ps 89:5-8). The armies of heaven or the "sons of God" (as in Job 1:6; 38:7; Ps 29:1; 89:6) show that God has agents. Of greater significance is the frequently mentioned "angel of Yahweh," who sometimes appears in human form but is nevertheless recognized as God (cf. Gen 16:7-14; 18:1-22; Ex 3:2-6). Nevertheless at times the "angel" is distinguished from Yahweh (Ex 33:2, 3). It is significant for the NT teaching about the Trinity and may have left enigmatic traces in Paul's writing (see Gal 4:14).

An entirely new factor was nevertheless introduced with the emergence of the Christian gospel, which led to a development of the monotheistic approach and ultimately to the doctrine of the Trinity. Of the Trinity there are many adumbrations in the NT, although it cannot be said that the doctrine is explicitly expounded in a formal way. It is significant that none of the NT writers sees the need to speculate about such a doctrine; they seem able to accord divine honors to Jesus without embarrassment (Dunn). They are content to present data that imply the divine nature of Christ and the Spirit and that naturally give rise to reflections about the unity of God (see Wainwright).

The Pauline evidence may be summarized under three different types of quasi-liturgical passages. First, there are a few passages where trinitarian formulae are used (e.g., 1 Cor 12:3-7, Eph 1:3-14; 2:18; 4:4-6; Tit 3:4-6) These passages are conceivably and suggestively linked with a baptismal and/or initiatory creed.

Another such passage is 2 Corinthians 13:13 (14), where Paul adds a benediction involving

God, the Lord Jesus Christ and the Holy Spirit. No distinction is made between them, and it is a reasonable assumption that Paul regarded them as coequal persons. (On the debate over the genitive, "fellowship of the Holy Spirit," see the commentaries.)

These sections are cast in triadic form. In Ephesians 4:4-6, we read of "one Spirit . . . one Lord . . . one God and Father." The threefold form occurs also in 1 Corinthians 12:3-7, where each person is introduced with the adjective *same* in the sequence Spirit, Lord and God, as in Ephesians 4. Under this category may be included Ephesians 1:3-14, where the flow of the eulogy is marked by a trinitarian format or a salvation-historical sequence of the plan of redemption from its eternal purpose to its execution in human experience (see Lincoln 1990, 8-44; Martin 1991, 13-20).

The second type consists of passages where the three persons are mentioned together but without any clear triadic structure. Samples of such passages are Galatians 4:4-6 ("God has sent the Spirit of his Son into our hearts"), Romans 8:1-4, 2 Thessalonians 2:13-14 and Titus 3:4-6. The close linking of Father, Son and Spirit in these passages cannot be regarded as accidental.

Third, actions that are normally attributed to God are ascribed to Christ (such as creation; see Col 1:15-20; 1 Cor 8:6) or to the Spirit (e.g., acts of power; e.g., Rom 8:5-11). These add a further dimension to the NT evidence. Although no systematic trinitarian doctrine is stated, Paul furnishes several hints that point in that direction. The problems that confronted later theologians do not seem to have occurred to him, especially as part of his "christological monotheism" or "realigned monotheism" (Dunn, 163) by which he was able to accommodate the risen Lord into his picture of the one God of his Jewish faith, now broadened and deepened to make space for the exalted Lord who in worship was greeted as on a par with Yahweh and worthy of divine honors and praise (Bauckham). In praise of the living Lord installed as head of the universe and the church, Pauline Christians evidently were expected to confess that Jesus could be worshiped alongside but not in competition with or to the exclusion of Israel's God. Hence the appellation *God* for the risen Christ trembles on Paul's lips (Rom 9:5; see Harris).

We have been discussing the adumbrations of the Trinity, but it is under the general heading of the unity of God and some comment must be made concerning this. It must at once be noted that nowhere in the NT is any concern shown over purely speculative ideas about unity. Statements can be found like "the Lord is the Spirit" (2 Cor 3:17) or "our Lord Jesus Christ . . . and God our Father . . . comfort" (sing. verb) in 2 Thessalonians 2:16 or a doxology to Christ as God (Rom 9:5; see the commentaries), without any apparent blurring of the distinction between them in the context. Undoubtedly there are deep mysteries in the NT conception of God, but what must strike the thoughtful reader is the absence of any attempt to explain the mysteries. Christian convictions were strong enough to maintain the divine nature of Jesus Christ and the Spirit without falling into the trap of postulating three gods. The conviction that God was active in Christ and in the Spirit prevented this from happening. It may be said that Paul does not work with a conceptual framework that would lead naturally to speculations about the essence of God. In a study of Paul's theology we cannot go further than the evidence we find. Yet the evidence lays foundations for the later developed doctrine. The problems that this later doctrine grappled with had their roots in the NT. Although Paul concentrates more on functions than relationships, as O. Cullmann's writings show, the latter aspect is not lacking.

4. Summary.

Our survey of the Pauline presentation of God has done no more than to erect signposts toward an understanding of what must always retain an air of profound mystery. No outline of names or qualities can present a total picture. But Paul gave abundant indication that what is necessary to know about God can be known. This is a basic assumption that colors his entire theological and missionary task (see Gilliland).

Moreover, in the titles and attributes of God found in the NT, there is a remarkable combination of what might at first appear to be opposites. The paradox of the love and wrath of God, his kindness and severity, his mercy and judgment, are examples of apparent antitheses or antinomies that nevertheless are perfectly balanced in the character of God. What in humans would be regarded as real antitheses and unrelieved paradoxes are postulated in God in a way that shows no awareness of any problem.

Another remarkable fact about the evidence

is that it includes transcendent and immanent aspects without any tendency to lay an overemphasis on either. There are no signs, in fact, that the problems that arise from such an overemphasis ever seriously troubled the minds of the early Christians. God is at the same time majestic and concerned about the human condition. He is never remote but is at the same time apart from his creation.

The relevance of a right doctrine of God for an approach to Pauline theology may be illustrated as follows. A God who cares for his creatures is the God who acts to redeem them. A true understanding of the incarnation and therefore of the person of Christ is impossible if a wrong notion of God is maintained (signally at Colossae). Similarly, if God were an angry deity who needed to be placated, this would naturally color any approach to the doctrine of the mission of Christ. Some indication of the havoc that can be caused within a theology based on wrong assumptions about God can be seen in such issues as the way Paul has been misread as supporting anti-Semitism or (to take a practical yet profound concern) recruited as an ally of the paternalistic-hierarchical structure that demotes and dehumanizes women due to a false deduction regarding male headship.

See also CHRISTOLOGY; CREATION, NEW CREATION; GNOSTICISM; HOLY SPIRIT; JUDGMENT; LORD; SON OF GOD.

DPL: IMAGE, IMAGE OF GOD; LOVE; MERCY; POWER; PRE-EXISTENCE; WRATH, DESTRUCTION.

BIBLIOGRAPHY. J. Abelson, *The Immanence of God in Rabbinical Literature* (London: Macmillan, 1912); J. Barr, "Abba Isn't Daddy," *JTS* 39 (1988) 28-47; idem, " 'Abba, Father' and the Familarity of Jesus' Speech," *Theology* 91 (1988) 173-79; C. K. Barrett, *Essays on Paul* (Philadelphia: Westminster, 1982); R. J. Bauckham, *God Crucified: Monotheism and Christology in the New Testament* (Grand Rapids: Eerdmans, 1998); idem, "The Worship of Jesus in Apocalyptic Christianity," *NTS* 27 (1981) 323-31; L. L. Belleville, *Reflections of Glory: Paul's Polemical Use of the Moses-Doxa Tradition in 2 Corinthians 3:12-18* (JSNTSup 52; Sheffield: Sheffield Academic, 1991); L. G. Bloomquist, *The Function of Suffering in Philippians* (JSNTSup 78; Sheffield: Academic Press, 1993); B. Byrne, *'Sons of God'— 'Seed of Abraham': A Study of the Idea of the Sonship of God of All Christians Against the Jewish Background* (AnBib 83; Rome: Biblical Institute, 1979); C. C. Caragounis, *The Ephesian Mysterion* (Lund: Gleerup, 1977); H. Conzelmann, *1 Corinthians* (Herm; Philadelphia: Fortress, 1975); O. Cullmann, *The Christology of the New Testament* (Philadelphia: Westminster, 1959); C. H. Dodd, *The Epistle of Paul to the Romans* (New York: Harper & Row, 1932); J. D. G. Dunn, *The Partings of the Ways* (Philadelphia: Trinity Press International, 1991); E. E. Ellis, *Prophecy and Hermeneutic in Early Christianity* (Tübingen: Mohr Siebeck; Grand Rapids: Eerdmans, 1978); G. D. Fee, *1 Corinthians* (NICNT; Grand Rapids: Eerdmans, 1987); D. S. Gilliland, *Pauline Theology and Mission Practice* (Grand Rapids: Baker, 1983); L. E. Goodman, *Monotheism* (Totowa, NJ: Allanheld Osmun, 1981); R. M. Grant, *Gods and the One God* (Philadelphia: Westminster, 1986); M. J. Harris, *Jesus as God* (Grand Rapids: Baker, 1992); A. E. Harvey, "The Use of Mystery Language in the Bible," *JTS* 81 (1980); G. F. Hawthorne, *Philippians* (WBC 43; Waco, TX: Word, 1983); R. B. Hays, *Echoes of Scripture* (New Haven, CT: Yale University Press, 1989); G. S. Hendry, "Reveal, Revelation" in *A Theological Word Book of the Bible,* ed. A. Richardson (London: SCM, 1950); L. W. Hurtado, *One God, One Lord: Early Christian Devotion and Ancient Jewish Monothesim* (Philadelphia: Fortress, 1988); L. J. Kreitzer, *Jesus and God in Paul's Eschatology* (JSNTSup 19; Sheffield: JSOT, 1987); D. W. Kuck, *Judgment and Community Conflict* (NovTSup 66; Leiden: E. J. Brill, 1992); A. T. Lincoln, *Ephesians* (WBC 42: Dallas: Word, 1990); idem, *Paradise Now and Not Yet* (SNTSMS 43; Cambridge: Cambridge University Press, 1981); idem, "Paul the Visionary: The Setting and Significance of the Rapture to Paradise in 2 Corinthians 12:1-10," *NTS* 25 (1979) 204-20; E. Lohse, *Colossians and Philemon* (Herm; Philadelphia: Fortress, 1971); R. P. Martin, *Colossians: The Church's Lord and the Christian's Liberty* (Exeter: Paternoster, 1972); idem, *2 Corinthians* (WBC 40; Waco, TX: Word, 1986); idem, *Ephesians, Colossians and Philemon* (Int; Louisville, KY: John Knox, 1991); idem, *The Spirit and the Congregation: Studies in 1 Corinthians 12-15* (Grand Rapids: Eerdmans, 1984); L. Morris, "The Apostle and His God," in *God Who Is Rich in Mercy,* ed. P. T. O'Brien and D. G. Peterson (Homebush West, NSW: Anzea, 1986) 165-78; idem, *The Biblical Doctrine of Judgment* (London: Tyndale, 1960); H. Moxnes, *Theology in Conflict: Studies in Paul's Understanding of God*

in Romans (NovTSup; Leiden: E. J. Brill, 1980);
C. Newman, *Paul's Glory-Christology: Tradition and Rhetoric* (NovTSup 69; Leiden: E. J. Brill, 1992); C. H. Powell, *The Biblical Concept of Power* (London: Epworth 1963); P. Rainbow, "Jewish Monotheism as the Matrix for New Testament Christology," *NovT* 33 (1991) 78-91; C. J. Roetzel, *Judgment in the Community: A Study of the Relationship Between Eschatology and Ecclesiology in Paul* (NovTSup; Leiden: E. J. Brill, 1972); E. P. Sanders, *Paul and Palestinian Judaism* (Philadelphia: Fortress, 1977); E. J. Schnabel, *Law and Wisdom from Ben Sira to Paul* (WUNT 2.16; Tübingen: Siebeck, 1985); C. A. A. Scott, *Christianity According to St. Paul* (Cambridge: Cambridge University Press, 1927); J. M. Scott, *Adoption as Sons of God: An Exegetical Investigation into the Background of ΥΙΟΘΕΣΙΑ in the Corpus Paulinum* (WUNT 2.48; Tübingen: Siebeck, 1992); R. Scroggs, *The Last Adam* (Oxford: Blackwell, 1966); A. F. Segal, *Paul the Convert* (New Haven, CT : Yale University Press, 1990); idem, *Two Powers in Heaven* (SJLA 25; Leiden: E. J. Brill, 1978); R. V. G. Tasker, *Biblical Doctrine of the Wrath of God* (London: Tyndale, 1951); M. M. Thompson, *The Promise of the Father: Jesus and God in the New Testament* (Louisville, KY: Westminster John Knox, 2000); A. W. Wainwright, *The Trinity in the New Testament* (London: SPCK, 1962); N. T. Wright, *The Climax of the Covenant* (Minneapolis: Fortress, 1991); idem, "One God, One Lord, One People," *Ex Auditu* 7 (1991) 46-48; idem, *The New Testament and the People of God* (Minneapolis: Fortress, 1992).

D. Guthrie and R. P. Martin

GOD III: ACTS, HEBREWS, GENERAL EPISTLES, REVELATION

"God" *(theos)* in the later NT documents continues to denote the unique deity of Israel's Scripture and tradition. Most every use of *theos* or its semantic or pronominal substitutes consequently carried with it the explicit commitment to an exclusive brand of Jewish monotheism—that is, that there is only one God, Israel's God, Yahweh. These same later NT documents, however, demonstrate that the identity of this God underwent a profound redefinition. The identity of Israel's one true God was enlarged to include Jesus of Nazareth.

Given such revision, it was not a foregone conclusion that Christianity would stay within the constraints dictated by Jewish monotheism (Harvey, 154-73). The temptations to entertain a whole host of other arrangements—from a full-fledged ditheism to supplanting Yahweh with Jesus—were ever present. The various christological debates and controversies of the first four centuries of the church can be read as a sustained struggle to bind the theological energy unleashed by the juxtaposition of Yahweh and Jesus within the worship of the church. Remarkably, Christianity did remain within the bounds of monotheism. Just as an unwavering commitment to an exclusive brand of monotheism provided the theological context for the Jewish way of living *(halakah)*, so too a christologically reformatted monotheism fueled the communal identity and eschatological ethics of the new Chris-tian movement. Monotheism proved to be as essential to Christianity's various conciliar confessions as it had been to Israel's *Shema* (Deut 6:4).

The crucial historical, theological and philosophical question then becomes, How did Christianity successfully effect the transition from "there is but one God" of Deuteronomy 6 to the Nicene affirmation of the three, "Father," "Son" and "Spirit," all within the bounds of monotheism? Although it was not until the second, third and particularly fourth centuries that Christian trinitarian reflection gathered momentum, the NT sets the trajectory for the course of Jewish monotheism in the Christian tradition. It is here that the later NT writers and the authors of the early second century take on a special significance, for they were the first to delineate the identity and mission of Jesus within Jewish monotheism. Moreover, the NT and early second-century documents inscripturate how the first Christians revised what they knew to be true about their God in light of Jesus. These documents are thus crucial for the theological trajectory that began to wrestle with Jesus' identity within the context of Jewish monotheism and God's identity in light of the veneration of Jesus.

1. Background
2. Acts
3. Hebrews
4. James
5. 1 Peter
6. 2 Peter and Jude
7. 1, 2 and 3 John
8. Revelation
9. Summary

1. Background.

Jewish monotheism formed the primary conceptual matrix for Christianity's understanding of God. In particular two aspects of Jewish monotheism were important for Christianity—the singularity of God (i.e., that there are no other gods aside from Yahweh) and the unity of the Jewish God (that there is no division within Yahweh).

1.1. The Shape of Jewish Monotheism. One way to approach the study of a deity is through a careful examination of the god's attributes (e.g., mercy, love, righteousness). However, the character, nature and attributes of Yahweh are primarily inferred only from the shape and tenor of his past and promised deeds. In turn Yahweh's actions, and thus by extension Yahweh's attributes, have meaning only when framed by the larger narration of Israel's story. It is the emplotment of all of Yahweh's deeds that imbues any individual event with revelatory and hermeneutical power. Monotheism thus becomes a necessary presupposition for and consequence of the narration of Israel's history: it is the same God who is responsible for all, from beginning to end. Jewish reflection upon its unique history implied and demanded one and only one God.

The OT repeatedly affirms the singularity of God and simultaneously opposes the multideity worldview of idolatrous paganism. The Decalogue states, "You shall have no other gods before me" (Ex 20:3 RSV; cf. Deut 5:6-7); the *Shema* declares, "Hear, O Israel: The LORD our God is one LORD" (Deut 6:4 RSV); and the prophet proclaims that "Before me no god was formed, nor shall there be any after me. . . . I am the LORD, and besides me there is no savior" (Is 43:10b-11 RSV; cf. Is 40:28-31; 44:6).

Israel openly asserted that this one God made the world and everything in it, that this one God had elected a people and that this one God providentially cared for them. That Yahweh had decisively and consistently acted on their behalf in the past emboldened Jews, even in the face of a historical crisis like the exile, to envision a new and better day. Jewish monotheism can be characterized as creational (it was Yahweh who created the world), covenantal (it was Yahweh who had given the promises) and providential (it was Yahweh who was directing the course of history), an exclusive monotheism that forged a dogged eschatological hope (Wright, 248-52).

1.2. Divine Agency Within the Matrix of Jewish

Monotheism. The documents of Second Temple Judaism demonstrate a proliferation of "divine agents" (Hurtado, 17-92). These heavenly figures can be divided into three sometimes overlapping categories: agents who are depicted as personified attributes of God (e.g., Wisdom, Word), as exalted patriarchs/matriarchs (e.g., Enoch, Moses, Jacob) or as principal angels (e.g., Michael, Melchizedek, Yaoel). Similar to other figures, these divine agents either originated in or were exalted to heaven; however, unlike other figures, these divine agents were depicted as bearing the marks and properties of divinity in unprecedented ways. In some cases these divine agents were described as performing deeds typically reserved for Israel's God— that is, creating the world and/or executing eschatological judgment and redemption.

The phenomenon of divine agency undermines any claim that Jewish monotheism had weakened during the Second Temple period. Instead of indicating transcendence and distance (Bousset), these divine agents actually demonstrate God's immanence and immediacy (Hurtado). Despite the exalted ways in which these figures could be described, divine agency did not compromise the piety of Jewish monotheism. Divine agents were never worshiped as god(s). Although the extravagant epiphanies could well have confused the line of demarcation between one of these powerful agents and the one true God, the angelic refusal tradition (in which angelic figures refuse to be worshiped) safeguarded Jewish monotheism by legitimating the veneration of the one true God alone (Stuckenbruck; *see* Worship).

If the monotheism of the biblical writings emphasized the singularity of the one true God (there is only one God, Yahweh; all others are mere idols), the writings of Second Temple Judaism preserved the unity of the one true God (despite the presence of powerful agents that share the marks of divinity, Yahweh is one). The singularity and unity of the creating, covenanting, and purposeful God formed the conceptual matrix for early Christian theological reflection.

2. Acts.

The book of Acts demonstrates that the supreme deity of the earliest followers of Jesus was none other than the God of Israel, that the identity of this God underwent a profound change and that belief in a Christian-style monotheism should not be confused with other theistic claims.

2.1. Lexical Observations. Acts (*see* Acts of the Apostles) employs six different constructions to denote the traditional deity of Jewish piety. The list includes "God" (*theos,* 159 times), "Lord" (*kyrios,* at least 31 times; see Mowery 1995, 89 and nn. 32-35), "Father" (*patēr* , 3 times), "Most High" (*hypsistos,* 2 times), "Sovereign" (*despotēs,* 1 time); "Deity" (*theios,* 1 time). Occasionally the terms are combined—for example, "Sovereign Lord" (Acts 4:24), "Lord God" (Acts 2:39).

Acts distinguishes between this God (i.e., the one worshiped by Jews and Christians) and other "gods" in the Greco-Roman world (Grant 1966). The list of other gods includes the god "called Great" (*hē kaloumenē Megale,* Acts 8:10), "the gods" (*hoi theoi*) Hermes and Zeus (Acts 14:11-12), "the great goddess Artemis" (*megalēs theas Artemidos,* Acts 19:27) and the god "Justice" (*hē dikē,* Acts 28:4) as well as unofficial or unsanctioned (demonic) deities—that is, "host of heaven" (*stratia tou ouranou,* Acts 7:42), "spirits" (*pneumata akatharta,* Acts 5:16; 8:7), or "Satan" (*ho satanos,* Acts 5:2; 26:20). While adamant about its brand of exclusive monotheism, Acts does demonstrate an awareness of competing and opposing claims.

2.2. Christian Monotheism as a Continuation of Jewish Monotheism. Acts assumes that its readers will identify its references to God as Israel's singular deity. There is not even the slightest hint otherwise. Repeated references to the "kingdom of God" (Acts 1:8; 8:12; 14:22; 19:8; 28:23; 28:31) not only link the story Acts narrates with the "first word" (Acts 1:1) told in the Gospel of Luke but also situates the narrative of Acts within the horizon of the Israel's story. The kingdom must belong to the one God about whom the prophets and Jesus preached. That Acts can summarize the preaching and teaching of the early church as "the word of God" (Acts 4:11; 6:2, 7; 8:14; 11:1; 12:24; 13:5, 7; 13:46; 17:13; 18:11), without pausing to identify which god, only reinforces this presupposed continuity. The "word of God" consists in a message about the one true God of Israel.

The disciples' continued veneration of the God of Israel also clearly documents the strength of early Christianity's unequivocal monotheistic commitment. This religious devotion included praising God (Acts 2:47; 3:8-9), glorifying God (Acts 4:21; 11:18; 21:20), magnifying God (Acts 10:46), lifting voices to God (Acts 4:24), singing hymns to God (Acts 16:25), giving thanks to God (Acts 27:35; 28:15) and offering prayer to God (Acts 12:5). The terms "God-fearer" (Acts 10:2, 22; 13:16, 26) and "worshiper of God" (Acts 16:14; 18:7, 13), while probably not technical, do refer to the worship of Israel's God. Acts consistently depicts the object of the disciples' preaching and worship as the God of Israel.

2.3. Images of God in Acts. Since the unstated theological assumption of Acts is that Israel's God is the God of early Christianity, it is not surprising to find God's picture painted with very traditional Jewish colors.

2.3.1. God as Creator. Acts several times depicts God as the creator of the world (*see* Creation, New Creation) and in each case echoes Genesis 1. The community of disciples addressed their prayer to the "Sovereign Lord, who made the heaven and the earth, the sea, and everything in them" (Acts 4:24 NRSV). Stephen's quotation of Isaiah 66:1-2 highlights the creative power of Israel's God (Acts 7:50). At Lystra Paul encourages his hearers to turn from idols to "the living God who made the heaven and earth and the sea and all that is in them" (Acts 14:15 RSV), while at Athens he begins his sermon by identifying the God of his preaching as "the God who made the world and everything in it" (Acts 17:24 RSV). The God of the earliest disciples is the God who made the world.

2.3.2. The Faithfulness of God. Acts repeatedly underscores God's covenant-keeping faithfulness. Peter, Stephen and Paul all clearly invoke the covenant promises made by Israel's God to Abraham (Acts 3:25; 7:3, 5-7) by identifying the God they preach and serve as the "God of Abraham, and of Isaac, and of Jacob, the God of our fathers" (Acts 3:13; 5:30; 7:32; 24:14; 26:6). The speeches of Acts specify the occasions when God demonstrably reaffirmed this covenant promise (Mowery 1990, 198). God rescued Joseph (Acts 7:9-10), secured Israel's release from Egyptian bondage (Acts 7:17; 13:17), promised a future deliverer like Moses (Acts 3:22; 7:37), endured Israel's rebellion during the wilderness wanderings (Acts 7:42; 13:18), led Israel in conquest over the nations (Acts 7:45; 13:19), swore an oath to David (Acts 2:30; 13:23) and reaffirmed his covenant promises to the prophets (Acts 3:18; 26:22). Even the risen Jesus charges his disciples to wait patiently for the complete fulfillment of God's covenant (Acts 1:4). The narrative force of these affirmations serves to characterize God as faithful to his covenant. But Acts presses further. The events of Jesus' life should also be understood as an act of God's covenant faithfulness. It is the "God of our fathers" who has now "raised" and "glorified" Jesus (Acts 3:13; 5:30); from David's posterity "God brought a Savior, Jesus"—just as was promised (Acts 13:23); the good news of Jesus' resurrection fulfills what was "promised to the fathers" (Acts 13:32-33). More than just another faithful act, the death (see Death of Christ) and resurrection of Jesus should be read as God's supreme act of covenant faithfulness.

2.3.3. God, the Sovereign Lord of History. God's resolute commitment to the covenant bespeaks a larger plan and purpose for the world. Acts portrays God as controlling all of history (Conzelmann, 149-63; Cosgrove). It was God who determined the temporal and geographical boundaries for the nations of the world (Acts 17:26). While past generations were permitted "to walk in their own ways" (Acts 14:16), God now requires undivided allegiance (Acts 17:31). God's sovereign control of history even includes the foreknowledge of the future (Acts 1:7).

Acts also portrays God as choreographing Jesus' life. God is the one who "sent" (Acts 3:26) or "brought" (Acts 13:23) Jesus to Israel. God is the one who "anointed" Jesus with the Spirit at his baptism (Acts 10:38; cf. 4:26-27); who, through signs and wonders, "attested" to Jesus' ministry (Acts 2:22); and who was "with him" (Acts 10:38). Even Jesus' death occurred in accordance with the definite plan *(boulē)* and foreknowledge *(prognōsis)* of God (Acts 2:23; see also Acts 3:18; 4:27-28; 20:28). God is the one who "ordained" Jesus to be the eschatological judge (Acts 10:42; 17:31). God is consistently pictured as controlling the life of Jesus from beginning to end.

Acts also sees providence at work in the community's mission to the Gentiles. Peter's Pentecost sermon (Acts 2:39), Paul's conversion (Acts 9:15; 21:21) and missionary endeavors (Acts 13:46; 18:6; 28:28 [quoting Is 49:6]), and the apostolic councils of the Jerusalem church (Acts 11:18; 15:7; 15:16-18 [quoting Amos 9:11-12; Jer 12:15; Is 45:21]) all show how the events of Jesus' life, death and resurrection have empowered the church to fulfill the task originally assigned to Israel. God's sovereign control of history and his covenant promises to Israel coa-

lesce in the predestined events of Jesus' life to bring about his intention to bless the nations with salvation (Acts 26:22-23).

The adventuresome character of Acts is due in large measure to the dramatic ways in which God intervenes on behalf of the community of followers within the story (see the extensive list provided by Pervo, 14-17). The external hazards of persecution, mob violence, imprisonment, punishment and travel, along with the internal threats of strife, deceit and prejudice, receive decisive resolution in God's many and multifaceted divine interventions. Through visions, miracles, sermons, angelophanies, christophanies and theophanies God consistently transforms external and internal threats into further growth and expansion (Newman). Acts depicts God as in control of every aspect of history.

2.3.4. God as Judge. The image of God as judge would be familiar to Jews, and thus the assertion in Acts that God had judged Egypt (Acts 7:7), the nations of Canaan (Acts 13:19) and even Israel (Acts 7:42) would not have surprised them. Neither would the portrayal in Acts of characters within the narrative as being aware of God's oversight (Acts 3:23; 4:19; 8:21; 10:4, 31, 33; 23:1; 24:16), for surely the God of Israel "knows the heart of all persons" (Acts 15:8). Acts portrays those outside of Christian circles as conscientiously avoiding being found "opposing God" (Acts 5:39) and records the rather severe judgment received by unsavory characters (e.g., Acts 5:5; 12:23). That God has "fixed a day in which he will judge the world in righteousness" (Acts 17:31) continues the OT's "day of the Lord" tradition. Acts states that God's eschatological, universal and impartial judgment will be executed "by a man who he has appointed" (cf. Acts 10:42), namely, Jesus of Nazareth, thus demonstrating how the tradition of divine agency was appropriated within Christianity.

2.4. Christian Monotheism as a Redefinition of Jewish Monotheism. The images enumerated meld the identity of God in Acts to that presupposed and evoked by the Jewish Scriptures. Acts, however, engages in a scandalous redefinition of God's identity.

2.4.1. The God of Israel Is the God Who Raised Jesus. The persistent refrain that it was God (i.e., the one true God of Israel) who raised, exalted and glorified Jesus (Acts 2:24, 32, 36; 3:13, 15, 26; 4:10; 5:30, 31; 7:37; 10:38, 40; 13:23, 30, 33, 37; 17:18, 31; 24:21; 26:8) rhetorically and theologically punctuates the narrative. By supplying the newest and ultimately most important bit of information about the God of Israel, these confessional fragments represent a determined effort by the early church, as depicted in Acts, to retrofit God's identity. The God of Israel is the God who raised the crucified Jesus. The historical implications of this claim are matched only by its hermeneutical ones: the resurrection unlocks the enigma of crucifixion; the cross and resurrection reveal the true significance of the earthly ministry and message of Jesus; the life of Jesus, rightly understood through the cross and resurrection, divulges the true intentions of Israel's God for the world. The resurrection of Jesus thus becomes the best commentary on God and his purposes for his people and the world.

2.4.2. Jesus as God. The resurrection of Jesus not only disclosed something new about the God of Israel but also simultaneously revealed the true stature of Jesus. The resurrection undeniably revealed Jesus' true identity as the divine Lord, the *kyrios* (Acts 2:36; Marshall, 161-69). Numerous times within the narrative does Acts specifically identify Jesus as the "Lord" (Acts 1:6, 21; 4:33; 7:59; 8:16; 9:5-6; 11:17, 20; 15:11, 26; 16:30; 19:5, 13; 20:21, 24; 21:13; 22:8; 26:15; in many others it is implied). By employing the same word used by the Septuagint to translate the divine name (i.e., Yahweh) as a title for Jesus, Acts comes close to binitarianism.

While it is true that Acts never applies *theos* to Jesus (unless the *kai* at Acts 7:55 is construed epexegetically—i.e., Stephen saw the "glory of God, even *[kai]* Jesus"), Acts does position Jesus as a divine being alongside Yahweh. First, Acts explicitly substitutes "Jesus" for "Yahweh" in several OT quotations (Joel 2:32 at Acts 2:21; Ps 110:1 at Acts 2:34-35; Ps 118:22 at Acts 4:11-12; and Amos 9:11-12, Jer 12:15 and Is 45:21 at Acts 15:16-18). Second, official, public, corporate religious acts are done "in the [divine] name of Jesus," including public repentance, conversion and baptism (Acts 2:38; 4:12; 8:16; 10:43; 10:48; 19:15; 22:16); religious healings and exorcisms (Acts 3:6; 16; 4:7, 10, 30); preaching and teaching (Acts 4:17, 18; 5:28, 40; 8:12; 9:27, 29); being appointed an official representative of the community (Acts 9:15); and suffering religious persecution (Acts 5:41; 9:16; 15:26; 21:13). Most importantly, religious devotion, the true test of monotheism, is directed to the name of Jesus (Acts 9:14, 21; 19:17; 22:16) or directly offered to

the risen Jesus (Acts 1:24; 7:59-60; 13:2; 19:17; see Bauckham 1992). The divine title *Lord,* the OT quotations, the use of the name of Jesus and religious devotion offered to Jesus all function to identify Jesus as participating in Yahweh's divinity.

2.5. Christian Monotheism in Opposition to Paganism. The geographical expansion of the Christian movement necessarily brought it into contact with other official and some unsanctioned competitors. Acts gives seven snapshots of Christianity's encounter with other religious construals. Philip's evangelistic efforts in Samaria (Acts 8:4-24) entangled him and Peter with the powers of magic. In his missionary activities on Cyprus, Paul had an encounter with magical powers (Acts 13:6-12). After healing a cripple at Lystra (Acts 14:8-20), Paul and Barnabas were confused with the pagan gods Hermes and Zeus. Paul's exorcism of a demon-possessed girl at Philippi (Acts 16:16-24) brought him into conflict with her owners. At Athens (Acts 17:16-34) Paul debated monotheism and resurrection with the philosophers gathered at the Areopagus. The success of Paul's apostolic ministry at Ephesus (Acts 19:1-40) undermined the cultic practices associated with Artemis. And at Malta (Acts 28:3-6) observers concluded that the god Justice had taken revenge upon Paul when he was bitten by a viper.

In each of these episodes Acts pits Christian monotheism against the surrounding paganism, graphically demonstrating that idols are not real (there is only one true God); that there are magical or demonic forces at work in the world (in direct opposition to the God of Christianity); that this magical world is intimately connected to economic gain by the practitioners (which contrasts with the benevolence associated with the new community); that Christianity's exclusive monotheism threatened devotion to other ethnic and nationalistic deities; and that Jesus should not be confused with other divine agents, be they pneumatic or human. Christianity, like Judaism, ardently and scandalously proclaimed monotheism to its pagan environment.

3. Hebrews.

The theological sophistication of Hebrews is matched by its literary elegance. The author's ability to refer to the theological language of levitical sacrifice balances a text thickly plotted with inventive scriptural interpretations, interlaced with elaborate analogies and structured by alternating genres of exposition and exhortation. At the same time that Hebrews presents a sustained theological argument about Jesus as Son and high priest, it also issues persuasive appeals to a community for repentance. The blended structural components of exposition and admonition yield complementary yet integrated pictures of God. While the expositional material focuses upon God in relationship to Jesus, the admonitions highlight God in relationship to the community. The literary and theological artistry in Hebrews unite in its intricate depiction of God.

3.1. Lexical Observations. God is the referent in all but one of the sixty-eight occurrences of *theos* ("God") and twelve of the fifteen occurrences of *kyrios* ("Lord"). That Jesus also bears both appellations (*theos,* Heb 1:8; *kyrios,* Heb 2:3; 7:14; 13:20) within the text of Hebrews confirms at the semantic level the kind of theological vitality that existed within the earliest church; both God and Jesus enjoyed the same status as divine beings (Heb 1:3, 8-9; see Harris, 205-28).

The titles "Majesty on High" (*megalōsynēs en hypsēlois,* Heb 1:3), the "Majesty in Heaven" (*megalōsynēs en tois ouranois,* Heb 8:1), the "God Most High" (*theos tou hypsistou,* Heb 7:1) and the "Father of Spirits" (*patēr tōn pneumatōn,* Heb 12:9) all emphasize that God sits atop a hierarchy of heavenly/angelic/pneumatic beings. The formulations "God of peace" (*ho theos tēs eirēnēs,* Heb 13:20) and "living God" (*theos zōn,* Heb 3:12; 9:14; 10:31; 12:22), while characteristic of Christianity (e.g., Mt 16:16; Jn 7:38; Rom 9:26; 15:33; 16:20; 2 Cor 3:3; Phil 4:9; 1 Thess 5:23; 1 Pet 1:23; Rev 7:2), locate author and readers in the broad stream of Jewish tradition. The circumlocutions "heaven" (Heb 3:1; 12:25) and "grace" ("throne of grace," Heb 4:16; "Spirit of grace," Heb 10:29) appear where "God" may be expected. Hebrews thus employs a rich and varied vocabulary in referring to God.

3.2. The God Who (Still) Speaks. Hebrews presents the reader with thirty-eight OT quotations (following the list printed in the UBS GNT) and thereby confronts the reader with a God who continues to speak in and through these citations. God is the grammatical subject in twenty-two of these quotations (Heb 1:5a, 5b, 6, 7, 8-9, 10-12, 13; 4:3, 4, 7; 5:5, 6; 6:14; 7:17, 21; 8:5, 8-12; 10:30a, 30b, 37-38; 12:26; 13:5; see Lane, cxvii), with the verb in the present tense, active voice,

being employed ten times (Heb 1:6, 7; 4:7; 5:6; 6:14; 8:8a, 8b, 9, 10; 12:26). Even a text that Hebrews ascribes to the Holy Spirit in its introductory formula (Heb 10:15) has God speaking in the quotation (Heb 10:16-17 [using Jer 31:33-34]), and one that is patently about God (Gen 2:2 quoted at Heb 4:4) Hebrews attributes to God. These OT citations position God as the ultimate authority of all Scripture, bestow a dynamic quality upon the text of the OT and bolster the community's awareness of the presence and nearness of God.

3.2.1. Hebrews 1:1-4. The opening hymnic/confessional exordium (Heb 1:1-4) parallels what God spoke to the ancestors through the prophets in the past with what God speaks to the community through the Son in the author's present. Hebrews situates this new word as God's final eschatological revelation by setting it within the prophetic sequence. The author also contrasts the Son (Heb 1:1-4) with the angels (Heb 1:5-14). The disparity between the Son and angels not only works on an ontological axis (Jesus is divine; angels are not) but also pivots on the eschatologically superior revelation delivered by the Son. The word God speaks through the Son is much preferred to that spoken through angels (Heb 2:2). God speaks his final word to the community through (the message about) his Son.

3.2.2. Hebrews 4:11-13. When at Hebrews 4:11 the readers are admonished not to fall into disobedience, the author grounds this admonition in the character and power of God's word (Heb 4:12-13). Like God (Heb 3:12; 9:14; 10:31; 12:22) the word is "living" *(zōn),* "active" *(energēs)* and "sharper than any two-edged sword" (Heb 4:12a; cf. Eph 6:17; Rev 1:16; 2:12). The author predicates divine qualities to the word through the use of physiognomic imagery: God's word pierces the division of the soul and spirit, of joints and marrow; it discerns the thoughts and intentions of the heart (Heb 4:12). The distinction between God and the "word" finally vanishes: to stand before God's word is to stand before "him" (Heb 4:13).

3.2.3. Hebrews 5:11-14. In Hebrews 5:11-14 the author employs four binary opposites to chastise the community. Instead of teaching others, the community has become dull of hearing. Instead of exhibiting competency in the "word of righteousness" (*logos dikaiosynēs,* Heb 5:13), they are in need of instruction in the "elementary principles of [God's] words" (*ta stoicheia tēs archēs tōn logiōn,* Heb 5:12). Instead of feasting on solid food, they can only stomach milk. Instead of experiencing maturity, they languish in adolescence. While the rhetoric is intended to shame the community, the passage also highlights the efficacy inherent in the divine message. Like God, the word demands attention and discipline and nurtures spiritual growth.

3.3. God in the Expositional Material. While it is common practice to divide Hebrews into expositional and hortatory sections (although the precise lines of division are often disputed), it has not been the norm to employ these divisions for theological ends. Recent work into the structure of Hebrews, however, advocates the separate treatment, at least initially, for the purpose of gaining a more precise theological profile (Guthrie).

The expositional material develops a spatial argument about Jesus that traces his journey from heaven to earth and back to heaven. The argument is logical in that each expositional unit depends directly upon the one that precedes it. This spatial and logical argument discloses two pictures of Jesus, as Son and as high priest (see Parsons), and consequently two corresponding pictures of God, as Father and as heavenly beneficiary.

3.3.1. God as Father. Although only explicitly used twice of God in the entire epistle (Heb 1:5; 12:9), "Father" *(patēr)* is one of the primary images for God. By frequently calling Jesus the "Son" (Heb 1:2, 5a [quoting Ps 2:7], 5b [quoting 2 Sam 7:14], 8 [in the introductory formula for Ps 45]; 2:6 [quoting Ps 8:4]; 3:6; 4:14; 5:5 [quoting Ps 2:7], 8; 6:6; 7:28; 10:29), Hebrews implicitly identifies God as "Father." The importance of "Father" for Hebrews can be seen in one of the epistle's opening OT citations in which God declares: "I will be a father to him [referring to Jesus], and he shall be a Son to me" (Heb 1:5b [quoting 2 Sam 7:14]).

God, as "Father," actively participates in the crucial events of Jesus' life. God "begot" (Heb 1:5) and "anointed" (Heb 2:9; cf. Heb 1:2) Jesus, making him "a little lower than the angels" (Heb 2:7, 9; cf. Heb 2:17). "Only by God's grace" did Jesus taste death for everyone (Heb 2:9; cf. Heb 9:28). God "completed"/"perfected" *(teleiōsai)* Jesus though suffering (Heb 2:10). God heard Jesus' cries in the garden and from the cross and always possessed the power to save

him from death (Heb 5:7). God "enthroned"/ "crowned"/"appointed"/"exalted"/"designated" Jesus (Heb 1:13; 2:9; 3:2; 5:5, 10; 7:26, 28; 8:1)— all references to the events of resurrection, which is only once (Heb 13:20) referred to explicitly—where he awaits God to make all enemies a footstool (Heb 10:13). God as "Father" and Jesus as "Son" help structure the expositional argument in Hebrews.

3.3.2. God as Heavenly Beneficiary. A second set of expositional texts, organized by the rubric of Jesus as high priest, picture God as the recipient of Jesus' activity. Jesus' life was one of faithful "obedience" and "service" to God (Heb 2:17; 3:2, 6; 5:8; 10:5-10; 12:2). In his death Jesus "offered" himself up as a sacrifice to God, "once for all" (Heb 2:17; 7:28; 9:14; 10:12). Jesus "passed through the heavens" (Heb 4:14) to "enter the true sanctuary" and "appear" before God (Heb 9:24). Jesus intercedes with God for those who "draw near" (Heb 7:25), being the mediator of God's new covenant with humanity (Heb 8:6; 9:15). As the "Father," God is actively involved in the course of Jesus' life; as the divine beneficiary, God passively receives the liturgical offerings and sacrifices rendered by his high priest, Jesus.

3.4. God in the Exhortations. The hortatory sections also contain two depictions of God— one emphasizing God's distance and one stressing God's accessibility.

3.4.1. The God Who Warns and Punishes. On five separate occasions Hebrews sternly cautions its readers about the divine consequences of persisting in sin.

If disobedience to the eschatologically inferior words delivered by angels received God's judgment, how can those who "drift away" from the message by the Son hope to escape (Heb 2:1-4)? Disobedience cannot be hidden from the "eyes of him" who knows and sees all (Heb 4:11-12). For those who finally apostatize there is nothing but judgment, because God "curses" the life that produces only "thorns and thistles" (Heb 6:4-8). Those who persist in sin should harbor no hope for forgiveness (Heb 10:26-31). They face a "terrifying prospect of judgment," "a raging fire," ready to fall upon God's "adversaries" (Heb 10:27). They should be forewarned: "It is a fearful thing to fall into the hands of the living God" (Heb 10:31). Hebrews 12:25-29 also cautions about rejecting "him who warns from heaven" (Heb 12:25). Theophanic imagery underscores the severity and certainty of impending divine judgment: "Yet once more I will shake not only the earth, but also the heaven" (Heb 12:26 [quoting Hag 2:6 LXX]). The readers are encouraged to respond with "worship," "reverence" and "awe" (Heb 12:28b), because God is a "consuming fire" (Heb 10:29; cf. Deut 4:24). Standing behind all five of the warning passages is a God who is holy and righteous and vows judgment for those who refuse him. Volatility and distance dominate when Hebrews pictures God as Judge.

3.4.2. The God Who Promises, Disciplines and Rewards. Hebrews also emphasizes the predictability and nearness of God. He is a God who promises, disciplines and rewards. God's promises provide the warranting basis for many of the author's exhortations. The admonition to "strive to enter that rest" (Heb 4:11) depends directly upon a God who promises a "rest" (Heb 4:1, 3, 4-5, 7, 9). The exhortations to "draw near" (Heb 10:22), "hold fast" (Heb 10:23) and "to stir up" (Heb 10:24) all acquire their rhetorical power from a God who is faithful to do all that he promises (Heb 10:23). Abel, Enoch, Noah, Abraham, Sarah, Isaac, Jacob, Joseph, Moses, and Rahab (as well as many others!) are examples of those who, even through they did not receive in their earthly life all that was promised (Heb 11:13-14, 39), were still faithful to God. Like this "great cloud of witnesses" the community should also "run the race with perseverance" (Heb 12:1-2). God promises; the community should persevere.

Discipline, like promises, should spur the readers on. In order to gain a perspective upon their own difficulties, the author invites the readers to consider those experienced by Jesus (Heb 12:3-4). The midrash on Proverbs 3:11-12 that follows (Heb 12:5b-6) identifies the community as God's children and God as their heavenly Father. It also interprets the difficulties they face as God's discipline. The community should not be dismayed when God treats them "as children," because discipline is a normal aspect of the parent-child relationship (Heb 12:7). The absence of discipline denotes illegitimacy (Heb 12:8). Since earthly fathers are held in respect for disciplining their children (Heb 12:9), the chastisement received from "the Father of spirits" should only inspire confidence, respect and holiness (Heb 12:10-11).

If the God of Hebrews promises and disciplines, this God also rewards. Those who seek to draw near should not think God "so unjust" so as to overlook their work and love (Heb 6:10). The author exhorts the community not to throw away their confidence, "which has a great reward" (Heb 10:35) but instead to develop endurance, so that they might "do the will of God and receive what has been promised" (Heb 10:36). Believing in a God who rewards is essential for moral transformation: "For whoever would draw near to God must believe that he exists and that he rewards those who seek him" (Heb 11:6 RSV). The hortatory material in Hebrews profiles God's volatility and his nearness, images strategically deployed to elicit the same response: repentance.

3.5. God, the Architect and Builder. Hebrews affirms that God designed and created this world. God founded the earth in the beginning, and the heavens are the work of his hands (Heb 1:10 [quoting Ps 102:25]). God is the one "through whom and for whom all things exist" (Heb 2:10), which is doubtless a monotheistic confession of the early church (cf. Rom 11:36; 1 Cor 8:6; 15:27-28; Col 1:16; Rev 4:11). God's "works were finished from the foundation of the world" (Heb 4:3b; cf. Heb 9:26), a fact understood only "by faith" (Heb 11:3). Such language pictures creation as a divine enterprise stretching back to eternity (cf. Mt 13:35; 25:34; Jn 17:24; Eph 1:4) and God as its architect.

4. James.

More than any other NT document James has been subject to the shifting opinions of its interpreters. This may largely be due to the unfortunate and inordinate influence wielded by Luther's negative evaluation of James as a "strawy epistle." While Luther's hesitation was based upon a perceived fall from Paul's doctrine of justification by faith, the absence (again, perceived) of an explicitly developed christology accounts for more recent uncertainty as to its point. So damning are the kerygmatic omissions that some consider James to be "wholly Jewish in language and thought" (Dunn, 212). Such an observation unfairly pits James's theocentrism against the christocentrism of other NT documents.

The charges of theological irregularities in James levied by some interpreters tell us more about the singular lack of information about the setting of the letter than they do about James's theology. James knows and employs the common core of apostolic theology (Sloan, 3-14), and, while admittedly more indirect, James is not entirely lacking direct and explicit christological claims (Mussner 1970, 111-17). James calls Jesus the "Lord" (*kyrios,* Jas 1:1; 2:1) and identifies him with God's divine presence, his Glory (*tou kyriou . . . tēs doxēs,* Jas 2:1; cf. 1 Cor 2:8). Despite the claims of some scholars, James admirably illustrates a profoundly theocentric perspective that is genuinely Christian.

4.1. Lexical Observations. All sixteen occurrences of *theos* ("God") in James refer to the one God of Judaism (Jas 1:1, 5, 13 [2x], 20, 27; 2:5, 19, 23 [2x]; 3:9; 4:4 [2x], 6, 7, 8). *Kyrios* ("Lord") appears fourteen times, and in five occurrences God is the clear referent (Jas 1:7; 3:9; 4:10, 15; 5:4). In two others Jesus is the clear referent (Jas 1:1; 2:1). The referent in the other seven occurrences of *kyrios* is uncertain, though the three occurrences in James 5:10-11 probably refer to God and on balance the other four (Jas 5:7, 8, 14, 15) refer to Jesus (Mussner 1981, 97). Three times James uses *patēr* ("Father") to refer to God, always in conjunction with or as part of other titles—"Father of Lights" (*patros tōn phōtōn,* Jas 1:17), "God and Father" (*tō theō kai patri,* Jas 1:27), "Lord and Father" (*kyrion kai patera,* Jas 3:9). Additionally, James uses the Isaiah's "Lord of Hosts" (*kyriou Sabaōth,* Jas 5:4; cf. Rom 9:29; it is used sixty-one times in Isaiah and only nine others in the entire OT) to refer to God. James also uses circumlocutions—"from above (*anōthen,* Jas 1:17; 3:15, 17) and "heaven" (*ouranos,* Jas 5:12) for God. If God and not Jesus (cf. Rev 3:20) is the referent, then James refers to God as "the Judge" (*ho kritēs,* Jas 5:9; cf. 5:12; Heb 12:23). James's multiple references to God endow his work with a powerful theocentrism.

4.2. A Wisdom Pneumatology? "Wisdom" (*sophia*) figures prominently in two important passages (Jas 1:5-8; 3:13-18), while echoes of it may be heard in two others (Jas 1:16-18; 2:1-3). James explicitly quotes Proverbs 3:34 at James 4:6 and implicitly alludes to other wisdom literature (Chester and Martin, 9 n. 8). Further, the parallels between wisdom in James and the Holy Spirit in other parts of the NT are also striking. Specific verbal connections can be made between the virtues of "wisdom" in James 3:13, 17 and those of the "Spirit" in Galatians 5:22-23—"meekness" (*prautēs*), "peaceableness"/"peace" (*eirēnikos/eirēne*) and "fruit" (*karpos*). This has led some (e.g., Davids, 56) to suppose James betrays a "wisdom pneumatology" that forms the major conceptual matrix and organizing principle of the text.

However, the connections between these two passages may be due to common dependence upon Jesus traditions rather than to an independent wisdom pneumatology. Further, James explicitly subordinates wisdom to God: Wisdom comes "from above" (Jas 1:17; 2:15). Thus a wisdom pneumatology does not run parallel with or control James's theological perspective; rather, James's reflection upon the one true God is the larger conceptual category into which specific comments about wisdom fit.

4.3. The Constancy of the One God. James no doubt approves of and accepts the exclusive monotheism of the Jewish Scriptures. Twice he plainly states that God is "one" (Jas 2:19; 4:12). However, James's interest in the one God of Jewish piety is of a different sort. His monotheistic exploration seeks to map the unchanging character of the one true God.

James describes God as the "Father of lights with whom there is not any variation or shadow of change" (Jas 1:17). "Lights" (*phōtōn,* i.e., the "stars") and "change" (*tropēs,* i.e., "solstice")—and possibly even "shadow" (*aposkiasma,* i.e., "eclipse"; see Dibelius and Greeven, 102-4)—are technical cosmological terms. James invokes the solar system to contrast the permanence of the Creator God with the instability of the creation. The heavenly bodies are subject to change; God is not. James applies this to the faith of the community. The constancy of God means that he is the author only of "good and perfect gifts" (Jas 1:17).

God's unaltering, equitable character can be seen in other of James's statements. God gives "freely" and "generously" to anyone who asks (Jas 1:5, 9, 17, 21). God will give the "crown of life" to anyone who endures (Jas 1:12). God neither tempts with nor is tempted by evil (Jas 1:13). God blesses anyone who is a hearer and a doer of the word (Jas 1:22-25). God's promises about the kingdom are inclusive, regardless of social or economic status (Jas 2:5). God applies the same law to everyone (Jas 2:8-13). God is jealous over anyone in whom his Spirit dwells (Jas 4:5; see commentaries on this problem text). God will draw near to anyone who seeks to draw near to him (Jas 4:8). God expects the same responses from all—submission (Jas 4:6), humility (Jas 4:10) and patience (Jas 5:8). God hears the prayer of the oppressed and the righteous (Jas 5:5, 16).

The one God's immutable character dramatically contrasts with humanity's duplicitous nature. Although created in God's likeness (Jas 3:9) to be "a kind of first fruit of his creatures" (Jas 1:18)—that is, to be like God—a doublemindedness (*dipsychoi,* Jas 1:8; 4:8) plagues humanity. Humanity doubts (Jas 1:6-8), denies (Jas 1:13-15), deceives (Jas 1:16-18, 26-27), forgets (Jas 1:22-25), discriminates (Jas 2:1-13; cf. 1:9-11) and slanders (Jas 3:6-12; 4:11-13); humanity is impetuous (Jas 1:19-21), controlled by selfish ambition (Jas 3:13-18; 4:1-10), arrogant (Jas 4:13-16), short-sighted (Jas 5:1-6) and impatient (Jas 5:7-11). Mired in fickleness, capriciousness and inconsistency, humanity fails to mime God's constant, true character.

4.4. Monotheism and Ethics. James offers a simple solution: believers should become as consistent as God. Word must always be matched by deed. But James does not simply preside over the marriage of monotheism to ethics, as if monotheism and ethics could legitimately exist independent of each other; for James a commitment to the one true God is at its core, and at the same time, a commitment to ethics.

By quoting the *Shema* (Deut 6:4) James demonstrates Christianity's continued confessional allegiance to Jewish monotheism. "You believe that 'God is one'; you do well" (Jas 2:19). While this text can be read as affirming God's singularity (there is no other god) or unity (there is no division with God) or both, James pursues another rhetorical goal. A monotheistic confession, while necessary, is not sufficient for Christian identity. There has to be more. Christianity moves beyond intellectual recognition and verbal confession—for even the demonic world does this in fear (Jas 2:19)—to a specific ethical program. The character of this one true God demands a certain relationship between confession and living. Believers' works should no more be separated from their faith than God's deeds are from his nature. Since there is no variance between God's nature and deeds, there should be none between a believer's faith (confession) and works (Jas 2:14, 16, 18b), a point amply illustrated by Abraham and Rahab (Jas 2:21-25). If there is separation, faith is "dead" (Jas 2:17, 20, 26).

James repeatedly illustrates the ethical obligation inherent in a monotheistic commitment. Genuine faith in God produces faithfulness, maturity and completeness in the believer (Jas 1:3). Embracing "the righteousness of God" outlaws the expression of human anger (Jas 1:20). Devotion to the one true God is to care for those who cannot care for themselves and to demonstrate moral purity (Jas 1:27). Christian "faith" (Jas 2:1) does not discriminate (Jas 2:1-13). Since God's wisdom is peaceable (Jas 3:17), those who are wise should make peace (Jas 3:18). That there is but one Lawgiver and Judge means that believers are not to judge each other (Jas 4:11-12). In imitation of God, the yes of a believer's life needs to remain a yes and the no a no (Jas 5:12). The singularity and constancy of the one true God elicits and demands a singular ethical resolve from those who would commit themselves to this God. Christian monotheism obligates the believer to the same relationship between faith and works that exists between God's nature and his deeds.

5. 1 Peter

First Peter identifies its readers as "visiting strangers" (1 Pet 1:1; 2:11) and "resident aliens" (1 Pet 2:11; cf. 1 Pet 1:17). Both terms imply that the recipients were experiencing political and social displacement (see Elliott). The ever-increasing friction with and ever-growing estrangement from the surrounding culture prompts the author to intertwine two themes in one letter, both of which are firmly anchored in the author's understanding of the one true God. First Peter preaches patience and endurance to those undergoing hardship because of their Christian identity. Support for this message is found in the christological shape of God's providence. First Peter also strongly advocates the maintenance of Christian distinctiveness in the face of a strong temptation to assimilate to the surrounding culture. The community is to be as holy as God is (based on Lev 17—26). God's providence and holiness are thus crucial for 1 Peter.

5.1. Lexical Observations. First Peter employs a closely circumscribed number of words for God. *Theos* ("God") appears thirty-nine times, and each use refers to the one God of the Scriptures. "Father" (*patēr*) is used of God three times (1 Pet 1:2, 3, 17). *Kyrios* (Lord) appears seven times; four of the references are to God (1 Pet 1:25, 2:3; 3:12 [2x]), all in OT quotations. Twice Jesus bears the title *Lord* (1 Pet 1:3; 3:15), and once the precise referent is unclear (1 Pet 2:13). First Peter also refers to God as the "faithful Creator" (*pistos ktistēs*, 1 Pet 4:19). Despite employing a small range of vocabulary for God, 1 Peter does possess a distinct image of God.

5.2. The Providence of God.

5.2.1. God's Election of Believers. First Peter applies God's providential care as a balm for the wounds inflicted by a world hostile to Christian faith. First Peter identifies its readers as God's "called" (*eklektos*, 1 Pet 1:1); they are God's "chosen race" (*genos eklekton*, 1 Pet 2:9). This calling occurred "according to God's foreknowledge" (*kata prognōsin theou*, 1 Pet 1:2) and unites the readers with other Christian communities—specifically the one in Babylon (Rome?)—as the "co-called" (*syneklektē*, 1 Pet 5:13). God's electing purposes help to locate and give self-identity to the estranged communities.

Election entails the experience of God's "mercy" in "new birth" (1 Pet 1:3, 23), the possession of a "living hope" (1 Pet 1:3; cf. 1 Pet 1:13, 21; 3:15), the promise of an "inheritance" no less magnificent than God himself (1 Pet 1:4; 3:9) and the constant protection of God's "power" (1 Pet 1:5). The effectual work of God's call commences with conversion, determines the shape of the Christian life and ensures final transformation (1 Pet 1:15; 5:10). For Peter, God's electing purposes embrace the beginning, middle and end of Christian experience.

5.2.2. God's Election of Jesus. What is true of every Christian is especially true of Jesus. His appearance on the stage of history was "destined" by God "before the foundation of the world" (*proegnōsmenou pro katabolēs kosmou*, 1 Pet 1:20). First Peter's exegesis of Isaiah 28:16 identifies Jesus as the "living stone," the "chief cornerstone" and the stone "specially chosen by God" (*para theō eklekton entimon*, 1 Pet 2:4, 6). God's electing purposes for Jesus included his death (1 Pet 1:2, 19; 2:21; 3:18), resurrection (1 Pet 1:21; cf. 1 Pet 1:3; 2:1; 3:18), exaltation (1 Pet 3:22) and future apocalypse (1 Pet 1:7, 13; 4:13; 5:1). Jesus is God's Elect One par excellence.

5.2.3. Election and Suffering. The juxtaposition of Jesus' election with that of believers implicitly suggests a connection between the two. The connection becomes explicit when the issue of suffering is raised. God's providential purposes worked through Jesus serve as a model and a guarantee of his providential care for all Christians.

Peter acknowledges that the community was undergoing a period of intense suffering (1 Pet 4:12; cf. 1 Pet 1:6-7; 3:14). Though probably not official persecution, the anguish was nonetheless real. Peter states, incredibly, that such difficulties are a natural consequence of God's calling (1 Pet 2:21); they are a "necessary" (1 Pet 1:6) and "required" (1 Pet 5:9) part of his "will" (1 Pet 3:17; 4:1-2, 19). What justification could there be for these extraordinary statements? Unlike Paul, who primarily uses physiomorphic eschatology, or Hebrews, whose author uses a journey motif, 1 Peter answers christologically the question that suffering puts to God's providence.

5.2.3.1. 1 Peter 2:18-25. First Peter admonishes servants to persist in respectful service to their masters despite the harsh treatment they receive (1 Pet 2:18), for anyone who patiently endures unjust suffering will find God's approval (1 Pet 2:19-20). Such moral stamina is required precisely because of the christological shape of the God's call: Christians "have been called to this [suffering], because Christ also suffered" (1 Pet 2:21). Jesus blazed the trail by not responding in kind but by completely trusting the "one who judges justly" (1 Pet 2:21). Jesus' response to unjust suffering (detailed in 1 Pet 2:22-24, based on Is 53) serves as a model for God's elect to follow.

5.2.3.2. 1 Peter 3:13-22. First Peter 3:13-22 also demonstrates that the interconnectedness of Jesus' election and that of believers is most apparent at the point of suffering. The passage opens with the rhetorical question about the ability of anyone to harm a Christian "zealous for the good" (1 Pet 3:13). But even if believers should suffer harm for the sake of righteousness, they will certainly enjoy God's blessing (1 Pet 3:14). First Peter then details what a proper response to suffering looks like—reverence, preparedness, gentleness and a clear conscious (1 Pet 3:15-16). Finally, Peter lays down his guiding principle: it is better for Christians to suffer for doing right than for wrong (1 Pet 3:17). This is so precisely "because Christ also died for sins once for all, the righteous for the unrighteous" (1 Pet 3:18). Peter's confessional justification (1 Pet 3:18-22) for patient endurance of unjust suffering (1) makes plain his christological belief, (2) promotes confidence in God's providential care and (3) celebrates God's victory over the demonic powers. Not only is unjust suffering a natural consequence of belonging to Christ but also the prospect of receiving God's blessing is no less certain than Jesus' resurrection.

5.2.3.3. 1 Peter 4:12-19. The christological shape of Christian suffering is most clear, however, in 1 Peter 4:12-19. Here Peter plainly states that a Christian shares in Christ's sufferings (*koinōneite tois tou Christou pathēmasin,* 1 Pet 4:13) and that sharing in Christ's suffering determines future joy (*hina kai en tē apokalypsei tēs doxēs autou charēte agalliōmenoi,* 1 Pet 4:13; cf. Rom 8:18). The present suffering/future glory shape of the passage follows the cross/resurrection shape of early Christian preaching and thereby confirms 1 Peter's theological indebtedness to the paradigmatic influence of the life of Jesus.

Peter's treatment of unjust suffering demonstrates that the destiny of believers lies within the destiny of Jesus. The prophetic predictions (1 Pet 1:11) and historical reality (1 Pet 2:21; 4:1, 13; 5:1) of messianic suffering become paradigmatic for all who follow in the steps of the Messiah. First Peter resolves the question that unjust Christian suffering puts to God's providence by pointing to the life of Jesus. Jesus is the divine exemplar (Christians should respond as Jesus did) and the guarantor (those who suffer unjustly yet patiently will enjoy the same eschatological blessings). God works his purposes in Christians in and through Jesus the Christ.

5.3. The Holiness of God. The emphasis upon suffering in 1 Peter encourages an adversarial picture of society, but that is not the whole story. Paradoxically running alongside the threat of persecution is the danger of assimilation (to avoid hardship?). Christians were tempted to return to or adopt a secular lifestyle. Peter insists that the boundary between the Christian community and society must remain distinct and recognizable. Crossing the line pollutes the purity of the community, a purity that is defined by and grounded in God's holiness.

First Peter systematically employs purity language to define community identity. The readers are to abandon their former life (1 Pet 1:14) and to pursue holiness in all their conduct (1 Pet 1:15). This 1 Peter justifies by quoting Leviticus 11:44-45, where God declares: "Be holy for I am holy" (1 Pet 1:16). In 1 Peter 2:11-12 Peter instructs the community "to abstain from passions of the flesh" and instead "to maintain good conduct among the Gentiles" in order that the outsiders might see the purity of their "good deeds." Christians are to submit "for the Lord's sake" to every human institution in order to silence de-

tractors (1 Pet 2:13-17). Peter instructs the community to refrain from living as the Gentiles do (1 Pet 4:3), because the Christians will one day have to give an account of their life to God (1 Pet 4:5). God's holiness defines what it means to be inside or outside the community.

God's holiness also builds cohesion within the community. Christians are to express "love" to one another (1 Pet 1:22), precisely because they have experienced God's "new birth" (1 Pet 1:23). Mutual submission (1 Pet 3:1, 7) should characterize marital relations because it is God who knows "the inner self" (1 Pet 3:4) and "hears" prayers (1 Pet 3:7). Love, hospitality and sacrificial service should guide the use of spiritual gifts (1 Pet 4:9-10) because it is God who gives, supplies and strengthens (1 Pet 4:11). Leaders are to tend the flock of God in a Christlike humility (1 Pet 5:1-5) because "God opposes the proud but gives grace to the humble" (1 Pet 5:6). The whole community should always be humble, sober, watchful and resistant (1 Pet 5:6-11), because the "God of all grace" will himself restore, establish and strengthen (1 Pet 5:10). To imitate God not only becomes a way of defining the boundary lines of the community but also strengthens bonds within it.

6. 2 Peter and Jude.

That 2 Peter and Jude bear a literary relationship with each other is hard to doubt (cf. Jude 4-13 and Jude 16-18 with 2 Pet 2:1-18 and 2 Pet 3:1-3). In all probability 2 Peter was dependent upon Jude. Further, both documents employ common topoi of Jewish apocalypticism and address similar situations, that is, problems with false teachers and teaching. Not surprisingly, then, both documents emphasize God's forbearance and judgment and do so in very similar ways.

6.1. Lexical Observations. Second Peter uses only four words to refer to God—"God" (*theos*), "Lord" (*kyrios*), "glory" (*doxa*) and "Father" (*patēr*). Six of the seven uses of *theos* are applied to God (2 Pet 1:2, 17, 21; 2:4; 3:5, 12). The other occurrence of *theos* refers to Jesus (2 Pet 1:1; see Harris, 229-38). Six of the fourteen occurrences of *kyrios* refer to God (2 Pet 2:9, 11; 3:8, 9; 3:10, 15), while the other eight refer to Jesus (2 Pet 1:2, 8, 11, 14, 16; 2:20; 3:2, 18). Once 2 Peter refers to God as the "majestic Glory" (*megaloprepous doxēs,* 2 Pet 1:17) and as "Father" (*para theou patros,* 2 Pet 1:17). The identical lexical situation prevails in Jude. All four occurrences of *theos* refer to God (Jude 1, 4, 21, 25). *Kyrios* is used seven times with two, possibly three, occurrences referring to God (Jude 5, 9, 14). Jude identifies God as "Father" *(patēr)* once (Jude 1) and, like 2 Peter, makes reference to God's glory (Jude 24).

6.2. God's Forbearance in 2 Peter. False teachers had undermined the stability of the church by calling into question the certainty of the parousia. The answer 2 Peter provides moves well beyond just reaffirming the certainty of the parousia; it addresses the issue of the delay, in light of the forbearance of God.

Second Peter begins by emphasizing God's beneficence. From the bounty of his "divine power" God gave "all" *(panta)* that could be given (2 Pet 1:3). The call includes "life and godliness" and a share in God's "glory and excellence" (2 Pet 1:3). He has provided an "escape" from the corrupting powers of this world and promised a share in his "divine nature" (2 Pet 1:4). All of this is mediated through the "knowledge" of him (2 Pet 1:3). The certainty and efficacy of God's gifts should never be doubted.

It is not what God has done but what he has apparently failed to do that has given an opportunity to the false teachers (2 Pet 2:1). Specifically, the fact that the end had not yet come allowed the false teachers to conclude that it would not come at all.

To counteract the appraisal of the parousia as simply a "cleverly devised myth" (2 Pet 1:16), 2 Peter points to Jesus' transfiguration. In that event the "majestic Glory" gave voice to his divine approval of Jesus (2 Pet 1:17). Second Peter interprets the transfiguration as a prolepsis of God's eschatological presence—Jesus received "honor and glory" from God—and thus a sure sign of the future apocalypse (2 Pet 1:19). This is a testimony still heard in the apostolic community (2 Pet 1:18) and verified by God's Spirit-inspired prophets (2 Pet 1:20-21). The transfiguration and the subsequent testimony mean that the parousia can hardly be described as a myth.

The false teachers also asserted that a day of judgment would never come. Second Peter rehearses past examples when God, despite the passage of time, judged the unrighteous and vindicated the faithful (2 Pet 2:1-10). God did not spare the disobedient angels (2 Pet 2:4), those who sinned during Noah's day (2 Pet 2:5) or the ungodly of Sodom and Gomorrah (2 Pet 2:6). However, God did rescue Noah out of the flood (2 Pet 2:4) and honored the endurance of Lot (2 Pet 2:7-8). Delay does not invalidate divine judgment, as the false prophets claimed; delay only witnesses to God's forbearance. God knows how to rescue and to punish (2 Pet 2:9), and thus to indulge one's passions (2 Pet 2:1-3, 10), as the false teachers encouraged, is not only eschatologically perilous but openly sneers at God's patience.

When the scoffers taunt, "Where is the promise of his coming?" (2 Pet 3:4a) and "All has remained the same since the beginning of creation!" (2 Pet 3:4b), they call into question God's intention and power to intervene in history. Such mockery deliberately ignores what is common knowledge: God's ability to create confirms his ability to judge (2 Pet 3:5-6).

Since the passage of time in no way undermines the certainty of God's promises—"with the Lord one day is as a thousand years, and a thousand years as one day" (2 Pet 3:8 [quoting Ps 90:6])—any perceived delay should be construed as an expression of God's mercy. God wishes that all should repent and that none should perish (2 Pet 3:9). God's forbearance is thus an expression of his saving purposes (2 Pet 3:15). The day of the Lord will come quickly enough, like a thief (2 Pet 3:10), and thus holiness and godliness should be the order of the day (2 Pet 3:11, 14).

6.3. The Judgment of God in Jude. Jude also seeks to contradict false teaching. The opponents advocate licentiousness ("ungodliness," Jude 4, 15, 18) apparently grounded in an overly realized eschatology. Jude instead mandates doctrinal purity (Jude 3) and moral sobriety (Jude 20-23) in the face of God's imminent judgment.

Jude begins by describing the readers as those having been "beloved by God the Father" (Jude 1b). Jude follows this with another reference to the goodness of God (Jude 3-4). But God's grace does not legitimate any sort of behavior (as the false teachers apparently taught). God's grace has limits. To appeal to God's grace as a cover for "licentiousness" is to "pervert" it and to "deny" the lordship of Jesus (Jude 4). Judgment awaits the ungodly, as it did for the disobedient of Israel (Jude 5), the disobedient angels (Jude 6) and the immoral of Sodom and

Gomorrah (Jude 7). The Lord's rebuke will most surely come upon those who reject and revile authority (Jude 8-10). "Woe to them!" (Jude 11), for the Lord will certainly come to judge (Jude 14; cf. *1 Enoch* 1:9). Jude even asserts that the ungodly false teachers are a sure sign of the end (Jude 17-18). The cure for such moral laxity is to stay within the "love of God" (Jude 21), for God is able to keep believers from falling and to finishing the process of eschatological transformation (Jude 24).

7. 1, 2 and 3 John.

The letters of 1, 2 and 3 John (*see* John, Letters of) seek to close social fissures opened by an amalgamation of erroneous teaching and practice of the gnosticizing kind. The letters encourage right belief and praxis, both of which are tied to the nature of the one true God.

7.1. Lexical Observations. Theos ("God") appears in 1 John sixty-two times, in 2 John twice (2 Jn 2, 9) and in 3 John three times (3 Jn 6, 11 [2x]). 1 John explicitly calls God "Father" *(patēr)* twelve times (1 Jn 1:2; 1:3; 2:1, 14, 15, 16, 22, 23 [2x], 24; 3:1, 14) and implies it in twenty-two other instances by identifying Jesus as the or his "Son." Second John refers to God as "Father" four times (2 Jn 3 [2x], 4, 9). Additionally, 1 John twice calls God the "One [who is] from the beginning *(ton ap' archēs,* 1 Jn 2:13, 14).

7.2. God as Light. "God is light and in him there is no darkness at all" (1 Jn 1:5). By juxtaposing "light" *(phōs)* and "darkness" *(skotia)* 1 John divides the world and human existence into two mutually exclusive domains. Specifically, 1 John allies "light" with "truth" (1 Jn 1:6), "love" (1 Jn 1:7; 2:10) and "forgiveness" (1 Jn 1:7). "Darkness" keeps company with lying (1 Jn 1:6), disobedience (1 Jn 1:6), ignorance (1 Jn 2:11) and spiritual blindness (1 Jn 2:11). Light invokes all the images associated with God and salvation; darkness, of sin and death.

John's Gospel identifies Jesus as the light that shines in a dark world (1 Jn 1:5), an illumination that bestows life upon all who are willing to identify with him (Jn 1:4, 9; 9:5; 12:46). First John also marks the transition from "darkness" to "light" at the advent of Jesus. "The darkness is (already) passing and the true light is already shining" (1 Jn 2:8). The "message" that the church first "heard" and continues to "preach" (1 Jn 1:5), the "word" that they had "from the beginning" (1 Jn 2:7), is the narration of Jesus' life,

death and resurrection. Adherence to this message of light demands spiritual transformation. The community is to "walk in the light as God is in the light" (1 Jn 1:7). Adherence to the message of light also requires confession (1 Jn 1:8), one that is not exhausted by words. To "hate" a fellow Christian is to betray the confession and demonstrates solidarity with darkness (1 Jn 2:9; cf. 1 Jn 2:1). To walk in God's light is to be forgiven, cleansed and unencumbered by the powers of evil (1 Jn 1:8; 2:10). The community is created and sustained by God's light.

7.3. God as Love. "God is love" (1 Jn 4:8, 16), God gives love (1 Jn 3:1; 4:7, 16), and God initiates love (1 Jn 4:10, 19; cf. Rom 5:8). God demonstrated his love in the sending of his Son (1 Jn 4:9) and most particularly in the Son's sacrificial death (1 Jn 3:16; 4:10). God's love permits knowledge of him (1 Jn 4:16), inspires belief and confidence (1 Jn 4:17) and conquers all fear (1 Jn 4:18).

God's love requires and enables love for one another (1 Jn 3:11, 16, 17, 23; 4:11, 19, 21; cf. 2 Jn 6; 3 Jn 11). Confession should be matched with compassion. "And this is his commandment: that we should believe in the name of his Son Jesus Christ and love one another" (1 Jn 3:23). To love authenticates the claim to saving knowledge of God (1 Jn 3:14; 4:8). To love demonstrates God's perfecting presence within (1 Jn 2:5, 10; 3:1; 4:12, 16; 5:1; cf. 1 Jn 2:14; 2 Jn 7, 9). "The one who does not love remains in the grip of death" (1 Jn 3:14; cf. 1 Jn 3:10). To love anything other than God (e.g., the "world") illustrates the absence of God's love (1 Jn 2:15; 3:17-18). To confess love for God and yet to hate others transforms the confession into a lie (1 Jn 4:20).

8. Revelation.

Revelation forms a fitting conclusion to the Christian canon: it narrates the final disposition of all things. Revelation's depiction of God equally satisfies: God faces opponents of great power—the dragon, the sea and earth beasts, Babylon—and soundly defeats them.

8.1. Lexical Observations. Revelation employs the most varied terminology in the NT to refer to the one true God. Standing at the head of the list are ninety-six occurrences of *theos* ("God"), *kyrios* ("Lord"), which appears twenty-three times (of which seventeen refer to God; the other occurrences refer to the risen Jesus [Rev 11:8;

14:13; 17:14; 19:16; 22:20, 21]) and *pater* ("Father"), which is used of God five times (Rev 1:6, 2:28; 3:5, 21; 14:1; cf. Rev 21:7).

The list widens to include constructions rarely or never used in other NT writings. "Almighty" *(pantokrator)* is used only once outside of Revelation (2 Cor 6:18), but within Revelation it is used of God nine times (Rev 1:8, 4:8; 11:17; 15:3; 16:7, 14; 19:6, 15; 21:23). Revelation uniquely entitles God "The King of the Nations"/"Ages" (*ho basileus ton ethnon/aionon*, Rev 15:3—depending on the textual reading), "The Sovereign [One]" (*ho despotes*, Rev 6:10; but cf. Lk 2:19; Acts 4:24), "The Holy and True [One]" (*ho hagios kai alethinos*, Rev 6:10), "The Lord of the Earth" (*tou kyriou tes ges*, Rev 11:4), "The One who was, is and comes" (*ho on kai ho en kai ho erchomenos*, Rev 1:4, 8; 4:8; 11:17; 16:5), "The Alpha and the Omega" (*ego eimi to Alpha kai to Ō*, Rev 1:8, 21:6; 22:13), "The Beginning and the End" (*he arche kai to telos*, Rev 21:6; 22:13) and "The First and the Last" (*ho protos kai ho eschatos*, Rev 22:13). On numerous occasions Revelation refers to God as "the One who sits/is seated upon the throne" (Rev 4:2, 3, 9, 10; 5:1, 7, 13; 6:16; 7:10, 15; 12:5; 14:3; 19:4; 20:11; 21:5). The unique ways in which Revelation refers to God corresponds to the singular importance of Revelation's message.

8.2. The Unseen Revealer. As a literary hybrid (the combination of letter, prophecy and narrative), Revelation communicates on several levels simultaneously. As a letter, Revelation addresses the situation and needs of specific congregations; as a prophetic work, Revelation dialogues with major historical events, albeit obliquely; and as a narrative, characters within Revelation's narrative (e.g., the angelic mediators, the Lamb, the unnamed voices or even the scroll) communicate with each other and the author. Revelation is something of a literary symphony.

Revelation wraps this complex enterprise within an apocalyptic disclosure. The book opens with the self-descriptive line "the revelation of Jesus Christ" (*apokalypsis Iesou Christou*, Rev 1:1), a phrase that should be read both objectively (i.e., "a revelation about Jesus Christ") and subjectively (i.e., "a revelation from Jesus Christ"). Jesus is both the author and the content of the apocalyptic visions given to John.

Revelation envelops Jesus' disclosure to John within yet another disclosure. The text stresses that what Jesus makes known to John is what

"God gave him" (Rev 1:1). It was God who gave this revelation to Jesus, who in turn gave it to John, who then obediently wrote it up for the communities where it should be read aloud. God therefore is the ultimate source of revelation—but, curiously, a source who is only rarely seen or heard.

While various heavenly beings are described in detail, including the risen Jesus (Rev 1:12-16) and the four living creatures (Rev 4:6-8), the only sort of descriptive accounting of God occurs when John likens his vision of the "One seated upon the throne" (Rev 4:2) to "jasper and carnelian" (Rev 4:3). John's approximation moves from the known (jasper and carnelian) to the unknown (God). Further, God only speaks twice within the entire narrative—the self-predication of Revelation 1:8 and the promises of Revelation 22:1-5. Thus even though God is the ultimate source (and therefore positioned as the most powerful agent in Revelation's story-world) and even though Revelation is putatively the most revelatory of all NT documents, the text never finally diminishes the mystery of God. What Revelation does make clear is that God is the all-powerful King who will judge evil and vindicate the righteous.

8.3. The Omnipotence of God. Simply naming God the "Almighty" (Rev 1:8, 4:8; 11:17; 15:3; 16:7, 14; 19:6, 15; 21:23) was not enough. The greatness of God's all-embracing power to be unleashed during the final days demanded elaboration.

8.3.1. God's Temporal Omnipotence. God is the One "who was, is and is to come" (Rev 1:4, 8; 4:8; 11:17; 16:5). God "lives for ever and ever" (Rev 4:9, 10; 10:6; 15:7; cf. Rev 1:6; 5:13; 7:2, 12). God is "The Alpha and the Omega" (Rev 1:8, 21:6; 22:13), "The Beginning and the End" (Rev 21:6; 22:13) and "The First and the Last" (Rev 22:13). While these sorts of declarations position God above and beyond time, Revelation also makes clear once and for all that the one God of the Scriptures intervenes within the flow of history to direct its course to a final and proper conclusion. The God who is beyond time controls time.

8.3.2. God's Cosmic Omnipotence. Revelation augments the picture of God's temporal power by linking it with his cosmic power. God created this world and everything in it (Rev 4:11; 10:6; 14:7). It is by his will that the world exists (Rev 4:11). He is the "Lord of the earth" (11:4). But

God's powers do not end there. The risen Jesus, "The Amen, the Faithful and True Witness," is the "beginning of God's [new] creation" (*hē archēs ktiseōs tou theou*, Rev 3:14; cf. Rev 1:5; Col 1:15, 18), and those who obediently follow this Lamb are its "first fruits" (*aparchē*, Rev 14:4; cf. Rev 11:11). God culminates his re-creation by refashioning a new heaven, a new earth and a new Jerusalem (Rev 21:1-2, 10). God's omnipotence includes his ability to create and recreate. God rules both chronos (time) and cosmos (the universe).

8.3.3. God's Theophanic Omnipotence. Revelation also strategically employs theophanic imagery to accentuate God's power. John's initial vision included God's throne from which spewed "flashes of lightning and voices and peals of thunder" (Rev 4:5). The unsealing of the seventh seal resulted in "peals of thunder, voices, flashes of lightning, and an earthquake" (Rev 8:5). The blowing of the seventh trumpet triggered "flashes of lightning, voices, peals of thunder, an earthquake and heavy hail" (Rev 11:19). The emptying of the seventh bowl of God was followed by "flashes of lighting, voices, peals of thunder, and a great earthquake such as had never been since men were on the earth, so great was that earthquake" (Rev 16:8). Not only does such rhetoric graphically depict God's power but the sequential intensification of theophanic imagery—at the very place where one might expect a detailed description of the parousia—moves the narrative forward toward the final theophany (cf. Rev 19:11-16).

8.3.4. God's Royal Omnipotence. Revelation explicitly identifies God as King only once (Rev 15:3) and makes reference to God's "kingdom" only twice (Rev 11:15; 12:10). However, Revelation refers to God's "throne" forty-two times. The throne thus becomes Revelation's major symbol for conveying God's royal power and authority.

God is explicitly identified as the One who sits/is seated upon the "throne" (Rev 3:21; 4:2, 3, 9, 10; 5:1, 7, 13; 6:16; 7:10, 15; 12:5; 14:3; 19:4; 20:11; 21:5). The throne is surrounded by a rainbow (Rev 4:3), seven torches of fire (Rev 4:5), a sea of glass (Rev 4:6) and a golden altar (Rev 8:3). From the throne spew flashes of lightning and fire (Rev 4:5), come unidentified voices (Rev 16:17; 19:5; 21:3) and flows a river (Rev 22:1). Revelation pictures all sorts of heavenly beings and angelic creatures as gathered around God's throne—i.e., the seven spirits/angels (Rev 1:4; 8:2), twenty-four elders (Rev 4:4; 5:11; 7:11; 11:16; 19:4), four living creatures (Rev 4:6; 5:11; 7:11; 19:4), the Lamb (Rev 5:6; 7:17), myriads of angels (Rev 5:11; 7:11), great multitudes from all the tribes of the earth (Rev 7:9; cf. 19; 1), innumerable people in white robes (Rev 7:15), the male child brought forth by a woman (Rev 12:5), the 144,000 (Rev 14:3) and all the dead, both great and small (Rev 20:12). At the throne these heavenly beings sing (Rev 4:6; 14:3), give thanks and praise (Rev 4:9), fall prostrate (Rev 4:10), worship (Rev 4:10; 5:13; 7:10, 11) and utter confessions/acclamations (Rev 7:10, 11; cf. 19:1). This extravagant imagery positions God as the most majestic, commanding and potent being in Revelation's hierarchy of beings.

8.3.5. God's Juridical Omnipotence. God's complete control is nowhere more evident than in the expression of his judgment. While Revelation makes explicit reference to God's judgments (Rev 6:10; 14:7; 15:4; 17:1; 19:8) or "plagues" (Rev 9:18, 20; 11:6; 15:1, 6, 8; 16:21; 18:4, 8; 21:9), it is the complex of events unfolding from the seven "seals" (Rev 4:1—6:17; 8:1-5), "trumpets" (Rev 8:2—9:21; 11:15-19) and "bowls" (Rev 15:1—19:10)—culminating in the judgment of the great harlot Babylon (Rev 18:1-24) and the great white throne (Rev 20:11-15)—that dramatically illustrate God's omnipotence. The all-powerful God of Revelation denies the evil powers of this world the final say: there is only one God powerful enough to render judgment.

Divine judgment is an expression of God's "anger" *(thymos)* and "wrath" *(orgē)*. No one will be able to stand the great day of God's wrath (Rev 6:17). God will answer the unrepentant nations with his wrath (Rev 11:18). Whoever worships the beast and opposes God will certainly "drink the wine of God's anger, poured unmixed into the cup of his wrath" (Rev 14:10; 16:19) and thereby experience eternal torment (Rev 14:11). God's judgment is nothing short of a "wine press" of his anger (Rev 14:19). The seven bowls are full of God's anger (Rev 15:7; 16:1), and only when the bowls are emptied shall God's anger cease (Rev 15:1). God's anger and wrath, however, should never be construed as indiscriminate vengeance. Revelation asserts that God's judgments are always "just and true" (Rev 16:5; 19:2).

8.4. The Worship of the Omnipotent God and the Crucified Lamb. Revelation weaves together the various images of God in the twelve songs/confessions that punctuate the narrative (Rev 4:8, 11; 5:13; 7:10, 12; 11:15, 17-18; 15:3-4, 5-6; 16:7; 19:1-3, 4). These songs/confessions celebrate God's "worthiness" (Rev 4:11) to receive "glory" (Rev 4:11; 5:13; 7:12; 19:1), "honor" (Rev 4:11; 5:13; 7:12), "power" (Rev 4:11; 7:12; 19:1), "blessing" (Rev 5:13; 7:12), "might" (Rev 5:13; 12), "wisdom" (Rev 7:12) and "thanksgiving" (Rev 7:12; 11:17). The songs/confessions affirm that "salvation" (Rev 7:10; 19:1) and "power" (Rev 11:17) belong only to God. The hymns extol God as the one who "reigns" (Rev 11:15, 17), "judges" (Rev 11:18; 15:4; 16:5; 19:2) and "rewards" (Rev 11:18; 19:2). God is "holy" (Rev 4:8; 15:4; 16:5), "just" and "true" (Rev 15:3; 16:5, 7; 19:2). In no other place in the NT are so many images for God brought together with such power.

Thus, in a book that venerates God's omnipotence in unprecedented ways, it is surprising to find that Revelation also openly encourages and models the worship of the enthroned Jesus. The opening doxology honors the risen Jesus as the one "who loves us and has freed us from our sins by his blood and made us a kingdom, priests to his God and Father, to him [i.e., to Jesus] be glory and dominion for ever and ever" (Rev 1:6). The new song sung by the elders and the creatures hallows the worthiness of Jesus (Rev 5:9). When the angelic hosts join the chorus, Jesus is again reckoned worthy to "receive power and wealth and wisdom and might and honor and glory and blessing" (Rev 5:12). The final song sung by every creature on earth culminates in worship being simultaneously given "to him who sits upon the throne and to the Lamb" (Rev 5:13; cf. Rev 7:10; 12:10). Revelation legitimates and promotes the worship of Jesus and God—and the worship of Jesus as God—and it does so at the very places where God is worshiped and with the very language that is used to venerate God. Revelation shows how the revision of Jewish monotheism occurred in context of Christian worship where OT psalms originally addressed to God, under the inspiration of the Spirit, were redirected to Jesus (Hengel, 81-83). The omnipotence of the only God was fully shared with the only one worthy enough to open the scroll.

9. Summary.

The NT employs a wide range of vocabulary to refer to the one true God. All the later NT authors employ *theos*, *kyrios* and *pater* to designate God. But any common lexical pattern ends there. Of the other twenty-eight separate titles noted here, only two titles appear in two or more authors—*hypsistos* in Acts and Hebrews and *despotes* in Acts and Revelation. When the NT authors speak, they tell of God's faithfulness, sovereignty, holiness, constancy, providence, forbearance, mercy, grace, love, anger and omnipotence; they explain God as Father, love and light; they write of a God who creates, builds, reveals, promises, saves, redeems, justifies, warns, disciplines, judges, vindicates and rewards.

Despite such wide-ranging vocabulary and imagery, the NT writers hold certain features of God in common (see Dahl, Bassler)—there is only one God who is the Creator and Giver of life, who rules, judges and mercifully redeems.

	Oneness	Creator of the World and the Giver of Life	Sovereign Ruler of the World	Righteous Judge	Gracious Merciful Redeemer
Acts	X	X	X	X	X
Hebrews	X	X	X	X	X
James	X		X	X	X
1 Peter		X	X	X	X
2 Peter		X		X	X
1, 2, 3 John				X	X
Jude	X			X	X
Revelation		X	X	X	X

The chart not only demonstrates commonality among the NT writers but also indicates the indebtedness of early Christianity to Jewish monotheism. The Jewish Scriptures, the Christian OT, bequeathed to Christianity the identity of the one true God.

Christianity did, however, recast Jewish monotheism in light of Jesus' death, resurrection and installation to God's right hand. Early on, Christians recognized the divine status of the risen Jesus, despite the high threshold that Jewish monotheism had established. Christians offered worship and prayers to Jesus (e.g., Acts, Revelation). Christians also began to call Jesus *theos* (e.g., Heb 1:8; 2 Pet 1:1). The trinitarian seeds planted within the later NT documents (Acts 2:33) were destined to flower into the great confessions of the church. The later NT documents demonstrate that the office of the one true God had been enlarged to include Jesus as worthy of worship and service.

See also CHRISTOLOGY; HOLY SPIRIT; LORD; WORSHIP.

DLNTD: CHRISTIANITY AND JUDAISM: PARTINGS OF THE WAYS.

BIBLIOGRAPHY. J. M. Bassler, "God (NT)," *ABD* (1992) 2:1049-55; R. J. Bauckham, *God Crucified: Monotheism and Christology in the New Testament* (Grand Rapids: Eerdmans, 1998); idem, "Jesus, Worship of," *ABD* (1992) 3:812-19; idem, "The Worship of Jesus in Apocalyptic Christianity," *NTS* 27 (1981) 323-31; W. Bousset, *Kyrios Christos* (Nashville: Abingdon, 1970); A. Chester and R. P. Martin, *The Theology of the Letters of James, Peter and Jude* (Cambridge: Cambridge University Press, 1994); H. Conzelmann, *The Theology of St. Luke* (Philadelphia: Fortress, 1961); C. H. Cosgrove, "The Divine *Dei* in Luke-Acts," *NovT* 26 (1984) 168-90; N. A. Dahl, "The Neglected Factor in New Testament Theology" in *Jesus the Christ: The Historical Origins of Christological Doctrine,* ed. D. H. Juel (Minneapolis: Fortress, 1991) 153-63; N. A. Dahl and A. F. Segal, "Philo and the Rabbis on the Name of God," *JSJ* 9 (1978) 1-28; P. H. Davids, *The Epistle of James* (NIGTC; Grand Rapids: Eerdmans, 1982); C. J. Davis, *The Name and Way of the Lord: Old Testament Themes; New Testament Christology* (JSNTSup 129; Sheffield: Sheffeld Academic Press, 1996); M. Dibelius and H. Greeven, *James* (Herm; Philadephia: Fortress, 1976); J. D. G. Dunn, *The Partings of the Ways* (Philadelphia: Trinity Press International, 1991); J. H. Elliott, *A Home for the Homeless: A Sociological Exegesis of 1 Peter* (Philadelphia: Fortress, 1981); R. M. Grant, *The Early Christian Doctrine of God* (Charlottesville: University of Virginia Press, 1966); idem, *Gods and the One God* (Philadelphia: Westminster, 1986); G. Guthrie, *The Structure of Hebrews: A Text-Linguistic Analysis* (NovTSup 73: Leiden: E. J. Brill, 1994); M. J. Harris, *Jesus as God: The New Testament Use of Theos in Reference to Jesus* (Grand Rapids: Eerdmans, 1992); A. E. Harvey, *Jesus and the Constraints of History* (Philadelphia: Westminster, 1982); M. Hengel, "Hymns and Christology" in *Between Jesus and Paul: Studies in the History of Earliest Christianity* (Philadelphia: Fortress, 1983) 78-96; L. W. Hurtado, *One God, One Lord: Early Christian Devotion and Ancient Jewish Monotheism* (Philadelphia: Fortress, 1988); W. L. Lane, *Hebrews* (WBC; Dallas: Word, 1991); I. H. Marshall, *Luke: Historian and Theologian* (Grand Rapids: Zondervan, 1970); T. N. D. Mettinger, *In Search of God: The Meaning and Message of the Everlasting Names* (Philadelphia: Fortress, 1988); R. L. Mowery, "Direct Statements Concerning God's Activity in Acts," *SBLSP* (1990) 196-211; idem, "Lord, God, and Father: Theological Language in Luke-Acts," *SBLSP* (1995) 82-101; F. Mussner, "'Direkte' und 'Indirekte' Christologie im Jakobusbrief," *Catholica* 24 (1970) 111-16; idem, *Jakobusbrief* (4th ed.; HTKNT; Freiburg: Herders, 1981); C. C. Newman, "Acts" in *A Complete Literary Guide to the Bible,* ed. L. Ryken and T. Longman III (Grand Rapids: Zondervan, 1993) 436-44; M. C. Parsons, "Son and High Priest: A Study in the Christology of Hebrews," *EvQ* 60 (1988) 195-218; R. I. Pervo, *Profit with Delight: The Literary Genre of the Acts of the Apostles* (Philadelphia: Fortress, 1987); P. Rainbow, "Jewish Monotheism as the Matrix for New Testament Christology," *NovT* 33 (1991) 78-91; A. F. Segal, *Two Powers in Heaven* (SJLA 25; Leiden: E. J. Brill, 1978); R. B. Sloan, "The Christology of James," *CTR* 1 (1986) 2-29; E. Stauffer, "θεός," *TDNT* 3:65-122; L. Stuckenbruck, *"Do Not Worship Me, Worship God!": The Problem of Angel Veneration in Early Judaism and Angelmorphic Aspects in the Christology of the Apocalypse of John* (WUNT; Tübingen: Siebeck, 1995); M. M. Thompson, *The Promise of the Father: Jesus and God in the New Testament* (Louisville, KY: Westminster John Knox, 2000); A. W. Wainwright, *The Trinity in the New Testament* (London: SPCK, 1962); N. T. Wright, *The New Testament and the People of God* (Minneapolis: Fortress, 1992).   C. C. Newman

GOLGOTHA. *See* DEATH OF CHRIST I.

GOSPEL (GENRE)

Discussion of the literary genre of the NT Gospels involves two basic issues: (1) the literary nature of the canonical Gospels as continuous prose narratives of Jesus' ministry and their relationship to other early Christian writings; (2) the relationship of the Gospels to their Greco-Roman literary setting. There are two practical purposes served in this discussion: (1) a better understanding of the place of the Gospels in the literary history of early Christianity and the Greco-Roman world; (2) a more intelligent interpretation of the Gospels as their features are illuminated by comparison with their literary background.

Until the 1970s there was practically a consensus that the Gospels constituted a unique literary genre in the Greco-Roman world and that any apparent analogies with other early Christian writings or from the wider Greco-Roman literary setting were irrelevant. This consensus has been challenged, however, and various scholars have argued that the Gospels are related to one or more types of Greco-Roman literature, most often biographical writings.

It is likely that both sides in the debate have a legitimate point. On the one hand, the Gospels share various characteristics of one or more types of Greco-Roman literature and in light of this can be likened to certain literary genres of that period. Moreover, we should expect that the NT authors would have been influenced by general literary conventions and practices of their day. Yet the NT Gospels also exhibit a certain uniqueness and thus form at least a partially distinctive category or subgenre. That is, the Evangelists, though influenced by their literary environment, seem to have produced works whose origin and characteristics are to be understood most directly in terms of the early Christian groups for which the Gospels were written.

1. Definition and Significance of Genre
2. The Scholarly Debate
3. The Genre of the Gospels
4. Conclusion

1. Definition and Significance of Genre.

A literary genre is a category or type of literature, such as biography or novel. Literary genres are not universal and static categories but have developed and changed over time, and genres popular in one age or culture may not be found in another. Even if a genre, such as biography, appears in more than one period or culture, the specific characteristics of the genre will often vary significantly in the different settings.

In seeking to determine a writing's genre, therefore, we must work with the genres and literary conventions relevant to the era of the writing. Thus, for example, the question of the genre(s) of the Gospels must be addressed by examining their characteristics in comparison with the types of literature current in the Greco-Roman setting or at least accessible to the authors. Genres are to be thought of in terms of clusters of characteristics or traits. The analysis of a work's relation to literary genres should involve comparison of all the characteristics of the

relevant genres and of the work in question. Emphasis on isolated characteristics of a work can produce misleading conclusions. A writing can be associated with a particular genre only to the degree that all the characteristics of the writing can be understood adequately in terms of the features of the genre.

The sorts of characteristics and factors to be considered in trying to determine a writing's genre include the following: formal features (e.g., structure, style, motifs, devices), author's intention, compositional process, setting of author, setting of intended use, and contents. Every reader brings expectations to a writing that shape the reading process and affect how the writing is understood. Acquaintance with the genre of a writing allows one's understanding of a writing to be guided in light of the features and intentions that characterize the genre. If an author sets out to write in accordance with the conventions and features of a particular genre, it may be comparatively easy to identify the genre of the writing.

But sometimes things are not so easy. For example, if an author adapts a genre to achieve a purpose not ordinarily associated with that genre, or if an author does not follow very methodically the full conventions of a given genre, it may be much more difficult to categorize the writing. In any case, identifying a writing's genre requires informed judgment that must be based on familiarity with the writing and its literary and social context.

2. The Scholarly Debate.

The question of the genre of the Gospels is basically a modern issue, characteristic of the modern historical investigation of the NT. Our cultural and chronological distance from the first-century setting and our modern desire to overcome this distance through accurate knowledge of the past fuel the attempt to analyze the Gospels in their literary context. It is interesting to note that the discussion of this topic has been related to wider developments in Gospel studies.

2.1. The Earlier Consensus. In 1915 C. W. Votaw argued that the Gospels can be likened to the popular biographical literature of the Greco-Roman era. But in 1923, in reply to Votaw, K. L. Schmidt argued influentially that the Gospels are a unique type of early Christian writing, not explainable by reference to any other type of literature of the ancient world. This position became the standard view among NT scholars, virtually unchallenged until recent decades.

Schmidt's case reflected in part the distinction made earlier by F. Overbeck, in which the NT was portrayed as relatively unsophisticated in comparison to the more polished literature of the classical authors and the Christian writings of the late second century and thereafter. Also, Schmidt reflected the approach of early form criticism, which tended to view the Gospels basically as collections of the Jesus traditions of early Christian communities and minimized the role of the Evangelists as authors. Moreover, form critics emphasized that the impetus for the Gospels was not literary but kerygmatic (from the Gk *kerygma*, "proclamation"). That is, form criticism emphasized that the Gospels embody the early Christian proclamation of the significance of Jesus and were written exclusively to serve this proclamation.

2.2. The Reopening of the Question. By the 1970s there was a renewed investigation of the relationship of the Gospels to Greco-Roman literature. This re-examination of the previous consensus seems to have arisen in part from developments in Gospel studies in the 1950s and subsequently that balanced the form-critical view of the Gospels as collections of tradition with emphasis on the role of the Evangelists as effective editors of the tradition (redaction criticism) and/or as authors who significantly determined the nature of their narratives of Jesus (recent literary criticism of the Gospels). Although some early contributions to the renewed question of the genre of the Gospels posited a classification of them as "aretalogies" (purported narratives of divine men in antiquity), this category has not proven viable for a variety of reasons (e.g., see Kee), including the lack of evidence for such a literary genre so defined in antiquity.

Scholars who now propose links between the Gospels and Greco-Roman literature focus on one of three genres: biography, history or novel. The modern discussion has also raised the question of whether the Gospels belong to one genre collectively or must be classified individually in different genres. Most of those who have addressed the genre of the Gospels, however, have tended to emphasize possible connections with the genre of Greco-Roman popular biography.

3. The Genre of the Gospels.

Proper consideration of the genre of the Gospels involves a variety of factors, and the variations among the four canonical accounts make it wise to treat them individually.

3.1. Basic Factors. There are formal features of the Gospels that must be considered. The Gospels are all narratives about Jesus that include examples of his deeds and sayings in a loose chronological framework that concentrates on the period between the beginning of his ministry and his death and resurrection. They are not impartial accounts; they all enthusiastically endorse Jesus and are quite negative in their treatment of any opposition to Jesus. In the case of Matthew and Luke, there are birth accounts attached that seem likewise intended to show dramatically the significance of Jesus (*see* Birth of Jesus).

The narrative mode of the canonical Gospels and their general shape as accounts of Jesus' ministry and death/resurrection set them apart from the surviving apocryphal Gospels. The latter form an assortment of writings about Jesus that include revelation/sayings collections (e.g., *Gospel of Thomas*), fanciful narratives of Jesus' childhood (the several so-called infancy Gospels), and other writings that may be likened a bit more to the canonical Gospels but are also shaped by different religious interests (e.g., *Gospel of Peter*). The distinctive form of the Gospels in comparison with other early Christian literature justifies viewing them as a group or sub group unto themselves in the literary history of early Christianity.

Though they exhibit distinguishing features as continuous narratives concerned with Jesus' ministry, the canonical Gospels can be likened to genres of Greco-Roman literature, particularly popular biography of that era (see, e.g., Aune 1987, 17-76). Indeed, in some cases there are specific formal features of a Gospel that directly reflect literary practices of the ancient setting (e.g., Luke's preface in Lk 1:1-4 and the prefaces to Greco-Roman literary works).

In addition to the narrative form of the Gospels, however, we should consider their contents. Here also, the Gospels can be likened to other examples of Greco-Roman biographical writings that promote a particular hero (see, e.g., Talbert "Biographies"; and Tiede). But the NT Gospels also diverge from general Greco-Roman literary culture. For example, though the Gospels may often reflect Greco-Roman themes, values and literary motifs (e.g., Luke's presentation of Jesus' death as heroic martyrdom, the motif of important teaching and events set at meal scenes, or the motif of the teacher and his disciples), more fundamentally the Evangelists invoke the OT (e.g., the many allusions and citations) and specifically early Christian beliefs in their presentation of Jesus (e.g., Jesus as Christ). These distinguishing features did not render their narratives more meaningful or harmonious with the literary and cultural tastes of the Greco-Roman world, and this indicates that the Evangelists were by no means simply patterning their narratives after genres of contemporary literature. Likewise, if we take into account the compositional process that probably lies behind the Gospels, there are general similarities with some types of Greco-Roman writings but also significant differences.

The Gospel writers did not invent the idea of narrating Jesus' ministry. We must surely grant some (in some places considerable) authorial contribution to the finished products. But, in many features of their form and in most of their contents (or all, depending on one's critical opinion), the Gospels reflect the Jesus tradition of Christian groups. That is, the immediate setting that shaped the work of the Evangelists was not the literary activities of the larger Greco-Roman era but the religious and social activities, needs and questions of early Christianity.

In the case of accounts of some figures associated with particular philosophical traditions (e.g., Socrates, Pythagoras), there may have been bodies of tradition about these individuals that were carried along in the groups that revered their memory. This would provide a general similarity to the Gospels' relationship to the Jesus tradition. Nevertheless, there appears to be no direct analogy to the rather considerable Jesus tradition available to the Evangelists, the massive preoccupation with proclaiming and teaching about Jesus and the rather exclusive claims made on his behalf in the early Christian movement.

The popularity of biographical writings in the Greco-Roman era may have conditioned the Evangelists to find the writing of their books about Jesus a worthy task. But the major reason biography-like accounts of Jesus appeared is that the early Christian message from the first was focused on Jesus as the personal vehicle of revelation and redemption (see, e.g., Stanton). The impetus, basic contents and general narrative complexion of the Gospels reflect primarily the Jesus-centered proclamation of early Christianity.

That the Gospels do not explicitly name their authors is evidence of their highly traditional nature. Contrary to the frequent literary practice of the Greco-Roman era, the Gospels do not convey their author's identities. The present superscriptions were added after the Gospels began to be circulated, probably when they were circulated as a fourfold collection. With the exception of Luke-Acts, the Gospels do not have such common literary devices as prefaces either. These things suggest that in general the Evangelists did not see themselves primarily as authors writing for a general audience, but more likely as "servants [hyperētai] of the word" (Lk 1:2).

Furthermore, the intended and characteristic use of the Gospels is somewhat distinctive. As indicated already, the Evangelists did not write for the general public but for the Christian groups with which they were associated. Suggestions that the Gospels were composed to fit some fixed lectionary schedule have been judged implausible. But the Gospels were apparently intended for corporate reading and teaching within Christian groups and quickly found a role in their liturgical activities. Although some Greco-Roman biographical writings may have been intended primarily for followers of a particular philosophical tradition, the close association of the Gospels with early Christian worship and proclamation suggests that we should see them as church documents with a certain biographical character rather than as biographies with a religious tone.

Furthermore, in Greco-Roman biography the central figure is glorified in terms of values that do not really derive from the figure or rest on his authority. Instead, the biographer shows the main character to be a model who embodies the virtues (sometimes the vices) already recognized by the writer and expected readers. The biographer seeks to show the essence of the main figure by recounting incidents and sayings that display and prove his character.

Although the Evangelists portray Jesus in ways that seem intended to dispose the Christian readers to find encouragement and inspiration to live as his followers, we can hardly say that the Gospels focus on the essence of Jesus' character or emphasize Jesus primarily as a model of particular virtues. In fact, they supply surprisingly little about Jesus' personality or character. The Evangelists were mainly concerned to show Jesus' significance in the divine purpose, not his virtues. Thus, in emphasis and aim, as in several other respects, the Gospels exhibit distinctive features that do not derive from Greco-Roman literary genres.

3.2. Mark. Mark is commonly regarded today as the earliest of the NT Gospels and the major narrative source of Matthew and Luke. Therefore it is important to try to understand the features of Mark and the forces that shaped this influential narrative. Matthew and Luke are called Synoptic Gospels because of their strong resemblance to Mark, making the question of the genre of Mark at least partially relevant for these other two Gospels as well.

It has long been recognized that Mark and the other Synoptics are composed of traditions about Jesus that circulated in the early churches and that can be classified into broad types of Jesus material (e.g., parables, miracle stories, chreia or pronouncement stories, passion narratives, etc.). These all exhibit in various ways rhetorical features of popular-level oral narratives as these were adapted in the proclamation and life of early Christianity. In the general narrative style of Mark as well, there is evidence of the continuing impact of oral narration. This indicates that the Gospels are not simply literary works but are constructed in close connection with the teaching and preaching activities of early Christianity.

Some scholars have noted that the plot or shape of Mark's story of Jesus reflects the general structure of Greek tragedy (introduction, rising action, climax/crisis, falling action, catastrophe, denouement), and a few have suggested that the Evangelist was influenced directly by this form of literature (e.g., Bilezikian, Standaert). But most scholars (e.g., Aune 1987, 48-49) believe that the resemblances are to a large extent coincidental and that Mark's plot reflects the broad narrative structure of pre-Markan Jesus tradition in which Jesus' ministry, death and resurrection were portrayed in terms of a general structure found in widespread literature of a variety of ancient cultures: a righteous person undergoes opposition, persecution and vindication. This judgment seems correct for not only Matthew and Luke but also John's Gospel, which is not usually thought to have been directly dependent on the Synoptics, reflect essentially this basic plot.

Some features of Mark and of Matthew and Luke as well are characteristic of ancient biography (e.g., anecdotal narrative style, absence of character growth), but there are no indications that the author was consciously shaping his work in the light of any literary precedents or patterns. If we ask, however, how the Evangelist came to compose a written narrative of Jesus in the form he did, it may be that very general literary influences can be included in the answer.

Surely the primary reasons Mark took pen in hand were the perceived needs of the Christians for whom he wrote, and the immediate influences on him stemmed from the religious circles in which the writer worked. But it may well be that the developing popularity of biography as a literary vehicle in the Greco-Roman era (see, e.g., Cox, Momigliano) helped make it seem logical or appropriate to the author to produce the first book narrating Jesus' ministry, though it is difficult to say whether such general influence was perceived consciously by the author. That is, the relevance of the genre of Greco-Roman biography for a historical explanation of Mark may be less in terms of direct or specific similarities and influence and more in terms of the general climate that contributed to the author's decision to serve Christ and Christians through his pioneering written work.

3.3. Matthew and Luke. In comparison with Mark, Matthew and Luke reflect a somewhat higher literary level and exhibit more features that can be compared with characteristics of Greco-Roman biographical literature. D. E. Aune refers to Matthew and Luke as early stages of the "literaturization," the more direct appropriation of literary tastes, that went on in early Christianity in the first few centuries.

In addition to their birth accounts, additional features such as the genealogies and postresurrection appearance/vindication scenes make Matthew and Luke seem closer to ancient biographies of figures described as sons of gods or divine. Also, Matthew and Luke have a more refined Greek style in comparison with Mark. In short, Matthew and Luke allow more scope for positing influence of the Greco-Roman literary environment. Nevertheless, like Mark, Matthew and Luke seem to have taken their major stimuli from and had their primary connections with the religious life of early Christianity. And the Christian matrix of these works has produced a profound adaptation of whatever Greco-Roman literary influences we can detect.

In Matthew, for example, Jesus is presented largely in terms of ideas, values and issues that stem from the OT and the Jewish and early Christian setting. The genealogy links Jesus with great figures of the OT and with the history of Israel. Like other subjects of Greco-Roman biography, Jesus is presented in Matthew as the great teacher. But in Matthew, Jesus' teaching is presented thoroughly in terms of the vocabulary and motifs of the Jewish and early Christian background, which are often noticeably different from those of the general literary culture. For example, the citation of numerous OT prophecies as fulfilled by Jesus probably reflects the narrative style of OT historical books (esp. 1 Sam—2 Kings), which likewise make fulfillment of the words of prophets a major device in their accounts.

P. L. Shuler has offered a definition of Matthew as a type of laudatory biography he calls "encomium biography," but this proposal is inadequate for several reasons. All ancient biographies were either laudatory and sought the same basic objectives as the rhetorical category of speeches called encomium or (occasionally) were condemnatory and critical. Shuler's category is not recognized in ancient sources and is too vague and broad to be of use. And Shuler is surely wide of the mark when he refers to Matthew as an attempt to relate the Evangelist's message "to the society in which he lived." The many indications that the Evangelist presumed an acceptance of the OT as Scripture and Christian beliefs and vocabulary as normative show that Matthew was written as an in-house document for the encouragement and edification of fellow Christians, not for the general public.

It is with Luke that scholars usually find the closest analogies to Greco-Roman literature. The author is believed to have drawn upon Mark as his major narrative source, but the use of a formal preface (Lk 1:1-4; cf. Acts 1:1) and chronologies (Lk 2:1-2; 3:1-2) are only two more obvious indications that this Evangelist consciously drew upon literary conventions of his time as well in composing his account. The scholarly attempt to categorize Luke in terms of a particular genre, however, has not resulted in agreement on what genre is preferable.

A major difficulty in reaching agreement is that one must take into account the second part of the Evangelist's work, the Acts of the Apostles.

C. H. Talbert has proposed that the combined work, Luke-Acts, is an integral work and represents a particular type of biography designed to show the valid succession of a tradition, in this case the tradition of Jesus in the ministry of the apostles featured in Acts. Others who agree that the genre of Luke must be decided in light of Acts have argued (e.g., Aune) that the two-volume work is an example of Greco-Roman historiography, in this case a history of the Christian message that begins with Jesus and continues on through to the Pauline Gentile mission.

S. M. Praeder, however, analyzed Luke-Acts as a Christian adaptation of the Greco-Roman genre of novel. Indeed, she regards all four canonical Gospels similarly, though she grants that their contents, setting and intended uses require that they be taken as forming a separate subgenre within the genre of "the ancient novel." Still others (e.g., Pervo) see as misguided the attempt to categorize Luke by reference to Acts and have urged that there is no reason why Luke and Acts cannot be linked to different genres. R. I. Pervo regards Acts as most closely related to the Greco-Roman genre of novel but seems to consider Luke an example of popular biography.

In view of these disagreements among scholars with special competence in Greco-Roman literature, perhaps the wisest course is to recognize the limitations inherent in approaching the Gospels, even Luke with its clear appropriation of Greco-Roman literary devices and techniques, in terms of Greco-Roman literary genres alone. To be sure, the author of Luke seems to have had direct acquaintance with formal literary conventions of the Greco-Roman era and unconsciously and consciously drew on them in producing Luke-Acts. But the same author also shows a rich familiarity with and the influence of other aspects of his more immediate background in early Christian circles, as shown in his linguistic style, which is much influenced by the LXX, and in various motifs drawn from the OT.

Also, in view of the fluidity in Greco-Roman literary genres and the influences of genres on one another, it is wise to be cautious about invoking a specific literary genre as the key to Luke or Luke-Acts on the basis of selected features of the work. For example, Greco-Roman historiography seems not to have conformed strictly to the standards espoused by the ancients who tried to define the literary genre. Popular historiography incorporated narrative features, such as fictional embroidering of events and dialogues, associated also with novels. Likewise, what may be termed historical novels affected a style like popular historiography. Biography too was not a tightly defined genre. Authors wishing to portray a great person had a variety of literary styles and approaches they could adapt.

In summary, Luke's appropriation of particular features of Greco-Roman literary practice can be demonstrated, and our grasp of the literary texture of Luke-Acts has been enhanced as a result. In spite of the scholarly disagreement mentioned, given the author's expressed intention (Lk 1:1-4) and taking Luke-Acts as a work of unified intention, the closest broad genre with which to compare Luke-Acts is probably Greco-Roman historiography. But Luke-Acts is a historical account with a sizable biographical component (Luke) and a certain amount of authorial freedom exercised in portraying dramatic scenes; and the whole was governed primarily by the ethos and needs of the Christians for whom the Evangelist wrote.

3.4. John. Not nearly as much scholarly effort has been spent on John's relationship to Greco-Roman literature. Talbert has classified John, with Mark, as an innovative example of a biography intended to correct a misunderstanding of the central character. But Talbert's categories are his own rather than those recognized by ancient writers, and his view of John as advocating a corrective christology is not widely shared.

Most scholars tend to see John as written mainly to consolidate a particular Christian community's tradition and to guide the community in the aftermath of a bitter conflict with Jewish synagogue authorities. John is broadly similar to the Synoptics and quite distinctive in features of contents, style and arrangement. In place of a birth account and genealogy, John 1:1-14 makes Jesus' birth the personal, historical manifestation of the divine Word *(logos)*. In place of the parables and pronouncement stories, there are extensive dialogs (e.g., Jn 3:1-21; 4:4-26) and discourses (esp. Jn 14–16) in which Jesus delivers teachings. The dialog was a well-established literary motif in Greco-Roman literature.

The narrative order exhibits differences from the Synoptics also (e.g., the temple incident in Jn 2), and the overall arrangement is distinctive (e.g., linkage of Jesus' movements with Jewish feasts) as is the vocabulary (e.g., "signs," "eternal life"). Nevertheless, John is much more easily compared with the other canonical Gospels than with any other type of ancient literature, non-Christian or Christian.

There are also interesting similarities between John and the Synoptic accounts in particular incidents such as the feeding account. The similarities show that common features were shared by different streams of the Jesus tradition. John seems to show also that the idea of a written narrative of Jesus' ministry suggested itself to more than one Christian independently in the latter decades of the first century. And it is likely that common factors, such as the general situation of the Christian movement at that time, plus, perhaps, the general literary climate, helped make the composition of a written account of Jesus' ministry seem an appropriate service to provide.

4. Conclusion.

Although there are numerous differences among them, the four canonical Gospels exhibit a basically similar type of Jesus literature: (1) connected narratives of his ministry, death and resurrection; (2) composed out of the Jesus tradition; (3) reflecting and serving early Christian proclamation; (4) intended for Christian readers and presupposing their beliefs and vocabulary. Their general formal characteristics and/or the beliefs they affirm set them apart from other early Christian literature, canonical and noncanonical, in varying ways and degrees. They thereby constitute a distinctive group of writings within early Christianity.

Similarities to other Greco-Roman narrative genres such as biography reflect the cultural setting in which the Gospels were written. The Greco-Roman genres provide partially analogous writings that help us understand better some particular features of the Gospels and may certainly help us see the literary expectations and categories through which non-Christian readers in particular may have viewed the Gospels. It is likely that the Evangelists consciously and, perhaps more often, unconsciously reflected features of Greco-Roman popular literature.

The Gospels are not fully explainable, however, simply in terms of the Greco-Roman literary setting or by linking them with literary genres of that era. The impetus for the Gospels derives from the religious complexion and needs of early Christianity, and their contents, presuppositions, major themes and literary texture are all heavily influenced by their immediate religious setting as well. In very general terms, the Gospels can be likened to other examples of Greco-Roman popular biography, but they also form a distinctive group within that broad body of ancient writings.

DNTB: APOCRYPHAL GOSPELS; BIOGRAPHY, ANCIENT; GENRES OF THE NEW TESTAMENT; SUETONIUS; TACITUS.

BIBLIOGRAPHY. D. E. Aune, *The New Testament in Its Literary Environment* (Philadelphia: Westminster, 1987); D. E. Aune, ed., *Greco-Roman Literature and the New Testament* (Atlanta: Scholars Press, 1988); G. G. Bilezikian, *The Liberated Gospel: A Comparison of the Gospel of Mark and Greek Tragedy* (Grand Rapids: Baker, 1977); R. A. Burridge, *What Are the Gospels? A Comparison with Greco-Roman Biography* (SNTSMS 70; Cambridge: Cambridge University Press, 1992); P. Cox, *Biography in Late Antiquity* (Berkeley: University of California Press, 1983); R. Guelich, "The Gospel Genre," in *The Gospel and the Gospels*, ed. P. Stuhlmacher (Grand Rapids: Eerdmans, 1991) 173-208; R. H. Gundry, "Recent Investigations into the Literary Genre 'Gospel' " in *New Dimensions in New Testament Study*, ed. R. N. Longenecker and M. C. Tenney (Grand Rapids: Zondervan, 1974) 97-114; H. C. Kee, "Aretalogies, Hellenistic 'Lives' and the Sources of Mark," in *Colloquy 12*, The Center for Hermeneutical Studies in Hellenistic and Modern Culture, ed. W. Wuellner (Berkeley, CA: Graduate Theological Union,1975); A. Momigliano, *The Development of Greek Biography* (Cambridge, MA: Harvard University Press, 1971); F. Overbeck, "Über die Aufänge der patristichen Literatur," *HZ* 12 (1882) 417-72; R. I. Pervo, *Profit with Delight: The Literary Genre of the Acts of the Apostles* (Philadelphia: Fortress, 1987); S. M. Praeder, "Luke-Acts and the Ancient Novel," *SBLSAP* (1981) 269-92; K. L. Schmidt, "Die Stellung der Evangelien in der allgemeinen Literaturgeschichte" in *Eucharisterion*, ed. H. Schmidt (Göttingen: Vandenhoeck & Ruprecht, 1923) 50-134; P. L. Shuler, *A Genre for the Gospels* (Philadelphia: Fortress, 1982); B. Standaert, *L'Evangileselon Marc: Composition et genre littéraire* (Bruge: Sint-Andriesabdijj, 1978); G. N. Stanton, *Jesus of Nazareth in New Testament Preaching* (SNTSMS 27; Cambridge: Cambridge University Press, 1974); C. H. Talbert, *What Is a Gospel?* (Philadelphia: Fortress, 1977); idem, "Biographies of Philosophers and Rulers as Instruments of Religious Propaganda in Mediterranean Antiquity" in *ANRW* 2, 16/2:1619-51; D. L. Tiede, "Religious Propaganda and the Gospel Literature of the Early Christian Mission" in *ANRW* 2, 25/2:1705-29; C. W. Votaw, *The Gospels and Contemporary Biographies in the Greco-Roman World* (Philadelphia: Fortress, 1970; reprint from *AJT* 19 [1915] 45-73, 217-49).
L. W. Hurtado

GOSPEL (GOOD NEWS). *See* KINGDOM OF GOD.

GOSPELS, HISTORICAL RELIABILITY OF

Different scholars come to widely divergent conclusions when they assess the historical reliability of the Gospels. About the only point on which virtually all are agreed is that the Gospels were written primarily for theological rather than historical purposes. In other words, Matthew, Mark, Luke and John above all wanted to commend their understanding of the person and work of Jesus to their first-century audiences. But most scholars also recognize that in order for the four Evangelists' representations of Jesus to be convincing, they had to match the course of events in his life. How much of a match is required and how much is actually present are questions that are both vigorously debated. This essay is written from the conviction that a fair assessment of the evidence supports a high degree of historicity. It must be stressed, however, that the Gospels have to be evaluated according to the historiographical canons of their day and not anachronistically compared with modern conceptions of what is and is not so-called reliable history.

1. External Evidence
2. Internal Evidence
3. Philosophical Considerations

1. External Evidence.

1.1. The Text of the Gospels. Non-Christian religions often allege that the Gospels as they now appear cannot be trusted because the text has been greatly corrupted. This allegation has virtually no evidence to support it. There are 2,328 manuscripts and manuscript fragments surviving from the earliest centuries of the Christian church and representing all portions of the Gospels. The earliest fragment of any portion of the NT currently in existence is the John Rylands papyrus fragment (P^{52}) of John 18:31-33, 37-38, which probably dates to about A.D. 125, or within about thirty years of the original composition of the Fourth Gospel. Twenty-one papyri containing major sections of one or more Gospels can be dated to the third and fourth centuries, while five virtually complete NTs survive from the fourth and fifth centuries. Compared with the numbers and ages of manuscripts that have survived for most other ancient documents, including many believed to contain reliable accounts of historical events, this evidence is overwhelming.

As a result, textual critics have been able to reconstruct a highly reliable prototype of what the original Gospel writers undoubtedly wrote. Estimates suggest that from 97 to 99 percent of the original text is securely recoverable. More than 54 percent of all of the verses in the Gospels are entirely free of textual variants, and the vast majority of those that remain have no bearing on questions of historicity. Modern editions of the Greek NT (Nestle-Aland; UBS) print the textual variants that have any significant effect on meaning, and most modern English translations use footnotes to alert readers to the most disputed texts (e.g., Mt 6:13b; Mk 16:9-20; Jn 7:53—8:11).

1.2. Archeology. Archeology has not played nearly as major a role in Gospel studies as it has for many other sections of Scripture. Occasionally the existence of previously unattested places or people has been demonstrated. For example, only in 1888 did the site of the pool of Bethesda become known (Jn 5:2), and excavations demonstrated that it contained five porticoes as described by John. So too, in 1961 the first reference in Roman sources to "Pontius Pilate, Prefect of Judea" was discovered in an inscription in Caesarea Maritimis. But for the most part, the type of information that the Gospels contain—narratives of actions and teachings of Jesus—do not lend themselves to archeological corroboration or contradiction. Since no one was able to tape-record them, there are no physical traces by which one can test the trustworthiness of the Gospel record.

1.3. Written Testimony Outside the Gospels. Virtually all biblical scholars acknowledge that there is enough information from ancient non-Christian sources to give lie to the myth (still, however, widely believed in popular circles and by some scholars in other fields—see esp. G. A. Wells) that claims that Jesus never existed. Most also recognize that only a paucity of the testimony of the Gospels can be corroborated by a comparison with other materials. Given that Jesus was not perceived by non-Christians as a significant political or military leader, this is not surprising. Ancient historians had little reason to consider that centuries later he would prove significant; even as the founder of a religious movement, he had little impact during his lifetime.

1.3.1. Greco-Roman Testimony. The third-century writer Julius Africanus cites a first-century Greek historian, Thallus, who referred to the darkness that occurred at the time of the crucifixion. Early in the second century the Roman legate Pliny the Younger wrote that Christians met regularly and sang hymns to Christ "as if to a god" (Pliny *Epp.* 10.96.7), in a way that suggested he realized that Jesus had been a human but doubted that he was a god. About the same time the Roman historian Tacitus clearly referred to "Christ who had been executed by sentence of the procurator Pontius Pilate in the reign of Tiberius" (Tacitus *Ann.* 15.44). Tacitus's Roman contemporary Suetonius speaks in one passage of "Chrestus" as the one at whose instigation a riot involving Jews and Christians in Rome broke out (Suetonius *Claudius* 25.4)—probably a garbled reference to Christ as the founder of Christianity.

1.3.2. Jewish Testimony. Jewish literature from the first centuries of the Christian era contains additional references to Jesus. Some have been censored, so once there were probably even more than now remain. A famous passage in the Talmud speaks of Jesus as "the Nazarene" who "practiced magic and led Israel astray" (*b. Sanh.* 107b). This reference is particularly interesting because it seems to admit that Jesus worked miracles, even though its interpretation of them differs from Christian belief. In several places Jesus is called the son of Pandera; the second-century Christian writer Origen explained that the Jews believed that Jesus was the child of Mary by an adulterous relationship with a Roman soldier by that name (Origen *Contra Celsum* 1.32). The name and legend could well have come from a corruption of the Greek word *parthenos* for "virgin" and thus provide indirect though corrupt testimony to the Gospels' claim that Jesus was not the natural child of Joseph but was virgin-conceived (*see* Birth of Jesus).

Again in the Talmud (*b. Sanh.* 43a) Jesus is said to have been hanged on the eve of the Passover. This text also teaches that "Jesus had five disciples, Mattha, Naqai, Nezer, Buni and Todah," possible references to Matthew, Nicodemus, an anonymous Nazarene, John and Thaddeus.

The most interesting of all of the Jewish testimonies to Jesus is the account in Josephus (*Ant.* 18.63-64). Here one learns that Jesus was a wise man who wrought surprising feats, taught many, gathered a large following and was crucified by Pilate. Extant copies of Josephus's writings also affirm that Jesus was the Messiah and that he was raised from the dead. Because Josephus was not a Christian, few people believe that he actually wrote these words; they may well have been added by scribes in later Christian circles that preserved his work. But the rest of his statements fit his style elsewhere and are most likely authentic. Josephus also offers independent corroboration of the ministry of John the Baptist (Josephus *Ant.* 18.117) and of James, the brother of Jesus (Josephus *Ant.* 20.200).

1.3.3. Other Christian Testimony. Outside the New Testament various apocryphal Gospels present additional teachings and deeds of Christ. Some of these are clearly legendary attempts to fill in the gaps in the Gospel record—stories of Jesus the child prodigy (e.g., the *Infancy Gospel of Thomas* and the *Protevangelium of James*) or additional details concerning his trial, death, descent into hell and resurrection (e.g., the *Gospel of Nicodemus* and the *Gospel of Peter*). Many emanate from Gnostic circles and purport to reveal secret teachings of Christ, often spoken after his resurrection in private conversation with the disciples (e.g., the *Apocryphon of John* and the *Dialogue of the Savior*). Two of these contain some sayings attributed to Jesus and often believed to be authentic, or at least as trust worthy as parts of the canonical Gospels (the Coptic *Gospel of Thomas* and the *Apocryphon of James*). But none of these extracanonical writings can be shown to date from before the mid-second century, so that the trustworthiness of the NT Gospels, which date from the first century, is in no way impugned. Though widely disputed, those documents from the Gnostic library at Nag Hammadi (esp. the Coptic *Gospel of Thomas*) that contain teachings of Jesus most closely paralleled in the NT are precisely those that are most clearly dependent on and inferior to the Synoptic Gospels (see Blomberg in *Gospel Perspectives*, vol. 5; Tuckett).

It has often been observed how little the Acts, epistles and Revelation reflect any awareness of the Gospel tradition. Only rarely is a teaching of Jesus quoted (but see Acts 20:35; 1 Cor 7:10; 9:14; 11:23-25; 1 Tim 5:18). Nevertheless, the epistles are filled with numerous allusions to Jesus' teaching (e.g., Rom 12:14; 12:17; 13:8-9; 14:10; 16:9; 1 Thess 2:14-16; 5:2), which suggests that such awareness was much more widespread than a superficial survey of Scripture discloses (see Stanton). The book of James contains allusions to the Sermon on the Mount in nearly every paragraph, while Acts reflects the basic outline of Mark in several of the longer speeches that summarize the gospel as preached by Peter and Paul (in Acts 10:36-41 and Acts 13:24-25 even more specific details are included).

1.4. Authorship. Many people have tried to assess the historicity of the Gospels in light of their authorship. It is often assumed that if the traditional ascriptions are correct, then these writers would have reflected firsthand eyewitness testimony in the case of Matthew and John, and secondhand in the case of Luke (cf. Lk 1:1-4). If the ascriptions are incorrect, as most modern scholars believe, then it is often assumed that the Gospels' historicity is impugned. But in fact eyewitnesses can err, accidentally or deliberately, while secondary sources can preserve accurate information reliably transmitted to them. For these reasons, the value of the debate over authorship for questions of historicity has probably been exaggerated.

Strictly speaking, the four Gospels are anonymous documents. The titles were added later, probably early in the second century when the texts were first gathered together as four versions of the one gospel. But the virtually unanimous early Christian testimony that associates them with Matthew, Mark, Luke and John (see, e.g., Eusebius *Hist. Eccl.* 3:39.4, 16; Irenaeus *Adv. Haer.* 3:1.1-2) should be treated very seriously. And even scholars who see the Gospels as written by anonymous Christians almost always date them within the first century. This is certainly well within a time period that would have permitted accurate information about the life and times of Jesus to have been preserved, even if it in no way guarantees such preservation.

1.5. Sources. An author, however close in time to the events he or she describes, is nevertheless only as reliable as his or her sources. The most common reconstruction of the literary interrelationship of the Synoptic Gospels has Matthew and Luke depending on at least two written sources—Mark and *Q, a hypothetical document accounting for material Matthew and Luke have in common which is not found in Mark (*see* Synoptic Problem). Q is usually dated to the 50s, and Mark is assumed to have utilized source material at least that old. With Christ's crucifixion no earlier than A.D. 30, the time gap between events and written accounts is reduced to about twenty years, a far cry from the centuries that were usually necessary for supernatural legends to attach themselves to other historical characters from antiquity (see Stein).

1.6. Oral Tradition. Any time lag between events and their recording allows for potential distortion. Despite all of the external evidence so far cited, many scholars doubt the reliability of the Gospels because they doubt either the ability or the interest of early Christians to have preserved accurately the story of Jesus' ministry as they passed it along by word of mouth. Several factors, however, support the likelihood that the Gospel tradition was carefully preserved.

(1) Jesus was perceived by his followers as one who proclaimed God's Word in a way that demanded careful retelling. (2) Over 90 percent of his teachings has poetic elements that would have made them easy to memorize. (3) The almost universal method of education in antiquity, and especially in Israel, was rote memorization, which enabled people accurately to recount quantities of material far greater than all of the Gospels put together. (4) Oral storytelling often permitted a wide range of freedom in selecting and describing details but required fixed points of a narrative to be preserved unchanged. (5) Written notes and a kind of shorthand were often privately kept by rabbis and their disciples, despite a publicly stated preference for oral tradition. (6) The lack of teachings ascribed to Jesus about later church controversies (e.g., circumcision, speaking in tongues) suggests that the disciples did not freely invent material and read it back onto the lips of Jesus. (7) The degree to which Jesus emphasized his imminent return, that is, to the exclusion of envisioning the establishment of an ongoing community of followers, has been exaggerated. Hence, the claim that the disciples would have had no interest in preserving the Gospel tradition until the second generation of Christianity is doubtful.

2. Internal Evidence.

2.1. The Intentions of the Evangelists. Gospel studies have often introduced a false dichotomy between history and theology. One group of scholars seeks to harmonize all of the data of the four Gospels in order to create a composite, comprehensive life of Christ that blurs the unique emphases of each Gospel in its own right. Another group so emphasizes the theological distinctives of each individual Evangelist that it rejects the possibility of constructing any kind of plausible harmony. The two clearest statements in the Gospels about their authors' intentions suggest that history and theology both played important roles (Lk 1:1-4; Jn 20:31). In fact, it is often precisely when one recognizes the theological emphases of a particular Gospel that one can understand why it differs from the others and can see those differences as complementary rather than contradictory.

Various studies of the Gospel genre (*see* Gospel [Genre]) have linked Matthew, Mark, Luke and John with apocalyptic, aretalogy (a Greco-Roman story of a divine man), tragedy or comedy, midrash (a Jewish form of interpretive rewriting of authoritative narrative) or parable, while many have viewed the Gospel as a new genre invented by Mark. But probably the best approach sees important parallels with the more historically reliable Jewish and Greco-Roman biographies and histories (see esp. Aune).

Ancient biographers and historians did not feel constrained to write from detached and so-called objective viewpoints. They did not give equal treatment to all periods of an individual's life. They felt free to write in topical as well as chronological sequence. They were highly selective in the material they included, choosing that which reinforced the morals they wished to inculcate. In an era that knew neither quotation marks nor plagiarism, speakers' words were abbreviated, explained, paraphrased and contemporized in whatever ways individual authors deemed beneficial for their audiences. All of these features occur in the Gospels, and none of them detracts from the Evangelists' integrity. At the same time, little if any material was recorded solely out of historical interest; interpreters must recognize theological motives as central to each text.

2.2. A Comparison of the Synoptics.

2.2.1. Agreement. The most striking feature one notices in comparing Matthew, Mark and

Luke is their similarity. Approximately 91 percent (c. 601 out of 661 verses) of Mark's information reappears in Matthew or Luke, and usually in both. An additional 235 verses appear in some form in both Matthew and Luke but not in Mark. Approximately 68 percent of the self-contained units of narrative common to Mark and either Matthew or Luke appear in the same sequence in each. Given the wealth of detail that could have been told about Jesus, the fact that these three Evangelists chose to follow such similar outlines (and almost certainly to borrow from one another in some kind of literary interrelationship) suggests that a relatively fixed manner of telling the gospel originated at an early date in the life of the church. This common *kerygma* ("proclamation") clearly enhances the case for the Gospels' historical reliability.

2.2.2. Disagreement. Nevertheless, numerous differences among the Synoptics appear whenever parallel accounts are laid side by side. For many critics these differences are of such a nature and number that no amount of external evidence can convince them of the Gospels' trustworthiness. Yet most of the differences are so minor that it seems unfair to refer to them as contradictions. Historians and biographers regularly add, omit or reword stories and portions of stories without necessarily falsifying them. At the same time, there are a handful of more glaring discrepancies that puzzle all readers. But plausible solutions have been suggested for all of them; fair-minded scholars must at least consider credible harmonizations before dismissing the whole process as impossible. In many instances it is precisely when one understands the varying theological concerns of the different Evangelists that one can appreciate how apparently discrepant accounts are complementary rather than contradictory (see Blomberg in Carson and Woodbridge). The following survey offers a representative sampling of seven major types of problems that appear, a few of the most famous illustrations of those problems and some possible solutions.

(1) The theologies of the Evangelists may seem to conflict. Mark portrays the disciples as without understanding following Jesus' walking on the water (Mk 6:52); Matthew has them worship him as the Son of God (Mt 14:33). In Mark, after stilling the storm, Jesus berates the disciples for their lack of faith (Mk 4:40); in Matthew he concedes that they have "a little faith" (Mt

8:26). Both tendencies are credible in light of the disciples' mixture of faith and disbelief elsewhere, and each fits into distinctive emphases of the Gospels in which they appear.

(2) One Evangelist may seem to correct his source. In Mark, Jesus' reply to the so-called rich young ruler seems to deny his goodness (Mk 10:18); Matthew rewords the comment so that Jesus merely inquires, "Why do you ask me about the good?" (Mt 19:17). Matthew is not contradicting Mark but trying to avoid a misinterpretation of him. Similarly, Luke reports Jesus as telling his followers to hate their parents (Lk 14:26); Matthew explains that this means they must love God much more than family (Mt 10:37).

(3) Events may appear in contradictory orders in different Gospels. Luke places Jesus' rejection in Nazareth at the beginning of his Galilean ministry (Lk 4:16-30); Mark locates it much later (Mk 6:1-6). Usually, it is best not to assume chronology unless it is explicitly indicated. Luke has topically relocated this story at the front of his Gospel to show the type of rejection Jesus would receive from his native people throughout his ministry. In the same way, Luke reverses the order of the second and third temptations of Christ to build toward a climax with Jesus in the temple in Jerusalem (Lk 4:1-13; cf. Mt 4:1-11). Both of these are key themes throughout his work.

(4) A passage may be so abbreviated that it seems to contradict a fuller parallel. Mark has Jairus and his companions come to Jesus twice, once to tell him of his daughter's illness and once to say that she has died (Mk 5:21-43). Matthew so compresses the account that Jairus comes only once and tells Jesus at the outset of the story that his daughter is dead (Mt 9:18-26). This type of literary abridgment was common in antiquity and not perceived as misleading or in error (cf. Lucian *How to Write History* 56). Similar telescoping appears in Matthew's account of the withered fig tree (Mt 21:18-22; cf. Mk 11:12-14, 20-21) and in Luke's account of Jesus' trial before the Sanhedrin, if Luke is not in fact using a different tradition altogether, rather than Mark (Lk 22:66-71; cf. Mk 14:53—15:1).

(5) Sayings of Jesus may appear in different contexts. The Sermon on the Mount (Mt 5—7) and the Olivet Discourse (Mt 24—25) gather together teachings that are scattered all around the Gospel of Luke. Some of these may simply

reflect Jesus' repeated utterances; others no doubt reflect the common practice of creating composite speeches. Again, no one questioned the integrity of ancient historians when they utilized a device that modern readers often find artificial. Yet again, both sermons may be excerpts of a much longer original.

(6) A unique event may be told twice in apparently contradictory ways. Many scholars see the feedings of the five thousand and the four thousand (Mk 6:32-44; 8:1-10) or the two anointings of Jesus (Lk 7:36-50; Mk 14:3-9) as doublets of the same events. In each case, these are probably better viewed as separate incidents.

(7) Names and numbers may appear to contradict each other. In Matthew Jesus heals two blind men along the Jericho road (Mt 20:30); in Mark he heals one (Mk 10:46). The latter does not exclude the former. In Mark Jesus exorcises a demoniac in the region near Gerasa (Mk 5:1); in Matthew it occurs in Gadara (Mt 8:28). The former is probably a city; the latter, a province.

2.3. The Synoptics and John. The Fourth Gospel stands out as distinct from the Synoptics in at least five principal ways. (1) Most of John's material is unparalleled in Matthew, Mark and Luke, and only rarely does a passage common to the first three Gospels reappear in John. (2) John seems to have a much higher *christology; only in his Gospel do explicit equations of Jesus with God ever appear (e.g., Jn 1:1; 10:30; 20:28). (3) The chronologies of John and the Synoptics are difficult to harmonize. Especially noteworthy are John's references to Jewish festivals, which indicate Jesus had at least a three-year ministry traveling back and forth between Judea and Galilee (in the Synoptics Jesus seems to visit Jerusalem for the first time the week before his death) and to the day of his crucifixion (apparently on Passover rather than the day after as in the Synoptics). (4) Other historical anachronisms seem to abound, most notably the reference to Jewish excommunication of Christians from the synagogues (Jn 9:22). (5) John's writing style differs markedly from that of the Synoptics; Jesus' language is indistinguishable from John's and Christ speaks in lengthy discourses rather than pithy aphorisms. As a result, even scholars who grant a substantial measure of historical reliability to the Synoptics usually view John as having so overlaid his material with theological interpretation that the Fourth Gospel has become largely worthless for the reconstruction of the historical Jesus.

However, major themes of John include the revelation of truth (see esp. Jn 19:35), the incarnation of the Logos in space and time (Jn 1:14) and the inspiration of the apostles by the Holy Spirit to enable them to remember what Jesus did and said (Jn 14:26; 15:26). John would undermine his own theological emphases if his historical information were in error. He must be given an opportunity to be viewed as reliable before he is assumed to be untrustworthy.

Each of the five distinctives noted above must be set in a proper context. (1) Information is no less reliable for not being multiply attested. John probably wrote either to supplement the Synoptics or in independence from them; either way he was not likely to repeat much of their material (Jn 21:25). (2) The Synoptics certainly know of Jesus' divine status even if it is not emphasized (Mt 1:18; Lk 1:35; Mk 14:62), while John also underlines Jesus' subordination to the Father (Jn 14:28). The christologies differ but do not contradict each other. (3) The Synoptics do not preclude a three-year ministry or additional visits to Jerusalem. The evidence suggesting Jesus' crucifixion on Passover in John (esp. Jn 13:1; 18:28; 19:14, 31) is better taken as referring to the week-long Passover festival rather than just the first day of that feast. (4) Closer analysis dispels allegations of anachronism. The reference to putting Jesus' disciples out of the synagogue does not refer to practice outside of Jerusalem or to any formal ban on Christians as occurred toward the end of the first century. (5) Historical accuracy does not require exact quotation, merely faithful paraphrase. John's extended discourses may reflect homiletical development of the teachings of Jesus, shorter parallels to which may usually be found in the Synoptics (cf. e.g., Jn 3:3 with Mk 10:15). They also often represent private teaching for the disciples, whereas the Synoptics tend to focus more on his public ministry. There is no doubt that history and theology are interwoven in more complex fashion in John, but once it is recognized that he is utilizing a more dramatic genre (see esp. Michaels), a good case can be made for the historical trustworthiness of the Fourth Gospel within the conventions of its genre (see Blomberg 2001; Robinson).

3. Philosophical Considerations.

3.1. Miracles and the Supernatural. For many readers the historicity of the Gospels is called into question simply because they are filled with *miracle stories about the supernatural deeds of Christ. Disbelief in the miracles usually stems from any one of three different objections. (1) Philosophers of science often allege that modern science has proved the impossibility of the supernatural. (2) Philosophers of history often argue that the evidence in favor of a miracle can never outweigh the evidence against it, so that a rational person may never conclude that testimony in behalf of a supernatural event is reliable. Unless someone has personally experienced the same kind of miracle, there is always a more likely explanation for someone else's claim that one has occurred. (3) Philosophers of religion often compare the miracle stories in the Gospels with those in other ancient religious and philosophical traditions and believe that all are equally suspect.

In fact, none of these claims can withstand close scrutiny. First, the proper domain of science is the realm of the repeatable, predictable and verifiable. Miracles by definition are nonrepeatable events. If there is a theistic God such as the Judeo-Christian tradition has affirmed, miracles are a natural corollary of his existence. Whether or not such a God exists cannot be determined by science. Second, personal experience is not a reliable criterion for determining truth. By that criterion evidence against the existence of ice would always demand that a primitive person in a tropical climate disbelieve it. Third, the testimony on behalf of other ancient miracles is usually not as strong, as consistent or as religiously significant as it is in the Gospels. Nevertheless, there is no reason to deny altogether the possibility of the miraculous in certain other ancient settings.

For many philosophers and theologians, the issue of the Gospels' credibility rests ultimately with the accounts of Jesus' resurrection. Several alternatives have been put forward to explain the origin of belief in the risen Lord. Those which have largely been abandoned in scholarly circles include the views that (1) Jesus never really died on the cross but later revived; (2) his body was stolen; (3) the women went to the wrong tomb and found it empty; and (4) mass hallucination.

More common is some form of the view that the disciples' belief in the abiding significance of Jesus' message and goals convinced them that he was still alive spiritually and that this belief

eventually became transformed, in Jewish categories, into the idea of a bodily resurrection. Had the Gospel begun in Hellenistic circles and later been transformed by Judaism, this view might be credible. But the direction of development was precisely the reverse. From the very outset belief in an empty tomb, and therefore a raised body, formed part of the Gospel tradition (see esp. 1 Cor 15:3-7), and in Jewish circles mere immortality of the soul was seldom affirmed. As long as one rejects a priori antisupernatural prejudices, the evidence may be seen to support a bodily resurrection of Jesus. All the proposed alternatives are even more incredible (see Ladd).

3.2 The Burden of Proof. Notwithstanding all of the evidence in favor of the general trustworthiness of the Gospels, many critics find little they can confidently endorse because they adopt a skeptical stance on the issue of the burden of proof. That is to say, they assume that each portion of the Gospels is suspect and reverse that verdict only when overwhelming evidence points to historical reliability. But this method inverts standard procedures of historical investigation; it applies more rigorous criteria to the biblical material than students of ancient history ever apply elsewhere.

Once a historian has proved reliable where verifiable, once apparent errors or contradictions receive plausible solutions, the appropriate approach is to give that writer the benefit of the doubt in areas where verification is not possible (see Goetz and Blomberg). Neither external nor internal testimony can prove the accuracy of most of the details of the Gospels; the necessary comparative data simply are lacking. But the coherence and consistency of material that cannot be tested with that which can be tested goes a long way toward inspiring confidence in the remaining portions of the texts.

See also BIRTH OF JESUS; GOSPEL (GENRE); MIRACLES, MIRACLE STORIES; RESURRECTION; TRIAL OF JESUS.

DJG: FORM CRITICISM; HISTORICAL JESUS, QUEST OF; REDACTION CRITICISM; SYNOPTIC PROBLEM; SYNOPTICS AND JOHN; TRADITION CRITICISM.

BIBLIOGRAPHY. K. Aland and B. Aland, *The Text of the New Testament* (Grand Rapids: Eerdmans, 1987); D. E. Aune, *The New Testament in Its Literary Environment* (Philadelphia: Westminster, 1987); C. L. Blomberg, *The Historical Reli-*

ability of the Gospels (Downers Grove, IL: InterVarsity Press, 1987); idem, *The Historical Reliability of John's Gospel* (Downers Grove, IL: InterVarsity Press, 2001); D. A. Carson and J. D. Woodbridge, eds., *Hermeneutics, Authority and Canon* (Grand Rapids: Zondervan, 1983); J. D. G. Dunn, *The Evidence for Jesus* (Philadelphia: Westminster, 1985); R. T. France, *The Evidence for Jesus* (Downers Grove, IL: InterVarsity Press, 1986); R. T. France, D. Wenham and C. Blom-berg, eds., *Gospel Perspectives* (6 vols.; Sheffield: JSOT, 1980-86); S. C. Goetz and C. L. Blomberg, "The Burden of Proof," *JSNT* 11 (1981) 39-63; G. R. Habermas, *Ancient Evidence for the Life of Jesus* (Nashville: Thomas Nelson, 1984); G. E. Ladd, *I Believe in the Resurrection of Jesus* (Grand Rapids: Eerdmans, 1975); R. Latourelle, *Finding Jesus Through the Gospels* (New York: Alba, 1979); idem, *The Miracles of Jesus and the Theology of Miracles* (New York: Paulist, 1988); I. H. Marshall, *I Believe in the Historical Jesus* (Grand Rapids: Eerdmans, 1977); J. R. Michaels, *Servant and Son* (Atlanta: John Knox, 1981); R. Riesner, *Jesus als Lehrer* (Tübingen: Mohr, 1981); J. A. T. Robinson, *The Priority of John* (London: SCM, 1985); G. N. Stanton, *Jesus of Nazareth in New Testament Preaching* (Cambridge: Cambridge University Press, 1974); R. H. Stein, *The Synoptic Problem* (Grand Rapids: Baker, 1987); C. M. Tuckett, *Nag Hammadi and the Gospel Tradition* (Edinburgh: T & T Clark, 1986); idem, "Thomas and the Synoptics," *NovT* 30 (1988) 132-57; G. H. Twelftree, *Jesus the Miracle Worker* (Downers Grove, IL: InterVarsity Press, 1999); G. A. Wells, *The Historical Evidence for Jesus* (New York: Prometheus, 1982); N. T. Wright, *The New Testament and the People of God* (Minneapolis: Fortress, 1992). C. L. Blomberg

GREAT HIGH PRIEST. *See* DEATH OF CHRIST III.

GRIESBACH HYPOTHESIS. *See* SYNOPTIC PROBLEM.

GUILT. *See* SIN.

H

HEAD COVERINGS. *See* WOMEN II.

HEADSHIP. *See* WOMEN II.

HEALING. *See* MIRACLES, MIRACLE STORIES.

HEBREWS, LETTER TO THE

Hebrews is a richly textured discourse addressed to a group of Christians who were experiencing a crisis of faith and a failure of nerve. The intended audience was almost certainly the members of a house church with a history of fidelity to Christ (Heb 10:32-34). These facts may be gleaned from the surface of the text. Although the character and location of the community addressed, the precise nature of the crisis to which Hebrews is a response, the circumstances and date of its composition, the literary genre of the discourse, and the purpose and plan of the work continue to be debated vigorously, no broad consensus has been reached.

All texts pose the challenge of reconstructing history from them. The only rational means by which this can be achieved is historical methodology, in which the historian's intuition is an essential component. This is particularly true in the case of Hebrews, which is distinctive in form and complex in literary structure. The early tradition concerning its authorship, purpose and intended audience is conflicting and unreliable. The evidence provided by the text lends itself to divergent interpretations. Any historical reconstruction must be proposed as tentative and exploratory in nature.

Patient interaction with the text and with the discussion it has prompted, especially during recent decades, supports the opinion that Hebrews is a sermon in response to circumstances in the life of the audience. The sermon throbs with an awareness of the privilege and the cost of Christian discipleship. It proves to be a sensitive pastoral response to the sagging faith of seasoned and weary individuals who were in danger of abandoning their Christian commitments. The writer sought to strengthen them in the face of a new crisis so that they would hold fast to their confession and stand firm in their faith. He warned them of the judgment of God they would incur if they were to falter in their commitments. His exhortations to covenant faithfulness and unwavering perseverance were grounded in a fresh presentation of the significance of Jesus and his sacrificial death. As high priest and Son of God in solidarity with the human family, he is the supreme exemplar of faithfulness to God and of endurance, whose death on the cross secured for his people unlimited access to God and the assurance of divine help that arrives at the appropriate time.

1. Authorship
2. Audience
3. Circumstances and Date of Composition
4. Integrity
5. Genre
6. Literary Structural Devices
7. Purpose and Plan
8. Structural Function of Old Testament Texts
9. Canonical Recognition
10. Concluding Observations

1. Authorship.

Hebrews is anonymous, and the identity of the author has been veiled from the earliest period of the church. Although it has been suggested that the author was Priscilla or some other woman, we are well advised to refer to the author as "he" in light of the masculine ending of the participle in Hebrews 11:32. The writer was known to the community he addressed (Heb 13:19), but the brief personal notes in Hebrews

13 are not specific enough to reveal his identity.

The author clearly was not Paul, though presumably he moved within the Pauline circle and expected to travel with Timothy (Heb 13:23). He classed himself as one who had not heard the Lord deliver the message of salvation (Heb 2:3-4). He was capable of writing some of the finest Greek in the NT, far superior in vocabulary and sentence construction to that of Paul. He also employs a distinctive range of images that are not found in Paul (Heb 2:1; 4:12, 13; 6:7-8, 19) and moves easily within the conceptual world of priesthood and sacrifice, emphases that are foreign to Paul's letters.

Among early church traditions we find the author of Hebrews identified as Paul, Barnabas, Luke or Clement of Rome. Contemporary scholars have suggested Apollos, Silvanus, the deacon Philip, Priscilla and Aquila, Jude, Aristion, and others (see Moffatt). This variety of opinion shows that the limits of our historical knowledge preclude any certainty regarding the writer's identity. We are left to conclude that Hebrews was composed by a creative theologian, one well trained in the art of expounding the Greek Scriptures, whose thought world was shaped by and whose vocabulary, traditions and theological conceptions were indebted to Hellenistic Judaism and the early Hellenistic church.

We may draw a number of plausible inferences regarding the author from the composition of Hebrews. He was structured in his thought patterns, stating a thesis and then developing it through analysis. His reasoning powers were exceptional, as illustrated by the majestic opening sentence (Heb 1:1-4) that sets the program for the entire discourse. He was evidently trained in rhetoric and understood speech as a medium of power to be used in the service of the gospel. He was able to deploy a rich vocabulary (169 of his 1,038 different words are found in the NT only in Hebrews) and a cultured diction. He had confidence in the persuasive power of oral speech as it is committed to the written text.

The writer's educational level may be compared with that of Philo of Alexandria and probably reflects training in a gymnasium or a private rhetorical school. Luke's description of Apollos as "an eloquent man" (Acts 18:24), a designation associated with formal rhetorical training and so used by Philo (see Philo *Poster. C.* 53; *Leg. Gai.* 142, 237, 310; *Vit. Mos.* 1.2), has

suggested to many scholars that Apollos was the author of Hebrews.

The writer was an intensely devout man whose subconscious mind was steeped in the cultic categories and language of the Septuagint. He was also a pastoral theologian who shaped early Christian tradition into an urgent appeal to a community in crisis. He was a gifted preacher and interpreter of salvation, a covenant theologian whose spiritual insight, scriptural exegesis and situational discernment provided encouragement, admonition and pastoral direction. He presents himself as a charismatic leader whose effectiveness did not depend on office or title. He at best wrote reluctantly, shaping his "word of exhortation" (Heb 13:22) as an effective substitute for his personal presence and immediate address. Our encounter with his discourse is fragmentary, for he does not present himself to us as he would have to his contemporaries.

2. Audience.

The attempt to establish a social and historical context for Hebrews is important for understanding its place within the life of an early Christian congregation. We must first sketch a profile of the audience on the basis of the evidence of the text.

2.1. The Audience in Profile. Hebrews was written with a specific local assembly in mind. The author is able to distinguish this assembly from its leaders and from other congregations in their social setting (Heb 13:17, 24), which was almost certainly an urban center (cf. Heb 13:14). This is borne out by the paraenetic concerns expressed in Hebrews 13:1-6, all of which are appropriate within an urban setting: hospitality to Christian "strangers" (Heb 13:2), empathetic "remembering" of Christians imprisoned or suffering ill treatment (Heb 13:3), concern for the sanctity of marriage and for sexual purity (Heb 13:4), and caution against greed and crass materialism (Heb 13:5-6).

The assembly was probably a house church (note "house" or "household" of God in Heb 3:6; 10:21) meeting in an ordinary room in a private home or apartment complex *(insula)*. The group was small, perhaps numbering no more than fifteen or twenty persons, though it was probably part of a larger network of local assemblies scattered throughout the city. Their numbers had recently been depleted through defections (Heb 10:25).

The roots of the congregation may be traced to a Hellenistic synagogue in the Jewish quarters of the city. Their primary source of authority is the Hebrew Bible in an old Greek version. Their familiarity with the biblical narratives makes it possible for the writer to refer to the story of Esau without elaboration (Heb 12:17). In the opening lines of Hebrews the writer can presume to establish contact by presenting the transcendent *Son of God in the distinctive vocabulary associated with divine *Wisdom in the traditions of Hellenistic Judaism of the Diaspora (cf. Wis 7:24-27)

Their spiritual, intellectual and social nurture in the Hellenistic synagogue is further borne out by the allusion to angels as the heavenly mediators of the old revelation (Heb 2:2). This notion, absent from Exodus 19—20 but hinted at in Deuteronomy 33:2 (cf. Ps 68:17), gained acceptance sometime prior to the first century and spread among Hellenistic Jews (cf. Acts 7:38, 53; Gal 3:19; Josephus *Ant.* 15.5.3 §136). The centrality of the figure of Moses in Hebrews corresponds with the veneration of Moses in Hellenistic Judaism (see *The Exodus* by the Hellenistic Jewish writer Ezekiel the Tragedian, preserved by Eusebius *Praep. Ev.* 9.29; and Philo *Vit. Mos.* 2.66-186; *Rer. Div. Her.* 182; *Praem. Poen.* 53, 56). In the Hellenistic Jewish tradition, Moses is the supreme exemplar of perfection because of his unique access to the unmediated presence of God, a feature that would explain Hebrews's sustained comparison of Moses and Jesus (see, e.g., Heb 3:1-6; 8:3-5; 12:18-29; 13:20).

2.2. Their Past Commitment and Present Crisis. The writer is well acquainted with the previous experience of his readers (see Heb 2:2-4; 5:11-14; 6:9-11; 10:32-34; 12:4; 13:7). They had been brought to faith through the preaching of some who had direct access to Jesus' ministry (Heb 2:3), and the testimony of these witnesses had been endorsed by the tangible evidence of "signs and wonders," "various miracles," and "gifts of the Holy Spirit" (Heb 2:4). The community's reception of the spoken word and their experience of the "powers of the age to come" (Heb 6:5) had confirmed that, as with Israel, God had constituted this Christian community by an act of revelation.

Those who first proclaimed the gospel to the community had become its first leaders (Heb 13:7). And although these first charismatic leaders were now deceased, the community's present response to their original proclamation is of utmost concern: "We must pay the closest attention, therefore, to what we have heard, so that we do not drift off course" (Heb 2:1).

Hebrews 2:1-4 is the first in a series of sections that addresses the audience in the light of their current situation (see Heb 3:7-4:13; 5:11—6:12; 10:19-39; 12:14-29). These sections form pauses in the discourse and are characterized by stern warning or urgent appeal. As such they also provide a window on the social and historical setting of Hebrews. The admonition in Hebrews 2:1-4, for example, implies that the readers had grown lax in their commitment to the basic Christian message of salvation, a situation that severely threatened the stability and integrity of the community. They are summoned to recognize the solemn import of the message and reaffirm their allegiance to it.

Throughout Hebrews the writer is pastorally concerned that the community might falter in its response to the claim of God upon their lives, a concern that extends to individual members (Heb 3:12, 13; 4:1, 11; 6:11; 12:15). The congregation was most likely varied in its experience, disposition and maturity (cf. Heb 12:13, 15), and the admonition to "encourage one another every day" (Heb 3:13) may presuppose a daily gathering of the household fellowship as the occasion for mutual encouragement.

The paraenetic unity of Hebrews 5:11—6:12 sheds further light on the circumstances. In Hebrews 5:11 the group is charged with spiritual lethargy ("you have become sluggish in understanding" [or, "hard of hearing"]), and this becomes the occasion for a resumed stress on the importance of listening to the voice of God (cf. Heb 2:1; 3:7-8, 15; 4:1-2, 7). This spiritual inertia and apathy must be checked before it undercuts their faith, hope and obedience.

The indictment of Hebrews 5:12, "You are at the stage of needing milk and not solid food," is probably ironical. Although interpreters often understand this as the author's considered estimation of his readers' current condition, this is difficult to reconcile with his determination to respond to them as mature believers (Heb 6:1, 3). It is more likely that he is employing biting irony to call them to acknowledge their maturity and thus reckon with their ethical, theological and social responsibilities as Christians in an urban society.

In Hebrews 5:13 the community is described as "unskilled in the word of righteousness." The meaning of this expression is unlocked by Polycarp's use of this precise expression in *Letter to the Philippians* 9.1, where, as in Hebrews, it is associated with a call to endurance. For Polycarp the "word of righteousness" is the paramount lesson in holiness that Christians must be prepared for the cost of discipleship, even if that cost extends to martyrdom. The use of the phrase in Hebrews 5:13 suggests that the threat of renewed suffering, perhaps even of martyrdom, has brought about a crisis of faith and a failure of nerve. In Hebrews 10:32-34 the writer appeals to their past and valiant commitment to Christ and to one another under the pressure of public abuse as a paradigm for their responding to renewed perils. But the indelible memory of past suffering and loss may account for some now deserting the assembly (Heb 10:25) and a general inclination to avoid contact with outsiders (Heb 5:12).

The likelihood of this threat of persecution is enhanced by the catalog of martyrs in Hebrews 11:35-38, crowned with the reference to Jesus, who endured a cross, disregarding the shame of crucifixion (Heb 12:2-3; 13:12). The use of agonistic (i.e., conflict-oriented) vocabulary is intentional (Heb 12:4), for it prepares readers to risk public identification with Jesus, bearing the shame he bore (Heb 13:12-13).

2.3. Their Social Location. Proposals for locating the audience have ranged from Jerusalem in the East to Spain in the West. But there are good reasons for placing them in or around Rome. The only NT parallel to "Those from Italy greet you" (Heb 13:24) is found in Acts 18:2. There the phrase "from Italy" is used of Aquila and Priscilla, who were currently in Corinth and had departed "from Italy," namely, Rome, because of the Claudian expulsion (see 3.3 below). Thus the most natural way of reading Hebrews 13:24 is as a greeting from certain Italian Christians who are currently absent from their homeland that is being communicated by the author to the members of the house church in or near Rome.

This judgment is supported by several additional lines of evidence: the allusions to the readers' generosity (Heb 6:10-11; 10:33-34) comport with the known character of Roman Christianity (cf. Ign. *Rom.* salutation; Eusebius *Hist. Eccl.* 4.23.10). The sufferings endured by the believers shortly after they came to faith (Heb 10:32-34) suggest the events surrounding the Claudian expulsion of A.D. 49 (Acts 18:2; Suetonius *Claudius* 25.4); the use of the term *hēgoumenoi* for leaders in the community (Heb 13:7, 17, 24) is found in early Christian documents associated with Rome (e.g., *1 Clem.* 21.6; *Herm. Vis.* 2.2.6; 3.9.7); and the first evidence of Hebrews' recognized authority comes to us from Clement of Rome, who throughout his letter produces striking parallels to Hebrews and is literarily dependent upon Hebrews in *1 Clement* 36.1-6.

This construction of social location cannot be proven, yet it provides a concreteness to Hebrews that other hypotheses lack, and it offers a plausible destination that may be tested exegetically. We may also fill out the picture by invoking what is known concerning the Jewish community and the early house churches in Rome. There is little doubt that Roman Christianity was originally Jewish. It is striking that the fourth-century commentator on Romans, Ambrosiaster, attests to Gentile Christians in Rome who came to faith through the evangelistic outreach of the original Jewish converts of the earliest Roman community (*Exposition of Romans,* prologue, 2 [CSEL 81.1.5-6]). By the time Paul wrote his letter to the Romans, there had been a significant influx of Gentile Christians in Rome, and the balance of power had shifted to Gentile leadership. In Romans 16:3-15 Paul gives us evidence for the existence of several house churches in Rome (see Rom 16:3-5, 10, 11, 14, 15).

Archaeological investigation has uncovered the remains of apartment complexes *(insulae)* several stories high that date to the second and third centuries. Incorporated into the walls or preserved below the floors of at least three of the existing titular churches in Rome are the remnants of large tenement houses. The ground floors would have been occupied by shops and the upper levels by prosperous families. Craftsmen and artisans such as Aquila and Priscilla might well have lived in such quarters, which served as workshop, residence and meeting place. From Paul's greetings in Romans 16:3-15 we may picture a number of relatively small household fellowships only loosely related to one another. Evidence indicates that even in the early second century the congregations of Rome were not centrally organized under the administrative authority of a single bishop. Ignatius insists on the importance of the office of bishop in six of his seven letters to churches, but he is silent on this matter in his letter to the Romans (Ign. *Rom.*, c. A.D. 110), presumably because there was no monarchical bishop in Rome. Shortly thereafter the *Shepherd of Hermas* refers only to "the elders who preside over the church" at Rome (*Herm. Vis.* 2.4.3; 3.9.7).

The setting we have sketched suggests why the Roman church may have been troubled by problems of diversity, disunity and a tendency toward independence. In Hebrews we see evidence of tension between the intended audience and the recognized leaders (Heb 13:17-18) and a pastoral concern to bring the two groups together (Heb 13:24). The members of the house church are not to regard themselves as an autonomous assembly or to isolate themselves from other household groups within the city, and as a countermeasure the writer asks them to convey his greetings "to all the saints" throughout the city (Heb 13:24).

3. Circumstances and Date of Composition.

3.1. Circumstances of Composition. In reconstructing the circumstances surrounding the composition of Hebrews, we are left to rely on the document itself. What is the precise relationship of the writer to his audience? The answer is difficult to discern, but in Hebrews 13:17-19 the writer identifies himself with the "leaders" of the community. He considers his pastoral responsibility, epitomized in his "word of exhortation" (Heb 13:22), to extend to the congregation. And his desire to be "restored to you sooner" (Heb 13:19) implies his personal acquaintance with them. His discourse (Heb 1:1—13:21) and personal note (Heb 13:22-25) are intended as a substitute for his presence until he can come in person (Heb 13:19, 23).

We have already noted that the assembly was in crisis. Their numbers had been depleted (Heb 10:25), and those who remained were subject to a loss of confidence in their convictions. Their former sense of identity as the new covenant people of God had been undermined, and in the writer's analysis they are no longer listening to the voice of God (Heb 2:1, 3; 3:7-4:14; 5:11; 12:25). Their formerly bold commitment in the face of public abuse, imprisonment and loss of property (Heb 10:32-34) has given way to discouragement (Heb 5:11; 6:12; 12:12-13) and a weariness of sustaining their Christian confession in the face of hostility (Heb 12:3-4).

The writer is alarmed at the group's attraction to traditions that he regarded as inconsistent with the word of God proclaimed by their former leaders (Heb 13:7-9). This may account for the tension between the community and their current leaders (Heb 13:1, 17-18), and it may also explain their apparent isolation and lack of accountability to the larger network of house churches (Heb 13:24). These factors would have exposed them to the corrosive impact of their sociopolitical and religious environment.

We should probably understand Hebrews to be addressing the concerns of second-generation Christians. The root of the problem may have been the delay of the parousia (Heb 10:25, 35-39), social ostracism and impending persecution (Heb 12:4; 13:13-14) or a general waning of enthusiasm and erosion of confidence (Heb 3:14; 10:35). A significant symptom was the faltering of hope (Heb 3:6; 6:11, 18-20; 10:23-25; 11:1), and the writer sensed the grave danger of apostasy among some members, which he defined as turning away from the living God (Heb 3:12) and subjecting Jesus Christ to public contempt (Heb 6:4-6; 10:26-31). Once the sacred covenant bond between God and his people was violated, they would be excluded from covenant fellowship. Weaker members might reject the grace of God and forfeit participation in the new covenant through personal carelessness (Heb 3:12-13; 4:1, 11; 6:4-8, 11; 10:26-31; 12:15-17, 25-29). These factors might well account for the urgent tone and pastoral strategies adopted by the writer.

3.2. Date of Composition: General Considerations. In assigning a date for the composition of Hebrews, we must first allow for the fact that the writer and his audience had come to faith through the preaching of those who had heard Jesus (Heb 2:3-4) and had subsequently served as leaders during the formative period of the community (Heb 13:7). Further, we learn that the present members had been believers for an extended time (Heb 5:12). If we allow that at least three or four decades have elapsed since the beginning of the Christian movement, the earliest date we can assign for the composition of Hebrews would be around A.D. 60.

In seeking to establish an upper limit for a date of composition we need to consider the use of Hebrews in *1 Clement* (see *1 Clem.* 17.1 for the use of Heb 11:37; *1 Clem.* 36.2-6 for direct literary dependence on Heb 1:3-5, 7; *1 Clem.* 36.3 for the quotation of Ps 104:4 [103 LXX] in the precise wording of Heb 1:7 [in variation from the LXX]). Internal evidence and external attestation indicate that *1 Clement* was composed some time between 80 and 140. Thus no firm inference concerning the date for the composition of Hebrews may be drawn from its use by Clement of Rome.

Some scholars have set an upper limit at 70, the year in which the Jerusalem temple was destroyed by Titus. This conclusion is based on the writer's referring to cultic activity in the present tense (e.g., Heb 7:27-28; 8:3-5; 9:7-8, 25; 10:1-3, 8; 13:10-11) and the presumption that cultic activity was being carried out in Jerusalem. But the writer shows no interest in the Jerusalem temple or in contemporary sacrificial praxis. In Hebrews 9:1-10, for example, the focus is on the tabernacle in the wilderness rather than the temple. Since the sanctuary is considered in relation to the old and new covenants and the contrast between the two, the writer refers to the tabernacle and its association with the old Sinai covenant rather than to the temple (see Heb 8:5). The use of the present tense evokes a sense of timelessness rather than indicating a continuing temple cult in Jerusalem. (Such use of a "timeless" present tense to describe the temple and its sacrifices after the temple had been destroyed may be observed in Josephus *Ant.* 4.8.17-23 §§224-57; *1 Clem.* 41.2; *Barn.* 7—8; *Diogn.* 3.) It has no bearing on the dating of Hebrews.

3.3. The Edict of Claudius. The most explicit reference to a specific event in the audience's past occurs in Hebrews 10:32-34. This description of the suffering endured is congruent with the hardships borne by the Jewish Christians who were expelled from Rome by the emperor Claudius in A.D. 49. Among them were the Jewish Christian leaders Aquila and Priscilla, who arrived in Corinth about 49 or 50 "because Claudius had commanded all the Jews to leave Rome" (Acts 18:2). This edict of expulsion is known from Suetonius, who in his *Lives of the Caesars* (A.D. 120) comments on Claudius's official actions toward certain foreign groups in Rome: *Iudaeos impulsore Chresto adsidue tumultantes Roma expulit* (Suetonius *Claudius* 25.4). This may be translated in either of two ways: "He expelled from Rome the Jews constantly making disturbances at the instigation of Chrestus," or "Since the Jews constantly made disturbances at the in-

stigation of Chrestus, he expelled them from Rome." Suetonius's comment can be interpreted to mean that either Claudius expelled only those responsible for the disturbances among the Jews, or the entire Jewish community in Rome was affected by the edict because they had been implicated in frequent rioting. The first translation is preferred because in Rome the Jewish community was divided into a number of district synagogues. In all probability the edict of expulsion was directed to the members of one or two specific synagogues, who would have been compelled to leave the city until there was a guarantee of no further social disturbances.

Although Chrestus was a common name among Roman slaves, signifying "good" or "useful," it was not a recognized Jewish name. The garbled reference to "Chrestus" is almost certainly evidence of the presence of Christians within the Jewish community of Rome. The confusion between *Chrestus* and *Christos* ("the Messiah") is understandable, since in antiquity the distinction in spelling and pronunciation was negligible. There is every reason to believe that the source of the disruptions was the Jewish Christian preaching of a crucified Jesus as Messiah. We can well imagine members of the Jewish community being thrown into violent debate, and this attracting the unfavorable attention of the imperial authorities. Claudius issued a decree of expulsion affecting those most directly involved (i.e., those Jewish Christians labeled under the name of *Chrestus*). Insult, public abuse and the loss of property were normal under the conditions of a decree of expulsion. If this reading of the evidence is correct, some of the recipients of Hebrews were Jewish Christians who had shared banishment from Rome with Aquila and Priscilla.

The date of the Claudian edict is contested, but the year A.D. 49 is plausible. It was in the period A.D. 47-52 that Claudius engaged in a campaign to restore the old Roman rites and to check the spread of foreign cults. Independent corroboration of this date is provided by the Gallio inscription from Delphi, which has made it possible to determine when Paul entered Corinth and made the acquaintance of Aquila and Priscilla, who had arrived in Corinth from Rome "only recently" (Acts 18:1-2). We conclude that the experience referred to in Hebrews 10:32-34 took place in A.D. 49.

Hebrews was written at a later time in which

a new crisis had emerged, posing its own threat to the welfare of the members of the house church. The fear of death (Heb 2:15), loss of heart (Heb 12:3) and the fact that the community had not yet contended to the point of bloodshed (Heb 12:4; cf. Heb 11:35—12:3) suggest a situation more serious than that under Claudius. This suggests the persecution and martyrdom endured by Roman Christians under Nero following the devastating fire of A.D. 64 (Tacitus *Ann.* 15.42-44). Christians then experienced the loss of life, not simply property. Hebrews appears to have been composed for members of a house church that had not yet borne the brunt of Nero's repressive measures, or less probably, for Jewish Christians who returned to Rome after that terrifying event. This suggests a tentative date of composition in the interval between the great fire of Rome (A.D. 64) and Nero's suicide in June 68. Incidental features of the text, such as the imminent expectation of the parousia (Heb 10:25, 36-39) or the notice of Timothy's release from prison (Heb 13:23), are consistent with this relatively early dating of Hebrews.

4. Integrity.

Few scholars have doubted the integrity of Hebrews 1—12, but questions have been raised concerning the authenticity of Hebrews 13 (for discussion, see Filson). The reasons are several: the chapter appears to begin abruptly and is marked by a sharp change in tone and theme; it appears to lack the writer's normal care to link a new section to the preceding unit of exhortation (Heb 12:14-29); the form of the chapter, marked by catechetical precepts characteristic of the paraenesis of Paul or Peter (e.g., 1 Thess 5:12-22; Rom 12:9-21; 13:8-10; 1 Pet 3:8-12), is without parallel in Hebrews 1—12; and its contents distinguish this section from the rest of the Hebrews.

Nevertheless Hebrews 13 exhibits the characteristic vocabulary and significant concepts, the appeal to the Pentateuch and Psalms and the elements of structure that are found in Hebrews 1—12. This constitutes a strong, cumulative argument for the authenticity of Hebrews 13.

A number of literary devices form a literary signature that identifies the author of Hebrews 13 as the author of Hebrews 1—12: the use of chiastic structure (Heb 13:2, 4, 10, 14, and 10-16); paronomasia, or play on words (Heb 13:2, 18, 20, 22); unusual word order designed to arouse attention (Heb 13:8, 11, 20); elegant style (Heb 13:17); linguistic rhythm (Heb 13:3); assonance (Heb 13:4, 5, 9, 13, 14, 16); alliterative arrangement of lines (Heb 13:5, 19); the use of syntax to display emphasis (Heb 13:3, 4, 5, 9, 11, 15, 18, 20) and the use of classical idioms (Heb 13:2, 5, 15, 17).

Hebrews 13 not only was composed by the same writer as Hebrews 1—12 but also was designed to accompany the preceding discourse. Its essential message can scarcely be separated from the primary concerns and conceptual themes expressed in Hebrews 1—12. The connection of Hebrews 13:1-21 to the preceding section (Heb 12:14-29) is established through Hebrews 12:28, where the community is called to serve God through thanksgiving. This concept of worship is an expansive one, and the varied aspects of life (Heb 13:1-21) are to be regarded as an expression of devoted service to God.

5. Genre.

The canonical ordering of Hebrews among the letters of the NT predisposes one to regard this document as a letter. This understanding of Hebrews can be traced back as early as the beginning of the third century and the Chester Beatty Papyrus (P46), where Hebrews is positioned after Romans and before 1 Corinthians and is identified by the superscription "To the Hebrews" (cf. the uncials B A C H I K P, where it appears after 2 Thessalonians and before 1 Timothy).

Hebrews does not possess the form of an ancient *letter. It lacks the conventional prescript of a letter and has none of the characteristic features of ordinary letters from this period. The writer offers no opening prayer for grace and peace, no expression of thanksgiving or blessing. Its beginning with a stately periodic sentence acclaiming the transcendent dignity of the Son of God through whom God spoke his final word (Heb 1:1-4) is more characteristic of rhetorical discourse that compels attention and engages a reader or auditor immediately. Hebrews begins like a sermon.

5.1. The Homily or Sermon Form. The writer confirms the sermonic genre when he describes the discourse as a "word of exhortation" (Heb 13:22), an idiomatic expression for a sermon in Hellenistic-Jewish and early Christian circles, where the public reading of Scripture was followed by preaching (cf. Acts 13:15 with Acts 13:16-41). Hebrews may be classified as a paraenetic homily in the Hellenistic-Jewish synagogue tradition. As such it is the oldest complete early Christian sermon that has been preserved. It possesses the eloquence of a discourse but the form of a homily. Like the paraenetic homilies of its period, Hebrews consists of strong encouragement and stern warning.

5.2. Defining the Genre. Recent research has identified a common form of Hellenistic-Jewish and early Christian oral sermon. The synagogue hortatory homily, or "word of exhortation," found in Acts 13:16-41 follows a threefold pattern: authoritative *exempla* (i.e., evidence in the form of biblical quotations, examples from the past or present, or reasoned exposition set out to commend the points that follow); a conclusion inferred from the preceding examples, indicating their relevance for the audience; a final exhortation. This threefold pattern can be found in many early Christian writings (Hebrews; *1 Clement;* other speeches in Acts; 1 Cor 10:1-14; 2 Cor 6:14—7:1; 1 Peter and 2 Peter, the letters of Ignatius; *Barnabas*) and in Jewish sources from the Hellenistic period (see Lane, lxxii).

This oral form was flexible and could be developed in a variety of ways. It could stand alone, as in Acts 13:16-41, or it could be extended in a cyclical fashion as the pattern is repeated in a longer sermon (e.g., Heb 1:5-4:16; 8:1—12:28; *1 Clem.* 4.1-13; 37.2—40.1; Ign. *Eph.* 3.1—4.2; 5.1-36; 7.2—10.1). Hebrews appears to follow a modified form of the latter pattern, creating in the process a complex sermonic text.

The study of Hebrews in light of Greco-Roman rhetoric, as outlined in the handbooks of Aristotle, Quintilian and Cicero, reveals the manner in which Hebrews addressed its hearers with the intent to persuade (cf. Aristotle *Rhet.* 1.2.1355B). Hebrews exhibits highly nuanced and sophisticated forms of proof. In its various hortatory cycles, in which complementary ideas are augmented with multiple arguments, the writer engages in what the rhetorical handbooks call amplification or refinement.

Even the lengthy interruption in the "word of exhortation" of Hebrews 5:1—10:18, where the writer turns from the established hortatory pattern to present an extended exposition, finds explanation in the rhetorical setting. The writer aims not only to exhort his audience but also to stimulate and fortify them in their present convictions on the basis of an exposition of the surpassing, unrepeatable priestly sacrifice of Jesus for the sins of the many.

An alternative approach takes note of the formal pattern that serves as a structuring device in important sections of Hebrews (Heb 3:1-4:16; 8:1—10:18; 12:1-13). The pattern consists of formal introduction (e.g., Heb 3:1-6; 8:1-6; 12:1-3), scriptural citation (e.g., Heb 3:7-11; 8:7-13; 12:4-6), exposition or thematic elaboration (e.g., Heb 3:12—4:13; Heb 9:1—10:18; Heb 12:7-11) and application (e.g., Heb 4:14-16; 10:19-21; 12:12-13). This pattern has left its partial imprint in other portions of Hebrews as well (e.g., Heb 7:1-28). This genre of "word of exhortation" (Heb 13:22; Acts 13:15), or "paraclesis" (i.e., "exhortation"), emerged in the hellenistic synagogue, where it served to actualize traditional Scripture for a Jewish community in a nontraditional environment. The writer of Hebrews adapted this form in order to confirm the values and commitments of a group of Christians who were experiencing social ostracism and alienation in their environment.

5.3. The Impact of the Sermonic Discourse. The writer of Hebrews skillfully projects the impression that he is present with the gathered audience, delivering the sermon. Until the postscript (Heb 13:22-25), he studiously avoids any reference to writing or reading, which would tend to emphasize his geographical distance from the audience. Instead the accent is on speaking and listening, and he directly identifies himself with the audience and establishes a sense of presence (Heb 2:5; 5:11; 6:9; 8:1; 9:5; 11:32).

As a gifted preacher, the writer skillfully employs alliteration, oratorical imperatives, euphonic phrases, unusual word order and literary devices, all calibrated for rhetorical effectiveness. The alternation between exposition and exhortation provides an effective vehicle for oral impact. As the discourse was read aloud to the gathered assembly, Hebrews would have communicated its point as much aurally as logically.

Interpreters should be aware of the difference between oral preaching and written discourse. The dynamic relationship between speaker and audience is distinct in each case. The writer expressly declares in Hebrews 13:22 that his "word of exhortation" has been reduced to writing. As such, it is available for study to a modern reader, taking on a life of its own independent of the audience for whom it was written. But it is clear that this was not the writer's intention. It is also clear that the writer would have preferred to have spoken directly with the men and women he addressed (Heb 13:19, 23). In the realm of oral speech, the speaker and the auditors are bound together in a dynamic relationship within a world of sound. Although forced by geographical distance and a sense of urgency to reduce his homily to writing, the writer of Hebrews never loses sight of the power of the spoken word.

5.4. Rhetorical Analysis. In Hebrews the voice of the writer is the voice of the speaker. It was essential to provide verbal clues to enable the audience to discern where one unit of the discourse ended and another began. These verbal clues were also necessary for the reader, because in ancient documents there was no indication where parts of a composition began or ended. Thus the organization of the argument was revealed by devices such as repetition, anaphora, *inclusio, responsio,* parallelism, catchwords (or "hook words") and the like. By attending to these clues, the one reading the discourse to the assembled group could give the discourse a coherent delivery. Hebrews was crafted not for the eye but for the ear, and its forceful, artistic prose provided the vehicle for the argument.

It is attractive to view Hebrews as a deliberative discourse since it consists of advising and dissuading (cf. Quintilian *Inst. Orat.* 3.8.6). Hebrews includes a rhetorical *prooemium* (prologue, Heb 1:1-4), *narratio* (necessary background information, Heb 1:5—2:18) with the *propositio* (a lucid thematic statement, or the statement that is to be proved, Heb 2:17-18), *argumentatio* with *probatio* and *refutatio* (argumentation with the presentation of proof and refutation, Heb 3:1—12:29), *peroratio* (peroration, Heb 13:1-21) and *postscriptum* (postscript, Heb 13:22-25) that identifies the discourse in Hebrews 1:1—13:21 as an exhortation or urgent appeal.

It is difficult, however, to classify Hebrews as a specific type of ancient rhetoric. Deliberative rhetoric attempts to persuade an audience to make a choice on the basis of some future benefit or to dissuade them from inappropriate action. This type of rhetoric agrees with the earnest pastoral character of much of Hebrews. Epideictic rhetoric, however, is concerned with reinforcing beliefs accepted by the audience. The tone is more instructive, seeking to buttress a set of convictions already embraced. This also is a feature of Hebrews and may be observed in the exhortation not to cast aside the confidence and hope once firmly held, for the One who had promised is faithful (e.g., Heb 3:6, 14; 10:23, 35-39; 11:11).

The state of research is such that no one has yet produced a structural analysis of the homily that conforms strictly to the type of rhetoric discussed in the ancient Greco-Roman handbooks. We must conclude that Hebrews resists being cast into any single mold of classical rhetoric. Although rhetorical devices are clearly discernible, an identifiable rhetorical structure is less evident. The writer of Hebrews (like Paul and Philo) was not bound by rhetorical conventions. He freely adapted rhetorical conventions to suit his purposes.

5.5. Discourse Analysis. As a written communication, Hebrews lends itself to discourse, or text-linguistic, analysis. As a technique of biblical criticism, discourse analysis is in its infancy. Discourse analysis is concerned with semantic cohesion, the relationships within a unit of discourse and the identification of unit boundaries within a discourse. Its primary goal is an understanding of the individual paragraphs that constitute the building blocks of a discourse. This is based on the premise that the paragraph, rather than individual semantic units like words, phrases or sentences, provides the key to understanding the total or main discourse. A writer organizes sentences to form larger semantic units (i.e., paragraphs) that are assigned a variety of semantic functions in the development of the discourse.

The fundamental assumption of discourse analysis is that written texts originate in a writer's conceptualization of a theme. This theme is given expression by linguistic choices (diction, grammar, style), which lend meaning and structure to paragraph units. In order to comprehend the writer's development of his theme, it is necessary to examine the text on the lexical, syntactic and rhetorical levels. Discourse analysis attempts to understand how a writer linguistically marked his paragraphs and embedded discourses (i.e., those identifiable, distinct units of discourse that have a beginning and an end) in the process of developing the main discourse.

One analysis of Hebrews has identified a discourse structure that may be broadly outlined as follows:

Thematic introduction (Heb 1:1-4)
Point 1 (embedded discourse 1,
   Heb 1:5—4:13)
Point 2 (embedded discourse 2,
   Heb 4:14—10:18)
Peak (embedded discourse 3,
   Heb 10:19—13:19)
Conclusion (Heb 13:20-21)
Finis (Heb 13:22-25)

According to this analysis, Hebrews comprises three major embedded discourses bracketed by an introduction and a conclusion. The formal closing at the end of the homily is unrelated semantically to the thematic development of the discourse (for further details, see Lane, lxxx-lxxxiv).

It must be emphasized that discourse analysis represents a purely linguistic approach that takes into account such factors as literary devices, shifts in genre, the semantic cohesion of individual sections, the functional role of subsections and the development of the discourse. It is not concerned with social or historical factors that may have affected the surface structure of the discourse. One of its major contributions to understanding Hebrews lies in its identification of techniques that not only effect a transition but also give cohesion to a unit of discourse.

6. Literary Structural Devices.

The literary structure of Hebrews is complex and elusive. The range of proposals concerning its literary structure attests to the artistic and literary complexity of this discourse. Nevertheless, the quest for a literary structure is legitimate and assumes that there were literary and rhetorical conventions for the orderly arrangement of a discourse and that in reducing the discourse to writing, verbal clues would need to be provided to assist the auditors in following the argument (see Lane, lxxxiv-xcviii).

The writer of Hebrews has used a number of literary devices to indicate the beginning and ending of unified sections. These verbal clues to the development of Hebrews may be enumerated as follows:

(1) Announcement of subject. The writer announces the primary theme just prior to the introduction of the unit in which the theme is developed. For example, in Hebrews 2:17 Jesus is designated a "merciful and faithful high priest in the service of God." These primary themes

are developed in inverse order. In Hebrews 3:1—5:10 the writer directs attention to Jesus as "faithful" (Heb 3:1—4:13) and then to Jesus as "merciful" (Heb 4:14—5:10).

(2) Transitional hook words. Hook words were a rhetorical device developed in antiquity to tie together two or more blocks of material. The introduction of a key word at the end of one section and its repetition at the beginning of the next served to mark formally the transition between the two units (e.g., "the angels" in Heb 1:4/5 joins the sections Heb 1:1-4/5-14).

(3) Change of genre. The writer alternates between exposition and exhortation throughout the discourse.

(4) Characteristic terms. The concentration of key vocabulary or of cognate terms within a unit of discourse frequently serves to articulate and develop a primary theme. For example, the term *angels* is found eleven times in Hebrews 1:5—2:16 and only twice after that. This density of usage serves to build cohesion in a block of material.

(5) *Inclusio*. Bracketing a unit of discourse by the repetition of a striking expression or key word at the beginning and close of a section provides an objective means of determining the beginning and end of a unit of discourse. For example, the repetition of the verb *to see* and the noun *unbelief* in Hebrews 3:12 and 19 marks Hebrews 3:12-19 as a discrete literary unit of commentary on the biblical text found in Hebrews 3:7-11.

7. Purpose and Plan.

The purpose and plan of Hebrews is integrally related to the literary structure of the document. The key issue is the distinctive role assigned by the writer to the expository and hortatory sections of the homily. How is the writer's essential purpose served by the blocks of exposition or of exhortation throughout the discourse? What is the intended relationship between the indicative and the imperative, between thesis and paraenesis, within the total work?

There are sound reasons for arguing that in Hebrews paraenesis takes precedence over thesis in expressing the writer's purpose. Argumentation serves exhortation. Hebrews may be designated a pastorally oriented sermon whose goal is given expression in the paraenetic sections of the discourse. When the writer characterized his entire discourse as paraenesis or paraclesis (Heb 13:22, "my word of exhortation" [*paraklēsis*]), he was identifying his work as an earnest, passionate and personal appeal. The writer's biblical and theological exposition is therefore subordinate to his paraenetic purpose. Hebrews was composed to arouse, urge, encourage and exhort the audience to maintain their Christian confession and to dissuade them from a course of action the writer regarded as catastrophic. The writer calls them to fidelity and obedience and seeks to prepare them for suffering.

The primary function of the exposition is thematic development. The primary function of the exhortation is to motivate the community to appropriate action. Exhortation confronts, with implications for obedience and disobedience. Exposition instructs, showing why obedience will be amply rewarded. In Hebrews, exposition provides an essential foundation for the exhortation and ultimately serves a hortatory purpose. The expository units of the discourse do not stand on their own but furnish the presupposition for the paraenesis. At the same time, the persuasive force of the exhortation is derived from the convincing thematic development in the expository sections of the sermon. The basis for the exhortation in Hebrews 2:1-4, for example, is provided in the demonstration of the superior dignity of God's Son in Hebrews 1:5-14.

As we have argued, the purpose of Hebrews is to strengthen, encourage and exhort the weary members of a house church to respond courageously to the prospect of renewed suffering in view of the gifts and resources God has lavished upon them. The plan of the homily complements its practical purpose. The finality of God's revelation in his Son is set forth in moving language (Heb 1:1-4). The transcendent dignity of the Son is superior both to the angels (Heb 1:5-14) and to Moses (Heb 3:1-6). Within this setting the writer warns his auditors against indifference to the gospel message they have heard (Heb 2:1-4) or blatant unbelief (Heb 3:7—4:13). The unique priesthood of Jesus is introduced in Hebrews 2:17—3:1 and Hebrews 4:14—5:10, and it is treated at length in Hebrews 7:1—10:18. Three contrasts are developed that demonstrate the superior dignity of Jesus as priest and sacrifice: the temporal, ephemeral character of the Aaronic priesthood is overshadowed by the eternal ministry of the priest like Melchizedek (Heb 5:1-10; 7:1-28); the priestly ministry in the tabernacle of the old covenant is superseded by the priestly ministry of Jesus in the heavenly sanctuary of the new covenant (Heb 8:1—9:28); the inadequacy of the sacrifices under the law is contrasted with the efficacy and finality of Jesus' sacrifice (Heb 10:1-18).

The thematic development of Jesus' priesthood and unique sacrifice is foundational to the paraenetic warnings concerning the peril of immaturity and apostasy, which can be avoided only through faith, endurance and hope (Heb 5:11—6:20; 10:19-39). The audience is exhorted to steadfast endurance and the exercise of eschatological faith that acts in light of the certainty of the future (Heb 11:1—12:3). The heroes and heroines of the past, whose faith was attested by God (Heb 11:1-40), are paraded before the audience. This appeal is then crowned by the supreme example of faith, Jesus (Heb 12:1-3). In the pastoral and theological climax to the sermon (Heb 12:14-29), the congregation is warned of the peril of refusing God's gracious word. A concluding exhortation summons them to a lifestyle of worship and unqualified identification with the confessing community (Heb 13:1-25).

Any analysis of the plan of Hebrews must reflect an intensive listening to the detail of the text. The analysis in figure 2 (p. 477) attempts to distinguish between thesis and paraenesis and to indicate the primacy of paraenesis in the discourse by italicizing the five warning passages that expose the danger to which the community was vulnerable (Heb 2:1-4; 3:7-19; 5:11—6:12; 10:19-39; 12:14-29). The passages listed in the right-hand column point out the extent to which Hebrews has been organized around paraenesis.

8. Structural Function of Old Testament Texts.

Every chapter in Hebrews is marked by explicit or implicit references to the OT text. The writer's use of Scripture expresses his firm belief in the continuity between God's speaking and action under the old and new covenants that has urgent ramifications for Israel and for the church. A detailed knowledge of the OT is indispensable for following what the writer of Hebrews was endeavoring to say, for he assumes on the part of his audience a deep familiarity with the detail of the biblical text.

The argument of Hebrews is focused upon a succession of OT themes and figures so as to draw out both the continuity and the discontinuity between the period prior to the coming of

Christ and the time of fulfillment in Christ. In the course of Hebrews a number of OT texts gain particular prominence. The rhetorical use of these OT texts defines the arrangement and the argument of Hebrews as a whole.

The writer appears to have arranged his argument as a series of six scriptural explications, each of which is framed by exhortation. He introduces a key biblical text, clarifies its eschatological significance and draws out the paraenetic implications for the community. This rhetorical strategy accounts for the arrangement of the entire discourse from Hebrews 2:5 to Hebrews 13:19. The argument is directed to the eschatological appeal for unqualified faithfulness in light of the fact that Christ's high-priestly ministry has now secured the promised "good things" (Heb 9:11). Once this is recognized, the structural organization is clearly perceived. It is evident that the paraenetic passages are grouped fairly uniformly in proximity to the six primary scriptural quotations (see figure 1).

This analysis demonstrates the consistency of the paraenesis in Hebrews 10:19—13:19 with the earlier sections of the discourse. It displays the same rhetorical arrangement and permits the argument of the homily to proceed directly to its crowning paraenetic conclusion.

An appreciation of the thematic development, of the form of certain segments and of the transitions between sections often depends on an understanding of the function of OT texts in defining the arrangement and argument in Hebrews.

The manner in which the writer makes use of the OT shows that he stands in the mainstream of Judaism and early Jewish Christianity. The distinctiveness of his interpretation of Scripture was determined by his Christian theology of the interrelationship of history, eschatology and revelation. But the principles that guided his approach to the OT text and the forms of exposition he adopted were drawn from synagogue preaching. It is safe to assume that his audience was thoroughly familiar with the approaches to the scriptural text that characterize this homily, for they also were conversant with the liturgy and preaching that were the mainstay of Hellenistic synagogues of the Diaspora.

Hebrews is a reminder that the OT remains a valid and significant witness to God's redemptive word and deed. Christians must appreciate

Section	OT Text	Placement	Paraenesis
Introduction			
1:1—2:4	Catena		2:1-4
First Point	"You Crowned Him"		
2:5-18	Ps 8	2:6-8	
Second Point	"Today"		
3:1—4:13	Ps 95	3:7-11	3:1-2, 12-14; 4:1, 11
Third Point	"A Priest Forever"		
4:14—7:28	Ps 110	5:6	4:14-16; 5:11—6:12
Fourth Point	"A New Covenant"		
8:1—10:31	Jer 31	8:8-12	10:19-29
Fifth Point	"By Faith"		
10:32—12:2	Hab 2	10:37-38	10:32-36; 12:1-2
Sixth Point	"Do Not Lose Heart"		
12:3—13:19	Prov 3	12:5-6	12:3-29; 13:1-19
Closing			
13:20-21			

Figure 1. Six primary OT texts

this witness in the light of God's decisive act of speaking through the Son (Heb 1:1-2). The words of the OT are invoked not for their significance in the past but for their significance in the present. For the writer of Hebrews, Scripture in its entirety remains a revelation of God's unalterable plan of redemption for the human family.

9. Canonical Recognition.
Hebrews asserted an intrinsic authority in the early church, both in the West and in the East. But there was reluctance to acknowledge it as

	Thesis	Paraenesis
1:1—2:18	**I. The Revelation of God Through His Son**	
1:1-4	A. God Has Spoken His Ultimate Word in His Son	
1:5-14	B. The Transcendent Dignity of the Son	
2:1-4		C. *The First Warning:* The Peril of Ignoring the Word Delivered by the Son
2:5-9	D. The Humiliation and Glory of the Son	
2:10-18	E. The Solidarity of the Son with the Human Family	
3:1—5:10	**II. The High Priestly Character of the Son**	
3:1-6		A. Consider That Jesus Was Faithful to God Who Appointed Him
3:7-19		B. *The Second Warning:* The Peril of Refusing to Believe God's Word
4:1-14		C. Strive to Enter God's Rest, the Sabbath Celebration for the People of God
4:15—5:10	D. A High Priest Worthy of Our Faith Because He Is the Son of God Who Is Compassionate	
5:11—10:39	**III. The Highly-Priestly Office of the Son**	
5:11—6:12		A. *The Third Warning:* The Peril of Spiritual Immaturity
6:13-20	B. A Basis for Confidence and Steadfastness	
7:1-10	C. Melchizedek, the Royal Priest	
7:11-28	D. Jesus, Eternal Priest like Melchizedek	
8:1-13	E. Sanctuary and Covenant	
9:1-10	F. The Necessity for New Cultic Action	
9:11-28	G. Decisive Purgation through the Blood of Christ	
10:1-18	H. The Ultimate Character of Christ's Single, Personal Sacrifice for Sins	
10:19-39		I. *The Fourth Warning:* The Peril of Disloyalty to Christ
11:1—12:13	**IV. Loyalty to God Through Persevering Faith**	
11:1-40	A. The Triumphs of Perseverance in Faith	
11:1-7	1. In the Antediluvian Era	
11:8-22	2. In the Patriarchal Era	
11:23-31	3. In the Mosaic Era	
11:32-40	4. In the Subsequent Era	
12:1-13		B. Display the Necessary Endurance
12:14—13:25	**V. Orientation for Life as Christians in a Hostile World**	
12:14-29		A. *The Final Warning:* The Peril of Refusing God's Gracious Word
13:1-25		B. Serve God Acceptably Within the Confessing Community

Figure 2. Analysis of Hebrews: The primacy of paraenesis

integral to the church's rule of faith and practice. In the West we find early evidence for the impact of Hebrews on the life of the Christian community in Rome through *1 Clement*. As we have earlier noted, *1 Clement* reflects a detailed literary acquaintance with Hebrews, and the manner in which he made use of Hebrews indicates that he recognized its authority (*1 Clem.* 9.3-4 [cf. Heb 11:5-7]; 12.1-3 [cf. Heb 11:31]; 17.1 [cf. Heb 11:37]; 19.2 [cf. Heb 12:1]; 21.9 [cf. Heb 4:12]; 27.2 [cf. Heb 6:18]; 36.1-6 [cf. Heb 1:3-13; 2:17-18; 4:15-16]; 43.1 [cf. Heb 3:2-5]).

The *Shepherd of Hermas,* an apocalyptic prophecy written in Rome between 120 and 140, appears to have known Hebrews. *Hermas* reflects questions raised in the Roman church concerning repentance and the possibility of "second" repentance. The writer of Hebrews is the only teacher in the period prior to *Hermas* who is known to have expressed precisely the eschatological singularity of baptismal repentance and of forgiveness. Since Hebrews was circulating within the Roman Christian community, the writer may have been the teacher from whom *Hermas* received the instruction concerning the singularity of repentance. *Hermas* developed its prophetic message concerning a second repentance in formal recognition of the teaching of Hebrews but in substantial contrast to Hebrews (*Herm. Vis.* 2.2.4-5). (Other passages in *Hermas* that appear to reflect an acquaintance with Hebrews are *Visions* 2.2.7 [cf. Heb 11:33]; *Visions* 2.3.2 [cf. Heb 3:13]; *Visions* 3.7.2 [cf. Heb 3:13]; *Visions* 4.2.4; *Similitudes* 9.13.7 [cf. Heb 11:33]; *Similitudes* 9.22 [cf. Heb 10:19-20].)

Justin Martyr clearly knew Hebrews (Justin *Apol. I* 12.9 [cf. Heb 3:1]; *Dial. Tryph.* 13.1 [cf. Heb 9:13-14]; 19.3 [cf. Heb 11:5]; 19.4 [cf. Heb 5:6; 6:20; 7:1-2]; 46.3; 56.1 [cf. Heb 3:5]; 67.9 [cf. Heb 12:21]; 96.1 [cf. Heb 7:17, 24]; 113.5 [cf. Heb 5:6, 10]; 121.2 [cf. Heb 4:12-13]). Hebrews was known and used by Irenaeus (Eusebius *Hist. Eccl.* 5.26.3), by Gaius of Rome (c. 200, Eusebius *Hist. Eccl.* 6.20.2) and by Hippolytus (*Refut.* 6.30.9), all of whom recognized that it was not Pauline in origin.

The absence of Hebrews from Marcion's *Apostolicon* (Tertullian *Marc.* 5) is sufficiently explained by its strong reliance upon the OT and upon Jewish thought forms. The Muratorian canon, which appears to date from the last quarter of the second century and provides a list of the documents received as authoritative by the

church in Rome, makes no mention of Hebrews. In the West, Hebrews was seldom quoted in the third century and in the first half of the fourth century.

Some church leaders in the West questioned the authority of Hebrews. Confusion over the distinction between authorship and authority was widespread. By the end of the second century and the beginning of the third, Roman opinion had crystallized in excluding Hebrews from the Pauline letter canon. The voice of Hebrews was muted for the church in the West. Even when its authority was formally recognized in the fourth century and Hebrews was admitted to the canon of sacred Scripture, there is little evidence that it exercised any considerable influence upon the thought, life and liturgy of the church in the West.

In the East the early Alexandrian fathers and the Eastern church in general appear to have recognized the intrinsic authority of Hebrews and attributed it to Paul. It is probable that in the East the superscription "To the Hebrews" was first added to manuscripts. Hebrews was known to Pantaenus (c. 180) and to Clement of Alexandria (c. 200) (Eusebius *Hist. Eccl.* 6.14.1-4). Pantaenus, Clement of Alexandria and Origen (Eusebius *Hist. Eccl.* 6.14.1-4; 6.25.11-14) acknowledge the presence of Hebrews among a collection of Paul's letters and sense the necessity of justifying that association. The arguments advanced by Clement and Origen to defend the legitimacy of this arrangement are a witness to recognition of the intrinsic authority of Hebrews in the East by the end of the second century.

Late in the fourth century, under the influence of Western fathers who had spent time in the East, an agreement was reached between East and West that Hebrews was a letter of Paul's (see Hilary of Poitiers *Trin.* 4.11). Jerome was aware of the diversity of opinion regarding Hebrews. Although he displayed caution in his citations of Hebrews, he had no reservations concerning its intrinsic authority and its right to be included in the NT (Jerome *Vir.* 5; *Ep.* 53.8; 129.3). Augustine recognized its authority and listed Hebrews among the letters of Paul (Augustine *Doctr. Christ.* 2.8; *Civ. D.* 16.22).

10. Concluding Observations.

The authority of a text is ultimately determined by the "performance" (i.e., its power to influence and effect change in the readers) of the text. Hebrews was preserved and transmitted because Christian leaders continued to use it, and positive results followed. The concern of the early church was with praxis, with piety, with an experienced, vital faith, with spiritual usefulness; and Hebrews demanded that its voice be heard.

The authority asserted by Hebrews early in the life of the church is a reminder that this document is more than a sensitive pastoral response relevant only to a specific occasion in the past. Rather, a specific occasion was a catalyst for creative and prayerful theologizing. More than that, it was a response to revelation. It conveys a word from God addressed to the church in response to the often harsh realities of Christian discipleship in a troubled world. Within the NT canon Hebrews is an essential witness to the decisive eschatological character of God's redemptive action through Jesus Christ and to the urgency of unwavering commitment to him.

Its canonical status reflects and confers normative status. The particular text was universalized, endowed with a life of its own so that it may address a variety of situations not identical with the situation that called forth the text. The authority of Hebrews to function as a rule of faith was recognized when Hebrews was used by the believing community for teaching, correcting, equipping and leading the community into the reality of the holiness that is indispensable to the enjoyment of the vision of God (Heb 12:14).

Hebrews has acquired a reputation for being formidable and remote from the world in which we live. Ironically, Hebrews is a call for ultimate certainty and ultimate commitment. It concerns itself with the issue of certainty by confronting ultimate questions about life and death with ultimate realities. Its presentation of the way in which God responds to the human family as the God who speaks, creates, covenants, pledges, calls and commits himself is intended to breathe new life into men and women who experience a failure of nerve because they live in an insecure, anxiety-provoking society. Hebrews is a scriptural gift to be appreciated especially when God's people find themselves prone to discouragement or distraction from any cause. It is a gift the church sorely needs.

See also ABRAHAM; CHRISTOLOGY; COVENANT, NEW COVENANT; DEATH OF CHRIST; WORSHIP.

DLNTD: ANCESTORS; ANGELS, HEAVENLY BE-INGS, ANGEL CHRISTOLOGY; JERUSALEM, ZION, HOLY CITY; JEWISH CHRISTIANITY; MELCHIZEDEK; MOSES; OLD TESTAMENT IN HEBREWS; PRIEST, HIGH PRIEST; PROMISE; REPENTANCE, SECOND REPENTANCE; RHETORIC, RHETORICAL CRITICISM; ROME, ROMAN CHRISTIANITY; SACRIFICE, OFFERINGS, GIFTS; TABERNACLE, SANCTUARY.

BIBLIOGRAPHY. **Commentaries:** H. W. Attridge, *A Commentary on the Epistle to the Hebrews* (Herm; Philadelphia: Fortress, 1989); F. F. Bruce, *The Epistle to the Hebrews* (rev. ed.; NICNT; Grand Rapids: Eerdmans, 1990); G. W. Buchanan, *To the Hebrews* (AB; Garden City, NY: Doubleday, 1972); P. Ellingworth, *Commentary on Hebrews: A Commentary on the Greek Text* (NIGTC; Grand Rapids: Eerdmans, 1993); G. H. Guthrie, *Hebrews* (NIVAC; Grand Rapids: Zondervan, 1998); D. A. Hagner, *Hebrews* (NIBC; Peabody, MA: Hendrickson, 1990); P. E. Hughes, *A Commentary on the Epistle to the Hebrews* (Grand Rapids: Eerdmans, 1977); S. J. Kistemaker, *Exposition of the Epistle to the Hebrews* (NTCom; Grand Rapids: Baker, 1984); W. L. Lane, *Hebrews* (2 vols.; WBC; Dallas: Word, 1991); J. Moffatt, *A Critical and Exegetical Commentary on the Epistle to the Hebrews* (ICC; Edinburgh: T & T Clark, 1924); V. C. Pfitzner, *Hebrews* (ANTC; Nashville: Abingdon, 1997). **Studies:** A. Cody, *Heavenly Sanctuary and Liturgy in the Epistle to the Hebrews: The Achievement of Salvation in the Epistle's Perspectives* (St. Meinrad, IN: Grail, 1960); M. R. D'Angelo, *Moses in the Letter to the Hebrews* (SBLDS 42; Missoula, MT: Scholars Press, 1979); D. A. DeSilva, *Despising Shame: Honor Discourse and Community Maintenance in the Epistle to the Hebrews* (SBLDS 152; Atlanta: Scholars Press, 1995); J. Dunnill, *Covenant and Sacrifice in the Letter to the Hebrews* (SNTSMS 75; Cambridge: Cambridge University Press, 1992); F. V. Filson, *"Yesterday": A Study of Hebrews in the Light of Chapter 13* (SBT 2/4; London: SCM, 1967); G. H. Guthrie, *The Structure of Hebrews: A Text Linguistic Analysis* (NovTSup 73; Leiden: E. J. Brill, 1994); D. M. Hay, *Glory at the Right Hand: Psalm 110 in Early Christianity* (SBLMS 18; Nashville: Abingdon, 1973); G. Hughes, *Hebrews and Hermeneutics: The Epistle to the Hebrews as a New Testament Example of Biblical Interpretation* (SNTSMS 36; Cambridge: Cambridge University Press, 1979); L. D. Hurst, *The Epistle to the Hebrews: Its Background of Thought* (SNTSMS 65; Cambridge:

Cambridge University Press, 1990); M. E. Isaacs, *Sacred Space: An Approach to the Theology of the Epistle to the Hebrews* (JSNTSup 73; Sheffield: JSOT, 1992); E. Käsemann, *The Wandering People of God* (Minneapolis: Augsburg, 1984); W. L. Lane, "Hebrews as Pastoral Response," in *The Newell Lectures* (Anderson, IN: Warner, 1996) 3:91-201; S. Lehne, *The New Covenant in Hebrews* (JSNTSup 44; Sheffield: JSOT, 1990); D. F. Leschert, *Hermeneutical Foundations of Hebrews: A Study in the Validity of the Epistle's Interpretation of Some Core Citations from the Psalms* (Lewiston, NY: Edwin Mellen Press, 1994); B. Lindars, *The Theology of the Letter to the Hebrews* (NTT; Cambridge: Cambridge University Press, 1991); J. C. McCullough, "Hebrews in Recent Scholarship," *IBS* 16 (1994) 66-86, 108-20; L. L. Neeley, "A Discourse Analysis of Hebrews," *Occasional Papers in Translation and Textlinguistics* 3.4 (1987) 1-146; D. G. Peterson, *Hebrews and Perfection: An Examination of the Concept of Perfection in the "Epistle to the Hebrews"* (SNTSMS 47; Cambridge: Cambridge University Press, 1982); D. J. Pursiful, *The Cultic Motif in the Spirituality of the Book of Hebrews* (Lewiston, NY: Edwin Mellen Press, 1993); J. M. Scholer, *Proleptic Priests: Priesthood in the Epistle to the Hebrews* (JSNTSup 49; Sheffield: JSOT, 1991); J. Swetnam, *Jesus and Isaac: A Study of the Epistle to the Hebrews in the Light of the Aqedah* (AnBib 94; Rome: Biblical Institute Press, 1981); K. J. Thomas, "The Old Testament Citations in Hebrews," *NTS* 11 (1964-65) 303-25; J. W. Thompson, *The Beginnings of Christian Philosophy: The Epistle to the Hebrews* (CBQMS 13; Washington, D.C.: The Catholic Biblical Association of America, 1981); A. H. Trotter Jr., *Interpreting the Book of Hebrews* (Grand Rapids: Baker, 1997); A. Vanhoye, *Structure and Message of the Epistle to the Hebrews* (Rome: Pontifical Biblical Institute, 1989); R. Williamson, *Philo and the Epistle to the Hebrews* (ALGHJ 4; Leiden: E. J. Brill, 1970).

W. L. Lane

HELL. *See* JUDGMENT.

HEROD ANTIPAS. *See* TRIAL OF JESUS.

HEROD THE GREAT. *See* JUDAISM AND THE NEW TESTAMENT; ROME.

HIGH PRIESTS. *See* JUDAISM AND THE NEW TESTAMENT.

HILLEL. *See* RABBINIC TRADITIONS AND WRITINGS.

HOLINESS OF GOD. *See* GOD I.

HOLY SPIRIT I: GOSPELS

In the Gospels the term *Holy Spirit* (along with "the Spirit," "Spirit of God," "Paraclete," etc.) is a referring expression for the power and presence of God in action, especially as the means of God's self-revelation.

1. The Holy Spirit in Intertestamental Judaism
2. The Holy Spirit in the Synoptic Gospels
3. The Holy Spirit in John

1. The Holy Spirit in Intertestamental Judaism.

1.1. As the Spirit of Prophecy. By far the most widespread understanding of the Spirit in Judaism is as "the Spirit of Prophecy" (a regular term for the Spirit, especially in the Targums), in other words the Spirit acting as the organ of communication between God and a person:

(1) affording charismatic revelation and guidance (numerous examples in Rabbinic Judaism and Targums; but see also, e.g., 4 Ezra 14:22; Philo [e.g.] *Som.* 2.252; *Bib. Ant.* 9.10; 31.9; Sir 48:24);

(2) affording charismatic wisdom (e.g., Targums to Ex 31:3; *Frg. Tg.* Num 11:26-27; *Tg. Onq.* Deut 34:9; *Jos. and As.* 4:9; Josephus *Ant.* 10.239; *Jub.* 40:5; Philo *Jos.* 117; *Vit. Mos.* 2.265; *Gig.* 24; Sir 39:6; Sus 45b [Theod]; Wis 7:7; 9:17-18; and cf. 1QH 12.11-13; 13.18-19; 14.12-13);

(3) less commonly, invasively inspiring prophetic speech (Targums to Num 11:26-27; Josephus *Ant.* 4.119; *Jub.* 25:14; 31:12; Philo *Spec. Leg.* IV.49; *Vit. Mos.* 1.175, 277; *Bib. Ant.* 28.6; etc.);

(4) rarely, invasively inspiring charismatic praise or worship (*1 Enoch* 71:11; *Ex Rab.* 23:2; *Tg. Neb.* 1 Sam 10:6; 19:20, 23; *Bib. Ant.* 32.14; *T. Job* 48—50).

It was generally held, though not universally, that the Spirit of prophecy had been withdrawn from Israel since the last prophets (*t. Soṭa* 13:3-4) because of the nation's sin (cf. *b. Sanh.* 65b), and (especially on the basis of Joel 2:28-32 [= MT 3:1-5]) that it would be poured out on all of the restored Israel at the end (cf. *Num Rab.* 15:25; *Midr. Haggadol Gen.* 140). This would bring Israel immediate knowledge of God and of his will and thus promote ongoing obedience fulfilling the hope of Ezekiel 36:27 (*Deut Rab.* 6:14; *Tg.*

Neb. Ezek 36:25-26: cf. *b. Ber.* 31b-32a). In the meantime the Spirit had afforded the repository of wisdom and revelation in Scripture.

1.2. As the Power of Creation and Miracle. It has sometimes been held that a Judaism that thought of the Spirit as the Spirit of prophecy could not conceive of it as the power of creation and miracle. This is at best a half-truth. While the Targums tended to translate Genesis 1:2 as "a wind from the Lord," the LXX renders *rûah ʾĕlōhîm* by *pneuma theou,* a collocation that elsewhere means "the Spirit of God" (e.g., Gen 41:38; contrast Gen 8:1 etc.). *Second Baruch* 21:4 unquestionably attributes the cosmos to the work of the Spirit (cf. Is 32:15), and there is a widespread attribution of animate creation to God's Spirit (cf. LXX Job 33:4; Ps 103:30; 32:6 and Jdt 16:14; Philo *Op. Mund.* 29-30; *2 Apoc. Bar.* 23:5; etc.) and some rare hints of resurrection life too (Ezek 37:9-10, 14; *2 Apoc. Bar.* 23:5; *m. Soṭa* 9:15; *Pesiq. R.* 1:6; *Cant. Rab.* 1.1.§9). The LXX and the Targums also retain the tradition that the Spirit empowered Samson's exploits (Judg 14:6, 19; 15:14) and might lift and/or transport prophets around (cf. 1 Kings 18:12; 2 Kings 2:16; Ezek 2:2; 3:12, 14; etc.), and, at 2 Kings 2:9-15, the power of Elisha's division of the waters is specifically traced by the Targumist to "the Spirit of prophecy" on him.

The Targums even extend the connection between Spirit and power in the Hebrew Bible by attributing to the Spirit of prophecy deeds the MT traces instead to "the hand" of the Lord (cf. Ezek 37:1). Of special interest is the tendency to trace the charismatic power of Gideon (Judg 6:34), Jephthah (Judg 11:29), Saul (1 Sam 11:6) and David (1 Sam 16:13-14) to "the Spirit of power" (as on Samson) rather than translating these passages with "Spirit of prophecy/wisdom" or "power of the Lord," which we might have expected if the relation between Spirit and miraculous "power" was thought to be problematic. Here the "Spirit of power" has become the equipment of Israel's "saviors," even the power miraculously to rout the enemy. Other examples of the Spirit understood as the power of miraculous deeds may be found outside the so-called biblical translations (e.g., *Lev. Rab.* 8:2; *Bib. Ant.* 27.9-10 and 36:2; Josephus *Ant.* 8.408 [and probably 8.346]; etc.).

1.3. As the Spirit on the Messiah. A major strand of Judaism anticipated a Messiah (*see* Christ) mightily endowed with the Spirit as the Spirit of prophecy (affording unique wisdom and knowledge of the Lord as the basis of dynamic righteousness) and the Spirit of power. The model is first David, then more especially the Davidic figure of Isaiah 11:1-4, endowed with the Spirit of wisdom, knowledge and power—and it is this combination, with strong echoes of the very language of Isaiah 11:1-4, that provides the messianic portrait in *1 Enoch* 49:2-3; 62:1-2; *Psalms of Solomon* 17:37; 18:7 (cf. 1QSb 5:24-25). Other rarer strands of Jewish messianic hope also involve Spirit-endowed figures, whether the Elijah-like prophet based on Malachi 4:5 (Sir 48:10); a priestly Messiah (e.g., 1QS 9:10-11; *T. Levi* 18); a prophet like Moses based on Deuteronomy 18:15-16 (e.g., 1QS 9:10-11); a Servant-Herald based on Isaiah 42:1-2 (*see* Servant of Yahweh); a Servant-Warrior derived from Isaiah 61:1-2 (e.g., 11QMelch), or some combination of these. In each case the quality of the endowment of the Spirit might be nuanced slightly differently but would combine wisdom, revelation and some kinds of acts of power.

2. The Holy Spirit in the Synoptic Gospels.

2.1. The Spirit in the Gospel Infancy Narratives.

2.1.1. Prophecy Restored in Israel. Luke alone portrays a number of prophetic activities in association with Jesus' conception, birth and infancy (*see* Birth of Jesus). Elizabeth and Zechariah experience the Spirit of prophecy in invasive prophetic speech (the invasive quality denoted here by the Lukan favorite idiom "filled with" the Holy Spirit) at Luke 1:41-42 and Luke 1:67, and as a result they give oracles of recognition and assurance of salvation. Simeon too receives charismatic revelation (Lk 2:26, and perhaps Anna at Lk 2:38), guidance (Lk 2:27) and prophetic utterance (Lk 2:29-35). This so closely tallies with the picture of the Spirit of prophecy in Judaism that it has been suggested Luke here creates an idealized picture of the epoch of Israel, to be succeeded by those of Jesus and the church (so Conzelmann), and that the deliberate likeness of the activities of the Spirit to those portrayed in Acts is intended by Luke to establish Christianity as the continuity and fulfillment of Judaism. However, although even the rabbis can exceptionally speak of individuals experiencing the Spirit of prophecy (only at *t. Pesaḥ.* 2.15; *Lev. Rab.* 21.8; *y. Šeb.* 9.1; *y. Soṭa* 1.4 and parallels?), the general belief in the full withdrawal of the Spirit until the end (see 1.1 above)

481

and the strongly christocentric focus of the Spirit's activities in Luke 1–2 (and it is exclusively those awaiting the messianic salvation of Israel that experience the Spirit), suggest rather that Luke portrays here the dawn of the eschatological (see Eschatology) restoration of the Spirit to pious Israel; not the period of Israel as such. This is further confirmed in what is said of *John the Baptist and Jesus.

2.1.2. The Spirit on the Baptist. The eschatological quality of the Spirit restored to God's people is evidenced in the unique features within the portrayal of John the Baptist as prophet. If he is the greatest (Lk 7:26-28), that is because he fulfills the role of the awaited Elijah to restore Israel in repentance before the eschatological visitation (Lk 7:27; Mal 3:1 [cf. Mal 4:5] denied by Conzelmann, but see Fitzmyer). Luke has carefully sculpted this understanding into the infancy narratives, not only in stepwise parallelism between John, the Prophet of the Most High (Lk 1:76), and Jesus, the Son of the Most High (Lk 1:32; see Son of God), who comes to effect the promised salvation, but also in the specific identification of John as the one who "will go before him in the Spirit and power of Elijah" to prepare the Lord's people (Lk 1:17, again strongly echoing the Malachi tradition). In Judaism the collocation "Spirit and power of Elijah" (probably pre-Lukan) would normally suggest a miracle-working prophet, but in the Lukan redaction it means rather that John preaches powerfully—according to Luke 7:21-23, miracles are what distinguish Jesus from John and are offered to John's disciples as evidence to their master that Jesus is indeed the Coming One. In accordance with his eschatological stature and role, the gift of the Spirit to John is unprecedented: he is "filled with the Holy Spirit" even from his mother's womb (Lk 1:15). Hence even *in utero* he recognizes with joy the bearer of the Messiah (Lk 1:41, 44) and from birth grows and becomes strong in the Spirit (Lk 1:80 [or possibly "in spirit"]).

2.1.3. The Spirit and the Conception of the Son of God. The eschatological quality of the Spirit restored to Israel is manifest especially in connection with its role in the conception of the Messiah (Lk 1:32-35). Here Luke is almost certainly dependent on tradition, for the same motif is witnessed independently, albeit briefly, in Matthew 1:18. The child born to Mary is to be hailed Son of the Most High and given the eschatological throne of David (Lk 1:32-33; see Son of David), because he will be no child of ordinary wedlock (Lk 1:35). As J. A. Fitzmyer now admits, following the semi-miraculous conception of John the Baptist to his aged parents (Lk 1:5-25), the ascending parallelism of the narrative requires that this means a virginal conception of Jesus by the creative activity of the Holy Spirit. The angelic oracle asserts that through the action of the Spirit (perceived as the new creation "power of the Most High" [cf. Lk 1:35b]) that which is born shall be "holy, the Son of God." As G. Schneider puts it, "Jesus is not merely filled with the Spirit, like John, rather his very being is attributed to the Spirit" (Schneider, 53).

While H. Leisegang's attempts to explain this striking assertion in terms of pagan prophetism have been decisively overturned (see e.g., Barrett 1966), it is usually explained instead (so Brown 1977) as a late development in Christian thinking which first attributed Jesus' divine sonship by the Spirit to the resurrection-exaltation (cf. Rom 1:4), then fed it back, first to Jesus' baptism, then finally to his birth. It is held that the notion of creation or new creation by the Spirit in a physical sense was unknown in pre-Christian Judaism and could only evolve with the resurrection belief. But the view is entirely conjectural: from the earliest confessions (Rom 1:3-4 and Gal 4:4-6) Jesus' birth is already a decisive christological moment, and there is no evidence Mark 1:10-11 and parallels were first understood in an adoptionistic sense. An understanding of the Spirit as new creation power of miracle is already clearly attested in the tradition of Jesus' miracles (see 2.4.2 below), and Judaism was not as devoid of the idea of the Spirit as the power of miracle, creation or resurrection as is alleged (see 1.2 above). Jesus and earliest Christianity would hardly have identified the power of resurrection specifically as God's Spirit unless Judaism already invited such an identification.

The outcome of Jesus' conception by the Spirit is portrayed in Luke 2:41-52, which is understood against the background of messianic hopes for a ruler endowed with wisdom (Is 11:2-4; *Pss. Sol.* 17:37; *1 Enoch* 49:2-3; etc.) and God's grace (cf. Lk 2:40). Already Jesus shows a wisdom that startles the leaders of Israel; knows a duty to his Father that transcends that to his parents (Lk 2:49) and a divine "sonship" (compare *ho patēr mou* ["my Father"] here with the same expression at Lk 10:22; 22:29; 24:49), the depths of which Luke underscores by the redactional notice in Luke 2:50 that Mary and Joseph did not understand the significance of what he said.

2.2. The Baptist's Promise (Mk 1:8 par. Mt 3:11; Lk 3:16). John contrasts his baptizing activity with that of one to come who "will baptize you with Holy Spirit-and-fire" (so the older Q version: Mark omits "and fire"). The "you" in question is all Israel, not merely the righteous, and syntactically "Holy Spirit and fire" is probably a hendiadys (i.e., one deluge consisting of Spirit and fire; not a baptism of Spirit for the righteous and one of fire for the wicked).

Speculation about whether the Baptist originally promised only judgment in the form of a baptism of fire alone (Bultmann 1963) or of "wind and fire" (Best, taking his cue from the winnowing image which follows in Q and the fact that Heb *rûah* can mean "wind" and "spirit"—but does one "baptize" with "wind"?) is as unverifiable as it is unnecessary. The concept of an eschatological deluge of Spirit and fire is understandable enough within apocalyptic Judaism. There, for example, we find an eschatological stream, deluge or flood of fire (a burning counterpart to Noah's: cf. Dan 7:10; 1QH 3:20-36; *1 Enoch* 67:13; 4 Ezra 13:10-11), destructive of the wicked, but purging the righteous (cf. *T. Isaac* 5:21-25; *T. Abr.* 13), and the connection of the Spirit with cleansing, purging, even "fiery" judgment was traditional (cf. esp. Is 4:4; 1QS 4:21-22; see Dunn 1972). This is not quite, however, a flood of Holy Spirit and fire, and in Judaism a flood of divine Spirit could only be anticipated from God, not from the Messiah, though 4 Ezra 13:8-11 comes close in anticipating a stream of flame and fiery breath from the Messiah. This is the main objection to the authenticity of the Baptist's promise as it stands: It is alleged that a promise of any human agent pouring out God's Spirit is simply inconceivable (*T. Jud.* 24:2-3 is suspect precisely as Christian interpolation).

But this probably misunderstands John's promise. He does not speak of the Messiah "bestowing" the gift of the Spirit. We have no need to posit that he went further than the traditional expectation of a messianic figure powerfully fulfilling Isaiah 11:1-4 (and Is 9:2-7—as in *1 Enoch* 49:2-3; 62:1-2; *Pss. Sol.* 17:37; 18:7; etc.). The arrival of such a figure to rule, with his decisively authoritative Spirit-imbued command, burning righteousness and dramatic acts of power, effecting judgment and salvation, would itself be sufficient to suggest the metaphor of his unleashing a deluge of Spirit and fire on Israel (cf. *Tg. Neb.* Is 4:4, where the "Spirit of judgment" and "Spirit of fire" become the Messiah's powerful command of judgment and of extirpation respectively).

The imagery here was clearly capable of being applied by the Evangelists (1) to the Spirit in Jesus' ministry, (2) to the continuation of his ministry through the church in Jesus' lordship over the Spirit and (3) to the final act of judgment and re-creation, without requiring to be applied exclusively to anyone. J. E. Yates is probably right to think Mark saw Jesus' baptismal reception of the Spirit and powerful ministry as fulfillment of the Baptist's promise but wrong to restrict it to that: because a climactic new phase in the revelation of Christ and of God's reign in Mark is initiated with the Easter events. Exegetes are right to suggest Luke saw the fulfillment of John's promise in Pentecost (Acts 1:5; 11:16) and Matthew in the eschaton (cf. "fire" in Matthew) but wrong to restrict it to this if it means denying Luke thought Jesus' ministry (empowered by the Spirit, precipitating eschatological judgment and salvation and casting "fire" on the earth [Lk 12:49]) already began to fulfill John's logion, and if it means denying that the final act of judgment and re-creation would further fulfill it.

2.3. The Spirit Comes in the Wilderness. The Gospels portray the Baptist as preparing the way of the Lord in the wilderness and appealing to Isaiah 40:3. This was to evoke an intertestamental Isaianic new exodus ideology: that God, through a Spirit-empowered Servant (Is 61:1-2, with certain Mosaic characteristics, cf. Is 42:1-7) would destroy Israel's enemies, which at the time were partly identified as the spiritual forces behind idolatry and Israel's blindness, and shepherd it along "the way" through a transformed wilderness to a restored Zion where he would rule. The ideology is widely reflected in Judaism (cf. 1QS 8:12b-16a; 9:17-20; 4Q176; Sir 48:24-25; *T. Moses* 10:1-8; *Pss. Sol.* 11; etc.) and is woven through the Spirit traditions.

2.3.1. Jesus "Receives" the Spirit (Mk 1:10-11 par. Mt 3:16-17; Lk 3:21-22). J. D. G. Dunn (1970, chap. 3) rightly observes that for the Evangelists Jesus receives the Spirit only after he comes out of the water (and for Luke, while he is praying); his baptism was not the first Christian sacrament. Strictly speaking, the Synoptic Gospels do not actually record an objective coming of the Spirit on Jesus but a vision ("the heaven(s) opened" is a standard formula to denote visionary experience: cf. Acts 7:56; 10:11; etc.; Mark's "heavens rent" simply heightens the Isaianic new exodus connections by using the language of Is 64:1). Within the structure of such visions what is seen and what is heard are mutually interpretive. Taken as a unity, the import of the vision is that from that time the Spirit will be with Jesus as the power to exercise the messianic task (thus the use of Ps 2:7 [Mk 1:11b and pars.]); particularly as the Servant-Herald of Isaiah 42:1-2 (Mk 1:11c and pars.; see also Is 53:7; 61:1-2). To see the Spirit descend as a dove most probably evokes the symbolism of the dove as a herald or trustworthy messenger (so *b. Git.* 45a; *b. Sanh.* 95a) and bearer of good tidings (cf. Gen 8:11) and so further interprets the Spirit on Jesus as the power to proclaim the messianic good news.

J. D. G. Dunn (following a long line of exegetical tradition from Büchsel and von Baer on) attempts to explain the gift here primarily in terms of Jesus' paradigmatic experience of the Spirit in eschatological sonship, new age "life," life of the kingdom of God, and so on, and only secondarily as empowering. But anyone holding the sort of messianic hopes outlined in §1.3. and §2.2. above would immediately recognize this primarily if not exclusively as messianic empowering. For Luke, Jesus already experiences a sonship to God deeper than that to which believers aspire, and any further dimension of sonship added by Jesus' reception of the Spirit at Jordan is of a more distinctively messianic rather than generally paradigmatic nature (see Turner 1981).

2.3.2. The Spirit and the Defeat of Satan in the Wilderness (Mk 1:12-13 par. Mt 4:1-11; Lk 4:1-13). The Spirit who comes upon Jesus in the wilderness now leads him deeper into the wilderness into the trial with Satan, but nothing is said of the Spirit's role in the encounter in Mark or Matthew. For Luke (Lk 4:1), however, the emphasis falls more on the one "full of the Spirit" now being led by God in the wilderness in a way that manifests the messianic empowering ("in the Spirit"). The final temptations echo Israel's in the wilderness, but while they "rebelled and grieved his Holy Spirit" there (Is 63:10), the new representative of Israel overcomes. Luke does not specify whether this is because the Spirit affords Jesus new depths of charismatic wisdom,

which is the basis of the hoped-for Messiah's redoubtable righteousness (*1 Enoch* 49:2-3; *Pss. Sol.* 17:37; 18:7; 1QSb 5:24-25; *Tg. Neb.* Is 11.1-2), but such is probably to be inferred. The redactional notice in Luke 4:14 that Jesus then returned "in the power of the Spirit" to Galilee not only highlights the "power" character of the gift of the Spirit to Jesus, but also may be intended to indicate that the successful encounter with Satan lies at the root of Jesus' later success in "healing all who were under the power of the devil" (Acts 10:38).

2.4. The Spirit in Jesus' Ministry.

2.4.1. The Messiah of the Spirit, Exorcisms and Blasphemy Against the Spirit. Matthew 12:28 (a Q saying) explicitly attributes Jesus' exorcisms to his empowering with the Spirit and concludes they manifest the inbreaking of God's reign (*see* Kingdom of God). This is striking as Judaism did not connect exorcisms with the Spirit or see them as evidence of the kingdom. The same assumption—that Jesus exorcises by the power of the Spirit—is made in the Markan tradition warning of blasphemy against the Spirit (Mk 3:28-30 par. Mt 12:31-32). This with the saying that immediately precedes may provide a clue to the connections of thought.

The most obvious OT background to the charge of "blasphemy against the Spirit" is Isaiah 63:10 with its accusation that the perverse and blind rebellion of the wilderness generation "grieved his Holy Spirit" and turned God into their enemy. Equally, the closest OT parallel to the parable of the strong man is widely recognized to be Isaiah 49:24-26, with its new exodus theme of the Yahweh-Warrior taking back the captives from warriors and plunder from the fierce—that is, releasing Israel—so that all humanity will know he is Israel's savior. By the intertestamental period these "enemies" from whom deliverance was awaited were none other than the powers of Belial, and the Messiah was the one who would act as God's agent in effecting the new exodus release (so esp. *T. Dan* 5:10-13 and 11QMelch, but see also *T. Zeb.* 9:8 and *T. Levi* 18:12). The new exodus hopes thus offer a plausible background to explain why the Messiah, already traditionally regarded as empowered by the Spirit to deliver Israel from its enemies, should be connected with exorcisms, and these in turn with the advent of God's reign. These hopes also provide an inviting background for labeling as "blasphemy against the Holy Spirit" the rebellious refusal to recognize such acts of redemption as God's work.

Luke has shifted the blasphemy against the Spirit saying to a different context (Lk 12:10-12). It probably still means obdurate and rebellious unbelief that opposes God's redemptive initiative, now in persistent antagonism to the gospel preached in the power of the Spirit (so Fitzmyer)—a theme that dominates Acts. Of the alternative suggestion (Schweizer etc.), that "blasphemy against the Spirit" denotes failure of the Christian to confess Jesus when prompted by the Spirit in situations of trial, there is simply no trace in Luke-Acts.

Luke 11:20 has also changed the Q saying to attribute exorcisms to "the finger of God" rather than to the Spirit. It is alleged Luke has made both these changes because he regarded the Spirit (as in Judaism) as "the Spirit of prophecy" and, for that reason, could not accept the Spirit was also the power of miracle. But this is based on a false antithesis (see 1.2 above), and Luke's changes are more readily explained in other terms. In Luke 11:20 the shift in terminology (a clear reference to Ex 8:19 [LXX Ex 8:15] is probably in the interest of Luke's prophet like Moses christology but still refers to the Spirit; cf. the parallel term "the hand of the Lord," which was interpreted to refer to the Spirit).

2.4.2. The Spirit and Miracles of Healing. To the extent that illness was regarded as directly and indirectly satanic (e.g., Acts 10:38; Lk 13:10-15; etc.), so we might expect healings to be regarded as part of the messianic deliverance; the acts of the Messiah endowed with the Spirit (cf. Mt 11:2) to liberate Israel from its enemies. The strong connection between healings and pronouncement of the inbreaking reign of God supports the view (notably Lk 9:2; 10:9, 11 par. Mt 10:7-8) and the Q tradition (Mt 11:5 par. Lk 7:21-22) that Jesus responded to the Baptist's doubt by highlighting the blind seeing, the lame walking, lepers cleansed, deaf hearing and "good news" being preached to the poor, thus evoking a medley of Isaianic new exodus texts (Is 29:18; 35:5-7; 42:18), including the most significant, Isaiah 61:1-2 (see 2.4.3 below). Matthew specifically and redactionally traces the healings to the Spirit bestowed on the Servant-Herald of Isaiah 42:1-2 (Mt 12:15-21). The occasional Elisha or prophet-like-Moses allusions in the miracle tradition of Luke (Lk 7:11-17; 9:10b-17, 28-36; 10:1-12; 13:32-33) should not be taken as providing a competing explanation but reflect a merging of prophetic and more traditional messianic views anticipated in the new exodus ideology and elsewhere.

2.4.3. The Interpretation of the Spirit in Terms of Isaiah 61:1-2. Via the redactional bridges of Luke 4:1 and Luke 4:14, Luke interprets the gift of the Spirit to Jesus in Luke 3:21-22 in terms of fulfillment of Isaiah 61:1-2 (Lk 4:18-21). The unusual text form of the citation and other non-Lukan features suggest he has received Luke 4:16-30 from a source, but Luke has given it programmatic significance.

The use of Isaiah 61:1-2 to explain the Spirit on Jesus has christological and soteriological significance. Isaiah 61:1-2 was understood in contemporary Judaism to encapsulate the new exodus hopes for a messianic Jubilee and "release" of "the poor" (i.e., Israel in need of salvation) from captivity to the powers of Beliar (compare 11QMelch; see Sloan). That the citation was under stood this way is indicated by the intercalation of the thematic "to set the oppressed free" from Isaiah 58:6. Jesus claims to be the one empowered by the Spirit to effect the "release" of Israel from the variety of forms of satanic oppression. That this includes healings and exorcisms is clear from Luke 7:21 (Lukan redaction) with Luke 7:22 (Q) and Acts 10:38 (which echo the language of Lk 4:18-21, see also, e.g., Lk 13:10-15). But that it also goes beyond these to include release from Israel's idolatrous "blindness" and "deafness" to God too (cf. Lk 8:4-15; Acts 28:26-27) is evident from the way Isaiah 61:1-2 shapes the Beatitudes (Mt 5:3-6; Lk 6:20-21).

Christologically, the use of Isaiah 61:1-2 and Isaiah 42:1-2 with a new exodus theme probably indicates a prophet-like-Moses motif rather than the more traditional regal Messiah. But the two are complimentary, not antithetical, and whether the Messiah is Davidic or Mosaic makes only slight difference to the pneumatology: both figures are expected to experience the Spirit in acts of power and deliverance, and both experience the Spirit in charismatic wisdom. A Mosaic motif enables an emphasis on the Spirit as the source of charismatic revelation, and on the outcome in foundational and authoritative teaching, more easily than the regal. In the final analysis, however, the Synoptics are surprisingly reticent to speak of Jesus receiving revelation (contrast the paucity of such reference in Luke [only Lk

3:21-22 (Lk 10:18?); 10:22] with the richness in Acts), and this is never specifically attributed to the Spirit. And while Jesus is presented as the giver of foundational teaching, the authority of the content is presented as his own ("I say to you"), rather than attributed to the Spirit. The Spirit has become the power that works through Jesus' words and deeds to affect others.

2.5. *Jesus' Promise of the Spirit.* As the Synoptics present Jesus giving minimal explicit teaching on the church, it is hardly surprising there is little on the gift of the Spirit.

Luke 11:11-13 probably belongs to the controversy within Jesus' ministry about the source of the power he demonstrates. It assures the disciples who have shared in this power on Jesus (cf. Lk 9:1; 10:17-19), that the Father does not give harmful gifts ("snake" and "scorpion" are symbols for evil powers, cf. Lk 10:19) when good gifts are sought. Similarly he gives a good spirit (*pneuma agathon: P*[45] L [etc.] is the reading that explains the rest), not an evil one as the opponents imply (Lk 11:14-23).

The only passage that specifically promises an activity of the Spirit in the disciples is that of Mark 13:11, Matthew 10:19-20 and Luke 12:11-12, where the Spirit is clearly the "Spirit of prophecy." That is, it affords charismatic revelation or wisdom to the persecuted disciple. This promise assumes the disciples will already have the Spirit promised by Joel (it is only the words of defense that are given "in that hour," not the gift of the Spirit itself). Luke's parallel saying (Lk 21:15) derives the necessary charismatic wisdom from the heavenly Lord instead, but it is clear Luke believes the means by which the charisma is received is the Spirit of prophecy—for he combines the wording of both promises in his description of Stephen's preaching at Acts 6:5, 10, which also shows he does not regard the activity as restricted to persecution contexts—and thus Luke 21:15 implicitly asserts Jesus' future lordship over the Spirit.

Relevant also are the two final commissioning passages: Matthew 28:18-20 and Luke 24:46-49. The former does not specify a promise of the Spirit to the disciples but is of interest as the one substantial hint of an emerging trinitarian understanding of the Spirit. Elsewhere the ideas do not necessarily move beyond Jewish traditional conceptions, but here the one divine name is spelled out in terms of Father, Son and Spirit. (J. Schaberg's rejection of the apparent trinitari-anism, on the grounds the Matthew passage is a midrash of Daniel 7:9-27, with the Holy Spirit replacing the multitude of angels, is hardly logical, even if the tradition history—itself questionable—is right.) Luke 24:49, strongly redactional in formulation, does not use the word *Spirit*, but the expression "the promise of the Father" clearly refers to Joel's promise through the verbal links Luke carefully establishes in Acts 1:8, Acts 2:17 and Acts 2:33. Though the activity of this gift will empower the mission to all nations, it is not to be thought of as a second blessing. Joel's promised gift of the Spirit of prophecy will become the means by which disciples experience the presence and guidance of their heavenly Lord.

3. The Holy Spirit in John.

In the Fourth Gospel the Spirit is to be understood primarily as a development of the Jewish understanding of the "Spirit of prophecy," redefined christologically and developed in a trinitarian direction.

3.1. *The Portrait of Jesus Endowed with the Spirit (Jn 1:32-34; 3:34-36; 6:63).* John's account jumps from the prologue, which proclaims Jesus the incarnate Logos who reveals the Father (Jn 1:1-18), to the Baptist's testimony concerning Jesus' reception of the Spirit (Jn 1:32-34), with no birth or infancy scenes. W. G. Kümmel, E. Schweizer, and others have claimed John plays down Jesus' endowment in favor of his own Logos christology—after all, he who has descended from the Father barely needs the Spirit to supply revelation (cf. Jn 3:12-13, 31-32). But F. Porsch and G. M. Burge have shown this to be misleading. The first glimpse we see of Jesus is through the testimony of the Baptist (apparently party to Jesus' vision) that he saw the Spirit descend on the Son and "rest/remain on him" (Jn 1:32-33—a reference to Is 11:2, or a way of saying the endowment was permanent or both?) and thereby identify him as the one who baptizes with the Holy Spirit. More significant is John 3:34-36. The elliptic John 3:34 means "Jesus utters the words of God because God gives him the Spirit without measure" (to make Jesus the one who gives the Spirit without measure here breaks the logic of the "because": with Burge, against Porsch). A deliberate contrast with the prophets seems intended (cf. *Lev. Rab.* 15:2, "The Holy Spirit who rests on the prophets, rests on them only by measure"). John's point is that the immeasurable gift of the Spirit (of revelation) to Jesus corresponds to the perfection of revelation through Jesus—it provides a revelation that transcends the Law and the Prophets. This is confirmed in John 3:35, where the result of the Father's love for the Son is that "he has given all things into his hands," that is, the totality of revelation given to the Son whereby he "utters the words of God" (Jn 3:34; cf. Mt 11:27!). John 3:36 now draws the natural conclusion: If the fullness of God's revelation is imparted through the Son, then to receive that revelation brings life. Correspondingly, to reject it is to reject God and so to remain under his wrath. It would seem then that John portrays the gift of the Spirit to Jesus at his baptism as the gift of full revelation and the power to impart it to others. This chimes with Jesus' claim in John 6:63 that his revelatory words *are* an experience of Spirit and life. The claim goes to the heart of John's soteriology.

3.2. Birth "from Above" and Birth of "Water and Spirit" (Jn 3). "Birth from above" (Jn 3:3; cf. Jn 3:31 for *anōthen* as "above" not "again") is a circumlocution for birth from God. The explanatory "birth 'of water and Spirit' " (Jn 3:5) is a hendiadys that must refer to a unitary event (so not natural birth followed by spiritual birth or John's baptism followed by reception of the Spirit, etc.), and it cannot be Christian baptism, of which Nicodemus could scarcely be expected to know. L. Belleville has shown the most probable explanation is the promise in Ezekiel 36:25-26 of eschatological cleansing and new creation in true filial obedience (which *Jub.* 1:23-25 already identifies as the gift of "sonship"). Jesus claims this essentially apocalyptic hope, and concomitant "eternal life," begins to be realized where people truly believe in the Son God has sent (Jn 3:14-18). By no means all "belief" in Jesus, however, is authentic (contrast Jn 2:23 with Jn 2:24; Jn 8:31a with Jn 8:31b-36; etc.). Even the claimed belief of the disciples (Jn 6:69) does not truly become authentic faith until after the glorification of Jesus in the cross (*see* Death of Christ) and resurrection (cf. Jn 16:25). The Spirit-imbued revelatory teaching of Jesus (Jn 6:63) plays a vital function in coming to true belief.

3.3. The Offer of "Living Water" (Jn 4:10, 13-14). Jesus' offer of "living (i.e., flowing) water" which truly quenches thirst and "wells up" like a spring in the believer "to eternal life" merges three kinds of symbolism: (1) the general use of flowing water as a symbol of God's eschatological salvation (e.g., Is 55:1; Zech 14:8; Ezek 47:1-12); (2) refreshing and life-giving water as a symbol for divine wisdom (Prov 13:14 ["a fountain of life"]; 18:4; Sir 24:21 ["Those who eat of me will hunger still; those who drink of me shall thirst for more"]), especially as revealed in the Law (Sir 24:23-29; CD 19:34, *Sipre Deut* 11. 22, §48) and (3) water as symbolism for the gift of the Spirit (Is 44:3; 1QS 4:21; etc.). That John intends the promise to be understood as the Spirit is evident from John 4:23 ("The hour is coming and now is" when true worshipers worship the Father "in Spirit and truth") and from his specific equation of the offer of living water with the Spirit in John 7:37-39. But it is particularly the Spirit as the revealer of divine wisdom through Jesus' Spirit-imbued teaching (cf. Jn 6:63b) that is meant at John 4:10, 13-14. Jesus, as Wisdom incarnate, imparts new revelatory wisdom that re-creates a person and brings "life," but he does so as the one to whom the Father has given the Spirit without measure (Jn 3:34). The combination of revelatory word and Spirit together that is the "living water" (cf. 1QS 4:21-22) effects the "birth from above."

3.4. The Redemptive-Historical Qualification on the Gift (Jn 7:37-39). John 4:10 and John 6:63b suggest the gift of life-giving Spirit-imbued revelation is available within the ministry of Jesus (cf. "the hour . . . now is" at Jn 4:23). This would appear to be supported by John 13:10, John 15:3 and John 17:17, which declare the disciples are already "cleansed" by Jesus' word, and by the implication of saying not *all* (who seem to) actually believe (Jn 6:64; cf. Jn 13:11)—to exclude Judas. But while these references indicate that Jesus' revelation is already beginning to transform the disciples, John provides a strong qualification of this.

3.4.1. John 7:37-39. In a context of the ceremony of water drawing and libation at the festival of tabernacles, interpreted in Judaism as a promise of the rivers of salvation to pour out from the temple (Isaiah 12:3, Ezekiel 47:1-12 and Zechariah 14:8 were read during the festival), Jesus invites the thirsty to drink from him instead. The invitation is supported by Scripture (apparently summarizing its message in the light of the fulfillment expected rather than citing; no OT passage corresponds verbally to John 7:38) that "out of his/its belly shall flow rivers of living water." Most modern exegetes (e.g., Brown

1966, Beasley-Murray, Burge) repunctuate John 7:37 to make Christ rather than the believer the source ("If anyone thirst, let him come to me, and let him drink who believes in me"). J. B. Cortes, however, argues strongly for the traditional view that the Spirit flows from the believer, the messianic community being thus seen as the embodiment of the eschatological temple from which the renewing waters stream (cf. Ezek 47:1-12; Zech 14:8)—with Jesus as the ultimate source. Either way, John 7:39 insists the promise relates to the gift of the Spirit (cf. *m. Sukk.* 5:55a) and affirms that this gift was not yet given, for Jesus was not yet been "glorified" (i.e., exalted through the cross, resurrection and ascension [Jn 12:23-24; 17:5]).

3.4.2. John 20:22. According to John 20:22, when Jesus appeared to the disciples, bid them peace and recommissioned them, "he breathed on them, and said to them, 'Receive the Holy Spirit' " (RSV). The verb *enephysēsen* means "insufflated" more readily than "breathed upon" and is a direct allusion to Genesis 2:7, where God breathed the breath of life into Adam (cf. Ezek 37:9). The implication is that it is only now, beyond the cross and vindication, that the Spirit-empowered revelation to the disciples achieves what had been begun within the ministry, namely, new creation transformation. Essentially the same point was anticipated at John 3:14-18, where the belief in the Son, which brings life, is specifically belief in the revelation of the Son afforded by the cross and vindication. Compare also John 6, where the divine wisdom Jesus' hearers are invited to eat and drink (Jn 6:35) is first spelled out as the unity of the Father and the Son in salvation (Jesus is the life-giving counterpart to the manna God gave in the wilderness) but then narrowed down to that divine wisdom expressed in the Son's revelatory death on behalf of humanity (Jn 6:51c-58). For John the fundamental problem of humankind is alienation from God expressed in unbelief, darkness and ignorance of God. What is needed to overcome it is a revealer, light and knowledge of God—which it is precisely the mission of the Son, empowered by the Spirit, to bring (Jn 8:28; 14:10; 15:22-24). His revelatory word frees (Jn 8:31-36); to "hear" it is to experience the Spirit transforming through it and to taste life (Jn 6:63b). But for John, the exaltation through the cross deals objectively with the sin that caused the fundamental alienation (contra Bultmann

and Forestell; see Turner 1990) and provides the supreme revelation of the unity of the Father and the Son in saving love. Correspondingly, only after the Easter event can the word of Jesus be released in full transforming power through the Spirit.

3.5. Jesus Promises the Spirit as "Another Paraclete" (Jn 14—16). In three passages (Jn 14:16-26; 15:26-27; 16:7-15) John speaks of a coming gift of the Holy Spirit (Jn 14:26), or "Spirit of Truth" (Jn 14:17; 15:26; 16:13: cf. *Jub.* 25:14; *T. Jud.* 20:1-5; 1QS 3:18-25), to act as a "paraclete" (*paraklētos:* Jn 14:16, 26; 15:26; 16:7).

3.5.1. The Meaning of Paraklētos. In Greek the word is formally a passive verbal adjective, "one called alongside" (especially to offer assistance in a court), and so an "advocate" (though not with the profession al legal sense of the Latin *advocatus*), and indeed later Rabbinic Judaism came to use *pĕraqlit* (a loan word) for "advocate" (cf. *Pirqe Aboth* 4:11). Because, however, the functions attributed to "the Paraclete" in John are primarily teaching, revealing and interpreting Jesus to the disciples (with forensic functions only explicit at Jn 15:26[?]; 16:8-11), other meanings of *paraklētos* have been championed. These include (1) "Comforter" (derived from *parakalein*, "to encourage" [so Davies]; but John does not use the verb, and this etymology should require an active not passive adjective); (2) "Exhorter" (so, roughly, Barrett 1950, deriving from *paraklēsis* and facing similar difficulties) and (3) "Helper" (so Bultmann 1971, by somewhat forced linguistic and conceptual association with [plural] "helpers" [arguably rather "bearers of light"] in alleged Mandaean background). But none of these have forensic functions. Those that have accepted the sense "advocate" have generally found the background in the angelic intercessor-defender figures of the OT and intertestamental literature and Qumran (*see* Dead Sea Scrolls) and (e.g., for the personal traits) their Michael mythology. (For a review of the complex discussion see G. Johnston [esp. chap. 7] and Burge [chap. 1]. To date these background studies illuminate various traits of John's portrait of the Paraclete rather than satisfactorily explaining the redactional whole.)

3.5.2. The Paraclete Is Modeled on Jesus. This point is made in Jesus' promise of "another Paraclete of the same kind" (*allos*) and in the deliberate parallelism between Jesus and what is promised of the Spirit. (1) Both "come forth"/

are "sent" from the Father into the world (Jn 3:16-17; 5:43; 16:27-28; 18:37 par. Jn 14:26; 15:26; 16:7-8, 13). (2) Both are called "holy" (Jn 6:39 par. Jn 14:26) and are characterized by "the truth" (Jn 14:6 par. Jn 14:17; 15:26; 16:13). (3) If Jesus is the great teacher (cf. Jn 13:13-14), the Paraclete will "teach you . . . all things" (Jn14:26). (4) Just as the Messiah bears witness to God and reveals all things (Jn 4:25-26; cf. Jn 1:18; 3:34-36; etc.)—supremely himself and the Father—so too the Paraclete will witness to and reveal especially the glorified Son (Jn 15:26-27; 16:13-14). And as Jesus set out to convince and convict the world, which nevertheless did not "receive" him (Jn 1:12 etc.), so too the Paraclete's task is to convince and convict the world (Jn 16:8-12), but the world does not receive him either (Jn 14:17; 15:18-26). The *Sitz-im-Leben* of these parallels is the usual concern of the Jewish genre farewell discourses, namely, to establish how the decisive initiative made by the man of God will be continued beyond his death. Jesus has acted as the Paraclete so far; the Spirit is to take over that role.

3.5.3. The Paraclete Will Mediate the Presence of the Father and the Glorified Son (Jn 14:16-26). Having assured them of the gift of the Spirit in John 14:16-17, in John 14:18-19 Jesus promises he will not leave the disciples desolate but will come to them in such a way that "the world" will not see him—he will manifest himself to any disciple who loves him (Jn 14:21). When this is pressed by Judas in John 14:22, Jesus reasserts that if a disciple loves him, he and the Father will come and make their home with him. This promise cannot refer to Jesus' "second coming," for then the world *shall* see, or to resurrection appearances that were neither dependent on the love of the disciples nor capable of being described as the coming of the Father and the Son to dwell with the disciple. As these affirmations are sandwiched by promises of the Spirit-Paraclete (Jn 14:14-17, 25-26), and as (in Judaism) the Spirit of prophecy was regarded as the presence of God in revelation, most exegetes infer that it is precisely the promised Spirit that will mediate the presence and self-revelation of Father and Son. Those who deny this (e.g., Beasley-Murray) do not tell us how Christ and the Father are supposed to "manifest themselves" to the disciple or explain why (if they can) John thinks the Spirit need be given at all. We conclude the Paraclete/ Advocate is the Holy Spirit in a special role,

namely, as the personal presence of Jesus in the Christian while Jesus is with the Father (so Brown), though without agreeing that John significantly collapsed the delayed parousia into his pneumatology.

3.5.4. The Paraclete as Teacher and Revealer (Jn 14:26; 16:12-14). The disciples cannot take in (Jn 16:12) or understand the significance of what Jesus has said and done until he is glorified (Jn 16:25). Consequently, the Spirit-Paraclete is given to remind them of Jesus' teaching (Jn 14:26) and to interpret it to them (e.g., Jn 2:22). The main task of the Spirit in John is to provide a particular sort of charismatic wisdom: to bring true comprehension of the significance of the historical revelation in Christ. The truth into which he leads (Jn 16:13) is not the later doctrines of the church but principally the truth that Jesus has incarnated and taught and concerning which Jesus would readily explain more at the Last Supper, if the disciples could only absorb it (Jn 16:12); the things of Jesus and which glorify him (cf. Jn 16:14). Even the promise of the Spirit declaring "the things that are to come" (Jn 16:13), in context of the Last Supper, refers primarily though not exclusively to the all-important coming events of the cross and exaltation, not the end. As Porsch put it: "Jesus brings the truth, and makes it present through his coming into the world; the Spirit-Paraclete opens up this truth and creates the entrance into it for believers" (Porsch, 300). The title of E. Franck's monograph on the Spirit-Paraclete—*Revelation Taught*—points to the centrality of this motif for John.

3.5.5. The Paraclete as "Advocate" and the Christian Mission. The reason why this Revealer-Teacher is called "another Paraclete" (= "advocate," Jn 14:16) is best clarified in terms of John's presentation of Jesus' ministry under the extended metaphor of a cosmic trial. The issue contended is whether or not Jesus truly is the final manifestation of God, very Son from the Father, whom to know is "Life" transcending the possibilities offered by Judaism (cf. Jn 20:31). As the sent one, Jesus has a mission to convince the world of God's saving truth, which he incarnates and reveals, and this mission dominates the Gospel (within Jn 5:31-47 alone Jesus points to five "witnesses" on his side): he is the chief advocate of the case with which the disciples have become identified. The impending removal of Jesus through cross and exaltation cannot be allowed to leave the disciples "as orphans" (correctly NIV; RSV's "desolate" misses the point)—that is, defenseless. Nor may the case be lost because reduced to silence. Rather the disciples are now "sent" as Jesus was "sent" (Jn 20:21; cf. Jn 17:17-18), and the Spirit from the heavenly Lord is given to them to take over the earthly Jesus' advocacy of the case (Jn 15:26-27; 16:7b-11). According to John 16:8-11, the Spirit-Paraclete will prosecute the case against the world by exposing it with respect to sin (that its unbelief is the essence of sin), righteousness (that its claim to righteousness is false [?]; or—more probably—that its verdict on Jesus is reversed by the exaltation) and judgment (that the power that engineered Jesus' death, and continues to oppose Christ, stands condemned in Jesus' vindication). But the connection with John 16:12-15 must be observed. The Spirit will convince the world of these things precisely by revealing the truth and by teaching its significance to the disciples. John 16:8-11 does not mean the Spirit offers independent witness; John knows of no witness by the Spirit that is not witness through the church. But equally the disciples only give their witness as ones to whom the Spirit has revealed Jesus and the significance of his life, death and resurrection. It is thus as teacher and revealer that the Spirit will also be Paraclete or Advocate. This does not mean John thinks the Paraclete is given as a second blessing of revelation and wisdom for missionary empowering but that he thinks the post-ascension gift of the Spirit is simultaneously the means by which the disciple "understands" the gospel and the means of ongoing knowledge of the presence and guidance of the Father and the Son. This itself constitutes the witness to Christ and so is "the Spirit of mission."

3.5.6. Concluding Theological and Critical Remarks. A minor debate continues as to when John thought the Spirit was first given as the "Paraclete" (whether at Jn 20:22 or beyond the period of the Gospel, when first the Spirit replaces Jesus). More theologically significant are the christological and trinitarian conclusions to be drawn. (1) Jesus' lordship over the Spirit expressed in his sending and commissioning of the "Paraclete" (Jn 15:26; 16:7) attests a fully divine Christology. (2) The portrait of the Spirit as a replacement figure, and one which goes well beyond the frequent but incidental personifications of the Spirit in Judaism, takes the pneuma-

tology in the direction of trinitarianism. Major differences center on the origin of the traditions about the Spirit—whether they are purely Christian creative midrash around Jesus' minimal teaching on the Spirit as an advocate in time of persecution (see 2.5 above) or more substantially derive from Jesus—but a convincing tradition history of the material would at present be very hard to establish. Nevertheless, it may be observed that the Johannine Spirit teaching, with its strong wisdom accent, is evidently rooted in the Jewish conception of the Spirit as the "Spirit of prophecy." No single formulation demonstrably moves beyond the circle of what could be expected if the Jesus we otherwise know from the Synoptics were to express his teaching in specifically pneumatological terms.

See also BAPTISM; BIRTH OF JESUS; CHRISTOLOGY; GOD; JOHN THE BAPTIST.

DNTB: HOLY SPIRIT.

BIBLIOGRAPHY. C. K. Barrett, *The Holy Spirit and the Gospel Tradition* (2d ed., London: SPCK, 1966); idem, "The Holy Spirit in the Fourth Gospel," *JTS* 1 (1950) 1-15; G. R. Beasley-Murray, *John* (WBC 36; Waco, TX: Word, 1989); L. Belle-ville " 'Born of Water and Spirit': John 3:5," *TJ* 1 (1980) 125-41; E. Best, "Spirit-Baptism," *NovT* 4 (1960) 236-43; R. E. Brown, *The Birth of the Messiah* (New York: Doubleday, 1977); idem, *The Gospel According to John* (AB 29; Garden City, NY: Doubleday, 1966, 1970); idem, "The Paraclete in the Fourth Gospel," *NTS* 13 (1966-67) 113-32; R. Bultmann, *The Gospel of John* (Philadelphia: Westminster, 1971); idem, *The History of the Synoptic Tradition* (Oxford: Blackwell, 1963); idem, *Theology of the New Testament* (2 vols.; New York: Scribner's, 1951, 1955); G. M. Burge, *The Anointed Community: The Holy Spirit in the Johannine Community* (Grand Rapids: Eerdmans, 1987); H. Conzelmann, *The Theology of St. Luke* (London: Faber and Faber, 1960); J. B. Cortes, "Yet Another Look at John 7:37-38," *CBQ* 29 (1967) 75-86; J. G. Davies, "The Primary Meaning of ΠΑΡΑΚΛΗΤΟΣ," *JTS* 4 (1953) 35-38; J. D. G. Dunn, *Baptism in the Holy Spirit: A Reexamination of the New Testament Teaching on the Gift of the Spirit in Relation to Pentecostalism Today* (Philadelphia: Westminster, 1970); idem, *Jesus and the Spirit* (Philadelphia: Westminster, 1975); idem, "Spirit and Fire Baptism," *NovT* 14 (1972) 81-92; J. A. Fitzmyer, *The Gospel According to Luke* (AB 28; New York: Doubleday, 1981, 1985); J. T. Forestell, *The Word of the Cross: Salvation as Revelation in the Fourth Gospel* (Rome: Pontifical Biblical Institute, 1970); E. Franck, *Revelation Taught: The Paraclete in the Gospel of John* (Lund: Gleerup, 1985); D. E. Holwerda, *The Holy Spirit and Eschatology in the Gospel of John* (Kampen: Kok, 1959); G. Johnston, *The Spirit-Paraclete in the Gospel of John* (Cambridge: Cambridge University Press, 1970); W. G. Kümmel, *The Theology of the New Testament* (Nashville: Abingdon, 1973); H. Leisegang, *Pneuma Hagion* (Leipzig: Hinrichs, 1922); M. R. Mansfield, *"Spirit and Gospel" in Mark* (Peabody, MA: Hendrickson, 1987); F. Porsch, *Pneuma und Wort: Ein exegetischer Beitrag zur Pneumatologie des Johannesevangeliums* (Frankfurt: Knecht, 1974); J. Schaberg, *The Father, the Son and the Holy Spirit: The Triadic Phrase in Matthew 28:19b* (Chico, CA: Scholars Press, 1982); G. Schneider, *Das Evangelium nach Lukas* (Gütersloh: Mohn, 1977); E. Schweizer, "πνεῦμα κτλ," *TDNT* 6:389-455; R. B. Sloan, *The Favorable Year of the Lord: A Study of Jubilary Theology in the Gospel of Luke* (Austin: Schola, 1977); C. Tuckett, "Luke 4,16-30, Isaiah and Q" in *Logia: Les Paroles de Jésus—The Sayings of Jesus,* ed. J. Delobel (Louvain: University Press, 1982) 343-54; M. M. B. Turner, "Atonement and the Death of Jesus in John—Some Questions to Bultmann and Forestell," *EvQ* 62 (1990) 99-122; idem, "Jesus and the Spirit in Lukan Perspective," *TynB* 32 (1981) 3-42; idem, "The Significance of Receiving the Spirit in John's Gospel," *VoxEv* 10 (1977) 24-42; idem, "The Spirit and the Power of Jesus' Miracles in the Lucan Conception," *NovT* 33 (1991) 124-52; J. E. Yates, *The Spirit and the Kingdom* (London: SPCK, 1963).

M. M. B. Turner

HOLY SPIRIT II: PAUL

The Holy Spirit is a prominent theme in Paul's letters and theology. This Spirit is the very Spirit of God that Israel knew and the OT testifies to, but for Christians the Spirit is also the Spirit of Christ, the presence of the risen Lord to believers, who imparts divine wisdom and power for spiritual growth and renewal, and empowers and impels Christian mission. The presence and working of the Spirit is an eschatological gift, or downpayment, of the age to come, enabling believers to overcome the opposition and challenges of this age and to live Christ-like lives that bear the "fruit of the Spirit." Further, the Spirit empowers the community with gifts that contribute to its growth, welfare and worship.

1. The Sources of Paul's Concept of the Spirit
2. The Spirit of God
3. The Spirit and Wisdom
4. The Spirit as Divine Power
5. The Spirit of Christ
6. The Spirit and Mission
7. The Spirit and the Christian's New Life
8. The Spirit and Eschatology
9. The Spirit and Worship

1. The Sources of Paul's Concept of the Spirit. Paul's concept of the Spirit has three main sources: the revelation in the OT canon, intertestamental Judaism and early Christian thought. In addition, Paul's experience and that of the Christian communities he founded no doubt played an important role in his thinking. It must be admitted that only three times in the OT (MT: Is 63:10-11; Ps 51:13) is the Spirit of God called "holy," but this designation became more common in the intertestamental period. The OT roots are evident in the fact that for Paul the Spirit is singular and unique. To speak of the Spirit is to speak of God's presence and power (Is 31:3; 34:16; 40:13). As God is one, so there is only one Spirit of God (1 Cor 12:4-6, 11, 13; Eph 4:4-6). However the term *spirit* (Heb *rûaḥ,* Gk *pneuma*) is increasingly used in later Jewish writing for angels or demons (usually in the plural) at Qumran, in rabbinic and apocalyptic literature (Sekki, chap. 5; Schweizer, 6:375-76). The Spirit is associated from an early time forward with prophecy (Num 11:29; 1 Sam 10:6; 19:20-24; Mic 3:8; Ezek 11:5; Joel 2:28-29; Sir 48:12, 24; cf. 1 Thess 5:19-20; 1 Cor 12:7-11). And, especially in the prophets, the Spirit has a moral character, being associated with justice, judgment and living in covenant (Is 4:4; 28:5-6; 59:21; 63:10; Ezek 36:26-27; 39:27-29; Ps 51:10-11; 143:10). The OT holds out a hope that this Spirit, as the power of prophecy, life and covenant keeping, will be a feature of the future messianic age of blessing (Is 32:15; 44:3; Ezek 36:25-27; 39:28-29; Joel 2:28-29), and this hope persisted into the Second Temple period (*Pss. Sol.* 17:37; 18:7; *T. Levi* 18:7; *T. Judah* 24:2). The Qumran sectarians apparently believed themselves heirs in some sense of this promise of the Spirit (Sekki, 79-84). This prophetic promise underlies Paul's view of the Spirit as a normal part of the Christian life.

The association of the Spirit with God's wisdom (cf. 1 Cor 2:10-11) is a thought found a few times in the OT (Ex 31:3; 35:31; Num 11:16-17; Job 32:8; Is 11:2; 42:1-4) and developed further in later Judaism (Wis 7:22–8:1; 1QH 9; 12:11-12, 31-35; in Philo the divine *pneuma* is the source of reason and wisdom in mortals, *Leg. All.* 1.42; *Gig.* 22-24, 27). Two other ideas that Paul inherits from his background, though they are not unique to Hebrew thought, are the association of Spirit with power (2 Kings 2:9-15; Judg 6:34-35; 14:19; 15:14-15) and with life, as the life-giving force that originates with God (Gen 1:2; 6:3; Ps 104:29-30; Job 32:8; Is 42:5; Ezek 37:4-14; on the Spirit in the OT and Judaism see *TDNT* 6:362-63, 365-67, 368-89).

Paul's concept of the Spirit is not, however, simply a continuation of the OT/Jewish viewpoint. For one thing the Spirit has a prominence in Paul's writings that far exceeds its place in the OT. In relative numeric terms, *rûaḥ* refers to the Spirit of God an estimated 90 times in the MT, and *pneuma* does so 100 times in the LXX. In contrast *pneuma* refers to God's Spirit 112 to 115 times (depending on the exegesis of some passages) in the much smaller corpus of Pauline letters.

The increased importance of the Spirit in Paul may be explained on the basis of the early Christian communities' experience of the Spirit in their midst, including Paul's experience, in the perception of God's immanence during worship, in the working of *miracles and the inspiration of prophecy, in the experience of boldness and wisdom to proclaim the gospel even through difficult circumstances, and in the feelings of joy. These experiences for the early Christians were evidence of the Spirit present and acting. And they understood their experience as the fulfillment of prophetic hopes that in the age of the Messiah, the Spirit would fall on "Israel" (Ezek 36:25-27; Joel 2:28-32; Paul cites from the latter passage in Rom 10:13). Paul shows awareness of this OT eschatological hope in referring to the "promise of the Spirit" (Gal 3:14; cf. Eph 1:13). The coming of the Spirit was also a sign for the early Christians that the risen Lord, Jesus, was indeed the Messiah (cf. Acts 2:14-24, 36, 38-39; Jn 16:7-11; see 5 below).

In contrast to much Hellenistic thought, Paul does not see the Spirit as a force or a being at the beck and call of the believer. Unlike "demons" or the magician's helping spirits, the Holy Spirit cannot be controlled by special incantations or actions. He is, however, present to aid the believer in living out God's will. And while in ancient magic supernatural aid was believed to be available only to the few with esoteric knowledge, regardless of their motives, the Spirit is given freely to all, on the sole condition of faith in Christ as Lord (1 Cor 12:3).

2. The Spirit of God.

An obvious but important fact is that Paul assumes the Holy Spirit is God's Spirit (*see* God). That is, it is not merely one of a host of intermediaries, but in accord with the OT and intertestamental Jewish literature it is assumed that the Spirit is singular, unique in power and in its relationship to God (e.g., 1 Cor 2:11; Rom 8:9, 11; 2 Cor 3:17; cf. Eph 4:4). Paul always speaks of the Spirit that is given to Christians in the singular: the Holy Spirit or Spirit of God (cf. Rom 8:9; 1 Cor 3:17; 12:4-6; 2 Cor 5:5; Gal 3:5). This singularity of the Spirit can be used as a theological argument for the unity of the church: "we were all baptized by one Spirit into one body . . . we were all given the one Spirit to drink" (1 Cor 12:13). Paul never speaks of God's giving spirits (plural) to believers (1 Cor 14:12 is best taken as Paul's quoting a Corinthian saying, "[we are] zealots for spirits," without endorsing the viewpoint it implies). The Spirit represents God as present among his people—in Paul often in connection with inspired speech, particularly proclaiming the gospel, but also prophecy, encouragement, exhortation and teaching, and with miracles (1 Cor 12:4-11; 1 Thess 1:5; Gal 3:1-5).

Paul never addresses directly the issue of the personality of the Holy Spirit. At times the Spirit and God may overlap, having seemingly identical functions, as in the distribution of spiritual gifts to different "parts" of the body of Christ (1 Cor 12:11, 18, 26). At times the Spirit is spoken of as distinct from God and Christ, as in the triadic formula of 1 Corinthians 12:4-6 or the blessing of 2 Corinthians 13:13 (14), or when God is said to send the Spirit or to seal believers by means of the Spirit (Gal 4:6; 2 Cor 1:21-22; 5:5; Rom 5:5). The Spirit may be described with personal characteristics. He may "lead" believers (Gal 5:18; Rom 8:14; cf. 8:4), "reveal" the mystery of the gospel and its implications (1 Cor 2:6-16; Eph 3:5) or help believers in prayer (Gal 4:6; Rom 8:15, 26-27; cf. 1 Cor 14:14-16). The Spirit has its "desires" (though the "flesh" does also, without the "flesh" necessarily being a personal force: Gal 5:16-17); and in Ephesians the Spirit may be "grieved" (Eph 4:30). None of these remarks are intended by Paul as comment directly on the personhood of the Spirit, but they are incidental to Paul's main point, which is usually more pragmatic than speculative. Some scholars think these remarks no more point to personhood than do remarks that seem to personalize the power of sin or of the flesh. Certainly Paul does not work with definitions of divine "persons" such as arose in later Christian theology. Nevertheless it seems that the seeds of such thought are present here. Whether or not Paul asserts the personhood of the Spirit, he is eager that his churches know what sort of personality the Spirit has: he has the character of God, and more precisely, of Jesus Christ (see 5 below).

3. The Spirit and Wisdom.

The Spirit is the only means by which God's wisdom may be communicated to humans, for only the Spirit knows God's mind (1 Cor 2:10-16). Paul denies that any sort of "wisdom" originating from below, from the side of humanity, may comprehend God and his workings. In 1 Corinthians 1:18—2:16 Paul attacks attempts by Corinthian Christians to "correct" the gospel by revising it in the light of contemporary intellectual currents, whether Jewish or Greco-Roman—specifically by denigrating the role of Jesus' death on the cross. In this passage Paul makes an important link between the Spirit, the cross and wisdom. The gospel foundations cannot be altered, for not only are human intellectual systems "foolish" in God's sight (1 Cor 1:18-25); the problem is even more radical. God's working remains mysterious, incomprehensible to the unredeemed, who reject it (1 Cor 2:6-8, 14).

It is precisely the crucified Savior who is the content of God's mysterious wisdom, a wisdom that cannot be grasped apart from the Spirit (1 Cor 1:23-24; 2:2, 6-12). So the Spirit remains as the only possible bridge to knowing God and to accepting the gospel. Those who try to tamper with the role of the cross or the foundational elements of the gospel only demonstrate that they are people without the Spirit, "carnal" (1 Cor 2:14; 3:1). This last remark is addressed to those at Corinth who regarded themselves as "the spiritual ones" and who were attempting to revise the apostolic message. When seen in its historical and literary context, this passage has continuing relevance for the church, which in every age is faced with demands by the dominant intellectual/religious forces to modify some aspect of the gospel core. First Corinthians 2:6-16 is not an announcement of mystical knowledge for a Christian elite; it is a defense of the apostolic gospel as most truly spiritual, and the Spirit as the one who communicates and expounds it.

4. The Spirit as Divine Power.

Paul inherits from the OT and intertestamental Judaism the concept of the Spirit as the power of God (see 1 above). He attributes his evangelistic success to the Spirit's effective presence and suggests more than once that miracles attended his own preaching, though he does not enumerate these (1 Thess 1:4-6; 1 Cor 2:4-5; Rom 15:18-19; Gal 3:2). He expects that at Christian meetings the Spirit will inspire not only the spoken word but "supernatural" skills and events as well (1 Cor 12:7-11; 14; Gal 3:5). Naturally this is only one facet of Paul's understanding of the Spirit and must not be taken in isolation. Never does Paul invoke the Spirit's work merely to impress or entertain. Most of the Pauline passages speaking of the Spirit's power relate it directly to the purpose of evangelism or to living the new life in Christ (on evangelism see 6 below; on the Christian life see 7 below). Other references include the Spirit's power in worship—again, not simply as display but as the power to inform and "build up" Christians (1 Cor 12:7; cf. 14:5, 19, 26) or to discipline and punish (cf. 1 Cor 5:3-5).

That the reception of the Spirit by believers is sometimes described with terms such as "fill" or "pour out (on)" has led several to claim that the Spirit was conceived by Paul and the earliest Christians as a fluid that physically fills the believer (e.g., Hunter, 92), though in the Pauline corpus "fill" is only one image of many, and it occurs just three times (1 Cor 12:13; Eph 5:18; Tit 3:4-5). Such language is evoked in part by purposefully echoing Septuagintal usage and is best understood as metaphor (cf. Joel 2:28-29, "pour out" the Spirit, echoed at Acts 2:33; and Mic 3:8, "I am filled with power, with the Spirit of the Lord").

In Ephesians the only explicit connection between Spirit and power has been internalized: it is for the "inner self" and is associated with the indwelling of Christ by faith (Eph 3:16-17). Elsewhere in Ephesians the author speaks of God's power (= the Spirit?) as the instrument of Christ's *resurrection (Eph 1:19-20). Similarly at 2 Timothy 1:7 the Spirit given to Timothy is to be the foundation for a divinely inspired boldness concerning the gospel and his association with the imprisoned Paul ("therefore do not be ashamed of the testimony about our Lord, nor of me his prisoner," 2 Tim 1:8), as well as the source of divine power to "suffer together [with Paul or with Christ?] for the gospel" (2 Tim 1:8). These functions are reminiscent of the role of the Spirit in the proclamation of the gospel (see 6 below).

5. The Spirit of Christ.

The Spirit has the character of *Christ. One notable aspect of Paul's teaching on the Spirit that distinguishes it from Israelite and Jewish faith is the intimate association of the Spirit with the risen Lord Jesus, the "Jesus character" of the Spirit (Dunn 1975, 318-26). Hence it is called the "Spirit of Christ" or the "Spirit of God's Son" (Rom 8:9; Gal 4:6). The Spirit transforms believers from the heart outward to have the character of their Lord Jesus Christ (2 Cor 3:3, 18; Eph 3:16-17). And to be in the fellowship of God's Son, Jesus Christ (1 Cor 1:9), is the same as having fellowship in the Holy Spirit (2 Cor 13:13 [14]; Phil 2:1; see Christology).

5.1. The Spirit of Christ and the Cross. Because the Spirit is Christ's, he is associated not only with power and blessing but also with the cross of Christ (1 Cor 2:1-16; see 4 above), with lowliness and service to others in line with the character of the master (1 Cor 12—13). The Corinthians have to be taught that to be a spiritual person may mean not glory but weakness and suffering (e.g., 2 Cor 4:7-18 with 2 Cor 3:7-8; 2 Cor 11:16—12:10). Jesus' earthly life is a pattern for the Spirit's working in believers: "For in fact [Christ] was crucified in weakness, but lives by God's power; and indeed we are weak in him, but we will live with him by God's power for your benefit" (2 Cor 13:4). In this verse God's power is tantamount to the Spirit of Christ. This Jesus-character of the Spirit explains why the supreme sign of the Spirit's presence, the principal element of the "fruit of the Spirit" (Gal 5:22), is love. God's greatest act of love was shown to creation in Christ's death for its redemption, and this love is "poured out" into believers' hearts by the presence of the Spirit (Rom 5:5-8).

5.2. The Spirit of Christ Relating to the Church.

Since his resurrection and ascension Jesus now relates to his church and to the world via the Spirit (see Eschatology). Christ can be experienced in this time before his return only through the Spirit. The Spirit marks Christians as members of Christ's body (1 Cor 6:15-20; 12:12-13; see Body of Christ); he signifies that believers do not belong to themselves but to the Lord who purchased them. Christ, as the church's Lord, leads it by means of the Spirit in prophecy, in the teaching and leadership gifts, or by other means. The Spirit's opposition to the flesh may be seen as one way the Spirit presents Christ's will to the individual. The link between Jesus and the Spirit is so intimate that for Paul it was impossible to have one without the other: "If anyone does not have the Spirit of Christ, that person does not belong to him" (Rom 8:9; cf. 1 Cor 12:12-13). All who have faith in Christ are on the basis of that faith assured of the eschatological gift of the Spirit (Rom 8:1-2, 9; Gal 3:1-2, 5; cf. Eph 1:13-14; 4:30; and Acts 2:33, 38-39). Hence to be a Christian is to be truly a "spiritual person" (*pneumatikon*, 1 Cor 2:10-16), indwelt by the Spirit.

"The first Adam became a living soul; the last Adam became a life-giving Spirit" (1 Cor 15:45) is not meant to be a simple identification of Christ with the Spirit; the point of the saying in the context of the discussion of resurrection is not christological but soteriological (Fee). Adam had life for himself as God's gift, but Christ is able to give life to others (the life of resurrection, of the age to come). And he is able to do this via the Spirit, with whom he is in some sense one (2 Cor 3:17; see Adam and Christ).

In light of the above, it is to be expected that the Spirit is known by the fact that he will promote the confession of Jesus as Lord (1 Cor 12:3). Anything contrary to that confession cannot be from the Spirit. This is the measure of the authenticity of any manifestation of the Spirit, taking precedence over ecstasy, glossolalia or any other supposed sign.

5.3. Distinctions Between the Spirit and Christ. At times the Spirit and Christ (as with the Spirit and God) seem to overlap or even become interchangeable, as in Romans 8:9-11, where "the Spirit of God," "the Spirit of Christ" and "Christ in you" all refer to the same reality (on 1 Corinthians 15:45 see 5.2 above). Christians may be said to be "in the Spirit" (Rom 8:9; Gal 5:25; cf. Gal 5:16; 1 Cor 12:3) or to have the Spirit in them (Rom 8:11; 1 Cor 3:16; 6:19; Gal 4:6), just as they may be "in Christ" (2 Cor 5:17) or have Christ in them (Gal 2:20). Second Corinthians 3:17 should not be taken as evidence for the identity of Jesus and the Spirit ("The Lord is the Spirit; and where the Spirit of the Lord is, there is freedom"). The first occurrence of "Lord" in that passage refers to the wording of Exodus 34:34 LXX (2 Cor 3:16), meaning that when those in this age "turn to the Lord [i.e., God]" as Moses did at Sinai, a veil of spiritual blindness is lifted from their eyes; only now "Lord" signifies "the Spirit" who is the key to knowledge of God. This is Paul's interpretation of the OT passage's meaning that he applies to his conflict with Jews and Jewish Christians. The next verse must also be understood in this context: it is the work of "the Lord who is the Spirit" to transform believers into the image of Christ, the last Adam, the pattern of a new humanity (2 Cor 3:18).

In the expression "Spirit of Christ" we cannot take the genitive "of" as simply an equal sign (i.e., an epexegetical genitive phrase, meaning "the Spirit that = Christ"). Paul can clearly distinguish the two: only Jesus is described as the Father's Son (Rom 1:3; Gal 4:4); only he had a human nature (Rom 1:3; 8:3; Gal 4:4; Phil 2:7); only Jesus Christ died "for our sins" (1 Cor 15:3; cf. Rom 5:8; 2 Cor 5:15), was raised and is said to be seated at God's right hand (Col 3:3; cf. Phil 2:9). Never are these said of the Spirit. In none of his extant letters does Paul spell out in detail how the Spirit and Christ are related, but a few clues to his thinking may be present:

(1) The Spirit comes only as a result of faith in Christ and is not otherwise a possession of humanity in general (Gal 3:1-2).

(2) The Spirit is known by the fact that he will promote the confession of Jesus as Lord in the church (1 Cor 12:3) and that he bears witness to the character of and the truth about Jesus (1 Thess 1:6 with 1:8; 4:7-8). The Spirit is recognized because he manifests the character of Christ in himself and in those in whom he dwells.

(3) The Spirit brings to believers in a personal or existential way the reality of their new relation to God as children (huioi), a reality that has been accomplished for them by Christ. "God sent his Son . . . to redeem those under Law, so that we might receive adoption as children [see Adoption, Sonship]. Because you are children, God sent the Spirit of his Son into our hearts crying 'Abba, Father!' " (Gal 4:4-6; cf. Rom 8:14-16).

(4) The coming of the Spirit for the church is a divine work that is historically subsequent to the work of Christ (Gal 4:4-6) and may be seen as dependent upon what he accomplished.

(5) The Spirit binds all believers to Christ: they are "one Spirit" with him (1 Cor 6:17) and have been baptized in or by the Spirit into the body of Christ, where they serve in the power of the Spirit and at his direction (1 Cor 12:4-13).

(6) On the basis of the 1 Corinthians 12, we see the Spirit as empowering, organizing and directing Christian worship and Christian community. This direction carries equal authority to that of God (1 Cor 12:11 with 18, 28) or Christ (by implication, since the "body" in which believers serve is Christ's). The functions of the Spirit in relation to Christ may in many ways be said to be analogous to Jesus' relationship to the Father as depicted in the Synoptics. The two may have identical functions, yet they are distinct. The Spirit, to use John's phrase, glorifies Christ (Jn 16:12-14; cf. 1 Cor 12:3), just as the earthly Jesus glorified the Father. The Spirit conveys the "mind of Christ" to believers; he communicates the will and direction of their Lord and an understanding of his gospel. The Spirit's work and the Spirit's coming to believers are dependent on the Son and ultimately on the Father. Yet the Spirit is not thought of as a lesser emissary, like one of the angels; he is in a real sense the presence of Christ with believers.

The Spirit has an important place in Paul's theology because it makes possible the uniting of the historical Jesus, who was raised from the dead, with the heavenly Lord, who is at the same time present with his people. The corporeality of a risen Jesus could be potentially troubling in two ways: (1) it might seem to give Jesus a corruptible nature (because he shared in material existence); and just as serious, (2) it might make Jesus a distant figure, exalted into heaven but separated from the feelings and needs of his people on earth. Paul avoids these pitfalls, preserving Jesus' exalted nature in a new body and at the same time his immanent presence with the faithful in the Spirit ("spiritual body," 1 Cor 15:44, does not mean "a body made of spirit" or bodiless existence; rather, it indicates a body fit for the existence of resurrection life—simultaneously corporeal and "spiritual"). To use a modern analogy, the Spirit might be compared with the lines connecting our homes to electricity or to telecommunication networks. These make possible the presence in our homes of power or of communication with other people, without having those people or the electricity plant physically present.

Some scholars believe Paul was the first Christian to link Jesus and the Spirit in this way. Although this is especially peculiar to Paul, there is evidence that he developed themes or linkages already present in early Christianity. For instance, in Acts receiving the Spirit is linked with faith in the risen Christ and confession of him as Lord (Acts 2:38; 4:29-31; 11:17; cf. Hunter, 95; Goppelt, 1:249), not to mention the gospel traditions about Jesus as the one who would baptize with the Holy Spirit (Mk 1:8 and par.). It is also notable that there is no evidence that any Palestinian or Jewish Christians ever opposed Paul's linking of Spirit and Christ in this fashion, though there was plenty of controversy on other points (one exception may be 2 Cor 11:4, which has the expression "different spirit/Spirit"; see the commentaries). This implies that Paul's stance was in harmony with early Palestinian Christianity, even if Paul developed and expanded its less articulated ideas.

6. The Spirit and Mission.

As the Spirit of Christ, the Holy Spirit has an intimate connection with the gospel message. The Spirit empowers and impels the Christian mission. This is vividly portrayed in Acts, where the coming of the Spirit is associated with the beginning of the post-Easter proclamation of the gospel (Acts 2), with its infusion of power (Acts 4:8, 31; 6:10; 8:29; 10:44) and with the directing of Peter, Paul and Barnabas at key points (Acts 10:19-20; 11:12; 13:2-5; 16:6-10). Paul writes to the church at Rome that he has been enabled to lead Gentiles to God "by what I have said and done—by the power of signs and miracles, through the power of the Spirit" (Rom 15:18-19 NIV). He can refer to the apostolic task as a "ministry of the Spirit" (2 Cor 3:8), no small part of which was evangelism. The Spirit accompanied his initial missionary preaching (1) by confirming the truth of the message in his hearers' hearts, (2) by empowering Paul to effect "signs and wonders" (Rom 15:18-19; cf. 2 Cor 12:12, which may, however, be a Corinthian expression; see the commentaries) and (3) by filling new believers in such a way that the Spirit's presence was unmistakable. In three of his letters, all to different communities, he reminds the read-

ers of their initial vivid experience of the Spirit in the context of hearing the gospel and conversion (1 Thess 1:4-6; Gal 3:1-3; 1 Cor 2:4-5). Paul assumes such initial encounters with the Spirit serve to confirm the reality of his readers' conversion and the validity of his gospel as being truly from God. The Spirit gives believers in turn boldness and wisdom to testify about Jesus (cf. 1 Thess 2:2 with 1 Thess 1:5-6).

7. The Spirit and the Christian's New Life.

Paul more than any other NT writer links the concept of the Spirit given to indwell believers with living the Christian life. The Spirit is not only the power of God convincing believers of the truth of the gospel, not only promoting its preaching, but the Spirit is the power of new creation to those who have come to faith in Christ (see Creation, New Creation). Christians who were formerly alienated from God have not simply been entered into the heavenly register of the redeemed; the Spirit indwells them and empowers them to live a life pleasing to God (Rom 8:1-4; 12:1; 1 Thess 4:1; to the Lord, 2 Cor 5:9; Eph 5:10). This life is described as being "led by the Spirit" (Rom 8:14) or "walking in the Spirit" (Rom 8:4; Gal 5:16, 25).

7.1. Flesh and Spirit. The opposite of walking in the Spirit is to be "in the flesh," and "flesh" is often contrasted with "Spirit" in Paul. Flesh represents the self in its fallenness: the egotism, self-assertion, willful ignorance of God's will or the outright defying of that will. Such defiance characterizes humanity in Adam under the old aeon. The Spirit is utterly opposed to the principles of flesh and sin, "for the flesh's way of thinking is death; but the Spirit's way of thinking is life and peace" (Rom 8:6). The Spirit within believers breaks the power of sin so that the Christian may be said to fulfill the Law (Rom 8:1-4, 12-15).

Just how pervasive the new dominion of the Spirit is in believers, according to Paul, and how far Paul expected the Spirit-led freedom from the dominion of sin and the flesh to be complete, is a matter of scholarly debate. A large part of the debate concerns the meaning of Romans 7 in the context of that letter. Calvin and several modern exegetes (Cranfield, Dunn) understand Romans 7:14-25 as referring to the experience of a believer and hence modifying the seemingly absolute statements of freedom from the power of the flesh in Romans 8:1-11. The

Christian, though redeemed, may still be described as "fleshly," "sold under sin" and helplessly subject to its power until the resurrection. Some interpreters would see Romans 7:14-25, along with Romans 7:7-13, as referring to life prior to conversion, with the inevitable victory of sin broken and deliverance shown in Romans 8. Others see Romans 7:14-25 as the experience of a convert who attempts to fight sin by personal willpower, a believer who is spiritually immature and needs to be pointed to the power of the Spirit (Rom 8) that is necessary to triumph over sin (Bruce, 193-98).

Whether Romans 7 is seen as referring to preconversion or postconversion, there is abundant evidence elsewhere in Paul of his awareness that believers can and do sin. This is presupposed by his many warnings against falling into sin and his exhortations to chose the path of life in the Spirit (Rom 8:12-14, a warning and implied imperative; 1 Cor 6:18-20; Gal 5:16-26; cf. Rom 6:12-16; 1 Cor 5:9-13; 10:11-13, 14, 18-22, 31; and esp. 2 Cor 12:21). Though Paul may express surprise and condemnation when members of his churches persist in sinful behavior (1 Cor 5:1-6, 11-12; cf. Rom 6:1-2, 11-12; Gal 6:7-10; Col 2:20-23), he is ready nevertheless to admonish those who are "spiritual" *(hoi pneumatikoi)* to deal pastorally and meekly with Christians who do sin (Gal 6:1-2).

Because of humanity's corporate participation in the fallen Adamic nature, the believer's present existence is one of struggle in a life lived in the era between two aeons. The pull of the old nature does not let up, even though the redeemed now belong to the future age, to the new humanity in Christ. "We also, who possess the Spirit as a firstfruits, groan within ourselves as we eagerly expect our adoption, the redemption of our body" (Rom 8:23). Christ's redemption will therefore eventually extend to the complete renewal even of the physical self, when at the parousia Christians are raised from the dead and receive "spiritual bodies" (1 Cor 15:42-54; 2 Cor 5:1-5; *see* Eschatology).

We should take seriously Paul's assumption in Romans 8 that such a choosing of the path of life, to walk in the Spirit and please the Lord, is possible in the present time. The Spirit provides new possibilities for humanity, and the Spirit's powerful presence characterizes the new existence that is the "indicative" (or statement of a factual condition) upon which the ethical "imperative" is grounded. This is not simply an objective, legal matter to be believed; Paul expected this living in the Spirit to affect their lives in the world in a concrete fashion. "I tell you, live by the Spirit and you will certainly not accomplish the desire of the flesh" (Gal 5:16; cf. 1 Thess 1:4-10; 4:3-8; Rom 8:4, 12-17).

This being in the Spirit expresses itself by the "fruit" of the Spirit: love, joy, peace, and so on (Gal 5:22-23). The image of fruit accords with the gracious character of the new possibility given by God, like the fruits of the earth that grow by his creative sustaining power. And in Galatians 5:22-23 this fruit is explicitly contrasted with "works of the flesh." If any proof of the Spirit's working and a believer's maturing is to be looked for on the basis of Scripture, surely it is to be found in the fruit of the Spirit, which displays the character of Christ being formed in a person. In 1 Corinthians 13 Paul criticizes the idea that any spiritual manifestation is of value apart from that most important token of the Spirit of Christ, love.

7.2. Spirit and Law. As the Spirit is opposed to the power of flesh, so we find Spirit and Law opposed in several places in Paul (*see* Law). This is primarily because the Law (i.e., Jewish Torah), though given by God, has become sidetracked by sin and the flesh, so that even Law keeping can become another sinful enterprise whereby humans idolize their efforts and keep the living God at bay; or alternatively, attempt to put God under obligation. The Law cannot be kept fully by unregenerate humans, for it is impossible for them to overcome the power of sin. When the Spirit enters in, he begins a transformation into the new humanity that is epitomized by Christ. The Spirit places believers in the position of fulfilling "the righteous requirement of the law" (Rom 8:4) because by his assistance they are able to carry out the original intent of the Law: to love and obey the heavenly Father (cf. Mt 5:48; 22:34-40).

A key function of the Spirit is its power to make the saving events of Jesus' life-death-resurrection present in an effective way for the believer (Wendland, 151, 136-37). The Spirit "presents" the Son to believers: "the one joined to the Lord is one Spirit with him" (1 Cor 6:17). God's sending the Spirit depends on and makes real to believers the sending of the Son (Gal 4:4-7). A similar connection may be observed in the prayer in Ephesians: "I pray to the Father . . .

that he may cause you to be strengthened with power . . . by his Spirit in the inner person, so that Christ may dwell in your hearts through faith" (Eph 3:14-17). Related to this function of making Christ and his benefits present to believers, Paul's understanding of the Spirit is continuous with his understanding of justification. The placement of Romans 8 in the letter's overall structure, as well as the argument of the chapter (cf. Rom 5:1-5 with Rom 8:1-4), confirms this. There is no doctrine of Christ without justification or without the Spirit, and no justification without Christ and the Spirit.

Why the ethical quality of Spirit? For Paul this ethical nature of the Spirit and of his effect on the believer originates from two main sources. The first is that, like the classical Israelite prophets, Paul sees the Spirit as having the ethical character of God (see 1 above), which he expresses in the appellative *holy*.

Paul argues in 1 Thessalonians 4:7-8 that whoever rejects the new lifestyle that is consecrated to God (1 Thess 4:3, 7) is rejecting "God who also gives his Holy Spirit to you" (1 Thess 4:8). The argument uses the fact that the Spirit is known as the Holy Spirit, supposing that therefore those in whom the Spirit dwells should be characterized by ethical purity. Similarly in 1 Corinthians 6:19-20, while showing the Corinthians why it is wrong and inconsistent for a Christian to use prostitutes, Paul musters the argument that "your body is a temple of the Holy Spirit within you, whom you have [received] from God."

A second reason for Paul's emphasis on the ethical nature of the Spirit is the fact that it is the Spirit of Christ. As mediator of the presence of Christ to the Christian, the Spirit promotes desires, attitudes and behavior that are in line with the person and teaching of Christ. He is at work creating the new nature of which Christ is the archetype and which believers will possess in its perfect form in the age to come (2 Cor 3:17-18).

7.3. The Spirit and the Church as Body of Christ. A person does not simply receive the Spirit as an individual. To claim Christ as Lord entails being "baptized by one Spirit into one body" (1 Cor 12:13; *see* Body of Christ). It means a calling into a corporate existence, becoming part of a new social network directed by the Spirit. Therefore the changes that the Spirit brings about, and the spiritual gifts that he supplies to the individual, are not for self-improvement only; believers are

to use these for the benefit of their fellow Christians (1 Cor 12:7; 14:5, 26). The Spirit is the unifying and creative force that brings about Christian community, expressed in the term *koinōnia*, which points toward a mutual sharing in the Spirit ("participation in" the Spirit) and a fellowship (i.e., community) created by the Spirit (2 Cor 13:13 [14]). Within this new fellowship the Spirit brings different gifts to different people, who are intended to come together and work with one another, like the diverse parts of a natural body, so forming Christ's body on earth to serve the Lord (1 Cor 12:4-31).

8. The Spirit and Eschatology.
Paul regards the Spirit given to believers as an eschatological sign signifying that God's promised salvation and restoration of his people has already begun. H.-D. Wendland speaks of "the thoroughly eschatological character of the *pneuma*" for Paul (Wendland, 134). This eschatological viewpoint has some precursors in the OT and rabbinic hope for the general giving of the Spirit in the future age and in perspectives of the Qumran literature (Sekki, 82-83). The difference for Paul is that the Spirit represents the inbreaking of the end time in the present.

An eschatological note is sounded in the idea of the Spirit as "first fruits" and as the "down payment" *(arrabōn)* for believers of what they will receive when the messianic kingdom has fully arrived, judgment is past and every enemy of God is defeated (Rom 8:18-25; 2 Cor 1:22; 5:5; Eph 1:13-14; 4:30). Thus in the present the Spirit is simultaneously a portion of the life and power of the future age and a sign pointing beyond the present, telling believers that the fullness of the messianic age has not yet arrived. "The creation waits in eager expectation for the children of God to be revealed . . . but also we who have the first fruits of the Spirit groan inwardly too, while we eagerly await [our] adoption, the redemption of our bodies" (Rom 8:19, 23). Throughout his letters Paul maintains this tension in his view of the Spirit: it is not itself the fullness of the kingdom of God, yet it is a foretaste of future "glory," continually pointing forward to the eschatological redemption of the body (Beker, 281-83). The Spirit is an inbreaking of the powers of the age to come and a guarantee of the reality of that age together with the believer's part in it.

This linking of the power and presence of

the Spirit with the future age is also manifest in the hope and joy that the Spirit inspires in believers (Gal 5:22; Rom 15:13). This hope is a confidence that believers will not be disappointed, that the down payment of the Spirit will indeed be one day confirmed by participation in God's glory and in the renewal of their entire existence alongside the renewal of all creation (Rom 5:2, 5; 8:23-25). Hence a "hope" that has reference only to this present existence is a cruel joke that ends in meaningless existence (1 Cor 15:19).

The Spirit is also the power of the future age present for believers in their struggle with the forces of this age that are at enmity with God—particularly the flesh and sin. Paul can at the same time say "by the Spirit we eagerly await through faith the hoped-for righteousness" yet also enjoin believers to "live by the Spirit, and you will not carry out what the flesh desires" (Gal 5:5, 16). For Christians in the Spirit are set free from the deadly powers of this age (Rom 8:2, 6). Hence we are brought back to ethics and to the Christ-nature of the Spirit, showing how for Paul all these facets are inextricably interwoven.

9. The Spirit and Worship.

Paul informs the Corinthian Christians that as a whole and individually, they are God's temple: "Do you not know that you [plural] are God's temple, and God's Spirit lives in you?" (1 Cor 3:16; cf. 1 Cor 6:19). This saying establishes that worship is not facilitated by a holy site, building or objects but by the presence of God's Spirit. "For it is we who are the circumcision, we who worship by the Spirit of God, who glory in Christ Jesus" (Phil 3:3). The place of worship is the human heart, cleansed, renewed and accompanied by the Spirit (cf. Jn 4:23-24), or the Christian community as the Spirit's shrine (1 Cor 3:16).

In 1 Corinthians 12 and 1 Corinthians 14 Paul discusses the significance and purpose of the Spirit's gifts to the body of Christ within the context of worship gatherings. This is the most extensive discussion of early Christian worship we have from the NT period. Paul points to the Spirit as the source of Christians' "gifts," whether they appear to be more supernatural or more normal. That the Spirit distributes these gifts means they are benefits given by God's generous grace and may not be used as tokens of one's spiritual status or achievement. They are given out as the Spirit wishes, not as humans

wish. We learn from 1 Corinthians 14 that the purpose of this direction by the Spirit is for Christians to be "edified" (1 Cor 14:1-5, 26)—a term that literally means "built up," as in the construction of a house. "To edify" pictures the Christians as those who learn, mature and are strengthened. Although Paul urges believers to attend to the way in which they use these Spirit-given abilities, ultimately the building up of the body is the work of the Spirit.

The most notable class of actions that the Spirit empowers in worship is that of inspired speech of various sorts. Prophecy is the most obvious (1 Cor 12:10; 14:1-5, 39); it involved instruction, moral exhortation and correction for the congregation (1 Cor 14:3). It is one of the most frequently mentioned of spiritual gifts, closely linked with the Spirit's presence, and Paul encouraged its practice. To denigrate or prohibit it would seem from 1 Thessalonians 5:19-20 to be equivalent to "quenching" the Spirit. Other gifts of inspired speech include a "word of knowledge" or wisdom (1 Cor 12:8; one or both may be equivalent to teaching, which is not mentioned in this list but is included at 1 Cor 12:28-29); teaching is viewed as inspired by the Spirit as well (1 Cor 12:28-29; 14:19, 26), as is prayer—whether "in the Spirit" or not (1 Cor 14:2, 14-19)—and glossolalia with its accompanying interpretation (1 Cor 14:1-5, 13-19, 39). Even the singing of hymns is in the overall context to be understood as something prompted by the Spirit, who leads the church in its worship, inspiring music and praise (1 Cor 14:15, 26). Ephesians 5:18-19 (cf. Col 3:16) also makes a link between being filled with the Spirit, edification and worship (psalms, hymns and songs of the Spirit).

These worship settings also demonstrate a concern for the mutual welfare and upbuilding of believers. Other supernatural events during worship are sometimes referred to by Paul in a general way. The reference of Galatians 3:5 to God's supplying the Spirit and working miracles among the Galatians most likely refers to the ongoing worship experience of their churches. And if, on the basis of what is said about the Spirit's work in 1 Corinthians 12:4-11, the gifts are always the Spirit's work, then we may look to the list in Romans 12:6-8 to highlight vividly how for Paul the Spirit inspires even mundane tasks such as administration and charity.

Outside 1 Corinthians there are surprisingly

few explicit references to the role of the Spirit in worship. Perhaps this is partly because nowhere else in Paul are problems with the worship assemblies of a church dealt with so extensively. Outside 1 Corinthians the most frequent aspect of worship associated with the Spirit is prayer. The Spirit who marks Christians as God's children inspires the confident *Abba* prayer of the redeemed (Rom 8:15-16; Gal 4:6). And he aids believers in their prayers, directing them to pray properly (Rom 8:26). At the same time the Spirit prays on behalf of those he indwells (Rom 8:27). In Ephesians also "access" to God in prayer is granted by the Spirit (Eph 2:18), and this praying in the Spirit is urged on believers as a constant practice (Eph 6:18). This is the mark of the church as true Israel, that the community prays and worships in the Spirit (Phil 3:3). Philippians 1:19 also associates the Spirit's provision with prayer.

Beyond these there are no other explicit connections between the Spirit and worship in Paul. A few other statements may depend upon an oblique reference to believers' experience of the Spirit in worship, such as the *Abba* prayer already noted. It is possible that references to the peace and joy generated by the Spirit are inspired partly by worship experiences (Rom 15:13), as are those to the love generated by the Spirit (Rom 5:5; Col 1:8), the fellowship created by the Spirit (Phil 2:1; 2 Cor 13:13 [14]) and the Spirit as a "down payment" (2 Cor 1:22; 5:5—as though it were a tangible evidence to believers), though these suggestions are only conjectures. One thing is sure: the Spirit plays an enormously important role in Christian worship and in every aspect of the believer's experience of God. We must remember the ad hoc nature of Paul's letters and assume that there is even more to be said about the Spirit's role in worship that he has not thought necessary to mention (hence the need, e.g., to supply the idea of the Spirit's inspiration in Rom 12:6-8 on the basis of what Paul says in 1 Cor 12).

We might summarize by saying that the Spirit empowers various believers with gifts that benefit others and that aid in worship; that he arranges the distribution of gifts according to their need and inspires believers to use them aright (1 Cor 14:37-40). This does not mean that everything done with the Spirit's aid in worship must necessarily be done spontaneously, for what is done with the mind (1 Cor 14:15), with purposeful and creative forethought or with faithfulness to apostolic tradition (as in teaching), may be just as inspired and spiritual as something done on the spur of the moment (cf. traditional formulas at 1 Cor 15:1-8; 1 Tim 3:16).

The Spirit encourages believers in prayer to have boldness in speaking to the God with whom they are now reconciled as beloved children. He initiates the impulse from below and brings the Father's loving response from above. Ideally, worship is a Spirit-led symphony of doxology, giving praise to God, proclaiming what he has done and is doing, and what the human response should be.

See also ADOPTION, SONSHIP; CHRISTOLOGY; ESCHATOLOGY; GOD; IN CHRIST; WORSHIP.

DPL: ETHICS; FELLOWSHIP, COMMUNION, SHARING; FIRST FRUITS, DOWN PAYMENT; FRUIT OF THE SPIRIT; GIFTS OF THE SPIRIT; HOLINESS, SANCTIFICATION; POWER; PROPHECY, PROPHESYING; SPIRITUALITY; TONGUES.

BIBLIOGRAPHY. J. C. Beker, *Paul the Apostle: The Triumph of God in Life and Thought* (Philadelphia: Fortress, 1980); F. F. Bruce, *Paul: Apostle of the Heart Set Free* (Grand Rapids: Eerdmans, 1977); R. Bultmann, *Theology of the New Testament* (London: SCM, 1952); C. E. B. Cranfield, *A Critical and Exegetical Commentary on the Epistle to the Romans* (2 vols.; ICC; Edinburgh: T & T Clark, 1975, 1979); J. D. G. Dunn, *Jesus and the Spirit* (Philadelphia: Westminster, 1975); idem, *Romans* (WBC; 2 vols.; Dallas: Word, 1988); E. E. Ellis, *Prophecy and Hermeneutic* (Tübingen: J. C. B. Mohr, 1978); G. D. Fee, *The First Epistle to the Corinthians* (NICNT; Grand Rapids: Eerdmans, 1987); idem, *God's Empowering Presence: The Holy Spirit in the Letters of Paul* (Peabody, MA: Hendrickson, 1994); L. Goppelt, *Theology of the New Testament* (2 vols.; Grand Rapids: Eerdmans, 1981, 1982); D. Hill, *Greek Words and Hebrew Meanings* (Cambridge: Cambridge University Press, 1967); A. M. Hunter, *Paul and his Predecessors* (rev. ed.; London: SCM, 1961); D. J. Lull, *The Spirit in Galatia: Paul's Interpretation of Pneuma as Divine Power* (SBLDS 49; Chico, CA: Scholars Press, 1980); R. P. Martin, *The Spirit and the Congregation* (Grand Rapids: Eerdmans, 1984); idem, "The Spirit in 2 Corinthians in Light of the 'Fellowship of the Holy Spirit' in 2 Corinthians 13:14" in *Eschatology and the New Testament*, ed. W. H. Gloer (Peabody, MA: Hendrickson, 1988); idem, *Worship in the Early Church* (London: Marshall, Morgan & Scott, 1964); P. Meyer, "The Holy Spirit in the Pauline Letters: A Contextual Exploration," *Int* 33 (1979) 3-18; C. F. D. Moule, *The Holy Spirit* (London: Mowbrays, 1978); A. Schweitzer, *The Mysticism of Paul the Apostle* (2d ed.; London: Black, 1953); E. Schweizer, "πνεῦμα κτλ," *TDNT* 6:396-451; idem, *The Holy Spirit* (London: SCM, 1980); A. E. Sekki, *The Meaning of Ruah at Qumran* (SBLDS 110; Atlanta: Scholars Press, 1989); H.-D. Wendland, "Das Wirken des heiligen Geistes in den Gläubigen nach Paulus," in *Pro Veritate: Ein theologischer Dialog,* ed. E. Schlink and H. Volk (Münster: Aschendorff, 1963) 133-56; W. Wright Jr., "The Source of Paul's Concept of *Pneuma,*" *CovQ* 41 (1983) 17-26.   T. Paige

HOLY SPIRIT III: ACTS, HEBREWS, GENERAL EPISTLES, REVELATION

There is a sense in which the OT was the age of law and prophecy, a period when the Spirit of God came powerfully upon or into the lives of a variety of people—priests, judges, kings, prophets and the like—but only sporadically and for a brief time in order to accomplish certain specific tasks on God's behalf for God's people. With the coming of Jesus Christ, however, the eschatological age dawned (see Heb 1:1-2); the age of the Spirit was inaugurated. Then not only did the Spirit come upon/into (Mk 1:10) Jesus at his baptism and remain with him throughout his life (cf. Lk 4:1), but later and as a consequence of Jesus' death (*see* Death of Christ), resurrection and exaltation, the Spirit was "poured out," in the fulfillment of Joel's prophecy (Joel 3:1-5), upon all of Jesus' followers—irrespective of gender, age, race or social status—and upon them permanently (see Acts 2:4, 17-20, passim). The age of hope had given way to the age of fulfillment, so that the gift of the Spirit is presently available to all who repent and believe in the name of Jesus Christ. The promised gift of the Holy Spirit belongs now to those who are near (Jews) and to those afar off (Gentiles) (Acts 2:38).

1. Etymology
2. Terminology
3. The Holy Spirit in the Life of Jesus
4. The Holy Spirit and the Church
5. The Holy Spirit and the Inspiration of Scripture
6. The Holy Spirit and the Trinity

1. Etymology.

In all the writings under consideration the word translated "Spirit" (i.e., the Spirit of God, the Holy Spirit), is the Greek word *pneuma* (the equivalent of its Hebrew counterpart, *rûaḥ*), whose fundamental meaning is "air in motion." This word encompasses such ideas as wind, gale, storm or blast (see Ex 14:21; 15:8; Gen 1:2, where von Rad translates *rûaḥ ʾĕlōhîm* [Spirit of God] as "Storm of God," von Rad, 49)—ideas of immense power, force and uncontrollable strength; or ideas of peace, quietness and refreshment, for *pneuma* may also be used to describe something as gentle as a breeze (see Gen 3:8). Significantly, *pneuma* also means "breath," the breath of one's mouth or nostrils and by extension the breath of life—the stuff of existence for all living beings (see Gen 2:7; Ps 104:29-30).

It is this word that OT, NT and early Christian writers attach to God in an attempt to describe him, to tell in part who he is: God is *pneuma,* wind, and as such he is invisible, irresistible, unpredictable, uncontrollable power. He is *pneuma,* breath, and as such he imparts life and vitality into every living creature. He is *pneuma,* air in motion, and as such is movement and action, energy at work, everywhere and always present to create and recreate, to sustain, to order, to renew, to revive. This Spirit of God is God, the living God, who infuses new life into his people, filling them with strength, wisdom, moral courage and power, heightening and enhancing their natural abilities, equipping them in an extraordinary fashion so as to take them beyond the borders of their limitations, preparing them to carry out significant moral and ethical roles in the course of redemptive history (Hawthorne, 14-23).

2. Terminology.

The titles most frequently used for this "breath of God" in the OT and in the OT apocryphal and pseudepigraphal writings are "the Spirit," "the Spirit of God" and "the Spirit of the Lord." The name "[the] Holy Spirit" occurs in only two places in the OT (Ps 51:11; Is 63:10-11) and somewhat more often in later writings (4 Ezra 14:22; *Asc. Is.* 5:14; cf. CD 2:11-13; 1QS 3:6-12). It becomes the standard term in rabbinical literature, meaning the Spirit of God as "an entity which stands outside [a person], and which comes to [that person] from God in special situations and under special circumstances" (Sjöberg,

6:381; for other, less frequently occurring titles see Is 11:1-2; Zech 12:10).

The NT and early Christian documents produce a plethora of titles by which attempts were made to catch in a net of words this elusive, universal, immediate, life-changing power that was daily being experienced by ordinary people. The Spirit of God, which many of Israel's teachers taught had fallen silent or had ceased to be active in the world or was no longer needed now that the Hebrew Scriptures were complete (see Davies, 208-15; Scott, 47, 50; but cf. Aune, 103-47), was once again observed to be present and active. It is as though the world had suddenly awakened to the fact that the longed-for universal age of the Spirit had dawned (see Joel 2:28-29), that the hoped-for new era when God's people would continuously be infused with, inspired and motivated by the Spirit had at last arrived (Is 61). It is no wonder, then, that some of our literature abounds with references to the Spirit and that the titles now are far more varied than before.

As in the OT, especially in Ezekiel, "Spirit" or "the Spirit" are titles frequently used in the NT and the apostolic fathers to designate the Holy Spirit (cf. Acts 6:3 with 6:5; 1 Pet 1:2; *1 Clem.* 42.4, passim). Surprising, however, is the fact that the familiar OT terms such as "the Spirit of God" and "the Spirit of the Lord" hardly occur in our literature. "The Spirit of God" appears in the NT only in 1 Peter 4:14 and 1 John 4:2; "the Spirit of the Lord" occurs only in Acts 5:9 and Acts 8:39.

Yet the excitement generated by the presence and power of the Spirit in the Christian community fostered an irresistible desire on its part to set forth in words the nature of this presence, to explain as clearly as possible the overwhelming significance of the Spirit, to try to make comprehensible the incomprehensible. This desire led to the creation of a variety of new terms to describe the person and work of the Spirit. Thus in addition to the aforementioned terms, the Spirit is called "the promise of the Father" (Acts 1:4; 2:33, 39; cf. Lk 24:49; Jn 14:16, 26; 15:26; Joel 2:28-29), "the Spirit of life" (Rev 11:11), "the Spirit of truth" (1 Jn 4:6), "the Spirit of grace" (Heb 10:29), "the eternal Spirit" (Heb 9:14), "the seven Spirits of God" (Rev 1:4; 3:1; 4:5; 5:6; see Bruce, 336), "the prophetic Spirit" and "the Spirit of prophecy" (Rev 19:10, calling attention to the Spirit as the inspirer of Scripture).

Another new and important title given to the Holy Spirit, yet one that would be easily understood, is "the Anointing" (*to chrismon,* 1 Jn 2:20, 27): "You have an anointing from the Holy One and all of you have knowledge," an allusion to the Holy Spirit that Jesus poured out upon his followers like an anointing oil (Acts 2:32-33; cf. 1 Sam 16:17-18). This anointing imparted to Christians a special gift of knowledge about God and about Christ and about their relation to God and Christ (see 1 Jn 3:24; 4:13).

The most common title for the Spirit is "[the] Holy Spirit": *hagion pneuma, to hagion pneuma, to pneuma to hagion*—rare in the OT but abundant in our literature. The reason for this radical alteration in terminology is not completely clear. Perhaps it is because now it is more fully understood that it is the Spirit who sets the people of faith apart ("set apart" is the fundamental meaning of *hagion,* "holy") from the profane world unto God and who consecrates them to God's service (cf. 1 Pet 1:2). More likely, however, it is because the Spirit was being dramatically experienced as the power of God by which God was effecting changes in the lives of human beings on a very large scale, transforming them from sinners into a holy people as God himself is holy (1 Pet 1:15-16; cf. Lev 19). That is, the Spirit was effectively working out in them God's "personal will directed to a religious and moral end" (Baumgärtel, 365), making them ethically and morally good people (cf. Ezek 11:19; 18:31; 36:26; Acts 2:1-41).

Perhaps the titles for the Spirit that call for the greatest reflection are those that bring the Spirit and Jesus close together in a dialectical pattern of identity and distinction, arising no doubt from the fact that "Christ and the Spirit are so closely associated in the life of Christians that their names are interchangeable" (Hendry, 24): "the Spirit of Jesus" (Acts 16:7; see Stählin, 229-52) and "the Spirit of Christ" (1 Pet 1:11). The preposition *of* in the expression "the Spirit of Jesus, of Christ" need not necessarily lead one to identify the Spirit with Christ, since at base the function of the preposition is only to describe a close relationship existing between the two and may simply convey an idea similar to that of the Fourth Gospel, in which the Spirit of Christ is the Spirit who witnesses to Christ (cf. Jn 14:26; 15:26; 1 Cor 12:3). But the ambiguity of the expressions obviously led some of the Fathers to go beyond this and say that the one is the other and not to make a distinction between

Christ and the Spirit (cf. Rom 8:9-10; 1 Cor 10:4; 2 Cor 3:18; see the confused and confusing passage in *Herm. Sim.* 5.6.5-7; also in the same vein, *2 Clem.* 9.5).

3. The Holy Spirit in the Life of Jesus.

The Gospel writers record decisive points in the life and ministry of Jesus, noting the presence of the Holy Spirit in each of these—his baptism, his temptation, his preaching, his exorcisms, and so on. Recording these events in this way, they make it clear that their intent was to describe the life of the Son of God become incarnate as that of a truly human person who was wholly guided and empowered by the Spirit (Hendry, 19). This theme is picked up in our literature and is clearly and succinctly summarized in Acts 2:22 and Acts 10:38. There it is stated that "Jesus the Nazarene was a man marked out by God with mighty works, wonders and signs which God did through him" (Acts 2:22), for "God had anointed him [made him Messiah] with the Holy Spirit and power"; as a consequence, "he always went about (*diēlthen*, see BDF 332.1) doing good [*euergetōn*] and healing [*iōmenos*] all who were overpowered by the devil because God was with him" (Acts 10:38; see Robinson, 125; Swete 1976, 59). The whole of Jesus' ministry is here regarded as "made up of a continuous series of acts of beneficence"—"God's decisive attack upon the (personally conceived) power of evil" (Barrett, 525)—performed by Jesus in the power of the Holy Spirit (cf. Is 61:1-2; 42:1; 11:1-3; see Hawthorne, 97-172).

The writer to the Hebrews alone describes the presence and power of the Holy Spirit at the death of Jesus. He writes, "Christ, who through the eternal Spirit offered himself without blemish to God" (Heb 9:14). Behind these words "lies the portrayal of the Isaianic Servant of the Lord, who yields up his life to God as a guilt offering for many, bearing their sin and procuring their justification. When this servant is introduced for the first time, God says: 'I have put my Spirit upon him' (Is 42:1). It is in the power of the Divine Spirit, accordingly, that the Servant accomplishes every phase of his ministry, including the crowning phase in which he accepts death for the transgression of his people" (Bruce, 205; cf. the enigmatic words of *Barn.* 7.2-3).

In the literature we are considering there are repeated statements that God raised up Jesus and freed him of the pains, or pangs, of death (Acts 2:24, 32; 3:15, 26; 4:10; 5:30-31; 13:33-34; 17:31; 1 Pet 1:21). But how did God do this? By what power did God effect this mighty act of resurrection?

It is possible to infer that the power by which God did this was the power of the Holy Spirit, especially when one considers that the Holy Spirit of God was present in every significant event of Jesus' existence—at his birth, in his life and ministry, and at his death. This inference is strengthened by the implication of the somewhat enigmatic creedal statement of 1 Peter 3:18, variously translated "He [Christ] was put to death in the flesh, but made alive [*zōopoiētheis*] in the spirit" (NRSV) or "He was put to death in the body but made alive by the Spirit" (NIV). This statement has been taken by some to be an unmistakable reference to Jesus' resurrection by the Spirit. The parallels with the two other creedal statements involving flesh-spirit distinctions (i.e., Rom 1:3-4; 1 Tim 3:16) confirm the contention that "spirit" here refers to that sphere of Christ's existence "in which God's Holy Spirit was supremely and most conspicuously at work" (Dalton, 129-30). "Jesus was 'put to death' by human hands, not by God, but it was God who brought him to life by the power of the Spirit (cf. 4:6)" (Michaels, 204; cf. *Mart. Pol.* 14.2).

Further, the possibility that God raised Jesus by the power of his Spirit seems to be an increasingly reasonable supposition upon noting the words of Luke's introduction of his second treatise to Theophilus: "I wrote about all that Jesus began both to do and to teach until the day in which he was received up after he had given commandment [cf. Mt 28:19-20; Lk 24:45-49; Jn 20:21-23] through the Holy Spirit to the apostles he had chosen" (Acts 1:1-2; see Robinson, 125). This is to say, that during the forty-day period after his resurrection and before he was taken up to heaven, Jesus continued to instruct his disciples, as he had done before, "by means of the Holy Spirit." Thus Jesus' entire time on earth, from his birth until his exaltation, which includes his resurrection, is bracketed by references to the presence and power of the Holy Spirit effectively at work in every significant event of his life (see Hawthorne, 184-94).

4. The Holy Spirit and the Church.

4.1. The Initial Coming of the Holy Spirit. From the beginning of time the Spirit of God has been present and active in the world (Gen 1:2). Never has there been a period in human history when this has not been so—the Spirit creatively at work bringing order, relief and life in the midst of chaos, suffering and death; the Spirit persistently and effectively reversing the process of destruction and decay; the Spirit in concrete ways acting "against the power of sin, despair, cynicism and death" (Welker, 340). If there was a time when the Spirit was thought to be absent, removed from the sphere of human affairs, no longer visibly evident (see Davies, 208-15; Scott, 47, 50), even then the Spirit was present and at work. There is, however, a difference in emphasis at different times with regard to the activity of the Spirit. The OT primarily focuses attention upon the presence and power of the Spirit in periods of national crisis and in the lives of select individuals. The NT, however, primarily focuses attention upon the presence and power of the Holy Spirit in the life of Jesus and then through him in the lives of all his followers.

After his resurrection Jesus told his disciples to wait in Jerusalem until they should receive the promise of the Father, the promise of the Holy Spirit (Acts 1:4-5; 2:33). This waiting period ended on the day of Pentecost (Acts 2:1), the fiftieth day after Passover (*hē pentēkostē [hēmera]* = the fiftieth [day]). Pentecost was the Jewish "feast of weeks" (Deut 16:9-12) or the "day of the first fruits" (Num 28:26), so called because it was when the first fruits of wheat harvest were offered to God (Ex 34:22; cf. Tob 2:1; Josephus *Ant.* 17.10.2 §254). Later Jewish writers viewed Pentecost as the commemoration of the giving of the law by Moses (Str-B 2:601). It is tempting to speculate about why this particular day was chosen to end the waiting period and mark the coming of the Holy Spirit—for example, as Pentecost was thought to commemorate the gift of the Law that resulted in the old covenant between God and his ancient people, so this same day was selected to celebrate the gift of the Spirit, based upon the life, death, resurrection and exaltation of Jesus that issued in a new covenant between God and his new or renewed people (see Schweizer, 411; *Jub.* 6:17-19; see also *Jub.* 1:1; 15:1; 44:4-5; Philo *Decal.* 33, 35; Philo *Spec. Leg.* 2.189). But such attempts have proved futile (see Lohse, 49-50; Barrett, 111). It appears that Luke was attempting only to state a fact, not make a theological statement.

Whatever may have been the significance of this particular day, Jesus' followers—no doubt the entire 120 (see Acts 1:15)—were together in one place. Then an unforgettable and decisive experience in the life of the church occurred—an event that was audible and visible. Luke describes it as a sound like the rush of a violent wind and as the appearance of divided tongues of fire resting on each of the persons present (Acts 2:1-3). It is not possible adequately "to translate this experience into terms which convey the true significance to us" today (Bruce, 54), but wind and fire are familiar biblical terms that call to mind the presence and power of God, of the Spirit of God, creatively at work in the world (cf. Ezek 37:9-14; Ex 3:2-6). Thus it is not surprising to read immediately after this description of such an extraordinary happening that "all of them were filled with the Holy Spirit" (Acts 2:4), which Peter interprets as the fulfillment of God's promise through the prophet Joel (Acts 2:17-21, quoting Joel 3:1-3) and as the direct result of the resurrected and exalted Christ lavishly bestowing on his church the gift of the Holy Spirit that he had received from his Father (Acts 2:32-33).

Only in Acts 2—nowhere else in the NT or apostolic fathers—is this founding gift of the Holy Spirit described. Only here is the initial fulfillment of Jesus' promise to his followers that they would be infused with supernatural power detailed. Only here is the permanent coming of the Holy Spirit to live in the lives of the faithful, to indwell the community of believers, the church, made known. What then is one to make of the so-called additional comings of the Spirit described in Acts 8:16 and Acts 10:44 = 11:15? To be sure, the Greek verb that is used in these texts, *epipiptō* (lit. "to fall upon") is similar in meaning to other verbs—*eperchesthai* (Acts 1:8, "to come upon"), *pimplēnai* (Acts 2:4, "to fill"), or *baptizesthai en* (Acts 1:5, "to be baptized in")—used by Luke of that initial giving of the Holy Spirit.

Was there then more than one initial gift of the Spirit to the church? If the answer is no, perhaps the subsequent events recorded in Acts 8 and Acts 10 can be explained not so much as new comings but rather as necessary demonstrations that this same Spirit was no longer exclusively for believing Israel but was now present and available to all who believe. In other words, these so-called comings were concrete, visible proofs that Samaritans (Acts 8:16) and Gentiles (Acts 10:44 = Acts 11:15)—people despised or looked down upon as outsiders by Israel—were now fully included among the recipients of God's gracious gift of the Spirit, proofs that the church, which from the beginning, though located only in Jerusalem, "is . . . a universal society in which universal communication is possible" (Barrett, 108). The Spirit once-for-all given at Pentecost to Jewish believers in Jerusalem is seen now to pervade every part of the believing community drawn from among all the nations of the world (Acts 1:8; 2:38-39).

4.2. On Receiving the Holy Spirit. To discuss the initial coming of the Holy Spirit upon the faithful in Jerusalem at Pentecost is one thing. But when and how does the Spirit come upon or into each new believer subsequently? How does each new believer receive the Holy Spirit? Of the writings being studied in this article only the book of Acts gives an answer to this question, and its answer is unclear.

Certain texts seem to connect baptism so closely with the Holy Spirit (Acts 2:38; 19:1-7) that interpreters have come to understand that baptism is a necessary prerequisite for the coming of the Spirit into the life of the believer, a rite of the church by which the faithful receive the Spirit (e.g., Luther: "This doctrine is to remain sure and firm, that the Holy Spirit is given through the office of the church, that is through the preaching of the gospel and baptism," quoted by Lenski, 109; see more recently, Conzelmann, 22: "Baptism and receiving the Spirit belong together").

But if it is true that the gift of the Holy Spirit is contingent upon baptism, it is remarkable that there is such a varying relation in Acts of baptism to the coming of the Holy Spirit. In Acts 2:38 baptism precedes the gift of the Holy Spirit, from which it could be argued that baptism is a prerequisite for receiving the Spirit. But in Acts 8:16 baptism and the coming of the Spirit are not connected, and in Acts 8:36-39 the Ethiopian eunuch is baptized without any mention of the Holy Spirit coming upon him (see also Acts 9:17-19; 16:14-17, 31-33; 18:8; but note the variant reading to Acts 8:39). In Acts 10:44 the Spirit falls upon Cornelius and his household before their baptism takes place, whereas in Acts 18:24-26 baptism appears to be an unnecessary or at least an unmentioned element in the instruction given to Apollos. Finally, in Acts 19:5-6 it appears that the Holy Spirit is not so much conferred upon those who believe by baptism as it is

by the laying on of the apostle's hands (see Barrett, 154).

There is, then, in Acts no consistent tie to enable one to say unequivocally that the Spirit is received at baptism. Nor do the apostolic fathers make any such connection between baptism and the giving of the Spirit (*Barn.* 11.11 excepted, although the translation there of the key expression, *en tō pneumati*, is open to question: "in our spirit" [Swete 1912, 19], "in the Spirit" [Lake, Loeb trans.]).

If our texts will not permit one to argue with complete confidence that water baptism (though important) is a prerequisite for the conferring of the Holy Spirit, it is possible to infer from them that whenever the Spirit "falls upon" or "fills" any person or group of persons it is because of their positive response to the divine person who encounters them in the gospel. For example, even while Peter was proclaiming the gospel to the receptive Cornelius and his household the Holy Spirit "fell upon all who heard the word" (Acts 10:44), an event that brought to mind the word of the Lord: "John baptized with water, but you will be baptized with the Holy Spirit" (Acts 11:15-16). Thus the all-important baptism is the baptism with the Spirit, namely, the coming of the Holy Spirit upon or into the community or into the life of individuals. This baptism is predicated upon and coincident with faith in Jesus—in his person, life, death, resurrection and exaltation (cf. Acts 8:12, 14-17; 16:14-17, 31-33; 18:8, passim).

It seems clear from comparing Acts 1:5 with Acts 1:8 and Acts 2:4 that baptism with the Holy Spirit and being filled with the Holy Spirit are to be equated. Nothing is to be found in the book of Acts (and Acts is the principal source of information about the person and work of the Spirit in the literature under discussion) to indicate that the Holy Spirit once imparted was ever taken away from those to whom it was given—church or individual. In fact "Luke [in Acts] believes that the gift of the Spirit is constitutive of the Christian life (see [Acts] 19.1-6; there is something wrong with a disciple who has not received the Holy Spirit)" (Barrett, 115).

What then is meant when Acts says that at a later time Peter and the other believers "were filled" with the Holy Spirit (Acts 4:8, 31; 13:52; see also Acts 9:17 with Acts 13:9)? Perhaps the answer to this question can be gained by comparing the Holy Spirit in the life of Jesus with that of the Spirit in the life of the church. Luke records that at Jesus' baptism the Holy Spirit descended upon him, filled him, was constantly leading *(ēgeto)* him during the forty days of his wilderness testing (Lk 3:21-22; 4:1-2) and was present with him throughout the remainder of his life (cf. Lk 4:14, 18), even at the cross (cf. Heb 9:4). Nevertheless, there are points noted by the Evangelists in the ministry of Jesus where it might be said that Jesus, "filled with the Spirit," healed, spoke, saw or rejoiced. That is, he who was filled with the Spirit at all times was especially inspired by the Spirit at special moments during his ministry. For example, Luke records that on one such occasion "the power [= Spirit, see Acts 1:8] of the Lord was at hand for him to heal" (Lk 5:17). Again, when the woman with an incurable menstrual flow purposefully touched Jesus' clothes, he knew "that power [= Holy Spirit] had gone out from him" (Lk 8:46). Jesus' disciples returned to him with word of their success over the forces of evil. At that instant, it would appear, the Spirit gave him a flash of insight to see in their successes Satan's fall like a lightning bolt from heaven, for Luke goes on to say that "at that time Jesus, full of joy by the Holy Spirit," began to praise God (Lk 10:17-21).

So it is with Peter and all other Christians, initially and continuously filled with the Holy Spirit from conversion. When they are faced with especially difficult and challenging experiences they need from the Holy Spirit a special endowment of insight, inspiration, effective speech, power and emotional strength successfully to carry out their mission in life.

4.3. The Work of the Holy Spirit. It has already been noted that believers in Jesus who were filled with the Holy Spirit from the inception of the church (Acts 2:4) were also "filled with the Spirit" at certain important junctures in life (Acts 4:8). That is to say, they were especially empowered by the Spirit to go beyond the limits of their innate human abilities so as to carry out a God-given mission in fulfillment of Jesus' words, "You will receive power [focused power, power to achieve some good end] when the Holy Spirit comes upon you" (Acts 1:8).

For example, it is the Holy Spirit who gives Peter, perceived as an "uneducated and ordinary" person, a special power of effective speech (Acts 4:8), so that even the learned elite are forced to recognize the unusualness of his eloquence (Acts 4:13). This power was not given solely to Peter in the history of the church, nor was it intended to be limited to him (Acts 6:10 with Acts 6:5; cf. Lk 12:11-12; see Swete 1976, 84).

Further, it is the Holy Spirit that gives humble men and women, when faced with real threats to their life and welfare, supernormal courage to speak the word of the Lord with boldness and carry to completion the task they believed God wanted them to accomplish regardless of the consequences (Acts 4:31; 7:54-56; 20:23).

The Holy Spirit on occasion lifts certain people in an ecstatic, trancelike state above their confining human limitations and heightens their natural faculties, intellectual and spiritual, so that they are able to see and know things other people cannot see and know (Acts 7:55; 10:19; 20:23; Rev 1:10; 4:2; 17:3; 21:10), to peer into the future and predict events yet to come (Acts 11:28; 21:12). Perhaps in a similar ecstatic manner, the Holy Spirit comes to the aid of God's people in prayer (Jude 20; cf. Rom 8:15-16, 26-37; Gal 4:6; Jn 4:23-24; Bauckham, 113; Dunn 1975, 245-46).

For whatever reason and in unspecified ways, the Spirit at times hinders people from doing what they intended to do or from going where they planned to go. The Spirit then turns them in quite different directions, giving them undreamed of work to accomplish (Acts 16:6).

The Spirit, living within believers, grants to them the possibility of a new understanding of existence, imparting to them right knowledge and instruction, so that they may come to realize that Jesus is the Christ (1 Jn 4:2, 6), know that God lives in them and they in God (1 Jn 3:24; 4:13) and recognize the difference between truth and error (1 Jn 2:20-21, 27; 4:6; see Bultmann, 80).

Still further, the Spirit is the silent, invisible one who sanctifies. The Spirit is the inner transformer of human lives, the one who acts through the preaching of the gospel to separate individuals from the world unto God (1 Pet 1:2; cf. 1 Pet 1:12) so that they no longer indulge themselves in immoral behavior (Jude 18-19) or engage their minds in attitudes hostile to God (Jas 4:4-5 and Martin's translation of Jas 4:5: "The Spirit God made to dwell in us opposes envy," 149).

Again, there are times when the Spirit constrains believers to achieve some worthwhile goal in life, as Paul felt constrained *(dedemenos)* by the Spirit to go to Jerusalem, while at the same time the Spirit warns them through other Christians or Christian prophets of impending disaster if they proceed as planned (Acts 20:22-23; 21:4, 12). Luke sees no contradiction in this, for to him it accords "with the common notion of prophecies and prodigies: they are fulfilled, but not to the exclusion of human decision. Paul 'must' go, but he freely affirms his destiny" (Conzelmann, 178).

It was the Holy Spirit who, in his inexplicable way, appointed "overseers to shepherd the church of God" at Ephesus (Acts 20:28). Thus one should be careful not to make too sharp a distinction between the charismatic age of the Spirit and the ecclesiastical age, the age of the organized church, as though the latter automatically excluded from its midst the presence and power of the Spirit (see also *1 Clem.* 42.4; Ign. *Phld.* presc. 7.1-2).

The Spirit continues to be the Spirit of prophecy, that is, the Spirit still inspires select men and women (see Acts 21:9), so that when they speak, they speak with power, so that they rank with the OT prophets in bringing to the people of God the word of God. Christian prophets resided in numbers in Syrian Antioch (Acts 13:1; cf. *Did.* 13.1); others were itinerant (Acts 11:28; 21:10; cf. *Did.* 11). All were authoritative figures within the church, for the Spirit spoke through them. They were to be respected, even feared, certainly obeyed. Nevertheless, they and their message could and should be put to the test (see *Did.* 11.7—12.11; *Herm. Man.* 1.7-17). This phenomenon of the Christian prophet survived at least into the fourth or fifth decade of the second century (Swete 1912, 25).

The Holy Spirit, present and living within believers, is the companion or author of joy even in the presence of the most adverse circumstances. For instance, Paul and Barnabas, persecuted and driven from city to city for preaching the gospel, nevertheless "were filled with joy and with the Holy Spirit" (Acts 13:52; see Swete 1976, 174).

When the church throughout Judea, Galatia and Samaria had endured fierce persecution and had come through it into an era of peace they found themselves living "in the comfort of the Holy Spirit" (NRSV; *paraklēsei tou hagiou pneumatos*, or as the NIV puts it, "encouraged by the Holy Spirit" (Acts 9:31)—a difficult word and phrase to translate. At times the noun *paraklēsis*

can mean (prophetic) exhortation, as in Acts 13:15; at other times comfort, as is possible in Acts 15:31; at still other times, encouragement. "Followed here by the subjective genitive *tou hagiou pneumatos* it is not wrong to allow it to refer to whatever it is that the Holy Spirit does, and this will include both the (messianic) consolation . . . and the stirring up and enabling of Christians to live as they should (cf. 1.8)" (Barrett, 474).

4.4. How the Holy Spirit Works in the Church. It is clear from the NT that the Holy Spirit is God/Christ powerfully, mysteriously, sometimes quietly and unobtrusively at work in and through the church. But it is not always clear how this work is carried out.

Sometimes supernatural means are used, which defy further definition or explanation, as when Luke says that the Spirit of the Lord "snatched Philip away," and he later found himself in Azotus.

The chorus that is repeated seven times in the Apocalypse, "Let anyone who has an ear listen to what the Spirit is saying to the churches" (Rev 2:7, 11, 17, 28; 3:6, 13, 22), may find its explanation in the opening phrase of each letter addressed to the seven churches: "To the angel *[angelos]* of the church . . . write," for *angelos* may refer not to some supernatural being but to mortals, for it also means "messenger." These messengers may have been prophets—human beings especially prepared by God, people sensitive and open to receiving God's word—who wrote to each of these churches an authoritative word of the Lord, because the Holy Spirit inspired them to write. Thus each letter was in essence the Spirit speaking to the particular church addressed. The same might be said of Acts 13:2—how did the Holy Spirit say to the church at Antioch, "Set apart for me Barnabas and Saul for the work to which I have called them"? Very likely the Spirit did so through the human voice of men or women—for there were prophets, people especially tuned to listening to the voice of the Spirit, in Antioch at that time (Acts 13:1). And when Luke goes on to say that Barnabas and Saul "were sent out by the Holy Spirit" (Acts 13:4), he meant for everyone to understand that the Spirit "sent them out" by means of the church.

That is to say, the Spirit infused God's people, who were praying and fasting, with the authority necessary to commission these two men by the laying on of their hands (Acts 13:3). How was it that the Holy Spirit told Philip to join the Ethiopian eunuch in his chariot? Perhaps he spoke to Philip in a human messenger *(angelos)*, "the messenger of the Lord" who told him to leave Samaria and go south (Acts 8:29 with Acts 8:26).

Sometimes the Spirit acts in people's lives, communicates with and directs them through dreams, trances (Acts 10:9-20) or ecstatic experiences (Rev 1:10). At other times the Spirit concurs with and confirms the verbal witness of the church by external, visible miraculous signs and wonders (Acts 5:32 with Acts 2:32-39 and Lk 24:48-49; cf. Heb 2:4).

Sometimes the Spirit speaks through disappointing circumstances that cause people in whom he lives to take a different but better course of action than that originally planned (Acts 16:6-7).

Perhaps it was by a still, small, inner voice of conviction that the Spirit testified to Paul that in every city imprisonment and persecution were waiting for him (Acts 20:23). Whatever can be said of God, namely, that he "moves in mysterious ways his wonders to perform," can also be said of God's Spirit. But whenever the Spirit commands, he gives the power to carry out that command; wherever he directs, he gives the strength to traverse that course, however difficult.

5. The Holy Spirit and the Inspiration of the Scripture.

In the OT the formulas that the ancient prophets repeated over and over again as introductions to their prophecies were "thus says the Lord" (Jer 9:23, passim), "the Lord has spoken" (Is 1:2, passim), "hear the word of the Lord" (Is 1:10, passim), "the word of the Lord came to me" (Ezek 33:1, passim), or the like. Such introductory formulas were intended to assure the audience that the message that came to them, whether spoken or written, did not originate with the prophet but with God. The word of the prophet was the word of the Lord and was to be received as such.

In the NT these older formulas for the most part have been replaced by the single formula "the Holy Spirit said" or its like. The writers of our literature perceive the Holy Spirit as God's pervasive influence in the life of certain persons, inspiring them, validating their message by his power as words that are sacred, authoritative and final. Notice Peter's remarks to the 120 disci-

ples after the resurrection and exaltation of Jesus: "Friends, the Scripture had to be fulfilled, which the Holy Spirit through David foretold" (Acts 1:16). These words of Peter give clear expression to the widespread belief of the early church about the OT as a whole—the Holy Spirit was its ultimate source; the Holy Spirit was speaking through persons, such as David, so that what was contained in the OT was the word of God, the word of the Spirit of God (see also Acts 4:25; 28:25; Heb 3:7; 9:8; 10:15). The remarks of the writer of 2 Peter 1:21 are apt at this point, even though the text is difficult to translate: "No prophecy of scripture is a matter of one's own interpretation, because no prophecy ever came by human will, but men and women moved by the Holy Spirit spoke from God" (NRSV, but see also the NIV). However one finally translates this verse, its message is clear: "The only point which the author of 2 Peter is concerned to deny is that the prophets themselves were the originating source of their message. To counter this view he affirms that the Holy Spirit was the source of their prophecy, enabling them to speak as God's spokesmen" (Bauckham, 234; cf. Philo *Rer. Div. Her.* 259; Philo *Vit. Mos.* 1.281, 286).

The universal testimony of the earliest church concerning the OT is that it is the word of God, because those designated persons who spoke or wrote its message spoke or wrote by inspiration of the Holy Spirit and thus spoke or wrote for God. God spoke to his people through David, Isaiah, Jeremiah and others by the Holy Spirit (Acts 4:25). But what of the NT? Luke was aware that the Holy Spirit was still speaking in the apostolic period (Acts 13:2; 20:23), and the writer to the Hebrews refers to the Holy Spirit not only to say that the scriptural account of the tabernacle and its priestly services was divinely inspired but also to say that the Holy Spirit was still speaking—in his day—and indicating that the way into the sanctuary could not be opened as long as the first tabernacle and its services still stood (Heb 9:8). Later, Clement seems more certain that the apostles shared the same inspiration as the OT prophets. He wrote that they "having therefore received their commands, and being fully assured by the resurrection of our Lord Jesus Christ . . . went forth with the certainty that the Holy Spirit gives preaching the good news" (*1 Clem.* 42.3). Again, of Paul he writes, "With true inspiration *(ep' alētheias pneumatikōs* he charged you concerning himself and Cephas and Apollos" (*1 Clem.* 47.3). From these few texts it is possible to infer that the Spirit was still speaking during the apostolic period, inspiring prepared persons to be God's voice in the world.

6. The Holy Spirit and the Trinity.

The trinitarian formula that appears in Matthew 28:19, "baptize . . . in the name of the Father and of the Son and of the Holy Spirit," surprisingly appears neither in Acts nor in any other of the apostolic writings being considered. Nor does even a suggestive summary appear here such as that found in 2 Corinthians 13:14: "The grace of the Lord Jesus Christ, the love of God, and the communion of the Holy Spirit be with all of you." Seemingly none of our NT writers was concerned to construct a full-blown doctrine of the Trinity. Nevertheless, all the necessary ingredients to do so were present in our texts from the beginning, gathered up in the experience of Jewish Christians: "their inherited conception of God as 'Father,' their new faith in Christ as the 'Son,' . . . and their experience of the Spirit which [had] been given as the earnest and guarantee of the coming New Age" (Grant, 1015).

As time passed and Christian writers had more time to reflect, a gradual pulling together of these elements into a unified whole began to take shape, although there was still no developed doctrine of the Trinity. Nevertheless, several writers in the postapostolic period bring together the words "Father, Son and Holy Spirit" in a single sentence (*1 Clem.* 46.6; 58.2; Ign. *Magn.* 13.1). The earlier expression "baptize . . . in the name of the Father and of the Son and of the Holy Spirit" reemerges in the *Didache* (7.1, 3), the earliest noncanonical writing to give the trinitarian form of baptism (Swete 1976, 19). Polycarp's prayer at his martyrdom is the earliest instance of a doxology that glorifies the Spirit together with the Father and the Son: "I praise thee for all things, I bless thee, I glorify thee through the everlasting and heavenly high priest, Jesus Christ, thy beloved child, through whom be glory to thee with him and the Holy Spirit, both now and for the ages that are to come. Amen" (*Mart. Pol.* 14.3; cf. also *Mart. Pol.* 22.1). From this time on Christian thinkers had the materials that enabled them to theorize about the mystery of the nature of the Godhead and hammer out the doctrine of the Trinity.

See also CHRISTOLOGY; GOD; MIRACLES, MIRACLE STORIES.

DLNTD: HOLY, HOLINESS; NEW BIRTH; PENTECOST; POWER; SIGNS AND WONDERS; SPIRITS; TONGUES.

BIBLIOGRAPHY. H. W. Attridge, *The Epistle to the Hebrews* (Herm; Philadelphia: Fortress, 1989); D. E. Aune, *Prophecy in Early Christianity* (Grand Rapids: Eerdmans, 1983); C. K. Barrett, *The Acts of the Apostles* (ICC; Edinburgh: T & T Clark, 1994) vol. 1; R. J. Bauckham, *Jude, 2 Peter* (WBC; Waco, TX: Word, 1983); F. Baumgärtel, "πνεῦμα κτλ (OT, Judaism)," *TDNT* 6:359-68; F. F. Bruce, *The Epistle to the Hebrews* (NICNT; Grand Rapids: Eerdmans, 1964); R. Bultmann, *The Johannine Epistles* (Philadelphia: Fortress, 1973); H. Conzelmann, *Acts of the Apostles* (Philadelphia: Fortress, 1987); W. J. Dalton, *Christ's Proclamation to the Spirits: A Study of 1 Peter 3:18—4:6* (AnBib 23; Rome: Pontifical Biblical Institute, 1965); W. D. Davies, *Paul and Rabbinic Judaism* (rev. ed.; Philadelphia: Fortress, 1980); J. D. G. Dunn, "Discernment of Spirits—A Neglected Gift" in *Witness to the Spirit: Essays on Revelation, Spirit, Redemption,* ed. W. Harrington (Dublin: Koinonia, 1979) 79-96; idem, *Jesus and the Spirit* (Philadelphia: Westminster, 1975); G. D. Fee, *God's Empowering Presence: The Holy Spirit in the Letters of Paul* (Peabody, MA: Hendrickson, 1994); F. C. Grant, "Trinity, the," *Dictionary of the Bible,* ed. J. Hastings (rev. ed.; New York: Scribners, 1963); M. Green, *I Believe in the Holy Spirit* (Grand Rapids: Eerdmans, 1975); G. F. Hawthorne, *The Presence and the Power: The Significance of the Holy Spirit in the Life of Jesus* (Dallas: Word, 1991); G. S. Hendry, *The Holy Spirit in Christian Theology* (rev. ed.; Philadelphia: Westminster, 1965); R. C. H. Lenski, *The Interpretation of the Acts of the Apostles* (Minneapolis: Augsburg, 1934); E. Lohse, "πεντη-κοστή," *TDNT* 6:44-53; R. P. Martin, *James* (WBC; Waco, TX: Word, 1988); J. R. Michaels, *1 Peter* (WBC; Waco, TX: Word, 1988); R. H. Mounce, *The Book of Revelation* (NICNT; Grand Rapids: Eerdmans, 1977); G. von Rad, *Genesis* (rev. ed.; Philadelphia: Westminster, 1976); H. W. Robinson, *The Christian Experience of the Holy Spirit* (London: Nisbet, 1928); E. Schweizer, "πνεῦμα κτλ, (NT)," *TDNT* 6:396-453; E. F. Scott, *The Spirit in the New Testament* (London: Hodder & Stoughton, 1923); E. Sjöberg, "πνεῦμα κτλ (Palestinian Judaism)," *TDNT* 6:375-89; G. Stählin, "τὸ πνεῦμα Ἰησοῦ (Apostelgeschichte 16:7)," in *Christ and Spirit in the New Testament,* ed. B. Lindars and S. S. Smalley (Cambridge: Cambridge University Press, 1973) 229-52; H. B. Swete, *The Holy Spirit in the Ancient Church* (London: Macmillan, 1912); idem, *The Holy Spirit in the New Testament* (reprint ed.; Grand Rapids: Baker, 1976); M. M. B. Turner, "The Significance of Receiving the Spirit in Luke-Acts: A Survey of Modern Scholarship," *TJ* (1982) 131-42; idem, "The Spirit of Christ and Christology," in *Christ the Lord,* ed. H. H. Rowdon (Leicester: Inter-Varsity Press, 1982) 168-90; H. P. Van Dusen, *Spirit, Son and Father* (New York: Scribners, 1958); M. Welker, *God and Spirit* (Minneapolis: Fortress, 1994).

G. F. Hawthorne

HOMILY. *See* HEBREWS, LETTER TO THE.

HOUSE CHURCH. *See* CHURCH II.

HOUSEHOLD, CHURCH AS. *See* CHURCH II.

HUSBANDS. *See* WOMEN.

HYMNS. *See* WORSHIP.

I

"I AM" SAYINGS. *See* JOHN, GOSPEL OF.

IMAGE OF GOD. *See* ADAM AND CHRIST.

IMMORTALITY. *See* RESURRECTION II.

IMPERIAL CULT. *See* RELIGIONS, GRECO-ROMAN.

IN CHRIST: PAUL

The phrases "in Christ (Jesus)" and "in the Lord" appear frequently in the Pauline letters. They are nearly absent from the other writings of the NT, except for pronominal references to Christ in the Johannine materials. This concentration of the expression in the Pauline letters has suggested to many interpreters that some or all of its occurrences represent a Pauline formula. It is often thought that such a formula was based on a local conception of Christ as a substance or person. But the variety of ways in which the phrases appear in Paul's letters indicates that they serve as a flexible idiom that may express instrumentality or mode of action as well as locality. While Paul sometimes joins the expression "in Christ" with the image of Christ as an inclusive figure, body or building, it is not derived from or limited to a corporate idea. Paul's language instead partakes of a common metaphorical use of space by which definition or exclusivity is represented. In varying ways, then, the expression "in Christ" conveys Paul's belief that God's saving purposes are decisively effected through Christ.

1. The Usage of the Expression
2. The Origin and Basis of the Expression
3. Theological Aspects of Paul's Usage

1. The Usage of the Expression.

A number of variations of the expression are possible for Paul, the most frequent of which are "in Christ," "in Christ Jesus" and "in the Lord." It is probable that the individual forms often represent differing nuances of meaning. The Pauline letters only once use "in Jesus" (Eph 4:21) and never "in Jesus Christ," although otherwise references to "Jesus Christ" regularly appear in the letters. The prominence of "Christ" in the phrase suggests an emphasis on the exalted status and saving role of the Messiah. The frequently attached name *Jesus* may call forth the idea of the earthly figure and his humanity. The alternative form "in the Lord" usually stresses the unique power and divine authority of Christ, and hence his right to demand obedience or his ability to deliver from other "powers" (e.g., Phil 1:14, 1 Thess 4:1). These distinctions in meaning may not always be present however (see, e.g., Rom 16:1-16).

Unlike the Johannine literature, which focuses on the mutual inherence of Christ and believers, Paul does not emphasize this reciprocal aspect. The idea that Christ is in or among believers appears in his letters (e.g., Gal 2:19; Rom 8:10; Col 1:27) but is only occasionally brought into association with the thought that believers are in Christ.

The expression is used over a triangular field of meaning rather than in a single, technical sense. At one corner of the field one finds the examples of the form "certain ones/churches (are) in Christ," where the phrase takes a local sense. At another corner one finds statements like "God was reconciling the world to himself in Christ" (2 Cor 5:19). Here Christ is viewed as the instrument of God's action, debate on the meaning of this verse notwithstanding. Sometimes "in Christ/the Lord" may stress the manner in which an action occurs ("I speak the truth in Christ," Rom 9:1). Paul's use of the phrases moves between these limits, generally exhibiting a lack of distinction between the three ideas of locality, instrumentality and modality (e.g., "your labor is not in vain in the Lord," 1 Cor 15:58).

As A. T. Robertson and others have observed, the instrumental use of the Greek preposition *en* ("in") is a metaphorical extension of the local sense (Robertson, 590). Even when "in Christ"/ "in the Lord" is used to describe an instrument or manner of action, Christ is understood as a defining sphere. The "in" phrases bear a more specific sense than the "through" phrases, as Paul's shift from the wording "through a human being" to "in Adam" and "in Christ" shows (1 Cor 15:21-22). Christ, and no other, is God's instrument for raising humans from the dead, just as death comes through Adam alone. A similar change of meaning emerges in 2 Corinthians 5:18-19, where Paul moves from affirming that he was reconciled to God through Christ to describing his preaching as asserting that God was reconciling the world to himself in Christ. In the second instance the exclusivity of the proclamation evokes a more definite idea.

Occasionally Paul describes believers or their actions as "in the Spirit" (e.g., Rom 8:9; 9:1; 14:17; *see* Holy Spirit). If we may take Romans 8:1-11 as the determinative context, it is clear that being "in Christ" leads to being "in the Spirit," not the reverse (Rom 8:1, 2). Those who belong to Christ have the indwelling Spirit of Christ and so are not "in the flesh" but "in the Spirit" (Rom 8:9).

Twice Paul refers to the Thessalonians as being "in God the Father and the Lord Jesus Christ" (1 Thess 1:1; 2 Thess 1:1). This unusual variation is part of Paul's concentration of references to God in the Thessalonian correspondence, stemming from his focus on eschatology and, perhaps, his awareness of their recent conversion from paganism. It may reflect a concern on Paul's part to preserve monotheism while asserting the efficacy of faith in Christ.

In Colossians and Ephesians the frequency of "in Christ/the Lord" increases sharply. Furthermore, a series of new spatial metaphors appears. The fullness of deity dwells in Christ bodily (Col 2:9). The divine purpose for creation, redemption and the consummation of all things is comprehended within the "sphere" of Christ (Eph 1:3-10). Believers have been placed in heaven by being placed in him (Eph 2:6; Col 3:1). They have been made part of a body of which Christ is the head (Eph 4:15-16). They are being built together as a temple (Eph 2:21-22). They have put on a new humanity (Eph 4:22-24; Col 3:10). All these images present Christ as the focal expression of deity and the divine purpose and consequently the basis of the life and unity of the entire church.

2. The Origin and Basis of the Expression.

The local or spatial sense of "in Christ/the Lord" has provided the starting point for most modern scholarly theories of its derivation. Generally these theories depend on a quasi-physical understanding of Christ in order to interpret the spatial sense conveyed by the phrases. Some scholars in the earlier part of the twentieth century claimed that Paul, equating Christ with the Spirit, understood him as an all-pervading fluid, like the air that we breathe and in which we live (e.g., Deissmann, Bousset). Others asserted that the background to the local idea lay in the myth of a redeemer figure found in gnostic writings (e.g., Käsemann). This thesis further provided the means for understanding Paul's statements about participation with Christ in death and resurrection: as a member of the redeemer's material body, one shared in his destiny. A. Schweitzer claimed to find the source of Paul's thought in an early Jewish expectation of a real, physical union of the elect with the Messiah.

During the latter decades of the twentieth century, scholars have tended to appeal to the broader notion of a corporate personality, which is thought to be found in the Hebrew Scriptures and early Jewish literature (e.g., Best, Moule). In this reading Christ is regarded as an all-encompassing "person" with whom the whole community of believers is united in experience and destiny. This frequently used but ill-defined idea has come under justified criticism in recent study (see Wedderburn, Porter).

In some measure the local and quasi-physical understanding of Paul's language has been tempered by several mid twentieth-century studies, especially those of F. Neugebauer and M. Bouttier. Neugebauer denied that "in Christ" or "in the Lord" had any spatial sense, arguing that these expressions convey instead the temporal idea of inclusion in the decisive saving event, Christ's death and resurrection. Bouttier was more impressed by the diversity of Paul's usage, finding instrumental and eschatological ideas as well as the inclusive (local) sense. These studies have brought an increased awareness that in many contexts the primary force of the phrase may be something other than locality.

It remains a question whether Paul's employment of a spatial metaphor demands any of the proposed corporeal images of Christ. Three crucial considerations argue against supposing that the idea of an organic reality lies behind his usage. Paul's references to "in Christ" and "in the Lord" appear to be a special extension of the common and almost unnoticed practice of symbolically representing exclusivity or definition as a locality. Paul, like the psalmist, rejoices and hopes "in the Lord" (e.g., Phil 4:4, cf. Ps 5:11; 9:2; 33:21, 22). He applies similar language to persons who do not fit the model of a universal corporate personality: the Israelites were baptized "into Moses" (1 Cor 10:2), God promised to bless the nations "in Abraham" (Gal 3:8, 9), he raised up Pharaoh to display his power "in him" (Rom 9:15), the Philippians have the struggle they saw and heard "in me" (Phil 1:30), the unbelieving husband is sanctified "in his wife" (1 Cor 7:14). Parallel representations may be found elsewhere in the NT (e.g., Mk 3:22; 14:6), in contemporary Jewish authors ("In him [God], and in no other, was their salvation," Josephus *Ant.* 3.1.5 §23), in secular papyri (e.g., "There is an additional debt from the price of grain 'in' Ptolemy," cited by Mayser, 2.396), and even in classical Greek sources of the fifth century B.C. (e.g., Sophocles *Ajax* 518, the captive Tecmessa to Ajax: "In you entirely, I am delivered"). The Greek preposition *en*, "in," may convey association or instrumentality, but the idea of a defining sphere remains in such instances. This wider use of spatial metaphor cautions against requiring a concrete local image behind Paul's language.

Moreover, although the attempt has been made (Schweitzer, Sanders), it is not possible to extend a quasi-physical image of union with Christ into Paul's larger theology. There is a breakdown of the metaphor, which reveals that it is not informed by some more definite corporeal understanding of salvation. Paul derives his ethical demands from what God has accomplished in Christ: "Clean out the old leaven, that you might be a new lump of dough, just as you are unleavened" (1 Cor 5:7); "You were once in darkness, but now you are light in the Lord: walk as children of light" (Eph 5:8). If Paul were operating with an organic concept of salvation, he might speak of degrees of mystical participation (e.g., a process of being filled with light) but not in the paradoxical formulation he offers here.

Paul's utilization of material symbols is robust yet diverse, suggesting a plurality of metaphors rather than a basic realistic idea. Paul's figure of the "body of Christ" is supplemented by his description of the community of believers as the temple of God (e.g., 1 Cor 3:16, 17; Eph 2:19-22). He plays upon the image of spirit-body dualism with his description of immersion and infusion with the Spirit uniting believers in one body (1 Cor 12:12, 13). He also occasionally links Christ with the indwelling Spirit (Rom 8:10; 1 Cor 15:45; probably Col 3:11; *see* Holy Spirit). Yet there is no absolute identification of the two (e.g., Rom 8:11). The statements rather represent metonymy: the Spirit is spoken of as Christ, because the Spirit is the means by which Christ's lordship is effected in believers (e.g., 1 Cor 12:3). It is noteworthy that the expression "in Christ" qualifies the idea of believers as the body of Christ, describing its sphere of validity: "We, who are many, are one body in Christ" (Rom 12:5). As R. H. Gundry has argued, the body here is a metaphor for the interdependence and unity of believers, not a real entity (Gundry, 223-44).

Although the corporate explanations are not satisfactory, it is clear that for Paul, in some real sense, believers share in Christ's death and resurrection. Life in Christ brings participation with him in his death and resurrection (Rom 6:1-11; 2 Cor 13:4; Gal 3:26-28). Paul's employment of Adam as an inclusive figure is of fundamental importance in tracing this aspect of his thought. Early Jewish parallels to Paul's references to Adam are especially close and reveal a conception of destiny based on divine pronouncement that matches Paul's statements. God ordained that the entire human race arise from one human being, to show that one who murders a single human being is guilty of destroying the whole world (*m. Sanh.* 4:5). With Adam's transgression, condemnation came on the whole of humanity (*4 Ezra* 3:21; *2 Baruch* 23:4; 48:42, 43). The judgment of God on the deed of the one decides the life or death of the many: as in Adam, so also in Christ, Paul argues (1 Cor 15:22, Rom 5:12-21). Solidarity with Adam stems from the divine will to bless or curse through him, not from physical descent, although in this instance the two converge. Paul's

513

dependence on this larger category is apparent in his interpretation of the divine blessing of the Gentiles "in Abraham," who were not the physical offspring of the patriarch (Gal 3:8, 9).

Paul's connection of Christ to Adam derives from his understanding of the universal scope of Christ's atoning work on the cross: "One died for all, therefore all died" (2 Cor 5:14, 15). Like Adam, therefore, Christ is the new beginning of humanity (Gal 3:28; Eph 4:22-24; Col 3:9-11). The idea that the destinies of the Messiah and the people of God are linked is not unique (e.g., Dan 7:9-27; 2 Baruch 30), but Paul's explicit messianic universalism is. For him, the figures of Adam and Christ are contrasted in all-embracing judgment and salvation.

The expression "in Christ/the Lord" probably came from earlier Jewish Christianity. The book of Acts provides evidence that, before Paul, the earliest believers in Jerusalem proclaimed Jesus as the decisive sphere of God's saving action (Acts 4:2, 12). And as Paul's reliance on a traditional statement in Romans 6:3 shows, prior to him participation in salvation had been expressed in baptism, through which one was transferred into the "realm of Christ." This language and these ideas came into special prominence and underwent further definition in Paul's letters.

3. Theological Aspects of Paul's Usage.

Although there is considerable overlap of the various types, the occurrences of the expression may be divided into five broad thematic categories:

(1) More than one-third of the 151 references affirm something that God has done or does through Christ for salvation (e.g., "the redemption which is in Christ Jesus," Rom 3:24). As we have noted, in Colossians and Ephesians this is expanded to include creation and its consummation.

(2) Approximately another third have to do with exhortation or commendation of behavior or character (e.g., "Rejoice in the Lord always," Phil 4:4; "Prisca and Aquila, my fellow workers in Christ Jesus," Rom 16:3).

(3) About twenty occurrences of the expression describe the present state of believers in view of Christ's saving work (e.g., "we, who are many, are one in Christ," Rom 12:5).

(4) A final dozen or so describe specific persons or particular situations in relation to salvation. Among these are six statements that simply affirm that certain ones are "in Christ" (Rom 16:7, 22, 1 Cor 1:30; Gal 1:22; 1 Thess 3:8; 2 Cor 12:2).

(5) Two references in Colossians have to do strictly with the nature of Christ (Col 1:19; 2:9).

The expansion of the phrases in the vocabulary of Paul's letters and churches is very likely the product of two basic concerns:

(1) In varying ways Paul found it necessary to assert the exclusivity or distinctiveness of God's saving action through Christ. To describe God as having acted "in Christ" or redemption as being "in Christ" succinctly conveyed this thought ("the gift of God is eternal life in Christ Jesus our Lord," Rom 6:23).

(2) It was also important to Paul to define how believers were to live under Christ's saving lordship. In statements that call for, describe or commend obedience, "in Christ/the Lord" communicates simultaneously the gift of salvation and the accompanying divine demand (e.g., "stand firm in the Lord," Phil 4:1). The phrases therefore became a vehicle for Paul to describe the life of faith under Christ's lordship in a world where other powers and temptations were present. To act "in Christ" is to act in faith and obedience in the face of false alternatives: "In Christ Jesus neither circumcision or uncircumcision has any force, but rather faith working through love" (Gal 5:6).

See also ADAM AND CHRIST; BODY OF CHRIST; CHRIST; CHRISTOLOGY.

BIBLIOGRAPHY. E. Best, *One Body in Christ: A Study of the Relationship of the Church to Christ in the Epistles of the Apostle Paul* (London: SPCK, 1955); W. Bousset, *Kyrios Christos* (Nashville: Abingdon, 1970); M. Bouttier, *En Christ: Étude d'exégèse et de théologie pauliniennes* (Paris: Universitaires de France, 1962); A. Deissmann, *Paul: A Study in Social and Religious History* (London: Hodder & Stoughton, 1926); R. H. Gundry, Soma *in Biblical Theology* (SNTSMS 29; Cambridge: Cambridge University Press, 1976); E. Käsemann, "The Theological Problem Presented by the Motif of the Body of Christ" in *Perspectives on Paul* (Philadelphia: Fortress, 1971) 102-21; E. Mayser, *Grammatik der griechischen Papyri aus der Ptolemäerzeit* (Berlin: Walter de Gruyter, 1934); C. F. D. Moule, *The Origin of Christology* (Cambridge: Cambridge University Press, 1977); F. Neugebauer, "Das Paulinische 'in Christo,' " *NTS* 4 (1957-58) 124-38; A. Oepke, "ἐν," *TDNT* 2:537-43; S. E. Porter, "Two Myths: Corporate Personality and Language/Mentality Determinism," *SJT* 43 (1990) 289-307; A. T. Robertson, *A Grammar of the Greek New Testament in the Light of Historical Research* (4th ed.; New York: Hodder & Stoughton, 1923); E. P. Sanders, *Paul and Palestinian Judaism: A Comparison of Patterns of Religion* (Philadelphia: Fortress, 1977); A. Schweitzer, *The Mysticism of Paul the Apostle* (London: Black, 1931); A. J. M. Wedderburn, *Baptism and Resurrection: Studies in Pauline Theology Against Its Greco-Roman Background* (WUNT 44; Tübingen: Siebeck, 1987); idem, "Some Observations on Paul's Use of the Phrases 'in Christ' and 'with Christ,' " *JSNT* 25 (1985) 83-97; N. T. Wright, "Ξριστός" as 'Messiah' in Paul: Philemon 6," in *The Climax of the Covenant* (Minneapolis: Fortress, 1991) 41-55.

M. A. Seifrid

INSPIRATION OF SCRIPTURE. *See* HOLY SPIRIT III.

INTERIM ETHIC. *See* ETHICS I.

ISAIANIC SERVANT. *See* SERVANT OF YAHWEH.

ISRAEL I: GOSPELS

The presence of the name "Israel" in the Gospels reminds us that Jesus lived among the people of the God of the OT Scriptures, that these same people played an important role in the unfolding history of *salvation and that Christ's saving work continues to possess particular relevance for them.

    1. Introduction
    2. Israel in the Gospels
    3. Jesus and Israel

1. Introduction.
The name Israel (Gk *Israēl*) occurs only thirty times in the four Gospels, and in no less than a third of these cases as part of another common expression, like "God of Israel" or "king of Israel." But the scarcity of the term itself is a little misleading, for the idea of Israel permeates the Gospels and comes through strongly in terms such as Jew *(Ioudaios)*, Hebrew *(Hebraikos)*, people *(laos)* and Israelite *(Israēlitēs)*. A score of other terms and ideas (such as "feast" and "Pharisee") similarly reveal the tremendous debt of the Gospels to the concept of Israel.

    For Jews of the first century the name Israel probably carried with it one or more of three basic associated ideas, all of which stemmed from their historical and religious consciousness: (1) reference to the election of Jacob (called Israel) and his progeny; (2) ongoing faithfulness to the divine covenants (notably circumcision); and (3) the theocratic ideal of Israel as it emerged in the people's history, particularly in the Davidic Golden Age. Such religious and historical associations would be largely foreign to Gentiles. Hence the rule in the ancient world that Israel was primarily a Jewish self-designation, while Jews was the name more familiar to Gentiles. In the mouth of Gentiles the term *Jews* frequently carried a deprecatory tone, although it was used in a positive, nationalistic sense by Israelites. In fact, the latter group may have opted for this name, since out of an apparent respect for the term there seems to have been a reticence among the Jewish people to employ Israel too freely. Israel seems to have been reserved as a term of self-dignity, religious privilege or purity of the people, or to refer to biblical Israel.

    There is no evidence up to this time that Israel had ever been used to define a geographic entity, even though a strong national and geographical constitution appears to have existed earlier on in biblical history. When the Gospels were written the people Israel was neither independent politically nor well-defined geographically, so the idea of a state of Israel was presently nonexistent, although it had a part in certain future hopes of the people. For the time, however, the capital, Jerusalem, and in particular the Temple, functioned as a unifying focal point. So the use of the term implied nearness to the capital and cultic center. In other words, those Jews living near Jerusalem were more commonly referred to as Israel, and in this way the term retained a certain geo-political nuance, although this could not have been the chief sense of the word. It was primarily a socio-religious term, a self-designation of God's people.

    When we come to the Gospels we see that the term likewise preserves a geopolitical nuance in some passages (Mk 15:32; Mt 2:20-21; 9:33; 10:23; Lk 4:25; 7:9; Jn 1:49; 12:13). Even these texts demonstrate, however, that the reference is primarily social (i.e., refers to a people: Lk 1:80; 2:25, 32, 34; 24:21; Jn 1:31; 3:10; cf. "sons of Israel," Mt 27:9; Lk 1:16; "God of Israel," Mt 15:31; Lk 1:68; "house of Israel," Mt 10:6; 15:24; "twelve tribes of Israel," Mt 19:28 par. Lk 22:30).

And yet the term is never simply ethnic. Israel is also a religious term. It frequently denotes a people with a particular religious identity. This religious element often takes on a negative content in the Gospels, associated with the rejection *by* Israel of the one sent *to* Israel. Yet in spite of this fact, the one consistent feature of the usage of the word in the Gospels—in continuity with its use in the Jewish world generally—is that it retains its dignity. It continues to imply privilege associated with *covenant, election and theocratic ideals. This is true even in a passage like Matthew 8:10 and its parallel Luke 7:9, where the surprise shown by Jesus (expressed in the word *oudeni/oude,* "not even") nevertheless implies a special dignity for Israel. Nor do the Gospels deviate from the traditional significance of the term as referring to the descendants of *Abraham (through Jacob). Never, for example, is the term used either of the church or of Gentiles. While Paul can distinguish between an ethnic and a spiritual Israel (Rom 9:6), the Gospels avoid the use of the term in anything but its traditional sense (granting, however, that Pauline-type ideas may be differently expressed).

It is clear, however, that our concern goes far beyond the usage of the term, for a whole theology of Israel can be found in the Gospels. The interpretation of this theology has seen important changes throughout its history. Among the earliest Christian exegetes the Israel of the Gospels received little attention and even less sympathy. Even up to modern times the Gospels have commonly been thought to pronounce the rejection of Israel in favor of a New Israel— namely, a *church consisting predominantly of Gentiles which superseded the Old Israel of the *law. This view eventually gave way to another, which recognized that it was not all of Israel which was rejected, for from that nation came a small remnant who formed the nucleus of the "True Israel." Sometimes the idea of a True Israel is used to refer to believing Jews, sometimes to Jewish and Gentile believers together, sometimes to believing Jews with a believing Gentile "addition." Simply expressed, the term "New Israel" implies some continuity with the idea of Israel, but a whole different people is intended; "True Israel," on the other hand, implies a new set of criteria for membership in the people of God (cf. "spiritual" Israel with Israel "according to the flesh," *kata sarka,* Rom 2:28-29; 9:3). In either case these terms by themselves might imply

that the significance of the historic nation Israel in the divine economy has come to an abrupt and decisive end. It should be noted that the term "True Israel," like "New Israel," is not found in the Gospels.

Interest in the place of Israel in the Gospels has, until lately, chiefly been that of the redaction critics. The perspective of many of these scholars is that while the Gospels do in fact portray the rejection of Israel, this notion largely emerged during the later debate between church and *synagogue rather than in the ministry of Jesus. (With this view the form critics would largely agree, with the exception that they place the same developments earlier on in the stages of oral transmission, rather than with the Evangelists as such.)

The most recent approaches to the question of Israel, however, have come from another discipline, that of historical-Jesus research. These new contributions have served to place Israel not at the perimeter as earlier, but in the very center of Gospel studies. By viewing Jesus as a Jewish restorationist preacher, they have also served to accentuate the rift already discerned by redaction criticism, between the historical ministry of Jesus and the portrayal of him in the Gospels. In attempting to answer the question of Israel and its salvation, we will first consider the redaction critics' findings in the Gospels before moving on to the larger question of Israel in Jesus research.

2. Israel in the Gospels.

The view that the negative attitude toward Israel in the Gospels originates in the synagogue/ church debate rather than in the ministry of Jesus itself takes its cue from passages like the parable of the tenants (Mk 12:1-2 par. Mt 21:33-46 and Lk 20:9-19), which ends with the moral that the owner of the vineyard will "give the vineyard to others" (seemingly indicating a transferral of the kingdom [*see* Kingdom of God] from Israel to the Gentiles). This parable is felt to depend on a highly developed *christology (cf. the important place of the son and his death in the parable), a christology that could only have originated long after the ministry of Jesus and presumably, therefore, amidst the conflict between Christianity and Judaism.

But while it may seem quite a straightforward matter to discard such pericopes as later Christian expansions of the ministry of Jesus, it is nevertheless much more difficult to eliminate the still large accumulation of sayings and oracles against Israel which remain after this process. For example, the *judgment of Israel motif is present in a large proportion of the Gospel material. The "killing of the prophets" theme (a theme, incidentally, which has been thought to explain and authenticate Jesus' own use of the parable of the tenants) is also present in every layer of the Gospel tradition, including the so-called triple tradition (*see* Synoptic Problem), Mark and Q (cf. Mt 8:11-12 par. Lk 13:28-29). Can all of this tradition be relegated to the Evangelists and their communities? This would appear to be the view of some extreme redaction critics.

2.1. Mark. While redaction critics have paid most attention to Israel's place in the other Gospels, Mark has not been ignored in this respect. The findings of Markan studies are summarized by the Jewish scholar S. Sandmel in his study of anti-Semitism in the Gospels. Like the other Gospels, large sections of Mark develop the central plot of Jewish conspiracy against Jesus. In the process the members of Israel are portrayed as extremely stubborn and imperceptive. Even the Jewish disciples in Mark are imperceptive, an observation first given significance by W. Wrede, the father of modern Markan redaction criticism. Only a Gentile centurion clearly understands who Jesus is (Mk 15:39; cf. 8:33). Some feel that this reflects an attack by Gentile or Galilean Christianity on the establishment in Jerusalem, or on Judaizers such as Paul confronted in his ministry, while others hold that it represents a categorical rejection of all of Judaism. Some scholars find evidence for the view that Mark therefore envisages God's decisive rejection of Israel: Israel is undeserving of salvation.

But it should be noted that it is never explicitly stated in Mark's Gospel that Israel as a people is rejected. The so-called conspiracy plot, as in the other Gospels, is essential to understanding the rejection of Jesus, explaining his death and accentuating the graciousness of God in sending Jesus to die for the "many" (Mk 10:45). Furthermore, this rejection by his own people serves as one more form of opposition, along with sickness and demonic oppression, over which Jesus is seen to triumph. Thus Mark has a theological-historical interest in this dramatic progression. Rather than portraying the rejection of Israel, Mark's Gospel contrasts God's sav-

ing initiative with the undeservedness, not only of Israel, but of those imperceptive Jewish disciples who will prove to be far from rejected. If Mark is guilty of theologizing in his Gospel, it is by presenting the received tradition in light of the saving event of the cross; it is not with a feeling of hostility toward Israel that he does so—such a judgment is a quite subjective one placed on Mark and on his community.

2.2. Matthew. The question of Israel in this Gospel and its sources is considerably more involved (*see* Matthew, Gospel of). While the Gospel is Pharisaic in tone, it is also highly critical of that group. Although Jesus restricts his ministry to Israel in Matthew (Mt 10:6; 15:24), according to some scholars the Gospel leads naturally and progressively to the conclusion that the Gentile mission is all that remains for its readers (cf. Mt 28:19)—Israel is rejected and there is no future for the nation. Others see a carefully constructed salvation history at work here: Whereas Mark merely characterizes Israel as reprobate and undeserving, Matthew speaks of the transfer of salvation to the Gentiles, something deliberately orchestrated and commanded by Christ. Matthew adjusts the wording of texts like Mark 3:7-12 (par. Mt 12:15-21) to highlight this transfer. He always emphasizes controversy and conflict. In this Gospel the blame for Jesus' death (*see* Death of Christ) is consciously assumed by an Israel who invokes on their race the ensuing punishment for this act (Mt 27:25, referring to A.D. 70, according to some).

W. Trilling considered such things evidence that Matthew envisaged a "True Israel," which displaced ethnic Israel, and that the Gospel came from a time when Jews and Christians were decisively split (A.D. 70-135). D. R. A. Hare, who studied Jewish persecution of Christians in this Gospel, concluded that while controversy was doubtless a part of Jesus' ministry, Matthew's situation was largely responsible for this element in his Gospel. The abundant references to Pharisees (Matthew even seems to insert them into his sources) reflects a late date when that group was prominent. Matthew envisaged not a "New" or "True" Israel, but a "Third Race" of Christians altogether. S. H. Brooks has recently added complexity to the debate by suggesting that there is evidence of several layers of material in Matthew, ranging from times of peaceful relations between the Christian community and Judaism to times of hostile opposition.

In spite of all the relevant observations made above, much of the same rationale for including the Jesus-Israel debate applies for Matthew as well as for Mark. There is no compelling reason to doubt that the struggles witnessed in Matthew were struggles *within* Judaism and reflect the kind of interaction with his people that Jesus experienced during his ministry. A true respect for Judaism is evidenced in the Gospel, where Jesus' teaching is rooted in and emulates Jewish teaching, making Matthew the most Jewish of the Gospels. While a few have interpreted the presence of extensive teaching material (the Sermon on the Mount in chapters 5–7) as a competing legal system in contrast to, and in defiance of, the law of Israel—a Christian system supplanting the Jewish one—this is only one way of interpreting the teaching material, and clearly a minority point of view.

As for the Pharisees, the little we know about this party suggests that their history extended over a much earlier period, hardly making it a controlling factor in the dating of Matthew's final redaction—a point which lately has been made by several scholars. Pharisees appear in every Gospel, if not as frequently as in Matthew. The invective against the scribes and Pharisees may represent nothing more than a focusing of blame on establishment-Judaism as Matthew knew it. More likely it reflects Matthew's characterization of Jesus' historical opponents (something we also find in John) since it was widely known that the Pharisees were notorious in their resistance to Jesus. This characterization may give us a clue to the relative dating of the Gospels but says little about their situation of writing. The theme of Israel's obduracy was taken up by Paul as early as A.D. 57 (Rom 9–11) and does not necessarily presuppose later synagogue/church debate. As with Mark, nothing explicit is found regarding the rejection of Israel.

2.3. Luke. Luke's Gospel is of special interest because of the author's apparent concern with salvation history—God's working among Jews and Gentiles (*see* Luke, Gospel of). H. Conzelmann stressed the discontinuity between Israel and the church created by this salvation history and postulated that Luke envisaged a New Israel. But in this Gospel the continuity between Israel and the Jesus movement is also obvious. The latter appears as the valid fulfillment of the former. Many scholars therefore feel that the church of Luke is depicted as the "True Israel."

But others deny that any sense of continuity is intended, or else that this continuity is meant to dignify Israel in any way. What takes place in Luke's view is a gradual shifting of God's people from Jews to Gentiles (cf. the prominent location of Lk 4:16-30, along with the story line of the companion volume *Acts, the Stephen episode in Acts 7 and the conclusion of Acts at 28:23-28). R. Maddox and J. T. Sanders are the most recent exponents of this view. The church is a New Israel, and the break with the Old Israel is complete. As a sign of this, Luke appears to transfer the term "people" (*laos*, a term for Israel) to the church (a view held earlier by Conzelmann). This Gospel has the entire Jewish populace united in condemning Jesus to death (Lk 23:2-5, 13-23).

It should be noted, however, that this latter passage may only reflect the perspective of Luke's source. Some feel that the Q source is itself responsible for Luke's negative view of Israel. Indeed Luke's special source (L), or Luke himself, emphasizes the dignity and hope of Israel (Lk 1:80; 2:25, 32, 34; 24:21).

The idea that the fate of Israel comes to rest either in a New Israel or a True Israel is clearly an interpretation placed on Luke. There is no need to adopt either view. Luke's interest was largely historical and apologetic. The common question of theodicy, "Why did so few from Israel respond to the Gospel?" is also dealt with by Paul in Rom 9–11 (cf. Rom 9:6, 19-20, 30; 11:1). According to Luke, many in Israel did believe. We should therefore probably follow scholars like J. Jervell who see Israel divided by the ministry of Jesus, some coming to repentance, others not. But Israel never transfers its name or status to Gentiles.

2.4. John. John's Gospel is notorious for its frequent (but strangely not consistent) derogatory usage of the term "the Jews" to speak of Jesus' adversaries. Long digressions on the unbelief of the Jews and Jesus' conflict with them appear in John 5–9. The Jews as a group are treated as resisters (Jn 5:10, 15, 18; 8:48, 52, 57; 10:24, 31). In their recalcitrance they even disown the universal Jewish confession of God as king (Jn 19:12-15). This categorical distrust of the Jews is widely felt to reflect a much later situation in the life of the church when excommunication from the synagogue for confessing Christians was officially sanctioned (cf. Jn 9:22), a view widely made known by J. L. Martyn's study of the relevant chapters and of the life setting of John's Gospel. By all appearances John's Gospel is no longer aware of the diversity of parties within early first-century Judaism. They are all lumped together as one group: "the Jews." Jews appear to the readers of this Gospel as outsiders (e.g., "your law," Jn 10:34).

But Jews also believe (Jn 11:45). And they are at times divided (Jn 10:19-21). *Israel* always remains a positive term (Jn 1:31, 47), and singular respect for Judaism is evinced (Jn 4:22). Other uses of "the Jews" are neutral (e.g., Jn 11:19; 18:20). The usage of "the Jews" seems therefore to demonstrate what has been described as a sense of remoteness rather than hatred. Considering the growing recognition among scholars of the Jewish background of the Fourth Gospel (*see* John, Gospel of), this remoteness is somewhat baffling. Perhaps the writer was a Jew, but he was writing for non-Jews. The important point is that this remoteness is also expressed in passages where Jews believe. This precludes the notion that Jews are recalcitrant because they are Jews.

While some feel that it is only the authorities who are singled out for criticism in the Gospel, the critique appears to be more widespread than that. The message seems to be that the structure of the religion of Judaism, as it was interpreted in contemporary Israel, had departed from the way of Israel historically, and this departure was reflected in the attitudes of many Jews (cf. Jn 2:18-20). There are strong indications in the Fourth Gospel of the underlying doctrine of the remnant (cf. Jn 10:1-18; 11:45; see 3.1 below).

2.5. Conclusions about Israel in the Gospels. Some of the tendencies noted by scholars in the individual Gospels may be significant, but these tendencies have been exaggerated. The teaching which is so often attributed to the developing tradition has a claim to go back to Jesus himself (see 3 below). The characterizations ("the Jews," "the scribes and Pharisees") often refer to a certain part of Israel that typically rejected Jesus, but the term *Israel* is never used for this group. While there are no clear statements that Israel is forever rejected by God, there nonetheless emerges through the Gospels the impression that, by the time of the Gospel writers at least, Israel had surprisingly little representation among the followers of Jesus. This needed to be explained from the events of Jesus' ministry, and the Gospels sought to fill this need. However, the theological, historical and soteriological motive—the need to explain how God brought salvation through rejection—was certainly still the dominating factor in the Gospel presentations.

3. Jesus and Israel.

3.1. Background for Jesus' Ministry to Israel. The most recent development in the study of Israel in the Gospels has come from the area of historical-Jesus research. Older, historically negative quests for the Jesus of history, like that of R. Bultmann, which divorced Jesus from his Jewish environment, have been abandoned in favor of a new Jewish Quest, or Third Quest, which attempts to place Jesus properly within his Jewish environment. This approach has been adopted by an impressive array of scholars both Jewish and Christian (among them: G. Vermes, B. F. Meyer, A. E. Harvey, J. Riches, G. Lohfink, E. P. Sanders, J. H. Charlesworth, J. P. Meier and N. T. Wright). Some adherents of this new school of Jesus research hold that the major presupposition for Jesus' ministry was the widespread eschatological doctrine of the restoration of Israel, and that Jesus both addressed this concern and understood his ministry in the light of the expectation.

G. Lohfink is a good example of the newly emerging restorationist perspective. He points to Jesus' deliberate choice of twelve disciples and to the significance of the miracles as evidence that Jesus intended from the beginning of his ministry to restore the nation. When his preaching failed to appeal to Israel, Jesus began to see that Israel's salvation would now only come through his own meritorious death which would result in the salvation of the "many" (Mk 10:45).

E. P. Sanders has notably presented Jesus as an eschatological restorationist preacher. Sanders maintains that in common with the rest of Judaism, Jesus assumed the salvation of all Israel. Jesus' preaching was in anticipation of the final restoration of Israel. This can be seen in the way Jesus predicted the destruction of the Temple (*see* Temple Cleansing) so that it could be replaced with the new eschatological Temple. In addition, the kingdom Jesus preached referred to the hope of a restored nation. Jesus' task, specifically, was gathering the sinners and outcasts of Israel so as to assure that all Israel would be included in this blessing (see also Wright).

Where such a position is adopted, it could easily lead to the view that the restoration which Jesus envisaged was a failure, for Israel turned away from him and the promised gathering of Israel did not take place. The view of restoration as the salvation of all Israel and the return of the dispersed Jews does not seem to match the results of Jesus' ministry. What can be said about Jesus as a preacher of Israel's restoration, especially when the Gospels provide such clear evidence that this restoration was a failure? Are we forced to accept the pathos and tragedy of A. Schweitzer's Jesus whose goals, even at the cost of death, were scarcely acquired?

The attempt to place Jesus within Judaism is a welcome trend. But restorationism was not so prevalent a movement in Judaism as the scholars of the Third Quest seem to maintain, at least in the way assumed by them. We can point to many groups in Judaism who indeed looked forward to restoration in the future but also maintained that only a faithful remnant would be saved in the present (see Elliott).

The doctrine of the remnant consists in the idea that many, perhaps most, of Israel has abandoned the covenant in such a way as to place themselves outside salvation and in danger of judgment. Such doctrines could be cultivated in Judaism because Israel was not a unified community at this time. It was severely divided within itself. As a result of so much intra-Jewish conflict, divisions between ethnic and religious Israel were drawn, each party claiming to be the remnant. We see the beginnings of the doctrine of segregation within Israel in Sirach (cf. Sir 8:17; 9:16; 11:9; 12:14; 13:1, 17-18; 22:13). 1 Maccabees implies throughout that God's retribution against sinful Israel finally outweighs his concern for their election, for they have broken the covenant (! Macc 1:43, 52-53; 9:23-25; 10:14). There is a clear distinction between the faithful and the apostates, and the righteous are in the minority (1 Macc 1:62-63; 3:15-19; 9:5-6). The rest are judged in the unfolding history (1 Macc 1:63-64). The apocalyptic writings and those of Qumran (see Dead Sea Scrolls) take this development further and speak clearly of a remnant of the faithful, or righteous, in Israel (1 Enoch 10:16; 83:8; 94:4; 99:10; Pss. Sol. 12:6; 4 Ezra 7:50-61; 8:2- 3; 2 Apoc. Bar. 48:33; 77:2-6; CD 1:4-5; 2:11-12; 3:19-20; 1QM 13:8; 14:8-9; 1QH 6:7-8; 4Q181) and of the judgment of the remainder of Israel (1 Enoch 5:6-9; 80:2-8; 81:7-9;

90:26-27; Jub. 15:34; Pss. Sol. 8:15-20; 12:6; 13:5-10; 4 Ezra 9:8-12; 2 Apoc. Bar. 24:1-25:2; CD 1:3-4; 1QS 4:11-14), for many in Israel, along with their leaders, have effectively broken the covenant (1 Enoch 94:2-5; 101:1-9; Jub. 23:19; 4 Ezra 7:22-24; 2 Apoc. Bar. 41:3; CD 1:12-2:1; 1QH 15:18-21; often they are implicated in the sin of the world, e.g., 4 Ezra 8:14-18). Accordingly, ideas of national election are questioned or played down (cf. 4 Ezra 3:11-17, 36). Occasionally the community of the remnant appears to take the name Israel for itself (1 Macc 1:53; 7:9, 22; 9:27, 51; Pss. Sol. 10:6; 1QS 5:22; 8:4, CD[B] 2:26; 1QSa 1:6; 1QM 10:9, 1QpNah 3:2-3), although as a rule the term still refers to the nation.

In spite of their sometimes-harsh remnant theology, these works also manifest a definite respect for the promises to Israel and a hope for the eventual restoration of all Israel (1 Enoch 90:30-36; Jub. 23:27-32; Pss. Sol. 8:28; 17:26-46; 4 Ezra 4:26-35; 6:26b-28; 13:12-13, 39-47; 2 Apoc. Bar. 29:3–30:3; CD 2:11-12). This restoration frequently includes the Gentiles (e.g., 1 Enoch 10:17, 21-22; 90:33), but the remnant is consistently at the center of this restoration. Israel is not restored except by joining the remnant (cf. e.g., 1 Enoch 90:30).

We can see therefore that a background had already been established for the kind of intra-Jewish strife recorded in the Gospels. Sociologically speaking, the most bitter battles are fought among siblings, especially when, as in the Jewish world of this time, the claims on God and salvation are mutually exclusive. It is notable that within one sectarian dispute one side was forced to adopt a negative view of the name "Judah" (cf. "Jew" in CD 4:3, 11; 8:3), suggesting a certain group which the author's community felt had corrupted the true faith of Israel.

3.2. Jesus and the Remnant of Israel. As scholars like B. F. Meyer have insisted, the remnant theme is undeniably present in the Gospels. While it is conceivable that the Evangelists have written their contemporary controversies between church and synagogue back into their Gospels, it is difficult to remove altogether from the tradition signs that Jesus faced controversy over Israel's salvation in his day and offered comments of the type that we now find in our Gospels. Specifically, Jesus' association with John the Baptist (see John the Baptist) reveals that he shared the warnings about the coming judgment upon Israel. It appears that Jesus not only warned about judgment but pronounced it (cf. Mt 11:20-24 par. Lk 10:12-15). His parables and the secrecy theme demonstrate that he shared the current practice of sheltering truth designed for the righteous from those who would misunderstand and abuse it. Sayings like that concerning Jesus' mother and brothers (an undeniably authentic tradition; Mk 3:31-35 par. Mt 12:46-50 and Lk 8:19-21) demonstrate that Jesus set his own criteria for membership in the covenant people of God. That Jesus often alluded to a "seed" in his parables may also mean that he shared the dualism of the sectarian groups who distinguished between the righteous and the unrighteous "seed" in Israel. Such a use of the concept of good and evil seed is well documented in Jewish literature (*1 Enoch* 80:2; *Jub.* 7:29; 16:26; 22:13, 27; 31:20; 4 Ezra 4:28-32; *2 Apoc. Bar.* 42:4-5; CD 2:11-12). The choice of the Twelve (*see* Disciples) who eventually assumed their role as apostles to Israel seems also to point in this direction, although there may be something to the view that Twelve pointed more to Israel's restoration than to its reduction to a remnant. The Twelve clearly did not compose the remnant. They were just a few of the wider circle of repentant in Israel who had committed themselves to John's baptism and to Jesus' own preaching of the kingdom. Response to the presence of this kingdom was doubtless the criterion by which these were saved and others were not.

This brings us to one of the chief objections to the idea that Jesus called a remnant. J. Jeremias strongly influenced the view that while many groups in Judaism considered themselves to be the chosen remnant, this was far too particularist a doctrine for the liberal-minded Jesus who preached against all forms of strict Judaism. Meyer responded that Jesus could have created an "open remnant," a remnant which did not establish social boundaries and was never clearly defined. All of this discussion, however, takes us away from historical questions to dogmatic ones. The fact remains that Jesus' group from the beginning was particularistic inasmuch as Jesus required faith and response to God's message preached by him. While Jesus' remnant did not possess a legalistic base, it did have an implicit christological one. (In a sense, then, this particularism was an anti-particularism, or a particularism not based on legal requirements.) As for Meyer's view of the "open remnant," it requires

that we deny any intentions by Jesus to foster community interaction—something which seems doubtful indeed (cf. e.g., Mt 18).

Then there is the persistent question whether Jesus intended, called or gathered a remnant, or whether this remnant was the unintended result of his divisive mission. It appears that there was nothing unintentional about Jesus' remnant ideas, providing we recognize the theological framework in which the idea of intention was operating. For human intention was considered subservient to divine determination in Jesus' day, and no one more than Jesus was aware of the inevitability of the working of God's word in Israel. In short, if the word of God created a remnant in Israel's past, it must be considered inevitable that such a remnant would be created by God's word to Israel through Jesus today. Such an idea would conform to the way Scripture so often appears to have molded Jesus' self-consciousness in the Gospels. It appears, therefore, not only that Jesus expected a remnant, but that he cooperated with its formation by intending, gathering and calling.

If Jesus possessed a remnant theology, what exactly did he have in mind? Was there to emerge a True Israel? Or a New Israel? A common view is that while Israel was denied salvation as an institution, individuals out of the nation might still be saved. But this is not the Jewish view of the remnant as seen in the OT or in the Judaism of Jesus' day. The remnant always relates back to Israel. There is implied in this doctrine an accountability or responsibility to Israel; the ties are not broken altogether. Through this remnant Israel is affirmed. There is certainly no New Israel, and the idea of a True Israel might falsely signify independence from ethnic Israel—a view not generally encouraged by Judaism.

3.3. Jesus and the Destiny of Israel. But what can we say about Jesus? Did he possess any hope for the restoration of Israel *kata sarka* ("according to the flesh")? Or did his view of the remnant of Israel override, or perhaps extinguish altogether, the hope for restoration? It is apparent that Paul still held the two ideas in tension in Rom 9–11. But a systematic statement such as we find there does not exist in the Gospels. In fact, there is no explicit statement to the effect that Jesus expected, either then or in the future, a restoration of Israel. Many scholars therefore argue that there is no doctrine of restoration in the

Gospels. And it is difficult to disagree with this conclusion.

However, some things might be considered as less direct evidence of the restoration of Israel before the idea is dismissed out of hand. We have already mentioned the possibility that the Twelve points to the hope that Israel will be fully restored through Jesus' ministry, since twelve is manifestly the number of the tribes of Israel. And Sanders's view that the announcement of a kingdom must in its context imply restoration, also carries conviction. Then we have evidence like Matthew 23:39 (par. Lk 13:35), where Jesus announces to Jerusalem, "I tell you, you will not see me (again) until you say, 'Blessed is he who comes in the name of the *Lord!' " Matthew, who places the saying after the Triumphal Entry, clearly implies the warm reception of the *Son of man by Israel at some future date.

On any accounting, the number of references to restoration in the Gospels is minimal. Can this be explained? Certainly if Jesus intended to restore Israel, all indications are that this was not expected immediately but in some indefinite future, and it was conditioned by the acceptance of his preaching—contrary to the view that Jesus was a restorationist (e.g., Sanders). In this case the most that can be said is that Jesus set in motion a (gradual?) restoration exemplified in his disciples. More likely, restoration was still a future hope. For the present, however, only a remnant would respond. In this way the judgment pronounced against Jesus' contemporaries can be taken seriously; restoration still remains valid only for those who accept the terms of salvation. In the Gospels the idea of the restoration of Israel is therefore overshadowed by the teaching about the remnant. For the relatively small group of Jesus' followers who found themselves in conflict with the rest of the Jewish world, this teaching would certainly have been the more urgent one.

Perhaps also by the time the Gospels were written, attention was turning from the hope for restoration to the influx of Gentiles into the kingdom. If Israel was not experiencing her restoration, Gentiles certainly were. In the Fourth Gospel unbelieving Jews are lumped together with the world; perhaps by analogy we can say that within the allusions to success in mission to the world, Israel herself is also to be included (cf. Jn 17:21; 21:11). This would amount to a restoration which affects Israel as well as the Gen-tiles—something quite in harmony with the Jewish restoration belief.

If Jesus did teach the restoration of Israel, he probably also had some view of the role the Gentiles would play in this restoration. Both the Gospels and the Jewish background encourage this assumption. It is less clear whether Jesus intended to remove all distinctions between Jews and Gentiles, or to uphold the special privilege of Israel.

Thus the idea of a future for Israel which includes their salvation is not incongruous with the message of Jesus and may be implied in certain texts of the Gospels. Such a restoration would clearly involve the future (or possibly gradual) acceptance of the message of the kingdom by Israel based on Jesus' work on their behalf (cf. Mk 10:45).

See also CHURCH; JUDAISM; LAW.

DJG: ANTI-SEMITISM; GENTILES; HISTORICAL JESUS, QUEST OF. *DPL:* RESTORATION OF ISRAEL.

BIBLIOGRAPHY. S. H. Brooks, *Matthew's Community: The Evidence of His Special Sayings Material* (JSNTSup 16; Sheffield: JSOT, 1987); J. H. Charlesworth, *Jesus Within Judaism* (New York: Doubleday, 1988); H. Conzelman, *The Theology of St. Luke* (New York: Harper & Row, 1961); M. A. Elliott, *The Survivors of Israel* (Grand Rapids: Eerdmans, 2000); D. R. A. Hare, *The Theme of Jewish Persecution of Christians in Matthew's Gospel* (SNTSMS 6; Cambridge: Cambridge University Press, 1967); A. E. Harvey, *Jesus and the Constraints of History* (Philadelphia: Westminster, 1982); A. J. Hultgren, *Jesus and His Adversaries. The Form and Function of the Conflict Stories in the Synoptic Tradition* (Minneapolis: Augsburg, 1979); J. Jeremias, "Der Gedanke des heiligen Restes im Spätjudentum und in der Verkündigung Jesu," *ZNW* 42 (1949) 184-94; J. Jervell, *Luke and the People of God* (Minneapolis: Augsburg, 1972); G. Lohfink, *Jesus and Community* (Philadelphia: Fortress; New York: Paulist, 1982); R. Maddox, *The Purpose of Luke-Acts* (FRLANT 126; Göttingen: Vandenhoeck & Ruprecht, 1982); J. L. Martyn, *History and Theology in the Fourth Gospel* (New York: Harper & Row, 1968); S. McKnight, *A New Vision for Israel: The Teachings of Jesus in National Context* (Grand Rapids: Eerdmans, 1999); B. F. Meyer, *The Aims of Jesus* (London: SCM, 1979); J. Riches, *Jesus and the Transformation of Judaism* (New York: Seabury, 1982); E. P. Sanders, *Jesus and Judaism* (London: SCM, 1985); J. T. Sanders, *The Jews in Luke-Acts* (London: SCM, 1987); S. Sandmel, *Anti-Semitism in the New Testament?* (Philadelphia: Fortress, 1978); K. H. Schelkle, *Israel im Neuen Testament* (Darmstadt: Wissenschaftliche Buchgesellschaft, 1985); W. Trilling, *Das wahre Israel* (3d ed.; München: Kösel, 1964); G. Vermes, *Jesus and the World of Judaism* (London: SCM, 1983); N. T. Wright, *Jesus and the Victory of God* (Minneapolis: Fortress, 1996).

M. A. Elliott

ISRAEL II: PAUL

Paul confesses openly that he is an Israelite, that he loves his kinfolk and desires their salvation. Despite their present rejection of the gospel, he refuses to regard them as irretrievably rejected by God. He sees them as bearers of a spiritual heritage that has now been opened up to Gentiles also. He never suggests that Gentiles have displaced Israel or that Israel has no role to play in God's future. Rather he sees God's gift to Israel as irrevocable and Israel as occupying an inalienable place in the divine economy of salvation.

1. Introduction
2. Definition and Terminology
3. The Extension of the Covenant with Israel to Gentiles
4. Israel as the Creation of God's Word
5. Israel's Fault
6. Israel's Dual Status: Beloved and at Enmity with the Gospel
7. Paul's Solution: The Restoration of Israel by Means of the Gentile Mission
8. Israel in Contemporary Perspective

1. Introduction.

Israel was the established name in Scripture for both the covenant people and the covenanted land. When Paul uses the term he is not using it simply as a general designation of those claiming physical descent from Abraham. Rather he uses it to designate them as the people of the covenant made with Abraham. Even when Paul refers to the Israel that has rejected his gospel, he can still use the title because he thinks of the people as a whole as a religious entity, the historic people of God. In Romans 2:17, 28-29 and Romans 3:29 Paul speaks of the "Jew," but in Romans 9—11 his clear preference is for "Israel"/ "Israelite." One gets the impression that when Paul wants to stress ethnic affiliation, he uses the term *Jew,* but when he comes to reflect upon their spiritual heritage, *Israel/Israelite* alone can

clearly designate this people as a religious entity.

2. Definition and Terminology.

2.1. Israel of God—New Israel. The main passages in Paul's letters where Israel is discussed are Galatians 6:16, Romans 9—11 and, to a lesser extent, 2 Corinthians 3:7, 13. In 1 Corinthians 10:18 Paul gives a brief reference to Israel to warn the Christians not to be presumptuous. In 2 Corinthians 3 a contrast is drawn between the old dispensation and the new—a contrast really between degrees of glory, showing how greatly the new excels the old. Also in 2 Corinthians 11:22 Paul, in the face of counterclaims, asserts that he is an Israelite. It turns out therefore that Romans 9—11 is the crucial text for our topic, and we must devote substantial attention to it. But first we need to consider Galatians 6:16 ("the Israel of God"), which some interpreters have regarded as the first reference to the church as "the new Israel."

At the conclusion of his letter to the Galatians, Paul concludes with a benediction. In Galatians 6:15 he has asserted that in Christ "neither circumcision counts for anything nor uncircumcision, but a new creation." By this he sought to repudiate and to relativize the claims of those who wanted to force his Gentile converts in Galatia to accept circumcision—the major purpose of his letter. He concludes with a sentence that the RSV translates as "Grace and mercy be upon all who walk by this rule, upon the Israel of God." This translation suggests that the latter phrase, "the Israel of God," is simply in apposition to the former and that Paul's benediction is thereby applied to all those Christians who, like him, regard circumcision as unessential. This would mean that Paul, already at this early stage in the NT era, identifies the Christian church as "the Israel of God" in opposition to the historical people of God. But this translation is unlikely for several reasons.

The basic problem is that the RSV translation has omitted the *kai* ("and") in the Greek text. The NRSV has corrected this error and now translates Galatians 6:15, "Peace be upon them, and mercy, and upon the Israel of God." The revised NEB unfortunately is similar to the RSV. If Paul had really wished to equate the Gentile believers with "the Israel of God," it seems strange that he first uses the phrase here at the very conclusion of his letter. And even if it is granted that the identification is made here between believ-

523

ers and the Israel of God, it is somewhat tenuous to hang so much on one doubtful translation since, apart from this passage, there is no other evidence until about A.D. 160 for the explicit identification of the church as "the Israel of God" or "new Israel." This isolated instance would be difficult to explain by itself. Why was it that no one in the next hundred years used this verse to identify the church as "the new Israel"?

It seems better to translate as P. Richardson has suggested: "May God give peace to all who will walk according to this criterion, and mercy also to his faithful people Israel" (Richardson, 84), or as the NIV translates, "Peace and mercy to all who follow this rule, even to the Israel of God."

From this brief survey of the references to Israel in Paul, there is no clear or explicit evidence prior to Romans 9—11 that suggests either an identification of the church with "the new Israel" or of a theory of displacement of the "old Israel" by the new. Only historical Israel can properly claim the title "Israel of God."

2.2. An Israel Within Israel? The attribution of the title *Israel* and the recognition of its heritage does not imply however that Paul is not fully conscious of the fact that the majority of the people of Israel were currently rejecting his message. The unique aspect of Paul's understanding of Israel is that it is beloved because of the fathers—the legitimate heir of the promises—and yet at the same time at enmity with the gospel. In order to give a satisfactory explanation of this state of affairs, Paul was forced to take a careful look at the history of Israel in the Scriptures. From this he came to a conclusion that some Jews would have considered radical, even blasphemous—that not all the descendants of Abraham are truly Abraham's children in the sense that they share the same kind of faith as their father Abraham.

Paul's thesis, which has been grossly misrepresented and which has led to unbalanced interpretations of the relation of Jew and Gentile in the gospel is not, on his premises, simply his novel creation. Within the nation of Israel God has always exercised his prerogative to select people to carry out his purpose. Every Jew admitted this; Ishmael was a child of Abraham, but no Jew believed that the Arabs, his descendants, were within the covenant. According to the OT, the children of faith were reckoned through the line of Isaac (Rom 9:8), and this was because the

birth of Isaac was not just a matter of ordinary physical generation but the result of the promise of God, accepted in faith by Abraham (Rom 4:18-22). So Paul insists that since in the biblical narrative there were already examples of descendants of Abraham who were not children of promise, then there ought to be no problem in acknowledging in his day that "not all those descended from Abraham are Israel."

It seems, at least on the surface, that Paul is guilty of redefining Israel to suit his own purposes. The issue centers on the definition of "the Israel of God."

In Romans 2:28-29 Paul had already asserted, "Not the outward Jew is a real Jew," a parallel to Romans 9:6b—"Not all offspring of Israel are Israel." It seems therefore that some such term as the "real Israel," "true Israel" or "inner Israel" is logically required to express Paul's intent. The true Israel is "of Israel" in terms of physical descent but not coextensive with historical Israel. (We note in passing that having introduced the concept of the "true Israel," we are then forced to introduce a neutral term, that is, "historical Israel," in order to avoid slipping into the easy equation of Israel with unbelieving or false Israel, that is, as a symbol of disobedience.)

Paul appears to operate with a fluid concept of Israel. This doubtless originates from ancient Semitic concepts of solidarity that modern individualism finds hard to understand because it is so far removed from much contemporary (Western) religious thought.

Paul's thought in Romans needs to be differentiated from his previous discussion in Galatians. There Paul distinguished two contrasting groups: "Israel of the flesh" and "Israel of the Spirit" (Rom 2:29). The closest parallel in Romans is Romans 4:14-16, where the terms used are *hoi ek nomou* ("those of the law") and *hoi ek pisteōs* ("those of faith"). But in this chapter the argument runs not on the pattern "either a or b" but "not only a but also b"—it is inclusive rather than exclusive. Paul insists that since the coming of faith in Christ, not only those who follow the law, the Jews, but also those of faith, Gentiles, may also be included in the people of God. It could be argued that Paul in Romans 9—11 first frees the concept of Israel from its absolute identification with all of Abraham's descendants and then, having loosed this connection, proceeds to include Gentiles also within "eschatological Israel."

But we must be careful about what Paul does and does not say. It is true that he argues that not all offspring of Israel are Israel. Then he continues from this to argue from Romans 9:22 and what follows that Gentiles may also be included in the people of God. Yet Paul never suggests a complete displacement of Israel by Gentiles however much he argues for the rights of believers. In the end he maintains that the children of God (tekna tou theou) are not merely children of fleshly descent (tekna tēs sarkos) but rather children of promise (tekna tēs epangelias, Rom 9:8).

Nor does Paul simply equate the Christian community with "spiritual Israel," "Israel kata pneuma," and the Jews with "fleshly Israel," "Israel kata sarka" (cf. Gal 4:29). His thought is more complex on this issue.

The problem with terms such as "true Israel," "spiritual Israel" or even "eschatological Israel" is that all of these may be misused to imply that the church is the only true Israel, and that historical Israel is no better than pagan nations, having forfeited its heritage absolutely. It is clear that despite Paul's making a radical distinction within Israel and thereby driving a wedge into the historical people of God, he would have insisted that part of historical Israel is also part of eschatological Israel.

3. The Extension of the Covenant with Israel to Gentiles.

It is beyond dispute that Paul could not have envisaged an eschatological Israel that contained none of the historical Israel. Paul's thinking is much more concrete and historically oriented than subsequent Gentile-Christian understanding makes it out to be.

Moreover, certain legal and theological factors have to be taken into account. If an inheritance is bequeathed to someone, one cannot legally displace the heir without breaking the terms of the agreement, the covenant. Gentiles have too easily presumed on their access to the heritage of Israel to which they have no inherent right. The theological factor involves our conception of God's faithfulness. If God is a faithful, covenant-keeping God, how then can Israel be fully and finally rejected? If, for whatever reason, Israel's promises are given to others, then Israel has failed and God also has failed in his purpose for Israel (Rom 9:6). Paul is therefore concerned to maintain that God is free and hence not determined by Israel, but also that he is committed to Israel in that he will achieve his purposes through this people whether in their cooperation or in their rebellion.

4. Israel as the Creation of God's Word.

The power and the creative freedom of God are emphasized by Paul in his discussion of Israel in Romans 9—11. By his call God created his people and by his word he accomplishes what he purposes. By this alone is Israel the people of God constituted and reconstituted. But this does not mean God uses his power in any arbitrary fashion. He does have the power to make children from stones, but what Paul claims in Romans 9:1-22 is that God selects not stones, nor even Gentiles, but those from within the people of Israel.

The freedom of the potter is absolute; he can make from the clay whatever vessel he purposes, whether for menial or honorable purposes, and the vessel cannot question the logic of its destiny. Yet we need to remember that God, the divine potter, uses the Jewish people as his clay. Granted, the Jew is not eo ipso "seed" (sperma) or "child of God" (teknon theou) but only becomes this through the calling (kalein) and reckoning (logizesthai) of God (Rom 9:7-8). Yet this people, as those historically in covenant with their Creator, occupy a unique position. Only since and because of the advent of Christ can Gentiles be included in the people of God through the extension of Israel's covenant; Israel's privilege and priority necessitate that the gospel to the Gentiles can only come by the way of Judaism. Thus Israel occupies an inalienable place in the purposes and plans of God; if Gentiles are to participate in these, they must acknowledge God's prior commitment to Israel and all that this entails (Eph 2:11-22 is an important recognition of this fact).

Until the coming of Christ, God, through his word of promise, creates Israel anew according to his purpose of grace. With the opening up of the promises to Gentiles also the possibility of a "new Israel" or a "renewed Israel" is now a reality. Thus Israel and the church are both the creation of the divine word. From this perspective there is no essential difference between them. However, historically and theologically, Paul wishes to maintain an awareness of the priority of Israel and warns Gentiles about being too presumptuous lest they forget God's prior engagement with Israel.

5. Israel's Fault.

The noninclusion of part of Israel is attributed by Paul to God's predestination and to Israel's failure (Rom 9:6-29). In Paul's thought these elements are neither contradictory nor mutually exclusive. Israel's fault is that most Israelites of Paul's time did not put their faith in Jesus Christ. He had become a stumbling stone to them (Rom 9:30—10:4). The reason for this failure to accept Christ has traditionally been regarded as a self-righteous attitude on the part of Jews. "They sought to establish their own righteousness" (Rom 10:3) has been understood to mean that Jews thought that righteousness could be achieved by their own effort, that is, by good works. Hence those who made that effort presumed they had succeeded and became self-righteous as a result. They had a zeal but a mistaken zeal (Rom 10:2).

E. P. Sanders in particular has written much to correct this general view of the fault of Israel. He argues that zeal as such is not wrong. They did not err in seeking righteousness, but they sought the wrong kind of righteousness—righteousness "of their own" in the sense that it was a righteousness peculiar to Jews as a people and the righteousness of a former dispensation prior to the coming of faith in Jesus Christ. The fault of this righteousness is its exclusivity and the "coming of faith" means that God's salvation is open to everyone who has faith, whether Jew or Gentile; there is no distinction (Rom 10:12). It seems, therefore, that Paul's gospel was an offense to many Jews who failed to understand and/or acknowledge the new day that had dawned in Jesus Christ. They saw Paul's work and message as an absolute threat to the future and well-being of Israel, and they opposed it bitterly as a result. But Paul did not perceive it thus—he sees the coming of Christ as confirmation (Gk *bebaian*, Rom 4:16) of the promises made to Abraham and as an extension of the covenant to include believing Gentiles along with the believing in Israel. He refuses to regard Israel as rejected but only as temporarily hardened by God until the full number of the Gentiles comes into the kingdom.

6. Israel's Dual Status: Beloved and at Enmity with the Gospel.

As we have noted already, Paul seems to have had a fluid concept of Israel because he saw the people as one corporate entity irrespective of the merits or failure of particular individuals. His perspective on Israel is historical and communal, as distinct from some modern views that are theological/symbolic and individualistic. But because his approach is historical and since he discusses the actual, empirical Israel, he has a problem of definition. Israel is opposed to the gospel; particular Jews are enemies of Paul and his message. But the Jews as a whole are the heirs of the promises given to Abraham and confirmed by the coming of Christ.

Paul does not shrink from the full seriousness of this dilemma. Israel's dual status is that it is rejecting the gospel but is still beloved because of the patriarchs.

Various solutions have been offered to this problem. A common one is that God has two different covenants—a covenant involving law-keeping for the Jews and a covenant based on faith alone for Gentiles. But Paul's solution differs from this. He neither minimizes the problem by claiming that all Jews will be saved apart from Christ nor by predicting another covenant to ensure their eventual salvation.

7. Paul's Solution: The Restoration of Israel by Means of the Gentile Mission.

The situation Paul faced near the end of his ministry was that Gentiles were willing to accept Christ but Jews were not. Some Jews probably still held fast to the traditional view of "Jews first and then the Gentiles," that the gospel could only be allowed to proceed to the Gentiles after Israel had already embraced it. Paul had possibly wrestled with this issue as he first heard the Hellenists proclaim the Christian message. But when he experienced his Damascus Road vision, he had to work out how his commission related to this perspective (*see* Conversion and Call of Paul). Working from the empirical evidence of the reality of the Spirit's work among the Gentiles, Paul came to the conclusion that the order of salvation had been changed. "To the Jew first" now means that while the irrevocable place of Israel is confirmed by the gospel, the order of entry for Jew and Gentile into the new community of faith is in fact reversed.

The new reality is that the Gentiles are preceding the Jews, and from this actual historical sequence Paul proceeds to argue a theology of the final salvation of Israel succeeding that of Gentiles (Rom 11:12). Just as the rejection of the gospel by Jews had caused it to spread to the

Gentiles, so now the reception of the gospel by Gentiles will ensure the turning back of the Jews. Paul came to this conclusion from scriptural, theological and empirical evidence. The empirical evidence of believing Gentiles and unbelieving Jews was plain to see.

The theological evidence Paul developed from his conviction of God's faithfulness. Paul was convinced that Christ's coming demonstrated that God is faithful and that he justifies the one who has faith in Jesus (Rom 3:26). The theology of a "righteous remnant" was frequently used in this discussion. God always retained a faithful remnant to ensure the final success of his purposes. The remnant could be seen as a sign either of judgment or of mercy, or even of both. In Romans 9:22-29 and Romans 11:2-6 Paul makes use of this theme. The RSV text of Romans 9:27, which quotes the prophet Isaiah, reads, "Though the number of the sons of Israel be as the sand of the sea, only a remnant will be saved." Although it could be disputed whether the introduction of "only" is justified, we have in the English version an example of the remnant theme reminding us of the divine judgment upon Israel. In Romans 11:2-6 there is no doubt that Paul sees the remnant as a sign of hope—of mercy rather than of judgment, although judgment is already presupposed. He again uses a scriptural example: Elijah mistakenly thought he alone was left of God's faithful people, but God reminded him that he had kept for himself seven thousand who had not bowed the knee to Baal. Paul concludes, "So too at the present time, there is a remnant, chosen by grace" (Rom 11:5). Paul interprets this present remnant, believing Jews, as first fruits of the coming harvest—it is a hopeful sign. Thus it would be appropriate to translate Romans 11:5 "so too at the present time—there is already a remnant." The existence of some Jewish believers becomes for Paul a pointer to the salvation of all Israel.

How this salvation would take place led Paul to ponder the Scriptures in the light of his own experience. There is a very real possibility that Paul's apostolic commission may have included a vision of the restoration of Israel. The image in Isaiah 49:1 of one set apart from his mother's womb is used by Paul in Galatians 1:15 (cf. Acts 13:47). The Servant's call in this passage ties together the twin aspects of his universal work—to be an agent of Israel's restoration and a light to the Gentiles. It is therefore inappropriate to view Paul as apostle to the Gentiles with no function in relation to Israel. It is more fitting to see him as the apostle to the Gentiles for the sake of Israel, so that there is a necessary connection between Paul's Gentile mission and the restoration of Israel.

It was, however, in Deuteronomy 32 that Paul found Scripture that suggested a way to lead rebellious Israel back to God. When Paul read in Deuteronomy 32:21, "I will make you jealous of those who are not a nation; with a foolish nation I will make you angry," he took this to mean that the Gentiles were "the foolish nation," the "no people." So he found here a clue that he developed to argue that his Gentile mission would indirectly bring Israel, through jealousy, to acknowledge the truth as he saw it.

R. B. Hays has convincingly demonstrated that in Deuteronomy 32 "Paul finds not only the prophecy of Israel's lack of faith and ultimate restoration but also the prefiguration of God's intention to 'stir them to jealousy' through embracing the Gentiles (Deut 32:43)." Hays goes on to comment, "It is hardly coincidental that Paul quotes both of these verses explicitly (Rom 10:19; 15:10)," and he concludes "Deuteronomy 32 contains Romans 'in nuce' " (Hays, 164). It would appear that Paul, faced with the hardened hearts of the majority of his people, found in Deuteronomy 32 a text that looked inexorably beyond present judgment to future hope. Despite a certain tendency among some scholars to regard Romans 9—11 as stressing *either* judgment or mercy upon Israel, it is plain that in the Deuteronomic tradition it includes both—"Note then the kindness and the severity of God" (Rom 11:22). The severity is for the sake of God's ultimate compassion, and it is perfectly fitting that Romans 11 ends not with the rejection but with the restoration of "all Israel" (Rom 11:25).

So despite Israel's present obduracy, the ongoing historical process of the Gentile mission will continue until their number is complete—perhaps when the gospel has been planted everywhere. The pilgrimage of the Gentiles (Is 2:2-5) will not succeed but rather precede the restoration of Israel—the nations do not come because they see Israel's glory, but Israel comes because it sees the salvation and glory Gentiles have in Christ. Paul was probably the first to propose this sequence but, as O. Hofius notes, Paul may have found support in certain OT texts that had already suggested it.

A number of items are closely interrelated in Paul's thought: "The Deliverer will come from Zion, he will remove ungodliness from Jacob"; all Israel—in the sense of the totality of the people (not necessarily every single individual)—will be saved, and this will usher in the resurrection of the dead.

This will be the final deliverance and vindication of Israel expected in Deuteronomy 32:36-43 and, significantly for Paul, when the Gentiles will rejoice with Israel (Deut 32:43). Most important of all, with the restoration of Israel it is not primarily Israel that is vindicated but the faithfulness and honorable name of God.

What emerges from all this is that Paul's mission cannot be viewed in isolation from Israel's restoration. The apostle views his Gentile mission as a catalyst to the present salvation of a remnant from within Israel and as an essential precursor to the eventual salvation of all Israel; it is only when the "full measure" of the Gentiles comes in that all Israel will be saved (Rom 11:25-26).

Thus in the reverse sequence to earlier traditions, Israel and the Gentiles will both share in God's salvation. Moreover, despite present or future separation between the church and Israel, in the end there can be no absolutely separate development because their destinies remain intertwined in the mysterious workings of God's eternal purpose. Thus Israel cannot achieve her restoration until "the fullness of the Gentiles," and the Gentiles cannot participate in the resurrection without the prior restoration of Israel.

8. Israel in Contemporary Perspective.

Paul's understanding of Israel is thoroughly eschatological. Modern Christians frequently do not share his perspective. They want to know precisely where contemporary Jews stand in relation to the *kingdom of God—judging more from the perspective of a realized eschatology. Paul was as conscious as anyone of the division between him and his unconverted kinfolk. But he viewed them in the perspective of God's ultimate purpose. From this perspective they are not rejected by God but rather they still remain potential members of his eternal kingdom (as all are).

The continuing existence of the Jewish people should not be viewed simply as a result of their failure to accept the Christian message, that is, as a result of their disobedience. Nor should they be viewed merely as a sort of living object lesson to Christians of the danger of "blind religiosity," as some extremists might describe them. We dare not insist that everything that happens in this world is directly caused by God, but it would be naive to suggest it is merely an accident of history that the historical people of God, the Jewish race, should continue to exist alongside Christianity.

See also ABRAHAM; COVENANT, NEW COVENANT; ESCHATOLOGY; JEW, PAUL THE; ROMANS, LETTER TO THE.

DPL: GENTILES; OLIVE TREE; RESTORATION OF ISRAEL; STUMBLING BLOCK.

BIBLIOGRAPHY. J. C. Beker, "The Faithfulness of God and the Priority of Israel in Paul's Letter to the Romans," in *The Romans Debate*, ed. K. P. Donfried (rev. ed.; Peabody, MA: Hendrickson, 1991); R. Bring, "Paul and the Old Testament: A Study of the Ideas of Election, Faith and Law in Paul with Special Reference to Rom 9:30—10:21," *Studia Theologica* 25 (1971) 21-60; P. M. van Buren, "The Church and Israel: Romans 9—11," *The Princeton Seminary Bulletin*, Supplementary Issue 1, *The Church and Israel: Romans 9—11* (1990) 5-18; W. S. Campbell, *Paul's Gospel in an Intercultural Context* (Frankfurt: Peter Lang, 1992); R. E. Clements, "A Remnant Chosen by Grace (Rom 11:5)," in *Pauline Studies: Essays Presented to F. F. Bruce,* ed. D. A. Hagner and M. J. Harris (Grand Rapids: Eerdmans, 1980) 106-21; C. E. B. Cranfield, *Romans* (ICC; Edinburgh: T & T Clark, 1979); idem, "The Significance of *dia pantos* in Romans 11:10," Studia Evangelica 2, *Texte und Untersuchungen* 87 (1964) 547-50; N. A. Dahl, "The Future of Israel," in *Studies in Paul: Theology for the Early Christian Mission* (Minneapolis: Augsburg, 1977) 137-58: W. D. Davies, "Paul and the People of Israel" and "Paul and the Gentiles: A Suggestion Concerning Romans 11:13-24," in *Pauline and Jewish Studies* (Philadelphia: Fortress, 1984) 123-63; E. Dinkler, "The Historical and Eschatological Israel in Rom 9—11: A Contribution to the Problem of Predestination and Individual Responsibility," *JR* (1956) 109-27; K. P. Donfried, ed., *The Romans Debate* (rev. ed.; Peabody, MA: Hendrickson, 1991); J. D. G. Dunn, *Romans* (WBC 38b; Dallas: Word, 1988); L. Gaston, *Paul and the Torah* (Vancouver: University of British Columbia, 1987); M. A. Getty, "Paul on the Covenants and the Future of Israel," *BTB* 17 (1987) 92-99; S. J. Hafemann, "The Salvation of Israel in Romans 11:25-32: A

Response to Krister Stendahl," *Ex Auditu* 4 (1989) 38-58; R. B. Hays, *Echoes of Scripture in the Letters of Paul* (New Haven, CT: Yale University Press, 1989); M. Hengel, *The Pre-Christian Paul* (Philadelphia: Trinity Press International, 1991); O. Hofius, "All Israel Will Be Saved: Divine Salvation and Israel's Deliverance in Romans 9—11," *The Princeton Seminary Bulletin*, Supplementary Issue 1 (1990) 19-39; idem, "Das Evangelium und Israel: Erwägungen zu Römer 9—11," *ZThK* 83 (1986) 297-324; D. G. Johnson, "The Structure and Meaning of Romans 11," *CBQ* 46 (1984) 91-103; E. Käsemann, "Paul and Israel" in *New Testament Questions of Today* (Philadelphia: Fortress, 1969) 183-87; R. D. Kaylor, *Paul's Covenant Community: Jew and Gentile in Romans* (Atlanta: John Knox, 1988); S. Kim, *The Origin of Paul's Gospel* (2d ed.; WUNT 2.4; Tübingen: Siebeck, 1984); R. P. Martin, *Reconciliation: A Study of Paul's Theology* (rev. ed.; Grand Rapids: Zondervan, 1990); W. A. Meeks, "Judgment and the Brother: Romans 14:1—15:13," in *Tradition and Interpretation: Essays in Honor of E. Earle Ellis*, ed. G. F. Hawthorne with O. Betz (Grand Rapids: Eerdmans, 1987) 290-300; L. Morris, *The Epistle to the Romans* (Grand Rapids: Eerdmans, 1988); J. Munck, *Christ and Israel: An Interpretation of Romans 9–11* (Philadelphia: Fortress, 1967); H. Räisänen, "Paul, God and Israel: Romans 9—11 in Recent Research," in *The Social World of Formative Christianity and Judaism: Essays in Tribute to Howard Clark Kee*, ed. J. Neusner et al. (Philadelphia: Fortress, 1988); P. Richardson, *Israel in the Apostolic Church* (SNTSMS 10; Cambridge: Cambridge University Press, 1969); E. P. Sanders, *Paul* (Oxford: Oxford University Press, 1991); idem, *Paul, the Law and the Jewish People* (Philadelphia: Fortress, 1983); A. F. Segal, *Paul the Convert: The Apostolate and Apostasy of Saul the Pharisee* (New Haven, CT: Yale University Press, 1990); K. Stendahl, *Paul Among Jews and Gentiles and Other Essays* (Philadelphia: Fortress, 1976); J. Ziesler, *Romans* (TPINTC; Philadelphia: Trinity Press International, 1989).

W. S. Campbell

ISRAELITE HISTORY. *See* JUDAISM AND THE NEW TESTAMENT.

J

JAIRUS'S DAUGHTER, RAISING OF. *See* RES-
URRECTION.

JAMES, LETTER OF

The letter of James is among the most neglected
books of the NT canon. Many believers and
their (especially Protestant) faith traditions still
agree with Luther's negative verdict of its usefulness for Christian formation, pointing out its
lack of reference to Christ and its apparent disagreement with Paul as good reasons for its marginal status within the church. During the
modern period of biblical studies, some interpreters have even viewed the book's more practical bent as inherently inferior when compared
with the theological profundity of Paul's correspondence. At the same time, others have come
to depend upon the book's wise solutions to everyday situations, which insist that a fully biblical religion requires more than mere confessions of orthodox faith. In this sense James
offers a complementary check and balance to
the accents of the Pauline letters, helping to
form a biblical witness that commends a firm
trust in the saving work of the Lord Jesus
(Pauline) and a practical wisdom patterned after
his life (James).

1. The Author(s) of James
2. The Audience(s) of James
3. The Literature of James
4. A Canonical Approach to James
5. The Gospel According to James
6. The Argument of James

1. The Author(s) of James.

1.1. Candidates for Authorship. The identities
of a book's author and his first audience are important considerations for any interpreter interested in a wide range of historical issues. For
instance, it is difficult to locate a composition in
its original world, to know something of what occasioned its writing, and when and how it functioned among its first readers without good
ideas of who wrote it and why.

The opening verse directly claims authorship
for "James, servant of God and of Jesus Christ"
(Jas 1:1). Yet the author's identity remains a contested issue of modern scholarship. Two critical
issues are at stake in this continuing discussion:
who is this James referred to in the letter's address, and is he necessarily the author of the
book? The evidence that may settle these issues
is historical and lacking: we have no other writing from James by which to compare its literary
style and subject matter; nor do we have a reliable contemporary of the author who confirms
the author's identity.

Even if one agrees that the book's superscription identifies its real author, there are still several Christian leaders named James to choose
from, including six mentioned in the NT. Some
have even added an "unknown James" to this
list (Moffatt), only by sheer conjecture. Among
those named by Scripture are two apostles, making them especially attractive candidates because of the close historical connection between
canonicity and apostolicity, a point embraced
for a time in the West, where some thought the
book was written by the apostle James, son of Alphaeus (cf. Mk 3:18; Acts 1:13). Yet memory of
his apostolic ministry outside of Scripture is lacking. In any case an apostolic credential does not
seem required for the author: the book's address does not appeal to an apostolic office for
personal authorization but rather to the more
modest relationship to God and the Lord Jesus
as their "servant." Origen and Jerome even held
that no apostle could have written James, which
disagrees so thoroughly with Pauline thought—
a point followed by Luther centuries later.

Most scholars suppose the only viable candidate remains James the Just, the brother of Jesus, a verdict that has modest support from ancient tradition (see Eusebius *Hist. Eccl.* 2.23.4). While he was not one of the Twelve, the biblical portrait of James commends him as a significant leader in earliest Jewish Christianity. Jesus even singled him out following the resurrection (1 Cor 15:7), apparently for an important ministry (see *Gos. Heb.* 7). It is not surprising, then, that Acts introduces James as Peter's successor in Jerusalem (Acts 12:17; Wall 1991), whose pastoral leadership over the Jerusalem church became increasingly strategic, first at the Jerusalem council (Acts 15:13-21) and then during his relations with Paul (Acts 21:17-26). Paul named James as the first of three "pillars" of the Jewish church (Gal 2:9), whose continuing observance of circumcision and laws of ritual purity undermined the gospel of his Gentile mission in Antioch (Gal 2:11-15).

In fact, the robust memories of James the Just were preserved well into the second century by the Jewish church, who viewed him the model disciple (Martin, xli-lxi). Eusebius even cites Hegesippus, a second-century Jewish believer from Jerusalem, who describes in some detail the moral and religious superiority of James (Eusebius *Hist. Eccl.* 2.23.4). Indeed, a substantial body of apocryphal (largely gnostic) Christian writings, written in his name by pseudepigraphers during the second and third centuries (*1 and 2 Apoc. Jas.*; *Ap. Jas.*; *Protev.* [= Book] *Jas.*; also, *Gos. Heb.*, *Epis. Pet.*), promote an exemplary, if not legendary, James whose vital piety and ascetic lifestyle corrected a church that had become too secular and middle-class for the taste of its more conservative Jewish and gnostic constituencies (Wall and Lemcio, 250-71). Almost certainly the canonizing church envisaged this James as the James of the biblical letter's address. Only his witness to Christ and abiding authority within earliest Christianity, singular among possible candidates, justify the canonical status accorded this controversial composition. Thus W. G. Kümmel concludes, "Without doubt James claims to be written by [the brother of Jesus], and even if the letter is not authentic, it appeals to this famous James and the weight of his person as authority for its content" (Kümmel, 412).

1.2. Authorial Style and Subject Matter. Did "this famous James" write the book in his name?

A majority of modern scholars think not and favor a postapostolic date and pseudonymity, even though there are significant allusions to James already in *1 Clement* and *Hermas* at the end of the first century (Davids, 8-9). They suppose the composition's superior Koine Greek and literary artistry, as well as the author's substantial knowledge of current Hellenistic philosophy, lie beyond the ability and provenance of this working-class Jew from Galilee (Reicke, Laws). James may have even employed a trusted and well-educated amanuensis, or secretary, a common practice then, who knew Greek well and who transcribed James's pastoral exhortations into a more suitable idiom and literary form for a wider Greek-speaking audience (Mitton) while retaining their original Semitic flavor.

This compromise solution is hardly necessary. One need only appeal to the mounting evidence that demonstrates a fairly active social intercourse between Hellenistic and Palestinian cultures during the late Second Temple period. Religious Jews, especially in Galilee, may well have been anti-Hellenistic during the days immediately before and after the fall of Jerusalem in A.D. 70 (*see* Judaism); however, Jew and Greek intermingled, if a little uneasily. Thus Acts describes a Jerusalem congregation that included Greek-speaking Jews and a pastor (James) who cites the Greek translation (LXX) of Scripture when instructing them (Acts 15:17-18; cf. Jas 4:6). Sharply put, James grew up in a Hellenized Jewish culture where Greek was used and perhaps learned well enough to write this book.

Others contend that the epistolary writer could not be the brother of Jesus, whose biblical portrait values aspects of the Jewish law that finally disagree with the thrust of the letter (Kümmel). This objection too has little merit. A growing number of scholars think that the Jewish-Christian theological cast and pastoral intentions of the letter mirror those same commitments of the biblical James. For example, his concerns for religious purity (Acts 21) and for the public performance of the biblical torah (Gal 2) are central concerns of this book (Jas 1:22-27; 2:8-26); and his commitment to the poor, which Paul mentions in Galatians 2:10, also reflects an important theme of the book (Jas 1:9-11; 2:1-7; 5:1-6). Even the conciliatory James of Acts 15 seems consistent with the spirit that undergirds this letter. Likewise, the traditions used by Luke to narrate the speech of James to the Jerusalem council (Acts 15:13-21) and the subsequent letter to Antioch (Acts 15:23-29) reveal a remarkable similarity in both substance and vocabulary to the letter of James (Adamson, 18-20). Further, the many apocalyptic images and themes found throughout James fashion a sociology of suffering and vindication similar to that of the Jerusalem community James pastored, according to Acts and the social world of first-century messianic Judaism. Noteworthy also are the many allusions to targumic and midrashic materials found in James, which follow his speech in Acts where James settles a crucial intramural conflict by a midrash on the biblical book of Amos (Acts 15:17-21).

The agreement between this James and the subject matter of the letter is also secured by more implicit evidence. Many suppose that dates of compositions can be calculated by images and ideas of Jesus, so that a more full-bodied or developed christology is contained in a later composition. By this reasoning the scant references to Jesus in James (Jas 1:1; 2:1), which does not include even an apparent allusion to his atoning death (see Death of Christ), is more easily explicable if James was written in the middle of the first century.

Finally, however, the most important consideration in this matter is whether the author is responding to controversial elements of Paul's teaching, including the relationship between faith and works and law and liberty. Since these combinations are found neither in Jewish sources nor in the earliest Christian traditions of the NT, some scholars assume the author is responding to ideas found in Paul's writings and only after their publication toward the end of the first century when they came into a wider circulation (e.g., Dibelius, Laws). Since James was executed in A.D. 62 by the Sadducean high priest Ananus II, these same scholars further presume that James the Just could not have written the letter of James.

Yet many are reluctant to find in favor of the author's dependence on the writings of Paul. Some find it impossible that any Christian reader of Paul's writings would criticize him so openly, especially at the close of the first century or beginning of the second when his writings already were being recognized as "Scripture" (2 Pet 3:15-16). Still others find the issue of literary dependency indeterminate (Mayor, Davids, Martin). Even if James and Paul mean the same

thing by "faith and works" or by "law and liberty," a view that remains contested among scholars, Paul could have as easily been responding to the kerygma of Jerusalem Christianity, especially in his Romans and Galatians where numerous parallels are found. In support one may appeal to the well-known contention of G. Bornkamm that Paul wrote Romans as his "last will and testament" in order to recall and respond to the controversies generated by his missionary work, particularly among believers in Jerusalem (Bornkamm, 17-31). While the ideas and precise argument of James may not predate Paul's Gentile mission and his corpus of NT writings, their status in earliest Christianity may be more current and certain than is often supposed. In short, there is no compelling reason to argue against the traditional position, which supposes a pre-Pauline date for this book and James the Just as its author (however, see 4 below).

1.3. Stages of Composition. Perhaps the persistent indeterminacy of this problem commends another solution that considers and integrates a wider field of available evidence. In this case J. Cantinat, more recently and cautiously followed by P. H. Davids, has suggested that the biblical form of James evolved in two discrete stages of composition (see Davids, 12-13). According to this hypothesis, James the Just is responsible for most of the book's raw material, delivered first as homilies and preserved by the Jewish Christian Diaspora (Jas 1:1; cf. Acts 8:4; 11:19). This may help explain the letter's "primitive" theological content.

These precious memories of James were then edited and written by another, probably although not necessarily after James's death, under the pressures of the educational mission of an expanding church. The editor who wrote James may have done so without a religious agenda of his own: his intent was to compile and preserve the most enduring "sayings of James" for future readerships. If required at all, this conjecture may help explain the letter's articulation of Jacobean Christianity in the literary and intellectual idiom of Hellenistic culture.

Editors, however, are rarely this objective. Even editors who do not overlay a peculiar theological perspective on that of another still must select material from available traditions when composing a new work—a self-critical act of interpretation. Further, the reworking of old traditions is typically occasioned by the requirements of new readers. The letter's careful literary design and theological coherence seem to reflect this very sort of editorial decision making: James is hardly the mere compilation of sayings, as some have suggested (see 3 below), or the exact copy of some former speech recalled. Indeed, if a two-stage composition is followed, one should probably assume that the editor had specific theological, sociological and literary intentions in mind, which are then reflected by the letter's final shape and subject matter.

For instance, the editor's arrangement of earlier traditions to combine Pauline catchwords (Jas 2:12-26) and to make strategic allusions to Jesus' ministry among the poor (Jas 2:1-5), along with the clever pairing of cited/alluded Scripture from Torah and wisdom (Jas 1:19-27), and from the prophets and wisdom (Jas 4:6-10; Jas 4:13—5:6), all intend to create a far richer context within which his audience could better hear and interpret the authoritative witness of James to the gospel. New audiences are addressed by a written composition unlike any sermon preached by James and in a fresh way that more effectively presents an inspired solution to their particular spiritual crisis. Even though the editor followed the core convictions of James the Just, his literary design accented certain theological convictions that were apropos for the new contingencies of his late first-century church, which occupied a very different geographical, linguistic and cultural turf than it did during the old days in Jerusalem. For these reasons the interpreter who decides in favor of the two-stage hypothesis of composition should consider the editor the real author of the letter of James and the late first century its true date of composition.

2. The Audience(s) of James.

The letters of the NT are occasional literature, most often written to defend or nurture the tentative faith of immature audiences. While the author's advice only rarely takes a narrative form, every letter tells a story, however implicit, of an audience's struggle to confirm its faith. In the case of James, the story is plotted by the suffering of Jewish believers whose devotion to the Lord and to one another is tested by various kinds of conflicts, both spiritual and social.

2.1. Identity of the Audience. The precise identity of the first readers of James is indeterminate and opinion remains divided. Lacking specific details of the readers' identity, most exegetes are content to locate them in either of two places: post-Pauline Diaspora or in prewar (A.D. 66-70) Palestine-Syria. All agree, however, that the proper place to begin this discussion is the letter's opening verse, which greets the audience as "the twelve tribes in the Diaspora." This enigmatic phrase, however finally understood, might then be employed to interpret subsequent references to the readership in the letter itself, resulting in a more detailed and focused picture.

If this opening phrase is taken at face value, the readers are probably Jewish believers ("twelve tribes") with an address in some Roman territory outside of Palestine ("in the Diaspora"), perhaps in Rome, Alexandria or even Syria toward the end of Domitian's turbulent reign (Reicke). If, however, the phrase is taken metaphorically, the scope of possible meaning and setting is significantly widened. On this basis some have created complex settings of social and spiritual conflict, which are then confirmed by the images of hostility found throughout the book.

In fact, a metaphorical reading of "the twelve tribes" agrees with use of the phrase by other biblical writers. The biblical prophets, for instance, use the phrase (or "tribes of Israel") as a reference to a future, restored Israel (Ezek 47:13, 22; Is 49:6; Zech 9:1). Paul contends that the "Israel of God" (Gal 6:16) is a spiritual rather than an ethnic people (cf. Rom 9—11; Gal 3—6) who belong to Christ (Rom 9:1-18) and are the true heirs of the biblical promise of salvation (Gal 3:21—4:7; cf. Jas 2:5). In a similar way the audience of James consists of those whose primary identity appears religious and eschatological rather than ethnic and national; that is, they form a spiritual people whose life is guided by God's word and whose destiny is the realization of God's promised blessing.

The metaphorical use of "Diaspora" is also attested in Jewish literature as a reference to believers, living in Palestine, but who are cut off from social and religious support systems (Overman; Maynard-Reid). In this case a reference to diasporic Jews need not place them in a geographical location but rather in a social world. Moreover, diasporic Jews were often driven from their homeland for political (e.g., criminals) and economic (e.g., unemployed workers or tax debtors) reasons; in this sense they were aliens at home and abroad. Even in Palestine the "homeland" was typically in the hands of wealthy landowners (Jas 5:1) who controlled the economic (Jas 5:4-6) and religious lives (Jas 2:2-7) of their poor workers, sometimes in venal and vicious ways (see 2.2 below).

In a similar way Scripture speaks of the Diaspora to accent this very kind of experience (cf. 1 Pet 1:1; Is 49:6) in which a people's present pain results from their separation from the plentiful land of divine blessing, whether the land of Israel or in heaven. In a religious sense present suffering discloses one's status as "alien and stranger" but more significantly the absence of promised salvation that is still in the future. Indeed, this theological understanding of place adds another layer of meaning to "the twelve tribes," whose future inheritance of the kingdom's blessings ameliorates the trials and tribulations of their present exile.

The haunting ambivalence between the audience's present suffering in the Diaspora and its future restoration as the twelve tribes underscores the spiritual crisis that has occasioned the writing and reading of this composition. Its thesis neatly follows: Even though belonging to the redeemed and restored Israel, believers continue to face the hardships and heartaches of the Diaspora that test their devotion to God (Jas 1:2-3). Their possible spiritual failure carries this future consequence: the forfeiture of promised blessing (Jas 1:12-15); the passing of their spiritual testing, enabled by divine wisdom, ensures the community's future salvation (Jas 1:16-21). The community's joyful consideration of present suffering (Jas 1:2), then, has in mind the prospect of a future restoration, when all is made complete and perfect and when nothing is lacked (Jas 1:4).

2.2. Social and Spiritual Worlds of the Audience. References to the first readers of this letter, however vague and even opaque, supply several details about the nature of the conflict that may help us tell their unrecorded story. They are believers (Jas 1:2) who are members of a Jewish Christian synagogue (Jas 2:1-2), who aspire to be "rich in faith" as heirs of the promised kingdom (Jas 2:5) and at the same time pursue worldly pleasures that they lack (Jas 4:1-5). A measure of their current suffering is due to their poverty. They are a congregation of "humble" means (Jas 1:9-11; cf. Jas 4:6-10), composed of members from the working-class poor (Jas 5:1-6) and from other social groups who are most neglected (Jas

1:27; cf. Acts 6:1-6), most oppressed (Jas 2:1-7; cf. Gal 2:9-10) and most poor (Jas 2:14-17).

Their enemies are the landed rich (Jas 5:1) and merchant middle class (Jas 4:13) who are members of a Jewish congregation attached to the local synagogue (Jas 2:2-4; cf. Jas 1:9). However, their exploitation of the poor, their greed and maliciousness, which so fundamentally offend the moral essentials of their biblical tradition (Jas 2:8-10), fortify the author's polemic against them. They are foolish to look in the "mirror" (= biblical law) and then turn away from it (Jas 1:22-24) without any further reflection of their own frailty (or their riches, Jas 5:1-3) under the eternal light of God's will (Jas 4:14-17) and the imminent coming of God's judgment (Jas 5:4-6, 7-9). Indeed, they have become "outsiders" (Jas 2:6-7) to God's reign (Jas 2:5) who no longer belong to "the twelve tribes" and cannot look forward in joy to their complete restoration. In demonstration of their outsider status they oppress the impoverished members of the Christian congregation (Jas 2:2), even using their political clout to exploit the working-class poor (Jas 5:1-6) and to demand favorable verdicts against them from the law court (Jas 2:6-7) and the synagogue court (Jas 2:3-4; Ward).

These outside pressures have created tensions inside the congregation that threaten its present unity and eschatological survival. The conflict that rages between believers is pluriform. Some disregard their own poor in favor of the rich and powerful outsiders (Jas 1:22—2:26); abusive speech between rival teachers undermines their teaching ministry and the congregation's spiritual formation (Jas 3:1-18); and hostilities between believers (Jas 4:1-2) and finally toward God (Jas 4:7-10) have their source in their frustration of not having the material goods they passionately desire (Jas 4:3-6).

Perhaps more troubling than this class conflict between rich and poor, which in turn threatens the solidarity of the congregation, is the spiritual or psychological conflict that threatens the believers' relationship with God. These same trials also occasion doubt about God's generosity (Jas 1:5-8) or even the self-destructive deception that God is to blame for the bad news of human life (Jas 1:13-16). Perhaps anxiety for personal safety prompts some believers to suppose that glib confessions of orthodox faith are sufficient for God's approval (Jas 1:22-27; 2:14-20), substituting them for a morally rigorous life that responds in mercy to the poor and powerless when they are exploited by the rich and influential (Jas 2:1-13; 2:21-26). An inward passion for lacking pleasure (Jas 4:1-2) gives one up to a consuming desire for things at the cost of relationships with God (Jas 4:6-12) and neighbor (Jas 4:3-5). Spiritual failure results from theological deception, when a faulty view of the word of God yields bad decisions and ultimately prevents participation in the new order (Jas 1:17-21; 2:12-13; 3:14-16; 4:11-12).

2.3. Social and Spiritual Tensions. To specify a locale in the first-century Roman world, whether Hellenistic or Palestinian, is extremely difficult to do with any precision. For this reason some continue to follow Dibelius's lead and contend that this form of literature (paraenesis) resists any reference to a particular historical contingency that may have occasioned the writing and first reading of this composition. One can speak perhaps of a moral culture that this literature helps to shape by its advice, which fixes the community's socioreligious borders within any hostile environment (Perdue, Elliot). Perhaps even the apocalyptic images found throughout this composition perform this same social role—images that anticipate a new cultural order that promises an alternative, more hospitable homeland for a poor and powerless people (Wall 1990).

Nevertheless, some continue to investigate James for a particular historical *Sitz im Leben* (life setting). The traditional position locates the author and his audience in prewar Palestine; the details gathered from the letter fit this setting well (Davids, 28-34). Of course, no one who accepts a literal Diaspora would subscribe to this provenance. Further, while the images and metaphors of nature are brought to sharper focus against a Palestinian backdrop (Hadidian), S. S. Laws, for one, remains unconvinced by this evidence and counters by pointing to Greek literature for similar images, even as others can point to Scripture as the source of these images.

However, if the diasporic setting is viewed as a metaphor of spiritual or social dislocation, the references to class strife between rich and poor proffers a more convincing line of evidence for a Palestinian provenance (Maynard-Reid). In Palestine, as throughout the Roman world, rural land and wealth were concentrated in the hands of a few wealthy farmers (Jas 5:1). Middle-class merchants (Jas 4:13) could but dream of a future

when they too could take their place among the landed gentry and share their life of luxury. Toward that end the merchants worked with the large landowners to control the agrarian marketplace, which only made the workers more dependent upon the landowner and the independent farmer's situation more difficult to endure.

Very little upward mobility was enjoyed between these classes, since Rome maintained a stratified society as a means of managing the masses. While the continuing exploitation of the poor by the merchant-farmer coalition was not encouraged by Rome, for fear of a worker strike, it was tolerated in order to maintain the fragile prosperity of the region. Especially during times of famine (see Jas 5:17-18; Acts 11:27-30), the economic pressures of field hands and harvesters became more intense and their economic well-being more precarious as landowners tried to maximize their profits (Jas 4:4-6). The result is that some lacked even the basic requirements of a humane existence (see Jas 2:15-16). The great majority of the Palestinian population was thus confined to working-class ghettos, living a hand-to-mouth existence without any hope of an improved life. Such historical determinism either gave rise to social rage and the potential of peasant rebellion or to religious sentiment deeply rooted in a "piety of poverty" and apocalyptic hope.

In addition, Martin contends, James was written for a community of poor people and their religious leaders who were suffering under Sadducean rule. His argument recognizes Josephus's historical record that James was executed in 62 by Ananus II, a Sadducean priest, at the height of tensions with the Jerusalem church; James might be read as another kind of record of that episode. His contention also makes considerable sense not only of the economic conflict mentioned in the letter (Jas 5:1-6; 2:6-7), since the landed aristocracy was essentially Sadducean if even religious, but also of the book's theological cast, since Sadducees also observed Torah (Jas 1:22-25; 2:8-13) and were deeply fearful of any apocalyptic-messianic movement—to which the readers of James belonged (Jas 2:1; Martin, lxiv-lxv). However, unlike the Zealots, whose *apocalypticism the Sadducees feared most of all, James takes his readers in a more spiritual and less violent direction, so that the struggles of the poor against the rich are then internalized as spiritual warfare with materialism (Jas 4:1-5).

3. The Literature of James.

3.1. James as Exhortation. Most scholars accept with some qualification Dibelius's important form-critical conclusion that James is a paraenesis, a genre of ancient moral literature characterized by various collections of moral sayings and essays, loosely held together by common themes and linking catchwords but without literary rhyme, theological reason or specific social location. The dominant mood of paraenesis is imperative; the primary exhortation is to live a virtuous life. Readers are often reminded of moral truth that all should accept (e.g., Jas 1:19; 3:1-8; 4:3-4) and of heroic exemplars (e.g., Jesus, Abraham, Rahab, Job, Elijah) whom all should imitate.

Even if one allows that James exhibits the conventions of paraenetic literature and has wide appeal, its final shape frames a carefully orchestrated witness to God that compels a faithful and Christian response to its claims. Since Dibelius, several interpreters have demonstrated that the composition develops along the lines of a specific rhetorical strategy (e.g., Johnson, Watson) that argues for a specific theological point. L. T. Johnson, who contends that James must be approached as an oral presentation, argues for a thematic and literary coherence that is organized by two competing worldviews between "friendship with the world" and "friendship with God" (1995, 13-15).

3.2. James as an Epistle. James may also be studied as epistolary literature. Even though omitting many features of the Pauline or Hellenistic epistolary form, the structure of James is still vaguely parallel to other NT letters: it opens with an address (Jas 1:1) followed by a thesis statement (Jas 1:2-21) that clarifies the letter's occasion and introduces the author's advice. It then sets forth various exhortations and oaths that promote Christian piety (Jas 5:7-8, 9-11, 12, 13-18) before the real purpose for writing is stated (Jas 5:19-20). Sandwiched between the opening thesis statements and concluding exhortations is the letter's main body (Jas 1:22—5:6), made of three extended essays on the wisdom of "quick to hear" (Jas 1:22—2:26), "slow to speak" (Jas 3:1-18) and "slow to anger" (Jas 4:1—5:6), which communicates more fully its pastoral message to an embattled readership.

Clearly the literary form of the main body of James differs in convention and substance when compared with the Pauline letters. However, its function is precisely the same: to provide the readers with a powerful interpretation of their present spiritual crisis and to offer them a practical solution that encourages their future salvation (see 4 below).

3.3. James as Wisdom Literature. The question of sources remains a thorny one: from whence comes this book's understanding of wisdom? In my view, wisdom is the orienting concern of this book by which all else is understood. James refers to wisdom as the divine "word of truth," which is graciously provided to a faithful people to make sense of their trials and to guide them through those trials in order to ensure their future destiny in the new creation (cf. Martin, lxxxii-lxxxiv). A strong case has been made that James shares in the moral world of the Greco-Roman world (Laws): the virtue of the community of the wise is aptly demonstrated during personal testing, when the actions of the wise result in personal and divine blessing (see Johnson 1995, 27-29). The well-known contrast between professions of trust and an embodied faith may be less a response to Pauline teaching and more a reflection of the contrast between eloquent speech and moral action found among certain Hellenistic moralists such as Epictetus.

The characteristics of a virtuous life, concentrated by the catalog found in James 3:17 and complemented by the book's accent on a life of patience, perfection, consistency and self-control, are common themes among current moral philosophies, especially Stoicism and Cynicism.

This article will seek to understand this same moral calculus and its various topoi under the light of Jewish wisdom literature. The theological subject matter of James is profoundly biblical, and the Greco-Roman literary patterns and moral topoi found in this composition are subsumed by the author's biblical vision. Morality, according to James, is concentrated by a believer's faith in God. It is not a virtue ethic, then, whose failure is vice and self-destruction. Rather, it is a theological ethic, since the lack of wisdom threatens the believer's relations with God and imperils the prospect of future blessing in God's coming reign on earth. For this reason James fits much more comfortably in Scripture than in an anthology of Hellenistic moral philosophy.

Of course, these two sources, Hellenistic and biblical, are not dissimilar in either form or content and are found integrated in Jewish intertestamental writings such as Sirach and Wisdom of Solomon, which no doubt formed a part of the wisdom tradition this author inherited. There are frequent parallels to the writings of Philo. James is a traditional wisdom, and its sensibilities are Jewish more than Greco-Roman. In passage after passage the crucial subtexts of this composition are not Greco-Roman but biblical—a perspective recently defended in Johnson's commentary on James.

For this reason the interpreter seeks after the relationship between James and its principal subtexts in Scripture rather than in the writings of Greco-Roman moralists and philosophy: James offers one tradent's reading of biblical wisdom (Jas 1:19; see 6 below). The overarching interpretive strategy of James is sapiential in that nonwisdom and extrabiblical traditions are strained through the filter of Jewish wisdom. In this sense, then, the testing addressed by James is spiritual and not personal, and this "way of wisdom" promises eschatological blessing (Jas 1:12) for those who live and act under the light of the Lord's coming triumph (Jas 2:5; 5:7-9).

3.4. James as Midrash. James is midrashic literature. While several exegetes have discovered fragments of existing Jewish midrashim employed by James (e.g., Ward, Johnson), few go as far as M. Gertner, who claims that the whole of James is a midrash on Psalm 12. More modest is the suggestion of Johnson, who finds examples of a halakic midrash on Leviticus 19 throughout James that anchors and warrants its moral vision (Johnson 1982).

Contemporary literary theory uses midrash as a metaphor of a literary text's reflexive interplay with another, earlier text. That is, a literary text is midrashic insofar as it interprets an earlier text as part of its own redaction and argumentation for a new audience and its particular situation. In this sense the primary indicator of biblical midrash is not a certain form of literature (e.g., halakic) that is produced by following certain rabbinical rules for commenting on Scripture. Rather, the primary indicator is a text's intertextuality, when the reader of a biblical text recognizes its citation, allusion or echo of another, earlier biblical text that then completes and commends its meaning. In my reading of the intertextuality of midrash, biblical

texts echo other biblical texts as literary cues that point us to those stories or topoi, persons or places in order to construct a fuller biblical context within which the strong interpreter reflects upon the theological meaning of the passage under analysis.

With this understanding of midrash in mind, then, similar words and ideas found in different parts of Scripture are cited, alluded to and echoed in James, and add a rich subtexture to its message—a message that is framed by a reflexive, mutually enriching conversation between James and these other biblical voices. Sometimes a meaningful contour is added to James by what is lacking from a biblical allusion. For example, the carefully worded reference to Rahab in James 2:25 presumes by what it omits that the reader knows the details of her story as told in Joshua 2. In this way James need not even mention Rahab's faith since her biblical story asserts that the works of her hospitality are the real stuff of true religion. Thus I have come to read James as the literary product of an author whose canon consciousness first elevates the status of his Bible as the central symbol of his religious life and then routinely appeals to it, sometimes in subtle ways, to justify the moral authority of what he advises his readership to be and do.

The dynamic quality of an intertextual reading of James is envisaged even when the exegete narrows one's frame of reference to the intratextuality of the book of James itself. Following the lead of G. Lindbeck, the full meaning of James is discovered when a text is analyzed within (intra-) the literary and theological context of the composition, when the composition serves as the privileged medium of its own interpretation. In this sense the book of James is approached as an autonomous text that supplies its own special "grammar," which makes sense of its own "text-constituted world" (Lindbeck, 136). From this intratextual perspective, then, a fuller meaning of its most important catchwords can be discerned by their repetition in different locations of the argument (for example, follow the author's use of "perfect" [Jas 1:4, 17, 25; 2:22; 3:2; cf. 2:8; 5:11]). These words acquire new and enlarged meanings by their repeated use, while at the same time their prior uses alert the interpreter to possible meanings that may well be obscured by their new literary and linguistic context. This literary feature of James is especially important, since it provides a kind of literary coherence that otherwise has seemed lacking to some.

Both features of the literary art of James mentioned above are also important features of persuasive speech in the Greco-Roman literary culture, which also contributed to the shaping of this composition's main body (Watson). Clearly the repetition of key words and ideas in a composition was one such feature of ancient rhetorical writing and speaking. By repeating catchwords throughout a composition or speech, for example, an author like the writer of James could organize and relate together different sections of a composition for his auditors. Especially important in this regard is the reflexive character of repetition, so that subsequent uses of a word or phrase would naturally expand and clarify how an auditor or a reader should understand an important thematic interest of the composition as a whole.

The use of prophetic exemplars in James also follows ancient rhetorical practice. In the case of James, references to familiar biblical personages (Abraham, Rahab, Job, Elijah) not only provided authoritative examples in support of the thesis—these were those who passed their spiritual tests. They provided role models for an eschatological community—these were those who received promised blessings from God. The use of these exemplars in James is more than rhetorical, since each calls attention to a biblical story that provides the primary subtext that in turn deepens the point James scores.

3.5. Literary Sources. The author's possible knowledge and use of NT traditions, specifically those found in the Synoptic Gospels and in the Pauline and Petrine letters, remains debated. While there are significant linguistic and thematic parallels between James and the major letters of Paul and 1 Peter—more numerous and certain than most scholars care to admit—the question of literary dependence remains indeterminate (see 1 above). The same can be said of the possible appropriation by James of Jesus' sayings found in Q (Hartin 1991) and then in Luke (Davids) and especially Matthew (Shepherd). In fact, the parallels between James and Matthew's Sermon on the Mount (par. Luke and Q) are remarkably close (e.g., Mayor, lxxxii-lxxxiv; Shepherd; cf. Hartin 1993). However, D. D. Deppe argues against a pre-Synoptic source by contending that the parallel sayings in James evince an even more primitive source and have

in any case a different literary form and function than they do for Q and the Synoptic Evangelists. In any case, B. Witherington correctly contends that James exhibits a more conventional, less prophetic theological conception than found on the lips of the Synoptic Jesus (Witherington, 236-47).

4. A Canonical Approach to James.

The canonical approach to biblical interpretation is interested in reading the whole of Scripture as the church's authoritative or canonical witness to God and so formative and normative of the church's understanding of God (Wall 1995). The interpreter recognizes this theological role more clearly when reflecting upon Scripture within its biblical and ecclesiastical contexts rather than in terms of the conventions of its "original" historical or literary environments. While historical and literary reconstructions of the "original" James have had some value in determining the full meaning of a biblical text, to presume that critical historical investigation determines its normative meaning is mistaken. The principal property of the biblical text is neither historical nor literary but theological. For the exegete to locate this composition within its first-century milieu and to fix its meaning there is to mistake the true referent of the biblical witness, who is God. If the interpreter's orienting concern toward Scripture is its authorized roles within the church, then all the various tasks and exegesis and interpretation will seek to understand a biblical writing as a resource for theological reflection and understanding.

Within its particular biblical *Sitz im Leben* the book of James supplies a distinctive and complementary witness to God, so that it functions neither as the single articulation of God's biblical word nor as an atonal voice that must be excluded from the chorus of voices that together harmonize on the word of God. In this sense, Christian faith is distorted by not taking the distinctive witness of James seriously. The special significance of this book's particular witness to God is best understood in relationship to the witnesses of other biblical books and collections, precisely because each understands God in different, although complementary, ways and forms, if finally by "mutual criticism" a more objective and discriminating faith.

Besides this overarching perspective on the

study of Scripture, important guidance is provided the interpreter by the title that introduces a book within its discrete canonical collection; by the arrangement of canonical writings within the canon as a whole; by the final literary form of a composition that best articulates that variety of God's word; by the author's use of his Scripture as a decisive clue to how the canonical audience should read his book as Scripture; and by the history of its interpretation, whenever a biblical writing "becomes canonical" as faithful interpreters pick it up again and again to comfort the afflicted or afflict the comfortable.

4.1. Title. Titles are properties of the canonical process and as such are indicators of a theological tradition and a practical role that continues to exercise authority in forming the faith and witness of Scripture's current readerships. Even if one is not convinced that James should be read as a literary letter, the ancient church recognized its divine inspiration precisely when using it as a letter. Thus the inscription, *Iakōbou Epistolē* ("the letter of James"), is added to this nonletter (or at least a literary letter different from those written by the Pauline school) to fit it into a wider collection of epistolary writings, all of which share a similar role in nurturing the faith of believers. That is, letters function as pastoral vehicles of instruction and exhortation, written for believers whose worship of God is threatened by personal hardship or theological confusion. The canonical audience orients itself to James from this perspective to read it as Christian Scripture.

The importance of authorship statements in the address of a biblical letter is not exclusively historical; rather, names found in titles and greetings also locate compositions in particular theological traditions, each of which provides an authoritative witness to God's saving activity in Christ Jesus. This particular title locates the composition of James in a particular genre of literature to underscore its practical role in forming Christian faith; it also places the theological subject matter of James in a particular theological tradition—that belonging to James of Jerusalem, the brother of Jesus. In turn, the name of James, found in its biblical title and epistolary address, assigns this writing to the revelation tradition founded by James—that is, a conservative variety of Jewish Christianity.

4.2. Placement Within the Canon. The placement of the letters within the NT and then of James among them is suggestive of the role this book continues to perform as part of the biblical canon. James is placed within a second collection of NT letters. While the relation between the four NT Gospels has long been a topic of scholarly investigation, few have considered the relationship between the two collections of NT letters as significant. What possible relationship do the non-Pauline letters have with the Pauline in forming our theological understanding (the intended role of Scripture), and how might this consideration aid the interpreter in discerning the special role James might perform within the Christian Bible?

Especially within Protestantism, primary attention has been concentrated upon the Pauline collection to investigate not only the meaning of individual letters but also the relationship between them. Partial justification for this keen interest in Paul's witness to the gospel is claimed by the ordering of the letters, since the Pauline corpus comes first. Yet this very Pauline priority has also led to a reductionism in the study of the second, non-Pauline collection of letters. For example, James is typically viewed as envisaging either a Pauline faith, although in alternative wording, or an anti-Pauline faith. In either case the more complementary character of the intracanonical relationship between James and Paul is seriously distorted, as is their integral witness to God's gospel.

Accordingly, one may suggest that a critical role performed by the second collection of (non-Pauline) letters is to enhance our understanding of the first (Pauline) by provision of an apparatus of checks and balances that prevents distortion of the full gospel (Wall 1992, 208-71). In light of the history of its interpretation, the interpreter is especially challenged to listen to James for a voice different from that heard when reading Paul. However, it is neither the voice of a ventriloquist nor the voice of an adversary but that of a colleague whose new perspective adds and even supplies a necessary balance to what has already been read and accepted from Paul (see 5 below).

4.3. The Canonical Audience. Even though their readerships constantly change, biblical letters allow for the continual adaptation of their practical message to every generation of believers. There is no guarantee that the current readers of James participate in any of the ancient worlds occupied by its first readers; nor should we expect to recover the full meaning of the words that James originally wrote. Precisely because James is canonical Scripture, readers must not interpret its meaning as belonging to a distant past. Not only does its central theme of spiritual testing seem pertinent, but also readers often number themselves among the rich and powerful who disregard the powerless or among the powerless who require and are given God's support against the powerful. James sometimes exposes the foolishness of believers who substitute facile confession for an embodied devotion to God or use malicious words to gain an advantage over a rival—both important topics of James. The wise words of James may sound a prophetic tone, sharply critical of business as usual and often inviting our repentance or a pastoral tone for those in need of the gospel's assurance. The point is this: the book of James has found a place in Scripture not only because it provides us trustworthy contours of our understanding about God but also because it illumines our walk before God, especially when considered an integral part of an inspired whole.

5. The Gospel According to James.

5.1. A Portrait of God. The old critical conclusion that James is not a theological writing has waned in recent years. At the very least, most scholars now acknowledge the importance of theological images and themes in communicating the message of this book. For instance, the portrait of *God that James envisages is rather robust. God is Creator who rules over all things (Jas 1:17) and who promises a new cosmic order (Jas 1:18) that is remade perfect and complete, lacking in nothing (Jas 1:4). In preparation for the coming triumph of the Creator, God gives only good gifts to the faith community (Jas 1:13-17), especially the gift of wisdom (Jas 1:5-6; 3:17), which is able to "save their souls" (Jas 1:21; 3:18). God also receives petitions for wisdom (Jas 1:5; 4:3) and healing (Jas 5:13-18). God is faithful to the promise of salvation (Jas 2:5; 4:6-10) and will reverse the status of the faithful poor and powerless in the coming age (Jas 1:9-11; 2:1-5). Because God is Savior and Judge of all creation (Jas 2:12-13; 4:11-12, 13-17; 5:1-9), God is worshiped (Jas 3:9-10; 4:7-10) and God's law obeyed (Jas 1:22-27).

5.2. A Story of God's Salvation. Biblical scholarship has recently underscored the narrative aspect of Scripture's theological subject matter—

in J. A. Sanders's tidy phrase, "God has a story too." The functional importance of this line of inquiry is twofold. First, it supplies biblical theologians with a framework for building a comprehensive and coherent treatment of Scripture's theological subject matter. Second, foundational stories function to facilitate a more personal and immediate identification between the biblical narrative and its contemporary audience.

One fruitful effort in this regard is by R. Hays, who contends that Paul's theological vision is narrative in cast. According to Hays, Paul's core theological convictions comprise a sequence of six events, beginning with God's promise of blessing to Abraham and concluding with the Lord's second coming. Between are those episodes that constitute the Christ event, climaxed by Jesus' messianic death and resurrection and their results in the faith community. While the Pauline accents are distinctive within the NT, the narrative theology of other contributors to the biblical canon, including James, follows a similar story line. Like Hays, E. E. Lemcio has isolated the basic ingredients of a "unifying kerygma" in every canonical unit (i.e., Gospels, Acts, Letters, Apocalypse) of the NT.

The fourfold Gospel frames and founds Scripture with a narrative substructure; that is, this story of Jesus becomes the interpreter's foundational presupposition in understanding the practical advice given and theological claims made by every subsequent book of the NT. From this perspective as well, James shares with other biblical writers a common story of God's salvation through Jesus Christ, which provides the structure and supplies the subject matter of a fully integrated biblical theology.

The story's inaugural event is (1) God's election of a people to save. James understands divine election in terms of social class: God chooses the poor as heirs of the promised kingdom (Jas 2:5). Their inheritance of the blessing first promised to the children of Abraham is not conditioned upon their national or ethnic identity but upon their devotion to God, whether they are "rich in faith" (cf. Jas 1:12; 2:5) as embodied by merciful deeds (Jas 2:8-26).

(2) God sends an agent of *salvation into the world in order to free people from the results of their sin. According to James, God "gives" "the word of truth" to these pious poor in order to enable the passing of their spiritual tests (Jas 1:2-3) and to restore them as part of the coming

order (Jas 1:4, 17-18). The subject matter of the divine word is proverbial wisdom (Jas 1:5), which demands that the community be "quick to hear, slow to speak and slow to anger" (Jas 1:19; see 6 below). This word of wisdom is capable of saving the community (Jas 1:21; 3:17-18) from all the foolishness (Jas 1:16) and filthiness (Jas 1:21) that bring forth death (Jas 1:14-15; 3:14-16; 5:19-20).

(3) God's word is disclosed in the messianic "faith of the Lord Jesus Christ" (Jas 2:1). Unlike Paul, who understands the faith of Jesus in terms of his messianic death and resurrection, James understands the faith of Jesus as exemplary of an observed wisdom ("the word of truth"). In particular, Jesus' devotion to God is confirmed by his just treatment of the poor neighbor, which God demands according to the "royal" law (Jas 2:8; cf. 1:27).

(4) The divine word, already made known in Scripture's wisdom and exemplified by Jesus, illumines "the way" to divine blessing for any believer who asks God for it (Jas 1:5) and does not doubt its efficacy (Jas 1:6-8). Further, this same word has taken root within (Jas 1:21) and so marks out the boundaries of the elect community of the poor (Jas 1:27). Membership in this community, and with it the prospect of future blessing, is maintained by those who observe the word (Jas 1:22-25; cf. 4:13-17), who teach it without jealousy (Jas 3:1-18) and who resist those internal passions that undermine its performance (Jas 4:1-10; cf. 1:14-15).

(5) The current crisis that provokes spiritual testing is occasioned by every struggle of remaining faithful to God in an anti-God world (Jas 1:2-3; 3:13-16). In the present situation, when the community's suffering indicates a real "lack" of God's good intentions for creation, James contends that the word of proverbial wisdom empowers the passing of the spiritual test, so that the "first fruits" of a new creation might even now be demonstrated in the community's life together (Jas 1:18; 3:17-18). In this restricted sense, the witness of the wise community anticipates the coming age: the true and approved religion is an ethical people, whose witness to God is measured by the purity of its collective and personal life (Jas 1:27; 2:14-16). Thus it is finally the public works of wisdom, which demands the community's merciful treatment of its own poor (Jas 1:22—2:26), purity of speech among its word brokers (Jas 3:1-18) and a denial of materialistic affections among its aspiring middle class (Jas 4:1—5:6) that form the essential identity of an eschatological people.

(6) The community's hope is concentrated by the story's conclusion, the Lord's imminent parousia from heaven (Jas 5:7-9), which ushers into history the ultimate good and perfecting gift from above. At this climactic "any moment" the eschatological community will be confirmed and vindicated: God will judge the foolish and bless the wise (Jas 2:13; 4:11-12; 5:4-6; 5:7-9; cf. Mt 7:24-27). James and Paul substantially agree on this final event. Both agree that divine judgment and blessing are finally creational activities, which bring about the new order of things (Jas 1:4; 1:18; 3:18; 5:7-8). Both agree that the Lord's parousia is imminent, so that the convictions of christological monotheism and the demands of public witness are made more urgently and embodied more readily. The time for repentance is short, because the time of judgment is at hand (Jas 5:7-9, 19-20).

6. The Argument of James.

6.1. Thematic Introduction (Jas 1:1-21). James is written to a community whose faith in God is threatened by a daily struggle with hardship (Jas 1:2-4). This "testing of faith" is provoked by a variety of external and historical circumstances or "trials." More importantly, every test occasions a theological crisis, when the believer is more easily deceived or confused about who God is and how God acts (Jas 1:5-8). Within a crucible of theological reflection, largely internal and spiritual (Jas 1:13-15), a decision is called forth that ultimately measures the believer's true devotion to God, whether one is fit to participate in God's coming reign (Jas 1:12). To remain faithful to God in the present is the way to receive promised blessings from God in the future.

The community's decision for or against God is rooted in a sense of moral freedom. What form will this freedom take? On the one hand the wise believer loves God and trusts that God is a consistently loyal Father who generously supplies the faith community with the "word of truth" that will guide the believer's pilgrimage on earth through the wilderness of trials and into the promised land of eternal life (Jas 1:16-18). The anticipated result of receiving this word, whose subject matter is proverbial wisdom (Jas 1:19-20), is an increased capacity to remain faithful to God during the testing of this age until the Lord comes in triumph over sin and death. The wise and faithful believer will enter into the coming age where all that is lacking is reversed and made perfect by the Creator, who alone completes humanity's material (Jas 1:9-11) and spiritual existence (Jas 1:21).

On the other hand, the foolish Christian believes that God is disloyal to the promise of new life and is responsible for the community's hardships (Jas 1:13-16). The fool supposes that God is responsible for humanity's hardship and intends one's death; however, this deception results in refusing the merits of God's advice (cf. Jas 1:21). Such doubt gives birth to spiritual failure when facing present hardships, and the eschatological result of present spiritual failure is the forfeiture of the "crown of life" that is the blessing of all those who endure (Jas 1:12).

6.2. The Wisdom of "Quick to Hear" (Jas 1:22— 2:26). In this first section of the main body of James, the wisdom of "quick hearing" is paired with biblical Torah: to "hear" is to "do the work" of Torah (Jas 1:22-25). More specifically, the wisdom of "quick hearing" means to obey the levitical laws pertaining to the merciful treatment of the neighbor (Jas 1:26-27). This portion of the Torah is defined as the wise thing to do in order to address a situation in which the material needs of the poorest and most marginal members of the faith community are neglected. The occasion for this neglect is the favored treatment of rich and powerful outsiders in the legal proceedings of the synagogue (Jas 2:2-4) and law courts (Jas 2:6-7). In this situation the biblical Torah demands jubilary justice in order to liberate the poor and powerless from their oppression (Jas 2:8-13).

The decision to favor these rich outsiders over poor insiders, even though perhaps a matter of short-term survival, fails the community's "test of faith" because God has in fact chosen the pious poor of the world to receive blessing (Jas 2:5). Further, favoritism of this sort envisages a compromise to the evils of the world order. Such is the nature of a theological failure that imperils the community's future salvation, which requires concrete works of mercy toward the poor (the social diaspora). Jesus was approved by God as "glorious Lord" (Jas 2:1) because he loved his poor and powerless neighbor according to the "royal law" (Jas 2:8). His example of divine mercy, which followed in the way of ancestor Abraham (Jas 2:21-24) and prostitute Ra-

hab (Jas 2:25), charts the way of wisdom for all which leads into eternal life.

The wise community is quick to hear and act upon what the Torah commands, knowing that it articulates God's will according to which all people will be either blessed or judged at the coming triumph of God's reign (Jas 2:12-13). If the Torah is centered on the command to love the neighbor, especially those who are like the "widow and orphan in distress," then it is foolish to favor the rich over the poor when the result is eternal retribution. According to Torah, faith in God is embodied by works of mercy: true religion is an ethical religion, not confessional orthodoxy (Jas 2:14-26). To profess devotion to God without a complement of merciful works is foolish (Jas 2:20). Such religion is worthless for either heralding or entering the age to come (Jas 2:17, 26).

6.3. The Wisdom of "Slow to Speak" (Jas 3:1-18). James's essay on the proverbial wisdom of "slow speaking" is especially suited for the "wilderness" (Jas 3:11-12), when the spiritual journey is most unstable (Jas 3:3-6), when the guidance of "wise and understanding" teachers (Jas 3:13) is most critical, but also when harsh things are more easily said. The peril of speech is made even more pointed by the inherent difficulty of controlling what is said (Jas 3:7-8).

Every social crisis embodies a theological crisis as well; that is, a crisis of faith in God as Creator (Jas 3:9-10). Slanderous speech, which curses the neighbor who should be loved (Jas 2:8), offends the good intentions of the Creator, who made people in God's image. The deeper logic of a creation theology is that God built certain patterns in the created order (Jas 3:11-12); in this sense profane speech will not yield spiritual results (Jas 3:15-16), whereas pure speech will (Jas 3:17-18).

That is, the result of speech that substitutes "earthly" wisdom (Jas 3:15) for "heavenly" wisdom (Jas 3:17) is "chaos" (Jas 3:16), which is opposite of the Creator's intentions for a restored creation (cf. Gen 1:2). Demonic speech destroys human relationships and prevents the sort of spiritual nurture that empowers the community's journey through present trials toward the future promise of a new order. The harvest of "pure and merciful" speech (Jas 3:17), which conforms to heavenly wisdom, is the blessing of peace for those "perfect" teachers (Jas 3:1-2) who practice it (Jas 3:18).

6.4. The Wisdom of "Slow to Anger" (Jas 4:1—5:6). James 4:1—5:6 interprets the meaning of the proverbial exhortation for believers to be "slow to anger." According to James, the source of the community's anger (Jas 4:1) is an inward passion for lacking material pleasures (Jas 4:2-3). The trial that imperils the community's participation in God's coming triumph stems from an inability to be content with one's humble conditions, coveting rather the material goods of others (Jas 4:4-5). This passion for things tests the community's dependence upon God, who resists the arrogant and exults those of humble means (Jas 4:6; cf. 2:5). The wise community humbles itself before God (Jas 4:7-10), who alone establishes the criterion for judge and salvation (Jas 4:11-12).

The foolish, however, continue to indulge in self-centered passion for material profit without consideration of God's will for human existence (Jas 4:13-17). Indeed, those who choose Mammon over God will also choose Mammon over people and treat their poor neighbor with inequity (Jas 5:4) and hostility (Jas 5:6). The misery of mistreated workers ironically foreshadows the misery of the rich in the last days, when they will lose their wealth (Jas 5:1-2) and lives (Jas 5:4) to an angry God.

6.5. Concluding Exhortations (Jas 5:7-20). James concludes as it opens, with a pair of integral statements. By recalling important catchwords and phrases from the opening statements, the author forms an *inclusio* with his thesis that frames the commentary on wisdom found in between. More than a retrospective on the way of wisdom according to James, this conclusion also supplies the principal motivation for following its advice: the coming of the Lord is near (Jas 5:7-9).

The concluding exhortations to endure the testing of faith, implicit throughout James, are made more urgent by the author's pointed assertions that the parousia is imminent. The community is encouraged to exercise patience (Jas 5:7-8), like Job (Jas 5:10-12) rather than his complaining friends (Jas 5:9), and to be vigilant in prayers for healing (Jas 5:13-16), like Elijah (Jas 5:17-18), in order to ensure participation in the coming triumph of God's reign.

The final verses (Jas 5:19-20) form a commission that calls the readers to a special mission for those foolish believers who have been deceived by falsehood and have departed from the "word of truth" that defines the way of wisdom. Their spiritual healing will result in salvation rather than condemnation at the end of the age. To be the church is to be wise when tested in knowing that the present testing of faith determines the future entrance into the age to come.

See also WISDOM.

DLNTD: FAITH AND WORKS; JEWISH CHRISTIANITY.

BIBLIOGRAPHY. **Commentaries:** J. B. Adamson, *The Epistle of James* (NICNT; Grand Rapids: Eerdmans, 1954); J. Cantinat, *Les épîtres de s. Jacques et de s. Jude* (SB; Paris: Gabalda, 1973); P. H. Davids, *Commentary on James* (NIGTC; Grand Rapids: Eerdmans, 1982); M. Dibelius, *James*, rev. H. Greeven (Herm; Philadelphia: Fortress, 1976); Z. C. Hodges, *The Epistle of James* (Irving, TX: Grace Evangelical Society, 1994); L. T. Johnson, *The Letter of James* (AB; New York: Doubleday, 1995); S. S. Laws, *A Commentary on the Epistle of James* (HNTC; San Francisco: Harper & Row, 1980); R. P. Martin, *James* (WBC; Waco, TX: Word, 1988); J. B. Mayor, *The Epistle of St. James* (Grand Rapids: Zondervan, 1954); C. L. Mitton, *The Epistle of James* (Grand Rapids: Eerdmans, 1966); J. Moffatt, *The General Epistles* (MNTC; London: Hodder & Stoughton, 1928); D. Moo, *James* (TNTC; Grand Rapids: Eerdmans, 1987); P. Perkins, *First and Second Peter, James and Jude* (IntC; Louisville, KY: John Knox, 1995); B. Reicke, *The Epistles of James, Peter and Jude* (AB; Garden City, NY: Doubleday, 1964); J. H. Ropes, *The Epistle of St. James* (ICC; Edinburgh: T & T Clark, 1916); G. M. Stulac, *James* (IVPNTC; Downers Grove, IL: InterVarsity Press, 1993); R. W. Wall, *The Community of the Wise: The Book of James* (NTC; Harrisburg, PA: Trinity Press International, 1997). **Studies:** G. Bornkamm, "The Letter to the Romans as Paul's Last Will and Testament" in *The Romans Debate*, ed. K. Donfried (Minneapolis: Augsburg, 1977) 17-31; A. Chester and R. P. Martin, *The Theology of the Letters of James, Peter, and Jude* (NTT; Cambridge: Cambridge University Press, 1994); C. E. B. Cranfield, "The Message of James," *SJT* 18 (1965) 182-93, 338-45; D. D. Deppe, *The Sayings of Jesus in the Epistle of James* (Chelsea, MI: Bookcrafters, 1989); J. H. Elliot, "The Epistle of James in Rhetorical and Social Scientific Perspective: Holiness-Wholeness and Patterns of Replication," *BTB* 23 (1993) 71-81; M. Gertner, "Midrashic Terms and Techniques in the New Testament: the Epistle of James, a Midrash on a Psalm," *SE*

3 (= TU 88 [1964]) 463; D. E. Gowan, "Wisdom and Endurance in James," *HBT* 15 (1993) 145-53; D. Hadidian, "Palestinian Pictures in the Epistles of James," *ExpT* 63 (1952) 227-28; P. J. Hartin, "'Come Now, You Rich, Weep and Wail . . .' (James 5:1-6)," *JTSA* 84 (1993) 57-63; idem, *James and the Q Sayings of Jesus* (JSNTSup 47; Sheffield: JSOT, 1991); R. B. Hays, *The Faith of Jesus Christ* (SBLDS 56; Chico, CA: Scholars Press, 1983); J. Jeremias, "Paul and James," *ExpT* 66 (1954-55) 368-71; L. T. Johnson, "Friendship with the World/Friendship with God: A Study of Discipleship in James" in *Discipleship in the New Testament*, ed. F. F. Segovia (Philadelphia: Fortress, 1985) 166-83; idem, "The Mirror of Remembrance (James 1:22-25)," *CBQ* 50 (1988) 632-45; idem, "The Social World of James," in *The Social World of the First Christians*, ed. L. M. White and O. L. Yarborough (Minneapolis: Fortress, 1995) 178-97; idem, "The Use of Leviticus 19 in the Letter of James," *JBL* 101 (1982) 391-401; J. A. Kirk, "The Meaning of Wisdom in James," *NTS* 16 (1969) 24-38; G. Kittel, "Der Jakobusbrief und die apostolischen Vater," *ZNW* 43 (1950) 54-112; W. G. Kümmel, *Introduction to the New Testament* (rev. ed.; Nashville: Abingdon, 1975); E. E. Lemcio, "The Unifying Kerygma of the New Testament," *JSNT* 33 (1988) 3-17; G. Lindbeck, *The Nature of Doctrine: Religion and Theology in a Postliberal Age* (Philadelphia: Westminster, 1984); P. U. Maynard-Reid, *Poverty and Wealth in James* (Maryknoll, NY: Orbis, 1987); J. A. Overman, "The Diaspora in the Modern Study of Ancient Judaism," in *Diaspora Jews and Judaism*, ed. J. A. Overman and R. S. MacLennan (SFSHJ 41; Atlanta: Scholars Press, 1992) 63-78; T. C. Penner, *The Epistle of James and Eschatology* (JSNTSup 121; Sheffield: Sheffield Academic Press, 1996); L. Perdue, "Paraenesis and the Epistle of James," *ZNW* 72 (1981) 241-56; J. A. Sanders, *God Has a Story Too* (Philadelphia: Fortress, 1979); A. M. Shepherd, "The Epistle of James and the Gospel of Matthew," *JBL* 75 (1956) 40-51; R. W. Wall, *Colossians & Philemon* (IVPNTC; Downers Grove, IL: InterVarsity Press, 1993); idem, "James as Apocalyptic Paraenesis," *RQ* 32 (1990) 11-22; idem, "Reading the New Testament in Canonical Context," in *Hearing the New Testament: Strategies for Interpretation*, ed. J. B. Green (Grand Rapids: Eerdmans, 1995) 370-93; idem, "Successors to 'the Twelve' According to Acts 12:1-17, " *CBQ* 53 (1991) 628-43; idem, "A Unifying Theology of the Catholic Epistles: A Canonical Approach" in *Catholic Epistles and the Tradition*, J. Schlosser (BETL, Leuven: Peeters, 2003); R. W. Wall and E. E. Lemcio, *The New Testament as Canon: A Reader in Canonical Criticism* (JSNTSup 76; Sheffield: JSOT, 1992); R. B. Ward, "Partiality in the Assembly: James 2:2-4; " *HTR* 62 (1969) 87-97; idem, "The Works of Abraham: James 2:14-26," *HTR* 61 (1968) 283-90; D. F. Watson, "James 2 in Light of Greco-Roman Schemes of Argumentation," *NTS* 39 (1993) 94-121; idem, "The Rhetoric of James 3:1-12 and a Classical Pattern of Argumentation," *NovT* 35 (1993) 487-64; B. Witherington, *Jesus the Sage* (Minneapolis: Fortress, 1994).

R. W. Wall

JERUSALEM, PAUL'S VISITS TO. *See* GALATIANS, LETTER TO THE.

JERUSALEM CONFERENCE. *See* PAUL IN ACTS AND LETTERS.

JERUSALEM TALMUD. *See* RABBINIC TRADITIONS AND WRITINGS.

JESUS AND PAUL

The relationship between Jesus and Paul poses a historical question with huge theological ramifications. Is Paul's theology in harmony and continuity with the teaching and ministry of Jesus, or is there an unbridgeable gulf between them? It is generally held that if it is to merit the title *Christian*, the Christian religion must be recognizably continuous with Jesus' message and the impact of his activity. Yet, at a popular and a scholarly level, many interpreters would argue that Paul, our earliest Christian witness, departed significantly from the message of Jesus and introduced an alien system of theology. This raises many important historical questions, but, since Paul has been so influential in later Christianity, it also constitutes a major theological challenge.

1. History of the Debate
2. The Teaching of Jesus in Paul
3. The Life of Jesus and His Example
4. Letters and Missionary Preaching
5. Revelation and Tradition
6. The Kingdom of God
7. Israel and the Law
8. Sinners, Outsiders and the Mercy of God
9. Suffering, the Cross and Vindication
10. Continuity and Development

1. History of the Debate.

1.1. Before 1914.

1.1.1. Ferdinand Christian Baur. When F. C.
Baur opened the modern era of Pauline studies in the nineteenth century, he argued that rigorous historical analysis of the NT indicated that there were significant differences among the various branches of the early Christian church. In particular he emphasized the differences between Paul on the one hand and the Jerusalem apostles and Palestinian churches on the other. The latter were more influenced by and more faithful to the original teaching of Jesus, whereas Paul was consciously independent of such traditions and differed widely from the teaching of Jesus, particularly in his christology and in relation to the validity of the law.

The questions raised by this thesis were discussed in various forms but became the center of an extremely lively debate in the twenty years preceding the First World War. The "Jesus and Paul" question became in these years a focal point of discussion at an academic and a popular level, as a number of scholars in Germany and France (H. H. Wendt, M. Goguel, M. Brückner, P. Wernle) suggested that there was a significant gulf between the teaching of Jesus and the theology of Paul. Some also argued that for all his organizational and intellectual gifts, Paul should not be allowed to obscure the essential religious truths expressed by Jesus. "Back from Paul to Jesus" became the slogan of such radical critics. Such views were highly alarming to traditional believers and to liberal Protestant theologians whose theological commitments depended on a synthesis of the teaching of Jesus and Paul.

1.1.2. William Wrede. This controversy became most sharply focused through the publication in 1904 of W. Wrede's *Paul*, a popular book, brilliantly composed and presenting the radical position with provocative force. Wrede argued that Paul's theology represented a religion of redemption whose centerpiece is the notion of a superhuman being (the Son of God) entering the world in order to break the hold of the powers that keep it in slavery. This theological structure, a system of ideas that he inherited preformed from apocalyptic Judaism, Paul merged with the story of the death and resurrection of Jesus. What was significant in Paul's religious experience and his system of thought was not the life and teaching of Jesus but only the fact that

Jesus was a man, that he died and was raised. Thus, as representative of humanity, Christ effected an objective salvation, now mediated to those who believe these dogmas and take part in the sacraments.

Wrede insisted that this thought structure was alien to current theological emphases on individual piety and, more particularly, was in a different world from the simple prophetic style of Jesus and the pure moral truths he had so memorably pronounced. Paul's conversion had been through an encounter with the risen Christ, not the earthly Jesus, and he was only able to describe Christ as a divine figure because he had not known Jesus. For all the points on which Paul and Jesus might agree, and however much Paul may have known about the teaching of Jesus, Paul was not deeply influenced either by the personality of Jesus or by the spirit of his thought. In all important respects, the theological system basic to Paul's thought was worlds apart from Jesus. Thus Wrede reached his oft-quoted conclusion that "Paul is to be regarded as the second founder of Christianity" (Wrede, 179). While Paul rescued the Christian faith from "pining away as a Jewish sect" he did so only by transforming it. One can readily appreciate the theological dynamite packed into this conclusion. The dilemma that it poses for Christian theology is encapsulated in Wrede's observation that "this second founder of Christianity has even, compared with the first, exercised beyond all doubt the stronger—not the better—influence" (Wrede, 180).

1.1.3. Response to Wrede. The response to Wrede and to similar radical views was vigorous, both from liberal Protestant theologians in Germany (A. von Harnack, A. Jülicher, A. Resch) and from more conservative voices in the English-speaking world (J. Moffatt, C. A. A. Scott, J. G. Machen). Among the common lines of defense were the following: (1) Paul knew a lot more of the teaching of Jesus than we are inclined to acknowledge and alludes to it often, even if he quotes it rarely. (2) Although Paul rarely refers to the life of Jesus in his letters, the salient facts and even the personality of Jesus must have figured largely in his initial missionary preaching. (3) The supposed gulf between Jesus and Paul in matters of theology has been greatly exaggerated; for instance, Jesus' attitude to the law was, in his own way, just as critical as Paul's, and the implicit christology in his claims

is not that far distant from the explicit divine titles and roles accorded him by Paul. (4) In many aspects of their theology Jesus and Paul were entirely at one, for instance, in their doctrine of the fatherly love of God, in their perception of eschatology and in their ethics. It could be argued that these were the kernel of the Christian religion and that any remaining differences were on merely peripheral matters. (5) It was argued by some scholars that even if Paul's theology was different from that of Jesus, in his religious experience he was at one with the spirit of Christ and showed clear signs of the influence of the personality of Jesus. (6) Finally, a variety of explanations could be put forward for the difference of atmosphere between the Gospels and the Pauline letters: Paul's rabbinic training (see Jew, Paul the), his different personal experience, the needs of the Gentile mission and of the battle against Judaizers, as well as the obvious fact that Paul inevitably views Christ from, as it were, the other side of the cross and resurrection. All these were appealed to as factors of purely external significance, not materially affecting the substance of the inner unity between Paul and Jesus.

By such means there was mounted a strenuous rebuttal of the notion of Paul as second founder of Christianity and any implication that he had perverted or substantially altered the gospel announced by Jesus. In the kernel of their thought, Jesus and Paul are in harmony and any development from Jesus to Paul constitutes no more than legitimate interpretation and explication.

1.1.4. Wilhelm Heitmüller and Albert Schweitzer. Just before the interruption caused by the First World War, two further contributions heralded important aspects of the debate in its next phases. In 1912 W. Heitmüller probed the question of the Christian sources of influence on Paul's thinking. Whereas previously Paul had been treated largely as an isolated figure, or as drawing what information he had about Jesus from the primitive Palestinian communities, Heitmüller drew attention to the Hellenistic Christian circles in which Paul was nurtured as a Christian. He suggested that Paul's relative neglect of the words and deeds of Jesus was not just an idiosyncrasy but was characteristic of the Hellenized forms of the Christian movement. This not only reinforced those in the history-of-religions school who argued that the really decisive influences on Paul's thought came not from Judaism but from Hellenistic culture. It also pinpointed an important issue in the historical question of continuity between Jesus and Paul: if the Hellenized wing of the early Christian movement already put more emphasis on the risen Lord than the earthly teacher, the problem cannot simply be framed as Jesus and Paul but must incorporate study of this third shadowy entity, Hellenistic Christianity.

By contrast, in his survey of Pauline scholarship, *Paul and his Interpreters* (1911), A. Schweitzer supported those who discerned the influence of Jewish apocalyptic on Paul. His interpretation of Paul's theology as molded by eschatological "mysticism" was not published until many years later (*The Mysticism of Paul the Apostle,* 1930), but already in his earlier survey it is clear that he considered Paul's thought to be fully explicable from its parallels in Jewish apocalyptic sources. The significance of this is that in his famous *Quest of the Historical Jesus* (1906) Schweitzer had demolished all the liberal attempts to write a biography of Jesus and had presented Jesus not as the spokesperson for liberal piety and morality but as an apocalyptic prophet working within a rigorous apocalyptic timetable. Schweitzer thus suggested a quite different solution to the Jesus and Paul question. Instead of the gulf between the liberal Jesus and a Hellenized or an apocalyptic Paul, Schweitzer suggested a relatively easy transition from the apocalyptic Jesus to an apocalyptic Paul, separated only by the fact that the eschatological events, to which Jesus had looked forward, Paul now saw as having at least begun in the resurrection of the Messiah.

1.1.5. Which Jesus and Which Paul? These contributions at the end of this period of fierce controversy serve to highlight one of its essential underlying problems. In any comparison between Jesus and Paul and any attempt to suggest continuities or correspondences between them, everything will depend on which Jesus is being compared with which Paul. Critical questions about the validity of the gospel material as evidence for the historical Jesus continued to be discussed (the majority discounted John but put confidence in Mark's Gospel). Yet most of the participants in the mainstream of this debate took it as axiomatic that the real Jesus was the Jesus of liberal theology, who preached simple but profound moral truths and highlighted in particular the fatherhood of God, the brotherhood of all humanity and the infinite value of the human soul. The essence of Christianity and of religion in general was contained in Jesus' call for the trusting devotion of the human soul in its God. With this Jesus on one side of the equation, it was simply a matter of arguing whether Paul, in his religion or his theology, had substantially altered or appropriately developed this essential religious vision. When Schweitzer and J. Weiss began to shake the foundations of the liberal picture of the historical Jesus, new possibilities for understanding the relationship between Jesus and Paul began to open up.

1.2. Rudolf Bultmann. In the next phase of the discussion, from the First World War to the 1950s, R. Bultmann's contributions were of decisive importance. As a major participant in the postwar theological backlash against liberal theology, he moved the debate forward in several significant ways, in his multifarious individual works on Jesus and Paul and in two seminal essays specifically on the Jesus and Paul question.

1.2.1. Bultmann's Jesus. Bultmann shared Schweitzer's perception of Jesus as an apocalyptic preacher who proclaimed the imminent arrival of the kingdom of God. In his form-critical work on the Gospels, Bultmann cast doubt on the historicity of much of the material, arguing that the Gospel accounts had been heavily influenced by the faith of the church in the period of oral transmission, as well as by the interests of the individual Gospel writers. This made it impossible, in his view, to reconstruct a convincing portrait of the personality of Jesus or the sequence of events in his life. But (contrary to popular opinion) Bultmann was still confident that he could draw the main contours of the message of Jesus; and that proclamation he saw as decisively molded by an eschatological outlook. The kingdom of God was not a matter of God's rule in the soul (Harnack) but described the moment when God would bring the corrupt world to an end. Jesus thus portrayed God in radical terms as Creator and Judge, and his apocalyptic language could not be dismissed as mere "husk"; thus "whoever finds Paul offensive and uncanny must find Jesus equally so!" (Bultmann 1936, 194).

1.2.2. Material Congruity with Paul. In his interpretation of the proclamation of Jesus, Bultmann broke decisively with the liberal emphasis on ethics and on Jesus as a teacher of timeless and universal truths. In probing the meaning of Jesus' eschatological message and the human situation portrayed in it, Bultmann saw Jesus as issuing a summons, a call to radical obedience. He took Jesus' critique of the Pharisees to represent an attack on any legalism that required only partial or external obedience. In his absolute demands Jesus calls for the total dedication of the self to the will of God as the individual surrenders his or her previous self-satisfaction. Moreover, he saw here a real point of correspondence with Paul's theology. At the center of Paul's critique of the law and in his theology of the cross, Bultmann saw a penetrating attack on Jewish legalism and on any attempt to secure salvation from purely human resources. "The real sin of man is that he himself takes his will and his life into his own hands, makes himself secure and so has his self-confidence, his 'boast'" (Bultmann 1929, 228). Thus, with interpretative insights derived from existential philosophy, Bultmann detected a material (*sachliche*) congruity between Jesus and Paul in their understanding of the human condition, even though Paul's theology was more theoretically explicated than that of Jesus. Even in christology Bultmann saw some element of similarity, since Jesus, although he "did not demand faith in his own person, did demand faith in his word. That is, he made his appearance in the consciousness that God had sent him in the last hour of the world" (Bultmann 1936, 195). It was thus inevitable that the proclaimer should become the proclaimed. The only difference, though it is significant, is that what Jesus proclaimed as an imminent act of God, Paul preached as an accomplished work of salvation.

1.2.3. Historical Continuity? Bultmann made an extremely important distinction between two aspects of the Jesus and Paul debate. It is one question to ask what correspondence there may be between the proclamation of Jesus and the preaching of Paul; it is quite another to inquire if Paul was, either directly or indirectly, influenced by the teaching of Jesus. In regard to this latter question, Bultmann saw very little historical connection between Jesus and Paul. He emphasized how little Paul quotes of the words of Jesus and that even if one allows for all possible allusions, they affect only Paul's ethics. "It is most obvious that he does not appeal to the words of the Lord in support of his strictly theological, anthropological and soteriological views" in which are contained "the essentially

Pauline conceptions" (Bultmann 1929, 223). In such respects Paul is not dependent on Jesus, and "Jesus' teaching is—at least in essentials—irrelevant for Paul." Thus while he saw some important elements of theological congruity between the proclamation of Jesus and the kerygma of Paul, Bultmann found very little by way of historical continuity between them.

1.2.4. The Historical Jesus and the Kerygma. Bultmann's treatment of our theme also made one further significant contribution. He took the Jesus and Paul question to be representative of a wider theological issue, namely, the relationship between the historical Jesus and the preaching of the church. This issue had been vigorously pressed in 1892 in M. Kähler's protest against the liberal lives of Jesus—that they attempted to substitute for the Christ of the church's faith a pale, historically uncertain and theologically irrelevant Jesus of history. As a "theologian of the word" Bultmann shared Kähler's conviction that the Reformation principle of justification by faith should be applied to theological method: theological truths could never be validated by the limited and insecure results of historical research but were secured by faith alone. Christian theology therefore could never confine itself to or even take its starting point from scholars' tentative reconstructions of the historical Jesus. The starting point is always the kerygma—that the crucified Christ was raised from the dead and is to be acknowledged as Lord.

Bultmann's interpretation of the NT gave strong support to this theology. In particular he argued that the lack of reference in Paul to the life and teaching of Jesus indicated that the only thing concerning the historical Jesus that was significant for the church's preaching and faith was that Jesus, the crucified one, was a historical fact. Everything else that was important about him theologically (e.g., that he died for us, that he was the preexistent *Son of God and that he is *Lord) was established by the resurrection and by the preaching of the church, not by the facts and events of Jesus' historical life. The significance of the historical Jesus for faith was simply that he lived (*Dass*), not how he lived (*Was*). In Paul's theology "one does not acquire knowledge about the Messiah: one either acknowledges him or repudiates him" (Bultmann 1929, 236). If Jesus is teacher or example, that is only as he is already acknowledged as Lord—"it

is not the exemplary character of the historical Jesus that makes him Lord" (Bultmann 1929, 239). Thus Bultmann considered the radical cry—"Back from Paul to Jesus"—theologically dubious. "All that one can do is to go to Jesus through Paul: that is, one is asked by Paul whether he is willing to understand God's act in Christ as the event that has decided and now decides with respect both to the world and to us" (Bultmann 1936, 201).

1.2.5. Bultmann's Significance. In this way Bultmann tackled the question of Jesus and Paul not merely at the historical level (how much was Paul actually informed about, influenced by or in agreement with Jesus) but also in the context of the larger theological issue of the relationship between the historical Jesus and Christian faith. It is the massive significance of this theological question, and the radical way it was posed and answered by Bultmann, which made his contributions to the debate so important.

It is worth emphasizing also the value of Bultmann's distinction between historical continuity between Jesus and Paul and theological congruity. Much of the discussion of the Jesus and Paul issue before Bultmann had confused these two matters, and some debate since has failed to heed his distinction. It has been easily assumed, for instance, that if agreements in motif or vocabulary between Jesus and Paul can be found which suggest some lines of continuity (e.g., that Paul drew on traditions of the teaching of Jesus in ethics or eschatology), that in itself is proof of close correspondence in their theological perspectives. As NT scholars have learned from many other areas of study, even if parallels are found between two sources, and even if those parallels represent dependence by one upon the other (they sometimes do not), these can be no more than surface phenomena that mask deep differences in the underlying structure of thought. Conversely, as Bultmann argued, significant congruity between the thought of Jesus and Paul need not imply continuity in the simple historical sense of traditions about Jesus being passed on to and received by Paul. One could still press a historical question as to how such remarkable congruity came about (Bultmann never addresses this), and it would be unwise to separate totally the questions of continuity and congruity. But there is nonetheless considerable value in recognizing the distinction between them.

1.3. From the 1950s to the Present Day. Bultmann's dominant position in German NT scholarship had the effect of depressing interest in the historical Jesus. Historically he cast doubt on our ability to recover anything like a rounded picture of the Jesus of history, and theologically he considered that the results would be largely irrelevant as far as the kerygma was concerned. But when he emphasized these points in a lecture in 1960 he was obliged to defend his position against a contrary trend already gaining ground even among his pupils. The tide had begun to turn, and it was bound to bring in with it a renewed interest in the old question of Jesus and Paul.

1.3.1. Joachim Jeremias. From the 1930s onward, resolutely independent of the Bultmannian school, J. Jeremias had been pursuing fresh and highly successful research on the historical Jesus. He believed that it was possible to recover the central facts about Jesus and even, in some cases, his *ipsissima verba* ("very words"). He also considered that the Jesus thus recovered was, in his consciousness of his status (as seen in the distinctive *Abba*), in his break with the law and in his redemptive interpretation of his death, entirely at one with later Christian preaching about him. In particular, Jeremias detected a crucial point of similarity between the Jesus who gave a welcome to sinners and outcasts and the Paul who preached the justification of the ungodly through the grace of God.

1.3.2. Werner G. Kümmel. At the same time W. G. Kümmel kept the Jesus and Paul issue alive with important essays on the theme. While considerably influenced by Bultmann's position and largely agreeing with him on Paul's lack of information about the life and teaching of Jesus, Kümmel analyzed the congruity between Jesus and Paul in terms less dependent on existentialist philosophy. In particular he argued that for Jesus the kingdom was not purely future but was already breaking in during his ministry. Whereas Bultmann (following Schweitzer) had seen an important distinction between Jesus pointing to the imminent future and Paul pointing to the immediate past, Kümmel saw Jesus and Paul as conditioned by a very similar tension between the presence of salvation and its future fulfillment (*see* Eschatology). The resurrection and the gift of the Spirit (*see* Holy Spirit) merely widened the effect of the salvation already present in Jesus—and present not just in his word (Bult-

mann) but also in his person. Thus for all the differences in formulation between Jesus' preaching and Paul's, Kümmel insisted that Paul's theology represents no fundamental alteration or falsification of the teaching of Jesus but only a proper reformulation of its fundamental ideas.

1.3.3. The New Quest. However, the Jesus and Paul debate could only take on new life with a widespread revival of research on Jesus. The 1950s saw renewed interest in the historical Jesus springing up even among Bultmann's pupils, most notably E. Fuchs, G. Bornkamm and E. Käsemann. While remaining true to the kerygmatic principle that the gospel can never be dependent on the uncertain results of historical research, Käsemann made out a powerful exegetical and theological case for what became known as the new quest for the historical Jesus. He warned against the dangers of "docetism" if the Christ preached in the gospel is not firmly linked to the historical Jesus and argued that Bultmann's reduction of this link to the mere historical existence of Jesus was too meager. If Christian scholars did not investigate the character of Jesus' ministry, others certainly would. More importantly, the Synoptic Gospels showed that an important strand of early Christianity did attempt to tie its preaching of the gospel to a life story of Jesus; and even if Paul's kerygma has much less interest in such things, it does focus on the earthly Jesus inasmuch as it emphasizes his crucifixion. Only in this way could Paul combat the Spirit enthusiasm of his converts, for he soon discovered in Corinth that an appeal to the Spirit alone was vulnerable to all sorts of misinterpretations (*see* Corinthians, Letters to the). Thus research into the historical Jesus, while not providing a historical basis for faith, is important as a criterion for distinguishing the true gospel from falsifications of it. In particular, Käsemann's interpretation of the historical Jesus as one who broke in a decisive way with the law and removed the distinction between sacred and secular realms gave support for his emphasis on the radical political and social significance of the gospel.

1.3.4. Eberhard Jüngel. Although the new quest of the 1950s and 1960s had rather limited results, it did open up again the historical questions about Jesus and thus serve to raise afresh the question of the relationship between Jesus and Paul. The most immediate result was a new presentation of the congruity between Paul and Jesus by E. Jüngel (1962). With a skillful combination of NT exegesis and theological expertise, and drawing effectively on the "new hermeneutic" of his mentor E. Fuchs, Jüngel compared the understanding of the kingdom of God that comes to expression in the parables with Paul's central theological affirmations about the righteousness of God. For all their differences as forms of speech, Jüngel detected an essential correspondence here. Just as in the parables, as "speech-events," God and his kingdom draw near to history and establish a new word over against the old word of the law, so Paul preaches the arrival of a new era that releases us from the slavery of the law and from the bondage of the past.

1.3.5. Omissions and Problems. The abstract character of Jüngel's thesis has perhaps made his work more accessible to theologians than to NT specialists. But it is remarkable that there has been virtually no new work on the question of theological congruity between Paul and Jesus in the thirty years since Jüngel's book. The reasons for this neglect are complex but certainly include the following.

(1) In general there has been a parting of the ways between theology and NT study. The theological dimensions of our topic that were so important to Bultmann and his immediate successors have simply eluded or failed to interest most recent NT scholars. At the same time theology has taken much less interest in the NT.

(2) To discuss the congruity between Jesus and Paul requires an analysis of their theologies that can isolate the dominant motifs and discern, within and behind these, the central dimensions of their thought. But in the present climate a large degree of uncertainty prevails concerning such matters regarding Paul and Jesus.

The Reformation interpretation of Paul, dominant in Germany and also in evangelical theology elsewhere, has long identified justification as the heart of Paul's theology, understanding his critique of the law as an attack on any attempt of the individual to earn his or her righteousness. At present, however, under the influence of K. Stendahl and E. P. Sanders, it is now highly debatable whether *justification by faith is so easily to be identified as the center of Paul's thought and whether its thrust is to be understood in such individualistic terms. The last

decade in particular has seen a considerable debate on Paul's theology of the law in which many influential voices present Paul's thought as confused or wholly confined to issues of practical significance in his Gentile mission. This leaves significantly fewer scholars than in previous generations who are confident about the central dynamic of Paul's theology and thus able to compare this with the central concerns of Jesus.

Meanwhile, although research on the historical Jesus has gained a new lease on life, it has largely cut loose from theological interests—in contrast to the close connections between the old quest and liberalism on the one hand and the new quest and Protestant existentialism on the other. Thus although there have been substantial advances made in recent years on the historical context of Jesus' ministry and the analogies between his impact on Israel and that of contemporary first-century Palestinian movements (e.g., by J. K. Riches, A. E. Harvey, G. Theissen, M. Hengel, M. J. Borg, Sanders), these have rarely been accompanied by the sort of theological engagement that seeks to pinpoint the core of Jesus' message and purpose. Although some consensus is emerging on the limits of a plausible picture of Jesus, there is continuing scholarly uncertainty about the authenticity of the sayings material in the Gospels and a large measure of disagreement about the extent to which Jesus challenged central aspects of Judaism. In particular, Sanders has forced a reconsideration of the two points at which Jesus' distinctive message has been most commonly discerned—his critique of the law and his welcome of sinners. Although many would take issue with Sanders on this, most scholars agree that the decisive questions in relation to the historical Jesus concern his purpose in relation to Israel and his impact on the religious, cultural and political complex of Palestinian Judaism.

But the more Jesus' life and preaching are placed within his Palestinian context, the harder it appears to find significant points of correspondence with the theology of Paul, which was forged in the light of the cross and resurrection and in the context of the Gentile mission. In fact, the present trend of NT scholarship is largely hostile toward the creation of theological syntheses in general, and any synthesis between Jesus and Paul in particular. It is the diversity, rather than the unity, of the NT that attracts most attention, and there is a general distaste for what are seen as apologetic attempts to paper over the cracks.

The conviction of many Jewish scholars—that Jesus can be accommodated within Judaism but Paul cannot—was famously propounded in the middle of the century by J. Klausner and has since been reiterated by G. Vermes and others. Although most Pauline scholars would resist the implication that Paul has been decisively influenced by non-Jewish (mystery-religion [*see* Religion, Greco-Roman] or Gnostic [*see* Gnosticism]) ideas, there is still a general willingness to concede that between the worldview of Jesus and that of Paul there is a considerable gulf. Whereas previous generations were concerned to rebuff Jewish arguments that Christianity was corrupted by Paul, the prevailing atmosphere of pluralism and of sympathetic sensitivity to Jewish perspectives has made Christian scholars less urgent and less polemical in their treatment of this issue.

1.3.6. Progress. If the last decades have seen little attempt to explore the possible congruity between the messages of Jesus and Paul, there has been considerable attention paid to the question of historical continuity. There has been renewed interest in the question of Paul's use of traditions about and from the historical Jesus. The conservative British school of thought had been maintained in W. D. Davies's influential *Paul and Rabbinic Judaism* (1948) in which he deduced from the quotations and allusions in Paul's letters that "Paul is steeped in the mind and words of his Lord" (Davies, 140). This was supplemented by the researches of the Scandinavian school (H. Riesenfeld, B. Gerhardsson), which stressed the careful preservation of Jesus material in the first generation. In the case of Paul, much hinges on the detection and evaluation of allusions to the teaching of Jesus. D. L. Dungan's careful analysis of *The Sayings of Jesus in the Churches of Paul* (1971) examined Paul's allusive use of the sayings of Jesus in 1 Corinthians 7:10 and 1 Corinthians 9:14. He suggested that the Corinthians were already familiar with such material and that there could be many other places where Paul alludes to Jesus' teaching. This has encouraged scholars to pursue further the question of Paul's dependence on eschatological material originating from Jesus and the possibility that Paul knows not just isolated sayings but whole blocks of material (D. Wenham, D. C. Allison, P. Stuhlmacher). New work on the character of echoes and allusions and the proper method for detecting them is being undertaken (M. Thompson), although it must also be acknowledged that a large number of scholars consider this whole enterprise as so fraught with uncertainty as to be of very limited significance.

The second aspect of continuity that presently commands attention is the question of the channel through which Jesus tradition could reach Paul. Most scholars acknowledge that Paul's contact with the immediate disciples of Jesus in the Palestinian churches was not extensive, although argument continues over the proper evaluation of Paul's first meeting with Peter (Gal 1:18). More interest focuses on the Hellenists, the radical Jewish-Christian group represented by Stephen and Barnabas, who were expelled from Jerusalem, became the target of Paul's persecution and seem to have been the most important influence upon him after his conversion. It is generally accepted that if there is any bridge between Jesus and Paul it must lie here. But we are hampered by our lack of direct and reliable evidence about this group. If, in historical terms, the Jesus and Paul question cannot be discussed without reference to the early church as a third entity, it is frustrating that it is precisely this decisive early period and this crucial Hellenist branch of the church that remain so shadowy.

2. The Teaching of Jesus in Paul.

As we have seen, there has been considerable debate about the extent and significance of Paul's use of the teaching of Jesus. There is no dispute about the occasions on which Paul explicitly quotes the words of Jesus (e.g., 1 Cor 7:10; 9:14; 11:23; 1 Thess 4:15—though the origin of this is uncertain). The argument generally focuses on the question whether in other places, where we can detect parallels with the Gospels, Paul is alluding to or echoing the teaching of Jesus (e.g., the cluster of possible allusions in Rom 12—14). Naturally, those who emphasize the gulf between Jesus and Paul minimize the number of plausible allusions; and those who see a close relation between them tend toward a maximalist reading. Of course, within the wider debate the issue is not just the number of occasions on which Paul quotes or alludes to Jesus' teaching. It also concerns the significance that

Paul attaches to the teaching of Jesus. Do the words of Jesus carry a special authority? If he does allude to them, why are they so often mixed in with other material and not specifically identified as the words of Jesus? Further, what significance would Paul's christology give to Jesus as a moral teacher?

3. The Life of Jesus and His Example.

The number of facts about Jesus' life that we could glean from Paul's letters is not large: he was born and lived under the law (Gal 4:4); he was of the line of David (Rom 1:3); he had brothers, one of whom was called James (1 Cor 9:5; Gal 1:19); he had a meal on the night he was betrayed at which he used certain words (1 Cor 11:23-25). There is no reference to the baptism of Jesus, to his many miracles and parables, to the disputes with Pharisees, the transfiguration or the temple incident; there is no indication of the setting of Jesus' ministry, no references to Galilee or Jerusalem. The only facts about Jesus that are constantly referred to are that he was crucified and that he was raised, although even here we must note the absence of detail about time, place and attendant circumstances. The mere fact of Christ crucified seems so to dominate Paul's perspective that everything else recedes into the background.

The cross is also central to Paul's depiction of Jesus' character and his moral example. There are references to the gentleness and meekness of Jesus (2 Cor 10:1) and to his love (Gal 2:20). These general character traits are illustrated not by any incidents in his life or by his treatment of others but by his self-giving on the cross. When Paul refers to the obedience of Christ (Rom 5:19; Phil 2:5-9) or to his grace in making himself poor (2 Cor 8:9), it appears that he has in mind the whole drama of the incarnation and the cross (*see* Christology) rather than any specifiable event in Jesus' life. And it is probably significant that in referring to the example of Jesus in bearing the burdens of others (Rom 15:3) Paul refers not to any words or deeds of Jesus but to the depiction in the Psalms of the suffering of the righteous.

All this suggests that it would be incorrect to claim that Paul was wholly ignorant of or uninterested in the life of the earthly Jesus. But his mind operates in terms of general characteristics rather than specific narratives, and he is concerned to bring out the significance of the

story of Jesus as a whole, interpreted in the light of the Scriptures. Alongside the references to his own example, Paul does appeal to the figure of Jesus as an example of obedience, self-giving and love. For instance, despite the objections of some scholars, part of Paul's purpose in citing the hymn in Philippians 2:5-11 does seem to be to provide a moral example. However, one may observe that such a generalized depiction of virtue is sometimes not as effective in moral exhortation as the dramatic narrative that illustrates the point. Other religious and philosophical groups in the Greco-Roman world cultivated stories of heroes (e.g., Moses, Pythagoras, Diogenes, Socrates) whose lives encapsulated the truths they propounded. One can thus understand the need for and the popularity of the detailed Gospel narratives alongside the generalized outlines provided by Paul.

4. Letters and Missionary Preaching.

Thus far we have been discussing the evidence of Paul's letters. But it is obvious that these provide only a partial picture of Paul's thought, and it has often been suggested that Paul may (or even "must") have provided a much fuller picture of the life and ministry of Jesus when he carried out his initial evangelism. To draw broad conclusions from the letters alone would thus be misleading. It has been suggested that the genre of a letter precludes the provision of detailed narratives, and the contrast between the Gospel and the letters of John is sometimes cited as a parallel here. There is also the general consideration that one would expect any preaching of Christ crucified to provoke requests for fuller information from interested and hostile audiences.

The problem here is our lack of evidence for the original preaching of Paul. Although Acts gives some of his sermons, scholars continue to debate how much these can be taken as evidence for Paul's preaching and the extent of their recasting by Luke; in any case, even the speech at Pisidian Antioch (Acts 13:16-41) provides very scanty information about the earthly Jesus. In his letters Paul does occasionally refer to the terms of his initial preaching (1 Thess 1:9-10; 1 Cor 2:2), but he does not give any hint of a fuller account of the life of Jesus. Further, in Romans, which Paul writes to a church he did not found and which sets out fully the gospel he preaches, there is none of the expected detail on the life of Jesus. To argue that Paul rarely referred to the life of Jesus because he does not say much about it in his letters is to argue from silence, and arguments from silence are always slightly precarious. Yet to assert that Paul did know much more than he says in his letters, and thus to have to provide one hypothesis or another to explain his silence, is perhaps an even more precarious procedure.

5. Revelation and Tradition.

There is an interesting contrast between Galatians 1 and 1 Corinthians 15 in the way Paul describes the origins of his gospel. In Galatians 1 he insists on his independence from all human authorities and in particular from the apostles in Jerusalem. He suggests that his call and his gospel were received directly through a revelation from Christ (*see* Conversion and Call of Paul) and that it was only some three years later that he had occasion to meet Peter. In 1 Corinthians 15, however, he reminds the Corinthians of the creedal formula he had passed on to them concerning the death and resurrection of Christ, and he says that he had himself received this piece of tradition. In this latter case we see Paul as one who inherits and treasures traditions from those who were Christians before him, including Palestinian eyewitnesses of the resurrection; in Galatians all the emphasis lies on what he himself has experienced in his call-revelation. The two passages thereby suggest different perceptions of how much Paul would be concerned to find out and pass on information about the earthly Jesus.

It would obviously be a mistake to set these two self-portraits in any absolute antithesis. In both passages rhetorical considerations explain a certain one-sidedness in Paul's presentation. It would be wrong to conclude from Galatians that Paul was averse to or embarrassed by information about the historical Jesus. As C. H. Dodd once quipped, it is hardly likely that at their initial meeting Peter and Paul spent a fortnight talking about the weather (Gal 1:18)! Yet it is also clear that Paul is extremely self-conscious about the manner of his calling. As one who had not seen or followed the earthly Jesus, his authority could rest only on the visionary calling he received on the Damascus Road. There he encountered the risen Christ, whose crucifixion he had previously counted the chief scandal to Jews like himself (*see* Jew, Paul the). It is under-

standable, then, that it is these facts about Christ, his crucifixion and resurrection, rather than details of his teaching or ministry, that impressed themselves most on Paul's mind.

Another verse often referred to in this connection is 2 Corinthians 5:16, where Paul writes: "So from now on we regard no one from a human point of view *(kata sarka);* even if we once knew Christ from a human perspective *(ei kai egnōkamen kata sarka Christon),* we know him thus no longer." For a while this verse became a central text in the Jesus-Paul debate, particularly since Bultmann interpreted it to support his view that Paul had little interest in the life of the earthly Jesus. Detailed discussion of whether the phrase *kata sarka* should go with the noun or the verb tended to obscure the fact that what is said here of Christ is said in the first half of the verse of everyone. One could hardly say that Paul was uninterested in the natural life and circumstances of everyone he encountered! Yet it is also clear in the context (with its talk of dying with Christ and of the new creation in Christ [*see* Creation, New Creation]) that Paul's perspective on everyone, including Christ, is determined by the world-shattering events of the cross and resurrection. For Paul these were not simply events that concluded Jesus' life; they constituted the death of an old aeon, together with its old ways of perception,and the opening of a new (*see* Eschatology).

In this sense, any information Paul may have had about the life and ministry of Jesus seems to have been overshadowed by the cross and resurrection. It is sometimes suggested that Paul makes little reference to the life and teaching of Jesus because he felt insecure in citing such facts, which could be used with more confidence by his Palestine-based opponents. It is also possible that stories of Jesus as a miracle worker were naively invoked by some of his enthusiastic converts, for instance the Corinthian Christians. But even if either or both of these hypotheses are true, it is more important that the structure of Paul's theology laid almost exclusive stress on the central facts about Jesus which had caused the dramatic shift in salvation history: that Jesus, the Christ, had been crucified but raised from the dead by God.

6. The Kingdom of God.

One theme that provides a particularly clear example of the difference between the theology of

Jesus and Paul is the *kingdom of God. On a surface level, in terms of vocabulary usage, it is immediately obvious that this terminology, which is so central to Jesus' message, plays a much reduced role in Paul. It is still a part of Paul's vocabulary (e.g., Rom 14:17; 1 Thess 2:12; Gal 5:21; 1 Cor 4:20; 6:9) but often in formulae that appear stereotyped and never in the central statements about salvation. It is possible that this reflects a merely superficial change of terminology and that, as Jüngel and more recently A. J. M. Wedderburn have argued, the basic concept is preserved in Paul's talk of the righteousness of God. However, it is also significant that where Paul uses metaphors of sovereignty, he does so characteristically by reference to the lordship of Christ (see Lord). In this connection 1 Corinthians 15:20-28 is particularly revealing with its reference to Christ's present reign, even though that is only preliminary and ultimately subordinate to the universal rule of God. This passage also makes it clear that Paul understands the lordship of Christ as a consequence of the resurrection.

This would suggest an important dissimilarity between the preaching of Jesus and the theology of Paul. If Jesus spoke of the kingdom of God as breaking in through his ministry, he pointed primarily to the effects of his preaching and healing. From the other side of the cross and resurrection, Paul understood the rule of God as focused in the risen Lord, and thereby he highlighted an event and emphasized a christology that are at most implicit in the teaching of Jesus. Given this undeniable difference in perspective caused by the events of the cross and resurrection, we must now consider whether there are still significant points of congruity between the preaching of Jesus and the theology of Paul that would allow us to hold them together as recognizably united in their fundamental concerns.

7. Israel and the Law.

Recent research on the historical Jesus has highlighted the question of his purpose and has focused attention on his relationship to the people of Israel. A consensus has emerged that understands his ministry as devoted to the restoration and reconstitution of Israel: he called twelve disciples, a symbol of the twelve tribes of Israel, in order to gather around himself the renewed core of the people of God. Jesus did not found a church because the church (Israel) was already in existence. But the restoration of Israel involved a fundamental challenge to its value system. Following on from *John the Baptist's call to repentance, Jesus challenged Israel to grasp and to practice the will of God in radical obedience. The object of his attack was not legalism in the sense of the self-satisfied performance of meritorious works but the narrowness of vision that confines the perception of the will of God within the boundaries of nation and tradition (see Law). When Jesus spoke of the kingdom of God he consistently broke apart traditional expectations. Although the evidence probably does not allow us to claim that he set himself against the authority of the Torah as a matter of principle, it is sufficiently clear that he challenged the nation to reconsider its priorities and interpreted the law in such areas as sabbath, purity and the love command in an open-ended fashion. To insist, for instance, that the sabbath rest was to be understood as an opportunity for the performance of acts of mercy was to shift the emphasis from the protection of Israel's way of life to its unique calling to demonstrate, even in the tense historical context of Palestine, the unlimited mercy of God.

Paul's theology also has as its focal point the question of God's purposes for Israel. It is now increasingly appreciated that Romans 9—11 is not an appendix but an integral part of the argument of that letter and that Paul's theology of justification has as its immediate horizon not the question of the salvation of the individual but of God's impartiality toward Jews and Gentiles. Paul then is also concerned with the reconstitution of Israel, the redefinition of the children of Abraham. For Paul, the context in which this is worked out is not the political and religious tensions of Palestine but the social environment of Jews and Gentiles in the cities of the Greco-Roman world. His unique calling to the Gentile mission and its remarkable success necessitated a rethinking of the sufficiency of the Torah as the standard of moral guidance—a much more radical reappraisal than we can detect in the teaching of Jesus. Paul looks back to Jesus as one who lived under the law (Gal 4:4) and his ministry as directed to "the circumcision" in order to fulfill the promises to the patriarchs (Rom 15:8). But he understands that fulfillment as now entailing a systematic redefinition of the "Israel of God" (see Israel) to include Gentiles, who enjoyed freedom from the law. Paul never invokes the life or teaching of Jesus as a model for his Gentile mission or his selective use of the law; in this respect it appears that he was aware of a significant point of discontinuity between Jesus and himself. But it may still be possible for us to claim that there is a real congruity between the dynamic of Jesus' challenge to Israel and Paul's law-free mission to Gentiles; this will require us to investigate more carefully the theological driving force of their respective ministries.

8. Sinners, Outsiders and the Mercy of God.

Recent discussion of Jesus and the sinners has highlighted the boldness of his association with those who were not just ignorant of the law but who willfully and repeatedly crossed the boundaries of acceptable Jewish behavior. Prostitutes and tax collectors (renowned for their dishonesty) were apparently among the company whom Jesus welcomed in table fellowship. The rationale for this controversial behavior is made clear in the parables of the lost (Lk 15) and the saying about the doctor (Mk 2:17): Jesus represents his ministry as the decisive opportunity of forgiveness, the moment when the kingdom of God, focused in his activity, is revealed as the unconditional and saving mercy of God. Instead of reinforcing the protective boundaries of the pure and the righteous, Jesus consciously redefined God's love in radically inclusive terms as welcoming the poor, the maimed, the tainted, the "unconvertible" and the enemy. In taking a Samaritan as the model of service to others, in finding the qualities proper to the people of God represented even outside its traditional boundaries (cf. Mt 8:10-12; Mk 7:24-30), Jesus hints that the mercy of God is not necessarily confined to the Jewish race, even if his primary concern is with the revitalization of Israel. In Paul's context sinners are not just disobedient Jews but also, and especially, Gentiles. His theology of justification is focused on the question of how even such Gentiles can be included in Abraham's family. The Gentile mission he pursues, together with his experience of transformation from persecutor of the church to apostle, lie at the root of his characteristic emphasis on the grace of God—a grace extended even to the weak, the enemy and the ungodly (Rom 4:5; 5:6-11; etc.). For all the differences of context and expression, and for all the complexities of the theological argumentation Paul employs, it is here, at the very heart of his theology, where Paul seems to be entirely in tune with the dynamic of the message and ministry of Jesus. For Jesus and Paul, the core of the good news consists in the radical demolition of restrictive boundaries in the free and gracious activity of a merciful God.

Since Paul never appeals to the example of Jesus in this regard, it is not clear how this remarkable theological congruity can be explained in historical terms. The most likely solution, well argued by Wedderburn, is that the Jewish Hellenist Christians whom Paul initially persecuted were influenced in their openness to Gentile converts by the memory of Jesus' controversial welcome of sinners and took inspiration from his open-ended emphasis on the merciful forgiveness of God. It was perhaps this atmosphere and these priorities that Paul then absorbed when he joined the Hellenist community that he had formerly tried to destroy.

9. Suffering, the Cross and Vindication.

There is good evidence that Jesus consciously adopted a life of poverty and self-denial and understood the measure of greatness to be in service. Because of the suspicion that the Gospel records of Jesus' words have been heavily influenced by subsequent events, many scholars remain agnostic on the question of whether Jesus predicted his death or what interpretation he may have given to it. However, there is some solid evidence in the well-attested tradition about the *Last Supper (see Lord's Supper) and in the logion in Mark 10:45 that Jesus knew his life of service would culminate in death and understood that death as being in some sense on behalf of many. Moreover, given the long tradition of reflection in Jewish theology on the fate of the righteous martyrs and their sure vindication by God, it is entirely plausible to attribute to Jesus some hope that God's purposes would triumph even in and through his impending death.

Looking back from the other side of the cross and resurrection, Paul's perspective is in some respects radically different: in the confidence of Christian experience of the resurrection, he detects the opening of the new era in the resurrection of Christ and his exaltation to the position of Lord. Yet he also sees the life and death of Jesus as characterized preeminently by service and obedience (Phil 2:5-11; Rom 15:3; 2 Cor

8:9). Moreover, like Jesus, he places the pattern of service and vindication, death and new life, at the very heart of the good news of the gospel. Just as Jesus saw the love of God as expressed in his self-giving for others and the essence of discipleship in losing one's life and finding it again (Mk 8:34-37), Paul's theology focuses on the "Son of God who loved me and gave himself for me" (Gal 2:20), and his dominant image of the Christian life is of "carrying about the dying of Christ in order that the life of Christ might be manifest in our bodies" (2 Cor 4:10). Like Jesus, although with more explicit focus on the cross, Paul sees this gospel pattern as presenting a radical challenge to the pride, defensiveness and self-sufficiency endemic in human nature (1 Cor 1:18-25; cf. Lk 10:25-37; Mk 10:35-45).

10. Continuity and Development.

As our survey of the history of debate has shown, there are important theological presuppositions lying behind many discussions of the Jesus and Paul issue. At one extreme lies Bultmann's assertion "that it is the Christ of the kerygma and not the person of the historical Jesus who is the object of faith" (Bultmann 1960, 17). The natural effect of this is to minimize the continuity between the historical Jesus and the theology of Paul and to lay all the emphasis on the Easter faith. At the opposite end of the spectrum is J. W. Fraser's concern that "we cannot rest content with the beliefs of Paul or others; it must be Jesus himself who provided the basis for and the impetus to the whole New Testament understanding of his saving person and work" (Fraser, 29). From this perspective it is important to find as much similarity and continuity between Jesus and Paul as possible.

In fact no one can deny that there are significant changes and developments between the message of Jesus and the theology of Paul. The events of Good Friday and Easter, and the momentum of the Gentile mission, made such developments inevitable and necessary. Moreover, quite apart from the different idioms and thought forms used by Jesus and Paul, their very different social and cultural contexts would have made it impossible for Paul simply to repeat the preaching of Jesus. The central question is whether in essence Paul's theology is harmonious with and a legitimate development of the message of Jesus. As we have seen, this question cannot be answered simply by discovering or de-

nying the presence of echoes of the words of Jesus in Paul. That issue, which lies on the level of historical continuity between Jesus and Paul, cannot by itself determine whether Paul's theology is congruous with that of Jesus. But there is sufficient evidence to show that, whether consciously or otherwise, Paul did develop the central insights of the teaching of Jesus and the central meaning of his life and death in a way that truly represented their dynamic and their fullest significance.

See also CHRISTOLOGY; ESCHATOLOGY; JEW, PAUL THE; KINGDOM OF GOD; LAW; LORD'S SUPPER.

DPL: IMITATION OF PAUL/OF CHRIST; JESUS, SAYINGS OF; PAUL AND HIS INTERPRETERS; RESTORATION OF ISRAEL; TRADITION. *DLNTD:* JESUS TRADITIONS.

BIBLIOGRAPHY. M. J. Borg, *Conflict, Holiness and Politics in the Teaching of Jesus* (New York and Toronto: Edwin Mellen Press, 1984); C. Brown, "Historical Jesus, Quest of," *DJG* 326-41; R. Bultmann, "The Significance of the Historical Jesus for the Theology of Paul" in *Faith and Understanding* 1 (New York: Harper & Row, 1966 [1929]) 220-46; idem, "Jesus and Paul" in *Existence and Faith* (London: Hodder & Stoughton, 1961 [1936]) 183-201; idem, "The Primitive Christian Kerygma and the Historical Jesus" (1960), in *The Historical Jesus and the Kerygmatic Christ,* ed. C. E. Braaten and R. A. Harrisville (New York and Nashville: Abingdon, 1964) 15-42; W. D. Davies, *Paul and Rabbinic Judaism* (Philadelphia: Fortress, 1948); D. L. Dungan, *The Sayings of Jesus in the Churches of Paul* (Oxford: Blackwell, 1971); J. W. Fraser, *Jesus and Paul* (Appleford, Berkshire: Marcham, 1974); W. Heitmüller, "Zum Problem Paulus und Jesus," *ZNW* 13 (1912) 320-37; J. Jeremias, *The Central Message of the New Testament* (London: SCM, 1965); E. Jüngel, *Paulus und Jesus* (Tübingen: J. C. B. Mohr, 1962); M. Kähler, *The So-Called Historical Jesus and the Historic Biblical Christ* (Philadelphia: Fortress, 1964 [1896]); E. Käsemann, "The Problem of the Historical Jesus" in *Essays on New Testament Themes* (London: SCM, 1964); idem, "Blind Alleys in the 'Jesus of History' Controversy" in *New Testament Questions of Today* (London: SCM, 1969); J. Klausner, *From Jesus to Paul* (London: Allen & Unwin, 1943); W. G. Kümmel, "Jesus und Paulus" (1939) and "Jesus und Paulus" (1963) in *Heilsgeschehen und Geschichte* (Marburg: N. G. Elwert, 1965) 81-106, 439-56; J. K. Riches, *Jesus and the Transformation of Judaism* (New York: Seabury, 1982); E. P. Sanders, *Paul and Palestinian Judaism* (Philadelphia: Fortress, 1977); idem, *Jesus and Judaism* (Philadelphia: Fortress, 1985); A. Schweitzer, *Paul and His Interpreters* (London: A & C Black, 1912); M. B. Thompson, *Clothed with Christ: The Example and Teaching of Jesus in Romans 12:1—15:13* (Sheffield: JSOT, 1991): G. Vermes, *Jesus and the World of Judaism* (Philadelphia: Fortress, 1984); A. J. M. Wedderburn, ed., *Paul and Jesus: Collected Essays* (JSNTSup 37; Sheffield: JSOT, 1989); D. Wenham, *Paul: Follower of Jesus or Founder of Christianity?* (Grand Rapids: Eerdmans, 1995); S. G. Wilson, "From Jesus to Paul: The Contours and Consequences of a Debate" in *From Jesus to Paul: Studies in Honor of Francis Wright Beare,* ed. P. Richardson and J. C. Hurd (Waterloo, ON: Wilfrid Laurier University, 1984); B. Witherington III, *Jesus, Paul and the End of the World: A Comparative Study in New Testament Eschatology* (Downers Grove, IL: InterVarsity Press, 1992); W. Wrede, *Paul* (London: Philip Green, 1907).

J. M. G. Barclay

JEW, PAUL THE

In recent years a significant change has taken place in Pauline scholarship. During the first half of the twentieth century the dominant history-of-religions school emphasized a Hellenistic approach to Paul: Paul was understood to be a Hellenized Jew of the Diaspora. For example, R. Bultmann and his followers reasoned the syncretistic Judaism of the Diaspora and the popular philosophy of the time constituted the background of Paul's thought. Today, however, NT scholarship finds more and more evidence for the Jewishness of Paul's life and thought. This change is part of a general movement in Christian scholarship to rediscover the Jewish roots of Christianity. Concurrently, Jewish scholarship shows a growing interest in reclaiming the Jewishness of Jesus and Paul. Accordingly, the following study emphasizes the Jewish dimension of Paul's life and thought.

Much of the current emphasis on the Jewishness of Paul focuses on his social world. It attempts to go behind his thoughts and words to matters of lifestyle and behavior. For example, Paul shared the apocalyptic hope of primitive Christianity: what did that mean in terms of everyday life, in terms of a group that lived outside the mainstream of life in the Roman Empire? Since the social study of Paul is now a field in itself, it is not possible here to do full justice to this aspect of Pauline scholarship.

A recent study by J. Neyrey, however, demonstrates how cultural anthropology sheds light on the Pauline letters and on Paul the Jew. According to Neyrey, Paul's early upbringing, or socialization, as a strict Pharisaic Jew conditioned his view of the world and reality. Consequently, Paul had a passionate concern for such categories as order, hierarchy and boundaries in matters of purity. Paul's concern for these categories was carried over to his postconversion (*see* Conversion and Call of Paul) perspective. Thus Paul was not an entirely new person after his conversion: his Jewish past continued to influence him. This continuity will be further illustrated in the following discussion.

1. Paul's Autobiographical Statements
2. Paul's Formal Education in Judaism
3. Paul's Apocalyptic Worldview
4. Paul's Self-Understanding as a Jew
5. Paul's Mysticism
6. Paul and Torah

1. Paul's Autobiographical Statements.

The proper place to begin a study of Paul the Jew is his autobiographical statements. The most pertinent autobiographical passage is Philippians 3:4-6. This is a polemical passage in which Paul explicitly emphasizes his credentials as a Jew. "If anyone else has reason to be confident in the flesh, I have more: circumcised on the eighth day, of the people of Israel, of the tribe of Benjamin, a Hebrew born of Hebrews; as to the law a Pharisee, as to zeal a persecutor of the church, as to righteousness under the law blameless." In this passage Paul makes the point that his Jewish credentials and his zeal for his religion could be matched by few other Jews or Jewish Christians.

Still haunted by a false dichotomy between Palestinian Judaism and that of the Diaspora, many Pauline scholars refuse to take such autobiographical statements at face value. The scholarship of a previous generation posited a pure, Torah-centered Judaism for Palestine and a syncretistic, Hellenistic Judaism for the Diaspora. And, since Tarsus was located in the Diaspora, Paul was subsumed under the category of syncretistic Hellenistic Jew.

In contrast to the older view, recent archeological and literary finds have demonstrated the rich variety in Palestinian Judaism in adherence to the law and in speaking languages other than Aramaic. Much the same variety is true of Diaspora Judaism, although Greek was the predominant language spoken. While Greek was the language of Alexandrian and Egyptian Jewry, the language situation in Syria was different; Syria later produced an Aramaic literature. Geographically, Tarsus is quite close to Syria. Also, Jerome reports that Paul's parents came from Gischala in Galilee. If Jerome is correct, Paul could very well have spoken Hebrew or Aramaic in his home.

Philippians 3:4-6, however, reports far more about Paul's Judaism than the fact that he claimed Jewish identity. For example, he claims to be a Benjaminite. Precisely what Paul was declaring by this assertion is not clear. Nevertheless, the following may have been involved in Paul's boast. Jerusalem and the temple were located within the tribal land of Benjamin. In the separation of the northern kingdom from Judah, Benjamin and Judah remained loyal to the Davidic kings. After the Babylonian exile, Benjamin and Judah were the center of the new community.

Next, Paul claims to be "a Hebrew born of Hebrews." Again, certainty is elusive in defining this phrase (cf. 2 Cor 11:22). He may have meant his blood was pure in that he had no Gentile ancestry. More probably, he was contrasting himself with Hellenists or Greek-speaking Jews. Thereby, he was saying that he was taught to speak Hebrew in the home. According to R. N. Longenecker, this interpretation gains in probability if Philippians is read in the light of 2 Corinthians 11:22. There Paul matches his qualifications against those of other Jews or Jewish Christians: "Are they Hebrews? So am I. Are they Israelites? So am I. Are they descendants of Abraham? So am I" (Longenecker, 22).

As a further cause for boasting in Philippians, Paul claims to be a Pharisee. Here the term was defined with precision. The expression "as to the law a Pharisee" refers to the oral law. The Sadducees held that only the written law was binding, while the Pharisees believed God had revealed the oral law as well as the written law. In Galatians 1:14 Paul writes that he was "extremely zealous . . . for the traditions of the elders." The Greek for traditions is a technical expression (*paradosis*) for the oral law. The

same Greek word occurs in Mark 7:5, where the Evangelist speaks of the "traditions of the elders." According to E. Rivkin, Paul thereby understood himself as a member of the scholarly class who taught the twofold law. By saying that the Pharisees sit on Moses' seat (Mt 23:2), Jesus was indicating they were authoritative teachers of the law. Consequently, the Pharisees claimed to believe that they were the true Israel who knew God's will for the world.

Another basic Pharisaic belief was the resurrection of the dead. If a member of the covenant community (a Jew) or a Gentile convert obeyed the oral and written law, that person could anticipate being raised to eternal life.

In summary, Paul was saying that he was a Hebrew-speaking interpreter and teacher of the oral and written law.

A further point should be made in reference to Paul's statement "as to righteousness under the law blameless" (Phil 3:6). The uneasy, guilt-ridden conscience of the West, as seen particularly in Martin Luther and his age, should not be read back into Paul's psyche (see Stendahl). The anxieties of one age are not those of another. Paul's biographical statements are best taken at face value—like the Pharisees in the Gospels he understood himself as zealous and righteous.

2. Paul's Formal Education in Judaism.

According to Acts 22:3 Paul received formal education in the Judaism of the time "at the feet of Gamaliel." This famous Gamaliel was either the grandson or son of the renowned Hillel, who was instrumental in drawing up the exegetical methods (*middôt*) by which Scripture should be studied (cf. *t. Sanh.* 7.11; *'Abot R. Nat.* [A] §37). Recently, some scholars have questioned the claim that Paul was trained under Gamaliel. The dispute cannot be recapitulated here, but a brief consideration of Jewish education in Paul's day illuminates the setting of Paul's early years (see Hengel, 1:78-83).

From the early Hellenistic period we have the renowned Ben Sira's description of his school, which was designed to teach wisdom to upper-class young men (*Sir* 51:23-28). Sometime later and well into the Hellenistic period there arose a movement to instruct the whole Jewish population in the law (*b. B.Bat.* 21a). This movement attempted to preserve Judaism from assimilation to Greek learning and language. Even later the attempt to instruct the whole people became a primary goal of Pharisaism. In Paul's generation a network of elementary schools taught the Hebrew Bible, primarily the Pentateuch, to boys who began school at the age of six or seven (*y. Ketub.* 32c, 4). More advanced schools taught young men to interpret the text of the Bible and to explain contradictions and problems found therein. The exegetical methods drawn up by Hillel were applied to interpreting the text of the Bible as well as to applying Pentateuchal laws to the contemporary needs of Jewish society.

Some insight into Paul's formal education is gained by considering his exegetical skills in a passage such as Romans 9:6-29, where Paul utilizes Hebrew Scripture, midrashic techniques and the exegetical traditions of his day. In this passage Paul is struggling with a problem faced by early Christians: Why have the majority of Jews rejected their own Christ? He states the issue in Romans 9:6: "But it is not as though the word of God had failed." He then turns to the Pentateuch for primary passages that address this issue. The initial text to which Paul appeals is Genesis 21:12: "Through Isaac shall your descendants be named" (Rom 9:7). A second supplementary text is cited from Genesis 18:10: "About this time I will return and Sarah shall have a son" (Rom 9:9). In the argument that follows, Paul cites other subordinate texts from the OT. These subordinate quotations are linked to the initial and secondary texts by the use of three catchwords: "descendants" (*sperma;* translated "children" in Rom 9:29), "named" (*kaleō*) and "son" (*huios; see* Adoption, Sonship). E. E. Ellis has outlined the pattern of the use of Scripture in the following manner (Ellis, 155).

Romans 9:6-7	Theme and initial text: Genesis 21:12
Romans 9:9	A second, supplemental text: Genesis 18:10
Romans 9:10-28	Exposition containing additional citations (Rom 9:13, 15, 17, 25-28) and linked to the initial texts by the catchwords *kaleō* ("name") and *huios* ("son") (Rom 9:12, 24-26, 27)
Romans 9:29	A final text alluding to the initial text with the catchword *sperma* ("descendants" and "children")

Paul employed a number of midrashic techniques in composing this unit. The use of a par-

allel secondary text to supplement and elucidate the primary text is frequently found in later classical midrashim. Also common is the use of a key term in the initial text and the conclusion of the composition, thereby forming a correspondence of beginning and ending in a discussion (*inclusio*). The use of key words to pull in other passages of Scripture is also well known. In Paul's composition the key word is not always found in the texts that have been quoted. Nevertheless, the key word is always found in the context of the quotation if not in the quotation itself. Similarly, later rabbis did not always quote the key word.

Other elements of midrashic form found here are introductory or citation formulas for Scripture, breaks in thought caused by dealing with an incorrect inference or an imaginary opponent (also found in the diatribe), and the use of words from the initial text in the exposition.

Perhaps the most significant element in this midrash-like unit is Paul's use of contemporaneous exegetical traditions that are preserved for us in later rabbinic works. An example from outside Romans 9:6-29 is found in 1 Corinthians 10:4, where Paul wrote: "For they drank from the supernatural rock which followed them." The biblical narrative contains no hint that the rock was mobile. How did Paul know this? As H. Conzelmann states (Conzelmann, 166-67), Paul was making use of a Jewish haggadic tradition that appears in a later work (*t. Sukk.* 3.11; cf. *b. Ta'an.* 9a; *Bib. Ant.* 11.14; Philo *Leg. All.* 2.86).

In Romans 9:6-29 the initial text (Gen 21:12) Paul employs was used in two different ways in later rabbinic works. First, the Babylonian Talmud quotes Genesis 21:12 in several places. The following passage from *Sanhedrin* 59b is typical:

> Circumcision was from the very first commanded to Abraham only. . . . If so, should it not be incumbent upon the children of Ishmael (Abraham's son)? For *in Isaac shall thy seed be called.* Then should not the children of Esau be bound to practice it?—*In Isaac* but not all Isaac. (Soncino edition)

Both Paul and the later Babylonian Talmud use the same text to show who belonged to Israel, and both associated Esau with this text. However, unlike Paul, the Talmud ties "in Isaac" to purely physical descent from Jewish parentage.

But what is even more striking is the way Paul and the later Genesis *Rabbah* exegete this same text. Here another factor in addition to physical descent is associated with the phrase "in Isaac." (In order to understand the following passage the reader needs to know that in the first-century Hebrew letters also had a numerical equivalent: since *bêt* is the second letter of the alphabet, it was also the symbol for the number two.) In *Midrash Rabbah* Genesis 53.12 we read:

AND GOD SAID UNTO ABRAHAM: LET IT NOT BE GRIEVOUS IN THY SIGHT . . . FOR IN ISAAC SHALL SEED BE CALLED TO THEE (XXI, 12): R. Judan b. Shilum said: Not 'Isaac', but IN ISAAC is written here. R. 'Azariah said in the name of *Bar Ḥutah* the *beth* (IN) denotes two, i.e., [thy seed shall be called] in him who recognizes the existence of two worlds; he shall inherit two worlds [God says]; 'I have given a sign [whereby the true descendants of Abraham can be known] viz. he who expressly recognises [God's judgments]: thus whoever believes in the two worlds shall be called "thy seed", while he who rejects belief in two worlds shall not be called "thy seed." (Soncino edition, 471)

In the above midrash the true descendants of Abraham believe in two worlds. This is precisely Paul's stance in Romans: physical descent alone is not enough; those who have a certain belief or type of faith are children of Abraham. In commenting on Romans 9:6-29 Paul writes the following in Romans 9:30-32:

What shall we say, then? That Gentiles who did not pursue righteousness have attained it, that is, righteousness through faith; but that Israel who pursued the righteousness which is based on law did not succeed in fulfilling that law. Why? Because they did not pursue it through faith.

Paul's view of faith is closely related to what we have observed in the *Midrash Rabbah*. As a Pharisee Paul had believed in the two worlds, that is, not only in this present world but also in the resurrection—the world to come. When Paul met the resurrected Christ on the Damascus Road, he interpreted Christ as the "first-fruits" of the general resurrection to follow. From that point on his belief in a general resurrection became concretized in a specific person through whom he had experienced reconciliation with God and all that the term "faith" meant for him.

Before drawing any conclusions, however, another piece must be added to the picture.

Genesis *Rabbah* is not the only later rabbinic work in which belief in two worlds is associated with Genesis 21:12. Much the same interpretation is also found in the Jerusalem Talmud, *Nedarim* 2:10. Here also the *bêt* means "two" and points to a Jew who believes in two worlds.

These two late Palestinian sources raise the possibility of the existence of a Palestinian exegetical tradition that associated the belief in two worlds with Genesis 21:12. As we have seen, the Babylonian Talmud does not know this tradition and construes Genesis 21:12 to mean physical descent alone.

Still, the question remains: How could Paul and this exegetical tradition (if such it was), found in sources published hundreds of years after Paul, have interpreted the same verse in such a remarkably similar manner? G. Vermes points us toward a solution (Vermes, chap. 6). He first rejects various possibilities: that the NT depends on the Talmud and Genesis *Rabbah* (they did not exist in NT times); that the later exegetical tradition was learned from Paul; and that the similarities are purely coincidental (there is too much overlap). Rather, he holds open the possibility that the NT and the later rabbinic exegetical tradition had a common source, namely, traditional Jewish teaching. Exegetical traditions lived for hundreds of years. Here Vermes would say that Paul knew the exegetical tradition associated with Genesis 21:12. This tradition lived in the schools of Palestine and later resurfaced in the Jerusalem Talmud and in Genesis *Rabbah*. And, of course, this opens the possibility that a Palestinian exegetical tradition was one source of Paul's doctrine of justification through faith.

In addition, another exegetical tradition was apparently associated with Paul's second text: "About this time I will return and Sarah shall have a son." Genesis 18:10 and the figure of Sarah were associated with the theme of the steadfastness of God's work in Genesis *Rabbah* and in other places (see Stegner, 47).

Paul's use of Scripture, of midrashic techniques and of contemporary exegetical traditions in Romans 9:6-29 yielded a highly sophisticated composition. It cannot have been the product of an uneducated mind. If he was not trained by Gamaliel, then he was taught by some other Jewish master. In any case, it seems clear that Paul received a formal education in the Judaism of the time.

3. Paul's Apocalyptic Worldview.

Did Paul's apocalyptic (*see* Apocalypticism) worldview constitute a central motif in his thinking and theology? In answering this question scholars sometimes begin by defining the term, then match their definition with passages from Paul and thereby conclude that apocalypticism did or did not constitute a central focus in his thinking. However, since definitions vary from one scholar to another, it is better to start with the centrality of Paul's belief in the resurrection of Jesus and work outward from there.

W. Pannenberg is surely correct in pointing out that in first-century Judaism the *resurrection could be expressed only in the language of the apocalyptic tradition (Pannenberg, 96). Indeed, the belief in a resurrection was part of the apocalyptic hope and worldview. For example, the disciples already had to have an understanding of resurrection before they could identify Jesus' empty tomb and appearances as constituting a resurrection. The hundreds of ossuaries (receptacles holding bones of the dead) discovered by archeologists in the environs of Jerusalem may be material evidence of this first-century Jewish hope in a future resurrection.

That the resurrection was a central element in Paul's message is a truism. First Corinthians 15 alone illustrates the point, and Paul again and again mentions resurrection: Christ's saving death and resurrection seem to have been the focus of his preaching.

Moreover, Jesus' resurrection is the first fruits that foreshadows and authenticates the resurrection of all those who belong to him (1 Cor 15:23). This resurrection will involve a transformation like the transformation that Jesus' body underwent in the tomb. Paul makes this point in Philippians 3:20-21: "We await a Savior, the Lord Jesus Christ, who will change our lowly body to be like his glorious body, by the power which enables him even to subject all things to himself." In apocalyptic fashion Paul is speaking of a bodily resurrection and transformation in so far as one can speak of a spiritual body as a body.

Further, the resurrection of Jesus as first fruit of the eschaton heightened the expectation for the general resurrection at the end of this age and the accompanying transformation of all creation (*see* Eschatology). Thus Paul believed the end of this age was very near. According to 1 Thessalonians 4:13-18, Paul expected to be alive (1 Thess 4:15) to see Jesus return. Then two related events would occur: first, the "dead in Christ will rise" and, second, the living will be transformed (so also 1 Cor 15:51). This raising of the dead and transformation of the living was to be accompanied by the transformation of nature and all creation: "the creation itself will be set free from its bondage to decay and obtain the glorious liberty of the children of God" (Rom 8:21). This is clearly apocalypticism.

Paul shared the apocalyptic belief in the two ages: this present evil age will be transformed by an act of God into the age to come, or kingdom of God (*see* Kingdom of God). Thus Paul says that "the whole creation has been groaning in travail" (Rom 8:22) and waiting "with eager longing for the revealing of the children of God" (Rom 8:19).

Perhaps the key ingredient in apocalypticism was the category of revelation. Most apocalyptic writings reveal the future. Paul also reveals the future.

In describing God's purpose for the future, Paul, like other apocalypticists, used the word *mystery* (*mystērion*, e.g., Rom 11:25). Paul's use of the term is Jewish and apocalyptic in background. Generally speaking, the Jewish apocalypses portrayed God's purposes for history as well as the nearness of the end of this age. They used the term *mystery* to designate a purpose or secret of God that could not be known by human reason but had to be revealed by God.

According to the mystery that Paul is revealing, God has formed a new people in Christ, and the unbelief of the Jewish people has caused the gospel to be preached to the Gentiles. However, in the end time "all Israel," presumably the Jewish people who do not believe in Christ, will be drawn to faith in him by God (*see* Israel).

Many interpreters conclude that Paul was speaking of a secret or revelation that he had received from God. Others are not sure. Regardless of how Paul received the mystery, this term was the common currency of apocalyptic language.

Nevertheless, in the use of traditional apocalyptic language and imagery there is a difference between Paul and other apocalypticists. In Paul the sharp separation between this age and the age to come is lacking. The resurrection of Jesus, more specifically, his crucifixion and resurrection, introduced a new factor into the equation. There is an overlap between the two ages: the new age is proleptically present in Christ's work of reconciliation. Indeed, the transformation of believers is secretly taking place within them: "And we all . . . beholding the glory of the Lord, are being changed into his likeness from one degree of glory to another" (2 Cor 3:18).

4. Paul's Self-Understanding as a Jew.

The previous discussion of the term *mystery* and its surrounding context in Romans 9—11 introduces another dimension of Paul's Jewishness, namely, his ongoing Jewish self-understanding. Romans 9—11 enables us to enter into Paul's self-understanding as a Jew better than any other Pauline passage.

In introducing his discussion in Romans 9:2-3 he shares his feelings for his "own people," his "kindred according to the flesh." He agonizes over the unbelief of the Jews as only a fellow Jew could. Troubled by the general Jewish rejection of "the Christ," Paul rejects the possibility that "the word of God has failed" (Rom 9:6). In Romans 11:1 Paul also rejects the proposition that God has "rejected his people." The solution is simple: the unbelief of the Jews has caused the gospel to be preached to the Gentiles, who in turn believed. While Paul was "an apostle to the Gentiles" (Rom 11:13), he cannot forget his own people. Indeed, the turning of the Gentiles to Christ causes the Jews to become jealous: "Inasmuch then as I am an apostle to the Gentiles, I magnify my ministry in order to make my fellow Jews jealous, and thus save some of them" (Rom 11:13-14). The very vigor with which Paul pursued his Gentile apostolate has suggested to some interpreters that Paul thought he was entering into the very eschatological purpose of God in saving all Israel. Paul not only had "unceasing anguish" for his "kinsmen by race," but he gave himself for their salvation, a side effect of his Gentile mission being the conversion of Jews.

At this point, recent scholarship has tended to take divergent paths. Some scholars hold that Paul is advocating a two-covenant people of God: the Gentiles approach God through faith, while the Jews approach him through Torah (Gaston, Gager, Stendahl). Surely, the majority of NT scholars are correct in holding that any two-covenant approach founders on the rock of Romans 10 (*see* Law).

If the Jews must come to faith in Christ in or-

der to be saved, how will God accomplish this? Paul knows the election of the Jews still holds (Rom 11:28-29), and he knows the secret plan (mystery) of God (note the elements of self-understanding implied here). After "the full number of the Gentiles come in," then "all Israel will be saved" (Rom 11:25-26). Will jealousy over the "full number of the Gentiles" turn the Jews to faith? Will the second coming of Jesus occasion such faith? Paul reveals God's overall purpose for Israel but not the details. Paul continued to understand himself as a believing-in-Christ Jew, privy to the plan of God.

Even the notion of the ingathering of the Gentiles at the end of the age was a part of Paul's Jewish heritage. In some apocalyptic scenarios the Gentiles would be converted in the end time and make a pilgrimage to Jerusalem. This expectation for the ingathering of the Gentiles seems to lie behind Romans 11:25. However, in the mystery that Paul is sharing, God has formed the Jewish Christians and the Gentile converts into a new people of God in Christ. As we have seen, the unbelief of the Jewish people had caused the gospel to be preached to the Gentiles.

5. Paul's Mysticism.

Contemporary scholarship is just beginning to explore Paul's mysticism. Paul's mysticism is Jewish mysticism and derives from Palestinian Judaism. It must be defined with care.

Paul's mysticism is as well defined by what it is not as by what it is. The attempt of a previous generation to identify Paul with the mystery religions (*see* Religions, Greco-Roman) of the Hellenistic world on the basis of his use of the Greek term *mystērion* was a failure. Further, the older discussion of Paul's Christ mysticism, related to his repeated use of the phrase *"in Christ," is not the issue contemporary scholars are addressing. Rather, Paul's mysticism is best defined by (1) the experience he describes in 2 Corinthians 12:1-4 and (2) his knowledge of God's eschatological plan (described above in connection with the term *mystery*). In 2 Corinthians 12:1 Paul boasts of "visions and revelations of the Lord." He goes on to describe his being "caught up to the third heaven" (2 Cor 12:2) and then "into Paradise" (2 Cor 12:3) where "he heard things that cannot be told, which man may not utter" (2 Cor 12:4).

What is the background for this kind of experience? An emerging scholarly consensus posits Merkabah mysticism (related to Ezekiel's vision of the throne chariot, or *merkābâ*, of God) as the background for Paul's experience (see, e.g., Bowker, Segal). G. Scholem (*EncJud*) associates early Merkabah mysticism with certain circles of Pharisees, particularly with Johanan ben Zakkai, who flourished around A.D. 70, and with the later Akiba.

Today, scholars are dating Merkabah mysticism earlier than Scholem supposed. Among the *Dead Sea Scrolls fragments of a so-called *Angelic Liturgy* were found (4Q400-407 = 4QShirShab). These fragments describe the divine throne chariot—a central theme of early Jewish mysticism. This find shows that Paul could have been acquainted with Merkabah mysticism, especially since he was Johanan ben Zakkai's contemporary.

This early Jewish mysticism was centered in Palestine and found expression in apocalyptic literature such as the Enoch tradition (e.g., *1 Enoch* 70—71; *2 Enoch* 22; *3 Enoch*). Certain Pharisaic circles focused on the first chapter of Ezekiel, which tells of the throne chariot (the *merkābâ*) of God. Scholem also reports that the early literature speaks of an "ascent to the Merkabah" (Scholem 1961, 46).

This form of early Jewish mysticism fits together with Paul's autobiographical statements. In Philippians 3:5-6 Paul tells us that he was a zealous Pharisee and blameless "as to righteousness under the law." In 2 Corinthians 11:22, a passage immediately preceding his description of his visions, Paul emphasizes his descent from Abraham: "Are they descendants of Abraham? So am I." Early Jewish mysticism was practiced in certain Pharisaic circles. Nevertheless, not every Pharisee was permitted to study Ezekiel 1 because of the dangers involved (cf. *m. Ḥag.* 2:1). If the exegete should see again the vision of the throne chariot and not be in a state of ritual purity, he might die: "You cannot see my face; for man shall not see me and live" (Ex 33:20). Hence Johanan ben Zakkai taught mystical contemplation only to "his most favored pupils." J. W. Bowker has emphasized the importance of the Jewish credentials of the exegete, such as his direct descent from Abraham. Paul's credentials well fit these requirements.

However, even more important than Paul's credentials for establishing a connection with Merkabah mysticism are the words he uses in 2 Corinthians 12:1-4. Three expressions stand out: being "caught up" *(harpazō)*, "the third heaven" *(tritos ouranos)* and "paradise" *(paradeisos)*. J. D. Tabor has shown that these words belonged to the vocabulary of Jewish mysticism and cites the first-century *Life of Adam and Eve* (25:3) as an illustration:

> And I saw a chariot like the wind and its wheels were fiery. I was carried off into the Paradise of righteousness, and I saw the Lord sitting and his appearance was unbearable flaming fire. And many thousands of angels were at the right and at the left of the chariot (*OTP* 2:266-8).

In this excerpt the mystic is not talking about the future but the dwelling of God in paradise, perhaps in the seventh heaven. Other visions associate paradise with the third heaven.

Finally, the book of Acts records that Paul experienced visions. While all visions are not the same, the overlap in vocabulary plus Paul's credentials indicate that his vision in 2 Corinthians 12:1-4 was the kind associated with Merkabah mysticism. Furthermore, Paul's apocalyptic worldview and his concept of mystery (revelation of God's future plan) are additional indications of his orientation to mysticism.

There is a fascinating interplay between the facets of Paul the Jew that we have examined so far. His autobiographical statements disclose his Pharisaism, his zeal and his righteousness under the law. His writings reveal his exegetical prowess and his appropriation of the exegetical traditions by means of which he interpreted the passages of the Septuagint. All this is evidence of his formal training in the Judaism of his day. Of course, this formal training was a precondition for his instruction in Merkabah mysticism. Moreover, his mysticism and his apocalyptic worldview fit together like hand in glove. Since revelation of God's plan for the future is an essential ingredient in apocalypticism, the one depends on the other.

Two striking observations emerge from the above summary. The first concerns how well Paul fits into the first-century, pre-A.D. 70 (Palestinian) Judaism that we know from other sources. For example, the same combination of zeal for the law, apocalyptic worldview and mysticism characterized the Qumran sectarians. While not an Essene, Paul stands forth as a devoutly religious Pharisee of the time. The second striking observation concerns how well the pieces all fit together into a harmonious whole. Heretofore Paul has been pictured as a marginal man, living uncomfortably in two worlds—the Hellenistic and the Jewish. Heretofore Paul has been pictured as a man characterized by conflicting goals and serious internal contradictions. This is not the picture that emerges from the above study.

Now we are ready to examine the element that shattered the unity of his preconversion synthesis—his relationship to Torah. Still, nothing more cogently depicts Paul the Jew than his continuing preoccupation with Torah. On the one hand, he cannot reject Torah altogether and, on the other hand, he cannot accept it as he formerly did.

6. Paul and Torah.

The literature on the subject of Paul and Torah, or law, is immense. Our purpose here is not to review this literature (see, e.g., Dunn, Sanders), but to outline the significant issues in the contemporary debate (*see* Law). Indeed, a new perspective on Paul and the law is coming into focus out of the contemporary debate.

The dilemma for scholarship is posed by Paul's apparently contradictory statements about the law. On the one hand, Paul appears to have had a positive view of the law: "So the law is holy, and the commandment is holy and just and good" (Rom 7:12). "Do we then overthrow the law by this faith? By no means! On the contrary we uphold the law" (Rom 3:31). On the other hand, Paul wrote negatively about the law and appears to have attacked the law: "By works of the law shall no one be justified" (Gal 2:16). "For Christ is the end [in the sense of termination] of the law, that every one who has faith may be justified" (Rom 10:4). Did Paul contradict himself?

According to the traditional view Paul made a radical break with the positive OT view of law. Paul rejected the law and saw Christ as the termination or end of the law. The traditional view is best articulated by R. Bultmann and other German Lutheran exegetes. The Jews obeyed the law to accumulate merit for themselves and thereby earn salvation. Indeed, the Pharisee was a worse sinner than most because the Pharisee best exemplified the human striving to assert independence from God and to be free of dependence upon God's grace.

E. P. Sanders has challenged this traditional interpretation of law in the name of covenantal nomism. After an exhaustive examination of the Jewish literature of the period, Sanders has challenged Bultmann's understanding of first-century Judaism: Bultmann has read Luther's conflict with Catholicism back into the first century. The covenant, the law, the special status as elect people of God (hence the term *covenantal nomism*) were all gifts of God's grace to Israel. The Jews did not have to earn what they already had: the law was simply the means of maintaining their covenantal status.

What then was Paul condemning when he spoke of "works of the law"? In answering this question, J. D. G. Dunn, who accepts Sanders's understanding of first-century Judaism, carries the argument further than Sanders. Dunn points out that the phrase "works of the law" occurs three times in Galatians 2:16. More importantly, the issue is table fellowship between Jewish Christians and Gentile Christians: in this context Paul was opposing Jewish Christians who insist on maintaining the food laws. The heart of the matter for Paul is the inclusion of Gentiles in the messianic community on an equal footing with Jewish Christians. The Jewish Christians wanted the Gentiles to become Jews before they could share in the table fellowship with observant Jewish Christians. Thus the issue was not merit-based righteousness so much as racial exclusiveness. According to Dunn, the problem for Paul was those observances of the law that set Jews apart from Gentiles.

For Dunn the issue Paul addressed was not how one was saved: the issue was sociological. The "works of the law" were circumcision, purity and food laws, and sabbath observance. In the ancient world the pagan writers regarded these very practices as distinctly Jewish. These "works of the law" marked "the boundaries of the covenant people" (Dunn, 193). Paul was saying no to the law inasmuch as it set boundaries for the covenant people. Thus Paul was saying no and yes to the law at the same time. According to Dunn, Paul said no to the law where it reinforced Jewish nationalism and exclusiveness, but yes to the law where it expressed the will of God.

How could Paul the Jew do this? How could he say no to some provisions of the law and yes to other provisions of the same law? The answer seems to lie in Paul's apocalyptic worldview. A shift had taken place from the old age to the new age in Christ. Law or Torah was superseded by Christ. Paul's statement in Romans 10:4 is crucial: "For Christ is the end of the law, that everyone who has faith may be justified." Paul was not speaking of "the end" as termination of the law but as the goal or fulfillment of the law. While the law still defined God's will, it no longer functioned salvifically. The new age had arrived, and the law had been superseded by God's new gift: Christ. Thus Paul can write in 1 Corinthians 15:20-22:

> But in fact Christ has been raised from the dead, the first fruits of those who have fallen asleep. For as by a man came death, by a man has come also the resurrection of the dead. For as in Adam all die, so also in Christ shall all be made alive.

The new perspective first advanced by Sanders and then furthered by Dunn does not answer all questions concerning Paul and Torah. But it does answer some. It tends to solve Paul's so-called contradictory attitude toward the law, as stated above. This new perspective also allows for some continuity between the generally positive attitude toward the law in the OT and Paul's attitude. Paul opposed the more nationalistic and exclusivistic parts of the law because God's new act in Christ had extended the covenant to Gentiles: Grace had superseded ritual and race.

Dunn's observation that Paul affirmed the law where it expressed the will of God is strikingly confirmed by the recent research of P. Tomson. For example, in 1 Corinthians 5:1-5 Paul writes about a man who "is living with his father's wife." The issue is forbidden sexual relationships according to Leviticus 18:1-18. Paul tells the church to excommunicate the man. Tomson discovers point-by-point agreement between Paul's discussion and later Jewish legal tradition that explicates forbidden sexual relationships. This is only one example of the continuity between Paul's ethical teachings and Jewish legal tradition.

Finally, this new perspective enables us to see Paul more clearly as a first-century Jew. Jewish scholars have long argued that Paul misunderstood Judaism and his view of the law differed from that of most first-century Jews. Actually, according to Dunn, the German Lutheran portrayal of Paul has been the problem. Paul was an authentic first-century Jew; there was no serious discontinuity between Paul and his Jewish past. He was a son of Abraham who objected to narrowing the covenant to the Jewish nation: Abraham was to be a blessing to all the families of the earth.

Among other questions that still remain is Paul's teaching directed toward Jewish Christianity. Was Paul asking Jewish Christians to abandon the boundary markers of the law in their own practice? Did he teach that they should cease circumcising their sons and observing the dietary laws in their homes? Or was he speaking about fellowship between Jewish Christians and Gentile Christians in such places as Antioch and other mixed congregations? The question can be asked more pointedly: Did Paul abandon the boundary markers ("works of the law") for himself? Or did he continue to observe them in so far as they did not interfere with his Gentile apostolate? At this point, there does not seem to be a clear answer to this question.

Only a few Jewish Christian voices have survived to tell us how Jewish Christianity reacted to Paul's views concerning the law. Whether those surviving voices are representative of the various groups composing Jewish Christianity, we do not know. However, these few voices, while they stressed the Jewishness of Jesus, regarded Paul as a villain (Flusser, chap. 13). Some Jewish Christians looked upon Peter as their leader, and others preferred James, the leader of the church in Jerusalem.

Do these few muffled Jewish Christian voices constitute the last Jewish pronouncements about Paul the Jew? We hope not. With the scholarly rediscovery of the Judaism of Paul's day, perhaps some Jewish voices contemporary with Paul will offer a more positive evaluation of Paul the Jew.

See also APOCALYPTICISM; CONVERSION AND CALL OF PAUL; ISRAEL; JUDAISM AND THE NEW TESTAMENT; LAW; PAUL IN ACTS AND LETTERS; RABBINIC TRADITIONS AND WRITINGS.

DPL: CIRCUMCISION; DIASPORA; HELLENISM; MYSTERY; MYSTICISM; OLD TESTAMENT IN PAUL; PURITY AND IMPURITY; QUMRAN AND PAUL; RESTORATION OF ISRAEL; VISIONS, ECSTATIC EXPERIENCE; WORKS OF THE LAW.

BIBLIOGRAPHY. **Texts:** Babylonian Talmud: Sanhedrin (Hebrew-English Edition of the Babylonian Talmud; London: Soncino Press, 1969); Midrash Rabba Genesis (The Midrash Rabba, 1 Genesis; London: Soncino Press, 1977); *Life of Adam and Eve, OTP* 2:266-68. **Studies:** J. C. Beker, *Paul the Apostle* (Philadelphia: Fortress, 1980); J. W. Bowker, " 'Merkabah' Visions and the Visions of Paul," *JSS* (1971) 157-73; H. Conzelmann, *1 Corinthians* (Herm; Philadelphia: Fortress, 1975); J. D. G. Dunn, *Jesus, Paul and the Law* (Louisville, KY: Westminster John Knox, 1990); E. E. Ellis, *Prophecy and Hermeneutic in Early Christianity* (Tübingen: J. C. B. Mohr, 1978); D. Flusser, *Jewish Sources in Early Christianity* (New York: Adama Books, 1987); J. Gager, *The Origins of Anti-Semitism: Attitudes Towards Judaism in Pagan and Christian Antiquity* (New York: Oxford University Press, 1983); L. Gaston, *Paul and the Torah* (Vancouver: University of British Columbia, 1987); G. F. Hawthorne, *Philippians* (WBC 43; Waco, TX: Word, 1983); M. Hengel, *Judaism and Hellenism* (Philadelphia: Fortress, 1981); R. N. Longenecker, *Paul, Apostle of Liberty* (Grand Rapids: Baker, 1976); J. Neyrey, *Paul, In Other Words: A Cultural Reading of His Letters* (Louisville, KY: Westminster John Knox, 1990); W. Pannenberg, *Jesus—God and Man* (Philadelphia: Westminster, 1968); E. Rivkin, "Pharisees," *IDBSup* 657-63; E. P. Sanders, *Paul and Palestinian Judaism* (Philadelphia: Fortress, 1977); G. G. Scholem, *Major Trends in Jewish Mysticism* (New York: Schocken, 1961); idem, "Merkabah Mysticism," *EncJud* 11 cols. 1386-89; A. F. Segal, *Paul the Convert: The Apostolate and Apostasy of Saul the Pharisee* (New Haven, CT: Yale University Press, 1990); W. R. Stegner, "Romans 9:6-29: A Midrash," *JSNT* 22 (1984) 37-52; K. Stendahl, *Paul Among Jews and Gentiles and Other Essays* (Philadelphia: Fortress, 1976); J. D. Tabor, *Things Unutterable: Paul's Ascent to Paradise in Its Greco-Roman, Judaic and Early Christian Contexts* (Lanham, MD: University Press of America, 1986); P. Tomson, *Paul and the Jewish Law: Halakha in the Letters of the Apostle to the Gentiles* (Minneapolis: Fortress, 1990); G. Vermes, *Jesus and the World of Judaism* (Philadelphia: Fortress, 1984). W. R. Stegner

JEWISH GNOSTICISM. *See* ADVERSARIES I.

JEWISH HISTORY. *See* JUDAISM AND THE NEW TESTAMENT.

JOHANNINE COMMUNITY. *See* JOHN, LETTERS OF.

JOHN, GOSPEL OF

The Gospel of John has long been prized by Christians for its distinctive portrayal of Jesus.

John characterizes Jesus as the light of the world; way, truth and life; resurrection; vine; good shepherd; and bread of life. John presents extensive narrative and sayings material found in no other Gospel, and it includes some of the best-loved stories in the Gospels, such as the encounter with the woman at the well and the raising of Lazarus, as well as some of the most familiar sayings of the NT, including Jesus' majestic "I am" statements. And yet controversy has long swirled around problems of John's origin, historicity and theology.

    1. Origin of John
    2. Structure of John
    3. Genre and Character of John
    4. Theology of John

1. Origin of John.

As with the other Gospels, there are questions about the purpose, intended readers, date and authorship of the Gospel of John. But with John these questions become particularly acute due to its unique content, distinctive presentation of Jesus and the significant differences between it and the other three (Synoptic) Gospels. In this section we shall briefly take up the questions of authorship, date, place of origin and purpose of the Gospel. We shall deal with related issues, such as the nature of the tradition found only in John and John's relationship to the other three Gospels in section 3 below.

1.1. Authorship. The Gospel comes to us anonymously, as do all the Gospels and, in fact, much ancient literature. The title "According to John" (*kata Iōannēn*) is derived from the tradition that the Gospel was written by the apostle John, the son of Zebedee. This tradition has been challenged for the following reasons: The evidence of the earliest sources and church fathers (external evidence) is deemed ambiguous, inadequate, wrong, legendary or polemical. Those statements within the Gospel that might allude to its authorship (internal evidence) are also ambiguous and perhaps even point away from authorship by one of the Twelve. The content of the Gospel suggests that it was not written by an eyewitness or by one of the twelve disciples of Jesus. We shall look briefly at the external and internal evidence for authorship and discuss the content of the Gospel in section 3 below.

1.1.1. External Evidence. There are full discussions of the problems of assessing the external evidence in the commentaries of Barrett, Beasley-Murray, Brown and Schnackenburg. None of these scholars holds to authorship by John, the son of Zebedee. Discussion of the issue usually begins with the following statement from Irenaeus (c. A.D. 130-200): "John, the disciple of the Lord, who leaned on his breast, also published the Gospel while living at Ephesus in Asia" (Irenaeus *Haer.* 3.1.1; quoted in Eusebius *Hist. Eccl.* 5.8.4.). Irenaeus also writes (in a letter to a friend, Florinus) of hearing Polycarp (d. 155) recount his interaction with "John and with the others who had seen the Lord, how he remembered their words, and what were the things concerning the Lord which he had heard from them," and of which he took notes "not on paper but in my heart" (Eusebius *Hist. Eccl.* 5.20.6-7; cf. 4.14.3-5). We have, then, in Irenaeus a man who claims to have traditions from John—whom Irenaeus assumes to be the apostle John, the son of Zebedee—mediated through Polycarp. But questions have been raised about the source and reliability of this information from Irenaeus, especially in light of the following facts.

Other Christian literature which we know to have had its origin or destination in Ephesus, such as the Epistle of Ignatius to the Ephesians, mentions no ministry of the apostle John there, although Ignatius does stress the church's ties to the apostle Paul. Although not inexplicable, the absence of any reference to John is odd if John was known to have ministered there and if his place was firmly fixed in Ephesus.

Irenaeus's testimony depends on secondhand information that he received as a young boy from the aged Polycarp. But it is possible that Irenaeus either did not remember or understand correctly Polycarp's references to "John." For Irenaeus also says that Papias was "a hearer of John and companion of Polycarp" (Irenaeus *Haer.* 5.33.4). But as Eusebius (*Hist. Eccl.* 3.39.33) notes, Papias—according to his own words—was not a "hearer of John" the apostle but of John the presbyter, who was living in Papias's day (Eusebius *Hist. Eccl.* 3.39.4). Perhaps this is the John meant by Polycarp as well.

Other testimonies to the apostolic authorship of the Gospel seem to be either legendary or polemical, such as Clement of Alexandria's (c. A.D. 155-220) famous assertion that after the other Gospels were written, "John, perceiving that the bodily facts had been made plain in the Gospels,

being urged by his friends, and inspired by the Spirit, composed a spiritual gospel" (Eusebius *Hist. Eccl.* 6.14.7). The Muratorian Canon (c. A.D. 180-200) provides a more elaborate version of the same tradition, in which the other apostles fast and pray with John and then urge him to act as their spokesperson and write a Gospel. Such stories seem to be nothing other than legends, intended, perhaps, to bolster the case for the apostolic authorship of the Fourth Gospel.

Mistakes in these testimonies, lack of corroborating evidence and fanciful narratives do not necessarily impugn the tradition of apostolic authorship, but neither do they inspire confidence in it. It will be seen that the internal evidence leaves us with similar ambiguity.

1.1.2. Internal Evidence. Evidence within the Gospel about its authorship is of two kinds: direct statements about the composition of the Gospel and statements about the "disciple whom Jesus loved" (commonly called the "Beloved Disciple"). These statements come together in John 21:24, where we read that "this is the disciple who is bearing witness to these things, and who has written these things; and we know that his testimony is true" (RSV), and John 21:20, where "the disciple" is identified as "the disciple whom Jesus loved, who had lain close to his breast at the supper" (RSV). Two questions arise. Does John 21:24 imply that "the disciple whom Jesus loved" is the author of the Gospel? Does the Gospel allow us to identify the Beloved Disciple as John, the son of Zebedee?

The first question concerns the proper interpretation of John 21:24, and several issues arise. First, what is the meaning of "these things" (*tauta*) to which the Beloved Disciple is "bearing witness" and that he "has written"? When taken in conjunction with the statements of John 21:25, that "there are also many other things which Jesus did" and that "the world itself could not contain the books that would be written" about all of these, it seems most natural to interpret John 21:24 as referring to the entire Gospel. And yet some scholars think that *tauta* refers only to John 21:21-23 (the false interpretation of Jesus' saying that must be refuted) or to John 21 (which appears to be an addendum; see 2.3 below).

But even if we take "these things" (*tauta*) as referring to the entire Gospel, does John 21:24 assert that the Beloved Disciple wrote the Gospel? That depends on the understanding of the phrase "who has written these things" (*grapsas tauta*), which may be rendered "has caused these things to be written," in which case the Beloved Disciple is indirectly responsible for the Gospel. Whoever wrote John 21:24-25 presumably did not write the rest of the Gospel, or at least the rest of John 21, since in John 21:24 the author (or authors) is testifying to the veracity of the Beloved Disciple's witness. The Gospel presents the Beloved Disciple as the witness on which it is based, but not necessarily as its author.

This leads us to the second question, whether the Beloved Disciple is John the son of Zebedee. "The disciple whom Jesus loved" is mentioned explicitly by that designation in John 13:23, as he is in John 19:26-27, John 20:1-10 and John 21:7, 20-24. Although John 19:34-37 does not speak of "the disciple whom Jesus loved," it is generally assumed that the witness mentioned there is the Beloved Disciple. John 18:15-16 is sometimes included here and, with greater reservations, John 1:35-36. We may summarize the data as follows. Nowhere does the Gospel identify the Beloved Disciple by name. Moreover, the Gospel does not explicitly refer to John, the son of Zebedee, though John 21:2 refers to the "sons of Zebedee." It is disputed whether the Gospel presents the Beloved Disciple as one of the Twelve. If we assume that only the Twelve were present at the Last Supper (*see* Last Supper), then the Beloved Disciple must be one of the Twelve. But this assumption is neither supported nor refuted by the Gospel, which refers to those at the Supper as "his own" (Jn 13:1) and his "disciples" (Jn 13:35), a term not limited in John to the Twelve. The Beloved Disciple is consistently presented as a model of faith and discipleship, leading some to assert that the Beloved Disciple is a purely ideal, and not historical, figure. His designation as "the disciple whom Jesus loved" puts him in a position of unique intimacy with Jesus, describing his relationship to Jesus on the same terms that Jesus' relationship to the Father is described (Jn 1:18). The suggestion that this veiled allusion is a way of preserving the author's modesty seems strained. It would be far less presumptuous to name oneself than to continually speak of oneself as enjoying the most intimate of relationships to Jesus. Others would more naturally bestow such a term of honor.

A common understanding of the Beloved Disciple is that he is a person who heard and followed Jesus, although he was not one of the Twelve. That there clearly were such persons is obvious from the rest of the NT (Acts 1:21-26). He exercised a role of leadership in one group of early Christian congregations, probably gathering a circle of disciples around him. One (or more) of his disciples wrote the Gospel, but who this author is remains unknown to us. He preserved, shaped and interpreted the witness of his master, the Beloved Disciple, who had in turn interpreted the teaching of the Master.

1.2. Date and Place. As with all the Gospels, it is difficult to fix the date at which John was written, especially since the process of writing and editing the Gospel—whether by one person or several—seems to have occurred over some period of time. The time at which the Gospel was actually published and circulated may be somewhat later than the time of writing.

1.2.1. The Date of the Gospel. Earlier in the twentieth century it was fashionable to date the Fourth Gospel in the second century, due to its developed theology, presumed dependence on one (or more) of the Synoptic Gospels, lack of evidence of its use by early second-century writers and lack of early manuscript evidence. But the discovery of Rylands Papyrus 457 (P^{52}), an Egyptian codex fragment containing John 18:31-33, 37, 38 and dated by scholars to the early second century, suggests that John cannot have been published later than the end of the first century or very early part of the second. A manuscript of a similar date, Egerton Papyrus 2, may have used John. Together with reevaluations of the theory of a linear development of NT theology, of the view that a high or developed christology must necessarily be late, and of John's use of the Synoptics, these manuscript finds have mitigated the force of the argument for a later date, although they do not solve the problem of dating. One date that has been widely accepted by scholars of all persuasions places the Gospel in the period A.D. 90-100. The earliest external witnesses date the Gospel in this period as well. However, there have always been scholars who have argued that the Gospel can easily be dated earlier, perhaps as early as A.D. 50-60, and that it ought certainly to be placed before the first Jewish-Roman war (A.D. 66-70). In recent studies, this theory has been advanced most forcefully by J. A. T. Robinson (1985). By "priority" Robinson does not mean that John is necessarily the first of the Gospels to be written but that it is closest to the "source," namely, to Jesus.

Yet, at the same time, John exhibits the deepest theological reflection of all the Gospels. In Robinson's words, John "got it right—historically and theologically" (Robinson, xiii). Robinson also argues for the reliability of the ancient tradition that the Gospel is written by John, the son of Zebedee, the Beloved Disciple, but this is not the real focus of his concern. Instead, he is primarily interested in probing the implications of his view for reconstructing the life of Jesus.

While scholars typically use only the Synoptic Gospels when reconstructing the ministry and teaching of Jesus, Robinson argues that John ought to be regarded as a witness on a par with the other Gospels—and even to be preferred over them. He argues that we should no longer assume that the Synoptics provide the historical touchstone for understanding Jesus, with John regarded always as secondary and only to be fitted into the Synoptic picture. Instead, we ought to reconsider whether the Gospel story is not often illumined and clarified when we begin with John, and fit the picture of Jesus given in the Synoptic Gospels into its framework.

It is the merit of Robinson's work to point out that while many scholars no longer hold that John uses the other Gospels, and that it therefore supplements or interprets them, they have nevertheless not given up the related presumptions and presuppositions with which they approach the Gospel of John. They continue to use the Synoptics as the norm against which John is measured. But Robinson makes a strong case for reconsidering the historical witness of the Gospel of John to the ministry of Jesus.

Those who hope to find in an early dating (Robinson puts the Gospel's final form at about A.D. 65) a vindication of John's historical accuracy will not be disappointed. However, one must realize that Robinson's arguments are aimed at getting an equal hearing for John alongside the other Gospels, as one of four sources for understanding the historical events of Jesus' life and ministry. Its witness cannot simply be added to that of the Synoptics but must be weighed along with theirs. Thus Robinson is not interested in harmonizing the four Gospels but in arguing for John's priority in reconstructing our understanding of Jesus. As an example, one may take the cleansing of the temple (see Temple Cleansing), which the Synoptics place toward the end of Jesus' life and John puts quite early. Robinson does not argue for two cleansings but rather

that on historical grounds there is good reason to prefer the Johannine dating rather than the Synoptic chronology.

Many of Robinson's arguments carry weight even if one does not adopt all his conclusions about individual points of exegesis or historical reconstruction. While most scholars have not been persuaded to follow Robinson, he has at least reopened the question of the date of the Gospel. Most scholars continue to place the date of the Gospel post-70, and probably sometime after A.D. 85 or so. But others will ask whether John cannot comfortably be placed early in the period A.D. 70-100 rather than toward the end of that period.

1.2.2. Place. According to tradition, the Gospel was published in Ephesus, but other large centers of Christian activity that also had significant Jewish populations and representatives of various Hellenistic religions, such as Alexandria and Syrian Antioch, have also been proposed. Indeed, some scholars see the traditions of the Gospel as stemming from Palestine but being shaped into their final form in other territory, where the influence of Diaspora Judaism and Hellenistic religions was greater.

1.3. The Life Setting and Purpose of the Gospel.

1.3.1. The Life Setting of the Gospel. There are various clues in the Gospel from which we may make some tentative deductions about situations that shaped the traditions and material within the Gospel as we now know it. The Gospel often refers to "the Jews," even when "the Jews" are distinguished from other persons who are obviously also Jewish (cf. Jn 1:19; 2:13; 3:25; 6:42; 7:2, 11, 13, 15, passim). Indeed, throughout the Gospel "the Jews" are set over against those who believe in Jesus as Messiah; that is, "Jews" are set over against Christians, not Gentiles, and the term is not used simply as an ethnic or racial characterization.

The Gospel manifests perhaps the sharpest polemic in the NT against "the Jews"—a polemic matched in force only by passages such as Matthew 23 (e.g., Jn 8:42-47). The intensity of the polemic may be a reaction to Jewish measures, and particularly to expulsion from the synagogue (Jn 9:22; 12:42; 16:2) of those who had become believers in Jesus. Some scholars have suggested that the reference to being expelled from the synagogue reflects the Jewish *birkat hamminîn* ("blessing against the heretics"), said to have been promulgated at Jamnia under Rabbi Gamaliel II about A.D. 85-90. In its full form this prayer invokes God's judgment upon all heretics, including Christians and sectarian Jews. However, some scholars judge it to have been formulated much later, perhaps as late as A.D. 135. In any case, it is questionable whether the actions described in the Gospel mirror those dictated by the "benediction." The NT and early Christian literature testify to strained and hostile relationships between Christians and Jews at an earlier date, beginning with the confrontation between Stephen and certain Jews in Jerusalem (Acts 6—8).

The Gospel is concerned for second-generation and subsequent believers who were not eyewitnesses (Jn 20:26-31), including Jews and Gentiles (Jn 7:35), the other "sheep not of this fold" (Jn 10:16; cf. Jn 7:35; 11:52). The situation and role of this community's life under the guidance of the *Holy Spirit is dealt with at length (Jn 14—16). There is reference to the need for unity and love within the community (Jn 15:12-17; 17:20-23), continued faithfulness to Jesus (Jn 15:1-11; 17:11-12), the possibility of persecution (Jn 15:18-25; 16:1-4), anxiety and turmoil (Jn 14:1-7, 18-21, 27-31; 16:4-6; 16:16-24), the role of the Spirit's instruction (Jn 14:15-17, 25-26; 16:7-15) and the community's mission in the world (Jn 14:12-14, 23-24; 15:26-27; 17:15-19).

We may speculate that the community whose life and struggles are reflected in the Gospel was a community made up of Jewish and Gentile Christians. Prior to the composition or at least final editing of the Gospel, a primarily Jewish-Christian church had experienced hostile conflict with the Jews of the synagogue, to the point of ostracism and alienation. By the time the Gospel is written the hostilities between Jews and Christians are behind it, and the church includes Gentile believers. It continues to experience the pressures of existence in this world and hence needs to be reminded of the words that Jesus gave to the church about its life and mission. This leads us to a discussion of the purpose of the Gospel.

1.3.2. The Purpose of the Gospel. The Gospel presents us with a statement of its purpose in John 20:31 (RSV): "These are written that you may believe that Jesus is the Christ, the Son of God, and that believing you may have life in his name." But this broad statement leaves many details to be filled in. Some scholars have interpreted this statement to mean that the Gospel is

an evangelistic document, designed to win converts, perhaps from Diaspora Judaism. But the sharpness of the polemic against unbelieving Jews in the Gospel counts against this hypothesis. Moreover, the statement that the Gospel is written in order "that you may believe" can also be rendered "that you may continue to believe," and much of the Gospel seems designed to encourage believers to persevere in faith.

The Gospel intends to present Jesus to second and subsequent generations of believers, those who did not "see signs" but have the Gospel's written account of them (Jn 20:30-31: "these are written"). By making clear who Jesus is and the salvation that he offers, the Gospel intends to encourage and strengthen believers in their faith in Jesus as the Messiah and Son of God. As part of its exhortative function, the Gospel endeavors to clarify the relationship of Jesus to Judaism by showing his superiority to the patriarchs of the Jewish faith (Jn 4:12; 6:32; 8:53-58), the replacement in his person of Jewish feasts and religious institutions (Jn 2:1-11, 19-22; 6:32-41; 7:37-39), and the relationship between the law and Moses on the one hand and Jesus Christ on the other (Jn 1:17; 5:39-40, 45-47; 7:19-23). Probably these traditions were shaped by disputes with the synagogue. Yet the Gospel clearly indicates the place that Gentile believers are to have in the community of faith.

Other theories, not necessarily incompatible with the broad statement of purpose outlined above, have been advanced as well. (1) An older view was that John is the Gospel in Hellenized form. While this theory has been questioned, due to a reevaluation of the influence of Hellenism on Judaism and of the character of the Gospel, there are unquestionably striking contacts with Hellenistic religion and philosophy (for example, in the Logos doctrine). (2) The Gospel endeavors to make clear the proper relationship between *John the Baptist and Jesus (Jn 1:6-8, 15, 19-28, 30; 3:22-30; 5:33-36; 10:40-42). Although some have interpreted these statements as an anti-Baptist polemic, directed against a group claiming John to be the Messiah, such an evaluation goes too far. The Gospel presents John positively as a witness—virtually equivalent to "disciple" in John—to Jesus. (3) Similarly, the Gospel repeatedly defines the role of the Beloved Disciple vis-á-vis that of Peter (Jn 13:23-25; 20:3-8; 21:7, 20-23), which has been taken as evidence of some conflict between the churches represented by the Beloved Disciple and by Peter. The Gospel does bolster the case for the Beloved Disciple's authority and distinctive role, perhaps to show that he was in no way inferior to Peter and the Twelve. (4) Some see in those verses of John that insist on the "flesh" of Jesus (Jn 1:14; 6:51-58) an antidocetic polemic. But the Gospel seems not so much intent on proving the true humanity or physicality of Jesus as it does in pressing the case for the heavenly origin and identity of the incarnate Word. These statements are not directed against docetists but against those who do not share the Christian confession of Jesus as the Word made flesh (Jn 1:14). (5) Others suggest that the Gospel contains an apologetic against or for the sacramental teaching of the church, and the material in John 6:51-58 certainly has eucharistic overtones. But it is difficult to discern a theology of the sacraments from the passages on water (which seem to refer more to the Holy Spirit than to baptism) and blood.

The Gospel may have been edited over a period of years to include materials that met changing or different circumstances. Its basic purpose, to tell the story of Jesus in such a way that his identity as Messiah and Son of God is made known to later generations, shines through, regardless of the many individual polemics and situations that may also have shaped the production of the Gospel. Indeed, the very structure of the Gospel points to the purpose of the Gospel to define who Jesus is, and to do so in categories that arise out of Judaism, but speak to a broader religious milieu as well.

2. Structure of John.

The Gospel is essentially divided into two main parts, with a prologue (Jn 1:1-18) and an epilogue (Jn 21). The first main part, John 1:19—12:50, was designated by C. H. Dodd as the "Book of Signs," and the second part, John 13—20, as "The Book of the Passion" or "The Book of Glory" (Brown). Each book ends with a summary statement (Jn 12:37-50; 20:30-31). All the signs or miracles of Jesus are narrated in the first part, while the second part begins with the *Last Supper and concentrates on the events leading up to and including the passion narrative and the resurrection appearances. "Book of Glory" is an apt designation for the second part of the book, since in Johannine theology Jesus' glorification occurs as he returns to the Father through his death, resurrection and ascension.

2.1. The Prologue (Jn 1:1-18). Parts of these verses appear to come from an early Christian hymn, or at least from creedal or confessional material of the church. And since some of the vocabulary (such as Logos and grace) does not appear again in the Gospel, some interpreters argue that the prologue was affixed to the Gospel after it was completed. But even if the prologue has underlying sources, as it stands, it introduces the main themes, movement and chief protagonist of the Gospel. Opening with an echo of Genesis 1:1, the prologue goes on to identify its protagonist as the "Logos," the Word of God, and thus places the drama in a cosmic setting and against an OT background. The prologue foreshadows the division between belief and unbelief so characteristic of the rest of the Gospel (Jn 1:10-11). This division rests on one's response to and understanding of Jesus Christ (Jn 1:12-13). The prologue argues for its confession of Jesus by prohibiting false evaluations of John the Baptist (Jn 1:6-8, 15), showing the relationship of Jesus to Moses and the law (Jn 1:17-18) and calling for belief in Jesus Christ as the Logos of God made flesh (Jn 1:1, 14). Throughout each episode of the Gospel the drama hinted at in the prologue is replayed as the various persons that Jesus encounters endeavor to understand who Jesus is. Some (the Samaritan woman, the man born blind, Martha, Thomas) eventually come to a confession that, if not phrased in the words of the prologue, is consonant with it, while others reject precisely the prologue's evaluation of Jesus Christ as the Word and Son of God (e.g., the disciples of Jn 6:66; the Jewish authorities of Jn 7:32, 35-52; 11:45-53).

2.2. The Book of Signs (Jn 1:19—12:50). The arrangement of much of the first part of the Gospel is topical and thematic. The placement of some events (e.g., Jesus' baptism) is due to chronological considerations, while that of others (the cleansing of the temple, the raising of Lazarus) may be due to theological reasons or for dramatic effect. John thus introduces early in the Gospel the theme that Jesus replaces, in his person, the religious observances of Judaism. With the narrative of the changing of the water to wine (Jn 2:1-11), Jesus is seen transforming the water set aside for the Jewish rites of purification into the wine symbolic of the presence of the messianic age (Amos 9:13-14; Hos 14:7; Jer 31:12).

The rest of the book of signs (Jn 2:12—12:50) refers to various feasts of the Jewish calendar (Jn 2:13; 5:1; 6:4; 7:2; 10:22; 11:55). These references serve to move the story along chronologically, as well as to introduce imagery from the ceremonies that become the backdrop for Jesus' self-revelation in signs and discourses, which provoke his disputes with opponents. Thus, for example, the sabbath (the probable feast of Jn 5:1) becomes the occasion for a sabbath healing and subsequent disputes about Jesus' authority to work on the sabbath, to give life and to raise the dead—all privileges deemed reserved for God (Jn 5). Near Passover Jesus feeds the five thousand and gives a long discourse on being the "bread from heaven," actions and words that recall the exodus from Egypt on the original Passover and the giving of manna to provide for the people of God (Jn 6). The Feast of Tabernacles included ceremonies that featured water and light, and it is at this feast that Jesus promises living water (Jn 7:37-39) and proclaims that he is the light of the world (Jn 8:12; 9:5). Following the climactic deed of the raising of Lazarus from the dead, there comes a transitional chapter (Jn 12) that summarizes the results of Jesus' ministry in terms of unbelief and belief. Jesus' public ministry is over, and he will now engage in extensive private instruction to his disciples (Jn 13—17).

2.3. Book of Glory (Jn 13—20). The Book of Glory is divided into three subsections: John 13, the Last Supper with the disciples; John 14—17, the so-called Farewell Discourses of Jesus to the disciples; (3) chapters 18—20, the narratives of the passion and resurrection. The Last Supper that Jesus eats with his disciples is apparently not a Passover meal but occurs twenty-four hours prior to the eating of the Passover. There is no institution of the Lord's Supper but rather the story of Jesus' washing the disciples' feet, which prefigures Jesus' sacrificial death and provides an example for the disciples to imitate in community. John 14—17 then provides exhortations about community life, instruction about the role of the Holy Spirit in teaching and guiding the community, warnings about persecution and trouble and encouragement to remain faithful to Jesus. John 17 is a prayer that the disciples will be kept safe and remain faithful. The passion narratives and resurrection appearances share features in common with the Synoptic Gospels, even though they have numerous incidents and scenes distinctive to John.

2.4. Epilogue (Jn 21). For several reasons the last chapter of the Gospel appears to many to be an appendix of additional narratives not included in the earlier draft of the Gospel. (1) The Gospel appears to end with the summary statement at John 20:30-31. (2) The additional resurrection appearance is more like a first appearance, since the disciples do not recognize Jesus, although they have previously seen and recognized the risen Lord. (3) The narrative of Peter's restoration seems out of place, for it would have belonged more naturally prior to the giving of the Spirit and commissioning of the disciples. (4) Finally, it appears that a new problem has arisen within the church, namely, the death of the Beloved Disciple. John 21 has been added to correct a rumor that circulated concerning a prophecy that Jesus had made about the death of the Beloved Disciple.

At least John 21:24-25 are added later. They may reflect the fact that the Beloved Disciple has recently died, although he was alive when the first edition of the Gospel was being written, as the present tense in John 19:35 suggests. His death appears to contradict Jesus' prediction that the Beloved Disciple would remain alive until he returned, but the author of the Gospel (or of these verses) notes that this is not what Jesus had said.

But most of John 21 deals not with the death of the Beloved Disciple but with Peter and with Jesus' prophecy about his death. Just as Peter denied Jesus three times, so now he is asked three times whether he loves Jesus. The commands to "tend my sheep" and "feed my lambs" may be reported to show that Peter's role was understood to be that of shepherd, whereas the Beloved Disciple is understood chiefly as a witness. Nevertheless, Peter was commanded above all else to "follow me" (Jn 21:19), just as the Beloved Disciple is shown doing in the next verse (Jn 21:20). Thus John 21 again contrasts Peter and the Beloved Disciple, includes Jesus' prediction about each disciple's death, and shows how the Beloved Disciple was ahead of Peter in recognizing and following Jesus. The chapter does not so much denigrate Peter as it shows that the role of each disciple is distinctive but not thereby inferior to that of the other disciple.

3. Genre and Character of John.

3.1. John and the Synoptics. The difference between John and the other Gospels is significant, and it raises the question of John's relationship to them. This question is not new, nor is it merely the product of modern biblical criticism. The assertion of the early Christian writer Clement of Alexandria that John is a "spiritual Gospel" while the others recount the "physical" or "bodily" facts (Eusebius *Hist. Eccl.* 6.14.7) was an early attempt to account for the differences between all the Gospels.

3.1.1. The Johannine Difference. The particular differences between John and the other three Gospels are striking and may be set out briefly.

3.1.1.1. Material and Content. In John we do not find: parables; demon exorcisms; healings of lepers; tax collectors; Sadducees; *table fellowship with sinners; infancy narratives; the temptation of Jesus; the transfiguration; the material in Matthew's Sermon on the Mount; or the institution of the Lord's Supper. By contrast, the following material is in John but not in any of the Synoptics: Jesus' *baptismal ministry at the Jordan; the encounters with Nicodemus and the Samaritan woman; the "I am" sayings, coupled with long discourses; most of the material in John 7—11 and John 14—17; the foot washing; and Jesus' conversation with Pilate. Of the Johannine *miracles only the feeding of the five thousand is found in the other Gospels.

3.1.1.2. Vocabulary. Whereas "kingdom of God" occurs often in the Synoptics, it occurs only twice in John, and the distinctively Johannine terminology (truth, witness, world, abide, love, believe, light, darkness, life, and Father and Son) occurs far less often in the other Gospels.

3.1.1.3. Chronology and Presentation of Jesus' Ministry. While in the Synoptics Jesus goes to Jerusalem only at the end of his life (except for Luke's account of Jesus' visit to the temple as a boy), much of the ministry in John occurs in Jerusalem and Judea. The *temple cleansing is placed early in the Gospel rather than toward the end; Jesus and John the Baptist minister at the same time; the anointing occurs prior to the triumphal entry; and the Last Supper appears to be eaten twenty-four hours earlier than in the other Gospels.

3.1.1.4. Messianic Secret. Whereas in the Synoptics Jesus is first confessed as Messiah by Peter well into the course of the ministry, in John, Jesus is acknowledged with various messianic titles—six times in the first chapter alone (Jn 1:29, 34, 36, 41, 45, 49)!

3.1.2. The Question of John's Relationship with the Synoptics. Prior to the twentieth century most interpreters assumed that John was familiar with the other Gospels and that his role was to supplement and interpret them. While this theory has a broad appeal, it is difficult to explain all the differences in detail and content as either supplementation or interpretation. Sometimes the theory that John wrote to interpret the other Gospels has been coupled with a denigration of its historical value (forcing a choice between John or the Synoptics in deciding historical questions), due to the problems and difficulties in reconciling the differences between John and the other Gospels. Some scholars have gone further, suggesting that John intended to replace or supplant the other Gospels. All of these theories depend on the assumption that John knew or was familiar with the other Gospels. But in the twentieth century that theory has been challenged.

The theory that John is independent of the other Gospels was carefully argued by P. Gardner-Smith and C. H. Dodd, and it has become widely, although not unanimously, accepted. On this theory John was composed without knowledge of, or reference to, the other three written Gospels. All the similarities between them can be accounted for by shared tradition, whether written or oral, which John used without access to the Synoptics. The differences are due to variant traditions—which does not rule out eyewitness recollection—and John's highly interpretative character.

While John may have known of the other Gospels, he did not use them as sources in the way that Matthew and Luke used Mark. Study of John ought not to proceed on the assumption that the Gospel intends to be a commentary on or elucidation of the other Gospels. Neither is it helpful to repeat older explanations that while the Synoptics are biography or history, John is doctrine or theology. At least some of the difference between John and the Synoptics is a difference of the degree to which the author's interpretation has shaped the story. This leads us to the question of the character of the Gospel of John.

3.2. The Historical Character of the Gospel of John. A recognition of the differences between John and the other Gospels and of John's intensely interpretative character raises the question of the nature of the historical tradition found only in John (*see* Gospels [Genre]). If, for example, all the other Gospels record Jesus as speaking in parables and often of the *kingdom of God, but never in "I am" sayings, how are we to assess the historicity of such utterances? We should note, first of all, that simply because information is found only in John is no reason to discard it as of no historical value (see esp. Robinson). Scholars consider it probable, for example, that Jesus' ministry lasted two to three years, as John implies; that he was in and out of Jerusalem, as the other Gospels hint (e.g., Lk 13:34); that some of the disciples of Jesus were first disciples of John the Baptist (Jn 1:35-37); and that Jesus and his disciples conducted a ministry of baptism (Jn 3:22).

There is also material in John that is similar or identical to that in the Synoptics but appears in different contexts or looks like a different story. Such material includes the charges of demon possession (cf. Mk 3:22-30 and Jn 7:20; 8:48-53; 10:19-20), the unbelief of Jesus' brothers (Mk 3:31-35 and Jn 7:5), challenges to Jesus' authority (Mk 2:1—3:6; 3:22-30; 11:27-33 and Jn 5:19, 26-27, 30) and titles such as "prophet" (Mk 6:15; 8:28 and Jn 6:14; 7:40), "Messiah" (Mk 8:29; 14:61 and Jn 1:17, 41; 7:41-42) and "Son of man" (Mk 2:28; 8:31, 38; 9:31; 10:33, 45; and Jn 1:51; 3:13-14; 5:27; 6:53, 62; 9:35; 12:34). Although most of the miracles are unique to John, they have analogies in the Synoptics.

Finally, John shows an elaboration and development of themes found in the other Gospels, such as Jesus' relationship to the Father, his messianic authority, the Holy Spirit and the meaning of Jesus' miracle-working activity.

Clearly, historical traditions and reminiscences lie behind John, and information from John should not be dismissed simply because it comes from John. Nevertheless, such information must be judiciously weighed in light of what we know about the interpretative character of all the Gospels and with awareness of the contours of Jesus' ministry as it is portrayed in the Synoptics.

Much of our understanding of the Gospel of John will depend on our prior definition and understanding of the genre of the Gospels (*see* Gospel [Genre]). Where the Gospels are understood to be interpretations of the life of Jesus, for specific purposes and audiences, John will be seen to fit that genre, even though it has exercised more freedom in reworking and interpreting the traditions upon which it is based. To a more marked extent than the Synoptics, John's Gospel consciously interprets the essence of Jesus' ministry and teaching in light of later theological reflection. John explicitly acknowledges the understanding gained after the resurrection (Jn 2:22; 7:39; 12:16; 13:7) and through the instruction of the Paraclete (Jn 15:26; 16:13, 14), and some of this insight is likely incorporated into the Gospel. In many respects, John is like one of the Pauline epistles, interpreting the meaning of Jesus' life and death in terms and categories that were not typical or characteristic of Jesus. As part of our canon of Scripture, the Gospel of John bears authoritative witness to Jesus, who he is, and what he means for Christians and for the world.

4. Theology of John.

4.1. Christology. One of the most striking features of the Gospel of John is its distinctive christology. Although John shares several important titles with the other Gospels, these are sometimes used in distinctively Johannine ways. In addition, there are other images and designations for Jesus peculiar to John. Following an overview of some of the more important titles, we will summarize the central features of John's picture of Jesus.

4.1.1. Word/Logos. The only other place in the NT that the title "Word (Gk *logos*) of God" appears is in Revelation 19:13. But the term was also used in Greek philosophical thought. According to Heraclitus (sixth century B.C.), the *Logos was the eternal principle of order in the universe. The Stoics saw the "word" as the mind of God, the principle of reason within the universe, controlling and directing all things. But the idea of God's word or God's speaking has a Jewish context as well. God created the world by speaking it into existence (Gen 1; Ps 33:6). In the prophetic books, "the word of the Lord" is nearly personified as it is described as coming to a particular prophet (Hos 1:1; Joel 1:1). The word heals (Ps 107:20), obedience to it brings life (Deut 32:46-47), and it is a light that guides people to God (Ps 119:105, 130).

The Johannine description of the Word (*logos*) has further affinities with the Jewish concept of Wisdom as well. In Proverbs 8, especially Proverbs 8:22-31, Wisdom is said to have existed in the beginning, prior to the creation of the world; it was God's agent in creation; it brings life and light to those who accept it; and it was rejected by most human beings. According to Sirach 24:8, Wisdom made its dwelling among human beings. The verb for "made its dwelling" is a cognate of the term used of the Logos's "dwelling" (*skēnoō*) in John 1:14. The actual term *word* (*logos*) is that found in the OT prophets in the Greek OT (LXX), but the characterization of that *logos* in John has striking correspondences to the biblical and apocryphal descriptions of wisdom.

The utility of the term *logos* to speak to the Jewish and Greek worlds is demonstrated by the Jewish writer Philo (born c. 20 B.C.), who attempted to explain Judaism in terms of Greek philosophy in order to give a rational account of the Jewish faith. Philo spoke of the Logos as an intermediary between God and his creatures, which gave meaning to the universe and was the instrument of God in creation. Like the rabbis, Philo speculated about the two "powers" of God (in the rabbinic writings, the "two measures," or *middôt*), and identified these "powers" with the names of God. In Philo these powers are frequently characterized as the creative power and ordering or ruling power of God. In commenting on Exodus 25:22, Philo describes the ark of the covenant, identifying the two cherubim with the two powers of God, in whose midst is the Logos, and goes on to say, "And from the divine Logos as from a spring, there divide and break forth two powers. One is the creative power through which the Artificer placed and ordered all things: this is named 'God.' And the other is the royal power, since through it the Creator rules over created things; this is called 'Lord'" (*Quaest. in Ex.* 2.68; see *Fug.* 95-98, 100-101)." In the Logos are the two powers of God, to create and to rule, and for this reason the Logos can be called "God" and "Lord" (cf. Jn 1:1; 20:28). In John the Logos is the agent of creation (Jn 1:3), and the incarnate Logos is the agent of God's judgment. And in John's Gospel, the Logos is confessed as Lord and God, an important designation for Jesus in Johannine theology.

4.1.2. God. The opening words of the Gospel raise the problem of Johannine christology in acute form when they say that the Word was with God, thereby implying a distinction between the Word and God, and that the Word was God (Jn 1:1-2). The designation of Jesus as "God" occurs once more, in John 20:28, when the risen Jesus is confessed as "Lord and God." Elsewhere, Jesus is accused of "making himself

equal to God" (Jn 5:18) and "making himself God" (Jn 10:33). While the pair of titles ("Lord and God") in John 20:28 may reflect the fact that the emperor Domitian (A.D. 81-96) sought to have himself addressed as "Lord and God," the absolute designation of the Word as "God" (in Jn 1:1) requires another explanation. What the Gospel means in introducing the Word as "God" must be understood in light of the strict monotheism of Judaism that became the heritage of Christianity as well.

Here the Jewish category of agency sheds light. In the rabbinic writings there is reference to the figure of the *šālîaḥ*, which means literally "one who is sent" (*see* Apostle). A *šālîaḥ* was a surrogate sent on a task or mission with specific instructions and authority to carry it out. According to the Talmud, a *šālîaḥ* could, among other things, carry out business transactions, make binding treaties and arrange marriages (*b. Qidd.* 41a, 42b-43a). A common saying in the rabbis was "the one who is sent is like the one who sent him" or "a man's agent is equivalent to himself" (*m. Ber.* 5:5; *b. B. Meṣ.* 96a; *b. Ḥag.* 10b; *b. Menaḥ* 93b; *b. Nazir* 12b; *b. Qidd.* 42b, 43a). Because the *šālîaḥ* may act on behalf of the one who sent him, when one deals with the *šālîaḥ* it is as if one is dealing with the one who sent that person.

Jesus is presented in the Gospel against the backdrop of the Jewish concept of agency and, furthermore, against the understanding that there is one chief agent through whom God acts. Such chief agents were variously understood to be a principal angel (Gabriel, Michael), an exalted patriarch (Enoch, Moses) or personified divine attributes (Wisdom, Word). Clearly the Word is understood as God's chief and exclusive agent in creation (Jn 1:3). He is shown exercising the divine prerogatives in judging (Jn 5:22, 27, 30; 8:16, 26; 9:39; 12:47-48), in raising the dead (Jn 5:21, 25-26, 28-29; 6:27, 35, 39-40, 50-51, 54-58; 10:28; 11:25-26) and in working on the sabbath (Jn 5:9-18; 7:21-23), deeds that, according to various Jewish authors, were permitted to God alone. Because Jesus is the chief agent of God, when one confronts him, one confronts God. When the concept of agency is coupled with speculation on the names or powers of God, we see that the name of "God" for the Word is intended to show that the Word exercises the divine prerogatives. As Jesus of Nazareth, the incarnate Word continues to exercise the divine prerogatives, and exactly these actions and this claim evoke hostility from the Jewish authorities, who charge Jesus with blasphemy (Jn 10:31-38).

4.1.3. "I Am." Unique to the Gospel of John are the "I am" sayings. In those "I am" statements with a predicate (bread of life, light of the world, vine) Jesus speaks of the salvation that he offers to human beings. The "I am" sayings without predicate (Jn 8:24, 28, 58) are more difficult to interpret. In the OT, "I am" sayings are found in contexts of God's revelation to Israel. "I am" also appears, apparently, as the name of God ("I am who I am"). But note that the LXX translation of this crucial passage in Exodus 3:14 is "I am the one who is" (*egō eimi ho ōn*), thus underscoring that the essence of God's being or nature is unique, divine existence: God is.

Clearly the absolute "I am" sayings of the Gospel intend to reveal something about Jesus' person, and to do so with a formula that alludes to the OT formula of divine revelation. Yet Jesus is not simply using a familiar divine name for himself. His statement would not have been heard as "I am Yahweh." Rather, as the "I am" statements especially in John 8 reveal, Jesus claims to share in God's eternal existence. He has life in himself (Jn 5:26), and the power to lay down his life and to take it up again (Jn 10:17-18). He also has the power to give life to those who keep his word (Jn 8:51; 17:2), thus exercising the unique life-giving prerogative of God. In John 8, one of the most heated disputes with his opponents, Jesus' claim "Before Abraham was, I am" (Jn 8:58) contrasts Abraham's kind of life which "came into being" (*genesthai*) with his own, which simply "is" (*egō eimi*; present tense). These claims resonate with what is perhaps the central theme of the Gospel: that Jesus has and mediates eternal life (Jn 20:30-31; and see Jn 3:16, 36; 4:14, 53; 5:21-26; 6:33, 35, 44, 51-58, 68; 8:12; 10:10, 17-18; 11:25; 14:6; 17:2-3).

There is, therefore, a reference to the divine OT "I am" in the claim of John 8:58, but it is allusive or indirect. Jesus does not say "I am the I am." In fact, in John 8:24 and John 8:28, when Jesus uses the absolute "I am," no one reacts, except in puzzlement. It is not until he claims, in John 8:48-58, to "have seen Abraham," that is, to share in eternal life, that the people react: now he is claiming to have or give what God alone has and gives. The Johannine "I am" statements link Jesus' work and person in the most intimate

relationship with the divine person and work. They are, therefore, closely analogous to the predicate "Word" and "God" (see 4.1.1. and 4.1.2. above).

4.1.4. Son of God. In the Gospel and Epistles of John, Jesus is called the **"Son of God" (huios),* while Christians are called "children of God" (*tekna*) who are "born of God." This distinction highlights the unique relationship of Jesus to the Father, which is further underscored by the Gospel's designation of Jesus as "the only Son" or "the unique Son" (*monogenēs*). (The KJV's translation of this term as "only begotten" is due to Jerome's translation of the Greek term with the Latin *unigenitus*—"only begotten"—which the KJV then echoed. Jerome was answering the Arian assertion that Jesus was "made" not "begotten.")

The frequent characterization of the Son as "sent" from the Father has a legal flavor. As Son, Jesus can function as a unique delegate (*šālîaḥ*) on his Father's behalf and, indeed, the "Father has given all things into the Son's hands" (Jn 3:35). Nevertheless, that Jesus is Son also underlines his dependence on and obedience to the Father (Jn 5:19, "The Son can do nothing of his own accord"; cf. Jn 3:34; 7:28; 8:26, 42; 10:32, 37; 12:49). All that the Son does, he does in perfect harmony with his Father's will. Thus the Gospel speaks of reciprocal knowledge of Father and Son (Jn 10:15). Because of this intimate and reciprocal knowledge, the Son reveals the Father (Jn 1:18; 8:38; 15:15; 17:25-26). When the Gospel speaks of the unity of the Father and Son, it points especially to their unity in the work of revelation and salvation (Jn 8:16; 10:25-30; 14:10-11; 17:10). That is to say, the actions and words of Jesus were truly the actions and words of God. In the incarnate Word we are confronted by God, and the designation of Jesus as "Son" serves to underscore the intimate connection between God and Jesus.

4.1.5. Messiah. In the NT John alone presents the transliterated form of the Hebrew or Aramaic term *messias* (Jn 1:41; 4:25); **"Christ" (christos)* is used seventeen times; and the compound "Jesus Christ" occurs twice (Jn 1:17; 17:3). Whether or not Jesus is the Messiah becomes a topic of conversation and controversy far more often than in the Synoptics. The Baptist denies that he is the Messiah (Jn 1:20; 3:28); Jesus' disciples acclaim him as Messiah quite early in the narrative (Jn 1:41); the Samaritans (Jn 4:29) and

Jews (Jn 7:25-31, 40-43, 52; 12:34) discuss messiahship; and the confession of Jesus as Messiah is met with expulsion from the synagogue (Jn 9:22; cf. Jn 16:2). Yet, like the Synoptic Gospels, Jesus does not announce himself to be the Messiah or answer plainly when asked whether he is the Christ (Jn 10:24). There is a secret to Jesus' messiahship in John, and that secret is revealed to the eyes of faith. John's use of the term *Messiah* still maintains its meaning of the one anointed by God as vice regent in the messianic kingdom, and John emphasizes Jesus' kingly role (Jn 6:14-15; 18:33-37). In some places it appears that Messiah is virtually equivalent to "Son of God" (Jn 20:31), emphasizing again the unique relationship to God that this appointed agent has.

4.1.6. Son of Man. Few problems have vexed scholars as greatly as that of the title or phrase *"Son of man" in the Gospels. The central features of John's portrait of Jesus as "Son of man" may be sketched. (1) As the Son of man, Jesus serves as judge in the final judgment (Jn 5:27), a usage paralleling the Synoptic statements that the Son of man will return in glory (Mk 13:26). (2) "Son of man" is particularly linked with death, especially when it is de scribed as Jesus being "lifted up" from the earth. (3) The Son of man reveals God by serving as the mediator between earth and heaven (Jn 1:51; 3:13; 6:27, 62). These three categories should not be kept distinct from each other, however, but are obviously closely related. Jesus' glorification and death are nearly synonymous in John, for Jesus' death is at the same time his lifting up to the Father in glory (Jn 3:14). Moreover, when he is lifted up, his work is brought to its climactic fulfillment as mediator between God and all humankind.

4.1.7. Prophet. The Gospel speaks of Jesus as "prophet," but the question is whether John accepts this designation for Jesus, regards it as correct but not ultimate or adequate, or rejects it. A prophet was a person who spoke with divine authority and by divine inspiration. When Jesus heals the man born blind, the man acknowledges him to be "a prophet" (Jn 9:17), thus confessing him to be "from God" (Jn 9:16). Jesus' feeding of the five thousand leads people to exclaim, "Surely this is the prophet who is to come into the world!" (Jn 6:14), and some wonder whether he is "the Prophet" (Jn 7:40). These acclamations honor Jesus not just as one among the prophets but as the Prophet who would ap-

pear in the end time, thus fulfilling the promise of Moses to the people in Deuteronomy 18:15, "The Lord your God will raise up for you a prophet like me." The expectation of a prophet like Moses was known among the Samaritans (cf. Jn 4:19) and the community at Qumran (4QTestim 5-8). Thus the confession of Jesus as a prophet acknowledges Jesus' divine commissioning and authoritative message, but the confession of Jesus as the Prophet points to his unique role as the final prophet of God. Here again Jesus is portrayed as the chief and unique agent of God.

We may summarize John's portrait of Jesus by noting the importance of the category of the agent as background. Jesus is the uniquely commissioned agent of God who, in his task of bringing the salvation of God to the world, exercises a unique, mediating function between God and human beings. Because Jesus is the designated agent of God, he also represents God to human beings in such a way that the Gospel can say that to encounter Jesus is to encounter God, to have seen him is to have seen the Father (Jn 12:45; 14:7-9), or to know and receive him is to have known and received the Father (Jn 8:19; 12:44; 13:20; 17:8; cf. Jn 15:23). As God's agent Jesus carries out a mission that mediates God's salvation to the world, as is manifested in the signs which he does.

4.2. Signs and Faith. According to John 20:30-31 the narratives of the signs were written down in order to lead to faith. And while the signs figure prominently throughout the Gospel, there are numerous problems surrounding our interpretation of the meaning and role of signs, including such issues as the definition of a sign, the function of signs and the relationship of signs and faith.

The term *sign* is not unique to John, although it is used differently than in the Synoptic Gospels. There a sign is either an act confirming the truth of what Jesus has said, which Jesus refuses to supply (Mk 8:11-12), or a portent of the end times (Mk 13:4, 22). In the Synoptics the *miracles are usually called "mighty deeds" (*dynamis*). But in John the miracles are regularly called "signs" (*sēmeia*). "Sign" need not, in and of itself, mean "miracle." In the OT, prophetic acts that signaled the coming of some future act of God, such as judgment, were called "signs." Thus some scholars think that in John the signs include the healings, feeding of the five thousand and changing of the water into wine—in short, the miracles—but possibly other acts as well, such as the temple cleansing or even the resurrection of Jesus. But for the broad spectrum of Jesus' activity, the Gospel reserves the word *works*.

Whereas the Synoptics narrate several dozen miracles, John recounts but a few. They are the changing of the water to wine (Jn 2:1-11), the healing of the official's son (Jn 4:46-54), the healing of the man at the pool of Bethesda (Jn 5:1-9), the feeding of the five thousand (Jn 6:1-13), the healing of the man born blind (Jn 9:1-12) and the raising of Lazarus (Jn 11:1-44). Some also include the walking on the water (Jn 6:16-21), the resurrection (Jn 20:1-18) and the catch of fish (Jn 21:1-8). The two healings each illustrate the truth of the statement, "The hour is coming, and now is, when the dead will hear the voice of the Son of God, and those who hear will live" (Jn 5:25 RSV). These signs show Jesus' life-giving power. Even more dramatically is this power manifested in Jesus' raising of Lazarus. The two "gift" or "supply" miracles (the changing of the water to wine and the feeding) strike a note of messianic fulfillment and abundance. The extravagant provision of wine at the wedding may allude to traditions that in the messianic age the yield of the vineyards would be enormous and spectacular (*1 Enoch* 10:19; *2 Apoc. Bar.* 29:5; Irenaeus *Haer.* 5.33.3). Similarly, the provision of bread in the wilderness calls to mind the promises of the return of the treasury of manna from on high in the age to come. Finally, the healing of the man born blind blends together favorite Johannine terms such as light and darkness, seeing and believing, judgment and guilt, in such a way that their symbolic import is obvious. But the healing on the physical level is not played down. One is to see in the magnanimous act of healing the generous grace of God and to see Jesus carrying out "the work of God."

We may define a sign as a manifestation, through the person of Jesus, of God's work in the world. Signs are not understood to prove Jesus' divinity—for, as the Synoptics make clear, miracles only raise the question of the source of one's power, whether demonic or divine—but to point to the fact that God works through him. Specifically, God works through Jesus to bring salvation to the world, a salvation not merely symbolized by the signs but also offered through the signs inasmuch as they are tokens of the eschatological activity of God in the world (*see* Eschatology). Thus the signs are revelatory of the glory of God inasmuch as they show God's power at work through the person of Jesus. Specifically, that power is understood as life-giving power, and Jesus' signs point to the fact that he offers life. It is appropriate to his life-giving work that his deeds involve the physical universe and the elements necessary for life (bread, water, wine, healing of the human body, restoration of life). Jesus offers bread which satisfies spiritual hunger and thirst even as he also offers that which meets the physical needs of hunger and thirst, and he does so because he is the agent of the God who creates and who rules, the Maker and Judge of all. Through Jesus, the incarnate Word through whom the world was made, God is at work restoring health and bringing salvation.

A sign is thus properly understood when it is seen as pointing to God's work through the person of Jesus to effect salvation. To have grasped this truth is to have come to faith. Signs thus serve an indirect role in mediating faith, but by no means are they discounted. Yet some interpreters have taken texts such as John 4:48 to point to a relativizing of the role of miracles in John. But the statement of John 2:11, that the disciples believed when they saw Jesus' glory, is programmatic for the Gospel's understanding of signs: Jesus' glory is revealed in the signs, and those who see the glory of Jesus (cf. Jn 1:14) have grasped the secret of his person and identity.

And yet it is difficult to detect a systematic understanding of the relationship between signs and faith in John. Sometimes those who are witnesses of a sign are also led to belief in Jesus (Jn 2:11; 4:53), so that seeing leads to believing. And yet some who see do not believe, including the Pharisees of John 9; perhaps the crowds of John 6; and, depending on how one reads the evidence, the crowds of John 2:23-25, Nicodemus (cf. Jn 3:1-2) and the man at the pool of Bethesda. The summary statement of John 12:37-38, "Although Jesus had done so many signs before them, yet they did not believe," characterizes them. They did not fail to believe that a miracle had been done; rather, they did not discern the meaning of the sign. Thus they did not "see signs" as manifestations of God's work through Jesus and of God's glory in Jesus—a work and glory understood to be unique to Jesus.

By contrast, there are those who do not see signs and yet believe. All the readers of the Gospel who were not also eyewitnesses fall into this category. Their faith is not superior to those who came to believe through Jesus' signs, but neither is it an inferior faith, and this is the point of Jesus' statement to Thomas, "Blessed are those who have not seen and yet believe" (Jn 20:29 RSV). Those who "see" the signs, "see" the secret of Jesus' person as the mediator of God's salvation to humankind.

4.3. Salvation. In Jesus' prayer there is a pithy statement that summarizes the Gospel's view of salvation: "This is eternal life: to know God and Jesus Christ whom [God] has sent" (Jn 17:3). Here several elements of the Johannine theology of salvation come to the fore and need to be examined. First is the restatement of the Gospel message in terms of "eternal life," a term found in the Synoptic Gospels but not nearly so dominant in those Gospels as it is here in John. Second, this verse apparently implies this eternal life is something that one has in the present. Third, eternal life comes about through or is equated with "knowing" (rather than believing, confessing, trusting), which seems to point to a cognitive dimension of salvation. Indeed, the previous discussion of the relationship of signs and faith underscores the importance of "seeing" and "understanding" in the Gospel of John, suggesting that salvation can be characterized as the response to the revelation that one sees. These elements can be examined in turn in order to come to a fuller understanding of the Johannine view of salvation.

4.3.1. Eternal Life. It would not be amiss to summarize the Son's mission and the theme of the Gospel of John in terms of "eternal life." The Son comes so that those who believe in him may be saved or receive eternal life, and the Gospel's purpose is phrased in similar terms. But it is more difficult to explain the origin of, and impetus for, John's use of eternal life. When compared with the other Gospels, John seems to give to "eternal life" the prominence that they accord to "kingdom of God." Some scholars have suggested that John uses "eternal life" in place of "kingdom of God" in order to accent the personal and individualistic aspects of salvation. Others suggest that "eternal life" can convey the inner experience of salvation more aptly than a term like "kingdom of God." Still other scholars have argued that John's preference for "eternal life" can be explained in terms of his historical setting: the Jewish "kingdom of God" has been reinterpreted for John's Hellenistic readership as "eternal life," perhaps emphasizing its timeless reality.

Of course the Synoptic Gospels do use the terms *life* and *eternal life* (Mt 19:16-17; Mk 10:29-30; Mt 19:29; Lk 18:29-30; cf. Mt 7:14; Lk 13:23-24; Mk 10:26; Mt 19:25; Lk 18:26). Already in the Synoptics "eternal life" and "kingdom of God" appear as virtual equivalents (Mk 9:43, 45, 47; 10:17-30; Mt 19:23-29; Lk 18:24-30). "Eternal life" translates *zōē aiōnios*, which literally means "life of the age" but was used in Jewish writings prior to, or contemporaneous with, the NT to mean "life of the age to come" (Dan 12:2; *Pss. Sol.* 3:12; 13:11; 14:10; *1 Enoch* 37:4; 58:3). The absolute "life" is used in the same way. The same situation obtains for the Gospel of John. "Life" and "eternal life" are used interchangeably and can also be used in place of "kingdom of God" to speak of the state of blessedness that one participates in through faith in Jesus. Thus the background against which one should understand the term "eternal life" is chiefly that of the Jewish view of the "life of the age to come" that the righteous are to inherit.

This "eternal life" or "life of the age to come" is the very life that God has, God's own kind of life, divine life. We may see how the adjective *eternal* fits the noun *life,* for God alone exists eternally. According to John, the Father "has life in himself" (Jn 5:26). Furthermore, the Father "has granted the Son also to have life in himself." The Son has life, then, in dependence on the Father, and as the Father has it. And believers have life insofar as they depend on the Father through the mediating work of Jesus Christ. Thus John sums up, "This is eternal life, that they know thee, the only true God, and Jesus Christ whom thou hast sent" (Jn 17:3 RSV). Here John does not state that knowing God precedes or is necessary for eternal life but that knowing God is eternal life. Those who know God in the present have an incorruptible fellowship with God that cannot be severed or impugned by death. This understanding of eternal life shows its affinities with the Synoptics' "kingdom of God." Both "kingdom of God" and "eternal life" come from God and are mediated through the agent of divine rule, Jesus Christ.

But what makes the Johannine statements about eternal life particularly striking is that they promise eternal life in the present (Jn 5:24-26). Attempts to argue that John relegates the reception of eternal life entirely to the future have not proved convincing. And yet it seems almost a contradiction in terms to speak of having "eternal life," the life of the age to come, in the present, for eternal life is that life which does not end—and yet John clearly expects the death and resurrection of believers. "Life" and "resurrection" are not simply synonyms in John. Nor should we understand eternal life as a purely spiritual or individualized reality. John does not abandon the Jewish conception of "eternal life" as entailing the gathering of the people of God, nor does he spiritualize the hope for the resurrection of the body. Eternal life is present now insofar as through Jesus knowledge of and fellowship with God is mediated. Thus eternal life is also the appropriation by faith of unseen yet present realities that shape one's life in this world and become more fully realized in the next.

But even as salvation is present to believers through faith in Christ, so judgment is effected in the present as well (Jn 3:16-21, 36). This facet of John's theology that emphasizes the present manifestations of salvation and judgment is known as realized eschatology. It is not unique in the NT, which stresses the present reality of salvation in Christ, but it is fair to say that in John the "realized" aspects of salvation receive greater emphasis. John's best-known image for the presence of salvation is that of new birth, of being "born again."

There is a play on words in the phrase "born again," for the Greek (*gennaō anōthen*) can be understood to mean either "born from above" or "born anew." Nicodemus's protest that one cannot enter into his mother's womb and be "born again" shows that he misunderstands the meaning of Jesus' assertion "you must be born from above," for Jesus refers to the importance of submitting to a new work of the Spirit in one's life. This statement is to be taken at the individual and corporate level. On the level of the individual there is a call to pay heed to a new work of the Spirit through Jesus and the community of faith and to be renewed by the working of the Spirit. But on the corporate level there is implicit also a statement about who the elect people of God are, for the imagery of new birth states that there is no continuous or automatic movement forward from Judaism to eternal life. Although salvation

is "from the Jews" in the person of the Messiah, Jesus, merely belonging to the Jewish people does not guarantee entry into life (Jn 3:36).

Not surprisingly, the Fourth Gospel also accents the role of human decision and faith, for it is through faith in Jesus that one becomes a member of the people of God, and not through descent or birth. However, faith is not to be construed as a natural human inclination, for those who come are those "drawn by God" or "taught by God" (Jn 6:44-45). John underscores the divine sovereignty in drawing people to faith as well as the human responsibility in responding to Jesus (Carson). Similarly, there is an emphasis on God's trustworthiness in keeping believers faithful, as well as an insistent call to "abide" or persevere in the faith. But the Gospel does not deal philosophically with questions about predestination and free will. Its chief concern is to show that Jesus was the divinely commissioned agent, endowed with the unlimited power of the Spirit (Jn 3:34), and that those who respond to Christ in faith are enlivened by the same Spirit of God (Jn 3:5-8). Conversely, those who do not come to Christ cannot justly claim to have the Spirit of God at work within them.

4.3.2. Salvation as Revelation. The Gospel's emphasis on coming to know or believe what Jesus makes known suggests that salvation consists in accepting the revelation that Jesus brings. The image that Jesus is the light of the world fits here as well, for "light" is frequently understood in the OT as an image for instruction and guidance. That Jesus is the light of the world (Jn 8:12; 9:5) means that he makes known the way in which people are to walk in order to have salvation. A similar statement is "I am the way, the truth, and the life" (Jn 14:6). The predicates in this statement can be read as making three distinct assertions about Jesus, or they can be subordinated, as follows: "I am the way, that leads to truth and life" (or, "I am the way and the truth that leads to life"), thus underscoring that what Jesus makes known is not a new concept about God but the path to God. When, at times, his revelation is set over against that of the OT Scriptures or patriarchs, and especially Moses, it does not invalidate what was made known there but rather shows that the revelation through the Son now fulfills and supersedes all other revelation. What Moses said was true, but now since the fullness of truth resides in the Son, those who claim to be "disciples of

Moses" are not disciples of the truth at all, inasmuch as they reject the one who is truth. Salvation consists in coming to accept the embodiment of truth in the person of Jesus, not in adhering to abstract formulations of truth about Jesus.

4.3.3. The Death of Jesus. Jesus' death as an atonement for sin does not figure prominently in John (*see* Death of Christ). There may be an allusion to atonement when the Baptist identifies Jesus as "the Lamb of God who takes away the sin of the world" (Jn 1:36). But even if the atoning function of Jesus' death is not highlighted, it is clear that the mission of Jesus is brought to fulfillment with his death. While John's characterization of the effects of Jesus' death shares certain traits with the Synoptic Gospels and with Paul, it has distinctive features as well. (1) John particularly accents the fact that Jesus' death serves to gather together the people of God (Jn 10:1-18; 11:46-52; 12:20-33; cf. Ezek 34). The Messiah was expected to gather together those scattered throughout the diaspora, and this expectation is found fulfilled in Jesus, even though that in-gathering is not understood in literal and physical terms. Even so, the gathering together of the "children of God scattered abroad" signals God's final salvation at work in the world. (2) Jesus gives his life so that others may have life. As one who has "life in himself" he can bestow on others the gift of life, but only through his death. (3) Jesus' death shows his love for his own (Jn 13:1), as well as revealing God's love for the world (Jn 3:16-17). In its manifestation of self-giving love, it becomes an example for his disciples (Jn 13:11-17; 15:13).

4.4. The Community and the Paraclete.

4.4.1. The Paraclete. The term *paraclete* (*paraklētos*) is unique in the NT to the Johannine literature and is ascribed once to Jesus in the Epistles (1 Jn 2:1) and to the *Holy Spirit in the Gospels. Scholars have debated the meaning and background of the term. The popular interpretation of the Paraclete as "one called alongside to help" is derived from analysis of the two parts of the compound Greek word: *para*, meaning "by" or "with," and *kaleō*, meaning "to call." Thus it is deduced that the Paraclete is one "called alongside (to help)." But if this is the function of the Paraclete in John, then this must be discerned from statements in the Gospel and not from dubious etymological arguments. Other interpreters relate the word

to *paraklēsis*, which means "exhortation" or "encouragement," hence the traditional rendering "Comforter." And yet in John the Spirit's functions are not primarily to comfort or console believers.

In 1 John 2:1 "paraclete" seems closest to "intercessor" (although some take it more in a forensic sense, close to defending attorney). The Paraclete may be understood in terms of the Latin *advocatus,* who was a legal assistant or friend at court, a person of sufficient reputation to influence the king, emperor or other sovereign.

As stated above, in 1 John the Paraclete is the risen Jesus, but in the Gospel the Paraclete is the Holy Spirit (Jn 14:26), the "Spirit of Truth" (Jn 14:17; 15:26; 16:13). But Jesus also promises that upon his departure he will send "another Paraclete" (Jn 14:16). While the Greek could be construed to read "another who will be a Paraclete," most scholars prefer the translation "another Paraclete," implying that the first is Jesus. It is thus often assumed that John states that the Paraclete-Jesus comes back to the disciples in the person of the Paraclete-Spirit. But while there is continuity and overlap between the ministries of Jesus and the Paraclete, there are important distinctions as well.

The functions of the Paraclete can be divided between his relationship to the world and his relationship to the disciples. With respect to the world, the Paraclete serves as an accuser, putting the world on trial, pronouncing it guilty of sin and worthy of condemnation (Jn 16:8-11; cf. 14:17; 15:18-26). But the Paraclete's functions with respect to the disciples are described positively. Above all, the Paraclete assumes the role of teacher (Jn 16:13), guiding the disciples into all truth by reminding them of what Jesus had said, where reminding seems to have the force not only of recollecting but of interpreting as well. Indeed, as stated earlier, much of the Paraclete-inspired truth is found in the Gospel of John. One cannot, then, speak of the role of the Paraclete without also turning to the Gospel's vision of the community in which the Paraclete plays such a central role.

4.4.2. The Community. Certainly the Gospel of John emphasizes the necessity of the individual appropriation of faith in God through Jesus Christ. However, the individualistic tenor of the Gospel is balanced by its stress on one's obligation within the community of faith. The community of which the believer becomes a part is

581

characterized by its unity and love. Its unity is modeled on the relationship between the Father and the Son and is thus characterized by an intimacy of love, as well as a common purpose in serving as the vehicle of bringing God's revelation and salvation to the world. We may say that the unity of which the Gospel speaks has two aspects. (1) It is contemporary, a unity among Christians of any one age or time; (2) it is historical, binding Christians to their predecessors in the faith. Both are of concern in the Gospel, as Jesus' high-priestly prayer for the community demonstrates. In fact the line most often quoted in ecumenical circles, "that they may all be one," refers to the unity that exists between believers of Jesus' day and those of second and later generations of believers. They are all, equally and together, the one people of God. A concomitant of the emphasis on unity is an accent on love, where love is understood as the peculiar bond of service and loyalty that unites Christians to their God and to each other.

The Christian fellowship is distinguished in Johannine thought from the "world" *(kosmos).* "World" has several shades of meaning, from the positive created order, to the sphere of human beings, to human beings as they are hostile to the revelation of God in Christ. It is in the last sense that the "world" is a force opposing, rejecting or indifferent to God and the people of God. For if God's people are characterized by their trust in God, then the world is marked by its lack of similar commitment. The church's role vis-á-vis the world is to bear witness to the truth through its proclamation and example in order that the world may know its guilt, repent and come to the light and be saved. While some scholars have painted the portrait of the Johannine church as a community alienated from its environment, hostile to unbelievers and without a sense of responsibility toward the world, the statements of the church's mission—even when the mission results in pronouncing judgment—cannot be overlooked as suggesting that the Johannine community retained its sense of mission.

See also JOHN, LETTERS OF.

DJG: ABIDING; "I AM" SAYINGS; LAMB OF GOD; LAZARUS; LIGHT; LOGOS; SYNOPTICS AND JOHN; VINE, FRUIT OF THE VINE; WORLD.

BIBLIOGRAPHY. **Commentaries:** C. K. Barrett, *The Gospel According to St. John* (2d ed.; Philadelphia: Westminster, 1978); G. R. Beasley-Murray,

John (WBC; Waco, TX: Word, 1987); R. E. Brown, *The Gospel According to John* (AB 29, 29A; Garden City, NY: Doubleday, 1966, 1970); F. F. Bruce, *The Gospel of John* (Grand Rapids: Eerdmans, 1983); R. Bultmann, *The Gospel of John: A Commentary* (Philadelphia: Westminster, 1971); D. A. Carson, *The Gospel According to John* (Grand Rapids: Eerdmans, 1991); E. C. Hoskyns, *The Fourth Gospel* (2d ed.; London: Faber & Faber, 1947); B. Lindars, *The Gospel of John* (NCB; Grand Rapids: Eerdmans, 1981); J. R. Michaels, *John* (San Francisco: Harper & Row, 1984); L. Morris, *The Gospel According to John* (NICNT; Grand Rapids: Eerdmans, 1970); R. Schnackenburg, *The Gospel According to St. John* (3 vols.; New York: Crossroad, 1980, 1982); B. F. Westcott, *The Gospel According to St. John* (London: J. Murray, 1881; repr. Grand Rapids: Baker, 1980). **Studies:** C. L. Blomberg, *The Historical Reliability of John's Gospel* (Downers Grove, IL: InterVarsity Press, 2002); P. Borgen, *Philo, John and Paul: New Perspectives on Judaism and Early Christianity* (Atlanta: Scholars Press, 1987); R. E. Brown, *An Introduction to the Gospel of John* (New York: Doubleday, 2003); G. Burge, *The Anointed Community: The Holy Spirit in the Johannine Tradition* (Grand Rapids: Eerdmans, 1987); D. A. Carson, *Divine Sovereignty and Human Responsibility* (Atlanta: John Knox, 1981); O. Cullmann, *The Johannine Circle* (Philadelphia: Westminster, 1975); R. A. Culpepper, *Anatomy of the Fourth Gospel: A Study in Literary Design* (FF; Philadelphia: Fortress, 1983); C. H. Dodd, *Historical Tradition in the Fourth Gospel* (Cambridge: Cambridge University Press, 1963); idem, *The Interpretation of the Fourth Gospel* (Cambridge: Cambridge University Press, 1953); P. D. Duke, *Irony in the Fourth Gospel* (Atlanta: John Knox, 1985); P. Gardner-Smith, *Saint John and the Synoptic Gospels* (Cambridge: Cambridge University Press, 1938); A. E. Harvey, *Jesus on Trial: A Study in the Fourth Gospel* (Atlanta: John Knox, 1976); M. Hengel, *The Johannine Question* (Philadelphia: Trinity Press International, 1989); R. Kysar, *The Fourth Evangelist and His Gospel: An Examination of Contemporary Scholarship* (Minneapolis: Augsburg, 1975); B. Lindars, *Behind the Fourth Gospel* (London: SPCK, 1971); J. L. Martyn, *History and Theology in the Fourth Gospel* (2d ed.; Nashville: Abingdon, 1979); L. Morris, *Jesus Is the Christ: Studies in the Theology of John* (Grand Rapids: Eerdmans, 1989); J. A. T. Robinson, *The Priority* *of John* (London: SCM, 1985); S. Smalley, *John: Evangelist and Interpreter* (Exeter: Paternoster, 1978); D. M. Smith, *Johannine Christianity* (Columbia: University of South Carolina, 1984); M. M. Thompson, *The God of the Gospel of John* (Grand Rapids: Eerdmans, 2001); idem, *The Humanity of Jesus in the Fourth Gospel* (Philadelphia: Fortress, 1988); R. A. Whitacre, *Johannine Polemic: The Role of Tradition and Theology* (Chico, CA: Scholars Press, 1982).

M. M. Thompson

JOHN, LETTERS OF

Three of the NT's twenty-one letters are associated with John. Even though they do not bear John's name, an impressive church tradition and unmistakable thematic connections with the Fourth Gospel have suggested that they stem from John, the author of the Fourth Gospel (*see* John, Gospel of).

Interest in the Johannine epistles has always been eclipsed by an untiring fascination with the Fourth Gospel. John's recasting of Jesus' life (compared with the Synoptic portrait), his theological probings into the essence of the incarnation and his theological contributions in christology, pneumatology and eschatology have all drawn expected attention. The Johannine epistles, however, are an enigma. While 2 John and 3 John have the usual features of ancient *letters, 1 John bears no such marks: it is more like a tract or a broadside aimed at a particular problem sweeping the church.

In recent years, however, scholars have taken a second look at the letters as one more avenue into exploring the composition and social history of the Johannine community. As early as 1979, R. E. Brown's *The Community of the Beloved Disciple* brought to general audiences suggestions about the Johannine community that had been offered elsewhere by J. L. Martyn (1968), O. Cullmann (ET 1975), R. A. Culpepper (1975), and others (for bibliography see Brown 1982, 140-43). Today it is commonplace to speak of the Johannine school, or community, or circle, from which the teachings of John about Jesus were preserved and penned (the Gospel of John) and where John's correspondence was preserved (1 Jn, 2 Jn, 3 Jn). Just as the Fourth Gospel yields information about Jesus, it also betrays the consciousness of the community that shaped and cherished it. Just as the opening paragraph of 1 John and the Fourth Gospel mirror each oth-

er, so too the concerns of the letters fit into the compositional history of the Gospel.

Therefore, in order for us to understand better the place of the letters of John, we would do well to reconstruct the social and theological history of the community as best we can from its surviving literature. There is considerable debate concerning the sequence of these four documents (Brown 1982, 14-35), but a consensus has emerged showing that they stem from the same community and, for many, they share the same author. Moreover, it is widely accepted that the problems addressed in the letters are reflected in the Fourth Gospel. A common compositional history argues that an early edition of the Fourth Gospel was followed by a theological crisis in the community. This crisis prompted a revision of the Gospel and the writing of 1 John. This explains, for instance, the parallels between the Gospel's prologue and that of 1 John, as well as parallels between 1 John and John 14—17, John's farewell discourse (Smalley 1984, xxix-xxx; see chart, Brown 1982, 757-59; Segovia). Finally, 2 John and 3 John were penned to address a subsequent local problem.

1. History of John's Church
2. Theological Struggle
3. John's Secondary Concerns
4. Authorship and Setting
5. Epistolary Structure

1. History of John's Church.

The Johannine literature does not provide us with chronological clues to reconstruct its life and setting. Nevertheless, we can confidently assume that these letters and the Gospel did not surface in a vacuum. It is not farfetched to assume that John—John the apostle, son of Zebedee, one of the Twelve—was a pastor and an evangelist who built churches in the Mediterranean world and was a custodian of traditions about Jesus. If this is the case, then the literature that survives this community, the letters and the Gospel of John, provide important evidence of the character of these Christians. These documents tell us about the development of thought among John's followers: their passions, their wars, even their history.

1.1. John's Earliest Community. Early traditions indicate that John planted churches in Ephesus. Eusebius, the fourth-century historian, quotes Irenaeus (130-200), bishop of Lyons, who tells us that John was a leading ecclesiastical figure in

Asia Minor (Eusebius *Hist. Eccl.* 3.23). He goes on to say that clergy from throughout the area would travel to Ephesus just to learn from John and hear his stories about Jesus. And how did Irenaeus know all this? Irenaeus says it was confirmed to him by Polycarp, the bishop of Smyrna, who in his younger years was instructed by John (Irenaeus *Haer.* 2.22.5). Similarly, Eusebius also preserves for us a letter by the bishop of Ephesus (Polycrates). In it the Ephesian bishop tells us that John who reclined near the Lord at the *Last Supper (Jn 13:25) was buried in Ephesus. Today two tombs still exist near this ancient city, both claiming to be the burial place of John.

While the early church was well known for its fanciful traditions about the apostles (see the Syriac *History of John),* many scholars do not count this story of John among them. John was a leading pastor whose memory of Jesus and whose recollection of his teachings gave him unique stature in antiquity.

John's community of believers lived on the frontiers of *Judaism. His church was heterogeneous: Jews who had moved into the Greek world lived alongside Greeks who knew little of the OT. Their common bond was a firm allegiance to Jesus, their messiah, and John was their leader. And yet because John and his "Christian message" were rooted in Judaism, it was natural that this community would live in proximity to the synagogues of his city. In fact it is here, in this relationship with the synagogue, that the Johannine community's story was forged.

1.2. The Fourth Gospel. The Gospel of John is a by-product of John's ministry. That is why it repeatedly anchors its message in John's "eyewitness" testimony (Jn 19:35; 20:24). Its text tells us about Jesus, to be sure, but the way its message is framed tells us about its author and his audience. This explains, for instance, why again and again the Gospel refers to "the Jews" (sixty-four times) as if they were the opponents of the church (neither Paul nor Luke writes with this same tone). Even though some have criticized the NT and especially the Fourth Gospel as anti-Semitic, such a view misrepresents the cultural and historical framework unique to these writings. In its earliest days John's congregation felt that it was under siege: external enemies particularly from the synagogue were in debate with them. This also explains the importance of

John's lengthy story in John 9: the blind man's expulsion from the synagogue may have meant a lot to John's Jewish followers who themselves were being expelled.

At its earliest stages (before the writing of the epistles) this community was cultivating an outlook of division: the world outside the church was a place of darkness, persecution and turmoil. In Jesus' prayer (Jn 17) there is not even a record of Jesus praying for the world: he simply prays for the survival and success of his followers. Stories that held deep meaning for the community ended up in the Johannine archive about Jesus: fights with Jewish leaders (see Jn 5, 8, 9 and 10), the continuing relevance of Jewish festivals like Passover (see Jn 6) and the ongoing importance of *John the Baptist (see Jn 1:35-51; 3:22-36) to name a few. We know, for example, that Ephesus had a community of people who were followers of John the Baptist but not of Jesus (see Acts 19:1-7). Did these groups debate? Did a story like John 1:35-51 encourage many of them to join the followers of Jesus?

In these earliest days the Fourth Gospel may have been a loose collection of stories preached by John (see Stibbe). These were the formative years of the community when prized stories about Jesus were being preserved and polished, when a collection of John's best memories and personal accounts were being written down. To be sure, this was a Gospel to be proud of: it gave generous amounts of teaching from Jesus, teaching that predicted the sort of persecution the church was having and yet promised an intimacy with Christ that made such suffering immaterial. This was a Gospel that described the *Holy Spirit in detail—that talked about conversion using terms like "rebirth" and "drinking living water" and "eating the bread of life." This was a Gospel that encouraged those believers prone to mystical experiences of the faith.

Indeed the Gospel of John was an empowering Gospel that shaped this Christian community so that it would expect dynamic spiritual experiences. Jesus and the Father were dwelling inside these spiritually reborn believers (Jn 14:23)! No other Gospel speaks like this. The Holy Spirit promised to provide them with incredible powers: power to recall Jesus' very words (Jn 14:26), power to work miracles greater than those of Jesus (Jn 14:12), power to have prayer answered (Jn 14:13-14) and power to confront a hostile world (Jn 16:7). They even had the power to forgive sin (Jn 20:23). Above all, the Spirit gave them the power of prophecy, to continue speaking with Jesus' voice, revealing new things not recorded in Scripture (Jn 16:13).

John's Gospel suggests that John's community was a pneumatic community. This is not to say that the Johannine literature provides a detailed working-out of the spiritual gifts as, say, Paul does in 1 Corinthians 12—14. Rather, the Johannine literature evidences a community that was alert to the centrality of the Spirit and ready to experience the Spirit in its fullness. Johannine theology laid the context in which a pneumatic/charismatic Christianity would flourish.

1.3. Problems in the Community: The Letters. But we can only speculate that something serious happened at a later stage of the church's life. The once-unified congregation began to tear apart from within. Threats that were once external now were found within the ranks of the fellowship. For John it must have been a crisis beyond belief. In 1 John 2:18 he even says that it is "the last hour" for the community.

Lengthy scholarly debate has centered on the identity of these dissenters. They were likely a select group of Johannine Christians who knew the Fourth Gospel well, claimed to be inspired by the Spirit and challenged John's understanding of Jesus Christ's personhood and work. And they were succeeding. The community was splitting, harsh words were being exchanged, and the vocabulary once reserved in the Fourth Gospel for those in "the world" now was being aimed at fellow Christians.

First John supplies our primary evidence for this division. In its chapters we have evidence of severe social conflict: the painful departure of the group (1 Jn 2:19-26) and warnings about "deceivers" and "liars" who twist the truth of Christ (1 Jn 2:22; 2 Jn 7). There were also severe theological debates (1 Jn 5:5-8) that were being fought among teachers claiming to be filled with the inspiration of the Holy Spirit (1 Jn 2:20-21; 4:1-6). The letter's repeated emphasis on love hints at the severity and desperation of the situation.

Brown believes that at this point the Fourth Gospel may have gone through a revision to correct some of these misunderstandings. The Gospel, for instance, gained its prologue (Jn 1:1-18), which emphasizes Jesus' full incarnation (Jn 1:14). These introductory verses have an uncanny resemblance to the opening verses of John's first letter (see 1 Jn 1:1-4). Some think that the event that inspired this "writing up" of the Gospel was John's death. John 21 implies that John has died even though his community thought that he would survive until Christ's second coming (see Jn 21:20-25). When John's disciples compiled their leader's story of Christ, they gave him a title of veneration that would make him famous: the Beloved Disciple (Jn 13:23; 19:26; 20:2; 21:7, 20).

Therefore we can say that in some respect John's letters are a response written in debate with those who may be misinterpreting the Fourth Gospel. For some scholars the epistles serve as a sort of commentary on the Gospel. Still other scholars would describe them as an epilogue to the Gospel designed to circulate with it so that erroneous interpretations would not be reached. S. S. Smalley prefers to describe 1 John as a paper that "sets out to expound Johannine teaching and ideas, now preserved in the tradition and theology of the Fourth Gospel, for the benefit of heterodox members of John's community who were also indebted to the teaching of the gospel but who were understanding it differently and, indeed, erroneously" (Smalley 1984, xxvii).

1.4. The Fate of the Johannine Church. But the Johannine church was not to survive the conflict. Second John and 3 John give a glimpse of the sort of crises that must have gripped one congregation. The larger Johannine community divided, with strong leaders taking the fellowship into *Gnosticism and Docetism while John's disciples remained in communion with the other NT churches of Paul and the apostles. The earliest commentaries on John (e.g., Heracleon) were written by Gnostics, a fact that shows how the Fourth Gospel was embraced in these heretical circles. The *Odes of Solomon* (if they are gnostic) likewise bear marks of Johannine influence. Even the Nag Hammadi texts seem to describe a dualism that would fit the secessionists of John's church quite well. Concepts such as light and darkness, sinlessness, divine birth, the Spirit of Truth and God's seed all appear in Nag Hammadi.

Hippolytus (c. 170-c. 236) describes how Johannine language was used by his gnostic opponents. This may explain why the orthodox church (the Great Church, as some label it) embraced the Fourth Gospel reluctantly. In fact there is a surprising lack of interest in the Johannine writings among the leading second-century writers. The church's gnostic opponents were using the Fourth Gospel or a form of it. As many scholars believe, it was the epistles of John—1 John in particular—that redeemed the Fourth Gospel for the NT we possess today.

2. Theological Struggle.

The Johannine epistles everywhere betray the marks of struggle and conflict. First John 2:18 describes antichrists in the world; 1 John 2:22 names them "liars" who are denying an orthodox christology. There is no doubt that the letters themselves were written in the midst of a severe and desperate theological debate.

2.1. John's Opponents. Who were these opponents whom John confronted? What were the issues that they debated? It is virtually impossible to name them specifically or label their movement, although some scholars attempt to do so (*see* Adversaries). Some even believe that John is confronting two separate groups in the letters (Painter; Smalley 1980). What we can do is outline their beliefs using the refutation that John has given us in his letters. But this is a difficult endeavor for a number of reasons. Writers rarely give a complete hearing to their opponents' views, and we have no first-hand information from John's adversaries. None of their writings have survived. Moreover, sometimes John opposes things that may not be on the agenda of his opponents. For instance, in 1 John 4:18 he says there is no fear in love because perfect love casts out fear. John may be taking an opportunity to chastise his followers and not necessarily addressing anyone else.

2.2. Theological Issues. John returns to two major subjects repeatedly as he writes: christology and ethical behavior. And it is likely that the two are intimately connected. The secessionists had embraced an aberrant form of christology that led them to make wrong judgments about Christian living.

2.2.1. Christology. The doctrine of Christ lived at the center of John's theological disputes. John says that his opponents hold the following beliefs: they deny the Son (1 Jn 2:23); they deny that Jesus Christ has come in the flesh (1 Jn 4:2; 2 Jn 7); they deny that Jesus is the Christ (1 Jn 2:22). These statements may be compared with affirmations in the epistles that buttress John's christology. It is likely that these verses are connected to the opponents' christological error:

Jesus is the Christ (1 Jn 5:1); Jesus Christ has come in the flesh (1 Jn 4:2); Jesus is the Son (1 Jn 2:23; 3:23; 5:11) or the Son of God (1 Jn 1:3, 7; 3:8, 23; 4:9, 10, 15); Jesus Christ came "by water and blood" (1 Jn 5:6).

From these statements a composite image begins to emerge. These are no doubt Christians who have begun to deviate from the traditionally received understanding of Jesus Christ. They affirm the idea of Christ but doubt if Christ became flesh and if the man Jesus was indeed the incarnation of God.

Today scholars have concluded that John's opponents embraced a high christology that elevated Christ's divinity at the expense of his humanity. The Hellenistic world commonly affirmed a cosmos populated by numerous deities. Elevating Christ into their company was easy given the tolerant, syncretistic outlook of the day. And yet this same Hellenistic world was predisposed to reject that such divinities would materially enter the world. Using a dualistic outlook, Christ was separated from the world, set apart with the divinities of heaven and there left to rule. One Christian variety of this view said that Christ may have "seemed" (Gk *dokein*, hence, Docetism) to appear in the flesh, but he did not. The notion that Christ would appear "in flesh" (Gk *sarx*) was ridiculous if not abhorrent. The strong emphases of John 1:14 and 1 John 1:1-3 are all salvos in John's theological struggle.

If the earthly life of Jesus Christ was now irrelevant, these people still claimed to have immediate access to God. In their view they had moved beyond the basic, elementary, orthodox teachings of Christianity and, inspired by the Spirit, could know God directly. I. H. Marshall describes them well: "They were like men kicking away the ladder on which they have climbed to the heights and leaving themselves without any visible means of support" (Marshall, 21). The very gospel that had given birth to their faith was being jettisoned. They are not abiding in the teaching of Christ but are going beyond it (2 Jn 8).

This tendency to divide the world along dualistic lines that separated reality into opposing forces (light/darkness, above/below, spirit/flesh, etc.) was quite common in the first century. Further, the notion of immediate revelation through divine knowledge (known as Gnosticism) was just coming to life. But the application of these principles to a Christian christology was something new.

2.2.2. Cerinthus. One of the first teachers to do so was Cerinthus. What we know about him is contained in the records of his opponents, particularly Irenaeus. In Irenaeus's *Adversus Haereses* (c. A.D. 180) we find an important story reported by Polycarp that bring Cerinthus and John together. Apparently John once was in the public baths at Ephesus and discovering Cerinthus there cried out, "Let us save ourselves; the bath house may fall down, for inside is Cerinthus, the enemy of the truth." Irenaeus goes on to say that John proclaimed his gospel in order to refute the errors of Cerinthus (Irenaeus *Haer.* 3.3.4; 3.11.1).

Cerinthus's theology is outlined for us by Irenaeus. Cerinthus may have been one of the first to carefully distinguish Jesus and Christ. He argued that Jesus was the earthly man of Nazareth well known for his piety and wisdom. Christ was a heavenly deity who descended on Jesus at his baptism and departed before the crucifixion (*see* Death of Christ). Thus the man Jesus, not the Son of God, died on the cross. Therefore, when we read 1 John 2:22 ("Who is the liar but the one who denies that Jesus is the Christ.") many commentators wonder if it is just this sort of distinction that John has in mind (see also 1 Jn 5:1, 11, etc.). Someone is saying that Jesus the man is not the Christ.

In summary, for John's opponents the incarnate Jesus Christ was no longer occupying the central place in Christian faith. At best these secessionists had a nominal interest in the Jesus of history and tradition and instead were looking to inspired spiritual experiences that lifted them above the conventional views of John.

2.2.3. Ethics. John's letters also evidence a sustained critique of the moral disposition of certain persons. This is not like the usual exhortations we find in Paul's writings, in which believers are warned against catalogs of sins (1 Cor 6) or dispositions of the heart (Gal 5). In the Johannine context a theological rationale had formed, making ethical behavior of no consequence for the Christian life. John mentions his opponents' views in a number of places:

they boast that they are "free from sin" (1 Jn 1:8, 10)

they boast that "they have fellowship" with God but walk in the darkness (1 Jn 1:6)

they boast that they "know God" but nevertheless are disobedient (1 Jn 2:4)

they boast that they "love God" but hate their brothers and sisters (1 Jn 4:20)

they boast that they are "in the light" but hate their fellow Christians (1 Jn 2:9)

John also repeats a number of affirmations that shed some light on the nature of the secessionists' ethical position:

to abide in God is to obey him—it is to walk as Jesus walked (1 Jn 2:6)

to sin willfully shows that you have not known God (1 Jn 3:3-6; 5:18)

whoever acts sinfully belongs to the devil (1 Jn 3:7-8, 9-10)

we should love one another (1 Jn 3:11-12, 17-18)

refusing to love your brother or sister means that you have not inherited eternal life (1 Jn 3:14-15)

God is love—and to know him is to love (1 Jn 4:8-10)

While christology was the main battleground in the community, the tangible expression of these disagreements came in the form of open conflict and hostility. Faulty christology spilled into unethical conduct.

What does John mean when he says that these people are "not obedient"? There is no evidence that they were living immoral lives. First John 2:15-16 is likely a general exhortation for the church not to be worldly. Instead, these people were not following the conventional authoritative teachings of the church. Since they denied the significance of Christ's incarnation, it stands to reason that they would deny the significance of his earthly teachings. Therefore they did not heed Jesus' words written in the Gospel. Likewise, if they denied their own sinfulness, they would feel no need for Christ's atoning death on the cross. Theirs was a "deeper" religion, a mystical faith, fueled by nontraditional insights gleaned from the Spirit (1 Jn 2:20-23; 4:1). They refused to conform to traditional teachings, and as a result they refused to submit to the leadership that bore those teachings.

The secessionists were not simply indifferent to those who disagreed with them. They were intolerant. This explains the repeated times that John refers to hating fellow Christians. Conflict resulted from their superior spirituality. These people had become elitist in their view of themselves. And those who sought to exhort them who could not catalog similar experiences for themselves had no credibility.

We must not read John's words about community love as applying merely to John's opponents, however. Too often we have characterized these unorthodox Christians as difficult, haughty and unremitting in their attitudes toward the church. John is also exhorting his followers to exhibit love because they are responding to the secessionists with equal hostility. And just because their theology is right by no means says that their angry attitudes are justified.

2.2.4. Incipient Gnosticism? This disposition to spiritualize the earthly career of Christ, giving it no great salvific importance, and to deny the spiritual importance of one's own physical, moral life had some currency in antiquity. Gnostic systems of religious thought were in intense debate with Christianity from about A.D. 150 to 300 (years after John's death) and yet the framework that would lead to these systems was already in place (*see* Gnosticism). This later literature speaks of a religion of enlightenment, of special knowledge, preserved only for the initiated. Believers were "reborn," creating a unique union with God that literally brought about a state of sinless perfection. "Sin" belongs to another nature, our material nature, which no longer matters in God's economy. Hence, enlightened spiritual experiences validated spirituality, while at the same time practical questions of moral conduct were deemed irrelevant.

Scholars who have compared the Johannine literature with second- and third-century gnostic writings find striking similarities of language and tone. For instance, when 1 John 3:9 talks about God's "seed" remaining in one born of God, this echoes the teaching of the Valentinian Gnostics who were great opponents to the orthodox church. In the nineteenth century this even led some to conclude that John was directly in debate with a fully developed gnostic religious system and hence to be dated much later. But this is not necessary. The predisposition to divide the world along material and spiritual lines (dualism), to seek spiritual enlightenment (mysticism) and to deny personal moral responsibility were well-established by the end of the first century. Colossians and the Pastoral Epistles bear similar witness to Christians who have some christological deviation and who disregard the value of practical moral conduct.

3. John's Secondary Concerns.

A number of secondary themes are found throughout the epistles. In some sense these appear by accident because they are a part of the refutation the author is making against his opponents. In most cases these are intimately connected with the two primary subjects under debate in his church: christology and ethics.

3.1. The Holy Spirit. If study of the Fourth Gospel was central to this community's spiritual formation, it comes as no surprise that the Spirit would play a pivotal role in discipleship. No gospel places as much emphasis on the Spirit as John's Gospel (Burge). In fact, the indwelling of Christ and the transformation of the believer are both framed in terms of Spirit experience in this literature (Jn 14:23-24; 3:1-8). Even the Lord's Supper is defined as an assimilation of Christ in Spirit (Jn 6:52-63). This is why John's community had strong pneumatic or ecstatic tendencies. His followers were confident of their anointing, and in his polemic against the secessionists he must take this pneumatic context into consideration.

In 1 John 4:13 John reassures his followers that possessing the Spirit is characteristic of those who "abide in God." Such abiding is not simply a matter of orthodox confession (1 Jn 4:15) or loving conduct (1 Jn 4:16), although these are important. Abiding in God is experiential: it is a personal experience with the Holy Spirit. Therefore, John's opponents (the false teachers) must buttress their authority with some pneumatic experience, some evidence that they have the Spirit too. This explains why in 1 John 4:1-3 the church is called to "test the spirits." These opponents are claiming to be prophets (1 Jn 4:1 labels them false prophets) who, under the inspiration of the Spirit, are making striking new claims about Christ.

This is a pneumatic context. It is interesting to note what John does not say. He does not employ his apostolic authority as, say, Paul does in Galatians to refute the Judaizers there. He does not leverage pastoral authority as power anchored in a position. Instead, he urges the church to test the spirits to see if they are affirming traditional beliefs about Jesus—thereby undercutting the authority of these prophets. His tactic therefore is characteristic of those struggling against rival leadership claims in a charismatic setting. One cannot deny the Spirit. One must teach discernment and urge believers to weigh claims made in the voice of the Spirit.

But John goes further. If these secessionists are claiming a superior spirituality, John reminds the church that each member has been equally anointed with the Spirit (1 Jn 2:20, 27). In other words, spiritual discernment is the task of every person. To be a Christian is to possess the Spirit, and no one may come along claiming exclusive spiritual insight. Thus 1 John 2:27 remarks, "As for you, the anointing you received from him remains in you, and you do not need to have anyone teach you." Christians must be well-grounded and confident in the authenticity of their own spiritual experience and not swayed by the seemingly more compelling experiences of others.

3.2. Discernment and Tradition. John reminds us that the church is the custodian of the truth. Foremost among John's concerns is the responsibility of the corporate community to discern false belief and practice, to distinguish between truth and error. While this theme is explicitly mentioned only in 1 John 4:1-6, nevertheless it is presumed throughout 1 John. The church must stand guard against any who would bring distortion or error (2 Jn 8).

But this presents a problem. How can we discern truth from falsehood? If a prophet urges something new under the authority of the Spirit how can it be weighed? In 1 Corinthians 14:29 Paul confronted a similar dilemma. His solution was to have the prophets weigh one another's words, thereby checking individual inspiration in a deliberative body. John nowhere uses that tactic, setting prophet against prophet. Instead, he believes that the church is accountable to the historic revelation given in Jesus Christ and passed down through the apostles. Individual inspiration, therefore, must be weighed against truth revealed in Scripture and tradition.

Throughout 1 John the author affirms that what was "from the beginning" should be the anchor for what we believe now (1 Jn 1:1; 2:13, 14; 3:11). In fact "from the beginning" becomes a refrain as John urges his readers to recall what they first learned and measure all else by it. "Let what you heard from the beginning abide in you. If what you heard from the beginning abides in you, then you will abide in the Son and in the Father" (1 Jn 2:24 NRSV). He says that his commandments are not new, but "old commandment[s] that you have heard from the beginning" (1 Jn 2:7; 2 Jn 5).

John is not merely giving a stubborn defense of tradition, as if older is better. By "the beginning" he refers to the historic coming of Jesus Christ and the preservation of that revelation. What was revealed in the incarnation must be the litmus test for all new theological insights. Thus in 1 John 1:1-3 John points to what he saw with eyes and touched with hands—the incarnate Christ. Historic christology must be the touchstone for all Christian belief. How do we know love? "God sent his son into the world" (1 Jn 4:9). Curiously, his exhortation in 1 John 2:12-14 twice reminds the fathers—those who are older—to rekindle their acquaintance with the ancient teachings, things the younger generation may no longer treasure.

This theological anchor in historic christology is reminiscent of what we read in the Gospel of John. In his Farewell Discourse, Jesus talks about the Spirit and the limits of what he will do. As Jesus' words cannot deviate from the Father's words (Jn 5:19), so too the Spirit will reiterate what Jesus has said in history (Jn 14:26). The Spirit "will not speak on his own, he will speak only what he hears" (Jn 16:13). In Christian faith Father, Son and Spirit provide a revelation that is self-consistent and harmonious. No later revelation contradicts what has gone before. John is affirming that Christian wisdom and truth, anchored in right christology, are cumulative and binding.

3.3. Love, Unity and Fellowship. The epistles of John as well as the Gospel of John place a high premium on the quality of Christian community. Jesus' command in John 13:34 and John 15:12, 17 made clear that love should be the hallmark of his followers. In John 17 Jesus prays for harmony and unity among his followers "so that they may be one" on the model of the oneness of the Father and the Son (Jn 17:20-23).

No doubt the schism in John's church has placed unity and love on the ecclesiastical agenda. He even makes love a command: Christians who love God must love their brother or sister in the church (1 Jn 4:21). This teaching John anchors "in the beginning" as well (1 Jn 3:11; 2 Jn 5), harking back no doubt to the Gospel. In 1 John 3:23 he almost sums up the Christian life giving two simple exhortations: belief in Jesus Christ and loving one another.

But John does not give an exhortation without offering some theological ground since there are indeed times when loving those who are unlovely seems impossible. God, he says, first loved us (1 Jn 4:19). Love, especially in difficult circumstances, cannot be fueled by human energy. Love originates from God when we apprehend the depth of his love for us (1 Jn 4:7a) and when we are born anew by his spirit (1 Jn 4:7b). For John, intimate knowledge of God is the same as enjoying the intimate reciprocity of God's love: he loves us, we love him, and this love spills over to those near us. In harsher terms, not to love is evidence, severe evidence, that someone does not know God and has failed to experience him fully (1 Jn 4:8).

If we are uncertain about God's profound desire for us, we need only look to God's love shown to us in Christ. Christ is the material expression of God's tangible love, and so once again John is making a claim for the value of historic, incarnational christology to address issues of ethics. Because Christ laid down his life for us, so too we ought to do the same for one another (1 Jn 3:16). 1 John 4:10 says it succinctly: "This is love, not that we loved God, but that he loved us and sent his Son as an atoning sacrifice for our sins."

John describes living in God's love, knowing him and obeying his commands as "walking in the light." This is one more metaphor for normative Christian discipleship. Therefore, in 1 John 1:7 he affirms that when people walk in the light together, when corporately they experience God's love, unity and fellowship result. Vibrant community is the natural outgrowth of people who genuinely live in God's presence. But the reverse is also true. When people exhibit hostility and division, when they "hate" (to use John's term), they prove that their lives are being lived "in the darkness" (1 Jn 2:9-11) or being lived "in death" (1 Jn 3:14). Such so-called Christians are "liars" and hypocrites (1 Jn 4:20). John spares no words for people who claim to know God but fail to exhibit genuine godliness.

There is an important nuance to John's teaching. To anchor our love in God's affection might inspire passivity. That is, we wait for God's love to mature and change us, to shape us, before we apply any effort to our own growth. If we cannot feel God's love, John would have us exhibit love toward others as a way to step into God's presence. In 1 John 4:12 he talks about the limits of our experience of God: "No one has ever seen God; but if we love one another, God lives in us and his love is made complete in us." Loving the unlovely or the difficult to love is an avenue, a mystical avenue, to discover God in our midst.

A concrete example of how this love might be expressed is in simple acts of charity among God's people. First John 4:17 remarks: "How does God's love abide in anyone who has the world's goods and sees a brother or sister in need and yet refuses help? Little children, let us love, not in word or speech, but in truth and action" (NRSV). In 3 John 10 we are even given a negative example of someone named Diotrephes who is lacking in the practice of Christian charity and hospitality, according to the elder.

Are there limits to love? Of course, John says that we must not love the world (1 Jn 2:15)—not meaning the people of the world (Jn 3:16) or God's creation (Jn 17:24). This instead refers to everything that is hostile to God and inimical to the truth of the gospel. But in 2 John 10 we have an interesting problem. John urges his followers not to welcome (to receive into fellowship) anyone who intentionally professes false doctrine. Could John be referring to the secessionists who have divided the church? While participation with the unbelieving world is a necessary facet of Christian discipleship, if we are to have integrity there must be a limit to tolerance. There are lines of personal social intercourse and public participation that Christians must not cross.

4. Authorship and Setting.

4.1. Authorship. While Christian tradition has attributed these letters to John the apostle, the Johannine epistles are anonymous with the exception that 2 John and 3 John call their author "the elder" (2 Jn 1; 3 Jn 1). Locating his identity would of course solve the mystery. The title may simply refer to a man of high esteem in the community, although good evidence shows us that the apostles were described as elders in antiquity (cf. 1 Pet 5:1).

The situation is sorely complicated by a reference in Eusebius (*Hist. Eccl.* 3.39.4) to two Johns, one clearly the apostle and the other possibly an elder who lived later (some have speculated that he was a disciple of the apostle John). Could the elder in our epistles be this second John? Marshall, however, has shown that this does not necessarily have to be the case and that even if two persons named John lived in this period, the attribution of epistolary authorship to the later man is purely hypothetical (Marshall, 42-48).

While 2 John and 3 John appear to come from the same pen, does 1 John originate with this author? Nowhere is he described as "the elder," who is so called in 2 John and 3 John. Careful comparisons of style and content show striking similarities among all three writings and suggest that common authorship is not at all unlikely (Brown 1982, 14-35, 755-59). A more compelling question is whether the same pen wrote the epistles and the Gospel of John. As early as the third century Dionysius the Great of Alexandria was making this claim based on similarities of content and style, and today the parallels between the Gospel and the letters is commonplace in NT studies. This is particularly true of 1 John and the Gospel. In fact, careful comparison of 1 John and the Gospel's Farewell Discourse (Jn 13—17) shows even more remarkable parallels. Parallels in style and content are comparable to those found in Luke and Acts or even Colossians and Ephesians. This has led the vast majority of scholars to affirm common authorship for 1 John and the Gospel. Those who disagree point to the absence of OT quotations in 1 John, stress on future eschatology, Jesus as paraclete (rather than the Spirit), 1 John's emphasis on Jesus' sacrificial death and the promotion of ecclesiastical authority. But for most, these objections have not been decisive.

4.2. Date. Since the epistles have been closely associated with the Fourth Gospel, those who would place the Gospel in the late first century locate the epistles anywhere from A.D. 90 to 110. However, arguments for such a late date now must bear the weight of serious criticisms, and increasingly the Gospel has been given an earlier time frame closer to A.D. 70 or A.D. 80. Allowing time for the development of the heresy described in the epistles, a date between A.D. 70 and A.D. 90 would not be unreasonable.

4.3. Location. The traditional view that the Johannine writings originated from Asia Minor is sound. The heresies addressed in the epistles (and perhaps the Gospel) are well-established in this area. Further, the Fourth Gospel is traditionally associated with Ephesus. We can also argue by inference. John 1:35-42, John 3:22—4:3 and John 10:41 suggest that the Johannine community was in a debate with followers of John the Baptist who had not affirmed the messiahship of Jesus. Acts 19:1-7 describes twelve such followers of the Baptist in Ephesus who find themselves at odds with the Christians in that city.

4.4. The Sequence of 1, 2 and 3 John. Since little supplemental information exists telling us about the circumstances of these letters, we cannot assume that they were written in the sequence in which they appear in our NT. Some scholars have rearranged the three letters in every conceivable configuration. Some have argued that 2 John precedes 1 John because the tone is quite different: in 2 John the false teachers are addressed mildly (2 Jn 7-9) while in 1 John the struggles are described more severely (1 Jn 2:19; 4:1-3). We can wonder then if the problems brought on by the secessionists are just beginning in 2 John (making it earlier) and only later come to blows in 1 John.

The differences in the epistles may be explained by geographical locale. That is, 1 John may be addressed to a community setting at the heart of the Johannine world, perhaps the center where the secessionists had launched their campaign. This would explain the personal nature of the letter as well as its intensity. By contrast 2 John may be addressed to outlying house churches not fully embroiled in the controversy. Perhaps this is why 2 John is more formal and detached in the way it addresses its readers (see 2 Jn 1, 5, 13) and essentially is a warning about what is to come (2 Jn 8-11). Another possibility is that 2 John and 3 John were cover letters that were accompanied by the more substantial treatise 1 John. Some believe that this fits 3 John particularly well since it is addressed to Gaius, and Demetrius, who is being commended to the church, may have been the letter's courier (3 Jn 12; cf. 3 Jn 8). But we cannot be confident about any of these theories.

It is no doubt best to view these letters as coming from the same approximate time period and addressing the same general crisis in the church. First John is the author's full broadside against his opponents. Second John and 3 John are personal notes that either accompanied 1 John or were sent separately to another destination.

5. Epistolary Structure.

Second John and 3 John have all of the usual features of first-century letters (*see* Letter, Letter Forms). The author and recipient are identified at the beginning, a blessing or prayer follows ("Grace, mercy, and peace will be with us," 2 Jn 3; "I pray that all may go well with you," 3 Jn 2) and there is a concluding greeting (2 Jn 13; 3 Jn 15; cf. Gal 1:1; 1 Thess 1:1). The letters also contain personal references and allusions that suggest they are intended for a specific, personal situation. Some even suggest that 3 John is the best NT example of first-century epistolary format.

The same cannot be said, however, for 1 John. In fact, of all twenty-one letters, 1 John is the least like a first-century letter. As B. F. Westcott wrote, there is "no address, no subscription, no name is contained in it of a person or place; no direct trace of the author, no indication of any special destination" (Westcott, xxix). No conclusion ends the document. First John 5:21 even sounds as if the writer's thoughts have been cut off. Further, no personal comments suggest that the author is writing a personal letter. This is highly unusual when we consider the intensely personal character of the crisis in the church. It is all the more unusual if we believe that the same author penned 2 John and 3 John. If so, then he clearly knew epistolary form.

This absence of form has rightly led many to suggest that 1 John is not a personal letter but a general treatise aimed at wide distribution. Some prefer to call it a sermon or an address. Perhaps it is a pamphlet, a brochure or an encyclical. Some prefer to think of it as a tractate engaged in some sort of polemic, a kind of manifesto that addresses specific theological issues across a general front. This may explain why John mentions thirteen times that "[he is] writing" and that twenty-two times he uses the plural "you".

The earliest patristic view understood that 1 John was a sort of introduction or explanation of the Fourth Gospel. It was not an exposition or a commentary but rather a correction, a clarification aimed at those who might distort its teachings. And in the end the Fourth Gospel would become more intelligible. This explains why John chooses an opening that deliberately imitates that of the Gospel and why in 1 John 5:13 his closing epilogue resembles John 20:31. Brown (1982, 116-29), who defends this view (following earlier scholars like Lightfoot), even finds a two-part structure to the epistle that imitates the two-part structure of the Fourth Gospel (cf. The Book of Signs, Jn 1—12; The Book of Glory, Jn 13—21).

5.1. The Structure of 1 John. Discovering a recognizable pattern or structure of thought in 1 John has proven impossible. Most scholars have sought to divide it into either two or three sections. Some commentators (Brooke, Dodd, Grayston, Houlden and Marshall) believe this is

pointless and find instead either spirals of cyclical thought or a list of unconnected units. According to this view, John's units link up with each other only casually and are "governed by an association of ideas rather than by a logical plan" (Marshall, 26).

The most famous threefold division belongs to R. Law, whose 1909 commentary argued that 1 John had three parts, each part offering three "tests of life:" righteousness, love and belief. The secessionists fail to acknowledge the importance of righteous behavior, do not love fellow Christians and deny belief in Jesus Christ, the Son of God. While such a theory's creativity is attractive it falls short in many places in the epistle, particularly in part three (1 Jn 4:7—5:13). Nevertheless, a number of current scholars have defended such a three-unit theory: A. E. Brooke (1912), E. Malatesta (1973), P. R. Jones (1970), M. Thompson (1992) and R. Schnackenburg (1965). Those who find a threefold structure appealing generally look for thematic divisions at 1 John 2:27/28/29 and at 1 John 3:22/24, 4:6 or 4:12.

A twofold or bipartite division has traditionally been less popular but today is commanding renewed attention. The French scholar A. Feuillet defended this view in 1973 and most recently Brown (1982) and Smalley (1984) have become its champion in their commentaries. Two observations argue for this structure. First, John makes two declarations in the Gospel (Jn 1:5; 4:6) that Brown suggests are keys to John's master plan: "God is light" (Jn 1:5) and "God is love" (Jn 4:6). Second, the Gospel of John, which enjoys a bipartite form, may be the structural model for this second Johannine writing. Similarities between the two writings have often been observed. Each begins with parallel prologues, and the bodies of each writing move from doctrinal truths to practical applications for life.

Smalley would prefer to divide the epistle at 1 John 2:29 and 1 John 3:1, which would employ a division popularly used by those making a threefold division in the epistle. Brown's divisions shown here provide proportionally sized halves for the epistle and also find parallel introductory lines for 1 John 1:5 and 1 John 3:11, "This is the message we have heard."

• Prologue, 1 John 1:1-4: The word of life which we have witnessed among us.

• Part 1, 1 John 1:5—3:10: God is Light—and we should walk accordingly.

"This is the message we have heard from him and proclaim to you."

    1 John 1:5-7: Thesis: walking in the light and walking in the darkness.

    1 John 1:8—2:2: First Exhortation: Resist sinfulness.

    1 John 2:3-11: Second Exhortation: Obey God's commands.

    1 John 2:12-17: Third Exhortation: Defy the world and its allure.

    1 John 2:18-27: Fourth Exhortation: Renounce those who distort the truth.

    1 John 2:28—3:10: Fifth Exhortation: Live like God's children.

• Part 2, 1 John 3:11—5:12: God is Love—and we should walk accordingly.

"This is the message you have heard from the beginning, that we should love one another."

    1 John 3:11-24: Love one another in practical ways.

    1 John 4:1-6: Beware of false prophets who would deceive you.

    1 John 4:7-21: Love one another as God loves us in Christ.

    1 John 5:1-4: Obey God and thereby conquer the world.

    1 John 5:5-12: Never compromise your testimony.

• Conclusion, 1 John 5:13-21: The boldness and confidence of those who walk in God's light and love.

5.2. The Structure of 2 and 3 John. Few interpreters have discovered a careful literary structure for these brief epistles. Like personal letters everywhere, they begin with a greeting and then develop one theme after another in a casual manner. Each letter is occasioned by the same concern: living the truth. This takes on two dimensions: it means loving those who abide in the family of God, and it means chastising those who would dismantle that family. In each case John warns against community destroyers—a theme grounded in the concerns about division well-known throughout 1 John.

2 John

    2 John 1-3: Personal Greetings

    2 John 4-6: Loving the Family of God

    2 John 7-11: Protecting the Family of God

    2 John 12-13: Closing

3 John

    3 John 1-2: Personal Greetings

    3 John 3-8: Loving Christ's Emissaries

    3 John 9-12: Exhortations About Diotrephes

    3 John 13-14: Closing

See also ADVERSARIES; CHRISTOLOGY; JOHN, GOSPEL OF.

DLNTD: DOCETISM.

BIBLIOGRAPHY. **Commentaries:** A. E. Brooke, *A Critical and Exegetical Commentary on the Johannine Epistles* (Edinburgh: T & T Clark, 1912); R. E. Brown, *The Epistles of John: Translated with Introduction, Notes, and Commentary* (AB; Garden City, NY: Doubleday, 1982); F. F. Bruce, *The Epistles of John: Introduction, Exposition, and Notes* (Old Tappan, NJ: Revell, 1970); R. Bultmann, *The Johannine Epistles: A Commentary on the Johannine Epistles* (Philadelphia: Fortress, 1973); G. M. Burge, *The Epistles of John* (Grand Rapids: Zondervan, 1996); C. H. Dodd, *The Johannine Epistles* (London: Hodder & Stoughton, 1946); K. Grayston, *The Johannine Epistles* (Grand Rapids: Eerdmans, 1984); J. L. Houlden, *A Commentary on the Johannine Epistles* (London: Adam & Charles Black; New York: Harper & Row, 1973); S. J. Kistemaker, *Exposition of the Epistle of James and the Epistles of John* (NTCom; Grand Rapids: Baker, 1986); R. Law, *The Tests of Life: A Study in the First Epistle of St. John* (Edinburgh: T & T Clark, 1909); I. H. Marshall, *The Epistles of John* (NICNT; Grand Rapids: Eerdmans; London: Marshall, Morgan & Scott, 1978); R. Schnackenburg, *The Johannine Epistles: Introduction and Commentary* (New York: Crossroad, 1965/1992); S. S. Smalley, *1, 2, 3 John* (WBC; Waco, TX: Word, 1984); J. R. W. Stott, *The Letters of John: An Introduction and Commentary* (TNTC; 2d ed.; Grand Rapids: Eerdmans, 1988); M. M. Thompson, *1-3 John* (IVPNTC; Downers Grove, IL, 1992); B. F. Westcott, *The Epistles of St. John: The Greek Text with Notes* (4th ed.; Grand Rapids: Eerdmans 1966, [1883]). **Studies:** C. K. Barrett, *Essays on John* (London: SPCK, 1982); R. E. Brown, *The Community of the Beloved Disciple: The Life, Loves and Hates of an Individual Church in New Testament Times* (New York: Paulist; London: Geoffrey Chapman, 1979); idem, "'Other Sheep Not of This Fold': The Johannine Perspective on Christian Diversity in the Late First Century," *JBL* 97 (1978) 5-22; idem, "The Relationship to the Fourth Gospel Shared by the Author of 1 John and by His Opponents" in *Text and Interpretation,* ed. E. Best and R. McL. Wilson (Cambridge: Cambridge University Press, 1979) 57-68; G. M. Burge, *The Anointed Community: The Holy Spirit in the Johannine Tradition* (Grand Rapids: Eerdmans, 1987); O. Cullmann, *The Johannine Circle*

(Philadelphia: Westminster, 1975); R. A. Culpepper, *The Johannine School* (Missoula, MT: Scholars Press, 1975); A. Feuillet, "The Structure of First John: Comparison with the Fourth Gospel," *BTB* 3 (1973) 194-216; P. R. Jones, "A Structural Analysis of I John," *RevExp* 67 (1970) 433-44; J. M. Lieu, *The Second and Third Epistles of John: History and Background* (Edinburgh: T & T Clark, 1986); idem, *The Theology of the Johannine Epistles* (NTT; Cambridge: Cambridge University Press, 1991); idem, "What Was from the Beginning: Scripture and Tradition in the Johannine Epistles," *NTS* 39 (1993); E. Malatesta, *The Epistles of St. John: Greek Text and English Translations Schematicallty Arranged* (Rome: Gregorian University, 1973); J. L. Martyn, *History and Theology in the Fourth Gospel* (Nashville: Abingdon, 1968); J. Painter, *The Quest for the Messiah: The History, Literature, and Theology of the Johannine Community* (Nashville: Abingdon, 1993); F. F. Segovia, "The Love and Hatred of Jesus and Johannine Sectarianism," *CBQ* 43 (1981) 258-72; S. S. Smalley, *John: Evangelist and Interpreter* (2d ed.; Downers Grove, IL: InterVarsity Press, 1998 [1978]); idem, "What about 1 John?" in *Studia Biblica 1978, 3: Papers on Paul and Other New Testament Authors,* ed. E. A. Livingstone (JSNTSup 3; Sheffield: JSOT, 1980) 337-43; D. M. Smith, "Johannine Christianity: Some Reflections on Its Character and Delineation," *NTS* 21 (1974-75) 222-48; M. W. G. Stibbe, *John as Storyteller: Narrative Criticism and the Fourth Gospel* (SNTSMS 73; Cambridge: Cambridge University Press, 1992); J. C. Thomas, "The Order of the Composition of the Johannine Epistles," *NovT* 37 (1995) 68-75; U. C. von Walde, *The Johannine Commandments: 1 John and the Struggle for the Johannine Tradition* (New York: Paulist, 1990); R. A. Whitacre, *Johannine Polemic: The Role of Tradition and Theology* (Chico, CA: Scholars Press, 1982).

G. M. Burge

JOHN THE BAPTIST

Numerous lines of evidence demonstrate the importance of John the Baptist, or John the Baptizer, as he is sometimes called in the NT (cf. Mk 1:4; 6:14, 24). All four Gospels associate John with or treat him as the "beginning of the gospel" (see also Acts 1:22). Jesus reportedly claimed that he was more than a prophet and, from a human point of view, the greatest human being (Mt 11:11 par. Lk 7:28; Mt 11:9 par. Lk 7:26). Unlike the case with other major NT figures such as the apostles, only the deaths of John and Jesus are given significant treatment in the NT (Mk 6:14-29 and par.). The author of Luke-Acts indicates that John was such a significant figure that he still had disciples or followers long after his death (Acts 18:25; 19:1-7). The Synoptic Gospels state that Jesus submitted to John's baptism, and the earliest Gospel suggests that at least initially Jesus preached a message similar to John's (Mk 1:14-15). Also, the Fourth Gospel suggests that Jesus assisted John for a time or followed his example in the wilderness, collecting disciples and supervising baptisms (Jn 3:22-36). During and at the end of his ministry Jesus expresses his own purpose and authority by comparing and contrasting himself with John and suggesting they are part of a single effort by God to reach his people (cf. Mt 11:16-19 par. Lk 7:31-35; Mk 11:27-33 and par.). Some traditions suggest that Jesus saw John as the eschatological prophet Elijah *redivivus* (Mk 9:12-13 and par.). Jesus apparently was thought by some to be John come back from the dead (Mk 6:14 and par.). According to the Synoptic Gospels Jesus did not begin his Galilean ministry until after John was imprisoned, which suggests that John's life and death influenced how Jesus acted.

1. John's Origins and Early Activities.
2. Jewish Expectations and Practices
3. John's Eschatological Message and Ministry
4. Jesus' View of John and His Ministry
5. The Death of the Baptist
6. The Baptist Movement in the Christian Era
7. The Christian Portrayal of the Baptist

1. John's Origins and Early Activities.

Luke alone informs us that John was born into a pious and priestly family, to parents well advanced in age (Lk 1). He also informs us that John's father, Zechariah, served in Herod's temple and that he and his family lived in a town in the Judean hill country (Lk 1:39). Luke 1:36 tells us that his mother, Elizabeth, was a female relative of Jesus' mother, Mary. The Greek word *sungenis* is a general term that could refer to an aunt or a cousin (Jn 1:33 suggests that the kinship may have been rather remote). In any case, Jesus grew up in Nazareth, John apparently in Judea.

Several considerations have led some scholars to conjecture that John may have been a part of the Qumran community from an early age (*see* Dead Sea Scrolls). The Qumran community had priestly connections, plus an interest in priestly matters and a priestly Messiah (1QS 5:2). John also had priestly connections, and John's parents may well have passed away when he was quite young. Apparently the Qumran community frequently adopted orphans (Josephus *J.W.* 2.120). The locale of John's ministry suggests a connection with Qumran. The Gospel tradition introduces John using Isaiah 40:3 (cf. Mk 1:2), a text that was also very important at Qumran (cf. 1QS 8:14). John's spartan diet and apparent ascetical behavior have analogies with Qumran (S. L. Davies). The Damascus Rule 12.13-14 in fact specifies how to eat honey and locusts. John's water rite has similarities to Qumran ablution rites. John's eschatological orientation and belief that the judgment of God would soon fall on Israel, with the possible exception of those who would repent, parallel Qumran. John's apparent belief that the religious leadership of Israel was hopelessly corrupt strikes a chord with some attitudes known to have existed at Qumran.

This list, however impressive, does not prove a connection between John and Qumran for several reasons. When we first meet John in the Gospels he is not, or is no longer, part of the Qumran community. Rather, he is undertaking his own ministry by calling the nation to repentance, not merely withdrawing from it as if it were hopelessly corrupt. There are major differences between John's water rite and the usual lustrations at Qumran (see 3.3 below), though there may have been an initiatory water rite at Qumran as well. John allows the clean and the unclean to come into contact with him (possibly even Gentiles, cf. Lk 3:14) and apparently does not believe in an already existing "righteous remnant" of Israel, that is, one that exists prior to submitting to his baptism. John was perceived by Herod Antipas to be a political threat in a way in which the Qumran community apparently was not. John's diet is what would be expected of any itinerant in the wilderness. At most, it suggests only either that John was consciously taking the prophetic mantle upon himself, as his dress suggested (cf. Zech 13:4, 2 Kings 1:8), and/or assuming a Nazirite vow. In any case, fasting, ascetic behavior and devotion to prayer (cf. Lk 11:1; Mt 11:18 and par.) were by no means unique to the Qumran community. Indeed, Jo-

sephus tells us of one Bannus (Josephus *Life* 11-12a) who ate and dressed much like John, lived in the Judean wilderness and stressed ritual ablutions. Thus, while John may have been connected with Qumran at one time, in the Gospels this is no longer the case (see Reicke).

2. Jewish Expectations and Practices.

2.1. Messianic Hope and the Baptist. In early Judaism, messianic hope took on a variety of shapes. Some Jews expected a particular messianic figure in the mold of David to come and retake the promised land by force for God's people (cf. *Pss. Sol.* 17). Some Qumranites seem to have expected two messianic figures—a priestly one and a kingly one (cf. 1QS 9:11; also *T. Levi* 18; *T. Reuben* 6:8). Still other Jews looked for an eschatological prophet like Moses (cf. 4QTest; 1QS 9:11; cf. also the Samaritan expectation of a *Taheb* who will be a Moses *redivivus*). There were those who looked for the coming of a messianic age in general without focusing on a particular messianic figure. Other early Jews, apparently including the Sadducees, seem to have had no messianic hopes.

P. W. Barnett has noted a pattern that various early messianic movements took. Whether one is talking about Theudas, or the Egyptian or the Samaritan—or a figure like Jesus—all seem to have drawn significant crowds in remote areas, whether in the Judean wilderness, near the Jordan or in remote areas of Galilee. All of them performed or promised to perform symbolic acts that had messianic overtones (i.e., divide Jordan, cause Jerusalem's walls to collapse, reveal the temple vessels on Mt. Gerizim, provide manna in the wilderness for the five thousand). Note that John the Baptizer preached in "the wilderness," particularly at the Jordan, drew great crowds and performed an act symbolizing a change in the status of at least some of God's people—water baptism.

Given that all messianic movements in early Judaism had some social and political repercussions, even if that was not always their design, it is easy to see how John the Baptist, who so far as we know made no messianic claims, could have been viewed as some sort of messianic figure. In addition, he could have been perceived as a threat to some of the governing authorities and, in light of Jewish views about martyrdom, John could have had an ongoing group of followers long after his death. All of these messianic figures, including the Baptist, implied and in some cases articulated a belief that things were not as they ought to be among God's people. Thus, at least by implication, the existing authorities, religious and political, Jewish and Roman, were indicted by the very existence of these movements. It is into this sort of environment that John and Jesus came raising messianic hopes and making various authorities uneasy, to the point that both were eventually executed.

One particular form of messianic hope that needs to be explored more fully in connection with John the Baptist is the belief that Elijah or one like him would come, signaling the advent either of the messianic age, or of the Messiah or both. Whether there was such an expectation, or at least whether it was widespread during the lifetime of John the Baptist and Jesus, has been disputed (cf. Faierstein; Allison; Fitzmyer).

One must consider a number of factors, however. Early Christians did associate John the Baptist with Elijah, as the Gospels attest. It is also clear that in Mark 9:11-13 and parallels we have a tradition indicating that the teachers of the Law taught that Elijah must come first to restore all things, but we are not told explicitly what the scribes thought he would come before—either the Messiah, or the day of the Lord or the Son of man rising from the dead. Nevertheless, it is unlikely that early Christians would have attributed a Christian interpretation of the eschatological Elijah figure to the scribes if there were no basis for this in fact. The tradition found in Malachi 3:1-4 (Mt 4:5-6) says explicitly that Elijah will come before the great and terrible day of the Lord, which presumably refers to the day of Judgment (this idea is also found in such texts as Sir 48 and possibly *1 Enoch* 90:31). A fragment from Qumran (4Q558 frag. 14) reads *lkn 'šlh l'lyh qd[m]*—"therefore I will send Elijah be[fore]"—but unfortunately it breaks off at this point. The baraita in *b. 'Erub.* 43a-b, which quotes the passage from Malachi and then comments on it, provides us with the earliest clear extracanonical evidence that Elijah would return before Messiah came. This tradition dates to the third century of the common era and may be much earlier, but since it is not associated with a particular Jewish teacher, we cannot be sure. Thus, there may have been a belief in Elijah as forerunner of Messiah in John's time, but we cannot be sure how widespread it was.

What is certain is that the Gospel tradition indicates that Jesus interpreted John the Baptist as an Elijah figure, and since this idea is found in at least two sources, it is very likely to be authentic (cf. Mk 9:12-13 and par.; Mt 11:14). It is also clear from Mark 9:12-13 that we have the sequence of first Elijah (John), then the *Son of man, with both suffering similar fates. The natural way to understand Mark 9:11 is to say that the scribes were claiming Elijah would be the first in a sequence of messianic comings, an idea the early church would hardly have predicated of the scribes if the church had invented it and also placed it on Jesus' lips (Allison).

Thus in the NT there are various traditions suggesting that John was viewed as an Elijah figure, and there is evidence that Elijah was expected as a precursor of the final eschatological work of God, and perhaps also of Messiah. At least two Gospels indicate Jesus viewed John in this light.

2.2. The End of Prophecy. There are some OT and some intertestamental traditions that suggest that after Zechariah, Haggai and Malachi, OT prophecy as we know it ceased (*see* Holy Spirit). Psalm 74:9 has been understood in this way, or one may point to 1 Maccabees 9:27, which speaks of the distress in the land since the prophets ceased to appear there (cf. 1 Macc 4:45-46; 14:41, *2 Apoc. Bar.* 85:3). Of later provenance are traditions in the Talmud that state explicitly that Haggai, Zechariah and Malachi were the last of the prophets.

Whether or not one agrees that the apocalyptic literature that came to the fore in the intertestamental period is a form of and the sequel to OT prophecy, there is no question that the classical prophetic movement had disappeared long before the beginning of the NT era. The apocalyptic literature was by and large pseudonymous in contrast to much of classical prophecy, and furthermore it was primarily a literary rather than oral phenomenon. The rabbinic notion of the *bat qôl* ("daughter of a voice"), an audible echo of the heavenly voice that formerly spoke to the prophets, also attests to a difference from the period of classical prophecy. Thus, when John the Baptist arrived on the scene around A.D. 28 (cf. Lk 3:1), he was probably perceived by some as a new and different figure, unlike anyone since the OT prophets and most like such classical figures as Isaiah, Jeremiah or Elijah.

2.3. Jewish Water Rites. The discussion about what precedents there may have been for John's baptism has been a heated one among scholars (*see* Baptism). This is in part the case because it is uncertain when proselyte baptism was first practiced by early Jews. In addition to the matter of OT water rituals having to do with ceremonial uncleanness, there is also the vexed question of what, if any, connection the Baptist may have had with the Qumran community (see 1 above). It is also possible that John's rite was something new and different, without precedent.

With regard to the matter of proselyte baptism, several considerations are relevant. The Mishna (*m. Pesah.* 8:8) records a dispute between the school of Hillel and Shammai concerning whether or not a newly circumcised proselyte may immerse himself and eat the Paschal meal. If this dispute goes back to Hillel and Shammai, then it predates John's ministry. The Babylonian Talmud (*b. Yebam.* 46a) also records a dispute between two first-century A.D. rabbis about proselyte baptism and its necessity. In view of the Jewish belief that Gentiles in general were unclean, the likelihood is strong that there was some rite of initiation such as proselyte baptism for female converts to early Judaism. Thus proselyte baptism probably did exist during John's era (but cf. Pusey, Betz, Badia and McKnight).

However, we must note several differences between John's practice and that of Jewish proselyte baptism. Apparently John was the active immerser when he offered his rite, but Jewish proselytes immersed themselves. John performed his rite primarily on Jews, who were never subject to Jewish proselyte baptism. Thus one may argue that John was practicing proselyte baptism on Jews, which suggests that he did not feel their heredity was an adequate safeguard from God's coming eschatological wrath. Indeed, it seems he felt Israel was lost, just like the Gentile world, unless they repented and received his baptism.

There are also salient differences between John's practice and the water lustrations mentioned in the OT and those found at Qumran, including the cleansing ritual in the *mikwâ*. John's rite, like proselyte baptism, was a unique and unrepeated ritual, so far as we can tell. There is no indication that John's rite had anything to do with purely ceremonial uncleanness caused, for instance, by touching a corpse. Apparently it is only or at least primarily moral uncleanness that is at issue in John's rite. John's baptism seems to have been an initiation rite,

not a rite to continue to maintain purity or cleanliness for one who was already basically in right relationship with Yahweh. There is no evidence that John required a probationary period before being immersed or any prior demonstration of one's earnestness to obey God other than the willingness to come forward and be baptized.

When one considers the Qumran initiatory water rite, the probationary period and self-immersion appear to distinguish the Qumran practice from that of the Baptist. Quite possibly the Baptist's rite was uniquely unrepeatable (Badia). Note that John may have been drawing on the ancient idea of trial by water ordeal, in which case the rite is connected with his proclamation about coming wrath and is a visible symbol of preparation for that coming event. One may compare the idea of circumcision being an act invoking the oath curse on oneself, and thus of being cut off by God, if one does not go on to obey the covenant.

2.4. Geographical Considerations. John ministered "in the wilderness," but the question is, Which wilderness? Was it Perea, as Josephus's account (*Ant.* 18.5) and John's death at the hands of Herod Antipas might suggest? Or was he ministering in the Judean wilderness adjacent to the Jordan? If full weight is given to John 1:28 and John 3:23, this might suggest a ministry in the north. R. Riesner (cf. McCown) has even suggested a ministry in Batanaea. What is clear is that John baptized in the Jordan, and our earliest Gospel, Mark, makes clear that Jesus was baptized by John in the Jordan (Mk 1:9-11— *hypo Ioannou* must mean "by John," distinguishing this rite from normal proselyte baptism). John may have worked his way up and down the Jordan valley (is this what "all the environs of the Jordan" means? cf. Mt 3:5 par. Lk 3:3). Perhaps he sometimes operated adjacent to the Judean wilderness or in Perea or used some of the streams that flow into the Jordan (if Aenon near Salim is near the Salem in Samaria).

Another consideration is whether or not John fully immersed those whom he baptized. If so, presumably he would have needed a body of water of sufficient depth to do so. The Greek verb *baptizō* does not in itself indicate a particular quantity of water, but if John saw his practice as a modification of proselyte baptism, then he may have totally immersed those who came to him. In any event, there is no reason to doubt that John stayed in the remote regions adjacent to the Jordan, as various different Gospel traditions suggest. Thus the description "the voice of one crying in the wilderness" was an apt one.

3. John's Eschatological Message and Ministry.

John the Baptist called his audience to repentance. One major theme of John's preaching was that Yahweh's eschatological wrath would soon fall on Israel. What is not clear is the relationship between John's preaching of repentance and his baptismal practice. Josephus (*Ant.* 18.5.2) suggests that repentance was seen as a prerequisite to receiving John's baptism. But Mark and Luke call John's rite a "baptism of repentance," which presumably means a baptism that expresses a willingness to repent and live a life that bears fruit corresponding to repentance (cf. Mt 3:8 par. Lk 3:8, 10-14).

That the association of repentance with John's water rite is historically authentic few would care to dispute, particularly in view of the difficulties this connection suggested for the Christian community when Jesus submitted to such a baptism. Only the First Evangelist suggests a motive for Jesus submitting to the rite— "to fulfill all righteousness" (Mt. 3:15)—which may mean to be obedient to God's plan for his life, to fully identify with the needs of God's people. Less probably it may mean he intends to fulfill all Scripture (Davies and Allison).

According to Mark, Q and John, John the Baptist expected a successor—the Coming One. It has been suggested that John expected Yahweh to come and bring in the day of the Lord, which is understandable in light of the prophecy in Malachi. However, the metaphor of untying the sandal (or possibly carrying the sandal), while it connotes the idea of being unworthy to be the servant of the Coming One, also suggests that John envisioned a human successor, one who would come and baptize with Spirit and fire (possibly an example of hendiadys—the fiery Spirit). This means that John did not see himself as the definitive revealer of God (O'Neill).

Did John see Jesus as this Coming One? John 1:29-34 seems to make this identification clear, but a likely authentic Q tradition (Mt 11:2-3 par. Lk 7:19) shows that John had doubts about such an identification even as late as the time of his imprisonment. Possibly these doubts were created by the fact that Jesus did not immediately bring down fiery judgment on Israel.

Other authentic elements in John's preaching probably include (1) an appeal to charitable and honest conduct (Lk 3:11-14), some of which Jesus also picks up in his proclamation (Mt. 5:40 and par.; *see* Sermon on the Mount); (2) a belief that being a descendant of Abraham was no guarantee of avoiding the wrath to come, if it was not also accompanied by repentance and its fruit; (3) preaching against immorality, such as that exhibited by Herod Antipas and Herodias in their incestuous union (Lk 3:19) and (4) the idea that the Coming One would gather in the wheat as well as burn up the chaff (Lk 3:17). This means that John conceived of a righteous remnant being created by the Coming One—a community of the faithful who would survive the coming wrath.

These themes do not suggest that John preached the coming dominion of God (Heb *malēkût Yahweh; see* Kingdom of God) in the same fashion as Jesus. Apparently he did not stress the aspect of good news entailed in the coming events. The summary in Mark 1:14 does suggest that Jesus was influenced, at least in his early Galilean preaching, by John (Witherington). This continuity in preaching between John and Jesus can also be found when one compares the likely authentic parable of the tares (Mt 13:24-30 and par.) to the Johannine preaching found in Matthew 3:7-10 and parallels (Catchpole). Serious attention should also be given to the hints in John 3:22-36 that historically Jesus assisted John or had a parallel ministry involving baptizing in the Judean wilderness prior to John's imprisonment and Jesus' Galilean ministry.

Thus, in this regard and also by virtue of the fact that Jesus' Galilean ministry begins after John baptizes Jesus (and probably after John was imprisoned), one may say that the origins of Jesus' call and ministry lie in the ministry of the Baptist, and perhaps after John's death, in Jesus' desire to continue and to build on some of John's main emphases. John therefore rightly deserves the place he is given in Mark 1 as the beginning of the gospel. This raises the question of Jesus' view of John and John's relationship to God's coming reign.

4. Jesus' View of John and His Ministry.

Jesus was not stinting in his praise of John. According to the Q tradition in Matthew 11:7-11 (par. Lk 7:24-28), John is called "the greatest person ever born" and "more than just another prophet." In view of the tendency in the early church to emphasize John's role as a forerunner in relationship to Jesus, subordinating the former to the latter, it is very likely that this Q tradition is authentic. In Matthew 11:7 we find confirmation of the setting of John's ministry—at the Jordan where there were reeds blowing in the wind. It is possible that in Matthew 11:8 we have an allusion to Herod Antipas, who is contrasted with John. The way in which this Q tradition is framed suggests that Jesus saw John as *the* great eschatological prophet, hence the description "more than just another prophet." This comports with traditions that intimate that Jesus thought of John as an Elijah *redivivus* figure. The quotation of Malachi 3:1 in Matthew 11:10 also confirms Jesus' viewpoint. John is one who prepares the way for God's eschatological activity.

The saying in Matthew 11:11 might seem strange—"yet he who is least in the kingdom of heaven is greater than he [John]" (RSV). Jesus is probably not talking about John being outside the kingdom and others in it; rather, he is talking about two ways of viewing people—from a purely human perspective and from a kingdom perspective. Judged from a purely human perspective, or if one is considering human origins, Jesus thought John was the greatest. Thus Matthew 11:12 is not in conflict with Matthew 11:11, for Matthew 11:12 suggests that the beginning of the advancement of God's eschatological dominion started when John came on the scene. A similar idea is also found in Luke 16:16 (possibly a variant of the same tradition found in Mt 11:12-13), where John is probably not said to be the last of the OT prophets but rather the one who inaugurates the news of the dominion of God breaking in (cf. Lk 3:18). The era of the Law and the Prophets lasted until John came on the scene. These conclusions also make sense of another difficult verse, Matthew 11:12b (par. Lk 16:16b), which suggests that the violence being done to John and Jesus as proclaimers of God's new activity is in fact violence against God's reign.

Yet for all the praise of John and close identification with John in this new work of God, Jesus also distinguished himself from John in several ways. John is seen as one who prepares the way and one who expects a successor. Jesus sees his ministry as part of that for which John prepared,

and he expects no successor to follow him. In their style of ministries Jesus sees a contrast between himself and John (Mt 11:19 par. Lk 7:33-34), and yet in both cases they suffered rejection by "this generation." When Jesus answered John's query from prison (Mt 11:2-6 and par.) he indicated another point of distinction—that is, Jesus' ministry was characterized by miracles, and Jesus sees the Isaianic prophecies about such happenings in the messianic age to be referring to his own ministry.

Although John and Jesus each had a ministry from God, there were points of discontinuity as well as continuity between the two men in their words, deeds and self-understanding. From a saying such as Matthew 11:19b it also appears that Jesus may have regarded himself as divine Wisdom personified, something we have no hint of in John's case (Witherington). In any event, the measure of the continuity between the two men is perhaps shown by the fact that Mark 6:14, 16 records a likely authentic tradition suggesting that some, including Herod, thought Jesus was John raised from the dead, which they believed explained Jesus' miraculous powers.

5. The Death of the Baptist.

Josephus and the Gospel tradition agree that John lost his life at the hands of Herod Antipas, the ruler of Galilee and Perea. If Josephus's account (*Ant.* 18.5.2) is to be believed, then it appears John was executed not long before the Nabatean war against Antipas. This likely means he died around A.D. 32 (Reicke). We also learn from Josephus that John was imprisoned in the Machaerus, a fortress in Perea east of the Dead Sea, and that he met his end there.

The Gospels do not contradict the testimony of Josephus, though it has been suggested that Mark thought the execution took place in Galilee (Mk 6:22). The text only says that the leading figures of Galilee were invited to Herod's birthday celebration, which could have been held either in Perea or Galilee. Josephus indicates that John was imprisoned and executed because Herod feared John might stir the people to insurrection. This is a believable rationale for Herod Antipas's action. Mark 6:20 (cf. Mt 14:5) also informs us that Herod was afraid of the Baptist, but Mark 6:17-29 goes on to relate that John was imprisoned because he had criticized Herod's incestuous marriage with Herodias. Further, it indicates that John was executed because Herodias nursed a grudge against the Baptist and devised a ruse to force Herod into executing the Baptist.

It may be that Josephus is only relating why John was imprisoned by Herod, not the cause of his execution, but if this is not the case then the Gospels disagree with Josephus on what led to the Baptist's death. It will be noted though that Josephus tends to analyze matters in terms of the political issues and forces involved, not in terms of matters of personal intrigue. Furthermore, from Josephus's account we would never have guessed the eschatological character of John's ministry or baptism, another factor Josephus downplays or eliminates in his account. Thus it is doubtful that Josephus should be considered a more reliable authority on the matter of John's death than Mark (Scobie).

6. The Baptist Movement in the Christian Era.

That John had a considerable number of disciples who followed his practices and preaching is indicated in various Gospel sources (cf. Jn 1:35; 3:25-36; Lk 11:1). The Johannine material suggests some of Jesus' first disciples were originally John's disciples (this idea is not found in the Synoptics). That John also had a following after his death is indicated by such texts as Acts 18:25 and Acts 19:1-7. Consequently, the possibility remains that the movement not merely endured but spread after John's death.

To this day there is a small sect called the Mandaeans in parts of Iraq and Iran who claim to have kept this movement going continuously into the modern era. Modern Christendom was first made aware of their existence when Christian missionaries encountered them in the seventeenth century. It is doubtful that the Mandaean literature, which dates back only to the eighth century, can help us discern anything about the historical John the Baptist, except to witness that his ongoing impact was considerably greater than Christians have sometimes thought.

In point of fact, John the Baptist is mentioned by various early Christian writers such as Justin Martyr, Tertullian, Hippolytus and Origen. He figures in several apocryphal Christian works such as the second-century Gospel according to the Hebrews, the Protoevangelium of James, and according to Epiphanius he is mentioned in the nonextant Gospel of the Ebionites. Mention should also be made of the references to John's disciples in the *Clementine Recognitions* 1.60, where one of John's disciples is said to claim that John was the Messiah (Farmer).

It is further witness to the ongoing fascination with John that in the twentieth century various scholars have thought they have discovered traditions in the NT that ultimately came from the Baptist's followers (for example, Kraeling). Few such conjectures have received widespread acceptance among scholars, though they are not totally implausible (e.g., in the case of Lk 1). What is much more certain is that John the Baptist made a major impression on all the canonical Gospel writers and that each sought to present him in a particular and somewhat distinctive way.

7. The Christian Portrayal of the Baptist.

It has sometimes been thought that the NT reflects an anti-Baptist polemic, based on the assumption that the Christian movement saw the Baptist movement as a competitor. However, W. Wink has shown that, far from polemics against the Baptist, what we find in the NT is an attempt to claim John for the Christian cause. This entails a rather full recognition of the importance of the Baptist so that his testimony about the Coming One may be given its full weight.

As one moves chronologically through the Gospels (Mark, Matthew, Luke, then John) one finds, with the possible exception of Luke, that John's words about Jesus become increasingly confessional. Yet even as early as Mark, John is already the beginning of the good news. Thus it must be considered doubtful that Christians were guilty of projecting some sort of later conflict between Christians and John's followers into the Gospels. It is hard to believe that the early church would create such a notable group of traditions that grant the Baptist an important role in the Gospel, given the tendency of the church increasingly to stress the uniqueness of Jesus. Wink urges that Jesus' positive evaluation of the Baptist led to the incorporation of these traditions in the Gospels.

7.1. John the Baptist from Four Perspectives. In terms of the editorial perspective of each Evangelist, several motifs are readily apparent.

7.1.1. Mark. Mark seems to portray the Baptist as Elijah incognito (paralleling the messianic secret). He also goes to some lengths to parallel the passion of John and Jesus, the only two figures whose deaths he gives significant attention to in his Gospel (*see* Death of Christ). It may be that Mark 6 has been sandwiched between the sending and return of Jesus' disciples because Mark has earlier indicated that the ministry of Jesus in Galilee is precipitated by John's removal from the scene (cf. Mk 1:14).

7.1.2. Matthew. The First Evangelist stresses that Jesus and John stand together against a hostile religious and political opposition to their ministries. It is interesting, however, that we do not find this parallelism in the uniquely Matthean material within the birth narratives (*see* Birth of Jesus).

7.1.3. Luke. The Third Evangelist places John within his broader schema of salvation history as a notable figure in the historical chain of events initiated by God's intervention into Israel's history at the turn of the era. He also places more explicit stress than either Mark or Matthew on John's ministry involving "good news" (Lk 1:19; 3:18). In this way he stresses more than the other Evangelists the continuity between Jesus and John, an emphasis seen in the material shared in common with Matthew and Mark and in the uniquely Lukan material in the birth narratives (*see* Birth of Jesus). Luke 16:16 need not be seen as being at odds with the attempt to depict John as one who is part of the new eschatological action of God amidst his people. In view of Luke 1:19 and 3:18, Luke 16:16 should probably be taken to mean that the period of the activity of the prophets had already ended when John came on the scene.

7.1.4. John. The Fourth Evangelist portrays John as the ideal and almost-Christian witness to Jesus (cf. Jn 1, 3) as God's Messiah and Lamb, stressing the subordination of John to Jesus (Wink). If this element of subordination and the idea of John as a preparer for the One who is to follow does go back to the Baptist, then it is not a case of the Evangelists relegating John to a position that he did not have in real life but rather highlighting and building on John's self-proclaimed role.

7.2. A Focus on Mark's Gospel. It is not sufficient simply to take cursory note of how the Evangelists have edited their sources about John the Baptist in service of their christological interests. It is equally important to gain a sense of the overall portrayal of the Baptist in each Gospel. Space does not allow us to develop fully the portrait of John in each of the four Gospels. Thus we will focus on one such sample—the

earliest, and in many ways most suggestive, portrait of the Baptist found in Mark's Gospel. Depending on how one reads Mark 1:1, it is possible that Mark intends to portray the story of the Baptist as "the beginning of the gospel of Jesus Christ, the Son of God." If this is so, it affects not only how one reads the rest of the portrayal of the Baptist in this Gospel but also how one understands what Mark means by "gospel." In what sense is the story of John part of the good news about Jesus? Is it just that he was the beginning of the good news of God's climactic saving activity or is something more intended?

In terms of the structure of Mark's Gospel, one notes that all the references to John are confined to the first eleven chapters of this Gospel. In fact, John appears only periodically in these chapters. He is not an ongoing figure in the flow of the narrative, nor does he link the pericopes together. After the initial paragraphs about John in Mark 1:2-11, followed by a brief reference to John's disciples fasting in Mark 2:18, John does not appear in the story again until Mark 6. There we hear the story of two rejections—that of Jesus in Nazareth and that of John by Herod Antipas, which leads to John's demise. It is striking that this substantial narrative in Mark 6 is introduced by the suggestion that Jesus might be John *redivivus* (Mk 6:14), which is very close to the way in which John is introduced into the Caesarea Philippi discussion at Mark 8:27-28. There Jesus asks his disciples, "Who do people say that I am?" to which the first reply is, "John the Baptist." Then in the following chapter, Jesus goes on to distinguish himself from John by implying that John is Elijah incognito (Mk 9:11-12), whom he says comes to restore all things. Yet in Mark 11:27-33, in the final clear reference to John, Jesus links his authority with John and his baptism.

Thus in the Markan schema, we seem to see the following pattern emerging. (1) John linked closely with Jesus and the Gospel (Mk 1). (2) John distinguished from Jesus in his practices as noted by outsiders (Mk 2). (3) Outsiders attempt to identify Jesus with John, even considering him as possibly John come back from the dead (Mk 6; 8). (4) Jesus distinguishes himself from John but in the process ascribes to him a significant role in the new saving activity of God—he is Elijah, the one who restores all (Mk 9). (5) In Jerusalem before the chief priests, scribes and elders, Jesus publicly implies some sort of identification of John and Jesus in regard to the matter of divine authorization (Mk 11).

This suggests that Mark's intention in using the Baptist material is not primarily to indicate that John bore witness to Jesus (as in the Johannine material) but rather as a foil to indicate who Jesus was not. This is accomplished in part by distinguishing Jesus' and John's activities and correcting the false impression of outsiders about their identities, and in part by having Jesus in two key places (Mk 9; 11) give testimony to who John really is, a testimony that balances that of John to Jesus in Mark 1. This suggests that for Mark, John *is* the beginning of the gospel, not merely because he was seen to be Jesus' forerunner, an Elijah figure, but also because Jesus bore witness to John.

Finally, it may be important that near the end of Mark's Gospel outsiders once again misunderstand Jesus and his words, this time assuming he was calling on Elijah (Mk 15:35). But Jesus had already spoken of "Elijah" as one who had come and gone as it was written of him (Mk 9). Thus the end of the Gospel, unlike its beginning, is a word not about Elijah or his coming or going. Rather, it is about the going and coming again of Jesus. To put it another way, the conclusion of the Gospel is about the death of Jesus, about the God on whom he called, and about that unique one for whom the divine witness is given: "Do not be amazed; you seek Jesus of Nazareth, who was crucified. He has risen; he is not here" (Mk 16:6). In the end, Jesus of Nazareth is not John *redivivus*. John's story finishes before the end of the Gospel, but as for Jesus of Nazareth, he comes back from the dead as himself—*that* is the end of the Gospel. The tension in the narrative is resolved by showing that the discontinuity between Jesus' and John's stories is more profound than the continuity.

It is no accident that in the new quest for the historical Jesus, scholars have seen the history of John the Baptist as a rather secure foundation on which to reconstruct an historical estimate of Jesus and his ministry. A major key to understanding the historical Jesus is a proper estimation of the elements of continuity and discontinuity between the ministries and messages of the two major figures in the Gospels—Jesus and John.

See also BAPTISM; ESCHATOLOGY; JUDGMENT.

DJG: ELIJAH AND ELISHA; HERODIAN DYNASTY.

BIBLIOGRAPHY. D. C. Allison, "Elijah Must Come First," *JBL* 103 (1984) 256-58; L. F. Badia, *The Qumran Baptism and John the Baptist's Baptism* (Lanham, MD: University Press of America, 1980); P. W. Barnett, "The Jewish Sign Prophets—A.D. 40-70: Their Intentions and Origin," *NTS* 27 (1981) 679-97; O. Betz, "Die Proselytentaufe der Qumransekte und die Taufe im Neuen Testament," *RevQ* 1 (1958) 213-34; D. Catchpole, "John the Baptist, Jesus and the Parable of the Tares," *SJT* 31 (1978) 557-70; W. D. Davies and D. C. Allison Jr., *The Gospel According to St. Matthew,* vol. 1 (ICC; Edinburgh: T & T Clark, 1988); S. L. Davies, "John the Baptist and the Essene Kashruth," *NTS* 29 (1983) 569-71; M. M. Faierstein, "Why Do the Scribes Say That Elijah Must Come First?" *JBL* 100 (1981) 75-86; W. R. Farmer, "John the Baptist," *IDB* (1962) 1:955-62; J. A. Fitzmyer, "More About Elijah Coming First," *JBL* 104 (1985) 295-96; C. H. Kraeling, *John the Baptist* (New York: Scribner's, 1951); C. C. McCown, "The Scene of John's Ministry and Its Relation to the Purpose and Outcome of His Mission," *JBL* 59 (1940) 113-31; S. McKnight, *A Light Among the Gentiles* (Minneapolis: Fortress, 1991); J. P. Meier, *A Marginal Jew: Rethinking the Historical Jesus,* vol. 2, *Mentor, Message and Miracles* (New York: Doubleday, 1994) 19-233; J. C. O'Neill, *Messiah: Six Lectures on the Ministry of Jesus* (Cambridge: Cochrane, 1980); K. Pusey, "Jewish Proselyte Baptism," *ExpT* 95 (1983-84) 141-45; B. Reicke, "The Historical Setting of John's Baptism," in *Jesus, the Gospels and the Church,* ed. E. P. Sanders (Macon, GA: Mercer University Press, 1987) 209-24; R. Riesner, "Bethany Beyond Jordan (Jn 1:28), Topography, Theology and History in the Fourth Gospel," *TynB* 38 (1987) 29-63; C. H. H. Scobie, *John the Baptist* (Philadelphia: Fortress, 1964); J. E. Taylor, *The Immerser: John the Baptist Within Second Temple Judaism* (Grand Rapids: Eerdmans, 1997); T. M. Taylor, "The Beginnings of Jewish Proselyte Baptism," *NTS* 2 (1955-56) 193-98; R. L. Webb, *John the Baptizer and Prophet: A Socio-Historical Study* (JSNTSup 62; Sheffield: JSOT, 1991); W. Wink, *John the Baptist in the Gospel Tradition* (Cambridge: Cambridge University Press, 1968); B. Witherington, *The Christology of Jesus* (Minneapolis: Fortress, 1990).   B. Witherington III

JUBILEES. *See* APOCRYPHA AND PSEUDEPIGRAPHA.

JUDAISM AND THE NEW TESTAMENT

Judaism in antiquity is a complex phenomenon, involving religious, social, economic, historical and ethnic aspects of the life of a people whose influence has greatly exceeded their power.

That influence is most obvious today in the literary remains of ancient Judaism, canonical and noncanonical, which continue to have a formative impact upon the very definition of human culture. But Judaism must not be equated directly with the religions of those Judaic sources that happen to remain; in order to assess those sources, to appreciate the significance of Judaism within the task of understanding Jesus and the NT and to gauge its influence more generally, a different approach is necessary. We need to uncover those religious systems of beliefs, reactions, social conventions, ways of thinking and habits of feeling that the literary sources and the history of the people manifest; moreover, those systems must be appraised with reference to their dramatic transitions over time, or not at all. The present article is to deal with Judaism through the time of the NT, that is, prior to the emergence of rabbinic Judaism (*see* Rabbinic Traditions and Writings). Judaism in the time of the NT can be appreciated only on the basis of its procession from earlier forms. Accordingly, we must first turn our attention to the root of Judaism, the religion of Israel, taking account of the delay between the emergence of that religion and the probable dates of its sources.

Judaism in every period is rooted in the notion that Israel is chosen. The perennial paradox in the study of Judaism is that the notion of election is more persistent than any definition of what Israel might be. We might be thinking of an extended family of Arameans that departed from Mesopotamia in order to settle westward, of their initial settlement in Canaan, of the migrant group in Egypt, of those who departed from Egypt, of those who struggled for control of the land of Canaan, of the nation and its eventual monarchy and consequent civil war, of the dispossessed peoples in Babylonia, of the ideal Israel that the Scriptures of the exile project and/or of those people in the land and in the Diaspora who read those Scriptures as their own, for whom Israel was and is an identification of self.

Each of the moments of the development of Israel named above and each of several other stages has been the object of particular, scholarly attention. But we may, as a convenience, cope with the topic of Judaism under four stages: the period of prehistory, between the scriptural Abrahamic family and the scriptural people led by judges; the period of nationalization and monarchy; the period of dispossession and the canonization of Scripture; and the period of radical pluralization, which is widely referred to today as early Judaism.

1. The Prehistory of Israel: From Family to People
2. Nationalization and Monarchy
3. Dispossession and Canonization
4. Radical Pluralization
5. Early Judaism and the New Testament

1. The Prehistory of Israel: From Family to People.

If the conviction of being divinely elect is a condition *sine qua non* of Judaism, then the traditional notion that Abraham is the father of all Jews is a useful point of departure. After all, he is remembered as being partner to the covenant involving God's gift of the land that would be called Israel and the sign of circumcision (Gen 15:1-21; 17:1-14). But the assumption of Genesis is that Abraham and the patriarchs are seminomadic, in the sense that they migrate and cultivate land. Just that style of living is what brings Israel, the children of Jacob, who was renamed in a struggle with God (Gen 32:22-32), down to Egypt. The emphasis throughout the patriarchal cycle is upon the literal kinship of the entire group that may be called Israel.

Moses is particularly associated with the liberation of Israel from Egypt, but, just as the quality of the sojourn in that land changed (see Ex 1:8-10), so did the constitution of the people. The estimate of more than a half million warriors in Numbers 1:45-46 may well be hyperbolic, but an increase of population during a period described biblically as of more than four centuries (Ex 12:40) meant that any system of strictly familial lineage was out of the question. Moses was therefore responsible not simply for the liberation from Egypt but also for the reconstitution of Israel as a people, rather than simply a family, on the basis of his revelation.

The Mosaic constitution or covenant would become paradigmatic for every age of Judaism that followed. Tribal lineage, on the assumption that the tribes were descended from the sons of Jacob/Israel, replaced familial lineage as the operative definition of the group, and that was an evolution that the weight of numbers alone probably effected. But the tribal arrangement by itself was unsystematic and needed to be balanced by a centripetal impulse in order for Israel to emerge as a functional entity. Moses is the emblem of centralized sacrifice and judgment. His claims upon Pharaoh are predicated upon sacrifice (Ex 3:18), and his relation to Jethro (or Reuel, in the passage in question), the Midianite priest, makes his cultic interests manifest (Ex 2:15b-22). The notion of the people sacrificing creates the notion of the people; apart from some common action, there would be families, extended families, villages and "stems" (or "staffs," as the tribes are called in the Hebrew Bible), but no organic whole.

The Mosaic constitution established the stem of Levi as the guardians of the sanctuary (Num 4:1-49) and assured that the conception of one God would be coextensive with the conviction of one people. If sacrifice was the charter of liberation, then a declension into multiple gods would return Israel to the division of Egypt (Ex 20:2, 3, 22-26). A corollary of the unity of God and his people is that there should be a single sanctuary, but in the premonarchial phase we can speak only of the preeminence of the pan-tribal shrine, since worship at other sites is also attested. At the same time, the tribal stems of Israel were coordinated at the cultic center in a system of judgment (Ex 18:13-26), so that disputes could be regulated and the appropriate integrity of Israel could be maintained. That Israel should be whole, an integer of divine revelation, becomes the central imperative of the Mosaic covenant.

Sacrifice, within the Mosaic system, is the place of meeting between God and Israel (Ex 24:1-11), such that only what is clean may be involved (Lev 11—15), and much of it passes to divine ownership (Lev 3:1-17). Not only parts of things offered but the cultic instruments (Ex 25—31) and the entire tribe of Levi (Num 3:45) are God's. Moreover, the declared aim of entry into the land of promise is to cleanse it of what is not acceptable to God. Everything else, people, beasts and property, is to be "devoted," that is, extirpated (Josh 6, 7). The pentateuchal emphasis upon that "devotion" (*ḥerem*) has confused some modern discussion. There has been a tendency to refer to the conquest of Canaan, but much of the language of destruction—which is undoubtedly present—needs to be under-stood in its sacrificial context, as a cleansing of the land.

Joshua and Judges reflect the situation in Canaan much more directly, in their stories of intertribal rivalries and wars, accommodations with the indigenous populations, the desire for booty and the problems inherent in the tendency to erect local shrines. Those glimpses into the turmoil in the midst of which the nation emerged have led to the evolution of distinct, scholarly theories concerning how Canaan was settled by Hebrew-speakers. M. Noth is associated with the theory of an amphictyony (such as existed in ancient Greece), an association of twelve tribes for cultic purposes. The number twelve is problematic, however. Greek amphictyonies of other numbers are known, and the number within Israel was largely theoretical, perhaps derived from sacrificial practice (see Josh 4:9, 20).

Levi was left out from the point of view of a geographical inheritance, and Joseph in standard lists could be counted three times, as Ephraim and the two half-tribes of Manasseh (Josh 17:17, 18; 22:1-6). Unusual lists, such as Judges 1:16-36, have the tribes deviate from the number, names and kinship presupposed ordinarily in the Mosaic covenant. In addition, the point of Levi within Israel is to provide a fixed arrangement of cultic personnel for a moving sanctuary, while in Noth's Greek analogy, tribes took turns in providing for a settled sanctuary. But with those crucial allowances, Noth's theory has been the most influential of the twentieth century. Crucial changes, however, have been suggested by G. Mendenhall and N. Gottwald. The former envisages the occupation of the land as an instance of peasants' revolt, while the latter thinks in terms of a union between disenfranchised local elements and migrants from Egypt in opposition to Canaanite hegemony.

The Israel that (dis)possessed the land of Canaan, then, was an amalgam of groups that claimed such affinity with Abraham, pursued the worship of God laid down by Moses and on that basis sought to rid the land of Canaan of all but its own. Its destruction of other material cultures, particularly urban cultures (as in the case of Jericho; Josh 6), was its hallmark. Leadership consisted in the intervention of judges who defended the possession of a given stem or stems, rooted out elements of Canaanite worship or attacked non-Israelite powers. The authority of the judges seems to have resided in their success in pursuing one or more of those aims, which success might be attributed to possession by the Spirit of God (see Judg 11).

2. Nationalization and Monarchy.

Judges takes a particularly dim view of the institution that obviously would have provided greater stability: the monarchy. The removable ark of the covenant, which provided the center of Israel's loyalty and devotion, was vulnerable to attack, and the unsystematic convention of judges, while it might answer to the occasional onslaught of disorganized foes, was no answer to the centralized attack of even a petty kingdom. But the book of Judges casts monarchy as an essentially apostate institution, in that it implicitly involves denying the sovereignty of the Lord (see Judg 8:22—9:57).

The prophet Samuel is portrayed as intimately connected with the rise of the monarchy in Israel. He is closely associated with the ark of the covenant and the priesthood of Eli. Evidently worship effects the proximity of the Lord, whose will Samuel is then held to interpret (1 Sam 3:1—4:1). Samuel is a fully priestly figure (and a judge, 1 Sam 7:15—8:2), in that he offers sacrifice himself, and it is notable that he does so in sites other than the central shrine (1 Sam 7; 9:3—10:24; 16). Assertions about the future are involved in his interpretation of God's presence in sacrifice, but interpretation is by no means limited to prediction. Samuel's period of prophecy corresponds to the capture of the ark in war and its removal to Ashdod, a city with a fixed temple for its god, Dagon (1 Sam 4, 5). The ultimate release of the ark, after it was held to cause harm to the inhabitants of any city in which it was held, ends the regular practice of bringing it into battle (1 Sam 7:1-2; cf. 1 Sam 14:18-22), and a desire for monarchy grows thereafter (1 Sam 8:4-22). Samuel resists but ultimately gives in, on God's behalf, to popular desire and anoints Saul (1 Sam 10). Saul is a physically big man (1 Sam 9:1-2), in the tradition of the judges, but also a failure. He usurps the function of sacrifice (1 Sam 13:8-15; 14:31-35); fails to devote what he should (that is, destroy captives and spoil that was incompatible with God's sanctity; 1 Sam 15); he also becomes ambitious for his own family (1 Sam 18—20). God, by means of Samuel, rejects Saul and anoints David (1 Sam 16:1-13).

2.1. The Davidic Monarchy. The Davidic monarchy becomes the object of a solemn oath in 2 Samuel 7, where the prophet Nathan promises God's protection of David's progeny. It is notable that the promise is occasioned by David's undertaking to build a temple. The offer itself is accepted but deferred: Solomon is to accomplish the task (2 Sam 7:13). But the function of the king in protecting, not leading, worship is established, and the role of prophecy as the guide of the king is confirmed. Precisely in those aspects, David differs from Saul, and the promise to David is integrated within the covenant generally.

The centralization of the sacrificial cult in David's city, Jerusalem (2 Sam 6), had both positive and negative effects, from the point of view of faithfulness to the covenant. Positive, because the new center became the focus of codification. In addition to the court history, an account of David's reign produced shortly after his death (2 Sam 9—1 Kings 2), the source known to scholarship as J was produced. J (named after its putative author or authors, the Yahwist [earlier spelled with a "J" in the Latin manner]) first linked in literary form the people of the Davidic kingdom with creation, the patriarchs, the exodus and the possession of the land. Earlier, shorter books had been compiled to be recited at cultic centers, so that a treaty, or regulations of purity or ethics, or alleged genealogical connections or victories or other formative events might be remembered in association with sacrifice. But a single center involved a collection of such materials during the tenth century, and an early attempt to present them more coherently, for presentation at Jerusalem for the feasts that were primarily celebrated there. But there is also a negative side to the settlement in Jerusalem. With monarchy there came the pressure to trade and compete with other cities: the multiplication of cults—and the de facto acceptance of their deities—was a feature of Solomon's otherwise auspicious reign (1 Kings 11).

First Kings lays the blame for the division of united Israel into Israel in the north and Judah in the south upon Solomon's apostasy (1 Kings 11:29-40), and there is a thematic link in Scripture between marriage to non-Israelite women and idolatry. But the kings, north and south, undermined their own authority by their recourse to slavery and their conspicuous consumption, not only their idolatry. The last aspect is nonetheless an especially emphasized feature in the careers of the worst kings. Ahab in the north, with his wife Jezebel, fomented the worship of Baal and was opposed by the prophet Elijah (1 Kings 16:29—22:40); in the south, Ahaz renovated the temple to look like the one in Damascus and may even have practiced human sacrifice (2 Kings 16:1-20). It is evident that the alliance of Ahab with Sidon and of Ahaz with Damascus was a formative influence in their respective religious policies.

2.2. The Prophetic Movement. Prophecy found its voice as a movement in its opposition to the monarchs it regarded as apostate. Prior to the crystallizing impact of that opposition, prophets appear to have been identified as those who spoke for God, often in association with worship in particular sanctuaries. Their prophetic ministry might to a greater or lesser extent involve unusual states of consciousness or atypical behavior, sometimes with the use of music and dance. But first the association with David, and then the antagonism of kings in the north and south, made of prophecy a startlingly coherent movement.

The emergence of prophecy as a literary genre is to be dated to the eighth century and the message of Amos. Fundamentally a prophet of doom against the northern kingdom, Amos foretold judgment against Israel's apostate kings, and the prophet Hosea vividly generalized that theme to include the nation as a whole. They were quickly followed in the south by Micah and Isaiah, and an urgent appeal for social justice became a hallmark of prophecy in the south.

The doom announced against the north by an Amos or a Hosea must have appeared idle during periods of prosperity, but when, in 722 B.C., the capital of the north was taken and the northern kingdom was subjected to a policy of exile, the prophetic message appeared to have been vindicated. The works of the northern prophets were preserved in the south, together with extensive pentateuchal traditions of Israel's beginnings that had been treasured in the north. There were those in the north, priests and prophets and scribes, who were not taken in by the royal attempt at syncretism. Nonetheless, the prophetic attack upon deceitful prophets and cultic hypocrisy is eloquent testimony to the power of that attempt.

Spurred on by the demise of Israel in the north, whose people were lost to history, the prophets in Judah attempted to purify the life of their people. Isaiah urgently argued against foreign alliances and insisted that fidelity to God alone would save Jerusalem; Jeremiah ceaselessly denounced faithlessness and was prosecuted for his trouble; Ezekiel's enactments of coming disaster won him a reputation as a crank. But in the reign of Josiah, a royal reformation backed much of the critique of the prophets (2 Kings 22:1—23:30; 2 Chron 34:1—35:27). Josiah restored worship in the temple according to covenantal norms; he centralized sacrifice, even of the Passover, in Jerusalem; he tolerated no foreign incursions. In his program he was guided by a scroll of the law, which was found in the temple during the restoration, a scroll that has since antiquity been associated with the present book of Deuteronomy, which presses an agenda of radical centralization and separation from foreign nations such as impelled Josiah. But in 609 B.C., Josiah was killed in battle in an attempt to block the alliance between Pharaoh Neco and the Assyrians at a place called Megiddo. The impact of his death may be gauged by the impact of that name upon the apocalyptic tradition (see 4.1.1 below), in the form Armageddon (Rev 16:16; cf. Zech 12:11).

3. Dispossession and Canonization.

3.1. Exile and the Vision of Classic Israel: The Pentateuch. The end of the kingdom of Judah came quickly after the death of Josiah. Culminating in 587/586 B.C., the Babylonian Empire, which had succeeded the Assyrians (see the prophetic book of Nahum), implemented a policy of exile, subsequent to their siege of Jerusalem and their destruction of the temple. Had the course of events then followed what happened to Israel, there would today be no Judaism to study. Paradoxically, however, the forces that must have seemed sure to destroy the religion of the covenant with the Lord instead assured its survival and nurtured its international dimension. During the Babylonian exile, priestly and prophetic movements joined forces to form a united program of restoration that put a form of Israel back on the map within a generation. Out of this restoration a vision of an ideal Israel, memorialized in the Pentateuch as we know it, emerged as a truly canonical standard for Judaism.

3.2. Restoration and New Visions for the Future: The Prophets. The dispossession of Judah to

Babylon set up the priestly and prophetic hegemony that made restoration possible. But just as the Pentateuch sets out particularly priestly concerns, the prophetic movement also brought a distinctive message to the canon. The prophets generally agreed with their priestly confederates that the land was to be possessed again, and postexilic additions to the books of Isaiah (Is 40—55), Jeremiah (Jer 23:1-8; 31) and Ezekiel (Ezek 40—48) constitute eloquent motivations for return to the land.

But the previous abuses of the kings and their sanctuaries made the prophetic movement insist that righteousness was the prior requirement of sacrifice and that the events of the recent past were a warning. A Zechariah might be happy to set out the hope of a priestly messiah beside the Davidic king who was to rule (Zech 3; 4), but the predominant emphasis fell on the crucial necessity of loyalty to the worship of God (Zech 8). Moreover, eschatology became characteristic of the prophetic movement, both in additions to biblical prophets, such as Isaiah and Ezekiel, and in fresh works, such as Joel and Malachi. The contemporary governance, whether Persian, Ptolemaic or Seleucid, and the present temple were provisional, until an anointed king and an anointed priest would rule properly. Just the image of a priestly orientation redefined by the prophets is seen in the career of Ezra in the books of Ezra and Nehemiah: prophet, priest and scribe become one in their insistence on the vision of classic Israel, centered on the restored temple.

The temple as restored (beginning in 520 B.C.) was, however, far from anyone's ideal. Some who remembered the splendor of Solomon's edifice are reported to have wept when they saw the results of the efforts under Ezra (Ezra 3:10-13). That imperfect focus nonetheless served to attract a permanent priesthood, and the notion of a canon provided focus to the prophetic movement. Now a body of literature, which could be interpreted, was held to provide the guidance that individual prophets formerly gave. It is notable that Ezra's ministry involved guiding Israel on the basis of scriptural interpretation. The scribe emerges as something of a judge: the dominant, religious personality, as the warrant of true prophecy and the arbiter of priestly conduct (Neh 8—13).

3.3. Voices from Outside the Priestly-Prophetic Hegemony: The Writings. But the appearance that scribal leadership was settled is more superficial than representative. Battles concerning the proper conduct of the cult and the proper personnel of the priesthood raged during the period of restored Israel, and powerful movements produced literatures outside of scribal control. While the final form of the Pentateuch and what are called the Former Prophets (Joshua—2 Kings) and the Latter Prophets within Judaism may be attributed to the hegemony of priestly and prophetic interests that has been described, the category of Writings (the last in the three biblical divisions of traditional Judaism), together with the Apocrypha and the pseudepigrapha, best characterizes other facets of the religion.

The book of Psalms represents a cultic piety centered on just those aspects that levitical instructions exclude: the music, dance, poetry, prayer and praise (the term *psalms, tĕhillîm,* means "songs of praise") that the temple attracted. They speak more eloquently of the emotional affect of and popular participation in sacrificial worship than does any other document in the Bible. Proverbs also represents a nonpriestly, nonprophetic focus of piety in restored Israel, defined by prudential wisdom. Job and Ecclesiastes are other examples within the canon.

Initially wisdom is understood to be an aspect of God, which by knowing one can become familiar with God. "Wisdom" in Hebrew is a feminine noun and came to be personified as a woman; by the time of Ecclesiasticus (or Ben Sira, from the early second century B.C.) and the Wisdom of Solomon (from the late first century B.C. or somewhat later), she is considered a fundamental means of access to God. The Wisdom of Solomon was composed in Greek, but the focus upon Wisdom is by no means unique to what is commonly called Hellenistic Judaism. Contacts with Egyptian and Babylonian inquiries into divine wisdom do probably date from the time of the Israelite and Judean kings, as part of their characteristic syncretism. But unlike idolatry and polygyny, Wisdom survived and prospered as a suitable and fertile means of communion with God after the notion of the unique covenant with Israel had triumphed.

In the case of Philo of Alexandria, whose lifetime straddled the end of the last era and the beginning of our own, the pursuit of wisdom became a philosophical articulation of Judaism; he contributed an awareness of how Judaism and

Hellenistic culture—whose contact is already obvious in the Apocrypha and pseudepigrapha—might be related. Philo is unusually learned in his representation of a basic development of the Judaism of his period. His simultaneously Greco-Roman and Judaic notion of the logos is a case in point (see Philo *Op. Mund.*).

3.4. Threats to Cultic Purity and Priestly Unity.

The question of the priesthood in the restored temple, meanwhile, became increasingly fraught. The Persian regime gave way to Alexander the Great. Among the dynasties of the generals who succeeded him, first the Egyptian Ptolemies and then the Syrian Seleucids largely maintained the enlightened settlement of the Persians. The Seleucid monarch Antiochus IV (surnamed Epiphanes) is commonly portrayed as a great exception to the policy, and he did unquestionably occupy Jerusalem and arrange for a foreign cult in the sanctuary in 167 B.C., which included the sacrifice of swine (a Hellenistic delicacy; 1 Macc 1:20-64; Josephus *Ant.* 12.5.4 §§248-56). But Antiochus intervened in the city at first as the protector of a high-priestly family, the Tobiads, who were then in dispute with the Oniad family (Josephus *J.W.* 1.1-2 §§31-35). Dispossessed, the latter group moved to Egypt, where a temple was built at Heliopolis, in a form different from the restored temple in Jerusalem (Josephus *J.W.* 1.1 §33; 7.10.2-3 §§420-32). The cult of Onias appears to have been of limited influence, but the mere existence in the period of restored Israel of an alternative cult, manned by legitimate pretenders to the high priesthood in Jerusalem, is eloquent testimony of deep divisions within the sacerdotal ranks and within Judaism generally.

4. Radical Pluralization.

Early Judaism may conveniently be dated from 167 B.C., with the entry of Antiochus's officer, named Apollonius (2 Macc 5:24-25), into Jerusalem and his desecration of the temple, but it is evident that the radical pluralization of Judaism prior to Jesus, and of which Jesus was a symptom and a result, is rooted in the flawed unity of restored Israel during the previous period. But Antiochus's campaign triggered a fissure of interests and a reconfiguration of those interests in a way that made pluralism the order of the day. The temple of Onias at Heliopolis is only one example, but one that shows that how sacrifice was offered, and by whom, was held by one familial group to be a better measure of the acceptability of worship than where sacrifice was offered.

4.1. The Rise of the Hasmoneans and the Response of the Faithful.

In Israel, however, there was another group, defined by a desire to remain loyal to sacrifice in Jerusalem by an appropriate priesthood and a resistance to the demands of Antiochus, known as "the faithful" (the famous Hasidim). Attempts have been made in the history of scholarship to identify the Hasidim with a particular sect of Judaism during the period of the Second Temple, such as the Essenes or the Pharisees, but the adjective *faithful* cannot usefully or legitimately be limited to any one specific group. In the context of reaction to Antiochus, however, the sense of the term clearly related to one's adherence to covenantal norms of sacrifice, as part of a vehement resistance.

Among the resisters was Mattathias, a country priest from Modin, whose son, Judas Maccabeus ("the hammer") introduced the most powerful priestly rule Judaism has ever known, which was known under the name of Hasmoneus, Mattathias's ancestor (1 Macc 2:1—9:18; Josephus *Ant.* 12.6.1 §265; 16.7.1 §187; 20.8.11 §190; 20.10.1 §§238, 247). Judas, as is well known, turned piety into disciplined revolt, including an alliance with Rome (1 Macc 8) and a willingness to break the sabbath for military reasons (1 Macc 2:41), which saw the restoration of worship within the covenant in the temple in 164 B.C. (1 Macc 4:36-61). After his death, his brother Jonathan was named high priest (1 Macc 10:20-21), and from that time until the period of Roman rule, the high priesthood was a Hasmonean prerogative.

Those events were too rapid for some and unacceptable in the view of others. In strictly familial terms, the Hasmoneans could not claim the high priesthood as a right, and therefore competition with other families of priests was a factor. Moreover, the suspension of the sabbath for military purposes (see Josephus *J.W.* 1.7.3 §146) and the arrogation of the high priesthood and the monarchy by the non-Davidic Hasmoneans seemed particularly vicious to many Jews (Josephus *J.W.* 1.3.1 §70). Antiochus had sanctioned apostasy, and the Hasmonean regime appeared to be compounding apostasy both in its initial resistance and its consolidation of power.

4.1.1. Apocalyptic Resistance.

The book of Daniel does not express overt opposition to the

Hasmoneans, but it does represent the less activist, apocalyptic stance that many pious Jews adopted as an alternative to the nationalistic and militaristic policy of the Hasmoneans. The eschatology of the prophets during the period of restored Israel is here transformed into a scenario of the end time, in which the temple would be restored by miraculous means, with the archangel Michael's triumph capped by the resurrection of the just and the unjust (Dan 12:1-4). Folk Judaism of the period also anticipated providential interventions, but Daniel elevates and specifies that anticipation until it becomes a program of patient attention and fidelity, warranted by both heavenly vision and the sage named Daniel of the Babylonian period (cf. Ezek 14:14).

4.1.2. Essenes. In the case of the Essenes, opposition to the Hasmoneans became overt. They pursued their own system of purity, ethics and initiation, followed their own calendar and withdrew into their own communities, either within cities or in isolated sites such as Qumran. There they awaited a coming apocalyptic war, when they, as "the sons of light," would triumph over "the sons of darkness": not only the Gentiles but also anyone not of their vision (*War Scroll* [1QM]; *Rule of the Community* [1QS]). The culmination of those efforts was to be complete control of Jerusalem and the temple, where worship would be offered according to their revelation, the correct understanding of the law of Moses (cf. CD 5:17—6:11). Their insistence upon a doctrine of two messiahs, one of Israel and one of Aaron, would suggest that it was particularly the Hasmoneans' arrogation of priestly and royal powers that alienated the Essenes.

4.1.3. Pharisees. Most of those who resisted the Seleucids or who sympathized with the resistance were neither of priestly families nor of Essene temperament. Nonetheless, the unchecked rule of the Hasmonean priests in the temple was not entirely acceptable to them. For that large group, the pharisaic movement held a great attraction. The Pharisees, in their attempt to influence what the Hasmoneans did rather than to replace them definitively, appear as much more conservative than the Essenes or competing priestly families. Their focus was upon the issue of purity, as defined principally in their oral tradition and their interpretation of Scripture. Since issues of purity were bound to be complicated in the Hasmonean combination of secular government and sacrificial worship, disputes were inevitable.

Josephus, for example, reports that the Pharisees made known their displeasure at Alexander Janneus by inciting a crowd to pelt him with lemons (at hand for a festal procession) at the time he should have been offering sacrifice (Josephus *Ant.* 13.13.5 §§372-73). Josephus also relates, from a later period, the teaching of the rabbis (probably Pharisees) who were implicated in dismantling the eagle Herod had erected over a gate of the temple (Josephus *J.W.* 1.33.2-4 §§648-55; *Ant.* 17.6.2-4 §§149-67). This gesture was less subversive of the established authority in the cult than what earlier Pharisees had done and more pointedly a challenge to Herod. Paradoxically, the willingness of the Pharisees to consider the Hasmoneans in their priestly function, in distinction from the Essenes, involved them not only in symbolic disputes but also in vocal and bloody confrontations. Alexander Janneus is reported to have executed by crucifixion eight hundred opponents, either Pharisees or those with whom the Pharisees sympathized, and to have slaughtered their families; but his wife came to an accommodation with the Pharisees that guaranteed them considerable influence (Josephus *J.W.* 1.4.6—1.5.3 §§96-114).

It seems clear that within the Hasmonean period, purity was a political issue and to some extent a symbol. The acquiescence of one of the dynasty to any pharisaic stricture implicitly acknowledged that the Hasmonean priesthood was provisional, and the pharisaic movement probably found its original political expression in opposition to that priesthood (Josephus *Ant.* 13.10.5-6 §§288-98). The Pharisees accepted and developed the notion that with the end of the canon, the age of prophecy in the classical sense had ceased (cf. 1 Macc 4:46). For that reason they plausibly saw Ezra as their source and their own interpretative movement as an extension of his program of restoration (cf. *m. 'Abot* 1:1-18; 2 Esdr 14). But in two vital respects, the Pharisees need to be distinguished from the reforms of Ezra. First, they identified themselves with no specific priestly or political figure. Their program was its own guide and was not to be subservient to any particular family or dynasty. Second, pharisaic interpretation was not limited to the Scriptures, nor was its characteristic focus scriptural: the principal point of departure was the recollection of earlier teaching of those called sages.

609

Ultimately, after the period of the NT, the ideology of the rabbis, as the Pharisees came to be called, had it that Moses conveyed two Torahs on Sinai, one written and one oral. Even before that understanding, however, the sages treated as normative the teachings of their predecessors in chains of tradition. It was not so much that oral tradition was set alongside Scripture as that oral tradition *was* Scripture until the canon could no longer be ignored as the functional standard of Judaism.

4.2. Judaism Under Roman Rule. Factionalism among the Hasmoneans, which resulted in rival claims to the high priesthood between Aristobulus and Hyrcanus, the sons of Alexandra, culminated in an appeal by both sides to Pompey, who obliged by taking Jerusalem for Rome and entering the sanctuary in 63 B.C. (Josephus *J.W.* 1.7.6 §§152-54).

4.2.1. Opposition and Accommodation. The *Psalms of Solomon* represents a common, pious expression of horror at the events of 63 B.C., which was probably shared by most Pharisees, whether or not the *Psalms* should be taken as specifically pharisaic. From that period and all through the reign of Herod and his relatives, the Pharisees' attitude to the government was ambivalent. Some appear to have engaged in a principled opposition to Roman rule and its representatives as such. Today that group is known as the Zealots, but the term is a misnomer.

The Zealots were a priestly group of revolutionaries, not rebellious Pharisees, who were associated with Eleazar, son of Simon, during the revolt of A.D. 66-73 (Josephus *J.W.* 2.20.3 §§564-65; 4.4.1 §§224-25). The rebellious Pharisees are also to be distinguished from the movements of prophetic pretenders who claimed divine inspiration for their efforts to free the land of the Romans (Josephus *J.W.* 2.13.4-6 §§258-65; 7.11.1-2 §§437-46). Other Pharisees normally accommodated to the new regime, but resisted—sometimes violently—Herodian excesses, such as the erection of a golden eagle on a gate of the temple (Josephus *J.W.* 1.33.2-4 §§648-55). Nonetheless, an apparently pharisaic group is called "the Herodians" (Mt 22:16; Mk 3:6; 12:13), which presumably signals its partisanship of the interests of the royal family as a considerable support of their teaching of purity. They may be associated with rabbis who enjoyed the protection of Herod and his house; the authorities referred to in rabbinic literature as the "sons of Bathyra"

(cf. *b. B. Mes.* 85a) may have been such a group.

Others still largely cooperated with the Romans and with the priestly administration of the temple, although they might fall out regarding such questions as whether the priestly vestments should be kept under Roman or local control (Josephus *Ant.* 18.4.3 §§90-95; 20.1.1-2 §§6-14) or the price of doves for sacrifice (*m. Ker.* 1:7).

4.2.2. The Fracturing of the Priesthood: Sadducees, High Priests and Priestly Nationalists. The priesthood, meanwhile, was fractured further in its response to the fact of Roman governance. Some priests, especially among the privileged families in Jerusalem, were notoriously pro-Roman. The story of sons of the high priest having the surgery called *epispasm* in order to restore the appearance of a foreskin (for gymnastic purposes) is well known (cf. 1 Macc 1:14-15; Josephus *Ant.* 12.5.1 §§240-41). There is little doubt but that such families, the most prominent of which were the Sadducees and Boethusians, were not highly regarded by most Jews (*b. Pesah.* 57a). They are typically portrayed in a negative light, as not teaching the resurrection of the dead (Josephus *J.W.* 2.8.14 §165; Mt 22:23; Mk 12:18; Lk 20:27; Acts 23:8), but the issue may have been one of emphasis. The Torah had stressed that correct worship in the temple would bring with it material prosperity, and the elite priests attempted to realize that promise. Appeal to apocalyptic schemes or revelations would never have been accepted by the Sadducees as equivalent to or comparable with the Torah. Arrangements in the temple gave them such consistent control that they became known as high priests, although there was only one high priest. But Josephus indulges in the plural usage, as well as the Gospels, so that it should not be taken as an inaccuracy: the plural is a cultic mistake but a sociological fact.

Caiaphas held a historically long tenure as high priest during the period (Josephus *Ant.* 18.2.2 §35; 18.4.3 §95), and the frequent change of personnel reflects the collective nature of the priestly leadership as well as Roman caution in respect of a post that might at any time have produced a national leader. Herod understood the possibilities of the high priesthood in that regard, which is why he had Jonathan and Hyrcanus, potential rivals (albeit relatives by marriage), murdered, and why he married Mariamne (Josephus *J.W.* 1.22.1-5 §§431-37; *Ant.* 20.10.1 §§247-49). His ambition was for a new

Hasmonean dynasty, and it appears that only the notorious greed of his sons, combined with his willingness to have them executed, thwarted its realization. As it was, Herod's grandson and namesake, king of Chalcis, did maintain the residual power of selecting the high priest, although as king of Chalcis he had no ordinary authority over Jerusalem (Josephus *Ant.* 20.1.3 §§15-16).

Several priests were also prominent in the revolt against Rome, however, and it should not be thought that such priestly nationalists, among whom were Joseph bar Matthias, better known as Flavius Josephus, emerged only at the end of the sixties (Josephus *J.W.* 2.20.3-4 §§562-68). The precedent of the Hasmoneans was there for any priestly family to see as a possible alternative to Roman rule, direct or indirect. Some priests were not only nationalists but also revolutionaries who joined with the Essenes or with rebellious Pharisees, although any alliance of priests with a prophetic pretender is perhaps not a likely supposition.

4.2.3. The Growing Influence of the Pharisees. The Pharisees' mastery of the oral medium made them the most successful—in terms of popularity—of the tendencies within pluralized Judaism. In the period before written communication was standard among the generality of Jews, the use of memorization and recitation was far more prominent. The Pharisees were in a position to communicate guidance in respect of purity, an emerging understanding of Scripture (in the targumim, whose development they influenced) and their own sense of the authority of the sages, without requiring general literacy. There is no reason to suppose, for example, that rabbis of the first century such as Hillel and Hanina ben Dosa were able to read fluently, although each was a formative member of the pharisaic, and therefore later of the rabbinic, movements. The Pharisees' willingness to live by craft rather than by status (cf. *m. 'Abot* 2:2)—the most prominent example being Hillel's menial labor (*b. Yoma* 35b)—also meant that they could move from town to town, promulgating their views. In some respects, their occasional itinerancy was comparable in Israel to that of the Greco-Roman philosophers of the Mediterranean world (Stoic, Pythagorean and/or Cynic).

The success of the Pharisees in small towns became all the more pronounced as their power was largely ceded to priestly interests in Jerusa-lem. Many local scribes, but not all, were likely Pharisees, and the majority would have to account for pharisaic views. Scribes are men who can read and write, a skill that in antiquity represented some social and educational attainment. In Israel, given the Roman encouragement of local government, scribes emerged in towns and villages as a focus of judicial and religious power; their role might be characterized as that of a judge or a magistrate. From the time of the writing of the Torah, it was accepted that both aspects of God's rule, the legal and the cultic, were articulated by Moses. The ability of the scribes to read and write made them ideal judges, adjuncts to priests, teachers and leaders of worship.

All those functions were probably discharged by an interactive group of scribes, people of priestly lineage, Pharisees and other elders in any given village. It was likely in the same place in a town that cases were settled, purity or impurity declared, lessons given and the Torah recited from the written form and from memory in Aramaic. There, too, disputes would take place among scribes, judges, priests, Pharisees and elders, concerning how the Torah was to be understood and applied. Later rabbinic literature tends to reduce the disputes of the period to the houses of Hillel and Shammai, but that is evidently a schematic presentation; because they lacked any central leadership in the period before A.D. 70, Pharisees differed from movement to movement, town to town, rabbi to rabbi, and to some extent even day to day.

4.2.4. The Sanhedrin. The structure of a local council also prevailed under Roman rule in Jerusalem, and the Greek term *synedrion* was applied to it and it has become known as the Sanhedrin, largely as a result of the Mishnah. Mishnah, a document of the second century, cannot be taken as a sure guide of events and institutions during the first century (*see* Rabbinic Traditions and Literature), but it does seem clear, from the Gospels and Josephus with the Mishnah, that the council in Jerusalem was largely controlled by the high priests. Elders or aristocrats of the city also participated, among whom were Pharisees, and some scribes who may or may not have been priests, elders or Pharisees. Whether there were seventy-one members of the Sanhedrin (as in rabbinic literature) cannot be known with certainty, and the extent of its capital jurisdiction is not known. But the Romans appear to have given the council the authority to order the execution of perpetrators of blatant sacrilege (Josephus *J.W.* 2.12.2 §§228-31; 5.5.2 §194; *Ant.* 15.11.5 §417).

The authority of the council of Jerusalem outside of the city followed the prestige of the city and the acknowledged centrality of the temple. But a ruling of the council there was not automatically binding upon those in the countryside and in other major cities; acceptance of a given teaching, precept by precept, was the path of influence. Pharisees also taught in and around the temple, the focus of their discussion of purity, and the Pharisees in Jerusalem were the most prestigious in the movement.

5. Early Judaism and the New Testament.

5.1. Jesus in the Temple Within the Context of Early Judaism. Hillel, an older contemporary of Jesus, is reported to have taught that offerings (as in the case of his own ʿōlâh, sacrifice by fire) should be brought to the temple, where the owners would lay hands on them and then give them over to priests for slaughter (cf. *t. Ḥag.* 2:11; *y. Ḥag.* 2:3; *y. Beṣa* 2:4; *b. Beṣa* 20a, b). His perennial and stereotypical disputants, the school of Shammai, resist, insisting that the animals might be handed over directly. One of the school of Shammai (named Baba ben Buta in the Babylonian Talmud and Tosefta), however, was so struck by the rectitude of Hillel's position that he had three thousand animals (a number specified only in the Jerusalem Talmud) brought to the temple, and he gave them to those who were willing to lay hands on them in advance of sacrifice.

Generally, the Haggadah (narrative, or instructional tale) concerning Hillel, Baba ben Buta and the sheep is characteristic of the pharisaic/rabbinic program. Moreover, the broad attestation of the story within the two Talmuds and its appearance in the Tosefta constitute an indication that it may reflect an actual dispute. Finally, although Hillel's disputants are stereotypical, it is striking that in *b. Beṣa* 20a, Hillel pretends the animal is a female, for a shared sacrifice rather than a sacrifice by fire, in order to get it by the disciples of Shammai. That is, the Babli's version of the story assumes that the followers of Shammai are in better control of what worshipers do in the temple than are followers of Hillel. The Haggadah is a far cry from the sort of tale, also instanced in rabbinic literature, in which Hillel is portrayed as the prototypical patriarchate of rabbinic Judaism.

In one sense, the tradition concerning Hillel envisages a movement opposite from that of Jesus in the temple (Mt 21:12, 13; Mk 11:15-17; Lk 19:45, 46; Jn 2:13-17): animals are introduced, rather than their traders expelled. But the purpose of the action by Hillel's partisan is to enforce a certain understanding of correct worship, and that is also the motivation attributed to Jesus in the Gospels. Hillel's Halakah, in effect, insists upon the participation of the offerer by virtue of his ownership of what is offered, an ownership of which the laying on of hands is a definitive gesture (cf. *b. Pesaḥ.* 66b and the abundant anthropological evidence for this sacrificial gesture, some of which is cited in Chilton 1992, 27-42). "The house of Shammai" is portrayed as sanctioning sacrifice without mandating that sort of emphatic participation on the part of the offerer. Although nothing like the violence of Jesus is attributed to Baba ben Buta, he does offer an analogy for a forcible attempt to insist upon correct worship in the temple on the part of a Pharisee.

Mishnah reflects a concern to control commercial arrangements connected with the temple, and such concern is also somewhat analogous to Jesus' action in the exterior court. The following story is told concerning one of the successors of Hillel (*m. Ker.* 1:7):

> Once in Jerusalem a pair of doves cost a golden denar. Rabban Simeon ben Gamaliel said: By this Place! I will not rest this night before they cost but a [silver] denar. He went into the court and taught: If a woman suffered five miscarriages that were not in doubt or five issues that were not in doubt, she need bring but one offering, and she may then eat of the sacrifices; and the rest is not required of her. And the same day the price of a pair of doves stood at a quarter denar each.

Although the story requires more effort to understand than does the one concerning Hillel, it rewards the attention required. The assumption of the tale is that a pair of doves might be offered by a woman as a burnt offering and a sacrifice for sin, in order to be purified after childbirth; the second of the two would be offered normally, while the first, in the case of poverty, might take the place of a yearling lamb (Lev 12:6-8). The story also assumes that miscarriages and unusual issues of blood akin to miscarriages should be treated under the category of childbirth, from the point of view of purity. That interest is characteristically pharisaic, as is the question of when the woman might be considered entitled to eat of offerings. The Pharisees defined purity as fitness to take part in sacrifice and in meals that in their teaching were extensions of the holiness of the temple.

Simeon's anger, which causes him to swear by the temple (cf. Mt 23:16-22), is therefore motivated to some extent by economic considerations, and his response is, like Jesus', to teach in the court of the temple, to which point such offerings would be brought. But his action there is far less direct than that of Hillel or Jesus. Instead of importing more birds or releasing those bought at an extortionate price, he promulgates a Halakah designed to reduce the trade in doves, no matter what their price.

If a woman may await several (up to five) miscarriages or flows of blood, offer a single pair of doves and be considered pure enough to eat of the animal offering, the potential revenue from sales of doves would obviously decline. In effect, Simeon counters inflationary prices with sacrificial monetarism. The political lesson was quickly appreciated (on the very day, if we believe the story), and prices went lower even than Simeon had intended. Presumably there was no reason for him to continue promulgating his view in the court of the temple, and both he and the traders were content with the settlement.

The dating of the Mishnah, as compared with the Tosefta, the *Yerushalmi* and the *Babli* (the Jerusalem and Babylonian Talmuds respectively) makes its material, when in any way comparable to the Gospels, of immediate interest to the student of Jesus' life and teaching. For all its complexity, the Haggadah in *Keritot* is vital for appreciating the sort of pharisaic intervention in the operation of the temple that was considered possible during the first century according to the testimony of the Mishnah. (Perhaps the story concerning Simeon is more complicated precisely because it is closer to particulars of pharisaic concern than is the Haggadah concerning Hillel and Baba ben Buta, which is available only in later sources.) Hillel, Simeon and Jesus are all portrayed as interested in the animals offered in the temple to the extent that they intervene (or, in the case of Hillel, a surrogate intervenes) in the exterior court in order to influence the ordinary course of worship. To that extent, it may be said that rabbinic traditions and writings provide a context within which it is possible to interpret a well-attested action of Jesus.

5.2. Paul and the Temple Within Early Judaism.

When Paul conceives of Jesus' death sacrificially, he does so as a sacrifice for sin (Rom 8:3). By the time he came to compose Romans, he had been referring to Jesus' death in that way for five years (cf. Gal 1:4, written about A.D. 53, following Papyrus 46 and Sinaiticus). Paul uses precisely the phrase used in the Septuagint to refer to a sacrifice for sin (*peri hamartias*; cf. Lev 16:3, 5, 6, 9, 11, 15). Paul cites the Hebrew Scriptures in a paradigmatically Septuagintal version, so that the identity of phrasing might alone be taken to suggest that he presented Jesus' death as a sacrifice for sin. In addition, Galatians and Romans conceive of Jesus' death in a manner congruent with the image of a sacrifice for sin. In Galatians 1:4 the purpose of his death is redemption from the present evil age, while Romans 8:3 contrasts God's sending his Son with the flesh of sacrifice.

But Paul did not conceive of that death as a replacement of the cult, for the simple reason that Paul believed he had a role to play within the service of the temple. His preaching of the gospel is depicted in Romans 15:16 as a kind of priestly service, in that it is to result in "the offering of the nations, pleasing, sanctified in the Holy Spirit." Contextually, Paul's characterization of his own ministry as sacrificial is associated with his "serving the saints in Jerusalem" (Rom 15:25), by means of a collection in Macedonia and Asia for the poorer community in return for its spiritual treasure (Rom 15:26, 27). That done, Paul expects to come to Rome "in the fullness of Christ's blessing" and to proceed to Spain (Rom 15:28, 29), there to engage in the same priestly service (cf. Rom 15:19). Paul's program is known conventionally as the collection, after Galatians 2:10; 1 Corinthians 16:1, 2; 2 Corinthians 8, 9; and Romans 15:26, and the assumption has been that the purpose of the program was purely practical: Paul agreed to provide material support in exchange for recognition by Peter, James and John (cf. Gal 2:9) and used priestly language as a rhetorical device.

Paul was unquestionably capable of using cultic language as metaphor. Romans 12:1 provides the example of the addressees being called to present their bodies as "a living sacrifice, holy and acceptable to God." Romans 15:16 can only refer to Paul's priestly service metaphorically, as the agency by which the offering of the nations might be completed, since Paul did not claim priestly lineage. But is "the offering of the nations" to be taken only as a metaphor? Paul may be capable of priestly service only in the figurative sense that he brings support to the community of Jesus' followers in Jerusalem, who in turn offer sacrifice within the temple. But the fact would remain that the offering of that community was a sacrifice according to the Torah in the direct and usual sense.

The hope of a climactic disclosure of divine power, signaled in the willingness of nations to worship on Mount Zion, is attested within Judaic sources extant by the first century. Chief among them, from the point of view of its influence upon the NT, is the book of Zechariah. It can be argued that Zechariah provided a point of departure for Jesus' inclusive program of purity and forgiveness as the occasions of the kingdom (see Chilton 1992, 113-36). Jesus is said to have mentioned the prophet by name (cf. Mt 23:34-36; Lk 11:49-51). The book programmatically concerns the establishment of restored worship in the temple, especially at the feast of Sukkoth (Zech 14:16-19).

"All the nations" are to go up to Jerusalem annually for worship (Zech 14:16), and the transformation of which that worship is part involves the provision of "living waters" from the city (Zech 14:8; cf. Jn 4:10, 14). That image is related to an earlier "fountain opened for the house of David and the inhabitants of Jerusalem in view of sin and uncleanness" (Zech 13:1). Here is the association of forgiveness and purity that is a feature of Jesus' program, as well as the notion of an immediate release, without any mention of sacrifice, from what keeps Israel from God. (There is also an indication of how the issue of Davidic ancestry might have featured in Jesus' ministry, aside from a formally messianic claim.) God is held to arrange the purity he requires, so that the sacrifice he desires might take place.

Zechariah features the commissioning of a priest (Zech 3; cf. Mt 16:18, 19), an oracle against swearing (Zech 5:3, 4; cf. Mt 5:33-37), a vision of a king humbly riding an ass (Zech 9:9; cf. Mt 21:1-9; Mk 11:1-10; Lk 19:28-40; Jn 12:12-19), the prophetic receipt of thirty shekels of silver in witness against the owners of sheep (Zech 11:4-17; cf. Mt 26:14-16; 27:3-10; Mk 14:10, 11; Lk 22:3-6). It is obvious that the connections between Jesus'

ministry and Zechariah do not amount to a completely common agenda in every detail, and Matthew reflects a tendency to tailor the fit between the two. But the similarities may be suggestive of Jesus' appropriation of Zechariah's prophecy of eschatological purity, as a final, more fundamental connection would indicate. The climactic vision of Zechariah insists that every vessel in Jerusalem will belong to the Lord and become a fit vessel for sacrifice. As part of that insistence, the text asserts that no trader will be allowed in the temple (Zech 14:20, 21). In the light of Zechariah, Jesus' occupation of the temple appears an enactment of prophetic purity in the face of a commercial innovation, a vigorous insistence that God would prepare his own people as vessels for eschatological worship.

Notably, the *Targum of Zechariah* specifically includes reference to God's kingdom at Zechariah 14:9, and that provides another programmatic link with Jesus. It is clear that Jesus understood the essential affect of sacrifice to derive from a purity and a forgiveness that God extended to Israel in anticipation of the climax of worship. In those understandings, Jesus was no doubt unusual in his immediate application of a prophetic program to the temple, but far from unique. His precise demands concerning the provision of animals as offerings, however, show how the issue of purity was for him pragmatic as well as affective. And it was in that pharisaic vein that he confronted the authorities in the temple with the claim that their management was a scandal and that the direct provision of animals by a forgiven, purified Israel was what was required for the experience of holiness and the reality of the covenant to be achieved.

Whether or not Jesus' program was a direct precedent for Paul's, the mere existence of Zechariah, which Paul alludes to (cf. Rom 8:36; 1 Cor- 2:11; 11:25; 13:5; 14:25), opens the possibility that Paul might have included an offering from the Gentiles in Jerusalem as a part of his program and therefore as part of his meaning in Romans 15:16. The reading of the *Targum of Zechariah* is particularly pertinent at this point, aside from the question of its relationship to Jesus' preaching. This section of the *Targum of Zechariah* is agreed to reflect the earliest development of the targumim, from the first century onward, and this theme is also represented independently of the book of Zechariah, within the book of Tobit (Tob 13:8-11). It is evident that within Hellenistic Judaism the consolation of Jerusalem and the sacrificial recognition of God as king by the nations were motifs that could be and were associated. The significance of the prominence of a similar theme in the *Targum of Zechariah* shows that the association was not merely Hellenistic and that it survived through the first century. More generally, *Jubilees* 4:26 establishes that the global range of the sanctuary was an expectation within early Judaism.

Targum Jonathan, together with Tobit and *Jubilees,* establishes clearly that an expectation of global worship in the temple was a feature of early Judaism, so that it is within the range of plausibility that Paul aimed to promote a literal offering of the nations by means of his collection for the needs of the church in Jerusalem. The book of Acts is at pains to exculpate Paul from the charge that he introduced Gentiles into the precincts of the temple (Acts 21:27-30), but precisely that accusation, mounted by Jews from Asia who were in a position to know what Paul intended (Acts 21:27), is what in Acts produces the attempt to kill Paul and his subsequent (as it turned out, definitive) arrest (Acts 21:31-32). The conflicted picture Acts conveys at this point may be said to be consistent with the finding from Paul's letters that he intended that Gentiles should be joined within the sacrificial worship of Israel.

Paul's assertion in Romans 3:25, that God appointed Jesus a cultic appeasement through faith in his blood, is therefore not to be understood as positing a formal replacement of the cult by Jesus' death. The standard references to similar usages in 2 Maccabees (2 Macc 3:33) and 4 Maccabees (4 Macc 6:28, 29; 17:20-22) ought long ago to have warned commentators against any reading that involves such notions. Second Maccabees 3:33 speaks of a high priest "making appeasement" by cultic means. Even 4 Maccabees, which is probably too late a composition to be used as representing the milieu that was the matrix of Paul's thought, maintains a distinction between God's pleasure in sacrifice and the means of that sacrifice. In 4 Maccabees 6:28, God is asked to be pleased with his people by Eleazar and on that basis to make his blood their purification and his life their ransom (4 Macc 6:29). Then, in 4 Maccabees 17, it is said of the seven brothers that, in the manner of Eleazar, they purified the homeland in that they be-

came a ransom for the sin of the nation (4 Macc 17:21). The language of purification and ransom is consistently used, in 4 Maccabees 6 and 17, to refer to the deaths of martyrs in cultic and salvific terms. That salvation did not involve the replacement of cultic sacrifice but its reestablishment in the temple.

Jesus for Paul in Romans 3:25 is a *hilastērion* because he provides the occasion on which God may be appeased, an opportunity for the correct offering of sacrifice in Jerusalem. Precisely that rectitude lies behind the emphasis upon God's righteousness. "The righteous" are held within the *Targum of Isaiah* to be the recipients of that joy whose epicenter is the sanctuary (cf. Is 24:16; 5:17; 66:24). More particularly, the establishment of correct worship in the temple is signaled in Daniel 8:14 as involving a divine justification. Danielic usage presents God as righteous (cf. Dan 9:7, 14, 16) and making righteous (Dan 9:24; cf. 12:3) an unrighteous nation (Dan 9:7, 16, 18).

5.3. Summary. The utility of the documents of early Judaism and rabbinic Judaism in assessing Jesus and Paul is qualified by three critical considerations, each of which has been instanced in the examples developed here. First, the relatively late date of rabbinic literature must be taken into account, although the continuities between rabbinic Judaism and Pharisaism during the first century rule out any global refusal to countenance analogies between the Gospels and rabbinica. Second, a recognition of the social and religious transformations involved in the emergence of rabbinic Judaism must alert the reader to the possibility of anachronistic attributions or to the presentation of early teachers as spokesmen of later theologies. And finally, the initial target of inquiry must be understood to be the recovery not so much of particular events and sayings paralleled in the Gospels but of the milieu of early Judaism, reflected indirectly both in the Gospels and in rabbinica, which was the matrix of the Christian faith.

See also APOCRYPHA AND PSEUDEPIGRAPHA, OLD TESTAMENT; RABBINIC TRADITIONS AND WRITINGS.

DNTB: FESTIVALS AND HOLY DAYS: JEWISH; HASMONEANS; HEBREW BIBLE; JEWISH HISTORY; MESSIANISM; PHARISEES; RABBIS; SACRIFICE AND TEMPLE SERVICE; TEMPLE, JEWISH; TORAH; THEOLOGIES AND SECTS, JEWISH; WRITING AND LITERATURE: JEWISH.

BIBLIOGRAPHY. E. Auerbach, *Moses* (Detroit: Wayne State University Press, 1975); J. Bright, *A History of Israel* (Philadelphia: Westminster, 1981); B. D. Chilton, "Aramaic and Targumic Antecedents of Pauline 'Justification,'" in *The Aramaic Bible: The Targums in Their Historical Context* (JSOTSup 166; Sheffield: Sheffield Academic Press, 1994) 379-97; idem, *The Isaiah Targum: Introduction, Translation, Apparatus and Notes* (ArBib 11; Wilmington, DE: Michael Glazier, 1987); idem, *The Temple of Jesus: His Sacrificial Program Within a Cultural History of Sacrifice* (University Park: Pennsylvania State University Press, 1992); S. J. D. Cohen, *From the Maccabees to the Mishnah* (LEC 7; Philadelphia: Westminster, 1987); W. D. Davies and L. Finkelstein, eds., *The Cambridge History of Judaism*, vol. 1, *Introduction; the Persian Period* (London and New York: Cambridge University Press, 1984); A. Finkel, *The Pharisees and the Teacher of Nazareth* (AGSU 4; Leiden: E. J. Brill, 1964); V. P. Furnish, *2 Corinthians* (AB; Garden City, NY: Doubleday, 1984); E. R. Goodenough, *An Introduction to Philo Judaeus* (BCJ; Lanham, MD: University Press of America, 1986); N. K. Gottwald, *The Tribes of Yahweh: A Sociology of the Religion of Liberated Israel 1250-1050 B.C.* (Maryknoll, NY: Orbis, 1979); L. R. Helyer, *Exploring Jewish Literature of the Second Temple Period: A Guide to New Testament Students* (Downers Grove, IL: InterVarsity Press, 2002); R. A. Kraft and G. W. E. Nickelsburg, *Early Judaism and Its Modern Interpreters* (The Bible and Its Modern Interpreters 2; Atlanta: Scholars Press, 1986); A. R. C. Leany, *The Jewish and Christian World 200 B.C. to A.D. 200* (CCWJCW 7; Cambridge and New York: Cambridge University Press, 1984); N. P. Lemche, *Early Israel: Anthropological and Historical Studies on the Israelite Society Before the Monarchy* (VTSup; Leiden: E. J. Brill, 1985); L. I. Levine, *The Rabbinic Class of Roman Palestine in Late Antiquity* (New York: Jewish Theological Seminary of America, 1989); M. McNamara, *Palestinian Judaism and the New Testament* (GNS 4; Wilmington, DE: Michael Glazier, 1983); G. E. Mendenhall, "The Hebrew Conquest of Palestine," *The Biblical Archaeologist Reader* 3 (1962) 100-120; J. Neusner, "Josephus' Pharisees: A Complete Repertoire," in *Josephus, Judaism and Christianity,* ed. L. H. Feldman and G. Hata (Detroit: Wayne State University Press, 1987) 274-92; idem, *The Pharisees: Rabbinic Perspectives* (SAJ; Hoboken, NJ: Ktav, 1984); M. Noth, *The History of Israel* (London: Adam & Charles Black, 1959); E. Schürer, *The History of the Jewish People in the Age of Jesus Christ* (175 B.C.-A.D. 135), ed. G. Vermes, F. Millar and M. Goodman (3 vols.; Edinburgh: T & T Clark, 1973-87); R. M. Seltzer, ed., *Judaism: A People and Its History* (New York: Macmillan, 1989); A. J. Tomasino, *Judaism Before Jesus: The Events and Ideas that Shaped the New Testament World* (Downers Grove, IL: InterVarsity Press, 2003); J. C. VanderKam, *An Introduction to Early Judaism* (Grand Rapids: Eerdmans, 2001); R. R. Wilson, *Sociological Approaches to the Old Testament* (Philadelphia: Fortress, 1984). B. D. Chilton

JUDAIZERS. *See* ADVERSARIES.

JUDAS. *See* TRIAL OF JESUS.

JUDE, LETTER OF

The letter of Jude is the last letter in what has become known as the "catholic" or "general letters" of the NT (i.e., James through Jude; Webb 1992). In this letter Jude warns his readers about false teachers and exhorts them to defend the faith. D. J. Rowston (1975) is correct in lamenting that Jude is "the most neglected book" in the NT. But careful study of it will richly repay the reader.

1. Literary Structure and Form
2. Character
3. Opponents
4. Authorship
5. Date
6. Recipients/Destination
7. Message

1. Literary Structure and Form.

Although Jude is one of the smallest letters of the NT, analysis of its structure reveals a carefully composed literary gem.

1.1. Epistolary Structure. While Jude has a letter opening (Jude 1-2) and a closing doxology (Jude 24-25), its epistolary character has been questioned (*see* Letter, Letter Forms). For example, R. H. Fuller considers Jude to be a tract, and the epistolary features to be "merely a conventional device" (Fuller, 160). But such a claim cannot really be substantiated because these features characterize the letter genre, and there are no formal means for distinguishing them as conventional devices or later interpolations (Bauckham 1988 *ANRW,* 3800). Furthermore, the body alludes to the epistolary character of the text (Jude 3); it also uses epistolary conventions (e.g., "I desire to remind you," Jude 5).

As an epistle, Jude's epistolary structure may be outlined as follows:

Letter Opening (Jude 1-2)
  Opening Address (Jude 1)
  Salutation (Jude 2)
Letter Body (Jude 3-23)
  Body Opening (Jude 3-4)
  Body Middle (Jude 5-23)
Letter Closing (Jude 24-25)

Due to the brevity of the letter, there is no body closing. J. H. Neyrey (1993, 27) views Jude 17-23 as the body closing because of the use of a disclosure formula (cf. Watson, 67). However, the phrase "but you, beloved" (Jude 17, cf. Jude 20) with an imperative is not actually a disclosure formula. Rather, this use of direct address and a command indicates a major transition within the body middle. In this instance Jude 20-23 brings the body to a fitting climax by addressing the purpose of the letter: how to contend for the faith (cf. Jude 3).

The body opening of a letter usually identifies the occasion for the letter and alludes to its purpose. Thus the body opening of Jude indicates that the occasion for the letter is Jude's realization that false teachers have entered the church (Jude 4), and the letter's dual purpose is to make his readers aware of them and their condemnation (Jude 4), as well as to exhort them to fight for the faith (Jude 3). As a body opening, Jude 3-4 lays the foundation for the discussion in the body middle (Jude 5-23). This relationship between the body opening and body middle produces a chiastic structure (cf. Bauckham 1983, 5-6):

A Appeal: need to contend for the faith (Jude 3)
  B Occasion for appeal: false teachers identified and condemned (Jude 4)
  B' Occasion for appeal: false teachers described and condemned (Jude 5-19)
A' Appeal: how to contend for the faith (Jude 20-23)

By concluding with a doxology, Jude does not follow the usual form for a letter closing. This form of the closing suggests that Jude envisions the letter being read to the Christian community gathered in worship, and he is addressing them with a sermon in letter form. This suggestion is confirmed by the midrashic style of

the letter's body (see below), and thus, as R. J. Bauckham (1983, 1) suggests, Jude is an "epistolary sermon."

1.2. Rhetorical Structure. Within the past twenty years scholars have begun to analyze NT texts in light of Greco-Roman rhetorical techniques and forms. While originally an oral skill used in speeches, rhetoric was later used in written texts as well, particularly in those forms of literature that were meant to persuade. Rhetoric was taught to Greco-Roman students and included instruction in selecting the appropriate arguments (called "invention"), arranging the material into the most effective outline (called "arrangement"), and developing appropriate language for effective communication (called "style").

In a helpful analysis, D. F. Watson (29-79) has applied rhetorical criticism to Jude's letter. All parts of a letter, including its opening and closing, may contribute to its rhetorical effectiveness. For example, while the identification of the readers in Jude 1 is necessary according to epistolary form, the description reassures the readers and contributes to their sense of good-will toward the author. Thus a letter opening may contribute to the rhetorical function of an introduction *(exordium)* while at the same time conforming to the epistolary form.

Watson's analysis (29-79, esp. 77-78; cf. Neyrey 1993, 25-27) results in the following rhetorical outline of Jude, to which has been added brief definitions of the Latin terms.

1. Introduction *(exordium;* Jude 3) (with Jude 1-2 as a quasi-*exordium)*
2. Narration *(narratio;* Jude 4)
3. Proofs *(probatio;* Jude 5-16 containing three proofs: Jude 5-10, 11-13, 14-16)
4. Conclusion *(peroratio;* Jude 17-23)
  Recapitulation *(repetitio;* Jude 17-19)
  Emotional Appeal *(adfectus;* Jude 20-23)
  (with Jude 24-25 as a quasi-*peroratio)*

While this is an informative analysis, its weakness is the combination of Jude 17-19 and Jude 20-23 as the conclusion *(peroratio).* Jude 17-19 as a unit contains the same formal characteristics as the earlier three proofs (example/text, application to the opponents), and so it should be considered a fourth proof in the *probatio.* The unit of Jude 20-23 does not really qualify as an *adfectus,* or emotional appeal; it is, rather, completing the appeal stated in Jude 3 by giving instructions for how to contend for the faith.

How to classify such paraenesis in NT letters is one of the questions still unanswered in the application of rhetorical analysis to biblical texts.

1.3. Midrash. E. E. Ellis (221-26; cf. Bauckham 1983, 4-5) first observed the midrashic style used in Jude 5-19, in which scriptural examples and quotations become "texts" that are then interpreted to apply to the situation facing Jude's readers. This midrashic pattern of text followed by interpretation is repeated four times in these verses. The first two texts are allusions to biblical stories (Jude 5-7, 11) which are then interpreted to apply to Jude's opponents (Jude 8-10, 12-13). The latter two are from authoritative though not biblical sources (Jude 14-15, 17-18) which are equally applied to the readers' situation (Jude 16, 19; cf. Bauckham 1990, 179-234).

This midrashic style may be compared profitably with the Qumran pesharim (scrolls interpreting biblical texts; from *pēšer*, "interpretation"; plural *pēšārîm*), particularly the thematic pesharim that comment on diverse texts that have been brought together because they address a common theme (e.g., 4QFlor; 11QMelch; in contrast to continuous pesharim, e.g., 1QpHab). Both similarities and differences may be noted between Jude and these pesharim (cf. Bauckham 1983, 4-5; Bauckham later suggests avoiding the term *midrash* because of potential confusion with rabbinic midrashim; cf. Bauckham 1990, 180 n. 2).

2. Character.

Jude has frequently been viewed as characterized by the early catholicism of the postapostolic era (e.g., Sidebottom, 77-78; Rowston 1971, 145-54; on date, see 5 below). As a category in which to understand the development of early Christianity, early catholicism has increasingly been called into question. But even if the characteristics of this category are granted for the sake of argument, Jude still should not be so characterized (e.g., Bauckham 1983, 8-9). The expectation of an imminent parousia has not faded (Jude 1, 14-15, 21, 24; cf. Webb 1996). Jude does not argue that the false teachers should submit to some form of ecclesiastical hierarchy; he does not even allude to such officials. There is no evidence of a developing Christian canon. The evidence for this characterization is based on two things: (1) Jude 17 is interpreted to imply a postapostolic date, but this is unnecessary (on date, see 5 below). (2) The reference to "the faith" in

Jude 3 (cf. Jude 20) is interpreted as referring to a defined set of crystallized doctrines. But there is no need to view this phrase as anything more than a synonym for "the gospel." And even Paul, writing in the 40s and 50s, used "the faith" in this way (e.g., Gal 1:23; cf. Neyrey, 55).

Rather than being early catholic, Jude is better understood as an *apocalyptic Jewish-Christian letter (e.g., Bauckham 1983, 8-11; Charles 1993, 42-64). This view is based on observing the midrashic style of argumentation (see above), the pervasive use of Jewish sources, especially apocalyptic ones (see 3.2 below), and the prominence of an apocalyptic worldview in the thought of the letter.

2.1. Literary Relationships. Packed within the twenty-five verses of this letter is an amazing number of literary allusions. Perceiving them aids the reader in appreciating Jude's literary richness.

2.2. Old Testament. While Jude does not quote any OT texts, a careful study reveals its extensive dependence on the OT, including its narratives (e.g., Israel's exodus and wilderness experience, Jude 5), theology (e.g., the people of God are "the called," Jude 1) and language ("feeding themselves," Jude 12, from Ezek 34:2; e.g., Rowston 1971, 37-48; Bauckham 1983; Charles 1993, 91-127).

The author is evidently aware of Greek versions of the OT because he picks up some of its distinctive terminology (e.g., "grumbler," Jude 16; Symm. Prov 26:22; Is 29:24; cf. Bigg, 310-11). But his primary text appears to be the Hebrew because he alludes to OT passages in which the Hebrew text makes his point, but the Greek translation does not support it. For example, Jude 12 refers to "clouds without rain, carried away by winds," which probably alludes to the Hebrew version of Proverbs 25:14 ("clouds and wind, but there is no rain"). But Proverbs 25:14 LXX reads "winds and clouds and rain appear," and lacks the vivid image Jude is using.

2.3. Jewish Traditions. While not quoting from the Hebrew canon, Jude is the only NT book to cite explicitly an extracanonical Jewish source. This is clearly the case in Jude 14-15, which quotes *1 Enoch* 1:9, and probably also in Jude 9, which may quote the now lost ending of the *Testament of Moses* (Bauckham 1983, 65-76). For some later Christians this was a problem. Tertullian saw this as an argument for *1 Enoch*'s authenticity (Tertullian *De Cult. Fem.* 1.3), while Jerome questioned Jude's canonicity (*Vir.* 4; cf. Bauckham 1990, 137-38). Given the other allusions to these and other Jewish apocalyptic texts in Jude and in some other NT books, it is evident that these works were popular in the milieu in which this letter was composed and read. If this is the case, then Jude's quotations should not be a problem to modern readers; it is similar to a minister in a sermon making a point by quoting a popular Christian writer who is a recognized authority on a subject.

Beyond these explicit quotations, Jude makes extensive allusions to *1 Enoch* and other Jewish writings and traditions of the Second Temple period (Osburn 1977; Charles 1991, "Jude's Use"; Charles 1993, 128-66). An appreciation of these allusions assists the reader in understanding what Jude is implying in his dense and compact work. The use of these Jewish traditions often moves an OT story or reference beyond that which may be understood from the OT itself. For example, Jude 11 refers to Cain, Balaam and Korah. Jude has probably brought these three characters together in this woe oracle based on similarities among them, which they have in later Jewish tradition. In the case of each of these three men, Jewish tradition viewed them as leading people astray through false teaching (e.g., Cain, Josephus *Ant.* 1.2.1 §61; Balaam, Philo *Abr.* 114; Korah, *Pseudo-Philo* 16:1; cf. 16:5; Josephus *Ant.* 4.2.3 §21). That such points are made allusively rather than explicitly suggests that such Jewish traditions were a natural part of the milieu of Jude's readers.

2.4. 2 Peter. It is evident that some relationship exists among Jude 4-13, 16-18 and 2 Peter 2:1-18; 3:1-3. Until the nineteenth century the predominant view was that Jude used *2 Peter as a source (e.g., Luther, 203; Bigg, 216-24), but more recently the predominant view has been reversed to 2 Peter having used Jude (cf. list in Bauckham 1990, 145), with very few holding the earlier view. A few interpreters have argued that Jude and 2 Peter are dependent upon a common source (e.g., Reicke, 189-90; Green, 58-64), and common authorship by Jude has also been argued.

More recent work using redaction criticism (e.g., Bauckham 1983) and rhetorical criticism (Watson 1988, 160-87) have strengthened the position that 2 Peter used Jude as a source, and this remains the most probable position. However,

the lack of precise verbal links between 2 Peter and Jude renders the position of a common source a possibility.

2.5. Christian Traditions. It has frequently been asserted that Jude is indebted to Paul's thought and terminology (e.g., Bigg, 311-12; Sidebottom, 72-73), such as Jude's self-description, "a servant of Jesus Christ" (Jude 1; cf. Rom 1:1), or use of the phrase "build yourselves up" (Jude 20; cf. 1 Thess 5:11; cf. the list of parallels in Rowston 1971, 60-61). The problem with this assertion is its assumption that parallels between Jude and Paul's letters are distinctively Pauline. But this assumption is questionable on two grounds. Paul makes use of common early Christian traditional materials, and many of the supposed examples of Jude's indebtedness to Paul may be better explained as traditional material common to early Christianity (Bauckham 1983, 8). Second, some of the common terminology may be better explained by the fact that Jude is addressing a situation similar to that which Paul sometimes faced (e.g., "worldly," Jude 19; cf. 1 Cor 2:14).

If Jude is not indebted to Paul in particular, it is more likely that he is indebted to early Christian tradition in general. This is the case not only with respect to his use of Christian terminology but also catechetical (Jude 20-21) and liturgical material (Jude 24-25).

2.6. Other. A few suggestions have been made that Jude is dependent upon Greek literature for certain traditions (e.g., Charles 1993, 162-63). The evidence substantiating this indebtedness is weak at best, and the imagery in Jude that is used to support this claim is better explained through links with Jewish apocalyptic literature (Osburn 1992, 302-3).

3. Opponents.

The opponents (*see* Adversaries) referred to in Jude have often been identified as Gnostics and considered to be similar to or the same as the opponents in 2 Peter (e.g., Green, 42-46). Older scholars tended to identify the opponents with a specific gnostic group (cf. the list in Bauckham 1988 *ANRW,* 3809; Osburn 1992, 310), but more recently those holding to a gnostic identity have not made a specific identification, referring instead to some form of incipient *Gnosticism (e.g., Sidebottom, 75-76; Kelly, 231). It is increasingly recognized that developed, second-century Gnosticism should not be read back into Jude, and the few defined features of Jude's opponents do not point in this direction. Other proposals for identifying Jude's opponents include political agitators in the employ of Rome (Reicke, 191-92), the Essenes, deviant Hebraists who have rejected OT ethical codes (Ellis, 235) or "Pauline" antinomians (cf. Bauckham 1993, 12). It has also been argued that Jude probably does not describe a specific heresy or that Jude is not combating actual opponents because the letter is a general "eschatological tract" preparing Christians everywhere for the imminent parousia. M. Desjardins, who blends Jude and 2 Peter, suggests that the communities were eschatologically minded and world denying, whereas the opponents were becoming less radical because of the delay of the parousia (*see* Eschatology).

Many elements of Jude's language about the opponents must be understood as rhetoric rather than as description; nevertheless, certain elements do provide some sense of their character. The internal evidence of Jude indicates that the primary characteristic of the opponents is antinomianism; they reject the moral authority of Christ (Jude 4) and the law (Jude 8-10). As a consequence, they engage in immoral behavior, particularly sexual immorality (Jude 6-8, 16, 18, 23). The authority for these opponents is their visionary experiences (Jude 8). Jude's rhetorical statement that they were "soulish" (lit.; i.e., functioning at a natural, human level) and were "devoid of the Spirit" (Jude 19) is probably countering their claim to prophetic inspiration. These opponents did not arise within the community but rather entered in from the outside (Jude 4), have been accepted by the community (Jude 12) and were perhaps supported by them as well (Jude 16). The influence they were having on the community (Jude 11-13) and Jude's use of shepherding imagery ("shepherding themselves," Jude 12) indicate that these opponents functioned as teachers. Their claim to prophetic inspiration supported their teaching role.

In light of these elements, Jude's opponents are most likely itinerant prophets whose charismatic experience led them to reject moral authority and to practice immorality. They also taught others to adopt these views and practices. There is no real indication of cosmic dualism underlying the thought of these false teachers, and so the evidence does not support the claim that these opponents are Gnostics. Other early Christian texts point to itinerant charismatic prophets being a problem for some churches (Mt 7:15; 24:11-12; 2 Pet 2:1; 1 Jn 4:1; 2 Jn 7-11; *Did.* 11-12; cf. Bauckham 1983, 11-13; Martin, 68-75), and it is against such that Jude is best understood to be writing.

4. Authorship.

Two related questions arise with respect to the authorship of this letter. First, what is the identity of the "Jude" referred to in Jude 1? Second, is the name "Jude" used pseudepigraphally or not?

4.1. The Issue of Jude's Identity. In the NT the name "Jude" refers to at least eight different men (the Greek is translated as "Judah," "Judas" or "Jude," depending on the person to whom reference is made). It is a common Jewish name held in honor because of its namesake, Judah, one of the twelve sons of Israel.

It is theoretically possible that this Jude is an otherwise unknown person and that the James referred to in Jude 1 is also unknown. But it is unusual to identify oneself as someone's brother, rather than using the name of one's father. As Bauckham (1983, 23) aptly observes, "The only theory which does explain it is that which identifies James as the James whom everyone knew." Equally, the phrase "brother of James" could be a later gloss, but without manuscript evidence such a proposal begs the question.

Some older scholars identified the author as one of the twelve apostles, Judas of James (Lk 6:16; Jn 14:22; Acts 1:13), equating Jude the apostle with Jude the brother of Jesus. The weaknesses of this view are that (1) the expression "Judas of James" would naturally be understood as "Judas, son of James" rather than "Judas, brother of James"; (2) Jude does not identify himself as an apostle of Jesus Christ in Jude 1; and (3) the disciple, Judas of James, is better understood to be a different person than Jude, brother of Jesus, because Jesus' brothers were not disciples during his lifetime.

A few scholars have identified Jude as the apostle Thomas who was known in the eastern Syriac tradition as Judas Thomas or Didymus Judas Thomas (e.g., Sidebottom, 69, 79; cf. *Gos. Thom.* title). The names Thomas and Didymus both mean "twin" in Syriac and Greek respectively, and thus in two works of this tradition the apostle Thomas was equated with the brother of Jesus named Jude, identified as his "twin," and so named Judas Thomas (cf. *Thom. Cont.* 138:1, 4, 7, 10, 19; *Acts Thom.* 10, 31, 39; cf. Jn 14:22 sy$^{s.(c)}$). But this equation is probably a later confusion (Klijn 1970; Gunther; Bauckham 1990, 32-36).

Another proposed identification is Judas called Barsabbas, who accompanied Paul, Barnabas and Silas to Antioch with the decision of the Jerusalem council (Acts 15:22, 27, 32; e.g., du Plessis; Ellis, 226-34). In this view the James in Jude 1 is identified with the brother of Jesus, but the term *brother* in Jude 1 is interpreted not as a blood brother but as a spiritual designation for those who were involved in ministry with the apostles in the Jerusalem church (cf. Acts 11:1). Acts 15:22 describes Judas called Barsabbas as a leader among the "brothers" (*adelphoi*). This identification of Jude is possible, but its weakness is that, if this particular Jude's identity was clarified by also being called Barsabbas, he did not use it in his letter.

Most scholars identify the author as the brother of Jesus (cf. Mt 13:55 par. Mk 6:3; Eusebius *Hist. Eccl.* 3.19.1—20.1; e.g., Bauckham 1983, 21-25) on the strength of the author's self-designation, "brother of James" (Jude 1). This Jude was not a disciple during Jesus' lifetime (Jn 7:5; cf. Mk 3:20-21), but, like his brother, James, he became a member of the early Christian movement after the resurrection of Jesus. The strength of this view is that it explains the evidence in Jude's letter in the simplest way. Its chief weakness is that Jude could have clarified who he was by identifying himself as "brother of Jesus Christ." It should be noted, however, that whereas the early church used the term "brother(s) of Jesus" (e.g., Mk 3:31; Acts 1:14; 1 Cor 9:5; Gal 1:19; *Gos. Thom.* 99; Eusebius, *Hist. Eccl.* 2.23.4; 3.19.1—3.20.1), it would appear that this expression was not used as a self-designation by these men (cf. Jas 1:1).

Of all these alternatives, the last two are the most plausible, with the identification of Jude as the brother of Jesus the more probable of the two.

4.2. The Issue of Pseudepigraphy. Ascertaining the probable identity of Jude does not address the second issue: whether or not this letter is pseudepigraphic. Scholars are divided on this point, with an increasing number in recent years proposing that the letter is pseudepigraphic (cf. list in Bauckham 1990, 174 n. 261). There are two main arguments for the pseudepigraphic character of Jude's letter. First, the letter should be dated quite late (after the death of Jude, about which nothing is known) because Jude 17 is interpreted to refer to the apostolic age as being in the past, and the letter is characterized by early catholicism opposing Gnosticism (e.g., Kelly, 233-34). But a careful reading of Jude 17 indicates that it is referring rather to the readers having heard the prediction by the apostles, probably at the time when this church was first established by these apostolic missionaries. In other words, Jude is bringing his readers back to their first instructions in the faith (cf. Jude 3, 5; with respect to Jude's letter not being characterized by early catholicism and the opponents not being Gnostics, see 2 above).

The second main argument for the pseudepigraphic character of Jude is the quality of the letter's use of language. It can be claimed that the letter's Greek is too good to have been written by a Palestinian Jewish peasant like Jude (e.g., Kelly, 233). But a couple of points call this argument into question. (1) While the letter is marked by a rich and varied vocabulary and it has quite clearly been carefully composed, the grammar itself is relatively unsophisticated. And much of this vocabulary echoes Jewish sources, so the language does not necessarily need to be entirely natural for this author. (2) In light of the increasing recognition of the bilingual character of Galilee, and that, if written by Jude, it was written after many years' experience in missionary activity, it is quite possible for someone like Jude to have used Greek competently (e.g., Bauckham 1983, 6-7, 14-16; Green, 48-52).

One objection to using Jude as a pseudonym is that he was too obscure a person for his name to be used in this way (e.g., Cranfield, 147-48; Green, 51-52). It may be noted, however, that, while Jude may be obscure to us, as one of "the brothers of the Lord" he would probably have been well known among Jewish Christians of the first century—the environment in which this letter arose (Rowston 1975, 559-60). However, the fact that the letter uses the self-description "servant of Jesus Christ" rather than "brother of Jesus Christ"—the description by which Jude would have been known in that environment—militates against the pseudepigraphic designation (Bauckham 1990, 176).

The evidence for the hypothesis of pseudepigraphy does not bear the weight placed upon it. The character and language of the letter is best explained as having come from the pen of Jude.

5. Date.

Scholarly opinion for the date of Jude varies widely, from the A.D. 50s and 60s (e.g., Ellis, 232-35; Bauckham 1983, 13; Green, 56), to the latter part of the first century; through the early second century (e.g., Sidebottom, 77); and even into the latter part of that century (for a complete survey of dates, see Bauckham 1990, 168-69 n. 237). The question of date is tied to a number of issues already discussed. If the letter is read as an early catholic, postapostolic document, then the later dates are more appropriate. But if, as discussed above, the letter is rather to be characterized by Jewish-Christian apocalypticism, then the door is open to considering an earlier date, though this characterization would not require an earlier date. The type of opponents (see 4 above) are not dissimilar to some that Paul faced in Corinth during the A.D. 50s.

If the letter is pseudepigraphic, then a later date is more appropriate; but if, as argued above, the letter was written by Jude, the brother of Jesus, then Jude's death provides a *terminus ad quem*. Unfortunately nothing is known about Jude's death, though Eusebius cites Hegesippus referring to grandsons of Jude who lived during the reign of Domitian (A.D. 81-96; Eusebius *Hist. Eccl.* 3.19.1—3.20.7). The citation begins, "Now there still survived of the family of the Lord grandsons of Judas, who was said to have been his brother according to the flesh" (Eusebius *Hist. Eccl.* 3.20.1), which may imply that Jude was dead at this time. Since Jude was probably one of the youngest of the brothers, falling near the bottom of the list of names (Mk 6:3 par. Mt 13:55), he could have lived well into Domitian's reign, and an estimate of some date shortly before A.D. 90 for his death is reasonable (Mayor 1978 [1907], cxlviii). Paul alludes to the brothers of the Lord engaged in missionary activity (1 Cor 9:5). If this includes Jude and is current with Paul's writing 1 Corinthians, then it would place Jude as engaged in ministry during the A.D. 50s. The tone of Jude's letter and Jude 3 in particular indicates that Jude is actively engaged in ministry, and this suggests a date earlier in his life rather than at its end.

If, as discussed above, Jude 17-18 does not support a postapostolic date but is instead an allusion to the readers' initial reception of the gospel and the establishment of their church, then these verses imply that the readers are still the first-generation Christians who were part of the church's founding.

This meager evidence suggests a date for Jude's letter between the A.D. 50s and the 80s, with the earlier half of this spectrum being more probable.

6. Recipients/Destination.

Little real evidence exists to address the questions of the recipients and destination of this letter. Given the pervasive use of Jewish traditions it is plausible to suggest the readers are Jewish Christians and Jude expects his readers to appreciate his allusions. But this evidence tells us more about the author than the recipients. By contrast, problems with antinomianism as evidenced in this letter were more common among Gentiles than Jews but not unknown among Jews (cf. Bauckham 1983, 16). Yet this tells us more about the opponents who have come from outside than the recipients themselves. Given Jude's knowledge of his readers (Jude 3) it would appear that he is personally acquainted with them and pastorally concerned for them. If they are within the sphere of his pastoral ministry, then the weight of probability is that they are predominantly Jewish Christians, but their problems arose because the context in which they lived may have been dominated by Hellenistic values.

Destinations proposed for this letter include Palestine (e.g., Kelly, 234), Syria, Egypt or simply unknown. All destinations could meet the suggestion made above that the readers were Jewish Christians living in a Hellenistic environment. One indirect piece of evidence is that Jude was accepted as canonical in Alexandria by the time of Clement, but the Syriac church did not accept it as canonical until the sixth century (Bauckham 1983, 16-17).

7. Message.

In light of the preceding discussion, especially on literary structure and form, the message of the letter may now be more fully understood (cf. Martin, 81-86).

Jude writes to address a specific situation facing his readers. He encourages them "to fight for the faith" (Jude 3) because false teachers "have infiltrated" them with a message and lifestyle, the implications of which Jude understands to be a perversion of God's grace and a denial of Christ's lordship (Jude 4). Jude's opponents, the false teachers, would not, of course, state matters in such blatant anti-Christian terms (if they had, they would probably not have been able to infiltrate this Christian community successfully). So before Jude can instruct them how to fight for the faith, he must convince his readers of the dangers of the opponents' teaching and lifestyle and of the certain divine judgment awaiting them (Webb 1996).

Jude accomplishes this latter task by means of four sets of examples or texts that he applies to his opponents. Each of these sets has some point of commonality between them and the false teachers. Consequently, Jude can then point to the theme of judgment found in all four sets and conclude that divine judgment is the fate awaiting "these" (Jude 7, 8, 10, 12, 14, 16, 19) false teachers. The first two sets are collections of examples from the past—OT narratives that were expanded in later Jewish traditions (see 3.2 above). In the first set the sins by and judgment of Israel in the wilderness, the disenfranchised angels, and Sodom and Gomorrah (Jude 5-7) are then applied to Jude's opponents (Jude 8-10). Similarly, in the second set the examples of Cain, Balaam and Korah (Jude 11) are applied to the false teachers (Jude 12-14). The third and fourth sets are quotations from authoritative sources that are applied in similar fashion as the first two sets. In the third set a prophecy of divine judgment from *1 Enoch* 1:9 is quoted (Jude 14-15) and then applied (Jude 16), and in the fourth set a quotation from early Christian apostolic tradition is cited (Jude 17-18) and applied (Jude 19).

Having denounced the errors of the false teachers and announced their certain judgment, Jude returns to the purpose at hand in Jude 20-23, namely, to instruct the readers how "to fight for the faith" (Jude 3). Their first concern must be to guard their own relationship with God (Jude 21; the verb "keep" in Jude 21 is also used in Jude 1, 6 [2x], 13), which entails fulfilling certain responsibilities (Jude 20) as well as maintaining an eschatologically oriented outlook (Jude 21). Their second concern is to assist those who have become tainted with this false teaching (Jude 22-23), while being careful not to be tainted with it themselves (Jude 23).

Jude's pastoral concern does not end with his advice in Jude 20-23 but concludes instead with a doxology (Jude 24-25) in which he returns to themes he alluded to in the letter's opening (Jude 1-2). As an expression of prayerful confidence, the doxology reassures the readers that God is able to preserve them not only through this situation but unto the parousia, at which time they will be able to stand and rejoice in God's presence.

See also ADVERSARIES; APOCALYPTICISM; ESCHATOLOGY; 2 PETER, LETTER OF.

DLNTD: EARLY CATHOLICISM; JEWISH CHRISTIANITY; NONCANONICAL WRITINGS, CITATIONS OF; RELATIVES OF JESUS.

BIBLIOGRAPHY. **Commentaries:** R. J. Bauckham, *Jude, 2 Peter* (WBC; Waco, TX: Word, 1983); C. Bigg, *A Critical and Exegetical Commentary on the Epistles of St. Peter and St. Jude* (ICC; Edinburgh: T & T Clark, 1901); C. E. B. Cranfield, *1 and 2 Peter and Jude* (TBC; London: SCM, 1960); M. Green, *The Second Epistle General of Peter and the General Epistle of Jude* (2d ed.; TNTC; Grand Rapids: Eerdmans, 1987); N. Hillyer, *1 and 2 Peter, Jude* (NIBC; Peabody, MA: Hendrickson, 1992); J. N. D. Kelly, *A Commentary on the Epistles of Peter and of Jude* (BNTC; London: A. & C. Black, 1969); S. J. Kistemaker, *Exposition of the Epistles of Peter and of the Epistle of Jude* (NTCom; Grand Rapids: Baker, 1987); S. J. Kraftchick, *Jude, 2 Peter* (ANTC; Nashville: Abingdon, 2002); M. Luther, "Sermons on the Epistle of St. Jude" in *The Catholic Epistles,* ed. J. Peli-kan and W. A. Hansen (*LW* 30; St. Louis: Concordia, 1967 [1523]) 203-15; J. B. Mayor, *The Epistle of St. Jude and the Second Epistle of St. Peter* (Minneapolis: Klock & Klock, 1978 [1907]); J. H. Neyrey, *2 Peter, Jude* (AB; New York: Doubleday, 1993); P. Perkins, *First and Second Peter, James, and Jude* (IntC; Louisville, KY: John Knox, 1995); B. Reicke, *The Epistles of James, Peter, and Jude* (AB; Garden City, NY: Doubleday, 1964); E. M. Sidebottom, *James, Jude, 2 Peter* (NCB; Grand Rapids: Eerdmans, 1967). **Studies:** R. J. Bauckham, "James, 1 and 2 Peter, Jude" in *It is Written: Scripture Citing Scripture: Essays in Honor of Barnabas Lindars, SSF,* ed. D. A. Carson and H. G. M. Williamson (Cambridge: Cambridge University Press, 1988) 303-13; idem, *Jude and the Relatives of Jesus in the Early Church* (Edinburgh: T & T Clark, 1990); idem, "Jude, Epistle of," *ABD* (1992) 3:1098-1103; idem, "The Letter of Jude: An Account of

Research," *ANRW* 2.25.5 (1988) 3791-826; J. D. Charles, "Jude's Use of Pseudepigraphical Source Material as Part of a Literary Strategy," *NTS* 37 (1991) 130-45; idem, *Literary Strategy in the Epistle of Jude* (London/Toronto: Associated University Presses, 1993); M. Desjardins, "The Portrayal of the Dissidents in 2 Peter and Jude: Does It Tell Us More About the 'Godly' Than the 'Ungodly' " *JSNT* 30 (1987) 89-102; E. E. Ellis, "Prophecy and Hermeneutic in Jude," in *Prophecy and Hermeneutic in Early Christianity* (Grand Rapids: Eerdmans, 1978) 220-36; R. H. Fuller, *A Critical Introduction to the New Testament* (2d ed.; London: Duckworth, 1971); J. J. Gunther, "The Meaning and Origin of the Name 'Judas Thomas,' " *Mus* 93 (1980) 113-48; S. J. Joubert, "Language, Ideology and the Social Context of the Letter of Jude," *Neot* 24 (1990) 335-49; A. F. J. Klijn, "John xiv 22 and the Name Judas Thomas" in *Studies in John: Presented to Professor Dr. J. N. Sevenster on the Occasion of His Seventieth Birthday* (NovTSup 24; Leiden: E. J. Brill, 1970) 88-96; idem, "Jude 5 to 7" in *The New Testament Age: Essays in Honor of Bo Reicke*, ed. W. C. Weinrich (Macon, GA: Mercer University Press, 1984) 1.237-44; K. R. Lyle Jr., *Ethical Admonition in the Epistle of Jude* (SBL 4; New York: Peter Lang, 1998); R. P. Martin, "The Theology of Jude, 1 Peter, and 2 Peter" in *The Theology of the Letters of James, Peter and Jude*, ed. A. Chester and R. P. Martin (NTT; Cambridge: Cambridge University Press, 1994) 63-163; J. B. Mayor, "The Epistle of St. Jude and the Marcosian Heresy," *JTS* 6 (1905) 569-77; C. D. Osburn, "The Christological Use of 1 Enoch 1:9 in Jude 14, 15, " *NTS* 23 (1977) 334-41; idem, "Discourse Analysis and Jewish Apocalyptic in the Epistle of Jude," in *Linguistics and New Testament Interpretation: Essays on Discourse Analysis*, ed. D. A. Black, K. Barnwell and S. Levinsohn (Nashville: Broadman, 1992) 287-319; D. J. Rowston, "The Most Neglected Book in the New Testament," *NTS* 21 (1975) 554-63; idem, "The Setting of the Letter of Jude" (Southern Baptist Theological Seminary; unpublished Ph.D. dissertation, 1971); D. F. Watson, *Invention, Arrangement and Style: Rhetorical Criticism of Jude and 2 Peter* (SBLDS 104; Atlanta: Scholars Press, 1988); R. L. Webb, "Epistles, Catholic," *ABD* (1992) 2:569-70; idem, "The Eschatology of the Epistle of Jude and Its Rhetorical and Social Functions," *BBR* 6 (1996) 139-51.

R. L. Webb

JUDGMENT I: GOSPELS

Judgment is the process whereby God calls people to account for their behavior and allots their destinies accordingly. The theme is prominent in the teaching of Jesus, which echoes many features found in the OT, apocalyptic and *rabbinic literature.

1. Terminology and Meaning
2. The Message of Jesus
3. Emphases of the Gospel Writers

1. Terminology and Meaning.

Like the English verb *judge*, the Greek word *krinō* can mean "form an opinion" (Lk 7:43). But normally in the NT it describes the passing of a sentence, either in a law court (Mt 5:40) or metaphorically with reference to divine judgment (Mt 7:1-2; Jn 5:22, 30). Often the focus is on the negative aspect of condemnation (Mt 7:1; Jn 3:17-18). The noun *krisis* normally refers to the act of judging (Mt 5:21-22; Lk 11:31-32), while *krima* connotes the verdict or sentence (Lk 23:40). But this distinction is sometimes blurred (e.g., *krima* in Jn 9:39). The influence of the LXX, where the word group usually translates *špt*, can be seen in Matthew 23:23 and Luke 11:42, where *krisis* means "justice," and in Matthew 19:28 and Luke 22:30, where *krinō* probably means "rule." Although the noun *judge* (*kritēs*) occurs in parables (Mt 5:25; Lk 18:2, 6), it is not used as a description of God in the direct sayings of Jesus.

Other expressions to be considered are "condemn" (*katakrinō*, Mt 12:41-42; *katadikazō*, Mt 12:37); "punishment" (*kolasis*, Mt 25:46); the *dik*-word group, translated variously as "punishment," "retribution," "vindicate," "justice" (Lk 18:1-8; 21:22); "visitation" (*episkopē*, Lk 19:44); and references to the "day" (*hēmera*) of judgment (Mt 7:22; 12:36; Lk 21:34; *see* Eschatology). In addition, there is a rich variety of parabolic images of judgment.

2. The Message of Jesus.

Jesus rejects the widespread idea that the wealth or suffering of individuals is God's reward for righteousness or punishment for sin (Mk 12:38-44; Jn 9:2-3). In Luke 13:1-5 the lesson to be learned from the sufferings of some Galileans at Pilate's hands and from the disaster in Siloam is not that the victims were especially wicked but that everyone must repent in the face of God's judgment.

2.1. Judgment on the Nation. Much of Jesus'

most vivid teaching consists of warnings to his contemporaries that an unrepentant Israel is heading for imminent historical catastrophe. According to the parable of the children in the marketplace (Mt 11:16-19), "this generation's" refusal to "play the game" with either *John the Baptist or Jesus shows its defiance of God. The phrase identifies Jesus' contemporaries with the rebellious generation of Deuteronomy 32:5, 20; Psalm 78:8 and Jeremiah 7:29. This is the last generation of a rebellious people, destined now to pay in full the accumulated debt of the nation's resistance to God (Lk 11:47-51; Mk 12:1-12). There is still time for a change of heart, but a strictly limited time (Lk 13:6-9).

Jerusalem and its religious leaders are the main target of these warnings. In the manner of an OT prophet, Jesus laments Jerusalem's failure to respond to his call and prophesies its desolation (Lk 13:34-35; 19:41-44). Judgment takes the form of God's abandonment of Israel to its enemies (see Jer 7:25-34; 12:7; 25:4-11; Hos 9:15-17; 10:13-15).

It has been argued, notably by C. H. Dodd and J. Jeremias, that several parables, which in the Gospels are addressed to disciples and relate to Jesus' final coming and the final judgment, were originally addressed by Jesus to his opponents or to the crowds and referred to the coming catastrophe for Israel (e.g., Mt 24:45—25:30). But since Jeremias concedes that Jesus expected a final judgment, it is better to allow that some parables allude to Israel's impending crisis, others to the final judgment of all people (see Marshall). But we may of course agree with Jeremias that Jesus gave no clue that the gap between Jerusalem's destruction and the final judgment would be extended for centuries.

2.2. The Final Judgment. Jesus speaks of a judgment of all people on the "day" when the Son of man comes to establish his kingdom in its fullness (Mt 7:22; Lk 17:30-35; see Kingdom of God). God is the judge (Mt 10:28). Jesus' role at the judgment is sometimes that of witness for or against the person judged (Mt 10:32-33), but sometimes he is the judge (Mt 7:21-23; 16:27). There is some force in the argument that in the earliest Son of man sayings Jesus is witness rather than judge and that the depiction of him as judge is therefore a later development. Yet the fact that the Son of man sits at God's right hand (Mk 14:62) shows how easily one concept could pass over into the other.

2.2.1. Judgment as Separation. The judgment involves a division between two kinds of people: "sons of the kingdom" and "sons of the evil one" (Mt 13:38), "wise" and "foolish" (Mt 7:24-27), "sheep" and "goats" (Mt 25:31-46), those who "enter into life" and those who are "thrown into hell" (Mk 9:42-48). This reflects the radical distinction between "the righteous" and "the wicked" found in much apocalyptic literature and in the Dead Sea Scrolls.

2.2.2. The Criterion and the Outcome of Judgment. Jesus maintains the Jewish emphasis on judgment according to works (Mt 7:21-23; 12:36-37; 25:31-46). He provides examples of particular kinds of deeds that will seal a person's condemnation, such as causing "little ones" to sin (Mk 9:42), lack of care for the poor (Lk 16:19-31; Mt 25:31-46), failure to forgive (Mt 18:21-35) and being judgmental toward others (Mt 7:1-2). His warnings of condemnation are almost never directed at those who, for example, commit adultery or collect taxes dishonestly, but at the pious who would exclude such people from the community (Mt 23:33; Lk 18:9-14).

In some judgment sayings, works are bound up with relationship or response to Jesus. In Matthew 7:24-27 we read, "everyone who hears these words of mine and does them is like a wise man." In Matthew 25:31-46 care for the needy or lack of it is taken as evidence of people's reaction to Jesus. Other sayings declare that reaction to Jesus will be the key criterion at the judgment. "All who acknowledge me before other people, the Son of Man will acknowledge them before the angels of God. Those who disown me before other people will be disowned before the angels of God" (Lk 12:8-9; cf. Mk 8:38; Lk 10:8-16; 11:29-32).

Luke 12:8-9 also indicates that just as the criterion of judgment is relationship to Jesus, so the outcome of judgment will be expressed in terms of relationship to Jesus or to God. It will involve acceptance into fellowship with God or rejection from that fellowship. Those who do not know him—who are not in genuine, obedient relationship to him now—will not know him then. In the parables of Matthew 25 and Luke 13:25-27 the outcome of the judgment is also expressed in terms of coming into or departing from God's presence.

Apart from the language of relationship, Jesus uses other more pictorial language to depict human destiny beyond the judgment. God's family will sit at the Father's table, while others are thrown outside (Lk 13:28-29). They will see God (Mt 5:8) and experience eternal life (Mk 10:30). A negative outcome is described as unquenchable fire or Gehenna (Mk 9:43, 45, 48; Mt 5:22; Lk 12:5). Those excluded from God's kingdom will "weep and gnash their teeth" (Mt 13:42, 50; Lk 13:28). It is not clear whether such language can be taken to imply eternal torment as traditionally understood. Such imagery, together with the reference to "eternal punishment" in Matthew 25:46, may be intended not so much to describe the specific character of punishment as to underline the irreversible and negative force of separation from God's presence.

It must also be noted that, in comparison with much Jewish literature (e.g., *1 Enoch* 21—22), Jesus' references to the destiny of the wicked are remarkably allusive and unspecific, and that such references occur mostly in exhortations to the hearer to respond to Jesus' message, not in descriptions of the fate of someone else.

2.2.3. The Main Thrust: Relationship Rather Than Retribution. The evidence suggests that Jesus' understanding of judgment focuses not on a strictly retributive justice, whereby rewards and punishments are recompense for human deeds. Rather, the focus is on relationship to Jesus or to God through him. The relationship chosen by people when confronted by the message of God's kingdom will be confirmed at the final judgment. When the language of judgment according to works is used, the character of the works is understood as evidence of a person's relationship to God or as showing whether the basic direction of one's life is toward him or away from him.

This perspective on Jesus' message is reinforced by three other images of judgment. The motif of the Two Ways, already familiar in Judaism (e.g., *1 Enoch* 94:1-4; 1QS 3:13—4:26), suggests that human destinies are not rewards or punishments imposed from outside but the inherent outcome of the choices people make (Mt 7:13-14). The image of treasure in heaven (Tob 4:3-10; *Pss. Sol.* 9:9; *2 Apoc. Bar.* 14:12; 24:1) pictures people's destinies as the end result of their desires. Those whose hearts are fixed on submission to God's rule will gain the riches of his kingdom (Mt 6:19-21; Lk 12:33-34). Finally, in the image of the banquet invitation (Lk 14:16-24), everything turns on the refusal of those invited to come to the feast. They have excluded themselves while the poor are open to the insistent gift of the host.

2.2.4. Conclusion. Jesus rejects speculation about many aspects of final judgment and its outcome. He is silent about the geography of God's kingdom or of Gehenna. Rather than speculate about the number of those saved (2 Esdr 8:1), he urges his hearers to make sure of their own entry into the kingdom (Lk 13:23-24). And he tempers stern warnings of judgment with a greater emphasis on the infinite care of God for his creatures (Lk 12:4-12). There are also hints that his suffering and death involve taking on himself the judgment of God on behalf of others (Mk 10:45; 14:36; 15:34).

3. Emphases of the Gospel Writers.

3.1. Matthew. In comparison with Mark and Luke, Matthew heightens the emphasis on judgment, reward and punishment. He increases the number of references to Gehenna and related images (Mt 5:22; 8:12; 13:42, 50; 22:13; 23:15, 33; 24:51; 25:30) and makes more prominent use of judgment as a sanction for behavior (Mt 6:1-6, 16-18; 18:35; 25:14-30). In keeping with this is the stress on judgment according to works (Mt 16:27, different from Mk 8:38). Peculiar to Matthew is the parable of the sheep and the goats (Mt 25:31-46) in which destinies are allotted according to deeds of mercy done, or not done, toward "the least of these brothers of mine." The older view, that this refers to general humanitarian concern, has been increasingly supplanted in recent studies by the view that the "brothers" are Christians, or Christian missionaries (see France, 264). Possibly Jesus' original reference was to suffering humanity in general, but this has been narrowed down in Matthew to a reference to Christian missionaries.

Matthew's Gospel highlights God's judgment on "this generation" of Jews, in particular Jewish leaders (Mt 23:29-36). They are the object of the series of "woes" in Matthew 23. Matthew alone adds to the parable of the wicked tenants the conclusion: "Therefore I tell you that the kingdom of God will be taken away from you and given to a nation producing its fruits" (Mt 21:43). Yet there are severe warnings for the church too, lest it follow the same path of disobedience. The parable of the wedding feast ends with the ejection of the replacement guest who has failed to meet the condition of being properly dressed (Mt 22:1-14). The criticism of scribes and Pharisees becomes a warning to "you," the hearers of the Gospel, to live circumspectly (Mt 23:2-12). For even religious works will count for nothing at the judgment if they are not "the will of my Father in heaven" (Mt 7:21-23). Only at the judgment will it be clear who truly belongs to God's kingdom (Mt 13:24-30, 36-43, 47-50).

3.2. John. The Fourth Gospel refers in only two places to the final judgment. When in John 12:48 Jesus says people will be judged on the last day by the word which he has spoken, the thought seems to be close to that of Mark 8:38. John 5:26-29 offers the traditional apocalyptic description of a final general resurrection and judgment. Christ is the judge (Jn 5:27). He judges according to works, and there are two possible outcomes—life and condemnation (*krisis,* Jn 5:29; for *krisis* and *krino* denoting condemnation cf. Jn 3:18; 12:31; 16:11). But these verses are set in relation to John 5:19-25, which emphasize a process of judgment already in operation: "whoever hears my word and believes him who sent me has eternal life, and does not come under condemnation, but has crossed over from death to life." Thus the verdict of the last judgment is a ratification of the life or death which people already experience because of their reaction to Christ.

This focus on judgment as a process already at work is entirely characteristic of John. Confronted by Jesus and his revelation of God, people react either by committing themselves in trust to him or by rejecting him (Jn 1:11-12; 3:16-21, 36; 5:24; 8:12-19; 9:39). The immediate outcome of faith is reception of eternal life (Jn 3:16, 36; 5:24; 12:50), which derives its quality from relationship to Christ (Jn 17:3). The experience of eternal life reaches its goal beyond death (Jn 11:25-26) or at the last day (Jn 5:29; 6:40, 51, 54, 58). Those who do not receive Christ are out of relationship to him. God's wrath rests on them (Jn 3:36); they remain in darkness and death (Jn 12:46; 5:24). Their condition is self-imposed: They prefer darkness, and that is what they get (Jn 3:19-21).

Whereas the Synoptics use colorful imagery such as kingdom and wedding, John prefers the more abstract language of love, knowing God, life and death. The overall effect of his presentation is to highlight the theme, which we have seen in the Synoptics, of judgment determined by response to the person and message of Jesus.

See also Apocalypticism; Eschatology.

DJG: Blessing and Woe; Hardness of Heart; Heaven and Hell.

BIBLIOGRAPHY. J. A. Baird, *The Justice of God in the Teaching of Jesus* (Philadelphia: Westminster, 1963); C. H. Dodd, *The Parables of the Kingdom* (New York: Scribner's, 1936); A. M. Fairhurst, "The Problem Posed by the Severe Sayings Attributed to Jesus in the Synoptic Gospels," *SJT* 23 (1970) 77-91; R. T. France, *Matthew: Evangelist and Teacher* (Grand Rapids: Zondervan, 1989); J. Jeremias, *The Parables of Jesus* (3d ed.; New York: Scribners, 1972); I. H. Marshall, *Eschatology and the Parables* (London: Tyndale, 1963); W. Strawson, *Jesus and the Future Life* (London: Epworth, 1970); S. H. Travis, *Christ and the Judgment of God* (Basingstoke: Marshall Pickering, 1986). S. H. Travis

JUDGMENT II: PAUL

Paul shares with his Jewish antecedents the conviction that *God as Creator has the right to call people to account for their behavior and allot their destinies accordingly.

1. Terminology and Meaning.
2. Continuity and Discontinuity with Judaism
3. Judgment and the Gospel of Christ
4. Judgment According to Works
5. Judgment of Christians

1. Terminology and Meaning.

Two main word groups occur frequently in Paul's letters. Like the English verb *to judge,* the Greek *krino* can mean "form an opinion" or "decide" (1 Cor 2:2), but it commonly refers to the assessment of human beings by others (1 Cor 4:5; 6:1) or by God (Rom 2:16). Related words include *krima* ("judgment," "sentence," Rom 2:2; 13:2), *katakrino* ("condemn," 1 Cor 11:32) and *katakrima* ("condemnation," Rom 5:16). Words derived from *dike* ("justice," "punishment," 2 Thess 1:9) include *ekdikesis* ("punishment," 2 Thess 1:8) and *ekdikos* ("punisher," Rom 13:4; 1 Thess 4:6). But Paul expresses his thought also in other images, such as wrath (*orge,* Rom 1:18), destruction (*phthora,* Gal 6:8), "paying back" (*antapodidomi,* 2 Thess 1:6) and reward (*antapodosis,* Col 3:24).

2. Continuity and Discontinuity with Judaism.

In many respects Paul takes over perspectives familiar in Jewish literature. Non-Christian Jews would find nothing strange in Paul's expectation of a final day of judgment (Rom 2:16) when all "will appear before God's judgment seat" (Rom 14:10) to be judged "according to their deeds" (Rom 2:6; 1 Thess 4:6; cf. *1 Enoch* 45:3; 4 Ezra 7:33-44; *see* Eschatology). But they would be shocked by his reversal of common Jewish assumptions about the outcome of judgment. Because God exercises impartiality in judgment (Rom 2:11), Jew and Gentile alike face the prospect of judgment and the possibility of salvation through Christ.

3. Judgment and the Gospel of Christ.

For Paul, the process of judgment is integrally related to his message of salvation through Christ. Although he can speak of God's righteous judgment (Rom 2:5; 2 Thess 1:5), God's wrath (Rom 1:18) and God's judgment seat (Rom 14:10), he regularly associates judgment with Christ. He cites with reference to Christ OT texts that originally referred to judgment by Yahweh (2 Thess 1:9-10, citing Is 2:10, 19, 21). He links judgment with the "day" of Christ's parousia (2 Thess 1:6-10; 1 Cor 4:3-5), when "we shall all appear before the judgment seat of Christ" (2 Cor 5:10).

The criterion by which people will be judged is their attitude or relationship to Christ: the key question is whether they "believe" in him, whether they "know" God and "obey the gospel of the Lord Jesus" (2 Thess 1:8, 10).

The outcome of the final judgment also is expressed in terms of relationship to Christ. Unbelievers will suffer "exclusion from the presence of the Lord" (2 Thess 1:9), while the destiny of believers is to be "at home with the Lord" (2 Cor 5:8). Paul is reticent about going further than this in describing human destiny. He does not use terms such as *Gehenna* (Mk 9:43, 45, 47) or the vivid imagery of some Jewish apocalyptists (*see* Apocalypticism). He prefers more abstract terms such as "life" (*zōē*) and "death" (*thanatos,* Rom 6:23), "destruction" (*olethros*, 1 Thess 5:3; *apōleia,* Phil 3:19; *phthora,* Gal 6:8). He is more concerned to warn of the danger of missing life in Christ than to explore the precise form that this loss might take.

4. Judgment According to Works.

Paul's focus on relationship to Christ is not in conflict with his affirmation of judgment according to works. For he understands people's deeds as evidence of their character, showing whether their relation to God is fundamentally one of faith or unbelief. Judgment according to deeds does not imply degrees of reward or punishment in accordance with the quantity of good or evil works done. In Romans 2:5-11 and elsewhere Paul distinguishes only two groups of people—those who do evil and those who do good—and only two possible destinies (see Snodgrass). When he writes that those whose lives are dominated by sinful acts "will not inherit the kingdom of God" (Gal 5:19-21; cf. 1 Cor 6:9-10; Eph 5:5; *see* Kingdom of God), he implies that if professing Christians persistently did evil rather than good they would show themselves not to be Christians and to be in danger of condemnation at the final judgment. Christians are not exempt from that judgment precisely because its function is to show, by the evidence of people's deeds, whether they are in relationship to Christ or not (2 Cor 5:10).

5. Judgment of Christians.

For Christian believers *justification by grace represents a real, though not irreversible, anticipation of the verdict of the final judgment. Through faith in Christ they have been accepted into relationship with God and are expected to bear the fruit of this relationship in their lives. At the final judgment the evidence of their deeds will confirm the reality of this relationship, which will then find its eternal fulfillment in God's presence.

Two passages in 1 Corinthians (1 Cor 5:5; 11:27-34) seem to express the conviction that when Christians are guilty of serious sin, God may use illness as a disciplinary judgment to provoke them to repentance. But it would be risky to conclude from this limited evidence either that (in Paul's view) God regularly deals with Christians' disobedience in this way or that Paul normally understands illness as an expression of divine judgment.

Some interpreters have argued, on the basis of texts such as 1 Corinthians 3:14-15 and 2 Corinthians 5:10, that Paul believed in a final assessment of Christians leading to degrees of reward in the future life. But these tantalizingly unspecific texts are an uncertain basis for such a doctrine. What they do make clear, however, is Paul's willingness to urge human accountability to God as a motive for Christians to take seriously their life and service.

See also APOCALYPTICISM; ESCHATOLOGY; JUSTIFICATION.

DPL: APOSTASY, FALLING AWAY, PERSEVERANCE; LIFE AND DEATH; REWARDS; SALVATION; WRATH, DESTRUCTION.

BIBLIOGRAPHY. K. P. Donfried, "Justification and Last Judgment in Paul," *ZNW* 67 (1976) 90-110; F. V. Filson, *St. Paul's Conception of Recompense* (Leipzig: Hinrichsche Buchhandlung, 1931); C. J. Roetzel, *Judgment in the Community* (Leiden: E. J. Brill, 1972); K. R. Snodgrass, "Justification by Grace—to the Doers: An Analysis of the Place of Romans 2 in the Theology of Paul," *NTS* 32 (1986) 72-93; S. H. Travis, *Christ and the Judgment of God* (Basingstoke: Marshall Pickering, 1986).   S. H. Travis

JUDGMENT III: ACTS, HEBREWS, GENERAL EPISTLES, REVELATION

The NT expectation of a final judgment is derived from biblical tradition and therefore is based on God's right as Creator to execute justice in the earth. The day of the Lord, in which righteous judgment will take place, is not a matter of calculation but of patient hope, faith and obedience. The coming day of judgment is integral to the gospel and to the comfort, warning and call to perseverance that proceed from it. Christ shall judge each one according to his or her deeds. The eternal destiny of each person shall be determined in this judgment.

1. The Background of the New Testament Understanding
2. The Day of Judgment in Acts, the Non-Pauline Letters and Revelation
3. The Context and Function of the Theme of Judgment in the Earliest Church
4. The Early Christian Concept of Judgment

1. The Background of the New Testament Understanding.

Early Christian belief in a final divine judgment represents a development of biblical faith in the one God of Israel, the Judge and Ruler of all the earth (e.g., Gen 18:25). The Psalms celebrate Yahweh as the righteous king who punishes the wicked and intervenes on behalf of the downtrodden (e.g., Ps 72:1-4). He has the sovereign right to determine justice and execute judgment (e.g., Ps 96—99). The prophets announce that divine visitation will bring punishment not only to the nations that oppose God but first and foremost to the disobedient within Israel (e.g., Is 1:1-31). The covenant renders Israel, the object

of divine favor, more and not less liable to judgment (e.g., Amos 3:2). Wisdom literature anticipates that deeds, whether good or evil, will receive recompense (Prov, passim). Ultimately the hope grew for a revelation of divine glory at the end of human history, including a judgment at which all human beings would be brought to account (e.g., Dan 12:2-3; *1 Enoch* 1:1-9; *4 Ezra* 7:70-74).

This understanding of final judgment characterized the message of Jesus. The Gospels record numerous instances in which Jesus warned of future punishment and—subject to the paradox of grace—promised reward for the faithful (e.g., Mt 19:27—20:16). His proclamation of coming judgment represented not a new teaching but a reassertion of the biblical tradition. Before him, *John the Baptist had announced that the impending wrath of God demanded repentance from all and insisted, like the classical prophets, that membership in the covenant nation was insufficient for deliverance from judgment (Mt 3:7-10). In continuity with John, Jesus issued a call to repentance in anticipation of the coming judgment with his announcement of the kingdom (Mk 1:15; 9:42-48; Mt 11:20-24; *see* Kingdom of God).

The authors of the NT writings and other early Christian literature likewise shared the conviction of many of their Jewish contemporaries that a final divine judgment was coming upon the world. Continuity with the biblical tradition, in which God the Creator and his claim upon his creatures is central, sets the NT understanding of final judgment apart from Egyptian and Greco-Roman conceptions of the afterlife (see in this regard *m. 'Abot* 4:22). Particularly in the latter, the torments of the wicked are of primary interest, a tradition to which Dante's *Inferno* was an heir. Some early extrabiblical writings, Jewish and Christian, from the first through fifth centuries show such influence, although they are not simple developments of Greek ideas (see Himmelfarb) and stand at a distance from the NT materials (e.g., *Apoc. Zeph., Apoc. Peter, Apoc. Paul;* with time attention shifted from future to postmortem punishment [Bauckham]). In contrast even the NT Apocalypse of John (Revelation), which vividly depicts the outpouring of wrath, focuses not on the experience of perdition but on the wickedness of humanity and on the certainty and justice of divine judgment.

2. The Day of Judgment in Acts, the Non-Pauline Letters and Revelation.

In the Hebrew Scriptures the predominant expression for the time at which God visits judgment on the earth is "the day of the Lord." The NT writers take up this term, give nuance to the basic phrase with varying forms and use it to signify the final judgment at the end of the present age (e.g., "the Day," Heb 10:25; "the day of visitation," 1 Pet 2:12; "the day of the Lord," 2 Pet 3:10; "the day of judgment," 1 Jn 4:17; "the great day," Jude 6; "the great day of wrath," Rev 6:16-17).

There is little basis in the NT for the thesis that a crisis resulted from the so-called delay of the parousia, that is, the supposed disappointment of the first generation of believers who are thought to have believed that Christ's coming (parousia) would certainly occur within their lifetime (see *inter alia* Moore). In 2 Peter, where the delay of the day of the Lord is treated explicitly as a theological problem, the challenge to Christian faith arises not from a failure of Christ to appear immediately but from a teaching that denied biblical faith more broadly considered (2 Pet 3:1-10). "Scoffers" have used the apparent continuity of the world from the time of the ancestors to advance what seems to have been a monistic, materialist view of the world. Such philosophy, the author declares, ignores the biblical witness to creation *ex nihilo*, the patriarchal deluge and the divine word that has determined a fiery end to the present order (2 Pet 3:5-7).

The tenor of the NT anticipation of the day of the Lord reflects that of numerous passages in the Hebrew Scriptures, particularly the Psalms, in which the faith of the righteous is proved in their patiently waiting in hope for God to act on their behalf (e.g., Ps 25; 27; 31; 37-39). The NT writings are distinct in their sense of imminence, but for them the nearness of the parousia is not subject to calculation. As with their biblical precedents, it is rather a matter of faith and obedience. Christ has appeared, in whom God's saving purposes have culminated (e.g., Acts 10:43; 1 Pet 1:20). With him the last days have arrived (e.g., Acts 2:17; Heb 1:2; Jas 5:3). Judgment now impends since no saving event will intervene before the end (e.g., Heb 10:26-27; 1 Pet 4:5, 6). The "day" will come unexpectedly upon the unbelieving and disobedient (e.g., 2 Pet 3:10; Rev 3:3; 16:15). Those who belong to Christ are to be prepared by their faith and upright behavior (e.g., Heb 10:35-39; 1 Pet 4:7; 1 Jn 2:28-29).

3. The Context and Function of the Theme of Judgment in the Earliest Church.

The expectation of a final judgment not only motivated the apostolic mission and witness of the earliest church but also is basic to all instruction, exhortation and comfort in the NT. The NT authors invariably address threats to the life and faith of Christians that bear the potential of bringing condemnation on them. Often such threats prompt the composition and sending of the letters, as is the case with Hebrews, 2 Peter and Jude, 1 John and Revelation. It is crucial to remember that the proclamation of the gospel included a call to repentance coupled with the warning of coming judgment (e.g., Acts 2:38-40; 3:19; 10:42; 11:18; 17:30-31; 26:19-20; cf. Rom 2:4; Rev 9:20-21; 16:9) and that new converts were instructed on the final judgment (Heb 6:1-2; cf. Acts 24:24-25). Frequently the prospect of facing divine judgment is joined to specific admonitions (e.g., Heb 6:10-12; 13:4; Jas 1:12; 2:12-13; 5:9). Christian leaders and teachers are singled out as being especially accountable to God (Heb 13:17; Jas 3:1; cf. 1 Pet 5:1-4). Strikingly, three NT letters conclude with encouragement to restore the disobedient in view of their perilous state (Jas 5:19-20; 1 Jn 5:14-17; Jude 22-23; see also 1 Pet 4:8).

It is equally clear, however, that the expectation of a final judgment alone does not adequately describe the NT writings. They bear as their central message the conviction that God through Christ has provided forgiveness and salvation at the final judgment (e.g., Acts 20:32; Heb 7:23-28; Jas 1:18; 1 Jn 4:17-21). Between these two beliefs there exists an inescapable tension (see 4 below). Here it is important to note that the NT writers regarded the judgment to come not merely as a basis for warning but as an offer of hope, comfort and encouragement. The author of Hebrews, for example, reminds his readers that God is not unjust. He will not forget the labor and love of believers (Heb 6:10). James assures his audience that those who endure trial will receive the crown of life that God has promised to those who love him (Jas 1:12; cf. Rev 2:10). The hope of divine deliverance underlies the Apocalypse of John (e.g., Rev 6:9-11; 7:13-17; 11:16-19; 19:1-4).

Of fundamental significance for Christian

theology and ethics is the broadly attested stance of the NT writers that judgment and retribution belong to God alone and that believers consequently are not to take vengeance themselves or to condemn one another (Mt 7:1; Rom 12:19-21; 14:10-12; Jas 2:4, 12-13; 5:9; cf. 1 Cor 5:1-13: church discipline is not thereby excluded). To assume such authority is to trespass upon the divine role itself, an act of hubris that even the angels of God do not dare (Jas 4:11-12; 2 Pet 2:11; Jude 9). Following the pattern of Christ, Christians are to entrust their rights to "the one who judges righteously" (1 Pet 2:21-23, 4:19; Jas 5:7-11; Rev 6:9-11).

4. The Early Christian Concept of Judgment.

A prominent and distinctive aspect of NT and early Christian teaching is the prospect that Christ will judge all humanity at his parousia. The formulaic description of Christ as the "one who is to judge the living and the dead" provides an indication of the centrality of this belief to early Christian thought (Acts 10:42; 2 Tim 4:1; 1 Pet 4:5; *Barn.* 7.2; Pol. *Phil.* 2.1). Judgment hinges on one's response to Jesus (Acts 13:40-41; 13:46; 18:6). Disobedience to the word that God has spoken in his Son brings a more severe punishment than rejection of Moses (Heb 4:12-13; 6:7-8; 10:26-31; 12:25). The book of Revelation stresses that it is supremely right that Jesus, who suffered innocently and thereby secured salvation, should be the agent of divine judgment (e.g., Rev 1:4-7; 5:9-10). Jesus' resurrection and ascension signify God's vindication of his messianic claims and place him in a role that otherwise was reserved for God alone (Acts 10:42; 17:30-31; see the christologically significant 2 *Clem.* 1.1). To some extent, parallels may be found within some circles of early Judaism in which the Messiah was expected to act as judge, yet in these instances no historical figure is in view (*1 Enoch* 62:1-16; 4 Ezra 13:1-58).

No less prominent is the theme of individual judgment according to works (Heb 9:27-28; Rev 1:7; 2:7; 2:23). Each one will be called to give an account for his or her deeds (Heb 4:13; 13:17; 1 Pet 4:5-6). The NT authors are careful to apply the prospect of judgment to Christians. As the judge of all, God will render his verdict impartially. Believers, although they name God as Father, must not presume upon grace (1 Pet 1:17-19; Heb 10:30; cf. Jas 2:9). Frequently the authors bring reminders that punishment will be meted out to those who practice immorality, greed and similar vices (Heb 13:4).

NT exhortations are frequently based on final recompense for obedience and hardly make sense apart from this prospect. Moreover, the NT writers regularly depict final punishment as corresponding to deeds done in this life, underscoring the manifest justice of the final divine verdict (*lex talionis,* Jas 2:13; 5:1-3; Jude 6; cf. Rev 2:10; 3:10). Measure-for-measure retribution is not unique to the biblical writings and appears with particular prominence in early Jewish and Christian "tours of hell." Yet since the biblical materials lack detailed descriptions of torment, they give greater prominence to the divine verdict, implicitly emphasizing the justice of God. The tours of hell instead portray a correspondence between deeds and gruesome destinies, suggesting an inherent connection between deed and outcome (cf. Himmelfarb).

The NT describes reward as intrinsically related to God and Christ, the object of hope and trust. Those who love Christ and consequently serve him now will be rewarded by seeing him in his glory. Moreover, such reward always paradoxically issues in glory to Christ, who has worked the believer's salvation. Nevertheless, the NT writers do not regard retribution as mere divine confirmation of human decision. Punishment and reward are actively imposed by God from without on the human being (contra Travis; see, e.g., Heb 10:26-31; Jas 5:1; 2 Pet 2:6).

If the cross has worked a right standing with God for the believer, how is it that the believer must yet face judgment? Between this prospect and the proclamation of forgiveness in Christ stands an irreducible paradox. Yet to a certain extent lines of convergence can be traced. In the first place, as we have noted, the NT writers anticipate that Christ will judge humanity. Faith in him is a moral act, the fundamental obedience that God requires of human beings (e.g., Heb 3:12-19; 1 Pet 1:3-9; 1 Jn 2:22-25). Furthermore, the NT writings display a deep confidence in the power of God to effect salvation for those who have received the forgiveness offered in Christ (e.g., Acts 20:32; Jas 1:9; 2 Pet 2:9; Jude 24). That is not to say that all uncertainty is removed from the visible community of Christians; otherwise the warnings of judgment would hardly make sense. The church on earth yet remains under testing. Nevertheless, where saving realities are present they manifest themselves in persevering faith and obedience, which secure the believer in the final judgment (e.g., Heb 10:39; 1 Jn 2:29—3:3; Rev 1:9).

Paul's understanding of the gospel therefore does not stand at odds with the rest of the NT. While there are distinctions that cannot be ignored, there is no final contradiction between Paul and James. James speaks of a final justification by faith with works (not by faith and works; Jas 2:22-24) and therefore thinks of works that proceed from faith. When Paul affirms that a person is justified by faith and not by "works of the law," he rejects the saving value of deeds of obedience apart from faith, which are always incomplete and proceed from the self-seeking heart of the fallen human being. Any claim to righteousness is thereby ruled out, and the whole of justification is located in the atoning work of the cross, which is grasped by faith alone. Paul thereby in no way diminishes James's demand for deeds of obedience. He too expects a judgment according to deeds (2 Cor 5:10). James speaks of the justification at the final judgment (Jas 2:14-26), while Paul speaks of a final justification worked already by the cross (e.g., Rom 3:21-26). The two loci stand in tension but not in contradiction. There is evidence in James's letter that he would embrace Paul's interpretation of the cross. He views the gospel as the source of life, on the basis of unconditioned divine mercy (Jas 1:18; 2:12-13). Paul and James share the expectation that acceptance of the gospel will issue in new obedience (Jas 1:21, "the word [i.e., gospel] implanted, which has the power to save"; Rom 6:19).

An immediate postmortem judgment, which is implicit in the parable of the rich man and Lazarus (Lk 16:19-31; but cf. Acts 10:42), is likewise suggested in a few NT passages such as the vision of the righteous martyrs (Rev 6:9-11; cf. Jas 3:6) and occasionally in Jewish and Christian sources (e.g., 4 Ezra 7:78-80; cf. 4 Ezra 7:104-5; *1 Clem.* 20.5; *2 Clem.* 19.4). This expectation does not eliminate the judgment of the last day, upon which the focus is set.

Understandably, judgment imagery similar to some of that employed in the NT may be found in the Greco-Roman world, including Egypt. Sometimes borrowing is evident (e.g., the imprisonment of angels in Tartarus, 2 Pet 2:4), but similarities do not necessarily constitute parallels or influence (contra Griffiths). The NT writers generally appeal more directly to biblical tradition, as do early Jewish writings. Probably the image of the opening of books in which deeds have been recorded derives from Daniel (Dan 7:10; e.g., Rev 20:12; *Jub.* 30:22; *1 Enoch* 98:8; *2 Bar* 24:1; *m. 'Abot* 2:1). The juxtaposed "book [of life]," which paradoxically contains the names of the elect, appears here as well (Dan 12:1; cf. Ps 69:28; Phil 4:3; Rev 3:5; 20:12; 20:15; cf. *Jub.* 30:23). Divine judgments in the past serve as patterns for what is yet to come, especially the deliverance of the righteous and the destruction of the wicked. The salvation of Noah through the flood prefigured *baptism, by which believers lay claim to forgiveness (cf. *1 Enoch* 54). Here baptism entails a self-judgment in anticipation of the eschaton (1 Pet 3:20-22; cf. 2 Pet 2:5; Heb 11:7). The destruction of Sodom and Gomorrah by fire serves as an example of what is coming on the ungodly (2 Pet 2:6; Jude 7; cf. Lk 17:29; Rev 14:9-11), just as the divine rescue of Lot prefigures the rescue of the righteous (2 Pet 2:7; cf. Lk 17:28-32).

In some passages of the NT the punishment of unbelievers is described as enduring eternally. There has been some recent debate over this matter, naturally involving the interpretation of various occurrences of the Greek word *aiōn*, which may signify "eon" or "forever," and the corresponding adjective *aiōnios*. Nevertheless, it is sufficiently clear that the adjective is regularly used in the sense of everlasting (see Sasse; Heb 5:9; 6:2; 9:12; 9:14; 9:15; 13:20; 2 Pet 1:11). Various references in which the noun is employed envision an everlasting punishment (Rev 14:9-12; 19:1-3; 20:10-15). Moreover, the anticipation of everlasting punishment is attested outside the NT (e.g., *1 Enoch* 91:12-16; *Pss. Sol.* 3:11-12). Explicit teaching of eternal punishment appears only occasionally in the NT, probably because it was an uncontested part of elementary Christian instruction (Heb 6:1-2). There is no indication that the NT writers derived the belief that punishment would be eternal from the presupposition that the soul is naturally immortal. They rather regard it as an expression of the justice of God (e.g., Rev 19:1-4).

See also APOCALYPTICISM; ESCHATOLOGY; JUSTIFICATION.

DLNTD: DAY OF THE LORD; HELL, ABYSS, ETERNAL PUNISHMENT; REWARDS; UNIVERSALISM; WRATH, DESTRUCTION.

BIBLIOGRAPHY. R. J. Bauckham, "Early Jewish Visions of Hell," *JTS* 41 (1990) 355-85; A. E.

Bernstein, *The Formation of Hell: Death and Retribution in the Ancient and Early Christian Worlds* (Ithaca, NY: Cornell University Press, 1993); S. G. F. Brandon, *The Judgment of the Dead: A Historical and Comparative Study of the Idea of Postmortem Judgment in the Major Religions* (London: Weidenfeld & Nicolson, 1967); D. Cohn-Sherbok, "Rabbinic Judaism and the Doctrine of Hell," in *Rabbinic Perspectives on the New Testament* (SBEC 28; Lewiston, NY: Edwin Mellen, 1990) 1-18; J. G. Griffiths, *The Divine Verdict: A Study of Divine Judgment in the Ancient Religions* (SHR 52; Leiden: E. J. Brill, 1991); M. Himmelfarb, *Tours of Hell: An Apocalyptic Form in Jewish and Christian Literature* (Philadelphia: University of Pennsylvania, 1983); A. L. Moore, *The Parousia in the New Testament* (NovTSup 13; Leiden: E. J. Brill, 1966); L. Morris, *The Biblical Doctrine of Judgment* (Grand Rapids: Eerdmans, 1960); C. F. D. Moule, "The Judgment Theme in the Sacraments," in *The Background of the New Testament and Its Eschatology*, ed. W. D. Davies and D. Daube (Cambridge: Cambridge University Press, 1956) 464-81; idem, "Punishment and Retribution," in *Essays in New Testament Interpretation* (Cambridge: Cambridge University Press, 1982) 235-49; H. Sasse, "αἰών, αἰώνιος," *TDNT* 1:197-209; P. Toon, *Heaven and Hell: A Biblical and Theological Overview* (Nashville: Thomas Nelson, 1986); S. H. Travis, *Christ and the Judgment of God: Divine Retribution in the New Testament* (Grand Rapids: Zondervan, 1987); G. Vermes, F. Millar and M. Black, "The Last Judgment," in *The History of the Jewish People in the Age of Jesus Christ* (175 B.C.—A.D. 135) (2 vols.; Edinburgh: T & T Clark, 1979) 2:544-47.   M. A. Seifrid

JUDGMENT SEAT OF GOD. *See* ESCHATOLOGY II.

JUSTICE. *See* RIGHTEOUSNESS.

JUSTIFICATION: PAUL

Since the time of the Reformation in the sixteenth century, considerable attention has been paid to the theme of justification in Paul. For Martin Luther the doctrine of justification was not merely the center and focus of Paul's thought; it was the "article by which the church stands or falls," the touchstone and heartbeat of all Christian theology and spirituality. That judgment has, however, been subject to intense scrutiny over the last two centuries. Recent discussion of Paul's understanding of justification has tended to focus on a number of major themes, each of which merits careful attention.

The purpose of this article is to explore and explain the present state of scholarly research on these questions. It will be clear, however, that these issues are not merely of scholarly interest; they are of vital importance to Christian evangelism and spirituality.

We begin by considering what Paul means by the term *justification* and how this differs from related terms such as *sanctification* and *salvation*.

1. The Meaning of the Term *Justification*
2. The Relation of Paul's Thought to That of Contemporary Judaism
3. Paul's Understanding of the Righteousness of God
4. The Relation Between Faith and Works in Paul's Thought
5. The Importance of Justification to Paul's Thought

1. The Meaning of the Term *Justification*.

The Pauline vocabulary relating to justification is grounded in the OT and seems to express the notion of rightness or rectitude rather than righteousness. The OT prefers the verb rather than the noun, presumably thereby indicating that justification results from an action of God whereby an individual is set in a right relationship with God—that is, vindicated or declared to be in the right. Paul echoes this emphasis, using the verb *dikaioō*, "justify," relatively often, but generally avoiding using the noun *dikaiōsis*, "justification" (Rom 4:25). The verb denotes God's powerful, cosmic and universal action in effecting a change in the situation between sinful humanity and God, by which God is able to acquit and vindicate believers, setting them in a right and faithful relation to himself.

How does justification relate to other Pauline soteriological terms? It is tempting to adopt a simplistic approach to the matter. For example, one could attempt to force justification, sanctification and salvation into a neat past-present-future framework (Donfried), as follows:

Justification: a past event, with present implications (sanctification).

Sanctification: a present event, dependent upon a past event (justification), which has future implications (salvation).

Salvation: a future event, already anticipated

and partially experienced in the past event of justification and the present event of sanctification, and dependent upon them.

But this is inadequate. Justification has future as well as past reference (Rom 2:13; 8:33; Gal 5:4-5) and appears to relate to the beginning of the Christian life and its final consummation. Similarly, sanctification can also refer to a past event (1 Cor 6:11) or a future event (1 Thess 5:23). And salvation is an exceptionally complex idea, embracing not simply a future event but also something that has happened in the past (Rom 8:24; 1 Cor 15:2) or is taking place now (1 Cor 1:18).

It is important to note that not all Paul's statements regarding justification are specifically linked with the theme of faith. The statements appear to fall into two general categories (Hultgren): those set in strongly theocentric contexts, referring to God's cosmic and universal action in relation to human sin; and those making reference to faith, which is the mark to identify the people of God. This is perhaps best regarded as a difference of emphasis rather than of substance. In its universal sense justification seems to underlie Paul's argument for the universality of the gospel; there is no distinction between Jews and Gentiles. But in its more restricted sense justification is concerned with the identity of the people of God and the basis of its membership.

Justification language appears in Paul with reference to the inauguration of the life of faith and its final consummation. It is a complex and all-embracing notion that anticipates the verdict of the final judgment (Rom 8:30-34) by declaring in advance the verdict of ultimate acquittal. The believer's present justified Christian existence is thus an anticipation and advance participation of deliverance from the wrath to come and an assurance in the present of the final eschatological (see Eschatology) verdict of acquittal (Rom 5:9-10).

2. The Relation of Paul's Thought to That of Contemporary Judaism.

In recent years a considerable debate on the relation of Paul's views on justification to those of first-century Judaism has developed, centering on the writings of E. P. Sanders. His first major writing to address this theme was *Paul and Palestinian Judaism* (1977), followed several years later by the more important *Paul, the Law and the*

Jewish People (1983). Sanders's work represents a demand for a complete reappraisal of our understanding of Paul's relation to Judaism (see Jew, Paul the). Sanders noted that Paul has too often been read through Lutheran eyes (a perspective in marked contrast to the Reformed standpoint, associated with Bullinger and Calvin, it stresses the divergence between the Law and the gospel). Luther argued that Paul criticized a totally misguided attempt on the part of Jewish legalists to find favor and acceptance in the sight of God by earning righteousness through performing works of the Law. This view, Sanders argued, colored the analysis of such Lutheran writings as those of E. Käsemann and R. Bultmann. These scholars, perhaps unwittingly, read Paul through Lutheran spectacles and thus failed to realize that Paul had to be read against his proper historical context in first-century Judaism.

According to Sanders, Palestinian Judaism at the time of Paul could be characterized as a form of "covenantal nomism." The Law is to be regarded as an expression of the covenant between God and Israel and is intended to spell out as clearly and precisely as possible what forms of human conduct are appropriate within the context of this covenant. Righteousness is thus defined as behavior or attitudes that are consistent with being the historical covenant people of God. "Works of the Law" are thus not understood, as Luther suggested, as the means by which Jews believed they could gain access to the covenant, for they already stood within it. Rather, these works are an expression of the fact that the Jews already belonged to the covenant people of God and were living out their obligations to that covenant.

Sanders puts it like this. He rejects the opinion that "the righteousness which comes from the law" is "a meritorious achievement which allows one to demand reward from God and is thus a denial of grace." "Works of the Law" were not understood as the basis of entry to the covenant but of maintaining that covenant. As Sanders puts it, "works are the condition of remaining 'in,' but they do not earn salvation." If Sanders is right, the basic features of Luther's interpretation of Paul are incorrect and require radical revision.

So what, then, is Paul's understanding of the difference between Judaism and Christianity according to Sanders? Having argued that Jews never believed in salvation on account of works or unaided human effort, what does Sanders see as providing the distinctive advantage of Christianity over and against Judaism? Having argued that it is not correct to see Judaism as a religion of merit and Christianity as a religion of grace, Sanders argues as follows. Judaism sees its hope of salvation as resting on "their status as God's covenant people who possess the law," whereas Christians believe in "a better righteousness based solely upon believing participation in Christ." Paul, like Judaism, was concerned with the issue of entering into and remaining within the covenant. The basic difference is Paul's declaration that the Jews have no national charter of privilege; membership of the covenant is open to all who have faith in Christ and who thus stand in continuity with Abraham (Rom 4).

Sanders's analysis is important, not least in that it forces us to ask hard questions about Paul's relation to his Jewish background and the relation between the idea of participating in Christ and justification. (Interestingly, Luther and Calvin made the notion of participating in Christ of central importance to their doctrines of justification, Calvin to the point of making justification the consequence of such participation). But is Sanders right? The debate over this matter continues and is likely to go on for some time. But the following points seem to be sufficiently well established to note.

First, Sanders is rather vague about why Paul is convinced of the superiority of Christianity over Judaism. Judaism is presented as being wrong, simply because it is not Christianity. They are different dispensations of the same covenant. But Paul seems to regard Christianity as far more than some kind of dispensational shift within Judaism. R. H. Gundry is one of a number of scholars to stress that salvation history does not account for all that Paul says, much less for the passion with which he says it.

Second, Sanders suggests that Paul and Judaism regard works as the principle of continuing in salvation through the covenant. Yet Paul appears to regard good works as evidential rather than instrumental. In other words, they are a demonstration of the fact that the believers stand within the covenant rather than instrumental in maintaining them within that covenant. One enters within the sphere of the covenant through faith. There is a radical new element here, one that does not fit in as easily

with existing Jewish ideas as Sanders seems to imply. Sanders may well be right in suggesting that good works are a condition for and a sign of remaining within the covenant. Paul, however, sees faith as the necessary and sufficient condition for and sign of being in the covenant, with works at best a sign of remaining within its bounds.

Third, Sanders tends to regard Paul's doctrine of justification in a slightly negative light, as posing a challenge to the notion of a national, ethnic election. In other words, Paul's doctrine of justification is a subtle challenge to the notion that Israel has special religious rights on account of its national identity. N. T. Wright, however, has argued that Paul's doctrine of justification should be viewed positively, as an attempt to redefine who comes within the ambit of the promises made by God to Abraham (Wright 1980 and 1992). Such ideas, which may subsequently be found developed in such essays as J. D. G. Dunn (1983), treat justification as Paul's redefinition of how the inheritance of Abraham genuinely embraces the Gentiles apart from the Law.

3. Paul's Understanding of the Righteousness of God.

There is a close semantic connection between the terms *justification (dikaiōsis)* and *righteousness (dikaiosynē)* in Paul's thought, making it essential to give at least a brief account of Paul's understanding of righteousness in the present discussion. The idea of the revelation of the righteousness of God is obviously of major importance to Paul's conception of the gospel (e.g., Rom 1:16-17). Before exploring this in any detail, a serious difficulty must be noted, arising directly out of the English language. English possesses two words that are regularly used to translate the Greek *dikaiosynē* and the Latin *iustitia*: "justice" and "righteousness." These words have very different associations in English. "Righteousness" tends to mean something like "personal moral uprightness" whereas "justice" tends to bear the meaning of "social and political fairness." The former has individualistic, the latter social and communal, associations. If *dikaiosynē tou theou* is translated as "the righteousness of God," the English translation can mislead us regarding Paul's intentions by imposing individualist ideas of righteousness upon God. There is no easy way of avoiding this difficulty other than noting that one could equally well translate the phrase as "the justice of God."

But what does the phrase mean? There is a distinguished history of interpretation of this term, going back to the first centuries of the Christian tradition. Augustine of Hippo argued that "the righteousness of God" did not refer to the personal righteousness of God (in other words, the righteousness by which God is righteous) but to the righteousness which he bestows upon sinners, in order to justify them (in other words, the righteousness that comes from God). This interpretation of the phrase seems to have dominated the Western theological tradition until the fourteenth century, when writers such as G. Biel began to reinterpret it in terms of "the righteousness by which God is righteous."

The interpretation of the phrase came to be of major importance at the time of the Reformation in the sixteenth century. Luther's theological breakthrough, probably dating from 1515, centers on the question of what it meant to speak of God as righteous. Luther initially believed that it meant that God was righteous and employed that righteousness to reward those who were obedient and punish those who were sinners. As Luther knew himself to be a sinner, he could not see how the revelation of the righteousness of God could conceivably be gospel—good news—for sinners. Gradually, he came to discover that it referred to the righteousness which God imputes to sinners, covering their sins and enabling them to be counted as righteous in the sight of God *(coram Deo)*.

This understanding of the nature of the righteousness of God has continued to find a place in the modern debate, especially on the part of Lutheran interpreters of Paul. Two such interpreters may be considered in detail—Bultmann and Käsemann.

Bultmann, basing his view especially on Romans 10:3 and Philippians 3:9, argued that the "righteousness of God" was not a moral but a relational term. Believers are counted as being righteous by means of their faith. The term "righteousness of God" represents a genitive of authorship. Whereas Judaism regarded the bestowal of this righteousness as part and parcel of the future eschatological hope, something that would happen at the end of history, Bultmann argued that Paul was declaring that this right-

eousness is imputed to believers in the present time, through faith.

Käsemann subjected Bultmann's interpretation to a penetrating criticism on a number of grounds. First, he argued that Bultmann had fallen into the trap of a radical individualism, based on his anthropocentric approach to theology. Bultmann was mainly concerned with questions of human existence; he ought, according to Käsemann, to have concentrated on the purpose of God. Furthermore, by interpreting "the righteousness of God" as a genitive of authorship, Bultmann had managed to drive a wedge between the God who gives and the gift that is given. Bultmann's approach isolated the gift from the giver and concentrated on the gift rather than on God. Käsemann comments thus: "The Gift can never be separated from the Giver; it participates in the power of God, since God steps on to the scene in the gift" (Käsemann 1969, 174).

This lack of balance could be recovered by understanding "righteousness" as referring to God rather than to that which he gives. Käsemann then argues that the "righteousness of God" refers to God in action. It refers to his power and to his gift. (Strictly speaking, then, Käsemann is not treating the "righteousness of God" as a statement about God's attributes but as a reference to God in action.) A cluster of phrases may help convey the sort of things that Käsemann has in mind here: "salvation-creating power"; "a transformation of [our] existence"; "the power-character of the Gift"; "a change of Lordship" (Käsemann 1969, 168-82). The basic theme that recurs throughout Käsemann's discussion is that of God's saving power and action, revealed eschatologically in Jesus Christ. It merges a number of central Pauline themes, including those of victory through Christ, God's faithfulness to his covenant and his giving of himself in power and action.

Käsemann's approach has been very influential in recent years, positively and negatively. Basing himself on Käsemann, P. Stuhlmacher argues that it is unacceptable to treat the "righteousness of God" as if it were a purely theocentric notion or an exclusively anthropocentric idea. It brings together elements of both, as the embodiment of the saving action of God in Christ that brings new life for believers in its wake. The righteousness of God is demonstrated and seen in action in the redemptive event of

Christ—in terms of God's faithfulness to his covenant and in terms of the salvific transformation of the believer.

A much more critical approach is adopted by K. Stendahl, who argued that Käsemann had neglected the importance of salvation history (often referred to in its German form, *Heilsgeschichte*) in his analysis. Stendahl suggests that Käsemann has virtually lost sight of the fact that Paul locates the event of justification in a specific historical context—namely, the history of God's dealings with his people, Israel. There is every danger that Käsemann's approach could lead to some kind of unhistorical mysticism by failing to see that Paul discusses justification within the context of "reflection on God's plan for the world." Drawing on a series of passages (most significantly, Rom 9—11), Stendahl argues that Paul seems far more interested in the way in which God enables salvation to come about through history (above all, through the history of Israel) rather than with the abstract idea of justification by faith.

Once more, an important debate is still under way and has yet to be resolved. J. Reumann helpfully suggests that four main lines of interpretation of the "righteousness of God" may be discerned, along with their respective champions, as follows:

1. An objective genitive: "a righteousness which is valid before God" (Luther).

2. A subjective genitive: "righteousness as an attribute or quality of God" (Käsemann).

3. A genitive of authorship: "a righteousness that goes forth from God" (Bultmann).

4. A genitive of origin: "man's righteous status which is the result of God's action of justifying" (Cranfield).

However, there is a general consensus on one point of major importance, which needs to be emphasized. The "righteousness of God" is not for Paul primarily a moral concept. Rather, it represents a profound statement about the relevance of God for the human situation. Especially in popular circles, there is often a disturbing tendency to use Pauline texts to construct a picture of God as some kind of moral rigorist and thus impose human conceptions of righteousness upon God. If Pauline exegesis has achieved anything, it is to remind us of the need to interpret Pauline phrases within their proper context, rather than impose supposedly self-evident interpretations on them.

4. The Relation Between Faith and Works in Paul's Thought.

It is sometimes remarked that justification by faith implies a devaluing of human works. Or does it? A long and distinguished tradition of interpretation, drawing its inspiration largely from Luther, has seen an absolute contradiction between faith and works. They are held to be mutually exclusive entities designating two radically opposed ways of thinking about and responding to God. The way of works is seen as oriented toward human achievement, centered upon human righteousness and based upon human merit. The way of faith is seen as radically opposite, oriented toward God's achievement in Christ, centered on the righteousness of God and based upon divine grace.

Yet this is an inadequate understanding of a complex aspect of Paul's understanding of justification. It is unquestionably a simple interpretation of Paul and possesses all the seductive attractiveness of simplicity. But it is not adequate. It fails to do justice to the nuanced understanding of the relation of faith and works within Paul's thought, most notably expressed in the terse statement that "not the hearers, but the doers of the Law will be justified" (Rom 2:13). Some interpreters (e.g., Bultmann) have sought to dismiss this as a vestige of Paul's Jewish phase. But this cannot be maintained in the face of the evidence.

Perhaps the most important issue to emerge from recent Pauline interpretation concerning the relation between faith and works centers on clarifying the relation between Paul's theme of "justification by faith" and "judgment by works." There seems to be an apparent contradiction here, the resolution of which is made considerably more difficult by the fact that Paul can speak of this future judgment negatively (as a warning against disobedience) and positively (as an encouragement for obedience). Sanders argues that Paul reproduces a characteristic first-century Jewish attitude, which could be summarized in the words "God judges according to their deeds those whom he saves by his grace." Justification by faith resonates with the accents of grace—so why are believers going to be judged on the basis of their works (e.g., Rom 2:12; 14:10; 1 Cor 3:15; 2 Cor 5:10), which resonates with the accents of human achievement? But this statement of the problem and its solution fails to deal with the fact that justification is not seen as an event in the past but as something with future reference (Rom 2:13; 8:33; Gal 5:4-5). It is not simply a case of being justified in the past and judged in the future; there is a "not yet" element to Paul's teaching on justification that Sanders cannot quite explain.

One possible explanation of the way in which justification and future judgment are related involves an enhanced sensitivity toward the different contexts that the Pauline letters presuppose (Watson). Paul's message of justification is directed toward various audiences with very different backgrounds. The one doctrine finds itself applied practically for very different ends. The Corinthians appeared to be living in a state of bad theology and spiritual arrogance; Paul's objective is to break down their arrogance by warning them of judgment. Paul does not intend the message of judgment to be his last word but rather the word they need to hear so long as they remain unaware of the full implications of the gospel. On the other hand, those who exist in a state of spiritual dejection or discouragement need reassurance of the unconditionality of grace. If this understanding of Paul is correct, it implies that the theme of judgment by works is not Paul's final word to his audience; it is his penultimate word, determined by the pastoral situation of his audience and intended to shake up those who exploit and thus distort the gospel proclamation of grace.

This attractive approach to the problem leaves one glad to have been reminded that Paul's letters have indeed been written to different audiences but profoundly uneasy concerning the idea of a "penultimate word of God." How does one know what is God's final word and which is merely his penultimate word? The idea of the finality of justification seems to be compromised.

Perhaps the simplest approach to the problem has the most to commend it. In one of his earliest writings, Paul uses the enormously important phrase "work of faith" (1 Thess 1:3). This would most naturally be understood as implying a genitive of origin—that is, "work which comes from faith." Faith is such that it does not merely produce obedience (Rom 1:5 speaks of the "obedience of faith"—that is, assuming a genitive of origin, the obedience that comes from faith) but also activity. Believers are thus justified on the basis of faith, seen not as a human work or merit but as an expression and re-

sult of the grace of God. And believers are judged on the basis of their works, seen as the natural outcome, result and expression of justifying faith. Believers are justified by faith and judged by its fruit. There is thus a strong connection between the past and future elements of justification—embracing faith and its outworking. Works are the visible demonstration of a real and justifying faith—not the dead faith of which James complained (Jas 2:14-24). And so these two moments of justification coinhere.

5. The Importance of Justification to Paul's Thought.

In conclusion, we may pose the question that continues to remain intensely controversial within Pauline scholarship: how important is justification to Paul's understanding of the gospel? Luther, as is well known, regarded it as central. While some modern writers have endorsed Luther's judgment, others have been more critical. The center of gravity of Paul's thought lies elsewhere, they argue. But where? It is one thing to suggest that justification is not the center of Paul's presentation of Christianity. But if it is not, what is? It is quite difficult to identify a center to Paul's thought, not least because there is disagreement among scholars as to what the idea of a center means: a principle of coherence? a summarizing principle? a criterion of authenticity? These difficulties stand in the path of any attempt to reach agreement on the importance of justification to Paul's thought.

Nevertheless, three broad positions may be discerned within recent scholarship on this question.

(1) Justification by faith is of central importance to Paul's conception of Christianity. Among those who adopt this position are G. Bornkamm, H. Conzelmann, Käsemann and K. Kertelge. As noted above, this position has strong historical associations with Martin Luther, and it is perhaps not surprising that it is echoed by many modern German Lutheran NT scholars. This school of thought tends to regard justification as the real theological center of gravity within Paul's thought and is critical of any attempt to treat it as being of lesser importance. Justification by faith is not simply concerned with clarifying the Christian gospel in relation to first-century Judaism; it addresses the fundamental question of how sinful human beings can find favor or acceptance in the sight of

a righteous God. Within this approach differences can nevertheless be discerned. Bultmann adopts a generally Lutheran position, stressing the positive importance of faith while interpreting Paul's justification language in terms of existentialist categories. C. E. B. Cranfield adopts a more Reformed stance, noting the continuing importance of the Law.

(2) Justification by faith is a "subsidiary crater" (Schweitzer) in Paul's overall presentation and understanding of the Christian gospel. The origins of this view may be traced back to the nineteenth century, especially to the writings of W. Wrede. Wrede argued that justification by faith was simply a polemical doctrine designed to neutralize the theological threat posed by Judaism. Having neutralized this threat, Paul was then able to develop the positive aspects of his own thought (which, for Wrede, centered on the idea of redemption in Christ). The real emphasis of Paul's thought thus lies elsewhere than justification. Among those who adopt this position, the following may be noted (along with their views on where the center of Paul's thought really lies): A. Schweitzer (the rising and dying of the believer with Christ), R. P. Martin (reconciliation with God) and Sanders (believing participation in Christ).

(3) A third view may be regarded as a compromise between these two views. Justification by faith is regarded as one of a number of ways of thinking about, or visualizing, what God has achieved for believers in and through Christ. The position adopted by J. Jeremias well illustrates this mediating function. The center of Paul's thought does not lie with justification as such; rather, it lies with the grace of God. But justification is one of a number of ways of describing this grace (in juridical terms of unconditional pardon and forgiveness). It is thus central in one sense (in that it is a way of expressing the core of the gospel) and not central in another (in that it is only one way, among others, of expressing this core).

This debate seems set to continue, and it is not clear whether there is any hope of a genuine consensus. It is perhaps worth noting that it is genuinely difficult to classify some approaches to Paul's theology in terms of this neat framework. Nevertheless, the first and second positions continue to attract supporters.

This, then, represents the state of present scholarship on the main aspects of Paul's theology of justification by faith. It is clear that it is one of the most interesting aspects of Pauline scholarship, attracting writers of considerable skill and commitment. It is likely that the years ahead will witness still further wrestling with this aspect of Pauline thought, to the considerable enhancement of academy and church; the former, as scholars seek to understand Paul, and the latter, as Christians seek to apply him to the tasks and opportunities of the Christian life.

See also JUDGMENT; LAW; RIGHTEOUSNESS.

DPL: CENTER OF PAUL; HOLINESS, SANCTIFICATION; PAUL AND HIS INTERPRETERS; WORKS OF THE LAW.

BIBLIOGRAPHY. G. Bornkamm, *Paul* (New York: Harper & Row, 1971); C. H. Cosgrove, "Justification in Paul: A Linguistic and Theological Reflection," *JBL* 106 (1987) 653-70; C. E. B. Cranfield, *A Critical and Exegetical Commentary on the Epistle to the Romans* (2 vols; ICC; Edinburgh: T & T Clark, 1975, 1979); K. P. Donfried, "Justification and Last Judgment in Paul," *ZNW* 67 (1976) 90-110; J. D. G. Dunn, "The New Perspective on Paul," *BJRL* 65 (1983) 95-122; R. H. Gundry, "Grace, Works and Staying Saved in Paul," *Bib* 60 (1985) 1-38; C. J. A. Hickling, "Centre and Periphery in the Thought of St. Paul," in *Studia Biblica 3: Papers on Paul and Other New Testament Authors*, ed. E. A. Livingstone (JSNTSup 3; Sheffield, Academic Press, 1978) 199-214; A. J. Hultgren, *Paul's Gospel and Mission* (Philadelphia: Fortress, 1985); E. Käsemann, *Commentary on Romans* (Grand Rapids: Eerdmans, 1980); idem, " 'The Righteousness of God' in Paul," in *New Testament Questions of Today* (Philadelphia: Fortress, 1969); K. Kertelge, *Rechtfertigung bei Paulus* (Münster: Aschendorff, 1967); A. E. McGrath, *Iustitia Dei: A History of the Christian Doctrine of Justification* (2 vols; Cambridge: Cambridge University Press, 1986); R. P. Martin, *Reconciliation: A Study of Paul's Theology* (Atlanta: John Knox, 1981); J. Reumann, *Righteousness in the New Testament* (Philadelphia: Fortress, 1982); E. P. Sanders, *Paul and Palestinian Judaism* (Philadelphia: Fortress, 1977); idem, *Paul, the Law, and the Jewish People* (Philadelphia: Fortress, 1983); M. A. Seifrid, *Christ, Our Righteousness: Paul's Theology of Justification* (NSBT; Downers Grove, IL: InterVarsity Press, 2000); idem, *Justification by Faith: The Origin and Development of a Central Pauline Theme* (NovTSup 68; Leiden: E. J. Brill, 1992); K. Stendahl, *Paul Among Jews and Gentiles* (Philadelphia: Fortress, 1976); P. Stuhlmacher, *Gerechtigkeit Gottes bei Paulus* (FRLANT 87; Göttingen: Vandenhoeck & Ruprecht, 1966); idem, "The Apostle Paul's View of Righteousness," in *Reconciliation, Law and Righteousness: Essays in Biblical Theology* (Philadelphia: Fortress, 1986) 68-93; idem, *Revisiting Paul's Doctrine of Justification: A Challenge to the New Perspective* (Downers Grove, IL: InterVarsity Press, 2001); N. M. Watson, "Justified by Faith, Judged by Works: An Antimony?" *NTS* 29 (1983) 209-21; D. V. Way, *The Lordship of Christ: Ernst Käsemann's Interpretation of Paul's Theology* (Oxford: Clarendon, 1991); S. K. Williams, "The 'Righteousness of God' in Romans," *JBL* 99 (1980) 241-90; N. T. Wright, *The Climax of the Covenant: Christ and the Law in Pauline Theology* (Minneapolis: Fortress, 1991); idem, *The Messiah and the People of God* (unpublished D.Phil. thesis, Oxford University, 1980); idem, "The Paul of History and the Apostle of Faith," *TynB* 29 (1978) 61-88; idem, *What Saint Paul Really Said* (Grand Rapids: Eerdmans, 1997); J. A. Ziesler, *The Meaning of Righteousness in Paul* (Cambridge: Cambridge University Press, 1972). A. E. McGrath

K

KING, GOD AS. *See* GOD.

KINGDOM OF CHRIST. *See* KINGDOM OF GOD
II.

KINGDOM OF GOD I: GOSPELS

The term "kingdom of God" or "kingdom of
heaven" signifies God's sovereign, dynamic and
eschatological (*see* Eschatology) rule. The kingdom of God lay at the heart of Jesus' teaching.
As proclaimed by Jesus, the kingdom of God
had continuity with the OT promise as well as
with Jewish apocalyptic thinking but differed
from them in important respects. For example, it
denoted God's eternal rule rather than an
earthly kingdom, its scope was universal rather
than limited to the Jewish nation, and it was imminent and potentially present in him rather
than a vague future hope, being inextricably
connected with his own person and mission.

    1. Terminology
    2. Old Testament Antecedents
    3. Judaism
    4. Jesus and the Kingdom of God
    5. The Gospels
    6. The Kingdom of God and the Church To-
      day

1. Terminology.

The Gospels use three terms to express the idea
of the kingdom of God: *hē basileia tou theou*
("the kingdom of God"), *hē basileia tōn ouranōn*
("the kingdom of [the] heaven[s]") and the absolute *hē basileia* ("the kingdom"). The equivalence of the first two expressions is indicated by
their content, context and interchangeability in
the Gospels. (The distinction between the kingdom of God as God's sovereignty, and the kingdom of heaven conceived as an otherworldly,
future reality, the former of which is the condi-

tion for entering the latter [Pamment], is without
exegetical basis). The Greek for "the kingdom of
(the) heaven(s)" is a literal translation of the
later Jewish *malēkût šāmayim* (e.g., *2 Apoc. Bar.*
73; *3 Apoc. Bar.* 11:2; *As. Mos.* 10; *Pss. Sol.* 17:4;
1QSb 3.5; *m. Ber.* 2.2, 5; *y. Ber.* 4a; 7b), where
"heaven" replaces "God" out of reverence, as
ʾădōnay ("lord," "master") had replaced *Yahweh*
("Lord") and *mākôm* ("place") in due time replaced *šāmayim* ("heaven") (Dalman, 91-101).
The kingdom of God is also referred to by the
absolute "kingdom" when the reference is obvious.

    The primary meaning of the Hebrew *malēkût*
(with synonyms), Aramaic *malkû* and Greek
basileia is abstract and dynamic, that is, sovereignty or royal rule. This is almost always the
case in the OT and Jewish literature when the
term is applied to God. The sense of realm—a
territorial kingdom—is secondary, arising out of
the necessity for a definite locus as the sphere
for the exercise of sovereignty.

2. Old Testament Antecedents.

The Gospels introduce the ministries of *John
the Baptist and of Jesus by stating that they proclaimed the nearness of the kingdom of God.
No word of explanation is ever offered, and the
conclusion must be that the idea of God's kingdom was well known.

    In contrast to this is the total absence in the
OT canonical books of the expression "kingdom of God." The expression occurs once in
Wisdom 10:10. Yet though the term is absent, the
idea is present throughout the OT. In a number
of instances Yahweh is presented as king (Deut
9:26 [LXX]; 1 Sam 12:12; Ps 24:10 [LXX 23:10];
29:10 [LXX 28:10]; Is 6:5; 33:22; Zeph 3:15; Zech
14:16, 17). At other places he is ascribed a royal
throne (Ps 9:4 [LXX 9:5]; 45:6 [LXX 44:7]; 47:8

[LXX 46:9]; Is 6:1; 66:1; Ezek 1:26; Sir 1:8) while occasionally his continuous or future reign is affirmed (Ps 10:16 [LXX 9:37]; 146:10 [LXX 145:10]; Is 24:23; Wis 3:8). In fact Psalm 22:28 (MT 22:29; LXX 21:29) says "the kingdom" (*hammĕlûkâ;* LXX *basileia*) belongs to the Lord.

The idea is not, however, confined to these texts with explicitly royal attributes; it underlies Yahweh's whole relation to Israel. The demand presented to Pharaoh to let Israel go is the demand of the lawful king over against the usurper. The covenant with Israel is the covenant that affirms the suzerainty of Yahweh over his people. In the conquest of Canaan Yahweh as king apportions to his people a country which he, as the creator and king of the earth, can dispose as he pleases. The rule of God over Israel is especially exemplified in the time of the judges, who functioned as his representatives. A crisis emerged with Israel's demand for a king (1 Sam 8:4-5), a demand that was interpreted as a rejection of Yahweh's rule (1 Sam 8:6-8). With the accession of David to the throne, however, the situation was somewhat normalized and the king was understood to reign as Yahweh's representative and be under Yahweh's suzerainty. In other words, the monarchy was looked on as the concrete manifestation of Yahweh's rule.

This explains the authoritative role of the prophets at the court (e.g., Nathan, Gad, Elijah). The promise to establish David's throne forever, despite the rejection of Solomon (1 Kings 11:11-14), led to the focus upon a future Messiah (*see* Christ) who would rule over David's kingdom in righteousness and prosperity (*see* Son of David). Thus the Davidic kingdom was somehow conflated with Yahweh's rule. The great ethical prophets portrayed Israel's unfaithfulness against the Creator and King (Lord) of the universe, who had been pleased to identify himself with Israel. The crisis became especially acute when the last vestiges of David's kingdom were swept away by the Babylonian captivity. The promise made to David for an everlasting kingdom was now in some circles radically reinterpreted.

No other writing of the OT has more to say about the sovereignty of God than Daniel, where the kingdom of God is the central theme. However, the conception of the kingdom of God by Daniel is transformed under the impact of the new situation. The divine sovereignty is set vis á vis human kingdoms. These are described as being under the control of the God of heaven, who allots the sovereignty in accordance with his will. In Daniel 2 the kingdom of God is described as a direct divine intervention. Its agent, in the form of a stone cut without hands, crushes the various human kingdoms, here symbolized by various metals and clay, and it grows until it (i.e., the kingdom, king and kingdom being interchangeable in Daniel) fills the whole earth. In Daniel 7 the symbolism changes to one of wild beasts portraying the ungodly character of the human kingdoms. The agent for the kingdom of God is a figure described as "one like a son of man" (*see* Son of Man). This figure assumes the royal rule of the spiritual powers at work behind the earthly potentates, and his saints are given the kingly rule of the monarchs under the whole heaven (i.e., the earthly potentates).

Thus Daniel not only portrays the kingdom of God divested of its Davidic, earthly, political character but also depicts its agent as a heavenly, transcendental being. The new situation has brought about not only a new concept of the kingdom of God but also a transformation of its agent (see Caragounis 1986, 61-80). These new ideas were of decisive importance in shaping future messianic thought and eschatology, not only in Judaism but also in Jesus' teaching.

3. Judaism.

The concept of the kingdom of God in early Judaism was shaped principally by three factors. At the basis was the OT idea of Yahweh's eschatological epiphany in judgment to punish the wicked (i.e., Israel's enemies) and reward the just (i.e., Israel). This was coupled with the idea of God's reign through his elect messianic king of Davidic descent, bringing in a time of untold bliss for the Jewish people. The second factor was Daniel's new understanding of the kingdom and its agent as transcendental, heavenly realities and the consequent deliverance of God's people in primarily dynamic terms. The third factor was the centuries-long Gentile rule over Palestine that intensified the longing for liberation, national identity and happiness (*see* Revolutionary Movements).

Although the term "kingdom of God" is rare in Judaism, the idea is almost ubiquitous, either explicitly as the kingdom of the Messiah or implicitly in descriptions of the messianic age. The two lines of messianic expectation to which Judaism was heir are reflected in the ambivalent descriptions of the messianic kingdom. This ambivalence, besides defying a strictly systematic presentation of kingdom teaching, also implies that motifs from both lines of thought are blended together to various degrees. The result is a variety of messianologies and kingdom conceptions, which are not always clearly demarcated from one another. In general, however, we may distinguish between two main tendencies in kingdom thinking: an earlier, political, this-worldly conception of a temporary, Davidic kingdom with Jerusalem as the center and the Jews as the primary beneficiaries—though sometimes encompassing the whole world—and a later, apocalyptic conception of an ultra-mundane, transcendental and everlasting kingdom, conceived in universalistic terms.

When the kingdom of God is considered as temporary, usually a judgment follows and a new world is posited, and a reign of God is looked for in heaven with greater bliss than that of the messianic kingdom. This view is sharply contrasted with the apocalyptic view, according to which the kingdom of God comes by a direct intervention of God and is transcendental and everlasting under a similarly transcendental and preexistent Messiah, described as Son of man (Daniel, the so-called Parables of *1 Enoch* 37—71, 2 Ezra). In this case the Messiah takes part in the judgment, which thus precedes the messianic kingdom. This kingdom is the final kingdom of God, which is to last forever.

But as is natural, even the later expectation for the most part utilizes the messianic categories of the earlier expectation, and this makes it more difficult to isolate the traits of the one from those of the other. The following is an attempt to illustrate briefly some of the main lines of thought in Jewish expectations of the kingdom of God without attempting to draw a strict demarcating line between the early and the later forms of the expectation or between the different standpoints within early Judaism.

Especially in works evincing Danielic influence, the inbreaking of the kingdom of God is preceded by a time of tribulation and upheaval in heaven and on earth (*Sib. Or.* 3:796-808; *2 Apoc. Bar.* 70:2-8; 4 Ezra 6:24; 9:1-12; 13:29-31; 1QM 12:9; 19:1-2; cf. Mt 24:7-12 par.). In rabbinic literature this came to be called the birth pangs of the Messiah (*b. Sanh.* 98b.; Str-B 1.950). The Messiah's appearance is sometimes preced-

ed by the coming of Elijah (Mal 3:1-4; Sir 48:10-11; cf. Mt 17:10 par.; *m.* '*Ed.* 8:7; Justin *Dial. Tryph.* 8) or of the prophet like Moses (Deut 18:15; 1QS 9:11; 4QTestim 5-8; Jn 1:21).

The Messiah is conceived variously. The traditional view of a fully human, Davidic Messiah (*Pss. Sol.* 17:5, 23; *Sib. Or.* 3:49) who conquers the wicked (*Sib. Or.* 3:652-56; *Pss. Sol.* 17:23-32) is frequent, while in works belonging to the Danielic tradition the Messiah is a preexistent, supernatural being with powers to judge the kings and the mighty, in short, all the enemies of God, and to vindicate the righteous (*1 Enoch* 46:1-6; 48:2-6; 62:5-7; 4 Ezra 12:32). Another difference is that according to *1 Enoch* 90:16-38 the Messiah will appear after the judgment, whereas in most other works (*Sib. Or.* 3:652-6; *Pss. Sol.* 17:14-41; *1 Enoch* 46:4-6; 62:3-12; 69:27-9; 4 Ezra 13:32-8; cf. Mt 25:31-46) he conquers or judges his enemies.

Echoing the sentiment of Psalm 2:1-3 a number of works presuppose a final assault by the ungodly against the Messiah (*Sib. Or.* 3:663-68; *1 Enoch* 90:16; 1QM 15—19; 4 Ezra 13:33-34) in order to thwart the establishment of the messianic kingdom. These powers are annihilated sometimes by God (*T. Mos.* 10:2-7; *1 Enoch* 90:18-19) or more often by the Messiah (4 Ezra 12:32-33; 13:27-28, 37-39; *2 Apoc. Bar.* 39:7—40:2), who is occasionally presented as a warrior (*Tg. Isa.* 10:27; Gen 49:11), and sometimes in judicial categories (*1 Enoch* 46:4-6; 45:3; 52:4-9; 55:4; 61:8-10; cf. Mt 25:31-46).

The establishment of the Messiah's kingdom involves the gathering of the scattered Israelites (LXX Bar 4:36-37; 5:5-9; Philo *Praem. Poen.* 28; 4 Ezra 13:39-47) and the restoration of Jerusalem (*Pss. Sol.* 17:25, 33; *1 Enoch* 53:6; 90:28-29; 4 Ezra 7:26). The messianic kingdom is understood to imply the ultimate reign of God over his people (*Sib. Or.* 3:704-6, 756-59; *Pss. Sol.* 17:1-4; 1QM 19:1; Šĕmôneh 'Eśrēh, 11 bĕrākâ), thus fulfilling the OT idea of God being king over Israel. The kingdom is centered on Palestine, with Jerusalem being "the jewel of the world" (*Sib. Or.* 3:423), though Jubilees (mid-second century B.C.) probably presents the first instance of a temporary messianic kingdom of one thousand years. This is brought about gradually by human moral or spiritual development, and during this time the powers of evil are restrained (*Jub.* 1:29; 23:26-30).

Similarly, the third book of the *Sibylline Ora-*

cles 762-71 (second century B.C.) exhorts to righteous living as the condition for God "to raise up his kingdom for all ages over men." The Messiah is described in *Sibylline Oracles* 5:414 (c. A.D. 100) as "a Blessed Man" from "the plains of heaven," perhaps reflecting Danielic influence. Under his reign there will be peace (*Sib. Or.* 3:702), fruitfulness and prosperity (*Sib. Or.* 3:744), in which even the animal world will share (*Sib. Or.* 3:788-95).

According to the *Testament of Moses* 10:1 (first century A.D.), God's kingdom "shall appear throughout his whole creation." However, the kingdom seems to be earthly and appears to lack a Messiah, being introduced by repentance (*T. Moses* 1:18; 9:6-7). The awaited kingdom will spell glory for Israel and punishment for the Gentiles (*T. Moses* 10:7-10).

The *Second Apocalypse of Baruch* describes the messianic kingdom especially in three visions (considered pre-70 A.D.). In the first vision (*Bar.* 27—30) the revelation of the Messiah will bring a time of prosperity for "those who are found in this land" and "have arrived at the consummation of time." In the second vision (*Bar.* 36—40) the Messiah will annihilate his enemy, the fourth empire, (reflecting Dan 7) and reign "until the world of corruption has ended . . . and the times . . . have been fulfilled." In the third vision (*Bar.* 53—74) prosperity and bliss follow the Messiah's annihilation of Israel's enemies. The kingdom is related to Israel's long-cherished hope, though the Messiah has supernatural status.

The two works bearing the clearest influence of the Danielic Son of man, the Parables of *1 Enoch* and the book of 4 Ezra, follow their source in associating the concepts of kingdom and Son of man. At several points in the parables the Son of man is portrayed as exercising the functions of judge and universal ruler (*1 Enoch* 46:4-6; 62:3-12; 63:4; 69:27-29, and the book closes with a description of the messianic age (*1 Enoch* 71:15-17, cf. *1 Enoch* 62:12-16; see Caragounis 1986, 84-119).

The book of 4 Ezra conflates the earthly with the transcendental Messiah (4 Ezra 12:32), who dies after reigning for four hundred years (4 Ezra 7:28-29; other versions have variously one thousand and thirty years). The Davidic descent of the Messiah is perhaps his way of stressing continuity in messianic thought, though the content is that of a transcendental Messiah, as seen, for example, from 4 Ezra 12:32-34 and

4 Ezra 13:26 (see Caragounis 1986, 119-31).

In the Qumran scrolls the term *malēkût* occurs over a dozen times, but probably only once of God's kingdom (1QM 12:7), most of the rest referring to Israel's kingdom. The idea of God's kingdom is, however, latent in the sectarians' belief that they constituted God's true people who were to fight the eschatological battle against God's enemies (*see* Dead Sea Scrolls; on Judaism generally, see Schürer 2:492-554).

4. Jesus and the Kingdom of God.

In the teaching of Jesus the discussion of the kingdom of God revolves around two questions: (1) the character and (2) the imminence of the kingdom of God. These two questions are interrelated and have been at the center of scholarly discussion during the past hundred years.

4.1. Jesus' Dynamic View. Jesus' conception of the kingdom of God had continuity with the OT promise as well as shared certain features with apocalyptic Judaism, particularly Daniel, but went beyond them in certain important respects. (1) The kingdom of God was primarily dynamic rather than a geographical entity. (2) It was connected with the destiny of the Son of man. (3) Entrance into it was not based on the covenant or confined to Jewish participation. And (4) whereas in apocalypticism it was a vague future hope, in Jesus it is definite and imminent; it demands immediate response.

With the apocalypticists Jesus held that the kingdom of God was no human achievement but an act of God. However, unlike them he did not expect the kingdom of God to follow on upheavals and catastrophes but to appear in a gentle, quiet and unobtrusive manner. The catastrophic element for Jesus lay in the upheaval his call caused to his followers' relations with their family, friends and even self. Jesus' followers should be willing to "hate" their life in order to be worthy of him, worthy of the kingdom of God.

4.2. The Kingdom as Present or Future—The Modern Debate. In modern discussion the kingdom of God in the teaching of Jesus has actualized three questions. What is its essence? How is it related to Jesus' person and work? When does it come?

In the past hundred years since the work of A. Ritschl and J. Weiss, the kingdom of God has been at the center of discussion, and the three questions above have received a variety of answers. Ritschl, influenced by Kant's idealistic philosophy, conceived of the kingdom of God in primarily ethical terms as the organization of redeemed humanity, whose actions are inspired by love.

The interest generated by Ritschl's work gave rise to several principal interpretations of the kingdom of God. The first interpretation was the individualistic, spiritual and noneschatological interpretation, which located the kingdom of God in the experience of a person's heart. This interpretation was associated with the liberal school, for which the essence of Christianity lay in certain general principles taught by Jesus, as the fatherhood of God and the brotherhood of all people (e.g., A. von Harnack, 1886; W. Herrmann, 1901). The second was the social gospel movement in Germany (C. Blumhardt, c. 1900; L. Ragaz, 1911) and especially in America with its emphasis on a present social order based on love and solidarity (S. Mathews, 1897; F. G. Peabody, 1900; particularly W. Rauschenbusch, 1912).

But the most important interpretation for the continued scholarly discussion was given by Ritschl's son-in-law, J. Weiss, in his epoch-making work *Die Predigt Jesu vom Reiche Gottes* (1892, ET *Jesus' Proclamation of the Kingdom of God*, 1971). Weiss reacted strongly against Ritschl's interpretation, emphasizing the future, eschatological and apocalyptic character of the kingdom of God that is opposed by the kingdom of Satan. The kingdom of God would erupt suddenly, be solely the work of God and sweep away the present order. The work of Weiss aroused a storm and with it an unprecedented interest in the theme of the kingdom of God. In the hands of A. Schweitzer the line Weiss had struck out became known as *Konsequente Eschatologie* ("consistent," "futuristic" or "thoroughgoing eschatology"). In due time this found its opposite pole in C. H. Dodd's realized eschatology. In the meantime G. Dalman (1898), by means of philology, demonstrated the dynamic character of the kingdom of God in Judaism and the NT, which has been the basic assumption of almost all subsequent discussions. According to Dalman the idea of kingdom of God has no territorial or geographical reference but expresses dynamically the kingly rule of God, which is basically eschatological. However, the theological interpretation was given by A. Schweitzer.

In his landmark works *The Mystery of the King-dom of God* (ET, 1925 [1901]) and especially in *The Quest of the Historical Jesus,* (ET, 1910 [1906]), Schweitzer interpreted not only Jesus' teaching, as Weiss had done, but also Jesus' whole ministry in consistently eschatological terms. Jesus was understood as an apocalyptic figure who expected the end to come during the mission of the Twelve (Mk 6:7-13 par.), wherefore he did not expect to see the disciples again. In this he was, however, mistaken. The end, and with it the kingdom of God, did not come. Having staked everything on this expectation and been proved wrong in his prediction of the end, Jesus decided to cast himself headlong to death in a final, heroic attempt to force God to set up his kingdom. Schweitzer's impact, particularly in Germany, can be gauged from the fact that his futuristic eschatology became the characteristic German line.

As a reaction to the one-sidedness of this German position, a number of British scholars like A. T. Cadoux (1930) and T. W. Manson (1931) (and even Germans like E. von Dobschütz and H.-D. Wendland) laid emphasis on the present element of the kingdom of God in the teaching of Jesus. Like Schweitzer, R. Bultmann thought that Jesus expected the kingdom of God to begin at his death and went up to Jerusalem to purify the temple in preparation for it. The kingdom of God is conceived by Bultmann as a future, eschatological, suprahistorical and supernatural entity, which places a person at the position of decision. But differently from Schweitzer, in Bultmann's demythologizing interpretation the kingdom of God is ever coming and thus ceases to be a future event that is and can be hoped for. Since the decision is a continual decision, the kingdom of God is not an event in time. Thus the kingdom of God, emptied of its content, transcends time without ever entering it. In short, Bultmann sees the kingdom of God primarily in existentialist fashion as the hour for the individual's decision.

However, the scholar who gave definitive form to this reaction was Dodd. In *The Parables of the Kingdom* (1935), Dodd interpreted the *ēngiken* of (e.g.) Mark 1:15 and its parallels in light of the *ephthasen* of Matthew 12:28 (par. Lk 11:20). His claim was that LXX usage translating the Aramaic of Daniel, Modern Greek idiomatic usage and the parables of the kingdom all lent their united support to his thesis that the kingdom of God was already a present reality during

Jesus' ministry. The decisive event had occurred in the coming of Jesus. Jesus' healings, particularly his casting out of demons, were proof that in Jesus' person and works the divine sovereignty had dealt the decisive blow to the kingdom of Satan and was indubitably a wholly present reality. In a sense Dodd identified the kingdom of God with the person of Jesus. This opened the way to viewing the kingdom of God as a timeless reality. "The absolute, the 'wholly other', has entered into time and space" (Dodd, 81). "The inconceivable had happened: history had become the vehicle of the eternal; the absolute was clothed with flesh and blood" (Dodd, 147). In Dodd's interpretation of the kingdom of God, "futurist eschatology disappears, and all that is left is 'the eschaton' as the Eternal" (Lundström, 121). To achieve this, Dodd played down the Gospel statements that presented the kingdom of God as future.

Dodd's influence has been far-reaching, forcing significant modifications upon the futuristic interpretation. This has led in the last forty-five years to a number of mediating positions according to which the kingdom of God is conceived as both present and future, with the German side inclining more toward the future and the British more toward the present aspect (e.g., W. G. Kümmel in *Verheissung und Erfüllung* [1945, *Promise and Fulfillment*, 1961], G. R. Beasley-Murray [1954, 312-16; 1986, 75-80], E. Jüngel, Schnackenburg, N. Perrin, D. C. Allison [99-114]). In a similar vein J. Jeremias, at the suggestion of E. Haenchen, speaks of the kingdom of God as *sich realisierende Eschatologie* ("an eschatology in process of realization"), a term preferred by Dodd but apparently never allowed to change his basic viewpoint. R. H. Fuller (25-27) interprets *ephthasen* as "has come," but understands it by way of the prophetic device of speaking of an event proleptically as though it had already taken place. For Fuller the powers of the kingdom of God were already making themselves felt in the deeds of Jesus by operating in advance, and his viewpoint received the label of proleptic eschatology. G. Florovsky and A. M. Hunter (94) speak of inaugurated eschatology, while G. E. Ladd argues from a rendering of *ephthasen* as "has come," for a fulfillment of the kingdom of God in history (i.e., in Jesus' ministry) as well as a full consummation at the end of history, and calls his position an eschatology of biblical realism.

Kümmel has been described as the scholar who came closest to a "genuine synthesis of realized and futurist eschatology in the teaching of our Lord" (Beasley-Murray 1954, 103). Thus, while duly recognizing the future character of sayings admitting an interval between the passion and the parousia (Mk 2:18-20; 8:38 par. Lk 12:8-9), he understands the *ephthasen* of Matthew 12:28, with Dodd, as "has come" and as implying that the eschaton was already active in Jesus. In Jesus' person and actions the future was already realized since he who was to usher in salvation at the end was already present. In this way the future of the kingdom of God and its coming were linked closely with the present, which had Jesus as its center. The kingdom of God was present in the person, teaching and works of Jesus. By faith in him people received the kingdom of God and the guarantee of its appearance. This guarantee implied that the kingdom of God is to be fulfilled in him. Thus promise and fulfillment are insolubly connected with each other. Ladd (123-24) criticizes Kümmel for failing to define precisely what the kingdom of God is. According to E. Grässer (7), what is understood as present by Kümmel is not the kingdom of God but its imminence.

R. Morgenthaler, R. Schnackenburg and Beasley-Murray (1986) all take *ephthasen* as "has come," though for Morgenthaler it only implies that the kingdom of God is around here but not actually present. For Schnackenburg it means that the kingdom of God is "connected with [Jesus'] person and his work" (Schnackenburg, 109). Although he speaks of the kingdom of God as something entirely eschatological and wholly supernatural, he also conceives of it in its salvific character as present and active in Jesus. The miracles of Jesus were "the kingdom of God in action." But it would be an overstatement to claim that the presence of the kingdom of God indicates something completed; the present kingdom functions as a precursor of the coming, perfected kingdom of God.

Beasley-Murray thinks that the meaning of "has come" for *ephthasen* in Matthew 12:28 and parallel is "unambiguously plain" and criticizes the defenders of futuristic eschatology for looking for "ways of muting its testimony" (Beasley-Murray 1986, 75-76). The miracles of Jesus, especially his driving out demons, speak eloquently of the presence of the kingdom. However, the arrival of the kingdom of God spoken of in Matthew 12:28 and parallel was not the same thing as its consummation, which Beasley-Murray, like Schnackenburg, Kümmel, Ladd, and others, considers as future.

A basically similar position is that of D. C. Allison. He follows the usual interpretation of *ephthasen* and thus subscribes to the present consensus that the kingdom of God is both present and future. The relation between present and future is explained by appealing to Jewish thought, which "could envision the final events—the judgment of evil and the arrival of the kingdom of God—as extending over a time and as a process or series of events that could involve the present. When Jesus announced that the kingdom of God has come and is coming, this means that the last act has begun but has not yet reached its climax; the last things have come and will come" (Allison, 105-6). And again, "For Jesus, the kingdom of God, the eschatological establishment of God's kingly rule, was due to come in its fullness soon" (Allison, 114).

It may then be concluded that those who emphasize the presence of the kingdom of God in Jesus' works of power also allow for a future perfection or consummation of the kingdom of God. Those who advocate the futurity of the kingdom of God allow for some kind of effect that the imminently near kingdom of God exercised in the ministry of Jesus. Both of these positions are attempts to explain important elements in the Gospel data.

Of rather different nature is the later work of N. Perrin, who retreated from his earlier positions (1963). Receiving impulses from literary critics like P. Wheelwright (1962), P. Ricoeur (1969), A. N. Wilder (1964), R. W. Funk (1966), D. O. Via (1967) and F. D. Crossan (1973), Perrin suggests that "kingdom of God" is not an idea or a conception but a mythical symbol (Perrin 1976, 33). He adopts Wheelwright's distinction of steno-symbol, which has fixed meaning—a one-to-one correspondence between symbol and referent as in apocalyptic language—and tensive symbol, which is open and multi-significant, having an inexhaustible set of meanings. Jesus' proclamation of the kingdom of God involved the tensive symbol, which, however, his followers turned to an apocalyptic steno-symbol, making the kingdom of God lose its rich variety of reference and instead refer to a particular event of universal experience. Perrin thinks that Jesus' whole teaching claimed "to mediate an experience of God as king, an experience of such an order that it brings world to an end" (Perrin 1976, 54). Though the symbolic and metaphorical aspects of the kingdom of God and its parables should be profitably explored, Perrin's analysis and claims can hardly be said to do justice to the biblical data or to have led to a deeper or more valid understanding of the kingdom of God. Not infrequently Perrin's position involves self-contradictions, and his categories are plainly inapplicable to the Gospel texts (see further the criticism of Beasley-Murray 1986, 338-44; Allison, 107-12).

4.3. The Imminence of the Kingdom. From the above it must have become clear that the interpretation of *ephthasen* of Matthew 12:28 and its parallel Luke 11:20, which is normally accepted as an authentic saying of Jesus, has played a most crucial role in discussions of the kingdom of God. This is so because it is the only kingdom saying in the Synoptics that apparently describes the kingdom of God as having arrived. Dodd was so certain of this meaning that he let it determine his interpretation of the *ēngiken*-type of sayings. The claim that the kingdom of God had arrived in Jesus' person and that it consisted of, or at least was active in, his driving out demons is hardly a satisfactory answer to the three questions regarding the essence, the arrival and the relation of the kingdom of God to Jesus' person and work. If the kingdom of God had come already, say, by the time Jesus uttered the saying in Matthew 12:28 and Luke 11:20, how is the remainder of Jesus' earthly existence to be understood? And what about the Son of man's duty "to give his life a ransom for many"? What is the significance of his death? And how did Jesus relate his death to the kingdom of God? To speak of a final or full consummation at a future point of time does not satisfactorily answer these questions. And to emphasize the coming of the kingdom prior to the time of the *ephthasen* saying raises the question of whether the death of Jesus is superfluous to that coming. Any viable solution must take account of the language used and the relation of the kingdom of God to the Son of man (4.5 below).

4.3.1. Ephthasen (Mt 12:28/Lk 11:20). The most indubitable fact is that the Synoptics present Jesus as having spoken of the kingdom of God as imminently near (*ēngiken*), just as John did (Mt 3:2). The problem that the *ephthasen* saying raises is due to its being interpreted in a dubious way. The *ephthasen* saying makes excellent sense if understood according to a well-attested but little-known and generally misunderstood Greek idiom. The aorist tense is sometimes used to emphasize the certainty and immediacy of an action that properly belongs in the future by describing it as though it had already transpired (Caragounis 1989, 12-23). In comparison with the *ēngiken*-type of sayings, the *ephthasen* logion implies an advance, but not quite the presence of the kingdom of God which, in the context of Matthew 12:28 and Luke 11:20, is still future. What Jesus is saying in effect is, "If it is by the Spirit/finger of God (rather than by Beelzebul, as you claim) that I drive out the demons (i.e., preparing for the coming of the kingdom of God by defeating the forces of evil), then the kingdom of God is about to break in upon you (and overtake you in your obstinate and unrepentant state)" (*see* Holy Spirit).

Ephthasen implies that the coming of the kingdom of God is so imminent that the kingdom of God may be considered as being virtually here. This means that the force of the saying is not purely informative, in which case the force of *eph' hymas* ("upon you") would have been lost, but one of warning, almost threat. This threatening force of *eph' hymas* shows clearly that the kingdom of God has not yet arrived. The relation of the *miracles of Jesus to the kingdom of God is that they bear witness to the warfare of the Son of man (i.e., the agent of the kingdom of God) against the powers of evil for the establishment of the kingdom of God. But the kingdom of God does not consist of those miracles. Jesus' miracles are only the preliminaries, not the kingdom of God (contra Dodd). The kingdom of God is the dynamic reign of God over his people. The saying looks forward to the cross.

4.3.2. Entos Hymōn Estin (Lk 17:21). Another saying often adduced as evidence of the presence of the kingdom of God is Luke 17:21. Here Jesus is represented answering the Pharisees' question about the time of the coming of the kingdom of God by saying, "the kingdom of God does not come with your careful observation, nor will people say, 'Here it is,' or 'There it is,' because the kingdom of God is within you" (*entos hymōn estin*) (NIV). The basic meaning of *entos* is "within," "inside," being the opposite of *ektos*, "without" (i.e., "outside"). This meaning is borne out by the entire Greek literary corpus, in-

cluding the papyri and Modern Greek. The attempt has sometimes been made to construe *entos hymōn* in the sense of "in your midst," "among you," "in your domain" or "within your grasp," in accordance with whether *hymōn* is interpreted of the Pharisees or of eventual followers of Jesus, in which case the *estin* ("is") is taken with future significance (i.e., "the kingdom of God will suddenly be among you," etc.).

An examination of the ancient Greek texts that have been appealed to for these meanings (e.g., Herodotus, Xenophon, Symmachus's translation of the OT, Papyri) shows that the meaning is regularly "within" and that the sense of "among" has been based on a few, sometimes obscure, instances in Aquila and Symmachus. P. Oxy 654, 16 (which is parallel to the *Gospel of Thomas*) has a saying similar to Luke's, where the meaning is unambiguously "the kingdom (of God) is within you." Luke's usage must be considered decisive. The sense of "among" occurs a good many times in Luke-Acts, but the expression is always *en (tō) mesō hymōn*, never *entos*. The *entos hymōn* is the opposite of *meta paratērēseōs* ("with [apocalyptic?] signs that can be observed") with its amplification " 'Here it is' or 'There it is.' " Therefore any interpretation that fails to set *entos hymōn* in its intended contradistinction to *meta paratērēseōs* fails to do justice to Luke's intention. Jesus is here trying to discourage apocalyptic speculations and calculations based on observable signs (*see* Apocalypticism). "Within you," therefore, seems to be Luke's way of expressing the inward nature and dynamic of the kingdom of God rather than referring to any actual presence in or among the Pharisees.

In the Synoptics there does not seem to be a single kingdom of God saying that unequivocally demands to be taken in the present sense. The kingdom of God is presented either timelessly (notably in the parables) or as the object of proclamation or in its demands (Mk 9 [10]x; Lk 17 [19]x; Mt 25 [31]x) or as something future from the standpoint of the utterance in Mk 5 [6]x; Lk 19 [21]x; Mt 19 [25]x; the figures in brackets fitting either category).

4.4. The Kingdom in Jesus' Teaching. The Synoptics present Jesus from the start as charged with one message, compelling and irresistible, the message that the kingdom of God was at hand. The impression is that the eschaton has drawn near, the long-promised kingdom of God

648

is about to appear and the hour of decision has come. The kingdom of God is presented in two ways: it forms the heart of Jesus' teaching, and it is confirmed by his mighty works (see e.g., Mt 4:23; 9:35). A third component is that the kingdom of God is inextricably connected with Jesus' person as Son of man (see 4.5 below).

4.4.1. The Conditions and Demands of the Kingdom. The first condition is to "repent and believe the gospel" (Mk 1:15; Mt 4:17). A childlike faith is a presupposition for entering into the kingdom of God (Mt 18:3; Mk 10:14 par.). The gospel is the good news about the sovereignty of God. God's eschatological, salvific act demands an undivided heart (Mk 12:29-30 par.). Therefore, it is not lip service or even the use of Jesus' name in performing miracles but the performance of God's will that opens the door to the kingdom of God (Mt 7:21-23). Nothing may stand in the way of the kingdom since no one who has put his hand on the plow and looks back is fit for the kingdom of God (Lk 9:62). The kingdom may demand the sacrifice of marriage and family (Mt 19:12) as well as of possessions (Mk 10:21-27 par.). At the other end, it holds the promise of repaying to a hundredfold (Mk 10:29-31 par.). The demand is radicalized still further when the would-be disciple is given the choice of either letting the tempting hand be cut off or the tempting eye plucked out for the kingdom of God, or keeping them and being cast into Gehenna (Mk 9:47 par.). The kingdom must be preferred to everything. All this illustrates the seriousness with which people must act with regard to the kingdom of God rather than superior or moral attributes qualifying for entrance into it. In other words, they must seek to enter in by the narrow gate (Mt 7:13-14); they must actively storm the kingdom (Mt 11:12).

4.4.2. The Ethics of the Kingdom. The *ethics of the kingdom of God are the ethics that God expects from those who are set to do his will. The ethical demands are scattered throughout Jesus' teaching but occur in more concentrated form in the *Sermon on the Mount (Mt 5—7; see also Lk 6:17-49). Here we see a continuation with the ethical teaching of the OT, although Jesus' requirements go beyond it by penetrating behind the letter to the spirit and intent of it. In the end, Jesus lifts up a performance motivated by pure love and devotion to God and love to one's neighbor. Thus, for example, the commandments "Do not murder," "Do not commit adul-

tery," "Do not break your oath" are only partial and particular aspects of the greatest commandment of all, namely, undivided love toward God and neighbor. Love is the fulfilling of all the commandments (cf. Mt 22:40); the logical conclusion would seem to be that love makes commandments superfluous.

4.4.3. The Parables of the Kingdom. Jesus spoke about the kingdom of God also through the medium of *parables. After centuries of allegorical interpretation of the parables, in which every detail was given a particular significance, A. Jülicher demonstrated that the parables had one essential point, the other details being the necessary trappings of the story. (Jülicher's principle should not be applied rigidly as there are occasions when more than one point may have been intended.)

The parables of the kingdom have been regarded as the most authentic element in Jesus' teaching and occur in concentrated collections in Mark 4 and Matthew 13. These parables illustrate different aspects of the kingdom of God: people's response to the message of the kingdom of God (the sower, Mk 4:3-9; Mt 13:3-9), the unobtrusive character of the kingdom of God as contrasted with the apocalyptic expectation of upheaval (the seed growing quietly, Mk 4:26-29), the immense growth of the kingdom from an insignificant beginning (the mustard seed, Mk 4:30-32; Mt 13:31-32, and the leaven, Mt 13:33), the mixed nature of those presently involved in the kingdom of God, who will be separated at the end (the weeds, Mt 13:24-30, with its probably later allegorical interpretation, Mt 13:36-43, and in all probability the dragnet, Mt 13:47-50) and the inestimable value of the kingdom of God, for which people must be prepared to give up everything (the treasure and the pearl, Mt 13:44-46).

Jesus' use of parables raises the question of their purpose or function. Matthew has the disciples raise the question (Mt 13:10). Jesus' answer, "To you it is given to learn the mysteries of the kingdom of heaven, but to those it is not given" (Mt 13:11), has given rise to many interpretations. The point of the explanation seems to be that, having rejected the message of Jesus when exposed to it, these "outsiders" (Mk 4:10) have willfully chosen to keep their eyes shut and their hearts hardened, that the continued message is now given in the form of half-revealing, half-concealing parables. But though the interpretation—and therewith the precise meaning—is denied to them, they still perceive their gist sufficiently well (cf. Mk 12:12 par.: "they knew he had spoken the parable against them"). It is not therefore an exaggeration to say that sometimes the parables have a polemical tone in addition to their use to illustrate the kingdom of God.

4.5. The Kingdom of God and the Son of Man. The kingdom of God should not be dissociated from the Son of man, who in Jesus' teaching, as in Daniel, is its agent. The destiny of the Son of man is therefore directly connected with the coming of the kingdom of God. The present activity of the Son of man, especially his casting out of demons, is an integral part of the proclamation of the kingdom of God. These activities should be seen not so much as indicating the actual occurrence of the decisive event of the kingdom of God but as the preliminary warfare of the Son of man against the evil powers in his work of making possible the entrance of the kingdom of God in human history. This warfare, the Son of man's attacks on the kingdom of evil, ought not to be construed in terms of the Hellenistic or Jewish exorcist's activity. Instead they should be connected with the Son of man's mission to "serve and to give his life a ransom for many" (Mk 10:45 par.). Otherwise the link between the kingdom of God and the cross becomes illegitimately obscured.

We would thus submit that it was the near prospect of a violent death (*see* Death of Christ), to which Jesus attributed atoning significance, that led him to change the *ēngiken* to *ephthasen* and thus characterize the coming of the kingdom of God as unprecedentedly certain and imminent. Viewed from this perspective, though the kingdom of God had come nearer than in the *ēngiken* type of sayings, it had not arrived, as the last pre-passion occurrence(s) of kingdom of God in all three Synoptics would seem to testify.

4.6. Potential Eschatology. By way of conclusion it may be said that during Jesus' ministry the kingdom of God is spoken of always as a future event. It is expected, hoped for and prayed for. But it is never said explicitly to have arrived, not even at the *Last Supper. What is present is the agent of the kingdom of God, Jesus. But because the agent of the kingdom of God is present and active through his teaching and mighty works, the kingdom of God may also be said to be potentially present. However, the decisive event for its coming, that is, for the release of its powers in salvific blessings, still lies ahead.

The term *potential* does not qualify the term "kingdom of God," but only the term "present in Jesus." Thus it should not be construed as in any way implying uncertainty as to the kingdom's coming. *Potential* simply means that the kingdom of God in Jesus' ministry is not present in any absolute or independent sense but only insofar as it is represented by Jesus. Its arrival and presence in its own right is depicted as a future event. Thus if we are to speak of eschatology in connection with the kingdom of God during Jesus' earthly ministry at all, then it is more accurate to speak of *potential eschatology.* This is an eschatology that has not yet begun to unfold itself in final, catastrophic events, but the eschaton is, nevertheless, in principle present in Jesus, because he, as Son of man, is the agent of the kingdom of God. Nonetheless, the ministry of Jesus and his teaching look forward to the awful and more immediate event of the cross, the event in which the Son of man fulfills his God-given mission for the arrival of the kingdom of God.

4.7. The Consummation. But even this decisive event (the cross-resurrection complex) does not exhaust the entire content or expectation of the promise. It seems to be the key event that makes possible the arrival of the kingdom of God in time, but also in principle its full manifestation and consummation that lies at the end of history (see Ladd, 307-28). In this regard the concept of the kingdom of God is parallel with the Johannine concept of eternal life and the Pauline concept of salvation. Precisely as those who put their faith in the atoning work of Christ are said to possess eternal life, to be in Christ or to be saved, in spite of the fact that eternal life or salvation are essentially eschatological concepts, so also believers may be said to have entered into the kingdom of God despite the fact that the kingdom of God, like eternal life and salvation, can be properly experienced only at the end of time.

5. The Gospels.

The Synoptic Gospels contain 76 different kingdom sayings, or 103, including the parallels:

(1) *Mark-Matthew-Luke* (Mk 4:11 par. Mt 13:11 and Lk 8:10; Mk 4:30 par. Mt 13:31 and Lk 13:18; Mk 9:1 par. Mt 16:28 and Lk 9:27; Mk 10:14 par. Mt 19:14 and Lk 18:16; Mk 10:15 par. Mt 18:3

and Lk 18:17; Mk 10:23 par. Mt 19:23 and Lk 18:24; Mk 10:25 par. Mt 19:24 and Lk 18:25; Mk 14:25 par. Mt 26:29 and Lk 22:18);

(2) *Mark-Matthew* (Mk 1:15 par. Mt 4:17);

(3) *Mark-Luke* (Mk 15:43 par. Lk 23:51);

(4) *Matthew-Luke* (Mt 5:3 par Lk 6:20; Mt 6:10 par. Lk 11:2; Mt 6:33 par. Lk 12:31; Mt 8:11 par. Lk 13:29; Mt 10:7 par. Lk 9:2; Mt 11:11 par. Lk 7:28; Mt 11:12 par. Lk 16:16; Mt 12:28 par. Lk 11:20; Mt 13:33 par. Lk 13:20);

(5) *Mark* (4:26; 9:47; 10:24; 12:34);

(6) *Matthew* (3:2; 4:23: 5:10, 19 [bis], 20; 7:21; 8:12; 9:35; 13:19, 24, 38, 41, 43, 44, 45, 47, 52; 16:19; 18:1, 4, 23; 19:12; 20:1, 21; 21:31, 43; 22:2; 23:13; 24:14; 25:1, 34);

(7) *Luke* (1:33; 4:43; 8:1; 9:11, 60, 62; 10:11; 12:32; 13:28; 14:15; 17:20-21; 18:29; 19:11; 21:31; 22:16, 29-30; 23:42).

In addition, Matthew has one more reference to "kingdom of God" (Mt 7:21) and one to "kingdom" (Mt 6:13) in part of the textual tradition. The Gospel data on the distribution of the various expressions is shown in table 1.

Table 1.

	Mt	Mk	Lk	Jn
Kingdom of God	5	14	32	2
Kingdom of Heaven	32	—	—	—
Kingdom	13	—	7	3
Total	50	14	39	5

The Johannine sayings have no parallels in the Synoptics. The three expressions "Kingdom of God" (KG), "Kingdom of Heaven" (KH) and "Kingdom" (K) are distributed according to table 2.

5.1. Mark. *Mark introduces the public ministry of Jesus with the summary statement that Jesus proclaimed the gospel of God, saying, "The time is fulfilled, and the kingdom of God is

at hand; repent and believe the gospel" (Mk 1:15). The position of the statement within the structure of Mark indicates that the proclamation of the kingdom of God was at the heart of Jesus' preaching. The saying announces the fulfillment of the time for the arrival of the kingdom of God. The kingdom of God is still future, but it has drawn near and already makes its demands for preparation to receive it: these are repentance and believing acceptance of the gospel. This saying does not give any clear indications whether "kingdom" refers to the national or to a more apocalyptic type of hope. The collocation of "repent" and "believe" might favor the second alternative, but even for the national hope Israel was expected to keep the Law flawlessly for at least one day (see *b. Ta'an.* 64a).

In Mark 4 Jesus' parabolic teaching is concerned with the mystery of the kingdom of God which is given to the group of Jesus' inner disciples, while to the outsiders the kingdom of God is being conveyed in dark, unintelligible parables (Mk 4:11). The description of the kingdom of God as seed sown, shooting up and growing quietly (Mk 4:26) implies that the kingdom of God here is conceived neither in nationalistic terms of open revolt and warfare for liberation nor in the style of apocalyptic upheavals. The emphasis in the similar idea expressed at Mark 4:30 is on the contrast between the insignificant beginning and the immense growth of the kingdom of God.

In an isolated logion at Mark 9:1 the kingdom of God is described as imminent, to occur within a generation or two. At Mark 9:47 in the context of resisting various temptations, the importance of entering the kingdom of God at any price—even losing one's eye—is underlined, and entering the kingdom of God is compared with entering "life" (Mk 9:43-44).

According to Mark 10:14 children should be allowed access to Jesus because the kingdom of

Table 2.

Gospel	Total	Peculiar	Mt-Mk-Lk	Mt-Mk	Mt-Lk	Mk-Lk
Mt	50	32: 20 KH	8: 5 KH	1 KH	9: 6 KH	—
		2 KG	1 KG	—	2 KG	—
		10 K	2 K	—	1 K	—
Mk	14	4 KG	8 KG	1 KG	—	1 KG
Lk	39	21: 17 KG	8 KG	—	9: 7 KG	1 KG
		4 K	—	—	2 K	—

God belongs to such as these. In fact, the kingdom of God demands a childlike faith (Mk 10:15).

In the group of sayings at Mark 10:23, 24 and 25, love of possessions is a hindrance to entering the kingdom of God, which demands the sacrifice of everything and implies being "saved" (Mk 10:26).

The scribe who recognized that the heart of Hebrew/Jewish religion lay in undivided devotion to God was told that he was not far from the kingdom of God (Mk 12:34). In the Last Supper (Mk 14:25) the kingdom of God is eschatological. In traditional Jewish imagery Jesus will feast with his own. Finally, at Mark 15:43 Joseph of Arimathea is described as awaiting the kingdom of God, presumably in the sense of the traditional hope of Israel.

5.2. Matthew. As implied above, *Matthew offers a richer and more nuanced picture of Jesus' teaching on the kingdom of God than Mark. For in addition to his nine Markan and his nine Q sayings, he has another thirty-two sayings peculiar to himself.

At the outset of his Gospel Matthew describes the preaching of John as being one of repentance in view of the nearness of the kingdom of heaven (Mt 3:2). The wording—probably stylized by Matthew to bring out the continuity—is placed on Jesus' lips by way of a summary of his proclamation from the time of John's arrest onwards (Mt 4:17). The summary character of Jesus' preaching is repeated at Matthew 4:23 and again at Matthew 9:35 along with the information that Jesus' preaching was accompanied by healing. The same emphasis occurs in the mission of the Twelve (Mt 10:5-8).

The kingdom of God figures at the first and last beatitude (Mt 5:3, 10), thus framing the collection of Beatitudes (an *inclusio*) and suggesting that they must be understood within its thought compass (note: *autōn estin* ["theirs is"] occurs only in these two beatitudes. The beatitude of Mt 5:11 is in different form [second person]). Humility and righteous suffering are necessary presuppositions for possessing the kingdom.

The three logia at Matthew 5:19-20 teach that even the least commandments affect people's relation to the kingdom of God and that scribal or Pharisaic (i.e., Jewish) religiosity is insufficient for entrance into it. The centrality of the kingdom of God is seen also in the Lord's Prayer, where its future coming constitutes the first petition (Mt 6:10). Some textual witnesses end the Lord's Prayer with the mention of the kingdom. If this uncertain reading were original, it would imply that here too, as in the case of the Beatitudes, the prayer occurs within the frame of the kingdom of God.

The radicalism associated with the kingdom of God is underscored at Matthew 6:33, where the interests of the kingdom of God are to go before all other interests. The Sermon on the Mount closes by emphasizing that entrance into the kingdom of God will depend not on mere lip service but on a faithful performance of God's will (Mt 7:21). Not only will there be a distinction among the Jews as far as entering into the kingdom of God is concerned, but with faith rather than descent as a condition, the door to it will be opened to many Gentiles, while many of the "children of the kingdom" (i.e., physical descendants of the Patriarchs) will be excluded (Mt 8:11-12; 21:43; 22:2).

In a dispute concerning John, Jesus declares him to be the greatest of those born but still lesser than the least in the kingdom of heaven (Mt 11:11), the kingdom being pictured as the final eschatological reality. John's crucial role in salvation history is underscored by the statement that his day marks a new period in the realization of the kingdom. From his time on the kingdom of God is proclaimed and is being stormed by those who are eager to get in. His coming has given the signal that the kingdom of God has now drawn near and people can prepare themselves by repentance and baptism (Mt 11:12). From Matthew 21:31 we understand that those most eager to enter the kingdom of God are precisely the ones considered furthest from it. The imminence of the kingdom of God is expressed in unprecedentedly strong terms at Matthew 12:28, where Jesus' miracles, wrought by the Spirit of God, are interpreted as a sign of it.

The chapter on the parables of the kingdom contains no fewer than twelve kingdom logia (see 4.4.3 above). The point made in Matthew 16:19, where Peter is given the keys of the kingdom, is probably in polemic against the Jewish dispensers of God's truth, who according to Matthew 23:13 not only would not enter the kingdom themselves but also closed the door to those who wanted to enter. The logion is often understood as the Christian counterpart to the Jewish way of speaking of authority in teaching as binding and loosing.

Matthew ascribes a kingdom to the Son of man (Mt 16:28; 20:21), which is thought of as being future. The disciples' questions as to who is greatest in the kingdom of heaven (Mt 18:1) elicits from Jesus the statement that a condition for entering into the kingdom and being greatest in it is childlike faith and humility (Mt 18:3-4). The kingdom belongs to such as these (Mt 19:14).

The kingdom of God illustrates God's forgiveness and demands a spirit of forgiveness from those who would enter it (Mt 18:23). It may demand abstention from marriage (Mt 19:12), and it demands being taken seriously and loved more than possessions (Mt 19:23-24).

The rewards of the kingdom are apportioned by different principles. Personal achievement is of little importance. In God's evaluation scheme the last can become first and the first last (Mt 20:1).

In the Olivet discourse the kingdom of God is presented in future, apocalyptic terms. Those who persevere faithfully to the end will be saved. But the end will not come until the gospel of the kingdom has been proclaimed throughout the world. The parable of the ten virgins (Mt 25:1) was intended to teach perseverance and watchfulness. This finds its fitting sequel in the great judgment, when the Son of man invites the faithful to inherit the kingdom that had been prepared for them from the time of the foundation of the world (Mt 25:34). The righteous are to go into its bliss, while the unjust are to go to everlasting torment. This picture bears the well-known features of apocalyptic thought.

The last occurrence of kingdom in Matthew is in connection with the Last Supper, when Jesus, looking forward to the eschatological feast in the Father's kingdom, promises to abstain from wine until that day.

5.3. Luke. *Luke's presentation of the kingdom of God is richer than Mark's but less nuanced than Matthew's, having no fewer than twenty-one sayings peculiar to himself.

The first mention of kingdom occurs at Luke 1:33 and is put on the angel's lips, when he brings Mary the message of the birth of the Messiah who is to sit on the throne of his father David, reigning forever as the definitive Messiah (*see* Birth of Jesus).

The first clear reference to kingdom in connection with Jesus' ministry occurs at Luke 4:43, in which Jesus' mission consists of the proclamation of the kingdom of God. This gives the saying the character of a summary statement and implies that Jesus' previous ministry too was concerned with the kingdom of God. The same is repeated at Luke 8:1.

In his Sermon on the Plain, Luke has a logion similar to Matthew's first beatitude, but the saying is here directed to the poor rather than the humble (Lk 6:20). This is in line with Jesus' sermon in Nazareth (Lk 4:18) and Luke's sociological interests. Luke also has the saying on the least in the kingdom of God being greater than John (Lk 7:28). In interpreting the parable of the sower, Luke too affirms that the knowledge of the mysteries of the kingdom of God are given to Jesus' disciples, but the rest must be content with unexplained parables (Lk 8:10).

Luke has a mission of the Twelve and a mission of the seventy-two. The Twelve were to proclaim the kingdom of God (Lk 9:2), while the seventy-two were to proclaim that the kingdom had drawn near (Lk 10:9, 11). The preaching of both groups was to be accompanied by healing. And the crowds that followed Jesus were instructed by him in the kingdom of God (Lk 9:11).

Luke connects the death of the Son of man with the coming of the kingdom of God and envisages the latter event as taking place within the lifetime of some who were present on the occasion (Lk 9:27). This indicates not only that the kingdom is thought of as future but also that its coming is fairly imminent. The urgency of the kingdom makes it imperative that those who aspire to it do not let anything stand in the way— even the death of relatives (Lk 9:60)—but must devote themselves wholly to it, never looking back (Lk 9:62).

As in Matthew the coming of the kingdom figures prominently in the prayer Jesus taught his disciples (Lk 11:2). In the Beelzebul controversy, Jesus' works of power accomplished through the finger (Mt: "Spirit") of God are a strong indication of the imminence of the kingdom (Lk 11:20).

The concerns of the kingdom of God are to affect all attitudes toward life. Undue worry about worldly matters is to be laid aside and the interests of the kingdom to be given priority. Then God will see to it that all legitimate needs are supplied (Lk 12:31). Trust rather than fear is to characterize Jesus' followers since God has been pleased to give them the kingdom (Lk 13:18, 20). Like Matthew, Luke makes it clear that entrance to the kingdom of God is not based on physical acquaintance with Jesus or physical descent, but it is based on accepting the conditions of the kingdom—entering through the narrow gate. This, while leaving out many descendants of Abraham, Isaac and Jacob, will open the door for many Gentiles to feast with the patriarchs in the kingdom (Lk 13:28-29).

The comment made by an outsider as to the blessed state of those who feast in the kingdom of God (Lk 14:15) leads to the parable of the great banquet, in which, with a view to the Jewish rejection of Jesus and his message, the point is made that those called first were not worthy and were replaced by the sordid mob of Gentiles. Luke does not record the incident of the man who had no wedding apparel.

Luke too considers John's ministry as the beginning of a new era distinguished from that of the Law and the Prophets. It is the era of the proclamation of the kingdom of God when all people have the chance to force their way into it (Lk 16:16). This shows that Luke does not share the apocalyptic view of the kingdom of God as being introduced suddenly following great eschatological upheavals. The subject is broached by the Pharisees. The answer is that the kingdom does not come in a way open to physical observation (Lk 17:20). No one will be able to point to it as being here or there. The kingdom of God is "within you" (Lk 17:21; see 4.3.2 above). The view of the kingdom advocated here is one in which God is at work quietly in those who have accepted his claims and faithfully take on them the yoke of his will.

The kingdom of God must be accepted in childlike trust (Lk 18:16-17). By contrast, those who put their trust in their riches will not be able to enter into it (Lk 18:24-25). But to those who forsake everything for the kingdom of God a rich reward is promised, not only in the life to come but even in this world (Lk 18:29-30).

By relating the parable of the pounds, Luke has Jesus correct the popular notion that the kingdom of God was about to break out in the apocalyptic way (Lk 19:11). The point is that Jesus' hearers had rather see to it that they administer faithfully what was entrusted to them and wait quietly for its full realization than speculate on the time of its full arrival. Luke generally discourages such speculation (cf. Acts 1:6-8). Even in the prediction of the destruction of Jerusalem, only general signs are given for the arrival in power of God's kingdom (Lk 21:31). It

is obvious that Luke thinks of the kingdom of God as something that in a way has drawn near, so that from John's time onward people can prepare for it and be actively engaged in it, while in its full power it is something future, promised to appear after the fulfillment of certain events. Thus the apocalyptic element is not altogether absent from Luke.

That the kingdom can be spoken of as a future event is confirmed by the Last Supper, where Jesus promises to abstain from further eating and drinking until he can do so in the kingdom of God (Lk 22:16, 18).

Occasionally the kingdom is ascribed to Jesus as given to him by the Father (Lk 22:29-30). The context is again eschatological.

Finally, the thief on the cross asks to be remembered by Jesus when the latter comes in his kingdom (Lk 23:42), and Joseph of Arimathea is described as a man waiting for the kingdom of God (Lk 23:51), though it is by no means easy to decide whether his expectation was for a mundane or a transcendental kingdom.

5.4. John. The kingdom of God plays no significant role in *John's Gospel, its place being taken by the typically Johannine concept of "eternal life" (seventeen times) or simply "life" (nineteen times). The equivalence of eternal life with kingdom of God is proved from the occasional interchange of the two terms in the Synoptics (Mk 9:43-47 par.; 10:17-30 par.; Mt 25:31-46) and has its roots in rabbinic tradition (see Dalman, 116-17, 156-58). John's avoidance of the term "kingdom of God" may be owing to his desire to avoid association with current apocalyptic hopes. It may also be due to his writing for non-Jewish readers to whom a typically Jewish conception might pose communication problems, and especially because the term had been in rather rare use in the church, where the emphasis had been laid on Christ's person and work (christology and soteriology) as well as on the church (ecclesiology).

The concept "kingdom of God" occurs twice in the story of Nicodemus, and the expression "my kingdom" occurs three times in Jesus' answer to Pilate. In the incident with Nicodemus no indication is given that the kingdom of God had been the main emphasis in Jesus' teaching or even a subject of discussion. But with Nathanael's confession, "Rabbi . . . you are the king of Israel!" (Jn 1:49), the reader is, however, not totally unprepared.

At John 3:3, 5 Jesus tells Nicodemus that spiritual regeneration is the condition to seeing or entering the kingdom of God. From this it becomes obvious that the idea bears no relation to the Jewish national hope. It is the sovereignty of God under which people place themselves by accepting the message of Jesus in faith and undergoing a spiritual rebirth.

In Pilate's interrogation Jesus answers the question "Are you the king of Israel?" (Jn 18:33) by explaining that "my kingdom is not of this world" (Jn 18:36, "my kingdom" being repeated three times). No clearer statement than this could be made to show that the kingdom of which Jesus thought had very little relation to Israel's national expectation. This accusation, which stemmed from the Jews as well as from the *titulus* on the cross, indicates that in John's Gospel the rejection and condemnation of Jesus depended to a large extent on the Jews' disappointment by Jesus' refusal to accept the role of the national, political Messiah (see also Jn 6:15, 26).

6. The Kingdom of God and the Church Today.

Does the concept of the kingdom of God have any relevance for the present proclamation of the church? Here we are confronted with the kind of dilemma that led Bultmann to launch his controversial demythologization program.

In his proclamation of the kingdom of God, Jesus was standing firmly on OT ground. At the same time, he was proclaiming a subject that made every Jewish heart throb. Yet Jesus took this concept and transformed it from a narrow-minded nationalistic hope to a universal, spiritual order in which humankind could find the fulfillment of its ultimate desires for righteousness, justice, peace, happiness, freedom from sin and guilt, and a restored relationship to God—an order in which God was king. Given the fact that the basic human problem of sin and alienation from God is as true today as it ever has been, the message of the kingdom of God ought to have as great a relevance today as it ever had.

The kingdom of God need not be demythologized. But it is instructive to note that the early church, addressing primarily Gentile converts, avoided using a term loaded with Jewish national or apocalyptic connotations that might introduce confusion, seeking instead other dynamic equivalents such as "eternal life" or "salvation" as more appropriate, though "kingdom of God" did not disappear entirely from its lips. The

church continued to proclaim the legacy of its Master, but in dynamic forms. Every age has to find its own appropriate forms for expressing the ever-relevant message of Jesus on the kingdom of God. The forms may change but the essence remains.

See also APOCALYPTICISM; CHURCH; ESCHATOLOGY; ETHICS; HOLY SPIRIT; PARABLE.

DJG: DEMON, DEVIL, SATAN; GOSPEL [GOOD NEWS]; HEALING; JUBILEE; LIFE; REVOLUTIONARY MOVEMENTS; SERMON ON THE MOUNT.

BIBLIOGRAPHY. D. C. Allison, *The End of the Ages Has Come: An Early Interpretation of the Passion and Resurrection of Jesus* (Philadelphia: Fortress, 1987); G. R. Beasley-Murray, *Jesus and the Future* (London: Macmillan, 1954); idem, *Jesus and the Kingdom of God* (Grand Rapids: Eerdmans, 1986); C. C. Caragounis, *The Son of Man* (WUNT 38; Tübingen: J. C. B. Mohr, 1986); idem, "Kingdom of God, Son of Man and Jesus' Self-Understanding," *TynB* 40 (1989) 3-23; 40.2 (1989) 223-38; G. Dalman, *The Words of Jesus* (Edinburgh: T & T Clark, 1902); C. H. Dodd, *The Parables of the Kingdom* (rev. ed.; London: Collins, 1961); R. H. Fuller, *The Mission and Achievement of Jesus* (SBT 12; Naperville, IL: Allenson, 1954); E. Grässer, *Das Problem der Parusieverzögerung in den synoptischen Evangelien und in der Apostelgeschichte* (BZNW nr. 22; Berlin: A. Töpelman, 1957); R. H. Hiers, *The Historical Jesus and the Kingdom of God* (Gainesville: University of Florida Press, 1973); A. M. Hunter, *The Work and Words of Jesus* (rev. ed.; London: SCM, 1973); J. Jeremias, *The Parables of Jesus* (New York: Charles Scribner's, 1963); E. Jüngel, *Paulus und Jesus* (4th ed.; HUT; Tübingen: J. C. B. Mohr, 1972); W. G. Kümmel, *Promise and Fulfilment* (2d ed.; SBT 23; Naperville, IL: Allenson, 1961); G. E. Ladd, *The Presence of the Future* (Grand Rapids: Eerdmans, 1974); G. Lundström, *The Kingdom of God in the Teaching of Jesus* (London: Oliver and Boyd, 1963); J. P. Meier, *A Marginal Jew: Rethinking the Historical Jesus*, vol. 2: *Mentor, Message, and Miracles* (New York: Doubleday, 1994); M. Pamment, "The Kingdom of Heaven According to the First Gospel," *NTS* 27 (1981) 211-32; N. Perrin, *The Kingdom of God in the Teaching of Jesus* (Philadelphia: Westminster, 1963); idem, *Jesus and the Language of the Kingdom* (Philadelphia: Fortress, 1976); H. Ridderbos, *The Coming of the Kingdom* (Philadelphia: Presbyterian and Reformed, 1962); K. L. Schmidt et al., "Βασιλεύς κτλ," *TDNT* 1:564-93;

R. Schnackenburg, *God's Rule and Kingdom* (New York: Herder and Herder, 1963); E. Schürer, *The History of the Jewish People in the Age of Jesus Christ (175 B.C.-A.D. 135)*, rev. and ed. G. Vermes et al. (3 vols.; Edinburgh: T & T Clark, 1973-87); A. Schweitzer, *The Quest of the Historical Jesus* (London: A & C Black, 1910); W. Willis, ed., *The Kingdom of God in Twentieth-Century Interpretation* (Peabody, MA: Hendrickson, 1987); N. T. Wright, *Jesus and the Victory of God* (Minneapolis: Fortress, 1996).

C. C. Caragounis

KINGDOM OF GOD II: PAUL

The whole of Paul's theology is conditioned by a perspective that sees the eschatological promises of God as having been inaugurated through the resurrection of Jesus Christ from the dead. An important feature of this eschatological worldview is the teaching concerning the kingdom of God, which overlaps somewhat with the teaching about the kingdom of Christ in the Pauline materials. This overlap also provides a fertile ground for demonstrating how christology and eschatology interlock in Paul's thought.

1. Statistical Evidence
2. Is the Kingdom Present or Future?
3. Is the Kingdom of God the Same as the Kingdom of Christ?
4. The Deliverance of the Kingdom to God the Father
5. Transferral into the Kingdom of Christ

1. Statistical Evidence.

While the idea of the kingdom of God or kingdom of Christ is foundational to the whole of Paul's thought, it is somewhat surprising to discover the comparative rarity of explicit references to "the kingdom" within the Pauline letters. The term *basileia* ("reign," "kingdom") occurs only fifteen times (Rom 14:17; 1 Cor 4:20; 6:9, 10; 15:24, 50; Gal 5:21; Eph 5:5; Col 1:13; 4:11; 1 Thess 2:12; 2 Thess 1:5; 2 Tim 4:1, 14, 18), while the verb *basileuō* ("to reign") occurs nine times (Rom 5:14, 17 [twice], 21 [twice]; 6:12; 1 Cor 4:8 [twice]; 15:25), and the verb *symbasileuō* ("to reign with") occurs in 1 Timothy 2:12. The phrase "kingdom of God" or its equivalent occurs a mere eight times within the Pauline letters (Rom 14:17; 1 Cor 4:20; 6:9; 15:50; Gal 5:21; Col 4:11; 1 Thess 2:12 ["his kingdom"]; 2 Thess 1:5). The reference to "commonwealth in the heavens" *(to politeuma en ouranois)*

in Philippians 3:20 might also legitimately be understood as a parallel expression. Another startling fact is that within the Pauline corpus the kingdom of Christ is only explicitly described in Colossians 1:13 and Ephesians 5:5. This is remarkable given Paul's firm commitment to the messiahship of Jesus Christ and the frequent association of the kingdom with God's Messiah in Jewish OT and pseudepigraphal literature (see Kreitzer, 29-91, for details). Several key issues arise as one considers the teaching about the kingdom within the Pauline letters.

2. Is the Kingdom Present or Future?

NT scholarship has long discussed the temporal nature of the kingdom of God as it is found in the sayings of Jesus. A general consensus has been reached, namely, that the primary message of Jesus was one of an inaugurated kingdom, one that had already begun in his life and ministry but was awaiting consummation in the future. Many of the questions about the temporal nature of the kingdom as it is found in the Gospel materials also surface within the Pauline letters, despite the paucity of references to the kingdom as such. At times Paul speaks of the kingdom of God as if it were a present reality capable of being experienced by the Christian believers. Notably, two texts are expressive of this, Romans 14:17 and 1 Corinthians 4:20.

At other times Paul speaks of the kingdom of God as if it were a future hope, something that had yet to be awaited by the Christian believers. A good example of this is 1 Thessalonians 2:12, a verse sandwiched between two declarations of the parousia of Christ (1 Thess 1:10; 2:19). In 2 Thessalonians 1:5 the kingdom of God is described in terms of its being God's future vindication for those who endure suffering for their faith.

Again, in keeping with the future dimension of the kingdom of God, Paul often speaks of it as something that will be inherited by the faithful if they demonstrate the necessary character (1 Cor 6:9-10; 15:50; Gal 5:21). The language of future inheritance is also found in Colossians 3:24 (cf. Col 1:12). A similar declaration about inheritance is made in Ephesians 5:5, with the slight alteration that the kingdom is here described as belonging to God and Christ.

In short, the kingdom of God is something that straddles the dimensions of time, being present and future (as Martin, 109-25, affirms). It is not possible to restrict Paul's teaching about the kingdom of God/Christ to temporal terms. It is true that he tends to speak of the ultimate revelation of the kingdom as a future event, but there is ample evidence to support the contention that the power of this eschatological kingdom is also at work in the life of the Christian community now. Indeed, G. Johnson in his comment on 1 Corinthians 4:20 goes so far as to suggest that "in the last analysis the so-called 'eschatological' dimension of the kingdom has been relegated to a fairly minor place, and its present fact has been translated instead into the great concept of spiritual life" (Johnson, 151). Thus the kingdom of God/Christ might even be described as "life in the Spirit" or "life within the Body of Christ," both much more prominent themes within the Pauline letters.

3. Is the Kingdom of God the Same as the Kingdom of Christ?

Some scholars have suggested that Paul maintains a distinction between the kingdom of God and the kingdom of Christ, usually by pointing to 1 Corinthians 15:20-28 as a key text and postulating that the passage hints at a temporary messianic reign on earth that gives way to the kingdom of God in the fullness of time. Such a suggestion parallels a similar distinction between the two kingdoms found in select Jewish and Christian apocalypses of the NT period, namely, the *Apocalypse of Weeks* (*1 Enoch* 93:1-10; 91:12-17); 4 Ezra 7:26-30; 12:31-34; *2 Baruch* 29:3—30:1; 40:1-4; and Revelation 20:4-6 (see Kreitzer for a discussion).

A literal interpretation of passages such as these has yielded a "chiliastic," or "premillennial," strand of eschatology in the history of the Christian church. Some interpreters, such as A. Schweitzer, have appealed to Paul as an advocate of precisely this position, noting that a necessary corollary is a doctrine of two resurrections, one for the saints who participate in the temporary, messianic kingdom and the second a general resurrection for judgment before the age to come. Effectively this means that the kingdom of Christ commences with the parousia and concludes with the arrival of the kingdom of God (the age to come), and that the reign of the Messiah is the interval between the two resurrections associated with these two events.

However, it is not clear that Paul maintains a rigid distinction between the kingdom of God

and the kingdom of Christ throughout his letters or that he anywhere teaches a doctrine of two resurrections, although Luke has Paul speak of a resurrection of "the just and the unjust" in Acts 24:15. Consequently, most scholars dispute that Paul can be legitimately described as consistently chiliastic in his eschatological viewpoint (if he can be described as chiliastic at all). They point out that more often than not Paul's description of the consummation of God's kingdom is simply associated with the future parousia of Jesus Christ, with no forced dichotomy implied between the two kingdoms. In other words, it is denied that 1 Corinthians 15:20-28 teaches a temporary messianic kingdom, and the passage is effectively harmonized with other passages (such as 1 Cor 15:51-56 and 1 Thess 4:13-18) that describe the parousia of Christ in greater detail (G. Vos is a classic proponent of this approach).

Usually those following this interpretation take Christ's rule over the "kingdom," which he is said to hand over to the Father in 1 Corinthians 15:24, to have begun at the cross. This interpretation has the benefit of offering a Paul who is entirely coherent and uniform in his schematization of the future, avoiding presenting Paul as hopelessly confused or inconsistent in his teaching. However, the passage in 1 Corinthians 15:20-28 is anything but clear in its expression, and it is easy to see how a chiliastic interpretation might be derived from it. The question then arises whether we need Paul to be wholly consistent in the way that he describes how the kingdom of God relates to the kingdom of Christ and the parousia. A much more realistic approach is to accept the idea that flexibility of expression is inherent within all eschatological literature, including Paul's letters. Harmonization of eschatological detail, even in the aid of rescuing Paul from what is perceived to be a damaging inconsistency, is not the answer. We may be able to iron out all of the eschatological tensions and wrinkles within Pauline theology but in the process distance ourselves from Paul.

How then is it that the "kingdom of God" gives way to the "kingdom of Christ" as an expression of eschatological hope? If the basis of Paul's eschatology is the OT proclamation of the kingdom of God, how is it that this kingdom becomes explicitly described as the kingdom of Christ? Almost certainly this transition takes place as a result of the close association of Jesus of Nazareth and the kingdom of God that he came to proclaim. We see examples of just this sort of christological shift of emphasis in the redaction of the Gospels, and it is likely that the Pauline materials follow suit in this regard. As B. Klappert remarks: "The phrase '*basileia* of Christ' and the equation of 'kingdom of God' with Jesus Christ are thus seen to be the result of the change-over from an implicit to an explicit christology" (Klappert, 387).

4. The Deliverance of the Kingdom to God the Father.

In 1 Corinthians 15:20-28 we have one of the most difficult passages within the Pauline corpus to interpret, one that is filled with apocalyptic imagery and language (E. Käsemann's interpretation of Pauline apocalyptic eschatology is heavily dependent upon these verses). Contained within the passage is a curious reference to "the kingdom": "Then comes the end, when he delivers the kingdom to God the Father after destroying every rule and every authority and power" (1 Cor 15:24). One of the most frustrating features of this highly compressed pericope is the ambiguity of the subject of the verbs. For example, who is the subject of *hypetaxen* ("he subjected") in 1 Corinthians 15:27? Is it God or Christ? If it is assumed to be God, as in the NRSV, then some difficulties of understanding arise within the rest of the passage. One is never quite sure who is subjecting what to whom. No doubt the referential confusion between God and Christ is partly due to the christologically motivated use of Psalm 110:1 and Psalm 8:7b in 1 Corinthians 15:25, 27 respectively (de Boer, 114-20, offers some discussion of this).

A related item of exegetical significance is the connection between "the kingdom" and "the created order" *(ta panta)* within the passage. M. J. Harris associates the resurrection of the dead and the coming of the kingdom with the re-creation of the created order (*see* Creation, New Creation); the kingdom, he says, "incorporate(s) the rational and the irrational universe" (Harris, 18). Clearly there is an important cosmological dimension to this passage in addition to the more traditional temporal one that has been the focus of scholarly attention in the past.

5. Transferral into the Kingdom of Christ.

In Colossians 1:13-14 we have an unusual reference to the kingdom of Christ: "He [God] has delivered us from the dominion of darkness and transferred us to the kingdom of his beloved Son, in whom we have redemption, the forgiveness of sins." The remarkable thing about this passage is that the transferral is described as an act already accomplished, as realized within the life of the believer. This departure from the more characteristic description of the kingdom of God/Christ as a future reality yet to be awaited has led some interpreters to question Pauline authorship of the letter (see the commentaries by E. Lohse, E. Schweizer and P. T. O'Brien for a discussion of this; *see* Colossians, Letter to the).

In conclusion, while the explicit expression "kingdom of God/Christ" is not widespread within the Pauline letters, the idea is a fundamental component of Paul's eschatological perspective and underlies the whole of his teaching. The same tension between the present and future dimensions of a kingdom theology found to be present in the teaching of Jesus within the Synoptic Gospels is also contained within the Pauline materials. Perhaps even more significant within the Pauline letters is the fact that the idea of the "kingdom of God" affords an important vehicle for Paul's developing christology wherein the "kingdom of Christ" begins to compete with "kingdom of God" as the focal point of theological concern.

See also APOCALYPTICISM; CHRISTOLOGY; CREATION, NEW CREATION; ESCHATOLOGY; JESUS AND PAUL; RESURRECTION.

DPL: EXALTATION AND ENTHRONEMENT.

BIBLIOGRAPHY. M. C. de Boer, *The Defeat of Death* (JSNTSup 22; Sheffield: Academic Press, 1988); M. J. Harris, *Raised Immortal: The Relation Between Resurrection and Immortality in New Testament Teaching* (Grand Rapids: Eerdmans, 1983); G. Johnson, " 'Kingdom of God' Sayings in Paul's Epistles," in *From Jesus to Paul: Studies in Honor of Francis Wright Beare*, ed. P. Richardson and J. C. Hurd (Ontario: Wilfred Laurier University, 1984) 143-56; E. Käsemann, "Primitive Christian Apocalyptic," in *New Testament Questions of Today* (Philadelphia: Fortress, 1969) 108-37, esp. 133-37; B. Klappert, "King, Kingdom," *NIDNTT* 2:372-90; L. J. Kreitzer, *Jesus and God in Paul's Eschatology* (JSNTSup 19; Sheffield: Academic Press, 1987) 131-64; R. P. Martin, *The Spirit and the Congregation* (Grand Rapids: Eerdmans, 1984); A. Schweitzer, *The Mysticism of Paul the Apostle* (London: A & C Black, 1931); G. Vos, *The Pauline Eschatology*

(Princeton, NJ: Princeton University Press, 1930) 226-60.

L. J. Kreitzer

KINGDOM OF GOD III: ACTS, HEBREWS, GENERAL EPISTLES, REVELATION

Most of the writings under discussion show that the kingdom of God continued to be a vital theme in the preaching of the church. They maintain several characteristics of Jesus' conception of the kingdom of God, although sometimes they express them in new ways in adjustment to their new salvation-historical and missionary situations.

1. Acts
2. Hebrews
3. General Epistles
4. Revelation

1. Acts.

1.1. The Kingdom of God as the Central Theme of Acts. In the introduction to the book of Acts, the second volume of his two-volume work, Luke summarizes the teaching that the risen Jesus imparted to his apostles during the forty days before his ascension as having been about "the kingdom of God" (Acts 1:3). Luke concludes the volume with Paul's preaching of the "kingdom of God" and "about the Lord Jesus Christ" in the heart of the Roman Empire (Acts 28:31; see also Acts 28:23). With this *inclusio*, linking the beginning of the book's message with its ending, Luke appears to indicate that his central theme in the second volume is the kingdom of God in continuation with that in his first volume, the Gospel of Luke. This is confirmed by his summaries of the messages of Philip and Paul in terms of the kingdom of God in the main body of Acts (Acts 8:12; 19:8; 20:25; see also Acts 14:22; 17:7).

Yet Luke's combination of "the kingdom of God" with "the name of Jesus Christ" and with "the Lord Jesus Christ" as the gospel of Philip (Acts 8:12) and of Paul (Acts 28:23, 31) suggests a shift: in the Gospel of Luke the gospel of Jesus was about "the kingdom of God," but in Acts the gospel of the apostles includes the Lord Jesus Christ along with the kingdom of God. In his summaries of the apostolic preaching, Luke has as the object of the verb *euangelizomai* not only the kingdom of God (Acts 8:12) but also the Lord Jesus Christ (Acts 5:42; 8:35; 10:36; 11:20; 17:18; cf. Acts 15:35). Using the verb *kēryssō* to

summarize the apostolic preaching, he likewise specifies as the object of the verb Jesus the *Christ or the *Son of God (Acts 8:5; 9:20; 19:13; see also Acts 17:3, 7) as well as the kingdom of God (Acts 20:25; 28:31). These phenomena, especially those in the various summaries of Philip's gospel (Acts 8:5, 12, 35), suggest that the preaching of the kingdom of God was in effect the preaching of Christ Jesus. As is well known, Jesus' gospel of the kingdom of God in the Synoptic Gospels is generally replaced with the apostolic gospel of Christ in the rest of the NT, and the preacher Jesus in the former becomes the preached Christ in the latter. In Acts, Luke also reflects this general change and in his own way shows how and why this has taken place.

1.2. The Future Kingdom of God. The final coming of the kingdom of God is expected to be an event in the future, but we are not to be anxious to know its "times or dates [which] the Father has set in his authority" (Acts 1:6-7). It will be the "times of refreshing" or the "times of restoration of all things," and it will take place with the second coming of Christ (*see* Parousia) when all Israel repents (Acts 3:19-21). So the kingdom of God represents the consummation of salvation, and we must maintain faith and bear sufferings patiently "to enter the kingdom of God" (Acts 14:22).

1.3. The Lord Jesus Christ, the Present Regent and Savior. However, Luke is more concerned with the reign of God in the present. God's reign takes place in the present through the exalted Christ and the Holy Spirit. In his earthly existence Jesus was the agent through whom God did miracles, wonders and signs, or displayed his saving reign (Acts 2:22-23). God has raised this Jesus from the dead and exalted him to his right hand to be his viceroy in fulfillment of the promise of Psalm 110:1 (Acts 2:32-35; 5:31). So "God has made this Jesus . . . both Lord and Christ" (Acts 2:36). In Acts the title *Lord (kyrios)* is applied to Jesus as well as to God, with the implication that Jesus Christ now exercises God's lordship on his behalf. This is the reason the apostolic preaching of the kingdom of God regularly involves preaching Jesus' messianic kingship or lordship or occasionally is replaced by the latter.

In the OT it is Yahweh as the *kyrios* who forgives the sins of his people and saves them, but now it is Jesus the *kyrios* who exercises this divine prerogative. In the OT it was by calling on the name of Yahweh the Lord that one was saved (e.g., Joel 3:5 cited in Acts 2:21), but now this Lord is none other than Jesus Christ. So it is through the name of "Jesus Christ who is Lord of all" (Acts 10:36), "the judge of the living and the dead" (Acts 10:42), that forgiveness of sins or salvation is obtained (Acts 10:43; see also Acts 3:16; 4:12, 30; 16:18; 22:16).

The exalted Lord Jesus Christ's exercise of divine kingship or lordship is manifested in his direction of the church's mission. As the *Son of Man or the Lord standing at the right hand of God, he receives the spirit of his martyr Stephen (Acts 7:56, 59). He arrests Saul/Paul near Damascus and calls him to be his apostle to the Gentiles (Acts 9:1-19; 22:3-16; 26:9-18), assures Paul of his protection (Acts 18:9), redirects his mission (Acts 22:17-21) and leads him to Rome (Acts 23:11). The Lord Jesus Christ opens Lydia's heart to appropriate Paul's gospel (Acts 16:14-15), makes Christian mission in Antioch successful and leads a great number of people to turn to himself by faith (Acts 11:21). In his exercise of divine lordship, Jesus Christ uses the agency and power of the Holy Spirit and the ministry of his apostles.

1.4. Through the Agency and Power of the Spirit. God's exaltation of Jesus at his right hand involved not only mandating him with his lordship but also giving him his Holy Spirit and making him the dispenser of the divine Spirit: "Exalted to the right hand of God, [the Lord Jesus Christ] has received from the Father the promised Holy Spirit and has poured [the Spirit] out" (Acts 2:33). So, if through his exaltation God the Father made Jesus his vicegerent to exercise his kingship or lordship on his behalf, at Pentecost the Lord Jesus Christ poured out the Holy Spirit to be his agent and execute his kingship or lordship on his behalf. While the Lord Jesus Christ remains at the right hand of God in heaven until his second coming for "the restoration of all things" or the consummation of the kingdom of God (Acts 3:19-21), on earth the Holy Spirit exercises his lordship on his behalf. Thus there is a trinitarian structure in the present manifestation of the kingdom of God: God the Father reigns through his Son (Acts 9:20) Jesus Christ, who in turn reigns through the Holy Spirit. Hence the direction of the church and the mighty saving acts that are ascribed to the Lord Jesus Christ are also ascribed to the Spirit. They are the Lord Jesus Christ's ex-

ercise of God's reign through the agency of the Holy Spirit. Therefore they may be ascribed to the Spirit as well as to the Lord Jesus Christ.

So the Lord Jesus Christ's direction of the church is through the agency and power of the Spirit. Before his ascension he gave instructions to his apostles through the Holy Spirit (Acts 1:2). But after his ascension the apostles received the Holy Spirit given by the Lord Jesus Christ, and the Holy Spirit empowered and directed their mission (Acts 1:5, 8; 2:33). While there are references to the Lord Jesus Christ's directing and empowering the apostles' mission, there are parallel references to the Spirit's directing and empowering the apostles' mission: Acts 8:29; 10:19; 11:12, 28; 13:2, 4; 15:28; 16:6, 7; 19:21; 20:22, 23; 21:4, 11. That the two kinds of statements refer to the same reality is suggested in Acts 16:6-7: the Holy Spirit who directed Paul to leave Asia for Macedonia is explicitly identified as "the Spirit of Jesus." Paul concludes from this experience "that God had called [him] to preach the gospel" to the Macedonians (Acts 16:10). Thus Acts 16:6-10 implies the trinitarian structure of divine lordship exercised in regard to the church's mission.

During his earthly existence Jesus actualized God's saving reign through his exorcism and healing ministry that he wrought through the power of the Holy Spirit (Lk 11:20 par. Mt 12:28; Acts 2:22; 10:38). Now, as the exalted Lord, he has poured out the Holy Spirit to his church (Acts 2:33). Those who believe in him and are baptized in his name are given the Spirit (Acts 2:38; 9:17-18; 10:43-44; 11:16-17; 19:5-6; see Baptism) and thus are made to enjoy the blessings of the eschatological power of God in the sphere of Jesus Christ's lordship.

Further, the exalted Lord Jesus' dispensing the Holy Spirit to his apostles had the purpose of empowering them (Acts 1:8) to preach the gospel effectively and to perform many exorcisms and healing miracles as demonstrations of the eschatological salvation. Such "signs and wonders" are often said to have been performed by the apostles "in the name of Jesus Christ" (Acts 3:6, 16; 4:30; 8:6-12; 16:16-18; cf. Acts 19:13-20) or are attributed directly to God (Acts 15:12; 19:11-12) or to the Lord (Jesus?) (Acts 14:3). However, not only from Acts 1:8 and Acts 2:33 but also from Acts 4:29-31, Acts 6:8 and Acts 8:5-19 the clear implication is that the apostles performed the healing miracles through the power of the Holy Spirit given by the Lord Jesus Christ. So the Holy Spirit is the agent who actualizes the Lord Jesus Christ's saving reign, which is in reality God's saving reign. We are to respond affirmatively to the rhetorical question of J. D. G. Dunn: "If the Kingdom's presence in Jesus was determined by the coming of the Spirit upon Jesus at Jordan, then may we, indeed must we not say that the Kingdom became present in the disciples by the coming of the Spirit at Pentecost in the same way?" (Dunn, 40).

1.5. The Lord Jesus and His Apostles. Along with the Holy Spirit, the church, especially the twelve apostles, is also the agent that actualizes the kingdom of God or Christ in the present, or to be more precise, the church led and empowered by the Holy Spirit fulfills this role. In his Farewell Discourse, the earthly Jesus promised to vest by way of a covenant *(diatithemai)* the kingdom to the Twelve, just as the Father had vested it by way of a covenant *(dietheto)* to him, so that they might participate in Christ's kingdom and become rulers and judges over Israel (Lk 22:29-30). Through his death, which was the sacrifice for establishing the new covenant (Lk 22:20), Jesus fulfilled this promise and created a new people of God with the Twelve as the nucleus, in typological correspondence to Israel with the twelve tribes. Thus by way of a covenant he constituted a new people of God, a new people under God's kingship. Then the risen Christ taught them about the kingdom of God (Acts 1:3), empowered them with the Holy Spirit and commissioned them to bear witness to the kingdom of God or Christ (Acts 1:8; 2:1-36).

The twelve apostles, represented by Peter, and others like Stephen, Philip, Paul and Barnabas go to Judea, Samaria and the Gentile world as far as Rome, proclaiming the kingdom of God or the lordship of Christ and demonstrating the salvation of the kingdom ("signs and wonders" of exorcism and healing) through the power of the Holy Spirit. Those who respond to their gospel by repentance and faith are incorporated into the sphere under the lordship of Jesus Christ (i.e., the kingdom of God) by being baptized in the name of the Lord Jesus Christ, and they receive the blessings of the kingdom, the forgiveness of their sins and the eschatological power of the Holy Spirit (Acts 2:38; 19:5-6; 22:16). Thus through the mission of the church the kingdom of God or Christ is extended.

*1.6. The Messiah, the Kingdom of David or Isra-*el, *and the Twelve.* Along with the title *Kyrios,* the "Christ" (= Messiah) is used to designate Jesus as the regent in the kingdom of God: God has exalted the crucified Jesus to his right hand and made him both Lord and Christ (Acts 2:33, 38). This exaltation as the Messiah means Jesus' enthronement on the throne of David in fulfillment of God's promise to David (Acts 2:30; 13:23, 32-39; cf. 2 Sam 7:12-14). As such it represents the restoration of "David's fallen tent" (Acts 15:16), and "the remnant" of the Jews who "seek the Lord" and "all the Gentiles who bear [Christ's] name" are the eschatological people of God, the restored kingdom of David or Israel, over which Jesus the Davidic Messiah reigns (Acts 15:17). The twelve apostles are set as his representatives so that they may rule and judge them in his name (Lk 22:30). However, this restored kingdom of David or Israel, is not to be thought of in terms of a Jewish nationalistic political system, as it was in some of the contemporary Jewish parties (Acts 1:6). Instead it is to be thought of in terms of a community of the Jews and the Gentiles who call on the name of the Lord (i.e., submit to the kingship of Jesus the Messiah, who represents the kingship of Yahweh [Acts 2:21]).

1.7. Conclusion. In Acts, Luke records the salvation history of God's exaltation of Jesus at his right hand to execute his lordship and kingship, of the Lord Jesus Christ's execution of God's kingship or lordship through the Holy Spirit and his church, and of the Jewish and Gentile believers being brought into the kingdom of God or Christ for salvation. Luke concentrates on the present manifestation of the kingdom but views it as a process toward the consummation, "the restoration of all things," at the parousia of Christ.

2. Hebrews.

2.1. The Kingdom of God. In Hebrews there is only one explicit reference to the kingdom of God: "Since we are receiving an unshakable kingdom, let us be thankful and so worship God acceptably with reverence and awe" (Heb 12:28). Here "kingdom" does not seem to refer to God's kingly reign, and the verse does not seem to have in view either our submitting to it or our sharing in it.

Throughout the epistle there is little teaching about God's kingly rule. Rather, "kingdom" seems to be used as a synonym for "the city of

God" (Heb 11:10, 16; 12:22), "the city that is to come" (Heb 13:14), "Mount Zion" or "the heavenly Jerusalem" (Heb 12:22), and the "fatherland" (Heb 11:14). Like these terms, "kingdom" seems to denote the place where God reigns and the believers are to obtain the blissful rest (*katapausis,* Heb 3:11, 18; 4:1, 3, 5, 10-11; *sabbatismos,* Heb 4:9), the consummation of their salvation.

To be sure, God's heavenly "throne" is referred to (Heb 4:16; 8:1; 12:2). In the formulation "the throne of the Majesty" *(megalōsynēs)* in heaven (Heb 8:1) there may be a connotation of divine power or sovereignty, and from the contrast between the cross Jesus endured and the divine throne Jesus eventually obtained (Heb 12:2) we may discern a similar connotation of the divine throne. However, in both cases the connotation cannot be said to be strong. In Hebrews 8:1 as well as in Hebrews 4:16 the cultic meaning of the divine throne is much more prominent than is its political meaning.

2.2. Jesus Christ Exalted to the Right Hand of God's Throne.

A similar phenomenon takes place with reference to Jesus Christ. It belongs to the central theme of Hebrews that Jesus Christ was exalted to sit at the right hand of God or his throne in fulfillment of Psalm 110:1 (Heb 1:3, 13; 8:1; 10:12; 12:2). Besides the fact that in several books of the NT, Psalm 110:1 functions prominently to substantiate the lordship or kingship that the exalted Jesus Christ has come to exercise on God's behalf, several factors in Hebrews point to a political connotation of the theme. (1) It is accompanied by references to God's appointment of Jesus as his Son, his "heir of all things" in fulfillment of Psalm 2:7-8 (Heb 1:2, 5; 5:5; 7:28) and 2 Samuel 7:14 (Heb 1:5), which were interpreted as prophecies for the messianic king in Judaism and in the early church. (2) Psalm 45:6-7 and Psalm 8:4-6 are applied to Christ respectively in Hebrews 1:8-9 and Hebrews 2:6-8 to emphasize his exaltation to universal kingship or lordship. Note especially the language of the former:

> Your throne, O God, will last for ever and ever, and righteousness will be the scepter of your kingdom.
>
> You have loved righteousness and hated wickedness; therefore God, your God, has set you above your companions by anointing you with the oil of joy.

(3) Christ is said to be "faithful as a son over God's house," in contrast to Moses, who was faithful as a servant (Heb 3:5-6). (4) The name *Melchizedek* is interpreted in terms of "king of Salem [or peace]" and "king of righteousness" (Heb 7:1-3), in whose order Christ is supposed to have been appointed the high priest (Heb 5:6; 7:13-28). These factors clearly indicate that in Hebrews there is an understanding of Jesus Christ as the messianic king who exercises divine kingship on God's behalf. Here may be involved something more than a simple reflection of the primitive church's common kerygma. The statement in Hebrews 2:3-4 appears to reflect Jesus' ministry of kingdom preaching and healing (e.g., Mt 12:28 par. Lk 11:20). Further, it is possible that the presentation of the consummation of salvation in terms of the sabbath rest in this epistle (Heb 4:9) reflects Jesus' ministry of healing on the sabbath as a proleptic actualization of the sabbath perfection or the restored creation in the kingdom of God.

However, it can hardly be said that the theme of Jesus' messianic kingship is expounded in the epistle. As little is said about the reign of the exalted Lord Jesus Christ over his people or the world as is said about God's reign. Since his exaltation to the right hand of God, Christ waits for his enemies to be made his footstool (Heb 10:13; cf. Ps 110:1). Beyond affirming his exaltation to universal kingship, this is all that is said about the exalted Christ's current political activity. Instead, the exaltation of Christ to the right hand of God is expounded almost exclusively in terms of his ministry as the high priest (cf. Davies, 388-89), just as God's throne in the heavenly sanctuary is almost exclusively interpreted in its cultic significance. Having entered the holy of holies once for all by his own blood, obtaining eternal redemption for us (Heb 9:12) and mediating the new covenant (Heb 8:6-13; 9:15-22), Christ now serves in the heavenly sanctuary as the high priest, interceding for us (Heb 2:17-18; 4:14-16; 7:25; 8:1-2; 9:24; 10:19-22).

2.3. Based on the Jesus Tradition?

Hebrews's exposition of God's throne in the heavenly sanctuary and of Christ's exaltation to the right hand of it chiefly in terms of their cultic significance, while retaining their political significance in the background, is based on the common conception of the temple both as the sanctuary where God is worshiped and as the palace from which God reigns (cf. Hengel and Schwemer). Jesus also combined the concept of the kingdom of God and the temple: he sometimes pictured the former in terms of the latter (cf. Aalen), and concluded his kingdom preaching with a sign-act for God's impending destruction of the Jerusalem temple and for his building a new temple (Mk 11:15 par.; Mk 14:58 par.).

Even if *cheiropoiētos* ("made with hands") or *acheiropoiētos* ("not made with hands") in Mark 14:58 should be inauthentic, the appearance of the vocabulary in Acts 7:48 and Hebrews 9:11, 24 as well as Mark 14:58 suggests that it was part of a common early church tradition to express with this vocabulary a contrast between the Jerusalem temple and the new worship made possible by Jesus Christ. Then it appears that the idea of Christ's entering "the greater and more perfect tabernacle that is not made with hands" (Heb 9:11), the heavenly reality of which the Jerusalem temple or its predecessor (the wilderness tabernacle) "made with hands" was only a copy and a shadow (Heb 8:2, 5; 9:24), reflects this common tradition.

Since Hebrews shows some awareness of the Jesus tradition (e.g., Heb 2:3-4; 5:7-8; 13:12), it is possible that beyond the common tradition the author was aware of Jesus' negative attitude to the Jerusalem temple and his claim to build a new temple as part of his kingdom preaching. Thus the genius of the author may lie in his systematic exposition of the cultic element at least secondarily present in Jesus' kingdom preaching (cf. Gaston, 65-243) in the light of Psalm 110:1, 4. If so, his gospel is also based ultimately on Jesus' gospel of the kingdom of God.

2.4. Already but Not Yet. The believers are to receive "an unshakable kingdom" (Heb 12:28), that is, "the heavenly Jerusalem," "the city of God." In the "kingdom," "city" (e.g., Heb 11:10) or sanctuary (Heb 6:19-20) of God there is to be the sabbath rest (Heb 4:9) and the festival that God's people celebrate with myriads of angels. They are at present on pilgrimage toward it, and they must press forward by faith and with perseverance, following Jesus Christ, "the pioneer and perfecter of our faith" (Heb 12:2). Yet by appropriating Christ's atonement and new covenant, in a real sense they "have [already] come to Mount Zion, to the city of the living God, the heavenly Jerusalem" to celebrate the sabbath in the festal gathering of angels and saints (Heb 12:22-23). Besides the tension between the "already" and the "not yet," a tension that is characteristic of NT eschatology as a whole, we may observe that this imagery is not far from Jesus'

favorite picture of a feast for the kingdom of God and from his actualization of the salvation of the kingdom of God through his healing ministry on the sabbath.

3. General Epistles.

In the rest of the General Epistles, the term "the kingdom [of God]" appears only in James 2:5 and 2 Peter 1:11; related concepts are found in 1 Peter 2:4-10.

In 2 Peter 1:11 the readers are exhorted to cultivate Christian virtues so that they may be "provided with an entrance into the eternal kingdom of our Lord and Savior Jesus Christ." It is possible that in 1 Peter 2 the ideas of the church as the "spiritual house" or the temple founded on the cornerstone or a foundation stone (1 Pet 2:4-8) and as "a chosen race, a royal house, a priesthood, a holy nation, a people for God's possession" (1 Pet 2:9; Ex 19:6) reflect what Jesus aimed at in his kingdom preaching and temple saying: to create a new, eschatological people of God or to build a new "temple."

Reminding the readers that God has chosen the poor "to be rich in faith and to inherit the kingdom he promised to those who love him" (Jas 2:5), James urges them to keep "the royal law" *(nomos basilikos)*, "Love your neighbor as yourself" (Jas 2:8). He also warns them with a contrasting picture of the rich: they are those who exploit others and slander the name of God (Jas 2:6-7). Here Jesus' language is clearly echoed in the idioms "the poor" (Lk 4:18; Mt 5:3 par. Lk 6:20) and "to inherit the kingdom" (e.g., Mt 5:5; 25:34).

Jesus' teaching is also clearly reflected: Jesus gave as the law of the kingdom the double command of love: love your God with your whole being and your neighbor as yourself (Mt 22:34-40 par.) and concretized it (e.g., in the Sermon on the Mount or Plain [Mt 5—7 par. Lk 6:20-49]). The rich violate this law of the kingdom, or "the royal law": instead of loving God, they slander the name of God and love rather the idol Mammon (cf. Mt 6:24 par. Lk 16:13) and so inevitably exploit their neighbors. In consequence, they are excluded from the kingdom of God. In contrast, "the poor" are rich in faith: they rely on God and love him, and so they love their neighbors too. Thus they prove themselves to be people of the kingdom of God, and they are to "inherit the kingdom" when it comes in its consummation. The contrast between the poor and the rich echoes closely the Beatitudes in the Lukan form (Lk 6:20-26). The poor will inherit the kingdom, it is implied, when the Lord comes as the judge, and so they are to wait patiently, as "the Lord's Parousia is at hand" (Jas 5:7-9).

4. Revelation.

"The kingdom of God" is the theme of Revelation, and so to study it is to survey the whole content of the book (*see* Revelation, Book of).

4.1. The Kingdom of God in Heaven. God, as "the Alpha and the Omega" and "the First and the Last," is the Creator and goal of all things and, as the *pantokratōr* ("all-sovereign" or "almighty"), is the sovereign Lord of the whole universe. He is "the One who sits on the throne" in heaven, and from there he directs the course of history. This fact is dramatically presented to the seer John in a vision described in Revelation 4.

In the vision, John sees God sitting on the heavenly throne and receiving the worship of the "four living creatures" and the "twenty-four elders." In the heavenly throne room, the prototype of the holy of holies in the earthly temple, the four living creatures, appearing respectively like a lion, an ox, a human being and an eagle, as representatives of all creatures, worship God on the throne. In their hymn the holiness of the eternal and sovereign God is highlighted. God the Creator and Ruler of the whole universe is properly hallowed (Rev 4:8). The "twenty-four elders," the angelic beings who make up the heavenly council and rule the heavenly sphere on God's behalf, also worship God, acknowledging the sovereign will and power of the Creator (Rev 4:11). So John sees that in heaven God's name is hallowed, he reigns, and his will is done (cf. Mt 6:9-10).

4.2. The Kingdom of Satan. However, on earth Satan (the dragon or serpent), the primeval adversary of God and the supernatural source of all evils, reigns, misleading all the nations with falsehood to worship him instead of the true God (Rev 12). John sees this reign of Satan taking a concrete form in the tyrannical and exploitative Roman Empire: the Roman imperial power incorporated in the emperor is the beast or sea monster that rules the world on behalf of the dragon (Rev 13; 17). The dragon, the beast and the second beast or land monster that persuades nations to worship the beast are a parody of the triune God, the Father, the Son and the Holy Spirit. The satanic trinity forces the nations to submit to the imperial cult by deceiving them with the wine of the harlot of Babylon (i.e., the ideology of *pax romana,* Rev 17), as well as by overwhelming them with the apparently invincible power of the Roman Empire (Rev 13).

Thus on earth the Roman emperor masquerades as god, and so the name of the true God is not hallowed, his reign is usurped, and his will is not done.

4.3. The Kingdom of God on Earth: The Christ Event (Already). God, "who is and who was," "is to come" to earth in order to establish his rightful kingship, destroying the satanic forces. This is the main message of Revelation. John is sure of this because he saw in a vision the heavenly reality of God's triumph through Jesus Christ, which is to be unfolded on earth (Rev 5). In a real sense God has already come and triumphed in Jesus Christ. As the one who bears his names ("the First and the Last," "the Alpha and the Omega" and "the Beginning and the End") and shares his throne, Christ is the agent of God who establishes God's kingship on earth. He is the one who turns "the kingdom of the world" into "the kingdom of our Lord and his Christ" (Rev 11:15). Christ is completely identified with God, so that God's future coming for salvation and judgment is none other than Christ's (Rev 22:12, 20).

This Christ has already come and conquered the satanic forces and is now enthroned in heaven (Rev 3:21). For Christ's conflict with the satanic forces and his redemption of humankind, John uses two metaphors: the messianic war and the exodus. Jesus is the Messiah, "the Lion of the tribe of Judah, the root of David" (Rev 5:5; 22:16) and has overcome the rebellious nations (cf. Ps 2:8-9) with a sharp two-edged sword issuing from his mouth (cf. Is 49:2; Rev 1:16; 2:12, 16; 19:11, 15, 21). Jesus is the Passover Lamb (Rev 5:6, 9-11) who by his blood has ransomed a people from all the nations of the world and "made them a kingdom and priests to serve God" (Rev 5:9-10; cf. Ex 19:5-6).

Jesus Christ has conquered the satanic forces by bearing a faithful witness to God and then by his death (*see* Death of Christ). Jesus Christ was "the faithful and true witness" to God even unto his death (Rev 3:14; cf. Rev 1:5; 12:17; 19:10). This must refer to Jesus' proclamation of the kingdom of God during his earthly life. But the decisive victory was by his death. This is made clear in the vision of Revelation 5 (Bauckham): in Revelation

5:5 it is declared that Jesus as the Davidic Messiah has triumphed, but in the subsequent verses this triumphant Messiah appears as a Lamb slaughtered, standing in the center of the divine throne and receiving the worship of the four living creatures and the twenty-four elders. Then a myriad of angels and eventually all creatures in the universe are seen joining in their worship and praising him for his triumph won through his sacrificial death. In Revelation 12:5-12 Christ's decisive victory over Satan through his death is depicted in two vivid pictures: Christ is enthroned in heaven while Satan is driven out of heaven and cast down to the earth.

This is in complete agreement with Jesus or the Gospels: Jesus Christ has triumphed over the satanic forces through his preaching of the kingdom of God and his sacrificial death on the cross. Again in full agreement with Jesus' own teaching or the testimonies of the Gospels, the result of Jesus' victory over the satanic forces is the creation of the people of God, a people he has ransomed from the kingdom of Satan and made "a kingdom and priests to serve God" (Rev 5:10). They are the people over whom God reigns as King, or they are the kingdom of God that has already come into being. In this way Jesus Christ has already brought about the kingdom of God.

Thus Jesus has fulfilled the OT or Jewish expectation of the Davidic Messiah. However, again in agreement with Jesus or the Gospels, John also reinterprets messiahship. Jesus' messianic victory was a victory over the evil forces of Satan (Rev 12:7-9) rather than the Gentile nations as such. The means of his victory was his witness to truth or to the true God and his sacrificial death rather than military conquest. And the people gathered into the kingdom of God to share in God's reign was not the Jewish nation but a new people of God who would hold faithfully to "the testimony of Jesus" or faithfully adhere to the kingdom of God that Jesus proclaimed (Rev 12:17; 17:6; 19:10).

By describing the vision of God enthroned in heaven and of Jesus Christ as the Lamb slain to establish his kingdom on earth (Rev 4—5), John presents an image of God who rules in self-giving love and righteousness over against the satanic forces, who rule by self-assertion and oppression. Because God reigns in love, his kingship means salvation for humankind, and the message of his coming to establish his king-ship is the gospel. Thus the message of John is the same as the gospel of Jesus, the Evangelists and Paul.

4.4. The Kingdom of God in or Through the Church (Now). The church or the people of God ransomed from the kingdom of Satan through Christ's sacrificial death is the kingdom of God present on earth (Rev 1:6; 5:10). The Christians make Christ's triumph over the satanic forces effective on earth. In parallel to the work of Christ, this role of the church is pictured in terms of the messianic war. The dragon, which has been conquered at Christ's death and cast down from heaven, now tyrannizes the world through the sea beast and the land beast. With Satan's authority and at his behest, the emperors and the local rulers of the Roman Empire make war against the church (Rev 12:13-13:18). The church is the army of the Messiah, numbering 144,000, drawn from the twelve tribes of Israel (Rev 7:4-8; i.e., 12 x 12 x 1,000—all symbolic ciphers). The risen Christ, the victorious Lamb, is present with his church (Rev 1:13; 2:1) and leads it as his army (Rev 14:1, 4; 17:14) into the battle against the satanic trinity, empowering the church with the Holy Spirit, which is his power operating in the world (Rev 3:1; 5:6).

Again in parallel to the work of Christ, the church's holy war against the satanic forces is cast in terms not of a military conquest but a witness to the kingship of God or Christ and Jesus' sacrificial death (Rev 11:1-13; 12:11). The Christians are an army, but an army of the Lamb slain (Rev 14:1-5). As such they participate in the Lamb's victory over the satanic forces through their martyrdom, which is their participation in the Lamb's sacrificial death (Rev 7:14). Their holy war consists in continuing the "testimony of Jesus" to the kingship of the true God (Rev 12:17; 19:10) and resisting the idolatry of the false god, the beast.

The persecution of the beast (the Roman imperial power) is fierce, and the deception of the harlot of Babylon (the ideology of *pax romana*) is seductive. Yet the church is empowered by the Spirit of prophecy (Rev 11:3-6; 19:10), and its faithful witness to the kingship of the true God and the Lamb unto death among all the nations brings about the conversion of the nations from idolatry to the worship of the true God (Rev 11:13; 15:2-4). Thus God's kingship is made effective over the nations at present through the church's witness.

665

4.5. The Consummation of the Kingdom at the Parousia of Christ (Future). However, there remain those who neither heed God's warning judgments (the two series of judgments: Rev 6:1-17; 8:1, 3-5; 8:2, 6-11; 11:14-19) nor accept the church's witness. They continue to be under the rule of the satanic trinity so long as the latter exists, blaspheming against God and coercing and deluding nations into their worship. The saints continue to suffer under their tyranny, and even the souls of those who have already been martyred must wait for the consummation of their salvation and the judgment of the wicked (Rev 6:9-11).

The consummation of salvation and judgment is to take place with the parousia of Christ. Christ will come as "King of kings and Lord of lords" (Rev 17:14; 19:16) and finish off the holy war against the satanic forces. There will be the final judgment (Rev 15:1, 5—16:21), in which Babylon, the satanic regime, will fall (Rev 16:16—18:24), the rulers of the world allied with it will be destroyed (Rev 19:17-21) and the wicked will be condemned (Rev 14:17-20; 17:12-14; 19:15). The satanic trinity of the dragon, the beast and the false prophet themselves will be destroyed (Rev 19:19—20:10). But the saints will be harvested into Christ's kingdom (Rev 14:15-16).

John depicts the destruction of the dragon, Satan, in two stages and accordingly the consummation of the salvation of the saints also in two stages. The dragon is first to be captured and locked in the abyss for a thousand years, and during that period only the martyrs are to be resurrected to participate in Christ's reign. Then Satan is to be released to muster Gog and Magog (from Ezek) for the final battle against God's people, only to be cast into the lake of fire forever. Together with Satan, death and hades are to be destroyed. This results in the general resurrection and the last judgment of all the dead (Rev 20:1-10). It is disputed whether this picture of the millennial kingdom of Christ should be interpreted in such a way as to be identified with any objective period in the eschaton (e.g., premillennialism and postmillennialism), beyond making the theological point that unlike the paradise of the *Urzeit*, the universe restored under God's kingship at the *Endzeit* is no longer vulnerable to Satan (Bauckham).

Then John depicts the consummation of the kingdom of God in terms of a new creation, "a new heaven and a new earth" and "the Holy City, the new Jerusalem, coming down out of heaven from God" (Rev 21:1—22:5). The new creation is more than just a restoration of the original creation. In it there will be "no longer any sea" (Rev 21:1), whereas in the first creation the "sea," the primeval source of evil (cf. Rev 13:1), remained as the potential threat to the cosmos (Gen 1:2; 7:11).

Filled with God's presence, the new creation will be the city of God, the new Jerusalem, and also the temple where God and the Lamb will be enthroned. There God will dwell with his people, and those who "conquer" by faith in Christ will be his people and will dwell with God. There will be no more death but only the fullness of life, as the "river of the water of life" will flow from the throne of God and the Lamb and the fruits of "the tree of life" will be available. There will be no more darkness, but the glory of God and the Lamb will enlighten the whole city. There will be no more satanic deception and impurity (Rev 21:27), but God's Word and his truth will prevail (Rev 19:11, 13). God's people as his children will inherit all these blessings and participate in God's reign, and the nations will come with their treasures to worship God and walk by his light, in fulfillment of the prophecies of the OT prophets and Jesus. So will the kingdom of God be consummated and God's intent in his creation and covenant be fulfilled.

4.6. Conclusion. Revelation presents a faithful interpretation of Jesus' gospel of the kingdom of God in the light of Christ's death, resurrection and exaltation and a creative contextualization of it to the latter half of the first century in which the Roman Empire appeared as the incarnation of the satanic kingdom.

See also ESCHATOLOGY; GOD; LORD.

DLNTD: ASCENSION; CREATION, COSMOLOGY; EXALTATION, ENTHRONEMENT; GLORY; HEAVEN, NEW HEAVEN; LAND IN EARLY CHRISTIANITY; MILLENNIUM; PAROUSIA.

BIBLIOGRAPHY. S. Aalen, " 'Reign' and 'House' in the Gospels," *NTS* 8 (1961-62) 215-40; R. J. Bauckham, *The Climax of Prophecy: Studies on the Book of Revelation* (Edinburgh: T & T Clark, 1992); G. R. Beasley-Murray, *The Book of Revelation* (Grand Rapids: Eerdmans, 1983); F. F. Bruce, *The Acts of the Apostles* (Grand Rapids: Eerdmans, 1990); P. H. Davids, *Commentary on James* (NIGTC; Grand Rapids: Eerdmans, 1982); J. H. Davies, "The Heavenly Work of Christ in Hebrews," *SE* 4 (1968) 384-89; J. D. G. Dunn, "Spirit and Kingdom," *ExpT* 82 (1970-71) 36-40; P. Ellingworth, *Commentary on Hebrews* (NIGTC; Grand Rapids: Eerdmans, 1993); L. Gaston, *No Stone on Another* (Leiden: E. J. Brill, 1970); M. Hengel and A. M. Schwemer, eds., *Königsherrschaft Gottes und himmlischer Kult* (Tübingen: J. C. B. Mohr, 1991); W. L. Lane, *Hebrews* (2 vols.; WBC; Dallas: Word, 1991); I. H. Marshall, *Luke: Historian and Theologian* (Exeter: Paternoster, 1970).

S. Kim

KINGDOM OF HEAVEN. *See* KINGDOM OF GOD I.

L

L TRADITION. *See* SYNOPTIC PROBLEM.

LAST ADAM. *See* ADAM AND CHRIST.

LAST SUPPER: GOSPELS

In the history of the Christian church a number of different terms have been associated with the Last Supper. Some of these, such as the "breaking of bread" (Acts 2:42, 46; 20:7, 11), the "eucharist" (Mt 26:27; Mk 14:23; Lk 22:17, 19; 1 Cor 11:24), the "table of the Lord" (1 Cor 10:21), "communion" (1 Cor 10:16) and the "Lord's Supper" (1 Cor 11:20) stem from the NT. Others, such as the "mass" (from the Latin ending of the Roman rite—*Ite, missa est*—"Go, you are dismissed") and the "Last Supper," do not.

Within the NT there are a number of references and allusions to the Last Supper (1 Cor 10:1-22; 11:20-22; Lk 24:30; Acts 27:35; Mk 6:41; 8:6; Jn 6:25-59; 19:34; Acts 2:42, 46; 20:7, 11), but the most important are the four accounts in Matthew 26:26-29, Mark 14:22-25, Luke 22:15-20 and 1 Corinthians 11:23-26, the latter being the oldest written account.

1. Earliest Church Tradition and Gospel Accounts
2. Historical Background
3. The Last Supper in the Context of Passover
4. The Four Words of the Last Supper
5. The Celebration of the Supper

1. Earliest Church Tradition and Gospel Accounts.

In Paul's first letter to the Corinthians, written sometime during the mid-fifties, he refers to a tradition that he received from the Lord. By this he means that ultimately the tradition of the Last Supper comes from Jesus, but by his use of the terms *received* and *delivered* it is clear that he is referring to a tradition that he was taught by the church. ("Received" and "delivered" were technical terms used to describe the passing on of oral tradition; cf. Lk 1:2; 1 Cor 15:3.) Whether this tradition was "received" from the church in Antioch (Acts 11:26) in the mid-forties or from the church in Damascus (Acts 9:19; Gal 1:17) in the mid-thirties is uncertain. The Gospel accounts date most probably from A.D. 65-90.

The four accounts of the Last Supper fall into two distinct groups representing two specific forms of the tradition. These are Matthew 26:26-29/Mark 14:22-25 and Luke 22:15-20/1 Corinthians 11:23-26. The two forms may be characterized as follows:

The Lukan account is the most unusual of the four. It alone mentions the cup before the bread (Lk 22:17) and has the word about the fu-

Matthew/Mark	Luke/1 Corinthians
"blessed" bread _____	"gave thanks" bread
"Take" _____	[lack "Take"]
"this is my body" _____	"this is my body + which is . . . you"
[lack "This do in my _____ remembrance"]	"This do in my remembrance"
"this" _____	"this cup"
"thanks" before cup _____	[lack "thanks" before cup]
reference to all _____	lack reference to all
drinking of the cup _____	[drinking of the cup]
"my blood of the _____ covenant"	"new covenant in my blood"
"which is poured out for __ many"	Luke has "which is poured out for you" [not in 1 Cor]

ture kingdom (*see* Kingdom of God) at the beginning of the supper (Lk 22:16) rather than at the end as in the other accounts. There is also a textual problem in the Lukan account in that a few significant manuscripts, mainly Codex Bezae and several old Latin manuscripts, omit Luke 22:19b and 20, " 'which is given for you. This do in my remembrance.' And the cup likewise after Supper, saying, 'This cup is the new covenant in my blood which is poured out for you.'" The main arguments in favor of this shorter text are (1) the unusual nature of the reading. It is clearly the more difficult reading, for it is unlikely that a scribe would have wanted to omit the more traditional ending. (2) It is a shorter reading, which on textual-critical principles would generally be the preferred reading. This is especially true here in the case of a Western noninterpolation (i.e., a reading not found in the Western family of manuscripts), and such shorter readings are contrary to the tendency of the Western scribal tradition. Nevertheless, the overall manuscript evidence favoring the inclusion of Luke 22:19b-20 is far too strong to be ignored, and it would appear that somewhere in the manuscript tradition a scribe was confused by the cup-bread-cup sequence in Luke and omitted the second mention of the cup.

2. Historical Background.
A number of historical issues present themselves in any proper understanding of the Last Supper. All four accounts indicate that the Supper was celebrated "on the night in which he was betrayed" (1 Cor 11:23). This is specifically stated in the Pauline version of the Last Supper, but each Gospel also indicates that on the night of the Last Supper Jesus announced his betrayal and went to Gethsemane, where he was betrayed (Mt 26:21-25, 36-56; Mk 14:18-21, 32-42; Lk 22:21-23, 39-53).

2.1. The Problem of Mark 14:12. In this verse we encounter a difficulty with regard to the dating of the supper. Mark states, "And on the first day of Unleavened Bread when they were sacrificing the Passover lamb, his disciples say to him, 'Where do you wish that we should go and prepare in order that you might eat the Passover?' " The Passover, which was the first day of the Feast of Unleavened Bread, was celebrated on the fifteenth of Nisan. The sacrifice of the Passover lambs, however, took place on the fourteenth of Nisan, when the ritual search for leaven took place. Most probably Mark is not using technical terminology here. In the more popular understanding this technical distinction was lost, for the beginning of the Feast of Unleavened Bread took place on the preceding day

when preparations such as the slaughtering of the Passover lamb and the search for leaven took place. Mark, in his description, has done what individuals today do when they speak of celebrating Christmas on Christmas Eve when presents are exchanged. Mark 14:12 is best understood in a similar way as a popular, inexact designation (cf. Josephus *J.W.* 5.3.1 for a similar reference to the fourteenth of Nisan as the beginning of the Feast of Unleavened Bread).

2.2. Was the Last Supper Associated with a Passover Meal? It is clear in all four Gospels that the crucifixion of Jesus took place on a Friday (Mt 27:62; Mk 15:42; Lk 23:54; Jn 19:31, 42). This, of course, means before 6 P.M. Friday, for in the Jewish reckoning of time this marks the end of Friday and the start of Saturday. The cardinal question regarding the date of the Last Supper involves whether it was in fact associated with a Passover meal. This would appear to be certain from Matthew 26:17-19; Mark 14:12-16 and Luke 22:7-15. But John 13:1, 29; 18:28; 19:31 give the impression that the trial and crucifixion took place before the Passover. Thus from John it appears that the Last Supper must have taken place on or before the fourteenth of Nisan. There have been numerous attempts to explain this. Some of these are:

(1) The Synoptic Gospels are correct. The Last Supper was a Passover meal. The term *Passover* in John 18:28 does not refer to the Passover lamb but to later feasts and sacrifices associated with the Feast of Unleavened Bread.

(2) John is correct. Jesus did not eat the customary Passover meal with his disciples but anticipated it and ate it earlier because he knew he would be dead at the time of the Passover. John 18:28, however, refers to the actual Passover.

(3) Both the Synoptic Gospels and John are correct, because the Passover was celebrated that year on two separate days.

Several objections have been raised against the view that the Last Supper was associated with a Passover meal. First, no mention is made of the Passover lamb. Second, the word used for "bread" in the account is *artos,* the usual word for leavened bread, which could not be used to designate unleavened bread. Third, the four cups used in the traditional Jewish celebration of the Passover are not mentioned.

These objections are not serious, however, for the accounts of the Last Supper are abbreviated summaries of what happened, and one would expect the accounts to focus on those things that were most relevant for its celebration. Furthermore, because the early church regularly celebrated the Last Supper apart from the yearly Jewish Passover festival, those aspects of the Passover that had little or no bearing on the Last Supper were soon dropped. As for the statement that *artos* could not be used to designate the unleavened bread of the Passover, this is simply incorrect. The general term for "bread," whether the Greek *artos* or Hebrew *leḥem*, was always used in the OT, the LXX, the Mishnah and the Targums to describe the shewbread, which consisted of unleavened bread. Other objections focus on whether the *trial of Jesus could have taken place on the day of the Passover.

The question of whether the Last Supper was a Passover meal needs to be clarified. The Last Supper was not a Passover meal. It was not celebrated yearly, and it involves only two elements—bread and wine. A literal Passover lamb is not involved, nor are other elements of the Passover meal. Whereas Matthew 26:26, Mark 14:22 and Luke 22:15-17 envision the Last Supper taking place within the time frame of a Passover meal, it is not for them a Passover meal. This is especially clear in Luke, for none of his references to the breaking of bread in Acts are associated with the Jewish Passover. Paul furthermore appears to separate the "cup" from the supper itself (1 Cor 11:25). Thus, whereas the Last Supper was associated with a Passover meal, and whereas the *Lord's Supper was probably associated in the early church with a meal (the "love feast"), it was never understood as being identical with these meals.

2.3. The Last Supper Associated with a Passover Meal. Several weighty arguments favor the view that the Last Supper was associated with a Passover meal. Some of these are:

(1) The Passover meal had to be eaten within the walled city of Jerusalem, and the Last Supper was eaten within the city walls.

(2) The Passover night had to be spent within greater Jerusalem, which included Jerusalem and the surrounding hills facing it. That night, unlike other nights, Jesus and the disciples spent in Gethsemane, within greater Jerusalem, and not in Bethany.

(3) Jesus and the disciples reclined as they ate (Mk 14:18). It was customary to sit at ordinary meals but to recline at the Passover.

(4) People in Israel usually ate two meals a day. The first was a breakfast around 10-11 a.m., and the second was the main meal in late afternoon. The Last Supper was eaten in the evening (1 Cor 11:23; Mk 14:17), which was what the Law required for the Passover (Ex 12:8).

(5) The Last Supper ended with a hymn (Mt 26:30; Mk 14:26), and it was customary at the end of the Passover to sing the last part of the Hallel Psalms (Ps 115-118).

(6) The interpretation of the elements was a customary part of the Passover ritual (Ex 12:26-27).

(7) It was also customary at the Passover to give some money to the poor, a practice that would explain Judas's leaving the gathering (Jn 13:29).

None of these arguments by itself is conclusive, but their overall weight argues strongly that the Last Supper was indeed associated with a Passover meal. They receive additional support from Paul's calling Jesus "Christ, our Passover" (1 Cor 5:7) and his reference to "the cup of blessing" (1 Cor 10:16), the name given to the third cup of the Passover meal. The suggestion that the Last Supper was a *qiddûš* or some other religious meal that was eaten on the eve of the sabbath and included a blessing over the bread and cup seems highly unlikely due to the numerous associations of the Last Supper with the Passover celebration. Indeed, the traditional materials that inform us about the *qiddûš* are post-Christian, and it was never celebrated twenty-four hours before the sabbath but early on the sabbath eve. There is even a question as to whether the *qiddûš* was a meal or simply a blessing pronounced at a meal. As to the Johannine dating of the Passover, it should be noted that this fits his theological emphases quite nicely, for John seeks to tie the death of Jesus closely with the Passover (cf. Jn 1:29, 35; 19:36; Ex 12:46; Num 9:12).

3. The Last Supper in the Context of Passover.

If, as has been maintained, the Last Supper took place at a Passover meal, any proper interpretation must seek to understand it in light of this particular context. The Passover was an elaborate ritual full of symbolism and redemptive history.

3.1. The Passover Elements. The meal consisted mainly of six elements.

(1) The most significant was the *Passover lamb,* which had to be roasted over a fire. All the

lamb had to be eaten that night. Nothing could be saved. The lamb of course reminded the participants of the first Passover in which the angel of death was kept from visiting the firstborn of Israel because they were protected by the blood of the lamb.

(2) The *unleavened bread* reminded them of the swiftness of God's deliverance. His salvation was so swift that the people of Israel did not have time to bake bread.

(3) The bowl of *salt water* reminded them of the tears shed in their captivity and the crossing of the Red Sea.

(4) The *bitter herbs* recalled the bitterness of their slavery.

(5) A fruit puree called *Charosheth* reminded them of the clay that they used to make bricks in their captivity in Egypt.

(6) Finally, there were four *cups of wine*, mixed three parts water to one part wine, which reminded them of the promises of Exodus 6:6-7. The third cup of blessing was probably the one Jesus used in the Last Supper (Lk 22:20; 1 Cor 10:16; 11:25). The fourth cup was followed by a benediction and singing.

3.2. The Passover Parallels. During the Passover meal someone, usually the youngest son, was designated to ask the question "Why is this night different from other nights?" At this point the host would retell the story of Israel's deliverance out of Egypt and the meaning of the various elements of the meal. As the host of the Last Supper, Jesus would have been the one who retold the story. Later, the parallels between the Passover and the Last Supper that Jesus was establishing would be quite apparent.

The Passover	The Last Supper
God remembered his _____ covenant	A new covenant is enacted
Slavery in Egypt _____	[Slavery to sin?]
Deliverance from Egypt ___	Forgiveness of sins (Mt 26:28)
Blood of Passover Lamb __	Blood of Christ (our Passover, 1 Cor 5:7; the lamb of God, Jn 1:29, 35)
Interpretation of elements_	Interpretation of elements
Call for continual _____ celebration	Call for continual celebration

4. The Four Words of the Last Supper.

Whereas some scholars have argued that the Pauline form is the most original, in general most scholars conclude that the oldest form is to be found in the Markan version. Among the more important reasons are that (1) the Markan account contains more Aramaisms than the Pauline account (e.g., "he took bread, and blessed, and broke it") and (2) it is easier to understand how the Pauline-Lukan version originated from the Markan form than vice versa. It would appear that the original form contained four elements or "words."

4.1. "This Is My Body." The addition of "which is [or "is given"] for you" in Luke and 1 Corinthians may be an interpretative comment to help explain the meaning of the bread for the believer. Yet even if these are not authentic words of Jesus, this comment is certainly implied and makes explicit what was implicit in Jesus' words. It is difficult to believe that the disciples did not interpret the "is" metaphorically. If asked "Where is the body of Jesus?" they would have pointed to Jesus rather than the bread. His frequent use of metaphorical language would have provided the context for understanding "is" nonliterally. This metaphorical interpretation of "is" is supported by the fact that they are still called "bread and cup" (1 Cor 11:26-28), an unlikely reference if the elements had undergone transubstantiation.

In the first word Jesus states that he has come to give his body—himself as a person—on their behalf (cf. Phil 1:20; Rom 12:1; 1 Cor 9:27). Later, the church would understand more fully what this meant and realize that the bread represents the incarnation when the "Word [who] became flesh" bore our sins in his body (1 Pet 2:24) in order to achieve the redemption of the world.

4.2. "This Do in My Remembrance." The authenticity of these words has been denied, primarily because they are not found in Mark and Matthew. Yet, if Jesus saw his death as sealing a new covenant and in the context of the continual repetition of the Passover, it would have been quite natural for him to have said that this new and more significant deliverance of the people of God by his blood should likewise be continually remembered. Furthermore, the practice of the early church in regularly celebrating the Lord's Supper, and on more than just a yearly basis like the Passover, can best be understood as due to Jesus having said something like "Do this in my remembrance." The Passover had as its purpose that "[Israel might] remember the day when [it] came out of the land of Egypt" (Deut 16:3). Jesus' vicarious death and his inauguration of a new covenant were to be remembered in like manner.

Exactly what this remembrance involves is debated. J. Jeremias has suggested that it involved the disciples petitioning God to remember Jesus and come to his rescue. The Last Supper thus focuses not on Jesus' mediation of humanity before God but rather on Jesus' followers seeking to intercede before God on Jesus' behalf. Another view is to understand this remembrance as a memorial in which the believer thinks back and reflects upon the death of Jesus. A third way of understanding this term is to interpret it as meaning "to proclaim." Through the Last Supper the church proclaims the death of Jesus. This view finds support in 1 Corinthians 11:26. This tends to make the purpose of the Last Supper evangelistic in nature. The Last Supper, however, is first and foremost meant for the church. Probably the best interpretation of this command is to understand it as ordering the continual recapitulation or recounting of the passion and parousia of Jesus Christ, even as the Passover meal recounted and represented the events of the exodus (Ex 12:1-20).

4.3. "This Is My Blood of the Covenant Poured Out for Many." At the third cup of the Passover meal, after the traditional blessing, "Blessed be thou, Lord our God, King of the world, who has created the fruit of the vine" or in lieu of it, Jesus said, "This is my blood of the covenant poured out for many." The imagery recalls Exodus 24:8, where Moses seals the divine covenant by pouring half of the "blood of the covenant" upon the altar and sprinkling the other half on the people. The covenant blood of Exodus 24:8 is understood in the Targums *Pseudo-Jonathan* and *Onkelos* as being given to "atone" for the sins of the people—as being expiatory in nature. Similarly, the Matthean addition "for the forgiveness of sins" (Mt 26:28) makes explicit what is already implicit in the expression "blood of the covenant" (cf. Heb 9:20-22; 10:26-29).

Although not directly quoted, Jeremiah 31:31-34, with its reference to a "new" covenant, is also alluded to in this word. Even as the Qumran community spoke of a "new covenant" (CD 6:19; 8:21; 19:33-34; 20:1-2; 1QpHab 2:1-4; 1Q28b 3:25-26; 5:21-22; 1Q34 frag. 3 2:5-6), Jesus perceived his mission as having inaugurated a new covenant that would be sealed by his sacrificial death. Even if "new" was not expressly stated by Jesus, it is implied. In this it recalls Jeremiah 31:34, which speaks of forgiveness of sins accompanying a new covenant. The centrality of forgiveness in this new covenant is also supported by the additional expression "which is poured out for many" found in the Markan and Matthean accounts. (The Lukan "for you" in Lk 22:20 is most probably a liturgical change introduced to balance the "for you" of Lk 22:19.) This recalls the expiatory and sacrificial self-giving of the suffering servant of Isaiah 53:12 who bears the sin of many (*see* Servant of Yahweh). It is illegitimate to interpret "many" as denoting a limited atonement, for the expression here means "transgressors"; that is, it refers to all, as the synonymous parallelism in Isaiah 53:12b-c clearly indicates.

This word indicates that Jesus, in referring to his "blood poured out," understood his death as sacrificial (Lev 17:11-14) and sealing a new covenant. It is difficult not to interpret this word along the lines of Mark 10:45, 1 Corinthians 15:3, 2 Corinthians 5:21 and other passages where Jesus gives his life—pours out his blood—as a vicarious atonement for sinful humanity. This and the first word indicate the voluntary nature of Jesus' self-surrender, but this word adds that this self-surrender involves a sacrificial death that establishes a new covenant. It also seems clear that the words "this *is* my blood" would not have been interpreted literally by any of the disciples in light of the OT prohibition against drinking blood (cf. Lev 3:17; 7:26-27; 17:14; etc.), for if one remembers the difficulty Peter encountered in Acts 10:6-16 with regard to non-kosher meat, it is difficult to conclude that the disciples would have had no qualms drinking what they thought was real blood. The fact that there is not the slightest hesitation or reservation mentioned in any of the accounts to drinking the cup indicates that they interpreted Jesus' words metaphorically. The cup—that is, the contents of the cup—symbolizes Jesus' death, his poured-out blood, shed as a sacrifice that seals a covenant.

4.4. "Until . . . the Kingdom of God." Even as the Passover celebration involved an anticipation and longing for the final day when Israel would share in the messianic banquet (Is 25:6-9; 53:12; cf. Is 55:1-2), so all four accounts of the Last Supper contain a word concerning the future. Though Luke's wording varies and is exceptional in its placement before the bread, the Synoptics bear unified witness to Jesus' words: "I say to you, I shall not in any way drink any longer from the fruit of the vine until that day when I drink it new in the kingdom of God." The Pauline word about the future does not come from Jesus' lips but is a comment from the apostle in which he says that when the church celebrates the Lord's Supper they "proclaim the Lord's death until he comes." In the Synoptics this word points triumphantly to the future messianic banquet when Jesus will eat once again with the disciples.

Elsewhere Jesus on various occasions referred to the joyous participation in the consummated kingdom as a sharing in the messianic banquet (Mt 8:11 par. Lk 13:29; Mt 5:6 par. Lk 6:21; Lk 12:35-38; Mk 7:24-30; *see* Table Fellowship). The feeding of the five thousand and the four thousand were probably also understood by the Evangelists as proleptic participations of the Last Supper and the eschatological banquet (Mt 14:19 par. Mk 6:41 and Lk 9:16 [Jn 6:11] and Mt 15:36 par. Mk 8:6). Luke in fact heightens the allusion to this by separating the reference to the fish in Luke 9:16. According to the Jewish tradition in *Mekilta Exodus* 12:42, Israel's future redemption would come on the night of the Passover. As a result the celebration of the Passover looked back to the greatest redemptive event of the OT and forward to the joyous anticipation of the coming of the messianic age. In a similar way, Jesus in the Last Supper points his disciples to the greatest redemptive event of the NT, which is soon to be a past event, and to the arrival of the kingdom in glory when he comes (1 Cor 11:26) and shares the messianic banquet with his followers (Mt 26:29; Mk 14:25; Lk 22:16).

Clearly, Jesus does not see his passion as a tragedy or error but the crowning act of his ministry in which he pours out his blood as the once-for-all sacrifice that secures redemption "for many" and ensures a glorious consummation in the future. Paul in his future word refers more specifically to the event that will bring about that consummation—the parousia. Thus the Last Supper, while not the realization of the messianic banquet, is a proleptic experience of it, a kind of earnest, or firstfruits, of that banquet.

4.5. Later Additions to the Last Supper. Within the four accounts of the Last Supper we find a number of liturgical and interpretative comments. This should not be surprising. While certainty is impossible, the following may be liturgical additions: "Take" (Mt 26:26; Mk 14:22); "eat" (Mt 26:26); "drink of it, all of you" (Mt 26:27); "and they all drank of it" (Mk 14:23); "In the same way also the cup, after Supper, saying," (1 Cor 11:25); "cup" (1 Cor 11:25; Lk 22:20); "For as often as you eat this bread and drink the cup, you are proclaiming the Lord's death until he comes" (1 Cor 11:26). Some interpretative comments that may have been added to the account are "which is for you" (Lk 22:19; 1 Cor 11:24); "given" (Lk 22:19); "This do in my remembrance" (Lk 22:19; 1 Cor 11:24; see 4.2 above); "new" [covenant] (Lk 22:20; 1 Cor 11:25); "for the forgiveness of sins" (Mt 26:28). In all these instances the intention of Jesus is not altered, but the additions either make explicit what is perhaps only implicit or make the format of the sacrament more liturgically serviceable.

Several additional interpretative comments are found within the NT concerning the Last Supper. In 1 Corinthians 10:3-4 Paul gives a warning against the danger of assuming that mere participation in the Lord's Supper and in Christian *baptism (1 Cor 10:1-2) guarantees the participant a favorable standing with God (see also Lk 13:26). Paul clearly rejects a crass sacramental view of the Lord's Supper. As in the case of circumcision, the Lord's Supper and baptism are of value when accompanied by faith and obedience (Rom 2:25). There is also a specific warning concerning the danger of partaking of the Lord's Supper "in an unworthy manner" (1 Cor 11:27-32).

5. The Celebration of the Supper.

Within Acts we find several references to the "breaking of bread" (Acts 2:42, 46; 20:7, 11; Lk 24:30). Although it is debated whether this refers to a celebration derived from the Last Supper, it is clear that the Evangelist understood it this way. This is evident from Luke's use of the expression "breaking of bread" (Lk 22:19). It is further supported by the fact that in Acts 20:7 we find the breaking of bread taking place in the context of church worship on the first day of the week. Thus for Luke these references to the "breaking of bread" are understood as the fulfillment of Jesus' command to "do this in remembrance of me" found in his Gospel. To interpret them as simply ordinary meals, or even as love feasts, would contradict Luke's normal practice of showing how the church in Acts carried out Jesus' teachings. Probably the breaking of bread normally occurred in the context of a love feast, but the similarity in wording with the Last Supper ("breaking bread") indicates that what is most important for Luke is the celebration of the Supper. The only difficulty with this understanding is Acts 27:39, but it is not serious enough to overcome the previous facts.

In the early church the celebration of the Supper was almost immediately separated from the Passover, for the "breaking of bread" was practiced far more frequently than once a year. There are indications that it was celebrated weekly (Acts 20:7, 11; 1 Cor 16:2) and even daily (Acts 2:46-47). No rate of frequency, however, is prescribed within the NT. In the earliest period of the church the supper was celebrated in connection with a "love feast" (Jude 12; Acts 2:42, 46; 1 Cor 11:20-22, 33-34). It may be that Acts 2:42 should be interpreted, "They were continuing in the teaching of the apostles, and in fellowship [the love feast], the breaking of bread [the supper] and prayers." Likewise, Acts 2:46 might be read, "and breaking bread [the supper] in their homes, they partook of food with glad and generous hearts [the love feast]." This practice stemmed from the fact that Jesus' Last Supper was associated with a meal (Lk 22:20; 1 Cor 11:25). Soon, however, it became completely separate due most probably to such problems as Paul mentions in 1 Corinthians 11:20-22, 33-34—where Paul refers to it as the Lord's Supper (*kyriakos deipnon*, 1 Cor 11:20)—and by the middle of the second century that separation was complete.

The Lord's Supper contains a two-dimensional focus. It recounts the passion of the *Son of man and his sacrificial death by which he seals a new covenant for humanity. One cannot celebrate the Lord's Supper without looking backward to the cross and the suffering of Christ, our Passover. As a result a certain pathos and sadness is present at this celebration. But there is a forward-looking dimension that does not permit the Lord's Supper to become simply a morbid recalling of the passion. Believers "proclaim the Lord's death until he comes." Since the final dimension of the supper looks forward to the messianic banquet, the Lord's Supper is not simply practiced; it is celebrated in faith. In this celebration the church believes, hopes and sings "*Marana tha*—Come, Lord Jesus" (1 Cor

16:22; Rev 22:20) and awaits the consummation when faith turns to sight at the table of the Lord.

See also LORD'S SUPPER; TABLE FELLOWSHIP.

DJG: FEASTS.

BIBLIOGRAPHY. W. Barclay, *The Lord's Supper* (Nashville: Abingdon, 1967); M. Barth, *Rediscovering the Lord's Supper* (Atlanta: John Knox, 1988); G. Bornkamm, "Lord's Supper and Church in Paul," in *Early Christian Experience* (London: SCM, 1969) 123-60; J. B. Green, *The Death of Jesus* (Tübingen: J. C. B. Mohr, 1988); J. Jeremias, *The Eucharistic Words of Jesus* (London: SCM, 1966); X. Leon-Dufour, *Sharing the Eucharistic Bread* (New York: Paulist, 1987); B. Klappert, "Lord's Supper," *NIDNTT* 2:520-38; H. Lietzmann, *Mass and the Lord's Supper* (Leiden: E. J. Brill, 1979); I. H. Marshall, *Last Supper and Lord's Supper* (Grand Rapids: Eerdmans, 1980); W. Marxsen, *The Lord's Supper as a Christological Problem* (Philadelphia: Fortress, 1970); G. Ogg, "The Chronology of the Last Supper," in *Historicity and Chronology in the New Testament* (London: SPCK, 1965) 75-96; J. Reumann, *The Supper of the Lord* (Philadelphia: Fortress, 1985); E. Schweizer, *The Lord's Supper According to the New Testament* (Philadelphia: Fortress, 1967); G. Wainwright, *Eucharist and Eschatology* (New York: Oxford University Press, 1981). R. H. Stein

LAW I: GOSPELS

What impact did the coming of Jesus the Messiah and the establishment through him of the *kingdom of God have on the authority and applicability of the Mosaic law? The question is at the heart of the Gospels. It played a critical role not only in Jesus' disputes with various Jewish groups but also in the development of the early church's self-understanding as followers of Jesus sought to define the relationship between the church and Israel.

Jesus, living in the overlap between the old covenant and the new, is generally obedient to the Mosaic law, but at the same time he makes clear that he has sovereign rights to interpret and to set aside that law. On this basis he criticizes the developing oral law for its focus on a casuistic literalness that denied the heart and purpose of the law. It is in the dual command to love God and neighbor that Jesus found the heart of the law, and he used these basic demands to interpret and apply the law in accordance with its author's intention. But Jesus was not simply a great expositor of the law. What is most characteristic of the Gospels is Jesus' claim to be the Lord of the law. Jesus manifests this claim in his implicit abrogation of several commandments within the law and in his independent yet authoritative proclamation of God's will for his followers. As Messiah and *Son of God, Jesus stands superior to the law. Nevertheless, Jesus never attacks the law and asserts its enduring validity. But it is only as taken up into Jesus' teaching, and thus fulfilled, that the law retains its validity. The law comes to those living on this side of the cross only through the filter of its fulfillment in Christ the Lord.

The general sketch drawn in the preceding paragraph is reproduced in each of the Gospels, though with considerable differences in clarity and emphasis. Mark highlights Jesus' abrogation of ritual aspects of the law, though he shows little interest in Jesus' ethical teachings. Matthew writes his Gospel for a community deeply concerned about the relation of Israel and the church and, consequently, about the relation of the law to Jesus' teaching. He therefore includes more of the teaching of Jesus on this issue than the other Evangelists, showing how Jesus both endorses the law and surpasses it. Luke in his own way strikes a similar balance, commending the piety of those who follow the law while showing that the continuing validity of the law lies mainly in its prophetic aspects. John's stance is polemical, as he puts Jesus and his claims on a collision course with the law and its institutions. Even here, however, the point is not so much that Jesus abrogates the law as to show that as Son of God he replaces it.

1. Introduction
2. Jesus
3. The Gospel Writers
4. Conclusion

1. Introduction.

The word *law* is the standard translation of the Greek word *nomos*. This word occurs thirty-one times in the Gospels, always in the singular, and with two possible exceptions—both in John 19:7—the word denotes the body of commandments given by God to the people of *Israel through Moses. Thus the law can be called "the law of the Lord" (Lk 2:23-24, 39) as well as "the Law of Moses" (Lk 2:22; Jn 7:23; cf. Jn 1:17, "the law came through Moses," and Jn 1:45, "Moses wrote in the law"). On five occasions the law is linked with "the prophets" (Mt. 5:17; 7:12; 11:13; 22:40; Lk 16:16; Jn 1:45—there is Jewish precedent for such a combination: cf. 4 Macc 18:10) and once with the prophets and "the psalms" (Lk 24:44). In most of these texts *nomos* refers to the Pentateuch, and the whole phrase denotes "the Scriptures." The Gospel writers also refer to the law with the words *commandment* (*entolē;* singular: Mt 15:3 par. Mk 7:9; Mt 22:36 par. Mk 12:28; Mt 22:38 par. Mk 12:31; Mk 7:8; 10:5; Lk 23:56; plural: Mt 5:19; 19:17 par. Mk 10:19 and Lk 18:20; Mt 22:40; Lk 1:6) and *decree (dikaiōma)* (Lk 1:6) or with a reference simply to "Moses" (Mt 8:4 par. Mk 1:44 and Lk 5:14; Mt 19:7 par. Mk 10:3; Mt 19:8 par. Mk 10:4; Mt 22:24 par. Mk 12:19 and Lk 20:28; Mk 7:10; Jn 7:22 [2x]: cf. "Moses and the prophets" in Lk 16:29, 31). By contrast, *graphē* ("Scripture") is never used to refer to the Mosaic law alone, while the verb *graphō* ("write": e.g., "it is written") is only rarely so used (Mk 10:5; 12:19; Lk 2:23; 10:26; 20:28; Jn 1:45; 8:17; 10:34).

The virtual identification of "law" with "Law of Moses" in the Gospels reflects OT usage and the Jewish milieu, in both of which the Law of Moses, the Torah *(tôrâ),* plays a central role. Obedience to the law was not the means by which the people of Israel attained their covenant relationship with God. It was their response to the gracious initiative of God, a response appropriate as a means of thanking and glorifying the God who had chosen them and necessary as the means by which the promises attached to the covenant would be actualized (see e.g., Deut 28:1-2, 9; 30:1-10, 15-16). In a development predicted in the Pentateuch (Deut 30:15-20) and identified by the prophets, Israel failed to obey the law and so broke the terms of God's covenant. Nevertheless, God affirmed his continuing faithfulness to his people and promises, announcing that he would establish a new covenant with his people, a covenant through which God's law would be "written on the heart" (Jer 31:31-34) and through which those very hearts would be transformed so as to make them obedient to the Lord (Ezek 36:24-28).

This pessimism about the law did not take root in early Judaism. While generalizations about the Jewish people as a whole are dangerous and usually misleading, it is clear that the most important Jewish groups in Jesus' day gave to the Mosaic law a place of central importance in the life of the people and in their relationship to the Lord. Some of these groups, most notably the Pharisees, sought to aid the Jews in their obedience to God's law by adding to the written law an oral tradition that would apply the written law to the new situations faced by Jews. This development cannot be traced in detail, but it was well underway in Jesus' day, as is clear from his reference to the "traditions of the elders" (Mt 15:2 par. Mk 7:3). Fueling this development were two central postulates: that the Jew must obey God and that the complete guide for that obedience is to be found in the Torah. The growth of an authoritative tradition such as this, which could, at a later date, be called *tôrâ* (e.g., *b. Šabb.* 31a), complicates the discussion of Jesus and the law. It is necessary, for instance, to determine whether Jesus' critical attitude toward certain commandments and customs embodies criticism of the written Law of Moses or of the oral traditions of the Pharisees.

2. Jesus.

From what the Gospels tell us of Jesus' behavior, he was generally obedient to the Law of Moses. He attends the major feasts in Jerusalem, pays the half-shekel temple tax (Mt 17:24-27), wears the prescribed tassel on his robe (Mt 9:20; cf. Num 15:38-41) and, whatever may be said about his disciples' behavior or his teaching, never clearly violates the sabbath. It is only in the case of Jesus' contact with unclean people in his healing ministry (e.g., touching a leper [Mt 8:3 par. Mk 1:41 and Lk 5:13]) that he could be considered in violation of the Law of Moses. Even in this case, however, the unusual nature of Jesus' healing activities makes it difficult to identify a clear-cut violation of the law.

The situation is different with respect to the oral traditions of the Jews. Jesus deliberately associates with people considered by strict Jews to be unclean (the tax collectors and sinners; cf. Mt 9:10-13 par. Mk 2:15-17 and Lk 5:29-32) and "works" on the sabbath by healing people who are in no danger of losing their lives (Mk 3:1-6 par. Mt. 12:9-14 and Lk 6:6-11; Lk 13:10-17; 14:1-6; Jn 5:2-47; 9:1-41). It is not, however, that Jesus consistently flouts the traditions, for he attends the synagogue on the sabbath and displays habits at mealtime and at prayer that are consistent with the traditions. What we, have, then, is a Jesus who does not go out of his way to break the traditions of his day but at the same time makes clear that he considers himself free to ignore them if need demands.

While we can conclude from Jesus' behavior that he did not endorse the "traditions of the elders" as authoritative, his general conformity to the written law allows no clear conclusions. Did Jesus obey the law because he considered it to be eternally valid? Or did he obey it as "old covenant" law, valid only until his death and resurrection should inaugurate a new covenant? Or was there a principle that Jesus applied to determine the validity of different commandments within the law?

2.1. Love and the Law. The principle most often cited in this regard is the love command. Jesus singled out love for God and love for neighbor as the two great commandments (Mt 22:34-40 par. Mk 12:28-34; Lk 10:25-28; cf. Jn 13:31-35), going so far as to assert that "all the law and the prophets depend" on them (Mt 22:40). Taken with Jesus' pronouncement of the golden rule (Mt 7:12), his insistence that "mercy" is more important than "sacrifice" (Mt 9:13; 12:7) and his humanitarian approach to the sabbath (Mk 2:27; cf. Mt 12:3-4 par. Mk 2:25-26 and Lk 6:3-4; Mt 12:12 par. Mk 3:4 and Lk 6:9; Lk 13:15-16), his highlighting of the love command suggests that it plays a significant role in his understanding of the law. But what is its role? Does love function to determine when the law is to be obeyed? What laws are to be obeyed? And what is the meaning and intent of the law?

Only this last role of the demand of love, that of determining the meaning and intent of the law, has any clear basis in Jesus' teaching. Never does he suggest that he or his followers are free on the basis of love to disobey an authoritative commandment of Scripture. Nor does he dismiss the validity of commandments according to whether or not they are loving. But Jesus does appeal to love in elucidating the meaning and application of the law. In contrast to the scribes, who insisted on literal and scrupulous observance of the commandments, Jesus sought out the intention behind the commandments and understood their meaning and the way they were to be obeyed in light of this intention (see Westerholm). And it is to love for God and love for others that Jesus appeals in clarifying God's intention in the law. This is what he means by claiming that "all the law and the prophets" (i.e., the OT in its commanding aspect; cf. Mt 5:17 and 7:12) "depend" on the commands of love for God (Deut 6:5) and love for neighbor (Lev 19:18). Jesus is not here teaching that love replaces the law or that love shows how we are to obey the law. Rather, as the greatest commandments within the law, they are the touchstone by which the intention and meaning of all the other commandments must be understood. Several incidents reveal this role of the love commands in Jesus' interpretation of the law.

When Jesus defends his befriending of tax collectors and sinners by appealing to Hosea 6:6 (Mt 9:13), his point is not that the moral law ("mercy") takes precedence over the ceremonial law ("sacrifice") or that being merciful to people is more important than obeying the law. Instead, his point is that one has failed to understand God's intention in the law if rigid adherence to oral tradition (i.e., prohibition of association with the "unclean") is retained at the expense of showing God's compassion on sinners.

The situation is similar in Matthew 12:7, where Jesus cites Hosea 6:6 to defend his disciples from the charge of breaking the sabbath: they are "guiltless" *(anaitios)* because their plucking of grain is not contrary to God's intention in giving the sabbath command. In the same incident Jesus also defends the disciples by citing the action of David and his followers (1 Sam 21:1-6). As they were fleeing from the wrath of Saul, David and his confederates ate the bread of the presence, "which is not lawful for any but the priests to eat" (Mt 12:3-4 par. Mk 2:25-26 and Lk 6:3-4). Jesus, it is sometimes alleged, cites this incident to show that human need takes precedence over obedience to the law. But only Matthew even mentions the fact that the disciples were hungry. And, in any case, their need could not have been great—surely Jesus does not encourage disobedience to the law to meet casual wants and desires! Rather, Jesus' purpose is quite different: by comparing his disciples with David's followers, he also compares himself with David, suggesting that if, in serving David, his followers were justified in doing what was illegal, so much the more were Jesus' disciples justified in breaking the sabbath halakah (*see* Rabbinic Traditions and Writings) in their service of the greater *Son of David. The focus is on *christology, not on the interpretation of the sabbath command. This christological interpretation is reinforced in Matthew by the comparison that immediately follows between Jesus and the temple (Mt 12:5-6).

In Mark's Gospel, however, Jesus' reference to 1 Samuel 21:1-6 is followed by the strongly humanitarian statement that "the Sabbath was made for humankind, not humankind for the Sabbath" (Mk 2:27). Some interpreters have found christology here also, arguing that "humankind" *(anthropos)* is a mistranslation of an Aramaic expression by which Jesus referred to himself as the *Son of man. There is no basis for this, however, and the saying fits well with similar pronouncements of Jesus such as, "it is lawful to do good on the Sabbath" (Mt 12:12; cf. Mk 3:4; Lk 6:9). Again, however, Jesus is not claiming that one can break the sabbath command when human needs dictate but that the sabbath command must be so understood as to include this basic purpose in its promulgation. The sabbath is truly obeyed only when its intention to aid human beings is recognized and factored into one's behavior. That is why, rather than being a violation of the law, Jesus' sabbath-day healing of a woman was a true fulfillment of that law ("it was necessary" *[edei]* that she be healed on the sabbath [Lk 13:16]).

For Jesus, then, love for God and for others, being basic to God's intention in giving the law, must always be considered in interpreting the meaning of that law.

2.2. Jesus' Use of the Law in His Ethical Teaching. The relatively few occasions on which Jesus cites the OT law in formulating his own demands is revealing of the independent authority with which Jesus speaks. True, Jesus believes that his teaching stands in continuity with the OT demand (see, e.g., Mt 5:17; 7:12). And he occasionally cites the OT in his teaching. But most of these citations come in conversation with Jewish opponents or inquirers in which the OT is appealed to because of its relevance to their situation. Jesus' teaching about the dual command of love is a case in point. He highlights these commandments in response to a question about which is the greatest commandment (Mt 22:36 par. Mk 12:28). Without minimizing the importance of these commandments, it is significant that in John's Gospel the commandment to love one another is a new commandment, authorized by Jesus without reference to the OT (13:31-35). Jesus also appeals to the prophets to establish priorities within the law (Hos 6:6 in Mt 9:13; 12:7; Mic 6:8 in Mt 23:23 [cf. Lk 11:42]).

Similarly, when questioned about the legitimacy of divorce, Jesus cites Genesis 1:27 and

Genesis 2:24 to correct the common overinterpretation of Deuteronomy 24:1-4 (Mt 19:3-12 par. Mk 10:2-10). Some interpreters have thought that Jesus is following a rabbinic procedure by which two apparently contradictory statements within the law could be harmonized. But rather than harmonizing the two, Jesus appeals to one over against the other. The original intention of God expressed in the Genesis texts is elevated over the Mosaic command that was given, Jesus says, because of "hardness of heart." Here Jesus appeals to the OT teaching about the origin of marriage as authoritative for his followers. It is not clear, however, that this should be considered as an appeal to the law. For Jesus' careful distinction between what God had said in Genesis and what Moses had said in Deuteronomy suggests that he cites Genesis not as part of the law, in the sense of the Mosaic command, but as a scriptural and hence authoritative statement of God's intention for marriage. Here Jesus makes an important distinction, one that runs counter to the tendency of Judaism in his day: the distinction between the books of Moses as Scripture and the Law of Moses that takes up a large portion of those books.

Another polemical use of the law appears in Jesus' debate with the Pharisees over ritual defilement. Jesus defends his disciples' behavior in this matter by calling into question the "traditions of the elders" generally (Mt 15:3-6 par. Mk 7:8-13). Jesus brands these traditions as contrary to the law they purport to expound and apply. From this we can conclude that Jesus expected the Jews of his day to observe the commandments under which they lived—beyond that we cannot go.

Slightly different is Jesus' rehearsal of Decalogue commandments when a young man asks him how he may attain eternal life (Mt 19:16-22 par. Mk 10:17-22 and Lk 18:18-23). Here, it could be argued, Jesus makes OT commandments basic to his own ethical demands. But such a conclusion would be too hasty. For Jesus imposes these commands not on a follower but on a seeker after eternal life. Does Jesus then view obedience to the law as a means of salvation? This is possible, although we would then want to question whether Jesus considered it possible for any human being to render an obedience adequate to that end. For the young man, after claiming to have observed all the command-

ments cited by Jesus, is still seen to be short of entrance into the *kingdom. But it is also possible that Jesus cites the commandments simply to initiate a discussion and to draw out this young man and that he is not teaching that eternal life can be gained by obedience to the law. In any case, it is significant that the climax of the narrative is Jesus' demand that the young man "follow me." This has been viewed as Jesus' further exposition of the real meaning of the commandments, but we question whether following Jesus in discipleship can be considered an exposition of any Mosaic command. Rather, whatever the role played by the commandments of the law, it is Jesus' demand that is crucial here. Jesus goes beyond the OT demand: it is following him, not obedience to the law, that is the door into the kingdom of God.

It is clear, then, that Jesus' direct use of the OT in his ethical teaching is minimal. Most of the references occur in polemical contexts where Jesus may be doing no more than assuming the reference point of his opponent. This does not necessarily mean that Jesus did not consider the OT law to be relevant for the new age that was dawning through his ministry and work. He may simply have assumed its continuing validity. Still, what is impressive in Jesus' teaching is the way in which he taught directly, and without reference to any other authority, what it was that God was demanding of his people. The Mosaic law, if not discarded, is generally ignored—and this signals an important shift from the OT and the Judaism of Jesus' day.

2.3. Abrogation of the Law? We have seen that Jesus does not generally use the law to formulate his ethics. But does he ever go so far as to pronounce invalid the law or commandments within the law?

2.3.1. Clean and unclean. When Jesus' disciples violated the scribal tradition about hand washing, he defended them in two ways (Mt 15:1-20 par. Mk 7:1-23). First, he criticized the scribal tradition generally, branding it a "human tradition" (Mk 7:8) that interferes with true worship of and obedience to God. He cites as an example the situation in which the scribes would insist that a person perform a vow, even if that vow were taken selfishly to avoid giving due honor to one's parents. Some interpreters have seen here a conflict between two parts of the written law—the command to honor oaths and the command to honor parents—but the text makes clear that the conflict is rather between the "commandment of God" and "human tradition." This text suggests, then, that Jesus did not endorse the developing oral law of the Pharisees. But Jesus' second line of defense goes further. In enunciating the principle that "there is nothing outside a person which by going into a person can defile them" (Mk 7:15; cf. Mt 15:11), Jesus casts doubt on the continuing validity of the entire ritual body of laws in the OT. Certainly, this is how Mark understands him: "Thus he declared all foods to be clean" (Mk 7:19). Doubt has been cast on the authenticity of this saying of Jesus, it being argued that the debates in the early church over this matter are hard to understand if Jesus had spoken so clearly on the issue. But Jesus' almost parabolic saying would hardly have been sufficient to settle the matter, and Mark's parenthetical interpretation reflects a later, clearer perspective. The contrast in this pericope between Jesus' upholding of one commandment—to honor parents—and his effective abrogation of others—concerning unclean foods—raises the possibility that Jesus distinguished between the so-called moral and the ceremonial law. There are hints of such a distinction in the Gospels, in Jesus' stress on the "weightier matters of the law" (Mt 23:23) and in his picking up the prophetic focus on inner obedience. Nevertheless, the distinction was unknown in the Judaism of Jesus' day, and we would have expected him to make the distinction much clearer had it been fundamental to his assessment of the OT law. Moreover, as we will see, Jesus' varying pronouncements about the law cannot be fit into a neat distinction between the moral and the ceremonial.

2.3.2. The Sabbath. The centrality of the sabbath for Jewish piety is reflected in the numerous conflicts between Jesus and the Jews over its observance: the Gospels record six separate incidents. Did Jesus abrogate the sabbath command, as some scholars claim? Answering this question is complicated by the need to distinguish between the Mosaic sabbath requirements and the extensive traditional regulations developed by the scribes in an effort to regulate sabbath observance. The OT prohibits work on the sabbath but gives few details about what constitutes work. It is this ambiguity that the scribal tradition seeks to clarify. Jesus and his disciples violated the scribal sabbath regulations by plucking grain (Mt 12:1-8 par. Mk 2:23-28 and Lk

6:1-5) and by healing people whose lives were not in danger (Mt 12:9-14 par. Mk 3:1-6 and Lk 6:6-11; Lk 13:10-17; 14:1-6; Jn 5:2-47; 9:1-41). Neither of these activities is a clear violation of the Mosaic sabbath rules, although Jesus' healing ministry is difficult to categorize. The most that can be said is that his initiative in healing on the sabbath, rooted in theological conviction—"it was necessary" for Jesus to heal on the sabbath (Lk 13:16)—stretches the sabbath commandment. But we have no evidence that Jesus ever violated, or approved of his disciples violating, the written sabbath commandment.

Jesus' teaching, however, is another matter. We have already discussed (see 2.1 above) Jesus' focus on humanitarian concerns in defending his sabbath behavior. Some scholars think that Jesus here abrogates or at least relativizes the sabbath by putting human need over observance of the command. As we have argued, this is not the case: Jesus' humanitarian emphasis is not intended to abrogate but to define the sabbath command. More telling is Jesus' christological defense for his sabbath activity. He justifies the disciples' grain plucking through a comparison of himself with David (Mt 12:3-4 par. Mk 2:25-26 and Lk 6:3-4) and the temple (Mt 12:5-6). He claims the Father's right to continue "working" on the sabbath (Jn 5:17-18). And in a succinct and clear statement of his position vis-à-vis the sabbath, he claims "the Son of man is Lord of the Sabbath" (Mt 12:8 par. Mk 2:28 and Lk 6:5). Here Jesus claims superiority over the sabbath, including the right to interpret, transform or even abrogate this central Mosaic institution. Nevertheless, Jesus never uses this authority to abrogate the sabbath, and whether the early church did so on the basis of Jesus' authority is another question.

2.3.3. Divorce. We have noted that Jesus responds to a question about the grounds for divorce by citing Genesis 1:27 and Genesis 2:24 (Mt 19:3-12 par. Mk 10:2-12; cf. Lk 16:18). He thereby bypasses the then-current debate about the interpretation of Deuteronomy 24:1-4 by using God's intention in creation to call into question the entire matter of an allowance for divorce. It is true that according to Matthew (Mt 19:9; cf. Mt 5:31-32), Jesus' position is not far from that of his near-contemporary Shammai and from Deuteronomy 24:1-4 as well. But what is important for our purposes is the logic with which Jesus arrives at his position. The Mosaic provision for divorce is simply swept aside as a concession to "hardness of heart." What is unclear is whether Jesus thinks that the inauguration of the kingdom through his redemptive work will take away that hardness of heart or whether he considers this condition to be one that will disappear only in the next life. The contrast between the creation intention of God and the Mosaic provision ("but from the beginning it was not so") favors the former. If this is so, Jesus questions the tacit approval of divorce within the Mosaic legislation.

2.3.4. The Antitheses. Matthew 5:17-48 is the most significant passage in the Gospels for determining the relationship between Jesus and the Mosaic law. Matthew 5:17-20 will be considered below (see 2.4 below); here we focus on Matthew 5:21-48, in which Jesus six times compares his teaching with what had been told to "the ancients." Many scholars are convinced that Jesus abrogates Mosaic commands in at least some of these comparisons.

The introductory formulae vary but appear to be variations of a single basic formula, seen fully in Matthew 5:21, 33: "you have heard that it was said to the ancients *(tois archaiois)* . . . but I say to you." The dative *tois archaiois* has occasionally been understood in an ablatival sense ("by the ancients") but is probably a pure dative, as we have translated it. Jesus' reference is probably to the generation that received the law at Sinai, although this does not exclude the possibility that oral traditions are included in the reference, for it was taught that the "oral law" had also been given at Sinai (cf. *m. ʾAbot.* 1:1-2). Similarly, the "you have heard" refers to the hearing of the law read in the synagogue, a reading that often incorporated traditional interpretations. The formula in itself, then, does not enable us to decide whether Jesus is citing the Mosaic law per se or the Mosaic law as interpreted and expanded by the scribes. Nor, while the nomenclature has become standard, is "antitheses" necessarily the best way to describe these six comparisons. The grammar allows at least three different nuances: (1) "you have heard, but I (in contrast to that) say to you"; (2) "you have heard, but I (in addition to that) say to you" or (3) "you have heard, and I (in agreement with that) say to you."

No abrogation of the law occurs in the first two comparisons (Mt 5:21-26, 27-30), but it is harder to know whether Jesus is expounding the true meaning of the commandments, deepening the commandments by extending them from the level of action to the level of attitude, or simply juxtaposing his teaching with that of the law. Against the first alternative, however, is the lack of clear evidence that the Decalogue prohibitions of murder and adultery included prohibitions of, respectively, anger and lust as well. Jesus, while not necessarily going beyond the Mosaic law and the scribal teaching, both of which prohibit anger and lust, goes beyond the actual commandments he cites.

Jesus' teaching about divorce in Matthew 5:31-32 is sometimes taken as part of the second comparison, but the abbreviated introductory formula in Matthew 5:31 suggests rather that it be considered a separate, third comparison. In our earlier discussion of Jesus' teaching on divorce (see 2.3.3 above), we noted that Matthew's exceptive clause (Mt 5:32: "except on the ground of unchastity") has the effect of bringing Jesus' teaching fairly closely into line with the Mosaic allowance. What effect this has on the actual commandment Jesus cites—namely, that a person who divorces his wife give her a "bill of divorcement"—is not clear, but it is probably stretching the matter to speak of an abrogation of the commandment here. Nevertheless, Jesus' teaching that an improper remarriage constitutes adultery goes beyond the OT. Jesus is not simply expounding the Mosaic legislation regarding divorce; nor does the idea of deepening fit the circumstances very well. He goes beyond the law in the seriousness with which he considers improper remarriages, and his basic agreement with Deuteronomy 24:1-4 over the appropriate grounds for divorce and remarriage is, as it were, incidental to the central point.

The fourth thesis cited by Jesus as a point of departure for his teaching is an accurate summary of the Mosaic requirements regarding oaths and vows (Mt 5:33). Oaths and vows were not carefully distinguished in the OT, both involving a pledge of truthfulness in connection with God. The rabbis reluctantly accepted the need for oaths and regulated their use, but the Essenes, who often had stricter requirements than the Pharisees or the rabbis, apparently did prohibit most oaths (see Josephus *J.W.* 2.135). Jesus' requirement seems absolute: "Do not swear at all" (Mt 5:34). But there is considerable debate about this, for the following delineation of examples appears to reflect the casuistic debates about oaths in the scribal tradition (see *m. Šeb.; m. Sanh.* 3:2; *t. Ned.* 1). This background, taken with the undoubted presence of hyperbole in Matthew 5, may suggest that Jesus simply intends to encourage absolute truthfulness (see Mt 5:37). Another possibility is that Jesus prohibits voluntary oaths. If Jesus is indeed prohibiting all oaths, then a technical abrogation of the Mosaic command requiring an oath in the court (Ex 22:10-13) occurs (Meier). But the uncertainty about Jesus' intention should make us cautious about claiming an abrogation of the law here. In any case, we see again that Jesus is neither expounding nor deepening the law but juxtaposing his own (perhaps more radical) demand with that of the law.

Of the six antitheses there is most agreement among scholars that the fifth, relating to the *lex talionis*, abrogates the Mosaic law. But this is not at all clear. The law of equivalent compensation is stated in three places in the Mosaic law (Ex 21:23-25; Lev 24:20; Deut 19:21), and in each case it has the purpose not of justifying but of restraining private retribution by establishing an equitable judicial guideline to which all could be held. Jesus does not question, nor does he uphold, this policy. He simply demands that his followers not use it as an excuse for retaliation. Jesus goes beyond the demands of the law, but he does not contradict it.

The final quotation in Matthew 5 differs from the others in including a clause not found in the OT—that one is to "hate one's enemy" (Mt 5:43). It has sometimes been argued that this requirement is a fair extrapolation from the fact that the scope of the love command (Lev 19:18) is restricted to the fellow Israelite (*rēʿ*) and from the frequent OT expressions of hostility to Israel's enemies. But this conclusion is not warranted, and we must consider the command to "hate your enemy" not as an OT requirement but as a reflection of current Jewish teaching in some circles, perhaps associated with the Essenes of Qumran. Jesus does not, therefore, abrogate Mosaic law by requiring love for one's enemy, but he does ask his followers to do something that the Mosaic law had not asked the people of Israel to do: love one's enemy. Once more, then, Jesus' teaching transcends without clearly revoking the OT law.

We find, then, that only one possible abrogation of the law—that having to do with divorce and remarriage—occurs in the antitheses. In the others, Jesus' teaching is juxtaposed with the Mosaic commands in a way that does not fit either of the popular categories: exposition or deepening. The dominant note, hinted at in the emphatic "I say to you" and recognized by the crowds at the end of the sermon (Mt 7:28-29), is the independent authority of Jesus, who presumes to announce God's will for life in the kingdom without support from any other source.

Jesus, then, abrogated some Mosaic laws— the food laws and possibly the divorce provisions—but this is not the dominant motif in his teaching. Jesus does not so much oppose the law as claim to transcend it. He is the Lord of the sabbath and claims the right to determine God's will without reference to the law.

2.4. Fulfillment of the Law. The best-known statement of Jesus with respect to the law comes in Matthew 5:17: "Do not think that I have come to abolish the law or the prophets: I have not come to abolish, but to fulfill them." To understand this claim, we must consider its following context (Mt 5:18-19) and the partial Lukan parallel to this context (Lk 16:16-17).

In Luke 16:16 Jesus announces a fundamental shift in salvation history: "The law and the prophets were until John: since then the good news of the kingdom of God is preached, and every one enters it violently." Especially in light of Luke 16:17 Jesus cannot mean that the significance of the OT is terminated; he must mean that John's coming has signaled a fundamental shift in the role and importance of "the law and the prophets." Matthew's parallel (Mt 11:13) adds an important nuance: "the law and the prophets prophesied until John." Here Jesus claims that the entire OT has a prophetic aspect, that the law itself has some kind of forward-looking element. This reference furnishes an important clue to the Matthean viewpoint on the law and helps us unravel the meaning of Matthew 5:17.

Study of Matthew 5:17-19 is complicated by the complex and debated tradition history of the verses. According to one viewpoint, for instance, each verse is to be assigned to a different stratum of the early Christian community, with none of them embodying the teaching of Jesus. However, while the verses may indeed come from different sources (e.g., Mt 5:18 may be from Q; cf. Lk 16:17) and while Matthew was undoubtedly responsible for their final arrangement in his Gospel, there is no compelling reason to deny their authenticity.

The key word in this paragraph is the word *fulfill* (*pleroō*, Mt 5:17). Its interpretation becomes the basis for, or expression of, divergent general interpretations of Jesus and the law. We speak of "law" because in Matthean usage the expression "law and the prophets" (cf. Mt 7:12; 22:40) and the parallels "law" (Mt 5:18) and "commandments" (Mt 5:19) refer to the commanding aspect of the OT. The clear connection with the comparisons of Matthew 5:21-48 also indicates that Jesus is focusing on the relationship between his teaching and the law. With these qualifications in view, the following are the most important interpretations of "fulfill." (1) Jesus fulfills the law by confirming its validity (presupposing that the Aramaic word *qûm* lies behind *pleroō*; Branscomb). (2) Jesus fulfills the law by adding to it (based on the alleged parallel to Mt 5:17 in *b. Šabb.* 116b; Jeremias). (3) Jesus fulfills the law by bringing out its full, originally intended meaning (Bahnsen). (4) Jesus fulfills the law by extending its demands (Davies). (5) Jesus fulfills the law by teaching the eschatological will of God that the law anticipated (Banks, Meier).

Methodologically, we should look for the meaning of *pleroō* by referring to Matthew's usage rather than to an alleged Hebrew or Aramaic original. For there is no way of confirming what that Semitic original may have been, and there is ample evidence that Matthew, while reproducing Jesus' intention, is responsible for the wording of the saying. The closest syntactical parallel to Matthew 5:17 is Matthew 3:15, where *pleroō* is also used in the active voice and is followed by a direct object. Focusing on this parallel, H. Ljungman argues that "fulfilling" the law must refer to Jesus' fulfillment of the Scripture as the means of bringing in eschatological righteousness. But the most distinctive use of *pleroō* in Matthew comes in the introductions to his eleven so-called formula quotations, most of which are unique to his Gospel. In these texts Matthew announces the fulfillment of a text, event or prophecy in the life of Jesus. The importance of this word in these contexts, combined with Matthew's striking reference to the law as "prophesying" (Mt 11:13), makes this prophetic use of *pleroō* the most likely source for our interpretation of Matthew 5:17. In a way analogous to his fulfilling Israel's history in his own departure from Egypt (cf. Mt 2:15) and his fulfilling the prophets' predictions in his life,

Jesus also fulfills Israel's law in his teaching. The entire OT, in all its parts, is viewed as the promise component in a promise-fulfillment scheme of salvation history, and the law cannot be excluded from this scheme.

We conclude, then, that the fifth alternative listed above—the eschatological will of God—is the best interpretation of Matthew 5:17. In response to rumors about his law-negating stance, Jesus assures his listeners that his teaching stands in continuity with the OT law. His teaching does not abolish the law but brings it to its intended eschatological climax. This view of Matthew 5:17 fits well with the antitheses that follow and which furnish specific examples of Jesus' fulfillment of the law (Mt 5:21-48). For, as we have seen (2.3.4 above), what Jesus does with the law in these six comparisons cannot all be explained by recourse to any single concept, such as exposition or deepening. What is common to each is a juxtaposition of OT teaching with Jesus' own, a teaching that transcends the OT teaching. Understanding "fulfillment" in the broad, salvation-historical sense that we have defended enables Matthew 5:17 to function as a heading to these comparisons, as indeed it was apparently intended to do.

Can this interpretation be reconciled with the context of Matthew 5:18-19? At first sight, no stronger endorsement of the eternal applicability of every commandment of the Mosaic law could be envisaged than what we have here. Agreeing with this assessment are those scholars who think that Matthew 5:19, or Matthew 5:18-19 together, is a creation of a conservative Jewish group within the early church. Matthew, they argue, has inserted this material into the present context in order to correct it. While it may well be that Matthew has been responsible for juxtaposing verses Matthew 5:18-19 with Mathew 5:17, we are not so sure that we must deny these sayings to Jesus. Can these verses be read in a way compatible with Jesus' teaching about the law elsewhere in Matthew's Gospel? Attempts to avoid the conclusion that Jesus here endorses the continuing applicability of every "jot and tittle" of the law, and so to reconcile Matthew 5:18-19 with Mathew 5:17 and Matthew 5:21-48, focus on three issues: the scope of the two *heōs* ("until") clauses in Matthew 5:18, the meaning of *nomos* ("law") in Matthew 5:18 and the antecedent of *toutōn* ("these [commandments]") in Matthew 5:19.

The first *heōs* clause in Matthew 5:18, "until heaven and earth pass away," must be compared with its counterpart in Luke 16:17: "It is easier for heaven and earth to pass away than for one dot of the law to become void." Luke apparently uses this verse to guard against an antinomian interpretation of Luke 16:16. Probably we are to understand the clause in Matthew in the same way; every detail of the law remains valid until the present world order passes away. Nevertheless, this conclusion in itself does not stand in contradiction to Matthew 5:17, for the nature of this validity must be probed further.

The second *heōs* clause, which many take to be Matthew's insertion, is more difficult to interpret, for there is no clear antecedent to *panta*, "all things," and the precise force of *genētai* is not evident. One possibility is that Jesus is teaching that the law will remain valid only until all the demands of the law are "done" or "obeyed." We may then infer that these demands were fully met by Jesus in his obedient life and sacrificial death and that the law is therefore no longer valid. But *genētai* is more likely to mean "happen" in this context, while *panta* probably refers to predicted events (cf. Mt 24:34-35). These events have been identified with Jesus' death and resurrection, with those things prophesied about Jesus generally or with all the components of God's plan for history. The lack of any restriction in this context favors the last of these alternatives. This being so, the second *heōs* clause is roughly parallel to the first, both maintaining that the law will remain valid until the end of history as we know it.

An assumption quite popular in some circles is that *nomos* in Matthew 5:18 refers only to the moral law. But no such restriction can be entertained. Not only is there no support for such a limitation in first-century Judaism, and little in the teaching of Jesus, but the reference to "jot and tittle" in Matthew 5:18 shows that no part of the law can be omitted from Jesus' purview.

Jesus, then, asserts in Matthew 5:18 (and in its parallel, Lk 16:17), that the whole Mosaic law will remain valid throughout this age. But valid in what way? Here it is appropriate to suggest that this must be understood in light of Matthew 5:17—the continuing validity of the law must be seen in terms of Jesus' fulfillment of it. In all its details the law remains valid, but the manner in which people are to relate to it has now been determined by the one who brought its fulfillment.

We are probably to understand Matthew 5:19 in a similar way. Indeed, some interpreters have taken *toutōn* to refer to what follows, in which case "these commandments" are the commands Jesus issues in Matthew 5:21-48. But there is little grammatical basis for this. "These commandments" are the detailed parts of the law of Matthew 5:18; the teaching of these commandments must take place in conjunction with the nature of Jesus' fulfillment of the law.

There is an undeniable tension between the stress on continuity with the law in these two verses and the stress on discontinuity that pervades Jesus' teaching about the law. Those who find the tension intolerable will declare these verses inauthentic. But we would argue that while some tension remains, the interpretation we have given makes credible Jesus' uttering all the statements in Matthew 5:17-19. Indeed, if tension is to be found, it is more likely to be an authentic reflection of the historical Jesus than the creation of the church or the Evangelist. Seen in this light, Matthew 5:18-19 reinforces the "I have not come to abolish" of Matthew 5:17. As Jesus proclaimed the beginning of the new era with its "new wineskins," he was aware of the danger that the newness could be pressed to the point of rupture with the OT. This he guards against by stressing, perhaps with some hyperbole, the continuing validity of the OT and its law for the life of the kingdom.

3. The Gospel Writers.

Jesus' stance on the law and his disputes with his Jewish contemporaries about this stance are so integral to his mission and message that none of the Evangelists can avoid the topic. Nor is there any indication that they wanted to. However, they do differ in the degree to which they are interested in this issue and the emphases they bring to it.

3.1. Matthew. As our previous discussion would indicate, Matthew shows more interest in Jesus and the law than do the other Evangelists. He alone records Jesus' claim to fulfill the law (Mt 5:17). In passages paralleled in Luke's Gospel, Matthew adds references to the law, most notably in the formulation of the so-called golden rule (Mt 7:12 par. Lk 6:31) and in the antitheses (Mt 5:21-48; cf. Lk 6:27-36; 12:57-59; 16:18). It is evident that Matthew writes to a community that is deeply concerned about the relationship between Jesus and the law, but there is scholarly debate about the exact nature of that community and the overall force of Matthew's teaching on this matter. This is partly because Matthew presents two different—potentially conflictive—emphases: endorsement of the law and transcendence of the law.

3.1.1. Endorsement of the Law. In our previous discussion (see 2.4 above) we noted the strength of Jesus' endorsement of the law as recorded in Matthew 5:18-19. But this passage is not alone. In Matthew 8:4 (with parallels in Mk 1:44 and Lk 5:14) Jesus insists that the leper whom he cleansed report to the priests and "offer the gift which Moses commanded, as a witness to them." In the story of the rich young man, Matthew accentuates more strongly the connection between obedience to the law and salvation by adding the saying "If you want to enter life, keep the commandments" (Mt 19:17). In Matthew 23:23 Jesus, while scolding the religious leaders for neglecting the "weightier matters of the law," nevertheless insists that they should continue to obey the law of tithing. Jesus in Matthew expects his disciples to bring gifts to the altar (Mt 5:23-24), to give alms (Mt 6:1-4) and to fast (Mt 6:16-18). And, in perhaps the strongest statement of its kind, Matthew presents Jesus endorsing the authority and teaching of the scribes and Pharisees (Mt 23:2-3). Here Jesus appears to endorse not only the Mosaic law but the oral law as well.

3.1.2. Transcendence of the Law. Along with these apparently strong endorsements of the law come equally strong indications of Jesus' transcendence of the law. Only Matthew records Jesus' claim to fulfill the law (Mt 5:17) and the antitheses, with their implicit criticism of the law (Mt 5:21-48). He, along with Mark and Luke, portrays Jesus acting with sovereign freedom on the sabbath and records his far-reaching claim to be "Lord of the Sabbath" (Mt 12:8). In a related development that many think to be central to Matthew's view of the law, there is a strong emphasis on love or concern for others as the embodiment of the law (Mt 7:12; 22:40).

3.1.3. A Synthesis. With these two strands of teaching in evidence, it is no wonder that some have seen Matthew as a conservative on the law, while others have seen him as antinomian. Others seek to do justice to both strands in Matthew by suggesting that he is fighting on two fronts—combating Jews and/or Jewish-Christian rigorists and Gentile-Christian antinomians (e.g., Barth). That Matthew was seeking to present a balanced teaching on the law against opposing tendencies is possible. But it is also possible to find a theological coherence in Matthew's teaching about the law if his salvation-historical perspective is considered.

Matthew makes clear that Jesus' death and resurrection mark a significant shift in salvation history. Prior to these events, as Jesus makes clear, his business is with "the lost sheep of the house of Israel" (Mt 15:24). After Jesus' mission is accomplished, however, the disciples are sent to "all the nations" with the good news (Mt 28:19-20). Similarly, Matthew shows that John's ministry ends the prophetic office of the OT (Mt 11:13). To some extent, then, Jesus' endorsement of the law in Matthew reflects only its continuing validity during the period before the new era is brought in. This is almost certainly the case in Matthew 8:4, Matthew 23:23, Matthew 5:23-24, Matthew 6:1-4 and Matthew 6:16-18. Jesus' endorsement of the teachings of the scribes and the Pharisees in Matthew 23:2-3 may also fall into this category, although we are probably to see irony here also (Jeremias).

Jesus never doubted the authority of the Mosaic law for the time preceding the entrance of the kingdom, and his instructions to followers living in that time will naturally include admonitions to obey those laws. Only those who think Matthew has rewritten everything in his Gospel for the consumption of the church in his day would have any difficulty with this. However, statements about Jesus transcending the law—and these represent the dominant thrust of the Gospel—reflect the fact that a new era of salvation history is indeed breaking in. This is an era in which Jesus' teaching will be the central authority for the people of God, and the law will play a role only as caught up in and re-applied by Jesus (Mt 5:17-19).

The relationship of the law to Jesus in Matthew is, then, only one segment of his salvation-historical, promise-fulfillment scheme. Through it Matthew integrates his stress on the continuity of the law—for the law looks ahead to and is incorporated into the teaching of Jesus—and on its discontinuity—for Jesus, not the law, is now the locus of God's word to his people.

3.2. Mark. In comparison with Matthew, Mark seems to display little interest in the issue of the law, as is revealed by the fact that the word never occurs in his Gospel. Nevertheless, many of those incidents that are fundamental in

Matthew's presentation of Jesus and the law are taken from Mark: the controversies over the sabbath (Mk 2:23-3:6) and ritual defilement (Mk 7:1-23), Jesus' teaching on divorce and remarriage (Mk 10:2-10), the story of the rich young ruler (Mk 10:17-22), and Jesus' teaching about the "great commandment" (Mk 12:28-34). Indeed, in three of these incidents Mark has important material not found in Matthew or in any other Gospel: the saying that "the Sabbath was made for humankind" (Mk 2:27), the editorial application of Jesus' teaching about defilement ("thus he made all foods clean," Mk 7:19) and the conversation between Jesus and a scribe after Jesus' identification of the greatest commandment, in which the scribe, with Jesus' approval, asserts that loving one's neighbor is "more than all the burnt offerings and sacrifices" (Mk 12:33). This material suggests that Mark may have had a particular interest in the supersession of the ritual law.

3.3. Luke. While Luke's perspective on the law cannot be understood apart from Acts, the second part of his two-volume work, we will concentrate on the Gospel. Here there is evidence that Luke is conservative with respect to the law (see Jervell), evidence that comes from what Luke has added to and omitted from the tradition. In adding to the tradition he portrays the piety of those involved in Jesus' infancy in legal terms (Lk 1:6; 2:22-24, 27, 37, 39, 42; *see* Birth of Jesus). Luke omits from his Markan source the episode concerning ritual defilement, the dispute about the law in its relation to divorce and remarriage and the teaching on the great commandment. In comparison with Matthew, Luke includes Jesus' teaching about the eternal validity of the law (Lk 16:17) but does not have the antitheses, Jesus' claim to have fulfilled the law or any reference to "weightier matters of the law." But these data do not justify the conclusion that Luke, in contrast to Matthew, upholds the Mosaic law.

First, comparisons with Matthew are difficult because we do not know whether Luke has omitted something in their common tradition or whether Matthew has added that which was not there. Second, Luke's omission of some of the Markan episodes suggests that he was not as interested in the law as were Mark and Matthew, but this is not necessarily indicative of a conservative attitude. Third, almost all of the positive evidence for a Lukan endorsement of the law

comes from the infancy narrative. But his purpose in portraying the people in this narrative as obedient to the law is simply to stress their piety and righteousness in accordance with the standards under which they lived. To conclude that Luke presents these people as exemplars of Torah piety for Christians generally is to go far beyond the evidence. Fourth, Luke adds to the tradition two sabbath healings by Jesus (Lk 13:10-17; 14:1-6) and, while they do not present Jesus annulling the sabbath, they share with the other sabbath incidents an emphasis on the sovereign freedom with which Jesus treated the sabbath.

Finally, Luke includes several sayings of Jesus that betray the same kind of salvation-historical perspective we have seen in Matthew. Luke 16:16 (with a parallel in Mt 11:12-13) is the most important: "The law and the prophets were until John; since then the kingdom of God is being proclaimed, and everyone is entering it violently." The debate about whether John is here included in the time of the "law and the prophets" or in the time of the kingdom is immaterial to our purposes. What is important is that Luke's Jesus affirms the cessation of the authority of the OT, in some sense, in the age of the kingdom. The important promise-fulfillment emphasis of Luke 24 (see Lk 24:25-27, 44), while not directly applied to the Mosaic commands, contributes to this Lukan salvation-history scheme. Rather than being a "conservative," Luke in his Gospel gives many indications that he views the law as belonging fundamentally to the past of the people of God (Blomberg).

3.4. John. True to its tendency, the Fourth Gospel follows its own course with regard to the law. In fact there is no single teaching about the law that is common to John and to any of the Synoptic Evangelists. Like the Synoptic Evangelists, however, John records two healings of Jesus on the sabbath (Jn 5:2-47; 9:1-41). In the first, Jesus' healing of a lame man sparks a debate about Jesus' authority to work on the sabbath. John betrays no interest in the meaning and intent of the sabbath command; he focuses exclusively on the christological claim: Jesus, as Son of God, has the same right to work on the sabbath as does the Father. The same christological focus is evident in the second incident, the healing of the man born blind. The Pharisees deny that Jesus is from God, because he sinned in performing the miracle on the sabbath (Jn 9:14-

16). Once again, Jesus' behavior, bound up as it is with his unique status, says nothing about his attitude toward the sabbath or the law generally.

Jesus' references to "your law" in disputes with the Jewish authorities (Jn 8:17; 10:34, although note the alternative reading) strike a much more polemical note. The use of the possessive pronoun creates some distance between Jesus and the law, although it is not clear if this is because Jesus stands with God over against the people, because he stands with John's Gentile readers against the Jews (as some interpret the circumstances of the Gospel) or simply because he wants to impress on the Jews their responsibility to hearken to their own law. Probably the last of these alternatives is the best (see Jn 7:51), in which case we learn little from it about Jesus' attitude to the law in John.

John shares with the Synoptic Evangelists an emphasis on the fulfillment of prophecy in Jesus' ministry and includes the law as a witness to Jesus on one occasion (Jn 1:45). We should note in this regard the way John shows Jesus replacing the great feasts and institutions of Israel—Passover (Jn 1:29 [?]; Jn 19:36 [probably]); the manna in the wilderness (Jn 6); tabernacles (Jn 7—8); Israel (Jn 15). Evidence that John included the law in this replacement scheme comes from terms, commonly associated with the law, that are applied to Jesus ("light," Jn 8:12; "bread of life," Jn 6:35; "living water," Jn 4:10), the designation of faith in Jesus as the one "work" that disciples are to do (Jn 6:29; in contrast to the "works of the law"?) and the Mosaic role that Jesus often assumes. It is precariously easy to read anything into John's symbolism that one wants, but there is enough evidence here to create the strong presumption that John wants to present Jesus as one who comes to fulfill for the church the role that Moses and the law performed in Israel.

The discontinuity between the law and Jesus seen in this replacement motif comes to clear expression in John 1:17: "the law came through Moses, grace and truth came through Jesus Christ." This discontinuity does not relate to the presence of grace in the OT as such, for John 1:16 indicates that Christians receive grace "in place of" (anti) the grace found in the old covenant. The discontinuity lies rather in the suggestion that the grace available for God's people in the OT does not come through the law and that it is only now in Jesus Christ that such grace can

be found. Moreover, in associating the law so closely with Moses and putting Christ firmly on the other side of the salvation-historical dividing line, John implies that in Jesus the law will no longer have the same position and significance that it had before.

4. Conclusion.

In different ways and with different emphases, all four Gospels reflect a dominant theme in the teaching of Jesus: his divine authority with reference to the law. Jesus was quick to clarify that his authority did not negate the role of the law in salvation history. But he also made it clear that this authority involved the right not only to exposit, add to or deepen the law but also to make demands of his people independent of that law. This being the case, it is quite inadequate and potentially misleading to think of Jesus as "the last great expositor of the law." The law, God's great gift to Israel, anticipated and looked forward to the eschatological teaching of God's will that Jesus brought. This teaching, not the law, is the focus of the Gospels, and the law remains authoritative for the disciple of Jesus only insofar as it is taken up into his own teaching.

See also ETHICS; RABBINIC TRADITIONS AND WRITINGS.

DJG: CLEAN AND UNCLEAN; COMMANDMENT; MARRIAGE AND DIVORCE; OATHS AND SWEARING; SERMON ON THE MOUNT.

BIBLIOGRAPHY. G. Bahnsen, *Theonomy in Christian Ethics* (Nutley, NJ: Craig, 1977); R. Banks, *Jesus and the Law in the Synoptic Tradition* (SNTSMS 28; Cambridge: Cambridge University Press, 1975); G. Barth, "Matthew's Understanding of the Law," in *Tradition and Interpretation in Matthew* (Philadelphia: Westminster, 1963); C. Blom-berg, "The Law in Luke-Acts," *JSNT* 22 (1984) 53-80; B. H. Branscomb, *Jesus and the Law of Moses* (New York: Richard A. Smith, 1930); D. A. Carson, ed., *From Sabbath to Lord's Day* (Grand Rapids: Zondervan, 1982); W. D. Davies, "Matthew 5:17, 18," in *Christian Origins and Judaism* (Philadelphia: Westminster, 1962); J. D. G. Dunn, *Jesus, Paul and the Law: Studies in Mark and Galatians* (Louisville, KY: Westminster John Knox, 1990); P. Fairbairn, *The Revelation of Law in Scripture* (Grand Rapids: Zondervan, 1957 [1869]); V. P. Furnish, *The Love Command in the New Testament* (Nashville: Abingdon, 1972); W. Gutbrod, "νόμος," *TDNT*

4:1036-85; J. Jeremias, *New Testament Theology: The Proclamation of Jesus* (New York: Scribner's, 1971); J. Jervell, *Luke and the People of God* (Minneapolis: Augsburg, 1972); H. Ljungman, *Das Gesetz Erfullen: Matth. 5.17ff. und 3.15 untersucht* (LUA 50S; Lund: Gleerup, 1954); J. P. Meier, *Law and History in Matthew's Gospel* (AnBib 71; Rome: Biblical Institute, 1976); D. J. Moo, "Jesus and the Authority of the Mosaic Law," *JSNT* 20 (1984) 3-49; S. Pancaro, *The Law in the Fourth Gospel* (NovTSup 42; Leiden: E. J. Brill, 1975); E. P. Sanders, *Jesus and Judaism* (Philadelphia: Fortress, 1985); idem, *Jewish Law from Jesus to the Mishnah: Five Studies* (Philadelphia: Trinity Press International, 1990); S. Westerholm, *Jesus and Scribal Authority* (ConBNT 10; Lund: C. W. K. Gleerup, 1978).

D. J. Moo

LAW II: PAUL

A well-attested feature of Jewish religion in Paul's time was the manner in which the Jewish way of life was being defined in oral and written form. The foundation of this material was the covenant that God communicated to Moses and made with the people of Israel at Sinai as it is preserved in the first five books of the Hebrew Bible. Jews of Paul's time, following biblical usage, frequently referred to these foundational writings as the "law" (Heb *tôrâ*, Gk *nomos*). After Paul's call to preach Christ to the Gentiles (Gal 1:15-16; Rom 1:5, 13-14; 15:18; cf. Acts 9:15; 22:21; 26:17) he thought extensively about the relationship between the Jewish law and faith in Christ. We find the results of that thinking primarily in the Thessalonian and Corinthian correspondence, in Galatians, Philippians and Romans, and to a lesser extent in Colossians, Ephesians and the Pastorals.

No area of Pauline studies has undergone more sweeping revision in the last half century than the apostle's view of the law. Compelling evidence has required a reassessment of Christian, and especially Protestant, assumptions about the law in Judaism and therefore about Paul's relationship to this single most important aspect of his ancestral faith. Some understanding of the nature of this revolution in Pauline studies is therefore an important prerequisite to a fresh reading of Paul's comments about the Jewish law.

1. The Struggle to Understand Paul's View of the Law

2. The Jewish Law in the Second Temple Period
3. The Jewish Law in the Context of Paul's Letters
4. Conclusion

1. The Struggle to Understand Paul's View of the Law.

During the period of the Renaissance and Reformation the Roman Catholic Church understood Paul's claim that "by works of the law no flesh shall be justified" (Gal 2:16) to mean that no one could attain eternal life without divine help. To the Catholic Church in the several centuries before and after Luther, this dictum did not seem to exclude good deeds from some role in salvation, and other passages in Paul's letters seemed to indicate that such works were necessary (Gal 5:6; Rom 6:13, 19; cf. Council of Trent, *Decree on Justification*, 6.10-11). Thomas Aquinas, therefore, believed that since human nature in itself required the transforming power of God's grace in order to inherit eternal life, humanity could not have been saved by its own merits even prior to the fall. After the fall, God's grace was even more necessary for salvation since humanity was now two removes from God (*Summa Theologica* 1-2.109.2). The OT law likewise operated at a human level and, as good as it might have been, was lacking the requisite grace of God that enabled people to keep its precepts (*Summa Theologica* 1-2.98.1-2). The new law of the NT contained this grace, however, and so Christians were able, by means of this grace, to do the works which merited for them eternal life (*Summa Theologica* 1-2.108.1; 111.2; 112.1; 114.1-9). Likewise, the Council of Trent claimed that justification was a process of cooperation with divine grace that began with repentance and continued in the form of obedience to the commandments of God and the church (Council of Trent, *Decree on Justification*, 6.10-11).

It was chiefly against this principle of cooperation between grace and works as it was expressed in the doctrine of the merits of the saints that the Reformers raised the banner of dissent. Prior to his protest against the Roman Catholic Church, Luther feared that neither his own good works, even if done out of love for Christ, nor the merits of his order could save him from God's terrible righteousness. Finally, after reaching a point of near despair, Luther began meditating on such texts as Psalm 31:1-2 and Romans 1:17 and discovered through them that the purpose of God's righteousness was not to condemn but to save the sinner. Rather than his angry accuser, God, as it turned out, was his rock of refuge and mighty fortress.

This experience informed Luther's reading of Paul's letters, especially Galatians. There he found ample evidence that no human activity, or "active righteousness," no matter how sincere or vigorous, could save people from God's wrath. Such salvation could come only through "passive righteousness"—a righteousness provided in its entirety by God and appropriated by faith in Jesus Christ. Luther took Paul's use of the word *law* in such passages as Galatians 2:16-21 as a cipher for God's righteous demands and all human attempts to be saved by them. These, he believed, could not save but only condemn and inspire terror: "no matter how wise and righteous men may be according to reason and the divine law," he says, "yet with all their works, merits, Masses, righteousness, and acts of worship they are not justified" (*LW*, 26:140, commenting on Gal 2:16). The role of the law is not to justify but to condemn and terrify (*LW*, 26:148-51). Salvation comes by another, entirely separate "law," the law of grace that gives righteousness to the believer apart from any effort and insulates him or her from the law's accusations. In the sphere of justification, therefore, the law has no place. By putting his or her faith in Christ, the Christian has climbed up into heaven and left the law far away on the earth below (*LW*, 26:156-57).

It is easy, when reading Luther, to concentrate on the theological argument with the Roman Catholic Church in which he is so energetically engaged and to miss a subtle hermeneutical impropriety in which the great Reformer and theologian has indulged. Especially in his lectures on Galatians, but elsewhere as well, Luther assumes that the Jews, against whose view of the law Paul was arguing, held the same theology of justification as the medieval Roman Catholic Church. This hermeneutical error would be perpetuated over the next four centuries and eventually serve as the organizing principle for mountains of Protestant scholarship on the OT and ancient Judaism.

It was frequently assumed among OT scholars, for example, that at least from the period of the restoration of the Jews to Israel under Ezra, the history of Judaism was a story of spiraling degeneracy into legalism, hypocrisy and lack of compassion. Similarly, when Protestant scholars discussed rabbinic Judaism they tended to assume that Paul's polemic against Judaism, interpreted through the lens of Luther's reaction against Roman Catholicism, provided a sound basis for systematizing the religion of the Mishnah, Talmud and related Jewish writings of a later era. F. Weber's description of Talmudic theology (1880) is typical. Keeping the many and peculiar commands of the law, said Weber, was the means by which the rabbis believed salvation was earned. The ordinary rabbi, therefore, believed that the goal of rabbinic religion was the search for reward on the basis of merit, that God was a stern judge and that approaching death brought with it the fear of losing salvation due to a lack of merit.

A large part of this portrait of ancient Judaism found its way into interpretations of the NT generally, and especially into expositions of Paul's writings. Widely used commentaries, such as that of W. Sanday and A. C. Headlam on Romans (reprinted seventeen times from 1895 to 1952) and influential books about the NT, such as R. Bultmann's description of *Primitive Christianity in Its Contemporary Setting* (1949; ET 1956) used this picture of Judaism as the backdrop for their explanations of NT theology. In Sanday and Headlam's commentary, for example, Paul's struggle with the law in Romans 7:7-25, which they take to be a self-portrait of his preconversion existence, is interpreted as the natural consequence of the "stern" rabbinic view of the law, which, they claim, "was fatal to peace of mind" (Sanday and Headlam, 189). Similarly, Bultmann, in a section of *Primitive Christianity* titled "Jewish legalism," claimed that the Jewish view of the law in the first century made "radical obedience" to God impossible because it held that once a certain list of commandments had been kept, one was in the clear and was free to do anything (Bultmann, 69). In addition, said Bultmann, it taught that God would punish sins strictly according to the law of retribution, that salvation was never a certainty and that even repentance and faith could be transformed into meritorious works (Bultmann, 69-71).

The Lutheran picture of ancient Judaism, now clad in the impressive robes of scholarship, did not go unchallenged among Jewish scholars. As early as 1894 the distinguished Jewish reformer C. G. Montefiore objected forcefully to what he viewed as the tendency of Christian theologians to paint rabbinic Judaism as a dark shadow against which Paul's theology could brightly shine. The rabbinic literature, pleaded Montefiore, reveals a compassionate and forgiving God, ready to lay aside even grievous infractions of the law at the slightest movement toward repentance by the offending party. It portrays rabbis, moreover, as those who regarded the law as a gift and delight, who placed a value on faith in God as high as Paul's, and whose daily prayer was "Sovereign of all worlds! not because of our righteous acts do we lay our supplications before thee, but because of thine abundant mercies" (b. Yoma 87b). "I wonder," Montefiore asked in an address before England's St. Paul Association in 1900, "if there is the smallest chance that you, unlike the theologians, will believe me when I say that all this business of the severe Judge and the stern law giver is a figment and a bugbear?"

Montefiore's critique of the Lutheran caricature of Judaism at first fell on deaf ears, but through the work of several influential scholars over the next seventy years, it gradually began to gain the ascendancy not only in Jewish circles but among nearly everyone working in the field. In 1927 G. F. Moore published a two-volume study of rabbinic theology that, in contrast to Weber's work, emphasized the role of grace, forgiveness and repentance in the earliest literature of rabbinic religion. This was followed in 1948 by W. D. Davies's detailed study of *Paul and Rabbinic Judaism*, in which Davies argued that Paul's doctrine of justification by faith apart from the law was only one metaphor among many, probably developed first in the heat of argument (Davies, 221-23), and that the apostle's letters revealed simply a Pharisee for whom the messianic age had dawned (Davies, 71-73; *see* Jew, Paul the).

Without question, however, the pivotal event in bringing Montefiore's complaint from the backwater to mainstream was the publication in 1977 of E. P. Sanders's *Paul and Palestinian Judaism*. Sanders's book was so powerful not because its approach was original but because Sanders addressed pointedly and exhaustively the distorted view of Judaism that Lutheran scholarship, and those under its influence, had produced. Sanders made his way step by step through the most influential works of modern NT scholarship in order to show that they dis-

paraged ancient Judaism as a religion in which salvation was accomplished by meritorious achievement. He then embarked on a lengthy journey through not only the rabbinic literature of the first two hundred years after Christ but through the Qumran literature, the apocrypha and the pseudepigrapha as well to determine how those documents answer the question, What must one do to be saved?

His conclusion was that in all of this ancient Jewish literature, with the exception of the atypical document 4 Ezra, salvation came not through achieving a certain number of meritorious works but through belonging to the covenant people of God. The proper response to the covenant was obedience, but means of atonement were readily available for those who did not obey fully. This "pattern of religion" Sanders called "covenantal nomism" (Sanders 1977, 75; 1992, 262-78), and, he claimed, it bears little resemblance to the descriptions of Jewish soteriology in most handbooks of Protestant biblical scholarship.

Largely as a result of this important work, most students of Pauline theology now believe that Montefiore, Sanders and other dissenters from the classic Protestant perspective have proven their case. The problem has now become what to do with Paul, who after all does seem to argue loudly against Jews who espouse justification by "works of the law." Montefiore's answer to this question in 1894 has become popular among some. He believed that Paul was an aberration whose neglect of the Jewish doctrine of repentance for infractions against the law was puzzling and whose Judaism, if Judaism at all, must have been heavily influenced by Hellenism. S. Sandmel claims similarly that "Paul's attitude toward the law is exactly the reverse of the views in all other surviving Jewish writings" (Sandmel 1978, 320) and that the origin of Paul's negative evaluation of the law lies to a large extent in ideas about the law that flourished in the fertile soil of Hellenistic Judaism. This brand of Judaism, Sandmel argues, often saw value in the law only as a guide to other religious ideals and so played down the importance of its literal observance. Paul, therefore, was predisposed to devalue the law because of his roots in a Judaism heavily influenced by Greek thought (Sandmel 1979, 48-53). This view reaches its extreme in the work of H. Maccoby, who, largely on the basis of Galatians 3:19 and Galatians 4:9-10, claims that

Paul's view of the law was derived from Gnosticism (Maccoby, 40-48).

This reading of Paul, as Davies observed long ago, blunders methodologically and historically by assuming neat divisions between the orthodox Judaism of Palestine and a supposedly deviant variety in the Diaspora. Such neat divisions apparently did not exist. Sanders, in *Paul and Palestinian Judaism* and in two subsequent books on Paul, takes the view articulated by Moore (Moore, 2.94) half a century before but not carefully worked out: Paul always began with the premise, which his experience had made certain to him, that Jesus was the Savior of the world, and worked backward from this premise to the conclusion that all the world, Jews included, needed to be saved through Jesus. In Sanders's view, therefore, Paul's theology represents a leap out of Jewish covenantal nomism into a different religion.

Sanders contends that Paul had no "theology of the law" but responded in various ways to various circumstances that threatened his mission of announcing to Jew and Gentile the necessity of participation in Christ for salvation. For practical reasons he considered those parts of the law that Gentiles viewed as particularly Jewish (circumcision, sabbath keeping and dietary observance) to be annulled. They would hinder the Gentile mission and would make it seem to Gentiles that the key to salvation was Judaism when in fact it was participation in Christ. When he felt compelled to give reasons for setting aside the law, he answered in various ways, some of them incompatible with others. His central explanation, however, seems to be that the law was given to condemn everyone so that everyone could be saved through Jesus Christ.

Nevertheless, Paul was still enough of a Jew psychologically to be uncomfortable with saying in every situation that the law was no longer valid. He had firm convictions about right and wrong, propriety and impropriety, derived from his Jewish upbringing. When asked to adjudicate on such matters, as he was for example by the Corinthians, the origin of his answers was often, ironically, the Jewish law (Sanders 1991, 84-100).

J. D. G. Dunn likewise has accepted the new consensus that Sanders's work represents but criticizes Sanders for not providing a plausible explanation of the fundamental Jewishness of Paul's letters. Sanders, Dunn charges, has so divorced Paul from Judaism that Paul's anguish over his unbelieving Jewish brothers and sisters in Romans 9:1-3 and his concern that Gentile Christians understand their spiritual indebtedness to Israel in Romans 11:17-24 are enigmas (Dunn, 188; *see* Romans, Letter to the).

The account of Paul that Dunn proposes as a substitute claims that Paul worked through the details of his view of the law in the heat of controversy with Jewish Christians who believed that Gentile Christians, in order to maintain a place in the covenant people of God, had to adopt the three "works of the law" that served as badges of national Israel: circumcision, sabbath keeping and dietary observance. Paul's polemic against "works of the law," then, is not directed against gaining salvation by doing good works but against believing that salvation was, at least in part, contingent upon belonging to national Israel and observing the law as a badge of that status (Dunn, 191-96). As a result, Paul's positive statements about the law are not inconsistent with his more negative statements, for the negative statements are directed against a nationalistic misuse of the law rather than against the law itself (Dunn, 200).

This reading of Paul, says Dunn, has numerous advantages. It acknowledges the legitimacy of Sanders's complaint against the Lutheran paradigm for understanding Judaism, but it gives a picture of Paul more plausible than Sanders's picture. Paul is now firmly rooted within first-century Judaism and his statements about the law, positive and negative, are held together by a consistent underlying conviction that the law, while good, can be misused as an instrument of national pride (Dunn, 200-203).

Another highly influential response to the new consensus comes from the pen of H. Räisänen. Like Dunn, Räisänen accepts Sanders's portrait of ancient Judaism and, like others, attempts to explain Paul's polemic against works of the law in light of this new perspective. He claims that Paul first developed his postconversion attitudes toward the law under the influence of the Hellenistic Christian community, a group that played down the necessity of the law's particularly Jewish aspects in the interest of winning Gentiles to Christianity. Later, in the heat of his Gentile mission and as a matter of convenience, Paul dropped the Law entirely from his evangelistic agenda without clearly thinking through the reasons why (Räisänen

1986, 300-301; cf. Räisänen 1983, 256-63).

Räisänen suggests that Paul produced his first attempts to explain the relationship between the law and faith in Christ when the Judaizers invaded his churches in Galatia. This group was antagonistic to Paul and produced a powerful case, based on straightforward arguments from the Hebrew Scriptures that Gentile Christians should adhere to the law and so become Jewish. Paul, convinced on the basis of his experience that such additions to the requirement of faith in Christ were unnecessary hindrances, then began to cast around for arguments to prove his conviction (Räisänen 1983, 256-63). In Räisänen's view he was less than successful. Instead of producing a convincing counterargument, he constructed a series of ad hoc statements, some mutually contradictory and others clear distortions of the Jewish view of the law.

The Paul of Räisänen's description provides an appropriate summarizing metaphor for the state of current scholarship on Paul's view of the law. The reexamination of Judaism that began with Montefiore and culminated in Sanders has shifted the ground beneath interpreters' feet so dramatically that no consensus on Paul's theology of the law has been able to emerge. Is this disarray ultimately the product of the disharmony between Paul's distorted picture of Judaism and Judaism as it existed? Could it be the result of internal disharmonies within Paul, and hence within his letters? An honest answer to these questions will require a fresh reading of Paul and of the Jewish literature of his era.

2. The Jewish Law in the Second Temple Period.

After the Babylonians destroyed Jerusalem, burned the temple and took many in Israel captive in 586 B.C., most Israelites in exile seem to have adopted the perspective of Jeremiah and Ezekiel and considered the experience as punishment for breaking the covenant God had made with them at Sinai. To the exiles, the Pentateuch's curses for disobedience to the covenant must have appeared to be a breathtakingly accurate prediction of the Babylonian invasion and subsequent exile (Lev 26:14-46; Deut 28:43-52, 64-67; 29:22-28; 31:14-29). Thus, when the Persians overran the Babylonians and subsequently allowed expatriate Israelites to return to their native land, the leaders of the return understandably resolved to adhere strictly to the

law and so to avoid future punishment for disobedience. Their Achilles heel prior to the exile, they believed, was their seduction into idolatry by foreign influences. The road to a restored covenant relationship with God, they reasoned, was a renewed determination to fence themselves off from harmful foreign influences by strictly obeying the law.

We can see these convictions clearly in Ezra-Nehemiah, where Ezra and Nehemiah express grave concern over Jewish intermarriage with the Gentile population of Palestine precisely because such actions could lead Israel once again into national apostasy and punishment (Ezra 9:10-15; cf. Neh 10:30). These convictions were still in place two and a half centuries later, as the book of Tobit reveals. There we read of Tobit's awareness that defeat and exile came to Israel as just punishment for breaking the Mosaic covenant (Tob 3:2-6) and of Tobit's determination, while living among Gentiles, to observe the Jewish marriage and dietary customs strictly (Tob 1:9-12; cf. Tob 4:12-13).

The belief that the law was the distinguishing mark of Israel as God's chosen people intensified in subsequent years as Hellenistic challenges to Israel's ancestral religion became more frequent and violent, especially under the Seleucid ruler Antiochus IV. The Maccabean books show that Antiochus attempted to force Israel into cultural conformity with the rest of his realm by forbidding the Jews to practice precisely those parts of their law that distinguished them from other peoples. He outlawed circumcision (1 Macc 1:48), made martyrs of those who refused to eat unclean food (2 Macc 6:18-31) and, most horrific of all, tried to force Jews to worship pagan gods (1 Macc 2:15-28).

Some Jews folded under such pressure, and a few even welcomed compromise as an opportunity for personal advancement, but many became more resolute than ever in their conviction that they would not again ignore God's law and consort with Gentile ways. They believed that if Israel were faithful to the Mosaic covenant, God would protect them no matter how overwhelming the foe, but that if they disobeyed the law, the Gentiles would defeat them in battle and they would cease to be, in any meaningful sense, God's covenant people (Jdt 5:17-21; 8:18-23; Pr Azar 6-14). So, like Daniel (Dan 1:1-21; 3:1-30) they determined not to break the law, especially observance of circumcision (*Jub.* 15:11-34), dietary restrictions (Jdt 10:5; cf. Jdt 12:2) and sabbath keeping (*Jub.* 2:17-33), for these aspects of the law separated them most clearly from the surrounding nations.

The politically minded among these strict adherents to the covenant of Moses turned to open rebellion against a succession of Seleucid rulers and eventually obtained political independence. Others, however, were content to wait upon God to establish the new covenant with his people that Jeremiah (Jer 31:31-34) and Ezekiel (Ezek 36:24—37:28) had predicted, a covenant in which God would give them a "new heart" and a "new spirit," removing their "heart of stone" and giving them a "heart of flesh" in its stead (Ezek 36:26). Thus the authors of *Jubilees* and of the Qumran documents frequently echo these passages (*Jub.* 1:22-25; 1QS 4, 5; 1QH 4, 5, 18; 4QShirShabb 2) and witness to a belief that these prophecies were being fulfilled within their communities.

Once the Maccabean family succeeded in throwing off Seleucid rule, observing the Jewish law was required of all who lived in the land, whether Jewish or not. Under John Hyrcanus I the Idumeans were forced to submit to circumcision and other legal requirements (Josephus *Ant.* 13.9.1 §§257-58), and Hyrcanus's successor, Aristobulus I, forced the Itureans to do the same (Josephus *Ant.* 13.11.3 §318). M. Hengel concludes appropriately that Hyrcanus and Aristobulus took these steps because they regarded all of ancient Israel as God's possession and viewed it as part of their mandate to purge the land of Gentiles, either by forcing them out or by forcing them to become Jews (Hengel, 197). Although written much earlier, Psalm 125:3 must have struck a resonant chord with them: "For the scepter of the wicked shall not stay upon the land apportioned to the righteous so that the righteous might not stretch out their hands to act wickedly." The evil influences of Gentiles in years past had led Israel into exile. That mistake would not be repeated.

By the first century A.D., the last of the Hasmoneans had nevertheless capitulated to Rome, and many Jews were happy within the limits of religious freedom that Rome allowed. Some radical groups arose, however, who claimed to be heirs to the zeal of the Hasmonean family and whose goal was to free Israel from the polluting presence of Gentiles. During the formative years of the early church these groups gained strength

until, prompted by the blunders and corruption of a quick succession of Roman procurators, their zeal burst into open rebellion against Rome in A.D. 66. Many of those involved in the revolt were concerned, like the Hasmoneans of old, to force conformity to the particularly Jewish aspects of the law on everyone who lived on the sacred land of Israel (see, e.g., Josephus *J.W.* 2.17.10 §454; *Life* 12 §§65, 67; 23 §§112-13).

Not all Jews during the five centuries from Ezra to the time of Paul took an approach this radical, and many sought to achieve some level of compromise with the Gentile world around them. In such writings as the Wisdom of Solomon, Ben Sira and Baruch, for example, the law was closely identified with "wisdom" and was found to encompass the insight that Gentile philosophers and theologians on occasion undeniably possessed. In the Wisdom of Solomon the Jewish law is said to be given to the world through Israel (Wis 18:4), and in Ben Sira and Baruch true wisdom and understanding are repeatedly coupled with observance of the commandments (Sir 1:26; 6:37; 9:15; 15:1; 16:4; 19:20; 21:11; 23:27—24:1; 24:23-29; 33:2-3; 34:8; 39:1-5; Bar 3:12; 3:36—4:1, 12). Despite these efforts to take Gentile thought seriously, however, there is no doubt that if a choice must be made, the law, not wisdom, should take priority (cf. Sir 19:20 with Sir 19:24). This literature, moreover, continues to express a profound sense of grief at the plight of oppression into which disobedience to the law has landed Israel (Sir 49:4-7; Bar 2:27—3:13; 4:12-13).

In other writings of the period the particularly Jewish aspects of the law were ignored (e.g., *Pseudo-Phocylides*), allegorized (e.g., *Letter of Aristeas* 139-69) or otherwise rationalized (see, e.g., Josephus *Ag. Ap.* §§2.173-74, 234; Aristobulus as quoted in Eusebius *Praep. Ev.* 13.12.9-16; 13.13.8) in an effort to emphasize to Gentile readers aspects of Judaism that would be most intelligible and attractive to them. Some Jews even spiritualized the distinctively Jewish aspects of the law to the extent that they felt literal observance was not necessary. According to Philo, who did not approve of their activity, this group focused its spiritualizing efforts on the laws of sabbath observance, festival participation and circumcision (Philo *Migr. Abr.* 450).

In sum, from at least the period of the exile in Babylon, most Jews realized that their subjugation to foreign powers was a direct result of their violation of the law given at Sinai. Many Jews believed, therefore, that the answer to their oppression was renewed commitment to separate themselves from the Gentiles around them by adhering to the law, especially to those aspects of the law that marked Israel as a separate people with a distinct way of life. Some within this group sought to cast off Gentile overlords and even to purge Gentiles from the land within the borders of Davidic Israel. Others, believing that God had begun to establish his new covenant within their communities, waited upon God to intervene eschatologically as he had promised in the prophets.

Another group, although probably no less committed to the law as the distinguishing mark of Israel, believed that contact with Gentile peoples and ideas was not only permitted but revealed that the best aspects of Gentile life were anticipated in the Mosaic law. Some Jews were willing to go still further and to become outwardly indistinguishable from monotheistic and morally upright Gentiles by spiritualizing at least the laws governing sabbath observance, festival keeping and circumcision. The scanty evidence for this last group probably indicates that their numbers were small and their influence insignificant. For most Jews of Paul's era, then, the law was the distinguishing mark of the Jewish people, to be kept at all costs in order to escape the curse that the law pronounced on the disobedient, and for some Jews the period in which this happened would mark the fulfillment of the prophetic promise of the new covenant.

3. The Jewish Law in the Context of Paul's Letters.

When we turn to Paul's letters we find a large measure of discontinuity, but also a surprising amount of continuity, between Paul and Second Temple Judaism on the place of the law in God's dealings with his people.

3.1. 1 and 2 Thessalonians. Paul's Thessalonian correspondence is widely neglected in the study of the apostle's view of the law. The word *nomos* ("law") does not occur in these letters, and they were written before Paul's heated disputes with the Judaizers over the law had taken place. It has in the past, therefore, seemed safe to move immediately beyond them to the more fertile ground of 2 Corinthians, Galatians, Philippians and Romans. The absence of the word *nomos* from the Thessalonian letters, however,

does not mean that we cannot glean some information from them about Paul's view of the law at this early stage in his letter-writing career. What we can glean turns out to be helpful in understanding Paul's view of the law in his later, more law-oriented correspondence.

As T. J. Deidun has pointed out (Deidun, 10-12), Paul's use of the phrase "the church of the Thessalonians in God the Father and the Lord Jesus Christ" in 1 Thessalonians 1:1 (cf. 2 Thess 1:1), and his description of the Judean Christians as "the churches of God" in 1 Thessalonians 2:14 come from the OT conception of "the church of God," a status that became Israel's on the day that they assembled to receive the law from Moses at Sinai (Deut 4:9-14; 9:10; 10:4; 18:16). Israel was to observe this law, according to Leviticus, because it gave them a holiness corresponding to the holiness of God who was present among them and because it distinguished them from the surrounding Gentile nations (Lev 11:45; 18:1-5, 24-30; 19:1; 20:7-8, 23-26). Presumably the new covenant prophesied in Jeremiah 31 and Ezekiel 36—37 would have a similar effect for God's people: it would serve to distinguish his people from the rest of the world.

This is precisely what we find in 1 Thessalonians, where the distinguishing mark of the Thessalonians is adherence to the "specific precepts" (*tinas parangelias*, 1 Thess 4:2) that Paul gave to them and that would mark them off from "the Gentiles who do not know God" (1 Thess 4:5; Deidun, 18-28). They are to be "set apart" (*hagiasmos*), for God's Holy Spirit dwells among them and they are taught by God (1 Thess 4:7-9; cf. Jer 31:34). The wicked figure who will arise in the eschaton can therefore be described as "the man of lawlessness" (*anomia*, 2 Thess 2:3, 7-8). Paul could hardly be unaware of the echoes that his description of the Thessalonian community contains of Leviticus and of Jeremiah.

Thus Paul views the Thessalonian congregation as a fulfillment of God's promise to establish a new covenant with his people, one in which the law would be written on hearts and obeyed. Although the congregation is predominantly Gentile (1 Thess 1:9), Paul regards it as parallel to the Israel of the Mosaic covenant, whose status as "the church of God" originated with the giving of precepts to mark them off as a distinct people. We cannot at this point discern the details of the relationship between the old covenant and the new in Paul's thinking; but that there are parallels between the patterns of the two covenants and that there are differences is clear. Both old covenant and new emphasize sanctity through behavior and for identical reasons; but the new covenant, unlike the old, is not ethnically determined.

3.2. 1 Corinthians. Paul's attitude toward the Jewish law comes into sharper focus when we move to 1 Corinthians. Although Paul uses the word *nomos* only eight times in this letter (nine if 1 Cor 14:34 is original), like the Thessalonian correspondence, a stance toward the law is presupposed in much of what Paul says in the letter about sanctity and ethics. Moreover, the few times that Paul explicitly speaks of the law provide excellent evidence for his attitude toward the law when the law is not a bone of contention between himself and his opponents, as it is in several of his later letters. For these reasons, 1 Corinthians provides a ripe field for gleaning information about Paul's view of the law.

The first two verses of the letter demonstrate that Paul's emphasis on the continuity between the people of God in the OT and the newly constituted people of God has not weakened since writing to the Thessalonians. Paul addresses the Corinthian believers as "the church of God . . . set apart in Christ Jesus, called to be separate" (1 Cor 1:2), once again echoing the Pentateuch's description of Israel's constitution as the people of God at Sinai. The theme is filled out in 1 Corinthians 3:10-17, where Paul describes the Corinthian church as God's temple, subject to the most careful maintenance, "for the temple of God, which you [pl.] are, is sacred" (1 Cor 3:17). Because they are God's congregation and God's temple, moreover, the Corinthians should distinguish themselves from "the Gentiles" by abstaining from sexual immorality (1 Cor 5:1; cf. 1 Thess 4:5) and separating themselves from those who claim to be part of God's congregation but refuse to shun immorality (1 Cor 5:10-13). Paul supports his argument for excommunicating those within the church who refuse to separate themselves from Gentile sexual misconduct by citing a saying that recurs many times in Deuteronomy and makes the same point with respect to Israel: "cast out the evil person from among you" (1 Cor 5:13; cf. Deut 17:7; 19:19; 22:21, 24; 24:7). He is also concerned that they not taint themselves with idolatry and, as N. T. Wright (120-36) has shown, Paul approaches the subject of eating meat offered to

idols from the standpoint of the great Jewish confession, drawn from the Torah, that there is but one God (1 Cor 8:4; cf. Deut 4:35, 39; 6:4).

Paul also demonstrates in 1 Corinthians that he is aware of the whole story of God's *covenant with Israel at Sinai, Israel's failure to keep that covenant, and of the promise of an eschatological covenant (*see* Eschatology). In 1 Corinthians, just as in 1 Thessalonians, he shows that he believes the churches coming into existence through his missionary work and on the basis of faith in Christ are the inheritors of this new covenant. These convictions come most clearly to the surface in 1 Corinthians 10, where, in the course of warning the Corinthian believers against idolatry, Paul reminds them of the story of Israel's failure and its miserable consequences and then makes the telling statement, "But these things happened to them as a pattern and were written in order to admonish us, upon whom the climax of the ages has arrived" (1 Cor 10:11). The Corinthian believers, then, appear in Paul's thinking to be eschatological Israel, the new "congregation of God" who stand in contrast to the Gentiles on one side and to "Israel according to the flesh" on the other (1 Cor 10:18, 32; cf. 1 Cor 12:2).

Most of the points in the letter at which Paul specifically refers to the law tally well with this picture of believers as the new Israel. In 1 Corinthians 7:19 Paul claims that what really matters in the busy era before Christ's return is not whether one is married or unmarried, slave or free, circumcised or uncircumcised, but whether one "keeps the commands of God," a phrase frequently used in the literature of Paul's era for "observing the Jewish law" (Ezra 9:4 LXX; Sir 32:23; Mt 19:17-19). In 1 Corinthians 9:8-9 he calls on "the Mosaic law" as an authority for his contention that he, like other preachers of the gospel, has the right to be supported by the community in which he works. In 1 Corinthians 9:19-23 he claims that he seeks to accommodate everyone, whether Jew or Gentile, whether "under the law" or not, although he is not "outside the law but within the law of Christ" (1 Cor 9:21). In 1 Corinthians 14:21 he calls upon "the law" to prove a point about the role of speaking in tongues in the church's worship (1 Cor 14:23). Clearly, for Paul, "the law" was valid in some form for members of the new covenant.

Already in these few references, however, we find clues that Paul's view of the law is complex.

How could Paul claim that what mattered was keeping God's commands but then say that circumcision, one of the law's most prominent commands, did not matter? What provoked him to say that he could observe or not observe the dietary scruples of "weak" Jewish Christians because he was not "under law" but that he was subject to "the law of Christ"? In what meaningful sense could Paul claim that the law was authoritative for believers when he ignored these central commands?

First Corinthians does not provide an explicit answer to this question, but if we add Paul's comments in 1 Corinthians 7:19 to those in 1 Corinthians 9:19-23 we can see a pattern that may help us to understand Paul's thinking about the law. In 1 Corinthians 7:19 the part of the law with which Paul is willing to dispense is circumcision; in 1 Corinthians 9:19-23 it is dietary observance (cf. 1 Cor 8:1-13; 10:1—11:1). Both of these aspects of the law, as we saw above in our study of the law in Judaism, were prized by many Jews as particularly Jewish laws, laws that marked the Jews off from the rest of the world as God's special people. It is precisely these highly prized and ethnically specific aspects of the law that Paul considers no longer valid.

If we pause to think about Paul's calling to be the apostle to the Gentiles we can see clearly the reason for his rejection of these laws: they served to limit membership in the people of God to ethnic Jews and those willing to convert to Judaism. As we have seen, Paul affirmed the law's commitment to separation of the people of God from the rest of the world. The crucial areas of separation, however, were now no longer the observance of dietary rules and circumcision but moral behavior motivated by God's sanctifying Spirit.

Paul's view of the law, however, is more complex still. Another element of its complex structure breaks through the surface in 1 Corinthians 15:56, his final reference to the law in this letter. Paul has been discussing the necessity of the bodily resurrection of believers and of Christ from the dead, and he has been trying to explain to Greeks unfamiliar with Jewish eschatology the eternal value of the body and what a bodily resurrection will be like. The climax of his argument comes in 1 Corinthians 15:54-55 with a paraphrase of Isaiah 25:8 and a quotation of Hosea 14:4: "Death has been swallowed up in victory. Where, O Death, is your victory? Where, O Death, is your sting?" Paul's next statement comes, like a bolt from the blue, with no warning: "the sting of death is sin, and the power of sin is the law" (1 Cor 15:56). Sin has not figured prominently in Paul's argument to this point, and law not at all. Why does Paul suddenly mention them here?

The surprise that the reader feels at encountering 1 Corinthians 15:56 demonstrates how firmly the law was connected with sin and death in Paul's mind. Like a runner unable to stop at the finish line, Paul is unable to stop his argument at its most rhetorically effective finish and runs ahead into other subjects that he associates with the law. This comes as a surprise not only because it raises a new subject within 1 Corinthians 15 but also because what Paul says about the law in this verse does not immediately appear to be compatible with what he has said about it elsewhere in the letter. Elsewhere it appears as an authority; here it is connected with sin and death, aspects of the present world that are evil and will pass away. How can Paul hold both positions?

First Corinthians does not answer this question for us. In Paul's next letter, however, we find some information that helps us to move toward an answer.

3.3. 2 Corinthians. By the time Paul wrote 2 Corinthians he had entered a period of stormy relations with the Corinthian believers, apparently aggravated by the arrival in Corinth of a group of Jewish Christians who opposed him. Despite this changed situation, Paul's attitude toward Jewish law in 2 Corinthians meshes well with our discoveries in the Thessalonian correspondence and in 1 Corinthians. We still find Paul, for example, appealing to the law as an authority when discussing how believers should conduct the practical affairs of everyday life (2 Cor 8:15, quoting Ex 16:18; 2 Cor 13:1, quoting Deut 19:15). In 2 Corinthians, as in 1 Corinthians, moreover, one passage does not seem to square with this picture of continuity between the Jewish law and the new Israel.

The topic under discussion in 2 Corinthians 3:1-18 is the contrast between Paul's style of ministry and that of his opponents. Specifically, Paul is concerned to refute the notion that letters of recommendation, such as his opponents carry, are necessary credentials for true apostleship (2 Cor 3:1; *see* Apostle). Paul claims to have letters of recommendation, but not ones written with ink or on tablets of stone. His letters were written instead with the Spirit of the living God on the tablets of the human heart (2 Cor 3:2-3). Letters were not written with ink on stone in Paul's time, but with ink on papyrus. Paul has, however, purposely mixed his metaphors in order to echo the prophetic passages dealing with the new covenant, in which God would replace his people's "heart of stone" with a "heart of flesh," put his Spirit in them (Ezek 36:26-27), and write his law "on [their] hearts" (Jer 31:33). Thus, in 2 Corinthians 3:6 Paul claims to be a minister of a new covenant, not like the old, written covenant that "killed" by properly bringing the covenant's curses down upon disobedient Israel, but like the covenant that Jeremiah predicted would at some future time bring forgiveness for sin and a renewed ability to know and to obey God.

Paul's implied conclusion to this argument is that written letters, such as his opponents carry (2 Cor 3:1-2), provide insignificant proof of apostleship when compared with the eschatologically significant "letters" that Paul can bring forward in the form of the Corinthian believers themselves, for the Corinthians joined the eschatological people of God through Paul's ministry and represent the long-awaited fulfillment of the prophetic promise.

In order to drive the point home even more forcefully, Paul in 2 Corinthians 3:7-11 comments on the superiority of the new covenant, of which he is minister and the Corinthians are proof, to the old. The old covenant, he says, was glorious, so glorious in fact that when Moses received the covenant stipulations from God, his face was "glorified" to the extent that the Israelites were not able to look at it (2 Cor 3:7; cf. Ex 34:29-30 LXX; *Tg. Onq.* Ex 34:29-30). If such glory attaches to "the ministry of death" (2 Cor 3:7) and "condemnation" (2 Cor 3:9), Paul says, how much more glorious must be "the ministry of the Spirit" and "righteousness" (2 Cor 3:8-9). In 2 Corinthians 3:12-18 Paul goes on to describe how Moses veiled his face to prevent the Israelites from seeing that its glory was fading and comments that the old covenant's obsolescence is still veiled from the unbelieving Jews of Paul's day (2 Cor 3:14).

When we compare 2 Corinthians 3:1-18 with Paul's appeal to the law as a guide to conduct in 2 Corinthians 8:5 and 2 Corinthians 13:1 we face the same problem we discovered in 1 Corin-

thians. Paul at times appears to say that the law is no longer valid since it is aligned with sin, death and condemnation (1 Cor 15:56; 2 Cor 3:7, 9), and at times seems to regard it, at least in some form, as authoritative. Are these two sides of a complex view of the law, or are they, as Räisänen and others believe, indications that Paul's view of the law is confused and contradictory?

One hint that these two approaches to the law form part of a complex but coherent position lies in the consistent presence of the two approaches in different letters. That 1 Corinthians and 2 Corinthians contain both attitudes, although the letters address different situations, shows at least that Paul did not simply make one type of statement when convenient in one situation and another type of statement when convenient in a different situation.

A second indication that Paul's view of the law is complex and coherent rather than ad hoc and contradictory lies in the nature of the negative statements. The most natural background for Paul's statements that the law is aligned with sin, death and condemnation is the widespread conviction among first-century Jews that the law had justly condemned Israel to Gentile domination for transgressing its commands. When Paul speaks of the "old covenant" as "made obsolete in Christ" (2 Cor 3:14), he may have in focus not everything the law contained but the law's sentence of condemnation upon Israel's transgression of the covenant. This reading gains some support from Paul's description of the Sinaitic covenant as "the ministry of death" (2 Cor 3:7), recalling precisely the penalty for breaking the covenant according to Leviticus 26:25 (LXX) and Deuteronomy 30:15, 19, and his further description, so appropriate in this context, of the Mosaic code as the "ministry of condemnation" (2 Cor 3:9). If this perspective is correct, then Paul does not say in these passages that every aspect of the Mosaic legislation was abolished but that God had abolished the law's just sentence of condemnation upon his people for their transgressions. As Paul puts it, "God was in Christ reconciling the world to himself by not counting their transgressions against them" (2 Cor 5:19).

In sum, we have discovered so far that Paul clearly believed that the promise of the new covenant had been fulfilled in the coming of Jesus Christ, that the people of God which this new covenant constituted included Gentiles as Gentiles, not Gentiles as converts to Judaism, and that this newly constituted people was, like the old people of God, separated from the world around it by their conduct. We have also found that the specific rules of this separation coincide in many cases with the rules in the Mosaic legislation and sometimes are quoted from that legislation word for word. Nevertheless, the Mosaic code, viewed from the standpoint of its historical role in justly condemning God's people for their sin, Paul says, has been abolished. For Paul, therefore, it is impossible to say that the Mosaic law, minus a few cultic and ethnic regulations, is still in force. To the contrary, since the Mosaic law was inextricably bound to a period of time in which the boundaries of God's people were virtually identical with the boundaries of the Jewish people and to a time in which God's people labored under a justly pronounced sentence of condemnation, it has come to its divinely appointed end (see esp. 2 Cor 3:13).

With these discoveries in mind we are now in a better position to understand the statements that Paul makes about the Jewish law in the letters where the law is a specific topic of debate. Our discoveries in the Thessalonian and Corinthian correspondence will help us to understand the more difficult passages in Galatians, Philippians and Romans.

3.4. Galatians. Paul's letter to the Galatians records the apostle's angry response to a group of fledgling churches that had come under the influence of Jewish Christians preaching "another gospel" (Gal 1:8-9). This group, evidently under pressure from zealous and violent Jews in Palestine (Gal 6:12), taught that it was necessary to become a full proselyte to Judaism in order to stand justified (*see* Justification) before God at the final day of reckoning. At issue in particular were the requirements that the Gentile Galatians observe circumcision (Gal 2:3; 5:2-6, 11-12; 6:12-13), Jewish holy days (Gal 4:10) and dietary restrictions (Gal 2:11-14).

The details of Paul's response are compressed and frequently difficult to understand, but it is clear that they flow out of the central convictions that a new era in God's dealings with his creation has dawned and that in this new era God has established a new covenant with a newly constituted people (Gal 1:4; 4:4; 4:24, 28; cf. Gal 3:17). Viewed from this perspective, the reintroduction of precisely those barriers that divided Jew from Gentile was nothing short of a defection from the new covenant and a return to the days of the old covenant with its divisions between people (Gal 2:15-21) and its legitimate curse upon Israel's miserable failure to keep the law (Gal 3:10-14). It was to nullify the effect of Christ's timely coming and death (Gal 4:4; 2:21; 5:4; cf. Gal 3:13-14), to deny the work of the eschatologically supplied Spirit (Gal 3:1-5) and to fall away from the graciously fulfilled promise of God (Gal 5:4). It was, in short, a prodigious error of timekeeping.

From this hermeneutical origin, Paul's discussion of the law takes two directions. The first, which not surprisingly consumes most of his energy, is that the national markers of circumcision, sabbath keeping and dietary observances, or "works of the law" as Paul calls them (Gal 2:11-16), cannot make one righteous before God. The reason for this is twofold. For one thing, Paul says, no one can keep the whole law. Paul's opponents demonstrate this by their inability to follow the law (Gal 6:13); the Galatians will discover it too if they undertake its yoke (Gal 5:3); and the historical experience of Israel with the curse of the law for disobedience proves it to be true (Gal 3:10-12, cf. Col 2:14). Why is it impossible to keep the law? Paul hints at what he thinks on this important issue in Galatians 2:16, when he says that "by works of the law no *flesh* shall be justified." The term *flesh* was probably suggested to Paul not only by the physical nature of the circumcisions that his opponents wished to perform on the Galatians but also by the use of the word to indicate human weakness in such biblical passages as Genesis 6:3, 12, Jeremiah 17:5 and Isaiah 40:6. Thus the term appears to be Paul's shorthand for humanity's vulnerability to sin (Gal 5:19, 24; 6:8). To elevate "works of the law" to the level of a requirement for living in a harmonious covenant relationship with God, Paul says, is to place such a relationship outside anyone's reach, whether Jew or Gentile, because the human inclination to disobey God prevents "any flesh" from obeying the law completely (Gal 2:16).

The second reason that "works of the law" cannot place one within this harmonious covenant relationship with God is that the covenant of which these works are part was temporary. Unlike the promise made to Abraham, which constituted a permanent covenant fulfilled in Christ (Gal 3:15-18), the Sinaitic covenant was established "on account of transgressions." By this last phrase Paul probably means that God gave the law at Sinai in order to reveal clearly Israel's sin, to transform it from something ill defined and inchoate into specific transgressions against God's will. Paul is probably alluding here to a well-known irony: at the very moment God gave the law to Moses on Sinai, Israel was on the plain below already violating its first stipulation (Ex 32:7-8; cf. *Bib. Ant.* 12.4, c. first century A.D.).

Paul's meaning becomes even clearer when he describes the Sinaitic covenant as a "pedagogue" *(paidagōgos)*, the family slave in the Greco-Roman world who served as guardian, disciplinarian and teacher of children until they reached maturity (Gal 3:23-25). Those under the pedagogue's charge sometimes remembered their caretaker fondly, but frequently in satire and in art he is depicted as a harsh figure, rod in hand, ready to punish any disobedience. As Galatians 3:23 shows, Paul's purpose for comparing the Sinaitic covenant with a pedagogue in this passage is twofold: to emphasize its purpose of identifying and punishing sin and to highlight its temporary nature.

From Galatians 4:1—5:1 Paul uses a series of metaphors to argue that those who want to live under the yoke of the covenant at Sinai are turning the clock back to an era in which Gentile and Jew were enslaved to sin. The concept that allows these various metaphors to hang together is that of slavery. First, Paul compares the Gentile Galatians' former existence under "the elemental things of the world" *(stoicheia tou kosmou)*, a phrase reminiscent of their former idolatrous practices, with the life of the young heir to a wealthy estate who, for the time being, is no different from a slave. For the Galatians to accept the yoke of the Sinai covenant was to return from the era of the eschatological Spirit to that former era in which sin dominated their lives (Gal 4:1-11). Next, Paul compares life under the Sinaitic covenant with Hagar, Abraham's female slave who gave birth to Abraham's first son, Ishmael (Gal 4:21-31). Hagar, he says, stands for the present Jerusalem (Gal 4:25), and to accept the Sinaitic covenant as binding is to turn away from the eschatological new Jerusalem, with its new covenant of freedom from the law's curse (Gal 4:24, 26), and to return to the "present" Jerusalem where the curse remains in force (Gal 4:25; cf. 4 Ezra 9:38-10:28; *2 Bar.* 4). It is, therefore, to accept Hagar the slave as one's mother and to live in slavery with her other children (Gal 4:25).

This extensive case against human ability to keep the Mosaic covenant and against that covenant's continuing validity does not, however, exhaust Paul's comments on the law in Galatians. In a few other passages, Paul's comments take a different direction. In Galatians 5:14 he tells his readers that "the whole law is fulfilled in one phrase, namely, 'You shall love your neighbor as yourself,' " and in Galatians 6:2 he encourages them to bear each others' burdens "for thereby you will fulfill the law of Christ." These statements seem surprising until we remember (1) that the Corinthian correspondence showed a similar pattern of regarding the Mosaic legislation as obsolete but then referring to the law in positive ways and (2) that in neither the Corinthian correspondence nor in Galatians does Paul say that each specific command in the Mosaic code is obsolete, but only the code viewed as a whole with its curses for disobedience and its barriers against Gentiles.

Paul's quarrel is with the imposition of old and temporary structures upon the new eschatological age of reconciliation—structures whose purpose was to condemn sin and to sequester the Jews from the Gentiles (cf. Eph 2:14-18). Some of the content of the Mosaic law emerges unscathed from Paul's critique, therefore, because it is untainted by the temporal nature of the curses and barriers. These aspects of the Mosaic law, Paul believes, are not only still valid but are fulfilled by believers when they walk in the Spirit (Gal 5:22-23; 6:2; cf. Eph 6:2).

3.5. Philippians. Although Philippians, unlike Galatians, was not written primarily to correct a mistaken notion of the role of the law in salvation history, the Galatian controversy was nevertheless ringing in Paul's ears as he wrote this letter. In Philippians 3:2-11, therefore, we find a warning against the same Jewish Christians who were trying to turn the clock back to an era in which circumcision, dietary requirements and sabbath keeping separated Israel from the Gentiles (Phil 3:2-3). Although the group did not yet pose an active threat to the Philippians (Phil 3:2 sounds more like a warning of possible rather than of present danger), Paul had seen enough of the damage they could do to warrant delivering a warning against them to one of his favorite churches (Phil 4:15-16).

Paul's warning, although brief, provides a helpful link between his compressed and forceful statements about the law in Galatians and his more carefully nuanced comments in Romans. In articulating his case against his opponents, Paul argues, as he had in Galatians, that to demand the fulfillment of these obsolete requirements is to place confidence in "the flesh," humanity's fallen and inadequate ability to do what God requires (Phil 3:3-4; cf. Gal 2:16). In explaining what he means, however, he takes a step beyond Galatians toward his later argument in Romans. To place confidence in one's fleshly circumcision, Jewish lineage and punctilious legal observance, he says, is to rely on one's own inadequate righteousness rather than on the righteousness that comes from God (Phil 3:5-6, 9; cf. Rom 2:1—3:20).

This new twist to his case against the reintroduction of the Sinaitic covenant is grounded in two biblical images. The first is the image of Israel's inadequate righteousness during the wilderness wanderings, in spite of which God led them into the promised land (Deut 9:1—10:11). As with Israel, Paul's righteousness was based on the broken Sinaitic covenant and therefore was an inadequate means of attaining salvation (lit. "the resurrection from the dead," Phil 3:9; cf. Rom 10:2-3). The second biblical image Paul uses is of God's powerful and effective action to rescue his people from their plight as exiles and to restore them to their land and to a peaceful relationship with himself. In Isaiah 46:13 and Isaiah 51:5-8 God refers to this saving activity as "my righteousness." Paul takes up this notion in Philippians 3:9 to say that the biblical expectations of an eschatological display of God's righteousness have been at least partially fulfilled in Jesus Christ, and so to cling to the old, inadequate righteousness based on a broken Sinaitic covenant is to put one's trust in "refuse" (Phil 3:8). This brief comment in Philippians on the relationship between the law, conceived as the Sinaitic covenant, and "the righteousness from God" will in Romans become a dominant theme.

3.6. Romans. Paul's view of the law in Romans, like his comments in Galatians, come into sharper focus if we understand something about the situation that provoked the letter. When Paul wrote Romans he was on the verge of delivering his highly prized collection of relief funds from his predominantly Gentile churches to the Jewish Christians in Jerusalem (Rom 15:25). He was concerned, however, that this offering, purchased at the price of considerable labor, would not be acceptable to the church there, and so he wrote to Rome, in part, to solicit that church's prayer support for his journey (Rom 15:30-32). Acts shows us that Paul's concern centered upon what some Jewish Christians in Jerusalem had heard about his view of the law (Acts 21:20-21). Similar rumors had also reached the Roman church, a community that, as A. J. M. Wedderburn (44-65) argues, had close ties to Jerusalem (Rom 3:8; 6:1; 6:15). Hence Paul's purpose in Romans was probably at least in part to correct misunderstanding about his view of the law.

As in Galatians, Paul makes positive and negative statements about the law. He maintains that "works of the law" cannot give righteousness and that the law, no longer apparently conceived as the Sinaitic covenant, can be fulfilled by Christians. In Romans, however, Paul articulates his critique of the Sinaitic covenant in a slightly different way from what he had in Galatians. In Galatians, Paul never mentioned boasting in the law (although see Gal 6:13-14), but in Romans his argument receives a new twist from the case it makes against "boasting" or "glorying" in the law as a special possession of the Jewish people (Rom 2:17, 23; 4:2; cf. Phil 3:3-6).

When Paul begins to describe the gospel that he wants "to preach to you who are in Rome also" (Rom 1:15), among his first points is that mere knowledge of what God requires does not provide one with a right standing before God. Only obedience to God's requirements, Paul says, can do that. He begins by discussing the Gentile world where many people sin against God (Rom 1:21-31) although they know his awesomeness, power, divinity (Rom 1:20), creative activity (Rom 1:25) and moral standard (Rom 1:32). Nevertheless, their knowledge goes unaccompanied by obedience, and so in spite of their knowledge, God punishes them precisely as their sins deserve (Rom 1:24, 26, 28).

Paul then turns to the Jewish world where God's impartiality (Rom 2:11) requires that the same standard of judgment hold true: "It is not the hearers of the law who are righteous in God's eyes, but the doers of the law who will be declared righteous" (Rom 2:13). This standard is so firm, says Paul, that in God's eyes it is appropriate for a Gentile who keeps the law in spirit but violates its letter by remaining uncircumcised (Rom 2:26, 29) to sit in judgment upon a Jew who boasts (Rom 2:23) in the possession of the law but does not obey it (Rom 2:14-29). Although this is a complex passage, its fundamental point is clear: it is no use for Jewish Christians to impose a standard upon Gentile Christians that the Jews have historically not been able to keep (cf. Rom 2:24 and Acts 15:10-11). The reason for this is that doing the "just requirements of the law" (Rom 2:26) and keeping it "inwardly" and "spiritually" (Rom 2:28-29) are what matters before God, not boasting in the possession of the law (Rom 2:23) and in outward marks like circumcision (Rom 2:25-26).

In Romans 3:9-20 Paul takes the further step of pointing out that no one, whether Jew or Gentile, fully does what the law requires. Instead, when measured against the standard that the law demands, all apologetic speeches must cease (Rom 3:19; cf. Job 29:7-10), for everyone stands condemned. All, Jew and Gentile, are "under sin" (Rom 3:9; cf. Rom 8:7), and boasting in possession of the law (Rom 3:27) or the careful observance of the Mosaic code's stipulations ("works of law," Rom 3:28) are of no use. The Mosaic covenant has been broken nationally and personally by Jew and Gentile, and only eschatological help from the covenant keeping God ("the righteousness of God," Rom 3:21) can remedy the situation. This has happened in Jesus Christ, because of whom all believers, whether Jew or Gentile, stand assured of a favorable verdict at the day of reckoning (Rom 3:21-26).

By this point in the argument Paul has largely made his case. Two important threads, however, remain loose and need attention. First, Paul must address the significant objection that he has nullified the law, which Paul believes to be God's Word (Rom 3:31). Paul answers this objection by appealing not to the Sinaitic covenant but to the narrative portion of the law and specifically to God's covenant with Abraham, the first "Jew." Paul observes that God reckoned Abraham righteous (Gen 15:6) prior to circumcision (Gen 17:11-14, 23-27) and then claims that circumcision served only as a seal upon a covenant already made on the basis of Abraham's faith. Hence faith, not "works" prescribed by the Mosaic code, bring righteousness (Rom 4:1, 1-5, 13), and Abraham serves as the prototype not only of the believing and circumcised Jew but of the believing and uncircumcised Gentile as well (Rom 4:11-12). In this way Paul demonstrates that, far from nullifying the law, "the righteousness of God" is consistent with the principle of faith found in the law.

A second problem Paul must address is why, if it lends no advantage to the Jew, did God give the law? Paul points out carefully that nothing he has said should lead to the conclusion that the law and sin are identical (Rom 7:7). To the contrary, the law is holy, righteous, good and spiritual (Rom 7:12, 14; cf. 7:22); it is only so closely allied with sin because it shows sin for the evil transgression that it is and condemns the transgressor. It accomplishes this, according to Paul, in three ways. First, it brings knowledge of sin by making God's will explicit so that people can know God's will and understand that they have not done it (Rom 3:20; 4:15; 5:13; 7:7, 21-23). Second, the law demonstrates how insidious sin is by suggesting to fallen humanity ways in which it can rebel against God (Rom 7:7-12; cf. 5:20). Finally, "the law brings wrath" (Rom 4:15; cf. Rom 1:18), for it contains a list of dire consequences that God ordains for those who disobey its commands. Not surprisingly, then, believers are "no longer under," have "died to" and have been "freed from" this "law of sin and death" (Rom 6:14; 7:4; 7:6; 8:2).

By this point in our study it should come as no surprise that while Paul can unambiguously speak of the abrogation of the Mosaic code, he can at the same time speak of the law's authority and of its fulfillment among believers. In Romans the tension between these two kinds of statements is at its sharpest, for along with comments about freedom from the law we read that the law is God's (Rom 7:22; 8:7), that it is "the law of the spirit of life in Christ Jesus" (Rom 8:2) and that believers fulfill its "just requirement" when they walk in the Spirit (Rom 8:4; cf. 13:8-10), something that unbelievers are not able to do (Rom 8:7).

Evidence from Paul's other letters has so far pointed toward a resolution to this tension in Paul's belief in two covenants, or two laws, one old and the other new. Romans 9:30—10:8 tends to confirm this view. Here Paul explains that most of Israel has failed to believe the gospel because they have pursued the law "as if it were a matter of works" (Rom 9:32), believing that in spite of God's eschatological provision for rescue from the broken covenant in Jesus Christ ("the righteousness of God," Rom 10:3), they could continue to cling to the law of Sinai as proof that they were God's people (Rom 10:3; cf. Phil 3:9). To demonstrate that clinging to the law in this way could not lead to salvation, Paul quotes two passages from "the law." The first, Leviticus 18:5, reminds the attentive reader that the Mosaic covenant promised life only to those who obeyed it (Rom 10:5), something that anyone who had read Leviticus 26:14-46 knew Israel had not done, and which Paul has just argued energetically that no individual has done either. This law, Paul says, has reached its climax *(telos)* in Christ (Rom 10:4; see Wright, 241) and has given way to a new covenant. The second passage features much of the vocabulary of Deuteronomy 9:4 and Deuteronomy 30:12, passages which in their original context spoke of obedience to the Mosaic law. In Paul's hands, however, they have been transposed into a different key and now speak of righteousness by faith in Christ (Rom 10:6-8; Hays, 73-83). The very law that has come to its climactic end *(telos)* in Christ can be taken up and remolded to fit the shape of the new covenant.

4. Conclusion.

If the portrait of Paul's view of the law painted here is correct, then at its heart was the conviction that the old covenant made with Israel at Sinai had passed away and the new covenant predicted by Jeremiah and Ezekiel had come. The change of covenants was necessary because no individual could keep the stipulations of the old covenant, a fact that Israel had demonstrated at the national level. The change was also necessary because after the covenant was broken, Israel used the law to erect barriers between itself and the Gentile world, barriers that to some became a point of pride and false security. The new covenant maintained the formal structure of the old, including its barrier of separation between those within and those outside. This barrier ceased to be national in character, however, and assumed instead dimensions dictated by the Spirit, dimensions that in their practical outworking coincided in many particulars with the old covenant. This new covenant, moreover, as the prophets had predicted, was written on the heart and could be kept by those who walked in the Spirit.

All of this means that Paul's view of the law was to a large measure discontinuous with the view of many Jews during his time. It is hard to imagine that the authors of Tobit and Judith, *Jubilees* and the Qumran Scrolls would have been comfortable in Paul's company. Yet the undeniable element of discontinuity can be overstressed. The conceptual world within which Paul worked would have been familiar to Paul's Jewish contemporaries. They knew that Israel suffered under "the curse of the law" in the form of Gentile domination because it had broken the covenant, and some of them at least looked for the answer to this plight in the promises of Jeremiah 31 and Ezekiel 36—37. The image of Paul, the aberration, as it appears in the work of Montefiore, Sanders and others, is therefore hardly fair.

Neither, if our reading is correct, is Räisänen's image of Paul the muddlehead. Paul's conviction that his churches formed the community of the new covenant, with all of the ramifications which that conviction entailed, remains consistent from his earliest correspondence to his latest, from his most placid to his most polemical. Paul did not produce his view of the law as an expedient in the heat of the moment. Rather, it bears the marks of a complex and carefully considered position, worthy of the most painstaking study and of the deepest theological reflection.

See also COVENANT, NEW COVENANT; ISRAEL; JEW, PAUL THE; JUSTIFICATION.

DPL: CURSE, ACCURSED, ANATHEMA; JUDAIZERS; LAW OF CHRIST; RESTORATION OF ISRAEL; WORKS OF THE LAW.

BIBLIOGRAPHY. R. Bultmann, *Primitive Christianity in Its Contemporary Setting* (Philadelphia: Fortress, 1956); D. A. Carson, P. T. O'Brien and M. A. Seifrid, eds., *Justification and Variegated Nomism*, vol. 1, *The Complexities of Second Temple Judaism* (Grand Rapids: Baker, 2001); W. D. Davies, *Paul and Rabbinic Judaism: Some Rabbinic Elements in Pauline Theology* (4th ed.; Philadelphia: Fortress, 1980); T. J. Deidun, *New Covenant Morality in Paul* (AnBib 89; Rome: Biblical Institute, 1981); J. D. G. Dunn, *Jesus, Paul, and the Law: Studies in Mark and Galatians* (Louisville, KY: Westminster John Knox, 1990); R. B. Hays, *Echoes of Scripture in the Letters of Paul* (New Haven, CT: Yale University Press, 1989); M. Hengel, *The Zealots* (Edinburgh: T & T Clark, 1989); H. Hübner, *Law in Paul's Thought* (Edinburgh: T & T Clark, 1984); H. Maccoby, *Paul and Hellenism* (Philadelphia: Trinity Press International, 1991); C. G. Montefiore, "First Impressions of Paul," *JQR* 6 (1894) 428-75; idem, "Rabbinic Judaism and the Epistles of St. Paul," *JQR* 13 (1900-1901) 161-217; G. F. Moore, *Judaism in the First Centu-*

ries of the Christian Era: The Age of the Tannaim (2 vols.; Cambridge, MA: Harvard University Press, 1927); H. Räisänen, *Paul and the Law* (WUNT 29; Tübingen: J. C. B. Mohr, 1983); idem, *The Torah and Christ: Essays in German and English on the Problem of the Law in Early Christianity* (SESJ; Helsinki: Finnish Exegetical Society, 1986); W. Sanday and A. C. Headlam, *A Critical and Exegetical Commentary on the Epistle to the Romans* (ICC; 5th ed; Edinburgh: T & T Clark, 1902); E. P. Sanders, *Judaism: Practice and Belief 63 B.C.E.-66 C.E.* (Philadelphia: Trinity Press International, 1992); idem, *Paul and Palestinian Judaism: A Comparison of Patterns of Religion* (Philadelphia: Fortress, 1977); idem, *Paul, the Law, and the Jewish People* (Philadelphia: Fortress, 1983); idem, *Paul* (New York: Oxford University Press, 1991); S. Sandmel, *The Genius of Paul: A Study in History* (Philadelphia: Fortress, 1979); idem, *Judaism and Christian Beginnings* (New York: Oxford University Press, 1978); F. Thielman, *From Plight to Solution: A Jewish Framework for Understanding Paul's View of the Law in Galatians and Romans* (NovTSup 61; Leiden: E. J. Brill, 1989); idem, *Paul and the Law: A Contextual Approach* (Downers Grove, IL: InterVarsity Press, 1994); P. J. Tomson, *Paul and the Jewish Law: Halakah in the Letters of the Apostle to the Gentiles* (CRINT 3.1; Minneapolis: Fortress, 1990); F. Weber, *Jüdische Theologie auf Grund des Talmud und verwandter Schriften, gemeinfasslich dargestellt* (2d ed.; Leipzig: Dörffling & Franke, 1897; 1st ed., 1880); A. J. M. Wedderburn, *The Reasons for Romans* (Edinburgh: T & T Clark, 1988); S. Westerholm, *Israel's Law and the Church's Faith: Paul and His Recent Interpreters* (Grand Rapids: Eerdmans, 1988); N. T. Wright, *The Climax of the Covenant: Christ and the Law in Pauline Theology* (Edinburgh: T & T Clark, 1991).   F. Thielman

LAW III: ACTS, HEBREWS, GENERAL EPISTLES, REVELATION

The relationship between Christians and the Mosaic Torah was one of the most disputed and complex issues in the early church. The law comes to the forefront in the Pauline writings (*see* Law II) and receives considerable attention in the Synoptics and the Gospel of John (*see* Law I). In the literature under consideration in this volume, the Mosaic law is not as prominent. For instance, the Mosaic law is not the subject of discussion in *Revelation, 1 and 2 Peter, Jude or 3 John (*see* John, Letters of). In 2 John 4—6 it is treated in a glancing way when the author commends keeping the commandments, but the relationship of commandments to the Mosaic law here is disputed. More promising, although frustratingly brief and ambiguous, are texts relating to the law in James and 1 John. The law crops up in Acts on a number of occasions and is prominent in the letter to the Hebrews.

1. James
2. 1 John
3. Hebrews
4. Acts of the Apostles

1. James.

James describes the law as "the perfect law of liberty" (Jas 1:25), "the royal law" (Jas 2:8) and "the law of liberty" (Jas 2:12). To what does the word *law (nomos)* refer here? Scholars have often remarked that James hails from conservative Jewish Christian circles, and thus one might think that the entire OT law is intended. For instance, the early Christian sect called the Ebionites demanded the observance of circumcision. But it is doubtful that the reference is to the whole OT law, for James nowhere commands believers to keep any part of the ceremonial law. For instance, he never says anything about circumcision, food laws and sabbath. And his letter would be a fitting place to address these matters, for he probably corrects a false understanding of Paul's view of *justification. So too the letter would be an appropriate place to counter the Pauline teaching on circumcision. His silence on this issue is likely to be an indication that he agreed with Paul that circumcision was unnecessary. Indeed, Acts 15:13-21 and Galatians 2:1-10 confirm that James did not believe circumcision should be required of Gentile converts. We may conclude then that James 2:10, "For whoever keeps the whole law, but stumbles in one matter, has become guilty of all," does not require adherence to the ceremonial law.

If *nomos* does not refer to the ceremonial law, to what does James refer? James 2:8-12 is the central text for answering this question. The "royal law" is in accord with the OT command to love one's neighbor as oneself (Lev 19:18). It seems, therefore, that the "royal law" is from the OT. James 2:11 substantiates this interpretation, for there the law is explained in terms of the prohibitions against murder and adultery (Ex 20:13-14; Deut 5:17-18). The "law" in James, therefore, seems to refer to the moral norms of the OT law, and love is the apex and heart of the law's requirement.

It is also instructive to note that James establishes a connection between "law" *(nomos)* and "word" *(logos)* in James 1:21-25. The readers are commanded to "receive the implanted word which is able to save your souls" (Jas 1:21) and to be "doers of the word" and not just hearers of it (Jas 1:22-23). In James 1:25 the doing of the word is explained in other terms, that is, abiding "in the perfect law of liberty." We conclude that doing the "word" and keeping the "law" are synonymous for James. The idea that the word is "implanted" and "saves" most likely reflects Jeremiah 31:31-34, a passage in which Jeremiah promises that the law will be written on the heart and that people will be enabled to keep God's commands when the new covenant is fulfilled. This is probably why James says the law is one of "liberty" (Jas 1:25; 2:12), for the implanting of the law indicates God has provided the strength to keep the law and that doing the word is a freeing and liberating experience, not a burden.

The reference to the "word" and the "law" in this text must also be explained in terms of the gospel of Jesus Christ, for it is this gospel that saves. Many scholars have rightly argued that the letter to James depends on the teaching of Jesus, especially the Sermon on the Mount (the *Didache* also witnesses to the tradition shared by Matthew and James, *Did.* 1.2-5). The "law of liberty" and "the royal law," therefore, cannot be separated from the message of the gospel and the teaching of Jesus. The moral norms of the OT law and the call to love are realized to their fullest extent in the teaching of Jesus of Nazareth and reflected in the teaching of James. It seems fair to conclude that the OT law is interpreted by James in the light of the Christ event, and it would even be fitting to say that the "law of Christ" is the authoritative standard for believers and that this law contains the moral norms of the OT law.

2. 1 John.

John often emphasizes that believers should keep God's commandments (1 Jn 2:3, 4, 7, 8; 3:22, 23, 24; 4:21; 5:2-3; 2 Jn 4, 5, 6). The content of the commandments is not specified in detail, except the command to love one another and to

believe in Jesus as Messiah (1 Jn 3:22-24; 4:21; 5:2; 2 Jn 4-6). The love commandment is presumably what John has in mind when he refers to the "old" command that is "new" in him (1 Jn 2:7-11). Jesus' call to love one another as he has loved the disciples (Jn 13:34-35) is likely the "old" command. John probably calls it old to emphasize that the message he imparts does not deviate from the truth they have always known (cf. 1 Jn 2:18-27). But love has now become a reality because of the coming of Jesus Christ, who has begun to dispel the darkness of the old age by introducing the light of the new age. John seems to be saying that the ability to love one another is a gift of the new age inaugurated by Jesus.

R. E. Brown has remarked that there is a close connection between "word" *(logos)* and "commandment" *(entolē)* in Johannine writings. This is borne out by 1 John 2:3-6, where knowing God is described in terms of keeping "his commandments" (1 Jn 2:3-4) and also as "keeping his word" (1 Jn 2:5; cf. 2:7). The "commandments" and the "word" probably hearken back to the "ten words" (Ex 34:28) Moses inscribed upon the stone tablets. Thereby John suggests that those who believe Jesus is the Christ and love their brothers and sisters fulfill the OT law, which is summed up in the Ten Commandments. John does not envision keeping the commandments in one's own strength. Those who do so "have been born of God" (1 Jn 5:1), signifying that his seed provides the power. And "the victory which overcomes the world is our faith" (1 Jn 5:4), indicating that our trust in God's power is the foundation of our obedience.

3. Hebrews.

The letter to the Hebrews contains an elegant argument for the supersession of the Mosaic law, in particular the obsolescence of the Aaronic priesthood and the OT sacrifices. The author's thesis is that Jesus is the Melchizedekean priest predicted in the OT (Ps 110:4). The fact that a new priesthood was anticipated demonstrates that the Aaronic priesthood was not intended to be permanent (Heb 7:11). And if a new priest has arisen, a new law must be enacted, "for when the priesthood is changed, of necessity there is a change of law also" (Heb 7:12).

The inferiority of the old priesthood is impressed upon the reader with a series of stunning contrasts. Aaronic priests served without an oath while Jesus received an oath (Heb 7:21-22). There were many priests in the old order because death prevented them from continuing to serve as priests, but Jesus abides as a priest forever since he always lives to make effective intercession for his people (Heb 7:23-25). Aaronic priests had to offer sacrifices for their own sins as fallible and flawed human beings, whereas the sinless Son offered up one effective sacrifice for the sins of all human beings (Heb 7:26-28). Aaronic priests stand daily since their work of atoning for sins is never finished (Heb 10:11), but the Son sits triumphantly at the right hand of God since his one sacrifice was definitive and effective (Heb 10:12-14). Similarly, the sacrifice of Jesus is infinitely superior to the sacrifices offered under the old covenant. Animal sacrifices have to be repeated since they do not cleanse the conscience from sin (Heb 10:1-2, 11), but Christ through one sacrifice has cleansed the conscience from sin forever (Heb 9:25-28; 10:12-14). Animals are brute victims whose blood is spilled, but they have no conception of the significance of their sacrifice (Heb 10:3-4); the Son as a human being offered himself voluntarily for the salvation of others (Heb 10:5-10).

When the author refers to the "weakness and uselessness" of the "former commandment" (Heb 7:18) and claims that "the law made nothing perfect," he is reflecting on its inability to effect forgiveness of sins and to bring believers into God's presence. This is evident in Hebrews 7:19, for the work of Christ on the cross was effective because through it "we draw near to God." It is here that the author finds fault with the old covenant; it could not accomplish forgiveness of sins (Heb 8:7-13; 10:16-18). The very promise that a new covenant would commence signals that the old is inadequate and doomed to obsolescence.

The author of Hebrews does not deny the historical validity of the old covenant, nor does he allegorize the laws of the OT so that they are robbed of their literal meaning, nor does he dismiss OT practices as absurd and irrational. He has a sense of salvation history that is remarkably lacking in the apostolic fathers such as *Epistle of Barnabas* and the *Epistle to Diognetus*. The OT priesthood, sacrifices and covenant are inferior to the new covenant according to Hebrews, but they played a positive role in redemptive history. The priests, sacrifices and tabernacle (Heb 8:1—9:28) functioned as types or patterns of the work of Christ. The content of OT revelation is not denigrated as in *Barnabas* but is ascribed a particular place in the history of salvation. OT sacrifices and priests played a proper role in their era, pointing to the fulfillment that would be enacted when the true priest and sacrifice arrived. Now that the fulfillment of the old covenant has arrived, returning to the old way deserves judgment, but the old way was instituted by God as a prelude and pointer to the salvation to come. For instance, the entrance into the land under Joshua anticipates the heavenly rest available for God's people (Heb 3:7—4:13). Similarly, resting on the sabbath anticipates the eschatological sabbath rest (Heb 4:3-11).

4. Acts of the Apostles.

The Lukan view of the law may be discerned from Luke's Gospel and Acts, but here we shall confine ourselves to Acts (*see* Law I, for a discussion of the Gospel of Luke). The Lukan theology of the law is a matter of debate. For instance, J. Jervell thinks that Luke's view is the most conservative in the NT, while S. G. Wilson argues that Luke is ambiguous on the question. One can understand why Luke would be designated as conservative, for the church in Acts seems to abide by the Torah. They worship in the temple (Acts 3:1-10), the charge that Stephen violates the law is false (Acts 6:11-14), and Stephen says the law contains "living words" (Acts 7:38; cf. Acts 7:53). Paul is portrayed as a law-abiding Jew: he accepts the apostolic decree (Acts 15:22-29), circumcises Timothy (Acts 16:3), takes a Nazirite vow (Acts 21:21-26; cf. Acts 18:18) and insists that he has never transgressed the law (Acts 24:14-16; 25:8; 28:17).

C. L. Blomberg and M. A. Seifrid (see also Turner) have convincingly argued that the most satisfying perspective from which to understand Luke's theology of the law is salvation history. The OT prophecies are fulfilled in the ministry, death and resurrection of Jesus (Acts 2:16-36; 3:11-26; 4:11; 8:32-35; 13:16-41; 15:13-21; 24:13-14; 26:22-23, 27; *see* Death of Christ). The Mosaic law was provisional but has been displaced now that the fulfillment of the law has come, Jesus the Messiah. Thus Paul proclaims in Acts 13:38-39 that forgiveness and justification are now available through Jesus Christ and that the law of Moses did not provide forgiveness or justification. Similarly, in Acts 15:10-11 Peter argues that the law was a yoke that the Jews could not bear. J. Nolland has rightly argued that the intention of the verse is not to say that the Mosaic law is an oppressive burden. Instead, the purpose is to say that no one could keep the law. Thus Peter concludes in Acts 15:11 that salvation is through the grace of the Lord Jesus Christ rather than through the Mosaic law.

The salvation-historical dimension of the law is also apparent in Acts 10:1—11:18 and Acts 15:1-29. In the former text Peter is enjoined in a vision to eat unclean foods. Peter is puzzled as to why he is commanded to violate the OT law that specifically prohibits consuming the foods that were represented in the vision (Lev 11:1-45; Deut 14:3-21), but the rationale for the vision dawns upon him as the story unfolds. Immediately after this ecstatic experience he was summoned to the house of Cornelius. As Gentiles, Cornelius and his friends were considered to be "unclean," and thus Jews could eat with them only if purity laws were observed. While Peter was explaining the gospel of Jesus Christ, God poured out his Spirit (*see* Holy Spirit) upon Cornelius and his friends to indicate that Gentiles could be part of the people of God without the imposition of the Mosaic law.

The relationship of Jews and Gentiles in the church came to a head in the apostolic council of Acts 15. The successful missionary tour of Paul and Barnabas (Acts 13—14) led to an influx of Gentiles into the church. Some Jewish Christians from the pharisaic wing of the church were concerned that the OT law and the distinctive place of the Jews were being abandoned since Gentiles were streaming into the church without being circumcised. They argued that circumcision was necessary for salvation (Acts 15:1, 5). A meeting of the church was called in Jerusalem to discuss this matter, and it was determined that Gentiles could be members of the church without being circumcised. The gift of the Holy Spirit to Cornelius and his friends played a decisive role in the debate (Acts 15:7-11), for if God gave the Spirit apart from circumcision, then it must not be required for entrance into the church. James argued that the OT Scriptures anticipated the inclusion of Gentiles apart from the imposition of the law (Acts 15:13-21). Acts 10:1—11:18 and Acts 15:1-29 demonstrate that Luke should hardly be characterized as the most conservative writer in the NT with reference to the law, for the OT law required circumcision and the ob-

servance of food laws. Luke sees these as passé now that the fulfillment of the OT law has arrived and the promise to Abraham that all nations should be blessed is becoming a reality.

The addition of the four requirements of the apostolic decree, namely, abstention from immorality *(porneia)*, blood, food contaminated by idols, and that which was strangled, seems puzzling. Has Luke introduced other requirements of the law after circumcision has been dismissed as necessary? The complexity of the apostolic decree warrants more discussion than is possible here, but these four requirements were probably retained as a means of facilitating fellowship between Jews and Gentiles. The church emphatically rejected the notion that Gentiles must observe the law (i.e., circumcision) in order to obtain salvation, but they were not opposed to the temporary observance of parts of the law as a way of preserving fellowship between Jews and Gentiles. Jewish sensibilities received some consideration at the apostolic council, while the idea that circumcision should be required for salvation was rejected.

It is probable that not all Jewish Christians concurred with or abided by the decision of the council. This seems confirmed by second-century evidence, for the Jewish Christian sect called the Ebionites (lit. "the poor") demanded the observance of the OT law and circumcision. Most of our information about the Ebionites derives from the early church fathers, but the sources are fragmentary and thus our understanding of Ebionism is partial and cannot be harmonized into a coherent unity. They rejected Paul's view of the law. Most Ebionites denied the virgin birth and all seem to have rejected the preexistence of Christ. Scholars debate whether the Pseudo-Clementines derive from the Ebionites, especially the *Sermons of Peter.* Certainty eludes us since the literary history and composition of the Clementine literature are complex. One interesting feature is that the Pauline view of the law is fiercely rejected by Peter in this literature. The Pseudo-Clementines may also reflect in places the views of the sect called the Elkesaites, for the latter required circumcision and sabbath observance, although they rejected OT sacrifices. Some scholars have suggested that the Ebionites are derived from the Elkesaites, but again this is hypothetical and cannot be established. The relationship of the Ebionites to the *Gospel of the Nazoraeans* has also been intensely studied, but unfortunately no firm conclusions may be drawn.

The law-abiding Paul of Acts has stimulated much discussion. Many scholars contend that the circumcision of Timothy by Paul (Acts 16:3) and his taking of a Nazirite vow (Acts 21:21-26) are historically incredible and betray Lukan theology rather than Pauline history. Several things should be said briefly in response to this. Lukan history and theology need not and should not be pitted against each other. Modern scholarship rightly stresses that Luke is a theologian, but theology and history are not mutually exclusive. Nor are the Pauline accommodations to the law in Acts foreign to the spirit of the Pauline letters. First Corinthians 9:19-23 indicates that Paul adopted a flexible stance on the law in order to advance his mission. Paul invariably resisted the imposition of the law on Gentiles for salvation, but he was not averse to some observance of the law by Gentiles to accommodate Jewish culture. The narrative of Acts 15—16 underscores this very point: circumcision is not required to be part of the people of God, yet Paul accedes to the circumcision of Timothy (Acts 16:3) in order to advance his mission.

See also COVENANT, NEW COVENANT; ISRAEL; RABBINIC TRADITIONS AND WRITINGS.

DLNTD: CIRCUMCISION; COMMANDMENTS; FOOD, FOOD LAWS, TABLE FELLOWSHIP; JEWISH CHRISTIANITY; OLD TESTAMENT.

BIBLIOGRAPHY. H. Attridge, *The Epistle to the Hebrews* (Herm; Philadelphia: Fortress, 1989); C. L. Blomberg, "The Law in Luke-Acts," *JSNT* 22 (1984) 53-80; R. E. Brown, *The Epistles of John* (AB; Garden City, NY: Doubleday, 1982); P. H. Davids, *The Epistle of James* (NIGTC; Grand Rapids: Eerdmans, 1982); C. J. Hemer, *The Book of Acts in the Setting of Hellenistic History* (WUNT 49; Tübingen: J. C. B. Mohr, 1988); M. Hengel, "Der Jakobusbrief als antipaulinische Polemik," in *Tradition and Interpretation in the New Testament: Essays in Honor of E. E. Ellis,* ed. G. F. Hawthorne and O. Betz (Grand Rapids: Eerdmans, 1987) 248-65; J. Jervell, *Luke and the People of God: A New Look at Luke-Acts* (Minneapolis: Augsburg, 1972); L. T. Johnson, "The Use of Leviticus 19 in the Letter of James," *JBL* 101 (1982) 391-401; R. P. Martin, *James* (WBC; Waco, TX: Word, 1988); D. J. Moo, *The Letter of James* (TNTC; Grand Rapids: Eerdmans, 1985); J. Nolland, "A Fresh Look at Acts 15:10, " *NTS* 27 (1980) 105-15; K. Salo, *Luke's Treatment of the Law: A Redaction-Critical Investiga-* tion (DHL 57; Helsinki: Annales Academiae Scientiarum Fennicae, 1991); M. A. Seifrid, "Jesus and the Law in Acts," *JSNT* 30 (1987) 39-57; O. F. J. Seitz, "James and the Law," *SE* 2 (1964) 472-86; M. M. B. Turner, "The Sabbath, Sunday and the Law in Luke/Acts," in *From Sabbath to Lord's Day: A Biblical, Historical and Theological Investigation,* ed. D. A. Carson (Grand Rapids: Zondervan, 1982) 100-157; S. G. Wilson, *Luke and the Law* (SNTSMS 50; Cambridge: Cambridge University Press, 1983). T. R. Schreiner

LAZARUS, RAISING OF. *See* RESURRECTION I.

LECTIONARIES, JEWISH. *See* WORSHIP.

LETTER OF ARISTEAS. *See* APOCRYPHA AND PSEUDEPIGRAPHA.

LETTERS, LETTER FORMS I: PAUL

The Greek word *epistolē* ("epistle," "letter") originally referred to an oral communication sent by a messenger. The term *letters* was a broad designation for different types of documents in the ancient world and could include a great variety of commercial, governmental and legal documents, as well as political and military reports, along with other sorts of correspondence, especially of a personal kind. Paul adapted the Greco-Roman letter models for Christian purposes. His letters, which have fascinated people for generations, were usually constructed along lines similar to that of Hellenistic letters. But the apostle, who had a sense of freedom in literary matters, was not tied to fixed models, and he often combined non-Jewish Hellenistic customs with Hellenistic Jewish ones.

1. Private Personal Letters?
2. The Form of the Pauline Letters
3. The Use of Other Literary Traditions

1. Private Personal Letters?

Since A. Deissmann's distinction between "letters," which were understood as natural, daily and situational, and "epistles," which were understood as mechanical, artistic and literary, there has been considerable scholarly discussion as to whether Paul's letters should be regarded as private personal letters or not. They were certainly private as opposed to literary essays, which adopted an epistolary form but were written for an unspecified, universal audience, and official letters, which were not written in the context of a personal relationship. Galatians, for example, is a highly personal letter written to a specific group of people in an immediate relationship with Paul. However inclusive is the address, "the churches of Galatia," this letter was sent to a relatively minor group in the Greco-Roman world (Hansen).

But Paul's letters were more than private. He wrote self-consciously as an *apostle, that is, as a representative of the risen Christ (note the emphasis on apostleship in Gal 1:1, 15, 16; 5:2) in order to instruct, give advice, encourage and reprimand (note 1 Thess 5:27 and 2 Thess 3:14-15 regarding the impact on the church at Thessalonica). Most of Paul's letters were addressed to communities of Christian believers and were intended for public use within the congregations. They were occasional, contextual writings addressing particular situations (though note Ephesians) and were the substitutes for Paul's personal presence. He was concerned with the life situation of his readers, but never in the impersonal way characteristic of many Hellenistic letters. Paul treated each situation as unique and important. At the same time, his letters set forth significant theological teaching and express a Christian understanding of life that reaches beyond the particular historical situation.

2. The Form of the Pauline Letters.

Many ancient letters, which were written by professional scribes, were highly stylized with each part basically determined by convention, regardless of the occasion. The general model of the Hellenistic letter included an opening, a body and a closing. The basic Pauline letter form, in which there was a normal progression rather than any stereotyped or mechanical framework, contained the following elements.

2.1. Opening. Paul's letters, which follow the usual Hellenistic letter openings of "A to B, greetings," regularly contain expansions of this basic pattern (e.g., Rom 1:1-7; Gal 1:1-5; 1 Thess 1:1; Tit 1:1-4), and these often point to the specific purposes of the letters. The identification of the writer (with coworkers often named) and addressees is followed by expanded descriptions of both in terms of their standing in relation to God in Christ. Paul usually identifies himself with epithets such as "apostle" and "servant," while the addressees are called "saints," "beloved" or "the church of God which is at." The usual Hellenistic greeting, *chairein* ("greeting"),

is replaced by *charis kai eirēnē* ("grace and peace"). This benediction is an affirmation regarding the grace and peace of God in which they already participate and a prayer that they may appreciate and experience these blessings more fully.

2.2. Introductory Thanksgiving or Blessing. On occasion the more intimate letters of the Hellenistic period began with a thanksgiving to the gods for personal benefits received. Paul adopted this Hellenistic epistolary model, frequently using it at the beginning of his letters as he expressed his gratitude to God, the Father of Jesus Christ, for what God had effected in the lives of these predominantly Gentile readers (e.g., 1 Cor 1:4; Phil 1:3; Col 1:3; 1 Thess 1:2; 2 Thess 1:3; Philem 4). But the apostle was no slavish imitator of this epistolary convention, since his structures were highly developed and sophisticated.

Two basic types of structure occurred in Paul's thanksgiving paragraphs. The first, which contained up to seven basic elements, began with the verb of thanksgiving and concluded with a *hina* clause or its equivalent that spelled out the content of the apostle's intercession for the readers (Phil 1:3-11; Col 1:3-14; 1 Thess 1:2—3:13; 2 Thess 1:2-12; 2:13-14; Philem 4-7; cf. Eph 1:15-19). The second was simpler in form. It also commenced with the giving of thanks to God and concluded with a *hoti* clause that noted the reason for this expression of gratitude (1 Cor 1:4-9; cf. Rom 1:8-10).

While the structure of the Pauline thanksgiving periods was Hellenistic, the contents, apart from their specifically Christian elements, showed the influence of the OT and Jewish thought. These paragraphs, which open with a statement of thanksgiving to God, have an epistolary function, that is, they introduce and present the main themes of their letters, usually setting the tone and atmosphere. Many have a didactic function so that either by fresh teaching or recall to instruction previously given the apostle sets forth theological matters he considers important (see esp. Col 1:9-14). An exhortatory purpose is also present in several of these passages (e.g., Phil 1:9-11). Further, the thanksgivings and petitions that are included give evidence of the apostle's deep pastoral and apostolic concern for the readers. At the same time Paul reports his actual thanksgivings and actual petitions for the readers.

Using a typically OT and Jewish prayer form

denoting praise (cf. the doxological conclusions to the books of the Psalter: Ps 41:13; 72:19-20, etc.), Paul introduces two of his letters (2 Cor 1:3-4; Eph 1:3-14; cf. 1 Pet 1:3-5) with an introductory blessing or eulogy (*eulogētos*, "blessed"). While his introductory thanksgivings focus on God's work in the lives of others, his *eulogies* praise God for blessings in which he himself participates. The formula with a Jewish background was apparently more apt when he himself came within the circle of blessing.

2.3. Body. The bodies of Paul's letters show considerable variety, for it is here more than anywhere else that they reflect the different epistolary situations. Apparently the apostle was more inclined to strike out on his own within the bodies of his letters and to be least bound by epistolary structures. There has been some difficulty in determining where the body section begins and ends (for example, in 1 and 2 Thess the body seems to have assimilated entirely to the thanksgiving). However, several possible openings have been identified through the *parakaleō* sentences ("I urge you my brothers," 1 Cor 1:10; 1 Thess 4:1; cf. Rom 12:1; 15:30), the disclosure formula ("I/we want you to know," Rom 1:13; Gal 1:11; Phil 1:12), the expression of joy (Philem 7), the expression of astonishment (Gal 1:6) or statement of compliance (Gal 1:8-9), while the close of the body was occasionally signaled by eschatological conclusions (Rom 11:25-36; 1 Thess 3:11-13) or the travelogue (see 2.4 below).

The clustering of various epistolary formulas at certain strategic points signals significant breaks or turning points in the letter (Mullins). A distinct transition from a more didactic section to a lengthy section of paraenesis is occasionally signaled by a closing doxology and one of the transitional formulas (e.g., Rom 11:36—12:1; Eph 3:21—4:1; 1 Thess 3:11—4:1). Paraenetic or exhortatory materials were by and large traditional materials (they included "household tables": cf. Col 3:18—4:1; Eph 5:22—6:9), deriving from the OT and Jewish literature as well as from Hellenistic moral traditions (cf. Phil 4:8-9).

Another typical feature of the bodies of Paul's letters is the "apostolic *parousia*" (i.e., presence), in which the apostle speaks of his travel plans, including his intention to be with his readers, and of his past and future contacts with them through his coworkers (1 Cor 4:17-21; 16:5-12; Phil 2:19-30; 1 Thess 2:17–3:11; Philem 22). Because he was unable to be with his readers, Paul's letters were a direct substitute for his personal presence and were "to be accorded weight equal to [his] physical presence" (Doty).

Epistolary *topoi*, that is, themes and constituent motifs of ancient letters, appear also in Paul's letters. These include the themes of letter writing (Rom 15:14; 1 Cor 4:14), health (2 Cor 1:8-11; Phil 2:25-30), domestic events (1 Cor 5:1-6:11; Phil 4:2-4) and reunion with the addressees (Rom 15:14-33; 1 Thess 2:17—3:13).

2.4. Closing. Paul used the typical closing greetings of Hellenistic letters in order to link the congregations with his own traveling ministry (cf. Rom 16:3-16, 21-23; 2 Cor 13:12-13; Col 4:10-17). However, he did not include the customary health wish or Greek word of farewell. Instead, a benediction (1 Cor 16:23; Gal 6:16, 18; Eph 6:23-24; 2 Thess 3:16, 18) or doxology (Rom 16:25-27; Phil 4:20; cf. Heb 13:20-21) served the same function. The final benediction, which brings the letter to a definitive conclusion, often gives expression to Paul's strong desire (e.g., that the grace of the Lord Jesus may be with them, 1 Cor 16:24) and strikes a note of confidence.

Other closing conventions Paul used include references to his writing a phrase or two in his own hand (1 Cor 16:21; Gal 6:11; Col 4:18; 2 Thess 3:17), his use of a secretary (Tertius, Rom 16:22; cf. Richards) and a holy kiss (e.g., Rom 16:16).

3. The Use of Other Literary Traditions.

Paul's letters exhibit not only a broad stylistic range; they also employ a variety of other literary traditions, including the contemporary rhetorical forms and modes of persuasion, chiastic structures, diatribe style, midrashic exegetical methods where appeal is made to the authority of the OT, as well as early traditional hymnic material and confessional formulas. Paul appears not to have been bound to any one stylistic convention, whether epistolary, sermonic or oratorical. The letter form that developed in the Pauline letters was richer than either the brief private letters or the more developed letter essays of Hellenism. We note briefly the following.

3.1. Liturgical Forms. The apostle's letters were intended to be read aloud to the congregations to whom they were addressed (1 Thess 5:27; Col 4:16). Perhaps this intended setting accounts for the inclusion of liturgical formulas in Christian letters. Recent scholarship suggests that the following belong to this category: (1) "grace" benedictions, (2) blessings (Rom 1:25; 9:5), (3) doxologies (Rom 11:36; Gal 1:5), (4) hymns (cf. Col 3:16) and (5) confessions and acclamations (Rom 10:9; 1 Cor 12:3).

3.2. Greco-Roman Rhetoric. Paul specifies his primary, apostolic task as the preaching of the gospel (Gal 1:16). When he writes his letters, he does so as a preacher of the gospel. His letters, though real, are nevertheless similar in many ways to oral speech. Accordingly, any epistolary analysis must be supplemented with a rhetorical analysis of his argumentation. The persuasive modes of the classical rhetorical handbooks were well known during Paul's day, and one did not have to be formally trained in rhetoric to use them. Each type of speech could consist of four elements: (1) *exordium* (introduction), (2) *narratio* (statement of facts), (3) *probatio* (argument) and (4) *peroratio* (conclusion). The introduction and conclusion were intended to influence the audience by securing their interest and goodwill and conclude by recapitulating the arguments and making an appeal. The body of the speech sought to establish the case. Most of the early Christian letters were written with a basically deliberative purpose. Apart from the opening and closing epistolary formulas, Paul's letters consist of three elements: in the first, which is conciliatory, he commends his readers for their past performance. The middle segment consists of advice, while the final section contains paraenesis (Aune).

R. N. Longenecker claims that in Galatians, as elsewhere in his letters, "Paul seems to have availed himself almost unconsciously of the rhetorical forms at hand, fitting them into his inherited epistolary structures and filling them out with such Jewish theological motifs and exegetical methods as would be particularly significant in countering what the Judaizers were telling his converts" (Longenecker, cxix).

See also GOSPEL (GENRE); RHETORIC.

DPL: BENEDICTION, BLESSING, DOXOLOGY, THANKSGIVING; DIATRIBE; HOUSEHOLDS AND HOUSEHOLD CODES; ITINERARIES, TRAVEL PLANS, JOURNEYS, APOSTOLIC PAROUSIA; HERMENEUTICS/INTERPRETING PAUL; LITURGICAL ELEMENTS; RHETORICAL CRITICISM.

BIBLIOGRAPHY. D. E. Aune, *The New Testament in Its Literary Environment* (LEC; Philadelphia: Westminster, 1987); G. J. Bahr, "The Subscriptions in the Pauline Letters," *JBL* 87 (1968) 27-41; A. Deissmann, *Light from the Ancient East* (2d ed.; London: Hodder & Stoughton); W. G. Doty, *Letters in Primitive Christianity* (Philadelphia: Fortress, 1973); R. W. Funk, *Language, Hermeneutic and Word of God* (New York: Harper and Row, 1966) 250-74; idem, "The Apostolic *Parousia*: Form and Significance," in *Christian History and Interpretation: Studies Presented to John Knox,* ed. W. R. Farmer, C. F. D. Moule and R. R. Niebuhr (Cambridge: Cambridge University Press, 1967) 249-68; G. W. Hansen, *Abraham in Galatians: Epistolary and Rhetorical Contexts* (JSNT 29; Sheffield: JSOT, 1989); R. N. Longenecker, *Galatians* (WBC 41; Dallas: Word, 1990); T. Y. Mullins, "Formulas in New Testament Epistles," *JBL* 91 (1972) 380-90; idem, "Topos as a New Testament Form," *JBL* 99 (1980) 541-47; P. T. O'Brien, *Introductory Thanksgivings in the Letters of Paul* (NovTSup 49; Leiden: E. J. Brill, 1977); E. R. Richards, *The Secretary in the Letters of Paul* (WUNT 2.42; Tübingen: J. C. B. Mohr, 1991); J. T. Sanders, "The Transition from Opening Epistolary Thanksgiving to Body in the Pauline Corpus," *JBL* 81 (1962) 348-62; S. K. Stowers, *Letter Writing in Greco-Roman Antiquity* (LEC; Philadelphia: Westminster, 1986); J. L. White, "Introductory Formulae in the Body of the Pauline Letter," *JBL* 90 (1971) 91-97; idem, *Light from Ancient Letters* (Philadelphia: Fortress, 1986); idem, *The Form and Function of the Body of the Greek Letter* (SBLDS 2; Missoula, MT: Scholars Press, 1972).

P. T. O'Brien

LETTERS, LETTER FORMS II: HEBREWS, GENERAL EPISTLES, REVELATION

The early church relied on the letter because of the necessity of communicating important matters of the gospel and the Christian community over long distances. There were several factors peculiar to the early church that influenced how these letters were written. Among many others, these factors included the understanding of relationships among Christians in terms of family ties, the unique authority of apostles and their successors, the desire persuasively to present the gospel and its consequences for practical living, and the influence of liturgical language. Early Christian letter writers, whose works are found within and without the NT, adapted the epistolary and rhetorical forms of the Greco-Roman world to create sophisticated, literary creations.

1. Classification of Early Christian Letters.

Early in the twentieth century A. Deissmann made the questionable distinction between non-literary, or documentary letters (situational, private), and literary epistles (for posterity, public, rhetorically sophisticated), a distinction that persists. He classified the letters of the NT as documentary, but rhetorical analysis of NT letters has demonstrated that they fall between his categories, being situational yet possessing rhetorical sophistication.

Ancient letters are of various types, depending on the contexts from which they arose and the purposes they served. The relationships of friendship, family and client-patron generated the bulk of ancient letters. Ancient epistolary handbooks classify letters into their many types, including friendship, family, praise and blame, and exhortation and advice. These are ideal types that can be elaborated and mixed with other types.

Ancient letters contemporary with those of the NT were influenced by rhetorical conventions. These letters can be classified according to the three species of rhetoric: judicial (accusation and defense), deliberative (persuasion and dissuasion) and epideictic (praise and blame). For example, accusing and apologetic letters are judicial, letters of advice and exhortation are deliberative, and letters of recommendation and praise are epideictic.

The more early Christian letters are compared with literary letters rather than with documentary letters (as has been the case in the past) the more their rhetorical sophistication is noted. Early Christian letters exhibit patterns of argumentation and arrangement as well as many stylistic features of Greco-Roman rhetorical convention used in literary letters. Rhetorical analysis has been helpful in determining the structure of the elusive body of the letter, which was least bound by letter conventions.

Early Christian letters generally are a mix of the ideal types of letters and rhetorical classifications and often are not adequately classified with any one letter type or rhetorical species. Hebrews and the General Epistles are usually classified as letters of exhortation and advice, but they show characteristics of other letter types as well. They have been classified in part or whole according to all three species of rhetoric. Determination of letter and rhetorical classification are interdependent, since letters were influenced by rhetorical conventions at various points.

2. The Form of Early Christian Letters.

Christian letters followed the conventions of Greek letters with some modifications attributable to Christian experience. Greek letters, especially the opening and closing, are governed by convention. They begin with the letter opening, or prescript, composed of this formula: sender (*superscriptio*) to recipient (*adscriptio*), greetings (*salutatio*). Christian letters typically expand the prescript by describing the sender and recipient in relation to God (e.g., "apostle," "chosen by God"). The Greek letter greeting uses a verb of greeting (*chairō*) and a wish for the recipient's health (*hygianō*), but in Christian letters these become "grace" (*charis*) and "peace" (*eirēnē*) respectively, often presented in the form of a benediction ("may grace and peace be yours").

The Greek letter greeting is usually followed by the sender's wish for the health of the recipient (*hygianō*), an expression of joy at the receipt of the letter from the recipients (*chairō*), a thanksgiving for good health and deliverance from disaster (*eucharisteō*, "to rejoice"), a report of a prayer for the addressees (*proskynēma*) and/or a mention that the sender remembers the recipients (*mneia*). In Christian letters these are often subsumed into the thanksgiving or a benediction, which introduces the key topics of the letter.

The body of Greek and Christian letters has three parts: the body-opening, body-middle and body-closing. The body-opening establishes the common ground between the sender and recipient by alluding to shared information or by disclosing new information. It provides the principal occasion or purpose of the letter that prompts the sender to write and introduces the main points the letter will develop. The purpose of the letter can be expressed in one of three ways: (1) a full disclosure formula giving the sender's wish or command that the recipients know something ("I want you to know that"), consisting of a verb of disclosure (*thelō, boulomai*) and a verb of knowing (*ginōskō*), (2) a motivation for writing (*graphō*) or (3) a petition that the audience take some course of action, composed of a verb of petition *(parakaleō, erōtaō)* and the reason for the petition.

The body-middle both develops the subject(s) introduced in the body-opening and introduces new material. It often begins with a disclosure formula that conveys that the sender desires or commands that the recipients know something. The body-closing accentuates and reiterates the principal motivation for writing and establishes bridges to further communication. It often begins with the imperative form of the disclosure formula using the verb *ginōskō* ("to know") followed by responsibility statements urging the recipients to be attentive to the content of the letter and to respond as desired. It may notify the recipients of the sender's intention to visit, which is motivated by a desire to talk face to face rather than to use pen and ink. It may also contain recommendation of a third party who will deliver the letter.

The letter closing or postscript maintains contact between sender and recipient and enhances their friendship. This is accomplished by using greetings *(aspazomai)*, a health wish and/or words of farewell. In Christian letters a doxology or benediction can replace the last two.

3. The Letter Form of Hebrews, the General Epistles and Revelation.

The degree to which the books of Hebrews, the General Epistles and Revelation conform to the conventions of the Greek and early Christian letter forms varies according to purpose and associated genres.

3.1. Hebrews. Hebrews has been identified as a Jewish-Hellenistic and early Christian homily or sermon influenced by classical rhetoric. More recently it has been classified as a written speech of encomium. It does not conform to the letter form; it does not even possess a formal letter prescript. It does have a postscript incorporating a benediction (Heb 13:20-21), a formal petition functioning as a responsibility statement *(parakaleō,* Heb 13:22), an announcement of the sender's plan to visit (Heb 13:23), greetings from the sender and secondary greetings from those with him *(aspazomai,* Heb 13:24) and a second benediction (Heb 13:25). The appeal to obey the exhortation given (Heb 13:22) indicates that seeking such obedience was the main reason for writing.

3.2. James. James is protreptic literature in letter form. It tries to persuade the recipients to live a particular life of virtue. It begins with a prescript that includes sender, recipients and greeting *(chairō,* Jas 1:1). The prescript indicates that James is a circular letter meant to be distributed to numerous churches ("twelve tribes of the Dispersion"). James does not exhibit a clear body-opening, middle or closing, nor does it have a postscript. However, James 1:2-27 acts like a body-opening in introducing topics that are developed in James 2:1—5:12, and James 5:13-20 acts like a body-closing in recapitulating some of those same topics. Also included in its letter form are diatribal elements (dialogue and question and answer in pursuit of truth), paraenesis (moral instruction) and three examples of a complete elaboration of an argument according to Greco-Roman rhetoric (Jas 2:1-13; 2:14-26; 3:1-12).

3.3. 1 Peter. First Peter conforms only partially to the ancient letter form. It begins with a prescript (1 Pet 1:1-2) containing a reference to the sender (Peter) and the recipients (exiles of the Diaspora), each with a theological description (1 Pet 1:1-2), and a greeting in the form of a benediction (1 Pet 1:2). The prescript is followed by a benediction substituting for the health wish or thanksgiving (1 Pet 1:3-9). The body of the letter (1 Pet 1:13—5:12) is not easily divided into body-opening, middle and closing. The body-opening begins with a petition in the form of a command to "set all your hope on the grace that Jesus Christ will bring you when he is revealed" (1 Pet 1:13). An imperatival petition often begins the body-opening. It gives the sender's main reason for writing, which the body of the letter will elaborate. The body-closing contains a motivation-for-writing formula and a responsibility statement that echoes the petition that begins the body-opening: "Stand fast in it [the true grace of God]" (1 Pet 5:12). The postscript (1 Pet 5:13-14) is comprised of greetings from a third party and the sender *(aspazomai;* 1 Pet 5:13-14) and a benediction (1 Pet 5:14).

First Peter has been identified as a diaspora letter modeled on those in the OT sent from Jews in Jerusalem to those in exile (cf. 1 Pet 1:1), but the diaspora letter is not a specific genre. First Peter is better identified as a circular letter sent to several congregations. Among other traditional materials, it incorporates a household code that describes the role of members of the household in relation to one another (1 Pet 2:18—3:7). Although it has been surmised that a catechism or a baptismal liturgy underlies the body of the letter, these features can be attributed to shared early Christian tradition.

3.4. 2 Peter. In a Jewish or Christian farewell speech or testament a dying community leader announces his death and exhorts the community to be faithful to its traditions after his death. The sender of 2 Peter creates the unusual combination of a testament in letter form. This allows the sender in the postapostolic era to portray the apostle Peter as communicating over time to the recipients.

Second Peter begins with the typical prescript referring to sender and recipients and a benediction (2 Pet 1:1-2). The letter prescript is followed by elements borrowed from the testament genre: the rehearsal of the traditions central to the community (2 Pet 1:3-11) and an announcement of Peter's death (2 Pet 1:12-15). This announcement functions as the body-opening of the letter (2 Pet 1:12-15). Reminding the recipients of the traditional teachings works like a full disclosure formula ("I wish you to know that") and a motivation for writing. The body-middle of 2 Peter (2 Pet 1:16—3:13) develops the motif of the coming of false teachers, so common to a testament, by refuting their main doctrines. The body-closing (2 Pet 3:14-18) is indicated by the vocative *beloved* and a responsibility statement (2 Pet 3:14). A doxology serves as the postscript (2 Pet 3:18).

3.5. 1 John. First John (*see* John, Letters of) does not exhibit the typical letter opening conventions needed to classify a document as a letter. The opening (1 Jn 1:1-4) is modeled on the prologue of the Fourth Gospel (Jn 1:1-18) and introduces topics to be developed in the remainder of the work. The closing of 1 John 5:13-21 reiterates main topics but does not contain letter closing conventions. The reason for writing (1 Jn 1:4, 5:13) is the only true letter convention to be noted.

3.6. 2 John. In contrast to 1 John, 2 John conforms to letter conventions. It begins with a prescript (2 Jn 1-3) referring to the sender (the elder) and the recipients (the elect lady), accompanied by theological description of the latter (2 Jn 1-2). A benediction replaces the greeting (2 Jn 3). Although it is not formally a thanksgiving, 2 John 4 functions as one as it rejoices in the recipient's welfare. The body-opening (2 Jn 4-5) begins with an expression of joy (*echarēn lian*), alludes to subject matter shared by both parties so as to provide a common basis for matters of the letter body (the commandment) and presents a petition. The petition is standard: 2 John 4 providing the background ("walking in the truth") and 2 John 5 providing the petition (*erōtaō*, "Let us love one another"; i.e., to continue to walk in the truth).

The body-middle (2 Jn 6-11) develops the concerns presented in the body-opening and introduces other concerns of equal importance. It is indicated by the presence of responsibility statements (2 Jn 8, 10) and the concluding short paraenetic section common to Christian letters (2 Jn 11). The body-closing (2 Jn 12) reiterates and accentuates what has been said. It presents the motivation for writing ("much to write"), forms a bridge to further communication and notifies the recipients of the sender's coming visit to discuss further issues. The letter closing sends traditional greetings from a third party (*aspazomai*, 2 Jn 13).

3.7. 3 John. Third John also follows letter conventions. The prescript refers to sender (the elder) and recipient (Gaius) but lacks the typical greeting (3 Jn 1). Although 3 John 2 contains a conventional health wish *(hygiainō)* within a report of a prayer for the recipients, both of which are typical of the prescript, the initial vocative, *beloved,* of 3 John 2 marks the transition to the body-opening (3 Jn 2-6). The body-opening contains an expression of joy over the welfare of the recipient (*echarēn lian*, 3 Jn 3-4) and a petition that expresses its purpose (3 Jn 5-6). The petition contains the petition proper ("you will do well," *kalōs poiēseis*, 3 Jn 6) and its background, beginning with the formula "you do faithfully" *(piston poieis*, 3 Jn 5-6), a variation of "you will do well" *(kalōs poiēseis).* The body-middle (3 Jn 7-12) contains responsibility statements (3 Jn 8, 11) and a recommendation of a third party carrying the letter (Demetrius, 3 Jn 12). The body-closing (3 Jn 13-14) presents a reference to writing and notifies the recipients of the sender's upcoming visit, techniques that enable the body-closing to form a bridge to further communication. The postscript consists of a benediction and greetings from the sender and a third party (*aspazomai*, 3 Jn 15).

3.8. Jude. It has been suggested that Jude is a homily in letter form or that it incorporates a midrash in Jude 5-19. At least it can be said that elements of these genres have been incorporated into a rhetorically complex letter that tries to prove that the opponents are the ungodly of whom the prophets spoke. Jude begins with a prescript containing reference to sender (Jude) and recipients, described in their relationship to God (Jude 1), and a benediction (Jude 2). The letter body (Jude 3-23) is divided into the body-opening (Jude 3-4), body-middle (Jude 5-16) and body-closing (Jude 17-23), all beginning with the transitional vocative *beloved*. The body-opening (Jude 3-4) begins with a reference to "the salvation we share," providing the common ground for the letter. It supplies the occasion for the letter as a petition (*parakaleō*, Jude 3) and its background (Jude 4). The body-middle (Jude 5-16) provides further background for the petition, beginning with a full disclosure formula that employs the idea of wishing *(boulomai)* the recipients know *(oida)* something. The body-closing (Jude 17-23) begins with the imperative form of the disclosure formula ("remember," *mnēsthēte*) and contains many responsibility statements in the form of exhortation. The postscript is a doxology (Jude 24-25).

3.9. Revelation. Revelation can be classified as several genres, including letter, prophecy and apocalyptic. It exhibits few features of the Greek letter tradition. After a brief prologue (Rev 1:1-3) there is a letter opening referring to sender (John) and recipients (seven churches of Asia, Rev 1:4), a benediction (Rev 1:4-5) and a doxology (Rev 1:6). After an epilogue (Rev 22:6-20) the letter closes with a benediction (Rev 22:21). The remainder of the book is dominated by the forms of the prophetic and apocalyptic genre.

Mention must be made of the letters to the seven churches in Revelation 2—3. These seven letters each have some forms of ancient letters, including reference to recipients (one of seven churches) and sender (Christ) in the prescript and a reference to knowing *(oida)*, which often begins the body-opening. However, D. E. Aune's careful analysis shows that the seven letters are to be classified as ancient royal or imperial edicts or proclamations, with the mode used being the paraenetic salvation-judgment oracles of early Christian prophecy.

See also GOSPEL (GENRE); RHETORIC.

DLNTD: HERMENEUTICS; LITURGICAL ELEMENTS; PSEUDEPIGRAPHY; RHETORICAL CRITICISM.

BIBLIOGRAPHY. D. E. Aune, "The Form and Function of the Proclamations to the Seven Churches (Revelation 2—3)," *NTS* 36 (1990) 182-204; R. E. Brown, "Appendix V: General Observations on Epistolary Format," in *The Epistles of John* (AB; Garden City, NY: Doubleday, 1982) 788-95 (deals with 2 and 3 John; see 86-92 on 1 John); J. D. Charles, *Literary Strategy in the Epistle of Jude* (Scranton, PA: University of Scranton Press, 1993) 20-64; A. Deissmann, *Bible Studies* (Edinburgh: T & T Clark, 1901) 3-59; idem, *Light from the Ancient East* (New York: Doran, 1927) 146-251; W. G. Doty, *Letters in Primitive Christianity* (Philadelphia: Fortress, 1973); J. A. du Rand, "Structure and Message of 2 John," *Neot* 13 (1979) 101-20; idem, "The Structure of 3 John," *Neot* 13 (1979) 121-31; F. O. Francis, "The Form and Function of the Opening and Closing Paragraphs of James and 1 John," *ZNW* 61 (1970) 110-26; R. W. Funk, "The Form and Structure of 2 and 3 John," *JBL* 86 (1967) 424-30; J. Lieu, *The Second and Third Epistles of John: History and Background*, ed. J. Riches (SNTW; Edinburgh: T & T Clark, 1986) 37-51; T. W. Martin, *Metaphor and Composition in 1 Peter* (SBLDS 131; Atlanta: Scholars Press, 1992) 41-79; S. K. Stowers, *Letter Writing in Greco-Roman Antiquity* (LEC 5; Philadelphia: Westminster, 1986); L. Thurén, *The Rhetorical Strategy of 1 Peter: With Special Regard to Ambiguous Expressions* (Åbo: Åbo Academy Press, 1990) 84-88; D. F. Watson, *Invention, Arrangement and Style: Rhetorical Criticism of Jude and 2 Peter* (SBLDS 104; Atlanta: Scholars Press, 1988) passim; idem, "A Rhetorical Analysis of 2 John According to Greco-Roman Convention," *NTS* 35 (1989) 104-30; idem, "A Rhetorical Analysis of 3 John: A Study in Epistolary Rhetoric," *CBQ* 51 (1989) 479-501; J. L. White, "Ancient Greek Letters," in *Greco-Roman Literature and the New Testament*, ed. D. E. Aune (SBLSBS 21; Atlanta: Scholars Press, 1988) 85-105; idem, *The Body of the Greek Letter* (SBLDS 2; Missoula, MT: Scholars Press, 1972); idem, *Light from Ancient Letters* (Philadelphia: Fortress, 1986); idem, "New Testament Epistolary Literature in the Framework of Ancient Epistolography," *ANRW* 2.25.2 (1984) 1730-56; idem, "Saint Paul and the Apostolic Letter Tradition," *CBQ* 45 (1983) 433-44.

D. F. Watson

LIBERTINES. *See* ADVERSARIES.

LOGOS. *See* JOHN, GOSPEL OF.

LORD I: GOSPELS

The term *kyrios* ("Lord"), which became for the early church the central Christian confession regarding Jesus (cf. Rom 10:9; 1 Cor 12:3; Phil 2:11), had a wide variety of uses in antiquity. It is necessary to explore some of them before examining how and whether Jesus, the earliest Christians and then the Evangelists used such a term or its Aramaic equivalent to say something essential or even extraordinary about the central figure of Christian faith.

1. Greek Usage
2. Jewish Background
3. The Origin of the Christian *Kyrios* Usage
4. Jesus as *Kyrios*
5. *Kyrios* in the Gospels
6. Conclusion

1. Greek Usage.

The term *kyrios* was used in religious and secular contexts in the NT era. On the one hand, national and mystery religions, especially in the East (i.e., Egypt, Syria, Asia Minor, but also in Greece and elsewhere), frequently used the term *kyrios* or its female equivalent, *kyria,* to refer to gods and goddesses such as Isis, Serapis or Osiris. For instance, we have evidence of the use of the term in countless papyri and inscriptions of Serapis (e.g., "I thank the Lord Serapis *(tō kyriō)* that when I was in peril on the sea, he saved me immediately," letter from Apion, soldier in the Roman navy, to his father, second century A.D.). Or again in a letter from a son to his mother, Nilus, in the second century A.D., we read, "I make intercession for you day by day to the Lord Serapis" *(tō kyriō)*. It is quite clear in these contexts that the term *kyrios* connotes a deity who can answer prayers and deserves thanks for divine help. This development seems to go beyond the use of *kyrios* in the period of classical Greek, where the term did refer to the great power a god had over a person or group of persons but does not yet seem to have been a divine title (cf. Pindar *Isth.* 5.53; Plato *Leg.* 12.13).

Equally important for our purposes is the fact that the Roman emperor was as early as the time of Nero called *kyrios* with the sense of divinity. Yet even though he was divinized, he was also known to be a human being. For instance, from an ostracon dated August 4, A.D. 63, we read, "In the year nine of Nero the Lord *(tou kyriou)*." Even before this time, however, in the eastern part of the empire and in Egypt in particular, the emperor was being called *kyrios* in a more-than-merely-human sense. Thus, for instance, Oxyrhynchus papyrus 1143, which dates to A.D. 1, speaks of sacrifices and libations "for the God and Lord Emperor" [Augustus]. Even in 12 B.C. we have an inscription to Augustus as *theos kai kyrios,* "God and Lord" (*BGU*, 1197, 1, 15).

As A. Deissmann (349-51) long ago argued, it is quite likely that the early church deliberately and polemically ascribed to Jesus titles that had already been applied to the emperor. The meaning of the term within the Pauline communities, namely, an absolute divine being to whom one belongs and owes absolute allegiance and submission, becomes all the more evident in light of the Pauline language of self-reference. Paul speaks of himself and others as *douloi,* "slaves," in order to indicate their relationship to Jesus "the Lord" (Rom 1:1; 13:4). This term may be distinguished from *misthios,* or *diakonos,* terms used for hired servants who had certain rights and privileges. The *doulos* who served a *kyrios* was not free but was the property of his or her lord. This was the normal terminology in various oriental religions to express the relationship of the adherent to the deity. No doubt to a significant degree this usage has derived from the more ordinary usage in the institution of slavery. The term *kyrios* had a perfectly normal, nonreligious sense in classical and *Koine* Greek, meaning "master" or "owner" of some property, including human property.

The vocative form *kyrie* frequently was just a polite form of address like the English term *sir.* This latter usage is in evidence not only in secular Greek literature but also appears at various points in the NT. For instance in Acts 9:5 (and par.) Paul addresses the heavenly Jesus with the term *kyrie.* Since he is asking whom he is addressing, it is unlikely that in this case the term means anything but "sir." Again in Mark 7:28 we find the use of *kyrie,* in all probability indicating a respectful form of address, not a confession of deity. Once again, in Luke 6:46 *kyrie kyrie* may refer to a respectful form of address, not a confession of divinity. Luke 6:46 seems to suggest that it is inconsistent to address Jesus in respectful terms as a great teacher but not do what he commands. It is not impossible, however, that the use of *mārî,* the Aramaic equivalent of *kyrie,* was, at least in the context of Jesus' inner circle of disciples, already taking on a deeper significance than a mere respectful form of address (see Vermes 109-15).

There may be a clear distinction between the use of the term *kyrios* and its near synonym *despotēs*. The latter term suggested arbitrariness while the term *kyrios* connoted the idea of legitimate authority (cf. Bietenhard, 510).

From these examples we can readily observe the scope of usage of the term *kyrios* in Greek literature. It can have a perfectly mundane use to refer to the master or owner of slaves or some other sort of property such as a household or business. The term in the vocative could also be used as a respectful way of addressing a person, in particular a superior, who was not one's owner or employer. This second sort of usage had become so conventional that it often meant little more than our use of the address "Dear Sir" in a letter. Yet early in the first century B.C., at least in the eastern part of the empire, the term *kyrios*, in the sense of divinity, was being applied not only to mythological gods like Serapis or Osiris but also to one particular human being, the Roman emperor. In such a context it is understandable why Paul might say there are many so-called gods and lords, yet for Christians there is but one Lord, Jesus Christ (1 Cor 8:5-6). Because of the use of *kyrios* in these more religious senses, W. Bousset argued that it was not until Christianity reached a mainly Greek or Hellenistic environment that the title *Lord* was applied to Jesus, and then under the influence of pagan usage. This conclusion can be shown to be incorrect by a study of the Jewish usage of *kyrios* and its Aramaic cognates. To this we now turn.

2. Jewish Background.

In the Septuagint (LXX) the term *kyrios* occurs more than 9,000 times, and in 6,156 occurrences it is used in place of the proper name of God, Yahweh. This amounts not to a translation of the personal name Yahweh but a circumlocution meant to aid in avoiding saying the sacred Tetragrammaton. There are, however, some doubts as to whether the original compilers of the LXX in every case translated the Tetragrammaton with *kyrios*. Some older manuscripts have the Hebrew *YHWH* in the Greek text at some places, and at least one LXX manuscript from Qumran uses *IAO* for the Tetragrammaton instead of *kyrios*. The copies of the LXX that do have *kyrios* for *YHWH* date from the fourth century A.D. on and appear to be Christian copies

with Christian modifications. Yet J. A. Fitzmyer has produced evidence that early Jews did use the Greek *kyrios* as well as *ʾādôn*, or *mārêh*, of Yahweh, and thus it is not impossible that early Jewish Christians transferred such a title from Yahweh to Jesus (Fitzmyer 1979, 115-42; 1981, 218-35). But we can no longer say with any assurance that this was done under the influence of the LXX. Examples of *kyrios* used of Yahweh can be found not only in Josephus and Philo but even as early as in the Wisdom of Solomon (27 times; cf. Wis 1:1, 7, 9; 2:13). Of special significance is Josephus's remark that early Jews refused to call the emperor *kyrios* precisely because they regarded it as a name reserved for God (Josephus *J.W.* 7.10.1 §§418-19).

When in the LXX and other early Jewish literature *kyrios* is used to translate the Hebrew word *ʾādôn*, it is a matter of translation and not a circumlocution. Some 190 times in the LXX *ʾādôn* is translated *kyrios* and refers to men who were lords or commanders in some sense. In fact there is also some evidence that *ʾādônay* was being used as a substitute for *YHWH* in some cases at Qumran in their Hebrew biblical manuscripts. Equally interesting is the use of *ʾādônay* in prayers of invocation at Qumran (cf. 1QM 12:8, 18; 1Q 34).

The Aramaic use of *mārêh* to refer to God as Lord can be traced back at least as early as Daniel 2:47 and Daniel 5:23, even though in these texts the term is not yet used in an absolute sense as a title. Evidence of a different sort comes to us from the Genesis Apocryphon (1QapGen). This Qumran document probably dates from about the turn of the era and provides us with examples of God being addressed in Aramaic as *mārî*, "my Lord." This is the only known example of this usage in Aramaic. However, it is quite common to find the more mundane use of *mārî* by a wife or servant of the husband or head of the household. *Mār* is the Aramaic word for "lord," but it is almost always found with various sorts of suffixes. In 11Q Targum of Job (11QtgJob) we have *mārêh* as a rendering of the Hebrew word *šadday* ("almighty"). There are also some fragments from Cave 4 from the Enoch literature where *mārêh*, or *māran*, is used of God (cf. *1 Enoch* 89:31-36), and the Greek version has *ho kyrios*. Further evidence of importance comes from the temple discovered at Gaza, which was called the Marneum, where a god called *mār* was worshiped (Johnson, 151).

L. W. Hurtado (1988) has amassed material demonstrating the complex nature of early Jewish thought on such subjects as divine agents. He has shown that there is plenty of evidence that in early Judaism the Jewish concept of the uniqueness of God could co-exist with the idea that God could give a unique place and role to a particular heavenly figure or agent. This included the idea that exalted patriarchs (e.g., Enoch or Moses) and principal angels (e.g., Michael) could speak and act for God with divine authority and power. This evidence is significant because it indicates a larger context of divine agency in early Judaism by which even the first Jewish Christians could have understood Jesus.

3. The Origin of the Christian *Kyrios* Usage.

Aramaic evidence of singular importance for our study can be found in 1 Corinthians 16:22 and in what is probably the earliest of extracanonical Christian works, the *Didache* (cf. *Did.* 10.6). Here Jesus is referred to as Lord by the earliest Aramaic-speaking Christians using the phrase *maran atha,* or more likely *marana tha* (cf. Rev 22:20, which is likely a Greek translation of this phrase. This last text makes clear that it is Jesus who is in view, as is also evident in 1 Cor 16:22-23). There are basically three ways the phrase *marana tha* could be rendered: (1) "Lord come," (2) "Our Lord has come" or (3) even as a prophetic perfect "The Lord will come." Whichever rendering one chooses, and (1) seems most likely, especially in view of Revelation 22:20, a person who has died is being referred to as Lord. Since the first translation is the most likely, C. F. D. Moule's (41) pointed remark bears repeating: "Besides even if 'our Lord' is not the same as 'the Lord' absolutely, and even if the Aramaic *mārêh* had been used mostly for humans and not for God (which we have seen reason to question) one does not call upon a mere Rabbi, after his death, to come. The entire phrase, *Maranatha,* if it meant 'Come, our Master!' would be bound to carry transcendental overtones even if the *māran* by itself did not."

It is not completely clear whether *marana tha* was used to invoke Christ's presence in worship or was a wish prayer for the return of Christ from heaven. Nevertheless, on the basis of strong evidence that the Aramaic-speaking Jewish Christians, during and likely before Paul's time (i.e., the earliest Jewish Christians), called Jesus "Lord" or at least "our Lord," we must reject Bousset's argument for the origin of the christological title *kyrios* in the Hellenistic mission of the early church.

It is striking that Paul, writing in the fifties to Greek-speaking Christians who very likely did not know Aramaic, does not bother to translate *marana tha.* This must surely mean that he assumes they understood the meaning of the phrase, which in turn suggests that it had long been a common invocation used by Christians. Consequently, the apostle sees no need to explain or translate it. The origins of the Christian use of the term *Lord* for Jesus must be traced at least back to the earliest Aramaic-speaking Jewish-Christians. Can it be traced back even further?

4. Jesus as *Kyrios.*

Several texts seem likely to go back to a historical setting during the lifetime of Jesus. They may raise the question whether and in what sense Jesus may have been called Lord during his early ministry. We have already dealt with texts where the vocative *kyrie* was used, and we will not return to them here, as they probably offer us little help. Of more importance may be a text like Mark 11:3, where Jesus tells his disciples to go and get him a colt to ride into Jerusalem and to tell whomever may question, "The Lord has need of it." The Greek reads *ho kyrios,* and presumably, if this goes back to an actual command of Jesus, it is a rendering of the Aramaic *mārêh.* There are several possible ways of looking at this text. Even if it does go back to an utterance of Jesus, *mārêh* could here mean either the owner or the master, in which case it would imply nothing about Jesus' divine status. Some commentators have speculated either that Jesus was the owner of the animal being requested (which the text does not really suggest) or that the owner of the animal was with Jesus and was loaning the animal to Jesus. This latter view also finds no clues in the text to give it credence. It is much more probable that the meaning here is much like what we find in Mark 14:14, where Jesus is reported to have said, "The teacher says, Where is my guest room?" If so, then "Lord" here may be no more than a respectful way of referring to a master teacher, just as we might speak of a master craftsman. It does suggest one who sees himself as having authority to command or commandeer certain things of people, whether they were disciples or not. It is not clear that this particular usage of *mārêh* bears more significance than this.

Support for this suggestion can be found in several places in the Fourth Gospel. Here we find that the two terms *teacher* and *lord* are juxtaposed (Jn 13:13-16). It should also be noted that in the primitive resurrection account in John 20 we find Mary Magdalene calling her deceased teacher "my Lord" (Jn 20:13), and when she recognizes the voice of Jesus speaking to her we hear the cry "Rabbouni" (Jn 20:16), which is translated "Teacher." This text also seems to suggest that Jesus was called not only *rabbî*, or *rabbûnî*, during his ministry, but he was probably also addressed by the term of respect *mārêh*, which would have connoted that Jesus was a great teacher who exercised authority over his disciples. The disciples looked to Jesus as master in that sense. Another piece of evidence that may support this line of reasoning is the use of slave and master language (Jn 15:15, 20) in referring to the relationship between Jesus and his disciples.

A much more crucial passage for our discussion is Mark 12:35-37. Here Psalm 110:7 is quoted, "The Lord said to my lord, sit at my right hand." Jesus then asks, "David himself calls him Lord: so how is he his son?" This text should not be abruptly dismissed as reflecting the later theology of the early church, especially inasmuch as there is extensive evidence that Jesus saw himself in messianic terms and at least indirectly made messianic claims (see Witherington 1990). Mark 12:35-37 reflects precisely the sort of allusive, or indirect, manner that Jesus seems to have used in public to indicate how he viewed himself. His method was to allude to his significance in such a way as to lure his audience into careful and deep reflection on this important matter. The form of teaching here is characteristic of early Jewish teachers. Taking a puzzling text, they would raise questions about it in such a way as to challenge common misconceptions about various matters, in this case the nature of Messiah as a *son of David.

Also favoring the authenticity of this tradition is the fact that it seems to suggest that Jesus challenges the idea that Messiah must be of Davidic origins, a fact that the early church went some lengths to demonstrate (e.g., Mt 1:1-20; Lk 1:27; 3:23-38). In the text as it stands Jesus is suggesting that Messiah is David's Lord, and as such he stands above and exists prior to David. This is

the reason Jesus raises the question of why the scribes call Messiah "David's son." The idea of preexistence, as Hurtado (1988, 41-50) has shown, was not uncommonly predicated of God's divine agents in early Judaism.

It is then not inconceivable that Jesus here could have alluded to himself not only as Messiah but even as preexistent Lord and been understood by his audience. V. Taylor (492-93) puts it as follows and deserves to be quoted at length:

Certainly a secret of Jesus concerning Himself is implied. His question is shaped by His estimate of Messiahship embodied in Himself. His purpose, however, is not to reveal this secret, which is and remains his own, but to expose the futility of Messianic hopes which do not rise above the earthly and human plane. . . . The allusive character of the saying favours the view that it is an original utterance; it half conceals and half reveals the 'Messianic secret'. It suggests, but does not state the claim that Jesus is supernatural in dignity and origin and that His Sonship is no mere matter of human descent. It is difficult to think that the doctrinal beliefs of a community could be expressed in this allusive manner. The intention in a doctrinal statement is that it should be understood, whereas the purpose of the saying is to challenge thought and decision. This is the very idiom of Jesus Himself as his message to the Baptist shows (Lk. vii.22f.). But demonstrably, it is not the tone or the method of primitive Christianity.

This means that ultimately the proclamation of Jesus as Lord goes back to something Jesus suggested about himself, albeit obliquely, during his ministry and in public. Yet this does not explain when and at what point Jesus' followers took the hint and really began to see Jesus in this light. We have noted that the evidence is at best scant that during his ministry Jesus' disciples thought of him as *mārêh* in any sort of transcendent sense (Lk 6:46 may suggest this). What then prompted the confession of Jesus as Lord? Here we may consider clues from several sources.

First, there is the matter of the primitive confessional material Paul uses in Romans 1:3-4. This text suggests that Jesus assumed new functions, authority and power as a result of his resurrection. Indeed, he was given the new title "Son of God in power" as a result of the resurrection. Another piece of evidence comes to us from what is probably a christological hymn Paul is quoting in Philippians 2:6-11. Here we are told that because of Jesus' giving up the status and prerogatives of "being equal to God" and taking on the form not merely of a human being but of a slave, being obedient to God's plan even to the point of death, he has now been highly exalted and given the name that is above all names. Jesus moves from being a *doulos* to the *kyrios*. In the context of the hymn, that name which is above all others is not Jesus, a name he already had, but the throne name he acquired when he assumed the functions of deity, ruling over all things. This name is *kyrios*. Acts 2:36, which may reflect some of the early apostolic preaching, says, "Let all the house of Israel therefore know assuredly that God has made him both Lord and Christ, this Jesus whom you crucified." In view of the fact that Luke readily calls Jesus *kyrios* in his Gospel, it is most unlikely that he would have created a text like this that suggests, if not states, that lordship is most appropriately predicated of Jesus after his death. This text seems to indicate that these titles are especially apt because of what God did for Jesus after he was crucified—namely, as Acts 2:32 states, "This Jesus God raised up, and of that we are all witnesses."

Another hint comes from John 20:18, which suggests that the earliest post-Easter proclamation of faith was, "I have seen the [risen] Lord." In short, the evidence suggests that the confession "Jesus is Lord" arose as a result of the earliest disciples' experiences of the risen Christ. Paul suggests that such a confession could not arise until after the Lord had risen and the Spirit (*see* Holy Spirit) had descended on Jesus' followers, for he says, "No one can say 'Jesus is Lord' except by the Holy Spirit" (1 Cor 12:3).

While the ultimate ground for the confession of Jesus as Lord seems to go back to something Jesus alluded to during his ministry, the formal point of departure for such a confession by the disciples was their experiences of the risen Lord on and after Easter Sunday, as well as their reception of the Holy Spirit. As best we can tell, the first to so confess Jesus seems to have been the person who first claimed to have seen Jesus risen—Mary Magdalene. In view of the negative view regarding a woman's word of witness that existed in many places in the first century, but especially in Palestine (see Witherington 1984), it is not credible that the early church invented

the idea that Mary Magdalene was the first to claim, "I have seen the Lord." The early witness list in 1 Corinthians 15:5-8 is indicative of the tendency in the early church to move in quite the opposite direction and claim the prominence of the Twelve and the apostles as witnesses of the resurrection.

We find further evidence that the experience of the risen Lord led to the full confession of Jesus' significance in John 20:28, where the climactic confession in a Gospel full of confessions is *ho kyrios mou kai ho theos mou* ("My Lord and my God"). It may be that this material is included here because the Evangelist, writing toward the close of the first century, knew of the Emperor Domitian's (A.D. 81-96) practice of naming himself in official correspondence *dominus et deus noster* ("our Lord and God"). The Fourth Evangelist may have been countering such a claim. But even if this is so, it seems rather clear that John wishes to convey to his audience that the true confession of Jesus first came about as a result of seeing the risen Lord, in the case of Mary Magdalene and Thomas. We conclude that Hurtado should be heeded when he says:

> Rather than trying to account for such a development as the veneration of Jesus by resort to vague suggestions of ideational borrowing from the cafeteria of heroes and demigods of the Greco-Roman world, scholars should pay more attention to this sort of religious experience of the first Christians. It is more likely that the initial and main reason that this particular chief agent (Jesus) came to share in the religious devotion of this particular Jewish group (the earliest Christians) is that they had visions and other experiences that communicated the risen and exalted Christ and that presented him in such unprecedented and superlative divine glory that they felt compelled to respond devotionally as they did. (Hurtado, 121)

Christological convictions and confessions were first generated by the experience of the risen Lord and his Spirit. This leads us to examine how the term *kyrios* came to be used by the Evangelists, who were likely composing their Gospels during the last third of the first century A.D.

5. *Kyrios* in the Gospels.

The Synoptic Gospels, and Luke in particular, include nearly the whole range of uses of the term *kyrios* as we have discussed it. There are 717 passages where the term *kyrios* occurs in the NT, and 210 of them can be found in Luke-Acts (another 275 are found in Paul). The fact that the majority of the uses of *kyrios* are found in the writings of Luke and Paul may be explained by the fact that they were in the main addressing Gentile audiences, or at least they were writing to areas where Greek language and culture were the predominant influences. In contrast to Luke, *kyrios* occurs only 18 times in Mark and 80 times in Matthew, while there are 52 instances in the Fourth Gospel.

5.1. Kyrios in the Synoptics. A sampling of the various uses not referring to Jesus can now be given. In Mark and the Q material God is never called *kyrios* except in Mark 5:19 and Mark 13:20. Neither Matthew nor Luke follows Mark in either of these examples. In the Lukan parallel to Mark 5:19 we find *ho theos* ("God"; Lk 8:39) instead of Mark's *ho kyrios*, and Matthew does not include parallel material. In the Matthean parallel to Mark 13:20 the First Evangelist uses the indirect form, "and if the days had not been shortened" (Mt 24:22), instead of Mark's, "And if the Lord had not shortened the days." This difference cannot be explained by the idea that Matthew and Luke do not call God *kyrios*, for quite clearly, especially in the birth narratives, both of these Evangelists do (cf. Mt 1:20, 22, 24; 2:13, 15, 19 with Lk 1:6, 9, 11, 15, 17, 25, 28, 38, 45, 58, 66; 2:9, 15, 22, 23, 24, 26, 39). We also find *kyrios* used of God in the resurrection material at Matthew 28:2 and in two passages unique to the Third Gospel, Luke 5:17 and Luke 20:37. *Kyrie* as a conventional address of respect is always used in the Gospels whenever a slave speaks to a master. However, it can also be found on the lips of Jews addressing Pilate (Mt 27:63), of workers speaking to the owner of a vineyard (Lk 13:8), of a son to his father when he works for him (Mt 21:30), of Mary to the gardener (Jn 20:15) and, finally, on the lips of a Syro-Phoenician woman addressing Jesus (Mk 7:28; Mt 15:27). The use of the doubled form, *kyrie, kyrie,* seems to reflect Palestinian usage (cf. Mt 7:21, 22; 25:11; Lk 6:46).

Kyrios can be used to refer to the lord or owner of some property or estate, such as the owner of a vineyard (Mk 12:9 and par.). We have already noted that Mark 11:3 and parallels likely reflects the same sort of usage. The term can also be used either of the master of a (free) steward (Lk 16:3) or of an owner of slaves (almost always with a qualifier like "his" or "my"; cf. Mt 18:25; 24:45; Lk 12:37, 42; 14:23). But we do not find the Gospels using *kyrios* either for the emperor or for any pagan deities.

There are, however, some examples where *kyrios* seems to refer to ability and the right to exercise authority and power. In these cases it amounts to a nontitular use without any transcendent implications. For instance, in Mark 2:28, when Jesus says the Son of man is lord of the sabbath, he means he is one who exercises authority over the rules that govern the sabbath. Of a similar nature is the nontitular use in Luke 10:2, where God is said to be the one who controls the harvest; he is "the lord of the harvest."

5.2. Kyrios in Luke. Regarding the absolute use of the noun *kyrios,* Matthew and Mark do not use the term in a transcendent sense within their narrative frameworks of the sayings of Jesus (Mk 11:3 is probably not an exception). But Luke does employ such a usage. For instance, in Luke 7:13 we read, "And the Lord (*ho kyrios*) had compassion on him." Or in Luke 10:5 the Evangelist writes, "And the Lord (*ho kyrios*) appointed seventy others." Luke, as a Gentile writing exclusively to a Gentile audience, shows no reticence in using *ho kyrios* of Jesus and thereby implying the transcendent religious sense of the term. This is not to say that Luke is being totally anachronistic, for he is usually careful not to place the term on Jesus' lips or on the lips of his interlocutors in a sense or manner that it would not likely have been used during the ministry of Jesus. Some probable exceptions are found in Luke 1:43, where Elizabeth speaks of Mary as "the mother of my Lord"; Luke 2:11, where Jesus is identified as "Lord" to the shepherds; and Luke 1:38, where Mary is called the handmaiden of the Lord, though here it seems to refer to Yahweh (*see* Birth of Jesus).

Numerous other references in Luke's Gospel indicate the Evangelist's regular use of *kyrios* within the narrative framework of his account of Jesus' ministry (cf. Lk 7:19; 10:1, 39, 41; 11:39; 12:42; 16:8; 17:5, 6; 18:6; 19:8a; 22:61; 24:3, 34). When he is speaking of Jesus, Luke is not reluctant to use the Christian title Lord. The implication may be that Luke is suggesting that at least in being, if not yet fully in action or recognition, Jesus was already the *kyrios*.

Luke does not seem to introduce the title into his Markan material (Lk 22:61 might be an exception). This raises the question of whether Luke found this frequent use of the titular *kyrios* in his own source material. However, where we find *kyrios* in material drawn from Q or L, it appears to be his own addition (cf. Lk 7:19; 10:1; 11:39; 12:42; 17:5-6). So on the whole it appears that most instances of the titular *kyrios* in the Third Gospel are a result of Luke's editorial activity (cf. de la Potterie). There is some justification then for H. Conzelmann's claim that for Luke, Jesus is first of all the *kyrios* who was given dominion by God and rules over the Christian community by means of the Spirit (176-79).

5.3. Kyrios in Matthew. In the First Gospel, strangers, enemies and Judas Iscariot always greet Jesus with *didaskale* or *rabbi,* but never with *kyrie,* while the disciples and those who seek out Jesus for healing never use the former terms but always address Jesus as *kyrie.* So while J. D. Kingsbury (1975) has perhaps made too much of Matthew's use of the vocative *kyrie,* there is some justification for including some of these instances in a discussion of Matthew's christology.

The First Evangelist is not shy of using *kyrios* of Jesus. For example, in Matthew 3:3 (following Mark 1:3) he quotes Isaiah 40:3 ("prepare the way of the Lord") and implicitly applies to Jesus a title originally referring to Yahweh. This reference, however, only becomes evident from what follows in the narrative, not from the quote itself. Within the temptation narrative, Matthew 4:7 ("You shall not tempt the Lord your God," Deut 6:16) might at first glance seem to imply that *kyrios* refers to Jesus. But even though it is Jesus who is being tempted, two factors tell against this reading: (1) In Matthew 4:10 Jesus uses the same language (quoting Deut 6:13) and there it is rather clear that Yahweh is in view; (2) Jesus is quoting Scripture against the devil and in both the quote that precedes and the one that follows the reference to God is a reference to someone other than Jesus the speaker.

Matthew 7:21-22 is a more promising case, even though the vocative is used. Here it seems clear that it is disciples who have prophesied and done miracles in Jesus' name that call Jesus "Lord, Lord." Yet it is also clear from this text that calling Jesus "Lord" and even doing deeds and proclaiming words in his name is insufficient if one does not also hear and heed Jesus' words and do the Father's will.

There is a notable stress on the lordship of Jesus as the First Gospel works to its climax. Thus for instance in Matthew 22:44 Jesus is clearly implied to be Lord, and in Matthew 24:42 Jesus refers to himself as "your Lord" (note the parallel with Son of man in Mt 24:39). This last example is not an instance of the absolute usage. But taken together with some of the other texts already cited and the fact that Jesus is speaking of this Lord in the language of the *yôm Yahweh* (day of the Lord), we should surely understand *ho kyrios* to mean more than "master" in this instance.

Kingsbury (1975) offers some helpful conclusions about the use of *kyrios* in Matthew, particularly his observation that the word is most often used in Matthew as a relational term—the master as opposed to the slave, the owner as opposed to the worker, even the father as opposed to the son (Mt 21:28-30). However, none of these examples comes from passages of christological significance. Yet it is telling that in the christological passages we have examined, the relational character of the term is indicated by (1) the use of the vocative "Lord, Lord" in Matthew 7:21-22; (2) the use of "*your* Lord" in Matthew 24:42; and (3) the use of "*my* Lord" in the citation of Psalm 110:1 in Matthew 22:44. Kingsbury has shown, however, that *kyrios* is not Matthew's premier title for Jesus. When it does bear christological weight it is usually explained or qualified by another title and thus at most it should be regarded as an auxiliary christological title in the First Gospel. We have also noted a certain allusive or indirect character in some of the christological passages (cf. Mt 3:3; 22:44).

5.4. Kyrios in John. John's christological use of *kyrios* is scant compared with Luke, yet more evident than in Matthew. The titles Son, *Son of God or Messiah/*Christ occur in John more frequently than Lord. This may seem surprising given the likelihood that it is the latest Gospel, written well after the confession "Jesus is Lord" would have been widespread in the church. While the address of the paralytic (vocative, *kyrie*) in John 5:7 should not be counted as having christological weight, John's reference to Jesus as "the Lord" in John 6:23 is a christological usage (if we do not follow the few Western manuscripts [D, 086, arm et al.] that omit the relevant phrase here).

Peter's address to Jesus, "Lord *(kyrie),* to whom shall we go?" (Jn 6:68), may be intended to be seen as more than a respectful form of address, especially in view of Peter's confession in John 6:69. A christological meaning is possible but not as likely in the address of the woman caught in adultery (Jn 8:11), though the pericope was not originally part of this Gospel. More clearly, the healed blind man clearly uses *kyrie* (Jn 9:36) as a respectful form of address. The editorial comment in John 11:2 provides us with a clear Christian use of *ho kyrios*. The blessing at the triumphal entry in John 12:13 (citing Ps 118:26) likely refers to God, not Jesus, as *kyrios*. John 12:38, citing Isaiah 53:1, should likely also be seen in this way.

Peter's address of "Lord" in John 13:6, 9, the narrative of Jesus' washing the disciples' feet, may have some christological implications in light of Peter's earlier use of the term in John 6:68-69. But we should not discount the possibility *kyrie* is here used as a term of respect for one's teacher. The same can be said of Peter's words in John 13:36-37 and Thomas's address in John 14:5. It may be of some significance that (1) Jesus does not call himself *kyrios* in the Fourth Gospel; (2) the Evangelist clearly does call Jesus *kyrios* in his editorial remarks and within the narrative framework; (3) up until John 20, whenever the term is found on a disciple's lips, it is always in the vocative, and none of these instances is clearly christological. The words of Mary Magdalene in John 20:13 ("my Lord"), which is not cast in the absolute form, is the first nonvocative use of *kyrios* by a character within the narrative, and even here it may not bear christological meaning.

This means that John 20:18, John 20:28, John 21:7, and possibly the multiple examples of the vocative in John 21:15-21 are the only clear references in this Gospel where a character in the narrative calls Jesus *kyrios* in the transcendent sense. This strongly suggests that the Fourth Evangelist is consciously trying to avoid anachronism in his use of this title and wishes to indicate that Jesus was only truly known and confessed to be Lord as a result of the disciples' encounters with the risen Lord.

6. Conclusion.

A somewhat clear development of the use of the term *kyrios* for Jesus of Nazareth can now be traced. The usage begins with indirect hints during the time of Jesus' ministry, through accounts of the experiences of the risen Lord, to the use of *marana tha* in early Palestinian Jewish-Chris-

tian contexts, to evidence of the christological use of the term in the narrative framework of Luke and John, and finally to the variegated use of the term in Acts. There it is used in combination with other names and titles, as a form of address to the exalted Christ, and in the transfer of reference from Yahweh to Jesus in quotes from the OT.

Interestingly, we do not find the use of the absolute or transcendent *kyrios* in the narrative framework of Matthew and Mark, and there is some attempt by Luke and the Fourth Evangelist to avoid anachronism by not placing the full Christian use of the term on anyone's lips during the ministry of Jesus. It is also significant that Luke-Acts and John intimate that the confession of Jesus as Lord arose as a result of the resurrection experiences. This did not prevent the Evangelists from sometimes calling the Jesus of the ministry "Lord" in their narratives, for it was "this same Jesus" whom God had raised from the dead who took on the tasks of Lord in earnest when he joined God in heaven. In other words, the continuity of usage of *kyrios* from before to after the death and resurrection in the Gospels reflects the belief in the continuity of personhood between the historical Jesus and the risen Lord.

The use of the term *kyrios* in a religious sense was sure to be taken to imply Jesus' divinity, especially in the eastern part of the Roman Empire and in Gentile contexts. The evidence suggests that this remarkable mutation in the Jewish concept of monotheism took place in the earliest Palestinian Jewish-Christian community as a result of some hints from Jesus and especially as a result of the experiences of the risen Lord shared by some of the eyewitnesses of the life of the historical Jesus. The evidence we have studied indicates that the high christology of the early Christian church was not a new development of the late first century A.D.

See also CHRIST; GOD; SON OF DAVID; SON OF GOD; SON OF MAN.

DJG: "I AM" SAYINGS; LOGOS; TEACHER; WISDOM.

BIBLIOGRAPHY. H. Bietenhard, "Lord," *NIDNTT* 2:510-20; W. Bousset, *Kyrios Christos* (Nashville: Abingdon, 1970); H. Conzelmann, *The Theology of St. Luke* (New York: Harper and Row, 1960); A. Deissmann, *Light from the Ancient East* (repr.; Grand Rapids: Baker, 1978); J. A. Fitzmyer, "New Testament Kyrios and Maranatha and Their Aramaic Background," in *To Advance the Gospel* (New York: Crossroad, 1981) 218-35; idem, "The Semitic Background of the New Testament Kyrios-Title," in *A Wandering Aramean* (Missoula, MT: Scholars Press, 1979) 115-42; W. Foerster, "κύριος κτλ," *TDNT* 3:1039-95; G. Howard, "The Tetragram and the New Testament," *JBL* 96 (1977) 63-83; L. W. Hurtado, *Lord Jesus Christ: Devotion to Jesus in Earliest Christianity* (Grand Rapids: Eerdmans, 2003); idem, *One God, One Lord: Early Christian Devotion and Ancient Jewish Monotheism* (Philadelphia: Fortress, 1988); S. E. Johnson, "Lord," *IDB* 3:150-51; J. D. Kingsbury, *Matthew: Structure, Christology, Kingdom* (2d ed.; Minneapolis: Fortress, 1989); idem, "The Title 'Kyrios' in Matthew's Gospel," *JBL* 94 (1975) 246-55; C. F. D. Moule, *The Origin of Christology* (Cambridge: Cambridge University Press, 1977); I. de la Potterie, "Le titre KYRIOS applique a Jesus dans l'Evangile de Luc," in *Melanges Bibliques en hommage au R. P. Rigaux*, eds. A. Descamps and A. de Halleux (Gembloux: Duculot, 1970) 117-46; V. Taylor, *The Gospel According to St. Mark* (New York: St. Martin's, 1966); G. Vermes, *Jesus the Jew* (New York: Harper and Row, 1973); B. Witherington III, *The Christology of Jesus* (Minneapolis: Fortress, 1990); idem, *Women in the Ministry of Jesus* (Cambridge: Cambridge University Press, 1984).

B. Witherington III

LORD II: PAUL

In Pauline writings as in the rest of the NT, "lord" usually translates the Greek term *kyrios*. The term connotes a superiority of the one to whom it is given. When *kyrios* is used vocatively to address a person *(kyrie),* it can be a purely respectful gesture, roughly equivalent to the English polite address "sir" or "mister" (Jesus is frequently addressed as *kyrie* with this sense in the Gospels). The term can also designate a person as "master" of his servants or followers and was applied to rulers as masters over their subjects. With this connotation of the term, *kyrios* is linguistically paired with *doulos* ("slave," "servant"). Also, *kyrios* was applied to deities, especially among Semitic and other Eastern peoples of the Greco-Roman period *(see* Worship), and came to be applied to Roman emperors in the late first century and beyond as emperor devotion was more strongly promoted. The Greek *despotēs*, also translated "lord" or "master," is

found a mere ten times in the NT, and in the Pauline corpus, mainly in household codes, only in writings whose authorship is disputed, where the term refers to a "master" in a social relationship (1 Tim 6:1, 2; Tit 2:9; 2 Tim 2:21).

Kyrios is used by Paul with reference to Christ most frequently, far less often to designate God, and in a very few cases to refer to humans in socially dominant roles such as masters of slaves. Along with the more frequently occurring "Christ" and the less frequently occurring "Son of God," *kyrios* ("Lord") is one of the major christological titles used by Paul.

Paul's secular use of *kyrios* for human masters and his religious use of the term for God reflect the applications of *kyrios* in the Greco-Roman world among Jews and Gentiles. It is Paul's use of *kyrios* with reference to Christ that marks Paul as Christian and has drawn the interest of scholars. The central questions have to do with the historical background and influences upon the application of *kyrios* to Christ, the origin of this use of the term in early Christianity, and its use and significance as a christological title in Paul *(see* Christology).

1. Background
2. Origins of Christian Usage
3. Pauline Usage
4. Summary

1. Background.

1.1. General. As with many other languages, so in ancient Hebrew, Aramaic and Greek, the terms for "master" or "lord" were used with reference to humans in socially superior positions and could also be used as designations for deities (for much more extensive discussion of the linguistic background, see Foerster and Quell). It is this use of *kyrios* as a title for deities that seems most relevant for appreciating Paul's application of the term to Christ. Paul alludes to the pagan use of *kyrios* for divine beings in 1 Corinthians 8:5 with his remark about "many gods *[theoi]* and many lords *[kyrioi]*" in the religious world of his day.

In the wider religious uses in Paul's time, two in particular have sometimes been pointed to as of direct significance for Paul's designation of Christ as *kyrios*: the use of *kyrios* for the deities of various so-called mystery cults and the application of the term in Roman emperor devotion. Various criticisms have been offered about such suggestions, however, which make it highly improbable that Paul's use of *kyrios* for Christ can be explained as stemming from these circles.

Both the mystery cults and emperor devotion achieved their zenith of popularity in the second century and later, well after the Christian use of *kyrios* for Christ was firmly established. Most importantly, a general and deeply felt antipathy toward and disdain of pagan religiousness were characteristic of Jews such as Paul and the others who made up the initial circles of Christian groups and who continued in leadership positions through the crucial first few decades. This makes it most difficult to understand how pagan religious usage of *kyrios* could have had any direct influence upon early Christian application of the term to Christ.

Consequently, more recent scholarship has tended to conclude that the pagan use of *kyrios* and similar terms in other languages is probably not the occasion or source that explains the early Christian application of *kyrios* as a title for Christ. Instead, the pagan religious use of the term simply illustrates the wider linguistic context within which the Christian use of *kyrios* is to be seen, showing that the term was widely seen as an appropriate appellation for revered beings and that pagans would have understood the term as connoting such reverence when Christians used it for Christ. But to understand why Paul and other early Christians acclaimed Christ as *kyrios* and what they meant when they did so, we must turn elsewhere.

1.2. Jewish. It is now clear to most scholars that it is the Jewish religious background of early Christianity that provides the most important linguistic sources and precedents for the use of *kyrios* as a christological title (see esp. Fitzmyer). There are two particular features of this Jewish religious background that are directly relevant: the religious use of translation equivalents to *kyrios* in Hebrew and Aramaic and the use of *kyrios* itself as a religious term by Greek-speaking Jews.

By the time of the origin of Christianity, it appears that religious Jews had already developed a widely observed avoidance of pronouncing the Hebrew name of God, Yahweh, and that various substitutes were used. Evidence of ancient Jewish texts suggests that substitutes for Yahweh were often used even in written references to God. In Hebrew, God was often referred to as "the Lord" using *ʾādônay*. And in Aramaic, as illustrated in documents from Qumran, the equiv-

alent term, *māryāʾ* (definite form of *mārêh*), was used similarly. That is, in Jewish circles of the first century, the Semitic equivalents to *kyrios* could be used to designate the God of the Bible, and in the absolute form ("the Lord") they could be used as substitutes for the holy name of God (Yahweh).

Among Greek-speaking Jews of the period, there likewise developed the practice of using Greek equivalents of *ʾādônay* to refer to God in place of using the sacred Hebrew name of God. Josephus, writing toward the end of the first century, seems to have preferred *despotēs* in place of God's name, but he may have wanted to avoid using *kyrios* on account of its having become one of the titles of the Roman emperors under whose sponsorship he worked. Philo, several decades earlier than Josephus, usually employed *kyrios* as the Greek substitute for Yahweh. The NT authors likewise more often than not use *kyrios* in citing OT passages where God's name appears in Hebrew, giving further evidence that Greek substitutes were used for God's name and that *kyrios* was a popular (preferred?) choice as such a substitute, functioning in Greek the same as Hebrew *ʾādônay* and Aramaic *māryāʾ*.

The occurrences of Yahweh in Hebrew characters *(yhwh)* or of the curious combination of Greek characters *pipi,* which seems intended to signal and to resemble the Hebrew characters for Yahweh, in certain early Jewish copies of the Greek OT cannot be used to gainsay these observations. It is almost certain that in the actual reading of these copies of the OT in Greek neither Yahweh nor the *pipi* device was pronounced, and that instead a substitute, very likely *kyrios,* was spoken, the sort of practice demonstrated in the NT and other first-century Greek writings that reflect the Jewish religious background.

To summarize, in addition to the general honorific sense of *kyrios* and the pagan religious application of the term to certain divine figures, there is the specific adoption of *kyrios* into the religious vocabulary of Greek-speaking Jews of the first century as a way of referring reverentially to God, which was paralleled to and likely facilitated by the use of *ʾādônay* and *mārêh* for God among Semitic-speaking Jews. And given the Jewish religious background and theological scruples of Paul and most Christians of the formative decades, the Jewish religious use of *kyrios* and its Semitic equivalents is to be seen as the most directly important linguistic datum in considering the use of *kyrios* in the NT. The Jewish uses of *kyrios* as equivalent to *ʾādônay* and even as a Greek substitute for Yahweh add significantly to the range of connotative possibilities to be reckoned with, especially when interpreting the application of the term to Christ.

2. Origins of Christian Usage.

The earliest Christian writings extant are Paul's letters, and they provide evidence for the origin of a practice of referring to Christ as Lord that antedates the apostle (cf. Kramer, whose treatment of this question, however, goes repeatedly against the evidence). From his earliest letters onward, Paul applies *kyrios* to Jesus without explanation or justification, suggesting that his readers already were familiar with the term and its connotation. This is shown also in the formulaic or linguistically routinized way that *kyrios* is applied to Christ in phrases such as "the Lord Jesus Christ" (e.g., 1 Thess 1:1), and "our Lord Jesus Christ" (e.g., 1 Thess 1:3), especially common in the letter openings and closings (*see* Letters, Letter Forms) that seem to employ greetings and benediction conventions from the liturgical life of Paul's churches. The frequently occurring reference to Jesus simply as "the Lord" (e.g., 1 Thess 1:6; 4:15) shows how the term had acquired such a familiar usage for Christ that no further identification was necessary. Paul's letters presume a familiarity with the term as a christological title from the earliest stages of his ministry.

And such a usage of the term is a priori unlikely to have been initiated by Paul peculiarly among his converts. This is confirmed by a number of data. Though Paul insisted on his special calling from God to evangelize the Gentiles and could even refer to "my gospel" (Rom 2:16), he was also at pains to insist that his proclamation embodied a view of Christ shared by Jewish Christians in Jerusalem (e.g., Gal 1–2; 1 Cor 15:1-11). His concise summary of faith in Romans 10:9-10, which focuses on Jesus' resurrection and status as *kyrios*, is presented as an uncontested core statement of Christian belief shared by Christians generally. In Paul's references to James and others as "brother(s) of the Lord" he seems to be using quasi-formal designations of Jesus' relatives that originated in Palestinian Jewish-Christian groups (see, e.g., Gal

1:19; 1 Cor 9:5), in which the risen Jesus was referred to as "the Lord."

But the most direct confirmation of the very early and non-Pauline origin of the reference to Jesus as "Lord" is found in the Greek transliteration of the Aramaic invocation formula, *maranatha*, in 1 Corinthians 16:22. Probably to be vocalized *marānāʾ ta*, it means "Our Lord, come!" This phrase derives from Aramaic-speaking Jewish Christians. It is used here by Paul without explanation or even translation, which suggests that it had been conveyed to the Corinthians earlier by him, likely as a sacred verbal link between Paul's Gentile Christians and their Palestinian predecessors and coreligionists, among whom the risen Jesus was addressed as "our Lord" (*marānāʾ* from *mārêh*). Paul's preservation of the Aramaic form of invocation of God as *abba* (*ʾabbāʾ*, Rom 8:15; Gal 4:6) is probably a parallel linguistic and liturgical link with Jewish Christians that Paul gave to his Gentile converts. It is interesting that Paul passed on to his converts the Aramaic liturgical terms used to address both God and Christ, showing the early "binitarian shape" of Christian devotion in both Aramaic-speaking and Greek-speaking churches.

Suggestions by W. Bousset that *marana tha* was an Aramaic translation of an invocation of Christ that originated among Greek-speaking Christians, or that the "Lord" addressed was not Christ but God, are rightly regarded today as utterly unpersuasive attempts to avoid the obvious historical force of the phrase, which is that the reverential address of Christ as "Lord" can be traced back to the earliest Jewish Christian groups. Furthermore, claims that the use of *mārêh* for Christ among Aramaic-speaking Christians cannot have connoted a reverence of him as divine but only a more general honorific connotation such as "master" are now refuted by Aramaic texts from Qumran in which forms of *mārêh* are used to refer to God. *Mārêh* seems to have been used similarly to the Hebrew *ʾādônay* and the Greek *kyrios*, including its use as an appellation for God.

When this semantic fact is combined with the observation that the *marana tha* phrase shows Christ addressed as *mārêh* in corporate prayer/invocation, it is difficult to avoid the conclusion that *mārêh* connotes a reverence of the risen Christ approaching, or on the level with, the reverence shown to God. And this means that

Christ first began to be reverenced as Lord among the earliest circles of Jewish Christians in terms and actions corresponding to what is slightly later presupposed and everywhere reflected in Paul's letters.

That is, the appellation of Christ as Lord, connoting a status like God's, seems to have its roots surprisingly early, in the earliest circles of the Christian movement, and is not to be the result of a gradual process of assimilation to pagan models of devotion to various deities. Nor can the attribution of *kyrios* to Christ and the view of him as divine be attributed to the influx of large numbers of Gentiles of pagan background into the Christian movement (contra Casey). Linguistically and historically, the reference to Christ as Lord with an exalted connotation seems to have erupted among Jewish Christians of Palestinian provenance. As was also true for Paul, they were somehow able to accommodate such reverence for Christ within their exclusivist monotheism inherited from their Jewish background, producing thereby a distinctive "binitarian" adjustment in this tradition (see Hurtado 1988; *see* God).

3. Pauline Usage.

3.1. Old Testament Citations. The first observation to make about Paul's use of *kyrios* concerns the figures to whom he applies the term. If, simply to avoid becoming entangled in another issue, we exclude the Pauline writings widely regarded as pseudepigraphical, there are a little more than 200 occurrences of *kyrios* to reckon with, and the following observations would not be altered if the excluded letters were included. In the overwhelming majority of these occurrences (about 180) Paul uses *kyrios* as an appellation for Christ, and it is this use of the term to which we must devote the greater part of the following discussion. But it is worth noting that Paul refers to God as *kyrios* also, though in several passages it is difficult to be sure whether the reference is to God or Christ.

The certain passages where Paul refers to God as *kyrios* are all in citations of the OT where God is mentioned in the OT text, and *kyrios* is Paul's Greek substitute/translation for the Hebrew Yahweh, the practice customarily followed also in the LXX. We may take God as certainly the referent in the following Pauline passages where *kyrios* translates Yahweh in the Hebrew text of the OT: Romans 4:8 (Ps 32:1-2);

Romans 9:28-29 (Is 28:22; 1:9); Romans 10:16 (Is 53:1); Romans 11:34 (Is 40:13); Romans 15:11 (Ps 117:1); 1 Corinthians 3:20 (Ps 94:11); and 2 Corinthians 6:17-18 (Is 52:11; 2 Sam 7:14). In addition, there are several passages where Paul cites the OT and modifies it by supplying an explicit reference to God as *kyrios* that is missing in the Hebrew and LXX: Romans 11:3 (1 Kings 19:10); Romans 12:19 (Deut 32:35); 1 Corinthians 14:21 (Is 28:11). In these latter passages Paul imitates the language of his Greek Bible and shows how familiar he was with *kyrios* as a Greek substitute/translation of Yahweh in referring to the God of the OT among Greek-speaking Jews and Christians. This makes the following passages all the more interesting.

In several places where Paul cites OT references that mention Yahweh, he clearly applies the OT citations to Christ: Romans 10:13 (Joel 2:32); 1 Corinthians 1:31 (Jer 9:23-24); 10:26 (Ps 24:1); 2 Corinthians 10:17 (Jer 9:23-24). There are two passages where the context makes it more difficult to be certain whether it is God or Christ to whom Paul applies the citation (cf. Capes, who argues these are references to Christ): Romans 14:11 (Is 45:23); 1 Corinthians 2:16 (Is 40:13). Moreover, there are a number of Pauline passages that may well incorporate allusions to OT passages that mention Yahweh where the *kyrios* Paul refers to is clearly Christ (e.g.): 1 Corinthians 10:21 (Mal 1:7, 12); 1 Corinthians 10:22 (Deut 32:21); 2 Corinthians 3:16 (Ex 34:34); 1 Thessalonians 3:13 (Zech 14:5); 1 Thessalonians 4:6 (Ps 94:2); 2 Thessalonians 1:7-8 (Is 66:15); 2 Thessalonians 1:9 (Is 2:10, 19, 21); 1:12 (Is 66:5). But surely the most striking allusive passage in Paul is Philippians 2:10-11, which is commonly seen as an appropriation of monotheistic language from Isaiah 45:23-25 concerning Yahweh to portray the eschatological acclamation of Christ as *kyrios* "to the glory of God the Father."

If we set aside the ambiguous passages mentioned above, we are still left with a considerable body of evidence that Paul applied to Christ OT language, even passages, that originally quite clearly referred to Yahweh. In these cases at least, it appears that Paul's appellation of Christ as *kyrios* connoted and was based on the conviction that Christ was somehow directly and uniquely associated with Yahweh. In Philippians 2:9-11 we read that God has bestowed on Christ "the name above every name." Whether the passage was composed by Paul or appropriated by him, either way he clearly approved of it as a christological statement. This phrase likely reflects the ancient Jewish reverence for God's name (Yahweh), which for ancient Jews represented God's unique status and being. The passage thus refers to a status and endowment given to Christ that can be compared only with God's status and attributes. This seems to be why Isaiah 45:23-25, originally portraying a universal acknowledgment of Yahweh, is drawn upon to predict a universal acknowledgment of Jesus as *kyrios. Kyrios* here must be the Greek equivalent of acclaiming Christ as bearing the OT name of God.

Another instance of Paul appropriating an OT passage allusively to make a christological point is in the much studied passage 2 Corinthians 3:15-18. Paul's statement "when one turns to the Lord the veil is lifted" (2 Cor 3:16) adapts phrasing from Exodus 34:34, where the *kyrios* is Yahweh, to refer to Christ. This application of *kyrios* to Christ is not simply wordplay but indicates that Paul sees Christ as the *kyrios* in divine terms. The following verses confirm this, where Christ the *kyrios* is linked with the divine Spirit (*see* Holy Spirit) and is referred to as the source of transforming "glory" (Gk *doxa* = Heb *kābôd*), one of the most important attributes of Yahweh in the OT and here borne by Christ (see also 1 Cor 2:8, which refers to Christ as "the Lord of glory"; and on the christological significance of *doxa,* see Newman).

Other evidence that Paul's reference to Jesus as *kyrios* can connote a direct association of Jesus with Yahweh is found in several passages where Paul uses the OT concept of "the day of the Lord [Yahweh]" to refer to the eschatological victory of Christ (on this see Kreitzer; *see* Eschatology). In 1 Thessalonians 5:2, 2 Thessalonians 2:2 and 1 Corinthians 5:5, Paul simply appropriates the OT phrase, though the context makes it clear that the *kyrios* whose "day" is coming is Christ. In other passages, Paul modifies the phrase to identify Christ explicitly as the *kyrios* (1 Cor 1:8; 2 Cor 1:14; cf. 2 Tim 1:18; 4:8). D. B. Capes studied Paul's application of *kyrios* to Christ, emphasizing especially those OT passages applied to Christ where the *kyrios* referred to was originally Yahweh. Unfortunately, his work is flawed at crucial points by his tendency to approach the Pauline texts in terms of the christological controversies of later centuries,

occasional distortion of the work of others (esp. Capes, 168-74, in his discussion of Hurtado) and dubious claims about pre-Christian Jewish readiness to accept the worship of figures other than God. Though he is not fully consistent, Capes tends to claim that Paul's application of OT Yahweh texts to Jesus means that Paul "considered Jesus to be one with God" (Capes, 165) and that for Paul Jesus was "identified with God" (Capes, 169). These are, however, unfortunate oversimplifications.

L. J. Kreitzer focused on the close association between Christ and God in Paul's eschatology and described a "referential shift" of the term *kyrios* in Paul (e.g., Kreitzer, 113), in which Christ is the referent acting in the role of God. Though Kreitzer intended nothing of the sort, his phrase could be misunderstood as implying an emphasis on Christ in Paul at the expense of God, leading to christomonism. Elsewhere (Kreitzer, 116), Kreitzer refers to a "conceptual overlap between God and Christ" in Paul, and this is perhaps a more appropriate way of putting the matter. Linguistically, we might also speak of Christ as enfranchised or incorporated quite prominently and uniquely into Paul's referential field in his use of *kyrios* as a divine title. And, as shown particularly in Paul's application to Christ of OT passages and eschatological actions that originally concerned Yahweh, when Paul refers to Christ as *kyrios* the term can carry a connotation of honor and status deliberately comparable with God's.

3.2. Creedal Use. Another particularly important collection of evidence concerning Paul's application of *kyrios* to Christ are the several passages commonly identified by scholars as "creedal," that is, passages probably reflecting early expressions of Christian faith in Christ. The term *creedal* is perhaps a bit misleading, however, for the phrases in question were neither intended as full confessions of early Christian beliefs nor were they the result of doctrinal deliberations. Instead, these faith expressions likely originated as acclamations in the setting of corporate *worship in Christian circles. The oldest surviving expressions of Christian faith, they all acclaim Christ as *kyrios.*

Perhaps the earliest reference to the acclamation of Christ in the Christian worship setting is 1 Corinthians 12:3. Here, in the midst of a lengthy discussion of proper behavior in Christian worship (1 Cor 11–14), Paul refers to the acclamation *kyrios Iēsous* and attributes it to the work of the Holy Spirit in Christian believers. We have noted earlier Romans 10:9-10, which is another reference to this early liturgical acclamation of Jesus as *kyrios Iēsous,* probably to be translated as "Jesus is Lord." In Romans 10:9-10 this acclamation is connected to belief in Christ's resurrection, which was the event that seems to have initiated the conviction that Christ had been given the unique heavenly glory referred to in proclaiming him *kyrios.* This passage shows that Jesus' resurrection continued to be regarded in early Christian groups as the historic basis and demonstration of his exaltation.

Another passage previously cited, Philippians 2:9-11, likewise must be considered again here. On the basis of the two previous passages just considered, Philippians 2:9-11 also seems to allude to the early Christian acclamation of Jesus as *kyrios,* projecting a future universal participation in this acclamation which now the Christian groups anticipate and prefigure in their worship gatherings.

Two more features of this passage are to be noted. First, the slightly longer formulation *Kyrios Iēsous Christos* (Phil 2:11) is found with some variation especially in Paul's letter openings and closings (commonly thought to reflect liturgical formulas used in his churches), such as Philippians 1:2. This fuller formulation shows that there were variations in acclamation wording (this one is likely an attempt at greater sonorousness and christological fullness) and demonstrates at the same time that the core acclamation remained the heralding of Jesus as "Lord." And, as mentioned already, the title here certainly seems to carry the connotation of Jesus having been given the name (thus status, honor and attributes) of God.

Second, the attempt at fuller christological expression in the acclamation formula is followed in Philippians 2:11 by a phrase conveying more explicit theological precision than the simple acclamation of Jesus as *kyrios.* Specifically, Philippians 2:11 makes the acclamation of Jesus as "Lord," which constitutes acknowledging that Jesus has been given the divine name, redound at the same time "to the glory of God the Father." As Kreitzer observed (Kreitzer, 161), this phrase is evidence that Paul sought to maintain the "integrity" of his monotheistic faith and reconcile it with the breathtaking status of Jesus reflected in the acclamation of him as the *kyrios.*

This concern is also reflected elsewhere in Paul in this sort of "clarifying word or phrase" (Kreitzer, 158) added to passages referring to Christ (e.g., 1 Cor 3:23; 11:3; 15:20-28).

In the final creedal passage to be considered here, 1 Corinthians 8:5-6, we see another example of how Paul reconciled Christ's exalted status with his inherited monotheism. In contrast to the Greco-Roman polytheistic environment (*see* Religions, Greco-Roman), Paul affirms a two-part confession of "one God *[heis theos]* the Father," and "one Lord *[heis kyrios]* Jesus Christ" (the latter phrase another example of the longer sonorous reference to Christ noticed above in Phil 2:11). The wording seems to be influenced by Deuteronomy 6:4, "Hear, O Israel: The Lord our God is one Lord" (*kyrios heis estin* [LXX], translating the Hebrew *Yahweh 'eḥād).* That is, Christ is included in a revised proclamation of God's uniqueness. By Paul's time, Jews were probably using Deuteronomy 6:4 as part of their confession of faith in the uniqueness of their God, the *Shema.* Paul may thus have intended an allusion to this Jewish confessional practice as well, to express the distinctively Christian version of monotheism in which Christ is the "one *Kyrios,*" the Greek title by which Yahweh was referred to among Greek-speaking Jews and in the Greek OT. This constitutes an acclamation of Christ in the most exalted degree.

At the same time, we must notice how Paul's two-part ("binitarian") statement of Christian faith in 1 Corinthians 8:6 places the acclamation of the "one Lord Jesus Christ" within and under a continuing commitment to a monotheistic faith. This is the significance involved in the careful use of prepositions in the statement that "all things," including the redemption of Christians, which is probably what is meant by "we," have come "from" *(ek)* the "one God the Father" and "through" *(dia)* the Lord Jesus Christ.

Nevertheless, although Paul fitted his view of Christ within his monotheistic faith, he clearly felt compelled to regard Christ in an amazingly exalted light, which resulted in a dramatically redrawn monotheism. Indeed, given Paul's fundamentally monotheistic commitment, it is difficult to imagine a more exalted status for Christ without replacing God with Christ, something scarcely imaginable for Paul.

D. R. de Lacey has described 1 Corinthians 8:6 as representing "a significant milestone in the development of New Testament Christology" (de Lacey, 203), and this is surely correct. It is, however, less certain that he is right to make the religious view it expresses Paul's unique christological handiwork, "his own radical re-interpretation of the creed of Israel" through which he "was able to steer the church down the road towards a truly trinitarian faith" (de Lacey, 202).

In Paul's personal history, to be sure, he experienced a "radical re-interpretation of the creed of Israel" as a result of his christophany experience in which God chose "to reveal his Son" to him (Gal 1:16). And Paul's "revelations" and gifts in thinking through their implications are not to be minimized. The wording of 1 Corinthians 8:6 with its allusions to Deuteronomy 6:4 and to Jewish recitation of the *Shema* may well show Paul's creativity of expression and rhetorical skill. But the "significant milestone" de Lacey refers to, the reverence for Jesus as *kyrios*, connoting his divine status but within the limits of the biblical tradition about God's uniqueness and supremacy, seems to have been arrived at by many other Christians in addition to Paul, including Jewish Christians not indebted to him for their faith.

The evidences of corporate acclamations of Jesus as *kyrios* considered above suggest that Paul's high view of Christ was representative of the Christians with whom he was acquainted and of the churches whose piety he knew. And, as shown earlier, we must include Jewish-Christian groups, both Greek-speaking and Aramaic-speaking ones, as those who confessed and invoked Christ as Lord in their gatherings and over their lives.

3.3. Appellation Formulas. In addition to the types of usages already mentioned, there are in the seven undisputed letters about another 170 occurrences of *kyrios* (of the approximately 200 total occurrences) that appear in several frequently recurring, somewhat fixed ways of referring to Christ. These may be seen sociolinguistically as "routinizations" in the religious language of Paul and early Christians which show how thoroughly familiar among them was the use of *kyrios* as a christological title.

Of these, in about sixty-five cases (decisions about textual variants in a number of passages will produce slightly differing counts) *kyrios* is used in connection with other christological terms in the following expressions: "Jesus Christ our Lord" (e.g., Rom 1:4; 5:21), "our Lord Jesus Christ" (e.g., Rom 5:1, 11; 16:20; Gal 6:18),

"Christ Jesus our Lord" (e.g., Rom 6:23; 1 Cor 15:31), "the Lord Jesus Christ" (e.g., 2 Cor 13:13) and "the Lord Jesus" (e.g., Rom 14:14; 1 Cor 11:23). These constructions are found especially but by no means exclusively in the opening and closing sections of Paul's letters, in greetings and farewells, where as already noted Paul is believed to use the greeting and benediction formulas used in early Christian worship assemblies. Here we probably have a glimpse of the deliberately sonorous phrasing of earliest Christian liturgical language.

Syntactically, in these expressions "Jesus," with and without "Christ," identifies the "Lord," and "Lord" defines who Jesus is for Christians and their relationship to him. That is, in these expressions the fundamental force of the term *kyrios* denoting the superior or "master," seems primary. Jesus is the "master" of Christians, to whom in turn they are his followers, his subjects bound to obey him.

The most frequently found use of *kyrios* in Paul (about one hundred times in the letters we are considering here) is as the designation of Jesus without any other title, simply "the Lord" (*ho kyrios*, e.g., Rom 14:6, 8; 16:2, 8, 11, 12, 13; 1 Cor 3:5; 4:4-5). It is as if "the Lord" is a shorthand way of referring to Jesus, and Paul feels he needs no identifying terms to indicate who is designated as "the Lord." As noted earlier, the reference to Jesus simply as "the Lord" seems to have had its equivalent (*māryā'*) in Aramaic-speaking Christian groups and was likely taken over by Paul from his predecessors in the faith. It is certainly the case that Paul nowhere shows any need to justify or explain such a way of referring to Christ, indirectly suggesting that this is a well-established custom already among Christians of his time.

As with the fuller constructions listed above, so in this absolute form, *ho kyrios,* used of Jesus, we are probably to see the primary connotation as "Lord" or "Master." That is, Jesus is the one whom the Christians are to regard as supreme, to whom they are obliged to give obedience, and whom they see as designated by God as the unique agent of redemption and judgment. Through his death and resurrection Jesus has now been given authority to exercise lordship (Rom 14:9, *kyrieuō*), which Christians recognize freely now in referring to him as Lord.

Yet it is well to remember that Paul and other Christians applied *kyrios* to Jesus at times with a far more specific connotation that was also more sweeping in import. As noted earlier, in some Pauline passages *kyrios* is applied to Christ with the effect of associating him directly with God, even implying that he shares in the divine name. It may be that this very profound and exalted meaning of *kyrios* was not consciously intended every time Jesus was referred to by Paul in expressions such as "the [our] Lord Jesus Christ" or even "the Lord." But it is reasonable to surmise that an undertone of the more exalted connotation was present even in these formulaic uses. That is, though the emphasis of the term might vary from one occasion to another, it is likely that the various connotations or emphases of *kyrios* mutually colored one another in the living use of the term by Paul and other Christians.

3.4. Contexts. In his study of Paul's christological titles, W. Kramer pointed out that the individual titles each tend to be used in particular kinds of statements and contexts. He noted that Jesus is referred to as *kyrios* especially frequently in hortatory passages in Paul. Kreitzer and Capes have confirmed that references to Jesus as *kyrios* tend to occur in certain kinds of contexts, especially in Paul's hortatory and eschatological passages. However, we should identify at least three types of statements in which Jesus is referred to as *kyrios*, each of which reflects an important way in which Paul and fellow Christians related themselves to Christ as Lord. Paul's usage is not rigid, but we can identify a tendency to refer to Jesus as *kyrios* more frequently in these contexts.

3.4.1. Paraenetic Contexts. It is certainly the case that Jesus is referred to as *kyrios* in passages where Paul deals with matters of Christian behavior. We may take Romans 14:1-12 as an example, where Paul urges believers who differ over scruples of food and calendar matters not to judge one another harshly. Whether they eat or refrain, whether they regard one day special or all days alike (Rom 14:5-8), Paul encourages them all to believe that their common motivation is that they act "unto the Lord." And he goes on to characterize Christian existence generally as living and dying "to the Lord" to whom they belong (Rom 14:9).

To cite another passage, in 1 Corinthians 6:13—7:40, where Paul deals with a number of questions of sexual relationships, he mainly refers to Jesus as "the Lord." Forbidding the use of prostitutes, Paul proclaims that the Christian's body is "for the Lord" (1 Cor 6:13). It is "the Lord" whose command he either can or cannot cite (1 Cor 7:10-12, 25) in responding to the questions sent to him from Corinth about married and unmarried people. (See also 1 Cor 9:14; 14:37 for references to commands of "the Lord.") Indeed, here as in other passages Jesus "the Lord" defines the realm of Christian existence. Christians are called "in the Lord" (1 Cor 7:22); single persons are able with fewer distractions to devote themselves "to the Lord" (1 Cor 7:32-35); and the widow may remarry only "in the Lord" (1 Cor 7:39, i.e., within the Christian fellowship).

In Romans 16:2-20 Paul repeatedly uses the phrase "in the Lord" in referring to people in the context of Christian fellowship and service to Christ (Rom 16:2, 8, 11-13). Compare his criticism of certain troublesome people who by contrast "do not serve our Lord Christ" (Rom 16:18). The phrase "the work of the Lord" can serve as Paul's way of referring to Christian involvement in promoting the gospel (1 Cor 15:58; 16:10). And Paul refers to his personal movements in his ministry as dependent on the will of "the Lord" (1 Cor 4:19; 16:7).

In 1 Thessalonians 1:6 the Thessalonians are congratulated for having become "imitators of us and of the Lord" in their obedience to the gospel despite affliction. And in 1 Thessalonians 4:1-12, where Paul exhorts the believers to observe ethical instructions previously given, he designates Jesus as "the Lord Jesus" (1 Thess 4:1-2) or simply "the Lord" (1 Thess 4:6).

We may summarize these examples as showing that Paul tended to refer to Jesus as "Lord" in contexts where Paul instructs his churches in Christian obedience, and, more generally, in referring to Christian life and relationships and the service involved in spreading the gospel message. As their *kyrios*, Jesus claimed the obedience of his followers and defined the sphere of their endeavor.

3.4.2. Eschatological Contexts. A second type of context and statement in which Paul tends to refer to Jesus as *kyrios* may be identified as eschatological. Consider, for example, the several references to the eschatological return of Jesus in 1 Thessalonians in which the term *kyrios* is used, either alone (four times) or with identifying terms ("the Lord," 1 Thess 4:15-17; "day of the Lord," 1 Thess 5:2; "our Lord Jesus Christ,"

1 Thess 5:23; "our Lord Jesus," 1 Thess 2:19; 3:13).

As another example of this usage, in 1 Corinthians 1:7-8 the Corinthians are described as awaiting the eschatological "revelation" and "day" of "our Lord Jesus Christ." And in 1 Corinthians 4:1-5 Paul refers to the eschatological coming of "the Lord" who will render final judgment over Paul and other ministers of the gospel (1 Cor 4:4-5). The little phrase "the Lord is near" in Philippians 4:5 is probably to be taken as a reference to the hope of Christ's imminent return. As 1 Corinthians 15:23 shows, with its reference to the eschatological "coming" of "Christ," there is some variation in the christological terms Paul uses in eschatological references as well as in other kinds of statements. But his general tendency was to use the title *Lord* in passages where Jesus' eschatological manifestation and victory are in view (*see* Eschatology).

To the passages cited here we must add the references listed earlier where Paul appropriates the OT concept/phrase "day of the Lord" to describe Jesus' eschatological appearance, sometimes modifying the OT phrase by the use of formulas such as "Lord Jesus Christ." In fact it is likely that the OT phrase "day of the Lord," and the hope it came to represent in ancient Jewish tradition, influenced Paul's tendency to use "Lord" in references to Jesus' return. And, given Paul's familiarity with the OT, it is also likely that we should see his references to the "day of the Lord (Jesus)" as indications that for Paul, Jesus was associated with God and would act in the eschatological role of God.

Thus, to refer to Jesus as *kyrios* in these eschatological statements probably connoted something beyond the basic meaning of "master." In such statements the "Lord" Jesus is clothed with the attributes and functions of Yahweh. His eschatological appearance would involve his judging all things and would bring divine victory over all evil. As Kreitzer has shown, pre-Christian Jewish writings show that there had already developed the notion of a messianic figure acting on God's behalf in eschatological redemption. In this the Pauline references to Jesus carrying out the role that originally was God's has a precedent. It is, however, significant that in Paul and the NT elsewhere Jesus not only acts in God's place in the projections of eschatological hope but also is frequently referred to as the "Lord" whose "day"

of eschatological triumph is anticipated. This association of Jesus with God, in eschatological action and in title, is not without parallel but seems comparatively more pronounced and consistent in the NT than in the pre-Christian Jewish references to principal agents of God's eschatological victory.

3.4.3. Liturgical Contexts. The third type of passage and setting to highlight with regard to Paul's use of the term *kyrios* for Jesus has to do with the worship life of earliest Christian groups. We have already mentioned Pauline passages identified as evidence of early acclamation formulas and practices by which Jesus was confessed liturgically as *kyrios* in Christian worship gatherings (probably collectively). And we have also noted that Paul's letter openings and closings, with their sonorous references to "the [or our] *kyrios* Jesus Christ" (or "Christ Jesus our *kyrios*") in statements of greetings and farewells, are commonly thought to echo the parlance of early Christian worship as well. The point to repeat here is that these uses of *kyrios* all derive from and give evidence of the setting of Christian worship gatherings as one of the earliest and most important contexts for and sources of the application of *kyrios* to Christ.

In further illustration of this we may consider 1 Corinthians 5:1-5, which concerns the man guilty of *porneia* ("sexual immorality") with "his father's wife." Paul calls for disciplinary action to be taken in the setting of the gathered church, and we are particularly concerned to note the way he describes the Christian gathering. We should probably punctuate 1 Corinthians 5:3-5 with a stop at the end of 1 Corinthians 5:3, taking "in the name of the Lord Jesus" in 1 Corinthians 5:4 as referring to the Christian assembly. Thus, 1 Corinthians 5:4-5 are to be read in the following fashion: "When you have assembled in the name of the Lord Jesus, I also present in spirit, with the power of our Lord Jesus you are to hand this man over to Satan for the destruction of his flesh that his spirit may be saved in the day of the Lord."

Though the occasion for this particular assembly may have been unusual, the terms Paul uses to describe the Christian gathering are probably typical, and the point to underscore here is how Jesus is repeatedly referred to as *kyrios*. They gather "in the name of the Lord Jesus," a probable allusion to an invocation and acclamation of Jesus as *kyrios* in the early Christian assembly for which we have already seen evidence. This phrase and the references to the "power" of the Lord and his eschatological "day" show that *kyrios* is here applied to Jesus with a connotation of transcendent attributes and functions such as are associated with God.

And both the use of *kyrios* to designate Jesus and the transcendent connotation of the title seem typical of the Pauline passages where early Christian worship gatherings are either referred to directly or are indirectly reflected in phraseology taken from this setting. As a final example we may examine 1 Corinthians 11:17-33. The sacred meal of the Christian gathering is "the Lord's supper" (*kyriakon deipnon*, 1 Cor 11:20; and cf. "table of the Lord" in 1 Cor 10:21; *see* Lord's Supper). Consistently Jesus is referred to as *kyrios* in the passage (1 Cor 11:23, 26, 27, 32). It is probably both the worship context and the allusion to the eschatological appearance of Christ ("until he comes") that account for the expression "the death of the Lord" in 1 Corinthians 11:26, a striking contrast to the more typical Pauline tendency to use "Christ" in references to Jesus' death (*see* Death of Christ).

We have, then, three main types of Pauline contexts in which he characteristically uses *kyrios* to designate Jesus, reflecting three early church settings in which particularly Jesus was referred to as *kyrios*. In the Pauline hortatory statements and passages the *kyrios* Jesus is the "master" whose teaching and example are authoritative for Christian conduct. In the references to eschatological expectations, the designation of Jesus as *kyrios* seems to reflect the conviction that Jesus has been designated *kyrios* in the eschatological role of God. Finally, in the Pauline references to early Christian *worship gatherings and in his liturgically influenced language, *kyrios* designates Jesus as the transcendent, exalted one who has been given the divine "name" and incorporated into the devotional and cultic life of early Christianity.

These three contexts are not to be separated entirely. We may distinguish varying emphases of the term *kyrios* as applied to Christ in each type of passage, but the connotations were also likely linked in the religious thought of Paul and early Christians generally. In some cases the link is explicit, as in Philippians 2:9-11, where the future universal acclamation, *Kyrios Iēsous Christos*, echoes and is anticipated in the Christian acclamation of Jesus in the worship setting.

Or we may again cite 1 Corinthians 11:26, where the present liturgical celebration of the death of the *kyrios* Jesus in the sacred meal is connected with his eschatological appearance. In Paul's references to early Christian worship, Jesus is the *kyrios* whose present authority over the church is real and inseparable from his future dominion over all things to be made manifest in the "day of the Lord."

4. Summary.

In any attempt to probe Paul's view of Christ, the term *kyrios* must be central. It functions in several ways and is enriched by several connotations in Paul. The term expresses the relationship of Christians to Jesus as subjects and followers to their master, as in the phrase "our Lord Jesus Christ." In Philippians 3:8 Paul speaks of this relationship in very personal terms with the reference to "Christ Jesus my Lord." As *kyrios,* Jesus' example and command are unquestionable authorities for Christian behavior in Paul's letters. Paul reflects the acclamation of Jesus as *kyrios* in the worship setting, which is understood by him as the pattern and anticipation of the universal acknowledgment of Jesus as Lord when he comes in eschatological glory. The divine glory of Jesus the Lord, however, has already been revealed to Paul. As a result, Paul views Jesus in incredibly exalted terms, permitting the application to Jesus of OT passages concerning Yahweh and the portrayal of *kyrios* Jesus as the agent of all creation and redemption (1 Cor 8:6). In short, in some cases at least, Paul's application of *kyrios* to Jesus connotes the conviction that Jesus had been given to share in the properties and honor of God's "name" (with all that represented in the OT and ancient Jewish tradition) and bore the very glory of God in such fullness and uniqueness that Jesus could be compared and associated only with God "the Father" in the honor and reverence due him.

See also CHRIST; CHRISTOLOGY; GOD; HOLY SPIRIT; SON OF GOD.

DPL: EMPERORS, ROMAN; EXALTATION AND ENTHRONEMENT; SAVIOR.

BIBLIOGRAPHY. W. Bousset, *Kyrios Christos* (Nashville: Abingdon, 1970 [1913]); E. D. Burton, *A Critical and Exegetical Commentary on the Epistle to the Galatians* (ICC; Edinburgh: T & T Clark, 1921) 392-417; D. B. Capes, *Old Testament Yahweh Texts in Paul's Christology* (WUNT 2/47;

Tübingen: J. C. B. Mohr, 1992); P. M. Casey, *From Jewish Prophet to Gentile God* (Louisville, KY: Westminster John Knox, 1991); L. Cerfaux, "*Kyrios* dans les citations pauliniennes de l'Ancien Testament," in *Receueil Lucien Cerfaux: Études d'exégèse et d'histoire religieuse de Monseigneur Cerfaux* (Gembloux: Duculot, 1954) vol. 1; O. Cullmann, *The Christology of the New Testament* (Philadelphia: Westminster, 1963 [1957]); N. A. Dahl, "Sources of Christological Language," in *Jesus the Christ*, ed. D. H. Juel (Minneapolis: Fortress, 1991) 113-36; D. R. de Lacey, " 'One Lord' in Pauline Christology," in *Christ the Lord: Studies in Christology Presented to Donald Guthrie*, ed. H. H. Rowdon (Downers Grove, IL: InterVarsity Press, 1982) 191-203; W. Foerster and G. Quell, "κύριος κτλ," *TDNT* 3:1039-98; J. A. Fitzmyer, "The Semitic Background of the New Testament Kyrios-Title," in *A Wandering Aramean: Collected Aramaic Essays* (SBLMS 25; Missoula, MT: Scholars Press, 1979) 115-42; L. W. Hurtado, *Lord Jesus Christ: Devotion to Jesus in Earliest Christianity* (Grand Rapids: Eerdmans, 2003); idem, "New Testament Christology: A Critique of Bousset's Influence," *TS* 40 (1979) 306-17; idem, *One God, One Lord: Early Christian Devotion and Ancient Jewish Monotheism* (Philadelphia: Fortress, 1988); W. Kramer, *Christ, Lord, Son of God* (SBT 50; London: SCM, 1966 [1963]); L. J. Kreitzer, *Jesus and God in Paul's Eschatology* (JSNTSup 19; Sheffield: JSOT, 1987); C. C. Newman, *Paul's Glory Christology: Tradition and Rhetoric* (NovTSup 69; Leiden: E. J. Brill, 1992).   L. W. Hurtado

LORD III: ACTS, HEBREWS, GENERAL EPISTLES, REVELATION

Any survey of the NT literature, particularly Paul's letters, will show the importance of the term *kyrios* for the early church (*see* Lord I). The faith of the early church involved confessing that Jesus is the risen and exalted *kyrios* (1 Cor 9:1; 12:3; Rom 10:9; Phil 2:9-11). That this confession was largely based on what was true about Jesus after his death (*see* Death of Christ) is shown by the fact that the term *kyrios*, when it is found in the dialogue portions of the Gospels as a mode of address to Jesus, almost without exception means "master" or "respected sir," not "divine being" (but see Mk 12:35-37; Witherington 1990).

Kyrios, like its Aramaic equivalent *mārêh*,

normally conveyed the idea of a human being who was superior to or over another human being or group of people. *Kyrios* tells us something about a person's position in relationship to other things or persons. This is shown by the fact that in social contexts *kyrios* is often paired with the term *doulos*, "slave" or "servant." The former is lord of and lord over the latter. It is not surprising that early Christians appropriated this terminology to speak of the risen Jesus. The term was commonly used in the Greco-Roman world to refer to exalted beings, including gods and demigods (cf. 1 Cor 8:5), and early Christians felt that their relationship to the risen Jesus was like that of the relationship of a *doulos* to a *kyrios* (cf. Rom 1:1 to 2 Pet 1:1). With this background we are prepared to consider the use of the term *kyrios* outside the Gospels and the Pauline literature.

The term *kyrios* is used in a variety of ways outside of the Gospels and the Pauline portions of the NT. In some cases it seems to have a simple functional connotation, indicating a role that Jesus or God plays, but in other contexts it seems also to imply something about who Jesus is, namely, one who can be placed on the Creator side of the Creator/creature distinction. This sort of distinction, however, has its limitations. A review of the relevant passages shows how *kyrios* can be used almost interchangeably of God and Jesus by early Christians. We will review the data beginning with the book of Acts, then turning to Hebrews, James and Jude, the Petrine epistles (*see* 1 Peter; 2 Peter), the Johannine letters (*see* John, Letters of) and the Apocalypse (*see* Revelation, Book of).

1. The Acts of the Apostles
2. Hebrews
3. James and Jude
4. 1 Peter and 2 Peter
5. The Johannine Epistles and the Apocalypse
6. Summary

1. The Acts of the Apostles.

The term *kyrios* appears 104 times in Acts, with at least 18 of these occurrences referring to God, 47 referring to Jesus, 4 referring to secular masters, owners or rulers, and the remainder referring to either Jesus or God, though in these instances it is not clear who is meant (cf. Kee, 19). Luke is familiar with the use of the term, even with the article, to refer to a secular ruler

(Acts 25:26, of Nero) or to an owner or a master of a slave (Acts 16:16, 19), but his interest lies elsewhere. We can be certain that *kyrios* refers to Jesus in some texts because the term is combined either with the name *Jesus* (Acts 1:21; 4:33; 8:16; 15:11; 16:31; 19:5, 13, 17; 20:24, 35; 21:13) or with the combined referent *Jesus Christ* (Acts 11:17; 15:26; 28:31). In other cases the context makes evident that Jesus is meant (e.g., Acts 9:5, 10, 11). In some instances, primarily in quotations of the OT that have the combination of *kyrios* with *theos*, it is evident that God and not Jesus is meant (Acts 2:39; 3:22). Some of the confusion could be resolved if we could know that Luke does not draw on the concept of the preexistent Son of God, but texts like Acts 2:25 may suggest he knows of such an idea. The remarkable quotation from Psalm 110:1 in Acts 2:34, in which God and Jesus are referred to as *kyrios*, shows how flexible Luke was prepared to be in his use of the term. It would be wrong, however, to conclude from such a text that Luke saw Jesus as merely the believers' Lord, for in Acts 10:36 he is called the Lord of all (*pantōn kyrios*). It was not merely the use of the term *kyrios* of Jesus that caused the parting of the ways between Christianity and early *Judaism. Christians also wished to appropriate the term and the OT texts in which *kyrios* had the more exalted sense of divine Lord (referring to Yahweh) and to apply those texts and their attendant concepts to Jesus (cf. Dunn 1991). In general, when an OT phrase or concept such as the "Day of the Lord" (Acts 2:20), "the angel of the Lord" (Acts 5:19; 12:11, 23), "the fear of the Lord" (Acts 9:31) or "the hand of the Lord" (Acts 13:11) appears in the text it is likely that "Lord" means "God" in such texts. The phrase "the Word of the Lord," especially if one takes it as an objective genitive (the Word about the Lord), appears to refer to Jesus (Acts 8:25; 13:44, 49; 15:35, 36; 19:20), as is likely the case with the phrase "the way of the Lord" (Acts 18:25). Further, the phrase "the name of the Lord" (Acts 9:28) likely refers to Jesus, especially in view of the clearer texts such as Acts 19:5, 13 and 17.

One of the keys to understanding Luke's use of *kyrios* in Acts is to recognize the narrative framework, which includes a historical component, in which he views all christological matters (on theology in a narrative framework see Witherington, *Narrative* 1994). The references to *kyrios* in Acts must be compared and contrasted to the material in Luke's Gospel, but what Luke says about Jesus depends on what point in the trajectory of his career Luke is discussing. One must ask whether Luke is referring to Jesus during his historical ministry or to what Luke believes to be true about Jesus after the resurrection and ascension.

For example, it is widely recognized that Luke uses the term *kyrios* in the narrative framework and in the editorial comments in his Gospel in a way the other Synoptic writers do not, while at the same time no character in the Gospel narrative calls Jesus *kyrios* unless it is under inspiration (Lk 1:43, 76), involves an angel (Lk 2:11) or involves Jesus obliquely alluding to himself (Lk 19:31, 34; cf. Fitzmyer 1981). However, as soon as the narrative gets beyond Easter, various human beings can and do use *kyrios* of Jesus (cf. Lk 24:34; Acts 10:36-38; Moule). This may be explained in part as an example of Luke's desire to avoid historical anachronisms, but it also shows that he does not wish to violate the internal logic of the narrative and so have characters get ahead of what they ought to be saying at a particular juncture in the story. The assertion that Luke is adoptionist in his christological thinking is based on texts like Acts 2:36— "God has made this Jesus whom you crucified both *kyrios* and Christ." The problem with this conclusion is that here, as elsewhere in Acts, Luke uses his christological language in a way that suits his narrative. From Luke's point of view Jesus did not in any full sense assume the roles of Lord and Messiah over all until after the resurrection and ascension. It was not that Jesus became someone different from who he was before but that he entered a new stage in his career or assumed new roles after the ascension (cf. Dunn 1980). Only as an exalted one could Jesus take on the tasks of Lord over all and universal Messiah.

Luke's basic interest is in the story of Jesus from his birth until he assumes and begins to exercise the role of Lord from heaven, though a text like Acts 2:25 may imply that Luke knew of the concept of the preexistent Lord (cf. Acts 2:24; Craddock). It is the narrative about Jesus and its progress that affects how the terminology is used, not a concern to settle a later debate about functional over against ontological christology. Furthermore, nice distinctions between being and doing would probably have seemed inappropriate to Luke. The Lord Jesus is able to do what he does because he is who he is. The roles he assumes are roles that are appropriate in Luke's mind for the exalted Jesus to assume. Jesus' lordship is viewed not as a mere honorary title but as a description of his status and activity since at least the resurrection.

The term *kyrios* is the most frequently used christological title in all of Luke-Acts, used almost twice as frequently as the term *Christ*. Of 717 occurrences of *kyrios* in the NT the vast majority are to be found either in Luke-Acts (210) or in the Pauline letters (275) (Bietenhard, 2:513). This emphasis in Luke-Acts comports with Luke's basic stress on God's sovereignty over and in history as it is expressed in the form of God's plan of salvation for the world that comes to fruition through Jesus (cf. Squires). Jesus is the one who expresses and in a sense executes this salvation plan by his acts in space and time and by his acts as the exalted Lord sending the Holy Spirit to work on earth in his behalf and place. It becomes clear that the basic connotation for Luke of the term *kyrios* is one who exercises dominion over the world and in particular over human lives and events. It is important not to underestimate the significance of the transfer of the term *kyrios* from Yahweh to Christ at various points in Acts. As J. A. Fitzmyer says, "In using kurios of both Yahweh and Jesus in his writings Luke continues the sense of the title already being used in the early Christian community, which in some sense regarded Jesus as on a level with Yahweh" (Fitzmyer 1981, 203). Acts indicates, as the Pauline epistles also suggest, that the basic confession of the early church was that Jesus is the risen Lord (cf. Acts 10:46; 11:16; 16:31; 20:21). It is Jesus the risen and exalted Lord whom people are called upon to turn to and believe in (Acts 5:14; 9:35; 11:17). This risen Lord confronts Saul on the Damascus road (Acts 9:10-17, 18:9), and to him believers must remain faithful (Acts 20:19). It is the Lord Jesus with whom the original disciples traveled (Acts 1:21), whose teaching Paul can quote (Acts 20:35) and who commissions people for ministry (Acts 20:24). In these texts the name *Jesus* seems to be appended to *kyrios* to make clear the identity of this Lord. The continuity of the Lord's identity before and after Easter makes it possible for Luke to refer to Jesus' earthly activity and teaching using the term *kyrios*, even though he knows that Jesus does not fully or truly assume the roles of exalted Lord until after Easter.

In other texts where the Lord God and not Jesus is meant by *kyrios* (Acts 2:39; 3:19, 22; 4:26; 7:31; 10:4, 33), these references are found either in the first few chapters of Acts or on the lips of Jews or apparent proselytes to Judaism. The further one gets into Acts and the more Christians speak for themselves, it is almost always Jesus who is referred to as the Lord. After the crucial apostolic council and decree (Acts 15), there is only one text in which *kyrios* seems clearly to refer to God and not Jesus: in the apologetic speech of Paul before the Areopagus (Acts 17:24). That is, in almost half of Acts, where Luke may have drawn on his own knowledge and travel accounts beginning in Acts 16, references to God as *kyrios* are strikingly lacking.

In some passages one could debate whether Jesus or God is the referent. For example, in Acts 2:47 "the Lord" is probably God (cf. Acts 2:34), but in a text like Acts 21:14 *kyrios* could refer to either Jesus or God (cf. Acts 21:13). In Acts 12:11, 17 (cf. Acts 12:5) the "Lord" seems to refer to God, as is more clearly the case in Acts 12:23. But in Acts 7:60, Acts 13:2 and Acts 16:14-15 it appears that it is Jesus who is prayed to, worshiped and believed in (cf. Kee, 20). This sort of ambiguity does not trouble Luke because in his view the terminology is equally appropriate when used of either God or Jesus, not least because he viewed Jesus as a proper object of worship and petitionary prayer.

2. Hebrews.

Of the sixteen references to *kyrios* in Hebrews only three refer to Jesus (Heb 2:3; 7:14; 13:20); the remainder refer to God. Of these thirteen references to God all but one (Heb 8:2) are found in quotations or paraphrases of several OT texts that are important to the writer's argument: Psalm 102:26, cited in Hebrews 1:10; Psalm 110:4, cited in Hebrews 7:21; Jeremiah 31:31-34, cited in Hebrews 8:8-11, and Jeremiah 31:33, cited in Hebrews 10:16; Proverbs 3:11-12, cited in Hebrews 12:5-6; and Psalm 118:6, cited in Hebrews 13:6. That the author does not see an allusion to Jesus as Lord in any OT texts is surprising, since the prologue (Heb 1:1-4) speaks of a role the preexistent Son of God played in the acts of creation (cf. Witherington, *Sage* 1994). This may in part be explained by the fact that the author does not indulge in midrashic contemporizing of the OT so much as he uses it for typology (cf. G. Hughes). The author of Hebrews feels free to refer to the earthly Jesus who announced salvation to his first followers as "Lord" (Heb 2:3), and even more tellingly he speaks of Jesus' ancestry as the ancestry of "our Lord." The closing benediction in Hebrews 13:20 refers to God bringing back from the dead "our Lord Jesus." Nothing here suggests an adoptionist christology, but equally clearly there is no stress on Christ's cosmic roles as Lord of the universe. The author rather focuses on the fact that Jesus is "our Lord," and wherever "Lord" refers to Jesus in Hebrews the subject is his historical roles and experiences (e.g., birth, proclamation, death and resurrection). One reason the author feels free to use the term *kyrios* of Jesus during his earthly ministry may be that he sees him as a perfect human being, without sin, and thus above all other mortals (cf. Hoekema).

3. James and Jude.

The usage of *kyrios* in James is easier to analyze than in some NT books. In thirteen instances *kyrios* is used, and in all but four it seems certain that the reference is to God, not Jesus. The references to the Lord Jesus Christ in James 1:1 and James 2:1 provide almost the only clear evidence that this homiletical document is a Christian one, if one did not recognize the echoes of the Sermon on the Mount in various portions of James (see Witherington, *Sage* 1994). In the context of a Christian document James 5:7-8 is also likely a reference to Christ's second coming. As for the other ten instances of *kyrios,* none reflect any theological meanings, insights or nuances that are specifically Christian in character or that could not be found in general in early Jewish sapiential literature. Thus it is God the Lord to whom one prays (Jas 1:5-7; 5:4—the "Lord Sabaoth" or "almighty") and whom one worships (Jas 3:9). The odd phrase "the Lord and Father" in James 3:9 is surely a reference to one person in view of the single article. It is to God the Lord that one submits or humbles oneself (cf. Jas 4:7 and Jas 4:10) and whose will determines the length of one's life (Jas 4:15).

The prophets spoke in the name of the Lord God (Jas 5:10), and it was the Lord who finally had compassion on Job (Jas 5:11). The final references to "Lord" (Jas 5:14-15) are ambiguous. Is it in the name of the Lord Jesus that one is to anoint the sick and to expect the Lord to raise them up, or is this also a reference to the Lord

God who responds to prayers and various forms of petition, as was seen in James 1:5-7 and James 5:4? The latter seems likely. The term *Lord* in James then normally refers to the One who is and has always been sovereign over the universe and has always been the object of prayer. The references to Jesus as Lord at James 1:1, James 2:1 and probably James 5:7-8 all refer to roles he assumed or will assume after the resurrection, hence the apt qualifier at James 2:1 ("our glorious Lord Jesus"). This way of putting the matter may refer to Jesus as risen in glory or Jesus as exalted to God's right hand or both. The writer of this document seems to reflect the earliest period of Christian thinking about Jesus, including the early fervency and hope for his imminent return.

The preceding makes for a striking contrast in terms of emphasis with the use of *kyrios* in another early Jewish Christian document—Jude. Here, with the probable exception of the reference to the Lord God in Jude 9, five other references to *kyrios* in this book apply to Jesus. It is textually uncertain as to whether "Lord" or "Jesus" should be read in Jude 5, but "Jesus" or perhaps "Joshua" is the better attested reference (cf. Metzger, 726). In Jude 4 Jesus is called "our sovereign *[despotēn]* and Lord." His second coming with the holy ones (angels?) is referred to in Jude 14, and he is three times called "our Lord Jesus Christ" (Jude 17, 21, 25). He is the one who not only is coming but also will bring the gift of eternal life to the believers (Jude 21). Jude 25 suggests that he is the one through whom one relates to and petitions the only God. Finally, the Lord's apostles or sent ones are referred to in Jude 17, the sole reference where "Lord" may be predicated of Jesus during his earthly ministry (cf. Bauckham).

4. 1 Peter and 2 Peter.

Of the eight references to *kyrios* in 1 Peter, one is an example of the mundane use of the term to refer to a human master (what Sarah called Abraham—1 Pet 3:6), and most of the remaining examples involve an allusion to or quotation of an OT text. For example, Psalm 34 is alluded to several times. At 1 Peter 2:3, Psalm 34:8 is quoted; and at 1 Peter 3:12, Psalm 34:15-16 is cited, accounting for two further examples of *kyrios*. While in the latter citation it seems clear that the Lord God is meant, at 1 Peter 2:3 the reference could be to Christ, whom the audience has now experienced and found good. More clearly, 1 Peter 3:15 is an appeal to acknowledge Christ as the holy Lord, a text that may include a possible allusion to Isaiah 8:13. If so, this provides us with another example in which OT texts are used homiletically to affirm what is true about Jesus (cf. Davies).

In 1 Peter 1:25 *kyrios* seems a clear reference to God, in view of the parallel "word of God" in 1 Peter 1:23. Again, an OT text, Isaiah 40:6-8, is being quoted. In the initial thanksgiving at 1 Peter 1:3 we find a clear distinction between God who is Father and "our Lord Jesus Christ." The text says that the one praised is both the God and Father of Jesus. What is less evident in 1 Peter is any connection of the *kyrios* references to a subtext of the story about the various stages in Jesus' career, though hints in this direction can probably be seen in 1 Peter 1:20 (preexistence) and 1 Peter 3:18-22 (suffering and atonement). When Christ is the subject, however, the focus is on what Christ now is and should be confessed to be. When God is the subject, *kyrios* is usually introduced because the author is citing the OT. Nevertheless, the writer is apparently not shy about using the OT to describe the exalted qualities of Christ as heavenly Lord—he is holy and good and as such is to be acknowledged and experienced (Krafft). Of the fourteen references to *kyrios* in 2 Peter, none clearly quote an OT text, but 2 Peter 2:9 and 2 Peter 2:11 are part of a recitation of the stories of God's judgments by flood and fire (Gen 6-8; 18-19), and in this context it is not surprising that *kyrios* refers to the Lord God. It appears too that when the author reflected on the day of the Lord, he thought of it in terms of the *yôm Yahweh* ("Day of the Lord") spoken of in the OT, and thus it is likely that *kyrios* in 2 Peter 3:8, 9, 10 and 15 refers to God (cf. 2 Pet 3:12; Witherington 1992 on the *yôm Yahweh*).

All the other references in this letter refer to Christ, as is made evident by the coupling of *kyrios* with either "Jesus" (2 Pet 1:2), "Jesus Christ" (2 Pet 1:8, 11, 14, 16; 3:18) or *sōtēr* (2 Pet 3:2). This writer has a penchant for coupling the term *kyrios* with the term *savior* (2 Pet 1:11; 2:20; 3:2, 18). In neither of the Petrine letters is there any major focus on the cosmic dimensions of Christ's lordship (but cf. 1 Pet 3:21-22). Rather, as the qualifier *our* shows, the focus is on Christ's rule and dominion over the Christian community and individual Christian life (esp. 2 Pet, but see also 1 Pet 1:3). Second Peter does

not reflect the ambiguity we have seen in some of the other NT documents in the use of *kyrios*. In each instance it is clear when Christ is and is not meant. This author does not show the subtlety of use of the OT to speak about lordship that the author of 1 Peter does.

5. The Johannine Epistles and the Apocalypse.

In view of the use of *kyrios* in the Fourth Gospel and the Apocalypse and considering the high christology one finds in 1 John, it comes as a surprise that there are no references to either God or Christ as *kyrios* in the Johannine epistles, nor any more mundane uses of the term. Accordingly we must turn our attention to the Apocalypse. There are twenty-one uses of *kyrios* in the Revelation; in this book, which is a pastiche of OT allusions and images with few direct quotations, the use of *kyrios,* particularly in the first half of the book, is like that found in the OT (cf. Black). Besides Revelation 7:14, where the vocative *kyrie* is little more than a term of respect meaning something like "sir," all the references prior to Revelation 11:8 seem clearly to refer to God and not to Jesus as Lord. John likes to use the phrase "the Lord God" (*kyrios ho theos;* Rev 1:8; 4:8; 11:17; 15:3; 16:7; 18:8; 19:6; 21:22; 22:5-6), and especially in a text like Revelation 21:22, where the term is used to distinguish God from the Lamb, it becomes clear that this phrase does not refer to Jesus, with only one possible exception. This phrase comes up particularly in contexts in which prayer or praise is being offered up to God, and it is sometimes combined with the term *pantokratōr* ("almighty"; Rev 15:3; 19:6; 21:22) to indicate the magnitude of God's sovereignty.

The first clear reference to Jesus as *kyrios* comes at Revelation 11:8, and this is made clear in two ways: by reference to the crucifixion and by the modifier *their* attached to "Lord." It is unclear with a text like Revelation 14:13 whether dying in the Lord refers to dying for Jesus, but in view of Revelation 14:12 this seems likely. Twice Jesus is acclaimed as King of kings and Lord of lords (Rev 17:14; 19:16) in a context where Christ's eschatological role of subduing the opposition at the end of history is stressed. He is not merely sovereign over the church but also will exercise his sovereignty over the nations of the world on behalf of the faithful. The more familiar early Christian usage "Lord Jesus" occurs twice at the end of the document, where Christ's second coming and a benediction in Christ's name is invoked (Rev 22:20-21). One of the most debatable issues in this book is whether at its beginning it is God or Jesus who is called the Lord and the Alpha and Omega (Rev 1:8), especially since the terminology comes up again in Revelation 21:6 and Revelation 22:7, and in the latter-most example it seems rather certain the reference is to the returning Lord Jesus (*see* Christology). However, everywhere else the phrase "the Lord God," especially when qualified by the term *Almighty*, does not refer to Jesus; most scholars think this is also likely the case in Revelation 1:8. Revelation 1:17 may suggest the opposite conclusion, however (cf. Rowland). The point of mentioning this ambiguity is that John, especially in a doxological context, is willing to predicate of Jesus what he predicates of the Lord God, because he sees them as on the same level, being divine and proper objects of worship, unlike the angels (cf. Rev 19:10). Jesus, like God's Spirit, is part of John's vision of what the Godhead is, without at the same time denying the oneness of God. In such circumstances it is understandable that some of the references to *kyrios* in this book could refer to either the Lord Jesus or the Lord God.

6. Summary.

In all these documents we have seen certain repeated patterns and a considerable variety in the use of the term *kyrios*. It is noticeable that only some of the canonical texts (e.g., Acts) seem to reflect an attempt to use the term *kyrios* in a way that reflects the narrative subtext about Jesus' earthly and heavenly career.

It is also noticeable that the more a document is influenced by the OT and Jewish ideas, the more the term *kyrios*, if it stands alone, is likely to refer to the Lord God, not the Lord Jesus. Yet this is only a trend, not a universal pattern. This lack of clear and universal patterns suggests it is well not to exaggerate the image of Jewish Christian communities developing their own theologies apart from Gentile Christians and their communities. Rather, one must think in terms of cross-fertilization; all early Jewish Christians were at least somewhat Hellenized, though a particular author will normally reflect his primary background and influences most of the time.

All this material suggests that Jewish ways of thinking about Jesus and God persisted well into the second century and that the high christology one finds in Ignatius of Antioch had precedents in earlier Christian documents that came to be seen as canonical, particularly the Pauline and Johannine ones. The old, neat dichotomies between early and primitive Jewish christologies versus later, higher and more Hellenistic christologies are too simplistic when one studies the material carefully, especially in view of the enormous importance of sapiential ways of thinking about Jesus from the beginnings of early Christianity (cf. Witherington, *Sage* 1994).

See also CHRIST; CHRISTOLOGY; SON OF GOD.

DLNTD: DOCETISM; LAMB; LITURGICAL ELEMENTS; LOGOS CHRISTOLOGY; LORD'S DAY; PREEXISTENCE; STONE, CORNERSTONE.

BIBLIOGRAPHY. R. J. Bauckham, *Jude, 2 Peter* (WBC; Waco, TX: Word, 1983); H. Bietenhard, "Lord," *NIDNTT* 2:510-20; M. Black, "The Christological Use of the Old Testament in the New Testament," *NTS* 18 (1971-72) 1-14; F. B. Craddock, *The Preexistence of Christ in the New Testament* (Nashville: Abingdon, 1968); O. Cullmann, *The Christology of the New Testament* (Philadelphia: Westminster, 1959); P. E. Davies, "Primitive Christology in 1 Peter," in *Festschrift to Honor F. W. Gingrich*, ed. E. H. Barth and R. E. Cocraft (Leiden: E. J. Brill, 1972) 115-22; S. H. Duffy, "The Early Church Fathers and the Great Councils: The Emergence of Classical Christianity," in *Jesus One and Many: The Christological Concept of New Testament Authors*, ed. E. Richard (Wilmington, DE: Michael Glazier, 1988) 435-86; J. D. G. Dunn, *Christology in the Making* (Philadelphia: Westminster, 1980); idem, *The Partings of the Ways Between Christianity and Judaism and Their Significance for the Character of Christianity* (Philadelphia: Trinity Press International, 1991); J. A. Fitzmyer, *The Gospel According to Luke 1—9* (Garden City, NY: Doubleday, 1981) 143-270; idem, "The Semitic Background of the New Testament Kyrios-Title," in *A Wandering Aramean: Collected Aramaic Essays* (Missoula, MT: Scholars Press, 1979) 115-42; W. Foerster, " κύριος κτλ," *TDNT* 3:1039-98; D. A. Hagner, *The Jewish Reclamation of Jesus: An Analysis and Critique of the Modern Jewish Study of Jesus* (Grand Rapids: Zondervan, 1984); A. T. Hanson, *Jesus Christ in the Old Testament* (London: SPCK, 1965); M. Hengel, *Between Jesus and Paul* (Philadelphia: Fortress, 1983); idem, "Christological Titles in Early Christianity," in *The Messiah: Developments in Earliest Judaism and*

Christianity, ed. J. H. Charlesworth (Minneapolis: Fortress, 1992) 425-48; A. A. Hoekema, "The Perfection of Christ in Hebrews," *CTJ* 9 (1974) 31-37; G. Hughes, *Hebrews and Hermeneutics: The Epistle to the Hebrews as a New Testament Example of Biblical Interpretation* (SNTSMS 36; Cambridge: Cambridge University Press, 1979); P. E. Hughes, "The Christology of Hebrews," *SWJT* 28 (1985) 19-27; L. W. Hurtado, *Lord Jesus Christ: Devotion to Jesus in Earliest Christianity* (Grand Rapids: Eerdmans, 2003); idem, *One God, One Lord* (Philadelphia: Fortress, 1988); D. L. Jones, "The Title *kyrios* in Luke-Acts," in *SBLSP* (1974) 2:85-101; H. C. Kee, *Good News to the Ends of the Earth: The Theology of Acts* (Philadelphia: Trinity Press International, 1990); H. Krafft, "Christologie und Eschatologie im 1. Petrusbrief," *EvT* 10 (1950-51) 120-26; R. N. Longenecker, *The Christology of Early Jewish Christianity* (SBT 2d series 17; Naperville, IL: Allenson, 1970); B. M. Metzger, *A Textual Commentary on the Greek New Testament* (New York: United Bible Societies, 1971); C. F. D. Moule, "The Christology of Acts," in *Studies in Luke-Acts*, ed. L. E. Keck and J. L. Martyn (Nashville: Abingdon, 1966) 159-85; R. C. Nevius, "*Kyrios* and *Iēsous* in St. Luke," *ATR* 48 (1966) 75-77; C. Rowland, "The Vision of Christ in Rev. 113ff. The Debt of an Early Christology to an Aspect of Jewish Angelology," *JTS* 31 (1980) 1-11; J. T. Squires, *The Plan of God in Luke-Acts* (Cambridge: Cambridge University Press, 1993); B. Witherington III, *The Christology of Jesus* (Minneapolis: Fortress, 1990); idem, *Conflict and Community in Corinth: A Sociorhetorical Commentary on 1 and 2 Corinthians* (Grand Rapids: Eerdmans, 1995); idem, ed., *History, Literature and Society in the Book of Acts* (Cambridge: Cambridge University Press, 1996); idem, *Jesus, Paul and the End of the World* (Downers Grove, IL: InterVarsity Press, 1992); idem, *Jesus the Sage: The Pilgrimage of Wisdom* (Minneapolis: Fortress, 1994); idem, *Paul's Narrative Thought World: The Tapestry of Tragedy and Triumph* (Louisville, KY: Westminster John Knox, 1994).   B. Witherington

LORD'S SUPPER I: PAUL

Abuses in the holding of the church meal at Corinth led Paul to remind the church of its real significance as a memorial of the Lord's sacrificial death on the basis of a tradition describing the Last Supper. Recent study has emphasized the importance of social factors in explaining the divisions between rich and poor in the church. These divisions led to the abuses and the response of Paul, which emphasized the meal as a focus of Christian unity and mutual love that does away with class and other human distinctions. Theories that the Pauline type of meal differed significantly from meals in other areas of the early church are improbable.

1. Introduction
2. Religious Meals in the Ancient World
3. The Church Meal in Corinth
4. Paul's Response to the Situation at Corinth
5. The Pauline Lord's Supper and Practice Elsewhere

1. Introduction.

In 1 Corinthians 10:1-3 Paul points out the danger that Christians who think that they stand secure in their faith may fall into severe temptation by participation in idolatry. The people of Israel, who had experienced a remarkable act of divine grace in being liberated from slavery in Egypt, nevertheless fell into idolatry and its accompanying immorality. This was to serve as a warning to the Corinthians. Paul strengthens the parallel he is drawing by tracing an analogy with the way in which the Israelites "were all baptized . . . [and] all ate the same spiritual food and drank the same spiritual drink." Just as their experience with the cloud and the sea is seen in terms of Christian *baptism, so too their eating and drinking must be seen as analogous to the Christian meal, which is referred to later in the same chapter (1 Cor 10:15-17). Here, then, we have the first explicit mention (though some scholars find a possible allusion in 1 Cor 5:6-8) by Paul of the church meal with its spiritual food and drink. And here, too, we have one of the few places where baptism and the Lord's Supper are linked together as the two rites practiced in the church. First Corinthians 12:13 refers purely to baptism in two parallel expres-sions and not to baptism with the Spirit (*see* Holy Spirit) and drinking the Spirit at the Lord's Supper, which is a totally unattested idea.

Later in the same letter Paul refers to a church meal called the Lord's Supper (1 Cor 11:20; cf. "the table of the Lord," 1 Cor 10:20) that was celebrated, manifestly on a frequent basis, in the church at Corinth. References in Acts indicate that an event called "the breaking of bread" was celebrated in the church at Jerusalem, "on the first day of the week" at Troas (Acts 20:7), and by implication in the other churches. Since at Corinth the collection of money for church purposes was also made on the first day of the week (1 Cor 16:2), it is reasonable to suppose that this day had special significance for the church and that a church meeting took place weekly on that day.

Details of what happened at the celebration, whether in the Pauline churches or elsewhere, are scanty, and it has often been commented that if there had not been abuses of the meal in Corinth, we might never have heard about it. However, the fact that the tradition cited by Paul in connection with the occasion contains a command by the Lord to his followers to "do this in memory of him" indicates clearly enough that it was regarded as a duty wherever this tradition was known.

For Paul the origin of the meal lay in the last meal of Jesus with his disciples "on the night when he was betrayed/handed over" to the Jewish authorities, and ultimately by God, and subsequently put to death (1 Cor 11:23). Paul based his understanding of the meal on this event. However, the nature and theology of the meal in the Pauline churches, and its relationship to the so-called Last Supper and to Christian meals in general, raise a number of problems.

2. Religious Meals in the Ancient World.

Communal meals were important in Judaism and Hellenistic religions. They served a social purpose in bringing the adherents together, and they functioned religiously in a variety of ways.

For the Jews in general each and every meal was religious to the extent that it was accompanied by the giving of thanks to God for the food. The main evening meal at the beginning of the Sabbath, which commenced at sunset on the previous day, had a special character, and there were special meals associated with Passover and other festivals. Within the religious movement associated with the Pharisees, small groups known as *ḥ̣ābûrot* met to celebrate meals as occasions for giving thanks to God and for self-dedication. Jewish daily meals began with a thanksgiving to God associated with the breaking of bread and concluded with a further thanksgiving. Festal meals on special occasions, including sabbaths, other festivals and guest meals, included wine, which was not drunk at ordinary daily meals. Thanks were offered for each cup of wine (Klauck 1982, 66-67). At the Passover meal a more elaborate procedure was followed. An important element was an explanation of the symbolism attached to the various parts of the meal, including the lamb, unleavened bread and bitter herbs. This verbal "proclamation" (cf. *katangellō*, 1 Cor 11:26) was intended to make the occasion a remembrance (Ex 12:14; 13:9; cf. *anamnēsis*, 1 Cor 11:24-25) of what God had done for his people.

The situation in the Hellenistic world has been described fairly exhaustively by H. J. Klauck (1982), who discusses in turn meals associated with religious offerings and sacrifices, meals held by associations, meals celebrated in the cult of the dead, meals associated with the various mystery religions in Hellenism and in Judaism, and cultic meals in Gnostic sects (*see* Gnosticism). He notes that the communal meals held by associations were particularly important and that they maintained a religious character. Individual Christian converts could well have been familiar with any of these types of meal and also with some of the practices of the different mystery religions (*see* Religions, Greco-Roman).

There was a complicated mix of religious practices in Corinth. Some members of the church were familiar with meals associated with pagan temples, and some of them believed that it was all right to continue to participate in these. It does not follow that they viewed what happened at these meals and the Lord's Supper in the same way. Further, it is important to note that the very strong explicit criticisms that Paul makes of the Corinthian church meal do not appear to be connected in any way with pagan beliefs or practices that had been carried over into it. It may be that the Corinthian Christians felt that participation in the meal of itself protected them from divine judgment, but Paul's instruction to them is not about misunderstanding the meal but about refraining from idolatry. Rather, the abuses at the meal were of a social character and reflected the practices of the secular world in general rather than of pagan religions in particular.

3. The Church Meal in Corinth.

Since Paul was the founder of the church, and since he refers to what he had told the church (undoubtedly during the visit to Corinth when the church was established), it follows that the church meal had been introduced by Paul but had developed characteristics in his absence from Corinth of which he could not approve. The church was meeting regularly to celebrate the Lord's Supper, but in such a way that Paul denied that the church meal could properly be called the *Lord's* Supper (1 Cor 11:20).

The basic problem appears to have arisen out of tensions in the church between the poor and the rich. Since there were no church buildings, meals were held in the houses of church members. The believers met together in groups of a maximum size dictated by the size of the houses that were at their disposal. It has been convincingly shown that the groups would have met in the homes of the rich, since they alone could accommodate them. These occasions were full meals with plenty of food and drink—at least for some members. The rich brought plentiful food, including meat, for themselves, whereas the poorer members had to make do with their own scanty fare.

Closer definition of what went on is disputed. The tradition about the Last Supper suggests that the eating of the bread and the sharing of the cup, which were given special significance by Jesus, were separated from one another by the meal (cf. the words "likewise after supper the cup," Lk 22:20 = 1 Cor 11:25). Nevertheless, the bringing together of the bread and the cup in the tradition and the way in which the words of interpretation were shaped symmetrically indicate that the specific "remembrance of the Lord's death" came to be seen as one action and that it followed the meal proper. However, there is dispute as to whether the juxtaposition had already taken place in Corinth when Paul wrote, and it has been argued that the order bread-meal-cup was followed at Corinth (Theissen; Lampe). Klauck (1982, 295) argues that since there is no indication that the poorer members of the church were excluded from participation in the bread, the meal must have preceded the use of the bread and cup.

One view of the matter is that the richer members came early and ate and drank copiously before (cf. Gk *prolambanō*) the arrival of the poorer members, who would have brought much scantier fare with them (Theissen). It is pointed out that the poorer people would have had to be content with bread and not much besides, whereas the rich would have had meat

and a variety of delicacies. Parallels from the Greco-Roman world indicate that there could be at least two levels of eating at one and the same meal, the rich thereby accentuating their difference from their poorer neighbors who also came at their invitation to the church meeting. Thus, although the rich opened their houses to the church, they did so in a way that emphasized social divisions. It perhaps needs to be mentioned that the fact that the problems at the meal reflected social divisions was recognized long before G. Theissen (see, e.g., G. G. Findlay, in *EGT* 2:879); what his research has done is to indicate more clearly how the rich carried over the practices of the secular world into the church and sinned against their poorer brothers and sisters.

Further research has taken up the analogy of Hellenistic meals to which a householder would invite guests; a meal was held in two stages, the main meal being followed by a "dessert" or "symposium," at which there could be further guests who had not been at the earlier stage (Lampe). P. Lampe argues that the "religious" gathering at Corinth corresponded to the "dessert and drinks" part of the meal and that it was preceded for the rich by the "main meal" to which each brought their own food (on the analogy of a Greek *eranos*). The poorer members of the church could not come so early (because of their work commitments) or bring food of the same quality.

An alternative view is that the rich were eating their meal in the presence of the poorer members and not sharing out the food with them (Winter; the problem at issue is whether Gk *prolambanō* in 1 Cor 11:21 signifies eating prior to other people or, as an intensified form of *lambanō*, "take," means simply "to devour").

Despite uncertainty over the precise circumstances, the main point stands out quite clearly. There was overindulgence on the part of the rich and feelings of envy on the part of the poor, who were made to feel inferior (cf. 1 Cor 12:15). For Paul this was inconsistent with the intended character of the meal. Hunger and drunkenness were out of place in a church meal. Rowdy festivity and social divisions alike ruined the occasion.

4. Paul's Response to the Situation at Corinth.
Paul's teaching in 1 Corinthians 11 was directed against these practices that meant that the meal

had lost its character as the *Lord's* meal. As far as practically stopping the abuse was concerned, he commanded that the church members should welcome one another when they came together for their meal. That is to say, the rich should welcome the poor and treat them (as indeed all members of the church should treat one another) courteously and graciously. The occasion was still to be a meal, but the implication may be that there was to be sharing of the food (Winter defends this sense for Gk *ekdechomai* in 1 Cor 11:33) so that nobody felt disadvantaged. Further, Paul laid down that the rich should eat privately in their houses if they wished to have a larger meal or more expensive fare and thus avoid importing social divisions into the meeting of the church. Thus Paul was not counseling that the occasion should cease to be a meal and become what it subsequently became in the church generally, namely, the token consumption of a morsel of bread and a sip of wine. He had further instructions that he promised to give verbally, but we shall never know what these were.

Paul's main point, which provided the theological undergirding for the practical advice, was made by citing the tradition that he had received concerning the meal and that he had previously passed on to the church by word of mouth. The language used indicates that it was a matter of an accepted, authoritative tradition. Paul says that he received it "from the Lord," which has been understood by some to mean that it came in the form of a private vision or communication directly from the Lord to Paul (Maccoby). It is far more likely to have been a piece of church tradition that had the authority of the Lord behind it (cf. the use of words of the Lord, doubtless handed down in church tradition to Paul, in 1 Cor 7:10; 9:14).

The tradition described what happened at the Last Supper, when the Lord took bread and the cup and distributed them to his disciples with accompanying sayings that interpreted them as representing his body and the new covenant in his blood; he gave directions that the disciples were to do "this" (i.e., repeat the practice) in memory of him. The meal was thus intended to be a memorial of his death, through which it would be proclaimed. It followed that conduct which was contrary to the spirit of self-giving seen in the death of Jesus would negate that proclamation. Hence it was the contempt

and lack of love for the poorer members of the church that specifically aroused Paul's anger.

The members of the church should stop before taking part in the meal to be sure that they were not committing this sin, which was a sin against the body and blood of Christ and would bring judgment on them. Such conduct was "unworthy" and represented a failure to "discern the body" (1 Cor 11:29). The use of "discern" (Gk *diakrinō*) here is difficult, and interpretation depends on whether "body" stands for "the body [and blood of the crucified Lord]" or for "the church" (Fee, 562-64). Either Paul is saying that people who eat unworthily are not recognizing that the food symbolizes the body (and blood) of Jesus or acting as befits the recipients of his salvation, or he is saying that they are failing to recognize that the people gathered together for the meal are present as the body of Christ (made one by sharing in the one loaf, 1 Cor 10:17) and must be treated in Christian love.

In any case, what Paul says here is reinforced by his earlier comment that the "many" who share in the one loaf at the supper are "one body" in virtue of doing so (1 Cor 10:16-17). He sees that those who share in the blood and the body of Jesus are thereby brought into a unity with one another where social distinctions cannot be allowed to exist. Opinions differ as to whether the communion with the body and blood of Christ signifies "a union (sharing) with the risen Christ" (Hauck, 805), or a common sharing between the members that binds them together on the basis of the Lord, his death and his resurrection (Fee, 564), or a common sharing in the benefits secured for them by the death of Christ (Barrett 1968, 232). However precisely we understand the phrase, Paul emphasizes that sharing in this meal and taking part in idolatrous meals are incompatible. His stress on the fact that believers are joined together as one by the church meal may suggest that any members who take part in idolatry are contaminating the whole community. But his main thought is probably, as in 1 Corinthians 6, the incompatibility of being joined to Christ and to what is sinful/demonic.

In 1 Corinthians 11 Paul develops the theological significance of the supper on the basis of the tradition. He reminds the readers that the body of Christ, represented by the bread, was "for you." This phrase forms part of a series of statements that teach that Christ died for other people (Rom 5:8; 8:32; 1 Cor 15:3; 2 Cor 5:15 [three times]; Gal 2:20; 3:13; Eph 5:2, 25; 1 Tim 2:6; Tit 2:14) and that occur throughout the NT (Mk 10:45 [Gk *anti*]; Jn 10:11, 15; 11:52; Heb 2:9; 9:24; 1 Pet 2:21; 3:18; 1 Jn 3:16). Thus the death of Jesus is seen as his self-giving in death on behalf and for the benefit of other people, so that they might be redeemed from sin and its judgment and be justified. Possibly his self-giving "for you" is intended also to be seen as exemplary (Winter, 79).

The cup is interpreted as signifying the new covenant in the blood of Christ. Against the background of Exodus 24:8 and Jeremiah 31:31-34 this indicates that the death of Jesus is the sacrifice that inaugurates the new covenant between God and his people, thus establishing the new people of God.

There has been much discussion, arising out of contemporary theological differences in the church, as to whether Paul's teaching indicates that the Lord is present at the supper. He appears to regard the food and drink as "spiritual," like the heaven-sent provision for the Israelites in the desert (1 Cor 10:3-4; Wedderburn, 234-39). Roman Catholic interpreters tend to find a presence of the Lord in the bread and the cup on the basis of "This is my body," whereas Protestant interpreters argue that the phrase means rather "This symbolizes my body." The debate turns on 1 Corinthians 10:20-21, where there appears to be an analogy between being partakers with demons through sharing in their cup and table and what happens at the Lord's Supper. However, there is no indication that the two events are precisely parallel, and in any case it is not suggested that the worshipers eat the demons or that the demons are present in the food. Rather, the parallel suggests that just as those who share in idolatrous feasts are brought into a relationship with demons, so those who share in the Lord's Supper are brought into a relationship with the Lord, who is present as host. This language of "host and guests" admittedly goes beyond what Paul explicitly says, but it fits in with the background concept of feasts held under the patronage of a god in paganism and feasts celebrated "in the presence of the Lord" in the OT and Judaism (see also Rev 3:20). There is no indication that Paul saw the event as sacrificial; it is likened not to the offering of an animal on an altar but to the eating of food at a table, where the partakers receive the symbols

that indicate that a sacrificial death has already taken place at Calvary. It is thus conceived of as a postsacrificial meal.

There is no explicit reference to the supper elsewhere in Paul. However, if 1 Corinthians was meant to be read as part of the proceedings at the church meal, the use of the curse against those who do not love the Lord (1 Cor 16:21) may be seen as reinforcing the sense of community among those who in the meal confessed their love of the Lord and their separation from others, specifically those who proclaimed another gospel (cf. the similarly placed warning in Rom 16:17-18 and Gal 1:8-9 for the use of the curse). The kiss of peace, mentioned at the end of several letters, will also have had significance as an expression of unity and love. Finally, the phrase *Maranatha*, which may be understood as a statement or a prayer, should be taken as an expression of longing for the final coming of Jesus as Lord rather than as a prayer for his presence in the Lord's Supper.

5. The Pauline Lord's Supper and Practice Elsewhere.

How is the Pauline material related to other teaching about the supper in the NT? The Synoptic Gospels uniformly witness to the occasion when Jesus met with his disciples for what is characterized as a Passover meal. He used this occasion to announce to them his imminent decease and to share with them the customary bread of the Passover and one of the cups of wine with accompanying statements that these symbolized his body and his blood. The precise wording of the accounts varies among the Gospels, with Matthew and Mark standing close to one another with essentially the same wording (Mark: "Take, this is my body; this is my blood of the covenant which is poured out for many"), and with Luke offering a form of words close to those preserved by Paul (Luke: "This is my body which is given for you; do this in remembrance of me; this cup is the new covenant in my blood, which is poured out for you"). The somewhat stylized nature of the accounts suggests that the wording had become "fixed" as part of a liturgical statement used in church meetings and was incorporated into the Gospels (*see* Worship).

The variation in wording between Matthew/ Mark and Luke/Paul has been variously explained. Perhaps the majority of scholars regard the Markan wording as the older, with the Lukan/Pauline as a development from it, but there is a sizable minority (to which the present writer would join himself) that sees the development moving in the reverse direction. Opinions further differ as to whether this tradition goes back to the historical occasion described or has been developed from a simpler form of words that was less pregnant with theological implications. The view that the whole account is a church creation, and that we know nothing historical about a final meal of Jesus with his disciples, need not be taken seriously (*see* Last Supper).

Communal meals were celebrated widely in the early church and are traced back by Luke to the earliest days of the Jerusalem church. There is nothing unlikely about this. The first Christians in a Jewish setting appear to have acted in a way analogous to the Pharisees or indeed to any Jewish group that met to eat together. The meal is referred to as "the breaking of bread"—with no mention of drinking wine. Although this phrase refers strictly to the opening act of a meal, the sharing of bread to the accompaniment of prayers of thanksgiving, it is clear that a proper meal is meant. The use of meal imagery in Revelation likewise shows that the religious significance of meals was recognized in its geographical area in Asia.

The question that now arises is whether there was uniformity of practice throughout the early church. Were there two or more types of meal in the early church, the one a rather more festive type of meal that was known as "the breaking of bread" and that was not a memorial of the Lord's death and not based on the tradition of the Last Supper, while the other was very much tied up with the use of bread and the cup to remember the Lord's death and was the kind of occasion advocated by Paul?

A theory of this kind was developed especially by H. Lietzmann, who argued that the original Jerusalem meal was replaced by the Pauline one. Other scholars have suggested similar theories. (Barrett 1985, 61, 67-68, thinks it possible that it was Paul who made the link between the church's weekly fellowship meal, celebrating the resurrection, and the Last Supper.) However, it has proved impossible to trace the independent existence of the putative Jerusalem meal. The most that can be said is that the phrase "the breaking of bread" in Acts may cover celebrations of the Lord's Supper and other church meals without wine, which was not normally

drunk at ordinary meals. The meal at Corinth included the breaking of bread, and it included the use of wine. Our sole witness for a Lord's Supper with bread only would be Luke, if that is what he is describing, and the close links of Luke with Pauline Christianity make it very unlikely that he intends to describe anything other than Pauline practice. The case that a post-Pauline writer is describing a "bread-only" meal current in his own time and reading it back into the days of the early church has no basis. Thus we have no historical evidence for the parallel existence of two different kinds of meal.

We therefore have to ask whether there is any evidence that might suggest an evolution in the early church meals from being simply fellowship gatherings to becoming memorials to the death of Jesus with an increasingly elaborate theological significance attached to them and reflected in the varying forms of the so-called words of institution. The Last Supper was a reinterpretation of a Passover meal, and this might have suggested an annual celebration of it rather than a weekly one. That some early Christians celebrated an annual "Christian Passover" emerges from 1 Corinthians 5:6-8, but this evidence also shows that Paul had no difficulty in holding together an annual Christian Passover and a weekly Lord's Supper (see Jeremias, 901-4). We are thus thrown back again on the question whether the account of the Last Supper is historically plausible and reliable and whether it influenced the church from its earliest days. So far as Luke is concerned, it is noteworthy that he describes the Emmaus meal with the risen Lord in a way that suggests that it was a pattern for what was to follow, and he describes it in terms that are reminiscent of the Last Supper. There were evidently no problems in his mind regarding the continuity between them.

The case for development has been defended by H. Maccoby. He states that at ordinary Jewish meals the opening action was the "breaking of bread" and the sharing of it among the participants with a prayer of thanksgiving in which God was blessed for his provision. However, at ceremonial meals on the sabbath and at festivals this action was preceded by the sharing of wine, with thanks given to God. He then argues that in the Jerusalem church the "breaking of bread" followed the pattern of ordinary Jewish meals. But the last meal of Jesus with his disciples followed the pattern of a festival meal with the order wine-bread, as attested in Luke and *Didache* 9—10. Originally it had a purely "apocalyptic" theme, as Jesus looked forward to the imminent inauguration of the kingdom of God. Then Paul had a vision in which he learned that at the Last Supper Jesus had distributed bread and wine (in that order!) and interpreted them with reference to his death. (This is the tradition received [directly] from the Lord to which reference is made in 1 Cor 11.) Hence arose the text of Luke that shows a secondary combination of the apocalyptic and eucharistic themes, and then the text of Mark, which almost entirely suppresses the apocalyptic aspect. Thus the Lord's Supper is a Pauline creation and is not to be confused with the breaking of bread in Acts.

Maccoby's theory comes to grief on various facts. There is no clear evidence in the NT for a church meal with the order wine-bread (1 Cor 10:16-17, to which he rightly does not appeal, has the inverted order to allow Paul to develop the significance of the one loaf), and the *Didache*'s evidence should not be preferred to that of earlier sources. It would be strange if the post-Pauline Acts were to ascribe to Paul a "breaking of bread" (Acts 20) that was different from the Pauline custom known to the author. Paul uses the term "breaking of bread" to refer to the Lord's Supper (1 Cor 10:16). And the phrase "the cup of blessing" (i.e., "the cup for which we bless God") used by Paul in 1 Corinthians 10:16 was used for the *third* cup at the Passover meal (Str-B 4:1, 72). The case, in short, is not convincing.

See also BAPTISM; BODY OF CHRIST; CORINTHIANS, LETTERS TO THE; LAST SUPPER; WORSHIP.

DPL: FELLOWSHIP, COMMUNION, SHARING; FOOD OFFERED TO IDOLS AND JEWISH FOOD LAWS; LITURGICAL ELEMENTS; LOVE FEAST; SACRIFICE, OFFERING; SOCIAL-SCIENTIFIC APPROACHES TO PAUL; TRADITION.

BIBLIOGRAPHY. C. K. Barrett, *The First Epistle to the Corinthians* (HNTC; New York: Harper & Row, 1968); idem, *Church, Ministry and Sacraments in the New Testament* (Exeter: Paternoster, 1985); G. D. Fee, *The First Epistle to the Corinthians* (NICNT; Grand Rapids: Eerdmans, 1987); F. Hauck, "κοινός κτλ," *TDNT* 3:789-809; J. Jeremias, "πάσχα," *TDNT* 5:896-904; H. J. Klauck, *Herrenmahl und Hellenistischer Kult: Eine religionsgeschichtliche Untersuchung zum ersten Korintherbrief* (Münster: Aschendorff, 1982); idem,

"Lord's Supper," *ABD* 4:362-72; P. Lampe, "Das korinthische Herrenmahl im Schnittpunkt hellenistisch-römischer Mahlpraxis und paulinischer Theologia Crucis (1 Kor 11, 17-34)," *ZNW* 82 (1991) 183-213; H. Lietzmann, *Mass and Lord's Supper* (Leiden: E. J. Brill, 1953-1979); H. Maccoby, "Paul and the Eucharist," *NTS* 37 (1991) 247-67; I. H. Marshall, *Last Supper and Lord's Supper* (Exeter: Paternoster, 1980); E. Schweizer, *The Lord's Supper According to the New Testament* (Philadelphia: Fortress, 1967); G. Theissen, *The Social Setting of Pauline Christianity: Essays on Corinth* (Philadelphia: Fortress, 1982); A. J. M. Wedderburn, *Baptism and Resurrection: Studies in Pauline Theology Against Its Greco-Roman Background* (Tübingen: J. C. B. Mohr, 1987); B. W. Winter, *After Paul Left Corinth* (Grand Rapids: Eerdmans, 2001).

I. H. Marshall

LORD'S SUPPER II: ACTS, HEBREWS, GENERAL EPISTLES, REVELATION

The term Lord's Supper, *kyriakon deipnon*, occurs in the NT only at 1 Corinthians 11:20 (*see* Lord's Supper I). When the Corinthian Christians gather "as a church *[en ekklēsia]*" (1 Cor 11:18), their assembly includes a meal to which belong the eating of the bread and the drinking of the cup that "proclaim the Lord's death until he comes" (1 Cor 11:26). It is not clear whether that bread and that cup framed the full meal, bread at the beginning and cup at the end (as would be the case if the Corinthian practice took the same pattern as the apostle Paul's account of Jesus' Last Supper, 1 Cor 11:23-25), or whether that bread and that cup both rather came together after people had otherwise eaten and drunk. It is certain that by their abusive behavior— "each goes ahead with his own meal, and one is hungry and another drunk" (1 Cor 11:21)—the Corinthians are, in the judgment of the apostle Paul and apparently of God also (1 Cor 11:27-34), denaturing "the Lord's Supper." Scholars generally agree that conduct such as that found at Corinth was the likely reason for an eventual separation between the *agapē*, or love feast (a designation full of irony in such circumstances), and the sacrament (to speak anachronistically for the apostolic period). In treating the NT and the early postapostolic writings, it will be necessary to speak of the *agapē* and the Eucharist together; as the second century progresses, a clearer distinction emerges between the love feast and the Holy Communion.

The Synoptic Gospels and Paul all report the institution by Jesus, at the Last Supper, of a rite with bread and wine as his own memorial (Mt 26:26-29; Mk 14:22-25; Lk 22:17-20, 29-30; 1 Cor 11:23-26; *see* Last Supper). The Acts of the Apostles mentions the meals at which the memorial actions probably took place in the primitive church. A few other echoes of the ritual meal are found elsewhere in the later NT writings. The most important evidence for developments in the second century is provided by the *Didache*, the letters of Ignatius of Antioch and the *Apologies* of Justin Martyr and of Tertullian.

1. The Breaking of Bread in Acts
2. The Non-Pauline Epistles and Revelation
3. The Early Postapostolic Period
4. *Agapē* and Eucharist Distinguished
5. Conclusion

1. The Breaking of Bread in Acts.

By noun or by verb Luke speaks five times in Acts of "the breaking of bread": Acts 2:42 and 46, as part of a description of the life of the Jerusalem church directly after the outpouring of the Spirit at Pentecost; Acts 20:7 and 11, in the narrative of Paul's visit to the assembly at Troas; Acts 27:35, in telling how Paul encouraged the ship's company to take food when in danger of shipwreck. The matter of "tables" in Acts 6:1-6 is also relevant.

In Jewish practice, bread was broken when God was blessed at the start of a meal. In primitive Christianity, the breaking of bread bore the special imprint it had acquired from its significant usage by Jesus. In the Gospel of Luke, in whose light Acts has particularly to be read, Jesus broke the loaves when he fed the five thousand (Lk 9:16); the Savior broke the bread when he gave it to his disciples at the Last Supper, saying, "This is my body which is given for you. Do this in remembrance of me" (Lk 22:19); and the risen Lord broke the bread at Emmaus (Lk 24:30) and was known to his two companions "in the breaking of the bread" (Lk 24:35). Around those highly significant occasions cluster then all the multiple words and deeds of Jesus involving food and drink that also give weight and texture to the observance that the church of Acts called by metonymy "the breaking of bread."

Jesus had pictured God's coming reign as a feast: "People will come from east and west, and from north and south, and sit at table in the kingdom of God" (Lk 13:29). Apart from the messianic act of already feeding the multitudes in anticipation of the kingdom, Jesus had been notorious also for eating and drinking with publicans and sinners (Lk 7:34; 15:1-2; *see* Table Fellowship); he thereby invited them to repentance (Lk 5:30-32), for the mere eating and drinking in his presence was no guarantee of salvation (Lk 13:22-30). At the Last Supper he spoke of himself as being among his disciples "as one who serves" (Lk 22:27), yet he was also able to promise them a place at his table in the kingdom that his Father had given him (Lk 22:28-30). After his resurrection, his appearance at Emmaus was not the only one in which he shared in a meal with his followers. He ate with the others in Jerusalem (Lk 24:36-43), and in Acts Luke gives Peter the summary statement that "God raised Jesus on the third day and made him manifest . . . to us who were chosen by God as witnesses, who ate and drank with him after he rose from the dead" (Acts 10:40-41). (Acts 1:4 implies the same, if *synalizomenos* is to be associated with *hals*, salt, and then understood as a reference to the risen Jesus' eating with the apostles, as in fact the Latin, Syriac and Coptic versions translate.) These, then, are the associations that accompany the meal assemblies perpetuated by the primitive church after the Lord's exaltation.

1.1. Acts 2:41-46. According to Acts 2:41-42, those who at Pentecost repented and were baptized were added to the company of those who "devoted themselves to the apostles' teaching and fellowship *[koinōnia]*, to the breaking of bread and the prayers." It is hard to determine the precise relationship among the elements in this foursome, chiefly because of the difficulty in specifying the meaning of the somewhat elastic word *koinōnia*. It has been suggested that the four items constitute a service, in liturgical sequence, of preaching, *agapē*, Eucharist and prayers (*see* Worship). Another suggestion is that *koinōnia* designates a collection of money or goods, so that "the breaking of bread" might then stand for either an *agapē* or the Eucharist or both. In any case, the context indicates that the believers shared several things together: not only apostolic instruction, the "breaking of bread" and prayers, but also attendance at the temple (Acts 2:46) and the distribution of material goods as need arose (Acts 2:44-45). Thus the breaking of bread is associated with a common faith, the common worship of God and a common life of mutual service; the "breaking" is for the purpose of "sharing," as X. Léon-Dufour insists *(le partage du pain)*, and so brings to expression the unity of the community in Christ. The breaking of bread took place in the homes of believers and in conjunction with a meal of which they partook "with glad and generous hearts" (Acts 2:46; cf. du Toit).

The joy that characterized these meals has led some scholars, notably H. Lietzmann, to postulate an original "Jerusalem-type" Lord's Supper in distinction from a Pauline type, where the apostle, perhaps in dependence on Hellenistic memorial meals, would have shifted the theme to the Lord's death. While different emphases may have marked the Christian meal at different times and in different places, it is unwise and unnecessary to exaggerate the difference between Jerusalem and Paul in this matter. According to Luke, the Jerusalem church was well aware that the redemption in which it rejoiced had been bought at the price of the Lord's crucifixion (Acts 2:23), while Paul may, in his reminder that the Supper proclaimed the Lord's death until he comes, have been correcting an overenthusiastic Corinthian supposition that the divine kingdom was already here. The joy *(agalliasis)* that marked the meals of the Jerusalem church was experienced by the Philippian jailer *(ēgalliasato,* Acts 16:34), who "set a table" *(parathēken trapezan)* for Paul and Silas after his baptism.

1.2. Acts 6:1-6. "Tables" had been an issue between the Greek-speakers ("Hellenists") and the Aramaic-speakers ("Hebrews") in the Christian community at Jerusalem (Acts 6:1-6). The primitive church inherited a Jewish tradition of provision for the poor and needy at festive meals, which would be extended to all the needy sisters and brothers in their regular gatherings (Reicke 1948). The Hellenists complained that their widows were not treated fairly in the distribution of food. The daily dole had apparently taken place under the general oversight, though not detailed supervision, of the apostles ("It is not right that we should give up preaching the word of God to serve tables"). The apostles proposed that seven other men be elected to the duty. Seven people with Greek names were chosen, and the apostles prayed and laid their hands upon them. Traditionally this event has been seen as

the origin of the diaconate as an order of ministry. The apostles could now devote themselves "to prayer and to the ministry of the word." Some have regretted the divergence between a preaching and a diaconal ministry. It is in any case sad that, as would be the case at Corinth, the sharing of food should be a divisive issue among Christians. Table fellowship—this time explicitly as a matter of theological principle between Jewish and Gentile Christians—would emerge as a question again in Acts 10—11, where the episode concerning the apostle Peter and the centurion Cornelius would be settled by the recognition that "to the Gentiles also God has granted repentance unto life" (Acts 11:18).

1.3. Acts 20:7-12. The next occurrence of "the breaking of bread" in the narrative of Acts falls during the apostle Paul's visit to Troas (Acts 20:7-12). The Christians "gathered together to break bread" on "the first day of the week." The assembly took place (the verb *synagō* is used) during the evening and night.

Whether it was the evening and night of our Saturday/Sunday or of our Sunday/Monday is uncertain. If Luke is using the Roman system of reckoning, which begins the day in the morning, then the meeting started on Sunday evening. If he is using the Jewish liturgical reckoning, however, the assembly would have started on the evening of Saturday, the beginning of "the first day of the week." It has been suggested that the Christian Sunday originated as a prolongation of the Jewish sabbath: Christians kept the sabbath by attending Jewish worship and then, because the sabbath no longer sufficed since it has been fulfilled by Jesus, they assembled in houses for specifically Christian worship as soon as the sabbath was over (Riesenfeld). If such a Jewish-Christian influence affected the church at Troas, then the assembly of Acts 20:7-12 would have taken place on Saturday/Sunday. But Sunday evening may have imposed itself on the earliest church, as the time for the main weekly assembly, on account of the memory of the meals that the risen Lord had shared with his disciples on the first Easter Sunday.

In any case, we find that Paul "prolonged his speech until midnight"; and only then, after incidentally reviving the hapless Eutychus, did the apostle "break bread and eat." This pattern of preaching and meal—recalling the risen Lord's exposition of the Scriptures to the two on the road to Emmaus and his being made known to them in the breaking of the bread (Lk 24:27-35)—may already show a regular practice of "word and table" in the main weekly assembly of the Christians.

1.4. Acts 27:33-38. The most intriguing case of "breaking bread" in Acts occurs during the story of Paul's shipwreck. Acts 27:33-38 reads:

> As day was about to dawn, Paul urged them all to take some food, saying 'Today is the fourteenth day that you have continued in suspense and without food, having taken nothing. Therefore I urge you to take some food; it will give you strength [lit. "this will be for your salvation"], since not a hair is to perish from the head of any of you.' And when he had said this, he took bread, and giving thanks to God in the presence of all he broke it and began to eat. Then they all were encouraged and ate some food themselves. (We were in all two hundred and seventy-six persons in the ship.) And when they had eaten enough, they lightened the ship, throwing out the wheat into the sea.

Strikingly, Paul's actions with the bread mirror those of Jesus at the Last Supper and presage what modern scholarship has called "the 'four-action' shape of the eucharist" (Dix): the apostle "took bread" (the "offertory"), he gave thanks (the "eucharistic prayer"), he broke the bread (the "fraction"), he ate (the "communion"). Paul was in this way presiding over a meal shared by a whole boatload of presumably heathen sailors and passengers, for there is no indication of two separate meals, one for Paul, Aristarchus and "the travel-diarist," and another for the heathen. Thus it is usually said that this cannot have been a Eucharist but was rather a case simply of Paul observing the Jewish custom of grace before food.

One modern exegete has tried to do more justice to the "eucharistic" tone of Acts 27:35. B. Reicke argued that Acts 27:33-38 is a further stylized account of an incident upon which Paul had already put a quasi-eucharistic stamp at the time of its happening. Paul had let the people on board participate in "a prefiguration of the Christian Eucharist as a potential preparation for later discipleship," and the author of Acts, understanding the episode in the same way, had used the story of what happened on the voyage to open up also the prospect of the work that Paul would do in the wider context of the mission when he reached Rome (cf. Acts 28:28-30).

It may be wondered whether even this interpretation goes far enough. Those on board a ship running on the rocks (Acts 27:29) were confronted by "the last things": it was a matter of life and death, both physically and, for the heathen, spiritually. The possibility should not be excluded that when the apostle proposed they should all take food, telling them, "This will be the saving of you" (Acts 27:34) and having already announced to them that their destiny was in the hands of his God whose will it was that there should be no loss of life among them (Acts 27:21-26), he then celebrated for them the meal that is life to all who will choose life. Certainly this episode provides the clearest instance of what J. Wanke sees as a eucharistic motif characteristic of Lukan meal stories: the Lord is present to protect and preserve his people.

2. The Non-Pauline Epistles and Revelation.

2.1. Jude 12. This verse may represent the only use in the NT of *agapē* in the sense of love feast (the regular meaning of *agapē* is simply "love"). In a closely related passage, the manuscripts in 2 Peter 2:13 are divided between *agapais* ("love feasts") and *apatais* ("pleasures," "dissipations"). I. H. Marshall suggests that the former reading may result from a later scribe's ironing out of a deliberate pun. In any case, the fiery epistle of Jude declares that the Christian assembly has been infiltrated by "ungodly persons who pervert the grace of our God into licentiousness and deny our only Master and Lord, Jesus Christ." They are said to be "blemishes on your love-feasts, as they boldly carouse together, looking after themselves."

2.2. Hebrews. It has been argued that "there is little or no evidence in Hebrews of involvement, on the part of the author or of the community of Christians to which the epistle was addressed, in eucharistic faith and practice" and indeed suggested that, for the writer, "the sacrifice of Christ was of a kind that rendered obsolete every form of cultus that placed a material means of sacramental communion between God and the worshiper" (Williamson). Other exegetes see the letter to the Hebrews as shot through with allusions to the Eucharist. It is certain that Hebrews contains language that the later Christian tradition has associated with the Eucharist.

Two verses are of particular interest: "Through [Jesus Christ] let us continually offer up a sacrifice of praise to God, that is, the fruit of lips that acknowledge his name. Do not neglect to do good and to share what you have, for such sacrifices are pleasing to God" (Heb 13:15-16). The "sacrifice of praise [and thanksgiving]" became a designation for the Eucharist; and John Chrysostom, in expounding the gospel story of the healed leper, commented that we offer thanks to God not because God has need of anything but in order to bring us closer to God (*Hom. Mt. 25*, Migne, *PG* 57.331). In the Hebrews passage the sacrifice is not limited to verbal confession of God's name but includes also sharing *(koinōnia)* and good works.

More generally, the letter to the Hebrews has been considered important in the Christian liturgical tradition for its description of Christ's continuing intercession after his entrance from Calvary into the Holy of Holies: the Eucharist is traditionally seen to represent in ritual mode the high-priestly work of Christ before the face of the Father. Moreover, references in Hebrews to "the blood of the covenant" resonate with the cup-word at the Eucharist, and in particular Hebrews 13:20 finds an echo in the words of consecration at the Roman Mass: "This is the cup of my blood, the blood of the new and everlasting covenant."

2.3. 1 Peter 2:3. The phrase from Psalm 34:8 echoed in 1 Peter 2:3 about "tasting the goodness of the Lord" has been used as a communion verse in traditional liturgies of the Eucharist. In the Petrine context it comes close to the notion of Christians as "a spiritual house," "a holy priesthood, to offer spiritual sacrifices acceptable to God through Jesus Christ" (1 Pet 2:5).

2.4. Revelation. At the beginning of Revelation, the seer says that he "was in the Spirit on the Lord's day" (Rev 1:10). Modern scholarship has suggested that the Apocalypse reflects the church's worship in which John found inspiration, either the Sunday assembly of the congregation or the annual Easter liturgy, depending on the sense of "Lord's Day." In traditional Christian rites for the Lord's Supper, participants have been summoned by the *Sursum Corda* ("Lift up your hearts") to join in the heavenly worship and add their voices to the angelic company in singing the *Sanctus:* "Holy, holy, holy, Lord God Almighty" (Rev 4:8). Besides the praise of God, life in the city of God includes the messianic feast, "the marriage supper of the Lamb." In the Roman Catholic Mass, the invitation to commun-

ion borrows from Revelation 19:9: "This is the Lamb of God. . . . Happy are those who are called to his supper." The Jesus of the Apocalypse extends the invitation: "Behold, I stand at the door and knock; if any one hears my voice and opens the door, I will come in to him and eat with him, and he with me" (Rev 3:20).

3. The Early Postapostolic Period.

3.1. Didache. The earliest nonscriptural material related to Lord's Supper and love feast probably comes from the *Didache,* or Teaching of the Twelve Apostles, which may belong around the turn of the first century, although scholarly dating of this text, rediscovered in 1875, varies between A.D. 60 and 200. Opinion is divided concerning the Jewish-style table prayers given in chapters 9 and 10. The text reads as follows:

About the thanksgiving, give thanks thus. First about the cup: "We give thanks to you, our Father, for the holy vine of your child *(pais)* David, which you made known to us through your child *(pais)* Jesus; glory to you for evermore." And about the broken bread: "We give thanks to you, for the life and knowledge which you made known to us through your child Jesus; glory to you for evermore. As this broken bread was scattered over the mountains, and when brought together became one, so let your church be brought together from the ends of the earth into your kingdom; for yours are the glory and the power through Jesus Christ for evermore." But let no one eat or drink of your thanksgiving but those who have been baptized in the name of the Lord. For about this also the Lord has said, "Do not give what is holy to the dogs."

And after you have had your fill, give thanks thus: "We give thanks to you, holy Father, for your holy name which you have enshrined in our hearts, and for the knowledge and faith and immortality which you have made known to us through your child Jesus; glory to you for evermore. You, almighty Master, created all things for the sake of your name, and gave food and drink to human beings for their enjoyment, that they might give you thanks; but to us you have granted spiritual food and drink and eternal life through your child Jesus. Above all we give you thanks because you are mighty; glory to you for evermore. May grace come, and may this world pass away. Hosanna to the God of David." If any is holy, let him come; if any is not, let him repent. Maranatha. Amen.

Although the introductory word is about "the thanksgiving" *(eucharistia)*, it is likely that the first two prayers, over the cup and over the bread, belong to an *agapē* (the order of cup before bread is perhaps to be found at the communal meal in the later church order reconstituted by modern scholarship and identified with *The Apostolic Tradition* of Hippolytus, although the text is very confused around chapter 25/26; cf. also perhaps 1 Cor 10:16-17). All food over which thanks have been said is sanctified (cf. 1 Tim 4:4-5), and so the application of the Lord's word from Matthew 7:6 ("Do not give what is holy to the dogs") does not necessarily imply a sacramental Eucharist. The rubric "after you have had your fill" implies that a meal has occurred before the next prayer. However, that prayer has a more redemptive cast than the previous ones, bringing it closer to the themes of the Eucharist proper; and the fourth-century compiler of *Apostolic Constitutions* VII was easily able to make it unmistakably sacramental in his adaptation of the text and in fact obviously understood all the prayers in the *Didache* in a sacramental sense.

Whatever may be the case with chapters 9 and 10 of the *Didache,* scholars are agreed that chapter 14 refers to what would be called "the Eucharist." The text reads:

On the Lord's day of the Lord, come together, break bread and give thanks, having first confessed your transgressions, that your sacrifice may be pure. But let none who has a quarrel with his companion join with you until they have been reconciled, that your sacrifice may not be defiled. For this is that which was spoken by the Lord, "In every place, and at every time, offer me a pure sacrifice; for I am a great king, says the Lord, and my name is wonderful among the nations."

The timing is for Sunday, although some scholars have wanted to make the rather strange turn of phrase refer only to Easter. The requirement for prior confession of sin may derive from Leviticus 5:5-6, while the requirement for reconciliation within the fellowship certainly comes from the saying of Jesus recorded at Matthew 5:23-24 (a text frequently evoked later in connection

with the Eucharist, e.g. by Irenaeus *Haer.* 4.18.1, and by Cyril of Jerusalem *Myst. Cat.* 5.3). The application of Malachi 1:11 concerning the "pure sacrifice" will be repeated in Justin (*Dial. Tryph.* 41; cf. 117) and Irenaeus (*Haer.* 4.17.5), and it will become a commonplace that the Eucharist is to be offered "always and everywhere" *(semper et ubique).*

3.2. Pliny's Letter. From the early years of the second century comes external and internal evidence, of a fragmentary kind, concerning the ritual meal practice of the Christians in Asia Minor. The imperial official Pliny reports to the emperor Trajan on his investigations into the group (Pliny *Ep.* 10.96).

On a fixed day [presumably Sunday], [the Christians were] accustomed to meet before dawn, and to recite a hymn antiphonally to Christ, as to a god, and to bind themselves by an oath *[sacramentum]*. . . . After the conclusion of this ceremony it was their custom to depart and meet again to take food; but it was ordinary and harmless food; and they had ceased this practice after my edict in which, in accordance with your orders, I had forbidden secret societies.

Some scholars have seen in the early morning meeting a garbled reference to the Eucharist, while the later gathering would have been for an *agapē.* The suspicion that Christians engaged in cannibalism recurred throughout antiquity, doubtless provoked by reference to communion in the body and blood of the Lord.

3.3. Ignatius of Antioch. The letters of Ignatius, bishop of Antioch (martyred about A.D. 110), contain several references to *agapē* and Eucharist. A passage in the *Letter to the Smyrnaeans* suggests that the Eucharist was held in conjunction with an *agapē.*

Let that be regarded as a valid Eucharist which is under the bishop or someone appointed by him. Where the bishop is present, there let the congregation gather, just as where Jesus Christ is, there is the catholic church. Without the bishop it is not lawful either to baptize or to hold a love-feast. (Ign. *Smyrn.* 8.1-2)

The writer's main concern here, in any case, is for the unity of the congregation, which is grounded christologically, sacramentally and ministerially:

Take care to observe a single Eucharist, for there is one flesh of our Lord Jesus Christ and one cup to unite us with his blood, and one altar, as there is one bishop with the presbytery and the deacons, my fellow servants, in order that what you do, you do according to God. (Ign. *Phld.* 4.1)

The sacramental reality corresponds to the reality of the incarnation:

[The Docetists] abstain from the Eucharist and prayer because they do not confess that the Eucharist is the flesh of our Savior Jesus Christ which suffered for our sins and which the Father in his goodness raised. (Ign. *Smyrn.* 7.1)

Ignatius speaks of "breaking the one bread," which is "a medicine of immortality, and an antidote against dying, but rather that one may live in Jesus Christ for ever" (Ign. *Eph.* 20.2).

4. *Agapē* and Eucharist Distinguished.

4.1. Justin Martyr. By the middle of the second century, Justin Martyr describes the church in Rome as holding a regular Sunday service of word and table, where the reading and exposition of the Scriptures are followed by prayers and the Eucharist of the Lord's body and blood. The description in chapter 67 of Justin's *First Apology* runs as follows:

And on the day called Sunday an assembly is held in one place of all who live in town or country, and the memoirs of the apostles or the writings of the prophets are read as time allows. Then, when the reader has finished, the president in a discourse admonishes and exhorts us to imitate these good things. Then we all stand up together and send up prayers; and as we said before, when we have finished praying, bread and wine and water are brought up, and the president likewise sends up prayers and thanksgivings to the best of his ability, and the people assent, saying the Amen; and the elements over which thanks have been given are distributed, and everyone partakes; and they are sent through the deacons to those who are not present.

And the wealthy who so desire give what they wish, as each chooses; and what is collected is deposited with the president. He helps orphans and widows, and those who through sickness or any other cause are in need, and those in prison, and strangers sojourning among us; in a word, he takes care of all those who are in need.

And we all assemble together on Sunday, because it is the first day, on which God transformed darkness and matter, and made the world; and Jesus Christ our Savior rose from the dead on that day; for they crucified him the day before Saturday; and the day after Saturday, which is Sunday, he appeared to his apostles and disciples, and taught them these things which we have presented to you also for your consideration. (Justin *Apol.* 1.67)

Several points are noteworthy, some of them capable of supplementation from other passages in Justin, particularly his description of the Eucharist celebrated after baptisms (*Apol.* 1.65):

(1) Sunday is the chosen day of the liturgical assembly as a commemoration and celebration of creation and of Christ's resurrection, the day marked by the risen Lord's appearances to his followers.

(2) The service includes reading from what became the NT ("the memoirs *[apomnēmoneumata]* of the apostles") as well as the OT ("the writings of the prophets"), and these Scriptures are expounded in a homily by the presider.

(3) The presider is not further identified, but if the practice follows that stipulated by Ignatius, it will be the bishop or someone appointed by him.

(4) Bread and wine are the food and drink, the wine probably being mixed with water (the word *krama*, "mixture," is used in *Apol.* 1.65).

(5) The presider improvises the eucharistic prayer ("to the best of his ability"), though probably according to certain guidelines. He "sends up praise and glory to the Father of all in the name of the Son and of the Holy Spirit" (*Apol.* 1.65). The people's assent ("Amen") is significant enough to be mentioned in both chapters.

(6) Only the baptized may participate in the Eucharist: "We call this food 'thanksgiving'; and no one may partake of it unless he is convinced of the truth of our teaching, and has been cleansed with the washing for forgiveness of sins and regeneration, and lives as Christ handed down" (*Apol.* 1.66). But it is important that Christians enjoy their privilege: "Everyone partakes, and [the bread and wine] are sent through deacons to those who are not present" (presumably the sick and the imprisoned are in mind).

(7) The reason for the restriction of communion to baptized believers and the purpose of their participation are spelled out in *Apology* 1.66:

For we do not receive these things as common bread or common drink; but just as our Savior Jesus Christ, being incarnate through the word of God, took flesh and blood for our salvation, so too we have been taught that the food over which thanks have been given by a word of prayer which is from him, (the food) from which our flesh and blood are fed by transformation, is both the flesh and blood of that incarnate Jesus. For the apostles in the records composed by them which are called Gospels, have handed down thus what was commanded of them: that Jesus took bread, gave thanks, and said, 'Do this for the remembrance of me; this is my body'; and likewise he took the cup, gave thanks, and said, 'This is my blood'; and gave to them alone.

(8) The material care for the needy recalls the situation in Acts 2:42-47. No *agapē* is mentioned by Justin, but later writers envisage that for some time the church continued a practice they saw as apostolic: "When the assembly *[synaxis]* was over, after the communion of the mysteries, they all went to a common banquet *[euōchia]*, the rich bringing their provisions with them, and the poor and destitute being invited by them, and all feasting in common. But afterwards this custom also became corrupt" (John Chrysostom *Homily 27 on 1 Corinthians*; Migne, *PG* 61.223-24).

4.2. Tertullian. In the late second century, Tertullian gives some account of the purposes for which Christians assemble ("The scriptures are read, psalms are sung, sermons are given, prayers are offered"; *De Anim.* 9); and to prayers, Scriptures and exhortations he adds, in the *Apologeticus*, the making of modest and voluntary contributions to the needy (*Apol.* 39.5-6). The fuller description contained in this latter writing includes also, by name, a love feast:

Our supper *(coena)* explains itself by its name, which is the Greek word for love [i.e., *agapē*]. Whatever it costs, our outlay in the name of piety is gain, for it is the needy that we benefit by that banquet *[refrigerio isto]*. . . . We taste first of prayer to God before we recline to food; we eat only what suffices hunger, and drink only what befits such as are chaste. We satisfy appetite as those who remember that even during the night they have to worship God. We converse as those who know that they are in the hearing of

their Lord. After water for washing the hands, and the lights have been brought in, everyone is called forward to sing praises to God, either from the Holy Scriptures or of his own composing. And this is a proof of the measure of the drinking. As we began, so the feast is concluded with prayer. We depart not like a pack of ruffians, nor in gangs of vagabonds, nor to break out into licentiousness, but with as much regard for our modesty and chastity as if we had been taking in a moral lesson rather than a supper. (Tertullian *Apol.* 39.16-19)

Here there is nothing specifically eucharistic, but in other writings Tertullian makes reference to what can only be the sacramental Eucharist: for example, "the sacrament of the Eucharist *[eucharistiae sacramentum]*" (*De Cor.* 3; *Marc.* 4.34); "the sacrament of the bread and the cup *[panis et calicis sacramentum]*" (*Marc.* 5.8); "the body of the Lord *[corpus domini]*" (*De Idol.* 7; *De Orat.* 19). There is no clear indication as to how this Eucharist was liturgically or ritually related to the assemblies in which the Scriptures, psalms, prayers, collection and *agapē* took place. His terms *convivium dominicum* (in *Ad Ux.* 2.4) and *coena Dei* (in *De Spect.* 13) could apply either to an *agapē* or to the Eucharist or to both.

5. Conclusion.

In the anonymous *Epistle to Diognetus*, dating perhaps from the middle of the second century, the author's description of the life of the Christians states: "They spread a common board *[trapezan koinēn paratithentai]*, though not a common bed [reading *koitēn]*" (*Diogn.* 5.7). Pictorial testimony to the importance of the common meal is borne by the frequency of table scenes in the mural paintings of the Christian catacombs, where loaves and fishes are also a recurrent motif. It is impossible to know whether the reference is to *agapē* or to Eucharist. In NT times the behavior of the participants at the meals varies from the idyllic to the problematic to the reprehensible. In the second and third centuries, apologists defend the community against accusations of debauchery and cannibalism by explaining the charitable nature of the love feast and the sacramental character of the memorial of the Lord under bread and wine. By the late fourth century we find Augustine and other African bishops and synods prohibiting the *agapē* on account of revelry (e.g.,

Augustine *Ep.* 22, to Aurelius; Migne, *PL* 33.90-92). At the same time, under the imperial establishment of Christianity, there sets in the decline from the regular participation in eucharistic communion that had been, according to Ignatius of Antioch and Justin Martyr, a hallmark of membership in the church.

See also BAPTISM; DEATH OF CHRIST; TABLE FELLOWSHIP; WORSHIP.

DLNTD: FOOD, FOOD LAWS, TABLE FELLOWSHIP; LITURGICAL ELEMENTS; LORD'S DAY; SACRIFICE, OFFERINGS, GIFTS.

BIBLIOGRAPHY. A. Bouley, *From Freedom to Formula: The Evolution of the Eucharistic Prayer from Oral Improvisation to Written Texts* (Washington, DC: The Catholic University of America, 1981); O. Cullmann, "The Meaning of the Lord's Supper in Primitive Christianity," in *Essays on the Lord's Supper,* ed. O. Cullmann and F. J. Leenhardt (ESW 1; Richmond, VA: John Knox, 1958); G. Dix, *The Shape of the Liturgy* (London: Dacre Press/A. & C. Black, 1945); A. B. du Toit, *Der Aspekt der Freude im urchristlichen Abendmahl* (Winterthur: Keller, 1965); P. F. Esler, *Community and Gospel in Luke-Acts* (SNTSMS 57; Cambridge: Cambridge University Press, 1987); J. L. Espinel Marcos, *La Eucaristia del Nuevo Testamento* (Salamanca: San Esteban, 1980); A. J. B. Higgins, *The Lord's Supper in the New Testament* (SBT 6; London: SCM, 1952); R. C. D. Jasper and G. J. Cuming, *Prayers of the Eucharist: Early and Reformed* (3d ed.; New York: Pueblo, 1987); J. Jeremias, *The Eucharistic Words of Jesus* (New York: Scribner's, 1966); A. A. Just, *The Ongoing Feast: Table Fellowship and Eschatology at Emmaus* (Collegeville, MN.: Liturgical Press, 1993); J. F. Keating, *The Agape and the Eucharist in the Early Church* (London: Methuen, 1901); H.-J. Klauck, *Herrenmahl und hellenistischer Kult* (Münster: Aschendorff, 1982); J. Kodell, *The Eucharist in the New Testament* (Wilmington, DE: Michael Glazier, 1988); J. Koenig, *The Feast of the World's Redemption* (Harrisburg, PA: Trinity Press International, 2000); X. Léon-Dufour, *Sharing the Eucharistic Bread: The Witness of the New Testament* (Mahwah, NJ: Paulist, 1987); H. Lietzmann, *Mass and Lord's Supper* (Leiden: E. J. Brill, 1953, 1979); I. H. Marshall, *Last Supper and Lord's Supper* (Grand Rapids: Eerdmans, 1981); P. H. Menoud, "Les Actes des apôtres et l'eucharistie," in *Jésus-Christ et la foi* (Neuchâtel: Delachaux & Niestlé, 1975) 63-76; B. Reicke, *Diakonie, Festfreude und Zelos in Verbindung mit der altchristlichen Agapenfeier* (Uppsala: Lundequistska Bokhandeln, 1948); idem, "Die Mahlzeit mit Paulus auf den Wellen des Mittelmeeres Act. 27, 33-38, " *TZ* 4 (1948) 401-10; J. Reumann, *The Supper of the Lord: The New Testament, Ecumenical Dialogues and Faith and Order on Eucharist* (Philadelphia: Fortress, 1985); H. Riesenfeld, "Sabbat et jour du Seigneur," in *New Testament Essays,* ed. A. J. B. Higgins (Manchester: Manchester University Press, 1959) 210-17; W. Rordorf et al., *The Eucharist of the Early Christians* (New York: Pueblo, 1978); M. H. Shepherd, *The Pascal Liturgy and the Apocalypse* (ESW 6; Richmond, VA: John Knox, 1960); G. Wainwright, *Eucharist and Eschatology* (London: Epworth, 1971; New York: Oxford University Press, 1981); J. Wanke, *Beobachtungen zum Eucharistieverständnis des Lukas auf Grund der lukanischen Mahlberichte* (ETS 8; Leipzig: St. Benno-Verlag, 1973); L. Wehr, *Arznei der Unsterblichkeit: Die Eucharistie bei Ignatius von Antiochien und im Johannesevangelium* (NTAbh n.s. 18; Münster: Aschendorff, 1987); R. Williamson, "The Eucharist and the Epistle to the Hebrews," *NTS* 21 (1975) 300-312.

G. Wainwright

LOVE ETHIC. *See* ETHICS.

LOVE FEAST. *See* LORD'S SUPPER II.

LUKE, GOSPEL OF

Luke's Gospel (*see* Gospel [Genre]) is the longest of the four Gospels. It is also the only Gospel with a sequel. By continuing his literary project into the *Acts of the Apostles, Luke introduces us not only to Jesus and his ministry but also to how that ministry relates to significant events in the early church. This enables Luke to discuss how God brought his salvation in Jesus, how the church preached Jesus and how it carried out its mission to Jew and Gentile.

Luke's two-part work highlights God's plan. It explains how Jews and Gentiles could become equals in a community planted by God, even though that community was rooted in a promise to Israel. More specifically, four issues would have posed problems for those who observed the church during Luke's time.

First was the question of salvation. How could Gentiles be included as God's people on an equal basis with Jews, extending even to matters like sharing *table fellowship and eliminating the necessity of circumcision?

Second was the apparent paradox of the claim that God's plan was at work while Jews, the most natural recipients for the gospel, were largely responding negatively. How could God's plan and God's messengers, especially Paul, meet so much hostility?

Third was the problem of explaining how the person and teaching of a crucified Jesus fit into this plan. How could Jesus continue to exercise a presence and represent the hope of God when he was physically absent? How could the church exalt an absent and slain figure and regard him as the center of God's work?

Fourth was the question of what it means to respond to Jesus. What is required, and what can one expect for such a commitment? How should men and women live until the day Jesus returns?

Luke's Gospel and its sequel deal with all of these issues. Luke's task is to reassure his readers of the place of Gentiles in the new community and the role of Jesus in God's plan (Lk 1:4).

1. Authorship, Origin and Purpose
2. Structure and Argument of Luke
3. Theology of Luke
4. Conclusion

1. Authorship, Origin and Purpose.

The Third Gospel and Acts do not directly identify their author. We are left to examine the internal and external evidence and draw the most plausible conclusion.

1.1. Internal Evidence for Authorship. Internal features draw our attention to two points. First, the author is not an eyewitness to most of the events in his two volumes, especially those tied to the ministry of Jesus (Lk 1:1-2). Rather, he has relied on his study of traditions derived from eyewitnesses and ministers of the Word (Lk 1:2-4). Second, he presents himself as a companion of Paul in the so-called we sections of Acts (Acts 16:10-17; 20:5-15; 21:1-18; 27:1—28:16). This latter feature, though its significance is debated, narrows the search for possible authors.

Interpreters have debated whether the "we" sections reflect the testimony of an eyewitness (Ellis) or are a literary device gauged to create the impression of an eyewitness (Haenchen and Vielhauer). Related to this issue is the question of how well the author of the Third Gospel knew Paul, since the we sections portray its author as a traveling companion of Paul. Those who reject such a connection attempt to compare the picture of Paul in Acts with the self-portrait of the Pauline epistles. They argue that the two pictures do not match in historical detail or in theological emphasis. In addition, the author fails to use the Pauline epistles to describe Paul's work and position (*see* Paul in Acts and Letters).

P. Vielhauer argues that the Lukan Paul is too dissimilar from Paul as we know him from his letters for the author of the Third Gospel to have been a companion of Paul. But J. Fitzmyer defends the connection, especially on the basis of the "we" sections in Acts, arguing that a creative literary device cannot explain how the units appear and disappear in such an arbitrary manner (Fitzmyer 1981, 1985). He also notes that several "sailing" references, which would be candidates for such literary insertions, lack them (Acts 13:4; 13:13; 14:26; 17:14; 18:18, 21; 20:1-2). He suggests that Luke may have been only a junior companion, in contrast to Irenaeus's famous claim that Luke was "inseparable" from Paul (Irenaeus *Haer.* 3.14.1). In addition, M. Goulder has suggested that Luke may have known and alluded to Paul's letter to Corinth and, to a lesser extent, the letter to Thessalonica. Others have defended the compatibility of the portraits of Paul found in Acts and the epistles (Bruce 1975/76). From the internal evidence of Luke-Acts it appears that the writer knew Paul and was at least a second-generation Christian.

1.2. External Evidence for Authorship. The Pauline letters name some of Paul's traveling companions: Mark, Aristarchus, Demas and Luke (Philem 24; Col 4:14). To this list one could add figures such as Timothy, Titus, Silas, Epaphras and Barnabas. Yet despite the wide selection of potential candidates, early-church tradition singles out one name as the author of these volumes: Luke. By A.D. 200 this tradition had become firmly fixed without any hint of contrary opinion.

Allusions to the Gospel appear early and exist in *1 Clement* 13.2; 48.4 (late 90s) and in *2 Clement* 13.4 (c. 150). In addition, a use of Jesus' teaching similar to that found in Luke 10:7 appears in 1 Timothy 5:18. Numerous texts comment on the authorship of Luke-Acts. Justin (c. 160) in *Dialogues* 103.19 speaks of Luke having written a "memoir of Jesus" and notes the author was a follower of Paul. The Muratorian Canon (c. 170-180) attributes the Gospel to Luke, a doctor, who is Paul's companion. Irenaeus (c. 175-195; *Haer.* 3.1.1; 3.14.1) attributes the Gospel to Luke, follower of Paul, and notes how the "we" sections suggest the connection. The so-called Anti-Marcionite Canon (c. 175) describes Luke as a native of Antioch in Syria (Acts 11:19-30; 13:1-3; 15:30-35), commenting that he lived to be eighty-four, was a doctor, was unmarried, wrote in Achaia and died in Boeotia. Tertullian (early third century; *Marc.* 4.2.2; 4.5.3) calls the Gospel a digest of Paul's gospel. Finally, Eusebius (early fourth century; *Hist. Eccl.* 3.4.2) mentions that Luke was from Antioch, a companion to Paul and the author of the Gospel and Acts. The unified voice of these traditions regarding authorship enhances the identification of the Gospel with Luke and makes Luke's connection to Paul very likely.

1.3. Luke the Man: A Gentile or a Semite? Most scholars see Luke as a Gentile, though they debate whether he is a pure Gentile or a non-Jewish Semite. An exception is Ellis, who argues that Luke was a Hellenistic-Jewish Christian. Ellis notes that Luke's knowledge of the OT is extensive; that Colossians 4:10-11, with its reference to those "not of the circumcision," suggests merely that he is a Hellenist; and that evidences of the use of Palestinian language show Luke's Jewish roots. But Ellis's reading of Colossians 4 is not the most natural one.

Fitzmyer suggests Luke was a Semite, arguing from the evidence of the Colossians 4 text; the shortened form of Luke's name, which was a Greek form of a Latin name; and the details of the church tradition, which place him in Antioch of Syria. This view is quite plausible.

However, most scholars have argued that Luke was a non-Semitic Gentile. They too argue from Colossians 4; note the allusion of Acts 1:19, which gives the Semitic name for Judas's field and then refers to it being in "their" language; and mention the attention given to Hellenistic locales and the concern for Gentiles. These latter two arguments are not strong, since one could attribute these same concerns to a Jew like Paul. In sum, Luke was very likely a Gentile, though it is unclear whether he was a Semite.

1.4. Sources of the Gospel and Its Tie to Acts. The problem of determining Luke's sources is intimately related to the complex issue known as the Synoptic Problem. Numerous approaches to this issue have been suggested, but in terms of Luke's Gospel alone, his preface demands a hypothesis that accounts for several sources.

1.4.1. Luke and the Synoptic Problem. While some scholars maintain the two-Gospel hypothesis, which supports the chronological priority of Matthew, followed by Luke and Mark (Farmer), today most scholars maintain some form of the two-document hypothesis (sometimes called the four-document hypothesis; *see* Synoptic Problem). This view argues for the priority of Mark and its use by Matthew and Luke, who also used a "sayings" source known as *Q. In addition, Matthew has special source material (M), while Luke has his special material (L). Thus the two common sources are Mark and Q, while L and M constituted separate sources for Luke and Matthew respectively. Luke would have used Mark, Q and L.

In all likelihood, Luke had access to Mark. Second, he had much special material (L). Third, he had traditions that also are reflected in Matthew, though often with some (even significant) divergence. In fact the Q material is so varied in character that some speak of a Matthean and a Lukan version of Q (see Marshall 1978, who often makes this distinction). This means that Q may not have been a fixed, written tradition, so much as a pool of widely circulating traditions. Given the amount of teaching and parables shared between Matthew and Luke, we cannot rule out the possibility that L and Q might have overlapped, with Matthew using Q and Luke using L. (Though we will use the symbol "Q," we note the potential ambiguity of this source or set of sources.)

1.4.2. Markan Material. A little over 410 verses of Luke, just short of 40 percent of the whole of Luke's Gospel, corresponds to Mark. Significantly, the Markan material tends to come in blocks, especially in sections that describe Jesus' ministry. This is one of the reasons Mark is seen as a fundamental source. A few texts related to Mark also have added to them material from Q or L (Lk 3:7-14; 3:23-38; 4:2b-13; 5:1-11; 19:1-10, 11-27; 22:28-33, 35-38; 23:6-16; 23:27-31; 23:39b-43; 23:47b-49).

1.4.3. Q Material. When one turns to Q material, the picture is more complex. Problematic texts involve those sayings or parables that one Gospel writer places in one location and the other Gospel writer includes in a very different location, those which one writer has together while another writer has separated or those in which an account is rendered in significantly different terms.

Almost 250 verses of material not found in Mark, or slightly over 20 percent of Luke's Gospel, might be called Q. The questionable Q texts tend to cluster in the central section of Luke's Gospel. This unit, Luke 9:51—19:44, is a combination of large amounts of L material with material having apparent parallels with Matthew. Given the amount of unique L material and the thematic character of some parts of this section, it is difficult to discern whether material is really from Q or from L.

Goulder has suggested a large amount of Lukan rewriting of Matthean material and has posited that little of L really comes from a source but is reflective of Lukan emphases and elaboration. The problem with this approach is it means that Luke handled Markan material in a manner completely distinct from the way in which he handled Matthew (or Q), since Luke did so little to change the substance of his Markan material.

1.4.4. L Material. The unique L material is represented in about 455 verses of Luke, or just over 40 percent of the entire Gospel. Clearly there is much in Luke that is not found in the other Synoptics. This material contains not only a unique portrait of Jesus' infancy but also many fresh sayings and *parables of Jesus.

Four *miracles are unique to Luke (Lk 7:11-17; 13:10-17; 14:1-6; 17:11-19). Several parables are indisputably unique to Luke (Lk 10:29-37; 11:5-8; 12:13-21; 15:8-10; 15:11-32; 16:1-8; 16:19-31; 18:1-8; 18:9-14). The ethical thrust of Luke's Gospel emerges in this material. An additional four parables having potential overlap with Matthew are cast in fresh light by Luke (Lk 12:39-46; 14:15-24; 15:1-7; 19:11-27). The breadth of topics in the Gospel and Luke's pastoral concern emerge in this unique or uniquely emphasized material.

1.4.5. The Third Gospel's Relationship with Acts. Luke structured his Gospel in anticipation of its sequel. This tie to Acts is seen in the repetition of the prologue (Lk 1:1-4; Acts 1:1; cf. Josephus *Ag. Ap.*). The relationship is seen also in the parallel themes that dominate the two volumes (Maddox; O'Toole). Jesus heals, and so do Peter and Paul. Jesus must travel to Jerusalem, while Paul must go to Rome. Jesus is slain by opposition, and so is Stephen. The account of the ascension also links the two volumes tightly together (Lk 24:49-53; Acts 1:1-11).

Efforts to note extensive parallels between Luke and Acts have generated scholarly discussion (Talbert). Some of these connections may be overdrawn and subtle, so each must be evalu-

ated on its own merit. But there is no doubt that Luke intends to show parallels between the time of Jesus and the time of his followers. From Luke's perspective, to understand the emergence of the church one must understand Jesus and the plan of God.

1.5. Luke as Historian. One other point emerges from an examination of Luke's use of sources. Although the issue of Luke as a historian has been strongly debated, it appears that Luke was careful with his material (*see* Gospels, Historical Reliability of).

By contrast, many scholars understand him to have handled his sources with great freedom, either for theological (Goulder, Haenchen, Dibelius) or sociological (Esler) reasons. Among the items under scrutiny are the association of Jesus' birth with a census by Quirinius (*see* Birth of Jesus), his chronological placement of the rebellion under Theudas, the authenticity of certain parables and sayings, the reality of the miracles, his portrait of the trials of Jesus (*see* Trial of Jesus), the details of Jesus' resurrection, the authenticity of the speeches in Acts, his portrayal of early church harmony, the uniqueness of the meeting with Cornelius, the reality of the Jerusalem council and his portrait of Paul. These details must be examined case by case, and judgments will inevitably vary. This is due not only to the complexity of the evidence but also to differences in the interpreters' philosophical worldviews. Nevertheless, where we can examine Luke's use of his sources, we find him trustworthy (Marshall 1988). Investigations into his descriptions of settings, customs and locales reveal a consistent concern for accuracy (Hengel, Hemer).

This does not mean Luke does not rearrange material for emphasis, summarize events in his own language or emphasize aspects of his received tradition. The Lukan speeches summarize and proclaim as well as report. Luke shows an interest in history and theology, twin emphases evidenced not only in his attention to the time sequence of events and teachings but also in their topical and theological relationship. He writes as a theologian and a pastor but is directed by the history that preceded him. To underemphasize any element in the Lukan enterprise, whether pastoral, theological or historical, is to underestimate the depth of his writing.

1.6. Purpose, Readership and Destination of Luke's Gospel. It is debated whether Theophilus

(Lk 1:4) was a Christian or was thinking of becoming one. Numerous possible intentions for Luke's writing the Gospel and its sequel have been suggested: (1) to explain why Jesus had not returned, (2) to provide a defense brief for Christianity, (3) to defend Paul before Rome, (4) to defend Paul before the community, (5) to combat gnosticism; (6) to evangelize, (7) to confirm the Word and the message of salvation, (8) to present a theodicy of God's faithfulness, (9) to provide a sociological legitimation of full fellowship for Gentiles and a defense of the new community. This plethora of credible suggestions is evidence of the complexity of the Lukan enterprise. Of all of these suggestions, those centering on God's role in salvation and the nature of the new community (views 7-9) are most likely to reflect Luke's most comprehensive agenda. An examination of the structure and theology of the Gospel will bear this out.

It is unlikely that Theophilus is only interested in becoming a Christian or is a Roman official who needs Christianity explained to him in order to accept it as a legitimate religion. Neither is Paul per se the object of defense. Too little of the Gospel deals with such legal and political concerns and too much focuses on issues other than evangelism. Paul's importance in the latter part of Acts is due especially to the mission and perspective he represents.

Luke 1:3-4 suggests that Theophilus had received some instruction. The amount of detail in Luke-Acts devoted to faithfulness, Jewish-Gentile relations and clinging to the hope of Jesus' return suggests a Gentile who was experiencing doubt about his association with the new community. This setting is also suggested in the controversy over table fellowship, the issue of Gentile inclusion, the detailed examples of how rejection was faced in the early church and the amount of attention devoted to ethical exhortation. Theophilus appears to be a man of rank (Lk 1:3). Having associated himself with the church, he is undergoing doubt whether he belongs in this racially mixed and heavily persecuted community. The Gospel openly includes Theophilus in the new community, calling him to remain faithful, committed and expectant, even in the midst of intense Jewish rejection.

Given the magnitude of Luke's effort, it seems clear that he did not write for Theophilus alone but for any who shared this tension. Any Gentile who felt out of place in an originally

Jewish movement would have recognized the reassurance Luke offers. Any Jew or Jewish Christian troubled by the lack of Jewish response to the gospel or the openness with which Gentiles were welcomed into it could see how God had given the nation multiple invitations to join in his renewed work. The Christian movement had not attempted to remove itself from Judaism; it had been forced out. This exclusion becomes clear in Acts, but Luke carefully details the seeds of opposition being sown in the official Jewish rejection of Jesus (Lk 9—13; 22—23). For Luke the new community extends its blessings broadly, true to Jesus' preaching (Lk 4:16-30; 5:30-32; 19:10; 24:44-47) and God's direction (Acts 10:34-43; 15:1-21; 22:6-11; 26:15-20).

1.7. Date. Several possibilities have been argued, but two factors set the outside limits for a possible date. The last event in Acts takes place in A.D. 62, thus establishing the earliest possible date for the completion of the two-volume work. On the other end, Irenaeus cites texts indisputably derived from Luke, thus setting the latest possible date as about 170 (*Haer.* 3.13.3; 3.15.1). Three possibilities present themselves.

1.7.1. Second Century. A date in the early to mid-second century has been argued on the basis of comparisons with material from Marcion, Josephus, Justin Martyr or the Pseudo-Clementines. But against this approach is the fact that the tone of Acts does not fit that of other letters of this period such as *1 Clement* (A.D. 95) and Ignatius (A.D. 117). In addition, it is hard to believe that such a late work would have ignored Paul's letters as much as Acts does. Finally, possible allusions in *1 Clement* to Acts 13:22 (*1 Clem.* 18.1); 20:35 (*1 Clem.* 2.1) and Acts 26 (*1 Clem.* 5.6-7) argue against this date. This factor also brings the upper limit for a date down to the mid-nineties.

1.7.2. After the Fall of Jerusalem. The most popular view is a date sometime after the fall of Jerusalem. The reasons set forth include the premise that Luke follows after Mark, which itself is a document of the sixties; the picture of Paul as a hero figure needed time to emerge; the portraits of churches like Ephesus require a period before the Domitian persecution of the mid-nineties; the Lukan apocalyptic discourse, with its description of siege and its focus on the city, presuppose the fall of Jerusalem and require a period after A.D. 70; the indications that Luke reflects a late, even "early Catholic," theology would place it toward the end of the first century.

Three of these arguments are not compelling in their force. It is not clear that Paul needed time to emerge as a hero. Evidence from his epistles agrees with Acts, suggesting that he was a central figure in the church who generated some following and controversy. The portrait of the churches that are not yet under Roman persecution can fit any time before Domitian or any time after Nero. The debate about early catholicism in Luke-Acts continues, but it is by no means apparent that the perspective of these volumes requires a late theology (Marshall 1988).

Two arguments have more substance. The suggestion that Luke follows Mark is likely. (Even if one thinks Matthew was written first, the problem remains.) But this argument creates no more difficulty for an early date than does the fact that the last event in Acts occurs in the early sixties. How long must Mark's Gospel have been in circulation before it could have served as a source for Luke?

The weightiest argument is that Luke's eschatological discourses (Lk 19:41-44; 21:20-24) assume a post-70 date. P. Esler has argued that the details of these discourses cannot be attributed simply to "what inevitably happens in war," because some of the features, such as building a circumvallation, the total destruction of the city or the marching off of all the captives were not the inevitable results of war. In so arguing, Esler has challenged C. H. Dodd's view that the language fits ancient military operations and parallels the LXX's descriptions of the sacking of Solomon's temple in 587 B.C. However, Esler has missed a key point of connection with the OT. The judgment exercised is directed toward covenant unfaithfulness. As such, Luke's picture of the total destruction of Jerusalem, including its siege and defeat, is what was to be expected of an act of God. There is no need to argue that the description of the fall of Jerusalem is language shaped in light of a past event.

The prediction of Jerusalem's fall is one that Jesus would have been capable of making solely on the basis of his knowledge of how God acts to judge covenant unfaithfulness. Luke has made no effort to update this Jesus tradition. He only clarifies that in the temple's collapse, the city is not spared either.

1.7.3. Before the Fall of Jerusalem. The third possibility is a date during the sixties. Arguments for this date include the picture in Acts that

Rome knows little about the Christian movement and is still uncertain about where it fits among the religions of the empire, which suggests a date in the sixties; the failure to note either the death of James (A.D. 62) and especially Paul (c. late 60s) would seem to indicate an earlier date; the silence about Jerusalem's destruction, even in settings where it could have been mentioned (e.g., Stephen's speech in Acts 6—7; Paul's trip to Jerusalem, Acts 21—23) is odd if the work was completed after 70; and the amount of uncertainty expressed about internal Gentile-Jewish relations fits a setting parallel to the Pauline epistles, which deal with similar tensions (Rom, Gal, 1 Cor 8—10).

This last argument is most significant and to date has not been thoroughly developed. Several aspects of Acts suggest that Luke was addressing the concerns of an earlier period. (1) It presupposes a racially mixed community in its attention to potentially offensive details about the law, table fellowship and other practices (Acts 6:1-6; 10-11, 15). (2) Its vigorous defense of the Gentile mission contrasts with the situation in the eighties when the Gentile character of the Christian movement was accepted. (3) It provides believers reassurance in the midst of intense Jewish pressure.

It is difficult to determine when in the sixties the account may have been written. Some argue that the ending of Acts indicates the date of completion. Others suggest that texts like Luke 11:49-51 presuppose the start of the struggle with Rome and suggest a date in the late sixties. The fact that Paul's death is not mentioned may be an indication that the work was completed in the early to mid-sixties rather than the latter third of the sixties. But the necessity for Luke to have received and incorporated Mark might suggest a date in the mid-sixties. Given that the Gospel would have preceded Acts, a mid-sixties date is slightly more likely. Luke might have left the end of Paul's career open-ended because that is where matters stood when he wrote.

2. Structure and Argument of Luke.
The Gospel may be viewed as follows, with the material devoted to Jesus' ministry being viewed geographically.

1. Introduction of John the Baptist and Jesus (Lk 1:1—2:52)

2. Preparation for Ministry: Anointed by God (Lk 3:1—4:13)

3. Galilean Ministry: The Revelation of Jesus (Lk 4:14—9:50)

4. Jerusalem Journey: Jewish Rejection and the New Way (Lk 9:51—19:44)

5. Jerusalem: The Innocent Slain and Raised (Lk 19:45—24:53)

2.1. Introduction of John the Baptist and Jesus (Lk 1:1—2:52). Following a preface in which Luke explains his task, the author launches into a comparison of John and Jesus, showing how both represent the fulfillment of promises made by God. *John the Baptist is like Elijah (Lk 1:17), but Jesus has Davidic roles to fulfill and possesses a unique supernatural origin (Lk 1:31-35). John is forerunner, but Jesus is fulfillment. Everything in Luke 1—2 points to the superiority of Jesus.

Jesus' birth (*see* Birth of Jesus) takes place in humble circumstances, but all the figures surrounding his birth are pious and responsive to the hope of God. Only the word of Simeon to Mary gives an ominous ring (Lk 2:34-35). Jesus is the salvation of God (Lk 2:30), but in the midst of hope is the reality that fulfillment comes mixed with pain. This section, dominated by OT allusions, opens the Gospel with the twin themes of fulfillment and divine direction. These themes continue throughout the Gospel.

2.2. Preparation for Ministry: Anointed by God (Lk 3:1—4:13). John and Jesus remain side by side as Jesus prepares for his ministry. John is the "One who goes before" (Is 40:3-5; Lk 3:1-6), while Jesus is the "One who comes" (Lk 3:15-17). John baptizes Jesus, but the main feature of the baptism is one of two heavenly testimonies to Jesus (Lk 3:21-22; cf. Lk 9:28-36). The heavenly testimony calls Jesus the "beloved Son in whom I am well pleased." This fusion of Isaiah 42 and Psalm 2 marks out Jesus as a regal, prophetic figure who as chosen servant of God brings God's revelation and salvation. The universal character of Jesus' relationship to humanity is highlighted in the list of his ancestors (Lk 3:23-38). He is "Son of Adam, Son of God." His first actions are to overcome temptations from Satan, something Adam had failed to do (Lk 4:1-13). So the section shows Jesus as God's anointed, a representative of humanity and one who is faithful to God.

2.3. Galilean Ministry: The Revelation of Jesus (Lk 4:14—9:50). This section focuses primarily on the teaching of Jesus and his miraculous works. Major teaching blocks include his syna-gogue declaration of the fulfillment of God's promise (Lk 4:16-30) and the Sermon on the Plain (Lk 6:17-49; *see* Sermon on the Mount). Both passages are unique to Luke. The synagogue speech represents Jesus' understanding of his mission, while the sermon represents his fundamental ethic presented without the concerns related to Jewish tradition (cf. Matthew's Sermon on the Mount).

In the synagogue speech (Lk 4:16-30) Jesus raises the note of fulfillment through his appeal to Isaiah 61:1 and Isaiah 58:6. God's promised anointing is fulfilled "today," which in the Lukan context looks back to Jesus' anointing with the Spirit (Lk 3). Here is a reminder of his regal role. He will bring salvation to all those in need: the poor, the blind and the captive.

In Luke 4—9, Luke juxtaposes Jesus' work with the gathering of disciples and the rising opposition. Jesus' ability to bring salvation is pictured in a series of miracles (Lk 4:31-44), while disciples are called to be fishers of humankind (Lk 5:1-11). The first hints of official opposition arise with the miracles suggesting his divine-like authority: the Son of man claims to forgive sins and heals on the sabbath (Lk 5:12-26). Levi, a hated tax collector, is called (Lk 5:27-28), and four controversies emerge, one of which involves the type of company Jesus keeps, while the others center on the sabbath (Lk 5:29—6:11). Jesus gives a mission statement: his task is to call the sick to repentance (Lk 5:32).

Subsequently, through a series of pericopae focusing on Jesus' calling of the disciples, his teaching and miracles, Luke concentrates on the question Who is Jesus? and the appropriate response to him. John the Baptist, perhaps doubtful because of Jesus' style of ministry, wonders if Jesus is the coming one. Jesus replies that his eschatological works of healing and preaching affirm his status (Lk 7:18-35; cf. Is 29:18; 35:5-6; 61:1). One is to respond to the Word, though many obstacles prevent response (Lk 8:4-15). Jesus' miraculous work over nature (Lk 8:22-25), over demons (Lk 8:26-39), and over disease and death (Lk 8:40-56) shows the extent of his authority and pictures his eschatological work. This section moves from teaching and demonstration of authority to confession and call to discipleship. Peter confesses Jesus to be the Christ (Lk 9:18-20). Now Jesus explains what kind of Messiah he will be: he will suffer (Lk 9:21-22). Those who follow him must have total commitment in order to survive the path of rejection that comes with following Jesus (Lk 9:23-27).

The second heavenly testimony to Jesus comes at the transfiguration (Lk 9:28-36). The divine voice repeats the endorsement made at the baptism with one additional note: "listen to him" (Deut 18:15). Jesus is a second Moses who marks out a new way.

2.4. Jerusalem Journey: Jewish Rejection and the New Way (Lk 9:51—19:44). This part of the Gospel is particularly Lukan, with more than 44 percent consisting of material found only in Luke. There is a high concentration of teaching and parable. In fact there are seventeen parables, fifteen of which are unique to Luke. The journey to Jerusalem is not a chronological, straight line, since Jesus in Luke 10:38-42 is near Jerusalem, while later in the section he is back in the north. Rather, it is a journey in time within the context of the necessity of God's plan. Journey notes punctuate the section (Lk 9:51; 13:22; 17:11; 18:31; 19:28, 44). Jesus travels to meet his appointed destiny in Jerusalem (Lk 13:31-35).

The thrust of this section is that Jesus initiates a new way to follow God. Its theme is "listen to him." Since his way is distinct from that promulgated by the Jewish leadership, this section discusses how Jesus' teaching relates to the Judaism of his day. The difference provokes great opposition, a theme that dominates Luke 9—13. All are invited to follow the new way, but some refuse. The seeds of discontent that will lead to Jesus' death are manifest.

The section starts with the disciples learning the basics of discipleship: mission, commitment, love for God, love for one's neighbor, devotion to Jesus and his teaching, and to prayer (Lk 9:51—11:13). In a critical section Jesus calls on the crowd to discern the nature of the times (Lk 12:49—14:24). Israel is turning away, and the time for it to respond, without facing judgment, is short (Lk 13:1-9, 31-35). Nevertheless, blessing will still come.

From this point on, most of the journey section concerns discipleship. In the face of such rejection disciples will need absolute commitment (Lk 14:25-35). Their mission is to seek the lost just as God does (Lk 15:1-32). God rejoices in finding lost sinners, so Jesus' call is to pursue them. Discipleship expresses itself in service to others, so it is generous with resources (Lk 16:1-31). In fact, one is accountable to God for how they are used. Though false teaching is a threat,

it is overcome with forgiveness of the brother or sister, deep faith and service (Lk 17:1-10). The disciple is to live in hope of the king's return. Then the promise of the kingdom, already inaugurated and present, will be consummated (Lk 17:11—18:8). His coming will be a time of severe judgment but also vindication. The disciple is to live humbly, giving all and trusting all to the Father (Lk 18:9-30).

Now Jesus turns to Jerusalem, renewing the display of his authority as he predicts his suffering and heals as the Son of David (Lk 18:32-43). Zacchaeus epitomizes the transformed sinner and rich man (Lk 19:1-10). He is a picture of the mission of Jesus; he is the lost one who is sought and saved (Lk 19:10). The parable of the pounds shows the need for faithfulness and the reality that the disciple as well as the nation is accountable to the king (Lk 19:11-27). Jesus enters Jerusalem as a king, but the leaders reject the claim (Lk 19:28-40). Jesus warns the nation that it has failed to respond to God's promise and faces judgment (Lk 19:41-44). Though opposition brings Jesus to his death, it brings far more tragic consequences on the nation of Israel.

2.5. Jerusalem: The Innocent Slain and Raised (Lk 19:45—24:53). In his concluding section Luke explains how Jesus died, why apparent defeat became victory and how God revealed who Jesus was. In addition, the task of disciples in light of God's acts becomes clear. Luke mixes fresh material with that found in the other Gospels.

The final battles in Jesus' earthly ministry occur here, recalling earlier confrontations in Luke 11—13. Jesus cleanses the temple (*see* Temple Cleansing), thereby indicating his displeasure with official Judaism (Lk 19:45-48). The leaders fail to embarrass Jesus in various controversies concerning his authority (Lk 20:1-8, 20-26, 27-40).

In the light of the nation's refusal to accept him, Jesus predicts the fall of the temple and of Jerusalem, events that are a foretaste of the end (Lk 21:5-38). The fall of Jerusalem will be a terrible time for the nation, but it is not yet the end, when the Son of man returns on the clouds with authority to redeem his people (Dan 7:13-14). Disciples are to watch and be faithful.

Luke 22—23 pictures Jesus' movement toward the cross. Jesus is betrayed and yet is innocent, but his death will initiate the new covenant and will be a sacrifice on behalf of others (Lk 22:1-20; *see* Last Supper). In his last discourse

Jesus announces the betrayal, points out that greatness is in service, appoints eleven to authority, predicts Peter's denials and warns of rejection (Lk 22:21-38). Jesus is in control even as his death approaches.

As Jesus prays, and thereby exemplifies for his disciples the trust they must have in the midst of rejection, he is betrayed and arrested (Lk 22:47-53). The trials center again on who Jesus is. The answer comes in Luke 22:69. Jesus "from now on" will be shown to be the exalted Lord who is seated with authority at the side of God. Messiahship means lordship (*see* Lord), authority over God's plan and salvation. Ironically and unwittingly, the Jewish leaders help bring these things to pass. Jesus is on trial, or so it seems; but in fact he is the judge (Lk 22:54-71; *see* Trial of Jesus).

But it is not the leaders alone who are guilty. As Pilate and Herod debate what to do about Jesus, the people are given the final choice (Lk 23:1-25). Despite Pilate's repeated protestations of innocence and Herod's similar reaction, the people ask for Jesus to be slain and Barabbas to be freed. Luke portrays Jesus' death with OT allusions picturing Jesus as an innocent sufferer who relies on God (Lk 23:26-56; Ps 22:8-9; 19; 69:22; 31:6; *see* Death of Christ).

Luke 24 presents three scenes of resurrection and vindication. Luke 24:1-12 announces the empty tomb, but the news of the excited women is greeted with skepticism. The angelic announcement directed the women to recall the predictions of suffering. The experience of the Emmaus disciples pictures the reversal the resurrection brought to the despairing disciples (Lk 24:13-36). Two disciples mourn the departure of the prophet of Israel who might have redeemed the nation. But Scripture and the revelation of Jesus show that God had a plan that included Jesus' death. God has indeed raised Jesus, vindicating Jesus and the divine strategy. Despair turns to joy when they understand the nature of God's plan and Jesus' role in it, a major note in Luke.

Just as Luke 1—2 opened with the hope of OT promises being fulfilled, so Luke 24 returns to the central theme of Jesus the Messiah as the fulfillment of God's plan and promise (Lk 24:36-53). Jesus' final Gospel appearance yields a commission, a plan and a promise. Reminding them yet again that Scripture foretold the suffering and exaltation of Messiah, Jesus tells the disciples that they are called as witnesses to preach repentance. The plan is to go to all the nations, starting from Jerusalem. The promise is the "promise of the Father," the coming of the Spirit (Lk 24:49). As the Baptist had promised (Lk 3:15-17), so it has come to pass.

3. Theology of Luke.

Our brief survey will outline the major strands and connections that show Luke's theological and pastoral concerns.

3.1. The God of Design and Concern: The Plan. At the center of Luke's concern to reassure Theophilus is the detailed discussion of God's plan. Luke emphasizes and enunciates this theme more than the other Synoptic Evangelists.

3.1.1. The Plan. A number of uniquely Lukan passages bring out this theme (Lk 1:14-17, 31-35, 46-55, 68-79; 2:9-14, 30-32, 34-35; 4:16-30; 13:31-35; 24:44-49), with one key text overlapping with the other Gospels (the inquiry of John the Baptist, Lk 7:18-35). In addition, Luke utilizes the suffering Son of man texts, a few of which are unique to him (Lk 9:22, 44; 17:25 [L]; 18:31-33 [L]; 22:22 [L]; 24:7 [L]). Acts also highlights the details of the plan (Acts 2:23; 4:27-28; 13:32-39; 24:14-15; 26:22-23). The major elements of the plan are the career of Jesus, the hope of the spiritually humble and needy, the offer of God's blessings, the coming of the new era, along with the suffering which comes to Jesus and the division which comes to Israel.

3.1.2. The Plan's Structure: Promise and Fulfillment. Supporting the theme of God's plan is the note of promise and fulfillment running throughout the Gospel and Acts, especially as it relates to the Scriptures. The appeal to the OT concentrates on three areas: christology, Israelite rejection/Gentile inclusion and justice in the end. The latter two themes are more prominent in Acts, as "the Way" (Acts 24:14) is presented and defended from various charges, particularly as it is represented by the efforts of Paul among the Gentiles. Nonetheless, the theme of Gentiles and non-Jews responding to the gospel, while Israel stumbles, is present in numerous texts (Lk 2:34; 3:4-6; 4:25-27; 7:1-10; 10:25-37; 11:49-51; 13:7-9, 23-30, 31-35; 14:16-24; 17:12-19; 19:41-44).

3.1.3. "Today" Texts. Various themes enhance the plan. The "today" passages show the immediate availability of promise (Lk 2:11; 4:21; 5:26; 13:32-33; 19:5, 9; 19:42; 23:42-43).

3.1.4. John the Baptist. John the Baptist is the

bridge stretching between the old era of promise and the new era of inauguration (Lk 1—2; esp. Lk 1:76-79; 3:4-6; 7:24-35; 16:16). Luke 7 is instructive here. John is the forerunner of Malachi's prediction, but beyond that John represents the greatest prophet of the old era (Lk 7:27). Nonetheless, the new era is so great that the lowest member of the kingdom is higher than the greatest prophet of the old (Lk 7:28). This passage presents the basic Lukan structure of the plan: the era of promise-expectation followed by the era of inauguration. The church's message of the gospel and Jesus' teaching on the end serve to clarify the timing and structure of the newly inaugurated era. The plan still has future elements to be realized (Lk 17:21-37; 21:5-38), but the basic turning point has come. So the second portion of the plan also has a subdivision, even though all of that era represents fulfillment. Those subdivisions are inauguration (Acts 2:14-40) and consummation (Acts 3:14-26), the "already and not yet."

3.1.5. Mission Statements. Other elements of the plan are seen in Jesus' mission statements where he outlines his task. Jesus has come to preach good news to those in need (Lk 4:18-19), to heal the sick (Lk 5:30-32) and to be heard, whether the message is communicated through him or his representatives (Lk 10:16-20). He has come to seek and save the lost (Lk 19:10). This career is reviewed in Acts 10:36-43.

3.1.6. Geographic Progression. The geographic progression also reveals the movement's growth under the plan. The basic outline of the Gospel from Galilee to Jerusalem shows this growth, as does the necessity of Paul's going to Rome in Acts (Acts 1:8; 19:21; 23:11).

3.1.7. "It Is Necessary." Many passages declare that "it is necessary" *(dei)* that something occur. In fact, 40 of 101 NT uses of *dei* occur in Luke-Acts. Jesus must be in his Father's house (Lk 2:49), he must preach the kingdom (Lk 4:43), and he must heal the woman tormented by Satan (Lk 13:16). Certain events must precede the end (Lk 17:25; 21:9). Jesus must be numbered among the transgressors (Lk 22:37). The Christ must suffer and be raised, and repentance for the forgiveness of sins must be preached. The necessity of the Son of man's suffering, already noted, is also a part of this theme. Acts continues to strike this chord (Acts 1:16; 3:21; 9:6, 16; 13:46; 14:22; 19:21; 23:11; 25:10; 27:24).

3.2. Christology and Salvation: Messiah-Lord,

His Teaching and Work, and the Blessings of the Plan Through Him. Jesus and deliverance stand at the center of the plan. Who is Jesus? What does he bring? How do we know he is God's chosen? These are central christological questions for Luke. In addition, there is the call to respond.

3.2.1. Christology: Messiah-Servant-Prophet to Lord. Luke carefully develops his portrait of Jesus, though this feature is not universally recognized. Some say that Luke's christology is more of a patchwork than a unified whole; it is a collection of a variety of traditions, "the most variegated in the NT" (Evans).

It is clear from a reading of Luke 1—2 that Jesus is introduced as a regal figure. The announcement to Mary and the remarks of Zechariah make the Davidic connection explicit (Lk 1:31-33, 69). In addition, the anointing of Jesus at his baptism appeals to a pair of OT passages, Psalm 2 and Isaiah 42, which bring together regal-prophetic images. The images of servant and prophet likewise come together in Simeon's remarks (Lk 2:30-35), but the idea of a leader-prophet is a dominant christological theme in Luke.

Jesus' sermon at Nazareth (Lk 4:16-30) likewise joins regal and prophetic motifs. Though Elijah and Elisha are elicited as parallels to Jesus' situation (Lk 4:25-27), for Luke the anointing of Isaiah 61:1 is in the aorist tense and looks back to the baptism with its regal-prophetic motifs. Even when the people recognize that Jesus is a prophet (Lk 7:16; 9:7-9, 19), it is qualified by Peter's confession that he is the Christ (Lk 9:20) and Jesus' further explanation that his work will inevitably be that of a suffering Son of man. In a tradition unique to his Gospel, Luke even relates Jesus' title as "Son" to Jesus' messianic role (Lk 4:41). The regal-prophetic mix reappears with the voice from heaven at the transfiguration (Lk 9:35; cf. Ps 2:7; Is 42:1; Deut 18:15).

When Jesus is presented as a prophet he is a leader-prophet, one like Moses, so that even here the note of rule and direction is fundamental. In short, Luke regards Jesus' messianic role as pivotal for christology. Jesus' messiahship needs clarification and careful definition, and it is placed beside other expectations, but his messiahship is a category around which the other concepts revolve.

The prophetic motif plays an important role in the woes against the scribes (Lk 11:47-51), the mourning for Jerusalem (Lk 13:31-35) and the conversation on the Emmaus road (Lk 24:19, 21). Yet even in texts like Luke 13:31-35, the appeal to Psalm 118 ("Blessed is he who comes in the name of the Lord") expands in the Lukan presentation into a regal allusion (cf. the triumphal entry, Lk 19:38), since "the one who comes" is for Luke fundamentally an eschatological and messianic deliverer (Lk 3:15-18; 7:22-23; 19:38). Again, on the Emmaus road the disciples mix their perception of Jesus as a prophet with the hope that Jesus might "redeem" the nation (Lk 24:21). For Luke the deliverer-regal imagery is never very far from the prophetic.

Luke develops the elevated status of Jesus as he draws his Gospel to a close. While the authority of the Son of man is introduced as early as Luke 5:24, this theme and his status as Lord become the focus of dispute in Luke 20:41-44, Luke 21:27 and Luke 22:69 (cf. Acts 2:30-36; 10:35). The significance of Psalm 110 and its reference to Jesus is of signal importance to Luke. Following a three-step progression that bridges Luke and Acts, the issue is raised (Lk 20:41-44), Jesus responds (Lk 22:69) and the message of Jesus' authority as Lord is proclaimed (Acts 2:30-36). The Synoptics share the first two texts, but Luke's sequence, ending with the detailed exposition of Acts 2, shows the importance of this dispute. Luke 22:69 makes it clear that "from now on" Jesus—the Messiah-Servant-Prophet—will exercise his authority as Lord at the right hand of God.

This is not to say that Luke does not use other titles alongside this basic portrait of Jesus' messiahship. Jesus is Savior, or one who delivers (Lk 2:11; 1:70-75; 2:30-32; Acts 5:31; 13:23-25), as well as Son of David (Lk 1:27, 32, 69; 2:4, 11; 18:38-39; Acts 2:25-31; 15:16) or King (Lk 19:38). He is the Son, who relates to God as Father, even as divine testimony declares (Lk 1:35; 2:49; 3:22; 3:38; 4:3, 9, 41; 9:35; 10:21-22). Yet he is also Son of Adam, who grows in grace (Lk 3:38; 2:40, 52; Acts 2:22). He is compared with Jonah (Lk 11:29-32, message of repentance) and Solomon (message of wisdom, Lk 11:29-32). As Son of man he not only suffers and is exalted but also ministers (e.g., Lk 5:24; 19:10). Another frequent title is Teacher (Lk 7:40; 8:49; 9:38; 10:25; 11:45; 12:13; 18:18; 19:39; 20:21, 28, 39; 21:7; 22:11). The portrait of Jesus is variegated, but it is organized as well. Jesus bears authority as well as promise.

3.2.2. The Kingdom in Jesus' Teaching and Work.

The Messiah brings the kingdom of God, God's rule manifested on earth (Lk 4:18, 43; 7:22; 8:1; 9:6; 10:11). Here is a complex theme in Luke's Gospel. The kingdom is present now, but it comes in the future. It includes earthly hope and yet has spiritual dimensions.

The kingdom as present reality is associated with Jesus' authority, well illustrated as he exercises his command over evil spiritual forces. This also reveals the spiritual character of the kingdom. Jesus can speak of the kingdom as "near" (Lk 10:9). And as the seventy (-two) disciples exercise authority over demons, he sees Satan fall (Lk 10:18-19). In fact, Jesus says that if he casts out demons by the finger of God, then the kingdom has come upon those present (Lk 11:20-23). Asked by Pharisees when the kingdom would come, he could say the kingdom is "among you" (Lk 17:21). The king, in one parable, departs "to receive a kingdom" (Lk 19:14-15). In his hearing before the council of Jewish elders, Luke makes it clear that from that point on Jesus will be at God's side (Lk 22:69). Finally, the appeal to Psalm 110 depicts the presence of a regal authority, ruling from the side of God.

But the kingdom is also future (see Eschatology). Luke 17:22-37 describes the judgment preceding its arrival. Here is the "not yet" aspect—the kingdom in consummation. Luke 21:5-38 also describes the "time of redemption." Here the imagery of the day of the Lord abounds as evil is decisively judged. Within the space of a few verses (Lk 21:25-27), allusion is made to a range of OT passages suggesting the cosmic disturbance associated with the day of the Lord (Is 13:10; Ezek 32:7; Joel 2:30-31; Ps 46:2-3; 65:7; Is 24:19 [LXX]; Hag 2:6, 21; Dan 7:13). OT hope and expectation is not dead, as Acts 3:20-21 also makes clear. Jesus will return to fulfill the rest of the promise, a promise that will show itself visibly on earth to all humanity, as well as in the eternal benefits given to believers.

So the kingdom is earthly; that is, Jesus will rule as a Davidide on the earth and bring about total deliverance as he executes his sovereignty over all. Such hope is most strongly expressed in the narrative and songs of Luke 1:32-33, 46-55, 69-75. The eschatological discourses and the remarks of Acts 1:11 and Acts 3:18-21 show that the future hope has not been absorbed in the theme of present inauguration but remains alive, connected to its OT roots. God is faithful and brings all of his promises to fruition.

But spiritual deliverance is also his. Zechariah's song (Lk 1:78-79) makes this clear by speaking of Jesus as the rising sun who shines on those in darkness and leads them into the path of peace. The promise of the Spirit (Lk 3:15-18; 24:49; Acts 1:8) and the hope of forgiveness of sins (Lk 24:47) also belong to this emphasis. Jesus' authority over demons and other forces show that he is able to bring such promises to pass.

Those who are most obviously subjects of the kingdom and benefit from its presence are the disciples (Lk 18:26-30). All of salvation's benefits are theirs. But potential beneficiaries also exist. Anyone who wishes to enter in is a potential beneficiary (Lk 13:23-30; 14:16-24; see 3.3.1 below). But there are also unwilling subjects who are accountable to him now and one day will face the reality of his rule (Lk 19:27; 21:24-27; Acts 3:20-26; 10:42; 17:30-31).

3.2.3. The Spirit. The Spirit as a central figure of redemption is viewed first as the one promised (Lk 3:15-18) and then as a testifier and enabler of Jesus (Lk 3:22; 4:16-18). Later the full promise finally comes and the Spirit falls on all believers (Acts 2:1-13). Acts 2:14-21 (cf. Joel 2:28-32) explains the event as the sign that the new era has come. The Spirit is the gift of the Father through the exalted Son. He is power or enablement from on high (Lk 24:49; Acts 2:30-36; 10:44-47; 11:15-16; 15:8). The Spirit's presence is evidence that Jesus is raised and that Jesus directs his new community from the right hand of God. Luke reassures Theophilus that though the Messiah died and is seemingly absent, he is pres-ent in the gift and presence of the Spirit he has sent (*see* Holy Spirit).

3.2.4. The Resurrection/Ascension. The key event at the center of God's provision of salvation is the resurrection/ascension. Among the Gospel writers, only Luke mentions and develops the ascension, an event that for him provides the link between Luke 24 and Acts 1 (its significance being further explained in Acts 2:23-24, 30-36; 3:14-15, 21; 4:10-12; 5:30; 17:31). A risen Savior is one who can rule and consummate his promise. He is the one who can forgive and signify forgiveness by bestowing blessings (Acts 2:21; 4:12; 10:43). Moreover, the ongoing reality of Jesus' authority is demonstrated in the activity of those who minister "in his name" (Acts 2:38; 3:6, 16; 4:6, 10; 8:11-12; 9:27-28;

10:48; 19:5). In short, the ascension shows that he is Lord.

3.2.5. Salvation in Jesus' Teaching and Work. Jesus brings promise and salvation. Salvation involves sharing in hope, experiencing the kingdom, tasting forgiveness and partaking in the enabling power of the Spirit. Just as Jesus' person reveals the character and ability of the bringer of blessing, his teaching and work explain and signify the desired results. Jesus was a teacher and wonder worker (Lk 4:14-15, 31-32, 44; 6:17-19; 7:22). As we have seen, his teaching focused on the offer of the kingdom. This opportunity is pictured as the release and healing of Jubilee (Lk 4:16-21; cf. Lev 25:10; Is 61:1-2), but it also includes a call to ethical honor reflecting the experience of blessing (Lk 6:20-49). The parables show the same dual concern. A few parables deal with God's plan (Lk 13:6-9, 23-30; 14:16-24; 20:9-18), and in some of these a meal or feast scene is employed. The feast displays not only the joy of salvation but also the table fellowship of the future, a reality in which the community can now partake without racial distinction (Acts 10—11; 15). There is to be unity among the people of God.

Beyond unity stands a call to an ethical way of life. The life of relationship with God, engagement in mission and ethical honor is to be dominated by love, humility, service and righteousness—the subject of most of the other parables (Lk 10:25-37; 11:5-8; 14:1-12; 12:36-49; 15:1-32; 16:1-8, 19-31; 18:1-8; 19:11-27). Jesus did not come just to rescue people for heaven but to have them come to know the transforming activity of God in their life. It is to this God that they are accountable. This is why commitment is so prominent in Jesus' teaching (Lk 9:21-26, 57-62; 14:25-34; 18:18-30).

3.2.6. The Cross. Thus far in our survey of Jesus' work and teaching, little has been said about the cross (*see* Death of Christ [Gospels]). This is because Luke gives Jesus' ascension and exaltation more prominence than he does the cross. Some scholars have gone so far as to deny that Luke ascribed a saving function to Jesus' death, arguing instead that Luke portrays Jesus as an example in his death. While Luke does employ exemplary elements in his narrative of Jesus' death, and thereby addresses the needs of a church under pressure, to view Jesus' death solely as an ethical example is to miss other Lukan emphases.

Though the cross is less prominent for Luke than for Paul, its significance moves beyond an ethical or historical function and occupies an important theological position in Luke's teaching. Jesus, as was noted in examining Luke 22—23, is the righteous sufferer. But two texts cast light on the meaning of his death. Luke 22:20 makes it clear that Jesus' death inaugurates the new covenant with God, while Acts 20:28 argues that the church was, in Paul's words, "purchased" with Jesus' blood. Covenant inauguration and a soteriological transaction take place in Jesus' death. Two other images reinforce this view. The substitution of Jesus for Barabbas portrays the fact that Jesus took the place of the sinner, an exchange made all the more poignant when Luke notes that the people "with one voice" shared in this unrighteous choice (Lk 23:18-25). Jesus' offer of paradise to the thief as they die together (Lk 23:43) shows that Jesus, despite his death, can offer life.

3.2.7. Miracles. Not only the resurrection but also the *miracles, in their display of the arrival of the new era, authenticate Jesus' role in the divine plan (Lk 7:22; Acts 2:22-24). In fact, the scope of Jesus' works of healing shows the breadth of Jesus' authority. He exorcises evil spirits, heals those generally called "sick" and cures a variety of specific conditions: a flow of blood, a withered hand, blindness, deafness, paralysis, epilepsy, leprosy, dropsy and fever. He resuscitates the dead and exercises power over nature. Jesus' work testifies to his person and task. The fact that Acts records the disciples continuing to perform some of these works shows that authentication continues (Acts 3:6, 16) and that Jesus' authority continues as well.

3.2.8. Jesus and Salvation. Luke's portrayal of Jesus is fundamentally concerned with his authority and then with the promise he brings. Jesus' saving work inaugurates the kingdom, delivers the sinner, forgives sin, provides the Spirit, calls for a committed and faithful life lived in the context of hope in the future consummation, and makes all accountable to God's plan. In fact, all the covenant promises of God are inaugurated by Jesus. Luke sets forth the Abrahamic promise of blessing to the peoples of the earth as realized in Jesus (Acts 3:22-26). So is the Davidic hope (Lk 1:31-33, 69; 22:69; Acts 2:25-36) and the hope of the Spirit associated with the coming of the new era and new covenant (Lk 22:20; Acts 2:14-21). Theophilus should be reassured that Jesus can and does deliver on such promises. But who makes up the new community and what is it to be? How does christology relate to the content and task of the new community for Luke?

3.3. The New Community. Within Luke's Gospel the new community formed around Jesus is not really an organized entity. There are the Twelve and the seventy(-two), but beyond these basic groups there is no formal structure. Rather, those who will become the new community of Acts are called disciples. In the Gospel this group is mostly Jewish, but there are a few hints that the benefits of Jesus' program can extend to Samaritans and non-Jews (Lk 3:4-6; 4:22-30; 7:1-10; 13:23-30; 14:16-24; 17:12-19; 20:15-16; 24:47). This multiracial theme becomes prominent in Acts, but more important to the Gospel is the fact that the message goes out to those on the fringe of society.

3.3.1. The Beneficiaries of Salvation. Luke focuses on the reception of the gospel message by outcasts: the poor, sinners and tax collectors. In addition, women come in for special treatment. For Luke, the poor are materially *and* spiritually impoverished. The spiritual element is clearly indicated in Luke 1:50-53 and Luke 6:20-23, where the poor and humble are related to God's covenant promise or to the treatment of God's prophets. The poor or rejected are mentioned in several texts (Lk 1:46-55; 4:18; 6:20-23; 7:22; 10:21-22; 14:13, 21-24; 16:19-31; 21:1-4). Sinners are also highlighted as the special objects of the gospel (Lk 5:27-32; 7:28, 30, 34, 36-50; 15:1-2; 19:7). Tax collectors, culturally understood as betrayers of their nation, are still noted as potential beneficiaries as well (Lk 5:27-32; 7:34; 18:9-14; 19:1-10).

Finally, Luke features the responsiveness of women (Lk 7:36-50; 8:1-3; 8:48; 10:38-42; 13:10-17; 24:1-12). Often it is not just a woman but a widow who is cited, since she represented the most vulnerable status within society (Lk 2:37; 4:25-26; 7:12; 18:3, 5; 20:47; 21:2-3). Whether in parable or by example, these women show that they are sensitive to the message of Jesus. Though on the fringes of first-century society, they are in the middle of Luke's story. Often they are paired with men (Lk 2:25-28; 4:25-27; 8:40-56; 11:31-32; 13:18-21; 15:4-10; 17:34-35; Acts 21:9-10), a feature suggesting that the gospel is for both genders, as well as all races and social strata.

In short, the makeup of the new community is to know no boundaries. The good news is available to all, but society's weak and vulnerable are often most suited to respond to its message of hope and reliance on God.

3.3.2. The Terms and Pictures of Response. Luke uses three terms to describe response to the message: "repent," "turn" and "faith." The term translated "repent" is rooted in the OT (Lk 11:32) word *šûb*, "to turn around." The Greek term *metanoeō* has to do with a change of mind. The point is that repentance involves a reorientation of perspective, a fresh point of view. When dealing with God's plan it entails seeing that plan in a new way and orienting oneself to it. For Luke the fruit of repentance expresses itself concretely. The particular expressions of repentance are illustrated in some material unique to Luke in which the Baptist replies to those who inquire, "What should we do then?" Repentance expresses itself in everyday life, especially in how men and women treat each other (Lk 3:7-14).

Four pictures of repentance stand out. Luke 5:31-32 develops the observation that those who respond to Jesus come as those seeking a physician. Just as a sick patient in need of medical attention is totally reliant on the skill of the doctor, so the one who repents comes to God as if for healing. Luke 15:17-21 portrays the repentance of the prodigal and indicates how a repentant heart makes no claims, being totally reliant on the mercy of the one entreated. Repentance involves a changed attitude toward sin, but the change primarily comes from recognizing that only God and his mercy can provide relief. Luke indicates the crucial role of repentance when, at the end of his Gospel, he summarizes the essence of the good news: "Repentance and forgiveness of sins will be preached in his name" (Lk 24:47). The parable of the tax collector who in the temple cries out "God, have mercy on me, a sinner" (Lk 18:9-14) demonstrates the repentant response, though the term *repentance* is not used (cf. Lk 19:1-10).

The word *turn* (Gk *epistrephō*), while rarely used in the Gospel (Lk 1:17; 17:4; 22:32), becomes prominent in Acts, where it pictures the fundamental change of direction that accompanies repentance (Acts 3:19; 9:35; 11:21; 14:15; 15:19; 26:18-20; 28:27).

"Faith" (Gk n. *pistis*, v. *pisteuō*) also describes actions that bring credit and benefit to the bearer. Faith for Luke expresses itself concretely, whether as the faith of the paralytic's friends (Lk 5:20), the faith of the centurion (Lk 7:9) or the faith of the sinful woman who anoints Jesus (Lk 7:47-50). The Samaritan leper and the blind man also have faith that Jesus can restore them to wholeness (Lk 17:19; 18:42). Faith believes, and so it acts. In Acts, those who responded were some times called "believers" to show the centrality of faith (Acts 5:14; 15:5). In short, faith is the recognition and persuasion that God had something to offer through Jesus—forgiveness and the blessings of promise—that one must actively embrace. Such people "call on the name of the Lord" (Acts 2:21; cf. Rom 10:13).

3.3.3. The Blessings of the New Community. Luke's Gospel employs various terms for the blessings on offer: forgiveness or release (Lk 1:77 and Lk 3:3 as tied to John the Baptist; Lk 4:18; 24:47; Acts 2:38; 5:31; 10:43; 13:38); life (Lk 10:25; 12:16, 21; 18:29-30); peace (Lk 1:79; 2:14; 10:5-6; Acts 10:36); and, as we have seen, the kingdom and the Spirit.

3.3.4. The Opponents of Salvation. In contrast to those who respond positively to the gospel, Luke identifies spiritual and human opponents of the new community. At the transcendent level the spiritual forces of evil stand resistant though powerless before the plan (Lk 4:1-13, 33-37; 8:26-39; 9:1; 10:1-12, 18; 11:14-26; 22:3). For Luke, God's struggle involves not only reclaiming humanity's devotion but also reversing the effects of the presence of evil forces.

On a human level the opponents are primarily the scribes and Pharisees. When Jesus claims authority to forgive sin and challenges the sabbath tradition (Lk 5:24; 6:1-11), their opposition becomes a regular feature of the narrative. The roots of this rejection go back to their refusal to respond to John the Baptist (Lk 7:29-30). In three instances where Jesus is seated at table with Pharisees, they are warned (Lk 7:36-50; 11:37-52; 14:1-24). In the journey section as well as in Jerusalem, it is the leaders who are at the center of Jesus' condemnation (Lk 11:37-52; 12:1; 14:1-4; 15:1-10; 16:14-15; 19:45-47; 20:45-47). While the few exceptions, such as Jairus (Lk 8:41) and Joseph of Arimathea (Lk 23:50-53), catch our attention, for the most part Luke sees the leaders standing opposed to Jesus and plotting his demise (Lk 6:11; 11:53-54; 20:19; 22:3-6, 31; 23:3-5).

The crowd's reaction to Jesus is mixed. They

have interest in Jesus, and yet their response to him is superficial and sometimes fickle. The transition occurs in Luke 9—13. Jesus offers many warnings to them in the crucial section of Luke 12:49—14:24. In addition he rebukes "this generation" in Luke 11:29-32, condemns various cities of Israel in Luke 10:13-16 and tells a few parables about the failings of the nation (Lk 13:6-9; 20:9-19). The crowd's eventual response typifies the general response of most in Israel. Their rejection brings warnings of judgment, but such warnings do not represent Jesus' anger. They picture prophetic regret, as when Jesus weeps for those he warns (Lk 19:41-44). In the end, the crowd shares in the responsibility for Jesus' death when they ask for Barabbas (Lk 23:18-25). At the final hour, on the road to the cross, Jesus delivers a prophetic message of judgment to the daughters of Jerusalem and their children (Lk 23:27-31).

The response of most of Israel is a tragic one. It was in line for blessing but has missed its day of visitation and now awaits judgment (Lk 19:44). Now it is the "time of the Gentiles" (Lk 21:24). Israel has not lost its place in God's plan, for the faithfulness of God's promise to it cannot be denied, but it is "desolate" until it acknowledges this Messiah (Lk 13:34-35; Acts 3:14-21). In Acts the nation is warned to change its mind about Jesus and repent (Acts 2:22-24; 5:27-32).

Luke has been accused of anti-Semitism (Sanders), but this is a harsh judgment. Luke is arguing that it was the new community that was persecuted by those who failed to respond to the message of hope. Jesus and the disciples consistently offered the gospel to the nation and suffered while making the offer. The disciples did not create the division and did not bring violence to the Jewish community. Those who responded to Jesus were forced out, as the persecution of Acts shows and as Jesus predicted (Lk 12:1-12). The new community was not anti-Jewish; it was pro-promise. Consistently in Acts the new community suffers great risk as it returns to the synagogue to offer hope to the nation. Such enemies were to be loved and prayed for, as Jesus made clear (Lk 6:27-36; 23:34; Acts 7:60).

3.3.5. A Source of Tension: The Issue of the Law. One of the primary causes of tension in the Gospel and in Acts is the new community's relationship to the law. At the same time, Luke's precise understanding of this issue has been a subject of ongoing debate in Lukan scholarship.

Some scholars have argued that Luke displays a very conservative attitude toward the law, conservative in the sense that the new community's existence and conduct is in keeping with the law. There is but one Israel, one covenant, one law and the Jewish-Christian community in particular, along with its associate Gentile Christians, are the true heirs of the OT promise (Jervell). More recently, Esler has argued that Luke maintains this position—untenable as it may be—out of the sociological motivation of legitimating the community.

Others (Wilson) suggest that Luke is ambivalent toward the law. Luke sees Jewish Christians keeping the law, while Gentiles are free from some of its demands (circumcision) and bound by others (idols, meat offered to idols, immorality).

Finally, it has been argued that Luke understands the law to be part of the old era but portrays the church as it slowly came to recognize that truth (Blomberg). Law was not regarded as binding, though the missionary praxis of the early church allowed its observance in matters where issues central to the new faith were not at stake. The latter view is well supported by the Gospel and Acts.

The law or its associated traditions, especially sabbath regulations (Lk 6:1-11, esp. Lk 6:4), are a central source of irritation in Luke's Gospel. It is important to note that the sabbath challenge comes after Jesus' proclamation that new wine must come in new wineskins and that those who like the old will not try the new (Lk 5:33-39). This remark was part of a dispute centered around Jesus' neglect of Jewish traditions related to cleansing. Jesus challenged the law, at least in terms of its first-century Jewish interpretation, and Luke regards this challenge as the catalyst for Jewish opposition.

Acts throws further light on Luke's understanding of law. The understanding that all foods are clean, the full table fellowship with the Gentiles and the refusal to circumcise Gentiles (Acts 10—11, 15) are vivid examples of the early church's rejection of some elements of the law and the tradition that grew out of it. Luke's clear recounting of early Christians being charged by Jews with denying Mosaic customs, as well as his description of the early community's struggle with the issue of keeping the law, shows an awareness of the ferment within the early community (Lk 13:10-17; 14:2-6; 23:2; Acts 6:11, 13; 15:1-5; 21:28; 25:8). Luke's understanding is that the law pointed to the promise (Lk 16:16; 24:43-47; Acts 26:4-23; cf. Acts 3:14-26, which cites Torah texts exclusively). While he openly describes the differences within the early church, the prevailing argument is that God gave evidence of his acceptance of Gentiles by pouring out the Spirit before they were circumcised (Acts 11:15-18) and gave a vision to Peter that commanded open table fellowship (Acts 10:1-33). Luke portrays taking vows and observing other elements of the law as optional, sometimes necessary for unity, but not to be confused with what is necessary for salvation (Acts 15:22-29; 21:17-26).

Luke's resolution is that Jewish Christians are free to observe such customs as long as they do not force Gentiles to do so. This distinction is crucial and not unlike the solution of Paul in Romans 13—14. On this view the law cannot be held as binding. The many texts in Acts dealing with this issue reveal some of the concerns Luke wishes to address. They also presuppose a racially mixed community struggling with its relationship to its ancient roots. Luke is honest about these differences and forthright about the complex solution and compromise that emerged out of the concern for the church's unity. Moreover, his account indicates his endorsement of the resolution.

3.3.6. The Pressure and the Plan. In the face of opposition, disciples were called to a strong commitment to Jesus, for it was inevitable that with a decision for Jesus, opposition would come. Indications of division and opposition come early in the Gospel (Lk 2:34-35) and are constant throughout (Lk 8:14-15; 9:21-23, 61-62; 12:4-9, 22-34; 22:35-38). The disciples are pictured as shrinking back from responding boldly, as Peter's denial exemplifies. But in Acts the presence of the Spirit enables them to become consistently bold so that they truly exemplify the steadfastness and faithfulness that should mark a disciple.

The exhortation to steadfast discipleship surely reveals a facet of the Gospel's origin. For Theophilus and other Gentiles, the pressure of conflict was the occasion for reassurance that they not only belonged in the new community but also that they would partake of God's plan and blessing.

3.4. The New Community: Mission, Ethics and Accountability. The new community had not cho-

sen to separate itself from Judaism. It had presented itself as the hope of the nation but had been forced to become distinct. However, its new experience of the Spirit set it apart from the Jewish community. The Spirit not only evidenced the presence of the ascended Lord in their midst (Acts 2:14-40; 11:15) but also enabled the new community to live by the principles Jesus had laid down—a life distinct from contemporary norms of piety and current cultural standards (Lk 12:1; 14:1-14; 22:24-27).

3.4.1. Faith, Dependence and Commitment. The community was called to a fundamental reorientation toward God, expressed as faith and repentance (see 3.3.2 above). This attitude of trust, so clearly indicated in Jesus' preaching, parables and encounters with individuals, not only begins the walk with God but also sustains it (Lk 5:31-32; 15:17-21; with Lk 12:22-32). Disciples are to be totally focused on their walk with God. The path is difficult and requires self-reflection, total commitment, daily dedication and cross bearing (Lk 9:23; 9:57-62; 14:25-35).

The community was called to mission. While Acts details the early missionary activity of the community, the call to preach repentance and forgiveness to all nations, beginning at Jerusalem, is spelled out in the Gospel (Lk 24:47). The parables of Luke 15:1-32 reflect the focus on the lost, as do the clear statements of Luke 5:31-32 and Luke 19:10. Jesus' disciples were to follow him in reaching out to others.

3.4.2. Love for God and One's Neighbor. Devotion to God is highlighted in Luke 11:1-13, a devotion expressing itself in dependent prayer. Devotion to Jesus is shown by Mary's choice to sit at Jesus' feet, absorbing his teaching and presence (Lk 10:38-42). In addition, the care of one's neighbor is also an expression of such devotion (Lk 10:25-37). In fact, what Jesus demonstrated, he calls his disciples to be: neighbors to all, without distinction of race or class.

3.4.3. Prayer. Jesus models and encourages prayer (Lk 11:1-13; 18:1-8; 18:9-14; 22:40). Prayer does not demand; it requests, humbly relying on God's mercy and will. It voices trust in God's care and provision of basic needs. It recognizes that in seeking forgiveness, men and women should be prepared to give it as well. And it looks with expectation to the eschatological consummation of God's kingdom.

3.4.4. Persistence and Watchfulness. Under the pressure of conflict and opposition, the community is to remain steadfast and faithful (Lk 8:13-15; 9:23; 18:8; 21:19; see 3.3.6. above). The church in Acts often exemplifies such persistence (Acts 4:23-31). This attitude is related in turn to patience and expectation. Disciples are to fear God, not mortals (Lk 12:1-12), recognizing that the Lord will return and that they are responsible to him (Lk 12:35-48; 19:11-27; 18:8). Like the seed on good soil, they hear the Word, cling to it and persevere to bear fruit (Lk 8:15).

It is here that eschatology makes its impact in Luke. Jesus represents the present and the future. The promises that remain unrealized will be fulfilled (Lk 17:22-37; 21:5-38). The judgment of Jerusalem is the guarantee and picture of the final judgment. The return will be a horrific period in which unbelieving humanity is severely judged and believers will suffer at the hands of unbelievers. Luke emphasizes that the coming of the Son of man places responsibility on disciples to be faithful and on all humanity to respond to the gospel. In Acts he will note that Jesus is the "judge of the living and the dead" (Acts 10:42; 17:31). While Luke indicates that the time of the return is unknown, it will come suddenly, and the disciples must be prepared (Lk 12:35-40).

3.4.5. Overcoming Hindrances to Discipleship. The Lukan view of wealth has been a topic of recent scholarly investigation (*see* Riches and Poverty). Warnings and parables about riches abound in Luke (Lk 8:14; 12:13-21; 16:1-15, 19-31; 18:18-25). But positive examples also exist (Lk 8:1-3; 19:1-10; 21:1-4; Acts 4:36-37).

Scholars have debated whether Luke decries wealth per se. Zacchaeus, who generously gives half of his possessions to the poor and repays those he has wronged, hardly seems to have divested himself of every asset. His example suggests that the issue is not what a person has but what a person does with his or her possessions. The disciples are said to have "left all" for Jesus (Lk 18:28-30), a remark that includes family as well as resources. Yet later in the Gospel, under the pressure of Jesus' arrest, they exhibit fear and denial. The issue with resources, as with the other demands of discipleship, is not the perfection of the response or the parting with one's last coin but the fundamental orientation of the response. Disciples are called to recognize that all of life belongs to God and comes from his hand. The rich man would not even consider Jesus' request to sell all, while the disciples and

Zacchaeus had entered into the process. In sum, Luke warns that the hindrances to discipleship include not only confidence in resources but also the fear of others' opinions (Lk 12:1-12) and the cares of life (Lk 8:14).

4. Conclusion.
Luke's Gospel is pastoral, theological and historical. The reality of God's plan affects how individuals see themselves and the community to which they belong. Old barriers of race are removed. New hope abounds. The message of Jesus is one of hope and transformation. Anyone, Jew or Gentile, can belong to the new community. At the center is Jesus, the promised Messiah-Lord, who sits at God's right hand exercising authority from above. He will return one day, and all are accountable to him. His life, ministry and resurrection/ascension show he is worthy of trust. Just as he has inaugurated the fulfillment of God's promises, so he will bring them to completion. In the meantime, being a disciple is not easy, but it is full of rich blessing that transcends anything else this life can offer. This is the reassurance about salvation that Luke offers to Theophilus and others like him.

See also ACTS OF THE APOSTLES; JOHN, GOSPEL OF; MARK, GOSPEL OF; MATTHEW, GOSPEL OF.

DJG: "L" TRADITION; MARY'S SONG; SIMEON'S SONG; ZECHARIAH'S SONG.

BIBLIOGRAPHY. **Commentaries:** D. L. Bock, *Luke 1:1—9:50* (BECNT; Grand Rapids: Baker, 1994; an expanded version of this article appears as the introduction of this commentary); idem, *Luke 9:51—24:53* (BECNT; Grand Rapids: Baker, 1996); F. Danker, *Jesus and the New Age* (rev. ed.; Philadelphia: Fortress: 1988); E. E. Ellis, *The Gospel of Luke* (NCB; 2d ed.; Grand Rapids: Eerdmans, 1974); C. A. Evans, *Luke* (NIBC; Peabody, MA: Hendrickson, 1990); C. F. Evans, *Saint Luke* (TPINTC; Philadelphia: Trinity Press International, 1990); J. Fitzmyer, *The Gospel According to Luke* (2 vols.; AB 28, 28a; Garden City, NY: Doubleday, 1981, 1985); J. B. Green, *The Gospel of Luke* (NICNT; Grand Rapids: Eerdmans, 1997); I. H. Marshall, *Commentary on Luke* (NIGTC; Grand Rapids: Eerdmans, 1978); L. Morris, *Luke* (rev. ed.; TNTC; Grand Rapids: Eerdmans, 1983); J. Nolland, *Luke 1—9:20* (WBC; Dallas: Word, 1989); idem, *Luke 9:21—18* (WBC; Dallas: Word, 1993); idem, *Luke 19—24* (WBC; Dallas: Word, 1993). **Studies:** C. Blomberg, "The Law in Luke-Acts,"

JSNT 22 (1984) 53-80; D. L. Bock, *Proclamation from Prophecy and Pattern: Lucan Old Testament Christology* (JSNTSup 12; Sheffield: Sheffield Academic Press, 1987); F. F. Bruce, "Is the Paul of Acts the Real Paul?" *BJRL* 58 (1975/76) 282-305; H. J. Cadbury, *The Making of Luke-Acts* (2d ed.; London: SPCK, 1958); R. Cassidy, *Jesus, Politics and Society: A Study of Luke's Gospel* (Maryknoll, NY: Orbis, 1978); H. Conzelmann, *The Theology of St. Luke* (New York: Harper & Row, 1960); M. Dibelius, *Studies in the Acts of the Apostles,* ed. H. Greeven (New York: Charles Scribner's Sons, 1956); C. H. Dodd, "The Fall of Jerusalem and the Abomination of Desolation," *JRS* 37 (1947) 47-54; P. F. Esler, *Community and Gospel in Luke-Acts* (SNTMS 57; Cambridge: Cambridge University Press, 1987); W. Farmer, *Luke the Theologian: Aspects of His Teaching* (London: Geoffrey Chapman, 1989); E. Franklin, *Christ the Lord: A Study in the Purpose and Theology of Luke-Acts* (London: SPCK, 1975); M. Goulder, *Luke: A New Paradigm* (JSNTSup 20; 2 vols.; Sheffield: Sheffield Academic Press, 1989); E. Haenchen, *The Acts of the Apostles* (Philadelphia: Westminster, 1971); C. J. Hemer, *The Book of Acts in the Setting of Hellenistic History,* ed. C. Gempf (WUNT 49; Tübingen: Mohr Siebeck, 1989); M. Hengel, *Acts and the History of Earliest Christianity* (Philadelphia: Fortress, 1980); J. Jervell, *Luke and the People of God* (Minneapolis: Augsburg, 1972); R. Maddox, *The Purpose of Luke-Acts* (FRLANT 126; Göttingen: Vandenhoeck & Ruprecht, 1982); I. H. Marshall, *Luke: Historian and Theologian* (3d ed.; Downers Grove, IL: InterVarsity Press, 1988); R. F. O'Toole, *The Unity of Luke's Theology: An Analysis of Luke-Acts* (Wilmington, DE: Michael Glazier, 1984); J. T. Sanders, *The Jews in Luke-Acts* (Philadelphia: Fortress, 1987); C. H. Talbert, *Literary Patterns, Theological Themes and the Genre of Luke-Acts* (SBLMS 20; Missoula, MT: Scholars Press, 1974); R. C. Tannehill, *The Narrative Unity of Luke-Acts: A Literary Interpretation,* vol. 1: *The Gospel According to Luke* (FF; Philadelphia: Fortress, 1986); D. L. Tiede, *Prophecy and History in Luke-Acts* (Philadelphia: Fortress, 1980); P. Vielhauer, "On the 'Paulinism' of Acts," in *Studies in Luke-Acts,* ed. L. E. Keck and J. L. Martyn (London: SPCK, 1966) 33-50; S. G. Wilson, *Luke and the Law* (SNTSMS 50; Cambridge: Cambridge University Press, 1983).

D. L. Bock

M, N

M TRADITION. *See* SYNOPTIC PROBLEM.

MACCABEES, BOOKS OF. *See* APOCRYPHA AND PSEUDEPIGRAPHA.

MAGI. *See* BIRTH OF JESUS.

MAGIC. *See* RELIGIONS, GRECO-ROMAN.

MAN OF LAWLESSNESS. *See* ESCHATOLOGY II.

MEN AND WOMEN. *See* WOMEN.

MARANATHA. *See* ESCHATOLOGY II; LORD I; WORSHIP.

MARK, GOSPEL OF

The Gospel according to Mark stands as one of the foundational documents of the Christian faith. Eclipsed for centuries as an abridged edition of the Gospels according to Matthew and Luke, this Gospel was rediscovered for its own sake in the nineteenth-century quests for the historical Jesus and rose to prominence in twentieth-century Gospel studies. Indeed, the number of written works on Mark over the past forty to fifty years certainly rivals and may well surpass that written on Matthew and Luke combined.

1. Introduction
2. Mark's Narrative Pattern
3. Mark's Theology
4. Mark's Ending
5. Mark's Purpose

1. Introduction.

The Gospel according to Mark has raised numerous questions about its significance, authorship, date, place, audience and genre. Some of these issues are more critical than others for a proper understanding of Mark as a Gospel. Certainly the rediscovery of Mark as a narrative text to be viewed as a whole rather than merely a collection of its constituent parts has done much to recapture the dynamic thrust of the thought of this Gospel.

1.1. The Significance of Mark. How does this Gospel serve as a fundamental document for the Christian faith? Two contemporary NT scholars—one in Germany and one in the United States—have attributed the story of Jesus found in all the Gospels to the creativity of the original author of this (B. Mack, *Myth of Innocence,* 1989) or its underlying (W. Schmithals, *Das Evangelium nach Markus,* 1979) Gospel. Mack goes so far as to attribute the "origin for the Christian view of Christian origins" to the genius of the writer of Mark's Gospel (Mack, 357). These extreme views stem in part from the broad consensus that Mark's Gospel was indeed the first Gospel and provided the literary basis for the Gospels of Matthew and Luke.

Did Mark create the story of Jesus for the church (e.g., Schmithals, Mack) or did Mark create the literary genre of the Gospel (the broad consensus of NT scholars) for the church? In other words, just how foundational was Mark's Gospel as a document in the early church?

1.1.1. "The Beginning of the Gospel." The first clue to the role of Mark's Gospel comes in the opening words: "the beginning of the gospel of Jesus Messiah [Christ], Son of God" (Mk 1:1). Taken as an independent heading, as found in most English translations, and punctuated with a period at the end, the meaning of "beginning" and "gospel" can be and has been debated. For example, does "beginning" refer to the Gospel as the "beginning (either as a point in time or as the rudimentary elements) of the gospel" or the "beginning section" of the Gospel of Mark—

that is, the opening verses? Does "gospel" then refer to the message preached by Jesus Messiah, Son of God (cf. Mk 1:14); the message about Jesus Messiah, Son of God as understood and proclaimed by the church; or the story that follows as the Gospel?

The common Jewish formula for a scriptural citation, "as has been written by," in Mark 1:2 removes these ambiguities. This citation formula always links what has gone before to what follows. It never begins a citation by referring forward to what follows (e.g., Mk 1:4-8). Therefore, instead of placing a period at the end of "the beginning of the gospel of Jesus Messiah, Son of God" (Mk 1:1), one must continue with "as has been written by the prophet Isaiah" (Mk 1:1-2). Accordingly, Mark opens by stating that "the beginning" (Mk 1:1) occurs "as has been written by the prophet Isaiah." References—explicit or oblique—to Isaiah in the following verses set the boundaries of "the beginning of the gospel . . . as has been written by Isaiah the prophet." Since Isaiah's promise underlies the coming of John the Baptizer (Mk 1:4-8, cf. Is 40; see John the Baptist), the baptism of Jesus (Mk 1:9-11, cf. Is 42:1; 61:1), Jesus' presence in the wilderness (Mk 1:12-13, cf. Is 40; 65) and Jesus' proclamation of the "gospel of God" (Mk 1:14-15, cf. Is 52:7; 61:1-2), 1:1-15 represents the "beginning of the gospel about Jesus Messiah, Son of God as has been written by the prophet Isaiah" (Mk 1:1-2).

If Mark 1:1-15 represents the "beginning of the gospel" in keeping with Isaiah's promise, then Mark 1:16—16:8 must be the rest of the "gospel concerning Jesus Messiah, Son of God" for which Mark 1:1-15 is "the beginning." In other words, Mark refers to the following story about Jesus, which begins with the coming of John the Baptizer (Mk 1:4) and runs to the statement of the women's fear (Mk 16:8), as the "gospel." The story about Jesus is the "gospel."

1.1.2. Gospel Narrative Before Mark. Paul's "gospel" by contrast does not focus on the story of the earthly ministry of Jesus. Rather, it centers on statements about what God has done through Jesus' death (see Death of Christ) on the cross and subsequent resurrection. Even the earliest Christian traditional expression of the "gospel" consists of creedal statements. "For I handed on to you [as tradition] of first importance what I in turn had received [as tradition]: 'that Christ died for our sins in accordance with

the Scriptures, and that he was buried, and that he was raised on the third day in accordance with the scriptures, and that he appeared to Cephas, then to the Twelve' " (1 Cor 15:2-5). Did Mark then, in place of this propositional gospel encapsulated in pithy formulas, create what he calls "the gospel about Jesus Messiah, Son of God," a gospel in narrative form that focused more on Jesus' earthly ministry as well as his death?

The answer may well lie in Peter's sermon in Acts 10:34-43. One finds in this brief summary the basic structure of the narrative Gospel common to Matthew, Mark, Luke and John. It sets the beginning with John the Baptizer and runs through Jesus' ministry, death, resurrection and appearance to witnesses, all accompanied by allusions to the Scriptures. In fact, the reference to preaching the gospel of peace of Isaiah 52:7 stands as the backdrop for this Gospel (cf. Acts 10:36).

If the outline of Peter's sermon in Acts 10:34-43 reflects an early Christian form of preaching the gospel, then Mark would not have been the one to create the gospel in narrative form in contrast to the more propositional statement of the gospel as found in Paul. The use of the narrative or story of Jesus as the "gospel," consisting of traditional materials about his work and words, would antedate Mark's writing of his Gospel and preclude his having created the actual form and content of his Gospel. Where does Mark's foundational contribution then lie?

1.1.3. Gospel Narrative as Literary Form. On the basis of intensive comparative studies, a scholarly consensus affirms that Mark's Gospel was the earliest of the four Gospels. Furthermore, Matthew and Luke appear to have used Mark's Gospel as the basis for writing their own. Luke 1:1 notes that "many have undertaken to set down an orderly account [a "narrative"] of the events that have been fulfilled among us." Whether John's Gospel was familiar with this or all three Synoptic Gospels is still debated, but his narrative does follow the same broad structure of Mark and the summary in Acts 10:34-43. Therefore, Mark's foundational contribution lies in his having written the first of our four Gospels. He was the first to put into written or literary form a narrative of Jesus as the Gospel. Finally, Mark was the first and only Evangelist to refer to his narrative as "the gospel" (Mk 1:1; cf. Lk 1:1; Mt 1:1). By the turn of the first century, the four Gospels were known as "the Gospel according to Matthew, Mark, Luke and John" respectively. Thus Mark's opening reference to his story as "the gospel" most likely set the stage for the use of that term as a literary designation for the four distinctive literary works we now call our Gospels.

1.2. Authorship. Who was the innovative author of this foundational Gospel? Like the other three Gospels, this one is anonymous and contains neither allusions (cf. Lk 1:1-4; Jn 21:24) nor clues to authorship. Perhaps the author assumed the readers' knowledge of authorship (e.g., Lk 1:1-4; Acts 1:1). More likely the anonymity reflects the author's understanding that his Gospel was hardly a creative literary product but rather was an expression of the gospel from God promised by Isaiah (Is 52:7; 61:1) and expressed in the teaching and stories of Jesus as preached in the early church (cf. Mk 1:1, 14). Since no single author could lay personal claim to creating this Gospel, the Gospel is anonymous.

Traditionally, however, it became known as the "Gospel according to Mark." Apart from this title, which with the titles of the other Gospels may date from the end of the first century, Papias, bishop of Hierapolis, provides the earliest documented testimony attributing a literary work to one named Mark. But Papias, whose five-volume work *Interpretation of the Lord's Sayings* (c. A.D. 120/30) was cited by Eusebius (*Hist. Eccl.* 3.39.15), claims to have learned this from another whom he calls the Elder: "And this is what the Elder said, 'Mark, who became Peter's interpreter, accurately wrote, though not in order, as many of the things said and done by the Lord as he had noted.' " The subsequent extant testimony of the late second century (e.g., the anti-Marcionite prologue; Irenaeus *Haer.* 3.1.1; Clement of Alexandria as cited by Eusebius *Hist. Eccl.* 6.14; cf. 2:15) appears to be derivative of this tradition.

Who was Mark? Despite the common occurrence of Mark (*Marcus*) as a Roman name, the association by Papias and the early church tradition of Mark with Peter has led to identifying the author as the "John Mark" known elsewhere in the NT (1 Pet 5:13; Acts 12:12, 25; 13:13; 15:37-39; in the Pauline corpus, Philem 24; Col 4:10; 2 Tim 4:11). Some more recent scholars have sought to distinguish between the Evangelist Mark, a companion of Peter (1 Pet 5:13), and John Mark, the associate of Paul in Acts and the

Pauline corpus. This distinction, however, requires special pleading. Apart from the absence of any solid basis for this distinction in the tradition, the mention of Silvanus and Mark in 1 Peter 5:12-13 makes clear that "Mark" was the "John Mark" of Acts and the Pauline corpus who with Silvanus (Silas) had also been a companion of Paul. Therefore, Mark was the companion of Peter and Paul, a member of the primitive community in Jerusalem that met in the upper room of his mother's home (Acts 12:12) where Jesus might have celebrated the Last Supper (cf. Mk 14:14-15; Acts 1:13-14; *see* Last Supper).

In any case, the question of authorship need not have a bearing on one's reading of the Gospel. The author makes no pretense of giving either his own or another's eyewitness account of any events of the Gospel. Furthermore, his identity neither assists one's understanding nor guarantees the accuracy of the details. Consequently, his identity remains merely a historical curiosity that the author fostered by his decision to remain anonymous.

1.3. Date. When did the author write this foundational document? According to our earliest tradition (anti-Marcionite prologue; Irenaeus *Haer.* 3.1.1, c. A.D. 160/80), Mark wrotuee after Peter's death in Rome, assumed to be about A.D. 64-65 during Nero's rule. Clement of Alexandria (Eusebius *Hist. Eccl.* 6.14.5-7) places the writing during Peter's time in Rome (c. A.D. 45-65). Most scholars, however, follow the earlier tradition and debate only whether he wrote before or after the fall of Jerusalem in A.D. 70.

The only relevant data in Mark may come in Mark 13:14, when read against the historical background of the Jewish war of A.D. 67-70. The Evangelist sets the discourse in Mark 13:3-37 in the context of the predicted fall of Jerusalem. Yet the reference to the "abomination of desolation" and the order for the Judeans to "flee to the hills" hardly makes sense after the destruction of the temple. Not only does the "abomination" lack a personal referent in the events of the destruction of the temple, but also the summons to "flee to the hills" makes little sense after Rome surrounded Jerusalem with a tight military blockade in A.D. 67-69 that prevented all entrance and exit. Perhaps a time about A.D. 66-67, before the final siege of Jerusalem but when the inevitable end of Jerusalem and the temple was in sight, corresponds more closely to the details than a date during or after the siege.

As with authorship, however, apart from Mark 13:14 one gains little advantage in interpreting Mark's Gospel by having a precise date for its inception. The story stands without any direct connection to any current historical events. The nature of Mark's story, with its primary focus on Jesus' life and teaching as constitutive of the plot, may account for Mark's reticence to read his day and times back into the story of an earlier period. Consequently, the specific date of Mark's Gospel is more an issue of historical curiosity than a necessity or even an aid for correctly understanding Mark's text.

1.4. Place. Where did Mark write this Gospel? Various locales, including Galilee, the Decapolis, Tyre, Sidon, Syria, the East and Rome, have been suggested. Traditionally, the anti-Marcionite prologue places it in the "regions of Italy," with Clement of Alexandria locating it in Rome during Peter's ministry (Eusebius *Hist. Eccl.* 2.15; 6.14.6). John Chrysostom (*Hom. Mt.* 1.3) even sets it in Egypt.

The diversity of proposed locales indicates how little evidence the Gospel gives in helping one determine its original setting. One of the strongest arguments for Rome or Italy, apart from the traditional association of the Gospel with Peter, lies in the numerous Latinisms, several of which Mark simply transliterates into Greek. Furthermore, Mark 12:42 explains the "widow's mite," a Greek coin, as being a *quadrans* and "inside the courtyard" of Mark 15:16 as being "the governor's headquarters." Both of the underlying Greek expressions would have needed little clarification for readers in the East, whereas they might be unfamiliar to an audience in the West and support a setting in Rome. The argument from language, however, is hardly conclusive, since many of the Latinisms do reflect semitechnical expressions common to military and trade and would be found in any area, such as the East, occupied by Roman forces.

As with date and author, the lack of explicit references supporting any one locale means that the issue of place has little to do with how one reads or understands the Gospel. Consequently, time and space locators in Mark belong strictly to the narrative rather than to the historical setting of when and where the Gospel was written.

1.5. Audience. As with place and date, one cannot specify the audience and occasion for this Gospel. The frequent explanation of Aramaic expressions as well as Jewish laws and customs may well indicate an audience unfamiliar with certain forms of Judaism. To say more goes beyond the limits of the text. Consequently, this generic quality of Mark gives it a universal character that addresses the modern disciple in much the same manner as it did its first readers. It is the "gospel concerning Jesus Messiah, Son of God" that summons one to "repent and believe the gospel" that God has acted and will act again to effect his sovereign, saving rule in and through Jesus Messiah, God's Son.

1.6. Mark as Story. Because the Gospels consist of episodes focusing on Jesus' ministry and teaching, the reader often concentrates more on the individual parts than on the whole. Such a reading has marked the popular reading of the Gospels on a personal and liturgical level. At the scholarly level much of twentieth-century Markan studies has specialized in decomposing the Gospel by delineating and analyzing the underlying traditional units, a study that has made us aware of the rich background of the Gospels' constituent parts. Yet Mark's opening statement about the "gospel concerning Jesus Messiah, Son of God" refers to the whole of Mark's narrative. The Evangelist wrote a story, a narrative. Consequently, aware of this rich traditional background, one needs to step back and look at the elements involved in this Gospel as a story in order to gain a better view of its message.

1.6.1. The Narrator's Role. The narrator provides the primary point of view for this story. As one who knows all the events of the story, the narrator also knows the thoughts, feelings, emotions and intentions of the story's many characters. Yet the narrator, distinguished from the author by such omniscience, never appears as part of the story or as one of the characters of the story. The story is told by one external to its events, who clearly shares the point of view of Jesus, who in turn shares God's point of view in the story. Therefore, one is led from the outset to trust the narrator.

1.6.2. Plot and Characters. The reader discovers the plot in the opening statement. It revolves around the "good news about Jesus Messiah, Son of God" expressed in the events of the story. In other words, the plot consists in Jesus' effective proclamation in word and deed of the "gospel" from God that God's promised redemptive rule was at hand summoning people to repent and respond in faith. Mark wanted the reader to respond in faith, "to think the thoughts of God" (Mk 8:33). This plot is carried by the ensuing conflict motif between Jesus and the demonic (e.g., Mk 1:12-13, 21-27), between Jesus and the Jewish authorities (e.g., Mk 2:1—3:6; 12:13-44), between Jesus and the Roman authorities (e.g., Mk 15:2-15), between Jesus and his family (e.g., Mk 3:20-21, 30-35) and even between Jesus and his disciples (e.g., Mk 8:14-21).

A corollary of this conflict motif is Jesus' identity. His identity is made explicit to the reader as "Jesus Messiah, Son of God" in Mark 1:1 with accent on the "Son of God," confirmed by God through the voice from heaven at the baptism (Mk 1:11) and the transfiguration (Mk 9:7), declared by the demons (Mk 1:25; 3:11-12; 5:7), confessed by Peter (Mk 8:27-29), personally affirmed by Jesus to the high priest (Mk 14:61-62), but declared openly without qualification for the first time at the crucifixion by the Roman centurion (Mk 15:39).

Yet apart from the demons the full significance of Jesus' identity escapes the other leading characters of the story. This failure to recognize who Jesus was comes through in the rejection of Jesus by the religious authorities (e.g., Mk 3:22-30; 14:63-65), his parents (e.g., Mk 3:21), his hometown (e.g., Mk 6:1-6) and even the misunderstanding of his disciples (e.g., Mk 4:35-41; 6:45-52; 8:31-33). Furthermore, Jesus' silencing of the demons and his disciples whenever his true identity is involved, as well as his exclusive use of the ambiguous "Son of man" to refer to himself, enhances this "messianic secret."

The other leading role in this story is played by the disciples, whose response to Jesus forms a major part of the plot. Called and privileged to be with Jesus (Mk 1:16-20; 3:7-12), privately taught by him (e.g., Mk 4:10-20, 33-34), commissioned to participate in his ministry (e.g., Mk 6:7-13, 30), they continually fail to understand him or accurately recognize who he really is and the implications of who he is for their discipleship (e.g., Mk 8:27—10:45). They waffle between having their mind on "divine things" and having their mind on "human things" (Mk 8:33).

1.6.3. Narrative Space and Time. The story covers an indefinite time span between Jesus' appearance at the Jordan to be baptized by John and his death during a Passover celebration in Jerusalem. The tight framework constructed from the movement around Galilee (Mk 1:16—7:23), then north and east of Galilee (Mk 7:24—9:29), back to Galilee (Mk 9:30-50) and on to the Trans-Jordan (Mk 10:1-52), ending eventually in Jerusalem (Mk 11:1—16:8), suggests a period of less than one year. One must not, however, assume that the author's desire to provide a connected narrative necessarily implies a short, chronologically arranged and comprehensive account of Jesus' ministry. The narrative space and time belong primarily to the story rather than to the events, as a comparison with the other Gospels, especially the Fourth Gospel, indicates.

2. Mark's Narrative Pattern.

A narrative often presents difficulties for one seeking to break it into discrete parts. This Gospel is no exception, as a quick review of the numerous suggested outlines in the commentaries will indicate. The edges are fuzzy at best, but a literary pattern suggests a threefold division (Mk 1:1-15; 1:16—8:26; 8:27—16:8), with the two larger parts (Mk 1:16—8:26; 8:27—16:8) divisible into three sections respectively.

2.1. Prologue (Mk 1:1-15). The Gospel opens with a prologue, or a "beginning of the gospel," set against Isaiah's promise (Mk 1:1-2). First, the coming, baptism and preaching of John the Baptizer (Mk 1:4-8) correspond to Isaiah's promise of a "voice in the wilderness" who "prepares the way of the Lord" as the precursor. Then Jesus' baptism accompanied by the coming of the Spirit (*see* Holy Spirit) and the voice from heaven echoes Isaiah 42:1 (cf. Is 42:1-2; 61:1) and sets the stage for his being for forty days in the wilderness (Mk 1:12-13), where he is sustained by the angels in the company of the wild animals (cf. Is 65:17-25). Finally, in summary fashion, having been anointed by the Spirit at his baptism and led by the Spirit into the wilderness, Jesus emerges to declare the "good news of God" that the "time has been fulfilled, God's redemptive rule has come" in keeping with Isaiah 52:7 and Isaiah 61:1. By introducing the ensuing story in this way, the Evangelist shows the "gospel concerning Jesus Messiah, Son of God" to be Isaiah's promised "good news" of God's salvation (cf. Is 52:7; 61:1).

2.2. Part One (Mk 1:16—8:26). Jesus' ministry in public as the "Messiah, Son of God" runs from Mark 1:16 to Mark 8:26. This part consists of three smaller sections that seem to have a similar literary structure. Each begins with a story about the disciples (Mk 1:16-20; 3:13-19; 6:7-13), and each closes with an ominous story of rejection or unbelief (Mk 3:1-6; 6:1-6; 8:10-21) followed by a summary (Mk 3:7-12; 6:6) or a story with the function of a summary (Mk 8:22-26) that is related to the theme of the respective section.

2.2.1. The first of these (Mk 1:16—3:12) might be called "new wine in old wineskins." After calling the first disciples, it moves from a day in Capernaum to a series of conflicts issuing from Jesus' authoritative ministry (Mk 2:1—3:6).

2.2.2. The second section (Mk 3:13—6:6) might be called the "mystery of the kingdom of God" as seen in Jesus' words (Mk 3:20—4:34) and deeds (Mk 4:35—5:43).

2.2.3. In the third section (Mk 6:7—8:26) Jesus' ministry extends beyond the purity boundaries of Galilee (cf. Mk 7:1—8:9), but the motif of misunderstanding emerges more forcefully from the public's and Herod's misconceptions about Jesus (Mk 6:14-16) to the disciples' failure to understand (Mk 6:45-52; 8:14-21), despite the feedings of the five and four thousand. The healing of the blind man from Bethsaida (Mk 7:22-26) appears to illustrate the disciples' myopic plight. Though seeing, they need the "second touch." Consequently, they form the primary focus of Jesus' ministry in Mark 8:27—16:8.

2.3. Part Two (Mk 8:27—16:8). The final part of Mark's story (Mk 8:27—16:8) clearly focuses on the death of Jesus Messiah, Son of God, and it also falls into three sections.

2.3.1. The first section (Mk 8:27—10:52) revolves around a threefold pattern of a Son of man passion prediction (Mk 8:31; 9:31; 10:33) followed by the disciples' failure to grasp the point that sets the stage for Jesus' teaching on discipleship (Mk 8:32-38; 9:32—10:31; 10:34-45). The healing of blind Bartimaeus (Mk 10:46-52) and his enthusiastic response of joining Jesus "on the way" stand as a counterpoint to the disciples and the earlier, belabored healing of the blind man of Bethsaida (Mk 8:22-26).

2.3.2. The second section (Mk 11:1—13:37) sets Jesus in and around the temple in Jerusalem, where the conflict mounts from his actions (Mk 11:1-19) and teaching (Mk 11:27—12:44) in the temple and across from the temple (Mk 13:1-37).

2.3.3. In the third and final section (Mk 14:1—16:8) one has the Last Supper, arrest, trial, crucifixion and burial of Jesus, "Messiah, Son of God" (Mk 14:1—15:47). Clearly one finds the climax of the Markan narrative in the ironic indictment of Jesus by the Romans as the "king of the Jews" (Mk 15:26), the taunts of the Jewish religious authorities of Jesus as "Messiah, king of Israel" (Mk 15:32) and the declaration by the Roman centurion that he indeed was the "Son of God" (Mk 15:39) after the temple curtain had been torn in two (Mk 15:38). On Easter morning the messenger at the tomb points beyond the story to Jesus' promised meeting with his "disciples and Peter" in Galilee (cf. Mk 14:28), despite their flight and denial (Mk 16:7-8).

Woven together from isolated units, preformed blocks of traditional units and an extended unit underlying the passion narrative (*see* Passion Narrative), Mark has composed a moving story full of action and pathos. Far more than a scissors-and-paste product, this narrative forms a dramatic whole that derives its power from its being the "gospel concerning Jesus Messiah, Son of God." It makes a theological statement—a statement about God—focusing on God's awaited redemptive activity in history through "Jesus Messiah, Son of God."

3. Mark's Theology.

The Evangelist wrote a story, not a theology. Consequently, in describing Mark's theology one must select the leading motifs of the story and ask about their theological meaning.

3.1. Kingdom of God. Mark programmatically summarizes Jesus' message at the outset of his Gospel in terms of the kingdom of God (Mk 1:14-15; *see* Kingdom of God). One would therefore expect a strong emphasis on the kingdom to follow in his narrative. Yet for Mark "kingdom of God" hardly stands out in Jesus' ministry. Matthew refers to the kingdom of heaven or of God approximately fifty times, Luke forty, but Mark only fifteen. Of these references, three occur in the parables of Mark 4:1-34, three in the sayings about children (Mk 10:14-15) and three in the discussion of the rich (Mk 10:23-25; *see* Riches and Poverty). The usages are neither defined nor uniform.

3.1.1. Kingdom as Future Expectation. In the discussion with the disciples following the story of the rich man, Jesus refers to the kingdom as something one will enter (Mk 10:23-25; so Mk 9:47 and Mk 10:15). The future moment (*see* Eschatology) also appears in Jesus' promise at the Last Supper about not drinking again until the

775

kingdom (Mk 14:25), in the description of Joseph of Arimathea as one "waiting expectantly for the kingdom of God" (Mk 15:43), in the anticipation of the seed parables (Mk 4:3-20, 26-29, 30-32) and above all in Jesus' assurance that some would "see the kingdom of God having come in power" (Mk 9:1). This future expectation correlates with the references to the coming of the Son of man in judgment in Mark 8:38, Mark 13:26-32 and Mark 14:62, and with the summons given the disciples to watch in Mark 13:33-37. The kingdom in Mark, therefore, maintains a distinctive future significance as the time of judgment and consummation.

3.1.2. Kingdom as Present Reality. At the same time, the possibility of a present reality of God's kingdom appears in the saying about receiving "the kingdom of God as a child" (Mk 10:14-15), the prerequisite for eventually entering the kingdom (Mk 10:15). Not only does one have here a difference in time between the kingdom present and the kingdom future, but also one has a different nuance in the meaning of the kingdom of God. To receive the kingdom as a child implies a personal experience of God's sovereign rule that qualifies one to enter into at least a fuller experience of God's sovereign rule or kingdom at a time in the future. In other words, to "receive the kingdom of God as a child" in the present does not exhaust the meaning or expectation of the kingdom of God in the future, nor does the anticipation of the future kingdom of God preclude an experience or reception of the kingdom of God in the present.

3.1.3. The Mystery of the Kingdom. This dual motif of the present and future kingdom of God correlates with Jesus' parables in Mark 4 about the "mystery of the kingdom of God" (*see* Parables). Each of the three seed parables (Mk 4:3-20, 26-29, 30-32) refers to the present and future dimensions of the kingdom. Indeed, for Mark the "mystery of the kingdom of God" (Mk 4:11) lies precisely in this revelation to the disciples ("to you has been given") of what until then had been hidden about the kingdom of God. God's sovereign redemptive rule has come into history like a vulnerable seed (Mk 4:3-9, 13-20) that grows inexorably until the day of harvest (Mk 4:26-29), whose beginning is infinitely small but whose end is magnificently grand (Mk 4:30-32).

3.1.4. The Inauguration of God's Sovereign Reign. This dual dimension of the kingdom present and yet future may well be deliberately reflected in the programmatic summary of Jesus' proclamation of the "gospel of God" (Mk 1:14) in Mark 1:15: "The appointed time has been fulfilled, the kingdom of God has come, repent and believe the gospel." As the parallel construction indicates, "the appointed time" and the "kingdom of God" have come to pass at a point in history. Yet the Greek verb *(ēngiken)* describing the "presence" of the kingdom usually denotes nearness rather than presence, in other words, "the kingdom of God has come near." The apparent tension between the parallel construction and the lexical meaning of the verb affirms that the kingdom of God has come into history, "the appointed time has been fulfilled," even though the full appearance is yet to come ("near"). Present and future dimensions are important for Mark. This programmatic summary at the outset of Mark's Gospel clearly indicates that the kingdom is the theme of Jesus' ministry.

For Mark, therefore, Jesus' ministry has to do with the inauguration of God's sovereign, redemptive rule, the kingdom of God, in history. The exorcisms of the demonic (e.g., Mk 1:21-27), healing of the sick (e.g., Mk 2:1-12), fellowship with sinners (Mk 2:13-17), feeding the hungry (e.g., Mk 6:34-44), even the programmatic calling of the Twelve (Mk 3:13-19), all give expression in Mark's story to Jesus' preaching of the "gospel of God, the time has been fulfilled, the kingdom of God has come" as found in the programmatic summary of Jesus' ministry in Mark 1:14-15. Yet Jesus' earthly ministry does not exhaust the meaning or expectation of the kingdom of God. As seen in the declaration of the coming of the kingdom in power, the references to the future dimension of the kingdom, the anticipation of the seed parables and the announcement of the coming judgment, Mark understood the kingdom to have a future chapter as well when God's redemptive rule will be revealed in the consummation.

3.2. Christology. The correlation of eschatology and christology in Mark is evident in the opening statement about the "gospel concerning Jesus Messiah, Son of God" (Mk 1:1). Although one might render "Jesus Messiah" as "Jesus Christ" (see most English translations), Mark's clear focus on Jesus as the "Messiah, Son of God" in his narrative, along with the programmatic summary of Jesus' ministry that centers on the coming of the kingdom of God, indicates that more was at stake in his use of

"Christ" than simply a proper name. Mark wants to affirm that Jesus is the Messiah, the Anointed One, who inaugurated God's kingdom through his ministry.

3.2.1. Messiah. That Jesus is God's Anointed One, the Messiah (*see* Christ), is confirmed for the reader at the baptism, the first appearance of Jesus in the story (Mk 1:9-13). The voice from heaven at the baptism (Mk 1:11) calls Jesus "my son," an echo of Psalm 2:7 ("You are my son, this day have I begotten you"). Since this psalm most likely was a royal psalm used at the coronation of the king in Israel, the royal connotation of Jesus as the anointed king, the Messiah, would naturally follow. At the same time, the voice also declares Jesus to be the one with whom "I am well pleased," an echo of Isaiah 42:1. This passage introduces the Servant (*see* Servant of Yahweh) whom God equips with the Holy Spirit (Is 42:1-2), an event portrayed in Mark 1:9-11 by the coming of the Spirit at the baptism. Therefore, when Jesus appears "proclaiming the gospel of God" in Mark 1:14, set against the promise of Isaiah (cf. Mk 1:1-2), the reader recognizes Jesus' coming not only to fulfill the promise of the coming evangel of Isaiah 52:7 who declares the good news of God's salvation and God's reign (i.e., the kingdom of God) but also to fulfill Isaiah 61:1 ("The Spirit of the Lord is upon me, because the Lord has anointed me to proclaim the good news"). Jesus then is the promised Anointed One (Messiah), as seen here by his calling, equipping and message.

Jesus' public ministry, as portrayed from the calling of the four disciples in Mark 1:16-20 to the healing of the blind man of Bethsaida in Mark 8:22-26, also demonstrates by word and deed his coming as the Messiah to announce and inaugurate God's promised redemptive rule in history. When Jesus asks the disciples then in Mark 8:27 who the people say he is, the answer reveals the public's awareness of God's work in him—but only as a prophet (Mk 8:28). When Jesus asks the disciples who they say he is, Peter responds correctly, "You are the Messiah" (Mk 8:29).

After the arrest and during the trial by the Sanhedrin, the high priest poses the question of Jesus' identity in terms of "the Messiah, Son of the Blessed" directly to Jesus (Mk 14:61), who answers affirmatively: "I am" (Mk 14:62). This led to the Sanhedrin's deliverance of Jesus to Pilate (Mk 15:1), who posed the same question in its more political form: "Are you the king of the Jews?" To which Jesus answered more cryptically, "You say so." Despite Pilate's subsequent equivocation (Mk 15:6-15), he eventually sentenced Jesus to death under the charge that he was the "king of the Jews" (Mk 15:16-20, 26). The Jewish leaders, the chief priests and the scribes then taunted the crucified Jesus as "the Messiah, king of Israel" (Mk 15:32). Yet Mark intends the reader to see the irony in Pilate's accommodating indictment and the disbelieving taunts of the religious authorities, since Jesus was indeed the "Messiah, king of the Jews." The transfiguration (Mk 9:2-9; cf. Mk 9:1), which comes subsequent to Peter's confession (Mk 8:27-29); Jesus' mode of entry into Jerusalem on a young donkey (Mk 11:1-11), which fulfills the promise of Zechariah 9:9 about the coming of Israel's lowly king; and especially Jesus' affirmative response to the high priest's question confirm for the reader that Jesus was indeed the "Messiah, king of Israel," whose coming had directly to do with the inauguration of the kingdom of God in history.

For Mark's narrative, however, Jesus' identity as Messiah can be clearly understood only in the light of the cross. No sooner did Peter correctly confess Jesus to be the Messiah (Mk 8:29) than Jesus announced that the Son of man must suffer, be rejected by the elders, chief priests and scribes, be killed, and rise again after three days (Mk 8:31). Peter's negative response (Mk 8:32) indicates the incongruity of such a possibility for the Messiah. Similarly, Jesus' instructions that Peter, James and John not disclose their experience of his transfiguration until after the resurrection (Mk 9:9) implies the necessity of his death as seen in the following dialogue (cf. Mk 9:11-13). Finally, it hardly comes as coincidental that Jesus' only explicit affirmation of his identity as "Messiah" takes place before the Sanhedrin (Mk 14:61-62) in the trial scene that leads directly to his sentence to death by Pilate under the indictment "king of the Jews," a view certainly implicit in Peter's confession (cf. Mk 8:32) and in the glory of the transfiguration (cf. Mk 9:1). Consequently, for the reader, the Jewish religious leaders' unbelieving mockery of the crucified "Messiah, king of Israel" declares in fact who Jesus really is.

Mark's narrative, therefore, affirms the early Christian traditional statement of the gospel, "Christ (the Messiah) died for our sins according to the Scriptures" (1 Cor 15:3; cf. Mk 10:45;

14:22-24). Yet as crucial as Jesus' death is to his identity as the Messiah for Mark, Jesus was not simply a dying Messiah, that is, a Messiah identified by his death. His earthly ministry, which led to Peter's confession "You are the Messiah," and his promised future role in the kingdom when he "will drink it [the fruit of the vine] new in the kingdom of God" on "that day" (Mk 14:25; cf. Mk 13:32) are also essential ingredients in Jesus' identity as Messiah. Mark's "gospel concerning Jesus Messiah" (Mk 1:1) is the "gospel from God" (Mk 1:14) relating Jesus' inauguration of God's kingdom—God's redemptive rule in history—in the present through a ministry culminating in his death and his continued role in the kingdom that is coming "in power" (Mk 9:1) in the future.

3.2.2. Son of God. Jesus is also seen as "the *Son of God" in Mark. In fact, some interpreters would say that "Son of God" is Mark's particular designation for Jesus. It stands in the opening line of the Gospel alongside "Jesus Messiah" (Mk 1:1). Though omitted by some early Greek manuscripts, "Jesus Messiah, Son of God" represents the preferable reading and stands in tandem in Mark's narrative with the climactic concluding confession of Jesus as "Son of God" by the Roman centurion at the cross (Mk 15:39). The identification of Jesus as God's Son in Mark 1:1 also finds its confirmation by the voice from heaven that declares at the baptism, "You are my son" (Mk 1:11). As noted above, this statement of sonship echoes Psalm 2:7, with its royal overtones consistent with the joint expression "Messiah, Son of God" in Mark 1:1. Yet the voice also refers to Jesus as "my beloved son," a qualification foreign to Psalm 2:7 but used in Genesis 22:2, 13, 16 (LXX) to refer to Isaac as *Abraham's "only" or "unique" son. Therefore, as God's "beloved Son," Jesus has a special role (= "anointed king," Ps 2:7) and relationship (= "my son, the only/beloved one," Gen 22) with God. The latter underlies the "beloved son" in the parable of the wicked vineyard keepers (Mk 12:1-12), the reference to "the Son's" lack of knowledge in Mark 13:32, and certainly Jesus' prayer to the "Father" *(Abba)* in Gethsemane (Mk 14:36).

Jesus' role and relationship as the Son of God may explain the demons' use of "Son of God" in addressing him. In the first miracle of Mark's Gospel, an exorcism (Mk 1:23-27), the demon addresses Jesus as "the Holy One of God," a designation suggesting a unique role and relationship of Jesus to God (Mk 1:24), though not specifically identifying Jesus as the Son of God. But in a statement summarizing the demons' response to Jesus in Mark 3:11 they consistently address him directly as "the Son of God," and in Mark 5:7 the Gerasene demoniac addresses Jesus as "the Son of the Most High God" (Mk 5:7). The Evangelist indirectly assures the reader of the validity of this identification by noting in Mark 1:34 that Jesus would not permit the exorcised demons to speak "because they knew him" and by noting in Mark 3:12 that Jesus ordered the demons, who had identified him as the Son of God, not to make him known. For Mark, the exorcisms as such point to Jesus' authority as the Son of God to defeat Satan and his forces, a demonstration of the establishment of God's redemptive rule by conquering the enemy or "binding the strong man" (Mk 3:22-27).

In the transfiguration scene, which follows Jesus' declaration that some standing with him would not "taste death until they see that the kingdom of God has come with power" (Mk 9:1), the voice from heaven declares to Peter, James and John: "This is my beloved son" (Mk 9:7). The context appears to affirm Jesus' role as the Messiah, whose revelation, along with the coming of the kingdom with power, are anticipated by Jesus' transfiguration and the disciples' experience on the mountain. Yet, as was the case with the demons, Jesus orders the disciples not to reveal what they had experienced, including his identity as God's Son, until after the resurrection (Mk 9:9).

In the high priest's question—"Are you the Messiah, the Son of the Blessed?" (Mk 14:61)—the two designations of "Messiah" and "Son of God" explicitly come together again. Since "Son of the Blessed" represents a Jewish circumlocution for "Son of God," one has here an echo of the opening statement about "Jesus Messiah, Son of God" (Mk 1:1). Obviously the high priest's question reflects the royal motif of sonship present in Psalm 2:7, whose roots extend back to Nathan's promise to David that his son would know God as "father" and God would know him as "son" (2 Sam 7:14).

After affirming that he was indeed the "Messiah, Son of the Blessed" (Mk 14:62), Jesus immediately warned the Sanhedrin that they would see "the Son of man seated on the right hand of power and coming with the clouds of heaven" (Mk 14:62). At that the high priest tore his clothes and charged Jesus with blasphemy (Mk 14:63-64). The basis for this charge has been disputed. It most likely has more to do with Jesus' follow-up response when he appeared to lay claim to God's role of judge (cf. the similar charge in Mk 2:7 for usurping God's right to forgive sins) than with his affirmative response to the question of his being the "Messiah, Son of the Blessed."

Finally, the passion narrative reaches a climax with Jesus' death, the rending of the temple curtain, and the response by the Roman centurion in Mark 15:37-39. In contrast to the Jewish religious authorities who stood at the cross mocking Jesus as the "Messiah, king of Israel" (Mk 15:32), the Roman centurion publicly declares, "Truly, this man was God's Son!" (Mk 15:39). In this way the two designations, "Messiah" and "Son of God," come together once again, both qualified and clarified by the cross. Mark's opening statement about the gospel concerning "Jesus Messiah, Son of God" has now come full circle in these words from the final scenes at the cross.

For Mark, then, Jesus is the "Son of God" in his role as "Messiah, Son of God" (Mk 1:1; 14:61-62; 15:32, 39). At the same time, as God's Son, Jesus has a special relationship with God that sets him apart (cf. Mk 1:11 and Mk 9:7, "my beloved son"; the Father and the Son, Mk 13:32 and Mk 14:36; and the "beloved son" of the vineyard owner, Mk 12:6). Nevertheless, the Roman centurion's climactic confession of Jesus as God's Son at the end of the passion narrative affirms for Mark and his readers that Jesus as "Son of God," like Jesus as "Messiah," takes on special coloring in the light of the cross.

3.2.3. Son of Man. Mark opens and concludes his narrative by identifying Jesus as the "Messiah, Son of God" (Mk 1:1; 15:32, 39; cf. Mk 1:11; 8:29; 9:9; 14:61-62), but the designation that occurs most frequently is "Son of man" (*see* Son of Man). Appearing only twice and in proximity in the first half of the Gospel (Mk 2:10, 28), the expression appears thirteen times from Mark 8:31 through Mark 14:62. Contrary to "Christ" and "Son of God," "Son of man" is used exclusively by Jesus and always with reference to himself in Mark's narrative and never with the accompanying qualifications or reticence that mark the use of the other designations.

Twice Jesus uses "Son of man" to refer to his authoritative earthly ministry—"to forgive sins

on earth" (Mk 2:10) and as "Lord of the Sabbath" (Mk 2:28). Each of these references in the first half of Mark's narrative do, however, carry an ominous tone. The former comes in the context of the charge of blasphemy, a capital crime (Mk 2:7). The latter comes in the context of sabbath conflicts that culminate in a conspiracy to have him killed (cf. Mk 3:6). Three times Jesus uses "Son of man" to refer to the future coming of the Son of man as judge at the consummation (Mk 8:38; 13:26; 14:62). And two of these references appear in the larger context of Jesus' impending death—Mark 8:38 follows the passion prediction of Mark 8:31 and the reference to taking up one's cross (Mk 8:34), while Mark 14:62 comes in the trial before the Sanhedrin and evokes the charge of the capital crime of blasphemy and its consequent death sentence (Mk 14:64).

It follows, therefore, that the bulk of the Son of man references in Mark have to do specifically with Jesus' impending suffering and death. Three occur within explicit passion predictions about the suffering and death of the Son of man (Mk 8:31; 9:31; 10:33). Five other usages echo motifs found in these passion predictions (Mk 9:9, 12; 14:21 [2x], 41). And Mark 10:45 explains the significance of the coming passion by declaring that the "Son of man came not to be served but to serve and to give his life as a ransom for many." Therefore, like "Messiah" and "Son of God," "Son of man" also stands under the shadow of the cross in the multiple, direct references to his coming death, a shadow that hangs over even the references to the Son of man's authoritative earthly ministry and his coming role as judge at the consummation.

However, in contrast to the use of "Messiah" and "Son of God" in Mark, Jesus publicly and without qualification refers to himself as the "Son of man" before friend and foe—the disciples (Mk 8:31, 38; 9:9, 12, 31; 10:33, 45; 13:26; 14:21, 41), the scribes (Mk 2:10) and the Sanhedrin (Mk 14:62). Furthermore, Jesus never cautions against the use of this designation as he does with the use of "Messiah" and "Son of God." Nor does he qualify it by the use of another clarifying designation or statement as he consistently does with "Messiah" and "Son of God." Yet the reader never doubts from the first to the last occurrence that "Son of man" refers to anyone but Jesus. Consequently, for Mark "Son of man" functions as a self-designation by Jesus, a way of referring to himself without any inherent christological overtones, as with "Messiah" or "Son of God."

If "Son of man" has so little christological weight, why then does Mark have Jesus refer to himself as the "Son of man"? One can only hazard a suggestion. First, Mark's use most likely has its roots in Jesus' ministry and choice of "Son of man" as a self-designation. Thus Mark would have been faithfully reflecting the tradition stemming from Jesus' practice of using "Son of man" as a self-designation. Second, the extensive scholarly discussion of the background and meaning of "Son of man" indicates at least the ambiguity surrounding its meaning and use. It hardly seems to have given a clear messianic signal to the hearer, certainly not in Mark's Gospel. This ambiguity was appropriate not only to the hiddenness that marked Jesus' christological identity during his earthly ministry but was especially appropriate to the "messianic secret" in Mark which the nuanced uses of "Messiah" and "Son of God" reflected. Therefore "Son of man" denoted a self-designation by Jesus but carried little of the christological or messianic overtones of "Messiah" and "Son of God" for Mark.

3.3. The Messianic Secret. Since W. Wrede's epoch-making work *The Messianic Secret* (*Das Messiasgeheimnis in den Evangelien*, 1901), Mark's emphasis on the "messianic secret" has highlighted the discussion of Mark's theology. Without doubt this motif stands out in Mark's Gospel when compared with the other Gospels. A closer look shows that it correlates with Mark's christology as seen above.

3.3.1. Silencing the Demons. We find this motif first in Jesus' response to the demons. In the first miracle, an exorcism, the demon addresses Jesus as "Jesus from Nazareth . . . the Holy One of God" (Mk 1:25). Jesus then rebukes the demon by silencing and exorcising him (Mk 1:26). On the surface Jesus' command of silence offers little out of the ordinary for an exorcism, since the use of a name and the counter by a silence command represent the common ingredients of the power struggle between a demon and a first-century exorcist. The use of the name was a common attempt by either the demon or the exorcist to gain power or control and the silence command was a move to overcome that attempt in the exorcism.

Yet in Mark the use of the name by the demon and the silence command hardly have their typical exorcistic function. First, the demons or the demon possessed in Mark's Gospel are never in a power position with Jesus. The exorcisms are marked by a total absence of the demons' struggle or resistance to Jesus. Furthermore, their immediate reaction to Jesus betrays the recognition of their subjugation or defeat from the outset (cf. "You have come to destroy us," Mk 1:24; their prostration before Jesus, Mk 3:11; 5:6; 9:20). Second, Mark reveals his understanding of the silence command to be a secrecy command in the summary statements of Mark 1:34 and Mark 3:11 where Jesus prohibits the exorcised demons from speaking "because they knew him" (Mk 1:34) to be the "Son of God" (Mk 3:10). Third, Mark's understanding that the silence command is a secrecy command rather than a part of the exorcistic pattern is further supported by the absence of any silence command in contexts where Jesus' identity was not an issue (cf. Mk 5:1-20; 7:24-30; 9:14-29). Consequently, Mark clearly qualifies the demons' correct identification of Jesus as the Son of God by having Jesus silence them, commanding them to keep it a secret.

3.3.2. Silencing the Disciples. Similarly, Jesus gives a silence command to his disciples who know who he is. In Mark 8:30 Jesus prohibits the disciples from making public that he is the Messiah, as correctly confessed by Peter (Mk 8:29) in contrast to the public's view of him as a prophet (Mk 8:27-28; cf. Mk 6:14-16). In Mark 9:9 he prohibits Peter, James and John from making known what they had experienced at the transfiguration, including the voice from heaven that identified Jesus as "my beloved son." But here we learn the temporal limits of this silence command. They were to keep this a secret only "until after the Son of man had risen from the dead." Consequently, Jesus' identity as the Messiah and Son of God could not be revealed publicly until after the cross and resurrection, a motif commensurate with Jesus' qualification of Peter's confession (Mk 8:29) by his announcement of the coming suffering, death and resurrection of the Son of man (Mk 8:31).

In other words, Mark's messianic secret corresponds to his portrait of Jesus as Messiah, Son of God whose true significance could be grasped only in the light of the cross. Mark's portrait consistently identifies Jesus as Messiah, Son of God in the light of his ministry on earth (cf. Mk 1:24; 3:11; 8:29) and his future glory (Mk 9:7; cf.

9:1). But he qualifies this identity by Jesus' death as the Messiah, Son of God (Mk 8:30-31; 9:9; 14:61-64; 15:25-32, 39). In so doing, the Evangelist accents Jesus' death as part of the significance of Jesus' identity as Messiah, Son of God without denying the corresponding aspects of his earthly ministry or his future role. Therefore, Mark's messianic secret qualifies Jesus' identity as Messiah, Son of God without attempting in any way to conceal who Jesus really is until a later time.

3.3.3. Broken Silences. But what about the times when the silence command is broken? In the healing of the leper (Mk 1:40-45) and the deaf stutterer (Mk 7:31-37), Jesus' silence command is explicitly broken (cf. Mk 5:20-21). And one can only assume the silence command to Jairus's family would be broken in view of the public awareness of the girl's death (Mk 5:21-43).

Yet in none of these instances is Jesus' identity per se at stake, only his actions. Furthermore, these actions involve a healing. Silence commands were also characteristic of healing stories outside the New Testament in the ancient world. They were intended to keep the means or healing formulas a secret. Obviously for Mark these silence commands no longer applied to Jesus' healing technique, since none is given in the cleansing of the leper (Mk 1:40-45) and the formulas *(Talitha cum* and *Ephphata)* are translated for the reader (Mk 5:41; 7:34). Rather, in these instances Jesus' silence command seems to evoke the opposite response in Mark 1:44-45 and Mark 7:36. When the opposite response is noted (cf. Mk 5:21-43), however, the contrary behavior results in large crowds (Mk 1:45; 8:1-8) and sets the stage for Jesus' next move in the story line (cf. Mk 6:1-6).

Therefore, these silence commands, once functioning as a part of the healing narrative, have little to do with the healing secret or the messianic secret in Mark and have more to do now with the story line of Mark's Gospel. These commands and their contrary behavior function as literary devices to set the stage by providing crowds for the next event in Jesus' ministry, a role not played by the other silence commands directed at the demons and the disciples.

3.4. Discipleship. Mark's emphasis on discipleship becomes evident from the place he gives the *disciples in the structure of his narrative. Not only does the story of Jesus' ministry open with the calling of Peter, Andrew, James and John (Mk 1:16-20), but also pericopes involving the disciples begin each of the three constituent sections (Mk 1:16-20 in Mk 1:16—3:12; Mk 3:13-19 in Mk 3:13—6:6; Mk 6:7-13 in Mk 6:7—8:26) of the second part of the Gospel. In the third part (Mk 8:27—16:8), the disciples form Jesus' primary audience within the section (Mk 8:27—10:52). They accompany Jesus to Jerusalem as his constant companions in the second section (Mk 11:1—13:37) and remain on the scene in the final section (Mk 14:1—16:8) until their flight highlighted by Peter's denial (Mk 14:50, 66-72). Despite their failure, the story ends as it begins, with a final reference to the disciples. The messenger at the tomb gives the women a message of hope for "the disciples and Peter" (Mk 16:7).

3.4.1. Who Are the Disciples in Mark? One finds both a narrower circle comprised of the Twelve who are called to be "with him" and specially commissioned to share in his ministry of teaching, healing and exorcism (Mk 3:13-14; cf. 5:18; 6:7-13, 30) and a larger circle who also are called (e.g., Levi, Mk 2:14), commissioned (e.g., Mk 5:19-20) "followers" (e.g., Mk 2:15-17). Both groups are beneficiaries of Jesus' miraculous works (e.g., Mk 1:40-45; 6:45-52), teaching (e.g., Mk 3:20, 31-35; 4:10-20) and company (e.g., Mk 2:15-17; 3:13-14; 3:20, 31-35). Yet most of the references to the disciples appear to denote the narrower circle and its members who are accorded special privileges (e.g., Mk 5:21-43; 9:2-8; 14:12-25) and given special teaching (e.g., Mk 7:17-23; 10:10-12; 13:3-37; 14:22-25).

3.4.2. The Failure of the Disciples. Nevertheless, Mark portrays the disciples in a less than positive light. They fail to understand Jesus' teaching in parables (e.g., Mk 4:13, cf. Mk 4:34; 7:18), on divorce (Mk 10:10-12) and especially about his coming death (Mk 8:32-33; 9:9-13, 32). They fail to understand what he does when he calms the storm (Mk 4:35-41) and walks on the water (Mk 6:45-52). Indeed, they fail to understand fully who he is, as seen by Peter's response to the passion prediction in Mark 8:31-33, a failure that constantly reappears throughout the section of Mark 8:27—10:52, as well as in their behavior at his arrest and trial.

3.4.3. The Leaven of the Pharisees and Herod. One pericope in particular portrays their halting relationship with Jesus, the warning against the leaven of the Pharisees and Herod (Mk 8:14-21). The warning comes at the end of the first half of the Gospel, which has focused on Jesus' public ministry (Mk 1:16—8:26), and follows the two feeding miracles (Mk 6:34-44; 8:1-9). And it is enclosed by a reference to Herod's question about Jesus (Mk 6:14-17) and the Pharisee's request for a sign (Mk 8:11-13). Within this context Mark points out the weakness in the disciples' faith relationship to Jesus.

First, recognizing their concern about having failed to bring sufficient provisions with them (Mk 8:14, 16), Jesus warns the disciples about the "leaven of the Pharisees and Herod" (Mk 8:15). Within the Markan context this can only refer to their failure, like Herod (Mk 6:16) and the Pharisees (Mk 8:10-12), to comprehend who Jesus really was. Second, Jesus specifically asks if they do not "perceive and understand" or if their "hearts are hardened" (Mk 8:17; cf. Mk 6:52), a trait ascribed earlier to the Pharisees for their failure to recognize Jesus for who he was (Mk 3:5). Third, citing the words of Jeremiah 5:21, Jesus asks if having eyes they do not see and ears they do not hear (Mk 8:18). These words echo the motif first sounded in the earlier citation of Isaiah 6:9 to describe "those outside" (Mk 4:12). Jesus' response to the disciples' concern about lack of sufficient provisions betrays a lack of faith (cf. Mk 4:35-41; 6:45-52) dangerously comparable to the response of Herod, the Pharisees and the outsiders, despite their having been "given the mystery of the kingdom of God" (Mk 4:11). Finally, Jesus asks the disciples specifically about the amount of leftovers from the feedings of the five and four thousand respectively (Mk 8:19-20) before concluding once again with the question "Do you not yet understand?" (Mk 8:21).

Although the disciples seem precariously close to the leaven of Herod and the Pharisees as they respond to Jesus in the hour of their own need (cf. Mk 4:35-41; 6:45-52), their special role, privilege and response in the previous Markan narrative has shown them to be different. Yet, as the next story about the blind man (Mk 8:22-26) indicates, their sight is at best partial. Their response to Jesus' teaching and his coming death in Mark 8:27—14:63 demonstrates even more clearly their need for the second touch.

3.4.4. The Cost of Discipleship. Indeed their response and behavior following the three Son of man passion predictions in Mark 8:27—10:52 become the basis for Jesus' teaching on discipleship in Mark 8:27—10:52. Their failure to recog-

nize his coming death in Mark 8:31-33; 9:31-32; 10:33-37 leads to Jesus' teaching about the cost of discipleship and the way of the cross (Mk 8:34-38), about status and kingdom conduct (Mk 9:33—10:31) and about the inverse nature of greatness illustrated ultimately by Jesus coming to serve as the Son of man (Mk 10:34-45). In this way Mark uses the disciples as a means of addressing what discipleship really means when lived in the already/not yet of God's redemptive activity in Christ. Just as the way of Jesus Messiah, Son of God had to be set in the light of the cross, so those who would follow Jesus must see discipleship, with all its privilege and promise, set on "the way" of Jesus Messiah, Son of God.

4. Mark's Ending.
As it now stands, Mark 16:8 offers the best attested ending of Mark's Gospel: "They went out and fled from the tomb, for they were trembling and astonished. They said nothing to anyone. For they were afraid." The abruptness of this ending and the resurrection appearances in the Gospels of Matthew, Luke and John (implied by the promise of Mk 14:28) have led to the conclusion that a more complete ending has been lost. The so-called shorter and longer endings (Mk 16:9-20) to Mark's Gospel represent attempts to provide an appropriate ending. Yet the external evidence drawn from the witness of the ancient manuscript traditions and the internal evidence based on vocabulary and style rule against the authenticity of any extant ending other than Mark 16:8 as it stands. The evidence, however, obviously cannot prove that Mark 16:8 was the original ending, since a longer ending could have been lost prior to the earliest manuscript evidence we possess.

Indeed, Mark hardly intended for his readers to think that his story of "the gospel concerning Jesus Messiah, Son of God" (Mk 1:1) ended with the women's failure. The evidence for this is varied: the transfiguration, followed by the command that the disciples not reveal it until after the resurrection (Mk 9:2-9), the promise of the coming of the Son of man in Mark 13:26 following a mission period entailing much suffering (cf. Mk 13:9-13), the warning to the Sanhedrin about the coming Son of man (Mk 14:62). All of these elements correspond to the anticipation of the future found in the parables of the kingdom of Mark 4:1-34 and make clear that Mark's story, the "gospel," does not end with Mark 16:8. The cross and the empty tomb are not the end. Jesus' role as Messiah, Son of God, has a future chapter. Furthermore, Mark's readers certainly knew of the resurrection appearances and the mission of the church. The conviction that the story continued on doubtless led to the so-called shorter ending: "They promptly announced to Peter all they had been told. After these things Jesus himself sent the holy and imperishable proclamation of the eternal salvation from East to West through them."

Yet when one looks at Mark's narrative from the standpoint of a literary text, the present ending fits his literary pattern quite well. The ultimate climax of Mark's story comes at the crucifixion and death of Jesus with the ironic taunts of the Jewish leaders and the declaration by the Roman centurion that show Jesus to indeed be the "Messiah, Son of God," as introduced in the opening statement (Mk 15:32-39; cf. Mk 1:1). Furthermore, the disciples have repeatedly failed throughout the narrative to grasp the total import of Jesus and his teaching. Their failure never altered Jesus' course as the "Messiah, Son of God" (cf. Mk 4:35-41; 6:45-52; 8:14-21; 8:27—14:63). Nor did this failure, as dangerous as it may have been for the disciples (cf. Mk 8:14-21), lead to Jesus' giving up on the disciples. In fact their most glaring failure comes in their flight at his arrest (Mk 14:50) and Peter's denial (Mk 14:66-72). Yet the message of Mark 16:7 is addressed to "the disciples and Peter."

The women, who enter the scene at the cross (Mk 15:40-41), note Jesus' place of burial (Mk 15:47) and come to the tomb to anoint him (Mk 16:1), pick up where the disciples left off. But they too "are afraid" (cf. Mk 4:41; 6:50). With a final touch of irony, one of Mark's favorite literary devices, the women fail to disclose (they "tell no one") Jesus' resurrection, even though commanded to do so (Mk 16:7). But the leper at the beginning of the Gospel proclaims what he has been commanded to "tell no one" (Mk 1:44-45; cf. Mk 8:36). On the one hand the present ending corresponds with Mark's portrait of the disciples, and on the other hand it leaves open the future fulfillment of Jesus' promise to meet the disciples in Galilee (cf. Mk 14:28) and the glorious future of the parousia (Mk 13:26-37).

5. Mark's Purpose.
Despite numerous attempts to find Mark's purpose in the theological struggles (e.g., christol-

ogy) or social circumstances of the early church (e.g., the fall of Jerusalem), the rather generic character of the story (lacking specific clues about place and date of authorship) and the narrative integrity of the Gospel makes such historical or theological reconstructions at best speculative. Taken on its own terms, the leading characters—Jesus and the disciples—and the nature of the conflict motif provide the best clues for understanding the author's design in writing this Gospel.

Once again we appeal to Mark 1:1 as a statement of what the author intended to do, namely, write the "gospel concerning Jesus Messiah, Son of God." For the Evangelist this Gospel clearly shows Jesus as coming to inaugurate God's sovereign rule, the kingdom, as seen in the programmatic summary of Jesus' ministry in Mark 1:14-15. At the same time God's sovereign rule, the kingdom, has a future component that will appear "in power" (Mk 9:1) when the Son of man comes to bring God's salvation to its consummation (Mk 13:26-37). But why did the Evangelist write this Gospel?

This "gospel" according to Mark corresponds to Isaiah's promised good news of God's rule and salvation (Is 52:7) as proclaimed by Jesus (Mk 1:14), but it contains within it the question of how God's promised sovereign rule could be present and future. In what sense was Jesus "Messiah, Son of God," since he was crucified rather than crowned in Jerusalem?

The confusion was no less intense in Mark's day than in Jesus' experience. Drawing on the disciples, who doubtless reflect the confusion of Jesus' followers, Mark uses them to illustrate the standpoint of his privileged and perplexed community. By focusing on who Jesus was in his repeated reminders throughout the narrative (e.g., Mk 1:11; 1:25; 1:34; 3:11; 5:7; 8:27-29; 9:7; 14:61-62; 15:39), the Evangelist reassured his readers that Jesus was indeed the "Messiah, Son of God." This was seen not only in his authoritative defeat of Satan, his forgiveness of sinners, his healing the sick, his feeding the hungry and his raising the dead, but above all in his death (e.g., Mk 8:27-31; 14:61-62; 15:39).

By emphasizing in the seed parables (Mk 4:1-20, 26-29, 30-32) that the kingdom is present but vulnerable; warning about troubling times (Mk 13:3-37); issuing silence commands; hinting of a mortal conflict; making explicit statements of coming death; the rejection of family, friends and the religious establishment; and, finally, setting the centurion's climactic confession in the light of the cross, the Evangelist warns his readers against any triumphalist reading of the Gospel. Mark's own readers needed to know that God had indeed acted decisively, "the time has been fulfilled" (Mk 1:15) in Jesus Messiah, Son of God, but the way of discipleship was also the way of the cross (Mk 8:34-38). Right thinking and right faith must issue in right living. Right living was the way of the cross.

We conclude that pastoral concern was foremost in Mark's mind as he wrote the "gospel concerning Jesus Messiah, Son of God." He wanted to address a community under duress, a duress that may well have given rise to questions about who Jesus really was and the nature of the kingdom he had come to inaugurate. This Gospel offered a renewed basis for their faith, made clear the trials and tribulations along the journey of that faith, and offered the hope of the kingdom future when the harvest, the full-grown mustard tree, the resurrection and the consummation of God's salvation would make all things right.

See also JOHN, GOSPEL OF; LUKE, GOSPEL OF; MATTHEW, GOSPEL OF.

BIBLIOGRAPHY. **Commentaries:** H. Anderson, *The Gospel of Mark* (NCB; Grand Rapids: Eerdmans, 1981); C. E. B. Cranfield, *The Gospel According to St. Mark* (CGTC; Cambridge: Cambridge University Press, 1963); J. R. Edwards Jr., *The Gospel According to Mark* (PNTC; Grand Rapids: Eerdmans, 2001); C. A. Evans, *Mark 8:27—16:20* (WBC 34b; Dallas: Word, 2001); R. T. France, *The Gospel of Mark* (NIGNTC; Grand Rapids: Eerdmans, 2002); D. E. Garland, *Mark* (NIVAC; Grand Rapids: Zondervan, 1996); R. A. Guelich, *Mark 1—8:26* (WBC 34a; Waco, TX: Word, 1989); R. H. Gundry, *Mark: A Commentary on His Apology for the Cross* (Grand Rapids: Eerdmans, 1993); M. D. Hooker, *The Gospel According to Mark* (BNTC; Peabody, MA: Hendrickson, 1991); L. Hurtado, *Mark* (NIBC; Peabody, MA: Hendrickson, 1983); W. L. Lane, *The Gospel According to Mark* (NICNT; Grand Rapids: Eerdmans, 1974); J. Marcus, *Mark 1—8* (AB; New York: Doubleday, 2000); D. E. Nineham, *The Gospel of St. Mark* (New York: Penguin, 1963); E. Schweizer, *The Good News According to Mark* (Richmond: John Knox, 1970); V. Taylor, *The Gospel According to St Mark* (2d ed; New York: St Martin's, 1966); B. Witherington III, *The Gospel of Mark: A Socio-Rhetorical Commentary* (Grand Rapids: Eerdmans, 2001). **Studies:** E. Best, *Following Jesus: Discipleship in the Gospel of Mark* (JSNTS 4; Sheffield: JSOT, 1981); idem, *Mark: The Gospel As Story* (Philadelphia: Fortress, 1983); M. Hengel, *Studies in the Gospel of Mark* (Minneapolis: Fortress, 1985); H. C. Kee, *Community of the New Age: Studies in the Gospel of Mark* (Philadelphia: Westminster, 1977); W. Kelber, *The Kingdom in Mark: A New Place and a New Time* (Philadelphia: Fortress, 1974); J. D. Kingsbury, *The Christology of Mark's Gospel* (Philadelphia: Fortress, 1989); idem, *Conflict in Mark* (Minneapolis: Fortress, 1989); A. T. Lincoln, "The Promise and the Failure—Mark 16:7, 8," *JBL* 108 (1989) 283-300; J. Marcus, *The Way of the Lord* (Louisville, KY: Westminster/John Knox, 1992); R. P. Martin, *Mark: Evangelist and Theologian* (Grand Rapids: Zondervan, 1973); W. Marxsen, *Mark the Evangelist: Studies on the Redaction History of the Gospel* (Nashville: Abingdon, 1969); R. P. Meye, *Jesus and the Twelve: Discipleship and Revelation in Mark's Gospel* (Grand Rapids: Eerdmans, 1968); C. Myers, *Binding the Strong Man: A Political Reading of Mark's Story of Jesus* (Maryknoll, NY: Orbis, 1988); E. J. Pryke, *Redactional Style in the Marcan Gospel* (SNTSMS 33; Cambridge: Cambridge University Press, 1978); D. Rhodes and D. Miche, *Mark As Story* (Philadelphia: Fortress, 1982); C. M. Tuckett, ed., *The Messianic Secret* (IRT 1; Philadelphia: Fortress, 1983); T. J. Weeden, *Mark: Traditions in Conflict* (Philadelphia: Fortress, 1971).   R. A. Guelich

MARKAN PRIORITY. *See* SYNOPTIC PROBLEM.

MARTYRDOM OF ISAIAH. *See* APOCRYPHA AND PSEUDEPIGRAPHA.

MARY, MOTHER OF JESUS. *See* WOMEN I.

MATTHEW, GOSPEL OF

The Gospel of Matthew quickly established itself as the early church's favorite Gospel—in part because of its organization and in part because of the topics it addresses. Not only does it contain the Sermon on the Mount, but it has memorable accounts of the birth of Jesus, his early struggle to survive, and selections of his teachings (speeches) that were amenable to catechesis and kerygma. No other Gospel connects itself to the Old Testament so markedly or offers an apparent dialogue with Judaism's perception of the early Christian movement.

1. The Origin of Matthew.

In order to find an adequate solution to the question of the origin of Matthew's Gospel, a series of interrelated questions must be answered: Who is the author or who are the authors? When was it composed? What is its relationship to the other Gospel traditions and Gospels? Satisfactory answers to each of these questions, however intertwined they may be, will yield the most probable solution to the mystery of Matthew's origin.

1.1. The Papias Logion. A strategic place to begin is with the traditional view that the apostle Matthew wrote a Gospel in Hebrew or Aramaic. This tradition stems from the testimony of Papias, bishop of Hierapolis in Phrygia (died c. A.D. 130). The record of Papias's statement about Matthew survives only in Eusebius (*Hist. Eccl.* 3.39.16). It reads, "Matthew collected *(synetaxato)* the oracles *(ta logia)* in the Hebrew language (*Hēbraidi dialektō*), and each interpreted (*hērmēneusen*) them as best he could." On first analysis the tradition of Papias appears to say that the apostle Matthew wrote a Gospel in Hebrew or Aramaic, and various translations were made of his work. So it was apparently understood, with minor modifications, in the early churches.

Irenaeus confirms this analysis, adding that the First Gospel was composed while Peter and Paul were founding the church in Rome (*Haer.* 3.1.1; from Eusebius *Hist. Eccl.* 5.8.2). Eusebius corroborates the Semitic origin in a legend concerning Pantaenus, who reportedly discovered a Semitic Matthew, supposedly brought to India or Arabia by Bartholomew (*Hist. Eccl.* 5.10.3). Origen affirms this tradition, adding only that the First Gospel was written for Jewish believers (*Hist. Eccl.* 6.25.4). In addition to passing on these traditions, Eusebius states that the occasion for the First Gospel was Matthew's departure from Palestine (*Hist. Eccl.* 3.24.6). Further support for this traditional understanding of the origin of Matthew can be found in Cyril of Jerusalem (*Cat.* 14), Epiphanius (*Haer.* 30.3) and Jerome (*Prol. in Matt.*; *Praef. in Quat. Ev.*; *Vir.* 3).

In more recent times, however, this tradition has been given several interpretations. First, some scholars have argued that the apostle Matthew penned an original Aramaic Gospel that was later translated into Greek by an unknown Christian (though some have contended that Matthew also translated the work). This Greek Gospel, it is argued, is substantially the same as the Aramaic Gospel (see Tasker).

Second, others have argued that Matthew composed an original Aramaic collection of the sayings of Jesus (sometimes clearly identified with Q), and this was later translated and augmented with Markan traditions, probably after A.D. 70 (see, with variations, the commentaries of Hill, Allen, Plummer).

Third, some scholars have challenged this interpretation of the early Christian evidence. In effect, these scholars contend that an original Aramaic Gospel is a faulty inference from the evidence, and this contention is buttressed with the arguments that at least substantial portions of Matthew were not penned by Matthew and that the linguistic evidence suggests that the Gospel was originally composed in Greek (see Bacon, Beare, Meier).

This variety of interpretations compels us to look again at Papias, the apparent source of most of the early church traditions.

First, in light of Eusebius's previous reference to Mark as an "arrangement of the Lord's oracles" (*Hist. Eccl.* 3.39.15), wherein the same word *oracles (logia)* is used as in the Matthean reference, it is most probable that *logia* in "Matthew collected the oracles *[logia]*" refers to the entire Gospel, rendering the second interpretation discussed above unlikely. Second, although a majority of scholars have inferred that "in the Hebrew language *[Hēbraidi dialektō]*" means a Gospel written either in Hebrew or Aramaic, recent scholarship has virtually overturned this interpretation.

It has been argued (1) that Matthew betrays no evidence of being a translated Gospel; (2) that the Greek expression *Hēbraidi dialektō*, when investigated carefully in its Asia Minor context, means not "in the Hebrew language" but "in a Hebrew rhetorical style" (Gundry, 619-20); (3) that the context shows that Papias is comparing Matthew's style ("orderly" and "in a Hebrew style") with Mark's style ("chreia form" *[pros tas chreias]*, "not, indeed, in order"; *Hist. Eccl.* 3.39.15); and (4) that "interpreted" (*hērmēneusen*) in Papias's statement (*Hist. Eccl.* 3.39.16) most probably refers to the explanation and communication of Matthew's style by others rather than its translation (Gundry, 619). Prior to this statement about Matthew, Papias, according to Eusebius, had said that Mark was Peter's interpreter *(hērmēneutes)*. This most likely refers not to Mark's translation of Peter's words but to his interpretation and composition of Peter's words into the form of a Gospel.

In conclusion, the most recent scholarship on the Papias logion suggests that the traditional rendering is insufficient and should be understood now in the following manner: In contrast to Mark's unordered, chreia-style Gospel, Papias contends, Matthew composed a more Jewish, orderly-styled Gospel. The original language, then, is of no concern to Papias. This suggests that the first interpretation is unlikely. In all likelihood our Gospel of Matthew was composed originally in Greek and in a Jewish style. But was the First Gospel composed by an apostle?

1.2. Was the Author the Apostle? Although there is an impressive list of scholars who argue that the First Gospel was apostolic (e.g., the commentators Tasker, Gundry, Carson), several arguments have been used to dispute that the First Gospel was penned by the apostle Matthew.

Foremost, it is argued that if the First Gospel used Mark as its primary source, it is most unlikely that an apostle (Matthew) would need to borrow from a nonapostolic source (Mark) (e.g., the commentators Allen, Beare; see also Bacon). This observation appears most penetrating when one observes that, assuming Matthew used Mark, the supposed apostolic author largely copied Mark's account of his own call (Mt 9:9-13 par. Mk 2:13-17). However significant this objection may seem, and however many esteemed scholars rely on this source-critical argument, it is not finally persuasive. If one grants that Peter somehow stands behind Mark—and early Christian evidence supports this view (Eusebius *Hist. Eccl.* 3.39.15)—thereby lending it some level of apostolic authority, then Matthew's use of Mark is hardly beneath apostolic dignity.

Second, it is argued that the author did not write the Gospel in Aramaic or Hebrew but wrote in Greek, and that therefore the author could not have been the apostle Matthew This argument has some important features. To be sure, it is now clear that our present Gospel is most likely not originally an Aramaic or Hebrew Gospel. In fact, it often betrays its Greek origin in Greek word plays (e.g., Mt 6:16; 21:41; 24:30) and its dependence on the Septuagint (Mt 1:23; 11:10;

12:21; 13:14-15; 21:16). However, evidence clearly pointing toward a Greek original is not proof of a Gentile or nonapostolic author. Matthew, having been a tax collector, would very likely have been quite versatile in several languages. The argument over language proves little.

Third, various scholars have pointed to features that suggest to them a Gentile author. These features include (1) the universalism of the First Gospel (Mt 2:1-12; 4:14-16; 12:21; 28:19) when coupled with the condemnation of the Jewish nation (Mt 20:1-16; 21:28-32, 43; 27:25); (2) the torture described in Matthew 18:34, which was not a Jewish practice (Jeremias 1972, 210-14); (3) the so-called misunderstood Hebrew parallelism of Matthew 21:5-7; and (4) various other non-Jewish features (Mt 5:43; 12:11-12; 27:5). For these scholars, these data point away from a Jewish (apostolic) author and toward a Gentile author. Without going into details regarding each of these pieces of evidence (and each of those listed in 2-4 is not easy to explain), it must be said that neither universalism nor a clear stance against unbelieving Judaism (see McKnight 1993) is evidence for non-Jewish authorship. There is nothing ideological in the First Gospel that is not also found in either the OT prophets or in the letters of Paul, sources that are clearly Jewish in origin.

A final argument lodged against apostolic authorship pertains to the date of the First Gospel. If we assume, as the majority of scholarship does, that Matthew used Mark, and if Mark was written in the late 60s, say A.D. 68-70 (but before the destruction of Jerusalem in A.D. 70; see Hengel, 1-30), then it follows that the First Gospel was written sometime after A.D. 70. Making allowance for enough time for Mark to circulate and gain authority, most scholars estimate that Matthew would have been written a decade later. If we grant that Mark could have been written as early as the mid-60s, we have the earliest possible date for Matthew between A.D. 75 and 80, with a date between A.D. 75 and 85 being widely held (Davies and Allison). Could the apostle Matthew have penned the Gospel that late? Perhaps so. Earliest Christian evidence does not suggest that Matthew died before A.D. 70, and so traditional authorship is not excluded even with a date as late as A.D. 85.

It follows from the preceding arguments that the traditional view that the First Gospel was authored by the apostle Matthew is a reasonable position. However, this conclusion is not without problems. Several issues caution against regarding the authorship of the First Gospel a settled matter. (1) The later one dates Matthew after the destruction of Jerusalem, the less likely it becomes that its author was the apostle. Furthermore, (2) its probable use of Mark and (3) its evidently Greek origin should give one pause. Further, (4) the several problems with respect to Jewish customs make one hesitate in coming to a firm conclusion regarding authorship. (5) If Matthew used Mark, it is at best peculiar that Matthew would have recorded his own conversion by copying Mark (cf. Mt 9:9-13 with Mk 2:13-17). Finally, (6) it needs to be noted that textual critics are agreed that the original copy of the First Gospel did not contain an ascription of authorship to Matthew. This means that the matter of authorship has nothing to do with canon or with interpretation of the original; it is an intriguing historical issue on which scholars have cast some illuminating but not yet definitive light.

2. The Structure of Matthew.

Over the last twenty years Matthean scholars have engaged in an important discussion centered on the structure of Matthew's Gospel (see Bauer, 21-55). A summary of this discussion will permit the reader to gain a glimpse of the First Gospel in its entirety. Four major models for understanding the structure of Matthew have been proposed. Following an overview of these models, a synthetic proposal will be presented.

2.1. Geographical-Biographical. The oldest, and perhaps simplest, is the geographical-biographical model. This proposal organizes Matthew according to a suggested outline of the life of Jesus as he moves through his Galilean and Jerusalem ministries. In his commentary on Matthew (1912), W. C. Allen proposed the following:

1. The Birth and Infancy of the Messiah (Mt 1:1—2:23)
2. Preparation for Ministry (Mt 3:1—4:11)
3. Public Ministry in Galilee (Mt 4:12—15:20)
4. Ministry in the Neighborhood of Galilee (Mt 15:21—18:35)
5. Journey to Jerusalem (Mt 19:1—20:34)
6. Last Days of the Messiah's Life (Mt 21:1—28:20)

Several features dominate this perspective on Matthew. (1) The view is harmonious with nineteenth- and early twentieth-century views of the life of Jesus; (2) the life of Jesus so predominates that a feature from Luke (the so-called travel narrative) finds its way into Matthew, though Matthew gives no serious attention to the travel (e.g., Mt 19:1—20:34); (3) the progress of Gospel studies in the last two centuries has drawn more and more attention to the various presentations of the Evangelists, and this aspect of Matthew has been completely neglected. Consequently, although many of the older commentaries used this essential outline (e.g., Plummer, McNeile), few would follow it today. Rather, it is recognized that this approach reflects a preoccupation of nineteenth-century Gospel studies: how to compose a life of Jesus.

2.2. Fivefold Discourse. Matthean scholarship changed when B. W. Bacon proposed his fivefold topical model (1918 and 1930). Bacon presented a new outline, one based on Matthew's clear alternation between narrative and discourse. Departing from the life-of-Jesus approach, he took a literary perspective. Moreover, Bacon argued, Matthew's use of five major discourses reveals a christological tendency: Jesus is a new Moses who gives a new law for the church. Bacon's proposal follows:

Preamble (Mt 1:1—2:23)

1. Book 1: Concerning Discipleship (Mt 3:1—7:29)
2. Book 2: Concerning Apostleship (Mt 8:1—11:1)
3. Book 3: Concerning Hiding Revelation (Mt 11:2—13:53)
4. Book 4: Concerning Church Administration (Mt 13:54—19:1a)
5. Book 5: Concerning the Judgment (Mt 19:1b—26:2)

Epilogue (26:3—28:20)

Apart from relegating the passion and resurrection narratives (Mt 26:2—28:20) to an epilogue, Bacon made a great advance for Matthean studies by paying attention to Matthew's structuring devices. Accordingly, we are indebted to Bacon when we call attention to Matthew's major structural marker for the discourses (Mt 7:28; 11:1; 13:53; 19:1; 26:1: "And when Jesus had finished these things . . ."). We must also credit Bacon with transforming the obvious alternation between narrative and discourse in Matthew from a banal observation to a significant key to Matthew's structural plan. However, Bacon's suggestion of a Pentateuchal pattern behind Matthew's five discourses has not been generally accepted, and further modifications have been made to his view (see esp. Farrer, Barr, Bauer).

2.3. Chiastic/Concentric. Anticipating the trend of literary analysis, C. H. Lohr proposed that Matthew's Gospel was arranged chiastically or concentrically. That is, each earlier section of the Gospel is related to a later section, and these sections are in turn arranged in reverse order from the center ("F" below):

1. Narrative: Birth and Beginnings (Mt 1—4) A
  2. Sermon: Blessings, Entering the Kingdom (Mt 5—7) B
    3. Narrative: Authority and Invitation (Mt 8—9) C
      4. Sermon: Mission (Mt 10) D
        5. Narrative: Rejection by this Generation (Mt 11—12) E
          6. Sermon: Parables of the Kingdom (Mt 13) F
        7. Narrative: Acknowledgment by the Disciples (Mt 14—17) E'
      8. Sermon: Community Discourse (Mt 18) D'
    9. Narrative: Authority and Invitation (Mt 19—22) C'
  10. Sermon: Woes, Coming of the Kingdom (Mt 23—25) B'
11. Narrative: Death and Rebirth (Mt 26—28) A'

Lohr's theory (and those who have modified his essential view; see Bauer, Combrink Rolland) has several important features. Besides recognizing Matthew's structural alternation between narrative and discourse, the proposal observes the connections between various sections of Matthew as well as the various topics that Matthew develops. However, Lohr's approach has been widely criticized for its failure to heed chronological features inherent to the text as well as its fancifulness in connecting various sections. One example will suffice: it may be structurally pleasing to say that Matthew 1—4 are birth and beginnings and Matthew 26—28 are death and rebirth, but this does not represent the theological and literary content of these important sections of Matthew. Any skilled literary artist or homiletician can find connections of this sort at the abstract level, but such constructions fail at the level of exegesis and details.

2.4. Biographical and Theological. The fourth proposal, a biographical and theological model, has commanded the most discussion as well as consent. This model, originally developed by N. B. Stonehouse and then improved by E. Krentz, has been fully worked out by J. D. Kingsbury and D. R. Bauer. In essence, this model recognizes an essential biographical aspect of the drama of Matthew's Gospel but sees it as subservient to an overall theological program. Matthew leaves clues to this structure through a superscription device: namely, at Matthew 4:17 and Matthew 16:21 Matthew uses an expression ("From that time on Jesus began . . .") that signals the outset of a new division. This provides a neat and useful threefold division to the Gospel.

1. The Person of Jesus Messiah (Mt 1:1—4:16)
2. The Proclamation of Jesus Messiah (Mt 4:17—16:20)
3. The Suffering, Death and Resurrection of Jesus Messiah (Mt 16:21—28:20)

The alternatives are clear: either the structural devices of alternating narratives and discourses or the repetition of the formula at Matthew 4:17 and Matthew 16:21 are to be given the structural priority. Scholars have argued that the additional use of the superscription formula at Matthew 26:16 as well as the essential use of Mark 8:31 at Matthew 16:21 (rather than a unique signal in Matthew) suggest that Kingsbury has gone too far in making Matthew 4:17 and Matthew 16:21 structurally determinative. In fact, it can be said that though Matthew 16:21 may have been a major turning point in Jesus' life, it is not a necessary turning point in Matthew's structural plot. Kingsbury has elevated to the level of a structuring device a Markan comment on the life of Jesus that Matthew has incorporated into his Gospel. In neither Gospel was it intended to play such a role.

2.5. Considerations for Determining Matthew's Structure. In light of the preceding survey, several features must be incorporated into any adequate proposal for understanding Matthew's structure.

First, it must determine the genre of the Synoptic Gospels and, in particular, the genre of Matthew (see Gospel [Genre]). P. L. Shuler has investigated this matter with respect to Matthew and has concluded that Matthew is essentially encomium, or laudatory, biography (see Shuler).

Second, the structure needs to reckon with the clear theological tendencies of the author. Both redaction critics and literary critics have expanded our knowledge of the nature of a Synoptic Gospel in highlighting the Evangelist's contributions and literary strategies. The implication of these approaches for structure is a recognition that the Gospels, however biographical, are directed by an author's theological and literary designs. The authors of the Synoptics are more than historians.

Third, at times the structure of sections of Matthew may well be determined by the traditions and sources Matthew inherited. Thus, while we see major innovation on the part of Matthew in Matthew 4—13 when compared with Mark, from Matthew 14 on we see very few deviations from the essential Markan structure. One gains the impression that church tradition had grown accustomed to what we now see in Mark and this tradition, rather than the Evangelist's designs, controlled the direction of Matthew's pen.

Fourth, at times sections in Matthew may be controlled more by theme than by chronology and historical succession. Hence Matthew, in the interest of a more thematic arrangement, may at times reorder and relocate traditions found elsewhere in Mark or Luke. When we look at Matthew's discourses and compare their material with the same material found in either Mark or Luke, we often find that Matthew's arrangement differs and that Matthew's pattern seems to be thematic. For example, the material Luke relates in the context of two different missions (Lk 9:1-6 [cf. Mk 6:6-13]; Lk 10:1-12) Matthew records as only one mission (Mt 9:36—11:1). It is apparent that Matthew has thematically grouped material around "missionary instructions" rather than paying strict attention to chronology. (In the same discourse of Matthew, compare Mt 10:17-25 with Mk 13:9-13; Mt 10:26-33 with Lk 12:2-9; Mt 10:34-36 with Lk 12:51-53; Mt 10:37-39 with Lk 14:26-27; 17:33.)

Fifth, for a structural proposal to be complete it must pay special attention to Matthew's redactional alterations and arrangements. Hence, in reading a red-letter edition of Matthew, it may at times be important to give special attention to the black letters to observe Matthew's authorial angle. Whether that redaction of Matthew pertains to smaller (cf. Mt 11:2,19 with Lk 7:18, 35; cf. Mt 8:1—9:35 with Mt 10:8 and Mk 6:7 or Lk 9:1-2) or larger (cf. the structural importance of Mt 4:23 and Mt 9:35) units, painstaking observations of details distinct to Matthew are significant for determining Matthew's overall structure.

2.6. A Proposed Structure. As Bacon and Lohr have observed, the most important literary and redactional feature of Matthew's Gospel is an alternation between narrative and discourse. Furthermore, five discourses stand out in relief on the Matthean landscape. These two features are crucial to Matthew's ordering of his material. The following outline organizes these two structural features under an essential biographical or chronological plot.

Prologue (Mt 1:1—2:23)
Introduction (Mt 3:1—4:11)

1. The Messiah Confronts Israel in His Galilean Ministry (Mt 4:12—11:1)
   1.1. Narrative: Introduction (Mt 4:12-22)
   1.2. Discourse: The Messiah's Call to Righteousness (Mt 5:1—7:29)
   1.3. Narrative: The Messiah's Ministry (Mt 8:1—9:34)
   1.4. Discourse: The Messiah Extends His Ministry (Mt 9:36—11:1)

2. The Responses to the Messiah: Rejection and Acceptance from Galilee to Jerusalem (Mt 11:2—20:34)
   2.1. Narrative: The Messiah Is Rejected by Jewish Leaders but Accepted by the Disciples (Mt 11:2—12:50)
   2.2. Discourse: The Messiah Teaches About the Kingdom (Mt 13:1-53)
   2.3. Narrative: The Messiah Is Rejected by Jewish Leaders but Accepted by the Disciples: Responses Intensify (Mt 13:54—17:27)
   2.4. Discourse: The Messiah Instructs on Community Life (Mt 18:1—19:1)
   2.5. Narrative: The Messiah Instructs on the Way to Jerusalem (Mt 19:2—20:34)

3. The Messiah Inaugurates the Kingdom of Heaven Through Rejection and Vindications: Jesus the Messiah Confronts Jerusalem (Mt 21:1—28:20)
   3.1. Narrative: The Messiah Confronts Israel in Jerusalem (Mt 21:1—22:46)
   3.2. Discourse: The Messiah Predicts the Judgment of Unbelieving Israel (Mt 23:1—26:2)
   3.3. Narrative: The Messiah Is Rejected in Jerusalem but Vindicated by God Through Resurrection (Mt 26:3—28:20)

This outline utilizes the guiding themes (see 3 below) of Matthew for its main points: Jesus as Messiah, kingdom, confrontation and so on. In addition, we make the following observations. First, it needs to be observed that Matthew has essentially two introductions, a prologue (Mt 1:1—2:23) and an introduction to the public ministry of Jesus (Mt 3:1—4:11). These two introductions stem from two essential traditions: the prologue is derived from Matthew's special material ("M"), and the second introduction is a conflation of Mark's introduction with Q traditions on John the Baptist and the temptation of Jesus. Thus the problem of two introductions is essentially a source-critical matter; Matthew had at his disposal two different ways to begin his Gospel, and he chose to use both.

Second, Matthew 4:23 and Matthew 9:35 are virtually identical in wording and bracket the material between them. In fact, Matthew 4:23 is an outline of Matthew 5:1—9:34: Jesus is described in Matthew 4:23 as one who teaches and preaches (Mt 5:1—7:29) and one who heals all diseases (Mt 8:1—9:34). It appears that Matthew 4:23 and Matthew 9:35 are a literary device used by Matthew to announce to the reader what is coming (Mt 4:23) in Matthew 5:1—9:34 and what has transpired (Mt 9:35). This device of beginning and ending a section with the same literary form is called an *inclusio*. Furthermore, the essential unity of the first major section, Matthew 4:12—11:1, is seen in that the last element of Matthew 4:23 and Matthew 9:35 is then used for describing what the disciples are to do—heal every disease and sickness (cf. Mt 10:1). In addition, Jesus' ministry of healing and casting out demons in Matthew 8:1—9:34 is then commanded of the disciples in Matthew 10:8. What needs to be noted here is that the missionary commands of Matthew (Mt 10:8) are much more complete than those of either Mark (Mk 6:7) or Luke (Lk 9:1-2), and the commands of Matthew are clearly a repetition of what Jesus has done previously.

Third, in light of these observations it follows that Matthew 4:12—11:1 is essentially a programmatic description of the ministry of Jesus directed toward those who wish to follow him as disciples. Put differently, in Matthew 4:12—11:1 Matthew presents Jesus in the fullness of his ministry, thereby enabling readers to decide how they will respond to him. It is therefore of no surprise that the section following Matthew 4:12—11:1 is primarily wrapped around various responses to Jesus (Mt 11:2—20:34).

Fourth, two sections in Matthew 11:2—20:34 are organized around the twin response to Jesus: rejection by leaders and acceptance by the disciples. These sections are Matthew 11:2—12:50 and Matthew 13:54—17:27, the latter section revealing deeper acceptance by the disciples (see Mt 16:21—17:27) and more radical rejection of Jesus by the leaders (see Mt 14:1-12; 15:1-20; 16:1-12). Between these two sections falls the third discourse (Mt 13:1-53). To title this the "Discourse on Parables" gives too much attention to form rather than content. Instead, Matthew 13 is concerned with Jesus' parabolic teaching about the nature of the "kingdom of the heavens" (Matthew's literal rendering of a Jewish equivalent to "kingdom of God," hereafter translated "kingdom of heaven"; see Kingdom of God). Here we see that the kingdom effects various responses (Mt 13:1-9, 18-23), comes silently and nonviolently (Mt 13:24-30, 31-32, 33, 36-43), calls for drastic commitment (Mt 13:44, 45-46) and has an ethical call that is rooted in God's final judgment (Mt 13:47-50). Buttressing these teachings are comments by Jesus on the privileged knowledge of the disciples (Mt 13:10-17) and the dawn of fulfillment in Jesus' parabolic teaching (Mt 13:34-35). Those who can understand Jesus' teachings about the kingdom of heaven are compared with scribes who understand all things (Mt 13:51-52).

Fifth, perhaps because of Christian familiarity with Jesus' final week, several comments need to be made about how to read Matthew 21:1—28:20. To begin with, in light of Matthew's theology and NT theology in general, readers need to bear in mind that this section is not just a rehearsal of the last week of Jesus for the convenience of historians or for the liturgical needs of church calendars. Rather, this section tells of the passion and vindication of Jesus that together bring about salvation for the world. From the Matthean perspective these climactic events inaugurated the kingdom of heaven more fully than had any other event or set of events since the advent of John the Baptist (Mt 3:2).

Furthermore, there is an essential unity to Matthew 21:1—25:46. Jesus enters Jerusalem as Messiah (see Christ) to display who he is (Mt 21:1-22). He enters into a contest with the Jerusalem authorities to demonstrate his wisdom and calling by God (Mt 21:23—22:46), and he then warns the nation that judgment is coming because it has rejected God's appointed Messiah (Mt 23:1—25:46).

Due to a keen interest in end-time eschatology, modern-day evangelicals have frequently separated Matthew 23:1-39 from Matthew 24:1—25:46. This separation usually leads to major interpretive errors. It is important to recognize that Matthew 23:1-39 leads into Matthew 24:1-36; the rejection of Jesus Messiah by the leaders prompts Jesus to predict the destruction of Jerusalem. Jesus predicts not the destruction of Judaism but the destruction of Jerusalem, thereby making it clear that he sees God's judgment directed primarily against the Jewish establishment centralized in Jerusalem (see Levine). It follows from this contextual tie (cf. Mt 23:36 and Mt 23:37-39 with Mt 24:1-3, 8, 33, 34 in their uses of "all these things") that the dominant concern of Matthew 24:1-36 is the destruction of Jerusalem in A.D. 70 and not a final tribulation at the end of history. Indeed, it is difficult to interpret Matthew 24:29 ("immediately") and Matthew 24:34 in any other way than as a primary if not total reference to the destruction of Jerusalem in A.D. 70 (see France, 333-48).

3. The Theology of Matthew.

By discussing Matthew's theology we do not imply that the evidence is sufficient for us to infer an entire systematic theology. Rather, what we find in the Gospel of Matthew is a record of the life of Jesus that has been shaped by Matthew in such a way that we can detect emphases and patterns of thought that are the author's. It is these patterns and themes that we describe when we outline Matthew's theology. Matthew certainly believed a great deal more than what we are able to infer, but these themes contribute to our understanding of biblical theology.

When scholars today discuss Matthew's theology as distinct from that of Mark, Luke or John, a subtle but significant difference is being made between the theology of the Evangelist and the teachings of Jesus. Whereas the expression "teachings of Jesus" describes all that Jesus taught as it is found in the four canonical Gospels and elsewhere (with little appreciable being added by sources outside the canonical Gospels), an analysis of Matthew's theology studies the particular contributions and shaping of tradition observable in this particular Gospel. Accordingly, in describing Matthew's theology the scholar looks for the Evangelist's beliefs as they are embedded in the First Gospel and considers what his beliefs meant in their cultural and religious contexts.

There are four major themes in the First Gospel: christology, or what the Evangelist believed about Jesus Christ, who is the center of Matthew's theology; the kingdom of heaven, which often reveals what he believed about God; salvation history, the conceptual and hermeneutical grid through which Matthew read and interpreted the past, present and future; and discipleship, the expectation laid upon humans in light of the dawn of the kingdom in Jesus Christ.

3.1. Christology. There have been three major approaches to Matthew's christology. First, many scholars have found in the titles Matthew ascribes to Jesus the decisive clues for constructing Matthew's christology. This approach usually revolves around the centrality of *"Son of God" (Kingsbury). This approach has the advantage of a clear organizational method for categorizing the evidence. But this method can neglect the fact that the titles ascribed to a person reveal only certain aspects of that person.

Second, others (esp. Hill, Verseput, France, Suggs) have argued that while "Son of God" is a central title, it must be supplemented by additional ideas in order to achieve a comprehensive and accurate portrayal of Matthew's christology.

Third, in essential support of traditional interpretation of Matthew, B. M. Nolan has argued that Matthew develops a "royal christology" with the predominant category for Jesus being "Messianic King and Son of God."

The first two approaches emphasize an aspect or title of Matthew's portrayal of Christ that is clearly present in the Gospel. But in each case the emphasis is reductionistic, whether or not the title is then augmented with other ideas. In what follows we propose that a larger synthesis, using titles and functions, describes more comprehensively and accurately the christology of Matthew.

We may summarize Matthew's christology as follows: Jesus is God's Messiah who fulfills OT promise, reveals God's will and inaugurates the kingdom of heaven through his public ministry, passion and resurrection, and consequently reigns over the new people of God.

3.1.1. Messiah. Even apart from the number of times the title occurs in the First Gospel (Mt 1:1,

16, 17, 18; 2:4; 11:2; 16:16, 20; 22:42; 23:10; 26:63, 68; 27:17, 22), for Matthew, Jesus is preeminently the Messiah. The use of the term *Messiah* for Jesus implies a confession that in Jesus the OT promises of restoration and salvation are coming to pass (cf. Mt 2:4; 26:63). For Matthew the term *Messiah* seems inherently to bear some concept of preexistence (Mt 2:4; 22:41-46). But primarily the Messiah fulfills the OT in his person and ministry (Mt 1:1—2:23; 5:17-48). Thus, according to Matthew's typological exegesis, Jesus is a sort of new Moses, he brings a new exodus, and he is a kind of new Israel (Mt 1:18—2:23; 3:3; see the commentary of Davies and Allison; France, 185-91). Further, he brings the fulfillment of the law and prophets (Mt 3:15; 5:17-48; 12:17-21; 13:35; 21:5, 16, 42; 22:44; 23:39; 26:31; 27:9, 35, 46) and has become the suffering and rejected Servant of Yahweh (Mt 3:17; 8:17; 10:35; 12:17-21; 13:14-15; 21:5, 42; 23:39; 26:31, 38; 27:9, 35, 46; *see* Servant of Yahweh).

As Messiah, Jesus is described at several crucial junctures in the Gospel as "Son of God." In fact, J. D. Kingsbury has contended in numerous writings that Matthew regards "Son of God" as the central and most theologically laden term used for Jesus. Thus at Matthew 3:17 the Father announces publicly "this is my Son" (cf. with Mk 1:11 and Lk 3:22: "you are my Son"); at Matthew 4:3, 6 the devil addresses Jesus as God's Son; at Matthew 11:27 Jesus refers to his special relationship to God as that of a son to a father. At Matthew 14:33 the men in the boat, on seeing a marvel beyond description, confess Jesus as God's Son. At Matthew 16:16, Matthew apparently glosses Peter's confession of Jesus as God's Messiah with "Son of the living God." At Matthew 17:5 the Father again announces to the inner circle that Jesus is the Son of God. At Matthew 24:36 Jesus reveals that, in spite of his privileged knowledge of God's will, not even he, the Son of God, knows the date of the parousia. At Matthew 26:63 the high priest explains the term *Messiah* with "Son of God." At Matthew 27:40, 43 the passersby appeal to Jesus as Son of God to tempt him to come down from his ignominious crucifixion. And at Matthew 27:54 the Gentile centurion confesses Jesus, in what is taken by many to be the climax of human perception in the First Gospel, to be the Son of God.

In light of the preceding survey, it is not surprising that many scholars have argued that "Son of God" is the most important title in Mat-thew. While one cannot doubt its crucial or central role as a title, the issue is not so much which title is more important but what the First Gospel asserts about Jesus in light of what he says, does and is called. Thus a more functional and less titular approach gives us a more comprehensive and accurate picture. And, while it may be true that "Son of God" is highly important, it remains the case that two of the instances of "Son of God" are explained by the concept of Jesus as God's servant (Mt 3:17—4:11; 16:16, 21).

As Messiah, Jesus is also the destined king of Israel, in spite of his crucifixion. To be Messiah is to be the king of Israel (Mt 2:2; 21:5; 27:11, 29, 37, 42). But even though Jesus is Messiah, king of Israel, he is a unique king because he is God's unique Son and reigns through his suffering (Mt 27:11, 29, 37, 42; cf. also the rejection inherent at Mt 2:1-12; see Hill, Gerhardsson 1974).

3.1.2. Teacher and Preacher. For Matthew, Jesus Messiah reveals God's will. Jesus Messiah teaches and reveals God's will in his public ministry, but his teaching and preaching are largely ignored or rejected. Although the terms have fallen out of favor with Matthean scholars, *teacher* and *preacher* are important categories for understanding the Jesus of Matthew. Even if it is clear that "teacher" (i.e., rabbi) is inadequate for fully comprehending the nature of Jesus' person and mission, Matthew evidently regarded this category as nonetheless vital for understanding him. Thus the structure of Matthew, punctuated as it is by five major discourses (nine chapters), leads the reader to think of Jesus as a great teacher, a special rabbi, a revealer of wisdom (esp. Mt 5—7; 13; 18). In scholarship's tendency to go beyond "teacher" for describing Jesus, it has bypassed this important category. To be sure, it is nondisciples in Matthew who describe Jesus as teacher (Mt 8:19; 9:11; 12:38; 17:24; 19:16; 22:16, 24, 36), while the disciples of Jesus never call him "teacher." However, Jesus describes himself as teacher (Mt 10:24, 25; 23:8; 26:18), and his ministry, according to Matthew, revolves around teaching God's will as revealed in the new age (Mt 3:15; 5:17-48; 11:27; 13:10-17; 23:8). As teacher, Jesus will suffer (Mt 10:24-25).

One of Jesus' messianic tasks is to preach the gospel of the kingdom of heaven (Mt 4:17, 23; 9:35), a message requiring repentance and obedience to God's will (Mt 4:17). Interestingly, as the preacher of the gospel, Jesus falls in line with the rejected prophets of Israel (Mt 5:10-12;

23:34-39; 24:14) and John the Baptist (Mt 3:1-2; 14:1-13). A motif running through Matthew's presentation of Jesus as revealer of God's will is the rejection of his teaching and preaching (Mt 11:1—12:50).

3.1.3. Inaugurator of the Kingdom. Another important feature of Matthew's christology is that Jesus Messiah inaugurates the kingdom of heaven, apparently in three moments or phases: in his public ministry, in his passion and in his vindicating resurrection. Each of these moments is important to the story line of Matthew and each is associated with the inauguration of the kingdom. Hence we have chosen to speak of three "moments" or "phases" of the inauguration of the kingdom of heaven in Matthew. In the First Gospel it is critical to recognize that Jesus' primary calling is to inaugurate the kingdom of heaven.

In his public ministry Jesus anticipates the kingdom's inauguration (Mt 4:17; *ēngiken* means "has drawn near but is not yet here"), but that kingdom begins to demonstrate its presence especially through Jesus' mighty deeds of wonder (*see* Kingdom of God). Thus Jesus points to his powerful miracles as evidence of the inauguration of the kingdom (Mt 11:2-6; 12:28; see Gerhardsson 1979; Held). As Son of David (*see* Son of David), Jesus is healer (Mt 9:32-34; 12:24), but it is also important to observe that Matthew connects Jesus' mighty works with his ministry as servant and his atoning sacrifice (Mt 8:16-17; 12:15-21; 27:51-53). In Jesus' public ministry we must also observe that Jesus' revelatory teaching and preaching are an integral aspect of the beginning of the inauguration of the kingdom of heaven as Jesus teaches the "ethic of the New Era" or, as others have put it, "kingdom ethics." These teachings (e.g., Mt 5:17-20) are an integral aspect of the dawning of the kingdom (also Guelich, 134-74).

In his passion, Jesus accomplishes the second phase of the inauguration of the kingdom of heaven (*see* Death of Christ [Gospels]). Even if it is a commonplace to observe that the Gospels have given much attention to the passion story of Jesus—and so we point to the cruciform nature of the earliest Christian story about Jesus—it is nonetheless important to incorporate this structure into our understanding of Matthew's theology. If it is true that Matthew anticipates to some degree the kingdom of God being inaugurated (cf. Mt 4:17; 20:28), it is reasonable to expect that the passion, the story of Jesus' rejection and death, will be an important phase in its inauguration.

We can observe the importance of the passion for Matthew's telling of the story of Jesus in the fourfold prediction of Jesus' death and rejection (Mt 16:21; 17:22-23; 20:18-19; 26:2). As mentioned above, even the mighty miracles of Jesus are seen as proleptic realizations of the kingdom on the basis of the passion ministry of Jesus (Mt 8:16-17). For Matthew, Jesus is the one who forgives sins (Mt 9:6) and the Son of man (*see* Son of Man) who will ransom many through his self-sacrifice (Mt 20:28). This latter passage clearly suggests an integral connection between the death of Jesus, the forgiveness of sins and the kingdom of God. And in the Last Supper, Matthew again makes similar connections: Jesus' blood, forgiveness, anticipation of the consummation of the kingdom (Mt 26:29).

When it comes to describing the passion, the Gospel writers are notoriously silent in their reflection on its soteriological significance. However, in Matthew we find several indications that Matthew, among other things, sees the kingdom of God being inaugurated through Jesus' passion and rejection (Allison, 40-50). First, the connection of Jesus' death (Mt 27:50) with the resurrection of the holy ones (Mt 27:51-53), with its clear allusion to Zechariah 14:4-5 (LXX), indicates for Matthew that Jesus' death breaks the bonds of death and inaugurates the general resurrection (a clear end-time, or kingdom, expectation). Second, the confession of the Gentile centurion (Mt 27:54) may well be a sign of the commencement of Gentile salvation that was to occur at the end of history (universalism; cf. Mt 2:1-12; 4:12-17; 8:5-13, 28-34; 12:38-42; 15:21-28; 21:33-46; 22:1-14; 24:14; 28:16-20). And Matthew tightens the connection between Jesus' death, the resurrection of the saints and the confession of the Gentile centurion and others with him by adding "When . . . they saw the earthquake and what took place" (Mt 27:54 RSV). Finally, the connection of the themes of Matthew 26:64 with their partial realization in Matthew 28:16-20 suggests another instance wherein the passion and rejection of Jesus are described as the inauguration of the kingdom of heaven. Thus Matthew's treatment of his traditions, as well as his addition of new ones, indicates that he sees the death of Jesus as an important phase in the inauguration of the kingdom of heaven.

In his resurrection, Jesus is vindicated, and this too is a phase in the inauguration of the kingdom. Matthew's narrative of the resurrection (Mt 27:62—28:20) gives indications of his seeing the resurrection of Jesus as the inauguration of a new epoch in history. The descriptive language of Matthew 28:2-4, with its report of the earthquake, the descent of the angel and the fear of the guards borrows heavily from language shared by texts rooted in Jewish eschatological speculation. As Allison has put it, "Matthew 28:2-4 appears to recount the events of Easter morning as though they were events of the last times" (Allison, 48).

Matthew's eschatological orientation becomes particularly apparent when we examine the Great Commission (Mt 28:16-20). There we observe massive reorientations in history, revealing clearly that a new epoch has dawned as a result of Jesus' resurrection. First, although it is true that prior to his resurrection the Father has given Jesus personal authority (Mt 5:17-48; 7:29; 21:23, 24, 27) and authority over sickness and demons (Mt 9:6, 8; 10:1), that authority is fully granted only after his resurrection (Mt 28:18: "all authority"). Christologically Jesus has moved from one acting with authority within the narrow confines of Palestine to one who possesses universal sovereign authority.

Second, as with Mark and Luke, throughout Matthew's Gospel Jesus is regularly vindicated in the face of opposition. Thus, in line with the essence of a pronouncement story, Jesus is victoriously vindicated as God's special messenger (e.g., Mt 12:1-8). It follows that the resurrection of Jesus is God's unique and final vindication of his Son following a momentary victory by his opponents (cf. Mt 27:39-44 and 28:1-10; Osborne, 73-98).

Third, Matthew's heavy emphasis on universalism (see 3.1.3. above) reaches its consummation in Jesus' command to disciple the entire world (Mt 28:19). The people of Jesus include those of all nations, all social levels and both genders (Levine, 165-92). What was previously prohibited (Mt 10:5-6, "Do not go among the Gentiles") is now the culminating command (Mt 28:19); those who were previously exceptions (Mt 8:5-13; 15:21-28) are now the focus. And, in continuity with the old era, the new era does not erase Israel from God's plan of salvation. On the contrary, the term *nations* includes Jews alongside Gentiles (see Levine, 185-92). A subtle reminder of Matthew's attempt to evangelize

Jews may be observed in Matthew's narrative of the guards at the tomb, the appearance of the angel and the women's encounter with Jesus (Mt 27:62-66; 28:5-7, 9-10). The manner in which this material speaks about Jews and addresses Jewish concerns demonstrates a clear apologetic tendency. The rescinding of the previous prohibition against evangelizing the Gentiles and the proclamation of a new duty of evangelizing the nations reveal that Matthew sees the resurrection of Jesus as inaugurating a new age.

Finally, it is no overstatement to say that the Great Commission envisions the formation of a new people of God, founded no doubt on the disciples of Jesus. This new people of God Matthew calls "the church" (Mt 16:18; 18:17). The commission to form this new people reveals that something new is happening as a result of Jesus' resurrection. Thus the final scenes of Matthew show Jesus now vindicated by God as Messiah, invested with all authority and commissioning the disciples to disciple the world.

Although the three phases of the inauguration of the kingdom sketched above are only different (chronologically distinct) aspects of the ministry of Jesus, they each contribute to the inauguration of that kingdom. In general, through Jesus God inaugurated the kingdom of heaven; in particular, God has done this through Jesus' public ministry, his passion and most climactically through his resurrection. But what is the kingdom of heaven?

3.2. The Kingdom of Heaven. In general, we can say the kingdom of heaven is God's reign through Jesus Christ over all people, and that those who repent and believe in Jesus enter into God's reign in the present. The experience of God's sovereign reign brings with it righteousness and joy as well as the hope of its future consummation in glory at the parousia of the Son of man (*see* Apocalypticism). An inevitable consequence of the conviction that the kingdom of heaven has come through Jesus Messiah is the judgment against any who do not respond properly to Jesus Messiah.

For Matthew the kingdom of heaven (literally, "kingdom of heavens"; *see* Kingdom of God) is present (Mt 6:33; 11:12; 12:28; 13:24-30, 36-43; 16:19; 23:13) and future (Mt 4:17; 5:19; 8:12; 16:28; 25:1-13; 26:29). This teaching of the kingdom's presence and its futurity has led a vast number of interpreters to speak of "inaugurated eschatology" in the teachings of Jesus and the

Evangelists (see Kingsbury, 128-60; Jeremias). This article operates from this understanding and maintains that the essential orientation of Jesus did not revolve exclusively around the presence of the kingdom of God but around its potentiality or futurity and the impact that its nearness was to make on the present. Interpreters disagree on the time of its full realization. The following presentation works from a view that sees the kingdom being inaugurated in three phases (public ministry, passion and resurrection, to which Luke adds Pentecost). We also assume that the kingdom of God has a future finality to it that can be described as the consummation of the kingdom.

In its present aspects the kingdom demonstrates itself in God's strength and power (Mt 10:7-8; 12:28; 16:28); is opposed by cosmic powers and their human allies (Mt 11:12; 13:24-30; 23:13); demands responsible, righteous behavior (Mt 4:17; 5:20; 6:33; 7:21; 13:44-45; 18:3, 23; 19:12, 23-24; 21:31-32; 24:14); is presently (for Jesus) Jewish but includes the unlikely or the marginal and will in the future be universal (Mt 5:3, 10; 8:11-12; 13:31-32; 19:14; 21:31, 43; 22:1-14; 23:13; 24:14); and warns of judgment on those who do not respond appropriately (Mt 16:19; 21:43).

In its future aspects the kingdom of heaven will be brought to consummation at the parousia of the Son of man (Mt 13:24-30, 36-43, 47-50; 16:28; 25:1-13); will begin with a judgment by God (Mt 8:12; 18:3; 19:23-24; 20:1-16; 22:1-14; 25:1-13); and will be characterized by God's final approbation of his people (Mt 5:19; 8:11; 11:11; 13:43; 18:1, 3, 4; 20:1-16; 25:31-46; 26:29). In spite of the importance of the kingdom of heaven for Matthew's theology, there has been very little scholarly discussion on the particular nuances of Matthew's view of the kingdom.

3.3. Salvation History. "Salvation history" is an expression scholars use to describe the manner in which God acts in the past, present and future in redeeming people from sin and calling them to become his own. In another sense, salvation history refers to the development of God's salvific purposes in history. In this latter sense the expression is used for tracing the history of God's actions for the salvation of persons. In Gospel studies the expression "salvation history" is used similarly to the second sense: it refers to how each Evangelist conceives of God's history of redemption.

3.3.1. Proposals for Understanding Matthew's View of Salvation History. The history of the discussion of Matthew's view of salvation history was initially shaped by H. Conzelmann's important study, *The Theology of St. Luke* (1960), which explored Luke's concept of salvation history. Conzelmann concluded that Luke saw salvation history as divided into three periods: Israel; Jesus, the "Center of Time"; and the church. Conzelmann's work on Luke has led Matthean scholars to debate whether or not Matthew saw history in two periods (Israel and Jesus/church) or three (Israel, Jesus, church). There have been four major approaches to Matthew's view of salvation history. R. Walker has argued that Matthew's scheme of salvation history is oriented around *mission*. Three major periods emerge: the prehistory of the Messiah; the calling of Israel through John the Baptist, Jesus and the resurrected Lord; and the Gentile mission beginning at A.D. 70. Essentially, Walker sees the history of salvation in terms of the mission to the world. A.-J. Levine also observes a mission pattern in Matthew, though she differs radically on how Matthew sees the future of Israel. Levine sees two axes in Matthew's salvation history, one temporal and the other social. The temporal axis moves through two periods, from Israelite privilege to universalism, and the social axis represents the incorporation of the marginal elements of a patriarchal society into the new people of God. Unlike Walker, Levine sees the major shift coming at the Great Commission, not at A.D. 70.

Second, an *ecclesiastical* orientation has been articulated by W. G. Thompson. Emphasizing the present situation of Matthew's church, Thompson's detailed analysis of Matthew 24:4b-14 has rendered three periods: Abraham and Israel; Jesus' offer to Israel and its Jewish opposition; and the church's offer to the Gentiles and its Gentile opposition. Thompson concludes that Matthew views the third period as largely future.

Third, Kingsbury has expounded a *christological* orientation to Matthew's salvation history, demonstrating the importance of integrating the various motifs in Matthew's theology. Kingsbury sees two periods: the time of Israel (ending with Mt 3:1) and the time of Jesus Messiah (beginning with Mt 3:1 and ending with the parousia). In the latter period there are three subperiods: John to Jesus, post-Easter times and the consummation of history at the end. Kingsbury bases his view on Matthew's nondistinction between Israel and the church, the "transparency of the disciples" (i.e., they are typological equivalents to the church of Matthew and not just historical figures) and the absence of time references related to the church. Although Kingsbury's analysis has thrown fresh light on Matthew's views, his neglect of significant events in Matthew's description of history and the future (including John the Baptist in Mt 11:11-12; the destruction of Jerusalem; the Gentile mission as seen from Mt 10:5-6 and Mt 28:16-20) call for a modification of his schema.

Fourth, an *apocalyptic* orientation has been utilized by J. P. Meier to explain the data in Matthew. Meier approaches Matthew from the perspective of Jewish apocalyptic, which sees major acts of God altering the course of history. Meier sees three periods: Israel; Jesus until the cross and resurrection; and the consummation, which includes the Gentile mission.

3.3.2. A New Synthesis. In presenting a modification and synthesis of the above views, several introductory remarks need to be made. First, the issue of whether there are two or three periods in Matthew's scheme of salvation history is a subordinate point to which the Evangelist seems oblivious. Second, Kingsbury is surely right in pleading for an integration of Matthew's view of history with his christology, particularly because the latter is the most important aspect of Matthew's theology. Third, one's view of the function of the canon as it relates to systematic theology or hermeneutics will undoubtedly influence how one perceives Matthew's view of salvation history. Among evangelicals, covenant theologians will tend to stress the continuities in Matthew's scheme, and dispensationalists will emphasize the discontinuities. Finally, one's view must derive from careful consideration of texts that speak in salvation-historical terms, texts that include Matthew 1:1-17; 3:1-12; 5:17-20; 9:14-17; 11:2-19; 16:13-28; 21:33—22:14; 23:1—25:46; 27:51-53; 28:1-10; 28:16-20.

The following outline of Matthew's concept of salvation history attempts to synthesize the data and the scholarly positions sketched above. There are six periods in Matthew's scheme: the time of anticipatory revelation and promise; the time of transition with John the Baptist; the time of the Messiah's inauguration of the kingdom of heaven; the time of Israel's decision; the time of all nations; and the time of the consummation.

3.3.2.1. The Time of Anticipatory Revelation and Promise. In Matthew's perspective the past, particularly the period from Abraham to David and then from David until the birth of Jesus Messiah (Mt 1:1-17), was a time of God's salvation but more especially the time of anticipatory promise. This period from Abraham onward pointed to, prefigured and awaited with promises the inauguration of the kingdom through God's Son. Thus the fulfillment of the OT in Jesus' ministry is an indication that the past is a time of promise and anticipation (Mt 1:23; 2:6, 15, 18, 23; 4:12-16; 12:15-21; 13:35). This past was a time in which revelation was restricted to one nation, Israel (Mt 4:12-16), and a time when God's law was incompletely revealed (Mt 5:17-48).

3.3.2.2. The Time of Transition with John the Baptist. Although scholars have debated whether Matthew 11:11-12 implies that John's ministry was prior to the inauguration of the kingdom or postinauguration, it may be said with fairness that John was the transitional prophet from anticipation to inauguration. Thus it is John who first announces the dawning of the kingdom and the call to the kingdom's righteousness (Mt 3:2; 21:28-32), who first announces the end of nationalism (Mt 3:7-10), who points to the kingdom's Messiah (Mt 3:11-12) and who, along with Jesus, "fulfills all righteousness" (Mt 3:15; *see* John the Baptist). Indeed, Jesus refers to John's transitional status by saying that he was greater than all humans prior to him but less than the "least" *(mikroteros)* in the kingdom of heaven (Mt 11:11). John marks a decisive turning point in God's redemptive plan (Mt 3:15; 11:12).

3.3.2.3. The Time of the Messiah's Inauguration of the Kingdom of Heaven and His Revelation of Its Ethical Standards. Jesus, however, is the one through whom the kingdom of heaven comes, and this stage in history must be seen as the center of history in Matthew's scheme. Jesus receives the Holy Spirit (Mt 3:16; *see* Holy Spirit) and is the object of Satan's attacks against the dawning of the kingdom of heaven (Mt 4:1-11; 11:12). Jesus not only announces the dawning of the kingdom (Mt 4:17) but also effects its powers (Mt 4:23; 9:14-17, 35; 11:2-6; 12:28, 43-45). He reveals God's radical will (Mt 5:1—7:29; 11:25-27; 13:10-17; 18:1—19:1; 23:1—25:46), and on the basis of revealing God's will, he forms a new people of God around him (Mt 4:18-22; 5:3-12; 6:9-13; 7:15-23; 12:46-50; 16:17-19; 18:1—19:1). He inaugurates the world mission (Mt 8:5-13;

10:18; 13:31-33; 15:21-28; 21:33-46; 22:1-14; 24:14; 28:16-20). Most especially, as we have already noted (see 3.1.3 above), it is Jesus who inaugurates the kingdom of heaven through his public ministry, passion and resurrection.

The following two points, the "time of Israel's decision" and "time of all nations," may not be separate periods for Matthew's view of salvation history. Instead, they may be two complementary aspects of the inauguration of the kingdom of heaven, one emphasizing the dilemma of Israel and the other the dilemma of the Gentiles.

3.3.2.4. The Time of Israel's Decision. It is clear that Matthew's Gospel no longer distinguishes humans along ethnic lines, as in Jew versus Gentile (see esp. Levine), but it is also clear that the Evangelist and probably his early Christian community were struggling with the place of Israel in salvation history. Matthew's approach is to demonstrate that the true people of God are those who believe and obey Jesus (Mt 12:46-50), those who are righteous according to Jesus' new standards (Mt 7:21-23). In asserting this, the First Gospel reveals that the privileged position of Israel as a nation, as seen in the time of anticipatory revelation, has been forfeited (Mt 21:43). This is not to say that all Jews are condemned (that would be a racial comment, bordering on anti-Semitism; see McKnight 1993) but that non-messianic Judaism is condemned. Further, it is to say that the former privileged position of the nation of Israel has been annulled and that all nations are now just as privileged as Israel formerly was (Mt 22:1-14).

The evidence of Matthew suggests that this privilege began to be lifted during the ministry of Jesus (Mt 10:13-15; 11:20-24) but was not completely lifted until the destruction of Jerusalem. For Matthew the destruction of Jerusalem is the highly important and visible demonstration of God's judgment on unbelieving Judaism and its leaders. The destruction of Jerusalem highlights the tearing down of the centralized power in Jerusalem, emphasizing a judgment on the leaders and elite within Judaism. We may perhaps be justified in seeing the period from Jesus until the destruction as the one generation for decision regarding Jesus as Messiah.

Three pieces of evidence point to the conclusion that the destruction of Jerusalem renders a finality to Israel's mission. First, Matthew emphasizes the exclusive nature of the missions of John the Baptist, Jesus and the Twelve to Israel (Mt 10:5; 11:16-19, 20-24; 15:24), showing that the time of the past, and of John, Jesus and the Twelve, was a time of mission directed almost exclusively toward Israel. Second, it is Matthew who highlights the significance of the destruction of Jerusalem in salvation history. The structure of Matthew's last chapters draws attention to the destruction as a judgment by God on unbelieving Judaism and its leaders (Mt 21:1—25:46; esp. Mt 23:34-39; 24:1-2, 34). We catch a glimpse of this position in two parables: Matthew 21:33-46 and Matthew 22:1-14. In the former, the lifting of the privilege is asserted (Mt 21:43), and in the latter, that lifting, graphically symbolized in the burning of the city, seems to be followed by a universal mission (Mt 22:7-10). Third, the Gentile mission, or all-nations mission (since it is not limited to Gentiles only), is portrayed as something crucial but future. The mission to all nations is yet future for the Twelve (Mt 10:18), since it is associated with end-time events (Mt 24:14), and Jesus will only later command its commencement (Mt 28:16-20).

Interestingly, Matthew gives no indication that the all-nations mission will take a central role prior to the time associated with the destruction of Jerusalem. While Jesus commands the mission after he is resurrected, the description of events between the resurrection and the destruction shows no traces of the importance of the all-nations mission. Rather, this is apparently the time for Israel's decision regarding Jesus.

3.3.2.5. The Time of All Nations. Again, the lines are not drawn clearly: as in the Abrahamic promise (Gen 12:1-3) and in periodic episodes in the OT (see Mt 1:1-17), so in the ministry of Jesus there are occasional receptions of Gentiles into the blessings of the covenant (perhaps Mt 2:1-12; 8:5-13; 15:21-28). Furthermore, the passion arouses a significant response of faith on the part of a Gentile (Mt 27:54). And Jesus' final commission commands a mission to all nations (Mt 28:16-20; see Levine, 165-92). However, even that commission is given special impetus by the destruction of Jerusalem, an event that turns the focus from Israel's decision to universal mission (Mt 21:33—22:14). Inasmuch as it was customary for Judaism at the time of Jesus to associate the fulfillment of the Abrahamic promise of universal salvation with the end times, it is perhaps not surprising that Matthew's Gospel makes the same connection.

At any rate, the inauguration of the kingdom of heaven in Jesus forces decisions on the part of Jews and Gentiles, with Jesus' program emphasizing the nonethnic character of the future subjects of God's kingdom. In light of Matthew's probable Palestinian origin and the time it took for the early church to incorporate Gentiles, we should not wonder at the ambivalence the First Gospel portrays with respect to the time of the all-nations mission and the place of Israel in God's new period of history.

3.3.2.6. The Time of the Consummation. As with many early Christian writers, the end of history focuses on the return of Jesus (sometimes as the Son of man), the final judgment and the glorious salvation that God's people will inherit. For Matthew, Jesus the Son of man will return and bring all ordinary history to a close (Mt 25:31-46). This end brings with it a universal and eternal judgment (Mt 8:11-12; 13:38-43; 16:27-28; 19:27-30; 24:37—25:46). This judgment is based upon a person's works (Mt 16:27-28) and that person's association with Jesus (Mt 10:32-33; 25:31-46). The salvation described in the First Gospel is characterized by endless table fellowship (*see* Table Fellowship) with the Father and Son (Mt 8:11-12; 26:29), the glory of God's new people (Mt 13:43) and the reign of the Twelve (Mt 19:27-30).

3.4. Discipleship. With the exception perhaps of Exodus or Deuteronomy, no other book of Christian Scripture is devoted as much to ethics as the First Gospel. The keynote of Matthew's view of discipleship is radical obedience to the teachings of Jesus, summarized at times with the term *righteousness* (Mt 5:17-20) and at others with *love* (Mt 22:37-40). *Disciples, or adherents (see Wilkins), are those who have radically conformed their lives to the teachings of Jesus. However, it must not be thought that Jesus expects perfection; indeed, in the pages of Matthew the disciples fail frequently. But a pattern is established in Matthew that has comforted countless followers of Jesus since then: failure is met by Jesus' stern rebuke; Jesus' rebuke gives way to instruction for future improvement; Jesus restores the repentant disciple (see Mt 14:15-21).

The importance of discipleship to Matthew can be seen in the final command of Jesus: "Go, make disciples in all the nations" (Mt 28:19; McKnight 1988, 111). A disciple is here defined as one who is baptized (*see* Baptism) and has been taught to obey all the teachings of Jesus (Mt 28:19-20). The essence of discipleship for Matthew is to form a new people of God that conforms to the entirety of the ethical demands of Jesus. For Matthew, orthopraxis has as much importance as orthodoxy. Being a disciple is equivalent to being a Christian and to being in a position of final approval by God. The distinction between Jesus as "Savior" and Jesus as "Lord" is a modern one and wholly foreign to the message of Jesus and the Gospels.

3.4.1. Called by Jesus. A disciple is one who has been called by Jesus. Whereas in Judaism (as we have come to know it) the prospective rabbinical student would seek out his teacher and volunteer to be his student, Jesus sought out his followers. These calls of Jesus are depicted by Matthew in an authoritative way (Mt 4:18-22; 9:9-13). At times he called disciples and others to deeper commitment (Mt 11:28-30; 15:13; 19:21). Because being a follower of Jesus meant adherence to Jesus, as a person and as a teacher, Jesus spoke harshly about superficial following (Mt 8:18-22; 19:16-22). Those who are called by Jesus share certain characteristics in their relationship to Jesus. First, they exercise faith in Jesus, whether understood as faith in Jesus' person as Messiah or in his ability to effect miracles (Mt 8:10, 13, 23-27; 9:2, 22, 28-29; 13:58; 15:28; 17:20; 21:21-22, 32). Second, they seek, receive and dispense the forgiveness of sins (Mt 6:12; 9:2-8; 9:10-13; 18:23-35). Third, they are privileged to receive the revelations of Jesus that pertain to the inauguration of the kingdom of heaven (Mt 11:25-27; 13:1-52; 16:12, 17-21; 17:1-13, 22-23; 20:17-19; 26:2). Fourth, those called by Jesus are commissioned in various ways, including evangelism (Mt 4:18-22; 10:5-8; 28:16-20), service to others (Mt 20:24-28; 23:11) and teaching (Mt 5:19; 13:51-52; 23:8-10; 28:20).

3.4.2. Radically Committed. Disciples of Jesus are marked by a radical commitment to the demands of Jesus. At times (apparently not always), the demand of Jesus challenged a person's pattern of life and so called them away from that pattern into the sphere of obedience to Jesus. For Matthew, there is no higher priority in life than obedience to Jesus, commitment to his righteousness and God's kingdom (Mt 6:25-34; 8:21-22; 10:21-22). At times this implies rejection (Mt 5:10-12) and relative loneliness (Mt 7:13-14).

In light of the prior demand of righteousness, following Jesus may involve great costs, including perhaps job (Mt 9:9), family (Mt 10:34-

39), economic security (Mt 19:16-30), physical comforts (Mt 8:18-22; 23:34-36) and social acceptance (Mt 10:24-25). Ultimately, the real cost of following Jesus involves the self, which must be offered to the Lord (Mt 16:24-28). All other costs are but consequences of this central cost.

3.4.3. Ethically Committed. Disciples of Jesus have an ethical commitment to the teachings of Jesus. Matthew uses a host of images and terms for proper behavior, including humility (Mt 5:3; 16:24-27; 18:1-5), peacefulness (Mt 5:9, 38-42; 17:24-27; 22:15-22, honesty (Mt 5:33-37), economic and material contentment (Mt 6:19-34), fearless obedience (Mt 10:26-33) and perseverance (Mt 24:36—25:46). The virtuous life for Matthew may be categorized under two central terms: love and righteousness.

3.4.3.1. Love. God loves all persons, and so Jesus' disciples are expected to be kind to all; they are not to observe ethnic and political lines in their treatment of others (Mt 5:44-45). God's nonparochial love is seen in his choice of certain women as part of the Messiah's heritage (Mt 1:1-17), in his prompting of the Gentile magi to be the first worshipers of the Messiah (Mt 2:1-12), in his choice of "Galilee of the Gentiles" as the arena of the Messiah's ministry (Mt 4:12-16) and in his generating faith in the heart of the centurion (Mt 8:5-13) and the Syro-Phonoecian woman (Mt 15:21-28). God's universal love becomes the capstone of the Gospel as Jesus commands the eleven to disciple all nations (Mt 28:16-20). Not only does God love all; he also responds to humans in mercy and forgives their sins against him (Mt 6:12; 9:1-8, 13; 12:7).

God's love, accordingly, becomes the paradigm for true human existence. The disciples of Jesus are to be loving toward all others. Jesus, according to Matthew, states that the greatest demand of the law is love (Mt 22:37-40) and sums up the ethical dimension of life with the golden rule (Mt 7:12). Consequently, the final judgment of God will be based on whether humans have been loving, acting mercifully to those in need (Mt 25:31-46) and whether or not they have been forgiving of others (Mt 18:23-35). Love for the disciple is the love of God, which manifests itself through the concrete behavior shown to others. Whereas in Matthew the term *love* primarily relates to one's relationship to others, the next term primarily relates to one's relationship to God and his will.

3.4.3.2. Righteousness. Although Matthew does use the term *righteousness* for conformity to OT Law (e.g., Mt 1:19), his primary interest is in Christian righteousness, that is, conformity to God's will as revealed by Jesus. The term, accordingly, is one that nicely bridges the transition now taking place in salvation history and one that surely provides a touchstone with Judaism.

Righteousness is a requirement for entrance into the kingdom of heaven. It outstrips the righteousness of the scribes and Pharisees because it is behavior that conforms to the standard of the new salvation-historical era that Jesus inaugurates (Mt 5:17-20). Thus righteousness is a virtue that Jesus praises (Mt 5:6, 10). Furthermore, the disciples of Jesus are not to do their righteous deeds (works done in obedience to God's will) in order to be seen (Mt 6:1-18). If righteousness is required for entrance into the kingdom, it must be pursued in the here and now (Mt 6:33). As examples of righteousness, Matthew presents Joseph (Mt 1:19), Abel (Mt 23:35), those who respond properly to the Son of man (Mt 13:43) and those who perform deeds of mercy (Mt 25:37, 46). The Great Commission, in essence, exhorts the eleven to raise up disciples of Jesus who are righteous; that is, disciples who live out the teachings of Jesus (Mt 28:20).

3.4.4. Recipients of God's Promises. Disciples of Jesus are recipients of God's rich promises. To those who follow Jesus in discipleship come the added blessings of receiving God's present and final promises. For the present, the disciple of Jesus is promised physical provisions (Mt 6:33; 19:29), rest for the soul (Mt 11:29) and Jesus' continual presence (Mt 28:20). For the future, the disciple is promised God's approval (Mt 6:1; 10:40-42; 16:27; 20:1-16), eternal life (Mt 19:29) and table fellowship with the Father and the Son (Mt 26:27-29).

See also JOHN, GOSPEL OF; LUKE, GOSPEL OF; MARK, GOSPEL OF.

DJG: "M" TRADITION; SERMON ON THE MOUNT/PLAIN.

BIBLIOGRAPHY. **Commentaries:** W. C. Allen, *The Gospel According to St. Matthew* (ICC; 3d ed; Edinburgh: T & T Clark, 1912); F. W. Beare, *The Gospel According to Matthew: A Commentary* (New York: Harper and Row, 1982); D. A. Carson, "Matthew," in *The Expositor's Bible Commentary* (Grand Rapids: Zondervan, 1984) vol. 8; W. D. Davies and D. C. Allison Jr., *A Critical and Exegetical Commentary on the Gospel According to Saint*

Matthew: Vol. 1, Introduction and Commentary on Matthew I-VII (ICC; Edinburgh: T & T Clark, 1988); R. T. France, *Matthew* (TNTC; Grand Rapids: Eerdmans, 1986); R. H. Gundry, *Matthew: A Commentary on His Literary and Theological Art* (Grand Rapids: Eerdmans, 1982); D. A. Hagner, *Matthew 1-13* (WBC; Dallas: Word, 1993); idem, *Matthew 14-28* (WBC; Dallas: Word, 1995); D. Hill, *The Gospel of Matthew* (NCB; Grand Rapids: Eerdmans, 1981); C. S. Keener, *A Commentary on the Gospel of Matthew* (Grand Rapids: Eerdmans, 1999); U. Luz, *Matthew 1—7* (Minneapolis: Augsburg, 1989); A. H. McNeile, *The Gospel According to St. Matthew: The Greek Text with Introduction and Notes* (London: Macmillan, 1915); J. P. Meier, *Matthew* (Wilmington, DE: Michael Glazier, 1980); A. Plummer, *An Exegetical Commentary on the Gospel of Matthew* (London: Clarke, 1909); L. Sabourin, *The Gospel According to St. Matthew* (2 vols.; Bombay: St. Paul, 1982); E. Schweizer, *The Good News According to Matthew* (Atlanta: John Knox, 1975); R. V. G. Tasker, *The Gospel According to St. Matthew* (TNTC; Grand Rapids: Eerdmans, 1961). **Studies:** D. C. Allison Jr., *The End of the Ages Has Come* (Philadelphia: Fortress, 1985); B. W. Bacon, "The 'Five Books' of Matthew Against the Jews," *The Expositor* 15 (1918) 56-66; idem, *Studies in Matthew* (New York: Henry Holt, 1930); idem, "Why 'According to Matthew'?" *Expositor* 20 (1920) 289-310; D. L. Barr, "The Drama of Matthew's Gospel: A Reconsideration of Its Structure and Purpose," *TD* 24 (1976) 349-59; D. R. Bauer, *The Structure of Matthew's Gospel* (Sheffield: Almond, 1988); H. J. B. Combrink, "The Structure of the Gospel of Matthew As Narrative," *TynB* 34 (1983) 61-90; A. M. Farrer, *St. Matthew and St. Mark* (London: Dacre, 1954); R. T. France, *Matthew: Evangelist and Teacher* (Downers Grove, IL: InterVarsity Press, 1989); B. Gerhardsson, *The Mighty Acts of Jesus According to Matthew* (Lund: Gleerup, 1979); idem, "Sacrificial Service and Atonement in the Gospel of Matthew," in *Reconciliation and Hope: New Testament Essays on Atonement and Eschatology Presented to L. L. Morris on His Sixtieth Birthday*, ed. R. Banks (Grand Rapids: Eerdmans, 1974) 25-35; R. A. Guelich, *The Sermon on the Mount* (Waco, TX: Word, 1982); H. J. Held, "Matthew As Interpreter of the Miracle Stories," in *Tradition and Interpretation in Matthew*, ed. G. Bornkamm (Philadelphia: Westminster, 1963) 165-99; M. Hengel, *Studies in the Gospel of Mark* (Philadelphia: Fortress, 1985); D. Hill, "Son and Servant: An Essay in Matthean Christology," *JSNT* 6 (1980) 2-16; J. Jeremias, *New Testament Theology: The Proclamation of Jesus* (New York: C. Scribner's, 1971); idem, *The Parables of Jesus* (2d ed.; New York: Scribner's, 1972); J. D. Kingsbury, *Matthew: Structure, Christology, Kingdom* (2d ed.; Minneapolis: Fortress, 1989); E. Krentz, "The Extent of Matthew's Prologue: Toward the Structure of the First Gospel," *JBL* 83 (1964) 409-15; A.-J. Levine, *The Social and Ethnic Dimensions of Matthean Salvation History* (Lewiston/Queenston, Lampeter: Edwin Mellen, 1988); C. H. Lohr, "Oral Techniques in the Gospel of Matthew," *CBQ* 23 (1961) 403-35; S. McKnight, *Interpreting the Synoptic Gospels* (Grand Rapids: Baker, 1988); idem, "A Loyal Critic: Matthew's Polemic with Judaism in Theological Perspective," in *The New Testament and Anti-Semitism*, ed. C. A. Evans and D. A. Hagner (Minneapolis: Fortress, 1993) 55-79; J. P. Meier, *The Vision of Matthew* (New York: Paulist, 1979); B. M. Nolan, *The Royal Son of God* (Göttingen: Vandenhoeck & Ruprecht, 1979); G. R. Osborne, *The Resurrection Narratives* (Grand Rapids: Baker, 1984); P. Rolland, "From the Genesis to the End of the World: The Plan of Matthew's Gospel," *BTB* 2 (1972) 155-76; P. L. Shuler, *A Genre for the Gospels: The Biographical Character of Matthew* (Philadelphia: Fortress, 1982); N. B. Stonehouse, *The Witness of the Synoptic Gospels to Christ* (Grand Rapids: Baker, 1979); M. J. Suggs, *Wisdom, Christology and Law in Matthew's Gospel* (Cambridge, MA: Harvard University Press, 1970); W. G. Thompson, "An Historical Perspective in the Gospel of Matthew," *JBL* 93 (1974) 243-62; D. Verseput, "The Role and Meaning of the 'Son of God' Title in Matthew's Gospel," *NTS* 33 (1987) 532-56; R. Walker, *Die Heilsgeschichte im ersten Evangelium* (Göttingen: Vandenhoeck & Ruprecht, 1967); M. J. Wilkins, *The Concept of Disciple in Matthew's Gospel* (Leiden: E. J. Brill, 1988).

S. McKnight

MEALS, COMMUNAL. *See* TABLE FELLOWSHIP.

MESSIAH. *See* CHRIST.

MESSIANIC KINGDOM. *See* APOCALYPTICISM; KINGDOM OF GOD.

MESSIANIC SECRET. *See* MARK, GOSPEL OF.

MESSIANISM. *See* APOCALYPTICISM; RABBINIC TRADITIONS AND WRITINGS.

MIDRASH. *See* RABBINIC TRADITIONS AND WRITINGS.

MIDRASH RABBAH. *See* RABBINIC TRADITIONS AND WRITINGS.

MILLENNIALISM. *See* APOCALYPTICISM; ESCHATOLOGY.

MIRACLES, MIRACLE STORIES I: GOSPELS

In biblical scholarship the English word *miracle* normally denotes a supernatural event, that is, an event that so transcends ordinary happenings that it is viewed as a direct result of supernatural power. In the Gospels such events are due to the exercise of God's power—whether directly or through human or superhuman agents—and reveal and/or effect his saving or judging purposes. Though some writers use *miracle* with enough latitude to include (predictive) prophecy, it is more common to restrict it to supernatural events in the space-time world. In contrast to *miracle, miracle stories* denotes relatively self-contained narratives in which an individual miraculous happening constitutes the, or at least a, major focus of the account. Unless one regards narratives describing angelophanies as miracle stories, Jesus is the subject of all such Gospel stories. Various summaries of Jesus' healings and exorcisms (e.g., Mk 1:32-34, 39) are not ranked as miracle stories since they do not relate individual miracles. Such texts will be subsumed under the broad category "miracle traditions."

1. Miracle Traditions According to the Gospels
2. Tradition History and Historicity
3. Significance of the Miracles

1. Miracle Traditions According to the Gospels.
In a sense the Gospels testify to the truth of Goethe's description of miracle as "faith's favorite child." For example, they narrate or refer to no less than thirty-four specific miracles (exclusive of parallels) performed by Jesus during his earthly ministry. In addition there are fifteen texts (again, exclusive of parallels) that narrate or refer to Jesus' miraculous activity (almost always healings and exorcisms) in summary fashion. Beyond this, there are miracles in which Jesus is the object of the miraculous action (including the virginal conception [*see* Birth of

Jesus], *baptism, transfiguration, *resurrection and *ascension) and several (at least seven) epiphanies of the risen Christ. When one includes the angelophanies, portents and texts that refer to the disciples' miracles, the degree to which miracles dominate the Gospels becomes apparent.

1.1. The Synoptic Gospels Compared with the Fourth Gospel. The miracle traditions of the Synoptic Gospels evince several affinities. It is especially noticeable that the triple tradition contains eleven accounts of miraculous deeds performed by Jesus (excluding the baptism and transfiguration pericope), whereas only two (possibly three) Johannine miracles (feeding of the five thousand; walking on the sea; healing of official's son[?]) have Synoptic parallels. (Of these, only the feeding of the five thousand appears in all four Gospels.) For the Synoptic Evangelists, Jesus' miracles are *dynameis,* "deeds of power." *Sēmeia,* "signs," used consistently in the Fourth Gospel, never denotes Jesus' miracles in the Synoptics (*see* John, Gospel of). Conversely, Jesus' antagonists demand a sign (Mk 8:11 par.), and future false Christs/prophets will perform "signs and wonders" (Mk 13:22; Mt 24:24). In Luke, however, this avoidance of "sign/s" for Jesus' miracles is insignificant; after all, the Evangelist repeatedly describes miracles of Jesus and the apostles as "signs and wonders" in Acts (e.g., Acts 2:22, 43). Matthew's convictions are more difficult to determine, though it seems clear that he regarded Jesus' resurrection as a sign—perhaps the only sign—of Jesus (Mt 12:39-40). Mark's Gospel never brings "sign/s" into positive connection with Jesus' ministry, but twice devalues it (Mk 8:11-12; 13:22). Perhaps Mark regarded the use of "sign/s" for Jesus' miracles as a flagrant contradiction of Jesus' refusal to furnish any sign (Mk 8:12). Furthermore, *dynameis* accords better with Mark's emphasis on Jesus as the strong and Spirit-filled *Son of God (e.g., Mk 1:7-8, 10; 3:27; 5:1-8; *see* Holy Spirit).

In the Synoptics, Jesus' miracles are closely related to his proclamation of the advent of the *kingdom of God. Especially in summaries and in pericope describing the mission efforts of the disciples, the preaching of the kingdom and the performance of healings and exorcisms are carefully coordinated (e.g., Mk 1:39 par.; Mk 3:14-15 par.; Mk 6:12-13 par.). In one saying of Jesus transmitted in Matthew and Luke this relationship is defined: "if it is by the finger [Mt:

"Spirit"] of God that I cast out the demons, then the kingdom of God has come to you" (Lk 11:20; Mt 12:28 NRSV). Thus the Synoptists regarded Jesus' miracles, perhaps especially his exorcisms (never mentioned in the Fourth Gospel), as one mode of God's assertion of his royal power, so that while the kingdom in its fullness still lies in the future, it has already become a reality in Jesus' words and works. Of course, the Synoptists' linkage between Jesus' miracles and the assertion of God's power against evil, demonic forces closely coheres with their use of *dynameis*, "deeds of power," for Jesus' miracles.

The noun *pistis*, "faith," or the verb *pisteuein*, "to believe," plays a fairly dominant role in the Synoptic miracle stories. However, unlike the Fourth Gospel, where miracles ideally result in *pistis*, the Synoptic narratives regularly present *pistis* on the part of the suppliants (or their representatives) as a prerequisite for receiving miraculous help (cf. e.g., Mk 2:5 par.; Mk 6:5-6 par.). This is not to say, however, that the Synoptic Evangelists failed to appreciate the ability of the miracles to engender faith. This is particularly true of Luke, as can clearly be seen in Acts (e.g., Acts 2:22; 13:6-12; 14:3; see Achtemeier).

Finally, the Synoptics agree in emphasizing the miracle-working of the disciples. Various texts note or imply that the disciples, commissioned and empowered by Jesus, effected exorcisms and healings as they helped Jesus proclaim the coming of the kingdom (e.g., Mk 3:14-15; 6:7, 12-13).

1.1.1. Mark. Mark can truly be called a Gospel of miracles, for the amount of narrative relating miraculous events in proportion to the entire Gospel is the highest among the canonical Gospels. The vast majority of these miracles are directly related to Jesus. In three cases (baptism, transfiguration, resurrection) Jesus is, as it were, the object of the miracle. In most cases, however, he is the subject, performing eighteen specific miracles. Also, as in the other Gospels, there are summaries of Jesus' miracle-working activities (Mk 1:32-34, 39; 3:10-12; 6:5, 54-56).

In the history of Markan interpretation scholars have often grappled with two interrelated issues: the so-called messianic secret and the function of Jesus' miracles within the Gospel as a whole (*see* Mark, Gospel of). Long ago W. Wrede argued that the injunctions to secrecy following some of Jesus' miracles (Mk 1:44; 5:43; 7:36;

8:26) were part and parcel of an early Christian effort to harmonize the contradiction between the original Christian belief that Jesus became Messiah upon his resurrection and a growing conviction that Jesus must have also been the Messiah during his earthly life. This tension is resolved if Jesus revealed himself to his disciples as the Messiah during his ministry but kept it a secret until his resurrection (cf. Mk 9:9).

Bultmann agreed with Wrede's analysis of the secrecy motif and further argued that within Mark, Jesus' miracles function positively as proofs that Jesus is the Messiah. And in Mark, he argued, the title denotes a mythological figure: the Son of God, whose being is permeated by the Spirit of God and whose divinity is revealed by stunning miracles.

While Bultmann's understanding remained dominant for a time, the 1960s and 1970s saw a spate of works arguing that Mark employed the messianic secret as a theological means of subordinating the significance of Jesus' miracles to the proclamation of his death (*see* Death of Christ) and resurrection. T. Weeden, for example, argued that Mark intended to attack heretical Christians whose christology is best subsumed under the rubric *theios anēr*, or "divine man." "In such a perspective Jesus is characterized as the epiphany of God . . . , who intervenes in human affairs to work miracles. . . . He is embued with the power and authority of God, and possesses supernatural knowledge and wisdom" (Weeden, 55). Correspondingly, these heretics practiced a type of discipleship whose primary criterion of success was "the quantity, magnitude, and spectacular character of their miraculous acts and pneumatic experiences" (Weeden, 60). True, in the first half of the Gospel Jesus behaves as a *theios anēr*, but this "*theios anēr* position is set up only to be discredited by Jesus once the disciples confess to that position" (Weeden, 164). Weeden, however, is unconvincing. The essential arguments against this type of interpretation are assembled, among others, by G. Theissen. He asks the obvious question: "Can Mark really have told sixteen miracle stories in order to warn against belief in miracles?" (Theissen, 294). In addition, the transfiguration (Mk 9:2-8) and three other miracles (Mk 9:12-29; 10:46-52; 11:12-14, 20-21) occur after the first passion prediction. Even the passion narrative contains miracles (Mk 15:33-38).

Table 1. The Miracles of Jesus

Markan Miracles	Mark	Matthew	Luke	John
Possessed Man in Synagogue	1:23-26		4:33-35	
Peter's Mother-in-Law	1:30-31	8:14-15	4:38-39	
Man with Leprosy	1:40-42	8:2-4	5:12-13	
Paralyzed Man	2:3-12	9:2-7	5:18-25	
Man with Shriveled Hand	3:1-5	12:10-13	6:6-10	
Calming the Storm	4:37-41	8:23-27	8:22-25	
Gadarene Demoniac(s)	5:1-15	8:28-34	8:27-35	
Raising Jairus's Daughter	5:22-24, 38-42	9:18-19, 23-25	8:41-42, 49-56	
Hemorrhaging Woman	5:25-29	9:20-22	8:43-48	
Feeding of Five Thousand	6:35-44	14:15-21	9:12-17	6:5-13
Walking on Water	6:48-51	14:25		6:19-21
Canaanite Woman's Daughter	7:24-30	15:21-28		
Deaf Mute	7:31-37	15:29-31		
Feeding of Four Thousand	8:1-9	15:32-38		
Blind Man at Bethsaida	8:22-26			
Demon-Possessed Boy	9:17-19	17:14-18	9:38-43	
Two Blind Men	10:46-52	20:29-34	19:35-43	
Fig Tree Withered	11:12-14, 20-25	21:18-22		

Miracles Found Only in Matthew and Luke				
Roman Centurion's Servant		8:5-13	7:1-10	
Blind, Mute and Possessed Man		12:22	11:14	

Miracles Found Only in Matthew				
Two Blind Men		9:27-31		
Mute and Possessed Man		9:32-33		
Coin in Fish's Mouth		17:24-27		

Miracles Found Only in Luke				
First Catch of Fish			5:1-11	
Raising Widow's Son at Nain			7:11-15	
Crippled Woman			13:11-13	
Man with Dropsy			14:1-4	
Ten Men with Leprosy			17:11-19	
High Priest's Servant			22:50-51	

Miracles Found Only in John				
Water into Wine				2:1-11
Official's Son at Capernaum				4:46-54
Sick Man at Pool of Bethesda				5:1-9
Man Born Blind				9:1-7
Raising Lazarus				11:1-44
Second Catch of Fish				21:1-11

In view of these and other objections it has become more acceptable to interpret Jesus' miracle-working in Mark more positively. It is doubtful that the command to secrecy following the miracles is cut from the same cloth as the command to keep Jesus' divine sonship/messiahship secret. Jesus, for example, frequently performs miracles in public (in synagogues, packed houses, etc.). Mark 1:43-45, which contains the first command to keep a miracle secret, in conjunction with Mark 1:38 shows that the leper's disobedience resulted in a frustration of Jesus' plans, namely, to preach in other towns (cf. also Mk 7:24 with 7:36). Thus Mark may well have understood the four prohibitions in practical, strategic terms.

Jesus' miracles portray him as he is described by the Baptist: the mighty one—mightier than John—who acts in the power of the Spirit (Mk 1:7-8). As such, he silences and expels demons (Mk 1:21-27; 5:1-20; 7:24-30; 9:14-29) since he has overpowered and bound the strong man, Satan (Mk 3:22-27). Wind and sea obey him (Mk 4:41), and power proceeds from him and immediately cures a woman beyond the help of physicians (Mk 5:29-30). Little wonder then that in Mark his miracles are called *dynameis*, "deeds of power." And yet this powerful Son of God treads the path to horrible suffering and death in Jerusalem. This juxtaposition naturally heightens the narrative tension and serves to underscore the enormity and humiliation of the self-offering of the Son of Man as a ransom for many (Mk 10:45).

Jesus' miracles are also closely connected to the proclamation of the coming kingdom of God and the related presentation of Jesus as a teacher. A comparison of Mark 1:21-27 with Mark 1:14-15 and 1:39 reveals a Jesus who repeatedly proclaimed/taught concerning the kingdom of God in various *synagogues and who exorcised demons. Similarly, Mark 3:20-29 implies that Jesus' exorcisms are to be construed as successful attacks of the reign of God against the kingdom of Satan. In the context of miraculous activity Jesus is addressed as "teacher" (Mk 4:38; 5:35; 9:17), and the teaching of Jesus and his apostles is closely linked to miracle-working (Mk 6:2, 30, 34-44). Thus Mark—as well as Matthew and Luke—viewed these miracles as episodic manifestations of the advent of the kingdom of God.

Bultmann was therefore correct in his assessment of the positive function of the Markan miracles. However, in light of Jesus' refusal to provide a sign to skeptics (Mk 8:11-13), it is perhaps more accurate to view them not as proofs of Jesus' messiahship (*see* Christ) but as means of re-presenting the messianic Son of God, through whose miraculous ministry, death and resurrection God had inaugurated his long-awaited rule.

To Bultmann's view of the Markan miracles as proofs for the divinity of Jesus belongs the later attempt to classify Mark as an aretalogy, a Hellenistic biographical narrative aiming to glorify and propagandize for a *theios anēr*. Although this hypothesis has become less popular, G. Theissen has argued that the structure of ancient miracle stories, pressing forward as they do toward wonder/acclamation, has heavily contributed to the overall structure of Mark's Gospel. Thus Mark, Theissen surmises, purposefully suppressed titles in the acclamations of the miracle stories in order to create a powerful tension only released in the centurion's confession: "Truly this man was God's Son" (Mk 15:39 NRSV). One should observe, however, that most ancient miracle stories do not conclude with titular acclamations. Moreover, Theissen unfortunately viewed the centurion's confession as enabled by miraculous cosmic signs (Mk 15:33, 38) rather than by Jesus' loud cry (Mk 15:37, 39). A titular confession prompted by the resurrection would have made his theory more plausible.

Mark, like the other Synoptists, presents *pistis* ("faith") as a precondition for the reception of a miracle. Mark's contribution, however, is to forge a close link between faith and struggle: *pistis* is concretely demonstrated when the one(s) seeking a miracle encounter(s) a barrier which is subsequently overcome through determined struggle (Mk 2:4-5; 5:27-34, 35-36; 7:27-29; 9:22-24; 10:47-52).

1.1.2. Matthew. Matthew, according to the two-source hypothesis (*see* Synoptic Problem), has taken over almost all of the Markan miracle traditions, although he has abbreviated the miracle stories. On the other hand, Matthew contains additions. The infancy story contains angelophanies and the account of the star, but most importantly the account of the virginal conception (Mt 1:18-25; *see* Birth of Jesus). Matthew lacks three Markan miracles from the period of Jesus' ministry (Mk 1:23-28; 7:31-37; 8:22-26), but contains six additional ones: Matthew 8:5-13; 9:32-33; and 12:22 belong to or have parallels in Q; Matthew 9:27-31 is very similar to Mark 10:46-

52; Matthew 14:28-33 and 17:24-27 are unique to Matthew. In the passion narrative Matthew adds that when Jesus died, an earthquake shattered the rocks and many saints emerged from their tombs (Mt 27:51-53). Likewise, only Matthew describes a later earthquake occurring when an angel descended and rolled the stone from Jesus' tomb (Mt 28:2). The Evangelist concludes his Gospel with a christophany in Galilee, another account peculiar to this Gospel.

When one examines Matthew's miracle traditions along with those of Mark and Luke, several Matthean predilections surface. Two such are the phrases "according to your faith be it done to you" (Mt 8:13; 9:29; 15:28) and "X was healed from that hour" (Mt 8:13; 9:22; 15:28; 17:18). Matthew is also fond of repetition (Mt 9:32-34/ 12:22-24; 9:27-31/20:29-34; 12:38-39/16:1-4). Is this also related to the doubling of Markan characters in Matthew 8:28 and 20:30?

Three Matthean changes vis-á-vis Mark result in a heightening of Jesus' dignity. Thus characters in Matthean miracle traditions are much more apt to address Jesus as "Lord" (kyrie: Mt 8:2, 6, 8, 25; 9:28; 15:22, 25; 17:4; 20:31, 33). Likewise, suppliants or witnesses "worship" Jesus (proskynein: Mt 8:2; 9:18; 14:33; 15:25). Finally, Matthew insists that Jesus performed a miracle for all who needed it, or that all the sick were brought to him (Mt 4:23-24; 8:16; 12:15; 14:35; 15:37).

Scholars have long noted that Matthew is a Gospel of fulfilled Scripture, and this concern has influenced its miracle traditions. The virginal conception fulfilled Isaiah 7:14 (Mt 1:22-23); Jesus' exorcisms and healings fulfilled Isaiah 53:4 (Mt 8:17); and Jesus' miracles described in Matthew 11:5 correspond to Isaianic prophecies. Furthermore, Matthew rewrites a Markan summary (Mk 3:7-12) so that Jesus no longer prohibits demons from revealing his identity but rather forbids the healed to make him known (Mt 12:15-21). This in turn is interpreted as a fulfillment of the unobtrusive and gentle ways of God's servant (Is 42:1-4; see Servant of Yahweh). The desire to show fulfilled prophecy may also explain the tendency to underscore Jesus' healing ministry (cf. Mt 4:23; 10:1, 7-8; 12:15-16 with their Markan counterparts; see also Mt 9:35; 14:14; 15:30; 19:2; 21:14-15). For this activity Matthew could adduce OT prophecies (Mt 8:17; 11:5; 12:18-21). Twice Matthew notes the accusation that Jesus performed his miracles by Beelzebul's power (Mt 9:34; 12:24; cf. 13:56). He also

knows that false prophets will try to legitimate themselves by miracles (Mt 7:15-23; 24:24). It is therefore very important for this author, perhaps a Jewish-Christian "scribe" (Mt 13:52) and certainly one vitally concerned about the fulfillment of the Law and Prophets (Mt 5:17-20), to show that Jesus' miracles were in accord with the Torah and thus were of divine origin. This subordination of miracle to Torah, rooted in Deuteronomy 13:1-5, has possibly influenced Matthew's decision to present the *Sermon on the Mount (cf. esp. Mt 5:17-20) prior to any individual miracle stories.

H. J. Held, observing Matthew's abbreviations and expansions of Mark, concluded that the Evangelist intended primarily to provide instruction to the church concerning christology, faith and discipleship. Christological themes have already been noted: Jesus' fulfillment of OT prophecy and his status as the Lord who is to be worshiped (see Worship). Instruction on faith is also important to Matthew, though Theissen has noted that Matthew's dropping of pistis from three Markan stories retold in Matthew 9:18-26; 17:14-21; 20:29-34 militates against "Held's view that the motif of faith is Matthew's critical principle of selection for including Markan miracle stories" (Theissen, 137). On the other hand, rebuke of the disciples for little faith does play a more prominent role in Matthew than in Mark (cf. Mt 14:31; 17:20). Finally, Held identified Matthean changes that evince an interest in the nature and demands of discipleship (e.g., Mt 9:8; 14:28-33).

Matthew made a noticeable change in the way his miracle stories are ordered within the overall story of Jesus' ministry. After a brief summary of Jesus' message and ministry (Mt 4:23-25), he initiates his account of Jesus' work with an extensive account of his teaching, the Sermon on the Mount (Mt 5—7). Only then does he narrate a series of miracle stories (Mt 8—9). Moreover, the Sermon and the narratives of the following two chapters appear to constitute one major unit in Matthew's structure, judging from the similar summaries (Jesus taught, preached and healed) which form an inclusio (Mt 4:23-25; 9:35-38). On the other hand, Kingsbury, noting the mention of Jesus' teaching and preaching in Matthew 11:1, envisions chapters 8—9 as part of a section comprising Matthew 4:17—11:1 in which Jesus conducts a Galilean ministry of teaching, preaching and healing. In turn, this section would constitute the first major subdivision of Matthew 4:17—16:20, over which he places the rubric "The Proclamation of Jesus Messiah" (Kingsbury, 17).

But what is the function of the miracles within this unit? There are ten miracles in Matthew 8—9, but the presence of pericopes that do not narrate miracles and the merciful nature of Jesus' miracles make it unlikely either that these chapters intend to present the Messiah of deed (alongside the Messiah of word) or that Jesus is being portrayed as the new Moses. The themes of faith and discipleship surface several times, but it is difficult to subsume every pericope in chapters 8—9 under either heading. J. Gnilka has suggested that the principal message concerns Jesus the Son of God and the *Son of David, who acts with grace toward his people and who is to be encountered in faith and in willing discipleship. Luz has recently proposed that chapters 8—9 recapitulate the history of the Matthean church. The attempt to comprehend the precise import of these two chapters will no doubt continue.

1.1.3. Luke. The contours of the miraculous in Jesus' life, according to Luke's Gospel, are interesting to trace. Like Matthew, Luke commences with birth narratives which relate angelophanies and the virginal conception. Gabriel, in fact, draws a direct link between this generation by the Holy Spirit and Jesus' identity as "Son of God" (Lk 1:35). Between Matthew's five and Luke's three angelophanies there is no overlap.

Luke's presentation of Jesus' miracles largely corresponds to those of Mark and Matthew, yet there are interesting modifications. All of the Markan miracles appear in sequence in Luke save the cursing of the fig tree (cf. Lk 13:6-9) and the five miracle stories within Luke's so-called great omission (Mk 6:45—8:26). Luke also includes a healing (Lk 7:1-10) and an exorcism (Lk 11:14) belonging to the Q material. And finally, Luke contains seven specific miracles unique to this Gospel, including the notice concerning the exorcism of seven demons from Mary Magdalene (Lk 8:2) and a report of the healing of the ear of the high priest's servant (Lk 22:51; cf. also Lk 5:1-11; 7:11-17; 13:10-17; 14:1-6; 17:11-19).

Luke, of course, concludes with the Easter story. However, in his story the women receive the Easter news from two men wearing dazzling clothes (Lk 24:4). Subsequently, Luke narrates two christophanies and refers to a third, all of which occur on Easter Sunday: an appearance to the Emmaus disciples (Lk 24:13-35), a reference to an epiphany before Simon (Lk 24:34) and an evening appearance before the eleven and others (Lk 24:36-49). At this point Luke shows more affinity with the Fourth Gospel than with the other Synoptics. Mark contains no resurrection appearances, and Matthew's only one is situated in Galilee. On the other hand, John notes a christophany to the disciples on Easter evening (Jn 20:19-23), and Magdalene has an encounter with two angels in white (Jn 20:11-13). Finally, Luke concludes his Gospel by narrating the ascension more fully described in Acts 1:1-11.

In various ways Luke left his stamp on the traditions passed on by him. For example, certain vocabulary preferences are evident. To convey the immediate occurrence of the miracles he prefers the literary term *parachrēma* (Lk 4:39; 5:25; 8:44, 47, 55; 13:13; 18:43) to *euthys* (Mk) or *eutheōs* (Mt). Like Matthew, he expands Mark's use of *kyrios*, "Lord," both in direct address (Lk 5:12) and as an appellation in the third person (Lk 7:13; 13:15), but his frequent use of *epistata*, "master," is unique (Lk 5:5; 8:24, 45; 9:33; 17:13). Luke also prefers the verb *iaomai*, "to heal" (Lk 5:17; 6:18-19; 7:7; 8:47; 9:2, 11, 42; 14:4; 17:15; 22:51), more than do his Synoptic counterparts.

Comparison with the other Synoptics also reveals characteristic emphases in the Lukan miracle traditions. For all the Synoptists the miracles of Jesus are *dynameis*, "powerful deeds," but Luke stresses that they are the result of the *dynamis*, "power," at Jesus' disposal (Lk 4:36; 5:17; 6:19; 8:46), which he shares with his disciples (Lk 9:1), and which therefore enables them to crush the enemy's *dynamis* (Lk 10:19). Perhaps this emphasis is related to Luke's inclination to describe illness as *astheneia*, a bodily "weakness" (Lk 4:40; 5:15; 8:2; 13:11-12). U. Busse, on the basis of such texts as Luke 4:39 and 13:11, 16, argued that for Luke all sickness was caused by demons. Perhaps, but Luke never expressly affirms this, and some healings are narrated without explicit mention of demons or exorcistic motifs.

It has long been recognized that Luke redacted his sources to emphasize the praying of Jesus, and twice this motif appears in Luke's miracle stories (Lk 5:16; 9:29; cf. 3:21). Theissen observed that Luke on three occasions records that Jesus prayed shortly before divine power was manifested through or in him (Lk 5:16-17; 6:12-19; 9:29). This shows, according to Theissen, that Luke views Jesus' *dynamis* as a dynamic, not a static, phenomenon and accords with a Lukan tendency to emphasize the work of God behind and above Jesus' ministry. Accordingly, in several miracle story endings the supplicant and/or the witnessing crowd "give glory to God" or in some other way acknowledge God's activity (Lk 5:25; 7:16; 9:43; 13:13; 17:15, 18; 18:43; 19:37).

One may deduce from Acts 3:22-23 and 7:37 (cf. Lk 9:35) that Luke views Jesus as the Mosaic prophet predicted in Deuteronomy 18:15, 18. This prophet christology also makes itself felt in the Gospel, especially in those passages which relate Jesus' prophetic status to miracle-working (Lk 7:16; 24:19). Luke seemingly borrows hues from the Elijah-Elisha narratives to paint his portrait of Jesus (Lk 4:25-27; 7:11-17; 9:62), but it is unlikely that he presents him, even in a qualified sense, as Elijah *redivivus* (cf. Mal 4:5-6). It is the Baptist who comes in the "spirit and power of Elijah" (Lk 1:17), and Jesus declares John to be the coming messenger of Malachi 3:1 (a figure probably generally identified as the returning Elijah of Mal 4:5-6; *see* John the Baptist).

Finally, Theissen has called attention to how Luke's salvation-history schema has influenced his retelling of the miracle stories. Just as God's plan of salvation, anticipated in the OT, reached its denouement in the "today" of Jesus' ministry (Lk 4:21), so those who witnessed the forgiving and healing of the paralytic declare, "We have seen strange things *today*" (Lk 5:26 NRSV [author's emphasis]). Likewise, those who are confronted with Jesus' raising of the widow's son exclaim that now at last in Jesus, "God has looked favorably on his people" (Lk 7:16 NRSV).

1.2. The Fourth Gospel. Miracle plays a dominant role in the Fourth Gospel, and especially in this domain the distinctive Johannine perspective becomes evident. Jesus' miracles, for example, are set within the context of the one grand miracle, the incarnation of the Logos (Jn 1:14). Thus the Fourth Gospel contains no birth narratives, but in its prologue directs the reader all the way back to the preincarnate Son.

As in the Synoptics, Jesus receives the Spirit at his baptism (Jn 1:32-34). The Fourth Gospel also agrees that Jesus performed many miracles during his ministry, but it narrates only seven—far fewer than in the Synoptics. The feeding of the five thousand (Jn 6:1-15), Jesus walking on the sea (Jn 6:16-21) and probably the healing of the nobleman's son (Jn 4:46-54) have Synoptic parallels, but the other four, including the raising of Lazarus (Jn 11:1-44), are unique. Alongside these seven "signs" and predictive prophecy (attested in all the Gospels), the Johannine Jesus displays supernatural knowledge of hidden realities (Jn 1:47-49; 2:24-25; 4:16-19; 5:6?; 6:64, 70-71; 13:1; 21:6). While not entirely absent from the Synoptics, this feature is more pronounced in John.

The premier miracle of the last half of the Fourth Gospel is Jesus' resurrection/return to the Father. As noted above, John's resurrection narratives have interesting points of contact with Luke's: the two figures who convey the Easter message to Mary/the women, a resurrection appearance to the disciples on Easter and explicit mention of Jesus' ascension (though apparently understood differently). Nevertheless, the following miraculous elements are unique to John: a christophany to Mary Magdalene (Jn 20:14-18), Jesus' bestowal of the Holy Spirit on his disciples on Easter evening (Jn 20:21-22), a christophany to his disciples a week later (Jn 20:26-29) and, yet later, an early morning christophany to seven disciples (Jn 21:1-23).

On one level the miracle stories of the Fourth Gospel are similar to those of the Synoptic tradition. Three have Synoptic parallels, and of the remaining four, two are healings (from lameness, blindness), one a "gift" miracle (the production of wine from water) and one a resuscitation (Lazarus)—three types that have Synoptic parallels. Nevertheless, the Johannine presentation is distinctive.

In the first place, while in the Synoptics Jesus' miracles are normally called *dynameis,* "mighty deeds," the Fourth Evangelist repeatedly calls them *sēmeia,* "signs." He emphasizes that Jesus performed many signs, but scholars generally agree that he chose to narrate only seven. Since these appear within the first twelve chapters, R. Brown chose to label these chapters the "Book of Signs." Also, Burge has noted that most of the twenty-seven instances of *ergon,* "work," in the Fourth Gospel refer to Jesus' signs, although "work/s" includes more than signs (Jn 14:10; 17:4).

Whereas in the Synoptics the *dynameis* are closely correlated with the kingdom of God, proclaimed and proleptically established in Jesus' words and deeds, the Johannine *sēmeia* are said to evoke faith in Jesus as the Christ, the Son of God (Jn 20:30-31). The framework of the Johannine signs (especially the "I am" sayings) shows that the Evangelist has by no means simply adopted a traditional linguistic usage (cf. e.g.,

Acts 2:22; Rom 15:19). "Signs" are precisely what the Johannine miracles are, for in very concrete, physical ways they point to the deep and crucial truth about Jesus (and God), namely, that he is the absolutely unique Son of God who descended from heaven to reveal the Father and through whose "lifting up" on the cross, resurrection and return to the Father believers receive the Holy Spirit and thus eternal life. The signs, in other words, point to the present glory of the exclusive mediator of eschatological salvation and also portend the salvation to be enjoyed by the beneficiaries of the completion of his messianic work (cf. Jn 7:37-39).

Second, among the Johannine signs there are no exorcisms. In fact, Jesus' exorcisms are not even mentioned in John. In the Fourth Gospel it is in the "hour" of Jesus that the devil, the ruler of this world, makes his supreme assault against Jesus (Jn 13:2, 27; 14:30), but through Jesus' "lifting up" he is "cast out" (Jn 12:31-32).

Third, while the Fourth Gospel knows that faith is a prerequisite for miracles (Jn 4:50; 11:40), its emphasis is on the hope that retelling the signs will engender faith (Jn 20:30-31). Thus in the Fourth Gospel Jesus takes the initiative in performing signs, in fact, many signs (Jn 7:31; 11:47; 12:37; 20:30) "which no one else did" (Jn 15:24). The Fourth Gospel does not devalue faith based upon witnessing or hearing about signs unless such faith is less than a commitment to Jesus as (what the Evangelist understands by) the Christ, the Son of God. On the other hand, the Fourth Gospel does critique the demand to see signs before coming to faith (Jn 4:48; 6:30; 20:24-29).

2. Tradition History and Historicity.

2.1. Miracles of the Birth Narratives.
In the Matthean infancy narratives there appear five angelophanies, the story of the star and the account of the virginal conception. This last-mentioned miracle is also presented in Luke, along with three angelophanies. Strictly speaking, there are no parallels between these two sets of angelophanies, though it is true that both Gospels contain an angelic announcement of Jesus' birth (Matthew's to Joseph; Luke's to Mary). Because there is such little overlap between these birth narratives (cf. Fitzmyer, 1.307), it is difficult to trace their tradition history. Alongside appeal to the Evangelists' own creativity, a bewildering assortment of oral and written sources have been postulated, but no consensus has emerged.

At any rate one thing is clear: assuming that Matthew and Luke independently composed their birth narratives, both were relying on older tradition containing the virginal conception and probably an angelic announcement of Jesus' birth. The tradition of the virginal conception, therefore, predates Matthew and Luke, but by how long? Some conclude that it is a late creation since no other NT author—including the earliest, Paul—betrays knowledge of it (except perhaps the author of the Fourth Gospel [Jn 8:41; cf. Mk 6:3]). But can one show the probability that a given author would have mentioned it had he known about it? Moreover, some explain this silence by appeal to a "birth secret" (cf. Lk 2:19, 51) which was not divulged until considerably later.

There have been various efforts to explain the origin of belief in the virginal conception without recourse to the supernatural, but each is beset with difficulties. It is not clear that Isaiah 7:14, either in the MT or LXX, speaks of a virginal conception, and a messianic interpretation of this text in pre-Christian times is not forthcoming. In an allegorical exegesis of the birth of Isaac, Philo (*Cher.* 43-52) employs the pagan notion that a woman might become pregnant through the spirit, power or breath of a god (Aeschylus *Suppl.* 17-19; Plutarch *Ser. Num. Pun.* 4; *Mor.* 9.114-19). Yet Philo only uses this notion to explain the generation of virtue in the soul; there is no evidence that he or any other Jew believed that Isaac or anyone else had been fathered by God's Spirit apart from a human father. That the tradition of Jesus' virginal conception arose from a direct assimilation to pagan stories of gods copulating with mortal women is virtually excluded by the intensely Jewish ambience of the birth narratives. In sum, historical analysis of the tradition that Jesus had no biological father can yield neither proof nor refutation.

2.2. Miracles Performed by Jesus.
Among NT scholars there is almost universal agreement that Jesus performed what he and his contemporaries regarded as miraculous healings and exorcisms. This judgment is based primarily on several sayings of Jesus which, when evaluated against widely recognized criteria of authenticity, prove to be utterances of Jesus (Mt 12:28 par. Lk 11:20; Mk 3:23; Lk 13:32; Mt 11:4-6 par. Lk 7:22-23; Mt 13:16-17 par. Lk 10:23-24). To this evidence one may add the fact that Jesus' exorcis-

tic and/or healing activity is attested in every stratum of Gospel material (Q, Mark, M, L, John) and in a variety of literary forms (sayings, miracle stories, summaries, controversy stories, the so-called legends and the passion narratives [Mk 15:31 par.]). Outside of early Christianity Jesus was also known as an exorcist/healer in the magical papyri (PGM 4.3019-30) and within later Jewish circles (e.g., *t. Ḥul.* 2:22-23). Despite the highly speculative reconstruction of Christian origins by B. Mack, who argues that Jesus was not a miracle worker, sober historical analysis will continue to affirm the high probability that Jesus performed healings and exorcisms.

Evidence that Jesus raised the dead and performed so-called nature miracles is less pervasive. Only Jesus' revivification of the dead is attested in a saying (from Q) which scholars have frequently judged authentic (Mt 11:4-6 par. Lk 7:22-23). However, since Matthew, Luke and John contain at least one revivification and/or nature miracle not found in Mark, it is highly improbable that all such stories in Mark are Markan creations. We can, therefore, safely say that revivification and nature miracles were attributed to Jesus at some point prior to Mark. Of course, those who deny in principle the possibility of supernatural events reject such miracles (with the exception perhaps of revivifications, which could be explained on naturalistic grounds). On the other hand, those who believe that Jesus was raised from the dead are naturally open to the possibility that some such miracles actually occurred.

While most scholars agree that Jesus performed exorcisms and healings (and possibly deeds regarded as revivifications), many would be wary about claiming that any one of the miracle stories of the Gospels is based on actual reminiscence. This obviously raises questions concerning the source(s) employed by the Evangelists. To the degree that one is sure of the traditional link between Mark and Peter, or that John Zebedee was the ultimate authority for the Johannine signs, one will be very open to the historicity of these stories. These two hypotheses, however, have been—perhaps unwisely—widely abandoned. At the very least, it is virtually certain, as we have seen, that some, if not all, of the Gospel stories antedate Mark. Among the traditions designated as Q there are two miracle stories (Mt 8:5-13 par. Lk 7:1-10 [Jn 4:46-54 is possibly a variant]; Mt 12:22-23 par. Lk 11:14).

Various scholars have also attempted to delineate prior oral or written catenae, or chains, of miracles that were incorporated into the Gospels. P. Achtemeier (1970, 1972), for example, argues that two such catenae lie behind the Markan miracle stories appearing in Mark 4:35—6:44 and 6:45—8:26. Many Johannine scholars have appealed to a signs source to explain the composition of the Fourth Gospel. Mack has endeavored to find at the root of all these catenae a Christian effort to transform Jesus into a miracle worker.

In reality, however, these source theories involve a high degree of speculation (cf. Koch), and Mack's reconstruction in particular is not likely to inspire confidence. Source analysis may help to show that the miracle stories had an existence prior to their inclusion in the Gospels, but this fact does not in itself yield a verdict on historicity (*see* Gospels, Historical Reliability of).

Skepticism concerning the probable historicity of any particular miracle story has also been fueled by the conviction that those who formulated these accounts assimilated Jesus to the typical miracle-working divine man *(theios anēr)* familiar to the Hellenistic world. Nevertheless, the *theios anēr* hypothesis and its implications for the tradition history of the miracle stories is much weaker than its advocates realize. It will suffice here to note that (1) one can posit several reasons why the earliest Aramaic-speaking church would have narrated Jesus' miracles (see 3.2 below), and that (2) in fact a significant number of respected Gospel scholars have argued that at least a few of the miracle stories circulated in the earliest church.

Though one would be hard pressed to prove that some of the miracle stories did not originate among Hellenized Christians, one can with confidence exclude few if any from the early Aramaic-speaking church. Such early circulation would not in itself prove historicity, but with all other things equal this fact would enhance the case for historical verity. R. Pesch has thoughtfully pointed to elements within healing and exorcism stories that argue for their historicity, though some may hesitate to agree that some narratives contain elements that make historicity improbable.

2.3. Resurrection/Discovery of the Empty Tomb.

Whether Jesus rose from the dead is a complex philosophical, theological and historical problem. This complexity is demonstrated in the work of W. Pannenberg, the theologian who more than anyone else in the latter half of the twentieth century pressed for recognition of the historicity and centrality of Jesus' resurrection. Of this fact, however, all historians are confident: that very shortly after Jesus was crucified, his disciples became convinced by multiple visionary appearances of Jesus (1 Cor 15:5-8) that God had restored his life and ushered him into the heavenly world. Thus the *resurrection belongs to the bedrock of Christian belief.

Many, however, would refrain from saying the same about the story of the discovery of the empty tomb. Bultmann argued that it was not part of the early passion narrative but a late apologetic. Some scholars have since credited Mark with its origin. Pesch (1974), on the other hand, has argued cogently that it formed the conclusion of the old Jerusalem passion narrative. Yet he maintains that it was not based on a historical report, but was freely constructed after a pattern attested in the Jewish as well as in the Greco-Roman world: the unsuccessful search for the translated or resurrected person.

It is true that difficult questions face the defender of the substantial historicity of the empty-tomb story. Why, for example, does the empty tomb tradition not surface in the early confessional statement quoted by Paul in 1 Corinthians 15:3-7, in his own words, or in the sermons of Acts? Yet an impressive list of exegetes have concluded that jettisoning a historical core for the empty tomb story presents even more formidable problems. When Jesus' resurrection was first proclaimed, why did the authorities not exhume the corpse? Even if it had decayed beyond recognition, its presence in Joseph's tomb—a detail with strong historical credentials—would have been damning. And if the authorities themselves had discovered it empty, would they have revealed it? And had they done so, would Christians have not heavily exploited that fact? Morever, if the empty tomb narrative had been freely constructed, would a few women have been chosen as witnesses of the opened and empty tomb? Why not some or all of the eleven disciples? Finally, as W. L. Craig has argued, the discovery of the empty tomb on Easter Sunday following Good Friday offers the only really satisfying explanation of the creedal affirmation, "He was raised on the third day." While belief in Jesus' resurrection does not necessarily hinge on the historicity of the empty-tomb story, a variety of historical considerations make the latter plausible.

3. Significance of the Miracles.

3.1. Miracles of the Birth Narratives.
As different as they are, the Matthean and Lukan birth narratives converge in situating Jesus' nativity in a matrix of miracles. In general the angelophanies underscore the importance of Jesus' birth for salvation history. Matthew's five dream-angelophanies reveal God's ability to uphold his divine plan, prophesied in Scripture, over against historical ambiguities and Herod's machinations. Specifically, the angelic annunciation of Jesus' birth (to Joseph [Mt] and Mary [Lk]) is appropriate for the messianic scion of David, just as angels heralded important figures of the past: Isaac, Moses (e.g., Josephus Ant. 2.210-16) and Samson.

Matthew's star, connected to the oracle of Numbers 24:17, portends the birth of "King David's greater Son" (cf. e.g., 4QTestim 12-13). According to Kee, Matthew's portents at Jesus' birth and death are to be interpreted in light of Roman historical tradition, in which such portents demonstrate the divine governance of history in the rise and fall of emperors. Thus the perceptive will see in the star a disclosure of God's purpose in history, centered upon Jesus the king.

The virginal conception, like the angelophanies and the star, exalts Jesus and links him to OT history and expectation. Several key Israelite figures (e.g., Isaac, Joseph, Samson, Samuel) were born to barren women blessed by God. On the other hand, none was born to a virgin. R. Brown has called attention to this same "step-parallelism" between the birth accounts of John and Jesus in Luke. Such a unique origin was fitting for God's eschatological plenipotentiary, to whom worship would be the appropriate response. At some point this miraculous conception was regarded as the fulfillment of Isaiah 7:14 (Mt 1:22-23; allusion in Lk 1:26-31)—a promise given to the "house of David"—and associated with the title Son of God (Lk 1:35).

3.2. Miracles Occurring in Jesus' Ministry.
Almost all scholars believe that Jesus saw a direct connection between the miracles he performed and his proclamation of the coming of God's kingdom (see Kingdom of God). In the opinion of advocates of consistent eschatology, Jesus viewed his miracles as signs that the kingdom of God was on the verge of bringing the present age to an end. C. H. Dodd, the principal voice of real-

ized eschatology, argued on the basis of his interpretation of Matthew 12:28 and Luke 11:20 that Jesus saw his miracles as actual expressions of God's reign, already fully present in his ministry. According to others, however, Jesus performed his miracles knowing that in his ministry the reign of God was being inaugurated, yet also intending his miracles to portend the cosmic renewal that the future consummation of the kingdom would entail.

This connection between Jesus' miracles and his message about the advent of the kingdom accounts for most, if not all, of the miracles attributed to him in the Gospels. According to Isaiah, in the future era of salvation—the "kingdom of God" in apocalyptic thought—the deaf will hear, the blind will see, the lame will walk and the mute will sing (Is 29:18-19; 35:5-6; 61:1). Beyond that, both the OT and intertestamental apocalyptic know that the "age to come" will mean resurrection for the dead (Is 26:19; Dan 12:1-3). Although the OT has little to say about demons or exorcism, several noncanonical apocalyptic authors expected the advent of the kingdom to spell doom for Satan and his demonic minions (*1 Enoch* 10:11-15; 54-55; 11QMelch; *T. Levi* 18:12; *T. Mos.* 10:1-2; cf. Mt 12:28; Lk 11:20).

One can even posit an eschatological/apocalyptic background for the so-called nature miracles. All three gift or provision miracles (feedings of five thousand and four thousand; Cana wine miracle) actualize and foreshadow the messianic feast (Is 25:6-9; *2 Apoc. Bar.* 29:4; Mt 8:11 par.), characterized by an abundance of bread—the eschatological equivalent of the manna miracle (*2 Apoc. Bar.* 29:7-8; cf. Jn 6:4, 14, 30-31; Rev. 2:17)—and wine (*2 Apoc. Bar.* 29:5-6). The two rescue miracles, Jesus' calming of and walking on the sea, are meaningful against the horizon of Yahweh's assertion of his sovereignty over the sea in creation (Job 26:12-13; Ps 74:12-15), the exodus (Ps 77:16-20) and the eschaton (Is 27:1; cf. Rev 21:1). As apocalyptic also looked for divine judgment on God's enemies, it is tempting to see in Jesus' cursing of the fig tree an acted parable threatening the Jewish nation with disaster in the absence of repentance (cf. Mk 11:13; Mic 7:1-6; Jer 8:13). Even the visionary experiences of Jesus' baptism and transfiguration fall within the orbit of apocalyptic eschatology insofar as (1) literature of the latter type often employed vision as a revelatory medium, and (2) the two visions in question have eschatological content.

The miracles of Jesus are, however, not only integrally related to the coming of the kingdom but also support and promote the identity of Jesus as God's eschatological agent, the Messiah (*see* Christ). It is admittedly difficult to produce pre-Christian texts in which the expected Messiah appears as a miracle worker, but considerable evidence suggests that by the first Christian century at least some Jews saw Moses and the saving events of the Exodus period as prototypical of the Messiah and the liberating events of his reign. This typology probably lies behind the sign prophets of Josephus, the reaction of the crowd in John 6:14-15, the behavior of the false christs of Mark 13:21-22 and parallels, and the description of the miracle-working of the Davidic Messiah of 4 Ezra 13:32, 50. One thing is certain: at least as early as Luke-Acts—and probably much earlier—Jesus was regarded as the predicted Mosaic prophet of Deuteronomy 18:15, 18 (Acts 3:22-23; 7:37), and thus his miracles appear as "signs and wonders" standing in a typological relation to those that Moses performed (Acts 2:22).

Other factors also contributed to the christological significance of Jesus' miracles: (1) they document qualities expected in the shepherd-Messiah—compassion and mercy (esp. emphasized in Mt); (2) they demonstrate God's approbation of Jesus and his ministry, on the basis of the deeply rooted scriptural principle that miracles (performed within the framework of divine revelation) legitimate divinely authorized agents; and (3), aside from pre-Christian messianic expectations, their transmission and repetition are inevitable, given the desire of early Christians to glorify and exalt their Messiah.

3.3. Resurrection/Discovery of the Empty Tomb. In the historical-theological context in which belief in Jesus' resurrection originated, certain implications of this divine action were present from the beginning: Jesus was truly God's Messiah, and his resurrection marked the inauguration of the eschatological resurrection, though an interval of time would separate Jesus' resurrection from that of believers (1 Cor 15:20-28).

The Gospels proclaim the resurrection by narrating both the story of the empty tomb and—collectively—at least seven epiphanies of the risen Christ. The empty-tomb story is narrated first, but the significance of the vacant tomb does not emerge until Jesus' continued existence is revealed by angelic mediation and/or a christophany. In light of these divine revelations, however, the mystery (or misinterpretation) of the empty tomb is clarified, for the dominant Jewish notion of resurrection would have required that the earthly body of Jesus be transformed into the glorified body, hence resulting in an empty tomb.

In conclusion, taken as a whole the Gospels testify that Jesus performed many miracles and in addition that breathtaking wonders marked both the beginning and end of his earthly life. While this composite picture does not admit of scientific proof, the evidence at hand is sufficient to challenge the honest inquirer to consider seriously the Christian conviction about the identity of Jesus, and to perceive in him and his ministry the inauguration of the reign of God expected in Jewish apocalyptic. For believers these expressions of God's royal and benevolent power constitute a continual reminder of the divine power available in weakness for the church militant and in unveiled glory for the church triumphant.

See also BIRTH OF JESUS; GOSPELS, HISTORICAL RELIABILITY OF; KINGDOM OF GOD; RESURRECTION.

DJG: AUTHORITY AND POWER; DEMON, DEVIL, SATAN; DIVINE MAN/THEIOS ANĒR; HEALING.

BIBLIOGRAPHY. P. Achtemeier, "The Lucan Perspective on the Miracles of Jesus: A Preliminary Sketch," *JBL* 94 (1975) 547-62; idem, "The Origin and Function of the Pre-Marcan Miracle Catenae," *JBL* 91 (1972) 198-221; idem, "Toward the Isolation of Pre-Markan Miracle Catenae," *JBL* 89 (1970) 265-91; O. Betz and W. Grimm, *Wesen und Wirklichkeit der Wunder Jesu* (ANTJ 2; Frankfurt: Peter Lang, 1977); B. Blackburn, *Theios Anēr and the Markan Miracle Traditions* (WUNT 2.40; Tübingen: J. C. B. Mohr, 1991); C. Brown, *Miracles and the Critical Mind* (Grand Rapids: Eerdmans, 1984); R. Brown, *The Birth of the Messiah* (Garden City, NY: Doubleday, 1979); idem, *The Gospel According to John* (AB 29, 29A; Garden City, NY: Doubleday, 1966, 1970); R. Bultmann, *History of the Synoptic Tradition* (rev. ed.; New York: Harper and Row, 1963); G. Burge, *The Anointed Community: The Holy Spirit in the Johannine Tradition* (Grand Rapids: Eerdmans, 1987); U. Busse, *Die Wunder des Propheten Jesus: Rezeption, Komposition und Interpretation der* *Wundertradition im Evangelium des Lukas* (FB 24; Stuttgart: Katholisches Bibelwerk, 1977); W. Craig, "The Historicity of the Empty Tomb of Jesus," *NTS* 31 (1985) 39-67; J. A. Fitzmyer, *The Gospel According to Luke* (AB 28, 28A; Garden City, NY: Doubleday, 1981, 1985); R. Fortna, *The Gospel of Signs* (SNTSMS 11; Cambridge: Cambridge University Press, 1970); J. Gnilka, *Das Matthäusevangelium* (HTKNT 1; Freiburg: Herder, 1986); H. J. Held, "Matthew as Interpreter of the Miracle Stories," in *Tradition and Interpretation in Matthew,* G. Bornkamm, G. Barth, H. J. Held (Philadelphia: Westminster, 1963); H. C. Kee, *Miracle in the Early Christian World* (New Haven: Yale University Press, 1983); K. Kertelge, *Die Wunder Jesu im Markusevangelium* (SANT 13; Munich: Kösel-Verlag, 1970); D.-A. Koch, *Die Bedeutung der Wundererzählungen für die Christologie des Markusevangeliums* (BZNW 42; Berlin: W. de Gruyter, 1975); U. Luz, "Die Wundergeschichten von Mt 8—9" in *Tradition and Interpretation in the New Testament: Essays in Honor of E. Earle Ellis,* ed. G. Hawthorne and O. Betz (Grand Rapids: Eerdmans, 1987); B. Mack, *A Myth of Innocence: Mark and Christian Origins* (Philadelphia: Fortress, 1988); J. P. Meier, *A Marginal Jew,* vol. 2: *Mentor, Message, and Miracles* (New York: Doubleday, 1994); W. Pannenberg, *Jesus—God and Man* (Philadelphia: Westminster, 1977); R. Pesch, *Jesu ureigene Taten?* (QD 52; Freiburg: Herder, 1970); idem, "Der Schluss der vormarkinischen Passionsge schichte und des Markusevangeliums: Mk 15,42—16,8," in *L'Évangile selon Marc: Tradition et Rédaction,* ed. M. Sabbe (Leuven: Leuven University, 1974) 365-409; G. Theissen, *The Miracle Stories of the Early Christian Tradition* (Philadelphia: Fortress, 1983); G. H. Twelftree, *Jesus the Miracle Worker* (Downers Grove, IL: InterVarsity Press, 1999); T. Weeden, *Mark—Traditions in Conflict* (Philadelphia: Fortress, 1971); D. Wenham and C. Blomberg, eds., *Gospel Perspectives 6: The Miracles of Jesus* (Sheffield: JSOT, 1986); W. Wrede, *The Messianic Secret* (Cambridge: James Clarke, 1971); N. T. Wright, *The Resurrection of the Son of God* (Minneapolis: Fortress, 2003).

B. L. Blackburn

MIRACLES, MIRACLE STORIES II: ACTS

Miracles, or divine interventions in the observed order of human events, are part of most biblical narratives. Acts contains twenty to twenty-five miracle stories, the latter figure including five summary statements referring to the working of multiple miracles. These stories serve to point to divine activity and to authenticate the teaching and mission of the divinely authorized agent. While the healing miracles are in continuity with the miracles of Jesus in the Gospels, they reflect an independent tradition; there are also a number of miracles unique to Acts, such as miraculous releases from prison, transportation and especially judgment.

1. Miracle Story Evidence
2. Critical Assessment of the Miracle Stories
3. Paul as a Miracle Worker
4. Judgment Miracles
5. Function of Miracle Stories

1. Miracle Story Evidence.

The miracles in Acts continue the miracle narratives in Luke. However, along with the similarities there are significant differences. Healing miracles are more prominent in Luke, while protection or deliverance miracles are more prominent in Acts. Yet both works have miracles in each of the categories described below (see 1.2-4 below), which makes Luke-Acts different from the other Gospels (i.e., none of the others have judgment miracles, except the cursing of the fig tree, while John is the only other Gospel with clear miracles of deliverance or protection).

When we examine the miracles in Acts we will divide them into four groups, combining exorcism and raising of the dead with healing miracles (Neirynck, 170-71, uses seven groups; Hardon, 303-5, uses five groups). To this we could add a fifth type of miracle, that of the ascension (Acts 1:9-11; so also Hardon), which is presented as a significant event of salvation history and is thus in a class apart from the other miracles.

1.1. Miracles of Inspiration. The most prominent miracle of inspiration is Pentecost (Acts 2:1-13), although one could group with this other references to glossolalia or prophecy (Acts 10; 19) as well as references to Peter, Paul or others laying hands on people and the Holy Spirit coming upon them (which appears to include some experiential component) and to guidance by visions, angels or God's Spirit. Many writers would not count any of these experiences among the miracles in Acts in that no physical phenomena are involved (e.g., Gen 4; 6), while others would count Pentecost since it involved observable

phenomena but not the miracles of guidance (e.g., Praeder, 108). Yet surely these distinctions are modern, not those of the author of Acts. For him all of these events are part of his evidence that God through his Spirit was directing and empowering the mission of the church (Stronstad, 49-74).

1.2. Miracles of Healing. The healing miracles (including the summary statements) are common enough that they can be best presented as in table 1:

Table 1. Miracles of Healing

Reference	Miracle	Agent	Result
Acts 2:43	Summary	Apostles	Evangelization (in context)
Acts 3:1-10	Lame man healed	Peter (and John)	Evangelization
Acts 5:12-16	Summary	Apostles/ Peter	Evangelization/high regard
Acts 6:8	Summary	Stephen	Hostility
Acts 8:4-8	Summary	Philip	Evangelization
Acts 9:10-19/ Acts 22:12-16	Blind receives sight	Ananias	Evangelization
Acts 9:32-35	Paralytic healed	Peter	Evangelization
Acts 9:36-43	Dead woman raised	Peter	Evangelization
Acts 14:3	Summary	Paul and Barnabas	Evangelization/division
Acts 14:8-18	Lame man healed	Paul	High regard
Acts 15:12	Summary	Paul and Barnabas	Context of evangelistic report
Acts 16:16-24	Spirit exorcised	Paul	Hostile attack
Acts 19:11-12	Summary	Paul	Evangelization/high regard
Acts 20:7-12	Dead man raised	Paul	Comfort
Acts 28:7-10	Man with fever healed	Paul	High regard

What one notes is that these miracles, dealing with diseases stemming from both spiritual and nonspiritual causes, concern a variety of anatomical regions (although not as wide a variety as in Luke, possibly indicating real if limited results of redemption; Pilch), and these miracles are normally connected to an evangelistic result or at least a rise in the status of the miracle workers (Praeder, 113-14).

1.3. Miracles of Protection or Deliverance. Each of the miracles of protection or deliverance in some way extricates a person from danger or difficulty, allowing the person to get on with the work of evangelization. While many scholars do not count Paul's deliverance from the shipwreck as a miracle, Acts announces it as divine deliverance (Acts 27:23-24), and so it appears miraculous from Luke's perspective. Furthermore, the survival of Paul from stoning could also be grouped with healing miracles (similar to the raising of Eutychus); what it shares with the protection or deliverance miracles is the absence of a named agent.

Table 2. Miracles of Protection or Deliverance

Reference	Miracle	Subject	Result
Acts 5:17-21 (26)	Release from prison	Apostles	Preaching
Acts 8:39	Man transported	Philip	Preaching
Acts 12:1-19	Release from prison	Peter	Fear?
Acts 14:19-20	Paul survives stoning	Paul	Continues mission
Acts 16:16-24	Release from prison	Paul and Silas	Evangelization
Acts 27:13-44	Deliverance from shipwreck	Paul	Effect on sailors
Acts 28:1-6	Deliverance from snakebite	Paul	High regard

1.4. Miracles of Judgment. The miracles of judgment are the most unusual miracles in Acts. These appear to be the opposite of the salvation or healing miracles. There is some question as to whether to include among these miracles Paul's being blinded on the Damascus Road (see 4 below).

Table 3. Miracles of Judgment

Reference	Miracle	Agent	Result
Acts 5:1-11	Couple dies	Peter	Fear
Acts 9:1-9/ Acts 22:6-11	Paul blinded	Jesus	Conversion/ call
Acts 12:19-24	Herod dies	Angel of the Lord	Word of God increases
Acts 13:6-12	Bar-Jesus blinded	Paul	Evangelization

2. Critical Assessment of the Miracle Stories.

The modern criticism of the miracle stories in Acts began with the *Tendenzkritik* of the past century, pointing out that in Acts, Peter and Paul work similar miracles. This led to F. C. Baur's assertion that Luke had deliberately modeled Paul on Peter to equate the two. In a related development B. Bauer, building on the work of others, argued that miracle stories about Jesus were the original out of which both Peter's and Paul's miracles were built. The significance of this issue of the Jesus-Peter-Paul parallelism became a much discussed topic in further critical works.

A second approach to the miracles, developing in the nineteenth century, was that of source criticism. Scholars such as E. Zeller and A. von Harnack viewed the miracles not as Luke's creation but as stemming from his sources. Usually the sources included a Petrine source for Peter's miracles (often viewed as legendary) and the "we" source for Paul's (sometimes viewed as historical). Without the controls found in Synoptic source criticism, no firm conclusions have resulted from this research.

With the coming of the twentieth century, M. Dibelius and R. Bultmann pioneered the form-critical approach to the miracles in Acts, classifying them similarly to the Gospel pericope (Conzelmann, 25). However, more recent criticism (J. Roloff and S. H. Kanda) has pointed to the differences between the miracles in Acts and the miracles of Jesus, particularly in the use of prayer and the divine name, and thus views them as similar to Jewish miracles (Neirynck, 172-202). The most recent research has focused on the function of miracles in the Lukan redaction (see 5 below).

The present critical consensus is that the miracles in Acts are rarely if ever directly built upon the miracles in Luke's Gospel (although this does not deny influence) but instead stem from independent tradition available to Luke (Praeder, 120; Schreiber, 140-43; Conzelmann, 25, 76, 164). There are in fact few verbal or structural parallels with Gospel miracles other than the essential terms needed to describe a given type of healing. The historical validity of the underlying tradition is variously evaluated, as is the degree to which Luke may have embellished it for theological reasons. What is clear is that the miracle summaries are Lukan, although they too may indicate his knowledge of a tradition of miracle working by Peter, Paul, Stephen and others.

3. Paul as a Miracle Worker.

The critical discussion of the miracle stories in Acts points out as a major issue the portrait of Paul. There is no question that Paul in Acts is said to work miracles. Five miracle narratives (including one judgment miracle) and three summary statements present Paul as a charismatic wonder-worker. Does not this picture of Paul stand at odds with Paul's self-presentation as "weak"? Could it be that this picture of Paul is a deliberate attempt to parallel Paul to Peter? Or is Paul being presented as a *theios anēr* (divine man)?

Five observations have been made about this issue. First, given that there was no unified "divine man" ideal in the ancient world, the use of the term *theios anēr* is itself problematic. Furthermore, the evidence usually cited points to persons who were viewed as having power in themselves and thus as revealing their own status through their wonders. Paul's miracles are normally connected to his message, and this message is about someone other than he, that is, Jesus or God, who is said to be the real power working the wonder (Adams, 247-52).

Second, while Paul is undoubtedly a miracle worker in Acts, his miracles are spread thinly over his ministry. Two are at the beginning of his first missionary journey (including the judgment miracle), one in the second missionary journey and one in the third. The final miracle is an incidental event after the final shipwreck. One can hardly say that the miracle stories are a major part of the picture of Paul. Only the miracle summaries give that impression.

Third, there is no reference to the miracles in the speeches of Paul, which is not true of the speeches of Peter (miracles form the basis for at least three of them). Thus miracles function differently in relation to Paul than they do in relation to Peter. With Peter they initiate evangelism

and are a theme of his preaching while with Paul they only accompany evangelism.

Fourth, Paul's letters also refer to Paul as a miracle worker. Twice he uses the vocabulary of the Lukan summaries and notes that "signs and wonders" were worked through him, which he identifies as the "signs of an apostle" (2 Cor 12:12; Rom 15:19). Elsewhere he makes passing reference to miracles having accompanied his ministry (1 Cor 2:4; 1 Thess 1:5; Gal 3:1-4). Therefore the Lukan summaries do not differ significantly from Paul's self-presentation of the presence of the role of the miraculous in his ministry.

Fifth, Acts does have a suffering Paul. He is chased from Damascus and Jerusalem (the former of which incidents he viewed as showing "weakness," 2 Cor 11:30-33). Later he was forced out of the various cities of his first missionary journey, being stoned in one of them. Much the same could be said for his second missionary journey. His third journey ends with Paul imprisoned for two years. On his way to Rome he experiences a storm at sea and a shipwreck. Acts ends with Paul still a prisoner. What becomes clear in Acts is that while there are miracles of deliverance, the miracles are not about Paul. They are about the gospel. Nothing stops Paul (or Peter) from presenting the gospel, flight and rejection serving to continue its spread. And even when the doors of the prison are shaken open, the main result is evangelization, for it is by political means rather than the miracle that Paul eventually leaves the prison. Luke's triumph is a triumph of God, not of Paul.

Given that the Pauline letters are occasional letters and thus do not discuss the whole of Paul's theology, and given the preceding data, it is arguable that Paul's self-presentation is compatible with Luke's perspective on the triumph of the gospel through Paul (so Jervell, Praeder).

4. Judgment Miracles.

Acts reports at least three and possibly five judgment miracles. The deaths of Ananias and Sapphira, the death of Herod and the blinding of Bar-Jesus clearly fall in this category. There is debate as to whether the blinding of Paul is an act of judgment. Some interpreters view this as a judgment on Paul, while others view it as a natural result of the encounter with a divine epiphany. If it is judgment, we have a fourth judgment miracle; if it is not, then we have a healing after an "accident." The fifth possible judgment miracle is the storm at sea culminating in the shipwreck, which Luke presents as the result of not heeding Paul's advice (Acts 27:9-10, 21-26); however, in this case divine intervention is indicated only as the cause of deliverance, not as the cause of the storm.

Judgment miracles are not unique to Acts, since one, the muting of Zechariah, is included in Luke (Lk 1:19-22, 62-65). However, this is the only judgment miracle in the Gospels (other than the cursing of the fig tree, which concerns an object rather than a person). Thus we can conclude that judgment miracles are part of Lukan theology, continuing OT precedents. For instance, F. F. Bruce (102) has noted that the judgment of Ananias and Sapphira functions similarly to the judgment on Achan in Joshua in that the community is warned against ignoring the presence of God in their midst. In all of the judgment stories someone is ignoring or opposing the activity of God. The results may be temporary (Zechariah, Paul, Bar-Jesus) or permanent (Ananias and Sapphira, Herod), but in each case God intervenes to stop the opposition and demonstrate his presence.

The function of judgment miracles, therefore, is similar to the function of healing miracles. Each of them results in either fear (i.e., awe in the face of God's action) or evangelization (conversion of Paul, spread of the Word, conversion of Sergius Paulus). Thus God is attributed a higher status (fear) or more people submit to him. His presence and his teaching have been authenticated, even though the process was a negative one (Gen). They also prefigure the final judgment, which Acts warns about on more than one occasion (Acts 2:40; 10:42; 17:30-31).

A function of one of the judgment miracles (Acts 13:6-12) is to differentiate miracle from magic. It is clear that historically *magic* was a polemic term that identified the person or activity so designated as socially or religiously unacceptable (Garrett 1989, 11-17, 31-32). Ethnographically, however, magic indicates the attempt to manipulate the world through the use of divine powers. This manipulation may take place through the use of a term of power or an incantation or other means at the disposal of the magician (Adams, 241-44).

Both of these types of definitions reveal aspects of Luke's methodology. Elymas Bar-Jesus and Simon Magus are both pictured as magicians, thus individuals with a source of power other than God in Jesus. Both meet their match in Paul and Peter, with a shaming of the alternative powers through a judgment miracle (the blinding of Elymas) and a miracle of inspiration (the giving of the Holy Spirit through Peter) respectively. This contest with magic is carried out most fully by Paul in Acts 19, where he exhibits "extraordinary" power, while Jewish exorcists get only shame in trying to usurp that power. The result is that the Ephesian believers forsake magic (burning their books; Fiorenza, 8-16; Conzelmann, 163). This contrast with magic is a subtheme of the contrast between God and pagan deities found in several places in Acts (e.g., Acts 14; 17; 19).

In that all of the miracles are referred to God's power rather than to power resident in the miracle worker, and in that technique goes almost unmentioned (other than in the references to Paul's "handkerchiefs"; Tobin, 278); there is also a deliberate, unannounced contrast between magic and miracle (although clear to anyone involved in magic). Miracle is not about technique or influencing God but about God's sovereign activity in spreading the gospel. Thus when Simon Magus wants to purchase Peter's "secret," he is rebuked, for his magical mindset is inimical to what Peter is about.

The contrast with magic is most clearly seen in the miracles of protection or deliverance, for none of them are brought about by the person they benefit. The various apostles appear surprised upon being released from prison. And when Paul is stoned or bitten by a snake, we do not learn of anything that he does to heal himself. In the shipwreck incident, far from being in control, he appears to need encouragement himself. When combined with the fact that Stephen and James are not delivered, these miracles reveal a power of God that is not under the control of God's agents but that sometimes works through those agents.

5. Function of Miracle Stories.

We have already mentioned the function of the miracle stories in Acts as part of the Christian apologetic that contrasted the divine miracles of Jesus and the apostles with the magic of the Jewish and Hellenistic worlds (Fiorenza). Beyond this function, the miracles also serve as indicators of divine intervention in the world. There are two types of direct statements concerning divine intervention in Acts: statements concerning God's intervention in creation, Israel's history, the life of Jesus and (more rarely) the eschatological future, all of which have miraculous aspects but are outside the narrative context, and statements concerning God's intervention in the narrative, both in terms of miracles of inspiration and in terms of signs and wonders (Mowery). In other words, it is through the miraculous, including the advent of the Spirit (which is often said to be the force behind the miracles), that God becomes the most important actor in Acts. Peter and Paul are visible on the stage but only as agents for God, Jesus or the Spirit.

This is Luke's reason why the gospel advances as it does. The various messengers are sent out by the Holy Spirit and directed by the Spirit as they are underway. When the gospel encounters obstacles, God overcomes them so that it is not stopped. This is the message behind the judgment miracles: someone has opposed God, and God will not be stopped. In these miracles God may act without a human agent (as in the case of Herod) or speak through a human agent (as in the case of Ananias and Sapphira, where divine revelation of the deceit comes through Peter), yet whatever the means, God is more to the fore than in the healing miracles. This is also the message behind the nondeliverance of Stephen (indeed, his vision—that is, divine intervention—triggers his death) and James and the deliverance of the apostles Peter and Paul on other occasions. Stephen dies, and the gospel spreads as the church scatters. Paul is sent on a mission, and chasing him out of town only spreads the gospel further. Even stoning the messenger cannot stop the progress of the gospel. Put him in prison, and the power of God converts the jailer. A storm at sea only serves to move him further toward Rome, for it was God who said that Paul would go to Rome. While the church does pray for Peter (we are not told if it was for his deliverance), in none of these cases are we told that a miracle is requested. God appears to decide whether to spread the gospel through a martyrdom or a miracle. Thus again the most important actor in Acts is God (Barrett, 277).

Related to God's central role is the function of miracles to authenticate the gospel message. According to Acts, Jesus was attested by signs and wonders (Acts 2:22), so it is no surprise when the apostles ask God to stretch out his hand to attest to their message through signs and wonders "through the name of your holy servant Jesus" (Acts 4:30). As the tables demonstrate (see 1.2-4 above), the various miraculous events are connected to evangelization either through a rise in the status of the messenger or through direct evangelistic effect. Peter's first miracle (and the one reported in the most detail) is accomplished not by Peter's skill (magic) but through faith in Jesus, for God has chosen to glorify Jesus (Acts 3:13, 16; 4:10). The miracle is the evidence that the message about the resurrected Jesus is true. Without the message, the miracle is at best an equivocal communication. In Acts 14 a miracle is misinterpreted (even though "faith to be healed" was present), and it is only with difficulty that the apostles can communicate enough of the truth to prevent pagan sacrifice. The miracle then is God's authentication of the message and the messenger.

Another function of the miracles stories in Acts is to advance the Lukan theology of *salvation. In Acts 3:1-10 the healing of the lame man parallels the offer of salvation in the following two speeches. Thus at the time of prayer the lame man outside the temple is healed ("saved"; the verb *sōzō* is used) through the power of Jesus mediated through the apostles. The man then enters and leaps about in the temple illustrating the fulfillment of salvation-historical hope (cf. Is 35:6). Along with the formerly lame man, the offer of salvation comes through the apostles to the people in the temple, presenting to them the fulfillment of salvation history in Jesus (Hamm, without endorsing everything he sees in the text). This serves as a grid through which to read the other miracles in Acts as limited outward demonstrations of eschatological salvation.

Finally, miracles serve to tie NT and OT salvation history together. We have already mentioned that the story of Ananias and Sapphira reminds one of the story of Achan in Joshua. That parallel (judgment among the people of God as they are taking a new promised land [the whole world]) shows the salvation-historical continuity Luke demonstrates in other ways. In the healing of the two mobility-challenged men, the salvation-historical hope of Isaiah 35:4 comes to the fore. Thus the OT and its hope is mirrored in the Lukan context. Salvation history is also seen in the parallels with Jesus. As Jesus drove out demons, so the disciples in Acts continue his conflict with Satan, driving out demons. As Jesus healed, so the disciples healed. They advance the new eon begun in Jesus. Yet they do not act exactly like Jesus, for Luke is conscious of his uniqueness. Jesus acted sovereignly, while the disciples act in his name or through the power of the Spirit he promised. In other words, their miracles point back to the Lord (and at times to the promise of his eschatological return), for it is Jesus who is and remains the real miracle worker even in Acts.

See also ACTS OF THE APOSTLES.

DLNTD: HEALING, ILLNESS; SIGNS AND WONDERS.

BIBLIOGRAPHY. M. M. Adams, "The Role of Miracles in the Structure of Luke-Acts," in *Hermes and Athena: Biblical Exegesis and Philosophical Theology*, ed. E. Stump and T. P. Flint (Notre Dame, IN: University of Notre Dame Press, 1993) 235-72; C. K. Barrett, *A Critical and Exegetical Commentary on the Acts of the Apostles* (ICC; Edinburgh: T & T Clark, 1994); F. F. Bruce, *The Book of Acts* (NICNT; Grand Rapids: Eerdmans, 1988); H. Conzelmann, *Acts of the Apostles* (Herm; Philadelphia: Fortress, 1987); J. C. Fenton, "The Order of the Miracles Performed by Peter and Paul in Acts," *ExpT* 77 (1966) 381-83; E. Schüssler Fiorenza, "Miracles, Mission and Apologetics: An Introduction," in *Aspects of Religious Propaganda in Judaism and Early Christianity*, ed. E. Schüssler Fiorenza (Notre Dame, IN: University of Notre Dame Press, 1976) 1-25; J. M. Ford, "The Social and Political Implications of the Miraculous in Acts," in *Faces of Renewal: Studies in Honor of Stanley M. Horton Presented on his Seventieth Birthday*, ed. P. Elbert (Peabody, MA: Hendrickson, 1988) 137-60; S. R. Garrett, *The Demise of the Devil: Magic and the Demonic in Luke's Writings* (Minneapolis: Fortress, 1989); idem, "Light on a Dark Subject and Vice Versa: Magic and Magicians in the New Testament," in *Religion, Science and Magic: In Concert and in Conflict*, ed. J. Neusner (Oxford: Oxford University Press, 1992 [1989]) 142-65; R. M. Gen, "The Phenomena of Miracles and Divine Infliction in Luke-Acts: Their Theological Significance," *Pneuma* 11 (1989) 3-19; D. Hamm, "Acts 3:1-10: The Healing of the Temple Beggar as Lukan Theology," *Bib* 67.3 (1986) 305-19; J. A. Hardon, "Miracle Narratives in the Acts of the Apostles," *CBQ* 16 (1954) 303-18; P. W. van der Horst, "Peter's Shadow," *NTS* 23 (1977) 204-12; J. Jervell, "The Signs of an Apostle: Paul's Miracles," in *The Unknown Paul: Essays on Luke-Acts and Early Christian History* (Minneapolis: Augsburg, 1984) 77-95; R. L. Mowery, "Direct Statements Concerning God's Activity in Acts," *SBLSP* 29 (1990) 196-211; F. Neirynck, "The Miracle Stories in the Acts of the Apostles: An Introduction," in *Les Actes des Apôtres*, ed. J. Kremer (Gembloux: J. Duculot, 1979) 169-213; L. O'Reilly, *Word and Sign in the Acts of the Apostles: A Study in Lukan Theology* (*Analecta Gregoriana* 243.82; Rome: Editrice Pontificia Universita Gregoriana, 1987); J. J. Pilch, "Sickness and Healing in Luke-Acts," in *The Social World of Luke-Acts*, ed. J. H. Neyrey (Peabody, MA: Hendrickson, 1991) 181-209; S. M. Praeder, "Miracle Worker and Missionary: Paul in the Acts of the Apostles," *SBLSP* 22 (1983) 107-29; S. Schreiber, *Paulus als Wundertäter* (BZNW 79; Berlin: Walter de Gruyter, 1996); R. Stronstad, *The Charismatic Theology of St. Luke* (Peabody, MA: Hendrickson, 1984); T. H. Tobin, "Miracles, Magic and Modernity: Comments on the Paper of Marilyn McCord Adams," in *Hermes and Athena: Biblical Exegesis and Philosophical Theology*, ed. E. Stump and T. P. Flint (Notre Dame, IN: University of Notre Dame, 1993) 275-81; M. Turner, "The Spirit and the Power of Jesus' Miracles in the Lukan Conception," *NovT* 33 (1991) 124-52.

P. H. Davids

MISHNAH. *See* RABBINIC TRADITIONS AND WRITINGS.

MISSIONARY, PAUL AS. *See* PAUL IN ACTS AND LETTERS.

MYSTERY. *See* JEW, PAUL THE.

MYSTERY CULTS/RELIGIONS. *See* RELIGIONS, GRECO-ROMAN.

MYSTICISM, JEWISH. *See* ESCHATOLOGY II; JEW, PAUL THE.

NAG HAMMADI LIBRARY. *See* GNOSTICISM.

NEW COVENANT. *See* COVENANT, NEW COVENANT.

NEW CREATION. *See* CREATION, NEW CREATION.

NEW ISRAEL. *See* ISRAEL.

NEW PERSPECTIVE ON PAUL. *See* JUSTIFICATION; LAW II; ROMANS, LETTER TO THE.

O, P

ONESIMUS. *See* PHILEMON, LETTER TO.

OPPONENTS OF PAUL. *See* ADVERSARIES I.

ORACLES. *See* RELIGIONS, GRECO-ROMAN.

ORIGINAL SIN. *See* SIN.

PAPIAS LOGION. *See* MATTHEW, GOSPEL OF.

PARABLES

The English word *parable* refers to a short narrative with two levels of meaning. The Greek and Hebrew words for "parable" are much broader. Jesus' parables are works of art and the weapons he used in the conflict with his opponents. They were the teaching method he chose most frequently to explain the *kingdom of God and to show the character of God and the expectations God has for people. Despite the tradition that argues Jesus' parables have only one point, many parables convey two or three truths, and there may be several correspondences between a specific parable and the reality it portrays.

1. History of Interpretation
2. Definition of *Parabolē* and Related Terms
3. Characteristics of the Parables
4. The Use of Parables Prior to Jesus
5. Distribution of the Parables in the Gospels
6. The Authenticity of the Parables
7. The Purpose of the Parables
8. Guidelines for Interpretation
9. The Teaching of the Parables

1. History of Interpretation.

A history of interpretation is virtually a prerequisite for studying Jesus' parables. That history must be framed in relation to the work of A. Jülicher, a German NT scholar whose two-volume work on the parables (1888, 1889) has dominated parable studies, even though it has never been translated.

1.1. Before Jülicher. Throughout most of the church's history, Jesus' parables have been allegorized instead of interpreted. That is, people read into the parables elements of the church's theology that had nothing to do with Jesus' intention. The best-known example of this is Augustine's interpretation of the parable of the good Samaritan (Lk 10:30-37), in which virtually every item was given theological significance. The man is Adam; Jerusalem is the heavenly city; Jericho is the moon, which stands for our mortality; the robbers are the devil and his angels who strip the man of his immortality and beat him by persuading him to sin; the priest and Levite are the priesthood and the ministry of the OT; the good Samaritan is Christ; the binding of the wounds is the restraint of sin; the oil and wine are the comfort of hope and the encouragement to work; the animal is the incarnation; the inn is the church; the next day is after the resurrection of Christ; the innkeeper is the apostle Paul; and the two denarii are the two commandments of love or the promise of this life and that which is to come (Augustine *Quaest. Evan.* 2.19). Similarly, Gregory the Great allegorized the parable of the barren fig tree (Lk 13:6-9) so that the three times the owner came looking for fruit represent God's coming before the Law was given, his coming at the time the Law was written, and his coming in grace and mercy in Christ. The vinedresser represents those who rule the church, and the digging and dung refer to the rebuking of unfruitful people and the remembrance of sins (Gregory the Great *Hom.* 31). Some, such as John Chrysostom of the school of Antioch and John Calvin, did not allegorize the parables, but until the end of the nineteenth century allegorizing was the dominant means of interpretation.

1.2. Jülicher. Although others before him had argued against allegorizing, Jülicher's two-volume work on the parables sounded the death knell on this interpretive procedure. Jülicher denied that Jesus used allegory (a series of related metaphors) or allegorical traits (where a point in the story stands for something else in reality). Where allegory or allegorical traits occur, such as in the parable of the sower and the parable of the wicked tenants, the Evangelists are to blame. Jülicher viewed Jesus' parables as simple and straightforward comparisons that do not require interpretation. They have only one point of comparison: between the image and the idea being expressed. That one point is usually a general religious maxim. The parables are extended similes, whereas allegories are extended metaphors. Like metaphors, allegories are inauthentic speech and must be decoded. Jesus' purpose was not to obscure; therefore his parables cannot be viewed as allegories.

1.3. After Jülicher. All subsequent studies of the parables have had to deal with Jülicher's views. There were early attacks on Jülicher's arguments, particularly by P. Fiebig (beginning in 1904), who argued that Jülicher derived his understandings of parables from Greek rhetoric rather than from the Hebrew world, where allegorical parables are common. Others recognized that Jülicher had thrown out allegory, a literary form, while the problem was allegorizing, the interpretive procedure of reading into the parables a theology that Jesus did not intend. Few interpreters today would accept Jülicher's descriptions of metaphor or his argument that the parables give general religious maxims. There have been devastating critiques of his description of allegory, but even so, people often still speak of one point for parables and are suspicious of any parts of Jesus' parables that have allegorical significance. In addition, there have been several stages through which parable interpretation has gone.

1.3.1. C. H. Dodd and J. Jeremias. The Dodd and Jeremias era of parable studies extends from 1935 to roughly 1970, although Jeremias's book on the parables is still influential. Jeremias's work was an extension of Dodd's, and both were influenced by Jülicher. Dodd and Jeremias tried to understand the parables of Jesus in their historical and eschatological context (*see* Eschatology). Both attempted to remove allegorical elements from the parables. Dodd under-

stood Jesus' message as realized eschatology: the kingdom had already arrived. Parables about harvest are not about a coming end time but about the time of Jesus' earthly ministry.

Jeremias sought to provide historical and cultural evidence for understanding the parables and, under the influence of form criticism, to ascertain a given parable's original form by stripping away allegorical features or other additions supplied by the early church. Typically this led to a reconstruction of the supposedly original form of a given parable. Almost invariably the context in the Gospels, the introductions, the conclusions, and any interpretive comments were considered secondary. Such shortened, de-allegorized forms are close to the versions of the parables in the *Gospel of Thomas*, a collection of sayings of Jesus dating probably from the second century. The relation of the *Gospel of Thomas* to the canonical Gospels, its date and its character are all debated. The fact that Jeremias and others had suggested shorter forms of the parables before the discovery of *Thomas* was made known has erroneously led some to argue that *Thomas* preserves the original form of some of the parables.

While granting the presence of the kingdom in Jesus' ministry, Jeremias described Jesus' message as an eschatology in the process of realization. In his parables, Jesus presented people with a crisis of decision and invited them to respond to God's mercy. Jeremias's influence has been so strong that N. Perrin argued that future interpretation of the parables should be interpretation of the parables as Jeremias has analyzed them (Perrin, 101).

1.3.2. Existentialist, Structuralist and Literary Approaches. Several modern approaches to parables have grown out of philosophical currents and partly out of dissatisfaction with the focus of Dodd and Jeremias on a historical approach. While seeking something more than the merely historical, however, these approaches still follow Jeremias in stripping off allegorical and interpretive additions. The new hermeneutic of E. Fuchs and E. Jüngel focuses on the power of Jesus' parables to bring to expression the reality to which they point. The parables are viewed as "language events" *(Sprachereignisse)*. In the parables, Jesus expresses his understanding of his existence in such a way that this existence is available to his hearers. The parables are a summons to this existence.

Similarly, G. V. Jones, A. N. Wilder and D. Via

all have focused on the artistic and existential character of the parables. Especially for Via the parables are not bound by the author's intention. They are aesthetic works that address the present because in their patterns is an understanding of existence that calls for decision.

K. Bailey's work on the parables is noteworthy because of his detailed focus on the rhetorical structure of the parables as well as his interpretation in light of the Palestinian mindset, a mindset he encountered as a missionary in Lebanon.

In the decade between 1970 and 1980, structuralist approaches dominated parable studies. Structuralists were not concerned for historical meaning or the author's intention. Rather, they sought to compare surface and deep structures of various texts; that is, they sought to compare the movements, motives, functions, oppositions and resolutions within texts. At times structuralist analyses have been helpful, such as J. D. Crossan's identification of the categories of advent, reversal and action as basic to understanding the parables. The kingdom of God comes as advent as a gift of God, as a reversal of a person's world and as an empowering for action. For the most part, however, structuralist studies have been dominated by technical jargon and have not provided much additional insight.

The 1980s witnessed several discernible shifts in parable studies, largely because of the influence of literary criticism. Although a concern for redactional emphases of the Gospel writers has been a focus since the 1950s, literary concerns have led to much more attention on the technique and purposes of the Evangelists in the composition of their works. Literary criticism has also tended to emphasize a reader-response approach in which a text's meaning is determined by the interaction of the reader with the text. This approach is highly subjective and yields a variety of meanings, all of which are considered correct. Such a polyvalent understanding of texts invites the interpreter to be a "trained player" and read texts with as many different associations as desired. For example, the parable of the prodigal son can be read in light of Freudian psychology in which the prodigal, the elder brother and the father reflect the id, the superego and the ego. It can be read just as legitimately in other contexts with this method. However, such subjective readings of the parables are not interpretations; they are retellings of the stories in new contexts. To understand the message of Jesus one will have to do justice to the historical context in which the parables were told.

1.4. Interpretations Based on Comparisons with Jewish Parables. An alternative trend in recent parable studies focuses on insights gained by studying early rabbinic parables. Comparing Jewish parables to Jesus' parables is not new. Fiebig had already done this in combating Jülicher's approach, and about the same time A. Feldman had collected Jewish parables that made such comparison easier. Now approximately two thousand rabbinic parables have been collected. In recent years several works have appeared that discuss parable theory in light of rabbinic parables and rethink previous theories and interpretations. Most important of these is the research of D. Flusser, a Jewish NT scholar whose primary work has not yet been translated into English. Flusser's work, and that of other scholars focusing on Judaism, challenges the conclusions not only of Jülicher but also of Jeremias, of the reader-response approaches and of much of NT scholarship. Flusser acknowledges a thoroughgoing editing of the parables by the Evangelists, but he is optimistic about the reliability of the Gospel material. He argues that the contexts of the parables are usually correct and that the introductions and conclusions to the parables are necessary and usually derive from Jesus. He views the *Gospel of Thomas* as dependent on the Synoptic Gospels and as unimportant for researching the words of Jesus.

The distance some recent studies have moved from the works of Jülicher and Jeremias is evidenced in C. Blomberg's treatment of the parables. Blomberg argues that the parables of Jesus, like the rabbinic parables, are allegories and usually have two or three points to make, depending on the number of main characters the parable has.

2. Definition of *Parabolē* and Related Terms.

The Greek word *parabolē* has a much broader meaning in the Gospels than the English word *parable*. It can be used of a proverb (Lk 4:23), a riddle (Mk 3:23), a comparison (Mt 13:33), a contrast (Lk 18:1-8), and both simple stories (Lk 13:6-9) and complex stories (Mt 22:1-14). This range of meaning derives from the Hebrew word *māšal*, which is usually translated by *parabolē* in the LXX (28 of 39 occurrences). In

addition, *māšal* can be used of a taunt, a prophetic oracle or a byword. A *māšal* is any dark
saying intended to stimulate thought.

The concept of a parable needs to be clarified beyond distinguishing the wide meanings
of the words *parabolē* and *māšal*. Four forms of
parables are often distinguished: similitude, example story, parable and allegory. A *similitude* is
an extended simile (an explicit comparison using "like" or "as"). It is a comparison relating a
typical or recurring event in real life and is often
expressed in the present tense. The parable of
the leaven (Mt 13:31-32) is a similitude. An *example story* presents a positive or negative character
(or both) who serves as an example to be imitated or whose traits and actions are to be avoided.
Either explicitly or implicitly the example story
says, "Go and do [or do not do] likewise" (cf. Lk
10:37). Usually only four Gospel parables, all in
Luke, are identified as example stories: the good
Samaritan, the rich fool, the rich man and Lazarus, and the pharisee and the tax collector. A
parable is an extended metaphor (an implied
comparison) referring to a fictional event or
events narrated in past time to express a moral
or spiritual truth. The parable of the banquet
(Lk 14:15-24) would fit this definition. In this
classification system an *allegory* is a series of related metaphors, and the parable of the sower
would be an example of an allegory.

Although this fourfold classification is popular, many scholars find it unworkable. Some object to the category "example story," but as long
as one does not overlook that more may be involved in these stories than merely providing an
example, this is a helpful classification. Clearly
these stories are different from other parables
in some respects. More troublesome is the supposed distinction between parable and allegory,
which is among the most debated issues in NT
studies. For some, such as M. Boucher, allegory
is not a literary form but a device of meaning;
therefore, all parables are allegorical either as
wholes or in their parts. Parables rarely have
only one correspondence between the story and
the reality being reflected, even though one
should not view interpretation of the parables as
the process of deciphering points. Parables are
best defined as stories with two levels of meaning; the story level provides a mirror by which
reality is perceived and understood. In effect,
parables are imaginary gardens with real toads
in them.

3. Characteristics of the Parables.

Parables tend to be brief and symmetrical. They
often make use of balanced structures involving
two or three movements. They typically omit unnecessary descriptions and frequently leave
motives unexplained and implied questions unanswered. They usually are taken from everyday
life, but they are not necessarily realistic. Because of hyperbole or elements of improbability
they often are pseudo-realistic and have elements that shock. For example, it is unlikely that
anyone in first-century Palestine would owe a
10,000-talent debt (several million dollars) as in
the parable of the unforgiving servant (Mt 18:23-
35). In addition, parables elicit thought. Twenty-
two parables start with a question such as "Who
from you?" or "What do you think?" Parables
frequently cause a hearer to pass judgment on
the events in the story and then require a similar judgment about religious matters. Often the
parables require a reversal in one's thinking.
The despised Samaritan is a neighbor; the tax
collector, not the Pharisee, is righteous. The crucial matter is placed at the end of the parables,
and correspondingly, "the rule of end stress" requires that the interpretation focus on the end
of the parable. Although the parable of the
wicked tenants has christological implications,
most parables are theocentric in that they focus
on God, his kingdom and his expectations for
humans. Consequently, the parables are often
invitations to changed behavior and discipleship. The degree to which the theological referent is transparent varies from parable to
parable.

4. The Use of Parables Prior to Jesus.

Jesus was not the first person to teach by parables and stories. There are Greek and Semitic
antecedents, but there is no evidence of anyone
prior to Jesus using parables as consistently, creatively and effectively as he did. There are so
many rabbinic parables similar to the ones Jesus
told that some scholars argue Jesus drew from a
fund of popular stories or at least that he drew
his themes and structures from such a fund. As
always with the rabbinic evidence, the problem
is that these writings are later than the time of
the NT. Because there is so little actual evidence
of teaching in parables prior to Jesus, some
scholars argue that Jesus' use of parables was
entirely new. There are no parables so far from
Qumran and none in the apocrypha and

pseudepigrapha (excluding the so-called Similitudes of Enoch, which are apparently later in origin). Virtually none of the rabbinic parables is from as early as the first half of the first century. In addition to the problem of date, rabbinic parables, all of which are in Hebrew rather than Aramaic, primarily are used as a means to interpret Scripture, whereas Jesus did not use parables this way.

The OT does provide seven parables that are antecedents to Jesus' parables: Nathan's parable to David about the poor man and his lamb (2 Sam 12:1-10); the woman from Tekoa's story about her two sons (2 Sam 14:5-20); the prophet's acted parable condemning Ahab (1 Kings 20:35-40); the song of the vineyard (Is 5:1-7); the eagles and the vine (Ezek 17:2-10); the lioness and her cubs (Ezek 19:2-9); and the vine (Ezek 19:10-14). Only Ezekiel 17:2-10 is explicitly called a *māšal*. In addition, Judges 9:7-15 and 2 Kings 14:9 contain fables. Of these OT parables only Nathan's parable of the poor man and his lamb is a true parallel to the parables of Jesus.

5. Distribution of the Parables in the Gospels.

Approximately one-third of Jesus' teaching is in parables. The Greek word *parabolē* occurs fifty times in the NT, and except for Hebrews 9:9 and Hebrews 11:19 all the occurrences are in the Synoptic Gospels. Parables appear in all strata of the Synoptics. If one accepts the four-source hypothesis of Gospel origins, parables make up about 16 percent of Mark, about 29 percent of Q, about 43 percent of M and about 52 percent of L (*see* Synoptic Problem). John does not have story parables, but it does have forms that would fit the broad sense of *māšal* such as the good shepherd (Jn 10) and the true vine (Jn 15). (John uses the word *paroimia* four times. This word is similar in some respects to *parabolē*.)

An exact number of the parables cannot be given since there is no agreement among scholars as to which forms should be classified as a parable. There are thirty forms explicitly labeled *parabolē*, but this includes proverbs (Lk 4:23), riddles (Mk 3:23), short sayings (Mk 7:15) and questions (Lk 6:39). There are at least forty parables on a more restricted definition, but as many as sixty-five if one includes such items as Jesus' saying about a person with a beam in his or her eye trying to get a speck out of the eye of another (Mt 7:3-5).

The parables are thematically arranged in the Synoptics. Mark has only four story parables: in Mark 4 the sower, the mustard seed and the seed growing secretly; and in Mark 12 the wicked tenants. Except for the seed growing secretly, Matthew and Luke have Mark's story parables, and both of them have the parables of the leaven and of the lost sheep. Matthew and Luke have parables about guests who reject invitations to a feast (Mt 22:1-14; Lk 14:16-26) and about servants who are entrusted with money to invest (Mt 25:14-30; Lk 19:11-27). However, the wording is not close in either of these parallels, and whether Matthew and Luke are reporting the same parables or only similar parables is debated. Jesus no doubt told some of the parables more than once and offered several variations on the same basic structure. Matthew has arranged most of his parables in Matthew 12—13, Matthew 18 and Matthew 20—25. He has at least twelve parables that are unique to him. Luke has placed most of his parables in Luke 10—19 of his so-called travel narrative. Luke has at least fifteen parables that are unique to him.

Fourteen parables occur among the sayings of the *Gospel of Thomas*, three of which are not recorded in the canonical Gospels. The *Apocryphon of James* also has three parables not recorded in the canonical Gospels.

6. The Authenticity of the Parables.

Even scholars who are persuaded that the Gospel parables include additions by the early church still view the parables as providing some of the most authentic and reliable teaching from Jesus. Supporting evidence for this confidence is strong:

(1) The parables reflect the clarity and eschatology of Jesus' preaching and his conflict with Jewish authorities.

(2) They reflect daily life in Palestine.

(3) Little evidence exists that parables were used frequently prior to Jesus.

(4) In view of the fact that parables do not appear in the NT outside the Gospels and rarely in other early Christian literature, the early church shows no propensity for creating parables.

At the same time, critical scholarship has gone to great lengths debating the authenticity of the parts and the whole of specific parables. The so-called Jesus Seminar has even produced a red-letter edition of the parables of Jesus that prints the wording of the parables in red, pink, gray or black, reflecting the opinions respectively that

Jesus said those words, said something like those words, did not say those words but expressed similar ideas, or did not say those words and the ideas are from a later time. Only three parables represented in the canonical tradition are printed entirely in black (the tower builder and the warring king, both in Lk 14:28-32, and the fishnet, Mt 13:47-50), and only four more in which all accounts are printed entirely in gray. (However, in these cases preference is often for the version of the parable in the *Gospel of Thomas*.)

While this underscores the confidence expressed in the parable tradition, the assumptions and procedures adopted by the Jesus Seminar and many other scholars are unacceptable. The Jesus Seminar, like so many earlier scholars, has succumbed to the tendency to find a Jesus who is amenable with modern expectations. Far too much preference is given to the *Gospel of Thomas*, which appears to derive from a second stage of the oral tradition. Furthermore, the rejection of the introductions and conclusions of the parables and of any allegorical significance is unjustified in light of recent research on Jewish parables. The oral tradition no doubt shaped the parables, and the Evangelists have clearly edited them in keeping with their stylistic tendencies and theological purposes. We can and should identify many such changes. However, any attempt to identify the *ipsissima verba* (the exact words) of Jesus is naive at best. The Gospels present the *ipsissima vox* (the very voice) of Jesus, and nowhere is that voice so clearly heard as in the parables.

7. The Purpose of the Parables.

Often it has been said that the parables of Jesus are not merely illustrations of Jesus' preaching but are themselves the preaching. Clearly, the parables are to engage and instruct, but it is not fair to say that the parables are themselves the preaching. Parables demand interpretation; they point to something else. They are not merely stories to enjoy. They hold up one reality to serve as a mirror of another, the kingdom of God. They are avenues to understanding, handles by which one can grasp the kingdom. Jesus told parables to confront people with the character of God's kingdom and to invite them to participate in it and to live in accordance with it.

Mark 4:10-12, however, seems to say the exact opposite. On the surface these verses argue that Jesus gives the secret of the kingdom only to his disciples. "To those outside all things are in parables in order that seeing they may see and not see, and hearing they may hear and not understand, lest they turn and it be forgiven them" (Mk 4:11-12). The latter part of this saying is from Isaiah 6:9-10.

An understanding of Mark requires attention to his technique, structure and theological emphases. Mark uses the technique of bracketing to provide insight into the individual sections of his Gospel. For example, the cleansing of the temple (Mk 11:15-19) is bracketed by the cursing of the fig tree (Mk 11:12-14) and the lesson drawn from the withered fig tree (Mk 11:20-25). Furthermore, the material in Mark 4:1-34 has been carefully arranged:

Mark 4:1-2—Narrative introduction telling that Jesus taught parables from a boat

Mark 4:3-9—The parable of the sower

Mark 4:10-12—Jesus alone with disciples, with whom he contrasts those who are outside

Mark 4:13-20—Interpretation of the parable of the sower

Mark 4:21-25—Parabolic sayings about hearing

Mark 4:26-32—Parables of the seed growing secretly and the mustard seed

Mark 4:33-34—Narrative conclusion summarizing the intent of this section

Some interpreters argue that this structure is chiastic, with the center of the chiasmus being the interpretation of the parable of the sower. (Chiasmus is a poetic a b b' a' pattern.) Note that in Mark 4:35-41 Jesus and his disciples are back in the boat. This section picks up chronologically where Mark 4:9 seems to have left off. Therefore, Mark 4:10-34 comprise a thematic arrangement by the author. Note also that Mark 3:31-34, with its focus on Jesus' family standing outside seeking him, and Mark 4:10-12, with its focus on those outside, bracket the parable of the sower, just as the parable of the sower and its interpretation bracket Mark 4:10-12.

The dominant theme in the whole chapter is hearing, which is mentioned thirteen times. Isaiah 6:9-10, which is quoted in a version similar to the targum on Isaiah, was a classic text on the hardness of people's hearts as they refused to hear God's prophetic word. Hardness of heart is an important theme for Mark and is even possible of Jesus' disciples. (Note Mk 8:16-21, which uses words similar to Is 6:9-10, but this time drawn from Jer 5:21 or Ezek 12:2.)

Table 1. The Parables of Jesus

Markan Parables	Mark	Matthew	Luke
Bridegroom's Guests	2:19-20	9:15	5:33-39
Unshrunk Cloth	2:21	9:16	5:36
New Wine	2:22	9:17	5:37-39
Strong Man Bound	3:22-27	12:29-30	11:21-23
Sower	4:1-9, 13-20	13:1-9, 18-23	8:4-8, 11-15
Lamp and Measure	4:21-25		8:16-18
Seed Growing Secretly	4:26-29		
Mustard Seed	4:30-32	13:31-32	13:18-19
Wicked Tenants	12:1-12	21:33-46	20:9-19
Budding Fig Tree	13:28-32	24:32-36	21:29-33
Watchman	13:34-36		12:35-38

Parables Shared by Matthew and Luke (Q)			
Wise and Foolish Builders		7:24-27	6:47-49
Father and Children's Requests		7:9-11	11:11-13
Two Ways/Doors		7:13-14	13:23-27
Leaven		13:31-32	13:20-21
Lost Sheep		18:12-14	15:1-7
Wedding Banquet		22:1-14	14:15-24
Thief in the Night		24:42-44	12:39-40
Faithful and Unfaithful Steward		24:45-51	12:42-46
Talents and Pounds		25:14-30	19:11-27

Parables Found Only in Matthew			
Good and Bad Trees		7:16-20	
Fishnet		13:47-50	
Wheat and tares		13:24-30, 36-43	
Treasure		13:44	
Pearl		13:45-46	
Unmerciful Servant		18:23-35	
Laborers in the Vineyard		20:1-16	
Two Sons		21:28-32	
Wise and Foolish Maidens		25:1-13	
Sheep and Goats		25:31-46	

Parables Found Only in Luke			
Two Debtors			7:41-50
Good Samaritan			10:25-37
Friend at Midnight			11:5-8
Rich Fool			12:13-21
Barren Fig Tree			13:6-9
Tower Builder			14:28-30
Warring King			14:31-33
Lost Sheep			15:1-7
Lost Coin			15:8-10
Prodigal Son			15:11-32
Unjust Steward			16:1-8
Rich Man and Lazarus			16:19-31
Humble Servant			17:7-10
Unjust Judge			18:1-8
Pharisee and Tax Collector			18:9-14

Parables Found Only in John
Good Shepherd 10:1-18 (cf. Mt 18:12-14; Lk 15:1-7)
True Vine 15:1-8

Several scholars have tried to soften the impact of Mark 4:12 by interpreting *hina* ("in order that") as expressing something less than purpose. T. W. Manson suggested *hina* was a mistranslation of the Aramaic *de*, which can mean "who." Accordingly, he would translate, "all things come in parables to those outside who see indeed, but do not know" (Manson, 76-78). Jeremias argued *hina* was shorthand for *hina plerothē* ("in order that it might be fulfilled"). Others suggest *hina* should be interpreted as "because" as in Revelation 14:13, especially since the parallel in Matthew 13:13 has *hoti* ("because"). Jeremias's suggestion is helpful, but these explanations are unnecessary. They only mark the difficulty people have with the possibility that Jesus told parables to prevent understanding. Scholars have often attributed this to Mark's parable theory rather than to Jesus. Mark, however, does not have a theory that parables prevent understanding (cf. Mk 12:12).

The intent of Mark 4:10-12 is clear if one pays attention to the context. The kingdom is a kingdom of the word, and the issue is how people hear and respond to the word. The parable of the sower is a parable about hearing. In Mark 4:10-12 the Evangelist shows what typically happened in Jesus' ministry. (Note the use of the Greek imperfect tenses in Mark 4:10-11 indicating what happened customarily.) Jesus taught the crowds, but his teaching called for response. Where people responded, additional teaching was given. The pattern of public teaching followed by further private teaching to a circle of disciples is used elsewhere by Mark (Mk 7:17; 10:10). The strong words in Isaiah 6:9-10 were not an indication that God did not want to forgive people. They were a blunt statement expressing the inevitable. People would hear but not really understand.

The hardness of heart and lack of receptivity that Isaiah encountered were mirrored in the ministry of Jesus. The issue is whether one's heart will be hardened or whether one will hear and respond obediently. Even receiving the message with joy is not sufficient (Mk 4:16). What is required is hearing that leads to productive living. That this is Mark's intent is clear from the summary in Mark 4:33: "With many such parables he was expressing the word to them, even as they were able to hear." The saying in Mark 4:22 is also an important guide to understanding Mark's intent: "Nothing is hid-

den except that it should be revealed." This saying seems to be Mark's understanding of the parables. Parables hide in order to reveal. Even though some would respond with hardness of heart and lack of hearing, Jesus taught in parables to elicit hearing and obedient response.

8. Guidelines for Interpretation.
The interpretation of the parables is not a scientific procedure, but guidelines can be offered to enhance understanding and prevent abuse of the parables.

(1) Analyze the sequence, structure and wording of the parable, including any parallels in the other Gospels. Plot the movement of the parable, and note any specific structure such as parallelism or chiasmus. For example, there are significant parallels between the prodigal and the elder son in Luke's parable of the prodigal son (Lk 15:11-32). Significant changes in wording between the various accounts need to be understood in light of the redactional purposes of the Evangelists. One should not assume any particular Gospel always gives the earliest version of a specific parable. Certainly one should not excise the introductions and conclusions to the parables.

(2) Note cultural or historical features in the parable that provide insight. Most of the parables contain such features that require investigation. For example, the impact of the parable of the Pharisee and the tax collector (Lk 18:9-14) is strengthened if one is aware that these two men probably went to the temple to pray at the time of the morning or evening atoning sacrifice. In effect, the tax collector prayed, "Let the sacrifice result in mercy for me."

(3) Listen to the parables in the context of the ministry of Jesus. Modern readers are often so familiar with the parables that they miss the shock that Jesus' hearers would have felt. We tend to have negative views of Pharisees and are not surprised to hear Jesus say that the tax collector was declared righteous instead of the Pharisee. Jesus' hearers would have assumed that the Pharisee was a righteous man and that the tax collector was a cheat. We are not surprised that a Samaritan helps a victim (Lk 10:30-37), but Jesus' hearers, like the scribe to whom he spoke, could hardly say "Samaritan" and "neighbor" in the same breath. Parables often force such reversals in our thinking.

(4) Look for help in the context, but know that the context of many of the parables has not been pre-

served. The parable of the wicked tenants (Mt 21:33-44 and pars.) must be seen in light of the question about the authority by which Jesus does his acts (Mt 21:23-27). By contrast, Matthew 13 provides a thematic grouping of eight parables on the kingdom, the contexts of which have not been preserved.

(5) Note how the parable and its redactional shaping fit into the plan and purposes of the Gospel in which it appears. Most of the parables have been arranged thematically by the Evangelists to highlight Jesus' message. With such arrangements the Evangelists show their own theological tendencies. For example, Luke's parables appear primarily in his travel narrative (Lk 9:51—19:48), which is chiastic in its structure. Luke is concerned about prayer, wealth and the outcasts. Not surprisingly, Luke has arranged parables on prayer in Luke 11:5-13 and Luke 18:1-14, on wealth in Luke 12:13-21 and Luke 16:1-31, on invitations to a feast (particularly invitations to outcasts) as reflective of the kingdom in Luke 14:7-24, and on the joy of recovering that which was lost in Luke 15:1-32. In addition to the kingdom parables in Matthew 13, Matthew has placed two parables in the context of his "ecclesiastical discourse" in Matthew 18:10-14, 21-35 and has also grouped three parables on Israel's rejection of God's invitation in Matthew 21:28—22:14 and seven more on eschatology in Matthew 24:32—25:46. Matthew and Luke differ on the placement of some of the parables as well. For example, Luke has the parable of the lost sheep (Lk 15:1-7) in a context dealing with the repentance of sinners, but Matthew has this parable in a context dealing with an erring disciple. Jesus surely told some of the parables more than once, but such variations may result from intentional editorial activity.

(6) Determine the function of the story as a whole in the teaching of Jesus and for the Evangelists. There may be more than one truth to the parable and several correspondences between the parable and the reality that it reflects. This is not, however, a license to allegorize. Some parables even have two climaxes. Note the parable of the prodigal, or more aptly titled the parable of the father and his two sons, in Luke 15:11-32 and the parable of the wedding feast in Matthew 22:1-14, although the latter could be a joining of two parables. Any correspondence between the parable and the reality it reflects will probably be limited to the main characters in the story. Details

should not be allegorized, and parables should not be pushed beyond their purpose. The goal is to hear the intention of Jesus as conveyed by the Evangelists. A helpful way to determine the function of a parable is to ask what question it seeks to answer. Sometimes the question is explicit, such as in the parable of the good Samaritan (Lk 10:25-37), which addresses the question Who is my neighbor? At other times the question is implicit, such as in the parables of the warring king and the tower builder, which address the question, Is it easy to be a disciple?

(7) Determine the theological significance of the story. What the parable teaches about God and his kingdom should be reflected elsewhere in the teaching of Jesus. There is no suggestion that we are to reduce the parable to theological propositions, but the parables do express theology. Again, the details of parables should not be pushed. For example, while Matthew 18:34 may underscore the seriousness of God's judgment, it does not mean that God has tormentors!

(8) Pay special attention to the end of the parable. The rule of end stress recognizes that the most important part of the parable is the conclusion where the parable often requires a decision or forces the hearer to reverse his or her way of thinking. The end of the parable of the wicked tenants (Mt 21:33-44) is a quotation from Psalm 118:22 that via a wordplay forces the religious authorities to realize that they, the "builders" of the Jewish nation, have rejected God's Son (*see* Son of God). Whatever else may be true in the parable of the lost sheep, the focus is on the joy at recovering that which was lost.

9. The Teaching of the Parables.

The primary focus of the parables is the coming of the kingdom of God and the resulting discipleship that is required. When Jesus proclaimed the kingdom he meant that God was exercising his power and rule to bring forgiveness, defeat evil and establish righteousness in fulfillment of the OT promises. In Jesus' person and ministry these acts were happening, and the kingdom was made available to people. The kingdom comes with limitless grace, but with it comes limitless demand. That is why it is impossible to speak of the kingdom without at the same time speaking of discipleship. While a number of Jesus' parables anticipate a future aspect of God's kingdom, much of the focus is on the kingdom as present and available to Jesus' hearers. The kingdom is both present and still awaits consummation in the future. With the focus on the kingdom as present comes an invitation to enter the kingdom and live according to its standards. Prayer and the use of wealth are two areas of kingdom living that are treated specifically in the parables.

9.1. The Kingdom as Present. A short parable in Matthew 12:29 is one of the strongest statements about the presence of the kingdom, and this parable also has christological implications. In response to the charge that he cast out demons by the power of Beelzebub (Mt 12:24), Jesus points to the activity of the Spirit (*see* Holy Spirit) in his ministry as proof that the kingdom is present (Mt 12:28). The parable in Matthew 12:29 argues that no one can enter and plunder the house of the strong man unless he first binds the strong man. Clearly, Jesus views his ministry as binding Satan and plundering his house.

While all the parables are kingdom parables in one sense, the parables in Matthew 13 are grouped specifically to provide insight into the kingdom. The parable of the sower indicates that the kingdom involves the presentation of a message and the necessity of a response that leads to productive living. Several parables in this section seem designed to answer questions from Jesus' hearers about his claims that the kingdom was present. The parable of the wheat and the tares seems designed to answer the question How can the kingdom have come if evil is still present? The kingdom is present and growing even in the midst of evil, and judgment will take place in the future. Therefore, the kingdom invites involvement and patience. The twin parables of the mustard seed and the leaven both address the question How can the kingdom be present if the results seem so small? The beginning may be small, but the effect will be large and extensive. The twin parables of the treasure and of the pearl underscore that the kingdom is of ultimate value and is to be chosen above all else. In his section on kingdom parables, Mark includes the parable of the growing seed (Mk 4:26-29), which stresses that the kingdom is God's work and not the result of human action.

Other parables also emphasize the present aspect of the kingdom. The parables of the banquet (Lk 14:15-24) and of the wedding (Mt 22:1-14) affirm that all is ready and people should come now (Lk 14:17; Mt 22:4). The banquet theme is used to express other points as well. These parables and several others point to the refusal of many of the Jewish people to respond to Jesus' message. With parables like that of the barren fig tree (Lk 13:6-9) they mark a crisis of decision that should lead to repentance. Furthermore, the banquet parables and parables like that of the prodigal son (Lk 15:11-32) in effect proclaim that God is having a celebration and ask people why they are not joining in.

The kingdom is revealed as an amazing expression of God's grace. The Gospels do not record that Jesus taught about grace, but no other word summarizes so well the effect of the kingdom. The invitation to outcasts in the banquet parables is obviously an expression of grace. The parables of the two debtors (Lk 7:41-43), of the lost sheep, lost coin and prodigal son (Lk 15), of the unmerciful servant (Mt 18:23-35), and of the laborers in the vineyard (Mt 20:1-16) all point to God's eagerness to benefit people by seeking them, forgiving them and accepting them. The parable of the laborers in the vineyard also offers a critique of those who think God's grace should be given out based on merit.

9.2. The Kingdom as Future. Jesus' teaching on the future aspect of the kingdom is seen most clearly in those parables that speak of judgment or of a master who returns to settle accounts. The parables of growth also point to the future as a time of harvest. Particularly in Matthew, parables of judgment point to a separation between those who were obedient, faithful, prepared or merciful, and those who were not. The first group enters the kingdom and experiences praise and joy. The other group suffers punishment or destruction. Either explicitly or implicitly, judgment is based on whether one has shown mercy. Not all judgment parables are about the future. Some speak of judgment that is more immediate, such as the parable of the rich man and Lazarus (Lk 16:19-31) or the parables that express the crisis facing the Jewish people (Lk 13:6-9). Even so, future judgment is a major theme in Jesus' parables.

Parables about the future are not intended to satisfy curiosity. They are intended to alter life in the present. By focusing on judgment and the Master's return, the focus of these parables is to encourage faithfulness, wisdom and preparation. These themes are expressed in the parable of the faithful and unfaithful servants (Mt 24:45-

51; Lk 12:41-48), the parable of the ten maidens (Mt 25:1-13) and the parable of the talents (Mt 25:14-30, with a possible parallel in Lk 19:11-27). These themes are also stressed in parables about the present (note especially Lk 16:1-13). Both present and future eschatology have as their goal right living in the present.

9.3. Discipleship. Since discipleship is the main purpose of Jesus' teaching, the parables focus on this theme frequently. In many cases discipleship is the assumed subject. Elsewhere the concern for discipleship is explicit. In the twin parables of the tower builder and the warring king (Lk 14:28-32), people are warned to consider the cost, for being a disciple is no easy task. The parable of the owner and his servant (Lk 17:7-10) views obedience as an expectation, something people should do, rather than something noteworthy. (Contrast the parable in Luke 12:37, which tells of a master serving his servants because they were faithful!) The parable of the two builders describes the wise person as the one who hears and does Jesus' teachings. As elsewhere, the wise person is the one who understands the eschatological realities and lives accordingly. Likewise, the parable of the two sons (Mt 21:28-32) stresses the importance of obedience over against the intent to do the Father's will. Where obedience is made specific, the focus is on the necessity of doing acts of mercy (note especially Mt 18:33; 25:32-46; Lk 10:25-37). One cannot experience the grace of the kingdom without extending that grace to others.

9.3.1. The Right Use of Wealth. While the use of money is a frequent subject in the teaching of Jesus, Luke has a particular focus on the right use of wealth. Several of the parables unique to him discuss this theme. The rich fool (Lk 12:16-21) thought only of his own enjoyment in the use of his wealth. He failed to consider the source of his wealth or the fact that life consists of much more than possessions. Luke 12:20 suggests that life is on loan from God and that we are accountable to him for it. The parables and sayings in Luke 16 provide some of the most direct teaching on wealth. The parable of the dishonest steward is debated because there is uncertainty whether his reduction of the amounts owed was a reduction of his own commission, the reduction of the illegal usurious portion that would go to his owner, or merely a rash act counting on the master's mercy. The intent of the parable is

still clear. Jesus' point in Luke 16:8-9 is that people in this world understand the shrewd use of resources better than his disciples understand the economics of the kingdom. Jesus' disciples should make friends for themselves by the right use of "unrighteous mammon," money that tends to lead to unrighteousness. By the right use of wealth in acts of mercy, they make friendships with eternal benefits (cf. Lk 12:33). The parable of the rich man and Lazarus poignantly makes the same point. This parable is not intended to provide a description of judgment so much as it is to underscore the eternal consequences of failing to show mercy. To be a disciple of the kingdom is to have one's priorities reorganized with regard to finances.

9.3.2. Prayer. Another redactional concern that Luke conveys through parables is his focus on prayer. Two of these parables, that of the friend at midnight (Lk 11:5-8) and the wicked judge (Lk 18:1-8), are contrasts between human responses to requests and the way God responds to prayer. The friend at midnight is not about persistence. The word *anaideia* in Luke 11:8, which is sometimes translated "persistence," means "shamelessness" and almost certainly refers to the boldness of the man knocking. The point of the parable is that if a human responds to such knocking, how much more will God respond to the prayers of his people (cf. Lk 11:13). Similarly, the unjust judge acts on behalf of the widow so that she will not keep pestering him. But the parable indicates that God is not like the unjust judge; rather, he will adjudicate the cause of his people quickly. Luke gives his readers confidence that God hears and responds to prayer. The remaining parable on prayer, that of the Pharisee and the tax collector, emphasizes the humility and repentance with which one should approach God.

See also KINGDOM OF GOD.

DJG: FORM CRITICISM; HARDNESS OF HEART; LITERARY CRITICISM.

BIBLIOGRAPHY. K. E. Bailey, *Poet and Peasant: A Literary Cultural Approach to the Parables in Luke* (Grand Rapids: Eerdmans, 1976); idem, *Through Peasant Eyes: More Lucan Parables, Their Culture and Style* (Grand Rapids: Eerdmans, 1980); C. L. Blomberg, *Interpreting the Parables* (Downers Grove, IL: InterVarsity Press, 1990); M. Boucher, *The Mysterious Parable* (Washington, DC: The Catholic Biblical Association of America, 1977); J. D. Crossan, *In Parables* (New York: Harper and

Row, 1973); J. D. M. Derrett, *Law in the New Testament* (London: Darton, Longman, and Todd, 1976); C. H. Dodd, *The Parables of the Kingdom* (London: Nisbet, 1936); D. Flusser, *Die rabbinischen Gleichnisse und der Gleichniserzähler Jesus; 1 Teil: Das Wesen der Gleichnisse* (Bern: Peter Lang, 1981); R. W. Funk et al., *The Parables of Jesus: Red Letter Edition* (Sonoma, CA: Polebridge, 1988); J. Jeremias, *The Parables of Jesus* (New York: Charles Scribner's, 1963); G. V. Jones, *The Art and Truth of the Parables* (London: SPCK, 1964); P. R. Jones, *The Teaching of the Parables* (Nashville: Broadman, 1982); A. Jülicher, *Die Gleichnisreden Jesu* (2 vols.; Tübingen: Siebeck, 1888-89); J. D. Kingsbury, *The Parables of Jesus In Matthew 13* (Richmond, VA: John Knox, 1969); W. S. Kissinger, *The Parables of Jesus* (Metuchen, NJ: Scarecrow, 1979); H. K. McArthur and R. M. Johnston, *They Also Taught in Parables* (Grand Rapids: Zondervan, 1990); T. W. Manson, *The Teaching of Jesus* (Cambridge: Cambridge University Press, 1935); N. Perrin, *Jesus and the Language of the Kingdom* (Philadelphia: Fortress, 1976); B. B. Scott, *Hear Then the Parable* (Minneapolis: Fortress, 1989); K. Snodgrass, *The Parable of the Wicked Tenants* (Tübingen: Siebeck, 1983); R. H. Stein, *An Introduction to the Parables of Jesus* (Philadelphia: Westminster, 1981); D. O. Via Jr., *The Parables* (Philadelphia: Fortress, 1967); C. Westermann, *The Parables of Jesus in the Light of the Old Testament* (Minneapolis: Fortress, 1990); B. H. Young, *Jesus and His Jewish Parables* (New York: Paulist, 1989). K. R. Snodgrass

PARACLETE. *See* HOLY SPIRIT I; JOHN, GOSPEL OF.

PARAENESIS. *See* JAMES, LETTER OF.

PAROUSIA. *See* APOCALYPTICISM; ESCHATOLOGY.

PASSION NARRATIVE. *See* DEATH OF CHRIST I; TRIAL OF JESUS.

PASSION PREDICTIONS. *See* RESURRECTION I.

PASSOVER. *See* LAST SUPPER.

PASTORAL LETTERS

First Timothy, 2 Timothy and Titus, termed the Pastoral Epistles since the eighteenth century, are, with Philemon, letters of the Pauline corpus addressed to individuals. Like other NT literature written under Paul's name, they employ the letter form to convey not just personal communications but primarily teachings and exhortations, some of them preformed traditions already in use in Pauline congregations (Ellis 1999). In the face of defections and of the depredations of false teachers, they emphasize instructions on ministry, church order and related themes in order to protect the apostle's congregations in Asia Minor and Greece during the final years of his life.

1. Canonicity and Authorship
2. Occasion and Date
3. Historical Setting
4. Composition: Literary Criticism
5. Outline
6. Themes

1. Canonicity and Authorship.
In the patristic church the reception of the letters into the NT canon was tied to their Pauline authorship for, as Serapion (died c. A.D. 211), bishop of Antioch, put it, "we receive both Peter and the other apostles as Christ, but pseudepigrapha in their name we reject" (Eusebius *Hist. Eccl.* 6.12.3). This judgment was virtually unanimous, explicitly witnessed by the Muratorian Canon and Irenaeus (c. A.D. 180; Irenaeus *Haer.* 1.16.3; 2.14.7; 3.14.1) and probably to be inferred from earlier quotations (cf. Theophilus *Autol.* 3.14; Polycarp *Phil.* 4.1) and allusions (cf. Ignatius *Eph.* 14:1). The Pastorals, along with 2 Thessalonians and Philemon, are lacking only in one incomplete manuscript of Paul's letters (P^{46}, c. A.D. 200) and were rejected only by certain heretical teachers: 1-2 Timothy by Tatian and Basilides (cf. Clement *Strom.* 2.11, end; Jerome *Commentary on Titus, Preface*) and all three by Marcion (cf. Tertullian *Marc.* 5.21). However, they encountered serious objections in the literary criticism of the nineteenth century.

1.1. The Baur School. In 1835 F. C. Baur, drawing upon earlier literary questions about the Pastorals, concluded that they reflected a post-Pauline context and identified them, in his Hegelian reconstruction of early Christian history, as second-century forgeries (see Ellis, "F. C. Baur and His School," in 1999). His views were elaborated by H. J. Holtzmann, who summed up the objections to Pauline authorship: (1) the historical situation, (2) the gnosticizing false teachers condemned, (3) the stage of church organization, (4) the vocabulary and style, and (5) the theological views and themes. Baur was ambivalent about the effect of his criticism on the canonicity of the Pastorals, but most of his followers thought that it should have no effect, asserting against the evidence that in antiquity pseudonymity was an innocent device (see Ellis, "Pseudonymity," in 2001, 17-29). They often attributed the Pastorals to disciples of Paul and cited as precedents the schools of Pythagoras and Plato, who wrote letters in the names of those philosophers. However, there is no evidence that a school of Paul existed after the apostle's death: The earliest postapostolic writers, such as Clement of Rome, Papias, Ignatius and Polycarp, cite or appeal to various apostles and display no knowledge of any "school" tendency to transmit only teachings of a particular apostle.

1.2. The Nineteenth-Century Debate. J. B. Lightfoot and T. Zahn countered the Baur school with the observations that (1) the changed historical circumstances and (2) the more advanced church organization were well accounted for if some years separated Paul's earlier letters from his writing of the Pastorals, that is, after his release from his first Roman imprisonment, a release well attested in *1 Clement* 5 (c. A.D. 95, Lightfoot) and in second-century literature (Muratorian canon; *Acts of Peter [Vercelli]*). Anticipating twentieth-century criticism, Lightfoot argued that (3) gnosticizing false teachers were already present during the ministry of Paul (cf. Ellis 1993, 89-95), and he also attributed (4) changes in vocabulary, style and (5) in theological emphasis to the origin of the Pastorals in the last years of the apostle's ministry.

In the nineteenth century both traditional and speculative scholars assumed that Paul penned his letters or dictated them verbatim. They consequently supposed that if the major letters were taken as a touchstone, the genuineness of the others could be determined by internal criteria of vocabulary, style and theological motifs. They differed only as to whether variations in such matters were sufficient to exclude Pauline authorship (the Baur/Holtzmann tradition) or lay within the literary range of a versatile writer like the apostle (the Lightfoot/Zahn tradition). The debate, which continued and developed through the twentieth century, was something of a standoff (Prior; Ellis 1979). However, the pseudepigraphal viewpoint was undermined by three new insights of twentieth-

century criticism: the role of the secretary; the function of cosenders; and the presence of a considerable number of preformed, non-Pauline pieces in almost all of Paul's letters.

1.3. Developments in the Twentieth Century. The problem of the Pastorals continued in the minds of many to lie in their vocabulary and style, in their more developed church order and in the difficulty of placing them within the Pauline missions in Acts.

1.3.1. Vocabulary. With respect to vocabulary it was not just the divergence from the terminology of the recognized Pauline literature but also the absence of many word groups common to Paul (e.g., *apokalyptō, energeō, kauchaomai, perisseuō, hypakouō, phroneō*) and the use of different terminology for the same concepts in eschatology *(epiphaneia* vis-á-vis *parousia),* church organization *(presbyteroi* vis-á-vis *prohistamenoi* and *poimenes)* and soteriology (cf. Dibelius). At the same time many Pauline expressions in these letters were evident to all.

Three attempts were made to resolve this problem. Writers in the Baur/Holtzmann tradition ascribed the Pauline traits to a conscious attempt by the forger to imitate Paul, either to gain apostolic authority for his deception (Donelson) or, reworking certain Pauline traditions, to offer under the apostle's name what he thought Paul might have taught had he been there (Wolter). Some in the Lightfoot/Zahn tradition contended that the role of the secretary and Paul's use of traditions composed by others accounted for the differences in the Pastorals' style, vocabulary and theological idiom (see 4 below). A few scholars early in the twentieth century argued that the Pastorals were genuine Pauline letters supplemented by second-century interpolations, mainly on church order (Harnack), or that they were early second-century products incorporating some genuine Pauline fragments (Harrison). The fragment hypothesis failed to convince very many because it could not explain why and how a forger would have used the fragments in such a strange way (Guthrie; Dibelius). The interpolation hypothesis was a possibility in its day. But with the advances in textual criticism and in the understanding of writing practices of the Greco-Roman world, it lost credibility.

As was the custom in antiquity (cf. Cicero *To Friends* 7.25.1; Richards, 6-7.), Paul retained a copy of his letters for subsequent reference (cf. 1 Cor 5:9-10; 2 Cor 7:8; 2 Thess 2:15) and because of the danger of loss or damage in transit (cf. Cicero *Friends* 16.18. end). It is also likely that he allowed the church where he was writing to make a copy of the letter for its own use and that he permitted or instructed the recipients to make copies for themselves or for neighboring congregations (cf. 2 Cor 1:1, Achaia; Gal 1:2; Col 4:16). In this way the apostle initiated, virtually at the outset, different textual traditions with inevitable variations in the wording of his correspondence.

Therefore, "it appears to be quite impossible that an interpolator, who anywhere in the stream of tradition arbitrarily inserted three verses, could force under his spell the total textual tradition (which we today have before our eyes in a way quite different from any generation before us) . . . so that not even one contrary witness remained" (Aland, 141). What is said here of Romans applies also to the Pastorals. Any theory that certain verses were later additions must produce some manuscript that omits the verses, or it will lack all historical probability. The sections that Harnack thought were later interpolations are not absent from any manuscript and were, therefore, in all likelihood a part of the Pastorals from the beginning.

1.3.2. Church Organization. The Baur tradition and also A. von Harnack supposed that the qualifications demanded for the ministry of bishop or overseer (= "elder"?; 1 Tim 3; 5; Tit 1) reflected a developed church order that was post-Pauline. It rested its case on the twin assumptions that the earliest congregations had no structured ministries and that early Christian theology and praxis moved forward gradually and stage by stage as a block. These assumptions were deeply embedded in nineteenth-century consciousness from theories of egalitarianism, of historical and social progress and of biological evolution. But they do not accord either with the variegated church order of the apostolic congregations or with the present-day recognition that development may be either gradual or extremely rapid.

From the beginning the congregations of all the apostolic missions had some measure of church order. The church at Jerusalem with its leadership of resident apostles, especially Peter (c. A.D. 33-42; Gal 1:18; Acts 2:14; 3:12; 5:3; 8:14; 9:32; 12:17) and James (c. A.D. 42-62; Gal 2:9; Acts 12:17; 15:13; 21:18) and elders (Acts 11:30; 15:2; 21:18; cf. Jas 5:14) had a more structured organization, probably similar to that of the synagogues and of the Qumran community (e.g., Lk 7:3; CD 13:9-10; 1QS 6:14-15, 19-20: *měbaqqēr, pāqîd*; cf. Schürer 2:427-39; Thiering; Weinfeld). According to 1 Peter (1 Pet 5:1-3; cf. 1:1; c. A.D. 64) and Acts (Acts 14:23; 20:17, cf. 20:28; c. A.D. 65), certain churches in Asia Minor and Greece founded by the Petrine and Pauline missions also had a recognized church order, even if the term *elders (presbyteroi)* in Acts is a Lukan idiom for ministries given different designations in Paul's earlier letters. These letters disclose established ministries of administrative and teaching leadership, although they identify them more often as activities (Rom 12:8; 1 Cor 12:28; Gal 6:6; 1 Thess 5:12-13) than as appointed offices (cf. Phil 1:1). The Pastorals give more prominence to appointed ministries and to the qualifications for them because, among other things, of the increasing threat to Paul's churches by false teachers (Ellis 1999, 314-18; idem, 1993, 113-15). They represent an understandable development of his earlier usage.

1.4. Conclusion. The role of the secretary (Richards, Roller) and the use of preformed traditions (see 4.3 below) in the composition of the Pastorals cut the ground from under the pseudepigraphal hypothesis with its mistaken nineteenth-century assumptions about the nature of authorship. They require the critical student to give primary weight to the opening ascriptions in the letters and to the external historical evidence, both of which solidly support Pauline authorship.

2. Occasion and Date.

Proponents of Paul's authorship of the Pastorals usually, though not always (Reicke, Robinson), presuppose the tradition that Paul was released from his first Roman imprisonment (Acts 28), rightly regarded by Harnack (1:240n) as "a certain fact of history," and afterwards had a second Aegean ministry in which 1 Timothy and Titus could be placed. The tradition is supported by two considerations: (1) second-century accounts underlying the *Acts of Paul* (9-11; c. A.D. 170-190) of the apostle's final trip to Rome and martyrdom under Nero on a route different from that in Acts 27-28 (Rordorf; Zahn, 2:84) and (2) very early evidence for a post-Acts 28 Pauline mission to Spain.

2.1. Paul's Mission to Spain. The probability of a missionary journey to Spain arises largely (1) from the anticipation of such a task in Romans

15:24, Acts 1:8 and Acts 13:47, and (2) from the evidence for it in *1 Clement* 5.7 (c. A.D. 70, cf. Robinson), the *Acts of Peter (Vercelli)* 1-3, 40 (probably Asia Minor, c. A.D. 160-180) and the Muratorian Canon (Rome, c. A.D. 170-190). The last two are independent witnesses to a widespread second-century tradition that Paul journeyed from Rome to Spain and, in the *Acts of Peter,* that he returned to Rome for martyrdom.

Clement of Rome knows of seven imprisonments of Paul, calls Paul and Peter "our good apostles," and, according to Irenaeus (*Haer.* 3.3.3; c. A.D. 180), Clement sat under their teaching. He speaks of Paul's preaching in the West, which for a writer in Rome would mean Spain or Gaul (cf. 2 Tim 4:10), and of his reaching "the extreme limits of the West" *(to terma tēs dyseōs).* The latter phrase, like "to the end of the earth" *(heōs eschatou tēs gēs,* Acts 1:8), referred in the usage of the time to the region of Spain around Gades (= Cadiz), where the apostle probably traveled after he was set free from his first Roman imprisonment (cf. Ellis 1991; idem, 2001, 53-63; "End of the Earth"). These sources are supported by later traditions of Paul's release and of his post-Acts 28 ministry (Eusebius *Hist. Eccl.* 2.22.1-8: *logos echei,* 2). Since Paul's Spanish sojourn was apparently unknown to Origen (cf. Eusebius *Hist. Eccl.* 3.1.3) and produced no churches in Spain that claimed Pauline origins, it may have been a brief mission (c. A.D. 63-64), undertaken soon after his release (cf. Zahn, 2:64-66), from which he returned to his churches in the Aegean area.

2.2. The Situation of 1 Timothy and Titus. The situation of 1 Timothy and Titus differs from that of Paul's earlier Aegean ministry (c. A.D. 53-58; cf. Kelly, 6-10). His mission had now extended to Gaul (2 Tim 4:10; Zahn, 2:25-26), and his congregations around the Aegean had multiplied and now encompassed Crete, Miletus and Nicopolis (Tit 1:5; 3:12; 2 Tim 4:20). They were increasingly endangered by a judaizing-gnostic countermission (1 Tim 1:3-7, 19-20; 4:1-2; 6:20; 2 Tim 4:3-4; Tit 1:10-16; cf. Ellis 1993, 92-93; 113-15) that included church leaders and probably former coworkers (2 Tim 1:15-18; 2:16-17; 3:6-9; 4:10; Tit 3:9-14). Some house churches were ravaged and near collapse, as Paul's instructions to Titus indicate: "Restore the things that remain, and appoint elders in each city.... For many deceivers . . . especially the circumcision party . . . are overthrowing whole houses" (Tit 1:5, 10-11).

This threat may have occasioned Paul's return from Spain.

To meet the problem, Paul adopted a new strategy for his writing. He continued as before to work from a hub city, perhaps Corinth (2 Tim 4:20), with several visits to a number of churches, for example, in Macedonia (1 Tim 1:3), Crete (Tit 1:5), Nicopolis (Tit 3:12), Miletus (2 Tim 4:20) and Ephesus (1 Tim 1:3; 3:14; 4:13; 2 Tim 1:15-18; 4:19; but see Zahn, 2:17-19). But he could not, as he did earlier (1 Cor 4:17; 2 Cor 7:6, 12-13; Eph 6:21-22; Col 4:7-8; cf. Phil 2:25), send a letter to each of the many congregations, along with a colleague to explain and apply it. Instead, he sent letters to trusted coworkers, Titus in Crete and Timothy in Ephesus, which served as instruments of personal communication and encouragement and also as vade mecums to give apostolic authorization for their teaching.

For the itinerary of his second Aegean ministry one is left largely to conjecture, for Paul's letters and other sources offer little help. The apostle probably returned there from Spain only in late A.D. 64 and labored in Crete (Tit 1:5) and Macedonia (1 Tim 1:3) as well as in Achaia for a year or so, spending the winter of 65-66 (or 66-67) at Nicopolis in Epirus (Tit 3:12; Zahn, 2:27-35, 66). He composed 1 Timothy and Titus fairly early in this period, probably in 65. In the late spring of 66 or 67 he visited Miletus, where he left Trophimus (2 Tim 4:20), and Troas, where he left his winter coat and a number of books and notebooks *(membrana),* which probably included copies of his previous letters and traditional materials useful in his teaching and in composing new letters (2 Tim 4:13, 20; cf. Richards, 158-60). From Troas, apparently, he departed for Rome with the intention of returning before winter.

2.3. The Situation and Date of 2 Timothy. Paul took his last missionary journey from the Aegean to Rome, where he was again imprisoned, wrote 2 Timothy and soon thereafter was beheaded on the Ostian Way (2 Tim 4:6-7; *Acts of Paul* 11; Eusebius *Hist. Eccl.* 2.25.5-8). He may possibly have been arrested in Ephesus (Spicq, 1:141) or Troas (Fee, 244-45) and taken to Rome as a prisoner. More likely, in accordance with second-century traditions used in the *Acts of Paul* (9-10), he returned to Rome a free man (Rordorf, 323; cf. Zahn, 2:67) to minister to a church that was suffering "repeated calamities and reverses" (*1 Clem.* 1.1) due to the continuing persecution of Nero. He may have traveled by the Egnatian and Appian Ways (Troas—Philippi—Apollonia—Brundisium—Rome), about a three-week journey, or again following second-century traditions, by a route from Troas via Philippi to Corinth and from there to Italy and Rome (cf. 2 Tim 4:20; Rordorf).

According to Eusebius's *Chronicle* (c. A.D. 303; cf. Jerome, *Vir.* 1; 5; 12), Paul was martyred together with Peter in the fourteenth year of Nero, 67-68. However, neither *1 Clement* 5 nor the *Ascension of Isaiah* (4:2-5; c. A.D. 90) suggests that both apostles died together, and Dionysius, bishop of Corinth (c. A.D. 170; cf. Eusebius *Hist. Eccl.* 2.25.8), says only that they were executed at about the same time. Probably Peter suffered death near the beginning of the Neronian pogrom in the winter or spring of 65 and Paul in late 67, or at any rate before the suicide of Nero on June 9, 68 (cf. Zahn, 2:61-67; Edmundson, 147-52; otherwise: Harnack, 1:240-43). If so, he would have composed 2 Timothy in the late summer or fall of A.D. 67.

3. Historical Setting.

3.1. Congregations. The churches had no special buildings in Paul's day, and they usually met in the homes of affluent members. Some of these homes could accommodate a (standing) congregation of between 100 and 200 people in the main room *(atrium)* or in a colonnaded garden *(peristylium)* further back in the house (cf. Ellis 1989, 139-45, 144). Paul's Aegean congregations had affluent members, as is evident also in the Pastorals from his comments on slaves and masters, and on proper attitudes for wealthy Christians (1 Tim 6:1-7, 17-19; cf. Rom 16:23; Eph 6:5-9). Such house churches are probably in view in the references to "households" (1 Tim 3:15; 2 Tim 1:16; 4:19; Tit 1:11; 1 Tim 5:13).

Pliny (*Ep.* 10.96.9-10; c. A.D. 110), governor of Bithynia-Pontus, reported that extensive conversions to Christianity had virtually emptied pagan temples of the province "for a long time" (c. A.D. 100 ?). In the mid-sixties the Pastorals suggest that conversions around the Aegean had already been extensive. Paul's earlier letters disclose that even in the fifties there were at least two house churches in Colossae (Philem 2; Col 4:15) and two in Ephesus (1 Cor 16:19; cf. 2 Tim 1:16; 4:19), and probably four at Corinth (Rom 16:23; 1 Cor 1:11; 16:15-16; Acts 18:7-8). There

were four or five at Rome (Rom 16:5, 10-11, 14-15; cf. Phil 4:22). When one house church is specified, at least one other is implied. While many numbered their members in the dozens, some probably had congregations of 100 to 150, including the household servants. The size and impact of the church at Ephesus is reflected by the uproar of the silversmiths (Acts 19:23-40), who would hardly have reacted so strongly to a minor threat to their sales.

In the mid-sixties the church at Rome suffered the martyrdom of "a great multitude" (*1 Clem.* 6.1; cf. Tacitus *Ann.* 15.44) and Paul's Aegean churches had suffered defections, as the Pastorals attest. However, in the decade of 57-67 the Pauline congregations of Greece and Asia had greatly increased in numbers and in area, and their total membership is probably to be counted in the thousands.

3.2. Coworkers. The coworkers of Paul include a number who are mentioned in Acts (Trophimus) and in his earlier letters: Apollos, Demas, Erastus, Luke, Mark, Priscilla and Aquila, Timothy, Titus, Tychicus. Others appear only in Titus (Artemas, Zenas) or in 2 Timothy (Claudia, Crescens, Eubulus, Linus, Onesiphorus, Pudens, Carpus ?), where they are workers in the church at Rome or participants in Paul's continuing mission outreach.

3.3. Opponents. The opponents represent the same type of opposition throughout the Pastorals (Kelly, 10-11; Dibelius, 65-67), that is only a more developed form of the false teaching that plagued Paul's and other apostolic missions virtually from the beginning. They originated as a "judaizing" segment of the ritually strict *Hebraioi*, that is, "the circumcision party" of the Jerusalem church (cf. Acts 11:2 with Tit 1:10), which combined a demand for Gentile adherence to the Mosaic regulations and an ascetic ritualism with a zeal for visions of angels and, at least in the Diaspora, with gnosticizing tendencies to promote an experience of a distorted divine wisdom and knowledge, and to depreciate matter and physical resurrection and redemption (cf. 1 Cor 15:12 with 2 Tim 2:18; *see* Gnosticism). At times their vaunted asceticism produced an arrogance primed for a subtle sexual licentiousness (cf. Gal 4:9; 5:13-21; Col 2:18, 23 with 1 Tim 4:3; 2 Tim 3:6-7; Tit 1:10, 15). While Paul argued that in the messianic age the OT ethical laws remained valid but its ritual laws were passé (Col 2:17; cf. Gal 4:9-10) and were no longer binding

(Rom 10:4; 13:8-10; Gal 3:24-25), his opponents argued that the ritual laws remained binding and yet they vitiated the ethical commands by their conduct (cf. Ellis 1993, 36-38, 51-52, 61, 80-115, 116-28, 230-36; *see* Law).

In the Pastorals the gnosticizing judaizers were known as "the circumcision party" (Tit 1:10) and continued their claim to be "teachers of the Law" (1 Tim 1:7), although they apparently no longer stressed, as in Galatians, the duty of circumcision. They forbade marriage, promoted food laws and claimed to impart a spiritual "knowledge" *(gnōsis)* whose source was, in the words of an oracle applied to them, demonic spirits (1 Tim 4:1-3; 6:20). They represented one stage of a continuing counter-mission, which appears in Ignatius *(Magn.* 8-11; *Trall.* 9; c. A.D. 110) as a kind of "Judaism crossed with Gnosticism" (Lightfoot) that denied not only Christ's resurrection but also his physical incarnation and death and that later in the second century developed or merged into the full-blown Gnostic heresies. While some of the opponents originated in the mission of "the circumcision party," others were teachers in Pauline congregations and defectors from a Pauline theology, including former associates or coworkers (1 Tim 1:3-5; 2 Tim 1:15-16; Tit 1:10-11).

4. Composition: Literary Criticism.

Literary questions about the Pastorals have addressed their letter form, the role of the secretary and, perhaps most significant, their use of preformed traditions (cf. Ellis 1999; Ellis 1989, 104-7).

4.1. Letter Form. Early in this century Paul's "letters," understood as nonliterary products intended solely for the addressees, were distinguished from more formal literary epistles intended for a larger circle (G. A. Deissmann). More recently they have been the subject of attempts to identify the "letter" as a literary genre *(see* Letter, Letter Forms). Deissmann's distinctions were at best oversimplified and probably mistaken, and the later attempts at classification were misleading (cf. Ellis 1999; but see Malherbe, *ANRW* 2:26.1, 192-93, 325-26). In fact, in antiquity letters could take virtually any form, as P. L. Schmidt points out *(KP,* 2:325), and according to Cicero *(Friends* 2.4) they were simply "of many kinds," although he classified his own as newsletters and as the "familiar and sportive, and the grave and serious."

The apostle's letters were intended to be used by more people than the immediate addressees (see 1.3.1 above) and were specifically to be "read in church" (Col 4:16; 1 Thess 5:27; cf. 1 Cor 7:1, 25; 8:1; 12:1; 16:1, 12). In the light of his Jewish background in which not even Targums but only canonical Scripture could be read "in church" *(b. Meg.* 32a; cf. Alexander, CRINT 2.1. 238-39), they were written and received as "the Word of God," that is, as inspired and normative authority for the churches (cf. 1 Thess 2:13 with 2 Thess 2:15). They were teachings of an apostolic prophet that, unlike other prophetic teaching and writing in the congregations, were not subject to "testing" or vetting by other prophets (1 Cor 9:3, *anakrinō;* 1 Cor 14:29, *diakrinō,* with 1 Cor 14:37-38). That is, they were teaching pieces clothed in the form of letters: Philemon addresses a specific personal question; others, like 1 Corinthians, give attention to immediate congregational problems or, like Romans and Ephesians, to more general theological motifs; 1 Timothy and Titus (and to some extent 2 Tim) are virtual manuals of tradition that have genre affinities with Qumran's *Manual of Discipline.* The apostle utilizes the letter form for a number of reasons, not least that by it he can combine personal communication and relationships with his primary purpose of teaching and upbuilding believers in the truth of the gospel of Christ.

4.2. Secretary. A secretary was a practical necessity in antiquity for all but the briefest letters, since the poor quality of pen, ink and paper made writing slow and laborious (cf. Quintilian *Inst. Orat.* 10.3.31; 10.3.19-22) and could require more than an hour to write a small page (Roller, 13-14, 6-9). The secretary ordinarily would record first on a wax or wood tablet in shorthand, which was used in first-century Greek and Latin writing (Richards, 24-43), and then would transcribe in longhand onto papyrus. Such a helper is explicitly mentioned in Romans 16:22 and is implied where Paul, in accordance with the custom, adds a marginal note (e.g., Philem 19a; 1 Cor 14:34-35; Ellis 1989, 67-68) or an ending (e.g., 1 Cor 16:21-24; Gal 6:11-18; Col 4:18; 2 Thess 3:17; cf. 1 Tim 6:20-21; 2 Tim 4:19-22; Tit 3:15) to a completed secretarial composition. For the Pastorals a secretary may be inferred from numerous verbal and stylistic peculiarities, and he has been plausibly suggested to be Luke (2 Tim 4:11; cf. Strobel, 210; Moule, 434; Spicq,

1:199; Knight, 51: perhaps; but see Metzger, 10-16). The secretary's work could range from taking dictation to being a coauthor, and in the Pastorals he appears to have had a greater input than in certain other Pauline letters (cf. Richards, 23-24, 193-94). However, more significant for the literary form of the Pastorals are the numerous preformed traditions, largely non-Pauline, that are employed in them.

4.3. Traditions. Traditions in the Pastorals have long been recognized in a few passages, such as the confession at 1 Timothy 3:16 and the five "faithful word" *(pistos ho logos)* sayings (see 4.4.1 below). In other passages they can also be identified by the use of acceptable criteria. Some preformed pericopes were composed by Paul and some by others whom he recognized to be prophetically gifted to mediate divine revelation.

Criteria to identify a cited or traditioned piece include (1) a formula that elsewhere introduces or concludes quoted material (e.g., 1 Tim 4:1; cf. Acts 20:23; 28:25; Heb 3:7); (2) the self-contained character of the passage; (3) a relatively large number of *hapax legomena* and an idiom and style that differ from the rest of the letter and from other writings by the same author; and (4) a strikingly similar passage in another writing where no literary dependence is probable. One criterion alone may not be significant since a different vocabulary or idiom may point only to a change of subject matter, to a different secretary or to a different time of writing. Also, a quotation might not be transmitted tradition (e.g., Tit 1:12), and transmitted traditions might be paraphrased and incorporated without a formula of quotation. Nevertheless, several criteria in a given passage provide guidelines for measuring probabilities.

4.4. The Classification of Traditions. Preformed pieces embrace a variety of topics and literary forms (cf. Ellis 1999). Among them are doxologies (1 Tim 1:17; 6:15-16), a vice list (1 Tim 1:9-10), congregational regulations for the conduct of wives (1 Tim 2:9—3:1a) and qualifications for ministries (1 Tim 3:1b-13), predictive prophecies (1 Tim 4:1-5; 2 Tim 3:1-5), confessions that are sometimes hymnic (1 Tim 2:5-6; 3:16; 2 Tim 1:9-10; Tit 3:3-7; cf. 1 Tim 1:15) and other hymns (1 Tim 6:11-12, 15-16; 2 Tim 2:11-13; Tit 2:11-14). Some of these are in the form of implicit and explicit midrash, that is, commentary on OT texts (1 Tim 1:9-10; 2:9—3:1a; 5:17-18; 2 Tim 2:19-21; cf. Ellis 1993, 188-97, 147-237: "prophecy as exegesis"). One passage combines midrash and a hymnic form (Tit 3:3-7), both of which are characteristic of early Christian prophecy (cf. Aune, 453-55; "the prophetic hymn").

Some traditions may also be identified and classified in terms of three formulas that introduce or conclude them: "faithful is the word" *(pistos ho logos),* "knowing this that" *(touto ginōskein/idein hoti)* and "these things" *(tauta).* Such passages are relatively independent of their contexts and are distinguished by other criteria listed above.

4.4.1. "Faithful Is the Word." This formula introduces (1 Tim 1:15; 4:9-10; 2 Tim 2:11-13) or concludes (1 Tim 2:9—3:1a; Tit 3:3-8a) five passages which, with the exception of 1 Timothy 2:9—3:1a, are confessional statements of Pauline soteriological themes, whose vocabulary is generally Pauline. The formula is absent from Paul's earlier letters (but see 1 Cor 10:13) and apparently had its origin among Jewish apocalyptic prophets or at Qumran (cf. 1Q27 1:8). However, it was employed in the Johannine mission (Rev 22:6) and came to be used by Paul and his co-workers during his Caesarean or first Roman imprisonment. On the analogy of Ben Sira's use of "faithful" (Sir 46:15; 48:22) to designate the prophecies of Samuel and Isaiah, the formula governs a word that is no mere saying but that is a prophetic word of God to the hearers. Therefore, the teaching elder (= bishop) is required to "hold to the faithful word" (Tit 1:9), and Timothy in his ministry is said to be nourished on such "faithful words" and is urged to mediate them to his congregations (2 Tim 2:11-13, 14). Given their Pauline themes and vocabulary, most "faithful Word" sayings were probably Paul's compositions, but 1 Timothy 2:9—3:1a (and perhaps Tit 3:3-8), composed by others, is a variant of a tradition used in common with the Petrine mission (cf. 1 Pet 3:1-5, 18-22; 1 Cor 14:34-35).

4.4.2. "Knowing This That." This and similar phrases do not always have a formulaic significance (e.g., 1 Thess 1:4-5), but they are sometimes used elsewhere as formulas to introduce a paraphrastic biblical quotation (Acts 2:3, cf. Ps 132:11; cf. Polycarp *Phil.* 4.1) and other cited traditions (Rom 6:6; Eph 5:5; cf. 1 Cor 6:9-10). In the Pastorals they are used as formulas to introduce a vice list paraphrasing the fifth to the ninth commandments (1 Tim 1:9-10) and a transmitted prophecy (2 Tim 3:1-5).

4.4.3. "These Things." This formula is found

at the conclusion of cited material and introduces its application to the current situation. It appears at the end of pericopes identified above as traditioned pieces (1 Tim 4:6, 11; 2 Tim 2:14; cf. Tit 1:15-16; 2:1). It also occurs at the end of a regulation on ministry (1 Tim 3:1b-13, 14; cf. Tit 1:7-9) that is distinct from its context (Harnack, 1:482-83; Kelly, 231) and of congregational and household rules (1 Tim 5:5-6, 9-10, 17-20; 6:1, 2; Tit 2:2-14, 15), which are probably also preformed traditions incorporated into the letters.

4.4.4. Conclusion. A number of other passages are probably reworked traditional material: hymnic confessions (1 Tim 2:5-6; 2 Tim 1:9-10), a doxology (1 Tim 1:17), a commission + doxology (1 Tim 6:11-16) and other sayings (1 Tim 6:7-8, 10a; 2 Tim 1:7). Together such preformed materials make up about 43 percent of 1 Timothy, 16 percent of 2 Timothy and 46 percent of Titus (Ellis 1999).

5. Outline.
5.1. 1 Timothy.
I. 1:1-20 Introduction
 1:1-2 Greeting
 1:3-20 A Charge to Oppose the Gnosticizing Judaizers
   1:3-7 Their Errors
   1:8-11 The Right Use of the Law
   1:12-17 Paul's Example
   1:18-20 Timothy Contrasted with the False Teachers
II. 2:1—4:10 Congregational Regulations
 2:1-8 Prayers and Their Purpose
 2:9—3:1a "A Faithful Word" for Husbands and Wives
 3:1b-13 Qualifications for Overseers and Ministers
 3:14-16 Their Purpose and Christological Basis
 4:1-10 A Prophetic Warning and Its Application
III. 4:11—6:2 Instructions for Timothy
 4:11—5:2 His Example to Others
 5:3—6:2 His Congregational Supervision: Widows, Elders, Slaves and Others
   5:23 A Personal Aside: Purity Does Not Require Asceticism
IV. 6:3-19 Final Admonitions
 6:3-10 Concerning False Teachers and Their Money Motives
 6:11-16 Concerning the Motives and Conduct of "The Man of God"
 6:17-19 Concerning Affluent Believers
V. 6:20-21 Admonition and Benediction in Paul's Hand

5.2. Titus.
I. 1:1-4 Greeting
II. 1:5—2:1 Instructions for Titus
 1:5-9 Qualifications for Overseers
 1:10—2:1 Concerning False Teachers
III. 2:2-15 Congregational Supervision and Its Basis
IV. 3:1-11 Responsibilities of Believers
 3:1-2 Concerning Civic Life
 3:3-8 Its Basis in a Faithful Word
 3:9-11 Concerning the False Teachers
V. 3:12-15 A Concluding Word
 3:12-13 Concerning the Coworkers
 3:14 A Repeated Admonition
 3:15 Greetings and Benediction in Paul's Hand

5.3. 2 Timothy.
I. 1:1-5 Greeting and Thanksgiving
II. 1:6—2:13 Appeal to Timothy
 1:6—2:7 For Faithful Witness in the Face of Opposition
 2:8-13 In the Light of Paul's Example
III. 2:14—4:5 Warnings Against False Teachers
 2:14-26 Avoid Their Vain Ways
 3:1-9 A Prophecy Concerning False Teachers and Its Application
 3:10-17 The Reason and Way to Counter False Teachers
 4:1-5 An Exhortation to Faithful Ministry
IV. 4:6-18 Paul's Situation and Prospects
 4:6-8 His Approaching Death
 4:9-16 His Need for Timothy to Come
 4:17-18 His Confidence in God's Presence and Final Redemption
V. 4:19-22 Greetings and Benediction in Paul's Hand

6. Themes.
The teachings of the letters are largely contained in the reworked and transmitted traditions and their application. They concern the errors of the false teachers and the proper response to them (1 Tim 1:3-20; 4:1-10; 6:3-10; Tit 1:10—2:1; 3:9-11; 2 Tim 2:14—4:5) and the strict qualifications for ministries in the light of the opponents' activities (1 Tim 3:1b-13; Tit 1:5-9). Not unrelated to this situation are other regulations on church order (1 Tim 2:1—3:1a; 5:3-25;

Tit 2:1-14) and on the conduct of believers (1 Tim 6:1-2; Tit 3:1-8). As is the case in the other Pauline letters, all the teachings are given a christological basis in salvation history (1 Tim 3:16; Tit 2:11-14), including Christ's identity with God (Tit 2:13), preexistence (1 Tim 1:15), human Davidic descent (2 Tim 2:8), faithful ministry (1 Tim 6:13), saving work (1 Tim 2:5-6a; 2 Tim 1:9-10), resurrection (2 Tim 2:8) and future coming and reign (1 Tim 6:14; 2 Tim 2:11-12; 4:8, 18).

DPL: CANON; CHRONOLOGY OF PAUL; CHURCH ORDER AND GOVERNMENT; EARLY CATHOLICISM; PAUL IN EARLY CHURCH TRADITION.

BIBLIOGRAPHY. **Commentaries:** M. Dibelius and H. Conzelmann, *The Pastoral Epistles* (Herm; Philadelphia: Fortress, 1972); G. D. Fee, *The Pastoral Epistles* (Peabody, MA: Hendrickson, 1988); D. Guthrie, *The Pastoral Epistles* (TNTC; 2d ed.; Grand Rapids: Eerdmans, 1990); H. J. Holtzmann, *Die Pastoralbriefe* (Leipzig: Engelmann, 1880); J. N. D. Kelly, *The Pastoral Epistles* (London: Black, 1963); G. W. Knight III, *The Pastoral Epistles* (NIGTC; Grand Rapids: Eerdmans, 1992); T. D. Lea and H. P. Griffen Jr., *1, 2 Timothy, Titus* (NAC; Nashville: Broadman, 1992); W. L. Liefeld, *1 and 2 Timothy, Titus* (NIVAC; Grand Rapids: Zondervan, 1999); W. Lock, *The Pastoral Epistles* (ICC; Edinburgh: T & T Clark, 1958 [1924]); I. H. Marshall, *A Critical and Exegetical Commentary on the Pastoral Epistles* (ICC; Edinburgh: T & T Clark, 1999); W. D. Mounce, *The Pastoral Epistles* (WBC; Dallas: Word, 2000); C. Spicq, *Les Épîtres Pastorales* (2 vols.; Paris: Gabalda, 1969); P. H. Towner, *1-2 Timothy, Titus* (IVPNTC; Downers Grove, IL: InterVarsity Press, 1994). **Studies:** K. Aland, "Neutestamentliche Textkritik und Exegese," *Wissenschaft und Kirche*, FS E. Lohse, ed. K. Aland (Bielefeld: Luther, 1989) 132-48; D. E. Aune, "The Odes of Solomon and Early Christian Prophecy," *NTS* 28 (1982) 435-60; F. C. Baur, *Die sogenannten Pastoralbriefe* (Tübingen: Gotta, 1835); L. R. Donelson, *Pseudepigraphy and Ethical Argument in the Pastoral Epistles* (Tübingen: Mohr Siebeck, 1986); G. Edmundson, *The Church in Rome in the First Century* (London: Longmans, 1913); E. E. Ellis, " 'The End of the Earth' (Acts 1:8)," *BBR* 1 (1991) 123-32; idem, *History and Interpretation* (Leiden: E. J. Brill, 2001); idem, *The Making of the New Testament Documents* (Leiden: E. J. Brill, 1999); idem, *The Old Testament in Early Christianity* (Tübingen: Mohr Siebeck, 1991); idem, "The Pastorals and Paul," *ExpT* 104 (1992-93) 45-47; idem, *Paul and His Recent Interpreters* (5th ed.; Grand Rapids: Eerdmans, 1979) 49-57; idem, *Pauline Theology: Ministry and Society* (Grand Rapids: Eerdmans, 1989); idem, *Prophecy and Hermeneutic in Early Christianity* (4th ed.; Grand Rapids: Baker, 1993); D. Guthrie, *Introduction to the New Testament* (rev. ed.; Downers Grove, IL: InterVarsity, 1990) 636-46; A. Harnack, *Geschichte der altchristliche Literatur*, Teil 2: *Chronologie* (2 vols.; Leipzig: Hinrichs, 1958 [1904]) 1:480-85; P. N. Harrison, *The Problem of the Pastoral Epistles* (London: Oxford University Press, 1921); J. B. Lightfoot, "The Date of the Pastoral Epistles" and "The Close of the Acts," in *Biblical Essays* (London: Macmillan, 1893) 399-437; W. Metzger, *Die letzte Reise des Apostels Paulus* (Stuttgart: Calver, 1976); C. F. D. Moule, "The Problem of the Pastorals: A Reappraisal," *BJRL* 47 (1964-65) 430-52; M. Prior, *Paul the Letter-Writer* (JSNTSup 23; Sheffield: JSOT, 1989); B. Reicke, "Chronologie der Pastoralbriefe," *TLZ* 101 (1976) 82-94; E. R. Richards, *The Secretary in the Letters of Paul* (Tübingen: Mohr Siebeck, 1991); J. A. T. Robinson, *Redating the New Testament* (London: SCM, 1976); O. Roller, *Das Formular der paulinischen Briefe* (Stuttgart: Kohlhammer, 1933); W. Rordorf, "Nochmals: Paulusakten und Pastoralbriefe," in *Tradition and Interpretation in the New Testament*. FS E. E. Ellis, ed. G. F. Hawthorne with O. Betz (Grand Rapids: Eerdmans, 1987) 319-27; A. Strobel, "Schreiben des Lukas? Zum sprachlichen Problem der Pastoralbriefe," *NTS* 15 (1968-69) 191-210; B. E. Thiering, "*Mebaqqer* and *Episkopos* in the Light of the Temple Scroll," *JBL* 100 (1981) 59-74; M. Weinfeld, *The Organizational Pattern and the Penal Code of the Qumran Sect* (Göttingen: Vandenhoeck & Ruprecht, 1986); M. Wolter, *Die Pastoralbriefe als Paulustradition* (Göttingen: Vandenhoeck & Ruprecht, 1988); T. Zahn, *Introduction to the New Testament* (3 vols.; Minneapolis: Klock, 1977 [3d ed. 1909, 1st ed. 1899]) 2:1-133.

E. E. Ellis

PAUL IN ACTS AND LETTERS

Paul's letters provide us with the primary evidence of the apostle, while the Acts of the Apostles offers the closest thing to an orderly account of Paul's life and ministry. These two independent sources allow us to draw a composite portrait of the many-sided personality we know as Paul the apostle—his career, his mission and his message.

1. Sources.

There are two main sources for our knowledge of Paul—his own writings and the Acts of the Apostles. These two sources are apparently wholly independent. Paul's writings display him as a letter writer—he is in fact one of the great letter writers of world literature—whereas Acts says nothing of him in this regard. The majority opinion is that Acts makes no use of his letters, although his authentic letters were all in existence (though not yet collected) when Acts was written.

A subsidiary body of source material includes the contemporary evidence bearing on social, political and religious life in those parts of the Mediterranean world where Paul moved and worked, from Judea to Rome.

1.1. Paul's Letters. Paul's letters provide primary evidence for our knowledge of the man himself. Most of them were written to churches he had planted, dealing with issues that had arisen in them during his absence. They are usually second-best substitutes for his presence and spoken word. In Galatians 4:20, for example, he expresses the wish that he could be with his readers so that they could gather the intensity of his emotions from the tone of his voice as they could not from his writing. On one occasion, however, he deliberately did not visit the church of Corinth when he could have done so because he could express himself more severely in writing than he could have done in speech: he evidently found it difficult to be severe in the presence of his friends and converts and wanted to spare both them and himself the embarrassment of a face-to-face confrontation (2 Cor 1:23—2:4).

The outstanding exception to the rule that Paul's letters were sent to his own churches is the letter to the *Romans. (The letter to the Colossians is not really an exception: it was sent to a church in Paul's mission field, one founded by his lieutenant Epaphras.) The letter to the Romans was sent to the Christian community in Rome, when Paul was about to pay his first visit to their city. He wished not only to prepare the Roman Christians for his visit but also to enlist their sympathetic involvement in his further ap-

ostolic enterprise, both in his projected evangelization of Spain and in the discharge and continuation of his commission to the Gentile world at large. The main letters of his apostolic prime—those to the Galatians, Corinthians and Romans, are sometimes called his four "capital" letters; they provide our chief source of information for the content and purpose of his message. The "captivity," or "prison," letters (Philippians, Ephesians, Colossians, Philemon) are so called because he appears to have been undergoing some kind of imprisonment when they were written. Traditionally, they have been dated during his two years of house arrest in Rome; this is most frequently held to be the case with Philippians, but arguments have been presented for dating *Philippians and the other captivity letters during his period of custody in Caesarea (Acts 24:27) or during the earlier, not explicitly recorded, imprisonment in *Ephesus.

One of the captivity letters, the personal note to Paul's friend *Philemon of Colossae, interceding for Onesimus, Philemon's slave and now Paul's convert, shares the same life setting as Colossians (see Col 4:9 with the references to Archippus in Philem 2 and Col 4:17). Another, the letter to the *Ephesians, is not associated with one particular church: the phrase "in Ephesus" (Eph 1:1), from which the traditional title is derived, is probably not part of the original text. This letter has the character of a testament to Paul's mission field, especially in proconsular Asia, viewing his ministry to the Gentiles as a means to the fulfillment of God's eternal purpose, to unite the universe in Christ.

The *Pastoral Letters (1 and 2 Tim and Tit), of uncertain date, include a number of personal notes (especially 2 Tim), but 1 Timothy and Titus largely resemble early manuals of church order, while 2 Timothy has the nature of a personal testament.

Paul's letters were regularly dictated to amanuenses (the name of one of these, Tertius, has been preserved in Rom 16:22). Paul was accustomed to authenticate them by adding the last sentence or two in his own hand (cf. Gal 6:11). Occasionally, but not usually, this autographic addition included his name (cf. 1 Cor 16:21; Col 4:18; 2 Thess 3:17; also Philem 19).

In the opening salutation Paul frequently associates with himself one or more friends who might be with him at the time of writing; only occasionally, however, does internal evidence suggest that one of these was a responsible joint author, like Silvanus in 1 and 2 Thessalonians or Timothy in Colossians. In 1 and 2 Thessalonians those passages are evidently Paul's where we find the singular pronoun "I" (e.g., "I Paul" in 1 Thess 2:18).

Most of Paul's letters are "occasional documents" in the sense that they were called for by some local need where Paul was not present to deal with the situation firsthand. Only once, to our knowledge, did he deal with a critical situation by letter in preference to on-the-spot action (2 Cor 1:23—2:4). Even Romans is an occasional letter because it was sent in view of Paul's plan to visit Rome as soon as he had completed the delivery of relief money to Jerusalem (Rom 15:23-32), although he took the opportunity to present the Roman Christians with an orderly statement of the gospel as he understood and preached it.

1.2. Acts of the Apostles. In the Acts of the Apostles, the second part of Luke's history of Christian origins (the sequel to the Third Gospel), Paul is introduced at an early stage. His call to be Christ's worldwide witness is first related in Acts 9:1-20, and from Acts 15:40 to the end of the book he dominates the narrative, until he arrives in Rome and spends two years there in custody. After the record of Acts ends we have only scanty and uncertain hints about the remainder of his life. If the author of Acts was, as seems most probable, an acquaintance and occasional companion of Paul, then Acts has claims to be recognized as a primary source of information about Paul.

Indeed, a collection of occasional letters written by some figure of history at crucial epochs in his career, will have a value and directness of their own, by giving his personal perspective on persons and events and (in a man who wore his heart on his sleeve, as Paul did) by providing insight into his mind and motives. Such a collection, however, cannot take the place of an orderly account of events in which he played a major part, written from the more objective point of view of a writer who had access to the material from reliable informants and from personal involvement, and set in the context of contemporary history.

1.3. Comparison of the Letters and Acts. Although these two main sources for our knowledge are apparently independent of each other, there are impressive parallels between their respective portrayals of Paul.

In both sources Paul supports himself by his own labors so as not to be financially burdensome to his friends and converts. His policy recorded in Acts of visiting the local synagogue first, in place after place to which he comes, is in line with his insistence in Romans 1:16 that the gospel is directed "to the Jew first." Besides, apostle to the Gentiles as he knew himself to be, he found that the Gentile sympathizers who attended the synagogue services presented the most promising nucleus for a Christian community. Plainly, he did not regard visiting the synagogue to make contact with them a breach of his agreement with the Jerusalem church leaders, by which they were to concentrate on evangelizing Jews and he and Barnabas on the Gentile mission (Gal 2:7-9). In any case, he was not the man to keep silent about Jesus while in Jewish company; he was under a debt to his kinsfolk by race as well as to all others (*see* Israel).

In Acts, Paul is the most adaptable of people. He is equally at home with Gentiles and religiously observant Jews. This is the Paul who in 1 Corinthians 9:19-23 claims to live like a Jew among the Jews, in order to win Jews, and like a Gentile among Gentiles, in order to win Gentiles.

From the point where he assumes a major role in the narrative of Acts, Paul is Luke's hero. He is indeed a man "of like nature" with other human beings (Acts 14:15), but in Luke's portrayal he dominates the situation. He is always sure of himself; he always triumphs. The Paul of the letters includes himself among his fellow Christians when he describes them as "more than conquerors" through Christ (Rom 8:27); but there is little triumphalism in his own account of his apostolic activity. He is "led in triumph" in Christ (2 Cor 2:14)—led in Christ's triumphal procession—and he can thank God that by his grace he has worked harder than any of the others called to the same evangelistic task (1 Cor 15:10), but even when he contemplates with satisfaction his preaching the gospel "from Jerusalem and as far round as Illyricum" (Rom 15:19), he claims no credit for himself but for Christ working through him. In himself he is a cheap, expendable earthenware vessel, but to that vessel the surpassing treasure of the gospel has been entrusted "to show that the transcendent power belongs to God" and not to Paul or any of his fellow preachers (2 Cor 4:7).

If he was a hero to Luke, Paul was no hero in

his own eyes. In his letters he is too often the prey of conflicting emotions, "fightings without and fears within" (2 Cor 7:5). He confesses that he has neither the self-assurance nor the self-assertiveness of some of his rivals—of those intruders, for example, who tried to supplant his authority in the church of Corinth. Those intruders may exploit his converts, while he himself hesitates to claim his rights among them as their spiritual father, and some of them despise him for his "weakness" (2 Cor 10:1—12:13). At times indeed he did assert his authority, although the reader of his letters may suspect (as some of his converts realized) that he found it easier to do this by letter from a distance than in words spoken face to face. The side of Paul shown in Acts is the side that can readily assert authority, the charismatic person of power. But Paul was a many-sided personality, and his letters expose many other sides than that shown in Acts. The most revealing side disclosed in the letters is probably that which says, "I will all the more gladly boast of my weaknesses, that the power of Christ may rest upon me. For the sake of Christ, then, I am content with weaknesses, insult, hardships, persecutions and calamities; for when I am weak, then I am strong" (2 Cor 12:9-10).

2. Paul's Career.

2.1. Family and Citizenship.
Paul was born into a religiously observant Jewish family of Tarsus in Cilicia, apparently in the first decade of the first century A.D. According to Jerome (*Vir.* 5), his family came from Gischala in Galilee (*see* Jew, Paul the). It traced its descent from the tribe of Benjamin, and Paul was given the name Saul, borne by the most illustrious member of that tribe in history—Saul, the first king of Israel. The name Paul, by which he is commonly called, was part of his triple name as a Roman citizen: it is the Roman cognomen Paullus.

It is not known for how many generations the family had lived in Tarsus, but the family business of tentmaking (or perhaps, more generally, leatherworking) evidently prospered. Paul was born a citizen of Tarsus—"a citizen of no mean city," in his own words (Acts 21:39)—and this implied a certain level of wealth. The property qualification for Tarsian citizenship was 500 drachmae (Dio Chrysostom *Or.* 34.23). In addition to the wealth requirement, the practice of Judaism must have been a further obsta-

cle in the successful quest for citizenship. If the citizens of Tarsus were organized into tribes, like the citizens of many Hellenistic cities, membership of such a tribe involved practices which Jews would have found offensive; possibly the Jewish citizens of Tarsus were enrolled in a tribe of their own, though there is no positive evidence for this.

But much more important than the family's possession of Tarsian citizenship was its acquisition of Roman citizenship—an honor rarely granted to provincials. Paul inherited Roman citizenship at birth: his father or grandfather may have been so honored for conspicuous services rendered to a military proconsul such as Pompey or Antony. Paul would have been registered as a Roman citizen by his father at the public record office in Tarsus. Roman citizenship carried with it several privileges of which Paul was able to avail himself during his career—the right to a fair trial, for example, exemption from degrading penalties like scourging, and most notably the right to appeal from the jurisdiction of a lower court to that of the emperor of Rome (Acts 16:37; 22:25; 25:11).

2.2. Education at Jerusalem.
Although he was born in a Greek center of culture, it was not in any of the schools of Tarsus that Paul was educated. It was probably at a later stage that he acquired the measure of literary knowledge and Stoic thought that is attested in his writings and speeches. By his own account he was educated according to his ancestral traditions, surpassing many of his contemporaries in the study and practice of Judaism (Gal 1:14). In his Jerusalem speech of Acts 22:3 he says more precisely that, while born in Tarsus, he was brought up in Jerusalem and "trained in the school of Gamaliel according to the strict interpretation of our ancestral law."

Gamaliel, a leading Jewish teacher of his day, is said by later tradition to have been head of the rabbinical school founded by Hillel, c. 10 B.C., if not indeed a member of Hillel's family. But the earliest traditions which reflect some direct memory of Gamaliel and his teaching do not associate him with the school of Hillel; they speak rather of others as belonging to the school of Gamaliel, as though he founded a school of his own. Even if Gamaliel was a follower of Hillel, however, it would not follow that Paul was a Hillelite. Paul's writings do not yield sufficient evidence to show certainty whether, before he became a Christian, he was a Hillelite or an adherent of the rival school of Shammai. His statement that anyone who submits to circumcision "is bound to keep the whole Law" (Gal 5:3) might be thought to reflect the stricter Shammaite doctrine, but such a conclusion cannot safely be drawn from a statement made in a polemical context. His zeal as a persecutor of the church presents a sharp contrast to the temporizing policy advocated by Gamaliel in Acts 5:34-39, but the explanation may simply be that Paul saw more clearly than Gamaliel the serious implications of the Christian movement for the life and health of Judaism.

2.3. Persecutor of the Church. According to his letters and to Acts, Paul was an active persecutor of the church before he became a Christian. He assaulted the infant church with the utmost violence in his attempt to destroy it (Gal 1:13). This was the negative aspect of his zeal for the Law and traditions of Israel, which perhaps found a positive outlet in the proselytization of Gentiles. His words, "If I . . . still preach circumcision, why am I still persecuted?" (Gal 5:11), have been thought to point in that direction.

When he says that he "persecuted the church of God" (1 Cor 15:9), it is natural to think primarily of the Jerusalem church. The "church of God" would hardly have been found as a recognizable body anywhere else than in Jerusalem in the first two or three years after the resurrection of Christ. This is plainly attested by the record of Acts, which describes him as "entering into houses, dragging out men and women and committing them to prison" (Acts 8:3), and, when the persecution led to dispersal, harrying the refugees even beyond the frontiers of the province of Judea. Reading between the lines, one can infer that "Hellenists" rather than "Hebrews" (cf. Acts 6:1) were the principal targets for this attack. The apostles remained unscathed in Jerusalem (Acts 8:2).

2.4. Call to Apostleship. It was while Paul was on his way to Damascus, armed with the high priest's commission, to round up some who had sought refuge from the persecution there, that he was confronted by the risen and exalted Christ, turned right around in his tracks and called to be Christ's ambassador to the Gentile world (*see* Conversion and Call of Paul). This personal encounter with Christ determined the whole course of Paul's subsequent thought and action.

Until that moment Paul had taken it as axiomatic that one who had died the death on which the divine curse was pronounced by the Law (Deut 21:23) could not be the Messiah, the elect one of God, as his followers claimed. Their claim was blasphemous. But now their claim was manifestly true. He had seen and heard Jesus, the crucified one, alive and glorified. But it was his devotion to the Law that had made him such a zealous persecutor—that is, as he now realized, his devotion to the Law had led him into the most sinful course of all: he had been fighting against God, his *Son and his people. The Law had done nothing to show him the sinfulness of his course. The Law had proved itself bankrupt. But Christ, whose grace wiped out his guilt and empowered him to be his special envoy, displaced the Law's former centrality in Paul's life. For him, henceforth, "to live was Christ" (Phil 1:21). It was then that Paul first knew himself to be set right with God through the redemptive act of Christ and not through his own works of righteousness. The very death which incurred the curse of God turned out to be the deliverance of the people of Christ from the curse of a broken Law (Gal 3:10-14).

2.5. Apostle to the Gentiles. Paul quickly responded to his call to evangelize the Gentiles by traveling to the nearby territory of the Nabatean Arabs, where his activity seems to have aroused the hostility of the authorities (Gal 1:17; 2 Cor 11:32-33). From there he returned to Damascus and then went up to Jerusalem to visit Peter. He also met James, the Lord's brother, all the other apostles being evidently absent from Jerusalem. It was doubtless during this visit that Paul learned how Jesus had appeared in resurrection to Peter and James, as he records in 1 Corinthians 15:5, 7. They in turn would hear how he himself had met the risen one.

After two weeks he returned to his native Tarsus and spent several years in the united province of Syria and Cilicia, actively propagating the faith he had once endeavored to root out (Gal 1:21-24). While he was thus engaged, he was invited by Barnabas to join him in directing the new forward movement which had recently been launched in Antioch on the Orontes, where Gentiles in large numbers were making a positive response to the gospel (Acts 11:19-26).

Paul claimed to be an "apostle of Jesus Christ"; where necessary, he insisted on this designation. But in what sense was he an apostle? The term is used in a variety of ways in the New Testament: Luke, for his part, generally confines it to the Twelve (with Matthias replacing Judas Iscariot). If a qualification for apostleship was to have remained in Jesus' company throughout his public ministry (Acts 1:21-22), then Paul did not satisfy that qualification. In one section of his narrative (Acts 14:4, 14) Luke uses the plural "apostles" of Barnabas and Paul together; this usage may have been taken over from his source at this point. Otherwise, he does not call Paul an apostle. Paul may very well have recognized Barnabas as an apostle. By "those who were apostles before me" (Gal 1:17) he probably means the Twelve; but he almost certainly looks on James, the Lord's brother, as an apostle (Gal 1:19), together with "all the apostles" who saw the risen Lord in sequence from James (1 Cor 15:7) and who seem to be distinct from the Twelve, mentioned along with Peter in 1 Corinthians 15:5. When he speaks of Andronicus and Junia, whose faith in Christ antedated his own, as "of note among the apostles" (Rom 16:7), he probably means that they were apostles themselves. (The "apostles," or envoys of the churches, mentioned in 2 Cor 8:23, are in quite another category.)

If to be an apostle is to have seen the risen Lord and to have been called and commissioned by him to be his witness and messenger, then Paul was preeminently an apostle of Jesus Christ, accredited as such by the apostolic "signs" which attended his ministry (1 Cor 9:1-2; 2 Cor 12:12). Paul was called and commissioned to be an apostle to the Gentiles (Rom 11:13; Gal 1:16), and his Gentile apostolate appears to have been acknowledged by the leader of the Jerusalem church (Gal 2:7-8). But there was no other witness at hand when the Lord commissioned him. Anyone who refused to recognize this apostleship could appeal to the absence of independent testimony.

Paul could produce nothing like the credentials of the Twelve. His credentials were the converts he had won and the churches he had planted—more than adequate credentials, in all conscience. He had worked harder and preached more extensively than any of those who had seen the risen Christ before he did; he had planted churches more widely and observed the harvest of the Spirit growing in the lives of those who had turned to Christ through his ministry. It is almost incredible that intruders

should invade his own mission field and try to persuade his converts that his apostolic standing was questionable, and that they should even find some to lend them an ear. In such situations Paul's argument was practical: his converts were the last people who could question his apostleship, for they owed their new existence in Christ to his apostolic ministry—they were its seal and guarantee (1 Cor 9:2). But what is important is not the title he held but the work he did. In the light of his achievement Paul can safely rest his case before the bar of history—not to speak of a more august bar which he kept constantly in view, as he set himself to discharge his commission in such a way that the day of Christ would reveal that he had "neither run in vain nor labored in vain" (Phil 2:16).

2.6. Conference at Jerusalem. The church of Antioch, a mainly Gentile church, was not long in being established. Its members showed their quality by sending a sum of money to the mother church in Jerusalem to help it at a time of food scarcity in Judea, appointing Barnabas and Paul to convey the gift (Acts 11:27-30). This may have provided an occasion for the conference described by Paul in Galatians 2:1-10. Barnabas and Paul were received by the leaders of the Jerusalem church, James (the Lord's brother), Peter and John, the three so-called pillars. It was agreed that Barnabas and Paul should continue to concentrate on the Gentile mission, while the Jerusalem leaders would devote themselves to gospel witness among Jews. It is not implied that two different versions of the gospel were involved: Paul laid his Law-free gospel before the Jerusalem leaders, and they evidently found it acceptable. The difference lay rather in the two mission fields and in the presentation of the message. The agreement concealed several ambiguities, and these might lead to tension if full confidence were not maintained between the two sides. At the request of the Jerusalem leaders, Barnabas and Paul undertook to remember the poor in the mother church—an undertaking which Paul took very seriously.

2.7. With Barnabas in Cyprus and Anatolia. On returning to Antioch, Barnabas and Paul were released by the church there to embark on a missionary campaign which took them to Cyprus and then to central Anatolia—to the Pisidian, Phrygian and Lycaonian regions of the Roman province of Galatia. The churches planted in the course of this mission in the cities of

Pisidian Antioch, Iconium, Lystra and Derbe are probably among the "churches of Galatia" addressed in Paul's letter to the Galatians.

The historicity of this campaign has been questioned: it has been interpreted as a "model journey," setting forth the way in which Luke conceived that a missionary campaign should be conducted, including the way in which the gospel should be presented both to a synagogue congregation, as in Paul's address at Pisidian Antioch (Acts 13:16-41), and to a pagan audience, as in Barnabas and Paul's confronting the idolatrous Lystrans with the revelation of the true God in his works of creation and providence (Acts 14:15-17). But the details of the journey, when examined in the light of historical geography, make a strong impression of factual truth. There is, moreover, a marked similarity between the missionaries' remonstrance against idolatry at Lystra and Paul's reminder to the Thessalonian Christians of how they had "turned to God from idols to serve a living and true God" (1 Thess 1:9).

2.8. Terms of Gentile Admission to the Church. When Barnabas and Paul returned to Antioch on the Orontes, they found themselves before long involved in controversy. The agreement recently concluded at Jerusalem was perhaps understood differently by the two parties. Paul apparently soon began to feel that its spirit was not being observed by the Jerusalem leaders. There was a clash between him and Peter at Antioch, when Peter was spending some time with the church there. To begin with, Peter ate quite freely with the Gentile Christians, but some messengers from James in Jerusalem persuaded him to change his ways and withdraw from table fellowship with Gentiles. In Paul's eyes the implications of Peter's conduct threatened the foundations of the gospel of grace. But other Jewish Christians in Antioch, including even Barnabas, sided with Peter, and Antioch could no longer provide Paul with a base for his missionary activity.

A disagreement on this scale, affecting the unity of the church and indeed the very nature of the gospel, could not be left unresolved: Peter himself, we may be sure, was not happy with the embarrassing situation in which he was placed. A meeting of the Jerusalem apostles and elders, commonly called the Council of Jerusalem, was convened to consider the issue, and observers from the church of Antioch were invited to attend. Those members of the Jerusalem church who maintained that Gentile converts should be circumcised and submit to Mosaic Law were given an opportunity to express their views, but the apostles and elders resolved that no such conditions should be imposed—that Gentile Christians should simply be required to abstain from eating blood or the flesh of animals sacrificed to pagan divinities, and from fornication, including perhaps marital unions within bounds forbidden by Jewish rules (Acts 15:23-29). If Gentile Christians agreed to those terms, the barrier to table fellowship would be removed; and most of them agreed very readily.

Peter must certainly have welcomed this resolution of the dilemma. When Paul, however, was later consulted by his converts at Corinth about the eating of meat sacrificed to idols, he replied that eating such meat was harmless unless it violated one's own conscience or scandalized a fellow Christian. As for the ban on fornication, Paul agreed that fornication contravened the order of creation and frustrated the purpose of God in creating the human race male and female.

2.9. In Macedonia and Achaia. One of the messengers chosen by the Jerusalem church to convey the findings of the Council to the Gentile churches of Syria and Cilicia was Silas or Silvanus, in whom Paul found a congenial companion. He invited him to join him in a missionary expedition to the west. Traveling by land through Asia Minor, they first visited the churches which Paul and Barnabas had planted a few years earlier. At Lystra Paul found Timothy, a young convert of his, whom he invited to accompany him; Timothy became his devoted and lifelong lieutenant. Their westward journey would have taken them to Ephesus, which may have been Paul's goal, but they were diverted from this course in circumstances which they recognized to be tokens of the Holy Spirit's (*see* Holy Spirit II) guidance, and proceeded in a northwest direction until they reached the Aegean Sea at Alexandria Troas. There they took ship for Neapolis in Macedonia.

In Macedonia they preached the gospel and planted churches in three cities, Philippi, Thessalonica and Berea; but after a short stay in each they were forced to leave when riotous demonstrations had been stirred up against them—in Philippi because of their alleged interference with citizens' property rights and in the other cities through the activity of opponents within the Jewish community.

Philippi and Thessalonica stood on the great Egnatian Way, linking the Aegean with the Adriatic; and Paul may have thought of going on to its western terminus and crossing over to Italy. This would have been one of the many occasions when he planned to visit Rome (as he tells the Roman Christians in Rom 1:13). If so, his inability to continue farther west was providentially ordered, for had he gone on he would have met Jews (including Jewish Christians) traveling east because of Claudius's expulsion edict of A.D. 49 (see Acts 18:2). As it was, Paul had to turn off the Egnatian Way, and soon found himself compelled to leave Macedonia altogether. He was taken away from Berea for his own safety by his friends in that city and, after a short stay in Athens, proceeded to Corinth.

Paul's brief mission in Macedonia proved in fact to have been amazingly successful; the churches of Macedonia gave him much cause for encouragement and thanksgiving. But at the time the Macedonian venture must have seemed a failure, in spite of the clear signs of divine guidance which led him and his colleagues to undertake it. He left Macedonia in deep depression and arrived in Corinth, as he confessed, "in weakness and fear and much trembling" (1 Cor 2:3). If Macedonia had shown itself so unwelcoming, Corinth would surely be more so: its public reputation promised no receptive soil for the gospel seed. But nevertheless Paul was able to spend eighteen months in Corinth, preaching the gospel and building up the church, with no serious molestation (*see* Corinthians, Letters to the).

Here Paul met Priscilla and Aquila, a married couple who had left Rome when Claudius expelled the Jews of the city. In them he found helpful and devoted friends for life (cf. Rom 16:3-5).

One serious attempt was made to put an end to Paul's activity during his Corinthian ministry. Some Jewish leader in the city charged him before Gallio, lately arrived as proconsul of the province of Achaia, of propagating a form of religion not authorized by Roman law. A decision by so authoritative an imperial officer would have much greater weight than a ruling by a city magistrate. Had Gallio sustained the charge, the progress of the gospel would have been impeded not only in Achaia but elsewhere throughout the empire. Having heard the charge, however, he concluded that it involved a dispute about interpretations of the Jewish Law and refused to take it up. Negative as Gallio's action was, it worked to Paul's advantage: he continued his work unhindered.

The mention of Gallio in Acts 18:12 provides a fixed point for the chronology of Paul's career. An inscription at Delphi, recording a directive issued by Claudius within the first seven months of A.D. 52, refers to Gallio as recently proconsul of Achaia. The implication is that he became proconsul in the early summer of 51. We know from other sources that because of poor health he did not remain in the office long. Paul's eighteen-month stay in Corinth may safely be dated between the fall of 50 and the spring of 52.

By the time the work in Corinth was finished, Paul had left behind a large and gifted Christian community, although there were times in the following years when he had to regret its deficiency in moral ballast.

2.10. In Ephesus and Proconsular Asia. Paul's next base of operations was the city of Ephesus, in the province of Asia, where he settled for the greater part of three years. Those years mark one of the most fruitful phases of his whole apostolic ministry. The evangelization of the province was accomplished through the activity of Paul and several of his colleagues. One of these, Epaphras, served as the evangelist of the Lycus valley, where his labors resulted in the founding of churches in Hierapolis, Laodicea and Colossae (Col 1:7-8; 4:12-13).

The work was not accomplished without hazards; some of these are recorded by Luke, and others are alluded to by Paul himself. They may have included one or two of the frequent imprisonments which he mentions in 2 Corinthians 11:23. It is doubtful, however, if any of his prison letters is to be dated during an Ephesian imprisonment. Luke describes in graphic detail the riotous demonstration against Paul and his preaching in the great theater of Ephesus (Acts 19:19-41). Paul's activity was perceived as an economic threat to those tradesmen who depended for their livelihood on the cult of Artemis, the great goddess of the city whose temple was one of the seven wonders of the ancient world. But the greatest personal danger which he encountered in those years, toward the end of his Ephesian ministry, is referred to by Paul himself in 2 Corinthians 1:8-10. He speaks of a situation so threatening that death seemed inevitable, and when, against all odds, deliverance finally came, he greeted it as a token of God's power to raise the dead. It has been argued that this perilous occasion was connected with the crisis resulting from the assassination of M. Junius Silanus, in the latter part of A.D. 54. The situation was probably so unfavorable for Paul that an appeal to Caesar, the course which normally lay open to a Roman citizen, would have been counterproductive.

It was almost certainly this experience that brought home to him the likelihood that he would not survive to witness the Lord's parousia (*see* Eschatology II). In earlier references to the Parousia and the attendant resurrection, he tends to include himself among those who would still be alive then; from now on he tends to include himself rather among those who will be raised from the dead. For the first time, so far as the evidence goes, he considers seriously what his condition will be immediately after death: his conclusion, as set out in 2 Corinthians 5:1-10, is that he will not remain in a state of "nakedness" for one moment; he will be "clothed upon" forthwith with the housing even now reserved for him in heaven. By "nakedness" he means the lack of all means of communication with the environment, and for Paul the believer's environment immediately after death is summed up in the words "at home with the Lord" (2 Cor 5:8).

Some Pauline students, notably C. H. Dodd, have envisaged what they describe as Paul's "second conversion" around this time. This is not simply a matter of the shift in eschatological perspective just mentioned: Dodd draws attention to a change of temper in the later letters. Paul is less sharp in his polemic, less insistent on his status, more relaxed in his attitude toward those fellow Christians who tried to make his apostolic task more difficult than it need be. The contrast has often been pointed out between Paul's unrestrained denunciation of the intruders in the churches of Galatia (Gal 1:6-9; 5:10, 12) and his charitable reference to those Christian opponents (in Rome, possibly) who thought they could rub salt into his wounds by taking advantage of his imprisonment to preach the gospel the more energetically (Phil 1:15-18). True, the difference in the two situations must not be overlooked, but the change of temper is unmistakable. Whether the change was gradual, or

precipitated by some crisis like that described in 2 Corinthians 1:8, cannot be said with confidence. But a passage like Philippians 3:7-16 helps us to "see most clearly what experience had made of this naturally proud, self-assertive, and impatient man" (Dodd, 81).

Another experience which profoundly influenced Paul's attitude to life was one which he dates several years before this, although it is only now—at the end of his Ephesian ministry—that he records it (2 Cor 12:2-10). A mystical experience left him with a physical disability, which he calls a "thorn in the flesh." Whatever its precise nature was, it evidently threatened to incapacitate him from continuing his apostolic activity, and he prayed three times that it might be taken away. Instead of having his prayer answered, he received the assurance that the grace of Christ would enable him to live with it; in fact, he learned to rejoice in it because it helped him to be more completely reliant on the power of Christ at work in his weakness.

2.11. The Collection for Jerusalem. Toward the end of his Ephesian ministry Paul was busily engaged in organizing in the churches he had planted east and west of the Aegean a collection for the relief of the chronic poverty of the Jerusalem church. On the occasion when he and Barnabas met James, Peter and John in Jerusalem, those three "pillars" urged on them that they should "remember the poor" in the mother church (Gal 2:10). Paul treated this as a solemn obligation both then and subsequently throughout his ministry. As for this special collection, one impelling force behind it was his strong desire to bind the Gentile churches and the Jerusalem church more closely together. The Gentile churches probably imagined that they could get along quite well without Jerusalem, and many members of the Jerusalem church looked with serious misgivings on Paul's preaching of a Law-free gospel and on the Gentile churches founded on the basis of that preaching. If a bond of gratitude, confidence and love could be forged between Jerusalem and the churches of his own mission field, Paul would feel that his ministry had been truly worthwhile. A generous gift would persuade the mother church that the Gentiles' commitment to the gospel was genuine and practical. So he urged his converts by letter and, where practicable, by personal visits to give as generously as possible to this good cause. He also encouraged a spirit of competition when, for example, he depicted the Macedonian churches' sacrificial generosity in glowing terms to the Corinthians, and praised the Corinthians' prompt response to the Macedonians.

In Paul's eyes, moreover, the delivery of the collection in Jerusalem would be the climax of his apostolic service thus far, the visible sign of that "offering of the Gentiles" which he planned to present to God in Jerusalem as the crown of his "priestly service" (Rom 15:16). He hoped to consummate his thanksgiving for the past and his dedication for the future by an act of worship in the Temple, where the Lord had appeared to him many years before and sent him "far away to the Gentiles" (Acts 22:21).

2.12. Arrest in Jerusalem; Trial in Caesarea; Journey to Rome. After his long and fruitful ministry in the province of Asia, Paul revisited the churches of Macedonia and Achaia. He and some of his colleagues, especially Titus, helped them to complete their contributions to the collection. It was probably at this time, too, that he traveled west along the Egnatian Way and turned north in the direction of Illyricum (Rom 15:19).

After spending the winter of 56-57 in Corinth he set sail for Judea in company with representatives of the Gentile churches appointed to carry their churches' contributions to Jerusalem. The presence of these men, Paul hoped, would be a further witness to the Jerusalem church of the divine blessing on his Gentile mission. But Paul's final visit to Jerusalem turned out disastrously. In the Temple precincts he was set upon by some of his old enemies from proconsular Asia who accused him of sacrilege (polluting the sacred area by bringing Gentiles into it). He was taken into custody by the commander of the Roman garrison in the Antonia fortress and sent to Caesarea to stand trial before the procurator Felix. After two years' procrastination on the part of his detainers, he exercised the privilege of a Roman citizen and appealed to have his case transferred to the hearing of the emperor in Rome, and was sent there to have his appeal dealt with. After two years under house arrest in Rome, he was summoned to appear before the supreme court when at last his case came up for hearing. What the outcome was cannot be determined with certainty. The record of Acts comes to an end just before the hearing. Paul's letter to the Philippians, written apparently when court proceedings were imminent, shows that he was equally prepared for a favorable or unfavorable outcome—acquittal (followed by liberty for further ministry) or conviction (followed by execution)—although he thought it more probable that he would be acquitted.

That he was in fact acquitted and eventually realized his hope of preaching the gospel in Spain is assumed or implied by several writers from Clement of Rome onward (Clement does not actually mention Spain, but it is difficult to see what else he could have meant by "the limit of the west" which, in *1 Clem.* 5.7, he says that Paul reached before he was "taken up into the holy place"). But it is not clear that any of these had firm evidence for this belief, other than an inference from Romans 15:23-29, where Paul speaks of his plan, after the delivery of the Jerusalem relief fund, to begin the evangelization of Spain and to visit Rome on the way.

There is a tradition (accepted by Eusebius and Jerome) that after being acquitted when his appeal was heard, Paul was arrested again and subjected to the more rigorous imprisonment and trial in Rome to which reference is made in 2 Timothy 1:16-18; 4:16-18. There was no acquittal this time; he was convicted and beheaded with the sword at the third milestone on the Ostian Way, at a place called Aquae Salviae, and buried on the site covered by the basilica of St. Paul Outside the Walls—a probably authentic location. These last proceedings against him may well have been an incident in Nero's proceedings against Christians about A.D. 65.

3. Paul's Missionary Policy and Message.

Paul's missionary policy was to win as much of the Gentile world for Christ as was possible within his lifetime, and when it began to be evident that the task would not be completed within his lifetime he tried—not without success, it appears—to bring the Christian community of Rome to share his vision.

3.1. The Mission of the Apostle. The carrying out of this policy did not require the presentation of the gospel to every individual in the areas which he evangelized; it did require the planting of local churches to serve as self-propagating cells in those areas (*see* Church II). His plan involved pioneer evangelism, preaching the gospel, as he said, "not where Christ has already been named" (Rom 15:20-21), but laying the foundation himself.

A combination of strategic planning and re-

c. 33	Call to apostleship; mission in Arabia (Gal 1:15-17)
35	Short visit to Jerusalem (Gal 1:18-20)
35-45	In Cilicia, Syria, Antioch
46	Conference with "pillars" in Jerusalem (Gal 2:1-10); famine relief delivered from Antioch (Acts 11:27-30)
47-48	Paul and Barnabas in Cyprus and Anatolia (Acts 13:4—14:28)
48/49	Council of Jerusalem; apostolic decree (Acts 15:6-29)
49-51/52	Paul and Silas/Silvanus in Macedonia and Achaia; churches of Philippi, Thessalonica, Berea and Corinth planted (Acts 16:9—18:18)
51/52	Paul's hasty visit to Jerusalem, Antioch and Anatolia
52-55	Paul in Ephesus (Acts 19:1—20:1)
55-57	Paul in Macedonia, Illyricum and Corinth (Rom 15:19; 16:23)
57	Last visit to Jerusalem; arrest and loss of liberty (Acts 21:17—23:35)
57-59	Imprisonment in Caesarea (Acts 23:35—26:32)
59-60	Journey to Italy (Acts 27:1—28:15)
60-62	House arrest in Rome (Acts 28:16-31)
? 62	Paul's hearing before Caesar
64	Great fire of Rome

Chronological table

sponsiveness to divine guidance was called for. The whole enterprise was undertaken "by the power of the Holy Spirit" (Rom 15:19), and the Spirit's guidance was experienced at special junctures, as when his steps were diverted from the westward road to Ephesus and directed toward Troas and so to Macedonia (Acts 16:6-10). Paul may have discerned the Spirit's overruling, too, in the repeated obstacles placed in the way of his plan to visit Rome up to the time of his writing to the church of that city (Rom 1:13; 15:22). On the other hand, he discerned supernatural interference from a different source at times: "Satan hindered us" is his explanation of the factors which prevented him from returning to Thessalonica after his forced and hasty departure from it (1 Thess 2:18).

When he wrote to the Roman Christians, he regarded his work east and west of the Aegean as completed: "I no longer have any room for work in these regions" (Rom 15:23).

His achievement during those years, as "from Jerusalem and as far round as Illyricum" he "fully preached the gospel of Christ" (Rom 15:19), is impressive on any showing. As R. Allen has put it, in A.D. 47 there were no churches in the provinces of Galatia, Asia, Macedonia and Achaia. Now, ten years later, these four provinces had been evangelized so thoroughly that Paul could speak of his work in that part of the world as done, and he was planning to repeat a similar program in the Western Mediterranean.

Paul's evangelistic work was thus extensive rather than intensive. He concentrated on the principal cities situated along the main roads, assisted at times by colleagues working either in those cities or in neighboring ones. During his Ephesian ministry, for example, his colleagues worked in outlying parts of the province of Asia (like Epaphras in the Lycus valley), while he himself was active in Ephesus, so that "all the residents of (proconsular) Asia heard the word of the Lord, both Jews and Greeks" (Acts 19:10).

3.2. The Mission of the Churches. The local churches planted by Paul throughout these provinces may have preserved some family likeness to the synagogue although, being based on a Law-free gospel, they were separate from the synagogue. In some measure they resembled other private associations for religious or charitable purposes, attested in various parts of the Hellenistic world. But Paul maintained a continuing pastoral care for them, for his aim was that each church should be an extension of his apostolic ministry. Once he had established a church and given it basic teaching, his hope was that he could pass on to another place in the confidence that it would take up his gospel witness and spread the message. Thus, only a few weeks after he left Thessalonica, he could praise the young church he had left behind there because, as he said, "not only has the word of the Lord sounded forth from you in Macedonia and Achaia, but your faith in God has gone forth everywhere" (1 Thess 1:8).

Such a church was not encouraged to think of itself as "a garden walled around," mainly concerned to prevent any encroachment by the surrounding wilderness; rather, it was its business to take over more and more of the surrounding wilderness.

The Roman world had to be evangelized as soon as possible. The time was limited. Paul knew himself to be the Lord's special agent in the enterprise. His was not the only mission to the Gentiles, but he "worked harder than any of them" (1 Cor 15:10). He might not live to finish the task, but he would do as much as he could while he could, planting one "colony of heaven" (Phil 3:20) after another, so that in every area within the apostolic sphere allotted to him Christ might be represented, proclaimed and glorified. The churches were to "shine as lights in the world" (Phil 2:15); thus an ever-increasing number of people would come to see "the light of the gospel of the glory of Christ" (2 Cor 4:4).

3.3. Apostolic Authority and the Churches. The Pauline churches do not appear to have been linked together in any formal or visible organization. Paul was their founding apostle, and it was through his apostolic authority that the authority of Christ, the Lord of all the churches, was conveyed to them and accepted by them. But the one example of anything that could be called organization among Paul's churches is his organizing of the relief fund for the poor of the Jerusalem church (1 Cor 16:1-4, etc.). The care and practical wisdom which are so manifest in the organization of the relief might have been exercised in organizing the life and administration of individual churches, or of groups of churches. But Paul evidently was little concerned about this kind of organization. He was concerned, indeed, that in each of his churches there should be some members who were qualified to provide spiritual guidance for the others. He preferred to let such an aptitude develop and become apparent in the course of time (weeks or months rather than years). And if he thought that a church was slow in recognizing the qualities of leadership in this person or that, he would draw attention to them. The church of Corinth is urged, for example, to take note of the household of Stephanus, who "have devoted themselves to the service of the saints," and to "be subject to such people and to every fellow worker and laborer" (1 Cor 16:15-16).

The Corinthian Christians were perhaps impatient of anything in the nature of authority. In the church of Philippi, on the other hand, an orderly administration of "overseers (bishops) and deacons" was established within ten or twelve years from its foundation (Phil 1:1). But even in writing to the Philippian church Paul can recommend a man like Epaphroditus as specially worthy of honor because of his self-sacrificing devotion to the work of Christ (Phil 2:29-30).

The Pauline churches tended naturally to have features in common, but no attempt was made to impose conformity by regulation. Paul deprecated one of his churches for stepping completely out of line with the others; but if it insisted on doing so, all he could say was, "If any one is disposed to be contentious, we recognize no other practice, nor do the churches of God" (1 Cor 11:16)—in other words, if there are those who are determined to be out of step, let them recognize that that is what they are.

Individual members might in an extreme case be excommunicated from the local fellowship, like the incestuous man at Corinth whose public life subverted the ethics of the gospel and brought the Christian name into disrepute in a permissive pagan city—though even so this drastic measure was designed for his ultimate salvation (1 Cor 5:5). But there was no means of unchurching a church—not that Paul would have contemplated such a self-defeating thing as the disowning of a group of his own spiritual children, the "seal" of his "apostleship in the Lord" (1 Cor 4:14-16; 9:2).

In all these things, discipline, administration and others, the presence and directive power of the Holy Spirit were so real to Paul that he implies them even where he does not explicitly mention them. If he did not trust his converts, corporately or individually, to advance along the lines he laid down for them, his "ways in Christ" (1 Cor 4:17), he trusted the Holy Spirit to work in his converts.

The Pauline communities were thus equipped to carry on his ministry in the world. They were not debarred by food restrictions or the observance of sacred days from sharing meals or other forms of social fellowship with their pagan neighbors (1 Cor 10:27-30). Only unambiguous idolatry or sexual immorality were barred. Not by segregation but by participation could they most effectively shine among their neighbors "as lights in the world, holding forth the word of life" (Phil 2:15-16).

3.4. Baptism and the Lord's Supper. *Baptism and the *Lord's Supper were two primitive institutions in the church which Paul "received" from those who were in Christ before him and which he perpetuated in the churches of his own founding.

Baptism was initiatory. It might have been inferred from Jesus' words to the apostles, "John baptized with water, but . . . you shall be baptized with the Holy Spirit" (Acts 1:5; 11:16), that baptism in water would be superseded by baptism in the Spirit; but in fact it turned out otherwise. Baptism in water acquired a new significance from its association with the gift of the Spirit. "In one Spirit," Paul reminds his Corinthian converts, "we were all baptized into one body, . . . and we were all watered (*epotisthēmen*) with one Spirit" (1 Cor 12:13). Baptism is no individual experience: "All of us who have been baptized into Christ Jesus were baptized into his death, . . . so that . . . we too might walk in newness of life" (Rom 6:3-4); "as many of you as were baptized into Christ have put on Christ; . . . for you are all one in Christ Jesus" (Gal 3:27-28). To be baptized in the Christian sense involves becoming a member of Christ corporate—through the Spirit sharing the life of the exalted Christ together with all others who are united with him by faith.

Paul might not have left us his understanding of the Lord's Supper if his converts, more particularly in Corinth, had not conducted themselves at times in such a way as to give the lie to its significance. It was a meal in which they celebrated from time to time their fellowship with Christ and with one another. But those members of the church who ostensibly participated in Christ at "the table of the Lord" and also felt free to share a meal in a pagan temple, under the patronage of the divinity worshiped there, effectively denied their Christian profession (1 Cor 10:14-22). So too, those who ostensibly celebrated their fellowship with their brothers and sisters in Christ at the common memorial meal but acted uncharitably or inconsiderately toward some of them, especially the poorer or underprivileged, were "guilty of profaning the body and blood of the Lord" and brought judgment, not blessing, on themselves by their eating and drinking (1 Cor 11:17-32).

Neither baptism nor the Lord's Supper serves as a supernatural prophylactic against divine judgment, somehow counteracting the law of sowing and reaping. They signify and seal God's pardoning grace, with its ethical implications in believers' lives; those who think that they stand firm must therefore take heed lest they fall (1 Cor 10:11).

4. Paul's Abiding Influence.

4.1. In the Early Centuries. Paul was venerated as a saint, apostle and martyr throughout most of the church after his death. There were indeed some judaizing traditions which execrated his memory—those, for example, whose influence can be traced in the pseudo-Clementine literature of the third and fourth centuries—but they did not affect the mainstream of Christian thought.

The Roman church laid a special claim to him because it was in Rome that he spent his closing days and consummated his apostolic career in martyrdom. His funerary monument on the Ostian Way was pointed out with some pride by Roman Christians toward the end of the second century as though it enhanced the apostolic authority of their church. Indeed, Paul was accorded the honor of being joint-founder, along with Peter, of the Roman church—an honor which Paul himself would have deprecated. And nearly all the churches with which he is associated in the NT record made the most of that association (only in Ephesus did his name tend to be overshadowed by that of "John, the disciple of the Lord").

But while Paul's memory was revered, his message was to a large degree simply not comprehended. To know oneself to be freely justified by the grace of God and to rejoice in the liberty of the Spirit were experiences enjoyed by all too few Christians in the post-Pauline generations. Ignatius of Antioch did not enjoy them, as he hoped that his final acceptance with God would be secure when his bones were crunched by the teeth of the wild beasts. On his more pedestrian level Hermas did not enjoy them, as he anxiously feared that by some misdemeanor or other he might have irretrievably forfeited the divine forgiveness.

Paul's Law-free gospel does not readily commend itself to many religious people who prefer to direct their lives, and the lives of others, by rules and regulations. So he was domesticated: the apostle who spoke so "dangerously" (as some thought) of freedom from the Law was transformed into a moralist, not to say a legalist. Until the end of the second century the one man known to us who understood what Paul meant by freedom from the Law was Marcion—and, in Harnack's words, "even in his understanding he misunderstood him" (*History of Dogma* I [London, 1894], 89). Marcion's heresy consisted largely in his pressing Paul's antithesis between grace and Law to what he judged to be its logical conclusion, to the point where the OT, together with the God revealed in the OT, was dismissed as irrelevant to the gospel of Christ, the revealer of the hitherto unknown Father. Because of his heresy, Marcion was unable to transmit his insight into Paul's message to the Christian world: Marcion's teaching was repudiated *in toto*.

Marcion refused to undergird the ethics of the gospel with legal sanctions. When Christian moralists like Tertullian, writing a couple of generations after Marcion's death, asked rhetorically why Christians might not, in the absence of such sanctions, abandon themselves to an extravaganza of sin, Marcion's only answer was "God forbid!" *(absit)*—an answer on which Tertullian poured scorn *(Marc. 1.27)*. It is plain that here Marcion was echoing Paul's indignant question, "Are we to sin because we are not under Law but under grace?" and reacting with the Pauline answer "God forbid!" (Rom 6:15). Perhaps Tertullian knew this quite well but could not resist the temptation to score a debating point. Even so, his argument invited the retort: "And is *your* only reason for abstaining from sin your fear of wrath to come?"

It was through the experience and thought of Augustine that an appreciation of Paul's gospel of grace revived in the church. When Augustine, in his friend's garden at Milan, heard a child singing "*Tolle, lege!*" ("Take up and read!"), it is no accident that it was words of Paul (Rom 13:13-14) that his eyes lighted on, flooding his soul with clear light and dispelling the darkness of doubt (A.D. 386). Others had written about the grace of God before Augustine, but none so fully and systematically and none in such depth. Augustine knew himself, as Paul did, to be the undeserving recipient of divine grace. This appears supremely in his *Confessions* (397-401) rather than in his more formal treatises on grace, in which at times the logic of his arguments and the demands of systematization threaten to impose limits on the inherently limitless freedom and sovereignty of the grace of God.

Even in the *Confessions*, however, a non-Pauline note is struck. In the *Confessions* Augustine has given us perhaps the first great essay in world literature on spiritual introspection. Augustine certainly found Paul speaking eloquent-ly to his own condition, but for this reason there has been an unwarranted tendency to suppose that Paul in his pre-conversion days was prey to the same kind of divided conscience as Augustine. Paul, in fact, gives no hint that he suffered from such an inward conflict. Even while he was actively persecuting the church he maintained a good conscience because he was convinced he was serving God. After his conversion, indeed, when he realized the sinfulness of the course he had been pursuing, he magnified the grace of God which had pardoned him and called him to be an apostle (see Stendahl, 78-96). So Augustine's transmission of the doctrine of grace to the Middle Ages was Pauline in part but not in purity.

4.2. In the Later Centuries. On the theological side, the sixteenth-century Reformation in Europe marked an unprecedented revival of the Pauline message, or at least of one important aspect of it. Martin Luther tells how he was frustrated in his attempt to grasp the argument of Romans by the expression "the righteousness of God" (Rom 1:17). This he took to mean "the righteousness whereby God is righteous and acts righteously in punishing the unrighteous." But when, with further study of Scripture, he "grasped the truth that the righteousness of God is that righteousness whereby, through grace and sheer mercy, he justifies us by faith," then, he says, "I felt myself to be reborn and to have gone through open doors into paradise" (*Luther's Works,* American edition 34 [Philadelphia, 1960], 336-37). As K. Stendahl points out, Luther, like Augustine, found relief from an inner conflict in Paul's message. Luther's conflict was spiritual whereas Augustine's was moral, and in neither respect did they reproduce an experience of Paul's, but God's justifying grace speaks to the widest variety of human conditions.

It may be that Luther's understanding of justification by faith took insufficient account of other aspects of the believer's participation in Christ, including the ethical aspects.

Luther's discovery played a full part in the Evangelical Revival of the eighteenth century, although other influences were also at work, so that it proclaimed a more comprehensive version of the gospel of Paul, in which there is an insistence on "scriptural holiness" alongside the acceptance of justification by faith.

The most important of these other influences was a booklet published in Scotland in 1677,

The Life of God in the Soul of Man, by Henry Scougal, a discovery and exposition of Paul's understanding of the Christian life as "a union of the soul with God, a real participation of the divine nature, the very image of God drawn upon the soul, or, in the apostle's phrase, it is 'Christ formed within us' (cf. Gal 4:19)."

It was the reading of *The Life of God in the Soul of Man* that led to George Whitefield's conversion in 1733, and it was another expositor of Paul who precipitated similar experiences in Charles and John Wesley in 1738. Charles was gripped by his first reading of Luther's commentary on Galatians; the words of Galatians 2:20 came home to him with power: "who loved *me* and gave himself for *me.*" A few days later took place John Wesley's Aldersgate Street experience, when he felt his heart "strangely warmed" as he listened to a reading from Luther's preface to Romans. In his own words, "I felt I did trust in Christ, Christ alone, for salvation; and an assurance was given me that he had taken away *my* sins, even *mine,* and saved *me* from the law of sin and death" (*Journal,* I, 103). This was Paul's gospel manifesting its abiding vital power in personal life, with profound consequences for social life. It was perhaps the combination of two essential elements in Paulinism—the initial appropriation of God's justifying grace and the progressive work of the Spirit, reproducing the Christlikeness in the believer's life—that gave the evangelical revival such a well-balanced quality: concentration on the one without the other produces a lopsided religion.

One might go on into the twentieth century and recall how Karl Barth, starting to read and expound Romans, felt like a man who, clutching in the dark at a rope for support, finds that he has pulled on a bell-rope and made a noise fit to wake the dead. When the first edition of his *Römerbrief* appeared in 1918, it fell, said a Catholic theologian, "like a bomb on the theologians' playground" (K. Adam).

The explosive force of this "bomb" was the voice of Paul himself; and in all the forward movements of the Spirit which we have surveyed, and in others too, it has been the voice of the authentic Paul, the Paul of the capital letters, that has sounded out, making effective his perennial message of liberation. Being dead, Paul continues to speak.

See also ADVERSARIES I; JEW, PAUL THE.

DPL: CHRONOLOGY OF PAUL; MISSION; PASTOR, PAUL AS; PAUL AND HIS INTERPRETERS; PAUL IN EARLY CHURCH TRADITION; SOCIAL SETTING OF MISSION CHURCHES.

BIBLIOGRAPHY. R. Allen, *Missionary Methods: St. Paul's or Ours?* (2d ed.; London: Word Dominion Press, 1930); C. K. Barrett, *Essays on Paul* (London: SPCK, 1982); J. C. Becker, *Paul the Apostle* (Philadelphia: Fortress, 1980); G. Bornkamm, *Paul* (New York: Harper & Row, 1971); F. F. Bruce, *Paul: Apostle of the Heart Set Free* (Grand Rapids: Eerdmans, 1977); W. D. Davies, *Paul and Rabbinic Judaism* (3d ed.; Philadelphia: Fortress, 1980); C. H. Dodd, "The Mind of Paul," in *New Testament Studies* (Manchester: Manchester University Press, 1953) 67-128; J. D. G. Dunn, *A Theology of Paul the Apostle* (Grand Rapids: Eerdmans, 1998); V. P. Furnish, *Theology and Ethics in Paul* (Nashville: Abingdon, 1968); J. J. Gunther, *Paul: Messenger and Exile: A Study in the Chronology of His Life and Letters* (Valley Forge, PA: Judson, 1972); R. Jewett, *A Chronology of Paul's Life* (Philadelphia: Fortress, 1979); S. Kim, *The Origin of Paul's Gospel* (2d ed.; Grand Rapids: Eerdmans, 1984); J. Knox, *Chapters in a Life of Paul* (New York: Abingdon-Cokesbury, 1950); G. Luedemann, *Paul, Apostle to the Gentiles: Studies in Chronology* (Philadelphia: Fortress, 1984); J. McRay, *Paul: His Life and Teaching* (Grand Rapids: Baker, 2003); J. Munck, *Paul and the Salvation of Mankind* (London: SCM, 1959); J. Murphy-O'Connor, *Paul: A Critical Life* (Oxford: Clarendon, 1996); E. P. Sanders, *Paul, the Law, and the Jewish People* (Philadelphia: Fortress, 1983); idem, *Paul* (Oxford: Oxford University Press, 1991); H. J. Schoeps, *Paul* (Philadelphia: Westminster, 1961); T. R. Schreiner, *Paul, Apostle of God's Glory in Christ: A Pauline Theology* (Downers Grove, IL: InterVarsity Press, 2001); K. Stendahl, *Paul Among Jews and Gentiles* (Philadelphia: Fortress, 1976); F. B. Watson, *Paul, Judaism and the Gentiles* (SNTSMS 56; Cambridge: Cambridge University Press, 1986); A. J. M. Wedderburn, ed., *Paul and Jesus: Collected Essays* (JSNTS 37; Sheffield: JSOT, 1989); D. E. H. Whiteley, *The Theology of St. Paul* (Oxford: Basil Blackwell, 1964); B. Witherington III, *The Paul Quest: The Renewed Search for the Jew of Tarsus* (Downers Grove, IL: InterVarsity Press, 1998).

F. F. Bruce

PAUL'S FAMILY AND EDUCATION. *See* PAUL IN ACTS AND LETTERS.

PAUL'S INFLUENCE. *See* PAUL IN ACTS AND LETTERS.

PAUL'S JOURNEYS. *See* PAUL IN ACTS AND LETTERS.

PENTECOST, DAY OF. *See* BAPTISM III; HOLY SPIRIT III.

PEOPLE OF THE LAND. *See* SINNERS.

PESHER. *See* DEAD SEA SCROLLS.

PETER. *See* DISCIPLES; PETER, FIRST LETTER OF.

PETER, FIRST LETTER OF

The Gospels consistently present the apostle Peter as leader and spokesperson among Jesus' disciples, a role he continues to play in the beginnings of the Christian movement as described in the first half of the book of Acts. It is not surprising, therefore, that two NT letters bear his name. The first of these, traditionally called "first" because the other, shorter letter explicitly calls itself the second (2 Pet 3:1), is a remarkably concise and powerful summary of Christian belief and practice.

1. Author and Readers
2. Integrity and Literary Structure
3. Historical and Social Situation
4. Theological Contributions to the Canon

1. Author and Readers.

First Peter follows closely the literary format of the letters of Paul, identifying author and readers in the first two verses of the letter and following the identification with a "grace and peace" formula. It differs from Paul's letters, except for Galatians and Ephesians, in being addressed not to one specific local congregation but to a circle of congregations spread over a considerable geographical area (in this respect, compare Revelation [*see* Revelation, Book of], esp. Rev 1:4-6, 10-11).

1.1. Peter as Implied Author. Just as Paul in five of his letters is "Paul, apostle of Jesus Christ," so this author identifies himself as "Peter, apostle of Jesus Christ" (1 Pet 1:1). Whoever the real author may be, he is writing as the apostle Peter. In the context of the NT canon it appears that Peter is here exercising the judicial authority Jesus gave him (according to Mt 16:19) to bind and loose or is carrying out the command of Jesus

(according to Jn 21:15-17) to feed or shepherd the Christian flock.

Little is made explicitly of this claim of apostolic authority in the rest of the letter. Only three times does the author write in the first person singular. In the first of these instances (1 Pet 2:11) he says "I appeal" *(parakalōn);* in the second, "I appeal to any elders among you," referring to himself not as an apostle but as a "fellow elder and witness to the sufferings of Christ and a sharer as well in the glory to be revealed" (1 Pet 5:1). On the surface this is a more modest claim, but its apparent purpose is to establish collegiality and common ground with the readers, precisely as a great authority figure might do. We might compare Peter with John the prophet describing himself to his readers as "your brother and sharer in the tribulation and kingdom and patient endurance in Jesus" (Rev 1:9; *see* Kingdom of God) or even to the angel who, addressing John, claimed to be a "fellow servant with you and your brothers" (Rev 19:10; 22:9). Such language presupposes a certain status and sense of personal authority on the part of the speaker, and this kind of authority is evident throughout 1 Peter.

In his third use of "I," Peter concludes, "I have written these few lines through Silvanus (whom I consider a faithful brother) to appeal *[parakalōn]* and give testimony that this is true grace from God" (1 Pet 5:12). Then he sends greetings from "the sister [congregation] in Babylon, chosen along with you, and Mark, my son" (1 Pet 5:13). The effect is to locate Peter geographically in "Babylon," probably a metaphorical name for Rome, as in Revelation, and to link him with two of Paul's companions, Silvanus (1 Thess 1:1; 2 Thess 1:1; 2 Cor 1:19) and Mark (Philem 24; Col 4:14; 2 Tim 4:11).

Because of his adoption of the Pauline *letter form and his references to Paul's companions, some interpreters have inferred that the author of 1 Peter wants to present Peter as a friend or an associate of Paul (compare the explicit reference to "our beloved brother Paul" in 2 Peter 3:15). This tendency to make the implied author a Paulinist is a matter of indifference in itself, though the idea is hardly verifiable. But when it leads interpreters to measure the letter by the standards of Paul's writings it fails to do justice to 1 Peter, for then that letter is found to be either lacking the great Pauline themes of justification by faith and life in the Spirit (*see*

853

Holy Spirit) or somewhat inconsistently as exhibiting a derivative brand of Paulinism. Instead 1 Peter should be read on its own terms as a significant independent witness to Christian faith and life.

Not only where he specifically refers to himself, but also throughout the letter, this author wears his identity as "Peter, apostle of Jesus Christ" rather lightly. Jesus called Simon Peter a "rock" (Mt 16:18), but in 1 Peter the "living Stone" is Jesus Christ himself (1 Pet 2:4). Jesus also said to Peter, "You are a scandal to me" (Mt 16:23), but in 1 Peter it is Jesus Christ who is "a stone of stumbling and a rock of scandal" (1 Pet 2:8)—not to the people of God but to unbelievers. The irony is unmistakable. Jesus designated Peter as shepherd to his flock (Jn 21:15-17), but again the author of 1 Peter assigns this role to Jesus, "the Shepherd and Guardian of your souls" (1 Pet 2:25). "Shepherd the flock of God that is in your care," he tells the elders (1 Pet 5:2), but he gives no particular significance to his own role as shepherd. Instead he and the elders together wait for Christ to be revealed, for Christ is the "chief shepherd" (1 Pet 5:4) to whom all sheep and all shepherds are accountable.

The implied author's claim to be "witness to the sufferings of Christ and a sharer as well in the glory to be revealed" (1 Pet 5:1) should not be understood as emphasizing Peter's eyewitness role in relation to either Jesus' life or his *death on the cross (e.g., as in 2 Pet 1:16-18). Strictly speaking, Peter was not an eyewitness to Jesus' sufferings because, with other disciples, he deserted Jesus in Gethsemane and was not present at the crucifixion. Moreover, this author is stressing that which he has in common with the elders to whom he is writing, not that which he can claim and they cannot. He is saying that like them and like the prophets of old (1 Pet 1:11) he bears his witness or testimony to the gospel of Jesus' suffering and vindication as he waits for the future glory to be revealed.

1.2. Peter as Real Author. Early church tradition, where it mentions this letter at all, is unanimous in identifying Peter as its real author. Papias of Hierapolis, writing in the mid-second century from within the general area to which the letter is addressed, accepts the letter's claim to come from Peter, to be written from "Babylon," which Papias understood as Rome, and to convey greetings from Mark, whom Peter called his "son" (1 Pet 5:13; see Eusebius *Hist. Eccl.*

2.15.2). Irenaeus too, who lived first in Asia Minor and then in Gaul, cited 1 Peter late in the second century as Peter's work (Irenaeus *Haer.* 4.9.2; 4.16.5; 5.7.2). The same is true of Tertullian in Roman North Africa (*Scorp.* 12) and Clement of Alexandria in Egypt (e.g., Clement *Paed.* 1.6; Clement *Strom.* 3.12). Origen, also from Alexandria, expressed in one breath acceptance of 1 Peter and doubt about 2 Peter: "Peter, on whom Hades shall not prevail, has left one acknowledged epistle, and, it may be, a second one, for it is doubted" (Eusebius *Hist. Eccl.* 6.25.8; this claims to be from a portion of Origen's commentary on John that is not extant).

Modern scholars, unlike the ancient church, do not universally accept this letter's claim to come from Peter's hand. Peter is indeed the implied author, but is he the real author? Some who hold that 1 Peter is pseudonymous (i.e., that a later author adopted Peter's name as a literary device) argue that the style is far too elegant for Simon Peter, the Galilean fisherman. In Acts 4:13, just after Peter had quoted Psalm 118:22 (the same text he quotes in 1 Pet 2:7), he and his companion, John, are described as "uneducated and ordinary men" (NRSV). Yet 1 Peter contains some of the finest Greek in the NT. Others, pointing to traditions about Peter's martyrdom about A.D. 64 in the persecution under Nero, contend that 1 Peter cannot have been written before that date.

The latter argument is precarious because no one knows when or how Peter died. The testimony of 2 Peter (2 Pet 1:12-15) is that he had ample time to prepare and plan for his departure and is consistent with the notion that he died a natural death. This testimony carries weight even if Peter did not write 2 Peter, for it reflects early Christian belief about Peter's death. The same is true of the reference to his death in John's Gospel (Jn 21:18-19), which is more like a riddle about youth and old age than a prediction of martyrdom. Only later traditions make Peter into a martyr (e.g., Origen, Tertullian, Eusebius and above all *Acts of Peter* 30—41; *1 Clement* 5.4, written from Rome near the end of the first century, is far from clear on the subject).

As to the letter's style, a number of scholars (Selwyn, Kelly, Davids, Marshall) have attributed its actual composition to Silvanus ("through Silvanus," 1 Pet 5:12), but the expression is more likely a commendation of Silvanus as the bearer of the letter—as in the letters of Ignatius to the

Philadelphians (Ign. *Phld.* 11.2), Smyrneans (Ign. *Smyr.* 12.1), Romans (Ign. *Rom.* 10.1) and Polycarp (Ign. *Pol.* 8.1), and of Polycarp to the Philippians (Pol. *Phil.* 14.1). Although this hypothesis has become popular among some scholars as a defense of Petrine authorship, its effect is to make Silvanus and not Peter the real author of the letter, just as Mark and not Peter was identified as author of the Gospel of Mark (*see* Mark, Gospel of, §1.2). At least one defender of this hypothesis allows the possibility that Peter "may have never even seen" the letter, "having given only the briefest of instructions" to Silvanus (Davids, 7).

The notion that Peter had help in the composition of this letter does not stand or fall with the theory about Silvanus. If 1 Peter is, as it appears to be, an encyclical on behalf of the church at Rome ("Babylon") to a wide circle of churches on the frontiers of the Roman Empire in five provinces of Asia Minor ("Pontus, Galatia, Cappadocia, Asia and Bithynia," 1 Pet 1:2), then the author would likely have had scribal help with vocabulary and style, and his helpers would likely have remained anonymous. The burden of proof is still on those who reject the letter's claim to come from Peter the apostle.

1.3. The Implied Readers. First Peter shows little or no knowledge of the circumstances of its readers because they are spread over a huge and distant geographical area, and all we can know about the readers is the way in which the author visualizes them. Like the readers of Paul's letters, these implied readers are Gentiles who have come to believe in Jesus. They are no longer slaves to "the impulses that once drove [them] in [their] ignorance" (1 Pet 1:14) but are "redeemed from the empty way of life that was [their] heritage" (1 Pet 1:18). They have given up their former "acts of immorality and lust, drunken orgies, feasts, revelries and lawless acts of idolatry" (1 Pet 4:3). Through Jesus Christ they have come to faith and hope in the one true God, the God of Israel (1 Pet 1:21). Christian salvation is theirs, but they lack a past and a sense of identity. The letter confers on them a Jewish past and a quasi-Jewish identity by claiming that certain titles of privilege once given to Israel are now theirs as well. They are "a chosen race, the king's priesthood, a holy nation, a people destined for vindication" (1 Pet 2:9a; cf. Ex 19:6; Is 43:20-21).

Just as in ancient Israel, such privileges carry corresponding responsibilities. Like the Jews, these Gentile Christians are a *diaspora*, a chosen people scattered and living as strangers in a hostile world (1 Pet 1:1). Their task is to "be holy in all [their] conduct" (*anastrophē*, 1 Pet 1:15) and in this way to "sound the praises of him who called [them] out of darkness to his marvelous light" (1 Pet 2:9). The society they live in is hostile, but Roman magistrates are fair (1 Pet 2:13-17). Their responsibility is to "show respect for everyone and love for the brotherhood, reverence toward God and respect for the emperor" (1 Pet 2:17). This will not keep them from being accused of wrongdoing (1 Pet 2:12; 3:15-16; 4:15-16), but the hope is that when they are, their accusers will either be "put to shame" (1 Pet 3:16) or will, "from observing your good works, glorify God on the day of visitation" (1 Pet 2:12).

The readers' life situation is not a local or specific one but rests on the author's generalization about the situation of Christians in Roman society at the time the letter was written. In the author's mind his readers represent all Christian believers everywhere. For this reason the classification of 1 Peter as one of the catholic or general letters is an appropriate one.

2. Integrity and Literary Structure.

2.1. Integrity. Efforts to call into question the literary integrity of 1 Peter have been largely rejected in recent years. Arguments that part of the letter (1 Pet 1:3—4:11) was originally a baptismal sermon for new converts or even a full baptismal liturgy (*see* Worship), common in an earlier generation (e.g., Cross), are seldom made today. Nor has C. F. D. Moule's suggestion of a break between 1 Peter 4:11 and 1 Peter 4:12 found much recent support. Moule argued that persecution, a rather remote possibility in 1 Peter 1:3—4:11, becomes an urgent matter in 1 Peter 4:12—5:11. Either the author received sudden news of a wave of persecution or deliberately planned two letters, one for congregations faced with social pressures but not outright persecution (1 Pet 1:1—4:11; 5:12-14) and a shorter, more urgent one for congregations already suffering the "fiery trial" (1 Pet 1:1—2:10; 4:12—5:14). All such theories are speculative and without support in ancient manuscripts.

2.2. Literary Structure. There is a discernible break in structure between 1 Peter 4:11 and 12, even though it does not call the letter's integrity into question. The break is marked by the direct address "Beloved" (NRSV) or "Dear friends" (NIV; *agapētoi*) in 1 Peter 4:12. The same personal address marks a similar break at 1 Peter 2:11. The two appeals divide the letter into three main parts followed by a postscript: 1 Peter 1:1—2:10; 1 Peter 2:11—4:11; 1 Peter 4:12—5:11.

The first part centers on the implied readers' identity as people of God, based on their spiritual rebirth (1 Pet 1:3, 22-23; 2:2-3) and consequent hope of salvation (1 Pet 1:5, 9-10; 2:3). Peter announces their identity programmatically in 1 Peter 1:1-2 and confirms it in 1 Peter 2:9-10, framing the whole section. Within this framework he interweaves a recital of what God has done and will do (1 Pet 1:3-12, 18-21, 2:4-8) with a reminder of their responsibility to live in hope as a holy people (1 Pet 1:13-16), in reverent fear of the God who saved them at infinite cost (1 Pet 1:17-19), with love for each other and a desire for God (1 Pet 1:22; 2:1-3).

The second section is an appeal to the implied readers (1 Pet 2:11) focusing on their responsibility to show reverence toward God, love for one another, and honor and respect for everyone, starting with the emperor (1 Pet 2:13-17). Peter urges peace and respect specifically toward those who denounce their Christian faith and accuse them of wrongdoing (1 Pet 2:12; 3:16). He envisions social conflict in the setting of the Roman household, among Christian slaves owned by non-Christian masters (1 Pet 2:18-25) and Christian wives married to unbelieving husbands (1 Pet 3:1-6). His so-called household duty codes (unlike those in Col 3:18—4:1; Eph 5:21—6:9) are oriented more to relationships of Christians with unbelievers, even in the same household, than with one another and stand at the heart of the letter's ethical demands. Christians are called to do good in the face of slander and threats (1 Pet 3:8-9), just as Christ did (1 Pet 2:22-23), with full assurance that God will vindicate them (1 Pet 3:16-17; 4:5-6) as he vindicated Christ in the resurrection and victorious journey to heaven (1 Pet 3:18-22). Peter then accents the responsibility of Christians toward God and one another by urging mutual love, ministry and hospitality within the believing community and concludes with a doxology (1 Pet 4:7-11).

The third section reiterates the themes of the second, with particular attention to congregations ruled by the older members, or elders. The address in 1 Peter 4:12 ("dear friends") anticipates 1 Peter 5:1, "To any elders among you I appeal" (cf. 1 Pet 2:11, "Dear friends, I appeal"). Peter's intent is to develop further the admonitions he began in 1 Peter 4:7-11 by spelling out more fully the mutual responsibilities of older and younger members of the congregations, at least those congregations that operated with such a distinction. But he digresses (1 Pet 4:12-19) in order to highlight again and with greater urgency the themes of the previous section in light of his stated conviction that "the end of all things is near" (1 Pet 4:7). Peter sees a "fiery ordeal" (1 Pet 4:12) breaking out and divine judgment beginning "from the house of God" (1 Pet 4:17). With Ezekiel he interprets this to mean that the judgment begins "from the elders" among the people (cf. Ezek 9:6). Therefore he starts with elders and their responsibilities (1 Pet 5:1-4) and moves on to the younger persons and thus to everyone in the congregations (1 Pet 5:5) in relation to the coming crisis (1 Pet 5:6-9). Again he concludes with a doxology (1 Pet 5:10-11).

Rhetorically, 1 Peter is best described as an appeal, or persuasive discourse. In his postscript (1 Pet 5:12-14) Peter seems to describe the letter as a combination of appeal and testimony (*parakalon kai epimartyrōn*, 1 Pet 5:12), but the two terms are not to be separated. Peter's "testimony" here is not so much the announcement of salvation that underlies his appeal (e.g., in 1 Pet 1:3-12) as the conclusion to the appeal itself. Specifically, it is Peter's solemn assurance that the letter he has just written is "true grace from God" (1 Pet 5:12). The letter is his demonstration of the principle that Christians should use their respective spiritual gifts in ministry to one another, "faithfully administering God's grace in its various forms" (1 Pet 4:10, NIV).

3. Historical and Social Situation.

For the past two hundred years biblical scholarship has tried to determine the precise historical situation out of which or to which individual books of the Bible were written. For the past twenty years or so, equal or greater attention has been given to the social situation or social world of biblical writings.

The difference between the two enterprises, at the simplest level, is that historical investigation deals with what is unique, datable and historically and geographically fixed about the life setting (*Sitz im Leben*) of these ancient works, while social scientific theory looks at factors that are not unique but closely paralleled in other times, places and different—sometimes very different—cultures. In the past, social-scientific study was done under the broad canopy of historical study, but the recent trend has been to separate the two, especially when historical investigation by itself proved inconclusive. In the case of 1 Peter the two disciplines are interrelated but not quite interchangeable.

3.1. Historical Setting. It has become commonplace to define the life setting of 1 Peter as one of suffering or persecution. This has tended to locate the letter historically in a time of known persecution in the Roman Empire, either under Nero (c. A.D. 64), on the assumption that Peter is the real author (Selwyn), or under Trajan in the early second century, on the assumption that the letter is pseudonymous (Beare). A third option, that it was written in Domitian's time (between A.D. 81 and 96), is less common, possibly because the evidence for persecution during that period is weak. But does the letter presuppose a situation of outright persecution? Peter's attitude toward the Roman Empire seems similar to Paul's: "Defer to every human creature for the sake of the Lord, whether to the emperor as sovereign or to magistrates as those sent by him to punish wrongdoers and commend those who do good deeds" (1 Pet 2:13). If anything, he is clearer and more explicit than Paul, who spoke vaguely of "governing authorities" or "those authorities that exist" (Rom 13:1, NRSV). It is difficult to imagine either Paul or Peter writing such words in a time of systematic persecution of Christians.

Yet Peter does refer to "various trials" or ordeals of faith, being "tested by fire" (1 Pet 1:6-7), even of "the fiery ordeal that is taking place among you to test you" (1 Pet 4:12, NRSV). At least some of his rhetoric is the rhetoric of persecution and martyrdom. Christ is the supreme example for Christians precisely as a vindicated martyr, the One who was "put to death in the flesh but made alive in the Spirit" (1 Pet. 3:18; cf. 2:21-24; 4:1-2).

Undeniably, Peter saw himself and his readers in danger, but not from the emperor or provincial governors, whose legitimate task it was "to punish those who do wrong and to praise those who do right" (1 Pet 2:14, NRSV). The threat he saw was from fellow citizens in Rome (and, Peter assumes, in the provinces) who did not share the implied readers' Christian faith and who consequently rejected their distinctive worship and lifestyle. Peter urges, therefore, "that by doing right you should silence the ignorance of the foolish" (1 Pet 2:15, NRSV). The persecution in view is the kind carried out not with fire or sword but with words—words of ridicule, slander and sometimes formal accusations of crimes against society (see 1 Pet 2:12; 3:13-17; 4:14-16).

Such persecution is difficult to locate either chronologically or geographically. It could fit almost any time and place in the Mediterranean world in the late first or early second century. The uncomfortable fact is that we know little or nothing of the historical setting of 1 Peter. It is possible that when Peter says the "time for judgment to begin from the house of God" has come (1 Pet 4:17), he has in mind the destruction of Jerusalem and the Jewish temple in A.D. 70 by the Romans ("Babylon," 1 Pet 5:13) and sees this event as heralding danger for all who worship the God of Israel, Christians as well as Jews. But there is no proof of this. Without clearer points of reference we cannot use contemporary history to illumine the text of 1 Peter.

3.2. Social Setting. Since the 1970s studies of 1 Peter (e.g., Goppelt, Elliott and Balch) have centered more on its social than its historical setting. Whatever its precise historical context, the letter speaks to a situation in which the implied readers are visualized as outsiders in the Roman Empire. Peter writes from a Christian community in "Babylon" (1 Pet 5:13), in Jewish tradition the place of exile and alienation, to Christians who are similarly in exile, a "diaspora" (1 Pet 1:1) scattered as strangers throughout the Roman provinces. For author and implied readers alike, dramatic differences separate their values from those of the societies in which they live.

The works of J. H. Elliott and D. Balch uncovered a tension in 1 Peter between "acculturation" (i.e., conforming where possible to dominant values) and "boundary maintenance" (i.e., the preservation of Christian distinctives in a hostile society). As one observer put it, the letter has two goals at once: "(1) the social cohesion of the Christian groups, and (2) the social adaptation of the Christian groups to their cultural setting. Without the first, Christian identity would have been lost. Without the second, Christians would have had no social acceptability, which is also necessary for survival and outreach" (Talbert, 148).

Christians did have some values in common with the culture of the Mediterranean world, notably the contrasting social realities of honor and shame. Virtually all recent studies of the social world of the NT deal in some way with honor and shame, and in no book of the NT is the contrast highlighted more than in 1 Peter. Both to those addressed in the letter and to their enemies in Roman society, honor was a desirable goal, perhaps the supreme goal in life, while shame was something to be avoided at almost any cost. The radical difference between Christians and their contemporaries lay in what constituted honor and what constituted shame.

Honor to the Romans involved the praise and esteem of fellow citizens, usually with some kind of public recognition of their good deeds either within the household or on behalf of the larger community. Individual deeds of honor brought honor to the family, the state, the emperor and the gods. Shame was the result of antisocial behavior that tended to undermine or discredit these same institutions and consequently to disgrace in the eyes of the community those guilty of such behavior.

According to 1 Peter, honor and shame are determined not by public opinion, the emperor or the Roman gods but solely by the God of Israel, who is Father of those who believe in Jesus and the universal Judge to whom all are accountable (1 Pet 1:17; 4:5). Not their acts of public service but their loyalty to God and faithful endurance of "various trials" are what Christians will exchange for "praise, glory and honor" at the future "revelation of Jesus Christ" (1 Pet 1:6-7). Jesus was slain as God's "faultless and flawless lamb," but God "raised him from the dead and gave him glory" (1 Pet 1:19, 21). Drawing on biblical language (Is 28:16), Peter compares Jesus with "a choice and precious stone, a cornerstone in Zion" and announces that "the person who believes in him will never be put to shame" (1 Pet 2:6). This honor (of never being put to shame) belongs to Christians (1 Pet 2:7), while to unbelievers Christ becomes "a stone for stumbling and a rock to trip over"—a fate to which they were "appointed" (1 Pet 2:8). The dualism of such texts is absolute: Christians are destined for honor and non-Christians for eternal shame.

Yet Peter's values also overlap those of the wider society, for he is willing at times to measure honor and shame by a person's responsibilities to family, the wider community and the state, as well as to God and fellow believers: "Honor everyone," he writes, "love the brotherhood, fear God, honor the emperor" (1 Pet 2:17).

Peter urges his readers to answer the slanderous words of their detractors with kind words and good conduct, "so that in a case [en hō] where they accuse you of doing wrong they may, from observing your good works, glorify God on the day of visitation" (1 Pet 2:12). His goal is not to undermine the social world in which his readers live but to win it over—or at least to win converts from it who will honor the Christian God and receive in return the honor that only God can give. Peter knows this will not always happen. He writes at times as if he suspects it may never happen. But regardless of the outcome, Christians must "always be ready to answer anyone who demands from you an accounting of the hope that is yours . . . out of humility and reverence, with a good conscience, so that in a case [en hō] where you are accused, those who denounce your good conduct in Christ may be put to shame" (1 Pet 3:15-16).

These imagined cases, or occasions when Christians are charged with wrongdoing or antisocial behavior, are for Peter the decisive tests of honor or shame respectively, whether for the accused Christians themselves or their accusers. "Let none of you suffer as a murderer or a thief," he concludes, "or any kind of criminal, or even as a busybody. But if you suffer for being a Christian, do not be ashamed, but glorify God in such a case" (1 Pet 4:15-16, where the text followed by the KJV is to be preferred). To be accused of criminal acts, as Christians occasionally were, or to be slandered as "busybodies" (self-appointed guardians of public morality), as they often were and still are, is no reason for shame, according to Peter. Shame is appropriate only when such charges are true.

Honor in 1 Peter is the reward not of suffering as a virtue in itself but of suffering for doing good. Peter is not encouraging either paranoia or masochism. Make sure, he says, that when you are denounced or accused it is not because you are guilty of wrongdoing or antisocial behavior but solely because of your Christian faith. The Roman ideal of honor and good citizenship is transcended and relativized but not negated. Christians are a counterculture in Roman society, sharing the commitments of other Romans and provincials to the household and the state as long as these commitments do not entail worship of the Roman gods.

At the time of writing, the author is confident of his readers' conduct. While martyrdom is not out of the question (1 Pet 4:6; 5:8-9), neither is it a major theme of the letter. Babylon is still the place of exile, not the throne of Satan or the antichrist, as in the book of Revelation. The stark dualism of 1 Peter is qualified by the realities of life in what we would call a pluralistic society. For Western Christians in the twenty-first century, this brief tract written within a culture not yet Christian becomes a relevant textbook on Christian living in a culture no longer Christian.

4. Theological Contributions to the Canon.

First Peter's place in the NT canon has been a humble one, given Peter's prominence as the rock on which the church would be built (Mt 16:18-19) and the shepherd whose responsibility it was to feed Christ's sheep (Jn 21:15-17). This could be because of the letter's brevity, or because Peter has only two NT letters bearing his name while Paul has twelve, or because 1 Peter has long been yoked with 2 Peter, whose authenticity was disputed from the start. Or perhaps the author's self-deprecating attitude toward his own identity as "Peter" (see 1.1 above) had a lasting influence on how his letter was read. For whatever reason, when Christians spoke of "the apostle," especially in connection with the canon, in the early centuries, they almost always meant Paul, not Peter.

Yet 1 Peter strikes a more even balance than Paul between the teaching and example of Jesus on the one hand and his death and resurrection on the other. More than any other NT letter, 1 Peter completes or extends the testimony of the four Gospels, especially Mark. It does so in three respects. First, it gives the reader a sense of living in a world where Jesus is no longer or not yet visible. Second, it accents Christian discipleship as a journey in Jesus' footsteps to the cross and beyond the cross to heaven. Finally, the victory over "unclean spirits" that began in Jesus' ministry continues in 1 Peter in his resurrection and ascension, assuring his disciples of vindication against their oppressors when he becomes visible once again.

4.1. The Hidden Christ. The "living hope" of Christians (1 Pet 1:3) is not the "coming" *(parousia)* of Jesus, but rather his revelation or apocalypse *(apokalypsis,* see 1 Pet 1:7, 13). When he is revealed, "salvation" (1 Pet 1:5, 9) and "glory" (1 Pet 4:13) will be revealed as well. Jesus appeared or was made visible in the world once and will be again *(phanerōthentes,* 1 Pet 1:20, 5:4).

These are clearly apocalyptic themes in that they deal with a decisive apocalypse or revelation. Yet 1 Peter is not an apocalyptic letter like the book of Revelation. It never calls itself an apocalypse, as Revelation does (Rev 1:1), nor does it claim that Peter, like Paul (Gal 1:12), received a direct revelation from Jesus Christ (contrast 2 Pet 1:16-18). The decisive revelation or apocalypse is future. The only other revelation mentioned was a sort of nonrevelation to the ancient prophets, telling them that their prophecies of Christ were not for themselves or their time but for a distant future that to Peter and his readers is present (1 Pet 1:10-12). 1 Peter is not so much an apocalytic as a preapocalyptic letter. Christians cannot see Jesus now (1 Pet 1:8), but they stand on the threshold of a great apocalypse in which they will see him in all his glory and joyfully embrace the salvation he holds in store for them.

4.2. Discipleship as a Journey. One might conclude from this that the revelation of Jesus Christ and of full salvation is something for which Christians simply wait. Peter's reference to "an indestructible, incorruptible and unfading inheritance reserved in heaven for you" (1 Pet 1:4) is open to such an interpretation. But this is not the case. Salvation is not something that comes to us but something standing at "the end" of an active life of faithfulness (1 Pet 1:9) and toward which we "grow" (1 Pet 2:2). Jesus is viewed not as one who comes to us but as one toward whom we are coming (1 Pet 2:4), first in conversion and then in a lifelong process of being "built into a spiritual house for holy priesthood" (1 Pet 2:5). Peter's favorite metaphor for this process is that of the journey, or "following in Jesus' footsteps" (1 Pet 2:21).

This is the metaphor of the Gospel writers, above all Mark (see Mk 1:16-20; 8:34), and presumably of Jesus. Paul preferred for the most part the nonmetaphorical notion of faith, or believing. Although it can be plausibly argued that Paul understood faith as the equivalent of following Jesus' example of faithfulness, it remained for 1 Peter to bring together Paul's notion of faith and the command of Jesus in the Gospels to follow him as disciples. Whatever "faith" means in Paul, in 1 Peter it includes faithfulness (see 1 Pet 1:5, 7, 9), and faithfulness means following Jesus on a journey to the cross—and beyond (1 Pet 2:21-25).

Already in Mark there is a hint that the journey extends beyond the cross. If it were only a journey to the cross it would be a failure, for the disciples deserted Jesus at his arrest (Mk 14:50). Yet when Jesus predicted their desertion (Mk 14:27), he added, "But after I am raised up, I will go before you [that is, lead you as a shepherd] into Galilee" (Mk 14:28). Ironically it was Peter who protested, "Even though all become deserters, I will not" (Mk 14:29), and it is Peter who seems to allude to the incident: "For you were going astray like sheep, but you have turned now to the Shepherd and Guardian of your souls" (1 Pet 2:25).

The situation of the implied readers corresponds to that of Peter and the original disciples. The journey of Jesus in 1 Peter reaches beyond the cross, beyond Galilee, to heaven itself. As the next chapter makes clear, Jesus not only was "put to death in the flesh" and "made alive in the Spirit" (1 Pet 3:18) but also has "gone to heaven, with angels and authorities and powers in submission to him" (1 Pet 3:22). Consequently the journey of Christian disciples is a journey to heaven as well, like the Christian pilgrimage in the letter to the Hebrews (e.g., Heb 11:10, 16; 12:22; 13:14) or the journey of Christian in John Bunyan's *The Pilgrim's Progress*. The goal of Jesus' faithful followers is nothing less than God's "marvelous light" (1 Pet 2:9) or "eternal glory" (1 Pet 5:10).

First Peter is not alone in the NT in accenting the truth that a believer's whole life (see 1 Pet 1:15, 17; 2:12; 3:1-2, 16) is a journey to heaven in the footsteps of Jesus. Yet its testimony stands as a serious caution against three popular misconceptions: that salvation is merely something that happened to Christian believers in the past, that their only responsibility now is to wait passively for the second coming and that "going to heaven" is something that begins when they die.

4.3. Victory over Evil Spirits. At one other point 1 Peter extends the Markan testimony to Jesus beyond Jesus' ministry on earth and into the time and circumstances of its implied readers. Mark's Gospel pays special attention to incidents in which Jesus drove "unclean spirits" out of those who were demon-possessed (see Mk 1:23-28, 32-34; 3:11-12; 5:1-20; 7:24-30; 9:14-29).

Although several of these stories are repeated in Matthew and Luke, exorcism has no place among the gifts and ministries mentioned by Paul in his letters and plays only a minor role in narratives of the early Christian mission (see Acts 16:16-18, 19:11-16).

Only 1 Peter develops the theme of victory over evil spirits in connection with Jesus' resurrection and ascension (1 Pet 3:18-22). On his way to heaven Jesus "made proclamation" to the spirits, described here as "disobedient spirits" and viewed as offspring of an unnatural union between women and evil angels (Gen 6:1-6; see *1 Enoch* 15:8-10 and the discussions of Dalton and Michaels 1988). In doing so he gained victory over these spirits on behalf of his followers. The implication drawn in 1 Peter is not that those who have passed (like Noah) through water, the saving water of baptism (1 Pet 3:20), now have the power to perform exorcisms but that they have nothing to fear from human oppressors in Roman society who (like the spirits) are "disobedient" to God (see 1 Pet 2:8; 3:1; 4:17). Peter's triumphant message is that Jesus Christ reigns from heaven over all "angels and authorities and powers" (1 Pet 3:22).

4.4. Conclusion. These and other features of 1 Peter not only justify its inclusion in the NT canon but also suggest that its importance within the canon has been underrated. Despite its association with 2 Peter by virtue of common attribution of authorship, all it has in common with 2 Peter is a strong emphasis on the coming judgment of God. Its more significant function in the NT is as a link or a bridge between the Gospels and the letters of Paul.

First Peter seems to signal such a function with its terse references at the end to Paul's companion Silvanus and to "Mark, my son" (1 Pet 5:12-13). Mark was for centuries a neglected Gospel, and if we begin to think of 1 Peter as a sort of companion piece to Mark, in keeping with Papias's tradition about Mark as the inscribing of Peter's memoirs (Eusebius *Hist. Eccl.* 3.39.15), it is perhaps not surprising that this short letter has been neglected as well. The abundance of recent studies may indicate that this "exegetical step-child" (Elliott's term) within the canon is on its way to the rehabilitation it deserves.

See also PETER, SECOND LETTER OF.

DLNTD: HOUSEHOLD CODES; OLD TESTAMENT IN GENERAL EPISTLES.

BIBLIOGRAPHY. **Commentaries:** P. J. Acht-emeier, *1 Peter* (Herm; Minneapolis: Fortress, 1996); F. W. Beare, *The First Epistle of Peter* (3d ed.; Oxford: Blackwell, 1970); E. Best, *1 Peter* (NCB; Grand Rapids: Eerdmans, 1971); P. H. Davids, *The First Epistle of Peter* (NICNT; Grand Rapids: Eerdmans, 1990); J. H. Elliott, *1 Peter* (AB; New York: Doubleday, 2001); L. Goppelt, *A Commentary on 1 Peter,* ed. F. Hahn (Grand Rapids: Eerdmans, 1993); F. J. A. Hort, *The First Epistle of St. Peter 1:1—2:17* (London: Macmillan, 1898); J. N. D. Kelly, *A Commentary on the Epistles of Peter and Jude* (HNTC; Harper & Row, 1969); I. H. Marshall, *1 Peter* (IVPNTC; Downers Grove, IL: InterVarsity Press, 1991); S. McKnight, *1 Peter* (NIVAC; Grand Rapids: Zondervan, 1996); J. R. Michaels, *1 Peter* (WBC; Waco, TX: Word, 1988); B. Reicke, *The Epistles of James, Peter and Jude* (AB; Garden City, NY: Doubleday, 1964); E. G. Selwyn, *The First Epistle of Peter* (2d ed.; London: Macmillan, 1947); D. Senior, *1 and 2 Peter* (NT Message 20; Wilmington, DE: Michael Glazier, 1980). **Studies:** D. Balch, *Let Wives Be Submissive: The Domestic Code in 1 Peter* (SBLMS 26; Chico, CA: Scholars Press, 1981); A. Chester and R. P. Martin, *The Theology of the Letters of James, Peter and Jude* (Cambridge: Cambridge University Press, 1994); F. L. Cross, *1 Peter: A Paschal Liturgy* (London: Mowbray, 1954); W. J. Dalton, *Christ's Proclamation to the Spirits: A Study of 1 Peter 3:18—4:6* (2d ed.; Rome: Pontifical Biblical Institute, 1989); J. H. Elliott, *1 Peter: Estrangement and Community* (Chicago: Franciscan Herald, 1979); idem, *A Home for the Homeless: A Sociological Exegesis of 1 Peter, Its Situation and Strategy* (Philadelphia: Fortress, 1981); T. W. Martin, *Metaphor and Composition in 1 Peter* (SBLDS 131; Atlanta: Scholars Press, 1992); J. R. Michaels, *Word Biblical Themes: 1 Peter* (Dallas: Word, 1989); C. F. D. Moule, "The Nature and Purpose of 1 Peter," *NTS* 3 (1956-57) 1-11; W. L. Schutter, *Hermeneutic and Composition in 1 Peter* (WUNT; Tübingen: Mohr Siebeck, 1989); C. H. Talbert, ed., *Perspectives on First Peter* (NABPRSS; Macon, GA: Mercer University Press, 1986); W. C. van Unnik, "The Teaching of Good Works in 1 Peter," *NTS* 1 (1954-55) 92-110; B. W. Winter, *Seek the Welfare of the City: Christians as Benefactors and Citizens* (Grand Rapids: Eerdmans, 1994).

J. R. Michaels

PETER, SECOND LETTER OF

Second Peter presents itself as a testament or farewell discourse of the apostle Peter, written in the form of a letter shortly before his death (2 Pet 1:14). Its object is to remind the readers of Peter's teaching and to defend this teaching against objections raised by false teachers who were casting doubt on the Christian expectation of the parousia and advocating ethical libertinism.

1. Literary Structure and Genre
2. Attribution to Peter and Date
3. Opponents and Response
4. Theological Character

1. Literary Structure and Genre.
The structure of 2 Peter can be analyzed as follows.

(A = apologetic; E = exhortation/denunciation; L = letter; T = testament):

(L^1) Address and Greeting (2 Pet 1:1-2)
(T^1) Theme: A Summary of Peter's Message (2 Pet 1:3-11)
(T^2) Occasion: Peter's Testament (2 Pet 1:12-16)
(A^1) First Apologetic Section (2 Pet 1:16-21)
Two replies to Objection 1: that the apostles based their preaching of the parousia on human-made myths (2 Pet 1:16-19)
Reply to Objection 2: that OT prophecies were the products of human minds (2 Pet 1:20-21)
(T^3) Peter's Prediction of False Teachers (2 Pet 2:1-3a)
(A^2) Second Apologetic Section (2 Pet 2:3b-10a)
Reply to Objection 3: that divine judgment never happens (2 Pet 2:3b-10a)
(E^1) Denunciation of the False Teachers (2 Pet 2:10b-22)
(T^4) Peter's Prediction of Scoffers (2 Pet 3:1-4) (including Objection 4: 2 Pet 3:4)
(A^3) Third Apologetic Section (2 Pet 3:5-10)
Two replies to Objection 4: that the expectation of the parousia is disproved by its delay (2 Pet 3:5-10)
(E^2) Exhortation to Holy Living (2 Pet 3:11-16)
(L^2) Conclusion (2 Pet 3:17-18)

Second Peter is clearly a letter, since it has a formal letter opening (2 Pet 1:1-2), and the conclusion (2 Pet 3:17-18), while not specifically epistolary in character, can function as a letter closing (*see* Letters, Letter Forms). Moreover, 2 Peter seems to be addressed to those churches or some of those churches to which

1 Peter had been addressed (2 Pet 3:1). As well as being a letter, 2 Peter belongs to the literary genre of testament, well known in the Jewish literature of the period (e.g., *T. Mos.; 1 Enoch* 91—104; *2 Bar* 57—86; 4 Ezra 14:28-36). In such testaments an OT figure, such as Moses or Ezra, knowing that his death is approaching, gives a final message to his people, which typically includes ethical exhortation and prophetic revelations of the future. In 2 Peter, four passages (marked T1-T4 in the analysis above [2 Pet 1:3-11, 12-16; 2:1-3a; 3:1-4]) particularly resemble the Jewish testament literature and clearly identify the work as Peter's testament. In 2 Peter 1:12-15, a passage full of conventional testament language, Peter describes the occasion for writing as his awareness of approaching death and his desire to provide for his teaching to be remembered after his death. The teaching is summarized in 2 Peter 1:3-11, which is a miniature homily, following a pattern used in farewell speeches. It plays a key role in the book as a definitive summary of Peter's ethical and religious instruction. There are also two passages of prophecy (2 Pet 2:1-3a; 3:1-4) in which Peter foresees that after his death his message will be challenged by false teachers.

The rest of 2 Peter is structured around the four passages that belong to the testament genre. It includes three apologetic sections (marked A1-A3 [2 Pet 1:16-21; 2:3b-10a; 3:5-10]) whose aim is to answer the objections the false teachers raise against Peter's teaching. There are four such objections, only the last of which is explicitly stated as such (2 Pet 3:4). In the other three cases the objection is implied in the author's denial of it (2 Pet 1:16a, 20; 2:3b). These apologetic sections give 2 Peter its polemical character as not simply a testamentary statement of Peter's message but also a defense of it against objections. Two passages (marked E1, E2 [2 Pet 2:10b-22; 3:11-16]) contrast the libertine behavior of the false teachers, denounced in 2 Peter 2:10b-22, with the holy living expected of the readers if they are faithful to Peter's teaching (2 Pet 3:11-16).

2. Attribution to Peter and Date.

The problem of the authorship of 2 Peter arises in part out of the form and structure. In the Jewish literature of this period, testaments were pseudepigraphal. They were attributed to OT figures long dead and were probably understood as exercises in historical imagination, putting into the mouth of these figures the kind of thing they might have been expected to say in farewell speeches. This establishes an initial presumption that 2 Peter is likewise a work written in Peter's name by someone else after his death, though it remains possible that the testament genre could have been used by Peter to write his own, real testament.

But it should be noted how the predictive character of the testament genre is used in 2 Peter. Nothing in the letter reflects the situation in which Peter is said to be writing; the work is addressed to a situation after Peter's death. Peter's two predictions of false teachers (2 Pet 2:1-3a; 3:1-4) function as pegs on which is hung the apologetic debate with these false teachers about the validity of Peter's message.

Moreover, whereas the testamentary passages speak of the false teachers in the future tense, predicting their rise after Peter's death (2 Pet 2:1-3a; 3:1-4; cf. 3:17), the apologetic sections and the denunciation of the false teachers refer to them in the present tense (2 Pet 2:3b-22; 3:5-10, 16b). It is hardly possible to read 2 Peter without supposing the false teachers to be contemporaries of the author with whom he is already in debate. The alternation of predictive and present-tense references to them (most obvious in 2 Pet 3:1-10, 16b-17) is therefore best understood as a deliberate stylistic device by which the author conveys that these apostolic prophecies are now being fulfilled. In other words, Petrine authorship is a fiction that the real author does not feel obliged to maintain throughout his work. In that case it must be a transparent fiction, a literary convention that the author expected his readers to recognize as such. (That the author inadvertently slips into the present tense, forgetting that he is meant to be referring to the false teachers from Peter's perspective in the past, is not plausible, because 2 Peter is a carefully composed work, and the alternation of future-tense and present-tense references to the false teachers follows a structural pattern.)

These considerations of literary genre are probably the most important elements in the scholarly consensus that 2 Peter is pseudepigraphal, from which only a few recent discussions of the work still dissent. The most cogent additional reasons for denying Peter's authorship are the Hellenistic religious language and ideas and the evidence for dating the work after Peter's death in the mid-60s (see below). While the use of Hellenistic religious language and ideas by a Palestinian Jew should no longer be regarded as incredible, nevertheless the use of Hellenistic religious terminology is a particularly striking feature of 2 Peter and is more easily attributed to a Christian of Diaspora Jewish or Gentile origin. However, since Peter could have employed a collaborator in writing the letter, this argument cannot be decisive. The dating of the work is probably more significant for the question of authenticity.

It has been common to regard 2 Peter as the latest of the NT writings, to be dated well into the second century, even as late as A.D. 150. But there is no good reason to postulate such a late date. The clearest evidence of a postapostolic date is 2 Peter 3:4, which indicates, in the context of raising the problem of the delay of the parousia (*see* Eschatology), that the first Christian generation, here called "the fathers," has died. The probability is that the letter was written when this had only recently become true, about A.D. 80-90. This was the time when those who had expected the parousia during the lifetime of the generation of the apostles would face the problem of the nonfulfillment of that expectation. There is no evidence that this particular issue continued to be felt as a problem in the second century, though John 21 may hint at the problem.

The literary relationship between 2 Peter and Jude is another consideration that could be relevant to the date of 2 Peter. There are such close resemblances (especially between Jude 4-13, 16-18 and 2 Pet 2:1-18; 3:1-3) that some kind of literary relationship seems certain. Some scholars have held that Jude is dependent on 2 Peter or that both depend on a common source, but most conclude that 2 Peter has used Jude as a source. However, this requires a late date for 2 Peter only if Jude is dated late.

If 2 Peter was written not by Peter but after Peter's death, why did the real author present the work as Peter's testament? Probably because his intention was to defend the apostolic message in the period after the death of the apostles (2 Pet 3:4) against teachers who held that in important respects the teaching of the apostles was discredited. Whereas they were claiming to correct the apostles' teaching, the author of 2 Peter regards it as normative for the postapostolic church. By writing in Peter's name he claims no authority of his own except as a faithful mediator of the apostolic message, which he defends against attacks. The form of the letter as an apostolic testament is therefore closely connected with its apologetic purpose as a vindication of the normative authority of the apostolic teaching. That the author chose to write Peter's testament is probably best explained if he was a leader in the Roman church, which had counted Peter as the most prestigious of its leaders in the previous generation.

3. Opponents and Response.

The false teachers whom the letter opposes have usually been identified as Gnostics, but this identification, as recent scholarship has recognized, is insecure (*see* Adversaries). The only features of their teaching that are clear from the author's refutation of it are eschatological skepticism and moral libertinism. The parousia had been expected during the lifetime of the apostles, but the first generation of Christians had passed away and in the opponents' view this proved the primitive Christian eschatological hope to have been mistaken (2 Pet 3:4, 9a). There would be no eschatological judgment (2 Pet 2:3b), no divine intervention to eliminate evil and to establish a world of righteousness. This attitude seems to have been based on a rationalistic denial of divine intervention in history (2 Pet 3:4b), as well as on the nonfulfillment of the parousia prophecy. But it also related to the ethical libertinism of the opponents. They claimed to be emancipating people from the fear of divine judgment and therefore from conventional Christian morality (2 Pet 2:19a). Evidently they felt free to indulge in sexual immorality and sensual excesses generally (2 Pet 2:2, 10a, 13-14, 18).

This teaching involved a critique of the traditional teaching inherited from the apostles. The opponents claimed that the apostles had invented the idea of the parousia (2 Pet 1:16a) and denied the inspiration of the eschatological prophecies of the OT (2 Pet 1:20-21a). Either they appealed to Pauline teaching about freedom in support of their libertine views or they considered that Paul's expectation of the imminent parousia discredited his teaching. The claim that they distort what Paul wrote (2 Pet 3:16b) could be taken in either of these senses.

There is no basis in 2 Peter for supposing that these teachings had a gnostic basis. There is no indication, for example, of the dualism that is a defining characteristic of gnostic thought. The views of the opponents are more plausibly understood as reflecting popular pagan attitudes and deploying pagan skeptical arguments, such as were used by the Epicureans, about eschatology and revelation. The opponents probably aimed to disencumber Christianity of elements that seemed to them an embarrassment in their pagan cultural context: its cosmic eschatology, alien to most Hellenistic thinking and especially embarrassing after the apparent failure of the parousia hope, and its ethical rigorism, which contrasted with more permissive attitudes in the cultural context.

In response to this challenge, the author of 2 Peter mounts a defense of the apostolic expectation of judgment and salvation at the parousia and of the motivation for righteous living this provides. His definitive summary of Peter's teaching (2 Pet 1:3-11) stresses the need for moral effort if eschatological salvation is to be assured. This positive statement is then backed up by apologetic arguments in the rest of the letter.

The author argues that the apostles' preaching of the parousia was soundly based on their witnessing of the transfiguration of Jesus, when God appointed Jesus to be the eschatological judge and ruler (2 Pet 1:16-18), and on the divinely inspired prophecies of the OT (2 Pet 1:19-21). OT examples prove that divine judgment does happen and prefigure the eschatological judgment (2 Pet 2:3b-10a). As God decreed the destruction of the ancient world in the flood, so he has decreed the destruction of the present world in the fire of his eschatological judgment (2 Pet 3:5-7, 10). The problem of the delay of the parousia is met by traditional arguments drawn from Jewish tradition: that the delay is long only by human standards, not in the perspective of God's eternity, and should be seen as God's gracious withholding of judgment so that sinners may repent (2 Pet 3:8-9; *see* Sin). Such arguments enable the author, at a time when the hope of the parousia had become problematic, not to let it fade by postponing it indefinitely but vigorously to reassert the traditional Christian hope and its relevance. Throughout 2 Peter the author is concerned that the hope for the vindication and establishment of God's righteousness in the future (2 Pet 2:9; 3:7, 13) necessarily motivates the attempt to realize that righteousness in Christian lives (2 Pet 3:11, 14).

4. Theological Character.

The distinctive theological character of 2 Peter is found in its remarkable combination of Hellenistic religious language and Jewish eschatological ideas and imagery. On the one hand, for example, the author summarizes Peter's teaching in a passage that in its religious and ethical terminology is perhaps the most typically Hellenistic in the whole NT (2 Pet 1:3-11). This can be seen in the ethical terms drawn from Hellenistic moral philosophy (2 Pet 1:5-7) and in the promise of escaping corruption and sharing divine nature (2 Pet 1:4). Such Hellenistic terminology is carefully situated in a context that gives it Christian meaning (e.g., the list of virtues in 2 Peter 1:5-7 is given Christian definition by its first and last items: faith and love) but seems nevertheless a striking and deliberate attempt to make contact with the Hellenistic religious environment. On the other hand, 2 Peter accurately and effectively reproduces the concepts and imagery of Jewish cosmic eschatology, especially in 2 Peter 3:3-13, which may be drawing directly on a Jewish apocalypse.

This combination of two different theological styles can be explained by the author's intention of interpreting and defending the apostolic message in a postapostolic period and a pagan cultural context. When he states the Christian message positively (2 Pet 1:3-11) he does so in terms that make contact with the ideals and aspirations of contemporary pagan culture. He is engaged in the task of translating the gospel into terms intelligible in a new cultural environment. But this is a delicate task that requires care lest the real Christian content of the gospel be lost. In the author's view that was happening in his opponents' version of Christianity. In their attempt to adapt Christianity to Hellenistic culture they were compromising essential features of the apostolic message, advocating mere pagan skepticism about eschatology and mere acquiescence in moral permissiveness.

In order to defend the gospel against this excessive Hellenization, therefore, the author resorts to sources, including the letter of Jude, and ideas close to the eschatological outlook of early Jewish Christianity. He sees that if Hellenized Christianity is not to become paganized Christianity, cosmic eschatology—the hope for the triumph of God's righteousness in the whole of his creation—has to be reasserted, along with the ethical motivation it provides. Second Peter thus maintains a careful balance between a degree of Hellenization of the gospel message and a protest, in the name of cosmic eschatology, against an extreme Hellenization that would dissolve the real Christian substance of its message. It is a valuable witness to the church's difficult transition from a Jewish (albeit Hellenized) context to a predominantly non-Jewish Hellenistic environment and from the apostolic to the postapostolic age.

This understanding of the theological character of 2 Peter, it may be claimed, does better justice to its content than the tendency of older scholarship to assign it to the category of early catholicism, a classification that has usually been at the same time a way of denigrating the book as a lapse from the theological standards of earlier (usually meaning Pauline) Christianity. This classification of 2 Peter requires attributing to it features of so-called early catholicism that cannot be found in the text—such as ecclesiological institutionalization and the crystallization of the faith into rigid formulae. It also fails to explain or to appreciate 2 Peter's deliberate and creative combination of Jewish eschatology and Hellenistic religious terminology.

See also ADVERSARIES; ESCHATOLOGY; JUDE, LETTER OF; PETER, FIRST LETTER OF.

DLNTD: EARLY CATHOLICISM; PAROUSIA; PSEUDEPIGRAPHY.

BIBLIOGRAPHY. **Commentaries:** R. J. Bauckham, *Jude, 2 Peter* (WBC; Waco, TX: Word, 1983); D. Horrell, *The Epistles of Peter and Jude* (EC; Valley Forge, PA: Trinity Press International, 1998); J. N. D. Kelly, *The Epistles of Peter and Jude* (BNTC; New York: Harper & Row, 1969); J. B. Mayor, *The Epistle of St. Jude and the Second Epistle of St. Peter* (London: Macmillan, 1907); D. J. Moo, *2 Peter, Jude* (NIVAC; Grand Rapids: Zondervan, 1997); J. H. Neyrey, *2 Peter, Jude* (AB; Garden City, NY: Doubleday, 1993). **Studies:** R. J. Bauckham, "2 Peter: An Account of Research," *ANRW* II.25.5 (1988) 3713-52; A. Chester and R. P. Martin, *The Theology of the Letters of James, Peter and Jude* (Cambridge: Cambridge University Press, 1994); T. Fornberg, *An Early Church in a Pluralistic Society* (ConNT; Lund: Gleerup, 1977); A. E. Harvey, "The Testament of Simeon Peter," in *A Tribute to Geza Vermes: Essays on Jewish and Christian Literature and History*, ed. P. R. Davies and R. T. White (JSOTSup 100; Sheffield: JSOT, 1990) 339-54; E. Käsemann, "An Apologia for Primitive Christian Eschatology," in *Essays on New Tes-*

tament Themes (London: SCM, 1964) 169-95; D. G. Meade, *Pseudonymity and Canon* (WUNT; Tübingen: Mohr Siebeck, 1986); D. F. Watson, *Invention, Arrangement and Style: Rhetorical Criticism of Jude and 2 Peter* (SBLDS 104; Atlanta: Scholars Press, 1988); A. Wolters, " 'Partners of the Deity': A Covenantal Reading of 2 Peter 1:4," *CTJ* 25 (1990) 28-44. R. J. Bauckham

PHARISEES. *See* JUDAISM AND THE NEW TESTAMENT; RABBINIC TRADITIONS AND WRITINGS.

PHILEMON, LETTER TO

Philemon is the shortest (335 words in Greek) and most personal of the letters belonging to the Pauline corpus. Despite the literary, historical and interpretive problems the letter raises for modern scholarship, it offers a fascinating window not only on a corner of the social world of the first century but also on Christian principles at work in a particular setting within the early church.

1. History of Interpretation
2. Continuing Questions of Interpretation
3. Theological Significance

1. History of Interpretation.

1.1. Historical-Critical Method. Although some older critical theories tended to question the letter's authenticity and purpose (F. C. Baur, for example, regarded it as a second-century "fictional romance" seeking to address the issue of slavery in the early church), the interpretation given by most commentators who follow the historical-critical method and the natural meaning of the text is that this letter was written somewhere between A.D. 58 and 60 while Paul was in a Roman prison. It appears that the letter is addressed to Philemon (Philem 1), who was a wealthy Gentile Christian in Colossae who became a believer under Paul's ministry (Philem 19). Its divisions include Paul's greetings (Philem 1-3); thanksgiving and prayer (Philem 4-7); intercession for Onesimus (Philem 18-22); final greetings and benediction (Philem 23-25).

The heart of the letter centers upon Onesimus, Philemon's slave who had somehow wronged his master (Philem 18), made his way to Paul in prison (Philem 9), was converted (Philem 10) and became a useful partner with Paul in the gospel (Philem 11, 13). But under the existing laws governing slavery, Paul knows that Onesimus must be returned to his rightful owner. In the letter, Paul implores Philemon not only to receive (Philem 17), forgive (Philem 18) and acknowledge Onesimus's new status as a fellow believer (Philem 16) but also to relinquish all claims upon Onesimus so that he can continue serving with Paul (Philem 13, 21).

In the opening greetings (Philem 1-3), Paul identifies Philemon as a "dear friend and fellow worker" (NIV). We have no way of knowing how the two became acquainted and whether Philemon 19 should be taken to imply that Philemon was converted by Paul. If so, it probably was during Paul's stay in Ephesus and in similar circumstances when Epaphras, another resident of Colossae, came under Paul's ministry (Col 1:7; 4:12). Nor is there any way of knowing whether Apphia was Philemon's wife and Archippus his son.

The thanksgiving and prayer (Philem 4-7) focus on Philemon, who is commended for his faith in Christ and his love for the saints. Both of these virtues have "refreshed" the saints and given joy and encouragement to the apostle. The accent is on Philemon's spirit of love and not on any specific actions. It is the same word that Paul uses in verse 20, where he anticipates the effect of Philemon's response.

Paul's request—or intercession—on behalf of Onesimus (Philem 8-22) takes the reader through a series of agonizing delays because Paul just does not seem to get to the point (the opening, "I appeal to you for my son Onesimus" in verse 10, is not completed until verse 17). But Paul is careful to use diplomacy and tact in handling this rather delicate matter. He needs to state the request strongly but yet have the decision be voluntary. He wants Philemon to act out of conviction, not out of compulsion (Philem 14). Thus Paul approaches Philemon as a friend and coworker and not with apostolic authority.

Although the circumstances surrounding Onesimus's arrival at the place of Paul's imprisonment and his conversion to the Christian faith are uncertain, this section clarifies the strong attachment that Paul has developed for his spiritual "son" (Philem 10) and "brother" (Philem 16) and the appreciation for Onesimus's ministry to him while under house arrest.

All this puts Paul on the horns of a dilemma: Onesimus, whose name means "useful," can be of value to his master only if he returns, and to Paul if he stays. In spite of Paul's tact in approaching Philemon, it is obvious that he wants Philemon to release Onesimus so that he can retain him for his own service. This appears to overshadow the other concern Paul had that Philemon forgive Onesimus and receive him as a Christian brother (Philem 16). Paul's confidence of his release and plan to visit Philemon (Philem 22) may be related to both of these requests. Could it be that Onesimus returned to Colossae before Paul, that he was forgiven by Philemon, and then released to Paul when the apostle visited Colossae?

The final greetings (Philem 23-25) are almost identical to the closing section of Colossians (Col 4:12-18). The plural form of "you" in the benediction ("The grace of our Lord Jesus Christ be with your spirit") carries a singular meaning and does not necessarily confirm the public nature of the letter.

The letter to Philemon and the letter to the Colossians are closely related (*see* Colossians, Letter to the). Both are written from the same place, addressed to the same church and were carried to Colossae by Tychicus (Col 4:8-9); both mention similar circumstances about Paul's imprisonment (Col 4:3; Philem 1, 13) and have an almost identical list of personal greetings. It is most likely that the two letters were kept together as Paul's correspondence to Colossae. Unfortunately, the relationship of these two letters was lost when the compilers of the NT separated them in the canon.

1.2. Knox's Reconstruction. J. Knox's provocative study of Philemon broke with the traditional interpretation at a number of points. First, he identifies Archippus as the recipient of the letter and thus Onesimus's master. The "work" (NIV) or "ministry" (RSV) that Paul admonishes Archippus to complete (Col 4:17) refers to the way he was to receive and handle Onesimus. Philemon is an "overseer" of the churches in the Lycus Valley with a probable residence in Laodicea. Second, he equates "the letter from Laodicea" that Paul wants read in Colossae (Col 4:16) as "the epistle to Philemon." Third, Knox believes that the restored slave Onesimus is the same person who became bishop of Ephesus and may have been responsible for collecting Paul's letters in the second century (Ignatius *Eph.* 1.3). This, claims Knox, could account for the preservation and inclusion of this brief and personal letter in the canon.

Reaction to Knox's reconstruction varies among scholars. While most regard it as novel, interesting and/or ingenious, much of his reconstruction is generally dismissed as lacking sufficient evidence to be taken seriously. It seems more natural to conclude that Philemon, the first person addressed in the letter, is the recipient and the one to whom Paul is interceding on behalf of Onesimus. Neither can the letter referred to in Colossians 4:16 be identified with certainty as our letter to Philemon. However, Knox's proposal regarding the preservation and function of this letter remains intriguing.

1.3. Rhetorical Criticism. This approach analyzes the letter of Philemon through the categories of ancient rhetoric. F. Forrester Church, for example, believes that Paul is employing such classical rhetorical devices as "pathos," "ethos" and "forensic rhetoric" in order to persuade Philemon to accept his request. "The key" to deliberative rhetoric, writes Church, "is to demonstrate love or friendship and to induce sympathy or goodwill, in order to dispose the hearer favorably to the merits of one's case" (Church, 19-20). In rhetorical categories, Philemon would be divided into the exordium (Philem 4-7), proof (Philem 8-16) and peroration (Philem 17-22).

This method does not necessarily challenge the interpretation of Philemon given above. Its proponents believe that it provides further insights into the shape and design of Paul's letters (see White; *see* Letter, Letter Forms). The fact that a common rhetorical device was used to "conceal the ultimate objective" so that the hearers or readers may find it for themselves may account for the ambiguous and puzzling way Paul makes his request to Philemon (Derrett).

1.4. Legal Analogies. S. Winter has examined Philemon for parallels to legal forms and language used in Paul's day and believes that there are significant analogies that help to explain certain phrases in the letter. Paul's appeal in Philemon 10 *(parakalō . . . peri),* for example, is like a formula used in legal petitions; *anapempō* in Philem 12 ("I am sending him . . . back to you") is a legal term better understood as referring Onesimus's case "to the proper higher authority"; and the idea of the partnership *(koinōnia)* between Paul and Philemon, notes Winter, has more of the elements of a "consensual association," a *koinōnia* in which partnership was legally binding. Paul's plea to Philemon is that Onesimus be received into this *koinōnia* as an equal partner (Winter 1987, 7).

1.5. Literary Criticism and the Social Sciences.

The most extensive and significant work on the letter to Philemon from this perspective belongs to N. Petersen, who draws upon sociological and anthropological models (those of, e.g., Levi-Strauss, Evans-Pritchard, Berger, Eco) and insights on the sociology of the NT (the writings of J. Elliott, B. Malina, W. Meeks and G. Theissen).

Petersen transfers the letter into a story in order to create a "narrative world" in which Paul is the narrator and Philemon the actor. This narrative is played out in the midst of two social realities—the church and the world. The heart of the letter, according to Petersen, centers upon the sociological categories of kinship and the tension Philemon faces when confronted with values of kinship in the world and in the church. Paul is forcing Philemon to decide between the two.

The historical and literary approaches outlined above are not mutually exclusive. Rather, they are positive attempts by several disciplines to discover the nature and purpose of this letter. And, even though the letter to Philemon may not necessarily be written as a legal or rhetorical document, there are insights, when combined with the historical-critical method, that are helpful.

2. Continuing Questions of Interpretation.

Scholarly debate continues around issues where the text is ambiguous or for which there is no conclusive proof. These include the recipient of the letter (Philemon or Archippus), the address of the recipient (Colossae or Laodicea) and the place of Paul's imprisonment (Rome, Ephesus or Caesarea). Speculation also abounds on how and where Onesimus was converted, if he was returned to Philemon, if Paul was able to retain him as a coworker and whether or not he became the bishop of Ephesus. Two major concerns, however, merit special mention.

2.1. Onesimus: "Runaway Slave" or "Sent Messenger"? The traditional interpretation among commentators is based on the inference that Onesimus was a runaway slave who probably stole something from his master (Philem 11, 18). This view was doubted by Knox, whose doubts are amplified by Winter who proposes that Onesimus was "sent" to Paul by the Colossian congregation in order to meet some of Paul's physical needs while Paul was under house arrest. Onesimus's departure and consequent separation (Philem 15) from Philemon need not imply that he ran away. The situation could be similar to the one that brought Epaphroditus from Philippi to Paul while Paul was in prison (cf. Phil 2:22-30).

Winter's conclusions are based on several observations: first, she believes that Paul's commendations of Philemon in the thanksgiving section (Philem 4-7) express the apostle's gratitude for sending Onesimus to him; second, she interprets certain phrases to mean that Paul's "hearing" of Philemon's faith (Philem 5) came from Onesimus, that the "good thing" (*pantos agathou,* Philem 6; see Wright) and the "sharing of your faith" (*koinōnia;* Wright, 6) is Paul's response to having Onesimus sent by Philemon (Winter, 3-4). Some of this exegesis is questionable and lacks support from the main body of the letter.

All this, however, does not necessarily mean that Onesimus was a runaway slave in the traditional sense of being a fugitive or deserter (cf. Bruce, 197). P. Lampe argues that the situation of Onesimus does not fit the legal category of a "fugitive" (*fugitivus*). Under certain conditions of Roman law governing slavery, it was possible for a slave to seek out an advocate or intercessor to mediate a grievance with the master. In this case Onesimus legally makes his way to the place of Paul's imprisonment to seek help (Lampe; Bruce, 197; Bartchy).

Is it reasonable to suggest the following scenario? Onesimus would have known Paul from the contacts that Philemon had with the apostle (in visits to Ephesus?) and may even have become Paul's friend. Some serious domestic grievance destroyed the relationship between slave and master, and Onesimus, who knew his civil rights, believed that Paul could intercede for him. While visiting with Paul and attending to his needs while he was under house arrest (Philem 11, 13), Onesimus became a believer (Philem 10). Paul, then, wrote this "letter of intercession" trusting that Philemon would forgive the wrong, cancel any debt ("owes you anything," Philem 18, 19), accept Onesimus as a "brother in the Lord" (Philem 16) and release Onesimus into Paul's service (Philem 21). We need not infer from Philemon 18 and 19 that Onesimus had stolen money from Philemon other than, perhaps, enough to finance his journey to Paul (cf. O'Brien, 299-300). It could also be that Philemon loaned Onesimus to Paul (a modification of the "sent" theory) so that the "debt" refers to time and not monetary compensation (Patzia, 114).

2.2. The Letter: Private or Public? Some scholars conclude that the brevity, personal appeal to one person and the delicate way Paul handles his request, confirm that this is a private letter. However, several factors favor its public nature. (1) The length exceeds that of most private letters. (2) The greetings are extended to more than one person and include a house church. (3) It was customary to read Paul's letters to the entire church in worship. (4) The legal and technical language are more characteristic of a public document than a private letter. (5) It has all the characteristics of Paul's longer letters addressed to churches, such as the inclusion of Timothy as a cosender, salutation, thanksgiving, body and greetings. (6) The designations "fellow worker" *(synergos),* "sister" *(adelphē)* and "fellow soldier" *(systratiōtēs)* in Philemon 1-2 suggest church titles.

Finally, one cannot help but feel that Paul's request and the issue of social relationships involves the entire Christian community and not just one person. E. Lohse, quoting Wickert, notes that "in the Body of Christ personal affairs are no longer private" (Lohse, 187 n. 9). "In short," concludes R. P. Martin, "this brief epistle is to be seen not so much as a private letter of Paul as an individual . . . but as an apostolic letter about a personal matter" (Martin, 144). In other words, Paul is referring his case to the entire church. This public nature may also account for its value in the collection and canon of Paul's letters.

3. Theological Significance.
The literary, historical and interpretative problems that remain should not detract from the beauty and meaning of this letter. It contains no explicit theological or ethical doctrines; it attacks no heresies in the church. Nevertheless, it presents a number of important truths that should not go unnoticed.

First, it opens a window on the nature of Paul's imprisonment and the personal relationship that he enjoyed with his friends and coworkers (Philem 23, 24; Col 4:12-14). It ends by showing the optimism that Paul had for his release and desire to visit his beloved friend Philemon.

Second, it provides a small commentary on slavery in the ancient world. When read together with Colossians 3:22—4:1, we begin to appreciate how conversion to the Christian faith broke down all social, racial and economic barriers (Patzia, 91-93). Although Paul does not speak directly for the abolition of slavery, this letter exemplifies, as much as any other writing of his, the truth of Galatians 3:28: "There is neither Jew nor Greek, slave nor free, male nor female, for you are all one in Christ Jesus" (NIV). A new relationship and partnership has been formed in this situation where master, slave and apostle are all part of one family in Christ (Philem 16). The church as a whole should be characterized by such virtues as love, forgiveness, equality and fellowship.

Third, it is a masterpiece of pastoral diplomacy. Paul's request is not reinforced by expressions of compulsion, constraint or coercion. The reconciliation between Philemon and Onesimus is based on the principles of Christian love and forgiveness and not Roman law or apostolic authority. The release of Onesimus for Paul's ministry must be a voluntary action leading to the highest good for all parties concerned. Paul is confident that he will succeed in motivating Philemon "to do even more" than he has requested (Philem 21).

Finally, as W. Barclay so aptly wrote, "here is one of the great romances of grace in the early Church" (Barclay, 316). Although we do not know how the story ended, there is enough reason to suspect that Paul's confidence (Philem 21) in Philemon was honored and that the former slave Onesimus, now a brother in Christ, continued to serve Paul.

See also COLOSSIANS, LETTER TO THE.
DPL: SLAVE, SLAVERY.

BIBLIOGRAPHY. **Commentaries:** W. Barclay, *The Letters of Timothy, Titus and Philemon* (Philadelphia: Westminster, 1960); M. Barth and H. Blanke, *The Letter to Philemon* (Grand Rapids: Eerdmans, 2000); F. F. Bruce, *The Epistle to the Colossians, to Philemon, and to the Ephesians* (NICNT; Grand Rapids: Eerdmans, 1984); J. D. G. Dunn, *The Epistles to the Colossians and to Philemon* (NIGTC; Grand Rapids: Eerdmans, 1996); J. A. Fitzmyer, *The Letter to Philemon* (AB; New York: Doubleday, 2000); E. Lohse, *Colossians and Philemon* (Herm; Philadelphia: Fortress, 1971); R. P. Martin, *Colossians and Philemon* (rev. ed.; NCB; Grand Rapids: Eerdmans, 1981); P. T. O'Brien, *Colossians, Philemon* (WBC 44; Waco, TX: Word, 1982); A. G. Patzia, *Ephesians, Colossians, Philemon* (NIBC; Peabody, MA.: Hendrick-

son, 1991). **Studies:** S. S. Bartchy, "Philemon, Epistle to," *ABD* 5:305-10; F. F. Church, "Rhetorical Structure and Design in Paul's Letter to Philemon," *HTR* 71 (1978) 17-33; J. D. M. Derrett, "The Function of the Epistle to Philemon," *ZNW* 19 (1988) 85; J. Knox, *Philemon Among the Letters of Paul* (New York: Abingdon, 1959); P. Lampe, "Keine Sklavenflucht des Onesimus," *ZNW* 76 (1985) 135-37; N. R. Petersen, *Rediscovering Paul: Philemon and the Sociology of Paul's Narrative World* (Philadelphia: Fortress, 1985); J. White, *The Structural Analysis of Philemon: A Point of Departure in the Formal Analysis of the Pauline Letter* (SBLASP; Missoula, MT: Scholars Press, 1971); S. Winter, "Methodological Observations on a New Interpretation of Paul's Letter to Philemon," *USQR* 35 (1984) 203-12; idem, "Paul's Letter to Philemon," *NTS* 33 (1987) 1-15; N. T. Wright, "ΞΡΙΣΤΟΣ as 'Messiah' in Paul: Philemon 6," in *The Climax of the Covenant* (Minneapolis: Fortress, 1991) 41-55.

A. G. Patzia

PHILIPPI. *See* PHILIPPIANS, LETTER TO THE.

PHILIPPIAN JAILER. *See* BAPTISM III.

PHILIPPIANS, LETTER TO THE

Philippians is a letter the apostle Paul wrote to the church in the city of Philippi in Macedonia, the first church he founded in Europe. It is the most personal of all of his letters. Although not a theological treatise, Philippians does have a great deal to say about God and his ways with people, about Christ Jesus, and about Christians and how they should live in this world. The terms *overseers* and *deacons* (Phil 1:1) occur here for the one and only time in Paul's letters, but without any elaboration on what these people did or about what kind of authority they exercised within the church.

1. Contents
2. Philippi and Its Citizens
3. The Church and Its Apostle
4. Some Critical Questions
5. Theological Themes

1. Contents.

The letter begins with a salutation that is like (e.g., "A to B, greetings!") and unlike (e.g., "from God our Father and the Lord Jesus Christ") letters that were typical of first-century letter forms (Phil 1:1-2).

869

Paul then thanks God for the Philippians, reminds them of his constant prayer and affection for them and of his confidence in God concerning them, gives a brief account of his imprisonment and the unexpected positive effects it has had, and informs them of the likelihood that he will be released from prison and reunited with them (Phil 1:3-26).

Paul turns from thanks to plead with the Philippians to live in a manner worthy of the gospel of Christ: harmoniously with one another; striving for the faith of the gospel; unafraid of opponents of the gospel; willing to suffer for the gospel; eager to imitate Christ Jesus in seeking the welfare of others with humility; carrying out responsibilities without murmuring or grumbling; and keeping themselves pure and holy, blameless children of God (Phil 1:27—2:18).

Paul tells them of his desire to send Timothy to them, but until he is able to do so, of his intention instead to send back to them Epaphroditus, one of their own people, their messenger to him—a man who had risked his life in order to bring their gifts to him (Phil 2:19—3:1).

The letter changes tone at this point. Paul now begins a bitter attack on those who would subvert the Philippians—upon people who are "enemies of the cross of Christ." He counters whatever influence they may have had with an assertion of his authority based not on status but sacrifice, taking the Christ of the Christ hymn as his model (cf. Phil 3:4-11 with Phil 2:6-11), not on his self-worth but the exceeding worth of Christ Jesus (Phil 3:2-21).

In conclusion, Paul pleads for unity in the church, especially among its leaders; gives his advice about how Christians are to feel and think and act; relieves the Philippians of any sense of guilt they may have had for those times when they were not able to send him aid; gives them thanks for their renewed generosity; and brings the letter to a close with a doxology to God, greetings to all and a benediction (Phil 4:1-23).

2. Philippi and Its Citizens.

Philippi was already an old and historic city when Paul arrived and later wrote his letter to the Christians there. Philip of Macedon had built it in 358-57 B.C. on the site of an ancient Thracian city located eight miles from the sea in a spring-filled, fertile region. He fortified it and named it after himself. Later, Philippi became part of the Roman Empire and was made one of the stations along the main overland route connecting Rome with the East. Destroyed by wars, it was rebuilt by the emperor Octavian, who established it as a military outpost, populated it with veterans of his wars, made it a Roman colony and gave it the *ius italicum*—the highest privilege obtainable by a provincial municipality. Consequently, as the citizens of Rome, so the citizens of Philippi could buy and sell property, were exempt from land tax and the poll tax, and were entitled to protection by Roman law. Thus it was that when Paul made his first journey to Europe, he purposely neglected the port city of Neapolis to begin preaching the gospel in the small but more important city of Philippi of the first district of Macedonia (Acts 16:12).

Philippi was inhabited predominantly by Romans, but many Macedonian Greeks and some Jews lived there as well. Its people were proud of their city, proud of their ties with Rome, proud to observe Roman customs and obey Roman laws, proud to be Roman citizens (cf. Acts 16:21). Twice in this brief letter Paul makes statements that capitalize on this fact: "Only conduct yourselves in a manner worthy of the gospel of Christ" (Phil 1:27), where the verb he uses for "conduct yourselves," *politeuesthe*, literally means "to live as a citizen, to live as freepersons," even "to take part in government." By choosing this word Paul seems to be appealing to their pride as Roman citizens and to be extending this idea now to the church, the new community to which they belong and of which they must be responsible citizens, abiding by its law of love. Paul's other statement is in Philippians 3:20: "For our citizenship [*politeuma*] is in heaven." Here again his choice of the word *politeuma* recalls what he said in Philippians 1:27 and suggests that once more he is reflecting on the civic status of Philippi as a Roman colony and reminding the Philippians that they now belong to a higher, more important, more enduring commonwealth. Choosing Philippi as the place to launch the gospel on European soil fitted in with Paul's mission strategy of selecting important cities of repute and strategic location as ideal centers from which the good news of the gospel might radiate out.

3. The Church and Its Apostle.

Paul came to Philippi as the result of a vision he had while he was in Troas. He saw a "man of Macedonia" and heard him say "Come over . . .

and help us." Immediately after the vision Paul and his party left off their attempts to go into Bithynia and decided instead to go into Macedonia, concluding that God had called them to preach the gospel there (Acts 16:9-10). According to Acts, the first convert to Christianity in Philippi was a woman, Lydia. Although Lydia was a pagan, she nevertheless was a God-fearing person who had been attracted to the lofty ideals of the Jewish religion (Acts 16:14). But when she heard Paul preach the gospel and, as Luke said, God opened her heart, she put her faith in Jesus Christ and along with her household was baptized (Acts 16:14-15). These people became the nucleus of the church at Philippi, and while meeting in the home of Lydia they showed great kindness in their generous hospitality to Paul and his companions, prevailing upon them to come and join this household and stay with them (Acts 16:15).

The only other Philippian converts mentioned in Acts were the Roman soldier, who guarded the jail where Paul had been put in prison, and his household (Acts 16:30-33). But the extraordinary circumstances in which the jailer became a Christian generated within him such affection for Paul and Silas that he washed their wounds, brought them into his house and spread his table with food for them to eat.

The reactions of these two people, one a distinguished and wealthy woman and one a Roman soldier, and of those around them toward the apostle set the tone for the relationship that was to endure between the church at Philippi and Paul. It is obvious from this brief letter, no doubt one of several he wrote to the Philippians (see Polycarp *Phil.* 3.2), that not only did he have a deep affection for the Philippians, but they as well for him (cf. Phil 1:7; 4:16). When he addresses them he does not do so as "Paul the apostle" but only as a servant of Christ Jesus—he had no need to convince them of his authority. This is not to say, however, that there were not things happening in this church that grieved Paul and against which he raised his voice. Apparently there were divisions between groups of people there (Phil 1:27; 2:2), with people who were selfish, conceited and looking out only for their own interests (Phil 2:3-4). There were people who were murmuring and grumbling (Phil 2:14) and people who could not get along with others (Phil 4:2)—and all within the church. In a gentle fashion, holding up before them the way of Christ, he graciously calls them back to harmony and mutual concern one for another.

Little else is known about the composition of the church in Philippi, but names such as Epaphroditus, Euodia, Syntyche and Clement—all mentioned by Paul as members of this church (Phil 2:25; 4:2-3)—indicate that this first Christian church on European soil was made up largely of Greeks. Furthermore, it is safe to infer that from its inception women played an important role in this church, even in its leadership. Not only was its first convert a woman, a woman of wealth and influence (Acts 16:14), but it is possible that all the other women who had met with Lydia for prayer by the riverside even before Paul came to Philippi (Acts 16:13) also were led to faith in Jesus Christ by her example and testimony. It is a fact worthy of note that of the four Philippians mentioned by name in this letter, two of them are women and are designated by Paul as women who worked hard alongside him in the proclamation of the gospel (Phil 4:3).

4. Some Critical Questions.

4.1. Authorship. Although the letter to the Philippians opens with the words "[From] Paul and Timothy" (Phil 1:1), it is clear that whatever may have been the reason for Timothy's name being linked together with that of the apostle, it was Paul alone who was responsible for this letter and its contents. The tone of the letter is far too personal to be otherwise. For example, Paul's use of the singular personal pronouns "I," "me," "my"—occurring fifty-one times in such a short letter—alone argues for this. But, in addition, Timothy's name reappears again only in Philippians 2:19 and not at all, as might be expected, in the final salutation. In effect, therefore, it is Paul alone who lays claim to being the author of Philippians.

Historically the church has accepted this claim without question—Polycarp of Smyrna, Irenaeus, Clement of Alexandria, Tertullian and others not only quoted from Philippians but also assigned it solely to Paul. In the nineteenth century, however, some thinkers began to doubt that Paul had written Philippians. The most articulate of these thinkers was F. C. Baur. Baur's historical studies led him to the conclusion that Paul wrote none of the letters that bear his name, including Philippians, except Romans, 1 and 2 Corinthians and Galatians. In spite of the great power and erudition with which Baur argued, his arguments were not convincing or widely adopted. Eventually they fell into disuse and essentially disappeared. From time to time, however, other scholars have attempted to revive his thesis, but with little or no success. It is thus safe to say that the vast majority of those who study the NT today are certain that Paul was responsible for Philippians and that the question of the genuineness of this letter has only historical significance.

4.2. Unity. Is Philippians a single letter, or is it a composite of several letters written by Paul? In the second century A.D. Polycarp, bishop of Smyrna, wrote to the church at Philippi mentioning that Paul had sent them "letters" (Polycarp *Phil.* 3.2). This remark of Polycarp's, combined with the following features within Philippians, are sufficient reasons for many to regard this single letter in reality to be two or more letters fused together into one: (1) the quiet, orderly preparation for the conclusion of the letter at Philippians 3:1; (2) the radical change of tone from the rest of the letter beginning at Philippians 3:2 and continuing through Philippians 4:3; (3) the observation that Philippians 3:1 fits together so exactly with Philippians 4:4; and (4) the fact that Paul waits to the end of the letter to thank the Philippians for their generosity to him.

The reasons for considering Philippians a composite letter are weighty—as are those against such a consideration: (1) The fact that there is a disjointedness about Philippians and that Paul does interrupt himself at Philippians 3:2 should not be surprising in a personal, conversational letter, perhaps not all written or dictated at one time, by a person accustomed to abrupt shifts of style without notice (cf. Rom 16:16-19; 1 Thess 2:13-16). (2) There are no Greek manuscripts, no matter how far back one goes, nor is there any early church father offering the slightest indication that Philippians ever appeared in a form different from that which now exists. (3) It is difficult to isolate one part of the letter from another because the same terms, word roots and motifs pervade all of its so-called parts. Furthermore, the development of Paul's argument in one part of the letter often depends on what he has said in another part (cf. especially Phil 2:6-11 with Phil 3:7-11; and Phil 2:6-11 with Phil 3:20-21; see Hooker, 331-33). (4) If Philippians 3:1 and Philippians 4:4 fit together so perfectly that Philippians 3 must be consid-

ered a separate letter, it is difficult to explain why any thinking scribe intent on unifying the various letters would have placed it here where it seemingly fractures the unity of the whole. The same goes for the so-called letter of thanks (Phil 4:10-20). Why would an intelligent scribe, desiring to weave the Philippian letters together into a single letter, place this particular "letter" at the end and not at the beginning?

There is thus no compelling reason to doubt that Philippians came fresh from Paul as a single letter and not as several letters later made into one by some anonymous redactor. Hence Philippians should be treated by interpreters as a unified whole.

4.3. Place and Date. The place and time of Paul's writing the letter to the Philippians are important questions with a bearing on the interpretation of the text, particularly the issues of the identity of Paul's opponents and the nature of their opposition.

4.3.1. Place. Before it is possible to determine the provenance of Philippians, several factors must first be kept in mind. (1) Paul was in prison when he wrote (Phil 1:7, 13, 17). (2) He faced a trial that could end in his death (Phil 1:19-20; 2:17) or acquittal (Phil 1:25; 2:24). (3) There was a praetorium where he was held (Phil 1:13), as well as people who belonged to Caesar's household (Phil 4:22). (4) Timothy was with Paul (Phil 1:1; 2:19-23). (5) Extensive, effective evangelistic efforts were going on around him (Phil 1:14-17). (6) Paul planned to visit Philippi when he was acquitted (Phil 2:24). And (7) apparently several trips—possibly as many as four—back and forth between Philippi and the place from which Paul wrote Philippians were made by different people within the time span of his imprisonment.

4.3.1.1. Rome. As the hypothetical place from which Paul wrote Philippians, Rome not only meets most of these criteria but also is the oldest and longest-held view, dating from as far back as the second century A.D. and the Marcionite prologues. Paul was a prisoner in Rome under house arrest for at least two years (Acts 28:30). Here he had soldiers guarding him (Acts 28:16), yet he was given a certain degree of freedom to receive guests and gifts and to write and send off letters (Acts 28:17, 30). Here he was free to preach the gospel (Acts 28:31). Here he would stand before Caesar and here his fate would ultimately be decided. Here were the praetorium (Phil 1:13) and "the people of Caesar's household" (Phil 4:22), which included the imperial guard and the slaves and free persons in the employ of the emperor. Here also was a church sufficiently large and not all that loyal to Paul, not having been founded by him, which might have divided into the factions Paul refers to in his letter (cf. Phil 1:14-17).

And yet to identify Rome as the place from which Paul wrote Philippians is not without its problems. (1) The distance between Rome and Philippi makes it difficult, some would argue, to fit the number of trips between these two cities into the time frame of Paul's prison term. (2) There is no indication in Acts that Timothy was with Paul in Rome, whereas Philippians 1:1 makes it clear that Timothy was with him wherever it was he wrote this letter. (3) Paul's intent was to visit Philippi upon his release from prison (Phil 2:24), and yet his earlier-stated plan was to quit the East and focus on mission fields in the West, especially Spain (Rom 15:24-28). (4) It has been inferred from Philippians 1:30 and Philippians 4:15-16 (see also Phil 2:12, 22) that Paul is stating here that he had not returned to Philippi since he and Timothy had founded the church there—a statement he could not have made were he writing from Rome, since he had been to Philippi twice between the establishment of the Philippian church (Acts 16) and his journey to Rome (Acts 20:1-6).

4.3.1.2. Ephesus. Modern scholarship has suggested that Ephesus was the place from which Paul wrote Philippians. The following reasons are given in support of this hypothesis. (1) Reference to the praetorium can point to the residence of any provincial governor in Ephesus or elsewhere (cf. Mt 27:27; Jn 18:28, 33). (2) Timothy was with Paul in Ephesus (Acts 19:22; Phil 1:1). (3) The distance between Ephesus and Philippi is minimal in comparison with that between Rome and Philippi and eliminates the time problem that requires several journeys back and forth between Philippi and the place of Paul's imprisonment. (4) Extensive evangelistic activity went on in and around Ephesus while Paul was there (Acts 19:10, 25-26; cf. Phil 1:12-14) as well as contention over Paul and his teaching (Acts 19:2-9; cf. Phil 1:15). (5) Paul refers to his being imprisoned on several occasions (2 Cor 11:23). Consequently, the fact that Acts makes no mention of his being put in prison in Ephesus is not necessarily an argument against the possibility that he was indeed imprisoned there (cf. 1 Cor 15:32; 2 Cor 1:8).

The Ephesian hypothesis, although it enjoys increasing popularity, is not without serious objections. (1) It rests mainly on inference from those texts just cited. (2) Nothing is said in Philippians about the "collection" for the poor in Jerusalem—a matter of immense importance to Paul during his Ephesian stay—and for Paul to accept gifts for himself from the church at Philippi during this period of fund raising for the Jerusalem church is inconceivable (Phil 2:25; 4:10-20). (3) The church in the city from which Paul wrote was a divided church—divided over him (Phil 1:15-17)—a fact that does not fit the picture of the church in Ephesus (Acts 19; 20:17-31). (4) Paul speaks rather harshly about all the Christians around him except for Timothy (Phil 2:19-21), a strange feature when his best friends, Priscilla and Aquila, were in Ephesus when he was (Acts 18:2, 18, 24-26; 1 Cor 16:19).

4.3.1.3. Corinth. Several factors suggest the possibility of Corinth as the place from which Philippians was written. (1) Corinth was in geographical proximity to Philippi, closer even than Ephesus. (2) A proconsul was in Corinth (Acts 18:12), and consequently a praetorium and a "household of Caesar" were there. (3) Apparently Paul wrote Philippians before his polemic with Jewish Christians who came from James in Jerusalem (cf. Gal 2:12), for there is no mention of his apostleship in this letter; thus it was probably written before 1 Corinthians (a letter Paul wrote from Ephesus) while he was still in Corinth. (4) The severe opposition Paul faced in Corinth, even mortal danger, and the night vision of encouragement that came to him because of it (Acts 18:10), paralleling that which came to him while in prison in Jerusalem (Acts 23:11), allows one to infer that Paul's enemies had had him arrested, put in prison and threatened with death. But comforted by this nocturnal call to courage he could be confident of release and could assure the Philippians of this fact (Phil 1:25; 2:24).

The objections to this hypothesis are similar to those raised against the Ephesian hypothesis. (1) The hypothesis is totally based on conjecture, and (2) Paul's harsh remarks about those around him (Phil 2:19-20) make no sense when one realizes that Priscilla and Aquila were also with Paul when he was in Corinth (Acts 18:1-2, 18).

4.3.1.4. Caesarea. Another suggested provenance for Philippians—that of Caesarea—

though late in its formulation, makes a great deal of sense and harmonizes with most of the essential facts. (1) Luke specifically says that Paul was imprisoned in Caesarea in the praetorium of Herod (Acts 23:35)—the residence of the Roman procurator and headquarters for the Roman garrison in Palestine. (2) Paul's imprisonment in Caesarea was a long one (Acts 24:27), allowing time for several communications to travel back and forth from Caesarea to Philippi. (3) Although Paul was kept in custody, he was nevertheless given considerable liberty with opportunity to be aided by his friends (Acts 24:23; cf. Phil 2:25-30; 4:10-20). (4) Philippians 1:7 implies that Paul had already been given a hearing and had made a defense for himself and his gospel, while Philippians 1:16 indicates that Paul still lay in prison in spite of his defense. This harmonizes with the events that took place in Caesarea (Acts 24:1-27), whereas the story of Paul in Rome concludes by describing him as a prisoner, leaving no hint that he had made any defense of any kind (Acts 28:16-31). (5) When Paul wrote to the Philippians he was confident he would be released from prison (Phil 1:24-26) and would visit them on his journey west (Phil 2:24; cf. Rom 1:13-15; 15:23-29). Here again is a close correlation between the statements in Philippians and those in Acts (Acts 19:21; 23:11). Paul's plans to move west were large in his thinking because he believed his work in the east was done (Rom 15:20, 23-24). To assume then that he later changed his mind and made plans to return east from Rome would be a perplexing assumption and one without foundation in fact. It is not unreasonable, however, to assume that Paul would want to return to Philippi on his way from Caesarea westward, in order to see his loyal and generous friends.

The objections to Caesarea are not sufficient to eliminate the assumption that this was the place from which Paul wrote to the Philippians. (1) The objection that the distance from Caesarea to Philippi is too great for the number of communications back and forth is overruled in part by the length of Paul's stay in the Caesarean prison. Too much, thus, may have been made of this matter of distance when considering either Rome or Caesarea. (2) The objection that wherever Paul was when he wrote Philippians he was facing the very real possibility of death is also not a valid objection to Caesarea (cf. Acts 21:31, 36; 22:22; 23:30). It is true that as a Roman

citizen Paul had the right of appeal to Caesar, but if the Jews could have proved that he had brought a Gentile into that part of the temple forbidden to Gentiles, thus desecrating their holy place, then even as a Roman citizen he would, under Jewish law, have been liable to death at the hands of the Jews (cf. Acts 25:11, and see Josephus *J.W.* §§5.193-94; Josephus *Ant.* §15.417).

Not all questions can be answered in this matter, and in reality there is no possibility of knowing with absolute certainty where it was that Paul wrote Philippians. Yet for the sake of trying to understand this letter, and especially in the interest of trying to identify the opponents mentioned in it, it may be argued that Caesarea fits the evidence as well as, or perhaps better than, any other theory of the letter's provenance.

4.3.2. Date. If Paul wrote the letter to the Philippians from Rome, then he wrote it sometime in the early 60s, between A.D. 60 and 63; if from Ephesus, between A.D. 54 and 57; if from Corinth, about A.D. 50. But if he wrote this letter from Caesarea, then he wrote it sometime in the period A.D. 58-60.

4.4. Adversaries. The adversaries mentioned in Philippians cannot be understood as a single group of people but as several (*see* Adversaries [Paul]). One group opposed Paul, and though they preached Christ, they did so for the purpose of adding to Paul's sufferings while he was in prison. These were fellow Christians, irrespective of such a hostile attitude on their part, for Paul calls them "brothers" (Phil 1:14-15). These Christians may have had a divine man theology that made them view such matters as humility, meekness, imprisonment and suffering—things that Paul advocated or was experiencing—as proof that he knew nothing of the triumphant power of Christ and hence was an unworthy candidate for a Christian leader who might be emulated. Or they may have been Judaizers, who taught not only the need for faith in Christ but the necessity also of keeping the Jewish law, including circumcision and regulations about food and drink, and who thus were at odds with Paul since he held tenaciously to the necessity of faith in Christ but rejected the necessity of keeping the law.

But there was also a second group of opponents—people very different from those in the group mentioned above. These had threatened the Philippians, had made them afraid because of their threats and had tried to undermine the firmness of the Philippians' faith in the gospel (Phil 1:27-29). Very likely this group was the same as those Paul would call "dogs," "evil workers," "mutilators" (Phil 3:2), "enemies of the cross of Christ" (Phil 3:18), people "whose end is destruction" (Phil 3:19). They can hardly be identified as Judaizers—that is, Jewish Christians—but rather as Jews, Jewish missionaries in particular, who aggressively pushed for converts at Philippi, even with force. They proclaimed a message that righteousness and perfection were attainable "now" (cf. Phil 3:12-15) by submitting to circumcision and complying with certain ritual laws (Phil 3:19)—a message that offered visible and tangible tokens of God's favor in the present, not in the future and invisible world. Paul's exceedingly harsh words in Philippians 3:2 probably reflect his frustration over the fanatical and unrelenting opposition he was encountering from the Jews in Jerusalem and Caesarea (Acts 21:37—26:32; cf. Acts 28:19).

4.5. The Christ Hymn. Philippians 2:6-11 is the prime example of an early Christian hymn. But who wrote it, and what was the source of the ideas expressed here? Many scholars consider that Paul was its author (cf. Martin 1960), and this has been the traditional view. The way in which this section dovetails so perfectly into Paul's argument in Philippians 2 and into the whole tenor of the letter does not immediately lead one to look for another writer. Some scholars, however, have seen features of style, vocabulary and doctrine in the hymn that suggest a composer other than Paul. But whether it was the work of Paul or some other Christian hymn writer makes little difference, since it fits Paul's purpose at this point, harmonizes with his thinking as he writes to the Philippians and is incorporated into his letter without reservation.

Scholars have looked in many different directions for the source of the ideas in this hymn. Some have suggested the background of the Gnostic "Redeemed-Redeemer" myth that describes the descent into this world of a "light-person," who comes to bring knowledge to the sons of light, appears in human form and endures misery, pain and suffering like other humans until he leaves this world and returns to the world of light (Bultmann, 1:167).

Others have looked to the Adam theme from the Old Testament. *Adam and Christ were hu-

man beings made in the image of God (Gen 1:26; Phil 2:6, "image" and "form" being treated as synonymous), but whereas Adam disobeyed and grasped after being like God, Christ obeyed God and instead of grasping for equality with God chose the way of servanthood and mortality. As a consequence the first Adam was cast out of paradise because of his self-seeking, but the last Adam, Christ, was exalted by God and given the highest place because of his self-giving (Dunn, 114-21; but contrast Wright).

Perhaps one does not need to look so far afield as these scholars have suggested. There is recorded in the Gospel tradition (Jn 13:3-17) an incident from the life of Christ that provides an almost perfect model for the movement of the Christ hymn of Philippians 2. Both the Fourth Evangelist and Paul begin what they have to say in a similar fashion. John starts his narrative by saying that Jesus washed his disciples' feet (the work of a slave/servant) because he knew that the Father had given everything into his hands and that he had come out from God and was going back to God (Jn 13:3; cf. Hawthorne 1983, 78-79). The Philippian hymn begins by stating "that Jesus, being in the form of God and yet not taking advantage of his being equal with God, took the form of a slave, and did the work of a servant" (Phil 2:6-8). The entire hymn preserves the descent-ascent motif that is prominent in the Gospel story (13:3-17) (Hawthorne 1987, 65).

5. Theological Themes.

Because of its theological themes, the influence of the letter to the Philippians on the church seems to be out of all proportion to its size. Perhaps this in large part is due to the exquisite Christ hymn (Phil 2:6-11), a hymn that elegantly sums up Paul's teaching about the person of Jesus Christ and of the nature of God (*see* Christology).

While providing a magnificent description of Jesus Christ—preexistent, equal with God, becoming incarnate, a human being, a servant, totally obedient to God, in turn exalted by God to the highest place in heaven or on earth, the object of *worship for all created beings to the glory of God the Father—this hymn also articulately describes who God really is. For Jesus Christ, who shared the very nature of God and acted out of that nature, showed by what he chose to do and by what he in fact did that God's true nature is not characterized by seizing, grasping or attaining but rather by sharing, by open-handed giving and by pouring oneself out for others in order to enrich them.

Whether or not Paul composed this hymn, it undoubtedly was an integral part of the letter and not a later interpolation because by it Paul provides the Philippians with the basis of his ethical appeal. He begs them to live humbly, generously, unself-consciously, while being thoughtfully concerned for the welfare of those around them (Phil 2:1-5), for this was the attitude that Christ Jesus possessed and that governed all of his conduct—an attitude to be emulated by all who call themselves by his name.

The Christ hymn is not the only factor contributing to the influence of Philippians. Here in this letter one also finds Paul's motto for life, which in turn has become the life motto for many Christians ever since: "For me to live is Christ; to die is gain" (Phil 1:21). These two statements, coupled with the one that follows, namely, that "to depart and to be with Christ is a very much better thing [than living]," have had great theological significance. They suggest that the condition of Christians who die in the Lord is one of conscious happiness beyond anything experienced on earth. If indeed they do make such a suggestion, they then raise the question of the need for the resurrection of the body or for a new body from heaven (see Cullmann; but see also Phil 3:20-21).

Furthermore, there is in Philippians the often-quoted remark of Paul, "work out your own salvation . . . for it is God who is at work in you" (Phil 2:12-13). This remark, rarely put in its context so as to be properly understood, has influenced the thinking of those who argue for the sovereignty of God and of those who champion the free will of human beings. In the context of Philippians 2, Paul is not using the word *salvation* to refer to eschatological salvation, the salvation of one's eternal soul, but rather to the health of the Christian community in Philippi. Torn apart by conceit, pride and selfishness (Phil 2:3-4), the Philippians hear in these words the urging of the apostle to follow the example of Christ (Phil 2:5-11), to humble themselves and to take the role of the servant, to work obediently at bringing healing (i.e., "salvation") to their church and to work at this task until it is accomplished. If they do this, they will discover that they have only been cooperating with God, who is already at work among them giving them

these desires for wholeness and the energy to fulfill their desires.

In all of Paul's letters, perhaps the most important statement having to do with the doctrine of sanctification is found in Philippians 3:8-16. Holiness described here is an ever-increasing apprehension of the surpassing worth of Jesus Christ by the Christian, with nothing whatsoever allowed to destroy or diminish this apprehension. In turn it is also an apprehension of the Christian by Jesus Christ. Both elements are present—the work of God or Christ, and the work of the Christian. Sanctification for Paul, therefore, allows room for growth, increase, advancement and progress on the part of the Christian (Phil 1:9, 25). As the many imperatives present throughout this letter indicate, sanctification demands progress (e.g., Phil 4:8-9; see Beker, 218-19).

Finally, the theme of joy that runs throughout Philippians has had a profound influence on Christians through the centuries, drawing them back to this letter again and again. Here one learns that joy is not so much a feeling as it is a settled state of mind characterized by peace, an attitude that views life—including all of its ups and downs—with equanimity. It is a confident way of looking at life that is rooted in faith in the living Lord of the church (Phil 1:25; 3:1; 4:4, 10). For Paul, joy is an understanding of existence that makes it possible for one to accept elation and depression, to accept with creative submission events that bring either delight or dismay, because joy allows one to see beyond any particular event to the sovereign Lord who stands above all events.

See also CHRISTOLOGY.

DPL: CAESAR'S HOUSEHOLD, IMPERIAL HOUSEHOLD; IMITATION OF PAUL/OF CHRIST; JOY.

BIBLIOGRAPHY. **Commentaries:** K. Barth, *The Epistle to the Philippians* (Richmond: John Knox, 1962); F. W. Beare, *A Commentary on the Epistle to the Philippians* (HNTC; New York: Harper, 1959); M. Bockmuehl, *The Epistle to the Philippians* (BNTC; Peabody, MA: Hendrickson, 1997); J.-F. Collange, *The Epistle of Saint Paul to the Philippians* (London: Epworth, 1979); G. D. Fee, *Paul's Letter to the Philippians* (NICNT; Grand Rapids: Eerdmans, 1995); idem, *Philippians* (IVPNTC; Downers Grove, IL: InterVarsity Press, 1999); G. F. Hawthorne, *Philippians* (WBC 43; Waco, TX: Word, 1983); J. B. Lightfoot, *St. Paul's Epistle to the Philippians* (London: Macmillan, 1894);

I. H. Marshall, *The Epistle to the Philippians* (EC; Valley Forge, PA: Trinity Press International, 1992); R. P. Martin, *The Epistle of Paul to the Philippians* (TNTC; Grand Rapids: Eerdmans, 1959); idem, *Philippians* (NCB; Grand Rapids: Eerdmans, 1976); J. H. Michael, *The Epistle to the Philippians* (MNTC; London: Hodder and Stoughton, 1928); P. T. O'Brien, *The Epistle to the Philippians* (NIGTC; Grand Rapids: Eerdmans, 1991); M. Silva, *Philippians* (WEC; Chicago: Moody Press, 1988). **Studies:** J. M. Bassler, ed., *Pauline Theology* vol 1: *Thessalonians, Philippians, Galatians, Philemon* (Minneapolis: Fortress, 1991); F. C. Baur, *Paul, the Apostle of Jesus Christ* (2 vols.; London: Williams and Norgate, 1875); J. C. Beker, *Paul the Apostle* (Philadelphia: Fortress, 1980); R. Bultmann, *Theology of the New Testament* (2 vols.; New York: Scribners, 1951); O. Cullmann, *Immortality of the Soul or the Resurrection of the Dead* (London: Epworth, 1958); J. D. G. Dunn, *Christology in the Making* (Philadelphia: Westminster, 1980); D. E. Garland, "The Composition and Literary Unity of Philippians: Some Neglected Factors," *NovT* 27 (1985) 141-73; G. F. Hawthorne, *Word Biblical Themes: Philippians* (Waco, TX: Word, 1987); M. D. Hooker, "Pistis Cristou," *NTS* 35 (1989) 331-33; L. Hurtado, "Jesus as Lordly Example in Phil. 2:5-11," in *From Jesus to Paul: Studies in Honor of Francis Wright Beare*, ed. J. C. Hurd and G. P. Richardson (Waterloo, ON: Laurier University Press, 1984); R. P. Martin, *An Early Christian Confession: Philippians 2:5-11 in Recent Interpretation* (London: Tyndale Press, 1960); idem, *A Hymn of Christ: Philippians 2:5-11 in Recent Interpretation and in the Setting of Early Christian Worship* (3d ed.; Downers Grove, IL: InterVarsity Press, 1997); R. P. Martin and B. J. Dodd, eds., *Where Christology Began: Essays on Philippians 2* (Louisville, KY: Westminster John Knox, 1998); D. F. Watson, "A Rhetorical Analysis of Philippians, and Its Implications for the Unity Question," *NovT* 30 (1988) 57-88; N. T. Wright, "Harpagmos and the Meaning of Philippians 2:5-11," *JTS* 37 (Oct 1986) 321-52.   G. F. Hawthorne

PHILOSOPHY

The subject matter of philosophy as it emerges in Greece from the beginning of the sixth century with Thales of Miletus (fl. c. 585 B.C.) is grouped around three basic questions: What is there?—that is to say, what is the world made of, what is its origin and what is its end, if any? What ought we to do?—that is, what are the bases, natural or conventional, of personal and social morality? How can we know?—that is, what is the criterion of knowledge, as opposed to opinion, and what are the laws of reasoning and of proof? From these basic philosophical questions arise in this historical order the topics respectively of physics, including metaphysics, ethics and logic. The earliest philosophizing was really physics in this broad sense, and much of what constitutes pre-Socratic philosophy has more to do with the origins of science than with philosophy in the sense relevant to this article.

1. The Pre-Socratic Period
2. Plato and Aristotle
3. Hellenistic Philosophy: Stoics and Epicureans
4. The Philosophies of the Roman Empire

1. The Pre-Socratic Period.

The term *philosophia*, or "love of wisdom," as well as much of the substance behind that term is an invention not of the earliest recorded philosophers, the Milesian school of Thales and his successors, but rather of Pythagoras (fl. c. 520) and his followers in southern Italy, around the end of the sixth century B.C. The significance of this neologism, in Pythagoras's mind, was that he felt, in contrast to the early physicists and other contemporary experts (who would have called themselves *sophoi*) that wisdom *(sophia)* properly belonged to God alone, and that humans could only aspire to being seekers after wisdom *(philosophos)*.

For Pythagoras and the tradition stemming from him, including that of Plato, this search for wisdom involved not only the postulation of certain principles but also the adoption of a distinct moral code, or way of life *(bios)*. In the case of the original Pythagoreans this *bios* meant a strictly regulated communal life, anticipating in many ways that of later Christian monastic communities; abstention from animal food because of a belief in reincarnation and the kinship of all souls, human and animal; and a series of taboos, such as that against the eating of beans, probably devised by Pythagoras to give his followers a sense of distinctness.

Such a degree of discipline, however, remained peculiar to the Pythagoreans. Their philosophical doctrines became widely influential through commending themselves to Plato. Pythagoras's chief philosophical insight was that the world was held together and given coherence by the operation of harmony and proportion, which could be expressed in terms of mathematical ratios. The dominant creative principle was One, or unity (the Monad), which acted on an archetypal, formless substratum, symbolized by the number Two (the Dyad). The union of these two generated primarily the whole system of numbers and secondarily the world of physical objects, which, for the early Pythagoreans, were to be regarded as numbers.

Pythagoras was also the first to give philosophical underpinning to the originally shamanistic notion of the soul as something separable from the body, which is not just an insubstantial shade but the true repository of the personality. For him, and for Plato after him, immortality for the soul was inextricably involved with reincarnation, into both human and (in the case of unsatisfactory humans) animal bodies. The problems about personal identity that this involves do not seem to have bothered ancient thinkers.

2. Plato and Aristotle.

Plato (427-347 B.C.) is the spiritual heir to Pythagoras, but in constructing his philosophy he was also much influenced by the intellectual challenges laid down by Parmenides of Elea (c. 515-445 B.C.) and Heraclitus of Ephesus (fl. c. 500 B.C.). Heraclitus seems to have been the first to view the world *(kosmos)* as a system: in constant flux but held together in a tension of opposites, by a force that he termed *logos* ("ratio," "reason," "word"). Parmenides focused on the problem of being, what must be the characteristics of what is, and declared that it must be one, eternal, uniform and motionless, and that only what is can be known: there can be no knowledge of what is not. The true subject of these mysterious pronouncements remained a puzzle for subsequent thinkers, but they make the best sense if they are taken to concern the totality of what is. To confuse matters, Parmenides also composed an account of the physical world, which for him was a realm of illusion. Plato took up the challenge thus posed by postulating first an intelligible realm of true Being, which fulfilled Parmenides' prescription, and served as home of the Forms, ideal archetypes of all physical reality, and then a sense-perceptible realm of Becoming, in which we dwell, which is in constant (Heraclitean) flux but held together

nonetheless by the system of Forms, which project themselves upon a material substratum in the form of geometrical structures (the basic triangles and their combinations described in his dialogue *Timaeus*).

However, Pythagoras is the dominant influence on Plato and his immediate successors, Speusippus and Xenocrates, under whom Platonism becomes properly a system. All their works have perished, but we can see from the titles that are preserved their formalizing tendency, of Xenocrates in particular, and that propensity for reinterpreting Pythagoras to accord with their doctrines that is the origin of Neo-Pythagoreanism. Speusippus advanced a doctrine of the first principle, that it is a unity beyond being, which finds no support in mainline Platonism before Plotinus but which seems to have found echoes in less orthodox Neo-Pythagorean and platonizing gnostic circles. Xenocrates, perhaps influenced to some extent by Aristotle, postulated as a first principle a monad that is also an intellect and whose contents were probably, though not certainly, envisaged as being the Forms (this is the case in the Platonism of such figures as Antiochus and Eudorus in the first century B.C.).

Plato's most distinguished successor, however, was his most dissident one, Aristotle (384-322 B.C.). Aristotle, son of a distinguished doctor from Stagira in the north of Greece, had joined Plato's Academy in 367 B.C., at the age of seventeen, and remained with him until his death, though showing an increasing tendency to argue with him on basic issues. After a period abroad, Aristotle set up his own rival school across town, the Lyceum, or Peripatos, in 335 B.C. Aristotle greatly advanced all departments of philosophy, metaphysics, physics, ethics and logic, but despite his polemical stance toward Plato, his disagreements with him chiefly concern the theory of Forms, the general tendency to mathematicize the universe (evident particularly in Plato's other successors) and the doctrine of the separable nature of the soul. Later Platonists managed to appropriate most of Aristotelian philosophy into a common Academic synthesis, even contriving to downplay his objections to the Forms and his denial of the separate existence of the soul. In the former case, he was held to be referring to the immanent form *(eidos)*, a projection into matter of the transcendent form *(idea);* in the latter, likewise, his analysis (in the *De Anima*) is thought to concern only the soul in its embodied mode—a triumphant exercise of the late antique philosophical conviction that great minds must at all costs think alike, as well as being entirely consistent with themselves!

Aristotle's doctrine of the supreme principle, or God, as a mind thinking itself becomes standard Platonic doctrine up to the time of Plotinus, when a doctrine stemming from Speusippus is reasserted, of a unitary first principle, above being and intellection, the self-thinking mind being relegated to second place in the universe. Such doctrines as those of the four causes, of matter, of potentiality and actuality, and the whole of Aristotelian logic, are also taken on board. In the sphere of ethics, the doctrines advanced in the *Nicomachean Ethics,* such as those of virtue as a mean, the moderation of the passions and contemplation *(theōria)* as the supreme purpose of human life, are accepted likewise. It was felt by later Platonists that in all these areas Aristotle was formalizing the common doctrine of the Academy.

3. Hellenistic Philosophy: Stoics and Epicureans.

During the Hellenistic era, dating broadly from the death of Alexander the Great in 323 B.C. to the defeat of Antony and Cleopatra by Augustus in 31 B.C., the cutting edge of philosophy was represented not by either the Academy (which after Polemon deviated into skepticism) or by the Lyceum (which after Aristotle's successor, Theophrastus, declined into antiquarianism and triviality) but rather by the rival schools of Stoics and Epicureans, the one founded by Zeno of Kition in Cyprus (335-263 B.C.), a creative admirer of the Cynic movement, the other by the Athenian Epicurus (341-270 B.C.), a dissident follower of the Atomists, but both based in Athens.

Of these, the Epicureans have little to offer from the perspective of Christianity—being materialists, constructive atheists (Epicurus held that the gods existed but were not concerned with humans) and devotees of pleasure as the highest aim of human life—except for their advancement of certain arguments that they developed against the existence of the traditional Greek gods, which are borrowed gratefully by the church fathers. The Stoics, by contrast, despite their materialism, are of great importance. In metaphysics, their conception of the *Logos,

or creative reason-principle of God, which is borrowed back by later Platonists as a demythologized version of the Demiurge of Plato's *Timaeus,* becomes crucial for the development of christological doctrine from the Fourth Gospel on and causes difficulties later about the relation of the Son to the Father.

In epistemology, the Stoics' most important contribution was to postulate the concept of the "cognitive impression" *(kataleptikē phantasia),* the essential feature of which was that it could not have come from anything other than that of which it did in fact come. On this basis they were able to construct a system involving propositions of which one could be certain, such as "gods exist" and "they exercise providential care over the world"—this in the face of the pervasive skepticism being advanced by the Platonic Academy of the time.

In ethics, too, the Stoics set up an ideal of the extirpation of the passions *(apatheia),* as against the less extreme Aristotelian ideal of their moderation *(metriopatheia),* which proved attractive both to many Platonists and to many of the church fathers. The Stoics propounded an ideal of the Sage as self-sufficient and impervious to the blows of fortune, an ideal that was in one way attractive to Christian ascetics but in another way antithetical to the Christian ideal of brotherly love and concern for one's fellow humans.

5. The Philosophies of the Roman Empire.

In the first century B.C., various important developments took place. The Platonist Antiochus of Ascalon (c. 130-69 B.C.), much influenced by Stoic thought, turned Platonism back to dogmatism in a way that was to prove fruitful for later ages, though a transcendental element derived from Neo-Pythagoreanism, which reestablished a supreme deity as immaterial and external to the physical world, needed to be added before the synthetic philosophical system known as Middle Platonism could emerge in the first centuries A.D. and exercise a significant influence on emergent Christianity. At the same time, a revitalized Stoicism, the most notable representatives of which were the Roman nobleman Seneca (c. 4 B.C.-A.D. 65), the freed slave Epictetus (mid-first to mid-second century A.D.), and the emperor Marcus Aurelius Antoninus (A.D. 121-180), popularized and developed the basic principles of Stoic ethics in such a way as to influence both Platonism and Christianity.

In many ways, the new synthesis developed by the third-century Platonist Plotinus (A.D. 204-269), taking in many concepts from both Aristotelianism and Stoicism but adding also a strongly transcendentalist element derived from the Neo-Pythagoreanism of Numenius (fl. c. A.D. 150) provided a stimulus for later Christian thinkers such as the Cappadocian fathers. In Plotinus we find for the first time, in a coherent form, the concept of a first principle superior to intellect, the One, adumbrated by Plato's successor Speusippus but overlaid then by the Aristotelian concept of God as a self-thinking intellect. This development, however, which becomes a distinguishing mark of later Platonism, was one that Christian thinkers were disinclined to follow, as it conflicted with the concept of a personal God. Only in the writings of the mysterious sixth-century Christian Platonist going under the name of Dionysius the Areopagite is this concept taken on board, with fantastic results.

For Plotinus, as for most other philosophers of the period, philosophy is a matter of seeking the best way of purifying the soul from the influences of the body and the external world and leading it back to its source in the intelligible world. Both his ethical theory and his epistemology are directed to that end. He expends much effort in trying to bring us to a realization of our true nature, being that of a strictly impassive soul immured in a body animated by a sort of emanation from this soul, which is the seat of "vulgar" consciousness, involving passions and sense perceptions but which does not properly constitute the core of our being. Such a scenario, while considerably more austere than the normal Christian view, presents a challenge that a number of the more Platonically minded fathers, such as the Cappadocians, found stimulating.

See also GNOSTICISM.

DNTB: ARISTOTLE, ARISTOTELIANISM; CYNIC EPISTLES; CYNICISM AND SKEPTICISM; EPICTETUS; EPICUREANISM; NEO-PYTHAGOREANISM; PLATO, PLATONISM; SENECA; STOICISM.

BIBLIOGRAPHY. A. H. Armstrong, *An Introduction to Greek Philosophy* (London: Methuen, 1947); idem, ed., *The Cambridge History of Late Ancient and Early Medieval Philosophy* (Cambridge: Cambridge University Press, 1967); J. M. Dillon, *The Middle Platonists* (Ithaca, NY: Cornell University Press, 1977); W. K. C. Guthrie, *A History of Greek Philosophy* (Cambridge: Cambridge University Press, 1962).   J. M. Dillon

PLATO, PLATONISM. *See* PHILOSOPHY.

PONTIUS PILATE. *See* TRIAL OF JESUS.

POVERTY. *See* RICHES AND POVERTY.

PRAISE. *See* WORSHIP.

PRAYER. *See* WORSHIP.

PRIESTS. *See* JUDAISM AND THE NEW TESTAMENT.

PRINCIPALITIES AND POWERS. *See* EPHESIANS, LETTER TO THE.

PROPHECY. *See* HOLY SPIRIT.

PROTO-GNOSTICISM. *See* ADVERSARIES; COLOSSIANS, LETTER TO THE.

PSALMS OF SOLOMON. *See* APOCRYPHA AND PSEUDEPIGRAPHA.

PSEUDEPIGRAPHA. *See* APOCRYPHA AND PSEUDEPIGRAPHA; DEAD SEA SCROLLS.

PSEUDEPIGRAPHY, NEW TESTAMENT. *See* EPHESIANS, LETTER TO THE; PASTORAL LETTERS.

Q, R

RABBINIC TRADITIONS AND WRITINGS

The documents of rabbinic Judaism—primarily Mishnah, Tosepta, Talmud, midrash and targums—were inscribed over several centuries following the NT era but contain earlier traditions, some of which date from the first century. Their particular value for students of the NT is that, when critically evaluated, they offer insights into the Jewish matrix of the birth of Christianity.

1. The Roots of the Rabbinic Movement
2. The Transition to Rabbinic Judaism
3. The Emergence of Rabbinic Literature
4. The Use of Rabbinica in Understanding Jesus and the Gospels

1. The Roots of the Rabbinic Movement.

In its earliest phase the rabbinic movement may be identified with Pharisaism. The Pharisees are portrayed by Josephus as being critical of the Hasmonean priesthood. Their expression was at first political (Josephus *Ant.* 13.10.5-6 §§288-98) and could extend to violent action, as in the demand that the counselors who advised Alexander Jannaeus to kill some of their sympathizers should themselves be executed (Josephus *J.W.* 1.5.2-3 §§110-14). At base, however, the orientation of the Pharisees was toward the achievement and maintenance of purity. The purity they strived for had to do fundamentally with making offerings, people and priests fit for the cult of sacrifice in the temple. For that reason the issues of the personnel of the priesthood, the sorts of animals and goods that might be brought, and their permissible proximity to all sources of uncleanness were vitally important.

1.1. Hillel. By the dawn of the present era the Pharisees found a distinguished teacher in Jerusalem in the person of Hillel. Hillel is justly famous for the dictum, uttered some twenty years before Jesus, "That which you hate, do not do to your fellow; that is the whole Torah, while all the rest is commentary thereon" (*b. Šabb.* 31a). The saying is striking, but it can also be misleading. In context Hillel is talking to an impatient proselyte who wishes to learn the Torah while he stands on one foot; his impatience has just won him a cuff with a measuring rod from Shammai, the rabbi with whom Hillel is programmatically contrasted in Mishnah. Obviously, Hillel has no overt desire to reduce the Torah on the grounds of principle, and he goes to tell the proselyte, "Go and learn it." In other words, the Gentile is told that the revelation to Moses is the expression of the best ethics, and for that reason the whole should be mastered.

In any case, Hillel was understood among the Pharisees as having come to prominence for adjudicating quite a distinct issue: whether the Passover could be offered on the Sabbath. Hillel first offers a scriptural argument for accepting the practice: since other forms of priestly service are permitted, so is the slaying of the lamb. His hearers are unimpressed until he simply states that he learned the position in Babylon, from Shemaiah and Abtalion, distinguished predecessors in the movement. Their authority is sufficient to displace the current leaders of Pharisaic opinion, the sons of Bathyra (cf. *t. Pesaḥ.* 4.13-14; *y. Pesaḥ.* 6.1; *y. Šabb.* 19.1; *b. Pesaḥ.* 66a).

The latter story may appear the more arcane, but it is also more redolent of Pharisaic culture. Hillel consistently involved himself in cultic questions and disputes in Jerusalem. His position also is said to have convinced another teacher, Baba ben Buṭa, to provide cultically correct beasts in great numbers for slaughter, with the stipulation (against the school of Shammai) that the offerer lay hands on the victim immediately prior to the killing (cf. *t. Ḥag.* 2.11; *y. Ḥag.* 2.3; *y. Beṣah* 2.4; *b. Beṣah* 20a, b; see 4.3 below).

Moreover, the basis of Hillel's authority was not so much—as has been seen above—any scriptural expertise as his mastery of what he had been taught by previous masters. Hillel embodies the Pharisaic principle that the "chains" of their tradition were normative for purity. Such chains were understood to have been developed from Moses to the Prophets, after that by Ezra and "the men of the great congregation," and then by teachers who were generally invoked as "pairs" (*m. ʾAbot* 1:1-18). The last "pair" was Hillel and Shammai, from which point the Pharisees acknowledged that division increased in Israel (*b. Soṭa* 47b; *b. Sanh.* 88b; *t. Soṭa* 14.9; *t. Ḥag.* 2.9; *t. Sanh.* 7.1; *y. Ḥag.* 2.2; *y. Sanh.* 1.4). The notion of primeval unity disturbed by recent faction is probably mythical, but it is plain that the Pharisees developed their oral tradition by means of a structured understanding of the past as well as by mnemonic techniques.

1.2. Pharisees. The term *Pharisee* is probably an outsiders' name for the movement, and may mean "separatist" or "purist"; participants in the movement appear to have referred to their ancient predecessors (after Ezra) as "the sages" or "the wise," and to their more recent predecessors and contemporaries as "teachers" (cf. *rab* in *m. ʾAbot* 1:6, 16; *sophistēs* in Josephus). The normal, respectful address of a teacher was "my great one" or "my master," *rabbî*. In the Gospels people address Jesus as "rabbi" more frequently than by any other title. Moreover, Jesus had a characteristic interest in purity, and a dispute concerning appropriate sacrifice in the temple cost him his life.

The Gospels as they stand allow the straightforward deduction that Jesus' followers called him "rabbi" (Mt 26:25, 49; Mk 9:5; 10:51; 11:21; 14:45; Jn 1:38, 49; 3:2; 4:31; 6:25; 9:2; 11:8); they likewise allow the straightforward inference that he is most naturally to be associated with the Pharisees of his period. But in the course of the twentieth century scholars have expressed reservations regarding this finding, bearing in mind the danger of identifying Jesus with the rabbinic movement after A.D. 70. The latter movement was more systematized than the Pharisees before A.D. 70, amounting to the established power within Judaism. Unfortunately, anxiety with respect to the danger of anachronism can result in the far greater error of locating Jesus within sectarian Judaism (as if orthodoxy existed in early, pluralized Judaism). Worse still, Jesus might be placed within no Judaism at all.

During the time of Hillel and Shammai, and until A.D. 70, Pharisaic teaching was targeted at the conduct of the cult in the temple, but its influence was limited. Nonetheless, Pharisees appeared to have succeeded reasonably well in towns and villages. Even in Galilee they urged local populations to maintain the sort of purity that would permit them to participate rightly in the cult. Josephus's fellow in the armed resistance against Rome and his archrival, John of Gischala, may well have been representing Pharisaic interests when he arranged for Jews in Syria to purchase oil exclusively from Galilean sources (Josephus *J.W.* 2.21.2 §§591-93). In any case, it does appear plain that some Pharisees supported the revolt of A.D. 66-70 while others did not. But while many priests and Essenes perished in the internecine strife of the revolt and in the war with the Romans, and while the aristocracy of scribes and elders in Jerusalem was discredited and decimated, the Pharisees survived the war better than any other single group. They were well accepted locally, had long ago accommodated to some marginality, and survived with their personnel and their traditions comparatively in tact.

Rabbinic literature itself personifies the survival of the movement in a story concerning Rabbi Yoḥanan ben Zakkai. According to the story Yoḥanan had himself borne out of Jerusalem on the pretense that he was dead, only to hail Vespasian as king. On his ascent to power Vespasian granted Yoḥanan his wish of settlement in the town of Yavneh, the group of Rabbi Gamaliel, and medical attention for Rabbi Zadok (cf. *b. Giṭ.* 56a, b). In that Josephus claims similarly to have flattered Vespasian (*J.W.* 3.8.9 §§399-408) and to have seen in his coming the fulfillment of messianic prophecy (*J.W.* 6.5.4 §§310-15), the tale is to be used with caution. But it remains expressive of the rabbinic ethos.

2. The Transition to Rabbinic Judaism.
With the foundation of academies such as the one at Yavneh after A.D. 70, one may speak of the transition of Pharisaism to rabbinic Judaism.

The rabbis, those who directly contributed to rabbinic literature and to the Judaism that is framed by that literature, belonged to a movement much changed from the popular puritanism of the Pharisees. Initially this was for reasons not of their own making.

2.1. The Wider Application of Tradition. The sort of leadership which a Yoḥanan ben Zakkai might offer became suddenly attractive in the absence of priestly, Essene or scribal alternatives. The target of the tradition's application became correspondingly wider. The Pharisaic/rabbinic program was applied not simply to issues of purity and sacrifice, but to worship generally, to ethics and to daily living.

Yoḥanan is explicitly attributed with the view that the world, which had been sustained by the temple, the law and deeds of faithful love, now was to be supported only by the last two of the three (*'Abot R. Nat.* 4). Moreover, on the basis of his tradition he specifically adjudicated how feasts might be kept in the gathering for reading, prayer and discussion which was called a "congregation," or "synagogue" (*kenēset*, also applied to buildings erected for the purpose of such gatherings; cf. *m. Sukk.* 3:12; *m. Roš Haš.* 4:1, 3, 4). The development of that sort of worship as a replacement for activity within the temple was not without analogy during the period prior to A.D. 70. Mishnah (*m. Taʿan.* 4:2) envisages a system in which priests, Levites and lay people alike gathered in local synagogues while their representatives were in Jerusalem.

The germ of such piety perhaps lay in the priestly system of courses of service that allowed for a substantial population of priests, divided into twenty-four courses. During the course of the week a given course was appointed to cover, a few priests were chosen to officiate in Jerusalem. Meanwhile, the remainder may have gathered and read the appropriate lections in the villages of Judea and Galilee where they normally lived (1 Chron 24:1-19; Josephus *Ant.* 7.14.7 §365-67). The inclusion of the faithful in Israel in such meetings was a natural development under the rabbis, and general meetings for prayer and instruction had long been a customary feature of Judaism in the Diaspora. It was therefore natural that worship in synagogues should develop as something of a replacement for worship in the temple.

2.2. The Consolidation of Power. However, the transition from Pharisaism to rabbinic Judaism was not accomplished immediately after A.D. 70, nor was it simply a matter of the same movement with the same personnel carrying on in a totally new environment. The environment was new, of course, and uniquely favored the emerging authority of rabbis. But the Pharisees of the period were sufficiently flexible to accommodate an influx of priests and scribes into their ranks after the destruction of the temple. The priestly interest of the Pharisaic movement, of course, was historically organic, and the references to priests in stories and teachings from the time of Yoḥanan (cf. Rabbi Yosi the Priest, *m. 'Abot* 2:8) and well into the second century is striking. Moreover, the consolidation of the rabbis' power after A.D. 70, predicated as it was on local influence, could only be assured by means of the control of local adjudication, as well as worship and study. The tendency of scribes to align themselves with the Pharisees, together with priestly adherents and sympathizers with the movement, assured the emergence and the success of the rabbis.

The triumph of rabbinic authority assured the continuing influence of the priests in decisions regarding purity, in blessings and in receipts of payment of redemption and of tithe. At the same time, scribal influence in the production of written materials and the convocation of formal courts is also striking. Nonetheless, the functional consolidation of the power of the old groups and factions was only achieved during the time of Rabbi Judah (toward the end of the second century) with the emergence of a patriarchate recognized and supported by the Romans.

2.3. The Priority of Learned Consensus. In the wake of A.D. 70 and the Roman confiscation of the tax formerly paid for the temple, neither Jerusalem nor its environs was amenable to the maintenance of a hub of the movement. During the second century centers in prosperous Galilee, such as Usha and Beth She'arim would eclipse even Yavneh. Later yet, metropolitan cities such as Sepphoris and Tiberias were the foci of leadership. There was at first nothing like a central leadership or even a common policy, but rabbinic Judaism was constituted in the Pharisaic, priestly and scribal quest for the purity of the nation. The health of the movement required a shift from the highly personal authority of the Pharisees to some notion of learned consensus.

Just that shift is reflected in a Talmudic story

concerning a great teacher, Rabbi Eliezer ben Hyrcanus. The story has it that, against a majority of his colleagues, Eliezer held that a ceramic stove, once polluted, might be reassembled, provided the tiles were separated by sand. The majority taught that the result would be unclean; such materials should never be used again. Eliezer's correctness was demonstrated by a tree that was uprooted at his behest, by a stream that ran backward at his command, by a building he similarly demolished, and by a voice from heaven. Despite all that, the majority held that its decision was binding (*b. B. Meṣ.* 59a, b). As the rudiments of an institution emerged, Eliezer's personal authority clearly diminished; the rabbis of the second century were to stress a rational, consensual achievement of purity, and by the time of the Talmud that was held to be a greater purity than charismatic authority could achieve.

2.4. The Failure of Popular Messianism. The historic concern for the temple as the actual focus of purity nonetheless resulted in a final and nearly disastrous attempt—encouraged by some rabbis—to free and restore the holy site. The most prominent rabbinic supporter of that attempt was Aqiba, a student of Eliezer's renowned for his expertise in the tradition. Aqiba supported the claims of one Simeon bar Kosibah to be the new prince of Israel, acting in conjunction with a priest named Eleazar. Simeon's supporters referred to him as Bar Kokhba, "son of a star," projecting onto him the messianic expectations of Numbers 24:17, while his detractors came to know him as Bar Koziba, "son of a lie." His initial success and military acumen is attested in letters he sent his commanders during his revolt and regime, which lasted from A.D. 132 until 135. This time the response of the empire was even more definitive than it had been in A.D. 70. The emperor Hadrian ordered the remnants of the temple taken apart and new shrines built in the city. Jerusalem itself was now called Aelia Capitolina, Jews were denied entry and Judea became Syria Palaestina.

The rabbis survived by disowning the aspirations embodied by Aqiba but keeping much of his teaching. "Aqiba, grass will grow out of your jaw, before the son of David comes" (*y. Ta'an.* 4.7; cf. *Lam. Rab.* 2.2.4); that is to say, the Messiah is to be of David (*see* Son of David), not of popular choosing, and his time cannot be pressed. But the greatness of the rabbinic response to national defeat and their consequent

redefinition of Judaism consisted less in their formulation of a particular teaching regarding messianism (which emerges in any case from time to time in many forms of Judaism) than in their textual constitution of a form of thought, discipline and life—the Mishnah.

3. The Emergence of Rabbinic Literature.

3.1. Mishnah. Rabbis such as Aqiba had taught their own norms, which came to be known as halakoth (*halākôṯ*, pl. of *halākâ*, "the way"), and had their disciples learn them by heart. A disciple (*talmîd*) might himself internalize what he learned (his teacher's *mišnâ*, or "repetition"; pl. *mišnâyôṯ*), and proceed to promulgate both it and his own halakoth. But after the failure of Bar Kokhba, the rabbis engaged in an extraordinary synthetic effort under Rabbi Judah ha-Nasi (or "the Prince," in stark contrast to Bar Kokhba's aspirations) to assemble the mishnayoth commonly held to be worthy.

Certain features of the work are both striking and of paradigmatic importance for rabbinic Judaism. First and foremost, the Mishnah represents earlier traditions forced into a dialectical relationship; argument exists in an eternal present between positions which earlier had been separated by time and/or geography. The principal contribution of Mishnah is precisely this invitation to dialectical reasoning concerning purity, unconstrained by history or chronology. However, it must be said that the often uneven synthesis is presented in a definite plan of tractates which typically address the topic of their title, arranged within orders (*sedārîm*). Each order presupposes the agricultural activity the rabbis came to see as normal for Israel. As rabbis, they implied, we speak of the purity we may achieve for a temple that should always have been, but we do so in the knowledge that the Israel we address and which supports us is more a collection of farms than a nation. Paradoxically, however, Rabbi Judah's move from Beth She'arim to Sepphoris signaled the emergence of rabbinic authority within cities, and in close association with Roman power. In reading the Mishnah, anachronism must be taken into account at several levels.

Among formative events in the history of Judaism, the radical centralization accomplished under Rabbi Judah ranks with Ezra's reform. But where Ezra's program was located in a particular city (which could only be Jerusalem),

Judah's was headquartered in one (whether Beth She'arim or Sepphoris) but located in the mind. The Mishnah that emerged was a pattern of reflection that enabled any rabbi anywhere to join in the reflection and the discipline of keeping or making Israel pure. Sanctity in that sense could become the project of the learned in any place. The emergence of Mishnah, of course, called into question its status as compared to Scripture, and the revolt under Bar Kokhba radically raised the issue of the status of those works which had promised the speedy rebuilding of the temple after A.D. 70 (cf. 2 Esdras and the Targum of Isaiah).

The priestly canon, represented (although oddly counted) by Josephus (*Ag. Ap.* 1.8 §39), had already called for the recognition of twenty-four books. The rabbis could both invoke the support of that group and control messianic yearnings by insisting that those who read books outside that canon would have no part in the world to come (*m. Sanh.* 10:1). Nonetheless, the issue of messianism was more accidental than systemic; it needed to be addressed by the rabbis—and it was definitively addressed—but the crucial matter was the relationship between Scripture and Mishnah. That relationship required several centuries to resolve.

3.2. Midrash. Midrash may be said to be a category of thought and literature that seeks the resolution of Scripture with the teaching of the rabbis. It is true—as is frequently reported—that the noun derives from the verb *dāraš*, meaning "to inquire," but that fact is largely beside the point. Formally, any midrash will cite the scriptural locus under consideration, somewhat in the manner of the pesherim of Qumran (*see* Dead Sea Scrolls), but typically exegesis is not the point of the exercise. Rather, the citation becomes an occasion to invoke the rabbinic teaching that may be associated with Scripture at that juncture. The relative autonomy of that teaching from any text is usually apparent in what are called the tannaitic or halakic midrashim. "Tannaitic" refers to the Tannaim ("the repeaters," the rabbis of the mishnaic period, although the ascription is traditional, derived from the Aramaic *tenā*', "repeat"), while "halakic" refers to the substance of their teaching. Such documents include two midrashim on Exodus, each called the *Mekilta* (which means "measure"); one is ascribed to Rabbi Ishmael and another (although it is clearly to be dated to a later period) to Rabbi

Simeon ben Yohai, both of whom lived during the second century. Leviticus receives similar treatment in *Sifra* (or *Sipra*, meaning "book"), and Numbers and Deuteronomy in *Sifre* (or *Sipre*, meaning "books").

The influence of Rabbi Ishmael is apparent in the attribution to him (as to Hillel earlier) of rules (*middôt*) of interpretation. The rules by no means govern what rabbis may teach, but they do represent the evolving grammar of the association of that teaching with Scripture. Formally, the *middôt* set out the patterns of similarity, analogy and logical categorization that might permit scriptural patterns to be adduced in support of a given teaching or assertion. Their application may be observed within rabbinic discussion, but they more aptly describe the sort of inference involved in interpretation than provide the program by which that association was effected. The clear impression conveyed by *Mekilta* (in both traditions), *Sifra* and *Sifre* is that the biblical text is an occasion for the exposition of fundamentally rabbinic ideas and modes of thought.

3.3. Tosefta. Despite the triumph of Rabbi Judah's experiment, the third century saw a crisis in the understanding of what might be done with Mishnah. The crisis is visible in two dilemmas. The first dilemma concerned Scripture, as discussed above. The second was even more basic, in that it involved how the discussion occasioned by Mishnah was to be handled. If the question of Scripture turned on the issue of the rabbis' authority in regard to the past as embodied in the canon, the latter question turned on the issue of their authority in regard to that of their successors. Mishnah considered a dialectic of eternal purity, but how was that dialectic, once it was consigned to writing, to be related to rabbinic discussion in the present? Both dilemmas receive a tentative treatment in the Tosefta (or Tosepta). The term means "addition," in that the corpus was seen as an addendum to the Mishnah in later centuries.

In fact, however, the Tosefta is to some extent a fresh Mishnah which incorporates the work of later rabbis and brings their views into a pattern of discussion with those of the Tannaim. Nonetheless, the Tosefta is essentially conservative in its reliance on the materials and the structure of Mishnah, and it does not promulgate the radical notion—adumbrated in *'Abot*, a tractate appended to the Mishnah around 250—that, alongside the Torah written in Scripture, Moses received an oral Torah which was passed on through the prophets and sages, and finally to the rabbis. Tosefta represents a greater comprehensiveness in its supplementation of the Mishnah. But it points to the necessity of the daring it lacks: To elevate rabbis not merely by including their teaching, but by permitting them to engage directly in dialogue with their illustrious predecessors in Scripture and memory.

3.4. Talmud. The relative comprehensiveness of the Tosefta did not assure its triumph. Mishnah was not superseded by it, nor by any subsequent work within the rabbinic tradition. Moreover, even the rabbis accorded Scripture privilege, in that the capacity to cite a text in order to demonstrate or illustrate a point was privileged. The problem of how to address the present with the eternal truth of the tradition (and vice versa) was met by means of an innovation.

The rabbis as expositors (Amoraim, from ʾamôrāʾ, "interpreter," as distinct from Tannaim, "repeaters") undertook to treat Mishnah as Scripture. That is, they generated a commentary on Mishnah, which became known as Talmud (*talmûd*, a noun meaning "learning"). The commentary (as in the case of midrash) is more a matter of using a text as an occasion on which to associate teaching than it is an exposition or exegesis. But the Amoraim triumphantly accomplished what the rabbis of the Tosefta did not: Mishnah was preserved, and at the same time its generative activity and logic was perpetuated in the present. The ideological advance that allowed that accomplishment was the doctrine that Torah was known orally, not only in writing.

3.4.1. The Jerusalem Talmud (c. A.D. 400). The Talmud of Jerusalem, or the *Yerushalmi*, was the last great product of rabbinic Judaism in Palestine (as it came to be called in the Roman period). Sociologically, it was difficult to maintain the sort of discipline of purity the rabbis practiced—and wished others to practice—in a territory recently vanquished by the Romans. The Hadrianic prohibition of circumcision may or may not have been a great impediment (depending upon time and place within the history of the empire), but the incursion of Roman institutions and culture, even at a local level, was a reality from the second century in a way it was not earlier.

Toward the end of the period of the Palestinian Amoraim, the very patriarchate which had sealed the victory of the rabbis in the redaction of Mishnah, appears to have become more aligned with the local aristocracy. Progressive urbanization was not congenial to the maintenance of rabbinic power in Palestine. Moreover, Babylonia during the third century saw the rise of the Sassanids and their form of Zoroastrianism, whose policy toward the practice of Judaism was relatively tolerant. The economic life of the Jews in Babylon, located in largely autonomous towns and villages and supported by agriculture, was better suited to the rabbinic ethos than the increasing syncretism of the Roman Empire from the second century. Particularly, the Sassanids encouraged or tolerated (in varying degrees over time) the formation of the academies in places such as Sura, Pumbeditha and Nehardea, which were the *dynamos* of rabbinic discussion.

3.4.2. The Babylonian Talmud (c. 6th cent.). The rabbis of Babylon gave Judaism its distinctive character, at least until the modern period. This character was and is conveyed in their monument (probably completed during the sixth century), the Babylonian Talmud, or the *Babli*. It is a more comprehensive and subtle treatment of the Mishnah than the *Yerushalmi*, often employing rich, narrative means that permit the contemporization of the rabbinic ethos. Each rabbi is here to some extent a Moses of his own, as when Moses himself is said to visit the academy of Aqiba and to observe to God that the discussion is so complex, his own unworthiness is obvious (*b. Menah.* 29b). But the rabbis are also respectful tradents, as when Rab Joseph of Pumbeditha, the blind master, acknowledges that without the Targum he would not understand Scripture (*b. Sanh.* 94b). Their knowledge and expertise is functionally infinite: a rabbi can be consulted regarding the vision of God's chariot, how to make love or to relieve constipation. Although the Talmud (and *Babli* for practical purposes is the Talmud) is vast, its very range is a succinct statement of its intent: To transform the whole of life with the light of the Torah as interpreted by the rabbis.

3.5. Targums and Midrash Rabbah. Their energy and their resources enabled the rabbis of Babylon to see to the completion of the standard recension of the targums and to the publication of as definitive a form of the midrash as was ever produced. *Midrash Rabbah* presents not only the biblical books used for festal and commemorative occasions (Esther, Ruth, Song of

Orders and Tractates in the Mishna, Tosepta and Talmud

Zeraʿim	**"Seeds"**	***Neziqin***	**"Damages"**
Berakot	"Benedictions"	*Baba Qamma*	"The First Gate"
Peʾa	"Gleanings"	*Baba Meṣiʿa*	"The Middle Gate"
Demai	"Produce not certainly tithed"	*Baba Batra*	"The Last Gate"
		Sanhedrin	"Sanhedrin"
Kilʾayim	"Diverse Kinds"	*Makkot*	"Stripes"
Šebiʿit	"Seventh Year"	*Šebuʿot*	"Oaths"
Terumot	"Heave Offerings"	*ʿEduyyot*	"Testimonies"
Maʿaśerot	"Tithes"	*ʿAboda Zara*	"Idolatry"
Maʿaśer Šeni	"Second Tithe"	*ʾAbot*	"Fathers"
Ḥalla	"Dough Offering"	*Horayot*	"Instructions"
ʿOrla	"Fruit of Young Trees"		
Bikkurim	"First fruits"	***Qodašim***	**"Hallowed Things"**
		Zebaḥim	"Animal Offerings"
Moʿed	**"Set Feasts"**	*Menaḥot*	"Meal Offerings"
Šabbat	"Sabbath"	*Ḥullin*	"Animals killed for food"
ʿErubin	"Sabbath Limits"	*Bekorot*	"Firstlings"
Pesaḥim	"Passover"	*ʿArakin*	"Vows of Valuation"
Šeqalim	"Shekel Dues"	*Temura*	"Substituted Offering"
Yoma (= Kippurim)	"Day of Atonement"	*Keritot*	"Extirpation"
Sukka	"Tabernacles"	*Meʿila*	"Sacrilege"
Beṣa (= Yom Ṭob)	"Festivals"	*Tamid*	"Daily Whole Offering"
Roš Haššana	"New Year"	*Middot*	"Measurements"
Taʿanit	"Days of Fasting"	*Qinnim*	"Bird Offerings"
Megilla	"Scroll of Esther"		
Moʿed Qaṭan	"Mid-Festival Days"	***Ṭoharot***	**"Cleannesses"**
Ḥagiga	"Festival Offering"	*Kelim*	"Vessels"
		Oholot	"Tents"
Našim	**"Women"**	*Negaʿim*	"Leprosy Signs"
Yebamot	"Sisters-in-Law"	*Para*	"Red Heifer"
Ketubot	"Marriage Deeds"	*Ṭoharot*	"Cleannesses"
Nedarim	"Vows"	*Miqwaʾot*	"Immersion Pools"
Nazir	"Nazarite Vow"	*Niddah*	"The Menstruant"
Soṭa	"Suspected Adulteress"	*Makširin (= Mašqin)*	"The Predisposers"
Giṭṭin	"Bills of Divorce"	*Zabim*	"They that suffer a flux"
Qiddušin	"Betrothals"	*Ṭebul Yom*	"He that immersed himself that day"
		Yadayim	"Hands"
		ʿUqṣin	"Stalks"

Songs, Ecclesiastes, Lamentations) but also the Pentateuch. The confidence of the rabbis of Babylonia in their own ethos was so great that the comment upon Scripture might include explicit narrative concerning rabbis, as well as exposition and discourse. *Midrash Rabbah* was likely completed during the eighth century, and it represents the confidence that Torah, whether in Scripture or Talmud, is fundamentally one. The interweaving of Scripture and rabbinic teaching is also represented in the homiletic midrashim of a later period: The *Pesiqta Rabbati,* the *Pesiqta de-Rab Kahana* and *Tanḥuma*

3.6. The Sefer Yesirah. The rabbinic period closes with the rise of Islam and the subsequent reaction of the Geonim, the successors of the rabbis who maintained and extended rabbinic Judaism with a distinctively academic, and sometimes rationalistic, bent. Increasingly their work is of a literary nature and takes the rabbinic canon as a fact that is to be acknowledged rather than achieved. Moreover, a tendency toward philosophy and esoterism becomes manifest.

The *Sefer Yesirah,* or "book of formation," is a good representative of a work that is transitional between the Amoraim and the Geonim, and was perhaps composed during the seventh century. It builds on a mystical tradition reaching back at least until Yohanan ben Zakkai, according to which it is possible to see the chariot (the *Merkabah*) of Ezekiel 1, and to know the structure of the creation. But where the rabbis held that such experiments were a matter for private exposition (and then under tight controls, cf. *b. Šabb.* 80b; *b. Ḥag.* 11b, 13a, 14b), the *Sefer Yesirah* commences a tradition of literary and rational esoterism that is more typical of the Qabbala of the Middle Ages than of the Judaism of the rabbis. The dialectic of the rabbis was rooted in the oral argument that produced their literature and which their literature was designed to serve. When the logic of literary discourse takes over, the constitution of the Judaism that is reflected is no longer, strictly speaking, rabbinic.

4. The Use of Rabbinica in Understanding Jesus and the Gospels.

Rabbinic literature plainly developed in a way that makes it unlike the Gospels; in social and religious terms, the writings of rabbinic Judaism and early Christianity are not directly comparable. For that reason the existence of an alleged parallel in rabbinica to a passage in the Gospels is not to be taken by itself as proof that Judaism was the origin of the motif at issue. (Sometimes, the term *parallel* is only useful when it is borne in mind that the adjective describes lines that do not in fact meet.) Moreover, the very program of the rabbis, of taking up a perennial discussion of purity and promulgating that as Torah, caused words or sayings to be ascribed anachronistically to their predecessors. The attribution of positions to any rabbi, particularly of the Tannaitic period or earlier, is to be used only with caution.

4.1. Anachronisms. The earlier reference (see 1.1 above) to Hillel's teaching concerning love is a case in point. Hillel was revered as the progenitor of the patriarchate and was even—over the course of time—endowed with Davidic ancestry (*Gen. Rab.* 98), which reinforced the claim to authority of any patriarch descended from him. By the time of the Amoraim a rabbi was understood

to render with his own halakah the functional equivalent of Torah, and that is precisely what Hillel does in the story. In a single stroke he defeats the glib request of the proselyte and the rude exclusivism of Shammai. Hillel becomes what any Amoraim wanted to be: a hero for the Torah who succeeded because he understood the force of the Torah. In that this story of Hillel is consistent with the ethos of the Amoraim and appears only at this stage of the *Babli* (*b. Šabb.* 31a), its emphasis on learning the whole of Torah should not necessarily be ascribed to Hillel himself.

4.2. Analogies. On the other hand, the ubiquity of a form of what is commonly known as the Golden Rule makes it unwise to deny Hillel may have said some thing such as ascribed to him in the *Babli.* The story as it stands may reflect the ethos of the Amoraim, but a statement of Hillel's may lie at its point of origin. Negatively formulated as an imperative against doing what one finds loathsome, the maxim appears to have circulated generally during the ancient period (cf. Confucius *Analecta* 15.23; Tob 4:15; *Ep. Arist.* 207; Eusebius *Praep. Ev.* 8.7 [for its citation of Philo]; *T. Naph.* [Hebrew] 1:6; *2 Enoch* 61:1, 2; Sextus *Sententiae* 89 [and 210b]). It has also influenced the form of the Golden Rule in *Didache* 1:2 (cf. Acts 15:20, 29 in Bezae; Rom 13:10): Whatever you wish not to be done to you, do not do to another.

Given that the proverbial form of the Rule (i.e., in the negative) is the form that predominates in Christian antiquity, there is no question of attempting to argue that Hillel's version specifically influenced Jesus' saying. Further, the negative form of the Rule is as common in the Christian tradition as in many others; there is no need or reason to posit some specific source (such as Hillel's dictum) for a conventional statement.

Indeed, the feature which may be significantly distinctive in the maxim as attributed to Jesus in Matthew 7:12 and Luke 6:31 is that its form is positive. Although the substance of the teaching is proverbial, and far from unique, there is unquestionably an unusual element in the application of its principle. The active desire to do to others the good one wants for oneself is evidently a more aggressive version of the imperative not to inflict the harm one would avoid. The significance of what is attributed to Hillel in the *Babli* is not that it can be established to provide a parallel to Jesus' teaching from the first century, but that it establishes by contrast that, in rabbinic Judaism and probably in the Pharisaic circles of early Judaism, the proverbial, negative form of the maxim was current. Even that marginal insight is only obtainable when *Babli* is read within the terms of reference of earlier documents. There is no question of a critically acceptable, direct comparison between Jesus and Hillel on the basis of the Gospels and the *Babli* alone.

4.3. Milieu. As has already been mentioned (see 1.1 above), Hillel is reported to have taught that offerings should be brought to the temple, where the owners would lay hands on them and then give them over to priests for slaughter (cf. *t. Ḥag.* 2.11; *y. Ḥag.* 2.3; *y. Beṣa* 2.4; *b. Beṣa* 20a, b). His perennial and stereotypical disputants, the house of Shammai, resist, insisting that the animals might be handed over directly. One of the house of Shammai (named Baba ben Buṭa in the *Babli* and Tosefta), however, was so struck by the rectitude of Hillel's position that he had some 3,000 animals (a number specified only in the *Yerushalmi*) brought to the temple and gave them to those who were willing to lay hands on them in advance of sacrifice.

Generally speaking, the haggadah (*haggaddâ*, "narration, instruction") concerning Hillel, Baba ben Buta and the sheep is more characteristic of the Pharisaic/rabbinic program than is the vignette containing the Golden Rule. Moreover, the broader attestation of the story within the two Talmuds and its appearance in the Tosefta indicate that it may reflect an actual dispute. Finally, although Hillel's disputants are stereotypical, it is striking that in *Beṣa* 20a (cf. *t. Ḥag.* 2.11) Hillel pretends the animal is a female for a shared sacrifice (*zibḥê šelāmîm*) in order to get it by the disiples of Shammai. That is, the Babli's version of the story assumes that the followers of Shammai are in actual control of what worshipers do in the temple. The haggadah is a far cry from the sort of tale in which Hillel is protrayed as the prototypical patriarch of rabbinic Judaism.

In one sense the tradition concerning Hillel envisages a movement opposite from that of Jesus in the temple (Mt 21:12-13; Mk 11:15-17; Lk 19:45-46; Jn 2:13-17; *see* Temple Cleansing): Animals are introduced rather than their traders expelled. But the purpose of the action by Hillel's partisan is to enforce a certain understanding of correct worship, and that is also the motivation attributed to Jesus in the Gospels. Hillel's halakah, in effect, insists on the participation of the offerer by virtue of his ownership of what is offered, an ownership of which the laying on of hands is a definitive gesture (cf. *b. Pesaḥ.* 66b). The house of Shammai is portrayed as sanctioning sacrifice, without mandating that sort of emphatic participation on the part of the offerer. Although nothing like the violence of Jesus is attributed to Baba ben Buta, he does offer an analogy for a forcible attempt to insist on correct worship in the temple on the part of a Pharisee.

Mishnah itself reflects a concern to control commercial arrangements connected with the temple, and such concern is also somewhat analogous to Jesus' action in the exterior court. The following story is told concerning one of the successors of Hillel (*m. Ker.* 1:7):

> Once in Jerusalem a pair of doves cost a golden denar. Rabban Simeon ben Gamaliel said: By this Place I will not rest this night before they cost but a [silver] denar. He went into the court and taught: If a woman suffered five miscarriages that were not in doubt or five issues that were not in doubt, she need bring but one offering, and she may then eat of the sacrifices; and the rest is not required of her. And the same day the price of a pair of doves stood at a quarter denar each.

Although the story requires more effort to understand than the one concerning Hillel, it rewards the attention required. The assumption of the whole tale is that a pair of doves might be offered by a woman as both a burnt offering and a sacrifice for sin in order to be purified after childbirth; the second of the two would be offered normally, while the first—in the case of poverty—might take the place of a yearling lamb (Lev 12:6-8). The story also assumes that from the point of view of purity miscarriages and unusual issues of blood akin to miscarriages should be treated under the category of childbirth. That association is characteristically Pharisaic, as is the issue of when the woman might be considered entitled to eat of offerings. The Pharisees defined purity as fitness to take part in sacrifice and in meals that—in their teaching—were extensions of the holiness of the temple.

Simeon's anger, which causes him to swear by the temple (cf. Mt 23:12-22), is therefore motivated to some extent by economic considerations. His response is, like that of Jesus, to teach in the court of the temple, where such offerings would be brought. But his action there is far less direct than that of Hillel or Jesus. Instead of importing more birds or releasing those bought at an extortionate price, he promulgates a halakah designed to reduce the trade in doves, no matter what their price.

If a woman may await several (up to five) miscarriages or flows of blood and then offer a single pair of doves and be considered pure enough to eat of the animal offering, the potential revenue from sales of doves would obviously decline. In effect, Simeon counters inflationary prices with sacrificial monetarism. The political lesson was quickly appreciated (on the very day, if we believe the story), and prices went even lower than Simeon had intended. Presumably there was no reason for him to continue promulgating his view in the court of the temple, and both he and the traders were content with the settlement.

The date of the Mishnah, as compared to the Tosefta, the *Yershalmi* and the *Babli*, makes its material, when in any way comparable to the Gospels, of immediate interest to the student of Jesus' life and teaching. For all its complexity the haggadah in the mishnaic tractate *Keritot* is vitally important for appreciating the sort of Pharisaic intervention in the operation of the temple that was considered possible during the first century. (Perhaps the story concerning Simeon is more complicated precisely because it is closer to particulars of Pharisaic concern than the later haggadah concerning Hillel and Baba ben Buṭa.) Hillel, Simeon and Jesus are all portrayed as interested in the animals offered in the temple to the extent that they intervene (or, in the case of Hillel, a surrogate intervenes) in the exterior court in order to influence the ordinary course of worship. To that extent we may say that rabbinic traditions and writings provide a context within which it is possible to interpret a well-attested action of Jesus.

4.4. Summary. The usefulness of the documents of rabbinic Judaism for interpreting Jesus and the Gospels is qualified by three critical considerations, each of which we have observed in the examples provided above. First, the relatively late date of the literature must be taken into account, although the continuities between rabbinic Judaism and Pharisaism of the first century suggest some analogies between the Gospels and rabbinica. Second, a recognition of the social and religious transformations involved in the emergence of rabbinic Judaism must alert the reader to the possibility of anachronistic attributions or to the presentation of early teachers as spokesmen of later theologies. And finally, we must understand that the initial target of inquiry is the recovery of the milieu of early Judaism. That is, we should seek not so much particular events and sayings paralleled in the Gospels but to recapture the matrix of the Christian faith, as it is reflected indirectly both in the Gospels and in rabbinica.

See also APOCRYPHA AND PSUEDEPIGRAPHA, OLD TESTAMENT; JUDAISM.

DJG: MIDRASH; PHARISEES; TARGUMS; TEACHER. *DNTB:* RABBINIC LITERATURE: MIDRASH; RABBINIC LITERATURE: MISHNAH AND TOSEFTA; RABBINIC LITERATURE: TALMUD; RABBINIC LITERATURE: TARGUMS; REVOLUTIONARY MOVEMENTS; TORAH; WRITING AND LITERATURE: JEWISH.

BIBLIOGRAPHY. W. G. Braude, *Pesikta Rabbati: Discourses for Feasts, Fasts, and Special Sabbaths* (New Haven: Yale University Press, 1968); W. G. Braude and I. J. Epstein, *Pesikta de-Rab Kahana: R. Kahana's Compilation of Discourses for Sabbaths and Special days* (Philadelphia: Jewish Publication Society, 1975); W. D. Davies and D. C. Allison Jr., *A Critical and Exegetical Commentary on the Gospel according to Saint Matthew* (ICC; Edinburgh: T & T Clark, 1988); I. Epstein, ed., *The Babylonian Talmud . . . Translated with Notes, Glossary, and Indices* (London: Soncino, 1936-1948); A. Finkel, *The Pharisees and the Teacher of Nazareth* (AGSU 4; Leiden: E. J. Brill, 1964); J. A. Fitzmyer, "The Bar Cochba Period," in *Essays in the Semitic Background of the New Testament* (SBLSBS 5; Missoula: Scholars Press, 1974) 305-54; H. Freedman and M. Simon, *Midrash Rabbah, Translated into English with Notes, Glossary and Indices* (London: Soncino, 1983); J. Goldin, *The Fathers according to Rabbi Nathan* (New York: Schocken, 1974); J. Z. Lauterbach, *Mekita de-Rabbi Ishmael* (Philadelphia: Jewish Publication Society, 1976); L. I. Levine, *The Rabbinic Class of Roman Palestine in Late Antiquity* (New York: The Jewish Theological Seminary, 1989); J. N. Neusner, *The Mishnah: A New Translation* (New Haven: Yale University Press, 1988); idem, *The Pharisees: Rabbinic Perspectives* (Hoboken: Ktav, 1973); idem, *The Peripatetic Saying: The Problem of the Thrice-Told Tale in Talmudic Literature* (BJS 89; Chico: Scholars, 1985); idem, *Sifre, An Analytic Translation* (BJS 138; Atlanta: Scholars Press, 1988-); idem, *Talmud of the Land of Israel* (Chicago: University of Chicago Press, 1982-); idem, *Torah: From Scroll to Symbol in Formative Judaism* (FJ: Philadelphia: Fortress, 1985); E. Schürer, *The History of the Jewish People in the Age of Jesus Christ (175 B.C.-A.D. 135)*, rev. and ed. G. Vermes and F. Millar (3 vols.; Edinburgh: T & T Clark, 1973-87).   B. D. Chilton

RAISING THE DEAD, MIRACLES OF. *See* RESURRECTION I.

REALIZED ESCHATOLOGY. *See* ESCHATOLOGY; KINGDOM OF GOD I.

RECONCILIATION. *See* DEATH OF CHRIST II.

REDEMPTION. *See* DEATH OF CHRIST.

RELIGIONS, GRECO-ROMAN

The traditional religions of Greece and those of Rome underwent significant changes in the Hellenistic and Roman imperial periods. Nevertheless it would be a mistake to minimize the influence of the traditional religion and traditional religious attitudes in NT times. Against the background of the old cults and their practices, certain expressions of the religious spirit attained new prominence or new manifestations in the period of the rise of Christianity: the imperial cult, the mysteries, oracles and healing, magic, demons, astrology and fate.

    1. Ancient Greek and Roman Religion
    2. Characteristics of Religion in the Hellenistic-Roman Age
    3. Civic Cult
    4. Imperial Cult
    5. Mysteries
    6. Other Features
    7. Concluding Observation

1. Ancient Greek and Roman Religion.

The difference between the traditional religion of Greece and that of Rome is typified by the fact that Greek religion derived from the myths in the epics of Homer and Roman religion was ascribed to the institutions of the lawgiver Numa. The Greeks dealt with their deities as they would with larger-than-life human beings, whereas Roman religion had a definite legal cast. The Greek deities were anthropomorphic,

displaying human passions, portrayed as human beings and taking an interest in and interfering in human affairs but differing from humans by being ageless and deathless, not limited by space and being above ordinary morality. Sacrifices did not require a professional priesthood and were governed by the bargaining spirit that "I give gifts to the gods and ask that they may do things for me" (see Plato *Euthyphro* 14C-E). Roman deities were less personalized powers (*numina*) that had specific and limited functions. Human relations with the divine were of a more contractual nature so that ceremonies had to be exactly followed, and many religious observances were performed for the people by the professional experts (*pontifices* and *augures*). The domestic cult in both Greece and Rome continued with great consistency. Meals began with a sacrifice of food and ended with a libation.

2. Characteristics of Religion in the Hellenistic-Roman Age.

The modern distinction between religion and the state did not operate. Since idolatrous practices permeated all aspects of life (politics, the military, the theater, athletics, business), Jews and Christians were at a severe social and economic disadvantage.

Syncretism was encouraged by the transplanting of Greek gods to foreign lands and the immigration of foreign gods into the Greek and Roman worlds, resulting in the identification of deities and borrowing of ideas.

Polytheism was tolerant, or nonexclusive; the exclusivism of Judaism and Christianity was highly offensive to the pagan mentality. There was an inclination toward monotheism, but even where a supreme god was acknowledged, the old gods were kept as subordinate powers.

The increased individualism of the Hellenistic age put more emphasis on chosen relationships at the expense of inherited relationships, but the chosen relationships continued to express the corporate or social side of religion.

Piety (Lat *pietas;* Gk *eusebeia*) had to do primarily with external rites rather than inner attitudes. The pious person was the one who performed the required duties properly.

Morality was not derived primarily from the religious cult. The literary tradition provided examples of what was and was not done, and philosophers assumed the role of teachers of popular morality. Some of the cults began to include moral regulations along with rules for ritual purity.

By the first century, psychological needs included a feeling of helplessness before fate, uncertainty about the hereafter, curiosity about the supernatural and a sense of the instability of human affairs.

3. Civic Cult.

Contrary to what is often said, the traditional civic cults remained vibrant in the early centuries of the Christian era. The decline of local autonomy in Hellenistic and imperial times seemingly led to an awakening of loyalty and pride in the civic cult. As the political importance of the Greek cities diminished, their glory became associated with their temples and gods. The patriotism of the leading classes found expression in commissioning the writing of local histories, the study of old customs and myths, the building of new temples, instituting festivals and setting up commemorative or celebratory inscriptions. The civic cults were nurtured by primary and secondary education, where Homer was the basic textbook. Thus the educational curriculum transmitted the traditional myths and with them the traditional values of Greek culture.

The civic authorities determined the selection of cult personnel, requirements for ritual purity, distribution of items brought for sacrifice, order of march in processions, and other such externals of cultic affairs, and these regulations were often inscribed on stone monuments. The essential requirement of a religious sanctuary was an altar for sacrifice. Grain or bread, vegetables, olive oil and wine were more common sacrifices than meat, but the latter was the principal sacrifice at the periodic (often annual) state-sponsored festivals, the main time the poorer people had meat in their diet. Roman sacrifices were accompanied by the burning of incense and the playing of a pipe *(tibia)*, with the priest wearing a veil over the head. The altar was outside the temple, which was the house of the deity, not an assembly hall for worshipers. The deity's presence was symbolized by the cult statue, the central point of focus in the temple. The periodic festivals, in addition to the public procession and sacrifices, often included games and contests. The principal occasion of private sacrifice was the votive offering, the gift brought to the deity in fulfillment of a vow, a central act of personal piety and religious life.

Two narratives in Acts illustrate important features of local civic cults. In the episode at Lystra (Acts 14:11-13), which may have its background in the story recorded by Ovid (Ovid *Met.* 8.620-724), note may be taken of the following items: the anthropomorphic nature of the gods, who appear in human form; the giving of Greek names (Zeus, the chief god, and Hermes, the messenger of the gods) to native deities; the priest assigned to a deity; the identification of the cult as "Zeus-Outside-the-City" (NRSV footnote), where the sanctuary was located; and the intention to sacrifice bulls (the most expensive sacrifice and so an indication of the perceived importance of the occasion) that are garlanded, a common decoration of the sacrificial animal.

In one of the episodes at Ephesus (Acts 19:23-41) other features related to civic cults stand out: once more the giving of a Greek name to a local deity (Artemis of the Ephesians is not the classical Greek goddess of the hunt but an Asia Minor mother goddess; although the fertility feature is not specifically attested for Artemis of the Ephesians, the analogy with other Anatolian mother goddesses suggests fecundity of nature but not sexual immorality); the alliance of the most important local deity with the civic magistrates (Acts 19:35, 38-39), provincial authorities (Acts 19:31, 38) and economic activity (Acts 19:24-27); the making of images of the deity for sale as souvenirs or as votive offerings (Acts 19:24); the use of acclamations (Acts 19:34); the designation of Ephesus as "temple keeper" *(nēkoros)* of Artemis (Acts 19:35); and a divine origin attributed to the image or symbol of the deity (Acts 19:35).

4. Imperial Cult.

Under the empire the principal local civic cult was often joined to the imperial cult. Giving divine honors to the rulers was the climax of civic cult in the Greco-Roman world, only now the city (Rome) was the world and the city was personified in the royal family. Precedents for the ruler cult were provided by the Near-Eastern view of kings as divine by reason of office and by the Greek cult of heroes, notable human beings who by reason of their achievements were elevated to the status of divinities. Alexander the Great and his successors received divine honors, and the Roman emperors succeeded to these honors in the Greek

East and ultimately received them in the Latin West as well. Such was the great power exercised by the rulers and such was the gratitude for the peace and prosperity brought by the emperor that only the honors shown to the gods seemed an adequate expression of homage. The social elite, who benefited the most from Roman rule, were especially active in promoting the ruler cult, and generally the impetus came from the provinces, but certain rulers like Caligula and Domitian insisted on receiving divine honors.

The external forms taken by the imperial cult included the dedication of altars and temples, erection of statues to the person in the appearance of a deity, commemorative inscriptions, sacrifices in the ruler's honor, instituting new festivals or renaming old ones and ascribing divine titles. Although miracle stories were often associated with the birth of the ruler, there seems to have been no expectation that the ruler would act supernaturally. Prayers and votive offerings to the ruler were rare or nonexistent. The imperial cult was an acknowledgment of what seemed almost supernatural power and an act of gratitude for benefactions received or an anticipation of them. It was an expression of the status of the ruler, of loyalty to him or her and of the unity of the subjects. Thus its importance was more political and social than religious.

The story of Herod Agrippa I (Acts 12:20-23) illustrates the hyperbole of court flattery to a king from those who expected benefits from him (cf. the fuller account in Josephus Ant. 19.8.2 §343-352). The Asiarchs mentioned in Acts 19:31 were members of the provincial council of Asia, who without necessarily being personally involved, oversaw the imperial cult as part of their duties. The book of *Revelation shows the greatest antagonism of any NT writing toward Rome and its embodiment in the imperial cult. The religious aspect of the beast who will be overthrown by the Lord stands out (Rev 13:1, 4-8, 11-15; 19:20). Astral imagery, associated not only with the gods of paganism but also on the coins of Domitian with the imperial family, is subordinated to Christ, who holds in his hands "the seven stars" (Rev 1:16), which are really the "angels of the seven churches" (Rev 1:20), and who is the true world conqueror (Rev 3:21). Revelation from its beginning counters the imperial ideology by asserting that Christ is "ruler of the kings of the earth" (Rev 1:5) and that he has made his people "to be a kingdom" (Rev 1:6, 9; *see* Kingdom of God). It gives great emphasis throughout to the royal rule of God (Rev 11:15, 17; 12:10; 15:3; 19:6), to Christ as "Lord of lords and King of kings" (Rev 17:14; 19:16) and to the rule of the saints (Rev 5:10; 20:4, 6; 22:5).

5. Mysteries.

The mysteries, secret cults in which the uninitiated could not participate, were a feature of classical Greek religion. One of the oldest and the most influential was the Eleusinian mysteries celebrated in honor of Demeter. They were a local mystery, in that a person had to go to Eleusis, near Athens, to receive the initiation. A site mentioned in the NT where local mysteries were celebrated is Samothrace (Acts 16:11), where were worshiped the "Mother of the gods" and the Cabiri, the latter in Roman times confused with the Dioscuri, Castor and Pollux, who were protective deities of sailors (Acts 28:11). Also known in classical times were the mysteries of Dionysus, which were not confined to one locality.

Several Eastern cults, when their devotees became part of the Greek world, copied the Greek practice of mystery initiations. Especially widespread were the Egyptian deities Isis and Osiris (the latter largely replaced by Sarapis in the Greek world). Two second-century sources attest their popularity: the philosophical interpretation of the cult myth by Plutarch (Plutarch *Iside* 12-21, *Mor.* 355D-359) and the circumstantial account of the initiation (without divulging its secrets) by Apuleius (*Met.* 11), who also describes other features of the religion.

Numerous archaeological remains attest the spread of the mysteries of Mithras, especially in the second and third centuries after Christ. Although worshiping the Persian god Mithras, Roman Mithraism seems not to have been derived from Persian religion. Mithras was associated with astrological phenomena and was worshiped as having control over celestial forces. There were seven grades of initiation, from the rank of "raven" to that of "father." That Mithraism initiated only men and that it placed an emphasis on loyalty perhaps account for its popularity with soldiers and government officials.

The mysteries flourished around the beginning of the Christian era, especially in the second century, because they conveyed an assurance of higher status, a sense of a closer relationship with the deity and the hope of blessedness in the hereafter. They have in common with Christianity a concern with salvation, but their salvation was from fate and the terrors of the afterlife, not from sin. The "dying and rising" of the deities in the mysteries, where it occurs, relates to the cycle of nature and was no true resurrection. The NT terminology of mystery has to do with the divine plan, previously hidden but now revealed. The Christian initiation was not secret. Where washings occur in the mysteries, this was part of the purification preliminary to the initiation, not the initiation itself as in Christian baptism. The mysteries were rather expensive and were for the few deemed already worthy, whereas Christianity invited everyone (as the pagan critic Celsus pointed out—according to Origen *Cont. Cels.* 3.59).

6. Other Features.

6.1. Oracles and Healing.
The sanctuary of Apollo at Delphi had been the principal site for receiving divine communications in classical times, but it was in decline at the beginning of the Christian era, a fact for which Plutarch sought explanations (*On the Obsolescence of Oracles, Mor.* 409E-438E). Its influence was partially inherited by daughter sanctuaries at Claros and Didyma in Asia Minor and Daphne near Antioch in Syria. By the beginning of the Christian era the oracles were no longer determinative of political and religious developments, but they continued to be consulted by cities on formal sacred affairs and by individuals on affairs of personal life. Delphi was also known by the name Pytho, from Python, the female serpent representing the earth goddess who was killed by Apollo, and his priestess through whom the oracles were given was known as Pythia; hence "Pythian spirit" was used for the power to utter oracular messages such as the fortunetelling by the slave girl in Acts 16:16).

Dreams were considered another important source of divine communication, a belief shared by pagans and Jews and a frequent medium of providential guidance in the book of Acts (Acts 10:10-16; 16:9-10; 23:11; 27:23-24).

Many of the healing sanctuaries were properly shrines for oracles. The most important healing deity in the Greco-Roman world was the hero Asclepius, son of Apollo. In addition to his important sanctuary at Epidaurus, he had healing sites at Cos, Corinth, Athens and Rome. Rivaling Epidaurus was the sanctuary of Asclepius at Pergamum (Rev 2:12-17; see Hemer), celebrated by the second-century orator Aelius Aristides in his *Sacred Tales*. The satirist Lucian of Samosata, also second century, tells the story of *Alexander the False Prophet*, who created his own healing and oracular sanctuary in Asia Minor and duped many people, in a narrative that reveals the religious mentality of the age as well as the author's rationalist criticism. The sanctuaries of Asclepius often worked in cooperation with the medical profession to effect healing, but there were also told miracle stories of the most extraordinary kind. The expectation that divine power works miracles of healing is evident in many passages in Acts (Acts 3:1-10; 8:4-7; 9:32-41; 14:8-11; 28:8-9), but these accounts are more sober than the propaganda stories for Asclepius and are related to the saving work of Jesus as carried out by his messengers.

6.2. Magic.
Religion and magic were considered distinct, but they are not easily distinguished in the ancient world. In spite of laws against its practice, magic was widespread. As a somewhat artificial modern construct, the word *magic* as applied to ancient religion is used for efforts to compel supernatural forces by means of certain material objects and verbal formulas. Curse tablets sought to bring punishment on an enemy, and amulets were used to ward off potential attacks by evil forces. An extensive magical literature is preserved on papyri, often containing, it seems, the recipe books of practicing magicians (see Acts 19:19).

The term *magic* was derived from the name of a Persian priestly tribe and was used by the Greeks to refer to strange rites and formulas and then as a semitechnical term for the activity of those considered magicians. The use in Acts 8:9-11 illustrates the association of magic with the supposed control of supernatural power. The title *magos* is used for Bar-Jesus (or Elymas), also called a "false prophet," in Acts 13:6, 8. The Jews were widely regarded in the Greco-Roman world as possessing magical power. This association is evident also in the story in Acts 19:11-20, appropriately occurring in Ephesus, a city known as a center of magical activity (see Arnold). The story illustrates the use of formulas of constraint in magic and the common belief that knowledge of the name of a supernatural power gave one control over that power (Acts 19:13), but it also exemplifies the different significance "the name of the Lord Jesus" had for Christians (Acts 19:15).

6.3. Demons and Superstition. By Hellenistic times the word *daimōn* had come to be used for intermediate divine beings that might be either good or bad. Plato's student Xenocrates had classified the kinds of demons; another Platonist, Plutarch, gives considerable information on demonology at the end of the first Christian century. The tendency by philosophers to blame the intermediate beings for bad things and for the less acceptable features of pagan religion prepared for the Jewish and Christian appropriation of *daimonion* for evil spiritual beings (Jas 2:19; 3:15; Rev 9:20; 16:14; 18:2).

The term *deisidaimonia* ("fear of the demons") became the common Greek term for "superstition" (see Plutarch *On Superstition, Mor.* 164E-171F). The word could have a neutral sense, even as *daimoniōn* ("divinities") does in Acts 17:18. Whether it is used in a neutral or a negative sense in Acts 17:22 depends on whether Paul is making a factual observation about the religiosity of the Athenians or is identifying with the philosophical criticism of Greek popular religion.

6.4. Astrology and Fate. Astronomy and astrology were not distinct in the ancient world. The belief that the movements of the heavenly bodies in absolute regularity control earthly events up to the smallest detail was developed by Greeks in Egypt in the Hellenistic age and began to be popularized under the early Roman Empire. The emperor Tiberius became so absorbed in astrology (Suetonius *Tiberius* 69) that he neglected the practice of religion, but few went that far. The religious aspect of astrology came from the identification of the planets with the traditional deities of Greece and Rome, but the planets themselves did not receive cultic devotion. The learned astronomy gave a new worldview that distinguished the sublunary world and the seven planets, characterized by change and corruption, from the supralunary world of the fixed stars, characterized by unchangability and perfection. Astrology became a principal support for the idea of absolute fate. Although some people gladly embraced this view, the popular religions were those that offered deliverance from fate—the mysteries of Isis and Mithras as well as Christianity.

7. Concluding Observation.

A snake was associated with many of the Greco-Roman deities. Among the forms that Zeus took, particularly in the household cult, was that of a snake. A snake was portrayed on the shield of Athena, the patron goddess of Athens, and a snake was associated with Apollo at Delphi. The snake entwined around a staff was the symbol of Asclepius, and, from confusion of that with the twin snakes on the herald's staff of Hermes, this symbol has continued in use by the medical profession. The protective spirit of the Greek household, the Agathos Daimon, was depicted as a snake, and a snake represented the genius, or life principle, of the family on Roman household altars. Considering the biblical associations of the snake with Satan (Rev 20:2), there is little wonder that Jews and Christians saw pagan religion as inspired by the devil.

See also GNOSTICISM.

DNTB: CIVIC CULTS; FESTIVALS AND HOLY DAYS: GRECO-ROMAN; IDOLATRY, JEWISH CONCEPTION OF; MAGICAL PAPYRI; MYSTERIES; POLYTHEISM, GRECO-ROMAN; PROPHETS AND PROPHECY; RELIGION, PERSONAL; RULER CULT; TEMPLES, GRECO-ROMAN.

BIBLIOGRAPHY. C. E. Arnold, *Ephesians: Power and Magic* (SNTSMS 63; Cambridge: Cambridge University Press, 1989); E. Ferguson, *Backgrounds of Early Christianity* (2d ed.; Grand Rapids: Eerdmans, 1993) 137-298; J. Ferguson, *The Religions of the Roman Empire* (Aspects of Greek and Roman Life; Ithaca, NY: Cornell University Press, 1970); A. J. Festugière, *Le Monde Gréco-Romain au temps de notre-Seigneur, 2: Le Milieu Spirituel* (Bibliothèque Catholique des Sciences Religieuses 7.2; Paris: Blond & Gay, 1935); D. Fish-wick, *The Imperial Cult in the Latin West* (2 vols. in 4 pts.; Leiden: E. J. Brill, 1987-92); D. W. J. Gill and B. W. Winter, "Acts and Roman Religion" in *The Book of Acts in Its Greco-Roman Setting*, ed. D. W. J. Gill and C. Gempf (BAFCS 2; Grand Rapids: Eerdmans, 1994) 79-103; F. C. Grant, ed., *Ancient Roman Religion* (The Library of Religion; New York: Liberal Arts Press, 1957); idem, *Hellenistic Religions: The Age of Syncretism* (The Library of Religion; New York: Liberal Arts Press, 1953); C. J. Hemer, *The Letters to the Seven Churches of Asia in their Local Setting* (JSNTSup 11; Sheffield: JSOT, 1986); H. C. Kee, *Medicine, Miracle and Magic in New Testament Times* (Cambridge: Cambridge University Press, 1986); R. MacMullen, *Paganism in the Roman Empire* (New Haven, CT: Yale University

Press, 1981); M. W. Meyer, *The Ancient Mysteries: A Sourcebook* (San Francisco: Harper, 1987); M. P. Nilsson, *Geschichte der griechischen Religion*, 2: *Die hellenistische und römische Zeit* (Handbuch der Altertumswissenschaft; Munich: C. H. Beck, 1950); A. D. Nock, *Conversion: The Old and the New in Religion from Alexander the Great to Augustine of Hippo* (Oxford: Clarendon, 1933); idem, *Essays on Religion and the Ancient World*, ed. Z. Stewart (2 vols.; Oxford: Clarendon, 1972); S. R. F. Price, *Ritual and Power: The Roman Imperial Cult in Asia Minor* (Cambridge: Cambridge University Press, 1984); J. Z. Smith, *Drudgery Divine: On the Comparison of Early Christianities and the Religions of Late Antiquity* (Chicago: University of Chicago Press, 1990); D. Ulansey, *The Origins of the Mithraic Mysteries* (Oxford: Oxford University Press, 1989); A. J. M. Wedderburn, *Baptism and Resurrection: Studies in Pauline Theology Against Its Greco-Roman Background* (Tübingen: J. C. B. Mohr, 1987).   E. Ferguson

RELIGIOUS MEALS. *See* LORD'S SUPPER I.

REMNANT OF ISRAEL. *See* ISRAEL.

RESCUE. *See* SALVATION.

RESTORATION OF ISRAEL. *See* ISRAEL.

RESURRECTION I: GOSPELS

Jesus assumed and taught an *eschatological doctrine of the resurrection of the dead, an event whereby the ungodly would be delivered to judgment and the godly receive eternal life. Moreover, Jesus performed miracles of resuscitation and, as he predicted, was himself raised from the dead. Both categories of events are regarded by the Gospel writers as eschatologically significant. But whereas the individuals Jesus raised from the dead were, technically speaking, resuscitated and would once again face death, the resurrection of Jesus from the dead was an event of cosmic consequence. Each of the Gospel writers portrays this event in a distinctive way, each developing their own themes and yet together affirming the reality of the empty tomb and risen Christ, and the eschatological significance of this unique event in the mission of Jesus.

1. Pre-Christian Antecedents
2. Resurrection and Afterlife in the Sayings of Jesus
3. Miracles of Raising the Dead

4. Jesus' Resurrection in the Four Gospels

1. Pre-Christian Antecedents.

1.1. Resurrection in the Old Testament. Evidence from the Hebrew Scriptures indicates that Israel did not dwell on the question of the afterlife until late in the OT period. Rather, they stressed the involvement of Yahweh in this life. The blessing of the righteous and punishment of the wicked were seen as taking place in the present age. Life and death were also related primarily to this life.

This does not mean that Israelites believed in annihilation after death. The OT maintains that in one sense death is the cessation of life—at death a person returns to the "dust" (Gen 3:19; Ps 90:3). In another sense it is not the absolute end of life, for existence continues—at death the person descends to Sheol *(šĕ'ôl)*, a term at times synonymous with "death" (Gen 42:38; Ps 89:48), the "grave" (Gen 37:35; Is 14:11) or the "netherworld" (Ezek 32:21; perhaps Ps 86:13). In some cases the dead are said to dwell in Sheol as *repāîm*, or "shades" (Job 26:5; Ps 88:10; Prov 9:18; Is 26:14)—possibly either a shadowy, wraith-like existence or a synonym for "the dead" (Ugaritic parallels favor the former). These references to *repāîm* and Sheol suggest a burgeoning view of the afterlife.

But while the OT does not give explicit witness to an early belief in existence after death, neither does it deny it. Moreover, two figures were "taken up" to be with God and do not experience death—Enoch (Gen 5:24) and Elijah (2 Kings 2:9-11). While these narratives do not theologically reflect on the implications of these events (we read that Enoch "was no more, for God took him"), later Judaism (cf. Heb 11:5) interpreted this as an "assumption" to eternal life. The incident in 1 Samuel 28:1-25, where Saul attempts to consult Samuel through the medium of Endor, provides further evidence for popular belief that death was not the end of existence.

Several OT statements affirm resurrection in the sense of a corporate preservation rather than individual afterlife. For instance, Hosea 6:1-3 states, "After two days he will revive us; on the third day he will restore us, that we may live in his presence." Similarly, Hosea 13:14 promises, "I will ransom them from the power of the grave; I will redeem them from death" (cf. RSV). In both cases the redemption of Israel from exile is envisaged in terms of deliverance from death (exile) to life (national restoration). In the same way Ezekiel's famous vision of the dry bones coming to life (Ezek 37:1-14) depicts the national reconstitution of Israel. Other passages are often used as evidence of a resurrection hope but seem to refer to rescue from life-threatening situations (Deut 32:39; 1 Sam 2:6).

The basic question is stated in Job 14:14, "If mortals die, will they live again?" A tentative answer is given in Job's response to Bildad in Job 19:25-27, "I know that my Redeemer [*gōʾēl*] lives, and that in the end he will stand upon the earth. And after my skin has been destroyed, yet in my flesh I will see God." It is likely that the "redeemer" is God and that the time of deliverance is after death, thereby constituting a confession of belief in life after death.

The Psalms contain many similar statements. In Psalm 49:15 clearly and in Psalms 16:10 and 73:24 implicitly, a belief in resurrection is apparent, though without any speculation regarding the form the afterlife will take. As G. E. Ladd put it,

> the hope is based on confidence in God's power over death, not on a view of something immortal in man. The Psalmists do not reflect on what *part* of man survives death— his soul or spirit; nor is there any reflection on the nature of life after death. There is merely the confidence that even death cannot destroy the reality of fellowship with the living God. (Ladd, 47)

The prophets provide additional testimony to a resurrection faith. In the so-called Isaiah Apocalypse (Is 24:1—27:13) there are two statements, Isaiah 25:8 and 26:19. The former says that Yahweh will "swallow up death forever" and is used by Paul of the resurrection (1 Cor 15:54). This leads to the affirmation of Isaiah 26:19, "But your dead will live, their bodies will rise. You who dwell in the dust, wake up and shout for joy." However, this resurrection is restricted to God's people. The next two verses (Is 26:20-21) speak of God's wrath upon "the people of the earth" but mention no resurrection to judgment. Less certain is Isaiah 53:10, which asserts that the Servant of Yahweh (*see* Servant of Yahweh), after being "assigned a grave with the wicked" (Is 53:9), will "see his offspring and prolong his days." Most agree that "prolong his days" refers to eternal life, but there is disagreement as to whether the song refers to an individual or corporate figure, the nation or the remnant.

The resurrection faith attested in the prophets climaxes in Daniel 12:1-3, 13. Here the first complete statement of a resurrection of the just and the unjust appears: "Multitudes who sleep in the dust of the earth will awake; some to everlasting life, others to shame and everlasting contempt" (Dan 12:2). There is some question whether "many" is restricted to Israel or the righteous remnant ("many *among* those who sleep") or refers to a general resurrection ("many, *namely* those who sleep"). Verse 13 adds the promise that "at the end of your days you will rise to receive your allotted inheritance."

In conclusion, the OT stresses the presence of God in the daily affairs of this life and tends thereby to ignore the larger issue of life after death. Nevertheless, it is not entirely silent, and several passages demonstrate that at a later period in Israel's history a belief in resurrection became more explicit. Two emphases emerge: (1) a close connection between the corporate and individual aspect of resurrection (i.e., national restoration and individual resurrection) and (2) a link between ethics and eschatology (i.e., resurrection is associated with reward and punishment).

1.2. Intertestamental Developments. While intertestamental Jewish literature witnesses to a great deal more speculation regarding the afterlife, there is clearly no uniformity in the views expressed. G. E. Ladd explains that this was due in part to the emphasis in Judaism upon Torah and orthopraxy (correct practice) rather than orthodoxy (correct doctrine) (Ladd, 52).

Indeed, like the Sadducees of Jesus' day (see Josephus *Ant.* 18.1.4 §16 as well as Acts 4:1-2; 2:1—3:8), some Jews did not believe in a resurrection. Jesus ben Sirach wrote in his first book that at death the person abides in Sheol, a place of unending sleep (Sir 30:17; 46:19) and silence (Sir 17:27-28); and immortality is restricted to the nation and the person's good name (Sir 37:26; 39:9; 44:8-15).

Other texts show the influence of Hellenism, speaking of the afterlife in terms of immortality without linking it to a physical resurrection. Fourth Maccabees, in describing the same seven martyrs mentioned in 2 Maccabees, seemingly substitutes an immortality of the soul where 2 Maccabees spoke of a physical resurrection (cf. 4 Macc 10:15 with 2 Macc 7:14; cf. also 4 Macc 9:22; 16:13; 18:23). Likewise, Wisdom of Solomon speaks of the righteous finding peace (Wis 3:1-4) and an incorruptible existence (Wis 2:23-24; cf. 5:5; 6:19; and Philo *Op. Mund.* 135; *Gig.* 14). In the last book of Enoch (*1 Enoch* 91—104; notice that the five books contain quite variant views on this topic) there is language that at first glance seems to suggest a physical resurrection (e.g., *1 Enoch* 92:3-5; 104:2, 4), but in *1 Enoch* 103:4 we learn that it is their "spirits" that will "live and rejoice" and will "not perish."

Of those texts that do speak of a resurrection, some restrict it to Israel or "the saints" (*1 Enoch* 22:13; 46:6; 51:1-2; *Pss. Sol.* 3:11-16; 13:9-11; 14:4-10; 15:12-15), while several from the first century and later attest to belief in the resurrection of the righteous and the wicked (4 Ezra 4:41-43; 7:32-38 cf. *T. Benj.* 10:6-9; *2 Apoc. Bar.* 49:2-51:12; 85:13). While the possibility of some Christian influence and interpolation cannot be discounted, the resurrection of the righteous and the wicked is itself essentially Jewish, reflecting the eschatology of Daniel 12:2-3. Finally, an extremely literalistic concept of bodily resurrection can be found in 2 Maccabees, which speaks not only of the raising of the body but even the restoration of missing limbs or other body parts (2 Macc 7:10-11; 14:46). Similarly, the *Sibylline Oracles* states that the resurrection body will be fashioned exactly after the earthly body (2 Macc 4:176-82).

Clearly intertestamental Judaism showed a much greater interest than does the Hebrew Bible in the question of the afterlife, with interest centering on the theme of God vindicating his people. In addition, a variety of viewpoints emerged. This variety is reflected in the beliefs of the various parties or sects within the Judaism of Jesus' time. The Sadducees rejected any idea of an afterlife (Acts 23:8; 26:8; Josephus *Ant.* 18.14; *b. Sanh.* 90b). The Pharisees taught a resurrection and eternal reward for Israel in the age to come, excluding only apostates (Acts 23:6-8; *b. Sanh.* 90b; *b. Ketub.* 111b). The Essene view on the matter was not clear, as exemplified in the Qumran scrolls (*see* Dead Sea Scrolls). Josephus asserts that they held to the immortality of the soul (Josephus *Ant.* 18.1.5 §18), but many scholars maintain that statements referring to the habitation of the faithful with the angels (1QS 2:25; 1QH 3:19-23; 11:10-14) should be understood as the sectarians' experience in this life rather than an eschatological hope.

2. Resurrection and Afterlife in the Sayings of Jesus.

Jesus followed in the tradition extending from Daniel to the Pharisees, teaching that there would be a twofold resurrection: the righteous to reward and the wicked to judgment. While a full tradition-critical study is beyond the scope of this article, it is helpful to view the relevant teaching of Jesus from a source-critical perspective (*see* Synoptic Problem).

2.1. Sayings of the Triple Tradition. The clearest discussion of resurrection in Jesus' teaching can be found in the triple-tradition story of his controversy with the Sadducees (Mk 12:18-27 par. Mt 22:23-33 and Lk 20:27-38). Even those who maintain that the final form is a later catechetical elaboration accept the first pronouncement ("become like angels") as authentic. Luke in particular stresses the contrast between the "people of this age" and those "worthy of taking part in that age and in the resurrection from the dead" (Lk 20:34-35), a distinct reference to eschatological views of an afterlife. Yet the major question is the significance of the phrase "like the angels in heaven." Some conclude from this that Jesus believed in a spiritual rather than physical resurrection or that he had a view, like some within Judaism, that in heaven there would be no consciousness of prior existence. However, this reads more into the passage than is intended, since the phrase is contrasting marriage on earth with marriage in heaven rather than teaching the state of the resurrection body.

Sayings on reward and judgment also appear in the triple tradition. The query of the wealthy young man in Mark 10:17 (par. Mt 19:16 and Lk 18:18), "What must I do to inherit eternal life?" is often understood as a desire to "enter the kingdom" in its realized presence (*see* Kingdom of God). While this is certainly part of the meaning, it does not exhaust its thrust. Jesus' final statement in Mark 10:30 (par. Mt 19:29 and Lk 18:30), "and in the age to come eternal life," forms an inclusio with the young man's question and clearly refers to the afterlife. There is both a present and future connotation in "eternal life" in Mark 10:17, 30 and parallels. The other side, resurrection to judgment, is found in the Gehenna warning of Mark 9:43, 45, 47 (par. Mt 18:8-9; omitted in Luke). Using successive metaphors of the hand, foot and eye, Jesus exhorts the disciples to disciplined resistance against temptation, lest one (Mark and Matthew both stress the singular "you") be cast into "hell, where the fire never goes out" (Mk 9:43; cf. "eternal fire," Mt 18:8).

2.2. The Passion Predictions. The best-known tradition is the threefold passion prediction of Mark 8:31; 9:31; 10:33-34 and parallels. Many interpreters have understood these as *vaticinium ex eventu* (prophecies written after the event), but the absence of the type of theological elaboration found in the creeds (e.g., "for our sins," "according to the scriptures" and the exaltation theme) makes it more likely that these are indeed historical reminiscences. The one constant in all three accounts is Jesus' prediction that "three days after" his death he would be vindicated by resurrection. The third-day theme (cf. 1 Cor 15:4) may reflect Hosea 6:2 ("on the third day he will raise us"), a more general allusion to the OT theme of the third day as a day of deliverance (cf. Gen 22:4; 42:17-18; Is 2:16; Jon 2:1), or more simply a reference on Jesus' part to a brief period of time.

Added to these direct predictions are the numerous parallel passages where Jesus presumes his future resurrection, such as: Mark 9:9 (tell no one of the transfiguration "until the Son of Man has risen from the dead"); Mark 12:10-11 ("the stone the builders rejected has become the capstone"); Mark 13:26 ("the Son of man coming in clouds with great power and glory"); Mark 14:25 ("when I drink it [the eschatological cup] anew in the kingdom of God"); Mark 14:28 ("after I have arisen I will go before you into Galilee") and Mark 14:62 ("you will see the Son of man sitting at the right hand of the Mighty One and coming on the clouds of heaven" [see Son of Man]).

One of the most remarkable prophecies of Jesus is not found in Luke but is recorded indirectly in Mark (Mk 14:58; 15:29) and a Matthean parallel (Mt 26:61; 27:40) and directly in John 2:19: "Destroy this temple, and I will raise it again in three days." John 2:21-22 explains that this direct prophecy of physical resurrection was not understood by the disciples until after the resurrection itself (ironically, the chief priests and Pharisees, according to Mt 27:63, correctly interpreted this saying before the disciples did). In summation, according to the Gospels Jesus clearly expected to be vindicated by resurrection.

2.3. The Q Tradition. The Q tradition contains similar teaching. The "sign of Jonah" (Mt 12:39-42 par. Lk 11:29-32) is problematic be-

cause only Matthew spells out the sign as a cryptic reference to the resurrection ("the Son of man will be three days and three nights in the heart of the earth," Mt 12:40). But it is just as likely that Luke has omitted the Q statement on resurrection (due to the difficulty of "three days and three nights" for his readers) as Matthew has added it.

There are also several Q passages on final reward and punishment, such as those found at the end of Matthew's Olivet Discourse. At the end of the exhortation to watchfulness (Mt 24:40-44 par. Lk 17:34-37) we have three successive short parables (men in the field, women grinding, two in a bed) demonstrating that "one will be taken, the other left." These form a severe warning regarding the sudden, unexpected separation at the Parousia (cf. Mt 24:44; cf. Lk 12:40) between those receiving salvation and those doomed for judgment. This contrast is further emphasized in the parable of the good and wicked servants (Mt 24:45-51 par. Lk 12:41-46), in which the faithful servant is given a share in Jesus' future authority while the wicked servant will be "dismembered" (Lk 12:46) and placed with the unfaithful. Finally, Matthew 10:28 and Luke 12:5 add a further saying on Gehenna, that the disciple should fear not those who can kill the body but the one who "can destroy both soul and body in hell." These passages show that Jesus followed Daniel 12:2 regarding the resurrection of good and evil alike, one to vindication and the other to judgment.

2.4. The M and L Traditions. The source material peculiar to Matthew (M) and Luke (L) adds further data. In the M tradition judgment will be universal; both good and evil people will be accountable "on the day of judgment for every careless word they have spoken" (Mt 12:35-37). While evil or "careless" speech is stressed, the "acquittal" or "condemnation" (Mt 12:37) of all speech is in mind. Two further parables address the radical separation of believer from unbeliever at the last judgment. The parable of the weeds in Matthew 13:24-30, 36-43 teaches that only at "the end of the age" (Mt 13:43) will the wicked finally be separated from the good, the former headed for "the fiery furnace" and the latter for glory (Mt 13:42-43). The parable of the sheep and the goats (also called "the judgment of the nations") has a similar theme but adds that the judgment will be determined also by the way the nations have treated God's people (the "least of these" of Mt 13:40, 45). The reward for the merciful will be "your inheritance, the kingdom prepared for you since the creation of the world" (Mt 13:34); the punishment for the merciless will be "the eternal fire prepared for the devil and his angels" (Mt 13:41).

Several L passages demonstrate the Lukan theme of the reversal of roles at the final resurrection. At the conclusion of the sayings on proper conduct at banquets (Lk 14:7-14), Jesus says that those who invite the poor (*see* Riches and Poverty) and the crippled "will be repaid at the resurrection of the righteous" (Lk 14:14). While there may be no thanks in this life, God will vindicate good deeds at the eschaton. The key is a life of servanthood that seeks the lesser rather than the greater place (Lk 14:8-11) and is oriented to the dispossessed rather than the wealthy (Lk 14:12-14).

This theme is taken further in the parable of the rich man and Lazarus in Luke 16:19-31. The rich man, who undoubtedly had a lavish earthly funeral, is described in terse clauses: "died and was buried and in Hades." The poor man, who seemingly is not buried at all, has exactly the opposite afterlife: "angels carried him to Abraham's side." There are two concurrent emphases in this parable: the reversal of roles at the final resurrection and the radical faith demands of the kingdom message. Similar warnings of final judgment are addressed to the rich and to all disciples in Luke 3:7-14; 6:24-26; 12:16-21, 32-34, 42-48; 16:8-9. The implications of this parable for a doctrine of the afterlife cannot be pressed too far. The picture of a compartmentalized "Hades" does not describe "the way it is" but is a feature of the parable probably derived from a popular Jewish conception of Sheol.

2.5. The Johannine Tradition. The Johannine tradition contains a few sayings that relate to the resurrection theology of Jesus and the early church. While the Fourth Gospel primarily sets forth a realized eschatology, a growing consensus of scholarship has detected a future eschatology within this characteristic Johannine matrix (*see* John, Gospel of). In John 5:28-29 Jesus speaks of the "coming time" when the dead will hear his voice and "come out—those who have done good will rise to live, and those who have done evil will rise to be condemned." The context centers on Jesus as the eschatological Judge in the present (Jn 5:19-24) and the future (Jn 5:25-30). Then in John 6:40, 44, 54—

within a context emphasizing the united sovereignty of the Father and Son in the salvation process (cf. "will never die" in Jn 11:25-26)—Jesus thrice repeats that he will "raise" the faithful "at the last day."

The other side is found in John 12:48, in which the unbeliever is warned that Jesus' words will "condemn him at the last day." Finally, Jesus promises in John 14:2-3 that he is "preparing a place" for his disciples and "will come back" to bring them to his side. Some have interpreted this of the Paraclete/*Holy Spirit "coming back" as Jesus' representative, but the consensus is that this is a reference to the Parousia. Bultmann and others have long argued that these futuristic passages were added by a later redactor, and that realized passages like John 12:31 and 16:11 (the judgment "*now*" of the "prince of this world") are original. Yet there is no reason why the two cannot stand side-by-side, with present salvation and future promise interrelated.

Jesus' teaching fits into the ongoing tradition from Daniel through the Pharisees, attesting to the physical resurrection of God's people to reward and of the resurrection of the ungodly to final judgment.

3. Miracles of Raising the Dead.
Jesus affirmed his belief in resurrection not only by his words but also by his deeds. In one sense these are not true resurrections but miracles of resuscitation, for the recipients would still face death at a later date. However, in the Gospels they are treated as harbingers of Jesus' coming resurrection, proof of God's (and Jesus') control over the power of death.

3.1. Jairus's Daughter. The most fully attested miracle of resuscitation is the raising of Jairus's daughter. Found in the triple tradition (Mk 5:21-24, 35-43 par. Mt 9:18-19, 23-26 and Lk 8:40-42, 49-56), it is intertwined in all three accounts with the healing of the woman with a hemorrhage. The movement from healing to resuscitation shows Jesus as lord over both chronic illness and death. The overriding concern is christological, seeking to demonstrate Jesus' lordship. That Jairus—a ruler or president of a synagogue and a man with great social and religious prestige—would prostrate himself before Jesus would be astonishing to a first-century reader and point to Jesus as a God-ordained prophet.

On the basis of Jesus' statement "She is not dead, but asleep," many interpreters have argued that this is a healing miracle. However, the details regarding the mourning of the relatives and professional mourners all point to the reality of the girl's death. Instead, Jesus' comment is a theological pointer to the miracle as an "awakening" from the dead. In all three Gospels this story is part of a complex of miracles (the stilling of the storm, the Gerasene demoniac) demonstrating the messianic authority of Jesus over all earthly and heavenly powers. Even the ultimate power of death is conquered by him.

3.2. The Widow's Son. A second account is the Lukan tradition of Jesus raising the son of a widow of Nain (Lk 7:11-17). Recalling the similar raising of the widow's son by Elijah (1 Kings 17:8-24), this is also part of a section dealing with Jesus' prophetic ministry (note the healing of the centurion's son that precedes and the dialogue regarding the Baptist that follows). The miracle concludes with expressions of awe and wonder which are anchored in the "rising" of a "great prophet" and especially in the statement that "God has visited his people" (Lk 7:16), the latter echoing the language of Zechariah's Song (Lk 1:68, 78) and the Lukan theme of salvific deliverance. Jesus' power over life and death is vividly portrayed.

3.3. Lazarus. The raising of Lazarus (Jn 11:1-44) is the concluding and most astounding sign-miracle of John's so-called Book of Signs (Jn 1:19—12:50). It also functions as a transition to the Book of Glory (Jn 13:1—20:31), with the plot of the Jewish leaders being clearly tied to this event (cf. Jn 11:53; 12:17-19).

Of the so-called resurrection miracles, the raising of Lazarus is most clearly connected with the question of the afterlife. This becomes evident in the dialogue with Martha (Jn 11:20-26) and its connection to the Johannine theme of eternal life as resurrection (cf. 5:19-30). In John 11:21, 25, 28-29 Jesus demonstrates the presence of resurrection both now (the *spiritual* dead hear his voice and live, Jn 11:25) and in the future (those in the grave come forth, Jn 11:28-29). This is actualized in Lazarus—Jesus raises him as a clear foretaste of the final resurrection—and emphasized in the juxtaposition of Martha's confession ("I know he will rise again in the resurrection at the last day," Jn 11:24) and Jesus' bold claim ("I am the resurrection and the life," Jn 11:25). In fact, John 11:25 is the theological culmination of John 5:21, "For just as the Father raises the dead and gives them life, even so the Son gives life to whom he is pleased to give it." Jesus is equated with the Father as the one who gives "resurrection and life," so uniting the Johannine themes of realized (raising the spiritually dead to life) and final (the resurrection at the last day) eschatology.

3.4. The Saints. Finally, the enigmatic raising of the saints in Matthew 27:51-53 provides a theological bridge from the cross to the empty tomb. In what is likely an allusion to Ezekiel's vision of the valley of dry bones (Ezek 37:1-14, esp. 13-14, "When I open your graves and bring you up from them . . . and you will live"), the brief story summarizes the effects of Jesus' death (judgment and the defeat of the powers of death; *see* Death of Jesus) and resurrection (the raising of the dead saints and their appearance in the holy city). Thus Jesus' passion and resurrection are inextricably linked as a single event in salvation-history, and the effect upon the raising and uniting of the true "saints" of God, both past and future, is guaranteed by this supernatural deed.

The question of the historicity of these miracles is beyond the purview of this study (for arguments pro see Harris 1990; con see Perkins; *see* Gospels [Historical Reliability]). But the claim that Jesus raised the dead on the basis of his prophetic and messianic office and as a harbinger of his own resurrection can at least tentatively be affirmed (*see* Miracles, Miracle Stories). Miracles of raising the dead permeate all the traditions behind the Gospels (Mark, M, L, John, possibly Q), and their historicity can be argued on the basis of the criterion of multiple attestation.

4. Jesus' Resurrection in the Four Gospels.

4.1. The Resurrection in Mark. With the growing consensus among Gospel scholars that Mark's Gospel concludes at Mark 16:8 with the words *ephobounta gar* ("for they were afraid"), Mark 16:1-8 has come to be regarded as a literary masterpiece (*see* Mark, Gospel of). Moreover, Mark 16:1-8 may be seen as a brilliant conclusion to the Gospel as a whole, bringing Mark's two major themes to culmination: the hidden epiphany of Jesus as Messiah and *Son of God; and discipleship, particularly the problem of discipleship failure.

The first unit (Mk 16:1-4) combines tradition and Markan redaction. Pre-Markan tradition can be found in the names of the women and the trip to the tomb at dawn. Yet the whole narrative is tied together in Markan fashion and presents some basic Markan themes, particularly in the misunderstanding of the women. The chronological notes provide an important transition from the passion to the resurrection. The action proceeds from the terrible events on "the day before the Sabbath" (Mk 15:42) to the decision to bring spices "when the Sabbath was over" and then depicts the trip itself.

Continuity is also provided by the names. There are three in Mark's passion narrative (Mk 15:40, 47; 16:1), with Mary Magdalene, Mary and Salome in Mark 15:40 and 16:1 and the two Marys in Mark 15:47. Luke adds Joanna (Lk 24:10), while Matthew only has the two Marys (Mt 28:1; though Mt 27:56 par. Mk 15:40 adds "the mother of the sons of Zebedee"). It is likely that tradition and redaction are again combined. The key to Mark's purpose is found in his use of *theorein* with each name list, thereby making the women official witnesses of the crucifixion events (Mk 15:40), the burial (Mk 15:47) and the empty tomb (Mk 15:47).

The purchase of the spices for anointing Jesus' corpse parallels both Joseph's purchase in Mark 15:46 and the anointing (pointing to his death) of Mark 14:3-9. It is ironic in this context, for the messianic connotations of the earlier anointings, signifying Jesus' death as the assumption of his office as royal Messiah, make this anointing unnecessary. Jesus has not only become Messiah but has already risen, so there will be no further anointing. Irony and misunderstanding continue not only in the women's desire to anoint Jesus' body but in their perplexity as to how they can find help to "roll away the stone" (Mk 16:3) which was "very large" (Mk 16:4). A narrative gap occurs in the passive "had been rolled away" of Mark 16:4, anticipating the supernatural intervention of the angel (Mt 28:2 explicitly names the angel as the agent) in Mark 16:5. In short, Mark 16:1-4 centers on the misunderstanding of the women (who play a role in Mark's discipleship theme) and directs the reader forward to the divine intervention that alone can solve the dilemma.

The angelic message (Mk 16:5-7) also contains both tradition (the angelophany, the exhortation not to fear, the implied rebuke, the basic proclamation of the resurrection and empty tomb) and redaction (their "amazement," *Nazarenos*, the command to go to Galilee). The "messianic secret," partially lifted in the centurion's cry of Mark 15:39 ("Surely this man was the Son of God"), is now completely disclosed. The women's astonishment and the angel's command not to fear belong to the genre of epiphany, and the message is a kerygmatic formula that completely removes any doubt as to who this "Nazarene" is, confirming the significance of the threefold passion predictions centering on the "Son of man." There is again a tension introduced into the contrast between the women's pious but ignorant purpose ("seeking" to anoint one who "is not here") and the stupendous significance of the reality of resurrection as announced.

The promise of Mark 16:7—that the disciples will see Jesus in Galilee—is the key to Mark's narrative and is intimately connected to the promise of Mark 14:28 (cf. also Mk 9:9) that the disciples' misunderstanding and failure would be reversed in a Galilee experience. Some (e.g., W. Marxsen) have argued that this refers to a Parousia expectation rather than a resurrection appearance, but the absence of a glory motif and the fact that both Galilee and the promise "you will see him" *(opsesthe)* are connected in Mark with the resurrection rather than Parousia make such an assumption unlikely. "Galilee" occurs thirteen times in Mark, usually in the context of Jesus' mission and its success (cf. Mk 1:14, 28, 39; 3:7; 15:40). Therefore, it implicitly promises the overcoming of their failure and the passing of the baton, thus launching the church's mission. This is exemplified further in the pre-Markan tradition (cf. Lk 24:34, 1 Cor 15:5) to "tell the disciples and Peter," which may well indicate the reinstatement of the disciples.

This makes the Markan ending all the more startling. The reader would expect the fear to have ceased in Mark 16:6, yet here the fear overpowers the women and forces them to disobey the angel's mandate. However, the stress is not on an act of disobedience but on the numbing effect of the overwhelming awe. In every sense Mark 16:8 concludes Mark's theme of discipleship failure, for the women parallel the many scenes of similar awe, silence and misunderstanding on the part of the disciples (e.g., Mk 6:52; 8:14-21; 9:6, 32; 10:32). If Mark 16:8 were to be considered alone, it would make an incredibly negative conclusion; we would be left only with the warning that believers today not repeat the failure of the disciples and the women. However, Mark's actual message is to be found in the interaction between Mark 16:7 and 8. The resurrection appearances are not related in the narrative because Mark's emphasis is on the presence of the Risen One in our Galilee. Awe and failure are very real experiences for every disciple, but Jesus is at all times waiting to remove that fear and to guarantee success in mission.

4.2. The Resurrection in Matthew. Matthew follows Mark's basic outline but adds a great deal of his own material, primarily the narrative of the guards at the tomb (Mt 27:62-66; 28:4, 11-15) and the story of Jesus' appearance in Galilee (Mt 28:16-20). In so doing he has fashioned an episode employing two sets of contrasting scenes, thereby demonstrating the intervention of God against all attempts to obstruct his salvific plan. This plan follows the similar structure of both the infancy and passion narratives, which for Matthew center apologetically on the power of God to overcome all obstacles. Matthew's resurrection narrative also emphasizes the twin themes of authority and mission/commission, utilizing the theme of recognition or coming-to-understanding. All of this summarizes major themes that have occurred throughout *Matthew's Gospel. Whereas Mark focuses on the failure of the disciples, Matthew in every episode (e.g., Mt 14:27-32; cf. Mk 6:52; Mt 16:12; cf. Mk 8:21) shows how the presence of Jesus allows the disciples to overcome their failure and attain understanding. The resurrection scene culminates this development in discipleship.

The first set of contrasting scenes (Mt 27:62—28:10) contrasts the priests' complex plot to post the guards and seal the tomb with the sovereign act of God in raising Jesus from the dead. There are certainly strong redactional overtones in the guard narrative of Matthew 27:62-66 as well as in the related episodes of Matthew 28:4, 11-15. Yet this does not mean that there was no tradition behind the story. This is suggested by the non-Matthean vocabulary such as *epaurion, paraskeuē, planos* and *asphalizō.* Moreover, historical problems such as the likelihood of the priests going to Pilate on the Sabbath are not as problematic as they first appear. Research into Sabbath exceptions at the time of Jesus shows that such an incident would have been allowed, so long as the individuals did not travel more than a Sabbath day's journey or enter the palace (cf. Jn 18:28). It seems likely that Matthew has developed tradition regarding the priests' request for

a setting of the guard in order to answer contemporary Jewish charges that the body had been stolen and to emphasize the sovereign power of God in the resurrection despite all such plots. Matthew has also removed Mark's stress on the women's misguided purpose to anoint the body of Jesus, emphasizing instead the theme of witness (cf. Mt 27:56, 61). In the Matthean setting the women's simple act of reverence is set in contrast with the priestly intrigue.

The supernatural intervention of God in the two scenes of Matthew 28:2-4 and 5-10 is remarkable. Matthew favors such eschatological scenes (see the earthquake *[seismos]* scenes of Mt 8:24 and 27:51 as well as angel scenes in Mt 1:20, 24; 2:13, 19) to emphasize the inbreaking of the messianic age by direct acts of God. The earthquake establishes continuity with the crucifixion (Mt 27:51); as in Acts 16:26 and Revelation 6:12; 8:5; 16:18 it is not so much a symbol of judgment as a positive sign of divine deliverance. The angel's act in rolling back the stone and sitting upon it also has apocalyptic overtones (cf. also his description in Mt 28:3, paralleling Dan 7:9; 10:6; *1 Enoch* 71:1; Rev 1:14-15; 10:1), depicting the dawn of a new age. The tomb has been opened, allowing all to witness the triumph of God.

Matthew has clearly departed from the simple portrait of Mark; yet his restraint can be seen by comparing Matthew 28:2-4 with the elaborate narration in the *Gospel of Peter* 9:35-45, in which two angels help the risen Lord from the tomb, "and the heads of the two reaching to heaven, but that of him who was led of them by the hand surpassing the heavens." Matthew has deliberately avoided describing the resurrection itself. The reaction of the guards, who faint and "become like dead men," provides a negative "witness" (that of opponents to God's plan) to the theophanic overtones of the scene. This is not the fear of reverence (like that of the women in Mt 28:9) but the terror that God's enemies alone will feel.

The angel's message (Mt 28:5-7) is more closely aligned with Mark. Yet there are significant redactional alterations. Matthew replaces Mark's "do not be alarmed" with "do not be afraid," probably to strengthen the contrast with the guards' terror. He also connects the announcement of Jesus' resurrection directly with the passion predictions by adding "as he said." Mark uses this phrase after the reference to

Jesus preceding them to Galilee, but Matthew at this point has the angel conclude his pronouncement with "Now I have told you," stressing the authority of the divinely commissioned messenger. The meeting in Galilee thus becomes more directly the result of the angel's proclamation than of Jesus' previous promise (as in Mark). Mark's startling ending is radically altered by Matthew, who in Matthew 28:8-10 has the women go forth "afraid yet filled with joy" and "run to tell his disciples." The appearance of Jesus to the women is attested independently in John 20:11-18 and stems from tradition. But Matthean elements may be observed in the stress on "joy" (cf. Mt 2:10; 13:20, 44; 25:21, 23), "worship" (Mt 2:2, 11; 4:9-10; 8:1; 9:18; 14:33; 15:25) and "my brothers," which indicates in a single word the forgiveness and reinstatement of the fallen disciples (cf. Jn 15:11-17; 20:17 for a similar emphasis). The repetition of the command to go to Galilee prepares for the climactic scene in Matthew 28:16-20.

The second set of contrasts is between the evil plot to spread lies in Matthew 28:11-15 and the great commission of divine truth in Matthew 28:16-20. The irony of the priestly deception in Matthew 28:11-15 is obvious; the very thing they had sought to prevent in Matthew 27:62-66 (i.e., the possibility that Jesus' body might be stolen) they are now forced to proclaim. Matthew's apologetic against this Jewish polemic (note "to this very day," Mt 28:15) is now made explicit.

The aptly named "great commission" of Matthew 28:16-20 belongs to the genre of commissioning narratives seen often in the OT and Jewish literature. It consists of two parts, a narrative introduction (Mt 28:16-18a) and a threefold saying composed of a statement of authority (Mt 28:18b), a commission (Mt 28:19-20a) and reassurance of the Risen One's continued presence (Mt 28:20b). It is very likely that the episode is based on tradition, since it parallels similar commissionings in Luke 24:47-49 and John 20:21-23, and contains elements pointing to a source in the tradition: "the mountain where Jesus had told them to go" (no such command occurs in Matthew); "but some doubted" (a major resurrection tradition but apparently out of place here); and "in heaven and on earth" (not found elsewhere in Matthew). However, the language and themes are so Matthean that it is impossible to separate redaction from tradition (nor would

we wish to limit historical trustworthiness to one but not the other).

Matthew has carefully crafted the whole to summarize many of the major themes in his Gospel. Some interesting points occur in the introduction, such as the meeting on a mountain, so important in Matthew as a place of revelation (cf. Mt 4:8; 5:1; 8:1; 14:23; 15:29; 17:1; 21:1); and the presence of doubt in the midst of the disciples' worship. This latter element probably continues the Matthean theme of the "little-faithed ones." *Distazō* occurs in the NT only here and in Matthew 14:31, where Jesus chides his disciples, "O you of little faith, why did you doubt?" But they respond (Mt 14:32), "Truly you are the Son of God." It is likely that the doubt means uncertainty rather than unbelief and that this is part of the message through out the First Gospel: Spiritual hesitation in the midst of worship is the constant struggle of every disciple. The answer can only be found when one applies the promise inherent in Matthew 28:18-20.

The key term in the commission itself is "all"—"all authority," "all nations," "all things," "always." In many ways this short homily could be labeled the "Allness of Yahweh" passed on to the mission of the disciples through the presence of the Risen One among them. The "authority in heaven and on earth given" to Jesus is a reflection of Daniel 7:14, and therefore the Risen Jesus is depicted as the exalted Son of man who now has universal authority over all of God's kingdom. The authority of Jesus in Matthew's Gospel is now extended to all of God's kingdom, heavenly as well as earthly. The mission to disciple "all the nations" (possibly also connected to Dan 7:14) echoes the church's participation in the God-given mission of Jesus, which was limited to Israel (Mt 10:5-6; 15:24) but is now extended to all people. There is considerable debate as to whether *ethnē* ("nations," "peoples") refers only to the Gentile mission (due to the common restriction of the term to Gentiles) or whether the addition of *pas* ("all") extends the reference to include Israel as well as the nations. Several recent studies on the scope of the universal mission in Matthew find the latter interpretation more likely. Moreover, in Matthew 24:9, 14 and 25:32 (the other three places where the full expression "all nations" occurs) it refers to "all people," including Jew and Gentile.

There are two concomitant aspects to the discipling process: baptism and instruction. Jesus' resurrection command becomes the basis of Christian baptism, which is here seen as an entrance "into" (*eis*, as Matthew normally observes the distinction between *eis* and *en*) the lordship and fellowship of the triune godhead. There is Matthean background in the trinitarian formula, summarizing the Father-Son (Mt 3:17; 11:27) and Son-Spirit (Mt 3:11, 16; 12:32) relationships. The second aspect, teaching, also concludes a major theme. Matthew's Gospel is organized around the five great discourse units of chapters 5—7, 10, 13, 18 and 23—25, and discipleship itself is defined as an ethical response to Jesus' demands. As in Matthew 5:17-20 and 24:35, Jesus' teaching is presented as the authoritative words of Yahweh and as the fulfillment of the Torah (*see* Law). The Torah of the Messiah has come, and in this new age the disciple will obey "all the commands" of Jesus.

The disciple's obedient response to Jesus' teaching is paralleled by the promise of Jesus' continued presence, building upon earlier promises of Jesus as the *Immanuel,* or "God with us" (Mt 1:23) and as the one present whenever "two or three are gathered" (Mt 18:20). Here we see the solution to the "little faith" of Matthew 28:17; namely, the powerful presence of the Risen One would sustain them in their weakness. Moreover, that presence is constant "to the very end of the age." Many have called this a "proleptic parousia," due to the apocalyptic overtones (again building upon Dan 7:14) in which Jesus' future or final coming is mediated to the church now.

4.3. The Resurrection in Luke. In Luke and John the basic approach to the resurrection changes, with the appearances centered in Jerusalem rather than Galilee. For Luke this lends the account a geographical focus in which Jerusalem becomes both an ending (for the life and ministry of Jesus) and a beginning (for the ongoing mission of the church). Luke's presentation prepares for the book of Acts, so the resurrection provides a transition from the ministry of Jesus to that of the early church. As many have noted, there is a salvation-historical perspective throughout. Moreover, there is a strong creedal emphasis, with constant commentary elucidating the significance of the events from the perspective of prophetic fulfillment (Lk 24:5-7, 25-27, 44-47). Finally, there is a strong polemic focusing on doubt and the reality of the resurrection. An emphasis on witness, including

proofs for the resurrection, is evident, but this is constantly met by perplexity and unbelief. Luke presents these themes in linear fashion, with all the events occurring on the same day in four stages: the empty tomb (Lk 24:1-12), the road to Emmaus (Lk 24:13-35), the appearance to and commissioning of the disciples at the meal (Lk 24:36-49) and the ascension into heaven (Lk 24:50-52).

Luke's empty-tomb narrative (Lk 24:1-12) follows Mark's general order but introduces some interesting redactional twists. It is debated whether Luke utilizes Mark and adds L material (the women entering the tomb, the two angels, the appearance to Peter in Lk 24:12, 34) or has followed a non-Markan source and inserted some Markan details. Whichever is the case, Lukan redaction is evident. He has an extensive discussion of the women's preparation and rest on the Sabbath (Lk 23:54-56), with four time notes (Lk 23:54a, 54b, 56; 24:1) that unite the burial and tomb event into a salvation-historical whole. The emphasis is not so much on the women's misunderstanding (as in Mark) as on God's work behind the scenes. The action leads to the direct pronouncement in Luke 24:3 that the women "did not find the body" in the tomb. The role of the women as witnesses is expanded; they "saw" not only the tomb but "how his body was laid" (Lk 23:55) and then were witnesses to the empty tomb. The significance is seen in the added note that it was "the body of the Lord Jesus" (though this is a "western non-interpolation," missing in the normally adventuresome Western family of manuscripts, most scholars agree that the phrase "of the Lord Jesus" is original to the text). This introduces Luke's characteristic theology of glory at the very outset of the resurrection narrative.

The women's perplexity in Luke 24:3 turns into fearful awe (Lk 24:4) as there are now two angels in dazzling apparel (pre-Lukan tradition, cf. Jn 20:12). The message itself (Lk 24:5-7) departs from the Markan form. There is no alleviation of their fear but rather a direct challenge and proclamation of the critical reality of the resurrection. "Galilee" in this pronouncement is not the place where Jesus will meet them but the place where Jesus had formerly predicted his passion and resurrection. In Luke Galilee is the place of authoritative witness; the women themselves are from Galilee (Lk 8:1-3), and Galilean disciples attest to the Jerusalem appearances in

Acts 1:11 and 13:31. In other words, the focus changes from the future to the past, and the repetition of the passion prediction in Luke 24:7, being derived from Luke 9:22, 44; 18:31-33, adds a promise-fulfillment thrust. In Luke 24:8 the women "remember," a Lukan emphasis pointing to an awakening faith (contra Dillon) in the salvific plan of God (especially in its connection with the divine "must" *[dei]* of Lk 24:7; cf. Lk 1:54, 72; Acts 11:16). Their understanding leads them to report "all these things" (including not only the angel's message but their own witness to the empty tomb). Unlike Matthew and Mark, this is not in response to an angelic commission (omitted by Luke) but is the direct result of their burgeoning faith (seen in the and . . . and [*kai* . . . *kai*] pattern of Lk 24:8-9). Luke reserves the list of names (even adding "the other women with them") for this point (Lk 24:10) in order to give greater stress to the women's function as witnesses to the reality of the resurrection. Yet the result is startling; the "apostles" (Luke uses this title six times in his Gospel [as opposed to once in Matthew and twice in Mark] to stress the point of continuity between the disciples and the apostolic band of Acts) not only doubt but "disbelieve," considering the women's testimony to be "nonsense."

This unbelief is a major emphasis in Luke's empty-tomb narrative, preparing for the overcoming of doubt via the direct presence of the Risen One in the next episode. To give added stress to this motif Luke incorporates (another Western non-interpolation that most today accept as authentic) a further episode from the tradition (the language shows similarities with Jn 20:3-10) regarding Peter's trip to the tomb (Lk 24:12). Peter's "perplexed" departure from the tomb mutes somewhat the disbelief of the disciples, but conclusively, for he provides continuity from the confusion of the women in Luke 24:4 to the "amazement" of the travelers in Luke 24:22. Full-fledged faith comes only after the sovereign intervention of the Risen One himself (Lk 24:16, 31).

This struggle of faith continues in the Emmaus Road journey of Luke 24:13-35. The interplay of tradition and redaction is difficult to detect since this story only occurs in Luke. However, while there is a great deal of Lukan redaction, there are few scholars who would identify this as a free composition. It is likely that a pre-Lukan form of this story formed the basis for a

portion of the later Markan appendix (Mk 16:12-13), and the names "Emmaus" and "Cleopas" would have been unlikely in a story freely created. Most critical scholars accept the pre-Lukan origin of at least Luke 24:13, 16, 28-31, and many would accept a historical nucleus behind the whole.

Viewed within its larger context, several themes emerge. As so often in Luke, geography dominates the structure. In this case the journey "from" Jerusalem is characterized by defeat, the return "to" Jerusalem by witness and victory. The turn-about through Jesus' instruction takes place "on the way." The reality of the resurrection is the goal of the story, with Luke 24:28-32 climaxing not only this episode but the empty-tomb narrative as well. This reality is particularly stressed in the proof-from-prophecy (Lk 24:25-27) as Jesus shows that he is more than a powerful prophet (the travelers' belief in Lk 24:19) but is indeed the fulfillment of the prophetic vision of a suffering and glorified Messiah.

The movement toward understanding is accomplished utilizing a non-recognition/recognition motif. During the first half of the story the travelers are "kept from recognizing" Jesus, a feature recalling the disciples' need for divine disclosure in order to understand the passion predictions (Lk 9:45; 18:34). This is undoubtedly intended to lead the reader to the opening of blind eyes via the proclamation of the Word (Lk 24:25-27, 32) and the breaking of the bread (Lk 24:30-31, 35). The spoken word controls the narrative of Luke 24:17-27 and includes a summary of the tomb events, thereby elaborating on the confession that Jesus was "the prophet powerful in word and deed" (Lk 24:19; cf. 24:20-24), and on the scriptural fulfillment motif (Lk 24:25-27).

Many see a parallel here with the Ethiopian eunuch story of Acts 8:26-39, each story following a similar pattern: a stranger opens up the Word for the traveller, leading to conversion. Yet the instruction in Luke 24 is actually "pre-evangelism," for while their hearts did "burn" as Jesus opened the Scriptures (Lk 24:32), the breaking of bread is the turning point of the Emmaus episode. It is here that God sovereignly opens their blind eyes (note the divine passive "were opened" in Luke 24:31, the counterpart to "were kept from recognizing him" in Lk 24:16).

It is debated whether this implies a eucharistic celebration. "Breaking of bread" is seen by some as a technical phrase for the eucharist

(Acts 2:42; 20:7; 1 Cor 11:20), and the order of events in Luke 24:30 (taking, giving thanks, breaking, distributing) might be reminiscent of the *Last Supper (cf. Lk 22:19). However, the motif could also be more general, alluding to the Lukan meal or *table-fellowship scenes that feature Jesus' instruction (Lk 5:29; 7:36; 11:37; 12:37; 13:29; 14:1, 8-9; 22:14; cf. esp. Lk 9:10-17 [the feeding of the five thousand] which also has parallels to this passage). On the whole, it is possible that both aspects are found here, especially when one realizes that the eucharist was a meal scene in the Gospels. Yet one cannot be dogmatic, and it may be table fellowship rather than eucharist which is intended. The final emphasis is on witness and culminates this theme, from the incredulity of Luke 24:11 to the faith response of Luke 24:34. Interestingly, the witness of the two disciples does not produce faith; rather, it confirms the faith that resulted from the report of the appearance to Simon. In other words, the reality of the resurrection is confirmed by a double witness, that of Peter and of the two disciples.

In Luke's Gospel Jesus' appearance occurs in Jerusalem rather than Galilee. Scholars have discussed at length the significance of the Galilee versus Jerusalem appearance traditions, especially since they do not occur together in any single Gospel account (Jn 21 is an appendix added later—see below). Many believe that the Galilee tradition is prior, since it is found in the oldest tradition (Mk 14:28; 16:7). However, this is not a necessary conclusion, for even in Matthew—where the Galilee appearance takes center stage—there is a "Jerusalem" appearance to the women (Mt 28:8-10). The redactional interests of the Evangelists may have been reason enough for them to center on one tradition. C. F. D. Moule (1957-58) presents a quite plausible thesis that as festival pilgrims the disciples would have remained in Jerusalem for the feast of unleavened bread (thus the appearances of Mt 28:9-10; Lk 24:13-49; Jn 20:11-29), gone back to Galilee for the interim between the feasts (Mt 28:16-20; Jn 21) and finally returned to Jerusalem for Pentecost (the ascension in Lk 24:50-53; Acts 1:6-11).

The appearance recorded in Luke 24:36-43 centers on the physical reality of the resurrection. Structurally, it is closely connected to Luke 24:13-35, for Jesus appears while the eleven are discussing the report of the two travelers. Again,

a pre-Lukan tradition lies behind the story. This is evidenced in the appearance itself (witnessed by three other disparate sources—1 Cor 15:5; Mk 16:14-15; Jn 20:19-21); the charges by the Risen One of "Peace be with you" (cf. Jn 20:19, 21, 26) and "Touch me and see" (cf. Jn 20:27); the doubt motif; and the apologetic proof.

The "peace" greeting (Lk 24:36) has theological overtones, paralleling the "peace" given by the seventy-two in their own mission (Lk 10:5-6) and possibly including the same type of messianic promise as the "peace is yours" of John 20. This is followed by a strong emphasis on the disciples' doubt, seen in the successive verbs of Luke 24:37-38: startled; frightened; thinking they had seen a ghost; troubled; doubting. This is a surprising development following the faith they evidenced in Luke 24:31-35, but it prepares for Jesus' startling proof of his resurrection in Luke 24:39-43. The movement from sight to touch to actually sharing a meal with them gives great stress to the continuity between the crucified and risen Christ (showing his nail-scarred hands and feet) as well as to the corporeality of the resurrection ("a ghost does not have flesh and bones, as you see I have," Lk 24:39; eating the fish in Lk 24:43). Some have interpreted this as Luke's interest in refuting a docetic heresy in his church, but the emphasis is on the nature of the Risen Christ ("I am he," Lk 24:39) rather than on false teaching.

The commission scene of Luke 24:44-49 blends a liturgical tradition of Luke 24:44 (paralleling the sermons of Acts), a commission tradition of Luke 24:47 (like Mt 28:19; Jn 20:21) and a Spirit tradition of Luke 24:49 (like Jn 20:22). The fulfillment theme recapitulates Luke 24:6-7, 25-27, but adds the Psalms to the Law and the Prophets; the Psalms are used frequently in Acts (cf. Acts 2:25-26, 34-35; 4:11, 25-26; 13:33-35) to anchor the creedal stress on humiliation-vindication. The commission deepens mission preaching with soteriological themes. In fact, as Marshall notes, the terms "repentance" (cf. Lk 5:32; 13:3-4; 15:7-8; 16:30; 17:3-4), "forgiveness of sins" (cf. Lk 1:77; 3:3; 5:17-18; Acts 2:38; 5:31; 10:43) and "preach" (Lk 3:3; 4:18-19, 43-44; 8:39; 9:2; 12:3) virtually sum up the Lukan doctrine of salvation. This mission is to be done "in his name" (a Lukan phrase denoting power and authority in mission) "to all nations" (the universal mission) "beginning at Jerusalem" (the origin of the mission, looking forward to Acts 1—5). Each phrase prepares for the launching of the church's mission in Acts (note that the concatenation of "Jerusalem," "witnesses" and "power" occurs again in Acts 1:8, the table of contents for that book).

The powerful witness probably includes not only the eleven but the 120 (including women, cf. Lk 8:1-3; 24:9-10; Acts 1:14-15). Both Luke and John (Jn 20:21-23) anchor this witness in the bestowal of the Spirit. In John this occurs on the first day of the resurrection, but Luke does not have this in mind; here Jesus points to the coming of the Spirit in Acts 2 ("Stay in the city until you have been clothed with power from on high"). In Luke-Acts the Holy Spirit is the means of continuity from the time of Jesus to that of the church.

The ascension in Luke furnishes a structural transition from Luke's Gospel to Acts. In fact, a good argument can be made that the ascension has been the goal ever since Luke 9:31, in which Jesus, Moses and Elijah spoke of his "departure" (exodos), which would be "fulfilled at Jerusalem," an event which would come most naturally at the ascension (cf. Lk 9:51). In Luke 24:50-53 the ascension takes on a doxological tone, with Jesus imparting a priestly blessing; in Acts 1:6-11 it has ecclesiastical implications, with the Risen Lord empowering and launching the church's mission. In Luke it provides an ending, and in Acts 1 it becomes a beginning. Thus ends the theme of Jesus' glory in Luke 24. The Risen Lord now becomes the Exalted One and like Elijah is taken up to heaven. A further transition to Acts is seen in the disciples, who "worship" and "with great joy" return to Jerusalem, remaining "continually in the Temple" (Lk 24:52-53). Each of these—worship, joy and temple—are major themes both in the Gospel and Acts. The disciples and the church continue the ministry of Jesus in these areas.

4.4. The Resurrection in John. The resurrection in the Synoptic Gospels functions as the culmination of Jesus' life; it is both vindication and exaltation, and the Gospel accounts in one sense anticipate it. John, however, takes the opposite tack. His entire Gospel is told from a post-resurrection point of view. The resurrection is not so much the time when Jesus assumes his *doxa;* rather, his entire life and ministry comprise *doxa.* The disciples are not depicted as having "hardened hearts" (cf. Mk 6:52; 8:17); instead, they "believe" because they perceive his

revealed glory (Jn 2:11). John replaces the Synoptic passion predictions with three sayings on the "Son of man lifted up" (Jn 3:14; 8:28; 12:31-32), which looks at the passion as exaltation. Jesus' life and death are pictured as resurrection events. The resurrection itself then becomes the final moment in this drama of glory, and as such it culminates the major emphases of the Fourth Gospel: christology and soteriology in John 20; mission and discipleship in John 21.

4.4.1. John 20. Each of the four episodes in chapter twenty exhibits a crisis of faith, as the participants struggle with the reality of the resurrection. In each the level of faith drops to a lower level, from the beloved disciple with his natural faith (Jn 20:8-9) to Mary's sorrow (Jn 20:11) to the disciples' fear (Jn 20:19) to Thomas' cynical demand (Jn 20:25). Yet with each crisis Jesus meets the need, and the results become increasingly greater, culminating in Thomas' faith-cry, "My Lord and my God" (Jn 20:28), which climaxes the christology of John. As in Luke, the four episodes occur on the same day, two in the morning (Jn 20:1-18) and two in the evening (Jn 20:19-29).

There are actually three scenes in John 20:1-18, as the race to the tomb (Jn 20:3-10) separates Mary's discovery of the empty tomb (Jn 20:1-2) from Jesus' appearance to her (Jn 20:11-18). Several clues point to a tradition lying behind the passage. Mary's "we" in John 20:2 is a relic of a Synoptic-like tradition where several women are present. There are also connections with Luke 24:12, 34 and the Peter-tradition. Most scholars believe that each part—the trips to the tomb by the women and the disciples as well as the appearance to Mary—stem from tradition. In John 20:1-10 there is a subtle shift from Matthew's polemical use of the belief that Jesus' body had been stolen. In this case it is not an apologetic but part of the motif of misunderstanding among Jesus followers; it is Mary, not the chief priests (Mt 27:62-66), who fears this, and she sets the scene for the race to the tomb. This motif is heightened by John's comment that it occurred "while it was still dark" (Jn 20:1). Darkness belongs to the Johannine light-darkness dualism (cf. Jn 3:2; 11:10; 13:30) and here symbolizes a time of misunderstanding (cf. Jn 20:9).

Yet misunderstanding is restricted primarily to John 20:1-2. In the trip to the tomb (Jn 20:3-10) John goes even further than Luke in giving the empty tomb an apologetic function. He does this in several ways. The so-called rivalry between Peter and the Beloved Disciple make both witnesses (cf. Deut 19:15) of the import of the empty tomb. Scholars have debated the significance of this rivalry: both race to the tomb, but the Beloved Disciple arrives first; the Beloved Disciple delays entering, but Peter goes directly into the tomb. Upon entering, the Beloved Disciple simply "sees and believes" while Peter by implication does not.

Some see the two disciples as symbolic of conflict within the Johannine community, but the consistently positive portrait of Peter throughout the Fourth Gospel makes this doubtful. In the scenes where the two are juxtaposed (Jn 13:23-25; 18:15-16; 20:3-10; 21:7-8), there is a certain rivalry, but not at the expense of Peter. Peter typifies the dilemma of all disciples in coming to grips with the significance of Jesus. He is filled with questions (Jn 13:23-24), uncomprehending (Jn 20:6-7) and lacking vision (Jn 21:7-8). Yet Christians of every age have identified with him. The Beloved Disciple is the archetypal disciple, the one whose authentic witness (cf. Jn 19:35; 21:24) and belief (Jn 20:8-9) provide a model for successful discipleship.

The extensive description of the graveclothes (Jn 20:6-7) first of all proves that the body would not have been stolen. No thief would have taken the time to roll up the grave cloths so neatly. Moreover, the presence of the wrappings is proof that Jesus had indeed risen from the dead (cf. Jn 11:44, with Lazarus "coming forth" still wrapped in the linens). Finally, the Beloved Disciple believes even without benefit of the witness of "the Scriptures" (Jn 20:9). Faith response is one of the primary themes in John and is consistently linked with seeing and knowing (note "see" in Jn 20:6, 8, 14, 18 and "know" in Jn 20:2, 9, 13-14; 21:4, 12, 15-17). The tension between seeing and knowing typifies the resurrection narratives of both chapters 20 and 21. Commitment to Christ is deepened when vision leads faith to knowledge. Here is the first step: vision leading to faith.

The dramatic scene in which the distraught Mary comes to understanding (Jn 20:11-18) takes us more deeply into this encounter with the significance of the resurrection. Here the angels do not play a revelatory role as in the Synoptics. They encounter her grief (note the centrality of "weeping" in Jn 20:11, 13, 15) and prepare for the presence of the Risen One. The repetition of question and response in the two scenes with the angels and Jesus (Jn 20:13, 15) produce a narrative tension. The reader would expect one of the two (the presence of angels or of the Risen Lord himself) to suffice. But her grief is too deep. This prepares for the marvelous removal of blindness from her eyes in John 20:16. The good shepherd (Jn 10:1-18) calls her by name (cf. "calls his sheep by name," Jn 10:3), and she recognizes him (cf. "his sheep follow him because they know his voice," Jn 10:4). The results are notably different from John 20:10, where the disciples simply return home in an anti-climactic conclusion to their trip to the tomb. Here Jesus commissions Mary as the first herald of the resurrection tidings.

However, the wording is difficult. First Jesus says, "Stop clinging to me," which could reflect a situation like Matthew 28:9 where the women "grasp" Jesus' feet. Yet John might have a deeper meaning in mind, with Jesus asking her not to "cling" to the old relationships (note she has just called him "my teacher"). The seeming contradiction between "I have not yet returned" and "I am (in the process of) returning" explains the tension. Jesus is no longer to relate to them as their teacher, for in the course of his appearances he is finishing his work and is on the verge of fulfilling the promise of the Farewell Discourse: To return to the Father so the promised Paraclete can come (Jn 13:1, 3; 14:4, 25-26, 28; 15:26; 16:5, 7, 17, 28; 17:13). All previous relationships have been transformed and so the disciples are now "brothers" (cf. Mt 28:10; cf. Jn 15:15); in this one word the forgiveness and reinstatement of the disciples is assured.

Yet Mary's message (Jn 20:18), as in the other Gospels, apparently has little effect. In the following scene the disciples are still cowering "for fear of the Jews" (Jn 20:19). There are quite a few similarities to Luke 24: "the first day of the week," "stood in the midst," "peace be with you," "showed them his hands and side," the commission to mission, the gift of the Spirit and the stress on forgiveness of sins. This is filled out with Johannine redactional emphases and is a unique, well-balanced story. Jesus, as he did with Mary, meets their fearful lack of faith head on. Mary needed to hear the voice of the good shepherd, but they need more—to recognize that he is indeed the same Jesus raised from the dead. Jesus not only supplies that need but promises them messianic peace; the threefold "peace is yours" (Jn 20:19, 21, 26) controls the second unit of the chapter and fulfills the promise of John 14:1, 27 and 16:23. It is more than the basic greeting *"shalom";* it culminates the significance of the resurrection as bringing the peace of God to the believer. As the disciples see Jesus' hands and side (pointing, as in Luke, to the reality of the physical resurrection) they experience not only peace but joy in fulfillment of Jesus' promise in John 16:20-22.

The commission of John 20:21-23 is especially rich theologically. After the repeated "peace is yours," Jesus in a sense graduates the disciples and gives them the degree of "sent ones" (fulfilling Jn 17:18). One of the pre-eminent concepts in Johannine christology is that of Jesus as "sent" by the Father. Based on the Jewish institution of a *šāliaḥ,* a messenger or envoy authorized to carry out functions on behalf of another (*see* Apostle), Jesus as the sent one is presented as the living representative who reveals the Father to the world. In the Farewell Discourse the Spirit/Paraclete is "sent" by the Father (Jn 14:16, 26) and the Son (Jn 15:26; 16:7). Yet this chain of revelation is not complete, for now in a sense the entire godhead is involved in "sending" the disciples. The place of the Spirit is seen in the "Johannine Pentecost" of John 20:22.

In fulfillment of John 7:39; 15:26 and 16:7, Jesus now "breathes" the Spirit into the disciples, enabling them to bear witness to the sin-sick world (cf. Jn 14:16-17; 15:26-27; 16:7-11). In comparison with Acts 2, this is a private in-filling of the disciples while the later event at Pentecost is a public empowering which launches the church's mission (see Benoit). The mission is primary also in John 20:23, a statement which, like its counterpart in Matthew 16:19, has occasioned great debate. The power to bind/retain and loose/forgive sins is a legal authority and depicts the disciples as full-fledged ambassadors of the new age, dispensing judgment or salvation, depending on people's acceptance or rejection of their message (cf. Jesus' authority as judge in Jn 5:22, 27; 8:15-16; 9:39). In Matthew this saying deals with church discipline, while here it centers on mission evangelism.

The final episode (Jn 20:24-29) centers on the cynical doubt of Thomas and presents this doubt in even stronger fashion than does Luke 24:10-11. Thomas's declaration that he would not believe unless he could not only see but touch the wounds in Jesus' hands and side is an extension of John 20:20 in which Jesus showed the disciples his wounds in order to allay their fear. In the Fourth Gospel Thomas is a hard-headed realist who exemplifies the disciples' lack of understanding (Jn 11:16) and their confusion (Jn 14:5). Here he sums up their doubts as well.

As in the other episodes of chapter 20, Jesus acquiesces to his need, and Thomas's response is astonishing, culminating the high christology of John's Gospel with his confession "(You are) my Lord and my God." This goes beyond affirming the reality of the resurrection to interpreting its significance. The resurrection proves the validity of the emphasis throughout—that Jesus is one with the Father and therefore divine (cf. Jn 1:1, 14; 3:18; 8:58; 10:30, 34-38; 12:45; 14:9; 17:11). Jesus' concluding statement in John 20:29 is at one and the same time an admonition (against the demand for empirical proof) and a recognition (that Thomas had now come to faith). Yet the focus, as in John 10:16 and 17:20, is on the beatitude regarding future believers who will come to faith without benefit of such signs. It is they who are truly "blessed" (by God).

In John 20:30-31 the centrality of faith will conclude not only the resurrection narrative but the Gospel as a whole. Many have debated (partly on the basis of textual evidence for both a present and aorist verb) whether "believe" here is primarily evangelistic (thus the Gospel would be intended more for nonbelievers) or didactic (thus intended for believers). But the Fourth Gospel as a whole is clearly meant both to strengthen the faithful and to call non-believers to faith.

4.4.2. John 21. Most scholars assert that this is an appendix written some time after the completion of the Fourth Gospel, perhaps because of a crisis in the church as eyewitnesses were passing from the scene (cf. Jn 21:18-23). The debate is whether it was penned by the Evangelist or by someone else. The latter is suggested by John 21:24-25, which seems to be the imprimatur of a church official attesting to the validity of the Beloved Disciple's witness. Yet the chapter's language, style and emphases parallel the rest of the Gospel (see Osborne), and one can tentatively equate the authors of chapters 20 and 21. Much like John 20, the chapter divides into four episodes (Jn 21:1-14, 15-17, 18-19, 20-23) followed by a conclusion (Jn 21:24-25).

Many scholars find two separate traditions (an appearance and a meal story) in the account of the miraculous catch of fish (Jn 21:1-14). Others (e.g., Bultmann) have argued for a unified tradition. In either case the author has once again combined tradition and redaction into a theological whole. The primary thrust is the power of the Risen One, which is made available to the church. While there is no overt mention of mission, the symbolism as well as general thrust of the chapter has led most scholars to apply this to the church in mission, both in terms of evangelism (Jn 21:1-8) and fellowship (Jn 21:9-13). Jesus' appearance by the Sea of Galilee is often linked with the similar miracle at the call of the disciples in Luke 5:1-11, which is thought to be a displaced miracle story. However, as Marshall points out, the differences outweigh the similarities, and it is better to see them as separate episodes. Nevertheless, the themes are similar, with Jesus asking for radical obedience and then granting an astounding catch of fish to demonstrate the new call to "catch" people.

The first theological element of the story (recalling the Emmaus journey of Lk 24) concerns a recognition scene. The disciples, after fishing all night and catching nothing, encounter a man whom they fail to recognize. Interestingly (unlike the calling of the disciples in Lk 5 or the story of the road to Emmaus in Lk 24), they fail to recognize Jesus even as they obey him (Jn 21:6). Only after the overwhelming catch does the Beloved Disciple recognize that it is the Risen Lord. As in John 20:8, the Beloved Disciple represents the quintessential disciple whose love gives him greater insight into spiritual truth. The order of events points the reader toward the significance of the Risen Lord for the success of all Christian endeavors.

The next aspect is the promised success of Christian mission under the power of the Risen Lord. This theme is premised on the great size of the catch—153 large fish (Jn 21:6, 11). Many ingenious solutions have been propounded for the significance of the 153 fish, but the majority today interpret it as a more general reference to the universally great results of the mission.

The final aspect is the meal scene, which many see as a eucharistic celebration. While there are similarities to the feeding of the 5,000 (cf. Jn 21:13 and 6:11), there is no clear textual hint that this involves eucharistic connotations

(while fish are used in second-century eucharistic services, there is no evidence that was used in the first century). The one thing that can be said with probability is that the emphasis is on a new level of fellowship (built upon a table-fellowship theme similar to that of Luke) between Jesus and his followers. This is seen in the strange statement that "none of the disciples dared to ask him, 'Who are you?' They knew it was the Lord" (Jn 21:12). On one level the old doubt is experienced (they "dared not ask"), but on a deeper level a new certitude has appeared (they "knew").

The reinstatement (or rehabilitation) of Peter (Jn 21:15-17) is certainly one of the better-known resurrection stories. Many a minister has preached from this text, distinguishing between the two levels of love (*philos* and *agapē*), but this is a misjudgment. In reality four sets of synonyms are used in the passage (two terms for "love" and "know," three terms for "feed" and "sheep"). And it can be demonstrated that in the Fourth Gospel both *philos* and *agapē* are used for the love between Father and Son, both for the love between Father/Son and disciples, and both for the love that characterizes the community. In other words, the terms in all four cases are meant to be understood synonymously, and the purpose is to show the theological richness of the terms and the breadth of love between Jesus and his followers. The basic message of this episode deals with pastoral responsibility: Love for Jesus can only be complete when the leader tends his flock. This may also be the rehabilitation of Peter because the question "Do you love me more than these?" may recall Peter's promise to surrender his very life for Jesus if necessary (Jn 13:37), and the threefold repetition parallels Peter's threefold denial.

The final two sections concern the martyrdom of Peter (Jn 21:18-19) and the fate of the Beloved Disciple (Jn 21:20-23). The two are linked by the discipleship command "follow me" (Jn 21:19, 22), and this may indeed be the primary thrust of John 21:18-23: whether one's life is cut short or one is given a long life in which to minister for the Lord, "What is that to you? You must follow me" (Jn 21:22).

Most scholars have accepted Bultmann's hypothesis that the prophecy of Peter's martyrdom adapts an alleged proverb regarding old age; like the elderly, Peter at the end of his life would be bound and led where he does not wish to go. This was a prophecy predicting "the kind of death (i.e., martyrdom) by which Peter would glorify God" (Jn 21:19). There has been extensive debate over whether "stretch out your hands" is a reference to crucifixion (tradition tells us Peter was crucified upside-down). Those who doubt such a reference argue that the order (stretching the hands followed by being bound and led) does not fit crucifixion. However, if the language is understood to depict the bearing of the crossbeam to the place of crucifixion, the objection disappears. As such, this fulfills not only Peter's promise to follow Jesus to the death (Jn 13:36-38; cf. 12:23-24, 31-33; 17:1 on the connection between death and glorifying God) but the Johannine emphasis on Jesus carrying his own cross (Jn 19:17). The command "follow me" thereby has two meanings, referring both to Peter's present pastoral duties (Jn 21:15-17) and to his death as an act of discipleship in which he follows even Jesus' martyrdom via crucifixion.

Peter's query regarding the destiny of the Beloved Disciple (Jn 21:20-21) would be natural under the circumstances. The note that the Beloved Disciple "was following them" (Jn 21:20) ties the two sections together and supports the thesis that the main idea is discipleship. Jesus' reply to Peter's query is surprisingly harsh in tone ("What is that to you?"). In other words, Peter should not worry about someone else's calling and fate; his responsibility is to his own path of obedience. Yet from another perspective Peter's is the greater privilege—that of "following" his Lord in martyrdom. Many scholars interpret John 20:23 (in light of Jn 20:24) as indicating that the whole of John 20:20-23 was written in light of the fact that the Beloved Disciple had died and the prophecy that he would live until the Parousia was unfulfilled. Yet this goes beyond the passage, which stresses, "*if I want him to remain*" (Jn 21:22-23). The message would be just as meaningful if the Beloved Disciple were approaching death and the church was concerned about the prophecy. Either way, the broader point remains the same: the key to the meaning of the resurrection for discipleship is a willingness to follow Jesus no matter what a person's God-ordained destiny might be.

See also DEATH OF CHRIST; ESCHATOLOGY; MIRACLES, MIRACLE STORIES.

DJG: BURIAL OF JESUS; HEAVEN AND HELL;

LIFE; PREDICTIONS OF JESUS' PASSION AND RESURRECTION.

BIBLIOGRAPHY. J. E. Alsup, *The Post-Resurrection Appearance Stories of the Gospel Tradition: A History-of-Tradition Analysis* (Stuttgart: Calwer, 1975); P. Benoit, *The Passion and Resurrection of Jesus Christ* (New York: Sheed and Ward, 1969); E. L. Bode, *The First Easter Morning: The Gospel Accounts of the Women's Visit to the Tomb of Jesus* (Rome: Biblical Institute, 1970); R. E. Brown, *The Virginal Conception and Bodily Resurrection of Jesus* (New York: Paulist, 1973); W. L. Craig, "The Empty Tomb of Jesus," in *Gospel Perspectives 2: Studies of History and Tradition in the Four Gospels*, ed. R. T. France and D. Wenham (Sheffield: JSOT, 1981); R. J. Dillon, *From Eye-Witnesses to Ministers of the Word: Tradition and Composition in Luke 24* (Rome: Biblical Institute, 1978); C. F. Evans, *Resurrection and the New Testament* (SBT 12; London: SCM, 1970); D. P. Fuller, *Easter Faith and History* (Grand Rapids: Eerdmans, 1965); R. H. Fuller, *The Formation of the Resurrection Narratives* (New York: Macmillan, 1971); P. Gardner-Smith, *The Narratives of the Resurrection* (London: Methuen, 1926); G. R. Habermas, *Resurrection of Jesus: An Apologetic* (Grand Rapids: Baker, 1980); M. J. Harris, *Raised Immortal: Resurrection and Immortality in the New Testament* (Grand Rapids: Eerdmans, 1985); idem., *From Grave to Glory: Resurrection in the New Testament* (Grand Rapids: Zondervan, 1990); S. H. Hooke, *The Resurrection of Christ As History and Experience* (London: Darton, 1967); B. J. Hubbard, *The Matthean Redaction of a Primitive Apostolic Commissioning: An Exegesis of Matthew 28:16-20* (Missoula, MT: Scholars, 1974); J. Kremer, *Die Osterbotschaft der vier Evangelien* (Stuttgart: Katholisches Bibelwerk, 1968); G. E. Ladd, *I Believe in the Resurrection of Jesus* (Grand Rapids: Eerdmans, 1975); K. Lake, *The Historical Evidence for the Resurrection of Jesus* (New York: Putnam's, 1907); P. Lapide, *The Resurrection of Jesus: A Jewish Perspective* (Minneapolis: Augsburg, 1983); X. Leon-Dufour, *Resurrection and the Message of Easter* (London: Chapman, 1974); R. Mahoney, *Two Disciples at the Tomb. The Background and Message of Jn 20. 1-10* (Frankfurt: Peter Lang, 1974); I. H. Marshall, "The Resurrection of Jesus in Luke," *TynB* 24 (1974) 55-98; R. Martin-Achard, *From Death to Life* (Edinburgh: Oliver & Boyd, 1960); W. Marxsen, *The Resurrection of Jesus of Nazareth* (Philadelphia: Fortress, 1970); C. F. D. Moule, ed., *The Significance of the Message of the Resurrec-*

tion for Faith in Jesus Christ (London: SCM, 1968); idem., "The Post-Resurrection Appearances in the Light of Festival Pilgrimages," *NTS* 4 (1957-58) 58-61; G. W. E. Nickelsburg, *Resurrection, Immortality, and Eternal Life in Intertestamental Judaism* (HTS 26; Cambridge, MA: Harvard University Press, 1972); G. O'Collins, *The Easter Jesus* (London: Darton, 1973); idem, *What Are They Saying about the Resurrection?* (New York: Paulist, 1978); idem, *Jesus Risen* (New York: Paulist, 1987); G. R. Osborne, *The Resurrection Narratives: A Redactional Study* (Grand Rapids: Baker, 1984); P. Perkins, *Resurrection: New Testament Witness and Contemporary Reflection* (New York: Doubleday, 1984); R. H. Smith, *Easter Gospels* (Minneapolis: Augsburg, 1983); K. Stendahl, ed., *Immortality and Resurrection* (New York: Macmillan, 1965); E. Sutcliffe, *The Old Testament and the Future Life* (London: Barnes, Oates & Washborn, 1964); N. J. Tromp, *Primitive Conceptions of Death and the Nether World in the Old Testament* (Rome: Pontifical Biblical Institute, 1969); J. Wenham, *Easter Enigma: Are the Resurrection Accounts in Conflict?* (Grand Rapids: Zondervan, 1984); U. Wilckens, *Resurrection* (Atlanta: John Knox, 1978); N. T. Wright, *The Resurrection of the Son of God* (Minneapolis: Fortress, 2003).　　　　G. R. Osborne

RESURRECTION II: PAUL

The resurrection of Jesus Christ from the dead is foundational to the Christian faith. It is referred to explicitly in seventeen books of the NT and is implicit in most of the remaining ten. Nearly all of the letters within the Pauline corpus refer to it (the exceptions are 2 Thess, Tit, Philem). Indeed, Romans 10:9 makes confession of the resurrection the equivalent of acceptance of the lordship of Jesus Christ and a necessary condition of salvation, and 1 Corinthians 15:14 demonstrates how closely connected it is in Paul's mind to his own kerygmatic ministry. In Romans 4:25 Paul decisively grounds the doctrine of *justification upon Christ's resurrection when he says that Jesus was "raised for our justification" *(dia tēn dikaiōsin hēmōn);* while in Philippians 3:11 he equates "knowing Christ" with knowing "the power of the resurrection." It is no surprise that the longest single chapter in the Pauline letters (1 Cor 15) is given over completely to a discussion of the resurrection.

The resurrection of Jesus Christ stands as the central motif in Paul's eschatology insofar as it inaugurates the age to come and provides the basis for future hope. The Christ event is, in the evocative words of J. I. H. McDonald: "the Archimedean point that has levered the world of Jewish religion into a new order" (McDonald, 28). The resurrection of Christ and the resurrection of the faithful on the last day are related, the hope of the latter being based upon the certainty of the former.

Two remarks about the resurrection of Jesus Christ as it is portrayed in the Pauline letters need to be made at the outset. First, it is important to note that Paul never attempts to prove the historicity of the resurrection to any of the congregations to which he addresses his letters (contra R. Bultmann's views on 1 Cor 15:3-8). He simply asserts the resurrection as a fact (presumably believed by them) and seeks to draw out its implications for their life and faith. Paul is not concerned with philosophical questions of how subjective faith and objective history interrelate; this is predominantly a post-Enlightenment issue which is driven by positivistic concerns not a part of Paul's outlook. Modern attempts to argue for the historical verification of the resurrection of Jesus Christ based upon the Pauline materials are therefore misdirected, even though they are generally motivated by the best apologetic concerns (G. E. Ladd offers a readable discussion of this issue).

Second, Paul nowhere describes the actual resurrection of Jesus Christ itself, nor does he seek to provide an account of it simply as a historical event to be put alongside other events of history. The resurrection is historical, yes, but it is also more than historical (or to use McDonald's term, "meta-historical"; McDonald, 138). What descriptions Paul does offer about the risen Christ are postresurrectional appearances of the Lord that are taken to be illustrative of the event and serve as circumstantial guarantees of its historicity. Thus he begins his longest discussion of the resurrection theme by citing a traditional formula that summarizes the kerygma (1 Cor 15:3-4) and then proceeds to list the witnesses to these postresurrectional appearances of the Lord Jesus (1 Cor 15:6-8). The appeal to pre-Pauline tradition highlights the centrality of the resurrection proclamation from the earliest period of the Christian movement (see Kloppenborg and Murphy-O'Connor for a discussion of this passage).

Both of these considerations should be kept

in mind in all apologetical concerns focusing on the resurrection as the basis of Christian faith.

1. The Origins of a Doctrine of Resurrection.

Most scholars agree that the doctrine of bodily resurrection is a fairly late development within the writings of Judaism. The first unambiguous declarations in the OT of resurrection from the dead occur in Daniel 12:2 and (possibly) Isaiah 26:19, although there are antecedents of it in the miracles of resuscitation performed through Elijah and Elisha (1 and 2 Kings), and in images of a national revival within OT prophetic literature (notably Hos 6:1-2 and the vision of the valley of dry bones contained in Ezek 37:1-14). A bodily resurrection from the dead is also proclaimed in a number of Jewish apocryphal and pseudepigraphal texts, including 2 Maccabees, 4 Ezra, *1 Enoch* and *2 Baruch*. There are also important background materials, at least to do with postmortem life, within the classical tradition of Platonism, usually as an image of the spiritual awakening or the transmigration of the soul (see Perkins, 37-69). The matter has been well researched by scholarship and need not be rehearsed here (see Nickelsburg and Greenspoon for detailed studies of Jewish background texts).

While Paul's letters are the earliest Christian writings to mention the resurrection of Christ, there is every indication that the idea was part of Jesus' own belief and expectation. All four Gospels record reference to it in virtually all strata (some may deny it is expressed in 'Q'). Paul may have taken over the centrality of the resurrection as a theological idea from Jesus himself (see Witherington), although it certainly was present within the Pharisaic party of Judaism of which he was a member.

2. Paul and Pharisaic Belief in the Resurrection.

Paul's membership within the Pharisaic party of Judaism is asserted in both his letters (Phil 3:5) and by Luke (Acts 23:6; 26:5). In Acts the dis- agreement between the Sadducees and the Pharisees over the doctrine of a bodily resurrection is a prominent theme (Acts 4:2; 23:6-8; 24:21; cf. Acts 26:6; 28:20). It is reasonable to assume that Paul accepted the traditional Pharisaic view of the resurrection of the body and understood his encounter of the risen Lord Jesus Christ in light of it. As R. J. Sider states, "as a good first-century Pharisee, Paul could not conceive of the resurrection of the dead in purely immaterial terms" (Sider, 438; for further discussion see Davies, 285-320).

3. Terminology of the Resurrection.

There are several different words and phrases which are used to describe the idea of resurrection or associated concepts within the Pauline letters. The verb *anistēmi* ("raise up") is used a total of five times with reference to the resurrection, both of Christ (1 Thess 4:14; cf. Rom 15:12) and of the believer (1 Thess 4:16; Eph 5:14). The verb *egeirō* ("raise," "cause to rise") appears a total of thirty-eight times with reference to the resurrection (Rom 4:24, 25; 6:4, 9; 7:4; 8:11 [2x], 34; 10:9; 13:11; 1 Cor 6:14; 15:4, 12, 13, 14, 15 [2x], 16 [2x], 17, 20, 29, 32, 35, 42, 43 [2x], 52; 2 Cor 1:9; 4:14 [2x]; 5:15; Gal 1:1; Eph 1:20; 5:14; Col 2:12; 1 Thess 1:10; 2 Tim 2:8); and the compound verb *exegeirō* ("raise up") once in reference to the resurrection of believers (1 Cor 6:14). In addition the noun *anastasis* ("resurrection") is used eight times (Rom 1:4; 6:5; 1 Cor 15:12, 13, 21, 42; Phil 3:10; 2 Tim 2:18) and the noun *exanastasis* ("resurrection") occurs once (Phil 3:11). These terms are used of both the resurrection of Jesus Christ himself and the raising of the believers which the Lord's resurrection guarantees (N. Dahl provides a chart detailing the use of the terms in the NT).

Some have argued that there is a difference in meaning between these two word groups (*egeirō* and *anistēmi*) and on that basis have attempted to trace a development in the use of the terms within the Pauline materials. L. Coenen, for example, suggests that a close examination "shows that *egeirō*, especially in the pass., is used predominantly for what happened at Easter, i.e. the wakening of the Crucified to life, while *anistēmi* and *anastasis* refer more specifically to the recall to life of people during the earthly ministry of Jesus and to the eschatological and universal resurrection" (Coenen, 276). However, an absolute distinction seems rather arbitrary and difficult to sustain (both 1 Cor 15:12-13 and 15:42 appear to use the two verbs interchangeably and Eph 5:14 includes both verbs within its citation of Is 60:1). It seems that Paul does not intend that any substantial difference be maintained between the two, although the use of *egeirō* may be more traditional and related to an underlying Palestinian source (it does appear frequently within passages often taken to contain creedal declarations such as 1 Cor 15:4).

In Romans 6:10 and 14:9 the verb *zaō* ("to live") is used with reference to Jesus' resurrection. It is similarly used in 2 Corinthians 13:4 and is explicitly contrasted with the verb *stauroō* ("crucify"); the verse also applies the verb *zaō* to the Christians who will share in Christ's resurrection. The compound verb form *syzēsomen* ("we will live with [him]") in Romans 6:8 and 2 Timothy 2:11, as well as *syndoxasthōmen* ("we may be glorified with [him]") in Romans 8:17 are used to the same end. The use of the verb *zōopoieō* ("to give life to") also builds on a resurrection idea and occurs six times (Rom 4:17; 8:11; 1 Cor 15:22, 36, 45; 2 Cor 3:6), usually within the context of the ultimate resurrection of the saints and the manifestation of the glory of God. Similarly the verb *synegeirō* ("to rise up together") in Colossians 2:12; 3:1 and Ephesians 2:6, as well as *synezōopoiēsen* ("he made alive together with [him]") in Colossians 2:13 and Ephesians 2:5 continue this theme, expressing the union of the church in Christ's death. The verb *anagō* ("to bring up") occurs once in Romans 10:7 with reference to the resurrection of Jesus Christ from the dead (*Christon ek nekrōn anagagein*, "to bring Christ up from the dead").

The use of *anabainō* ("to go up, ascend") in Ephesians 4:8, 10 and *anelēmphthē* ("he was taken up") in 1 Timothy 3:16 may also reflect an underlying resurrection theme, demonstrating how closely connected is the language of ascension and resurrection. This is particularly evident in pre-Pauline materials, such as those contained in Romans 1:4; 8:34; Philippians 2:9 and 1 Thessalonians 1:10 (W. Baird discusses this at some length).

4. Images of the Resurrection.

It is important to note that the English phrase "resurrection from the dead" evokes a rather different mental picture than does its Greek equivalent *anastaseōs nekrōn* (Rom 1:4; cf. Phil 3:11, which has *ek nekrōn*, lit. "out from the dead

ones"). In English something of the dynamism of the phrase is lost due to the fact that we take "dead" to be a state of being or the place of habitation of those who are departed, almost as if it were a singular, abstract noun. In Greek, however, the noun behind *nekrōn* is a plural one, which means the phrase *anastasis nekrōn* may be translated literally as "resurrection from out of dead ones" (cf. Phil 3:11). The Greek expression contains a much more dynamic image, conjuring up a picture of "the standing up from the midst of corpses," and lending weight to the somatic nature of the resurrection body. But it is essential to observe that Paul does not proclaim a "resurrection of the flesh," as subsequent Christian writers were to do (including the author of *2 Clement* and Justin Martyr). Paul maintains a distinction between *sarx* (*"flesh") and *sōma* ("body") when it comes to his teaching about the resurrection.

It is important to show that Paul draws upon several different ideas in an effort to communicate the meaning of this resurrection, which he describes as "a mystery" (*mystērion*) in 1 Corinthians 15:51. The wide variety of images employed is revealing in its own right; demonstrating the limitations of language when it is put into the service of attempting to describe the indescribable. There is an open-endedness, a flexibility of expression, within Paul's description of the resurrection that is both exhilarating and frustrating to interpreters. The images may be discussed under eight headings.

4.1. Resurrection as Transformation. At several points Paul uses the language of transformation in his description of the future resurrection awaited by the Christian. In Philippians 3:10 a participial form of the verb *symmorphizō* ("to take on the same form") occurs in precisely this context: "that I may know him and the power of his resurrection, and may share his sufferings, becoming like him [*symmorphizomenos*] in his death." At the conclusion of the same chapter the image is expanded and linked directly with the revelation of the Lord Jesus Christ as Savior from heaven (Phil 3:20). In Philippians 3:21 the language of transformation appears twice: "(Jesus Christ) will change [*metaschēmatisei*] our lowly body to be like [*symmorphon*] his glorious body." One of the clearest expressions of resurrection as transformation occurs in 1 Corinthians 15:51-52, where the apostle twice uses the verb *allagēsometha* ("we shall be changed") to describe what awaits the believing community at the parousia of Christ. This future transformation is described in verse 52 as instantaneous (*en atomō en rhipē ophthalmou*, "in a moment, in the twinkling of an eye"). Such transformation language is different in emphasis from that contained in passages from earlier letters, such as 1 Thessalonians 4:13-18, where a spatial metaphor ("caught up together") dominates the action associated with the parousia. J. Gillman describes the shift such a difference represents as a move from the implicit to the explicit and suggests the "rapture" imagery of 1 Thessalonians 4 is fully compatible with the transformation motif in 1 Corinthians 15.

It is important to note that in 1 Corinthians 15:51-54a Paul is dealing with the matter of the transformation of those who happen to be alive at the parousia of Christ. Here the apostle teaches a universal transformation of all who are in Christ, both living and dead, but maintains that this does not mean that all will be resurrected. Only those who have died are in need of resurrection; for those who are alive at the parousia the transformation is sufficient to grant immortality in the age to come. Some NT commentators, notably J. Jeremias (following the lead of A. Schlatter), have taken the contrasting phrases in 1 Corinthians 15:50b-c to imply a similar distinction between those believers alive at the parousia and those who have already died (see 4.3 below for additional details). In any event the future transformation is clearly in view in 1 Corinthians 15.

By contrast we find eschatological transformation being described as *presently* taking place in 2 Corinthians 3:18. Here the present passive verb *metamorphoumetha* ("we are being transformed") is used in the midst of an extended passage in which Paul contrasts the glory of Moses with the glory of Christ (2 Cor 3:12—4:6). A similar use of the verb occurs in Romans 12:2, again emphasizing the present process of transformation.

The suggestion that transformation can be dualistically conceived (both present and future) demonstrates the tension inherent within Pauline eschatology as a whole. Despite this E. E. Ellis insists that Paul does not really present us with a true dualism since *moral* transformation is a present process, while *mortal* transformation awaits the granting of the resurrection body at the parousia of Christ; what unites the

two aspects of transformation is a corporate existence, the fact that the believer is "in Christ." The idea of resurrection as expressing the present spiritual transformation of the believer in Christ can also be found in Romans 6:1-11; 2 Corinthians 4:10-12; 5:15; 13:4; Galatians 5:24-25; 6:14-15; Colossians 2:12 and Ephesians 2:5-6 (as Harris, 101-5, argues). Once again the close connection between the believers' unity with Christ in his resurrection and their ethical conduct is asserted.

4.2. Resurrection as Incorruption. In the midst of his extended treatise on the subject in 1 Corinthians 15, Paul uses a number of contrasting terms and images to describe how resurrection life differs from the present order of existence. Included are the contrasting pairs, perishable/imperishable (1 Cor 15:42); dishonor/glory (1 Cor 15:43); weakness/power (1 Cor 15:43); physical body/spiritual body (1 Cor 15:44); man of dust/man of heaven (1 Cor 15:47-49). In 1 Corinthians 15:50 Paul again asserts the first of these contrasting pairs, perishable/imperishable, when he says: "flesh and blood does not inherit the kingdom of God, nor does the perishable inherit the imperishable." The relevant Greek terms (*phthora* and *aphtharsia*) provide quite a powerful image and are better translated as "corruptibility" and "incorruptibility" respectively. The term *aphtharsia* occurs seven times in the NT, all within the Pauline corpus (Rom 2:7; 1 Cor 15:42, 50, 53, 54; Eph 6:24; 2 Tim 1:10), while four of the seven instances of the cognate term *aphthartos* ("imperishable") in the NT are also found in Paul's letters (Rom 1:23; 1 Cor 9:25; 15:52; 1 Tim 1:17). There is a close connection between *aphtharsia/aphthartos* and the resurrection of Jesus Christ throughout, a vivid demonstration of the eschatological significance of the term.

In addition to the instances occurring within the extended discussion on the resurrection in 1 Corinthians 15, the revelation of *aphtharsia* through the destruction of death by means of Christ's resurrection is the focus of the assertion in 2 Timothy 1:10; *aphtharsia* is associated with eternal life in Romans 2:7; and *aphthartos* is used figuratively of the resurrection body within the confines of an athletic image in 1 Corinthians 9:25. Exceptions include Ephesians 6:24, where the term *aphtharsia* is used to describe Christian love of the Lord ("*undying* love"), and Romans 1:23 and 1 Timothy 1:17, where *aphthar-*

tos is used as an attribute of God.

J. Jeremias offers an interesting, if disputed, interpretation of 1 Corinthians 15:50, suggesting that a distinction be made between the metamorphosis of the living believer (1 Cor 15:50b) and the deceased one (1 Cor 15:50c), and that a contrast be drawn between Paul's language of corruption/incorruption and mortality/immortality. In effect Jeremias says that the phrase "flesh and blood cannot inherit the kingdom of God" refers to those who are alive at the parousia, and argues that "nor does the perishable inherit the imperishable" refers to those who have died before the parousia and are presently corpses in decomposition. He goes on to suggest that a similar distinction between the living and the dead is found in 1 Corinthians 15:50-53. However, the proposed distinction is almost certainly a forced one (or at least a limited one), and most scholars have not followed Jeremias in rigidly maintaining it (H. Conzelmann is a good representative of those who disagree with Jeremias).

An essential part of Jeremias's argument is the use of another term in 1 Corinthians 15:53-54, immortality *(athanasia)*, a term usually used to describe, as in 1 Timothy 6:16, an attribute of God himself (Harris, 273-75, provides a full terminological discussion of *aphtharsia* and *athanasia*, both of which he renders as "immortality"). Some have taken the language of investiture in 2 Corinthians 5:2-4 also to imply this distinction between the deceased believer and the believer who is alive at the parousia of Christ.

4.3. Resurrection as Immortality. Paul uses another interesting term to describe the resurrection in 1 Corinthians 15:53b-54. Here he describes it as the mortal nature *(to thnēton)* taking on immortality *(athanasia)*. The resurrection is the means whereby Christians gain immortality, and death is, in the poetic image drawn from Isaiah 25:8, "swallowed up in victory." The distinction between *athanasia* and *aphtharsia* is not always easy to define, but the association of both with the resurrection of the body is sure. Harris argues persuasively that while immortality (either *athanasia* or *aphtharsia*) and resurrection are intimately linked, the former is consistently presented as a *future* possession granted at the parousia of Christ to those who belong to him. In any event, immortality and resurrection both belong in Paul's thinking and are seen as related but distinct ideas (as Harris notes). Both are grounded in Paul's belief that the eschatological hope of the believer is somatic in nature and future in temporality.

4.4. Resurrection and Exaltation. In several places in Paul's letters there is a close connection drawn between Jesus' resurrection from the dead and his exaltation to the right hand of God. Several of the passages which juxtapose these two images are considered by many to reflect pre-Pauline traditions, namely Romans 1:3-4 and Philippians 2:9-11. In the case of the Philippian hymn the fact that there is movement from the death of Christ (Phil 2:8) to his exaltation (Phil 2:9-11) is somewhat unusual. This has caused many to consider that the original Christian proclamation about the resurrection was in fact a theological message of his vindication before God and not a historical message about his bodily resurrection from the dead. However, such a distinction is falsely conceived (as Harris points out). Exaltation is clearly set forth as following the resurrection at several other places within the Pauline letters (Rom 8:34; Eph 1:20; 2:6; Col 3:1). While it is true that resurrection and exaltation should not be viewed as synonymous, there is an essential theological linkage between them. The exaltation is not so much a theological interpretation of the resurrection as the inevitable consequence of it, the logical result to which it is leading. As Harris states, "[Jesus'] resurrection was the prerequisite and means of his exaltation and the exaltation was the outcome of his resurrection" (Harris, 85-86).

Strictly speaking, Paul does not relate detailed descriptions of Christ's physical ascension as such; in the NT this is found only in Luke/Acts and in veiled terms using traditional material (such as 1 Tim 3:16). Rather, Paul's letters tend to express the postresurrectional state of Jesus Christ in terms of both the Lord's exaltation and his glorification. Paul does, however, imply that the believers will experience a physical ascension to heaven at the parousia (1 Thess 4:16-17).

4.5. Resurrection and Glorification. The ultimate revelation of the glory of God is a well-established feature of Jewish eschatology. Paul also uses the language of glorification at several points to describe the implications of the resurrection for the Christian believer. 1 Thessalonians 2:12 associates the kingdom of God and glory, while 2 Thessalonians 2:14 unites the Christian calling and the future attainment of the glory of Jesus Christ. In Romans 5:2 the hope of sharing in the future glory of God is a matter of rejoicing for Paul, and in 2 Corinthians 4:17 he uses the poetic phrase "the eternal weight of glory" *(aiōnion baros doxēs)* to describe what lies in store for the faithful believer. In Romans 8:11-17 and 2 Corinthians 4:10-18 both "mortal bodies" *(ta thnēta ta sōmata)* and "mortal flesh" *(thnētē sarx)* are spoken of being eventually glorified as a result of the union between Christ and his church. In Romans 8:30 Paul even uses a series of aorist verbs, including *edoxasen* ("he glorified"), to proclaim the certainty of salvation based upon the union between Christ and believers. This description of the glorification associated with the resurrection as something in the past anticipates the language of the later letters (Col 1:27; 3:1, 4).

4.6. Resurrection and Eternal Life. In Galatians 6:8 we have an illustration of sowing/reaping used by Paul in which the Spirit is said to impart eternal life to the believer. This image is certainly eschatological in meaning and is probably best taken to be synonymous with future resurrection life. The phrase "eternal life" *(zōē aiōnios)* also occurs in passages concerned with the results of belief in Jesus Christ (Rom 5:21; 6:22-23; 1 Tim 1:16; 6:12; Tit 1:2; 3:7) and with the righteous final judgment (Rom 2:7). Whereas some images of resurrection in Paul clearly allow the focus to be on the present dimension of life in Christ, the granting of eternal life in all its fullness is (like immortality) something that lies in the future.

4.7. Resurrection and Conformity to the Image of Christ. The "image of Christ" is a key means of expressing christological truth in Paul, particularly within the bounds of the Adam/Christ analogy *(see* Adam and Christ). The assertion that the believer is also in the process of being conformed to the image of God (in Christ) is mentioned at several points (Rom 8:29; 2 Cor 3:18; Col 3:10). In each instance there is an overlap of imagery involved; "conformity to the image of Christ" is the Christian's eschatological goal and as such might be taken to be an overlap with resurrection. This is further evidenced by the fact that in 1 Corinthians 15:49 the Christian's resurrection hope is described as "bearing the image of the man from heaven." The heavenly dimension of Paul's eschatological thought is an important ingredient within his understanding of cosmic redemption (as Lincoln argues).

4.8. Resurrection and Redemption of the Body.

Paul's teaching about the bodily resurrection arises out of a Jewish anthropology in which the "soul" (Heb *nepeš*; Gk *psychē*) is the animating principle of human life. In mainstream Jewish thought human beings do not *have* souls, they *are* souls. This anthropological underpinning has tremendous implications for a doctrine of the resurrection in that it refuses to surrender the somatic component of a human being. Resurrection involves the redemption of the physical body, although (as we noted above) the somatic nature of that resurrection existence gives scope for some of Paul's most creative thinking in 1 Corinthians 15:35-49. Given this background it is perfectly understandable how in Romans 8:23 Paul describes the effects of the resurrection in terms of the ultimate "redemption of our bodies" *(tēn apolytrōsin tou sōmatos hēmōn)*. A similar idea is expressed in Philippians 3:20-21, this time where the resurrection body of the believing community is closely tied to that of the risen Lord Christ. Other instances of the idea of redemption *(apolytrōsis)* within the Pauline corpus (Rom 3:24; 1 Cor 1:30; Eph 1:7, 14; 4:30; Col 1:14) should be seen within the context of the resurrection of Jesus Christ and its implications for both humankind and the cosmos.

5. Co-Crucifixion and Co-Resurrection in Christ.

So certain is Paul of the unity that exists between Christ and his church that the believers can be described (within the confines of the image of baptism) as participating in Christ's death and resurrection (Rom 6:3-4, 8; Gal 3:27; Col 2:12). A similar declaration is contained in Colossians 3:1 where the verb *synegeirō* ("to raise up with") is used in a first-class conditional clause (assuming the truth of the statement). This union with Christ in his death and resurrection also means that Christian existence (the resurrection life) can be described as "walking in newness of life" (Rom 6:4; cf. Rom 8:13; 2 Cor 5:15; Gal 5:24). Similarly in Philippians 3:10 Paul associates "knowledge of Christ and the power of his resurrection" with participation in his sufferings, pointing to the importance of Christ's resurrection for an ethical lifestyle that endures trial. The aim of such conduct, Paul continues, is the attainment of the resurrection (Phil 3:11). In 2 Corinthians 4:10 another provocative image is used when Paul describes the believer as carrying the death of Jesus around bodily so as to manifest the resurrection.

6. The Resurrection: Some Issues of Interpretation.

Historically speaking, several important theological questions have been raised concerning resurrection. These issues particularly involve the exegesis of key Pauline passages or the interpretation of particular themes. Early evidence of the importance of Paul in these interpretative matters can be seen in the fact that Gnostic writings very often based their teaching on materials contained in his letters. It would be true to say that the complicated Pauline teaching about the resurrection body became one of the mainstays for the beliefs of Gnostic Christians in the second and third centuries. A classic Gnostic text that wrestles with these issues in typically Pauline language is the *Epistle to Rheginos*, an anonymous work otherwise known as *The Treatise on the Resurrection* (see Pagels).

Three issues call for reflection:

6.1. The Resurrection and the Messiahship of Jesus.

Several important passages within the Pauline corpus associate the messiahship of Jesus with his resurrection from the dead (Rom 1:3-4; 1 Cor 15:4; 2 Tim 2:8; *see* Christ). Although it would be going too far to suggest that for Paul the resurrection is the act that inaugurates Jesus' messiahship, it certainly would be true to say that his messiahship is vindicated and proclaimed by means of it. Indeed, it is possible to see the resurrection of Jesus as demonstrating not only his messiahship but his cosmic lordship (as Beasley-Murray argues; *see* Lord).

Nonetheless, it is possible to believe in the resurrection of Jesus from the dead without necessarily affirming that this divine act confirmed his messiahship. This may come as a surprise to many Christians since the two are sometimes taken to be equivalent. A good example of this viewpoint is the Jewish scholar P. Lapide, who accepts the historicity of Jesus' bodily resurrection, but does not therefore describe himself as a Christian (by definition, one who affirms Jesus as Messiah). For Lapide the resurrection of Jesus is part of God's preparatory work, making the world ready for the future revelation of the Messiah. The example of Lapide is a case in point for the too-casual assumption that the resurrection of Jesus is at the same time the self-evident proclamation of him as Messiah. At the same time, Lapide's argument offers an interesting insight into one of the peculiarities of modern NT interpretation. In an age when many competent Christian scholars find reason to deny the historicity of the bodily resurrection of Jesus and yet retain their Christian faith, here we have a Jewish scholar who strongly affirms the bodily resurrection and yet seeks to claim no faith on the basis of it. It is a salient lesson about the messianic content of the resurrection faith as Paul proclaims it.

6.2. The Resurrection and the Empty Tomb Motif.

All four Gospels mention the empty tomb within their resurrection narratives (Mt 28:6; Mk 16:6; Lk 24:2; Jn 20:4-7). On the other hand, while Paul does explicitly mention the burial of Jesus (1 Cor 15:4; cf. Rom 6:4), he nowhere mentions the empty tomb in connection with the resurrection. C. E. B. Cranfield, however, feels it is "almost certainly implied" (Cranfield, 168) by the mention of Christ's burial between "died" and "he was raised" in 1 Corinthians 15:4. It could simply be an accident of circumstance that Paul never mentions the empty tomb, although R. H. Stein has put forward the suggestion that the omission is due to apologetic concerns on the part of Paul: "When it came to the resurrection appearances, the apostle could argue on equal terms with the other disciples. He, too, had seen the Lord! He could not, however, say the same about the empty tomb" (Stein, 12).

In any event, within the NT the empty tomb is never adduced as proof of the resurrection of Jesus from the dead. This has led some to drive a wedge between the resurrection of Jesus and the evidence of the empty tomb, with a view to denying the historicity of the resurrection itself. The resurrection is capable of thereby being "spiritualized," and its basis in history is seriously undermined if not jettisoned altogether. In recent years in Britain this line of argumentation has been popularly associated with the former Bishop of Durham, David Jenkins (see Harris [1985] for details). The guarantee of the resurrection (so the argument goes) is not the empty tomb but the presence of the risen Lord in the lives of the believing community (see Harris, 37-44, and Walker). The Pauline materials, particularly 1 Corinthians 15, are at the heart of much of this modern discussion. It is unlikely that Paul would have accepted the truth of the resurrection of Jesus from the dead without also accepting that a corollary of this is an empty tomb.

Barrett's comment succinctly makes the point about how faith in the historicity of the empty tomb must be delicately poised: "Faith . . . would be destroyed by the discovery of the dead body of Jesus, but it cannot be created simply by the discovery of an empty tomb" (Barrett 1968, 349).

A growing number of scholars affirm the historicity of the empty tomb and Paul's knowledge of it (see, e.g., Craig 1985). The reason that the empty tomb is not explicitly discussed in Paul should not be taken as evidence of its historical unreliability, but of its unimportance as a matter of Christian proclamation.

6.3. The General Resurrection. Paul nowhere explicitly discusses a general resurrection for *all* people, although there are indications scattered throughout the letters that all (both believers and nonbelievers, the living and the dead) will face judgment (Rom 2:6-11; 2 Cor 4:5; 5:10; 2 Thess 1:6-10; 2 Tim 4:1). The nearest place that Paul comes to suggesting a general (or universal) resurrection is in 1 Corinthians 15:22: "in Christ shall all be made alive" *(en tō christō pantes zōopoiēthēsontai)*. However, this declaration comes in the midst of Paul's Adam/Christ analogy and must be so interpreted (it is "all *in Christ*" who will be resurrected). Some have based a Pauline belief in general resurrection upon the words attributed to the apostle in Acts 24:15, but this is viewed as methodologically suspect by many. The idea of a universal resurrection cannot be dismissed out of hand, however. D. C. Allison argues that the whole of early Christianity, including Paul, associated Christ's rising from the dead with a general resurrection and understood the Lord's resurrection to have inaugurated the onset of it (Allison is attempting to counter interpretations that overemphasize the importance of a realized eschatological viewpoint in early Christian belief).

See also CHRISTOLOGY; ESCHATOLOGY; JUDGMENT.

DPL: BODY; DYING AND RISING WITH CHRIST; EXALTATION AND ENTHRONEMENT; IMMORTALITY; INTERMEDIATE STATE; LIFE AND DEATH; POWER.

BIBLIOGRAPHY. D. C. Allison, *The End of the Ages Has Come* (Philadelphia: Fortress, 1985); W. Baird, "Ascension and Resurrection: An Intersection of Luke and Paul" in *Texts and Textuality: Critical Essays on the Bible and the Early Church Fathers*, ed. W. E. March (San Antonio: Trinity University Press, 1980) 3-18; C. K. Barrett, *The First Epistle to the Corinthians* (New York: Harper & Row, 1968); idem, "Immortality and Resurrection," in *Resurrection and Immortality: Aspects of twentieth-century Christian belief*, ed. C. S. Duthie (London: Samuel Bagster, 1979) 68-88; idem, *Essays on Paul* (London: SPCK, 1982); P. Beasley-Murray, "Romans 1:3f: An Early Confession of Faith in the Lordship of Jesus," *TynB* 31 (1980) 147-54; R. Bultmann, "The New Testament and Mythology," in *Kerygma and Myth I & II*, ed. H. W. Bartsch (London: SPCK, 1972) 1-44; H. C. C. Cavallin, *Life After Death: Paul's Argument for the Resurrection of the Dead in 1 Cor 15* (ConB 7.1; Lund: Gleerup, 1974); L. Coenen, "Resurrection," *NIDNTT* 3.259-309; W. L. Craig, "The Bodily Resurrection of Jesus," in *Gospel Perspectives 1: Studies of History and Tradition in the Four Gospels*, ed. R. T. France and D. Wenham (Sheffield: JSOT, 1980) 47-74; idem, "The Historicity of the Empty Tomb of Jesus," *NTS* 31 (1985) 39-67; C. E. B. Cranfield, "The Resurrection of Jesus Christ," *ExpT* 101 (1990) 167-72; O. Cullmann, *Immortality of the Soul or Resurrection of the Dead?* (London: Epworth, 1958); M. E. Dahl, *The Resurrection of the Body* (London: SCM, 1962); W. D. Davies, *Paul and Rabbinic Judaism* (4th ed.; Philadelphia: Fortress, 1980); J. D. G. Dunn, "I Corinthians 15:45—last Adam, life-giving spirit," in *Christ and Spirit in the New Testament: Studies in Honour of C. F. D. Moule*, ed. B. Lindars and S. Smalley (Cambridge: Cambridge University Press, 1973) 127-41; idem, *The Evidence for Jesus* (Philadelphia: Westminster, 1985); E. E. Ellis, "II Corinthians V.1-10 in Pauline Eschatology," *NTS* 6 (1959-60) 211-24; J. Gillman, "Signals of Transformation in 1 Thessalonians 4:13-18," *CBQ* 47 (1985) 263-81; L. J. Greenspoon, "The Origin of the Idea of Resurrection," in *Traditions in Transformation: Turning Points in Biblical Faith*, ed. B. Halpern and J. D. Levenson (Winona Lake, IN: Eisenbrauns, 1981) 247-317; M. J. Harris, *Raised Immortal: The Relation Between Resurrection and Immortality in New Testament Teaching* (Grand Rapids: Eerdmans, 1983); idem, *Easter in Durham: Bishop Jenkins and the Resurrection of Jesus* (Exeter: Paternoster, 1985); J. Jeremias, "Flesh and Blood Cannot Inherit the Kingdom of God," *NTS* 2 (1955-56) 151-59; J. Kloppenborg, "An Analysis of the Pre-Pauline Formula I Cor 15.3b-5 in the Light of Some Recent Literature," *CBQ* 40 (1978) 351-67; G. E. Ladd, *I Believe in the Resurrection of Jesus* (Grand Rapids: Eerdmans, 1975); P. Lapide, *The Resurrection of Jesus: A Jewish Perspective* (London: SPCK, 1984); A. T.

Lincoln, *Paradise Now and Not Yet* (SNTSMS 43; Cambridge: Cambridge University Press, 1981); J. I. H. McDonald, *The Resurrection: Narrative and Belief* (London: SPCK, 1989) 25-51; C. F. D. Moule, "St Paul and Dualism: The Pauline Conception of the Resurrection," *NTS* 13 (1966-67) 106-23; J. Murphy-O'Connor, "Tradition and Redaction in 1 Cor 15.3-7," *CBQ* 43 (1981) 582-89; G. W. E. Nickelsburg, *Resurrection, Immortality and Eternal Life in Intertestamental Judaism* (HTS 26; Cambridge, MA: Harvard University Press, 1972); E. Pagels, *The Gnostic Gospels* (New York: Random House, 1982) 35-54; B. A. Pearson, *The 'Pneumatikos-Psychikos' Terminology in 1 Corinthians* (Missoula, MT: Scholars, 1973); P. Perkins, *Resurrection* (London: Chapman, 1984); R. J. Sider, "The Pauline Conception of the Resurrection Body in I Corinthians XV.35-54," *NTS* 21 (1974-75) 428-39; R. H. Stein, "Was the tomb really empty?" *Themelios* 5 (1979) 8-12; D. A. Walker, "Resurrection, Empty Tomb and Easter Faith," *ExpT* 101 (1990) 172-75; B. Witherington, *Jesus, Paul and the End of the World* (Downers Grove, IL: InterVarsity Press, 1992); N. T. Wright, *The Resurrection of the Son of God* (Minneapolis: Fortress, 2003).   L. J. Kreitzer

RESURRECTION III: HEBREWS, GENERAL EPISTLES, REVELATION

The resurrection of Jesus Christ from the dead is referred to explicitly in three of the NT documents considered here. It is difficult to imagine that the remaining documents could have been written without an underlying conviction that Jesus was risen and accessible to Christian believers. In the second century the resurrection of Jesus and of believers continued to be a significant theme in Christian writings. Divergent interpretations of it marked the emerging divide between orthodox and gnostic streams in the church.

1. Terminology of Resurrection
2. Hebrews: Resurrection and Exaltation
3. 1 Peter: Hope of Vindication
4. Revelation: "I Was Dead and Am Alive For Ever"
5. Other New Testament Literature
6. Conclusions

1. Terminology of Resurrection.

Like the English verbs *raise* and *rise,* the verbs used in the NT do not refer exclusively to the raising of people from among the dead (see,

e.g., Heb 7:11, 15; Jas 5:15). The only occurrence in these documents of *egeirō* with reference to the resurrection of Jesus is 1 Peter 1:21. *Anastasis* refers to Jesus' resurrection in 1 Peter 1:3; 3:21; to a general future resurrection in Hebrews 6:2; 11:35; and to what John calls "the first resurrection" in Revelation 20:5-6. The verb *zaō* ("live") describes Jesus' resurrection in Revelation 1:18 and Revelation 2:8 and "the first resurrection" in Revelation 20:4-5. *Zōopoieō* ("make alive") denotes Jesus' resurrection in 1 Peter 3:18. Finally, *anagō* is used of God "bringing back" Jesus from the dead in Hebrews 13:20.

2. Hebrews: Resurrection and Exaltation.

For the writer of Hebrews "resurrection of the dead" is part of basic Christian instruction (Heb 6:2). The linking of resurrection with "eternal judgment" suggests that he envisages a future universal resurrection, of the righteous to eternal life and of the wicked to condemnation (cf. Dan 12:2; Jn 5:28-29; Acts 24:15). Later he sees restoration to physical life (*egeirein*, Heb 11:19; *anastasis*, Heb 11:35) as a picture of the future resurrection of the faithful to eternal life.

Jesus' resurrection is mentioned explicitly only once, in the prayer of Hebrews 13:20-21. Elsewhere the focus is on his exaltation to the right hand of God. The writer's distinctive emphasis on Jesus' exaltation rather than on resurrection is a natural consequence of his concentration on Christ's work as high priest foreshadowed in the ritual of the Day of Atonement. Just as the high priest of the OT entered the holy of holies with the blood of the sacrificial victim, so the crucified Jesus appeared at God's right hand in the heavenly sanctuary (Heb 9:11-12). In this pattern stressing Jesus' exaltation to heaven there is no separate place for his resurrection. It is presupposed (cf. the linking of these two themes in Rom 8:34; Eph 1:20; Col 3:1; 1 Pet 3:22). Christ's exaltation to God's right hand presupposes his resurrection from the dead; his resurrection was the way to exaltation.

Theologically, Jesus' resurrection-exaltation is linked with other key themes in Hebrews. It demonstrated God's acceptance of his atoning sacrifice (Heb 10:12; 13:20-21). It confirmed his divine sonship (Heb 1:3-5, 13; *see* Son of God), his high priesthood (Heb 5:5-10; 8:1) and his status as the last Adam (Heb 1:13—2:9, combining Ps 110:1 with Ps 8:4-6; see Dunn, 108-13).

The connection between Jesus' past resurrection and believers' future resurrection is hinted at in the unique description of Jesus in Hebrews as "forerunner" (*prodromos*, Heb 6:20). Meanwhile he "is permanently alive to plead their cause" (Heb 7:25). The knowledge that he went via the cross to God's right hand inspires them to remain faithful, confident that they will share his destiny.

The question of the timing of future resurrection is raised by the reference to "the spirits of the righteous made perfect" (Heb 12:23). This is commonly taken to mean dead believers (cf. *1 Enoch* 22:9), waiting in an intermediate state to receive resurrection bodies at Christ's second coming. However, Hebrews 12:22-24 seems to portray the ultimate encounter with God in the heavenly Jerusalem rather than in a preliminary or an intermediate state. Hence the "spirits" are probably the righteous in their ultimate state, in their "spiritual bodies" (1 Cor 15:44). If this is so, the text does not address the question whether there is an interim, disembodied state between death and the Parousia (see further Peterson, 163-67).

3. 1 Peter: Hope of Vindication.

The resurrection of Jesus is the foundation of hope for the author of 1 Peter and for his readers in churches facing persecution (1 Pet 1:3, 21; 3:15). The key passage is 1 Peter 3:18-22, which is widely regarded as drawing on primitive liturgical traditions, especially in 1 Peter 3:19-21 (see Michaels, 197-99).

Christ was "put to death in the flesh but made alive in the spirit" (1 Pet 3:18). The contrast between flesh and spirit has sometimes been taken to imply a dualism within Christ's human nature or a contrast between his divine and human natures. These terms, however, denote not two parts of Christ but two spheres of existence. His earthly life ended in death, but that was succeeded by his risen life in what Paul calls his "spiritual body" (1 Cor 15:42-44; note the similar contrast between flesh and spirit in Rom 1:3-4; 1 Tim 3:16; and discussion in Dalton, 124-34; Michaels, 204-5).

1 Peter 3:21-22 leads the readers' thought from Jesus' resurrection to his exaltation to God's right hand (cf. 1 Pet 1:21; Eph 1:20-22). So whatever the meaning of the intervening passage about his preaching to the spirits in prison, the focus is on his vindication by God and his lordship over all things.

For Peter's readers, God's vindication of Jesus gives them solid hope that he will also vindicate them. Through Jesus' resurrection God has given to believers new birth, a secure inheritance to be revealed at the last time (1 Pet 1:3-4), conveyed through baptism (1 Pet 3:21). Because God has called them in Christ to eternal glory they may stand firm in suffering (1 Pet 5:10).

The author maintains the typically Pauline tension between salvation already experienced and salvation yet to be received in its fullness (e.g., in 1 Pet 1:3-9). The link between baptism and resurrection in 1 Peter 3:21 echoes the language of Romans 6:1-14. But because he addresses Christians in the context of persecution, Peter uses the theme of resurrection with more focus on the future than does Paul in Romans. Although Jesus' resurrection means that believers enter into new life now, it inspires a greater hope that God will in the future bring them through suffering to glory.

4. Revelation: "I Was Dead and Am Alive For Ever."

The threat of persecution and the promise of vindication shape John's message also in *Revelation. The death of believers for their witness (*martyria*) to Christ has already occurred, and for others it will occur (Rev 2:10, 13; 6:9-11; 12:11; 17:6; 20:4).

The book is introduced with a vision of the risen Christ, "the first and the last and the living one" (Rev 1:18; cf. Rev 2:8). Since "the first and the last" is a title of God in Isaiah 44:6 and Isaiah 48:12 (cf. Rev 1:8; 21:6), the resurrection points to Christ's participation in the eternal being of God and his rule over creation (Bauckham 1993 *Theology*, 54-58).

More specific references to resurrection indicate the centrality of this theme in John's thought. Jesus is introduced as "the firstborn from the dead and the ruler of the kings of the earth" (Rev 1:5). This phrase combines the idea that Christ pioneered for others the way to resurrection (cf. Col 1:18; "firstfruits" in 1 Cor 15:20) with the language of Psalm 89:27, where the Davidic king is described as "my firstborn, the highest of the kings of the earth." By virtue of his resurrection Jesus is already establishing God's rule over earthly powers (cf. Rev 5:3-5).

The risen Lord has begun to fulfill the hope of establishing God's rule over the earth, so that ultimately God will through him make all things new (Rev 21:5). In the new heaven and new earth God will live with his resurrected people (Rev 21:3-4). John nowhere speaks of resurrection bodies, but the imagery of Revelation 21—22 would hardly fit with the notion that God's people are permanently disembodied spirits (see Charles, 1:81-83, 176, 184-88, 210, 213-14; 2:127-28, for the argument that in Revelation white robes represent resurrection bodies). He does not speculate about the separation or reassembly of bodies and spirits or souls but speaks simply of the death and resurrection of persons (Bauckham 1993 *Climax*, 62-70). John's hope, like the Jewish hope out of which it sprang, is not merely for the resurrection of individuals but also for resurrection of God's people in fellowship with each other in a renewed world.

Two related passages require special attention. According to Revelation 6:9-11, those who have been killed because of their faithful witness are told that they will be vindicated against their persecutors when the full number of martyrs is complete. Like some Jewish apocalyptic texts, this passage refers to dead saints awaiting resurrection as "souls" (*psychai*; cf. *1 Enoch* 22:3; *2 Bar.* 21:23). The text provides some support for the concept of an intermediate state, though the fact that the "souls" are described as wearing robes shows that they are not purely spiritual entities. Probably John's concern is not to teach about an intermediate state but to speak of the eschatological delay during which the church must continue its witness (Bauckham 1993 *Climax*, 55-56).

The promise of Revelation 6:9-11 finds its fulfillment in the millennium (Rev 20:4-6). The souls of the martyrs "came to life *(ezēsan)* and ruled with Christ for a thousand years." John comments that those who take part in this "first resurrection" *(anastasis)* are protected from "the second death" (eternal, spiritual death, cf. Rev 20:14). In contrast with them, "the rest of the dead did not come to life until the thousand years were completed." (For the view that in Revelation 6:9-11 and Revelation 20:4-6 John is concerned exclusively with Christian martyrs, see Beasley-Murray, 293-94. For the view that a wider group of believers is implied, see Harris, 178-79, 228; Mealy, 110-15.)

After the thousand years there is a scene of universal judgment, for which all the dead are gathered before God's throne (Rev 20:11-15). This must be the "second resurrection" implied by the earlier reference to the "first resurrection" (Rev 20:5). But it may be significant that John refrains from calling their standing before God for judgment a resurrection. Perhaps, like Paul, he prefers to reserve resurrection language for the raising of people to eternal life with Christ.

5. Other New Testament Literature.

In the shorter letters resurrection language hardly occurs, though there are occasional promises of "eternal life" (Jude 21), "a new heaven and a new earth" (2 Pet 3:13), entry into "the eternal kingdom" (2 Pet 1:11) or into "the presence of his glory" (Jude 24). In James, Jesus Christ is "our glorious Lord" (Jas 2:1) who promises "the crown of life" to those who remain faithful under testing (Jas 1:12).

Though 1 John (*see* John, Letters of) retains the Fourth Gospel's stress on eternal life as a present possession (1 Jn 3:15; 5:11-12), there is also an important future perspective. "We know that when he appears we shall be like him, for we shall see him as he is" (1 Jn 3:2). There are uncertainties of interpretation. For example, is "he" God or Christ? Shall we be "like him" in character, or in form or appearance? Though most commentators take John to refer to transformation of character at the parousia, it is likely that his focus is on the prospect of having resurrection bodies like that of Christ (cf. Phil 3:21; Col 3:4).

6. Conclusions.

Most of this literature expresses, like Paul, the central importance for Christian faith of the resurrection of Jesus and the expectation of the resurrection of believers. But there is no sustained reflection on the nature of resurrection such as we find in 1-2 Corinthians.

Like Paul, these writers see Jesus' resurrection as the prototype of the resurrection of believers. They focus on resurrection as God's vindication of those who suffer for Christ's sake. They make no sharp distinction between Christ's resurrection and his exaltation. They offer only limited material on the timing of the resurrection of believers or the nature of an intermediate state. While there is implicit affirmation of the idea that all the dead will be raised for final judgment, no writer explicitly speaks of a resurrection for judgment. Evidently, like Paul, they prefer to reserve the term *resurrection* for

God's raising of Jesus and of believers to eternal life in his presence.

See also CHRISTOLOGY; ESCHATOLOGY.

DLNTD: ASCENSION; CREATION, COSMOLOGY; EXALTATION, ENTHRONEMENT; GLORY; HEAVEN, NEW HEAVEN.

BIBLIOGRAPHY. R. J. Bauckham, *The Climax of Prophecy: Studies on the Book of Revelation* (Edinburgh: T & T Clark, 1993); idem, *The Theology of the Book of Revelation* (NTT; Cambridge: Cambridge University Press, 1993); G. R. Beasley-Murray, *The Book of Revelation* (NCB; London: Marshall, Morgan & Scott, 1974); R. H. Charles, *A Critical and Exegetical Commentary on the Revelation of St. John* (2 vols.; ICC; Edinburgh: T & T Clark, 1920); W. J. Dalton, *Christ's Proclamation to the Spirits: A Study of 1 Peter 3:18—4:6* (Rome: Pontifical Biblical Institute, 1965); J. D. G. Dunn, *Christology in the Making* (London: SCM, 1980); M. J. Harris, *Raised Immortal: The Relation Between Resurrection and Immortality in New Testament Teaching* (Grand Rapids: Eerdmans, 1983); D. M. Hay, *Glory at the Right Hand: Psalm 110 in Early Christianity* (Nashville: Abingdon, 1973); J. W. Mealy, *After the Thousand Years: Resurrection and Judgment in Revelation 20* (Sheffield: Sheffield Academic Press, 1992); J. R. Michaels, *1 Peter* (WBC; Waco, TX: Word, 1988); P. Perkins, *Resurrection: New Testament Witness and Contemporary Reflection* (New York: Doubleday, 1984); D. Peterson, *Hebrews and Perfection* (SNTSMS 47; Cambridge: Cambridge University Press, 1982); J. M. Robinson, "Jesus: From Easter to Valentinus (or to the Apostles' Creed)," *JBL* 101 (1982) 5-37.

S. H. Travis

REVELATION, BOOK OF

The book of Revelation is acknowledged to be a closed book by the majority of modern readers. This is largely due to the unfamiliarity of the prophetic books in the OT, the almost total ignorance of Jewish apocalyptic writings and the historical setting of the book that determines its content. In this article we shall endeavor to clarify these features and so enable the message of the last book of the Bible to be grasped.

1. Genre
2. Date
3. Historical Situation
4. Content and Structure
5. Authorship
6. Expectation of Antichrist
7. Purpose of the Revelation

8. Significance of the Revelation for Today
9. Revelation in the Earliest Post-New Testament Writings

1. Genre.

1.1. Apocalypse. The book of Revelation is the only work of its kind in the NT, but there were many like it in the ancient world, written especially by Jews but later also by Christians. These were called apocalypses, which is a Greek term from the verb *apokalypsis* meaning "to uncover," "to reveal" or "to disclose" what is hidden. The characteristic motive of such works was to keep alive the flame of faith in difficult times and to maintain hope in the coming of the day of the Lord and of the kingdom of God (*see* Kingdom of God). Accordingly, the apocalyptic movement is commonly viewed as the child of prophecy. Jewish apocalypses, however, were not entirely concerned with the eschatological hope of their people, for they frequently contain descriptions of the heavens and the earth and their inhabitants, including angelic and demonic powers. Nevertheless it is the eschatology of the apocalyptic writings that is most commonly in mind when one speaks of apocalyptic literature.

The most notable example of apocalypse in the OT is the book of Daniel, which became the model for subsequent apocalyptic writings. Other prophetic works, however, contain features that are related to apocalyptic thought and mode of expression. Ezekiel, for example, is sometimes called "the father of apocalyptic." Many passages in Isaiah 40—55 anticipate the apocalyptic style and content, along with Isaiah 25—27 and Zechariah 9—14. All these and other passages from the OT prophets contain representations of the intervention of God for the salvation of his people.

The book of Revelation opens with the words, "The Revelation of Jesus Christ that God gave him." We cannot be certain as to whether John intended to describe his work as an apocalypse. Was he implying that this revelation, given by God to Jesus (Rev 1:1-2), provided the definitive declaration of that which other writings of this kind sought to give? The nature of that which follows may be thought to justify it. If this admission is acknowledged, it would be of utmost importance in interpreting the language and symbolism of the book. Much of the teaching of Jesus is conveyed in *parables; the book of Revelation employs parabolic pictures for setting forth its representation of the past, present and future of history. An understanding of the use of such parables in related literature is invaluable for their interpretation in John's apocalypse. The pictorial language of Jewish apocalypses is rooted in the OT, and in turn the authors of the OT used imagery familiar to the nations of the Middle East. John the prophet was evidently acquainted with all that background, for it is recognized by virtually all scholars that his work reflects a mind soaked in the OT, and his language is dominated by it. A knowledge of this background is a prerequisite for a right understanding of his book.

1.2. Prophecy. The second sentence of the Revelation reads, "Happy is the one who reads [to others] and they who listen to the words of the prophecy and keep the things that are written in it." It is evident that John is aware that he was commissioned by the Lord to write this prophecy and that he is numbered among the prophets of God. As such he will have realized that he stands in the succession of the prophets of the new covenant. More than once this is mentioned in his book. The epilogue relates how John fell at the feet of the angel who had showed him the visions he had seen in order to worship him, but this he was forbidden to do: "You must not do that! I am a fellow servant with you and your brothers the prophets, and those who keep the words of this book. Worship God" (Rev 22:8-9). In Revelation 19:10 the angel tells John, "I am a fellow servant with you and your brothers who hold the testimony of Jesus . . . for the testimony of Jesus is the Spirit of prophecy." That appears to mean that the Holy Spirit who inspires prophecy enables prophets to bear witness to the revelation that Jesus brought and brings. It accords with the description of the content of the Revelation in its first sentence, where it is stated to be "witness to the word of God and the testimony of Jesus" (Rev 1:2). In light of these statements, indeed of the content of the entire book, we are to recognize that the Revelation is the work of the Spirit, who from Pentecost on has enabled Christians to bear prophetic witness to "the word of God and the witness of Jesus." That witness includes God's word concerning his will for humankind in the present and in the future.

It is evident, accordingly, that John's work is not to be viewed either as an apocalypse or as a prophecy, as though those terms were mutually exclusive; rather one should acknowledge that it has the features of both; that is, his work is to be defined as an apocalyptic prophecy and/or a prophetic apocalypse.

1.3. Letter. After the first paragraph, John greets his readers in the conventional manner of one writing a *letter (Rev 1:4-5). Correspondingly he concludes the prophecy with a benediction such as is normal in the NT epistles (Rev 22:21). Moreover, John was commanded to write what he was about to see and to send the work to seven churches in the Roman province of Asia (Rev 1:11). All these churches have a short letter addressed to them. The letter always includes the exhortation, "Let anyone who has an ear listen to what the Spirit is saying to the churches" (e.g., Rev 2:11).

It is clear that the seven letters were intended for the benefit of all the seven churches addressed. Significantly, the cities in which the seven churches were located were centers of civic administration and of postal distribution in their areas. It was therefore possible for copies of the whole prophecy to be dispatched to churches in other cities of the province. NT letters were clearly intended to be read to gathered congregations; the same applies to the entire book of Revelation, as is clear from the beatitude in Revelation 1:3 and from the epilogue in Revelation 22:6-21. If, then, the book of Revelation was a letter to the churches of Roman Asia, it is manifest that it was addressed to their situations.

In this respect, Revelation stands in contrast to the opening paragraph of *1 Enoch*, which states that what the prophet saw was "not for this generation, but for a remote one which is to come." The situations and needs of the churches to which John wrote were as truly in John's mind as the situations and needs of the churches to which Paul and other Christian leaders wrote. The recognition of this fact has important consequences for the interpretation of the whole work. The prophet was bidden to write to the churches of Roman Asia in view of events that were developing in their time and to prepare them for their future. Just as the rest of the letters in the NT require the circumstances of the churches to which they were addressed to be known for understanding their content, so it is with the book of Revelation. Failure to grasp this fact has led innumerable readers to misinterpret the book by identifying the figures and events described in it with persons and events of their own times. Such misunderstanding is corrected by every effort to perceive the situation addressed in the book and its message for those living in it and for all subsequent generations.

1.4. Liturgy. Not a few books in the NT reflect liturgical elements in them, especially prayers and hymns and confessions of faith (*see* Worship). One thinks of Ephesians 1 and the prayer of Ephesians 3:14-21; the christological hymn in Philippians 2:6-11 and that in Colossians 1:15-20; the short snatch of a hymn in Ephesians 5:14 (thought by some scholars to have been composed for the celebration of baptism) and the various "faithful sayings" of the Pastoral Epistles. The book of Revelation has more such songs scattered through its pages than does any other writing in the NT. Their substance and contexts led M. H. Shepherd to suggest that the early paschal liturgy of the churches formed the model for Revelation. This interpretation has not found acceptance by most scholars, but the presence of liturgical forms in so many sections of the book is important; their combination with other liturgical forms should be acknowledged.

1.5. Drama. In the Greek tradition, worship and drama are closely linked. The presence of the many hymns in the book of Revelation has encouraged some interpreters to see in the book a drama of the end time. J. G. Bowman observed that the book is made up of seven acts and seven scenes. The hymns have a similar function to the choruses in Greek drama: they throw light on the visions of the book. This E. Schüssler Fiorenza acknowledges: "They [the hymns of Revelation] function in the same way as the chorus in Greek drama, preparing and commenting upon the dramatic movements of the plot"; but she asserts that Revelation is not a drama (Schüssler Fiorenza, 166), and with this most concur while readily admitting that the book is a remarkably dramatic work.

2. Date.

Two chief possibilities as to the time of writing Revelation have been and still are maintained by scholars, namely, either in the turbulent period shortly after the death of Nero (A.D. 68-69) or toward the end of Domitian's reign, about A.D. 95.

The former view is held on the basis of the likelihood that John had endured the fearful persecution of Christians by Nero and also because there is no clear reference in the book to

the destruction of Jerusalem in A.D. 70. If Revelation 11:1-2 is interpreted literally, it can indicate that Jerusalem had been under prolonged attack and that the altar and outer court of the temple either had been seized or could not be kept from the Roman forces, whereas the sanctuary itself continued to be preserved by God.

In the latter chapters of the book Rome is called "Babylon" (see Rev 14:8; 16:19; 17:5; 18:2, 10, 21). The most probable reason for giving the name *Babylon* to Rome was that as Nebuchadnezzar, king of Babylon, had destroyed Jerusalem in 586 B.C., so Rome had done in recent times. The dirge over Babylon in Revelation 18 views the current tyrant city as another Babylon. The apocalypses 4 Ezra and *2 Baruch* were written at the end of the first century of the Christian era and also gave the name of Babylon to Rome for the same reason.

In Revelation 13:3 (cf. Rev 13:14) it is stated that one of the heads of the "beast," the antichrist, had received a deadly wound, but he lived again and was empowered by Satan to rule the empire (cf. Rev 17:8). This appears to refer to the contemporary belief that the wounded "head" was Nero and that he had not been killed, whether by himself or another, but had escaped and would return to rule the empire. Revelation 17 has a developed form of this notion and represents the belief that the beast Nero had risen from the dead and would come with a confederate army from the East and destroy Babylon the Great. This expectation would require a later date than the death of Nero.

The majority opinion as to the date of Revelation is that of Irenaeus, who wrote concerning the book, "That was seen no very long time since, but almost in our own day, toward the end of Domitian's reign" (Irenaeus *Haer.* 5.30.3). Eusebius cited this judgment with approval (Eusebius *Hist. Eccl.* 3.18-20; 5.8.6). This assessment of the date of Revelation suits other evidence of the character and contents of the book, above all the delineation of the antichrist as another Nero.

The explanation in Revelation 17:9-11 as to the meaning of the seven heads of the beast has been investigated with a view to determining the date of Revelation, but in vain. Two meanings are given in the text, the one identifying the seven heads with the seven hills of Rome, the other representing seven emperors. Both explanations are secondary, since they are applications to a contemporary situation of an ancient myth or saga of the seven-headed monster of the deep who opposed the powers of heaven. The list of emperors up to Domitian is Julius Caesar, Augustus, Tiberius, Gaius, Claudius, Nero, Galba, Otho, Vitellius, Vespasian, Titus, Domitian—twelve in all. Of these John states that five have fallen, one is (the sixth), one is to come (for a short time only), the eighth is one of the seven and will be the antichrist. Starting from Julius Caesar, John would be writing in Nero's reign, but the difficulties discussed remain. The simplest solution is to assume that the "five" that have "fallen" represent the majority, the sixth is the reigning emperor, Domitian; the seventh will reign for a short time and the antichrist will follow.

3. Historical Situation.

3.1. The Imperial Cult in Roman Asia. It is imperative to bear in mind that the churches for which Revelation was written were situated in the province of Roman Asia and that the emperor cult (i.e., the worship of the emperor) was enthusiastically adopted in that area, possibly more than elsewhere in the Roman Empire. L. L. Thompson pointed out that the imperial cult had its high point in the reign of Augustus: "Language praising him is lofty and is similar to that offered to the gods" (Thompson, 159). All the cities of the seven churches had the worship of the emperor in their midst. In many cities annual festivals were held, especially on the emperor's birthday, and such festivals were supported by people from all walks of life. Thompson, however, urges that the importance of the worship of the emperor for the early Christians should not be exaggerated. In his view the greater issue revolved around Christians' relation to adherents of traditional religious cults rather than their relation to the cult of the emperor, for sacrifices were made in connection with them also (*see* Religions, Greco-Roman).

Domitian, in whose reign Revelation is believed to have been written, has had the reputation of being a monster, who carried to an extreme the imperial cult. He is said to have erected an immense number of statues of himself, demanded that he be addressed as "our Lord and God" *(dominus et deus)* and embarked on a vicious persecution of the churches. Thompson has investigated the truth of these claims

and come to the conclusion that they are false. The portrait of Domitian was drawn a few years after his death by a circle of writers around Pliny the Younger, which included Tacitus, Dio Chrysostom and Suetonius. After Domitian's assassination Nerva became emperor, but his reign lasted only two years (A.D. 96-98). He was succeeded by Trajan, who recognized his need of writers and orators who could promote his ideas. He found them in Pliny and his friends. They pursued a common policy of exalting Trajan by contrasting him with Domitian. Pliny, for example, wrote of the pleasure of being appointed consul during September, a month of triple rejoicing "which saw the removal of the worst of emperors [Domitian], the accession of the best [Nerva] and the birth of one even better than the best" (i.e., Trajan; see Pliny *Panegyr.* 92.4).

On this procedure Thompson comments: "Propagandists for a new age have to sharpen both edges of their two-edged sword; both the ideal present and the evil past have to be exaggerated" (Thompson, 115). Contrary to the claim that Domitian demanded to be addressed as "our Lord and God," Statius reports that when Domitian was acclaimed as *Dominus* at one of his Saturnalia he forbade those who did so to address him in this manner (Statius *Silvae* 1.6, 81-84). There are no references to Domitian as *dominus et deus* on any inscriptions, coins or medallions from the Domitianic era. Certainly there were people who referred to Domitian as *dominus et deus,* but Thompson urged that one must reckon with popular opportunism among those seeking benefits from the emperor (Thompson, 105-6).

If Thompson has made a strong case for clearing Domitian's name as a monster obsessed with his inherited divinity, with others he has underestimated the threat of the emperor cult to the churches and instead has imputed to John the prophet an obsession with Jewish apocalyptic. While recognizing that apocalyptic writings have frequently been due to crises precipitated by persecution, Thompson denies that such action of governing authorities in Roman Asia existed in John's day. He cites the concept of "perceived crisis" put forward by J. J. Collins: that is, the apocalyptist sees in the situation in which he lives a crisis that is nonexistent but is "perceived" through interpreting his situation from the viewpoint of apocalyptic beliefs (J. J.

Collins, 2-8). Far from being an objective analysis of society at that time, Thompson affirms, "First century Roman life was . . . one of the most integrated, peaceful, meaningful periods of history for most of those who lived in the empire. This confusion of a particular social location with society as a whole is not uncommon in the study of early Christianity" (Thompson, 237 n. 10).

When one bears in mind that Roman society was dependent on sixty million slaves, many whose life of slavery was largely due to conquest of their countries by Rome's armies, the compulsion of many male slaves to become gladiators for the entertainment of crowds in the amphitheaters and female slaves to become prostitutes, such a statement is beyond comprehension. John the prophet refers to these in his doom song over the fall of Babylon as he concludes his list of the trades of the city with the words, "cattle and sheep, horses and chariots and bodies and souls of men" (Rev 18:13). He was no small-minded man, limited to an isolated congregation in a restricted area. He exercised an influential ministry over a group of churches in what was probably the most Christianized area of the Roman Empire in the late first century A.D. He was in a position to know what happens when emperors take measures against subjects whose conscience forbids them to acknowledge his divinity; for example, the action of Antiochus Epiphanes to compel the Jews to forsake their religion and adopt that of the rest of his domain, including sacrificing to himself as the representative of Zeus; Caligula's attempt to set his statue in the temple of Jerusalem and the panic caused by that among the Jews of Jerusalem; and the appalling cruelty of Nero in his persecution of Christians in Rome during John's lifetime.

John knew the teaching of the book of Daniel and its attitude to rulers who claimed to be not only divine but above the gods. Not that he interpreted the reigning emperor as holding that notion of himself, but it is evident that he saw in the enthusiastic pursuit of the emperor cult a preparation for the emergence of an antichrist who would not only declare war on the church but, astonishingly, destroy the empire (see Rev 17:12-17).

3.2. Persecution. Earlier beliefs that Domitian had already begun a severe persecution of the church are not borne out by Revelation. References such as Revelation 2:10 and Revelation 2:13 indicate a present hostility toward Christians but speak of a future increase of such opposition. Nevertheless, the fact that John had been removed to Patmos is evidence that the governing authorities in Roman Asia were taking action against the Christian church. John had been banished to Patmos because of his powerful ministry of the word of God and witness of Jesus and therefore was viewed by the authorities as a dangerous leader of the Christian sect. His perception of the nature of the imperial cult accordingly was conditioned by his experience, not his prejudice.

4. Content and Structure.

4.1. Introduction (Rev 1). The opening chapter forms an introduction to the book, with a prologue (Rev 1:1-8) and a vision of the risen Christ given to the prophet John (Rev 1:9-20). The former makes known the origin and nature of the book, pronounces the first of seven beatitudes in the work on its readers and hearers, gives a greeting from the triune God, a doxology to Christ and two prophetic sayings stating the theme of the book. The vision that follows contains a commission to John to write what he sees to seven churches in Roman Asia. The description of the risen Lord echoes that of the Ancient of Days in Daniel 7:9 and the powerful angel in Daniel 10:5-6.

4.2. Letters to Seven Churches (Rev 2—3). A series of seven letters to the churches named in Revelation 1:11 is given in Revelation 2—3. They are very brief, reminding us of the eight short oracles of Amos 1—2. The letters have an identical structure: an introductory statement from the risen Christ, drawn from the opening vision and usually pertinent to the contents of the letter; praise for the good qualities of the church and/or criticism of its faults; a promise to the victor relating to the blessings to be bestowed in the kingdom of Christ; and an exhortation to listen to what the spirit is saying to the churches.

4.3. Vision of the Heavenly Throne Room (Rev 4—5). As the vision of Christ in Revelation 1 leads into the seven letters, so the vision of heaven in Revelation 4—5 leads into the main body of Revelation. It initiates the process of events leading to the unveiling of the final kingdom of God (Rev 6—19) and at the same time determines the symbolism of the first series of messianic judgments (Rev 6:1—8:5).

4.4. Seals, Trumpets and Bowls (Rev 6—16). At this point we have to make a decision on how to interpret the relation of the three series of judgments that dominate the major part of the Revelation (Rev 6:1—19:10), portrayed under the symbolism of the opening of seven seals of the document in God's hands (Rev 6:1—8:5), the sounding of the seven trumpets (Rev 8:6—11:19) and the outpouring of seven bowls of wrath (Rev 15—16). These three series of judgments in Revelation have been interpreted as following in chronological sequence (see, e.g., Charles, 1:xxi-ii; Farrer 1964, 9-23; Court, 74-75; Rowland, 416).

There is, however, one major feature of the three series of judgments that makes this interpretation difficult to accept: each of the three series concludes with a description of the day of the Lord, which leads to a revelation of the final kingdom of God. The first series of judgments is closely paralleled with features of the eschatological discourse of Mark 13, although ostensibly it employs the imagery of four riders on horses, adapted from Zechariah 1 and Zechariah 6. The fifth seal reveals the cry of martyrs beneath the throne of God, "How long?" But the sixth seal brings the judgments to a climax as it tells of a great earthquake, the sun becoming black as sackcloth, the moon as blood, the stars falling to earth, the sky vanishing like a rolled up scroll, and every island and mountain being removed from its place. The kings and the mighty call on the rocks of the mountains to fall on them and hide them from the face of God and the wrath of the Lamb, "for the great day of their wrath has come, and who is able to stand?" The passage is made up of citations from OT prophetic descriptions of the day of the Lord (e.g., Is 13:10, 13; 34:4; Zeph 1:14-15), the meaning of which is not the destruction of the universe but a pictorial representation of the terror of the universe when the God of heaven steps forth to judge the world (cf. the last judgment scene, Rev 20:11).

In Revelation 6:12-17 the end of the rebellion of humankind in history has been reached. With the opening of the seventh seal in Revelation 8:1-5 the prayers of the martyrs beneath the throne of God and of the saints on earth are answered, and the accompaniments of the coming of Christ in his kingdom take place (with Rev 8:5 cf. Rev 11:19; 16:17-18).

The judgments of the seven trumpets are described in a similar fashion as those at the opening of the seven seals. The judgments of the first four trumpets are adaptations of those on Egypt at the exodus. They are followed by the announcement of three woes to come on earth, but the third woe is withheld until later, and instead a song of triumph that celebrates the consummation of the kingdom of God is sung in Revelation 11:15-18:

"The kingdom of the world has become
the kingdom of our Lord and of his Christ,
and he will reign for ever and ever."
The twenty-four elders then fall on
their faces and worship God:
"We give you thanks, Lord God Almighty,
who is and who was,
for you have taken your great power
and begun your reign."

Observe that whereas the elders in Revelation 4:8 sing to him "who was, and who is, and who is to come," they now sing of him "who was, and who is," for God has come, and his reign of ultimate salvation in the fulfilled kingdom of God has begun.

The same goal has evidently been reached on the completion of the outpouring of the seven bowls of wrath. A voice from the temple and the throne proclaims, "It is done" (Rev 16:17; cf. Rev 21:6, where the cry signifies that the completion of God's purpose in creation has arrived). It would appear that with the end of each series of messianic judgments, the end of history that precedes the triumph of the kingdom of God has also arrived. A corollary of this element of parallelism is that the period of divine judgments is not elongated into an interminable series of punishments but is a comparatively short period of intensified judgments executed by the Lord of history.

It is, however, important to note that John has linked the three series by a technique that has been variously described as "overlapping or interweaving" (Bauckham 1994, 8-9), "interlocking" (A. Y. Collins 1976, 16-18) or "intercalation" (Schüssler Fiorenza, 172-73). Between the silence in heaven and the offering of prayers to God for the kingdom's coming, the seven angels who are to sound the trumpets are introduced (Rev 8:1-5). After the sounding of the seventh trumpet the opening of the temple of God in heaven is mentioned, and thereby the ark of the covenant is seen (Rev 11:19). Similarly, Revelation 15:5-6 tells of the opening of the temple of the tent of witness in heaven out of which proceed the angels with the seven last plagues, so bridging the extensive gap of Revelation 12—14 (Bauckham 1994, 8-9). By this method of repetition and development John builds up to the advent of Christ in an awe-inspiring climax.

4.5. Interludes: Glimpses of the Church and Its Conflicts (Rev 7; 10:1—11:13; 12—14). Between the three descriptions of the messianic judgments are set episodes that throw light on what happens to the church during the period of tribulation and also the nature of its task.

In Revelation 7, between the opening of the sixth and seventh seals, occur two visions, the first of which recounts the sealing of God's people for protection in the time of trial (cf. Ezek 9:1-11), the second giving a proleptic description of their joy in the final kingdom of God. Likewise, between the sixth and seventh trumpets a more extensive interlude takes place in which John is confirmed in his prophetic ministry (Rev 10) and an oracle reveals the church's vocation to carry out a powerful prophetic witness expected of Elijah and Moses in the last days (Rev 11:1-13). Revelation 12—14 provide the longest interruption in the judgment visions; these chapters set the opposition between the emperor worship and the church in the context of the age-long conflict between the powers of darkness and the God of heaven.

4.6. The City of Antichrist and the City of God (Rev 17:1—22:5). One would have expected that after completing the description of the messianic judgments, John would portray at once the coming of the Christ and his kingdom. Instead, he reveals the doom of the antichristian empire as it falls prey to its own forces of destruction (Rev 17—18) and the praise of God's people and heaven's hosts over it (Rev 19:1-10). Then John is free to describe the coming of Jesus to defeat the enemies of God by his all-powerful word (Rev 19:11—21:3); the kingdom of Christ in the world (Rev 20:4-6); the last vain attempt of Satan to overthrow that kingdom (Rev 20:7-10); the last judgment of the human race (Rev 20:11-15); the new heaven and earth (Rev 21:1-8); and the city of God, the new Jerusalem (Rev 21:9—22:5).

It is important to observe that, strictly speaking, the story of salvation, the new exodus, ends at Revelation 21:8 with its depiction of the new creation. The description of the city of God, the bride of the Lamb, is given in a deliberate contrast to the antichristian city described in Revelation 17. The book of Revelation reaches its climax as the story of the harlot and the bride. It is in truth a tale of two cities!

4.7. Epilogue (Rev 22:6-21). The concluding paragraphs of Revelation sum up and press home on the conscience of the readers and hearers the practical lessons of the book. It primarily emphasizes the authenticity of the book as a true revelation from God and the nearness of the fulfillment of its message.

5. Authorship.

The author makes himself known in the first sentence of Revelation as "his [God's] slave, John." The use of that term *slave* jolts the modern reader, as it did the translators of the King James (Authorized) Version, for although the term frequently appears in the original languages of both Testaments, it occurs once only in the KJV OT (Jer 2:14) and once in the KJV NT (Rev 18:13). Paul began his letter to the Romans, "Paul, a slave of Christ Jesus, called to be an apostle." John wrote in the same way, but whereas he often refers to himself in his book, he never speaks of himself as an apostle (contrast 1 Cor 1:1; 2 Cor 1:1; Gal 1:1; Eph 1:1; Col 1:1).

From the latter part of the second century it was assumed that the Fourth Gospel (*see* John, Gospel of), the letters of John (*see* John, Letters of) and the book of Revelation were all written by John the son of Zebedee. Nevertheless, from early times it was recognized that there are difficulties in that assumption, notably with respect to the differences between the Revelation and the Gospel. The issues were clearly stated by Dionysius, bishop of Alexandria in the third century. He had been disturbed by the spread of millennial teaching in his diocese and wished to discourage it. He therefore sought to establish first that the Revelation is not to be interpreted literally and then to demonstrate that the book could not have been written by John the apostle. He adduced three reasons for the latter position.

First, the author did not claim to be the Beloved Disciple, or brother of James, or an eyewitness and hearer of the Lord, as John the Evangelist did; many Christians had the name John, and there were two Christian leaders of that name in Roman Asia and two tombs in Ephesus that were acclaimed to be the tomb of John.

Second, there are many contacts of thought between the Gospel of John and letters of John, but the Revelation is utterly different from both: "It scarcely, so to speak, has a syllable in common with them."

Third, the style of the Gospel and letters is different from that of the Revelation; the former are written in excellent Greek, but the latter is often ungrammatical and uses barbarous idioms.

While Dionysius has been applauded for his insight in the critical evaluation of the Revelation, the issues are much more complicated than he realized. That he was right on the last point there is no doubt: John does break rules of Greek grammar frequently but not always through lack of knowledge; it has been said that for every solecism in Revelation there is an example of correct linguistic usage (note, e.g., John's refusal to decline the divine name after a preposition in Rev 1:4, immediately followed by the correct use in relation to the seven spirits before God's throne). It is now generally recognized that behind the Revelation is the mind of a Semitic author, one whose native language is Hebrew or Aramaic, but how that relates to the style and language of the book is uncertain.

R. H. Charles held that John thought in Hebrew and wrote in Greek (Charles, 1:cxliii). H. H. Rowley maintained that John's first language was Aramaic and that he thought in Aramaic as he wrote in Greek (a view he communicated in a letter to this author). C. C. Torrey affirmed that John wrote his book in Aramaic and someone else translated it into Greek very literally out of reverence for the master (Torrey, 158). If Torrey's view were adopted, it would complicate discussion on the linguistic differences between the language and style of the Gospel and Revelation. Ironically, however, C. F. Burney wrote a book entitled *The Aramaic Origin of the Fourth Gospel* (Oxford: Oxford University Press, 1922) to demonstrate that the Gospel of John was written in Aramaic and later translated into Greek! It will be appreciated that recent scholars are wary of accepting that whole books of the NT were originally written in Aramaic and translated into Greek. In this case the argument has reached stalemate.

Dionysius's statement that Revelation has scarcely a syllable in common with the Gospel and letters of John is an exaggeration. Part of the problem of determining the relation between the Gospel and Revelation is precisely their differences and likenesses. Both works alone, for example, use the term *logos* (the

"Word") of Christ, both see in the Lamb of God a coalescence of the concept of the apocalyptic Warrior Lamb and the Passover Lamb (see Beasley-Murray 1978, 124-26; and 1986, 24-25, 354-55). Moreover the terms for "witness," "life," "death," "thirst," "hunger" and "conquer" in a spiritual or moral sense occur so frequently in the Gospel and Revelation as to suggest a positive relationship in the area of soteriology between the two works.

Yet these two books almost uniquely express the minds and personalities of two authors. Their works were composed with utmost care and in a peculiarly intricate manner. It is increasingly agreed that the Fourth Gospel contains material that not only has been thought over carefully but also has been preached a great deal through the years, and it displays a firsthand knowledge of rabbinic thought and Greek philosophical theology. Revelation comes from a mind imbued with the OT but also reflects a firsthand knowledge of apocalyptic literature, so that John finds it natural to express himself in this mode of writing.

How then are we to account for the relationships between the two works? Their authors must have been well acquainted. Of late the postulate of a school of John has been put forward to explain the origin of the Johannine writings, which is a highly plausible hypothesis. There is, however, a further feature about this problem: it never occurred to Dionysius that the son of Zebedee may have been John the prophet and not the author of the Gospel.

H. B. Swete, in his discussion on the authorship of Revelation, was impressed with the kinship between the character of John the apostle as he appears in the Synoptic Gospels and what one would expect of John the prophet. He and his brother James were named by Jesus "Boanerges," that is, "Sons of Thunder" (Mk 3:17); John forbade one who was not a member of the apostolic group to cast out demons in the name of Jesus; he wanted to call down fire from heaven on Samaritans who would not give Jesus and his disciples hospitality (Lk 9:52-55); he was a witness of the transfiguration of Jesus and of his resurrection. Swete therefore was inclined to view John the apostle as the author of Revelation and to divorce the problem from that of the authorship of the Fourth Gospel, but he wished to keep an open mind on the issue (Swete, clxxx-clxxxv).

M. Kiddle, forty years later, adopted a similar attitude and stated, "The authorship of the Revelation may prove to be the one mystery of the book which will never be revealed in this world" (Kiddle, xxxvi). W. G. Kümmel, yet another generation after Kiddle, wrote, "We know nothing more about the author of the Apocalypse other than that he was a Jewish Christian prophet by the name of John" (Kümmel, 331). Do we need to know more? In no other book of the Bible is the identity of the author of so little importance, for it is not, as earlier editions of the Bible had it, "The Revelation of St. John the Divine," but the revelation of Jesus Christ to his servant John. The question of authorship is settled not by the name of the person who received the Revelation and wrote it down but by the nature of the work, which in the providence of God completes the canon of the Scriptures as its crown.

6. Expectation of Antichrist.

We have already observed the connection between the emperor cult and the anticipation of the appearance of an antichrist who shall rule not only the empire but also the world. This expectation dominates Revelation 12—14 and Revelation 16—17, passages in which the apocalyptic style reaches its height in Revelation. The imagery of a woman clothed with the sun, with the moon beneath her feet and twelve stars above her head, and a dragon in the sky that throws a third of the stars down to earth clearly reflects ancient sources. These were known not only to writers of the OT but also to all the nations of the Middle East and were utilized in many ways. Common to all of them was the concept of a monster of the sea who fought the gods of heaven and sought to overthrow them. The imagery is clear in such a passage as Isaiah 27:1: "The Lord with his cruel and great sword will punish Leviathan the fleeing serpent, Leviathan the twisting serpent, and he will kill the dragon that is in the sea." The vision of the world empires in Daniel 7 that are symbolized by beasts that emerge from the sea, culminating in a fearful adversary of God and man, is an application of that same imagery to a contemporary tyrant who not only oppressed God's people but also sought world domination.

This symbolism was applied frequently in the OT as a cartoon for oppressive rulers, all of whom were doomed to be overcome by Israel's God, the Lord of heaven and earth. That cartoon was applied by the prophet John to the awaited antichrist emperor. It must be emphasized, however, that John did not look upon the reigning emperor as the antichrist; rather he viewed the emperor cult as preparing the way for an antichrist who would exploit it to the full, in a comparable manner as Paul in 2 Thessalonians 2:7 spoke of "the mystery of lawlessness" as already at work in the world. More precisely, John applied the dragon symbol to Satan (Rev 12), to the antichrist (Rev 13), and to the city and empire over which he ruled (Rev 17).

But John goes further in that he conjoins the antichrist concept with the contemporary expectation of the return of Nero to Rome. This is seen first in his description of the antichrist as smitten by a deadly wound and coming to life after it (Rev 13:3), and then by Revelation 13:18: "Let anyone with understanding calculate the number of the beast, for it is the number of a person. Its number is 666." The possibility of representing a name by a number lies in the fact that Hebrew and Greek did not have separate signs for numbers but used instead letters of the alphabet, so that "a" = 1, "b" = 2, "c" = 3, and so on. On this basis any name could be calculated by adding up the values of its letters. A. Deissmann, for example, cites a graffito on a wall in Pompeii reading, "I love her whose name is 545" (Deissmann, 275).

Through the centuries many names that add up to 666 have been suggested as the answer to the puzzle set by John, but in recent years a large measure of agreement has arisen that the name John had in mind is Nero Caesar in Hebrew. If one asks how Greek-speaking congregations could have known that, the answer is that it almost certainly arose among Hebrew- and Aramaic-speaking Jews; they had no reason to love Nero (the Roman-Jewish war began in his reign), and it would have become common knowledge among the churches, just as *Abba* and *Maranatha* became known among them all. Confirmation of this is found in an alternative reading of Revelation 13:18 in some manuscripts; that is, 616, which is the Hebrew number of the Latin form of Nero. By contrast it was early known among Christians that the name Jesus in Greek totals 888, which represents an advance upon perfection (777), as the antichrist shows a consistent falling below it. That indicates that the antichrist of Satan falls as far short of being the deliverer of humanity as the Christ of God exceeds all the hopes of humanity for a redeemer.

As to the historic Nero, Suetonius reported that when Nero learned that the Roman senate had proclaimed him a public enemy and troops were on their way to capture him, he committed suicide by slitting his throat and was buried in the tomb of his family (Suetonius *Nero* 49-50). This lack of a public burial for Nero led to widespread doubt that he really had died and contributed to the supposition that he had fled to the East. No fewer than three claimants to be Nero rose in subsequent years, one in the year following his death (A.D. 69), the second in A.D. 80 and the third in A.D. 88-89; this last one almost convinced the king of Parthia that he was Nero and nearly led to an invasion of the Roman Empire. Whereas earlier it was often supposed that Nero was still alive, a generation later it was thought that he had risen from the dead and would return to take vengeance on Rome. That is so expressed in the third, fourth and fifth books of the *Sibylline Oracles*.

John made use of this widespread expectation. In Revelation 13:3 he wrote that one of the beast's seven heads "was as it were slaughtered to death," a peculiar way of stating it, "and its deadly wound was healed." This is a reminiscence of Revelation 5:6, where the Lamb is described as "standing as it were slaughtered." The Christ of Satan is plainly a parody of the Christ of God, in this as in all other respects (see Rissi 1966, 66). The adaptation of the Nero anticipation to the coming antichrist appears again in Revelation 17:7-18 but with a different emphasis, in that the beast represents the empire and the antichrist. On the one hand, the beast on which the woman sits "was, and is not, and is to ascend from the abyss and go off to destruction" (Rev 17:8), and on the other hand it is said, "The beast who was and is not is the eighth [head], and is of the seven, and he goes off to destruction."

In light of Revelation 13 the eighth king is plainly Nero, in whom the nature and the destiny of the antichristian empire were embodied. Both share in the likeness of the dragon (Satan), both oppose the Lord and his people, both belong to the "abyss," and both are doomed to suffer the fate of those who make war on the Lamb (Rev 16:14). But one major difference is apparent in the representations of the antichrist in Revelation 13 and Revelation 17: in the former,

the empire receives a boost from the antichrist, so that all in the world, apart from those whose names are written in the Lamb's book of life, receive the mark of the beast and worship him (Rev 13:8, 16-18). In Revelation 17 the fears of many are fulfilled, and the Christ of Satan persuades the kings of the East to join him in attacking "Babylon the Great," and the city is destroyed and burned with fire (Rev 17:15-17). Such is the outcome of the emperor cult. The beast and his allies remain in the hand of the God they defy, and by the impulse of the devil they fulfill the words of God (Rev 17:16-17; on this see Bauckham 1994, 329-417).

One point must be clarified concerning John's use of the so-called Nero myth. There is no question that John looked for Nero literally to return from the dead to fulfill the role of the antichrist. He utilized the current expectation to portray the works of the antichrist as those of *another* Nero, and that for a good reason: Nero was the first Roman emperor to persecute the Christian church, and he did so with such bestial cruelty as to provide a pattern for the beast of Satan to follow in his war with the Lamb (Rev 11:7-10; 13:7; 17:12-14). By his presentation of antichrist as another Nero, John has made it clear that the cult of the emperor is a projection of what will take place when the seeds of its beginning reach their full harvest. It could not be otherwise. The emperor cult, as R. J. Bauckham observed, was a deification of power (Bauckham 1994, 451-52). History, not least in the twentieth century, shows that such deification is capable of reappearing with appalling results. Humankind ignores that to its peril.

7. Purpose of the Revelation.
E. F. Scott described the Revelation as "a trumpet call to faith" (Scott, 174). For the Christians of John's generation, especially in Roman Asia, the exaltation of Rome and the popularity of the emperor cult made the living of the Christian life difficult and the future dismaying, in light of the pressure to join the majority in the celebration of Caesar's divinity and the readiness of informers to report to the authorities their refusal to do so. Yet to yield to such pressure entailed the denial of the Christian faith in its entirety, which was unthinkable. John therefore wrote at the behest of the risen Lord to strengthen the faith and courage of believers, to nerve them for battle with antichristian forces in the world and

to help them to bear witness to the one true Lord and Savior.

The whole book of Revelation is rooted in its portrayal of God Almighty as the Lord of history and his redemptive activity in Christ. So surely as Jesus has accomplished the first and most important stage in the redemption of humanity, so he will complete his appointed task of bringing to victory the kingdom of God and thereby the total emancipation of humanity from the powers of evil. The followers of the Lamb cannot expect to avoid sharing his sufferings; hence the call early in the letters to the churches: "Be faithful until death, and I will give you the crown of life" (Rev 2:10). And that will be to participate in life eternal in the company of God and the redeemed in the eternal city of God.

8. Significance of the Revelation for Today.

The book of Revelation has been an inspiration for the church through the ages, above all when it has known the fierce opposition of ruling authorities. From time to time, however, it has been criticized as a sub-Christian book. R. Bultmann, to cite one example, considered that it presents "a weakly Christianized Judaism" (Bultmann 1955, 2:175). Bultmann's criticism reflects his rejection of all apocalyptic, yet he is aware that the NT presents the atonement as involving both the love and judgment of God. This is seen especially in John 12:31-32 but also in John 3:16-21; on the latter Bultmann made the striking comment, "There would be no judgment at all were it not for the event of God's Love" (Bultmann 1971, 154).

A. Y. Collins cites D. H. Lawrence as asserting that the book vents the anger, hatred and envy of the weaker against the strong, against civilization and even against nature (cited by A. Y. Collins 1984, 169). Lawrence's evaluation of Revelation is typical of his outlook on life, but it is disturbing that Christian exegetes should adopt such a view. Collins considers that John sought to overcome the tension between reality and faith, what is and what ought to be. Faith includes that God is ruler of all, Jesus is King of kings and Lord of all and that in the messianic kingdom all Christians will rule with him. The reality is the power of Rome and the powerlessness of Christians, their fear of denunciation before Roman authorities, their recollection of Nero's persecution, the destruction of Jerusalem and the banishment of John. This led to aggressive feelings of envy of the wealthy, frustration about the emperor cult and desire for vengeance for the violent acts of the empire. But these violent images were transferred to God and Christ in Revelation; hence Jesus will make war with the sword of his mouth against followers of Balaam, Nicolaitans and Jezebel ("fellow Christians"!) as well as the generals and rich and strong (Rev 6:15-17) and the armies that follow antichrist (Rev 19:21; see A. Y. Collins 1984, 156-57).

Much more is written in this vein, which requires more space to answer than is possible here. A few points, however, need to be made. If it is a question of realism, John the prophet has it. The followers of Balaam, the Nicolaitans and Jezebel are not broadminded Christians but those affected by the antinomianism of emerging Gnostics, and their influence had to be opposed. The hostility to the emperor cult is inevitable in any generation, and use of the cartoons derived from the ancient Middle East religions is justified. Regarding the violence in applying the latter, it is essential to recall the tradition of hyperbole used by the OT prophets. An outstanding example is seen in Zephaniah's language. In Zephaniah 1:2-6 the judgments of God are described in terms that involve the destruction of all living creatures on the day of the Lord. That language is repeated in Zephaniah 3:8: "In the fire of my passion all the earth shall be consumed." This is immediately followed by Zephaniah 3:9: "At that time I will change the speech of the peoples to a pure speech, that all of them may call on the name of the Lord and serve him with one accord."

Such contradiction of utterance cannot be taken literally, but the judgment and salvation of the Jews and Gentiles is seriously meant, as the rest of the book makes plain. The like holds good in Revelation, as Revelation 11:10 and Revelation 15:3-4, the survival of earth's inhabitants in the millennium, Revelation 20:4-6, and the kings of the earth bringing their gifts into the new Jerusalem (Rev 21:24-27) indicate. The picture of the city of God in Revelation 21:9—22:5 goes far beyond abating alleged anger and envy of Christians; its ultimate motive is to reveal the fulfillment of God's purpose for his creation in a redeemed humanity in fellowship with himself. In declaring this revelation the prophet John was truly led by the spirit (Rev 19:10). The church today will do well to give heed to the appeal that appears in every one of the letters to the seven churches: "Let anyone who has an ear listen to what the spirit is saying to the churches."

9. Revelation in the Earliest Post-New Testament Writings.

A number of the apostolic fathers indicate the influence of the book of Revelation in their works, though not all do so. *Didache, 1 Clement,* the letters of Ignatius and the letter of Polycarp to the Philippians show little or no reflection of Revelation and are more concerned with the life of the church, its order and *worship. The conclusion of the *Didache* (*Did.* 16) has an "apocalyptic postscript," but it clearly echoes the eschatological discourse of the Gospels (Mark 13 par.) rather than the Revelation. The *Epistle of Barnabas* adopts the interpretation of creation in six days as a figure of the cosmic week of history: the latter lasts for six thousand years and is followed by the sabbath rest of the kingdom of God (*Barn.* 15). This could well be one of the traditions that contributed to John's picture of the millennium. It is also found in *2 Enoch* 33, a book possibly of the same period as Revelation.

The *Visions* of the *Shepherd of Hermas* are also in the apocalyptic tradition. They concern the life of the church and are therefore close to Revelation. The like may be said of the *Similitudes* of *Hermas,* especially in the prominence given to angels, who are represented as responsible for creation, and a good and an evil angel are set over people (*Herm. Man.* 6.2.1; *Herm. Vis.* 3.4.1).

Papias above all was enthusiastic about the millennium. His famous statement relating to the extraordinary fruitfulness of the earth in that time is attributed to "the Lord" as made known by "presbyters who saw John." Vineyards will have "ten thousand vines, and each vine ten thousand branches, and each branch ten thousand shoots, and on every shoot will be ten thousand clusters, and in every cluster ten thousand grapes, and every grape when pressed will yield twenty-five measures of wine." Such growth will apply to wheat grains, fruit trees, seeds and herbs, and animals who eat them will be peaceable to each other and to man (reported by Irenaeus *Haer.* 5.33.3-4). A related but less extravagant statement is found in *1 Enoch* 10:19.

L. Gry suggested that Papias's concept of the millennium was gained from the followers of

Ariston and the elder John. It is evident that Papias's ideas were widespread in the church of his time and led to the endeavor of Dionysius to diminish the influence of Revelation. Nevertheless, the millennial interpretation of Revelation 20 was firmly held by Justin Martyr, Irenaeus, Hippolytus and Victorinus. Origen, however, was "the vehement opponent of millenarianism" (Beckwith, 323). Tyconius in his commentary followed in Origen's steps, and Augustine buried chiliasm by his doctrine of the millennium as the age of the church. Needless to say, the doctrine of the earthly kingdom of Christ has been resurrected in later centuries and espoused by many interpreters.

See also APOCALYPTICISM; ESCHATOLOGY.

DLNTD: ANTICHRIST; BABYLON; BEASTS, DRAGON, SEA, CONFLICT MOTIF; BOWLS; HEAVEN, NEW HEAVEN; JERUSALEM, ZION, HOLY CITY; LAMB; LITURGICAL ELEMENTS; MARTYRDOM; MILLENNIUM; OLD TESTAMENT IN REVELATION; PAROUSIA; PERSECUTION; PROPHECY, PROPHETS, FALSE PROPHETS; SCROLLS, SEALS, TRUMPETS; VISION, ECSTATIC EXPERIENCE; WRATH, DESTRUCTION.

BIBLIOGRAPHY. **Commentaries:** D. E. Aune, *Revelation* (WBC; Dallas: Word, 1997-2000); G. K. Beale, *The Book of Revelation* (NIGTC; Grand Rapids: Eerdmans, 1998); G. R. Beasley-Murray, *The Book of Revelation* (rev. ed.; NCB; Grand Rapids: Eerdmans, 1978); I. T. Beckwith, *The Apocalypse of John* (New York: Macmillan, 1919); M. E. Boring, *Revelation* (IntC; Louisville, KY: John Knox, 1989); G. B. Caird, *The Revelation of St. John the Divine* (HNTC; New York: Harper & Row, 1966); R. H. Charles, *A Critical and Exegetical Commentary on the Revelation of St. John* (2 vols.; ICC; Edinburgh: T & T Clark, 1920); A. M. Farrer, *The Revelation of St. John the Divine* (Oxford: Clarendon, 1964); J. M. Ford, *Revelation* (AB; New York: Doubleday, 1975); W. J. Harrington, *Revelation* (SacP 16; Collegeville, MN: Liturgical Press, 1993); C. S. Keener, *Revelation* (NIVAC; Grand Rapids: Zondervan, 2000); M. Kiddle, *The Revelation of St. John* (MNTC; New York: Harper, 1940); G. E. Ladd, *A Commentary on the Revelation of John* (Grand Rapids: Eerdmans, 1972); H. Lilje, *The Last Book of the Bible* (Philadelphia: Muhlenberg, 1957); J. R. Michaels, *Revelation* (IVPNTC; Downers Grove, IL: InterVarsity Press, 1997); L. Morris, *The Revelation of St. John* (2d ed.; TNTC; Leicester: InterVarsity Press, 1987); R. H. Mounce, *The Book of*

Revelation (Grand Rapids: Eerdmans, 1977); G. R. Osborne, *Revelation* (BECNT; Grand Rapids: Baker, 2002); E. F. Scott, *The Book of Revelation* (London: SCM, 1939); J. P. M. Sweet, *Revelation* (Philadelphia: Westminster, 1979); H. B. Swete, *Commentary on the Book of Revelation* (3d ed.; London: Macmillan, 1909). **Studies:** D. E. Aune, "The Apocalypse of John and the Problem of Genre," *Semeia* 36 (1986) 65-96; R. J. Bauckham, *The Climax of Prophecy* (Edinburgh: T & T Clark, 1994); idem, *The Theology of the Book of Revelation* (NTT; Cambridge: Cambridge University Press, 1993); G. R. Beasley-Murray, *John* (WBC; Waco, TX: Word, 1986); J. G. Bowman, "The Revelation of John: Its Dramatic Structure and Message," *Int* 9 (1955) 436-53; R. Bultmann, *Gospel of John* (Oxford: Blackwell, 1971); idem, *Theology of the New Testament* (New York: Scribners, 1951, 1955); A. Y. Collins, *The Apocalypse* (Wilmington, DE: Michael Glazier, 1979); idem, *The Combat Myth in the Book of Revelation* (HDR 9; Missoula, MT: Scholars Press, 1976); idem, *Crisis and Catharsis: The Power of the Apocalypse* (Philadelphia: Westminster, 1984); J. J. Collins, *The Apocalyptic Imagination* (New York: Crossroad, 1984); J. M. Court, *Myth and History in the Book of Revelation* (Atlanta: John Knox, 1979); A. Deissmann, *Light from the Ancient East* (Grand Rapids: Baker, 1978 [repr.]); A. M. Farrer, *A Rebirth of Images* (Westminster: Dacre, 1949); L. Gry, "Henoch X,19 et les belles promesses de Papias," *RB* 53 (1946) 197-206; C. J. Hemer, *The Letters to the Seven Churches of Asia in Their Local Setting* (Sheffield: JSOT, 1986); W. G. Kümmel, *Introduction to the New Testament* (Nashville: Abingdon, 1975); J. R. Michaels, *Interpreting the Book of Revelation* (Grand Rapids: Baker, 1992); S. Moyise, *The Old Testament in the Book of Revelation* (Sheffield: Sheffield Academic Press, 1995); M. Rissi, *The Future of the World: An Exegetical Study of Revelation 19:11—22:15* (SBT 2d ser.; London: SCM, 1972); idem, *Time and History* (Richmond, VA: John Knox, 1966); C. C. Rowland, *The Open Heaven* (New York: Crossroad, 1982); E. Schüssler Fiorenza, *The Book of Revelation: Justice and Judgment* (Philadelphia: Fortress, 1985); M. H. Shepherd, *The Paschal Liturgy and the Apocalypse* (Richmond, VA: John Knox, 1960); L. L. Thompson, *The Book of Revelation: Apocalypse and Empire* (Oxford: Oxford University Press, 1990); C. C. Torrey, *Documents of the Primitive Church* (New York and London: Harper, 1941).

G. R. Beasley-Murray

REVOLUTIONARY MOVEMENTS. *See* JUDA-ISM AND THE NEW TESTAMENT.

RHETORIC

Throughout the history of biblical studies, especially in the early *church fathers, in German biblical criticism of the eighteenth through the early twentieth centuries, and most recently in the latter part of the twentieth century, the study of rhetoric has been seen as an important background for interpreting the NT. By rhetoric it is usually meant ancient rhetorical theory, which emerged as a specific field of study during the Greek and Roman empires, what is often called classical rhetoric. The Greeks in particular developed *technē logōn* ("art of words/speech"), which was the exploration of human communication through language. This interest in communication is evident in early Greek literature like Homer's *Iliad* and in Greek drama. Various social constructs that emerged in the Greek city-state also contributed to the importance of oral communication with the lawcourt, political assembly and public ceremonies as key contexts for oral discourse. It was in the fourth century B.C. that this oral discourse came to be labeled as *rhētorikē* ("rhetoric"), defined in particular as *peithō* ("persuasion") (Plato, *Gorg.* 453a2).

This article will examine classical rhetoric in order to evaluate its importance as a historical communicative context for the NT.

1. History and Development of Classical Rhetoric
2. The Practice of Rhetoric in the First Century A.D.
3. Jewish Rhetoric
4. The Distinctives of Christian Rhetoric
5. Relevance for New Testament Interpretation Today

1. History and Development of Classical Rhetoric.

1.1. The Sophists and Early Greek Rhetoric (Fifth Century B.C.). In fifth-century Athens, a group of teachers who came to be known as Sophists set themselves up as instructors in wisdom and eloquence in order to help male Athenians succeed in civic life. Their focus was on bringing thought or ideas to expression through techniques of proof or devices of argument revealing the two sides to every question. Their teaching style mostly included imitation of good literature or speeches and memorizing certain rhetorical formulaic devices. Aristotle criticizes their style for lacking art and being unsystematic (Aristotle *Soph. Elench.* 183a-184b).

Some of the key figures are Protagoras, Antiphon, Gorgias and Isocrates, the latter two being the more influential. Gorgias (485-380 B.C.) linked eloquence and virtue as companion qualities. The Gorgias style used parallelism and antitheses expressed in ornate schemes or figures of speech marked by their clever and poetic sound patterns: making the ideas sound good was persuasive. His model speeches that are extant include *The Encomium of Helen* and *The Defense of Palamedes*. Isocrates' (436-338 B.C.) main contribution was to establish rhetoric as a key educational method (see his *Antidosis*). He also laid the foundation for three of the major elements of rhetoric: invention (the thought), arrangement (ways to join them together) and style (ways to adorn the speech) (Isocrates *Soph.* 13.16-17). He downplayed the ornate style of Gorgias and developed the periodic style in which the main subject and/or verb are withheld until the end of the sentence, creating suspense in the listener.

The sophistic approach to rhetoric—wisdom as eloquence is persuasive—continued as a prominent school of rhetoric throughout the history of rhetoric. In fact, there was a period known as the second sophistic, which began around the early second century A.D. In an environment of repressed freedom of speech due to empire politics, rhetoric moved toward oratorical excess in which the emphasis was on style and delivery rather than on content.

1.2. Plato (427-347 B.C.). The move away from the sophistic style to a more philosophical (and moral) rhetoric was inaugurated by Socrates. His pupil, Plato, perfected the Socratic method: using questions and answers in dialogue or dialectic to move toward the truth of an idea. He wrote two works that had an emphasis on rhetoric, *Gorgias* and *Phaedrus*. The earlier work, *Gorgias*, focuses on the orator and by implication contains a fairly negative perspective on rhetoric suggesting it is mostly art without knowledge, a form of flattery that produces pleasure in an audience and plays on the ignorance of the audience (see especially, *Gorg.* 462-66). In the *Phaedrus* there is a more sustained and focused discussion of rhetoric as a subject (see esp. *Phaedr.* 260-64). Plato recognizes the potential for rhetoric to "lead the soul" if practiced with

the correct principles: knowledge, logic, structure (unity of the parts).

1.3. Aristotle (394-322 B.C.). It is in the writings of Aristotle, particularly *Rhetoric*, that rhetoric as a topic is given systematic treatment. Most significantly, rather than positing rhetoric against dialectic (as in Plato's *Gorgias*), he suggests that rhetoric is a counterpoint to dialectic. By so saying, he elevates rhetoric as part of philosophy. *Rhetoric* is not an easy work to understand as it appears unpolished, with an elliptical style, possibly indicating it was a set of lecture notes. Internal contradictions also suggest this and possibly imply the influence of editorial hands in the extant text. Nonetheless, it remains a most significant and foundational treatise. Book 1 is essentially an introduction. He first establishes rhetoric as art (again contra the *Gorgias*) with concomitant uses. Next he sets forth a practical definition of rhetoric: "the ability in each case to see the available means of persuasion" (Aristotle *Rhet.* 1.2.1355b25-26). He sets out proofs as artistic (ethos, pathos and logos) and inartistic (direct evidence). He divides logical proofs into two types: examples (used in inductive arguments) and enthymemes (deductive syllogisms). Next, he proposes a theory of three categories of topics. Finally, he identifies the three genres, or species, of rhetoric: deliberative (a judgment about the future, usually with respect to an action), judicial (a judgment about the past) and epideictic (demonstration in the present of what is honorable). It is his concept of genres that influences almost all future theory on rhetoric. Book 2 examines material premises in depth, first as they relate to the three kinds of discourses, then as they establish ethos, then pathos, followed by a more general discussion. Book 3 looks in detail at forms of argument, in particular, enthymemes. Book 4 studies the language (or style) for presenting proofs. Book 5 discusses arrangement of proofs. Though there is a great deal that is significant, much of the terminology, definitions and categories are not found in later rhetorical theory, possibly due to the book's lack of circulation until his personal library was rediscovered in the first century B.C.

1.4. Development of Technical Rhetoric in the Roman Period (First Century B.C. to Second Century A.D.).

1.4.1. Rhetorica ad Alexandrum. While handbooks on rhetoric are alluded to as early as the fifth century B.C. through to the late classical and Hellenistic periods, the only extant one of this time is *Rhetorica ad Alexandrum* (late fourth or early third century B.C.). It also is important to mention Hermagoras of Temnos, who apparently wrote on rhetorical theory in the late second century B.C. but whose work is lost. From Cicero and Quintilian we know he developed a theory of *stasis*, which sought to determine the question at issue in a speech; this is at the heart of rhetorical invention. Hermagoras provides a key transition from Greek to Roman rhetoric. It is during the Roman period that follows (first to fourth centuries A.D.) that the theory of rhetoric becomes standardized through the influence of handbooks and influential rhetoricians.

1.4.2. Rhetorica ad Herennium. One of the most important works on rhetorical theory in the Roman period is *Rhetorica ad Herennium* (late first century B.C.), written in Latin. It is the earliest extant text that sets out the standard five elements of the practice of rhetoric: invention (identifying the subject, thesis or position to be adopted, and the arguments to be used), arrangement (ordering the components into an effective whole), style (configuring and enhancing the components through the choice of words, figures of speech and various devices), memory (memorizing the speech for effect and naturalness) and delivery (use of the voice and gestures).

One of the important aspects of arrangement was the theory regarding the standard form for the rhetorical speech. Based primarily on the judicial genre, the standard pattern consisted of six parts (Quintilian *Inst. Orat.* 3.9.1-6): *exordium, narratio, partitio, probatio, refutatio, peroratio.* The *partitio* is sometimes seen as part of the *narratio,* and the *refutatio* as part of the *probatio.* The *exordium* is like an introduction, which seeks to set the scene, favorably dispose the audience and establish the ethos of the speaker. The *narratio* is a statement of the case at hand, clarifying the specific question or *stasis* to be addressed. The *partitio,* or *propositio,* establishes the proposition. The *probatio,* or *confirmatio,* marshals arguments in order to confirm through conventional strategies and topics the case being argued. The *refutatio* attacks the proof of the opponent's argument by anticipation or through a response. The conclusion, or *peroratio,* recapitulates the main arguments and appeals for their accep-

tance. Rhetorical criticism then includes the attempt to analyze a speech or text by identifying its various parts (Mack, 41-48).

1.4.3. Cicero (106-44 B.C.). Cicero, who stands in this same tradition, combines sophistic and philosophical rhetoric with technical elaboration. He wrote seven influential works on rhetoric, chief of which are *De Inventione* and *De Oratore.* Cicero not only influenced the theory of rhetoric but also espoused and embodied the duties of a civil orator.

1.4.4. Demetrius. Another important work of this time is Demetrius's *De Elocutione* ("On Style"), which is pseudonymous and of uncertain dating but most likely from the first century B.C. It is primarily a study of the four kinds of style: elevated, plain, elegant and forceful. Unusually, and of interest for NT studies, the section on plain style includes a discussion of letter-writing. He defines a letter as one half of a dialogue, but distinctive from conversation in its more studied character (Demetrius *Eloc.* 224).

1.4.5. Marcus Fabius Quintilianus (c. A.D. 40-96). Quintilian is credited with the longest Latin writing on rhetoric, *Institutio Oratoria,* or *Education of the Orator.* He was a teacher of rhetoric and held an official government-sponsored chair of rhetoric in Rome. After retirement he published his lectures as a treatise extending over twelve books. His work is important because it represents the culmination of technical rhetoric in its standard, even canonical tradition, showing little distinctive innovation but solid and helpful insight on rhetorical theory in general. His work also gives a helpful historical perspective by often providing a historical survey of the subject he discusses. Interestingly, he reveals his direct dependence on both Cicero and Greek classical rhetoric. In Books 1 and 2, he sets the study of rhetoric in a complete educational context from birth to the grammar school, and he outlines the required training and education for a good rhetorician. In Books 3 through 11, he traverses the standard fivefold elements of rhetorical theory and practice. In Book 12 he describes the perfect orator. He gives a very sophistic definition of rhetoric himself, "the knowledge of speaking well" (Quintilian *Inst. Orat.* 2.15.34). For Quintilian, Cicero is the ideal rhetor: "Cicero is not the name of a man, but of eloquence" (Quintilian *Inst. Orat.* 10.1.112).

2. The Practice of Rhetoric in the First Century A.D.

2.1. Rhetoric and Hellenistic Society. It is difficult to discern how widespread the knowledge and practice of rhetoric was in the Greco-Roman world. In the upper spheres of Hellenistic society, among the free citizens and the wealthy, rhetoric played a key role. But this sector of society would comprise, at most, 10 percent of the population, probably less. And the extant literature of this period on this subject tends to be from the important political and cultural urban centers like Athens, Rome, Alexandria or Antioch. As the three genres of rhetoric imply, the main areas of life where important rhetorical oratory operated were the courtroom, the civil assembly and the important public civil and religious celebrations. To those who inhabited this realm of social life, rhetoric was perceived as being everywhere (Dio Chrysostom *Disc.* 27.6; Juvenal *Sat.* 15.110-12). Life in the provinces and rural parts of the empire probably did not experience the place of rhetoric in the same way as the major centers, but there is good archaeological evidence of Hellenistic cities with amphitheaters, gymnasia and markets where speech making was important. Whatever the experience of formal rhetorical theory and practice in Hellenistic society, it did influence many forms of communication.

It must be asked, however, how much the 90 percent knew and understood about rhetorical theory and practice. Even though literacy was more widespread than once thought, the literacy was limited and often very function specific, like letter writing or business accounts. No doubt effective communication was important to all people, and imitation of communication skills and forms of discourse, such as those possibly overheard in the marketplace, would have occurred even without specific technical knowledge and training.

2.2. Rhetoric as Part of the Education Program. An important factor that contributed to the high profile of rhetoric in the upper social spheres was its place as a primary subject in the education program. It is difficult to determine how early in the education of children aspects of formal rhetorical theory were introduced. Between the ages of twelve and fourteen, Hellenistic education appears to have included various composition exercises known as "first exercises," or "preliminary exercises," later known as *progym-*

nasmata. Essentially, a student would begin copying and later imitating various kinds of literature in order to learn a variety of writing techniques and literary or rhetorical concepts, such as fable, tale, chreia (or anecdote), proverb, refutation/confirmation, etc. As each stage was mastered, the exercises increased in length and complexity (see Theon [first century A.D.], Hermogenes of Tarsus [second century A.D.] and Aphthonius of Antioch [fifth century A.D.]). These exercises were the building blocks for the more advanced exercises of declamation, the creation and performance of complete practice orations on assigned topics, either political (*suasoriae*) or judicial (*controversiae*). These advanced were mostly in the next stage of education between the years of sixteen and eighteen. Declamation also became a form of public entertainment during the Roman Empire.

It is clear that mastery of oral communication was very important to the education program, but this program, especially after the age of twelve, was primarily for the wealthy or elite. When certain Latin writers of the first century A.D. discuss the popularity of rhetoric (as in Pliny *Ep.* 3.18.7), they are referring to the interests of the wealthy—it was the people with both the leisure and money who could linger in the marketplace or attend the courtroom or assembly to listen to speeches. So while rhetoric was pervasive in Greco-Roman society, it is unlikely that formal rhetorical theory and skills were widespread among the general population.

3. Jewish Rhetoric.

3.1. Jewish Argumentation. There is no real evidence that Greco-Roman classical rhetorical theory or practice pervaded Jewish literary or oral discourse, though this remains an important area of future research. Jewish discourse had its own literary genres and forms of argumentation. The area where there may be some cultural interchange and influence through rhetoric is the midrashic practice of Halakah (*see* Rabbinic Traditions and Writings). This consisted of applying a statement of law given in the Bible or from oral tradition (midrash) to some aspect of daily life. The process involved oral discourse in which the rabbis and students engaged in lecture, disputation and discussion.

3.2. Rhetorical Analysis of Jewish Oral Discourse. Looking at practice through the rhetorical terms, such as argument, proof, style, delivery and memory, several insights emerge. Generally, argumentation included citing respected authorities, authoritative writings and presentation of facts from life. Proof, as such, was practiced, centered on quoting an accepted scale of authorities. The best style was the clear, logical presentation of correctly cited sources, with the ability to reason out conclusions from them. There is limited use of figures and tropes, but generally the use of such rhetorical devices is condemned. Delivery was based on a loud and clear voice with precision in pronunciation. Though the speaker often planned around the subject area, it appears such discourse was generally extempore with the interruption of questions and arguments providing unplanned diversions. Because of the unpredictable interruptions, memory did not play an important part except through the recall of memorized biblical and Mishnaic material. Reconstructing the practice of such oral discourse is difficult because the sources, generally related to Talmudic writings, postdate the NT period. It is also questionable whether it is appropriate to speak of this form of Jewish discourse in classical rhetorical categories, but it does elucidate the distinctives of Jewish oral argumentation from Greco-Roman rhetoric.

4. The Distinctives of Christian Rhetoric.

4.1. The Appeal to Authority. The general modes of discourse in the NT—Gospels, various forms of epistles and the Apocalypse—are not recognized forms of rhetorical discourse according to the ancient Greco-Roman rhetorical handbooks. Nevertheless, it is clear that the NT texts are written to be persuasive. The question is the means of that persuasion and its distinctive character, if any. In general, the one distinction which many commentators note with regard to Christian rhetoric is its appeal to authority. This authority has been variously defined: *God, Jesus, *Holy Spirit, Hebrew Scripture, Christian tradition. In terms of rhetoric, an additional key question is whether there is a different rhetorical strategy or appeal in the different genres of the NT writings (Kennedy 1984; Mack).

4.2. Radical Christian Rhetoric. G. A. Kennedy, a classical scholar, has posited a definition of Christian rhetoric over against classical rhetoric: "Christian preaching is thus not persuasion, but proclamation, and is based on authority and grace, not on proof" (Kennedy 1980, 127). In a later book, Kennedy refined this wholesale distinction of Christian rhetoric from classical rhetoric to a notion that within the scriptural writings there is Christian rhetoric that uses classical rhetorical persuasion and there is radical Christian rhetoric (Kennedy 1984, 6-8). Still using the idea of Christian rhetoric as proclamation, Kennedy notes that some parts of the Bible "give a reason why the proclamation should be received and thus appeals, at least in part, to human rationality" (Kennedy 1984, 7). Radical Christian rhetoric is different in that it does not appeal to rational argument: "When a doctrine is purely proclaimed and not couched in enthymemes I call the technique radical Christian rhetoric" (Kennedy 1984, 7).

4.3. Distinctive Argumentation. Taking a different approach, B. Mack and A. Eriksson have noted that Christian rhetoric uses authoritative appeals to the Christian kerygma or Christian traditions as a core conviction (Mack, 96-98; Eriksson, 273-76). Where Mack and Eriksson depart is that Mack sees this appeal as outside the cultural conventions of Greco-Roman rhetoric, that is, outside the norms of rationality (Mack, 96-97), and Eriksson sees this appeal as according to such cultural convention, at least in terms of the use of logos, ethos and pathos, and more particularly as appeal to special topics (Eriksson, 273-76). T. Olbricht refers to the distinctive nature of Christian rhetoric as "church" rhetoric (Olbricht, 226-27). By this term Olbricht is hardly dismissing Aristotelian rhetoric; rather, he is asserting that Greco-Roman rhetorical theory is insufficient for fully understanding the nature of Christian rhetoric. But Olbricht, like Mack, Eriksson and even Kennedy, notes that Christian rhetoric is distinctive in that it operates within a particular worldview: "God (through God's son and the Spirit) carries out divine purposes among humans" (Olbricht, 226). Olbricht is happy to use Aristotelian rhetorical theory to analyze Christian rhetoric, but he recognizes that it may not be completely sufficient to ascertain the full gamut of persuasive strategies within the NT writings. What all these scholars agree on is that there is a distinctive form of argumentation, but the question is the degree of correspondence with Greco-Roman rhetorical convention. The question regarding the distinctive nature of Christian rhetoric in the NT writings remains an open question.

5. Relevance for New Testament Interpretation Today.

5.1. Different Rhetorical-Critical Approaches to the New Testament.
The study of the NT that attempts to analyze the rhetoric of the different NT texts is called rhetorical criticism. Assessing the rhetoric of the NT depends on the perspective one adopts about the influence of Greco-Roman rhetorical practice on the NT writings and about the nature of rhetoric. The primary debate is whether the writers themselves intended to use Greco-Roman rhetorical practice or whether they implicitly mirrored the communication context of the Hellenistic period that is to some degree rhetorical in the classical sense, or whether it is entirely inappropriate to use the categories of Greco-Roman rhetoric to analyze the NT writings. Another way to approach the question regarding the rhetorical nature of the NT is to use classical rhetorical categories to analyze the persuasive and argumentative form of the texts, either because that is the intention of the writers or because that was the universal communication practice of the time or because such categories provide a universal or heuristic means for analyzing any argumentation in any age (Stamps, 135-51). An interesting and growing rhetorical-critical perspective is socio-rhetorical criticism, which attempts to interpret and evaluate the rhetoric of the NT as a means to create a new sociocultural construct and as a text within a culture of social and literary convention and ideology (Robbins). There are others who adopt a modern rhetorical perspective to analyze the argumentation, forsaking classical rhetorical categories (Amador).

5.2. Rhetoric and the Genre of the New Testament Writings.
Part of the debate concerning the rhetoric of the NT is focused on the genre of the NT writings (Porter, 507-632). As noted above, epistles, or *letter writing, seemed to be excluded from Greco-Roman rhetorical theory and practice. The Gospels, whether a unique genre or an adapted Greco-Roman genre like *bios* (*see* Gospel [Genre]) also stand outside classical rhetorical theory because of the primary use of narrative discourse. Similarly, Revelation as an apocalypse or revelatory prophetic letter (*see* Apocalypticism) is not a common form of Greco-Roman rhetorical discourse. If these issues regarding genre are so, it is questionable whether such classical rhetorical conventions should be used to analyze the NT texts.

There is no way to solve the debate as to the extent Greco-Roman rhetorical theory and practice has influenced the NT writings. At present, NT rhetorical criticism is practiced from several different perspectives. Rhetoric is part of the literary and communication context of the Hellenistic world that played some role, whether to a large degree or small degree, in the writing of the NT.

See also GOSPEL (GENRE); LETTERS, LETTER FORMS.

DNTB: ARISTOTLE, ARISTOTELIANISM; BIOGRAPHY, ANCIENT; CICERO; DIATRIBE; EDUCATION: JEWISH AND GRECO-ROMAN; EPISTOLARY THEORY; GENRES OF THE NEW TESTAMENT; LETTERS, GRECO-ROMAN; LITERACY AND BOOK CULTURE; SCHOLARSHIP, GREEK AND ROMAN. *DJG:* RHETORICAL CRITICISM. *DPL:* RHETORIC; RHETORICAL CRITICISM. *DLNTD:* RHETORIC, RHETORICAL CRITICISM.

BIBLIOGRAPHY. J. D. H. Amador, *Academic Constraints in Rhetorical Criticism of the New Testament: An Introduction to a Rhetoric of Power* (JSNTSup 174; Sheffield: Sheffield Academic Press, 1999); R. D. Anderson Jr., *Ancient Rhetorical Theory and Paul* (rev. ed.; CBET 18; Leuven: Peeters, 1998); A. Eriksson, "Special Topics in 1 Corinthians 8—10," in *The Rhetorical Interpretation of Scripture: Essays from the 1996 Malibu Conference,* ed. S. E. Porter and D. L. Stamps (JSNTSup 180; Sheffield: Sheffield Academic Press, 1999) 272-301; G. A. Kennedy, *Classical Rhetoric and Its Christian and Secular Tradition from Ancient to Modern Times* (Chapel Hill: University of North Carolina Press, 1980); idem, *A New History of Classical Rhetoric* (Princeton, NJ: Princeton University Press, 1994); idem, *New Testament Interpretation Through Rhetorical Criticism* (SR; Chapel Hill: University of North Carolina Press, 1984); D. Litfin, *St. Paul's Theology of Proclamation: 1 Corinthians 1—4 and Greco-Roman Rhetoric* (SNTSMS 79: Cambridge: Cambridge University Press, 1994); B. L. Mack, *Rhetoric and the New Testament* (GBS; Minneapolis: Augsburg Fortress, 1990); J. J. Murphy, ed., *A Synoptic History of Classical Rhetoric* (Davis, CA: Hermagoras, 1983); T. S. Olbricht, "An Aristotelian Rhetorical Analysis of 1 Thessalonians," in *Greeks, Romans and Christians: Essays in Honor of A. J. Malherbe,* ed. D. Balch, E. Ferguson and W. Meeks (Minneapolis: Fortress, 1990) 216-37; C. Perelman and L. Olbrechts-Tyteca, *The New Rhetoric: A Treatise on Argumentation* (Notre Dame, IN: University of Notre Dame

Press, 1969); S. E. Porter, ed., *Handbook of Classical Rhetoric in the Hellenistic Period 330* B.C.-A.D. *400* (Leiden: E. J. Brill, 1997); V. K. Robbins, *The Tapestry of Early Christian Discourse: Rhetoric, Society and Ideology* (London and New York: Routledge, 1996); D. L. Stamps, "Rhetorical Criticism of the New Testament: Ancient and Modern Evaluations of Argumentation," in *Approaches to New Testament Study*, ed. S. E. Porter and D. Tombs (JSNTSup 120; Sheffield: Sheffield Academic Press, 1995) 129-69; B. Vickers, *In Defence of Rhetoric* (Oxford: Clarendon, 1988); D. F. Watson and A. J. Hauser, *Rhetorical Criticism of the Bible: A Comprehensive Bibliography with Notes on History and Method* (BIS 4; Leiden: E. J. Brill, 1994).   D. L. Stamps

RHETORICAL CRITICISM. *See* RHETORIC.

RICHES AND POVERTY I: GOSPELS

In the first-century Palestinian world the main classes were a relatively small wealthy class and a large, poor, peasant and artisan class, in some contexts referred to as "the people of the land." Judaism dealt with this social disparity by accepting it and encouraging the wealthy to give alms to the poorest of the poor. Jesus, however, saw wealth as a hindrance to entering the *kingdom of God and pronounced a blessing on those poor who were seeking God. He taught his followers a radical ethic of giving based on trust in God and the coming of the kingdom (i.e., an eschatological perspective) and lived out in the context of the new community of disciples. The texts indicate that Jesus is to be understood from within this eschatological perspective as a Jewish sage, not as a lawgiver or a teacher of an unattainable ideal.

1. Rich and Poor in First-Century Judaism
2. Rich and Poor in the Teaching of Jesus
3. Eschatology and the Ethic of Jesus

1. Rich and Poor in First-Century Judaism.

The material in the Gospels on rich and poor is set against a background of the social world of Jesus' day and the response that Judaism was making to that world. It was not without reason that Jesus has more to say on this topic than on almost any other he chose to address.

1.1. The Social World of First-Century Judaism. In the first-century Palestinian world there were essentially two major groups of people, the rich and the poor. The rich included especially the

wealthy high-priestly clans. Consisting of four extended families, they must be distinguished from the lower clergy (e.g., Zechariah of Luke's birth narrative) who were in general poor and felt oppressed by the high-priestly group. It was the chief priests who not only profited from the sacrifices offered in the Temple (the lower clergy officiated for only two weeks a year, while the high-priestly clans were always present) but also controlled the considerable commerce associated with that sacrifice and other religious activities (e.g., the activity noted in Mk 11:15-19).

Another wealthy group was the Herodian family and retinue, whose political power was easily translated into wealth. It has been estimated that Herod and later his family may have owned more than half the land in his dominions. Gifts of land to faithful followers were not unusual.

The third group of wealthy people were the remnants of the older Jewish aristocracy (although much of their land was confiscated by Herod and his sons) and individuals who had become rich through trade, tax farming or the like. To be considered truly rich one had to own land, so a person would purchase landholdings as he became wealthy, but such a person would not farm his own land. Instead, he rented it to tenant farmers and spent much of his time on civic and religious affairs in the city (principally, Jerusalem). This system led to the abuse of tenants and hired laborers, which mistreatment was seen by the wealthy as perfectly legal, but was viewed by the poor as totally unjust (cf. Jas 5:1-6).

A final group of wealthy people were the prosperous merchants who had not yet joined the land-owning aristocracy, although like them they controlled much of the economic life of the country. Both the land-owning and non-land-owning groups were deeply resented by the people of the land. It was no accident that during the Jewish revolt of A.D. 66-70, when the common people got the upper hand in Jerusalem, one of their first acts was the burning of the debt records and the slaughter of many of the aristocrats.

Religiously and socially then, the four groups of wealthy people could be split into two groups: (1) observant Jewish leaders and (2) those wealthy persons associated with the Herodians and Romans, whose power gained them a certain acceptance, but who were considered to be moral outcasts (i.e., "Jews who have made themselves Gentiles"), although obviously one dared not despise them too openly. Both groups at times used their power to oppress the lower classes. The less religious group did it through sheer abuse of power. The observant group justified their oppression through legal interpretation, which in the eyes of Jesus was viewed as more culpable, for it appeared to put God on the side of injustice.

Although there was a small middle class of some of the skilled artisans, land-owning medium-sized farmers and merchants (and socially, although not economically, the lower clergy), the second major social group was the poor, the peasants, the "people of the land" (ʿam hā-ʾāreṣ, although the Hebrew term was also used with a broader meaning, as will be seen below). This group included several subgroups.

The best-off were the small landowners, who tended to lead a precarious life which depended on the harvest. A bad year or two could spell the loss of their land to the wealthy neighbor who lent them seed after the first crop failure. It could also mean the starvation of their family. The tenant farmers were next best-off, although they had to pay their landlord his due before providing for their own families. Worst off were those without land (and without the skills of artisans), the hired laborers and the beggars. They were the truly poor. Their hand-to-mouth existence was considered hardly worth living. Mixed in among these various levels of poorer people were such trades as fishermen and carpenters, whose social level depended on their relative prosperity, even though they were landless. Zebedee, for example, appears to have been relatively prosperous, for he had hired workers on his boats, not simply family. Jesus' family, on the other hand, offered the sacrifice of the poor when he was born (Lk 2:24), but it is possible that when established back in Galilee they may have had a higher (if still modest) standard of living, which skilled work could at times command.

Cultural differences existed among the "people of the land" in that some (perhaps eight percent of the population) were urban-dwellers and thus closer to the life and values of the urban elite, while the rest (i.e., ninety percent of the people) were villagers, a step removed from the urban centers. A village carpenter, for example, would probably have been viewed by his urban fellow-carpenter as a "rustic," for his values would have been more those of the small land-

owner than those of the urban elite.

There were other minor classes in Jewish society. There were some slaves, although in Palestine hired laborers were preferred since slaves had to be cared for in bad years and Jewish ones then released in the Sabbath year. Furthermore, Gentile slaves might convert to Judaism and receive all the rights of Jewish slaves. Slaves tended to be house-servants in the city. There were also Jews who were forced (or chose) to drop out of respectable society and become outcasts ("Jews who had made themselves Gentiles"): tax collectors, hired shepherds, tanners, prostitutes. All except the tax collectors were among the poor, but the tax collectors, even if financially well-off, were never counted among the higher classes.

The poor in Judaism, then, included first of all those who owned no land (a definition based on the OT categories of poor, principally the Levite, the foreigner, the widow and the orphan). But because some non-landowners were wealthy, there was in the NT period also a secondary definition of poor in financial terms (reflected in *m. Peʿa.* 8:7-8, which was recorded by A.D. 250). However defined, the poor lived on the edge of existence even in the best of times, for to be in an agricultural economy without owning sufficient productive land to provide security is to be economically marginal. Yet the first century was not the best of times. Even if they managed to scrape by in normal years, the first century included years of famine, especially in the 40s (Josephus *Ant.* 20.2.5 records one incidence). This threat could never be far from any of the poorer people. Then there were Roman (or Herodian) taxes to pay and on top of that the Law prescribed a tithe (which could amount to from seventeen to twenty-three percent of one's gross income). It is no wonder that the "people of the land" in general were looked down on by the religious as lax in their observance of the Law.

This laxness was not universal in that many of the later rabbis and even the great Pharisaic teachers of Jesus' day appear to have been poor, at least during their time of study and in some cases throughout their life (teachers did not charge for their teaching). Yet most of the Pharisees were urban-dwellers, while most peasants in the village lacked the zeal and discipline of the rabbis or their closeness to the high culture. Their legal observance (and knowledge of the

Law) was minimal and based on village tradition. On the one hand, the choice for them often appeared to be between the piety proclaimed by city-dwellers and starvation. On the other hand, even if they had a desire to follow the Law exactly, their hand-to-mouth existence left little time for study and meditation or for being sure all food was kosher and the tithe (in its Pharisaic sense) meticulously paid.

Thus, virtually all poor peasants were considered among "the masses" or the "people of the land" (*'am hā-'āres*) which was for the Pharisees more a religious than a socioeconomic classification. In the OT it indicates either those who are not aristocrats (the earlier OT material) or non-Jews living within the traditional Jewish land (Ezra-Nehemiah). In rabbinic literature (thus beginning in the NT period) it frequently refers to those who are not observant of the Law as opposed to the Pharisees (and later rabbis). Virtually all rural peasants were included within this category, for, as we have noted, the Pharisees were predominantly town-dwellers. As a result, this pejorative term could include not simply the economically poor, but also somewhat better-off individuals (including the tiny middle class) and even the wealthy, unless they made the effort to follow the Pharisaic concept of purity. In general practice, however, it usually designated the semi-observant masses, the peasant population.

1.2. The Response of Judaism to Social Inequality. Judaism in general did not have any problem with wealth. Possessions were not viewed as evil. Indeed, because of the OT stories of Abraham, Solomon and Job, there was a tendency to connect wealth with the blessing of God (the piety-prosperity equation), but while for the most part this attitude continued in the first century, it was modified in two directions. On the one hand, the empirical observation was made that wealth tended to beget greed and the abuse of power. And in a society in which the supply of wealth was believed to be limited, any gathering of wealth that was not clearly from God was suspected of being done through such abuse (cf. Malina 1981, 75-78). In fact, in the light of the experience of the *righteous under the Seleucid rulers and later the Hasmoneans and Herods, it even appeared that most wealth was gained by injustice and that righteousness tended to make one poor. Some intertestamental writers questioned if there were any wealthy people who

were righteous (Sir 31:3-10). On the other hand, the same authors made it clear that a wealthy person could be righteous or honorable (especially if the wealth had been inherited) and the way that he or she could demonstrate this righteousness was through charity. Thus in Jewish tradition Abraham and Job were singled out as being wealthy persons who were righteous because they excelled in generosity (see *Jub.* or *T. Job*).

The real problem in first-century Judaism was that of poverty, especially the poverty of the righteous. Some anthropologically oriented scholars argue that the poverty that was a problem was that caused by the loss of one's inherited position, whether that position was economically rich or poor. This resulted in the OT categories of poor as noted above (cf. Malina 1981, 84). However, although this may have been true for the OT period, it does not completely fit that of the NT. A number of rabbinic sayings note the economic misery of the life of the poorer peasant (e.g., *Lev Rab.* 34:6 on Lev 25:25; *b. B. Bat.* 116a; *b. Sanh.* 151b). As it was later expressed, "There is nothing in the world more grievous than poverty—the most terrible of all sufferings. Our teachers said: all sufferings are on one side and poverty is on the other" (*Ex R.* 31:12 on Ex 22:24). Furthermore, the Jesus tradition (e.g., Lk 6) contrasts the poor, not with the greedy or the wicked (as in the OT), but with the rich, showing that economic issues had become more important. James also exhibits this pattern. Economic lack was a problem, even if inherited social status was not ignored.

The first response of Judaism to the poor was to encourage the voluntary sharing of wealth, for outside of assistance from a person's extended family, charity or almsgiving was the only form of social assistance available. Governments of that day only intervened, if at all, when mass starvation was threatened (and in those cases the motives were to preserve future tax revenues and prevent social unrest). Almsgiving included (1) private charitable actions (e.g., giving to a beggar, forgiving a debt, providing for the proper burial of an impoverished person), which in the case of the wealthy could include significant aid to large areas (Queen Helena of Adiabene, for example, sent major food aid to Jerusalem in the 40s); (2) group charitable actions (i.e., those organized through a village council of elders or a synagogue); (3) religious charity (e.g., the charitable fund collected and distributed through the Temple). Later Judaism would develop a highly organized system of collection and distribution of charity. In the first century, however, individual initiative in almsgiving was the primary force.

The giving of alms was therefore viewed by Judaism in general as a very important righteous work in the eyes of God. In fact, in rabbinic Judaism only meditation on Torah could have outranked charity as a righteous deed. Deeds of charity were seen as greater than all the commandments (*b. B. Bat.* 9a, b) and defended the giver before God whenever Satan tried to accuse him (*Ex Rab.* 31:1). In other words, almsgiving was so significant that the term "righteousness" became synonymous with the giving of alms. Because of this, "The poor do more for the wealthy than do the wealthy for the poor," for the poor provide the righteous with a means of gaining merit with God (*b. Šabb* 151b). On the negative side, evil comes upon Israel because of the neglect of obedience to the OT laws of giving to the poor (*m. ʾAbot* 5:9). One does not know exactly how much of this attitude can be attributed to the time of Jesus, but charity was certainly highly ranked: "Upon three things the world stands: the Law, worship [i.e., the service of God, including obedience], and deeds of loving-kindness [i.e., alms giving and other charitable acts]" (*m. ʾAbot* 1:2); in fact, charity is equivalent to sacrifice and atones for sins (Sir 35:1-2; 3:3-4).

At the same time, at least in rabbinic circles, the giving of alms was not viewed as a means of changing a person's social status, but as a means of rescuing him or her from the misfortune into which they had fallen and restoring them to their former station in life. Differing social status itself was not viewed as a problem. Thus a peasant who needed alms would not be supported at the same level as an impoverished aristocrat. For example, there is the (possibly apocryphal) story about Hillel, a contemporary of Jesus, who upon discovering that an impoverished member of a noble family was traveling, arranged that he be provided with a horse. But there was no servant to run in front of the man, so the rabbi himself took the role so the man could travel in the style appropriate to his rank (*b. Ketub.* 67b). This is certainly charity, but it is a charity that took social rank into account. Thus, while almsgiving was not to raise persons above their normal social rank, it might restore a noble person to his or her rank and fortune (e.g., an appropriately generous dowry might be provided so that a woman might marry at her accustomed status level).

Yet at the same time, there was, as noted above, a social status below which life was miserable. Thus, we find that people who fall below a certain level (defined in *m. Peʾa* 8, some discussions of which are first century) are always subjects of charity, whether it is their inherited status or not. In other words, once people were separated from inherited land the traditional social distinctions began to break down and economic ones started to take their place.

Charity was covered by a number of areas of Jewish Law, not simply the encouragements to almsgiving. Observant Jews not only gave the poor tithe in the third year and alms throughout the year, but also allowed the poor to glean in their fields and left their fields fallow one year in seven with the poor being allowed to gather what grew of itself. The repeated OT theme of caring for the poor was not lost in later Judaism, even if it was regulated.

At the same time, there was a recognition that even with plenty of charity the rich and powerful would tend to oppress the righteous. In other words, in this world righteousness tended to make one poor. This led to two final responses. First, the community of the righteous was in all likelihood the community of the poor (this identification is made explicitly in the *Dead Sea Scrolls and in the Pharisaic *Psalms of Solomon*). It is this community that must exercise generosity. Second, wealth will come to the righteous, but not in this age. God will redress all wrongs in the age to come, when the righteous poor of this age will reap the reward of their charitable deeds. This eschatological piety-prosperity equation is also important in considering the teaching of Jesus.

2. Rich and Poor in the Teaching of Jesus.

Jesus fits into the social situation of first-century Palestine as we have come to know it. He himself belonged to the people of the land as the son of a carpenter who owned neither inherited land nor land he had acquired himself (Mt 8:20; Lk 9:58). He was not an officially recognized teacher, but a charismatic leader with a ragtag group of followers (which explains the negative response to him in Nazareth, where his class origins were well known, Mk 6:3). He accepted the outcasts of society and was frequently found associating with the poor. This provides the immediate context for his teaching.

That teaching is reported in the Synoptic Gospels (the Fourth Gospel having relatively little to say on this topic). While Mark has some significant narratives and sayings on the issue, the vast majority of the teaching is found in *Q material, blocks of which occur in Matthew 6 and in Luke 6, 12 and 16. Of the two Gospels Luke has both more material than Matthew and a stronger form of the material which both include. For example, Luke includes woes along with his Beatitudes (Lk 6:20-26), which sharpen the teaching by explicitly stating the obverse. Therefore it can be said fairly that Luke has a special interest in the topic (which is the reason that most of the studies on Jesus' economic teaching focus on Luke), although the same general attitude is shared by Matthew and perhaps also by Mark. The three Evangelists give a consistent picture of Jesus' attitude toward wealth and poverty. Furthermore, the viewpoint they share is consistent with the ancient Mediterranean view that goods are limited and that collection of wealth by some implies the loss of basic subsistence for others. Yet Jesus does not accept inherited wealth to the same degree that his contemporaries did.

2.1. The Danger of Wealth. While Jesus never looks on possessions *per se* as evil (he was not a dualist), for him wealth was not something safe, but a dangerous substance. In many of his sayings it is personified as Mammon (which in the Aramaic of Jesus' day meant simply "possessions" and could be viewed as evil or neutral, depending on its modifiers) and functions exactly as the idols did in the eyes of ancient Hebrew prophets in that it seductively draws people away from total allegiance to God. For example, in the parable of the sower (Mk 4:18-19) it is "the deceit of wealth and the desires for other things" that come in and choke the word, making it unfruitful, just as if it had been snatched by Satan or burned out by persecution. Here wealth is personified and acts with effects similar to that of personal evil (i.e., Satan), although in a slower, less dramatic way. It draws the person away from God.

The issue is not simply a matter of giving both possessions and God their proper place. Both God and possessions (i.e., Mammon) claim a person's service. Mammon's claim is evident:

wealth must be preserved; daily bread must be earned. Yet Jesus categorically rejects that there is a proper service of Mammon: It is impossible to serve both money and God (Mt 6:24).

This impossibility is underlined by his next point, for, far from being a mark of divine favor, wealth makes it impossible to enter the kingdom. This constitutes a total denial (at least in the terms of this world) of the piety-prosperity equation. This idea is presented in a number of ways. The Markan story of the rich young man ends in all three Synoptics with the comment, "It is easier for a camel to go through the eye of a needle than for a rich man to enter the kingdom of God" (Mk 10:25). This clearly means that the salvation of the rich is an impossibility. Can such folk never be saved? "All things are possible with God," responds Jesus to the shocked question of his disciples. Luke follows his version of this story with the Zacchaeus narrative (Lk 19:1-10), which shows the impossible taking place. But this does not leave Zacchaeus rich (i.e., his possession of riches is not neutral), for in the process Zacchaeus gives up his wealth. It is only when he announces this intention that Jesus responds, "Salvation has come to this house today."

Jesus also emphasizes the impossibility of serving both God and money in his parable of the rich man and Lazarus (Lk 16:19-31). Abraham says to the rich man in Hades, "In your lifetime you received your good things . . . but now . . . you are in agony." This fits with the woe of Luke 6:24, "Woe to you who are rich, for you have already received your comfort." In the parable the woe receives a literal pictorial presentation, showing that to hold on to one's comfort today is to risk damnation tomorrow.

Finally, the parable of the rich fool (Lk 12:16-21) emphasizes once again that one cannot serve both God and Mammon. The rich man in the story, who simply has the good fortune of a bumper crop, prudently takes the excess of the present and stores it for the future, rejoicing that his future will be free from financial worry. That worldly prudence qualifies him in Jesus' eyes as a fool. The mere possession of this windfall condemns him. He has stored up for himself instead of giving to the poor (and thereby becoming "rich toward God").

2.2. The Only Healthy Use of Wealth Is in the Care of the Poor. In both of the parables cited above there are implied alternatives to the behavior of the rich. The first man could have cared for Lazarus, having both the means (the parable notes that he had plenty) and opportunity (Lazarus lay at his gate and was known to the rich man, cf. Lk 16:23-24). As for the rich fool, Luke defines what is meant by being "rich toward God" when a dozen verses later he concludes the section on the topic of wealth with, "Sell your possessions and give to the poor" (Lk 12:33). This interpretation of what one is to do with surplus is a consistent theme in the teaching of Jesus (and of the rest of the NT). If one has more than enough, the best thing to do with it is to give it to those who have less than enough and so invest in heaven.

Another example of this teaching is found in Luke 16:9 in which Jesus states, "Make friends for your selves by means of unrighteous Mammon ["worldly wealth" NIV], so that when it is gone, they will welcome you into eternal dwellings." In context this probably means that one should care for the poor with one's wealth ("make friends for yourselves") so that when one dies ("when it is gone," left behind at death) those poor welcome their benefactor into heaven ("eternal dwellings").

This teaching, of course, is in line with the Judaism of the period. Wealthier persons demonstrated their righteousness by caring for the poor, just as Job and Abraham (or, for Christians, perhaps Joseph of Arimathea or Barnabas) had done before them. Within their Mediterranean culture this both demonstrated the virtue of their class and showed that their wealth was not gained by injustice. Jesus differed from the Judaism of his day not in the high value he placed on charity but in the extent of the charity he required and the basis on which he founded his demand.

2.3. God Has a Special Interest in the Poor. Jesus was no ascetic. There is no glorification of poverty for its own sake nor a masochistic enjoyment of want. Indeed, Jesus consistently pictured the consummation of the kingdom as a time of plenty, and he was known as a person who enjoyed a party (e.g., Mt 11:19, not to mention Luke's well-known banquet theme; *see* Table Fellowship), so he was certainly not against good food and drink, even if he might be a guest who could make a host uncomfortable.

At the same time Jesus clearly stated that God has a special interest in the poor, a teaching that builds on God's care of the poor in the OT. For

example, in both Luke and Matthew one finds him describing his mission in terms of Isaiah 61:1-2 with specific reference to the poor having good news announced to them (Mt 11:5; Lk 4:18-21). These poor are surely the "people of the land" to whom he sends his disciples in Matthew 10:6-7. And it is on these poor that he pronounces, "Blessed are you poor, for yours is the kingdom of God" (Lk 6:20). While Matthew 5:3 has a different version of the saying, "Blessed are the poor in spirit," the sense is similar once one realizes that in Luke Jesus is addressing the poor who are following him and in Matthew he is speaking of the poor who display the (OT) spirit of the poor, that is, those who are seeking and depending on God (cf. 1QM 14:7, where the Hebrew equivalent of this phrase occurs).

Some scholars, however, question whether these are the materially poor or the metaphorically poor. Is not the phrase "I am poor and oppressed" used in the Psalms by individuals who are materially well-off? Has not the term *poor* become by the time of Jesus simply a synonym for Israel as an oppressed and helpless people? Certainly, as noted above, there is a spiritual qualification of the poor being addressed. It is also clear that in such intertestamental works as the *Psalms of Solomon* and the Dead Sea Scrolls, the term "poor" had come to designate the Pharisaic and Dead Sea communities respectively as the pious remnant of Israel. Finally, it is clear that some among Jesus' band of disciples were not poor to the extent of being destitute, even if they were not necessarily well-off (e.g., Peter and Andrew owned a house; James and John came from a reasonably prosperous family; Matthew/Levi, while not necessarily a wealthy tax collector, is reported to have afforded a feast for Jesus).

Yet, taking all of this into account, the term "poor" always carries with it a sense of the experience of oppression and helplessness or, as B. Malina put it, the inability to maintain inherited status. A person who was comfortable and secure would not be termed "poor." The disciples had left their relative security to identify with the insecurity of Jesus. The sects who referred to Israel as "the poor" were in fact experiencing oppression by the ruling classes. Even in the Psalms the term is used only if the psalmist feels helpless; he may in fact have money, but it is of no use to him in his need. In his helplessness he calls upon God to look on him with the special concern that the Law and Prophets proclaim God has for the poor. Thus the so-called metaphorical use of "poor" is not entirely metaphorical; it always contains an element of real suffering and insecurity, even if the suffering is not necessarily economic, but is instead a physical threat.

In the case of the two Beatitudes, groups experiencing real impoverishment are blessed. While one could be materially poor without receiving this blessing because of not following Christ or having the right spirit, there is no intention in either these or any similar passages that one can hold onto wealth or other security and yet claim such blessings because one's spirit is "poor." It is significant that the blessings are never pronounced on the rich, either in this passage or elsewhere. And in Luke this distinction is underlined by a curse on the rich three verses later (because "you have already received your comfort;" i.e., because they have maintained their wealth, not because of any other injustice). Again, it is "the poor, the maimed, the blind and the lame" whom God is inviting to his messianic banquet, while the wealthier people (who can afford to purchase fields and oxen) are excluded (Lk 14:21).

If people have their own security, they have no need for the "good news" Jesus preaches to the poor. Jesus not only quotes from Isaiah 61:1-2, with its theme of good news to the poor, release for prisoners, sight for the blind and release for the oppressed, he enacts it in his ministry. He gives sight to the blind and releases those who are bound and oppressed (which in Luke refers to his casting out demons, although the freedom of his new community of disciples was surely experienced as another form of release). And while there are wealthy people who receive the kingdom, the only ones mentioned in the Gospels are those like Zacchaeus, who are engaged in acts of generosity (and thus identify with the suffering). Those who refuse to so humble themselves are turned away.

Is Jesus then proclaiming a time of Jubilee (Lev 25:8-55) when he proclaims "the year of the Lord's acceptance"? Does this mean a time of economic redistribution of wealth? While this possibility is attractive and while Luke certainly sees the ideals of Sabbath and Jubilee years realized in the early church (Acts 4:34; cf. Deut 15:4), this is unlikely. Such an interpretation hangs on too narrow a linguistic base and focus-

es Jesus' concerns too exclusively on economic and class issues. There is a realization of the Jubilee ideal, but in terms much broader than those envisioned in the OT literature and without its specific regulations.

The language of Jesus is not class language, which would include all materially poor Israelites within it and exclude all materially rich Israelites. If that were the case, he would surely have had to define how poor one had to be to qualify. But at the same time it is not spiritual language, which speaks only of an inner condition without reference to outer circumstances. Rather, it refers to those actually experiencing oppression and helplessness in one form or another, or those identifying with this group by giving up their own security and generously sharing what they have.

2.4. Caring for the Poor Earns Eternal Reward. If God has a special concern for the poor (which is clear even in the OT where God proclaims himself the special protector of the classic Israelite poor—the widow, the orphan and the alien), one would expect that his followers would also display this concern. Jesus argues for such a conclusion by noting that it is treasure in heaven that is lasting (Mt 6:20; Lk 12:32-34; Luke makes it clear that people put treasure in heaven by "sell[ing] your possession and giv[ing] to the poor," while Matthew is content to simply use the phrase which was well known to his Jewish audience). The reason given for such radical action is that the heart naturally follows the treasure, so treasure in heaven means a heart fixed on heaven, while treasure on earth equally means a heart fixed on earth. Jesus' own practice must have followed his advice, for John 13:29 indicates that almsgiving ordered by Jesus was what the disciples suspected Judas was about when he left them. It was apparently a customary action, for it is presented as a natural assumption on the part of the disciples.

Charity, however, is not simply a matter of making sure that one's heart is in the right place or getting rid of a dangerous substance. It earns a reward. Just as the rich man is condemned for not practicing charity toward Lazarus and the rich fool for not putting treasure in heaven, so in the context of a banquet the promise is held out to those who invite the poor to their feasts: "You will be repaid at the resurrection of the just" (Lk 14:14). It is likely that Jesus is here applying Proverbs 19:17, "He who is kind to the poor lends to the Lord, and he will reward him for what he has done."

2.5. Radical Trust in God Is the Basis for the Ability to Give Up Wealth. The call of Jesus is radical with its point-counterpoint of "do not invest on earth—do invest in heaven," but it is based in an equally radical promise, "Seek first his kingdom and his righteousness, and all these [material] things shall be yours as well" (Mt 6:33). Likewise, the promise "Fear not, little flock, for it is your Father's good pleasure to give you the kingdom" precedes "Sell your possessions" in Luke 12:32-33. Those who are convinced that their heavenly Father will indeed care for them are also those who are able to give freely. Conversely, the lack of trust in the Father (including doubting the goodness of his will) leads to the need to provide for one's own security, to serve Mammon.

Jesus suggests that even on the level of creation people ought to realize that they can trust God, for if God cares for the birds without their providing for their own security and if he clothes the lilies with beauty, surely he is more concerned about his human children (Lk 12:22-31). Furthermore, human anxiety and attempts at providing for security are useless anyway (Mt 6:27). Instead, what counts is the assurance that "your heavenly Father knows that you need them all" (Mt 6:32; Lk 12:30). Renunciation flows out of security, not out of demand. But security is rooted in the knowledge of the Father, not in what is physically present.

It is at this level that the Fourth Gospel supports the teaching on rich and poor found in the Synoptics. While the language of wealth and poverty is almost entirely absent (occurring only in two passages in Jn 12—13), the language of radical trust in God is not. For example, John's Jesus argues that after the resurrection, "my Father will give you whatever you ask in my name." This asking and receiving is so that "your joy will be complete" (Jn 16:23-24). Such joyful dependence on the Father, underlined multiple times in the surrounding chapters along with the insistence that the Father loves them, is the foundation on which the carefree generosity of the Synoptics is based.

2.6. The Primary Context of Renunciation Is in the New Community. Jesus' whole life and teaching took place within the context of the social world of first-century Judaism in which a person was embedded in a social matrix, a community.

Within modern Western individualism, much of what Jesus taught on wealth and poverty appears to be nonsense. But given that his followers assumed that Jesus was correct in his teaching that the kingdom of God had come, it made good sense. As the Pharisees, the Dead Sea community and even the Zealots invited people to join a supportive community that pointed to the new order that was coming, so Jesus invited those who accepted his message into a new social world. They were to become his followers, part of the renewed community. The disciples left what they had, but they did so to follow Jesus, to be part of his band. The rich young ruler is not called simply to sell what he has and give to the poor, but to do that and then "follow me." In other words, the call of Jesus to radical generosity is at one level an individual decision, but its context is that of a call to community in line with the function of voluntary communities within his society.

Much of the teaching of Jesus can only be understood within this context. For example, the parable of the sheep and goats (Mt 25:31-46) is entirely related to community. People are certainly judged according to their charitable acts (all of the acts mentioned would have been viewed in Judaism as varieties of almsgiving), but the focus is on their acts of charity toward "one of the least of these brothers of mine" and not toward the poor in general. While it is clear that the charitable actions of Jesus and his followers (especially their healings and other miracles) extended beyond their own group, most of the concrete actions named have to do with actions toward his followers. This is true even for the offering of the proverbial "cup of cold water."

Likewise, the promises of Jesus are primarily addressed to his followers. The "you poor" of Luke 6 is put into the context of his "looking at his disciples." The Beatitudes of the Sermon on the Mount are spoken when "his disciples came to him." There is no blessing spoken to poor who are not disciples, although there is some type of blessing for anyone, rich or poor, who, though they are not his disciple, comes to the aid of a disciple (Mk 9:41; Mt 10:40-42).

Finally, the blessings pronounced by Jesus are primarily received within the context of the eschatological community (i.e., the band of disciples). When Peter notes that, unlike the rich man, "we have left everything to follow you," Jesus responds that he and the other disciples will receive "a hundred times as much in this present age" and "in the age to come, eternal life" (Mk 10:28-30). The reception of "one hundred times as much" (with persecutions added) refers not to an individual's personal reward but to their sharing in the wealth of the community. In anthropological terms, they receive a new network of dyadic relationships. It is as the disciples form a new extended family that each receives a larger family than they left behind. It is as the discipled community shares among itself that each member has access to much more than they gave up. Conceivably, this could also be said about heavenly reward. Certainly, at least on the level of temporal reward, without this community emphasis the teaching of Jesus easily degenerates into an ethic of personal fulfillment.

3. Eschatology and the Ethic of Jesus.
It is well known that Jesus' teaching was set within a context of expectation of the kingdom. Jesus came announcing that the time of fulfillment had come and that the kingdom of God was at hand. Each of the promises about the provision of the Father as well as the blessings of the Beatitudes, contains the command to seek the kingdom or the promise of the kingdom. God had broken into history in a decisive way; now was the time for radical change.

Given this context it is possible to read the ethic of Jesus in four different ways. First, following A. Schweitzer and others, we might view it as an interim ethic established in the face of the soon-to-appear kingdom. This perspective views Jesus' teaching about rich and poor as totally conditioned by his end-time expectation, an expectation that was not fulfilled. Thus the ethic was irrelevant to later generations in the church. Yet it does not appear that this was the position taken by the first interpreters of Jesus, for the Gospels were certainly written a generation into the Christian movement and such works as the Epistle of James demonstrate a relatively literal application of the teaching of Jesus.

Second, we can view it as an ideal ethic designed either to force Jesus' contemporaries to confront their own inability and their need for grace (so in part, R. Guelich) or to take effect when the kingdom would be consummated. The test of this position is to observe whether or not Jesus' disciples practiced his teaching literally or whether Jesus himself accepted it as an unat-

tainable ideal for them. Furthermore, one can ask whether the early church so understood Jesus (recognizing that the Gospels were their books and that they were responsible for shaping the tradition).

Third, is to see Jesus as giving a literal guideline to a particular group of followers. For communal Anabaptists this was a literal rule binding on all Christians who wish to walk in the way of full discipleship. For monastic orders this "gospel perfection" was only incumbent on the religious who wished to forsake the world and live the fullness of Christian life. In either case there is the implication that those who do not divest themselves of wealth and give to the poor are at best second-class followers of Jesus.

Fourth, we might understand his teaching as an ethic to be lived in the light of eschatology. The premises for this reading are: (1) the kingdom is in fact the wave of the future in the sense that, although it is unseen (except in the various signs of its coming), it is actual and the present observable features of this age are going to pass; (2) the Father in fact does love and care for his own; and (3) the Holy Spirit (promised in the Gospels) frees the follower of Jesus to respond to his demand. In light of these factors the application of Jesus' teaching on rich and poor to life in Christian community makes sense.

Related to the consideration of any of these positions is the fact that it is unlikely that Jesus is giving a new Law. In fact, only the third of these positions would suggest something like that. In the Gospels one discovers that Peter still owned a house (Mk 1:29) and that women of means continued supporting Jesus, apparently not ridding themselves of wealth in one act (Lk 8:3). They evidently understood Jesus to be speaking in the black-white hyperbole of a Jewish sage (as in Proverbs) or storyteller, rather than in the stark literalism of a lawgiver.

In fact, these and other examples show two things. First, while the disciples "left all" and followed Jesus, they did not necessarily renounce their possessions totally, although their decision did involve considerable economic loss and risk as well as trust in Jesus. Second, their joyful and generous giving was precisely that. It was not a rule enforced on them. For example, the narrative of the anointing at Bethany (Mk 14:1-9; it is found in all Gospels except Luke, who at best has it in quite a different form) shows quite a different type of generosity. The anointing of

Jesus "for burial" was certainly a radical act of giving (even an act of charity, if the burial idea was in any way conscious in the woman's mind, which is unlikely), but it was enacted toward Jesus, not toward the poor (which offended the disciples, and in John's Gospel especially offended Judas). There is certainly no suggestion that it would have been good for the woman to have kept the ointment for her own security. The issue for the Evangelists is the proper direction of the extravagant act. Jesus suggests that he took precedence over the poor; the eschatological moment took priority over all other demands. This is hardly the word of a lawgiver in any conventional sense.

The test of these positions, then, is threefold. First, we must look within the Gospels and ask how Jesus' contemporaries could have interpreted his message, a task that has been attempted in part above. Second, we must look at the Gospels (and perhaps along with them Acts as being of one perspective with Luke) and, realizing that they were foundation documents for Christian communities, ask if there is anything in them or in the NT epistolary literature that might direct us toward understanding this teaching as anything other than a command of the Founder to be practiced. Third, we must look at the early interpretations of the Christian tradition (e.g., Paul in 2 Cor 8—9; 1 Tim 6; James) and see if they agree with the perspective of Jesus or in some way mitigate the sharp edges of his teaching (*see* Riches and Poverty II & III).

None of these considerations will remove the aspect of eschatology from Jesus' teaching on rich and poor. But they will show how eschatology (and, in Paul and others, the gift of the *Spirit as the down payment on the eschatological future) was related to ethics in the early Christian tradition. We will then be better able to interpret that tradition for today.

See also ETHICS; RIGHTEOUSNESS.

DJG: TAXES.

BIBLIOGRAPHY. E. Bammel, "πτωχός κτλ," *TDNT* 6:885-915; C. L. Blomberg, *Neither Poverty nor Riches: A Biblical Theology of Possessions* (NSBT; Downers Grove, IL: InterVarsity Press, 1999); R. A. Cassidy, *Jesus, Politics, and Society* (Maryknoll, NY: Orbis Books, 1978); B. Chilton and J. I. H. McDonald, *Jesus and the Ethics of the Kingdom* (Grand Rapids: Eerdmans, 1987); P. H. Davids, "New Testament Foundations for Living More Simply" in *Living More Simply*, ed. R. J.

Sider (Downers Grove, IL: InterVarsity Press, 1980) 40-58; J. R. Donahue, "Two Decades of Research on the Rich and Poor in Luke-Acts" in *Justice and the Holy: Essays in Honor of Walter Harrelson*, ed. D. A. Knight and P. J. Paris (Atlanta: Scholars Press, 1989) 129-44; J. Eichler et al., "Possessions, Treasure, Mammon, Wealth," *NIDNTT* 3:829-47, 852-53; H.-H. Esser and C. Brown, "Poor," *NIDNTT* 3:820-29; R. T. France, "God and Mammon," *EvQ* 51 (1979) 3-21; R. A. Guelich, *The Sermon on the Mount* (Waco, TX: Word, 1982); M. Hengel, *Poverty and Riches in the Early Church* (London: SCM, 1974); L. J. Hopps, *Being Poor: A Biblical Study* (GNS 20; Wilmington: Michael Glazier, 1987); J. Jeremias, *Jerusalem in the Times of Jesus* (London: SCM, 1969); L. T. Johnson, *Sharing Possessions: Mandate and Symbol of Faith* (Philadelphia: Fortress, 1981); D. B. Kraybill, *The Upside-Down Kingdom* (Scottdale, PA: Herald, 1978); H. Kvalbein, "Jesus and the Poor," *Themelios* 12 (1987) 80-87; B. J. Malina, *Christian Origins and Cultural Anthropology* (Atlanta: John Knox, 1986); idem, *The New Testament World: Insights from Cultural Anthropology* (Atlanta: John Knox, 1981); idem, "Wealth and Poverty in the New Testament and Its World," *Int* 41 (1987) 354-67; W. E. Pilgrim, *Good News for the Poor* (Minneapolis: Augsburg, 1981); J. S. Pobee, *Who Are the Poor? The Beatitudes As a Call to Community* (RBS 32; Geneva: WCC, 1987); D. P. Seccombe, *Possessions and the Poor in Luke-Acts* (SNTSU; Linz: Fuchs, 1982); T. E. Schmidt, *Hostility to Wealth in the Synoptic Gospels* (JSNTSup 15; Sheffield: JSOT, 1987); L. Schotroff and W. Stegemann, *Jesus and the Hope of the Poor* (Maryknoll, NY: Orbis, 1980); E. Schürer, *The History of the Jewish People in the Age of Jesus Christ* (Edinburgh: T & T Clark, 1979); A. Verhey, *The Great Reversal: Ethics and the New Testament* (Grand Rapids: Eerdmans, 1984); J. H. Yoder, *The Politics of Jesus* (Grand Rapids: Eerdmans, 1972). P. H. Davids

RICHES AND POVERTY II: PAUL

Neither the appropriate use of riches nor the plight of the economically deprived are dominant concerns for Paul, who usually spiritualizes the vocabulary of riches. Where Paul does display concern about economic issues, his teaching for the most part reflects standard Jewish piety.

1. Riches
2. Poverty

1. Riches.

The lack of attention in the Pauline letters to the rich and to the appropriate use of riches is remarkable. The subject is common in intertestamental Jewish wisdom literature and among contemporary Greco-Roman moralists, and of course the Synoptic Gospels and James evince considerable concern about the dangers of wealth (see Riches and Poverty I & III). The evidence of Acts (e.g., Acts 16:14; 17:12; 18:7-8) and analysis of names mentioned in Paul's correspondence (e.g., Rom 16:1-23) suggest that there were many early converts who were well-to-do. Yet Paul scarcely touches on the subject of riches, and the only extended treatment is 1 Timothy 6:6-10, 17-19.

Admittedly, the use of wealth falls somewhat outside the scope of the interpersonal and intercommunity issues most characteristic of Pauline ethics. It is possible that Paul's own "freedom from worldly concerns" (1 Cor 7:28-35; 8:1-13), his "contentment in any state" (Phil 4:10-13), rendered him less aware of the issue for others. Conversely, he may have been so sensitive to the issue that he gave instructions only verbally to individuals. Still, the fact that Paul was an itinerant who presumably lived with minimal possessions and yet required nothing like this for others, suggests that his expectations for rank-and-file believers were modest by comparison.

1.1. The Spiritualization of Riches. Among writers roughly contemporary with Paul, only Philo of Alexandria approaches Paul's spiritualization of the vocabulary of wealth. The character of God in his bestowal of salvation is described in terms of his "riches," especially in Romans (Rom 2:4; 9:23; 10:12; 11:33) and Ephesians (Eph 1:7, 18; 2:4, 7; 3:8, 16; cf. Phil 4:19; Col 1:27). Accordingly, God "enriches" the saints (Rom 11:12; 1 Cor 1:5; 2 Cor 6:10; 9:11; Col 2:2; 3:16; Tit 3:6).

In 2 Corinthians 8:9 Christ is said to have moved from wealth to poverty in order to make others "rich" spiritually. Christ's "impoverishment" here is usually understood as a reference to his exchange of a heavenly state for an earthly state at the Incarnation, but it is possible that it reveals a literal renunciation of wealth on the part of Jesus—or at least highlights the low economic level endured in his earthly ministry. Paul uses a similar line of argument in 2 Corinthians 6:10, contending that his own (economic) poverty leads to the (spiritual) wealth of the Corinthians.

The inconsistency between Paul's titular status as a Roman citizen (probably indicative of a prosperous family) and his life as an itinerant evangelist may provide a clue to his other-worldly view of riches: in Christ (see In Christ), as worldly measures of value are transformed, so worldly terminology must be redefined. 1 Timothy 6:17-19, with its wordplay on "rich," may represent the fullest development of Paul's thought in this regard.

1.2. Economic Level of Paul's Constituency. 1 Corinthians 1:26 indicates that "not many" Corinthians were in positions of power or nobility, but recent studies have shown that it is a mistake to take this as an indicator of a low economic level in the Pauline churches. "Not many" allows for significant exceptions (cf. Acts 18:7-8; Rom 16:23), and people could possess riches without prestige or rank. Indeed, Paul criticizes members of the church for social pretensions (1 Cor 11:19) and social prejudice (1 Cor 11:17-22), and his extended appeal for financial aid assumes their ability to support the cause of helping the Jerusalem poor (2 Cor 8—9; esp. 2 Cor 8:13-15). The emerging consensus is that Pauline churches represented a fair cross-section of urban society: few extremes on either end of the socioeconomic scale, and a preponderance of artisans and traders at various levels of income. Those with money but without other means of status may have been attracted to Christianity in part as a status-enhancing mechanism within the local community.

1.3. Responsible Use of Riches. The personal economic ethic of the Pauline corpus reflects standard Jewish piety of the period. This includes warnings against greed (1 Cor 5:11; 1 Tim 3:8; Tit 1:7), avoidance of poverty by industry (Rom 13:8; 1 Thess 4:11-12; cf. 2 Thess 3:6-12), priority in giving to one's own household (Gal 6:10; 1 Tim 5:8; cf. Acts 11:27-30) and liberality toward others (Rom 12:8, 13; 1 Cor 16:2; 2 Cor 8:2; Eph 4:28). The focus of liberality for Paul is the collection for the saints, which appears to have taken the place of the Jewish Temple tax as a Pauline expression of solidarity with the Jerusalem church (Rom 15:25-29; 1 Cor 16:1-4; 2 Cor 8—9; perhaps Gal 2:10). More specifically, the rich themselves are enjoined to generosity, which will result in spiritual blessings in this life (2 Cor 9:10-15; Phil 4:14-

20) and the next (1 Tim 6:19).

Along with these Jewish features, there are also some Greek elements in Paul's teaching (especially in 2 Cor 8—9). The warning against "love of money" (1 Tim 3:3; 6:6-10; 2 Tim 3:2) is common in contemporary Greek literature. In Philippians 4:11-13 Paul argues for "self-suffi-ciency" in all circumstances (*autarkēs*, Phil 4:11; cf. 1 Tim 6:7-8), a term common among Stoics and Cynics. In Cynic practice and in later Chris-tian monasticism, *autarkeia* implied not only spiritual freedom or detachment but also volun-tary reduction to a minimal economic level. Paul's teaching—and certainly his example—al-low for such a radical degree of liberality on the part of the rich. Indeed, 1 Corinthians 13:3 al-ludes to those who "give away all" (provided they have love). But the fact that Paul does not make explicit such a demand suggests that his expectations for liberality are limited to such expressions of solidarity as the collection and provision for the subsistence of needy believers (Eph 4:28).

2. Poverty.

Paul has even less to say about the poor than he does about the rich. This may be due to Paul's own detachment, as suggested above. It may also be due in part to the lack of direct relevance of poverty to the Pauline churches. Among the ur-ban artisans, traders and even slaves who com-prised the early communities, there may have been very few who were poor by first-century standards; that is, without any means of liveli-hood apart from charity.

2.1. Responsibility to the Poor. To the extent that poor people can be found, they are the ap-propriate recipients of Christian liberality (Eph 4:28; cf. Acts 11:27-30), and Paul himself affirms that it is part of his commission to "remember" the poor (Gal 2:10; cf. instructions about widows in 1 Tim 5:3-16). The instructions regarding work in 1 Thessalonians 4:11-12 and 2 Thessalo-nians 3:6-12 imply a negative view of poverty that results from laziness. Elsewhere, we might infer a measure of sympathy for the plight of the needy from Paul's injunctions to kindness and love for fellow believers, but poverty per se is not a concern. Paul draws attention to his own pov-erty not to call for financial assistance, which he forgoes (1 Cor 9:15; 2 Cor 11:10), but to high-light the spiritual riches his ministry bestows (2 Cor 6:10; cf. 1 Cor 4:9-13). He draws attention

to the poverty of the Macedonians only as a rhe-torical device to highlight their exemplary gen-erosity (2 Cor 8:2).

2.2. "The Poor Among the Saints in Jerusalem." Romans 15:26 affirms the gifts of Macedonia and Achaia to "the poor among the saints at Jerusalem" (RSV). Since this is clearly a refer-ence to the Pauline collection, which is not de-scribed elsewhere as social relief, it may be best to take the expression here as explicative: "the poor *who are* the saints in Jerusalem." This is consistent with the use of the title *poor* as a self-designation of the Jews, especially the Qumran sectaries (see 1QpHab 12:3, 6, 10; 1QM 11:9, 13; 4Q171 37:2-10; cf. Ps 69:32; 72:4), in con-temporary literature. In this sense it is not *pri-marily* an economic designation but a signifier of the longing for the *spiritual* riches of salva-tion. This is in line with Paul's spiritualization of the terminology of riches, and it may indi-cate a noneconomic connotation in the refer-ence to Paul's remembering the poor in Galatians 2:10. On the other hand, if believers in Jerusalem, or a subgroup of them, had suf-fered economically, the title may indicate eco-nomic deprivation. Some may have suffered from despoliation at the hands of antagonistic Jews (Heb 10:32-34), from famine (Acts 11:27-30) or from voluntary depletion of capital (Acts 4:32-37).

See also ETHICS.

DPL: COLLECTION FOR THE SAINTS; SOCIAL SETTING OF MISSION CHURCHES; SUFFERING.

BIBLIOGRAPHY. E. Bammel, "πτωχός κτλ," *TDNT* 6:885-916; D. Georgi, *Remembering the Poor* (Nashville: Abingdon, 1992); C. L. Blomberg, *Neither Poverty nor Riches: A Biblical Theology of Possessions* (NSBT; Downers Grove, IL: InterVar-sity Press, 1999); F. Hauck and W. Kasch, "πλοῦτος κτλ," *TDNT* 6:318-32; M. Hengel, *Property and Riches in the Early Church* (Philadel-phia: Fortress, 1974); B. Holmberg, *Paul and Power* (Lund: CWK Gleerup, 1978); L. E. Keck, "The Poor Among the Saints in the New Testa-ment," *ZNW* 56 (1965) 100-129; R. M. Kidd, *Wealth and Beneficence in the Pastoral Epistles* (SBLDS 122, Missoula, MT: Scholars Press, 1990); W. Meeks, *The First Urban Christians* (New Haven: Yale University Press, 1983); K. F. Nickle, *The Collection: A Study of Paul's Strategy* (London: SCM, 1966); G. Theissen, *The Social Setting of Pauline Christianity: Essays on Corinth* (Philadel-phia: Fortress, 1982). T. E. Schmidt

RICHES AND POVERTY III: ACTS, HEBREWS, GENERAL EPISTLES, REVELATION

As seen in Acts, Hebrews, the general epistles and Revelation, the abundance or lack of material possessions was not a dominant concern for Christians of the first century. Most paraenetic statements are continuous with Jewish piety rather than the radical statements of the Gospels. More distinctively Christian developments include a stress on hospitality and an exchange of prayers on the part of the poor for the beneficence of rich believers.

1. Acts

2. Hebrews, General Epistles and Revelation

1. Acts.

Two key summary passages, Acts 2:43-45 and Acts 4:32-37, focus on the unity of believers in the first Jerusalem church. With respect to material possessions, the passages contain two distinct features: that property was held in common (Acts 2:44; 4:32) and that possessions were sold to prevent anyone from being needy (Acts 2:45; 4:35). These features appear to represent a departure from the radical renunciation demanded of disciples in the Gospel (e.g., Lk 5:11; 14:33; 18:22), but it may be a way to meet that demand (cf. Lk 8:3; 12:33; 16:9; 19:8). Material giving in Acts may assume what is stressed in the Gospels—that is, the need of the disciple to express complete dependence on God—but the focus is on the need of community members. This is consistent with the praise given to other people who give charitably to the needy (Acts 9:36; 10:2, 4; cf. Acts 6:1-6) and the condemnation of those who would put money above the needs of others (Acts 5:1-11; 8:14-24). It is also consistent with the Hellenistic ideal of friendship or unity of mind, often expressed in terms of common possessions, but here the practice is driven by the Spirit (*see* Holy Spirit) rather than by friendship.

Some scholars have suggested that community of possessions is not mentioned in early Christian writings after Acts 4 because it failed as a social experiment or because it was a temporary measure to help itinerant pilgrims who left when it became apparent that the eschaton was delayed. But a more likely implication of silence following such a glowing description of early church communal life is that believers failed to sustain their initial level of obedience.

2. Hebrews, General Epistles and Revelation.

The Pastoral Epistles and Hebrews reflect what we might term middle-class values. These letters share an interest in contentment with one's current economic status (1 Tim 6:6-10; Heb 13:5b) and condemn love of money (1 Tim 6:10; 2 Tim 3:2; Heb 13:5a; cf. Tit 1:7) without condemning those who possess much. The recommendation to the rich is "to do good, to be rich in good works, generous, and ready to share" (1 Tim 6:17-18 NRSV). All believers are enjoined to practice hospitality (1 Tim 5:10; Heb 13:2, 16).

The letters of Peter and John contain little relevant material. Peter warns against mercenary motives in ministry (1 Pet 5:2; 2 Pet 2:14-15) and John recommends generosity toward needy believers (1 Jn 3:17); both command hospitality (1 Pet 4:9; 3 Jn 5-8).

*James and *Revelation evince more of the critical attitude toward the rich and praise for the poor that are characteristic of the Gospels, but this does not mean that the audience is from the lowest stratum of society. Diatribes against the rich in James 5:1-6 appear to be directed toward non-Christian oppressors, but other passages (Jas 1:10-11; 2:1-7; 4:13-15) imply the presence of affluent believers. Moreover, both rich and poor are described as "they" in relation to the recipients of the letter (Jas 2:1-7). James tells poor believers to boast that they will soon be "lifted up" and rich believers to boast that they will soon be "brought low" (Jas 1:9-11). The boasting is in the transitoriness of their wealth as compared to the permanence of the coming kingdom, but James does not allow humility to remain at the level of attitude. "Doers of the word" (Jas 1:22) must care for the needy (Jas 1:27) and renounce worldly pleasures (Jas 4:3-10).

In Revelation Jesus commands the church of Laodicea to turn from its boast that "I am rich" to "buy from me gold refined by fire" (Rev 3:17-18 NRSV), a possible allusion to Gospel passages (Mt 13:44-45; Lk 16:9) in which "buying" is a metaphor for renunciation of possessions. Elsewhere in Revelation earthly riches are associated with the powers of evil, and Revelation 18 offers a lengthy woe against Babylon, who "glorified herself and lived luxuriously" (Rev 18:7 NRSV). Although the depiction of commercial enterprise is to some extent a metaphor for spiritual rebellion, the recommendation for believers is plain: "Come out of her, my people, so that you do not take part in her sins" (Rev 18:4 NRSV).

Revelation closes with a contrasting description of a heavenly kingdom made of gold, crystal and jewels (Rev 21:1—22:6). This too is metaphorical, a representation in prophetic language of a community perfectly ordered by God. But in its almost ironic depiction of unimaginable material riches as the reward for those who renounced the same on earth, it partakes of a tradition going back at least to Job and continuous with Matthew 5:3-5, 2 Corinthians 8:13-15 and Revelation 2:9: "I know your affliction and your poverty, even though you are rich" (NRSV).

See also ETHICS; JAMES, LETTER OF.

DLNTD: HOSPITALITY; SOCIAL SETTING OF EARLY NON-PAULINE CHRISTIANITY.

BIBLIOGRAPHY. C. L. Blomberg, *Neither Poverty nor Riches: A Biblical Theology of Possessions* (NSBT; Downers Grove, IL: InterVarsity Press, 1999); L. W. Countryman, *The Rich Christian in the Church of the Early Empire: Contradictions and Accommodations* (Lewiston, NY: Edwin Mellen, 1980); R. Garrison, *Redemptive Almsgiving in Early Christianity* (Sheffield: JSOT, 1993); J. Gonzalez, *Faith and Wealth: A History of Early Christian Ideas on the Origin, Significance and Use of Money* (San Francisco: Harper & Row, 1990); M. Hengel, *Property and Riches in the Early Church* (Philadelphia: Fortress, 1974); L. T. Johnson, *Sharing Possessions: Mandate and Symbol of Faith* (Philadelphia: Fortress, 1981); P. U. Maynard-Reid, *Poverty and Wealth in James* (Maryknoll, NY: Orbis, 1987). T. E. Schmidt

RIGHTEOUSNESS I: GOSPELS

In biblical thought the idea of justice or righteousness generally expresses conformity to God's will in all areas of life: *law, government, *covenant loyalty, ethical integrity or gracious actions. When humans adhere to God's will as expressed in his law, they are considered just or righteous. Jesus taught that those who conform their lives to his teachings are also just or righteous.

1. Terminology, Meaning and Context
2. The Message of Jesus
3. The Emphases of the Gospel Writers

1. Terminology, Meaning and Context.
English words related to justice and righteousness are usually used to translate the *dik-* word group found in the NT. The use of *dik-* in the NT reflects the LXX's usual translation of the He-

brew *ṣdq* (righteous) word-group with the Greek *dik-*. In the OT the *ṣdq* word group essentially refers to "conduct in accordance with the requirements of a particular relationship," whether that be the covenant which imposes obligations on both God and his people or the world order set up by *God, with which humanity must live in accordance. Hence, though she acted sinfully in playing the harlot, Tamar is said to be "more righteous" than Judah because she acted in the interest of a social standard—Judah's obligation to provide offspring for her deceased husband (Gen 38:26). In several instances the *ṣdq* word group is translated in the LXX by other Greek terms, including *eleēmosynē* (almsgiving) and *krisis* *(judgment). However, it is not just the *ṣdq* word group that conveys the idea of righteousness and justice in the Hebrew OT; the concept also embraces *mišpāṭ* (judgment, ordinance), *hesed* (lovingkindness), *tôrâ* (command) and *tāmîm* (perfect, complete).

Whereas in English "justice" emphasizes conformity to a society's standards, "righteousness" usually denotes conformity to God's standards or religious norms. However, these distinctions are not helpful when "justice" and "righteousness" are used to translate biblical terms (e.g., Job 22:6-9, 23; Ezek 45:9; Amos 4:1-3). In conveying biblical thought, the two English terms are inseparable in that it is God's will to which a person conforms, whether that will is expressed in predominantly social or religious categories. In this article "justice" will be used exclusively for the social implications of God's will; "righteousness" will be used for the broader meaning of the concept. However, in many instances a clear distinction cannot and should not be made.

Throughout Jewish literature we find two dominant ideas: God is righteous and his people are to be righteous in their behavior. The righteousness of God, primarily understood as his impeccable holiness and the conformity of his actions to that holy nature, is commonplace in Jewish thought (Is 45:21; Ps 22:31; 40:10; 51:14; 71:15-24; Hos 10:12; Amos 5:21-24; Mic 6:5; 7:9; *Pss. Sol.* 2:15; 8:23; Bar 5:1-2; *Sib. Or.* 3:704; Josephus *Ant.* 2.6.4 §108; 11.3.6 §55; 1QS 1:21; 10:11, 25; 1QH 12:19; 14:15; *Sipre Deut* 307 [on 32:4]; *m. Sota* 1:9). In addition, as recent scholarship has shown, righteousness attributed to God's people refers to moral behavior conforming to God's will (Gen 18:19; Lev 19:36; Deut 6:25; Is

5:16; Ps 1:4-6; *Pss. Sol.* 2:34-35; 3:3-12; 15:1-13; Philo, *Leg. All.* 2.18; *Migr. Abr.* 219; 1QS 1:5, 13; 3:1; 1QH 2:13; 4:30, 31; 7:14; *Sipra Qedoshim pereq* 11:6 [on Lev 20:16]; *t. Pe'a* 4.19; *t. Sanh.* 1.3-5). These twin themes of divine and human righteousness should inform our approach to the use of righteousness in the Gospels.

Biblical statements about the necessity of righteousness sometimes seem to imply a righteous status attained by works (Gen 18:19; Mt 5:20). But in the context of biblical thought righteous behavior is generally the result of *salvation and is required of those who participate in the covenantal blessings. Throughout the OT, as well as Jewish literature from the time of Jesus, righteousness refers to behavior conforming to the will of God. Paul's doctrine of *justification, an eschatological righteousness imputed to believers in view of Christ's work, is largely con- fined to Paul's letters and should not be read into the texts of the Gospels simply because the terminology of righteousness appears.

2. The Message of Jesus.

Jesus describes as righteous those who conform to God's will as revealed both in the OT and in his own teachings. The foundation for Jesus' teachings on righteous behavior is that the *kingdom of God has been inaugurated in his own person and ministry (Lk 7:18-23; 11:20). Since God's kingdom is a righteous kingdom (Ps 97—99; Is 11:1-5; *1 Enoch* 62:1-16), when Jesus inaugurates the kingdom he brings righteousness to pass and expects righteous behavior from his followers. Participation in the kingdom of God entails an ethical obligation (Mk 1:15), just as covenantal participation required obedience in OT religion (Lev 19:36; but 24:17-8) and in later Judaism (*see* Ethics).

Today many scholars argue that Jesus probably did not use the vocabulary of righteousness with any frequency. Since the vocabulary is found relatively infrequently in our Gospels, this view deserves consideration. However, evidence for the presence of the concept of righteousness in Jesus' teaching should not be limited to the occurrence or frequency of the vocabulary of righteousness. From the evidence of the Gospels, Jesus' teaching stressed that his followers must conform their lives to God's will. Thus it may be argued that the idea of righteousness, if not the terminology, is found everywhere in the teachings of Jesus: in his demand for repen-

tance, in his blessings for good works, in his practice of social mercy and in his consistent concern for personal holiness. Furthermore, the usage of the terminology of righteousness in the Gospels conforms to what we know of its usage in Judaism at the time of Jesus.

Since some of the references to righteousness in the *Gospels undoubtedly come from the vocabulary of the Evangelists themselves or their tradition (e.g., Mt 3:15), we cannot always be certain that the term was used by Jesus in a particular setting. But if Matthew, Luke or John used the term *righteousness* where Jesus did not, they are faithfully reflecting the message of Jesus, laying stress on what they considered needful for their audiences to hear.

2.1. Righteousness in the Mission of Jesus and John. Jesus and John (*see* John the Baptist) show clear continuity in their messages of righteousness. Jesus views his mission as intimately tied with John's as together they accomplish all righteousness by submitting to God—John as baptizer and Jesus as the one baptized (Mt 3:15). Furthermore, John's essential message was a call for righteous behavior (Mt 21:32; Mk 6:20) manifesting itself in repentance (Lk 3:7-9), mercy and the pursuit of justice (Lk 3:10-14). Jesus builds on John's message in his own call for repentance (cf. Mt 3:2 and 4:17).

2.2. Righteousness As Conformity to Old Testament Law. Jesus is described as righteous, just or innocent in the sense that he performs all that God's will requires. We may assume that God's will in this case is that described in the OT (Lk 23:47; Mt 27:4, 19, 24). Jesus also describes as righteous those whose behavior is in conformity to God's laws found in the OT. Thus "righteous" describes those who anticipated the Messiah (Mt 13:17) and those who were martyred (23:29, 35). In the OT (Gen 15:6; Ps 1:4-6; 11:7; 72:1; Is 1:16-17) and in Jewish literature (*Pss. Sol.* 3:3-12; Philo *Leg. All.* 2.18; Josephus *Ant.* 6.5.6 §93; 1QS 1:13, 15; CD 1:19-21; *m. Sota* 1:9) righteousness commonly characterizes those who adhere to God's commands in faith and obedience.

2.3. Righteousness As Conformity to Jesus' Teachings. Jesus goes beyond the OT as a standard for righteousness by describing as righteous those who obey his own teachings. In so doing, Jesus redefines the term in a manner parallel to what we find in the *Dead Sea Scrolls, where the instruction of the Teacher of Righteousness sets a new standard for the sectarian community at

Qumran (CD 4:7; 20:20-21; 1QpHab 2:2; 7:3-5).

In using his own teachings as the basis for righteousness, Jesus reveals that the OT law and Prophets (Mt 5:17) are being fulfilled in his own teachings and that he is the Messiah (*see* Christ). Jesus fulfills the law and so reveals a new standard of conduct (Mt 5:20). Henceforth the righteousness of God's people is determined by conformity to the teachings of Jesus, which in turn fulfill the OT revelation of God's will. Jesus expects his followers to be righteous in their conduct (Mt 5:6, 10), to do God's will (Mt 7:12, 13-27) and to pursue justice (Mt 23:23 [*krisis*]; 25:37; Jn 7:24). According to Jesus, only those who are righteous are finally acceptable to God (Mt 10:41; 12:37; 13:43, 49; 25:46; Lk 14:14; Jn 5:30). Again, this righteousness is not an outward conformity to the law or an appeal to ritual observances, but the necessary fruit of commitment to Jesus as Messiah and *Lord. The link between commitment and obedience is illustrated by Jesus' words at the end of the Sermon on the Mount: "Everyone then who hears these words of mine and does them . . ." (Mt 7:21-27). Particular manifestations of righteousness (Mt 6:1) include almsgiving (Mt 6:2-4), prayer (Mt 6:5-15) and fasting (Mt 6:16-18).

As for those who claim to have conformed to the standards of the Jewish legal traditions, Jesus—tongue in cheek—describes them as "righteous" (Mt 9:13; Mk 2:17). The righteousness of the Pharisees and scribes is not considered sufficient (cf. Lk 5:30, 32; 15:7; 18:9; 20:20; Mt 23:28) for at least two reasons: (1) their hearts are not right (Mk 7:6-7; Mt 5:28) and (2) their standard is no longer adequate since God has fulfilled the OT law in Jesus (Mt 5:17-48). However, for the one whose heart is right and whose standard is the fulfilled law of Jesus, their commitment to obedience is to be complete (Mt 5:48). The word *perfect* in Matthew 5:48 speaks of the response of the whole heart, a total or thorough commitment to God's will—not sinless perfection. For Jesus the pursuit of righteousness is obeying God's will in all its aspects (personal, social and communal) and is to be the first priority of his followers (Mt 6:33).

3. The Emphases of the Gospel Writers.

Among the Gospel authors only Matthew and Luke give prominent place to the vocabulary of righteousness; Mark only uses the adjective *dikaios*, and that only twice (Mk 2:17; 6:20),

while John uses *dik-* terminology five times (see 3.3 below).

3.1. Matthew. There is little doubt that Matthew has reworked some important traditions and added the term *righteousness*, emphasizing behavior that conforms to the new standard revealed in Jesus (cf., e.g., Mt 5:6 with Lk 6:21; Mt 6:33 with Lk 12:31). Indeed, some scholars see Matthew's hand in each occurrence of the word. Matthew places particular emphasis on righteousness as conformity to Jesus' teachings.

3.1.1. Righteousness as Conformity to Old Testament Law. As the wording of Matthew 3:15 indicates ("it is proper for us to fulfill all righteousness"), together John the Baptist and Jesus fulfill God's will for them in its entirety and so bring all of God's demands to a salvation-historical climax. The favored Matthean expressions, "fulfillment" and "all righteousness," set the tone for both John's work (Mt 21:32) and Jesus' life (Mt 27:19) and teachings (Mt 5:20). They do all that God has called them to do, and in so doing they fulfill all righteousness. John is later described as the one who came "in the way of righteousness," meaning he proclaimed and performed God's will (cf. Mt 21:31 and 3:1-10). Some interpreters have understood the fulfillment of righteousness in Matthew 3:15 as meaning "to bring about God's prophetic and eschatological plan of redemption." In either case the OT revelation of God's will is in view.

In addition to John the Baptist and Jesus, Matthew describes others as righteous in their obedience to OT law, including Joseph (Mt 1:19) and various OT saints (Mt 13:17; 23:29, 35).

3.1.2. Righteousness as Conformity to Jesus' Teachings. The Sermon on the Mount is a revelation of Jesus' teachings on righteousness, explaining what it is to do God's will and perform good works (Mt 5:6, 16, 17-20, 21-48; 6:1-18, 33; 7:12, 13-14, 16-21, 23-27). The thrust of the Sermon points to the importance of righteousness for Matthew.

For Matthew, Jesus' pre-eminent demand of his disciples is to do God's will—to exhibit righteousness (cf. Mt 5:20, 48; 7:13-27). Accordingly, entrance into the kingdom is conditioned on moral righteousness. In light of its Jewish background and its Matthean context, the beatitude on those who hunger and thirst for righteousness should be understood as a blessing for those who desire to do God's will, who strive to conform to his standard (Mt 5:6). However, some scholars understand this as a blessing on those who are longing for eschatological (*see* Eschatology) vindication or salvation. According to this interpretation, righteousness may be a gift of righteous conduct granted them in the last day or the fulfillment of their longing to see God's righteousness established on earth. But in light of the behavioral grounds for the blessings in Matthew 5:3-11, it is more likely that righteousness in Matthew 5:6 refers to the habit of doing God's will. Those who have been persecuted because of righteousness (Mt 5:10) are those who suffer for obedience to God's will as revealed by Jesus. Hence the grounds for their persecution is their loyalty to Jesus as much as it is their good works.

The righteousness expected of Jesus' disciples is a righteousness that is vastly superior to the righteousness of the scribes and Pharisees (Mt 5:20). Matthew 5:20 is often understood to mean that, whereas the Pharisees and scribes taught a righteousness that was merited by their quantity of good deeds, Jesus taught a righteousness that was given by God. Hence, Jesus' righteousness is superior. But today there is a growing consensus among scholars that the debate Jesus had with the scribes and Pharisees was not over earning merit before God. Rather, it was about Jesus' place in God's plan for redemption. Consequently, the righteousness Jesus demands is superior, not because scribal and Pharisaic righteousness is necessarily an attempt to earn salvation, but because Jesus demands behavior that conforms to God's standard as revealed by himself. The point-counterpoints of Matthew 5:21-48 explicate the nature of the surpassing righteousness that Jesus reveals. This righteousness is messianic (Mt 5:17), deeper (Mt 5:27-30) and innovative (Mt 5:38-42). The usage of "righteousness" in Matthew 5:20 is similar to the usage of the term in the Qumran literature: it is an eschatological righteousness pertaining to a particular group of God's people. Those who are marked by the righteousness of Jesus will be approved by God and will enter the kingdom (Mt 5:6, 10; 6:33; 7:21-23; cf. 12:36-37).

For Matthew, righteousness is behavioral. The "practice of piety" referred to in Matthew 6:1 is immediately related to the giving of alms in Matthew 6:2. Matthew 6:1 sets the theme for Jesus' instruction on religious behavior such as almsgiving, prayer and fasting (Mt 6:2-18). In some manuscripts Matthew 6:1 reads "almsgiving" *(eleēmosynēn)* instead of "practicing your piety" *(dikaiosynēn)*. Interestingly, rabbinic sources show that the Hebrew and Aramaic terms for almsgiving *sĕdāqâ)* and righteousness *(sedeq)* are closely associated, though in this case the more general term is most likely intended, setting the stage for the specific instructions of Matthew 6:2-18 (see Przybylski).

Though some scholars have suggested that the righteousness pursued in Matthew 6:33 is a gift from God—eschatological salvation (much like Pauline usage)—many interpreters today understand it as moral behavior which includes the establishment of justice (cf. Mt 6:10 with 5:6; 6:33). The fact that pursuing righteousness is joined so closely with seeking God's kingdom—submitting to God's reign and seeking to realize it in this world—favors a behavioral sense here as well. Thus submission to God through seeking his kingdom unleashes God's provisions (Mt 6:33).

Matthew further highlights the behavioral focus of righteousness in the examples of Joseph (Mt 1:19), Abel (Mt 23:35) and other OT saints who are finally acceptable to the Father because they have lived faithfully (Mt 5:45; 12:37; 13:43, 49; 25:37, 46). On the other hand, Matthew emphasizes the absence of the proper kind of righteousness in the Pharisees and Jewish leaders, who either feign their religiosity or have not perceived the new standard set forth in Jesus' teachings (Mt 5:20; 9:13; 23:28).

It is unclear whether the "righteous person" of Matthew 10:41 refers to a special class of leaders (e.g., teachers) among Jesus' followers or to anyone who is simply obedient to his commands. Jesus' final words explicitly call for all future disciples to obey his commands (Mt 28:20) and, in keeping with Matthew's emphases, we may assume that those who do so are righteous.

3.2. Luke. Luke seems to focus less attention on whether the standard of righteousness is derived from the OT or Jesus, placing his emphasis on the pious, merciful and just behavior that is the fruit of those who are ultimately approved by God. In several passages, Luke describes righteousness as conformity to God's law (Lk 1:6; 2:25; 23:47, 50). Zechariah and Elizabeth are described as "righteous before God" because they obeyed the Lord's commandments blamelessly (Lk 1:6). The angel tells Zechariah that John, the promised fruit of Elizabeth's womb, will turn many from disobedience to "the wisdom of the just"—a life of obedience to God's commands that conforms to God's wisdom (Lk 1:17). Simeon is described as "righteous and pious" because of his trusting hope that God would eventually save his people (Lk 2:25). Joseph from Arimathea was publicly known for his piety because he was one who lived according to God's commandments (Lk 23:50). In Acts a similar evaluation is given of Cornelius (Acts 10:22). These people embody proper OT faith—a faith that obeys God's will, trusts in his salvation and waits for him to vindicate his purposes. Luke's concept of righteousness includes a dominant element of piety as well as social mercy and justice (Lk 14:14; cf. also Lk 12:57; 23:41). The importance of righteousness in Luke is illustrated in Luke 14:14 (cf. Acts 24:15): It is the righteous who will be raised in the last day and enjoy fellowship with the Father.

This leads to Luke's heavy emphasis on social reversal (Lk 1:53; 6:20, 24; 12:16-21; 16:19-26) and economic justice (Lk 3:11, 14; 4:18; 5:11; 7:24-25; 12:33; 14:33; 16:13; 18:22). Those who finally will be declared righteous before God are humble, trusting *sinners (Lk 1:6, 17; 2:25; 18:14; 23:50). On the other hand, Luke, as Matthew, emphasizes the severe condemnation that befalls the self-righteous, who in their pride desire to be noticed. These Luke ironically describes as "righteous" (Lk 5:32; 10:29; 15:7; 16:15; 18:9; 20:20).

Finally, whereas in Matthew and Mark the centurion at the cross confesses Jesus as the *Son of God, in Luke he describes Jesus as *dikaios*—meaning "righteous," "just" or "innocent" (Lk 23:47; *see* Death of Christ). This speaks indirectly of the injustice dealt Jesus by the authorities. The innocent or righteous character of Jesus is a theme Luke further emphasizes in Acts. Peter accuses the Jewish crowds of denying the holy and righteous one and asking for a murderer in his place (Acts 3:14; cf. 7:52). Paul, when describing his conversion, says that Ananias told him that he was appointed by God to see the "Just One" (Acts 22:14)—referring to Jesus as vindicated and exalted in spite of his humiliating death in Jerusalem. Like the OT saints and their worthy successors in people like Zechariah, Elizabeth and Simeon, Jesus devoted his entire life to God and obeyed God's commands. Because of his obedience he was crucified.

For Luke the innocence of Jesus is more than a political or legal statement. It almost certainly connects Jesus with the *Servant of Yahweh described in Isaiah 52:13—53:12 who both suffers and is exalted. In Acts 3:13-14 the themes of suffering and the righteous one are joined. Likewise, Luke 22:35-37, 39-46 shows traces of the theme of Jesus as the Suffering Servant. At the cross, when the centurion confesses Jesus as "righteous" (Lk 23:47), Luke is once again indicating that Jesus is the innocent, law-abiding Servant of Yahweh who brings salvation.

3.3. John. Out of the five uses of *dik-* terminology in the Fourth Gospel, the adjective *righteous* is applied once to God (Jn 17:25) and twice to judgments made either by Jesus (Jn 5:30) or the crowd (Jn 7:24). John 16:8, 10 is the most notable use of "righteousness" in John, though scholars do not agree on the meaning of these verses. God has sent his Spirit (*see* Holy Spirit) into the world to convince the world either (1) of its inadequate righteousness and consequently its need to turn to Christ or (2) of the righteous vindication of the Son in spite of his condemnation by the world. The Spirit will continue the work that Jesus performed in exposing sin (Jn 16:8, 10).

In inaugurating the kingdom of God and salvation, Jesus revealed that his followers were to be characterized by the pursuit of righteousness and justice. This is so central to Jesus' message that he states that without a righteous status/ character one will not enter the kingdom of God. Though righteous character is expressed in righteous behavior, a righteous status is not obtained by good works. Rather, the person who is committed to Jesus in discipleship and has entered the kingdom of God can and should be expected to show righteousness in character and actions.

See also ETHICS; KINGDOM OF GOD; RICHES AND POVERTY; SALVATION.

DJG: DISCIPLESHIP; FASTING; PRAYER; SERMON ON THE MOUNT/PLAIN.

BIBLIOGRAPHY. E. Achtemeier et al., "Righteousness in the Old Testament, Jewish Literature, and the New Testament," *IDB* 4.80-99; D. Hill, *Greek Words and Hebrew Meanings: Studies in the Semantics of Soteriological Terms* (SNTSMS 5; Cambridge: University Press, 1967); B. Przybylski, *Righteousness in Matthew and His World of Thought* (SNTSMS 41; Cambridge: Cambridge University Press, 1980); G. Quell and G. Schrenk, "δίκη κτλ," *TDNT* 2.174-225; J. Reumann et al., *Righteousness in the New Testament* (Philadelphia: Fortress, 1982); E. P. Sanders, *Paul and Palestinian Judaism* (Philadelphia: Fortress, 1977); H. Seebass and C. Brown, "Righteousness, Justification," *NIDNTT* 3.352-77; N. Snaith, *The Distinctive Ideas of the Old Testament* (Philadelphia: Westminster, 1964); P. Stuhlmacher, *Reconciliation, Law, and Righteousness: Essays in Biblical Theology* (Philadelphia: Fortress, 1986); J. A. Ziesler, *The Meaning of Righteousness in Paul: A Linguistic and Theological Inquiry* (SNTSMS 20; Cambridge: Cambridge University Press, 1972).

S. McKnight

RIGHTEOUSNESS II: PAUL

The study of righteousness in the Pauline corpus has focused on the righteousness of *God and the related doctrine of the justification of the sinner. Though the centrality of these concepts in Pauline thought has in recent times been questioned (Schweitzer, Fitzmyer, Sanders; *see* Justification), they have in the past been the object of vigorous discussion, especially since these terms have been widely affirmed as a key to Paul's understanding of *salvation. But while there has been broad scholarly consensus about the significance of these terms in Paul's thought, there has not been agreement as to the precise meaning these terms have in Paul's usage.

1. Terminology, Background and Issues
2. Righteousness in Paul
3. History of Interpretation
4. God's Righteousness as Relation-Restoring Love

1. Terminology, Background and Issues.

The voluminous discussion has been focused largely on two questions: (1) how is the genitive construction *dikaiosynē theou* ("righteousness of God") to be interpreted, and (2) what does it mean in the overall context of Paul's thought? Is it to be understood in the so-called objective sense (somewhat straining the grammatical definition of objective genitive but frequently used by commentators to label this sense), that is, the righteousness that is valid before God? Or is it to be interpreted as a subjective genitive, referring either to God's own righteousness, describing his being (he is righteous) or God's action (God acts justly)? Further, is righteousness, or God's righteousness through *Christ, received by impartation or imputation? Does this righteousness give juridical standing, a new status, or a new nature? And from the human side, is the

righteousness of God experienced as ethical power, a new relationship with God, or a change of lordship? Is Paul using these terms within the context of Greco-Roman jurisprudence, where righteousness means "justice" or "righteous *judgment" (in a legal sense), or is he using them in light of OT meanings (see Wright, 101, for chart of interpretations)?

1.1. Philological Concerns. In the interpretation of the theme "righteousness of God," the problem begins when one considers the meaning of words. Words neither exist by themselves without a context, nor are texts written as free-floating packages of meaning without a historical basis or a place in their cultural milieu. The language Paul used was Greek, but as a Jew he participated in a culture that was Hebrew as well as Greco-Roman. Since Paul quotes passages of the OT throughout his letters, one must understand Paul as writing within the tradition of the Hebrew Bible. By reason of Paul's frequent use of the Septuagint version of the Hebrew Bible, the same concepts in the LXX should be given due consideration. In English translation the words "righteousness" or "justification" are used to translate the Greek *dikaiosynē*. These words may or may not connote the same meaning as the Greek term. These are just some of the linguistic issues that lie at the foundation of interpretation. If one couples the linguistic possibilities with various theological presuppositions, the interpretive options increase.

1.1.1. Etymology.

1.1.1.1. Hebrew. G. Quell provides an excellent introduction to the issues that are at the basis of the Hebrew understanding of righteousness. The concept of righteousness in the Hebrew Bible emphasizes the relational aspect of God and humanity in the context of a covenant. Among the various Hebrew word groups associated with righteousness, *ṣedeq* ("straightness," "justness," "rightness") and *ṣĕdāqâ* ("justice," "straightness," "honesty") suggest a norm. In the LXX *dikaiosynē* ("righteousness") is used eighty-one times for *ṣedeq*, 134 times for *ṣĕdāqâ*, and six times it renders freely the adjective *ṣaddîq* ("just," "righteous," "honest"). There are eight instances in which *dikaiosynē* ("righteousness") renders *ḥesed* ("loving-kindness," "mercy," "piety," "goodwill"; e.g., Gen 19:19). Other Hebrew words meaning "genuine," "good," "evenness," "purity" and "simplicity" are occasionally translated by *dikaiosynē*. *Dikaios* ("observant of right," "righteous," "fair") renders the Hebrew *ṣaddîq* 189 times. In sum, of the predominant Hebrew terms the root *ṣdq* is the only one to be rendered mainly by *dikē* ("right," "law") and its derivatives, especially *dikaiosynē*, while other synonymous Hebrew terms such as *ḥesed* are not given their due when the LXX translates them by *eleos* ("pity," "mercy"), which introduces an emotional element not present in the Hebrew. *Dikaiosynē* would have been a more accurate rendering of these words as well.

The common Hebrew word for righteousness is *ṣedeq*, or its feminine form *ṣĕdāqâ*, which occurs in the OT 117 and 115 times respectively. The Hebrew meaning of justice means more than the classical Greek idea of giving to every one their due. Usually the word suggests Yahweh's saving acts as evidence of God's faithfulness to the covenant. For this meaning of righteousness of God, *dikaiosynē* is not as flexible as the Hebrew word.

In the Tannaitic literature of rabbinic Judaism there was a theological and semantic shift restricting *ṣedeq* and *ṣĕdāqâ* to proper behavior, with *ṣĕdāqâ* being used primarily for almsgiving (Przybylski, 75). God's righteousness was increasingly understood as God's willingness to protect and provide for the poor. This association was already present within the Hebrew Bible; for example: "They have distributed freely, they have given to the poor; their righteousness endures forever" (Ps 112:9).

1.1.1.2. Greek. The richness of the Hebrew usage is generally well reproduced in the LXX (Quell). Of the relatively few instances in which *ṣedeq*, *ṣĕdāqâ* and *ṣaddîq* are not translated by *dikai-* words, *eleēmosynē* and *eleos* ("alms," "mercy") are employed for *ṣĕdāqâ* (cf. LXX Is 1:27; Ziesler, 59-60). Similar evidence of this is found in the NT at Matthew 6:1, where the variant readings of later MSS read *eleēmosynēn* for *dikaiosynēn* (see Przybylski, 78).

1.1.1.3. Latin. In the Western Roman Empire, the Old Latin versions of the NT displaced the Greek NT, and Paul was consequently understood via the Latin translation. The Old Latin and later Latin Vulgate rendered *dikaiosynē* by *iustitia* ("justice"). The legal connotation of this term in Roman Law was superimposed on the word *dikaiosynē*, which Paul had employed. The Roman legal understanding of justice was in a distributive sense: to give to each their due, the bestowal of rewards and punishments according to merit. The OT sense of righteousness as grounded in covenantal relationship was weakened, and its place was taken by the courtroom image of the sinner before God's tribunal. Although righteousness in the OT had a legal aspect, it was that of a litigant being adjudged righteous by God before his or her enemies. The biblical image of the covenant between God and humanity faded into the background, while the Latin context called to mind stark legal realities of the court. The shift in language from Hebrew to Greek to Latin resulted in an alteration in theological content as the words that were employed either overlaid the earlier meaning or signified something new in the receptor language.

1.1.1.4. English. Modern English partakes of a double portion of Indo-European languages: a Germanic base from Anglo-Saxon as well as Latinate words from the Norman Conquest. Because of this characteristic of English, one can say either "to be righteous" (from the Anglo-Saxon verb *rightwisen* meaning "to make right, to rightwise"), or "to be justified" (a verbal form derived from *ius, iuris* and *iustitia*, meaning "to be declared just"). The semantic ranges of the two are not identical.

1.1.2. Worldviews.

1.1.2.1. Hebrew. An essential component of Israel's religious experience was that Yahweh was not only *Lord of *Law but also the one who was faithful to it. God was faithful to the covenant. God's righteousness was shown by saving actions in accordance with this covenant relationship. A person was righteous by acting properly in regard to the covenant relationship with Yahweh. One's relationship with others reflected the relational aspect of the *covenant with Yahweh. Righteousness was understood in terms of being in proper relation to the covenant rather than in terms of "right" or ethical conduct as determined by some abstract standard. When Judah says of Tamar, "She is more righteous than I," he is referring to her being righteous in her pursuit of covenantal, familial responsibility (Gen 38:26).

1.1.2.2. Greco-Roman. The gods of the Greco-Roman pantheon were thought to be subject to forces beyond their control (*see* Religions, Greco-Roman). This understanding later degenerated into a sort of inexorable fate to which even the gods were subject (*see* Worship). The Hellenistic theory of universal law meant that both the gods and humanity had to comply with these overarching norms in order to be righteous. Giving others their due was the basis of righteousness; one acted in accordance with a norm (Plato). In Greek thought, righteousness was a virtue. According to Aristotle, righteousness was the correct functioning of all the virtues. In Roman Civil Law, justice *(iustitia)* was done when one acted toward another in accordance with one's respective status established by tradition and the Roman legal corpus.

1.2. Old Testament Background. While the OT uses righteousness terminology in numerous contexts involving all areas of life, the touchstone of righteousness is Israel's covenantal relationship with Yahweh. It is based on the standard of God's covenant faithfulness. Righteousness is not primarily an ethical quality; rather, it characterizes the character or action of God who deals rightly within a covenant relationship and who establishes how others are to act within that relationship. "Shall not the judge of all the earth do what is right?" (Gen 18:25). The covenant faithfulness of God, the righteousness of God, is shown by Yahweh's saving acts. This salvation is variously experienced as Israel's victory over enemies, or personal vindication of one's innocence before God in the presence of one's enemies, and it involves both soteriological and forensic elements.

In the classical prophets of the eighth century there is a greater emphasis on the juridical and ethical views of *ṣedeq.* Amos, on behalf of the poor, associates righteousness with doing justice (*mišpāṭ,* Amos 5:7, 24; 6:12). Corrupt judges who do not judge rightly do not reflect the righteousness of the covenant relationship. Their oppression of the poor is the antithesis of righteousness. Hosea, emphasizing divine love, links righteousness with loving-kindness and mercy as well as justice (Hos 2:19; 10:12). Micah refers only to God's righteousness as being his faithfulness to act within the covenant to save *Israel from her enemies and to vindicate the penitent (Mic 6:5; 7:9). Isaiah associates the righteousness of the people and God's righteousness with just decisions (Is 1:26; 16:5; 26:9). God's faithfulness to deliver Israel is seen in the Servant of the Lord and Cyrus as God's chosen leaders/deliverers (Is 42:6; 45:8, 13, 19). Covenant relationship is the basis of righteousness (Is 51:1). God promises to bring righteousness, which is often understood as deliverance or vin-

dication (Is 51:5, 8; 62:1, 2). In sum, the covenant understanding of righteousness in the classical prophets relates persons to the living God and his covenantal purposes in restoring order to his *creation, not to an abstract norm of conduct (see Scullion).

1.3. Intertestamental Literature.

1.3.1. LXX. The Hellenistic idea of righteousness as a virtue, a meeting of the norm, was replaced with the idea of meeting God's claim in this covenant relationship (Schrenk). Thus the semantic range for *dikaios* in LXX Greek was enlarged due to the influence of the Hebrew background. In fourteen instances the Hebrew word *ṣĕdāqâ,* which could have been translated by *dikaiosynē,* was rendered by *eleēmosynē* (meaning "pity," "mercy"; e.g., Is 1:27; 59:16; Ps 34[35]:24). This added emotional element also limited the semantic value of *dikaiosynē* in later Judaism to almsgiving.

1.3.2. Apocrypha. In addition to the understanding of righteousness in the Hellenistic manner as personal virtue, there are Stoic virtues "associated" with righteousness: integrity, courage, constancy, even in the midst of personal woe, and self-control. In the apocryphal works there is an increasing interest in good works and the merits of the righteous. Tobit's farewell advice to his son Tobias portrays charity *(eleēmosynē)* as bringing safety rather than fulfilling the prayers of the poor: "For charity delivers from death and keeps you from entering the darkness" (Tob 4:10). In Tobit the focus is on the individual rather than on the community. We further find an emphasis on the relation between suffering and righteousness (Wis 3:1-5). The belief that the merits of some will assist others to gain righteousness appears in the Maccabean literature (2 Macc 12:38-45).

1.3.3. Pseudepigrapha. In the apocalyptic literature such as the *Testaments of the Twelve Patriarchs,* the *Book of Enoch* and *Jubilees,* the idea is prominent that the righteousness of God will characterize the end time (e.g., *T. Dan* 5:7-13). In this literature God not only is faithful to the covenant, but beyond the present difficulty God will vindicate the covenant people in the eschatological future.

Characteristic of apocalyptic is an added sense of the distinction between the righteous and the unrighteous. And righteousness is seen as an eschatological reality in that Yahweh will vindicate the righteous (*1 Enoch* 95:7). The righteousness of God will be shown in the vindication of the persecuted righteous. Thus there is a coupling of the motif of the suffering righteous with the traditional Hebrew understanding of God as the one who vindicates (Ps 26; 31:14-18).

1.3.4. Qumran. In the documents from Qumran we find references to God's righteousness providing salvation and forgiveness. "And when I stumble, the mercies of God are always my salvation. When I stagger because of the evil of my flesh, my justification is in the righteousness of God which exists forever" (1QS 11:12). In the *Thanksgiving Psalm*, the righteousness of God shows God's faithfulness to the community: "You forgive the unjust and purify people from guilt by your righteousness" (*ṣĕdāqâ*, 1QH 4:37). In *The War of the Children of Light*, Yahweh is able to bring them to the joys of future vindication through the righteousness of God (1QM 18:8). "Essentially it means the covenantal faithfulness of God which is being revealed especially in the eschatological warfare for the rule of God's justice" (Kuyper).

2. Righteousness in Paul.

The noun "righteousness" (*dikaiosynē*), its related adjective "righteous" (*dikaios*), and the verb "to justify," "to pronounce/treat as righteous" or "put right" (*dikaioō*) are found in the Pauline writings over 100 times. The sheer volume of occurrences in their various usages and meanings indicates the central place they had in the theology of the apostle.

We will present the meaning of Paul's language of righteousness/justification in its various contexts, bearing in mind that not every instance of "the righteousness of God" carries the same meaning. We will then proceed to explain these terms within the history of interpretation, the currents of contemporary scholarship, and summarize our own conclusions regarding this central Pauline affirmation.

2.1. Dikaiosynē. Paul uses this word both in relationship to God and to human beings. In the latter case its ultimate origin is without exception the character and/or action of God. The term is used in various contexts or associations.

2.1.1. Righteousness Declared. A distinctive usage is found where Paul states that righteousness in believers is the result of a word, or declaration, of God. In Romans 4, where Paul interprets *Abraham's relationship with God as a scriptural foundation for his understanding of

believers' "justification by faith" (explained in Rom 1—3), righteousness is said to be "reckoned to" (RSV) or "credited to" (NIV) Abraham by God on the basis of Abraham's believing/trusting in God (Rom 4:3, 5, 6, 9, 11, 22), rather than on the basis of his works. In Galatians 3:6 Abraham's faith in God is "reckoned to him as righteousness." Here Abraham's trusting submission to God is evaluated as "righteousness."

2.1.2. Righteousness as Gift. Closely related are those usages where righteousness is stated to be a gift of God reigning in the believer (Rom 5:17, 21). Here it is seen as a new reality which dominates or directs the life in Christ (cf. Rom 8:10). According to Galatians 2:21, this righteousness results from God's grace, for if it were possible to achieve it via obedience to the Law, Christ's death would have been in vain. In Galatians 3:21 righteousness (in us, or as our new situation "in Christ") is equated with life, which the Law is powerless to produce.

2.1.3. Righteousness of Faith. Righteousness, based on God's word and work in Christ, a gift of God's grace, comes to believers in the context and through the instrumentality of faith. Where righteousness and faith are related by Paul, it is almost always contrasted with a legalistic, or Law-oriented, righteousness. Thus in Romans 4:11, 13-14 the "righteousness of faith" is said to be based neither on circumcision nor on the deeds of the Law. In Romans 9:30-32; 10:4-6, 10 the righteousness that comes by faith is contrasted with that which is based on the Law and the doing of the works of the Law. Only the former leads to life, to salvation. Philippians 3:9 speaks of the righteousness that results from faith in Jesus, rather than "my own righteousness" based on Law. This righteousness by faith is of course the righteousness from God, "which depends on faith." This conviction is affirmed by Paul in contrast to his own former experience where, on the basis of Law-based righteousness, he judged himself as "blameless" (Phil 3:6). Such moral perfectionism as that which Paul had by pedigree and personal endeavor does not, however, bring one into right relationship with God. According to Titus 3:5 believers are saved, not because of deeds done in righteousness (here righteousness means "legal obedience"), but by God's merciful, atoning work in Christ.

2.1.4. Righteousness of Obedience. A final context is the use of righteousness in an ethical sense, characterizing the life of obedience of those who have been justified. Romans 6:13, 18, 19, 20 contrast lives/bodies as instruments or slaves of wickedness with lives yielded to God as instruments of righteousness. What is clearly in view here is the expected result of life lived in relationship with Christ, right living that is in keeping with God's purposes. Righteousness (together with peace and joy) is that which marks the believer's relationship with others (rather than judging or offending others) and is the result of God's reign.

This view of righteousness is expanded in a number of Pauline passages. In 2 Corinthians 6:7, 14 it is given as a mark of the Christian life (acting rightly, justly, morally), in contrast with evil, falsehood, inequality (*see* Ethics). Righteousness is that quality of life which bears fruit in generous giving (2 Cor 9:10) or in purity and blamelessness (Phil 1:11). In Ephesians 4:24 righteousness is paired with holiness as resembling God, in contrast to corrupt, deceitful living. It is one of the marks of those who are "children of light" in distinction from those who perform "unfruitful works of darkness" (Eph 5:9). In the Pastorals there are the exhortations to "aim at righteousness" (1 Tim 6:11; 2 Tim 2:22) and to receive "training in righteousness" (2 Tim 3:16); the context is clearly that of moral, ethical living. Finally, on the basis of faithful service, "the crown of righteousness" is granted at the eschatological judgment by God, "the righteous judge" (2 Tim 4:8).

2.2. Dikaios. The adjective *dikaios* ("upright," "just," "righteous") is ascribed to both human beings and to God. When applied to persons, it defines them as those whose lives are in keeping with God's purposes (Eph 6:1); who live before him in faithfulness (Rom 1:17; Gal 3:11); who are obedient to God's commands (Rom 2:13; 3:10; 1 Tim 1:9); live good, upright, virtuous lives (Rom 5:7; Phil 4:8; Tit 1:8); and exercise fairness and justice (Col 4:1).

Several times God is defined as "righteous" in his nature and action as the just one, the one who can be counted on to mete out justice and do what is right (Rom 3:26; 2 Thess 1:5-6; 2 Tim 4:8). Related to this is the conviction that God's Law is "holy, righteous and good" (Rom 7:12).

Paul's conviction (Rom 5:19) that Christ's obedience to God (in contrast to Adam's disobedience) will result in "many being made righteous" must be understood within the context of God's Law, which reveals the righteous purposes

of God. In terms of God's will for humanity, the goal of God's work in Christ is to transform humans into those who are righteous, whose lives are aligned with God's purposes, and who, therefore, are in conformity with the image of Christ (2 Cor 3:18).

2.3. Dikaioō. The verbal form of the noun *righteousness*, (*dikaioō*, to justify? RSV, NIV, NEB; to put right? TEV) is used almost always to describe that divine action which affects the sinner in such a way that the relation with God is altered or transformed (either ontologically, as a change in nature; or positionally, resulting from a judicial act; or relationally, as one who was alienated and is now reconciled [see 3 below]). Everywhere this action of God, emerging from his nature as the righteous one, is seen as an act of grace and takes place in the context of the exercise of faith, or trust or believing in Jesus.

Romans 3:21-31 is the most thorough statement of this distinctive Pauline theme. Its validity is grounded by Paul in the story of Abraham (Rom 4). Further reflection is given to it in such central theological texts as Romans 5:1, 9 and Galatians 2:17; 3:8, 24. The negative formulation of this truth is in the contrasting affirmation that no one is justified "by the Law." In Romans 3:20; 4:2 and Galatians 2:16; 3:11 Paul states categorically the impossibility of receiving this justifying action of God by means of successfully keeping the requirements of the Law.

There are several texts where this action of God is addressed not to the sinner but to those who are already "justified." The setting for this action is always eschatological judgment (Rom 2:13; 8:33; Gal 5:4-5). The issue in these instances is not salvation (either by works or by faith). Rather, those who have been justified (by grace through faith) appear before "the judgment seat of Christ" (2 Cor 5:10) where "the empirical reality of one's life before God as 'works' will be revealed and evaluated" (Cosgrove, 660; *see* Judgment).

2.4. Dikaiosynē Theou. The concept of God's righteousness, its nature, function and result, is central to Paul's teaching on the justification of the sinner. The genitive construction *dikaiosynē theou*, "righteousness of God" (Rom 1:17; 3:5, 21, 22; 10:3; 2 Cor 5:21), or *dikaiosynē autou*, "his righteousness" (Rom 3:25, 26), or *hē ek theou dikaiosynē*, "righteousness from God" (Phil 3:9) are found ten times. Most of these are located in

Romans, Paul's fullest discourse on God's redemptive work in Christ.

Romans 1:16-17 is foundational for understanding the meaning of this concept. For Paul the gospel—the event of the life, death and resurrection of Christ—is the historical manifestation of divine redemptive power. In that gospel "God's righteousness is revealed." Here God's righteousness and the gospel (God's saving work in Christ) are virtually synonymous (with the revelation of the saving righteousness of God being contrasted with the revelation of the wrath of God in Rom 1:18). Faith responds to God's act of righteousness, and life results.

In contrast to human faithlessness and wickedness (Rom 3:3-5) God remains faithful, and in that faithfulness his righteousness is manifested. This faithfulness (or righteousness) is given its historical particularity (according to Paul's sustained presentation in Rom 3:21-31) in the sacrificial atonement of Christ's death (Rom 3:24-25). It is explicitly stated that in this redemptive act God's righteousness has been manifested (Rom 3:21, 25, 26; *see* Death of Christ).

In all three passages in Romans (Rom 1; 3; 10), as well as in Philippians 3:9, the apprehension of God's righteousness and of its coming into the sphere of human experience is related to faith in Jesus and understood as a gift of God's grace. In addition, all the texts explicitly include a rejection of "works of the Law" as a valid instrument for attaining or receiving this righteousness of, or from, God.

The use of "righteousness of God" in 2 Corinthians 5:21 is in a context which does not share all the elements of those in Romans and Philippians. References to the instrumentality of faith or works are absent here. The context is the new creation brought into being through God's work in Christ (2 Cor 5:17). This new creation consists of those who have been reconciled to God (2 Cor 5:18-19) and who at the same time become instruments of that reconciling work within the yet-existing old creation (2 Cor 5:19-20). Paul climaxes this passage with the affirmation that the purpose of Christ's identification with us in our sin-bound existence (2 Cor 5:21a) is so that we, in relationship with Christ, "might become God's righteousness" (2 Cor 5:21b). It is highly significant for the overall understanding of this term that Paul does not say that we in Christ "might become righteous" or "might receive God's righteousness," but rather "that we might become God's righteousness" (see 4 below).

3. History of Interpretation.

A. E. McGrath's study of the history of the doctrine of justification is instructive for discerning some of the reasons why the West has understood Paul's theology of God's saving action in Christ largely in terms of justification rather than relying on the varied richness of the biblical understanding of salvation in Christ. Several complex reasons for this include the interest in Paul evidenced by the rise in Pauline scholarship during the theological renaissance of the twelfth century, especially the use of Pauline commentaries as vehicles of theological speculation. Coupled with this, the Western church had a high regard for classical jurisprudence, which made possible the semantic relationship between *iustitia* (justice) and *iustificatio* (justification), and allowed theologians of High Scholasticism to find in the cognate concept of justification a means of rationalizing the divine dispensation toward humankind in terms of justice. Luther interpreted the scholastics as understanding the righteousness of God as that by which God punishes *sinners (WA 54.185.18-20). Therefore, Luther could not see how the gospel revealing the righteousness of God could be "good news." Luther's "discovery" of the free imparting of the righteousness of God to believers is instructive in explaining why the Reformation came to be perceived as inextricably linked with the doctrine of justification. The Roman Catholic desire to establish a Catholic consensus on this issue resulted in the discussion at the Council of Trent of the reconciliation of humanity to God under the aegis of the doctrine of justification.

3.1. Patristic-Medieval: East. In the East, Paul's concept of the righteousness of God and the justification of the sinner was not a prominent means for understanding God's saving acts in Jesus Christ. J. Reumann notes that the apostolic fathers maintain the biblical view of righteousness as what God does, but they show a greater interest in the human response. Rather than giving importance to the righteousness of God and justification, Eastern Christianity emphasized the divine economy and the condescension of the Son, which led to human participation in the divine nature understood as deification (rather than justification). McGrath sees the theological differences between East and West as due to their different understandings of the work of the *Holy Spirit: the West tended to subordinate the work of the Holy Spirit to the concept of grace interposed between God and humanity; the Eastern church holds to the immediacy of the divine and one's direct encounter with the *Holy Spirit expressed as deification. With this emphasis it is natural that the Eastern Church did not evidence the Western commitment to justification as the fundamental soteriological metaphor.

3.2. Patristic-Medieval: West. In the Latin fathers and Origen, the righteousness of God is understood as distributive justice: God gives to all their due, rewarding the good and punishing the wicked. The Reformers turned to Augustine for his views on the righteousness of God.

3.2.1. Augustine. Augustine thought the righteousness of God was not the righteousness characterizing God's nature, but rather that by which God justifies sinners. His idea of faith involved an intellectual aspect: to believe is to affirm in thought. Augustine coupled faith with love (Augustine *Serm.* 90.6; 93.5; *Ep.* 183.1.3). The love of God is the theme dominating his view of justification, whereas the Reformers would coin the slogan *sola fide* ("by faith alone") to characterize justification and their understanding of the righteousness of God. In his work *On the Trinity*, Augustine makes the statement that true justifying faith is accompanied by love (*De Trin.* 15.18.32). In his comments on 1 Corinthians 13:2 he remarks that genuine faith always works through love (recalling Gal 5:6: see Crabtree). Augustine, along with some Greek fathers, underscored the gift aspect of justification. He believed that one's nature was changed through this gift.

3.2.2. Roman Catholicism. In the Roman tradition the righteousness of God was understood more as that which was demanded by God. The medieval understanding of the nature of justification referred not merely to the beginning of the Christian life, but to its continuation and ultimate perfection, in which the Christian is made righteous in the sight of God and the sight of others through a fundamental change in nature (McGrath). The prevailing pre-Reformation view in the West of the righteousness of God was that of a distributive justice whereby God judges justly according to God's holiness. A common theological position was that righteousness of God was a subjective genitive, God's holiness being the norm by which all would be judged. Luther's personal struggle with the inexorable righteousness of God resulted in an understanding of the righteousness of God that was deeper than his tradition had grasped. In Catholic thought, justification was not considered something in the present as much as a process leading to the ultimate future judgment.

3.3. The Reformation. Generally the Reformers and their theological heirs have interpreted the righteousness of God as a so-called objective genitive (see 1 above) in all instances in Paul's writings, with the possible exceptions of Romans 3:5, 25, 26. The righteousness of God was understood from the viewpoint of the individual, as that righteousness which God gives to people, and on the basis of which the sinner is approved by God. The theocentric OT meaning of the righteousness of God in the sphere of covenant relationship was displaced by an anthropocentric focus. The reformers and their successors often interpreted the righteousness of God from the human aspect because they had replaced the biblical basis of covenant relationship with the Hellenistic theory of universal law, which both God and humanity had to fulfill in order to be regarded as righteous. The emphasis on the individual under universal law rather than in covenant relationship contributed to the later "legal fiction" theory whereby those who believe in Jesus are justified, deemed righteous, even though they are not actually righteous. In this view faith in Jesus takes the place of actual righteousness.

3.3.1. Luther. Luther's concern was personal and pastoral. The fine theological distinction maintained by the Roman Catholic magisterium did not "trickle down" to village parishes. Luther interpreted the righteousness of God distinctively as a so-called objective genitive, rendering the Greek term *dikaiosynē tou theou* in Romans 1:17 as righteousness "which counts before God." Luther states the righteousness of God is the cause of salvation, and thus it is not the righteousness by which God is righteous in himself but the righteousness by which we are made righteous by God. This happens through faith in the gospel. Luther points to Augustine for the sense that the righteousness of God is that by which God imparts and makes people righteous. Luther emphasized the immediacy of justification. A person is at once just and unjust: this suggests a composite view of Luther's new understanding of the righteousness of God, in addition to the traditional understanding of the distributive justice of God.

For Luther, works are the result of the righteousness given by God. Sanctification is a process that will not be consummated in this life. Luther clearly separated justification from regeneration and sanctification. This perspective gave rise to the understanding of justification as a new status before God: "Thus in ourselves we are sinners, and yet through faith we are righteous by God's imputation. For we believe Him who promises to free us, and in the meantime we strive that sin may not rule over us but that we may withstand it until He takes it from us" (WA 56.271). In Catholic thought, God responds to those who do what they can by giving them enabling grace which then leads to saving grace. Luther broke with this tradition in that he found that God provided the preconditions for justification (see Watson).

3.3.2. Calvin. Calvin in his *Commentary on Romans* presents his understanding of the righteousness of God in Romans 1:17 as that which is approved before God's tribunal. Calvin associated sanctification with justification and described sanctification in terms of being in Christ. According to Calvin, God communicates his righteousness to us. In a nearly mystical sense, through faith Jesus communicates himself to those who believe. Works have no place in the justification of sinners. Calvin refutes the notion of a fiction involved in the justification of sinners. God provides all that is necessary. He cautions not to understand righteousness as a quality; we are righteous only insofar as Christ reconciles the Father to us. Calvin, more so than Luther, emphasizes the relational aspect of the righteousness of God. Luther's view of the righteousness of God seems to contain the aspect of acquittal. Calvin emphasizes the marvelous nature of the communication, or imparting, of God's righteousness to us.

3.4. Post-Reformation. Just as the Western Church experienced the scholasticism of the twelfth century, Protestant Orthodoxy shifted from Calvin's christological emphasis to other matters, such as predestination, federal theology and the perseverance of the saints. Lutheranism shifted its emphasis from justification of sinners and the righteousness of God to deal with these developments within the Reformed camp. The Pietist movement within Lutheranism was a reaction against a strictly forensic understanding of righteousness. The pastoral aspects of Pietism later influenced Lutheranism to emphasize practical aspects of righteousness, reflecting an interest in promoting personal piety.

John Wesley argued for the Pietist position in his emphasis on personal righteousness subsequent to justification. In his sermon on "The Lord Our Righteousness" he adheres to imputation but understands the Holy Spirit to have a sanctifying aspect on the believer. The believer's basis of justification is the righteousness of Christ "implanted in everyone in whom God has imputed it." He maintains there is no true faith—justifying faith—which does not have the righteousness of Christ for its object. Wesley sees faith in Jesus' death, and hence the imputation of his righteousness, as the cause, end and middle term of salvation.

3.5. Currents of Recent Discussion. The variations within the history of interpretation reflect two basic views: (1) that God's righteousness is a quality of God (or Christ) imparted, making the sinner righteous; (2) that God, the righteous one, declares the sinner to be righteous in a legal transaction (imputed). These dominant views have increasingly been challenged. J. Reumann contends that there is a stronger basis in Christian hymnody for these views than in the NT. For Paul does not speak of Christ's merits or God's righteous essence being so imputed to us. G. E. Ladd contends that forensic (declared) righteousness is real righteousness because our relationship with God is just as real as one's subjective ethical condition. One is in fact "righteous" (defined as right relationship with God) based on what has been done for us objectively in Christ. The ethical content follows on its heels. Ladd maintains that righteousness as acquittal and right conduct belong together.

H. Cremer (1900) launched scholarship in a new direction by pointing to the OT understanding of *ṣĕdāqâ* ("righteousness") as covenant faithfulness, and seeing this meaning as the subjective genitive, not in the ontological sense, but as referring to God's saving activity as Redeemer.

Some scholars, such as R. Bultmann, attempt to combine both the objective and subjective aspects of the righteousness of God, suggesting a "genitive of the author" to describe God's righteousness which is given to believers as the basis of one's relationship with God. The righteousness of God is the gift which makes possible this new existence for the individual. His existential interpretation involves the kerygmatic reality of the individual: one continues to appropriate God's "rightwising" verdict in obedient existential decision and becomes what one is declared to be. Bultmann's inattention to OT background and to Paul's apocalyptic understanding of history results in an anthropocentric and individualistic orientation of the righteousness of God.

There have been various attempts to reevaluate the meaning of the righteousness of God in Paul's writings (see bibliographical details in Brauch). In 1954 J. Bollier, a critic of the legal fiction theory of justification, suggested that God requires a person to be righteous, to recognize God's sovereignty and to submit to God's Lordship. Under the old covenant as well as the new, God has graciously offered faith as the way a person may recognize God as one's Lord and so gain God's approval. Faith is the appropriate human response to the self-revelation of God. Faith actually is righteousness, for it is the way in which one may fulfill this obligation toward God within the covenant relationship. Thus Paul speaks of the "righteousness of faith" in Romans 4:11, 13. Bollier opts for a subjective genitive, maintaining that the righteousness of God is God's own inherent righteousness rather than the righteousness of which God is the author and which he approves. Anticipating E. Käsemann, Bollier further posits that this righteousness of God has a transcendent as well as an immanent aspect, for one is directly affected by the manifestation of this righteousness.

E. Käsemann has had a great impact on the discussion. Although he sees the righteousness of God in Romans 3:5, 25-26 as referring to God's character, he emphasizes that Paul's view of the righteousness of God accents its gift-character against the backdrop of Jewish apocalypticism. "The gift itself has the character of power, salvation-creating power" (Käsemann). The gift is never a personal possession separated from the giver. In this way Käsemann captures the eschatological nature of the relationship of God with creation in a forward orientation toward the consummation of God's saving acts in Jesus Christ. God's faithfulness is faithfulness to the creation, not simply to the individual (cf. Bultmann). God's sovereignty over the universe is established eschatologically in Jesus. A person within that framework experiences a change in

lordship. Johannine and Pauline language now go hand in hand, since by "abiding" in Jesus, believers become what they are. The righteousness of God is God's power in Christ reaching out to the world. Salvation is experienced in the sphere of Christ's lordship, which is entered in response to God's righteousness (Käsemann; on this see Way, 177-236).

The subjective genitive is also maintained by two of Käsemann's students, C. Müller and P. Stuhlmacher. Müller (1965) agrees with Käsemann, but places his emphasis on the eschatological victory of God, the final cosmic trial at which creation submits to God (see Eschatology). God's ultimate victory reveals his righteousness and is acknowledged by humanity. That final victory is anticipated in the present, where God's lordship is a reality in everyday life. P. Stuhlmacher stresses the saving aspect of the righteousness of God in that the creator makes right the world on account of his creation-faithfulness, even by raising the dead. The righteousness of God is God's creating power fostering faith and recreating the world. Stuhlmacher sees the righteousness of God as the center of Pauline theology whereby Paul shows a complete correlation between judicial and ontological ideas of righteousness. Thus justification refers to a divine creative activity, the actualization of the righteousness of God as a "Word event," which creates a new being at baptism. Stuhlmacher understands justification for Paul to mean the obligating, renewing call of the individual, by the power of God, into the realm of encounter with God that has been opened by Christ. The renewed calling culminates in service.

The Roman Catholic scholar K. Kertelge follows a similar line of thought to Stuhlmacher. The righteousness of God denotes God's redemptive activity and not God's gift of righteousness to us that leads to salvation. This reality consists of nothing except the new relationship between God and humanity created by God, which from the divine side is lordship and from the human side is obedience. For Paul the present and the future character of God's eschatological redemption are essentially identical, because both have their basis in the Christ event. Righteousness is by faith, not as a possession, but as a relationship in which one acknowledges God's claim upon one's life.

H. Brunner understands the OT material regarding righteousness to refer to a comprehensive order corresponding to God's will, which encompasses both nature and humanity. In Paul the theme is the change from alienation to reconciliation (2 Cor 5:17-21), from the old world to the new, from the old creation to the new. Humans are re-created by Christ: his death means his subjection to sin, namely the power of alienation from God; but it also means believers' becoming "God's righteousness." They become transformed by God's power into the people of the reestablished created order, the reconciled new world of God's people of the new covenant. In Romans 1 Paul speaks of the will of the creator being obscured by human rejection, but the gospel has revealed God's power for redemption. The righteousness of God is God's redemptive saving act. God's saving action has always been at work, as evidenced in the OT, but has now been clearly revealed in the Christ event. For those who believe in Christ, the reality and power of sin have been put aside. God's new created order, which is the removal of the alienation of sin, has been brought into being. To be righteous or declared righteous is neither a juridical act nor an ontological transformation, but a state of being restored to right relationship with God because the alienating reality of sin has been set aside.

4. God's Righteousness as Relation-Restoring Love.

The history of interpretation, including the recent perspectives sketched above, reveals two facets; (1) that the understanding of the righteousness of God has been largely dominated by Greek and Latin categories, where righteousness as a quality of God's character is either given to us and makes us righteous, or is the basis for God's judicial pronouncement, declaring us righteous; (2) that the more recent discussion, in seeking to take more seriously Paul's grounding in the OT, has found the earlier understanding to be an inadequate explication of Paul's meaning. Particularly important has been the insistence on the OT covenantal context of the righteousness of God as an interpretive background for the Pauline formulations.

Within that OT context, and beside other meanings and nuances (Brunner), the idea of God's righteousness appears prominently in salvation texts, where God's redemptive action toward his covenant people is defined by this term. It is God's righteousness which saves from enemies, from threatening situations, from the state of alienation from God. In such settings God's righteousness is frequently defined by the terms "steadfast love" and "faithfulness" (e.g., Is 11:5; 16:5; Ps 5:7-8; 89:13-14; 98:2-3). These relational attributes are in some contexts virtually synonymous with "righteousness" and "salvation" (e.g., Ps 85:7-13). Thus God's righteousness may be rendered as "saving deed" or "relation-restoring love."

Paul's use of "righteousness of God" may best be understood against the background of this particular OT concept. For Paul, "unrighteousness" results from disobedience, whether of persons generally, who refuse to acknowledge God (Rom 1:28), and obey unrighteousness and disobey truth (Rom 2:8), or of God's people who refuse to acknowledge God, and are disobedient within the covenant relationship (Rom 3:3-5; 10:21).

It is the reality of alienation, defined synonymously as "faithlessness" (Rom 3:3) and "unrighteousness" (Rom 3:5), which Paul knows to have been addressed by the revelation (Rom 1:16-17) or manifestation (Rom 3:21-26) of God's righteousness. In both texts the concrete historical expression of "God's righteousness" is the event of Christ: defined in Romans 1:16 as "the gospel" and "the power of God for salvation"; and in Romans 3:24 as "the redemption which is in Christ Jesus."

Paul contends that God is faithful to his creation/covenant relationship (Rom 3:3-4), his action is righteous (Rom 3:26) and it is this action in response to his rebellious creation which Paul therefore calls the righteousness of God. The term designates that act of God which restores the broken relationship. "Righteousness" in this context is not an attribute of God, but designates God's forgiving love and redemptive intervention in the world through Christ.

The righteousness of God, understood as God's relation-restoring love, is central to Paul's argument in Romans 3:21-26. The incarnation of the righteousness of God in the redemptive work of the cross leads to forgiveness; and forgiveness restores broken relationships. Because this is purely the act of God, Paul calls it a gift. Since a gift is ineffective unless appropriated, it must be "received by faith." The result of this gracious act of God is the justification ("setting right") of the sinner. The passage says nothing about an essential or judicial transaction; rather, it declares the restoration of the divine-human relationship through what Christ did by his death.

The language of "submitting to the righteousness of God" in Romans 10:3 confirms Paul's understanding of it as God's relation-restoring intervention. The attempt to establish one's own righteousness—one's own position before God—is a rejection of the coming of God's righteousness in Christ, God's way of saving the world. For to submit means to acknowledge one's severed relation with God and to confess the lordship of Christ (Rom 10:7; *see* Lord).

The difficult expression of 2 Corinthians 5:21, that in (relationship with) Christ "we might become the righteousness of God" further underlines a relational rather than a judicial or ontological meaning. The text is concerned with reconciliation to God in and through Christ and calls those who are reconciled to become instruments of that reconciling work (2 Cor 5:18-19). In that context, the phrase "to become God's righteousness" means that believers become participants in God's reconciling action, extensions of his restoring love.

For Paul, then, God's righteousness is God's saving deed. In continuity with OT expressions of God's righteousness as God's faithfulness and steadfast love toward Israel, Paul sees this divine action finally expressed in the life, death and *resurrection of Jesus. The acceptance of that divine condescension through the act of faith justifies us (makes us right) with God. Righteousness is present in this restored relationship when life is lived in conformity with God's purposes.

See also CREATION, NEW CREATION; ESCHATOLOGY; GOD; JUDGMENT; JUSTIFICATION; LAW; ROMANS, LETTER TO THE; SALVATION.

DPL: CENTER OF PAUL'S THEOLOGY; CROSS, THEOLOGY OF THE; EXPIATION, PROPITIATION, MERCY SEAT; FAITH; LOVE; MERCY; PAUL AND HIS INTERPRETERS; PEACE, RECONCILIATION; RESTORATION OF ISRAEL; TRIUMPH; WRATH, DESTRUCTION.

BIBLIOGRAPHY. O. Betz, "Der gekreuzigte Christus: unsere Weisheit und Gerechtigkeit der alttestamentliche Hintergrund von 1 Kor 1—2," in *Tradition and Interpretation in the New Testament*, ed. G. F. Hawthorne with O. Betz (Grand Rapids: Eerdmans, 1987) 195-215; P. Blaser, "Paulus und Luther über Gottes Gerechtigkeit," *Catholica* 36 (1982) 269-79; J. A. Bollier, "The Righteousness of God," *Int* 8 (1954) 404-13; M. T. Brauch, "Perspectives on 'God's Righteousness' in Recent German Discussion," in E. P. Sanders, *Paul and Palestinian Judaism* (Philadelphia: Fortress, 1977) 523-42; H. Brunner, "Die Gerechtigkeit Gottes" *ZRG* 39 (1987) 210-25; R. Bultmann, "ἔλεος κτλ," *TDNT* 2.477-87; C. H. Cosgrove, "Justification in Paul: A Linguistic and Theological Reflection," *JBL* 106 (1987) 653-70; A. B. Crabtree, *The Restored Relationship* (London: Carey Kingsgate, 1963); H. Cremer, *Die Paulinische Rechtfertigungslehre im Zussammenhang ihrer geschichtlichen Voraussetzungen* (1900); J. A. Fitzmyer, *Pauline Theology* (Engelwood Cliffs, NJ: Prentice-Hall, 1967); E. Käsemann, " 'The Righteousness of God' in Paul," in *New Testament Questions of Today* (Philadelphia: Fortress, 1969) 168-82; K. Kertelge, *"Rechtfertigung" bei Paulus* (NTAbh n.s. 3; 2d ed.; Münster: Aschendorf, 1971); idem, "δικαιοσύνη," "δικαιόω," *EDNT* 1.325-34; L. J. Kuyper, "Righteousness and Salvation," *SJT* 30 (1977) 233-52; G. E. Ladd, "Righteousness in Romans," *SWJT* 19 (1976) 6-17; E. Lohse "Die Gerechtigkeit Gottes in der Paulinischen Theologie," in *Die Einheit des Neuen Testaments* (Göttingen: Vandenhoeck & Ruprecht, 1973) 209-27; A. E. McGrath, *Iustitia Dei: A History of the Christian Doctrine of Justification* (2 vols. Cambridge: Cambridge University Press, 1986); R. K. Moore, "Issues Involved in the Interpretation of *Dikaiosyne Theou* in the Pauline Corpus," *Colloquium: The Australian and New Zealand Theological Society* 23 (1991) 59-70; C. Müller, *Gottesgerechtigkeit und Gottesvolk* (FRLANT 86; Göttingen: Vandenhoeck & Ruprecht, 1964); J. Piper, "The Demonstration of the Righteousness of God in Romans 3:25, 26," *JSNT* 7 (1980) 2-32; B. Przybylski, *Righteousness in Matthew and His World of Thought* (SNTSMS 41; Cambridge: Cambridge University Press, 1980); G. Quell and G. Schrenk, "δίκη κτλ," *TDNT* 2.174-225; J. Reumann, "Justification of God: Righteousness and the Cross," *Moravian Theological Seminary: Bulletin* (1964) 16-31; idem, "Righteousness (Early Judaism-New Testament)," *ABD* 5.736-73; idem, *Righteousness in the New Testament: Justification in the United States, Lutheran-Roman Catholic Dialogue* (Philadelphia: Fortress, 1983); idem, "The 'Righteousness of God' and the 'Economy of God': Two Great Doctrinal Themes Historically Compared," in *Askum-Thyateira*, ed. G. Dragas (London: Thyateira House, 1985) 615-37; L. Sabourin, "Formulations of Christian Beliefs in

Recent Exposition on Paul's Epistles to the Romans and Galatians," *RSB* 1 (1981) 120-36; A. Schweitzer, *The Mysticism of the Apostle Paul* (London: A & C Black, 1931); J. J. Scullion, "Righteousness (OT)," *ABD* 5.724-36; M. A. Seifrid, *Christ, Our Righteousness: Paul's Theology of Justification* (NSBT 9; Downers Grove, IL: InterVarsity Press, 2000); M. L. Soards, "The Righteousness of God in the Writings of the Apostle Paul," *BTB* 15 (1985) 104-9; P. Stuhlmacher, *Gerechtigkeit Gottes bei Paulus* (FRLANT 82; Göttingen: Vandenhoeck & Ruprecht, 1965); idem, *Reconciliation, Law, and Righteousness* (Philadelphia: Fortress, 1986); P. Watson, *Let God Be God* (London: Epworth, 1953); D. V. Way, *The Lordship of Christ: Ernst Käsemann's Interpretation of Paul's Theology* (Oxford: Clarendon, 1991); S. K. Williams, "The 'Righteousness of God' in Romans," *JBL* 99 (1980) 241-90; N. T. Wright, *What Saint Paul Really Said* (Grand Rapids: Eerdmans, 1997); J. A. Ziesler, *The Meaning of Righteousness in Paul: A Linguistic and Theological Inquiry* (SNTSMS 20; Cambridge: Cambridge University Press, 1972).

K. L. Onesti and M. T. Brauch

RIGHTEOUSNESS III: ACTS, HEBREWS, GENERAL EPISTLES, REVELATION

In the biblical tradition the noun *righteousness* and the adjective *righteous* normally denote the character, behavior and status appropriate to the *covenant relationship *God formed with the world through *Israel. God demonstrates righteousness through faithfulness to his promises, while humanity expresses righteousness in and through loyal obedience. "To justify" denotes the activity of "putting right" (in the case of God) and "being put right" (in the case of humans). This "being put right" can be ethical (i.e., "to be transformed"), forensic (i.e., "to be declared right") or relational (i.e., "to be reconciled").

Despite a long and cherished history in Christian theology (see McGrath), the varied theological nuances of righteousness language within the Bible have sometimes been overlooked. Part of the problem is that English employs two word families ("righteousness"/ "righteous" and "justify"/"justification") to translate only one family of words in Greek—the noun *dikaiosynē*, the adjective *dikaios* and the verb *dikaioō*. Because the word *justification*

has obtained prominence as a legal term in English, there is a strong temptation to read juridical connotations into any occurrence of a *dik-* stem word in Greek. The forensic interpretation of the Protestant slogan "justification by faith alone" has further blinded readers to the diverse and often ethical uses of righteousness language. Moreover, the supposed anthropological orientation of righteousness in Paul has unfairly truncated the meaning of justification: as the antidote to a guilty conscience, it primarily relates to the resolution of an individual's existential crisis (Stendahl). However, the kaleidoscopic contextual meanings and the variegated theological uses of the noun *dikaiosynē*, the adjective *dikaios* and the verb *dikaioō* mean that righteousness or justification cannot be reduced to a single theological concept. Righteousness justification language is one of the many ways that early Christians sought to convey the meaning and significance of God's saving deeds wrought in Jesus.

Thus it is not surprising to find that in the later NT documents, language about righteousness or justification falls into four, broad domains of usage: a theological domain (to speak of God), a christological domain (to define the person and work of Jesus), a soteriological domain (to describe the means and consequences of *salvation) and an ethical domain (to depict the character and behavior associated with spiritual transformation). Informing and guiding the use of language about righteousness or justification in each of these domains is an eschatological perspective common to early Christianity.

1. The Righteousness of God
2. Jesus, the Righteous One
3. Justification by Faith as a New Pattern of Religion
4. Righteousness and Ethics
5. Righteousness and Eschatology
6. Summary

1. The Righteousness of God.

Given the supposed foundational character of "righteousness of God" (*dikaiosynē theou*) as God's saving activity in Paul's thinking (Rom 1:17; 3:5, 22; 10:3; 1 Cor 1:30; 2 Cor 5:21; cf. Phil 3:9; see Käsemann, Stuhlmacher), it is remarkable that the phrase so rarely appears in post-Pauline Christianity. Outside of Paul the phrase occurs only twice (Mt 6:33; Jas 1:20; on 2 Pet 1:1, see 2 below).

James states that the "anger of man does not work the righteousness of God" (Jas 1:20). There are three ways to understand the phrase *dikaiosynēn theou*. (1) Human anger does not produce *(ergazetai)* the proper moral disposition or behavior *(dikaiosynēn)* within humans (see discussion in Davids, 93). (2) Human anger does not achieve *(ergazetai)* the level of perfection that God demands *(dikaiosynēn)*, especially that demand to be revealed at the last *judgment (Ziesler 133, 135). Or, preferably, (3) human anger does not bring into being *(ergazetai)* the state of affairs that God desires *(dikaiosynēn)*. By tying together the moral, forensic and eschatological senses, this last reading conceptually links the "righteousness of God" here with the *"kingdom of God" in the teaching of Jesus (Martin, 48). This reading also reveals that James is not reacting against Paul's notion of *dikaiosynē theou* (cf. Dibelius, 111). James stands much closer to *Matthew, where righteousness is indicative of God's kingdom (Mt 6:33; cf. Przybylski, 89-92).

The closest we come to Paul's rich and highly charged notion of *dikaiosynē theou* is in 1 John. The author claims that "If we confess our sins, he [God] is faithful and just *[pistos estin kai dikaios]* and will forgive our sins and cleanse us from all unrighteousness" (1 Jn 1:9). The paralleling of *dikaios* with *pistos* points to God's activity of forgiving sins and echoes his longstanding commitment to honor repentance and sacrifice (e.g., Ex 34:6-7). God's faithfulness thus becomes synonymous with his righteousness (Schnackenburg, 83).

The other uses of righteousness with reference to God are all clearly forensic. Paul in his Areopagus speech (Acts 17:31) declares that God has a fixed day in which he will "judge the world in righteousness" *(krinein . . . en dikaiosynē)*. This quotation of Psalm 95:13 (LXX) positions God in a traditional role as judge. 1 Peter (1 Pet 2:23) depicts Jesus as trusting the one (i.e., God) "who judges justly" *(tō krinonti dikaiōs)*. Three times in Revelation (Rev 16:5, 7; 19:2; cf. Rev 15:3) it is said of God that his judgments are "just" *(dikaios)*.

2. Jesus, the Righteous One.

Righteousness language is also applied to Jesus. In fact, various traditions entitle Jesus the "Righteous One" *(ho dikaios)*. In their speeches Peter, Stephen and Paul all name Jesus the "Righteous One" *(ho dikaios)*. Peter (Acts 3:14) charges his Jewish listeners with having denied "the Holy and Righteous One" *(ton hagion kai dikaion)*. Stephen (Acts 7:52; cf. Heb 10:37-38) understands the prophets as preaching about the "coming of the Righteous One" *(tēs eleuseōs tou dikaiou)*. Ananias (Acts 22:14) interprets Paul's christophany as an apocalyptic appearance of the "Righteous One" *(ton dikaion)*.

Jesus' priestly role as an advocate with the Father earns him the title "Jesus Christ, the Righteous" *(Iēsoun Christon dikaion)*, a confession common within the Johannine community (1 Jn 2:1, 29; 3:7). 1 Peter also names Jesus the "Righteous One" *(dikaios)* in an early confession of faith (1 Pet 3:18), and Hebrews applies Psalm 45:7 to Jesus to show that God's Son "loved righteousness and hated lawlessness" (Heb 1:9).

The special endowment of a figure with one of God's attributes (e.g., wisdom, holiness or glory) or the outright personification of an attribute were important ways Jews portrayed divine mediation (Hurtado, 41-50). In Second Temple Judaism, God's attribute of righteousness was often personified or given as a special endowment to some heavenly figure (e.g., *1 Enoch* 38:2; 53:6; 1QM 1:8; 17:8; 1QMyst 5-6; 1QIsaa 51:5; 11QPsaa 26:11; see Baumgarten, 219-39). Entitling Jesus the "Righteous One" positions him as God's chief agent.

As the "Righteous One," Jesus manifests what P. G. Davis calls the "triple pattern" of divine mediation. Jesus' substitutionary death (1 Pet 3:18) represents the legacy pattern, emphasizing the soteriological consequences of his past mediatorial deeds. Jesus' continuing role as an advocate with God the Father (1 Jn 2:1) reveals an interventionistic pattern, emphasizing the efficacy of his present mediatorial deeds. And the revelation of Jesus as a righteous judge at the parousia (Rev 19:11; cf. Acts 7:52) displays the consummation pattern, emphasizing the forensic character of his future mediatorial deeds. Thus while the title "Righteous One" closes the gap between God and Jesus (i.e., Jesus is marked as a special agent of God because he embodies one of God's attributes), the mediatorial deeds ascribed to Jesus as the "Righteous One" also represent a significant innovation: the concentration of the triple pattern of mediation in Jesus—a rarity in Judaism (Davis, 502)—highlights his unique status. The title "Righteous One" may well have been one of the earliest ways that Christians expressed their belief in the divinity of Jesus (Longenecker, 47).

One reading of 2 Peter's opening address supports such a view. There the author affirms that the readers have obtained a "faith in the righteousness of God and *Christ" (pistin en dikaiosynē tou theou hēmōn kai sōtēros Iēsou Christou, 2 Pet 1:1; cf. 2 Thess 1:12; Tit 2:13). Since it is best to understand both theou and sōtēros as appellations of Jesus (Brown, 184; Cullmann, 314), this text refers to Jesus as God (not to Jesus and God). The resulting translation would be "faith in the righteousness of our God and Savior, Jesus." 2 Peter then seems to endorse a belief in the righteousness (= divinity or divine status) of Jesus (cf. Harris, 237). Like the attributes glory and wisdom, righteousness not only associates Jesus with God as his chief vizier but also helps demarcate Jesus as God (the embodiment of God's divine presence).

3. Justification by Faith as a New Pattern of Religion.

E. P. Sanders helpfully outlines the way in which Palestinian Judaism worked. He describes a fivefold soteriological pattern: Jews believed (1) that they were elected by grace; (2) that God gave the commandments as a gift; (3) that obedience to the commandments brings blessing while disobedience brings cursing; (4) that repentance and atonement for sin (5) will yield God's forgiveness. Sanders terms this pattern of religion "covenantal nomism." Within this pattern of religion, righteousness was seen as a way of maintaining the covenant relationship and never as a means of obtaining or earning a relationship with God (Sanders, 205, 544).

This makes Paul's theology of *justification distinctive. For Paul, in direct contrast to Judaism, both "righteousness" and "faith" were used as entry terms: *justification by faith was the means of obtaining a right relationship with God. Furthermore, Paul insisted that a person initially justified by faith remains so through faith (Gal 3:1-3; Col 2:6-7; see Gundry). Paul, for all of his indebtedness to Judaism, conceptualized a completely new pattern of religion. The clarity and force of Paul's soteriological innovations make an examination of statements about justification in other Christian writers all the more intriguing.

3.1. Acts. Acts twice depicts Paul as preaching about righteousness or justification. In his Ar-

eopagus speech (Acts 13:38-39) Paul declares that through Jesus God forgives sins and that belief in Jesus "justifies" (dikaiountai) when the law was unable to do so (ouk . . . dikaiōthēnai). Justification here describes the movement from being unsaved to being saved, and consequently fits closely to the pattern of religion envisioned by Paul (see esp. Rom 8:2-4). In his defense before Felix, Paul again preaches about "faith in Christ Jesus" (Acts 24:24). This "faith in Christ" is further defined as "righteousness [dikaiosynēs], self-control and judgment" (Acts 24:25). As Acts styles it, Paul's christocentric preaching consisted in a message about salvation (righteousness), *ethics (self-control) and eschatological judgment (but see Reumann, 141). "Righteousness" here again describes "entrance" into salvation.

3.2. Hebrews. The use of righteousness language in two short comments about Abel and Noah in Hebrews allows a glimpse of that author's soteriological pattern. "By faith" Abel offered a better sacrifice and thereby "received approval as righteous" (emartyrēthē einai dikaios), in that God accepted his gift (Heb 11:4; cf. 1 Jn 3:12). Noah became an "heir of righteousness that comes by faith" (tēs kata pistin dikaiosynēs egeneto klēronomos) when he constructed the ark (Heb 11:7; cf. 2 Pet 2:5). Although it does not employ the formula "justified by faith," Hebrews, in its retrofitting of these two OT stories, represents a perspective that coheres with Paul's (Lane, 2:340; cf. Bacon, 14). Abel and Noah exemplify the faith praised at Hebrews 11:1 and Hebrews 10:37-38 (quoting Hab 2:4; Bruce, 71-72) and illustrate that faith serves as the only legitimate ground for righteousness.

3.3. James. Ever since Luther, James 2:14-26 has long plagued interpreters with its apparent contradictions with Paul at the point of justification. However, a close reading of James's *rhetoric reveals that this passage complements rather than contradicts Paul.

James's opponents contend that faith and works can legitimately be separated from each other (Jas 2:18; see Martin, 82-84). James responds by arguing for the interdependence of faith and works (Jas 2:18). Through an ironic appeal to the "faith" of demonic powers, James shows that "faith" is a necessary but insufficient basis for enjoying salvation (Jas 2:19). "Faith apart from works is barren" (Jas 2:20). James finds proof for this in the figure of *Abraham (Jas 2:21-22). In the offering of his son Isaac

(Gen 22:1-14) Abraham "was justified" (*edikaiōthē*). Faith "was active" (*synērgei*) in Abraham's works, and works "completed" (*eteleiōthē*) his faith. Genesis 15:6—"Abraham believed God, and it was reckoned to him as righteousness [*dikaiosynēn*]"—was fulfilled (*eplērōthē*) in Genesis 22 (Jas 2:23). Thus for everyone, and not for Abraham alone, the presence of justifying faith is demonstrated by works (Jas 2:24). To this James provides a second example, that of Rahab, whose faith was also completed in her works (Jas 2:25). James finally reiterates his point that faith apart from works is "dead" (Jas 2:26)

James is obviously seeking to correct something in early Christianity that he saw as an error (Reumann, 150). Specifically, James is responding to opponents who had either misunderstood Paul or improperly radicalized Paul's teaching of "justification by faith alone" (Davids 51, 130-31). Because of his opponents' misuse of the words, "faith" and "justify" take on different meanings for James than they do for Paul. Faith in James refers to intellectual assent, whereas for Paul faith means the commitment of one's life, which includes a change in one's behavior. Thus what Paul means by faith (as in Gal 5:6) is functionally equivalent to James's faith-as-demonstrated-by-works formula. For James the verb *justify* (Jas 2:21, 24, 25) bears a demonstrative meaning, whereas *dikaioō* in Paul should be read most often as forensic declaration.

What James and Paul do agree on is that "faith" and "justify" are entry terms (Sloan, 8-9), that complete and utter commitment to God is the means of justification and that good works should follow initial justification.

3.4. 1 John. 1 John (*see* John, Letters of) makes nearly the same point as James: righteous deeds are evidence of salvation. (This lends credence to the theory that [Paul's?] teaching on justification by faith alone had been greatly misunderstood; see 2 Pet 3:16.) The author explicitly ties the practice of righteousness (*ho poiōn tēn dikaiosynēn*) with conversion (1 Jn 2:29; 3:7, 10). Good works become the mark of conversion. While not specifically connecting righteousness or justification with faith, 1 John does ground the practice of righteousness with *christology. "He who does right is righteous, as he [Jesus] is righteous" (1 Jn 3:7). Laying claim to righteousness involves a christoformic pattern of living.

4. Righteousness and Ethics.

In the later documents of the NT the noun *dikaiosynē* and the adjective *dikaios* always have an "ethical content" (Ziesler, 141). This ethical content can be expressed in many ways. Righteousness language can refer to the character of a human (2 Pet 2:8; Rev 22:11); behavior (Acts 10:35; 1 Pet 2:24; 3:13-14; 1 Jn 3:12); a person's status, which is grounded in behavior (Acts 10:22; 1 Pet 4:18; 2 Pet 2:7-8; Jas 5:16); or to the process of moral transformation (Heb 12:11; Jas 3:18; 2 Pet 2:21).

5. Righteousness and Eschatology.

The soteriological and ethical uses temporally anchor righteousness or justification language to the writers' past or present. However, early Christianity also employed righteousness language to describe what the future was to be like. The new heavens and new earth will be a place in which righteousness dwells (2 Pet 3:13). The righteous person should look forward to the age to come, despite the prospect of a righteous judgment (Acts 17:31; Rev 19:11). The future will entail a resurrection of both the just and the unjust (Acts 24:15). The future will be a time of final salvation for the righteous (1 Pet 4:18), a time in which final transformation (Heb 12:23) and reversal will occur. Because the future kingdom is immanent, there is an ethical urgency for the righteous to practice righteousness (Rev 22:11).

6. Summary.

Teaching about righteousness or justification formed part of early Christian catechesis. Along with hope and love, righteousness was, according to Barnabas (Barn. 1.6), one of the "three basic doctrines of the Lord" (*tria dogmata kyriou*). Christians were to be skilled in the "word of righteousness" (Heb 5:13). This instruction emphasized God's righteousness (his faithfulness and his righteous character), Jesus as the Righteous One (his unique status and past, present and future deeds), the proper place of faith and works in salvation, and a hope for a future in which righteousness will rule. Early Christianity's use of the language of righteousness or justification is as diverse as it is evocative.

See also ABRAHAM; COVENANT, NEW COVENANT; DEATH OF CHRIST; ESCHATOLOGY; GOD; JUDGMENT; LAW.

DLNTD: FAITH AND WORKS; FORGIVENESS;

OBEDIENCE, LAWLESSNESS.

BIBLIOGRAPHY. B. W. Bacon, "The Doctrine of Faith in Hebrews, James and Clement of Rome," *JBL* 19 (1900) 12-21; J. M. Baumgarten, "The Heavenly Tribunal and the Personification of *Sedeq* in Jewish Apocalyptic," *ANRW* 2.19.1 (1979) 219-39; R. E. Brown, *An Introduction to New Testament Christology* (New York: Paulist, 1994); F. F. Bruce, "Justification by Faith in the Non-Pauline Writings of the New Testament," *EvQ* 34 (1952) 66-77; J. Buchanan, *The Doctrine of Justification* (Edinburgh: T & T Clark, 1867); H. Chadwick, "Justification by Faith and Hospitality," *TU* 79 (1961) 281-85; O. Cullmann, *The Christology of the New Testament* (Philadelphia: Westminster, 1959); P. H. Davids, *The Epistle of James* (NIGTC; Grand Rapids: Eerdmans, 1982); P. G. Davis, "Divine Agents, Mediators and New Testament Christology," *JTS* 45 (1994) 479-503; M. Dibelius and H. Greeven, *James* (Herm; Philadelphia: Fortress, 1976); R. H. Gundry, "Grace, Works and Staying Saved in Paul," *Bib* 66 (1985) 1-38; M. J. Harris, *Jesus as God: The New Testament Use of* Theos *in Reference to Jesus* (Grand Rapids: Baker, 1992); L. Hurtado, *One God, One Lord: Early Christian Devotion and Ancient Jewish Monotheism* (Philadelphia: Fortress, 1988); E. Käsemann, " 'The Righteousness of God' in Paul," in *New Testament Questions of Today* (Philadelphia: Fortress, 1969) 168-82; W. L. Lane, *Hebrews* (2 vols.; WBC; Dallas: Word, 1992); R. N. Longenecker, *The Christology of Early Jewish Christianity* (London: SCM, 1970); A. E. McGrath, *Iustitia Dei: A History of the Christian Doctrine of Justification* (2 vols.; Cambridge: Cambridge University Press, 1986); R. P. Martin, *James* (WBC; Waco, TX: Word, 1988); B. Przybylski, *Righteousness in Matthew and the World of His Thought* (SNTSMS 41; Cambridge: Cambridge University Press, 1980); H. Räisänen, "Righteousness by Works: An Early Catholic Doctrine? Thoughts on 1 Clement," in *Jesus, Paul and Torah: Collected Essays* (JSNTSup 43; Sheffield: JSOT, 1992) chap. 8; J. Reumann, *Righteousness in the New Testament* (Philadelphia: Fortress, 1983); E. P. Sanders, *Paul and Palestinian Judaism* (Philadelphia: Fortress, 1977); R. Schnackenburg, *The Johannine Epistles* (New York: Crossroad, 1992); R. B. Sloan, "The Christology of James," *CTR* 1 (1986) 3-29; K. Stendahl, "The Apostle Paul and the Introspective Conscience of the West," in *Paul Among Jews and Gentiles* (Philadelphia: Fortress, 1976) 78-96; P. Stuhlmacher, *Gerechtigkeit Gottes bei Paulus* (2d ed; FRLANT 82; Göttingen: Vandenhoeck & Ruprecht, 1966); J. A. Ziesler, *The Meaning of Righteousness in Paul: A Linguistic and Theological Enquiry* (SNTSMS 20; Cambridge: Cambridge University Press, 1971).

C. C. Newman

RIGHTEOUSNESS OF GOD. *See* RIGHTEOUSNESS II.

RISING WITH CHRIST. *See* RESURRECTION II.

ROMAN EMPIRE. *See* ROME.

ROMAN PROVINCIAL ADMINISTRATION. *See* ROME.

ROMANS, LETTER TO THE

Romans is both the least controversial of the major NT letters and the most important. Least controversial, at any rate, in the "who wrote what when to whom" questions that make it so difficult to gain a firm handle on most of the other NT writings. It is most important as being the first well-developed theological statement by a Christian theologian that has come down to us, and one that has had incalculable influence on the framing of Christian theology ever since—arguably the most important work of Christian theology ever written. This double feature of Romans is important since it means that discussion of the letter can quickly leave behind such preliminary questions and can focus on its substantive theological content without too much distraction from nagging introductory unknowns.

1. Author, Date and Place of Origin
2. Recipients
3. Purposes
4. Literary Form and Coherence
5. Issues at Stake
6. Argument of the Letter

1. Author, Date and Place of Origin.

1.1. Author. There has never been any dispute of real significance over the authorship of Romans. It was written by Paul (Rom 1:1). More to the point is what the letter tells us about this Paul—particularly his sense of commissioning (*see* Conversion and Call of Paul) as an apostle and consequent commitment to preaching the gospel (Rom 1:1, 5, 12-17; 15:15-24). It is the fact that Paul the Jew, or preferably, Paul the Israelite (Rom 11:1), believed himself thus commissioned as apostle to the Gentiles (Rom 11:13), which gives the letter its distinctive character and cutting edge.

1.2. Date. As to date, the most significant fact is that Paul wrote his letter at a time when he thought he had completed a major phase of his work—his evangelization of the northeastern quadrant of the Mediterranean (Rom 15:19, 23). The information that he was about to embark on a visit to Jerusalem (Rom 15:25) ties in with the larger picture in Acts of a final visit to Jerusalem at what proved to be the close of his work in Asia Minor and Greece (Acts 20). This certainly points to a date in the mid-50s (A.D. 55-57), though a minority of scholars has argued implausibly for a date as early as 51/52. The fact that in Romans 13:6-7 Paul felt it necessary to provide a theological rationale for paying taxes may also reflect some unrest in Rome on questions of taxation early in Nero's reign, that is, about the same period (56-58; Tacitus *Ann.* 13). The issue of precise date, however, is of minor significance beside the clear implication that the letter marks a climax in Paul's missionary work.

1.3. Place of Origin. The correlation of Romans 15:25 with Acts 20 also suggests the place of origin, since Acts 20:3 speaks of three months spent in Greece at the beginning of the final journey to Jerusalem. That suggests Corinth, Paul's main headquarters in Greece, and fits with the information provided by Romans 16: Phoebe came from Cenchreae, one of Corinth's ports (Rom 16:1-2); and Gaius and Erastus (Rom 16:23) probably lived in Corinth (1 Cor 1:14; *NewDocs* 4.160-61). More to the point, a period of three months centered in a single location would give Paul the time to reflect, compose and dictate what is the most carefully thought through and constructed of his letters.

2. Recipients.

There is as little dispute over the "to whom" question. The reference to "Rome" in Romans 1:7 is omitted by some manuscripts, but such omission is best explained by subsequent generalizing usage of a letter intended originally for a more specific audience. The more important issue is who the Christians in Rome were, and why Paul, who had never visited Rome, should think it necessary to write to them.

2.1. "Jews First . . . " The fact is that we do not know how Christianity began in Rome and who,

strictly speaking, its founding apostles were. We do know, however, that there was a large Jewish community in Rome in the first century, estimated at between forty thousand and fifty thousand. We also know that there was an active Christian mission among "the circumcised" (Gal 2:9). Even the Gentile mission must have found its most fruitful ground among the Gentile proselytes and God-fearers who attached themselves to many Diaspora synagogues, as indicated also by Acts and Paul's continuing identification with the synagogue implied by 2 Corinthians 11:24. Furthermore, we have the interesting information that many Jews were expelled from Rome in (probably) A.D. 49 because of disturbances "instigated by Chrestus" (Suetonius *Claudius* 25.4), where "Chrestus" is almost universally taken as a reference to Christ. And the number of slave names among those greeted in Romans 16 (at least fourteen out of twenty-four) suggests that not a few of those descended from the Jewish captives brought to Rome, particularly following Pompey's subjugation of Palestine in 62 B.C., came to believe in Jesus as Messiah.

The obvious implication, then, is that Christianity first took root in Rome within and among the many Jewish *synagogues of Rome. This would explain how Peter could plausibly be regarded as the founder of the church in Rome, and, more to the point, why Paul's letter is so dominated by the motif "to Jew, but also to Gentile" (Rom 1:16; 2:9-10; 3:9, 29; 9:24; 10:12).

2.2. " . . . Also Gentiles." That Gentiles were drawn in to the church at Rome sooner or later in the earliest years is clearly implied in the letter, particularly Romans 11:13-32 and Romans 15:7-12 (see also Rom 1:6, 13; 15:15-16). That means being drawn in to share in an essentially Jewish patrimony, inevitably raising questions as to Jewish and Christian identity. This alone is sufficient to explain some of the characteristic elements and themes in the letter: for example, "who/what is a Jew?" (Rom 2:25-29); who are "the elect of God"? (Rom 1:7; 8:33; 9:6-13; 11:5-7, 28-32); and the climactic position of Romans 9—11 and Romans 15:8-12. Whether the disturbances within the Jewish community of 49 were between Jews who believed Jesus to be Messiah ("Chrestus") and those who denied it, or between Jews who welcomed Gentiles and those, including Christian Jews, who did not, we cannot tell.

Moreover, if many Christian Jews were

among those expelled in A.D. 49 (see Acts 18:2), we may draw the further inference that the Roman churches were at that time shorn of much of their Jewish leadership and membership. Gentile leadership would have become more the norm. And when Christian Jews began to return to Rome as Claudius's rescript began to lapse, some tensions between old and new may well have arisen. This is just the circumstance that seems to be reflected in the exhortations in Romans 14:1 and Romans 15:1, 7.

2.3. The Social Context. Two other factors are important in filling in the background behind the letter, so far as that is possible. One is that the Jewish community was influential in Rome and deeply despised, not to say hated, by the most influential voices of the Roman intelligentsia. This was partly because of its sheer size, partly because of the preferential treatment they had received from Julius Caesar and Augustus, and, probably more important, because of the numbers of Gentiles who were attracted to Judaism. These will also no doubt have been factors in the tensions between Jew and Gentile evident in the letter and will help explain such emphases as Romans 1:16 and Romans 12:14—13:7.

We also know that the Jewish community had no central authority in Rome, as was the case in Alexandria. This indicates a more fragmented organization and, probably, a fair diversity among the different synagogues. Corresponding to this is the implication that the Christian community was equally lacking in organizational homogeneity (implied by the unusual fact that Paul does not speak of the "church," singular, in Rome). As we know the names of ten or so synagogues, so we know of several house churches (five may be implied in Rom 16:5, 10-11, 14-15).

All this suggests that the Christian groups formed something of a spectrum (some more Jewish in composition, some more Gentile, most mixed), which overlapped substantially with the spectrum of synagogues. Paul knew enough of the people and the circumstances (Rom 14:1—15:7; 16:3-15) to frame his teaching and paraenesis accordingly. Among other things he would be aware that his letter would be read not to one huge gathering of Christians (apart from anything else, such a gathering would be too dangerous in an imperial capital nervous of unlicensed gatherings), but repeatedly to the various house churches, where different facets of his exposition would resonate with different

force among the different congregations. This would help explain the combination of general teaching and specific exhortation that is a feature of the letter.

3. Purposes.

Among introductory questions related to Romans, the liveliest discussion in recent years has centered on Paul's purpose(s) in writing it. Three purposes in particular have been strongly canvassed.

3.1. A Missionary Purpose. This emerges especially from Romans 15:18-24, 28: Paul as "apostle to the Gentiles," eager to bring in "the full number of Gentiles" (Rom 11:13-15, 25-26), writes to the capital of the Gentile empire.

Some interpreters draw the inference that Paul was seeking to evangelize Rome (Rom 1:13-15). This cannot mean that he did not recognize a Christian presence already in Rome (contrast Rom 1:8; 15:14). It has been argued on the basis of Romans 15:20, however, that he saw the Roman churches as lacking an apostolic foundation and sought to fill the gap. But this is equally unlikely, since Paul regarded church founding as an apostolic work (1 Cor 9:1-2), and the slight embarrassment evident in Romans 1:11-12 is just what we would expect from Paul writing to churches in whose founding he had played no part.

More plausible is the thesis that Paul wrote to Rome with a view to the churches there providing a support base for his projected mission to Spain. This is what Paul says explicitly (Rom 15:24, 28), and there is no cause to doubt it; the church in Philippi in particular had already served in such a role. In that case the letter would be Paul's attempt to set out the gospel that he had preached so successfully so far and that he intended to preach in Spain (Rom 1:16-17). At the end of the first or preceding phase of his great missionary strategy (Rom 15:19, 23) he uses the opportunity to set out in complete terms the theology of the gospel on the basis of which he would be asking the Roman Christians for support.

3.2. An Apologetic Purpose. The implication of such passages as Romans 1:16, Romans 3:8 and Romans 9:1-2, not to mention the repeated recourse to diatribe style, is that Paul felt himself and his understanding of the gospel under attack and needing to be justified. Hence the obvious conclusion has been drawn that the letter functions as Paul's apology for his gospel and therefore also as a self-apologia, since his whole life's work was bound up with the gospel he preached.

The apology is directed to Rome; by means of the unusually expanded introduction of Romans 1:2-6, including what seems to be a common creedal formula in Romans 1:3-4, Paul presents his calling card and his *bona fides*. Was this because he looked to the Roman Christians for support in the next phase of his mission (to Spain)? Or did he already have an inkling that the Christian groups in Rome, the imperial capital, were bound in due course to become increasingly influential in relation to Christian work elsewhere in the empire? Also plausible is the suggestion that Paul set out a full statement of his gospel as a dress rehearsal for his self-defense in Jerusalem, and thus he hoped to recruit the Roman congregations to his support in any confrontation in Jerusalem. The likelihood of such a confrontation, and not simply with his "unbelieving" fellow Jews, was very much in his mind, as is clearly indicated in Romans 15:31. Whether he thought the Roman congregations could actually send support or was asking for their prayers (a real support in Paul's eyes) is left unclear by Romans 15:30.

3.3. A Pastoral Purpose. In recent years Romans 14:1—15:6 has assumed a central significance in attempts to clarify Romans' purpose: that Paul was writing to heal potential or real divisions among the churches in Rome. This makes good sense of the exhortations of Romans 14:1 and Romans 15:7, especially when set against the background sketched earlier (particularly 2.2 above). Such attempts have been weakened by too casual identifications of "the weak" and "the strong" as simply Jews and simply Gentiles and by hypothesizing too clearly distinct groups and too sharp differentiations between Jews and Christians. The probability is rather (see 2.3 above) that there were Jewish synagogues attended by God-fearing Gentiles and Christian Jews and Gentiles. It is also probable that there was a diverse spectrum of Christian groupings, some with more Gentiles (Gentiles more dominant, though not necessarily less attracted to the synagogue) and others with more Jews (Jews more dominant, though not necessarily more conservative toward Jewish traditions and customs).

This would help explain the character of the letter as a whole, and of Romans 14:1—15:6 in relation to the rest. Namely, Paul set out to explain the "both Jew and Gentile" character of the gospel and of the promises to Israel, not exclusively, but also not least, to encourage his Roman auditors to work out in the experience of every day what the gospel and these promises must mean in practice. Above all it would give proper significance to what is obviously a climactic expression and rounding-off conclusion of the letter's main theme in Romans 15:7-13. In contrast, attempts to read Romans 12:1—15:13 as generalized, all-purpose paraenesis, lifted in part from Paul's experiences with the Corinthian church, hardly explains the distinctiveness of Romans' paraenesis or the passion with which Paul writes or the climax of Romans 15:7-13.

In addition, assuming that Romans 16 is part of the original letter, it is evident that Paul had some close contacts with various members of the Roman churches and would therefore have a fair knowledge of the character of the Roman churches and of their circumstances. From Romans 16 we can also see that Paul was writing to introduce and commend Phoebe (Rom 16:1-2), but that would be a subsidiary purpose and of itself could hardly explain the whole letter.

3.4. The Purposes of Romans. The fact that each of the above reasons for Romans can find such clear support from within the letter points to the obvious conclusion: that Paul had not one but several purposes in view when he wrote. Such a conclusion is more or less required by the character of the letter; no single suggested reason on its own can explain the full sweep of the document. On the contrary, it was presumably because Paul had several purposes in view that he found it desirable to set out his understanding of the good news of Christ so fully, including its practical implications. As he stood at one of the most important transition points in his whole ministry he saw the need and the desirability of such a fully worked-out statement— to indicate to others clearly what was the gospel he preached, why as a Jew he preached it, and how it should come to expression in daily life and community. It is the completeness of the statement, as required by the multiplicity of purposes served, that lifts the letter above the immediacy of the circumstances in which and for which it was written, and gives it, if not a timeless quality, at least its timeless significance.

4. Literary Form and Coherence.

4.1. The Literary Form. A second area of debate in recent years has been over the literary character of the letter. Much of it has been inconclusive and a somewhat pointless dispute about suitability of categories drawn from other literary and rhetorical forms—"epideictic" (demonstrative), "deliberative" (persuasive), "ambassadorial," to name but three. But since these are hardly pure types themselves, and since different categories can be and have been applied to Romans, the point of the exercise becomes unclear. The fact is that whatever conventions Paul knew or used, the form he constructed is distinctive and unique in character and content. That being said, the inquiry into literary form and rhetorical parallels has contributed several points of significance to current understanding of Romans.

4.1.1. Introduction and Conclusion. One is greater clarification of the letter character of the document indicated by its beginning and end. The literary parallels show that Paul was quite aware of current conventions and that he was concerned to use a medium that would, at least initially, be familiar to his audience, however much he adapted it to his own ends. He writes, therefore, as the wise teacher, leading his audience through familiar forms to the real point of the letter. Equally important for the modern commentator, the literary parallels to the writing's introduction and conclusion show not only how Paul conformed to convention but also where and how he departed from it. The more standard were these conventions, the more distinctive his additions and modifications would be seen to be by his auditors. In particular, the considerable elaboration (Rom 1:2-6) of the normal greeting (Rom 1:1, 7) would indicate clearly enough to a literate audience what the thrust of the letter was to be.

4.1.2. Epistolary Framework and Body. Another point to emerge from the study of literary form is the importance of the relation between the epistolary framework and the body of the letter. It is not simply a matter of recognizing that the framework is important for interpreting the whole (Romans is not merely a dogmatic treatise, beginning at Rom 1:17). As we have already noted, the insertion of Romans 1:2-6 into the normal greetings structure gives these verses the force of a prologue to the whole letter. So too the fact that Romans 1:16-17 serves as the climax

to the introduction and the thematic statement for what follows indicates a concern on Paul's part to integrate the framework into the body of the letter. The same conclusion follows from Paul's repetition of his travel plans (Rom 1:8-15; 15:14-33), as indeed of his self-claims to the grace of God in Romans 1:2-6 and Romans 15:14-15, that is, after as well as before the body of the letter. Thus he indicates that the intervening exposition is an expression of that grace (cf. Rom 1:12) and the theological basis of the specific request for support with which he concludes the restatement of his travel plans (Rom 15:30-33).

4.1.3. Diatribe. The third point of significance to emerge from studying Romans as a rhetorical form is the renewed appreciation of the diatribe style used by Paul (dialogue with an imaginary interlocutor)—a feature at key phases in his argument (Rom 2:1-5, 17-29; 3:27—4:2; 9:19-21; 11:17-24). Characteristic of the diatribe is the attempt to criticize arrogance and correct pretension. S. K. Stowers in particular has pointed out that the typical function of the diatribe was not as polemic against an opponent but, in a philosophical school context, as a critical questioning of a fellow student intended to lead him to the truth. Thus awareness of contemporary rhetorical convention alerts the modern reader to the danger of reading passages like Romans 2 as the expression of out-and-out polemic against an opponent or as indicating a complete break between two monolithic entities, *Judaism and Christianity. What the diatribe passages indicate, rather, is Paul engaged in a critical dialogue with his fellow Jews and fellow Christian Jews about the significance of the new "philosophical sect" within Judaism (Christianity) as to its relation with its parent Judaism and with the other Judaisms of the time.

4.2. Literary Coherence. The a priori likelihood that Paul used or adapted material or themes that he had used in earlier teaching (cf., e.g., Acts 19:8-10) has resulted in various suggestions that some of this previous material can be distinguished as coherent blocks: for example, Romans 5—8 as a distinct homily, or Romans 9—11 as preformed material incorporated here somewhat awkwardly. Such hypotheses can never be proved or disproved since there is no clear line of distinction between re-use of oral patterns never before written down and re-use of written material. All we need say is that the various sections of the argument of Romans cohere with sufficient closeness and with such a high degree of integration that such hypotheses add nothing to our understanding of the letter. The same degree of coherence and integration, however, tells decisively against more complex dissections of the text or elaborate theories of substantial redaction, which unfailingly create more problems than they solve or leave us with a simplistic and monochrome Paul.

The one major issue raised by textual criticism is whether Romans 16 belonged to the original text dictated by Paul. A strong minority opinion continues to hold that Romans 16 was a separate letter written to Ephesus. This is unlikely. In particular, a letter ending with Romans 15:33 and without a "grace" benediction (Rom 16:20) would be quite unlike Paul; Romans 16:1-23 has all the marks of an epistolary conclusion; and it is hardly implausible that Paul should know so many in Rome, as the greetings indicate. The Jewish community was substantial, and the movements of Prisca and Aquila indicate that there was a fair amount of travel to and from Rome, as might be expected in relation to the imperial capital.

The presence of Romans 16:25-27 at different places in the manuscript tradition (also after Rom 14:23 and after Rom 15:33), however, suggests that shorter forms of the letter were circulated. The consensus is that under Marcionite influence the letter was abbreviated (to Rom 1:1—14:23), to which Romans 16:25-27 was then added to provide a fitting conclusion. Early copyists would also see less point in transcribing all the names of Romans 16 and probably circulated a more general version ending at Romans 15:33, to which Romans 16:25-27 was also added. It is equally understandable that the very fitting conclusion, Romans 16:25-27, should likewise become attached to the full version in successive copyings. At all events, there is a strong consensus that Romans 16:25-27 is a later addition to the letter.

5. Issues at Stake.

5.1. The New Perspective on Paul. Traditionally Romans has been treated as a work of systematic theology, "a compendium of Christian doctrine," in Melanchthon's words, a more or less timeless statement of what the gospel means. But the recent recognition that the letter is related to the particular emphases and circumstanc-

es of Paul's mission (see 3 above) carries with it the corollary that the issues addressed in the letter must also have been conditioned in greater or less measure by the same emphases and circumstances. What is at stake in Romans is not the gospel in general or in the abstract but the gospel in particular as embodied by Paul's life and work—a Jewish gospel for Gentiles, and the strains and tensions that stemmed from that basic conviction.

This perspective on the letter has been reinforced by the new perspective on Paul and on the Jewish context from which he emerged. Traditionally in Protestant exegesis, Judaism has been seen as the foil to Christianity, as that which Christianity brought to an end or showed to be bankrupt, as that from which Paul was converted when he became a Christian. Read in that light the antitheses in Romans, particularly between sin and grace, death and life, law and faith, though surprisingly less so between *flesh and Spirit (see Holy Spirit), appeared as antitheses between Judaism and Christianity. "The Jew" became the classic type of religion gone wrong, of religion understood in terms of human achievement rather than as the expression of gratitude for, and response to, the initiative of divine grace.

Now, however, more scattered protest against such stereotyping of "the Jew" and Judaism has reached a climax, particularly in English-speaking scholarship from the Christian side, in the work of E. P. Sanders. It is he who more effectively than anyone else in the English-speaking world has succeeded in getting across the message that early Judaism at its heart was a religion of grace: its starting point, God's free choice of Israel and rescue from slavery; its system that focused on repentance, atonement and forgiveness; its emphasis on Law keeping, the appropriate response of gratitude and faithfulness on the part of the elect people. From this new perspective the theological issues at stake in Romans take on a different hue. In that sense Sanders marks a new epoch in the study of Paul, and commentaries on Romans can be categorized as pre- and post-Sanders—at least to the extent that one can assess work on the theology of Romans by whether it takes serious account of the new perspective, even if to disagree with it.

5.2. The New Perspective on Romans. In light of the new perspective on Paul the issues at stake in Romans receive a fresh clarity. The various themes are already sounded in the substantial elaboration of the more common introduction (Rom 1:2-7): (1) the gospel of God; (2) continuous with the prophecies of the Holy Scriptures; (3) focusing on Jesus, *Son of David and *Son of God; (4) with his resurrection marking out a new eschatological epoch (*see* Eschatology); (5) and his lordship (*see* Lord) validating its outreach, not least by Paul, to all the Gentiles; (6) among whom the Roman believers in particular are to be counted as numbered among the elect and beloved people of God. Hence the overarching emphasis on the gospel for Jew and Gentile already noted (see 2.1-2 above) is sounded in the initial thematic statement (Rom 1:16) and in the climax of Romans 15:7-12. Hence also the repeated emphasis is on the gospel for all—"all who believe" (Rom 1:16; 3:22; 4:11; 10:4, 11-13), "all injustice" (Rom 1:18, 29), all under sin (Rom 3:9, 12, 19-20, 23; 5:12), "all the seed" (Rom 4:11, 16), "all Israel" (Rom 11:26). The issue is not so much the universality of human need and of the gospel's sufficiency as whether and how the gospel, Jewish in origin and in character, reaches beyond the Jewish nation to include the nations beyond ("all" = Gentile as well as Jew, Rom 1:18—5:21). And conversely, the issue is whether the gospel now drawing in Gentiles in such numbers remains a Jewish gospel and is still the gospel for the Jews ("all" = Jew as well as Gentile, Rom 9—11).

Of course this is a particular expression of the larger theological claim about the universality of human sin and of the gospel's provision, and it is wholly legitimate to validate such a larger theological claim from Romans. But it is important to recognize that the larger claim is derived from this particular expression, that is, to recognize its historical specificity, including the continuing Jewish character of the Christian gospel, and to be alert to the possibility that individual elements in this particular expression are determined primarily by that context and thus are less amenable to generalization.

5.3. The Faithfulness of God. Within this overarching emphasis (Jew and Gentile) several other key themes in the letter fall into place. One is the issue of theodicy ("the gospel of God"). This is indicated at once in the centrality of "the righteousness of God" (particularly Rom 1:17; 3:5, 21-26; 4:1-25; 9:30—10:13). The theme is through-and-through Jewish, its Pauline usage in direct

continuity with the usage of the Psalms and Isaiah 40—66. The issue is twofold. (1) How the saving action to which God committed himself on behalf of *Israel includes those outside Israel. The answer is given partly in terms of the correlated thematic word *faith:* that this always was the human medium through which God exercised his saving righteousness (so again particularly Rom 4:1-25 and 9:30—10:17, also Rom 14:22-23). And partly in terms of the new, climactic phase in God's purpose (the same purpose) marked by Christ's ministry (particularly Rom 3:22-26 and again Rom 9:30—10:13).

(2) What the Jewish gospel for Gentiles says about the faithfulness of God to his original promises to Israel. This theme is obscured somewhat by the fact that the Jewish motif of divine faithfulness is translated into Greek in two different ways: God's faithfulness (Rom 3:3; but perhaps also Rom 1:17 and Rom 3:25) and God's truth (particularly Rom 1:25; 3:7; 15:8). The issue is clearly articulated in Romans 3:1-8, but Paul is able to address it in detail only in Romans 9—11, where it is posed in the key question of whether the word of God has failed (Rom 9:6). The importance of Romans 15:7-13 (here Rom 15:8) as summing up Paul's concerns and thus indicating what these concerns were in the letter is again underlined.

Somewhat surprisingly, *christology does not seem to be part of the issue. It is fundamental to the gospel (Rom 1:3-4), but the fulcrum expression of it in Romans 3:21-26 is brief, probably makes use of preformed material, and seems to be noncontroversial (hence the brevity). The christology as such seems to be common ground. The universal significance of Christ is the presupposition of Romans 5—8 rather than the theme. And though Christ is presented as the stumbling stone in Romans 9:32-33, it is striking that in the final resolution to the problem of Israel's unbelief a distinctively Christian (as distinct from Jewish) messianism is lacking (Rom 11:26; *see* Christ). Characteristic of the letter at this point is, once again, the climax of Romans 15:8: "Christ has become the servant of the circumcised for the sake of God's truth (faithfulness)."

5.4. The Subtheme of the Law. The other theme that falls into place in the light of the new perspective is the role of the *law in Romans. The traditional view tended to see the law as belonging wholly on the negative side of the antitheses posed by Paul—a hostile power, like sin and death (understandably in view of Rom 5:20 and Rom 7:5), characterizing Judaism as legalistic, a religion of achievement, giving ground for human pride (cf. Rom 3:27-28; 9:11, 32; 11:6). The fact that Paul seems equally concerned to mount an apologetic in relation to the law (Rom 3:31; 7:7-25; 8:3-4; 13:8-10) fitted ill with this understanding, but on the traditional view it was not easy to see any solution. The new perspective has shaken up the negative side of the equation, but for some (Sanders, Räisänen) the result has been only to increase the incoherence of Paul's overall position.

However, within the new perspective on Paul and on Romans (see 5.1-2 above), a more coherent solution is possible. For where the primary issue is the tensions caused by a Jewish gospel being offered to Gentiles, the problem of the law is likely to relate to that issue. The law is then most naturally seen as a principal hindrance that prevents Gentiles from accepting the gospel. And so we find in Romans. It is the Jewish claim to have the law and thus to have a privileged position before God (Rom 2:12-29) which focuses the problem of Israel's election (Rom 3:1). It is the Jewish boast in this privileged status as marked out by their obedience to the law that Paul seeks to counter by his focus on faith (Rom 3:27-31; 4:1-25). It is the law, not as evil, but as weak and used as a cat's-paw by sin, that he attempts to defend (Rom 7:7—8:4). It is the law typified by Jewish works and a focus of Jewish zeal that Paul sees to have been ended by Christ, not "the law of righteousness" (Rom 9:30—10:4); "the law of sin and death," not "the law of the Spirit of life" (Rom 8:2-4). Properly understood in the new light of Christ, therefore, what the law calls for is not the "works" that mark off Jew from Gentile—particularly, though by no means exclusively, circumcision and food laws (Rom 2:25-29; 4:9-12; 9:10-13; 14:1-12)—but love of neighbor (Rom 13:8-10; 14:13—15:6).

In a word, then, it is not the law as expression of human achievement that Paul questions, but the law as expression of Jewish privilege. The solution to the problem of the law in Romans lies not in a demonizing of the law; nor in throwing up one's hands at Paul's "contradictions"; nor in distinguishing ceremonial law from moral law, though Paul's teaching can be worked out in these terms. Paul's concern was more with a nationalizing of the law than with

its ritualizing. It was because the law could be so identified with Israel, and that identification focused so much in distinctive Jewish rites (particularly circumcision and food laws), that Paul found it necessary to distinguish fulfillment of the law's requirements from doing such works. Evidently, in the tensions caused by his proclamation of a Jewish gospel to Gentiles, it was only by so arguing that he could defend both features of the gospel—its Jewish character and its openness to all nations.

6. Argument of the Letter.

We are now in a position to appreciate the thrust and movement of Paul's thought in Romans. Since the main body of the letter is set out so systematically, a brief survey of it provides an invaluable synopsis of Paul's theology as he stood at this climax to his missionary career.

6.1. Introduction (Rom 1:1-17). We have already noted how the expanded greetings (Rom 1:1-7) allow Paul to introduce his theme while still at the stage of friendly introductions (see 5.2 above). We also noted that the personal explanations that follow, with their typical features of thanksgiving and prayer (Rom 1:8-15), root the letter as a whole firmly into the particular historical setting of its composition and lead into the key thematic statement for what follows (Rom 1:16-17). Here the principal terms of the letter are clearly enunciated—the gospel as God's power for salvation, all who believe, Jew first and Greek, the righteousness of God being revealed from faith to faith—together with the supporting OT text (Hab 2:4).

6.2. The Human Condition—Gentile and Jew (Rom 1:18—3:20). In a manner followed in subsequent centuries by countless restatements of the Christian gospel or monographs on theology, Paul finds it necessary to define the human condition to which the gospel provides an answer.

6.2.1. Human Beastliness (Rom 1:18-32). Paul begins by characterizing what classically has been described as human depravity (*see* Sinners, Sin, Guilt). That is now too heavy or distancing a formulation, particularly when we appreciate that he rounds off his indictment with a description that includes the everyday nastiness and petty selfishnesses of human pride and ruptured relationships (Rom 1:29-31). Such negative features mark the breakdown of human society, features which all people of goodwill would deplore ("what is not fitting," Rom 1:28). The gospel starts by taking such things seriously (Rom 1:32).

Two other elements help explain the build-up to that climax. One is the strong echo of the Adam stories in Genesis 2—3 (Rom 1:19-23). The basic flaw in the make-up of human society is that the human creature has failed to live in accord with its creatureliness, has failed to acknowledge its dependence on God, has sought to usurp the role of the Creator. The consequence has been the opposite—not a rise above human creatureliness but a fall below humanity to a level of beastliness, marked by idolatry, unnatural sexual practices and the nastiness already mentioned. The other is the strong echo of characteristically Jewish polemic against Gentiles and particularly Gentile religion (Rom 1:24-27)—precisely as characterized by idolatry and debased sexuality (cf. Wis 11—15). Thus at once Paul highlights the tension between Jew and Gentile as central to his concerns.

6.2.2. Jews Too (Rom 2:1-29). Romans 2 has caused more difficulties than any other chapter for commentators, particularly because it seems to envisage final justification as depending on human deeds rather than on faith and because its argument seems to depend on a far too sweeping indictment of Jews at large. The key is to note that the chapter is framed, on the one side, by a typically Jewish attack on Gentile lifestyle (Rom 1:18-32) and, on the other, by a protest that Jewish privilege has been undermined (Rom 3:1). What is in view in Romans 2, therefore, is almost certainly the very sense of Jewish privilege and distinctiveness that was so clearly echoed in Romans 1.

This is confirmed by the first appearance of the characteristic diatribe form in Romans 2:1-5. Paul thus engages not with any imaginary onlooker but precisely with the typical Jew who would commend the typically Jewish indictment of Romans 1. The echoes of such Jewish reasoning as we find in *Psalms of Solomon* 15:8 and Wisdom 15:1-6 (Rom 2:3-4), as well as the explicit quotation of the Jewish theologoumenon in Romans 2:6, confirm that Paul has in view a Jewish rationalization that could justify or excuse in itself what it condemned in others (Rom 2:1-11).

The picture becomes clearer in Romans 2:12-16 as Paul attempts to undermine the confidence of those who think that because they have the law they are advantaged in the judgment over those without the law. On the contrary, Jewish teaching is precisely that doing the law is more important than merely hearing it; the argument is *ad hominem.* The pride and presumption of "the Jew," by virtue of possessing the law, becomes explicit in Romans 2:17-24. The intention of the forthright indictment of the typical Jewish interlocutor is not to condemn all Jews out of hand but rather to argue that when the typical Jew breaks the law in his presumption he undermines the whole basis of his privileged position. The point is brought to sharpest focus in circumcision, that which is so much the mark of "the Jew" that Jews as a whole can be called simply "the circumcision." The failure to distinguish an outward, ethnic identity marker from the hidden work of the Spirit in the heart and to play down the importance of the former in favor of the latter means that the typical Jew is in no better (indeed, maybe worse) standing before God than the Gentile (Rom 2:25-29).

6.2.3. Awkward Corollaries (Rom 3:1-8). Such an uninhibited attack on Jewish self-confidence in Israel's privileged status before God raises problems that Paul cannot ignore—particularly in relation to Israel's election, and thus also to God's faithfulness to the people he chose. It is to be noted that Paul does not wish to query the fact of that election, but also that his one-sentence defense of God's faithfulness looks beyond God's role as Israel's covenant partner to his role as Creator and Judge. Thus he hints that the resolution to the tensions of "Jew and Gentile" will be to set Israel's covenant status before its God within the larger picture of the world's status before its Creator. But such lines of thought can only be hinted at here.

6.2.4. Conclusion: All Under Sin (Rom 3:9-20). The summary gathers all humanity under the same indictment. But the target is still primarily Jewish presumption that "the Jew" is exempt. Thus the catena of OT texts that follows (Rom 3:10-18) consists mainly of passages that assume that those condemned are "them" and not "us." Paul's point is that such an assumption is an expression of the power of the sin it condemned. The trust in privileged position, the boast in the law (circumcision especially) as marking out Jew from Gentile, is an expression of the fleshliness (in this case, ethnic identity) that distances humankind from God (Rom 3:19-20).

6.3. The Gospel Answer (Rom 3:21—5:21). Again, providing a pattern for countless sermons and monographs, Paul, having indicted humanity as a whole, turns to the answer given by the gospel.

6.3.1. Through Faith in Christ (Rom 3:21-26). In a remarkably brief section (compared with the length of the indictment) Paul points to the death of Christ as the answer. The logic is not spelled out in any detail (why faith in Christ should provide the answer) and seems to draw on an accepted Christian formulation. So the answer must have been an already established Christian conviction that Paul did not need to elaborate.

Significant, however, is the emphasis again on complete continuity with what had gone before (Rom 3:21; Christ's death as a sacrifice, Rom 3:25). Presupposed, therefore, is the Jewish theology of sacrifice and of the need for an unblemished animal to act as a sin offering, with the probable implication that the animal's death served to put away or cover the sin or indeed to kill off in a representative way the sin-affected offerer. For a reason not given in the text, Christ's death could be seen not just as such a sacrifice, but as a climactic sacrifice that was effective for all humankind past and present, Gentile as well as Jew, and thus by implication as a sacrifice that ended all further need for sacrifice and as such became the means by which all human relationship with God could be restored (*see* Justification).

6.3.2. To Jew and Gentile (Rom 3:27-31). Indicative of Paul's concern is the way he immediately (Rom 3:27) picks up the theme of "the Jew's" boasting indicted in Romans 2:17, 23. As already clearly implied, it is a boasting in Jewish privilege and prerogative that Paul condemns, a boasting that in effect regards God as "the God of Jews only" (Rom 3:29). The twin recognition that God is one (the Jewish credo) and that God accepts human beings on the basis of faith shatters any such presumption. This universalism, Gentile as well as Jew, is what is now effective through the death of Jesus Christ (Rom 3:21-26). But since it is also (properly speaking) a Jewish universalism, it does not contradict the terms of the initial offer of that grace to Israel; that is, the gospel of Jesus Christ stands opposed to the law characterized by the works of Jewish prerogative but confirms the law as calling for the obedience of faith (Rom 3:31).

6.3.3. Abraham as a Test Case (Rom 4:1-25). To sustain this central claim Paul takes up the challenge of the precedent provided by "father Abraham." The test case was crucial, since *Abraham was widely regarded within Judaism as the model of piety. Already it was being said that he had observed the law in its as-yet-unwritten state (e.g., Gen 26:5; CD 3:2). In particular, he was regarded as a paradigm of faithfulness to the covenant, because he came through so strongly when he was tested in the matter of the offering of Isaac (e.g., Jdt 8:26; Sir 44:19-21). It was in the light of this faithfulness that Genesis 15:6 was understood: Abraham was counted righteous on the basis of this faithfulness (1 Macc 2:52; so Jas 2:22-23).

Paul's response is to expound Genesis 15:6 afresh: "Abraham believed God, and it was reckoned to him for righteousness." This is one of very few extended expositions of a text from a first-century Jew, Philo excepted, and can thus be counted as a classic example of early Jewish midrash. It proceeds by first announcing the text (Rom 4:3), then analyzing each of the key words in turn—"reckoned" (Rom 4:4-8) and "believed" (Rom 4:9-21)—and finally restating the text thus expounded (Rom 4:22) with its corollary (Rom 4:23-25).

"Reckoned," Paul notes, must have a different meaning in describing a divine-human relationship from its use in a human contract—a claim somewhat fortuitously but appropriately confirmed by the verb's appearance in Psalm 32:1-2. The exposition of "believed" is more tortuous but builds on three points: the fact that Abraham's believing was prior to and fully effective before he was circumcised (or subsequently "tested") (Rom 4:9-12); the fact that it was faith in promise (Rom 4:13-17); and the fact that the promise was so impossible of fulfillment by any degree of Abraham's contriving (or faithfulness; Rom 4:17-21). This believing could be only trust in God, confidence in God's power alone, that and nothing more—faith, not faithfulness. The faith called for in the gospel is precisely the same faith in the life-giving power of God (Rom 4:23-25).

6.3.4. Conclusion: What This Means for Individual Believers (Rom 5:1-11) and for Humankind (Rom 5:12-21). Having made his case that the gospel of God's acceptance is for all through faith, Paul rounds off this central section of his argument by spelling out the consequences. For individual believers it means peace with God, an experience of grace that will shape the character through suffering, and a secure basis of hope for the future (Rom 5:1-11). The initiative of God, its overwhelmingly gracious character, and the experience of that love already manifested in Christ's death and in the gift of the Spirit, is the firm rock on which the believer can face present and future in complete confidence. This is the same confidence that Abraham had displayed in his paradigmatic believing.

Christ's death thus marks a whole new beginning, not just for individuals but for all humankind (Rom 5:12-21). The tragedy that began to unfold with Adam, as implied in Romans 1:19-23 (see 6.2.1 above) and Romans 3:23, has been answered by another story (*see* Adam and Christ). The disobedience of Adam was the ancient way of explaining how the harsh reality of sin and death entered the world and gained such domination over it. But now the obedience of Christ has opened the way and provided another model for human existence. Sin and death need not have the last word in human affairs.

These two men—Adam and Christ—sum up in themselves the two chief possibilities for humanity. That is also to say that they sum up the argument from Romans 1:18 onwards—from the condemnation of life "in Adam" and under the domination of sin and death, to the offer of life "in Christ" under the reign of grace. The whole opening section of the body of the letter (Rom 1:18—5:21) thus has an impressively rounded and global quality—from Adam to Christ as a comprehensive summary of human history. But the passage also brings to the fore the negative factors brought into play by Adam, sin and death, with the role of the law as a further complicating factor (Rom 5:20-21); and what effect the gospel has on them requires further clarification.

6.4. The Problem of Sin, Death and the Law (Rom 6:1—8:39). Paul has essentially set out two principal alternatives for human existence and indicated that the individual believer can in effect transfer from one to the other in terms of basic motivation and character formation. The question at once arises, whether the transfer can be total. Paul's answer is summed up in terms of an already/not-yet formula (*see* Eschatology). Something decisive has already happened (Rom 5:1-11), but so long as life lasts within the transitoriness and weakness of this bodily existence, the outworking of that decisive act of God is not yet complete. That is to say, sin and death continue to exert an influence that believers cannot

escape and to which they are in some measure (the measure of his human Adamness) still subject but that they must continue to resist in the strength of the Spirit.

This is the basic line that Paul elaborates in the next three chapters—in relation first to sin, then to the law, and finally to *flesh and death. In each case he begins by stating clearly the new reality already made effective by God's action in Christ before going on to indicate how the new reality must be lived out in the "not-yet" conditions of the still sinful flesh—the indicative of God's grace as the inspiration and enabling of human commitment and obedience.

6.4.1. The Problem of Sin (Rom 6:1-23). The claim that grace had more than accounted for sin gives rise to the ribald response: if sin results in grace, then the more sin the better. Paul's answer is to point to the decisive cut-off point for sin and death in the death of Jesus. Sin and death could reach as far, but no farther: "the death he died, he died to sin once and for all" (Rom 6:10). For those who have identified themselves with Christ in his death (through *baptism), therefore, there can be no question of tolerating or cooperating with sin. The motivating center of their living is now directed toward and determined by the Christ on whom sin has no hold whatsoever.

Sin remains a reality, however, for believers have not yet shared fully in Christ's resurrection; they still must experience the outworking of fleshly corruption and death. Sin thus still has a foothold in them, and its wiles and enticements must be resisted until that end. But in the temptation of the not yet, the already of Christ's victory is the basis and source of strength to resist and overcome, to live out their initial commitment in the renewed commitment of every day.

6.4.2. The Problem of the Law (Rom 7:1-25). Underlying the first critique of Paul's gospel outlined in Romans 6:1 was a Jewish suspicion that Paul's gospel meant abandoning the law. It was precisely the law that served as a bulwark against the power of sin, did it not? But Paul's attack on Jewish presumption as focused in works of the law could easily be heard by his fellow Jews (and modern commentators!) as an attack on the law itself. It is this problem that Paul now addresses.

He begins, once again, by stating his position in bald terms. The Jewish law is so much identified with the period before Christ that the new possibility of existence brought about by Christ is like a being freed from the law. In terms of the earlier indictment (Rom 2—3), the law has become the occasion for Jewish presumption, and thus the instrument of the very sin that it was intended to thwart. Thus the transfer from old to new, from Adam to Christ, from sin and death to grace, has become also a transfer from the legal code that defines Israel to the new life of the Spirit.

But surely such a treatment of the law is tantamount to identifying the law with sin. Paul's answer is that the law is not to blame. It—and the "flesh" (*sarx*, i.e., human frailty and finitude)—have been manipulated by sin. The reality of the already/not-yet tension between what has begun with and in Christ and the salvation yet to be completed is reflected in a double split—in the individual who yearns to do the will of God but yet remains in "the flesh," and in the law, which expresses the will of God but is still the tool of sin and death.

6.4.3. The Problem of the Flesh and Death (Rom 8:1-39). The third restatement of the outworking of the gospel for the individual once again begins with strong emphasis on the divine indicative. What was impossible for the law in the face of the power of sin and death and the weakness of human flesh, God has accomplished in Christ. Those who have received the Spirit of Christ thus have a completely other base of operations than simply the flesh. It is from this base that they must live and act. They must live out the reality of the sonship that they already experience through the Spirit and share with God's Son (Rom 8:1-17).

This does not mean that the flesh has been left behind or that death has been avoided. On the contrary, the reality of the human condition means continuing weakness and, not least, suffering, a condition that will continue until the completion of the redemption process in the resurrection of the body. The present tension is uncomfortable, but it is one shared with the whole of creation, likewise caught in the overlap of the ages between what has been and what will be, between Adam and Christ. And it is made bearable by the fact of the Spirit already present, already active in and through that weakness, the ground of a sure hope (Rom 8:18-30).

The section is rounded off with a shout of glowing assurance, all equivocation and qualification put aside. Whatever the continuing power of sin and death, the continuing weakness of the flesh, and the continuing hostility of this age, God's triumph is sure. God's purpose in Christ has already secured the victory. Neither death nor any other power can separate believers from the love of God in Christ (Rom 8:31-39).

6.5. What of Israel? (Rom 9:1—11:36). The issue of Jew and Gentile that dominated the first two main sections of the letter (Rom 1:18—5:21) had been largely lost to sight in the last section (Rom 7 apart) as Paul focused on the outworkings of the gospel in global (Adam/Christ) and personal terms. But the language used had again and again been drawn from that of Israel's covenant promises (*see* Israel). And the final assurance of God's faithfulness to his elect begged the whole question of God's faithfulness to his earlier covenant partner, Israel. As the problem of the law indicated, a division of history into before and after Christ ran the danger of dumping Israel as a whole into the Adam phase. What then of God's promises to Israel? How could the faithfulness of God to believers be asserted while his faithfulness to Israel was being thus discounted? This is the issue that Paul now addresses in one of the most tensely argued passages in all his writing.

6.5.1. Introduction (Rom 9:1-5). Paul begins by reasserting his personal concern for his own people and reminding his readers of Israel's covenant privileges in which they were now participants—that is, in Israel's covenant privileges.

6.5.2. The Call of God (Rom 9:6-29). He then proceeds to state his primary thesis: God's word to Israel has not failed. The failure has been (by implication on Israel's part) to recognize the character of Israel's election and calling—that is, what constituted Israel as Israel. That election was a wholly gracious act of God without respect for physical descent or for the works that had come to be seen as marking out covenant identity.

The negative side of this view of election is that there is a non-Israel—those whose function is to highlight the gracious character of Israel's election. This harsh, almost predestinarian view of history is Paul's attempt to explain what he sees to be the simple fact of a chosen people within a hostile world, that the overall picture has many darker hues. The main point of the discussion, as becomes steadily more apparent, however, is not to dictate a doctrine of predestination but to undermine Israel's own doctrine of predestination. It is Jewish confidence that

Gentiles are by definition non-Israel that he seeks to challenge. By citing Israel's Scriptures, as now also being fulfilled through his mission, Paul is able to argue that whoever non-Israel might be, the chosen people include Jews and Gentiles.

6.5.3. Israel's Failure (Rom 9:30—10:21). Israel's failure, then, has been to understand its calling and privileges in a too narrow and restrictive way—a law understood in terms of works rather than faith, a righteousness understood as exclusively theirs from which Gentiles were excluded. The coming of Christ has put an end to such misunderstanding. He is the prophesied "stone of stumbling" in whom all may believe. The faith that is the only possible response to the completely gracious character of God's calling cannot be restricted within the confines of an exclusively Jewish law. It now finds expression more fully in the word of preaching that is truly universal in scope, the call for faith in Jesus as Lord. This is the word that is now being preached, not least by Paul himself, and that is being accepted by Gentiles. Israel, failing to recognize that this universal outreach expresses the same gracious character of its calling, is refusing to receive this gospel and thus is fulfilling its own Scriptures.

6.5.4. The Mystery of God's Faithfulness (Rom 11:1-32). The fact is that in the already/not-yet overlap period, Israel is as much split as the believer or the law (Rom 7:7-25). There are some within Israel who have recognized the gracious character of Israel's election and responded in terms of that grace, like the Gentile believers. But the bulk have failed to recognize that standing with God is a matter of grace from start to finish. Ironically, unbelieving Israel thus finds itself in the role of non-Israel, the negative role filled by Esau and Pharaoh in Romans 9:13 and 17.

And thus begins to become clear the mystery of the divine purpose of mercy and judgment. As it was necessary for Pharaoh to play his negative role in order for the graciousness of God's redemption of Israel to be made clear, so it has been necessary for the bulk of Israel to refuse the gospel in order that the gracious character of the gospel for Gentiles as well as Jews might be made plain. Paul's hope is that the sight of so many Gentiles entering into Israel's covenant blessings will spur Israel to jealousy; that is why he pursues his mission to the Gentiles with such dedication. If Israel's failure has brought such blessing to Gentiles, what will be the blessing for the whole world when Israel as a whole accepts its own heritage in Christ (Rom 11:11-16)!

This in turn indicates that an equivalent warning to the Gentile believers is called for. The degree to which the blessings of Israel have passed to Gentiles gives no more cause for pride and presumption to the latter than Israel's original election did to Jews. God has not discarded Israel and started afresh. Gentiles are incorporated into Israel and remain part of Israel only so long as they maintain the fundamental grace-faith character of the relationship (Rom 11:17-24).

The fact of the divine faithfulness is that God's original calling of Israel remains constant, and constant in terms of grace and faith. The mystery of the divine faithfulness is that the pre-Christian Jew-and-not-Gentile expression of election and the current Gentile-and-not-Jew response to the gospel are both phases in the larger divine purpose. God's purpose is that all Israel be saved. The perplexing disobedience shown in this phase of God's purpose is but the preliminary, and in some sense the means to realizing the ultimate purpose of showing mercy to all.

6.5.5. A Concluding Hymn of Adoration (Rom 11:33-36). Fittingly, Paul rounds off this exposition of high theological ideal and hope with a hymn of praise to the one creator God, that is, of Jew and Gentile.

6.6. The Practical Outworking of the Gospel (Rom 12:1—15:13). Having thus redefined the Israel of God it becomes necessary to spell out how this Israel should live. Israel defined simply in terms of the Jewish people knew at once the answer: the law provided the guidelines for life lived within the covenant. But Paul's earlier critique and redefinition of the role of the law (Rom 2:1-3:31; 7:1-25) must have left his auditors wondering where to find the guidelines for Christian living.

6.6.1. The Basis for Responsible Living (Rom 12:1-2). Paul therefore begins by calling for a commitment in daily living that is the Christian's equivalent to the discipline and order previously provided by the Jerusalem cult. Such committed openness to the Spirit of God allows the possibility of immediacy of knowledge of the divine will that the Scriptures had always held out as the ideal.

6.6.2. The Community of Faith (Rom 12:3-8). In the new order the social equivalent of corporate Israel (Judaism) is the *body of Christ. Life within ethnic Israel had involved the usual representative roles and functions of any national body. The body of Christ has its equivalent roles and functions, as determined and enabled by the Spirit. No member should think that he or she lacks a role or that there are only a few set roles to which all must aspire.

6.6.3. Love as the Norm for Social Relationships (Rom 12:9-21). As for the Christians' mutual relationships and relationships with the wider world, the norm is given by love. Paul illustrates what this will mean in practice. Then, turning to the wider relationships with outsiders, he draws on the accumulated wisdom of Diaspora Judaism on how to live within strange and hostile societies. Here peaceable good-neighborliness must be the rule.

6.6.4. Live as Good Citizens (Rom 13:1-7). In particular, and particularly living as they do within the imperial capital, the Roman Christians should endeavor to be as fully law-abiding as possible—including the payment of taxes levied on them.

6.6.5. Love Your Neighbor (Rom 13:8-10). The whole exhortation is summed up in the love command. It will be no accident either that this was also recognized within the rest of Judaism as a summary of the law, or that the Gospels recall Jesus as giving it similar prominence (Mk 12:31, etc). Here, in other words, Paul indicates his desire to show that the law still provides guidelines for living and how it does so—that is, by hearing it in the light of Christ's teaching and ministry.

6.6.6. The Imminence of the End as Spur (Rom 13:11-14). Ever in the background of Paul's thought was the confidence that the already/not-yet overlap period would not be long drawn out, in terms either of personal salvation (Rom 7:24; 8:23) or of Israel's salvation (Rom 11:13-15). The same perspective should help provide a spur to live out of the new reality and motivation of being in Christ and not in terms of the self-indulgent, decaying flesh.

6.6.7. The Problem of Food Laws and Holy Days (Rom 14:1—15:6). The whole issue expounded in principle and practice in the preceding chapters comes to particular focus in an issue that was bound to create tensions in any mixed community of Jews and Gentiles. Wherever there were Jews who continued to identify themselves with the heritage of the Maccabees and the Judaism of the succeeding decades, observance of the food laws was bound to be a matter of personal and national integrity (see, e.g., 1 Macc 2:62-63). The same would apply to Gentile proselytes or God-fearers who had found themselves religiously by identifying with the Judaism of the synagogue. Such Christians would find it hard to dispense with the Jewish food laws. Other Jews, like Paul, would have come to regard such works of the law as too restrictive of the grace of God and would have abandoned them in greater or lesser degree. Many Gentiles converted under such preaching would see no reason to subscribe to these laws. In mixed communities, where table fellowship was a fundamental expression of community, the tensions set up by these differences would be considerable. Presumably, Paul knew of such tensions from his personal contacts in Rome, particularly within churches in Rome now mainly Gentile in character to which Christian Jews were returning after the period of expulsion under Claudius. The issue, it should be noted, was a serious one, since bound up with it was the whole question of the identity of the new movement—as a sect within Judaism, or what? Hence the prominence given to it by Paul.

Paul in effect addresses the two main groupings in turn. To the "weak," that is the more scrupulous, law-abiding (mainly) Christian Jews who were defined as "weak" by the others who saw strength in their liberty from such scruples, Paul gives a simple warning: Do not make your conscience the measure for others; recognize that God may be heard speaking differently to different people on such matters; you cannot condemn those whom Christ accepts (Rom 14:3-12).

To the self-styled "strong," whose views Paul shares, Paul's advice is that they should hold strongly to conclusions reached in faith but that they should be willing to limit their liberty of practice if there was a real danger that their freer practice would cause genuine distress and harm to the faith of other members (Rom 14:13-23). The model for such behavior is Christ (Rom 15:1-6)—a confirmation that the teaching and example of Jesus provided the basic hermeneutic for this earliest Christian reinterpretation of the law.

6.6.8. Summary (Rom 15:7-13). Paul neatly integrates this plea to mutual acceptance and tolerance into the overarching theme of the whole letter. Christ was a Jew, to confirm God's faithfulness to the Jews and to open the door of grace and faith to the Gentiles, in fulfillment of God's overall purpose as indicated in Scripture.

6.7. Conclusion (Rom 15:14—16:27). Paul rounds off his letter by reverting to the themes of the introduction. He describes in more detail his mission, indicating its continuity with the cultic ministry of the Jerusalem temple and the successful conclusion of its eastern phase. Then he turns again to his plans for the future, indicating more clearly his reasons for wanting to visit his readers in Rome and the reasons for his delay. He ends by indicating his alarm at the possible outcome of his visit to deliver the collection in Jerusalem and asking for their prayers (Rom 15:14-33).

The final section is a note of commendation for Phoebe, deacon and patron of the church in Cenchreae, and a lengthy list of greetings to those he knows personally or by name in the Roman churches, among whom several women leaders are prominent. A final stereotyped warning about dangers of dissension and a few greetings from others brings this most important of Paul's letters to a close (Rom 16:1-23).

See also ABRAHAM; ADAM AND CHRIST; ISRAEL; JUSTIFICATION; LAW; PAUL IN ACTS AND LETTERS.

DPL: CENTER OF PAUL'S THEOLOGY; OLIVE TREE; PAUL AND HIS INTERPRETERS; RESTORATION OF ISRAEL; ROME AND ROMAN CHRISTIANITY; WORKS OF THE LAW.

BIBLIOGRAPHY. **Commentaries:** C. K. Barrett, *Romans* (BNTC; 2d ed.; London: Black, 1991); B. Byrne, *Romans* (SacP; Collegeville, Minn.: Glazier, Liturgical Press, 1996); C. E. B. Cranfield, *Romans* (2 vols.; ICC; Edinburgh: T & T Clark, 1975, 1979); J. D. G. Dunn, *Romans* (2 vols.; WBC 38; Dallas: Word, 1988); J. A. Fitzmyer, *Romans* (AB; New York: Doubleday, 1993); E. Käsemann, *Romans* (Grand Rapids: Eerdmans, 1980); D. J. Moo, *The Epistle to the Romans* (NICNT; Grand Rapids: Eerdmans, 1996); T. R. Schreiner, *Romans* (BECNT; Grand Rapids: Baker, 1998); N. T. Wright, "The Letter to the Romans," *NIBC* 10.393-770; J. Ziesler, *Romans* (TPINTC; Philadelphia: Trinity Press International, 1989). **Studies:** W. S. Campbell, *Paul's Gospel in an Intercultural Context: Jew and Gentile in the Letter to the Romans* (Frankfurt: Peter Lang, 1991); K. P. Donfried, ed., *The Romans Debate. Revised and Expanded Edition* (Peabody, MA: Hendrickson, 1991); J. D. G. Dunn, *The Partings of the Ways: Between Christianity and Judaism and Their Significance for the Character of Christianity* (Philadelphia: Trinity Press International, 1991); idem, *The Theology of Paul the Apostle* (Grand Rapids: Eerdmans, 1998); N. Elliott, *The Rhetoric of Romans. Argumentative Constraint and Strategy and Paul's Dialogue with Judaism* (JSNTSup 45; Sheffield: JSOT, 1990); D. B. Garlington, *Faith, Obedience and Perseverance: Aspects of Paul's Letter to the Romans* (WUNT 79; Tübingen: Mohr Siebeck, 1994); K. Haacker, *The Theology of Paul's Letter to the Romans* (NTT; Cambridge: Cambridge University Press, 2003); R. D. Kaylor, *Paul's Covenant Community: Jew and Gentile in Romans* (Atlanta: John Knox, 1988); B. W. Longenecker, *Eschatology and the Covenant: A Comparison of 4 Ezra and Romans 1—11* (JSNTSup 57; Sheffield: JSOT, 1991); M. D. Nanos, *The Mystery of Romans: The Jewish Context of Paul's Letter* (Minneapolis: Fortress, 1996); H. Räisänen, "Paul, God and Israel: Romans 9—11 in Recent Research" in *The Social World of Formative Christianity and Judaism,* ed. J. Neusner et al. (Philadelphia: Fortress, 1988) 178-206; E. P. Sanders, *Paul and Palestinian Judaism* (Philadelphia: Fortress, 1977); idem, *Paul, the Law, and the Jewish People* (Philadelphia: Fortress, 1983); S. K. Soderlund & N. T. Wright, eds., *Romans and the People of God* (Grand Rapids: Eerdmans, 1999); K. Stendahl, *Final Account: Paul's Letter to the Romans* (Minneapolis: Fortress, 1995); S. K. Stowers, *The Diatribe and Paul's Letter to the Romans* (SBLDS 57; Chico, CA: Scholars Press, 1981); F. B. Watson, *Paul, Judaism and the Gentiles: A Sociological Approach* (SNTSMS 56; Cambridge: Cambridge University Press, 1986); A. J. M. Wedderburn, *The Reasons for Romans* (Edinburgh: T & T Clark, 1988); N. T. Wright, *The Climax of the Covenant: Christ and the Law in Pauline Theology* (Edinburgh: T & T Clark, 1991).

J. D. G. Dunn

ROMANS IN PALESTINE. *See* ROME.

ROME

Rome was the chief city in Italy and the capital of the Roman Empire. Because of its prestige and importance its name is used both for the city and for Roman civilization.

1. Historical and Cultural Background of the City and the Empire
2. The City of Rome in the First Century A.D.
3. The Romans in Palestine

1. Historical and Cultural Background of the City and the Empire.

1.1. The Roman Republic. Rome began as a small settlement on the east bank of the Tiber River. Traditionally founded by Romulus by about 753 B.C. and ruled by kings, Rome became a republic in 509 B.C., governed by a senate under two consuls. It rapidly expanded, conquering its neighbors and establishing the dominance of its language, Latin. In the third to second centuries, Rome became a naval power, defeating its rival Carthage in two Punic wars. The Romans also gained ascendancy in the East with the defeat of Antiochus III of Syria and the conquest of Macedon and Greece (in 146 B.C. Corinth was sacked). By this time Rome had a highly efficient and well-disciplined professional army.

After class struggles, political rivalries and civil wars, the republic came to an end in a contest for power, initially among Pompey, Crassus and Julius Caesar (assassinated 44 B.C.), and then between Marc Antony and Octavian, who emerged victor at Actium (31 B.C.). In 27 B.C. Octavian, taking the surname Augustus, or "venerable" (cf. Lk 2:1), "restored the republic." This was the beginning of an empire that was to last for many centuries.

1.2. The Early Empire. For the purposes of studying the background to the NT, only the first phase of the Roman Empire, notably the Julio-Claudian and Flavian dynasties, is of direct importance. Knowledge of this period is indebted especially to Tacitus's *Annals* and *Histories*, Suetonius's *Lives of the Caesars*, Cassius Dio's *Histories* and Josephus's *Jewish War* and *Antiquities*, and to inscriptions, papyri and data derived from coins and other material remains (see Balsdon; Jones and Milns; Avi-Yonah).

Augustus (27 B.C.-A.D. 14) is rightly famous for establishing and maintaining peace (the *pax Romana*, although this was not kept without a price; see Wengst); for his efficient administration, including legal and financial reforms; his upholding of traditional Roman values and morality; and his patronage of the arts. Modest in his lifestyle, he preferred to be known as *princeps*, "first citizen," rather than *imperator*, "emperor." The principate of his stepson Tiberius (A.D. 14-37) proved more tyrannical and ended in a reign of terror. The evils of autocratic power became still more evident under Gaius (Caligula, A.D. 37-41), who may have been insane. He offended the Jews by ordering his statue to be placed in the temple at Jerusalem (the Syrian legate Petronius averted a confrontation by delaying tactics). After Gaius's assassination, Claudius's reign (A.D. 41-54) provided stability with the development of the civil service, the strengthening of the empire and the generous extension of Roman citizenship. He continued Augustus's policy of allowing the Jews freedom of worship and was a friend of Herod Agrippa I, whom he set up as king (see 2.2 below). In the later part of his reign, he expelled the Jews from Rome, an event that Suetonius (*Claudius* 25.4) claims was precipitated by disturbances caused by Chrestus ("at the instigation of Chrestus" [*impulsore Chresto*], perhaps a distortion of "Christ," although this is not certain; see Stern, 113-17). Nero's eccentric and extravagant reign (A.D. 54-68) was marked by a great fire at Rome, probably accidental but attributed to Christians. It led to the first concentrated Roman persecutions of Christians.

On Nero's death different military factions fought over the succession (A.D. 68-69, the Year of the Four Emperors), until Vespasian, a plebeian and commander of the army in the East, emerged victorious (reigned A.D. 69-79). This period saw the Jewish revolt of A.D. 66 to 70 with the brutal sack of Jerusalem by Vespasian's son Titus, who commemorated the event by his arch in Rome. After this, Judea became an imperial Roman province. Titus reigned only two years (A.D. 79-81) and was followed by his brother Domitian (A.D. 81-96), an efficient administrator who carried out a public building program. But his rule, like that of Tiberius, ended in a reign of terror. He claimed the title "lord and god" (Suetonius *Domitian* 13) and was responsible for a major persecution of Christians. In contrast, the reigns of Nerva (A.D. 96-98) and Trajan (A.D. 98-117) brought peace and stability.

One can understand why the Romans are famous for their military and administrative abilities, their law and their skills in architecture, engineering and road building. Deeply indebted to Greece in the areas of literature, philosophy and the creative arts, they nevertheless had their own gift for the lucid expression of ideas in precise and elegant language (see Howatson; Bandinelli). Traditionally the Romans valued family life and the virtues of *gravitas* ("dignity") and *pietas* ("devotion" or "dutifulness"). But like all peoples they had their darker side, and many instances are recorded of corruption, sexual immorality, brutality and murder. One should be wary of either idealizing or denigrating them as a people or in terms of their accomplishments.

1.3. Roman Religion and Politics.

1.3.1. Religion and Politics. Roman religion was originally animistic, involving the spirits of the woods, springs and mountains. The Romans also worshiped anthropomorphic gods such as Jupiter, Juno, Mars and Minerva, whom they identified with their Greek counterparts. They came successively under the influence of the Etruscans, the Greeks and various Eastern peoples and imported foreign cults, including those of Cybele, Isis and Mithras, so long as these were compatible with state policies. Roman religion and the state's policies toward religion affected the reception that the Roman people gave to foreign religions, including Judaism and Christianity, since Roman religion was closely bound up with the government of Rome. A good example of this linkage is emperor worship, which seems to have originated in the East, where Hellenistic monarchs had long been recognized as divine saviors. In the empire it became a focus and test of political loyalty (Pliny *Ep.* 10.96-97), even though at Rome it was at first restricted either to the deceased emperor (cf. the earlier worship of ancestors) or his "genius" (guardian spirit). In the provinces and later at Rome also, the emperor often shared his cult with the goddess Roma, personification of the power and spirit of Rome.

[R. B. Edwards]

The tie between religion and politics was felt in other ways, however. The priests of the state religion served as advisors to the senate. They were consulted for discerning the divine will through signs and purifying significant areas *(augures),* setting the calendar and establishing religious law *(pontifices),* making war in religiously correct ways *(fetiales)* and keeping and interpreting the Sibylline Books *(duoviri* [later *decemviri] sacris faciundis).* Priests, by their function of interpreting foreign books, especially in the third century B.C., called for the acceptance of certain foreign religions into Rome. At the end of the republican age the *haruspices* (lit., "soothsayers") were organized as a priestly college. Its members were trained to discern the divine will from the entrails of sacrificial animals.

Everywhere in first-century Rome there were reminders of the gods. On the hill known as Capitolium a large temple was dedicated to Jupiter, Juno and Minerva in the first year of the republic. Though it burned in 83 B.C., a new temple was built in 69 B.C. This was repaired and embellished by Augustus in 26 and 9 B.C. The temple therefore dominated the city when Christianity first made inroads there. On the southern border of the political center, the forum, were temples of Saturn, the Castores, Vesta and the office spaces of the *pontifices* and another member of their priestly college, the *rex sacrorum* ("king of sacred things," a religious post representing the ancient kings of Rome). Privately, the *lares* (shrines for dead family members) and *di penates* (gods of the family cupboard) were constant reminders in the home of the connection in the Roman religious mind between this world and the other.

Participation in religious ritual was a way of life for Romans. The possibility of choosing a religion and joining a group defined only for its religious identity was unknown. Groups that were organized solely for religious purposes, with the exception of vocational priesthoods in the state religion, Jewish synagogues, and later the churches, were unknown. Though there were *collegia* named after certain deities, the members of such associations were joined by a common occupation or ethnic background. The churches in Rome arguably showed their faith as the organizing principle more than synagogues, since the churches likely consisted of a greater variety in ethnic and class backgrounds.

1.3.2. Legal Orientation. In public and in private, Roman religion was in essence the performance of ritual; hence there was great emphasis on the proper observance of ritual (Pliny *Nat. Hist.* 13.10). The priesthoods were closely linked with the legislative government; this fact and the elaborate rules within Roman religion point to the essential legal character of religion. Far from espousing a personal relationship with the gods, Roman religion taught that if one followed the rituals correctly, a contract would be made that obtained the "peace of the gods" *(pax deorum;* cf. Rom 5:1-2, where Paul states that believers have "peace with God" on the basis of faith).

Since the Romans considered religion as essentially a legal matter, it is possible to interpret Paul's presentation of his gospel in the letter to the Romans in legal terms (*see* Romans, Letter to the): God's general moral law (Rom 2:14-16), Torah (Rom 3:21; 10:4) and political law (Rom

13:1-7). Paul's focus on questions of law (Rom 2:12-27; 4:13-16; 7 passim) and his acknowledgment that his readers "know law" (Rom 7:1) may not simply reflect the Jewish preoccupation with Torah or the high percentage of secular lawyers in Roman society but Paul's recognition that Romans viewed religion as a matter of law. The Roman emphasis on legal etiquette in religion presupposed that the gods were rational, a point not shared with most foreign cults introduced to Rome. The religious vow of 217 B.C. (Livy *Hist.* 22.10) illustrates how a Roman priest could treat the gods as rational bargaining partners, much as one person would reason with another. Paul's letter to the Romans emphasizes being rational in religion. The rational God hands over those who ignore him "to an unfit mind" (Rom 1:28); acting against one's mind is perceived as acting against God (Rom 7:20-24); and presenting one's body to God is reasonable religion, accompanied by a renewed mind (Rom 12:1-2).

1.3.3. Roman Policies and Attitudes to Foreign Religions. As one of the later foreign religions to seek entrance into Rome, Christianity inherited stereotypes and government policies developed from past encounters between the Roman government and foreign religions, such as Judaism. Any study of church-state relations not only must begin with the state religion of Rome but also must include the reception Rome gave to the foreign religions that antedated Christianity, since foreign religions could not be introduced in Rome without official approval from the senate, and Romans viewed religion as a concern of the state. Since the late republic, Rome looked at all foreign religions with much suspicion. At the same time, it was ready to attempt the introduction of a foreign religion when it perceived that cults offered a solution to an unmet need in Rome. For example, the Asclepius cult (known in Rome as *Aesculapius*) was brought from Epidaurus to Rome when in 293 B.C. the Roman priests who kept the Sibylline Books called for its importation to quell a plague. Its temple on the island of Tiber was dedicated on January 1, 291 B.C. The minor deity Hygieia was also worshiped there, to whom the Romans later attached the name of their Italian goddess, Salus.

The official importation of a new cult did not mean that the state religion was abandoned. There was no mechanism in Roman religion for abolishing any traditional practice. Rather, new cults were brought to Rome and new interpretations of state religion were made as history progressed. Religious exclusivism, such as was found in Judaism and Christianity, was therefore unheard of to the Roman religious mind. While initially more tolerant, Rome was more cautious regarding new religions after events in 186 B.C. that raised the government's suspicions about foreign religions. In this year, the Roman senate forbade the practice of the Dionysian *orgia*, or *bacchanalia*. The Dionysus cult had entered Rome from Campanian Italy. In response to the senate's measures (*CIL* 1.196; *ILS* 18), the people of Rome reacted violently, and an outbreak of crime spread through the city (Livy *Hist.* 39.8-18). This incident, known now as the Bacchanalia, helped shape the Roman stereotype that foreign religions inevitably brought disorder. Hence, when Christianity entered Rome, it too was viewed with suspicion.

[M. Reasoner]

1.4. Roman Provincial Administration. The first Roman provinces, in the West, were acquired in the third century B.C. After Rome's expansion into the East, Asia (i.e., western Turkey), Cilicia and Bithynia were added, followed by Syria and Egypt. Augustus annexed several more provinces, and Claudius added Britain (A.D. 43).

Under the empire, provinces were of two kinds: public or consular, governed by proconsuls under the authority of the senate (these were generally the richer and more settled provinces); or imperial, governed by legates, appointed by the emperor (mostly frontier provinces, such as Syria, where legions were stationed). Both these types of governor were of senatorial rank. There was a third class of governors, known as prefects or procurators, of lower equestrian rank, who were in charge of smaller provinces (e.g., Judea). These were often experts in financial administration. All governors had judicial and military powers. The number of troops available might be quite small (e.g., one cohort, consisting of three hundred to six hundred men) but in frontier provinces could rise to three or four legions (a legion consisting of some three thousand to six thousand infantry and one hundred to two hundred cavalry). Governors could not be prosecuted for mismanagement until after their term of office.

Roman provincial government has been described as "supervisory rather than executive" (Sherwin-White, *ISBE* 3:1027), which meant that few Roman officials were involved, detailed administration being in the hands of municipal authorities or, in the case of Judea, councils of elders grouped into toparchies. Revenue was raised by a system of tax farming. Local laws and religious customs were usually respected as long as they did not interfere with smooth government. Roman citizens came under Roman law. Citizenship could be granted both to whole communities and to individuals (e.g., to men with long service in auxiliary units of the army) and was passed down from father to son. In the Eastern provinces members of the wealthy upper classes often acquired their citizenship through influence.

[R. B. Edwards]

2. The City of Rome in the First Century A.D.

2.1. Size and Character. With a population of about one million people, the city of Rome in the first century drew people from every corner of the empire and beyond. During Augustus's reign an urban police force (*cohortes urbanae*) and fire prevention units (*vigiles*) were added to keep order in the growing city. Like the great cities of today, Rome was the place to visit in the imperial period. Paul's declaration that he had intended many times to visit the Roman Christians before writing his letter to them (Rom 1:13) was therefore similar to what any provincial would say before making final arrangements for a trip to Rome.

From at least the third century B.C., Rome had been a drawing point for people of a variety of ethnic backgrounds. The immigration of provincial Italians and Greeks that was occurring under the republic was eclipsed in the early principate by immigration from Syria, Asia Minor (modern Turkey), Egypt, Africa, Spain, and later Gaul and Germany. Juvenal's statement that "long ago the Orontes has overflowed into the Tiber" (Juvenal *Sat.* 3.62) shows his perception of the high number of Semitic people living in first-century Rome. Record of a Jewish presence in Rome dates from 139 B.C., and it is known that the number of Jewish residents in Rome increased when, in 62 B.C., Pompey brought back a large number of Jewish captives for use as slaves. By the time Cicero defended Flaccus in 59 B.C., it appears that the Jews were a significant political interest group in Rome (Cicero *Flac.* 66). In the civil war that began in 49 B.C., the Jews in Rome and throughout the Mediterranean world supported Julius Caesar against Pompey, thus explaining why Jews mourned the death of Caesar in 44 B.C. (Suetonius *Julius* 84.5). It is estimated that there were at least forty thousand Jews in Rome during the first century A.D. Literary sources from the late republic and early empire show, however, that these foreign residents in Rome (*peregrini*) were not fully accepted and experienced racial discrimination. Africans were reportedly despised (Livy *Hist.* 30.12.18; Sallust *Iug.* 91.7), the Jews were the victims of such discrimination (Cicero *Flac.* 66-69; Horace *Sat.* 1.9.71-72), and even Greeks received slurs (Cicero *Ep.* 16.4.2; *Tusc.* 2.65; *De Orat.* 1.105; 2.13).

2.2. Judaism in Rome. Scholars disagree whether Judaism had been accorded the status of a legal religion (*religio licita*), but it appears that Jews were given tacit permission to meet for religious purposes in their synagogues, and the Jews' observance of the sabbath was not used to their disadvantage. It is true that Jews were expelled from Rome in 139 B.C. (Valerius Maximus *Fact. ac Dict.* 1.3.2), in A.D. 19 (Josephus *Ant.* 18.3.5 §§81-84; Tacitus *Ann.* 2.85.5; Suetonius *Tiberius* 36; Dio Cassius *Hist.* 57.18.5) and in A.D. 49 (Suetonius *Claudius* 25.4; Acts 18:1-2; some scholars think this expulsion took place in A.D. 41). The first two cases were probably a Roman response to active proselytizing by the Jews, but the third was perhaps due to unrest within the Jewish community about Christianity (see 1.2 above). But these expulsions were not permanent measures, and at least in the latter two cases probably did not apply to Jews who were Roman citizens.

Judaism in Rome was also closely tied to Judaism in Jerusalem. Around 140 B.C., the high priests in Jerusalem sent emissaries to Rome in order to offset the power of the Seleucids. Later, ruling priests in the first century politically endorsed Julius Caesar (and not Pompey, who had entered the temple in 63 B.C.), and Herod the Great was in political alliance with Augustus. In the first century A.D., princes in the family of Herod such as Agrippa II, who would later hold the rights of appointing high priests in Jerusalem, were reared in Rome under imperial patronage. Far from being an unruly cousin of Judaism in Jerusalem, then, Judaism in Rome was rather a devoted son. Within the synagogues of Rome, Christianity first gained its inroads there.

2.3. Christians in Rome. Although Christianity first appeared as a sect of Judaism, the Roman church by the time of Paul's initial visit (A.D. 60) was already making its break with Judaism, a break that must have been complete by A.D. 64, when Nero focused persecution on Christians, blaming them for the fire in the city. The churches in Rome represented a body of Christianity that Paul could not ignore. Their strategic potential came from their close connection with Jerusalem, their location in the world capital and their connections with the rest of the empire through people groups represented in Rome's congregations.

2.3.1. Origins. The connection between the Jews in Rome and Jerusalem and the Jewish element within early Roman Christianity lead to the probable conclusion that Christianity was brought to Rome by Jewish Christians from Palestine. This is confirmed by the note that Jews from Rome were in Peter's audience in Jerusalem at Pentecost (Acts 2:10). Jewish Christians most probably entered into dialogue with fellow Jews, and this resulted in tumultuous encounters and some conversions. One such encounter possibly occurred in A.D. 49, when Claudius expelled the Jews from Rome. Suetonius's brief description of this event is generally taken to mean that the Jews were arguing among themselves about Christ. As a result, Priscilla and Aquila, two Jewish Christians, left Italy when Claudius expelled the Jews from Rome (Acts 18:2).

The Jewish component in early Roman Christianity suggests that house churches may have developed in association with various synagogues, indicating that Christianity in Rome arose not in a single church but in a plurality of house churches. Paul's greeting in the letter to the Romans is given not to a church (cf. 1 Cor 1:2; 2 Cor 1:1) but to "all those who are in Rome, beloved of God, chosen saints" (Rom 1:7). Paul still used the singular "church" to describe the Christians who met in Rome, while acknowledging that they did so probably in a variety of places.

2.3.2. Jewish Presence. Because of its likely origin in the synagogues of Rome, Jewish Christianity retained a close connection with its Jewish roots in Jerusalem. Paul's letter to the church is evidence for this (Rom 1:16; 3:1-30; 9-11). Half a century later, when Tacitus describes Christianity, he links it to Judea (Tacitus *Ann.* 15.44.2). Roman Christianity must have included a distinctly Jewish element. Theologically such a presence within the church most representative of the world's peoples forced Paul to outline his gospel in a manner that accounted for God's dealings with all people (Rom 2:1-16; 15:7-13). A letter and visit to this church provided apologetic opportunities for Paul to defend himself to people with close ties to the groups that most criticized and resisted Paul's ministry, the Judaism and Christianity of Jerusalem. Thus, for the Romans, Paul defends his theology (Rom 6:1-2) and mission strategy (Rom 15:14-24). His upcoming visit to Jerusalem is explained and addressed to them as a worthwhile and spiritual endeavor (Rom 15:25-32). While Roman Christianity was primarily composed of Gentiles, as Paul's letter shows, it is probable that there was an ethnically Jewish presence in the Roman churches.

2.3.3. Servile Presence. Since many Jews first came to Rome as slaves, it is likely that some of the Jews within the Roman churches were of the servile classes (either slaves or freedmen and freedwomen). The slaves in Rome were primarily of foreign origin in the first century of the principate. While there were some freeborn foreigners in Rome, the possibility that many were servile foreigners fits with Suetonius's conviction that Nero administered Roman law properly when crucifying Christians (Suetonius *Nero* 16.2; 19.3), since Roman law prohibited crucifixion of its citizens. Further evidence for the servile nature of the Roman church are the references to those of certain "households" (Rom 16:10-11), a standard euphemism for the servile classes.

2.3.4. Asceticism. G. La Piana has suggested an ascetic element within the first-century Roman church. This seems fully in accordance with extrabiblical evidence and indications in Paul's letter to the Romans. Vegetarianism was taught in the school of Quintus Sextius in the early first century. The philosopher Sotion led Seneca to practice vegetarianism for a time (Seneca *Ep.* 108.22). Another philosopher who was influential during the reign of Nero, Musonius Rufus, also taught vegetarianism (*Peri Trophes,* ed. Hense, 95). Vegetarianism is reflected in *1 Clement* 20.4, while asceticism in dress is mentioned in *1 Clement* 17.1. Biblical evidence for asceticism in Roman Christianity comes from Hebrews 13:9 and Romans 14:1-3, 21. In the latter reference the strong and weak are differentiated within the Roman church by different postures toward ascetic practice. The mind/body dualism common to ascetics is found in Romans 1:24; 6:19; 7:23-24; 12:1-2. The ascetic tendencies of Roman Christianity were later worked out in one of its leaders, Tatian (fl. in Rome A.D. 160-172). The ascetic movement within the Roman church at the time Paul wrote his letter may well have prompted him to delineate an ethic of responsibility in which the strong in conscience was to respect the weak, more ascetic, Christians (Rom 14:14-17; 15:1-3).

2.3.5. Influence. By the time Paul wrote Romans, it is clear that the Roman church was ascendant in influence among churches of the Mediterranean world. Paul's uncharacteristic desire to visit the church in Rome that he had not founded (Rom 1:9-13; cf. 15:20) and his need for the Roman church's endorsement and support (Rom 15:22-24) show the influence that this church carried in the Mediterranean world. The influence of the Roman church is also seen in *1 Clement,* a letter written as early as A.D. 96, in which the Roman church expects its directives to its sister church in Corinth to be followed (*1 Clem.* 7.1-3; 62.1-3; 65.1).

Though the church in Rome was not founded by an apostle, Paul is associated with its early history. As apostle to the Gentiles, he considered this within his sphere of ministry (Rom 1:11-15). One's understanding of the relationship that Paul had with Roman Christianity before his visit in A.D. 60 affects one's conception of early church history and hence one's interpretation of the letter to the Romans. While it is true that Romans is the most systematic of Paul's letters, its occasional nature cannot be denied. The influence that Roman Christianity enjoyed likely meant that Christians throughout the empire knew something about the Roman church. Paul's statement "your faith is announced throughout the whole world" (Rom 1:8) is probably more than epistolary flattery. Paul met Christians from Rome at least by A.D. 50, after Aquila and Priscilla had come to Corinth from Rome (Acts 18:1-2; cf. Rom 16:3-5). Christians in Pauline circles no doubt had associations with other Christians in Rome. While Romans 16 has been assigned an Ephesian destination by T. W. Manson, later works by H. Gamble, P. Lampe and W.-H. Ollrog have demonstrated the integrity of this chapter with the rest of the letter. On the basis of Romans 16, then, it is probable that Paul knew a number of people in Rome. The letter is written in order to strengthen an existing relationship.

By the time Paul arrived in Rome in about A.D. 60 (Acts 28:14-16) in order to stand trial before Nero's representative, the praetorian prefect, Nero had murdered his mother, his advisor Burrus had died, and Seneca had retired. Rumors were probably spreading that the imperial government did not seem as stable as in the earlier part of Nero's reign. According to tradition, Paul was freed after his first trial. From the testimony that Paul "reached the limits of the West" (*1 Clem.* 5.7), it is possible that Paul then reached Spain as intended (Rom 15:24). It is then most likely that Paul was arrested and imprisoned again at Rome, where he was executed sometime between A.D. 64 and 67. *First Clement* 5.2-5, in citing "pillars of the church," mentions Peter first and then Paul as examples of endurance under suffering. Today one can see a carving of both apostles baptizing their jailers in the Mamertine Prison (Rome's state prison), testimony to the tradition that both men suffered for their faith in Rome. The details of Paul's second trial (if he had one) and martyrdom are unknown. Tradition tells us that he was beheaded on the Ostian Way at about the same time and place as Peter (Eusebius *Hist. Eccl.* 2.25.7-8).

[M. Reasoner]

3. The Romans in Palestine.

3.1. To Herod the Great. The history of the Roman government of Palestine is complex. In 66 to 63 B.C., Pompey conducted his celebrated Eastern campaign, during which he was called into Palestine by the two sons of Salome Alexandra in their dispute over the succession. He captured Jerusalem and entered the temple but ordered its cleansing and reinstated Hyrcanus as high priest. After this, Syria became a Roman imperial province, with the Decapolis and Samaria, now freed from Jewish rule, under its wing. Judea, Galilee, Idumea and Perea were retained by the Jews as client kingdoms, dependent on Rome. Julius Caesar appointed Antipater procurator of Judea. His son Herod, who had been governor of Galilee, won from Rome the title King of the Jews, a title which he had to make a reality by force of arms. Herod reigned from 37 to 4 B.C.; he extended his territories and restored the Jerusalem temple on a lavish scale, including Greco-Roman architectural features. Herod was both a lover of Hellenism and an admirer of Roman culture. He encouraged Hellenistic education and social mores; he built theaters, amphitheaters and other civic amenities such as aqueducts. Under his rule, Judea was materially prosperous. But he was also violent and cruel. The massacre of the innocents at Bethlehem (Mt 2; *see* Birth of Jesus), though not confirmed by external sources, is consistent with his character.

3.2. After Herod the Great. On Herod's death his kingdom was split into three with Herod Antipas as tetrarch of Galilee and Perea (4 B.C.-A.D. 39); Philip tetrarch of Trachonitis and Iturea (4 B.C.-A.D. 34); and Archelaus ethnarch in Judea, Idumea and Samaria (4 B.C.-A.D. 6; cf. Mt 2:22; Lk 3:1). Archelaus's rule ended in riots, and he was banished. Judea now came under the control of Roman governors.

Pontius Pilate was governor of Judea from A.D. 26/27 to 36. Tacitus (*Ann.* 15.44) refers to him as procurator and mentions that "Christus" was put to death by him when Tiberius was emperor. However, an inscription from Caesarea, the Roman capital of Judea, shows that his title was more correctly *prefect*. He was of equestrian rank, presumably a former military tribune, and had five cohorts of infantry and a cavalry regiment under his command. He had absolute authority in his own province but was responsible to the legate in Syria. Josephus and Philo say that his governorship was marred by bloodshed, including a massacre of some Galileans (possibly alluded to in Lk 13:1) and the slaughter of many Samaritans in an ugly incident that resulted in protests to the legate Vitellius in Syria and Pilate's recall to Rome. According to Eusebius he later committed suicide.

In A.D. 41, Herod Agrippa I, who had previously governed northern Palestine and Galilee, was made king of the Jews (cf. Acts 12), but in A.D. 44 Palestine reverted to Roman governors. In A.D. 66 to 70 the tragic Jewish war erupted, with the siege and fall of Jerusalem in A.D. 70. The Jewish patriots held out at Masada until A.D. 73 and committed suicide rather than submit to Rome. In A.D. 132 to 135 the Bar Kokhba revolt finally sealed the fate of Judea, and Jerusalem became a Roman colony (Aelia Capitolina) inhabited by non-Jews.

In Palestine the Jewish leaders and people varied immensely in their attitudes to the Romans. The Herodian rulers and their party were naturally pro-Roman. The high priests also generally favored cooperation, as did the Sadducees. At least some of the Essenes withdrew to the desert, while the Zealots worked for armed rebellion. The Pharisees saw as their first loyalty absolute adherence to the Mosaic law and traditions, so they refused to take an oath of loyalty to Herod (Josephus *Ant.* 17.42); some actively resisted Roman rule, but others were more acquiescent. The common people must have simply scraped a living in a society where there was great inequality between rich and poor and much scope for oppression.

[R. B. Edwards]

See also HEBREWS, LETTER TO THE; JUDAISM AND THE NEW TESTAMENT; PAUL IN ACTS AND LETTERS; RELIGIONS, GRECO-ROMAN; ROMANS, LETTER TO THE.

DNTB: ROMAN ADMINISTRATION; ROMAN EAST; ROMAN EMPERORS; ROMAN EMPIRE; ROMAN GOVERNORS OF PALESTINE; ROMAN LAW AND LEGAL SYSTEM; ROMAN MILITARY; ROMAN POLITICAL SYSTEM; ROMAN SOCIAL CLASSES.

BIBLIOGRAPHY. L. Adkins and R. A. Adkins, *Dictionary of Roman Religion* (New York: Facts on File, 1996); W. T. Arnold, *The Roman System of Provincial Administration* (Oxford: Blackwell, 1906); M. Avi-Yonah, *Gazetteer of Roman Palestine* (*Qedem* 5; Jerusalem: Hebrew University, 1976); J. P. V. D. Balsdon, *Rome: The Story of an Empire* (London: Weidenfeld & Nicolson, 1970); E. Bammel and C. F. D. Moule, eds., *Jesus and the Politics of His Day* (Cambridge: Cambridge University Press, 1984); R. B. Bandinelli, *Rome, the Center of Power* (London: Thames & Hudson, 1970); M. Beard and M. Crawford, *Rome in the Late Republic* (London: Duckworth, 1985); K. R. Bradley, *Slaves and Masters in the Roman Empire: A Study in Social Control* (New York: Oxford University Press, 1987); R. E. Brown and J. P. Meier, *Antioch and Rome: New Testament Cradles of Catholic Christianity* (New York: Paulist, 1983); M. Cary, *A History of Rome Down to the Reign of Constantine* (2d ed.; London: Macmillan, 1967); M. P. Charlesworth, *Documents Illustrating the Reigns of Claudius and Nero* (Cambridge: Cambridge University Press, 1951); G. Edmundson, *The Church in Rome in the First Century* (London: Longmans, Green, 1913); V. Ehrenberg and A. H. M. Jones, *Documents Illustrating the Reigns of Augustus and Tiberius* (2d ed.; Oxford: Clarendon, 1955); S. Freyne, *Galilee from Alexander the Great to Hadrian* (Wilmington, DE: Michael Glazier, 1980); J. Ferguson, *The Religions of the Roman Empire* (Ithaca, NY: Cornell University Press, 1970); H. Gamble Jr., *The Textual History of the Letter to the Romans* (Grand Rapids: Eerdmans, 1977); P. Garnsey and R. Saller, *The Roman Empire: Economy, Society and Culture* (Berkeley: University of California Press, 1987); T. R. Glover, *The Conflict of Religions in the Early Roman Empire* (London: Methuen, 1909); F. C. Grant, *Roman Hellenism and the New Testament* (Edinburgh: Oliver & Boyd, 1962); M. Grant, *The Twelve Caesars* (London: Weidenfeld & Nicolson, 1975); R. M. Grant, *Early Christianity and Society* (London: Collins, 1978); M. C. Howatson, ed., *The Oxford Companion to Classical Literature* (2d ed.; Oxford: Oxford University Press, 1989); A. H. M. Jones, *Augustus* (London: Chatto & Windus, 1970); idem, *Cities of the Eastern Roman Provinces* (Oxford: Clarendon, 1937); B. W. Jones and R. D. Milns, *The Use of Documentary Evidence in the Study of Roman Imperial History* (Sydney: Sydney University Press, 1984); N. Kokkinos, *The Herodian Dynasty: Origins, Role in Society and Eclipse* (JSPSup 30; Sheffield: Sheffield Academic Press, 1998); L. J. Kreitzer, *Striking New Images: Roman Imperial Coinage and the New Testament World* (JSNTSup 134; Sheffield: Sheffield Academic Press, 1996); P. Lampe, *From Paul to Valentinus: Christians at Rome in the First Two Centuries* (Minneapolis: Fortress, 2003); G. La Piana, "Foreign Groups in Rome During the First Centuries of the Empire," *HTR* 20 (1927) 183-403; idem, "La Primitiva Communità Cristiana di Roma e L'epistola ai Romani," *Ricerche Religiose* 1 (1925) 209-26; 305-26; H. J. Leon, *The Jews of Ancient Rome* (Philadelphia: Jewish Publication Society of America, 1960); J. H. W. G. Liebeschuetz, *Continuity and Change in Roman Religion* (Oxford: Clarendon, 1979); A. Linder, *The Jews in Roman Imperial Legislation* (Detroit: Wayne State University Press, 1987); E. Lohse, *The New Testament Environment* (Nashville: Abingdon, 1976); R. MacMullen, *Christianizing the Roman Empire (A.D. 100-400)* (New Haven, CT: Yale University Press, 1984); idem, *Paganism in the Roman Empire* (New Haven, CT: Yale University Press, 1981); idem, *Roman Social Relations 50 B.C. to A.D. 284* (New Haven, CT: Yale University Press, 1974); T. W. Manson, "St. Paul's Letter to the Romans—and Others," in *The Romans Debate*, ed. K. P. Donfried (Minneapolis: Augsburg, 1978) 1-16; M. McCrum and A. G. Woodhead, *Select Documents of the Principates of the Flavian Emperors Including the Year of Revolution A.D. 68-96* (Cambridge: Cambridge University Press, 1966); F. Millar, *The Roman Empire and Its Neighbors* (2d ed.; London: Gerald Duckworth, 1981); idem, *The Roman Near East 31 B.C.-A.D. 337* (Cambridge, MA: Harvard University Press, 1993); T. Mommsen, *The Provinces of the Roman Empire from Caesar to Diocletian* (2 vols.; London: Macmillan, 1909); M. P. Nilsson, *The Dionysiac Mysteries of the Hellenistic and Roman Age* (Salem, NH: Ayer, 1985); idem, *Imperial Rome* (London: Bell, 1926); J. A. North, "Conservatism and Change in Roman Religion," *PBSR* 44 (1976) 1-12; idem, "Religion in Republican Rome," in *CAH* 7.2:573-624; W.-H. Ollrog, "Die Abfassungsverhältnisse von Röm 16," in *Kirche*, Festschrift for G. Bornkamm, ed. D. Lührmann and G. Strecker (Tübingen: Mohr Siebeck, 1980) 221-44; A. M. Rostovtzeff, *Social and Economic History of the Roman Empire* (2d ed.; 2 vols.; Oxford: Clarendon, 1957); R. K. Sherk, ed., *Rome and the Greek East to the Death of Augustus* (Cambridge: Cambridge University Press, 1984); idem, *The Roman Empire: Augustus to Hadrian* (Cambridge: Cambridge University Press, 1988); A. N. Sherwin-White, "Provinces, Roman," *ISBE* 3:1026-28; idem, *Roman Society and Roman Law in the New Testament* (Oxford: Clarendon, 1963); M. Stern, ed., *Greek and Latin Authors on Jews and Judaism*, vol. 2 (Jerusalem: Israel Academy of Sciences and Humanities, 1980); A. Watson, *The Law of the Ancient Romans* (Dallas: Southern Methodist University Press, 1970); K. Wengst, *Pax Romana and the Peace of Jesus Christ* (London: SCM, 1987); R. L. Wilken, *The Christians as the Romans Saw Them* (New Haven, CT: Yale University Press, 1984); M. H. Williams, *The Jews Among the Greeks and Romans: A Diasporan Sourcebook* (London: Duckworth, 1998).

R. B. Edwards and M. Reasoner

ROME, CHRISTIANITY IN. *See* ROME.

ROME, CITY OF. *See* ROME.

S

SABBATH COMMANDMENT. *See* ETHICS I; LAW I.

SACRIFICE. *See* DEATH OF CHRIST.

SADDUCEES. *See* JUDAISM AND THE NEW TESTAMENT.

SALVATION I: GOSPELS

The term *salvation* (with its associated word group) has become widely used in Christian theology to express the provision of *God for our human situation of need and sin. The word group has a less prominent theological role in the Gospels but nevertheless is important in expressing the effects of the ministry of Jesus. The present article is largely confined to the use of the word group and does not develop the broader concept of salvation at length.

1. Overview of Linguistic Usage
2. Background to the Usage in the Gospels
3. Salvation in the Individual Gospels
4. The Understanding of Salvation in the Gospels

1. Overview of Linguistic Usage.

1.1. The Verb Sōzō. According to Louw and Nida the verb *to save (sōzō)* has three meanings in the NT: (1) "To rescue from danger and to restore to a former state of safety and well being"; (2) "to cause someone to become well again after having been sick"; (3) "to cause someone to experience divine salvation—'to save.' "

The verb is found frequently in the Gospels (Mt 15 x; Mk 14 x + Mk 16:16; Lk 17 x; Jn 6 x; the sayings in Mt 18:11 and Lk 9:56 are not found in the oldest MSS; Mk 16:16 is part of a later addition to the Gospel). It has various senses.

1.1.1. The Synoptics. (1) The verb means "to deliver" from danger. So in Matthew 8:25 and 14:30 it is used of rescue from the danger of drowning. In Matthew 27:40 (par. Mk 15:30); 27:42b (par. Mk 15:31b and Lk 23:35b); 27:49; Luke 23:37, 39 it is used of Jesus being delivered from dying on the cross (presumably by miraculous means or by Elijah coming to help him). It is probably in this same general sense that reference is made to Jesus "saving" others (Mt 27:42a par. Mk 15:31 and Lk 23:35a).

In the passive the verb can mean "to come" or "to be brought safely through" a period of danger to life (Mt 10:22 and 24:13 par. Mk 13:13; cf. Mt 24:22 par. Mk 13:20).

A more metaphorical use is found in Luke 19:10, where Jesus is like a shepherd who seeks out and saves the lost [sheep] from danger of death.

(2) The verb often has the meaning "to heal" (namely, from disease). It is so used in Matthew 9:21 (par. Mk 5:28); 9:22a (par. Mk 5:34 and Lk 8:48); 9:22b; Mark 5:23; 6:56 (par. Mt 14:36, Gk *diasōzō*); 10:52 (par. Lk 18:42); Luke 7:50; 8:36, 50; 17:19 (note also Lk 7:3, Gk *diasōzō*). In some of these cases the reference is to deliverance from the power of evil spirits by exorcism or to the raising of the dead (*see* Resurrection). In Mark 3:4 (par. Lk 6:9) "to save a life" (Gk *psychē* may have the sense "person" here) is contrasted with killing. The phrase is used in the context of healing in a broad sense of doing whatever is needed to promote life and health, and the thought is probably of physical life.

(3) In the story of the conversation between Jesus, the rich young man and the *disciples, the phrases "to inherit eternal life," "to enter the kingdom of God" (*see* Kingdom of God) and "to be saved" appear to be used synonymously (Mk 10:17, 23-25, 26; cf. Mt 19:16, 23-24, 25; Lk 18:18, 24-25, 26). What might be regarded as a technical usage of spiritual salvation is found in Luke

13:23 ("are 'the saved' few?") and in Luke 8:12 ("so that they may not believe and be saved"). Jesus is so named according to the angel of the Lord in Matthew 1:21 because "he will save his people from their sins."

In a paradoxical saying, Jesus talks about people who want to save their lives and lose them (Mt 16:25 par. Mk 8:35a and Lk 9:24a) in contrast to those who lose their lives and (thus) save them (Mk 8:35b par. Lk 9:24b).

(4) In some passages the language is ambiguous, and it is not clear whether the reference is purely to physical and mental health and well-being or also to spiritual salvation (e.g., Lk 7:50, "Your faith has saved you"; note that this phrase is used elsewhere of physical healing: Mk 5:34 par. Lk 8:48; Mk 10:52 par. Lk 18:42; cf. Lk 8:50; 17:19).

1.1.2. John. The usage in John is similar to that of the Synoptics.

(1) In John 12:27 Jesus prays about the possibility of being delivered from having to undergo the cross. In John 10:9 he refers to people being like sheep who enter the sheepfold and live in safety.

(2) In John 11:12 Lazarus is thought to be asleep (i.e., in a coma) and therefore capable of being healed.

(3) Jesus is said to have come to save the world (Jn 3:17), and he refers to this as his purpose in 12:47. He speaks of his hearers being saved in 5:34.

1.2. The Verb **Rhyomai.** Meaning "to rescue, deliver," *rhyomai* is used much less frequently, generally with reference to deliverance from extreme danger, such as death or falling into the hands of enemies. In Matthew 27:43 it is found in the satirical quotation of Psalm 22:8 by the Jewish leaders to Jesus on the cross. In Luke 1:74 deliverance from enemies is part of the salvation awaited by Zechariah. In Matthew 6:13 the disciples are encouraged to pray for deliverance from the evil one (or from evil).

1.3. The Noun **Sōtēr.** *Sōtēr,* meaning "savior," is used by Mary with reference to God in Luke 1:47, and Jesus is so designated at his *birth by the angel of the *Lord to the shepherds (Lk 2:11). In John 4:42 the Samaritan people who have responded to Jesus declare that he is "the Savior of the world" (Jn 4:42).

1.4. The Noun **Sōtēria.** *Sōtēria,* a noun meaning "salvation," can refer to the process of saving or to the result. It is found in Luke 1:69 where Zechariah declares that God has raised up "a horn of salvation," and then defines God's gift more closely as "salvation [deliverance] from our enemies." Later in the same hymn the task of his son John (*see* John the Baptist) is defined as giving to his people "the knowledge of salvation through the forgiveness of their sins." Jesus comments that his visit to Zacchaeus has brought "salvation" to his household (Lk 19:9). And Jesus tells the woman of Samaria that "salvation is from the Jews" (Jn 4:22).

1.5. The Noun **Sōtērion.** Another word meaning "salvation," *sōtērion,* is found in Luke 2:30 where Simeon says that his eyes have seen God's salvation, and in Luke 3:6 where the Evangelist himself quotes Isaiah 40:5, "And all humanity will see God's salvation." According to Louw and Nida this word signifies rather "the means by which people experience divine salvation."

1.6. Salvation in a Spiritual Sense. This survey demonstrates that the spiritual sense is clearly present in Matthew (1:21) and Mark (10:26), but that it is most prominent in Luke, who alone of the Synoptic Evangelists develops the use of the nouns alongside the verb. One interesting fact which emerges is that the "literal" meaning of the word can be either broadly to "rescue" or to "heal," and both of these meanings can underlie the "spiritual" usage of the terminology. Louw and Nida (1.241 n. 4) comment that on the whole, Bible translators have used words reflecting the former meaning, but that there has been a shift to using words reflecting the latter meaning or to using words that signify more "to restore, recreate." Thus the accent has shifted from the action of God or the newness of what he creates to the restoration of what has been lost or marred.

2. Background to the Usage in the Gospels.
The Gospels were written at a time when the *church had already developed a special vocabulary to refer to Christian experience. We may envisage a two-way process whereby the vocabulary of the Christians will have been influenced by that of Jesus and, conversely, the diction of the Gospels may have been influenced by that of the church. The modes of expression of Jesus and his followers will also have been influenced by their heritage in the OT and Judaism, and to some extent also by the need to speak in terms that would be readily understood in the wider world.

The extensive and readable survey by E. M. B. Green considers the background to the NT use of the concept. There is a considerable amount of material in the OT where the corresponding Hebrew words are often used of deliverance in times of conflict, especially war. But the idea of deliverance is much wider and refers to being set free from all kinds of perils and dangers to life and even more generally to the state of well-being which God desires for his people. The Israelites naturally looked to God as their supreme and ultimate deliverer from all kinds of trouble and distress. He is the Savior *par excellence* (cf. Ps 27:1 and frequently).

The term *savior* was well known in the Greco-Roman world as an epithet for gods in their roles as helpers of humanity and particular communities; the god Asclepius was particularly important as the healer of the sick at various shrines. It was also used of statesmen, and when a religious cult of rulers developed, *savior* was one of the honorific titles used in this connection.

3. Salvation in the Individual Gospels.

3.1. Matthew.

3.1.1. Salvation from Sin. Right at the outset, Matthew's Gospel announces that "Jesus" is to be so-called because he will save his people from their *sins. In this context the "people" is a designation for Israel which is regarded as a sinful nation. Deliverance from sin is associated with the response of the people to John the Baptist (Mt 3:6) and with the sovereign declarations of Jesus as the *Son of man (Mt 9:2, 5, 6). At the *Last Supper Jesus declares that his blood is to be poured out for the forgiveness of sins (Mt 26:28). He also states that he has come with a mission to sinful people (Mt 9:10-13; cf. 11:19). The significance of "saving" is not spelled out in detail, but the three references to forgiveness indicate clearly enough what is probably in mind. One would naturally think of delivering people from the effects of their sins, but at the same time enabling them not to sin is in mind. In the ironic summary on the lips of the Jewish leaders at the crucifixion: "He saved others" (Mt 27:42a), the verb is used in a broad sense and is not to be limited to the sense of saving a person from death (Mt 27:42b). However, it is unlikely that we are to find a spiritual significance on the level of the original speakers.

3.1.2. Salvation as Physical and Spiritual. The references to deliverance from impending death at sea and to the cure of physical ailments need not necessarily imply anything further than this. However, a number of factors may suggest a different understanding.

First, there is the fact that stories in the Gospels about physical "salvation" may well have been used in the church with a symbolic significance; thus the story of the disciples in the boat during a storm has been taken to symbolize the church in the world suffering tribulation. In this case it is the followers of Jesus who cry out to the Lord to "save" them in the difficulties of life, and the answer to their prayers may lie in the removing or mitigating of their trials, or their being brought safely through them, or their being brought to final salvation despite even death itself. The collocation of healing a paralyzed man and forgiving his sins may equally have led to seeing healing as symbolic of spiritual forgiveness and salvation.

Second, there is the fact that the formula translated elsewhere in the Gospels as "your faith has healed you" is used once in Luke (7:50) of a sinful woman who had experienced forgiveness. Here the formula is naturally translated as "your faith has saved you" (so NIV), which is essentially the same as Ephesians 2:8 (cf. Acts 15:11 [if translated with F. F. Bruce, "we believe (so as) to be saved"]; 16:31; Rom 10:9; Jas 2:14; in the longer addition to Mark [16:16] the same church terminology is to be found). In view of the ambiguity of the formula when taken out of a healing context, it is quite probable that early Christians were led to see healing as symbolic of salvation and to draw the parallel between healing by faith and salvation by faith.

Third, no hard and fast line was drawn between the physical and the spiritual in the ancient world. In fact, the same is often true today. If Christians pray for God to "bless" somebody, it is often hard to say whether they are thinking of successfully carrying through some piece of business or aspect of daily life, or enjoying some kind of sense of divine favor or doing some aspect of Christian ministry and service success fully. It would therefore be hard to distinguish between a physical healing and the healing of the "inner person" (cf. Lk 17:19, where it is not clear whether the statement refers purely to the cure of the leprosy).

It is therefore likely that the healing stories in the Gospels were understood as accounts of a process that involved the whole person and not merely a physical or mental healing.

3.1.3. Salvation Despite Persecution. Matthew 10:22 and parallels could refer to being brought through persecution in physical safety; however, the reference to possible death in verse 21 suggests that the verse is about standing firm in loyalty to Jesus despite persecution, and that standing firm leads to "final salvation." However, in Matthew 24:22 (par. Mk 13:20) the force could be that if persecution went on too long, nobody would survive alive, and therefore there would be nobody left alive to welcome the *Son of man at his coming. The saying cannot mean that nobody would stand firm to the point of martyrdom. Here, then, we have two different uses of the word quite close to each other.

3.1.4. Final Salvation. Similarly, Matthew 19:25 and parallels must refer to "final salvation." It is about a future state of being saved as opposed to being lost, and in the imagery of the Gospels signifies entry to the heavenly banquet instead of exclusion, a welcome by the Son of man and entry to the heavenly kingdom instead of rejection and consignment to eternal fire (*see* Judgment). This raises the question whether "being saved" refers exclusively to a future state in the next world, or whether it can also refer to those who are already sure of entry to the kingdom.

3.1.5. Saving and Losing One's Life. In Matthew 16:25 and parallels there is an important set of sayings about saving and losing one's life. The difficulty here is partly caused by the ambiguity and uncertainty of the word *life* (Gk *psychē*), which can refer to the "soul" as distinct from the body (and hence signify an individual person), or to "life" or to one's "real life." Jesus appears to be saying that those who try to "save" (i.e., preserve) their lives, either in the sense of avoiding martyrdom or by holding fast to the things that give them pleasure and satisfaction in this world, will in the end "lose" their lives, either by finding that death cannot be kept at bay or that attachment to earthly things leads to loss at the final judgment and hence in the next world. On the other hand, those who are prepared to say "no" to their self, possibly even by dying, for the sake of Jesus (Mark adds "and the gospel"), find that they will "save" their lives in the sense that they will attain to the kingdom of God and enjoy the blessings that are really worth having (cf. the parallel in somewhat different wording in Mt 10:39 par. Lk 17:33).

3.2. Mark. The picture in Mark's Gospel is simpler than in Matthew. The one significant reference not paralleled in Matthew is Mark 3:4, where Jesus comments on the lawfulness of doing good and "saving life" on the sabbath in the broad sense of healing a sick man. The phrase stands in contrast to "killing" and is pointedly directed against what Jesus implies to be the secret intentions of his critics who attack him for healing on the sabbath. Otherwise, Mark lacks the programmatic text found in Matthew 1:21, and only in Mark 10:26 is there an explicitly theological use of the term.

3.3. Luke. The case is different with Luke. He has the same broad pattern of usage as the other two Gospels, but there is a special emphasis on salvation that is not found in them.

3.3.1. The Overture to the Story of Salvation. This is clear above all from the birth stories (*see* Birth of Jesus), which function like an overture, setting out the main themes of the following drama, but doing so with their own distinctive music. One of the most characteristic tones here is that of salvation, with six significant references.

The note is first struck in Luke 1:47, where Mary, as the mother-to-be of the Messiah, aligns herself with the people of God and rejoices in God her savior. The development of her song makes it clear that he is savior both of her and of the people. God's action is depicted in terms of powerful action against the mighty and the proud and on behalf of the poor and humble. These sets of terms connote respectively those who are opposed to God and those who trust him to provide for their needs. Further, God's action is seen as forming part of a long history of merciful concern for the people of his choice.

In the second song, that of Zechariah, the nature of salvation is brought out more clearly. Again, the note of powerful intervention is struck—"a horn of salvation" (Lk 1:69)—and it is associated with the coming of the Messiah (*see* Christ). Again we hear of God's action against the powerful wicked people making it possible for his people to serve him righteously without fear of attack (Lk 1:71). But above all Zechariah speaks of an experience (Gk *gnōsis*, "knowledge") of salvation which is closely associated with the forgiveness of sins (Lk 1:77). What Matthew 1:21 says with the utmost brevity Luke expresses on a broader canvas. It is not surprising after all this that when Jesus is born, the lofty language used to describe him refers not only to his Davidic links, to his messiahship and his position as Lord, but also to his being a savior (Lk 2:11). And the whole drama is summed up in the comment of Simeon that he has seen the salvation which the Lord has prepared—a salvation which is for all peoples (NIV "for all people" [singular] is not sufficiently literal), including the Gentiles (Lk 2:30-32).

3.3.2. Salvation as the Mission of the Son of Man. The notes of this overture are intended to stay in our ears as we continue to listen to Luke's Gospel, and other uses of the "salvation" terminology should resonate with what we have already heard. Luke repeats a good deal of what we have already found in Matthew and Mark. We may note that in recounting material parallel to that in Mark he has added a reference in 8:12 to the way in which the devil snatches away the word from some hearers "so they may not believe and be saved" (Lk 8:12). Here the language of the early church is echoed, and Luke is clearly referring to the experience of spiritual salvation, which comes through hearing the word of God. The same is true in Luke 13:23 where Jesus is asked whether "the saved" are few. This question should be interpreted in the light of Matthew 7:13-14, which speaks of the many people who tread the road to destruction and the few who find the way to life, and of the equating of terms which we saw in Mark 10. This is confirmed by the context, which refers to the coming feast in the kingdom of God.

Luke's theology of salvation is summed up in Luke 19:10 where the Son of man's mission is to seek and to save the lost. The language is that of shepherding and refers to the rescue of sheep from death in various possible ways. The metaphorical usage of such language to refer to God's care of his people was well established and is echoed here. In consequence of the coming of Jesus to him, it can be said that salvation has come to Zacchaeus's house there and then (Lk 19:9). It is thus a present experience involving the *table fellowship between Jesus and Zacchaeus and the commencement of a new way of life in which the latter abandons the sinful habits of the past. Jesus emphasizes that even though Zacchaeus is a sinner, yet he is one of the lost sheep of the house of Israel and therefore a rightful object of his mission.

3.4. John. In the Gospel of John salvation is associated with the mission of the *Son of God and is placed in direct contrast with the possibility of condemnation and perishing. To be saved is thus the opposite of being judged and destroyed. It is the same as to gain eternal life (Jn 3:16-17; cf. Jn 12:47). Salvation is not confined to the Jewish people. It is for the world, and this includes the Samaritans, whom Jewish orthodoxy regarded as excluded from God's favor; it is they who confess that Jesus is the "savior of the world" (Jn 4:42), even if it is true that salvation comes to the world "from the Jews." It follows that testimony to Jesus is what can lead people to experience salvation (Jn 5:34). The shepherding metaphor is also used to express the role of Jesus in this Gospel, but here Jesus functions as the door through which the sheep enter into the safety of the fold and so are free from the dangers outside. (The metaphor is not to be pressed; the sheep can go freely in and out in safety; the implication is that those who "belong" to the sheepfold are assured of the protection of the shepherd wherever they are.)

4. The Understanding of Salvation in the Gospels.

Enough has been said to show that "salvation" is not a dominant word group in the Gospels in the same way as, say, the "kingdom of God" is. This is particularly obvious in Mark. Matthew associates the coming of Jesus with his role as a savior, but does not develop the terminology significantly. Luke makes much of the theme in the birth narratives, and never altogether loses sight of it thereafter, but the terminology can scarcely be said to be prominent. In John the word group occupies a minor but significant role, alongside other word groups that receive much greater attention.

It is obvious that the Evangelists are here reflecting the historical realities of the situation, that this was not a word group used greatly by Jesus, especially in its full theological sense. Nevertheless, it is arguable that the Evangelists have correctly represented the situation in that they recognized that the mission of Jesus was ultimately concerned with salvation. Jesus announced the kingdom of God with its attendant blessings; the language of salvation spells out what this means in terms of the benefits for humankind.

Several themes emerge from the Gospels:

(1) Salvation is closely related to Jesus and his mission. It is a comprehensive term for the

benefits brought by the sovereign action of God through the Messiah.

(2) It is thought of as a future experience, identical with entry into the kingdom of God and gaining eternal life, but it is also a present experience resulting from personal encounter with Jesus.

(3) God brings salvation through Jesus for his people *Israel. The implication is that, although they are God's people, they are not enjoying the fullness of life which he wishes for them. This is due both to the effects of evil in the world at large (e.g., the action of enemies) and the workings of illness and death.

(4) Individuals are not by their sinfulness cut off from the possibility of gaining the salvation intended for God's people. On the contrary, this fact establishes their need. Nor in fact is salvation in principle limited to the Jews. There are hints that it is for all peoples, although within the ministry of Jesus there are only occasional contacts with Samaritans and other non-Jews.

(5) The linking of healing with faith and the wider use of the "your faith has saved you" formula indicate that the reception of salvation was associated with faith, understood in a broad sense as recognition of Jesus as God's sovereign and powerful agent and a commitment to him.

(6) Turning aside from evil is part of the process of salvation. Zacchaeus in fact not only abandons his former dishonest practices but pledges himself to a new way of life which involves giving to the poor.

(7) In presenting Jesus as the savior, the Evangelists are assigning to him a role which Judaism reserved for Yahweh (see God). Although the term could be applied to earthly leaders (the judges), it was used predominantly of Yahweh, and the echoes of OT passages about Yahweh's saving activity indicate that his role is now assigned to Jesus. The term savior was not previously applied to the Messiah in Judaism. At the same time, it is implied that Jesus stands over against other human figures (such as the Roman emperor) who were regarded as saviors.

See also CHRISTOLOGY; KINGDOM OF GOD; LUKE, GOSPEL OF.

DJG: FAITH; FORGIVENESS OF SINS; GENTILE; HEALING; LIFE.

BIBLIOGRAPHY. W. Foerster and G. Fohrer, "σῴζω κτλ," TDNT 7.965-1024; A George, Etudes sur l'oeuvre de Luc (Paris: Gabalda, 1978) 307-20 (= "L'emploi chez Luc du vocabulaire de salut,"

NTS 23 [1977] 308-20); E. M. B. Green, The Meaning of Salvation (London: Hodder & Stoughton, 1965); J. P. Louw and E. A. Nida, Greek-English Lexicon of the New Testament Based on Semantic Domains (New York: United Bible Societies, 1988); I. H. Marshall, Luke: Historian and Theologian (3d ed; Grand Rapids: Zondervan, 1989); J. Schneider and C. Brown, "Redemption etc.," NIDNTT 3.205-21; W. C. van Unnik, "L'usage de sozein 'sauver' et de ses dérivés dans les Evangiles synoptiques," in La formation des Evangiles, ed., J. Coppens (Bruges: Desclée de Brouwer, 1957) 178-94 (= W. C. van Unnik, Sparsa Collecta [Leiden: Brill, 1973] 16-34).

I. H. Marshall

SALVATION II: PAUL

Salvation is a general term, denoting deliverance of varying kinds. It may be used of the healing of disease, of safety in travel and of preservation in times of peril. It may apply to people or to things. In the OT, when Israel was threatened by hostile nations, the term is used of God's protection. In the Gospels it is often used of Jesus' healings ("Your faith has saved [i.e., healed] you"). But the term is also used for deliverance from sin and for the ultimate deliverance when the saved enter bliss with Christ at the end of the age.

In the Pauline writings the important thing is deliverance from *sin and from the consequences of sin, though it is much more common for Paul to speak simply of salvation than to say what people are saved from. He uses the verb sōzō ("to save") twenty-nine times (which is more than anyone else in the NT), the noun sōtēr ("savior") twelve times (exactly half its NT occurrences), sōtēria ("salvation") eighteen times, sōtērion ("salvation") and sōtērios ("bringing salvation") once each. He uses rhyomai ("to rescue") eleven times. Such statistics show that Paul is interested in the concept of salvation, more so, indeed, than any other NT writer.

Salvation has a wide range of meaning and there are different emphases in different parts of the NT. In the Gospels, for example, we often have stories of Jesus doing *miracles accompanied by such words as "your faith has saved you." In such contexts salvation has a strong physical component (though we would be wise not to exclude a spiritual component even in such passages). But this is not a Pauline usage (except in a few possible places, e.g., 1 Tim 2:15:

see 3 below). For Paul "salvation" refers to what Christ has done in his great saving act for sinners; all the Pauline passages bear on this act in some way. It is central to the Pauline understanding of Christianity, for salvation is the very purpose of the incarnation of the Son of God: "Christ Jesus came into the world to save sinners" (1 Tim 1:15). Salvation is a comprehensive word bringing out the truth that *God in *Christ has rescued people from the desperate state that their sins had brought about.

1. "God Our Savior"
2. Human Agents in Salvation
3. Who Will Be Saved?
4. Salvation in the Past
5. Salvation Now
6. A Future Salvation

1. "God Our Savior."

In the Pastoral Letters there are several references to "God our Savior" (1 Tim 1:1; 2:3; Tit 1:3; 2:10; 3:4), or to "Christ our Savior" (2 Tim 1:10; Tit 1:4; 2:13; 3:6). No great deal of difference should be made between these two groups of passages, for the accepted NT teaching that God acted in Christ is summed up in Paul's own words: "God was in Christ reconciling the world to himself" (2 Cor 5:19). From one point of view it is clear enough that salvation originated with the Father, and from another it was the Son who did what was necessary to bring about salvation.

Paul writes that God did not destine the Thessalonians for wrath but for salvation "through our Lord Jesus Christ" (1 Thess 5:9). It is Jesus who "delivers us from the wrath to come" (1 Thess 1:10), or to put it slightly differently, it is "through" Christ that believers shall be saved from the wrath (Rom 5:9). Paul develops this thought by saying that sinners were God's enemies but that they have now been reconciled through the death of the Son and, having been reconciled, "we will be saved in his life" (Rom 5:10). It is unlikely that we should understand the apostle to mean that the death of Jesus effects one form of salvation and his resurrected life another. He is referring to one great act of salvation involving the death and the *resurrection of Jesus, a salvation that delivers the saved from wrath and gives them continuing life. If the preposition "in" is significant, Paul is saying that our full salvation means being saved "in" the life of Christ. As he often speaks of being "in" Christ, this may well be the meaning

here. It is explicit when he writes of people obtaining salvation "in Christ Jesus" (2 Tim 2:10). He can also refer to the importance of the Scriptures which can make us "wise unto salvation through faith in Christ Jesus" (2 Tim 3:15).

That salvation has its origin in God is brought out by speaking of God's "call": God "saved us and called us with a holy calling" (2 Tim 1:9). The idea of call is an important one for Paul, and here it brings out the truth that salvation comes as a result of a prior divine initiative. Or it may be linked with grace to bring out the fact that salvation is for all (Tit 2:11). This means that salvation is available to all, not that every individual is saved.

Paul uses a number of expressions that bring out the thought that salvation comes "through" the Christian message. Thus God was pleased to save believers "through the foolishness of what was preached" (1 Cor 1:21). Later in the same letter Paul makes known "the gospel . . . through which you were saved" (1 Cor 15:1-2). In both cases the preaching clearly means the preaching of what Christ has accomplished in dying for sinners. They are saved by what he has done. Paul can equate "the word of truth" with "the gospel of your salvation" (Eph 1:13), which underlies the reliability of the gospel proclamation. The gospel tells of divine truth. And it tells of divine action. The reference to the person who "will be saved, but so as through fire" (1 Cor 3:15) envisages a believer who has achieved so little in the Christian life that on the day of *judgment his or her work will be "burned up." But, being on the foundation Christ laid, that person will be saved. It is Christ who brings salvation, not human effort. It is the sure foundation, not the uncertain work, that is ultimately important.

Nowhere does Paul speak of a salvation brought about by human effort. He does indeed speak of himself and his coworkers as being "afflicted" for the salvation of the Corinthians (2 Cor 1:6; cf. Col 1:24), but this means no more than that the evangelists had to undergo troubles to bring the message of salvation to people; it certainly does not mean that their troubles merited the salvation of their hearers. This passage also speaks of the apostle as being encouraged, but it was not the encouragement Paul received that brought salvation. Salvation always comes from God. Another passage indicates that the troubles of the early believers were a token of their salvation (Phil 1:28).

Paul uses the language of salvation to bring out aspects of the great truth that when sinners could do nothing to escape the results of their evil deeds, God took action to deliver them. "By grace you have been saved," he writes to the Ephesians (Eph 2:8), an expression that follows "and he has made us alive in Christ when we were dead in our transgressions" (Eph 2:5). The implication is that sins bring death, but that Christ brings life to people who are dead in sin. So we find that it is "not of works of righteousness that we have done, but according to his mercy he saved us" (Tit 3:5).

The initiative in salvation is with God: "God chose us . . . for salvation" (2 Thess 2:13). Indeed almost every passage dealing with salvation could be cited, for characteristically Paul (like the other NT writers) puts before his readers information about a salvation in one sense already brought about by Christ, and in another sense to be consummated in the age to come. In neither is there the slightest suggestion that human effort avails. It is relevant that Paul prays for the salvation of *Israel (Rom 10:1), for if their salvation is a matter for prayer, then clearly it is to be a gift of God. Salvation is brought about by God in Christ. Christians are "the saved" (1 Cor 1:18; 2 Cor 2:15), not "saving ones" or people saved by their own efforts. This is so also when faith is linked with salvation (Rom 10:9; 1 Cor 1:21; Eph 2:8), for faith means trusting in Christ or in God, not relying on one's own efforts.

2. Human Agents in Salvation.

There are some passages where human agency is named in the bringing about of salvation, though this, of course, does not mean that people can save one another. When Paul, for example, speaks of himself saving some of the Israelites (Rom 11:14), he does not mean that his efforts will effect salvation but only that he brings a message that he hopes will cause some of his own nation to turn to God and thus enter the salvation God alone can give. A similar comment should be made about a woman saving her husband and a man saving his wife (1 Cor 7:16). Paul is not claiming that people can effect the salvation of family members, but rather that a Christian wife or husband can so live as to cause the partner to turn to God and receive salvation from him. Paul sees the principle as of universal

application among Christians. He concludes a passage on eating food offered to idols by telling his correspondents that whatever they eat or drink, indeed whatever they do, they should do all things for God's glory. He claims that he himself pleases everyone in all he does; he does not look for personal profit, but for that of the many "in order that they may be saved" (1 Cor 10:31-33).

Timothy is urged to remain in "the teaching." By doing this he will save himself "and those who hear you" (1 Tim 4:16). The reference to "the teaching" shows that the writer is not referring to some meritorious activity, but to the teaching that Christ is Savior. And those who hear this will be with Timothy in salvation. Again there is the thought of human effort leading to the salvation of other people. But it is God in Christ who saves.

3. Who Will Be Saved?

The fact that salvation is a divine deliverance does not mean that everybody will be saved. Paul quotes from Isaiah the words, "If the number of the children of Israel be as the sand of the sea, it is the remnant that will be saved" (Rom 9:27). The article is important; Paul does not say "a" remnant but "the" remnant. He is referring to the biblical remnant, the remnant that God has spoken of through his prophets. This remnant is the real people of God, and salvation comes to them, not to the multitudes of the nation, careless as these multitudes are about the things of God.

We should notice that while Paul looks to God to bring salvation to *Israel, this does not mean that he sees himself as excused from doing anything to help his nation. Indeed, he regards his ministry to the Gentiles at any rate as in one respect a means of commending the gospel to the Jews. He refers to his position as "the apostle of the Gentiles" and trusts that his labors in that capacity "will provoke my own flesh and I will save some of them" (Rom 11:13-14). "My own flesh" is unusual in the sense of "member of the same nation," but it emphasizes Paul's sense of kinship with the nation Israel. And he is expressing the hope that the success of his labors among the Gentiles will have its effect on the Jews so that "some of them," too, will be saved.

He regards it as a principal count against the Jews that they forbade the Christian preachers "to speak to the Gentiles so that they might be saved" (1 Thess 2:16). In another context he speaks of becoming "all things to all people so that by all means I may save some" (1 Cor 9:22). It is clear that for the apostle the bringing of salvation to people everywhere was of the first importance and that, though his own ministry was largely to the Gentiles, this did not mean that he had ceased to care about Israel. His agonizing over his nation in Romans 9—11 should never be forgotten.

We should probably understand the statement that God wills "all people to be saved" (1 Tim 2:4) in this connection. It is the negation of all exclusivism, be it that of the Jews or of the later *Gnostics (who confined salvation to those who had special enlightenment). "All" is to be understood in the same way as it is in the following sentence, which speaks of Christ as giving himself "as a ransom for all" (1 Tim 2:6). We should certainly not take it in the sense that God sets his will on the salvation of the whole human race and is disappointed. Another passage of the same sort is that in which God is referred to as "the Savior of all people, especially believers" (1 Tim 4:10). We should perhaps understand "Savior" here as "Preserver" (for God does "save" us all in some sense), but the emphasis on believers shows that the salvation that matters comes only to people of faith. We should remember that the Philippians were exhorted, "With fear and trembling work out your salvation" (Phil 2:12). The plural may mean that the whole church is being exhorted to work hard at its spiritual well-being. If it is applied to the individual the meaning must be much the same. Paul never sees salvation as the result of the individual's own efforts, and it would be perverse to find such a meaning here (see Hawthorne, 98-100).

In a very difficult passage we are told that "the woman was deceived" (a reference to Eve), but that "she will be saved through the childbearing . . . if they abide in faith" (1 Tim 2:14-15). The plural shows that Paul is speaking of Christian women generally, not confining his remarks to Eve, but it is not easy to see how childbearing brings salvation ("this would be a very odd form of salvation by works," Ward, 53). Some interpreters have held that we should emphasize "the" childbearing (i.e., the bearing of *the* child) and see a reference to Christ, others that Christian *women are assured of safe delivery. Paul later speaks of people who forbade marriage (1 Tim 4:3), and it may well be that he is opposing false teaching and saying that women will be saved (provided, of course, that they "abide in faith and love and sanctification," 1 Tim 2:15) in the normal course of life, giving birth to children in marriage.

4. Salvation in the Past.

There is a sense in which salvation has already taken place. Paul can say, "In hope we were saved" (Rom 8:24), where the past tense looks back to the beginning of the Christian life.

"By grace you have been saved through faith and this not of yourselves; it is the gift of God, not of works lest anyone should boast. For we are his workmanship, created in Christ Jesus" (Eph 2:8-10). This is the typical position in Paul's writings. Salvation is something brought about by God (or Christ) and there is nothing human endeavor can do to produce this result. Paul piles expression on expression to emphasize the truth that salvation has been achieved by God only; it is never the result of human initiative or human achievement. We see this also in the reference to Christ as "the head of the church" and as "the Savior of the body" (Eph 5:23).

There is both a backward and a forward look when Paul writes, "For we were saved in hope, but hope seen is not hope" (Rom 8:24). This intriguing passage recognizes that there is a sense in which salvation is in the past: "we were saved." Paul looks back to the death of Christ for sinners and to the faith repentant sinners exercised when they came to Christ. But he also speaks of hope, and that points to the future when believers will experience to the full all that salvation means.

Salvation is past when the apostle says that God, "when we were dead in trespasses, gave us life in Christ—by grace you have been saved" (Eph 2:5). A little later he repeats the essential thought, "By grace you have been saved through faith" (Eph 2:8), where again the perfect tense points to a salvation already accomplished. The aorist of an event in the past is found when we read, "Not from works of righteousness that we have done, but according to his mercy he saved us" (Tit 3:5). Again, Christ "delivered us from the power of darkness" (Col 1:13). Paul leaves his readers in no doubt as to the reality of salvation as an accomplished fact. It happened in the past.

5. Salvation Now.

But in another sense Paul emphasizes that salvation is here and now. The gospel is "the power of God for salvation" and God's *righteousness is being revealed in it (Rom 1:16-17). The tenor of the apostle's writings and the manner of his living show that this is a reference to a present happening. Again, he quotes Isaiah 49:8, referring to God's help in a day of salvation, and proceeds, "Look, now is the acceptable time; look, now is the day of salvation" (2 Cor 6:2). The doubled "now" conveys a sense of urgency; salvation is not to be deferred to some convenient time in the future. Salvation is now. The gospel must be accepted now.

A present salvation is meant when Paul speaks of the gospel as "the power of God to us who are being saved" (1 Cor 1:18), and when he refers to "those being saved" (2 Cor 2:15). "With the mouth one confesses for salvation" (Rom 10:10) is another indication of a present salvation, not only one that is looked for in the future. This is probably the case also with the "godly grief" that "works repentance" leading to salvation (2 Cor 7:10). Salvation is in the present when Paul asks rhetorically, "Who will deliver me from this body of death?" and answers, "Thanks be to God through Jesus Christ our *Lord" (Rom 7:24-25). Paul is referring to this mortal body and to the constant temptations to sin that such a body provides. And he exults in the deliverance Christ brings. In the battle of life, salvation may be said to be the "helmet" (Eph 6:17), or the helmet may be "the hope of salvation" (1 Thess 5:8). Either way, salvation is now a critical part of the Christian's armor.

The apostle's attitude to the salvation of Israel also reveals a longing for something to happen now. He speaks of his affectionate goodwill toward his nation and adds that his prayer is for their salvation (Rom 10:1). While, of course, there is an eschatological dimension to the salvation for which he prays, the emphasis in this passage is present: he wants Israel to be saved now! That salvation is present is seen in another reference to Israel, namely that it is due to Israel's transgression that salvation has come to the Gentiles (Rom 11:11).

6. A Future Salvation.

Paul is certain that salvation is a present reality and that it is a life-changing experience. But he is equally certain that the best we know of it now does not exhaust the subject. He looks for a future salvation when "all Israel will be saved" (Rom 11:26), or again when he urges, somewhat mysteriously, that a certain sinner be "delivered to Satan for the destruction of the flesh so that the spirit may be saved in the day of the Lord" (1 Cor 5:5; *see* Eschatology). There is much that is obscure to us in this passage, but salvation "in the day of the Lord" certainly looks for the ultimate salvation. This is very clear also in the apostle's reference to our citizenship as being in heaven, "from where we await a Savior, the Lord Jesus Christ" (Phil 3:20). The idea that salvation is nearer than when we first believed (Rom 13:11) also points to a future happening. The statements that "all Israel will be saved" and that "the Deliverer will come out of Zion" (Rom 11:26) may be understood of the present or of the future. Whichever way we take them, there can be no doubt that Christ is the deliverer and that he is seen as having full heavenly authority.

Paul does not see this future salvation as coming to all, and we must remember that there are passages in which, for example, he sets those who are saved over against "those who are perishing" (1 Cor 1:18; 2 Cor 2:15; 2 Thess 2:10). "The wrath" (Rom 5:9) from which Paul is saved points forward to the ultimate disaster. Judgment day will test realities. The work of some will survive the fire, whereas that of others will be burned up; of such a one Paul says, "That person will be saved, but so as through fire" (1 Cor 3:15). Paul is here referring to believers and pointing to the difference between those who have built well and those who have built badly. But anyone who has built on the foundation Christ laid will be saved. Clearly this is the future salvation.

In his treatment of "the man of lawlessness" at the end of the age, Paul says that the Lord Jesus will destroy that wicked one. He also says that this evil being will operate "with every deceit of unrighteousness in them that are perishing, because they did not receive the love of the truth so that they might be saved" (2 Thess 2:10). This is an unusual way of putting it but is a reminder that "the love of the truth" is important. Right up to the last days people will perish because they did not love the truth.

Paul looks forward to the day when the Lord "will save me into his heavenly kingdom" (2 Tim 4:18). That also is the implication of the remark that the justified "will be saved through him from the wrath" (Rom 5:9). There is a future dimension in salvation, which is important, for Paul is clear that ultimately sinners will face the wrath of God. But there is ultimate deliverance for those who have put their trust in God. Paul quotes the prophet Joel for the assurance that "Everyone who calls on the name of the Lord will be saved" (Rom 10:13). "Calls" does not mean calls in a superficial manner, as of one who simply wishes to avoid the personal consequences of sin. "Calls" here means a genuine calling on the Lord which proceeds from the conviction that God can and will save and that the caller is in desperate need.

From all this we see that *salvation* is the comprehensive term that includes a multiplicity of aspects. Sometimes more than one of these aspects occur together, as when the apostle says that Christ *has delivered* us "from so great a death" and who *will deliver*, and adds that this is the one "on whom we have set our hope that he *will still deliver*" (2 Cor 1:10). For Paul it was important that sinners be delivered from the condemnation their sin deserved, and he gives a good deal of attention to *justification, the process of acquittal when believers stand at the bar of God's justice. But he also thinks of the present power of the *Holy Spirit in the lives of believers; salvation includes an ongoing triumph over the forces of evil. And Paul looks forward to the end of this age and sees salvation as having its effect throughout eternity. We should not think of salvation as simply negative, as "deliverance from . . ." It is that, but it is more. It involves wholeness, wellness, health, goodness. Thus Paul says that Christ "delivered us from the power of darkness," but immediately adds, "and transferred us into the kingdom of his beloved Son" (Col 1:13).

See also CREATION, NEW CREATION; DEATH OF CHRIST; ESCHATOLOGY; ISRAEL; JUSTIFICATION.

DPL: GENTILES; GRACE; HOPE; PEACE; RECONCILIATION; RESTORATION OF ISRAEL; SAVIOR; TRIUMPH; UNIVERSALISM; WRATH, DESTRUCTION.

BIBLIOGRAPHY. W. Foerster and G. Fohrer, "σῷζω κτλ," *TDNT* 7:965-1024; E. M. B. Green, *The Meaning of Salvation* (London: Hodder & Stoughton, 1965); R. Haughton, *The Drama of Salvation* (London: SPCK, 1976); G. F. Hawthorne, *Philippians* (WBC 43; Waco: Word, 1983); D. Hill, *Greek Words and Hebrew Meanings: Studies in the Semantics of Soteriological Terms* (SNTSMS 5; Cambridge: Cambridge University Press, 1967);

W. L. Liefeld, "Salvation," *ISBE* 4:287-95; H. R. Mackintosh, *The Christian Experience of Forgiveness* (London: Nisbet, 1927); L. Newbigin, *Sin and Salvation* (London: SCM, 1956); C. A. A. Scott, *Christianity According to St. Paul* (Cambridge: Cambridge University Press, 1927); R. A. Ward, *Commentary on 1 & 2 Timothy & Titus* (Waco: Word, 1973).   L. Morris

SALVATION III: ACTS, HEBREWS, GENERAL EPISTLES, REVELATION

With the noun *salvation (sōtēria)* is directly associated the verb *save (sōzō)* and rather more obliquely the noun *savior (sōtēr)*. In both the Septuagint and secular Greek the first two are connected with the notion of physical deliverance (e.g., from peril, illness or death). "Savior," however, issues from the vocabulary of the ruler cult of the Greco-Roman kingdoms of the NT era. According to the Priene inscription from Asia Minor, "Providence . . . has sent to us . . . a savior . . . who has put an end to war . . . Caesar [Augustus]" (Spicq, 3:353). Throughout the NT this word group lends itself metaphorically to the notion of eschatological salvation. The title *sōtēr* is applied to both *God and the *Son he sent into the world for its salvation.

1. Acts of the Apostles
2. Hebrews, the General Epistles and Revelation

1. Acts of the Apostles.

The underlying idea of physical deliverance from both illness and death may be seen at several points (Acts 4:9; 14:9; 7:25).

The more prominent idea, however, is metaphorical as applied to eschatological salvation. This appears early in the narrative, on the day of Pentecost, when, in light of the Holy Spirit's coming, Peter quotes Joel 2:32 (LXX): "Whoever calls on the name of the *Lord will be saved." The Spirit's arrival is evidence that the Lord, uncorrupted by death, is risen and ascended and that the gate to salvation, as heralded by the prophets, is now open. Hence, "save yourselves," Peter exhorted his hearers; day by day the Lord added "those who were being saved" (Acts 2:40, 47). Peter makes clear that only in Jesus Christ of Nazareth, crucified but risen, is salvation to be found (Acts 4:12). He is the Savior whom God has exalted to his right hand (Acts 5:31). Against those who asserted that circumcision was a prerequisite to salvation Peter declared that both Gentiles and Jews will be saved "through the grace of the Lord Jesus Christ" (Acts 15:1, 11). The apostolic word is the announcement but also, as apprehended by the hearers, the means of salvation (Acts 11:14).

In the second part of Acts, Paul, speaking as a Jew to a synagogue audience, stated that "to us has been sent the message of this salvation." This is the good news about a descendant of King David, Jesus, whom God has brought to *Israel as a "savior," whom, uncorrupted by the grave, God has raised up alive (Acts 13:26, 23, 30-41). But this message, rejected by those Jews, was also for the Gentiles. Indeed, God had appointed Paul to be a "light for the Gentiles," to bring God's salvation to them (Acts 13:47). Paul's emphasis in his preaching on salvation may be seen in the Philippian soothsayer's parroting of the message, "These men . . . proclaim to you the way of salvation" (Acts 16:17). This is borne out by the jailer's question "What must I do to be saved?" to which Paul replied, "Believe on the Lord Jesus Christ and you will be saved" (Acts 16:30, 31).

In short, we learn from the ministries of the apostles Peter and Paul in Acts that salvation is in fulfillment of OT prophecy, has become a present but exclusive reality in the death for sins and the resurrection from the dead of Jesus of Nazareth, the descendant of David, and is apprehended by receiving the apostolic message.

2. Hebrews, the General Epistles and Revelation.

The language of salvation appears often in this literature, though with different nuances.

2.1. Hebrews. In the letter to the Hebrews we find several references to physical salvation from death (Heb 5:7) and from the deluge (Heb 11:7). According to Hebrews, eschatological salvation belongs to the future (Heb 1:14), at the appearing of the *Son of God (Heb 9:28). In Hebrews, faith is the active expectation of the salvation, a hope that unceasingly and against all odds presses forward toward it (Heb 11:1-40 passim). Such faith is exercised in obedience to the good news, promising salvation (Heb 2:3; 4:1-6). This salvation is in the presence of the God who is holy, whither the incarnate Son of God has already arrived in virtue of his faith and obedience. Thus he is the "file leader" (*archēgos*) of his people, the exemplar of perseverance and obedience, to be followed after in

the path to God's salvation (Heb 12:2). Nonetheless, access to this salvation is not by self-effort but "through" the One who is high priest forever, after the order of Melchizedek (Heb 7:25). He is the "source" of eternal salvation to all who obey him (Heb 5:9), having offered for all time a single sacrifice for sins (Heb 10:12).

2.2. James. In the letter of James only the verb *save* is employed. It is the soul that is saved, and it is saved from death and from being "destroyed" (Jas 1:21; 4:12; 5:20). Thus salvation is eschatological. According to James, it is the Lawgiver and Judge, that is, God, who both "saves and destroys" (Jas 4:12). Nonetheless, the Lord, that is, the Lord Jesus Christ who is to come (Jas 5:7), will "raise . . . up" those who offer the prayer of faith, a deliberate double meaning, pointing to both physical healing and final *resurrection (Jas 5:15). How is one saved, according to James? It is by a lively faith that is authenticated by works; an empty or hypocritical faith will not save (Jas 2:14).

2.3. 1 Peter, 2 Peter and Jude. The language of salvation is important in 1 Peter. Such salvation is a present reality in Jesus Christ, who was predestined before the foundation of the world but who has been made manifest at the end of times (1 Pet 1:20), who "bore our sins on the tree" and who was raised from the dead as "a living hope [of salvation]" for those who believe in him (1 Pet 2:24; 1:3). This salvation, which will be "unveiled in the last time" (1 Pet 1:5), is entered into now through the preaching of the good news (1 Pet 1:12, 23). *Baptism, a response to the gospel, "saves," though not by its water but by the inner reality of a cleansed conscience in relationship with the God who is holy, through the resurrection of Jesus from the dead (1 Pet 3:21). As not yet revealed, this salvation is the goal or end point of faith (1 Pet 1:9), a salvation for which the "newborn" is nourished by the "pure spiritual milk" of the gospel (1 Pet 2:2).

There is an alternative to this eschatological salvation. It is the judgment of the living and the dead by God, who is holy (1 Pet 4:5; 1:15), upon "the passions . . . of ignorance" (1 Pet 1:14; 4:2). Quoting Proverbs 11:31 (LXX), Peter asks, "If the righteous man is scarcely saved, where will the impious and sinner appear?" (1 Pet 4:18).

Only once in 2 Peter does this language appear: "And count the forbearance of the Lord as salvation" (2 Pet 3:15). Here Peter is alluding to the salvation of which his "beloved brother Paul" wrote (in Rom 2:4?), "as he does in all his letters." Peter recognized the importance of salvation in the writings of the apostle Paul. In a context relating to the sudden, unheralded coming of the Day of the Lord and its *judgment, Peter is teaching that God's withholding of salvation is an expression of divine forbearance, providing space and opportunity for people to find salvation.

Second Peter, like the Pastorals, is marked by a number of references to "savior." Unlike the Pastorals, however, in which both God and the Lord Jesus Christ are called the, or our, Savior, 2 Peter confines this title to Jesus Christ. This usage may have been a polemical rebuttal of the contemporary application of this title to the Roman emperors; Jesus Christ is the true Savior. This possibility is strengthened by Peter's bracketing with "Savior" other imperial titles, "God" and "Lord" (2 Pet 1:1, 11; 2:20; 3:2, 18). Against pretentious and often evil rulers Jesus is God, Lord and Savior through whom we "escape the corruption that is in the world because of passion and become partakers of the divine nature" (2 Pet 1:4). This is salvation, which "is granted to us by way of God's precious and very great promises" (2 Pet 1:4).

Jude, unlike 2 Peter, applies the title *Savior* to "the only God our Savior" (Jude 25). Thus "our common salvation" is to be attributed to God, who saved a people out of Egypt. The alternative to this salvation is a "punishment of eternal fire" in the "judgment of the great day" (Jude 5, 6, 7). Thus Jude warns, "Save some by snatching them out of the fire" (Jude 23).

2.4. Johannine Literature. The letters of John (*see* John, Letters of) have only one example from the word group: "the Father has sent the Son as the savior of the world" (1 Jn 4:14; cf. Jn 4:42). In a parallel passage John's meaning becomes clear: "God . . . sent his Son to be the expiation *(hilasmos)* of our sins" (1 Jn 4:10; cf. 1 Jn 2:2). The Son of God, Jesus Christ the righteous, is the Savior because by his death he has propitiated the wrath of God toward sins or has covered sins (cf. Rom 3:25). Access to this salvation is by means of the apostolic proclamation of the message of the incarnation and death of the Son of God (1 Jn 1:2-3; 2:1-2).

In the Revelation, salvation belongs to *God, who "sits on the throne" of history and whose "judgments are just and true" (Rev 7:10; 19:1).

Sharing that throne with God is the Lamb (Rev 7:10; 19:1), an indication of the divine sovereignty of the Lamb (cf. Rev 4:11; 5:1-5, 7, 13). Although Revelation is interested in the unfolding of history leading to God's final, apocalyptic conclusion (Rev 16—22), that history and its consummation are in light of the salvation that is a present reality. The present and the future, which are awesome in their evil, unfold out of the already completed salvation of God in the death and resurrection of the Lamb (Rev 5:7-13). "Now the salvation . . . of our God and the authority of his Christ have come" (Rev 12:10). Thus, despite appearances to the contrary, "the kingdom of the world has become the kingdom of our Lord and of his Christ" (Rev 11:15; cf. Rev 1:6; 2:8). Those who "follow the Lamb" in his faithful witness and in purity of life (Rev 14:3-5) already have this salvation, already have begun to reign with Christ, as a kingdom and priests to God (Rev 1:6; 20:4, 6) and will not be subject to the "second death" (Rev 2:11; 21:7).

In the General Epistles and the Revelation, for the most part salvation is eschatological in its realization, is a present reality in Jesus Christ, fulfills the expectations of the OT and is made available by the word of God. The letter of James is silent as to its present reality and the OT expectations.

See also BAPTISM; CHRISTOLOGY; DEATH OF CHRIST; ESCHATOLOGY; RIGHTEOUSNESS.

DLNTD: ASSURANCE; FORGIVENESS; GRACE; NEW BIRTH; REDEMPTION; REPENTANCE, SECOND REPENTANCE; SAVIOR.

BIBLIOGRAPHY. W. Foerster and G. Fohrer, "σῴζω κτλ," *TDNT* 7.965-1003; E. M. B. Green, *The Meaning of Salvation* (London: Hodder & Stoughton, 1965); J. N. D. Kelly, *Early Christian Doctrines* (London: Black, 1980); A. McGrath, *Christian Theology: An Introduction* (Oxford: Blackwell, 1994); I. H. Marshall, *Luke: Historian and Theologian* (Exeter: Paternoster, 1970); D. G. Peterson, *Hebrews and Perfection* (SNTSMS 47; Cambridge: Cambridge University Press, 1982); W. Radl, "σῴζω," *EDNT* 3.319-21; K. H. Schelkle, "σωτηρία," *EDNT* 3.327-29; C. Spicq, *Theological Lexicon of the New Testament* (3 vols.; Peabody, MA: Hendrickson, 1994) 3.344-57; B. H. Throckmorton, "Σῴζειν σωτηρία in Luke-Acts," *SE* 6 (1973) 515-26.   P. W. Barnett

SANHEDRIN. *See* JUDAISM AND THE NEW TESTAMENT; TRIAL OF JESUS.

SAVIOR. *See* SALVATION.

SERMON ON THE MOUNT. *See* ETHICS I; LAW I; MATTHEW, GOSPEL OF.

SERVANT OF YAHWEH: GOSPELS

Four passages in Isaiah 40—55 are conventionally designated as the "Servant Songs" on the understanding that they together present a distinctive vision of a particular "Servant of Yahweh" or "Suffering Servant" to whom is entrusted a special mission on behalf of his people. This figure was one of those used by NT writers to illuminate the mission of Jesus.

    1. The Servant of Yahweh in the Book of Isaiah

    2. Jesus as the Servant in the Gospels

1. The Servant of Yahweh in the Book of Isaiah.
B. Duhm in 1892 isolated Isaiah 42:1-4; 49:1-6; 50:4-9 and 52:13—53:12 as the "Servant Songs." Others have wished to extend their limits or even add part of Isaiah 61 as a fifth Song. Many earlier scholars assumed that these passages had an origin independent of their present context in the book of Isaiah, but more recent scholarship has generally agreed that they belong integrally to the text of Isaiah 40—55 and must not be interpreted independently of that context. The idea of *Israel as God's Servant is not confined to these passages, but in them, and especially in Isaiah 53, there is a new and striking concept of a Servant whose role of vicarious suffering brings healing and deliverance to the people.

It is explicitly Israel who is here described as God's Servant (Is 49:3), as in much of the surrounding context (Is 41:8-9; 43:10; 44:1-2, etc). But in some parts of the Songs, notably in Isaiah 53:4-6, 10-12, the Servant is portrayed as an individual over against Israel and as suffering on its behalf.

This ambiguity as to the identity of the Servant, and whether he is intended to be understood as a corporate or an individual figure (or indeed whether there is a unified "Servant figure" in Isaiah at all), has led to intense debate among interpreters, ancient and modern.

Any statement about Jewish interpretation around the first century A.D. must be tentative, as the documentary evidence for Jewish thought at that period is minimal, and need not be typical of common belief. But while Jewish writers could apply phrases from these passages to various historical figures as well as to Israel corporately, there is also evidence that by NT times they were understood by some to refer to a future individual who would act as God's agent for his people's restoration—in other words, a messianic figure. (Jeremias, *TDNT* 5:682-700, presents sufficient evidence for this, though his survey has rightly been criticized as one-sided.)

This is particularly clear in the Targum on Isaiah 53, which explicitly identifies the Servant as "the Messiah" even though its author is so hostile to the idea of messianic suffering that each reference to suffering is carefully reinterpreted or transferred to the people or to some other subject. The messianic identification is apparently too firmly entrenched to allow the targumist the easy option of an alternative identification as Israel or as some historical figure. NT references especially to Isaiah 53 presuppose such a messianic interpretation.

2. Jesus as the Servant in the Gospels.
Christian devotion has always found in Isaiah 53 an unrivalled portrayal of the vicarious and redemptive suffering of Jesus, which offers perhaps a clearer presentation of the classic Christian doctrine of the atonement than any single passage in the NT.

A number of scholars have questioned, however, whether the figure of the Servant of Yahweh did in fact play any significant role in the development of Christian understanding of the mission of Jesus in the NT period. This has been argued by C. K. Barrett and C. F. D. Moule, and most fully by M. D. Hooker. Hooker has shown that some alleged references to the Servant passages are at least questionable and has rightly emphasized that even where such reference is undeniable, the focus is not so one-sidedly on the Servant's role of vicarious redemption as later Christian usage might expect. But she has not convinced most scholars that the Servant figure was not an important factor in the earliest *christology. In particular, no equally plausible source has yet been suggested for Jesus' conviction that it was his mission to suffer and die because this was "written" (*see* Death of Christ).

The direct use of the title "Servant" *(pais)* [of *God] for Jesus does not occur in the NT outside the early chapters of Acts (Acts 3:13, 26; 4:27, 30). But the Servant passages of Isaiah are quoted several times, and their language and ideas underlie some of the most central statements about Jesus' mission.

2.1. The Synoptic Tradition in General. Each of the Synoptic Gospels identifies Jesus at his *baptism by means of a direct pronouncement by God, subsequently repeated at the Transfiguration, "You are [this is] my beloved Son, with whom I am pleased" (Mk 1:11; 9:7). While the term *servant* is not used, almost all commentators agree that the words are a deliberate echo of the introduction to the first Servant Song (Is 42:1). Jesus' mission is thus marked out at the outset, and in the most authoritative way possible, as that of the Servant.

More specific allusions to Isaiah 53 occur in two key sayings about the redemptive significance of Jesus' coming death. Mark 10:43-44 defines greatness for Jesus' disciples in terms of accepting the role of a servant, and Mark 10:45 goes on to reinforce this demand by Jesus' own example: "The Son of man came not to be served but to serve, and to give his life as a ransom for many." Here it is not only the language of *service* which recalls the Isaiah passages but more specifically the idea of vicarious death, of ransom and the phrase "for many," which echoes the language of Isaiah 53:11-12. And at the *Last Supper Jesus' words over the cup use similar terminology about his blood being poured out "for many" (Mk 14:24). (For a detailed analysis of the verbal and conceptual links between these passages and the Servant Songs, see France 116-23.)

Other verbal allusions have been claimed with much less plausibility, but more important than any verbal echo is the frequently repeated concept of the mission of the *Son of man as one which fulfills the will of God by means of his rejection, suffering and death because these things are "written" about him (Mk 8:31; 9:12, 31; 10:32-34; 14:21, etc.). While some have argued that Daniel 7 supplies an adequate background for this concept (in the oppression of the saints which precedes their vindication, symbolized in the figure of "one like a son of man"), Jewish understanding of the human figure of Daniel 7:13-14 was in fact consistently of a majestic, victorious figure. That this "Son of man" should suffer and be killed was a striking paradox, and no more probable source for this innovative theology can be suggested than the suffering of the Isaianic Servant. A suffering

Messiah might have been derived from some of the psalms of the righteous sufferer or from the pierced and rejected shepherd of Zechariah 11—13, but no passage in the OT offers so clear a prediction of messianic suffering as Isaiah 53, and we have seen above that this passage is clearly echoed in some key pronouncements of Jesus on his mission.

It is on such grounds that many believe that Isaiah's Servant figure was a major factor in Jesus' understanding of his own mission and the crucial basis on which his followers found it possible to make sense of his death as the fulfillment of Scripture. The main Markan texts for this belief have already been cited, but each of the other Evangelists in his own way develops the theme of Jesus as the Servant of Yahweh.

2.2. Matthew. Two of Matthew's eleven formula quotations are drawn from Isaiah's Servant Songs. In Matthew 8:17 Jesus' healing ministry is seen as fulfilling Isaiah 53:4, "He took our weaknesses and carried our diseases," while in Matthew 12:15-21 Jesus' withdrawal from public attention is understood in the light of the first Servant Song, Isaiah 42:1-4, which is quoted in full. There is no doubt then that it is important for Matthew that Jesus fulfills the role of the Isaianic Servant of Yahweh. Yet it is remarkable that neither of these passages refers to the distinctive role of redemptive suffering, either in the specific words cited or in the aspect of Jesus' ministry to which they are applied. Jesus' earthly ministry of healing and deliverance, and his non-confrontational demeanor, are no less a fulfillment of the Servant's mission than his vicarious death.

Another possible allusion to Isaiah 53 has been seen in Matthew 3:15, where the divine designation of Jesus in terms drawn from Isaiah 42:1 is preceded by the justification of his baptism as "fulfilling all righteousness." This notoriously obscure pronouncement may be understood not only as referring to the Servant's representative role, thus leading Jesus to identify himself with repentant sinners, but also as a rather cryptic allusion to Isaiah 53:11, "The righteous one shall make many to be accounted righteous." The same idea of identification may also lie behind Matthew's mention that Joseph of Arimathea was a "rich" man (Mt 27:57), thus recalling Isaiah 53:9, "They made his grave . . . with a rich man in his death."

2.3. Luke. In the canticles of Luke 1 the designation "Servant of God" is applied not to Jesus but to Israel (Lk 1:54) and to David (Lk 1:69). And while Matthew has almost exact parallels to Mark 10:45 and 14:24, the Lukan equivalents do not share the same clear allusions to the language of Isaiah 53 (though the language of "service" is still emphasized in Lk 22:26-27). This might suggest that Luke is less interested than Mark and Matthew in the Isaianic Servant as a model for Jesus' ministry. But we should not forget that it is the same Luke who subsequently records the actual title "Servant of God" used for Jesus (Acts 3:13, 26; note, however, that David is also described as God's *pais* in 4:25). (Cf. the verbal parallels between Acts 3 and Is 52:13—53:12 [LXX]: Acts 3:13/Is 52:13; Acts 3:13/Is 53:6, 12; Acts 3:14/Is 53:11.) And it is Luke also who presents the only formal citation from Isaiah 53 in the Synoptic Gospels: the clause "And he was numbered among the lawless" (from Is 53:12) is introduced by the formula, "This which is written must be fulfilled in me," and followed by the further affirmation, "For what is [written] about me has its fulfillment" (Lk 22:37). There is no doubt, then, that for Luke the mission of the Servant in Isaiah 53 is a blueprint for that of Jesus; the Servant is Jesus.

The OT passage which in Luke's Gospel most prominently defines Jesus' ministry is Isaiah 61:1-2, the text of Jesus' Nazareth sermon in Luke 4:16-27. This Scripture, Jesus declares, is now being fulfilled in his ministry (Lk 4:21). Isaiah 61 is not, of course, one of Duhm's Servant Songs. But it shares with Isaiah 42:1-4 several important themes concerning the ministry of the one anointed by God for the work of delivering his people, and many commentators have understood the passages as related in their essential content, even if not in a formal literary sense. It is not unlikely that Luke, in recording Jesus' sermon on Isaiah 61, was thinking of his mission as the Servant of Yahweh.

2.4. John. John also has a formal citation from Isaiah 53. In John 12:38 the unbelief of the Jews is explained by the text, "Who has believed our report? And to whom has the arm of the *Lord been revealed?" (Is 53:1). Inasmuch as this unbelief in Isaiah is a mark of the paradoxical nature of the Servant's appearance and experience, and Jesus' ministry was similarly open to misunderstanding and rejection, a parallel is here drawn between Jesus and the Servant, which in the light of other Christian references

to the Servant seems entirely appropriate. But it must be admitted that the focus at this point in John is not on the redemptive mission of the Servant or of Jesus, but rather on the mere fact of Jewish unbelief.

Another possible allusion to Isaiah 53 may be found in John the Baptist's description of Jesus as "the lamb of God who takes away the sin of the world" (Jn 1:29, 36). The Servant is compared in Isaiah 53:7 to a lamb led to the slaughter, and the whole tenor of the chapter is on the taking away of the sins of the people through his suffering and death. The phrase "the lamb of God" can be related to several different lambs in OT and later Jewish thought, but most of these (e.g., the Passover lamb, the lamb of the daily offering or the messianic lamb of later apocalyptic) do not directly support the idea of taking away sin, so that it is reasonable to see the Servant figure as making a major contribution to this image.

2.5. Conclusion. The above evidence suggests that while the figure of the Servant of Yahweh was not necessarily the most prominent in the christological thinking of all the Evangelists, they all accepted it as an appropriate and illuminating model for Jesus' mission of vicarious suffering and death for the sins of his people, and also (at least for Matthew) in his wider ministry of healing and deliverance. It was Jesus' own consciousness that he had come to fulfill the role of the Servant which gave scriptural backing to his revolutionary new conception of the Messiah's role as one of rejection, suffering and death rather than of earthly victory and glory. And it was this model that eventually enabled his disciples to come to terms with his death as not defeat but achievement, the basis of the *salvation of the people of God.

See also CHRIST; DEATH OF CHRIST.

DJG: OLD TESTAMENT IN THE GOSPELS; PASSION NARRATIVE; RANSOM SAYING.

BIBLIOGRAPHY. C. K. Barrett, "The Background of Mark 10:45," in *New Testament Essays,* ed. A. J. B. Higgins (Manchester: Manchester University Press, 1959) 1-18; O. Cullmann, *The Christology of the New Testament* (rev. ed.; Philadelphia: Westminster, 1963) 51-82; R. T. France, *Jesus and the Old Testament* (London: Tyndale, 1971) 110-35; B. Gerhardsson, "Sacrificial Service and Atonement in the Gospel of Matthew," in *Reconciliation and Hope,* ed. R. Banks (Grand Rapids: Eerdmans, 1974) 25-35; J. B. Green,

"The Death of Jesus, God's Servant," in *Reimaging the Death of the Lukan Jesus*, ed. D. D. Sylva (BBB 73; Frankfurt am Main: Anton Hain, 1990) 1-28, 170-73; M. D. Hooker, *Jesus and the Servant* (London: SPCK, 1959); J. Jeremias, *New Testament Theology, Vol. 1: The Proclamation of Jesus* (New York: Scribner's, 1971) 286-99; D. Juel, *Messianic Exegesis: Christological Interpretation of the Old Testament in Early Christianity* (Philadelphia: Fortress, 1988); O. Michel, I. H. Marshall, "παῖς θεοῦ κτλ," *NIDNTT* 3.607-13; C. F. D. Moule, *The Phenomenon of the New Testament* (London: SCM, 1967) 82-99; C. R. North, *The Suffering Servant in Deutero-Isaiah* (2d ed.; Oxford: Oxford University Press, 1956); W. Zimmerli, J. Jeremias, "παῖς θεοῦ," *TDNT* 5.654-717.   R. T. France

SEVENTY, THE. *See* APOSTLE; DISCIPLES.

SHAMMAI. *See* RABBINIC TRADITIONS AND WRITINGS.

SHEMA. *See* CHRISTOLOGY; WORSHIP.

SHEPHERDS. *See* BIRTH OF JESUS.

SIGNS. *See* JOHN, GOSPEL OF; MIRACLES, MIRACLE STORIES.

SIN I: PAUL

There are more than thirty words in the NT that convey some notion of sin, and Paul employs at least twenty-four of them. He makes very little use of the "guilt" terminology in the psychological sense, but it may fairly be said that many of the things he says about sin include the thought that sinners are guilty people. After all, to commit a sin is to be guilty of that sin. While it cannot be said that Paul has a morbid preoccupation with sin, it can be pointed out that he recognizes that the evil that people do is a barrier to fellowship with *God and that unless some way is found of dealing with the problem of sin, all people as sinners face a time of moral accountability (Rom 2:16; 1 Cor 4:5; 2 Cor 5:10). But with this we must also say that Paul's prevailing attitude is not one of unrelieved gloom and pessimism. Rather, he continually rejoices that in *Christ sin has been defeated so that the believer has nothing to fear in this world or the next. (For the argument that Paul's thought moves "backward," from the solution of salvation in Christ to human plight, see Sanders 1977, 442-47; 474-511; cf.

Wright, 258-62.)

Paul presents a massive treatment of the problem of sin in his letter to the Romans, where he uses the noun for "sin" *(hamartia)* forty-eight times, the noun "trespass" *(paraptōma)* nine times, the verb "to sin" *(hamartanō)* seven times, "sinner" *(hamartōlos)* four times, "bad" *(kakos)* fifteen times, and "unrighteousness" *(adikia)* seven times. In addition, Paul uses a number of other words with similar meanings which individually do not occur frequently, but which when taken together add up to a significant part of Romans. This concentration of words about evil cannot be paralleled elsewhere in the NT. In this very weighty letter the problem of sin is examined very closely and some important statements are made in the light of his programmatic announcement of the good news of God in Romans 1:16-17.

Paul does not define sin, but clearly he does not see it as primarily an offense against other people; for him, sin is primarily an offense against God (cf. Rom 8:7; 1 Cor 8:12). The disruption of a right relationship with God has its results in hindering right relationships with people, but it is the offense against God that is primary.

1. The Fall
2. The Universality of Sin
3. Sin and the Law
4. The Effects of Sin
5. The Death of Jesus
6. Christian Opposition to Evil
7. Overcoming Sin
8. The Judgment of Sin

1. The Fall.

Paul does not give much attention to the origin of evil; he does not, for example, speak in set terms of the fall as though he could *explain* the origin of evil. The one place where he describes the stage setting of humankind's fall is 2 Corinthians 11:3 (cf. 1 Tim 2:13-15), which in common with Jewish thinking traces Adam's fall to Eve's influence (cf. Sir 25:24; *Life of Adam and Eve* 3). But he has an important treatment of Adam (Rom 5) in which he makes it clear that he accepts the truth that sin was no part of the original creation. Romans 8:19-23 may suggest that the cosmos is affected by man's, or even Satan's, downfall. He sees sin as having been brought into the world by Adam and as having been practiced by the whole human race ever since, for "all have sinned" (Rom 3:23). All commit their own sins, to be sure, but in some way all are also caught up in the sin of Adam, for "by the one man's trespass the many died" (Rom 5:15). Paul does not see sin as part of human nature as God created it. God is not responsible for a flawed creation. It is this that made Adam's sin so serious. It meant the bringing of sin into a creation that originally was unflawed. Paul could have expressed himself in the words of 4 Ezra 7:118: "O Adam, what have you done? For though it was you who sinned, the fall was not yours alone, but ours also who are your descendants" (NRSV). Yet Paul never apostrophizes in this way.

2. The Universality of Sin.

As he begins Romans the apostle has a strong argument in which he shows that Jews and Gentiles alike are all "under sin"; he quotes Scripture, "there is none righteous, not even one" (Rom 3:10). The whole human race is involved in sin. Paul does recognize that people on occasion act kindly and do good (Rom 2:7-10, 14). But that is not a problem. Sin is. And it is no minor problem, for it covers the whole human race and has calamitous consequences for every sinner (see Hooker).

3. Sin and the Law.

As a faithful Jew Paul had accepted the *Law as a gift from God, a mark of divine favor. But as a Christian he came to recognize that the Law taught some uncomfortable things about sin. The Law makes all the world guilty before God: "As many as are of works of Law (i.e., depend on the Law) are under a curse" (Gal 3:10). Through the Law comes the recognition of sin (Rom 3:19-20); indeed, Paul would not have known what sin is apart from the Law (Rom 7:7). He does not see the function of the Law as the prevention of sin, and he can even say that it multiplied sin (Rom 5:20). Its function was to make clear what sin is; its sharp definition of right and wrong made it plain that many things were sinful which people in every age have been quite prepared to overlook. The Law could not bring them *salvation, but it could bring them to Christ so that they could be justified by faith (Gal 3:24; cf. Wright, 193-216, who understands the role of the Law as concentrating sin on Israel so that it might be dealt with in the Messiah, Israel's representative, once and for all).

4. The Effects of Sin.

Paul sees a link between sin and death; indeed he says that "death came through sin," and further that, since all have sinned, death comes to all (Rom 5:12). He recognizes that although some people's sins are not like Adam's transgression, nevertheless death reigned over all the race (Rom 5:14; cf. 5:21) because all humankind seems to be represented in Adam (Rom 5:12; on this verse see commentaries and Williams). Elsewhere he says simply, "the wages of sin is death" (Rom 6:23). He was once alive apart from the Law, but "when the commandment came, Law sprang into life and I died" (Rom 7:9-10; cf. Gen 4:7). In Romans 7:11, 13 Paul repeats the thought that sin, conceptualized as a power (perhaps with the intimation that sin is like a demon, or monster), killed him. Indeed, the theme of sin as an alien, potent and active power recurs in Romans 5—7 (cf. Rom 5:12, 21; 6:6, 11, 12, 14, 16-18, 20; see Sanders *ABD*; Beker, 213-34; Röhser). In Ephesians Paul reminds his readers that they had been dead in their "trespasses and sins" (Eph 2:1). The apostle leaves no doubt that sin is death-dealing, cutting people off from that life that is life indeed (Eph 4:18).

Paul brings out the seriousness of sin in another way by insisting that sinners are slaves to sin (see Martin). They may fancy that when they commit an evil act, they are free and are doing what they choose to do, but Paul would not agree. He reminds the Romans that in their pre-Christian state they were "sin's slaves" (Rom 6:17, 20). He says that he himself is "fleshly, sold under sin" (Rom 7:14) and "captive to the law of sin" (Rom 7:23). Echoing Ovid, he remarks that he wants to do good, but he still does evil (Rom 7:19). With the mind he may serve the Law of God, but with the flesh he is "a slave to the law of sin" (Rom 7:25). Even when he wants to do good, evil is with him, indeed sin "dwells" in him (Rom 7:20-21).

Sin creates a gulf between sinners and God, as Paul makes clear in Romans 1:21-25. He specifically speaks of being "alienated from the life of God" (Eph 4:18), and says that the Colossians had been "alienated and enemies in their minds and engaged in evil works" (Col 1:21). In any case, it is obvious enough that when created beings sin against their creator, they erect a barrier between God and themselves.

They also disrupt relationships with one another as, for example, the list of sins in Romans 1 makes clear: covetousness, envy, murder, strife, deceit, insolence, covenant breaking and the rest. Humans may be united in sin, but that does not make them united to one another.

Paul offers a unique insight in pointing to an alienation from creation that sin brings and on which he dwells in Romans 8:19-23. Informed by this teaching, Christians do well to care for their environment, not only because of the urgings of modern secular environmentalists, but because this is God's world and Christians look forward to the time when the whole creation "will be freed from the bondage of corruption" (Rom 8:21).

Throughout his writings it is clear that Paul sees sin, however it may be described, as a serious matter and as something that is to be found throughout the whole human race. He sees this as persisting to the end, for when he is dealing with the end time he speaks of the coming of an evil being he calls "the man of lawlessness" (2 Thess 2:3; traditionally he is called "the man of sin"). Clearsightedly, Paul sees sin as operative throughout the human race and as something that will last through the whole of the race's history.

If he sees sin as universal through the whole human race, he also sees it as pervasive through the whole human person. People have sometimes regarded sin as to be found in the bodily functions only, the "heart" or "mind" or "spirit" being unsullied. But there is no way this can be derived from the apostle. It is true that he says that the sexual sinner "sins against his own body" (1 Cor 6:18). He also speaks of the *flesh as opposed to the Spirit and goes on to give a dreadful list of "the works of the flesh" (Gal 5:17-21). But his list includes such things as enmity and envy, which make it clear that he is speaking of sins of the human spirit as well as of those of the human flesh. Paul's writings as a whole demonstrate that he saw sin as involving the whole person, not one part only. To take an example at random, "the love of money" is not a fleshly activity, but it involves "all kinds of evil" (1 Tim 6:10).

5. The Death of Jesus.

Paul has a great deal to say about the death of Jesus, far more in fact than any other NT writer. And he frequently says that the Savior's death was due in some way to sin. Thus he says that

Christ "died for our sins" (1 Cor 15:3; this creedal statement, he says, "is of first importance"), and that he "gave himself for our sins" (Gal 1:4). He tells the Romans that Jesus "was delivered up for our offenses" (Rom 4:25), and again that "the death he died, he died to sin once for all" (Rom 6:10). There is not the slightest doubt that for Paul the death of Jesus was connected with humanity's sins, both in that human sins put Christ to death and that his death was designed to deal with sins.

He further says that Jesus' death was for sinners: Christ "died for ungodly people" (Rom 5:6). In a noteworthy passage Paul tells us that "God shows his own love for us in that while we were still sinners Christ died for us" (Rom 5:8). "His own love" is important; it would be easy to say that the cross demonstrates the love of Christ, but Paul is making the point that, while that is true, it is also true that the love of the Father is demonstrated in the death of the Son. And this death took place "while we were still sinners." It is not that we were somehow cleansed from sin and then the divine love was manifested. That divine love worked sacrificially to deal with the problem of human sin. In two further noteworthy statements Paul says, "one died for all" (2 Cor 5:14) and Christ "died for us" (1 Thess 5:10). The former statement brings out the truth that the death of Jesus is of universal application, the second that it is efficacious for believers. Paul can carry this latter thought a little further with his moving reference to "the *Son of God who loved me and gave himself up for me" (Gal 2:20). The influence of Isaiah 53 as well as early creedal formulations is evident in these Passion texts (see Popkes).

In an important passage Paul says, "Him who knew no sin he [i.e., the Father] made sin for us so that we might become the *righteousness of God in him" (2 Cor 5:21). This is often misquoted as a passive, "was made sin," which leaves the impression of an impersonal process. But Paul is referring to what the Father did as well as to the Son's saving action. The Father is involved in the solution to the problem of sin as well as the Son. It is important to be clear on this. Paul does not regard the Father as an indifferent spectator in the process of dealing with sin. He was there and the saving act was in accordance with his will. "Made sin" is not an easy expression but it surely indicates an identification with sin and sinners. Christ's death (like the offering of Is

53:6) was the sacrifice that takes away sin.

Paul writes to the Colossians that in Christ we have "the forgiveness of sins" (Col 1:14). The expression is in apposition with "the redemption" and clearly points us to the cross again. It means much to the apostle that Christ has dealt with all the evil human beings have done and has brought forgiveness of sins to believers.

6. Christian Opposition to Evil.

Paul recognizes the pervasiveness of sin, yet he does not acquiesce in its inevitability. Constantly he urges believers not to give way to evil, but rather to do what is good. He prays that the Corinthians may do no wrong (2 Cor 13:7), and he urges the Colossians to put to death the evil that is within them (Col 3:5). He urges the Romans not to retaliate when evil is done to them but rather to overcome evil with good (Rom 12:17, 21), and he has a very similar exhortation for the Thessalonians (1 Thess 5:15). It is important to bear in mind that love, which of course should characterize all Christians, does not keep accounts of wrongdoing (1 Cor 13:5).

Paul does not confine himself to denouncing evils in the strictly religious area. He informs Timothy that "the love of money is a root of all kinds of evil" (1 Tim 6:10). He urges the Romans to do what is good and so to merit the approval of rulers (Rom 13:3) and reminds them that love works no evil to a neighbor (Rom 13:10).

7. Overcoming Sin.

That sin is all-pervasive and that Christ has died to deal with its effects are two points that Paul makes with some emphasis. He also has a number of statements that make it clear that he does not envisage Christians as people who continue to sin (Rom 6:1, 15; Gal 5:13), though with the added knowledge that their sin is forgiven. He is well aware that sin is so firmly rooted in human nature that in this life it is presumptuous to claim to be free of every sin. But he is also clear that "sin will not lord it over you" (Rom 6:14), adding, "for you are not under Law but under grace." It is not the submission to some set of rules (like the Jews with their claim to have kept the Law as an identity marker or badge of election) that marks the Christian, but the presence of the grace of God. It is by grace that the believer is saved, and it is by grace that the whole Christian life is lived. Indeed Paul can go as far as to say that Christians, now freed from sin's domination, have "become slaves of righteousness" (Rom 6:18).

8. The Judgment of Sin.

Sin inevitably leads to final judgment. Some anticipation of the future is a present judgment, for to commit sin means to make oneself a sinner. The dreadful consequence of being a sinner is brought out in the threefold "God gave them up" in Romans 1:24, 26, 28, with its horrifying lists of the consequences of sin here and now. Paul further makes it clear that "the wages of sin is death" (Rom 6:23). He also points out that we reap what we sow and that to sow to the flesh means to reap corruption (Gal 6:7-8). This means that sin brings *judgment here and now.

But Paul also insists that sin will be finally dealt with at the judgment at the tribunal of Christ, a truth he brings out forcefully in, say, Romans 2:1-12, 16. This judgment is part of Christian truth and points to the final dealing with evil (1 Cor 4:4-6).

See also ADAM AND CHRIST; DEATH OF CHRIST; FLESH; JUDGMENT; JUSTIFICATION; LAW; RIGHTEOUSNESS.

DPL: CONSCIENCE; CURSE, ACCURSED, ANATHEMA; FORGIVENESS; HOLINESS, SANCTIFICATION; IDOLATRY; LIFE AND DEATH; MAN OF LAWLESSNESS AND RESTRAINING POWER; NEW NATURE AND OLD NATURE; PURITY AND IMPURITY; SATAN, DEVIL; VIRTUES AND VICES; WRATH, DESTRUCTION.

BIBLIOGRAPHY. J. C. Beker, *Paul the Apostle* (Philadelphia: Fortress, 1980); R. Bultmann, *Theology of the New Testament* (2 vols.; New York: Scribners, 1951, 1957); C. E. B. Cranfield, "On Some Problems in the Interpretation of Rom 5:12," *SJT* 22 (1969) 324-41; W. Günther and W. Bauder, "Sin," *NIDNTT* 3.573-87; M. D. Hooker, "Adam in Romans 1," in *From Adam to Christ: Essays on Paul* (Cambridge: Cambridge University Press, 1990); S. Lyonnet and L. Sabourin, ed., *Sin, Redemption and Sacrifice* (AnBib 48; Rome: Pontifical Biblical Institute, 1970); B. F. Malina, "Some Observations on the Origin of Sin in Judaism and St. Paul," *CBQ* 31 (1969) 18-34; D. Martin, *Slavery as Salvation* (New Haven: Yale University Press, 1990); L. Morris, *The Epistle to the Romans* (Grand Rapids: Eerdmans, 1988); W. Popkes, *Christus Traditus: Eine Untersuchung zum Begriff der Dahingabe* (ATANT 49; Zurich: Zwingli

Verlag, 1967); G. Quell et al., "ἁμαρτάνω κτλ," *TDNT* 1.267-335; G. Röhser, *Metaphorik und personifikation der Sünde* (WUNT 2.25; Tübingen: J. C. B. Mohr, 1987); E. P. Sanders, *Paul and Palestinian Judaism* (Philadelphia: Fortress, 1977); idem, "Sin, Sinners (NT)," *ABD* 6.40-47; J. Schneider, "παραβαίνω κτλ," *TDNT* 5.736-44; C. Ryder Smith, *The Bible Doctrine of Sin* (London: Epworth, 1953); F. R. Tennant, *The Origin and Propagation of Sin* (Cambridge: Cambridge University Press, 1902); idem, *The Concept of Sin* (Cambridge: Cambridge University Press, 1912); A. J. M. Wedderburn, "The Theological Structure of Romans 5:12," *NTS* 19 (1972-73) 339-54; N. P. Williams, *The Ideas of the Fall and of Original Sin, Bampton Lectures, 1927* (London: Longmans, 1927); N. T. Wright, *The Climax of the Covenant: Christ and the Law in Pauline Theology* (Minneapolis: Fortress, 1991). L. Morris

SIN II: ACTS, HEBREWS, GENERAL EPISTLES, REVELATION

Sin and wickedness are concepts frequently mentioned in the later NT writings by means of a number of different Greek words. The major words used for sin and wickedness are *kakos* and *ponēros*, two general words for evil or bad behavior; *adikia*, a general word for evil or sin; *hamartia*, a more specific term for sin often involving the breaking of God's *law; *asebeia*, a term for impiety; and *parabasis*, a specific word for sinful disobedience; and their cognates. Although in some contexts it is possible to distinguish clear meanings for these words, there is also a large amount of overlap, so much so that it is better to distinguish various senses of sin and wickedness rather than usage of individual lexical items.

Sin and wickedness are condemned as inappropriate and even law-breaking behavior in relation to one's fellow humans and *God. Often sin and wickedness are contrasted with positive qualities, such as goodness and love. This dualism is in keeping with the hortatory moral and paraenetic nature of much of this writing. The results of sin and wickedness are the severing of human and divine relationships and consequent punishment, including final judgment and condemnation.

1. Sin and Human Behavior
2. Sin and Christ
3. Sin and Love of God
4. Sin and Final Judgment

1. Sin and Human Behavior.

One of the fundamental distinctions in this body of writings is the opposition of good and evil, usually in terms of acts or behavior. In the opposition, good is to be preferred and is a reflection of maturity, obedience and seeking to do good things, while evil is to be shunned and is a reflection of immaturity, disobedience and the doing of wrong (e.g., Heb 5:14; Jas 2:9; 1 Pet 2:14; 3:8-12). In many contexts evil is directly equated with sin and wickedness, since it is behavior that contravenes God's goodness and righteousness (Heb 1:9; 3:12; 8:12; Jas 1:13; 4:17; 1 Pet 2:1, 16; 3:12; 3 Jn 11).

In these writings humans are often categorized by their sinful or evil behavior. Instruction is given not to be the kind of person who is found doing wicked or evil things (e.g., Acts 3:26; 8:23; Heb 12:1; Jas 2:4; 4:16; 2 Pet 2:13, 15; 3 Jn 11; Rev 2:2), who has an evil conscience due to impurity (Heb 10:22) or even who welcomes one who does evil into his house (2 Jn 11). In James some sin is depicted not as outright disobedience to God's law but as the result of desire that has been allowed to give birth to sin and then leads to death (Jas 1:15; 5:20). The classic example of this process may well be the evil that Cain did to his brother Abel (1 Jn 3:12). Because Cain belonged to the evil one (see also 1 Jn 2:13, 14; 5:18, 19), he did the evil deed of killing his brother, whose actions were righteous.

In Hebrews as well as in James, a clear exposition of sin as disobedience to God's law is given. The book resonates with the language of the OT temple and the cultus (e.g., purification, Heb 1:3; atonement, Heb 2:17; as well as the law as a shadow of that which was coming, Heb 10:2-4, 8). Analogies are drawn with the priesthood performing its functions in relation to sin offerings (Heb 5:1, 3; 10:11; 13:11), in which the priest's role is now taken by *Christ (Heb 2:17). The author goes further and not only equates the priestly function with Christ but also depicts Christ himself as the singular sacrifice itself (Heb 7:27; 9:28; cf. Rev 1:5) that removes any further need for sacrifice to remove sin (Heb 9:26). The result is forgiveness of sins—their never being remembered (Heb 8:12; 10:18). Hebrews 9:15 well summarizes the discussion of sin in the book when it speaks of Christ as the mediator of a new covenant with the reward of an eternal inheritance, since Christ died to free humans from their sins committed under the earlier covenant.

2. Sin and Christ.

In several passages in this body of writings, comments are made regarding the sinlessness of Jesus Christ, which stands in opposition to sinful human behavior. These passages have raised theological issues regarding the possibility of Christ's sinning—for example, whether he was perpetually sinless, whether he was ever able to sin, or whether he achieved sinlessness and was exalted in his attained sinless state.

In Hebrews 4:15 the author states that humans do not have a high priest who is incapable of sympathy with their weakness but have one who has been tempted in every way, just as humans are. Nevertheless he was without sin. It is this phrase, "without or apart from sin," that has caused the most difficulty. Sin in the context of Hebrews seems to revolve around Jesus' response to temptation rather than some kind of inherent sinless nature or his kinship with fallen humanity. The assertion seems to be that Christ resisted temptation at every stage of his life, so that when he is offered without blemish before God (Heb 9:14), this reflects not a final or an achieved blamelessness but the perfection of one who had always resisted temptation.

There is the same sense in 1 Peter 2:22, when the author quotes Isaiah 53:9, stating that Christ committed no sin and no deceit was found in him. This allows the author of 1 Peter to state in 1 Peter 3:18, the opening verse of the most important christological section in the letter, that Christ's death was that of a righteous person dying for the unjust concerning their sins (*see* Death of Christ).

3. Sin and Love of God.

An assumption of this part of the NT is that impiety and godlessness are forms of sinfulness and are to be rejected (Jude 4, 15, 18; 2 Pet 2:5, 6; 3:7). God is angry at sin, both in the past with disobedient angels (2 Pet 2:4) and the Israelites (Heb 3:17) and with contemporary Christian behavior. This dynamic is well illustrated in 1 John, a letter concerned to explicate the ethical mandate incumbent on those who have seen and known Christ. The letter exemplifies what it means to love God in terms of loving behavior toward others (see also 1 Pet 4:8).

Several passages in 1 John imply that sinlessness is achievable, while other passages recognize the factuality of human sinfulness. R. E. Brown lists seven possible solutions to the problems raised by these passages, although none is entirely convincing. For example, a standard distinction between the present and aorist tenses of the Greek verb, whereby although humans might continue the occasional one-time sin (aorist tense) they do not persist in sin (present tense), runs afoul of usage in the book. For example, 1 John 3:4, 6 and 8 use the present tense to describe actual sinful acts, and the perfect tense is used in 1 John 1:10 to make the opposite statement regarding sin.

A more plausible solution, and one not dependent on the Greek tense forms, is that a balance is being struck in the letter between the ideal of one not sinning, and thus being consistent with one's confession of Christ, and the reality of persistent human sinfulness. The ethical ideal is tempered by moral reality, although without neglecting the provision for forgiveness. In the argument of the letter, the reality is stated before the ideal. In 1 John 1:8-10 the author states that if we say that we have no sin, we deceive ourselves. If we say that we do not sin, we make God a liar, and his word is not in us. The ideal is established in such passages as 1 John 3:6, where the author says that everyone who abides in Christ does not sin, and everyone who does sin has not seen him; and 1 John 5:18, where he states that everyone who is begotten from God does not sin. Sin is clearly seen here as a breaking of divine law (1 Jn 3:4). Although those abiding in Christ know the demand of loving behavior through obedience, they will inevitably fail. Nevertheless, all is not lost. The solution of the dilemma is found in Christ. In 1 John 2:1, after stating that he is writing so that his audience may not sin, the author says that if they sin, they have an advocate with the Father, Jesus Christ the righteous. It is Christ who cleanses and forgives from all sin (1 Jn 1:7, 9; 2:12; 3:5), since he is the propitiatory sacrifice for sins (1 Jn 2:2; 4:10).

4. Sin and Final Judgment.

In a few passages in these NT writings there are explicit statements regarding the ultimate and final *judgment of sinners and the wicked. These passages impress the reader with the seriousness of sin and wickedness in the light of God and his demand for righteous behavior.

These passages often utilize apocalyptic imagery in painting a picture of final judgment. For example, Hebrews 2:2-3 asks the rhetorical question that if the message of angels was that every violation of God's law and every act of disobedience received punishment, how can Christians expect to escape if they ignore the call of *salvation? Similarly, Hebrews 10:26 says that those who keep on sinning can expect God's judgment. Revelation 18:4-8 and following draw a contrast between those who share in Babylon's sin and those who do not. Those who do can look forward only to trouble, including repayment for their sins in terms of ultimate death and fiery consumption meted out by a judging God.

Although this kind of apocalyptic language is fairly frequent in *Revelation, one of the most concentrated passages with such imagery is 2 Peter 2:9-16. After discussing how God has not spared others in the OT, the author asserts that God certainly knows how to rescue the godly from their trials and to hold the unrighteous for their day of punishment. He then depicts such unrighteous people in a lengthy catalog of their vices, including blasphemy and other sins so wicked that not even the angels would dare do the same. But these people will be paid back for their sins. The author describes this in anticipation of the day of the Lord, when the ungodly will be destroyed (2 Pet 3:7).

See also FLESH.

DLNTD: CONSCIENCE; FORGIVENESS; JUDGMENT; OBEDIENCE; REDEMPTION; VIRTUES AND VICES.

BIBLIOGRAPHY. R. E. Brown, *The Epistles of John* (AB; New York: Doubleday, 1982); A. Chester and R. P. Martin, *The Theology of the Letters of James, Peter and Jude* (NTT; Cambridge: Cambridge University Press, 1994); R. B. Edwards, *The Johannine Epistles* (NTG; Sheffield: Sheffield Academic Press, 1996); W. Günther, "Sin," *NIDNTT* 3.573-85; J. Lieu, *The Theology of the Johannine Epistles* (NTT; Cambridge: Cambridge University Press, 1991); B. Lindars, *The Theology of the Letter to the Hebrews* (NTT; Cambridge: Cambridge University Press, 1991); D. Peterson, *Hebrews and Perfection* (SNTSMS 47; Cambridge: Cambridge University Press, 1982).

S. E. Porter

SINNERS: GOSPELS

In the Gospels the term *sinner* is used in two ways—to describe the individual who is opposed to *God and his will, and by Jesus' opponents to describe those outside their group and to whom Jesus offers the gospel of *salvation. The nature and identity of these sinners has been a topic of scholarly investigation.

1. Terminology and Meaning
2. Usage in the Gospels
3. Jesus and Sinners
4. Conclusion

1. Terminology and Meaning.
Sinner is the English word most frequently used to translate the Greek term *hamartōlos*, an adjective related to the verb *hamartanō*, "to *sin," and the nouns for *sin*, *hamartēma* and *hamartia*. Within the LXX the Greek term *hamartōlos* occurs approximately ninety-four times, corresponding to five roots in the MT: *ḥṭʾ* (15x: e.g., Num 32:14), *ḥnp* (1x: Prov 11:9), *ḥrš* (1x: Ps 128:3), *rʿ* (1x: Prov 12:13) and *ršʿ* (74x: e.g., 2 Chron 19:2). In the Aramaic Targums there is evidence that a broader term, *ḥwbʾ*, meaning "debtor" or "sinner," is the natural counterpart of *hamartōlos* in the LXX. In the *Targum on Isaiah* "debtors," or "sinners," are punished by Messiah (*Tg. Isa* 11:4) and destroyed by the *Lord (*Tg. Isa* 14:4-5), but are also capable of repentance (*Tg. Isa* 28:24-25). *Hamartōlos* corresponds most frequently in the LXX with the Hebrew *rāšāʿ*, "wicked one." Especially in the Psalms, *rāšāʿ* is used in parallel with almost every Hebrew word for sin, evil and iniquity, and functions also as an adjective to designate the actions and conduct of a type of person (cf. Ps 10:4, 7; 36:1; 49:6, 13; 50:16-17). The *rāšāʿ*, "wicked one," is usually placed in antithetic parallelism to the *ṣaddîq*, "righteous one" (cf. Ps 1:6). This is the common meaning of the term in the early writings within Judaism as well (e.g., Sir, *1 Enoch* [G[a]] 22:10-14).

The word *sinner* also occurs in what we may call factional contexts to designate those who are outside the boundary of the group who use the term. In these cases wickedness, by definition, is conduct outside the boundary, conduct which is unacceptable to those inside. "Sinner" could thereby be used more or less as a synonym for "Gentile" (Ps 9:17; Tob 13:8; *Jub.* 23:23-24). But as Judaism developed, those boundaries could also be drawn *within* the people of *Israel as well, with "sinner" used to designate those for whom a particular faction showed disapproval. Thus "sinners" could be apostate Jews (1 Macc 1:34; 2:44, 48), Jews who wrongly reckoned the months and the feasts and the years (*1 Enoch* 82:4-7), Jews who did not hold to the sectarian interpretation of the Qumran community (CD 4:8; 1QS 5:7-11; 1QH 7:12; *see* Dead Sea Scrolls), Jewish opponents of the "devout" (*Pss. Sol.* 1:8; 2:3; 7:2; 8:12-13; 17:5-8; 23) or Jews with different interpretations of ritual purity requirements (*As. Mos.* 7:3, 9-10).

2. Usage in the Gospels.

Hamartōlos occurs forty-seven times in the NT, thirty-three times in the Gospels, never in Acts, fourteen times in the epistles and never in Revelation. Although the term occurs thirty-three times in the Gospels, those occurrences are clustered in thirteen pericopes, ten of which have the substantive form and three of which have the adjectival form. For the most part the term appears to be enmeshed in traditional materials which the Evangelists have adopted. Of the thirteen Gospel accounts in which the term occurs, one appears in all three Synoptic Gospels, a so-called triple tradition (the *table fellowship dispute: Mt 9:10; 11, 13 par. Mk 2:15, 16 [twice] and Lk 5:30, 32), one is shared between Mark and Matthew (the arrest in the Garden: Mt 26:45 par. Mk 14:41), and one is a passage shared between Matthew and Luke, being thereby designated as Q material (the contrast between John the Baptist and Jesus: Mt 11:19 par. Lk 7:34).

Matthew refers to "sinners" on only three occasions: the triple tradition (Mt 9:10, 11, 13 par. Mk 2:15, 16 [twice] and Lk 5:30, 32), the passage shared with Mark (Mt 26:45 par. Mk 14:41) and the passage shared with Luke/Q (Mt 11:19 par. Lk 7:34). Similarly, Mark refers to sinners on only three occasions: the triple tradition (Mk 2:15, 16 [twice] par. Mt 9:10; 11, 13 and Lk 5:30, 32), the passage shared with Matthew (Mk 14:41 par. Mt 26:45) and one triple-tradition incident in which only Mark uses the adjectival form of the term ("this sinful generation": Mk 8:38 par. Mt 16:26-27 and Lk 9:26). John does not share with the Synoptics any references to sinners, and he refers to sinners in only one pericope (the healed blind man interacts with the Pharisees: Jn 9:16, 24, 25, 31).

Luke has the most extensive references to "sinners." He refers to them on ten occasions: the triple tradition (Lk 5:30, 32 par. Mk 2:15, 16 [twice] and Mt 9:10, 11, 13), the passage shared with Matthew/Q (Lk 7:34 par. Mt 11:19) and eight incidents found only in Luke. Of those

eight, one incident is triple-tradition material in which only Luke has included the term (the angels' testimony, Lk 24:7), and two incidents have material similar to Matthew (not Q material), but only Luke uses the term (love of one's enemies, Lk 6:32, 33, 34 [2x]; parables about the lost ones, Lk 15:7, 10). In five of the eight incidents the term occurs in material unique to Luke's Gospel (Peter's confession, Lk 5:8; Simon the Pharisee and the woman called a "sinner," Lk 7:37, 39; Galilean martyrs, Lk 13:2; parable of the Pharisee and the tax collector, Lk 18:13; Zacchaeus's calling, Lk 19:7).

3. Jesus and Sinners.

One of the most distinctive features of Jesus' message and ministry is the promise of *salvation to sinners. Not only is there much material that includes that message, but it is found in diverse forms—ranging from sayings and *parables to reports of Jesus' activity and accusations against him. Jesus is said to have associated with sinners (Mk 2:15, 16 par.) and to have sought out the sinner as one who was lost (e.g., Lk 15:7, 10). Jesus flatly declares that one aspect of his ministry was "not to call the righteous, but sinners" (Mk 2:17 par.). One encounters no difficulty understanding the general use of "sinner" in the Gospels to designate the person who commits acts of sin defined by *Law, as is likely the case of the sinful woman in Luke 7:36-50. But in the Gospel accounts the term "sinner" also designates a narrow segment of the people. A well known combination, "tax collectors and sinners," appears to specify an identifiable segment of the people called "sinners" as being linked with "tax collectors" (Mt 9:10, 11, 13 par. Mt 11:19 par. Lk 15:7). On several occasions the Pharisees are placed in contrast with "sinners," apparently an identifiable segment of the people held up for special criticism by the Pharisees (cf. Mt 9:10, 11, 13 par. Lk 7:37, 39; 15:1, 2; 18:13; Jn 9:16, 24, 25). Recent scholarly investigation has attempted to identify the segment of people called "sinners."

3.1. Sinners Are Those Who Do Not Observe Sectarian Rituals. J. Jeremias is representative of a widely held interpretation which identifies the sinners as the common people, the *'ammê ha'āreṣ*, who are disapproved of by the Pharisees. This interpretation suggests that the people known as "sinners" are viewed from a double perspective in the Gospels. From the perspective of Jesus' opponents the term *sinner* was coined to express contempt for Jesus' following. Jesus' opponents were primarily Pharisees, whom Jeremias makes virtually coextensive with the *haberîm*, the brotherhood which insisted on ritual purity for table fellowship. They considered Jesus' following to consist primarily of the disreputable, the *ʿammê hāʾāreṣ*, the uneducated, whose religious ignorance and moral behavior stood in the way of their access to salvation. Other derogatory names used by these opponents to refer to Jesus' followers included: "the little ones" (e.g., Mk 9:42); "the simple ones"; "babes" (e.g., Mt 11:25).

Hence, "sinners" are those who have offended the exclusivism of the Pharisees' purity laws (especially table fellowship) and/or their rigorous observance of the Law. Although from the perspective of Jesus' opponents the followers of Jesus are called sinners, from Jesus' perspective they are called "the poor" or "those who labor and are heavy laden" (e.g., Mt 11:5, 28)—those disenfranchised from the religious, social and political life of Israel.

3.2. Sinners Are Those Wicked Ones Who Are Outside the Law.

E. P. Sanders is representative of a challenge to Jeremias's view. Sanders argues that the OT equivalent for *hamartōloi* is *rĕšaʿîm* (or the Aramaic equivalent), and that it is virtually a technical term. He suggests that it is best translated "the wicked," and it refers to those who sinned willfully and heinously and did not repent. When placed with "tax collectors," the two names stand for "traitors": the tax collectors are those who collaborated with Rome, and the sinners are the wicked who betrayed the God who redeemed Israel and gave them his Law.

Sanders further argues that the Pharisees were not primarily a table-fellowship group who were offended by Jesus' offering salvation to those outside their fellowship. Rather, they were a party devoted to the Torah in its oral explication. The sinners were not simply impure common people (*ʿammê hāʾāreṣ*) but the wicked who were offered inclusion in Jesus' company without being required to undergo the normal repentance required by the Law. Jesus allowed them to become his followers and remain "wicked ones." This put Jesus into conflict with all of the leaders of Israel, who focused on the Law as the center of religious and social life.

The strength of Sanders's argument is that it replaces a simplistic caricature of Judaism. Jeremias's view paints the Pharisees as hopelessly formalistic, to the degree that they were so incensed at Jesus' offer of salvation to the common people that they were willing to put him to death (*see* Trial of Jesus). But Sanders's alternative, that Jesus offered sinners salvation without any thought of them changing their behavior, is not true to the Gospel portrait of Jesus.

3.3. Sinners Are Those Opposed to God's Will.

A number of passages in the Gospels indicate a broad use of the term *sinner* to indicate a person opposed to the will of God. An important perspective is found in Mark 14:41 (par. Matthew 26:45), where Jesus, announcing his impending arrest, says, "the Son of Man is betrayed into the hands of sinners." This is ultimately directed at the chief priests and scribes and elders who had arranged the arrest (Mk 14:43 par. Mt 26:47). What makes the leaders of Israel sinners is that they are opposing the will of God as worked out in Jesus' ministry. Luke's story of the angels at the tomb echoes these words with the adjectival use of *hamartōlos* (Lk 24:7).

In Mark 8:38 Jesus' words about "this adulterous and sinful generation" are not addressed to any particular segment of the people, but to the people of Israel as a whole who have rejected him. In Luke 5:8 Simon Peter's reaction to Jesus' miraculous catch of fish is to confess that he is a sinful man. His confession comes in the presence of one whom he calls "Lord," indicating, at least, that Peter recognizes his own humility in the presence of the activity of God in Jesus.

Luke 13:1-2 tells the story of Galilean pilgrims put to death by Pilate while in Jerusalem to make sacrifices in the Temple. Jesus, using the term sinner, counters the common Jewish belief that calamity in life was the result of past sin. This is a general sense of the term sinner, since the expectation is that the judgment would ultimately have been from God and, hence, punishment for a sin against God. This is especially borne out in verse 4, where the parallel term is *opheiletai*, used in the sense of a debtor or sinner against God.

These Synoptic passages demonstrate a use of the term in nonfactional contexts, and point to a broad use of the term to designate a person opposed to the will of God. This understanding of "sinner" is corroborated in the Fourth Gospel. In the story of the controversy with the Pharisees, the man who has been healed of blindness says, "We know that God does not listen to sinners, but if any one is a worshiper of God and does his will, God listens to him" (Jn

9:31). Here the implication is that the sinner is one who does not worship God and does not do God's will. Although in the preceding context the Pharisees have emphasized Sabbath observance (Jn 9:16, 24, 25), the healed man implies a broader use of the term, not just specifying the nonobservant person.

4. Conclusion.
The use of "sinner" in the LXX and early Jewish literature is helpful for understanding the divergent usage of the term in the Gospels. The common use of the term was to indicate a "wicked one," often placed in antithetic parallelism with the "righteous one." But the term was also used in factional contexts, both to speak of Gentiles *outside* the boundaries of Israel, and within the context of factional rivalry *within* Judaism. These two emphases accord with the use of "sinner" in the Gospels. There are a significant number of passages that have a broad use of "sinner" to designate "one opposed to the will of God." There are a number of other passages that are factionally oriented.

Jeremias focuses primarily on the group of passages that pit the Pharisees against the sinners. Despite Sanders's objections, the strength of Jeremias's argument is that it gives proper attention to the factional use of the term in Judaism. J. D. G. Dunn has suggested that the Pharisees were a sect with clear ideas of the character of life and conduct required to maintain the covenant *righteousness* of the people of God. As such they were highly likely to regard as sinners those who disagreed with them and who lived in open disregard of this righteousness—as had the groups behind the apocalyptic Enoch traditions, the *Psalms of Solomon* and the Dead Sea Scrolls. The Pharisees firmly believed in the authority of their developing oral traditions, and those who were opposed to their practices were considered to be opposed to God.

Sanders tends to rely most heavily on those passages that align the tax collectors with the sinners. He has criticized Jeremias for downplaying the strength of the term and for making it simply an equivalent term for non-Pharisees. The Pharisees were not as rigid on matters of purity as were the Essenes. They did not necessarily regard all non-Pharisees as sinners—perhaps only those who made light of Pharisaic concerns. Nevertheless, the more members of the Jewish community moved away from Phari-

saic standards, the more likely the Pharisees would dub them sinners.

While Sanders goes too far in pressing the term always to mean blatant lawbreakers, when the Pharisees used the term *sinners* they meant one who was opposed to the will of God as reflected in their understanding of *halakah,* the rabbinic laws governing life. Behind the objections and charges leveled against Jesus was the central fact that he was ignoring and abolishing boundaries that more sectarian attitudes had erected *within* Israel. Hence, from the standpoint of Jesus' opponents a person was a sinner as long as he or she did not conform to the expectations of the sect. From the standpoint of Jesus, a person was a sinner as long as he or she remained opposed to the will of God. Once a person accepted the offer of forgiveness and made a commitment of faith to follow Jesus, he or she became a *disciple of Jesus. Jesus' offer of salvation to sinners apart from factional observance was a threat to the very foundation and way of life of sectarian Jews, yet it was at the heart of the gospel he came announcing.

See also DISCIPLES; ISRAEL; SALVATION; TABLE FELLOWSHIP.

DJG: CLEAN AND UNCLEAN; DISCIPLESHIP; PHARISEES.

BIBLIOGRAPHY. I. Abrahams, "Publicans and Sinners," *Studies in Pharisaism and the Gospels,* First Series (1917, 1924; New York: KTAV, 1967); R. G. Bratcher, "Unusual Sinners," *BT: Technical Papers* 39 (1988) 335-37; B. D. Chilton, "Jesus and the Repentance of E. P. Sanders," *TynB* 39 (1988) 1-18; J. D. G. Dunn, "Pharisees, Sinners, and Jesus," in *Jesus, Paul and the Law: Studies in Mark and Galatians* (Louisville: Westminster/John Knox, 1990) 61-88; W. Günther, "Sin," *NIDNTT* 3.573-87; J. Jeremias, *New Testament Theology: The Proclamation of Jesus* (New York: Charles Scribner's Sons, 1971); G. H. Livingston, "רָשַׁע (rāšāʿ)," *TWOT* 2.863-64; A. Oppenheimer, *The 'Am Ha-Aretz: A Study in the Social History of the Jewish People in the Hellenistic-Roman Period* (ALGHJ VIII; Leiden: E. J. Brill, 1977); K. H. Rengstorf, "ἁμαρτωλός," *TDNT* 1.317-35; A. J. Saldarini, *Pharisees, Scribes and Sadducees in Palestinian Society: A Sociological Approach* (Wilmington, DE: Michael Glazier, 1988); E. P. Sanders, *Jesus and Judaism* (Philadelphia: Fortress, 1985); N. H. Young, " 'Jesus and the Sinners': Some Queries," *JSNT* 24 (1985) 73-75.

M. J. Wilkins

SIRACH. *See* Apocrypha and Pseudepigrapha.

SON OF DAVID: GOSPELS

When used as a christological title in the Gospels, "Son of David" points to Jesus as the royal Messiah (*see* Christ) in the line of David. As such he fulfills the promises God made to David regarding the eternal reign of David's "offspring" (e.g., 2 Sam 7:12-16), and he acts as the unique agent in bringing the rule of *God (*see* Kingdom of God) to the earth, a rule that is characterized by *salvation and blessing. In contrast to major streams of popular messianic expectation, Jesus refused to establish his kingly rule through political ascendancy or military conquest. Rather, this Davidic king wielded his royal power by attending to the needs of the poor and oppressed, and by suffering and dying in order to bring salvation to his people.

In comparison with christological titles such as Son of God and *Son of Man, Son of David plays a relatively minor role in the NT. It seems to be used always with reference to Jesus' earthly existence, never of his heavenly or exalted state. Moreover, it appears in just eleven passages, all of them within the Synoptic Gospels. Nevertheless, the idea of Davidic sonship is often present even when the phrase itself does not occur, as when Jesus is described as "King." The concept of Son of David contributed to the early development of the church's *christology, and within the Synoptic tradition it provided specific content for the more general christological categories of Christ and Son of God.

1. The Old Testament and Judaic Background
2. The Son of David and the Historical Jesus
3. The Son of David in the Christology of the Gospels

1. The Old Testament and Judaic Background.

The expectation of a Davidic Messiah had its beginnings during the Exile, for central to the notion of such a Messiah is the re-establishment of the throne of David and the deliverance of Israel from its (foreign) oppressors. This expectation resulted from a combination of disappointment and confidence: disappointment at the destruction of Jerusalem and the suspension of the Davidic dynasty, and confidence in the faithfulness of God who had made an everlasting *covenant with David to establish David's kingdom forever through his offspring (2 Sam 7:10-16; cf. Ps 89:1-

4, 19-37; 132:11-12). Prophets such as Jeremiah, Ezekiel, Haggai and Zechariah spoke of the Davidic "righteous branch" who would soon appear to reconcile the people to their God, re-establish Israel in the land, cleanse the land of foreign oppressors as well as unrighteous Israelites, and cause peoples from all over the earth to flock to Jerusalem where they would behold the glory of Yahweh (Jer 23:5-8; 30:21-22; Ezek 37:21-23; Zech 3:8-10; 6:12-15; Hag 2:21-22). These prophets thought of an entirely earthly figure, a mortal man, who would inaugurate a dynasty that would continue forever through his descendants (Ps 89:3-4; Jer 17:25; 33:15-18).

Although there was much diversity in messianic speculation among individual Jewish groups, a general consensus emerged within later Judaism that the Messiah would be Davidic along the lines set out by the exilic prophets. A representative statement of Jewish messianic expectations is *Psalms of Solomon* 17—18 (a Pharisaic composition written around 50 B.C.). According to this description the "Son of David" (the title appears here for the first time) will (1) violently cast out the foreign nations occupying Jerusalem (*Pss. Sol.* 17:15, 24-25, 33); (2) judge all the nations of the earth (*Pss. Sol.* 17:4, 31, 38-39, 47) and cause these nations to "serve him under his yoke" (*Pss. Sol.* 17:32); (3) reign over Israel in wisdom (*Pss. Sol.* 17:23, 31, 42) and *righteousness (*Pss. Sol.* 17:23, 28, 31, 35, 41; 18:8), which involves removing all foreigners from the land (*Pss. Sol.* 17:31) and purging the land of unrighteous Israelites (*Pss. Sol.* 17:29, 33, 41) in order to eliminate all oppression (*Pss. Sol.* 17:46) and gather to himself a holy people (*Pss. Sol.* 17:28, 36; 18:9).

Although the Davidic Messiah is still pictured as an earthly figure, his rule obviously takes on eschatological and universal dimensions not found in the prophets. Essentially the same description of the Davidic Messiah appears at Qumran (1QM 11:1-18; 4QFlor 1:11-14; 4QPBless 1-7; 4QTestim 9-13; *see* Dead Sea Scrolls) and in the Pseudepigrapha (4 Ezra 12:31-32; *T. Jud.* 24:1-5).

2. The Son of David and the Historical Jesus.

The Gospels reveal that Davidic expectations along the lines of *Psalms of Solomon* were very much alive in Jesus' milieu. Jesus was executed on the charge that he claimed to be the king of the Jews (or of Israel; *see* Death of Christ), thus inciting political and military rebellion against Rome (Mk 15:2, 26; cf. Mk 10:46—11:10). The request from James and John for seats on the right and left of Jesus suggest that the disciples viewed Jesus' kingdom in terms of political authority and social supremacy (Mk 10:35-45). Moreover, the question posed by the disciples in Acts 1:6 indicates a nationalistic understanding of the kingdom. Jesus himself was aware of the popular expectations surrounding the Davidic Messiah and seems to have struggled with them (Mk 8:32-33; Mt 4:1-11; 27:32-44; Jn 6:15).

On only one occasion did Jesus specifically raise the issue of Davidic sonship: Mark 12:35-37 and its parallels. There is general scholarly consensus that Jesus did not wish, in this passage, to deny the Davidic sonship of the Messiah. Certainly the Evangelists who included this pericope in their Gospels did not understand it in that sense. Rather, Jesus engaged here in the rabbinic form of argument known as *haggadah*, according to which an apparent contradiction between two passages is presented and discussed in such a way that the truth of each is affirmed. Here Jesus (implicitly) sets all those passages that teach the Davidic sonship of the Messiah over against Psalm 110:1, which on the surface seems to contradict this teaching. In this way Jesus indicated that (1) the Messiah is the Son of David and (2) the Messiah is a transcendent being, whose glory and authority far surpass that of David. "Son of David," therefore, is an accurate but not fully adequate description of the Messiah.

Although Jesus accepted the Davidic sonship of the Messiah, he rejected the nationalistic and militaristic conceptions of the Son of David which were so much a part of Jewish expectations. As far as Jesus was concerned, the kingdom does not come by violence (Mt 11:12), nor is it characterized by oppressive, authoritarian rule (Mk 10:42-44). On the contrary, Jesus as Son of David is presented as he who acts mercifully to blind Bartimaeus (Mk 10:46-52). He seems to have viewed himself as one who dies on behalf of his people (Mk 8:31; 9:30-31; 10:32-34; 15:1-32), and indeed on behalf of all peoples ("the many," Mk 10:45). Those who participate in his kingdom follow him in the way of submission and sacrificial service (Mk 8:34-38).

This new understanding of the Son of David explains the reticence of Jesus concerning his Messianic and Davidic status. At no time did he claim to be the Son of David. As O. Cullmann points out, even Jesus' answer to the question Pontius Pilate put to him regarding his kingship was, in the Aramaic original, equivocal and ambiguous (Mk 15:2; *see* Trial of Jesus). The most natural interpretation of Jesus' reserve on this point is that he wished to avoid any tendency on the part of the people to view him as a nationalistic and military leader (Lk 22:47-53; Jn 6:15; 18:33-38).

3. The Son of David in the Christology of the Gospels.

Matthew gives greater prominence to "Son of David" than do the other Gospel writers. The title appears four times each in Mark and Luke, but ten times in Matthew. The phrase does not occur at all in the Fourth Gospel (but cf. Jn 7:42).

3.1. Mark. The reader is introduced to Jesus as Son of David in the story of Bartimaeus (Mk 10:46-52). Twice this blind beggar cries out, "Son of David, have mercy on me" (Mk 10:47-48); and in response to his pleas Jesus heals him (Mk 10:52). The fact that Jesus fulfills Bartimaeus's request to the letter suggests that the Markan Jesus accepts this title. This story indicates that (1) Jesus is in the lineage of David; (2) he fulfills Jewish expectations that the Son of David would bring wholeness to the oppressed; and (3) he wields his royal power by humbly submitting to those in need rather than by "exercising authority," like the rulers of the Gentiles (Mk 10:35-45).

Mark employs the healing of Bartimaeus as an introduction to the triumphal entry (Mk 11:1-11; cf. 10:52). As such, Jesus enters Jerusalem as the Son of David. By presenting Jesus as one who enters on his kingship riding a colt (Zech 9:9; cf. 2 Kings 9:13), Mark indicates that Jesus is the type of Davidic king described by Zechariah: a humble savior who brings peace and blessing to the nations. Although the people properly hail Jesus as the Davidic prince who brings God's kingdom of salvation to them (Mk 11:9-10), subsequent events indicate that the people have an entirely different understanding of this kingdom and of the Son of David who introduces this kingdom than does Jesus. In the *passion narrative the crowds reject Jesus' conception of a suffering and dying king who saves others by refusing to save himself (Mk 15:6-15, 25-39).

This section of Mark comes to a climax in the question regarding "David's son" (Mk 12:35-37). Mark has indicated that Jesus is the Son of David. Now he suggests that Jesus is much more than Son of David. Given Mark's accent on Jesus as *Son of God (Mk 1:1, 11; 9:7; 15:39), he is probably contending here that Jesus should be viewed primarily as Son of God, and in only an ancillary way as Son of David. Mark employs "Son of David" in such a way that it might contribute its own specific content to the broader conception of Jesus' divine sonship, a christological category which (in Mark) emphasizes the suffering and death of Jesus.

3.2. Matthew. Matthew has appropriated the four references to Son of David that he found in his Markan source, and he has introduced an additional six, presumably from his own hand. An examination of Matthew's use of this title indicates that he employs it with deliberation and consistency.

For Matthew, Jesus can function as Son of David because he is of the lineage of David (Mt 1:1-17). But Matthew immediately encounters a problem with this assertion; for he attempts to trace Jesus' Davidic ancestry through Joseph, while maintaining that Jesus was not, in fact, the biological son of Joseph. Jesus has been conceived not by Joseph but by the *Holy Spirit (Mt 1:16, 18-25; see Birth of Jesus). The reader is thus confronted with a question: How can Jesus be the Son of David through Joseph if he is not the natural son of Joseph? The answer: Joseph, son of David, adopts Jesus by giving him his name (Mt 1:20-25). The fact that Jesus is adopted by Joseph in no way makes Jesus' Davidic lineage questionable. In Jewish circles a child became a man's son not so much by physical procreation itself as by acknowledgment on the part of the man. Nevertheless, Jesus is Son of David by adoption, but Son of God by conception (Mt 2:15; 3:17).

But Jesus is not simply a son of David; he is *the* Son of David. As Son of David, Jesus is the Messiah-king in the line of David who has been sent by God specifically to the people of Israel, not in order to exercise oppressive rule over them (Mt 20:20—21:17) but to bring them salvation and deliverance by healing them of their diseases. Three times persons in need of healing cry out to him, "Have mercy upon me [us], Son of David" (Mt 9:27; 15:22; 20:31). In all instances Jesus grants the healing they seek. Moreover, on two other occasions Jesus' healings induce persons to speak about him in terms of "Son of David" (Mt 12:23; 21:15).

These passages have a double function. On the one hand, they make a positive statement about Jesus, demonstrating that Jesus fulfills the messianic expectation that the Son of David would bring wholeness to the oppressed, and that those who have faith to confess that Jesus is the Jewish Messiah will experience the blessings of the eschatological age. On the other hand, they make a negative statement about Israel. As J. D. Kingsbury has observed, only the "no-accounts" of Jewish society, and on one occasion a Gentile, appeal to Jesus as Son of David and are thereby healed. The crowds, however, generally respond to these healings with doubt (Mt 12:23), and the religious authorities respond with anger (Mt 21:15) and blasphemy (Mt 12:22-32). Matthew thus uses "Son of David" to point to Israel's rejection of its Messiah and to highlight the blindness and guilt that attended this rejection on the part of Israel as a whole.

The fact that Matthew gives more attention to "Son of David" than do the other Evangelists has led some scholars, such as G. Bornkamm and C. Burger, to argue that Son of David is the chief christological category in Matthew. Yet in the question regarding David's son, Matthew suggests that Jesus' Davidic sonship is secondary to another type of sonship (Mt 22:41-46; cf. Mk 12:35-37). No doubt Matthew has in mind that Jesus' divine sonship takes precedence over his Davidic sonship. In Matthew's Gospel Jesus is presented primarily as Son of God, the eschatological figure in whom God has drawn near to dwell with his people (Mt 1:18-25; 3:17; 16:16; 27:54), and in only a secondary and supportive way as Son of David.

3.3. Luke. Luke records the birth of Jesus in Bethlehem, "the city of David" (Lk 2:4, 11), to a woman betrothed to Joseph, "of the house and lineage of David" (Lk 2:4). Yet Luke gives relatively little attention to the title "Son of David." It appears only in passages which he takes over from Mark. In one of these passages (the question regarding David's son, Lk 20:41-47) Luke suggests that although Jesus is the Son of David, his Davidic sonship is subordinate to another christological category, probably that of Son of God (Lk 1:26-35; 3:23-38).

Nevertheless, the concept of Davidic sonship does appear in Luke's Gospel. As Son of David, Jesus is the royal heir to the throne of David (Lk 1:32-33). In him the promises which God made regarding the establishment of David's kingdom and the consequent salvation of *Israel find fulfillment (Lk 1:54, 68-75; 4:16-30; 19:28-40).

Jesus' Son of David is the one whom God has designated to usher in his kingdom, and the one through whom God exercises his will over his people Israel (including those Gentiles who by faith become part of the true Israel of God, Lk 1:30-32; cf. Acts). Luke emphasizes, even more than Mark and Matthew, that this Davidic king and the kingdom he inaugurates are not characterized by military revolt or political aspirations, but involve rather the salvation of God's people from demonic oppression (Lk 4:16-19; 11:14-23; 18:35-43) and the establishment of a community which fulfills the will of God (Lk 23:1-15, 32-49).

See also CHRIST; SON OF GOD; SON OF MAN.

DJG: GENEALOGY.

BIBLIOGRAPHY. G. Bornkamm, "End Expectation and Church in Matthew," in *Tradition and Interpretation in Matthew*, ed. G. Bornkamm et al. (Philadelphia: Westminster, 1963) 15-51; R. E. Brown, *The Birth of the Messiah* (Garden City, NY: Doubleday, 1977); C. Burger, *Jesus als Davidssohn* (FRLANT 98; Göttingen: Vandenhoeck & Ruprecht, 1967); O. Cullmann, *The Christology of the New Testament* (Philadelphia: Westminster, 1963); J. M. Gibbs, "Purpose and Pattern in Matthew's Use of the Title 'Son of David,' " *NTS* 10 (1963-1964) 446-64; F. Hahn, *The Titles of Jesus in Christology* (London: Lutterworth, 1969); J. D. Kingsbury, *Jesus Christ in Matthew, Mark, and Luke* (PC; Philadelphia: Fortress, 1981); idem, "The Title 'Son of David' in Matthew's Gospel," *JBL* 95 (1976) 591-602; E. Lohse, "υἱος Δαυίδ," *TDNT* 8.478-88; S. Mowinckel, *He That Cometh* (New York: Abingdon, 1955). D. R. Bauer

SON OF GOD I: GOSPELS

"Son of God" is arguably the most significant christological title in the NT. The title or its equivalents ("the Son," "my Son," etc.) occur more than 124 times in the NT, and may be the foremost christological category in each of the Gospels. The NT characteristically describes Jesus' relationship to *God in terms of divine sonship. The concept itself carries a variety of meanings, including commissioning to special work, obedience, intimate fellowship, knowledge, likeness, and the receiving of blessings and gifts.

1. Divine Sonship in the Old Testament, Judaism and Hellenism
2. Divine Sonship in the Life and Ministry

of the Historical Jesus
3. Divine Sonship in the Christology of the Gospels

1. Divine Sonship in the Old Testament, Judaism and Hellenism.

The notion of divine sonship appears in the OT with regard to three persons or groups of persons: angels (Gen 6:2; Job 1:6; Dan 3:25), *Israel (Ex 4:22-23; Hos 11:1; Mal 2:10) and the king (2 Sam 7:14; Ps 2:7; 89:26-27). When used of Israel and the king, sonship emphasizes belonging in a special way to God, election to perform the service of God (i.e., to obey God) and the experience of God's love, mercy, protection and gifts.

Although there are relatively few OT references to the king as son of God, this usage stands closer to the meaning of the title in the NT than do references to angels or even to the people as a whole. There are two emphases in the divine sonship of the king that set it apart from the sonship of the people. First, the king in his capacity as son of God exercises authority over both the people of Israel and the nations (see esp. Ps 2). Second, the divine sonship of the king has its basis in the *covenant God made with David in 2 Samuel 7:4-17 (cf. Ps 89:19-45), thereby (1) restricting royal divine sonship to descendants of David, (2) laying the foundation for relating the concepts of *Son of David and Son of God, and (3) infusing the notion of royal Son of God with the ideas of immutable divine promise, decree and covenant.

It is clear that the OT does not speak explicitly of the Messiah or of a specifically messianic figure as Son of God. This seems generally to be the case in postbiblical Palestinian Judaism as well. The expression refers to angels (*1 Enoch* 69:4-5; 71:1; *Jub* 1:24-25) and miracle workers (esp. Honi the circle-drawer [*b. Ta'an.* 24b; *b. Ber.* 17b; *b. ḥul.* 86a] and Ḥanina ben Dosa [*m. Ta'an.* 3:8]; see Vermes), but many passages that once were cited as evidence for the messianic use of Son of God have been discounted as later interpolations or mistranslations of the word for "servant."

There are three passages in the literature from Qumran (*see* Dead Sea Scrolls), however, which may connect the idea of Son of God to the Messiah: 4QFlor 1:10-14 applies 2 Samuel 7:11-14 to the Messiah; 1QSa 2:11-12 could be read in terms of God begetting the Messiah; and 4QpsDan A[a] (=4Q246) is reported to read "he shall be hailed as the Son of God, and they shall call him Son of the most High" (Fitzmyer). In spite of the sparsity of references that relate the Messiah to divine sonship, the observations that (1) messianic hope in the period was almost always linked to an ideal Davidic king (who in the OT is described as Son of God) and (2) some NT statements seem to assume a connection between Messiah and Son of God (e.g., Mk 14:61; Mt 16:16) suggest that the Messiah as Son of God was not totally foreign to Palestinian Judaism. Yet the Messiah was not understood primarily in terms of Son of God.

The consideration that Son of God was not a typical messianic designation in Palestinian Judaism and that Hellenism was acquainted with descriptions of heroes, philosophers, rulers and miracle workers who were designated sons of god has led many historians to argue for the Hellenistic origin of the title as applied to Jesus. These historians claim that Hellenistic Christians were responsible for the confession of Jesus' divine sonship, and that they understood Jesus to be Son of God along the lines of the "divine man" (*theios anēr*; *see* Divine Man/*Theios Anēr*), a heroic miracle-worker. This understanding of the origin of the title in *christology is today generally rejected, since (1) the Hellenistic concept stands in tension with the NT emphasis on the uniqueness of Jesus' divine sonship as well as with the NT insistence that the divine sonship of Jesus involves primarily suffering and death (*see* Death of Christ) rather than the performance of *miracles; (2) the notion of "divine man" was not as pervasive or uniform as once thought; and (3) there is no explicit connection in Hellenistic sources between "divine man" and persons held to be "sons of the gods." It is thus preferable to look to the OT and Palestinian Judaism for the religious background to the divine sonship of Jesus.

2. Divine Sonship in the Life and Ministry of the Historical Jesus.

The issue of divine sonship in the thinking and ministry of the historical Jesus revolves around two questions: Did Jesus consider himself to be the Son of God; and if so, how did he understand this role?

2.1. Did Jesus Consider Himself to Be the Son of God? According to the Synoptic Gospels, Jesus understood himself and his mission according to divine sonship and clearly implied that he

was the Son of God. Yet there are two sets of data that may challenge the historicity of the Gospel accounts at this point.

The first challenge comes from the almost total absence in literature from Palestinian Judaism of a connection between messianic expectations and the title "Son of God." This observation has led to the conclusion that neither Jesus nor his contemporaries would have thought of the Messiah in terms of Son of God, and that the christological confession of divine sonship must have arisen with the Hellenistic church, which was responsible for introducing its confession into the traditions of Jesus' earthly ministry. But we noted above that although specific references are few, there is reason to believe that the Messiah was in fact sometimes understood in terms of divine sonship.

The second challenge involves statements in the NT which may be understood as linking the divine sonship of Jesus to his resurrection/exaltation, thereby suggesting that Jesus became Son of God at that point (esp. Acts 13:33; Rom 1:3-4). Many scholars have argued that this was the original understanding of the divine sonship of Jesus and that the early church gradually pushed the inauguration of Jesus' status as Son of God back to the Transfiguration, then to the baptism and finally to either virginal conception (*see* Birth of Jesus) or preexistence.

Virtually everyone agrees that Romans 1:3-4 reflects an early creed that Paul has included in order to establish a point of theological contact between himself and his Roman readers. It is often claimed, furthermore, that the pre-Pauline formula lacked the phrase "in power," and thus signified that Jesus became Son of God at the *resurrection. By adding this phrase Paul has transformed the meaning of the statement so as to imply that Jesus had been Son of God all along, and that at the resurrection he became Son in a new sense. But some scholars (e.g., Dunn) have argued that "in power" may have been part of the pre-Pauline formula. Moreover, even if the original formula lacked this phrase, it is possible to construe *horisthentos* of verse 4 as "designated" (so RSV) rather than "appointed," thus indicating that in the resurrection God declared Jesus to be what he had been during his earthly ministry. But ultimately the interpretation of this verse turns on prior decisions regarding the connection of Messiah with the Son title in earliest Christianity. Those who deny such a connection see a dichotomy between the earthly Jesus as Son of David and his postresurrection status as Son of God, while those who affirm the connection between Son and Messiah argue that Davidic sonship implies divine sonship.

Acts 13:33 represents a similarly ambiguous case. On the surface this quotation from Psalm 2:7 seems to intimate that Jesus was "begotten" as Son of God at the resurrection. But it is possible to maintain with Marshall that both the flow of thought in Paul's sermon and the analogy with Wisdom 2:13-18 indicate that Psalm 2:7 was employed not to establish Jesus' divine sonship on the basis of his resurrection, but rather to prove that in the resurrection God confirmed the *righteousness of his obedient Son. Thus the passage links sonship to the obedience of the earthly Jesus and not to the event of the resurrection. We conclude, then, that there is no firm evidence in the NT for the view that Jesus entered into his role as Son of God at the resurrection.

Virtually all critics agree that Jesus addressed God as *Abba*, "Father," and typically referred to God by this designation when teaching his disciples. These phenomena are firmly embedded in the earliest strata of Gospel tradition, and throughout the Synoptic Gospels it is almost exclusively the way Jesus speaks of God and his relationship to God. This does not necessarily imply, however, that every reference to "Father" in our Gospels was spoken by the historical Jesus; the wide disparity in the number of occurrences in the four Gospels suggests that at points the Evangelists may have inserted the designation into traditions they inherited.

Scholarly debate has focused on those passages in which Jesus refers to himself as the Son. A strong claim for authenticity can be made especially for Mark 13:32; 12:6; and Matthew 11:27/Luke 10:22. In the case of Mark 13:32 it is unlikely that the early *church would have created a saying that asserted the ignorance of Jesus. The objections raised to the authenticity of the parable of the tenants (Mk 12:1-12) are not convincing. The fact that the parable contains some allegorical elements does not necessarily exclude it as coming from Jesus; and the argument that it contradicts Jesus' reticence to speak publicly about his sonship fails to take seriously the oblique nature of this reference to the "son." The reference to the "sending" of the son in this passage does not suggest preexis-

tence (as in Paul), but points rather to the calling, mission and eschatological significance of Jesus. A more difficult passage is Matthew 11:27/Luke 10:22. In the face of claims that this statement reflects a relatively late—even Johannine—*christology, Jeremias has successively argued that its language, style and structure reflect Semitic usage and that the relationship between Father and Son found here accords with Jesus' statements regarding the Father encountered throughout the Synoptic Gospels.

A focus on these three statements does not imply that other passages in which Jesus speaks of himself as the Son have no historical validity. R. J. Bauckham has argued for the historical value of many of the Son sayings in the Fourth Gospel, following O. Cullmann's hypothesis that behind much of the sayings material in this Gospel stands independent tradition passed on by the "beloved disciple" and preserved by the Johannine circle. Nevertheless, the task of assessing the historical character of Johannine material is extremely complicated, and it is therefore preferable to concentrate on the earliest strands of the Synoptic tradition.

2.2. How Did Jesus Understand His Divine Sonship? An examination of the authentic sayings of Jesus regarding the "Father" and the "Son" reveals the following emphases.

2.2.1. Personal Intimacy with the Father. It points to intimate personal fellowship between Jesus and God. Jesus experienced this intimate fellowship especially through prayer, and consequently addressed God in prayer almost exclusively as "Father" (Aramaic *'Abba;* Mk 14:36; cf. Rom 8:15; Gal 4:6). Jeremias has argued that Jesus was apparently the first Jew to address God in prayer as *'Abba* (Jewish prayers typically used the obsolete and formalized Hebrew term *'Abi*), and that *'Abba* was a term of familiarity and intimacy, having originally developed from the speech of children ("daddy"). Subsequent scholarship has been unable to contradict the claim that this prayer language of *'Abba* was original with Jesus. Although Jeremias's employment of etymological considerations is questionable (Barr), his distinction between formal prayer speech, which suggests distance, and the more colloquial expression used to address earthly fathers bears the weight of critical scrutiny.

Jesus' use of *'Abba* prompts the question as to how and when Jesus came to understand himself and his messianic role in terms of this intimate filial relationship with God. The attempt to reconstruct Jesus' messianic self-consciousness is notoriously difficult. Nevertheless, the tradition itself suggests that Jesus may have become conscious of his divine sonship at the point of his *baptism. In the earliest form of the baptism account the divine voice addresses Jesus directly in the second person: "You are my beloved Son" (Mk 1:11). If this experience did not initiate Jesus' Son-consciousness, it confirmed and informed it.

2.2.2. Obedience to the Will of God. This reference to the baptism leads to a second emphasis: Absolute obedience to the will of God understood in terms of the Suffering Servant (*see* Servant of Yahweh). The divine speech at the baptism accentuates obedience: "With you I am well pleased." Moreover, the heavenly voice alludes to Psalm 2:7 and Isaiah 42:1, thereby bringing together the concepts of divine sonship and the Servant of Yahweh. Thus divine sonship is defined in terms of obedience, and obedience is described in terms of the image of the Servant. Although intertestamental Judaism sometimes connected the Messiah with the Servant of Yahweh, it failed to link vicarious suffering of the Servant to the Messiah. But there is no doubt that Jesus made this connection, and he seems to have based the connection on his understanding of his role as Son of God. Jesus' construal of his divine sonship in terms of obedient submission to suffering and death emerges also in his prayer in Gethsemane (Mk 14:32-42).

2.2.3. The Unique Son of God. The foregoing implies a further emphasis in Jesus' speech involving his divine sonship: it is exclusive. Jesus is Son of God in a unique sense. In his capacity as Son of God, Jesus has the power to bring his followers into an experience of divine sonship, but Jesus consistently distinguishes between the sonship of disciples and his own sonship. He speaks of "my Father" and "your Father," but never "our Father" (the "our" of the Lord's Prayer [Mt 6:9] is what the disciples are to say).

It is clear that in the authentic statements from the Synoptic Gospels Jesus did not speak of his divine sonship in terms of preexistence or focus on ontological realities (such as his divine "nature"). Rather, Jesus emphasized the elements of personal relationship and active function.

3. Divine Sonship in the Christology of the Gospels.

Although there is wide disparity in the number of occurrences of "Son (of God)" and "Father" in the four Gospels, each of the Gospels gives significant attention to Jesus' divine sonship, and may in fact present "Son of God" as the preeminent christological title.

3.1. Mark. "Son (of God)" appears in Mark's Gospel only eight times and "Father" (referring to God) only four. Yet these titles surface at crucial points in Mark and play a role in the christology of the Gospel that surpasses their few occurrences (*see* Mark, Gospel of).

Scholars have generally recognized the importance of this title for Mark's christology, but they have assessed its function differently. Many authorities have linked the title to the concept of divine man, described above, arguing that in this Gospel Jesus became Son of God at his baptism when the Spirit descended upon him, thus providing him with divine power according to which he performed miracles and exorcisms. There is, however, a division among scholars who hold this divine man theory: some maintain that the Evangelist himself espoused such a christology, while others contend that Mark presented this portrait of Jesus as divine man only to correct it by presenting Jesus above all as the suffering Son of man. Indeed, scholars such as Perrin have argued that because the title Son of God could be linked to the divine man concept which Mark himself rejects, Mark has subordinated this title to that of *Son of man, which unambiguously points to Jesus' suffering and death.

The difficulties of employing the concept of divine man in NT christology were discussed above. In addition to these problems it should be observed that Mark gives unqualified approval to the title Son of God and understands this title primarily in terms of Jesus' obedient suffering and death. There is no evidence that Mark holds Son of God and Son of man in tension, nor that he gives prominence to the latter over the former.

Mark indicates the importance of this title for his christology by placing it within the general heading to the Gospel (Mk 1:1). The specific meaning of Jesus' divine sonship begins to come to expression in the account of the baptism (Mk 1:9-11), where the heavenly voice declares, "You are my beloved Son, with you I am well pleased."

This pericope indicates that God views Jesus primarily in terms of divine sonship and that Jesus' role as Son of God involves especially obedience to his Father. As mentioned above, the heavenly declaration alludes to Isaiah 42:1 and thus links the divine sonship of Jesus to his role as the Suffering Servant of Yahweh.

God makes this announcement to Jesus alone; at this point in the narrative, only God and Jesus are aware that Jesus is Son of God. In Mark 3:11 and 5:7 the demons address Jesus as "Son of (the Most High) God" (cf. Mk 1:24, 34), which seems to indicate they were privy to the divine communication at the baptism. Nevertheless, Jesus does not wish his divine sonship to be publicly announced and consequently commands the demons to be silent. The observation that Jesus also commands silence from those who were healed (Mk 1:43-44; 5:43; cf. 7:24) suggests the reason for this messianic secret. The Markan Jesus does not wish to be proclaimed as Son of God until it is clear his divine sonship involves not spectacular miracles but suffering and death. Hence, the secret of Jesus' divine sonship is revealed only gradually.

In Mark 9:7 the divine communication originally voiced at the baptism is repeated in the presence of the inner circle of the *disciples, but they will not understand what it means until after the resurrection (Mk 9:9-13). In Mark 12:6, in the course of the *parable of the tenants, Jesus speaks of the sending of a "son"; the religious authorities apparently understood Jesus to be referring to himself, since at the trial before the Sanhedrin they accuse him with the question "Are you the Christ, the Son of the Blessed?" (Mk 15:39; cf. 12:12). Yet they remain ignorant of Jesus' identity as Son of God, for they reject the very idea as a blasphemous claim (see Trial of Jesus).

It is only in Mark 15:39 that the secret of Jesus' status as Son of God is fully revealed to humans. As the centurion faces the cross he declares, "Truly this man was the Son of God." By bringing his Gospel to a climax with this christological confession at the cross, Mark indicates that Jesus is first and foremost Son of God, and that Jesus is Son of God as one who suffers and dies in obedience to God (cf. Mk 14:36). Yet this title relates not only to Jesus' earthly mission but also to his resurrection (Mk 12:10-11; cf. 9:9) and Second Coming (Mk 8:38; 13:32), for Mark emphasizes that it is precisely Jesus crucified as Son

of God who is raised (Mk 16:6) and will return in glory (Mk 14:61-62).

3.2. Matthew. Although various scholars have seen Matthew's focus in different titles, many today would argue that Son of God is the preeminent christological title in *Matthew. The First Evangelist retains virtually all of Mark's statements regarding the sonship of Jesus and the fatherhood of God, while adding ten references to Jesus as Son (of God) and forty references to God as Father. According to Matthew's Gospel, Son of God is the only adequate christological confession, and one can come to this understanding of Jesus solely through divine revelation (Mt 16:13-17; cf. 27:51-54).

Although Matthew begins by connecting Jesus' divine sonship to his virginal conception (Mt 1:18-25), he does not develop the notion of the divine nature of Jesus, but focuses instead on more functional aspects of Jesus' sonship. In this Gospel Jesus is Son of God primarily in the sense that he perfectly obeys the will of his Father, especially the will of God that the Messiah must suffer and die.

The emphasis on obedience to the will of the Father appears already in the baptism narrative (Mt 3:13-17). As in Mark, the heavenly voice expresses divine approval. But Matthew goes beyond Mark in stressing the obedience of Jesus: Jesus submits to baptism "to fulfill all righteousness" (Mt 3:15; see Righteousness); and immediately after the baptism Jesus is tempted in his capacity as Son of God, and as Son of God he refuses to yield to Satan's temptations (Mt 4:1-11; see Temptation of Jesus). Here Jesus is tempted to manifest his divine sonship through the performance of spectacular signs but chooses instead to demonstrate his sonship through submission to the Father's will.

This reference to temptation indicates that the Matthean Jesus struggles with the will of God regarding the nature of his messianic role. In Matthew 16:22-23 Peter assumes the role of Satan in that he, like Satan in the wilderness temptations, would turn Jesus aside from obedience to the Father's will for the Messiah and would encourage Jesus to construe his sonship in ways other than obedient suffering and death. In Gethsemane Jesus voices his desire to avoid the "cup" of suffering, but as Son of God he yields to the will of his Father (Mt 26:39, 42). Indeed, Matthew presents the event of the crucifixion as the ultimate temptation for Jesus as well as the climactic expression of his sonship. Jesus is condemned to death on the charge that he claimed to be the Son of God (Mt 26:63). Twice the passersby tempt Jesus to demonstrate his divine sonship by the sign of coming down from the cross (Mt 27:40, 43). But, as in his earlier temptations, Jesus refuses to yield to such appeals and dies as the righteous one who places his trust in God (Mt 27:43). In response to the obedience of Jesus his Son, God himself provides the signs (Mt 27:51-53), which prompt the centurion to declare, "Truly this was the Son of God" (Mt 27:54).

In addition to this focus on obedience to the will of God, there are three related dimensions to Jesus' divine sonship in Matthew: (1) As Son of God, Jesus knows the Father and his will and has unique authority to interpret that will (Mt 5:17-48; 7:28-29; 11:25-27). (2) Because Jesus is Son of God his disciples also become sons of God who address God as "Father." Their sonship, like his, is characterized above all by obedience to God's will (Mt 12:50). (3) Because Jesus remained the obedient Son until the end, his Father has given him "all authority in heaven and on earth" (Mt 28:18); he now reigns as Son (Mt 28:19; 24:36) and will return in that capacity (Mt 10:32; 16:27; 25:31-46).

3.3. Luke. The divine sonship of Jesus receives relatively less attention in Luke than in the other Gospels. Luke's allusions to Jesus as Son of God are for the most part taken over from tradition, and in fact Luke omits some references to Jesus' divine sonship found in Mark (Mk 13:32; 15:39). Still, the concept plays a significant role in Luke's Gospel. In fact, some scholars argue that it is the foremost christological title in this Gospel (e.g., Kingsbury).

Luke establishes the basic contours of Jesus' divine sonship in three passages at the beginning of the Gospel. The annunciation to Mary highlights several dimensions of Jesus' divine sonship (Lk 1:32-35). First, Jesus is Son of God as one who has been conceived by the Holy Spirit. Although Luke is moving toward understanding divine sonship in ontological terms (i.e., the divine nature of Jesus), he does little to develop his *christology along these lines. Rather, Luke suggests that the conception of Jesus by the Spirit (see Holy Spirit) forms the basis of Jesus' intimate personal relationship with God, a theme that stands at the center of the presentation of divine sonship throughout the Gospel (Lk 2:49;

10:21-22). Indeed, by having Jesus address God as "Father" on the cross, Luke indicates that even at that point in Jesus' life his intimate fellowship with God continues unabated (Lk 23:34, 46). Second, as Son of God Jesus inherits the *kingdom that God had promised to the Son of David, thus pointing to transcendent rule and authority (cf. Lk 22:28-30). Third, as Son of God Jesus is holy, set apart for the special service of bringing salvation to the people of God (Lk 1:68-69; 2:11; 19:9-10).

The second key passage for understanding Jesus' divine sonship is the genealogy (Lk 3:23-38). The genealogy begins by describing Jesus as the "supposed" son of Joseph, suggesting that he was not actually the son of Joseph but Son of God through divine conception (Lk 1:32-35). But this statement also points to the mystery of Jesus' divine sonship: God (Lk 3:22; 9:35), the devil (Lk 4:3, 9) and demons (Lk 4:41; 8:28) address Jesus as Son of God, but humans do not. They suppose him to be son of Joseph (Lk 4:22), that is, he is explicable in purely human terms. Consequently, they tend to remain blind to his transcendent power and authority. Moreover, Luke traces the genealogy of Jesus through *Adam to God (Lk 3:38), thus indicating that as God's Son Jesus has power to bring all humanity to its destiny as sons of God.

The temptation narrative (Lk 4:1-13) demonstrates that Jesus' divine sonship involves perfect obedience to the will of the Father (Lk 2:49; 23:47) and the exercise of authority over Satan and the forces of evil (Lk 10:17-19; 11:17-23; 13:11-17).

3.4. John. The Fourth Gospel places the divine sonship of Jesus at the center of its christology (see John, Gospel of). The Gospel speaks of "Son (of God)" twenty-nine times and refers to God as "Father" over a hundred times. Moreover, John expressly states that the purpose of his Gospel is to confirm his readers in the belief that "Jesus is the Christ, the Son of God" (Jn 20:31). Although John incorporates most of the main elements in the Synoptic presentation of Son of God, his portrait of Jesus' divine sonship is distinct from that found in the Synoptic Gospels.

One of the points of distinction between the Synoptic portrayal of Jesus as Son of God and that of the Fourth Gospel involves the preexistence of the Son. While the Synoptics nowhere describe Jesus' sonship in terms of preexistence, John begins his Gospel by linking the "Word" *(logos),* operative at creation, to the Son (Jn 1:1-18); and at subsequent points in the Gospel, Jesus Son of God speaks of his preincarnate existence (Jn 8:56-58; 17:5, 24). Yet John relates Jesus' divine sonship primarily to his earthly functioning. This Gospel emphasizes that God *sent* his Son into the world (Jn 3:17; 10:36; 17:18), and that he has come from the Father (Jn 3:31; 6:33-42) and is about to return to the Father (Jn 13:1-3; 14:28; 16:28; 20:17). He thus reflects God's person and glory (Jn 1:14; 14:6-11).

Jesus' role as Son of God is characterized by the following four elements. First, Jesus Son of God perfectly obeys the will of his Father (Jn 4:34; 5:30; 6:38; 7:28; 8:29); even his coming into the world reflects his obedience to the Father's will (Jn 8:42). Second, as Son of God Jesus shares the work of the Father (Jn 5:19; 9:4; 10:37), including those tasks belonging uniquely to God: giving life to the dead (Jn 5:21, 24; 6:40) and performing *judgment (Jn 5:22, 27-29; 8:16). Indeed, Jesus says nothing except what he has heard from the Father (Jn 3:32-34; 12:49-50; 15:15) and does nothing except what he has seen the Father do (Jn 5:20; 8:38). The works he does are actually the Father's works performed through him (Jn 5:17; 9:4; 10:32). Third, as Son of God Jesus enjoys intimate fellowship with the Father. John describes this intimacy in spatial terms: "in the bosom of the Father" (Jn 1:18). Specifically, this relationship involves (1) "knowing" the Father and his will (Jn 4:22-23; 6:45-47; 8:55; 15:15); (2) sharing in all that the Father has (Jn 16:15); and (3) enjoying special access and influence with the Father (Jn 14:13-16). Fourth, the relationship between the Father and the Son is characterized by love: The Father loves the Son (Jn 3:35; 5:20; 10:17; 17:23) and the Son loves the Father (Jn 14:31). The Father expresses his love for the Son by giving to the Son all things (Jn 3:35; 13:3), especially those who come to the Son (Jn 6:37, 44, 65; 10:29; 17:2).

All of this implies that the divine sonship of Jesus is unique; he is Son of God in a sense not true of anyone else, even believers. John calls attention to this uniqueness by designating Jesus the "only" *(monogenēs)* Son (Jn 1:14, 18; 3:16) and by constantly employing the absolute forms "the Father" and "the Son." In John's Gospel the disciples are never called "sons," nor do they address God as "Father." Only once is God described as the "Father" of disciples (Jn 20:17),

and there the distinction between "my Father" and "your Father" is emphasized.

The proclamation that Jesus is Son of God forces the decision of faith. Persons are called to believe that Jesus is the Son whom God has sent into the world, and the decision they make regarding this call to belief will determine the quality of their present existence as well as their eternal destiny (Jn 3:17-21, 36; 5:24; 11:26). Believing in the Son is the "work" which God requires. This belief involves, specifically, obeying the Son (Jn 3:36), coming to the Son (Jn 14:6) and honoring the Son (Jn 5:23). Such belief will result in salvation (Jn 5:34) and life (Jn 6:40, 47; 20:31).

See also CHRIST; GOD; SON OF DAVID; SON OF MAN.

DJG: DIVINE MAN/*THEIOS ANĒR.*

BIBLIOGRAPHY. J. Barr, " 'Abba' Isn't 'Daddy,'" *JTS* 39 (1988) 28-47; R. Bauckham, "The Sonship of the Historical Jesus in Christology," *SJT* 31 (1978) 245-60; O. Cullmann, *The Christology of the New Testament* (Philadelphia: Westminster, 1963); J. D. G. Dunn, *Christology in the Making* (Philadelphia: Westminster, 1980); J. Fitzmyer, "The Contribution of Qumran Aramaic to the Study of the New Testament," *NTS* 20 (1973-74) 382-407; F. Hahn, *The Titles of Jesus in Christology* (London: Lutterworth, 1969); L. W. Hurtado, *Lord Jesus Christ* (Grand Rapids: Eerdmans, 2003); J. Jeremias, *The Prayers of Jesus* (Philadelphia: Fortress, 1978); M. de Jonge, *Christology in Context* (Philadelphia: Westminster, 1988); J. D. Kingsbury, *Jesus Christ in Matthew, Mark, and Luke* (Philadelphia: Fortress, 1981); idem, *The Christology of Mark's Gospel* (Philadelphia: Fortress, 1983); I. H. Marshall, *The Origins of New Testament Christology* (rev. ed.; Downers Grove, IL: InterVarsity Press, 1990); W. von Martitz, "υἱός, υἱοθεσία," *TDNT* 8.334-40; N. Perrin, *A Modern Pilgrimage in New Testament Christology* (Philadelphia: Fortress, 1974); R. Schnackenburg, *The Gospel according to St. John* (New York: Crossroad, 1987); G. Vermes, *Jesus the Jew* (Philadelphia: Fortress, 1973); B. Witherington, *The Christology of Jesus* (Minneapolis: Fortress, 1990). D. R. Bauer

SON OF GOD II: PAUL

The divine sonship of Jesus is a major component of Paul's *christology, though in Paul's letters the references to Jesus as God's "Son" (seventeen times in the entire traditional Pauline corpus and only four instances of the full title "Son of God") are considerably fewer than Paul's many designations of Jesus as *"Lord" and *"Christ." Some have alleged that the idea of Jesus' divine sonship was an appropriation of pagan religious traditions, and that Paul thereby presented Jesus after the fashion of Greco-Roman cult deities (*see* Religions, Greco-Roman), but the evidence concerning the pagan religious background and Paul's use of the divine "Son" language goes against this.

Paul did not employ the language of divine sonship primarily to claim that Jesus was divine. Essentially Paul's references to Jesus as God's "Son" communicate Jesus' unique status and intimate relationship with God. But the contexts of these references supply several additional and more particular nuances to the term. In some passages Jesus is presented as God's regally enthroned Son, drawing on OT traditions of the Davidic king as "Son" of God (e.g., Ps 2:6-7). In others Paul seems to allude to the offering of Isaac (Gen 22) to represent Jesus' death as the supreme act of redemptive love (e.g., Rom 8:32). Also, Paul presents God's Son as the one sent forth to provide the standing with God for which the Torah was incapable. And Paul also portrays Jesus' divine sonship as the pattern for, and basis of, the enfranchisement of Christians as "sons of God."

1. Background
2. Jesus
3. Jesus' Divine Sonship Outside Paul
4. Paul's Usage

1. Background.

1.1. Pagan. In older history-of-religions scholarship, as represented by W. Bousset, Paul's references to "the Son of God" were taken as intended to denote Jesus as a divine being after the fashion of allegedly prominent pagan traditions about sons of gods with which Paul's Gentile converts would have been familiar (Bousset, 206-10). Though others (e.g., Schoeps) have repeated this viewpoint, it is not persuasive in light of the main body of scholarly analysis which has on the whole confirmed Paul's fundamental conceptual indebtedness to his Jewish tradition and his disdain for pagan religion (e.g., Blank, Hengel, Kim).

Moreover, Bousset's idea that to communicate his message among his pagan converts Paul misguidedly appropriated pagan traditions that produced a fundamentally new christology is not borne out by a careful reading of what Paul says about Jesus or by the relevant evidence from Greco-Roman pagan religion. As A. D. Nock (1972) and M. Hengel (21-41) have shown, it is difficult to find true Greco-Roman parallels that would account for Paul's view of Jesus as God's "Son" or render it more intelligible to Paul's Gentile converts. The human race could be referred to as offspring of Zeus or other gods, but this generality seems irrelevant to the particular significance Paul attached to Jesus as God's unique Son. A great man (e.g., Alexander the Great) might be styled as a son of a god, but this appears to have been essentially an honorific gesture in recognition of some quality in the man such as wisdom or military prowess, and it is not clear that the man so designated was really thought of as anything other than an exceptionally impressive human being. In fact the designation "son of god" was not common in Greco-Roman paganism and seems to have been used as a title only by Roman emperors (Latin *divi filius* rendered in Greek as *theou huios*). The deities of the so-called "mystery cults," for example, to which the early history-of-religions school attached such importance, were not referred to as "sons of god." Any influence of Roman emperor devotion upon early christology was probably much later than Paul and likely involved Christian recoil from what was regarded as blasphemous rather than as something to be appropriated (e.g., Cuss). Nock's judgment concerning the Pauline use of "Son of God" still holds: "the attempts which have been made to explain it from the larger Hellenistic world fail" (Nock 1964, 45).

1.2. Jewish. Consequently, most scholars have turned to the Jewish sources as more directly relevant background for Paul's references to Jesus' divine sonship. In Paul's Bible, the OT, the language of divine sonship is used with three types of referents. In passages that likely reflect an older usage, angels are referred to as "sons of God" (e.g., Gen 6:2-4; Deut 32:8; Ps 29:1; 89:6). Although in a number of cases in the LXX the Hebrew or Aramaic phrase "son(s) of God" is rendered in Greek as "angel(s) of God" (e.g., Deut 32:8; Job 1:6; 2:1; Dan 3:25), this is not consistently done (cf. Deut 32:43 LXX), showing that heavenly beings could still be referred to as "sons of God" among Greek-speaking Jews of the Greco-Roman period.

In some OT passages the Davidic king is referred to as God's "son" (2 Sam 7:14; Ps 2:7; 89:26-27). Psalm 2:7 refers to God having "begotten" the king, but it appears that this poetic language was a way of asserting his divine legitimation, with his enthronement being taken as a kind of divine adoption.

Royal Davidic traditions issued into Jewish messianic hopes of Paul's time. There is, however, no unambiguous evidence that the expression "son of God" was a messianic title, and it is difficult to say how widely the concept of divine sonship was a part of messianic expectation. The document known as 2 Esdras, or 4 Ezra, has several references to a messianic "son" of God in the surviving versions of this writing (e.g., Latin *filius* in 7:28; 13:32, 37, 52; 14:9), but it is now commonly accepted that these all are Christian translations of the Greek term *pais* ("servant"), which in turn may have rendered the equivalent Hebrew term ʿ*ebed*. Similarly, 2 Baruch 70:9 refers to "my Servant, the Anointed One."

The Qumran text 4Q174 (4QFlorilegium) contains a commentary on 2 Samuel 7:11-14, where God promises to make David's descendant God's "son," and the commentary applies the passage to the royal messiah. Since first notices of its existence in 1972, the Qumran document 4Q246 has received a great deal of attention because it refers to a ruler who will be acclaimed with the titles "son of God" and "son of the Most High," the same titles given to Jesus in Luke 1:32-35 (see, e.g., Fitzmyer, 90-94). Owing to the fragmentary nature of the document, it is difficult to be certain, but the eschatological flavor makes it quite possible that this document furnishes further evidence that the attribution of divine sonship, including the use of the title "son of God," was part of the messianism of at least some Jews (see Collins, 154-72).

One of the ways Philo refers to the *Logos is as God's "firstborn son" (e.g., Philo *Som.* 1.215; *Conf. Ling.* 146), but there seems to be no direct connection between this and Paul's use of the term for Jesus. Instead, Philo exhibits an independent appropriation of an OT designation of the king (Ps 89:27) and of Israel (Ex 4:22), which, however, may illustrate how biblical imagery and concepts could be adapted to later religious belief, as seems to be the case also in the NT.

In fact the most common applications of the concept of divine sonship in ancient Jewish texts are with reference to the righteous individual, righteous Jews collectively and Israel as God's chosen people. In a number of OT passages Israelites are called God's "sons" (Deut 14:1; Is 1:2; Jer 3:22; Hos 1:10) and collectively God's "firstborn" (Ex 4:22) and "son" (Hos 11:1). And in extracanonical Jewish texts these applications are frequent: Wisdom 2:18; 5:5; Sirach 4:10; *Psalms of Solomon* 13:9; 18:4 (righteous individuals); Wisdom 12:21; 16:10, 26; 18:4, 13 (Israel). In *Joseph and Asenath,* likewise, the righteous Israelites are called "sons" of "the living God" or "the Most High" (*Jos. and As.* 16:14; 19:8), and Joseph (who seems to be an idealized representation of the righteous Jew or of Israel) is acclaimed several times as "son" and "firstborn son" of God (*Jos. and As.* 6:3-5; 13:13; 18:11; 21:4; 23:10).

Vermes (206-11) has cited rabbinic texts in which ancient Jewish holy men are referred to as a "son" of God in the sense of being especially favored by God. With due caution about using such late texts to illustrate first-century Jewish religion, we may take the rabbinic figures Vermes cites as examples of the application to particular righteous individuals of the category of divine sonship as affirmed in Wisdom of Solomon and Sirach mentioned earlier.

2. Jesus.

It is widely accepted among scholars that Jesus spoke of God as "Father" (Aramaic ʾ*abbā*ʾ) in ways that expressed unusual familiarity and intimacy, and that he conducted himself in ways that reflect a profound sense of a special status and responsibility toward God. It is reasonable, therefore, to consider whether these features of Jesus' ministry might have influenced the view of Jesus as God's Son in Paul and early Christianity. For the present purpose we can make only a few relevant observations.

First, it seems likely that Jesus' own religious parlance and practice would have been of intense interest and relevance for his followers, both during Jesus' ministry and, especially in light of the conviction that he had been resurrected, in the early years afterward. Second, Paul's preservation of the Aramaic term *abba* in his Greek-speaking churches and his use of it in contexts mentioning Jesus' divine sonship (Rom 8:15; Gal 4:6, the earliest Christian references to the term) are probably best accounted for as indications that traditions about Jesus' relationship with God were known and were in fact influential in shaping the early Christian view of him as God's Son.

Early christology of course was mainly driven by the conviction that the crucified Jesus had been *resurrected and exalted to heavenly glory. But it is likely also that the traditions stemming from Jesus' ministry encouraged especially the identification of him as God's "Son," though the meaning attached to that identification seems to have grown far more exalted in the light of his resurrection and heavenly glorification than was ever explicit or even possible in Jesus' own ministry.

3. Jesus' Divine Sonship Outside Paul.

3.1. Pre-Pauline Tradition. A number of scholars have argued that Paul's references to Jesus' divine sonship show earmarks of "pre-Pauline" belief in Jesus as God's "Son," especially Romans 1:1-4; 1 Thessalonians 1:10; Galatians 4:4-6; and Romans 8:3. It is, however, misleading to speak of a christological "formula" of the divinely-sent-forth Son in Paul, which some have alleged in Romans 8:3 and Galatians 4:4. These two Pauline references use different Greek verbs, and have in common only the concept of the Son being divinely sent from God, an obvious enough way of referring to a figure seen as operating on a divine mandate.

As for Romans 1:3-4, M. Hengel (59) and J. M. Scott (236) have noted that attempts to reconstruct the actual wording of a pre-Pauline creedal statement from Romans 1:3-4 have amounted to unverifiable (and divergent) hypotheses. Nevertheless, the passage may well preserve basic pre-Pauline convictions about Jesus as Davidic heir by physical descent *(kata sarka)* now "appointed *[horisthentos]* the Son of God in/with power *[en dynamei]*" by virtue of his resurrection *[ex anastaseōs]*. Likewise, 1 Thessalonians 1:9-10, which refers to Jesus as God's Son who has been resurrected to heavenly status and will come as deliverer from eschatological wrath, is widely regarded as evidence of "pre-Pauline" divine-Son christology. But if these passages do preserve pre-Pauline tradition, Paul's appropriation of the traditions shows that he saw no essential discontinuity between his view of Jesus and that of his predecessors and of the Jewish-Christian churches such as the one in Jerusalem.

3.2. After Paul. Jesus' divine sonship is of considerable importance in the Synoptic Gospels, which were written after Paul's letters, and

carries varying connotations in each of the Evangelists (*see* Son of God I). In Matthew, Jesus' divine sonship, though infrequently mentioned, has a very strong messianic connotation and connection (e.g., Mt 16:16), and the disciples acclaim him as God's Son (e.g., Mt 14:33). A similar messianic connotation to divine sonship appears in Luke (e.g., Lk 1:32-35). In Mark, however, the claim is closely connected with the secrecy of Jesus' true (transcendent) identity and (with the ironic exception in Mk 15:39) only God (Mk 1:11; 9:7) and demons (e.g., Mk 3:11; 5:7) recognize Jesus' divine sonship.

Jesus' divine sonship is important also in *Hebrews, where his status as Son distinguishes him above prophets (Heb 1:1-2) and also angels (Heb 1:3-14; 2:5). Indeed, in Hebrews 1:2 the Son is "heir of all things," giving his sonship a cosmic-scale significance.

It is, however, in John that Jesus' divine sonship has a transcendent connotation expressed with an explicitness and emphasis unmatched in any other NT writing. From the Baptist's confession (Jn 1:34) to the climactic purpose statement in John 20:31, the Fourth Evangelist emphasizes that Jesus is to be recognized as God's Son. And he makes it explicit that the Son is of heavenly origin (e.g., Jn 1:14; 17:1-5). In John, Jesus' claim to be God's Son amounts to a claim to divinity, as illustrated by the charges of blasphemy from Jewish characters in the story (Jn 5:18; 10:36; 19:7).

This Johannine emphasis flowered in the faith of Christianity subsequently, for "Son of God" became the most favored way of referring to Jesus as divine and was used to distinguish Jesus' divinity from his human nature, as seen already in Ignatius (*Eph.* 20:2). As Dunn has noted, no other christological expression "has had both the historical depth and lasting power of 'Son of God' " (Dunn, 12). But we must be careful to determine Paul's connotations in referring to Jesus as God's Son without reading into it the way the term was used by later Christians.

4. Paul's Usage.

In the thirteen writings attributed to Paul in the NT, the title "the Son of God" is neither fixed nor frequently used, appearing only four times and in varying Greek word order (Rom 1:4; 2 Cor 1:19; Gal 2:20; Eph 4:13). In the remaining thirteen references to Jesus' divine sonship, we find "his Son" (Rom 1:3, 9; 5:10; 8:29, 32; 1 Cor 1:9;

Gal 1:16; 4:4, 6; 1 Thess 1:10), "his own Son" (Rom 8:3), "the Son" (1 Cor 15:28) and "the Son of his love" (Col 1:13). The conviction that Jesus is God's Son was apparently what mattered to Paul, not so much the christological title or fixed verbal formulas to express that conviction.

In all of his references to Jesus as God's Son, Paul uses the Greek definite article, not always easily represented in translations. The connotation of the definite article is that Paul views Jesus' divine sonship as unique, and does not accord Jesus membership in a class of other figures who may be regarded as sons of God such as we encounter in the Jewish or pagan sources (e.g., angels, the righteous, great men, wonder workers; but see 4.5 below).

It is also important, as Hengel has pointed out, that Paul refers to Jesus as God's Son mainly (eleven times) in Romans and Galatians (Hengel, 7). Both the comparative infrequency and the distribution of Paul's references to Jesus as God's Son suggest that for Paul Jesus' divine sonship did not constitute an appropriation of a pagan mythological concept as the crucial means of justifying the worship of the man Jesus among Gentile converts (contra Bousset, 208-9). Instead, Paul refers to God's Son in terms adapted from the Jewish background to make boldly exclusivist christological assertions in ways and contexts that interact directly with traditional Jewish concerns. These included the Torah (*see* Law), the unique significance of *Israel, messianic hopes and the fundamentally monotheistic outlook which Paul continued to share and promote in his churches (*see* God).

From the entire fabric of Paul's christology, it is apparent that Paul saw Jesus as participating in God's attributes and roles, as sharing in the divine glory and, most importantly, as worthy to receive formal veneration with God in Christian assemblies (*see* Worship). So we may say that the one Paul called "the Son of God" was regarded by him as divine in some unique way. But neither in the Jewish background of Paul nor in his own usage (unlike John's) did the language of divine sonship in itself attribute divinity. In Paul's Jewish tradition to call a human figure God's "Son" meant primarily to attribute to him a special standing, status and favor with God. Paul's references to Jesus as the "Son" of God meant that Jesus possessed a unique standing, status and favor with God.

In order to determine specifically what Jesus'

sonship connoted for Paul, we must look more closely at the references in question. We shall concentrate on references in the letters whose Pauline authorship is almost universally accepted (though Col 1:13 and Eph 4:13 in fact fit the categories established in the undisputed letters). We shall try to establish Paul's meaning by paying attention to the contexts.

4.1. The Gospel and the Son. In Romans 1:9 Paul refers to "the gospel of his [God's] Son," an unusual phrase in Paul (in addition to the numerous references to "the gospel," cf. "the gospel of God," Rom 1:1; 15:16; 2 Cor 11:7; 1 Thess 2:2, 8, 9; and "the gospel of Christ," Rom 15:19; 1 Cor 9:12; 2 Cor 2:12; 10:14; Gal 1:7; Phil 1:27; 1 Thess 3:2). It appears that the phrase is connected with the nearby references to Jesus as God's Son (Rom 1:2-4), and with the larger discussion in Romans in which Jesus' divine sonship is mentioned a number of times (seven of the seventeen instances in the traditional Pauline corpus; cf. 2 Cor 4:4, where the unique phrase "the gospel of the glory of Christ" appears to be linked similarly with the contextual discussion of Christ's divine glory in 2 Cor 3:12—4:6). But, though unique here in Paul, "the gospel of his Son" shows that Paul could refer to his message and ministry as concerned with Jesus' divine sonship. And the prominence given to Jesus' sonship in Romans and Galatians further suggests that the identification of Jesus as God's Son was more important to Paul than might at first be assumed, especially in portraying Jesus' redemptive significance in theocentric contexts and vis-á-vis Jewish religious themes.

This suggestion is underscored by Paul's description in Galatians 1:15-16 of the experience that turned him from opponent to apostle of Jesus: God "was pleased to reveal his Son to me [*en emoi*]" (Gal 1:16). To be sure, Paul elsewhere refers to having seen "Jesus the Lord" (1 Cor 9:1) and includes himself in a list of those to whom "Christ" appeared (1 Cor 15:1-8). But Galatians 1:15-16 indicates that the experience in question included the realization that Jesus is God's unique Son *(ton huion autou)* and that his calling was to proclaim God's Son (Gal 1:16) specifically among the Gentiles. Paul had certainly already heard Jewish-Christian claims about Jesus, which he probably regarded as repugnant glorification of a false prophet, and which likely formed part of his reason for zealously opposing Jewish Christians in the name of Jewish tradition (Gal 1:13-14). In ancient Jewish tradition to hail a despised figure as a son of God was to accede to the figure's divine legitimation and *righteousness (e.g., Wis 2:12-20; 5:1-8). Paul's reference to the revelation that Jesus is the Son of God *(ton huion autou)*, therefore, can be taken as connoting that the experience involved for Paul a direct reversal of his view of Jesus, from false prophet to God's unique representative.

4.2. The Royal Son. In several passages Paul portrays Jesus in a royal status and role, drawing upon OT Davidic traditions and applying them to Jesus as royal-messianic "Son" of God. We have already noted two of these passages as possible evidence of "pre-Pauline" christology. In Romans 1:3-4 there are echoes of 2 Samuel 7:12-14. As "seed *[sperma]* of David," Jesus was "raised up *[anastasis]* from the dead" by God (cf. the LXX of 2 Samuel 7:12: "I will raise up *[anastēsō]* your seed *[to sperma sou]*"). And Jesus' appointment in power as divine Son in Romans 1:4 may echo God's promise in 2 Samuel 7:14, "I will be father to him and he will be to me a son." As well, we may have here an allusion to Psalm 2:7, where God announces that he has "begotten" the king as his Son (a symbolic description of the king's enthronement). And Paul's reference to his mission to secure "obedience of faith among all the nations/Gentiles *[ethnesin]*" (Rom 1:5) may allude to God's promise to the royal "Son" in Psalm 2:8 to give "the nations *[ethnē]* as your inheritance."

In 1 Thessalonians 1:9-10, as in Romans 1:4, Jesus' sonship is mentioned in connection with God having resurrected *[ēgeiren]* him from death. Although we do not have allusions to OT Davidic passages here, nevertheless as the divine Son who delivers from (divine) eschatological wrath (1 Thess 1:10), Jesus is given a messianic role that can be compared with messianic expectations at Qumran and in such documents as *Psalms of Solomon* 17—18. This eschatological flavor, plus the contrast between pagan "idols" and "the living and true God" (1 Thess 1:9), all reflect strongly the Jewish religious background, providing further indication that the divine "Son" here who acts on God's behalf is, as in Romans 1:3-4, God's messianic representative.

Another reference to God's Son with a royal-messianic flavor is found in 1 Corinthians 15:24-28. Royal imagery abounds, with mention of a "kingdom" (1 Cor 15:24), Christ reigning (1 Cor 15:25) and the putting of all "enemies under his feet" (1 Cor 15:25, an allusion to Ps 110:1, a Davidic royal psalm frequently cited and alluded to in the NT). After "all things" (including death, 1 Cor 15:26) have been subjected to this royal Son, he will then "be subjected" to God (1 Cor 15:28), a thought which further shows that the Son here is not a new and rival deity after the fashion of pagan mythology but functions (as the OT king and the messiah figures) on God's behalf. And, if Colossians be accepted as from Paul, the reference in Colossians 1:13 to "the kingdom of the Son of his [God's] love" likewise alludes to Jesus in royal-messianic dress.

Certainly the scope and basis of Jesus' sonship in Paul's references are far beyond that of the OT Davidic kings. In Jewish messianic expectations it is perhaps only in the "Elect One" of *1 Enoch* (37—71) who sits on God's throne and seems to be clothed with transcendent attributes that we find anything approaching Paul's references to Jesus, the glorious and heavenly Son. And there is absolutely no parallel for the idea that the messianic figure was to be resurrected and thereby constituted God's Son who exercises divine power and authority. But in the passages considered, Paul uses motifs, language and imagery from the Jewish royal-messianic tradition in expressing these bold beliefs about Jesus' exalted place in God's plan.

4.3. The Sacrificed Son. In at least three other passages Paul refers to Jesus as God's Son explicitly as given over, or having given himself, to redemptive death. A striking example is Romans 8:32, where Paul says that God "did not withhold his own Son but gave him up for us all." The statement is made even more stunning theologically if one notices that "gave up" *(paradidōmi)* is the same verb Paul uses sonorously three times in Romans 1:24-28 to refer to God giving up sinful humanity to judgment, making Jesus' death just as much a deliberate and solemn act of God as the divine wrath against human *sin spoken of in Romans 1. In Romans 8:32, however, the Son is given up for the sake of sinful humans, and provides assurance that they will not be condemned and separated from God.

But what is the significance of designating as God's "Son" the one given over in Romans 8:32? In Romans 4:25 Paul uses the verb *paradidōmi* to refer to "Jesus our Lord" being given up to death "for our transgression," and in Romans 8:34, shortly after the statement we are examining, Paul mentions "Christ Jesus who died," illustrating Paul's flexibility in language and christological titles referring to Jesus' death. The reason for the choice of "Son" in Romans 8:32 seems to be that Paul here wishes to emphasize God's personal investment, so to speak, in Jesus' sacrificial death: It is the death of God's Son (see Schweizer, 384).

Paul appears to have used a bold scriptural allusion to underscore this point. The phrase "did not withhold [ouk epheisato] his own Son" in Romans 8:32 seems intended to recall the words of the angel to *Abraham, "you have not withheld [ouk epheisō] your son, your only son" (Gen 22:12, 16), likening thereby God's offering up of Jesus to Abraham's offering of Isaac.

It is this emphasis on what Jesus' death represented for God that also likely accounts for Paul's reference to "the death of his [God's] Son" in Romans 5:10. The context illustrates Paul's general tendency to use the title "Christ" in references to Jesus' death (Rom 5:6, 8; and cf. the fuller "our Lord Jesus Christ" in Rom 5:11), especially in christocentric statements that portray the death as an act of Jesus. But Romans 5:10-11 has a theocentric focus on reconciliation of God's "enemies" to God, and on God-directed rejoicing (Rom 5:11) in consequence of this reconciliation. That this has taken place through the death of God's Son emphasizes how much God has been directly involved in accomplishing this reconciliation.

In Galatians 2:20 Paul refers to "the Son of God who loved me and gave himself up [paradidōmi] for me," a statement emphasizing Jesus' active role in a larger christocentric context (Gal 1:15-21). The textual variant, "God and Christ" in place of "Son of God," though supported by several important Greek manuscripts, is probably a corruption of the original text. And so we are left to try to determine the significance of mentioning "the Son of God" here when seven other times immediately preceding and following Galatians 2:20 Paul calls him "Jesus Christ" (Gal 2:16), "Christ Jesus" (Gal 2:16) and "Christ" (Gal 2:16-19, 21).

The expression "the Son of God" emphasizes the very high divine favor and honor of the one whose love and self-giving is stated. And this description of Jesus also implicitly makes God a party to Jesus' redemptive actions, as is confirmed in the following statement (Gal 2:21) where Paul refers to "the grace of God" in connection with Jesus' death.

Given that Romans 8:32 shows that Paul could liken the death of God's Son to the offering of Isaac, it is also possible that Paul's reference in Galatians 2:20 to the self-giving of the Son of God shows an acquaintance with Jewish tradition about the story. Though the Genesis account is silent about Isaac's attitude, ancient Jewish tradition attributes to him an eager willingness to offer himself in obedience to God (e.g., Pseudo-Philo *Bib. Ant.* 18:5; 32:2-4; 40:2; Josephus *Ant.* 1.13.2-4 §§225-36).

4.4. The Son and the Torah. Scholars frequently point to Romans 8:3 and Galatians 4:4 as examples of a christological "formula" in which the Son is referred to as "sent" by God. But, as has already been indicated, the identification of a verbal "formula" in these passages is dubious. It is far more relevant that both of these references to the Son being sent are in contexts dealing with the Torah, the Jewish law. The sending of the Son in Romans 8:3-4 is precisely to overcome the inability of the Torah to save as described in Romans 7, and to make possible the fulfillment of the Torah's "just requirement" in the freedom of the Spirit given through the Son. And Galatians 4:4 mentions the Son being sent forth "to redeem those who were under the *law" (the limitations of which are emphasized in Galatians 3:1—4:1) and to make possible their "adoption as sons."

As well, in Romans 8:3 and Galatians 4:4 Paul emphasizes that the divine Son appeared in human form, which may allude to the idea of Jesus being an "incarnation" of the "preexistent" Son. But the humanity of the Son also means that the divinely initiated deliverance from the Torah's condemnation was effected by the Son within the sphere of human existence, specifically through his death.

4.5. The Son and God's Sons. Though he consistently designates Jesus as the divine Son with an exclusivity connoted, in several passages Paul implicitly or explicitly refers to the enfranchisement of the redeemed into fellowship with Jesus and into a filial relationship with God patterned after Jesus' sonship (on this see esp. Byrne). Galatians 4:5 gives as the purpose of the sending of the Son "that we might receive sonship [huiothesia]" (*see* Adoption, Sonship), and the following verses refer to Christians as God's "sons" (huioi) who have received "the Spirit of his Son," who join the Son in calling on God as "Abba, Father," and are now God's heirs. (And, as Gal

3:27-28 makes clear, the "sons" of God include both female and male on equal terms [hence one can, with the NRSV, translate *huioi* as "children"].)

In Romans 8 as well, Paul explicitly connects Jesus the Son with the sonship of Christians. After referring to the sending of the Son in Romans 8:3, Paul mentions the bestowal of the Spirit (Rom 8:5-13, explicitly linked with Jesus, "the Spirit of Christ," Rom 8:9), and refers to Christians as "sons of God" (Rom 8:14) who call to God as "Abba, Father" (Rom 8:15) and are "fellow heirs with Christ." And in Romans 8:18-27 Paul elaborates both present and future consequences of divine adoption. Then comes Romans 8:28-30, a very theocentric passage emphasizing God's redemptive initiative, in which the redeemed are said to have been "predestined to be conformed to the image of his Son, in order that he might be the firstborn within a large family" (Rom 8:29 NRSV). That is, the one divine Son here is the prototype as well as the agent through whom others are enfranchised as sons of God. The uniqueness of Jesus the Son is not restrictive but redemptive. The term *firstborn* may allude to Exodus 4:22, applying to Jesus a title of Israel and connoting that he has become the basis of God's reconstituted people that includes both Jew and Gentile.

The remaining Pauline references to the Son reflect this idea of God enfranchising others through the unique Son into a standing likened to his. First Corinthians 1:9 describes Christians as called by God into the "fellowship/participation *[koinōnia]* of his Son," which suggests that their status is both dependent on the Son and also a partaking in his filial status. And 2 Corinthians 1:19-20 probably is to be seen as alluding to something similar. The divine "yes" is in Jesus, the Son of God (2 Cor 1:19), because "all the promises of God find their Yes in him" (2 Cor 1:20). And this means that Christians are enfranchised as God's own through the Son (2 Cor 1:20) and given the Spirit as guarantee of full eschatological salvation (2 Cor 1:22). (The "knowledge of the Son of God" in Eph 4:13 is probably also an allusion to the idea of the redemption of the elect being patterned after Jesus' divine sonship.)

This idea of other sons or children of God is interesting in light of the strong connotation of the uniqueness of Jesus' divine sonship we have noted earlier. The resolution to the apparent tension seems to be that Paul consistently refers to the sonship of Christians as derived sonship, given through and after the pattern of Jesus, whereas Jesus is the original prototype, whose sonship is not derived from another.

See also ADOPTION, SONSHIP; CHRIST; CHRISTOLOGY; DEATH OF CHRIST; GOD; HOLY SPIRIT; LORD.

DPL: EXALTATION AND ENTHRONEMENT; FIRSTBORN; IMAGE, IMAGE OF GOD; PRE-EXISTENCE.

BIBLIOGRAPHY. J. Blank, *Paulus und Jesus* (SANT 16; Munich: Kösel, 1968); W. Bousset, *Kyrios Christos* (Nashville: Abingdon, 1970 [1921]); B. Byrne, *"Sons of God"—"Seed of Abraham"* (AnBib 83; Rome: Pontifical Institute, 1979); J. J. Collins, *The Scepter and the Star* (New York: Doubleday, 1995); O. Cullmann, *The Christology of the New Testament* (London: SCM, 1963); D. Cuss, *Imperial Cult and Honorary Terms in the New Testament* (Paradosis 23; Fribourg: University of Fribourg, 1974); J. D. G. Dunn, *Christology in the Making* (2d ed.; London: SCM, 1989); J. A. Fitzmyer, *A Wandering Aramean: Collected Aramaic Essays* (SBLMS 25; Missoula, MT: Scholars, 1979); M. Hengel, *The Son of God* (Philadelphia: Fortress, 1976); L. W. Hurtado, *Lord Jesus Christ* (Grand Rapids: Eerdmans, 2003); S. Kim, *The Origin of Paul's Gospel* (2d ed; WUNT 2/4; Tübingen: J. C. B. Mohr, 1984); W. Kramer, *Christ, Lord, Son of God* (SBT 50; London: SCM, 1966); O. Michel, "Son," *NIDNTT* 3.607-68; A. D. Nock, " 'Son of God' in Pauline and Hellenistic Thought," in *Essays on Religion and the Ancient World*, ed. Z. Stewart (Oxford: Clarendon, 1972) 2.928-39; idem, *Early Gentile Christianity and its Hellenistic Background* (New York: Harper & Row, 1964); H. J. Schoeps, *Paul* (Philadelphia: Westminster, 1961); E. Schweizer et al., "υἱός, υἱοθεσία," *TDNT* 8.334-99; J. M. Scott, *Adoption as Sons of God* (WUNT 2/48; Tübingen: J. C. B. Mohr, 1992); G. Vermes, *Jesus the Jew* (New York: Harper & Row, 1973). L. W. Hurtado

SON OF GOD III: ACTS, HEBREWS, GENERAL EPISTLES, REVELATION

Application of the title "Son of God" to Jesus underwent considerable change in early Christianity. In the earliest Christian communities it was primarily a functional expression, taking an image from extant OT and Jewish thought and applying it in a generally imprecise way to articulate the meaning of the *Christ event. In combination with insights drawn from other images (notably of the divine logos), "Son of God" was gradually invested with more metaphysical understandings until it eventually became the church's preferred christological title.

In the past this development engendered heated debate. The history of religions school highlighted the terminology of divine sonship as a leading example of the intrusion of alien categories in Christianity, and while there is still some peripheral argument about the possible influence of Gnostic categories, for example, most recent discussion has focused on theological concerns over whether the *church made an appropriate contextualization of its original faith in Jesus when it adopted the Son of God terminology. Was the notion of divine sonship alien to the teaching of Jesus and the beliefs of the first disciples, or did it make explicit in the context of Hellenistic culture what was already implicit in the Jewish culture within which the church originated?

1. Jewish Background
2. The Title and Its Development

1. Jewish Background.

The generic term "son of God" had a wide currency in ancient culture. It could as easily be applied to the heroes of traditional Greek mythology (often referred to as sons of Zeus) as to Egyptian pharaohs or Roman emperors.

Within Jewish culture the term was applied to Israel itself (Ex 4:22; Jer 31:9; Hos 11:1; Wis 9:7; 18:13; Jub. 1:24-25; *Pss. Sol.* 17:30), to leading individuals in the nation (Deut 14:1; Is 1:2; 43:6; Jer 3:22; 31:9; Hos 1:10; Wis 2:13-18; 5:5; 12:21; 16:10, 26; 18:4; Sir 4:10; 51:10; *Pss. Sol.* 13:8-9; 18:4; 2 Macc 7:34; Philo *Conf. Ling.* 145-47; Philo *Spec. Leg.* 1.318), to angels and other heavenly beings (Gen 6:2-4; Deut 32:8; Job 1:6-12; 2:1-6; 38:7; Ps 29:1; 89:6; Dan 3:25; *1 Enoch* 13:8, 106:5), to the king (2 Sam 7:14; 1 Chron 17:13; 22:10, 28:6; Ps 2:7; 89:26-27; 4Q174; 4Q246; cf. Philo *Som.* 1.215; Philo *Conf. Ling.* 146), to the Messiah (2 Esdr 7:28; 13:32, 37, 52; 14:9 may be later Christian interpolations; 1QSa 2:11-12; 4QFlor 1:10-13; 4QPsDan A), and later to individual rabbis (*m. Taʿan.* 3:8; *b. Taʿan.* 24). It did not, however, denote a divine figure descending from heaven as the bearer of *salvation, except insofar as angels were messengers or agents of God or Philo's application of it to the divine logos could be so understood. On the contrary, when the status "son of God" was conferred on

someone it was a recognition of a particular achievement. We therefore need to allow the literature itself to define the nature and scope of the term's meaning for early Christians.

2. The Title and Its Development.

2.1. General. Within the literature considered in this article, "Son of God" is absent from James while 1 Peter 1:3 and Jude 1 describe God as Jesus' Father (but without corresponding imagery of "son"). Revelation 2:18 has only a peripheral reference.

2.2. Son of God as Functional Eschatological Image. Acts uses "father" to describe God's relationship with Jesus (Acts 1:4, 7), but "Son of God" is not among the many christological titles in the early chapters (unless Acts 8:37 is accepted as genuine, against the best manuscripts). It first appears in Paul's postbaptismal message (Acts 9:20) as a synonym for "Messiah" (Acts 9:22; cf. Acts 17:4; 18:5; 24:24). Acts 13:33, however, contains a typical eschatological use of the term, in which Jesus' status as Son of God is conferred as a result of the *resurrection, in much the same way as are the titles *"Lord" and "Messiah" (Acts 2:36). This usage is widespread throughout the earlier NT, usually associated (as here; see also 2 Pet 1:16-18) with a reference to Psalm 2:7, which celebrates the status of the king as God's adopted son. There is an implied connection with belief in Jesus as Davidic king and Messiah, though understood in the functional sense that if Jesus was Messiah, then such imagery could appropriately be applied to him. There is no suggestion that Jesus was intrinsically related to *God apart from his accomplishment as eschatological Messiah and not a hint of later notions such as preexistence.

2.3. Son of God from Functional Savior to Incarnational Idea.

2.3.1. Hebrews. Hebrews represents an important transition from early images of sonship to later metaphysical beliefs. Jesus as Son of God is a key theme and a basic confession of faith (Heb 4:14). "Sonship" can be almost synonymous with the perfection and totality of salvation (Heb 4:14–5:9; 6:6; 7:3, 28; 8–9), rooted in the assumption that Jesus achieved this status through suffering and resurrection (Heb 5:8; 6:6; 10:29) and with the language of divine begetting (Ps 2) providing the frame of reference. However, other passages go well beyond this, identifying the Son as the agent of *creation, sharing God's own nature in language that is clearly related to philosophical categories applied elsewhere to the divine logos (Heb 1:2-4). In Hebrews 3:2-6 Jesus is "appointed" (like Moses), but as the Son he has a greater ontological (as distinct from functional) significance, a contrast that occurs again when Jesus' priesthood is compared to that of Melchizedek. While being "Son of God" is the typological fulfillment of Melchizedek's priesthood, this status also identifies Jesus with a preexisting ideal type, which explains why he is of greater significance than Melchizedek (Heb 5:6; 7:13, 15-17).

Little is known for certain about the background to *Hebrews, but the author is clearly searching for relevant philosophical categories as a vehicle for Christian belief; hence the occurrence of a more obviously incarnational Son of God *christology. At the same time, Hebrews preserves the language of adoption while making no attempt to combine the two: they stand together in an unintegrated symbiosis. Jesus as Son is the heavenly (ideal world) archetype in comparison with which other (this world) claims are inadequate. As the church moved into a Hellenistic milieu with a Platonic worldview, it was natural for Jesus' eschatological significance to be described in these terms. For Hebrews, however, the starting point is the Platonic worldview, not reflection on the significance of Jesus per se. This fact explains why there is no concept of the personal preexistence of the Son who is Jesus but only the abstract theological idea of preexistence, which then demands explanation by reference to the more traditional category of sonship through adoption or achievement. Again, later concerns about ontological or metaphysical substance do not occur. In this sense Hebrews appears to represent a midpoint between the Christ event and its explanation in purely OT categories and the later development of a fully fledged, incarnational christology.

2.3.2. Johannine Literature. In the Johannine literature Son of God language is central. It defines the purpose of the Fourth Gospel (Jn 20:31) and is even more prominent in 1 John (it does not appear in 2-3 Jn, though 2 Jn 3, 9 use Father/Son imagery of Jesus and God; see John, Letters of). There is still a clear connection between Jesus' status as Son and his death and resurrection (1 Jn 1:7; 3:8; 4:10).

As in Hebrews, belief in Jesus as Son appears as the functional equivalent of a dependable salvation (1 Jn 5:18-21). But there is in addition a more cognitive, theological content to such belief, which serves to distinguish truth from error (1 Jn 2:22-27; 3:23; 4:2, 9-12; 4:14-15; 5:5, 9-12; see Adversaries). This entails metaphysical propositions, including belief that God and the Son are one and that the Son as a human being came from heaven. John's Jesus is Son of God not primarily because of his exaltation or even as a by-product of the application of Platonic terminology to his functional importance but because he always had a personal existence with God that was of the same quality and purpose in this preexistence in heaven as it was during his lifetime on earth. This understanding probably emerged not from John's intrinsic concept of sonship but from a combination of that with the logos Christology that also features strongly in this literature. This association of preexistence with sonship goes further than does Hebrews, though 1 John still shows no interest in speculation about the precise ontological relationship between Jesus and God (yet the prologue, 1 Jn 1:1-4, comes near to that) and therefore never asks what oneness between Father and Son might mean.

See also CHRISTOLOGY; GOD.

DLNTD: SONSHIP, CHILD, CHILDREN.

BIBLIOGRAPHY. O. Cullmann, *The Christology of the New Testament* (London: SCM, 1963); C. J. Davis, *The Name and Way of the Lord: Old Testament Themes, New Testament Christology* (JSNTSup 129; Sheffield: Sheffield Academic Press, 1996); J. D. G. Dunn, *Christology in the Making* (London: SCM, 1989); F. Hahn, *The Titles of Jesus in Christology* (London: Lutterworth, 1969); J. A. Grassi, "From Jesus of Nazareth to Christ, the Son of God," *Bible Today* 61 (1972) 826-34; M. Hengel, *The Son of God* (London: SCM, 1976); J. Hick, ed., *The Myth of God Incarnate* (London: SCM, 1977); P. E. Hughes, "The Christology of Hebrews," *SWJT* 28 (1985) 19-27; L. W. Hurtado, *Lord Jesus Christ* (Grand Rapids: Eerdmans, 2003); J. Knox, *The Humanity and Divinity of Christ* (Cambridge: Cambridge University Press, 1967); W. Kramer, *Christ, Lord, Son of God* (London: SCM, 1966); J. T. Lienhard, "The Christology of the Epistle to Diognetus," *VC* 24 (1970) 280-89; H. L. MacNeill, *The Christology of the Epistle to the Hebrews* (Chicago: University of Chicago Press, 1914); J. Macquarrie, *Jesus Christ in Modern Thought* (London: SCM, 1990); P. S. Minear,

"The Idea of Incarnation in 1 John," *Int* 24 (1970) 291-302; E. Schweizer, "Variety and Unity in the New Testament proclamation of Jesus as the Son of God," *AusBR* 15 (1967) 1-12.

J. W. Drane

SON OF MAN: GOSPELS

The person whose name was Jesus (perhaps more closely defined as "Jesus of Nazareth" or as "Jesus the son of Joseph" [Jn 1:46; 6:42] to make clear which holder of the name was meant) is known by various forms of words in the Gospels and the NT generally. To some extent these forms of words are interchangeable, but clearly some of them are used with specific functions and in specific contexts.

The phrase "the Son of man" *(ho huios tou anthrōpou)* is such a form of words. It is the phrase used more frequently than any other (except "Jesus" itself) to refer to Jesus in the Gospels. It occurs in all four Gospels and only once outside them (Acts 7:56; Heb 2:6 [quoting Ps 8:5] and Rev 1:13; 14:14 [alluding to Dan 7:13] have "a son of man"). Within the Gospels it is found only in sayings ascribed to Jesus; the only clear exception is John 12:34, where the people quote Jesus' phrase back at him and ask to whom he is referring.

This evidence shows that "the Son of man" functions as a self-designation of some kind; it never became a way for other people to refer to Jesus, and it thus played no part in the confessional and doctrinal statements of the early church, unlike "Christ," *"Lord" and *"Son of God."

1. Usage in the Gospels
2. Jesus and the Son of Man
3. Conclusion

1. Usage in the Gospels.

In what kind of situation is the phrase used? Why does Jesus sometimes say "I" and sometimes "the Son of man"? There is manifestly some flexibility in usage, as is seen by comparing:

Luke 6:22 with Matthew 5:11
Matthew 16:13 with Mark 8:27
Luke 12:8 with Matthew 10:32

1.1. The Gospel of Mark. Broadly speaking, we can trace a pattern in the Gospel of *Mark, where the phrase occurs fourteen times (Mk 2:10, 28; 8:31, 38; 9:9, 12, 31; 10:33, 45; 13:26; 14:21a, b, 41, 62).

1.1.1. The Present Authority of Jesus. Jesus speaks of his authority to forgive sins (Mk 2:10) and of his lordship of the sabbath (Mk 2:28). In both cases the context makes it clear that it is the authority of Jesus that is at issue; he exercises it there and then; and it is an authority that would normally belong to *God or to somebody authorized by him. It is possible that the phrase might signify "human" in a generic sense (i.e., any particular member of the species; see further below), but it is doubtful whether a Greek reader would take this sense from the phrase.

1.1.2. The Suffering and Resurrection of Jesus. Jesus speaks of the impending suffering, *death and *resurrection of the Son of man in a series of predictions which emphasize that this must happen in accordance with the Scriptures; he speaks of the mission of the Son of man as being to serve others and to give his life as a ransom for many, and he speaks of himself as the Son of man in references to his impending betrayal and arrest (Mk 8:31; 9:9, 12, 31; 10:33, 45; 14:21a, b, 41). The threefold repetition of the prediction in Mark is particularly impressive. The sufferings of Jesus are clearly linked to his role as the Son of man; they are not mentioned explicitly without some reference to him as the Son of man.

1.1.3. The Future Coming of Jesus. There are three references to a future coming of the Son of man "in clouds with great power and glory" to gather his chosen people and reject (literally "be ashamed of") those who were ashamed of Jesus (*see* Apocalypticism); this coming is associated with his being seated on the right hand of God (Mk 8:38; 13:26; 14:62). Mark 13:26 and 14:62 are clearly reminiscent of Daniel 7:13-14, where a figure "like a son of man" comes with the clouds of heaven, appears before God and is given everlasting sovereign power and dominion (*see* Kingdom of God).

Allusions are also made to Psalm 11:1 and possibly to Zechariah 12:10. What is said in other passages in the OT about a future coming of God himself in *judgment (Zech 14:5) is here attributed to the Son of man as his agent.

1.1.4. The Suffering, Vindicated and Authoritative Son of Man. With this background now coming into focus, it is possible to argue that for Mark the teaching that he attributes to Jesus identifies him as the figure prophesied by Daniel who will come as God's agent to gather his people and act as judge. But already as a human figure Jesus acts with the authority that is inherent in this role. If we ask how the suffering and rejection of the Son of man fit into this picture, two (not necessarily exclusive) answers may be given. The first is that in Daniel 7 the Son of man is seen as the representative of "the saints of the Most High" who suffer defeat and oppression at the hands of their enemies (Dan 7:21, 25). The second is that the language used in Mark 9:12 and 10:45 and in the crucifixion narrative suggests that the Son of man undergoes the experiences of the "righteous sufferer" and the "rejected stone" in the Psalms (Ps 22; 69; 118:22) and the *Servant of Yahweh (Is 52:13—53:12) who suffers but is vindicated by God. Thus, not surprisingly, motifs from several OT passages which were regarded as providing the pattern for the destiny of Jesus are coalesced to give a picture of him as the suffering, vindicated and authoritative Son of man.

It also emerges that in Mark, Jesus prefers this way of describing himself to other possibilities. It is notable that, when Jesus is identified as the "Christ" (Mk 8:29-30; 14:61-62; and implicitly in Mk 13:21-22; 9:41 is an exception), he responds by speaking of what "the Son of man" will do. This curious fact suggests that Jesus almost wishes to replace the concept of Messiah (or Christ) by that of the Son of man. The reasons for this are not clear.

1.2. The Gospel of Matthew. The picture in the other two Synoptic Gospels is not markedly dissimilar. The phrase is used thirty times by *Matthew.

Matthew takes over thirteen of the usages in Mark (Mt 9:6; 12:8; 16:27; 17:9, 12, 22; 20:18, 28, 24:30b; 26:24a, b, 45, 64) and adds it editorially four times (Mt 16:13; 16:28; 24:30a (?); 26:2). He shares it with Luke eight times (Mt 8:20 par. Lk 9:58; Mt 11:19 par. Lk 7:34; Mt 12:32 par. Lk 12:10); Mt 12:40 par. Lk 11:30; Mt 24:27, 37, 39, 44 par. Lk 17:24, 26, 30; 12:40), and it is found in passages peculiar to Matthew five times (Mt 10:23; 13:37, 41; 19:28; 25:31).

Matthew's new uses of the phrase fall into the same general pattern as in Mark. In a series of sayings that he shares with Luke, the Son of man is an object of derision for associating with sinners (Mt 11:19) and invites his followers to share his homeless situation (Mt 8:20). There is more detailed teaching on the future coming of the Son of man, which will be unexpected and catastrophic for those who are not ready for him

(Mt 24:27, 37, 39, 44). The saying, which compares the way in which people treat Jesus now with the way in which they will be treated at the judgment (Mk 8:38 par. Mt 16:27), appears a second time in an expanded form in Luke 12:8-9; but in the corresponding saying in Matthew (Mt 10:32-33) the verbal contrast between Jesus and the Son of man is dropped and Jesus speaks of himself in the first person throughout. (Similarly, Mt 5:11 speaks of persecution for the sake of "me," whereas Lk 6:22 has "the Son of man.") Another interesting fact is that a saying which in Mark 3:28 speaks of forgiveness being extended to the sons of men for their sins and blasphemies except against the Holy Spirit, appears in Luke 12:10 in the form that if a person speaks against the Son of man he will be forgiven but not if he speaks against the Spirit (*see* Holy Spirit). Matthew 12:31-32 combines these two sayings (by substituting "men" for "the sons of men" in the Markan saying). The way in which the Evangelists understood this saying is debated, but it seems probable that they saw a contrast between speaking against Jesus on earth, when people might be forgiven for not recognizing who he really was, and opposition to the Holy Spirit by people (possibly disciples) when there should be no doubt that to do so was to take sides against God.

In the teaching peculiar to Matthew, the Son of man is especially understood as the coming savior (*see* Salvation) and judge (Mt 13:41; 19:28). In Matthew 10:23 Jesus tells his disciples that they will not finish the cities of *Israel until the Son of man comes. Matthew may have seen this as a reference to the fall of Jerusalem understood as the coming of the Son of man in judgment.

The general tendency in Matthew is thus to emphasize the identity of Jesus as the coming Son of man and as a figure who is rejected on earth.

1.3. The Gospel of Luke. Luke uses the phrase twenty-five times. He has equivalents to nine of the texts in Mark (Lk 5:24; 6:5; 9:22, 26, 44; 18:31; 21:27; 22:22, 69). He has the ten texts from Q, which he shares with Matthew (the eight texts listed above with Lk 6:22 and 12:8). This leaves six occurrences peculiar to Luke (Lk 17:22; 18:8; 19:10; 21:36; 22:48; 24:7). In these fresh sayings we hear of the Son of man's mission to save the lost (Lk 19:10), his betrayal by Judas (Lk 22:48; cf. Mk 14:21b) and his sufferings and resurrection (Lk 24:7—a report of what

Jesus had said earlier by the two angels at the tomb), and of his future coming (Lk 17:22; 18:8; 21:36). It is evident that the picture in Luke is very similar to that in the other Gospels. A notable omission by Luke is the ransom saying in Mark 10:45. There is a similar saying about "service" in Luke 22:27, but it does not use "the Son of man" nor the idea of ransom. Again there is no essential difference from the general picture given in Mark.

1.4. The Gospel of John. When we turn to the Gospel of John we get a picture with similarities and differences. The phrase is used thirteen times. We can readily find references that correspond to those of the passion and resurrection of Jesus in the other Gospels. But in John the reference is to the "lifting up" of the Son of man *(hypsoō).* The verb is ambiguous and can refer to "being lifted up" on a cross or to "being exalted" (Jn 3:14; 8:28; 12:34a, b). Jesus can thus refer to the final events in his life as the glorification of the Son of man (Jn 12:23; 13:31). Jesus also speaks of the authority to judge which has been committed to him as the Son of man (Jn 5:27), and of the power of the Son of man to grant life (Jn 6:27). These functions are summed up in his appeal to the blind man who had been healed to believe in the Son of man (Jn 9:35). And the life-giving function also appears in the reference to eating the flesh of the Son of man (Jn 6:53), a phrase which doubtless reflects the language of the *Last Supper but stresses the need for a spiritual partaking. Finally, there is the concept of the Son of man coming down from heaven (Jn 3:13) and ascending to where he formerly was (Jn 8:28); linked to this is the difficult saying about the angels ascending and descending on the Son of man (Jn 1:51).

2. Jesus and the Son of Man.

It is clear that the expression is used in much the same way in each of the Synoptic Gospels but that in John it is used in a wider manner. The crucial question is to what extent this usage corresponds with that of Jesus himself. We have already seen that the Evangelists can add the expression to their sources or subtract it from them. But much more far-reaching questions have been raised by modern scholarship concerning the origin of the phrase.

2.1. Son of Man and Messiah? Some scholars dispute whether Jesus expressed verbally any consciousness of being the Messiah or a messi-

anic type of figure. It would follow that he could not have used "the Son of man" as a messianic self-designation. Or, it is claimed, Messiah and Son of man represent two different types of figure and, if Jesus identified himself as the former, he could not have identified himself also with the latter.

Both of these claims are very doubtful. The evidence that Jesus acted in messianic ways is convincing (*see* Christ): why otherwise did his followers recognize him as the Messiah? This makes the view that he could not have referred to himself in a messianic fashion most improbable. Further, while it is true that the traditional Jewish Messiah is an earthly figure, whereas the Son of man has transcendent features, the role assigned to the latter is messianic in that he is given dominion and authority as the representative of God's people. This indicates, incidentally, that the claim that the Son of man is not associated with the kingdom of God in Judaism is without foundation.

2.2. Present and/or Future Son of Man? It has been observed that in those sayings where Jesus talks about the future activity of the Son of man, he is not necessarily talking about himself, and that in one or two sayings (Mk 8:38 par. Lk 12:8-9; Mk 14:62) there appears to be a distinction drawn between Jesus, presently active on earth, and the Son of man, active in the future at the last judgment. On the assumption that the early *church would not have created such a distinction, it is argued that such sayings have strong claims to authenticity. It is then further argued that originally Jesus envisaged the Son of man as a figure distinct from himself. It then follows that sayings which identify Jesus as the Son of man must either be compositions by the early church or have had the phrase added to them at a later stage. If this argument is valid, it fits in with the view that Jesus did not refer to himself in messianic terms.

Despite the wide popularity of this view among scholars influenced by R. Bultmann, it cannot be upheld. Essentially, the claim is being made that the future Son of man sayings have been reinterpreted by the early church to refer to Jesus. But there are various arguments against this view.

The crucial sayings (Mk 8:38 par. Lk 12:8-9; Mk 14:62) can be interpreted much more naturally as sayings in which Jesus draws a contrast between himself as a figure whose authority is not recognized and the Son of man as a figure whose authority cannot be gainsaid. The apparently odd switch from the first person to the third person is to be explained by the incorporation of an allusion to Daniel 7:13-14.

The theory requires that the authenticity of a very large number of occurrences of the expression as self-designations of Jesus be surrendered for no better reason than that they stand in conflict with a couple of texts whose interpretation in terms of another coming figure is highly uncertain. The fact that in so many other texts "Son of man" cannot be other than a self-designation must seriously damage the claim that the "future" texts originally spoke of a figure other than Jesus.

2.3. Son of Man as a Self-Designation of Jesus. Two lines of argument raise the question whether Jesus could have used "the Son of man" as a title to refer to himself.

2.3.1. The Interpretation of Daniel 7. In the vision of Daniel there appear four great beasts like various animals and a figure "like a son of man." This last phrase should undoubtedly be translated "like a man" (so NEB). The Aramaic phrase is used to designate a particular member of a species, and (as in Hebrew) "man" and "son of man" can be used interchangeably to refer to an individual. The force of *like* is that the figure is not a man but is like a man, just as the beasts are "like" different animals. In the interpretation of Daniel's vision the beasts represent four kingdoms and (implicitly) the manlike figure stands for "the saints of the Most High," the (faithful) people of Israel. It can therefore be argued that the manlike figure is a symbol for a collective entity. On the other hand, it is equally plausible that the manlike figure stands for the ruler of God's people, just as the beasts appear to represent both kingdoms and their rulers. There is no doubt that in subsequent interpretation the manlike figure was regarded as a messianic individual. This is true of *1 Enoch* 37-71 and also of *4 Ezra* 13 (where the actual phrase is not used, but the dependence on Dan 7 is clear). Nevertheless, it can be argued that in no sense is "a (son of) man" a title in Daniel 7.

2.3.2. Son of Man as an Aramaic Idiom of Self-Reference. There is a further idiom involving the use of the phrase "son of man." It occurs in a number of Aramaic texts with the sense of "an individual man" but with some kind of reference to the speaker. The precise way in which this happens is debated.

(1) It has been argued that the phrase is used to make statements that are true of people in general and therefore of the speaker in particular (M. Casey). It is thus a kind of self-designation, but what is said is not true exclusively of the speaker. (For example, in the Palestinian Targum Cain says: "Behold thou hast cast me forth this day on the face of the ground, and from before you, Lord, it is not possible for the son of man *[bar nāš]* to hide.")

(2) It has also been claimed that a speaker could use this expression to make statements that were true of himself in particular (G. Vermes). Against this interpretation it is argued that in every case cited a general or generic reference is possible. The idiom in fact seems to have arisen out of the use of the phrase to mean "a man" and hence "any man" to refer to the speaker, inasmuch as he is a man.

(3) However, there are cases where the reference is manifestly not to "everybody" but to people in a particular class, and therefore it is more accurate to say that it refers to such people, a group to which the speaker belongs (B. Lindars). (Thus: "When E. Hiyya ben Adda died . . . R. Levi received his valuables. This was because his teacher used to say: 'The disciple of *bar nāšâ* is as dear to him as his son.'" Here the expression plainly refers to the group of teachers.) It is suggested that the idiom was used as a form of self-reference in cases where the speaker wished to show modesty or to speak of matters (such as his own death) that were distasteful—in any case, in sayings where he wished to avoid speaking directly in the first person.

2.4. Evaluating the Options. The current opinion seems to favor view (3) as the appropriate explanation of the idiom. Those who hold this view then argue that there are a number of sayings in the Gospels that can be understood as examples of this usage. Jesus says something that is true of himself inasmuch as it is true of a group of people to whom he belongs.

2.4.1. Analyzing the statements as idiomatic self-references, M. Casey, B. Lindars and G. Vermes (the three major scholars who have done work in this area) have each determined which Son of man sayings are authentic. Their results may be compared in table 1.

Vermes has the largest number of authentic sayings because he includes sayings that are true only of the speaker (Jesus). His selection, as with that of Casey and Lindars, is reached by rejecting the sayings that reflect the influence of Daniel 7. Casey and Lindars agree substantially in their more limited selection.

Table 1: Son of Man Sayings as Self-Designation: Their Authenticity According to Casey, Lindars and Vermes

		Casey	Lindars	Vermes	Comments
Mark	2:10	*	*	*	
	2:28	*		*	
	8:31			*	(Mark only)
	8:38	*			
	9:9			*	
	9:12	*		*	
	9:31		*	*	(Lindars: core only)
	10:33			*	
	10:45	*	*	*	(Lindars v. 45b)
	14:21a,b	*	*	*	(Lindars v. 21a)
	14:41			*	
Matthew	8:20	*	*	*	(par. Lk 9:58 Q)
	11:19	*	*	*	(par. Lk 7:34 Q)
	16:13			*	(diff. Mk 8:31)
	26:22			*	
Luke	11:30		*	*	(par. Mt 12:40 Q)
	12:8	*	*		(diff. Mt 10:32 Q)
	12:10	*	*	*	(diff. Mt 12:32 Q)
	19:10			*	
	22:48	*			
	24:7			*	

There are instances where the Casey/Lindars approach to the sayings is plausible. Mark 2:10 could mean that there is a class of people with authority to forgive, including Jesus. (But the people comment with surprise that no human can forgive sins; only God can do so.) In Mark 2:28 the sabbath is made for humanity, and therefore people in general, including Jesus, have authority over it. In Matthew 11:18 Casey finds a group of people, including Jesus, who eat and drink with tax collectors and *sinners and who are attacked by the Pharisees. (But the text seems to be comparing two individuals.) In Matthew 8:20 Jesus says that there is a group of people, including his disciples and himself, who have no homes, and therefore a prospective disciple must expect the same situation. This

is the most cogent example, but it must be observed that Jesus could be saying that, if he himself as a messianic figure is rejected, so too will his *disciples be (cf. the identical argument in Mt 10:25b; Jn 15:18, 20b). The other examples lack all cogency.

2.4.2. The effect of the approach in question is to deny that Jesus thought of himself in terms of the Son of man of Daniel 7. According to Lindars, "it carried no christological meaning as such" (Lindars, 170). Jesus remains a figure possessed of some authority, totally committed to his vocation, a prophet who believes that to speak against him is to speak against God, and by their response to him people will stand or fall at the last judgment.

However, the fact that the Lindars/Casey theory simply fails to work, in that it can credibly explain such a tiny handful of sayings, must raise serious doubts about it. There is more to be said for Vermes's understanding of the sayings, according to which Jesus used the idiom to speak of himself with modesty or to avoid a direct reference to his own death.

2.5. Clarifying the Picture. According to C. Colpe, some of the sayings are generic. That is, Mark 2:10 comments on the fact that Jesus, as a human, can forgive; in Matthew 11:18-19 John is contrasted with "a human," namely Jesus. And in Matthew 8:20 Jesus says that even animals have dens but a human such as he, Jesus, has nowhere to lay his head (Colpe, 430-33). What appears to be essentially the same view is upheld by R. Bauckham, who thinks that the phrase is used indefinitely rather than generically to mean "somebody, a person," and that it could then be used as an oblique self-reference.

We are left with a problem in that the Aramaic usage remains unclear. But it is arguable that the sayings in the Gospels are evidence that the underlying Aramaic phrase could have been used on occasion to refer to the speaker only.

This leaves us with a number of sayings where the allusion to Daniel 7 is clear. J. D. G. Dunn has suggested that Jesus began by using the Aramaic idiom to refer to himself and then recognized in the use of the same phrase in Daniel 7 an allusion to the vindication which he expected from God. This led to the use of Daniel 7 on a broader scale in his sayings, and to the development of the term as a means of referring to himself as the authoritative messianic figure. Thus in some sayings Jesus will simply have used a self-designation, but in others he was making a conscious allusion to Daniel 7. No doubt early Christians would have understood most if not all of his sayings as references to himself as the figure of Daniel 7. The point is that not all uses of the term would necessarily have conveyed the same sense on the lips of Jesus.

To adopt this position is not necessarily to claim that all occurrences of the phrase or all the texts in which it occurs are authentic sayings of Jesus as they stand. We have to reckon with the activity of the Evangelists in adding the phrase (and also in replacing it by a personal pronoun or other equivalent; see the examples cited above). It is also possible that similar activity took place even before the writing of the Gospels.

One particular problem is raised by Mark 3:28-29 and its parallels (Mt 12:31-33; Lk 12:10). It seems certain that we have two variant forms of the same basic saying. The hypothetical original said that there was forgiveness available for sins and blasphemies for/against "the son of man." Mark's tradition took this to mean forgiveness for humankind (collective use), but the Q tradition took it to refer to blasphemies against the man (Jesus). On this view, the Markan tradition understood the Aramaic phrase in a way that was probably not the meaning as originally intended, but, although the reference to blasphemy against Jesus dropped out, it was implicitly included in that the saying promised forgiveness of all blasphemies except those against the Spirit. In its Aramaic form, the saying probably did not refer to Jesus as "the [Danielic] Son of man," and therefore the problem detected by modern readers as to what is the difference between speaking against the Son of man and against the Holy Spirit disappears. It is one thing to speak against Jesus under the humble appearance of a man, but it is another thing to speak against the manifest work of the Spirit (in Jesus or in anybody else).

3. Conclusion.

It emerges that two things happen in the Son of man texts.

3.1. Son of Man as Divine and Human. On the one hand, there is the phrase itself and the associations it would have for hearers and readers. In the Gospels as we have them, it points the reader to the figure in Daniel 7, who is a person with sovereign authority, a messianic figure identified in *1 Enoch* and 4 Ezra with the Messiah, God's Son and Elect One. Such a figure would be seen as in some sense divine in that he comes from heaven, and the description of him in Daniel 7 could be taken as an apotheosis, or "deification." He would be associated with the people of God, and in that sense the Son of man can be regarded as a corporate figure. (But the view that "Son of man" is a symbol for a corporate group which then becomes individualized in Jesus is to be rejected.) His associates are bound up with his destiny. But it must be emphasized that it is doubtful whether all of these associations would be present for the original hearers of Jesus and would have been intended by him every time he used the phrase. It is because of this dual origin of the phrase that it can be used to refer both to the humanity of Jesus and also to his divine origin. Jesus can use the term to refer to himself as a human over against God (Mk 2:10, 28), but also to indicate his divine origin. In the latter case, "Son of man" is a veiled way of expressing his relationship to God (Kim).

3.2. The Son of Man's Mission. On the other hand, this self-designation becomes the vehicle for teaching about the activity and fate of Jesus. He appears in the Synoptic Gospels as a figure of authority on earth who is not accepted by many people. He has a divinely ordained destiny, expressed in the Scriptures, which involves betrayal, rejection, suffering, death and resurrection. He has a future role in which he "comes" and brings salvation and judgment. In the Gospel of John there is greater stress laid on the fact that he comes from God and returns to be with him.

3.3. Son of Man as Jesus' Self-Designation. When Jesus refers to his own role, he adopts this term rather than "Messiah" or "Son of God." After the resurrection it never entered into Christian usage as a way of referring to Jesus or as a confessional term (not even in Jn 9:35-36 is it actually used by a believer; Acts 7:56 is a unique usage, probably a deliberate echo of Jesus' own words). It was recognized as a self-designation, and it was replaced by other terms which expressed its significance with greater clarity. It was in any case a term that would not have been meaningful for non-Jews. Since modern readers on the whole do not pick up the original nuances of the term (whether as a self-designation or as an allusion to Dan 7), the example of the early church in not using it remains valid for today. There is indeed a grave danger of using "Son of man" as a means of referring to the humanity of Jesus, as opposed to his divinity (expressed by "Son of God"), whereas in fact the Danielic background suggests a figure closely associated with the Ancient of Days.

We may conclude that in Aramaic "Son of man" was not a title but a self-designation used in certain specific contexts. Jesus used it in this way. However, in Daniel 7 the phrase was used nontechnically to refer to somebody "like a man," and hence the phrase came to be a means of reference to the person so described. Jesus took over this sense of the phrase, and thus identified his role with that of the figure in Daniel 7. Consequently, the phrase came to be used as a title of dignity for Jesus, although the memory of the fact that the idiom was used as a self-designation prevented it from being taken over by his followers.

See also CHRIST; KINGDOM OF GOD; LORD; SERVANT OF YAHWEH; SON OF DAVID; SON OF GOD.

BIBLIOGRAPHY. R. J. Bauckham, "The Son of Man: 'A Man in my Position' or 'Someone,' " *JSNT* 2 (1985) 23-33 (with a reply by B. Lindars, ibid. 35-41); C. C. Caragounis, *The Son of Man* (WUNT 38; Tübingen: J. C. B. Mohr, 1986); M. Casey, *Son of Man* (London: SPCK, 1979); idem, "General, Generic and Indefinite: The Use of the Term 'Son of Man' in Aramaic Sources and in the Teaching of Jesus," *JSNT* 29 (1987) 21-56; C. Colpe, "ὁ υἱός τοῦ ἀνθρώπου," *TDNT* 8.400-77; J. D. G. Dunn, *Christianity in the Making*, Vol. 1: *Jesus Remembered* (Grand Rapids: Eerdmans, 2003) 724-62; idem, *Christology in the Making* (Philadelphia: Westminster, 1980); S. Kim, *The Son of Man As the Son of God* (Grand Rapids: Eerdmans, 1983); B. Lindars, *Jesus Son of Man* (Grand Rapids: Eerdmans, 1983); H. E. Tödt, *The Son of Man in the Synoptic Tradition* (Philadelphia: Westminster, 1965); G. Vermes, *Jesus the Jew* (New York: Harper, 1973).

I. H. Marshall

SONSHIP. *See* ADOPTION, SONSHIP.

SPIRIT OF CHRIST. *See* HOLY SPIRIT II.

STOICS, STOICISM. *See* PHILOSOPHY.

SUBSTITUTIONARY ATONEMENT. *See* DEATH OF CHRIST.

SUFFERING SERVANT. *See* SERVANT OF YAHWEH.

SUPERSTITION. *See* RELIGIONS, GRECO-ROMAN.

SYMPOSIUM. *See* TABLE FELLOWSHIP.

SYNAGOGUE

The synagogue was the regular Jewish assembly for prayer and worship. Jesus is depicted as teaching and performing miracles in synagogues in Galilee (Mt 4:23; Lk 4:15), especially in Nazareth (Mt 13:54; Mk 6:2; Lk 4:16) and in Capernaum (Mk 1:21; Lk 7:5; Jn 6:59). The synagogue in the latter city was probably built by the centurion (Lk 7:5), whose servant Jesus healed.

The synagogue continues to play an important role in the early church and is mentioned frequently in the book of Acts, occurring some nineteen times. Although Paul is depicted as visiting and preaching in synagogues routinely, he never uses the word in his epistles. The word occurs rarely in the remainder of the NT writings, appearing only once in James, in reference to Christian assembly (Jas 2:2), and twice in Revelation, in reference to a "synagogue of Satan," an assembly, perhaps Jewish (they "say that they are Jews and are not, but lie"), that opposes the Christian community (Rev 2:9; 3:9).

1. Names and Origin
2. Offices
3. Services and Other Activities
4. Remains of Buildings
5. Interior

1. Names and Origin.

"Synagogue" is a word derived from the Greek *synagōgē*, which meant originally an assembly such as of the Jews meeting for worship. In the Septuagint it is used, for example, in Exodus 12:3 of the whole congregation of Israel. It came to mean local gatherings of Jews and then the building where Jewish congregations met. Especially after the destruction of the Temple in Jerusalem in A.D. 70, synagogues became the centers of both religious and communal activity wherever there was a *minyan*, or quorum, of ten Jewish men. The Talmud claimed that there were 480 synagogues in Jerusalem before A.D. 70. The

Pilgrim of Bordeaux (fourth cent. A.D.) reported but seven left in his day.

The Greek word *proseuchē*, literally "prayer," was also used as a synonym for synagogues in inscriptions, papyri, Philo and Josephus. Whether the occurrence of this word in Acts 16:13 designates a synagogue or a prayer meeting at Philippi is a matter of dispute. Another Greek word used in one papyrus for a Jewish place of prayer is the term *eucheion*. In one passage Josephus (*Ant.* 16.6.2 §164) quotes the term *sabbateion* to mean "synagogue." In later Hebrew tradition the synagogue was called variously *bêṭ ṭĕpillâ*, "house of prayer"; *bêṭ midrāš*, "house of study"; and *bêṭ kĕnēsseṭ*, "house of assembly."

Though a few scholars (e.g., J. Weingreen) have stressed the pre-exilic roots of the synagogue, most would ascribe its rise to the postexilic period. Many would place this development in the Jewish exilic community in Mesopotamia.

The earliest possible inscriptional evidences are references to *proseuchē* in inscriptions and papyri from Ptolemaic Egypt (E. Schürer), the earliest of which dates to the reign of Ptolemy III Euergetes (246-221 B.C.). This text refers to the foundation of a *proseuchē* at Schedia some twenty miles from Alexandria. Another text from the same reign refers to a *proseuchē* at Arsinoë-Crocodilopolis in the Fayum. The existence of a synagogue at this town is also confirmed by a land survey (P. Tebt. 86). An inscription from Ptolemy VII (145-17 B.C.) refers to the dedication of "the pylon," the monumental gate, of a synagogue (Griffiths, 10).

Some scholars who dispute the interpretation of references to these *proseuchai* in Egypt as synagogues, maintain that the synagogues as an institution developed in Palestine in the second century B.C. with the rise of the Pharisees (J. Gutmann).

2. Offices.

Jairus, whose daughter Jesus healed (Mk 5:22, 35, 36, 38; Lk 8:49), was the head of the synagogue (Gk *archisynagōgos*). Luke 8:41 has Jairus listed as one of the *archōn tēs synagōgēs*, "leaders of the synagogue"; Matthew 9:23 refers to him simply as an *archōn*. From Luke 13:10-17 and from passages in Acts (18:1-17), we can infer that such an officer was responsible for keeping the congregation faithful to the Torah.

The relative esteem in which the "head of the synagogue" was held in Jewish society is re-

vealed in a passage from the Talmud (*b. Pesah.* 49b): "Our rabbis taught: Let a man always sell all he has and marry the daughter of a scholar. If he does not find the daughter of a scholar, let him marry the daughter of [one of] the great men of the generation. If he does not find the daughter of [one of] the great men of the generation, let him marry the daughter of a head of a synagogue. If he does not find the daughter of a head of a synagogue, let him marry the daughter of a charity treasurer. If he does not find the daughter of a charity treasurer, let him marry the daughter of an elementary school teacher, but let him not marry the daughter of an *'am hāʾāreṣ* ("people of the land") because they are detestable and of their daughters it is said, 'Cursed be the one who lies with any manner of beast' (Deut 27:21)."

The word *archisynagōgos* appears in thirty Greek and Latin inscriptions. In three cases from Smyrna and Myndos in western Turkey and from Gortyn on Crete the term is used of women. B. Brooten has argued that these and other titles (*presbytera*, "elder," *hiereia*, "priestess") were not just honorific but referred to women leaders. One inscription to an infant as an *archisynagōgos* was certainly honorific.

A group of elders would direct the activities of the synagogue. The *archisynagōgos* was probably chosen from among them. An almoner would collect and distribute alms. The *ḥazzān*, or "attendant," was the one who took care of the Scripture scrolls. Jesus gave back the Isaiah scroll to such an attendant (Gk *hypēretē*, Lk 4:20). The *ḥazzān* also announced the beginning and the end of the Sabbath by blowing the *šôpār*, or ram's horn. In later practice the *ḥazzān* was paid and lodged at the synagogue as a caretaker.

3. Services and Other Activities.

We know that the later synagogue services included such features as the recitation of the *Shema*ʿ ("Hear O hear," Deut 6:4-9; 11:13-21; Num 15:37-41), prayer facing Jerusalem, the "Amen" response from the congregation, the reading of excerpts from the scrolls of the Torah (Acts 15:21) and of the Prophets, translation of the Scriptures into Aramaic paraphrases, a sermon and a benediction (cf. Neh 8).

It became customary to recite while standing the *Shemoneh Esreh*, or "Eighteen Benedictions," as a prayer. Toward the end of the first century A.D. a nineteenth was added, which was actually a curse against the *mînîm,* or heretics, namely the Christians. Any male could be called on to pray or to read the portions from the Torah or the Prophets *(haptārôt).* On one occasion Jesus read from the scroll of the prophet Isaiah (61:1-2) in the synagogue at Nazareth. Any competent individual could also be called on to give the sermon (cf. Acts 13:15, 42; 14:1; 17:2).

Jesus refers to the custom of the teachers of the law and the Pharisees sitting in Moses' seat (Mt 23:2). Such a seat of honor has been found at Chorazin. Stone benches along the walls were reserved for dignitaries The general congregation may have sat on mats or carpets.

Though synagogues in the Middle Ages had segregated galleries for women, there is no evidence for such segregation in ancient synagogues. In the NT the presence of women in the congregation is attested inasmuch as Jesus healed a crippled woman as he was teaching in a synagogue (Lk 13:10-17).

As the major community building, the synagogue was not only used for services on the Sabbath, Mondays, Thursdays and festival days, but also for various community functions. Children would be taught there by the *ḥazzān.* Funds could be kept in a communal treasury at the synagogue.

Offenders could be judged before the elders in the synagogues and flogged forty stripes save one by the *ḥazzān* (Mk 13:9; 2 Cor 11:24). Apostates could be excommunicated (Jn 9:22; 12:42; 16:2).

4. Remains of Buildings.

It is estimated that we have archeological remains for over one hundred synagogue sites from Palestine and for about twenty from the Diaspora. There are relatively few archeological evidences for synagogues in Palestine from either the first or the second century A.D. An inscription of Theodotus from Jerusalem, which has usually been dated prior to A.D. 70, refers to the establishment of a hostel for pilgrims and may possibly be related to the synagogue of the Freedmen (i.e., former slaves, Acts 6:9). It reads as follows: "Theodotus, son of Vettenos, the priest and *archisynagōgos,* son of a *archisynagōgos* and grandson of a *archisynagōgos,* who built the synagogue for purposes of reciting the law and studying the commandments, and the hostel, chambers and water installations to pro-

vide for the needs of itinerants from abroad, and whose father, with the elders, and Simonides, founded the synagogue."

A building (12 x 15 m.) at the Herodian fortress of Masada has been identified as a first-century synagogue by Y. Yadin. It is equipped with benches and two rows of columns. The building's entrance was oriented toward Jerusalem. Yadin found an ostracon with the inscription "priestly tithe" at the site. He argues that Herod had originally constructed the building as a synagogue for his Jewish followers. The Herodian building was later reused by the Zealots until the fall of Masada in A.D. 73 to the Romans. Pits in this building served as a *genîzâ,* or storage, for discarded Scriptural scrolls (Deuteronomy and Ezekiel). Nearby were *miqwā'ôt,* or stepped pools, for ritual purification.

A *triclinium* (dining room) at Herodium was transformed into a synagogue by the Zealots. The building measures 10.5 x 15 m. with benches along the walls. A *miqwâ* is near the entrance. This building is similar in appearance to that at Masada. S. Guttman believes that a building at Gamla in the Golan heights, which he uncovered in 1976, is also a first century A.D. synagogue.

But the alleged synagogue uncovered at Magdala in 1975 by V. Corbo and S. Loffreda has turned out to be part of a villa. No remains are visible from a first-century building excavated at Chorazin and identified by some scholars as a synagogue. The basalt synagogue that is visible at Chorazin is from a much later period. (In the Diaspora a building on the Aegean island of Delos has been identified as a synagogue dating from pre-Christian times.)

The most splendid synagogue remains in Palestine are those of the white limestone structure at Capernaum. On the basis of coins, the Franciscan excavators have dated this building to the fourth or fifth century A.D.; Israeli scholars still prefer to date it to the second or third century. In 1981 V. Corbo uncovered dark basalt walls underneath this synagogue, which he has identified as the remains of an earlier synagogue. He dug a trench within the nave and exposed a basalt wall for a length of 24 m. (78 ft.). The walls are nearly four feet thick. The floor was a cobbled pavement made up of black basalt. Pottery associated with the floor establishes its date as the first century A.D. Corbo has identified this structure as the synagogue built by the centurion, which Jesus attended (Lk 7:1-5; see J. F. Strange and H. Shanks).

No certain synagogue remains from the second century have been identified except for those at Nabratein, though Catholic excavators have claimed to have discovered a synagogue of "Jewish Christians" (third-fourth cent.) at the site of the Church of the Annunciation in Nazareth. They also identify several architectural fragments from the Franciscan monastery in Nazareth as derived from a synagogue (second-third cent.).

Most synagogue remains are from the Late Roman and Byzantine eras (A.D. 300-600), including about fifteen from Galilee and a similar number from the Golan Heights. The synagogues are of three architectural types: (1) Broad House, with the bema, or platform, on the southern long wall, such as at Khirbet Shema; (2) the Basilica type, as at Capernaum and Chorazin; (3) the Basilica with an apse at Beth Alpha.

5. Interior.

These later synagogues were elaborately decorated with symbols such as the lampstand *(měnôrâ)*, palm frond and citron. They were provided with a bema, or platform, for the reading of the Scriptures, and a niche for the display of the ark, or chest *('ărôn)*, for the biblical scrolls. In 1980 E. and C. Meyers discovered the fragment of such an ark niche from Nabratein. This pediment is decorated with reliefs of rampant lions, and a scallop shell with a hole for the chain of a perpetual lamp.

Many of the Byzantine synagogues were lavishly decorated with mosaics, including four mosaics of the zodiac at Hammath Tiberias, Beth Alpha, Na'aran and Husifa. The mosaic at Hammath Tiberias has a central panel with *Helios* (sun) on his chariot and figures reflecting the four seasons at the corners.

We also have three examples of lists of the twenty-four priestly courses *(mišmārôt)*, which hung in synagogues. Most synagogue inscriptions are of donors. The third-century A.D. synagogue at Dura Europos on the Euphrates River even had paintings on its walls depicting biblical narratives.

Because of the scant remains of synagogues from first-century A.D. Palestine, some scholars have argued that Luke-Acts is anachronistic when it refers to synagogue buildings. But this is to underestimate the fragmentary nature of the archaeological evidence and to disregard not only the testimony of the NT but also of Josephus (*Life* 277, 280), who speaks of a *proseuchē*, which was a large building at Tiberia (cf. also Jos. *J.W.* 2.14.4 §285; *Ant.* 14.10.23 §258; 19.6.3 §300). Philo's report of the anti-Semitic mob's attacks on *proseuchas* in Alexandria in A.D. 38 (*Leg. Gai.* 132) clearly refers to synagogue buildings.

See also JUDAISM; TEMPLE; WORSHIP.

DNTB: DIASPORA JUDAISM; HOMILY, ANCIENT; JEWISH COMMUNITIES IN ASIA MINOR; LITURGY: RABBINIC; TEMPLE, JEWISH.

BIBLIOGRAPHY. B. Brooten, *Women Leaders in the Ancient Synagogue* (Chico: Scholars Press, 1982); M. J. S. Chiat, *Handbook of Synagogue Architecture* (Chico: Scholars, 1982); L. L. Grabbe, "Synagogues in Pre-70 Palestine," *JTS* n.s. 39 (1988) 401-10; J. G. Griffiths, "Egypt and the Rise of the Synagogue," *JTS* n.s. 38 (1987) 1-15; J. Gutmann, ed., *Ancient Synagogues: The State of Research* (Chico: Scholars, 1981); idem, ed., *The Synagogue: Studies in Origins, Archaeology and Architecture* (New York: KTAV, 1975); M. Hengel, "Proseuche und Synagoge," in *Tradition und Glaube: Festgabe für Karl Georg Kuhn,* ed. G. Jeremias, H. W. Kuhn, and H. Stegemann (Güttingen: Vandenhoeck & Ruprecht, 1971) 157-84; F. Huttenmeister and G. Reeg, *Die antiken Synagogen in Israel* (2 vols.; Wiesbaden: L. Reichert, 1977); L. Levine, *The Ancient Synagogue: The First Thousand Years* (New Haven: Yale University Press, 2000); idem, ed., *Ancient Synagogues Revealed* (Jerusalem: Israel Exploration Society, 1981); idem, *The Synagogue in Late Antiquity* (Philadelphia: American Schools of Oriental Research, 1987); I. Levinskaya, "A Jewish or Gentile Prayer House? The Meaning of ΠΡΟΣΕΥΧΗ," *TynB* 41 (1990) 154-59; E. M. Meyers, "Synagogues of Galilee," *Archaeology* 35.3 (1985) 51-58; E. Schürer, *The History of the Jewish People in the Age of Jesus,* rev. and ed. G. Vermes et al. (Edinburgh: T & T Clark, 1979) 2:423-54; H. Shanks, *Judaism in Stone: The Archaeology of Ancient Synagogues* (New York: Harper & Row, 1979); J. F. Strange and H. Shanks, "Synagogue Where Jesus Preached Found at Capernaum," *BAR* 9.6 (1983) 24-31; J. Weingreen, "The Origin of the Synagogue," *Hermathena* 98 (1964) 68-84; Y. Yadin, *Masada* (New York: Random House, 1966). E. Yamauchi

SYNOPTIC PROBLEM

In reading the four Gospels it is apparent that three of them resemble one another and one does not. A brief time spent in any synopsis of the Gospels will indicate that Matthew, Mark and Luke share a number of striking similarities. The "Synoptic Problem" is the name that has been given to the problem of why the Gospels of Matthew, Mark and Luke look so much alike. Why are they so similar in content, in wording and in the order of events found within them?

1. The Similarity of the Synoptic Gospels
2. The Existence of a Literary Relationship
3. Various Literary Explanations
4. The Griesbach Hypothesis
5. The Two-Document Hypothesis
6. Problems with the Two-Document Hypothesis
7. The Value of the Solution of the Synoptic Problem

1. The Similarity of the Synoptic Gospels.

1.1 Similarity in Wording. The similarity of wording can easily be seen by comparing various parallel accounts found in these Gospels. This is best done by using a synopsis. Some helpful passages to compare are:

Matthew 19:13-15
Mark 10:13-16
Luke 18:15-17
Matthew 22:23-33
Mark 12:18-27
Luke 20:27-40
Matthew 24:4-8
Mark 13:5-8
Luke 21:8-11

1.2. Similarity in Order. Another area of similarity can be found when one compares the order of the various accounts (pericopes). Note:

Matthew 16:13—20:34
Mark 8:27—10:52
Luke 9:18-51/18:15-43
Matthew 12:46—13:58
Mark 3:31—6:6a
Luke 8:19-56

1.3. Similarity in Parenthetical Material. There also exists common parenthetical material. Note for example: "let the reader understand" in Matthew 24:15 and Mark 13:14; "he then said to the paralytic" in Matthew 9:6/Mark 2:10/Luke 5:24; "For he had said" in Mark 5:8/Luke 8:29.

1.4. Similarity in Biblical Quotations. At times we find the exact same form of an OT quotation.

This would not be unusual if that form were identical either with the Hebrew OT or the Greek translation of the OT known as the Septuagint, but when we find an identical quotation of the OT which is different from both the Hebrew OT and the Greek OT, this similarity requires some sort of explanation (cf. Mk 1:2 par. Mt 3:3 and Lk 3:4; Mk 7:7 par. Mt 15:9).

2. The Existence of a Literary Relationship.

There have been various ways in which people have sought to explain the similarities mentioned above. One attempt has been to explain their similarity as due to the inspiration of the Gospels. The similarity is due to the *Holy Spirit having guided Matthew, Mark and Luke. Such an explanation, however, does not really solve the problem, for those who posit this explanation usually maintain that the Gospel of John was also inspired. Yet John does not look like the Synoptics. If all four Gospels were written under the superintendence of the Holy Spirit, this superintendence cannot at the same time explain why some Gospels look alike and why another does not.

A second attempt to explain this similarity involves the argument from history. Matthew, Mark and Luke look alike because they are accurate historical records of what Jesus said and did. Without denying that the Synoptic Gospels do provide an accurate account of what Jesus said and did, it must be pointed out that at times we find a different ordering of the events and a different wording. In these instances are we to assume that the sayings and incidents are not historical? An incident in Jesus' ministry could be recounted correctly in different ways and in association with various events. Furthermore, a saying of Jesus in his native tongue, which was Aramaic, could be translated into Greek in several different ways.

These two explanations do not explain adequately the kind of similarities we find in the Synoptic Gospels. Some other explanation must be sought. As early as 1796, J. G. von Herder sought to explain the Synoptic Problem by positing a common oral tradition used by Matthew, Mark and Luke. This explanation was developed more fully by J. K. L. Gieseler in 1818. According to this explanation the disciples created this oral tradition, which soon became fixed in form. Some time after it was translated into Greek, this common tradition was used by the

Synoptic writers. Thus Matthew, Mark and Luke look alike because they all follow the exact same oral tradition.

There is little doubt that there was a period when the Gospel traditions circulated orally. Whether there ever was a period in which these traditions circulated only orally, how long that period lasted, the extent to which Matthew, Mark and Luke were influenced by the oral tradition, etc., have not been and may never be resolved. But can this explanation elucidate adequately the degree of similarity found in the Synoptic Gospels? This does not appear to be the case. At times the degree of similarity seems to require more than just a common oral tradition. More importantly, a common oral tradition is not able to explain the similar editorial comments that we find. Why do we find in the exact same location a word from the writer to his audience—"let the reader understand" (Mt 24:15/Mk 13:14)? Even more difficult for this explanation is the extensive agreement in the order of the material. Thus, although one does not want to minimize the influence of a common oral tradition on the writers of the Gospels, it would appear that the similarities we encounter require the existence of some sort of a literary relationship.

3. Various Literary Explanations.

If a literary relationship exists between the Synoptic Gospels, then the next question that must be investigated is the nature of that literary relationship. One explanation, originating with F. Schleiermacher (1817), suggested that the disciples had taken notes (memorabilia) of Jesus' words and deeds. These eventually were collected and arranged topically. From these collected memorabilia the Synoptic Gospels arose. This "fragmentary hypothesis" never received much support, for like the oral hypothesis it was not able to explain the extensive agreements in order.

Another theory is that of a so-called Ur-Gospel ("primitive" or "original" Gospel). According to G. E. Lessing (1776) and J. G. Eichhorn (1796), there existed an early written Gospel in Aramaic. This was translated into Greek and went through several revisions. The similarities we find in the Synoptic Gospels are due to the common use of a Greek translation of this "Ur-Gospel." The differences are explained by their use of different Greek recensions. The main

problem with this argument is that as one sought to reconstruct what this Ur-Gospel looked like, it began to look more and more like an Ur-Markus, that is, an earlier noncanonical form of the Gospel of Mark. This in turn began to look more and more like the canonical Gospel of Mark.

A more likely literary explanation is to see some sort of interdependence between the Synoptic Gospels themselves. The three most common explanations involving interdependence are:

Matthew wrote first, Mark used Matthew, Luke used Mark (Augustine).

Matthew wrote first, Luke used Matthew, Mark used Matthew and Luke (J. J. Griesbach, 1783 and 1789; W. R. Farmer, 1964).

Mark wrote first, Matthew used Mark, Luke used Mark. Matthew and Luke also used another common source—"Q" (H. J. Holtzmann, 1863; B. H. Streeter, 1924).

Of these three theories the most viable are the latter two: the Griesbach hypothesis and the two-document hypothesis.

4. The Griesbach Hypothesis.

This hypothesis, which argues that Matthew was the first Gospel written, that Luke used Matthew and that Mark used both Matthew and Luke, was first proposed by H. Owen in 1764. It received its name due to its advocacy by J. J. Griesbach. It has been revived and received considerable impetus recently as the two-Gospel hypothesis through the work of W. R. Farmer, J. B. Orchard and H.-H. Stoldt. Its early popularity and demise were associated with the rise and fall of the Tübingen Hypothesis (i.e., Matthew, Thesis; Luke, Antithesis; Mark, Synthesis). The strength of the Griesbach Hypothesis is that it appears to explain several aspects of the Synoptic Problem.

4.1. The Strengths of the Griesbach Hypothesis.

4.1.1. It Agrees with the Church Tradition. The early church tradition is quite unanimous in claiming that Matthew was the first Gospel written (Irenaeus, Eusebius, Augustine). Clement of Alexandria stated that the Gospels with genealogies were written first. Augustine furthermore called Mark an abridgment of Matthew. Whereas the priority of Mark was unknown in the early church, the priority of Matthew was assumed. It is clear that the Griesbach hypothesis fits this early tradition concerning the Synoptic Gospels better than the two-document hypothesis. It also fits better the order of the Gospels in the NT canon.

4.1.2. It Can Explain All the Gospel Agreements. In comparing the various agreements between the triple tradition (parallel passages in Matthew, Mark and Luke) we find that frequently we have Matthew-Mark agreements against Luke, Mark-Luke agreements against Matthew and even Matthew-Luke agreements against Mark. The Griesbach hypothesis can explain these quite simply: the Matthew-Mark agreements against Luke result when Luke deviates from his Matthean source but Mark does not; the Mark-Luke agreements against Matthew result when Luke deviates from his Matthean source and Mark follows Luke rather than Matthew; the Matthew-Luke agreements against Mark result when Luke follows Matthew and Mark deviates from both his sources. With regard to the latter the Griesbach hypothesis is strong where the two-document hypothesis is weak. It can easily explain the Matthew-Luke agreements against Mark, whereas the two-document hypothesis struggles with how Matthew and Luke can agree independently against their Markan source when they did not know each other, that is, when one did not use the other.

4.1.3. It Explains the Markan Redundancies. Within Mark we find at least 213 cases of redundancy such as: Mark 1:32 ("When evening came, as the sun was setting"); Mark 1:42 ("And immediately the leprosy left him and he was cleansed"); Mark 4:21 ("Is a lamp brought in order to be placed under a bushel basket or under a bed?"); etc. The Griesbach hypothesis suggests that this can best be explained by understanding that Mark tended to act with respect to his sources in the same way as the early scribes and copyists of the NT. When they found two different readings in their sources, they tended to harmonize them by including both. Mark's redundancies are therefore due to his having conflated his two sources when he came across different readings. Thus Matthew 8:16, "When evening came," and Luke 4:40, "While the sun was setting," become in Mark 1:32, "When evening came, as the sun was setting"; Matthew 5:14, "They do not set under a bushel basket," and Luke 8:16, "Nor set it under a bed," become in Mark 4:21, "Is a lamp brought in order to be placed under a bushel basket or under a bed?"

Other evidence for the Griesbach hypothesis, such as there being no need for the postula- tion of an additional hypothetical source such as "Q," could also be mentioned.

4.2. Problems for the Griesbach Hypothesis. A number of problems encountered by the Griesbach hypothesis have led many scholars to consider the two-document hypothesis a more viable option for explaining the Synoptic Problem. Two of these, the arguments in favor of the priority of Mark and the difficulty of claiming that Luke used Matthew, will be discussed at length below (see 5.1 and 5.2.1 below). There are several additional weaknesses.

4.2.1. The Griesbach Hypothesis Also Conflicts with the Church Tradition. Whereas the church tradition is unanimous in stating that Matthew was written before Mark and Luke, that tradition in the same breath also argues that Matthew was written in Aramaic (or Hebrew). Yet it is clear that our present Matthew is not a simple translation from Aramaic (or Hebrew) into Greek. Thus the Matthew of church tradition does not fit the Greek Matthew of the Synoptic Problem. If therefore the tradition at this point is either incorrect or speaking of a predecessor (or source) of our Greek Matthew, this greatly weakens the value of the church tradition for solving the Synoptic Problem (*see* Matthew, Gospel of).

Other aspects of the church tradition also cause difficulty for the Griesbach hypothesis. These include Papias's statement that Mark had as his main source the "memoirs" of Peter and wrote his Gospel independently of Matthew, and the views of Origen, the Anti-Marcionite Prologues and Augustine that Luke was written last.

4.2.2. Certain Gospel Agreements Are Best Explained by the Priority of Mark. Whereas the Griesbach hypothesis can explain all the Gospel agreements, in numerous instances the particular explanation of why two Gospels agree against the other is not persuasive. This is particularly true with regard to Matthew-Mark agreements against Luke, and Mark-Luke agreements against Matthew. In the abstract the Griesbach hypothesis can explain such agreements easily, but when one seeks to explain why Mark and Luke agree against Matthew and why Mark and Matthew agree against Luke, the explanations are often quite unconvincing (see 5.1.6 below). In general the attempts on the basis of the Griesbach hypothesis to explain Luke's use of Matthew and Mark's use of Matthew and/or Luke are less convincing than the explanations of how

Matthew and Luke used Mark according to the two-document hypothesis. Clearly the vast majority of redaction-critical investigation in the Synoptic Gospels has been based on the view that Matthew and Luke used Mark. Attempts to do redaction-critical work on the basis of a Matthean priority are meager and less convincing.

4.2.3. The Markan Redundancies Can Be Explained by the Two-Document Hypothesis. At first glance the argument that the 213 examples of Markan redundancy are due to his conflation of Matthew and Luke appears convincing, but on closer examination it is clear that out of these 213 examples only 17 are clear cases of redundancy in which Matthew has only one half of the redundancy and Luke has the other. (In 39 instances Matthew and Luke have the same parallel redundancy and lack the other; in 37 instances they possess neither redundant parallel; in 60 instances Matthew has one or both parallels and Luke has neither; in 26 instances Luke has one or both parallels and Matthew has neither; in 11 instances Luke has both parallels and Matthew has one; in 17 instances Matthew has both parallels and Luke has one; and in 6 instances Matthew and Luke have both parallels.) Thus we are essentially speaking of only 17 possible examples of conflation and not 213.

The attempt of the Griesbach hypothesis to see the Gospel of Mark as being typified by conflation is furthermore compromised when it at the same time speaks of Mark as an abridgment of Matthew and Luke. These supposed tendencies are essentially contradictory. The harmony of Tatian called the *Diatesseron* (c. 150) is an early example of conflation at work. But when one compares the portions of the *Diatesseron* derived from the Synoptic Gospels, they are considerably longer than any of the Synoptic Gospels. Mark, on the other hand, is considerably shorter than either Matthew or Luke. It is therefore quite unlike this early example of conflation. The Markan redundancies are therefore not a convincing argument in favor of the Griesbach hypothesis. It may even be that they can be better explained by the two-document hypothesis (see 5.1.2 below).

5. The Two-Document Hypothesis.

The explanation that has come to dominate Synoptic studies during the last century and a half has been the two-document hypothesis. This theory argues that Mark was the first Gospel written and that it was used independently by Matthew and Luke. It also argues that along with Mark, Matthew and Luke used another common source that has been called "Q." Evidence for the priority of Mark and the existence of "Q" follow.

5.1. The Priority of Mark.

5.1.1. Mark Is the Shortest Gospel. Of the three Synoptic Gospels, Mark is the shortest in length: It contains 661 verses; Matthew contains 1,068; Luke contains 1,149. When their content is compared, 97.2 percent of Mark is paralleled in Matthew and 88.4 percent is paralleled in Luke. It is easier to understand Matthew and Luke using Mark, and choosing to add additional materials to it, than to think of Mark using Matthew, Luke or both, and deciding to omit so much material. Why would he have omitted the birth accounts, the *Sermon on the Mount, the Lord's Prayer, various resurrection appearances, etc. It is easier to understand Matthew and Luke choosing to add this material to their Markan source than Mark choosing to omit so much material. The suggestion that Mark may have desired to produce a shorter, more abridged account stumbles over the fact that the common accounts in the Synoptic Gospels are generally longer in Mark. If Mark wanted to write an abbreviated account of Matthew and/or Luke, why would he choose to make the stories in his abridged account longer? These are contrary tendencies. When one seeks to abridge a work, one generally does so not only by eliminating certain materials but by abridging what one decides to keep.

5.1.2. Mark Has the Poorest Greek. There is a consensus that the Greek of Mark is poorer than that of either Matthew or Luke. It is easier to understand Matthew and Luke using Mark and improving on his Greek than to think of Mark copying the better Greek of Matthew and/or Luke and making it worse. There are numerous examples of peculiar Markan expressions.

(1) Mark contains various colloquialisms (Mk 10:20, "I have observed," aorist middle; 2:4, "bed" as *krabatton*) and grammatical problems (Mk 4:41, "hears" as a singular verb; 16:6, "see" as a singular verb; 5:9-10, "he begged" for the plural "we").

(2) Mark has Aramaic expressions (Mk 3:17; 5:41; 7:11, 34; 14:36; 15:22, 34) that are not found in Matthew or Luke. It is much easier to see Matthew and Luke omitting these Aramaic

expressions and giving their Greek counterparts than to see Mark choosing to abridge Matthew and/or Luke but adding Aramaic expressions that his Greek readers did not understand.

(3) Mark is frequently redundant. On numerous occasions (there are 213 examples), Mark has a redundant expression such as, "When evening came, as the sun was setting" (Mk 1:32; cf. also Mk 1:42; 2:25-26; 4:21; 15:24). It is easier to understand why Matthew and/or Luke would seek to eliminate such redundancies than to understand why, in abridging Matthew and/or Luke, Mark would have added them.

5.1.3. Mark Has Harder Readings. At times we find in Mark a saying that creates a theological difficulty but do not find this difficulty in Matthew and/or Luke. In Mark, for example, we find apparent limitations of Jesus' power (cf. Mk 1:32-34; 3:9-10; 6:5-6 with par.). At other times we find theological difficulties in Mark but not in Matthew or Luke (cf. Mk 10:17-18; 3:4-5; 2:25-26). In Mark 10:17-18 we have Jesus saying, "Why do you call me good? No one is good but God alone." It is easy to see why Matthew would want to change this to "Why do you ask me about what is good? There is One who is good." The changing (or explaining) of Mark's harder readings by Matthew and/or Luke is much easier to understand than Mark choosing to make the easier reading in Matthew and/or Luke more difficult.

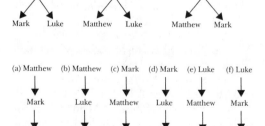

5.1.4. The Lack of Matthew-Luke Verbal Agreements Against Mark. If one observes the various kinds of agreements in the Synoptic Gospels, it is clear that, whereas we have numerous Matthew-Mark agreements against Luke, and Mark-Luke agreements against Matthew, there is a paucity of Matthew-Luke agreements against Mark. Assuming the simplest kind of interdependence in which one Gospel writer used one other Gospel writer, we have the following possibilities.

All other possible combinations of interdependence require that either Matthew "knew" (in the sense of "used") Luke or that Luke "knew" Matthew. As we shall see, this is most unlikely (see 5.2.1 below).

Given the fact that accounts of the triple tradition seldom show Matthew and Luke agreeing against Mark in their wording, explanations (1) and (3) cannot explain this. Furthermore (1), (c) and (e) cannot account for the Mark-Luke agreements, and (3), (b) and (d) cannot explain the Matthew-Mark agreements. Only explanations (2), (a) and (f) can explain the abundance of Matthew-Mark and Mark-Luke agreements and the lack of Matthew-Luke agreements. However, the arguments given earlier argue against (a) and (f).

5.1.5. The Lack of Matthew-Luke Agreements in Order Against Mark. Similar to the preceding argument, but involving the order of the materials, is the observation that when Matthew differs from the order of the accounts found in Mark, Luke never agrees with Matthew. Likewise, when Luke differs from the order that we find in Mark, Matthew never agrees with Luke against Mark. This observation by K. Lachmann (1835) has sometimes been thought to be an absolute proof for the priority of Mark. This, however, is not a proof of Markan priority, for with the Griesbach hypothesis in which Matthew was written first, Luke used Matthew, and Mark used both Matthew and Luke, we can explain such agreements in order. Lachmann, however, added to this observation the fact that, whereas both Matthew's deviation from Mark and Luke's deviation from Mark are understandable, a Markan deviation from the order of Matthew and Luke is much less so. In light of this observation, there is no reason to refer to this as the "Lachmann Fallacy."

5.1.6. Certain Literary Agreements Are Best Explained by a Markan Priority. There exist in the Synoptic Gospels certain literary agreements that are best explained on the basis of Matthew and Luke having used Mark. For instance, in Matthew 9:1-2/Mark 2:1-5/Luke 5:17-20, Matthew has, as he does frequently elsewhere (cf. Mt 8:5-13; 9:18-26), abbreviated the Markan account and omitted the reason why Jesus saw the faith of the paralytic and his friends. In Matthew

27:15-22/Mark 15:6-13/Luke 23:18-21, Luke has abbreviated the account and omitted the explanation of the Barabbas episode by not referring to the custom of releasing a prisoner at the time of the Passover. In Matthew 3:13-16/Mark 1:9-10/Luke 3:21-22, Matthew has sought to change the wording of Mark and has, by changing the verb *baptized* to the participle "having been baptized," mistakenly placed the word *immediately* with the verb "went up." The result, although understandable, has Jesus immediately coming up out of the water rather than immediately seeing the heavens opened. In Matthew 19:16-17/Mark 10:17-18/Luke 18:18-19, Matthew has sought to eliminate the difficulty created by Mark's "Why do you call me good? No one is good but God alone." Instead he has "Why do you ask me about what is good?" However, his next verse indicates that his source spoke about God being good—not "good" in an abstract sense, for he adds, "There is One who is good."

These and other literary agreements are more understandable on the basis of Matthew and Luke having used Mark than on the basis of any other theory of interdependence.

5.1.7. The Argument from Redaction. Probably the most significant argument today in favor of the priority of Mark involves redactional studies. It is undeniable that the great majority of redactional investigations of the Synoptic Gospels proceed on the basis of the priority of Mark. It is easier, for example, to understand why Matthew added his emphasis on Jesus as the "Son of David" to the Markan account than to understand why Luke and Mark would have chosen to omit this reference (cf. Mt 12:23; 15:22; 21:9, 15). Similarly, it is easier to understand Matthew having added his famous "this was to fulfill . . ." in Matthew 1:22; 2:15, 17; 4:14; 8:17; 12:17; 13:14, 35; 21:4; 27:9 to his Markan source than to understand why Mark and Luke would have chosen to omit them. Five of the last six references reveal this clearly, for the parallels in Mark and Luke lack this reference. To assume that Mark and Luke used Matthew and chose to omit these references is most difficult to comprehend. On the other hand, Matthew's having added them to his Markan source is easily understandable.

We also discover that certain Markan stylistic features, when found in Matthew, appear almost exclusively in the material that Matthew has in common with Mark. The famous Markan use of "immediately" occurs forty-one times within his Gospel. In Matthew it occurs eighteen times. Of these eighteen times, fourteen occur in the material he shares with Mark. The other four occur in his M (Matthew's special material) and Q material. However, of the 18,293 words which are in Matthew, 10,901 have parallels in Mark. A total of 7,392 do not have a parallel. This means that there is one "immediately" for every 778 words in the material Matthew has in common with Mark, but there is only one "immediately" for every 1,848 words in the non-Markan material (M and Q). The more frequent appearance of the word *immediately* in the material Matthew has in common with Mark is more easily explained by his use of Mark, where this word is found in abundance, than by any other explanation.

Another Markan stylistic feature is his use of an editorial "for (*gar*)" clause to explain something to his reader (see Mk 1:16, 22; 5:28; 6:17-18 etc.). Within Mark we find thirty-four such clauses; within Matthew we find ten, but all ten appear in the material he shares with Mark. Not one is found in the remaining material. If Matthew used Mark, the presence of these editorial "for" clauses is understandable. But why would they be only in one area of the Matthean material, the material he shares with Mark, if Matthew did not use Mark?

5.1.8. Mark's Theology Is Less Developed. When one compares the common material in Matthew, Mark and Luke, it is obvious time and time again that the materials in Matthew and Luke are theologically more developed. Mark, for example, uses the term "Lord" (*kyrios*) for Jesus six times, but in Matthew we find it used not only in the same six instances but in an additional twenty-four. Fifteen of these instances are found in material where Mark lacks this term. The same can be said of Luke, who uses this title even more frequently. It is easier to understand how Matthew and Luke would have added this title to their Markan source than to understand why Mark would have chosen to eliminate it if he were using Matthew and/or Luke. The same can be said for the title "Christ."

5.1.9. Conclusion. The reason why most scholars maintain the priority of Mark is not based on any one argument listed above. Rather, the priority of Mark is based on the entire collection of arguments. The weight of any one argument may not be convincing, but together they are quite convincing, and the best available hypothesis for explaining the Synoptic

Problem is that Matthew and Luke used Mark in the composition of their Gospels. Being a "hypothesis," absolute proof is by definition lacking, and the Synoptic Problem must always remain open to a better hypothesis if one should become available.

5.2. The Existence of "Q." Once the priority of Mark has been accepted, we are faced with another problem. This involves the common material found in Matthew and Luke that we do not find in Mark, the so-called Q material. Some examples of this are: Matthew 6:24/Luke 16:13; Matthew 7:7-11/Luke 11:9-13; Matthew 11:25-27/Luke 10:21-22; Matthew 23:37-39/Luke 13:34-35. How is this common material to be explained? We shall discuss below the suggestion that Matthew and Luke obtained this material from various oral traditions, but the simplest explanation is that either Matthew used Luke or that Luke used Matthew to obtain this material. There are a number of reasons, however, why it is unlikely that Luke used Matthew. (The theory that Matthew used Luke is held by few, and most of the arguments given below also demonstrate that Matthew did not use Luke.)

5.2.1. Matthew and Luke Did Not Know Each Other. This is evident from several lines of evidence.

(1) *Luke lacks the Matthean additions to the triple tradition.* When we find an account in the triple tradition and Matthew has something in the account not found in Mark, we never find that Matthean addition in Luke (cf. Mt 8:17; 12:5-7; 13:14-15, etc.). If Luke used Matthew, why do we never find any of these additions in Luke? The easiest explanation is that Luke did not use Matthew. (The same can be said about Lukan additions to the triple tradition. They are never found in Matthew.)

(2) *The "Q" material is found in a different context in Luke.* The Q material is arranged in Matthew into five blocks of teachings surrounded by six blocks of narrative. As a result we find: Narrative (Mt 1—4); Teaching (Mt 5—7); N (Mt 8—9); T (Mt 10); N (Mt 11—12); T (Mt 13); N (Mt 14—17); T (Mt 18); N (Mt 19—22); T (Mt 23—25); N (Mt 26—28). It should also be noted that each of these five teaching sections end similarly with "and when Jesus finished these sayings" (Mt 7:28; 11:1; 13:53; 19:1; 26:1). Luke, however, has lumped the Q material into two sections: Luke 6:20—8:3; 9:51—18:14. It is difficult to understand why, if Luke used Matthew, he would

have wanted to destroy the framework of the Q material in Matthew for his arrangement.

(3) *At times the Q material is less developed in Luke.* If Luke had used Matthew, one would expect that the form of the material in Luke would generally be more theologically developed than the corresponding material in Matthew. We do not find this, however. At times the Q material in Luke is clearly less developed. (Cf. Lk 6:20, "poor"; 21, "hunger now"; 31, no reference to "Law and the prophets"; 11:2, "Father"; 14:26, "hate.")

(4) *The lack of Matthew-Luke agreements in order and wording against Mark.* If Luke used Matthew, it is difficult to understand why his order never agrees with Matthew against Mark and why there are so few verbal agreements in Matthew-Luke against Mark.

(5) *The lack of M material in Luke.* By definition the *M material consists of the material in Matthew not found in either Mark or Luke. If Luke used Matthew, it is difficult to explain why he did not include some of this material. Such an argument from silence is always questionable. Nevertheless, knowing some of the theological interests of Luke, it is difficult to understand why, if he used Matthew, he did not include such material as the coming of the wise men (Mt 2:1-12). To have Gentiles present at the birth of Jesus would have fit his universal emphasis quite well. Likewise, the exclusion of such stories as the flight to Egypt and the return to Nazareth (Mt 2:13-23); the story of the guards at the tomb (Mt 27:62-66) and their report (Mt 28:11-15); and the unique Matthean material concerning the resurrection (Mt 28:9-10, 16-20) is inexplicable.

On the basis of the above arguments, it seems reasonable to conclude that Luke did not know Matthew (and Matthew did not know Luke). As a result, some other common source has been posited. The origin of "Q" as a symbol for this common material found only in Matthew and Luke is debated, but most probably it comes from the first letter of the German word *Quelle*, which means source.

5.2.2. Was Q a Written Source? If we assume that Matthew and Luke used a common source alongside Mark, was this source written or oral? The main arguments in favor of a written Q involve the exactness in wording of some of the Q parallels. The exactness in wording is at times quite impressive (cf. Mt 6:24 par. Lk 16:13, where twenty-seven of twenty-eight words are exactly the same; Mt 7:7-8 par. Lk 11:9-10, where all twenty-four words are exactly the same). Is this exactness better explained on the basis of a common written source? On the other hand, at times some of the Q material is not very exact.

Another argument frequently put forward for a written Q involves an agreement in order. At times one can observe a certain degree of order between the Q material in Matthew and Luke, but these agreements in order are not sufficient to require a common written source. Some have also sought to find a common order between the Q material in Luke and the Q material in each of the five Q sections in Matthew, that is, the order of Q in Luke is compared to Matthew 5—7, then to Matthew 10, to Matthew 13, etc. The argument from order has been convincing to some scholars but not to most.

A third argument for Q being a written source is the presence of doublets (double accounts of the same incident) in Matthew and Luke. This supposedly demonstrates that they used two separate written sources—Mark and Q. At best, however, if such doublets exist, they prove the use of a second common source, but this could have been oral or fragmentary written sources. A further attempt to prove that Q was a written source has been the effort to demonstrate that there is a common vocabulary and style in the Q material, which reveals that it comes from a common written source. This attempt, however, has not been convincing.

The Two- (or Four-) Document Hypothesis

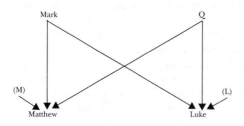

5.2.3. Summary. The Q hypothesis is not without its problems, but it possesses fewer difficulties than alternative hypotheses. As to its form, it is difficult to determine if the Q material came to Matthew and Luke as a single written source, as several written sources or from a common oral tradition. That Matthew and Luke did not know each other seems fairly certain. This,

along with the argument for Markan priority, favors some sort of a two-document hypothesis in which Matthew and Luke used Mark and probably a written Q. A related version of this is the four-document hypothesis, which assumes that the unique material found in Matthew (the M material) and Luke (the L material) came from two additional written sources.

6. Problems with the Two-Document Hypothesis.

The major alternative to the two- (or four-) document hypothesis is the Griesbach hypothesis (see 4 above). This hypothesis explains well the major problem facing the two-document hypothesis—the existence of Matthew-Luke agreements against Mark. Along with various agreements in omission created by their abbreviation of Mark, and the agreements which came about by their improvement of Mark's grammar, there are several significant Matthew-Luke agreements against Mark (cf. Mk 1:7-8; 2:12; 3:24, 26-29; 5:27; 6:33; 8:35; 9:2-4, 18-19; 10:29; 14:65, 72 and the Matthew-Luke parallels).

Although the Griesbach hypothesis can explain these agreements better than the two-document hypothesis, we must not forget that the reverse is true concerning all the arguments for Markan priority and against Matthew and Luke knowing each other. These arguments are far more numerous and weighty. As to the Matthew-Luke agreements against Mark, several explanations can be offered.

6.1. Overlapping Traditions. The Q material and Mark must have overlapped in certain places. At times Matthew and Luke may have preferred the Q readings over Mark and thus created a Matthew-Luke agreement.

6.2. Textual Corruption. We know that the early scribes had a tendency to make parallel accounts in the Gospels conform to one another, and since Matthew was the best-known and most frequently used Synoptic Gospel, it may be that some early scribe copying Luke may have changed his Lukan text to conform to the reading in Matthew. In such instances, the result would be a Matthew-Luke agreement.

6.3. Overlapping Oral Tradition. It may also be possible that at times Matthew and Luke knew a form of the oral tradition that was more familiar to them than the wording in their Markan source and so chose, quite independently of each other, to word their accounts according to the oral tradition. Again, a Matthew-Luke agreement would have resulted.

Among the several other possible reasons for a Matthew-Luke agreement are: coincidental modifications of Mark's grammar; coincidental omissions of Markan material; the common use of a different Mark and coincidental modifications of difficult passages in Mark.

7. The Value of the Solution of the Synoptic Problem.

The solution of the Synoptic Problem proves to be of value in several ways.

7.1. Historical Criticism. In seeking the solution to this problem great impetus was provided by the desire to find the oldest and, it was assumed, best historical source for investigating the life of Jesus. It was hoped that once the basic source of the Synoptic Gospels was discovered, scholars would possess a historical source uncluttered with the theology of the early church, which would then be the basis for the quest for the historical Jesus. Mark, it was thought, provided this source. Today we realize that Mark, like the other Gospels, is not an objective biography of the life of Jesus in any modern sense of the word (*see* Gospel [Genre]). What biography would omit the first thirty years of a person's life? And what Gospel writer is "objective"? It is evident, therefore, that this quest for a completely objective biography of the life of Jesus was doomed from the start.

The solution of the Synoptic Problem, however, has provided certain tools that are useful for historical investigation. The criterion of multiple attestation is based on the premise that several witnesses are better than one, and if a teaching of Jesus is witnessed to in Mark, Q, M, L and John, then we have five different sources that witness to its historicity (*see* Gospels [Historical Reliability]). Another useful tool is the criterion of divergent patterns from the redaction. Because of the application of the two-document hypothesis, Synoptic scholarship today is better acquainted with the literary style and theological emphases of the different Evangelists. It is quite apparent that if an Evangelist included something in his Gospel that seemed to conflict with his own emphasis, he witnessed to that tradition being very old and well-known.

7.2. Redactional Investigation of the Gospels. By observing how Matthew and Luke used Mark

and Q, we are better able to understand their theological emphases. Thus we are better able to comprehend the meaning of their works. One only needs to compare the following examples with their parallels to see how they help reveal the theological emphases of the Gospel writer: Luke 5:17; 6:27-28; 11:13; Matthew 8:15; 13:35; 15:22.

7.3. Hermeneutical Insights. It is frequently helpful to observe how one Evangelist interpreted his source, for the Evangelists were closer in time, situation, language and thought-world to their contemporaries than we. As a result, we can at times find help in interpreting a difficult text by observing how they interpreted this text. For example, it is evident from Matthew 10:37-38 that Luke's command to "hate one's parents" (Lk 14:26) means that his disciples must love Jesus more. One can also gain insight on how particular teachings of Jesus can be applied by observing how the Evangelists seek to apply them to their situation. A good example of this is the parable of the lost sheep (Lk 15:3-7 par. Mt 18:10-14).

See also GOSPEL (GENRE).

DJG: FORM CRITICISM; L; M; REDACTION CRITICISM; SYNOPTICS AND JOHN; TRADITION CRITICISM.

BIBLIOGRAPHY. A. J. Bellinzoni, Jr. et al., *The Two-Source Hypothesis: A Critical Appraisal* (Macon, GA: Mercer University Press, 1985); W. R. Farmer, *The Synoptic Problem: A Critical Analysis* (New York: Macmillan, 1964); A. M. Farrer, "On Dispensing with Q" in *Studies in the Gospels* (Oxford: Blackwell, 1955) 55-88; J. A. Fitzmyer, "The Priority of Mark and the 'Q' Source in Luke" in *Jesus and Man's Hope* (Pittsburgh: Pittsburgh Theological Seminary, 1970) 131-70; M. Goodacre, *The Case Against Q* (Harrisburg, PA: Trinity Press International, 2002); idem, *The Synoptic Problem* (Sheffield: Sheffield Academic Press, 2001); J. C. Hawkins, *Horae Synopticae* (Oxford: Clarendon, 1909); J. S. Kloppenborg, *The Formation of Q: Trajectories in Ancient Wisdom Collections* (Philadelphia: Fortress, 1987); T. R. W. Longstaff and P. A. Thomas, *The Synoptic Problem: A Bibliography 1716-1988* (Macon, GA: Mercer University Press, 1988); F. Neirynck, *The Minor Agreements of Matthew and Luke Against Mark with a Cumulative List* (Leuven: Leuven University Press, 1974); B. Reicke, *The Roots of the Synoptic Gospels* (Philadelphia: Fortress, 1986); R. H. Stein, *The Synoptic Problem* (Grand Rapids: Baker, 1987); B. H.

Streeter, *The Four Gospels* (London: Macmillan, 1951); H.-H. Stoldt, *History and Criticism of the Markan Hypothesis* (Macon, GA: Mercer University Press, 1980); G. M. Styler, "The Priority of Mark," in C. F. D. Moule, *The Birth of the New Testament* (3d ed.; New York: Harper & Row) 285-316; C. M. Tuckett, "The Argument from Order and the Synoptic Problem," *TZ* 36 (1980) 338-54; idem, *The Revival of the Griesbach Hypothesis: An Analysis and Appraisal* (Cambridge: Cambridge University Press, 1983). R. H. Stein

SYNOPTICS AND JOHN. *See* JOHN, GOSPEL OF.

T, U, V

TABLE FELLOWSHIP: GOSPELS

One distinctive feature of Jesus' ministry was his practice of a radically inclusive and nonhierarchical table fellowship as a central strategy in his announcement and redefinition of the inbreaking rule of God. In so doing, Jesus challenged the inherent exclusivism and status consciousness of accepted social and religious custom and presented a living parable of a renewed *Israel.

1. The Significance of Shared Meals
2. The Historical Jesus and Table Fellowship
3. Jesus' Table Praxis According to Mark
4. Jesus' Open "Symposia" According to Luke
5. Conclusion

1. The Significance of Shared Meals.

It would be difficult to overestimate the importance of table fellowship for the cultures of the Mediterranean basin in the first century of our era. Mealtimes were far more than occasions for individuals to consume nourishment. Being welcomed at a table for the purpose of eating food with another person had become a ceremony richly symbolic of friendship, intimacy and unity. Thus betrayal or unfaithfulness toward anyone with whom one had shared the table was viewed as particularly reprehensible. On the other hand, when persons were estranged, a meal invitation opened the way to reconciliation. Even everyday mealtimes were highly complex events in which social values, boundaries, statuses and hierarchies were reinforced. Anyone who challenged these rankings and boundaries would be judged to have acted dishonorably, a serious charge in cultures based on the values of honor and shame. Transgressing these customs consistently would make a person an enemy of social stability.

The extended family was the usual context in which meals were consumed. Coming together to eat became the occasion for sensing again that one was an integral, accepted part of a group. Beyond the household, people generally preferred to eat with persons from their own social class. Such meals of like with like reinforced the systems of social stratification, with the seating arrangements further signaling the relative status of each guest. People invited their social, religious and economic equals, that is, those who were in a position to return the favor in a relationship of balanced reciprocity.

In Israel a very salient social division had been created by the existence of a priestly class obliged by Torah (Lev 17—26) to live in a special state of ritual purity for at least six weeks a year while preparing to serve and then serving in the temple. Keeping this obligation led to a certain physical and social distance between priestly families and all other Israelites, whom the priests regarded as more or less unclean.

During the heavy-handed Hellenization that led to the Maccabean revolt (167-164 B.C.), many Jews, including an alarming number of leading priests, compromised both their purity and their identity by sacrificing to pagan gods and adopting Greek customs. In reaction, those who came to be known as Pharisees, remembering the call to separation from pagan ways that characterized the restoration of Israel after the Exile (cf. Ezra 10:11; see Judaism), exhorted all Jews to intensify their holiness and sense of unique identity by voluntarily living according to the priestly laws of ritual purity every day of the year. Although they did not reject the priesthood or the temple cult, in light of the priests' and the temple's vulnerability to impurity, the Pharisees sought to renew Israel by shifting the locus of holiness to their homes. This resulted in a special focus on the purity of one's everyday food and of one's companions at every meal.

The Pharisees regarded their tables at home as surrogates for the Lord's altar in the temple in Jerusalem and therefore strove to maintain in their households and among their eating companions the state of ritual purity required of priests in temple service (Neusner). The food had to be properly tithed, prepared and served but in itself did not symbolize any event (Passover was an exception). Pharisees prescribed no special prayers or unusual foods for their meals. But they did insist on eating only with companions who had "undefiled hands" (Mk 7:2-4), that is, with persons in a state of ritual purity (cf. Ex 30:19-21). The Pharisees longed for the time when all of Israel would live in such a state of holiness. They believed that Israel's identity and blessed future depended on it.

This is the context in which Jesus' practice of a radically open table fellowship is remembered in the NT. The exclusive and hierarchical meal practices of other Jewish groups, such as the Essenes, play no explicit role in any early Christian document. The Synoptic Gospels are consistent in specifically presenting Jesus in sharp contrast to Pharisaic practice as a teacher and healer who in God's name welcomed at the table an astonishing variety of both reputable and disreputable persons. This strongly suggests that Jesus' open table fellowship was a strategy used to challenge social and religious exclusivism wherever it was accepted as normal or officially sanctioned (Koenig, 20).

2. The Historical Jesus and Table Fellowship.

There is a high level of scholarly agreement that Jesus practiced a radically inclusive table fellowship as a central strategy in his announcement and redefinition of the in-breaking rule of God (*see* Kingdom of God). Although a few writers have challenged the historicity of Jesus actually eating with "toll collectors and sinners" (Smith 1989), the evidence for such an intentionally and symbolically open table is quite strong, being found in multiple sources and in various traditional forms. The sources include Mark, the Synoptic sayings source (*Q), Luke's unique material and probably the *Gospel of Thomas*. The forms include controversy stories (Mk 2:15-17 par. Mt 9:9-13 and Lk 5:29-32), kingdom parables (Lk 14:15-24 par. Mt 22:1-13; *Gos. Thom.* 64), pronouncement stories (Lk 7:36-50; 19:1-10), brief sayings (Mt 8:11-12 par. Lk 13:28-29; 14:12-

14), opponents' criticisms (Mt 11:18-19 par. Lk 7:33-34) and a summary (Lk 15:1-2).

Scholars have called particular attention to the odd saying of Jesus found in the Synoptic Sayings Source (Q), Matthew 11:16-19 and its parallel Luke 7:31-35. The presentations of this saying reveal little if any post-resurrection idealization of Jesus; thus they seem to offer an authentic glimpse into Jesus' own milieu by noting the people's criticism of *John the Baptizer as one who "has a demon" and of Jesus as "a glutton and a drunkard, a friend of toll collectors and sinners." The charge against John is unique in the NT and seems strange in light of the early Christians' memory of the claim that Jesus was possessed by a demon (Mk 3:22 and par.). The charge against Jesus is also unique and must have been an embarrassment for the early church, especially since the insult is not rebutted in this passage.

In no other Christian tradition is Jesus' open table fellowship denounced so sharply, and here the memory may be of Jesus' own caricature of the responses to John and him from their Galilean contemporaries. By expressing the spirit of their responses in pointed self-insults, Jesus may have intended to take the wind out of his critics' sails (Koenig, 23). In any case, the circumstances of the historical Jesus, rather than those of the post-resurrection Christian communities, provide the most plausible context for this sort of serious wordplay. Supporting this judgment is the unique use of *friend (philos)* in this saying. The term appears nowhere else on Jesus' lips as a self-designation, nor is it used in any other charge against him. To be reproached as a "friend of toll collectors" places Jesus plausibly in a Galilean context, where Herod's toll collectors were shunned by most people not so much because of their ritual impurity as because of their reputation for dishonest gouging of both rich and poor.

It is thus highly probable that Jesus did associate frequently with such immoral people, at the table and elsewhere. And as one who claimed to speak for God, his indiscriminate behavior greatly offended a wide spectrum of people who had been injured by the likes of Levi (Mk 2:13-17). In his message and table praxis, eating with anyone who would eat with him, Jesus challenged the central role played by table fellowship in reinforcing boundaries and statuses widely believed to be sanctioned by God. His use of table fellowship as a divine tool for undermining boundaries and hierarchies made him an enemy of social stability in the eyes of leading contemporaries.

Furthermore, a strong case may be made for the historicity of Jesus' criticism of hierarchical human relationships, found in Mark, Luke's unique material and Matthew's unique material, and remembered in the form of pronouncement stories (Mk 9:33-37 par. Lk 9:46-48; Mk 10:42-45 par. Mt 20:25-28 and Lk 22:24-30), parables (Lk 14:7-11; 18:9-14), brief sayings (Mt 23:11-12) and symbolic narrative and comment (Jn 13:3-16). Such status differences were reinforced at social meals, so that the meal settings for Jesus' challenge of this social practice, which are emphasized by Luke 14:7-11; 22:24-30 and by John 13:3-16, would have rung true for their readers in the ancient world.

Of the Evangelists, Mark and Luke seem particularly concerned about the role of meals in the congregations of their readers. They express this concern by presenting the traditions regarding Jesus' criticism of traditional rankings at meals and his offensively inclusive table fellowship with unique and striking emphases.

3. Jesus' Table Praxis in Mark.

Mark presents Jesus' table praxis as a metaphor for Christian discipleship in general; the disciples' growing inability to comprehend the significance of Jesus' meal strategy is symbolic of their failure to understand the nature of Jesus' entire mission (Klosinski). For Mark the Last Supper is the climactic last meal at which discipleship collapses completely. Mark emphasizes the rule of God and Christian discipleship together as the basis for an alternative community that practiced a social ethic undermining boundaries and subverting traditional categories of status and hierarchy. For this community the primary social virtue was serving (slave's work), symbolized by serving each other at an inclusive table, with Jesus himself as the prime example (Mk 10:43-45; see Jn 13).

Mark dramatizes Jesus' strategy in his story about the celebration following Levi's positive response to Jesus' call to discipleship (Mk 2:15-17; see Mt 9:10-13 and Lk 5:29-32). At this banquet (Mark's Greek implies that they were reclining at a formal meal) Jesus and his "many followers" crossed significant social boundaries by eating with "many toll collectors and sin-

ners," provoking sharp criticism from the scribes of the Pharisees (were they also invited?). This sets up Jesus' general observation that "those who are well do not need a physician but those who are sick do. I didn't come to call the righteous, but sinners."

In Mark 7:1-23 Pharisees accuse some of Jesus' disciples of eating with "defiled hands" and presumably of not caring if the hands of their table companions were unwashed, that is, of practicing open table fellowship and ignoring the boundaries set by the traditions of the elders. Jesus defends their praxis by arguing that the ritual purity of one's body or one's food is irrelevant to God. The important matter is how one treats others. Yet the disciples are presented as resistant and missing the point, requiring special instruction (Mk 7:17-19).

Thematically related to these passages is the feeding of the five thousand (Mk 6:30-44; Mt 14:13-21; Lk 9:11-17; Jn 6:5-13), which is the only miracle tradition attributed to Jesus that is present in all four Gospels (see also the feeding of the four thousand in Mk 8:1-9 par. Mt 15:32-39). Common to all four writers was a meal tradition made extraordinary by the very large number who shared in an unexpected abundance for which Jesus was the host. The food was shared with all who were present, without any boundaries or tests of purity. Unique to Mark is his apparent intention to link the feedings of the five thousand and the four thousand to Jesus' final meal with his disciples, suggested by Jesus' "blessing, breaking and giving" of bread in all three passages.

In Mark's presentation of the Last Supper (Mk 14:18-25) the disciples' increasing inability to understand Jesus and his mission climaxes in betrayal. At this last occasion of table fellowship before his crucifixion, Jesus continued to practice the forgiveness that had characterized his earlier table praxis. Mark stresses that Jesus and his betrayer dipped their bread in the common bowl together; Judas, not Jesus, withdrew his hand from the table (Bartchy, 56). At the only meal in the narrative which Jesus and the Twelve celebrate together by themselves, all followed Judas in turning the bread of forgiveness into the bread of abandonment. Only the women, including the unnamed disciple who anointed Jesus for his burial while he reclined at the table in the home of Simon the Leper, remained faithful (Mk 14:3-11; 15:40-41). For Mark and his community, faithful discipleship is based on understanding what Jesus was about when he shared bread at his table and then living according to his serving praxis.

4. Jesus' Open "Symposia" in Luke.

Luke gives more attention to table etiquette, table fellowship and the households in which these meals were eaten than any other NT writer (see Luke, Gospel of). He highlights offering hospitality and sharing food as occasions which display the sharp contrast between the radical inclusiveness of Jesus' mission and the various degrees of exclusiveness demanded by his competitors for renewing Israel, the Pharisees and scribes, who repeatedly charged Jesus with "receiving sinners and eating with them" (Lk 15:1-2).

Among scholars who have studied meals in the ancient world, a consensus has begun to develop that Luke's unique presentation of Jesus as a teacher in the context of meals was influenced by his awareness of the symposium tradition that was popular in Greco-Roman literature (Smith 1987). According to that tradition, with the *Symposia* of Plato and Xenophon as archetypes, the symposium was the drinking and talking party that followed a formal banquet. It provided not only for eating with one's peers but also for exchanges of wit and discussion of serious subjects of mutual interest. Many of Luke's readers would have experienced symposia as the central social activity of such groups as the popular funeral clubs, trade associations and philosophical schools. At these formal meals the diners reclined around a central table on couches most commonly arranged in a U-shape called a "triclinium." Since one's position at the table displayed one's rank relative to the other guests, the host used special care in assigning positions of honor, beginning at the right of the entrance.

Luke 14:7-11 presents Jesus reclining (Luke's Greek implies a formal banquet setting) and teaching at the table of a Pharisee whose many guests had sought out the positions of honor. In this parable unique to Luke, Jesus urges the guests not to seek honor but to defer to others, "for everyone who exalts himself will be humbled, and he who humbles himself will be exalted" (Lk 14:11), a saying which both Matthew 23:12 and Luke 18:4 present in settings without meals. The structure of Luke 14 suggests further influence of the symposium genre, not only in

the ambiance of a dialogue (Lk 14:7, 12, 15), but also in the specific mention of the host, the guest of honor and main speaker (Jesus), the invited guests and the uninvited guests (Lk 14:13, 23, 25; 15:1).

Perhaps the most striking evidence for Luke's interest in the symposium format is the meal setting provided in Luke 22:24-27 for the antihierarchical tradition found in Mark 10:35-45. While reclining at the Last Supper with his disciples, Jesus speaks strong words to them about who among them was to be regarded as the greatest, then asks: "For which is greater, one who reclines at the table, or one who serves? Is it not the one reclining? But I am among you as one who serves!" With such words Luke must have hoped to motivate his readers to modify their own traditional meal praxis.

Luke 7:36-50 and 11:37-52 provide further evidence for this Hellenistic emphasis on meals as the context for Jesus' teaching, describing two more occasions at which Jesus reclined at the table and taught in a Pharisee's house. Luke uses these settings to dramatize the sharp contrast between Jesus' radically inclusive message, reinforced by his table praxis, and the exclusive boundaries of purity set by the Pharisees and scribes that circumscribed their own meals.

Unique to the tension-filled meal setting of the special tradition in Luke 7:36-50 (but see also Mk 14:3-9) is the presentation of a woman described as a "sinner" who intruded into the meal hosted by Simon the Pharisee. Jesus and Simon are shown disagreeing strongly about the appropriateness of her presence. She clearly felt at home in the company of Jesus, who had forgiven her many sins; and she lavished attention on him in ways that highlighted Simon's failure to show the customary marks of hospitality. In view of the immediately following and unique listing of Mary called Magdalene, Joanna, Susanna and "many" other women, both as supporters of Jesus' itinerant ministry in Galilee and as traveling companions (Lk 8:1-3), it is likely that Luke intended here to emphasize that Jesus welcomed all kinds of women at his table (see Women). Note also Luke's unique presenting of Jesus' welcoming Mary as his student in the context of a meal about to be served (Lk 10:38-42).

The order of the symposium pattern seems to be reversed in Jesus' post-resurrection meal with two disciples in Emmaus (Lk 24:13-35). For although the meal is described formally as one at which they reclined, the discourse came first, while they were on the road. And although the two had invited Jesus, he quickly became the host. Luke drew on both Mark and the Synoptic sayings source (Q) for traditions about Jesus' eating with "toll collectors and sinners" and developed this theme by characterizing Jesus' entire ministry as a special mission to the poor, the captives, the blind, the oppressed and society's outcasts.

Luke especially uses meal imagery as a major means of conveying Jesus' good news. Central elements of this theme are recalled in Luke's unique story of Jesus' eating with Zacchaeus, described as both a chief "toll collector" and a "sinner" (Lk 19:1-9) in a scenario probably intended to remind the reader of Jesus' remarkably inclusive meal at Levi's house (Lk 5:27-32). And in Luke's presentation of the great banquet (Lk 14:15-24), a parable from the sayings source, Jesus' table companions under the rule of God include "the poor and maimed and blind and lame" (Matthew's version in Mt 22:10 mentions "both bad and good" guests). Luke's emphasis was probably "hard bread" for the elite Christians among his readers. For participation in such a socially inclusive community might well have cut them off from their prior social networks on which their status depended. From the perspective of Luke and Acts together, God intends this new community to offer reconciliation and solidarity among Jews and Gentiles, men and women, rich and poor.

5. Conclusion.

Apparently, one goal of Jesus' strategy of inclusive table fellowship was presenting himself and his followers as a living parable of how a renewed Israel could indeed live together from God's abundance (Koenig 28). He presented the rule of God, using images of food, drink and home as a roving banquet hall by which God sought Israelites to be guests and then hosts. At this table they were offered reconciliation with God, a true home, and a spiritual and material abundance as the basis for offering all these good things to each other, to others yet to come and even to enemies. A saying of Jesus, probably preserved in the Synoptic sayings source, linked the practice of inclusive table fellowship with the final consummation: "Many will come from east and west and recline at table with Abraham,

Isaac and Jacob in the kingdom of Heaven" (Mt 8:11 par. Lk 13:29; see Is 25:6-8).

See also LAST SUPPER; RICHES AND POVERTY; SINNERS.

DJG: BREAD; PROSTITUTE; TAXES.

BIBLIOGRAPHY. S. S. Bartchy, "Table Fellowship with Jesus and the 'Lord's Meal' at Corinth" in *Increase in Learning: Essays in Honor of James G. Van Buren,* ed. R. Owens and B. Hamm (Manhattan, KS: Manhattan Christian College, 1979) 45-61; M. J. Borg, *Conflict, Holiness and Politics in the Teachings of Jesus* (New York: Edwin Mellen, 1984) 71-143; J. Jeremias, *The Eucharistic Words of Jesus* (rev. ed.; New York: Scribner's, 1966; repr. Philadelphia: Fortress, 1977); L. E. Klosinski, "The Meals in Mark" (Ph.D. diss., Claremont Graduate School, 1988); J. Koenig, *New Testament Hospitality* (Philadelphia: Fortress, 1985); H. Moxnes, "Meals and the New Community in Luke," *SEA* 51 (1986) 158-67; J. Neusner, 1982. "Two Pictures of the Pharisees: Philosophical Circle or Eating Club?" *ATR* 64 (1982) 525-38; J. H. Neyrey, "Ceremonies in Luke-Acts: The Case of Meals and Table-Fellowship" in *The Social World of Luke-Acts,* ed. J. H. Neyrey (Peabody, MA: Hendrickson, 1991) 361-87; D. E. Smith, *From Symposium to Eucharist* (Minneapolis: Fortress, 2003); idem, "Table Fellowship as a Literary Motif in the Gospel of Luke," *JBL* 106 (1987) 613-38; idem, "The Historical Jesus at Table," *Society of Biblical Literature 1989 Seminar Papers,* ed. D. J. Lull (Atlanta: Scholars, 1989) 466-89.

S. S. Bartchy

TALMUD. *See* RABBINIC TRADITIONS AND WRITINGS.

TARGUM. *See* DEAD SEA SCROLLS; RABBINIC TRADITIONS AND WRITINGS.

TEMPLE. *See* JUDAISM AND THE NEW TESTAMENT; TEMPLE CLEANSING; WORSHIP.

TEMPLE ACT. *See* TEMPLE CLEANSING.

TEMPLE, CHURCH AS. *See* CHURCH II.

TEMPLE CLEANSING

The incident in the temple is recorded in all four Gospels (Mt 21:10-17; Mk 11:11, 15-17; Lk 19:45-46; Jn 2:13-17), although each Gospel writer has interpreted the event in a distinctive way. Precisely because it is attested in all four

Gospels, many believe that the incident traces to an event in Jesus' ministry although there is considerable debate about its meaning. This article will first examine the incident as interpreted by each of the Evangelists before suggesting what the incident might have meant in the context of Jesus' ministry.

1. The Temple Incident in the Four Gospels
2. The Temple Incident in the Ministry of Jesus

1. The Temple Incident in the Four Gospels.
Assuming that Mark is the earliest of the Gospels and that both Matthew and Luke used Mark, we will examine Mark first and then compare it with the Matthean and Lukan versions of the incident (*see* Synoptic Problem). While John's version of the incident has obvious affinities with the Synoptic accounts and may have grown out of a common tradition, it most likely was not drawn from Mark.

1.1. Mark: The Symbolic Destruction of the Temple. The following table will set the temple incident in its Markan context:

(1) Entry (Mk 11:11)
(2) Framing A (fig tree) (Mk 11:12-14)
(3) Incident in temple (Mk 11:15-17)
(4) Outcome (Mk 11:18-19)
(5) Framing B (fig tree) (Mk 11:20-26)

Mark frames the incident in the temple with the cursing of the fig tree so that the two episodes comment on each other. Seen in light of the fig tree episode, the temple incident is not so much a cleansing as a symbolic destruction. Because it has been unfruitful like the fig tree, the temple itself will be withered away to its very roots.

Peculiar to Mark is the separation of the entry from the temple incident by a full day. Jesus first enters Jerusalem and, coming to the temple, "scrutinizes *(periblepsamenos)* everything" before returning to Bethany for the night. The verb is distinctively Markan (six of its seven NT uses occur in Mark) and, when used in reference to Jesus, connotes casting a critical or discerning eye (Mk 3:5, 34; 5:32; 10:23). The first visit prepares the reader for Jesus' return. By depicting two visits to the temple, Mark creates a place for the first portion of the fig tree episode which otherwise would have interrupted the triumphal entry (Mk 11:1-10).

When on the following day Jesus enters the temple, he "throws out" *(ekballein)* the buyers and the dealers and "throws over" *(katestrepsen)* the tables of money-changers and the chairs of the dove sellers (Mk 11:15). His actions seem directed against all dealers in sacrifices as well as their customers, who include, no doubt, pilgrims visiting Jerusalem in fulfillment of their Torah obligation. In particular, Jesus singles out both the money-changers, who convert the varied currencies brought by pilgrims into the Tyrian coinage required by temple authorities for payment of the temple tax, and the dove dealers, who provide sacrifices for the poor.

Many have interpreted these actions as a cleansing of the temple, although the nature of the cleansing has been disputed. Was Jesus preserving the spiritual nature of the temple by purging it of commercial transactions? Or was he objecting to the abuse of the merchants who took advantage of the pilgrims through overcharging? Or was Jesus protesting the involvement of the priesthood in the commerce of the outer court?

Read in this framework, Mark 11:16 has been taken to mean either that Jesus forbade people from taking shortcuts through the temple's outer court or that he prevented anyone from bringing an unconsecrated vessel into that courtyard. In either case, Jesus would be expressing a desire to restore the holiness of the temple because he believed in its sanctity.

Problems with these readings of Mark 11:15-16 abound. The dealers and money-changers were performing an essential service for pilgrims and other worshipers. Indeed, without their infrastructure of services, it would be difficult to see how the temple sacrifices could have continued. Moreover, the moneychangers charged a modest commission to convert currency into the Tyrian coinage required by the temple, and the dealers in sacrifices provided unblemished and ritually acceptable victims. It is difficult to interpret Jesus' assault on them as cleansing the temple of crass commercialism. Nowhere does Jesus exhibit the zealous loyalty toward the temple ascribed to him by those who read the passage in this way. Finally, all such readings conflict with the Markan framing.

What reading then respects the framing and accounts for Jesus' action? The incident makes good sense as a symbolic prophetic action in which Jesus dramatizes the rejection of both the temple authorities and the economic systems that supported and enhanced their control over its functions. "Throwing out" and "throwing over" represent a rejection not a cleansing. If *skeuos* in verse 16 refers to sacred cult vessels (Jesus would not permit anyone to carry a sacred vessel through the courtyard), then Jesus' actions are complementary. He would permit no business as usual, either in the subsystems that support the temple or in the cultic activities themselves.

Jesus' pronouncement, drawn allusively from Isaiah 56:7 and Jeremiah 7:11, reinforces this reading. It declares God's will in making the temple a source of access to Yahweh for all peoples and denounces the perversion of that purpose by those who have made it "a cave of social bandits" *(spēlaion lēston)*. The use of Isaiah 56:7 probably reflects Mark's concern for the Gentiles, while the allusion to Jeremiah's temple sermon constitutes a prophetic oracle of doom. The reason for the destruction of the temple is made clear.

When the incident is understood as a prophetic act signaling the rejection and destruction of the temple, then the reaction of the chief priests and scribes is understandable. They seek a way to destroy Jesus.

1.2. Matthew: Cleansing the Temple. The following table indicates how Matthew places the incident in his narrative:
(1) Entry (Mt 21:10-11)
(2) Incident (Mt 21:12-13)
(3) Outcomes:
    (i) Matthew 21:14-17
    (ii) Matthew 21:18-22
    (iii) Matthew 21:23-27

Matthew removes the cursing of the fig tree as a framework for the incident in the temple. This allows him to elaborate on the entry itself. When Jesus enters Jerusalem, "the whole city was shaken" *(eseisthē,* Mt 21:10). The language is seismic and thereby casts his entry in the imagery of a theophany. This is no demonstration limited to Jesus' followers as in Mark. The entire city takes note, though its citizens are puzzled, asking "Who is this?" But what Jerusalem does not know, the crowd does: This is "the prophet Jesus from Nazareth of Galilee." The implicit opposition of the crowd to Jerusalem indicates that this is a positive affirmation not a deficient christology. "The prophet Jesus" may identify Jesus as the fulfillment of the promise made in Deuteronomy 18:15.

Matthew follows Mark in describing the initial actions of Jesus in the temple. Jesus "threw out" the sellers and buyers and "threw over" the tables of moneychangers and dove sellers. However, he omits Mark 11:16 altogether, perhaps because its meaning was unclear. The pronouncement of Jesus is likewise streamlined. The phrase "for all nations" is omitted from the compound quotation, thereby intensifying the accusation against the temple authorities whose leadership has led the temple away from its divine purpose (see Gundry, 412-13).

The justification for the indictment is illustrated in the special Matthean material that follows (Mt 21:14-16). Having denounced the perversion of the temple, Jesus restores its purpose by healing the broken and the outcast. His miraculous powers are hailed by the children in the temple in fulfillment of Scripture (Ps 8:2) but draw a predictably negative response from the temple leaders.

Taken together, the healings and the controversy they generate reflect a typical Matthean pattern: Jesus acts—his opponents protest—Jesus quotes Scripture. They also depict the fulfillment of the purpose for which the temple was given, a purpose frustrated by the very chief priests and scribes who object indignantly to what Jesus says and does. The blind, the lame and the children on the temple Mount parallel the crowds at the entry just as the puzzled city parallels the temple authorities. Matthew portrays a great reversal: the insiders are either ignorant or indignantly obstinate, while the outsiders respond graciously to God's Messiah (*see* Christ) as he restores the temple.

Two other outcomes follow rapidly from the incident and its aftermath. The fig tree episode (Mt 21:18-22) confirms the reversal of insider and outsider, especially the judgment on the temple insiders, while the dispute over authority must now be read in the light of the entire temple incident. The episode of the question about authority (Mt 21:23-27) hearkens back to the healings as well as the disruptions in the temple's outer court.

1.3. Luke: Preparing the Temple. Again, it will be helpful to study the temple incident in its Lukan narrative context.
(1) Frame: weeping over the city
    (Lk 19:41-44)
(2) Incident (Lk 19:45-46)
(3) Outcomes:
    (i) Luke 19:47-48

(ii) Luke 20:1-8

(iii) Luke 20:9-19

Most strikingly, Luke has muted the entire incident. Jesus "began to throw out the dealers." Missing are the references to buyers, moneychangers and dove sellers. Moreover, the pronouncement is directed to them alone in such a way that it appears as though Jesus is objecting to their commercial activity, presumably because it detracts from the divine purpose of the temple as a house of prayer.

The immediate outcome is that Jesus "was teaching daily in the temple courtyard" to the enthusiastic people (*laos,* not *ochlos* "crowd") who listen to his every word. Luke portrays Jesus clearing away the activity of the buyers, preparing the temple so that he can restore the temple courtyard as a place of teaching. The twin themes of that teaching are spelled out in the two pericopes that follow, the question about authority (Lk 20:1-8) and the parable of the wicked tenants along with its associated sayings (Lk 20:9-19). The former pericope establishes Jesus' authority for teaching on the temple, while the latter specifies the indictment against the current authorities.

The entire episode is introduced by Jesus' prophetic lament over Jerusalem (Lk 19:41-44), which concludes by revealing the reason for the turmoil and devastation that awaits city and temple alike. "You did not grasp the critical moment *[kairon]* of your visitation." The contrast between the deadly visitation of siege armies in Luke 19:43, 44 and the gracious visitation of Jesus is stark. The failure to understand one leads to the fatal outcome of the other.

For what then does Jesus prepare the temple? In light of its subsequent destruction, prophetically glimpsed in the lament, was Jesus preparing the temple for its destruction? No. Understood in the context of Luke-Acts, the incident was preparing the temple for its role as the starting point of a new movement away from Jerusalem announced in the pattern of witness found in Luke 24:47 and elaborated in Acts 1:8. Jerusalem and the temple would no longer be the goal of pilgrimage but the launching pad of a new mission.

1.4. John: The Cleansing and Replacement of the Temple. The incident in John occurs at the beginning of Jesus' ministry during his first trip to Jerusalem.

(1) Entry (Jn 2:13)

(2) Incident (Jn 2:14-17)

(3) Challenge (Jn 2:18-22)

The entire episode is self-contained, being separated from the miracle at Cana by John 2:12 and from subsequent events in Jerusalem by John 2:23-25.

Significant differences exist between the Johannine and the Synoptic versions. Jesus' actions are more extreme in John. He makes a whip to drive out the sellers of sheep and oxen, along with the moneychangers whose coins he pours out onto the temple courtyard. But he treats the dove sellers more leniently, simply ordering them to leave with their wares.

The pronouncement itself contrasts "the house of my Father" with "a house of trade," and the scriptural allusion is to Zechariah 14:21. The allusion to Zechariah certainly helps one to interpret the consequent challenge and call for a sign as well as Jesus' response (Jn 2:18-19). The prophecy of Zechariah refers to the eschatological Day of the Lord (*see* Apocalypticism) when the temple would become the center of worship for all peoples. On that day, "there shall be [no] trader in the house of the Lord of hosts" (Jn 14:21). So Jesus' actions appear to be informed by a purifying zeal (cf. Ps 69:9) to convert God's house into its eschatological form. In this context John 2:19 is a promise to perform such an act. It carries the sense "even if you were to destroy the temple, in just three days I would raise a better one in its place."

But John intrudes by reinterpreting the saying of Jesus to refer to his resurrection (Jn 2:21-22), and with the narrator's reading of the saying the purification theme becomes a replacement motif. For John's community Jesus' body is the temple that has replaced the temple of former times.

2. The Temple Incident in the Ministry of Jesus.

Given the diversity among the Gospel writers, it is not surprising that scholars have argued over both the meaning and the details of the incident in Jesus' ministry. Consensus does seem to place the incident at the end of Jesus' ministry rather than at the beginning, thereby favoring the Synoptics over John, but beyond this point, agreement ends.

Although varied, the interpretations of the incident do fall into four basic categories: (1) it is a *religious* event intended to cleanse the temple of impurities, whether commercial or sacerdotal; (2) it is a *messianic* event intended to include the Gentiles in the scope of the temple's activities; (3) it is a *prophetic* event intended to announce the destruction of the temple and its eschatological restoration; (4) it is a *political* event intended to disrupt the commercial and sacerdotal activities of the temple because they had become oppressive and exploitative. Whatever approach or combination of approaches interpreters may take, however, they must resolve some basic questions about the scope, purpose and content of the event. These can best be examined by looking at its two component parts, Jesus' actions and his pronouncement.

2.1. The Actions of Jesus in the Temple. For some scholars the incident recounts Jesus cleansing the temple and reclaiming it for its spiritual purpose as a house of prayer. For others, the event is an assault on and attempted political takeover of the temple. Between these extremes, scholars like R. A. Horsley and E. P. Sanders read the event as a symbolic prophetic action, limited in scope, but condemning the temple.

Sanders concludes that Jesus either prophesied or threatened the destruction of the temple as a prelude to its eschatological restoration. Horsley sees the action as an attack on the oppressive political and economic system that found its center in the temple. More than a symbolic action, it involved violence against the exploiters of the people. Both agree that the demonstration was sufficiently limited in scope so that it would not attract the attention of the temple police or the Roman troops stationed in the Antonia fortress, yet noteworthy enough to elicit concerted action against Jesus.

2.2. Jesus' Pronouncement in the Temple. The saying is highly debated, most scholars judging it to be Markan or pre-Markan but not traceable to Jesus. G. W. Buchanan, for instance, argues a Markan setting by identifying the *lēstai* of the saying with the "brigands" who seized the temple during the revolt against Rome. Others argue that the saying in John 2:19 may reflect Jesus' words more closely than the Markan saying.

If the prophetic-political readings of the passage are correct, however, they suggest a possible reading of the saying recorded in Mark that could place it in the context of Jesus' ministry. If this were the case, then Jesus would be declaring that the true social bandits were not the deviants operating out of caves in the Judean wilderness but the prominent officials of the temple built over the sacred cave on the temple Mount. Their exploitative and oppressive domination of the people through taxation and tribute represent the real social banditry of the time, even though it was masked as piety and religious obligation. Understood in this way, the saying fits the action, and both delineate Jesus' prophetic judgment of the temple that would set the authorities against him and lead to his crucifixion.

DJG: TEMPLE; TRIUMPHAL ENTRY.

BIBLIOGRAPHY. C. K. Barrett, "The House of Prayer and the Den of Thieves" in *Jesus und Paulus: Festschrift für Werner Georg Kümmel,* ed. E. E. Ellis and E. Grasser (Göttingen: Vandenhoeck & Ruprecht, 1975) 13-20; G. W. Buchanan, "Mark 11:15-19: Brigands in the Temple," *HUCA* 30 (1959) 169-77; B. Chilton, *Temple of Jesus* (University Park, PA: Pennsylvania State University Press, 1992); J. D. M. Derrett, "The Zeal of the House and the Cleansing of the Temple," *DRev* 95 (1977) 79-94; V. Eppstein, "The Historicity of the Gospel Account of the Cleansing of the Temple," *ZNW* (1964) 42-58; C. A. Evans, "Jesus' Action in the Temple: Cleansing or Portent of Destruction?" *CBQ* 51 (1989) 237-70; R. H. Gundry, *Matthew: A Commentary on His Literary and Theological Art* (Grand Rapids: Eerdmans, 1982); N. Q. Hamilton, "Temple Cleansing and Temple Bank," *JBL* 83 (1964) 365-72; R. H. Hiers, "Purification of the Temple: Preparation for the Kingdom of God," *JBL* 90 (1971) 82-90; R. A. Horsley, *Jesus and the Spiral of Violence: Popular Jewish Resistance in Roman Palestine* (San Francisco: Harper & Row, 1987); C. Roth, "The Cleansing of the Temple and Zechariah," *NovT* 4 (1960) 174-181; E. P. Sanders, *Jesus and Judaism* (Philadelphia: Fortress, 1985); N. T. Wright, *Jesus and the Victory of God* (Minneapolis: Fortress, 1996) 413-28.

W. R. Herzog II

TEMPLE DESTRUCTION. *See* JUDAISM AND THE NEW TESTAMENT; TEMPLE CLEANSING.

TEMPTATION OF JESUS. *See* LUKE, GOSPEL OF; MATTHEW, GOSPEL OF.

TESTAMENT OF JOB. *See* APOCRYPHA AND PSEUDEPIGRAPHA.

TESTAMENT OF MOSES. *See* APOCRYPHA AND PSEUDEPIGRAPHA.

TESTAMENTS OF THE TWELVE PATRIARCHS.
See Apocrypha and Pseudepigrapha.

THANKSGIVING, INTRODUCTORY. *See* Letters, Letter Forms.

THESSALONIANS, LETTERS TO THE

Paul and Silas, accompanied by their assistant, Timothy, took the first steps toward the establishment of a Christian community in Thessalonica as part of the first Christian mission to the province of Macedonia. Thessalonica was one of the major cities of the Roman Empire. The missionaries' subsequent contact with the Thessalonian church included two letters (*see* Letters, Letter Forms), which are probably the oldest Christian documents that we possess. Despite their brevity and their relative lack of significantly developed theological themes compared with the other letters in the Pauline corpus, the two letters to the Thessalonian Christians have become the object of much scholarly examination, particularly in the areas of rhetorical criticism, sociological analysis and the early development of Pauline theology.

  1. Contents of the Letters
  2. The City of Thessalonica
  3. The Pauline Mission
  4. The Writing of the Letters
  5. Literary and Historical Questions
  6. Early Pauline Theology

1. Contents of the Letters.

Both 1 and 2 Thessalonians identify themselves in their prescripts (1 Thess 1:1; 2 Thess 1:1-2) as co-authored by Paul, Silas (called Silvanus in the letters) and Timothy. But we can probably assume on the basis of Paul's later letters (and see 1 Thess 3:6) that Paul at least played the leading role in their composition.

1.1. 1 Thessalonians. In 1 Thessalonians Paul thanks God for the Thessalonian Christians, remembering in particular how they "received the word" preached by Paul and his coworkers "in the midst of much suffering" (1 Thess 1:6) and thus became an example for others who would hear the gospel (1 Thess 1:7-10). He goes on to recall for them the difficult circumstances and the earnest sincerity that characterized the initial apostolic mission (*see* Apostle) to Thessalonica (1 Thess 2:1-12). He does so apparently to set forth himself and his coworkers as examples of

blamelessness for his readers. Paul then returns to thanksgiving for the Thessalonians' reception of the gospel. He sets them on one side of a divide between God's suffering people and the persecuting rejectors of God's Word, the latter exemplified by the "the Jews" (1 Thess 2:13-16). He then tells of how his love for them and concern for their steadfastness has led him and his coworkers to seek renewed contact with the Thessalonians. Now, with Timothy successfully returned from Thessalonica, news of their steadfastness has arrived and has brought rejoicing (1 Thess 2:17—3:10).

A prayer for continued contact, love and blamelessness (1 Thess 3:11-13) closes out the first major section of the letter (1 Thess 1—3). In this section Paul has drawn strong continuities between the Gentile Christians of Thessalonica (see 1 Thess 1:9) and others among the people of God, including the OT prophets (1 Thess 2:15) and especially the missionaries who brought the gospel to Thessalonica. By this emphasis on their place in the people of God and their links with the apostolic mission, Paul gives the Thessalonian Christians a way of thinking about themselves that will enable them to stand with certainty in the adversity that they are experiencing. This in turn lays the foundation for the second major section of the letter, in which Paul will repeatedly refer to traditions and instructions that the Thessalonians have received from the missionaries (1 Thess 4:1, 2, 9, 11).

The second section (1 Thess 4—5) begins with an exhortation to holy living (1 Thess 4:1-12), the main focus of which is sexual morality. Paul then deals with Christ's return (1 Thess 4:13—5:11; *see* Eschatology), which provides the basis for an exhortation to alert and sober living; to faith, love and hope; and to mutual encouragement (1 Thess 5:4-8, 11). His main motivation in penning this eschatological section appears, however, to have been concern on the part of some Thessalonian Christians about the fate of those of their number who had died before Christ's return (1 Thess 4:13-18; *see* Resurrection). The letter closes with general admonitions and benedictions (1 Thess 5:12-28).

1.2. 2 Thessalonians. Paul's thanksgiving in 2 Thessalonians (2 Thess 1:3-12), like that in 1 Thessalonians, mentions the Thessalonian Christians' characteristic steadfastness in suffering and their example to others. Once again eschatology is the framework in which Paul views their suffering and their accomplishments.

Second Thessalonians also reveals that central to Paul's concerns for the Thessalonian Christian community were questions regarding eschatology (2 Thess 2:1-12). Here the problem seems to be that some believed that "the day of the Lord" had already occurred (2 Thess 2:2). Paul answers this belief by speaking of events that must take place before "that day" (2 Thess 2:3-12). As in 1 Thessalonians, having answered these initial concerns Paul returns to thanksgiving for the Thessalonians (2 Thess 2:13-17). A particular problem addressed in the general admonitions in 2 Thessalonians (2 Thess 3:1-15) is the refusal of some in the church to work (2 Thess 3:10-12); here the practice of the apostolic missionaries is offered as an example of labor and economic self-sufficiency (2 Thess 3:7-9). The letter closes with benedictions and Paul's personal greeting (2 Thess 3:16-18).

2. The City of Thessalonica.

Thessalonica was a populous city enjoying good fortune throughout most of the Hellenistic and Roman period. It was founded at or near the site of Therma at the head of the Thermaic Gulf, now called the Gulf of Salonika, about 315 B.C. by Cassander, formerly a general of Alexander the Great. As an important military and commercial port, it became the principal city of Macedonia. It was designated the capital of one of the four administrative districts into which Rome divided Macedonia in 168 B.C. In 146 B.C. it became the capital of the now-unified province of Macedonia. In the same year the Egnatian Way, connecting Asia Minor with the Adriatic Sea (and Rome beyond the Adriatic), was put through. It was on this road that Paul and his coworkers traveled from Philippi to Thessalonica (Acts 17:1). In return for its support of Antony and Octavian, Thessalonica became a free city in 42 B.C. It remained the most important and populous city of Macedonia into the third or fourth century A.D. As Salonika it is the second largest city of modern Greece and still an important seaport.

Archeological sites in the city include parts of the Roman city wall, a first-century Roman forum and an older Hellenistic agora, a hippodrome, three spans of the triumphal arch of Galerius, and a number of Byzantine churches. The Vardar Gate, which spanned the Egnatian Way at the west side of the city as the arch of Galerius spanned it at the east end of the city, was dismantled in the nineteenth century. An inscription from the gate, dating from the late first century B.C. to the early second century A.D., uses the Greek word *politarchēs* ("civic official"), otherwise found only in the Acts account of the Pauline mission to the city (Acts 17:6). Inscriptional evidence of Jewish settlement in the city dates from the late Roman period; a Samaritan synagogue inscription dates from an earlier period, perhaps the third century B.C.

3. The Pauline Mission.

3.1. The Account in Acts. The Jewish setting of the initial Christian mission to Thessalonica is prominent in Acts (Acts 17:1-10). The mission of Paul and Silas, which took place mostly or entirely in a Jewish synagogue, was focused on proving to Jews from their Scriptures that Jesus was the Messiah (*see* Christ). The first converts included some Jews, a large portion of the local Gentile worshipers of the God of Israel and a number of prominent women, who were probably also among the Gentile worshipers of Israel's God. Opposition to the mission began at the initiative of Jews (Acts 17:13), though it quickly spread to Gentiles, first to an unruly mob and then to the city officials. Apart from the difficulty it brought on the new Christian community, this opposition made it prudent for Paul and Silas (and Timothy, though he is not mentioned in Acts) to move on. Thus Jews who opposed the Pauline mission were successful before the officials in blaming their intended victims, the Christians, for a disturbance that the Jews had created.

But Paul's letters to the Thessalonian Christians do not seem, at first examination, to support the account in Acts of the beginnings of their church. Despite Paul's argument in person from the Scriptures (so Acts 17:2-3), neither letter quotes the OT; there are only occasional vague echoes, the most significant being of Daniel 11:36 in 2 Thessalonians 2:4. This is not what we would expect from a writer steeped in the Scriptures, the writer of Galatians and Romans, least of all when that person was writing to people who had only recently been all habitués of a synagogue. Furthermore, the readers are reminded how they turned "from idols" to await God's Son (*see* Son of God) from heaven (1 Thess 1:9-10). Nowhere in the letters is it even hinted that any of the readers had any positive and meaningful contact with Judaism before they met Paul and Silas, much less that any of them were Jews. (The contrast is at least less certain with regard to their opponents: In Acts the opposition is ultimately both Jewish and Gentile; in 1 Thessalonians the opponents are the Christians' "own countrymen" [1 Thess 2:14], and this designation might well include some Jews.) For these reasons it has been thought by many that the account in Acts of the mission in Thessalonica is inaccurate or at least that it is part of its author's broader portrayal of Paul's mission strategy and of Jewish-Christian relations (cf. Acts 13:44-50; 14:19; 18:12-17; etc.).

3.2. The Picture Suggested by the Letters.

The account in Acts might indeed describe only one side of a mission that also and even more significantly touched Gentiles who had not been influenced by Judaism. By referring to his physical labor in both letters (1 Thess 2:9; 2 Thess 3:7-9), Paul gives us a clue concerning this other side of the mission: His workplace may have been where many non-judaized Gentiles in the city heard the gospel. This would be in accord with the methods used by other preachers and popular philosophers of the day (Hock, 38-41; Malherbe 1987, 17-20). That Paul did enter into some sort of craft-business arrangement in Thessalonica (as in Corinth, Acts 18:2-3) suggests a longer stay in the city than the three weeks or a little more that might be inferred from Acts (Acts 17:2). It was more than once that the Philippian Christians sent Paul material assistance while he was in Thessalonica (Phil 4:15-16); this points to the same conclusion.

But it may be that the situation was more complex not only than Acts suggests but also than what we might infer from the letters by themselves. Perhaps Paul sought to downplay what Jewish influence there was on some of the Thessalonian Christians. As it is, the belief structure reflected in the letters is a messianic-apocalyptic form of Judaism (see Apocalypticism; Eschatology), even though the letters never refer to the Jewish Scriptures. They also include a strongly worded anti-Jewish polemic (1 Thess 2:14-16) and emphasize or perhaps even exaggerate the pagan origin of the addressees (1 Thess 1:9)—possibly because of the circumstances under which the Thessalonian church began or because of Paul's reaction against Judaism coming out of his call to Christian faith and apostleship (on the latter cf. Gager, though

he does not extend his argument back to 1 Thessalonians).

Any attempt to say more about the Thessalonian Christians on the basis of the letters must reckon with the observation that Paul apparently preached a message with a strong eschatological orientation and that this orientation was apparently taken to an extreme by some members of the community (1 Thess 4:13—5:11; 2 Thess 2:1-12; Simpson 1998). Perhaps this eschatological excitement was great enough to prompt charges of political subversion (Acts 17:6-7). Sociological study of eschatologically focused, or millenarian, groups has emphasized that a new experience of relative deprivation arising from changes within society's structures and patterns of relationships generally lies behind this kind of eschatological interest. Paul's preaching of the gospel offered just such an eschatological faith. Was there a social situation at Thessalonica that would have made Paul's gospel attractive?

Even if the Thessalonian Christians were not at ease with the status quo, we would be mistaken to suppose that all of them were at the bottom of society. Indeed, W. A. Meeks suggests (Meeks, 173-74) that some of Paul's converts would have been people of some wealth experiencing "status inconsistency" or "status dissonance" because their social standing did not match their wealth. This inconsistency lay behind their attraction to the eschatological faith preached by Paul. A community consisting of poor and rich persons is suggested by two lines of evidence: the decision of some to quit working (2 Thess 3:11) and references in Acts to "leading women" and to the householder Jason (Acts 17:4-5).

R. Jewett (Jewett, 113-32) has suggested specific social factors at Thessalonica that may have played a role in certain Thessalonians responding to Paul's message. Jewett speaks of the absorption of the Cabirus cult into the city cult of Thessalonica during the first century A.D. (see Donfried 1985). The Cabirus cult was a local eschatological redeemer cult once popular among the lower classes and with some superficial structural similarities to the Christian gospel. Some of the Cabirus cult's original adherents, having lost what their recently co-opted faith had provided for them, may have found a suitable substitute in the gospel. Jewett also points to changes in Thessalonian society that had occurred with the shift to Roman power and the coming of new people who bore governmental and commercial power. This shift in power would have contributed to a social situation in which Paul's eschatological gospel would been viewed with favor.

However we picture its origin, the Thessalonian church apparently remained stable and on friendly terms with Paul and his coworkers: Acts 20:4 mentions two men of Thessalonica among the representatives of the Gentile churches accompanying Paul on his last journey to Jerusalem. Second Timothy 4:10 mentions a Demas who deserted Paul and went to Thessalonica; this brief note is not enough to imply that the church there had become disaffected from the apostle.

4. The Writing of the Letters.

The letters to the Thessalonian Christians were apparently written not long after the departure of Paul, Silas and Timothy from Thessalonica and their arrival in Athens (1 Thess 2:17; 3:1; Acts 17:10-15). Paul's attempts to return to Thessalonica were hindered (1 Thess 2:18), perhaps by the guarantee that he would not come back, a guarantee forced out of the Thessalonian Christians by the city officials (Acts 17:9). But he did manage to send Timothy back (1 Thess 3:2).

A written message no doubt accompanied Timothy, but we do not have it, unless it is what we call 2 Thessalonians (which would then be the earlier of the two letters; so Wanamaker, 37-45; see below on the order of the letters). At any rate, 1 and perhaps 2 Thessalonians were written after Timothy's return from Thessalonica with good news concerning the stability of the Christian community there (1 Thess 3:6). Paul still hoped to return to Thessalonica (1 Thess 3:10-11). In the meantime he and his associates sent these two letters to encourage and exhort the fledgling church to attempt to clear up some confusion concerning the eschatological expectation that they had proclaimed and to address a problem of vagrancy on the part of some members.

The Thessalonian letters have often been viewed as arising out of a situation of particular ideological conflict. This situation has usually been defined under the influence of the interpretation of other, more clearly polemical letters of Paul (in different ways by, e.g., Schmithals, 123-218, and Jewett, 149-57). But such an approach is often part of an incorrectly monolithic

picture of Paul's opponents or of ancient religious currents (*see* Gnosticism). Furthermore, it is usually dependent on tenuous connections drawn between Pauline exhortations and other statements and phenomena in the ancient world or between the different letters of Paul (e.g., 1 Thessalonians and 2 Corinthians) and on a questionable identification of some parts of the Thessalonian letters as polemical (see 5.1 below). We are on the most secure ground if, generally speaking, we think of the problems in the Thessalonian church as arising from the possibilities within Pauline Christianity, not from any ideological corruption emanating from outside the community.

Within that framework, it does appear that an overrealized eschatology was advocated by at least some in the Thessalonian church. The eschatological confusion Paul addresses was apparently centered upon questions concerning the time remaining before the expected return of Jesus. Some members of the community had already died, and those remaining were unsure how the dead could benefit from Christ's return (1 Thess 4:13-18). In this situation some of the community had perhaps found solace in believing that the expected eschatological return had, in some sense or another, already occurred (2 Thess 2:1-3; *see* Resurrection).

Paul does not indicate the reasoning that lay behind the refusal of some to work (1 Thess 4:10-12; 5:14; 2 Thess 3:6-12) or even that there was reasoning behind it. He does not even say or clearly imply that this pattern of behavior arose subsequent to their conversion to Christianity. So the common suggestion that this vagrancy was motivated by their new eschatological beliefs and that it was thus another manifestation of the eschatological confusion addressed in the letters (e.g., Marshall, 117, 218) is little more than a guess.

It has also been suggested that the problem of Christian preachers claiming support from their audiences was showing its face in this refusal to work (Trilling 1972, 96-98). But this problem, in which Paul wished to avoid any suggestion of involvement, whether in Corinth or in Thessalonica (1 Thess 2:9; 2 Thess 3:7-9; 1 Cor 9), and which the *Didache* (*Did.* 12) addresses, was associated with itinerant preachers. The letters to the Thessalonians, however, address a problem of vagrancy among the resident members of the community.

It has commonly been thought that 1 Thessalonians 2:1-12 answers charges that Paul and his associates were hypocritical, motivated not by loyalty to God and love for the Thessalonians but by love for money (e.g., Bruce, 27-28), or that it responds to charges that Paul neglected charismatic gifts (cf. 1 Thess 1:5; 2 Cor 10:10; 11:6; Schmithals, 139-40, followed by Jewett, 102-3). But it has been shown that this passage is merely an example of a common ancient rhetorical pattern in which the speaker or writer provides an example to be emulated by describing his own behavior in antithetical terms ("not that, but this") (Lyons, 184; Malherbe 1970, 1983).

It has also been claimed that some aspects of the hortatory material in 1 Thessalonians addressed specific problems in the Thessalonian Christian community (e.g., Jewett, 100-102 on 1 Thess 5:19-22, 103-4 on 5:12-13; Bruce, 87 on 1 Thess 4:3-8). It is clear that this is the case for the problem of vagrancy in 2 Thessalonians and, by extension, in 1 Thessalonians. But in the other exhortations, those concerning adultery and other forms of sexual immorality (1 Thess 4:3-8), and respect for church leaders (1 Thess 5:12-13, perhaps with 2 Thess 3:14-15), Paul is using standardized exhortations expressed in rhetorically normal patterns with no suggestion that particular problems are addressed.

5. Literary and Historical Questions.

5.1. Form Criticism and Rhetorical Criticism.
Most of Paul's letters contain an "epistolary thanksgiving" after the salutation (e.g., Rom 1:8-15; 1 Cor 1:4-9; Phil 1:3-11), and in this they resemble other Hellenistic letters (see Letter, Letter Forms). Both 1 and 2 Thessalonians are anomalous in that they have what can be described as two thanksgiving sections each (1 Thess 1:2-10; 2:13-16; 2 Thess 1:3-4; 2:13-14), and later in 1 Thessalonians we encounter another renewal of thanksgiving (1 Thess 3:9-10). The presence of two thanksgivings in 2 Thessalonians is taken as evidence that it is a non-Pauline imitation of 1 Thessalonians (see below on the question of its authorship).

In 1 Thessalonians, however, this anomaly has been dealt with by adjustments of the normal form-critical categories (e.g., by speaking of the interpenetration of letter body and thanksgiving), by identifying 1 Thessalonians as the result of conflation of two letters (Schmithals) or by identifying 1 Thessalonians 2:13-16 as a post-Pauline interpolation into Paul's letter (e.g., Pearson, Schmidt). The interpolation view has also focused on the contrast between what Paul says in 1 Thessalonians 2:14-16 about "the Jews" and the high regard he shows for non-Christian Jews in Romans 9—11, including his statement regarding their future salvation (Rom 11:26). The interpolation view has also focused on other arguments based on the content and structure of the second thanksgiving.

It is usually taken for granted that the strongly worded polemics we see in 1 Thessalonians 2:13-16 arose out of a highly combative situation, but this assumption is undermined by the evidence for the general use of strongly worded polemics in the ancient world, including within Judaism and the church (see Johnson). Furthermore, Romans 9—11 seems to build on a negative assessment of the present situation of non-Christian Jews (particularly Rom 11:7-10). And if form criticism takes its place as a descriptive, rather than defining, tool, then it becomes difficult to build on it any argument for interpolation (or for regarding 1 Thess as a product of conflation). The same can be said regarding arguments that other passages in the Thessalonian letters were interpolated (e.g., 1 Thess 5:1-11).

Form criticism allows us to isolate the uniqueness, and therefore the special concerns, of the first three chapters of 1 Thessalonians, which are, in the most general terms, Paul's desire to return to thanksgiving as he thinks about his initial work among the Thessalonians (see Simpson 1990). The renewal of thanksgiving in 2 Thessalonians 2:13, however it may be described in form-critical terms, allows the writer to contrast "those affecting you" (2 Thess 1:6) and "those perishing" (2 Thess 2:10) with the addressees and to bracket words about the former with thanksgiving for the latter.

Generally, rhetorical criticism of the letters has consisted of identifying the ancient rhetorical components (e.g., exordium, partitio, narratio, etc.) of the letters and viewing the purposes of the sections and of the letters as wholes as the generalized functions associated with the rhetorical terms. In this way the letters are thought of as oratory set within epistolary frameworks. The increasing attention to the rhetorical structure of the letters has not led to complete agreement (see Jewett, 63-87, 221, 225; Wanamaker, 48-52). But it has allowed for more flexible approaches and new ways of understanding the functions of and relationships among the different parts of the letters, including 1 Thessalonians 2:13-16, particularly in comparison with thematic and form-critical analyses. Rhetorical analysis has also raised anew the question of the genre and focus of each of Paul's letters. The disagreements described above with regard to the purpose of 1 Thessalonians 2:1-12, for instance, have come increasingly to be described in rhetorical terms.

5.2. The Authorship of 2 Thessalonians. Many scholars working with the Thessalonian letters have concluded that though Paul and his coworkers wrote 1 Thessalonians to the Thessalonian Christians, a post-Pauline Paulinist wrote 2 Thessalonians, using the genuine letter as a model. The arguments for this view have usually been centered around an understanding of 2 Thessalonians as a conscious correction of an overheated apocalypticism partly inspired by the genuine letter. Second Thessalonians 2:2 and 2 Thessalonians 3:17 are regarded as attempts to cover the tracks of the forgery and to denounce 1 Thes-salonians, and the direct appeal to apostolic authority in 2 Thessalonians 2:15 is seen as a mark of a post-Pauline setting.

But the difference in eschatology between the two letters has been exaggerated. That the parousia would be unexpected (1 Thess 5) and that signs would precede it (2 Thess 2) were, in fact, beliefs held together in the earliest church (e.g., Mk 13). 2 Thessalonians 3:17 would be, as a false claim to authenticity, far from convincing, since no other Pauline letter has anything like it. The appeal to apostolic authority in 2 Thessalonians 2:15 is not stronger, just more explicit, than what we find in 1 Thessalonians.

W. Trilling's influential arguments against Pauline authorship of 2 Thessalonians have shifted attention away from eschatology and the references to a previous letter and focused on other issues: (1) a number of stylistic and theological differences between 2 Thessalonians and 1 Thessalonians together with the other unchallenged Pauline letters, (2) the difference in tone between the two letters and (3) the lack of personal references in 2 Thessalonians.

The claim of 2 Thessalonians to be written by Paul and his coworkers still does not face any argument that, taken by itself, comes close to making post-Pauline authorship a compelling conclusion. Trilling's separate arguments, particularly that from stylistic differences, have carried little weight with some scholars who have examined them in detail. The different tone of the letters, which must be related to the lack of personal references in 2 Thessalonians, might point, not to different addressees but to differing amounts of information about the same situation—which, under the assumption that both are Pauline, brings up the question of their chronological order.

5.3. The Order of the Letters. The canonical order of 1 and 2 Thessalonians matches the most-favored view of their chronological order but is of no importance as an argument for it, being based simply on the length of the letters. What does matter is, first, the differences in how the same concerns are addressed in the two letters and, second, whatever clues about movements of people and letters can be found in the two letters. Is it more likely that the manner in which the concerns with eschatology and vagrancy are addressed developed from 1 to 2 Thessalonians, or the reverse? What shall we make of the references to persecution as, it seems, an experience of the past in 1 Thessalonians (1 Thess 1:6; 2:14; 3:3) but presently occurring in 2 Thessalonians (2 Thess 1:4-7)? Timothy no doubt carried some written communication with him on the journey described in 1 Thessalonians 3:2-8; was it what we call 2 Thessalonians? Or is 1 Thessalonians the letter mentioned in 2 Thessalonians 2:2? Has a deteriorating situation led from the friendly and grateful-to-God tone of 1 Thessalonians to the more official tone of 2 Thessalonians, or did a better understanding of the situation (through Timothy's report; cf. 1 Thess 3:6) lead to that more thankful tone?

Strong arguments can be built for the priority of both 1 Thessalonians (Jewett, 24-30) and 2 Thessalonians (Wanamaker, 37-45). Which came first is a question for which we do not have a clear answer. Therefore, we have no sure basis on which to build a theory of the setting of the letters. As is so often the case, what is available to us is the content of the letters and not knowledge of their origin in the amount that we might desire.

6. Early Pauline Theology.

Much of the value of 1 and 2 Thessalonians as documents of Pauline theology is based on their apparent closeness to Pauline mission preaching. The two letters are addressed to a church that has been in existence just a short time. Much of both letters speaks of the work of proclamation to which the church owes its beginnings, and little of their content is prompted by special situational concerns, at least in comparison with other letters of Paul. To a large extent they seek merely to encourage the members of the new Christian community in their new standing. Even where they do respond directly to special situational concerns—in the eschatological sections and in the words about the obligation to work—they do so in language that was probably used in the primary gospel proclamation and which is certainly no more than an expansion of themes in that proclamation.

First Thessalonians 1:9-10 in particular allows us to see something of the general pattern of Paul's early preaching to Gentile audiences. The focus of this preaching was on the one God and Jesus, the coming one, the mediator to humankind of divine redemption (cf. Acts 17:23-31; 1 Cor 8:6). The one God was essential to any Judaism, and the message of the apocalyptic end of the age was at home in much of Judaism, though, of course, the place of Jesus (see Jesus and Paul) in Paul's preaching went beyond most Judaism.

First Thessalonians 1:9 also shows that Paul's preaching of Jewish monotheism (see God) included the standard Jewish polemics against pagan idolatry (cf., e.g., Jer 10:1-10; Wis 13-15). This one God Paul identified as the "Father" of Jesus and of Christians (e.g., 1 Thess 1:2-3, 9-10). Paul the preacher also spoke of Jesus' death (1 Thess 1:6; 2:15; 5:10), resurrection (1 Thess 1:10; 4:14) and expected eschatological return (1 Thess 1:10; 2:19; 3:13; 5:23—these references apart from the specific eschatological sections of both letters; see Eschatology). The main motivation given for accepting Paul's message (for "receiving the word of God," 1 Thess 2:13) was that faith in Jesus, "our deliverer from the wrath to come," is the way of escape from coming divine judgment (1 Thess 1:10; 5:9; 2 Thess 2:13).

Though the letters do not make explicit any developed christology, Jesus, "the Lord," is placed alongside God the Father as the source of the Thessalonian church's existence (1 Thess 1:1; 2 Thess 1:1), as the guide of the apostolic mission (1 Thess 3:11) and as the giver of Christian comfort and hope (2 Thess 2:16). He is also seen as a model member of the suffering people of God, along with the prophets, the apostles

and the Thessalonian Christians (1 Thess 1:6; 2:15). But his suffering and death have a greater significance: it is that which brings about believers' eternal life "together with him" (1 Thess 5:10, 17).

This prospect of life with Christ (2 Thess 2:1-2) sets apart Christians as people who have hope (1 Thess 4:13, 18). This life will begin with the divine initiative in Jesus' descent from heaven and the archangel's call (1 Thess 4:16; cf. 1 Cor 15:52); believers who have died will be resurrected and those living will be lifted up into the clouds so that both may share life with him (1 Thess 4:14-17; 5:10). This, the coming of Jesus and "our assembling together with him" (2 Thess 2:1), will be preceded by a manifestation of evil so great that it will attempt to take the place of God as the one who is worshiped, backing its claims with miracles and so convincing unbelievers (2 Thess 2:3, 9-10). Such evil is already at work, though its effectiveness is now limited (2 Thess 2:6-7). When it does come to its full manifestation, it will do so only as part of God's plan for judgment (2 Thess 2:11-12) and only to be destroyed by Christ in his coming for believers (2 Thess 2:8).

Christ's coming will be unexpected by unbelievers, and no timetable can be set for it (1 Thess 5:1-3). For believers it is not only the focus of hope but also the fundamental motivation for right living and the building up of the community (1 Thess 5:4-11). Nothing in the details of Paul's moral exhortations to the Thessalonians is distinctively Jewish or Christian; all of it could be found among Gentile preachers and moral philosophers of the time (see Malherbe 1987). But for Paul the basis of ethical exhortation is different: It is God's call "into his own kingdom and glory" (1 Thess 2:12; cf. 2 Thess 1:11), God's will (1 Thess 4:3), knowledge of God through the Christian proclamation (1 Thess 4:5) and expectation of God's ("the Lord's": perhaps Jesus') judgment (1 Thess 4:6). The call was to holiness (1 Thess 4:3-4, 7; cf. 5:23) and to a relationship with God enjoyed by those who partake of his Spirit (1 Thess 4:8; 5:19; 2 Thess 2:13).

Faith in the gospel had brought about a community that was to be focused on mutual love (1 Thess 3:12; 4:9; 2 Thess 1:3) and admonition (1 Thess 5:11; 2 Thess 3:15). The spread of the gospel to new areas was a major concern of the church and, even more, of its missionaries (1 Thess 1:8-9; 2 Thess 3:1). The letters grant little insight into the church structures that had emerged by this early stage, but Paul makes clear that the missionaries and the local leaders were regarded as having authority in the lives of believers. A significant function of local and apostolic leaders was providing ethical example and exhortation (1 Thess 2:11-12; 5:12-13; 2 Thess 3:4, 14-15), but this responsibility was borne also by the rank and file of church members (1 Thess 5:11). The centrality in Paul's theology of the suffering of the proclaimers of the gospel, particularly of Paul himself, apparently received much of its formation in connection with the church of Thessalonica (see especially 1 Thess 2 and cf. in particular 2 Cor 10-13; Phil 3; Gal 4:12-19; 5:11). Imitation is the link between those coming to faith and their suffering leaders and predecessors in the faith (1 Thess 1:7; 2:14; cf. 2 Thess 1:4), and suffering is the inevitable experience of the preachers and the Christian community (1 Thess 3:3-4).

See also ESCHATOLOGY.

DPL: MAN OF LAWLESSNESS AND RESTRAINING POWER.

BIBLIOGRAPHY. **Commentaries:** E. Best, *A Commentary on the First and Second Epistles to the Thessalonians* (BNTC; Peabody, MA: Hendrickson, 1988 [1972]); F. F. Bruce, *1 and 2 Thessalonians* (WBC; Waco, TX: Word, 1982); A. J. Malherbe, *The Letters to the Thessalonians* (AB; New York: Doubleday, 2000); I. H. Marshall, *1 and 2 Thessalonians* (NCBC; Grand Rapids: Eerdmans, 1983); L. Morris, *The First and Second Epistles to the Thessalonians* (NICNT; Grand Rapids: Eerdmans, 1959); E. J. Richard, *First and Second Thessalonians* (Collegeville, MN: Liturgical Press, 1995); C. A. Wanamaker, *1 and 2 Thessalonians* (NIGTC; Grand Rapids: Eerdmans, 1990). **Studies:** J. M. Bassler, ed., *Pauline Theology*, vol. 1: *Thessalonians, Philippians, Galatians, Philemon* (Minneapolis: Fortress, 1991); R. F. Collins, *Studies on the First Letter to the Thessalonians* (BETL 66; Louvain: Peeters/Louvain University); K. P. Donfried, "The Cults of Thessalonica and the Thessalonian Correspondence," *NTS* 31 (1985) 336-56; K. P. Donfried and J. Beutler, *The Thessalonians Debate: Methodological Discord or Methodological Synthesis?* (Grand Rapids: Eerdmans, 2000); J. G. Gager, "Some Notes on Paul's Conversion," *NTS* (1981) 697-704; R. F. Hock, *The Social Context of Paul's Ministry: Tentmaking and Apostleship* (Philadelphia: Fortress, 1980); F. W. Hughes, *Early Christian Rhetoric and 2 Thessalonians* (JSNTSup 30; Sheffield: JSOT, 1989); R. Jewett, *The Thessalonian Correspondence: Pauline Rhetoric and Millenarian Piety* (FF; Philadelphia: Fortress, 1986); L. T. Johnson, "The New Testament's Anti-Jewish Slander and the Conventions of Ancient Polemic," *JBL* 108 (1989) 419-41; G. Lyons, *Pauline Autobiography: Toward a New Understanding* (SBLDS 73; Atlanta: Scholars Press) 177-221; A. J. Malherbe, "Exhortation in First Thessalonians," *NovT* 25 (1983) 238-56; idem, " 'Gentle as a Nurse': The Stoic Background to 1 Thess. II," *NovT* 12 (1970) 203-17; idem, *Paul and the Thessalonians: The Philosophical Tradition of Pastoral Care* (Philadelphia: Fortress, 1987); W. A. Meeks, *The First Urban Christians: The Social World of the Apostle Paul* (New Haven, CT: Yale University Press, 1983; B. A. Pearson, "1 Thessalonians 2:13-16: A Deutero-Pauline Interpolation," *HTR* 64 (1971) 79-94; D. Schmidt, "1 Thess 2:13-16: Linguistic Evidence for an Interpolation," *JBL* 102 (1983) 269-79; W. Schmithals, *Paul and the Gnostics* (Nashville: Abingdon, 1972) 123-218; J. W. Simpson, "Problems Posed by 1 Thessalonians 2:15-16 and a Solution," *HBT* 12 (1990) 42-72; idem, "Shaped by the Stories: Narrative in 1 Thessalonians," *ATJ* 53 (1998) 15-25; W. Trilling, *Untersuchungen zum zweiten Thessalonicherbrief* (Leipzig: St. Benno, 1972).

J. W. Simpson Jr.

TIMOTHY, FIRST LETTER TO. *See* PASTORAL LETTERS.

TIMOTHY, SECOND LETTER TO. *See* PASTORAL LETTERS.

TITUS, LETTER TO. *See* PASTORAL LETTERS.

TORAH. *See* JEW, PAUL THE; LAW.

TOSEFTA. *See* RABBINIC TRADITIONS AND WRITINGS.

TRADITION. *See* PASTORAL LETTERS.

TRESPASS. *See* SIN.

TRIAL OF JESUS

The trial and *death of Jesus, in addition to being a celebrated problem of jurisprudence, is the focal point of the gospel story and thus assumes paramount importance as a historical and theological issue. Opinions are sharply divided over a wide range of historical, literary and legal aspects of the trial. However, the Jewish and Roman background supports a traditional approach to these questions, namely: after a religious trial before the Sanhedrin, which found Jesus guilty of blasphemy, the Jewish leaders brought a charge of sedition before Pilate, who conducted a political trial and had Jesus crucified.

1. Roman and Jewish Sources
2. New Testament Witnesses
3. Passion Narratives
4. Legal Issues
5. Theological Significance

1. Roman and Jewish Sources.

As a fact of history the trial and death of Jesus of Nazareth is a matter beyond dispute. It is better attested and supported with a wider array of evidence than any other comparable event known to us from the ancient world (Harvey, 11). This datum, so prominent in the apostolic preaching and in the written Gospels, is featured in reports of the historical Jesus in non-Christian sources; these notices, meager though they are, confirm the historical character of the NT's witness to Christ crucified. They furnish no details of the trial itself that are of independent value but, much in the manner of some NT references, make summary statements of what happened.

An official Roman record of the trial of Jesus was probably made at the time and subsequently lost. Imperial Rome received dispatches from the provinces at regular intervals, which included reports of major events. Among the *acta* entered in these official registers (Cassius Dio *Hist.* 57.21.5; 67.11.3) were trials and executions ordered by Roman governors. Such archives of Jesus' trial were reported to exist in the middle of the second Christian century: "That these things happened you may learn from the 'Acts' which were recorded under Pontius Pilate" (Justin Martyr *Apol.* 1.35.9; cf. 1.48.3; and Tertullian *Marc.* 4.17.19; Eusebius *Hist. Eccl.* 2.2.1-4). The later *Acts of Pilate* (fourth century A.D.) is a cycle of pious legends which probably appeared when the archives were no longer available.

On the Jewish side the situation is less certain. The rabbinic law directing two court clerks to write down the speeches pleading for acquittal and conviction (*m. Sanh.* 4:3) may reflect first-century procedures, but there are no allusions to such recordings in the case of Jesus. The Jewish

folklore about the last days of Jesus, called *Toledoth Jeshu*, is medieval in origin and has no historical value. A number of rabbinic and historical texts, however, lay fair claim to be worthy of credence and have been studied intensively.

1.1. Talmud. A common theme runs through all the Talmudic (*see* Rabbinic Traditions and Literature) references to Jesus: He was executed as a dangerous teacher, a seducer, or *mēsît*, who led Israel astray. A notable text from the Babylonian Talmud (*b. Sanh.* 43a) preserves a saying handed down from the earliest period (a *baraita* from the Tannaim, A.D. 70-200): "Jesus was hanged on Passover Eve. For forty days before the execution took place, a herald went forth and cried, 'He is going forth to be stoned because he has practiced sorcery and enticed Israel to apostasy. Anyone who can say anything in his favor, let him come forward and plead on his behalf.' But since nothing was brought forward in his favor, he was hanged on Passover Eve." The emphatic point is that the trial and execution, carried out under Jewish and not Roman procedures, were absolutely fair. Putting aside the questionable details in the account, the attempt to justify Jewish involvement in the death of Jesus is remarkable and stands in contrast to modern Jewish research on the trial. Other Talmudic statements are similar: "Jesus the Nazarene practiced magic and led Israel astray" (*b. Sanh.* 107b; cf. *b. Soṭa* 47a; *y. ḥag.* 2.2). Also, a series of disputed passages which refer to an executed heretic, a certain Ben Stada (*b. Sanh.* 67a; *t. Sanh.* 10.11; *b. Šabb.* 104b; *y. Sanh.* 7.16; *y. Yebam.* 16.6; *y. Šabb.* 12.4; *t. Šabb.* 11.15), in all likelihood is linked to the false-prophet tradition about Jesus (Catchpole, 64).

1.2. Josephus. The well-known passages about Jesus, the so-called *Testimonium Flavianum*, are widely regarded to be genuine, with some obvious Christian interpolations. The authentic text (see Josephus *Ant.* 20.9.1 §200) underscores the leading role of Pilate and the complicity of the Jewish leaders in the trial of Jesus: "On the accusation of our leading men, Pilate condemned him to the cross, but those who were attracted to him from the first did not cease to love him" (Josephua *Ant.* 18.3.3 §64). The Slavonic version of Josephus has fueled much speculation, but its embellished accounts of Jesus' life and death are legendary expansions of the Greek originals.

1.3. Tacitus. The information provided by

Tacitus, who wrote between A.D. 115 and 117, is very sketchy and may be derived from Josephus: "They got their name from Christ, who was executed by sentence of the procurator Pontius Pilate in the reign of Tiberius" (Tacitus *Ann.* 15.44.2). For Roman readers the pertinent information about the Christians, whom Nero had blamed for the fire in Rome (A.D. 64), was the identity and death of their namesake. Another allusion to Roman knowledge of the crucifixion appears in the Christian writer of the early third century, Julius Africanus; he cites (*PG* 10.89) one Thallus, a freedman of Tiberius who wrote a history (c. A.D. 50) now lost, for the opinion that the darkness and earthquake attending the cross were to be explained as an eclipse, inferring that Thallus mentioned the crucifixion in book three of his history.

1.4. Mara bar Serapion. A Syriac letter written from prison by Mara bar Serapion to his son cautions that misfortune overtakes those who persecute wise men, such as Socrates, Pythagoras and Jesus: "What advantage did the Jews gain from executing their wise King? It was just after that that their kingdom was abolished. . . . Nor did the wise King die altogether; he lived on in the teaching he had given." The date of Mara bar Serapion is uncertain; the only extant copy of the letter is seventh century, but historical clues place its origin in the first three centuries, perhaps as early as A.D. 73 (Blinzler, 36). The author was probably a pagan and, if first century, provides independent testimony to Jewish responsibility for the execution of Jesus.

In summary, the literary evidence confirms three facts: (1) Jesus was crucified by Roman authority under the sentence of Pontius Pilate (Josephus, Tacitus); (2) the Jewish leaders made a formal accusation against Jesus and participated decisively in the events leading to his execution (Josephus, Mara); and (3) Jewish involvement in the trial was explained as a proper undertaking against a heretic or seducer who led Israel astray (Talmud).

2. New Testament Witnesses.

The centrality of the cross in apostolic preaching gave rise to trial summaries which are found outside the passion narratives, primarily in sermons and creedal formulas. They were part of the earliest Gospel tradition proclaimed by the apostles and handed down to their converts (Acts 1:3; 1 Cor 15:3); these kerygmatic summaries disclose the contours of a written passion narrative in its earliest stages of formation.

2.1. Letters of Paul. The language of "handing over" (*paradidōmi*) describes Jesus' voluntary death as a divine necessity (Rom 4:25; 8:32; 1 Cor 11:32; Gal 2:20; Eph 5:2). The proximate agents of the crucifixion can be the "rulers of this age" (1 Cor 2:8; Col 2:15) or, from another point of view, the "Jews, who killed both the Lord Jesus and the prophets" (1 Thess 2:14-15). Paul alludes directly to the trial when he says that Christ Jesus "witnessed the good confession before Pontius Pilate" (1 Tim 6:13). Other epistolary texts emphasize the innocence of Jesus and the plight of those who caused him to suffer (1 Pet 2:22-24; Heb 6:6; 10:26-29; Rev 1:7).

2.2. Acts of the Apostles. Speeches in Acts provide eleven passages which relate to the trial. (1) The events in Jerusalem were part of a divine plan fulfilling the prophetic Scriptures (Acts 2:22-23; 3:17-19; 4:10-11, 25-28; 13:27-29). (2) Being ignorant of who Jesus was, the Jews in Jerusalem and their leaders delivered up and disowned him in the presence of Pilate (Acts 3:13, 17; 13:27). (3) The crucifixion was carried out by the Romans, but the Jews, specifically the leaders of the Sanhedrin, were chiefly responsible: "You killed him, having him crucified by the hand of godless men" (Acts 2:23; cf. 2:36; 3:15, 17; 4:10; 5:28, 30; 7:52; 10:39; 13:27-28). (4) In a prayer of the church the circle of conspiracy is widened to "both Herod and Pontius Pilate along with the Gentiles and the peoples of Israel" (Acts 4:27).

The writings and sermons preserved in the letters and Acts concur in the assertion that the handing over of Jesus to death was taken at the initiative of the Jews in Jerusalem and their leaders; moreover, the Gentile authorities bear equal responsibility whenever they are addressed. Whatever else may be said, the human actors played out a divine drama, doing what God's hand and purpose had predetermined to happen (Acts 4:28; cf. 2:23; 3:18; Rom 8:32; 1 Cor 2:7).

2.3. Gospel Predictions. What were hints earlier in the ministry of Jesus (e.g., Mk 2:18-22; Jn 7:6-8) become explicit predictions of impending death on the last journey to Jerusalem (Mk 8:31; 9:31; 10:33-34; cf. Mt 16:21; 17:22-23; 20:18-19; Lk 9:22, 44; 18:31-33). The three Synoptic predictions in the triple tradition converge with the apostolic proclamation on the basic points of importance: (1) the trial and death of Jesus is ordained of God; "the Son of man must suffer many things" (Mk 8:31) is a "must" *(dei)* of divine necessity (cf. Lk 17:25; 24:6-7) issuing from the will of the Father (Mk 9:11; 12:10; Mt 12:39; Lk 9:31; 24:26, 44); (2) the "handing over" of Jesus is a betrayal to the Sanhedrin in Jerusalem (the chief priests, scribes and elders), which condemns him to death (Mk 8:31; 10:33; cf. 12:1-12; Lk 24:20, chief priests and rulers deliver him up to the sentence of death); and (3) the ultimate suffering, that is, his mockery, being spit upon, scourging and death, comes at the hands of Gentiles, namely, the Roman authorities (Mk 10:34; Lk 18:32).

Lack of explicit details in the Markan predictions (e.g., no mention of Pilate or the cross) counts against the view that these sayings are prophecies after the fact created by the early church. They are better explained as seminal utterances which were elaborated in apostolic preaching. The impetus to proclaim the scandal of a crucified Messiah lies in the memory of Jesus' own words (Lk 24:44-49; 1 Cor 11:23-26).

3. Passion Narratives.

Our best sources of information are the accounts of the passion story in the four Gospels (Mt 26—27; Mk 14—15; Lk 22—23; Jn 13; 18—19), where the documents exhibit their highest degree of similarity. How is their striking relationship to be explained? The evidence tips in favor of the answer, vigorously contested in some quarters, that a connected passion narrative of some length circulated before the writing of the Gospels and underlies the work of the Evangelists. The further inference that Luke and John are independent witnesses to this earlier tradition, seen in their departures from the Markan-Matthean scheme, is less certain but can be strongly supported (Jeremias, Green).

This approach to the formation of the four passion narratives is based on the following observations: (1) the four Gospels narrate a unified story of some twenty pericopes, with minor transpositions, beginning with a plot which converges on the arrest of Jesus; (2) OT motifs of the Servant of the Lord (Isaiah; *see* Servant of Yahweh), stricken shepherd (Zechariah) and righteous sufferer (Psalms; *see* Death of Christ) link Jesus' death to the fulfillment of the Scriptures (cf. Mk 14:49) in a pattern distinctive of earliest Christian preaching; (3) the "handing

over" theme found in kerygmatic summaries and dominical sayings emerges in the betrayal and trial scenes (Mt 26:2, 46; 27:2; Mk 14:10; 15:1, 15; Lk 23:25; Jn 19:16); (4) the shared vocabulary of Luke with Mark decreases from 50 percent to 27 percent in the passion narratives; and (5) Luke and John agree together on numerous details that are absent from Mark and Matthew (e.g., Pilate's three verdicts of not guilty, Lk 23:4, 14, 22 par. Jn 18:38; 19:4, 6). On these grounds we will proceed to consider key episodes in the passion story, giving full weight to the testimony of each Evangelist.

3.1. Plot to Destroy Jesus. The enemies of Jesus hatched their plot during the earliest controversies in Galilee and Jerusalem (Mk 3:6; Jn 5:18), but their intention was forestalled until the final week when Jesus' triumphal entry, the cleansing of the temple (*see* Temple Cleansing) and head-on disputes prodded them into action (Mk 11:18; 12:12; 14:1). John records that Jesus lived under a constant death threat (Jn 7:1, 19, 25; 8:37; 11:16) and escaped a series of attempted arrests and stonings (Jn 7:30, 32, 44; 8:20, 59; 10:31, 39; cf. Lk 4:29-30). The popularity of Jesus with the crowds (Mt 7:28-29; Jn 4:1) precluded an open arrest by the religious leaders for fear of a riot but spurred their resolve to delay no longer: "See, this is getting us nowhere. Look how the whole world has gone after him" (Jn 12:19 NIV).

3.1.1. Proscription and Warrant. A crucial decision had been made weeks before, recounted in John 11:47-57. After the stir caused by the raising of Lazarus, "the chief priests and the Pharisees convened a meeting of the Sanhedrin" (Jn 11:47) in order to deal with Jesus. The high priest Caiaphas, an unwitting prophet, persuaded them that Jesus must die on behalf of the nation, thus keeping peace in the homeland and restoring the scattered people of God. The council, having formally decided to kill Jesus (Jn 11:52), issued a warrant for his arrest and solicited informers to come forward (Jn 11:57). This distinctive passage, filled with semitechnical terms, marks the beginning of the legal process and, in effect, makes Jesus a fugitive from Jewish law (Bammel 1971, 33-35). An ongoing prosecution instigated by the Jews and led by Caiaphas helps to explain what appears to be a precipitous rush to judgment in the Synoptic account of Passover night.

3.1.2. Passover Treachery. The Synoptic time

note, "after two days was the feast of Passover" (Mk 14:1 par. Mt 26:2 and Lk 22:1), appears to refer to a subsequent meeting of the council at the palace of Caiaphas. Here the discussion centered on a covert plan, as Luke puts it, "the how" (*to pōs*, Lk 22:2) of getting rid of Jesus without causing an uproar during the feast (cf. Mt 26:4; Mk 14:2). The question was how to implement the resolution already passed (Jn 11:52, 57). An unexpected visitor brought what they hoped for: Judas Iscariot, one of Jesus' disciples, agreed to collaborate for a sum of money. In turn he would "look for an opportunity to hand Jesus over to them without drawing a crowd" (Lk 22:6; cf. Mt 26:14-16; Mk 14:10-11).

Matthew and Mark tell the story of the anointing in Bethany (Mt 26:6-13; Mk 14:3-9) before the conspiracy visit by Judas with no hint of connection. John may well give the link: the indignation expressed among the disciples at the expensive waste of perfume (Mt 26:8; Mk 14:4) was voiced by Judas himself (Jn 12:4). The act of devotion by the woman contrasts to and leads to the act of treachery by the man. A sinister motive lies underneath the monetary concerns in the priests' contract and the anointing episode; Luke and John concur that Satan had entered the heart of Judas (Lk 22:3; Jn 13:2, 27).

3.2. Arrest in Gethsemane. The fateful Thursday evening begins with the intimacy of the Last Supper shattered by the talk of betrayal and the exit of Judas into the "night" (Jn 13:30). The scene is dominated by Jesus' knowledge that what will happen is God's plan: "The Son of man now goes as it has been decreed, but woe to that person by whom he is betrayed" (Lk 22:22; cf. Mt 26:24; Mk 14:21, "as it has been written about him"; *see* Son of Man). The predictive element heightens when Jesus leaves the table. The Synoptics focus on the scattering of the disciples and the approaching defection of Peter (Mt 26:31-35; Mk 14:27-31; Lk 22:24-38), while John relates the farewell discourses (Jn 14:1—17:26). As he frequently had done (Lk 22:39; Jn 18:1-2), Jesus walked with the disciples across the brook Kidron into a garden, a place on the Mount of Olives named Gethsemane (Mt 26:36 par. Mk 14:32). The calm of the upper room here gives way to burdened prayer as the cup of death looms before Jesus, an agony made all the greater by the sleeping disciples. The hour had come; the betrayer was at hand.

3.2.1. Judas's Betrayal. The actual arrest happened quickly. After Judas identified Jesus by a prearranged signal, a customary kiss of greeting (Mt 26:48-49; Mk 14:44-45; Lk 22:47-48), the armed crowd from the temple Mount laid hands on him. Since the authorities knew Jesus by face ("I was daily with you," Mk 14:49 par.), the approach with a kiss was more than simple identification; it was calculated to allay suspicion and to point out Jesus in the surrounding darkness. Theories suggesting that Judas betrayed who Jesus was or something he said have little support in the texts; more likely, he divulged the whereabouts of Jesus at a time and place when a quiet seizure was possible (cf. Mk 14:11; Jn 11:57) and guided the arrest party to the spot (Lk 22:47; Acts 1:16, "guide"). John's language, "Judas having received *[labōn]* the cohort and the officers of the chief priests and the Pharisees" (Jn 18:3), does not imply that Judas took charge but rather that he procured and escorted the band.

3.2.2. Flight of the Disciples. A flurry of resistance was offered by a sword-wielding disciple who cut off the ear ("right ear," Lk 22:50; Jn 18:10) of the high priest's servant—according to John it was Simon Peter who attacked Malchus. Jesus intervened, commanding Peter to stop ("Put your sword back in its place," Mt 26:52 par. Jn 18:11), and healed the servant's ear (Lk 22:51). Matthew alone records the sayings on perishing by the sword and the twelve legions of angels standing ready to help (Mt 26:52-54). The ironical question "Have you come out to arrest me, as you would a robber, with swords and clubs?" (Synoptics), a reply of peaceful surrender, exhausted the courage of the disciples. They deserted Jesus and fled. All four Gospels understand these events in the light of prophecy, as fulfillment of the Scriptures (Mt 26:54, 56; Mk 14:49), the hour of darkness (Lk 22:53) and the word of Jesus (Jn 18:9). The unique tradition in Mark of a young man who fled naked (14:51-52) may be the Evangelist's own modest signature.

3.2.3. Company and Commander. The Synoptics describe the personnel who arrested Jesus as a crowd sent from the Sanhedrin (chief priests, elders and scribes; Mk 14:43; Mt 26:47; "a large crowd"), and Luke puts the chief priests and elders at the scene along with the temple police (*stratēgoi*, constables or court officers, Lk 22:52). The impression of a solely Jewish initiative, however, diminishes in John who twice dis-

	Matthew	Mark	Luke	John
1. Jesus led to the high priest's house	26:57	14:53	22:54	18:13-14
2. Peter follows into the courtyard	26:58	14:54	22:55	18:15
3. Peter's denials begin	26:69-71a	14:66-68	22:56-57	18:16-18
4. Jesus interrogated by Annas				18:19-23
5. Jesus tried before Caiaphas at night	26:59-66	14:55-64	[22:67-71]	18:24
6. Peter's final denial at cockcrow	26:71b-75	14:69-72	22:58-62	18:25-27
7. Jesus abused and mocked by captors	26:67-68	14:65	22:63-65	
8. Jesus before the Sanhedrin at dawn	27:1	15:1a	22:66-71	18:28b
9. Jesus led to Pilate	27:2	15:1b	23:1	18:28a

Figure 1. Order of events in Jewish trial of Jesus

tinguishes "the company" (*speira*, 18:3, 12) of soldiers and its "commander" (*chiliarchos*, 18:12) from the Jewish detachment. These are the regular terms for the cohort and tribune of the Roman army (cf. Mt 27:27; Mk 15:16; Acts 10:1; 21:31; 27:1 NASB) and strongly suggest Roman participation in the arrest (*pace* Blinzler, Bammel, Catchpole). Objections to this view are not convincing: (1) the definite article with *speira* denotes the garrison regularly stationed at the Antonia fortress during festivals (cf. Josephus *J.W.* 2.12.1 §224; *Ant.* 20.5.3 §106; Acts 21:31); (2) the phrase does not demand that the entire cohort of 600 soldiers came to the garden; (3) pursuit of a "robber" (*lēstēs*, bandit, freedom fighter, revolutionary) by a heavily armed force was a matter for Roman jurisdiction (cf. Mk 15:7, 27; Jn 18:40); and (4) remanding a prisoner in Roman custody to a Jewish court is paralleled in the case of Paul (Acts 22:30). The first action against Jesus, instigated by agents of the Jewish court, was in collaboration with the Roman authorities.

3.3. The Jewish Proceedings. The Gospels report that swiftly following the arrest, probably before midnight, the Jewish leaders began an interrogation and trial of Jesus, arguing the case throughout the night and returning a death verdict at daybreak. The sequence and relationship of these blocks of narrative material are the most complex in the passion story. Alleged discrepancies have prompted some scholars to be dubious of the entire account of the Jewish trial, even to the point of denying that a formal trial before the Sanhedrin ever happened (Lietzmann, Winter). A composite version of the proceedings must bring together four graphic scenes: (1) an initial examination by Annas in John, (2) Peter's denials of Jesus in all four Gospels, (3) a nighttime trial before Caiaphas in Matthew and Mark and (4) a Sanhedrin trial at dawn in Luke.

3.3.1. Preliminary Hearing Before Annas. John writes that Jesus was led "first" (implying knowledge of a second hearing, Jn 18:13) to Annas, where he was briefly questioned about "his disciples and his teaching" (Jn 18:19) and struck in the face by a displeased captor (Jn 18:20-23). The atmosphere is not that of a trial but of a roughshod interrogation by a notable examiner to get incriminating evidence. Based on a straightforward reading of verse 24, "Annas then sent him, still bound, to Caiaphas the high priest," the examiner must have been Annas, a former high priest (A.D. 6-15) and father-in-law to his successor, Joseph Caiaphas (A.D. 18-36). The preceding passage twice then calls Annas the "high priest" (Jn 18:19, 22) and locates the denial scene at his residence (Jn 18:15). The Synoptics, on the other hand, place Jesus and Peter in the house and courtyard of Caiaphas (Mt 26:57-58 par. Mk 14:53-54 and Lk 22:54-55). A few minuscules and versions (225 1195 syr[s, h, p] Cyril of Alexandria) solve the problem by rearranging of verse 24 after verse 13 in John's account, thereby making Caiaphas the unnamed high priest in verses 15-23. A similar effect is gained by translating the aorist *apesteilen* (v. 24) with a pluperfect force, "Now Annas *had sent* him bound" (KJV, NIV mg). Neither expedient, however, is necessary: (1) Annas, as other high priests, would have kept the dignity and title of the office for life (Josephus *Ant.* 18.2.2 §34; *m. Hor.* 3:4), (2) that Caiaphas should defer to the elderly father-in-law is fully in keeping with the influence and power of Annas (cf. Lk 3:2; Acts 4:6) and (3) as for location, a more feasible conjecture is that Annas and Caiaphas were in wings of the same residence somewhere in the upper city (cf. Josephus *J.W.* 2.17.6 §426).

3.3.2. Peter's Denials. While Jesus was inside the high priest's residence until about 3 a.m. (the time of cockcrow for Jerusalem in April), Peter was outside (Mt 26:69; Jn 18:16) in the courtyard below where Jesus was being held (Mk 14:66). The four Gospels show this coincidence emphatically but in differing ways: Mark and Matthew intercalate the night session led by Caiaphas before the denial scene (Mk 14:55-65 par. Mt 26:59-68); John breaks up the scene itself, placing the Annas interrogation after the first denial (Jn 18:19-24); Luke tells Peter's story without interruption (Lk 22:55-62) but places him within sight of Jesus' withering gaze when the cock crowed. "And the Lord, having turned, looked straight at Peter" (Lk 22:61). By intertwining the two scenes the Gospels stress not only simultaneity (the connectives may be rendered "meanwhile," cf. NEB) but the gravity of Peter's act. While Jesus faced his accusers and denied nothing he truly was, Peter cringed before his accusers and denied everything.

3.3.3. Nighttime Trial Before Caiaphas. Was then Jesus formally tried during the night? This has been the crucial question in trial research. John, who mentions delivery to Caiaphas (Jn 18:24), and Luke, who describes only a mockery and beating at night (Lk 22:63-65), are silent on the issue. Luke does however report a morning session of the Sanhedrin, probably in the council chamber (*eis to synedrion,* Lk 22:66), where Jesus was questioned by the entire body (Lk 22:67-71). Matthew and Mark are quite definite that Caiaphas, in the company of "the chief priests and the whole council," held a nocturnal

interrogation with all the earmarks of a formal trial (Mt 26:59-68 par. Mk 14:55-65).

First, the required evidence ("false testimony," Mt 26:59) was sought in order to prosecute Jesus on a capital charge. From among several false witnesses who failed to agree at all, two eventually contrived the charge that Jesus had threatened to destroy the temple and rebuild it in three days (Mt 26:61; Mk 14:58; cf. Jn 2:19). Then the high priest himself, driven by Jesus' unwillingness to answer the charge, pressed for an admission of guilt, "Are you the Christ, the Son of the Blessed?" (Mk 14:61 par. Mt 26:63, "Son of God"). In Mark the explicit reply, "I am" (implicitly in Matthew and Luke), followed by the future Son of man saying (Mk 14:62; cf. Mt 26:64; Lk 22:69), linked Jesus' identity to three elevated titles, Messiah (*see* Christ), *Son of God and *Son of man. This claim constituted blasphemy in the eyes of the court, and "they all condemned him to be worthy of death" (Mk 14:64; Mt 26:66).

Although specific time notices are lacking, it is difficult to dislodge the timing of the trial in Matthew and Mark. They both report a summation of the proceedings in "early morning" (*prōi,* Mt 27:1; Mk 15:1), thus a time frame is fixed unless one treats the passage as an awkward insertion or a curious doublet. Again, the quaint detail of lighting a charcoal fire in the courtyard indicates a commotion that kept people awake during the night (Sherwin-White, Bruce) and puts Jesus before Caiaphas while Peter warmed himself (Mk 14:54, 66; Lk 22:55, 61; Jn 18:18, 24- 25).

3.3.4. Morning Decision of the Sanhedrin. Luke's record of the morning session ("as day was dawning," Lk 22:66) strikingly echoes most of the nighttime dialogue found in Matthew and Mark, except the questions are put by the entire body (plural subject throughout) and no witnesses are called, although Luke 22:71, "Why do we still need testimony?" implies their presence. The morning assembly described by Mark and Matthew is not so much another trial as a culmination of the preceding events during the night. The descriptive phrases mean "to take counsel, reach a decision" (*symboulion* + *poiein,* Mk 15:1; + *lambanein,* Mt 27:1; cf. 12:14; 22:15; 27:7; 28:12) and refer to the legal formulation of charges against Jesus, not to a second council meeting (Sherwin-White, 44).

Has one or the other of the Synoptics dislocated a single Jewish trial in the narrative sequence, or were there two sessions of the Sanhedrin, one at night and a second in the morning? Among those who defend the historicity of the Sanhedrin trial, the former option of a single trial is widely accepted, but its timing is debated: (1) a single morning session, according to Luke, the night setting being a Markan literary technique (Catchpole, Black, Robinson); or (2) a single nighttime session extending to dawn, following Mark and Matthew, with Luke telescoping the trial summary to the morning (Blinzler, Smalley, Sherwin-White). Luke's narrative does not fill the night with trial activity but does retain a nocturnal mocking and abuse by those guarding Jesus (Lk 22:63-65). A minor agreement here with Matthew, the tag line in the blind man's bluff, "Who is the one who hit you?" (Lk 22:64 par. Mt 26:68; omitted in Mk 14:65), hints at Luke's knowledge of the nighttime trial. Since the morning assembly went to Pilate with expanded allegations (Lk 23:2), the entire Sanhedrin may well have rehearsed the previous night's dialogue (Lk 22:66-71) in order to devise the sedition charge. Luke's arrangement shows that these political accusations were obtained by a legally convened Sanhedrin in a religious prosecution.

The probable order of events surrounding the Jewish trial can be tabulated as figure 1. The Gospels present events 3 and 6 as occurring simultaneously with 4 and 5; in Matthew and Mark the trial and mockery scenes (5 and 7 conflated) are the erratic blocks of material in the narrative order, whereas Luke (placing 7 at night) and John have the sequence intact.

3.4. The Roman Proceedings. The narratives of the trial before Pilate depict a separate prosecution aimed to secure a death sentence under terms of Roman law. The Sanhedrin, knowing well that blasphemy was not a capital offense in the eyes of Rome, urged the governor that Jesus had committed treason against the state. Like the structure of the Jewish trial, the four Gospels feature a Roman interrogation, condemnation and mockery of Jesus, but there are fundamental differences at each stage: (1) the questioning centers on the issue of kingship; (2) when Pilate proposes to release Jesus their king, the crowds shout for Barabbas instead, and under increasing pressure Pilate hands Jesus over to be crucified; and (3) Roman soldiers also mock and abuse Jesus, as did the Jewish constables, but in

contempt of his kingship. Three independent stories accentuate the officials: Luke prefaces the Barabbas scene with an account of the examination by Herod Antipas (Lk 23:8-12), while in Matthew's interludes we see Pilate warned by a troubled wife and washing his hands (Mt 27:19, 24-25).

The trial in John's account is extended with great dramatic effect. Whereas Jesus remains silent in the Synoptics (Mt 27:14; Mk 15:5; Lk 23:9), most of John is a private dialogue between Jesus and Pilate on kingship. The scene shifts in seven episodes between frontstage, the outside court where "the Jews" waited, and backstage, the inner Praetorium where Jesus was held. Pilate's shuffling back and forth (cf. Jn 18:29, 33, 38b; 19:1, 4, 9, 13) gives the impression of a vacillating judge who finally condemns an innocent "King of the Jews." A tragic irony emerges in John as well as the Synoptics: the "pretender" who went to the cross actually was the king, the crucified Messiah (cf. Jn 19:15; Mk 15:12-13; 1 Cor 2:8).

3.4.1. Accusation Before Pilate. The reason why the Jews came to the Roman authority is made clear by John: "It is not lawful for us to put anyone to death" (Jn 18:31). The Synoptics also assume that only Pilate was able to authorize the execution demanded by the Sanhedrin; moreover, he did not simply ratify the Jewish decision but made a new investigation of the case, asking for the charges against Jesus, "What accusation are you bringing against this man?" (Jn 18:29; cf. Mt 27:12; Mk 15:3; Lk 23:2). Luke gives the precise wording in a threefold form: leading astray the nation, forbidding payment of taxes to Caesar and claiming to be the Messiah, a king (Lk 23:2; cf. 23:5, stirring up the people; 23:14, inciting the people to rebel). The obvious political overtones of this accusation explain Pilate's first and uppermost question, "Are you the King of the Jews?" (Mt 27:11; Mk 15:2; Lk 23:3; Jn 18:33). The force of Jesus' reply, "The words are yours," eases some of the procurator's anxiety about sedition and revolution.

3.4.2. Transfer to Herod Antipas. The crowd protested Pilate's first attempt to dismiss the charge with the complaint that Jesus began his seditious activity in Galilee, the tetrarchy of Herod Antipas. Having learned that Jesus was a Galilean under Herod's jurisdiction, Pilate made a hasty arrangement ("Herod and Pilate became friends with one another that very day," Lk

23:12) to put Jesus before his old adversary (Lk 23:6-12; cf. 9:7-9; 13:31-32). The examination, carried on with a circus-like barrage of questions from Herod and "full-pitched accusations" (Lk 23:10) from the chief priests and scribes, stalled when Jesus would not answer; the sham ended in a staged ridicule of Jesus' kingship, by sending him back to Pilate dressed in a regal, shining robe (Lk 23:11). What Pilate had hoped to gain is not clear, but he interpreted Jesus' return as an acquittal (Lk 23:15).

The whole affair, plausible enough in itself, fully accords with what we know of the situation at the time: (1) the tetrarch's father, Herod the Great, had exercised unusual privileges of extradition (Josephus *J.W.* 1.24.2 §474), and Antipas himself had the ear of the emperor Tiberius (Josephus *Ant.* 18.2.3 §36; 18.4.5 §104); (2) procurators often used a *consilium*, a body of legal advisors or friends, to reach a verdict (Acts 25:12, 26; Justinian *Digest* 4.8.3; *SIG* 3 780.25; cf. Bickerman, 110); (3) advice or judgment sought in Jerusalem from a Herodian official would have been advantageous for Pilate whose relations with Antipas and Galilee needed repair (Lk 23:12b, "previously they had been enemies"; cf. Lk 13:1) and (4) although not required to do so, Pilate likely wanted a transfer to Herod's jurisdiction (available in the legal custom of home venue, or *forum domicilii*) to rid himself of a troublesome case (Sherwin-White, 28-31).

3.4.3. Release of Barabbas. The second stage of Pilate's trial in all four Gospels is an attempt to free Jesus by means of a Passover amnesty, the so-called *privilegium paschale* (Passover privilege), which failed and led to the release of Barabbas instead (Mt 27:15-26; Mk 15:6-15; Lk 23:13-25; Jn 18:39-40). Matthew and Mark introduce Barabbas at the beginning of the incident, building up the intervention of the crowd on his behalf. With the Jewish leaders stirring the people (Mt 27:20; Mk 15:11) to ask for Barabbas, Pilate's appeal for Jesus, "Do you wish that I release to you the King of the Jews?" (Mk 15:9) was futile. Luke and John stress Pilate's resolve to set Jesus free (Lk 23:20; Jn 19:12) because he had found "no basis for a charge against him" (Jn 18:38; cf. 19:4, 6; Lk 23:14, 22). The governor intended, after Jesus was punished by flogging (Lk 23:16, 22; Jn 19:1), to invoke the amnesty custom for his release; however, the crowd wanted Jesus crucified. The crescendo of shouts, "Crucify him! Crucify him!" depicted by all four

Evangelists in two distinct phases (Mt 27:22-23; Mk 15:13-14; Lk 23:21-23; Jn 19:6, 15), was decisive for Pilate.

The Gospels contain all we know about Barabbas, a revolutionary (*lēstēs*, Jn 18:40; "robber" KJV, RSV) who had committed murder in a Jerusalem insurrection (Lk 23:19, 25; Mk 15:7) and likely had followers in the Praetorium crowd. His name, the Greek form of an Aramaic surname *Bar-ʾAbbā*, means "son of Abba" (or literally, "son of the father"); it occurs in Aramaic texts from the fifth century B.C. down to rabbis of the Amoraic period (e.g., *ḥiyya bar ʾAbbā*, *Lev. Rab.* 3.1). The form *ʾAbbāh* is attested as a personal name on a funerary inscription near Jerusalem dated about the time of Jesus (*MPAT* §68); if the man had a son, he would have been called Barabbas in Greek. The variant *Barrabbas* (with two r's meaning "son of the teacher") read by Origen and Jerome is improbable. A better case has been made for the Caesarean text of Matthew 27:16-17 (Q 700* f[1]syr[s, pal] geo[2] Origen[pt]) which supplies a first name, "Jesus Barabbas" (cf. NEB). Some commentators who adopt this reading suggest that Pilate mistook shouts for Jesus Barabbas as a plea for Jesus of Nazareth and eventually had to ask which one the crowd preferred (Mt 27:21). The variant, however, is weakly supported and probably arose from conjecture about the two names, still an irrepressible desire in some modern critics (e.g., Winter, 142-43).

The Barabbas incident and the paschal amnesty in particular are often dismissed as nonhistorical, "nothing but a figment of the imagination" (Winter, 134). The objections to the episode, based on the lack of evidence for such a custom in antiquity, do not carry sufficient weight. In the provincial cities, acclamation of the people (*acclamatio populi*) played a significant role in Roman legal administration (Strobel, 126-27); there are numerous examples of Roman magistrates who heeded a crowd's wishes at the tribunal (e.g., Tacitus *Ann.* 1.44.4; Justinian *Digest* 49.1.12; 48.8.16; see Bickerman, 103, 133-34). This custom is well illustrated by an incident in Egypt (A.D. 85) where the Roman governor released the accused, saying, "You deserve to be scourged *[mastigōthēnai]* . . . , but I will deal more humanely with you and will release you to the crowds *[ochlois]*" (Papyrus Florentinus 61.59-65; cf. Blinzler, 207). The political situation for Pilate was acutely unstable because of a series of clashes with the Jews (cf. Philo *Leg. Gai.* 38 §§301-302), so he would have been inclined to placate them on this occasion. He did not want a bad report in Rome, and the Jews traded on his insecurity as a "friend of Caesar" (Jn 19:12), a title weighted with political intrigue during the last stages of Tiberius's reign (cf. Tacitus *Ann.* 6.8; Philo *Flacc.* 6 §40; *NewDocs* 1978, 75). No clear evidence has yet come to light for a regular amnesty at a feast, but a provision stated in the Mishnah may be relevant: "They may slaughter the Passover . . . for one whom they have promised to bring out of prison" (*m. Pesaḥ.* 8:6). This much-discussed text may refer to an evening release from a Jewish prison (Jeremias, 73), but it must have occurred with regularity to become a topic of rabbinic legislation, and a Roman detention cannot be ruled out (Blinzler, 218-21; Robinson, 261). These analogies favor the historical plausibility of the Gospel account much more than the explanations that try to derive the story in purely theological terms.

3.4.4. Scourging, Mockery and Death Sentence. The Barabbas scene closes in the Synoptics with Jesus sentenced to death by crucifixion (Mt 27:26; Mk 15:15; Lk 23:24-25). Matthew and Mark add the temporal participle, "having scourged [Jesus]," so that this punishment precedes the final sentence; then both relate the mockery by Roman soldiers in the Praetorium, where Jesus wore a crown of thorns and purple robe (Mt 27:27-31; Mk 15:16-20). Once again John sketches in the details which the Synoptics have summarized. Following the scourging and mockery in the Fourth Gospel, Jesus is brought before the Jews by a frustrated Pilate, who attempts to shift responsibility from himself ("You take him yourselves and crucify him," Jn 19:6). Amidst the insistent cries of "Crucify! Crucify!" a clear theological gravamen against Jesus finally emerges: "We have a law, and by that law he ought to die, because he made himself the Son of God" (Jn 19:7). Pilate retires in fear and in another exchange warns Jesus that he has power even at this stage in the proceedings to free him or to crucify him, but the governor's good intentions quickly turn to appeasement once the Jews question his loyalty to the emperor ("after he heard these words," Jn 19:13). Then, at a place called the *Lithostrōton* ("stone pavement"), the formal sentence of death is spoken from the judgment seat *(bēma)* where Pilate sits (the intransitive sense of *ekathisen* in v. 13, "Pilate sat

down," is preferred over the idea that Pilate "set Jesus down" as a jest). Roman law required the magistrate to pronounce a capital sentence from the judgment seat (Mommsen, 447). John, in agreement with the other Evangelists, marks this point in the trial narrative with a judicial use of *paredōken;* Pilate "handed over" Jesus to the condemnation of the cross (Jn 19:16 par. Mt 27:26; Mk 15:15 and Lk 23:25).

John's order of events—scourging, mockery, sentence—leaves little reason to question its correctness. The placement of the mockery after the sentence in Matthew and Mark has a dual function. It summarizes Pilate's decision and emphasizes the role of the Roman soldiers who carried out the order: "Then the soldiers of the governor took Jesus into the Praetorium . . . and they led him away to crucify him" (Mt 27:27, 31 par. Mk 15:16, 20; note the ambiguous "they" in Lk 23:25-26 and Jn 19:16, where the NIV supplies "soldiers"). That Pilate attempted to end the trial by having Jesus flogged conforms to Roman practice. Scourging could be inflicted as the first stage of capital punishment (Josephus *J.W.* 2.14.9 §306; 7.6.4 §200; Livy *Hist.* 1.26; 33.36) or, as it is in the Gospels (Lk 23:16, 22; Jn 19:10), an independent penalty followed by release or imprisonment (cf. Acts 16:23; 22:24; Josephus *J.W.* 2.13.7 § 269; Philo *Flacc.* 10 §75; Justinian *Digest* 48.2.6). A notable parallel is the case of Jesus bar Ananias, a strange prophet of doom who spoke against Jerusalem and the temple; after a trial and flogging by the Jewish authorities, he was charged before the procurator Albinus (A.D. 62), who released him as a madman, only when he had him "flayed to the bone with scourges" (Josephus *J.W.* 6.5.3 §304). The details of the Gospel narratives are, on the whole, in remarkable accord and are fully intelligible in light of the legal situation in Roman Palestine.

4. Legal Issues.
The modern history of trial research, both the Jewish and Christian contributions, entails a legal debate which has largely run its course (Catchpole, 221-60). Interest has shifted to literary and redactional questions, sometimes with negative results (e.g., continued dissection of the Gospel narratives will yield no reliable details because of the "conflicting evidence and the unpersuasive accounts," Sanders, 300). The major work of this kind by P. Winter categorizes the trial pericopes in three redactional levels (Win-

ter, 190-93): primary tradition, secondary tradition and editorial accretion. The upshot of Winter's analysis, indeed his thesis, eliminates the bulk of the Jewish trial, allowing only a brief, morning deliberation of the Sanhedrin as primary tradition, and posits a Roman trial and sentence on political grounds. While elaborated as redactional insights, these literary judgments revert to the historical premises shared by Winter with earlier studies of J. Juster and H. Lietzmann. Their assumptions of pro-Roman bias in the Gospels advance the argument only slightly and, in net effect, still turn on legal issues which can be summarized as follows:

1. Since the Sanhedrin retained the power of capital punishment, Jesus would have been executed by stoning if the Jewish court had in fact found him guilty of blasphemy and pronounced the sentence.

2. A nocturnal session of the Sanhedrin, convened in the high priest's residence on a feast day, violates Jewish legal procedure and was contrived by Mark to shift blame away from the Roman government.

3. The crucifixion of Jesus, a penalty never used by the Jews, indicates a political crime, that a Roman court found him guilty of sedition and excludes the possibility that religious charges were also preferred.

Each of these assertions has faced spirited challenge from both the literary and historical points of view (see Strobel, 21-61; cf. Sherwin-White, Kilpatrick, Blinzler, Catchpole, Betz). The crucial points of discussion pertain to the judicial competence of the Sanhedrin, the relevance of the Mishnaic law code and the procedures of the Roman provincial court.

4.1. Judicial Powers of the Sanhedrin. Did the Sanhedrin in the time of Jesus retain the right to sentence and execute criminals? Much hangs on this question, which admits no easy solution. The standard view, that the "Roman government retained for itself the right of life and death" (Mommsen, 240), implies a curtailment of the Sanhedrin's powers as John 18:31 precisely states: The Jews might pass a death sentence but the power to execute lay in the hands of the Roman procurator alone (Lohse, 865). Few had disputed this assessment of matters, notably the Jewish scholar J. Salvador (1838) and the Christian J. J. I. von Döllinger (1860), until the influential work of Juster (1914), who carefully assembled the pertinent evidence demonstrat-

ing that the Sanhedrin could and did execute capital offenders (Juster 2:127-45). Prominent endorsement of Juster's interpretation (Lietzmann, 258-60; Winter, 12-26; 110-30; Burkill, 80-96) initiated a critical debate which has yet to subside ("neither theory can be effectively proved," Schürer, 2:222). However, in the items of evidence cited below, the balance of interpretation leans toward Mommsen and the traditional view.

4.1.1. Roman Sanctions. While still competent to try religious cases, the prerogatives of the Sanhedrin changed with the beginning of direct Roman rule in Judea: (1) Coponius, the first governor (A.D. 6), was sent out by Augustus with full powers "extending to capital punishment" (Josephus *J.W.* 2.8.1 §117; cf. *Ant.* 18.1.1 §2); (2) Tannaitic tradition confirms that "the right to try capital cases was taken from Israel forty years before the destruction of the temple" (*y. Sanh.* 1.1; 7.2; cf. *b. Sanh.* 41a; *b. 'Abod. Zar.* 8b); (3) the Jewish death penalty was reinstated a week after the Romans lifted the siege of Jerusalem in September A.D. 66: "On the twenty-second of the month [Elul] the execution of malefactors began again" (*Meg. Ta'an.* 6).

4.1.2. Religious Concessions. Among concessions granted the Jews, violations of religious law were investigated and punished by the Sanhedrin (cf. Acts 4:5-23; 5:21-40; 26:10-11), but it cannot be shown that stipulations involving the death penalty were independent of Roman authority: (1) the warning inscription on Herod's temple (*CII* §1400; Josephus *J.W.* 5.5.2 §194; *Ant.* 15.11.5 §417; Philo *Leg. Gai.* 31 §212; *m. Kelim* 1.8), indicating that a Gentile, even a Roman citizen, caught trespassing in the inner temple court would be put to death, had Roman approval (Josephus *J.W.* 6.2.4 §126); (2) the same can be said of the death penalty prescribed for unlawful entry of a Jew, even the high priest, into the Holy of Holies (Philo *Leg. Gai.* 39 §307); (3) the Jewish authorities surely brought Jesus bar Ananias before Albinus (Josephus *J.W.* 6.5.3 §§300-305) to get an execution, since they had already scourged him; (4) reiterated attempts by the Sanhedrin to extradite Paul point to an illegal murder plot, not to legal competence (Acts 23:15, 20-21; 24:6-8; 25:3, 7-11), and even if capital charges were pressed in Jerusalem, it would have been before the Roman procurator Festus (Acts 25:9, 20).

4.1.3. Jewish Executions. During the period A.D.

6-66 executions carried out on orders of the Sanhedrin, prima facie testimony for the court's competence, turn out to be disruptions of normal legal process: (1) the burning of a priest's daughter convicted of adultery (*m. Sanh.* 7:2) happened during the reign of Agrippa I (A.D. 41-44), as did the execution of James, brother of John (Acts 12:2), when Judea had independent status; (2) during the interval between Festus and his successor, Albinus (A.D. 62), the high priest Ananus convened the Sanhedrin and had James, the Lord's brother, stoned to death (Josephus *Ant.* 20.9.1 §§200-203), an illegal undertaking for which Ananus was deposed from office; (3) the episode of the woman taken in adultery (Jn 7:53—8:11), a scene of mob violence, hardly qualifies as due process and proper sentence; (4) the stoning of Stephen, admittedly the strongest piece of evidence for the Juster-Lietzmann thesis, follows a Jewish trial (Acts 6:11-14) and exhibits required procedures (Acts 7:57-58); however, the trial was interrupted and ended without proper sentence—an act of lynch law—suggested by the death lament for Stephen (Acts 8:2), a custom forbidden in the case of legally executed offenders (*m. Sanh.* 6:6; Josephus *Ant.* 4.8.6 §202).

The theory of two (or three) Sanhedrins, a political one named in Greek sources and a religious one, the esteemed Great Sanhedrin *(Beth Din)* in rabbinic writings, offers a tidy solution to the legal problem: the political institution of the Gospels *(synedrion)*, a court of priests responsible for Jesus' condemnation, is distinct from the Great Sanhedrin whose interests lay only in religious matters. The sources, however, seem to be unaware of multiple institutions, and the theory creates more difficulties than it resolves (Schürer, 2:207-8; Lohse, 863). It is more probable that a single institution, the Sanhedrin, was allowed a limited criminal jurisdiction, both to police the temple area and to maintain Jewish law, whereby death sentences could be pronounced, but execution was kept strictly in Roman hands (cf. Blinzler, 165; Sherwin-White, 41-42; Catchpole, 254). The legal situation then offers little reason to doubt a Sanhedrin prosecution of Jesus that eventually led to a Roman court.

4.2. Violations of Mishnaic Law. Hints of illegality in the Gospel narratives (Mt 26:59; Mk 14:59) have been fully exploited in modern inquiries where no less than twenty-seven breaches of the Jewish legal code have been alleged.

How many of the procedural rules in the Mishnah tractate *Sanhedrin* (see Schürer, 2:225-26) applied before A.D. 70 is difficult to say; some at least are purported to be independently attested in the time of Jesus. Recent discussion has accordingly limited itself to five violations of the Mishnaic code in the trial of Jesus: (1) it was improperly convened in the high priest's house (*m. Sanh.* 11:2); (2) met during the night (*m. Sanh.* 4:1); (3) on a Sabbath eve or feast day (*m. Sanh.* 4:1); (4) reached a guilty verdict on the same day (*m. Sanh.* 4:1; 5:5); and (5) based on inadequate grounds for blasphemy (*m. Sanh.* 7:5). Whether one argues that a Sadducean code was current in the days of Jesus (Blinzler) or that some aspects of the later Mishnaic law were operative (Lohse), it is unwarranted to assume that an illegal trial could not have happened; justice does not always outweigh expedience (cf. Jn 11:50).

4.2.1. Time and Place of the Sessions. Our sources disagree about the precise location of the Sanhedrin's regular assembly, but it is clearly distinct from the courtyard and palace of the high priest (Mt 26:3). The Mishnah locates it, the Hall of Hewn Stone, inside the inner forecourt of the temple (*m. Sanh.* 11:2; *m. Mid.* 5.4; cf. *b. Yoma* 25a), whereas according to Josephus, the *boulē* ("council chamber") stood outside the upper city on the western slope of the temple Mount (Josephus *J.W.* 2.16.3 §344; 5.4.2 §144; 6.6.3 §354). Certainly by the time of Paul's trial, the Sanhedrin met outside the temple because Roman soldiers, who were forbidden to enter the inner court, appear in the council chamber (Acts 22:30; 23:10). The rabbinic tradition is that the chamber was moved "forty years before the destruction of the temple" (*b. Sanh.* 41a; *b. 'Abod. Zar.* 8b). If the Sanhedrin still met within the temple area during the time of Jesus, access may have been delayed by the fact that the gates of the temple, only on the night of Passover, were opened at midnight (Josephus *Ant.* 18.2.2 §29; cf. *m. Mid.* 1:1, normally locked all night). This would have dictated the initial choice of the high priest's residence and explain the impression of movement and double session in the trial accounts (Jn 18:13, 24; Mk 15:1; Mt 27:1). In any event Luke 22:66 reports the morning session in the council chamber as a new location (cf. Lk 22:54) and corresponds to the framework of the other narratives (*pace* Winter, 27-30).

The rule that no trials could be held on a Sabbath (Josephus *Ant.* 16.6.2 §163; Philo *Migr.*

Abr. 16 §91; CD 10:18) probably also applied to festival days in Jesus' time (*m Beṣa* 4:4; 5:2); further stipulations that "in capital cases they hold the trial during the daytime . . . but a verdict of conviction not until the following day" (*m. Sanh.* 4:1) meant also that no trial could begin on the eve of a Sabbath or of a festival day. These latter regulations, however, may date from the Tannaitic period when the Pharisees were keen to prevent miscarriages of justice (Blinzler, Catchpole). Their date notwithstanding, an exception is made for the convicted *mēsît*, a seducer to idolatry or false prophet (Deut 13:1-11). In such a case the verdict was passed on the day of the trial (*t. Sanh.* 10.11), and based on Deuteronomy 17:13, the execution took place in Jerusalem on a feast day: "bring them to the Sanhedrin in Jerusalem and keep them in custody until the feast and carry out the sentence on the feast" (*t. Sanh.* 11:7; cf. *m. Sanh.* 11:4). This procedure may explain the haste with which the Sanhedrin acted to have Jesus crucified on 15 Nisan (a Synoptic chronology; cf. Jeremias, 78-79); be this as it may, a strong caution should at least be entered against the notion of wholesale illegality.

4.2.2. Charge of Blasphemy. However obscure the particulars may be, the Sanhedrin eventually convicted Jesus of a specific crime: blasphemy (Mk 14:64 par. Mt 26:65). The blasphemer, "one who curses God" (Lev 24:15), was liable to death by stoning under OT Law, but again to provide a legal safeguard the rabbis formulated a rather narrow definition: "The blasphemer is only guilty if he pronounces the name of God distinctly" (*m. Sanh.* 7:5). Nothing uttered by Jesus in the trial records fits this strict requirement, but the term on the lips of Caiaphas had wider significance in the NT period (cf. Philo *Vit. Mos.* 2.37-38 §§204-6; Josephus *Ant.* 4.8.6 §202). Blasphemy referred to acts or words that violate God's power and majesty, a claiming of prerogatives belonging to God alone (Kilpatrick, 10-11; Juel, 103-7). The Evangelists clearly use the word with this meaning (Mk 2:7; Jn 10:33-36), and parallels occur in pagan Greek and the rabbis (*t. Sanh.* 1.2; *b. Sanh.* 38b; cf. Bickerman, 86-88). Since the blasphemy charge was broad enough to encompass several wrongs, what offense lay behind the conviction of Jesus? No single proposal put forward has won a consensus (see Catchpole, 126-48), but it seems that discrete items are linked together. We suggest that the blasphemy charge had three components: chris-

tological claims, threats against the temple and false prophecy, any one of which could carry a death warrant.

First, the utterances of Jesus in the trial itself were decisive: (1) an open avowal of messiahship ("I am," Mk 14:62), a claim without precedent in Judaism until Simon bar Kochba (A.D. 132-35) provoked immediate outrage; (2) Jewish messianism had embraced the concept of sonship (4QFlor 1:10-11; *Pss. Sol.* 17:27, 36; 18:6, 8; *see* Son of God), but when unified in the person of Jesus with the glorious Son of man, enthroned at God's right hand (cf. Dan 7:13; Ps 110:1; *Midr. Pss.* 1:40 §9 [Ps. 2:7]), the titles "Messiah" and "Son of God" gave him an exalted status the Sanhedrin found intolerable. In John 19:7 the overriding complaint even to Pilate was that Jesus claimed divine sonship.

Second, blasphemous overtones were heard in the accusation that Jesus threatened to destroy and rebuild the temple: (1) Stephen was charged with blasphemy for "speaking against this holy place," having also reportedly said that "this Jesus of Nazareth will destroy this place" (Acts 6:11, 13-14), so that a threat to the temple was tantamount to blasphemy; (2) Jesus' temple prophecy (Mk 13:2, 14; Lk 19:43-44) was probably misconstrued (Mk 14:57-59; 15:29) along the same lines of confusion reported in John 2:19-21; (3) talk of restoring the temple also invited the messianic question (see Sanders, 77-90; Green, 276-81; Juel, 198) since in Jewish eschatology the Messiah builds a new temple (4QFlor 1:1-7; *1 Enoch* 90:28-29; 4 Ezra 9:38—10:28; *Tg. Neb.* Is 53:5; *Tg. Neb.* Zech 6:12-13).

Finally, some elements of the Gospel narratives may be traced to a false-prophet tradition: (1) two marks of a false prophet—he leads others astray (Deut 13:2-6), and he presumes to speak in the Lord's name a message that does not come true (Deut 18:22)—fit the two queries by Annas about Jesus' disciples and teaching (Jn 18:19); (2) the mockery of Jesus after the trial, "Prophesy!" (Mk 14:65), is the horseplay of guards who no longer fear his words (cf. Deut 18:22); (3) the subversion charge put before Pilate, leading the people astray (Lk 23:2, 5, 14), is stated in terms of Roman politics, but on the religious side it echoes Jewish claims that Jesus was a deceiver (Mt 27:63; Jn 7:12, 47) betraying his people with misleading words (cf. Deut 13:5-8, 13; *m. Sanh.* 7:4; 11:1).

4.3. Roman Trial and Penal Law. A further

point of dispute stresses the nature of the penalty stemming from the charge in the Roman trial. Death by crucifixion, it is objected, was exclusively a Roman mode of execution reserved for political offenders. Therefore, the sentence carried out against Jesus was not based on religious charges from the Jews. We are asked to conclude that the Gospel portrayal of a religious accusation before Pilate was impossible, indeed that the account of a previous Jewish trial was "contrived to conceal that Jesus had been condemned and executed on a charge of sedition" (Winter, 34; cf. 79, 90; Lietzmann, 258-60; Lohse, 869). The evidence of Roman trial procedures in the first century shows this to be an unwarranted deduction, and the basic premise of the argument regarding crucifixion in the province of Judea has been brought into question.

4.3.1. Trials in the Provinces. We have no formal descriptions of capital trials in the Roman provinces between Cicero's *Verrines* (70 B.C.) and the *Letters* of Pliny (c. A.D. 110). The standard exposition depends on scattered excerpts from classical jurists of the second and third centuries of the empire compiled in the *Digest* of Roman law (Mommsen, 234-45). Under Augustus, in order to expedite the legal process, capital trials were usually conducted by provincial governors who could grade the penalty (cf. Justinian *Digest* 48.19.16). This procedure, named *cognitio extra ordinem* or *extraordinaria*, by and large replaced the jury court (Sherwin-White, 13-23), which had operated within the procedures and penalties stipulated by the fixed order of law (*ordo*). By contrast, the governor himself heard the formal accusation so that he could investigate the case by personal inquiry (*cognitio*), and he was free to choose any procedure he thought fit—determine the issue, hear the evidence and prescribe the penalty—without legal restriction (*extra ordinem*). The earliest evidence for trial by *cognitio* is the fourth edict of Augustus to the province of Cyrene (7/6 B.C.), which requires that in capital cases "the one who governs the province has the duty of conducting the investigation and rendering judgments himself" (*SEG* 9.8; *FIRA* 1.68 [ET: *TDGR* 6:27]).

The governor Pliny provides a good example: after the famous orator Dio Chrysostom placed a statue of the Emperor Trajan near his family burial plot, he was accused by an enemy of a treasonable act. The accuser, one Flavius Archippus, petitioned Pliny for a *cognitio* before the judgment seat (Pliny *Epp.* 10.81.3); Trajan dismissed the case when Pliny, faced with a *cognitio* of such magnitude, wrote to ask for direction in the matter (Pliny *Epp.* 10.82). Such trials follow a regular pattern, clearly attested in the case of Paul as well as Jesus: (1) the charges were drawn up and a formal accusation was brought by *delatores*, "accusers" (Mk 15:1; Lk 23:2; Jn 18:29); (2) the governor heard the case *pro tribunali*, "before the judgment seat" (Mt 27:19; Jn 19:13); (3) in the absence of a defense (Mt 27:14; Mk 15:5; Jn 19:10), a *condemno*, or "guilty," verdict was certain, and some form of punishment had to be prescribed (Lk 23:15-16, 22; Jn 19:6).

4.3.2. Charge of Sedition. The first question Pilate asked Jesus in the Roman trial, "Are you the King of the Jews?" indicates a shift of charge from the religious to the political. The issue of kingship in Pilate's court would raise the alarm of sedition (Jn 19:12; cf. Josephus *Ant.*17.10.8 §285, on bandit "kings"), an act deserving crucifixion (Justinian *Digest* 48.8.3.4; 48.19.38.2). Sedition, or inciting people to rebel, came under the treason crimes headed "offense against majesty" (*laesa maiestatis*), which were applied to all sorts of "misconduct." During the principate, especially under Tiberius, trials for lese-majesty were exploited as a convenient means to dispose of enemies, and many far-fetched examples are found (Suetonius *Tiberius* 61.3; Tacitus *Ann.* 1.72-74; 3.49, 70; Cassius Dio *Hist.* 59.3.6; Pliny *Epp.* 10.82; *Digest* 48.4.5). The nature of the alleged crime and its penalty would have been obvious to Pilate, even while he harbored doubts about the guilt of Jesus. The placard which he inscribed and refused to change, "The King of the Jews" (Jn 19:19-22), shows both the fixed reason for the condemnation (a *titulus* normally hung on the victim or was carried before him; cf. Suetonius *Caligula* 32.2; *Domitian* 10.1; Cassius Dio *Hist.* 54.3.7; Eusebius *Hist. Eccl.* 5.1.44; Josephus *Ant.* 14.3.1 §36), and a mocking affirmation of Jesus' claims to the chief priests.

Suggestions that Jesus was involved with a Zealot plot to overthrow the Romans are groundless (see Bammel-Moule). The Sanhedrin would also have known that a sedition charge was "a surer way of securing the death of Christ" (Smalley, 1054), and the morning session was likely occupied with recasting the indictment in acceptable terms for Pilate. The Lukan account of multiple charges, common in trials of the Flavian period (cf. Sherwin-White, 35), amounts to a political version of the blasphemy findings. The connection avowed is that Jesus held the kingly pretensions of the Jewish messiah, "saying that he himself is Christ a king" (Lk 23:2). This phrase is the crucial link between the religious and political charges, and it explains much of Pilate's dilemma. Even the ambiguous "Son of God" phrase to a Roman ear, when voiced by a crowd demanding that its law be respected (Jn 19:7), has fearful political implications for a governor already embroiled in the violation of Jewish customs. There is every reason to believe that the sedition alternative carried the day only because of the religious fervor behind it.

4.3.3. Penalty of Crucifixion. It is commonplace in trial research, even to opposing sides of the debate (cf. Blinzler, 247; Winter, 96), that the Jews never practiced crucifixion as a mode of execution. The episode when Alexander Jannaeus "hung up alive" 800 Pharisees, abhorred as that "never done in Israel before" (4QpNah 1:7-8; cf. Josephus *J.W.* 1.4.6 §97), is taken as the exception which proves the point. This consensus ought now to be revised in light of the Qumran *Temple Scroll* which interprets Deuteronomy 21:22-23 as crucifixion: "You shall hang him on the wood so that he dies" (11QT 64:8, 10-11). The OT ruled that after a capital offender had been executed by stoning, the cursed body was to be publicly exhibited by hanging on a tree (cf. *m. Sanh.* 6:4; 7:4; 9:3), but in the Scroll text hanging is clearly the cause of death. Those liable to this penalty are described in six phrases: (1) one who informs against his people, (2) betrays his people to a foreign nation, (3) does evil to his people, (4) one who commits a capital offense, (5) flees away to the Gentiles and (6) curses his people Israel (11QT 64:7, 9b-10a). Such accusations are reminiscent of those made against Jesus (Bammel 1984, 442), and although the regulation is sectarian in character, we must reckon with the wider possibility that other Jews in the first century had equated the practice of crucifixion with the law of Deuteronomy 21:23, viz., to bury the body before sunset (cf. Josephus *J.W.* 4.5.2 §317; *t. Sanh.* 9.7; Acts 5:30; 10:39). The Mishnaic criminal code excludes crucifixion (four methods in *m. Sanh.* 7:1: stoning, burning, beheading and strangling), but a thesis based on the assertion that no Jews in Jesus' time would have sought his death on the cross strains the evidence (see Betz, 603-12).

5. Theological Significance.
A lamentable feature of Christian reaction to the trial of Jesus across the centuries has been an odious persecution of the Jews for putting Jesus to death. It has been maintained above that the Evangelists did not invent the fact of Jewish involvement, but the NT never says that the Jews alone, least of all every succeeding generation, were responsible for the cross. The perennial instinct to kindle anti-Semitism by the findings of historical scholarship is deplorable in all its forms. The theological stance of the Gospels indicts us all, Jew and Gentile alike: "He was numbered with the transgressors" (Lk 22:37), yet "this man has done nothing wrong" (Lk 23:41).

See also DEATH OF JESUS.

DJG: GETHSEMANE.

BIBLIOGRAPHY. E. Bammel, ed., *The Trial of Jesus* (SBT, 2d ser., 13; 2d ed.; London: SCM, 1971); E. Bammel and C. F. D. Moule, eds., *Jesus and the Politics of His Day* (Cambridge: Cambridge University Press, 1984); O. Betz, "Probleme des Prozesses Jesu," *ANRW* 2.25.1 (New York: De Gruyter, 1982) 565-647; E. J. Bickerman, "Utilitas crucis" in *Studies in Jewish and Christian History* (AGJU 9; Leiden: E. J. Brill, 1986) pt. 3.82-138; M. Black, "The Arrest and Trial of Jesus and the Date of the Last Supper" in *New Testament Essays* (Manchester: Manchester University Press, 1959) 19-33; J. Blinzler, *The Trial of Jesus* (3d ed.; Cork: Mercier, 1961); D. L. Bock, *Blasphemy and Exaltation in Judaism and the Final Examination of Jesus* (Tübingen: Mohr Siebeck, 1998); F. F. Bruce, "The Trial of Jesus in the Fourth Gospel" in *Gospel Perspectives 1: Studies of History and Tradition in the Four Gospels* (Sheffield: JSOT, 1980) 7-20; T. A. Burkill, "The Competence of the Sanhedrin," *VC* 10 (1956) 80-96; D. R. Catchpole, *The Trial of Jesus* (SPB 18; Leiden: Brill, 1971); J. B. Green, *The Death of Jesus* (WUNT, 2d ser., 33; Tübingen: J. C. B. Mohr, 1988); A. E. Harvey, *Jesus and the Constraints of History* (London: Duckworth, 1982); J. Jeremias, *The Eucharistic Words of Jesus* (New York: Scribner's, 1966); D. Juel, *Messiah and Temple* (SBLDS 31; Missoula: Scholar's, 1977); J. Juster, *Les Juifs dans l' Empire Romain* (2 vols.; Paris: Geuthner, 1914); G. D. Kilpatrick, *The Trial of Jesus* (London: Oxford University Press, 1953); H. Lietzmann, "Der Prozess Jesu," *Kleine Schriften II* (TU 68; Berlin: Akademie, 1958; repr. of 1931) 251-63; E. Lohse, "συνέδριον," *TDNT*

7:860-71; T. Mommsen, *Römisches Strafrecht* (vol. 1, pt. 4; Leipzig: Duncker & Humblot, 1899); J. A. T. Robinson, *The Priority of John* (London: SCM, 1985); E. P. Sanders, *Jesus and Judaism* (Philadelphia: Fortress, 1985); E. Schürer, *The History of the Jewish People in the Age of Jesus Christ (175 B.C.-A.D. 135)*, rev. and ed. G. Vermes, F. Millar (3 vols.; Edinburgh: T & T Clark, 1973-86); A. N. Sherwin-White, *Roman Law and Roman Society in the New Testament* (Oxford: Oxford University Press, 1963); S. Smalley, "Arrest and Trial of Jesus Christ," *ISBE* 2:1049-55; A. Strobel, *Die Stunde der Wahrheit* (WUNT 21; Tübingen: J. C. B. Mohr, 1980); P. Winter, *On the Trial of Jesus* (SJ 1; 2d rev. ed.; New York: De Gruyter, 1974).

B. Corley

TRINITARIANISM, EMERGING. *See* CHRISTOLOGY; GOD; HOLY SPIRIT; WORSHIP.

TRUE ISRAEL. *See* ISRAEL.

TWELVE, THE. *See* APOSTLE; DISCIPLES.

TWO-DOCUMENT HYPOTHESIS. *See* SYNOPTIC PROBLEM.

TYPOLOGY. *See* ADAM AND CHRIST.

UNION WITH CHRIST. *See* BAPTISM II.

UR-GOSPEL. *See* SYNOPTIC PROBLEM.

VIRGIN BIRTH. *See* BIRTH OF JESUS.

W, X, Y, Z

WEALTH. *See* RICHES AND POVERTY.

WICKEDNESS. *See* SIN.

WISDOM. *See* CHRISTOLOGY; JAMES, LETTER OF.

WISDOM OF BEN SIRA. *See* APOCRYPHA AND PSEUDEPIGRAPHA.

WISDOM OF SOLOMON. *See* APOCRYPHA AND PSEUDEPIGRAPHA.

WIVES. *See* WOMEN.

WOMEN I: GOSPELS

All four Gospels contain information on Jesus' relationship to women and the involvement of women in Jesus' life and ministry. Jesus accepted and affirmed as persons of worth various women who were neglected or rejected within his society. Jesus taught women and included them among his disciples. Women also participated in the proclamation of the gospel. Many women associated with Jesus are known by name. Among the four Gospels, Luke evidences the greatest interest in Jesus' relationship with women and their involvement in his life and ministry. The contacts and involvements between Jesus and women need to be set within the social and cultural contexts of the first century A.D. The Gospel data on Jesus and women lead also to discussions about the significance of this data for women in ministry, leadership and authority within the church.

    1. Women in the Social-Cultural Contexts of the First Century A.D.
    2. Women as Persons of Dignity and Worth
    3. Women as Disciples
    4. Women as Proclaimers
    5. Women Specifically Named
    6. Women in the Perspective of Each Gospel
    7. Conclusions and Significance

1. Women in the Social-Cultural Contexts of the First Century A.D.

In very general terms Jesus lived in social-cultural contexts (the Jewish context and the larger Greco-Roman society) in which the male view of women was usually negative and the place of women was understood to be limited for the most part to the domestic roles of wife and mother. Women were perceived by extant male writers to be responsible for most (all?) sin, and especially for sexual temptation and sin. There are, on the other hand, clear indications from literary and nonliterary sources that there were positive roles for women as well.

The extant male literary sources of ancient Judaism, which reflect a class and gender perspective, present a fairly consistent pattern of a negative view toward women (see Swidler 1976). For example, Josephus, the first-century A.D. Jewish historian, states that the Law holds women to be inferior in all matters and that therefore women should be submissive (Josephus *Ag. Ap.* 2.25 §201). Philo, the first-century A.D. Alexandrian Jewish philosopher and biblical commentator, refers throughout his writings to women and female traits as examples of weakness (e.g., Philo *Op. Mund.* 151-52; *Quaest. in Gen.* 1.33). Philo argues that women ought to stay at home, desiring a life of seclusion (Philo *Spec. Leg.* 3.169-77; *Flacc.* 89). Sirach, a proto-Pharisaic work from about 180 B.C., presents women either as good wives or as problems. It even states that "better is the wickedness of a man than a woman who does good; it is woman who brings shame and disgrace" (Sir 42:14 NRSV). According to the rabbinic Tosefta, which may well in this case reflect first-century A.D. tradition, a Jewish man prayed three benedictions each day, including one in which he thanked God that he was not made a woman (*t. Ber.* 7:18).

Such texts reflect social reality to some extent and set a framework of societal expectation for the behavior and relationships of men and women.

This negative picture within Judaism was greatly shaped and influenced by Greek and Greco-Roman androcentrism and misogynism. However, as some have argued (e.g., Meyers), women's place in Israel began to decline with the emergence of a bureaucratic monarchy, prior to Greek influence.

However, there are, in spite of the lack of literary evidence from women, substantial indications that positive roles did exist for women within Judaism, even if limited. Especially important is the evidence that some women held the office of ruler or president of synagogues in ancient Judaism (see Kraemer). Significant religious roles for women are also indicated by the portrayal of Job's three daughters as those who speak the language of angels in the *Testament of Job* and in the traditions about Beruriah, a second-century A.D. rabbi (see Swidler 1976). Women as strong leaders are portrayed in the Hellenistic Jewish story of Judith and in the rule of Salome Alexandra as queen in Judea (approximately 76-67 B.C.). There is also substantial nonliterary evidence that shows that Jewish women often took initiative for their lives and activities in spite of the male orientation and domination prevalent in the culture (see Kraemer). These positive roles and opportunities constitute Jewish evidence for the significance of women in ancient Judaism.

Thus, it is important for Christians not to set a "Christian" Jesus over against his Judaism and Jewish context as the deliverer of women and thus engage in a subtle form of anti-Judaism. Christians can hardly deny that the history of the church shows that it, as much as any human social reality, has neglected and oppressed women over many centuries.

Yet, as a Jewish male in an androcentric, patriarchal society, Jesus' respect for women as persons of dignity and worth and his inclusion of them as disciples and proclaimers in his life and ministry were very significant in their first-century context for women and their place and activity in ministry in the earliest churches and is important as a heritage for Jewish and Christian people today.

2. Women as Persons of Dignity and Worth.

According to the Gospels Jesus clearly regarded women as persons of dignity and worth by his many healings of women, by his acceptance and forgiveness of undesirable and ritually unclean women, and by his implicit challenges to male sexual devaluation of women.

2.1. Women Healed by Jesus. Jesus healed various unnamed women: Peter's mother-in-law (Mt 8:14-15; Mk 1:29-31; Lk 4:38-39); the daughter of Jairus and the woman with the twelve-year flow of blood (Mt 9:18-26; Mk 5:21-43; Lk 8:40-56); and the eighteen-year crippled woman (Lk 13:11-17) whom Jesus called a "daughter of Abraham," probably an important status marker for a woman (see further the discussion of Lk 8:1-3 in 3.1 below). In addition, Jesus raised the son of the widow of Nain (Lk 7:11-17). In most of these stories Jesus touched or was touched by the woman involved. This is particularly important in terms of the woman with the twelve-year flow of blood, since she would have been considered ritually unclean according to levitical law (Lev 18).

2.2. Women's Sexual Integrity Affirmed by Jesus. According to two Gospel stories, Jesus accepted and forgave two women understood to be guilty of sexual sins. In Luke 7:36-50 a woman, called a sinner, anoints and kisses Jesus' feet in the home of a Pharisee. Jesus accepted her actions as those of love and declared: "Your faith has saved you; go in peace" (Lk 7:50). In the story of the woman caught in adultery (Jn 7:53—8:11; although not found in any of the oldest Greek manuscripts of the NT, most scholars regard this as an authentic story about Jesus) Jesus said: "Neither do I condemn you; go, and sin no longer" (Jn 8:11). This Jesus did in the presence of male critics who had brought only the woman, of the two involved, to Jesus.

Also to be noted in this connection is Jesus' encounter with the Samaritan woman (see 4.2 below), who is presented as one living in adultery. The male disciples are offended that Jesus is talking with a woman but dare not ask him why (Jn 4:27), indicating their negative sexual assumptions.

In fact, one saying of Jesus makes the general statement that "tax collectors and sexually immoral women [*hai pornai;* often translated "prostitutes"] will enter before you [religious leaders] into the kingdom of God" (Mt 21:31; *see* Kingdom of God). Jesus notes that such persons had already responded to the preaching of John the Baptist (Mt 21:32).

In one saying of Jesus in the Sermon on the Mount (Mt 5:27-30) concerning adultery, Jesus places the blame for lust on men, something rather unusual in ancient Mediterranean cultures.

In the Matthean account of Jesus' debate with the Pharisees on divorce (Mt 19:3-9), reference appears to be made to the dominant position that men could divorce their wives for virtually any reason (see "for any cause" in Mt 19:3; see Josephus *Ant.* 4.8.23 §253; *Life* 76 §426; *m. Git.* 9:10). Jesus responds by placing Deuteronomy 24:1-4 in a secondary position to Genesis 2:24 (Mt 19:5-6), which affirms the concept of "one flesh," giving sexual equality to women and men.

2.3. Women as Positive Examples in Jesus' Teaching. Jesus often used women as positive examples in stories and events for those who have responded to God with appropriate faith. Such regard prepares the way for women as disciples and proclaimers (as described in 3 and 4 below).

Women are used, sometimes in parallel with men, to describe the faithful and faithless at the time of the arrival of the future kingdom (Mt 24:41; Lk 17:35; Mt 25:1-13). A woman and her leaven are central in a parable about God's kingdom (Mt 13:33; Lk 13:20-21).

More important are the instances in which women portray persons of faith: the widow of Zarephath (Lk 4:26; see 1 Kings 17—18); the Syrophoenician or Canaanite woman (Mt 15:21-28; Mk 7:24-30); and the persistent widow (Lk 18:1-8). Faith is also an explicit feature of the women in the stories noted above (2.1. and 2.2.), of the woman who anoints Jesus' feet (Lk 7:50) and of the woman with the twelve-year flow of blood (Mt 9:22; Mk 5:34; Lk 8:48). The story of the "widow's mite" (Mk 12:41-44; Lk 21:1-4) presents a woman as one who fulfills Jesus' requirements, made especially clear in Luke, of discipleship with reference to material possessions.

The parable of the lost coin (Lk 15:8-10) presents a woman as the finder who rejoices with a party, the same role portrayed by the shepherd and the father in Luke 15. In all three cases this person images God who rejoices over repentant sinners (see also Mt 23:37; Lk 13:34 in which Jesus likens his concern for Jerusalem to that of a mother hen for her young).

3. Women as Disciples.

The Gospels indicate that women were among the followers (= disciples) of Jesus and were taught by him with the understanding that they could respond with obedience and commitment to the word of God.

3.1. The Women Who Followed Jesus. All four Gospels attest to the fact that a group of women followed Jesus in Galilee and to Jerusalem where they were present as faithful and active at the crucifixion (*see* Death of Christ), burial and resurrection of Jesus (Mt 27:55-56; 27:61—28:1; Mk 15:40-41; 15:47—16:1; Lk 23:49; 23:55—24:1; Jn 19:25-27; 20:1).

The verb used to designate their following of Jesus is *akoloutheō* or its compounds, a term that occurs more than seventy-five times in the Gospels and normally means following Jesus in the sense of being a disciple. This lexical evidence confirms the narrative presentation of women as disciples of Jesus, although some scholars would argue that when this term is used of women it does not designate discipleship.

Luke describes these female disciples in the Galilean context (Lk 8:1-3). He notes that the women were traveling with Jesus and the Twelve and that they were providing for them as well, which is probably an indication of their upper-class status and comparative wealth. These women apparently became disciples of Jesus as a result of the healing they had received from him. Luke mentions three by name, Mary Magdalene, Joanna and Susanna, and notes that there were also many others.

The mention of these women in the Jerusalem context repeats the name of Mary Magdalene and adds the names of Mary the mother of James the younger and Joses (Joseph), Salome and Mary the wife of Clopas (Jn 19:25), who may be the same person as Mary the mother of James and Joseph. Also noted are the mother of Jesus (Jn 2:5; 19:26-27 also attest to her discipleship), her sister, and the mother of the sons of Zebedee (who may be the same person as Salome).

Luke, whose Gospel alone mentions these women in the Galilean and Jerusalem contexts, also notes in Acts 1:14 that certain women, most likely those he has described in Luke 8:1-3 and in the *passion narrative, are present in the upper room in Jerusalem, along with Mary the mother of Jesus. Presumably, then, these female disciples were among the 120 followers of Jesus

(Acts 1:15) who waited for and received the *Holy Spirit on the day of Pentecost, fulfilling the prophecy of Joel that "in the last days . . . I will pour out my Spirit upon all flesh, and your sons and your daughters shall prophesy" (Acts 2:17; see Joel 2:28-29). The mention by Luke of Tabitha (Acts 9:36), also known as Dorcas, designated as a disciple, and Mary the mother of John Mark (Acts 12:12) as the one (leader?) in whose home believers were meeting, may indicate additional women by name who were followers of Jesus.

3.2. Mary of Bethany as a Disciple. According to Luke 10:38-42, Mary assumed the posture of a disciple by sitting at Jesus' feet (see Acts 22:3; *m. 'Abot* 1:4), listening to Jesus' word *(logos)*. In spite of the objections of Mary's sister Martha, based on the traditional female obligation to prepare the meal, Jesus affirmed Mary's choice: "Mary has chosen the better part which will not be taken from her" (Lk 10:42). Presumably, the "better part" refers to Jesus' teaching on the kingdom that characterizes Luke's central section of the Gospel (Lk 9:51—19:28) in which this story occurs.

Some interpreters have understood the story to present an image of women as silent learners rather than as active participants or speakers in the life of the church, indicating a redactional stage that reflects an alleged retreat from a more positive, egalitarian role for women in the very earliest years of the church. However, it is more likely that the story of Mary presents the image of women as disciples in equal partnership with men.

The presentation of Mary in John 11:28-33, 45; 12:1-8 may also point to her role as a disciple of Jesus, although it is not as clear as it is in the Lukan story. Martha's confession in John 11:27, parallel to Peter's confession in John 6:69 and in the Synoptic tradition (see Mt 16:16), indicates her discipleship as well.

3.3. Motherhood and Obedience. Two Gospel pericopes contain a similar saying of Jesus in which response and obedience to God's word (discipleship) appear to be placed above motherhood, the traditional role for women (Mt 12:46-50 par. Mk 3:31-35 and Lk 8:19-21; Lk 11:27-28). In the common Synoptic story Jesus says, "My mother and my brothers and sisters are those who hear the word *(logos)* of God and do it" (Lk 8:21). In the incident reported only in Luke, Jesus says in response to a woman's affir-mation of his mother: "Blessed rather are the ones who hear and keep the word *(logos)* of God" (Lk 11:28).

4. Women as Proclaimers.
The Gospels present three occasions in which women were proclaimers of Jesus: the Lukan infancy narrative (Lk 1—2), the story of the Samaritan woman (Jn 4:4-42) and the accounts of the women at the tomb in the resurrection narratives.

4.1. The Women Who Interpreted Jesus' Birth. In the Lukan infancy narrative (Lk 1:5—2:40) there are five persons, three of whom are women (Elizabeth; Mary, the mother of Jesus; and Anna; Zechariah and Simeon are also named), who speak by the power of the Holy Spirit or as a prophet in order to provide a divine interpretation of the meaning of Jesus' birth for the history of God's salvation (*see* Birth of Jesus).

Elizabeth (Lk 1:41-45) is filled with the Holy Spirit and pronounces a blessing on Mary, including designating her as "the mother of my Lord." Mary (Lk 1:26-38, 46-56), assuming her to be the speaker of the Magnificat (Lk 1:46-55), declares the saving work of God in language and structure similar to Hannah's prayer in 1 Samuel 2:1-10. Anna (Lk 2:36-38) is a prophet who praises God and speaks about Jesus to all who have been waiting for the redemption of Jerusalem. In the structure of Luke's Gospel these three women, along with Zechariah, Simeon, the angel Gabriel (Lk 1:26-38) and the angels who speak to the shepherds (Lk 2:8-15), proclaim Jesus' place in God's salvation, giving theological understanding and perspective to the event of his birth.

4.2. The Samaritan Woman. After Jesus' discourse with the Samaritan woman (Jn 4:7-26) she returns to her city and recounts her experience with Jesus: "Many of the Samaritans from that city believed in him, because of the word of the woman that he told me all that I did" (Jn 4:39). The Johannine account does go on to note that the Samaritans then have a direct encounter with Jesus' word *(logos)*, which they understand as the basis for their faith (Jn 4:40-42).

4.3. The Women as Witnesses to Jesus' Resurrection. All four Gospels report that the female disciples of Jesus were the first ones to receive the angelic account of Jesus' resurrection and commission to go and tell the male disciples of this event (Mt 28:1-8; Mk 16:1-8; Lk 24:1-12; see Jn

20:1-13). According to Luke (Lk 24:10-11, 22-24) the men did not believe the report of the women (see also Mk 16:11 in the long addition to Mark).

Further, the Gospels of Matthew and John and the long ending of Mark report that Jesus appeared first to Mary Magdalene (Jn 20:14-18; Mk 16:9-11; in Mt 28:9-10 the other Mary [see Mt 27:61; 28:1] is with Mary Magdalene; this other Mary is presumably Mary the mother of James the younger and Joseph, mentioned in Mt 27:56). In the Matthean and Johannine accounts Mary Magdalene is commissioned by Jesus to tell the male disciples what she has seen and heard.

It has often been noted that Paul, who provides the earliest written account of resurrection appearances of Jesus (1 Cor 15:3-8), does not mention the role of the women. It is often assumed that this is due to a Jewish understanding of the inadmissibility of the testimony of women in legal contexts (see Josephus *Ant.* 4.8.15 §219) and the argument Paul wishes to establish.

The first known pagan written critique of Christianity, that of the middle Platonist Celsus entitled *The True Word* (c. A.D. 175), builds on the Gospels' report of women as the first witnesses and proclaimers of Jesus' resurrection. Celsus, citing his alleged source, says that a hysterical female (and perhaps someone else) was the witness to Jesus' resurrection, which Celsus then discounts (*apud* Origen *Contra Celsum* 2.55). Origen responds (c. A.D. 225) to Celsus by saying that there were other witnesses in addition to the woman and that the Gospels do not say that she was hysterical (Origen *Contra Celsum* 2.59-60). Celsus's attack on Christianity shows how clearly and firmly the role of the women as the first witnesses of Jesus' resurrection was in the Gospel tradition and early church. It may be worth noting how important this theme is to the history of the discussion of the significance of Jesus' relationship to women for the church. In what may be the first book published in English in defense of women's preaching, Margaret Fell refers to the role of Mary Magdalene in the title of her book: *Womens Speaking Justified, Proved and Allowed of by the Scriptures, . . . And how Women were the first that preached the Tidings of the Resurrection of Jesus, and were sent by Christ's Own Command, before He ascended to the Father, John 20.17* (London, 1666).

4.4. Women in Noncanonical Gospel Traditions. Women are frequently presented as disciples and leaders, especially in resurrection narratives, in various noncanonical apocryphal and gnostic Gospels (e.g., *Gos. Thom.* 21, 61, 114; *Dial. Sav.*; see the comments on Mary Magdalene in 5.6 below).

This data is a witness to the strength of the Gospel tradition of the involvement of women as disciples and proclaimers of Jesus. It may also suggest, according to some scholars, that in some second-century A.D. circles, women had more options for involvement among Gnostic groups than in the orthodox church, which was increasingly excluding women from leadership. This understanding is, however, debatable and fraught with problems of social-historical analysis.

5. Women Specifically Named.

In the Gospels seventeen women are specifically named (some of them may, however, be the same person; see especially 5.8, 5.10 and 5.11). The amount and character of information concerning them varies as does their relationship to Jesus. What follows is an alphabetical list of these women with the Gospel references and basic information provided.

5.1. Anna. Anna was a prophet mentioned only in Luke 2:36-38. She spoke in the temple of the infant Jesus to all who were waiting for the redemption of Jerusalem. She was the daughter of Phanuel of the tribe of Asher and a widow who spent most of her time in the temple. It is not clear whether she was eighty-four at the time of the story or whether she had been a widow for eighty-four years (probably fourteen at marriage, plus seven years of marriage plus eighty-four years as a widow = one hundred five years of age, the age reached by Judith, a hero in Israel [Jdt 16:23]).

5.2. Elizabeth. Elizabeth, mentioned only in Luke 1, was of priestly descent and the wife of the priest Zechariah, mother of John the Baptist and a relative of Mary the mother of Jesus. Elizabeth was filled with the Holy Spirit and greeted Mary as the mother of her Lord.

5.3. Herodias. Herodias, noted in Mark 6:17-29, Matthew 14:3-12 and Luke 3:19-20, was the granddaughter of Herod the Great, the daughter of Aristobulus, the wife of Herod (called Philip in the Gospels), the mother of Salome and the mother-in-law of Philip the tetrarch (Josephus *Ant.* 18.5.1 §§110-11, 136). She conspired to have Herod Antipas kill John the Baptist (Josephus *Ant.* 18.5.2 §§116-19).

5.4. Joanna. Joanna is mentioned in Luke 8:3 and Luke 24:10 as one of the female disciples of Jesus who followed him in Galilee and to Jerusalem, and as one of the women who first received the message of Jesus' resurrection. She is identified as the wife of Chuza, a steward of Herod (Antipas), about whom nothing else is known.

5.5. Martha. Martha lived in Bethany and was the sister of Mary and Lazarus. She is described in Luke 10:38-42 and in John 11:1-44 and John 12:2. Martha, in contrast to Mary in both stories, was the one who prepared the meals for Jesus as a guest in their home. In the Lukan story Martha objects to Mary's involvement as a disciple of Jesus. In the Johannine story Martha makes a disciple's confession of Jesus as the Messiah (*see* Christ), the *Son of God (Jn 11:27).

5.6. Mary Magdalene. Mary Magdalene, from the Galilean town of Magdala, was a prominent disciple of Jesus who followed him in Galilee and to Jerusalem. She is always listed first in groups of named female disciples and was the first person to whom the resurrected Jesus made an appearance (Mt 27:56, 61; 28:1; Mk 15:40, 47; 16:1 [16:9]; Lk 8:2; 24:10; Jn 19:25; 20:1, 11, 16, 18). Her status is attested by the numerous references to her in early apocryphal and gnostic Christian literature (see Grassi and Grassi; e.g., the Nag Hammadi *Gos. Phil.* 59, 6-9).

5.7. Mary of Bethany. Mary was the sister of Martha and Lazarus and lived in Bethany (Lk 10:38-42; Jn 11:11-45; 12:1-8). She was a disciple of Jesus, commended by him for choosing the "better part" (see 3.2 above). She, according to the Johannine story, anointed Jesus' feet with costly perfume (the parallel stories in Mt 26:6-13 and Mk 14:3-9 do not name the woman; the story in Lk 7:36-50 is set in a different time and place). Jesus defended her act of devotion as an act of discipleship.

5.8. Mary the Mother of James the Younger and Joseph (Joses). This Mary is mentioned as one of the female disciples of Jesus (Mt 27:56; Mk 15:40, 47; 16:1; Lk 24:10) who was among those who received the first message of Jesus' resurrection. She is probably to be identified with the "other Mary" of Matthew 27:61 and Matthew 28:1, based on the Markan and Lukan parallel texts (see 5.11 and also 5.10 below).

5.9. Mary the Mother of Jesus. Jesus' mother is mentioned by name in the Synoptic Gospels (Mt 1—2; 13:55; Mk 6:3; Lk 1—2). John refers to her as Jesus' mother without ever noting her name (Jn 2:1, 3, 5, 12; 6:42; 19:25-27). Mary is prominent in the birth narratives and functions as God's obedient servant (see Lk 1:42, "Blessed are you among women") and as an interpreter of God's saving work (the Magnificat in Lk 1:46-55). Jesus' conversation with her in John 2 does not indicate disrespect but rather shows John's emphasis on Jesus' authority and responsibility for his mission and implies Mary's discipleship. Mary is understood to be a disciple (see Jn 19:25-27; Acts 1:14).

5.10. Mary the Wife of Clopas. This disciple of Jesus is mentioned only in John (Jn 19:25), along with Mary the mother of Jesus, her sister and Mary Magdalene at the cross of Jesus (*see* Death of Christ). Due to the names in the parallel texts in Matthew 27:56 and Mark 15:40, there is some possibility that this Mary is to be identified with Mary the mother of James and Joseph (see 5.8 above; see also 5.11 below).

5.11. The Other Mary. The "other Mary" is a designation that appears only in Matthew 27:61 and Matthew 28:1. She was one of Jesus' disciples at the cross and the resurrection. The parallel texts in Mark 15:47 and Mark 16:1 and the data of Matthew 27:56 and Luke 24:10 suggest that the "other Mary" is probably to be identified with Mary the mother of James and Joseph (see 5.8 and also 5.10 above).

5.12. Rahab. Rahab is mentioned in the Matthean genealogy of Jesus (1:5; see Josh 2; 6). She was considered an important woman in the Jewish and early church traditions, as suggested here and attested in Hebrews 11:31 and James 2:25. She is one of four women mentioned in Matthew's genealogy (see 5.13, 5.16 and 5.17 below). All of these women were Gentiles; their mention here may signify God's mercy and point to the Gentile mission (cf. Mt 28:18-20). They may also point to Mary as indicative of God's choice of unexpected women in the history of salvation.

5.13. Ruth. Ruth is mentioned in the Matthean genealogy of Jesus (Mt 1:5; see 5.12 above).

5.14. Salome. Salome is mentioned in Mark 15:40 and Mark 16:1 as one of Jesus' disciples at the cross and the resurrection. Due to the parallel to Mark 15:40 in Matthew 27:56, it is possible that Salome was the wife of Zebedee and thus the mother of James and John, two of Jesus' twelve disciples.

5.15. Susanna. Susanna is one of Jesus' disciples mentioned only in Luke 8:3. Nothing else is known of her.

5.16. Tamar. Tamar is mentioned in the Matthean genealogy of Jesus (Mt 1:3; see Gen 38; Ruth 4; 1 Chron 2:4; see 5.12 above).

5.17. The Wife of Uriah. Uriah's wife, Bathsheba, is mentioned in the Matthean genealogy of Jesus (Mt 1:6; see 2 Sam 11; 12:24; 1 Chron 3:5; see 5.12 above).

6. Women in the Perspective of Each Gospel.

Another way of viewing the data on Jesus and women is to look at the individual approach of each of the four Gospels. Among the four, Luke evidences the greatest interest in material that relates to women in the life and ministry of Jesus.

6.1. Matthew. The Gospel of Matthew contains stories about the healing (Mt 8:14-15; 9:18-26) and faith (Mt 9:22; 15:21-22) of women, as well as stories in which women are involved that define the kingdom (Mt 13:33; 24:41; 25:1-13). Four Gentile women are included in the genealogy of Jesus (Mt 1:3, 5-6). The sexual integrity of women is upheld in the discussions of lust (Mt 5:27-30) and divorce (Mt 19:3-9), and the inclusion of sexually immoral women in the kingdom is noted for the preaching of John the Baptist and Jesus (Mt 21:31-32).

The discipleship of women, including their involvement in proclamation, is noted both in a general saying of Jesus (Mt 12:49-50) and in the *passion and *resurrection narratives (Mt 27:55-56; 27:61—28:10).

Matthew is the only Gospel that tells the story (Mt 27:19) of Pilate's wife who, because of a dream, attempts to dissuade Pilate from being involved with Jesus.

6.2. Mark. The Gospel of Mark probably has the least amount of data about Jesus and women, yet Mark, with the rest of the Gospels, presents women as among the disciples of Jesus. Mark contains stories about the healing (Mk 1:29-31; 5:21-43) and faith (Mk 5:34; 7:24-30) of women.

The discipleship of women is noted in a general saying of Jesus (Mk 3:31-35), in the story of the widow who gave all her money (Mk 12:41-44), and in the passion and resurrection narratives (Mk 15:40-41; 15:47—16:8; see also Mk 16:9-11).

6.3. Luke. The Gospel of Luke shows the greatest interest in women in the life and ministry of Jesus, including numerous accounts and stories about women unique to its presentation. Luke also gives the specific names of more women in Jesus' life than do the other Gospels. This interest is continued in Acts (for Jesus' female disciples see Acts 1:14).

Luke relates stories about the healing (Lk 4:38-39; 8:1-3, 40-56; 13:11-17; 17:11-17) and faith (Lk 4:26; 7:36-50; 8:48; 18:1-8; 21:1-4) of women, many of which are unique to Luke. Women are important in two parables unique to Luke (Lk 15:8-10; 18:1-8) and are mentioned in two stories about the kingdom of God (Lk 13:20-21; 17:35).

The place of women in discipleship is particularly stressed by Luke in general statements (Lk 8:19-21; 11:27-28), in the story of Mary and Martha (Lk 10:38-42), and in the reports of the female disciples who traveled with Jesus (Lk 8:1-3) and are described in the passion and resurrection narratives (Lk 23:49; 23:55—24:12). Again, some of these accounts are unique to Luke (Lk 8:1-3; 10:38-42; 11:27-28).

Woman are prominent as proclaimers in the infancy narratives (Elizabeth, Mary the mother of Jesus, Anna; Lk 1—2) and in the resurrection narratives (Lk 24:10-11, 22-24).

6.4. John. The Gospel of John portrays in particular the discipleship of the mother of Jesus (Jn 2:1-12; 19:25-27), the Samaritan woman (Jn 4:7-42), Mary and Martha (Jn 11:1-45; 12:1-8) and Mary Magdalene (Jn 19:25; 20:1-18). Both the Samaritan woman and Mary Magdalene are proclaimers of Jesus in John, and both receive extended attention in the Johannine narratives.

7. Conclusions and Significance.

Jesus' respect for and inclusion of women as disciples and proclaimers provided the foundation for the positive place of women in the earliest churches and their ministry.

In fact, the baptismal formula reflected in Galatians 3:28 and its statement that in Christ "there is neither . . . male nor female" is probably rooted in the traditions of Jesus (see MacDonald). This indicates the formative role of Jesus in Paul's theological vision for the church's inclusive character.

The fact that there were no women among the Twelve is often cited as evidence that Jesus did not intend women to exercise leadership or authority in the church. However, it would not have been culturally possible to have included women in that most intimate group of Jesus' followers. It is remarkable and significant enough that many women, at least eight of whom are known by name and often with as much or more data as some of the Twelve, were included as disciples and proclaimers during Jesus' ministry (not to mention Elizabeth and Anna in Luke 1—2). It has often been observed that all of the Twelve were Jews, yet the early church, as it developed in other social contexts, included Gentiles in leadership. Thus the precise composition of the Twelve should not be pressed too far.

More significant is the fact that the Twelve did not constitute or provide the model or framework for leadership or authority in the early church, apart from the very earliest days in the Jerusalem church. Rather, what was significant for the character of leadership in the early church was Jesus' call to discipleship and its definition in terms of service, and the fact that men and women were among Jesus' followers as disciples and proclaimers.

It sometimes is noted that Jesus did not appoint any women to office. But neither did Jesus appoint any men to office (apart from the case of Peter, and that did not determine church structure apart from initial leadership in the Jerusalem church). The structures of leadership and authority in the early churches, especially those of Paul, for which the best evidence is available, were somewhat fluid and unstructured. In such contexts women did exercise leadership and authority (twelve women are known by name among Paul's coworkers in ministry; see Rom 16:1-16; Phil 4:2-3; 1 Cor 1:11; Col 4:15; Acts 16:14-15, 40).

See also BIRTH OF JESUS; RESURRECTION.

DJG: DIVORCE; MARY'S SONG; PROSTITUTE.

BIBLIOGRAPHY. L. J. Archer, *Her Price Is Beyond Rubies: The Jewish Woman in Graeco-Roman Palestine* (JSOTSup 60; Sheffield: Sheffield Academic Press, 1990); S. S. Bartchy, "Jesus, Power and Gender Roles," *TSFBul* 7.3 (1984) 2-4; R. Bauckham, *Gospel Women: Studies in the Named Women in the Gospels* (Grand Rapids: Eerdmans, 2002); R. E. Brown, "Roles of Women in the Fourth Gospel," *TS* 36 (1975) 688-99 (reprinted in *The Community of the Beloved Disciple* [New York: Paulist, 1979] 183-98); E. S. Fiorenza, *In Memory of Her: A Feminist Theological Reconstruction of Christian Origins* (New York: Crossroad, 1983); K. Giles, "Jesus and Women," *Interchange* 19 (1976)

131-36; A. Gill, "Women Ministers in the Gospel of Mark," *AusBR* 35 (1987) 14-21; C. M. Grassi and J. A. Grassi, *Mary Magdalene and the Women in Jesus' Life* (Kansas City: Sheed & Ward, 1986); J. B. Hurley, *Man and Woman in Biblical Perspective* (Grand Rapids: Zondervan, 1981); T. Ilan, *Jewish Women in Greco-Roman Palestine* (Peabody, MA: Hendrickson, 1996); W. Klassen, "The Role of Jesus in the Transformation of Feminine Consciousness," *JCSR* 7 (1980) 182-210; J. Kopas, "Jesus and Women: Luke's Gospel," *TToday* 43 (1986) 192-202; R. S. Kraemer, *Maenads, Martyrs, Matrons, Monastics: A Sourcebook on Women's Religions in the Greco-Roman World* (Philadelphia: Fortress, 1988); R. G. Maccini, *Her Testimony Is True: Women as Witnesses According to John* (JSNTSup 125; Sheffield: Sheffield Academic Press, 1996); D. R. MacDonald, *There Is No Male and Female: The Fate of a Dominical Saying in Paul and Gnosticism* (HDR 20; Philadelphia: Fortress, 1987); C. Meyers, *Discovering Eve: Ancient Israelite Women in Context* (New York: Oxford University Press, 1988); G. R. Osborne, "Women in Jesus' Ministry," *WTJ* 51 (1989) 259-91; L. Swidler, *Biblical Affirmations of Woman* (Philadelphia: Westminster, 1979); idem, *Women in Judaism: The Status of Women in Formative Judaism* (Metuchen, NJ: Scarecrow, 1976); R. A. Tucker and W. Liefeld, *Daughters of the Church: Women and Ministry from New Testament Times to the Present* (Grand Rapids: Zondervan, 1987); B. Witherington III, *Women in the Ministry of Jesus: A Study of Jesus' Attitudes to Women and Their Roles As Reflected in His Earthly Life* (SNTSMS 51; Cambridge: Cambridge University Press, 1984). D. M Scholer

WOMEN II: PAUL

No NT writer has been more criticized for his allegedly negative portrayal of women than the apostle Paul. Although Paul's view that "there is neither male nor female in Christ" (Gal 3:28) has been hailed as revolutionary, he has been viewed conversely as merely a child of his culture in other texts in which he appears to subordinate or denigrate women (e.g., 1 Cor 14:34-35). Whether Paul merely reflects his culture's views of women or significantly differs from them (positively or negatively) can only be determined by examining some of the most debated Pauline passages in light of his culture.

1. Paul and Men's and Women's Roles in General

2. Paul and Women's Head Coverings
3. Paul and Wives' Submission
4. Paul and Women's Ministry

1. Paul and Men's and Women's Roles in General.

Paul's letters are occasional letters, that is, they were occasioned by specific circumstances and thus address certain situations as responses to them. Paul's earlier letters (mainly those undisputedly attributed to him) do not deal specifically with women, men or marriage very frequently, but the topic does come up, especially in 1 Corinthians 7.

In 1 Corinthians 7 Paul addresses Christians who, like a few groups in their culture, have come to value the single lifestyle; their view, however, has created certain complications. One complication is that some of those valuing the single lifestyle are already married, and their pursuit of celibacy within marriage provides a danger of sexual temptation to their spouses and possibly themselves as well (1 Cor 7:2, 5; cf. 1 Cor 7:9). Paul may be citing a Corinthian position in 1 Corinthians 7:1, but in 1 Corinthians 7:2-5 Paul's language is quite sensitive to hearers of both genders: he addresses husbands and wives on equal terms. Jewish marriage contracts stipulated certain duties required of husbands and wives, but Paul focuses on one duty relevant here: intercourse. What is significant is that it is not simply a duty for husbands, as in some Jewish texts; it is a reciprocal duty (1 Cor 7:3-4). Both the Jewish contracts and Paul show special sensitivity for the wife's feelings in this matter, however, quite in contrast with Greek culture's emphasis on male sexual gratification (Keener 1991, 67-82).

Another complication of their lifestyle is that some Christians now wanted to divorce, either due to lack of sexual fulfillment or, more likely, to pursue a celibate lifestyle (or, like Cynic philosophers, a lifestyle free of the encumbrance of marriage yet not of sexual relations; cf. 1 Cor 6:12-20). In response Paul cites a saying of Jesus: divorce is not permissible (1 Cor 7:10-11; cf. Mk 10:11-12). Having appealed to Jesus' prohibition of divorce, however, Paul goes on to qualify it, without in any sense feeling that he is challenging its authority; it was widely understood that general statements of principle needed to be qualified in certain situations (especially since Jesus' Jewish teaching style often included hy-

perbole, i.e., rhetorical overstatement; see Keener 1991, 13-28). It is true that the believer is not allowed to initiate the breakup of his or her marriage; if, however, the believer is forced into the situation (Paul's example here covers abandonment and being divorced against one's will; either spouse could unilaterally divorce the other under Roman law), the believer is "not under bondage" (1 Cor 7:15), for there is no guarantee of the unbeliever's conversion (1 Cor 7:16).

Paul's "not under bondage" echoes the exact language of Jewish divorce contracts, meaning that the divorce was valid and persons were "free" to remarry (see Keener 1991, 50-66). To read "not under bondage" as anything other than freedom to remarry is to ignore how all first-century Jewish readers would have understood it (not to mention ignoring the synonym in 1 Cor 7:27, 39). Throughout this initial discussion on divorce, Paul is careful to maintain his balance of inclusive language, involving husband and wife equally in spiritual responsibility and freedom.

After exhorting his readers that it is better to remain in their present state (i.e., he prefers remaining single, and more strongly advocates avoiding divorce; cf. 1 Cor 7:17-24), he explains that virgins are probably better off remaining single (1 Cor 7:25-38), although he acknowledges that this is only better for those who are fit for it (1 Cor 7:36; cf. 1 Cor 7:9). In this context he again returns momentarily to the issue of divorce. Digressions were common in antiquity in general and Paul in particular, and the flow of thought in the immediate context leaves no doubt that 1 Corinthians 7:27-28 refers to divorce: "Are you married to a wife? Do not seek a divorce. Are you divorced [the same Greek word as in the preceding line] from a wife? Do not seek to be married again. But if you do remarry, you have not sinned; and the same is true for one who has not been married before." Here Paul's language is temporarily less inclusive, but his point is meant to cover both genders: by 1 Corinthians 7:32-34, he values the spiritual devotion of men and women equally.

First Corinthians 7:36-38 may be relevant to our discussion if it refers to parentally arranged marriages, as is likely; but scholars are almost evenly divided as to whether a virgin's father or fiancé is addressed here. If the former is in view, Paul simply addresses the father in the cultural situation which then prevailed: parents arranged their children's marriages, usually with input from the children. If the latter is in view, we have no earlier cultural parallels to the situation addressed here. On either reading, however, Paul apparently suggests sensitivity to the girl's wishes (1 Cor 7:36).

We must now turn to the more specific questions of head coverings and authority relationships in marriage and in the church, the most frequent issues of debate concerning women's roles in Paul.

2. Paul and Women's Head Coverings.

Some commentators have managed to deny Pauline authorship to nearly all the controversial passages in Paul concerning women, but the textual evidence for this attempt in 1 Corinthians 11:2-16 is so weak that few scholars support it; most writers have concerned themselves instead with the more rigorous task of understanding the text. The text clearly refers to a custom of women covering their heads, at least in worship; often a shawl (covering only the hair) was employed for this, but in some places face veils were also used. There are so many contexts in which head coverings were used, however, that one must question which context Paul addresses. For instance, people covered their heads due to mourning or shame, but since this practice was used for both men and women, it is unlikely that Paul has this practice directly in view.

Greek women had traditionally been secluded in the home to a great extent, and there is not much evidence for frequent head coverings among them in this period, certainly not among the well-to-do. East of Greece, however, the custom was prevalent, including in Palestine and southern Roman Asia (e.g., Tarsus; see MacMullen); further, Roman women, like Roman men, covered their heads in worship, in contrast to Greek women and men. The Corinthian church, located near a major port and born in a synagogue (Acts 18:4, 7-8), probably included a number of Eastern immigrants for whom the covering was an important practice. Evidence from Egypt indicates that many Jewish women covered their heads outside Palestine, even if they were Hellenized in many other respects (Philo; *Jos. and As.*). But more was probably involved than merely a clash of cultural icons; the head covering was a cultural issue, but it symbolized certain values that went deeper than the symbol itself.

Women's hair was a prime object of male lust in the ancient Mediterranean world (Apuleius *Met.* 2.8-9; *Sifre* Num. 11.2.3); societies that employed head coverings thus viewed uncovered married women as unfaithful to their husbands, that is, seeking another man (cf. *m. Ket.* 7:6; virgins and prostitutes, conversely, were expected not to cover their heads, since they were looking for men). Women who covered their heads could thus view uncovered women as a threat; uncovered women, however, undoubtedly viewed the covering custom as restrictive and saw the way they dressed their hair as their own business. Significantly, the uncovered women probably included the cultured women of higher status, whose family homes hosted most of the house churches. Statues show that well-to-do women pursued fashionable hairstyles and uncovered heads, styles that poorer women probably considered seductive. Given the class conflict in the Corinthian church evident from other passages in 1 Corinthians (e.g., 1 Cor 11:21-22; see Theissen), this would easily have flared into a major issue of controversy (see Keener 1992, 22-31; cf. Thompson)

Both the book of Acts and Paul's letters present him as a skilled debater, conversant in the logic and rhetoric of his culture. In ancient rhetoric, one's arguments for a position need not be the same as the reasons for which one held the position. Paul's purpose in advising head coverings may have been the unity of the church, but his arguments are those that would work best to persuade his readers. He proposes four main arguments for his position: family values, the creation order, the example of nature and propriety as dictated by custom.

First, Paul argues from family values and a pun (plays on words were common in ancient argumentation, Jewish and Greek): the husband is the wife's head, so if she dishonors her head by uncovering it in a culture where that is dishonorable, she dishonors her husband (1 Cor 11:2-6). By drawing an analogy between uncovered and shaven heads (this is the rhetorical technique *reductio ad absurdum*: Paul says, "If you want to be uncovered, why don't you go all the way with it?"), Paul reinforces this sense of shame; when a woman's hair was cut short or shaved, it was a great dishonor and symbolized the loss of her femininity.

Although Paul is arguing from a play on words, modern interpreters have often fastened on the single word *head* (Gk *kephalē*) and debated what Paul meant when he called the husband the wife's "head." Some scholars have argued that the term means "authority" or "boss"; the Hebrew for "head" *(rō'š)* could mean this, and occasionally *kephalē* means this in the Septuagint (Grudem; Fitzmyer). Other scholars have disputed this meaning, noting that the translators usually bent over backward to avoid translating the Hebrew *rō'š* with the Greek term *kephalē; kephalē* does not normally mean "authority" or "boss" in Greek. These latter scholars often argue for the meaning "source," which it does mean in some texts (Mickelsen in Mickelsen, 97-117; Scroggs, 284). Scholars favoring the "authority" meaning, however, respond that "source" is an even rarer meaning of *kephalē* in the Septuagint than "authority." Both groups of scholars are undoubtedly right in what they affirm but may fall short in what they deny; the term sometimes means "source" and sometimes means "authority," at least in "Jewish Greek" influenced by the rhythms of the Septuagint.

The question is, what sense should be attributed to the term in 1 Corinthians 11:3? Given the allusion to Adam as Eve's source in 1 Corinthians 11:8, it is very likely that Paul speaks of the man (Adam) as his wife's "source," just as Christ had created Adam and later proceeded from the Father in his incarnation (in which case 1 Cor 11:3 is in chronological sequence; see Bilezikian, 138). In Ephesians 5:23, by contrast, the wife is to submit to her husband as her "head," that is, one in authority over her, although the husband is simultaneously expected to define headship in terms of his sacrificial service for his wife. Even Ephesians 5, however, does not give us a transcultural view of the husband's authority; the husband's authority in this passage reflects the status of women in a society where they were already subordinate to their husbands and modifies it in a more progressive direction (see 3 below).

Second, Paul argues from the creation order (1 Cor 11:7-12); essentially Paul says, "Adam was created before Eve, therefore women should wear head coverings." This argument does not work well on modern logic but undoubtedly made the point admirably to the Corinthians. Although Paul knew from Genesis 1:26-27 that man and woman together represent God's image (cf. Rom 8:29; 2 Cor 3:18), he points out that woman, taken from man, also reflects man's glo-

ry (1 Cor 11:7) and therefore can distract men from worship; this may relate to the danger of typical male lust in that culture. But once Paul has made his argument from the creation order, he takes it back: it is true that woman comes from man, but it is also true that men come from women; both are dependent on one another in the Lord (1 Cor 11:11-12). Although Paul only needs woman's derivation from man to support his point, he qualifies his argument so that no one will press more meaning into it than he intends: he uses this only as an ad hoc argument for head coverings, not for everything one might extrapolate from it.

Paul concludes argument two with an allusion so brief that it has generated a considerable variety of interpretations: "Therefore it is proper for a woman to exercise authority over her head [not to have authority 'on' her head, as in many translations; see Hooker], because of the angels" (1 Cor 11:10). The angels may be (1) lusting angels, as in the most common Jewish interpretation of Genesis 6:2 (cf. also 2 Pet 2:4; Jude 6; probably 1 Pet 3:19-22), although Paul presumably would have made more of these angels here and elsewhere in his writings had he believed them a current threat; (2) angels who were present for worship, as witnessed in texts from Qumran, who might be offended by a breach of propriety that culturally signified disregard for one's family's honor; or (3) angels who ruled the nations but whom Christians would someday judge; in this case, Paul is exhorting the women to recognize their authority over their heads but to use it responsibly (cf. 1 Cor 6:3). In any case, the Greek construction indicates that Paul recognizes the woman's authority over her head; he reasons with her to cover it for the sake of propriety, but his argument is no more forceful than this.

Third, Paul argues from nature, that is, from the natural order of things (1 Cor 11:13-15). Stoics normally argued from nature, and other writers often joined them. Paul may here be arguing from current Greek and Roman custom (other peoples in Paul's day and Greeks in an earlier period wore their hair long), although "nature" usually means something stronger than this; or he may be arguing that women's hair naturally grows longer than men's.

Finally, Paul employs a classic argument of early Jewish and other Greco-Roman rhetoric: "That's just the way things are done" (1 Cor

11:16). One group of philosophers, called the Skeptics, only accepted arguments from custom; most other thinkers accepted this as a supporting argument. With arguments that related to all his readers (those influenced by Jewish, Stoic and perhaps some Skeptic thought), Paul concludes with an argument related to his real purpose for writing the arguments: to avoid contention (cf. Keener 1992, 31-47, for further documentation for this section).

A few points are clear here. One is that Paul engages the issues with which his congregation is struggling, including gender issues from the culture. He also upholds the importance of the Christian family and church unity; further, while providing arguments for propriety of dress to keep the church unified, he seeks to persuade the women who hear his letter read in the church to keep these arguments in mind without questioning their right to dress as they will (1 Cor 11:10), a far cry from stronger arguments elsewhere in the letter (1 Cor 4:18—5:5; 11:29-34). Perhaps most significant for our discussion, however, is what he omits: Paul nowhere in this text subordinates the woman, failing even to touch on that issue.

3. Paul and Wives' Submission.

Although several Pauline passages address the subordination of women in the home (Eph 5:22-33; Col 3:18; 1 Tim 5:14; Tit 2:4-5), we will examine in detail only the longest of these passages, since all four share the same cultural milieu, and the two references in the Pastorals may reflect the social situation depicted in our treatment of 1 Timothy 2:9-15 below. (That the social situation influences the directives is clear from a sample comparison of, say, 1 Tim 5:14 and Prov 31:10-31.)

3.1. The Social Situation. Before examining Paul's meaning in Ephesians 5:22-33, we should note that even the most restrictive interpretation of this passage would portray Paul as no more conservative than his culture in general. Although women were experiencing some upward mobility in this period (anything would have been an improvement over classical Athens!), and women in some areas (e.g., urban Roman Asia and Macedonia) experienced more freedom than in other areas, women nowhere enjoyed the social freedom recognized as their right today.

Influential ancient male attitudes toward women often sound harsh to modern ears; to some early Jewish teachers, women were inherently evil (cf. Sir 42:12-14; *m. 'Abot* 2:7); Josephus claims that the Law prescribes their subordination for their own good (Josephus *Ag. Ap.* 2.24 §§200-201). Philo complains that women have little sense (Philo *Omn. Prob. Lib.* 117) and praises one exception, the empress Livia, for becoming "intellectually male"! Likewise, Plutarch, one of the more progressive writers on the subject, positively suggests that women can learn philosophy from their husbands but negatively bases this on the datum that they will pursue folly if left to their own devices (Plutarch *Bride and Groom* 48; *Mor.* 145DE). Such attitudes naturally affected their treatment in ancient households, where men always held the power. Roman law vested complete authority over wife, children and slaves to the male head of the household, known as the *paterfamilias*. The wife's quiet submission was viewed as one of her greatest virtues throughout Greco-Roman antiquity (e.g., Sir 26:14-16, 30:19; Greek marriage contracts).

Perhaps due to the proliferation of female infanticide (this detail is debated), there seems to have been a shortage of women in Greek society, and the marriage of men in their thirties to girls in their early and midteens was thus a standard practice. Until their thirties men normally had intercourse with slaves, prostitutes or one another; when men in classical Athens married, many of them found their wives (just entering puberty) less intellectually challenging than prostitutes. While the situation was not this dismal throughout the Empire of Paul's day, and tomb inscriptions testify to an abundance of genuine love between husbands and wives, the very structures of ancient society militated against husbands perceiving their wives as potential equals.

From the time of Aristotle, in fact, it had been customary for moral philosophers to advise their male readers how to govern wives and other members of the household properly; these instructions have come to be known as household codes (or in their German title common in scholarly literature, the *Haustafeln*). Aristotle and many subsequent moralists classified the three main categories subordinate to the male householder as wives, children and slaves (Aristotle *Pol.* 1.2.1, 1253b); although he allowed that the character of their subordination differed (male children, for instance, required less subordination as they grew older; cf. Aristotle *Pol.* 1.5.12, 1260b), he argued that their subordination was a matter of their nature, not merely of culture (on women, Aristotle *Pol.* 1.2.12, 1254b). Such moral themes appealed to the Romans, whose culture emphasized duty and order and who were suspicious of any potential threats to their social order (e.g., the socially disruptive cult of Dionysus in the second century B.C.).

In the first and early second centuries, many aristocratic Romans (e.g., Petronius, Juvenal) found reason to disparage religious groups from the East, especially when these groups converted Roman women and subverted traditional Roman values. In the first century major scandals concerning women misled by Jews and followers of Isis in Rome led to severe reprisals from the government (Tacitus *Ann.* 2.85; Josephus *Ant.* 18.3.4 §§64-80). To prove that they were not subversive to traditional Roman family values, suspected groups often produced their own sets of household codes modeled after those of the moral philosophers: instructions as to how each householder should govern his wife, children and slaves (Josephus *Ag. Ap.* 2.25-31 §§201-17; see Balch for a thorough treatment of household codes from Aristotle through Josephus).

3.2. Ephesians 5:22-33. Some scholars have argued that the original Paul (as reflected in Rom 16:3-15; Phil 4:2-3) preserved Jesus' spirit of egalitarianism, but the second and third generations of his disciples (reflected in Colossians and Ephesians, and the Pastorals, respectively) increasingly subordinated women's roles to fit the standards of their culture. While such a view has some evidence to support it, it rests on two hypotheses requiring proof: first, that the later canonical Pauline writings are not genuine; and second, a particular reading of these later letters. The text of Ephesians does not support the contention that its writer has become more chauvinistic than the Paul of the earlier letters.

Assuming that Ephesians is written by Paul, it is written by a prisoner in Rome well aware of Roman attitudes toward Eastern cults like worshipers of Isis and Dionysus, plus Judaism in its Christian and non-Christian forms (what we today call Christianity and Judaism, respectively). Paul is also well aware that the social ostracism Jews and Christians often faced could become much worse if the outcome of his own trial set a negative precedent for Christians elsewhere (cf. Phil 1:7, addressed to a congregation that in-

cludes some Roman citizens like himself). Like representatives of other mistrusted religious groups in the Roman Empire, Paul had good strategic reason to uphold traditional Roman family values.

At first sight, it may appear that Paul does just that. Given the social situation, it is hardly surprising that Paul presents household codes in their familiar three basic categories: relations between wives and husbands, children and fathers, and slaves and masters. But contrary to our expectations, Paul significantly adapts the list. Yes, wives, children and slaves are to submit, and thus to silence cultural objections to the gospel (submission here is "for the Lord's sake," Eph 5:21; 6:5-8). But for Paul a truly Christian ethic compatible with Jesus' teaching and example of servanthood goes beyond this: the male householder is also to submit. That Paul requires this of the *paterfamilias* is implied in a number of ways, and the distinction between his view and the more usual ancient injunction that the householder govern should have been clear to ancient readers.

First, Paul begins this three-part structure in a very unusual way. As the climax of his exhortations describing a Spirit-filled life (Eph 5:18-21), Paul calls on all believers to submit to one another (Eph 5:21). It is true that the following context delineates different ways to submit according to differing societal roles; but the very idea of mutual submission strained the common sense of the term *submission:* householders were sometimes called to be sensitive to their wives, children and slaves, but they were never told to submit to them. That Paul envisions the same sort of mutual submission to cover the slave and master relationship is clear from his exhortation in Ephesians 6:9: after explaining how and why slaves should submit (Eph 6:5-8), he calls on masters to "do the same things to them," an idea which, if pressed literally, goes beyond virtually all other extant writers from antiquity.

Second, the duties are listed as reciprocal duties. Whereas most household codes simply addressed the head of the household, instructing him how to govern other members of his household, Paul first addresses wives, children and slaves. Far from instructing the *paterfamilias* how to govern his wife, children and slaves, he omits any injunction to govern and merely calls on him to love his wife (undoubtedly a common practice, but rarely prescribed), to be restrained in disciplining his children and to regard slaves as equals before God. This is hardly the language of the common household code, although some ancient philosophers also exhorted moderation and fair treatment of subordinates. The wife, children and slaves are to regulate their *own* submission voluntarily.

Third, Paul does not describe the duties that are attached to submission. An ancient reader could therefore have been tempted to read a wife's submission as meaning all that it could mean in that culture—which, as we have noted above, involves considerably more subordination than any modern Christian interpreters would apply to women today. (Applying the text in this way would return women to rarely being able to attend college, to disallowing them voting privileges, etc.) However, Paul does define the content of the wife's submission once, in quite a strategic place: at the concluding summary of his advice to married couples. The wife is to "respect" (Eph 5:33) her husband. Although the term usually translated "submission" could be used in the weaker sense of "respect," household codes demanded far more of wives than mere respect; Paul's view of women's subordination even in this social situation could not be much weaker than it is.

Finally, the wife's subordination to her husband is directly parallel to the slave's subordination to his or her master. In both cases one submits as "to Christ"—who is compared with a slave's master no less than with a wife's husband. Most interpreters recognize today that Ephesians 6:5-9 does not address the institution of slavery; it simply gives advice to slaves in their situation. Like some Stoic philosophers, Paul could recommend securing one's freedom where that was possible (1 Cor 7:21-22); like the rare philosophers whom Aristotle chastised for suggesting that slavery was against nature and therefore wrong, Paul clearly regarded the subordination of humans as unnatural (Eph 6:9). Whereas the OT enjoined children's obedience to morally sound parental instruction (Deut 21:18-21), the OT nowhere explicitly enjoins the submission of wives and slaves, although they regularly appear in subordinate cultural roles, which God sometimes contravened. Paul does call on wives and slaves in his culture to submit in some sense, but he does not thereby approve of the institutions of patriarchal marriage or slavery, both of which are part of the authority of

the *paterfamilias* and the household codes he here addresses.

That Paul's instructions to wives and slaves are limited to wives and slaves culturally subordinated to the male householder has often been noted (e.g., Martin, 206-31; Giles, 43). The objection that Paul could have rejected the institution of slavery but clearly would support the institution of marriage (Knight, 21-25) simply begs the real question. It is not the institution of marriage per se but the institution of patriarchal marriage that Paul addresses here; that was what appeared in the household codes. Paul elsewhere calls on believers in normal circumstances to submit to all who are in authority (Rom 13:1-7), as Peter does (1 Pet 2:13-17), but this does not mean that he regards the particular authority structures (e.g., kingship) as necessary for all cultures. Because Paul's instructions specifically address institutions as they existed in Paul's day, interpreters of Paul who do not insist on reinstituting slavery or the monarchy should not insist on patriarchal marriages that subordinate wives, either. Indeed, given Paul's weak definition of the wife's submission as "respect" (Eph 5:33; see above), it appears that Paul advocated her submission in only a limited manner even for his social situation.

4. Paul and Women's Ministry.

4.1. Passages in Which Paul Approves Women's Ministry. Although some Greek and Roman women became philosophers, higher education in rhetoric and philosophy was usually reserved for men. In a society where most people were functionally illiterate (especially much of the rural peasantry, estimated at perhaps 90 percent of the Empire's population), teaching roles naturally would fall on those who could read and speak well. Nearly all of our Jewish sources suggest that these roles were, with rare exceptions, limited to men.

Although inscriptions from ancient synagogues indicate that women filled a prominent role in some synagogues (see Brooten), the same inscriptions indicate that this was the exception rather than the norm. Our sources indicate that most Jewish men, like Philo, Josephus and many later rabbis, reflected the prejudice of much of the broader Greco-Roman culture. Josephus (*Ant.* 4.8.15 §219) and the rabbis in most cases dismissed the trustworthiness of women's witness, and, with the possible exceptions of

Beruriah, wife of R. Meir, and the women followers of Jesus (Mk 15:40-41; Lk 8:1-3; 10:38-42), women seem never to have been accorded the role or status of teachers or their disciples (see Swidler). While the roles of women varied from region to region, certain Pauline passages make it clear that he was among the more progressive, not the more chauvinistic, writers of his day.

In a brief letter of recommendation at the conclusion of Romans, Paul commends the bearer of his letter, whom the Romans may trust to explain it to them (Rom 16:1-2). Phoebe is "servant" of the church at Cenchrea, the port city of Corinth; the term may refer to a "deacon" *(diakonos)*, apparently a person with administrative responsibility in the early church, but in Paul's letters it usually refers to a minister of God's word, such as himself. He also calls her a "helper" of many, a term that normally referred in antiquity to patrons, some of whom were women. As a patron, she would own the home in which the church met and hold a position of honor (see further Keener 1992, 237-40).

In Paul's following greetings (Rom 16:3-16), he lists about twice as many men as women but commends more than twice as many women as men. This may indicate his sensitivity to the opposition women undoubtedly faced for their ministry in some quarters. Among the most significant ministers he lists is Prisca (a diminutive form of Priscilla), possibly mentioned before her husband, Aquila, because of her higher social status (Rom 16:3-4). Luke also portrays her as a fellow minister with her husband, joining him in instructing another minister, Apollos (Acts 18:26).

Paul also lists two fellow apostles (this is the most natural way to construe "notable among the apostles," since Paul nowhere else appeals to commendations from "the apostles"), Andronicus and Junia. Junia is clearly a feminine name, but writers inclined to doubt that Paul could have referred to a female apostle have proposed that this is a contraction for the masculine Junianus. But this contraction does not occur in our inscriptions from Rome and is by any count quite rare compared with the common feminine name; the proposal rests on the assumption that a woman could not be an apostle, rather than on any evidence inherent in the text.

In another letter Paul refers to the ministry of two women in Philippi, who, like his many male fellow ministers, shared in his work for the gospel there (Phil 4:2-3). Macedonia was one of the regions where women were accorded more prominent religious roles (Abrahamsen), and this may have made it easier for Paul's women colleagues to assume a position of prominence (see also Acts 16:14-15).

Paul, who ranks prophets second only to apostles (1 Cor 12:28), assumes the existence of prophetesses and demands only that they, like other women in the congregation, cover their heads (1 Cor 11:5). In this he follows the tradition of the OT (where women filled the prophetic office far less than men but nonetheless could assume positions of prominence and authority, e.g., Ex 15:20; Judg 4:4; 2 Kings 22:13-14) and other elements of early Christianity (Acts 2:17-18; 21:9).

These passages alone establish Paul among the more progressive writers of his culture, but other passages must be examined before one can determine *how* progressive he was. It is these passages, therefore, that have stirred the greatest controversy.

4.2. Passages in Which Paul Seems to Restrict Women's Ministry. Although both the following passages have been subjected to a bewildering array of interpretations, neither of them is universally held to be Pauline. Not only the authorship of 1 Timothy but also that of 1 Corinthians 14:34-35 has been called into question. On the basis of (admittedly slender) textual evidence, some prominent text critics have denied that the latter passage is Pauline, thinking that it was inserted instead by a later hand (Fee, 699-705). While this position is possible, the passage can be explained as a Pauline digression on a specific aspect of church order relevant to the Corinthian church.

Some interpreters have argued instead that Paul here quotes a Corinthian position (1 Cor 14:34-35), which he then refutes (1 Cor 14:36), but 1 Corinthians 14:36 does not read naturally as a refutation of 1 Corinthians 14:34-35. Others have suggested that the church services were segregated by gender like the synagogues, thus rendering any communication between the sexes disruptive, but this view is refuted by the architecture of synagogues in this period (Brooten) and that of homes like those in which the Corinthian church met. Still other scholars, examining the context, have suggested that Paul is addressing Corinthian women abusing the gifts of the Spirit, or a problem with judging prophecies. While both of these views can be argued from the context, ancient writers in general and Paul in particular were fond of digressions, and 1 Corinthians 14:34-35 may simply represent a digression concerning a specific issue of church order, distinct from other matters of church order in the context.

More likely is the view that Paul is restricting the only kind of speech directly addressed in these verses: asking questions (Giles, 56). It was common in the ancient world for hearers to interrupt teachers with questions, but it was considered rude if the questions reflected ignorance of the topic (see Plutarch *On Lectures*). Since women were normally considerably less educated than men, Paul proposes a short-range solution and a long-range solution to the problem. His short-range solution is that the women should stop asking the disruptive questions; the long-range solution is that they *should* be educated, receiving private tutoring from their husbands. Most husbands of the period doubted their wives' intellectual potential, but Paul was among the most progressive of ancient writers on the subject. Paul's long-range solution affirms women's ability to learn and places them on equal footing with men (see more fully Keener 1992, 80-85).

Whatever reconstruction one accepts, however, two points are clear. First, Paul plainly does not enjoin total silence on women, since earlier in the same letter he expects them to pray and prophesy publicly along with the men (1 Cor 11:4-5); he thus must enjoin only the silencing of a particular form of speaking. Second, there is nothing in the context to support the view that Paul refers here to women teaching the Bible. The only passage in the entire Bible that could be directly adduced in favor of that position is 1 Timothy 2:11-14.

In 1 Timothy 2:8-15 Paul (on authorship, *see* Pastoral Letters) apparently addresses the proper decorum of men and women in prayer. Paul first addresses the men in the Ephesian churches, who are apparently involved in conflict inappropriate for worshipers of God (1 Tim 2:8). Then, in a more lengthy passage, he turns to problems with the women in these congregations. As noted above, women of the lower economic ranks in the East frequently covered their heads, but the urban congregations of Ephesus would have included women of higher social status, who would flaunt their status by the or-

nate ways they decorated their hair. To poorer women in the congregation, the wealthier women's wardrobe represented ostentation and potential seduction, so Paul rules against it, borrowing language common among moralists of his day (1 Tim 2:9-10; Scholer, 3-6; Keener 1992, 103-7).

After calling on the women in the congregation to adorn themselves properly, he forbids them to "teach in such a way as to take authority" (reading "teach," *didaskō*, and "take authority," *authenteō*, together as many scholars do, although they could also be read as separate prohibitions). The precise meaning of the rare Greek term here used for "take authority" has been questioned. Some scholars suggest that it normally means simply "have authority" and that the passage thus excludes women from exercising any authority in the church. Other scholars have shown that it is often used more strongly than that in this period and may mean "seize authority"; on this reading, Paul merely forbids women to grasp for authority overbearingly, in the same way he would have forbidden it to men. Still other scholars have appealed to other examples within the semantic range of the term to argue for meanings like "domineer in a murderous way" or "proclaim oneself originator." Since some second-century Gnostics saw Eve as the originator of man, 1 Timothy could be refuting a Gnostic myth (Kroeger and Kroeger argue this case with impressive erudition and even suggest that part of this passage quotes a Gnostic source in order to refute it). This case works well if 1 Timothy is written by another writer in Paul's name in the second century (which many scholars believe, although Kroeger does not); if it was written by Paul or his amanuensis, however, the term probably means to "have authority" or (more likely) "seize authority."

The social situation of the letter may represent a more fruitful basis for resolving the meaning of the text than the broad lexical possibilities, however; Paul and his readers assumed this situation when reading the text, and the situation that elicited Paul's response is thus part of his intended meaning. Clues in the text indicate the following situation: male false teachers (1 Tim 1:20; 2 Tim 2:17) had been introducing dangerous heresy into the Ephesian church (1 Tim 1:4-7; 6:3-5), often beginning by gaining access to its women, who would normally have been difficult to reach because of their greater restriction to the domestic sphere (2 Tim 3:6-7). Because the women were still not well trained in the Scriptures (see above), they were most susceptible to the false teachers and could provide a network through which the false teachers could disrupt other homes (1 Tim 5:13; cf. 1 Tim 3:11). Given Roman society's perception of Christians as a subversive cult, false teaching that undermined Paul's strategies for the church's public witness (see above on Eph 5—6) could not be permitted (cf. 1 Tim 3:2, 7, 10; 5:7, 10, 14; 6:1; Tit 1:6; 2:1-5, 8, 10; cf. Padgett, 52; Keener 1991, 85-87; Verner).

Whether because the women were uneducated and thus particularly susceptible to error or because their seizing authority would have injured the church's witness in a tense social situation, or (most likely) both, the specific situation Paul addresses invites his specific response. Paul again provides a short-range solution and a long-range solution. The short-range solution is: they should not take ruling positions as teachers in the church. The long-range solution is: let them learn. Again, Paul affirms their ability to learn, and he proposes educating them as a long-range solution to the current problem. That they are to learn "quietly and submissively" may again reflect their witness within society (these were characteristics normally expected of women), but it should be pointed out that this was the way all novices were supposed to learn and also characterizes the desired behavior of the whole church (1 Tim 2:2). That Paul addresses these admonitions to the women rather than to the men is as determined by the social situation as his admonition to the men to stop disputing (1 Tim 2:8); he hardly wanted the women to dispute but addressed only those involved in the problem.

This solution might be so obvious as to render debate superfluous, except for Paul's following argument, in which he appears to predicate his admonitions to women on the roles of Adam and Eve (1 Tim 2:13-14). What one must ask is whether Paul adduces these examples as the basis for his point, or merely as an ad hoc argument to support it. His argument from the creation order is no more straightforward here (1 Tim 2:13) than it was when in 1 Corinthians 11:7-9 he used it to contend that women should wear head coverings. His argument from Eve's deception is even more likely to be ad hoc. If he argues that Eve's deception prohibits all women from teaching, he is arguing that all women, like Eve, are more easily deceived than all men; if the deception does not apply to all women, neither could his prohibition of their teaching. It is far more likely that Paul instead uses Eve to illustrate the plight of the particular women he addresses in Ephesus, who are easily deceived because they are untrained. Paul elsewhere uses Eve for *anyone* who is deceived, not just women (2 Cor 11:3). Finally, it is possible that 1 Timothy 2:15 is meant to qualify the preceding verses, though there is considerable debate on its meaning (salvation coming through Mary's childbirth, perhaps as the new Eve; through women submitting to traditional roles like childbearing; or simply a woman being brought through childbirth safely, challenging the curse in Eden).

Other passages in Paul that clearly demonstrate his approval of women's ministry of God's word (above) indicate that 1 Timothy 2:9-15 (if, as we assume here, it is genuinely Pauline) cannot prohibit women's ministry in all situations but is limited to the situation in Ephesus and perhaps some other congregations facing similar crises in this period of the church's history. Pauline texts addressing the roles of women in church and home suggest that Paul be ranked among the most progressive of ancient writers.

DPL: AUTHORITY; COWORKERS, PAUL AND HIS; HEAD; HOUSEHOLDS AND HOUSEHOLD CODES; MARRIAGE, DIVORCE, ADULTERY, INCEST; SEXUALITY, SEXUAL ETHICS.

BIBLIOGRAPHY. V. A. Abrahamsen, "The Rock Reliefs and the Cult of Diana at Philippi" (Th.D. diss., Harvard Divinity School, 1986); D. L. Balch, *Let Wives Be Submissive: The Domestic Code in 1 Peter* (SBLMS 26; Chico, CA: Scholars, 1981); G. Bilezikian, *Beyond Sex Roles: What the Bible Says About a Woman's Place in Church and Family* (Grand Rapids: Baker, 1986); B. J. Brooten, *Women Leaders in the Ancient Synagogue: Inscriptional Evidence and Background Issues* (Chico, CA: Scholars, 1982); G. D. Fee, *The First Epistle to the Corinthians* (NICNT; Grand Rapids: Eerdmans, 1987); J. A. Fitzmyer, "Another Look at *KEPHALE* in 1 Corinthians 11.3," *NTS* 35 (1989) 503-11; J. Gardner, *Women in Roman Law and Society* (Bloomington: Indiana University Press, 1986); K. Giles, *Created Woman: A Fresh Study of the Biblical Teaching* (Canberra: Acorn, 1985); W. A. Grudem, "Does *kephale* Mean 'Source' or

'Authority Over' in Greek Literature? A Survey of 2,336 Examples," *TJ* n.s. 6 (1985) 38-59; N. A. Hardesty, *Women Called to Witness: Evangelical Feminism in the 19th Century* (Nashville: Abingdon, 1984); M. D. Hooker, "Authority on Her Head: An Examination of I Cor. XI.10," *NTS* 10 (1964) 410-16; T. Ilan, *Jewish Women in Greco-Roman Palestine* (Peabody, MA: Hendrickson, 1996); P. K. Jewett, *Man as Male and Female: A Study in Sexual Relationships from a Theological Point of View* (Grand Rapids: Eerdmans, 1975); C. S. Keener, *And Marries Another: Divorce and Remarriage in the Teaching of the New Testament* (Peabody, MA: Hendrickson, 1991); idem, *Paul, Women and Wives: Marriage and Women's Ministry in the Letters of Paul* (Peabody, MA: Hendrickson, 1992); G. W. Knight III, *The New Testament Teaching on the Role Relationship of Men and Women* (Grand Rapids: Baker, 1977); R. S. Kraemer, *Maenads, Martyrs, Matrons, Monastics: A Sourcebook on Women's Religions in the Greco-Roman World* (Philadelphia: Fortress, 1988); R. C. Kroeger and C. C. Kroeger, *I Suffer Not a Woman: Rethinking 1 Timothy 2:11-15 in Light of Ancient Evidence* (Grand Rapids: Baker, 1992); M. R. Lefkowitz and M. B. Fant, *Women's Life in Greece and Rome* (Baltimore, MD: Johns Hopkins University Press, 1982); R. MacMullen, "Women in Public in the Roman Empire," *Historia* 29 (1980) 209-18; C. J. Martin, "The Haustafeln (Household Codes) in African American Biblical Interpretation: 'Free Slaves' and 'Subordinate Women,' " in *Stony the Road We Trod: African American Biblical Interpretation*, ed. C. H. Felder (Minneapolis: Fortress, 1990) 206-31; W. A. Meeks, "The Image of the Androgyne: Some Uses of a Symbol in Earliest Christianity," *History of Religions* 13 (1974) 165-208; A. Mickelsen, ed., *Women, Authority and the Bible* (Downers Grove, IL: InterVarsity Press, 1986); A. Padgett, "The Pauline Rationale for Submission: Biblical Feminism and the *Hina* Clauses of Titus 2:1-10," *EvQ* 59 (1987) 39-52; J. Peradotto and J. P. Sullivan, eds., *Women in the Ancient World: The Arethusa Papers* (SUNY Series in Classical Studies; Albany: State University of New York, 1984); S. B. Pomeroy, *Goddesses, Whores, Wives, and Slaves: Women in Classical Antiquity* (New York: Schocken, 1975); B. Rawson, "The Roman Family," in *The Family in Ancient Rome: New Perspectives*, ed. B. Rawson (Ithaca, NY: Cornell University Press, 1986) 1-57; S. Safrai, "Home and Family," in *The Jewish People in the First Century*,

ed. S. Safrai et al. (CRINT 1.2; Philadelphia: Fortress, 1976) 728-92; D. M. Scholer, "Women's Adornment: Some Historical and Hermeneutical Observations on the New Testament Passages," *Daughters of Sarah* 6 (1980) 3-6; R. Scroggs, "Paul and the Eschatological Woman," *JAAR* 40 (1972) 283-303; A. B. Spencer, *Beyond the Curse: Women Called to Ministry* (Peabody, MA: Hendrickson, 1989); L. Swidler, *Women in Judaism: The Status of Women in Formative Judaism* (Metuchen, NJ: Scarecrow, 1976); G. Theissen, *The Social Setting of Pauline Christianity* (Philadelphia: Fortress, 1982); C. L. Thompson, "Hairstyles, Head-Coverings and St. Paul: Portraits from Roman Corinth," *BA* 51 (1988) 101-15; D. C. Verner, *The Household of God: The Social World of the Pastoral Epistles* (SBLDS 71, Chico, CA: Scholars, 1983).

C. S. Keener

WOMEN III: ACTS, HEBREWS, GENERAL EPISTLES, REVELATION

The vigorous participation of women in the life of the early church is attested by a considerable body of evidence, both literary and archaeological. Many of these women are nameless; frequently they are designated by the category of their ministry or by their social or marital status. Sometimes there are hints of deep involvement in leadership that cannot be demonstrated with surety. Nevertheless those possibilities deserve to be acknowledged and explored.

1. Women as Leaders in Acts
2. Paul's Ministry Among Women in Acts
3. Priscilla: A Test Case
4. Women in Prophetic Ministry
5. Women in Evangelistic Traditions
6. Women as Leaders of House Churches
7. Widows and Disenfranchised Women
8. Married and Unmarried Women

1. Women as Leaders in Acts.

Throughout Acts there is a careful inclusion of women as well as men, both as believers (Acts 5:14; 8:12; 17:4, 12) and as objects of persecution (Acts 8:3; 9:2-3; 22:4). No fewer than eleven women are specifically named, and five are involved in church-related ministries. After the ascension of Christ, Mary the mother of Jesus and her female associates are included in the decision making to select Judas's replacement among the Twelve (Acts 1:14). The qualifications for an apostle are that the individual traveled with Jesus throughout his ministry and witnessed the resurrection (Acts 2:21-22). Although a woman is not chosen for the office, Luke's record makes it clear that some of Jesus' female followers fulfill the specifications (Lk 8:1-3; 23:49, 55-56; 24:1-10). At a different level, one woman, Dorcas, is specifically called a "disciple" because her ministry of social and spiritual outreach rendered her invaluable to the nascent church. And upon her untimely death, she was restored to the community that so sorely needed her services (Acts 9:36-41).

2. Paul's Ministry Among Women in Acts.

Luke particularly notes the response of women to the apostle Paul. Upon Paul's arrival at Antioch of Pisidia, he was welcomed into the synagogue and encouraged to return the next sabbath (Acts 13). The congregation, composed of Jews, proselytes and God-fearers, took offense at the disruptive behavior of the Gentiles who attended the worship service on the succeeding sabbath. Those who were accustomed to worshiping in the orderly Hebrew fashion were angered at the *ochlos* of the heathen. (The Greek term can be used for a crowd and for the disorderly behavior of which it is capable; see Acts 19:26; 24:12.) The well-bred women (*euschēmonai*) who participated in the sober life of the synagogue were particularly incensed, perhaps by the conduct of the heathen women, and insisted upon Paul's expulsion from the city (Acts 13:50).

Repugnance for the outrageous and abandoned worship patterns of non-Jewish women was a familiar literary and artistic theme (e.g., Juvenal *Sat.* 6; Plutarch *Mul. Virt.* 13, *Mor.;* Diodorus Siculus 4.3.2). Drunkenness, indecent and destructive conduct, obscenity, nudity, promiscuity and ritual cries were significant components in their cults. Some of these elements are well illustrated in the famous fresco of a Dionysiac initiation at the Villa of the Mysteries in Pompeii. In certain ecstatic religions of the area (see 1 Cor 12:2), women engaged in the tearing apart of young animals and consuming of the flesh while it was still raw, warm and quivering. It would be exceedingly difficult to incorporate such individuals into a worshiping community without seriously affronting the sensibilities of others.

At the end of Paul's first missionary journey, he and Barnabas were summoned to Jerusalem to determine how Gentiles might be integrated into faith communities composed largely of Jews and proselytes. Certain practices were proscribed, especially idolatry, immorality and the consumption of blood (Acts 15:20, 29). Armed with these interdictions, Paul returned to all of the churches visited on the first journey and explained the decision of the Jerusalem council (Acts 15:36). Thereafter he was highly successful with the very sort of well-bred women who objected so vehemently to his missionary endeavors in Antioch of Pisidia. His first contact in Philippi was mainly feminine, and Lydia, the first convert, became the leader of a house church (Acts 16:12-15, 40). Although Paul had received a vision of a man from Macedonia calling him to move in a new direction, the first objects of his ministry were women.

Prominent Hellenistic women received Paul's message gladly in Thessalonica (Acts 17:4) and in Berea, where the response of the women is noted before that of the men (Acts 17:12). In Athens, the intellectual center of the ancient world, a woman named Damaris was converted. She was probably one of the highly cultured courtesans (*hetairai*) attached to the various schools of philosophy, but her presence in the academic circle of the Areopagus indicates that she was well equipped to follow Paul's argument and to draw her own conclusions (Acts 17:34).

3. Priscilla: A Test Case.

In Acts 18 we first encounter Priscilla, a major woman associate of the apostle Paul and a strong proponent of the gospel in her own right. Married to a Jew from Pontus in Asia Minor, she was apparently a native of Rome, from whence the couple were driven by persecution under the emperor Claudius. The name of her husband, *Aquila,* though sometimes borne by citizens of Rome, was more commonly a slave name and may indicate that he was an enterprising freedman. *Priscilla* was a name more frequently given to patrician women, perhaps denoting non-Jewish birth and a higher social status.

Husband and wife received the apostle Paul into their home, their business operation (that of tent making) and into Christian fellowship and ministry. They may well have extended their hospitality to Timothy and Silas as well (Acts 18:5). Priscilla and Aquila's mobility in missionary travel may indicate that they owned a string of family enterprises at Rome (Acts 18:2; Rom 16:3-5), Corinth (Acts 18:2), Ephesus (Acts

18:18-19) and perhaps other points as well. Such branch businesses at far-flung locations are well documented in the ancient world.

At the end of Paul's first visit to Corinth, Priscilla and Aquila accompanied the apostle on his journey to Ephesus. The text here places Priscilla's name before that of her husband (Acts 18:18, as well as at Acts 18:26; Rom 16:3; 2 Tim 4:19), apparently indicating that her ministry and influence were more forceful than his. After Paul's departure, Priscilla and Aquila encountered in the synagogue Apollos, a brilliant Jewish thinker whose knowledge of the gospel was incomplete, despite a powerful command of the Scriptures. Again Priscilla's name stands first as the couple took him aside, perhaps actually into their home for a season, in order to give him the instruction he lacked. The term "expounded" *(exethento)* implies a careful examination of the Scriptures (compare the use of this same verb in Acts 11:4 and Acts 28:23). Though Apollos's basic understanding was adequate, a more complete level of instruction was supplied by the highly capable Priscilla and her husband.

Apparently Priscilla was possessed of a fine mind and an excellent education in order to have so affected the learned Apollos. Thereafter he was able to "debate daily with the Jews, powerfully demonstrating from the Scriptures that Jesus was indeed the Christ" (Acts 18:28). For this reason Chrysostom dubbed Priscilla "a teacher of teachers," noting that she did the same evangelistic work as her husband (PG 60.281D) and recognizing in her a greater zeal (PG 62.658A; 51.187).

When Apollos wished to continue his evangelistic outreach in Greece, the Ephesian believers, among whom Priscilla and Aquila were foremost, furnished him with letters of recommendation. The reception that he was accorded is surely an indication of the confidence that the Christian community reposed in Priscilla and Aquila. They were apparently well known and revered throughout the Pauline world as "fellow laborers" who had risked their lives for the sake of the apostle (Rom 16:3-4).

A. von Harnack was one of the first to suggest that Priscilla and Aquila might be the authors of the epistle to the *Hebrews, a suggestion that found support from J. H. Moulton, F. M. Schiele, A. S. Peake, J. R. Harris and others. Harnack reasoned that if Priscilla were perceived as the primary author, there might be a tendency to suppress this fact. As indicative of scribal prejudice against women, he cites Codex Bezae's elimination of the conversion of Damaris in Acts 17:34 and its change of "not a few of the honorable Greek women and men" (Acts 17:12) to "of the Greeks and the honorable, many men and women." Codex Bezae also reverses the order of Acts 17:4, placing the mention of the men before that of the women. In such a climate the ascription of a woman author might well disappear from sight.

Although the letter bears unmistakable signs of close association with Paul, it is not by the apostle and is a document in the NT to which no authorship is ascribed. The writer belonged to Paul's inner circle and enjoyed a relationship of collegiality with Timothy (Heb 13:23). He or she had not known Jesus but rather received his teachings from others with direct experience (Heb 2:3). The apostolic tone bespeaks the level of influence and authority wielded by the composer of the epistle (Heb 13:17-23).

The writing team or person was familiar with the persecutions that had been experienced in Rome and was demonstrably influenced by the thought of Philo of Alexandria, the Jewish philosopher who had visited Rome in A.D. 40. Priscilla and Aquila would be the Pauline associates most likely to have gained a familiarity with Philo.

The authors had been leaders in the community addressed by the letter and possessed an intimate knowledge of its members' lack of spiritual maturity (Heb 5:11-12). Steeped in Jewish Scriptures, they write of the ritual of the tabernacle but give no hint of an acquaintance with temple procedure. A Jew who had visited Jerusalem would almost inevitably have included allusions to temple practice. Priscilla and Aquila are unusual among Paul's coterie in never being recorded as traveling to Jerusalem.

Harnack observed that the author or authors move easily from a first person singular to first person plural in a manner that may suggest a team effort rather than the work of a single individual. The use of a masculine singular to refer to the writer at Hebrews 11:32 may indicate male input, while the marked sympathy for women may point toward the interests of Priscilla (Heb 11:11, 31, 35). In contrast to the reference in Genesis to Sarah's laughter of unbelief at the promise of a son in her old age (Gen 18:11-15), the account in Hebrews emphasizes her faith as she faced the challenges of conception, gestation and birth (Heb 11:11). The record in Exodus describes the activities of the mother of Moses in concealing his birth and preserving his life (Exod 2:2-9), but here the parental action of husband and wife is noted (Heb 11:23). Priscilla might well have empathized with the faith of a non-Jewish woman, Rahab, as she exercised the ministry of hospitality to the people of God (Heb 11:31). Harnack's theory cannot be substantiated but is worthy of respectful consideration.

4. Women in Prophetic Ministry.

Women are full recipients at the outpouring of the *Holy Spirit (Acts 2:37-38) at Pentecost as foretold by the prophet Joel. His promise that "your daughters shall prophesy" (Joel 2:28-32) is fulfilled in the ministry of Philip the evangelist's prophesying daughters as reported in the account of the apostle Paul's visit to their home (Acts 21:8-9). Later tradition maintained that Philip journeyed with his daughters to Hierapolis, where he engaged in evangelistic endeavors that led ultimately to his martyrdom. The daughters continued in ministry, two of them being buried at Hierapolis. According to Papias, these women collected traditions about the life of Christ, and Papias maintains that his knowledge of two Gospel events derived from these women (Eusebius *Hist. Eccl.* 3.31, 37, 39).

Besides the women prophets at Corinth (see Wire), another female prophet was based in Asia Minor, a citizen of Thyatira. Her teachings are regarded as erroneous (Rev 2:14). Significantly she was condemned not for her gender but for the harm she caused. Like the Nicolaitans of Pergamum (Rev 2:14-15), she instructed her followers to eat meat offered to idols and to practice ritual fornication (Rev 2:20). Her doctrines were regarded as "the deep things of Satan" (Rev 2:24) and were perhaps an early form of gnostic Ophitism. She was threatened with retribution for her lack of chastity (Rev 2:22-23) and for the misleading of God's people. Perhaps as early as the mid-second century, Montanist women in Phrygian Asia Minor were to take up this tradition of prophesying. As support for their ministry, they claimed the precedent of Deborah, Huldah, Anna, the daughters of Philip and an unknown prophet named Ammia.

5. Women in Evangelistic Traditions.

Among the nonbiblical traditions preserved of the apostles, few are better attested than that of Paul's empowerment of women in ministry. Before his call to the church of Antioch, he appears to have engaged in widespread evangelism in Asia Minor (Acts 11:25-26; 15:41). Consistent with Paul's designation of seven women as his fellow laborers (Rom 16:3, 6, 12, 15; Phil 4:2-3) are later accounts of women established in ministry. Pliny the Younger, writing from Asia Minor to the emperor Trajan in A.D. 112, tells of interrogating two leaders of the Christian community, slave women called *ministrae* ("deacons" or "ministers"; Pliny *Ep.* 96-97).

The most interesting story, however, is that of Paul's commissioning his young convert Thecla to become an apostle to Seleucia, close to his native city of Tarsus. Her story is contained in *The Acts of Paul and Thecla,* a composition usually placed in the mid-second century (MacDonald). W. M. Ramsay, however, insisted that the work "goes back ultimately to a document from the first century" (Ramsay, 375-76), though embellished with later accretions. As he saw it, at least some of the features necessitate an intimate knowledge of a first-century environment and throw "light on the character of popular Christianity in Asia Minor during the period" (Ramsay, 403).

The site of her ministry *(Aya Theckla),* one of the best attested in Christian antiquity (Festugière, 21-22), was continuously occupied as a place of pilgrimage and monastic community until the Turkish invasion in the fifteenth century. Part of the apse still stands above the great sanctuary built over the original cave where she established her ministry. The little underground chapel adjoining the cave bears evidence of masonry dating to the first century (Herzfeld and Euyer). The consistent attachment to the site of the same feminine name indicates the involvement of a strong woman leader in the early Christianization of Seleucia.

6. Women as Leaders of House Churches.

From the biblical texts we know the names of female leaders more often than we know the names of male leaders of house churches. Women who exercised the grace of hospitality received into their homes traveling missionaries and those seeking a place of Christian worship and fellowship. The mother of John Mark, a widow, opened her doors to a prayer meeting even in the danger-filled atmosphere of Jerusalem as the execution of Peter was expected the next day. The practice of assembling there must have been a regular one, for Peter threaded his way to her house after his miraculous release from prison (Acts 12:5-17). The gatekeeper, a trusted slave woman named Rhoda, recognized his voice and ran to the others for permission to allow him to enter. Although the participants at the prayer meeting initially challenged the credibility of her story, she remained steadfast in the midst of their opposition. At Rhoda's insistence the door was opened, Peter received and the slave woman vindicated. Her critically responsible position as guardian of the gate during a time of intense persecution bespeaks her importance to the Christian community and its confidence in her. Through this house church, whose leaders were Mary and Rhoda, Peter sent his message to the believers of Jerusalem (Acts 12:17).

The home of Lydia, the first European convert, became the center of the nascent Christian community in Philippi; and it was here that Paul and Silas repaired after their release from prison. B. Witherington observes, "At the two points in Acts where Luke clearly tells us of a church meeting in a particular person's home, it is in the home of a woman" (Witherington 1990, 213). We read also of house churches in the homes of Chloe, Nympha, and Priscilla and Aquila (Col 4:15; 1 Cor 1:11; 16:19; Rom 16:3-5). Women with enough space in their homes thus provided a needed function in their hospitality and in caring for the congregational life that developed in their homes.

In the case of Lydia, her workroom as well as her house may have served the purposes of the gospel. Like Priscilla, she was involved in the textile industry and operated a business, manufacturing coveted purple cloth. We are specifically told that all of her household were baptized (*see* Baptism), including her domestic staff. The women's workroom, as well as the house, offered prime opportunities for the propagation of the gospel in the early centuries of the church (den Boer).

The Johannine epistles (*see* John, Letters of) reveal the importance of the hospitality extended by influential Christians to traveling missionaries and evangelists who might bring spoken and written messages (3 Jn 5-10; see also *Did.* 11—12; Rom 12:13; 1 Pet 4:9; Heb 13:2). Leaders of a house church in a community might control the purity of the gospel message by their selec-

tion of appropriate emissaries to receive into their homes (3 Jn 8). To welcome in a false teacher imperiled the spiritual life of the entire believing community (2 Jn 10-11).

Thus house churches became the fundamental bases for the furtherance of the gospel in their respective communities, with the hosts becoming "fellow laborers" (3 Jn 8). D. W. Riddle has suggested that not only did these leaders further the spread of the kingdom but also these households served as collecting stations for oral and written traditions that would later be preserved in the writings of the NT. The role of women leaders of house churches is thus far more significant than might appear at first glance.

Although the majority of biblical scholars have maintained that the "elect lady" to whom 2 John is addressed represents a church rather than an individual, a few are of the opinion that a specific woman is addressed (A. T. Robertson, A. Clarke, A. Plummer, C. C. Ryrie, A. Ross, D. W. Burdick). If that is the case, she must have been a leader of a house church somewhere near Ephesus. It was her duty to defend her children against heresy. Her appellation, *Kyria Eklektē*, is ordinarily translated "elect lady," though Kyria was a proper name attested in Asia Minor, actually a Greek rendering of the Aramaic Martha (Harris). The text of 2 John also contains greetings from an "elect sister" along with her children (2 Jn 13), either a sister congregation or another woman leader of a house church. A. Spencer points out that an entire congregation cannot be addressed as the lady and her children (Spencer, 110-11). In 1 John and 3 John, the children represent the flock while the leaders are indicated as separate individuals.

7. Widows and Disenfranchised Women.

Throughout Luke-Acts, disadvantaged women are shown a special sympathy, so that Paul heals a deranged slave woman at the risk of his own safety (Acts 16:16-24). Several slave women are given positions of particular responsibility in the nascent church: Rhoda is doorkeeper of a house church, and two slave women of Bithynia are leaders of the Christian community and are specifically called ministers or deaconesses. As required by Roman law in the case of slaves, their testimony is obtained under torture and vindicates the harmless nature of Christian worship (Pliny *Ep.* 96).

A particular sensitivity is demonstrated toward widows or those suffering deprivation. Aware that widows of Hellenistic Jews are receiving less help than those of Palestinian background, the leaders of the early church form an order of deacons to insure an equitable distribution (Acts 6:1-6; cf. Mk 12:40; Lk 18:2-5). Dorcas's ministry is specifically said to have extended to widows, who were welded into a responsive and godly fellowship of caring (Acts 9:36-41; for the view that Dorcas was the leader of an order of widows, see Viteau).

James the brother of Jesus enjoins upon believers a concern for widows (Jas 1:27), while the first epistle to Timothy provides these bereaved women with rules of conduct as well as legitimation and empowerment for an organized ministry of outreach and intercession (1 Tim 5:3-16). Ignatius begs Polycarp to take special care of widows and to assume their guardianship (Ign. *Pol.* 4). Ecclesial widows were supported by the gifts of church members in return for their spiritual and social services. Polycarp recognizes their presence in the Philippian congregation (Pol. *Phil.* 6.1) and provides instructions for the proper attitude and deportment in the fulfillment of their duties. They were to be discreet, to avoid tale bearing, spite, gossip, greed and false allegations. They were also to give themselves to constant prayer for everyone because "they are an altar of God" (Pol. *Phil.* 4).

Ignatius of Antioch appears to be addressing women belonging to a definite office when he writes to "virgins who are called widows" (Ign. *Smyrn.* 13.1). Witherington suggests that *widow* became a technical term for "all unmarried women dedicated to chastity and the Lord's work, including those who have never been married" (Witherington 1988, 201; see also Stählin, 9:451). Grapte was to give the widows special instruction about the message of Hermas (*Herm. Vis.* 2.8.3.), while Hermas was to give himself to the care of widows and orphans (*Herm. Man.* 8.10). Especially in the East, widows would later become a part of the ordained clergy, attached to local churches and committed to a ministry of prayer and good works.

8. Married and Unmarried Women.

The marital status of women is of considerable interest to the writers of the early Christian literature. Married women appear in Acts as fully mature persons, required to take responsibility for their actions. Sapphira is held accountable along with her husband for the deception that they conspire to perpetrate (Acts 5:1-10). Priscilla participates equally in the leadership and exercise of the ministry that she shares with her husband. Even the Herodian queens listen to Paul's message with interest (Acts 24:24; 25:13, 23; 26:20). Though viewed in secular historical sources as concubines and oft-married pawns of power-hungry rulers, they appear in Acts as persons of power and integrity, capable of making their own moral and spiritual decisions.

As Jesus had warned (Mt 10:35-36; Lk 14:26), embracing the new faith did not always make for harmonious family relations, though sometimes it strengthened the bonds. Domitilla, the niece of the emperor Domitian (reigned A.D. 81-96), was exiled; her husband, also apparently a Christian, was executed (Suetonius *Dom.* 10.15.17; Dio Cassius *Hist.* 67.14). Justin Martyr (Justin *Apol. II* 2) tells of a woman whose profligate husband denounced her as a Christian and secured the punishment of her instructor.

Virginity in dedicated women commands a special respect. The four prophesying daughters of Philip were virgins, while the widow Anna, the sole prophet on hand to proclaim the birth of the Messiah, lived all but seven years of her life as a celibate. Thecla, convert and follower of the apostle Paul, made celibacy a condition of her apostolic calling. Such tendencies are precursors of the asceticism that was later to pervade the early church.

The *Shepherd of Hermas* displays a knowledge of a practice known as syneisakatism, the living together of a man with a woman "as brother and not as husband" (*Herm. Sim.* 9.11.3; cf. *Herm. Vis.* 1.7.2). Though they might occupy the same bed as the man, the women (called *subintroductae* or *agapētai*) were ostensibly virgins, committed to gospel ministry. The apostle Paul may refer to this arrangement when he speaks of the virgin who is free to serve Christ rather than her husband and of the man who "keeps his virgin" (1 Cor 7:34-37). One advantage of such a "spiritual marriage" was that it afforded material security, male protection and freedom from marital responsibility to a single woman intent on Christian service (McNamara).

According to a tradition known to Clement of Alexandria, the wives of the early apostles accompanied them in their travels in order to spread the gospel more effectively (Clement of

Alexandria *Strom.* 3.6; cf. Ambrosiaster *PL* 17, c496). An indication of this shared ministry may be found in the declaration of 1 Peter 5:13, "the fellow elect lady who is in Babylon greets you along with Mark my son."

While some scholars have suggested that the allusion is a personification of an entire congregation, it does not seem congruent in juxtaposition with the direct mention of Mark, who is attending Peter in Rome. It was Mark who had duly recorded the fact of the apostle's marriage in the Gospel that bears his name (Mk 1:29-31). Since "Babylon" was a widely used code name for Rome, J. A. Bengel, E. T. Mayerhoff, K. R. Jachmann, H. Alford, A. T. Robertson and others suggest that this may be a reference to Peter's wife, who is known to have journeyed with him in his missionary travels (1 Cor 9:5). Clement of Alexandria even preserved an account of the encouragement that Peter offered her as she was led to a martyr's death (Clement of Alexandria *Strom.* 7.11.63). C. Bigg observed that it would be natural for a woman who had shared in her husband's ministry to wish to send her own greeting to churches that she too had served in the gospel. He finds Peter's inclusion of a message from his wife "a noble and distinctive feature of St. Peter's character and . . . a touch of nature which speaks strongly in favour of the genuineness of the Epistle" (Bigg, 77).

Like Sarah as she forsook a settled existence for a life of wanderings (1 Pet 3:6), Peter's spouse persevered as a steadfast companion to found a new community with a new and living faith. Men and women throughout the Roman Empire faced this same challenge when they embraced Jesus Christ as Savior and Lord of their lives and became indeed "children of Sarah."

DLNTD: HOUSEHOLD CODES; HOUSEHOLD, FAMILY; MARY; MINISTRY; WOMAN AND MAN.

BIBLIOGRAPHY. C. Bigg, *A Critical and Exegetical Commentary on the Epistles of St. Peter and St. Jude* (ICC; Edinburgh: T & T Clark, 1961); W. den Boer, "Gynaeconitis, a Center of Christian Propaganda," *VC* 4 (1950) 61-64; A. J. Festugière, *Sainte Thècle, saints Côme et Damien, saints Cyr et Jean [extraits] saint George* (Paris: A. and J. Picard, 1971); R. Gryson, *The Ministry of Women in the Early Church* (Collegeville, MN: Liturgical Press, 1976); A. von Harnack, "Probability About the Address and Author of the Epistle to the Hebrews," in *The Bible Status of Woman*, ed. L. A. Starr (New York: Revell, 1926) 394-414; R. Harris,

"The Problem of the Address in the Second Epistle of John," *Expositor* (1901) 194-203; E. E. Herzfeld and S. Euyer, *Miriamlik und Korkyos: zwei christliche Ruinenstätten des Ruhen Kilikiens* (MAMA 2; Manchester: Manchester University Press, 1930); D. R. MacDonald, *The Legend and the Apostle: The Battle for Paul in Story and in Canon* (Philadelphia: Westminster, 1983); M. L. McKenna, *Women of the Church: Role and Renewal* (New York: P. J. Kennedy and Sons, 1967); J. A. McNamara, *A New Song: Celibate Women in the First Three Christian Centuries* (New York: Harrington Park Press, 1985); W. M. Ramsay, *The Church in the Roman Empire Before A.D. 170* (London: Hodder & Stoughton, 1893); D. W. Riddle, "Early Christian Hospitality: A Factor in the Gospel Transmission," *JBL* 57 (1938) 141-54; A. B. Spencer, *Beyond the Curse: Women Called to Ministry* (Nashville: Thomas Nelson, 1985); G. Stählin, "χήρα," *TDNT* 9:40-65; J. Viteau, "L'institution des diacres et des veuves—Actes 6:1-10, 8:4-40, 21:8, " *RHE* 22 (1926) 532-36; A. Wire, *The Corinthian Women Prophets: A Reconstruction Through Paul's Rhetoric* (Minneapolis: Augsburg Fortress, 1990); B. Witherington III, *Women and the Genesis of Christianity* (Cambridge: Cambridge University Press, 1990); idem, *Women in the Earliest Churches* (SNTSMS 59; Cambridge: Cambridge University Press, 1988).

C. C. Kroeger

WOMEN IN LEADERSHIP AND MINISTRY. *See* WOMEN.

WORKS OF THE LAW. *See* JUSTIFICATION; LAW.

WORLD. *See* JOHN, GOSPEL OF.

WORSHIP I: GOSPELS

The Gospels do not speak often of worship. The various Greek terms that might be considered its equivalents (*latreia, leitourgia, proskynēsis,* etc.) and the many technical terms connected with worship do not frequently appear in them. Moreover, many references to worship occur almost in passing; the time and place of a healing miracle, the sabbath in a synagogue, for example, might be given. While the references to worship are often incidental, however, worship itself is by no means peripheral. It is there in the Gospels in much the same way as the air that Jesus and the disciples breathed. It is so omnipresent that it is more assumed than mentioned.

One may speak of worship in the Gospels in two ways: of the worship practices of Jesus and the disciples and what one may infer about the worship practices of the early Christian churches in which the Gospels were composed. The Gospels are not as directly informative about these last matters as the Acts of the Apostles or the various epistles but can nevertheless make a useful contribution to our knowledge of Christian worship in the NT era. This article will discuss those two areas and also the theory that the Gospels were shaped according to the lectionary of OT readings in use in that period.

1. The Worship of Jesus and the Disciples
2. The Worship of the Early Church
3. The Gospels and Jewish Lectionaries

1. The Worship of Jesus and the Disciples.
Jesus and his disciples were, of course, Jewish. As such he and they took part in the religious life of the Jewish people (*see* Judaism and the New Testament). It is a reasonable assumption that the religious practices of his people were acceptable to Jesus except for those cases in which the Gospels record an attack against them.

There were three great foci of Jewish worship in the period: the home, the *synagogue and the temple. Of the first the Gospels speak very little. We know it was Jesus' custom, as with all pious Jews, to bless God before sharing bread (*God* rather than *bread* should be supplied as the object of the verb *bless* in such cases). The Synoptic Gospels also describe the *Last Supper as a Passover meal, implying that Jesus shared the practices of the Jewish home in this respect as well. It was also his custom to pray, usually in private. He also commended to his disciples the practice of private prayer (Mt 6:6). It is especially noteworthy that in his prayers all four Gospels report that Jesus addressed God as "Father" (probably the Aramaic 'Abba'). Sometimes the simple address "Father" appears; sometimes a qualifying term expressing the transcendence of God is linked with it. Beyond this, little can be said.

It is also clear that Jesus shared in the corporate worship life of Israel in the synagogues of Galilee. Jesus' word concerning private prayer (Mt 6:6) should not be interpreted as criticism of corporate worship; the focus is on hypocrisy and ostentation. It is in the synagogue that Jesus habitually teaches and preaches. He is apparently a welcome guest at the assemblies of his native province. Only in Luke 4:16-30, Luke's account

of the rejection at Nazareth, is there any description, even in passing, of the synagogue service. There Jesus is invited to read the lesson, apparently a perfectly normal procedure, in itself not surprising. Only the subsequent interpretation of the reading of Isaiah 61 provokes outrage.

During the time of Jesus, synagogue services were held three or perhaps four times on the sabbath. The normal pattern of the synagogue service appears to have included the recital of the *Shema*, a combination of Deuteronomy 6:4-9; 11:13-21 and Numbers 15:37-41, the *Tephillah*, also known as the *Amidah*, or the *Shemoneh Esreh*, a lengthy and elaborate corporate prayer, and the reading and interpretation of Scripture, perhaps on the basis of a lectionary. There is no comment about these matters in any of the Gospels. The worship of the early church tended to carry on the worship practices of the synagogue. While that affinity is chiefly the result of factors other than Jesus' precept and example, it is hard to imagine the early church carrying on a form of worship so reminiscent of the synagogue if Jesus had condemned such worship. In this instance the argument from silence seems compelling.

With respect to the temple the picture is more complex. The temple is held in esteem by the Synoptic Gospels, especially by Luke, who places much of his infancy narratives (*see* Birth of Jesus) and much of the early portions of Acts within its precincts. It is rightly a house of prayer (Mk 11:17 and par.) and, inasmuch as prayer was indeed a regular part of the temple liturgy, it could rightly be considered of value. It is worthy of note that Acts represents early Christians such as Peter and John (Acts 3:1-3) frequenting the temple for prayer. Paul, at the urging of James, even involves himself indirectly with the sacrificial cult (Acts 22:17-26). Jesus is willing to pay the tax that maintains it, although the willingness springs mainly from a desire to avoid unnecessary offense (Mt 17:24-27). In John also much of the action of the Gospel takes place within the temple. It is the spiritual center of Judaism and "salvation is of the Jews" (Jn 4:22). Yet it is not truly necessary for right worship. John asserts most vigorously that in the new age inaugurated by Jesus right worship is "in spirit and in truth" (Jn 4:23). Moreover, it will, after all, be destroyed with not one stone standing upon another (Lk 21:6). The clear implication is that the temple is no longer essential.

The chief difficulty here lies, it seems, in the temple's reason for being, the sacrificial system. A consideration of a key pericope, the cleansing of the temple, may be useful here (Mt 21:1-11; Mk 11:15-19; Lk 19:45-48; Jn 2:13-22; *see* Temple Cleansing). This heavily symbolic action may be more than a reaction to the excesses and the corruption involved in the system. The money-changers, the animal sellers and the animals are necessary if the system is to function. Driving them out may therefore symbolize a rejection of not only the corruption associated with the sale of sacrificial animals but also the sacrificial system. The temple functions rightly not as a place of sacrifice but as a "house of prayer" (Mk 11:17 and par.). The temple is a convenient and appropriate place for worship but, inasmuch as the sacrificial system is no longer valid in the new age inaugurated by the life, *death and *resurrection of Jesus Christ, it is not an essential place for worship of the God of Israel.

Perhaps this last point is best symbolized by the rending of the veil of the temple at the moment of Jesus' death on the cross (Mt 27:31; Mk 15:38; Lk 23:45). The old system with its limited and carefully regulated means of access to God has died. The Gospels and indeed the NT as a whole have a new and utterly different worldview with respect to the relationship between God and humanity. The distinction between the sacred and the common is radically altered, not by the decrease of the realm of the holy as in modern secularization but in the sacralization of that which had formerly been considered common (cf. Acts 10 and the Letter to the Hebrews). All human religious practices are diminished in significance because the new age is breaking into the world in Jesus Christ. Old practices are therefore necessary no longer; old ways of speaking about the worship of God no longer suffice (*see* Kingdom of God).

One's estimate of the accuracy of these various reports concerning the worship attitudes and practices of Jesus will be very much influenced by one's general attitude with respect to the historical reliability of the Gospels (*see* Gospels, Historical Reliability of). There is a considerable consistency between the reports about the attitudes and practices of Jesus on the one hand and those of the early church on the other. This would render these reports suspect in the eyes of a critic devoted to the criterion of dissimilarity (the principle that suggests one may safely accept as historical primarily those sayings or reports that are dissimilar from the Jewish background of Jesus' time and from the teaching or practices of the later church). The application of the criterion seems out of place in this instance, however. While one may doubt the historicity of specific pericopes, there seems no reason to doubt the accuracy of the general picture of Jesus' practices and attitudes with respect to worship presented by the Gospels.

2. The Worship of the Early Church.

The Gospels also provide us with information concerning the worship of the early church or, to put it more precisely, with the early churches known by the Evangelists. It is important not to speak with excessive precision regarding the worship of the early church. The NT era is marked by a very considerable diversity in many areas of Christian life, including worship. Moreover, one may not safely read back into the first century practices and attitudes typical of the third century, an era concerning which our knowledge of worship practices is more extensive. Generalizations concerning worship in this period are difficult and dangerous.

It is also reasonably clear that early Christian worship owes much to Jewish worship, especially that of the synagogue. Recent scholarship is not, however, willing to speak about Jewish liturgical forms and practices in the NT era as precisely as did a previous generation.

With some caution, however, a few observations may be made with respect to early Christian worship. Some passages in the Gospels may come from the worship of the early church. The Gospels may, for example, provide several examples of early Christian praise. In the infancy narratives of the Gospel of Luke we find three magnificent psalms of praise, the songs of Mary (Lk 1:46-55), of Zechariah (Lk 1:68-79) and of Simeon (Lk 2:29-32). These are identified by many scholars as hymns of the early Jewish-Christian church inserted by Luke to enrich his narrative. These hymns are so Jewish in their vocabulary and form that it is difficult to prove beyond reasonable doubt that they are in fact Christian. The Jewishness of these psalms suggests, as one might expect, that Jewish Christians, at least, continued to offer praise in much the same manner as they had always done.

One may recall at this point the manner in which the Evangelists speak so acceptingly of synagogues with little of the ambivalence one notices with respect to the temple. The word *synagogue* is sometimes actually used to describe the assemblies of Christians (cf. Jas 2:2 and various extracanonical sources). All this may tend to support, though it cannot prove, the contention that early Christian worship was in many ways a continuation of Jewish worship.

Luke's hymns are not the only examples of praise in the Gospel. The angelic acclamation of Luke 2:14 and the various forms of the human acclamation at Jesus' entry into Jerusalem (Mt 21:9 and par.) are other examples of the explosion of praise that seems to have accompanied the early years of Christianity. These ejaculations of praise, perhaps best labeled "victory shouts," are not dissimilar to certain fragments of praise in the book of Revelation. Perhaps all these materials are clues to the kind of praise offered in the first years of Christianity.

The prologue to the Fourth Gospel (Jn 1:1-18) probably contains another early hymn. Scholars differ as to the exact extent of the original hymn embedded in these verses (at least the references to John the Baptist are interpolated by the Evangelist) but widely agree that a hymn is actually present. In this case praise overlaps with confession of faith. Communities define themselves by means of the praise they offer as well as by the doctrines they profess. This impressive hymn may have functioned in precisely that manner for the community of the Beloved Disciple (*see* John, Gospel of).

With respect to prayer there also appears to be a continuity between material in the Gospels and the practice of the early church. The Lord's Prayer was certainly used by early Christians. The *Didache*, an early Christian manual of instruction, provides a version of the prayer almost identical to Matthew's and enjoins repetition of the prayer three times a day. This appears to be a continuation of the practice of pious Jews who recited the *Tephillah* three times daily. We know, likewise, that early Christians followed Jesus' example in addressing God as *Abba,* Father (Rom 8:15; Gal 4:6).

The accounts of the *Last Supper (Mt 26:26-30; Mk 14:22-26; Lk 22:14-23; cf. 1 Cor 11:23-25) reflect in their variety not only the events of the night before the crucifixion but also the eucharistic practices of the Evangelists' churches. For example, Mark and Matthew have separate prayers over both bread and cup, whereas in

Luke and in Paul the two prayers were apparently combined into one prayer of thanksgiving, the pattern that has endured in the liturgies of later centuries. It also appears that the actual words of interpretation, "This is my body," were not part of the prayers, as in many later liturgies, but were associated with the sharing of the elements. The words are addressed to the disciples rather than to God (note the second-person-plural verb forms). Moreover, in each case the words for prayer (either *eucharisteō,* "to give thanks," or *eulogeō,* "to bless"; the two appear to be synonymous in this context) are aorist participles. This form, which normally indicates the action of the participle, precedes the action of the main verbs of the sentence.

3. The Gospels and Jewish Lectionaries.

Various scholars have advanced in different forms a remarkable theory that the Gospels were shaped and some of their pericopes created to meet the needs of Christian worship. The theory begins with the unchallenged observation that Christian churches appear to have continued the synagogue practice of reading and interpreting the Torah and the Prophets. It is then argued that the churches also observed the Jewish sacred calendar and followed a fixed Jewish lectionary. The Evangelists, it is affirmed, ordered the various pericopes of the Gospels not according to the life of the historical Jesus or according to their own theological programs but according to the texts of the Law and Prophets of the hypothetical lectionary. So, to give but one example, the Emmaus road story of Luke 24, in which the risen Christ eats with two unknowing disciples, corresponds to the hypothetical reading of Genesis 18—22 on the fourth sabbath of the month of Nisan, chapters that include accounts of the Lord, under the form of three men, eating with Abraham and the unknowing Lot. In some cases, it is alleged, the Evangelists created pericopes of the Gospels according to the rather elastic rules of midrash, a Jewish method of interpretation of Scripture, to provide correspondences in the life of Christ to the prescribed readings of the day.

The hypothesis is daring and far-ranging. In some cases most of the NT and large sections of the OT are explained according to this principle. The hypothesis has not met with wide approval, however. The exact shape of Jewish lectionaries of the period and the degree to which they were fixed is uncertain. The reconstructions employed are therefore highly speculative. When one comes to examine particular Gospel passages OT texts other than the supposed lectionary readings often seem to be more clearly connected with the passages in question. Some proponents ignore evidence accumulated over decades of painstaking scholarship of sources underlying our Gospels and grant a degree of creativity to the Evangelists that few have found likely. In short, the hypothesis is more ingenious than it is persuasive.

See also SYNAGOGUE.

DJG: MARY'S SONG; PRAYER; SIMEON'S SONG; TEMPLE; ZECHARIAH'S SONG.

BIBLIOGRAPHY. R. T. Beckwith, "The Daily and Weekly Worship of the Primitive Church in Relation to Its Jewish Antecedents," *EvQ* 56 (1984) 65-80, 139-58; P. F. Bradshaw, "The Search for the Origins of Christian Liturgy: Some Methodological Reflections," *StudLit* 17 (1987) 26-34; J. D. G. Dunn, *Jesus and the Spirit* (Philadelphia: Westminster, 1979); idem, *Unity and Diversity in the New Testament* (Philadelphia: Westminster, 1977) 124-49; M. D. Goulder, *The Evangelists' Calendar* (London: SPCK, 1978); F. Hahn, *The Worship of the Early Church* (Philadelphia: Fortress, 1973); I. H. Marshall, *Last Supper and Lord's Supper* (Grand Rapids: Eerdmans, 1981); R. P. Martin, *Worship in the Early Church* (rev. ed.; Grand Rapids: Eerdmans, 1974); A. Millgram, *Jewish Worship* (Philadelphia: Jewish Publication Society of America, 1971); L. Morris, *The New Testament and the Jewish Lectionaries* (London: Tyndale, 1964).

S. C. Farris

WORSHIP II: PAUL

While there is no formal definition of what the worship of God means or entails in biblical literature, it can safely be said that in both Testament ages worship originates in the understanding of God as Creator and Redeemer. (The scriptural references that follow are drawn mainly from the Pauline corpus.) God is hailed as the sovereign Lord who brought the world into existence (Rom 4:17) and is the author of all that is (Rom 11:36; 1 Cor 8:6). He acted through the agency of his Son (Col 1:15-20; *see* Son of God) to create and to rescue, taking action in salvation to restore the universe once it had fallen from its original state and to save humankind implicated in sin (Rom 5:1-21; 8:18-23).

Notes of praise are sounded to herald the dawn of a new age of God's reconciling and renewing activity (2 Cor 5:17-21), and the church of Jesus Christ is viewed as the object of redemption (Eph 1:1-14) and the locus where God's saving activity is rehearsed and displayed (Eph 3:9-10). The scene is both terrestrial and set in the heavenly realms, brought together by the work of the regnant Christ who is at once the unifier of heaven and earth and the means by which earth's praises connect with the heavenly, angelic worship.

The key, then, to worship in the Pauline churches is found in Paul's central affirmations concerning the primacy of divine grace to meet the human and cosmic need and the pivotal role assigned to Jesus Christ, the once-crucified and now risen, ascended and glorified Lord, as head of the church and ruler of all creation (Phil 2:6-11; cf. 1 Tim 3:16). These twin assertions lie at the heart of Paul's practice of worship, seen in his praises, prayers and confessions of faith and addressed in the kind of celebratory activity in which he expected his congregations to engage.

1. Paul's Contemporary Setting
2. Pauline Teaching

1. Paul's Contemporary Setting.

1.1. Greco-Roman Religion and Cult. The ministry of Paul was set in a culture and civilization that had long since acknowledged the place of the gods and goddesses and responded to the elemental awareness of the divine (in the sense of *numen,* divine influence or eerie sensation felt by worshipers). In the ancient Greek world the deities of Homer and Hesiod were accepted as superior beings, linked with virtues and requiring obedience. They formed a society located on Mount Olympus and were presided over by Zeus, the father and king of the gods. Paul's tribute in 1 Corinthians 8:5 refers to deities "in heaven," presumably of the Homeric pantheon, and "on earth," relating to manifestations of the divine in fertility spirits or possibly deified kings and rulers.

At the center of traditional Greek religion was the idea that the gods were guardians of the moral order and were to be reverenced by offerings in a cultus as well as by prayer to secure a favorable "lot" in this world and in the underworld of Hades. The largely unpredictable "fate" awaiting the departed contributed to an uncertainty and fear that made worship at the shrines and temples a fitful experience. The linkage of the cultus with the cycle of nature and the desire for good harvests made religious practice an important feature of everyday life. But it added only to the uncertainty of life should the harvests fail and the herds be stricken with disease. A lot of traditional religion had a prophylactic element, that is, to ensure prosperity by warding off disease and danger.

The advent of Rome as a military and world-embracing power gave opportunity for the Homeric deities to be associated with the national aspirations and later the ruling emperors. The Roman genius for government and political action promoted a sense of duty to the state and obligation on the part of the citizens. Hence religion took on its function according to its true etymology, that is, *religare* in Latin, meaning "to bind," namely, humanity to the gods. Religious observances, domestic and on state occasions, served this wider interest. There was a corporate and a contractual obligation, and traditional and customary ways of life were related to the various gods and their consorts in a nonexclusive, syncretistic way. Notions of uncertainty were reinforced by the admission that *tychē* ("luck," "chance") was at the heart of things, and the gods were often treated in a superstitious manner as averters of one's fortune. Household gods (the *lares* and *penates*) were regarded as guardians of hearth and home against evil influences or capricious "fate." A wonderfully revealing picture of the Superstitious Man is drawn by Theophrastus in his *Characters* (for text and comment see Martin 1978, 2:36-38).

Hymns, prayers, votive offerings and sacrifices, at festival time and in conjunction with the shrines, are attested, with various deities being appealed to as a source of life and welfare and a giver of healing (notably of the cult of Asclepius) and prosperity. Divine guidance was sought at centers such as Delphi, where the oracle in the hands of the priestesses of Apollo yielded direction to the inquirer. Tributes of praise called aretalogies are on record, addressed to the deities such as Apollo and Zeus (the notable Cleanthes's *Hymn* is a fine example; cited in Martin 1978, 2:42).

With the world-shaking conquests of Alexander in the fourth century B.C. the ancient world was to know changes of an irreversible character. Life was never to be the same, and notably in the matter of religious influence and

worship. Two factors came into play: (1) There were political confusions that followed in the wake of Alexander's global influence and its sudden decline. The wars and the disturbances of the balance of power brought an unsettlement to the lives of ordinary people across the Mediterranean world and the Syrian Levant. This contributed to the sense of futility that fell across the spirit of Hellenistic society in the decades prior to Paul's mission. (2) But there was a more serious dimension to the human condition in Paul's world that directly influenced the sense of worship.

A new view on the cosmos had been introduced by Greek scientists, with direct repercussions on the traditional theology of Homer that located the deities on Mount Olympus. At a single stroke they were rendered otiose as far as endeavoring to locate them in a mundane sphere; they were banished to the outer regions of starry space. With the fateful exploiting of these astrological and theological novelties by the astrologers and occult practitioners from the oriental world, religion entered a new phase, one largely of pessimism and despair. Once the existence of personal gods and goddesses was either denied (but with little evidence of atheism in the modern philosophic sense) or "demythologized" (by reducing and explaining away their personal identity, as in Plato), no alternative seemed left but the sad conclusion that all things happen by chance. The next move was that the goddess *Tychē* (luck) was placed on the throne vacated by Zeus (Pliny *Nat. Hist.* 2.5.22: "We are so much at the mercy of chance that Chance is our god"). So it came about that everything in the cosmos—earthly, subterrestrial and in the heavenly sphere—was placed under the control of the star gods that controlled and determined the lot of humankind. Men and women were made to feel impotent and helpless, and religion was marked by a "failure of nerve" (to use Murray's phrase).

But escape was promised and sought along certain paths, all with their distinctive ethos and practice of worship. First, fellowship with a mighty god who was stronger than "necessity" was offered in the mystery religions that practiced an elaborate initiatory rite, as part of a baptismal and meal-event cultus. Second, the worship of Serapis, Isis and the healer Asclepius included the promise that worshipers could gain victory over their fate and be given hope. Third, by a life of renunciation and asceticism as well as the practice of magic, a yearning for salvation and harmony with the eternal world was expressed and celebrated in praise, ritual, sacrament and experience—with special emphasis on a knowledge of secret lore that would offer a passport to a union with the divine and a bridging of the gap that separated the worlds above and below. What Paul in Acts 17:22 said of the Athenian philosophers would be true of a wider constituency representing men and women throughout the Greco-Roman world: "I see that in every way you are very religious."

1.2. Jewish Practices.

1.2.1. Temple and Home. During the period when Palestine came under the influence of Alexander, the most notable change to Jewish worship was registered by the increasing Hellenization of Jewish ancestral culture. Greek influence, especially in education and thought forms, can be seen in the life of the *synagogues. Although there were many challenges to Israel's theocracy, especially emerging from the Maccabean struggle of the mid-second century B.C., once the political threat was withdrawn, the cultural changes to Jewish life served only to enhance belief in one God and the sanctity of his house, the temple at Jerusalem. Henceforth the creed of "one God, one land" would be embedded in all kinds of liturgical praise.

The Jerusalem shrine remained the focal point of national worship, since (it was said) the world rests on the threefold foundation of Torah, temple service and the practice of almsgiving (*m. 'Abot* 1:2). The Law was the basis of postexilic Judaism, and its central place in the liturgy was unchallenged. It provided a divine revelation of all needed truth, and its study and obedience was the gateway to salvation and holy living. The temple was the focal point for corporate worship and offered the physical meeting point at which the celebration of the annual festivals and feasts could take place. The latter were prescribed in the Law and were obligatory to all Jews living in Israel and the Dispersion. Three great pilgrim feasts (Passover, Pentecost and Booths, or Tabernacles) could only be observed in the holy land. The result was that loyal Jews came to Jerusalem to share in these occasions (see Acts 2:5-11; and for Paul, Acts 20:16).

Part of the Jewish way of life was sabbath observance. The seventh day of creation was regarded with special esteem as God's gracious gift to his people and a time of gladness. It was often thought of as a picture of the age to come, as well as imposing an identity marker on Jews as a separate people in society. Domestic worship made much of preparation for sabbath, a duty that fell to the Jewish mother and housewife, notably in lighting the sabbath lamp as a symbol of her role in providing a model of godly living.

At Passover this motif was particularly prominent in a solemn searching out of leaven as a prelude to paschal observance that allowed only unleavened bread to be in the home and kitchen (see Paul's application in 1 Cor 5:1-13). Passover commemorated the deliverance of Israel from Egypt, with a personal rehearsal and dramatization of the redemption in every age, and a pointing ahead to Israel's hope of Messiah's coming to set them free (*m. Pesah.* 10). These two ideas of commemoration and anticipation were to be taken over in the Pauline account of the *Lord's Supper, set in a Passover framework (1 Cor 11:17-34).

The annual Day of Atonement was, in reality, a fast whose details are elaborated in the Mishnaic tractate *Yoma* based on Leviticus 16. Paul makes little use of this language, except at Romans 3:24-26, which may be an edited form of a Jewish-Christian credo (for details, see Martin 1989, 81-89).

In Colossians 2:16, 23 Paul knows the ways in which cultic practices, part Jewish, part pagan, can distort what are for him the essentials of faith. His employment of temple cultus ideas and idioms is invariably spiritualized with some important results: The temple becomes the new temple of God's habitation in the church (Eph 2:21) as the *body of Christ (1 Cor 3:16-17; 6:19-20) and the shrine of the Spirit (*see* Holy Spirit). And the sacrificial idioms are now linked to the worship of the Spirit (Rom 12:1-2) and the tangible expressions of giving to the apostolic mission (Phil 4:18-20) and to the collection for the Jerusalem poor (2 Cor 8—9; on the profusion of cultic terms now lifted into a new setting see the commentaries).

1.2.2. Synagogue. The two loci of Jewish worship so far considered are the temple and the home. In the latter category we must remember that Christian church buildings did not appear until the fourth century. Up to that point Christian believers met for worship in their houses, a practice that goes back to the scenes in Acts 2:42, 46-47; 16:15, 34, 40; 20:7-12 as well as an attested feature of Pauline house churches (see Col 4:15-16; Philem 2; cf. Rom 16:5; *see* Church).

The third setting for Jewish worship was the synagogue. Itself the venue for much that characterized Jewish community life and affairs in the first century A.D.—as a school, a law court and a town forum—the synagogue originated (it is assumed) in the historical development of Judaism as a meeting place for worship on the sabbath and other set days in the week, usually market days. The format of worship is largely known from later sources, once Jewish sages had codified and elaborated the distinctive role of the synagogue in maintaining the national way of life. But, even if precise details are not given in any contemporary document, some valuable sources of information are provided in Luke 4:15-21 and Acts 13:13-43. Three main elements formed the genius of synagogue worship: praise, prayer and instruction. As Paul's understanding of Christian worship, notably at Corinth (1 Cor 12—14), is often thought to incorporate those features, it is worth turning to observe the chief emphases.

Praise. Corporate praise is the note that opens the service. The later Talmudic principle is thus enunciated: We "should always first utter praises, and then pray." It is illustrated in the synagogue liturgy for morning prayer called ʿ*Alenu:* "It is our duty to praise the Lord of all things." Worship is thereby directed to the covenant God of Israel as maker of all things and One worthy to receive the homage of his people.

Prayers. These prayers fall into two parts. The first group contains two special concerns. The *Yôsēr* (meaning "he who forms") takes up the theme of God as Creator, while the ʾ*Ahăbâ* (a term for love) is related to the fact of God's love for Israel and requires their answering pledge of love to him. In prayers like these, God is "blessed," that is, his name is honored and extolled with some following description of his attributes and character. Hence, "Blessed are you, O Lord, who chose Israel your people in love." In Paul's letters the exordium, or opening, will often announce God's activity as an incentive to praise and supply reasons for the invocation of blessing (2 Cor 1:3-7; Eph 1:3-10) as well as communicate the epistolary theme to be developed in the body of the letter. Part of the reason for this rhetorical feature is to secure a good relationship with his readers by inviting them to join in a rehearsal of praise. Part also is in the re-

minder that Paul's letters were meant to be read out in public assembly as the congregations gathered in homes for a liturgical service and assembly (see 1 Cor 5:3-5; Col 4:16; 1 Thess 5:27; Philem 2).

In synagogue worship, immediately following these prayers comes the Jewish creed, the *Shema,* which is both a confession of faith and a glad benediction. The title for the *Shema* derives from the opening word in Deuteronomy 6:4: "*Hear (šĕmaʿ),* O Israel, the Lord our God is one Lord." The term *one* emphasizes the unity and sole reality of God that has always been a central Jewish affirmation. It receives, then, a special prominence in the liturgy—as, indeed, it is picked up and carried forward into Pauline theology (Rom 3:30; 1 Cor 8:6; 12:5; Gal 3:20; cf. 1 Tim 2:5) and doxology (Rom 11:36; Phil 2:9-11). (On Paul's wrestling with Jewish monotheism as a frame for his christology, see Hurtado; *see* God.)

The second division of synagogue prayers begins with a reminder that God's promises are sure and dependable. Such a reminder is expressed in the prayer titled "True and firm" (cf. 2 Cor 1:18-22 for Paul's exploiting of this conviction as an apologetic ploy; and in Rom 3:4; 2 Cor 11:31; Gal 1:20 he can call on the same attribute of God, in doxological form). At this juncture the synagogue leader summons a member of the assembly to lead in the "Prayer proper," that is, the Eighteen Benedictions (*šĕmōneh ʿeśrēh*), which laud the character of God in blessing as his benefits and mercies to Israel are recalled. The Eighteen Benedictions cover a wide range of themes. They are partly an expression of praise, partly supplication for those in need (exiles, judges, counselors and the chosen people). In the Pauline corpus a parallel may be seen in 1 Timothy 2:1-4, as well as in Paul's concern for good government and a stable social order (Rom 13:1-7; Col 3:18—4:6; cf. 2 Thess 3:6-13).

Instruction. Once the prayers are said, the service assumes a form and shape that has given the synagogue its distinctive ethos. Indeed, the Jews themselves call the synagogue a "house of instruction" *(bêt hamidrāš),* for nothing is more in keeping with Jewish worship than the emphasis that is placed on Scripture reading and exposition. Instruction is given by two means. First, the Law and the Prophets are read by members of the congregation who come up to the rostrum to share the task. Historically, as the ancient language of Hebrew was not understood by all the people present, a translator would turn the Scripture lessons into the vernacular, usually Aramaic. Second, a homily followed that was based on the passages read (e.g., Lk 4:20-21; Acts 13:15-16; 1 Tim 4:13, 16 for duties devolving upon the Pauline pastor). Any person in the assembly who was considered suitable was invited to deliver this sermon, as in the instances at Nazareth and Pisidian Antioch. The service concluded with a benediction and congregational "Amen" (attested to in 1 Cor 14:16; 2 Cor 1:20) to confirm the truthfulness of all that the service has conveyed to the faithful who utter a word of agreement and application in line with the OT precedent (e.g., Neh 5:13).

The issue of whether psalm singing was a feature in Palestinian synagogues is still unresolved (Bradshaw, 22-24). There is no clear attestation. It has been proposed (Hengel, 78-79) that in contrast to Hellenistic synagogues in the world of the Diaspora, where singing is reported and confirmed by Philo of the sect of the Therapeutae (*Vit. Cont.* 80) and at Qumran (1QS 10:9; 1QH 11:3-4), singing was not allowed by the Pharisees. They would have regarded the practice as heretical, since it was practiced by groups they judged to be deviant. By contrast again, Paul's one description of a rudimentary worship service (at Corinth) includes the use of religious song as a "hymn" *(psalmos)* brought to the assembly (1 Cor 14:26; cf. Eph 5:19-20; Col 3:16-17). If strict etymology is the determining factor, *psalmos* would suggest compositions akin to the Hebrew Psalter, the headings for which in the LXX read *psalmoi* (cf. Lk 24:44). But in a Hellenistic environment such as Corinth there is no certainty that *psalmos* would be interpreted according to its LXX background, and in any case the "hymn" of 1 Corinthians 14:26 seems clearly to be a newly produced composition made available by a gifted member of the church. Such tributes were evidently meant to be sung (as in 1 Cor 14:15), though the rubrics of Colossians 3:16 and Ephesians 5:19 emphasize that the melody is to find an echo "in the heart" and be a true expression of inner devotion, not just an unthinking act of praise. The musical terms in 1 Corinthians 13 do not appear as germane to our knowledge of early Christian praise (see Smith).

A final word may be added on the question of Jewish holy days. Obviously the sabbath took pride of place, observed on a weekly cycle as a token of God's creatorial work and as a factor in redemptive history (Deut 5:12-15). The displacement of the Jewish seventh day by the Christian "first day" of the week is a thorny matter, since it seems that the transition was made only slowly. There can, however, be little doubt that the locus shifted from a memorial motif (Ex 20:8) to a day of celebration as a direct consequence of an appreciation of what Jesus did "on the first day." He was raised to new life and shared a meal with his followers as the living Lord (cf. the Gospel accounts of postresurrection appearances, and the *Gospel of the Hebrews* with its record of a dominical word to James, "My brother, eat your bread, for the Son of Man is risen from among those who sleep"). As far as the Pauline records go, there is an awareness that "the first day of the week" is the time for the Corinthian gathering (1 Cor 16:1-2), which will involve the bringing of money to the assembly. J. Héring's proposal that the first weekday was a payday at Corinth is not likely to command assent (Héring, 183). Paul more likely is investing a secular day with theological overtones as a tribute to the day as "the Lord's," just as he can commandeer the place of the agape-Lord's Supper as "the Lord's table" (1 Cor 10:21; see Rordorf, 274-75).

According to Acts 20:7-12, the believers at Troas gathered "on the first day of the week" in order to share a meal and to hear Paul speak. Evidently this was an evening-time occasion since (1) the hapless Eutychus was overcome by sleep as he sat at the window, and (2) Paul's resumed speech took him and his audience to daybreak before they dispersed. Later developments in the post-Pauline church gave a more reasoned conviction to the holy day as the start of a new age (*Barn.* 15.9; *Did.* 14.1; Rev 1:10) and placed the setting of the worship at dawn (Trajan-Pliny correspondence [*Ep.* 10.96] dates the *synaxis* "before daylight"), probably to herald the sunrise in christological terms (cf. the early Christian hymn, "Hail, gladdening light").

Yet the cameo of Acts 20:7-12 did play a more determinative role in the evolution of Christian worship, namely, it set a pattern of the twofold shape of the liturgy—the preaching and the breaking of bread, the *missa catechumenorum*, open to all, followed by the *missa fidelium*, restricted to the believers—that by the mid-second century (Justin *Apol. I* 66) became standard procedure. The dual pattern of a liturgy of the Word and a liturgy of the upper room, as it is sometimes called, goes back to its genetic origin in Acts 20 and Paul in 1 Corinthians 11—14, with one also directly traceable to the synagogue and the other taking its rise from the eucharistic tradition (1 Cor 11:23-26) Paul inherited and passed on to the Corinthians.

2. Pauline Teaching.

There is no systematized statement of what Paul understood to be a fitting worship practice, nor is there anything resembling a set of rubrics in later service books. Paul's teaching is scattered throughout his correspondence, and while there are some suggestions that he incorporated parts of a set pattern of worship (see the bold attempt of Cuming to construct a NT order of service) there is nothing definite. The one possible indication is seen in 1 Thessalonians 5:16-24, which is capable of being arranged in lines, each line purporting to be a service heading. (The arrangement, first proposed by J. M. Robinson, is set down by Martin 1975, 135-38, and since approved in part by Hill, 119-20. But see now the cautions voiced in Bradshaw, 30-55.)

In 1 Thessalonians 5:16-22 short sentences are carefully constructed. The verb stands last, and there is a predominance of words beginning with the Greek letter *p*, thus producing a rhythm. The sequence is noteworthy. First the note of glad adoration is sounded ("Rejoice always"). Prayer and thanksgiving are coupled—a linkage that derives from the synagogue. Christians are counseled to give the Spirit full rein, especially in allowing prophetic utterances to be heard (cf. *Did.* 10.7), but cautioned that they must test the spirits. Above all, nothing unseemly must enter the assembly, suggesting a control on unbridled worship practices. The closing part of this putative "church order" has a comprehensive prayer for the entire group (1 Thess 5:23) and an expression of confidence in God (1 Thess 5:24).

Parallels with 1 Corinthians 14 are suggested, with praise and "hymning" linked, and prayer and thanksgiving joined (1 Cor 14:13-18). There is the need to control prophecy and Spirit-inspired speech, especially by women prophets (1 Cor 14:34-36). And in both accounts the need for good order prevails (1 Cor 14:40).

Procedurally it is easier to set down Paul's teaching under simpler headings, namely, (1) evidence for the use of liturgical components in his churches; (2) corrective measures Paul took to deal with what he regarded as abuses and distortions; and (3) extrapolation of his theology of worship from the data thus displayed. These are not separate issues and will be treated in passing as well as in sections.

2.1. Evidence of Worship Forms and Speech. At a later stage we shall need to clarify the ways Paul took over preformed liturgical pieces and allusions to incorporate them into the epistolary flow of his writing (see 2.1.1 and 2.1.2 below). It will become clear, we hope, that he did this to establish a rapport with his readers who were not always well disposed to him, his apostleship and his theology. If he can demonstrate acquaintance with a shared creed or well-accepted hymn, he has immediately put himself on common ground, even if he found it needful to redact the tradition to underscore a point or bring it into line with his own position. Yet another possible reason for his citing of liturgical specimens is seen in the use he intended for his letters. They were his alter ego, making up for his enforced absence yet conveying the immediacy of his person to those whom distance or circumstance kept apart (see 1 Cor 5:1-12; Col 2:5). To draw on a common fund of hymn, prayer, baptismal reminder or catechesis would again make his presence vividly known to his readers who often apparently concluded he had forgotten (2 Cor; Phil) or deserted them (1 Thess).

2.1.1. Traditional Forms. One of the most obvious indices of Paul's borrowing from the liturgical treasury comes at 1 Corinthians 16:22. The strange-sounding *maranatha* would be equally as puzzling to the Corinthian Greek speaker as to the modern reader. The expression lies in the text without comment, translation or application. Its very meaning is a source of debate, either "the Lord is coming" or "our Lord, come!" are possible, with recent linguistic discussion (see Fitzmyer) tipping the scale in favor of the second rendering (as in Rev 22:20). The use of an Aramaic prayer call can only be satisfactorily explained on the assumption that it belonged to the liturgical vocabulary of an early Palestinian or bilingual setting. It became embedded in the liturgy of the *Didache* (10.6) as part of a service preparatory to the Lord's table (as it may function in the letter ending of 1 Cor 16:22-24: see Bornkamm and J. A. T. Robinson). It must surely reflect current usage at Corinth; else why would Paul deliberately confuse his readers with an unexplained term? The significance, however, is what counts. The evidence of this ancient watchword throws a flood of light on the way Jewish Christians worshiped their Lord. Here is the earliest recorded Christian prayer, ascribing to the church's Lord highest honors and giving indication of a cult centered on him. It also indicates that those who had previously invoked the name of their covenant God in the synagogue liturgy now came to apply the same divine title to Jesus the Messiah.

"Calling on the name of the Lord" was also an appellation used to describe the initiation of believers (Rom 10:12-17) and a self-designation of the church (1 Cor 1:2) as a group of men and women who prayed to the Lord (Jesus; cf. 2 Cor 12:1-10; Acts 7:55-60; 9:14; 22:16). Prayers to Jesus and in the name of Jesus were easily associated in a way we may find paradoxical, but the tension was evidently allowed to remain in Pauline circles, while strict monotheism and a worship directed to the risen Lord stood together with little attempt to correlate them (cf. Phil 2:9-11).

Triadic forms of prayer-praise-confession were also permitted to appear side by side (e.g., 2 Cor 1:20-21; 1 Cor 12:4-11; Eph 4:4-6), as the persons of the Godhead (as they later were formulated) were associated with various ministries and offices. In Ephesians 1:3-14 there is (on one reading of the text) a trinitarian format as the Father is said to choose believers, the Son of his love to redeem and the Spirit to authenticate salvation in human experience by applying the experiential seal (Eph 4:30; cf. 2 Cor 1:20-22; 5:5 in baptism?).

Specific forms of prayer and praise occur mainly in the opening sections of Paul's epistles and have been intensively studied (see Schubert; O'Brien). The consensus is that Paul used this device to state the epistolary context of what was to follow and to encourage mutual goodwill by establishing friendly relations with his readers (Gk. *philopronēsis*). Linguistic evidence in constructions like the stringing together of participles, the use of relative pronouns and the fulsome expressions (e.g., Eph 1:6, "to the praise of his glory") all seem to indicate Paul's indebtedness to a liturgical vocabulary (e.g., 2 Cor 1:3; Col 1:9-14; Eph 1:3-14; 1:15-23; on the Greek forms of blessing God, see Bradshaw, 44-45).

2.1.2. Hymns and Creeds. The habit Paul has of inserting hymnic and/or creedal pieces into the epistolary sequence of his writing is well known, and there are certain criteria that betray the presence of quoted material. Though there has recently been some resistance to this idea of Paul's taking over preformed hymnic, poetic or confessional matter (see Lash), the main conclusions already established by E. Stauffer (338-39) and O. Cullmann in their seminal discussions (and now supplemented by monographs such as Deichgräber) do not seem to be shaken. The combined data of unusual and dignified vocabulary, use of rhetorical features such as participles, relative pronouns and figures of speech, and the way in which the hypothetically inserted material can be detached from the context—all these signs point to Paul's drawing on traditional forms in order to buttress his hortatory appeal (e.g., Phil 2:6-11 in the setting of Phil 2:1-4, 12-13) and to use "the story of Christ" to serve as a paradigm for ethical action (2 Cor 8:9, again in context of generous giving and service).

The main examples are Philippians 2:6-11; Colossians 1:15-20; 1 Timothy 3:16 (most recently grouped together and studied by Fowl). Aside from the paraenetic function served by those citations, attention is focused on the insight these hymnic compositions give into a Christian cultus in the Pauline churches.

The ruling motif may be said to be the cosmological-redemptive work of Christ, the church's Lord who came from God and as God. He achieved a cosmic reconciliation by his death and exaltation, thereby uniting the disparate realms of heaven and earth (and so meeting the need evident in Greco-Roman religion, as noted earlier) and causing his triumph to be acknowledged in the underworld of demons and cosmic powers (thereby bringing all parts of the universe under his sway). The twin emphases of his preexistence with God and his role in creation, and his eschatological subjugation of all alien powers, especially the "elemental spirits" (*stoicheia tou kosmou*, Col 2:8, 20), served to assure the church that no hostile power can come between God and the world (Rom 8:38-39). The problem addressed in these hymnic/confessional tributes to the lordship of Christ (Rom 10:9-10; Phil 2:11) is that posed by Gnostic dualism, which made parts of the universe alien and hostile (*see* Gnosticism). God's rule in Christ, now established, and celebrated in song and creed, was the Christian response. Paul's unique contribution was (1) to anchor redemption and reconciliation in the deed of love at the cross, not in a cosmic fiat (Phil 2:8; Col 1:20; cf. Col 2:15) and (2) to steer the church that sang these hymns and uttered these confessions away from a false triumphalism that denied the continuing reality of evil as it telescoped the future into the present (*see* Eschatology). In its place Paul inserts the eschatological proviso of a "not-yet" factor (1 Cor 15:20-28) and maintains that hymns of triumph offered in worship must be tempered by a realistic assessment of ongoing struggle in anticipation of a future reign, now begun but not yet fully and finally achieved. The element of tension remains in Paul's soteriology, and some of the warning signs in his handling of worship problems are directed to this false emphasis, only too apparent when worship is unrestrained and too exuberant, as at Corinth (1 Cor 4:8; 12-14).

One specimen of Pauline hymnody (in Eph 5:14) is a reminder that not all worship forms were strictly theocentric and directed to the praise of God. Here the introductory words, "Therefore it is said," read as though they were added expressly to prepare for a citation of a familiar passage (otherwise unknown; not in the OT). Style, with a swinging trochaic rhythm and a rhetorical device whereby the ends of the first two lines match by assonance, prove this to be a carefully composed hymn. But it is addressed to believers, presumably newly converted and probably recently baptized, to call them to action and to promise them Christ's illumination. The idioms of awake/sleep and resurrection/death, along with light/dark indicate the setting in an initiatory rite to which these lines are the accompanying chant. They are words that would indelibly fix the meaning of baptism on the minds of the new believers.

2.1.3. Baptism. The appreciation of *baptism was evidently an important feature in the catechetical instruction offered to recent converts and adherents in the churches on a Pauline foundation. Sometimes (at Corinth) there was need to disabuse the people of wrongheaded notions regarding the practice of baptism (1 Cor 1:13-17; 10:1-17; 15:29). More prominently, Paul takes for granted the reality of what baptism entailed, and builds on it (Rom 6:1-14; Col 2:12). For Paul, baptism that is the believing, obedient individual's response to the word of the gospel

(Rom 1:16; 10:9-10) was regarded as the means of entry into the community of the new Israel, akin to the role played by circumcision in a faith context (Rom 2:27-29; 1 Cor 7:19; Col 2:11-12). So 1 Corinthians 12:13 and Galatians 3:27 are most naturally to be understood. Membership of the elect community was signified by the rite of passage involving the use of water as lustration and initiation. Paul can therefore base an ethical appeal on the reality of his readers' having been baptized (Rom 6:15; 13:14; Col 3:10; cf. Eph 4:24). Their being identified with Christ in his death and new life is reenacted in baptism and is to be played out in the call to "die daily" (2 Cor 4:11-12). At baptism there is for Paul a genuine sacramental action in which God is at work (Col 2:12). God applies to believers the saving efficacy of Christ's death and resurrection in which they died and were raised and puts them in a sphere of divine life (Gal 2:19-21) in which sin is conquered (Rom 6:7, 9-11). Henceforth, the Christian is bidden to work out the implications of what baptism means (Rom 6:12-14), just as the circumcised Israelite needed to make good his circumcision by a life of obedience within the covenant. The importance of confession at baptism (Rom 10:9-10; Eph 5:25-27) is thus given prominence. But sacramental action can be misrepresented when it is confounded with a gnosticized fiat without moral considerations. Hence the warnings Paul gives in 1 Corinthians 10.

2.1.4. Lord's Supper. Paul took over and enriched several traditions to do with a supper meal (*see* Lord's Supper), held in obedience to the Lord's intention "in the night he was handed over" to death (1 Cor 11:23). At an earlier (i.e., pre-Pauline) stage of development it looked as though the framework of the supper consisted of the following elements: a common meal based on Jewish table-fellowship custom and incorporating, we presume, the Jewish prayers for food and drink (with a Christian flavor seen in *Did.* 9-10); and, as bread and cup were taken, following the pattern of the upper room model, the Lord's presence was recalled "in remembrance of me." The simple rite pointed beyond itself to a future hope in the coming *kingdom of God. What Paul did in direct response evidently to social problems at Corinth was to enrich and apply these basic ideas with one practical consequence, namely, the separation of the love feast (of a shared meal) from a more solemn eucharistic service. The reason for this disjunction lay in the abuses prevalent at Corinth, where too much food and drink led to indulgence, and the late arrival of the poor believers meant that they would not share in the social meal (1 Cor 11:17-22). Divisions within the community had led to a breakdown in *koinōnia* and a refusal to accept one another in a Christian way (1 Cor 11:18-19, cf. 1 Cor 1:10-11; 3:3-4, 21). Paul finds the answer to this malady in a reemphasis on the "one bread" which betokens "one body" (1 Cor 10:16-17), and shows the way whereby the horizontal dimension of "fellowship in the body and blood" of the Lord sounds the death-knell to the party spirit and selfish concern for one's own interests.

The motif of "remembrance" is present in the Pauline account (1 Cor 11:24-25). He goes on to interpret this in the words "you proclaim the Lord's death." Equally, the future hope is stressed and held out in the reference "until he comes" (1 Cor 11:26). Both Pauline additions are to be understood against a Passover background (cf. 1 Cor 5:1-8) and enhance for Paul the soteriological emphasis of Christ's dying for sins (1 Cor 15:3-5; Rom 5:1-10; 2 Cor 5:18-21; Gal 3:13) to procure a redemption greater than the exodus deliverance and the eschatological reminder that the end is not yet (1 Cor 15:20-28) but will come at the Lord's parousia (1 Cor 16:22; *see* Eschatology). The latter will be a final coming and an anticipation of the ultimate reality as he visits his people at the table.

2.2. Paul's Corrective Measures. The Pauline teaching on worship includes the unusual feature that certain beliefs and practices in his churches caused him to enter a set of protests with a view to reformation and correction. His countermeasures fall into two categories.

First, certain creedal and hymnic texts were taken over and edited in the process by Paul before he saw fit to include them in his epistolary instruction. Additions such as those in Philippians 2:8, "even the death of the cross," and Colossians 1:18, "the church" to explicate the sense of "he is the head of the body," show the thrust of these revisions, namely, to enforce the centrality of the cross and to counteract any gnosticizing emphasis. In the creedal Romans 3:24-26 he evidently redacted a Jewish-Christian atonement formula to highlight the universality of faith.

Then, at Corinth Paul confronted a volatile situation in which worship had become completely disorganized and marred by features he reprobated. His concern was to (1) check undue exuberance caused by a false concept of "spirit" (1 Cor 12:1-3; *see* Holy Spirit) and a realized eschatology that denied a future eschaton on the mistaken assumption that the kingdom was here in its fullness (1 Cor 4:8; 15:20-28); and (2) to insert controls to maintain good order, to curb unrestricted glossolalia without interpretation, to elevate prophecy to a high office, and to silence the unguarded and alien utterances of women (prophets) in the assembly (for details see the commentaries and Martin 1984, chaps. 5-7).

2.3. Paul's Distinctives. The way Paul tackled the problems at Corinth was primarily to accentuate the positive elements in Christian worship. In the main he did this by introducing the three-fold criteria to test all spiritual gifts (*charismata*) that were exercised in the worshiping assembly (cf. Dunn, 293-97; Martin 1982, 194-200). They were:

(1) The firm nexus between the Jesus tradition and the Christ of experience (1 Cor 12:1-3) placed the cross at the center (1 Cor 5:6-7; 11:26) and indicated that the church lives always between the times of the two advents and in a state of unfulfilled expectation that only the parousia and final kingdom will bring to fruition. In the interim believers have the Holy Spirit to indwell and inspire them in worship (1 Cor 3:16-17; 6:19; 12:3), and he is the first fruits of the coming redemption that is promised but not yet actualized. No view of baptism that promotes the notion of an already attained resurrection can be right for Paul since it denies the futurity of resurrection hope (Phil 3:10-15).

(2) The primacy of love (Gk. *agapē*, found in Paul 75 times out of 116 NT occurrences) means that all spiritual exercises stand under the power of an energy that is God's gift in Christ (Rom 5:1-10; 2 Cor 5:14) and is to regulate and direct all the motions and demonstrations of worship into channels that are consonant with the divine character and design for his people's lives (Eph 5:1-2).

(3) The goal of worship on the horizontal plane is edification (Gk. *oikodomē*), which, for Paul, is more than a feeling of well-being or an ecstatic experience. Rather, *oikodomē* (in 1 Cor 14:3, 12, 17, 26; cf. 1 Cor 12:7) is a determined effort to promote God's will in human lives, our neighbor's no less than our own (1 Cor 8:9; 10:33; Rom 15:2 in the liturgical context of Rom

15:5-6; Phil 2:3-4 in the context set by the hymn of Phil 2:6-11). At worship, believers are actively to seek the good of the entire church and thereby to glorify God (1 Cor 10:31) and enjoy his presence, while at the same time recalling that God is really among them in holy judgment and renewing grace (1 Cor 14:25; cf. 1 Cor 5:3-5; 11:29-32; 16:22).

See also BAPTISM; LORD'S SUPPER.

DPL: BENEDICTION, BLESSING, DOXOLOGY, THANKSGIVING; HYMNS, HYMN FRAGMENTS, SONGS, SPIRITUAL SONGS; LITURGICAL ELEMENTS; PRAYER.

BIBLIOGRAPHY. G. Bornkamm, *Early Christian Experience* (London: SCM, 1969); P. F. Bradshaw, *The Search for the Origins of Christian Worship* (London: SPCK, 1992); A. Cabaniss, *Pattern in Early Christian Worship* (Macon, GA: Mercer University Press, 1989); G. J. Cuming, "The New Testament Foundation for Common Prayer," *StudLit* 10 (1974) 88-105; R. Deichgräber, *Gotteshymnus und Christushymnus in der frühen Christentum* (Göttingen: Vandenhoeck & Ruprecht, 1984); G. Delling, *Worship in the New Testament* (London: Darton, Longman & Todd, 1962); C. W. Dugmore, *The Influence of the Synagogue on the Divine Office* (London: Oxford University Press, 1944); J. D. G. Dunn, *Jesus and the Spirit* (Philadelphia: Westminster, 1975); J. A. Fitzmyer, "Kyrios and Maranatha and Their Aramaic Background," in *To Advance the Gospel* (New York: Crossroad, 1981) 218-35; S. E. Fowl, *The Story of Christ* (Sheffield: Academic Press, 1990); F. Hahn, *The Worship of the Early Church* (Philadelphia: Fortress, 1975); M. Hengel, "Hymns and Christology," in *Between Jesus and Paul* (Philadelphia: Fortress, 1983) 78-96; J. Héring, *Commentary on First Corinthians* (London: Epworth, 1962); D. Hill, *New Testament Prophecy* (Atlanta: John Knox, 1979); L. W. Hurtado, *One God, One Lord* (Philadelphia: Fortress, 1988); C. J. A. Lash, "Fashionable Sport: Hymn-Hunting in 1 Peter," *SE* 7 [TU 126] (1982) 293-97; R. P. Martin, *Carmen Christi: Philippians 2:5-11 in Recent Interpretation and in the Setting of Early Christian Worship* (SNTSMS 4; Cambridge: Cambridge University Press, 1967; Grand Rapids: Eerdmans, 1983) [= *A Hymn of Christ: Philippians 2:5-11 in Recent Interpretation and in the Setting of Early Christian Worship* (Downers Grove, IL: InterVarsity Press, 1997)]; idem, *New Testament Foundations*, vol. 2 (Grand Rapids: Eerdmans, 1978); idem, "Patterns of Worship in New Testament Churches," *JSNT* 37 (1989) 59-85; idem, *Reconciliation: A Study of Paul's Theology* (Grand Rapids: Zondervan, 1989); idem, *The Spirit and the Congregation: Studies in 1 Corinthians 12—15* (Grand Rapids: Eerdmans, 1984); idem, *Worship in the Early Church* (Grand Rapids: Eerdmans, 1975); idem, *The Worship of God* (Grand Rapids: Eerdmans, 1982); C. F. D. Moule, *Worship in the New Testament* (London: Lutterworth, 1961); G. Murray, *Five Stages of Greek Religion* (Oxford: Oxford University Press, 1925); P. T. O'Brien, *Introductory Thanksgivings in the Letters of Paul* (Leiden: E. J. Brill, 1977); J. A. T. Robinson, "The Earliest Christian Liturgical Sequence," in *Twelve New Testament Studies* (London: SCM, 1962) 154-57; J. M. Robinson, "Die Hodajot-Formel in Gebet und Hymnus des Frühchristentums," in *Apophoreta*, ed. W. Eltester (Berlin: Töpelmann, 1964) 194-235; W. Rordorf, *Sunday: The History of the Day of Rest and Worship in the Earliest Centuries of the Christian Church* (London: SCM, 1968); P. Schubert, *Form and Function of the Pauline Thanksgivings* (Berlin: Töpelmann, 1939); W. S. Smith, *Musical Aspects of the New Testament* (Amsterdam: Kok, 1962); E. Stauffer, *New Testament Theology* (New York: Macmillan, 1956).

R. P. Martin

WORSHIP III: ACTS, HEBREWS, GENERAL EPISTLES, REVELATION

What could be said of worship as it may be understood from the evidence of the Pauline literature (*see* Worship II) is equally valid in reference to the non-Pauline literature. That is, based on the traditions of belief and praxis inherited from Judaism, Christian understanding and praise of God expressed itself in acknowledging him as Creator and Redeemer. God is still hailed as the sovereign Lord whose fiat brought the world into existence (Heb 11:3; Rev 4:11) through the mediation of the cosmic *Christ (Heb 1:2; Jn 1:3) and by whose will the creation is sustained (Rev 4:11; cf. Col 1:15-18). The same God has acted savingly in the coming of Christ to rescue and restore the lost creation. Revelation 5:9-14 expresses this jubilation in lyric form, while the cosmic backdrop of the new age Christ has inaugurated is seen in Ignatius's "song of the star" (Ign. *Eph.* 19.1-3; on this text as a Christ-hymn see Lohmeyer, 64; with further comment in Martin 1997, 10-13). In a crisp, creedal formulary, the incarnational-redemptive tag is given in 1 Peter 1:20 in a context of Christ's sacrifice (1 Pet 1:18-19) and victory (1 Pet 3:21-22). Praise is thus directed to Israel's God, known as the Father of Jesus Christ (1 Pet 1:3) and the Father of those whose trust is in him (1 Pet 1:17; Heb 2:10-13; 1 Jn 1:3; 2:1, 13; 3:1) and who are part of the new creation that celebrates his grace (Jas 1:18) in hymns and in worship speech and acts (Rev 1:12-18; 19:10; 22:8-9; for such texts that forbid worship when angelomorphic beings were regarded as rivals to the one God, see Stuckenbruch). This article will survey the evidence from these and other NT texts, as well as from post-apostolic writings, for patterns of early Christian worship, viewed geographically, from the NT era to the middle of the second century.

1. Encouragements and Cautions
2. Method and Approaches
3. The Pauline Legacy
4. Evidence from Syria-Palestine
5. The Rome-Asia Minor Axis
6. Johannine Patterns and Their Influence
7. Some Conclusions

1. Encouragements and Cautions.

Just as scholars, by applying form-critical methods to the Pauline letters, have identified several passages as liturgical, so by means of these same techniques parts of 1 Peter, Hebrews, James and Revelation have been treated as embodying worship forms and fragments. Indeed, theories that have tried to understand whole NT books as emanating from a liturgical setting and incorporating rudimentary service directives have been proposed. This has tended to bring the entire approach into disrepute, with accusations of "pan-liturgism," that is, the misplaced confidence of being able to "detect reverberations of liturgy in the New Testament even where no liturgical note was originally struck" (Moule 1961, 7; cf. Dunn 1990, §36). One notable example will illustrate the danger. Reasoning back from the Passover celebration that may underlie Hippolytus's order in the *Apostolic Tradition* (c. A.D. 215, at Rome), M. H. Shepherd (1960) proposed that the parallel structure he perceived in Revelation contained the framework of a fully developed baptismal liturgy, made up of interrogations; preparatory fastings, leading to the initiation itself; lessons from the Law, the Prophets and Gospel, with psalmody and a baptismal eucharist. Aside from the debated issue of whether all these elements of worship are seen in Hippolytus, it raises much skepticism to think that the

entire Apocalypse is a virtual transcript of a paschal initiation rite, composed as a running commentary on what was happening liturgically. Much the same can be said for F. L. Cross's equally imaginative reconstruction of the scenario behind 1 Peter as a baptismal liturgy.

To remain unconvinced by these somewhat outlandish proposals, which have not withstood critical scrutiny, however, does not cast doubt on the more reasoned bids to discover snatches of hymnic and confessional forms, baptismal images and reminders, eucharistic prayers and catechetical instructions in several places of the NT corpus. Alert to the dangers of seeing liturgical data everywhere, we are not precluded from investigating the literary, stylistic and contextual shape of the passages under review with a view to placing them in a suitable *Sitz im Leben* of the churches' worshiping life and practice, if that placement throws light on their origin and gives an extra dimension to their point.

Two other considerations, moreover, pose a warning as we seek to deduce what worship was like in the congregations reflected in our texts. One is the temptation to harmonize. In the case of the Pauline materials, the task of constructing a picture of the worshiping life of his communities was not hampered by an impossible diversity. Churches on the Pauline foundation, while different in cultural background and outlook and facing several problems, were at least kept together by their common allegiance to Paul and his colleagues and belonged together as a corpus within a manageable time frame. The biblical books under review in this article have no such unifying thread and represent a wide spectrum of diverse cultures, interests, compositions and challenges, to say nothing of the multiform nature of the literature in its genre (Acts, epistles, apocalypse) we are seeking to encompass. Given these inconcinnities, to collate the worship styles and practices with their meanings across such a wide terrain into an intelligible picture is almost an impossible venture. And to seek to harmonize the different features and findings so as to yield a common pattern is to run the risk of a false harmonization that will only distort the evidence and give a wrong impression. When we attempt a summing up, this caveat will need to be borne in mind and a question mark will need to be reasserted against those attempts to find in too detailed a way a basic liturgical unity within the late apostolic period (see Cullmann, 7-36; Bradshaw 1992, 37).

The other pitfall is that mentioned in P. F. Bradshaw's handbook, *The Search for the Origins of Christian Worship,* which by its title confesses to the tentative nature of any reconstructions of early worship and the danger of reading back from the later liturgies the evidence that all too easily we profess to find in the earlier NT documents. This method was the outstanding feature of H. Lietzmann's celebrated monograph, *Mass and Lord's Supper* (ET 1953, 1978), which sought to work backward from the service books and later manuals to the more fragmentary and disputed data. As a technique this may be defended, but it exposes the readers to a false impression that Christian worship developed in a linear fashion and that we can trace the lines of development with unbounded confidence.

2. Method and Approaches.

The merit, however, of Lietzmann's approach was that it gave due respect to the origins of worship patterns in the differing geographic areas from which such service books came, using a technique that W. Bauer also employed in the same period as Lietzmann's work appeared (Bauer in 1934; Lietzmann's *Messe und Herrenmahl* in 1926). While the Bauer-Lietzmann approach is open to criticism in several of its aspects (see Turner, T. A. Robinson), there is less criticism when a similar appreciation of geographic spread is seen to underlie B. H. Streeter's works. There is no denying that early Christianity expanded across key areas of the ancient world from the Syrian Levant to centers and hinterlands of the Greco-Roman provinces, including Rome.

Equally it is true that the configurations of Christian life and worship, along with the more important aspects of belief and praxis, changed according to the places that spawned the literature emanating from such regions. Granted that in several cases the tie-in between location and literature is problematic, and we have to rest content with informed guesswork and sometimes speculation, yet it is undeniable that the pluriformity of expression of teaching and expected lifestyle represented in the documents of the later NT and its developments into the so-called apostolic fathers is an attested reality. It provides a suitable framework for the evolution of worship styles and practices. The close connectedness of belief and worship, incidentally, is

now an obvious datum on the principle *lex orandi, lex credendi* (how a person prays is an expression of that person's beliefs). The data will amply illustrate this linkage as we proceed to pass the evidence under review according to hypothetical geographic stemma, or lineages.

The functionality of this approach will, we hope, be clear, and its serviceability seen in that it obviates the more simplistic way of treating the NT books one by one and/or in canonical sequence. An alternative approach might have been to follow the lead of H. Koester and J. M. Robinson with their proposed trajectories or lines of development as we pass each aspect of worship practices under review and observe, for example, how baptism was understood from its chronological beginnings in the post-Pentecost church(es) to the second-century congregations of Ignatius, Justin and the Marcionite conventicles. This method might well have served the readers' interests, were it not for the possible misleading impression it would give that early liturgical observances developed in a system of end-on evolution. The truth rather is that often the local conditions that emerged in distinct and distinctive regions provided pressure points that shaped the growth or malformation of worship no less than the rise of "heresy and orthodoxy." This was the case until what emerged as "normative Christianity" (to use Hultgren's nomenclature) began to be dominant and was seen to be so in light of the embryonic creedal statements embodied in the traditions and the *regula fidei* from the mid-second or late-second century onward. In each case the items cherished as normative took shape within the setting of the cultural climate of the place on the map as well as under the constraints of local problems and their solutions.

3. The Pauline Legacy.

The contributions to the topic that stemmed from Paul's correspondence with his congregations have been noted elsewhere (*see* Worship II). In summary, these distinctives were related to the need to regulate the use of spiritual gifts in a situation such as Corinth that had become chaotic and unbridled. Paul's response is given in terms of a practical reiteration of the tension between the already and the not-yet elements in Christian salvation. Believers are now in God's realm where Christ's lordship is acknowledged in worship (1 Cor 12:3). Yet the fullness of their redemption is set in the future, at the parousia, when God's final kingdom will be established (1 Cor 15:28). The worship cry "God is really here" (1 Cor 14:25) needs to be heard in this context, uniting the reality of present salvation and its necessary futurity at the end time, which will usher in the *resurrection of the dead (1 Cor 15:42). In the interim of the church's life "between the times," the emphases Paul makes are in terms of an exercise of love and thankfulness for God's acts in Christ and the altruistic call to build up the body of believers (1 Cor 14:3, 12, 17, 26; 1 Cor 12:7).

These same emphases, boldly remarked in his Corinthian correspondence (*see* Corinthians, Letters to the), come over into Paul's later writings, whether treated as his final reflections from a Roman prison near the end of his days or as the legacy he bequeathed to his followers who published letters to churches that claimed to be on a Pauline foundation, at Colossae, Ephesus and its environs (*see* Colossians, Letter to the; Ephesians, Letter to the). As might well be expected, there are fresh emphases since new situations have emerged. In particular the need to consolidate the *church, now dubbed "the pillar and bulwark of the truth" (1 Tim 3:15), is evident in the face of new doctrines, and its witness needs to be safeguarded against false teachers who deny the future resurrection. So in baptismal confessions (2 Tim 2:11-13; Tit 3:4-7), sometimes prefaced by the formula of a "trusted word," and in christological hymns (e.g., 1 Tim 3:16, introduced by "we confess") the Pauline gospel is reasserted as deserving of all acceptance (1 Tim 1:15). This is accompanied by the cardinal teachings of one God and one mediator (1 Tim 2:5-7), known to be Paul's strong conviction. Jewish-Christian prayer language is scattered through these letters (e.g., 1 Tim 1:17), partly to demonstrate the church's close ties with its roots and partly to restate the Jewish belief in the goodness of God's creation, which is hallowed by prayer based on Psalm 24:1 (1 Tim 4:4-5).

The baptismal teachings in Colossians-Ephesians have given rise to debate, chiefly on the issue of whether they mark a divergence from Paul's careful distinction as we saw between what is true now (we are being saved) and the future hope (we shall be saved—in hope of the parousia, Rom 5:9-10; 6:1-14). Colossians emphasizes the present possession of *salvation (Col 1:12-14) and reconciliation (Col 1:21-22),

with the hymn of Colossians 1:15-20 inserted to celebrate the completeness of the universe's restoration to harmony with the Creator's will and the pacification of the evil powers (Col 2:15). Believers have entered into the benefit of Christ's cosmic triumph at baptism (Col 2:12-13) with no explicit eschatological proviso of what still awaits completion at the parousia. But the eschatological hope, while it is muted, sounds in Colossians 3:3, so it may be fairly claimed that Colossians reflects the true Pauline tradition at this point.

Less confidence is engendered, however, in the case of Ephesians. Here the implied baptismal setting of Ephesians 1:13-14, where "the seal of the Spirit" became a shorthand expression for a person's baptism (Lampe), though it does look on to the future possession of salvation, seems rather to situate the church's hope in the present (Eph 2:1-10; 5:14) and to reflect a fading of an imminent parousia. The church is already raised to the heavenly places (Eph 2:6) where the regnant Christ has begun his rule (Eph 1:22-23, a creedal fragment, it is believed). This noble prose poem celebrates Christ's lordship in exalted, hieratic terms drawn from the worship idioms of the Asian churches. Such an eclipse of the apocalyptic denouement, associated with Christ's return from heaven, may well be explained by the unique occasion of Ephesians, if its purpose is more doxological than edificatory or polemical. The nuances of liturgical language have given rise to the idea of the church as already triumphant and transcendent in its heavenly glory now and indeed as taking its place within the creedal confession (Eph 4:4-5), as though the church professes belief in itself—a forerunner of the sentence in the Apostles' Creed ("I believe in . . . one, holy, catholic, apostolic church")—and has its place in salvation history securely grounded on a true apostolic base (Eph 2:20; 3:5).

4. Evidence from Syria-Palestine.

4.1. Jerusalem. It is not easy to separate out from the data and descriptions in the book of Acts what is objective historical reporting of church life and practice in the holy city and the holy land, with extensions to the Syrian province from Damascus to Antioch (Acts 8:1; 9:19; 11:19-29; 13:1-3), and what is Luke's conscious bid to idealize the scenes in the interests of his own theological viewpoints. Perhaps the truth lies in a mediating position. Assuming that the writing of Luke is meant to have an edificatory purpose (so Haenchen, 103-10; Marshall, 33), it would be natural to suppose that the author recalls the early days of the church not in a nostalgic vein but in order to point out certain lessons for the church of his day. He tells the story, based on reliable eyewitness testimony, he believed (Lk 1:1-4; Acts 1:1), of how it was in the beginning when the Spirit first came on God's new *creation. He raises the cry *ad fontes:* back to the fountainhead of the church's early moments, yet he does so with a view to recapturing the past as he retells it so as to make it speak to his present. Luke's successive pictures of the church at worship are arranged to drive home a single point—that worship in his church needs to recover the emphases and features that marked the first generation, with the Holy Spirit's power in evidence (Acts 4:31; 13:1-3), giving rise to great freedom and joy (Acts 2:46, 47) and fidelity to apostolic norms (Acts 2:42).

Initiation into the community life is by baptism—based on ritual baths in distinctive Judaisms, both mainline and sectarian (Qumran, Therapeutae)—in the name of Jesus (Acts 2:38). This was a practice that spread with the expansion of the message to embrace disciples in Samaria (Acts 8:12), in Caesarea (Acts 10:47-48), in Damascus (Acts 9:18 and par.) as well as more remote, unspecified regions like the Gaza strip (Acts 8:36; Acts 8:37 mg. in the Western reading offers a fuller account of the baptismal interrogation and response). Initiation "in the name" of Jesus (Christ) was evidently meant to confess his messianic headship of the new community and the place individuals had in this messianic group as a mark of the new age he brought. Little further theologizing of baptism is found, though Acts 19:1-7 poses the problems associated with groups that had known only John's baptism. If Acts 10 (baptism and receiving the Spirit in the home of Cornelius) is meant to imply a Gentile Pentecost (cf. Lampe, chap. 5; Dunn 1970, 80-82; 1975, 154-56), then the baptism of John's disciples accompanied by the imposition of hands and gifts of tongues and prophecy may well have indicated to Luke's readers how "disciples" become full-blown believers in Jesus as Lord.

On face value the record in Acts gives cameo pictures of the worshiping/communal life in Jerusalem (notably at Acts 2:41-47; 4:32-35) as ideal scenes, meant to challenge and rebuke later loss of "apostolic simplicity." Features that marked out the earliest community fresh from its Pentecostal experience and radiating the Spirit's joy (Acts 2:26 based on Ps 16:8-11; cf. Acts 2:46) include above all the theme of exultant praise, whether the locale is the temple (Acts 3:1-10) or private residences (Acts 1:3; 2:46; 9:11, 36-43; 10:1-8, 24; 12:12). Prayers were offered for guidance (Acts 1:23-25) and for courage in the face of threats and dangers (Acts 4:23-31), though the reference to "the prayers" (Acts 2:42) suggests a continued adherence to the Jewish temple liturgy (Dugmore).

The "apostles' teaching" has been customarily regarded as a sign of early catechetical instruction, while "fellowship" indicates either a generalized reference to common life or, more specifically, to the material contributions expected, but not demanded, of each member (Acts 4:32; 5:1-11, Jeremias once believed Acts 2:42 referred to the offering as *koinōnia* but changed his mind; see Cullmann, 120). The "breaking of bread" is a Jewish expression for a meal, presumably a communal social event in which food was shared and eaten as a sign of mutual love (hence the name *agapē*, see Jude 12 where intruding teachers have "defiled" such convivial gatherings; and 2 Pet 2:13, if *agapais* is read in place of *apatais;* see Bauckham 1983; Ign. *Smyrn.* 8.2, *Acts of Paul and Thecla* 5, 25 shows how the practice persisted into later decades). If *Didache* 9-10 gives the text of prayers at the love-meal (see 4.2 below), how such meal occasions were understood may be revealed, and the way the agape functioned as a prelude to the later solemn eucharist of the Lord's sacrifice (*Did.* 14.1) is evident, perhaps explaining the link in 1 Corinthians 11:17-22 as a preparatory rite of sharing, paving the way for the solemn Pauline meal in 1 Corinthians 11:23-26.

Special mention should be made of the invocatory prayer, *maranatha* (found untranslated in its Aramaic form in 1 Cor 16:22; *Did.* 10.6). It may be claimed that here we have the oldest surviving prayer specimen, with one possible exception: an inscription on an ossuary found in Jerusalem with the wording "Jesus (let the one who rests here) arise," thereby invoking Jesus as Lord of resurrection (so B. Gustafsson, *NTS* 3 [1956-57] 65-69, but this interpretation of the graffito is contested; see J. P. Kane, *PEQ* 1971, 103-8). *Maranatha* is a composite word, almost certainly to be divided as *māranāʾ tāʾ* (Fitzmyer) and meaning "Our Lord, come," expressing a prayer call for the Lord (i.e., Jesus) to be present either at the eucharist (Cullmann) or the eschaton. The evidence at this point is finely balanced; *Didache* 10.6 is part of a meal liturgy while Revelation 22:20 ("even so, come, Lord Jesus") looks to be a variant of *maranatha* and is eschatological. The setting is perhaps not exclusively one or the other; what counts is the existence of a cultus, however rudimentary, where the risen Christ is invoked in prayer as a forerunner of later, more developed invocations and hymns.

If we are safe in including as representative of early Jewish Christianity the letters of James and Jude, the picture may be enlarged. Jude's epistle is notable for its fulsome liturgical ending (Jude 24, 25). This feature provides a window into how Christian praying matched human need in one of the earliest NT letters emanating from Palestinian Christianity (Bauckham). The idioms in these two prayer verses correspond exactly to the felt need of the com-munity, exposed as it was to dangers from antinomian intruders (Jude 4) and the threat of apostasy from a common faith (Jude 3, 22; Martin and Chester, 80-81). Links with Davidic heritage represented by the holy family (Jude 1) and the catechetical apostolic traditions (Jude 17) show affinity with the situation mirrored in the *Didache*. The teaching office of prophets and leaders is the bulwark against some influences boasting of ecstatic experiences and a trust in immediate spiritual inspiration (Jude 8; Martin and Chester, 83-84).

James's letter may well embody early Judaic traditions (Davids) that go back to Palestinian communities. Such traditions and teachings may conceivably have been carried to Antioch in Syria, where an editor fashioned them into our existing letter with its excellent Greek and literary flourishes. Liturgical practices may reflect this dual setting and include a heavy emphasis on prayer in faith (Jas 1:6), especially for an individual's healing by elders at prayer (Jas 5:13-16), once confession and forgiveness are realized and oil applied (on the possible significance of the use of oil here, see Martin 1993, 124-26). The church has an honored teaching office (Jas 3:1-12) with possible suggestions of ecstatic speech as causing problems (Martin 1988, 103, 123-24). The "excellent name" (Jas 2:7) is one invoked in baptism; and it is proposed that James 2:2, 3

conceals the presence of a church/synagogue "doorkeeper," known in the later church as *ostiarius* (Cabaniss 1954, 29).

4.2. Antioch-Syria. The material associated with the northern part of Syro-Palestine is more plentiful—if we are permitted to base our conjecture of appropriate documents from this region on some recent findings, then the NT books will include the redacted version of James and Matthew's Gospel, to which we may add *Didache* and Ignatius's letters. In listing these Christian writings it is interesting that the first three are joined by at least one shared feature: they depend on and draw from the oracles/teachings of the Lord that modern research has identified as "source strand" in the Synoptic Gospels, namely, Q. Antioch has been identified since Streeter's time as the most likely place where this collection of the Lord's sayings was assembled and used. The three main documents do not belong to the same literary category. Matthew shares the genre "gospel" (Mt 1:1). The *Didache* is a church order-cum-"manual of discipline" incorporating earlier and common traditions known as the "Two Ways" (*Did.* 1-6; *Barn.* 18-20). James is usually classified as paraenetic miscellany (Dibelius, 3), but it has been editorially completed to conform to the rhetorical genre of "epistle" with a superscription (Jas 1:1) and letter-close (Jas 5:12-20). Yet all three documents do possess common elements (cf. Shepherd 1956) and each, along with the logia source (Q; see Hartin), may be justifiably located in congregations in the same geographic region, namely, around Antioch on the Orontes.

For our purposes we may note the following items in the worship life of these communities. (1) Much is made of the role of the teacher, who is to be honored (Mt 13:52; *Did.* 4.1-4; 13.2; 15.2; Jas 3), with due caution that no one should aspire to the office too hastily (Mt 23:1-12; Jas 3:1). (2) Baptism is administered in the triune name as a distinct development from initiation in the name of the (Lord) Jesus found in Acts (see Mt 28:18-20; *Did.* 7.1-3; Jas 2:7 may allude to baptism in referring to the "worthy name" called over messianic believers). (3) Prayers couched in language and idioms directly indebted to Jewish synagogue worship (Mt 6:7-13, which incorporates the prayer "Our Father"; see Charlesworth), were given in its Matthean form in *Didache* 8.2-3 with instructions to pray thus thrice daily. In James 1:13-16 the use of prayer is treated as a pastoral issue. All documents emphasize the role of corporate praying based on God's role as heavenly parent (Mt 5:16; 6:9; 16:17; *Did.* 9.1; 10.1; Jas 1:17, 27; 5:13-18), with special stress laid on the need for mutual forgiveness and confession leading to reconciliation and absolution (Mt 5:21-26; 6:12, 14-15; 18:21-22, 35; *Did.* 1.4; 2.7; 4.3-4; 14.1-3; Jas 2:8; 4:11; 5:16, 19-20). Fasting is a token of true worship, along with almsgiving (Mt 6:1-4, 16-18; *Did.* 1.5-6; 4.5-8; 7.4; 8.1-3; 13.3-7; Jas 1:27; 2:15, 16 on giving to the needy). (4) Confession of belief in the one God (a hallmark of Jewish Christianity derived from the *Shema* of Judaism, Deut 6:4) runs through these documents (Mt 19:17; 22:37; 23:9; *Did.* 6.3 against idolatry; Jas 2:19).

(5) Special attention is drawn to the observance of the eucharistic service based on the Last Supper words in Matthew 26:26-29 (*see* Lord's Supper). In the main, these dominical statements conform to the Markan wording, with the important exceptions that the cup word is enlarged to connect the "blood of the covenant" represented in the cup with the forgiveness of sins ("which is poured out for many for the forgiveness of sins"). It has been surmised that for theological reasons, since remission of sins was evidently a live issue in the Matthean community, the Evangelist has transferred the promise of forgiveness from the Markan version of John the Baptist's role (Mk 1:4; cf. however, Mt 3:4-6) to his version of the Last Supper. He did so in order to relate forgiveness more intimately with the impending death of the Lord (*see* Death of Christ). The sacrificial motifs expressed in Matthew's upper-room account links with *Didache* 14.1-3, which is best taken to refer to the church's Sunday eucharist in contradistinction to the teaching expressed in the prayers of *Didache* 9-10, which are more suitably explained in reference to an agape meal. They contain no allusion to the Lord's death (unless "broken bread," *klasma,* makes this connection, but it is more likely drawn from the non-eucharistic setting of Jn 6) and are patterned on the Jewish table prayers (*birkath hammazon;* for these examples of grace after meals see Jasper and Cuming, 9-10) in spite of the occasion being titled as *eucharistia* in *Didache* 9.5. A convincing datum is in *Didache* 10.1 ("But after you are filled [with food]"), which suggests that the meals in view in *Didache* 9-10 are taken to satisfy natural hunger, not to serve as sacramental reminders.

The issue, however, is still unresolved (see Srawley, 18-25; Bradshaw 1992, 132-37, for a conspectus of opinion). The safest conclusions are that both canonical Gospel and the *Didache* are tentative data for the deep roots of the liturgy in Jewish covenantal theology, and the patterns of table fellowship and solemn celebration have some intimate connection with the synagogue service and the table graces of the Jewish tradition, into which the Matthean Jesus has injected overtones of his atoning sacrifice. *Didache* 14 only faintly echoes this in its allusion to sacrifice/offering, which is drawn from Malachi 1:11, 14.

(6) Set in the dialogical form of the prayers in *Didache* 10.6 is the versicle/response:

Let grace come, and let this world pass away
Hosanna to the God of David.
If any one is holy, let that person come!
If any is not, let such repent.
Marana tha [our Lord, come!]
Amen.

The framework suggests a call to self-scrutinizing (already the table is "fenced" in *Did.* 9.5, citing Mt 7:6) before the congregational meal is taken, akin to the rubrics implied by Paul in 1 Corinthians 11:27-34; 16:22, 23 (see Bornkamm 1969; J. A. T. Robinson). What comes through in this dialogue is the immediacy of judgment/invitation and welcome stemming from the presence of the Lord with his people. He comes to meet them and greet the penitent with offers of his grace now as a prelude to his coming at the last day (*Did.* 16.7, 8, noting Mt 24:30), an eschatological note sounded in Matthew 26:29 and frequent in James 5:7-11. Yet it is the awareness of the living Lord in the midst of his own that shows how these Syrian Christians have grasped the genius of early worship as an encounter with the risen Christ who comes to meet those gathered in his name (Mt 18:20; 28:20; a variant is seen in *Gos. Thom.* 30, cf. 77) as their call to him is "Hosanna," that is, "Save now!" "Blessed is he who comes in the Lord's name. Hosanna in the highest!" (Mt 21:9).

Ignatius of Antioch picks up this last-mentioned realization exactly in his dictum: "Wherever Jesus Christ is, there is the universal church" (Ign. *Smyrn.* 8.2), as if to emphasize the unrestrictedness of the risen Lord who comes to join his people as they sing their hymns through Christ to the Father (Ign. *Eph.* 4.2) and recognize that he is dwelling in them (Ign. *Eph.* 15.3) as members of God's Son (Ign. *Eph.* 4.2). The earlier description (Ign. *Eph.* 4) offers the attractive picture of a Christian assembly in which "by your concord and harmonious love Jesus Christ is sung," with its suggestion that Christ is not only the mediator but also the object of hymnic praise (so Kroll, 19; Bauer 1924, 204). Granted that Ignatius is using the features of the liturgy—notably unison, harmony, the right key as in music (*eine Tonart,* so Dölger, 127)—to drive home the need for church unanimity and a closing of ranks behind and in submission to the ecclesiastical leaders (Ign. *Eph.* 5.3), it still affords some confirmation of the centrality of Christ in his depictions of worship.

Specimens of Ignatian hymnody are seen in *Ephesians* 7.2 (Kroll, 20, points to the Semitic coloring, the elevated style, the antithetical sentences and their interrelatedness to suggest a snatch of creedal-hymnic material; cf. Norden, 256-57). Thus we read:

[there is] One physician,
who is both flesh and spirit,
born and yet not born.
God in man, true life in death,
both from Mary and from God,
first, subject to suffering,
then, impassible,
Jesus Christ our Lord.
(Ign. *Eph.* 7.2)

This antithetical pattern occurs also in Melito's homily and is amplified in Ignatius's *Letter to the Ephesians* 19, expounding the "silence" of *Ephesians* 15.2, in which three mysteries were accomplished: the virginity of Mary, her giving birth and the Lord's death. He was revealed to the "Aeons" (Bultmann, 1:177) and in the appearance of his natal star, which illumined the heavens with indescribable brightness and attracted the veneration of the constellations, including the sun and the moon, the new age was born. "When God appeared in human form to bring the newness of eternal life," all the cosmos was affected, with the ancient (demonic) astral powers overthrown and death itself defeated.

This celebration of Christ's victory and reign was evidently meant to be sung in veneration as the planetary powers too join in a chorus (Ign. *Eph.* 19.2), once we link the text with Ignatius's *Letter to the Romans* 2.2: "You form a chorus of love in singing to the Father in Christ Jesus."

A similar confession-like tribute to Christ is offered as part of Ignatius's antidocetic polemic (e.g., in Ign. *Trall.* 9.1-2; cf. Ign. *Smyrn.* 1.1-3.3), which again may be cast in verse form (by Norden, 266). This christological text rehearses the movements of Christ's birth, earthly career, condemnation "under Pontius Pilate" (pointing to the Apostles' Creed), death on the cross (attested by all the powers, heavenly and demonic, Phil 2:10 in Paul providing the exact wording) and resurrection. All these events are connected by the adverb *truly* and, as a result, lay the foundation for "true" life in the church's resurrection.

Ignatius's recourse to creedal and hymnic forms obviously have a polemical thrust, yet they do throw light on how he conceived of congregational worship in the centers to which he wrote. His great fear was that of the churches' becoming fragmented and being dissipated by schism. Hence his call is to rally round the bishop and his officers (Ign. *Phil.* 3.1-3), which leads him to lift up the central role of the eucharist as the church's focal point, with the *episkopos* as the indispensable ministrant (Ign. *Smyrn.* 8.1-2; *Pol.* 6.1-2). Moreover, the eucharist for Ignatius now takes on a quasi-magical significance, seen most starkly in *Ephesians* 20.3, which calls it "the medicine of immortality, the antidote that we should not die, but live forever in Jesus Christ." Again, it is possible the constraints of false teaching which in turn led to rebellion against "the bishop and the presbytery" drove Ignatius to this strongly worded eucharistic teaching, since the sentence is introduced by the renewed call to unity based on "breaking one loaf" (cf. 1 Cor 10:17 in Paul).

When Ignatius writes of worship practices, mainly of baptism, confession, creedal formulas and the eucharist, it is difficult to know whether he is describing traditions current at Antioch where he was bishop or the various centers through which he passed or to which he was headed. We may assume some common cultic practices since he makes these allusions the basis of his appeal, all set in a trinitarian frame (Ign. *Magn.* 13.1), typifying the threefold clerical ministry (bishop, elder, deacon).

5. The Rome-Asia Minor Axis.

Interestingly the parameters of this section are set by two scenes that represent an early cameo of worship in Asia Minor (Acts 20:7-12) and nearly a century later a more detailed description of how worship was understood in Rome about A.D. 150 (Justin *Apol. I* 67). While these two accounts are separated in time and by background, what is significant is the common elements they share: (1) The time is "the first day of the week," later to be known as "the day called Sunday" (Justin *Dial. Tryph.* 41.4; 138.1). *Barnabas* 15.3-9 gives the theological reasoning behind this shift from sabbath to the day following, "the eighth day," when Jesus rose and was made manifest and ascended to heaven, thereby claiming the day of celebration as his own (Rev 1:10; *Did.* 14.1; *Gos. Pet.* 12.50) as the risen Lord who greeted his people at a Sunday eucharistic meal, in accordance with the Gospel evidence (Jn 20:19; Lk 24:30, 41-43; cf. Acts 1:3-4; Rordorf 1992; McKay).

(2) The nature of the assembled company is understood as a "gathering" (*synēgmenōn* in Acts 20:7, a verbal form from which "synagogue" is derived; cf. Jas 2:2; Heb 10:25 for this verb/noun) as people come together, with the emphasis falling more on their associating than on a consecrated building or space. At this time Christians met in house congregations. Special structures are to be dated from the third/fourth centuries, with the earliest, best-attested example at Dura-Europos in Syria, about A.D. 256 (Hopkins). Yet the format and ethos of synagogue worship (see Morris, with a more cautious approach in McKay) carried over into the Christian synaxis (a technical term for such a gathering, as the word implied).

(3) The setting in Acts 20 suggests a two-part arrangement of public speaking (by Paul) and a meal (Acts 20:11) with some more discourse to follow. This interrelation of sermon and sacrament provided the basis for the later development of the liturgy of the Word followed by the liturgy of the upper room. One of the clearest illustrations of this dual rhythm is in fact provided in Justin, who proceeds in his description: "The memoirs of the apostles or the writings of the prophets are read. . . . When the reader has finished, the president in a discourse urges and invites [us] to imitate these noble things. . . . And, as we said before [Justin *Apol. I* 65 refers to the presenting of bread and a cup of water-and-wine, over which prayers of thanks are offered, regarded as consecrated, and then shared and distributed to those absent], when we have finished the prayer, bread is brought, and wine and water," followed by prayers and the offering. Justin sums up: "We all hold this common gathering on Sunday."

The stark simplicity of these details captures some of the basic ingredients of worship in the period about A.D. 50-150, with suitable variations that are distinctive to each part of the Rome-Asia Minor axis.

For what developed in Asia we need to turn to the Johannine writings. Yet the witness in the cognate epistles, Colossians-Ephesians in the Pauline corpus, must find a place in any appreciation of how worship was practiced in the churches of Paul's foundation. Colossians 3:16-17 (par. Eph 5:19-20) provides evidence of congregational assemblies who met to admonish one another in instruction ("in all wisdom"; cf. 1 Cor 12:8 for "utterances of wisdom" as a spiritual charism) and to sing hymns (evidently christological compositions) along with psalms (perhaps drawn from the Hebrew psalter or Jewish-Christian canticles) and "songs of the Spirit" (cf. *Odes Sol.* 14.7). All such tributes were intended to express thanks to God, and so formed part of the genre *hodayah/eucharistia*, which Bradshaw (1982, 30-37; 1992, 44) maintains with some cogency, was more characteristic than the *berakah/eulogia* type in early Christianity. Expressions of praise occur in Colossians 1:3, 12-14 with the longer, more stately and measured version in Ephesians 1:3-14, which rehearses the ground plan of salvation history in a trinitarian frame (Martin 1992, 13-15). Indeed the first three chapters of Ephesians have been viewed as based on a transcript of praise familiar in the Asian congregations and as celebrating the characteristic themes of the success of the Pauline gospel in repelling challenges to it (cf. 1 Tim 1:15) and the pivotal role of the apostle as its chief exponent.

Hymnic specimens are clearly to be seen in these letters. Colossians 1:15-20 has evidently been subject to authorial redaction, and it is just possible (if not likely) that it incorporates a pre-Christian version in praise of Gnostic redemption (Käsemann 1964: see critique in the commentaries). As it stands, it announces the universal reconciliation that rests on Christ's redemptive work (Col 1:20) and includes his authority as head of the ecclesial body (Col 1:18). Both these themes are important in the polemical use made of them, as seen in Ephesians 2:11-22 (incorporating, it may be, a pre-Pauline version) and in the teaching of true headship as Christ's role as heavenly bridegroom is unpacked (Eph 5:32). Moreover, Ephesians 5:14

contains one of the clearest evidences of baptismal hymnody in the Asian churches, with its swinging, trochaic rhythm and its motifs of paraenesis and application sounded in the wake-up call to move forward in Christ's light that first shone on the baptismal candidate, who is cleansed in water (Eph 5:26).

Clearly in these twin epistles we are in touch with the vibrant worshiping life that pulsated through these communities as the author(s) faced threats to Paul's apostolate and authority in Asia. The use of liturgical idioms (such as "to the praise of his glory," Eph 1:6, 12, 14), baptismal recall (in Col 1:12-14; 2:11-14; Eph 5:26) and eucharistic language (*eucharisteō*, "to thank," is a frequent idea in Ephesians), along with creedal expressions (e.g., Eph 4:4-6) and samples of prayer speech, all give indications of the letters as steeped in a liturgical atmosphere. They were meant to be read out in congregational assembly (Col 4:16) and passed on to neighboring churches, evidently at worship gatherings when their pastoral and didactic appeal would be most effective in catching the mood of praise and exultation (especially Ephesians, as in Paul's opening benedictions generally; see O'Brien) and bidding the hearers to participate in and thereby to accept the truth claims they make.

Ignatius, also reflecting the life setting of the Asian churches, followed in this tradition of letter-writing habits. As we observed, many of his allusions to music, creed and adherence to the teachings are cited to repel what he regarded as error and seem to have the scenario of the churches at worship in view. Indeed, H. Schlier (48-49) regards Ignatius's *Letter to the Ephesians* 4 as showing his acquaintance with Paul's representation of the church's gathering for worship in canonical Ephesians 5:15-21.

It could also be submitted that the ordering of church life in the Pastoral Epistles, equally of Asian provenance, could have led to Ignatius's view of a strictly hierarchical government of bishop and presbyters and deacons (see 1 Tim 3:1-3; Tit 1:7-9), who are shown to be faithful in maintaining discipline and repulsing deviance from apostolic-Pauline norms by inculcating sound teaching and promoting worship in a proper manner (1 Tim 4:11-16). False notions must be exposed and denounced by Timothy's recourse to the church's confessions of faith and creedal formulas (1 Tim 3:16, whose intro-

ductory sentence is a sign of the six-line, hymnic-poetic christological tribute that follows; 2 Tim 2:11-13). Worship functions in the pastors' congregations as a stabilizing, boundary-fixing marker (see MacDonald), whose effect is to close ranks within an inward-looking community. This body of literature evinces a trait, shared alike by Ignatius and Ephesians, of the church's assuming a role in salvation history centered on itself as an article of its faith (Eph 4:4, and often in Ignatius; cf. 1 Tim 4:15). We are here on the threshold of ecclesiastical history, where the church itself is part of God's salvific plan (Eph 3:10) and sees no incongruity—indeed it rejoices in this—that it professes to believe in itself. "I believe in . . . one, holy, catholic, apostolic church" is a sentence ready to be inserted in the creed.

If we wanted to see how the church's liturgical acts were becoming integrated into its understanding of its message and mission, the thrust conveyed in the letter to the *Hebrews would provide encouragement. By common consent, this sermon-like (Heb 13:22) document reflects Roman Christianity in the post-A.D. 70 decades of the first Christian century. The author's purpose is stated with clarity: it is to show the finality and superiority of the new economy brought by Christ who is ministrant (Heb 2:10-13; 8:2) and sacrifice (Heb 9—10) in the new sanctuary. Repeatedly his arguments and appeals are punctuated with liturgical idioms, often drawn from the levitical prototypes but always suffused with and corrected by Christian overtones (e.g., Heb 13:10-16). The language of offering and sacrifice is pressed into service in order to highlight the immeasurable greatness of the new covenant, based on the better sacrifice of Jesus (since it was made once for all) and the better effectiveness (securing a full and final forgiveness). Yet the high priestly ministry of Jesus continues in a heavenly sanctuary (e.g., Heb 7:25; 9:24; 13:10, sometimes taken in a eucharistic sense, see Dunnill, 240-42), and the implied call is made that the church is to share in this worship of God through him who is the perfect worshiper (Heb 2:11-12; 13:12-16).

This is an aspect of worship here receiving its emphasis in a unique way in the NT but with repercussions that were later to be enlarged and felt in the decades (e.g., *1 Clem.* 36.1; 40.1-5) and centuries to come. Worship is both "through Christ" (Heb 13:15) and "in Christ," making the church one with his self-offering (Heb 7:25) so that its sacrifices of praise are joined with the one offering that is both complete (once for all, *eph' hapax*) and ever-renewed as it is freshly appropriated by and mediated to the believing community. Hebrews 13:17 mentions the leaders who serve the community; *1 Clement* 41-44 reflects debate over the rightful authorities in the church (at Rome?), who should succeed the apostles in presenting the church's "sacrifices and services" (*1 Clem.* 40.2); namely, the credibility of other approved persons who as overseers have "offered the sacrifices" (*1 Clem.* 44.4).

The audience of Hebrews needs to catch this vision of itself as an eschatological people sharing in the heavenly host's triumph (Heb 12:22-24; the realized eschatology in these verses puts this part of Hebrews in touch with the "already accomplished" emphasis in Ephesians) and equally to face the stern realities of its life on earth as pilgrims and strangers (Heb 11:13-16; see Johnsson, Käsemann 1984). The way to win, for this author and the readers, is to remain committed to early baptismal pledges (e.g., Heb 4:14; see Bornkamm 1963) and keep the lines of communication with God, established in corporate worship, open (Heb 4:16) and intact (Heb 10:19-25). The temptation to withdraw from public assembly is evidently strong in time of testing (Heb 10:32-39), so the author makes adherence to the assembly a focal point of resistance and renewal, thereby giving to worship its pragmatic value and socializing dimension.

A parallel side to the way worship is seen to provide identity markers for the new Israel and to build confidence is evident in another document also associated with Rome. In *1 Peter the addressees are facing a loss of faith but for a different set of reasons. In Hebrews, where hope plays a key role (Heb 6:9-20; 11:1), the conflicts were domestic and internal, and there was theological questioning about the imminent parousia (Heb 10:37-39). The call to hope in 1 Peter (1 Pet 1:3, 13, 21; 3:5) is couched against a different background. Here the hostility is directed to the churches in Pontus-Bithynia (1 Pet 1:1) from outside (1 Pet 2:12; 4:1-6), and there seems to be no debate about their final salvation at an expected appearing of the Lord (1 Pet 1:5, 13; 4:7). The root problem faced in 1 Peter is the loss of social identity and the sense of rootlessness that has come to people who, from their pagan environment, have joined the church and accepted

its mores and manners. Their physical sufferings are raising problems to do with theodicy as they seek to understand and make sense of life's contrarieties and uncertainties when their newfound faith is tested (1 Pet 1:6; 2:19; 4:12).

The author's response in this hortatory document (1 Pet 5:12) is to impart social identity to the readers as those belonging to the "people of God," stretching back to Abraham and Sarah (1 Pet 3:5, 6) and onward to the complete "household of faith" soon to be realized (1 Pet 2:4-10; 4:17-19). The author offers assurance that God's plans do not miscarry as the churches come to see how Christ's victory over all his enemies is one to be shared by his followers who walk in his steps (1 Pet 2:21; 3:18-22; see Martin and Chester, 100 n. 26). Liturgical emphases play their role in enforcing these precise points, notably in the poetically structured passage (1 Pet 2:1-10; see commentaries, esp. Selwyn) that celebrates the church as God's new Israel in which erstwhile strangers and alienated people find their new home as worshipers and family; and in the christological hymn of 1 Peter 3:18-22, whose original form may well have looked like this:

Who suffered once for sins,
To bring us to God;
Put to death in the flesh,
But made alive in the spirit,
In which *he went* and preached to the spirits
 in prison,
[But] *having gone* into heaven he sat at the
 right hand of God,
Angels and authorities and powers under his
 control.

The intricacies of debate over this obscure passage are many (see commentaries by Reicke, Dalton, Boismard for basic treatments—all reacting to Bultmann's seminal work of 1947; for survey and bibliographical references, see Martin 1978, 335-44; Martin and Chester, 95, 110-17). For our purposes it is enough to seek to inquire how the cited lines functioned as a hymn. The key to this problem is suggestively to observe that the section encompasses a drama of Christ's odyssey, framed by two occurrences of the verb "to go" (represented in italics above). He *went* to visit the realm of the demonic; he *went* after his triumph to take his place on the universe's throne, with all cosmic powers held in subjugation. So the journey motif is the key, unlocking the chief problematic issue, which is to know how relevantly such a piece of christological suprahistory would affect the lives of Peter's readers, who are also reminded of their baptism (in turn typified in the ark by which Noah's family was saved in a generation Jewish thinkers regarded as the worst imaginable and the cause of demonic influence in the world). In Christian baptism—a thought conceivably inserted by Peter into the preformed creed-hymn—there is an appropriating of Christ's identification with dark powers and his subsequent victory over them.

Here baptism receives a treatment that ostensibly links it with Paul (in Rom 6; cf. Col 2:12; 3:1). Yet it adds a dimension of considerable pictorial, even mythological, effect. It proclaims that believers share in Christ's achievement in its horror and its glory. He made himself one with human enslavement to evil and then in his triumph over it (see Martin 1994, 114-17, referring to Rev 1:18), thus connecting its kinetic-dramatic theology with other hymns, notably Philippians 2:6-11, as well as the scenario in *Gospel of Peter* 10.41-42 and *Acts of Pilate* 5.1—8.2, in the section Christ's Descent into Hell, and of course the Apostles' Creed statement (at Rome, c. A.D. 150, as a baptismal creed; Kelly): "crucified, dead, and buried; he descended into Hades. The third day he rose again and ascended into heaven." The Christus victor theme reaches its zenith in the acknowledgment and proclamation that in baptism all demonic agencies that would tyrannize over the church and hold it prey are overcome, since Christ knew their power to hurt and their being reduced to impotence. The logical and liturgical outcome of this theologoumenon will be the use of exorcistic and renunciation formulas as a prelude to the actual baptism seen in Hippolytus's *Apostolic Tradition* (Jasper and Cuming).

6. Johannine Patterns and Their Influence.
If we are correct in assuming the presence in the Rome-Asia axis of styles of worship that looked to Paul's and Peter's deposits of teaching to inform them, with the universally accepted practices of baptism as initiatory rite and the Lord's Supper as celebratory of Christ's resurrection victory and set in a structure that tended to respect the authority of leaders, then in the Johannine literature the emphasis falls elsewhere (*see* John, Letters of).

The powerful influences seen in the Pastorals, the *Didache*, Ignatius and *1 Clement*, with their concerns over set prayers (the permission of *Did.* 10.7, "allow the prophets to give thanks at will," needs to be read in light of *Did.* 15.1-2, which shows that itinerant prophets are on the way out and are to be succeeded by "bishops and deacons," as in Ign. *Smyrn.* 8; *1 Clem.* 44), regular ministries, orderly worship (*1 Clem.* 20) and an incipient sacramental system (Ign. *Eph.* 20) seem to brook no challenge. Yet there is another strand that mirrors a reaction in the Asian churches in which the Johannine influence is strong. This body of literature (John's Gospel, Johannine Epistles and to an extent the Apocalypse) speaks to a situation where there are competing emphases, partly christological, partly ecclesiological, in the "community of the beloved disciple" (Brown). We may even postulate a threat to worship, as John's disciples feared it. Both the Johannine Gospel and Epistles raise a warning against the trend to overinstitutionalize. John senses the danger of suffocating the Spirit by placing too much emphasis on creedal orthodoxy, relying too heavily on structural forms and limiting the spontaneity that we saw to be evident in Luke's depictions. It is a moot point whether John's protest may be directed to just such a situation as that envisaged in the Pastoral Epistles, *1 Clement* and later in Ignatius.

At all events, for John the way forward is to stress the believer's individual participation in true spirituality, as he dubbed it. (1) Worship is "in the Spirit" (1 Jn 3:24) as in reality and is largely independent of outward forms, locations and ceremonials (Jn 4:20-24). The water of Jewish purification rituals is marvelously transformed into the wine of the new age, where Jesus' glory shines out as the universal logos (Jn 2:1-11).

(2) Love of God and his family members is the real test of authentic spirituality (1 Jn 3:1-18; 4:7-21), over against creedal rigidity and a blind trust in sacraments. The antisacramentalism alleged in the Fourth Gospel (Bultmann 1971) is a timely, if overstressed, protest against the opposite viewpoint of O. Cullmann, who sees baptism, unction and the eucharist everywhere on almost every page. There is no explicit institution of the Lord's Supper in John 13, which does, however, have an upper-room meal. But the Evangelist has incorporated a discourse set in the synagogue at Capernaum (Jn 6) as though to stress that the eucharist has an individualized,

inner meaning that is nothing less than a feeding on Christ the bread of life, just as John's earlier chapter (Jn 4) had depicted Jesus as the giver of living water to an individual woman of Samaria. The same note is struck in Revelation 3:20: "If anyone hears my voice, I will . . . eat with that person."

(3) It cannot be fortuitous that this body of literature lacks completely the term *church (ekklēsia)*. (Revelation is the exception, and it is notable for its inclusion of liturgical-hymnic tributes linking the old Jewish worship [Rev 4:8, 11; 7:12; 15:3-4] to the new age of Messiah's redemption [Rev 5:9-14] and victory [Rev 12:10-12].) Yet for John, believers do form a society under the imagery of a flock (Jn 10:1-16; cf. Jn 11:52) and the vine (Jn 15:1-11), but inevitably in such images the important thing is the personal relationship the believer sustains to the Lord. As the sheep hear the shepherd's voice when he calls each by name (Jn 10:3-5; cf. Heb 13:20; 1 Pet 5:2-4 has the chief shepherd with many undershepherds to tend the flock, and Peter will assume such a role in Jn 21), so there is no possibility of life unless the separate branches are linked to the parent stem of the vine (Jn 15:4, 5). John's view of the church governs his concept of worship. The church is made up of individual believers (Moule 1962) who are joined one by one to the Lord by the highly personal ties of baptism and new birth (Jn 3:1-6). The worship they offer springs from the experience of an enriched individualism: "the individual's direct and complete union with Jesus Christ sets its stamp on the ordering of the (Johannine) church" (Schweizer, 124). This is true also of its liturgy, remarkable for its absence of set forms and a Johannine passing over of much that other Christians elsewhere may have taken for granted.

7. Some Conclusions.

The above survey of worship materials and patterns, drawn from literature of a wide time span and diverse geographic and cultural spread, cannot pretend to be comprehensive. The soundings we have taken are at best, we hope, typical of the regions mentioned. Yet the picture is still incomplete and the settings proposed conjectural. It is difficult therefore to plot a trajectory or suggest a developing pattern with any convincing coherence. The bold attempt as proposed by G. J. Cuming (*SL* 10 [1974] 88-105),

ranging from salutation (grace and peace) by way of intercessions, Scripture readings to doxology, kiss of peace and dismissal, is hardly convincing (see Martin 1992, 190 n. 6). A lot of the material emerges from the socially conditioned pressures on writers and congregational addressees. The most we can hope for is to plot certain nodal points along the way. And as these are observed, we can submit that certain trends are visible.

7.1. Growing Systematization of Order. In the later Pauline/deutero-Pauline literature there is a growing move to systematization based on various factors: the squelching of charismatic fervor seems the inevitable concomitant of the growing emphasis on instruction/teaching roles (themselves in response to deviant notions that challenged the legacy of Paul's doctrine, e.g., in the Pastorals and Colossian-Ephesians). The rise of churchly concerns over order and fixity put a brake on immediacy and spontaneity in worship that we see at Corinth. Paul had sounded the caution, "let all things [in the worshiping assembly] be done in seemly fashion and in good order" (1 Cor 14:40, a phrase evidently picked up in *1 Clem.* 40, *panta taxei poiein opheilomen*); and the growing strength and authority accorded to duly appointed leaders (in the Pastorals and Eph 4:11-16; see commentaries; Martin 1992) tended to focus the spotlight on the hierarchical controls required to ensure that unity was promoted (Ign. *Smyrn.* 8, for instance) and the episcopal office maintained (*1 Clem.* 44). Along the way from the picture of congregational egalitarianism to the recognition of a settled ministry (a transition point seen in *Did.* 9-15), we may note the recourse made to apostolic teaching (Acts 2:42; Jude 17; *Did.* incipit; Heb 13:7; cf. Heb 2:3; the Johannine letters, *1 Clem.* 42) to repel false ideas that began to rear their head.

7.2. Emerging Trinitarian Focus. The occasional nature of much of the liturgical language, called out by the contingencies of congregational problems and challenges, should not blind us to some well-attested constants. Among these we may include (1) the appreciation of God as the holy object of Christian adoration and praise. The legacy of the OT-Judaic traditions is not overlooked but carried forward and enriched by an emerging trinitarian faith; for example, the "thrice holy" of Isaiah 6:3 is heard in Revelation 4:8, though the history of the *Sanctus* in the eucharistic liturgy is still a complex issue (cf. *1 Clem.*

34.6; Spinks, especially 46-54). All the documents in our period highlight the transcendence and worthiness of God, without which worship (as classically understood) fails.

(2) As a counterbalance, God is praised as intimately near in Christ his Son, whose true incarnation, death for sinners and resurrection victory over all evil forces are pivotal events in salvation history (cf. creedal-hymnic forms in 1 Pet; Heb 1:1-4; 1 Jn 4:1-6; 5:20; Rev 5:1-14; Ign. *Eph.* 19). This prepares the ground for a doctrine of the priestly office of the exalted Christ as intercessor and participant in the church's offices (Heb 7:25; *1 Clem.* 40; 59—62.3; *1 Clem.* 61.3 is an interesting specimen of prayer speech with nine pairs of parallel lines [in *1 Clem.* 59.3] consisting of divine predications and hymnic sentences [J. M. Robinson] offered through "Jesus Christ the high priest and guardian of our souls through whom be glory and majesty"). The Pauline verse (Eph 2:18) is sometimes hailed as encapsulating the essence of early worship in its trinitarian format (Crichton, 18, 19) and as offering a "basic morphology that cannot be violated if liturgical theology is to be Christian" (Hoon, 115). The data that begin with Paul's borrowing of formulas like 2 Corinthians 13:13 (14) take on this shape in Matthew 28:19, 20; Acts 2:33; Hebrews 9:14; 1 Peter 1:2; *Didache* 7.1-4; and Ignatius's *Letter to the Trallians* (incipit) on the road to full-blown trinitarian creeds (in Irenaeus and beyond; see Wainwright).

7.3. Placing the Risen Lord Alongside the Father. The place of the risen Lord in early Christian worship is still hotly debated (see representative positions held in Jungmann, Harris, Bauckham 1981, France, Hurtado 1988, Casey). From allusions that are at best inferential (Jn 14:14 RSV mg.; cf. Jn 16:23) or incidental (Acts 7:59; *1 Clem.* 21.6) to others that precisely speak of invoking the living Christ (1 Cor 16:22; Rev 22:20; *Did.* 10.6) or else set the exalted one at the center of a cultus on a par with Israel's covenant God (Rev 5:12-14; cf. 3:21; see Guthrie, Thompson), the line moves inexorably to a placing of Jesus alongside the Father as worthy of worship and the coauthor of salvation blessings for the church and the world. The title "God," so reticently applied to Jesus in the NT literature (though see Harris for the maximum value to be extracted from such verses as Heb 1:8; 2 Pet 1:1; 1 Jn 5:20) may well have received fresh impetus from the role cast for him in the Christians' as-sembly when, as Christians met on an appointed day (i.e., Sunday, so called in Justin *Apol. I* 67 as the day after Saturday before daybreak *[stato die ante lucem]*), hymns were sung antiphonally "to Christ as to God" *carmen quasi Deo* (Pliny *Ep.* 10.96.7 for this text, c. A.D. 112; see Cabaniss 1989, 11-18).

See also BAPTISM; GOD; LORD'S SUPPER.

DLNTD: CENTERS OF CHRISTIANITY; HYMNS, SONGS; LITURGICAL ELEMENTS; LORD'S DAY; PRAYER; TEMPLE.

BIBLIOGRAPHY. R. J. Bauckham, *Jude, 2 Peter* (WBC; Waco, TX: Word, 1983); idem, "The Worship of Jesus" *NTS* 27 (1981) 323-31; W. Bauer, *Die apostolischen Väter* 2 (Tübingen: J. C. B. Mohr, 1924) 204; idem, *Orthodoxy and Heresy in Earliest Christianity* (Philadelphia: Fortress 1971 [1924]); G. Bornkamm, "Das Bekenntnis im Hebräerbrief," in *Studien zu Antike und Urchristentum* (2d ed.; Munich: Kaiser, 1963) 188-203; idem, *Early Christian Experience* (London: SCM, 1969); P. F. Bradshaw, *Daily Prayer in the Early Church* (New York: Oxford University Press, 1982); idem, *The Search for the Origins of Christian Worship* (New York: Oxford University Press, 1992); R. E. Brown, *The Community of the Beloved Disciple* (New York: Paulist, 1979); R. Bultmann, *The Gospel of John* (Philadelphia: Fortress, 1971); idem, *Theology of the New Testament* (2 vols.; New York: Scribner's, 1952, 1955); A. Cabaniss, "The Epistle of Saint James," *JBR* 22 (1954) 27-29; idem, *Pattern in Early Christian Worship* (Macon, GA: Mercer University Press, 1989); M. Casey, *From Jewish Prophet to Gentile God* (Louisville, KY: Westminster John Knox, 1991); J. H. Charlesworth, ed., *The Lord's Prayer and Other Prayer Texts from the Greco-Roman Era* (Valley Forge, PA: Trinity Press International, 1994); J. D. Crichton, "A Theology of Worship," in *The Study of Liturgy,* ed. C. Jones, G. Wainwright and E. Yarnold (2d ed.; New York: Oxford University Press, 1992), 3-29; F. L. Cross, *1 Peter: A Paschal Liturgy* (London: Mowbray, 1964); O. Cullmann, *Early Christian Worship* (SBT 10; London: SCM, 1953) 7-36; P. H. Davids, *Commentary on James* (NIGTC; Grand Rapids: Eerdmans, 1982); M. Dibelius, *James* (Herm; Philadelphia: Fortress, 1976); F. J. Dölger, *Sol salutis: Gebet und Gesang im christlichen Altertum* (2d ed.; Münster: Aschendorff, 1925); C. W. Dugmore, *The Influence of the Synagogue on the Divine Office* (London: Oxford University Press, 1944); J. D. G. Dunn, *Baptism in the Holy Spirit* (Philadelphia: Westminster, 1970); idem, *Jesus and the Spirit* (Philadelphia: Westminster, 1975); idem, *Unity and Diversity in the New Testament* (2d ed.; Louisville, KY: Westminster, 1990); J. Dunnill, *Covenant and Sacrifice in the Letters to the Hebrews* (SNTSMS 75; Cambridge: Cambridge University Press, 1992); J. A. Fitzmyer, "The Aramaic Language and the Study of the New Testament," *JBL* 99 (1980) 5-21; R. T. France, "The Worship of Jesus," in *Christ the Lord,* ed. H. H. Rowdon (Downers Grove, IL: InterVarsity Press, 1982) 17-36; D. Guthrie, "Aspects of Worship in the Book of Revelation," in *Worship, Theology and Ministry in the Early Church,* ed. M. J. Wilkins and T. Paige (Sheffield: Academic Press, 1992) 70-83; E. Haenchen, *The Acts of the Apostles* (Philadelphia: Westminster, 1971); M. J. Harris, *Jesus as God: The New Testament Use of Theos in Reference to Jesus* (Grand Rapids: Baker, 1992); P. J. Hartin, *James and the Sayings of Jesus* (Sheffield: JSOT Press, 1991); P. W. Hoon, *The Integrity of Worship* (Nashville: Abingdon, 1971); C. Hopkins, *The Discovery of Dura-Europos* (New Haven, CT: Yale University Press, 1979); A. J. Hultgren, *The Rise of Normative Christianity* (Minneapolis: Augsburg/Fortress, 1994); L. W. Hurtado, *Lord Jesus Christ: Devotion to Jesus in Earliest Christianity* (Grand Rapids: Eerdmans, 2003); idem, *One God, One Lord* (Philadelphia: Fortress, 1988); R. D. Jasper and G. J. Cuming, *Prayers of the Eucharist: Early and Reformed* (London: Collins, 1975); J. Jeremias, *The Eucharistic Words of Jesus* (3d ed.; Philadelphia: Fortress, 1977); W. G. Johnsson, "The Pilgrimage Motif in the Book of Hebrews," *JBL* 97 (1978) 239-51; J. A. Jungmann, *The Place of Christ in Liturgical Prayer* (New York: Alba, 1965); E. Käsemann, "A Primitive Christian Baptismal Liturgy," in *Essays on New Testament Themes* (Philadelphia: Fortress, 1982 [1964]); idem, *The Wandering People of God* (Minneapolis: Fortress, 1984); J. N. D. Kelly, *Early Christian Creeds* (5th rev. ed.; London: A. C. Black, 1977); H. Koester and J. M. Robinson, *Trajectories Through Early Christianity* (Philadelphia: Fortress, 1971); J. Kroll, *Die christliche Hymnodik bis zu Klemens von Alexandreia* (Darmstadt: Wissenschaftliche Buchgesellschaft, 1968 repr.); G. W. H. Lampe, *The Seal of the Spirit* (2d ed.; London: SPCK, 1967); H. Lietzmann, *Mass and Lord's Supper: A Study in the History of the Liturgy* (Leiden: E. J. Brill, 1953-1978); E. Lohmeyer, *Kyrios Jesus: eine Untersuchung zu Phil 2.5-11* (2d ed.; Heidelberg: Winter, 1961 [1928]); M. Y. MacDonald, *The Pauline Churches* (SNTSMS 60; Cambridge: Cambridge University Press, 1988); I. H. Marshall, *Acts* (TNTC; Grand Rapids: Eerdmans, 1980); R. P. Martin, *Ephesians, Colossians, Philemon* (Int; Louisville, KY: Westminster, 1992); idem, *A Hymn of Christ* (Downers Grove, IL: InterVarsity Press, 1997 [1967, 1983]); idem, *James* (WBC; Waco, TX: Word, 1988); idem, "New Testament Worship: Some Puzzling Practices," *AUSS* (1993) 119-26; idem and A. Chester, *The Theology of the Letters of James, Peter and Jude* (NTT; Cambridge: Cambridge University Press, 1994); H. A. McKay, *Sabbath and Synagogue: The Question of Sabbath in Ancient Judaism* (RGRW 122; Leiden: E. J. Brill, 1994); L. Morris, "The Saints and the Synagogue," in *Worship, Theology and Ministry in the Early Church,* ed. T. Paige and M. J. Wilkins (Sheffield: Academic Press, 1992) 39-52; C. F. D. Moule, "The Individualism of the Fourth Gospel" *NovT* 5 (1962) 171-90; idem, *Worship in the New Testament* (London: Lutterworth, 1961); E. Norden, *Agnostos Theos* (Stuttgart: Teubner, 1956); P. T. O'Brien, *Introductory Thanksgivings in the Letters of Paul* (NovTSup 49: Leiden: E. J. Brill, 1977); J. A. T. Robinson, *Twelve New Testament Studies* (SBT 34; London: SCM, 1962) 154-57; J. M. Robinson, "Die Hodajot-Formel im Gebet und Hymnus des Frühchristentums," in *Apophoreta: Festschrift für Ernst Haenchen,* ed. W. Eltester (Berlin: Töpelmann, 1964) 194-235; T. A. Robinson, *The Bauer Thesis Examined: The Geography of Heresy in the Early Christian Community* (Lewiston, NY: Mellen, 1988); W. Rordorf, "Sunday," in *Encyclopedia of the Early Church,* ed. A. de Berardino (New York: Oxford University Press, 1992) 2:800-801; idem, *Sunday* (London: SCM, 1968); H. Schlier, *Die Verkündigung im Gottesdienst der Kirche* (Würzburg: Werkbung-Verlag, 1953); E. Schweizer, *Church Order in the New Testament* (SBT 32; London: SCM, 1961); E. G. Selwyn, *The First Epistle of St. Peter* (London: Macmillan, 1947); M. H. Shepherd, "The Epistle of James and the Gospel of Matthew," *JBL* 75 (1956) 40-51; idem, *The Paschal Liturgy and the Apocalypse* (Richmond, VA: John Knox, 1960); B. D. Spinks, *The Sanctus in the Eucharistic Prayer* (Cambridge: Cambridge University Press, 1991); J. H. Srawley, *Early History of the Eucharist* (2d ed.; Cambridge: Cambridge University Press, 1947); B. H. Streeter, *The Primitive Church* (London: Macmillan, 1929); L. T. Stuckenbruch, "A Refusal of Worship of an Angel: The Tradition and Its Function in the Apocalypse of John," *SBLSP* (1994); M. M. Thompson, "Worship in the Book of Revelation," *Ex Auditu* 8 (1992) 45-54; H. E. W. Turner, *The Pattern of Christian Truth* (London: Mowbray, 1954); A. W. Wainwright, *The Trinity in* *the New Testament* (London: SPCK, 1962).

R. P. Martin

WRATH, DIVINE. *See* JUDGMENT.

Glossary of Terms

These definitions are largely extracted from Arthur G. Patzia & Anthony J. Petrotta, *Pocket Dictionary of Biblical Studies*, InterVarsity Press, 2002.

abomination of desolation. A phrase taken from the prophecy of Daniel (Dan 11:31; 12:11) where the prophet states that the temple will be the site of some future abominable and revolting act.

adoptionism. In NT studies, the view that the man Jesus was "adopted" by God as Son rather than the Son preexisting with the Father.

agraphon. A Greek term for an "unwritten saying" (pl. *agrapha*) attributed to Jesus but not found in the canonical Gospels.

allegory. A literary form in which a story is told for what it signifies rather than for its own sake.

amanuensis. A scribe or secretary hired to write (usually a letter, in NT studies) from dictation or from an outline (from Lat *manu,* "hand").

Amoraim. Designation of the rabbinic teachers in both Palestine and Babylon during the third to sixth centuries A.D. (the Hebrew term means "speakers" or "interpreters").

anonymous. Literally, "nameless" (from the Gk *a,* "without," + *onoma,* "name"); used in NT studies usually with reference to the authorship of a document.

antinomian. In NT studies, a term characterizing early Christians who thought that salvation by faith in Jesus Christ freed them from all moral obligations, some of whom drew the conclusion that they could sin with impunity (Gk *anti,* "against," + *nomos,* "law").

antitheses. In NT studies, the six contrasts between Moses' and Jesus' teaching presented in the Sermon on the Mount in Matthew 5:21-48, where each antithesis is introduced by the formula, "You have heard that it was said," followed by the antithetical response, "But I [Jesus] say to you."

antitype. The "fulfillment" or counterpart of a type. *See* typology.

aphorism. A brief definition (Gk *aphorismos*), statement, pithy saying or formulation of a truth.

apocalypse. Literally, an "unveiling" or "revelation" (Gk *apokalypsis,* Rev 1:1), a literary style or genre in which "secrets" are revealed about the heavenly world or the end of the age.

apocalyptic. An adjective variously used with reference to the literary genre of apocalypse or its underlying religious perspective (e.g., apocalyptic eschatology). *See* apocalypse.

apocalypticism. A term usually used to refer to a social movement or belief system that produces apocalyptic literature. *See* apocalypse.

Apocrypha, the. The name given to a variable collection of books that were thought to contain "hidden" truths (from the Gk *apokryptō,* "to hide, conceal"). They are, with slight variations, included in the canons of the Roman Catholic and Orthodox churches. *See* deutero-canonical books.

apocryphal. An adjective sometimes used to refer to the Apocrypha but often of a text or saying of doubtful authority or truthfulness.

apophthegm. A transliteration of the Greek "to speak one's opinion freely" (pl. *apophthegmata*), used of proverbial and wisdom sayings of Jesus that were transmitted orally before being written down and incorporated into the Gospels.

apostolic fathers. A collection of post-apostolic Christian writers or writings of the late first and early second century that did not achieve canonical status but were valued by the early church (e.g., *1 Clement, 2 Clement, Epistle to Diognetus, Epistles of Ignatius, Didache, Shepherd of Hermas*).

apostolic parousia. The idea that even though Paul is not personally present in one of the churches, his apostolic authority is nevertheless present and should be felt through either his letter to the church or a designated envoy such as Timothy.

Aqedah. A rabbinic term referring to the story and the interpretations of Abraham "sacrificing" Isaac as narrated in Genesis 22, where Isaac is bound and placed on an altar (*'āqêdâ* means "binding" [of Isaac]).

Aramaism. Influences on the language, form and content of Greek (or other) texts from the Aramaic language.

aretalogy. A term describing the miracles, great deeds, supernatural powers, powerful acts and virtuous qualities of a god or a "divine man" (Gk *aretē*, "virtue").

Aristeas, Letter of. A document purportedly describing the circumstances surrounding the translation of the OT into Greek, or the Septuagint.

Augustinian hypothesis. The opinion of Augustine that the current canonical order of the Gospels (Matthew, Mark, Luke, John) is the actual chronological order in which they were composed.

autograph. The original (from the Gk *autographos*, "written in one's own hand") manuscript or document of an author's work.

B.C.E. Abbreviation for "Before the Common Era," an alternative to B.C. properly used in Jewish and Jewish-Christian contexts.

canon. An authoritative list or collection of religious literature, in this case biblical books (from Gk *kanon*, "measuring rod, standard").

C.E. Abbreviation for "Common Era," an alternative to A.D. properly used in Jewish and Jewish-Christian contexts.

chiasm. Derived from the Greek letter X, *chi*, a rhetorical device whereby parallel lines of a text correspond in an X pattern, such as A-B-C-B-A (in this case the center of the chiasm is C, and on either side line A will correspond to line A and so forth).

chreia. A technical term (pl. *chreiai*) from ancient Greek rhetoric meaning pithy phrases or short sayings (epigrams) and actions told about or in honor of an important person and useful for daily living.

coherence, criterion of. A criterion of authenticity whereby a saying of Jesus is judged to be authentic if it "coheres" or agrees in form and content with other material judged to be authentic by other criteria, such as dissimilarity or multiple attestation. *See* criteria of authenticity.

consistent eschatology. The view associated with Albert Schweitzer that Jesus' eschatological view was that the end of this age was imminent and that Jesus' sayings must be consistently interpreted in this vein.

covenantal nomism. A term coined by E. P. Sanders to describe his understanding of the essential pattern of Second Temple Judaism: "that one's place in God's plan is established on the basis of the covenant and that the covenant requires as the proper response of man his obedience to its commandments, while providing the means of atonement for transgression"

(*Paul and Palestinian Judaism*, p. 75). This is contrasted with the more traditional (Protestant) view that Jews regarded the law as a means of "earning" righteousness.

credo, creed. A formal or confessional statement of faith usually drawn from the cultic/religious life of believing communities (Lat *credo*, "I believe").

criteria of authenticity. The various tests NT scholars use to determine the historical authenticity of the sayings of Jesus in the Gospels. *See* coherence, criterion of; dissimilarity, criterion of; multiple attestation, criterion of.

criticism. An informed and rational analysis of the origin, nature, history and meaning of written works such as the NT literature. The term in itself does not imply finding fault. There are a variety of forms of criticism. *See* form criticism; literary criticism; redaction criticism; textual criticism; tradition criticism.

cult. A term used for public worship in general, particularly the festivals, rituals, sacrifices and other practices in service to God or the gods (Lat *cultus*, "reverence"). In biblical studies the term (and its adjective *cultic*) is used without the pejorative connotations associated with its use as a label for new religious movements.

Cynics. Adherents to the philosophical movement founded by Diogenes of Sinope (c. 400-325 B.C.). Cynicism was more a way of life than a system of philosophical principles.

deuterocanonical books. Literally "second(ary) canon," books or portions of books not included in the Hebrew canon but found in the Greek OT and commonly called the Apocrypha (*see* Apocrypha, the). To different extents, these books are found in the Roman Catholic and Orthodox canons of Scripture.

deutero-Pauline. Literally, a "deutero" ("second") Paul, the term is used of epistles explicitly attributed to Paul but whose authorship is questioned because of certain linguistic, theological and historical factors (e.g., 2 Thessalonians, Colossians, Ephesians, 1 and 2 Timothy, Titus).

Diaspora. A collective term for Jews living outside the land of Israel in places such as Babylon, Egypt and Asia Minor, originally through enforcement by a conquering nation, such as in the Babylonian exile of 586 B.C.

diatribe. A form of rhetoric identified by short ethical discourses, rhetorical questions and dialogues, and argumentative speech, in which the author or speaker debates with an imaginary person (interlocutor) in order to instruct the audience.

dissimilarity, criterion of. A criterion of authenticity by which sayings of Jesus are judged to be authentic if they are "dissimilar"—that is, distinct or unique from sayings or beliefs common to the early church or Second Temple Judaism. *See* criteria of authenticity.

docetism. An early Christian heresy emerging in the first century that denied the full humanity of Jesus and thus the reality of his sufferings and death.

double tradition. Those sayings of Jesus that are common to Matthew and Luke. *See* triple tradition.

early catholicism. A technical term for a later stage of the early church which is based on the hypothesis that the church developed from a rather loosely organized charismatic community under the direction of the Holy Spirit during the apostolic age to a rather formal or "institutionalized" community in the postapostolic age.

Ebionites, Ebionism. A Jewish-Christian sect whose name is derived from the Hebrew or Aramaic term for "the poor" and is first mentioned in the writings of Irenaeus, a second-century church father. The precise profile of this group is debated, but they are notably characterized by their adherence to the law and the Jewish way of life, and an adoptionist christology.

eschatology. A Greek-derived term meaning the study of, or belief about, the end of the age (Gk *eschatos,* "last [things]").

Essenes. One of the sects of Jews (along with the Pharisees and Sadducees, among others) that existed in Palestine during the NT period.

Eusebius (c. 260-340). Bishop of Caesarea, commonly referred to as "the father of church history" because of his *Ecclesiastical History.*

exegesis. The interpretation of a passage on its own terms (Gk *exēgeomai,* "to lead, draw out"), sometimes contrasted with reading one's beliefs into a passage, or eisegesis.

farewell discourse. In biblical and extrabiblical literature a farewell speech (often including instructions and warnings) delivered by someone about to die and addressing a group of family members, friends or disciples.

form criticism. An interpretive approach that seeks to uncover the oral tradition that is embedded in the written texts we now possess and to classify

them into certain categories, or "forms," and thus discover the history of their development within the early church (German *Formgeschichte* or *Gattungsgeschichte*).

four-source hypothesis. Also known as the four-document hypothesis, the theory that the Synoptic Gospels are based on four discrete sources: Mark, Q, L and M.

General Epistles. Non-Pauline NT letters thought to address the whole church (also called Catholic Epistles): James; 1-2 Peter; 1, 2, 3 John; Jude.

genre. A literary type, species or form (from the French word for "style"). Gospel, letter and apocalypse are NT genres.

Griesbach hypothesis. The theory, named after Johann Jakob Griesbach (1745-1812), that Matthew, rather than Mark, was the earliest Gospel to be written, and that Matthew was used by Mark and Luke to compose their Gospels.

Hasmoneans, Hasmonean dynasty. The family name of the Maccabean priestly and kingly family who ruled over Israel from the 160s B.C. until the Romans captured Jerusalem in 63 B.C. *See* Maccabees, Maccabean revolt.

Hauptbriefe. A German term (*Haupt,* literally "head" or "primary" + *Briefe,* "letters") referring to four primary letters of Paul: Romans, 1 and 2 Corinthians and Galatians.

Hellenism. The Greek-inspired cultural influences (e.g., ideas, customs, government, architecture, language, literature, art) that were disseminated throughout the Mediterranean world by Alexander the Great (d. 323 B.C.) and his successors.

Hellenistic Judaism. That sector of Judaism most profoundly influenced by the values and culture of Hellenism.

hermeneutics. A theory of interpretation or the study of theories of interpretation.

Herodians. A Jewish party that favored the dynasty of Herod.

historical criticism. An approach to the biblical text that seeks to determine the historical origins of a text as well as (where it pertains) "what really happened." The *historical-critical method* refers to the principles and tools of historical criticism used to reconstruct the historical context and original meaning of a text.

historical Jesus. The life and teachings of Jesus as determined by historical-critical methods. This ongoing modern enterprise is often called the Quest of (or for) the Historical Jesus.

household code. A "rule" or "table of rules" found in the NT as elsewhere in Greek literature, and dealing with domestic relationships: husband and wife, children and parents, slaves and masters (Eph 5:21—6:9; Col 3:18—4:1; 1 Pet 2:18—3:7).

inclusio. A technical term for a literary framing or bracketing device (Lat "confinement") in which the opening phrase or idea of a passage is repeated at the end.

intertestamental period. The historical period of Jewish history roughly between the OT and the NT, or between the postexilic period, ending about 400 B.C., and the first century A.D. Today many scholars refer to this same general period with the term "Second Temple Judaism."

Jacobean. Of or relating to James (Heb "Jacob") or his writings.

Johannine. Of or relating to John or his writings.

Josephus. A first-century Jewish historian (c. A.D. 37/38-110) whose primary works *Antiquities of the Jews*, *Jewish Wars* and *Vita* (*Life*) are important sources for understanding the historical and religious world of Palestine during the Roman rule.

Judaizers. A group of Jewish Christians who believed that all Gentile Christians should "live like Jews" (Gal 2:14) by embracing Jewish customs.

L tradition. Gospel material that is exclusive to Luke and possibly drawn from an independent source.

literary criticism. An approach to the biblical text that recognizes its literary nature and seeks to interpret it according to the methods of literary study.

liturgical element. A fragment of wording from a hymn, creed, prayer, benediction, doxology or acclamation that was used in early Christian worship and may now be detected within NT literature.

Lukan. Of or relating to Luke and his writings.

M tradition. Gospel material that is exclusive to Matthew and possibly drawn from an independent source.

Maccabees, Maccabean revolt. The leaders (most prominently Judas Maccabeus, or "the Hammer") and the Jewish revolt they led against their Seleucid overlords in 167-164 B.C.

manumission. The release of a person from slavery or bondage.

Markan. Of or relating to Mark and his Gospel.

Matthean. Of or relating to Matthew and his Gospel.

midrash. A specific form of Jewish biblical exposition or the genre characterized by this form. The term *midrash* (pl. *midrashim*) is a form of the Hebrew verb *dāraš*, "to seek, investigate."

mirror reading. The technique of reading a text for reverse images of the author's adversaries. The idea is, for example, that what Paul opposes at Corinth his opponents uphold, and from this evidence a profile of his opponents may emerge.

Mishnah. A corpus of Jewish legal material that achieved written form around A.D. 200 and is based on rabbinic tradition of discussion and interpretation of biblical laws.

multiple attestation, criterion of. A criterion of authenticity whereby sayings or actions of Jesus are judged to be authentic if identical or similar sayings or actions are attested in multiple and distinct Gospel sources (e.g., in the four-document hypothesis, Mark, Q, M, L). *See* criteria of authenticity.

mystery religions. The name given to a range of religious cults of ancient origin and syncretistic tendencies and practices (involving secret initiations) that prevailed in the Mediterranean world from the eighth century B.C. to the fourth century A.D.

Nag Hammadi Library. A collection of mostly Gnostic documents (in "book," or codex, form) dating from the fourth century A.D. and discovered about 1945-1946 near Nag Hammadi, a city in Upper Egypt.

pantheon. The collective body of gods of a particular people.

Papias. An early church father (c. A.D. 70-160), bishop of Hierapolis in Phrygia, whose work (including comments on Gospel authorship) is preserved only in fragments.

paradosis. A transliteration of the Greek *paradosis*, meaning "that which is handed down," and thus a technical term for tradition.

paraenesis. A transliteration of the Greek *parainesis*, meaning "exhortation" or "advice," and a technical term of form criticism referring to exhortation or admonition.

parousia. A transliteration of the Greek *parousia*, meaning "coming, arrival" and typically referring to the second coming and presence *(pareimi)* of Christ at the end of the world (1 Cor 16:22; Rev 22:7, 12, 20).

Pastoral Epistles/Letters. A collective term for

1 and 2 Timothy and Titus, which are written to individual "pastors" rather than churches and are broadly concerned with pastoral issues.

Pauline. Of or relating to the apostle Paul or his writings.

pericope. A short literary unit that has integrity even when "cut off" or "cut out" (Gk *perikoptō)* from a longer passage.

pesher. From the Hebrew word meaning "interpretation," a distinct style of commentary found especially in the Dead Sea Scrolls, in which a verse of Scripture is interpreted with reference to the interpreter's own time and situation (e.g., the Qumran community), which is usually viewed as the last days.

Petrine. Of or relating to the apostle Peter or his writings.

Pharisees. One of the chief sects of Judaism in NT times, noted for their belief that the oral Torah was revealed on Sinai in addition to the written Torah, and for applying priestly laws of ritual purity to everyday living in their pursuit of the restoration of a pure Israel.

Philo of Alexandria (c. 20 B.C.—A.D. 50). A Hellenistic Jewish philosopher, statesman, exegete and contemporary of Jesus and Paul, whose numerous works shed light on the thought world of Hellenistic Judaism.

Pliny the Younger (c. A.D. 61/62-113). A Roman writer and administrator of the Roman province of Bithynia during the rule of the emperor Trajan (A.D. 98-117).

pre-Pauline. Material (e.g., creeds, hymns) or ideas originating with others and incorporated by Paul into his thought and letters. The point is that the material or ideas existed before Paul *used* them and not that they predated Paul's lifetime or conversion.

proselyte. A person who is converted to another religious faith and becomes a member of that community.

proto-Gnosticism. An early or incipient form of Gnosticism which may have been present during the NT period.

Pseudepigrapha. A collection of ancient Jewish and Hellenistic writings that were written during the Second Temple period but are not part of the canonical OT or the Apocrypha, and are frequently attributed to great figures of the past (see James Charlesworth, ed., *The Old Testament Pseudepigrapha,* 2 vols.).

pseudonymous. A "false" claim of authorship for a literary work. In Second Temple Jewish literature there was a literary convention of attributing contemporary works to great figures of the distant past.

Q source. A hypothetical document consisting of a collection of Jesus' sayings that are common to Matthew and to Luke but not Mark (Q from German *Quelle,* "source").

Qumran. A site on the northwest shore of the Dead Sea whose ruins are associated with the Dead Sea Scrolls discovered in its immediate vicinity in 1947.

realized eschatology. The idea that the kingdom of God in Jesus' teaching is not future but "realized" in the person and mission of Jesus.

redaction criticism. An approach to a text (chiefly the Gospels in NT studies) that seeks to show how authors/editors have selected, shaped and framed sources in composing their work and communicating their point of view.

rhetoric. In NT studies, ancient Greek and Roman theories regarding effective oral or written discourse which may have been utilized by NT writers.

rhetorical criticism. An approach to the biblical text that focuses on the way language is used, particularly in accord with ancient rhetorical theory/practice, to persuade an audience.

Sadducees. A major sect of Judaism during the NT period, principally made up of the wealthy priestly class and noted for their denial of the resurrection of the dead.

Samaritans. Natives of Samaria, the province to the north of Judea, and the disparaged Jewish "cousins" whose religious beliefs and practices were based on the five books of Moses (Samaritan Pentateuch).

Sanhedrin. An administrative council or assembly (Gk, *synedrion)* of Jewish leaders. A tractate of the Mishnah is devoted to the organization and procedures of such a council.

Second Temple period. The period of Jewish history and literature extending from the completion of the second temple in 516 B.C. (or from Cyrus's decree in 538 B.C. to rebuild the temple) to the fall of Jerusalem and destruction of Herod's temple by the Romans in A.D. 70. Often used as a synonym for the intertestamental period.

Septuagint. Oldest Greek translation of the Hebrew Bible, usually abbreviated as LXX (for its legendary seventy translators) but inclusive of books outside the Hebrew canon (*see* Apocrypha).

1151

Sitz im Leben. German term translated literally as "setting in life" or "life situation" used chiefly in form criticism to speak of the social setting within the early church that enabled parables, sayings and stories of Jesus to take the shape in which the Evangelists inherited them.

socioscientific criticism. The application of sociological, anthropological, political and sociocultural theories to biblical texts in order to understand the communities in which they arose (in this case, early Christianity).

source criticism. An approach to texts (in NT studies, particularly the Gospels) that seeks to discover the literary sources of a document.

syncretism. A blending of varied and often contradictory tenets and practices from various belief systems into one system, or simply adapting and assimilating foreign ideas and practices into one's belief system.

synopsis (of the Gospels). A book that organizes the parallel material in the Synoptic Gospels (Matthew, Mark, Luke), and sometimes the Gospel of John, into vertical columns so that students and scholars can easily observe the similarities and differences between them.

Synoptic Gospels. The Gospels of Matthew, Mark and Luke, which "see together" the story of Jesus.

Synoptic Problem. The "problem" of how to account for the similarities and differences that exist between the three Synoptic Gospels.

Talmud. A definitive compendium of rabbinic law consisting of the Mishnah and its commentary, the Gemarah, and appearing in two different editions: the Babylonian and the Jerusalem (or Palestinian) Talmuds.

Targum. An Aramaic interpretive translation of the Hebrew Bible (from the Hebrew word meaning "interpretation").

textual criticism. The scholarly discipline of establishing a given text (the NT text, in this case) as close to the original material as possible or probable. Textual critics of the NT arrive at their conclusions by studying ancient manuscripts, versions and translations.

Torah. The first part of the Hebrew canon of Scripture, corresponding to the Pentateuch, or five books of Moses. The Hebrew name Torah *(tôrâ)* is effectively translated as "instruction," though it was translated into Greek as *nomos* and thus came into English as "law."

tradition. Oral or written material that is transmitted from one person or group to another, though usually within a particular community.

tradition criticism. An approach to a text that seeks to explain the ways various traditions within a text developed over the course of their oral transmission (from German *Traditionsgeschichte* or *Überlieferungsgeschichte*).

triple tradition. Material that is common to the three Synoptic Gospels: Matthew, Mark and Luke.

two-source hypothesis. A theory that attempts to explain the composition of the Synoptic Gospels by positing that Matthew and Luke used materials from two distinct sources, Mark and Q.

typology. The study of the pattern of correspondences between persons, objects, events or institutions within a text (Gk *typos*, "pattern"), typically between the OT and NT (e.g., Rom 5, where Adam is a type of Christ, who is the antitype).

vice and virtue catalog. A listing of vices and virtues by a NT writer (e.g., Gal 5:19-21), adopting a device of ethical instruction found in Stoic philosophy.

Zealots. A first-century Jewish revolutionary movement.

Articles Index

"In a time of universal deceit, telling the truth is a revolutionary act."

~ George Orwell

TABLE OF CONTENTS

FOREWORD

The Orphan Conspiracies: 29 Conspiracy Theories from The Orphan Trilogy, by James & Lance Morcan, contains hard-to-find knowledge. This book is based on the political, scientific and financial insights contained in the Morcans' bestselling international thriller series *The Orphan Trilogy*.

Throughout *The Orphan Trilogy*, James & Lance merge fact with fiction by incorporating real-world theories on known individuals and organizations. Now, with this non-fiction companion volume, they provide detailed analysis for each one of those controversial theories.

In many ways, this exhaustively-researched book is the secret history of the 20th Century and the early 21st Century. But more than a history lesson, it also discloses exactly what is happening right now behind the scenes – in underground bunkers, in the corridors of power, in prime banks and meetings of the global elite.

Currently, the world is in a desperate state due to environmental pollution, depletion of natural resources and food supplies, and economic inequalities. To solve these problems and to reach the next level of Mankind, a "new innovation of technology" is required. But nowadays innovative technologies such as cold fusion, and radical energy sources, including sonoluminescent-triggered fusion and anti-gravitational propulsion, are either being withheld or blocked by governments, old-fashioned science academia and multinational corporations.

I believe that the Big-Bang Theory and the Evolution Theory, as well as Einstein's Special Relativity Theory which does not allow for the existence of faster-than-light (superluminal) phenomena, all have flaws in them and must be replaced by new theories that can give Mankind a more concise view of our Universe. But the fact is exceptional discoveries and theories that challenge official science have been ignored by the Establishment for decades.

I was employed for many years as a senior research scientist developing naval underwater weapon systems at the Technical Research and Development Institute of the Ministry of Defense, Japan, and I often suspected there existed extraordinary technologies developed by the world's superpowers. I am of the opinion that most of these technologies have been concealed from the public's eyes.

The world's governments have many classified layers and outsiders rarely gain access to their hidden secrets. And certainly no common man can get confirmation of the existence of exotic technologies.

I was also part of a team of scientists in the Advanced Space Propulsion Investigation Committee (ASPIC), which was organized by the Japan Society for Aeronautical and Space Sciences in 1994. ASPIC's purpose was to study all kinds of non-chemical space propulsion systems instead of conventional rocket systems for space missions to nearby planets, the Moon and the outer Solar System. This included field propulsion systems which utilize zero-point energy, the electro-gravitic effect and the non-Newtonian gravitic effect predicted in Einstein's Theory of Gravity.

During my time with ASPIC, I strongly felt that some of the gravity control systems could have been realized, or had already been realized, but were being overshadowed by existing science. Such radical space technologies never reach the public because unknown groups do not wish humanity to have access to the highest knowledge or the most advanced scientific inventions. Perhaps this suppression is out of fear that the masses may be able to explore our Solar System and the Universe beyond it.

Whatever the case, it seems they want us to stay at ignorant levels forever.

This book is also about the purposeful bankrupting of nations around the world, the inherently corrupt monetary system and the scam of modern banking – all of which have obviously become major vices of our era. I believe that financial domination is one of the main methods used to enslave the people of this world.

I expect readers of this book will be surprised by the level of knowledge imparted in its pages, especially with its revelations of exotic technologies, financial injustices, political deceptions and suppressed scientific discoveries. I also expect readers will be inspired by the lifting of the veil that occurs when long-guarded information is absorbed.

Lastly, I sincerely hope that the publication of this book contributes to a global awakening which assists the future creation of new scientific theories and technologies – including space propulsion systems – that are not currently on the mainstream scientific agenda.

-Dr. Takaaki Musha

Director of the Advanced-Science Technology Research Organization (Japan)
Editor-in-Chief, Journal of Space Exploration (Mehta Press)
Former senior research scientist at the Technical Research and Development Institute of the Ministry of Defense, Japan.

Introduction

This book was borne out of reader curiosity for it was not something we ever intended to write. Nor was a non-fiction work something we ourselves would have naturally considered penning given we are novelists and feature filmmakers who specialize in writing and producing drama and works of fiction.

However, when *The Ninth Orphan*, the first book in our international thriller series *The Orphan Trilogy*, was published readers began commenting on or asking about the truth behind the real-life mysteries highlighted throughout. Since then, readers' emails and social media posts have escalated with the publication of *The Orphan Factory* and *The Orphan Uprising*, books two and three in the trilogy.

For those who haven't read the novels, *The Orphan Trilogy* is a series that's partially set in the boardrooms of real organizations such as the CIA, MI6, the FBI, the NSA and the UN; it features controversial theories about public figures, including President Obama, Queen Elizabeth II as well as the Clinton, Marcos and Bush families; and it illuminates shadow organizations *rumored* to exist in today's world.

In many ways, the trilogy merges fiction with reality. Or, as Amazon reviewer I.A.Wilhite, Ph.D., said of *The Ninth Orphan*: "The authors manage to weave political intrigue, espionage, and eugenics into an exciting fabric of mystery and entertainment. The reader can't but believe that the novel may not be only a work of fiction."

This book (*The Orphan Conspiracies*) bridges the gap between fiction and fact. It fully explores the real-world suppositions, assumptions and theories we included in our fictional universe and provides answers to the questions our readers have been asking.

The storyline of *The Orphan Trilogy*, which took about a decade to write, forced us to research all sorts of alternative concepts and seek out connected and learned individuals who could enlighten us. This comprehensive process not only enabled us to tell a layered and intelligent story, but also to acquire underground knowledge not easily accessible. Knowledge which we share, in depth, in this book and which upon reading we expect will enable, indeed encourage, the average reader to look at the world in a new light.

The challenge we face, of course, is that the subjects explored in this book are often in direct contrast with the way most of us view the world, and they invariably contradict the official line – the *line* that politicians, corporate leaders and other persons of influence convincingly peddle – that most of us have been conditioned to accept without questioning since childhood.

It's our experience that people are prepared to entertain unfamiliar hypotheses when they are incorporated into novels or movies, but are considerably less open-minded when there's no cozy fictional plot to soften the digestion of such concepts.

To counter this, we have avoided speculation wherever possible and have, for the most part, written about subjects that can be backed with hard facts. These facts include evidence substantiated in court cases, declassified government files, mainstream media reports and well-documented quotes from respected leaders in their fields. Wherever we do briefly deviate into mere speculation, we point that out so the dividing line between fact and rumor is always clear.

The other challenge in presenting this book is that many of the controversial topics we tackle can loosely be described as *conspiracy, conspiracies* or *conspiracy theories*. As a result, we will no doubt be categorized by many as *conspiracy theorists*.

Unfortunately, these have become dirty words and phrases in our culture. Any time a concern is raised by an individual who has been labeled a conspiracy theorist it's usually dismissed by most government spokespersons, mainstream media journalists and the public at large as paranoia, or worse, delusional.

And for the most part, those critics and skeptics are correct!

Probably 95% of conspiracy theories out there are pure crackpot stuff with not a shred of evidence to support them. We are talking the-moon-is-made-out-of-cheese type of theories. Such absurd concepts are espoused by conspiracy theory extremists who we refer to throughout this book as the *Tinfoil Hat Network* – those who wear tinfoil-lined hats to block mind control frequencies they believe are being beamed their way!

Although nutty notions certainly provide good entertainment value, they also undermine those serious conspiracy theories which warrant investigation.

A good example of theories deserving airtime is the contention that there were no Weapons of Mass Destruction in Iraq, which most Western governments have now acknowledged to be true. It was initially brought up by conspiracy theorists *before* the West's invasion of Iraq. Their claims were ignored, of course.

If society was prepared to listen to such individuals without pre-judging them, perhaps future wars could be averted.

Once you understand and accept that there are two types of conspiracy theorists – the *Tinfoil Hatters*, or lunatic fringe, and the more logically-minded – it becomes easy to distinguish between them.

You can spot the Tinfoil Hatters a mile off. They either present silly ideas like Marilyn Monroe being born a man or more dangerous ones like the Holocaust-never-happened – a theory which almost always has its roots in anti-Semitism. The more logically-minded, or sane, conspiracy theorists present more believable and potentially true ideas like there being cover-ups surrounding the deaths of JFK and Princess Diana – theories most Americans and Brits now believe likely, according to mainstream polls.

As WikiLeaks' founder Julian Assange succinctly put it: "There are conspiracies everywhere. There are also crazed conspiracy theories. It's important not to confuse these two."

Worth noting, also, is that when members of the Establishment mock conspiracy theories, they invariably quote the most bizarre premises that only the most paranoid and unstable in conspiracy circles – yes we refer to the Tinfoil Hatters – actually believe. This has proven to be very effective in undermining the more credible conspiracy theorist who may discover an awkward truth about an administration, a corporation or a well-known individual.

German novelist, pacifist and Nobel Peace Prize-recipient Hermann Hesse was labeled an eccentric and a traitor for resisting the ideologies of a popular candidate who was making waves in Germany's political scene in the early 1930's. As a result of Hesse's rebellious stance against fascism, and especially against the new wave of anti-Semitism, the critically-acclaimed author was soon blacklisted by all major newspapers in the nation and had his books banned and systematically burned by that same leader's political party.

As the politician swept into power and his party began beating the drums of war, Hesse continued to speak out in support of Jewish people and, living in exile outside of Germany, helped others flee from the brutal regime.

The political party was, of course, the Nazi Party and the individual who Hesse opposed was the charismatic Adolf Hitler.

If a new, charismatic politician with intentions as evil as Hitler's entered the political scene today and someone discovered that politician's plans and revealed them to the public, would their theories be listened to any more readily than Hermann Hesse's were?

By consistently reminding the public of the majority of conspiracy theorists who are clearly one missed-medication away from being locked up in asylums, the global elite are also able to discredit the 5% who may have stumbled on to something legitimate.

So the key with conspiracy theories is not to throw out the baby with the bathwater like the Establishment is relying on you to keep doing. In other words, don't discard good info or intel with the bad.

A large number of conspiracy theories initially scoffed at have since been proven to be true. Examples include: *the Gulf of Tonkin Incident* – the fabricated event that started the Vietnam War; *Watergate* – the proven allegation that US President Richard Nixon spied on Democrats; *MK-Ultra* – the Central Intelligence Agency's extensive mind control program was a conspiracy theory for over two decades until partially declassified in 1975; and *the Dreyfus Affair* – the 19th Century travesty involving the wrongful conviction of artillery officer Alfred Dreyfus by the French Government who later admitted to framing Dreyfus.

More recently, after years of claims by conspiracy theorists that the fabled *Area 51*, in Nevada, existed, the US Government and the CIA released declassified documents that clearly show it does exist and has existed all along.

We do not profess to be authorities on any of the subjects in this book. Nor do we get into absolutism. On the contrary, we believe very few people alive today can know for sure the whole truth about any of the complex topics we cover.

Our attitude when researching or writing about such topics has always been: *We know very little*. We took that approach when putting this book together. In our opinion that's the best way to tackle conspiracy theories or, indeed, any contentious incidents, policies or claims not publicly acknowledged or admitted to by officialdom.

Many people are programmed to instantly dismiss all conspiracy theories while others are just as ready to gullibly believe every theory fed to them. Both approaches are different sides of the same coin, and that coin is absolutism.

Believing in absolutes is a recipe for dogmatism and ignorance. The middle-path of open-mindedness combined with healthy skepticism seems to be the wisest route to take in our opinion.

Although "Conspiracy Theories" features in this book's title, many of the subjects we cover are actually *conspiracy fact*. Meaning they've already been confirmed as true by the appropriate authority or validated by the release of declassified documents and the like, but strangely remain categorized as *conspiracy theories* because confirmation of their validity has been ignored or at the very least not widely reported by mainstream media.

The conspiracy facts in our thriller series were noted by Louisiana-based author, historian and renowned US war veterans' advocate Remy Benoit. "A page turning, frightening high action journey into the world of corrupted power," Ms. Benoit says of the trilogy in her review, "that goes beyond conspiracy theories to tortured reality."

Even though the pages of this book contain rare and extraordinary information, it's surprising how much of it is verifiable and freely available in the public domain – there to be discovered as long as you know what you're looking for.

In recent years, various celebrities have been branded conspiracy theorists by mainstream media outlets and government departments. These public figures include Martin Sheen, Mark Ruffalo, Rosie O'Donnell, Sharon Stone, Spike Lee, Bruce Willis, Oliver Stone, Willie Nelson, Mos Def, Charlie Sheen, Juliette Binoche, Billy Corgan, Russell Brand, David Lynch, Randy Quaid, Ron Paul, Joe Rogan, Roseanne Barr, Phil Donahue, Jim Carrey, Geraldo Rivera, Robbie Williams, Sean Stone, Prince, Jesse Ventura, Dave Chappelle, Shirley MacLaine, Jim Corr, Henry Rollins, Woody Harrelson and Michael Moore.

This partial list of famous individuals with alternative viewpoints illustrates how being a conspiracy theorist isn't as rare as it used to be, and may even be trending toward the norm depending on how the term is defined.

That's not surprising given the balance of power between the state and the individual has swung to an unprecedented degree in favor of the state. Every day, it seems, more civil liberties are being eroded in the name of *national security*.

Events like the bailout of financial institutions ahead of regular citizens during the global financial crisis and the unwelcome post-9/11 foreign conflicts have left many citizens in the West second-guessing their governments.

Surveys have also shown that a big percentage of the public feel they're being manipulated by corporations, banks, international interests and the media as well as by politicians who appear to have less respect for voters than ever before. It's almost as if the public sense there must exist within government little-known powerbrokers who are not *for the people*, but against them.

We believe these trends in society explain why *The Orphan Trilogy* has proven to be so popular and why it has established a loyal fan base of readers worldwide.

In all likelihood, the number of people labeled *conspiracy theorists* is going to increase exponentially. Internationally, they probably already number hundreds of millions and so can no longer be dismissed as lunatics on the fringes of society.

Therefore, if questioning the motivations of political administrations and reminding you of the well-documented nefarious activities of the global elite make us conspiracy theorists, then hell, we'll accept that label and wear it with pride.

Before you read on, we'd also ask you to keep in mind that we are two working-class guys. We know all about the injustices that come with being humble citizens living in so-called democratic nations where democracy has all but vanished. We are tired of seeing honest, hard-working people being screwed over by greedy, corrupt corporations and are incensed by the spineless political leaders who permit them to commit such crimes.

Our mission in writing this book is twofold: to expose the global agenda designed to keep the power in the hands of a select few (the top 1%) and to empower the masses with essential knowledge that's been withheld from them until now.

From what we've observed, nearly all other conspiracy theory books have either been by established conspiracy theory authors and written almost exclusively for like-minded people, or they've been penned by academic-types with a high-brow intellectualism that only other academics can decipher.

This book, on the other hand, is written for the lower classes and the homeless, the outcasts and the marginalized, the abused and the victimized, the unpaid and the underpaid, the overworked and the out-of-work, the refugees and the poor, the uneducated and the undereducated, the forgotten and the lonely, the misunderstood and all the other underdogs of society who together, collectively, form *the majority* – or the 99%, if you will.

Contrary to what we, the people, have been told, *we* are the power; *we* have supreme authority because *we* are the masses and true power always resides with the masses, never with the global elite who, by their very nature, have always been a vulnerable minority and will always continue to be...

As long as the masses realize that, of course.

James Morcan & Lance Morcan (March, 2014)

FALSE FLAG OPERATIONS

"Why else do you think we are permanently at war in various regions all over the world? And why is it the citizens of this country, one of the richest on earth, get poorer each year?"

−The Orphan Factory

One of the recurring themes throughout *The Orphan Trilogy* is that the global elite will continue to profit any way they can. That often means orchestrating wars all over the planet. And to create wars there don't need to be any genuine enemies, only *perceived* enemies. If enough citizens believe their national security's in jeopardy then politicians who propose wars will receive the support they need.

Of course, the public are reliant on the media to inform them of the facts regarding potential threats. And therein lies the problem.

In early 2013, the world was told North Korea was on the verge of starting a nuclear war. This sparked a certain amount of fear worldwide while on social media reaction to the rumored nuclear threat bordered on something closer to hysteria.

Notwithstanding Kim Jong-un's Democratic People's Republic of Korea is a brutal regime that has committed untold human rights violations against its own people, it appeared then as now an unlikely threat to world peace. Despite the 25 million-strong rogue state having declared itself a nuclear power, it seemed in all probability to be just that – self-declared and nothing more. The vast majority of nuclear and regional experts agreed that North Korea's arsenal amounted to only a handful of crude devices and they concluded the country was unlikely to have nuclear-armed missiles capable of reaching the United States.

Furthermore, the overwhelming consensus was that to become a true nuclear power, North Korean scientists would need a lot more bomb fuel than they had access to at that time.

Siegfried Hecker, an American nuclear scientist who has regularly been granted access to North Korea's nuclear facilities, said the rogue nation lacked the materials to be a nuclear threat. Posting on the website of Stanford University's Center for International Security and Cooperation in April 2013, Hecker said: "North Korea does not yet have much of a nuclear arsenal because it lacks fissile materials and has limited nuclear testing experience."

Other similarly qualified commentators expressed near identical viewpoints. However, none of these expert opinions seem to have been taken into account by Western media outlets. Instead, most ran with the sensationalist angle that a nuclear war was a possibility. Some journalists even went so far as to mention the potential for World War Three by bringing China into the equation and assuming it would side with North Korea in any international conflict.

Less than a month or so later the news story had completely fizzled.

From what we can ascertain, the whole episode was essentially the media hyping up a decades old stand-off between North Korea and the West.

This brief but high profile news story drove us to question whether any wars have arisen from sensationalism or propaganda.

Conventional wisdom suggests all international armed conflicts since WW2 were inevitable and the millions of soldiers and civilians who have been killed during this period were sacrificed for some greater good. Certainly that's the commonly-held belief about conflicts Western nations – America and Britain in particular – have been involved in.

But is this really true?

If wars create vast sums of money for the global elite, is it possible the Soviets, the Viet Cong and Muslim extremists were, or are, also fabricated enemies of the West along with North Korea? Or at least exaggerated threats?

We also questioned whether there are enough *natural* enemies left in the 21st Century to organically lead to wars involving superpowers. After researching the history of false flag operations, we would have to say *no*. Otherwise, why would there be a need for any of these false flag attacks? If the purported aggressors were invading other nations in broad daylight then surely there'd be no need to fabricate anything.

A false flag operation is basically the act of committing a terrorist event or an act of war and having others blamed for it. In recent times those *others* are usually oil-rich countries like Iraq, geographically or strategically important nations such as Cuba, or drug-abundant states like Afghanistan.

False flag terrorism is employed by governments and intelligence agencies all over the world. It is cleverly orchestrated propaganda designed to provoke specific reactions from the masses in the build-up to war. *Sowing the seed*, they call it, where – in agricultural terms – the ground is prepared for the harvest that will most assuredly follow. The harvest in this case being war, or more to the point, the spoils of war.

The powers-that-be understand that to create the appropriate atmosphere for war, it's necessary to create within the general populace a hatred, fear or mistrust of others regardless of whether those *others* belong to a certain group of people or to a religion or a nation.

Essentially, the global elite's modus operandi when it comes to creating the perfect environment for wars can be summed up in two words: *manufacturing consent*.

"In war, truth is the first casualty."
–Aeschylus, Greek dramatist (525 BC - 456BC)

ANCIENT ROME

Roman emperor Nero is believed by many historians to be responsible for one of the earliest false flag operations. Those historians claim that Nero was the perpetrator of the Great Fire of Rome in 64 AD in which a third of the ancient city was torched.

The emperor's ulterior motive, they say, was to build *Domus Aurea*, an enormous building that would include the Colossus of Nero – none other than a massive bronze statue of himself! Before the fire, the Senate had blocked the emperor's proposal to destroy a third of the city to make way for this complex.

According to Roman historian Tacitus (56 AD – 117 AD), Nero told the Roman population that the Christians, *whom Rome was at war with*, were responsible for the fire.

While not everyone agrees with Tacitus, no-one disputes that Nero got his way in the end. The impressive Domus Aurea was built in the heart of ancient Rome precisely where the great fire had cleared away the aristocratic dwellings. Naturally, the complex included that statue of himself – the mighty Colossus of Nero.

NAZIS FRAMING COMMUNISTS

Another fire was responsible for one of many Nazi false flag operations.

In 1933, the Reichstag, the seat of the German parliament, was set ablaze. Adolf Hitler immediately stated he had evidence that communist terrorists started the fire. Most Germans readily accepted that – influenced no doubt by the month-long, Nazi-sponsored street violence that preceded the fire. The violence achieved its aim of creating a *Red Scare*, or a fear of communists, within the general populace.

The following day, Hitler and his party persuaded the elderly and senile President von Hindenburg to sign the *Reichstag Decree*. The decree, which was supposedly a defence against future terrorist acts, suspended almost every major civil liberty afforded German citizens at that time.

Despite the Nazi party's attempt to blame the fire on a group of communists, the communists were later acquitted by the German government itself.

Most historians agree that members of the Nazi Party were responsible for the fire in the Reichstag. The Hitlerites did this in stealth of course, using one Marinus van der Lubbe, a mentally disturbed arsonist hungry for fame, as their patsy. They'd received a tip-off that van der Lubbe planned to burn the building down. Not only did the Nazis let him do it, they encouraged him and even helped by leaving gasoline in parts of the building.

"All propaganda must be presented in a popular form and must fix its intellectual level so as not to be above the heads of the least intellectual of those to whom it is directed."

–Adolf Hitler, Mein Kampf

THE US MILITARY'S PROPOSAL TO KILL AMERICANS

In 1962, the US Government's Department of Defense and Joint Chiefs of Staff proposed carrying out acts of terrorism on American soil to justify military intervention in Cuba.

Hard to swallow or believe, we know, but it's on the record. Numerous military and intelligence documents recording these disturbing false flag proposals, known as *Operation Northwoods*, have since been declassified.

Operation Northwoods remained a secret for 35 years. The sinister proposal first came to the public's attention in November 1997 when The John F. Kennedy Assassination Records Review Board declassified various top secret military records, which included the Northwoods documents. The following year, the National Security Archive published further revealing information on Northwoods.

A (since declassified) 'Top Secret' memo dated March 13, 1962, addressed to the Secretary of Defense and signed by then-Chairman of the Joint Chiefs of Staff makes for interesting reading. Its subject line reads: *Justification for US Military Intervention in Cuba.*

Item No. 1 on that memo reads: "The Joint Chiefs of Staff have considered the attached Memorandum for the Chief of Operations, Cuba Project, which responds to a request of that office for brief but precise description of pretexts which would provide justification for US military intervention in Cuba."

Operation Northwoods' plans included the sinking of US war ships, shooting down hijacked passenger planes, killing innocent American citizens, letting off bombs and orchestrating other violent terrorist acts in major cities including Washington DC and Miami.

Every event would be blamed on Fidel Castro and the Cuban regime. The Joint Chiefs of Staff's logic was that these events would help gain enough support from the American public and the world at large for a US military invasion of Cuba.

Fortunately, President Kennedy immediately rejected the Northwoods proposal and fired one of its main proponents, Lyman Lemnitzer, who was then Chairman of the Joint Chiefs of Staff.

The following year, Kennedy was assassinated in Dallas, Texas, while Lemnitzer was appointed Supreme Allied Commander of NATO.

Go figure!

In his 2001 book *Body of Secrets*, US political journalist and bestselling author James Bamford wrote that Operation Northwoods "called for innocent people to be shot on American streets; for boats carrying refugees fleeing Cuba to be sunk on the high seas; for a wave of violent terrorism to be launched in Washington, D.C., Miami, and elsewhere. People would be framed for bombings they did not commit; planes would be hijacked. Using phony evidence, all of it would be blamed on Castro, thus giving Lemnitzer and his cabal the excuse, as well as the public and international backing, they needed to launch their war".

Sadly, Bamford is one of the few well-known political commentators to write about Operation Northwoods. When the documents were declassification in 1997, they were almost universally ignored by the media.

Apparently on-the-record discussions within the US Government about murdering its own citizens as propaganda to create a war were not deemed newsworthy.

Nine knew from experience it was simply about those powerful few, the secret elite, who manipulated the world's nations. On his many international assignments over the years, he had discovered the so-called evil countries were all too often controlled by the same people who ran the countries fighting to **liberate** *them.*
  –The Ninth Orphan

THE FALSE FLAG THAT BEGAN THE VIETNAM WAR

On August 4, 1964, President Lyndon Johnson alerted his fellow Americans on national television that North Vietnam had attacked the American destroyer *USS Maddox* in the Gulf of Tonkin.

Not long after, Congress passed the *Gulf of Tonkin Resolution*, which gave Johnson the green light to begin military operations against North Vietnam. American troops were soon stationed in Vietnam and neighboring countries, and the war that would dominate an era began.

However, President Johnson and his Secretary of Defense, Robert McNamara, successfully hoodwinked the American people because North Vietnam never initiated a sea battle with the *USS Maddox* as the Pentagon had claimed, and the so-called unequivocal evidence of a second attack by the North Vietnamese is now commonly acknowledged as being a false report.

A National Security Agency (NSA) report on the Gulf of Tonkin Incident, declassified in 2005, concluded that *USS Maddox* had engaged the North Vietnamese Navy on August 2, 1964, but (and this is a big but) "The *Maddox* fired three rounds to warn off the communist boats. This initial action was never reported by the Johnson administration, which insisted that the Vietnamese boats fired first."

Regarding the all-important second attack on August 4 – which effectively caused the Vietnam War – the NSA report concluded there were no North Vietnamese Naval vessels present during the entire incident: "It is not simply that there is a different story as to what happened; it is that no attack happened that night."

If an organization as biased as the NSA says no attack ever happened then it seems very safe to say the Gulf of Tonkin Incident was nothing but a phantom attack on the US Military. It was carefully crafted propaganda devised to manufacture consent for all-out war.

In this instance that propaganda ended up costing approximately 60,000 American lives and three million Vietnamese lives.

*Factual reporting is all too often propaganda designed
to provoke certain reactions from the masses.*
–The Orphan Factory

According to our research, WW2 was one of the last legitimate wars. Legitimate in that there was probably no other alternative but war. Nearly all other wars since – especially the Gulf Wars,

Vietnam, The Falklands War and the various Afghan wars – have simply been money-spinners spawned by the fear of fabricated enemies or at least unproven enemies.

This all leads to other questions.

Were communists ever a valid threat? When the US pulled out of Vietnam, why didn't the much hyped *Domino Theory* ever occur? Why weren't most other Asian countries overrun by communism as this theory stated was inevitable?

Is it realistic to have a war on 'terror' instead of a conventional war against a recognizable nation or group of nations? Can bearded nomads living in caves in Afghanistan or Pakistan really be a genuine threat to superpowers? And can isolated and impoverished nations like North Korea prevent world peace if the rest of the world wants peace?

Would North Korean president Kim Jong-un actually order his military to fire nuclear weapons and incite war? If so, what would be in it for North Korea when they'd obviously be committing suicide by inviting the rest of the world to immediately invade them? Can a leader of any nation really be that stupid?

And why is it leaders of such fiercely independent nations as Cuba, Venezuela, Iran and Libya are usually portrayed as madmen while the likes of George W. Bush are said to be completely sane?

Maybe world leaders and the invisible puppet masters who pull their strings are not that different to Rome's Emperor Nero all those centuries ago.

And it appears the world has not learnt from the well-documented false flag deceptions of the past, for as at the time of writing, news reports are surfacing that imply a new arms conflict between Russia, the Ukraine and the United States is possible.

Although the disagreement over the disputed region of Crimea appears to be a little more complicated than the North Korea issue, the usual signs of propaganda also seem to be being disseminated by warmongers. Echoing almost verbatim the alarmist news reports on North Korea a year earlier, talk of a return to the days of the Cold War, or even the possibility of

World War Three, are being mentioned in the media in regard to this standoff in the Ukraine.

We certainly don't pretend to have all the answers, but we agree with whoever it was who said we should all study the past to understand the present.

Of course, we could be totally wrong in our assumptions concerning wars. In which case, North Korea really may be about to nuke us all! If that's true, the best advice we could give you is to put this book down immediately and spend what's left of your precious life in party mode.

2

THE SECRET HISTORY
OF MIND CONTROL

*Some of America's highest profile assassins – including the
likes of John Lennon's killer Mark David Chapman and
Robert Kennedy's assassin Sirhan Sirhan – claimed they
were CIA-programmed killers hypnotized by MK-Ultra.
The media portrayed them as crazed lone gunmen, so
naturally the public paid little attention to their claims.
Kentbridge, however, knew it was possible some of these
men were mind controlled soldiers, or Manchurian
Candidates, carrying out assassination orders their
conscious minds were not even aware of.*

–The Ninth Orphan

In our trilogy, the orphans are up against – amongst other things –
mind control programming. Most don't realize they are under the
spell of mind control. They simply know they are fighting against
something dark which lies deep within, hidden in their psyche.

In *The Orphan Uprising* our lead character Number Nine, aka
Sebastian, goes up against a legion of mind-controlled orphans he
grew up with. Nine only escapes the sinister tentacles of
brainwashing when helped by an FBI agent who specializes in
deprogramming mind control victims.

On the surface, our series' plot may sound like far-fetched
science fiction. However, the reality is mind control is a
documented fact.

Manipulating the thoughts and behaviour of unsuspecting victims has been occurring for at least 60 years. From declassified files from governments, intelligence agencies and the military, to media reports and scientific journals, to interviews with psychiatrists involved in experiments, mind control is on-the-record and official.

It's worth considering here what British author and pacifist Aldous Huxley wrote in his 1958 non-fiction work *Brave New World Revisited*: "It is perfectly possible for a man to be out of prison, and yet not free – to be under no physical constraint and yet to be a psychological captive, compelled to think, feel and act as the representatives of the national state, or of some private interest within the nation, wants him to think, feel and act."

Huxley was alluding to the dark art of mind control, suggesting who the architects of this malicious behavior modification were and implying its extensive possibilities.

During the course of researching this subject for *The Orphan Trilogy* we uncovered the little known history of mind control, and it's something of a long, spooky rabbit hole to say the least. By reading and analyzing court cases, doctors' reports and declassified documents, we became aware of the often disastrous impact mind control programs have had on the lives of innocent civilians over the decades.

MIND CONTROL IN THE THIRD REICH

Most of the earliest reports of mind control come from Nazi Germany. In fact, many researchers have surmised that all subsequent mind control programs – including British, Russian and American programs – have firm roots in these early German experiments and applications.

"Hitler's philosophy and his concept of man in general were shaped to a decisive degree by psychiatry," according to Dr. Thomas Roeder and his co-authors Volker Kubillus and Anthony

Burwell in their 1995 book *Psychiatrists: The Men Behind Hitler*. They wrote: "An influential cluster of psychiatrists and their frightening theories and methods collectively form the missing piece of the puzzle of Hitler, the Third Reich, the atrocities and their dreadful legacy."

Lebensborn was one of numerous Nazi programs that incorporated mind control techniques. The SS-backed program, which was a pet project of senior Nazi party member Heinrich Himmler, was set up in 1935 with the goal of increasing the Aryan population. It involved kidnapping thousands of very young children who were deemed to be "racially pure". Some were orphans, some were not. They were sent to camps built specifically for the mind control tactics which would come to be known as *Eindeutschung* – meaning *Germanization*. Basically, it amounted to brainwashing the children to think like Nazis, even if they were not German.

SS officer Doctor Josef Mengele, infamously nicknamed the *Angel of Death* for his horrific human experiments at Auschwitz, is said to have been employed in the *Lebensborn* program, albeit quite secretively.

Doctor Mengele conducted one of the earliest studies on trauma-based mind control during his tenure at the Auschwitz concentration camp. Some researchers say that the Angel of Death's mind control methodologies became the primary brainwashing techniques used to reprogram the young children in *Lebensborn* facilities Europe-wide.

These advances in mind control techniques and technologies didn't disappear with the fall of Nazi Germany. When the Soviets and the Americans invaded the country and divided the spoils, they both inherited these sophisticated mind control breakthroughs.

BLUEBIRD

Project Bluebird was the CIA's first official behavior modification program. Created in 1949, its purpose was to study behavior modification, interrogation and general mind control as well as interrelated subjects.

Bluebird was an umbrella project spawned from the US Government's super-secret *Project Paperclip*. Also known as *Operation Paperclip*, it was a sinister venture that brought hundreds of Nazi scientists to America immediately after World War Two. They were spirited into the US, often with new identities. Many were experts in brainwashing and other mind control methods. Some were even known war criminals, prosecuted during the Nuremberg Trials.

Yes you read that right: the US Government's mind control programs stem directly from the horrendous psychiatric experiments the Nazis conducted during the Holocaust.

Again, this may all sound very far-fetched, but we implore you to do the research if you can't believe it. Paperclip is on-the-record, and fascist methodologies really did worm their way into nations throughout the West. (See chapter 12 for the history of Project Paperclip).

The sad thing was Seventeen would remain completely unaware she was being exploited, such were the ramifications of the insidious mind control programs.
                                        –The Ninth Orphan

ARTICHOKE

By 1950, Project Bluebird had morphed into *Project Artichoke*, which was a forerunner to the better known *Project MK-Ultra*.

Artichoke included non-consensual medical experiments in which elite psychiatrists created new identities in some people, amnesia in others and inserted false memories into the minds of the remaining subjects.

Professional magician John Mulholland was quietly recruited by Artichoke administrators to hypnotize subjects and prepare them for mind control experiments. In the early 1950's, he stopped performing magic shows, citing health problems. However, it was later revealed Mulholland had actually become an intelligence agent for the Central Intelligence Agency.

The following excerpt from a now declassified CIA memo dated 1952 summarizes the agency's motivations with Artichoke: "Can we get control of an individual to the point where he will do our bidding against his will and even against fundamental laws of nature, such as self-preservation?"

MK-ULTRA

The most documented government mind control program worldwide is *Project MK-Ultra*. This human research operation in behavioral engineering began in the early 1950's and was run through the CIA's Scientific Intelligence Division. It continued for a quarter of a century, and it used American and Canadian citizens as its test subjects, usually without their knowledge or consent.

Doctor Sidney Gottlieb was in charge of MK-Ultra from its inception until the mid-1960's. By all accounts a callous and eccentric individual, Gottlieb was the inspiration for Peter Sellers' title role in Stanley Kubrick's 1964 black comedy *Dr. Strangelove*.

Many researchers have deduced that the CIA's goal was to create real-life Manchurian Candidates. We'd have to agree, although there are probably wider applications of effective mind control than producing programmed assassins.

As a result of the United States' Freedom of Information Act, tens of thousands of government documents relating to Project

MK-Ultra have been obtained by independent researchers. Other documents regarding MK-Ultra have also been officially declassified.

The project finally came to the American public's attention in 1975 when it was discussed in the US Congress.

President Gerald Ford also set up a commission to investigate MK-Ultra and other CIA activities. This led to Senate hearings on MK-Ultra in 1977 during which Senator Ted Kennedy stated: "The Deputy Director of the CIA revealed that over 30 universities and institutions were involved in an extensive testing and experimentation program which included covert drug tests on unwitting citizens at all social levels, high and low, native Americans and foreign."

Seemingly following the same mind control protocols laid down by the Nazis, the CIA selected people from the most vulnerable sectors of American society to experiment on – orphans, the mentally ill, prisoners, the poor, the handicapped. Basically those who didn't have a voice or the wherewithal to seek help.

CIA doctors involved in MK-Ultra experiments incorporated various methods to manipulate people's brains and alter their mental states. These included disruptive electromagnetic signals, sensory deprivation, hypnosis, electroshock, sexual abuse and drugs, especially LSD.

Equally disturbing, the list of infamous people connected to, or rumored to be associated with, MK-Ultra almost reads like a who's who of the worst American criminals in the 20th Century.

Lawrence Teeter, the lawyer representing Robert F. Kennedy's assassin, Sirhan Sirhan, proposed that his client was an MK-Ultra victim. Teeter stated Sirhan displayed all the signs of being hypnotized before and after RFK's assassination.

Enough evidence exists to conclude that Theodore Kaczynski, otherwise known as the Unabomber, participated in MK-Ultra experiments conducted at Harvard University from 1959 to 1962. Although these Harvard experiments appeared relatively benign, they were surreptitiously sponsored by the CIA and that seems tantamount to a smoking gun.

Oklahoma City bomber Timothy McVeigh – a decorated Gulf War veteran – claimed to have been implanted with some kind of microchip while serving in the US Army. He also claimed he was yet another victim of MK-Ultra's vast web.

Interestingly, the US Army Major and mind control victim that Denzel Washington played in the 2004 remake of *The Manchurian Candidate* also had a microchip implanted in his body. Perhaps in a case of art imitating life, Washington's character was also a decorated Gulf War veteran who served in *Operation Desert Storm*, just as McVeigh did.

The 1978 Jonestown massacre in the jungles of Guyana is considered by various independent investigators to have been a large scale MK-Ultra experiment. Until 9/11, the Jonestown tragedy had the dubious distinction of being the greatest loss of American civilian lives in one single act. (See more on Jonestown in chapter 10).

There are also possible MK-Ultra links to Ronald Reagan's would-be assassin John Hinkley, Jr., as well as John Lennon's killer Mark David Chapman. Suspiciously, a copy of *The Catcher in the Rye* was found on both men upon their arrest – suspicious as J.D. Salinger's classic novel is said by many to be a mind control trigger device for MK-Ultra victims. (See chapter 27 for more on *The Catcher in the Rye*).

In 1976, more than two decades after MK-Ultra began, President Gerald Ford prohibited "experimentation with drugs on human subjects, except with the informed consent, in writing and witnessed by a disinterested party, of each such human subject."

However, repeated rumors suggest the MK-Ultra program continues – probably under another codename and perhaps as a Black Op rather than a government-sanctioned project.

For example, some say mind control technologies were employed during the First Gulf War on Saddam Hussein's million-strong Iraq army. This theory suggests the US army unleashed a type of advanced mind interference weapon so that Iraqi soldiers would lose their sanity and therefore surrender without much resistance or bloodshed. Although the Iraq army did surrender relatively quickly and there were reports of unusual goings on, it must be noted this Gulf War theory is not remotely proven and remains mere speculation.

At the civilian level, more MK-Ultra victims continue to come forward. In 1995, there were new US congressional hearings on MK-Ultra, which included statements made by mind control victims and the therapists who treated them.

Kentbridge's guilt stemmed from the fact he'd reluctantly agreed to enter his orphans into the MK-Ultra program – and while they were still very young. Naylor had convinced him at the time Omega needed a way to control its orphans if any of them ever rebelled.

–The Ninth Orphan

BRAINWASHING RUMORS

The self-proclaimed mind control victims have gotten weirder and weirder in recent years. They include those who claim they have been *Eyes Wide Shut*-style sex slaves under mind control their entire lives.

A word of caution is needed when considering these recent and highly sensational mind control claims. Firstly, it must be taken into consideration that those who are mentally unstable can latch on to reported projects like MK-Ultra as a way of validating their existence or else attempting to circumnavigate their mental illness. Secondly, mind control reports in the 21st Century have become a lot more hazy. They should not be compared to the highly documented mind control projects of the 20th Century – like MK-Ultra.

That's not to say some of these more recent reports are aren't true. However, the problem is the whole mind control subject has now become entangled in celebrity worship and conspiracy theorists with hidden agendas.

MONARCH

The Internet and sites like YouTube are awash with conspiracy theories about one of MK-Ultra's rumored, yet so far unproven, spin-off programs – *Project Monarch*. Conspiracy theorists say Monarch involves, among other things, the control of famous artists in Hollywood and in the music industry in particular. The apparent aim being to negatively influence the masses.

Celebrities mentioned in connection with Monarch include dead icons like Marilyn Monroe, Whitney Houston, Michael Jackson, Brittany Murphy, Jim Morrison, Jimi Hendrix and even Elvis Presley. Living stars supposedly in the program include almost every major celebrity alive – to our eyes at least. Stars that conspiracy theorists mention time and again include Britney Spears, Tiger Woods, Lady Gaga, Jay-Z, Megan Fox, Nicki Minaj, Paris Hilton, Katy Perry, Beyoncé, Miley Cyrus and Rihanna. And that's just the tip of the iceberg in terms of names bandied around.

The key fact is Project Monarch's existence is not verified by any declassified documents or any other official government materials for that matter. This is confirmed by Michael Barkun, a professor emeritus of political science at Syracuse University, who states in his 2003 book, *A Culture of Conspiracy: Apocalyptic Visions in Contemporary America*, that "scholarly and journalistic treatments of MK-ULTRA make no mention of a Project Monarch".

Monarch is therefore far more speculative than MK-Ultra and other documented mind control programs. Frankly, Monarch tends to undermine those proven mind control projects.

You also have to factor in that small but vocal segment of society who are completely obsessed with celebrity and can never get enough stories about their favorite icons. Consider the countless conspiracies on Elvis let alone Michael Jackson, Princess Diana et al. Famous figures like these seem to attract conspiracy theories like moths to the flames. And certain fans of theirs – perhaps with sycophantic tendencies – seem programmed (no pun intended) to create or add to myths surrounding these celebrities.

Whenever celebrities die, the conspiracy theorists inevitably go into overdrive. All the speculation about the death of *Fast and Furious* star Paul Walker in late 2013 is possibly a good example of this disturbing phenomenon.

Although conspiracy theorists have arguably come up with some interesting circumstantial evidence on certain celebrities, it's very possible Project Monarch is entirely fictitious. Or put another way, it could easily be a load of BS!

Naylor, who had always lusted after the seventeenth-born orphan, had misused his powers and treated the blue-eyed blonde as his personal sex slave. He'd resorted to using the MK-Ultra voice-commands to induce her to do whatever he asked. No-one else was aware of this. Not even his victim. In the process, after years of abuse, Seventeen had finally cracked. In medical terms, she had suffered a mental breakdown; in truth, she'd become yet another victim of MK-Ultra, and of Naylor.

–The Orphan Uprising

In the last 15 years or so, there has been a spate of popular movies released featuring mind control and including the incredible history of Project MK-Ultra. Examples include Stanley Kubrick's *Eyes Wide Shut*, *The Men Who Stare at Goats* starring George Clooney, *Conspiracy Theory* with Mel Gibson, the *Bourne* series starring Matt Damon and *The Manchurian Candidate* with Denzel Washington.

Conspiracy theorists say these films spilled quite a few secrets and point to Kubrick's Illuminati symbolism and mind controlled sex slaves in *Eyes Wide Shut*, the hypnotic triggers in *The Manchurian Candidate* as well as the post-assassination amnesia in the *Bourne* movies. Many of these cinematic moments do indeed appear to be based on actual MK-Ultra reports.

On the flip side, Hollywood tends to embellish certain real-world conspiracies for the sake of entertainment. Unfortunately, these embellishments end up being added into the melting pot of mind control lore. When the public are so easily influenced by movies, books and other forms of entertainment, it often makes it difficult to distinguish fiction from reality.

As novelists and filmmakers ourselves, we are guilty of this as well. And here's an inside tip about the entertainment industry: When it comes to bending the truth to assist a story's plot versus staying completely true to the facts, we can assure you any dramatist will always select the former. Mark Twain's old saying "Never let the truth get in the way of a good story" still reigns in Hollywood.

And, of course, we could be totally wrong in all our assumptions concerning mind control. In which case, you can now relax in the knowledge that your thoughts are indeed your own. No governments or corporations are waging war on your mind. You're just being paranoid!

Just in case though, maybe keep wearing that tinfoil hat until all the facts are in...

PUPPET MASTERS PULLING STRINGS

"Bilderberg pulls the strings of every government and intelligence agency in the Western world."

–The Ninth Orphan

What do President Bill Clinton, David Rockefeller, Prince Charles, Bill Gates and Prime Minister David Cameron, plus the founders and CEO's of Google, Facebook and Amazon all have in common?

Each has attended meetings of *the Bilderberg Group*, an invitation-only organization whose annual conferences for the most part remain mysteriously off the record.

In *The Ninth Orphan* we shine a light on the little known Bilderberg Group and portray it as being America's, and the world's, shadow government. We present Bilderberg members as an elite club who pull the strings of various administrations around the globe.

Is there any truth behind this supposed political conspiracy?

Well, that depends on who you ask.

Independent researchers have long claimed the Bilderberg Group undermines democracy and influences everything from nations' political leaders to the venue for the next war; the politicians and industrialists who attend say it's nothing more than a think-tank, conducted without media coverage so the world's most powerful can speak freely.

Certainly, it's easy to see why conspiracy theories plague the group.

BILDERBERG HISTORY

The Bilderberg Group takes its name from the Hotel de Bilderberg, in Oosterbeek, in the Netherlands, where the organization's first meeting took place in 1954. Ever since, every Bilderberg conference has had almost complete media blackouts despite being held at prominent five-star resorts.

Independent researchers point out this dearth of media coverage is highly unusual given the veritable who's who of world leaders and movers-and-shakers in attendance each year. Certainly some high ranking journalists have written articles on Bilderberg conferences, but overall the events are ignored by mainstream media outlets.

AMERICAN BILDERBERGERS

Within the last few years, Google's former CEO and now Executive Chairman Eric Schmidt, Facebook co-founder Chris Hughes as well as Jeff Bezos, founder and CEO of Amazon.com, have all attended Bilderberg conferences. In 2010, Microsoft founder and the world's richest man Bill Gates attended his first Bilderberg conference at the Hotel Dolce, in Sitges, Spain.

Other notable US political figures to have officially attended Bilderberg meetings include former Director of the CIA David Petraeus, former Treasury Secretary Timothy Geithner, former Chairman of the Federal Reserve Ben Bernanke, former Secretaries of State Henry Kissinger, Alexander Haig, Colin Powell and Condoleezza Rice, President Gerald Ford as well as current Governor of Texas Rick Perry.

THE LOGAN ACT

Some political analysts say all American attendees of Bilderberg conferences have been in direct violation of *the Logan Act* – a federal law which prevents US citizens and representatives from making policy decisions in secret with foreign government officials.

However, the catch is that no Bilderberger has ever acknowledged engaging in policy-making during the meetings and there is no conclusive proof that any of them do.

GLOBAL BILDERBERGERS

On the international roster, Bilderbergers have included leaders of almost every Western nation, Swiss bankers, EU Commissioners and Royalty. Among past and present attendees are current Canadian Prime Minister Stephen Harper, former British Prime Ministers Tony Blair, Gordon Brown and Margaret Thatcher, the King of Spain Juan Carlos I and the Duke of Edinburgh, Prince Philip.

In 2013, current British Prime Minister David Cameron came under fire from the British press for attending a Bilderberg conference in Watford, England. On June 7, 2013, leading UK newspaper *The Daily Mail* reported that Cameron would "take part in a debate on the global economy" and that Downing Street said they "will not give details of what is discussed".

Prime Minister Cameron also refused to provide any details of the time and day he would attend the conference – and this only a short while after promising the British public he would lead the "most open and transparent government in the world."

In recent years with the economic rise of the East, the Bilderberg Group has for the first time begun inviting leading business and political figures from Asia, especially Japanese and Chinese citizens.

Nine had heard whisperings that the secretive Bilderberg Group was effectively the World Government, undermining democracy by influencing everything from nations' political leaders to the venue for the next war. He recalled persistent rumors and confirmed media reports that the Bilderberg Group had such luminaries as Barack Obama, Prince Charles, Bill Gates, Rupert Murdoch, Tony Blair, Bill and Hillary Clinton, George Bush Sr. and George W. Bush. Other Bilderberg members sprung forth from Nine's memory bank. They included the founders and CEOs of various multinational corporations like Facebook, BP, Google, Shell and Amazon, as well as almost every major financial institution on the planet.

–The Ninth Orphan

OBAMA, MURDOCH AND THE BUSH/CLINTON CLANS

In addition to the aforementioned Bilderbergers, who are all confirmed to have participated in at least one conference, there's also a raft of other powerful figures *suspected* of having attended the group's annual meetings.

For whatever reason, it appears some world leaders decide it is better for their reputation to meet other Bilderbergers secretly rather than officially. Some critics have speculated this may because these people wish to maintain their façade of being for *the people* rather than the elite. Or put another way, they don't want it known that they represent the 1% instead of the 99%.

One such figure may be President Obama. Shortly before becoming the US President, Barack Obama was strongly rumored to have met with key Bilderberg members at or near their conference venue in Chantilly, Virginia, in 2008.

Veteran Bilderberg observer, Jim Tucker, phoned Obama's office during the presidential election campaign to confirm whether he had attended the conference. A campaign spokeswoman refused to discuss the matter, but would not deny that Obama had attended.

Other rumored attendees include media mogul Rupert Murdoch and US presidents George Bush, Sr. and George W. Bush.

Hillary Clinton also denies having attended any Bilderberg meetings despite reported sightings of her at the locations of the 2006 (Toronto) and 2008 (Virginia) conferences.

Bill Clinton, however, was an official attendee of the 1991 Bilderberg conference in Germany while still a little known Governor of Arkansas; the following year he won the US Presidential Election.

The former US President has since reluctantly answered questions regarding his confirmed involvement with the secretive organization.

Some of the more independent thinkers in the media had compared Naylor's unexpected rise to the top of the CIA ladder to that of Barack Obama and Bill Clinton – both of whom had a speedy ascension to the White House, catching many political analysts by surprise.
–The Ninth Orphan

THE COUNCIL ON FOREIGN RELATIONS

The Council on Foreign Relations is worth a brief study – if only to compare with the Bilderberg Group.

Another elitist, invitation-only organization which operates in almost total secrecy, the council has an equally impressive membership. Among its most famous members are Joe Biden,

George Soros, George H.W. Bush, Richard Branson, Bill and Hillary Clinton, Rupert Murdoch, Oprah Winfrey and Angelina Jolie.

It should be noted that many members of the Council on Foreign Relations have also attended Bilderberg conferences and the two organizations are apparently closely aligned.

On September 6, 2011, less than a month after the paperback edition of *The Ninth Orphan* was first published, one of us (Lance) received an email out of the blue from a senior member of the council.

Note that we are not naming this individual to ensure his/her right to privacy. Some parts of the email have also been redacted to further protect the individual's identity.

From: [surname redacted, first name redacted]
Date: Tue, Sep 6, 2011 at 11:51 AM
Subject: The Bilderberg Group
To: Lance Morcan, Sterling Gate Books

Dear Lance,

I have been a member of the Council on Foreign Relations (CFR) for over [redacted] years. Most of CFR's meetings at NYC headquarters and at CFR's building on F St., a block from the White House, are off the record. For decades, the far right has accused CFR of being a leftwing conspiracy. This is dwaddle in all its unrationed splendor. CFR's membership spans the political horizon from liberal to conservative. Similarly, the Bilderberg Group hears all points of view off the record. This format allows policy-makers to speak more freely. The same rule applies to diplomats when they speak to journalists. Officially, on the record, they can only reflect well known Administration views. Off the record, they can depart from the official line when they feel the Administration has adopted a misguided policy.

[Name redacted]

Whether this long serving CFR member sent this email to protect his/her own interests, or whether this individual genuinely believes elitist groups deserve total privacy, is not clear.

Either way, we strongly feel this Council on Foreign Relations member is misguided in his/her opinions. Obviously he/she has profited from being a CFR member all these years and without naming the industry (again, to protect their right to privacy), let's just say this person is at the very top of their particular field.

Here are some excerpts from our reply to this senior CFR member:

To clarify, we are essentially apolitical and most definitely not related to any of the far right groups you mention. We are not coming from either side of the political spectrum as, according to our research, there are no clear political sides anymore. Left vs. Right is an out-dated concept and an oversimplification of 21st Century politics, in our opinion. As we write in THE NINTH ORPHAN: **Democrats and Republicans were essentially the same party with different faces and that was why, no matter how many promises each leader made, significant change rarely transpired.**

Your comment that CFR membership spans the political horizon from liberal to conservative further cements our belief that the world's leading power players (from various political parties) have agendas beyond the administrations and nations they belong to. That's getting more and more obvious to more and more people we think.

We did read your email carefully and certainly understand the points you make in your email. However, your opinions on this subject actually contrast from many political commentators.

Consider, for example, this excerpt from an article the Washington Times ran on November 2, 2008: **More worrisome are open questions about the sources of Mr. Surroi's considerable wealth and relationships with certain foreign interests. How much control and influence does Mr. Surroi's financial benefactor, the political activist and multibillionaire George Soros, have over him? And why is the shadowy Bilderberg Group of old foreign policy lions from the United States and Europe apparently assisting him with access to their network and trying to prepare him for bigger things?**

Similarly, the Washington Post has also run articles on the Bilderberg Group, questioning their motives. For example, in an article about Vernon Jordan's relationship with then President Bill Clinton, the Washington Post ran the following on January 27, 1998: **After all, it was Jordan who first introduced then-Gov. Clinton to world leaders at their annual Bilderberg gathering in Germany in 1991. Plenty of governors try to make that scene; only Clinton got taken seriously at that meeting, because Vernon Jordan said he was okay.**

To our eyes, the Washington Post and the Washington Times are strongly implying that if certain individuals make the Bilderberg scene (as Clinton did) then great things can happen for them. It could easily be argued those "great things" are unconstitutional or undemocratic in the strictest sense.

We believe the American people, and the citizens of all Western nations, have the right to know about every single thing their representatives do on their behalf. After all, elected officials are merely representing those who hold the true power (the people).

Does the average US citizen know the Bilderberg and Council on Foreign Relations membership of the majority of America's elite?

This CFR member never replied again and we still don't know why he/she chose to email us in this fashion.

Our correspondence with this influential individual reminds us of a line in the 2000 feature film *The Skulls*, which perfectly encapsulates our assessment of organizations like the Bilderberg Group and the CFR: "If it's secret and elite, it can't be good."

People come up with all kinds of reasons to justify clandestine activities. Some say the masses are not smart enough and need wise old men to covertly influence voters. Others argue knights of the round table-style groups are needed to ensure the ill-informed public are not allowed to have too much power.

No matter how the invisible power players spin things, the truth is supporters of such elitist groups are deceiving themselves and others with such justifications.

The bottom line is: *Any time a secret group usurps the collective will of the people, it's wrong. Period.*

One small confirmation of the dangers of secretive and elitist organizations comes from within police forces in the US and UK, and relates to Freemasonry. Senior American and British police chiefs have gone on the record recommending that police officers should not be permitted to join any Masonic lodge. The police chiefs concerned invariably cited fears that Freemason police officers would have conflicts of interest. That's to say officers may at times put the interests of Freemasonry ahead of their police work.

Such dangers are obviously magnified a hundredfold when it comes to high ranking politicians being members of unaccountable organizations like the Bilderberg Group and the CFR.

*Bilderberg's modus operandi reinforced in his mind the
complexity of the global hierarchy. He didn't know if
Omega controlled the Bilderberg Group or vice versa,
but the situation reminded him that no matter how
much anyone thought they knew about the New World
Order elite, there were always higher levels in the
plethora of secret societies and shadow organizations
that ruled the planet.*

–The Ninth Orphan

So what does all this mean exactly? Is it just a pile of the usual circumstantial evidence that seems to conveniently support many conspiracy theories? According to Belgian magnate and former Bilderberg chairman Étienne Davignon, that is exactly the case. In the January 22, 2011 edition of *The Economist*, Davignon said Bilderberg Group meetings allowed attendees to speak off-the-record and share opinions with major figures – without the risk of casual comments being taken out of context by the media.

Those of Davignon's school of thought propose that all conspiracy theories surrounding Bilderberg simply arise because of the group's strict methods of ensuring absolute privacy of participants involved. Then again, it's hard to believe the only decisions the world's elite make at these exclusive resorts each year is what to order for dinner or what time to play golf!

There's also another possibility, or theory, in this discussion. It would lie about half way between the two extremes covered so far in this chapter.

This possibility would suggest that the powerful individuals who attend Bilderberg conferences have no devious intentions. On the contrary, all they really desire is to have informal chats with others at their own business or political level.

However, this would also suggest that in imperceptible ways leaders of different nations end up influencing each other's policymaking. And therefore a globalist agenda would still end up circumventing democracy in the nations represented – albeit subtly and possibly without the awareness of conference attendees.

If this theory is true then the darker intentions would lie with the lesser known individuals running the Bilderberg Group. These *invisible puppet masters* would be using Bilderberg attendees to orchestrate world events to their liking. It could be argued that the carrots the organization dangles – especially assistance in climbing business or political ladders – tug at the personal ambitions of those attendees.

But, of course, we could be totally wrong about everything we wrote about the Bilderbergers in *The Orphan Trilogy*. In which case, you can go back to trusting your elected politicians and believing they have no ulterior motives and really do have your best interests at heart…

INTERNATIONAL BANKSTERS

Fletcher Von Pein was one of the twelve founders of the Omega Agency. He was also a powerful banker and a majority shareholder in the US Federal Reserve which, despite its misleading name, had zero government ownership and was actually a private corporation owned by the global elite.

–The Orphan Factory

Since the Global Financial Crisis of 2007-2008, many around the world have been questioning whether there are certain figures and groups manipulating financial markets behind the scenes. This speculation intensified with the ensuing government bailouts of privately owned banking institutions ahead of the millions of citizens facing bankruptcy.

There has been a growing awareness in the masses of large-scale financial corruption by the elite – or *the 1%*, if you will.

The public are not stupid. What the average person lacks in specific knowledge of money markets, they make up for in spades with street smarts and life experience. And the masses have now caught on to what has been going on for decades, if not centuries, with the bankers of the world.

In *The Orphan Factory*, one of the founding members of the Omega Agency – the shadowy organization that created the orphans – is a senior banker of the US Federal Reserve, aka *the Fed*. We made this character choice as we believe the banking elite are some of the most powerful and influential people around. They shape the world far more than politicians do. After all, money can buy administrations. Some would even argue money can buy elections as well.

If one day proven to be correct, the conspiracy theory surrounding the Federal Reserve is one that may explain a variety of unusual occurrences in financial markets over the years.

In a nutshell, this theory contends that the Fed is an institution that acts independent of the US Congress, has zero transparency or accountability, and even determines its own monetary policy.

Bankster definition: A portmanteau or blend word derived from combining "banker" and "gangster". Usually referred to in the plural form "banksters" to refer to a predatory element within the financial industry.

WHAT IS A CENTRAL BANK?

A central bank is a financial organization responsible for overseeing the monetary system of a nation. It manages a country's currency, sets interest rates and steers an economy toward inflation targets.

If a nation's central bank is managed without internal corruption and without interference from foreign countries, it should be a stabilizing force. In theory, a central bank can shield an economy from volatility in financial markets.

But the operative word is *corruption*.

Numerous economists and historians, and vociferous politicians like Senator Ron Paul and Governor Jesse Ventura, have opined that the global elite had been aiming to control the resources of the US for centuries. Creating an American central bank privately owned by an international banking cartel seemed to be the most efficient way to achieve this aim.

A SHORT HISTORY OF
CENTRAL BANKING IN THE US

In 1791, *the First Bank of the United States* was set up apparently because the Government had a massive debt left over from the Revolutionary War known as the American Revolution. Many researchers say this was the earliest attempt by banking families of the global elite to create a *privately-owned* US central bank, masquerading as a federally-owned entity.

Although the bank had numerous opponents in the political arena, it only controlled 20% of the nation's money supply – unlike the Fed today which manages 100% of the nation's money supply and not a 'penny' less.

American Founding Father and the nation's third President, Thomas Jefferson, was one of the most vocal critics of the First Bank of the United States. He argued the bank was unconstitutional, citing the 10th Amendment.

Jefferson also hinted that a central bank would lead to a monopoly instead of a free market. He said, "The existing banks will, without a doubt, enter into arrangements for lending their agency, and the more favorable, as there will be a competition among them for it; whereas the bill delivers us up bound to the national bank, who are free to refuse all arrangement, but on their own terms, and the public not free, on such refusal, to employ any other bank."

This experiment in US banking ended in 1811 when the bank's charter expired. Because of the institution's many critics, Congress decided not to renew its charter.

Six years later, in 1817, *the Second Bank of the United States* was brought into being as major international banking families continued to push for an American central bank. This bank was also quite temporary, with President Andrew Jackson ending its existence only 15 years later.

However, the global elite's bankers did not give up and in the early 20th Century started formulating ideas to create the US Federal Reserve System as we know it. One of the group's breakthrough ideas came during a secretive meeting at a hunting lodge on Jekyll Island, off the coast of Georgia, when they decided not to call the new bank a central bank. History had shown America did not want a central bank.

After much brainstorming, the deceptive *Federal Reserve* name was agreed upon – presumably because it was assumed this name would fool the public into thinking it was a government-owned bank.

Although representatives of this shadowy banking cartel were open to co-managing this new central bank with Congress, all agreed the bank's members had to be *private banks that would own all of its stock.*

Von Pein's family was a little known, but highly
influential entity within American banking circles.
Banking Royalty, some called it. His grandfather had
been one of the chief orchestrators of the Federal Reserve
Act of 1913, which effectively took ownership of the
bank from the American people.

–The Orphan Factory

FEDERAL RESERVE ACT OF 1913

In 1913, the banksters finally succeeded in creating a US central bank with the passing of the Federal Reserve Act. This bill, which had already been soundly defeated several times, appears to have come to fruition only because of well-orchestrated timing: the Federal Reserve Act was slipped through a skeleton Congress on December 23, 1913 when most of the bill's opponents had already left Congress for the holidays.

The Federal Reserve System, which was first devised in that

secret meeting on Jekyll Island, was now codified by Congress and remains in effect to this day.

Fact: The Federal Reserve is the central bank of the United States, though not a part of the US Government.

Say what?

It's not a part of the government, *at all*.

But it says Federal! Surely it cannot be a privately owned organization?

The Fed is not a part of the government, *at all*.

Critics of the Federal Reserve say its sole purpose is to strip wealth from honest, hardworking American citizens and make the world's leading banking clans even richer.

John Hylan, Mayor of New York City from 1917 until 1925, made some extraordinary statements in a speech he delivered in 1922. What Mayor Hylan said seems to confirm a grand conspiracy was indeed devised for the American banking system by the global elite.

"The real menace of our Republic is the invisible government, which like a giant octopus sprawls its slimy legs over our cities, states and nation," said Mayor Hyland. "To depart from mere generalizations, let me say that at the head of this octopus are the Rockefeller-Standard Oil interests and a small group of powerful banking houses generally referred to as the international bankers. The little coterie of powerful international bankers virtually run the United States government for their own selfish purposes. They practically control both parties, write political platforms, make catspaws of party leaders, use the leading men of private organizations, and resort to every device to place in nomination for high public office only such candidates as will be amenable to the dictates of corrupt big business."

Only nine years after the Federal Reserve System was created, Mayor Hylan already seemed to be aware that this "invisible government" of "powerful international bankers" was controlling the US Government.

JFK VS THE FED

Less than six months before he was assassinated, President Kennedy had begun formulating a new Federal Reserve Act, which many say would have restored the Fed to a fully-fledged US Government bank.

A little-known Presidential decree – *Executive Order 11110* – was signed by Kennedy on June 4, 1963. It would have deprived the Federal Reserve of its ability to loan money to the US Government at interest. By signing the document, President Kennedy was attempting to put an end to the Fed – or at least the Fed as we know it.

Without going into the specifics of Executive Order 11110, it arguably could have stopped the US from reaching its record-level national debt. As of the time of writing, the country's national debt is a crippling 17 trillion dollars – that's US$17,000,000,000,000 – and has increased at approximately 2 billion per day for the last 18 months.

Instead, JFK was assassinated as we all know. But what is less known is *the United States Notes* the President had issued as part of the executive order – notes which were designed to replace the Federal Reserve Notes – were immediately taken out of circulation.

To this very day, the Federal Reserve Notes remain in circulation as the currency all Americans use.

And, of course, what also remained post JFK was a central bank only nominally under the Government's control.

Von Pein understood the entire monetary system was a gigantic Ponzi scheme and could be tampered with accordingly. He and his Federal Reserve cronies controlled interest rates, inflation and the printing of paper money. Thanks to him, funds from the Fed could be consistently funnelled into the Omega Agency via a multitude of offshore bank accounts.

–The Orphan Factory

THE FED IN THE 21ST CENTURY

It has been estimated by independent researchers that eight banking families, including the Rockefeller family, own 75% to 85% of the shares in the Federal Reserve Bank. Many of the individuals in those families are also politicians. They include Republicans and Democrats, so clearly political allegiances make no difference. That's no surprise as it's almost common knowledge that the same financiers bankroll the campaigns of the two dominant parties in American politics.

Interestingly, most of the shareholders of the Fed are also members of the Bilderberg Group and/or the Council on Foreign Relations.

After more than a century of these elite banksters having their way with little opposition, there has in recent times been a groundswell of resistance against the Fed. This resistance began as a grassroots movement early in the 21st Century and has really caught on in the last few years.

Two of the main reasons for the Federal Reserve conspiracy theory reaching popular consciousness were Ron Paul's presidential campaigns and the *Occupy* movement, that protest movement against economic and social inequality.

Congressman Ron Paul, a long-time critic of the Fed, said the following at the Republican GOP debate in Dearborn, Michigan, on October 9, 2007:

"What's happening is, there's transfer of wealth from the poor and the middle class to the wealthy. This comes about because of the monetary system that we have. When you inflate a currency or destroy a currency, the middle class gets wiped out... which is created by the Federal Reserve system benefit. So the money gravitates to the banks and to Wall Street."

And even more to the point, in a CNBC debate with Faiz Shakir on March 20, 2008, Ron Paul was asked to explain why he believes the Federal Reserve should not exist. Paul answered as follows:

"First reason is, it's not authorized in the Constitution, it's an illegal institution. The second reason, it's an immoral institution, because we have delivered to a secretive body the privilege of creating money out of thin air; if you or I did it, we'd be called counterfeiters, so why have we legalized counterfeiting? But the economic reasons are overwhelming: the Federal Reserve is the creature that destroys value. This station talks about free market capitalism, and you can't have free market capitalism if you have a secret bank creating money and credit out of thin air. They become the central planners, they decide what interest rates should be, what the supply of money should be."

Only a few years later, the Occupy Movement became headline news around the world after a series of dramatic protests. To paraphrase, the international protest organization's mission statement is to rally against inequality in all forms, especially economic inequalities. The Occupy Movement also aims to make the spread of wealth more evenly distributed amongst all sectors of society.

2011's *Occupy Wall Street* struck a chord with the masses, and the movement's ideals spread like wildfire from there. Less than a month after the Wall Street occupation began in New York City, there were protests all across America, and even more impressively in 82 countries worldwide.

During Occupy Wall Street, *End the Fed* and *Audit the Fed* were popular slogans used by protestors, and the mainstream media reported on these. *We are the 99%* proved to be an even more popular Occupy slogan – so much so that it soon became a worldwide catchphrase used by charities, television advertisers and common citizens.

Primarily off the back of the awareness gained from the Occupy Wall Street movement and Ron Paul's 2008 and 2012 presidential campaigns, campaigners' desire that the Federal Reserve System be audited sparked nationwide interest.

In 2012, a bill inspired by this movement was passed through the House of Representatives with overwhelming bipartisan support. Called 'Audit the Fed', the bill was introduced into the House by Ron Paul.

However, in late 2013, Paul's son Rand Paul launched an initiative to pass the same bill into the Senate. This debate is still ongoing as of writing, but it does not look likely to become law. Although the bill has some support in the Senate, Rand Paul currently faces stiff opposition from the likes of recently instated Federal Reserve Chair Janet Yellen and President Obama, to name but two.

Why are leaders so scared of having an audit of a supposedly federal organization?

Perhaps it's because there has never been a true, comprehensive audit of the Federal Reserve since the institution began in 1913…

"We have in this country one of the most corrupt institutions the world has ever known. I refer to the Federal Reserve Board and the Federal reserve banks. The Federal Reserve Board, a Government board, has cheated the Government of the United States out of enough money to pay the national debt. The depredations and the iniquities of the Federal Reserve Board and the Federal reserve banks acting together

have cost this country enough money to pay the national debt several times over. This evil institution has impoverished and ruined the people of the United States; has bankrupted itself, and has practically bankrupted our Government."
–*Congressman Louis T. McFadden. 10 June, 1932*

What do all these quotes, facts, opinions, rumors and conjecture mean regarding the financial system?

Admittedly, the points raised in this chapter simply lead to more questions than answers – that's always the hallmark of a good conspiracy theory!

Questions such as:

Is the Federal Reserve designed to be the biggest money laundering institution in the world?

Are there really powerful groups operating behind the scenes who manipulate governments, economies, journalists and elections with effortless ease? If so, how are they able to hide their deceitful activities?

Do journalists purposefully obscure the truths surrounding the Fed in order not to upset the powers that be? Or is the average journalist simply unaware of the history of the Fed?

And finally, remember that we could be totally wrong about everything we wrote on the Federal Reserve here and in *The Orphan Trilogy*. In which case you should probably bank all that cash you keep under your mattress and let it start earning interest!

5

Genius Techniques of the Elite

*The purpose of having the orphans study all these diverse
fields was not for them to just become geniuses, but to
become polymaths – meaning they would be geniuses in a
wide variety of fields. Whether they were studying the
sciences, languages, international finance, politics, the arts
or martial arts, they would not stop until they'd achieved
complete mastery of that subject. Kentbridge himself had
encyclopedic knowledge about almost everything, and
expected nothing less from his orphans.*

–The Ninth Orphan

It has long been speculated that secret societies, mystery schools, intelligence agencies and other clandestine organizations have advanced learning methods superior to anything taught in even the most prestigious universities. Methods which are only ever taught to the chosen few – initiates who have all sworn an oath to keep the group's syllabus *in house* and never reveal any of the teachings to outsiders.

On the rare occasions the public get wind of advanced learning techniques – usually via information leaked to the Internet, sometimes via published books – those techniques are seldom tested or given the attention they deserve and so largely remain in obscurity. One reason for this could be they're often not comprehensible because whoever is behind them has withheld the overall curriculum.

There's many a tale of mysterious figures from secretive groups mastering skills, languages and even complex career paths so quickly that most would say it's impossible. But that opinion assumes we know of, or have access to, all the learning methods known to man.

If we are to assume there are superior learning methods not taught in our mainstream education system then this naturally leads to other questions. What if your child's top-notch education is actually a second-rate education? Or, if you are a student, what if that professor you look up to is no genius, but just a tool of an inferior learning institution?

None of this is to disrespect formal education. It plays a vital role in society and the betterment of Mankind, and only a fool would doubt the importance of getting a good education.

Nor are we suggesting there isn't the odd learning institution that teaches at least some accelerated learning techniques, although such establishments would probably exist on the fringes of mainstream education.

The *Montessori* education system is possibly one such example as it allows children to have greater freedom of expression and to learn in playful and organic ways. Successful alumni of the Montessori system include Jeff Bezos, the founder of Amazon, as well as Wikipedia founder Jimmy Wales and the co-founders of Google, Sergey Brin and Larry Page.

In general however, accelerated learning methods are more likely to be found outside the modern education system. Let's face it, wherever in the world you go, real prodigies are the exception not the norm in the present system. Those rare individuals society labels geniuses are almost always *freaks of nature* and are naturally *gifted* rather than being diligent students who became geniuses because of their education.

In *The Ninth Orphan*, Nine is a pure genius and exhibits a level of intelligence rarely if ever seen in any character in literature. He has a photographic memory, can read entire books in five minutes flat and speaks dozens of languages. Plus he learns new skills extremely fast and is highly adaptable – so much so that he's nicknamed *the human chameleon*.

How Nine reached that level of intelligence, though, is merely implied or hinted at in this first book in the series.

In its prequel, *The Orphan Factory*, we had to design an education system that would reveal exactly how Nine grew up to become that smart. This was quite a challenge as our setting was no Ivy League college. Rather, it was the Pedemont Orphanage, a rundown institution in Riverdale, one of Chicago's poorest neighborhoods.

We had to do a lot of research into radical types of learning. Highlights from that research are covered in this chapter.

Having both gone through the traditional education system and finding it laborious and uninspiring, we found it fun to write about an alternative and more accelerated form of learning in our trilogy. Even so, it took several years of study before we felt confident enough to write about what it would take to create youngsters with intellects as advanced as those of our Pedemont orphans.

We predict, or sincerely hope, that formal education will one day be reflective of what occurs within the fictional Pedemont Orphanage – minus the assassination training of course!

"I'll be a genius and the world will admire me. Perhaps I'll be despised and misunderstood, but I'll be a genius, a great genius."
– Salvador Dalí. Written in his diary at the age of 16.

POLYMATHING ON CHICAGO'S FAR SOUTH SIDE

A book critic who reviewed *The Ninth Orphan* criticized our protagonist Nine for having an IQ, or intelligence quotient, higher than Einstein's. The strong implication in the review was that this was a ridiculous character decision we (the authors) had made.

That all sounds like a valid criticism on the surface, but had this critic gone beyond his own sphere of knowledge and done a little research he would have discovered there are many people whose IQ's have been recorded to be higher than Einstein's. American author Marilyn Vos Savant, for example, has an IQ of 192; Russian chess grandmaster and former world champion Garry Kasparov has an IQ of 194. Incidentally, Einstein's IQ was estimated in the 1920's to between 160 and 190.

But wait, there's much more when it comes to the world of super geniuses...

Quite a few individuals have tested in excess of a 200 IQ score, including South Korean civil engineer Kim Ung-yong (210), former child prodigy and former NASA employee Christopher Hirata (225) and Australian mathematician Terence Tao (225-230).

And last but not least is American child prodigy, mathematician and politician William James Sidis who had an IQ of 250-300. He graduated grammar school at age six, went to Harvard University at age 11 and graduated *cum laude* at the age of 16. Sidis, who died in 1944, could fluently speak 40 languages by the time he reached adulthood.

Remember, the average IQ is 100 and approximately 50% of those tested score between 90 and 110. According to the book *IQ and the Wealth of Nations* by Dr. Richard Lynn and Dr. Tatu Vanhanen, the top five countries in terms of average IQ's of their citizens are Hong Kong (107), South Korea (106), Japan (105), Taiwan (104) and Singapore (103). Further down the list, China, New Zealand and the UK share equal 12th position with a 100 average, while the US is in 19th position with an average citizen IQ of 98.

However, many scholars in the 21st Century now believe IQ scores aren't everything and it's likely areas of intelligence exist that cannot be measured in any test. This is possibly substantiated by the number of successful and iconic individuals who recorded very low IQ scores. These include the once highly articulate and outspoken boxer Muhammad Ali who, as a young man, scored only 78 – an IQ so low it supposedly denotes a mild mental disability!

And of course, the list of the world's so-called most intelligent *excludes* extremely bright individuals in impoverished parts of the world where IQ's are rarely tested. The Indian mathematical genius, Srinivasa Ramanujan (1887-1920), was an example of such incredible geniuses who defy all explanation.

Born into poverty in Erode, India, Ramanujan discovered extraordinary mathematical formulas, despite being self-taught with no formal training in mathematics. He changed the face of mathematics as we know it and left many highly-educated and acclaimed Western mathematicians completely gobsmacked.

Furthermore, the other high-IQ individuals mentioned earlier are only in the top bracket of those who *agreed* to undergo IQ tests *and* allow their scores to be published. It's quite conceivable certain elite individuals belonging to secret societies, mystery schools or intelligence agencies do not reveal their IQ scores. That secret intelligence factor was the basis for our fictional Pedemont orphans who we either state or imply have IQ's of around 200 or higher.

As a result of the accelerated learning techniques within the diverse curriculum that begins before they can even walk or talk, the orphans can assimilate and retain phenomenal amounts of information. By their teens, the child prodigies possess greater amounts of knowledge than even adult geniuses. They are able to solve complex problems, are fully knowledgeable about almost any current world subject or historical event, and are to all intents and purposes organic supercomputers and human library databases.

Again, our orphans are exposed to highly advanced learning methods so that they will have at their disposal all the necessary skills and information to be able to overcome life-and-death problems that may arise on future espionage assignments. They're taught there is no challenge or question that cannot be overcome, solved or answered as long as they fully utilize the power of their minds.

Each child at the Pedemont Orphanage eventually becomes a *polymath* – a person who is beyond a genius. It's a word we use throughout the trilogy as we felt it best describes the orphans' off-the-scale intellects.

A polymath is actually a *multiple-subject genius*. However, the criteria for a polymath is someone who is an expert in vastly different, almost unrelated fields. For example, an artist who works in the film, theatre and literary industries and who is a masterful actor, screenwriter, novelist, film director and film producer would *not* qualify as a polymath as those fields are all artistic mediums and closely related.

Rather, a polymath is someone who has excelled in, or completely mastered, a variety of unrelated or loosely related subjects. These could be as diverse as economics, dance, architecture, mathematics, history, forensic science, cooking and entomology.

And before you go calling yourself a polymath, don't forget you must be an expert in each field. Unfortunately being a jack-of-all-trades and master-of-none doesn't count.

One of the best examples of a polymath is Leonardo da Vinci. Born in Italy in 1452, he was a sculptor, painter, architect, mathematician, musician, engineer, inventor, anatomist, botanist, geologist, cartographer and writer. Although Leonardo received an informal education that included geometry, Latin and mathematics, he was essentially an *autodidact*, or a self-taught individual.

The man who many have called *the* most diversely talented person who ever lived, left behind an array of masterpieces in the painting world alone, including *The Last Supper*, *Mona Lisa* and *The Vitruvian Man*.

The subconscious was always favored over the everyday conscious mind, which was considered too slow to be effective.
–The Orphan Factory

OUTRUNNING THE CONSCIOUS MIND

Developing a genius mindset essentially comes down to two things: operating at speed and using the subconscious mind more than the conscious. This intuitive or relaxed approach to study is the polar opposite of traditional and mainstream forms of education. Apart from some artistic subjects like music or dance, learning institutions generally require pupils to concentrate hard at all times. In other words, students have no choice but to always use their conscious minds, thereby suppressing the great reservoir of the subconscious.

When we are forced to think s-l-o-w-l-y like this our brain functions at well below optimum levels. That's why school students often feel exhausted as studying in this fashion is incredibly draining. But how can we feel mentally drained when neuroscientists and brain researchers agree we each only use a tiny percentage of our brain?

Those who have read *The Orphan Trilogy* will recall our orphans often go into a daydream state whenever they need answers to life-and-death situations. This is because when you defocus you allow your intuitive self, or your subconscious mind, to *deliver* you the answers you need. It just happens, without reaching for it.

We've all experienced pondering a problem all day long only to find we *receive* the solution when forgetting about the problem and thinking of something else. When we stop concentrating so hard, we allow our subconscious to flourish, and those who do this more than others are often called geniuses.

As head of the Pedemont Orphanage, Tommy Kentbridge says to his students in *The Orphan Factory*, "The subconscious mind is where all higher intelligences exist. Every genius throughout history – Tesla, Einstein, Da Vinci – tapped into the infinite power of their subconscious minds."

Studies have shown the subconscious mind can process around 11 million bits of information per second. The conscious mind, however, can only process about 15 to 16 bits of information per second. Quite a difference!

One of the best ways to bring the subconscious mind into the equation is to *outrun* the conscious mind by going so fast it literally can't keep up. So, at Chicago's Pedemont Orphanage, our orphans do everything at speed. They're also taught how to learn things indirectly instead of directly. By skirting around the edges of complex subjects, the children never get information overload or lose their way.

As we wrote in *The Ninth Orphan*, "In the tradition of Leonardo da Vinci and history's other great polymaths, the children were taught how to fully understand anything by using an advanced mental technique where they would simply *life* their minds into comprehension."

To life your mind into comprehension is once again the polar opposite of modern education systems which imply there's only one way to learn: consciously and with intense concentration.

While this indirect way of learning may sound flaky, it is actually backed up by hard science and is not remotely mystical. This approach is about brainwaves and understanding, or recognizing, the optimal state for learning. When you hit the right groove, it's possible to learn quickly and in a satisfying, even enjoyable, fashion.

It is that singularity of mind top sportsmen and martial arts masters achieve. Psychologists sometimes refer to this ultimate mental state as *the zone*, but it's really just about having the most effective brainwaves for learning.

Any time study feels laborious the student is most likely in the beta brainwave, which occurs when the conscious mind is governing. A beta-dominant mind is the perfect recipe for mediocrity and boredom.

The subconscious mind comes into play in other less common brainwaves such as alpha, gamma, theta and delta. These brainwaves have also been shown to be activated when test subjects are laughing, daydreaming, meditating, singing, dancing or spontaneously moving about. Now how many math or English teachers would tolerate those activities in their classrooms?

What if there really is a much quicker, less methodical way of learning that allows you to learn without learning?

Sounds paradoxical, doesn't it?

All the activities the orphans participated in were performed well beyond average speed, be it playing chess, reading books, doing martial arts or learning languages. Kentbridge and specially recruited tutors would push their young charges at accelerated speeds so their conscious minds couldn't keep up. Only when they outran their conscious minds like this could the subconscious kick into action.

–The Orphan Factory

SPEED-READING

One of the most important skills our Pedemont orphans possess is the ability to speed read. Having vast amounts of knowledge, or being *walking encyclopedias*, is a common trait in geniuses, and even more so in polymaths.

Probably the simplest way to gain this amount of knowledge is to learn to read very, very fast.

Speed-reading is therefore at the core of the radical education program we designed in our conspiracy thriller series. However, our orphans' technique is much more advanced than the majority of speed-reading programs currently available to the public. Many such programs simply offer complementary reading skills rather than allowing for a whole new way to absorb the written word.

As we say in *The Ninth Orphan*, "It wasn't so much speed-reading as mind photography – a technique where the practitioner taps into the brain's innate photographic memory. The orphans were taught how to use their eyes and open their peripheral vision to mentally photograph the page of a book, magazine or newspaper at the rate of a page per second. Then they'd consciously recall every detail as if they'd read the material at normal, everyday reading speed. Tens of thousands of books, on all manner of subjects, were sent to the Pedemont Orphanage to keep up with the children's prolific reading habits."

The technique we wrote about was inspired by the most sophisticated speed-reading methods in the real world, as well as analysis of renowned speed-readers. It's also based on the brain's scientifically proven ability to pick up things subliminally and rapidly. By incorporating peripheral vision and photographic memory, it's possible to pick up or *photograph* entire pages at a time rather than one word at a time.

This method enables the Pedemont orphans to read at the rate of about 20,000 words per minute. That's many times faster than most readers can manage. In fact, the average reading speed is only 300 words per minute, or about one page per minute.

Although some skeptics – along with one or two book critics who reviewed our series – have expressed doubt over whether the human brain can absorb such vast quantities of data all at once, speed-reading is not fiction. And it has some famous devotees.

Various US Presidents were confirmed or rumored speed-readers. They include Theodore Roosevelt, Franklin Roosevelt, John F. Kennedy and Jimmy Carter.

Theodore (Teddy) Roosevelt, a self-taught speed-reader, is reported to have read a book before breakfast every single day while serving as president. Teddy's recall was said to be perfect and he could often quote from the books he read.

Kennedy studied under American speed-reading expert Evelyn Wood who could read at an impressive 6000 words a minute. JFK claimed he could read at around 2000 words per minute with a very high comprehension rate.

Carter, who also studied speed-reading during his time in the White House, took courses with his wife Rosalynn.

The fact that Dwight D. Eisenhower said "Don't be afraid to go in your library and read every book" may well allude to the fact he was yet another US president who could speed read. Who else but a speed-reader would have the time or ability to read *every* book in their local library?

Bestselling author, life coach and motivational speaker Anthony Robbins practices speed-reading and recommends it to audiences, personal clients and his readers.

In 2007, when J.K. Rowling's *Harry Potter and the Deathly Hallows* was published, six-time world champion speed-reader Anne Jones was the first to read it. Jones finished the 200,000-word, 759-page hardcover book in 47 minutes flat. Immediately afterwards, she completed a book review and sent it out to media outlets to prove her total comprehension of the story.

Jacques Bergier, French Resistance fighter, spy, journalist, chemical engineer and author of the bestselling book *The Morning of the Magicians*, was a born speed-reader. He started reading magazines and newspapers as a toddler, and by the age of four was fluent in three languages. By the time he reached adulthood, Bergier was reading 10 books a day.

New Yorker and State University graduate Howard Berg was listed in the 1990 Guinness Book of World Records as the world's fastest reader. His reading speed was clocked at a remarkable 25,000 words per minute. Berg says his skill was developed out of boredom. He spent his childhood in the library, which was apparently the only place in the world that interested him.

Autistic savant Kim Peek is one of the world's foremost speed-readers. The real-life inspiration for Dustin Hoffman's character in the 1988 movie *Rain Man*, Peek reads at between 10,000 and 20,000 words per minute and has a 98% comprehension rate. His method is to read two pages simultaneously, one with each eye. Spending most of his days in the public library in Salt Lake City, Utah, Peek has read many thousands of books.

Of all the examples of speed-readers, living or deceased, Peek's methods are closest to those described in *The Orphan Trilogy*. We sincerely hope in years to come scientists will figure out exactly how Peek so readily absorbs information from books so that children can be taught the technique the world over.

Since the term *speed-reading* was coined by Evelyn Wood more than 50 years ago, the skill has featured in various TV series and Hollywood movies. In the 1996 feature film *Phenomenon*, lead character George Malley, played by John Travolta, exhibits extraordinary speed-reading skills. Dr. Spencer Reid, one of the main characters on the hit TV series *Criminal Minds*, is also a speed-reader.

There's a speed-reading scene in the 2004 spy film *The Bourne Supremacy*, starring Matt Damon, in which CIA agent Pamela Landy, played by Joan Allen, is seen reading agency files at rapid speeds. Landy uses her finger to run up and down over text on each page. This finger pointing method is a real speed-reading technique known as Meta Guiding. In *Good Will Hunting* – another Matt Damon movie – Damon, who plays natural-born genius Will Hunting, is seen alone in his apartment flipping through page after page of a book without pause. Whether these two films on the actor's resume are just a coincidence or whether he's a speed-reader himself, is anyone's guess.

BRAINWAVE ENTERTAINMENT

As mentioned, brainwaves are a crucial part of accelerated learning techniques. It's proven that when individuals move out of normal waking brainwaves (beta) into other brainwaves (alpha, theta, delta and gamma) they enter the ideal state in which to absorb new information. Whether the learning is analyzing complex equations, or memorizing facts, or becoming an expert in martial arts, it makes no difference.

Our children at the Pedemont Orphanage use brainwave generators and biofeedback machines to reach the optimal frequency for study. This method of altering the mind is known as *brainwave entrainment*.

Gamma brainwaves, which are the highest frequency brainwave, are held in high regard at the orphanage. As we wrote in *The Orphan Factory*: "The children performed mind photography in uncommon brainwaves for regular wakeful consciousness. In this case it was predominantly gamma waves, and it allowed them to tap into the genius of their subconscious minds."

Besides being present while learning languages or forming new ideas, Gamma waves are also vital for recalling memories. And the faster the gamma brainwave, the faster the memory recall is – yet another advantage in doing things at speed.

SLEEP-LEARNING

Even at night, the Pedemont orphans' education continues through hypnopædia, or sleep-learning. Audio courses play through headphones they wear while asleep and our orphans are able to learn new subjects like high finance or foreign languages.

Hypnopædia comes from the Greek *hypnos*, meaning 'sleep', and *paideia*, meaning 'education'. Although still not conclusive, some research has shown the subconscious mind is very receptive to absorbing knowledge whilst we sleep.

There are numerous references to hypnopædia in Aldous Huxley's 1932 dystopian novel *Brave New World*. Thirty years later, this unusual learning method was also mentioned in *A Clockwork Orange*, another dystopian novel, by Anthony Burgess. The popularity of these bestselling novels coincided with the release of positive results of preliminary studies into sleep-learning, ensuring that hypnopædia became relatively well known around the world and interest in it blossomed.

However, from the early 1960's onwards, more in-depth scientific studies were conducted in laboratories in the US and the UK, disproving the theory that humans could learn during sleep.

Even though many students in numerous countries kept claiming they achieved better exam results after listening to audio recordings on subjects whilst asleep, official studies simply did not confirm this. As a result, hypnopædia was discredited for about 50 years and slipped into obscurity in scientific and education circles.

Only in the last few years has the potential learning method resurfaced. Recent studies are beginning to contradict earlier experiments and it may not be long before hypnopædia is proven to be a reality.

For example, on August 29, 2012, *The Huffington Post* ran a news article under the headline *Sleep Learning May Be Possible: Study*. The article mentioned a new study by researchers at the

Weizmann Institute of Science, which demonstrated test subjects learnt new information while asleep.

In an interrelated experiment, scientists at Illinois' Northwestern University discovered that taking a 90-minute nap immediately after studying helps solidify knowledge in the brain. They taught new things – both physical and mental – to people and then tested them on how well they remembered and applied the knowledge taught. There were two groups involved – one whose members slept after learning and one whose members stayed awake the whole time. Those who slept in the lab after studying showed significantly better mastery of the subject matter when tested.

So hypnopædia is once again on the scientific radar and it will be interesting to see the results of future studies.

With the help of virtual reality and biofeedback technologies, the orphans were taught how to guide their minds to reach certain brain frequencies – like Alpha, Theta and Delta – at will. The purpose of slipping into these particular frequencies was to allow the right brain to take over, as opposed to the left-brained consciousness dominant in most people. Whenever the orphans needed to access their higher intelligences, they would enter a daydream and simply intuit the answers. That way, they could bypass thinking, and just know. Within the Omega family, intuition was favored over logical thought patterns.

–The Ninth Orphan

BRAIN GLAND ACTIVATION

Activating dormant brain glands is another technique used inside the Pedemont Orphanage.

All individuals have a certain amount of dormant or underutilized brain areas. Every human brain ever mapped scientifically has shown at least some inactive cells and neurons. This area of neuroscience, especially concerning little known brain glands, may hold the answer as to why we only use such a small percentage of our brains.

As we wrote in *The Orphan Factory*: "Rare earth magnets were embedded inside each helmet for the purpose of activating certain brain glands. Glands that were dormant in the average person."

Neuromagnetic helmets and similar brain stimulation technologies are not just confined to the realms of fiction.

Transcranial direct current stimulation, or TDCS, is a brain stimulation technique. It's carried out by applying a helmet or cap to the individual's head. TDCS targets specific parts of the brain with low voltage electrical currents. This allows for the alteration of electrical states of neurons in targeted areas of the brain.

TDCS is in its infancy, but early studies have shown it enhances motor skills, memory recall and concentration. As a result, the US military now employs TDCS to assist fighter pilots, snipers and other personnel.

Transcranial magnetic stimulation, or TMS, is a similar non-invasive brain enhancement technology except it uses magnets instead of electricity. TMS's magnetic fields are capable of altering neurons in targeted areas of the brain.

Neuromagnetic helmets and similar devices have been nicknamed 'zap caps' and preliminary studies show they have the potential to improve brain function in numerous ways.

POLYGLOTTING IN THE PEDEMONT ORPHANAGE

The Pedemont orphans all speak a large number of languages and are therefore *polyglots*. Although we never actually specify how many, it's implied in our trilogy that each orphan can speak dozens of languages. They also have the ability to learn new ones quickly, and more than once we show our orphans, or orphan-operatives, mastering languages in the days leading up to a new mission.

While this may seem far-fetched, there have been persistent reports of CIA agents mastering languages within one week. If true, this is most likely a direct result of *classified* learning techniques or brain technologies not available to the general public.

In 2004, British autistic savant Daniel Tammet shocked Icelandic peoples when he appeared on live television to demonstrate his *overnight* mastery of their notoriously complex language. Tammet spoke fluent Icelandic, having only studied the language for seven days.

VIRTUAL REALITY TRAINING

Virtual reality is another advanced learning technology utilized within the walls of the orphanage. However, we specify it's not virtual reality as most of us know it.

This excerpt from *The Orphan Factory* explains what we are getting at: "Like most Omega technologies, it was a technology that was decades ahead of official science, and although virtual reality was widely known and available to the public, this military version had been suppressed from the masses because of its incredible power."

Although a suppressed form of the technology lies very much in government cover-up theories, known virtual reality systems have already been proven to be effective in a wide variety of diverse fields. Learning via this technology's computer-simulated environment is currently used the world over in the military, medical, aviation and architectural sectors to name but a few.

Virtual reality allows users to practice as if they are actually engaging in activities in the real world. The difference between reality and virtual reality can sometimes be so small it's indistinguishable to the human brain.

Or to put it another way, as we state in *The Orphan Factory*:

"Carrying out assignments under the influence of this particular software was no different to performing them in real life – at least not as far as the mind was concerned."

SUPERLUMINAL PARTICLES

The physics of faster-than-light (also known as *superluminal*) phenomena may also hold great potential for accelerated learning.

In his 2014 book *Superluminal Particles and Hypercomputation*, leading Japanese scientist Dr. Takaaki Musha claims that the superiority of the human brain is due to the superluminal particles generated in the microtubules of the brain.

The blurb for *Superluminal Particles and Hypercomputation* mentions that the book "describes a series of theoretical explorations probing the possibility that superluminal particles exist, and if so the consequences their existence may hold for biology and computing. Starting from the standpoint of a model of the brain based on superluminal tunneling photons, the authors included in this volume have described theoretically the possibility of a brain-like computer that would be more powerful than Turing machines, would allow non-Turing computations, and that may hold the key to the origin of human consciousness itself".

A former senior employee of Japan's Ministry of Defense where he developed naval weapon systems, Dr. Musha claims this generated superluminal field connects individuals with the outer field of the Universe and he contends this may explain human consciousness as well as the collective mind of Mankind.

Dr. Musha's theory relates to the quantum mechanics scale known as *decoherence*, which measures the time to maintain the quantum coherence between particles. If the decoherence time is long in an individual's brain, it permits the person to connect to the outer superluminal field easily.

"I think that the activity of superluminal particles can be

maintained by the structure of the metamaterial in the microtubules," says Dr. Musha. "The metamaterial has a non-natural property such as negative refractive index, which permits superluminal evanescent photons to move loosely in the nervous system. If this structure malfunctions in an individual, many problems can occur such as Alzheimer's disease."

Dr. Musha believes decoherence time can possibly be extended by mental training. If this is true, then genius abilities like photographic memory could result from the right sort of training.

If an individual's brain can connect with the superluminal field which is part of all other living organisms, then it may be possible for that individual to come from an awareness of what has been termed the *universal brain*. Dr. Musha claims this could explain the extraordinary abilities of the human mind, such as the enigma of Indian mathematical genius Srinivasa Ramanujan.

Superluminal Particles and Hypercomputation also proposes that the true nature of the human electromagnetic field may be similar to that of the Universe as a whole.

Dr. Musha continues, "The ancient Indian Vedas texts have lent a comparable view of unified consciousness with a key difference being the process of human ascension from stage to stage. Instead of oneness with the Universe, the Vedic vision of consciousness emphasizes the importance of attaining knowledge and pure intelligence.

"This is similar to the Vedic concept that the totality of our consciousness is comprised of three levels: the subconscious, the conscious, and the superconscious mind. These levels of consciousness represent differing degrees of intensity of awareness. Intuition and heightened mental clarity flow from superconscious awareness. The conscious mind is limited by its analytical nature, and therefore sees all things as separate and distinct.

"We may be puzzled by a certain situation, because it seems unrelated to other events, it's difficult to draw a clear course of action. By contrast, because the superconscious mind is intuitive and sees all things as part of a whole, it can readily draw solutions."

Dr. Musha also believes that if science can utilize superluminal particles for computer technology, it will one day be possible to build a hypercomputer system which has its own consciousness – like the HAL 9000 computer in the Stanley Kubrick film, *2001: A Space Odyssey*.

OTHER GENIUS TECHNIQUES OF THE ELITE

The Orphan Trilogy covers numerous other advanced learning methods, Baroque music being one. This form of classical music is played to our orphans from when they are babies in the womb right through their childhood. Baroque and classical music in general – especially the works of Mozart – have been shown to aid students when learning new things or recalling information.

In *The Orphan Factory*, the orphans lie in enclosed flotation tanks, also known as isolation tanks. This is called *sensory deprivation*. Brainwaves are altered while in this deeply relaxed state, making the floating participants very receptive to new information.

The ingredients of real-world flotation sessions are simply water and salt, and the individual floats alone for about an hour inside the tank.

Celebrities known to have used such flotation tanks include Robin Williams, John Lennon, Jeff Bridges and Susan Sarandon. William Hurt, the star of *Altered States*, a 1980 feature film about isolation tanks, is another celebrity said to have practiced sensory deprivation in his private life.

Various sports teams, including the Philadelphia Eagles and the Dallas Cowboys have also used flotation tanks, as have Olympians such as American track star and nine-time gold medal-winner Carl Lewis.

There are references to chess throughout the trilogy. Our orphans play rapid-fire matches known as *Lightning Chess* in which entire games are completed in 10 minutes or less. This is based on the theory that by playing the board game from a young age, certain parts of a child's brain develop quicker than normal, especially areas relating to strategy. Playing Lightning Chess and multiple games simultaneously once again relates to thinking so fast that the conscious mind must yield to the superior subconscious.

And finally, a mysterious substance known as *Ormus* is given to the orphans every day at the Pedemont Orphanage. By ingesting it, the children activate their entire DNA/RNA cellular system, which not only unlocks their physical body's true potential, but also stimulates their conscious, subconscious and unconscious minds.

Often referred to as *White Gold* or *White Gold Powder*, Ormus is a real substance discovered by science several decades ago. As it has been said to balance both hemispheres of the brain and therefore allow for *whole brain learning*, some believe Ormus to be a natural (legal) version of the smart drug Bradley Cooper's character took in the 2011 movie *Limitless*. Studies have proven whole brain learning is the ideal state for gaining new knowledge. (See Chapter 9 for more on White Gold).

From the examples given in this chapter alone, it should now be clear there have always been individuals learning at speeds many or most mainstream educationalists would have us believe are not possible. From US presidents like JFK and Roosevelt, to CIA agents and great polymaths such as Leonardo da Vinci, to savants like Kim Peek and Daniel Tammet, history's full of people achieving intellectual feats well beyond the norm.

We concede it cannot be proven that elite groups are withholding some of the most advanced learning methods from mainstream society. Hence it remains a 'conspiracy theory'. Even so, it's pretty obvious that little known, accelerated learning techniques do exist.

But remember, we could be totally wrong about everything we

wrote on the genius mindset here and in *The Orphan Trilogy*. Also, it's probably time to admit neither of us has ever done an IQ test...Nor do either of us have any formal education qualifications besides completing high school...So for all we know we could both be as thick as bricks! If that is the case, you'd be wise not to drop out of school or spend any time researching the accelerated learning methods we've outlined in this chapter.

6

THE MULTI-TRILLION DOLLAR WW2 COVER-UP

The rogue operative was here to trade the flash drive he'd brought with him from the Philippines. The flash drive's contents specified the exact location of Yamashita's Gold – a long lost treasure hoard Nine had located.

–The Ninth Orphan

The Ninth Orphan starts in the Philippines where Nine is sent on a mission to discover a treasure trove worth US$250 billion. It turns out this find is merely the leftovers of a much bigger treasure – a multi-trillion dollar booty, in fact.

Yamashita's Gold, also known as *Yamashita's Treasure*, is alleged stolen treasure squirreled away by the Japanese during their occupation of the Philippines in World War Two. Named after General Tomoyuki Yamashita, the war loot is said to have been hidden in caves and underground complexes throughout the islands of the Philippines.

The rumored treasures remain unconfirmed by the Japanese, Filipino and all other governments in Asia and the West to this very day. However, the majority of international investigators – Asian investigators included – believe Yamashita's Gold exists, or existed, at least to some degree.

The investigators' belief is supported by a Hawaii Supreme Court finding in 1998 and a subsequent US Ninth Circuit Court of

Appeal ruling, but more about those *legal bombshells* later in this chapter.

Between Japanese army records, international court hearings, eyewitness accounts and treasure finds throughout the Philippines over the decades following WW2, there seems to be more than enough substance to build a case for the existence of Yamashita's Gold. It ties in with a wider conspiracy about the war in the Pacific as well as the West's involvement with Asian countries since WW2.

Some independent researchers have even suggested the legendary Asian treasure hoard is one of the primary reasons for the volatility in global currencies and economies in recent decades.

RICHES WITHOUT EQUAL

Japan gained enormous wealth when it invaded China and a dozen or so other Asian countries during WW2. Besides the Philippines and China, other countries and territories Japan occupied include Korea, Hong Kong, Guam, Taiwan, Portuguese Timor, Thailand, Burma and French Indochina – a large French colony now part of Cambodia, Laos and Vietnam – as well as Singapore, Brunei and other British colonies in the lands now known as Malaysia and Indonesia.

To say the Japanese Empire was vast would be an understatement. In terms of accumulated wealth and total population under its control, it was one of the largest empires in the history of the world.

Essentially, within the space of a few short years, Japan systematically stripped every conceivable wealth from the bulk of Asia. At the behest of Emperor Hirohito, the Imperial Army methodically pillaged everything of value they could find and almost literally left no stone unturned. This included ransacking museums and government treasuries, banks, royal palaces, temples, churches and mosques, and even the private homes of wealthy families.

The conquering Japanese were primarily after gold, a commodity that was not in short supply in Asia at that time. In fact, the elite ruling families in Asian countries had been collecting and storing gold – often hidden in ancestral tombs and the like – for up to 4000 years.

Japanese soldiers looted bullion by the truckload, and very little of the precious metal escaped their grasp. Accounts of them extracting gold fillings from the teeth of corpses is but one of many examples of their ruthless meticulousness.

In addition to these incalculable amounts of gold, gigantic quantities of diamonds, silver, platinum, precious gems, royal jewels and religious artifacts were also stolen. These colossal treasure troves were shipped to the Philippines in preparation for transportation to Japan. However, as the war in the Pacific intensified, the ever-increasing presence of Allied ships and US submarines made the transport of such treasure problematic for Japan. As a result, most of it had to be hidden in the Philippines.

That done, the treasure sites were booby-trapped by the Japanese to protect the riches they contained. The plan was to recover the assets after the war's end. Of course, the Japanese assumed they'd be victorious over the Allied war machine.

Some researchers and treasure-hunters claim there are Imperial Japanese army maps in existence that reveal the whereabouts of these treasure sites. A series of the most important locations, known as *Trillion Yen sites*, contained gold and other precious metals valued during the war at one trillion yen. That's 1,000,000,000,000 yen!

Taking inflation into account, one trillion yen in 1945 currency equates to approximately US$250 billion dollars, or a quarter of a trillion, *per site* in today's money. That's why we specify this figure in *The Ninth Orphan* as being the value of the treasure site Nine finds on behalf of his shadowy employers.

Initially, there were dozens of Trillion Yen sites in the
Philippines, but Naylor had confirmed that after the
waves of bounty hunters – first the Americans under
General MacArthur, then Marcos decades later – only
one such site remained. Despite many attempts to find
the location, it had remained undiscovered until Nine
found it. The crafty orphan had somehow uncovered the
elusive site's location in the province of Benguet.

–The Ninth Orphan

THE BRITISH CONNECTION

The bulk of Asia's wealth wasn't the only treasure that made up Yamashita's Gold. Great Britain inadvertently *contributed* also.

Britain's little known link with the treasure dates all the way back to Hitler's rise in the 1930's. Fearing Germany was going to invade the UK, it's believed Britain shipped the bulk of its gold reserves – including the Royal Family's massive stockpile – to Singapore, which was under British rule at the time. When Singapore abruptly fell to the Japanese in 1942, Britain lost almost all its gold supplies overnight.

It has been asserted that Britain's lost bullion never made it to Japan either and was instead buried in the Philippines along with the treasures from all the other Asian countries.

SUPRESSING THE TRUTH

Several Yamashita investigators have estimated that Japan's total war plunder amounted to more than 300,000 tons of gold and other treasures. Nobody knows what proportion was gold, but it's worth noting the estimated total of the entire world's gold *officially* mined throughout human history is only 174,100 tons.

That puts Yamashita's Gold into perspective; it amounted to a massive percentage of the world's total (mined) gold reserves.

One school of thought says leading nations conspired to withhold this plundered gold from the global marketplace after WW2. Those who subscribe to this theory argue that if ever that much gold flooded the market, or was even acknowledged, it would completely devalue gold overnight. Not to mention destabilize various currencies.

Whatever the case, it's a fact that a gold discovery of this magnitude would have virtually destroyed the value of monetary gold, or gold held by governing authorities as a financial asset, worldwide. Remember, up until 1971, a *gold standard* existed in most countries, including America. This meant most nations' currencies were based on, or pegged to, a fixed quantity of gold.

As the US Government was the biggest holder of monetary gold, acknowledging the existence of Yamashita's Gold would have seriously devalued America's reserves and potentially its standing as the dominant economy.

If the truth about the finds in the Philippines had been publicly acknowledged, it would also have paved the way for substantial claims from those Asian countries the gold and other treasures originally belonged to. This would have promoted more rapid economic growth in the likes of China, Taiwan, Korea and Thailand than they experienced in the decades following WW2.

Many believe the US and other Western powers, including Britain and her Commonwealth realms, conspired to keep the existence of Yamashita's Gold hush-hush while, at the same time, those powers used the gold to further their own agendas. It's suspected those agendas include funding *black ops* to overthrow various governments and tampering with financial markets.

It is said every British Prime Minister and every US President since 1945 have known about the treasure hoard and have shaped their foreign policies around it.

Major financial institutions, including some of the world's top banks, as well as international funding organizations are also said to be part of this conspiracy to suppress the truth about the existence of Yamashita's Gold.

Many oil researchers have postulated that oil companies operate in much the same way. As George C. Scott's character says to Marlon Brando's character in the 1980 oil-themed movie *The Formula*: "You're not in the oil business. You're in the oil *shortage* business."

That same formula (creating the illusion of a shortage) can equally apply to the devious management of precious metal and diamond markets. The 2006 political thriller film *Blood Diamond* starring Leonardo DiCaprio also touched on this issue.

Few knew more about Yamashita's Gold than Naylor did. His own father had served in the Philippines under General MacArthur and, at the end of World War Two, had witnessed the earliest discoveries of Japan's massive plunder. Naylor had also confirmed that the former president of the Philippines, Ferdinand Marcos, had obtained much of his personal fortune from later discoveries.

–The Ninth Orphan

I SHALL RETURN
(FOR THE GOLD)

In 1942, US General Douglas MacArthur was forced to leave the Philippines as the nation was overrun by Japanese. MacArthur told journalists, "I shall return."

Over 10,000 American troops stationed in the Pacific had

already surrendered to the Japanese and MacArthur had been left without any reinforcements. Fearing for his general's safety, President Roosevelt had ordered him to leave the Philippines.

MacArthur's famous words *I shall return* meant a lot to the Filipino people who clung to the hope they'd eventually reclaim their freedom.

In October, 1944, after leading a series of strategically brilliant air and sea attacks against Japanese forces, General MacArthur stood on Philippine soil once more. "I have returned," he told emotional Filipinos who had not forgotten his promise.

Unfortunately, like most fairy tales spun during wartime, the true motivations in MacArthur's case were probably not quite as straightforward or innocent as they appeared to be.

He did return after leading the Allies to defeat the Japanese and kick them out of the Philippines. However, MacArthur may have been so keen to return to collect the riches he knew the Japanese had concealed all over the rugged island nation.

It is said that Charles Willoughby, the general's Chief of Intelligence, had earlier in the war found evidence of the vast treasures buried throughout the Philippines. According to this theory, Willoughby and his staff had confirmed there were almost 200 Yamashita sites throughout the Philippines, including the all-important Trillion Yen sites.

Various independent researchers have concluded that MacArthur worked closely with the CIA immediately after WW2. Their goal: to locate and retrieve as many of the Yamashita treasure hoards as possible.

Among those independent researchers are prolific authors Sterling Seagrave and Peggy Seagrave who wrote in their 2003 book *Gold Warriors: America's Secret Recovery of Yamashita's Gold* that General MacArthur "used war loot to create a trust fund for Hirohito at Sanwa Bank" and "also set up the secret M-Fund".

The Seagraves go into convincing detail about the evidence they apparently uncovered, proving MacArthur's post-WW2 success in secretly recovering the bulk of Yamashita's Gold for America. The authors also mention MacArthur's right-hand man

Charles Willoughby who they say "paid war criminals to rewrite history and manipulate Japan's government," immediately after the war as part of the covert operation.

The Marcos Family

Imelda Marcos has said repeatedly over the years that her deceased husband and former President of the Philippines, Ferdinand Marcos, gained much of his considerable personal fortune by looting riches from various Yamashita treasure locations.

For example, Manila-based newspaper *The Bulletin* ran an article on February 3, 1992, with the headline *Marcos widow claims wealth due to yamashita treasure*. The article states "Imelda Marcos today claimed for the first time the basis of her late husband's wealth was Japanese and other gold he found starting at the end of World War II."

Imelda told the newspaper, "From what I heard and I was told, the late President Marcos went to the United States in 1945 to sell some of the gold."

In addition to Imelda's statements, numerous investigators believe there was a joint venture between President Marcos and the US intelligence community who, it seems, had developed *gold rush fever*. It has been claimed Marcos arranged for CIA aircraft and even US Navy warships to transport the bullion into a worldwide network of offshore banks in various tax havens.

After Ferdinand Marcos was overthrown in 1986, the Philippine Government began an enquiry into Marcos' activities undertaken during his term in power. Known as *Operation Big Bird*, its goal was to recover the rumored tens of billions in secret assets of Ferdinand and Imelda Marcos, which apparently included scores of Swiss bank accounts.

On April 7, 2013, beneath the headline *Secret accounts*, Manila's *The Philippine Star* newspaper reported that Operation Big Bird failed to uncover the Marcos billions as they were too creatively stashed away in Swiss bank accounts. The Marcos's had used a combination of pseudonyms and nameless, number-only Swiss accounts to make their fortune almost impossible to uncover.

The Philippine Star article also mentioned that the couple's daughter, Imee Marcos, was embroiled in a new tax haven scandal. Ongoing investigations showed she held "secret accounts" in the British Virgin Islands, a tax haven known for ironclad bank secrecy. The article went on to speculate whether Imee's accounts were a residue of her parents' controversial empire.

THE ROXAS BUDDHAS

Probably the single biggest piece of evidence to support the existence of the rumored Yamashita's treasure was a lawsuit filed in a Hawaiian state court in 1988. It involved Filipino treasure hunter Rogelio Roxas and the former Philippine president, Ferdinand Marcos. The lawsuit was for theft and human rights abuses, and named Marcos and his wife Imelda as the perpetrators.

In 1961, Roxas claimed to have met a former member of the Japanese Imperial Army who showed him maps revealing the location of a major treasure site. He also said he met another Japanese man who worked as General Yamashita's interpreter and had seen a chamber full of bullion, including numerous gold Buddha statues.

Armed with maps and eyewitness accounts, Roxas began searching in earnest for the site.

Ten years later, in 1971, Roxas claimed to have discovered the underground chamber on the outskirts of Baguio City. Inside it, he found a 3-foot tall gold Buddha, which weighed approximately 1000 kilograms, and rows of staked boxes full of bullion. Roxas reportedly took one box, which was said to contain 24 solid gold bars from the chamber, as well as the gold Buddha and hid them in his home.

Roxas also claimed that President Marcos soon heard about his discovery and ordered him to be arrested and beaten. The booty he'd recovered, along with all the remaining contents of the underground chamber, was confiscated for Marcos' personal possession.

After Roxas protested vocally and spoke about his ill treatment to journalists, Marcos incarcerated him for over a year. Upon release, Roxas laid low until Marcos was stripped of his presidency and kicked out of the Philippines in 1986. Then, in 1988, Roxas filed the lawsuit against Marcos and his wife seeking damages for the human rights abuses and the theft of his Yamashita discovery.

Befitting an international intrigue novel, Roxas died on the eve of trial and Ferdinand Marcos, who by then was living in exile in Hawaii, also passed away the following year.

Some researchers believe Roxas was murdered. This theory is supported by the research of Yamashita experts Sterling Seagrave and Peggy Seagrave in their aforementioned book *Gold Warriors: America's Secret Recovery of Yamashita's Gold*, in which they state that Roxas did indeed discover a "solid gold Buddha looted from Burma" and, "after President Marcos stole it", that "Roxas was tortured and murdered to silence him".

However, in a twist, Roxas was not completely silenced. Shortly before dying he gave a disposition testimony that was used as evidence in the ensuing court case.

In 1996, the Roxas estate received what was at that point the largest judgment ever awarded – US$22 billion. The inclusion of added interest boosted that amount to US$40.5 billion. Then, in 1998, the Hawaii Supreme Court reversed the damages award even though it held there was sufficient evidence to support the jury's finding that Roxas had indeed found the treasure and that Marcos had seized it.

However, the court also held that the award for the chamber-full of gold was too speculative as there was no evidence of either quantity or quality. Instead, the court ordered a new hearing based solely on what Roxas had removed from the underground chamber, which were just the single golden Buddha and the box of gold bars.

After more protracted legal proceedings, the Roxas estate finally obtained a closing judgment against the now widowed Imelda Marcos. Roxas' estate obtained a US$6 million judgment regarding the claim for human rights abuse.

That lawsuit ultimately concluded that Roxas had found the treasures he said he had and *that it was likely part of the legendary Yamashita's Gold*. The complex case was concluded by the US Ninth Circuit Court of Appeal summarizing the allegations leading to Roxas' final judgment as follows: "The Yamashita Treasure was found by Roxas and stolen from Roxas by Marcos' men."

This was astonishing considering that neither the US Government nor any other government had ever acknowledged the existence of the Yamashita treasure hoard.

❧ ❦ ❧

Besides *The Ninth Orphan*, there have been various references to Yamashita's Gold in popular culture over the years. In 1993, an episode of the American TV show *Unsolved Mysteries* screened in the US, questioning what happened to the treasures amassed by General Yamashita; international bestselling author Clive Cussler wrote about Yamashita's Gold in his 1990 adventure novel *Dragon*; the treasure hoard also features heavily in the 2013 horror movie *Dead Mine*, which is primarily set in abandoned Japanese military bunkers in South-East Asia.

Treasure hunters from around the world continue to flock to the Philippines each year to find what remains of the Yamashita hoard. Some of them include descendants of Japanese WW2 veterans who served in the Philippines. There have also been reports of Japanese citizens purchasing land throughout the country in places they believe the treasures are still buried.

But, of course, we are dramatists, not historians. Therefore, we could be totally wrong about everything we've written on Yamashita's Gold. In which case, you would be advised to cancel that treasure-hunting expedition you've booked for the summer and stick to playing the lottery!

7

Suppressed Science

*They all wore neuromagnetic helmets. These would stay
on their heads until morning. The orphans understood
the device they wore was an example of the almost
infinite number of scientific breakthroughs made by the
military and secret organizations – breakthroughs the
public were never privy to.*

–The Orphan Factory

In January 2014, it was reported by *The New York Times* and other
mainstream media outlets that America's National Security
Agency (NSA) uses secret technology to remotely input and alter
data on computers worldwide – even when targeted PC's or
laptops are not connected to the Internet. This suppressed
technology, which uses radio frequencies to spy on computers,
only came to the public's attention due to leaked NSA documents
from former agency contractor-turned whistleblower Edward
Snowden.

This begs the question: Is it a regular occurrence for
governments, intelligence agencies and the military to withhold
scientific breakthroughs from the public?

If so, how many other suppressed inventions exist in the
world's ironclad vaults of power?

And what if most of the technologies readers and cinemagoers
are presented with in bestselling books and blockbuster movies
are not science fiction, but science fact? What if they currently
exist on the planet, but are suppressed from the masses?

Imagine for a moment a reality where all the technologies that futurists have predicted have already been invented and are currently being used by a privileged few.

There have been numerous reports of scientific inventions that never saw the light of day even though they were perfected and ready to go on the market. Rumors of these radical inventions date back to the post-Industrial Revolution period in the late 1800's and early 1900's, and have persisted right up to and including the present day.

Were a documentary film ever to be produced based on the conspiratorial history of suppressed technologies, the individuals featured would include everyone from inventors who either suddenly died, went missing or faded into obscurity, to tech investors who were mysteriously thwarted to scientists who lost their patents without receiving any valid explanation.

A COVERT CIVILIZATION

If such technologies do exist, that would likely confirm there is a *Splinter Civilization* that secretly and autonomously resides on our planet right now. Such a group's membership would probably be a combination of high-ranking military personnel, senior intelligence agents as well as shadowy government figures and many of the global elite already named or alluded to in previous chapters. Although all citizens of various nations and speaking different languages, they would be united by the common goal of attaining mass power, or a New World Order.

Because of its almost infinite sources of funding – mostly derived from black ops appropriations – this Splinter Civilization would have in its possession technologies that would make a layman's mind boggle. The covert civilization would use inconceivable, stealth-like weaponry to wage quiet wars on vulnerable nations. Such weaponry could even facilitate alteration of the weather and the creation of so-called acts of nature.

And of course, *contractors* commissioned by faceless

middlemen employed by the shadowy members of this splinter group would, one way or another, silence any investigative reporters or citizen journalists who come close to uncovering evidence of its existence.

Sounds like a theory we should reserve for one of our future movies or novels?

You'd be right, except for one important point. Many of these suppressed technologies have been reported by former engineers and other employees of the Military Industrial Complex. And the list of whistleblowers is an extensive and impressive one that dates back decades.

Based on the reports of those same whistleblowers, it appears suppression of scientific technologies is done for various reasons. Sometimes it's about governments wanting to achieve or maintain superior military might. Other times it's for financial reasons.

Few would deny it's in the interests of corporations that financially benefit from current technologies to block newer, more advanced technologies ever reaching the marketplace. Though immoral, that would make good business sense as it's an unwritten rule that corporations squash competitors and quash competition.

In the course of writing *The Orphan Trilogy*, we researched numerous scientific inventions rumored to exist somewhere in the world right now. Covering the entire history of suppressed science would require a whole book rather than this single chapter. Therefore, we will focus only on several rumored technologies, albeit ones that potentially hold great significance for humanity.

THE ELECTRIC MAGICIAN

Most secret technologies are rumored to be based on the works of the brilliant Croatian-born Serbian-American scientist Nikola Tesla (1856-1943). An inventor, physicist and electrical engineer, he is surely history's most underrated scientist. In fact, when researching suppressed science, it often seems as if all roads lead back to the man who was nicknamed *the Electric Magician*. To attempt to verify the Splinter Civilization's existence and ultimately understand its nature, we all must first comprehend what Tesla achieved in his eventful lifetime, including his tragic last few years.

In terms of *official* science, he is probably best known for designing the modern alternating current (AC) electricity supply system as well as his theoretical work used in the invention of radio communication. He's also referred to by many as *the godfather of wireless technology*, having first demonstrated wireless energy transmission in 1891.

After migrating to the US, Tesla worked for light bulb inventor Thomas Edison and fellow inventor George Westinghouse before branching out on his own. He began conducting more radical experiments involving remote-controlled devices, artificial lightning and thunder, early X-Ray testing, robotics, electric cars and lasers, and he even investigated whether it was possible to collect vast amounts of energy from the earth's atmosphere.

As revolutionary as Tesla's known inventions and experiments sound, it's his long-rumored suppressed inventions that have spawned countless conspiracy theories. Claims surrounding him include everything from perfecting free-energy technologies to being responsible for the mysterious 1908 Tunguska explosion in Siberia.

Tesla's high-frequency power experiments are also said to be the scientific foundations of HAARP, a controversial military-funded research program. (Read more on HAARP later in this chapter).

During his later years, between the First and Second World Wars, Tesla worked on a directed-energy weapon (DEW) he called a *teleforce gun*. 21st Century researchers now refer to this device as the *Tesla Death Ray*. Many believe it was stolen and used by the military; and many believe it remains in use today – possibly in a more advanced form.

As per one of his theses currently stored in the Nikola Tesla

Museum, in Belgrade, Serbia, the inventor described his DEW device as being a "superweapon that would put an end to all war." He also said it could stop fleets of airplanes and entire armies dead in their tracks.

Tesla claimed he was spied on by the US War Department as well as agencies of the Soviet Union and various European nations as a result of this fantastical invention. Decades later, Tesla's Death Ray and other works were referenced in a weapon patent taken out by Columbia Universty and MIT-educated physicist Dr. Bernard Eastlund.

As much of Tesla's material is no longer available to the public, it's impossible to prove or disprove his most radical science. Certainly his overall career is barely studied at learning institutions today and he is not held in the same high regard as scientists like Newton or Einstein. This despite Tesla obtaining approximately 300 patents worldwide for his inventions of such diverse things as alternating current generators, fluorescent lights, exotic power systems and even flying machines.

Whatever the case, there's enough evidence to conclude Tesla was hounded by the energy power brokers – Edison and American financier J.P. Morgan in particular – of the late 19th and early 20th Centuries. These figures recognized Tesla's technologies as a serious threat to their financial empires and, in Edison's case, to his scientific legacy as well.

When Tesla died in 1943, the US Government confiscated all his research material and immediately classified much of it. However, in recent years, through the Freedom of Information Act, some of that research has been declassified, leading to a resurgence of interest in Tesla.

Various independent investigators and freelance scientists claim they can identify irrefutable connections between Tesla's inventions and the most advanced technologies used by the military today.

"As an eminent pioneer in the realm of high frequency currents... I congratulate you on the great successes of your life's work."
–Albert Einstein, from a letter to Tesla for his 75th birthday in 1931.

FREE ENERGY AIN'T FREE, BABY!

As mentioned, there can be numerous reasons for suppressing inventions or discoveries. But financial gain is likely to be top of the heap. And few scientific breakthroughs could bankrupt large corporations like free-energy technologies would.

In a nutshell, this conspiracy theory suggests technologies have already been invented to provide for all the world's energy needs *for free*. Some of these suppressed inventions are apparently capable of generating their own power seemingly out of nothing. *Quantum vacuum zero point energy* is one example. Other devices are said to have the ability to extract energy from pre-existing reservoirs in nature.

Perpetual energy is a viable technology conspiracy theorists tell us, but unfortunately, it seems, there's also a perpetual war against it. For as long as energy companies exist, they will never allow such inventions to reach the public. After all, these technologies would decimate the oil, gas, electricity, nuclear and automobile industries overnight.

This theory asserts that by propagating the lie that expensive energy systems are the only options available, big corporations are able to control one of the planet's most lucrative fields.

Electrical engineer Thomas Henry Moray (1892-1974) claimed to have developed a working device for extracting free electricity from what he termed radiant energy waves of the atmosphere. He called his invention the *Moray Valve* and stated it was an effective extractor of an inexhaustible energy source. The scientific establishment immediately dismissed the device as a hoax. However, Moray claimed he received death threats and was even shot at in an effort to prevent his free-energy technology ever seeing the light of day.

Dr. Eugene Mallove was an MIT and Harvard-educated scientist, cold fusion advocate and publisher/editor of *Infinite Energy* magazine. He also founded the New Energy Foundation. Mallove's 1991 book *Fire from Ice: Searching for the Truth Behind the Cold Fusion Furor* outlined the science he believe proved the existence of cold fusion, a hypothetical free energy source derived from nuclear reactions. In particular, the book detailed a controversial experiment conducted in the late 1980's by one of the world's eminent electrochemists, Martin Fleischmann, and his partner Stanley Pons. Mallove believed the pair had invented an apparatus that successfully replicated cold fusion on several occasions.

Fire from Ice asserts that the results of the experiment and the apparatus had been suppressed. As a result, Mallove was ridiculed by mainstream physicists and lost his credibility in scientific circles. In 2004, he was killed at one of his residences in Connecticut. A decade of court proceedings followed in a complex murder trial that finally wrapped up late 2013. The judge ruled his death the result of a botched robbery. Cold fusion devotees however, claimed Mallove's death was all part of a conspiracy to silence him and bury cold fusion technologies.

Interrelated with free-energy are theories that very cheap energy is also possible. *Dirt cheap*, in fact. For example, there are various conspiracies dating back to the 1920's surrounding light bulb technology. Some investigators believe that leading corporations suppressed long-lasting light bulbs, forcing customers to regularly replace bulbs.

In 1972, Texan bulldozer-driver Richard Clem claimed to have invented a vegetable-oil turbine capable of traveling 115,000 miles on only eight gallons of chip fat. Ford Motors immediately threatened to sue Clem for installing his engine in his Ford Falcon. As he attracted more press coverage for his invention, Clem reported he'd received death threats. He refused to yield to pressure and vowed to get his prototype engine out into the world. However, Clem died of a heart attack shortly thereafter. His family believe he was murdered.

In the 1990's, reports began to surface in Japan that an engineer had developed a magnetic motor engine that powered itself. The inventor's name was Teruo Kawai and he reportedly had his device verified as workable by Hitachi engineers. However, Kawai claims Yakuza gangsters then threatened him and his associates, forcing them to relinquish the technology.

This brings us back to Nikola Tesla. As stated earlier in this chapter, many investigators have suggested he invented and perfected radical energy devices that could have provided free-energy to the entire world. These investigators also say the world's ongoing energy crisis is a total fabrication and that the problem was actually solved a century ago by Tesla.

Judging by the man's character at least, creating a non-profit energy device doesn't seem out of the question as Tesla was known to be a pure scientist disinterested in financial matters. Besides raising enough cash to fund his ambitious experiments, he had no record of chasing or making profits. By all accounts, he cared more about the world at large and wanted to use his scientific genius to benefit humanity. In fact, everything he did had some element of a social cause about it. As Tesla once wrote, "The desire that guides me in all I do is the desire to harness the forces of nature to the service of mankind."

In the early 1900's, American industrialist J.P. Morgan financed Tesla to construct a tower that would transmit wireless communications across the Atlantic. This experiment involved research into the Earth's ionosphere at a facility called Wardenclyffe, in Shoreham, New York. It entailed using the Wardenclyffe tower to employ naturally occurring frequencies to transmit data like voice messages, images and text. However, the experiments took Tesla in unexpected directions and many researchers believe he discovered and then harnessed a free, universal supply of energy from the ionosphere.

The inventor had apparently not only found a way to extract electricity, but also to rebroadcast this electricity *wirelessly* to neighboring towns. Besides being free, he deemed it to be a safe, renewable and clean form of electricity.

Tesla's mission suddenly shifted and he became obsessed with perfecting this newfound free-energy technology. His goal was to get it out to the world to empower individuals everywhere.

The Electric Magician expected J.P. Morgan would share his desire to assist Mankind with this incredible scientific discovery. He was grossly mistaken.

When J.P. Morgan was informed of Wardenclyffe's potential to harness an almost limitless amount of energy and freely broadcast it to anyone in the world, he realized it would damage his own electricity empire. As a result, the industrialist instantly terminated all of Tesla's funding. This effectively shut down the project as Tesla had lost his primary funder.

"Humanity is not yet sufficiently advanced to be willingly led by the discoverer's keen searching sense. But who knows? Perhaps it is better in this present world of ours that a revolutionary idea or invention instead of being helped and patted, be hampered and ill-treated in its adolescence – by want of means, by selfish interest, pedantry, stupidity and ignorance; that it be attacked and stifled; that it pass through bitter trials and tribulations, through the strife of commercial existence. So do we get our light. So all that was great in the past was ridiculed, condemned, combated, suppressed – only to emerge all the more powerfully, all the more triumphantly from the struggle."
–Nikola Tesla

THE SAGA OF THE ELECTRIC CAR

Believe it or not, electric and hybrid technologies for motor vehicles have existed since the early to mid-19th Century. Hungarian engineer and priest Ányos Jedlik has been attributed by many as designing the first electric motor in 1828. Jedlik invented a small model car that was powered by his motor.

However, the world's first recognized electric motorized vehicle, a locomotive that used electromagnets and a battery, was constructed by American inventor Thomas Davenport, in Vermont, in 1835. Around this same period, other inventors built basic electric vehicles and demonstrated them in public all over the world.

By the 1880's, the first practical electric cars were invented. European governments, including those of France and the UK, agreed to provide support and infrastructure to the electric car market. This enabled early automobile manufacturers to mass produce such vehicles. Soon, electric cars were being driven by consumers Europe-wide.

By the 1890's, electric vehicles hit the US market and proved to be very popular with American motor enthusiasts. In New York City, in 1897, a fleet of electric, battery-powered taxi cabs took New Yorkers around the city's streets. The cabs were nicknamed *hummingbirds* because of the eerie humming sound they made.

In 1899, a Belgian-built, futuristic, rocket-shaped electric racing car called *La Jamais Contente* set a world record for land speed, traveling at 66 miles per hour. The vehicle remains on display at an automobile museum in Compiègne, France.

By the early 20th Century, electric cars were becoming even more popular than gasoline-powered cars. For example, of all the automobiles in New York, Boston and Chicago in 1900, one third of them were fully electric while less than one fifth were powered by gasoline – the remainder being steam-powered.

So what the hell happened to the electric car? we hear you ask.

It's a valid question, for how can we have landed on the Moon in the intervening century or so that has elapsed since electric cars first become popular, and yet not have fully mastered this comparatively basic technology?

And speaking of the Moon, the first manned vehicle to drive on its surface was ironically an electric vehicle, the *Lunar Rover*, which was originally used in 1971 during the Apollo 15 mission.

Conventional wisdom says battery life and vehicle speeds are the problems that prevent electric cars being more widely sold. Conversely, many independent investigators have suggested electric cars were, and continue to be, quashed by bigger entities for monetary reasons.

If the electric car is another example of suppressed technology then oil corporations are the obvious culprits. After all, oil companies are known to purchase nearly all patents on proven efficient battery technology. Many argue this is to guarantee motor vehicle owners remain dependent on oil.

Besides the oil industry, other potential collaborators in this conspiracy include the US Government and its military – both of whom are commonly acknowledged to have major interests in the oil business. It's conceivable they could have conspired to kill off electric cars or any other technology that avoids continued dependency on gasoline. Even more so when you consider war is big business and oil fuels – both figuratively and literally – many a war. This would probably hold true for the governments and military regimes of Britain, Russia and many other nations.

The conspiracy theory of bigger players crushing electric car inventions gained mainstream awareness in 2006 with the theatrical release of Sony's documentary film *Who Killed the Electric Car?* It was notably produced by Hollywood producer/screenwriter Dean Devlin, who has a history of making conspiracy-themed films such as *Independence Day*, *Universal Soldier* and *Stargate*. Interviewees and apparent believers in the film's explicit suppression theory included Martin Sheen, Mel Gibson and Ralph Nader.

Who Killed the Electric Car? chronicles the release and eventual destruction of General Motors' EV1, a battery-powered electric vehicle that was tested on the market in the mid-1990's. The film rather convincingly argues that the oil industry, in collusion with automobile manufacturers and the US government, prevented the mass public from being given a chance to purchase the EV1.

Nikola Tesla claimed to have invented a highly efficient electric motor that contained rotating magnetic fields. Like most of Tesla's more radical inventions, his version of an electric car was never made available to the public. However, his discovery of the rotating magnetic field was eventually utilized for various modern electromechanical technologies such as generators and induction motors.

Twenty-first Century Silicon Valley start-up Tesla Motors is one of the more innovative companies producing electric cars. Their name, as you may have guessed, highlights the ongoing influence of Nikola Tesla's works. One of the latest model Tesla cars, the *Model S*, is equipped with a 300-mile range battery pack, potentially silencing the argument once and for all that electric vehicles have limited range due to battery life.

Although manufacturing very fast and reliable vehicles, Tesla Motors tends to produce premium vehicles with higher purchase prices than the average gasoline-run car. Unfortunately, this discounts much of the mainstream public from buying them, although the company is certainly worth keeping an eye on. With expected economies of scale, the prices of Tesla Motors' vehicles are likely to become more affordable in time. If they don't, be warned that will give rise to yet another conspiracy theory!

So, after roughly 180 years of this technology, the electric car surprisingly remains a niche automobile on the road today. However, in the last few years there has at least been a global resurgence of interest in electric cars. This revival has been primarily fueled (excuse our pun) by a few forward-thinking governments, celebrities and environmental organizations – not to mention customer demand.

Filmmaker Chris Paine, who directed *Who Killed the Electric Car?*, released a new documentary entitled *Revenge of the Electric Car*. This updated story of one of the most environmentally friendly vehicle technologies appropriately premiered on Earth Day, April 22, 2011 at the Tribeca Film Festival in New York City.

On January 5, 2014, *National Geographic* ran an article on its daily news website reporting that the world's first fully electric Formula racing championship series will soon be launched. The event, known as the FIA Formula E Championship, will take place in 10 cities including Berlin, Miami, Beijing, Monte Carlo, Los Angeles and Rio de Janeiro. Virgin Group founder and long-time environmentalist Sir Richard Branson, as well as electric car enthusiast and film star Leonardo DiCaprio are among a host of big names who have already been announced as taking part in the event.

Could the world finally be ready to embrace the electric car and make it the dominant vehicle on the planet?

WHETHER *THEY* ARE ALTERING THE WEATHER

Near the Arctic Circle, 200 miles north-east of Alaska's capital Anchorage, exists the site for the High Frequency Active Auroral Research Program – better known by its acronym, HAARP.

This controversial ionospheric research program, which officially speaking is not an intelligence or military program, has been shrouded in mystery since its inception. Little wonder HAARP has been the subject of ongoing heated debate in both mainstream and alternative media outlets.

Managed by the Air Force Research Laboratory and the Office of Naval Research, the program also receives scientific input from renowned academic learning institutions such as Stanford, MIT and UCLA. According to the US Government, HAARP is nothing but a field of antennae in remote Alaska constructed to improve telephone communications and monitor the ionosphere. Supposedly it's just *a little research project*, yet it has cost American taxpayers over a quarter of a billion dollars and counting. But hey, who's counting?

The fact that HAARP is being so heavily sponsored by the likes of the US Department of Defense, the Defense Advanced Research Projects Agency (DARPA), and the US Navy and Air Force, does not seem to reflect the Pentagon's line that it's a research program and nothing more. And why are many of America's top scientists and engineers also involved?

Critics of HAARP include Native Americans, Alaskan residents and neighboring Canadians, environmentalists, a small, but vocal group of scientists and engineers, and naturally, conspiracy buffs. The latter theorize HAARP is everything from a weather manipulation device to a broadcaster of mind-control frequencies to a weapon of mass destruction capable of creating hurricanes, earthquakes and tsunamis. Nobody seems to know for sure. What else is new in this book?

Is there any truth behind all the wild theories surrounding HAARP? To find out, you probably need to consider the past – and as we previously warned, all roads in the world of suppressed science lead back to Nikola Tesla.

The Alaskan site certainly has shades of Tesla's early 20th Century Wardenclyffe facility in New York State. And that's not where the connections to the Electric Magician end. Many say HAARP is a continuation of Tesla's technologies and discoveries. After all, HAARP's official purpose is to study the ionosphere, and nobody studied the ionosphere more than Tesla did.

As mentioned earlier, Tesla's Death Ray invention was referenced in a weapon patent taken out by Dr. Bernard Eastlund (1938-2007). The Texan physicist took out three US patents many believe were used to construct HAARP.

Even though the US Government denies any connection, numerous researchers concur that the Texan physicist's designs were nearly identical to the Alaskan facility. In particular US Patent #4,686,605. In this patent, Eastlund describes a weapon that could alter the ionosphere, transmit electromagnetic radiation, modify the weather, knock out power grids, bring down airplanes and eavesdrop on, or destroy, communications of foreign enemies.

In what may be the smoking gun, the US patent for Eastlund's invention is now owned by ARCO Power Technologies Inc., which is a sub-company of ARCO-Atlantic Richfield, a defense company hired by the Pentagon to build HAARP.

Admittedly, that's all circumstantial evidence and it could be entirely coincidental. Then again, HAARP has almost as many coincidences flying around it as does the theory that Oswald alone killed JFK, which by the way does anyone still actually believe? Either HAARP naturally attracts controversy, or there's a monumental cover-up going on as to the true nature of this 'ionospheric research program'.

Manipulating the weather sounds a bit far out, doesn't it? But consider that weather modification technologies were officially banned by the United Nations in the 1970's. For the UN to go to that trouble four decades ago, you could reasonably assume the concept of inflicting category five hurricanes or famines on enemies by altering the weather was close to becoming a scientific possibility. Or, who knows, maybe such technologies already secretly existed.

An intriguing 1996 US Air Force paper titled *Weather as a Force Mutliplier: Owning the Weather in 2025* detailed the military's attempts to turn the weather into a weapon by learning how to control it. Another document, delivered at the 1997 Intersociety Energy Conversion Engineering Conference, stated that "The effects of HAARP on the weather are completely unknown". It went on to make the point that "heating the jet stream over Alaska could have profound results on the weather in Denver or Miami".

A year later, in 1998, the European Parliament's Committee on Foreign Relations, Security and Defence Policy demanded an independent tribunal investigate the "legal, ecological and ethical implications" of the "global concern" that is HAARP. The US didn't play ball and no such investigation ever eventuated.

According to some, HAARP can cause blackouts of entire regions. The technology was believed to be responsible for the extensive power cuts that hit US states and Canadian provinces in August 2003, leaving around 50 million people without power in major cities including New York, Toronto, Ottawa and Detroit. Adding substance to this theory is the University of Tokyo's recording of a HAARP test-firing only 11 minutes before the blackout occurred.

If theorists are to be believed, HAARP's bad karma gets worse. *A lot* worse.

Theories abound surrounding HAARP's possible

responsibility for Hurricane Katrina's assault on New Orleans in 2005. On one conspiracy theory website, abovetopsecret.com, there was a chart illustrating extreme and supposedly *unnatural* fluctuations in the Earth's atmosphere during the days of August 24 and 25, which was precisely when Katrina was forming. *Above Top Secret* forum members claimed such fluctuations could only be caused by HAARP.

Other disasters that theorists have blamed on HAARP include the 2004 Indian Ocean Tsunami, the Haiti earthquake in 2010 and the Pakistan floods of the same year, the 2011 Japanese earthquake and tsunami, and the ensuing Fukushima nuclear disaster, as well as Typhoon Yolanda in the Philippines in 2013.

If HAARP is behind any of these catastrophes then the aforementioned Splinter Civilization has a massive amount of blood on its hands. The combined death toll of all these events is in the millions and many, many more were left injured or homeless.

Counting against this mega conspiracy theory, however, is the fact that HAARP is relatively transparent. Its program is unclassified, documents relating to its environmental impact are in the public domain and it has an open day for the general public twice a year. Hell, you can even call the facility at Gakona, Alaska, and what's more somebody will answer your call! In case you've gotten a sudden case of HAARPitis, here's their phone number: (907) 822 5497.

Whatever the case, one thing's for sure: HAARP ain't the little high school science experiment the US Government would have the world believe it is.

"Nikola Tesla is proof that real greatness surpasses national borders and differences."
–US President George W. Bush in a message to then President of Croatia, Stjepan Mesić. As quoted in "Nikola Tesla's anniversary and ancestry" in The New Generation on December 24, 2006.

Assuming it is true that certain scientific breakthroughs are kept from the masses by some kind of Splinter Civilization, it's our belief that nothing is more important than releasing details of these inventions. If used for good works, such technologies would have the potential to eradicate poverty in Third World nations and increase living standards throughout the rest of the world.

Tesla's inventions and ideas in particular should be declassified so that the scientific community can study his work in its entirety – something it has never been able to do. This step may be a necessary one if our society is ever to evolve beyond scarcity and corporatocracy, and move toward total sustainability.

But, hey, we ain't scientists, so you probably shouldn't be listening to us. All the technologies we wrote about in our trilogy may have been based on nothing other than fabrications by mad inventors. For all we know, the inventors mentioned in this chapter may have been nothing more than disgruntled scientists, frustrated that they could never quite nail their inventions.

So maybe it's best you keep on assuming that latest-model smart phone or tablet you're holding really is 'cutting edge' technology.

8

THE QUEEN'S INVISIBLE RICHES

Despite the absence of Queen Elizabeth II's name in
annual Forbes Rich Lists, everyone in the room was aware
the Queen was one of the wealthiest people in the world, if
not the wealthiest. However, hers and the House of
Windsor's assets and income were mostly non-declared.
–The Orphan Factory

In December 2013, Elizabeth Alexandra Mary Windsor, better known as Her Majesty Queen Elizabeth II, made world headlines over a trivial incident at London's Buckingham Palace. It was reported the Queen was irate over policemen deployed to the palace who repeatedly helped themselves to nuts meant for guests.

Newspapers around the world ran headlines such as: "Queen not so nuts about 'snacking' policemen" and "Britain's Queen Elizabeth goes nuts over nibbles at Buckingham Palace".

Such headlines are typical portrayals of Her Majesty, implying she's an eccentric old lady and some relic of another era. She is regularly presented as being nothing more than a symbolic figurehead who, apart from attending functions when duty calls, does little but walk her corgis and sip tea all day.

It's also a commonly held belief that the Queen's House of Windsor clan is a Royal Family in decline, desperately clinging to the past.

This concept would have been further solidified no doubt by an *Agencies* report dated January 29, 2014, advising that "the

Queen's household finances are at a 'historic low' with just 1 million pounds sterling in reserve, with courtiers advised to take money-saving tips from the Treasury".

The same report advises that "the parliamentary public accounts committee found the Queen's advisers were failing to control her finances while her palaces were crumbling".

However, there is another take on this iconic lady who is one of history's longest reigning monarchs. This alternative viewpoint suggests the public have been deceived into believing the Queen is just a vestige of the once powerful British Empire and no longer has any real authority.

According to this conspiracy theory, the Windsors have not yet passed their peak. On the contrary, they are richer and more powerful than ever. The only difference is they now *reign*, not *rule*. But that's merely semantics, these conspiracy theorists argue, for the Queen actually makes a myriad of executive decisions and freely operates above presidents and prime ministers.

Contrary to the myth that the British Royals were no longer all-powerful, it was common knowledge within Omega and other organizations in the know that they remained one of the most dominant forces on the planet. The Royals were totally comfortable with the mass populace believing they'd passed their heyday. That belief allowed them to control things behind the scenes with effortless ease. And control they did, in every way imaginable.

–*The Orphan Factory*

UNDECLARED FORTUNES

It has been purported by financial researchers and alternative media outlets that there are individuals whose net worth would dwarf whoever tops the Forbes Rich List at any given time – net worth the likes of Bill Gates, Warren Buffett or Carlos Slim Helu could only dream about.

This may be hard to fathom, but it's important to consider two points when analyzing the finances of the global elite.

Firstly, without being able to inspect the bank accounts of billionaires, Forbes and similar *Rich List* publishers can only make crude *guesstimates* of individuals' true worth. As a result, their lists are anything but official and their accuracy is questionable – something the billionaire community is quick to point out.

Secondly, beyond those individuals and sums mentioned on the Rich Lists, there exists what is often referred to as *invisible* or *hidden wealth*. This involves non-disclosed fortunes that are virtually impossible to detect. The planet's invisible wealth is comprised of undeclared income stashed away in offshore tax havens and Swiss bank accounts, secret *Old World* money and black market economies in which criminal enterprises conduct their business.

The criminal enterprises referred to include illegal drugs and arms dealing. One such arms dealer is Saudi Arabian Adnan Khashoggi who some banking and financial commentators estimate had a massive personal fortune of between US$2 trillion and US$7 trillion in the 1980's.

However, the world is still waiting for its first *official* trillionaire, and Khashoggi's fortune was only ever estimated by Forbes and the likes to be worth between $400 million and several billion. If the rumors of Khashoggi's multi-trillion dollar personal fortune were true then there's an extremely wide gulf separating unofficial and official estimates of his wealth.

The 2005 feature film *Lord of War*, directed by Andrew Niccol and starring Nicolas Cage and Ethan Hawke, is said to have been inspired by Russian arms dealer Viktor Bout. Like Khashoggi, Bout is rumored to have amassed a huge personal fortune impossible to estimate. Cage's character, a Ukranian-American arms dealer, is shown in the movie to be above the law with apparently unlimited money and resources.

Former Philippine President Ferdinand Marcos is another individual strongly rumored to have profited from the black market. As mentioned in chapter 6, many who have investigated Marcos, including politicians in the current Philippine government, say much of his wealth was secured from discoveries of Yamashita's Gold. As the existence of those treasures was never acknowledged by any government, it's conceivable President Marcos could have amassed a large fortune impossible to trace or estimate. Some investigators say his secret bank accounts amounted to *trillions* of dollars.

If this sounds totally unbelievable, consider the television interview Imelda Marcos gave in 2009 for the BBC TV travel series *Explore*. While being filmed inside her lavish home in the Philippines, Imelda told BBC presenter Simon Reeve that her late husband was heavily associated with gold mining companies and also traded in gold. The former First Lady then presented Reeve with an official document. Although she would not allow the document itself to be filmed, Reeve confirmed it was a Certificate of Deposit made by Ferdinand E. Marcos in a bank in Brussels, Belgium, for the amount of *Nine Hundred and Eighty Seven Billion United States Dollars.* For those who don't have a good math brain, that's only 13 billion short of a trillion bucks.

If true, this sum in Marcos' Belgium bank account alone would be almost 13 times more than Bill Gates' total current fortune. The legacy of the former president becomes even more staggering when considering that this was just one of his bank accounts; the Philippine government has confirmed through investigations of its own that Marcos had many such secret accounts in banks all over the world.

Sticking with the idea that there are individuals worth far more than the names topping official rich lists, some say the Queen is one of the wealthiest people, if not the wealthiest, in the world. In *The Orphan Factory* we run with this theory by referring to secret Royal assets and undeclared income of unimaginable proportions.

The special agent had often told his orphans that in her capacity as the reigning monarch of the Commonwealth nations, the Queen had legitimate business interests in the pharmaceutical, banking and mineral industries in most or all of those countries. No small cheese considering those nations included mineral-rich Canada and Australia as well as India and numerous African states.

–The Orphan Factory

THE MIGHT OF THE COMMONWEALTH

To get a sense of how wealthy and powerful the Queen really is, you must first study the Commonwealth and Her Majesty's role as head of it. Previously known as the British Commonwealth, the Commonwealth is basically what's left of the old British Empire that once ruled much of the world. As the various territories, or *colonies*, gained their independence, most became member states of the Commonwealth.

Queen Elizabeth II has been Head of the Commonwealth since her accession to the throne in 1952. As the multi-country union was only formally constituted in 1949, the Commonwealth and the Queen are in many ways inseparable.

With almost a third of the world's population and a quarter of the Earth's land mass, the Commonwealth spans all seven continents. In 2012, this intergovernmental organization produced almost $10 trillion in Gross Domestic Product, or GDP. In terms of population, wealth, mineral resources and land mass, the Commonwealth forms a big chunk of the planet.

Today, 53 countries remain in the Commonwealth. Members include such powerhouse nations as the United Kingdom, Canada, India, Australia, South Africa, Malaysia and Pakistan.

Other nations include Bangladesh, Singapore, Kenya, Nigeria, New Zealand, Sri Lanka, Cameroon, Jamaica and numerous other Caribbean countries.

In addition to being head of the Commonwealth of Nations, the Queen is the constitutional monarch of 16 sovereign states known as *the Commonwealth realms* where her powers are magnified.

For example, her official title in Australia is as follows: "Elizabeth the Second, by the Grace of God, *Queen of Australia* and Her other Realms and Territories, Head of the Commonwealth."

Her title as Queen and Head of Canada is almost identical to her title in Australia.

In a similar vein to the US Federal Reserve, the central banks of various Commonwealth realms such as New Zealand, Canada and Australia are officially titled 'Crown corporations' and by and large operate *independently* of those countries' governments. Some commentators have argued this banking loop-hole allows the Queen to quietly but methodically maintain control of these nations' finances.

The House of Windsor's business activities were, of course, under the radar and not on the record, just as its operations in larger Commonwealth nations like Australia and Canada were also never reported.

–The Orphan Factory

The Queen's representatives in Commonwealth realms like Canada, Australia, Jamaica and New Zealand are known as Governor-Generals, reflecting Her Majesty's supreme authority. What most citizens of these countries don't realize is that the Queen's powers extend *over and above* elected prime ministers.

This little known fact reared its ugly head in 1975 when Australia's elected Prime Minister Gough Whitlam was unceremoniously removed by then Governor-General Sir John Kerr. This was done at the behest of the Queen.

Prime Minister Whitlam had this to say to the press after being dismissed from office: "Well may we say God save the Queen, because nothing will save the Governor-General!"

Some researchers speculated the Whitlam Government's policies were interfering with the Queen's extensive business interests in Australia. It's plausible policies that were called radical, Far Left and anti-business – as Whitlam's policies were labeled by Australian and international media – could curtail profitability of Her Majesty's vast enterprises.

Besides the Queen's orders to dismiss Prime Minister Whitlam from office, there is a thread of evidence to suggest the CIA was also involved in Whitlam's dismissal.

In 2010, a similar political event occurred in Australia when Kevin Rudd, the country's elected Prime Minister, was abruptly replaced by fellow Labour Party MP Julia Gillard even though his popularity with the public was at a record high. Many citizens protested and some political analysts claimed it was unconstitutional to remove an elected PM from office. The Governor-General, however, did not intervene.

Interestingly, Rudd was in the process of implementing legislation to increase taxes on offshore mining companies to withhold more of the nation's mineral riches for the Australian people. This legislation would have included higher taxes for Rio Tinto, the multi-national metals and mining corporation the Queen owns the majority of shares in.

As well as being able to replace prime ministers, Her Majesty has the authority in Commonwealth countries to dissolve Parliament and call elections any time she so desires, refuse to approve any legislation she doesn't agree with and even pardon convicted criminals.

The leaders of all 53 Commonwealth countries officially swear an *Oath of Allegiance* to the Queen. Those who do not swear this oath are deemed unfit for office. Besides politicians, all public servants, lawyers, judges, police and military personnel are also forced to swear this oath. And new citizens of Commonwealth nations must swear an oath of allegiance to the Queen.

Bottom line is the Queen has absolute power throughout much of the mighty Commonwealth. Furthermore, she is *unelected* and *unaccountable*.

The reality was the Windsors had their fingers in many pies and had a huge say in global affairs. At home, they dictated to the British Parliament, and no elected Prime Minister could take up office without first pledging total allegiance to the Queen and future King. To Kentbridge's way of thinking, that proved Britain was no more a democracy than was the United States.

–The Orphan Factory

THE QUEEN'S POSITION IN MODERN BRITAIN

In her native Britain the Queen also has more powers assigned to her than the average journalist, and certainly the average British citizen, seems to realize. This lack of awareness of the Queen's true powers is possibly due to the fact that she rarely exercises her authority and only seems to do so when there's no alternative.

Nevertheless, the powers she has could be argued to be undemocratic given she is non-elected and received her authority by birth – all of which sound like the antithesis of a democracy.

This sentiment was echoed by Graham Smith, chief executive of *Republic*, a British group which campaigns for an alternative to the monarchy. In an article published by CNN (London) on June 1, 2012, Smith described the British Monarchy as being highly "secretive".

"Having recently lobbied successfully to have itself removed entirely from the reaches of our Freedom of Information laws," Smith stated, "it lobbies government ministers for improvements to its financial benefits and for its own private agenda."

Smith continued, "The queen and Prince Charles must be

asked for consent before our elected parliament is able to debate any legislation that affects their private interests ... The "Crown" is the supreme authority in this country – not the people. The Crown has vast powers that cannot be challenged in a court of law and those powers are exercised by the queen on the instruction of our prime minister".

The CNN article also mentioned the Queen's ability to appoint government ministers and other public servants, as well as "the power to go to war, sign treaties and change the law through the little-understood Privy Council".

Conspiracy theorists believe the Queen's imperceptible wealth – the unknown element that apparently forms the bulk of her true net worth – goes hand in hand with her rarely acknowledged political powers in Britain and throughout much of the world.

According to this theory, the Queen's overall wealth can essentially be compartmentalized into three separate categories: the Monarch, her visible fortune and, lastly and most importantly, her invisible fortune.

THE MONARCH

Much of Her Majesty's net worth is said to be derived from the Commonwealth and includes millions of acres of Crown land and thousands of Crown companies. In Britain alone, the Monarch's assets are colossal. On May 8, 2011, British newspaper *The Telegraph* reported the Crown Estate consisted of "a vast property empire dating back to the records of William the Conqueror in the Domesday Book of 1086".

The Monarch's diverse UK assets range from Ascot Racecourse to London's prime real estate district of Regent Street to shopping malls and industrial estates. It also owns a large percentage of Britain's forests, farmland and estates, and the majority of Britain's coastline, not to mention the rights to *all* the land's gold and silver discoveries.

As the reigning British Monarch, the Queen is also the

Supreme Governor of the Church of England, which may or may not carry financial rewards either directly or indirectly. For Christian readers this may seem to be a blasphemous statement, but consider the vast financial empire of the Vatican. Granted, the Church of England is not the Catholic Church, but it could still be enormously wealthy in its own right with centuries-old assets.

Officially speaking, the Monarch's assets and revenues are separate to the Queen's personal net worth. *However*, the two overlap and are not mutually exclusive.

VISIBLE PERSONAL FORTUNE

The Queen's *known* fortune was initially accumulated by indulging in *tax-free* investing during her first 40 years on the throne. In 1992, a law change required Her Majesty to pay taxes like any other British citizen. However, that did not curtail her business activities in the slightest.

Queen Elizabeth's empire includes hundreds of residences worldwide, including palaces and castles; there's also yachts, race horses, fleets of Bentleys and Rolls-Royces, tens of thousands of old masterpiece paintings and other prized artworks, the world's biggest collection of jewels, a gold carriage and billions of shares in blue chip multinational companies; Her Majesty's investment portfolio includes large shareholdings in major companies like Rio Tinto, General Electric, British Petroleum, Royal Dutch Shell and many other multinational corporations.

Now how many of the world's so-called wealthiest do you think have these kinds of assets? And keep in mind, all this is merely her *known* fortune. It has been claimed by many researchers that these official assets comprise a small percentage of her overall wealth.

*Kentbridge had also told the orphans it was a
commonly held belief within Omega that the Queen
bankrolled and reaped the rewards from other far more
secretive ventures worldwide. As for the exact nature of
those other ventures, nobody in the agency knew.*

–The Orphan Factory

INVISIBLE PERSONAL FORTUNE

In a case of *but wait there's more*, the Queen's hidden assets are rumored to dwarf her known ones, which would likely make her the richest person on earth.

The majority of the Queen's wealth is said to be inherited money. After all, the British Royals descend from elite European families in a centuries-old empire that reaped the spoils of Ancient Rome, the Crusades and splits in the Vatican.

We are talking *serious* Old World money here. The Queen's ancestors not only owned untold mineral resources throughout the known world, but were also instrumental in setting up the earliest banks and controlling money supplies and lending. And the British House of Saxe-Coburg and Gotha – since renamed the House of Windsor – actively supported and profited from nefarious but extremely lucrative historical events like the opium trade in China as well as slave-trading.

Certain theorists suggest gold alone in the Royal Family's possession is said to be worth well over a trillion pounds.

Some investigators, journalists and even EU politicians have over the years claimed the family's *dirty business* didn't end with the Opium Wars or the trading of African slaves. They've suggested the House of Windsor also participates in the industries of drug trafficking, arms trading and landmine manufacturing, using middle men or intermediaries in order to never leave any royal trace.

For example, *The Guardian* reported on March 30, 2012 that the candidate for the 2012 French presidential election, Jacques Cheminade, accused the Queen of amassing a drug money fortune. The article summarized Cheminade as theorizing that "Queen Elizabeth II owes her fortune to drug money".

"There are many other sources," the French politician was reported by *The Guardian* as saying, "but it's a series of trafficking operations within which, yes, there were drugs."

Speculation that the Queen is the richest person alive also points to the long-rumored existence of bank accounts in the name of Her Majesty in various tax havens. The plot of Roger Donaldson's 2008 heist thriller *The Bank Job*, starring Jason Statham, may vaguely allude to these secret offshore bank accounts. This true story film highlights a grand conspiracy involving MI5, elite bankers and the British Royals. Perhaps tellingly, it shows the Queen's younger sister, Princess Margaret, in a scandalous situation in the Caribbean island nation and *renowned tax haven* of Trinidad and Tobago.

Some independent researchers even say the Crown technically owns the City of London, the world's finance capital. Tied into this theory is the idea that the Windsors are senior players in the manipulation of global financial markets.

It's also worth noting the Queen has proven herself to be a highly effective investor and is regularly advised by her close circle of elite bankers, billionaire industrialists and leading politicians. She is exposed to State secrets and other privileged information.

When Her Majesty balances Royal duties and personal investing, we wonder whether she ever finds herself veering into *conflict of interest* territory?

Perhaps she never worries about such matters because British laws protect the Monarchy from prosecution or even any form of investigation. The Queen is therefore completely immune to such accusations.

This point was touched on by British pioneer organic farmer and social activist Julian Rose in an article he wrote for the non-profit news site *Activist Post* on June 12, 2012.

"The wealthiest woman in the World," Rose wrote, "Elizabeth Windsor owns one sixth of the land mass of our planet. A big Estate, it consists of Canada, Australia and the United Kingdom plus many more smaller 'Commonwealth' fiefdoms. Her Crown Estate does not attract Inheritance or Capital Gains Tax … According to Lord Halsbury in *Laws of the Land* 'The sovereign can do no wrong and no laws can be brought against her'."

When attempting to figure out the Queen's true net worth, you must also factor in that her husband, Prince Philip, is the unofficial leader of the mysterious *Club of the Isles*. A cagey oligarchy of European industrialists and aristocrats, the club is rumored to preside over approximately US$10 trillion in global assets. Companies said to be associated with the Club of the Isles include Royal Dutch Shell, The Bank of England, Lloyds Bank, SmithKline Beecham, General Electric, Barclays Bank, Rio Tinto, HSBC, BHP Billiton and DeBeers.

Some claim Prince Philip's highly secretive organization dominates the world's oil, banking, pharmaceutical and mining industries.

Researchers who believe there is a vast reservoir of undeclared Royal assets, have estimated the Queen's worth between US$11 trillion and US$30 trillion. Compare this to the world's official richest person who, as at the start of 2014, was Microsoft founder Bill Gates. Forbes' estimate of his worth was a paltry US$76 billion. Some would say that's how much the Queen makes annually in bank interest alone.

Naylor himself claimed to have witnessed one of the Queen's offshore bank accounts whose value was in the hundreds of billions.

–The Orphan Factory

"ALL THE DEMOCRACIES ARE BANKRUPT NOW"

In an informal, but recorded chat with President Reagan aboard the royal yacht *Britannia* off the coast of Florida in 1991, Queen Elizabeth II said something intriguing. Responding to Reagan's expressed desire to cut costs and scale back government, Her Majesty replied, "Well, you see, all the democracies are bankrupt now".

That was a surprisingly opinionated socio-economic commentary for an old lady some would have us believe is out of touch with the modern world. And starting a sentence with "Well, you see" when addressing the 40th President of the United States of America seems patronizing as, indeed, does her tone throughout the entire filmed discussion. At least to our ears it does.

Immediately after *informing* Reagan that "all the democracies are bankrupt now," Her Majesty added, "because of the way the services are being planned for people to grab".

In the footage, Reagan can be seen nodding enthusiastically. No doubt he'd found a like mind in the Queen as he was notorious for keeping a tight reign on America's purse strings during his time in office, especially with respect to social services.

Reagan's political stance during his two terms in office had been mirrored on the other side of the Atlantic, in Britain, where British PM Margaret Thatcher drastically slashed public services and welfare for the poor.

It's not too much of an assumption to believe the Queen's opinions on the dangers of providing people with welfare services stems from Britain's ugly class system. A system which for centuries dictated that the elite – including and especially the Royals – were *entitled* to almost everything and the commoners and the poor were left with scraps.

Judging by her comments, the Queen did not – and perhaps to this day does not – understand that welfare keeps millions afloat. It was, and is, the compassionate lifeline that civilized societies provide to assist those in genuine need. Yes, abuse of social welfare is rife, but the politics known as *Thatcherism* and *Reaganism* were not called brutal without reason.

Such comments about the *lower classes* by the Queen are not a one-off when it comes to the Windsors. In fact, they have sadly been echoed numerous times by the likes of the Queen's husband Prince Philip and their son and first in line to the throne, Prince Charles, Prince of Wales.

ROYAL WELFARE BENEFITS

The welfare benefits the Queen spoke so disparagingly of to President Reagan don't seem to include those received a little closer to home. For the fact is, the Windsors receive their own form of welfare. It's known as *the Sovereign Grant* and is paid for by the British Government.

That's right. The Windsors' lavish lifestyle is paid for by the British people!

However, the Government prefers to use the term "paid for by Parliament" rather than explicitly pointing out that taxpayers are the ones who foot the bill.

The Sovereign Grant, which until 2011 was known as *the Civil List*, amounts to multi-millions in annual handouts to the Queen and her family. This includes several million to Her Majesty annually as well as smaller but still sizeable payments to almost every other senior member of the Windsor family. A large percentage of the funds pays for salaries of Royal staff. The scheme also includes direct payments to distantly related Royals for performing official duties and attending functions.

The Civil List dates back to 1689 when Parliament, on the accession of William and Mary, agreed to pay the Royal Family 600,000 British Pounds Sterling for Royal expenses. These were enormous sums in the 17th Century and it's worth noting that before this date such expenses were paid almost entirely from the Monarch's hereditary revenues.

Royal corruption in regards to the Civil List was not uncommon. For example, during his reign from 1760-1820, King George III used his annual sum of almost a million pounds sterling as a political weapon by rewarding his supporters in Parliament with under-the-table bribes and pensions.

Besides the Sovereign Grant, the British Parliament also forks out hundreds of millions more every year to preserve the Monarch. These expenses include maintenance fees for Buckingham Palace, the Royal yachts and the Royal train, airfares and other travel expenses as well as round-the-clock security. The aforementioned 2012 CNN article written by Graham Smith also mentioned the Monarchy costs British taxpayers £202 million, or approximately US$340 million, annually.

These vast sums of taxpayer money that are paid to the already flush Windsors reflect the warped priorities of the British welfare system – a system which deprives many impoverished families of all but the barest of essentials.

Of course, the *grasping people* Her Majesty alluded to in that informal talk with President Reagan don't comprise the beneficiaries of the Sovereign Grant. In the Queen's mind, a social security system for her uber-rich Royal clan is obviously much more moral and necessary than providing for the poor and those in genuine need.

Little wonder the Windsors have often been accused of being snobby elitists by the British public at large.

AMERICA'S RELATIONSHIP WITH ROYALTY

It has been claimed by various conspiracy theorists that all American Presidents are subservient to the House of Windsor and surreptitiously look after the interests of the British Royals. Some also claim that every US President in history – right up to and including Obama – is related by blood to the Windsors.

Whatever the case, it's worth remembering America was founded upon a strong rebellion against Royalty and all it stood for. Hence the Founding Fathers adding that the United States was to be a nation "of the people, by the people and for the people" in the Constitution. No doubt they were mindful of the elitism of Britain where unelected families ruled the masses.

However, in recent decades many Americans seem to have become besotted by Royalty – especially since the glamorous Princess Diana and her sons Prince William and Prince Harry arrived on the scene. Not to forget William's beautiful wife Kate Middleton and the new addition to their family.

Possibly, this infatuation has something to do with the fact that the US does not have any royals, and there's a celebrity factor in British and European Royal Family members the American public can't get enough of.

Yet, conversely, millions of the working class people in Britain either dislike or are indifferent to the Royals.

That has always been the way in Britain where the Royals are generally loved by the upper and middle classes, but often despised by the lower classes who claim the Royal Family's sadly out of touch with them. This phenomenon could be seen whenever Queen Elizabeth's great-great-grandmother, Queen Victoria, appeared in London in the 19th Century. The crowds would boo and shout insults at her. Historians believe this is one of the reasons Victoria fled to Balmoral, the Royals' country estate in Scotland.

English actress Dame Helen Mirren, who won an Oscar for her portrayal of Queen Elizabeth II in the 2006 international box office hit *The Queen*, probably best summed up the Royals from the British public's perspective. In an interview given on the eve of the release of *The Queen*, Mirren had the following to say: "I still loathe the British class system, and the Royal family are the apex of the British class system. It's a system that I absolutely hate."

Like most Third World countries, Guyana was susceptible to interference by influential nations. In this case, it was Britain which was intent on capitalizing on the wealth – such as it was – of one of its former colonies.

–The Orphan Factory

PRINCESS DIANA'S BUTLER

At Buckingham Palace in December 1997, Princess Diana's butler Paul Burrell requested a meeting with the Queen. Burrell believed he'd found evidence of a possible conspiracy surrounding his former employer's recent death and wanted to inform Her Majesty.

The following year, at a London Inquest into Diana's death, Burrell stated that the Queen had warned him to "be careful" during their meeting of the year before. Burrell said the Queen had told him, "There are powers at work in this country of which we have no knowledge."

Who those mysterious *powers* were, the Queen apparently did not elaborate. The former butler said he had no idea what Her Majesty was referring to, but he agreed to back off the case nevertheless.

Perhaps the faceless people the Queen eluded to confirms her standing at or near the zenith of the global elite, and perhaps she's part of the "powers at work" that she referred to. If so, Her Majesty would obviously never reveal this to such a *lowly* person as Lady Diana's butler.

(See chapter 23 for more on Princess Diana's death).

At the end of the day, the Queen's true wealth is probably too vast, complex and hidden for any outsider to ever accurately calculate. Therefore, her true net wealth, and that of her descendants, will probably forever remain a mystery.

And, of course, we could be totally wrong about everything we've written about the Queen and the British Royals. In which case it would probably be best you accept that invitation to Buckingham Palace...

If you do, please write to us and let us know what it was like to meet the Royal Family because we are pretty sure our own ship has sailed in that regard – especially now that this book has been published!

9

ELIXIR OF LIFE

As the White Gold dissolved under their tongues, not
one of the orphans gave the substance a second thought.
They'd been taking the powder all their lives and gave it
no more consideration than they gave drinking water or
breathing air.

–The Orphan Factory

As mentioned in chapter 5, *Ormus* – aka *ORME, White Powder Gold* or simply *White Gold* – has been shown to balance the hemispheres of the brain and therefore accelerate learning speeds.

But that's just the tip of the iceberg when it comes to this unusual scientific discovery which, we admit, sounds like something out of an episode of *The X-Files*.

In *The Orphan Factory* we refer to how daily consumption of Ormus assists the orphans in every facet of their life, from enhancing mental alertness to developing physical strength and endurance to promoting good health.

Few mainstream scientific studies have thus far been conducted on the mysterious substance. But even if a tenth of what proponents of White Gold say is true, the potential for humanity is remarkable.

Preliminary studies have shown it to assist in a variety of diverse fields including agriculture, engineering and aeronautics. For example, small studies have been conducted by universities to evaluate Ormus' effects on various fruits and vegetables, and the results are impressive. Farmers and growers worldwide have also reported increased growth in crops, nuts, fruits and vegetables as a result of using Ormus.

However, it is the superconductor's effects on humans that have prompted most interest. Slowing aging, assisting mental wellbeing, replacing gray hair, improving eyesight, re-growing missing teeth, increasing body immunity and correcting damaged DNA are but a few of the astonishing claims surrounding the substance.

Ormus test results are apparently off the charts and defy the laws of science. White Gold experts explain this by saying the substance exists in the realms of quantum physics and hyperdimensional theory. Skeptics, however, say Ormus more appropriately exists in the twilight zone and its benefits are nowhere near conclusively proven.

Consumers of the little known substance, which is created in different forms by hundreds of commercial manufacturers worldwide, come from all sectors of society. Examples range from sportsmen looking for legal performance enhancers to terminally sick people seeking alternative cures for illnesses modern medicine cannot cure. A-List Hollywood stars are also among those who regularly ingest Ormus.

DISCOVERY

Ormus was discovered in 1975 by David Hudson, an Arizona cotton farmer and wealthy businessman. Hudson came across the substance while conducting analysis of natural resources on one of his farms in Arizona. He ended up devoting his life and millions of dollars to researching the strange substance, which he linked to Biblical and ancient Egyptian alchemy.

It was an unusual-looking white powder that the farmer discovered by chance on his farm. When he put the powder out to dry in the hot Arizona sun, it radically changed – from powder to oil!

After conducting scientific analysis of the substance, Hudson confirmed it seems to have odd properties that defy the laws of nature. For example, Ormus' elements, which include gold, copper and iron, frequently morph into other elements and the substance becomes an electromagnetic superconductor under certain conditions.

Hudson claimed to have knowledge of secretive Government-funded studies of Ormus. He said these experiments took place in laboratories throughout the US and the Soviet Union in the 1980's. If such experiments did take place, they've never been made public.

In the late 1980's, Hudson was issued a British patent by the UK Intellectual Property Office for the Ormus product he formulated from his initial discovery. At the same time, he coined a term for the exotic elements he patented – *Orbitally Rearranged Monoatomic Elements*, or *ORME*.

Shortly thereafter, Hudson was informed he no longer had the patent. He claims no clear reason was given and, soon after, he received a visit from the US Department of Defense.

Hudson then enigmatically became reclusive and made few if any public appearances for about 20 years. Nor did he make any comments about Ormus during that period. Only in the last two to three years has he ventured into the public arena again, giving lectures about his discovery.

It's worth considering the following excerpt by Barry Carter – arguably the world's foremost expert on Ormus and one of the few who personally knows David Hudson – from an article Carter wrote on the subtleenergies.com website: "It is my firm belief that, once it becomes widely known, the discovery of the ORMUS materials will be heralded as the greatest scientific discovery in human history."

As he watched his manufactured orphans consume their prescribed allocations of the substance, Doctor Pedemont pondered its scientific make-up. Besides gold, he knew it contained a number of other metals including rhodium, iridium, copper and platinum which, like the gold portion, all existed in their non-metallic states.

–The Orphan Factory

Scientific properties

Ormus is a complex concentrate of chemical elements. Besides gold, it contains a number of other metals including rhodium, iridium, copper and platinum. These metals are said to exist in the monoatomic state, or *m-state* – an unusual high-spin state of matter where metals don't form bonds or crystals but remain single atoms.

Incidentally, Ormus' non-scientific name White Powder Gold refers to the fact that when processed its appearance is reminiscent of cocaine powder.

M-state elements are naturally abundant in seawater, and the pure sea salt in seawater is said to be responsible for these rare, high-spin particles. Ormus properties are also said to be present in most rocks as well as trees.

In addition, various researchers have independently claimed to have found Ormus elements embedded in the DNA structure of animals and plants as well as in humans' brain, skin, nails, hair, blood and in all the organs.

Different methods for obtaining Ormus elements have been devised in recent years – the easiest and most common of which involves combining ocean water, lye water and distilled water in the right fashion. This method is said to be so simple it can be done by anyone in their own home.

Supposed formulas, or *recipes*, have been posted on various websites online. However, it's not clear whether these formulas lead to the same Ormus elements as those David Hudson discovered.

Tut's tail

In 2003, US citizen Dana Dudley found a stray male cat which she named *Tut*. Dudley adopted Tut and allowed him to sleep on the back porch of her home. Later, Tut's tail was cut off in an accident.

Dudley, who happened to be an Ormus user, decided to treat Tut with the substance to see if it would help the injured cat. Every day, she placed Ormus in Tut's food and also hand-fed some to him. It wasn't long before she was able to report that Tut had begun growing a new tail.

In 2007, Dudley posted before-and-after photos online of Tut. In the latest photos, the cat's tail looked normal and appeared to have completely regenerated. These before-and-after photos have been shared and reposted on various websites, and they remain online for all to see.

As of writing, Tut is still alive and Dudley reports he is a very happy and active cat.

ORME's biological results were outstanding. As well as balancing both hemispheres of the brain, the product had also been proven to activate so-called Junk DNA, and the orphans' regular consumption of it allowed them to move, fight and think as efficiently and effectively as almost any adult.

–The Orphan Factory

HEALTH BENEFITS

As mentioned, Ormus can be taken in order to improve a person's health. In its powdered form, it's usually ingested sublingually, or under the tongue. When taken this way, it goes straight into the bloodstream. Alternatively, in its liquid state, White Gold can be drunk as a potion or else applied topically to the skin.

Not long after he discovered Ormus and began analyzing it, David Hudson said the substance could repair the body on a genetic level. Others have since postulated that Ormus is a universal cure for *all* forms of disease, including cancer and AIDS. Proponents also say the substance can correct errors in the DNA and even activate Junk DNA.

It's worth mentioning that most commercial manufacturers of Ormus have numerous testimonials from customers. Testimonials on the manufacturers' websites claim cures for all sorts of serious illnesses, including mental disorders, diabetes, heart disease and osteoporosis. Various anti-aging results have also been reported.

Again, though, it should be stressed none of these health benefits have been proven scientifically. It's anybody's guess whether Ormus users experienced the placebo effect or whether there simply haven't been enough mainstream studies conducted to support users' claims.

Only time will tell.

Dispensing a phial to the last of the orphans, the doctor then handed another to Kentbridge who promptly emptied its contents under his tongue. As the biological effects were known to be similar for everyday people like him, Kentbridge thought it couldn't hurt. He'd been consuming it for over a decade – ever since Doctor Pedemont had assured him it would correct most of his damaged DNA and keep his body in shape. White Gold also had anti-aging benefits, something Kentbridge figured he would need in future if he was to keep up with the orphans.

–The Orphan Factory

HOLLYWOOD STARS ON ORMUS

Since its discovery, White Gold has been used by a raft of Hollywood stars. It's especially popular with middle-aged starlets – not surprising given the substance's purported anti-aging benefits and the fact Hollywood is notorious for casting young, or at least youthful-looking, actresses for most major roles.

Gwyneth Paltrow is probably the most vocal Ormus user in the Hollywood community. On the website alchemicalelixirs.com a testimonial (of hers) appears as follows:

Gwyneth Paltrow said: August 10th, 2009 5:27 pm

Dear Brendan, congratulations on your wonderful website, I must admit I am a little bit jealous that our little secret about your incredible ORMUS is now available to the world. I know I can`t stand in the way of human evolution and I am proud of you for your part in raising awareness and the planets consciousness through your ORMUS, god bless you, love Gwyneth x PS can you send me another few bottles of your latest brew my stash is running low thanks xx

Alchemical Elixirs, which also lists Jennifer Aniston and Audrey Tautou among its clients, is just one of many Ormus manufacturers and suppliers that names film stars, business executives, top sportsmen and famous musicians among its customers.

Like most of the substances and technologies Doctor Pedemont employed to perfect his orphan creations, the produce was not known to official science. Although the scientific community was aware of Arizona cotton farmer David Hudson's accidental discovery of ORME back in 1975, they had been denied the opportunity to test the latest strains. Indeed, they never knew of their existence. Pure White Gold Powder, the rarest and most effective strain, had been completely withheld from mainstream scientists and from the public at large. That way, elite groups like the Omega Agency could use it in total secrecy to profit from its unquestionable benefits and to further their own agendas.

–The Orphan Factory

A SUPPRESSED VERSION

Following on from the suppressed science covered in chapter 7, there have been rumors the Ormus that the public has access to is not the same as that which David Hudson discovered. The elements in the White Powder Gold that he discovered were said to become invisible at times, whereas nothing that radical appears to have been reported by Ormus users who source their product from known suppliers. No customers have disappeared that we know of!

If it's true there's a suppressed and more powerful type of Ormus, it probably relates to the top-secret lab experiments Hudson claimed the US and Soviets conducted in the 1980's.

In *The Orphan Factory* we refer to a conspiracy theory which claims the US Military tested Ormus extensively. This theory contends that the Military Industrial Complex observed that the substance exhibited a cloak of invisibility, and signals in its presence were corrupted.

As we wrote in *The Orphan Factory*: "The military had discovered an unexpected but useful side-effect of White Gold: when smothered on vehicles and planes, they became invisible to radar and satellite technologies, and all transmission devices failed to emit signals effectively."

Nine, our novel's young hero, escapes from his masters by using Ormus to avoid radar detection. But that's another story.

The agency had hired physicists, chemists and biologists to conduct laboratory experiments and design a version of ORME specifically for the orphans. They used various technologies to monitor the effectiveness of the powder, including dark-field microscopy of the blood and EEG tests on the brain.

–The Orphan Factory

THE REAL GOLD OF THE ANCIENTS

Some say Ormus is the *elixir of life* that ancient peoples spoke of and that was lost to Mankind for several thousand years. Apparently, the *Ancients* variously referred to the precious powder as, among other things, *the Fruit of the Tree of Life, the Gold of the Gods* and *the Philosopher's Stone*.

The mythical elixir of life was said to be a substance that would maintain life, or at least eternal youth, indefinitely. It has been said that the elixir of life was sought by alchemists for many centuries after it was lost. Subscribers to this theory say the Ancients had recognized this substance would cure all diseases and enable extraordinary life-spans for humans.

There have been rumors in conspiracy circles that Ormus was found in the King's Chamber of the Great Pyramid of Giza in Egypt. But again, this is not remotely proven.

☙ ❦ ❧

For around US$100 or less you can try Ormus for yourself by ordering it direct from any one of the various commercial enterprises that manufacture or supply it. It appears the manufacturers all use different formulas and, in the tradition of alchemists, those formulas for the most part seem to remain secret.

Any mainstream studies into Ormus will be worth keeping an eye on.

For the time-being, however, the substance remains shrouded in mystery and it's very hard to find the truth amongst the hype. This task is not made any easier with all the quasi-science commercial manufacturers are using to support their claims. No doubt the composition of their products is far removed from the properties of farmer Hudson's original discovery.

If you are thinking of purchasing a batch of Ormus, there are a couple of things to keep in mind. Besides the stunning testimonials surrounding White Gold, it's worth noting numerous users have also reported taking it and noticing no tangible results.

So it's a case of buyer beware and *always consult your doctor.*

By the way, we had to insert the italicized disclaimer above for legal purposes – such is the litigious nature of our society!

And, lastly, we could be totally wrong about everything we wrote or implied about Ormus / aka White Powder Gold. In which case, best you don't throw out your anti-wrinkle cream just yet...

10

JONESTOWN: SUICIDES OR MASS MURDER?

The Trojan Horse Sterling had referred to reflected his belief that the truth about Jonestown had never been revealed to the American people. A belief shared by his fellow co-founders. They were certain that while there were undoubtedly suicides at Jonestown, the event could more accurately be described as a mass murder that resulted from an experiment of sorts carried out by various US agencies.

–The Orphan Factory

The Peoples Temple Agricultural Project was a predominantly American residential community in Guyana, South America. Branded a cult by the media, it was more commonly known as *Jonestown* in deference to its leader, Jim Jones, a former communist and drug addict, and son of a Ku Klux Klansman.

The community made world headlines on November 18, 1978, when it was announced 918 people at Jonestown, including 200 children, had died. All but two Peoples Temple members died from cyanide poisoning in what was labeled "revolutionary suicide" by Jim Jones himself.

Besides the suicides at Jonestown, several surviving Temple members murdered five others, including California Congressman Leo Ryan at the nearby Port Kaituma airstrip.

Jonestown remained the largest loss of American civilian life in a single non-natural disaster until the deaths that occurred in the US on 9/11 in 2001.

Everything covered so far in this chapter is the *official* version of what occurred at Jonestown. However, there have long been rumors of MK-Ultra experimentation with the commune before the tragic incident occurred, and CIA involvement before and after the incident. Crucial sources, including Jonestown survivors as well as local officials first on the scene, appear to radically contradict the mass suicide story.

If something other than the mass suicide the history books inform us happened in 1978 at Jonestown, then what did occur? A dark social experiment, wholesale murder, CIA assassinations, mind control implementation gone wrong, or what? These, and more, have been touted as fact by independent researchers over the years.

In *The Orphan Factory*, we explore these theories when Nine and another orphan-operative attempt an assassination, deep in Guyana's Amazon rainforest, of a survivor of the Jonestown tragedy.

What struck him most were the discrepancies in the body count, and Omega's research people had come up with some interesting theories on that.

–The Orphan Factory

JONESTOWN DISCREPANCIES

Unusual anomalies within the US Government's official version of Jonestown raise alarm bells as they do seem to point to a conspiracy. In fact, there were so many conflicting reports that it was, and is, difficult to make head or tail of the event.

The Guyanese army, whose soldiers were among the first on the scene, reported only 408 Temple members had died by their own hand. Then the *New York Times* reported the actual number was around 500.

US Military personnel arrived several days later and the body count quickly rose – from 700 to a final tally of 909. No official explanation was ever given for these differing body counts although one US official was quoted as saying, "Guyanese cannot count."

There were also conflicting reports on the causes of death. The *New York Times* had reported the first medical official to arrive on the scene said he'd witnessed numerous gunshot wounds on victims. That didn't tally with the official story that the majority had committed suicide by drinking cyanide. And no-one seemed to know exactly how many people were in Jonestown at the time. Therefore, reports listing 33 survivors couldn't be verified.

Local newspaper the *Guyanese Daily Mirror* reported that around 60 to 80 American Green Berets and several hundred members of the UK's SAS Black Watch were performing military exercise drills in the jungles surrounding Jonestown at the exact same time the mass suicides or the massacre – depending on your take – occurred.

Was that a coincidence or does it as some suggest point to a sinister outside party, or parties, being responsible for the deaths?

Another anomaly in the official version as told by the US Government was that the bodies lay neatly arranged in rows and showed no signs of the heavily twisted rigidity known to be induced in cyanide suicides.

In the coroner's court, Guyanese pathologist Dr. Leslie Mootoo stated the bodies looked like they'd been murdered and, in his opinion, were not suicides at all. Dr. Mootoo also said that while he did find gunshot wounds on a small percentage of the victims, he found needle marks on the vast majority.

Needle usage would directly contradict the cyanide story as the official story says the cyanide was taken orally.

The US Army, however, said the cause of death was irrefutably cyanide suicides. Interestingly, it was only after mounting pressure from family members of the deceased back in America that the Army finally agreed to perform some autopsies – seven out of 900 deaths to be precise. Those token autopsies were clearly too few to gain true insight into what caused the deaths.

ASSASSINATION OF A CONGRESSMAN

Californian Congressman Leo Ryan had flown down to Guyana to investigate strange irregularities at Jonestown shortly before the incident.

In the Federal Bureau of Investigation's Vault the following description is listed under the code name *RYMUR (The Leo Ryan Murder/Jonestown Investigation)*: "On November 18, 1978, while investigating human rights abuses by a large cult led by James Warren "Jim" Jones (1931-1978), Congressman Leo Ryan (1925-1978) and several companions were murdered by Jones' followers. Ryan had traveled to "Jonestown," the cult's compound in the South American country of Guyana, at the behest of his constituents, some of whom had family members in the cult. Following Ryan's murder, Jones ordered his followers to commit mass suicide; more than 900 bodies were later found, most having died by taking poison. The FBI, charged with investigating violence against public officials, opened a probe into the murder of Ryan (hence the case name RYMUR) and provided other support and investigative assistance in relation to the mass casualties."

It has been claimed by some Jonestown researchers that Leo Ryan, who had been a vocal critic of the CIA for years, had discovered the community was not being run by Jim Jones, but by the CIA; instead of allowing Ryan to return to the US to inform congress, the CIA killed him then shut down the entire Jonestown program by instigating a massacre.

CIA FINGERPRINTS ON THE CRIME SCENE

Jonestown member George Blakey, who was a chief aid to Jim Jones, was later identified as a CIA agent. Blakey purchased the land on which Jonestown was built. That, together with his CIA involvement and the community's tragic end, could reasonably point to it being some kind of bizarre agency experiment.

What Blakey did immediately after the apparent Jonestown massacre lends weight to this theory. Within days, he reportedly moved to the nearby tax haven of Trinidad where he withdrew US$5 million from a Credit Suisse bank account.

In another CIA connection, US Embassy official Richard Dwyer was with Leo Ryan at the time of the airfield shootings and was later confirmed to have been a CIA agent. The first report of the "mass suicide" was made via radio a couple hours after the deaths occurred. Nobody has ever confirmed who made the radio reports, but perhaps tellingly, Richard Dwyer was the only person at Jonestown known to have a working radio.

Intriguingly, on the suicide tape recording of the last few minutes before the deaths occurred within the commune, Jim Jones can clearly be heard saying, "Get Dwyer out of here. Take him out of here now before something bad happens to him." This implies Jones and the CIA were in cahoots as the cult leader would not allow anyone else to leave the commune.

Many independent researchers also believe the suicide tape was heavily edited to disguise the unmistakable sound of gunshots. If true, this also points to murders, not suicides.

"Most of the deaths were undoubtedly the work of MK-Ultra brainwashed moles operating inside the Peoples Temple community."

–The Orphan Factory

THE MK-ULTRA THEORY

There are numerous theories suggesting Jonestown was a CIA test site for brainwashing and mind control. It has been claimed that Leo Ryan visited Jonestown because he'd uncovered evidence that Jonestown was a large-scale MK-Ultra experiment.

In a potential red flag supporting this theory, the psychoactive drugs found in Jonestown included most of those used in the MK-Ultra program.

Many investigators have theorized that Larry Layton, a senior member of Jonestown, was also an undercover CIA agent. In what could be a telling connection, Layton's father was in charge of the US Army's Biological Weapons Research unit. Mere coincidence? Or was Jonestown a "research experiment" conducted by the military?

Another thread that could link Jonestown with an MK-Ultra experiment is that US citizens were taken from mental hospitals and children were taken from orphanages in America and placed in the commune. (You'll recall from the declassified CIA documents mentioned in chapter 2 that it's on the record mental patients and orphans were experimented on against their will under the MK-Ultra program).

Why such a massacre had occurred, the Omegans could only speculate. Some thought it may have been to stop a large-scale emigration out of America to a fabled Utopian society; others wondered if it was intended to create fear in the populace – fear of cults, fear of Communism, fear of anything foreign; and still others believed it was to create a precedence whereby any groups labelled a cult would be vilified without due diligence by the public.

–The Orphan Factory

"A WACO BETA TEST"

The 1993 Waco massacre of members of the Christian sect, the so-called *Branch Davidians*, in Texas, shares much in common with

Jonestown: there were conflicting reports regarding cause of death, psychoactive drugs were found on the property and there was confusion surrounding cult leader David Koresh's intentions. In fact, Waco had a whole host of eerily similar discrepancies, not to mention traces of CIA involvement and possibly mind control operations as well.

As we wrote in *The Orphan Factory*; "MK-Ultra victims included the Branch Davidians at the Waco compound in Texas," and "Jonestown was a Waco beta test."

The US Government's own reports emphasize that Koresh had repeatedly insisted suicide was not an option for him or his fellow community members. As with Jonestown, the commonly held belief that the entire religious community at Waco wanted to die doesn't seem to hold true upon closer inspection.

"It suited the authorities that mainstream media reported the Jonestown tragedy as a mass suicide," Naylor continued. "The American public readily accepted that, shocking though it was. But make no mistake. It was primarily mass murder and the Peoples Temple was effectively turned into a slaughter house."
–The Orphan Factory

In addition to what's been covered in this chapter, there have been several other prominent conspiracy theories concerning Jonestown, including one which plays on the communist connections with the cult and claims the Soviets were responsible.

Some have even theorized the Jonestown massacre was some kind of sick "racial cleansing" experiment. As most Jonestown victims were black, some have argued it was a eugenics purification test conducted by white racists to prepare for even greater ethnic casualties in years to come. (See chapter 15 for more on eugenics).

Another strange thing about Jonestown was Jim Jones' corpse.

The Peoples Temple leader was known to have tattoos all over his chest. Yet the photos of his corpse found after his supposed suicide shows a chest free of tattoos.

America's House Foreign Affairs Committee (HFAC) concluded the massacre was entirely due to Jones' "extreme paranoia" and there was no outside interference from the CIA or otherwise. Strangely though, 5000 HFAC documents on Jonestown remain classified to this day.

If the old adage *Where there's smoke there's fire* is true then Jonestown must have been a cover-up of some kind. And it does seem unlikely anyone could convince more than 900 people to willfully commit suicide, especially when so many were young children.

Then again, our assumptions could all be wrong as brainwashing doesn't only belong in the domain of intelligence agencies. Fanatical, brainwashed cult members all over the world have committed mass suicides. (Remember the *Heaven's Gate* suicides?). And by all accounts Jim Jones was a megalomaniac. So it's possible he killed himself and his devotees followed suit as per the official story. And who's to say Jonestown members didn't believe their leader was guiding them all into heaven?

11

MEDICAL INDUSTRIAL COMPLEX

Nurse Hilda was also aware that Francis' DNA would be useful in some of the illicit scientific experiments the agency's medical people were carrying out on human guinea pigs in its various underground labs. One of its many legitimate businesses, KaizerSimonsKovak, just happened to be the world's number one pharmaceutical company, and Omega was anxious to protect its market share and the huge revenues it generated. Those same revenues helped finance Omega's activities.

–The Orphan Uprising

In book one in *The Orphan Trilogy*, we show Nine discovering an underground orphanage and witnessing the most horrible medical and scientific experiments imaginable being conducted on young orphans; in book three in the trilogy, we show one of the world's leading pharmaceutical companies kidnapping orphans and placing them in clandestine orphanages all over the world.

These are obviously fictional incidents, but they were inspired by some of the horrific medical experiments that have been reported over the years – since and including the Nazi era of heinous medical experimentation on concentration camp inmates. Naturally, being dramatists, we sensationalized things a fair bit in the trilogy...

Or did we?

You don't need to be a genius to know that corruption is rife in the world's most lucrative fields. It seems few in positions of power have the ability to resist the temptation of generating vast sums of money via devious if not downright dishonest means.

Whether it be profiting from *manufactured* arms conflicts, manipulating financial markets or creating the illusion of a scarcity of minerals and resources, history proves greed is often the rule and not the exception when it comes to the global elite's pursuit of wealth – or, perhaps more pertinently and disturbingly, when it comes to their pursuit of greater wealth.

Many argue that the medical sector is no different. This seems a strange accusation given most in this field, including doctors, nurses and hospital staff, embark on their careers out of a compassionate and genuine desire to care for the sick.

Unfortunately, there are powers-that-be whose motives are not so noble. Collectively and unofficially called *the Medical Industrial Complex*, they comprise a surprisingly large number of individuals, corporations, government health services and, dare we say it, hangers-on. Those in the latter category include the likes of health systems consultants, insurers, banking executives, accountants, lawyers, construction experts and even realtors.

Other key players in this complex include hospitals, the medical academic establishment, hospital supply and equipment companies, and of course the drug companies – let's not forget them.

To put the Medical Industrial Complex into perspective, consider this: modern medicine is one of the largest and most profitable industries on the planet. Someone who should know described it as America's biggest industry. Not sure it's as big as the *war industry*, but if it ain't, it must be a close second.

At the time of writing, Americans were transfixed, bemused and frustrated by the partisan squabbling surrounding President Obama's attempts to sort out the country's healthcare provisions once and for all.

One who summarizes America's health problems better than most is William A. Collins, a former state representative and former Mayor of Norwalk, Connecticut. In an article dated August 21, 2013, on OtherWords.org, Collins says in the US, the health industry's big players focus on making as much money as possible.

Collins also says, "The providers devise the system, making profits a high priority. Patients that can't contribute to profit margins are shunted off to government services or ignored... The network of handshakes and private agreements that links hospitals to medical device manufacturers and drug reps inflates our health cost just as much as the insurance and Big Pharma... Fortunately, the main offenders can be clearly labeled. Chief among them are the health insurers and the drug manufacturers. Big Pharma wields an army of lobbyists and administers large doses of campaign contributions to their friends in Congress".

For those not familiar with the term *Big Pharma*, it's the nickname given to the major pharmaceutical conglomerates which collectively form this multi-trillion dollar industry. Many believe Big Pharma can be compared to the most corrupt banks, media monopolies or oil corporations.

If you haven't worked it out already, the conspiracy theory we explore in this chapter contends that Big Pharma and other participants in the Medical Industrial Complex put profits ahead of patients' wellbeing and dollars ahead of lives.

CONSPIRING TO QUASH ALTERNATIVE MEDICINES

If Big Pharma is the Devil in this medical conspiracy theory, then natural/alternative medicine would probably be God.

Many of those in the medical fraternity instantly label treatments in the traditional, natural or holistic health fields as *quackery*. This word is even used to describe Traditional Chinese Medicine and the Indian Ayerveda, two medical systems which are far older than Western medicine and globally just as popular.

One sign that the Medical Industrial Complex may view natural/alternative medicine as a financial threat is the sweeping law changes it has forced upon the alternative health market in recent years. Today, most nations now have laws requiring any health substance with medicinal claims to be legally defined as "drugs". This includes herbal remedies and various other *non-drug* medicines of natural origins. Critics say such laws prevent wider distribution of natural health products and give Big Pharma ever more control.

In the US, these laws are monitored by the Food and Drug Administration (FDA), an organization which conspiracy theorists argue is at the very top of the Medical Industrial Complex. That's right folks, the same FDA that allows genetically-modified Monsanto organisms in your food supply and the same FDA that allows your kids to consume Aspartame in soft drinks is the organization responsible for telling Americans how they can and cannot treat their illnesses.

It has been repeatedly argued by natural health proponents that major pharmaceutical companies, along with their supportive cronies in governments, conspired to pass these laws to force the public to only use modern medicines that are pharmacological, patented and profitable.

Call us crazy, but we think any product with 100% natural and non-synthetic ingredients such as herbs, veggies and roots should be in a totally separate category to synthetic, laboratory-made pharmaceutical drugs.

Many alternative health researchers also claim that little funding is granted for research into natural or traditional cures because Big Pharma cannot patent things which occur organically in nature.

One such example is the work of high-profile American chemist and Nobel Peace Prize-recipient Linus Pauling (1901-1994). He received no support from the medical establishment for radical health discoveries he claimed he discovered when experimenting with mega-doses of Vitamin C. Despite his illustrious credentials, Pauling was also labeled a quack for his claims that the natural, *unpatentable* Vitamin C could cure a whole host of diseases, including cancer.

However, it appears Pauling may have the last laugh, albeit posthumously. Several high profile studies in the last few years suggest his theories on high dose Vitamin C being an effective anticancer agent may indeed be correct.

SUPPRESSED CURES

As covered in chapter 7, there seems to be more than enough evidence to support the claim that at least some scientific breakthroughs are suppressed. Unfortunately, it appears this also happens within modern medicine where cures for various illnesses mysteriously vanish or are quashed by the medical establishment.

This suppression theory supports the assertion that Big Pharma needs sick people to prosper. Patients, not healthy people, are their customers. If everybody was cured of a particular illness or disease, pharmaceutical companies would lose 100% of their profits on the products they sell for that ailment.

What all this means is because modern medicine is so heavily intertwined with the financial profits culture, it's a *sickness industry* more than it is a health industry.

"The cancer industry world wide is estimated at a 200 billion dollar a year industry. There are many in various associated positions within that industry who would be without a job if that cash flow dried up suddenly with the news that there are cheaper, less harmful, and more efficacious remedies available. Big Pharmacy would virtually vanish."
–Paul Fassa. Article excerpt in Natural News, September 24, 2009.

FINDING (HIDING) A CURE
FOR CANCER

In the West at least, cancer is the biggest natural killer. Some fatality estimates have been as high as 20,000 cancer patients worldwide dying every day. When a cancer cure is finally found it will save millions of lives and will be the medical discovery of this era.

In the last few decades, hundreds of billions of dollars have been spent internationally on cancer research. In the US alone, since President Nixon launched his 'War on Cancer' program in 1971, tens of billions in government funding have been granted to cancer researchers.

However, there are theories out there which suggest there has already been a cure, or many cures, discovered for cancer. These popular conspiracy theories suggest the Medical Industrial Complex have a huge financial incentive to suppress cures so they can continue to provide their own costly treatments for cancer patients.

If true, that would be a callous and unforgiveable business model, unnecessarily costing countless lives.

There are many case studies that support the theory. Here's a sample of those.

In the 1920's, Canadian nurse Rene Caisse developed a natural concoction of herbs called *Essiac*. She claimed it could cure cancer and garnered many testimonials from satisfied patients said to be cancer-free after taking the product. Laboratory tests did not confirm Essiac offered any benefits whatsoever, but conspiracy theorists argue the lab tests were rigged and that Big Pharma flexed its muscle to shut Caisse down.

In the 1940's, German-born American physician Max Gerson (1881-1959) developed a nutrition-based cancer treatment called *Gerson Therapy*. After repeatedly claiming his therapy cured cancer, Doctor Gerson had his medical license suspended and he died while still under suspension. Although now a maligned and mostly forgotten cancer treatment in America, it remains popular in Mexico where there are Gerson clinics in operation, treating local and foreign cancer patients.

In the 1950's, American coal miner Harry Hoxsey promoted his family's century-old herbal recipe, which he touted as a cancer cure. He set up clinics in 17 states around America before all were closed down by the FDA. Hoxsey made a rare documentary film in 1957 called *You Don't Have to Die*, which detailed his cure and covered the patients he treated with it. There's a more recent documentary titled *Hoxsey: How Healing Becomes a Crime*, which chronicles his battles with 'organized medicine'.

In the 1980's, Italian medical doctor, chemist and pharmacologist Luigi di Bella (1912-2003) claimed to have developed a cure for cancer known as *Di Bella Therapy*. The formula was a combination of vitamins, drugs and hormones.

The American Cancer Society says on its website that numerous studies showed Di Bella Therapy "may have had a negative effect compared to the outcome for similar patients receiving standard treatment".

However, there are some alternative medical researchers who believe Di Bella therapy was a legitimate cancer cure that was permanently quashed by the medical establishment.

Despite the extremely negative press garnered in Italy and the rest of the world there are, or were, cancer patients who swore by Di Bella Therapy and gave testimonials. For example, on the website beatingcancercenter.org is the following statement: "For about three years, the patient has been following the Di Bella therapy without side effects, improving the quality of life and going back to work."

Luigi di Bella himself consistently stated that pharmaceutical companies were conspiring against him.

The list of other supposed cancer cures said to have been suppressed is long enough to fill a whole book. These range from *Cannabidiol*, the little-known medical compound found in Marijuana, to a treatment that involves ingesting nothing other than regular household baking soda.

If you have cancer or know anyone who has been diagnosed with the disease, Massimo Mazzucco's 2010 documentary film *Cancer: The Forbidden Cures* is a good starting place for those searching for natural cures.

Of course, *always consult with your doctor first.* (And in case you're wondering, this is another disclaimer we had to include for legal reasons!).

To be fair, the natural health sector has attracted its share of quacks, too, so *all* theories of cures should be treated with a degree of skepticism until proven. However, automatically riding roughshod over claims of natural cures, especially where those claims are supported by glowing, bona-fide testimonials, is not the answer any more than gullibly believing them all is.

There are those who may argue that Big Pharma could also make money out of cures for cancer and that it would be a lot easier than suppressing cures. To counter that, many independent medical researchers say long-term or ongoing cancer treatments, like chemotherapy, would be far more profitable than delivering single-visit cures. It has been estimated that the average cancer patient spends tens of thousands of dollars on standard treatments with some even spending hundreds of thousands.

Again, Big Pharma's *repeat customers* are sick people. From a financial perspective, cured people are of little use.

As the cancer industry alone is a multi-trillion dollar industry for Big Pharma, it seems believable that if any cure was to be suppressed for financial gain it would be a cancer cure.

*Like all companies in the legal drug trade,
KaizerSimonsKovak needed to test new drugs before
releasing them onto the market. While its competitors
tested their new drugs mostly on rats, mice and
monkeys, KSK had the advantage of being able to test
them on humans. No KSK employee, or indeed anyone
outside Omega, was aware of that, however. All testing
was contracted out – to another Omega-owned
company. And its modus operandi was far from legal.*
    –The Orphan Uprising

HUMAN GUINEA PIGS

On May 14, 2013, German news magazine Der Spiegel ran an article about international drug companies conducting illegal tests on impoverished citizens in India. The article stated, "The practice is forbidden, but the use of subcontractors makes it difficult to detect".

In 2008, it was revealed that over a two-and-a- half-year period of testing medicines at the All India Institute of Medical Sciences (AIIMS), 49 babies had died during clinical studies. *The Times of India* reported this incident in no uncertain terms in an August 19, 2008 article headlined *49 babies die during clinical trials at AIIMS*.

Such experimentation is in direct violation of the World Medical Association's *Declaration of Helsinki*, which requires subjects in tests to be shielded from harm. However, in the AIIMS scandal the accused international drug manufacturers denied all responsibility for, or even any involvement in, the tests on the babies.

Besides India, it's common for Big Pharma to carry out illegal testing of medicines and drugs on human subjects in Russia, Brazil and China. So maybe showing orphans being used to test pharmaceutical drugs on in *The Orphan Uprising* is not that far-fetched after all.

He deliberately avoided using the term human guinea pig, preferring test subject to convey what was in store for Francis. It sounded more benign.

–The Orphan Uprising

Sinking natural health products in a sea of red tape? Suppressing cancer cures? Turning humans into lab rats? Cynically targeting babies, impoverished people, psychiatric patients, prisoners and others who don't have a voice for unethical medical testing?

Even if a fraction of the conspiracy theories explored in this chapter are true, it appears something has run amuck in the medical field – within Big Pharma and other key players in the Medical Industrial Complex in particular. For obvious reasons we can't name names, but one thing's for sure…You know who you are!

But we ain't doctors, so what do we know? Oh, and did we mention we forgot to take our medication whilst writing this chapter? Hmmm, maybe that's why we're feeling so paranoid…

12

The Fourth Reich

"The fascists. They took over this country straight after World War Two. Kennedy was the last president who knew anything about this. All those who followed him have been kept in the dark."

–The Orphan Factory

History reminds us that communism was already a dominant political force even before the echoes of World War Two had faded. After the war, as the Soviet Union began to encroach on more and more nations, communism and the threat of nuclear war were the West's two big fears.

However, there is a lesser known school of thought that says fascism actually posed an even bigger threat post-WW2.

On the surface, this theory doesn't make much sense for officially speaking fascism was all but expunged from the Earth when the Allies demolished the Nazi war machine. From then on, the only fascist remnants appeared to be obscure far-right political parties as well as the odd white supremacist or anti-Semitic group.

But that's just on the surface and what the history books tell us.

Alternative versions that lie beneath commonly accepted 20th Century history claim many Western nations – the US in particular – only missed out on becoming fascist states by a whisker. Such ideas pose the almost unthinkable question: what if Nazism morphed into something else and continued underground, in another guise, in the West?

Fascist ideologies, practices and technologies didn't vanish with the death of Hitler and Nazi Germany, this radical conspiracy theory suggests. Instead, they actually *grew* in popularity with fascist supporters springing up in senior positions of power in various Western governments. However, this theory asserts that fascism became harder to detect because of its more subtle implementation, which perhaps indicates this new breed of fascists learnt from the failures of the Third Reich.

Sounds ridiculous, doesn't it?

We thought so too...until we came across a little known US Government program whose declassified files reveal damning evidence of co-operation between Nazi party survivors and the highest ranking American politicians.

PROJECT PAPERCLIP

As stated in chapter 2, America's mind control programs stemmed from the US Government's *Project Paperclip*, but it wasn't just Nazi brainwashing techniques the Americans inherited. They also seized Nazi scientists whose number included known war criminals.

The top secret project, also known as *Operation Paperclip*, was a nefarious undertaking that allowed Nazi scientists to migrate to the US without prosecution. Some had studied brainwashing and other mind control methods first-hand in the concentration camps; many were rocket scientists who had been directly involved in the development of Germany's feared V-1 and V-2 rockets. The latter's contribution would pave the way for NASA and the Moon landings, and also for America's Intercontinental Ballistic Missile program.

Project Paperclip was as much about denying German scientific expertise to the Soviet Union and Britain as it was benefiting US science, defence and space programs. This was happening as the Cold War loomed don't forget and an uncertain world was being carved up by superpowers. It was a three-way grab (for the spoils) between the Americans, the Soviets and the Brits.

Remember, Nazi Germany's scientific breakthroughs were nothing short of revolutionary. Although it didn't last long, the Nazi era was arguably the most accelerated scientific period in history, especially when suppressed or little known Nazi inventions are taken into account. History reminds us how easily the Third Reich dominated Europe despite being greatly outnumbered by the combined Allied forces. The Germans ruled the land, sea and air, and it was obvious to all they had superior technologies.

The Allies learned the hard way that Nazi engineers and scientists had made incredible breakthroughs in various fields. These included semi-conductors, plasma physics, ballistic missiles, laser technologies, electromagnetic weapons, computers, astrophysics, infrared night vision and miniature electronics to name but a few. While some of these breakthroughs were commonly known, others remained classified and were kept secret for decades.

A *BBC News* report dated November 21, 2005 nicely summarizes the situation that existed at the close of WW2. That report states: "The end of World War II saw an intense scramble for Nazi Germany's many technological secrets. The Allies vied to plunder as much equipment and expertise as possible from the rubble of the Thousand Year Reich for themselves, while preventing others from doing the same".

The report continues: "The range of Germany's technical achievement astounded Allied scientific intelligence experts accompanying the invading forces in 1945".

That *BBC News* report also reminds us "It was the US and the Soviet Union which, in the first days of the Cold War, found themselves in a race against time to uncover Hitler's scientific secrets".

Project Paperclip was America's solution to this problem. Supposedly named after the paperclips that were used to attach the files of the recruited German scientists, the project was the brainchild of America's Joint Intelligence Objectives Agency (JOIA), a sub-committee of the Joint Chief's of Staff of the US Armed Forces.

Project Paperclip's architects viewed their secret endeavor as the solution to harnessing Nazi scientists' superior knowledge and expertise, and positioning America as the world leader in science and technology.

MK-Ultra, the CIA's far-reaching mind-control program, was an umbrella project spawned from the US Government's super-secret Project Paperclip, a sinister venture that involved bringing dozens of Nazi scientists to America immediately after World War Two.

–The Ninth Orphan

PAPERCLIP NAZIS GET THEIR GREENCARDS

The recruitment of Nazi scientists began as soon as the war ended although the project itself wasn't officially signed off by President Harry Truman until three months later.

It should be noted that while Truman stipulated that scientists who were active in the Nazi Party, or who actively supported it, should not be recruited, such limitations would have precluded the recruitment of the most eligible prospects.

Declassified files show that Truman's orders were ignored. All recruits were cleared to work in America after their backgrounds were *cleaned up*. US authorities created fake resumes, removing any mention of Nazi involvement, and entire false identities were designed for the highest profile war criminals.

Those same declassified files also indicate that, at one point, around 10,000 Nazis were living undercover in America. (Some estimates are as high as 15,000). Many were awarded citizenship.

Imagine how many descendants of those Nazis reside in the US today. It's quite possible some are reading this book right now.

Tom Bower's 1987 book, *The Paperclip Conspiracy: The Hunt for the Nazi Scientists*, provides an insightful look at the history behind the project and reminds readers how quickly morals can be set to one side to meet an apparent need – in this case the need for scientific knowledge. The author cites official WW2 files as his main source of information.

WORLDWIDE ASYLUM FOR NAZI SCIENTISTS

Reviewers of Bower's book have picked up on a key point he makes – notably that the Americans, Soviets and Brits were fiercely competing to secure Nazi scientists for themselves and were prepared to overlook the fact some, or possibly many, were known war criminals.

Various international media reports have also confirmed Britain and other countries outside the US were extremely active in pursuing Nazi scientists.

For example, *The Guardian* newspaper edition of August 17, 1999 reports that Britain secretly organized the recruitment and transfer to Australia of scores of leading Nazi scientists and weapons specialists after the close of WW2.

Quoting declassified Australian Government papers, *The Guardian* says the German scientists sent to Australia under a top secret project codenamed *Operation Matchbox* included SS and Nazi party members.

The article also states: "The leading Nazi-hunting watchdog, the Simon Wiesenthal Centre, in Jerusalem, yesterday demanded an investigation into the recruitments ordered by Britain and the US, and said Australia was a haven for 'holocaust perpetrators and mass murderers'."

The same newspaper, on August 29, 2007, reports that,

contrary to general assumption, German scientists and technicians were forcibly evacuated from Germany to Britain for more than two years after cessation of hostilities. In other words, they didn't volunteer. From what we can deduce, the same applies to those who ended up working in the US and the Soviet Union.

WELCOME MAT ROLLED OUT FOR WAR CRIMINALS

In the post-war years in the US, Project Paperclip remained hush-hush and only a select few knew of its existence. It wasn't until much later the American public learned the truth – or part of the truth at least.

A US Justice Department report dated December 2006 states: "In the 1970's, the public was shocked to learn that some Nazi persecutors had emigrated to the United States. There were calls for their expulsion and legislation was passed to facilitate their deportation. OSI (the Office of Special Investigations) was created in 1979 to handle the caseload".

In the report, the Justice Department goes to great lengths to explain that the obstacles to success in prosecuting these Nazi war criminals were formidable. It lists numerous reasons supporting this opinion – not the least being that so much time had passed and many of the recruits had died.

Several prominent US newspapers have claimed that the Justice Department report reveals OSI investigators learned some of the Nazis were knowingly granted entry to the US even though government officials were aware of their pasts. Some journalists have observed that America, with its proud history of providing sanctuary for the persecuted including Holocaust survivors, had ended up giving asylum to some of their persecutors.

A *New York Times* article dated November 13, 2010 takes the Justice Department to task for sitting on its report for so long. The article states: "The 600-page report, which the Justice Department has tried to keep secret for four years, provides new evidence about more than two dozen of the most notorious Nazi cases of the last three decades".

However, it's the article's intro that caught our eye. It reads: "A secret history of the US Government's Nazi-hunting operation concludes that American intelligence officials created a safe haven in the US for Nazis and their collaborators after WW2 and it details decades of clashes, often hidden, with other nations over war criminals here and abroad".

While over 300 Nazi migrants have either been deported or refused visas to America since OSI's formation, the Justice Department's report leaves no doubt the US Government collaborated with notorious war criminals and knowingly granted them entry into the US.

The CIA doesn't escape censure either. Its "use of Nazis for postwar intelligence purposes" comes under the spotlight in the report.

So WHO WERE THESE PAPERCLIP NAZIS?

There's obviously too many Paperclip Nazis to name them all, but here's a few confirmed names that kept popping up in our research.

Rocket engineer and prominent Nazi Arthur Rudolph was a major player in the development of Germany's V-2 rocket before being brought to the US. Rudolph subsequently worked for the US Army, developing missile systems, and for NASA, helping pioneer America's space program. After being investigated for possible war crimes, he struck a deal with the US Government that enabled him to depart the country without being prosecuted (in the US). One of the accusations leveled at him was that he'd worked thousands of slave laborers to death – an accusation he denied.

Engineer Georg Rickhey was awarded the War Merit Cross for

his work overseeing Germany's production of the V-1 and V-2 rockets. After being brought to the US, he was sent back to Germany to face accusations of having cooperated with the Gestapo and the SS. However, lack of evidence saw him acquitted and he returned to continue his work in the US.

Physiologist Hubertus Strughold, Chief of Aeromedical Research with the German Luftwaffe, subsequently worked at a high level in medical positions in NASA and the US Air Force. Strughold was bestowed the unofficial title of 'the father of space medicine' for his studies of the effects of spaceflight on astronauts. Before and after his death, he became the subject of several investigations into alleged war crimes, suffering significant damage to his reputation. One allegation leveled against him was that he was involved in Dachau Concentration Camp experiments, including one in which camp inmates were exposed to freezing conditions.

Since Strughold's death, debate has raged between former colleagues and between fellow scientists. Some insist his involvement with the Nazis should preclude any honors being bestowed upon him while others claim there was no evidence to prove he was guilty of the crimes he was accused of.

Perhaps the most prominent Nazi import was rocket scientist Wernher von Braun who is referred to as 'the father of rocket science'. Herr von Braun spearheaded Nazi Germany's development of rocket technology, and later, in company with key members of his team, became a leading figure in America's rocket program. Along with his protégé Doctor Hermann Oberth, he was an integral part of America's first Moon-landing.

In the biography of von Braun on NASA's official website, readers are advised the scientist engineered the surrender of 500 of his top rocket scientists, along with plans and test vehicles, to the Americans. He worked with the US Army for 15 years developing ballistic missiles before being sent to the US and eventually becoming a naturalized American.

Given that mind control as we know it was first mastered during Hitler's reign, it's no surprise Nazi psychiatrists were also among those brought into the US post WW2.

As Dr. Thomas Roeder and co-authors Volker Kubillus and Anthony Burwell revealed in their 1995 book *Psychiatrists: The Men Behind Hitler*, psychiatry was highly valued in the Third Reich. From declassified Paperclip files it's obvious the science of the mind was equally valued by US authorities.

What's insane is that after the American public had paid an enormously high price to win WW2, US taxpayers then paid for Josef Mengele's protégés to live and work in America.

This means that Doctor Mengele's dark scientific legacy not only included the countless victims of the Holocaust experiments he conducted, but also the thousands of American and Canadian casualties of the MK-Ultra program.

When considering Project Paperclip's influence on modern mind control programs, the doctor's moniker *The Angel of Death* suddenly becomes even more relevant.

"What national security permits the removal of fundamental power from the hands of the American people and validates the ascendancy of an invisible government in the United States? That kind of national security, gentlemen of the jury, is when it smells like it, feels like it, and looks like it, you call it what it is: Fascism! I submit to you that what took place on November 22, 1963 was a coup d'etat."
–Monologue delivered by Kevin Costner and written by Oliver Stone in JFK (1991)

UNIT 731 - THE JAPANESE AUSCHWITZ

It seems there was another post-WW2 program remarkably similar to Project Paperclip, involving Japanese scientists and war criminals rather than the Nazis. The US was a key player in this program, too. As a comparative example, it's worth studying to better understand why Western superpowers protected known war criminals throughout the mid-late 20th Century.

This program involves a ghastly human experimentation project at the infamous *Unit 731*, an isolated Japanese Biological Warfare research facility located in what was then Manchuria, a Japanese puppet state, but is now Northeast China. The experimentation project was the brainchild of the notoriously cruel General Shirō Ishii, a scientist who was effectively Japan's equivalent of Dr. Joseph Mengele.

Researchers at Unit 731, which facilitated secret biological and chemical warfare research, mainly used captured Chinese and Russian subjects for their horrific medical experiments. However, their *human guinea pigs* also included American, Australian, New Zealand and British prisoners of war.

General Ishii's *medical testing* at the secret Manchurian facility included high-voltage electric shock experiments, cyanide poisonings, frostbite studies, biological weapons testing including anthrax, heroin and other drug tests, and injecting prisoners with bacteria from plague-infected fleas procured from mice; live dissections on prisoners were also common and the victims were not even given any painkillers while their bodies were slowly dissected.

The prisoners were referred to as "monkeys" in scientific papers, even though it was common knowledge amongst the Japanese military and in political circles that the test subjects were in fact humans. Tens of thousands of victims died at Unit 731 and its sister sites.

Although less widely reported than Mengele's medical research at Auschwitz, many historians have compared the hideous medical experiments at Unit 731 to the Nazi medical experiments during the Holocaust.

Parallels with Project Paperclip are numerous. Declassified documents have revealed that after the war ended, large-scale collaboration occurred between America and scientists of Unit 731. What's more, the insidious Japanese research became the basis for many US military operations – and like the Nazi scientists protected by Project Paperclip, many of Unit 731's scientists went on to have prominent careers after the war.

Just as the Nazis had made incredible scientific breakthroughs during the war years, it appears Japan was another scientific giant of the era. Germany and Japan obviously got the jump on the rest of the world in the area of medical research by being able to ruthlessly experiment on as many human subjects as they wanted. And this informative and valuable research was desired by both the US and the Soviet Union at the start of the Cold War.

Japan's scientific breakthroughs most likely explain why General Ishii and all the other Japanese scientists involved in Unit 731 were never tried for war crimes by the US or by any other Allied nation.

A US intelligence cable advised the War Department that the Japanese scientists, "headed by Ishii did violate rules of land warfare," but that "this expression of opinion is not a recommendation that group be charged and tried as such."

Further evidence of the United States' intentions is evidenced by the actions of General Douglas MacArthur. While serving as Supreme Commander of the Allied Forces, MacArthur wrote to Washington DC on May 6, 1947 as follows: "Statements from Ishii probably can be obtained by informing Japanese involved that information will be retained in intelligence channels and will not be employed as 'War Crimes' evidence."

The following year, in exchange for all their biological warfare research, MacArthur orchestrated a deal with the scientists of Unit 731, including General Ishii, whereby they were secretly granted complete immunity from prosecution. Claims of the horrors Allied POW's endured at the hands of their Japanese captors were from that point on ignored, and the ensuing Tokyo War Crimes trials omitted reference to Ishii and his staff.

In the decades immediately after the war ended, the Japanese and American governments continuously denied any conspiracy surrounding the legacy of Unit 731.

However, another file from General MacArthur's headquarters confirms the ugly truth. In it, MacArthur states that in studying

General Ishii's work, "utmost secrecy is essential in order to protect the interests of the United States and to guard against embarrassment".

Like the US, the Soviets also appear to have secured some of the Japanese scientists' human experimentation research, for after WW2 a biological weapons facility was built in Sverdlovsk, in the Soviet Union. The Sverdlovsk facility and practices within it are said to have been almost a carbon copy of what was detailed in Unit 731 documents.

Many conspiracy theorists as well as a number of biological weapons researchers claim the US military secretly began testing germ warfare on American citizens without their knowledge. These tests, which were apparently conducted from the 1950's onwards, are said by some to be based on the science of Unit 731, and include tests still classified by the CIA and the US Army's Chemical and Biological Warfare laboratories.

The suspicion lingers that many of the US military's covert biological warfare operations since WW2, including the Vietnam War's *Operation Ranch Hand*, may be related to Unit 731 – and Gulf War Syndrome could also be the result of biological warfare directly inspired by General Ishii's germ warfare experiments.

If by chance *Chemtrails* – that favorite Tinfoil Hat theory which suggests governments release chemical agents into the skies above populated areas – is one day proven to be a reality, then the Japanese experiments could be the basis for these as well.

Along with Yamashita's Gold and Project Paperclip, Unit 731 and its aftermath – including America's involvement – remained one of the best kept secrets of the post war era. The public finally learned about this dreadful secret in 1993 when then US Defense Secretary William Perry declassified army and intelligence records relating to the extensive cover-up of the Japanese human experimentation project.

❧ ❧ ❧

To refocus on Project Paperclip, there's no doubt that bringing Nazi scientists into the US fast-tracked its scientific programs.

However, it's our opinion the project had political and moral ramifications for American society as well.

As we wrote in chapter 2, mind control was a fascist technology that appears to have enabled assassinations of many important American figures. And in chapter 7, we mentioned how a Splinter Civilization appears to have suppressed advanced technologies and used them for their own ends – much as the Nazis hid secrets from the German people before and during WW2.

Just as science and psychiatry were such a large part of the Third Reich, Project Paperclip had profound effects on American and Western society as a whole. In fact, it could easily be argued fascism subtly wormed its way into government ideologies the world over.

Added to this concern is the fact that there are still a large number of *classified* Project Paperclip documents in existence. If their contents are more controversial than, or even as controversial as, those of the declassified documents, the mind boggles at what secrets they hide. What else were the Nazi recruits used for and how many more war criminals were admitted to the US at war's end? Let's not forget the UK and Australia either; they had their Project Paperclip equivalents as did Russia.

At least one conspiracy theory author claims Josef Mengele briefly lived and worked in the US before being transferred to South America. Mengele's name appears in no Paperclip documents, however. At least not in any declassified documents.

If and when the remaining files are ever declassified, they may reveal even greater collusion between Nazi Party survivors and the US Government. In fact, we suspect they will. Otherwise, why do they remain classified?

Perhaps it's not too big a stretch to suggest that Nazi ideologies continue to the present day behind the veil of supposedly free societies and governments.

Some conspiracy theorists go even further and suggest *the Fourth Reich* – a long-predicted successor of the Third Reich – has already been achieved. And in the United States, no less!

Citing evidence of high-ranking survivors of Germany's Third Reich being given sanctuary in the West through top-secret operations like Project Paperclip, this theory suggests Nazi practices like human experimentation, media manipulation, military aggression and *1984*-style government controls on citizens have become a reality.

We don't claim to have all the answers on this subject – or any answers for that matter.

But one thing's for sure: Project Paperclip, not to mention Unit 731, deserves more attention from historians and mainstream media than it currently receives.

13

THE PRICE OF A FREE MEDIA
13

What made it worse was Helen wasn't just any old journalist. She was a student reporter unconnected to any of the mainstream media outlets – outlets Omega could usually control as a result of the moles the agency had planted in their midst. No, Helen and her university newspaper could not be bought or controlled. She was a free agent, able to investigate whatever took her fancy, and The Daily Illini newspaper was free to publish whatever it wanted to.

–The Orphan Factory

There's no escaping the media. Whether radio, television, newspapers, magazines, billboards, feature films, documentaries, online news or social media – it's *everywhere*.

If media in all its forms is compromised then frankly, we're all screwed!

One of us (Lance) writes from personal experience on this subject: as a former journalist, newspaper editor and public relations consultant with experience in television, radio, print and online reporting, he has observed the workings of the media from the inside over the past 45 years.

You don't need to be a former journalist however, to realize that manipulating the media is akin to poisoning a nation's water supply – it affects all of our lives in unimaginable ways.

Journalists are the barometer of a nation's freedom of speech. If they are threatened, gagged or otherwise silenced then who is going to ask the tough questions and keep the authorities honest?

"No President should fear public scrutiny of his program. For from that scrutiny comes understanding; and from that understanding comes support or opposition. And both are necessary. I am not asking your newspapers to support the Administration, but I am asking your help in the tremendous task of informing and alerting the American people. For I have complete confidence in the response and dedication of our citizens whenever they are fully informed. I not only could not stifle controversy among your readers--I welcome it. This Administration intends to be candid about its errors; for as a wise man once said: "An error does not become a mistake until you refuse to correct it." We intend to accept full responsibility for our errors; and we expect you to point them out when we miss them."
–President John F. Kennedy, speech to the American Newspaper Publishers Association. April 27, 1961, New York City.

In *The Orphan Factory*, our novel's lead female character Helen Katsarakis is a student journalist in Chicago. When she learns the shocking truth of the Pedemont Orphanage and starts to write about it, her life is suddenly endangered. Without giving away any spoilers, let's just say the powers that be swing into action to prevent her story ever reaching the masses.

Helen's character was partly a plot device designed to ask tough questions about the modern media. In particular, questioning the commonly held belief that here in the West we have a free press.

So, what's the truth? Do we really have a free press or are our journalists, or *journos*, being dictated to and told what they can and can't report on? Are certain topics suppressed from the public's consciousness by those who own or greatly influence the media? Are there any free-thinking, free-speaking journos left – alive and not retired that is?

TAKING ON THE ESTABLISHMENT

Few journos ever seriously challenge the Establishment. Why? Because it's usually not in the best interests of their employers – the select few media barons who run mainstream media these days. (More about them later).

The upshot of this is, while their turn of phrase may be eloquent, most journos just report on issues their masters are happy to allow to be aired publicly. This makes them little more than parrots for the Establishment. Unfortunately, few realize that.

The tragedy of this is major issues remain hidden and the public are continually being denied access to the truth.

Any journo who takes on the Establishment and interrogates officialdom about questionable policies – such as committing troops to new theaters of war – is quickly brought to heel. If the journo persists, he or she risks being branded a traitor, or unpatriotic at least.

In June 2013, former Minnesota Governor, Navy Seal and professional wrestler-turned political activist Jesse Ventura told *The New York Times*, "You're not unpatriotic for criticizing your government." Elaborating, Ventura said, "I know from experience, the only way you get good government is for the citizens to hold its feet to the fire."

Of course, holding an administration's feet to the fire relies on total freedom of speech, and a truly free media is a major part of that.

We know from personal experience it takes balls to ask the hard questions. Questions such as why Western nations are embroiled in perpetual wars and spending gazillions on military budgets when so many of their citizens are living hand to mouth on or below the poverty line.

What's needed is uncompromising, in-depth, insightful reporting where journos don't shy away from applying the metaphorical blowtorch to world leaders, politicians and business moguls. This would be in stark contrast to the staged interviews we are more commonly shown where handpicked journos rarely deviate from script.

True journalism is about uncovering and reporting on the truth. Nothing more, nothing less. In today's fast-moving world, where corruption, violence and grief are never far away, it's difficult to think of a more important job.

NEWS REPORTING OR STORYTELLING?

Traditional journalism, where reporters deliver information in a balanced and unbiased fashion, is rapidly fading into obscurity. This is especially evident on television where high profile reporters become bigger than the story, delivering news with large dollops of personality and wit – almost as if they are actors. And is it our imagination or are TV reporters becoming younger and more glamorous every year?

To our eyes, on major world issues at least, it seems very little factual-based news reporting occurs these days. Instead, it's nearly all opinion-based and *colored* to some degree.

Unfortunately, mainstream news has become *infotainment*, sharing more in common with the entertainment industry than with traditional journalism. Gossip, characterizations and injections of drama are subtly infused with facts, altering the truth in a similar way to how dramatists twist true stories to create greater excitement.

Another useful analogy here may be documentary movies. Although as filmmakers we only produce feature films, we know a lot of doco filmmakers and many tell us *storytelling* is just as prominent in reality-based productions as it is in dramatic ones. This makes sense because when a doco enters post-production after the filming period, the director has hundreds of hours of footage to sift through in the editing suite. The film then has to be edited down to around 90 minutes and there are often any number of stories a director can tell, depending on what is edited out, what is left in and what is highlighted.

In theory, documentary filmmakers are able to remain totally unbiased and allow the material to dictate the most relevant story to them. But only the very best are able to achieve this. All too often the filmmakers' own beliefs end up convincing them to tell stories that don't actually reflect the heart of the material.

Similarly, subjective storytelling is now almost as common in the news media as it is in feature films, TV dramas, novels or theater shows. Journalists at their worst are self-centered storytellers who either knowingly or unknowingly bend truths into *stories* that match their personal beliefs or those of their employers.

What is scarier however, is when entire media organizations craft fictional stories out of the truth to influence the masses on a grand scale.

THE KINGMAKERS

Media tycoons are among the most powerful and influential individuals on the planet as they and their minions shape society's opinions. It's no coincidence that a large percentage of the members of the Bilderberg Group, the Council on Foreign Relations and other such elitist organizations are media moguls. If it's true that nothing is more potent than an idea, then those who control the media can direct minds en masse.

Australian-born tycoon Rupert Murdoch has built a media empire unlike any other in history. His far-reaching enterprises incorporate major newspapers, television networks, book publishers and film production companies throughout the UK, the US, Australia and Asia. It's estimated that 40% of American television viewers are watching Murdoch-owned stations at any given time.

It has been reported in the mainstream media on several occasions that no Prime Minister of the UK or Australia takes office without consulting Murdoch first. Then again, if he controls the media wouldn't Murdoch have censored such reports? In which case wouldn't that make a mockery of this whole conspiracy theory? Ah well, you can't win 'em all!

There are parallels, albeit on a smaller scale, in Italy where former Italian Prime Minister Silvio Berlusconi owns much of the Italian media. During his controversial term as PM, critics argued many of Berlusconi's newspapers and TV channels promoted his far-right political ideologies.

Bottom line is: the media, like anything else, can be bought. Everything, it seems, has its price. Even the *free* press.

THE TREND TOWARDS MEDIA CONSOLIDATION

Some commentators say the world's six biggest media empires, between them, largely control what news we see, hear or read in the Western world. Others say the 10 biggest media empires control our news. Either way, the ramifications are frightening, wouldn't you agree?

The respected news and entertainment site Elite Daily, which calls itself "The voice of Generation-Y", makes the following claim: "With media oversight being taken for granted in recent years, media concentration has been a trend that's been rolling along with few signs of stopping. As a result, many of your favorite media entities have been consolidated and all work under the same umbrella corporation. If you think, for example, one channel offers better content than the other, you might be surprised to learn that you've stuck with the same company and are just now loyal to another one of its assets."

Elite Daily has identified the following as the world's 10 largest media conglomerates: Bertelsmann SE & Co. KGaA, Gannett Company Inc., CBS Corporation, British Sky Broadcasting Group Plc., Liberty Media, News Corporation, Viacom, Time Warner Inc., The Walt Disney Disney Company and Comcast Corporation.

In the early 1980's, some 50 companies owned 90% of American media. Now, 90% of US media is owned by just six corporations: Disney, Viacom, GE, CBS, Time Warner and Rupert Murdoch's NewsCorp.

Each of these conglomerates has fingers in many pies. Take Time Warner for example. It has major stakes in film and TV companies like New Line Cinema, CNN, TNT, Warner Bros. Pictures, HBO, Cinemax, Cartoon Network and Castle Rock plus magazines like People, Time, Sports Illustrated, Fortune and Marie Claire.

The problem with such media monopolies, especially when they are heavily entangled with politics as Murdoch's outlets are, is that censorship or even disseminating misinformation becomes a very real possibility.

If you believe the TV networks, newspapers and other media outlets owned by such conglomerates are regularly delivering balanced, unbiased news, you're dreaming. Each has its own agenda and recent history has shown those agendas aren't always honorable. Regrettably, and all too often, journalistic ethics come a distant second to corporate profits.

You only need to consider the events surrounding Rupert Murdoch's News of the World phone-hacking scandal to be reminded that media conglomerates and their owners don't always act honorably or have the public's best interests at heart.

For anyone who has been living under a rock since that controversy broke, Murdoch employees working in some of his British newspapers hacked the phones of leading politicians, businessmen and celebrities, resulting in a public outcry against News Corporation and Murdoch.

"There is very grave danger that an announced need for increased security will be seized upon by those anxious to expand its meaning to the very limits of official censorship and concealment. That I do not intend to permit to the extent that it is in my control. And no official of my Administration, whether his rank is high or low, civilian or military, should interpret my words here tonight as an excuse to censor the news, to stifle dissent, to cover up our mistakes or to withhold from the press and the public the facts they deserve to know."

–President John F. Kennedy, speech to the American Newspaper Publishers Association. April 27, 1961, New York City.

CENSORING THE TRUTH

Censorship involves limiting free expression and controlling information. Most Westerners tend to associate the word *censorship* with art – especially film. However, in less democratic regions of the world, censorship is all pervasive with North Korea being one of the best, or worst, examples of this in recent years.

Censorship is also alive and well in the West, although it is done in far more subtle ways. Sometimes it relates to that modern day ailment known as *corportocracy*, or the control of economic and political systems by corporate interests; sometimes it relates to government meddling where administrations or individual politicians derail what should be a free press.

Reporters Without Borders, a global freedom of press organization, recently announced in its annual Worldwide Freedom Index that the US has one of the highest levels of media censorship in the Western world. From their research, conducted in 2013, they reported that journalists in the UK, Canada, Australia, Ireland and New Zealand experience greater freedoms of speech than in the US.

The index reflects the level of freedom that news organizations, reporters and citizens enjoy in each country, and the efforts made by governing bodies to respect this freedom.

Given the US was founded on the greatest constitutional freedom of expression in history (the First Amendment) it's sad to see it only managed 32nd place on the Worldwide Freedom Index – behind the likes of Ghana and Suriname.

"Without debate, without criticism, no Administration and no country can succeed--and no republic can survive. That is why the Athenian lawmaker Solon decreed it a crime for any citizen to shrink from controversy. And that is why our press was protected by the First Amendment – the only business in America specifically protected by the Constitution – not primarily to amuse and entertain, not to emphasize the trivial and the sentimental, not to simply "give the public what it wants" – but to inform, to arouse, to reflect, to state our dangers and our opportunities, to indicate our crises and our choices, to lead, mold, educate and sometimes even anger public opinion."
–President John F. Kennedy, speech to the American Newspaper Publishers Association. April 27, 1961, New York City.

SPIN DOCTORS

A conservatively estimated 90% of all news items aired in the media – whether in print, radio or television – on any given day are *placed* items. (Placed news items are articles contributed by individuals, companies and organizations outside the media). An estimated 75% of all news items are placed by *spin doctors*, or public relations consultants.

Journos and PR gurus will know what we're talking about, but for outsiders we accept these stats are hard to get your head around.

Incidentally, many if not most spin doctors are former journos, so they know firsthand how the media works and they have well established journalistic networks to tap into. Very handy when it comes to placing stories.

What makes it difficult to accurately assess the amount of news that is placed or contributed, is that many such items appear under a journo's byline. All too often the journo may only change one para, sentence or word – or nothing at all – before recycling the story for publication under his or her name. Sad but true.

In the case of *news* items sourced from PR firms, the reality is those firms are handsomely paid by their (usually) corporate clients to publicize the clients' products and services. In some cases their non-corporate clients may be lobby groups, politicians, political parties, government departments, armed forces or other such entities each with their own barrow to push. All too often, the truth is secondary to the message. Also sad but true.

Mainstream media frequently serves as a public relations agency for the global elite, including politicians, bankers and Fortune 500 members. As a result, the so-called news has become a junkyard for propaganda. Such an environment is open slather for the spin doctors.

"News is what somebody somewhere wants to suppress; all the rest is advertising."
–Lord Northcliffe, British publisher (1865-1922)

MEDIA MANIPULATION

News stories often deliver one viewpoint, or one dominant viewpoint, so the audience will likely draw one particular conclusion. This can be done so cleverly we are usually none the wiser – unless we're on the lookout for such subterfuge.

Politicians and political parties are very aware of this, as are our military leaders. *Media manipulation* they call it – off the record of course. To sell their message to the public, they need to use the media to their advantage. Sometimes they go direct, oftentimes they use the spin doctors.

A classic example of this was how the US Administration used the media to convince the American public Iraq was hiding weapons of mass destruction before the troops were sent in. How wrong they were, but how effective their advance publicity was. It was swallowed hook, line and sinker by most Americans and, indeed, by much of the Western world. Certainly, Britain and others weren't slow to send their troops in to Iraq either. And it's worth noting this was initially a conspiracy theory, but now even mainstream media outlets commonly accept this was fabrication or at least exaggerated *spin* to start a war.

Clearly, the media can be used by political administrations as a propaganda tool.

The 1922 speech of former New York City Mayor John Hylan we quoted from in an earlier chapter is worth quoting from again: "These international bankers and Rockefeller-Standard Oil interests control the majority of the newspapers and magazines in this country. They use the columns of these papers to club into submission or drive out of office public officials who refuse to do the bidding of the powerful corrupt cliques which compose the invisible government."

OPERATION MOCKINGBIRD

From the 1950's to 1970's, the CIA covertly funded a number of leading domestic and foreign journalists from numerous major media outlets like The Washington Post, Time, The New York Times and CBS to publish CIA propaganda. This was known as *Operation Mockingbird* and was first brought to the public's attention in 1975 by The Church Committee.

Senator Frank Church, after whom the committee was named, claimed that misinforming the world cost American taxpayers around US$265 million a year. Some of that cost was wages as many of the CIA's *journalist-spooks* drew a CIA salary over and above their official media salary. Talk about serving two masters!

After the initial revelations, Congress admitted in 1976 that the CIA maintained a network of several hundred foreigners "who provide intelligence for the CIA and at times attempt to influence opinion through the use of covert propaganda."

The CIA also admitted that these individuals provided the agency with direct access to many media outlets.

Although restraints have since been applied to the CIA's media-related activities, to this day the agency makes no secret it continues to welcome the voluntary cooperation of reporters.

The CIA's involvement with media doesn't end there. In 1977, Washington Post journo Carl Bernstein, of *Watergate* fame, reported that "more than 400 journalists...in the past 25 years have secretly carried out assignments" for the CIA.

Intelligence agencies' approach to manipulating news media is probably best summed up by a comment a senior CIA employee made to Bernstein: "One journalist is worth twenty agents."

Besides messing with news media outlets, the agency has also been known to dabble in other forms of media. For example, the 1954 animated film *Animal Farm*, based on George Orwell's classic novel, was secretly funded by the CIA. In fact, three-fifths of the movie's half a million dollar budget was financed by the agency via one of its shell corporations, Touchstone Inc.

On the film's listing on the Internet Movie Database (IMDb) site, the following is mentioned under the trivia section: "The CIA obtained the film rights to "*Animal Farm*" from Orwell's widow, Sonia, after his death and covertly funded the production as anti-Communist propaganda. Some sources assert that the ending of the story was altered by the CIA (in the book, the pigs and humans join forces) to press home their message".

"The speed of communications is wondrous to behold. It is also true that speed can multiply the distribution of information that we know to be untrue."
–Edward R. Murrow (1908-1965), American broadcast journalist

THE POWER OF THE INTERNET

The Internet is expanding at a faster rate than most of we mere mortals can understand. Someone seriously compared its rate of growth to the speed of light, though we suspect he's prone to exaggerating. Even so, its growth is impressive, that much we know.

Impressive, too, is the growth and power of online news and especially social media. Nowhere has this been better demonstrated than during the *Arab Spring*, the revolution that is sweeping the Arab world. Since 2010, Egyptians, Libyans and more recently Syrians have effectively used the Internet both to access foreign news during media blackouts and to get news and images to the outside world as dramatic events unfolded in their respective countries.

Just as the Internet offers society many advantages and disadvantages so, too, does online journalism. On the one hand, alternative thought-provoking news and ideas can be aired online whereas they'd never see the light of day in a metropolitan daily newspaper or other conventional media outlets.

On the other hand, there are fewer checks and balances online where anyone can write just about anything and get away with it.

This duality of online news is exemplified by the rise of freelance journalists using the Internet to their advantage. *Citizen journos* we call them.

Some of these citizen journos are qualified reporters who, for various reasons, have chosen to go it alone. Many may prefer the autonomy that comes with freelance writing, others may have become disillusioned with traditional mainstream reporting. Some are good, some are bad and some should probably be shot. The latter, who are usually inexperienced or wannabe journalists, often pretend to present unbiased news stories. In reality, they have radical agendas be they political, religious, racist or whatever. These agendas, incidentally, aren't always apparent when you visit their blog sites.

It's also important to remember that mainstream media are major players on the Internet. Almost all major newspapers, television and radio networks have online news portals to recycle their news to reach audiences far beyond their traditional catchment areas.

Despite the Internet's faults, more and more people are viewing it as the only source for truthful information. Politicians and business moguls are aware of this and are actively lobbying to restrict or censor this medium so they can continue to manipulate, or better still control, public opinion.

Those same politicians and moguls are very mindful of initiatives like the *Occupy Wall Street* movement whose members are so heavily reliant on social media to spread their message. Young people are becoming more switched on, too. They're increasingly favoring alternative websites and citizen journos over mainstream media when it comes to receiving news and information.

So, what are we to believe when we search online or open that newspaper or switch on that radio or TV set for our daily dose of news?

Unfortunately there's no easy answer. As we keep saying, retain a healthy skepticism and don't believe everything you're told. The truth *is* out there…somewhere!

14

ABOVE THE PRESIDENT

It was true Isabelle was the daughter of a politician and therefore must have had an inkling of how Western alpha male-style governments functioned, but the world he operated in was beyond governments. Nine was one of the few who knew the truth. He understood world leaders were simply opportunists placed in so-called positions of power to carry out the agendas of the real power-players who always remained behind the scenes.

–The Ninth Orphan

The President of the United States is regularly referred to as the most powerful person on Earth. This holds true for the current president, Barack Obama, as it has for all other American presidents in recent decades.

Certainly, the US is the world's biggest economy and has the largest military force. It's arguably the last legitimate superpower left – not forgetting that China has all the hallmarks of a future superpower – and the US President, as commander-in-chief of America's armed forces, is in charge of the world's biggest nuclear arsenal as well.

So, surely if anybody would qualify as the most powerful person on the planet, then it would be the President.

Right?

Um…well…maybe wrong, actually.

What the hell are you guys talking about? we hear you ask.

Obviously the President is the most powerful person in the world! For pete's sake, you guys better retire now if you can't see that!

We hear you, we hear you. But just hold on a moment.

Appearances would certainly suggest he's the most powerful person – especially when America's dominant military, political and economic position is taken into account. But appearances can be deceiving.

It's important to remember the US President isn't only accountable to himself: he is, first and foremost, accountable to others – and we're not just referring to the American people.

Many a political conspiracy theory has at its cornerstone the idea that whoever the US President is at any given time is merely a pawn. An employee, if you will, representing the real power players who lurk in the shadows but rule with absolute authority.

This theory requires us to believe the President has secret allegiances with *invisible* people – invisible to anyone below the Presidency that is – who micromanage him.

If true, the President's decision-making power would be farcical; he'd simply be the person who presses the button – not the one making the decision to drop the bomb or send in the drones or bring home the troops.

Too big a stretch, you say?

Maybe, but stick with us…

Contrary to the media circus which portrayed politicians as all-powerful figures, Kentbridge knew from experience the vast majority of US Government officials – elected or otherwise – were puppets who only had the illusion of power. This included Presidents. These public figures all understood the game and were happy to go through the motions, carrying out orders that came from above – from the likes of the Omega Agency – so they could fulfill their own egotistical ambitions.

–The Ninth Orphan

Consider the "vast right-wing conspiracy" First Lady Hillary Rodham Clinton mentioned in 1998 in relation to the sex scandal involving her husband President Bill Clinton and White House intern Monica Lewinsky. Mrs Clinton's choice of words seem odd if you stop to consider she was talking about the man considered by many to be the world's most powerful at that time.

Surely such a man would be immune to attacks from minnows of the right wing Republican opposition. Or did Mrs Clinton's seemingly innocent comment allude to something, or someone, other than Republicans? Could she have been referring to shadowy figures in some invisible government who wanted to bring her husband down, or at least curtail some of his *wayward* policies?

Could her use of the word *conspiracy* in her statement have been a cryptic clue?

BOZOS IN THE WHITEHOUSE

George W. Bush is probably the US President whose intelligence has been most questioned. Certainly he's up there with Presidents Ford and Reagan. His frequent gaffes, or *Bushisms*, and his apparent inability at times to clearly answer even the simplest of questions raised alarm bells in the minds of many Americans.

George W's Bushisms include publicly congratulating ostracized FEMA director Michael Brown for his handling of the Hurricane Katrina emergency in 2005 despite the fact that Brown had received extreme nationwide criticism over his handling of the disaster; a year earlier, while talking about *the War on Terror*, Bush said America's enemies "never stop thinking about new ways to harm our country and our people, and neither do we." And in a speech in 2002, he famously remarked, "There's an old saying in Tennessee... I know it's in Texas, probably in Tennessee... that says, fool me once, shame on... shame on you... Fool me... you can't get fooled again!"

In case you're interested, there are hundreds of Bushism compilation videos, or *Greatest Hits*, that can be viewed on YouTube.

Rightly or wrongly, the moniker *Dubbya* forever became synonymous with stupidity and ignorance.

Was this man really bright enough to run the United States of America? Was he capable of making the myriad of complex decisions required of presidents every day?

During Ronald Reagan's presidency it was rumored he slept more than he worked, especially during his second term. As a former actor, perhaps Reagan understood better than most his White House role was less about making decisions and more about delivering lines and following scripts the powers-that-be wrote.

If even half the tales surrounding lazy or inept presidents are true then that may provide some insight into whether the US President is the most powerful person on Earth or, indeed, if he has any real power at all.

It has always intrigued us that no President ever asked Congress – on the record at least – to establish exactly who manages America's money supply? And why are the suspicious activities rumored to be swirling around the Federal Reserve never – officially at least – investigated? Could it be that Presidents promise to support global banksters before running for office?

When there is such a long and detailed history of false flag operations, why has no recent President seriously questioned the validity of intelligence reports claiming the existence of WMD's or the incidence of terrorist attacks in certain countries? Could it be these Presidents are also in the pocket of the *Military Industrial Complex*, that powerful combination of America's armed forces, legislators, political factions, defence contractors and money men?

The farewell speech of Dwight D. Eisenhower, the 34th President of the US and the only Army General ever to be elected President, is perhaps telling in this regard. In his speech, which was delivered in a television broadcast on January 17, 1961, Eisenhower warned America against the ever-increasing political influence of the Military Industrial Complex.

"We must guard against the acquisition of unwarranted influence, whether sought or unsought, by the military-industrial complex," said Eisenhower. "The potential for the disastrous rise of misplaced power exists and will persist. We must never let the weight of this combination endanger our liberties or democratic processes."

President Eisenhower also pointed out that the nation annually spent on "military security alone more than the net income of all United States corporations" – a fact which possibly holds true to this day, depending on definitions of where military security starts and ends.

Eisenhower's speech could be construed as suggesting his Presidential powers were diluted because of the influence of the Military Industrial Complex and/or other such entities. His warning that Americans must guard against the complex's "acquisition of unwarranted influence" certainly suggests that.

Kentbridge was certain all of the US presidents since JFK had been puppets. The lack of any real decision-making power presidents had was reflected in a long-running joke within the agency: One could place a monkey in the White House Oval Office and everything would run just fine.

–The Orphan Factory

THE INVISIBLE GOVERNMENT

Government, as we all know, is the system by which people, states or countries are governed.

Here's an alternative definition that's popular with conspiracy theorists: *Government* is a system certain nefarious people and organizations can hide behind and achieve even more than they could if legitimately elected to office. These immoral parties include unelected officials and secret societies who are collectively known in some circles as *the Invisible Government*.

It's quite possible there's an Invisible Government operating in

America today with some unknown entity pulling the strings of elected politicians and officials – in which case the Government that's portrayed in the media is just a front for some shadowy group.

If it's conceivable the Invisible Government is controlling, or at least has influence over, the banking system, the media and radical science, then why couldn't it have influence over the President, too?

There are also theories that there are 40 levels in US intelligence *above top secret*, of which the President only has clearance to about Level 20. No such theories have ever been proven, however.

We realize there are a lot of *what ifs* in our analysis, but it's important to remember we are dealing with 50 shades of subtlety when it comes to trying to ascertain how the world really operates. Those shadowy groups, secret societies and faceless people pulling strings in the financial, military, scientific, medical, industrial and political sectors don't take out front page newspaper ads to advertise their agendas or their modus operandi.

So it's up to us, average *Jo Citizen*, to read between the lines, think outside the square and question everything we're told.

If you think we're scaremongering, cast your eye over the quotations scattered throughout this chapter and, indeed, throughout this book – from JFK in particular – warning of secret societies and the like.

"There exists a shadowy government with its own Air Force, its own Navy, its own fundraising mechanism, and the ability to pursue its own ideas of national interest, free from all checks and balances, and free from the law itself."

–Daniel K. Inouye, US Senator from Hawaii. Testimony given to the Senate Select Committee on Secret Military Assistance to Iran and the Nicaraguan Opposition (Iran-Contra hearings) in 1987.

THE USUAL (AND UNUSUAL) SUSPECTS

If it's not the President and the official Government then who is really running the United States of America?

As the old saying goes, *follow the money trail*. That would surely make our aforementioned friends, the good ol' global banksters, prime suspects.

At the very least, bankers and financial services suppliers would have to be part of the Invisible Government, if indeed it does exist. They could be compared to the outer layer of an onion: peel back a layer or two and you'd likely find covert organizations running the banks.

And if that theory holds true, secret societies like the Freemasons and Skull and Bones would probably be to the fore.

Other major players in an Invisible Government could comprise the global elite groups mentioned in previous chapters, including the Bilderberg Group and the Council on Foreign Relations (CFR).

Now let's introduce another little known group into the equation…

THE BOHEMIAN CLUB

Bohemian Grove is a 2700-acre campground in Monte Rio, California, owned by an obscure Californian men's art club called *the Bohemian Club*, which can trace its foundation back to 1872.

According to Wikipedia, "In mid-July each year, Bohemian Grove hosts a two-week, three-weekend encampment of some of the most powerful men in the world."

Past and present members of this bizarre, invitation-only club, where grown men act like boys in the woods and conduct pagan rituals, include Richard Nixon, George H. W. Bush, Ronald Reagan and apparently every other Republican President since Calvin Coolidge. Other Bohemian members include or included

Jack London, Henry Kissinger, Walter Cronkite, David Rockefeller Sr., Donald Rumsfeld and Henry Ford.

Observers say the Bohemian Club is like the Bilderberg Group and the CFR in that it undermines democracy by holding closed meetings.

In a *Los Angeles Times* article dated May 26, 1987, it was reported that Richard Nixon once sent his fellow Bohemian Grove members a statement saying, "Anyone can aspire to be President of the United States, but few have any hope of becoming president of the Bohemian Club".

Nixon's also on record as commenting several times that attending Bohemian Grove was crucial to becoming the US President. For example, in his 1978 book, *Memoirs*, he says, "in many important ways it marked the first milestone on my road to the presidency".

If elitist groups like Bohemian Club, the CFR and the Bilderberg Group select and groom candidates to become Presidents of the US then isn't it safe to assume they also dictate certain policies once their alumni are in the White House?

"The very word "secrecy" is repugnant in a free and open society; and we are as a people inherently and historically opposed to secret societies, to secret oaths and to secret proceedings."
–President John F. Kennedy, speech to the American Newspaper Publishers Association. April 27, 1961, New York City.

SECRET AFFILIATIONS OF US PRESIDENTS

From our research into the history of American politics, one detail kept rising to the surface time and again: All recent US Presidents pledged allegiance to at least one secret society or elitist organization before they ran for office.

Freemasonry and Skull and Bones are two of the most common secret societies, while the Bilderberg Group, the Trilateral Commission, the Bohemian Club and the CFR seem to be the main elitist organizations on any serious presidential candidate's to-do list.

What follows are the secret affiliations of the previous eight Presidents before Obama. This list dates back over half a century to the 1963 assassination of JFK, but excludes President Kennedy himself who appeared to belong to no such societies, organizations or fraternities.

George W. Bush (Bohemian Club, Skull and Bones), Bill Clinton (Mason, Skull and Bones, Bilderberg, CFR, Trilateral Commission), George H. W. Bush (Mason, Skull and Bones, Bohemian Club, Trilateral Commission, CFR, Skull and Bones), Ronald Reagan (Bohemian Club, Mason), Jimmy Carter (Trilateral Commission, CFR), Gerald Ford (Mason, Bilderberg, Bohemian Club, CFR), Richard Nixon (Bohemian Club, CFR), Lyndon B. Johnson (Mason, CFR).

What this amounts to is that recent US Presidents have all been *owned* in one way or another before they even set foot in the White House Oval Office to serve their terms.

The one potential omission in this disturbing trend is Barry Soetoro – more commonly known as Barack Obama. We refer of course to the name Obama sometimes used in Indonesia where he spent part of his childhood. Soetoro was his stepfather's surname and Barry was the nickname he used throughout college.

However, to get back to the point, it may well be President Obama is ultra-secretive about his membership of elitist organizations and secret societies.

Sourcing accurate information on Obama's background is tricky. There's a huge amount of so-called evidence online, painting Obama as a fraud. But if you take the time to research the individuals making such claims you will quickly establish they are often racially motivated.

Given that racism still exists in the 21st Century, the amount of fabricated evidence on America's first black President is hardly surprising. Even so, there have been intriguing reports that point to the possibility of Obama being a member of various elitist, non-governmental groups.

For example, on March 5, 2007, conspiracy website *Above Top Secret* included statements from an anonymous Freemason who claimed to have befriended Obama years earlier at a Masonic lodge in Illinois. However, the lodge in question could find no record of Obama ever having attended.

Shortly before Obama was elected to the presidency, the June 2, 2008 issue of *Newsweek* included a photograph with an article that appeared to show a Masonic ring on the future president's finger. The image sent the Tinfoil Hat Network into a frenzy. However, there's no conclusive proof that the finger is Obama's.

And as mentioned in Chapter 3, there have been persistent rumors the Hawaii-born Obama has also attended at least one Bilderberg meeting – namely the conference at Chantilly, Virginia, in 2008, which also took place shortly before he became the US President.

So it remains inconclusive as to whether Obama is a tool or not. Either he's squeaky clean as his administration presents him to be, or he has covered his tracks so well that his membership of secret or elitist organizations cannot be proven conclusively.

Given the consistently nefarious behavior of the world's elite, we certainly know which way we'd be placing our bets regarding Obama. We just cannot believe that any average, honest, law-abiding American citizen can get anywhere near the presidency without shaking hands with corrupt powerbrokers, signing deals with banksters and generally bending over backwards for the global elite.

Certainly there were obvious differences in policies between the various leaders, and an America run by a Bush, an Obama or a Clinton would have distinct contrasts. Those variables didn't concern the secret elite rulers, however. As long as the Omega Agency and other clandestine groups ensured each administration sold out on the most lucrative issues – oil, banking, drug trafficking, arms sales – they couldn't care less whether a political party poured a few more measly bucks into healthcare or schools.

–The Ninth Orphan

A DIY GUIDE TO BUYING AMERICAN PRESIDENTS

For the sake of exploring this theory of *owning* Presidents and Administrations, let's create our own secret society right here and now, and let's call this covert, invitation-only organization *Pegasus*.

Pegasus members are a group of elite families whose combined wealth is worth trillions of dollars. Yet they feature on no rich lists for their wealth is created and expanded by high finance deals that are beyond governments and tax systems, and involve clandestine transfers in the murky world of offshore banking.

This consortium's members, who now make up the Invisible Government, have infiltrated every aspect of the current Administration by conducting a silent *coup d'etat* that went unreported.

Pegasus can afford to *buy* candidates upfront before they run for office. They also gain coercive influence over the key figures in all the major parties.

Pegasus can't lose if they back all the major political parties. Although it seems the Left side of the political spectrum is the antithesis of the Right, they understand there really is no Left or Right, or even any political parties. *There is only Pegasus.*

So while it appears as if voters have a choice, the reality is they don't – at least not a choice that matters a whole lot.

Although political parties often seemed poles apart, in reality they all bowed to this higher order of power. Kentbridge had long since understood Democrats and Republicans were essentially the same party with different faces and that was why, no matter how many promises each leader made, significant change rarely transpired.

–The Ninth Orphan

THE POLITICAL APATHY OF TODAY'S YOUTH

Young people today seem to be coming around to the idea it really doesn't matter which politician or political party you vote for; and they're catching on that it doesn't even matter if you don't vote because they have realized modern elections are just a way for the 1% to appease the 99% – a way to keep the masses in line by making them *believe* they've had their say, thereby perpetuating the lie that democracy continues.

More and more young people have twigged that modern politics is all a big game. Perhaps this is because they're more likely to source their information from the Internet, social media, alternative media and citizen journalists. They sense that leaders in power – be they presidents or prime ministers – are simply caretakers who serve a term or two before the next caretaker steps in to carry on with the charade.

The question is, are today's youth enlightened people or cynics who don't respect the democracy their forefathers fought for?

Perhaps authors Dan Cassino and Yasemin Besen-Cassino answer that question in a roundabout way in their 2009 book *Consuming Politics: Jon Stewart, Branding, and the Youth Vote in America*. They say, "The political apathy of today's youth can be seen largely as a result of this disengagement from the parties".

The Cassinos continue, "Different groups within the general category of young people are looking for different things within the political world, and won't become engaged in politics until they see those things".

Politicians would be well advised not to hold their breath for youth to engage in politics any time soon. Today's youth are the first generation to have realized for real change to occur, it must happen on an individual level rather than at an administrative level.

As Hollywood star Mark Ruffalo told Luke Rudkowski, a young American social activist and founder of grassroots media organization *We Are Change*, in a 2011 interview, "It's not going to happen from above. We are the change that we're waiting for".

Ruffalo continued, "Anything worth a damn that's ever happened on behalf of the people has always come up from the people and forced itself onto the power above. And that's the way it always is and that's the way it's always going to be".

Hear, hear, Mr. Ruffalo.

"Let's pick up from yesterday's teachings on the Gulf War," Kentbridge began. He wrote Iraq 1990-1991 on a blackboard. "Now that the West has control of Iraq's massive oil reserves, President Bush will be replaced."
The chalk squeaked as he wrote Bill Clinton on the board. "Bill Clinton will be our country's next President. The election later this year is just a formality. The result has already been decided."

–The Orphan Factory

Since winning the US Presidency, Barack Obama has been criticized for breaking almost every promise he made to the American people before running for office. And although he promised the opposite, his policies turned out to be almost a carbon copy of those of his predecessor George W. Bush – at least in terms of the big issues such as fighting unnecessary wars and protecting banksters ahead of everyday citizens.

Obama's supporters insist his intentions were honest. Maybe they were and maybe he really believed he'd be the boss instead being a small cog in a giant wheel.

Then again before being elected Obama had little track record in Congress of voting against the major issues like Big Pharma or banking chicanery. As political activist Ralph Nader pointed out when he ran against him in the 2008 Presidential campaign, the man formerly known as Barry Soetoro was hardly a revolutionary.

So maybe Obama knew all along he'd just be another puppet for the Establishment and was happy to play along.

Or maybe the likes of JFK was speaking through a hole in his head when he warned Americans about "secret societies, secret oaths and secret proceedings," and maybe Eisenhower was speaking through a hole in his when he warned of "the potential for the disastrous rise of misplaced power."

It's likely none of us will ever know for sure.

15

THE SCIENCE OF RACISM

Supervising the eerie experiment was Omega's own Doctor Frankenstein – better known as Doctor Pedemont, the brilliant biomedical scientist responsible for the radical science behind it. Over the past few years, with the help of his team of geneticists, Doctor Pedemont had painstakingly selected the fetus' genes from thousands of sperm donations combined with the genes of his female subjects. The donations had come from another medical experiment referred to as the Genius Sperm Bank.

–The Orphan Factory

Eugenics, or the science of improving a population by controlled breeding to increase the occurrence of desirable heritable characteristics, has been around since the mid-1800's. *Social engineering* some call it.

Genocide. Sterilization of the mentally ill, blacks, homosexuals and other *undesirables*. Euthenasia. Forced pregnancies and birth control. Racial segregation. Compulsory abortions. Genetic screening. These are examples of eugenics practices and policies adopted to varying degrees by various countries until commonsense prevailed and *most* countries banned such practices.

Although we don't specifically tackle eugenics or racial issues in *The Orphan Trilogy*, we use these early eugenics experiments as inspiration for the cold and ruthless way our fictional orphans are genetically engineered. Products of the *Genius Sperm Bank*, a real-world eugenics experiment, the orphans all have the genes of carefully selected white male donors.

In all three books in the trilogy, we also mention eugenics and cover very similar issues. Numerous book critics have referenced this wretched history of eugenics in their reviews for our series.

What's scary is that some independent researchers believe eugenics is not just a thing of the past.

The motivation behind the Genius Sperm Bank, which had been initiated over a decade earlier, was to advance the breeding of super-intelligent people. The bank was stocked full of semen donations solicited from many of the world's most intelligent men.

–The Orphan Factory

A SHORT HISTORY OF EUGENICS

Early eugenicists blamed genetics on polluting Mankind's gene pool. They cited everything from alcoholism and prostitution to homosexuality and feeble-mindedness as examples of defective genes, and favored elimination ahead of treatment.

Eugenics' original proponents were active throughout much of Europe, but it was in the US that eugenics really struck a chord – before the rise of Nazi Germany that is.

In the early days, the American eugenics movement received the financial backing of the likes of the Rockefeller Foundation and the Carnegie Institution as well as many high profile individuals such as Winston Churchill, H.G. Wells and Theodore Roosevelt. Eugenics was taught at many learning institutions and by the early 1900's eugenic policies were introduced into legislation.

The *Carnegie* name crops up an awful lot in the shameful history of eugenics.

As Edwin Black states in his book *War Against the Weak: Eugenics and America's Campaign to Create a Master Race*, in 1904, the Carnegie Institution established a laboratory complex on Long Island that stockpiled millions of index cards on ordinary Americans as researchers carefully plotted the removal of families, bloodlines and whole peoples.

And in 1911, a Carnegie-sponsored study explored solutions to ridding the population of people with defective genes. While euthanasia was shelved as one possible solution, marriage restrictions, racial segregation and forced abortions were deemed most acceptable.

Incidentally, euthanasia was only temporarily shelved as a possible solution. Proponents considered the timing wasn't yet right to suggest so drastic a measure.

COMPULSORY STERILIZATIONS

Indiana passed the world's first eugenics-motivated sterilization law in the early 20th Century. Thirty US states soon followed Indiana's lead by making it legal to sterilize those deemed genetically inferior, especially psychiatric patients.

Those with certain types of mental illness weren't the only ones sterilized en masse, however. Promiscuous women, prostitutes and females with perceived negative sexual orientations like bisexuality or lesbianism were often sterilized by authorities, while for men sterilizations were regularly done to curb excessive aggression in certain types of criminals.

Outside the US, various countries including Brazil, Belgium, Sweden and Canada implemented the policy of sterilizing citizens ruled not worthy of reproduction.

During the years that eugenics legislation was in effect in the US, around 65,000 American citizens were forcibly sterilized. Although compulsory sterilization has been considered a human rights violation in most parts of America since WW2, the laws were not overturned in many states until decades later. Virginia, for example, did not overturn its sterilization law until 1974.

FINAL SOLUTION

To quote author Edwin Black again, he says eugenics was the racist pseudoscience determined to wipe away all human beings deemed 'unfit,' preserving only those who conformed to a Nordic stereotype. "Elements of the philosophy were enshrined as national policy by forced sterilization and segregation laws, as well as marriage restrictions, enacted in 27 states (of America)...The grand plan was to literally wipe away the reproductive capability of those deemed weak and inferior."

Apparently, gas chambers were suggested, on the record, as the final solution for dealing with the unfit!

Do the words *gas chambers* and *final solution* sound familiar?

LINKS BETWEEN AMERICAN AND NAZI EUGENICS

Although eugenics flourished in Nazi Germany, the ideal of a blond-haired, blue-eyed master race wasn't Adolf Hitler's. It may surprise many to know that, in *Mein Kampf*, Hitler credited America with helping formulate his ideas on eugenics, and he admitted he'd studied the laws of US states to familiarize himself with selective reproduction and other eugenics issues.

Our research indicates it's no exaggeration to say American eugenics policies inspired eugenics programs in Nazi Germany.

If that's not disturbing enough, during the early days of the Third Reich, American eugenicists publicly praised Hitler's plans to introduce and enforce sterilization (of *unsuitable* people) and other such eugenics policies!

Funding also flowed from the US to Nazi Germany for eugenics programs. For example, The Rockefeller Foundation financed numerous German eugenics experiments, including one that Josef Mengele worked on before he carried out his notorious human experimentations in Auschwitz.

The website for Crichton University provides a succinct summary of the history of eugenics in the US and the links between American eugenics and Nazi Germany. It points out that, "Eugenicists across America welcomed Hitler's plans as the logical implementation of their own research" and "10 years after Virginia passed its 1924 Sterilization Act...the Superintendent of Virginia's Western State Hospital complained...the Germans are beating us at our own game."

America's influence on the Nazi government was also confirmed by senior eugenics leader C. M. Goethe who, after visiting Germany in 1934, wrote the following to a fellow eugenicist: "You will be interested to know that your work has played a powerful part in shaping the opinions of the group of intellectuals who are behind Hitler in this epoch-making program. Everywhere I sensed that their opinions have been tremendously stimulated by American thought...I want you, my dear friend, to carry this thought with you for the rest of your life, that you have really jolted into action a great government of 60 million people."

Of course Hitler took eugenics to a whole new level in a way probably no American envisaged. He hijacked the term *Final Solution* and decided genocide was the best method of permanently eradicating his long list of 'undesirables' from the European gene pool.

It's not known whether this America-Germany eugenics connection went full circle when Nazi scientists were brought into the US post-WW2 during the CIA's *Project Paperclip* operation.

*Benefiting from the efforts of some of Omega's elite
operatives, Doctor Pedemont had unlawfully obtained
hundreds of samples from the Genius Sperm Bank. Then,
taking the best of the sperm donations, he'd artificially
inseminated the very women who were now in the
process of giving birth. This meant each child that was
about to be born effectively had one mother and
numerous fathers.*

–The Orphan Factory

EUGENICS CONSPIRACIES

Since its beginnings, opponents of Eugenics have linked it to racial hatred. And rightly so, most would argue.

In America alone, eugenics often targeted minority ethnicities.

For example, Nobel-prize winning electronics pioneer, eugenics advocate and notorious racist, Dr. William Shockley (1910-1989), once proposed to pay black persons with IQ's lower than 100 a cash incentive of $1000 to have themselves sterilized. There was no mention of sterilizing white persons with IQ's lower than 100, of course.

However that is tame compared to the dark rumors swirling around modern eugenics. These rumors say the practice is not in decline but is actually being used to eradicate *genetic degenerates* by the millions.

Such ideas stem from conspiracy theories floating around which suggest certain viruses – like SARS, Ebola and Swine Flu – were created by pharmaceutical technicians in labs.

Some conspiracy theorists even claim HIV/AIDS is a man-made disease rather than a freak of nature. These theories suggest HIV was originally either a biological warfare virus that escaped from a laboratory by accident, or was released on purpose, as a tool for population control and eugenics implementation. The culprits are said to be shadowy, elitist organizations with New World Order ambitions.

Extreme accusations indeed, but perhaps not without some form of precedence.

From 1932 until 1972, the US Public Health Service deceptively conducted a clinical study known as the Tuskegee syphilis experiment. The notorious study was designed to monitor the progression of syphilis in African-American men who were led to believe they were receiving free treatment from the Government for the sexually transmitted disease. The infamous 40-year experiment involved medical professionals surreptitiously refusing treatment to black patients infected with syphilis.

Revelations by whistleblowers of the Tuskegee syphilis experiment led to US law changes concerning patient protection and informed consent for medical studies.

Several prominent African-American celebrities have made comments in public about the Tuskegee experiments, including comedian and film star Dave Chappelle whose grandfather was a Tuskegee survivor who was permanently blinded as a result of the experimentation.

Shortly after the Hurricane Katrina disaster in New Orleans, leading film director Spike Lee mentioned the Tuskegee experiment on an episode of the TV series *Real Time with Bill Maher*. Lee alluded to a racial conspiracy in the Katrina aftermath by comparing the Government's apparent lack of response to African-American communities with the ill treatment of patients in the syphilis experiment.

Various groups, including the Nation of Islam and the Black Panthers, believe the CIA purposefully infected African-Americans with HIV. Reminiscent of Tuskegee, this is said to have been carried out under the guise of hepatitis vaccinations. Those who subscribe to this theory have suggested HIV was spread by some pro-eugenics splinter group to decimate the black race, both in the US and in Africa.

The concept of AIDS being a sinister experiment seems to be

reasonably accepted in the African-American community at least. In 2005, *The Washington Post* did a survey on the subject, questioning 500 African-Americans. The newspaper reported over 50% of those surveyed believed HIV was man-made and over 25% believed it was created in a US Government laboratory.

In Nigeria, there have been theories amongst locals that the World Health Organization (WHO) was spreading HIV via polio vaccines. As a result, there has been a decrease in the amount of Nigerians vaccinated against polio in recent years as many parents choose to keep their children away from WHO needles.

In 1986, American Physician Doctor Robert Strecker stated that HIV was not only a man-made bio-weapon created by the US military, but that it was disseminated by the WHO in Africa in the 1970's by inserting the killer virus into smallpox vaccines. Strecker's theory went on to suggest the distribution of HIV did not stop with Africa, but continued in the US. According to the doctor, the outbreak of AIDS in America was caused by government-sponsored hepatitis B vaccine experiments in San Francisco, New York City and Los Angeles in the late 1970's and early 1980's. The vaccines were said to be contaminated with HIV and were apparently only given to gay men and African-American men.

Although *TIME* magazine and most other mainstream media outlets condemned Strecker's theory, it has since been supported by several prominent doctors and scientists. One of the supporters included Doctor Alan Cantwell who authored the 1988 book *AIDS and the Doctors of Death: An Inquiry into the Origin of the AIDS Epidemic.*

South Africa's former president, Thabo Mbeki, has claimed HIV/AIDS is a grand conspiracy involving the CIA and Big Pharma.

But probably the most famous supporter of the theory that AIDS is some kind of Unit 731-style biological weapon is the 2004 Nobel Peace Prize laureate and environmental and political activist Wangari Maathai (1940-2011).

The Kenyan was quoted by Nairobi-based newspaper *The Standard* in 2004 as saying AIDS was "deliberately created by

Western scientists to decimate the African population". This lead to a flurry of world headlines including this one by *Radio Free Europe Radio Liberty* on December 10, 2004, 'Africa's First Female Nobel Peace Laureate Accepts Award Amid Controversy Over AIDS Remarks' and this one on the same day in *The New York Times*, 'Nobel Laureate Seeks to Explain AIDS Remarks'.

Maathai was also reported in a December, 2004 edition of *TIME* magazine as saying, "I do know things like that don't come from the moon. I have always thought that it is important to tell people the truth, but I guess there is some truth that must not be too exposed ... I'm referring to AIDS. I am sure people know where it came from. And I'm quite sure it did not come from the monkeys".

As UNICEF has called AIDS "the worst catastrophe ever to hit the world" the idea that certain governments or agencies created the virus to attack minority groups is hard to even consider, let alone believe. Personally, we feel this theory is veering into the sort of crackpot conspiracy ideas promoted by the Tinfoil Hat Network. Then again, as Spike Lee was alluding to in his TV interview, history is riddled with malicious, eugenics-style medical experiments like Tuskegee, so you never know.

Here's hoping this HIV/AIDS conspiracy theory ain't true!

NORTH KOREAN EUGENICS

As far as governments go in the modern world, North Korea is known to practice eugenics. The neo-Stalanist regime is committed to protecting *racial purity* and sees eugenics as the way to breed a stronger population and eradicate *degenerates* who carry supposedly weak genes.

An October 21, 2006 article in UK newspaper *The Telegraph* reported the UN had uncovered "subhuman gulags" in North Korea where the disabled and mentally ill were locked up.

The rogue state operates a "rigorous system of eugenics" according to the article, for those "deemed subnormal, ranging from the disabled to dwarves."

The Telegraph also reported the gulags were designed so that "those who do not conform to the state's designation of normal do not pass on their genes by having children."

Apparently, in North Korea those deemed abnormal are locked up for life. Marriages are allowed at segregation camps, but reproducing is not. There have also been reports of turning these 'abnormals' into laboratory guinea pigs for testing chemicals and germ agents.

In the Western World, the disturbing trend toward designer babies, the unofficial use of euthanasia by some medical professionals and the treatment of elderly people in some rest homes are just a few examples of present-day eugenics in operation – albeit tame examples compared to the genocide and forced relocation of many thousands of people occurring in some Third World countries.

American Christopher Langan, who claims to have an IQ between 195 and 210 and is also known as *the world's smartest man*, has often been reported as being a eugenics supporter. The RationalWiki website describes a YouTube video in which "Langan talks about how he wishes he could implement a benign form of eugenics involving mandatory birth control and health screenings, and how breeding as much as we like isn't necessarily a free right, and that people have to be trained to not abuse their freedoms, especially at the expense of future generations."

Hopefully the 1997 sci-fi film *Gattaca* does not prove to be an accurate prophecy for eugenics implementations to come. Written and directed by Andrew Niccol and starring Ethan Hawke and Uma Thurman, the film presents a future society where nearly all children are conceived by genetic engineering technologies to ensure they do not inherit bad genes from their parents. Any persons born outside this society's eugenics program are labeled faith births, degenerates or invalids, and are heavily discriminated against.

And then there's the whole issue of human cloning. We

considered that too *out there*, and too far beyond our level of knowledge or understanding, to include in this book. However, we must at least acknowledge human cloning as it is a major theme of *The Orphan Trilogy* – in particular book three in the series which reveals the powerful Omega Agency's cloning plans have come to fruition, allowing the organization to conduct medical experimentation on live humans.

Given the well-documented history of eugenics, and the persistence of its known adherents into the 21st Century, it is possible the controversial science continues underground. The secret use of eugenics could include classified experiments similar to the programs described and shown in *The Orphan Trilogy* and *Gattaca* where humans are genetically engineered for perfection.

Then again, maybe (hopefully) we've been writing conspiracy thriller novels so long our fears regarding eugenics are closer to the fiction we write than reality! If our concerns have no basis then it's quite possible our critics are right and we really do see conspiracies *everywhere* in the real world.

16

BANKRUPTING THE THIRD WORLD

*To achieve this NWO and expand the super-secret
Omega Agency, the founding members knew they needed
to create enormous wealth in the quickest possible time.
The easiest way to do that, in their view, was to siphon
as many mineral riches as they could out of Third World
countries. It was an age-old practice, tried and tested,
but never before attempted on the enormous scale
Omega was gearing up for.*

–The Orphan Factory

The media regularly reminds us of the billions of dollars in aid First World governments and international aid organizations grant annually to impoverished Third World nations.

The official story goes that Western nations are extremely generous in assisting the development of the Third World. And few would argue with this summary as even when countries like the UK, Germany or the US are in an economic slump, they are never shy of giving vast sums to poorer nations in times of need.

This is especially true when it comes organizing relief efforts for natural disasters. Major catastrophes like the Pakistan floods, the Haiti earthquake and the Indian Ocean tsunami are recent examples of massive amounts of aid being raised almost overnight.

What if all this aid is not charitable, but completely selfish? What if it isn't actually giving, but taking? What if all the generosity has serious strings attached – strings designed to fleece vulnerable nations?

And what if the International Monetary Fund (IMF), the World Bank and other such financial aid organizations are all gigantic scams designed to subjugate Third World countries?

Sounds ridiculous, *right*?

Wrong, many globalization commentators would contest.

Before we expand on this alternative version of international aid, we'd like to separate the aforementioned aid organizations and their ilk from the genuine aid and charity organizations. They are too many genuine organizations to list here, but they include the likes of Save the Children, Red Cross, Doctors Without Borders, CARE, Oxfam and Refugees Internationals. Whilst some of these organizations have their critics, most people would agree their intentions are noble, the services they deliver invaluable – often lifesaving – and the people delivering those services extremely conscientious and passionate about what they do.

The alternative version of international aid suggests that money given or *loaned* by international aid organizations like the IMF and the World Bank is no different to banks dolling out credit cards to individual customers. And just as banks offer credit to customers so that they (the banks) can make money, this theory also suggests these big, so-called aid organizations are purely profit-motivated and not remotely charitable.

Let's explore this comparison a little deeper…

Banks know that some customers will pay off their credit cards quickly without incurring much interest. They also know a small percentage will have to be written off as bad debts, and they allow for this in their profit forecasts. However, the vast majority of customers who take on new credit cards will be indebted to the bank for months, years or even for the rest of their lives. Some of these customers will manage, barely, while some will be completely snowed under and one step away from bankruptcy.

Banks make the bulk of their profits by keeping most of their customers in this perpetual cycle of paying off interest, and that's why they regularly offer customers more credit – even, or *especially*, customers who are already having trouble getting themselves out of the debt cycle and who can least afford it.

Following this analogy, on the international stage the World Bank, the IMF and Western governments are the equivalent of smaller, personal banks, and impoverished Third World nations are the equivalent of customers accepting and using credit cards. Overall, the rules are virtually identical – foster a reliance on credit amongst those you lend to then ensure the interest rates are so extreme the debt can never be paid off.

Once poor Third World nations are beholden to lenders, First World governments and their allied corporations regularly demand favors in return. Those favors include relinquishing political control or simply turning a blind eye to the plunder of natural resources, or both. Manipulating the power structure of countries is done in a multitude of ways, including rigging elections, making under-the-table payments and organizing political assassinations.

When these nations are crushed, enslaved even, beneath mountains of debt, this creates enormous ongoing revenues for the lenders through high interest rates. It also allows for untold injustices to be perpetrated by major multinational corporations – injustices such as oil companies pumping toxins into rivers, logging companies destroying entire forests, pharmaceutical giants performing illegal human experimentation, manufacturers hiring people to work in inhumane conditions in sweat shops, and in some cases employing child labor.

"Western governments tax their citizens to fund the World Bank, lend this money to corrupt Third World dictators who abscond with the funds, and then demand repayment which is extracted through taxation from

poor Third World citizens, rather than from the
government officials responsible for the embezzlement.
It is in essence a global transfer of wealth from the poor
to the rich. Taxpayers around the world are forced to
subsidize the lavish lifestyles of Third World dictators
and highly-paid World Bank bureaucrats who don't
even pay income tax."
–Ron Paul's statement at the World Bank Hearing, May 22, 2007

OVERSHADOWING INDIVIDUAL NATIONS

Some of these dirty economic tactics used against vulnerable nations are examples of modern imperialism in action. This is especially true with the US, which as previously alluded to is in many ways the world's last remaining superpower. With hundreds of military bases worldwide and untold intelligence agents strategically placed in almost every country on Earth, the American empire is unlike any other.

Unfortunately, America's foreign activities all too often result in large amounts of collateral damage.

If we are ruffling any patriotic feathers in this chapter then you're viewing it all wrong because the reality is no powerful country – be it the US or the UK, Russia or France – is immune to financial domination from the likes of the World Bank and the IMF. The recent financial austerity measures placed upon EU nations like Portugal, Greece and Spain are prime examples of this.

There's no reason to suggest if a country like the US slipped into a deep enough economic recession that corrupt international financial organizations would not swoop to enslave Americans in a web of debt. In fact, many conspiracy theorists, and more than a few economists, believe this is already happening to America.

The key point is nearly all the decisions to commit these destructive acts against Third World countries are made *above* governmental level. And above countries, too. For it's not about governments or countries, and it never was. It's simply about the powerful global elite who secretly rule the media, the politicians, the political parties, the governments and ipso facto, the countries.

The privileged individuals and families who comprise the global elite will happily bankrupt their own countrymen, decimate their own community and evict their neighbors from houses in their desperate bid to increase their wealth.

"About 21,000 people die every day of hunger or hunger-related causes, according to the United Nations. This is one person every four seconds ... Sadly, it is children who die most often. Yet there is plenty of food in the world for everyone. The problem is that hungry people are trapped in severe poverty. They lack the money to buy enough food to nourish themselves. Being constantly malnourished, they become weaker and often sick. This makes them increasingly less able to work, which then makes them even poorer and hungrier. This downward spiral often continues until death for them and their families."

–Official statement on the poverty.com website as at February 2014

END POVERTY NOW - OR LATER ...OR MUCH LATER

If you haven't picked up on it already, we believe world poverty can be fixed. And fixed quickly.

Some of you may be doubting our sanity about now. At the very least, you'll be thinking we are underestimating the task at hand, and that poverty's far too big a challenge to solve any time soon.

But consider this for a moment: the *United Nations Development Program* estimated in 1998 that it would only cost an additional US$40 billion above current aid payments at the time to completely eradicate poverty as we know it. This figure was broken down as per the following necessary (US dollar) payments: $13 billion extra for every person on Earth to have enough food as well as access to basic health care; an additional $12 billion to cover reproductive health for all women worldwide; $6 billion extra to provide basic education for all; and an additional $9 billion to provide clean water and sanitation for every man, woman and child on the planet.

Now that $40 billion figure was in 1998 dollars, of course, and the world's biggest problems have arguably gotten worse since then. So let's allow for inflation and let's also assume the UN underestimated the amount required.

Let's say $200 billion dollars, or five times what the UN estimated, is needed over and above current aid payments. To our eyes, that seems a small price to pay for what would undoubtedly be the greatest moment in human history.

Two hundred billion is also a fraction of the cost governments of major nations like China, the US, Russia and the UK spend on their annual military budgets. By some estimates, the Afghanistan conflict alone has cost America more than a trillion dollars, with all wars since 9/11 said to have cost America several trillion dollars. However, waging wars is clearly a far bigger priority than ending poverty.

"It's an amazing thing to think that ours is the first generation in history that really can end extreme poverty, the kind that means a child dies for lack of food in its belly. That should be seen as the most incredible, historic opportunity but instead it's become a millstone around our necks. We let our own pathetic excuses about how it's difficult justify our own inaction. Be honest.

We have the science, the technology, and the wealth.
What we don't have is the will, and that's not a reason
that history will accept."

–Bono, interview to the World Association of Newspapers for
World Press Freedom Day. May 3, 2004.

PROFITING FROM WAR

Ever wonder why peace in certain countries like Afghanistan, Iraq and the Democratic Republic of Congo is never achieved no matter how many thousands of international peacekeepers are sent?

The answer may be that despite appearances, the world's powers-that-be don't actually want peace in those countries to be achieved any time soon.

Engaging in diplomatic talks and sending in UN peacekeepers is just a farce, apparently. According to our research, it's far more lucrative for the global elite to keep wars going so the invaders can plunder resources for as long as they can. If we are correct in this analysis, then maybe wars like Afghanistan, Iraq and Vietnam were not about winning, but something else. Something much more sinister.

More than any other region on the planet, Africa's probably the best example of these vicious, imperialistic strategies. Unfortunately for Africa it has many, many resources the outside world wants, needs and will kill to get its hands on. Resources like its vast water reserves, unlimited land, oil and precious metals such as gold, diamonds, cobalt and uranium to name a few. Not to mention the continent's wildlife and cheap human labor.

U2's lead singer Bono possibly summarized it best in a 2004 speech he gave at the University of Pennsylvania when he said, "Africa needs justice as much as it needs charity."

In *The Ninth Orphan*, we wrote the following pertinent paragraphs about the African continent:

As the seemingly well-intentioned French journalist spoke

about Africa's *scarcity* and its *limited resources*, Nine smiled to himself almost condescendingly. He considered such statements an absolute joke. Africa did not, nor did it ever have, *limited resources*.

Nine knew something the journalist obviously didn't: Africa was the most abundantly resourced continent on the planet bar none. Like the despots who ruled much of the region, and the foreign governments who propped them up, he knew there was more than enough wealth in Africa's mineral resources such as gold, diamonds and oil – not to mention the land that nurtured these resources – for every man, woman and child.

He thought it unfortunate Africa had never been able to compete on a level playing field. The continent's almost unlimited resources were the very reason foreigners had meddled in African affairs for the past century or more. Nine knew it was Omega's plan, and that of other greedy organizations, to siphon as much wealth as they could out of vulnerable Third World countries, especially in Africa.

The same organizations had the formula down pat: they indirectly started civil wars in mineral-rich regions by providing arms to opposing local factions, and sometimes even helped to create famines, in order to destabilize African countries. This made the targeted countries highly vulnerable to international control. Once the outside organizations had divided and conquered, they were then able to plunder the country's resources.

The defeated eyes of the starving children on screen reminded Nine of his fellow orphans growing up in the Pedemont Orphanage. Although he had never experienced malnutrition, he knew what it was like to be born into a living hell.

Sadly, since *The Ninth Orphan* was published in 2011, not much has changed in Africa; international governments, multinational corporations and the likes of the World Bank and the IMF continue to profit from Africa's vulnerability.

Wars in numerous African countries continue to go unchallenged and untold millions are raped, killed, maimed and starved while the rest of the world just looks on. It has become such a repetitious story in Africa that wars in the region rarely make international headlines anymore.

Divide and conquer. That's the global elite's proven strategy when it comes to its treatment of Third World countries in Africa and indeed throughout the world. Or, to put it another way, order out of chaos is the global elite's favored tactic. They engineer chaos by financing both sides of revolutions, movements and civil wars then create *order* by providing *solutions* to governments and citizens in these war-torn countries.

To quote the British group *James* from their 2008 song *Ha Ma*: "War is just about business."

CONFESSIONS OF AN ECONOMIC HIT MAN

One of the best testimonies toward this conspiracy against Third World nations is John Perkins' 2004 bestselling book *Confessions of an Economic Hit Man*. The book mentions how it's no longer necessary to invade other countries to plunder their resources. Now there are other easier ways to achieve this.

Much of the old invade-and-occupy strategy has been replaced by economics. As JFK once said, it's now about "infiltration instead of invasion," and there are many ways to successfully infiltrate a nation. It can be done by owning politicians and thereby subtly implementing policies, or it can be done by buying a nation's media and feeding that nation's citizens propaganda.

Confessions of an Economic Hit Man describes how mysterious independent contractors known as economic hit men cheat poor countries all over the world out of trillions of dollars. They're paid large sums to creatively influence and/or bribe leading politicians in developing nations to make policy changes that suit multinational corporations. These policy changes usually revolve around either giving up the developing nation's resources to offshore interests or accepting large Halliburton-esque building contracts.

Perkins describes how the main job of an economic hit man is to persuade the leaders of Third World nations to accept multi-billion dollar development loans from (guess who?) the IMF and World Bank – that's right, the usual suspects!

Once economic hit men have carried out a *hit* on a nation, the US doesn't need to invade that nation or, indeed, do anything more. The profits automatically flow into the US while all the hard work is done by the impoverished citizens of the targeted nation.

Perkins claims he was formerly one of these economic hit men and was hired by America's National Security Agency (NSA) to carry out hits against vulnerable and mineral-rich Third World countries.

As Perkins writes in the book's preface: "Economic hit men (EHMs) are highly-paid professionals, who cheat countries around the globe out of trillions of dollars. They funnel money from the World Bank, the US Agency for International Development (USAID), and other foreign *aid* organizations into the coffers of huge corporations and the pockets of a few wealthy families who control the planet's natural resources. Their tools included fraudulent financial reports, rigged elections, payoffs, extortion, sex, and murder. They play a game as old as empire, but one that has taken on new and terrifying dimensions during this time of globalization. *I should know; I was an EHM.*"

As a result of his tenure of many years as an EHM, of which he expresses much guilt, Perkins claims in the book that the developing nations he worked in were in the end crippled economically and virtually remote-controlled politically.

Interestingly, in the epilogue to the 2006 edition of *Confessions of an Economic Hit Man,* Perkins writes that the supposedly generous offer by G8 nations to wipe all Third World debt was a trick. He states the catch was that to erase all their debts these countries would be forced to privatize almost all their assets, including electricity, water, education and health. Perkins argues this would potentially leave these countries worse off in the long run.

In 2009, a documentary film titled *Apologies of an Economic Hit Man* was released. It includes poignant interviews with Perkins. The film, which was directed by Stelios Kouloglou, was shown at film festivals around the world.

Perkins' confessions serve as an important reminder that the *winner takes all* mindset at the root of capitalism is a poison if left unchecked. That's not to say capitalism is bad per sē, or that a more refined version of it cannot work effectively. Nor does it mean the world should move toward socialism or communism, which have both proven throughout history to be just as disastrous. But surely the world's recent financial catastrophes and the bankrupting of individuals, families, small businesses, communities and entire nations, must make even the most ardent capitalist examine his or her beliefs.

"We are opposed around the world by a monolithic and ruthless conspiracy that relies primarily on covert means for expanding its sphere of influence – on infiltration instead of invasion, on subversion instead of elections, on intimidation instead of free choice, on guerrillas by night instead of armies by day. It is a system which has conscripted vast human and material resources into the building of a tightly knit, highly efficient machine that combines military, diplomatic, intelligence, economic, scientific and political operations. Its preparations are concealed, not published. Its mistakes are buried, not headlined. Its dissenters are silenced not praised. No expenditure is questioned, no rumor is printed, no secret is revealed."
–President John F. Kennedy, speech to the American Newspaper Publishers Association. April 27, 1961, New York City.

We accept that a lot of the ideas in this chapter seem very extreme. Many of our readers will no doubt find it hard, or perhaps impossible, to believe world leaders could view nations like Haiti, Somalia and Cambodia as being nothing other than money-spinners.

In attempting to understand how the global elite think, we would draw your attention to *National Security Memorandum 200*, a recently declassified document headed 'Implications for Worldwide Population Growth for US Security & Overseas Interests' and dated 10 December 10, 1974. In it, National Security consultant (and favorite of *old boy* networks like Bilderberg, CFR and Bohemian Grove) Henry Kissinger, states, "Depopulation should be the highest priority of US foreign policy towards the Third World," to secure mineral resources for the US.

Exactly how depopulation of the Third World was to be accomplished wasn't specified in the document. Kissinger may have favored obvious methods like keeping certain countries in perpetual states of war, famine and scarcity. Or the depopulation he encouraged could perhaps be achieved through something much more nefarious – possibly even something along the lines of the purposeful spread of AIDS, which was a conspiracy theory mentioned in chapter 15.

Either way, Kissinger's statement is both scary and profound. If depopulation is on the table then fleecing the Third World of all its riches and keeping its citizens impoverished actually seems benign by comparison.

But listen, maybe we just don't understand the world we're in. Who knows, perhaps the mad pursuit of profits at all costs will eventually rid the world of poverty, and maybe certain economists, Far Right politicians and libertarians are right when they say *unregulated* capitalism is the answer.

Possibly that free market approach will give everybody the opportunity to become super rich no matter where they live – in which case perhaps pure capitalism without any social reforms whatsoever isn't the *bullet to the head* that we common people think it is...

NEW WORLD ORDER

"Marcia Wilson was a good example of Omega's core strategy for creating a New World Order. It involved placing their people, or moles, in positions of power within the CIA, the NSA, the Pentagon, the White House and global organizations like the UN, the IMF and the World Bank. This enabled Omega to pull some of the strings of these organizations and to direct American, and world politics, to an extent."

–The Ninth Orphan

Almost every conspiracy theory in recent years at least references the New World Order (NWO) in some way.

There are various versions of the *NWO Theory*, depending on who is telling it and what their agenda may be – if they have an agenda, which they usually do! However, in the simplest of terms, the theory suggests the global elite are subtly directing our civilization toward a totalitarian one world government.

This is apparently being orchestrated by leading politicians, including heads of state, who are implementing policies to allow for a one world government that will eventually replace sovereign nation-states. Once a reality, such a governing body so empowered would naturally set laws that reflect the global elite's core philosophies.

Methods used by the global elite to action this NWO plan are said to embrace many of the subjects covered so far in this book, including media propaganda, central banking and engineering wars with false flag attacks.

It all sounds possible – at least within the context of this book – right?

The only problem is, NWO conspiracy theories are often trumpeted by those who are more than a few pennies short of a pound and have trouble distinguishing fantasy from reality.

Those commonly peddling one world government ideas include anti-Semites blaming Jewish people for every problem under the sun, religious zealots who believe the NWO will bring about apocalyptic scenarios, UFO gurus warning an alien invasion is imminent, and indeed all those other conspiracy extremists who together form our beloved Tinfoil Hat Network.

So, all this talk of a NWO is a bunch of BS then. Right?

Um…maybe. Or maybe not.

"The only salvation for civilization lies in the creation of a world government"

–Albert Einstein

MONEY TALKS

If any group had the authority to direct the planet towards a NWO, it would be the world's financial elite.

Many independent researchers have said the bulk of the world's money supply is in the hands of less than 1000 families. Yep you read that right: *the bulk of the world's money supply is in the hands of less than 1000 families.*

These families would include the Rockefellers, the British Royals, the Marcos and Bush clans as well as other elite dynasties mentioned in this book. Their fortunes consist of Old World money, invisible money and blood money.

In a similar vein, David Rothkopf's 2008 book, *Superclass: The*

Global Power Elite and the World They Are Making, states that the world is governed by a group of 6000 elite individuals.

And according to Oxfam's 2014 economic briefing, the wealth of the top 1% in the world amounts to US$110 trillion. That's 65 times the total wealth of the bottom half of the world's population.

Another staggering statistic from Oxfam's briefing was that, collectively, the financial worth of the world's 85 wealthiest people approximately equals that of the poorer half of the world's total population. In other words, and *get this* – the richest 85 individuals have as much wealth as the 3.5 billion or so people who make up 50% of the world's population and who are categorized as the poorest on the planet!

What if those 85 *Rich Listers* got together – assuming they or their representatives haven't already – and agreed on certain things? Things like lobbying for a one world currency, for example, or anything else that fits their definition of a better world? With their financial clout and inherent power, would they not be capable of creating a New World Order of sorts?

Kentbridge continued, "There are different types of New World Order scenarios. One would be a world government ruled by a totalitarian regime like the Nazis were working toward. That would obviously be destructive. Another scenario would be one in which a fairer world is created. That's what we are aiming for. We can unite everybody worldwide and create everlasting peace."

–The Orphan Factory

In *The Orphan Trilogy*, we refer to two secret organizations, the Omega Agency and the Nexus Foundation, whom we describe as having ambitions to create a NWO on their terms. Omega and Nexus are inspired by shadow organizations rumored to exist in today's world – shadowy, real-world organizations, which according to conspiracy theorists are hell-bent on achieving a NWO.

But beyond works of fiction, is there any truth behind this conspiracy theory?

We got no idea. Why ask us? We have no answers, remember? We're merely dramatists posing a number of questions, but we can theorize of course. (You may have noticed by now we tend to specialize in that).

A NWO BY INCREMENTS

There is a *theory* that suggests the NWO will be achieved in stages.

Firstly, blocks of countries such as the African Union, the European Union and the proposed North American Union between the US, Canada and Mexico combine.

Secondly, before you know it, global organizations pop up all over the show, including the World Bank, the United Nations and the International Monetary Fund – their presence and power magnifying with each passing day.

Thirdly, and last of all, a one world government is formed. Then, apparently, it's too late to do anything about it and the global elite have won, according to conspiracy theorists.

Imagine waking up to headlines announcing that your nation's government has relinquished the reigns of power to a one world government. Hells bells!

The global elite may have completed steps one and two (above), but step three, the formation of a one world government, has so far eluded them.

So, if this is a game of soccer, it's currently 2-0 to the global elite, according to you-know-who. However, it ain't game over yet.

THE DOLLAR BILL CONSPIRACY
THEORY

Probably the most high profile and best known reference to the NWO, in America at least, is the much-touted *US One Dollar Bill Theory*. As many a proud member of the Tinfoil Hat Network will tell anyone who is half-listening to them, written on the US dollar bill is a Latin Phrase that translates as *New World Order*.

We even heard a well-known conspiracy theory radio show host tell his audience, "As everybody knows, it's a fact that the words New World Order are written in Latin on the dollar bill."

Apparently, many American school kids accept this as fact as well.

The only problem is the Latin phrase *novus ordo seclorum*, which has been on the reverse side of the Great Seal of the United States since 1782, and on the reverse of the dollar bill since 1935, doesn't translate to *New World Order*; it actually translates to *New Order of the Ages*.

Instead of a New World Order and toppling of nation-states, New Order of the Ages is commonly acknowledged by experts as being a reference to a new era of the United States of America, suggesting the nation will go from strength to strength. This appears to directly contradict the NWO claim, as nations are supposed to get weaker not stronger in the build-up to a one world government.

However, conspiracy theorists, especially the Tinfoil Hatter extremists, continue to claim that the direct Latin translation is just a smokescreen and the dollar bill does in fact allude to a coming NWO.

It seems the word *mistranslation* isn't part of the vocab of the Tinfoil Hat Network's members.

Kentbridge passionately believed that Omega – or the
Light, as Naylor sometimes referred to the agency – was
America's, and the world's, only hope of ever unifying. And
unification was the only solution for he was also aware
that while the public was dividing and conquering itself by
focusing on banal, media-driven conflicts such as
Neoconservatives versus Liberals, democracy versus
terrorism and the West versus the rest, destructive covert
outfits were slowly but surely growing stronger. The
special agent also understood how groups like Nexus
fostered and benefited from the climate of fear perpetuated
in television broadcasts and newspaper headlines. As long
as Americans were consumed by fear of evildoers, whether
these be communists, terrorists, religious extremists or any
other potential enemy, he knew they would never realize
the greatest enemy of all was operating within – within
the West, within America, within their own Government.
–The Orphan Factory

PUPPET MASTERS PULLING
STRINGS AGAIN

As we've revealed in earlier chapters, most of America's if not the
world's senior leaders have pledged allegiance to at least one elitist
organization such as the Bilderberg Group, Bohemian Grove,
Freemasons or the Council on Foreign Relations. The NWO concept
is interrelated with these secret handshakes and closeted meetings.

Remember those invisible puppet masters we referred to in
chapter 3? And the little known founding members of those
organizations we name above? And the people who are rumored to
be manipulating the higher profile members of those same
organizations?

Well, if a NWO exists, those puppet masters would likely be the orchestrators of it. They would be the ones quietly but diligently setting up the beginnings of a one world government.

In 2001, one of the founders of the Bilderberg Group and likely puppet master Denis Healey said: "To say we were striving for a one-world government is exaggerated, but not wholly unfair. Those of us in Bilderberg felt we couldn't go on forever fighting one another for nothing and killing people and rendering millions homeless. So we felt that a single community throughout the world would be a good thing."

As they watched and listened to the recorded speech, the orphans noted something which the vast majority of political commentators, and certainly the public at large, had never picked up on. That something was that President Bush subtly mentioned the phrase New World Order several times throughout his speech.

–The Orphan Factory

BUSH'S NEW WORLD ORDER SPEECH

NWO came to some prominence in 1990 when President George H. W. Bush said in a speech to Congress, "Now, we can see a new world coming into view. A world in which there is the very real prospect of a new world order".

Conspiracy theorists claimed this was the President announcing – albeit in code – the elite were one step closer to creating a one world government that would dominate the planet and eliminate all dissenters, starting with the Iraqi people.

"It is not my intention to doubt that the doctrine of the Illuminati and the principles of Jacobinism had not spread in the United States. On the contrary, no one is more satisfied of this fact than I am".

–George Washington

ILLUMINATI

Author Dan Brown's 2003 mega bestseller *The Da Vinci Code* introduced many in the mainstream to the Illuminati, even though a thousand and one NWO theories had referred to this mysterious group well before the novel ever hit bookstore shelves.

But like the novel, the infamous Illuminati secret society is a mixture of fact and fiction. And probably more fiction than fact.

The (true) Illuminati story begins in Europe with historical records showing the Order of the Illuminati was founded by German professor Adam Weishaupt, in Bavaria, in 1776. The underground organization was a type of breakaway group that separated from European Freemasonry, with most of the founding members being recruited from German Masonic Lodges. In 1785, the order was destroyed from within by agent provocateurs working for the Bavarian Government, which feared secret societies could eventually overthrow the ruling Bavarian Monarchy.

Unfortunately, that's where the facts and historical evidence surrounding the Illuminati end. Virtually every other supposed piece of Illuminati evidence that conspiracy buffs put forward is debatable at best and pure fantasy at worst.

In the late 1700's and early 1800's, there were many prominent figures who surmised that the Illuminati may have somehow survived and masterminded key historical events, including the French Revolution.

But again, there's no evidence of this.

However, those rumors are nothing compared to more recent rumors, which reflect fear and paranoia.

Between the First and Second World Wars, as fascism advanced, various rampant anti-Semitics said the Illuminati served elite Jewish bankers who, they claimed, were dividing Europe to gain financial control and create a Jewish type of NWO. It's possible some of these Illuminati theories aided in creating a furtive and fertile environment for the likes of the Nazi Party to assume power so easily.

In the early 21st Century, Illuminati folklore has blossomed, perhaps off the back of *The Da Vinci Code*, or maybe it has more to do with increases in mental illness cases!

The supposed mind control program *Project Monarch*, which we covered in chapter 2, is closely tied in with modern Illuminati theories. If you Google phrases like *mind controlled celebrities* or *Hollywood stars and the music industry*, you'll find countless conspiracy theories referring to the Illuminati and its numerous "Monarch slaves".

Music stars in particular are said to be Monarch victims, and common names bandied about include Beyoncé, Lady Gaga, Nicki Minaj, Britney Spears, Katy Perry, Miley Cyrus and Rihanna. What's more, they all supposedly use Illuminati symbolism in their music videos.

None of the Tinfoil Hatters ever seem to consider that these ancient Illuminati symbols could have simply been hijacked by modern and infinitely less powerful groups. This is what Dan Brown seems to be getting at in his Robert Langdon novel *Angel's & Demons*, when he writes, "It means that when organized philosophies like the Illuminati go out of existence, their symbols remain... available for adoption by other groups. It's called transference. It's very common in symbology. The Nazis took the swastika from the Hindus, the Christians adopted the cruciform from the Egyptians".

Furthermore, any death of an A-List celebrity is always claimed to be Illuminati-orchestrated, according to conspiracy extremists. For example, on February 2, 2014, the day Academy

Award-winning actor Philip Seymour Hoffman tragically died, YouTube was awash with hastily compiled videos featuring titles such as "Philip Seymour Hoffman Murdered by Illuminati" and "PHILLIP SEYMOUR HOFFMAN...ILLUMINATI SACRIFICE?"

None of those who promote such theories ever seem to question whether the Illuminati still exists. Nor do their followers, it seems. Again, the last confirmation of the Illuminati's existence was in 1785. Something tells us if they still were around, there would have been at least one verification of their presence in the more than two centuries that have since elapsed.

Nor do these conspiracy theorists ever seem to acknowledge there's not a shred of evidence to prove Project Monarch exists. Instead, Monarch gets lumped in with the highly documented CIA mind control program MK-Ultra. This is rather deceitful to say the least.

Some celebrities, including Jay-Z, Kim Kardashian and Howard Stern, have fought back against the *keyboard warriors* who make such videos or write such blogs, by issuing media statements and publicly denying they are members of the Illuminati.

Unfortunately, when such high profile names defend themselves like this, it only seems to add fuel to the Illuminati fire.

"For more than a century ideological extremists at either end of the political spectrum have seized upon well-publicized incidents such as my encounter with Castro to attack the Rockefeller family for the inordinate influence they claim we wield over American political and economic institutions. Some even believe we are part of a secret cabal working against the best interests of the United States, characterizing my family and me as internationalists and of conspiring with others around the world to build a more integrated global political and economic structure — one world, if you will. If that's the charge, I stand guilty, and I am proud of it."

–David Rockefeller from his 2002 autobiography Memoirs.

So where does all that leave us when it comes to deciding whether or not a New World Order exists?

Dunno. (Surely by now you realize we don't have any answers to offer)!

If you really want our opinion – and we are not quite sure why on earth you would – we'd have to say there does seem to be a NWO, or the beginnings of one at least, but it's probably in a different form than most conspiracy theorists imagine. (And we use the word *imagine* advisedly). Ever the optimists, we'd like to think it's in a form that will facilitate sharing of nations' resources, elimination of wars and poverty, and promotion of peace and cooperation worldwide.

But maybe – quite possibly in fact – there is no NWO in the making and maybe there never was. In which case, we'll keep this note to ourselves handy and read it every time we sit in front of our keyboards: *Remove our tinfoil hats before we write anything.*

18

SADDAM HUSSEIN: FABRICATED ENEMY?

Kentbridge spun around from the blackboard and held up an infamous photograph of former US Secretary of Defense Donald Rumsfeld shaking hands with Iraqi President Saddam Hussein. The special agent gave the photo to Eleven, a stunning brunette orphan who had been genetically engineered for beauty. She looked at the image before sharing it with the other orphans.

–The Orphan Factory

In the Federal Bureau of Investigation's vault the following description of former Iraqi leader Saddam Hussein is listed as follows: "Saddam Hussein (1937-2006) was the president of Iraq from 1979-2003. In 2003, coalition forces invaded Iraq and deposed Hussein. In 2006, he was tried by the Iraqi Interim Government and convicted of the retaliatory executions of 148 Iraqi Shiites. He was executed on December 30, 2006."

The FBI summary goes on to mention the "Iraqi Special Tribunal concerning Hussein's commission of crimes against humanity, war crimes, and genocide."

Describing Saddam as a war criminal and an enemy of the West sounds to us like a fair summary that few would argue with.

As Steve Pickering, then intern with the Washington Peace Center (WPC), wrote for the center in a June 1998 article: "The history of Iraq under Saddam Hussein is one of harsh oppression, with widespread abuses of human rights, and frequent torture and murder of political opponents, or just those who displease him."

However, even with the knowledge of Saddam's confirmed atrocities, it seems there's little doubt the US was in bed with him for decades before his eventual removal from power if the assertions of various independent researchers are correct.

To this day, those assertions remain theories – unproven in the eyes of many.

At the heart of such theories is the idea that the West needs enemies to lambast in the media in order to engineer wars. Once a leader like Saddam has been condemned, or at least heavily derided, through media propaganda the masses hardly blink when false flag attacks are attributed to those who have been labeled dictators, despots and war criminals.

"Saddam's military machine is partly a creation of the Western powers," according to American investigative journalist Murray Waas, who extensively researched and wrote about the Gulf Wars and earlier Middle East conflicts.

As is the case with many conspiracy theories, the theories surrounding Saddam Hussein are often extreme and unprovable. Some go so far as to say that Saddam, along with Osama Bin Laden, was CIA-trained; others suggest the real Saddam was killed long before he was *officially* put to death, and the man who was executed in 2006 was one of the Iraqi leader's doubles.

There's enough evidence to suggest the Iraqi leader had at least one double. But to our knowledge there's no evidence to prove that the man they executed wasn't the real deal.

However, at the very least, there's a question that needs to be asked. It is: Why did Ronald Reagan, George Bush, Donald Rumsfeld and Dick Cheney all have extensive dealings with Saddam Hussein?

THE IRAN-IRAQ WAR

During the Iran-Iraq War (1980-1988), it has been widely reported that governments of the US, Germany, France, the Soviet Union and the UK all sold Saddam vast quantities of weapons, including everything from missiles and armored vehicles to nerve gas and fighter planes.

Again, *war is just about business* to the global elite. And wars in the Middle East are big business.

Officially, the US was neutral in the Iran-Iraq conflict. Certainly, all White House and Pentagon statements made during that period confirm this supposed stance.

However, a US interests section cable since declassified under the Freedom of Information Act appears to radically contradict the official role of America in the conflict. It describes presidential envoy Donald Rumsfeld's planned meeting with Saddam Hussein. Expected talking points for the meeting included the Iran-Iraq War – a war which the cable states the US "would regard any major reversal of Iraq's fortunes as a strategic defeat for the West".

It wasn't just the US that profited from the Iran-Iraq War, of course. Numerous sources claim various industrialized nations were arming both sides during the conflict. For example, *the Washington Times* claimed that "France has been sleeping with Saddam for decades."

THAT INFAMOUS PHOTOGRAPH

One of the potential pieces of evidence that possibly confirms Saddam Hussein was a pawn of the West is a mysterious photograph he appears in with former US Secretary of Defense and then private businessman Donald Rumsfeld. This photo was taken in December 1983, at the height of the Iran-Iraq War, when

Rumsfeld met with Saddam on behalf of President Ronald Reagan. The meeting took place in the Iraqi dictator's Baghdad palace.

This has become a much talked about photo in conspiracy circles, primarily because Saddam Hussein's atrocities were known to the US Government by this point and the Reagan Administration claimed it fostered zero ties with Iraq.

Declassified documents reveal the main motivations of Rumsfeld's semi-secret meeting with Saddam were to discuss how to increase Iraqi oil production via new pipelines in the region and preventing arms sales to Iran by foreign countries – potential outcomes of which were both deemed beneficial to US interests.

In *The Orphan Factory*, our orphans are shown the photo of Rumsfeld and Saddam during a lecture in the fictitious Pedemont Orphanage. The following excerpt from this passage provides what we believe could be an accurate summation of the background to that historic photo shoot:

"That photo was taken in Baghdad in 1983 during the Iran-Iraq War," Kentbridge stated. "Officially, Donald Rumsfeld was sent as special envoy of President Reagan. The thing is though, people, Saddam was already a known war criminal by that stage."

When the revealing photo reached Nine, he studied it before flipping it over. On the reverse side was a handwritten question. It read: *Saddam Hussein = CIA Puppet?*

Nine turned the photo over again and inspected Rumsfeld's smiling face. The handshake looked suspiciously like a deal had gone down. Nine couldn't be certain, but nothing would surprise him given the game he understood secret organizations such as Omega orchestrated on the world stage.

The ninth orphan also understood that *game* **often involved an official story – usually presented to the media via politicians – that created a believable enough smokescreen to conceal the truth. And he was learning the truth nearly always had to do with money and power.**

In his 2006 memoir *Known and Unknown*, Rumsfeld denies any wrongdoing in the 1983 meeting with Saddam. He states his meeting with the Iraqi President "has been the subject of gossip, rumors, and crackpot conspiracy theories for more than a quarter of a century... Supposedly I had been sent to see Saddam by President Reagan either to negotiate a secret oil deal, to help arm Iraq, or to make Iraq an American client state. The truth is that our encounter was more straightforward and less dramatic."

However, various official US Government documents fly in the face of Rumsfeld's denials. For example, one declassified document points out that a major issue discussed in the meeting between Rumsfeld and Saddam was the "expansion of Iraqi pipeline facilities". Another declassified document – a cable from Charles H. Price II to the Department of State retrieved from the US Embassy in the UK – states that Rumsfeld encouraged "arrangements that might provide alternative transshipment routes for Iraq's oil, including pipelines through Saudi Arabia or to the Gulf of Aqaba in Jordan."

Beyond the photo itself, video recordings of the 1983 Rumsfeld-Saddam meeting have been posted on YouTube and other Internet sites in recent years. In these videos, Rumsfeld looks surprisingly at home in the Iraqi dictator's grand palace – as you'll see for yourself if you check them out.

"Conspiracy means there is more than one player knowingly engaged. But with that term (conspiracy), you think of all the people with the tin foil on their heads before you think of what it really means. So these people are often discounted before you even hear them ... I think the best way to hide is to do it in broad daylight and in public. So, a lot of your present-day conspiracies are literally major multi-national corporations working with governments, including America's, to extract minerals from countries with ridiculous contracts to oil."
–Henry Rollins. Excerpt from an interview with the Swerve
Magazine.

THE GULF WARS

In 1989, President George H. W. Bush signed a National Security Directive ordering closer ties with Iraq. Yet conversely, around the same time, Bush condemned Saddam Hussein in press interviews – like the one in which he accused the Iraqi leader as being "worse than Hitler."

The following year, in 1990, the First Gulf War began and the US invaded Iraq.

It was one of the most surreal wars ever, and few if any journalists seemed to be able to accurately describe what caused it. Other than the obvious, that is. We refer of course to Iraq's invasion of Kuwait – something countries do to each other with frightening regularity and with little or no interference from the international community.

Someone said the First Gulf War was like a movie without a screenwriter. Can't remember who it was who said that. Wait a minute…oh yes, it was us! Certainly, it seemed to lack a coherent storyline or plot.

Some journos observed that the war was about overthrowing a dictator, which didn't happen if you recall, while others said it was fighting to free the Iraqi people, which didn't happen either.

As former Pentagon defense analyst Pierre Sprey told Congress, "The shallow, Nintendo view of the war on TV was false. It was created by hand-picked video tapes and shamelessly doctored statistics."

Let's return to the June 1998 article Washington Peace Center intern Steve Pickering wrote for the center. It was curiously headlined *The Making of an Enemy: Saddam Hussein*. In this insightful article, which was written in the interim between the First and Second Gulf Wars, Pickering goes to great lengths to acknowledge the Iraqi leader's war crimes, but also mentions US "foreign policy propaganda" and states the US had reasons for "demonizing Saddam Hussein". He claims those reasons had nothing to do with fighting for the freedom of the Iraqi people.

In the article, Pickering goes on to describe how throughout the period of the Iran-Iraq conflict "United States foreign policy was firmly in support of Iraq". During this time, the Soviet Union, the UK, the US and various other major nations, all saw their (mainly oil) interests being threatened. As "the war shifted in Iran's favor," these superpowers and industrialized nations suddenly realized if Iran defeated the Iraqi regime, "Iraq would have become a mirror of the political situation seen in Iran".

"In order to tip the scales back in the favor of Iraq," Pickering continues, "the international community began to supply technologically advanced weapons, credit facilities and important military information to Iraq."

Pickering also explains how the West saw its Middle Eastern interests threatened again in 1990 when Iraq invaded Kuwait. Only this time, Iraq was in the position Iran had formerly been in where they were the ones threatening Western interests.

And thus, Pickering concludes, Western media suddenly informed the public of "the horrors of Saddam Hussein, of his despotic control, of his endless paranoid quest for power".

From the many years he'd spent in the Omega Agency, the special agent understood there were no obvious good guys or bad guys on the world stage. Contrary to the PR spin generated within Congress and spoon-fed to the well-meaning American public by a gullible or at least malleable media, Kentbridge also knew there were no clear sides anymore. As he often told the orphans, patriotism was a useless emotion because the modern world was no longer shaped by countries or governments. In fact, nations had long since been superseded by the vast spider web of elite conspirators spanning the globe.

–The Orphan Factory

THE IRAQ WAR

The plot thickens when we come to the Iraq War (aka the Second Gulf War). That's the conflict that followed the George W. Bush Administration's erroneous allegation that Saddam Hussein's Iraq was hiding weapons of mass destruction (WMD).

Conspiracy theorists and opponents of that war are pretty unanimous in their opinion of the WMD allegation. Most view it as a trumped-up justification to invade Iraq. Whether those two factions are right or wrong about that is still up for debate. However, we all know that weapons of mass destruction were never found despite the best efforts of the Bush Administration and the UN weapon inspectors on the ground.

Further allegations leading up to the American-led coalition's invasion of Iraq in 2003 included the never-proven and apparently unfounded accusation that Saddam was harboring al Qaeda terrorists and, of course, that old chestnut that the Iraqi Government was responsible for the most despicable human rights abuses.

There's no doubting the validity of the latter allegation. Under Saddam, Iraq had a terrible and well documented reputation for abuses of human rights. *However*, the same could be said of numerous other countries – then and now.

Remember Rwanda? In just three months, in 1994, an estimated 800,000 Rwandans (mainly Tutsis) were killed in one of the worst cases of genocide in the 20th Century.

But where were the Coalition Forces then? They were conspicuous by their absence. Could it have something to do with the fact that Rwanda has few natural resources and little strategic value?

Iraq on the other hand was, and is, almost literally swimming in oil. According to Wikipedia, Iraq has 143 billion barrels of proven oil reserves, which ranks it second in the world behind Saudi Arabia for reserves of the precious *black gold*.

Starting to get the picture?

Even Saddam Hussein's capture and subsequent execution in

2006 sparked a flood of conspiracy theories, throughout the Middle East in particular.

Theories to emerge from the Arab world have ranged from Saddam being an agent of America, waging war against Iran to help out the US, and even the suggestion that Saddam was already a prisoner of the Americans who, for PR reasons, opted to delay his *capture.*

This last conspiracy theory was highlighted in WND Weekly's online news site beneath the heading *The mother of all conspiracy theories.* In an article dated December 19, 2003, WND quotes Middle East Media Research Institute senior analyst Dr. Nimrod Raphaeli who, it says, "explains the dramatic flowering of fanciful explanations for Saddam's capture".

Dr. Raphaeli is quoted as saying, "Almost every calamity that adversely affects the Arab world prompts conspiracy theories that are quickly woven into intricate shapes and patterns to demonstrate innocence and blame others for the calamity. In recent times this was demonstrated by conspiracy theories surrounding the September 11th attack and the terrorist attacks inside Saudi Arabia. The capture of Saddam Hussein served as yet another new cause celebre generating, to paraphrase Saddam's own words, 'the mother of all conspiracies'."

※ ※ ※

It seems clear there's enough smoke to indicate the presence of fire regarding the West's demonizing and *usage* of Saddam Hussein, in particular by the US. And that fire would prove that at least some of the conspiracy theories regarding the Iraqi leader and the Gulf Wars are true, or at least very close to the mark.

Then again, we've never been to Iraq and we don't have a direct line to the White House. Nor do we know anyone in the Bush family. So again we ask, why listen to us?

19

BENEATH THE SURFACE

"The secret facility was not only off limits to the general public, it was completely off the US Government's radar. In fact, like everything else connected with Omega, knowledge of its existence was beyond any government."

–*The Ninth Orphan*

In 1998, one of us (James) took a guided tour through the Pentagon, the US Department of Defense headquarters in Arlington County, Virginia. It was quite an eye-opener.

The tour guide was a young military staffer and the other 50 or so tour party members included a chubby, garrulous boy of about eight or nine who spoke with a southern drawl and was constantly eating. Between mouthfuls of food, the boy interrupted the tour guide's running commentary in a loud voice, asking, "What about the levels below the Pentagon, sir?"

The tour guide politely but firmly replied, "Son, there are no levels below the Pentagon, what you see is all there is."

That reply seemed to satisfy the boy until about five minutes later he repeated the question and received a near identical response. This same question-same answer pattern continued for the remainder of the tour, visibly raising the young staffer's aggravation levels every time he was interrupted and forced to answer the persistent boy.

In all likelihood the boy had watched TV shows or movies

referencing the conspiracy theory which insists there are miles of tunnels, subterranean levels and underground bunkers below the Pentagon, suggesting what's seen above ground is merely the tip of the iceberg.

If you're wondering how the previously mentioned Splinter Civilization with all its suppressed technologies, manpower and equipment could exist without the mass public's knowledge then consider what's below the surface. Literally.

That's right folks, we're talking about the hidden *black world* beneath our feet – another favorite theory of a million and one members of the Tinfoil Hat Network, but also a theory many genuine researchers buy into as well.

In our international thriller series – you guessed it, *The Orphan Trilogy* – the shadowy Omega Agency's secret headquarters are one mile below ground. This decision for the storyline was inspired by longstanding rumors of military bunkers and enormous underground facilities not known to the general public.

One book critic commented at the end of her review of our series as follows: "Quite thought-provoking books, too, when you ponder on what the world's super powers are really up to in their underground bunkers!"

That comment got us thinking. What the hell are the powers-that-be doing below ground and why are they building such facilities?

In the course of researching this particular book, we came across a number of convincing sources that appear to confirm the existence of at least some secret subterranean facilities. These sources include declassified US Government files, university reports, Wikileaks' documents and eyewitness accounts from common citizens who stumbled across such bases, as well as interviews with, and testimonials from, former military personnel who claim to have worked in underground bunkers.

Like most theories covered in this book, we still don't necessarily have any definitive answers to offer. That's the nature of conspiracy theories, folks. Nevertheless, sifting through the myriad of reports, whispers and rumors of underground facilities sure was enlightening, sobering and fun all at the same time!

"Omega's HQ did not show up on any maps or satellite images. That was because it was a subterranean facility hidden deep beneath an abandoned hydro dam in south-west Illinois. Built in 1978, the existence of the underground facility was unknown to the American public. More importantly, it was unknown to the US Government, or any other government for that matter."
                                            –The Orphan Factory

D.U.M.B.

Remember in chapter 7 we covered examples of suppressed science – like Nikola Tesla's technologies and other little-known inventions that we suggested the Splinter Civilization may have in their possession? Well, if we are correct and a more scientifically advanced *offshoot* of humanity co-exists on the planet right now, then it's a safe bet they maintain their secrecy by going about most of their business in underground bases. And not only in America, but most likely all over the world.

Where else short of colonizing another planet could they hide the required plant, machinery and equipment – and the manpower to operate it – away from the prying eyes of Joe Citizen, investigative journalists and inquisitive everyday people like us?

Worth noting is that security at the entrances to *known and acknowledged* underground facilities is at least equal to security at the border checkpoints that separate nations. This seems to add some weight to the theory that we are dealing with a Splinter Civilization and this small but powerful group have purposefully divided themselves from official society, or from the world as we know it. More correctly, the global elite have separated *us* from their society because they're able to operate in both worlds – above and below ground.

We accept the concept of such a breakaway group may still seem hard to fathom, but consider once more the aforementioned comments given by Daniel K. Inouye, US Senator from Hawaii, in his testimony at the 1987 Iran-Contra Hearings. "There exists a shadowy government," Inouye said, "with its own Air Force, its own Navy, its own fundraising mechanism, and the ability to pursue its own ideas of national interest, free from all checks and balances, and free from the law itself."

According to our research, this Splinter Civilization was able to grow so powerful and remain largely below the radar due to a number of complex events, which all intersected mid to late last century.

One was the apparent arrival of extra-terrestrials en masse, allegedly commencing around the time of the widely reported yet still classified Roswell UFO incident in New Mexico in 1947.

Another was the scientific improvements in tunnelling and digging technologies from the 1950's onwards. Again, one of us (Lance) can speak with a little authority on this, having gone through the Mount Isa Mines school of mining in the Outback of Queensland, Australia, working as an underground miner back in the late 1960's and following mining developments around the world with interest ever since.

The third reason was the Cold War whose 'national security' demands and the resulting unhealthy culture of secrecy it gave rise to encouraged governments to be less accountable to their citizens.

These coinciding factors all created a *perfect storm* for underground bases to be built and managed by the Military Industrial Complex and intelligence agencies as well as private corporations.

Those who have researched unacknowledged subterranean facilities are almost unanimous in their belief that the bases are funded by black budgets financed by a combination of banksters, drug wars and profits from (mainly mineral) resources plundered from unwitting Third World countries.

The US program for building these underground bunkers is

known as DUMB, or Deep Underground Military Bases. DUMB has apparently been in operation since the late 1940's and there are now said to be hundreds of such bases in almost every state in mainland America.

MAYBE THAT FAT KID WASN'T SO DUMB AFTER ALL

In the 21st Century, it's basically common knowledge and certainly widely accepted that the Pentagon has multiple levels of enormous bunkers and an immense network of tunnels beneath its visible exterior.

It makes complete sense, too. You'd expect the Department of Defense's HQ of the world's greatest superpower would have multiple access routes and escape tunnels to accommodate sudden evacuations and other emergencies.

It's a similar situation in Washington D.C. where it has been widely reported by mainstream media that there's a vast tunnel system below the capital. And it's our understanding that at any given time there are at hundreds of security personnel patrolling the tunnels, on foot or with the aid of motorized vehicles, beneath the city.

Very likely many of D.C.'s tunnels lead to and from the White House. The often-told stories of Marilyn Monroe being sneaked in and out of the White House via underground tunnels to meet with JFK would seem to confirm this. Such tales reveal the capital's extensive tunnel system enabled Marilyn to be the President's mistress without much scandal – for a period, at least.

"The covert underground infrastructure serves many functions. Among these are strategic storage of materials and weapons, clandestine research and production facilities, alternant basing for military personnel and equipment, surface environment control systems (atmospheric lensing, synthetic earthquakes, weather modification, civilian population control, etc)."

–Dr. Steven J. Smith. *Excerpt from the paper* Underground Infrastructure – The missing forty trillion dollars.

UNDERGROUND CITIES

By all appearances, the US Government is building underground cities in preparation for a coming catastrophe they seem certain is imminent. Whether the elite believe it will be some kind of nuclear apocalypse or a religious, Armageddon-type scenario, nobody knows. At least, nobody we know knows.

In episode 4 of the third season of *Conspiracy Theory with Jesse Ventura*, former Minnesota Governor Ventura and his son Tyrel Ventura, along with Sean Stone, son of Oscar-winning filmmaker Oliver Stone, travel to the Ozarks, a mountainous region of the central United States, to investigate rumors of underground developments there. They find the entrance to what appears to be an underground city being built inside a mountain.

Despite heavy fortifications – and no doubt aided by Ventura's status as former Governor of Minnesota – the team gain vehicular entry to the massive underground facility, which they discover covers an area of 50 square miles! As they drive around freely, they quickly deduce it is indeed an underground city in the making, complete with offices, warehouses, manufacturing plants, indoor farming facilities as well as stockpiles of food, water and crude oil.

"It's like they've got door-to-door transportation for the chosen few when it's time to move inside and weld those doors shut. I don't necessarily think it'd be a good place to live, but it would be a good place to survive."
–Jesse Ventura, from episode 4, season 3, of Conspiracy Theory with Jesse Ventura.

WHAT'S HAPPENING BELOW GROUND?

There's a long list of claims regarding the nefarious activities conducted by the global elite and their *pawns* in these underground bases. Some say they have clandestine prisons where officially designated *missing persons* and others who have dropped off the grid are held captive; some believe human-alien joint ventures are taking place in these bases to further black technologies or to advance certain species.

When it comes to suppressed science, the hit sci-fi television series *Warehouse 13*, which at the time of writing is still on TV and into its fifth season, probably best portrays the secret science bunker concept. The basic plot has two US Secret Service Agents assigned to a top-secret government warehouse to protect scientific discoveries and radical technologies invented by Nikola Tesla and others – none of which the public are aware. The premise of a largely underground warehouse storing suppressed discoveries and inventions is based on conspiracy theories that have been swirling around for decades.

There have also been reports from former military engineers and government geologists about supersonic transportation systems underground. Who knows, maybe the global elite travel between cities and countries below ground, utilizing the underworld's rumored faster transportation methods?

It has also been claimed that radical biological experiments take place in the Splinter Civilization's underworld. The kind that the laws of the land above ground don't allow – such as unsanctioned forms of genetic engineering, human cloning and illegal drug testing by pharmaceutical corporations. Some conspiracy theorists who believe complex viruses like HIV/AIDS, SARS and Ebola are all manmade, have even theorized that these viruses are manufactured and tested in underground facilities before being unleashed above ground.

Neo-Nazi technologies are also said to exist below ground. This apparently dates back to the Project Paperclip scientists who, as we mention in chapter 12, were secretly ushered in to America immediately after WW2. Werner von Braun, the German-turned naturalized American and Godfather of NASA's space rocket program, is one that many researchers have named in relation to underground bases. These Nazi Paperclip scientists were supposedly crucial to the development and construction of the underground bases and tunnels that now exist beneath American soil.

If that sounds farfetched, remember it's well-documented that von Braun and other Paperclip Nazis built V2 rockets for Hitler in large underground missile facilities in their German homeland in the 1940's.

Wildest of all, are the numerous conspiracy theories that maintain many of these underground bases – of which there are rumored to be thousands worldwide – are full of captive men, women and children. Some suggest the captives may have been *taken* from above ground, which may partially account for the hundreds of thousands of missing persons reported annually around the world who are never found; others suggest the captives are human clones designed to spend their lives enslaved underground to further the global elite's agendas; and still others suggest some captives are used as human guinea pigs in radical science experiments conducted by scientists working for the Splinter Civilization.

And then there's the intriguing statements made by one Philip Schneider, an American geologist who, until his untimely death, also claimed to be an ex-government military engineer. Schneider said while he was involved in constructing additional bunkers in one underground base in New Mexico, he discovered aliens conducted horrific experiments on people detained in bunkers miles below the earth's surface. (More on Schneider later in this chapter).

About now you may be asking, "Why are these guys talking about aliens as if their existence on earth is a documented fact?" Or if you've read *The Orphan Trilogy*, you may be thinking, "There's no mention of aliens in those novels, so why are you guys suddenly hitting me with all this ET stuff now?"

Fair questions, but keep in mind we have no strong opinion either way as to whether aliens are with us or even if they exist. All we are doing is repeating the conspiracy theories out there concerning underground bases. It just so happens a lot of rumors and reports – some reliable, some not – on such bases involve either aliens or alien technologies. In many instances, the theories surrounding underground bunkers and aliens cannot be separated.

"It is the most well kept 'secret' of all time! The earth is a much grander, mysterious and wondrous place than anyone could ever imagine in our wildest dreams! If true, an entire 'second' earth exists right below our feet! Not just in the US but nearly every point on this earth hosts an entire network of caverns of vast size and depth; honey-combed thru out the planet! There is a vast and deep underground world where advanced technology can be used freely. Where people can escape to and where all manner of secrets can be kept. Some very important testimonies and documents are available from certain 'military' sources (confirming) that this is real!"
–ArraiEl (Yahoo member), published on the Yahoo Voices website on 25 October 2011 in an article titled Deep Cavern Systems Worldwide.

COMBINING ADVANCED TECHNOLOGIES
AND MOTHER NATURE

While the vast majority of underground bases are said to have been constructed by the Military Industrial Complex, it seems most are also built inside or directly above natural, pre-existing cave networks. Either that or the constructors have made use of miles of abandoned mine tunnels and shafts.

This would make sense as those who design and build such bases would naturally look to utilize the best of nature and man – and possibly extra-terrestrial civilizations as well.

When it comes to American underground bases, this may not be as crazy as it first seems as much of mainland America is dotted with sinkholes, abandoned mines and enormous caves and cavern networks.

The word *cave* usually conjures up images of small caverns or fissures in the ground. But the reality is there are giant underground caves extending many, many miles underground. Some are said to be *bottomless* – and who are we to argue? For all we know, a cave or cave system could start in the wilds of Montana and end in Alaska.

Many caves, including one nicknamed the *Subterranean Grand Canyon*, are so vast only their entrances have been explored, while others – it's universally agreed – have yet to be discovered let alone explored. And many of these giant cave systems contain rare rock formations and unusual geology, significant underground rivers, lakes and seas with unique species of *cavefish* in them, as well as abundances of gemstones, crystals and gold. The *Er Wang Dong* cave system, in China, even has its own climate system complete with clouds and rain!

One example of the scale of underground cave systems is the extensive system known as *Craighead Caverns* in Sweetwater, Tennessee. According to Wikipedia, Craighead Caverns are "best known for containing the United States' largest and the world's second largest non-subglacial underground lake, *The Lost Sea*. In addition to the lake, the caverns contain an abundance of crystal clusters called anthodites, stalactites and stalagmites, plus a waterfall."

The Lechuguilla Cave in New Mexico is another example. Only officially discovered in 1986, Lechuguilla is the seventh-longest *explored* cave in the world with 138.3 miles of confirmed cave networks, although more sections of the cave continue to be found.

Given the scale of these naturally-occurring subterranean cavities, perhaps the theory of building in, around or on top of such geological systems when constructing underground bases would not only seem prudent, but practical.

It's also worth noting that access to many of the world's largest caves, including the Lechuguilla Cave, is restricted to approved scientific researchers and government employees. This fact may dovetail with the conspiracy theory that says some of the largest caves are either controlled by the government or lie below completely restricted lands like Nevada's Area 51, for example. Then again, denying public access to such caves could simply be a matter of safety or conservation concerns, or both.

MOUNT WEATHER

An hour's drive from Washington D.C. is *Mount Weather*, a massive underground complex in the state of Virginia. It's basically a military base within a hollowed-out mountain.

As UK newspaper *The Guardian* reports in an article dated August 28, 2006, the underground emergency operations facility was "originally built to house governmental officials in the event of a full-scale nuclear exchange". However, with the Cold War over, the article went on to speculate that "as the Bush administration wages its war on terror, Mount Weather is believed to house a 'shadow government' made up of senior Washington officials on temporary assignment".

No outsiders have ever been allowed inside Mount Weather, but Richard Pollock, an author and a regular contributor for

Progressive Magazine, interviewed several individuals who claimed to have previously been employed on site within the mountain. The interviewees said the base had its own lake with fresh spring water, independent power generation, cafeterias, hydroponic gardens, hospitals and transportation system as well as residential apartments. They also said Mount Weather has its own fire and police departments and, as you can no doubt imagine, its own laws too.

Taking the speculation about a shadow government in *The Guardian* article one step further, Pollock reported the underground facility has its own replica government, which apparently is every bit as comprehensive as the official government above ground.

DULCE BASE

One of the most commonly referred to sites mentioned by underground base researchers is an unconfirmed one said to exist below the small and almost entirely Native American-populated town of Dulce, in New Mexico.

There are many stories of government collaborations with aliens in *Dulce Base* where all manner of exotic research is apparently conducted within its seven or more vast subterranean levels and numerous tunnel offshoots. By all accounts this includes advanced mind control and psychotronic warfare experiments as well as genetic engineering.

Some Dulce researchers believe levels 5 and below are occupied entirely by alien personnel and house technologies also alien to this planet. The deepest sections of the underground base are apparently connected to an extensive cave system, which as we've mentioned seems to be common theme for most underground bases.

Dulce is believed to have interconnected bases in New Mexico, including the rumored ones at Sandia Base and White Sands, with tunnel systems linking them all. Perhaps tellingly, part of the aforementioned almost 140 mile-long and still not fully discovered cavern system known as The Lechuguilla Cave is said to extend under some of the bases Dulce connects to.

Dulce Base first came to the public's attention in 1979 when New Mexico businessman Paul Bennowitz was convinced he had intercepted communications between antigravity flying machines and underground installations in the area. In the 1980's, Bennowitz claimed he'd discovered the Dulce Base. The story spread like wildfire in conspiracy circles and the UFO community in particular.

In the 1990's, US commercial airline pilot John Lear, the son of *Lear Jet* designer William P. Lear, also claimed he had confirmed the existence of Dulce Base, *independently* of Bennowitz. However, this is tempered by the writings of political scientist Michael Barkun. The professor emeritus of political science at New York's Syracuse University believes that Cold War underground missile installations in New Mexico falsely excited ufologists and conspiracy theorists. In Barkun's opinion there's nothing else there to support rumors of an underground base at Dulce or rumors of supposed human-alien collaborations.

But many Dulce locals, as well as quite a few independent researchers, continue to maintain there is a large site beneath the town.

Norio Hayakawa, a New Mexico resident who has independently studied Dulce Base for decades, wrote an article dated March 28, 2007 on the Rense.com website, which detailed his extensive research into the Dulce rumors over the years.

Hayawaka mentions in the article how in 1990 he worked with a visiting Japanese television crew to attempt to confirm the alleged existence of an "underground U.S./alien joint bio-lab" beneath Dulce. He also mentions that when interviewing locals with the Japanese TV crew, he and the Japanese were detained by the town's Police Chief, Hoyt Velarde, without any valid reason being given. According to Hayawaka, Chief Velarde warned them, "Don't you ever ask any more questions regarding such a base. I have nothing to do with it and I do not want to talk about it!"

Hayawaka implies that Velarde's choice of words seemed to indicate the Dulce Base was known to the police.

Upon returning to Dulce in 2007 to investigate further, Hayawaka says "the son of the former head of the Dulce Police Department took me to the site of *Project Gasbuggy*. Project Gasbuggy was a rather 'strange' 1967 government project which involved a large underground nuclear explosion (29 kilotons of TNT) deep inside the high plateau area 25 miles south of Dulce, allegedly to release natural gas from deep under the ground. It was a joint project with El Paso Natural Gas Company. What is not frequently mentioned in association with this curious project was that the huge nuclear explosion had created, deep, huge underground extensive caverns all over the area along with extensive natural "tunnels"."

Unsurprisingly, Dulce Base has featured regularly in popular culture, including an episode of *Conspiracy Theory with Jesse Ventura* titled *Ancient Aliens*, Pittacus Lore's bestselling young adult book series *The Lorien Legacies*, an episode of the History Channel program *UFO Hunters*, the 2012 video game *Ghost Recon: Future Soldier* and the comic series *The Invisibles* in which Dulce Base is shown to house a secret vaccine for AIDS.

THE MONTAUK PROJECT

The abandoned Montauk Air Force Station in Camp Hero State Park, Montauk Point, Long Island, NY, has long been the source of many an exotic conspiracy theory, most of which usually involve underground locations. For example, it's rumored that Paperclip Nazi scientists worked at the mysterious Long Island military facility commonly known as *Montauk*.

The area takes its name from the region's original inhabitants, the Montauk Indians, who according to the courts no longer exist as a tribe even though remaining Montauk tribal members insist they do still exist. But that's a whole other conspiracy theory!

Many independent researchers have described Montauk as a

secret research facility where they claim psy-ops like remote viewing and time travel experiments took place for decades before the site was eventually shut down. Some conspiracy theorists even say there was a more advanced version of the infamous *Philadelphia Experiment* conducted at Montauk. You may recall the original experiment allegedly rendered a US Navy vessel invisible to enemy radar and listening devices – a story denied by the US Navy. These top-secret experiments were known as *the Montauk Project* and were reportedly carried out in nine subterranean levels beneath the abandoned Air Force station.

Quite a few Montauk Point locals have reported sightings of high-tech equipment being taken underground, and tunnels and subterranean bases beneath the region have long been rumored within the tightknit community.

In the 2010 TV documentary *Inside Secret Government Warehouses*, produced by the US cable network Syfy, the filmmakers went to Montauk to see if they could confirm the existence of underground facilities. No tunnels or underground facilities were found. However, ground-penetrating radar devices were also used and, although not completely conclusive, they appeared to show evidence of some kind of underground chamber directly below ground – a conclusion confirmed by the independent radar technicians operating the devices.

The TV crew also revealed a vast network of tunnels beneath nearby historic resort hotel Montauk Manor. Many commentators believe these tunnels lead directly to the Air Force station and were built as part of the mysterious Montauk Project.

OTHER CONFIRMED AND RUMORED UNDERGROUND BASES

Cheyenne Mountain is NORAD's confirmed underground bunker at Colorado Springs, in Colorado. It was developed during the Cold War complete with missile defence systems and advanced space technologies, and is still in operation today. The North

American Aerospace Defense Command (NORAD) facility is basically a self-sustained *city* built inside the mountain. Some conspiracy theorists say tunnels extend from Cheyenne Mountain to other underground bases around the nation including Denver and Dulce Base.

Denver International Airport (DIA) is said to have an underground base concealed directly below its tarmac. Around the airport there are numerous fenced-in areas covered in barbed wire. To our eyes at least this seems a tad unusual even for an international airport. What's also strange about DIA is there are Masonic symbols everywhere and freaky artwork depicting cities ablaze, women in coffins and dead babies adorning the airport's walls.

Supposedly, there's also an underground base below the town of *Kokomo*, Indiana. For over a decade, Kokomo locals have reported hearing a hum coming from below ground – a hum that's so extreme some have become sick. It has even forced some residents to leave town. Following numerous complaints, the mysterious humming sound has been formally investigated, but investigations have not revealed a likely cause.

After living with the problem for many years and sharing information on the grapevine, many Kokomo locals now believe the hum is actually vibrations caused by machinery operating far below ground. This tallies with the beliefs of independent underground base researchers who insist large-scale subterranean excavations and tunnelling are occurring beneath Kokomo.

Many have also claimed there's a vast underground complex beneath *Area 51*, in Nevada, and that it also contains (perhaps literally) out-of-this-world technologies. (See chapter 29 for a detailed analysis of Area 51).

"Since the early 1960's, the American citizenry have been the unwitting victims of government fraud, perpetrated on a scale so vast that it staggers the imagination ... The

*total amount exceeds 40 trillion dollars ... The government
has built an entirely new underground civilization ... In
this new society, there is no poverty, no crime or illicit
drug use. In this new society, healthcare is affordable,
energy is free, public transport is efficient. And you, the
American tax payer have paid for it all."*
–Dr. Steven J. Smith. Excerpt from the paper Underground
Infrastructure – The missing forty trillion dollars.

SECRET UNDERGROUND SITES AROUND THE WORLD

Mezhgorye is an enormous underground military facility in
Russia's Ural Mountains, close to the city of Mezhgorye. The
sprawling subterranean facility apparently required more than
10,000 workers to build it and spans over 400 miles! The military
site has never been acknowledged by the Russian Government, or
by the Soviet one before it. However, America received
intelligence confirming its existence in 1992, according to an
article *The New York Times* ran in 1996.

Some underground researchers believe the *Vatican* also holds
subterranean secrets. And we're not speaking of the known
basement areas like the Vatican empire's Necropolis or the Secret
Archives, but rather an ancient network of tunnels, chambers and
mysterious buildings miles beneath it.

Down in the hidden bowels of the sovereign Catholic state,
bizarre ceremonies are said to be performed by Vatican cardinals,
bishops and priests. Ceremonies which have nothing to do with
Catholicism and everything to do with the religions of ancient
Egypt and Babylon. But that, too, is a whole other conspiracy
theory and something probably best left to bestselling author Dan
Brown.

The mother of all underground bases may actually exist in the
Southern Hemisphere. In the heart of Australia, the underground
facility known as *Pine Gap* is known about, yet not known about.

Officially a joint defence and satellite tracking station, it has been reported by local media that nobody in the Australian Federal Parliament, not even the Prime Minister, has any meaningful information about the US-run base. Local Outback residents have reported seeing massive quantities of food and supplies being delivered for what could be an enormous city below ground. Apparently Pine Gap was constructed on top of the deepest drilling hole in Australia and is about five miles deep.

THE CURIOUS CASE OF PHILIP SCHNEIDER

One of the most out-there, yet hard-to-dismiss testimonials supporting the existence of underground bases and the rumored ET's some of them hide, is that of American Philip Schneider (1947-1996). Although very few records exist on the man and his military career, Schneider stated he was a geologist and former government military engineer. More controversially, he also claimed to have been involved in a firefight that broke out with Extra-terrestrials while he was building additions to the underground military base at Dulce, New Mexico, in 1979.

Schneider said he was one of only three survivors in the humans vs. aliens battle in which 66 US Delta Force soldiers were killed. Although Schneider survived, he had severe flesh wounds and burns to his entire body – wounds he claimed were the result of some kind of radiation weapon the ET's fired at him.

In the mid-1990's, Schneider began giving lectures all over the world about what he said was the absolute truth regarding ET's living below Earth's surface. During one such lecture, at the Preparedness Expo in November of 1995, he said, "Right now military technology is about 1200 years more advanced than public state technology."

During another lecture, Schneider mentioned how in 1954 the Eisenhower administration disregarded the Constitution by signing a treaty with the ET's. The treaty was apparently named

The 1954 Greada Treaty. In the same lecture, he mentioned a human-looking alien who was "one of the aliens who has been working for the Pentagon for the last 58 years." He then produced a photograph of this supposed alien and showed it to the audience and the cameraman filming the lecture.

Providing a possible insight into the Splinter Civilization's monetary resources, Schneider claimed that since 1940's the US Government had spent almost *one quadrillion dollars* building hundreds of underground bases all over America.

In the course of delivering these lectures – some of which were filmed and are available for anyone to see on the Internet – Schneider displayed visible injuries, including missing fingers and chest wounds, which he claimed were a legacy of the battle with the ET's. To back up his statements, Schneider also produced what he claimed were classified photographs, ancient alien fossils and non-Earth metal ores retrieved from Dulce Base.

In his last recorded lecture, Schneider told his audience there had been 13 murder attempts on his life by government agents intent on preventing him continuing to inform the public of the existence of ET's. He said he was speaking out because, "I love my country more than I love my own life."

Schneider was found dead in his apartment in Wilsonville, Oregon, on January 17, 1996, several days after he'd died.

As with everything else in Schneider's life, his death was also shrouded in mystery. Initially, the Clackamas County Coroner's office said he'd died of either a stroke or a heart attack. Then they changed their story to suicide. It's also worth noting that all the geologist's documents relating to underground bases, as well as the alleged alien artifacts that he'd begun showing to audiences, went missing and have never been seen since.

Cynthia Drayer, Schneider's ex-wife, is one of many who firmly believe Schneider was murdered to prevent him from leaking anything more about the ET-human interactions occurring below ground.

An interesting footnote to Philip Schneider's life is that he claimed his father, Oscar Schneider, revealed to him on his deathbed that he was not the German Jewish immigrant he'd always proclaimed to be, but was actually an ex-Nazi. Schneider's father also apparently revealed he was a Paperclip scientist. Actually, make that a *pre*-Paperclip scientist as he was hustled in to America at the *start* of WW2 to conduct scientific research for the US Government long before Project Paperclip even existed.

Schneider's father went on to tell him that as an American scientist he was involved in the Philadelphia Experiment. He also told his son about other exotic and clandestine government projects that may have included early underground bases, although Schneider couldn't be sure.

Schneider said he was shocked his father revealed all this to him on his deathbed. By all accounts there wasn't time to compare both of their experiences before Schneider Senior died.

Whether Schneider's father was in any way responsible for the top-secret military clearance levels his son attained or indeed whether Philip Schneider's own claims about working in underground bases are true, remain pure speculation and will probably never be proven or disproven.

As one would expect, without undeniable evidence or absolute proof left behind to confirm Schneider's story, there are as many skeptics as believers. The former include some who insist they've debunked all his claims about underground bases and ET's.

On the other hand, it could reasonably be argued undeniable evidence is exceedingly difficult to obtain when it comes to proving the Splinter Civilization exists and is in our midst.

"The North Atlantic seems to be very significant and is possibly the largest sea base in European waters. Other reported underwater bases are in South America waters – in the areas of Puerto Rico and Brazil – in Antarctica and other deep unobserved areas of ocean."
–Tony Dodd. Former British police officer.

UNDERSEA BASES

Could there also be secret military facilities under our ocean floors?

In 1969, the Stanford Research Institute in Menlo Park, California, published a report titled *The Feasibility of manned in-bottom bases*. The report states, "The construction of thirty in-bottom bases within the ocean floors is technically and economically feasible … The cost of such a base program would be about $2.7 billion".

Now keep in mind that was in 1969. So given the multi-trillion dollar black budgets numerous researchers claim the US Government and its agencies have access to annually, who is to say undersea bases weren't financed and built as long ago as the 1970's?

Interestingly, the Stanford Research Institute's 1969 report also states that deep submergence vehicles would need to be developed to build undersea bases. The following year it was announced Lockheed had launched deep sea vehicles with the necessary capabilities to do just that.

According to a lecture that independent researcher Dr. Richard Sauder gave at the Xcon 2004 conference, there could easily be US-built undersea bases in the Persian Gulf, the North Sea and the Gulf of Mexico.

Dr. Sauder, author of the 1996 book *Underground Bases and Tunnels: What is the Government Trying to Hide?*, also spoke of the US Navy's undersea test and research center off the coast of Andros Island, in the Bahamas. He speculated that the facility, which is known as AUTEC (Atlantic Undersea Test and Evaluation Centre), could be a front for an undersea complex of secret bases.

On May 1, 2008, UK newspaper *The Telegraph* ran an article about China's underwater sea bases. The article, which contained satellite imagery of base openings on Hainan Island, China, states there's "a network of underground tunnels at the Sanya base on the southern tip of Hainan island". The article also states that the tunnels allow Chinese submarines to travel out into the ocean from the base completely undetected.

"Of even greater concern to the Pentagon," the article continues, "are massive tunnel entrances, estimated to be 60ft high, built into hillsides around the base ... While it has been known that China might be developing an underground base at Sanya, the pictures provide the first proof of the base's existence and the rapid progress made".

Although likely to be more complex and costly to build than bases beneath land, undersea bases would obviously provide even more secure hideaways for the Splinter Civilization to go about their business. It's unlikely China and the US would be the only countries building undersea bases for their naval advancements and other purposes.

We'd be remiss not to add that a few conspiracy theorists – most likely of the Tinfoil Hat variety – believe that senior Nazis built an undersea *colony* beneath Antarctica and even lived there after WW2 ended.

This base was supposedly at or off the coast of New Swabia, which was explored and claimed as a territory by Germany just before WW2 – in early 1939. The Antarctic region was named after that expedition's ship, the *Ms Schwabenland*. However, the region's official exploration is where the facts end and the (possibly lunatic) theories begin.

One such theory insists that hundreds of Nazi flying saucers were stored in the New Swabia undersea colony. Not only that but a secret *nuclear* war occurred there in the late 1980's between the US and the surviving Nazis, causing the ozone hole over the South Pole and "false" global warming issues!

You gotta love the Tinfoil Hat Network. What they lack in anything resembling evidence, they make up in spades for with blockbuster-style entertainment.

❀ ❀ ❀

Admittedly, we have no idea how many of these undersea and underground bases are real and how many are pure fiction. Nor do we know the extent of activity in the *known* subterranean bases or whether ET's are present.

Anyone desperate enough to learn the truth could approach scientists, engineers and military personnel who have worked at confirmed underground bases and try to prize information out of them. Truthseekers could also go to areas where subterranean bases are rumored to exist and use ground penetrating radar devices to see if manmade levels, structures and machinery show up below.

However, anyone considering such action should probably keep in mind that the line between independent investigator and conspiracy crackpot is often a thin one... Actually, maybe we should have kept that in mind ourselves before we agreed to write this book!

20

Hidden Messages

According to their music teacher, the mind became like a sponge when listening to the symphonies of Mozart and other Baroque composers. Nine, however, suspected there were subliminal messages embedded in the music. Sometimes he thought he caught whispers of Naylor's voice underneath the music and worried he was being brainwashed.

–The Orphan Factory

Subliminal messages are any sensory stimuli that occur below an individual's threshold of conscious awareness. What this means is messages can be sent to your mind without you being aware of the fact.

The concept of information being transmitted to individuals without their consent or awareness is interrelated with other subjects explored so far in this book, especially mind control in chapter 2 and media manipulation in chapter 13.

Subliminal messaging – also known as subliminals – is nothing new. The technique has been around at least since the advent of radio and television.

Although there was great concern about subliminals when they first came to the mass public's attention in the 1950's, fears soon waned as experts assured all and sundry that the ever so subtle messages were relatively ineffective or else did not work at all.

By the late 20th Century, a whole host of scientific studies had concluded subliminals were not remotely effective.

Over the decades, however, there have been many groups in society who continued to maintain concerns over the wide usage of subliminals. Conspiracy theorists naturally expressed the greatest fears, but civil libertarians, media watchdogs and worried parents also raised issues.

Adding fuel to the whole debate is the fact that new science of the early 21st Century is also beginning to raise alarm bells regarding the influence and effectiveness of subliminals. It turns out the subtle method of advertising may be a little more persuasive on the mind than experts told us it was in the 20th Century.

Perhaps even *a lot* more persuasive...

"I saw a subliminal advertising executive, but only for a second."

–Steven Wright, American comedian

CONCEALED MESSAGES IN ADS

It's no secret that advertisers and programmers have long inserted *hidden* messages that consumers receive unknowingly.

There are numerous well-known incidents of subliminals being used in media advertising. A CBS News article headed *The 10 Best Subliminal Ads Ever Made* (dated October 20, 2011) provides some interesting examples.

The known history of this advertising technique essentially began in 1957, when market researcher James Vicary inserted subliminal messages into screenings of a film at a movie theater in New Jersey. The subliminals instructed cinemagoers to eat popcorn and buy Coca-Cola. According to Vicary, sales for both Coke and popcorn went through the roof.

Vicary's cinema experiment coincided with the publication of Vance Packard's bestselling book *The Hidden Persuaders*, which highlights subliminal tactics used by advertisers.

These developments prompted many others with an interest in influencing minds to begin researching this new technique. And so the subliminal movement was born.

SHOULD IT BE LEGAL?

Subliminal messaging has been banned in some countries including the UK and Australia, but it remains legal in most countries.

Although legal in the US, subliminal messaging is frowned upon – officially at least. The Federal Communications Commission (FCC) warns it will revoke any broadcaster's licence where the use of subliminals is proven, and high profile American broadcasters and television networks pay lip service to the intent behind the FCC's warning and to their expressed desire to protect listeners and viewers from subliminals.

Since the 1950's, numerous proposed laws to ban subliminal advertising have been introduced to the US Congress, but all have perished in committee without making it to the floor of either the House or Senate for a vote. Several states, including California, have at times discussed anti-subliminal advertising laws, but none have enacted those laws. The usual excuse given by lawmakers is that as research has failed to conclusively prove subliminal advertising is effective there's no need to pass such laws.

There is a school of thought in America that there's a conspiracy – in which the big corporations and ad agencies are key players – to convince the public that subliminal advertising doesn't work.

DO SUBLIMINALS WORK?

Advertisers and others have gone to great lengths to assure us subliminals do not work, trotting out the results of "exhaustive studies," "consumer poll results" and "extensive research" that point to the results of subliminal messaging being fairly ambiguous at best. One study quoted by Wikipedia claims "subliminal messages produce only one-tenth of the effects of detected messages".

However, there is credible research that shows subliminal stimuli often sparks actions someone intended to perform. In other words, actions can be subliminally prompted if someone was already planning to carry out that action, but it will not force them to do something they weren't already thinking of doing.

Conspiracy theorists go much further than that and often state or imply many or even most of our everyday actions are the result of subliminal messages we have seen or heard. They argue we receive so many subliminals throughout our lives that it has a cumulative effect which, when added up, amounts to mind control.

So there you have it: the two extremes. As is often the case, the truth may be somewhere in the middle. Or is it?

Many independent researchers have come to the shocking conclusion that we are being bombarded with so many subliminals every day it's virtually impossible not to be influenced by them in some way.

And science may be beginning to support the claims of these researchers. For example, very recent studies involving *functional magnetic resonance imaging* (fMRI) have revealed that subliminals activate crucial regions of the brain including the hippocampus, the amygdala, the primary visual cortex and the insular cortex. These latest scientific studies directly contradict 20th Century research.

Our own research has revealed major corporations – in the US especially – are investing tens of millions of dollars into subliminal advertising each year. Some are even hiring subliminal experts to covertly influence consumers into buying their products and services.

Which begs the question: why do these corporations so frequently use subliminal advertising and spend so much of their precious marketing campaign budgets on it if they don't believe it sways customers and boosts sales?

A similar question could be asked of politicians and political parties who attempt to sway voters with subliminal advertising. American voters have long been concerned about the incidence of such advertising on their television and computer screens leading up to elections.

POLITICAL MANIPULATION

Often quoted is the television advertisement promoting George W. Bush during the 2000 election campaign. When a photo of his opponent, Vice President Al Gore, appeared on screen, a subliminal flashed across the screen with the word 'RATS'. This has since been acknowledged as a purposeful subliminal insertion by the ad company and campaign managers responsible for the ad.

With media advertising per candidate in the US presidential elections now costing north of US$250 million, you can imagine how much television ads cost – even back in 2000. Whatever the actual cost of the subliminal component of the infamous George W. Bush ad, it was an expensive addition to spend on a technology that supposedly does not work.

Then again…who was it who won that election?

Subliminal researcher Martin Howard claims the US Government uses the underhand advertising technology as a way to mind control the American public.

In his 2005 book *We Know What You Want: How They Change Your Mind*, Howard states that by "using the universal tools fear, patriotism, and phrase repetition, these high flying spin doctors can easily sway the population. The most successful public relations campaigns aim to change public perception without our awareness of the campaign. They are typically launched by governments, institutions and countries who need to change their public image, restore their reputation or manipulate public opinion. There are PR firms today who advise dictatorships, dishonest politicians and corrupt industries to cover up environmental catastrophes and human rights violations."

The previously mentioned 1957 book *The Hidden Persuaders*, by Vance Packard, explores the manipulation techniques used to sway voters toward a certain political candidate. According to Packard, these techniques often include subliminal messages. The bestselling book also questions the morality of such techniques.

SUBLIMINAL SPECIALISTS

The little known individuals who specialize in subliminal marketing and advertising are often referred to as either *influence consultants* or *subliminal influencers*. However, the former title is more common, perhaps because the word *subliminal* has bad connotations.

These specialists work in the field known as *subliminal branding* and are quietly employed by major corporations to create subliminally effective marketing campaigns for the mediums of television, radio and especially the Internet and social media. Or put another way, these *penetrators of the subconscious* insert subliminal messages into ads in ways known to strongly influence those who are exposed to them.

It all sounds quite similar to the 2010 sci-fi thriller *Inception*, which stars Leonardo DiCaprio and was directed by Christopher Nolan. In the blockbuster film, DiCaprio's character plants ideas into unsuspecting targets' minds.

The main difference between *Inception* and the real-world usage of subliminals is that the movie is about influencing the subconscious minds of people while they are asleep.

On the other hand, neuroscientists tell us the brain produces similar hypnotic brain waves when watching television, films or listening to music as it does when asleep. In other words, it is in a *highly* suggestible state and is wide open for influencing, or some would say for *manipulating*.

There's one final point worth mentioning regarding the high-flying influence consultants hired by multinational corporations. Whilst researching them, we noticed an intriguing and perhaps disturbing theme: most either had an employment history in the hypnosis, brain wave entrainment or mind control fields, or else had strong interests that often bordered on fixations with these subjects.

It appears these *masters of subliminal science* may have a little too much in common with the likes of the psychiatrists and scientists who formulated MK-Ultra and other insidious mind control programs.

SUBLIMINALS, DRUGS AND ROCK 'N' ROLL

Of course, subliminal messages are not just visual. They've traditionally been inserted into radio broadcasts and even into pop music.

Pop and rock bands have been known to use something called *Reverse Speech*, which is another form of subliminals. It involves infusing subliminal messages into songs, often contradicting the song's apparent message.

The Beatles and *U2* have both been accused of using reverse speech in the lyrics of their songs. However, it was British band *Judas Priest* – renowned as one of the best heavy metal bands of all time – who hit the headlines when, in 1990, they were taken to court by parents who claimed the band had inserted evil subliminal messages in albums and songs, negatively influencing their children toward destructive behavior. The parents of one of two young men involved in a suicide pact alleged the *Judas Priest* song 'Better By You, Better Than Me', from the 'Stained Glass' album, contained the subliminal command "Do it" that triggered their son's suicide attempt.

At trial's end, the ruling was the so-called command was in fact an accident resulting from the wrong background lyrics being used.

CARTOONS

Perhaps the widest current use of subliminals is found in children's television shows, including animation programs.

Opponents of subliminals have long been critical of the amount of sex and violence secretly contained in children's cartoons. Some well publicized instances – such as the subliminal insertion of the word 'SEX' in the movie, *The Lion King,* and similar subliminal messages in Disney films – have been satisfactorily explained as mistakes or coincidences. Others have been quite deliberate – such as the case of one Ken Sobel, a New Yorker who was viewing a videotaped episode of the animated series *Alf* when something made him freeze the screen. What he saw disturbed him.

Across the screen, in front of images of the Statue of Liberty and the American flag, was the word 'AMERICA' in large letters. It occupied precisely one frame – too fast for the average person to see if played at normal speed, but not too fast for Mr. Sobel who had the presence of mind to freeze-frame it at that crucial point.

A subsequent NBC investigation into the incident resulted in the series' animators admitting to deliberately inserting the image in the cartoon. Their admission didn't stop there. The same animators admitted to placing other images in their cartoons.

That there are many other examples of such *indiscretions* is alarming given young minds are so impressionable and easily manipulated. Few would disagree that children's cartoons, films, videos and television series should be free of anything resembling subliminals. Unfortunately, we live in an age where the mighty dollar comes ahead of such considerations.

Incidentally, although NBC and most of their competitor networks publicly condemn subliminal messages in advertising, none appear to monitor their ads to ensure they're subliminal-free. Nor do their policies make mention of subliminals in their on-air programs.

NEW FRONTIERS

Online media has led to a proliferation of subliminal messages. Subliminals are tailor-made for insertion into video and even online text and animation – and there's little or no legislator oversight.

And when you consider the worldwide explosion of screens with video game machines, computer tablets, ATM machines, smart phones and wearable technology devices like *Google Glass*, you start to get the idea how many possibilities there are for subliminal ad predators to take advantage of.

"Advertising, music, atmospheres, subliminal messages and films can have an impact on our emotional life, and we cannot control it because we are not even conscious of it."
–Tariq Ramadan, The Quest for Meaning: Developing a Philosophy of Pluralism.

In recent years, with the evolution of the Internet, including video sites and social media, the Tinfoil Hat Network has gone into overdrive with conspiracy theories surrounding subliminals. They claim subliminal messages *are used by the Illuminati via their mind controlled Project Monarch music artists to lead the world into an era of Satanism that will in turn lead to a global Apocalypse.*

If nothing else, Tinfoil Hatters are always sensationalists. No matter where they conjure up their outlandish conspiracies, be it in their local asylum or in their mother's basement, they never fail to shock. Ya gotta give 'em that – and ya gotta love 'em!

21

REAL-LIFE
MANCHURIAN CANDIDATES

Because of their sublime genes, the orphans were all incredible specimens and often referred to by their creator, Doctor Pedemont, and by Naylor, Kentbridge and the rest of their Omega masters, as post-humans. Their DNA was different to anyone else's and by their teens they were superior in many ways to the rest of the population, being smarter, faster, stronger and more adaptable.

–The Ninth Orphan

In 1959, Richard Condon's classic psychological thriller *The Manchurian Candidate* was published. The book's plot revolves around the son of a leading American political family being brainwashed into becoming a communist assassin without his knowledge or consent.

Ever since then, the title has become a catch-phrase amongst conspiracy theorists who swear they've got *evidence* to prove governments around the world have such mind-controlled assassins at their disposal.

They often list the likes of Lee Harvey Oswald, Sirhan Sirhan, Jack Ruby, Mark David Chapman and James Earl Ray as being likely Manchurian Candidates; and they point out that nearly all these men, as well as numerous other infamous lone gunmen, claimed after being captured that they were patsies who were being mind-controlled.

However, the reality is programmed killers only exist in the realms of fictional stories and in the warped minds of those wearing tinfoil hats. There is no hard evidence to confirm the existence of Manchurian Candidates.

At least that's what the authorities would have us believe.

From a very early age, Nine had been aware Omega's motivation for manufacturing himself and the other orphans was to create the world's most effective espionage agents. The mysterious figures who ran the Omega Agency knew from experience that family ties and espionage didn't go together. In fact, they were a recipe for disaster. The shadow organization's hierarchy needed operatives who were unencumbered by family ties, who could undertake any mission, anywhere on earth, no matter what the sacrifice.

–The Ninth Orphan

In books one and two of *The Orphan Trilogy* we describe how the clandestine Omega Agency creates the most advanced intelligence operatives and assassins – *super spies* if you like.

Twenty-three genetically engineered orphans are *nurtured* from childhood, through their teenage years and into early adulthood with one end goal in mind: to turn them into the ultimate spies. The methods used range from providing advanced training in everything from speed reading, math and science to languages, martial arts and military strategies to isolation tank, biofeedback and virtual reality sessions. So by the time our orphans reach their early teens, they're already faster, stronger and more resilient, learned and intelligent than most adults.

Not content to rely on their charges' *natural* ability in the field – on assignment that is – their Omegan masters program them using mind control technologies so the orphans, or orphan-operatives, can effectively be remote-controlled. Any who try to flee Omega can quickly be reined in courtesy of a microchip implant embedded in the forearm of each; the microchip emits an electronic signal, allowing the orphans' masters to see their whereabouts at any time no matter where in the world they are.

MK = MIND KONTROL

The plot to our series could accurately be described as being very far-fetched, were it not for one thing: the officially acknowledged, real-life MK-Ultra program.

To recap, *Project MK-Ultra*, the most documented government mind control program uncovered yet, began in the early 1950's, using unwitting American and Canadian citizens as its test subjects. We know this as a result of the many thousands of US Government documents that have been publicly accessed courtesy of the Freedom of Information Act, and the release of other formerly classified documents relating to MK-Ultra.

These revelations generated considerable publicity, debate, research – both official and unofficial – and a number of feature films, documentaries and television series.

Then there are the rumored Manchurian Candidates said to have been brainwashed by US Military factions, with heavy CIA involvement, to carry out assassinations or other such acts for those who have programmed them.

Incidentally, the best description we've found of a Manchurian Candidate is someone with an artificially created multiple personality; that personality has various identities; if one identity performs an act and gets caught, another identity takes over and the original identity has no recollection of the act he (seems it's always a man) committed, so the information remains hidden from interrogators.

Mind control expert and award-winning author Dr. Alan Scheflin has for years claimed that, thanks to the CIA, MK-Ultra is still alive and well in America and that declassified documents show the CIA is creating a new kind of weapon. Scheflin, whose books include *The Mind Manipulators*, leaves little doubt the *weapon* he refers to is a Manchurian Candidate and, he says, such people aren't responsible for their actions because they're being controlled.

Scheflin's assertions are confirmed by renowned psychiatrist Dr. Colin A. Ross, president and founder of the Colin A. Ross Institute for Psychological Trauma, who says he used the Freedom of Information Act to source US Government documents that show the CIA and different branches of the military continue to be active in the mind control business.

This revelation contradicts the US Government's official statements which say there have been no further mind control programs since MK-Ultra was shut down in 1973.

Dr. Ross likens the selection of Manchurian Candidates to the selection process for the military's documented radiation and germ warfare experiments that were conducted on soldiers who were always unaware of the dangers involved. He says the declassified documents he has sourced on mind control experiments reveal volunteers received huge amounts of electric shocks, which permanently wiped out their memories.

MIND GAMES

Assassins experiencing amnesia is a subject that's been explored in various bestselling novels and blockbuster movies, including Robert Ludlum's *Bourne* novels and subsequent film adaptations.

In the 2007 feature film *The Bourne Ultimatum*, which stars Matt Damon and was directed by Paul Greengrass, a surprise twist delivered via flashbacks in the film's third act reveals that Jason Bourne had actually volunteered to become an assassin. These flashbacks show Bourne has had his identity fractured and his memories erased after having been put through a series of trauma-based psychological trials that eventually broke down his original personality.

Such works of fiction are clearly inspired by conspiracy theories which insist this is how mind-controlled assassins are created.

Numerous sources – some reliable, some not – report that Manchurian Candidates are subjected to receiving large amounts of LSD and other drugs, isolation, interrogation, hypnotism, and food and sleep deprivation as well as electric shocks. It seems trauma-based torture is used to program inductees and to promote the development of alternate psyches, or personalities, which would enable them to function *normally* and then to kill on command but have no recollection of their actions.

This fracturing of the psyche is said to be conducive to creating the phenomenon that has been termed *sleeper assassins*.

According to such theories, the first psychiatrists employed to master mind control studied mental patients who had been diagnosed with Multiple Personality Disorder, which medical science has since renamed Dissociative Identity Disorder. Many of those psychiatrists are said to have been Paperclip Nazi doctors who were brought to the US after conducting radical psychiatric experiments on patients during the Holocaust – the same doctors whose victims not only included Jews, Gyspies, political agitators and homosexuals, but also the mentally ill.

THE (REAL) MAN WHO
STARED AT GOATS

One of the more colorful characters circulating rumors of hypnotized assassins is former head of US Army Intelligence, Major General Albert Stubblebine III, who masterminded the army's psychic warfare program back in the early 1980's. Yes, the same Stubblebine the Third who famously tried to create a soldier who could levitate and walk through walls, and who – on the record – said he believed American soldiers could win all wars if they could walk through walls!

In case you still doubt Stubblebine's credentials to speak on this subject, he's the officer that the central character of the 2009 feature film *The Men Who Stare at Goats*, is based on. Is there a higher accolade than that? Still not convinced? Well, the central character was played by none other than George Clooney. Happy now?

According to Stubblebine, that story had its origins in his office when he was asked to develop the minds of people so that if they stared at a goat long enough its heart would explode. What's more, he claims he has seen evidence that such a thing is possible, and he says he's positive that the creation of Manchurian Candidates continues in America today.

We are not sure how seriously Albert Stubblebine III should be taken. Our first impressions are that he's one sandwich short of a picnic.

Perhaps the *Encyclopedia of American Loons* should have the last say on Stubblebine. In a blog post dated January 13, 2013, the encyclopedia claims: "He is currently heartily insane, but seems to have been batshit crazy even before he tried to walk through walls".

In a final diagnosis, the post ends: "I guess one could make an argument that the world needs hapless, elderly men called 'Albert Stubblebine' who are constantly befuddled by their failure to walk through solid walls".

Then again, Stubblebine achieved the esteemed military rank of Major General and was the head of US Army Intelligence for many years. Those things don't normally happen to *loons*.

"The victim of mind-manipulation does not know that he is a victim."
–*Aldous Huxley, excerpt from his 1958 non-fiction book*
Brave New World Revisited.

DOCUMENTED CIA SLEEPER ASSASSINS

On December 2, 2010, *Russia Today* ran an article headed *CIA creating real life Manchurian Candidates?* The news outlet's report details the statements of a group of US military veterans who claimed their government had created sleeper assassins long ago. Decades ago in fact.

The vets were quoted as saying that from 1950 until 1975 experiments on themselves and other US soldiers were conducted at the Army's Edgewood Arsenal in Maryland where "the government messed with their minds, implanted microchips and electrodes" during "mind control experiments".

"They are alleging," the article continues, "top secret CIA, military and even university scientists experimented on them with the purpose of implanting remote control devices in their brains to eventually turn them into robot-like assassins".

Documents, which according to the article include declassified research papers from the Office of Naval Research as well as results of experiments conducted at Harvard and Yale, show how hypnosis and electro-implant experiments were first conducted on animals. This involved inserting electrodes into the brains of dolphins, cats and dogs. By all accounts, the tests were a success in that the scientists conducting them were able to control the actions of the laboratory animals via remote transmitters.

The next stage of testing was on humans – volunteers who apparently weren't clear about what they were letting themselves in for – and proved equally successful. The individuals were mind controlled via the electrode brain implants and carried out a range of actions that signals beamed to their brains instructed them to do.

In what's likely to be a case of art imitating life, the electrode implants used, on the record, by the US Government for brainwashing soldiers echoes the 2004 remake of *The Manchurian Candidate* starring Denzel Washington and Liev Schreiber. In that film, Schreiber's character has electrodes implanted in his brain by neuroscientists.

The aforementioned mind control expert Dr. Colin A. Ross says the account of the US military veterans who were experimented on, as well as the official government documents detailing the experiments, all prove "this is absolutely documented fact."

"People can be in a sleeper state indefinably," Dr. Ross adds, "but of course this is all secret and classified."

Although more recent mind control science remains classified, creating sleeper assassins all sounds very possible given what is known to have occurred during MK-Ultra. In fact, it not only sounds possible, but highly likely. After all, if the long-desired Manchurian Candidate phenomenon was proven to be a reality decades ago, something tells us senior intelligence agents wouldn't just say to each other, "Oh well, we proved it's possible, but we won't send any mind controlled assassins out into the field as that would be immoral."

According to our research, it's very probable sleeper assassins are in existence all over the world today, quietly carrying out *hits* for the global elite. Given mind control has been a documented fact for well over half a century, the powers that be must surely now have all the science needed to create as many brainwashed assassins as they require.

*"Our orphans exist on the frontiers of modern science,"
the doctor said proudly. "They each have two more
chromosomes than the average person. For all intents
and purposes, they are post-humans. Superior in every
way to the rest of the population."*

–The Orphan Factory

THE PHYSICAL SIDE OF
THE EQUATION

Besides the psychological manipulation said to be needed to create programmed killers, the human body must also be enhanced. Manchurian Candidates would be of no use to intelligences agencies if they were not physically capable of carrying out complex assassinations. It is one thing to have a malleable brain, but quite another to have the body and physical skills of a killing machine.

Common claims to emerge regarding the physical training inductees receive in these black op programs include harsh trials of strength, martial arts and weapons training, feats of endurance and wilderness survival tests, and even flying various aircraft. The result is super soldiers who are trained to extremely advanced levels in numerous disciplines – much like our fictitious orphan polymaths in *The Orphan Trilogy*.

Beyond physical training, forcibly altering and enhancing assassins' bodies would be another likely way to create the ultimate killing machines. This could be achieved by genetic engineering ensuring none of the usual genetic imperfections would exist in the Manchurian Candidates' bodies.

Administering advanced substances – of the chemical variety or otherwise – could also be a way to manufacture such individuals. Steroids would be the obvious one, but that's probably too simplistic an approach for designing elite assassins.

The 2012 film *The Bourne Legacy*, which stars Jeremy Renner and Rachel Weisz and was directed by Tony Gilroy, shows the CIA improving their operatives by altering their DNA with top-secret drugs. In the film, Weisz plays a CIA chemist employed to create the drugs that make Renner's character and other operatives superior to average humans, not only intellectually, but also physically.

We explore a similar theme in *The Orphan Trilogy* by showing the orphans regularly ingesting the mysterious Ormus aka White Gold. Unlike the substance given to the spies in *The Bourne Legacy*, Ormus is not a manufactured laboratory drug but a naturally occurring substance that exists in the real world. It allows the orphans to run as fast and fight as well as any adult.

For all anyone knows, Ormus may actually be one of the substances being used by the world's elite assassins.

THE GOVERNOR TO THE RESCUE

Perhaps the most high profile investigation into MK-Ultra and mind controlled operatives has been conducted by Jesse Ventura, former Governor of Minnesota, who is probably America's – and possibly the world's – best known conspiracy theorist.

The Governor fronts *Sleeper Assassins*, a 2010 episode of the popular US television series *Conspiracy Theory with Jesse Ventura*. In the episode, he and his team of investigators present a fairly compelling case that Manchurian Candidates in the form of programmed killers do exist in present-day America.

Ventura, who by dearth of his political status had – and to an extent still has – access to official documents, facilities and personnel at the highest levels, informs his audience the US military has been experimenting with mind control since the 1950's.

Jesse Ventura – Sleeper Assassins starts with Ventura telling viewers he has uncovered a Government plot to turn ordinary citizens into programmed killers.

"I've also seen how hypnosis, torture and other techniques can make ordinary people do things they otherwise couldn't do," he says. "I met a man who says they did it to him. All the high-profile assassins who fit this same pattern...believe the government turned them into weapons. Could this be a coincidence? I don't think so."

The most intriguing point of the episode is when Ventura interviews whistleblower Robert Duncan O'Finioan, a self-professed former Manchurian Candidate who candidly reveals the methods used to *take over* his mind and reveals the types of missions he undertook whilst under the influence of mind control.

O'Finioan, who is said to have unusual body strength, martial arts talents and alter egos that can be triggered, also claims he and others like him were "taken" and "genetically enhanced with implants" and "turned into something more than a normal human being" – so they almost literally became fighting machines.

O'Finioan appears to be the go-to guy for any conspiracy theorist wanting to add credibility to his or her theory on Manchurian Candidates. He shows up on numerous websites and, it appears, he was and maybe still is the subject of at least one planned book and film.

An item dated January 2007 on the popular ProjectCamelot.org site catalogues an interesting interview conducted with O'Finioan and his friend Dave Corso who, the writer claims, "are both part of Project Talent, an unacknowledged MK-ULTRA military program".

The article continues: "Their joint testimony strongly suggests that the US military has a program of super soldiers, not only those like Duncan (O'Finioan) – with psychic abilities and uncommon strength – but also those in command, who were trained to spot military talent and were skilled in psychotronics, that is: mind control...

"Controller and soldier? ... Their relationship is unclear. But somewhere in the murky waters of the past, two men, from vastly different backgrounds, have come together as friends only to discover that what brings them together may be far more mysterious and sinister than either is prepared to remember".

Since that interview, O'Finioan is on the record as saying an MRI scan he had following a car accident caused a cranial implant to malfunction, removing barriers in his mind that had previously kept memories hidden. He claims those memories leave no doubt that he was a killing machine used for termination assignments and that he was also a victim of MK-Ultra.

O'Finioan's own blog site at duncanofinian.com makes for an interesting read also. In an entry dated January 21, 2014, the man himself posts an open letter from "the survivors of Project Talent" addressed to, among others, President Obama, the US Senate, Congress, the UN and several other organizations. He encourages subscribers to distribute the letter far and wide.

The letter reads: "We, the survivors of MK ULTRA and all of its sub-projects – Project Talent being one of them – are coming to you, the leaders of the free world, for redress. We request immediate action on this matter, as we have waited long enough for our respective governments to take notice of the torture that was illegally and secretly forced upon us as children by the same said governments."

In the same letter, the writers make a number of other requests – including the following: "We ask for acknowledgement of all that was done to us, both as children and adults, by the governments who committed these illegal acts against us, as well as recognition of duties that we performed for our respective countries in the name of freedom and national security… And finally, we request that all black projects which use children cease immediately… The torture of children can in no way ever be condoned by any country for any reason. It is our highest wish to have a public announcement that these projects using children will be stopped."

The same blog site features an August 2013 OffPlanet Radio interview with one John Stormm, another self-professed survivor of Project Talent and fellow victim of MK-Ultra. He claims he was one of the first batches of *infants* to be inducted into the MK Ultra program.

"I was subjected to torturous physical, mental, genetic, psychological and chemical conditionings, designed to make me into an unstoppable hunter/seeker/assassin," says Stormm. "A master of what the CIA used to refer to as 'the happy accident'. An untraceable stealth weapon capable of fracturing skulls, necks, spines, ribs or whatever and in a split second, leaving a corpse that can be easily set up to appear as a car wreck or household accident that leaves no embarrassing fingers pointed or homicide investigations."

Storm claims that in the late 1960's he was trained and used as a remote viewer in an MK Talent portion of the program, and by 1970, had taken on some of his first combat roles.

To achieve its New World Order plans, the Omega Agency needed people who could make use of their primordial instincts, who wouldn't question the morality of orders and who would kill without hesitation. Operatives of that caliber were priceless.

–The Ninth Orphan

Getting back to Governor Jesse Ventura and that *Conspiracy Theory* TV episode, before his director can shout *Cut! It's a wrap!* Ventura informs viewers he's convinced there are more programmed killers out there. "Let's just hope their sites are aimed at the enemy," he says.

Let's hope he's right about that!

22

Blood Minerals

Ongoing conflicts had made exploitation of coltan ore problematic, and much of it was mined illegally and smuggled out of the country by militias from Rwanda and other neighboring countries. As a result, Congolese coltan represented only about a tenth of the world's total production even though the DRC was believed to have seventy percent of known coltan reserves.

–The Orphan Uprising

In *The Orphan Uprising*, Nine (aka Sebastian) has reason to cross Zambia's northern border into the Democratic Republic of the Congo (DRC) – previously and variously known as the Belgian Congo, Congo Free State, Congo-Leopoldville, Congo-Kinshasa and Zaire – in central Africa.

Nine's target is a coltan refinery owned and operated by American conglomerate Carmel Corporation. The corporation is a fictitious entity, but the precious metallic ore known as coltan – official name *columbite-tantalite* – is very real.

This precious ore is found in large quantities in the DRC's disputed eastern regions. When refined, the result is metallic tantalum, a heat-resistant powder capable of holding a high electrical charge – properties that are essential for the creation of electronic elements known as capacitors.

These capacitors are included in the manufacture of mobile phones, digital cameras, laptop computers and in communications technology generally, making coltan an indispensable part of the burgeoning and extraordinarily profitable communications and technology sectors. Hence its value.

DRC'S ESTIMATED MINERAL WEALTH US$24 TRILLION

As chance would have it, the DRC is believed to have seventy to eighty per cent of known coltan reserves worldwide. It also has around one third of the world's known diamond reserves and is rich in other precious metals, too. With reserves of untapped mineral deposits estimated at US$24 trillion, it's little wonder the DRC is considered by some to be one of the wealthiest countries in the world, if not the wealthiest, in terms of natural resources.

Now here's the rub: the Democratic Republic of the Congo has been beset by war and is one of the most violent, unstable and poverty stricken nations on the planet.

In an article on the *All Africa* online news site dated November 21, 2013, the Congolese war (which incorporates the back-to-back First and Second Congo Wars) is said to have "killed over six million people since 1996," and "is the deadliest conflict in the world since the Second World War. If you add the number of deaths in Darfur, Iraq, Afghanistan, Bosnia and Rwanda over the same period, it would still not equal the millions who have died in the Democratic Republic of Congo".

Fatalities are just one side of the conflict, however, with rape also being used as a "weapon of war", the article goes on to mention. Women and young girls raped during the conflict are estimated to number in the hundreds of thousands.

It's a sad truth that conflict over control of the DRC's mineral wealth accounts for much of the violence. Hence the term *conflict minerals* used to describe coltan, diamonds, gold, copper, cobalt and other precious minerals in the DRC and, indeed, throughout much of Africa.

To Nine's way of thinking, the problems surrounding the
exploitation of coltan in the DRC epitomized the problems
the entire African continent faced in capitalizing on the
huge untapped wealth that lay beneath its surface.
Corruption, political unrest and outside interference from
non-African countries ensured the continent that should be
the world's wealthiest remained the poorest.

–*The Orphan Uprising*

A PLETHORA OF REBEL MILITIAS

In the DRC, the link between its vast mineral resources and financing the various militia groups running riot is impossible to ignore. And coltan plays a key role in this never-ending conundrum.

Ongoing conflicts have made exploitation of the DRC's coltan ore problematic to put it mildly. As a result, Congolese coltan represents only about a tenth of the world's total production even though it has the lion's share of the precious metal within its borders.

A UN Security Council report leaves no doubt much of the country's coltan is mined illegally and smuggled out by rebel militias from neighboring Rwanda, Burundi and Uganda. Monies *earned* by these forces finance the ongoing conflict.

So who are these militia groups who are holding the DRC to ransom?

According to South African investigative site *Daily Maverick* there's a plethora of rebel militias "all of whom are capable of causing varying degrees of chaos" in the eastern DRC.

In a report on the main rebel factions operating there, *Daily Maverick* states: "The M23 rebel movement has been the strongest in recent years, closely followed by the Democratic Forces for the Liberation of Rwanda (FDLR), a motley but dangerous band of

Rwandan refugees (some on the run from their role in the Rwandan genocide) and ethnic Hutus, dedicated to their own survival and the eventual overthrow of the Rwandan government".

The report continues: "Their existence is thought to be a major factor in Rwanda's involvement in the conflict in the eastern DRC (that and the region's vast, lucrative mineral supplies, of course) and the group has a horrendous record when it comes to respect for human rights".

As for the amount of money at stake, the Rwandan Army was rumored to have raised around US$250,000,000 from illegal coltan sales in just 18 months. The Rwandans have denied this of course.

"The continent that contains the most poverty also contains the most wealth."
–Bono, from a speech given at the G8 summit held in Chicago, IL, in May 2012.

AN UNNECESSARY WAR

It has been widely acknowledged that the brutal war in the DRC is primarily and directly related to the massive demand in the developed world's countries for the minerals required for their military and electronic industries.

Coltan reserves are not abundant around the world like many other precious metals are. For instance, no coltan mining is undertaken in the US, which is totally reliant on imports of the precious material. The DRC is by far the easiest and cheapest place for the US to import coltan from.

Coltan mining is declining in Canada. And although China has some coltan, it has nowhere near enough to provide for its own high demand for the commodity. Both countries are in a very similar position to the US in this regard.

If the likes of North America and China dealt with alternative coltan suppliers – such as Australia – that would prove far less profitable than dealing with the DRC whose Third World conditions and lack of protections in place guarantee coltan can be sourced at rock bottom prices.

As mentioned in Chapter 16, fleecing the Third World has been a reality for decades if not centuries. Mineral-abundant Third World nations, which should be some of the richest on Earth, are all too often among the poorest. Many argue that the poverty of these nations can usually be blamed on wars strategically *engineered* by developed nations and Superpowers – wars that are also armed and funded by the developed world.

There is no greater example of this ugly phenomenon than in Africa, and the DRC has regularly been referred to as *the poorest country in the world* by international aid agencies.

As well as engineered wars that last for many years, the DRC is also raped financially over and over again. The World Bank loans the country billions annually and special clauses in the loan agreements allow for multinational companies to *take* virtually all the DRC's enormous mineral resources for a pittance.

Meanwhile, the DRC is left indentured to the World Bank, forever attempting to pay off crippling interest rates. Almost none of the nation's mineral wealth flows back to its people.

CHILD LABOR

To add to the problem, many tens of thousands of children in the DRC are employed as miners – oftentimes in coltan mines. The work is primitive, dirty and dangerous.

Workers dig large craters in riverbeds to access the coltan. They then mix water and mud in big tubs to encourage the heavy coltan to settle on the bottom – much like gold miners did panning and sluicing for gold in years gone by. The mines management calls it *child labor* and officially employs children as young as 12 for this work; the outside world views it as slave labor, which is exactly what it is of course.

As most mobile phones contain coltan, it's not too dramatic to say there's blood on *your* cell phone – the blood of Congolese workers who are dying in their hundreds of thousands in a conflict that continues to claim many lives. There's no doubt the demand for coltan is financing the conflict in the DRC and helping to promote the evil that is child/slave labor.

In an October 31, 2010 article by the leading Pakistani media outlet *The Express Tribune*, columnist Fatima Najm asks if "Pakistan's 100 million cell phone users know their devices may be soaked in Congolese blood".

Najm says within each of those phones are small amounts of coltan that add up to a lucrative illegal trade. "The explosive growth in the wireless industry means that demand for these tin ores collectively results in the rape and torture of hundreds of thousands of innocent Congolese people a year".

The columnist points out that Congo is resource-rich, and its mighty river system has the potential to power all of Africa's electricity needs. "Experts say stability in Congo could translate into peace and progress for all of Africa, but at least five neighboring countries have proxy militias battling each other in Congo for control of valuable tin ores".

BLOOD COLTAN NOT AS SEXY AS BLOOD DIAMONDS

Najm makes an interesting comparison between Congolese coltan and diamonds, advising it's logical to assume that "given the widespread violence attributed to coltan...one would imagine it would be destined for the same sort of notoriety as blood diamonds".

Alas, not so, it would seem. 'Blood diamonds' obviously sounds a whole lot sexier than 'blood coltan' to Western media, moviegoers and the general public.

Predictably, smart phone manufacturers and the like have been quick to distance themselves from the whole murky business. Some publish disclaimers, denying that they source coltan from militia's operating in the DRC; many claim the supply chain for coltan mined in the DRC is so complex it's impossible to ascertain whether it has been legally or illegally mined and supplied.

To be fair, several high profile manufacturers in the US and elsewhere are sourcing their coltan from outside the DRC and, indeed, outside central Africa until such time as the legitimacy of mining operations there can be more clearly established. However, they're in the minority.

Cell phone consumers and others have long been questioning the legitimacy of products. For the most part, it appears their questions are falling on deaf ears. Perhaps it's time to ask more questions – and ask them louder.

There has been a campaign in recent years to try to force the big multinational companies to disclose whether or not they use Congolese conflict minerals. However, it's often impossible to prove where such minerals come from.

Just as crafty banksters frequently transfer vast sums of money between various offshore tax havens to conceal their money trail, corporations that profit from ultra-cheap Congolese *conflict minerals* have middle men – usually warlords – who smuggle minerals from country to country so it's extremely difficult to trace their origins.

Of course, the problem of conflict minerals isn't limited to the Democratic Republic of the Congo; it exists throughout much of the African continent. Equally, the problem isn't limited to Africa.

Perhaps the last word on this vexing issue should go to *The Guardian* contributor Zobel Behalal, a peace and conflict advocacy officer, who reminds us that in Burma the mining industry was militarized for several decades, with the national army controlling mining sites, business operations and exportation, while in Colombia tantalum, wolframite and gold mines as well as their respective business concerns are controlled and taxed by armed groups.

Writing in The Guardian, Behalal says, "Products that have funded conflicts can only reach the international market with participation of the businesses that buy and use them. Bloomberg revealed that BMW's, Ferraris, Porches and Volkswagens contain tungsten and wolframite that come from businesses under the control of the FARC Colombian rebels".

Behalal insists these aren't isolated cases.

"The trade of natural resources continues at the expense of violence and human rights violations. There is an urgent need to create a win-win contract between the economic factors and the local populations in order to create real and sustainable development in countries rich in natural resources.

"Due diligence must be enforced as a mandatory requirement throughout the supply chain of natural resources."

Nine was aware the continued siphoning of coltan, as well as cobalt and diamonds, from the eastern Congo was part of a wider conspiracy to destabilize the country.

–The Orphan Uprising

It's our contention governments, big corporations, industries and business moguls of the West and elsewhere in the developed world are very aware of what's going on in Third World countries like the DRC. At best they pay lip service to the need to stamp out the conflict minerals business; at worst they knowingly encourage the trade in conflict minerals.

There does seem to be enough evidence – anecdotal and otherwise – surrounding the trade of coltan sourced in the DRC to suggest most are content to turn a blind eye to the exploitation of natural resources and the human cost of the conflict minerals business. To our eyes at least, this evidence is overwhelming. So overwhelming that, of the 29 conspiracy theories highlighted in *The Orphan Trilogy*, the blood minerals conspiracy is probably among those most likely to be true.

But hey, what do we know?

23

MYSTERIOUS DEATHS

She couldn't even hear Kentbridge's voice now. All she could hear was her beating heart. She emptied her lungs of air then, between heartbeats, gently squeezed the trigger. The shot shattered the silence. Staring through his binoculars, Nine waited for what seemed an eternity before he saw the results of Seventeen's shot. In fact it was only two seconds, maybe three. The target's head seemed to explode, like a ripe melon. "Target is down!" he exclaimed as Ezekiel fell to the ground.

–The Orphan Factory

In book two of our trilogy, two orphan-operatives are tasked as young adults with carrying out a political assassination deep in Guyana's Amazon rainforest. There's much at stake: a successful mission will enable the global elite to control the country's natural resources.

Political assassinations are probably much more common than we realize. Take for example the 2013 news reports that Hugo Chávez, President of Venezuela and long-time perceived enemy of the West, had died of cancer.

Could Chávez's death have been a creative form of assassination as his supporters have alleged?

The US weekly newspaper *American Free Press* poses that exact question in an article dated May 20, 2013 in which it suggests Chávez may have been "deliberately infected with a carcinogenic agent".

Conservative estimates suggest the CIA has assassinated, or attempted to assassinate, more than 50 foreign leaders over the years, so why not Chávez? And how many leaders of other nations died suddenly, or under unexplained circumstances, before they could implement their long-planned policies?

"How many more political murders disguised as heart attacks, suicides, cancers, drug overdoses? How many plane and car crashes will occur before they are exposed for what they are?"
–Monologue delivered by Kevin Costner and written by Oliver Stone in JFK (1991).

From our research we'd have to say it seems distinctly possible that many of *the most* influential and socially-driven individuals of the past half-century or so died as a result of carefully crafted assassination plots. It's hard to deny that an alarming number of those who stood for peace, not war, were either killed by deranged lone gunmen or else died in suspicious circumstances. We refer of course to the likes of JFK, Martin Luther King, Benazir Bhutto, Bobby Kennedy and John Lennon, to name but a few.

Could the long list of victims even include the mother of an heir to the British Royal throne?

DEATH OF A PRINCESS

In 1997, in a dark tunnel in Paris, France, Princess Diana along with her partner Dodi Fayed were killed in a horrific car crash. Numerous inquiries and investigations all determined the crash was an accident and not a murder, but conspiracy theories stick to Diana's death as much as they do to JFK's assassination.

And much like JFK's death, alternative theories are not just believed by conspiracy theorists or those on the fringes of society. In fact, various polls conducted by the likes of the BBC, CNN and CBS have consistently shown that a quarter to one third of Britons and Americans believe the princess's death was no accident.

Dodi Fayed's father, Egyptian business magnate Mohamed Al Fayed, also believes Diana, as well as his son, were murdered in that tunnel in Paris.

In an article in *The Guardian* dated February 19, 2008 and headlined *Nazi Philip wanted Diana dead, Fayed tells inquest*, the article begins, "Mohamed Al Fayed branded Prince Philip a "Nazi" and a "racist" in the high court today as he detailed his belief that his son Dodi and Diana, Princess of Wales, were "murdered" in a conspiracy initiated by the royal family and carried out with the involvement of Tony Blair, the security services and others".

The Harrods store-owner informed the inquest Diana had told him she was pregnant and had agreed to marry his son, according to the same article.

Mohamed Al Fayed's comments lend weight to what is probably the most widely believed conspiracy theory on Diana's death: that the British royal family had Diana murdered to avoid a marriage between the mother of the future King of England and an Egyptian Muslim, not to mention the arrival of a Muslim-British Royal baby.

It was never confirmed if Diana was pregnant or not as, strangely, no autopsy was conducted.

As mentioned in chapter 8, Diana's former butler Paul Burrell stated the Queen had once warned him, "There are powers at work in this country of which we have no knowledge". Burrell also told an inquest in 1998 that an unnamed British royal had once warned Diana, "You need to be discreet, even in your own home, because they are listening to you all of the time".

And then in 2003, Burrell published one of Diana's letters in the *Daily Mirror* newspaper, revealing that she wrote, "This particular phase in my life is the most dangerous. Xxxxxxx (name redacted) is planning an accident in my car, brake failure and serious head injury in order to make the path clear for Charles to marry."

And those words proved to be eerily prophetic in terms of the way she died, if not the reasons why.

The Daily Mirror reported that Diana had actually named the person (Xxxxxxx) she believed was plotting against her, but that the newspaper decided not to publish the individual's identity for fear of a lawsuit.

Piers Morgan, then editor of the Daily Mirror, said of Diana's predictive letter, "I think everybody who thought it was accident will think to themselves, well hang on a second, could it be that these wild allegations have any substance?"

Also in chapter 8 we refer to rumored dirty businesses the House of Windsor engages in, such as the arms trade and landmine sales. The latter, in particular, has been a focal point for conspiracy theorists; the fact that Princess Diana fought tirelessly against landmines through her charitable work for the anti-landmine organization the Halo Trust put her at risk and may explain why she was murdered, according to these theories.

However, there's no proof that the Windsors profit or profited from landmines or other criminal enterprises, so this conspiracy theory seems much more speculative than some others surrounding Diana's death.

One of the other more *out there* conspiracy theories is that Osama bin Laden was responsible for killing Diana. This theory suggests the terrorist leader had gotten wind of the Princess' pregnancy and upcoming marriage to Dodi and was concerned she'd be a bad influence on Muslim women.

There appear to be seemingly infinite plot holes in this particular theory. Plot holes such as how did Bin Laden know Diana was pregnant and why would he even care given he was reportedly so busy blowing up the West.

Besides these questions, the most important question relating to Bin Laden is: Was the terrorist leader still alive in 1997?

OSAMA BIN LADEN

Officially, Bin Laden died in 2011 in Pakistan – but was that really him? Or was Bin Laden just a fabricated and much-needed bad guy *manufactured* by the Military Industrial Complex to enable it to *legitimately* wage the so-called War on Terror?

In the FBI's Vault records, the following is mentioned on the Muslim leader's file: "Usama (or Osama) Bin Laden, founder of the al Qaeda terrorist organization, was born in Saudi Arabia in 1957. On March 10, 1984, Bin Laden and others killed two German nationals. On March 16, 1998, authorities in Tripoli issued an arrest warrant for him for murder and illegal possession of firearms. Bin Laden was also wanted for the August 1998 bombing of U.S. embassies in Kenya and Tanzania. He was killed by U.S. forces in May 2011."

Furthermore, FBI records clearly label Bin Laden as the mastermind of 9/11, and as a result he inherited the mantel of *Most Wanted* during the War on Terror.

To most in the West – mainstream media included – the US Navy Seals' termination of Bin Laden in Pakistan is where the terrorist leader's story ends, but not for any conspiracy theorist worth his or her salt. They would argue there are too many unanswered questions and cute coincidences surrounding the man's death – and surrounding his life, too, for that matter.

And conspiracy theorists aren't the only ones raising questions. Media reports throughout the Middle East, India, Pakistan and Afghanistan have been awash with quotes from locals purporting to know the truth about Bin Laden. These reports speculate everything from his dying years earlier, even before 9/11, to still being alive and free today.

The Express Tribune, of Pakistan, reported that polls showed two-thirds of Pakistanis did not believe US reports stating Navy Seals had assassinated Bin Laden, and less than a quarter believed he was responsible for the 2001 terrorist acts on American soil.

More recently, Western media has joined in the speculation. For example, leading UK newspaper *The Daily Mail* ran an article on February 12, 2014 headed, *U.S. special forces ordered the destruction of Osama bin Laden's death photos two weeks after top secret seek and destroy mission to kill him.* And *The Wall Street Journal* reported that an Egyptian bank manager formerly associated with the Muslim extremist claimed to be certain Bin Laden had died many years before the US announced they'd killed him.

Several prominent American celebrities have also publicly voiced their skepticism surrounding US claims regarding Bin Laden's demise.

Shortly after Bin Laden's death was announced, former US Navy Seal Jesse Ventura made an interesting observation in a television interview that aired on CNN in June 2011. He reminded viewers of earlier reports stating "Bin Laden was on a dialysis machine 10 years ago." Ventura added, "Experts have said the disease he suffered from is generally fatal within two years. How did he manage to survive 10?"

And back in 2007, American hip-hop artist and film star Mos Def appeared on *Real Time with Bill Maher* where he called Bin Laden a "boogeyman" and implied his whole existence was nothing more than a fabrication by the US Government to blame 9/11 on.

But let's return to the crux of the *story*...After more than a decade of failing to find Bin Laden, suddenly he's tracked, located and then killed? All in one evening? And on top of that, there's not one shred of evidence to prove any of this occurred?

As President Obama and his team of intelligence advisors watched real-time footage of Bin Laden's termination in the comfort of the White House's situation room, it was reported the then-director of the US National Counterterrorism Center, Michael Leiter, was first to speak. Apparently, Leiter said, "Holy shit!"

That's not all he said, but bear with us. We just want to draw out the suspense a little.

"I don't need facial recognition," Leiter reportedly added. "We just killed Bin Laden!"

So clearly, nobody on American soil knew for a fact it was Bin Laden.

What about in Pakistan then? Surely, *someone* confirmed they'd just taken out the most wanted man on the planet?

Well, you'd think so, wouldn't you? But this is where it gets a little murky.

After what seemed a surprisingly short period of time, a White House spokesman informed the world's media that Bin Laden's body had been flown to the USS Carl Vinson aircraft-carrier in the Arabian Sea where it (the body) was cast overboard in a weighted bag. The spokesman said this was all done "in conformance with Islamic precepts and practices".

What the...?

Did we hear that right? Instead of keeping evidence *in conformance with Western precepts and practices*, the United States of America vetoed its own laws and diligently adhered to the customs and religious rituals of the world's most wanted terrorist and those of the country that harbored him?

Again: *What the...?*

Remember, the bodies of Saddam Hussein's sons, Uday and Qusay, were kept for 11 days before finally being buried. America didn't go out of its way to follow Islamic protocols on that occasion, and nobody in the West complained about that.

But wait, it gets stranger still.

The Obama Administration released an image to the media showing President Obama, Hillary Clinton and other members of the National Security team watching the raid *live*. According to the Administration, the footage came from a camera attached to a Navy Seal's helmet. However, this was contradicted when CIA director Leon Panetta emphatically stated the feed had gone dead "for around 20 to 25 minutes" during the raid.

If the CIA director is correct, does that mean the photo of Obama, Clinton and others was staged in order to sell a *story*? What other conclusion could be drawn?

American anti-war activist Cindy Sheehan, whose son was killed on duty in Iraq, also questioned how the US had matched Bin Laden's DNA with a member of the terrorist's family in less than 24 hours. "The only proof of Osama being dead again that we were offered," Sheehan wrote on her Facebook page as CNN reported on May 5, 2011, "was Obama telling us that there was a DNA match between the man killed by the Navy SEALs and OBL. Even if it is possible to get DNA done so quickly, and the regime did have bin Laden DNA lying around a lab somewhere -- where is the empirical proof?"

Sheehan concluded her Facebook post, "I am sorry, but if you believe the newest death of OBL, you're stupid."

Wikipedia accurately summarizes the persistent conspiracy theory surrounding the terrorist leader as follows: "Doubts about bin Laden's death were fueled by the U.S. military's disposal of his body at sea, the decision to not release any photographic or DNA evidence of bin Laden's death to the public, the contradicting accounts of the incident (with the official story on the raid appearing to change or directly contradict previous assertions), and the 25-minute blackout during the raid on bin Laden's compound during which a live feed from cameras mounted on the helmets of the U.S. special forces was cut off".

Maybe all this smoke around Bin Laden's demise doesn't indicate a fire. And maybe all the perceived plot holes were caused by an unfortunate series of coincidences and misunderstandings – the type that lead to conspiracy theories blossoming out of nothing.

Hmmm…Those are big maybes.

"An ideal form of government is democracy tempered with assassination."

–Voltaire

MLK

On April 4, 1968, civil rights leader Martin Luther King (MLK) was shot dead in Memphis, Tennessee. After a large-scale international investigation, small-time criminal and WW2 war veteran James Earl Ray was captured and charged with the murder. Ray entered a guilty plea and on March 10, 1969 he was convicted for the murder and sentenced to 99 years.

So that's it? How can anyone create a conspiracy theory on this case when the convicted murderer pleaded guilty, we hear you ask?

Well, it's complicated. Ain't it always! And numerous unanswered questions remain.

For example, why did Memphis police withdraw MLK's police protection the day before he was killed? This despite the civil rights activist having received more than 50 death threats and being the known target of many groups all over America.

Also, James Earl Ray later recanted his confession and attempted to gain a new trial. Like Lee Harvey Oswald, he claimed he was a patsy.

Need more convincing evidence to support this conspiracy theory? Don't worry, it's coming, but we like to release it slowly…again, to build the tension.

Even the 1977-78 House Select Committee on Assassinations found there was a "likelihood" that Ray did not act alone. This supports the contention of many that there was a major conspiracy to murder MLK. The House also discussed whether the CIA had been involved in the murder as the agency's antagonism toward him was well documented.

Besides the CIA, the African-American's long list of enemies included no less than FBI director J. Edgar Hoover who is said to have hated MLK's guts.

In 1993, a surprising twist occurred when Loyd Jowers, owner of the Memphis bar opposite the motel where MLK was shot, made a confession of sorts. Jowers told ABC TV that he'd been asked – by Memphis police as well as government agents – to aid the planned assassination.

Perhaps most tellingly, MLK's family never believed James Earl Ray was responsible for the murder. King's wife Coretta Scott King and their son Dexter Scott King are on record as saying they believe in a far-reaching assassination conspiracy involving the FBI, the CIA, the US Army and even President Johnson.

Dexter met with James Earl Ray in prison and believed him to be innocent. He pushed for a retrial, but Ray died the following year (1998) of Hepatitis C before any retrial could take place.

On the night of MLK's death, Robert F. Kennedy (RFK), New York's then Senator who was on the US Presidency campaign trail, chose to deliver the sad news to the people of Indianapolis in person. The Indianapolis police department warned RFK they wouldn't be able to provide adequate protection should the crowd riot, which they felt likely given he'd be speaking in an African-American neighborhood.

RFK was unfazed. He delivered a profound speech to the people of Indianapolis in which he shared his own personal sufferings following the assassination of his brother JFK. He also spoke of the need to follow in Martin Luther King's footsteps.

"What we need in the United States is not division," RFK said. "What we need in the United States is not hatred. What we need in the United States is not violence and lawlessness, but is love and wisdom and compassion toward one another, a feeling of justice toward those who still suffer within our country, whether they be white or whether they be black."

After RFK's heartfelt speech that evening, Indianapolis was quiet and mourned MLK's passing in peace while major cities throughout America experienced a wave of riots.

Two months after giving that speech, RFK was also assassinated.

"RFK MUST DIE"

It seems likely MK-Ultra or a Manchurian Candidate, or possibly both, may have been involved in the 1968 assassination of Robert F. Kennedy, the US Presidential candidate most political analysts agree would have been elected President had he lived.

As mentioned earlier, *The Orphan Factory* climaxes with a political assassination in the Amazon jungle. Nine and Seventeen, the orphan-operatives charged with carrying out the assassination, tell themselves over and over in their own minds, "Quamina Ezekiel must die." They are not sure why they're repeating this phrase to themselves; the implication is they're under the influence of mind control.

In the writing of that sequence, we include mind control triggers based on alternative theories surrounding some of the most well-known lone gunmen of the 20th Century. But more than any other real-world assassination, this section of our novel was directly inspired by reports of RFK's convicted killer, Sirhan Sirhan.

By all accounts, on the fateful evening of June 5, 1968, the Palestinian-Jordanian assassin appeared to be in a hypnotic state at the scene of the crime – the Ambassador Hotel in Los Angeles. Many believe Sirhan Sirhan was a Manchurian Candidate diligently following instructions his conscious mind was not even aware of.

The prevailing professional opinion is RFK's assassin has never been able to remember *anything* of that night – not entering the hotel, not the killing itself and not leaving the hotel in handcuffs. *Nothing*.

Apparently, Sirhan Sirhan's's only vague memory fragment, if it can be described as that, was said to be a vision of a typewriter he remembered observing all night long as it automatically typed a series of orders for him to follow.

All the evidence at hand seems to indicate Sirhan Sirhan was a brainwashed assassin or, at the very least, he was in a hypnotized state when he pulled the trigger of his .22 caliber revolver.

We refer to his memory blackouts; the reports of multiple witnesses claiming he looked like he was in "a trance"; the psychiatrist who testified at the ensuing court case that Sirhan Sirhan was in a trance state on the night of the crime; and especially the diaries found in his home by the LAPD – diaries whose pages were filled with Sirhan's scribbled handwriting.

Over and over, the words "RFK must die" filled the pages of those diaries. Handwriting analysis indicated the writing was *automatic writing*, meaning Sirhan Sirhan was not conscious of what he was writing.

Another curious fact supporting the hypnotism and mind control theory was that the Jordanian passport-holder had earlier joined the Rosicrucians, an occult group also known as *the Ancient Mystical Order of the Rose Cross*. When several psychiatrists assessed him to be in a hypnotized state after the assassination, Sirhan Sirhan's Rosicrucian membership was treated by many as suspicious, especially as trance and hypnotism are a known part of the group's teachings.

Defence attorney Dr. Bernard Diamond tried to dismiss his client's undeniable hypnotized state by claiming Sirhan Sirhan must have hypnotized himself.

If the assassin was a Manchurian Candidate, the range of suspects could include anyone from the CIA or the Mafia to occultists or the Military Industrial Complex. Many believe the latter to be the culprit, especially as Kennedy had stated he would immediately end the Vietnam War were he to become President.

In a 2011 parole hearing, Sirhan Sirhan's new lawyer, Dr. William Pepper, said his client had been "hypno programmed" and he alluded to the Manchurian Candidate theory.

Ezekiel's head was in the center of the crosshairs of Seventeen's telescopic sight. As she prepared for the shot, the only sound she could hear was Kentbridge's voice in her mind. Her mentor sounded like a broken record. Quamina Ezekiel must die. Quamina Ezekiel must die. Quamina Ezekiel must die.

–*The Orphan Factory*

THE SMILING POPE

Pope John Paul I, who was nicknamed *the Smiling Pope* due to his forever-cheerful demeanor, was elected the Catholic Pope on August 26, 1978. Just 33 days later, at 5am on September 28, John Paul I was found dead, marking the end of one of the shortest reigns in papal history.

Initially, the Vatican stated his body was discovered by papal secretaries, and that John Paul I was found propped up in bed still holding a copy of Thomas Kempis' book, *Imitation of Christ*, which he'd apparently been reading. Then the Vatican's story suddenly changed. They now said their first statement had in fact been wrong and John Paul I was actually discovered by a nun.

What was also strange in regard to the death of the Smiling Pope was the speed of events that unfolded afterwards. Not long after the nun *apparently* found John Paul I, a papal doctor declared the Pope had died of a heart attack, and that was that; by 5.15pm that same day, the Vatican's embalmers arrived on the scene and immediately began work on the corpse before any autopsy could be done.

If you think all this sounds worthy of a Dan Brown novel, you're not alone.

Conspiracy theories abound on John Paul I's death. Possible conspirators include international banksters operating within the Vatican Bank, Freemasons and even the Vatican itself. In fact, that's the most common theory – that it was an *inside job*.

Despite his constant smile, Pope John Paul I was apparently hell-bent on reforming the Vatican, and many have argued the Catholic powers that be were simply protecting their position by assassinating him.

Top of the Smiling Pope's to-do list was said to have been fixing the large scale corruption he believed existed within the Vatican Bank. The same religious financial institution which only a few decades earlier had lucrative collaborations with Benito Mussolini's fascist regime and Adolf Hitler's Nazi Party, and had strayed into many other areas not generally associated with the Holy Spirit, was about to be brought into line.

According to this murder theory, Vatican banksters weren't too keen on being reformed. Nor did they resonate with the possibility of being forced to confess their sins, so they sent the Pope to an early grave.

In a case of circumstantial evidence, the President of the Vatican Bank in 1978 was American archbishop Paul Marcinkus who just happened to be seen walking briskly through the Vatican at dawn and around the exact time Pope John Paul I had died. That could obviously be a coincidence, but then again Marcinkus wasn't known for early morning walks.

Conspiracy theorists also say the Pope was assassinated by non-money men in the Vatican for other planned radical reforms, including allowing for Catholics around the world to practice contraception.

If Pope John Paul I didn't die of natural causes, the common consensus between researchers and even many Catholics is that there are more than enough dark factions operating within the Vatican to have carried out such a murder.

"It's difficult to believe that the death was natural," said an aide to the French Archbishop Marcel Lefebvre, "considering all the creatures of the devil who inhabit the Vatican."

Hell, if American Presidents can be assassinated by their own countrymen while in office, is it really so hard to believe a Catholic Pope could be killed by members of the Vatican?

MARILYN MONROE

Hollywood icon Marilyn Monroe was found dead on August 4, 1962 with enough drugs in her bloodstream to kill 15 individuals, according to the Los Angeles County Coroner who also declared her death a suicide. Or, more accurately, Dr. Thomas Noguchi wrote "probably suicide" on the coroner's report he filed.

The world famous sex symbol's demise has attracted almost as many conspiracy theories as have the deaths of her reported lovers JFK and RFK. Some argue suicide does not make sense considering Monroe was about to reunite with baseball star and first husband Joe DiMaggio who was said to be the love of her life.

One of the many mysteries surrounding Monroe's death was the amount of time it took for anybody to alert the police. The nearest police station to her home in Brentwood, Los Angeles, was only three miles away and yet the police weren't summoned until the following day (August 5) at 4.30am – a full six hours after Monroe's publicist and other associates had been called to the house and found her dead.

On arrival at the film star's residence, one policeman reportedly took one look at the pill bottles neatly arranged next to the bed, as well as the perfectly aligned position of Monroe's body on the bed, and said it was "the most obviously staged death I have ever seen."

In other oddities, the housekeeper had already removed all of the deceased's bed linen by the time the police arrived; all Marilyn's diaries had mysteriously vanished; despite all the pill bottles by her bed, an autopsy revealed her stomach contained no tablet residue whatsoever; and perhaps most alarmingly, her body was covered in bruises.

According to conspiracy theorists, Monroe didn't commit suicide, but was killed by global elitists for knowing too much. The sex symbol's affairs with both JFK and RFK have been well-documented and some say the Mafia, who financially backed the Kennedy family, were responsible for killing her because she'd become an embarrassment to President Kennedy. CIA memos and FBI records since leaked and/or declassified appear to confirm she may have been killed for knowing too much.

In the end though, Monroe's death remains a mystery and we are unlikely to ever know with absolute certainty how she died.

As Donald Wolfe, author of *The Last Days of Marilyn Monroe*, said, "People don't really want to know what actually happened to her. I think they would prefer the mystery, because what really happened to her is a rather dark story".

JOHN LENNON

Most people old enough remember exactly where they were when they heard the news that John Lennon was shot dead in New York City on December 8, 1980. The murderer was Mark David Chapman – yet another lone gunman who stood glassy-eyed at the crime scene waiting for the police to arrive. A witness to the shooting asked him if he was aware what he'd just done. "I just shot John Lennon," Chapman calmly replied.

In the court case that followed, Chapman's defence team included psychiatrist Dr. Bernard Diamond. Recognize that name? That's right, he's the very same psychiatrist who assessed Sirhan Sirhan's mental state and, as per his assessment of RFK's assassin, Dr. Diamond stated Chapman was completely insane. Little mention was made of the fact that Chapman was a former World Vision employee who worked as a children's counsellor in refugee camps in Asia and the Middle East.

Author Fenton Bresler put forward the theory in his book *Who Killed John Lennon?* that while Chapman was working in Beirut he fell into the orbit of CIA agents who drugged and brainwashed him as part of the ongoing MK-Ultra program.

What is known is shortly after beginning his charity work in Beirut, Chapman began to exhibit mental illness and was hospitalized as a result. Who he associated with from that point on is not known.

Assuming Chapman was yet another Manchurian Candidate and Lennon wasn't killed randomly, then who on earth would have wanted to kill the peace-loving singer?

Most conspiracy theorists and many researchers point the finger at the US Government for singer-songwriter Lennon was a known threat to the political order of that time. This threat was primarily due to two reasons: his fearless opinions that he gave freely to the press and the sheer size of his following, which was almost unprecedented.

FBI records and other Government files on Lennon indicate the Establishment viewed him as a very dangerous activist. For example, FBI director J. Edgar Hoover personally wrote on Lennon's file: "ALL EXTREMISTS SHOULD BE CONSIDERED DANGEROUS."

Another such file said the ex-Beatle, who by then was a US resident, was able to "draw one million anti-war protestors in any given city in 24 hours". That is some *serious* influence, and judging by the declassified files it's obvious the Military Industrial Complex viewed Lennon as a potential stumbling block to their plans for future wars.

Sean Lennon, the son of John and Yoko, told the *New Yorker* in April 1998 that his father "was dangerous to the government" and "If he had said 'Bomb the White House tomorrow,' there would have been 10,000 people who would have done it. These pacifist revolutionaries are historically killed by the government".

The only thing counting against this whole premise is that Lennon was killed in 1980 – long after the likes of JFK, RFK, MLK and others were killed and long after the civil unrest of the 1960's and early 1970's had faded. It was a different political and social climate by then with less foreign wars and less volatility within America. Some have even argued that Lennon's star power was waning, at least slightly, by 1980.

Of course, it's not known what Lennon was planning at the time of his death, and for all anyone knows the authorities may have gotten wind of some radical peace movement he was hatching.

To add yet another curiosity to the mix, while Chapman patiently waited for the police to arrive and arrest him, he stood at the scene of the crime reading a copy of *The Catcher in the Rye*. Many conspiracy theorists believe that finding this particular book in the hands of an assassin is no mere coincidence. Regardless, it must have been a macabre sight to see Lennon lying dead on the ground with his murderer standing over him happily reading J.D. Salinger's classic novel. (See chapter 27 for more mysteries surrounding *The Catcher in the Rye*).

NOVEMBER 22, 1963.
DALLAS, TEXAS.

Of all conspiracy theories, the cover-up after JFK's assassination in Dallas, Texas, is one that nearly everyone believes.

All the evidence screams foul play – from eye witness testimonies contradicting the official report to the ridiculous *Magic Bullet* explanation, the suspected murders of numerous witnesses and suspects, the Dallas doctors' conflicting reports on the body and the official Government line. Not to mention Lee Harvey Oswald's still classified 1962 tax return, something many researchers believe can be attributed to the *fact* that Oswald was receiving US Government cheques and was on their payroll.

But really, what is there to say about JFK's assassination that hasn't been said before? It's the mother of all conspiracies and has spawned a million theories. We certainly won't add to them, except to say the official explanation provided by the US Government seems about as realistic as the plot of a bad B-movie.

In the interests of doing some serious investigative reporting – *finally*, we hear you say! – we uncovered these immortal words uttered by action movie star Bruce Willis in May 2007 to *Vanity Fair*: "They still haven't caught the guy that killed Kennedy. I'll get killed for saying this, but I'm pretty sure those guys are still in power, in some form … The entire government of the United States was co-opted."

Yippee ki yay, Mister Willis, yippee ki yay!

Okay, that's enough investigative reporting for the moment.

"It would certainly be interesting to know what the CIA knew about Oswald six weeks before the assassination, but the contents of this particular message never reached the Warren Commission and remain a complete mystery."
–Jim Garrison, former District Attorney of Orleans Parish, Louisiana.

As many a Tinfoil Hatter has pointed out over the years, the most infamous assassins of the 20th Century all had three names, including Lee Harvey Oswald, Mark David Chapman, James Earl Ray. *What about Sirhan Sirhan*, we hear you ask? Him too, actually, as his full name, which was rarely reported by the media, was Sirhan Bashira Sirhan.

So what does this three-name assassin point prove? Absolutely nothing, of course.

Remember, the hallmark of a good conspiracy theory is it cannot be proven! It's a weird coincidence nevertheless. And coincidences seem to be the norm when it comes to the deaths of the most famous, influential and politically-threatening figures of recent decades…

24

SECRET PRISONS

*Mountain Retreat was the code-name for the secret CIA
prison Naylor had instructed Seventeen to transfer
Isabelle to. It was situated in the isolated and
mountainous Canillo region, in the country of Andorra.
The highly secretive Andorran facility was part of the
global internment network that had been established
after 9/11 to deal with suspected terrorists. Even after
the bad press received in 2005, when it was leaked to the
world's media that the CIA had secret prisons all over
Europe, new prisons, or black sites, had been set up.*

–The Ninth Orphan

If there is a Splinter Civilization on the planet right now, in
addition to having suppressed technologies, underground bases
and trillions of dollars in black budgets at their disposal, they
may also have secret prisons around the world. These could be
used to incarcerate any who threaten to expose this breakaway
group's existence or otherwise thwart their New World Order
plans.

Those who buy into this mega conspiracy believe it was
uncovered, in part at least, when mainstream media outlets
reported that the CIA covertly operates numerous prisons all over
Europe that are in defiance of EU laws in every respect.

Many believe those prisons that have been exposed to date are merely the tip of the iceberg. They also warn there are signs the global elite could be building thousands of such incarceration centers – referred to as *concentration camps* by the most outspoken critics – in preparation for some kind of anarchistic or apocalyptic scenario.

Sounds a bit tinfoil hattish, right? Er…yes we'd have to agree!

Mind you, what do we mere mortals really know about what the global elite get up to when they're not attending Bilderberg conferences or sailing their luxury yachts? Whenever any of us receive small fragments of news, like intelligence agencies managing illegal prisons in Europe, we assume that's the extent of their unlawful activities and that justice will prevail now that such practices have been exposed.

But could that be a naïve assumption?

Seventeen knew why Naylor wanted Isabelle at this particular black site. Hidden amongst snow-covered mountains, the modern, nondescript Mountain Retreat facility was regarded as the most secure and secretive CIA prison on earth. As the van arrived at the detention center, Seventeen went through a strict security check to confirm she was a CIA employee. Once screened, she was cleared to drive Isabelle inside.

–The Ninth Orphan

THE CIA'S GLOBAL INTERNMENT NETWORK

Much changed after 9/11. Some said the world would never be the same again – and for many that was true…

Wars broke out, international travel became problematic, civil liberties were reined in, and words and phrases like rendition, extraordinary rendition, black sites, WMD, weapons of mass destruction, ghost detainees, unlawful enemy combatants, Guantanamo Bay and the War on Terror came into common usage.

The term black sites intrigued us. So we looked into these and were alarmed by what we discovered.

In military jargon, a black site is where a classified and unacknowledged defence project, or black project, is conducted. Such sites have earned notoriety following revelations that the CIA operates black sites for the purpose of detaining (illegally in the opinion of many) so-called unlawful enemy combatants – ostensibly to aid its War on Terror.

Mounting mainstream media speculation on the existence of such sites back in the mid-2000's undoubtedly forced the hand of President George W. Bush who announced in September 2006 that secret CIA prisons did exist. He also confirmed that many of the detainees held in those prisons were to be transferred to Guantanamo Bay.

In The Ninth Orphan, our heroine Isabelle is transferred to a black site that may or may not exist in the tiny European principality of Andorra, high in the Pyrenees Mountains between Spain and France.

While the Andorra site was a figment of our collective imagination, it's not beyond the realm of possibility it could have existed for similar black sites are believed by many to have sprung up post 9/11 throughout Europe and on other continents.

A report by The Washington Post dated January 23, 2014 caught our eye. Here's an excerpt from that report:

"The CIA prison in Poland was arguably the most important of all the black sites created by the agency after the Sept. 11, 2001, attacks. It was the first of a trio in Europe that housed the initial wave of accused Sept. 11 conspirators, and it was where Khalid Sheik Mohammed, the self-declared mastermind of the attacks, was waterboarded 183 times after his capture.

"Much about the creation and operation of the CIA's prison at a base in one of the young democracies of Central Europe remains cloaked in mystery, matters that the U.S. government has classified as state secrets".

As long ago as 2005, The Washington Post reported that "The hidden global internment network is a central element in the CIA's unconventional war on terrorism. It depends on the cooperation of foreign intelligence services, and on keeping even basic information about the system secret from the public, foreign officials and nearly all members of Congress charged with overseeing the CIA's covert actions".

Poland, the UK and Romania are just three of the European countries black site watchers have named among the 30 countries rumored to hold (between them) scores of detainees on behalf of the US. Those same sources claim American ships have also been used as floating prisons, boosting the likely number of black sites to more than 90 worldwide.

Add to that an EU report stating the CIA operated over 1200 flights ferrying alleged terrorist suspects to and from "detention centers" in Europe, and it's a no-brainer that EU countries have played their part in this game.

COMBATTING A DEARTH OF INFORMATION

Exactly how the game is played is open to conjecture as there is no single source of reliable information. Not outside of the CIA at least, and the agency ain't talking – not to us anyway.

From all reports it appears there could be hundreds of detainees at any given time – the majority being *ghost detainees* apprehended in Europe and transported to other countries as part of an extraordinary rendition process.

Most interest, however, surrounds those classed as unlawful enemy combatants – the most important of whom are detained at sites that are totally off the grid. Those not so important have been transferred by the CIA to friendly agencies in other countries.

Commonly acknowledged estimates of numbers of detainees could be conservative in the extreme if unsubstantiated media reports are correct. For example, in *The Observor*, June 13, 2004,

South East Asia correspondent Jason Burk reports: "The United States government, in conjunction with key allies, is running an 'invisible' network of prisons and detention centres into which thousands of suspects have disappeared without trace since the 'war on terror' began".

The report goes on to mention "secret operations that by-pass extradition laws" and adds that the "astonishing traffic has seen many, including British citizens, sent from the West to countries where they can be tortured to extract information".

In an item published on PBS.org, reporter Stephen Grey, author of *Ghost Plane: The True Story of the CIA Rendition and Torture Program*, says the US Government needs to account for the fate of more than 500 prisoners handed over to the United States since 9/11 by Pakistan. "All were rendered into U.S. custody without any extradition procedures," he says.

As an aside, in the same article Grey claims the CIA's rendition program is nothing new and has been going on for decades.

"Rendition began in 1883 when Frederick Ker was kidnapped in Peru by the Pinkerton Detective Agency and rendered back to Chicago to face trial for grand larceny," he says. "The tactic was endorsed by the Supreme Court... These renditions...were renditions to courts of law...very different from the CIA's current covert program of extraordinary rendition, in which terror suspects are sent not to justice but into the hands of rough allies."

After the negative press that has surrounded Guantanamo Bay, horror stories have emerged of prolonged and intentional use of torture and abuse of detainees. Released prisoners claim they were subjected to many forms of torture, ranging from beatings and sleep deprivation to sexual abuse and temperature extremes. Add to this suicides and attempted suicides by detainees, and you get the idea it's a sorry state of affairs.

The allegations of torture and abuse at Guantanamo Bay and other black sites have been given credence by official reports from respectable organizations such as the International Committee of the Red Cross and Amnesty International. However, it's clear much information is being withheld from the public.

"Miss Alleget, I'm not going to kid you." Seventeen
pulled up a chair and sat only a meter from Isabelle.
"This place makes Guantanamo Bay seem like paradise.
But if you co-operate and answer all my questions, I
won't have to torture you."

–The Ninth Orphan

OTHER BLACK SITES

As mentioned, there are theories that black sites go far beyond the clandestine CIA prisons, and secret prisons can be found all over America and, as also mentioned, throughout the world.

Many Americans will be familiar with the Federal Emergency Management Agency conspiracy theory that insists FEMA has set up hundreds of secret prisons – also referred to by some as *concentration camps* – throughout the US to detain anyone deemed to present a threat to national security.

This theory may seem extreme to the common individual, but conspiracy theorists assure anyone who will listen that they have uncovered enough evidence to prove concentration camps are being built on American soil and are being managed by the military.

Apparently, these clandestine facilities will be used to detain dissenting American citizens once the *one world government* officially swings into action. But not everyone agrees…

According to RationalWiki.org, "FEMA concentration camps exist in the mind of a particularly loopy bunch of conspiracy theorists who believe that mass internment facilities have been built across the continental United States by the Federal Emergency Management Agency, in preparation for a future declaration of martial law."

RationalWiki goes on to say: "There are several videos purporting to show footage of the camps, as well as shots of ominous-looking fences and webpages listing locations of over 800 camps, allegedly all fully guarded and staffed full-time despite being completely empty."

One of the videos RationalWiki undoubtedly refers to is an episode Governor Jesse Ventura made for his *Conspiracy Theory* television series. Shot in 2010 and titled *Police State FEMA Camps*, it was unaccountably pulled off air, but (at the time of writing) it can still be viewed on YouTube. It highlights so-called *fusion centers* and FEMA camps which, according to the program, have been set up "to imprison innocent Americans" who have been spied on and rounded up by "the secret government".

COMPARISONS WITH NAZI DEATH CAMPS

One of several informants Ventura's team interviews describes *fusion centers* as "command centers for a network of concentration camps – similar to the Nazi concentration camps – for US citizens who don't toe the line". This is supported by footage of several modern establishments that do look suspiciously like concentration camps, complete with tight security and razor wire fences.

As the program's voice-over would have us believe, "Jesse Ventura uncovers a plot to force martial law on law abiding citizens, replace 50 states with 10 giant prison sectors, fill up hundreds of concentration camps with people like you and me, and pull the trigger with a disease pandemic."

In support of these assertions, Ventura and his TV crew visit one establishment where, from the cover of trees, hundreds of new plastic coffins can be seen stockpiled row upon row inside the perimeter fence, ostensibly in preparation for one of the pandemics referred to above. Soon after the arrival of Ventura's team, trucks arrive and start transporting the coffins away, leaving viewers to draw their own conclusion.

The coffins, incidentally, are referred to by officialdom as "plastic grave-liners".

The fact that this particular episode of *Conspiracy Theory* was pulled off air, allegedly in response to Government pressure, would seem to lend some weight to the message Ventura was trying to get across. Certainly, it does give pause for thought.

Interestingly, the name *Halliburton* keeps cropping up in the video in relation to the coffins and the fusion centers that feature in it. Halliburton Company, of course, is the multinational corporation that George H.W. Bush, Dick Cheney and George W. Bush are connected with. Yes the same corporation involved in controversies dating back to the Iraq War. Anyway, Halliburton is named as the designer of the fusion centers, and one of its (unnamed) associate companies is said to have supplied the coffins.

Ventura interviews retired FBI agent Mike German who is especially critical of the fusion centers and their management. A 16-year veteran of the FBI, where he served as a Special Agent in domestic terrorism, bank fraud and public corruption investigations, German says the centers have no oversight or guidelines, and he agrees with Ventura that their management and purpose are undemocratic.

It should be noted that not all conspiracy theorists have bought in to Governor Ventura's assertions regarding the FEMA camps and fusion centers.

TopSecretWriters.com's Ryan Dube calls Ventura's assertions fear-mongering. Dube says, "True researchers not only track down leads in…documents and by conducting interviews, but more importantly they do not jump to conclusions based on shabby evidence. True conspiracy researchers remain honest with readers and viewers regarding what is actually known, and what remains unknown. Unfortunately, these are lessons that Jesse Ventura… never learned."

Dube describes as "all lies" claims that the centers are spying on every American who speaks out against the government and that huge piles of "coffins" are being stored for future mass genocides. "It does legitimate conspiracy researchers…a great disservice to spread fear-mongering and disinformation in an effort to increase ratings and create misdirected fear among the American population," he says.

Using documentation TopSecretWriters obtained, apparently on request, from the Department of Homeland Security Office of Intelligence and Analysis, Dube attempts to debunk core theories that Ventura highlights in the program.

"In fact, the effort by the DHS in creating these centers," according to Dube, "was to allow local law enforcement to respond more quickly whenever someone is spotted casing out a bridge, a bank, or a high rise building as part of planning for another terrorist attack."

Given Homeland Security would be first in the firing line if Governor Ventura's allegations about the real purpose of the centers and camps were ever proven correct, we are not sure if the department is the most reliable source of information in this debate. Nevertheless, we accede that many Americans – possibly most – will accept Homeland Security's word as gospel on this issue.

Regardless, images of prison-like camps and stockpiled items that look suspiciously like plastic coffins would appear to undermine the official explanation.

Seventeen didn't even glance at any of the detainees as she pushed Isabelle along. Having worked as an interrogator and torturer at several CIA prisons around the world, she knew all about the secret internment program. She understood some of the detainees were major terrorist suspects while others were considered less important, having limited intelligence value and little direct involvement in terrorism. Isabelle had been classified as among the latter group, the cover story being that she was the former lover of a low-level Al Qaeda figure. This allowed the CIA and Omega to detain the Frenchwoman legally.

–The Ninth Orphan

MARTIAL LAW IN EFFECT

On February 3, 2014 *The Huffington Post* reported, "U.S. Supreme Court Justice Antonin Scalia told law students at the University of Hawaii on Monday that the nation's highest court was wrong to uphold the internment of Japanese-Americans during World War II, but he wouldn't be surprised if the court issued a similar ruling during a future conflict".

The article goes on to mention that Scalia told staff and students at the university "you are kidding yourself if you think the same thing will not happen again".

Inspired by Scalia's comments, Aaron Dykes and Melissa Melton, creators of alternative news site TruthstreamMedia.com, wrote in an article dated February 5, 2014, "Martial Law has already been established on paper, and a Supreme Court Justice now warns that the nation's highest court would back executive orders to intern Americans, as it did during WWII."

The TruthstreamMedia.com article asks how quickly would the Obama Administration or a future President use the powers of Executive Order to hold Americans in actual camps in the event of future crisis – be it natural disaster, false flag terrorism, economic collapse or a large-scale war.

"This is particularly pertinent," Dykes and Melton continue, "given that acts of legislation such as H.R. 645 have been introduced to establish 'National Emergency Centers' for times of crisis and that hundreds of facilities in major metropolitan areas across the country have been designated for use as FEMA camps and readied for mass population processing and control... these authors have covered several of these facilities and relevant drills, and the intent is becoming very clear."

Formalities over, Seventeen wheeled the prisoner along a corridor which took them past still more cells. Isabelle saw Muslim detainees dressed in orange overalls. Some

*were praying, others were being interrogated by CIA
personnel. She caught a glimpse of a bearded Arab man
with fresh wounds on his bare chest. Isabelle sensed this
prison was one big torture chamber. She shuddered as
the thought of what her abductor and the guards had in
store for her.*

–*The Ninth Orphan*

So, who do you believe? The "particularly loopy bunch of conspiracy theorists" RationalWiki refers to, or the politicians who either deny existence of the FEMA camps or assure us their existence is solely to safeguard the interests of law abiding citizens?

Tough choice isn't it? Not sure the word of any of the above can be fully trusted.

Where do we stand on this? we hear you ask. (Our hearing is highly attuned to such questions even if they're only whispered in your thoughts)!

On the question of FEMA camps specifically, we'd have to say on the strength of our research there's no doubt they exist, but their true purpose remains debatable. Certainly, for Americans at least, there are sufficient rumors and innuendo to warrant a degree of nervousness, caution and alertness.

On the question of secret prisons, or so-called black sites, since the veil of secrecy was lifted – in part anyway – off various CIA prisons in Europe, and their true purpose was officially acknowledged, there's no doubting the existence of these sites. What's still in doubt is the number of black sites, their locations and how many suspects are detained within their walls.

As for other secret prisons, clandestine containment centers, illegal holding pens – call them what you will – around the world, it would be naïve to deny their existence. We need only consider the fate of political dissidents in countries like North Korea to know there are probably hundreds if not thousands of secret prisons around the globe.

Just between us, we are quietly hoping we don't end up in such an establishment as a result of the release of this book into the public domain! In case we do, *please* put in a good word for us. Assure our jailers we are only members of that particularly loopy bunch of conspiracy theorists we referred to earlier and are a threat to no-one but ourselves! We have a long list of friends – and an even longer list of *former* friends – who can vouch for that.

25

DRUG WARS

They'd arranged to meet with an Omegan mole who worked in the Clinton administration. He was helping them with a new Omega Agency operation involving the Kosovo War, which had just broken out in Europe. Naylor and his cronies were seeking to use Kosovo as a transit route for Afghan heroin bound for EU countries. Despite the official news stories being circulated by mainstream media, Omega knew the extremely lucrative heroin trade was behind the war.

–The Orphan Factory

In book two in *The Orphan Trilogy* we highlight the direct link many commentators and researchers are convinced exists between the Kosovo War and heroin.

The above excerpt from *The Orphan Factory* was inspired in part by a discussion rumored to have taken place at the 1996 Bilderberg Group conference in Toronto, Canada. Its confirmed elite attendees included David Rockefeller, Henry Kissinger and Margaret Thatcher, and the discussion was said to have ended with the decision to create the Kosovo War.

If true, we can only imagine how the discussion went...

Bilderberger #1 may have said in passing that another war was needed to support the Military Industrial Complex.

Bilderberger #2 may have mentioned that Kosovo had significant mineral reserves – since valued at more than 13 billion

Euros – including silver, zinc, cobalt, lead, bauxite and lignite worth tapping into.

Bilderberger #3 may have replied that the value of those reserves paled into insignificance next to the value of oil reserves of Middle East countries, and the gold and diamond reserves of several African countries.

"Yeah, true, we gotta think big," Bilderberger #4 may have added.

After some head scratching, Bilderberger #5 may have reminded his or her fellow Bilderbergers that Kosovo lay smack bang in the middle of the infamous *Balkan Route* through which billions of dollars of heroin passed annually into western Europe from Turkey, Iran and Afghanistan. And his or her associates may have quickly deduced that whilst the value of Kosovo's mineral resources may not warrant going to war over, the value of its drug trade – then believed to be worth around US$300 billion – was something else entirely.

That imaginary discussion highlights one of the most disturbing conspiracy theories surrounding illicit drugs – in particular heroin and opium – and the disturbing role these drugs have played in recent wars.

THE DRUG BEHIND A HUNDRED WARS

Dope. Tar. White Nurse. Black Pearl. Hero. Big H. Snow. Boy. Junk. Smack.

These are just a few examples of the seemingly inexhaustible slang terms people use when referring to heroin. Some, like *China White* or *Mexican Mud*, reflect location; others, like *Dragon* or *White Girl*, reflect popular songs while most are simply insider terms for those in the know.

It's worth noting the difference between heroin and opium because the two are often confused and because both are often referred to in the conflicts we wish to highlight – namely the Kosovo and the Afghanistan wars.

Opium comes from the opium poppy (also known as Papaver Somniferum in scientific circles), whereas heroin is a semi-synthetic opioid analgesic, not an opiate.

Most will be familiar with the Opium Wars that date back to the late 1830's and involved Britain illegally trafficking opium into China and making enormous financial sums as a result.

What's less known is that heroin has been a cause of many a conflict – between countries, tribes and drug cartels – since it was first produced on a commercial scale as a *wonder drug* in the late 1890's.

THE KOSOVO WAR

The brief but bloody Kosovo War was fought over 1998-99 between the ruling Federal Republic of Yugoslavia and the Kosovo Liberation Army (KLA) who, you may recall, received military support from NATO. Essentially, it was a conflict between the Orthodox Serbians and the Kosovo-Albanians.

Armed with weapons smuggled in from Albania, the KLA attacked Yugoslav authorities in Kosovo, sparking a campaign of retribution by Serbs, which resulted in the confirmed deaths of many hundreds of KLA sympathizers – fighters and civilians – and a mass exodus of refugees.

NATO then lent its weight to the conflict by participating in an aerial bombardment of Yugoslavia, attracting widespread controversy and condemnation, and prompting more than a few conspiracy theories. Even China chipped in, claiming the US was flexing its military muscle and expanding its presence and influence in Europe.

Some critics of the NATO campaign, which occurred during President Bill Clinton's tenure, even labeled it a diversionary tactic to deflect attention from Clinton's recent embarrassing dalliance with Monica Lewinsky in the White House.

All of these accusations were met with denials by the Clinton Administration, although the denials rang hollow in the face of the UN Security Council's refusal to sanction NATO's aggressive military involvement in the conflict.

"How many wars do you want to have in your lifetime? How many bombs are you going to drop? I just think it looks like we've become a warrior nation ... We are dropping bombs on crowded cities at night where old people and children are sleeping, and we're watching it on CNN ... What are we doing with all these wars? How are we safer? ... You can't use an anti-war platform to get elected. So maybe that explains why it's so easy for us to go to war. Norman Solomon has written a book War Made Easy. Essentially he says, if the president of the United States wants a war, he can have one. I believe that totally. It's very, very hard to dissent."
–Phil Donahue, interview on Piers Morgan Tonight that aired on
CNN January 7, 2012

THE HEROIN CONNECTION

It's the role heroin played in the Kosovo War that has intrigued many independent researchers.

Kosovo lies in the center of the Balkan Route through which nearly all Afghan heroin (the world's most popular variety) passes through on its way to greater Europe and beyond, including the United States. The extraordinary value of the Balkans' drug trade has been estimated to be worth anywhere from US$500 billion to one trillion dollars annually.

There's speculation the Western-backed KLA was heavily involved in this profitable business, adding fuel to the theory that the desire to control heroin trafficking was the underlying cause of the Kosovo War.

Certainly, Kosovo Albanians are prime movers in the region's illegal drug trade – second only to the Turkish mafia, according to US Drug Enforcement Agency officials who, in 2000, estimated that Kosovo Albanians controlled nearly half of Europe's heroin. Those same officials said as much as 6 tonnes of heroin passed through the Balkan Route every month.

In an article by *The Guardian* dated March 13, 2000, columnist Maggie O'Kane said international agencies fighting the drug trade were warning that Kosovo had become "a smuggler's paradise" and "Nato-led forces, struggling to keep the peace a year after the war, have no mandate to fight drug traffickers…who are running the Balkan route with complete freedom".

In the same article, a former Yugoslav narcotics official described Kosovo as "the Colombia of Europe". The official says, "The Kosovo mafia has been smuggling heroin since the mid-1980's. But since the Kosovo War, they have come into their own."

Perhaps the foremost authority on drug wars is Canadian economist Dr. Michel Chossudovsky, author of *The New World Order*, whose extensive commentaries clearly convey that "the expensive Yugoslav conflict" was "directly linked to the multi-billion drug war".

In an exclusive interview dated June 30, 1999 in cannabisculture.com, Dr. Chossudovsky says, "Drugs serve political interests … They help finance covert intelligence operations … the Vietnam War, the generals in Haiti, the Contras, Colombian paramilitaries … Many groups are funded with drug money that serve geopolitical interests. And there is usually covert support provided by the CIA to these groups.

"It is well documented the KLA is financed by the drug trade. It also has links to the CIA, German intelligence and Islamic terrorist organizations. So Islamic terrorist organizations the West has labeled as its enemies are co-financing the KLA alongside NATO. It's a totally absurd situation".

Dr. Chossudovsky also alludes to drug profits being laundered to buy arms in post-war Kosovo.

OPERATION ENDURING FREEDOM
AKA OPERATION OPIUM

Dr. Chossudovsky also believes heroin is a primary motivating factor in the war in Afghanistan – the war the American administration calls *Operation Enduring Freedom.* In an article published in RonPaulForums.com and dated June 25, 2013, he says, "Since the US-led invasion of Afghanistan in October 2001, the Golden Crescent opium trade has soared."

In the same article, Dr. Chossudovsky says in the previous four years there was a surge in Afghan opium production. He quotes UNODC (the UN Office on Drugs and Crime) figures which reveal that poppy cultivation in Afghanistan in 2012 covered an area of more than 154,000 hectares; he also quotes a UNODC spokesperson as confirming in 2013 that opium production is heading toward record levels.

Dr. Chossudovsky is also extensively quoted in the GlobalResearch.com site, which provides some of the most credible, in depth research and reporting on the Afghan drug trade.

Under the tell-all heading "The Spoils of War: Afghanistan's Multibillion Dollar Heroin Trade", Global Research carries yet another article by Dr. Chossudovsky. It was first published in May 2005. In it he states:

"Heroin is a multi-billion dollar business supported by powerful interests...One of the 'hidden' objectives of the war (in Afghanistan) was precisely to restore the CIA-sponsored drug trade to its historical levels and exert direct control over the drug routes.

"Immediately following the October 2001 invasion, Opium markets were restored. By early 2002, the opium price...was almost 10 times higher than in 2000."

Readers are reminded that "prior to the Soviet-Afghan War (1979-1989) opium production in Afghanistan and Pakistan was directed to small regional markets" and "there was no local production of heroin."

Dr. Chossudovsky claims "the Afghan narcotics economy was a carefully designed project of the CIA, supported by US foreign policy".

History lends some weight to the doctor's claims. Out of the chaos that followed the Soviet-Afghan War, the ruling Taliban decreed that opium production be significantly curbed. That ruling was followed by another ordering that opium cultivation cease totally.

There has been considerable speculation that America's invasion of Afghanistan was prompted by this development. Whether true or not, one result of that military action is not in doubt: the opium ban was quickly lifted and Afghan opium production rapidly rose to record levels.

Of course, this could be passed off as coincidental. An innocent result of an invasion that saw Afghanistan's war lords back in control and opium growth thriving once again. Indeed, that's the official line and that's how many perceive it.

However, if commentators and researchers are united about any one thing it's that the CIA is inexorably linked to Afghanistan's illicit drug trade and has been, in the words of one commentator, "since the agency funded Taliban fighters to oppose the Soviets".

(PROFITING FROM) THE WAR ON DRUGS

The motivations for creating these drug wars, if indeed that's what they are, is the massive profits the global elite can derive from their well-documented drug trafficking.

Which begs the question: why are drugs so profitable? Essentially, many argue, it's because they are *illegal*. By making drugs a criminal enterprise, it creates an enormous black market economy where drugs fetch far greater prices than they would if legal.

Many authors and independent media outlets have repeatedly suggested *the War on Drugs* is a money-making scheme and doesn't actually prevent drug usage or reduce the number of addicts. They point to countries like Portugal, the Netherlands and the Czech Republic, which have all decriminalized drug usage to varying degrees and have subsequently experienced a decrease in the amount of drug-related crime and a reduction in the incidence of drug addiction.

In an article dated January 23, 2014 and headed *World leaders slam war on drugs as 'a disaster'*, CNBC comments that the "decades-long war on drugs has failed and the world's lawmakers need to consider decriminalization".

Former UN Secretary General Kofi Annan is quoted in the article as saying the War on Drugs "has been a disaster and has inflicted enormous harm … Drug use is not down. It's time for a different approach. Drugs have destroyed many people, and the wrong government and policies have destroyed many people".

Possibly interrelated to the theory that drugs are prohibited to fuel the highly profitable international drug trade, is the privatization of prisons that has occurred in America and throughout much of the Western world in recent decades. Something that started happening around the same time the War on Drugs began.

Privatized prisons could be viewed as an adjunct to the previous chapter, which covered secret prisons. In the West at least, these privately-owned, non-government facilities can't be classified as secret prisons in that they are not *off-the-grid* or unknown to the government. However, according to conspiracy theorists, they are secretive in so far as they don't disclose their true agendas.

Once prisons are privatized, they need prisoners to make a buck or they'll go out of business. That's the economic reality. Some critics of the privatized prisons business claim that it's open to corruption and suggest that private companies running these prisons have been known to collaborate quietly with law enforcement officials to ensure their prisons are full of inmates.

The obvious candidates to target – after murderers, rapists and drug-pushers of course – are drug-users, according to those who promote this theory. If true, then the War on Drugs may also be a scam designed to put users in prison and keep them there.

Remember, it's a fact that a large percentage of prisoners around the world have committed *victimless crimes* involving drugs. And like the War on Drugs itself, the privatized prison system is highly profitable.

Could it be this *war* and these privatized prisons are some kind of two-fold, money-making scheme of the elite? Or are we getting a bit paranoid here?

"I've seen people I love die from this disease (drug addiction). Now we have a chance to at least demonstrate that this isn't what people feel about this issue anymore ... People don't want drugs to be illegal anymore, they don't want their heads of politicians buried in the sand."
–Russell Brand, from television interview on February 13, 2014 on the UK's Channel 4.

If this entire conspiracy theory on drug wars is wrong, fictitious, over-egged or, heaven forbid, just plain loony, another scenario is very possible: this scenario is that drugs are simply one of the many fortuitous and spontaneous spoils of war, and while the global elite may not actually be starting wars to financially benefit from drug-trafficking they sure as hell do alright out of it.

Even in mineral-rich and oil-rich war-torn regions like the Middle East, illicit drugs and the huge profits to be made from them are a nice added bonus, wouldn't you agree?

And even if there is no ulterior motive surrounding the War on Drugs – a very big IF – the bottom line is the drug prohibition program hasn't remotely worked; the international drug trade is expanding, not contracting, and drug usage is increasing worldwide.

We don't remotely support drug use. The horrors that illicit drugs inflict on individuals and on society in general are there for all to see.

However, the problem is one that may be with us forever because it does seem that drugs and profits cannot be separated, and history shows that where large profits are to be made, corruption flourishes.

Meanwhile, excuse us for one moment. It's time for us to take our medication again!

26

GREENLAND AKA CONSPIRACYLAND

On arriving at Thule Air Base via Air Greenland and passing through the various US Air Force security checks, Nine's first port of call was his guest house in the tiny settlement of Thule. Then, after checking in and taking delivery of a rental car, his next port of call, quite literally, was the nearby Port of Thule. Located as it was above the Arctic Circle, it was the world's northernmost deep water port. And, like all of Greenland's west coast ports and settlements, it was also ice-free in summer, which suited Nine just fine for what he was planning.–The Orphan Uprising

Greenland is the setting for an important section of our final book in *The Orphan Trilogy*. There's a series of life-and-death action sequences in this northern outpost of Denmark as Nine, our hero, attempts to find his kidnapped son who he fears is being experimented on at a secret research facility.

We initially selected the enigmatic, mostly inhospitable and largely ice-covered landmass which, for some unknown reason, is called Greenland. It seemed an ideal place for the Splinter Civilization to house secret technologies and conduct medical experimentation on children – if indeed such a civilization exists. However, in the course of researching the icy subcontinent we were pleasantly surprised to discover a wide variety of unusual and unexplained events have occurred there throughout its colorful history. Events that have fueled many a conspiracy theory…

Re-evaluating what he knew about the base, the former operative was aware it was home to the 21st Space Wing's global network of sensors that provided space surveillance and missile warning to the Air Force Space Command and the North American Aerospace Defence Command. It also served as a ballistic missile early warning site and since 2002 had been home to the 821st Air Base Group.

–The Orphan Uprising

THULEGATE

In *The Orphan Uprising*, Nine arrives in disguise at Thule Air Base, the US Air Force's northernmost base located as it is above the Arctic Circle in Greenland's northwest, in search of his abducted son.

Home to the 21st Space Wing's space surveillance and missile warning sensors, the Air Base has attracted its share of controversy – as has Thule itself with conspiracy theories dating back to ancient times.

The location's name itself is shrouded in mystery. Various interpretations of *Thule* have confused it with other northern destinations including Iceland and Scandinavia, and in medieval times Thule was associated with distant places beyond the known world. So it's ripe for conspiracy theories, mired as it is in ancient mythology.

Situated less than 1000 miles from the North Pole, Thule's a magnet for you know who. (Our old mates the Tinfoil Hatters)! However, once in a blue moon, the Tinfoil Hat Network's stalwarts promote some way-out conspiracy theory that turns out to be true; and Thule's the scene of *Thulegate*, one of their most treasured conspiracies. Treasured because it miraculously ended up being proven true, also proving the old adage that if you take enough wild stabs in the dark, occasionally you'll get lucky!

Tinfoil Hatters now rightfully refer to Thulegate as *conspiracy fact*. Yet still, sadly for them, few buy in to any of their other theories, including the Moon being manmade, the ruling elite are all reptiles, that germs do not exist, blah, blah, blah.

Thulegate relates to the *documented* January 1968 crash of an American B-52 nuclear bomber on the ice sheet near the Thule Air Base. Apparently, the bomber was carrying four nuclear warheads, which the Pentagon maintained were destroyed in the crash. However, a *Daily Mail* report (updated on November 11, 2008 in its *Mail Online* site) debunks this, confirming what conspiracy theorists had speculated all along – that one or more of the warheads hadn't been destroyed.

Excerpts from the *Daily Mail* report follow:

"Greenland is a self-governing province of Denmark, but the carrying of nuclear weapons over Danish territory was kept secret, according to the BBC investigation...One of the missions went wrong and a bomber crashed into the ice a few miles from the air base.

"A declassified US government video, obtained by the BBC, documents the clear-up and gives some idea of the scale of the operation.

"The Pentagon had maintained that all four weapons had been 'destroyed', but declassified documents obtained...reveal investigators realized only three of the weapons could be accounted for."

The report continues, "The underwater search (for the missing weapon) was beset by technical problems...Eventually the search was abandoned.

"A nuclear scientist has told the Daily Mail: 'We really don't know what has happened to this bomb'."

According to the ApacheClips.com military media site, "The incident caused controversy at the time and in the years since. It highlighted the risks Thule Air Base posed to Greenlanders from nuclear accidents and potential superpower conflicts."

The ApacheClips.com article continues: "The accident... signaled the immediate end of the airborne alert program, which had become untenable because of the political and operational risks involved.

"Scott Sagan, a political science academic and writer, postulated that if the aircraft had crashed into Thule Air Base, the missile early warning system and the redundant warning aircraft would have been knocked out simultaneously, potentially leading NORAD to conclude incorrectly that a nuclear attack had started."

So the B-52 incident turned out to be another good example of something that started out as a conspiracy theory and ended up as fact.

When a B-52 nuclear bomber crashed and burned on the ice near Thule Air Base in 1968, the Pentagon classified all documents relating to the crash. Since then, media reports on America's northernmost Air Force base had been unaccountably few and far between.

–The Orphan Uprising

PROJECT ICEWORM

Many independent investigators believe Thulegate was the tip of the iceberg – please excuse the pun, but we couldn't resist – in a large-scale Cold War nuclear program the US Military was conducting *beneath* Greenland's surface.

The ambitious program, which was apparently managed by the US Army, went by the codename *Project Iceworm* and involved the construction of a series of nuclear missile launch sites beneath the Greenland ice sheet and conveniently within striking distance of the Soviet Union.

These top-secret sites were constructed under the ice so that the Danish Government would remain unaware of them as America did not have permission to build nuclear missile sites in Greenland.

As covered in chapter 19, the global elite have numerous underground bases – some of them confirmed despite being off-limits to non-military personnel or to anyone beneath the highest levels of government. That confirmation has usually come via reluctant acknowledgement from the Military Industrial Complex, persistent investigative reporting by a handful of brave journalists or, last but certainly not least, publication of declassified documents.

This accounts for those clandestine subterranean bases we now know of. However, there are persistent rumors that hundreds more such secret underground facilities exist around the world.

Many conspiracy theorists believe the US Army had, or still has, several underground cities – yes cities – beneath the Greenland ice sheet where all manner of secret technologies are being developed and maintained. If there is a Splinter Civilization that has more advanced technologies than official science is aware of then the icy, inhospitable Danish-governed country with a population of less than 60,000 people would seem to the best place this side of the Moon for safekeeping of such technologies.

One of those underground sites whose existence has been confirmed is a former US Army facility in Greenland known as *Camp Century*, which was part of *Project Iceworm* and was also previously just a conspiracy theory. (It's about here our Tinfoil Hat readers start cheering wildly)! The Camp Century site beneath the Greenland ice sheet was selected by US Army engineers in May, 1959. Construction began in 1960 and it was soon a fully-fledged subterranean city that ran entirely on nuclear power.

Camp Century has long been declassified and is now an Arctic research facility. The US Army's activities there were officially abandoned in 1966, reportedly due to the unstable conditions that existed beneath the ice. However, given the B-52 incident occurred only two years later, in 1968, a skeptic could be forgiven for linking it with Project Iceworm and also for wondering whether the project was actually axed.

Continuing with the Cold War theme, in an article headed *US Army's top secret Arctic city under the ice*, Curezon.org claims, "It eventually came out that the ultimate objective of Camp Century was of placing medium-range missiles under the ice – close enough to Moscow to strike targets within the Soviet Union."

Curezon also mentions a now declassified US Army film showing "the nuclear-powered construction process of Camp Century, beneath the ice of central Greenland".

The article continues: "Details of the missile base project were classified for decades, first coming to light in January 1997, when the Danish Foreign Policy Institute (DUPI) was asked by the Danish Parliament to research the history of nuclear weapons in Greenland during the Thulegate scandal.

"A report confirmed that the U.S. stockpiled nuclear weapons in Greenland until 1965, contradicting assurances by Danish foreign minister Niels Helveg Petersen that the weapons were in Greenland's airspace, but never on the ground. The DUPI report also revealed details of Project Iceworm, a hitherto secret United States Army plan to store up to 600 nuclear missiles under the Greenland ice cap…

"Danish workers involved in the clean-up operation claimed long-term health problems resulting from their exposure to the radiation."

Incidentally, the declassified US army film referred to in the article is freely available to watch online, having been uploaded to various video sites.

In the comments section beneath one such website that posted video footage of Camp Century, one viewer wrote, "The machinery and the whole project makes me think of the Thunderbird animations."

Who knows, maybe the underground facilities in the popular British science fiction TV series *Thunderbirds* were inspired by Camp Century or other similar confirmed or rumored subterranean bases of the global elite.

It's unlikely any of us will ever know how far the Splinter Civilization's rabbit holes extend beneath our feet. And whenever we see sprawling underground cities in sci-fi movies and television episodes, or read about them in novels, most of us still think, *This plot sounds far-fetched* or *The scientific concepts are ridiculous.* Right?

Why on earth Omega had chosen Thule as the location
for one of its secret medical labs, Nine could only guess.
He assumed its isolation was one reason. No doubt the
security afforded by the Air Force base was another.

–The Orphan Uprising

THE THULE SOCIETY

One of the oldest conspiracy theories relating to the name Thule dates back to *The Oera Linda Book*, a 19th Century manuscript written in Old Frisian and purported to have been compiled as long ago as AD 803. After being translated into German in the 1930's, leading Nazi Party member Heinrich Himmler latched onto the book because of its apparent references to the origins of the Aryan race.

Infamous German occultist group *the Thule Society*, which was later absorbed into Hitler's National Socialist German Workers Party, also accepted the book's contents as absolute fact. The Thule Society's followers believed in an ancient landmass known as *Hyperborea*, which they said was near the North Pole and was exactly where modern Greenland is. These Nazi mystics identified a place called *Ultima Thule* as the capital of this mythological and Atlantis-like continent of the Prehistoric World.

The translation of *The Oera Linda Book* has since been branded a hoax. Nevertheless, the book's contents continue to be a subject for speculation.

The blog site TIA MYSOA (This Is Africa – My Simple Online Abode) reminds followers *The Oera Linda Book* became known as *Himmler's Bible* and was also dubbed the *Nordic Bible*. It states: "Hoax or no hoax, this book articulates the first known example of the concept of root races, and I was quite surprised to read how accurate this old manuscript described a black maiden...by the name of Lyda...The description of the three earliest races, Lyda (black), Finda (yellow) and Frya (white) are provided in a section of the manuscript…"

Warning: If you are a member of the Tinfoil Hat Network, we strongly suggest you check that your hat is firmly attached to your head about now…

Often associated with the Thule Society is *the Vril Society*, another German occultist group said to comprise an alien super race known as *Vril-ya* whose intention was, or is, to join forces with superior beings they believe reside below ground on planet Earth. Believers insist the end goal for the Vril-ya and their subterranean allies is to rule the planet's surface one day.

Meanwhile, the Tinfoil Hatters would have us believe the Vril Society developed Vril-powered spacecraft that the Germans used to explore space and to transport fleeing Nazis to the Moon and beyond.

According to the SabotageTimes.com site, "People fully bought into this work of fiction as being gospel truth… They met in secret and reportedly performed bizarre séance-like rituals in a bid to awaken the Vril people and gain control of their powerful elixirs, all in a bid to help them take over the world."

The SabotageTimes report continues, "Although farfetched, when the war ended hundreds of Nazi blueprints were found by the allies, some actually detailed how to build propulsion aircrafts shaped like flying saucers."

The report concludes, "Captured Nazi turned American scientist Wernher von Braun said when asked about how the Nazis became so advanced: 'We had help from them' and pointed upwards."

If the quote is accurate, it's not to be sneezed at. Don't forget von Braun is the *Father of Rocket Science* referred to in chapter 12 – the same gentleman America awarded the National Medal of Science to in 1975.

It just goes to show that in amongst the flood of extravagant claims made by hardcore conspiracy theorists little gems can be found that at the very least warrant further thought if not further investigation.

Nine was also aware of the strange events said to have occurred at or near Thule over the years. Conspiracy theories abounded. In the early Twentieth Century, the tiny settlement inspired the underground Nazi occult organization known as the Thule Society. Its membership was rumored to include Adolf Hitler and numerous other Nazi leaders.

–The Orphan Uprising

KOREAN WAR VETERANS EXPERIMENTED ON?

In our research of various theories concerning Greenland, we came across one conspiracy author who claimed that in the early 1950's American soldiers wounded during the Korean War were secretly hospitalized in undisclosed bases in Greenland. According to the author, this was because the US Government considered its citizens weren't ready to see battle casualties so soon after WW2.

The same author also asserts those veterans were experimented on, resulting in the deaths of some.

However, we've searched far and wide and can find no credible sources confirming, or even suggesting, that wounded Korean War vets were taken to Greenland instead of being repatriated (to the US). So it's entirely possible this theory could come under the category of a desperate conspiracy author running out of ideas and fabricating shocking theories just to keep selling books.

On the other hand, who knows? Stranger and darker things have happened in the history of governments, and that includes the US Government. If it is true it wouldn't be the first time American soldiers, and indeed soldiers of many other nations, have been experimented on without their consent.

"Before anyone passes judgment, may I remind you, we are in the Arctic."
–Fox Mulder (played by David Duchovny) in
Season 1, Episode 7 of The X-Files.

ALIEN ARTIFACTS IN THE ICE

The first season of *The X-Files* television series features an episode called *Ice*, which is set in the Arctic. Delta Air Park, in Vancouver, Canada, was selected by location scouts as the venue for filming because its flat and tundra-like terrain resembles the Arctic environment. At least it does through the lens of a camera.

An impressive 10 million American viewers watched the episode when it first aired in November, 1993. The high-rating, well-reviewed episode has the series' leads David Duchovny and Gillian Anderson as FBI Agents Fox Mulder and Dana Scully, investigating the mysterious deaths of research scientists in the Arctic. The pair soon discover evidence of extraterrestrial, parasitic organisms that take over their hosts and cause those infected to commit extremely violent acts.

A true story, of sorts, in Greenland was reportedly the inspiration for the episode's writers Glen Morgan and James Wong who conjured up the plot in association with the series' creator Chris Carter. Morgan said a *Science News* article about scientists in "Greenland who dug something 250,000 years old out of the ice" gave him the idea.

Of course, if anything like that TV episode actually occurred and alien origins were discovered beneath Greenland's ice sheet, the powers that be are not saying.

Various similarly-themed conspiracy theories reference abandoned ET civilizations discovered in Greenland by the global elite. Warning: more puns ahead… However, all these theories have grown cold, or are completely frozen, due to a total lack of evidence.

A HOLLOW CONSPIRACY THEORY

We doubt there are any gems to be found in the following theory, though it has a surprisingly high number of adherents. It was drawn to our attention by The Atlantean Conspiracy website, which refers to "that mother of all conspiracy theories – the *Hollow Earth Theory*".

A February 2013 article on the site refers to "various testimonies" of the likes of "Admiral Byrd's trips to the poles" and other explorers' accounts of the land beyond the poles as "evidence pointing towards a Hollow Earth theory".

The article states: "Nowadays only government-approved teams are allowed anywhere near the poles, but historically almost every explorer who has traveled to the poles has recorded that as you get closer, it gets warmer, the snow and ice disappear, and greenery and wild-life reappear. Even modern-day explorers continue finding driftwood, pollen, animals, and insects the closer they get to the poles.

"In Greenland animals should migrate south for the winter, but in fact they all migrate north, and northern winds in Greenland are actually warmer than Southern winds during winter. In Northern Russia there are constantly large animal bones and driftwood coming ashore from the North as well. The poles are no-fly zones and compasses start going haywire as soon as explorers sail/fly near them.

"During earthquakes the Earth behaves much more like a hollow body than a solid one, ringing like a bell with after-shocks spreading out like ripples in a pond. This behavior is indicative of a Hollow Earth and something which plate tectonics theory falls short of adequately explaining."

The article invites readers to "view some of the evidence" in the videos it provides links to.

The idea of an alien civilization living inside the earth is a favorite of the Tinfoil Hat Network. Nazi mystics were also believers in the theory, and Lord Edward Bulwer-Lytton's 1871 novel *The Coming Race* was said to be Adolf Hitler's favorite book. The early science fiction story describes a mysterious free energy source called Vril and also describes in great detail the life of inhabitants living in the so-called Hollow Earth.

These days, given science has progressed and we now know so much more about the planet's properties and nature, Hollow Earth believers are held in much the same regard as Flat Earth subscribers.

We've only scratched the surface of conspiracy theories involving Greenland. Many of them get even zanier than the ones covered in this chapter.

Other Greenland conspiracy theories presented as fact by the Tinfoil Hat Network include: the landmass being the real Atlantis; factories near the North pole with three-foot tall alien workers who manufacture human sweat which nourishes them; Adolf Hitler being alive and well and living in a Nazi-populated city beneath Greenland's ice sheet; and Greenland's flag being a secret Illuminati symbol.

Seriously, does anyone believe this stuff?

27

THE CATCHER IN THE RYE ENIGMA

27

Now alone with Seventeen, Naylor stared intently at the young blonde operative. She was as motionless as a statue, staring right through him. She'd been like this for the past couple of minutes, but she didn't know that. Her eyes had glazed over and she was in some kind of trance. She held a copy of the novel, The Catcher in the Rye.

–The Ninth Orphan

The 1951 novel *The Catcher in the Rye*, by J.D. Salinger, is arguably the most controversial book of all time.

Nicknamed the 'Bible of teenage angst', the classic novel, which is frequently labeled immoral by different groups, has been banned in various parts of America over the decades. From 1961-1982 it was the most censored book in libraries and high schools across the US. School principals have branded it communist propaganda and teachers have been fired for assigning it to students.

But the main controversy, and indeed the most common reason for it being banned, was that it either directly inspired or was associated with some of the most infamous crimes of the 20th Century.

Presidential assassins and would-be Presidential assassins, stalkers and murderers of film stars and music icons are among the known deranged individuals who were obsessed with Salinger's book, which many claim to be an assassination trigger device.

The murderers, stalkers and their victims and targets, who are all either confirmed or rumored to be part of the *The Catcher in the Rye* mystery, include John Lennon, Ronald Reagan, Robert John Bardo, Lee Harvey Oswald, Bobby Kennedy, Madonna, Martin Luther King, Mark David Chapman, Jack Ruby, Rebecca Schaeffer, Jodie Foster, JFK, John Hinckley Junior, James Earl Ray and Sirhan Sirhan.

The allegation pointed at Salinger is that he craftily implanted coded messages into the book that act as post-hypnotic suggestions or mind control triggers. In turn, these enable the CIA handlers to *activate* Manchurian Candidates for planned assassinations.

Many believe the novel was part of the CIA's extensive mind control program MK-Ultra and that while future assassins are being brainwashed they are forced to read the book over and over until it is embedded in their minds.

These ideas and others have been covered in pop culture, especially in the 1997 film *Conspiracy Theory*, in which Mel Gibson's character carries a copy of Salinger's book with him at all times. The cleverly-written film, which at first appears to be a lightweight romantic comedy co-starring rom-com queen Julia Roberts, becomes more intense as the story progresses and it's revealed Mel Gibson's character is entwined with the CIA and is a mind control victim of the agency's MK-Ultra program.

Season three of the TV series *Criminal Minds* features an episode called *Limelight* in which the character of David Rossi, played by Joe Mantegna, mentions having once interviewed serial killer Ted Bundy who told him, "If you wanna stop people from becoming like me, don't burn Catcher in the Rye."

An episode of the animated TV series *South Park* also covers the mind control theory in a humorous way when one of the show's young characters reads the book then picks up a knife and starts saying, "Kill John Lennon, kill John Lennon." The boy is disappointed when his father informs him the former Beatle was assassinated years earlier.

But seriously, can *The Catcher in the Rye* really wake MK-Ultra *sleeper assassins* from their slumber?

"A substitute teacher out on Long Island was dropped from his job for fighting with a student. A few weeks later, he returned to the classroom, shot the student, unsuccessfully, held the class hostage and then shot himself. Successfully. This fact caught my eye: last sentence, Times; A neighbor described him as a nice boy – always reading Catcher in the Rye. The nitwit, Chapman, who shot John Lennon said he did it because he wanted to draw the attention of the world to The Catcher in the Rye and the reading of the book would be his defense. And young Hinckley, the whiz kid who shot Reagan and his press secretary, said if you want my defense all you have to do is read Catcher in the Rye."
–Monologue delivered by Will Smith in the film Six Degrees of Separation (1993)

It must be noted the idea that assassination codes are buried deep in Salinger's book is one of the oldest conspiracy theories around and has often been explored over the decades. In fact, many readers familiar with *Catcher* conspiracies may think all the theories have already been proven to be false and there's no need to drag them up yet again.

However, given what we've unearthed in compiling this book (*The Orphan Conspiracies*) thus far – especially the unique revelations on the history of mind control, the effectiveness of subliminal messages, the latest scientific studies on the brain, the Americanized Nazis in *Project Paperclip* and the recently declassified documents on real-life Manchurian Candidates – we believe some of the theories swirling about Salinger's classic deserve another look.

"I shoot people in this hat."
– J.D. Salinger, The Catcher in the Rye

INTRODUCING... THE *CATCHER* CRIMINALS

The mother of all *Catcher* incidents is probably Mark David Chapman's assassination of John Lennon on December 8, 1980. As widely reported, and as mentioned in chapters 21 and 23, the killer stood over the ex-Beatle's corpse after shooting him and patiently read a copy of Salinger's classic while waiting for police to arrive and arrest him.

Not long before the murder, Chapman had wanted to change his name to the novel's narrator and anti-hero *Holden Caulfield* – so enamored was he with this fictitious character; inside the very copy of the book Chapman had purchased on the day of the murder, police found he'd written, "To Holden Caulfield, From Holden Caulfield, This is my statement"; and during the court case that followed, Chapman read a passage from the novel when addressing the judge and jury during his sentencing.

In the FBI's Vault the following is mentioned under the file *Attempted Assassination of President Ronald Reagan*: "On March 31, 1981, John W. Hinckley, Jr., shot President Ronald Reagan and several others in a failed assassination attempt. The FBI conducted an extensive investigation, named REAGAT."

Just like Mark David Chapman, Hinckley did not attempt to flee the crime site and seemed content to be arrested. After the assassination attempt, which besides wounding President Reagan also left White House Press Secretary James Brady permanently disabled, detectives found a copy of *The Catcher in the Rye* on a coffee table in Hinckley's hotel room.

Before the attempt on Reagan's life, Hinckley had relentlessly stalked actress Jodie Foster for a number of years. He reportedly became obsessed with the Hollywood star after first seeing her in Martin Scorsese's 1976 film *Taxi Driver*. Even to this day, more than three decades later, Foster has hardly ever spoken of the incident and has been known to walk out of interviews when Hinckley's name, or the Reagan assassination attempt, is mentioned.

The shooter, whose full name was John Warnock Hinckley Jr. (maintaining the three-name lone gunman theme), tried to assassinate Reagan because he said he thought that would impress Jodie Foster. It was later revealed that during his stay in the Washington D.C. psychiatric hospital St. Elizabeths, Hinckley had exchanged letters with serial killer Ted Bundy and sought the address of mass murderer Charles Manson.

Another *Catcher* fan was Robert John Bardo, yet another three-name assassin, who murdered American actress and model Rebecca Schaeffer on July 18, 1989. Like Mark David Chapman, Bardo was carrying a copy of Salinger's book on him at the scene of the crime.

The one-time stalker of Madonna and child actress Samantha Smith, Bardo stalked Schaeffer before finding her alone at her home in Los Angeles. He shot the star of *My Sister Sam* TV series in the chest then threw his red paperback copy of the book onto the roof of a nearby building as he fled.

As for JFK's killer Lee Harvey Oswald, *The Catcher in the Rye* was found in a raid on his Dallas, Texas apartment after the assassination. His other books included George Orwell's *Animal Farm* and Adolf Hitler's *Mein Kampf*. Although unconfirmed, it has been claimed by a few sources that Oswald was very keen on Salinger's novel, which apparently was his favorite.

Criminals not officially acknowledged but rumored in conspiracy circles to have been directly influenced by *Catcher* include RFK's assassin Sirhan Sirhan, Lee Harvey Oswald's killer Jack Ruby, Martin Luther King's murderer James Earl Ray, cult leader and killer Charles Manson, the Washington Sniper John Allen Muhammad, Jonestown founder Jim Jones, the Boston Strangler Albert DeSalvo, the unidentified Zodiac Killer, the Unabomber Ted Kaczynski, serial killer Ted Bundy and the Oklahoma bomber Timothy McVeigh.

Even if none of these killers were inspired by Salinger's novel, the list of murderers and other criminals whose possession of, or obsession with, the book has been proven is surprisingly lengthy and throws up a thousand unanswered questions.

Isn't it also possible, probable or even highly likely other criminals have been inspired by *The Catcher in the Rye*? How many assassins disposed of their copies after committing murders or other crimes – as Robert John Bardo tried to do? Maybe others were as obsessed with the book as Mark David Chapman was, but subsequent investigations failed to uncover those details? After all, not every criminal keeps a diary or records of their personal library of reading material.

As one book reviewer wrote on Amazon.com in a review of Salinger's classic: "There may be countless other criminals and stalkers who have identified with the book's main character, Holden Caulfield."

Minutes earlier, Naylor had hypnotized Seventeen using the MK-Ultra voice commands he'd recently received from Langley. For years, he'd wanted to have his way with Seventeen. Receiving the orphans' MK-Ultra codes had presented him with the perfect opportunity. It was perfect because she would never remember a thing. The copy of The Catcher in the Rye *he'd given her was all part of the mind control program. The book acted as an additional control mechanism to activate hypnotism triggers in the brain.*

–*The Ninth Orphan*

A LITERARY PSY-OP?

In *The Ninth Orphan*, Nine and his fellow orphans have a triggering device which happens to be the names of all the planets in the solar system – Mercury, Venus, Earth, Mars, Jupiter, Saturn, Uranus, Neptune, Pluto. When the orphans hear or read those words in precisely that order, they immediately fall into a hypnotized state as a result of their MK-Ultra programming. That's all their handlers have to do to gain total control of their charges and force them to do *anything*, even kill.

This phrasing technique we included in our novel was based on declassified CIA documents, as well as published research on hypnotism, revealing how mind control has been shown to work. It's only one of many techniques used, but one that crops up again and again in the documented evidence of successful mind control experiments.

Accepting for a moment that *Catcher* is such a triggering device, it would likely set off MK-Ultra subjects by having carefully phrased words in strategic parts of the book. Nobody outside of the sleeper assassins and their intelligence agency handlers would be able to recognize such phrases as being abnormal, especially if crafted by such a skillful writer as Salinger.

Richard Condon's 1959 classic novel *The Manchurian Candidate* uses only one card, the Queen of Hearts, out of an entire deck of cards as a triggering device for activating the mind control programs in the story's main characters. If the mind controlled subjects are shown a deck of cards, card by card, they're hypnotized simply because the Queen of Hearts happens to be in the deck. Keep in mind there are 52 cards in a deck, so about 98% of cards in the deck aren't related to the mind control program at all.

Similarly, 98% of Salinger's book would simply be literature and probably have nothing to do with nefarious intelligence agency programs like MK-Ultra. It wouldn't have upset the flow of the novel if Salinger, or perhaps his publishing house editor, had inserted a few brief triggering devices, or phrases, at the behest of the CIA or FBI or other such agency.

If the novel contains mind control triggers there are two obvious possibilities regarding exactly who inserted them.

One is that Salinger didn't deliberately insert such triggers in *Catcher* and had no knowledge his book would be used for mind control. Instead, it was simply used by intelligence agencies, without his permission, as a triggering device to prompt chosen subjects to kill. This would likely have been achieved during the brainwashing process of subjects by repeating certain sentences from the book over and over. It may also be true that the likes of the CIA simply selected the novel as the perfect story to brainwash lone gunmen given its themes of alienation and angst.

The second possibility is that Salinger knowingly inserted mind control phrases into the novel and worked in collusion with high ranking officials in the US intelligence community. Following this theme Salinger along with his advisors, or controllers perhaps, planted excerpts of neurolinguistic writing designed to *speak* to an assassin's brain.

How could any ordinary writer achieve that? Such a question assumes Salinger was an ordinary writer…

Fearing Isabelle was beginning to see his real self, Nine turned his back on her and looked down at the copy of
The Catcher in the Rye he held.
–*The Ninth Orphan*

THE AUTHOR'S SECRETIVE LIFE

J.D. Salinger was by all accounts a recluse and, of all the 20th Century's masters of literature, he's probably the one least is known about. This is due in part to his extreme desire for privacy. A good example of this was the reported act of painting his forest cabin in camouflage colors so nobody could find him!

Despite living until 2010, some 59 years after *The Catcher in the Rye* was first published and became a phenomenal worldwide bestseller, he never published another novel.

Salinger's last published work, the short story collection *Hapworth 16, 1924*, came out in 1965. From that point on he continued to write, but his writing remained for his eyes only. Calls from his millions of fans eager to read more of his works apparently fell on deaf ears.

Besides being reclusive, many have labeled him eccentric and even mean-spirited. There are numerous colorful stories about him. These include him regularly drinking his own urine, becoming enraged whenever his infant children cried, being a hypochondriac, telling one of his wives never to disturb him "unless the house is burning down", exploring Dianetics (later renamed Scientology) and meeting its founder L. Ron Hubbard, and having his photo removed from all his books' jackets.

However, what many conspiracy theorists believe holds the key in the whole mystery surrounding *Catcher* is Salinger's life before he wrote the book. During and immediately after World War 2 to be precise.

And like many subjects in this book, the controversies linked to Salinger's masterpiece appear to lead directly back to the Nazis.

What few of Salinger's fans ever fully comprehend is the man's extensive military and intelligence employment history. Employment that included working for the OSS – the forerunner to the CIA – on highly classified projects in Europe post-WW2.

According to the 1988 unauthorized biography *In Search of J.D. Salinger*, by Ian Hamilton, Salinger worked for the Defense Intelligence during WW2 and served with the Counter Intelligence Corps. His main duties, Hamilton wrote, involved interrogating captured Nazis.

And on September 3, 2013, *The Telegraph* ran an article headlined *JD Salinger's five unpublished titles revealed, and how Second World War shaped his thinking*. According to the article, one of Salinger's unpublished books is "about his time interrogating prisoners of war when he served working in the counter-intelligence division". That book, incidentally, has the revealing title, *A Counterintelligence Agent's Diary*.

Equally intriguing is another unpublished Salinger book titled *A World War II Love Story*, which according to the same article claims is "based on his brief marriage to Sylvia, a Nazi collaborator, just after the war".

Ian Hamilton's *In Search of J.D. Salinger* also mentions that as the war came to a close Salinger was an active participant in the deNazification of Germany.

Now let's think about that word for a moment...*deNazification*.

That word could very well mean Salinger was actively involved in the genesis of *Project Paperclip*, that clandestine program we detailed in chapter 12, which involved smuggling hundreds of Nazis into America and using them to progress the US intelligence and scientific sectors. After all, declassified files have since revealed that much of America's (and the Soviet Union's) efforts in deNazifying Europe in truth amounted to gathering up all the Nazi regime's incredible scientific technologies, not to mention its scientists.

In fact, some researchers have gone as far as saying the process was more of a *reNazification* than a deNazification. Or, put another way, fascism continued, stronger than ever, but in another form and leaping across oceans to far-away countries like America.

As we've shown in earlier chapters through declassified documents and mainstream media reports, some of the *Paperclip Nazi* scientists squirreled into the US after WW2 were charged with developing America's earliest attempts at mind control. This was due to the fact that the Nazis had made tremendous progress in the science of the mind – primarily because of the horrific experiments they conducted on *live* prisoners during the Holocaust.

Declassified documents also prove these Americanized Nazis had a major influence on the intelligence community in the West post-WW2, especially with US mind control programs which had fascist science written all over them.

Given Salinger's top-secret wartime experiences, some conspiracy theorists have connected the dots. They assert that he planted mind control triggers in *The Catcher in the Rye* using the advanced knowledge he was exposed to in his dealings with Nazi scientists. This theory suggests the book was written in such a way that it could be used in MK-Ultra and the CIA's earlier mind control projects such as *Project Artichoke*.

These are wild theories indeed. However, given what we now know (and are still learning) about how advanced Nazi mind technologies were, and how much they shaped the modern US intelligence community, these theories should not be wholly dismissed.

Whatever the case, the actual reason for Salinger's reclusiveness may have been because of what he knew, or what he had been forced to do, in this so-called deNazification process after WW2. This idea is potentially supported by Hamilton's biography, which argues that Salinger had post-traumatic stress disorder due to wartime activities that left him a forever disturbed individual.

Seventeen frowned when she noticed the top button of her blouse was undone. Her gaze strayed to the copy of The Catcher in the Rye *on her lap. The orphan had no recollection of picking up the book at any stage. In fact, she'd never even read it. All she knew about the novel was it had been found on the men behind the assassination and attempted assassination of John Lennon and Ronald Reagan respectively, and its author, J.D. Salinger, had significant ties to the CIA.*

–The Ninth Orphan

MORE ON THE MAN WHO KILLED JOHN LENNON

On February 9, 1981, *The New York Times* ran an article stating Mark David Chapman was preparing to plead insanity at the upcoming trial in which he was accused of murdering John Lennon. The article mentions Chapman had developed an unhealthy "obsession" with *Catcher* and "in a handwritten statement delivered to The New York Times last week, Mr. Chapman" had "urged everyone to read the novel, a copy of which was in his possession when he was arrested".

Chapman had apparently told the NY Times that reading the book would "help many to understand what has happened".

The newspaper also reported that the accused's statement

ended with: "My wish is for all of you to someday read 'The Catcher in the Rye.' All of my efforts will now be devoted toward this goal, for this extraordinary book holds many answers. My true hope is that in wanting to find these answers you will read 'The Catcher in the Rye.' Thank you."

The accused's statement was signed "Mark David Chapman – The Catcher in the Rye."

During the trial that followed, Chapman continued to promote the book. At times he would open up a copy and begin reading intently for all to see the book's cover. On other occasions he would stand up excitedly and shout to everyone in the court, imploring them to read the novel.

It also came out during the court case that shortly before the assassination Chapman would sit in his room chanting the mantra, "THE PHONY MUST DIE SAYS THE CATCHER IN THE RYE!" as well as "JOHN LENNON MUST DIE SAYS THE CATCHER IN THE RYE!"

These phrases are eerily similar to Sirhan Sirhan's documented diary entries in which he repeatedly wrote "RFK MUST DIE!"

Another parallel is that the word *phony* in the aforementioned mantra was borrowed from *Catcher*, once again indicating that Chapman's murder of Lennon was somehow inspired by the book.

There is also an urban legend which says John Lennon himself was in the middle of reading the novel the week he was killed. There's no solid evidence to confirm this, and if Yoko Ono knows, she isn't saying.

What can be confirmed is Mark David Chapman's ties with World Vision. As mentioned in chapter 23, it's a little known fact that Chapman was a former World Vision employee and children's counsellor who worked in refugee camps all over the world. Contrary to media reports, he was by all accounts formerly a good citizen who exhibited no signs of mental illness.

As some researchers have speculated, Chapman may have been drugged by CIA agents and forced into their MK-Ultra program while doing aid work for World Vision in Beirut. Some conspiracy theories claim this MK-Ultra program included setting up mind control triggers by repeating certain sentences from *Catcher* for long, sustained periods.

But that's not where the World Vision link to Salinger's novel, or its deadly aftermath, ends...

THE HINCKLEY-BUSH-REAGAN CONNECTION

Surprisingly, World Vision crops up again with Reagan's attempted assassin, John Hinckley, Jr., whose father, John Warnock Hinckley, Sr., was president of World Vision United States.

The gunman's father was also a multi-millionaire Texas oilman and President and Chairman of the independent oil and gas exploration firm Vanderbilt Energy Corporation. Considering he belonged to such a wealthy and prominent family, it seems rather odd that John Hinckley, Jr. was always portrayed by the media as some kind of vagabond who did nothing but stalk Jodie Foster and read *Catcher* all day.

What was also rarely if ever reported was that Hinckley Sr. was a major financial contributor to the failed 1980 Presidential campaign of the Vice President, George H. W. Bush, the man who would have become President sooner had Reagan been killed in the assassination attempt.

But the Bush-Hinckley family ties don't end there. Oh no, not by a long shot...

Hinckley's older brother, Scott, had a dinner date scheduled at the home of Neil Bush, the Vice President's son, the day after the assassination attempt on Reagan. A March 31, 1981 news headline by Associated Press confirmed this: *Bush Son Had Dinner Plans With Hinckley Brother Before Shooting.*

George H.W. Bush's other son, George W. Bush, also admitted to journalists that he may have had dealings with Scott Hinckley who was Vice-President of Vanderbilt Energy, but could not remember either way.

Obviously this is all very circumstantial, but then again...What are the odds that the family of the convicted shooter of the President were intimately tied to the Vice President's family and were also Texas oil tycoons who part-financed the Vice President's unsuccessful presidential campaign against the President?

And why were so few of these facts ever reported by the mainstream media?

Some conspiracy theorists have asked if John Warnock Hinckley Jr.'s actions mirror the plot of Richard Condon's *The Manchurian Candidate*? And if so, was *The Catcher in the Rye* used to transmit the appropriate assassination triggers?

In the book *George Bush: The Unauthorized Biography*, published in 2004 by Progressive Press, Webster Griffin Tarpley and Anton Chaitkin imply that at least the former may have been the case.

Tarpley and Chaitkin state, "For Bush, the vice presidency was not an end in itself, but merely another stage in the ascent towards the pinnacle of the federal bureaucracy, the White House. With the help of his Brown Brothers, Harriman/Skull and Bones network, Bush had now reached the point where but a single human life stood between him and the presidency ... In the midst of the Bush-Baker cabal's relentless drive to seize control over the Reagan administration, John Warnock Hinckley Jr. carried out his attempt to assassinate President Reagan".

The writers continue by asking whether Hinckley was "part of a conspiracy, domestic or international? Not more than five hours after the attempt to kill Reagan, on the basis of the most fragmentary early reports, before Hinckley had been properly questioned, and before a full investigation had been carried out, a group of cabinet officers chaired by George Bush had ruled out a priori any conspiracy".

And ever since, all levels of the US Government, from the White House and FBI down, have maintained that there was no conspiracy involved in the assassination attempt on President Reagan.

When one journalist put all these seemingly connected events to the White House, Bush spokeswoman Shirley M. Green replied on March 31, 1981 that it was all just "Bizarre happenstance, a weird coincidence."

It's also worth noting that none of the Bush family, not the Vice President or Neil Bush or George W. Bush, was ever questioned by the FBI regarding their string of connections with the Hinckley family. If a formal FBI investigation was conducted, you would assume interviewing Vice President Bush and his sons would have been a logical starting point.

Maybe the eighth grade pupil at Alice Deal Junior High School, in Washington D.C., accurately summarized the assassination attempt best when responding to a task set all the students the day after the assassination attempt. Asked to express their views on the incident, the pupil told teachers, "It is a plot by Vice President Bush to get into power. If Bush becomes President, the CIA would be in charge of the country."

Perhaps the young Hinckley also accurately summarized the whole incident. Scribbled notes found in his cell during a random search described a political conspiracy involving either the Left or the Right and orchestrated to attempt to assassinate the President. Unfortunately, this potential evidence was never brought up in the court case.

Reporting on the trial, the media fixated on three points: Hinckley's stalking of Jodie Foster, the defense team's promotion of the *insanity* argument, and the fact that the first thing detectives saw when they busted in to Hinckley's hotel room after the shooting was his copy of *The Catcher in the Rye*.

FORMERLY BANNED, NOW REQUIRED READING

These days, *Catcher* is 'required reading' in most high school English courses in the US and throughout much of the Western world. This despite the fact it has been banned by various schools and libraries, and criticized by numerous parent and teacher groups as being immoral literature due to its use of profanity and themes of excessive rebellion and alienation.

The fact it's now required reading has inspired some conspiracy theorists – most probably of the Tinfoil Hat variety –

to envisage a grand conspiracy in which mind control is being conducted on a mass scale in order to corrupt, pacify or otherwise control today's youth.

Reclusive *Guns N' Roses* lead singer Axl Rose took part in an online chat on December 12, 2008 on the GNR fan community site. When a fan asked him about a song he'd written called *Catcher N' The Rye* on GNR's new album *Chinese Democracy*, Axl's responses seem to indicate he believed the theory that the novel can incite violent acts when read by certain individuals.

"For me," he said, "the song is inspired by what's referred to sometimes as Holden Caulfield Syndrome ...I feel there's a possibility that how the writing is structured with the thinking of the main character could somehow re-program, for lack of a better word, some who may be a bit more vulnerable, with a skewed way of thinking."

Axl also mentioned he felt that the novel is "utter garbage" and said he agrees "wholeheartedly that it should be discontinued as required reading in schools".

THE ARGUMENT AGAINST THE *CATCHER* CONSPIRACY

We concede that we and others may be reading too much into the murders that some connect with Salinger's classic novel. It could be argued that, at best, those murders are only loosely related to *Catcher* for it was, after all, a critically acclaimed masterpiece and one of the biggest selling books of the 20th Century.

Given its worldwide popularity, the fact that the book was found in the possession of a few killers – a handful at most – could just be pure coincidence.

Today, if some new Presidential assassin or serial killer had a copy of *The Da Vinci Code* or a *Harry Potter* book in their possession, would anyone blink? And even though religious books such as the Bible, the Qur'an (Koran) and the Torah have inspired innumerable assassins, madmen and terrorists – some well known, some not – surely that doesn't mean there are insidious mind control programs infused in their writings?

What about Mark David Chapman? we hear you ask.

Yes, the man was completely obsessed with the book, but then again so, too, were countless other (normal) young people around the world in the decades following its publication. Many commented they felt as if Holden Caulfield was voicing their own inner reality and the angers and frustrations they felt in their own lives. And for those who are insane, as Chapman appeared to end up, a work as brilliantly and intensely written as Salinger's novel was bound to reach the darkest corners of their brains, encouraging those individuals take the story too literally, or out of context, or both.

People who are mentally ill often obsess over all kinds of artworks – such as Michael Jackson's music, Stanley Kubrick's movies or Andy Warhol's paintings – believing there are dark messages embedded in those works, instructing them to kill. It's simply a case of criminal minds latching on to warped ideas and dark concepts in popular culture. And certainly *Catcher* is not the only novel to inspire murders, and it won't be the last.

As Aidan Doyle wrote on December 16, 2003 in a Salon.com article entitled *When books kill*: "A copy of 'The Turner Diaries' was found in Timothy McVeigh's car when he was arrested. The novel was written by a leader of the National Alliance and tells the story of a white supremacist group that overthrows the government and subsequently eradicates nonwhites as well as race traitors. The narrator destroys FBI headquarters by detonating a truck loaded with ammonium nitrate and fuel oil. McVeigh used a similar mechanism to destroy the federal building in Oklahoma City, killing 168 people."

The same article also mentions it's not just books that have inspired killings. "A \$246 million lawsuit was lodged against the makers of the game *Grand Theft Auto III* by the families of two people shot by teenagers allegedly inspired by the game. Such movies as 'Natural Born Killers,' 'A Clockwork Orange' and 'Money Train' have routinely been accused of inspiring copycat crimes."

It has been estimated more than 100,000,000 people have read

Catcher. With only a few crazy incidents attributed to it, you could reasonably argue this is not a bad record and certainly isn't enough to justify outlandish conspiracy theories.

୧ ୧ ୧

As mentioned, the alleged conspiracy surrounding *The Catcher in the Rye* has already been studied ad nauseam and the general consensus by experts is that it is a mere coincidence that these criminals committed such horrific crimes after reading the book.

But how many of the so-called experts know about MK-Ultra and the highly documented history of mind control? And how many are aware of the intelligence community's experiments proving Manchurian Candidates are indeed possible?

We're certainly not implying we are experts, but it's a fact that most who have analyzed *Catcher* conspiracy theories have been authorities in either literature or criminology with highly specific knowledge in their chosen fields. Perhaps to more accurately assess this subject a prerequisite would be to have a broader knowledge of such topics as the way intelligence agencies operate, the dark history of assassinations and suspicious lone gunmen, and Project Paperclip's Americanized Nazis as well as understanding how advanced the science of mind control really is.

We ain't saying *Catcher* is definitely a mind control mechanism for those who have been brainwashed by intelligence agencies. But at the very least, the book had an accidental and unintended influence on some of the most heinous and high profile crimes of the 20th Century. And to us that seems very convenient or coincidental or suspicious – take your pick.

Just like any good story, maybe there's a few facts hidden within the fiction and a healthy dose of fiction buried amongst the facts. Perhaps J.D. Salinger never bothered to publicly comment on the crimes associated with his book as he liked the mystery that surrounded it.

And on that note let's allow the man himself have the final word...

"It's partly true, too, but it isn't all true," Salinger wrote in *The Catcher in the Rye*. "People always think something's all true."

28

EXPERIMENTS ON ORPHANS

*"I'm one of twenty-three orphan prodigies. We were
created using genetic engineering technologies that have
been suppressed from the mainstream. I'm at least half a
century ahead of our times in terms of official science. The
embryologists who created me selected the strongest genes
from about a thousand sperm donors then used in-vitro
fertilization to impregnate my mother and other women."*
–The Ninth Orphan

Experimentation on orphans features prominently throughout
The Orphan Trilogy – not surprising given our central characters
are products of the Pedemont Orphanage, a secretive institution
on Chicago's impoverished South Side, where experimentation is
the rule, not the exception.

Keen to maintain at least a level of believability, we spent a
considerable amount of time researching this somewhat unsavory
and unpalatable topic. What we found makes for disturbing reading.

Records of experimentation on children and orphans are often
indistinguishable, and for good reason: in many if not most cases the
children involved are, or were, orphans. Those who weren't technically
classed as such were from one-parent families where, for one reason or
another, that parent – usually the mother – was absent or negligent. In
which case the child might as well have been an orphan.

Those records date right back to biblical times – to experiments
performed on young Jewish prisoners in the *Book of Daniel*.

To remain reasonably contemporary, we chose to limit most of our research to the 1930's onwards.

The man tried to shut out the voices from his childhood which now echoed in his head. He could hear the other orphans calling his name. Nine! Suppressed memories of his time spent at the Pedemont Orphanage surfaced from the depths of his psyche.

–The Ninth Orphan

The very first case that caught our eye was tame compared to others that followed, but nevertheless was devastating for those children involved. Popularly known as *The Monster Study*, it entailed conducting an experiment on 22 children – including 10 orphans – in Davenport, Iowa, in 1939.

The brainchild of one Wendell Johnson, himself a stutterer, at the University of Iowa, the experiment was conducted by grad student Mary Tudor who was tasked with giving half the children positive speech therapy and half negative speech therapy. Those in the former group were praised for their speech fluency while those in the latter were ridiculed and told they were stutterers.

Most disturbingly, many of the orphan children in the 'negative' group suffered psychologically and developed permanent speech problems even though they were once normal speaking children.

The experiment, which was cynically described as *The Monster Study* by Johnson's peers, coincided with news of Nazi experiments on Jewish and other children early in World War Two, and so was kept hidden from the public at large.

In a New York Times article dated March 16, 2003, columnist Gretchen Reynolds says Johnson's findings about the nature of stuttering, once it has begun, remains the accepted wisdom to this day. "The disorder does respond to conditioning, and once established, stuttering can have a ruinous momentum. Often, the worse someone stutters, the more he fears speaking, and the worse his speech becomes."

Reynolds adds, "It is an ugly thing, after all, to experiment on orphans. And Johnson's admirers, who still are legion, struggle to understand why he proposed and designed the project."

No doubt many assumed Johnson believed it was okay to sacrifice a few to help the many other children who stuttered. *The ends justify the means* mindset has been the impetus behind many a cruel medical or social experiment.

Wikipedia reports that the University of Iowa publicly apologized for The Monster Study in 2001. It quotes University of Iowa assistant professor of speech pathology [name redacted] as saying "we still don't know what causes stuttering, but the 'Iowa' way of approaching study and treatment is still heavily influenced by Johnson, but with an added emphasis on speech production".

Well that's all fine and dandy, but what about the experiment's subjects? By all accounts the State of Iowa awarded six of the orphan children close to US$1 million for lifelong psychological and emotional scars caused by six months of torment during the study. And before her death, Tudor expressed deep regret, claiming Johnson should have done more to reverse the negative effects on the orphan children's speech.

Too little, too late, we say.

Peering down through the vent, Kentbridge couldn't believe his eyes: the vent opened up into an underground base occupied by children – boys and girls. No more than five or six years old, they seemed to be hypnotized and moved around like zombies. As some moved out of sight, others came into Kentbridge's line of vision. Dozens of them. The senior agent looked aghast at Nine, then returned his attention to the macabre scene below.

–The Ninth Orphan

THE LEBENSBORN PROGRAM

The Monster Study pales into insignificance next to the horror stories that have come out of Nazi Germany – such as the *Lebensborn Program*, which we touched on briefly in Chapter 2.

To recap, Lebensborn was just one of many Nazi programs incorporating mind control techniques and was a pet project of Heinrich Himmler. The aim of the SS-backed program was to increase the Aryan population and it involved kidnapping thousands of very young children – including orphans – who were deemed to be 'racially pure'. They were interned in camps where they were subjected to mind control tactics and brainwashed to think like Nazis.

In the respected German news site, Spiegel Online International, columnist David Crossland reported (in November 2006) that after decades of hushed shame, the children of the Lebensborn program to create a blond, blue-eyed master race have started to speak out.

"Topic number one is the painful search for their true parents," said Crossland. "And then that nagging question: Was my father a war criminal?"

Crossland observed that the children of the Nazis' Lebensborn ('Spring of Life') program to create an Aryan master race were starting to go public with their plight and were renewing efforts to find out who their true parents were.

Reports from a variety of sources reveal the Nazis kidnapped children from Russia, the Ukraine and throughout Europe. Poland and Yugoslavia figure prominently with estimates of the number of Polish children kidnapped ranging from 20,000 to 200,000.

By all accounts the children were tested then placed in one of three groups, including one for those not wanted. The unfortunate members of that group were killed or dispatched to concentration camps.

Unfortunately, such horrors didn't end with Nazi Germany.

It gradually dawned on Nine that Francis' abduction could somehow be connected to the Black Forest orphanage or one of the other underground medical labs Omega was rumored to be operating elsewhere in the world. Whilst with Omega, Nine had heard the rumors that the agency was conducting illegal scientific experiments on genetically enhanced children at various isolated labs. He'd seen it for himself in Germany, and didn't doubt for a minute there could be others.

–The Orphan Uprising

THE DUPLESSIS ORPHANS

In the 1940's, the government of Quebec, Canada, in league with the Roman Catholic Church, began falsely certifying thousands of orphans as mentally ill and confining them in psychiatric institutions.

Why? The short answer: money.

It happened during the tenure of Quebec Premier Maurice Duplessis in the 1940's and 1950's when a change in government policy saw higher federal subsidies paid out to hospitals than to orphanages. One shameful result of this was indecent numbers of healthy children were hastily diagnosed as psychotic to capitalize on the increased subsidies.

As *CBC Canada* reports on its *CBC Digital Archives* site, the diagnoses were always swift – the children went to bed orphans and woke up psychiatric patients.

Here's excerpts from that report:

"Some children allegedly endured lobotomies, electroshock, straitjackets and abuse. For the rest of their lives they would struggle to bring attention to their story and demand compensation. They called themselves *the Duplessis Orphans*.

"Born out of wedlock and deemed "children of sin," thousands of Quebec children were cut off from society and sent to orphanages... Many were improperly diagnosed as mentally incompetent. The diagnosis would be a lifelong sentence; the orphans endured a difficult and sometimes abusive childhood...the orphans...have organized and are seeking compensation. With each day, more and more people are coming forward with claims of abuse."

Among those survivors seeking compensation, some have asked the Quebec government to exhume bodies in an abandoned Montreal cemetery thought to hold the remains of orphans subjected to medical experiments. The survivors are pushing for autopsies to be performed.

Naylor inspected the documents. They included files and photos Nine had uplifted from the Berlin journalist Naylor had ordered him to execute a year earlier. Among them were graphic photos of orphans who had been subjected to horrific scientific experiments.

–The Ninth Orphan

SYPHILIS TESTING IN GUATEMALA

Now here's an experiment that defies belief. It involved the proven and acknowledged infection of Guatemalan orphans, schoolchildren, psychiatric patients, prison inmates and many others with venereal diseases in the late 1940's by – wait for it – American public health doctors!

Through the late Nineties and early 2000's rumors of deliberate infection of Guatemalans became whispers until finally, in 2005, hard evidence of what one senior US health official described as "a dark chapter in the history of medicine" was produced.

The world learned that for years American public health

doctors deliberately infected hundreds of Guatemalans with syphilis and other venereal diseases. Apparently, the reason for this was to test the effectiveness of penicillin on those infections.

International Rights Advocates claim more than 5000 Guatemalans were experimented on and, in the course of those experiments, over 1000 were infected with venereal diseases.

One experiment entailed syphilis-infected prostitutes sleeping with prisoners in Guatemalan prisons. It transpires that prisoners not infected were administered the bacteria by injection or other means. While those who contracted syphilis were given antibiotics, it remains unclear exactly how many – if any – were cured.

The experiments, funded by America's National Institutes of Health, were facilitated by Guatemalan health officials without the informed consent of subjects. Reports show at least 80 deaths resulted – with some estimates being much higher.

In October 2010 the US Government officially apologized for the actions of American citizens involved in the whole ugly business.

In a joint statement, Secretary of State Hillary Rodham Clinton and Health and Human Services Secretary Kathleen Sebelius said: "Although these events occurred more than 64 years ago, we are outraged that such reprehensible research could have occurred under the guise of public health. We deeply regret that it happened, and we apologize to all the individuals who were affected by such abhorrent research practices."

In a twist to the revelation, the New York Times issue of October 1, 2010 reported – beneath the banner headline *U.S. apologizes for syphilis tests in Guatemala* – that "The public health doctor who led the experiment, John C. Cutler, would later have an important role in the Tuskegee study."

The study referred to was the US Public Health Service's unethical and infamous Tuskegee syphilis experiment that saw African-American males with syphilis deliberately left untreated for 40 years (from 1932 to 1972). But that's a whole other story.

Getting back to the Guatemala experiments, a (US) Presidential

Commission for the Study of Bioethical Issues concluded that, after an intensive nine-month investigation, "The Guatemala experiments involved gross violations of ethics...It is the Commission's firm belief that many of the actions undertaken in Guatemala were especially egregious moral wrongs because many of the individuals involved held positions of public institutional responsibility."

Our research into this experiment has not uncovered reports of successful prosecutions against any of the American health officials or medical staffers involved in this travesty. Nor has it revealed whether any of the experiment's subjects have received compensation for the atrocities committed. We can only assume the answer is *No* to both those questions.

DISPROVEN ALLEGATIONS

In a series of articles first published in the early to mid-2000's, dogged journalist Liam Scheff, who has been described by at least one mainstream US media outlet as a 'HIV denialist', claimed cruel AIDS experiments on children – usually orphans – were being conducted in New York's Incarnation Children's Center (ICC).

Scheff claimed his investigations revealed the children were being force-fed numerous drugs after allegedly testing positive to HIV/AIDS tests.

The allegations were vehemently denied by ICC staffers, and a subsequent New York State Department of Health investigation found none of the allegations could be substantiated. The department also indicated that the accusers appeared to subscribe to the unpopular theory that HIV does not cause AIDS.

One major media outlet pointed out that the allegations came from one person (Scheff) and weren't backed up with real names or evidence of any kind.

When Scheff couldn't get any traction for his allegations with mainstream media, he turned to online media to air his grievances.

Okay, so what does this have to do with experiments on orphans? Apparently...nothing at all. We mention it only to remind any readers who may consider themselves conspiracy theorists how important it is not to believe every conspiracy theory out there.

By the same token, if you've picked up anything from the preceding chapters, you'd have to agree only a fool would automatically accept as gospel everything officialdom tells us.

Nine went on to explain the notes he'd recovered from the journalist left no doubt Omega was manufacturing a new breed of genetically-superior orphans. Kentbridge's mind was racing as Nine brought him up to speed. The program had obviously changed out of sight since The Pedemont Project. Why wasn't I told? Now, it appeared, the emphasis was on radical medical experimentation.

–The Ninth Orphan

Liam Scheff's apparently fictional allegations are eerily reminiscent of some of our fictional musings in *The Orphan Trilogy* – in particular in books one and three, *The Ninth Orphan* and *The Orphan Uprising* – in which the ninth-born orphan visits clandestine orphanages and medical labs on three continents.

And besides all the true accounts of orphan experimentation covered in this chapter, what if there are more advanced, secretive experiments on orphans and children generally that we never hear of?

Again we ask, where does the fiction end and the truth begin?

29

AREA 51: HUMAN OR ALIEN TECHNOLOGIES?

*Nine was aware the base was supposedly connected to,
or even part of, the fabled Area 51. Like most other
Americans, he'd heard the rumors surrounding Area 51 –
such as its anti-gravity machines and other suppressed
technologies and inventions. He had no idea whether
there was any truth in the rumors. Whether the US
Government secretly worked in collaboration with
extraterrestrial civilizations was of no concern to him
anyway. All he cared about was finding his son.*

–*The Orphan Uprising*

If we are right in our assumption that there is a Splinter Civilization – an elite offshoot of humanity that has kept incredible secrets and hoarded advanced technologies – then *Area 51* is one of the red flags signaling its existence.

After decades of denials and calling all conspiracy theorists deluded, the US Government has finally admitted the famed Area 51, in the Nevada desert, does exist.

The top secret Cold War test site adjoining Nellis Air Force Base, northwest of Las Vegas, has long been fodder for speculation the authorities have covered up reported sightings of UFO's and aliens. Until recently the government has denied its existence.

Now a newly declassified CIA document confirms the existence of Area 51. The document states the contentious zone was used as a testing range for the government's U-2 spy plane during the Cold War.

However, there's no mention of the controversial Roswell incident, which UFO believers claim was an alien space ship that crashed in New Mexico in 1947 and not a weather balloon as the authorities insisted. Supporters of the theory allege that Area 51's hangars were used to hide evidence of alien bodies recovered from the spaceship.

The CIA asserts government secrecy surrounding Area 51 was simply about ensuring a new spy plane – the U-2 reconnaissance aircraft – remained hidden from prying Soviet eyes. Plausible considering the aircraft was designed specifically for high altitude snooping on the Soviets.

The agency's report explains the "tremendous increase in reports of unidentified flying objects" as an "unexpected side effect" of high altitude testing of the U-2. This increase was due to the aircraft's silver wings reflecting the rays of the sun, according to the official explanation.

However, this doesn't explain the Roswell incident or the many other reported UFO, and indeed alien, sightings in and around Area 51 over the years.

It's easy to dismiss such sightings as the ramblings of zealous conspiracy theorists. However, in the wake of the US Government's belated and official admission that Area 51 does exist, maybe those reports shouldn't be dismissed quite so readily.

"You know, there aren't six people in this room who know how true this really is."
–President Ronald Reagan. Conversation with Steven Spielberg at the White House on June 27, 1982 during a Presidential screening of E.T. the Extra-Terrestrial.

We visit Area 51 and Nellis Air Force Base in *The Orphan Uprising*. Our research for that novel raised more questions than answers –

questions we'll probably never know the answers to.

Of all the explanations those in the conspiracy community want regarding Area 51, probably the most pressing is whether the global elite are housing *human* or *alien* technologies there.

If either was admitted to, that would be equally extraordinary.

Say what? Well, if the anti-gravity flying machines witnessed by so many in and around Area 51's airspace are manmade then that confirms the Splinter Civilization are almost light years ahead of known science – and they have technologies the common man could scarcely comprehend.

If on the other hand UFO's are of alien origin, that implies the global elite are collaborating with an ET civilization – and this may explain why classified technology has progressed at such a rapid rate since around the time of Roswell.

THE CIA FINALLY COMES CLEAN

As mentioned, for decades Area 51 was said to exist only in the furtive and skeptical minds of conspiracy theorists. Then Russian satellite photos of the facility were leaked and shared far and wide online. But still the US Government continued to maintain there was *no such place as Area 51* and blamed conspiracy theorists as being responsible for *spreading lies*.

Each and every US administration maintained this position until August 16, 2013…

That was a day the Tinfoil Hat Network had something to celebrate, for on that date the you-know-what hit the fan when the world's media reported that the CIA had officially announced the existence of Area 51.

This significant acknowledgement came by way of declassified documents procured via a public records request lodged by George Washington University's National Security Archive. The documentation included a CIA history of Area 51's top secret U-2 spy plane program. Where references to Area 51 had been redacted in earlier documentation released by the CIA, it was named for all to see in the latest documents.

In the outpouring of media commentary that followed, a ForeignPolicy.com editorial piece sums up the revelations better than most – to our eyes at least – describing Area 51 as "a touchstone of America's cultural mythology."

The editorial continues:

"It (Area 51) rose to notoriety in 1989, when a Las Vegas man claimed he had worked at the secret facility to discover the secrets of crashed alien hardware, spawning two decades of conspiracy theories and speculation about little green men. But the facility's history -- and the history of the strange, secret aircraft that were developed there -- extends back to 1955. Since its inception, the government has obliquely acknowledged its existence only a handful of times, and even the CIA's 1996 declassified history of the OXCART program -- the development of the SR-71 Blackbird at the secret site -- refers only to tests conducted in "the Nevada desert." The government has never publicly discussed the specific facility ... until now."

While the declassified documents acknowledge the Nevada site was a testing ground for surveillance during the Cold War, conspiracy theorists will be disappointed there's no mention of UFO's or aliens.

UFO sightings and conspiracy theories have dogged Area 51 since its inception. Time travel, advanced weapons programs and enormous underground bases, as well as the recovery of downed alien spacecraft and interaction with the occupants of those craft are just some of claims made by conspiracy theorists.

Of all the conspiracy claims surrounding Area 51, one stands out above all others: Roswell.

ROSWELL

The *Roswell event* occurred near Roswell, New Mexico, in 1947 when a mystery craft crashed on a ranch and debris was recovered. That much at least is true. The official explanation – courtesy of the United States Armed Forces – is the debris was the result of a secret US military Air Force surveillance balloon crashing.

Interestingly, the very first official explanation – issued by an Army spokesman – was that the mystery craft was "a flying disc." That was quickly *corrected* in an Air Force statement advising that Roswell Army Air Field personnel had recovered a downed weather balloon at the crash site.

However, it's the unofficial explanations that most interest us. They obviously interest a lot of others, too: the public at large have been intrigued by the enduring theories the incident spawned – the most prominent being that the mystery craft was in fact a spaceship and that it contained extraterrestrial life.

A 1995 feature-length doco titled *The Roswell Incident* provides a compelling overview of the incident, inclusive of very persuasive eye-witness accounts. It's accessible via Top Documentary Films' website.

Top Documentary Films' splurge for the doco begins:

"In the summer of 1947, there were a number of UFO sightings in the United States. Sometime during the first week of July 1947, something crashed near Roswell.

"W.W. (Mack) Brazel, a New Mexico rancher, saddled up his horse and rode out with the son of neighbors Floyd and Loretta Proctor, to check on the sheep after a fierce thunderstorm the night before. As they rode along, Brazel began to notice unusual pieces of what seemed to be metal debris, scattered over a large area. Upon further inspection, Brazel saw that a shallow trench, several hundred feet long, had been gouged into the land."

The doco reports the crash site was quickly sealed off by the military, but not before the discovery of four alien bodies outside a damaged spacecraft – at a second crash site – that was largely intact.

Sounds far-fetched? Many think so. Even a few high profile UFO commentators dismiss the Roswell-related alien body claims as implausible.

Then again, it's one of the oldest conspiracy theories around and it shows no sign of going away any time soon. One reason for this could be the eyewitnesses who claim, or claimed, to have observed the aftermath of the crash are in the main very credible and convincing.

"For some years I have had good reason to believe that world governments, headed by the Americans, not only have contact with alien races, but have reciprocal agreements with them, allowing certain species to come and go around our planet without hindrance."
–Tony Dodd. Former British police officer.

AREA 51 ACCOUNTS FROM US GOVERNMENT EMPLOYEES

Numerous insiders from the US military and intelligence communities have stated that the technologies at Area 51 are of extraterrestrial origins. These individuals are, or were, for the most part former military employees, and in many cases they died after giving testimony!

Coincidences perhaps?

Probably the best known of these insiders is one Bob Lazar who claims he was employed as a scientist in the late 1980's to study recovered ET technologies housed at a top-secret facility known as *S4*, which is said to be in, or bordering, Area 51.

Lazar, who is an electronics expert and a former document photo processor, says he had to pass strict military tests before being permitted to study the recovered ET craft. His assignment was to determine how humans could fly the craft and how more such craft could be constructed.

The scientist claims the craft he studied had extraordinary super physics abilities. It could bend the fabric of space and time, thereby making it capable of defying Einstein's *Theory of Relativity* by teleporting and time traveling.

After studying the first craft, Lazar says he was put to work on other spacecraft. Yes you read that right: *other spacecraft*.

In total, over the 12 months Lazar worked at Area 51, he claims he experimented with nine different extraterrestrial vehicles. Apparently these craft used a unique fuel – one that Lazar called *Element 115* – that allowed the Beings who created them to travel across the universe at or somewhere near the speed of light.

Potentially supporting Lazar's testimonial, Element 115 was discovered on August 28, 2013, prompting various news outlets and scientific journals to run stories on the discovery that same day. These included an article by National Geographic headed *Meet 115, the Newest Element on the Periodic Table*. It mentions how the "extremely heavy element was just confirmed by scientists in Sweden".

UFO website openminds.tv also posted an article the same day, mentioning Lazar's claim of 23 years earlier. "Element 115 received attention in 1989 when Area 51 whistleblower Bob Lazar asserted that extraterrestrial spacecraft at Area 51's S4 facility were powered by the element."

Another intriguing case is the deathbed testimonial of an ex-CIA employee who convincingly reveals what he insists is the truth regarding extraterrestrials' involvement with humanity. The recorded interview was conducted by American television host and UFO author Richard Dolan, and filmed on March 5, 2013 at an undisclosed location somewhere in mainland America.

The dying man, who remained unnamed presumably to protect his family, claims to have been hired by the CIA when he was a young man in the 1950's. He says he was first employed to investigate UFO's in the top-secret *Project Blue Book*, another former conspiracy theory which has since been proven to be legitimate in the light of declassified CIA documents.

The elderly gentleman, who – unless he's the world's greatest actor – was clearly on his deathbed, also speaks of being sent to Area 51 on behalf of President Eisenhower where he not only witnessed ET anti-gravity technologies, but also says he met a real, live Grey Alien.

A May 3, 2013 article, again on the *Open Minds* UFO investigation website, accurately summarizes the aforementioned interview – referring to the unnamed interview subject as 'Anonymous' – (abridged) as follows: "Facing impending kidney failure, this individual felt compelled to disclose secret information he feels is too important to keep secret … 'Anonymous' alleges that, after an invasion threat … President Dwight Eisenhower, he and his superior at the CIA were allowed inside the secretive Area 51 in Nevada to gather intel and report back to the president. There, 'Anonymous' describes seeing several alien spacecraft, including the craft that crashed in Roswell, New Mexico. Then, he and his superior were taken to the S-4 facility southwest of Area 51 where they observed live extraterrestrials."

Footage of the testimonial was first shown to the public on May 3, 2013 at the Citizen Hearing on Disclosure, at the National Press Club, in Washington, DC.

UFO researcher and bestselling author Peter Robbins, who attended the Citizen Hearing, watched the recorded testimony at that event. Robbins wrote the following on his Facebook account after the screening: "In my opinion, if it can be confirmed by any relevant supporting documentation, this moving and fascinating account does qualify as an authentic 'death bed' testimony from an individual who convincingly claims to have been a CIA officer deeply involved in the matter of crashed and/or recovered craft, and at one time a liaison between the Agency and the President."

The filmed testimonial has since been uploaded by various YouTube users and has been watched by millions of people, prompting many to comment that their "gut feelings" tell them the elderly gent is telling the truth, and also that it would be very hard to fake being that sick. Although some think it's a fabrication, the consensus – judging by comments left below the uploaded versions of the testimonial – supports the unnamed man's testimonial.

Finally, it should be noted that the man's testimonial, which has not yet been verified as either true or false, dovetails with a long-held popular theory which suggests the US Government entered into an agreement with an ET civilization. According to this theory, a deal was struck up with President Eisenhower and these other Beings whereby the US would be the beneficiaries of their advanced technologies provided the ET's could visit the US and elsewhere on Planet Earth at will to carry out whatever their agenda may be.

Some conspiracy theorists say that alien agenda includes abducting humans. Interestingly, the self-proclaimed former CIA agent who gave the deathbed testimonial also mentions that Eisenhower agreed to allow the aliens to abduct humans, including US citizens, as part of the agreement he signed with them.

"In our obsession with antagonisms of the moment, we often forget how much unites all the members of humanity. Perhaps we need some outside, universal threat to make us recognize this common bond. I occasionally think how quickly our differences worldwide would vanish if we were facing an alien threat from outside of this world. And yet I ask – is not an alien force already among us?"

–President Ronald Reagan at the UN General Assembly. September 21, 1987, Geneva, Switzerland.

CLOSE ENCOUNTERS OF THE FOURTH KIND

Even though the subject does not directly relate to Area 51, we would be remiss not to discuss alien abductees – those who have been abducted by aliens or those who *imagine* they have, depending on your take – in this chapter. After all, Area 51 is only part of the bigger question we are exploring here: that is, are all the accounts of anti-gravity flying saucers the result of alien or human technology?

Although we haven't personally devoted much time to researching abductees' claims, we have by chance been personally involved with one of the most incredible, and supposedly true, stories of alien abduction ever told.

Around 2005-2006, we took out an option to the film rights of the 1998 book *Coevolution: The True Story of a Man Taken for Ten Days to an Extraterrestrial Civilization*, by fellow New Zealander Alec Newald whom we interviewed at length and subsequently wrote a treatment for a feature film screenplay adaptation of his book.

We believed the planned film would take the alien and space genres to a whole new level. Unfortunately, scheduling conflicts with our filmmaking slates prevented us from devoting the time required to produce the movie.

As the book's full title suggests, *Coevolution* is about *The True Story of a Man Taken for Ten Days to an Extraterrestrial Civilization*. Here's the book's blurb sourced from the popular reading social network Goodreads.com:

"One Monday in mid-February 1989, Alec Newald set off on what should have been a three-hour drive from Rotorua to Auckland, New Zealand. Instead he became a missing person for ten days. Newald claims that during those ten days he was taken by friendly aliens to their home planet, which he describes in full and awesome detail (for) part of this book -- an amazing first-person account of a growing but still unexplained phenomenon."

Alec writes at length in the book how after being returned to Earth he was mysteriously contacted by agents of unnamed international intelligence agencies, even though he'd told nobody about his alien abduction. These agents harassed, threatened and tortured Alec in their belief he wasn't divulging all the information he had about this ET civilization. They also advised him he would, in the interests of self-preservation, be best to never publicly divulge what he experienced.

But that didn't deter Alec, who describes himself as a stubborn individual – and he wrote the book about his other worldly experience.

Coevolution contains detailed drawings of the friendly ET's he claims he met, as well as sketches of their spacecraft, their advanced technologies and the planet they took him to. He also has in his possession crystals and other rock formations he says he brought back from the planet.

We had no way of verifying this, but the rocks were strange and like none other we'd seen. Of course, we were essentially approaching the planned film adaptation from a storytellers' perspective – meaning we believed it would make a very entertaining movie and didn't give a lot of thought as to how likely it was true.

What we can say is Alec, who is a professional sailmaker by trade, believes 100% this happened to him. As an apparently sane and balanced individual, he presents a very convincing case. However, in considering such extraordinary claims, we must remember the mind is a very complex thing; its workings can deceive even the most stable individual, especially in times of stress or other outward influences.

Worth noting, especially for sci-fi fans, is Alec's claim that we humans are the ancestors of aliens and they, in turn, are our descendants from the future who have mastered time travel. Apparently, the ET's Alec befriended are close to extinction as a result of decisions their ancestors (we Earthlings!) made. They therefore regularly time travel back into their past to positively influence present-day humanity so they can improve their own reality.

And on top of all those complex themes, Alec also recounts in his book a love affair with one of the female aliens who he describes as having out-of-this-world beauty – figuratively and literally!

As filmmakers, we felt *Coevolution* would make an explosive and contentious sci-fi movie worthy of a Steven Spielberg blockbuster. We still feel that way. It's our hope that either a feature film or at the very least a feature-length documentary on it is eventually produced, exploring the mystery of Alec Newald's missing 10 days in the year 1989.

"I heard you had reports this morning of an unidentified aircraft. Don't worry it was just me."
–George W. Bush speaking to the Military Academy in Roswell, New Mexico, January 22, 2004

THE ARGUMENT FOR MANMADE TECHNOLOGIES

There's no denying the Roswell event unearthed some convincing *evidence* and very credible eye witnesses, and there have been innumerable reported UFO sightings from around the world since that incident.

A likely explanation for those sightings in and around Area 51 air space in particular is that they are in fact man-made machines – such as the once-secret U-2 spy plane – primarily originating in the Cold War in which America was a willing participant.

Since the U-2's development and subsequent *unveiling*, the public have become familiar with other cutting-edge aviation developments – such as the Stealth Bomber.

But what else *out there* is manmade?

Rumors of government-sponsored craft capable of traveling at unearthly speeds and resembling flying saucers have been around since World War Two. That includes the legendary Nazi *foo fighter* flying saucers, which scores of Allied pilots reported witnessing in-flight.

Given the many thousands of UFO reports logged around the world every year, such rumors shouldn't be dismissed too lightly. Certainly, manmade craft would be a more logical explanation for UFO sightings than alien craft. Not because it's unlikely there's life beyond our planet. Rather, because it could be argued it's unlikely other beings have discovered our little corner of the universe just yet.

This thinking suggests the odds of the Earth being discovered are astronomical given the size of our universe. It's a rather large 28 billion light-years in diameter, according to scientists, although that doesn't take into account the universe's expansion since this book underwent its final proofing.

Furthermore, if there's one thing our research has taught us, it is that it's naïve to believe *the latest* technology in the public domain is truly the latest. There are numerous examples of products or technology being introduced as new, or cutting-edge, whereas they had already been secretly used – for years in many cases – by the military or by certain government agencies, or both. The Internet was one such case, first being used for a number of years by the military before eventually being released to the public.

If we can accept that, we should be able to accept that there are new technologies, both in development and in existence right now, the average person couldn't even begin to imagine.

DISINFORMING THE PUBLIC

Perhaps the ET and UFO movements are simply disinformation – i.e. deception, propaganda or half-truths.

Persuading everyone to believe in aliens compels us to look *up* to the skies. And while we are all waiting for *Little Green Men* to arrive, the shadowy people in the Splinter Civilization effortlessly go about their secret work by advancing their suppressed inventions at a rate of knots.

This *disinformation counter-conspiracy theory* suggests that, collectively, accounts of ET's coming or crashing or even living amongst us conveniently form the perfect cover story. It's a story that is spread by intelligence agencies which encourage, and even surreptitiously finance, Hollywood film studios to make mega-budget movies about aliens and alien invasions.

Maybe the widespread acceptance by many that aliens have

arrived on earth at some point – or at least a willingness to consider such a thing is possible – can be blamed on Hollywood. More likely, it can be attributed to the fact that we have been given so little of the big picture. (No pun intended).

If the Splinter Civilization's suppressed technologies were revealed in their entirety to the public at large, would everyone still believe UFO's *must be* of extraterrestrial origin?

Take Nikola Tesla's technologies alone. If these were suddenly declassified and opened up to public scrutiny, would we still be so quick to automatically assume that any alien civilization is superior, scientifically or otherwise, to our own? For all anyone knows, humanity may be the most scientifically advanced civilization in the entire universe.

"The phenomenon of UFOs does exist, and it must be treated seriously."
–*Mikhail Gorbachev, 'Soviet Youth' speech, May 4, 1990.*

EINSTEIN'S *UNIFIED FIELD THEORY*

Strengthening the case for UFO's being manmade and of earthly origins, is the history of *electrogravitic propulsion*. It's a history that's either known, little known, rumored or usually unknown – depending on who you talk to.

According to American linguist and bestselling author Charles Berlitz, there was a rumor at Princeton's Institute for Advanced Study that Albert Einstein did indeed complete a version of his *Unified Field Theory for Gravitation and Electricity* – even though officially it remains a never-completed theory.

At first, this theory was published in German and appeared in a few scientific journals. In his papers, Einstein called his purported mathematical proof of the connection between the forces of electromagnetism and gravity as being "highly convincing".

However, this work was withdrawn as incomplete, although no published reason is given save that Einstein suddenly grew dissatisfied with it.

British mathematician Lord Bertrand Russell considered Einstein's *Unified Field Theory* complete, but felt that "Man is not ready for it and shan't be until after World War III."

Thus the Unified Field Theory on the connection between gravity and the electromagnetic field has remained unproven until the present time.

Leading Japanese scientist and former high-ranking employee of Japan's Ministry of Defense, Dr. Takaaki Musha, published an article in the 2004, Issue 53 edition of the *Infinite Energy Magazine* relating to this very question. The article, which covers a unique formula Musha developed for the link between electromagnetism and gravitation, was titled *The possibility of strong coupling between electricity and gravitation.*

After publication of the article, Dr. Musha claims he was contacted by Doctor (name redacted) from the Institute for Nuclear Research and Nuclear Energy, in Bulgaria. The Bulgarian scientist, whose name we have withheld due to our inability to reach him for comment before this book's publication, was already working on a similar formula to Dr. Musha's.

According to Dr. Musha, the Bulgarian's "formulation proves it is possible to create an unbalanced acceleration by creating intense electric and magnetic fields in a dielectric or ferromagnetic medium. These predicted coupling effects for electromagnetic and gravitational fields would be static and thus they should be able to produce a net force to *propel a spaceship*."

The Bulgarian scientist wrote two papers on his formula in 1994.

"However," Dr. Musha claims, these "papers were rejected by two well-known science journals."

The strong implication is that there was a cover-up or else mainstream science was just not prepared to consider such theories on anti-gravity.

T. T. Brown, who discovered this electrogravitic effect first, conducted several experiments during the 1950's and succeeded to generate thrust without the reliance on a surrounding medium, such as air, by applying high voltages to materials with high dielectric constants. Around this time, US aerospace companies also become involved in such research, but their results are mostly classified.

In the late 1980's and early 1990's, a rash of observer *sightings* of unidentified, high-speed, high-flying air vehicles continued, but the US Government repeatedly denied it had developed an aircraft to replace the Mach 3-plus Lockheed SR-71 strategic reconnaissance platform – indicating it (the government) was content to let the public assume the sightings were of the SR-71.

In the 1990's, a quest for an antigravity propulsion system was conducted by the USAF Science Applications International Corp. on behalf of USAF's then Astronautics Laboratory at Edwards AFB. (Area 51 is a detachment of Edwards ABF, which is responsible for testing of advanced flying vehicles). British multinational defence and aerospace company BAE Systems also provided internal resources for its own anti-gravity studies.

However, there was no significant progress in this area. At least not officially.

In the late 1990's, Dr. Musha says he worked with the Honda Corporation Research Institute in Japan and conducted an experiment to confirm the electrogravitic effect. Astonishingly, Dr. Musha claims he and the Honda Corporation obtained a positive result.

Dr. Musha also says, "In Dr. Thomas Valone's 1993 book *Electrogravitics Systems: Reports on a New Propulsion Methodology*, Dr. Paul LaViolette claimed that electrogravitic technology was developed under US Air Force black projects since late 1954, and it may now have been put to practical use in the B-2 Advanced Technology Bomber to provide an exotic auxiliary mode of propulsion."

Dr. Musha continues, "An electrogravitic drive of B-2 could allow it to fly at a sufficiently high speed at high altitude, or even space, and it could fly around the world without refueling in an antigravity mode."

What all this means is that science, and especially suppressed or classified science, may have long-ago evolved to the point where building anti-gravity spacecraft has been entirely possible.

Possible, that is, *without any assistance from ET civilizations.*

> *"I've been working with Paul Hellyer. He's the minister, the ex-minister of defense, Canada, under Trudeau. He is upset because the Americans are planning the weaponization of space, as though they (ET's) are enemies ... It came out of a project called Project Paperclip, in which – and this is what Eisenhower warned us against – the sustention of the Military Industrial Complex. In order to extend the power and the funding of the Military Industrial Complex, you have to be afraid of things. Number one was communism. If that petered out, number two is terrorism. That's here for a while. Number three is asteroids. And number four is extraterrestrials."*

–Shirley MacLaine. Excerpt from an interview with Larry King on Larry King Live that aired on CNN on November 9, 2007.

REVERSE ENGINEERING

There's a third scenario in the human vs. alien debate regarding anti-gravity technologies.

This scenario would see a combination of the two extremes – meaning it isn't fully human technology and isn't fully alien, but a hybrid. The theory suggests alien technology somehow arrived on earth in the mid-20th Century in an event like the Roswell crash. A flying saucer was found and then reverse-engineered by reproducing the alien manufacturer's product after careful study.

The aforementioned claims of Area 51 employee Bob Lazar

would fit this theory. Besides Lazar, many other ex-military personnel have claimed the US did indeed successfully reverse-engineer recovered ET spacecraft and eventually learn how to manufacture such anti-gravity craft en masse.

"I have contact with certain diplomats who not only confirm meetings have been taking place between some government officials and an alien race, but have been receiving assistance from this race to advance technology to enable us to meet hostile aliens on a level playing field. My contacts have been present at these meetings and have met these aliens who are benevolent towards us but will not act with aggression towards any life form unless in self defence, but they are prepared to help us advance our technology."
–Tony Dodd. Former British police officer.

POPULAR CULTURE'S INFLUENCE ON AREA 51 MYTHS

The rumors swirling around Area 51 have given it a life of its own and have resulted in numerous films, TV programs, comics and video games.

Previously, these were readily identifiable as fiction because, for starters, they portrayed a place that didn't exist – not officially at least. We refer, of course, to Area 51.

However, now that we know Area 51 does exist – and has existed all along – perhaps the likes of the 1994 TV movie *Roswell*, starring Martin Sheen, the Roland Emmerich-helmed *Independence Day*, starring Will Smith, and the Steven Spielberg-produced TV mini-series *Taken*, starring Dakota Fanning, will be viewed in a different light...

But are such dramatizations any closer to the truth than the stories the world governments' *spin merchants* have fed to us about UFO sightings these past decades? If there is a Splinter Civilization currently operating under the surface – both figuratively and literally – then perhaps it's not in the global elite's interests to shatter the ET myths perpetuated by conspiracy theorists and Hollywood film studios. Perhaps it serves the Splinter Civilization's agenda just fine.

"The reality is that they (aliens) have been visiting earth for decades and probably millennia and have contributed considerably to our knowledge."
–Paul Hellyer (Canada's former Minister of National Defence) from an interview with the Canadian Press in 2010.

So what is the truth regarding the anti-gravity spacecraft that Area 51 appears to be concealing? Are such technologies manmade or alien, or a combination of the two?

In short, we have no idea! The next person's opinion is as good as ours.

If you really want our guess, and it most certainly would be a guess, we think there are enough eyewitness accounts and testimonials from former military and intelligence personnel to suggest aliens not only exist, but have already visited Planet Earth. And it's our guess the highest levels of the world's governments are aware of this.

Perhaps it would be wise to defer to former Canadian Defence Minister Paul Hellyer, the man nicknamed *The highest-ranked alien believer on Earth*, who has said on the record that extraterrestrials are already living among us, but refuse to share their most advanced technology because of humanity's refusal to stop wars.

The now retired politician and engineer claims to have directly witnessed UFO technology and confirmed the existence of alien beings on earth through his high-level political and military contacts in Canada and the United States.

On January 1, 2014, Hellyer told news outlet *Russia Today* he believes there are about 80 different species of ETs, some of whom "look just like us and they could walk down the street and you wouldn't know if you walked past one … I would say that nearly all are benign and benevolent and they do want to help us, there may be one or two species which do not."

Hellyer also told *Russia Today* that aliens are not that impressed by humans. "They don't think we are good stewards of our planet, we're clear cutting our forests, we're polluting our rivers and our lakes, and we're dumping sewage in the oceans, and we're doing all sorts of things which are not what good stewards of their homes should be doing."

Canada's former Defence Minister has repeatedly begged governments around the world to disclose ET technology for the benefit of Mankind, in particular technology that could resolve the problem of climate change.

For example, on February 28, 2007, he told the *Ottawa Citizen*: "I would like to see what (alien) technology there might be that could eliminate the burning of fossil fuels within a generation... that could be a way to save our planet... We need to persuade governments to come clean on what they know. Some of us suspect they know quite a lot, and it might be enough to save our planet if applied quickly enough."

If Hellyer is correct in what he says, this further confirms the existence of the Splinter Civilization we have theorized on and speculated about throughout this book. His comments also support our contention that nothing's more important for the planet right now than releasing all the scientific breakthroughs and technologies that are currently being suppressed or otherwise classified by the Splinter Civilization.

Whether these technologies are of alien origin (*a la* Roswell) or are of the human variety (*a la* Tesla), we firmly believe they could not only solve climate change, as Hellyer suggests, but also solve an infinite number of other critical problems that currently plague the planet.

The danger is if the collective thinking of the public at large remains closed to the possibility of such technologies existing, the likelihood of these problems being solved any time soon looks remote.

A major mind-shift is required. That doesn't mean buying into every conspiracy theory out there, but it does mean keeping – or adopting, whichever the case – an open mind so that all possibilities can be considered.

CONNECTING THE DOTS

When we set out to write this book it was not our intention to add more negativity to the world, or to depress or frighten readers: rather, we were simply aiming to find an overarching, all-embracing *truth* in our research into the 29 conspiracy theories covered in our thriller series, and then relay that truth to readers through our writing.

However, the subject matter required honesty to be effective, and it's an inescapable fact that at this time in the Earth's history there are some dark secrets being whispered in the corridors of power.

Such matters should not be ignored, for as Carl Jung said, "One does not become enlightened by imagining figures of light, but by making the darkness conscious."

In shedding light on the crimes perpetuated by the global elite and all their subtle and often heavily-disguised offshoots, we trust this book will contribute toward a greater awareness in society the world over. If knowledge is indeed power, then we fervently hope the light we shed on these particular conspiracy theories will empower people everywhere – in every nation.

Of all the statistics we uncovered during our research, one in particular has stayed in our minds throughout the writing process: *21,000 people die every day (one person every four seconds) from starvation.*

That's a sickening figure considering our research has also shown there is more than enough wealth in the world for everyone to at least receive the basic necessities. And contrary to mainstream media reports, there is very little *true* scarcity in the world.

You will recall in chapter 6 we mentioned those running the oil and precious metals industries purposefully foster a belief that there's a critical shortage of resources in the world. And we advised how films like *The Formula* and *Blood Diamond* are based on the global elite's devious approach to managing those resources. You'll also recall that chapter contains examples of how creating the illusion of scarcity is intrinsically linked with an excessive desire for profits – a desire that will stop at nothing. Not even the loss of human lives.

Well, it's like that with *everything* in our world at present.

Such illusions are constantly being fed to us as if they are proven facts – the illusion that wars are unavoidable, that there's not enough wealth to go around, that the Third World cannot organically sustain itself, that terrorists are everywhere...

As we covered in chapter 13, mainstream media is a big part of this grand deception. This should come as no surprise considering the bulk of the world's news outlets are owned by only a handful of media tycoons who all belong to secretive, elitist and unaccountable organizations such as the Bilderberg Group and the Council on Foreign Relations.

It's becoming obvious to most that mainstream media is nothing but a megaphone for the global elite to present biased news that's designed to *align* the masses with their agenda.

Take the *Overpopulation Theory* – a pet hobbyhorse of virtually every powerful individual in the Establishment.

"A total (world) population of 250-300 million people, a 95% decline from present levels, would be ideal."

Ted Turner. Quote from an interview in 1996 with Audubon
magazine.

THE POPULATION DEBATE

The supposed need to depopulate the planet for the good of Mankind is a theory that has been peddled by every elitist from the Rockefellers, to Bill Gates and Ted Turner, to US Presidents like George W. Bush and Bill Clinton, to Prince Charles and other British Royals. The latter includes the Queen's husband Prince Philip who once infamously remarked, "If I were reincarnated, I would wish to be returned to Earth as a killer virus to lower human population levels."

Let us also not forget Henry Kissinger's aforementioned comment in the recently declassified National Security Memorandum 200 document in which he states, "Depopulation should be the highest priority of US foreign policy towards the Third World," *to secure mineral resources for the US.*

The motivations behind depopulation suggestions may actually be a desire to create a modern form of eugenics, albeit masquerading as something more benign. That may sound a rather extreme accusation, but keep in mind it was only a generation or two ago that the global elite were bona fide supporters of draconian eugenics programs.

How many remain adherents of this insidious science, but choose to keep their beliefs to themselves now that eugenics has been universally vilified?

Many independent researchers, ourselves included, believe the proposed global population control measures really are a politically correct version of the once government-sponsored eugenics programs.

In our opinion, racial hatred is the likely impetus behind this new version of eugenics. As Edwin Black reminds us in his book *War Against the Weak: Eugenics and America's Campaign to Create a Master Race*, "Eugenics was" a "pseudoscience," and "In its extreme, racist form, this meant wiping away all human beings deemed 'unfit,' preserving only those who conformed to a Nordic stereotype".

There are clues that would seem to confirm that domination of non-white races remains a part of the agenda. The biggest clues are the countries and peoples that are being singled out for supposedly propagating too fast.

Have you noticed how those powerful figures who promote the "urgent need" for depopulation are almost always, if not always, referring to Third World countries or developing nations in Africa, Asia and Latin America – and not countries like the UK, France, Germany, Russia or the US whose citizens are predominantly Caucasian?

Could it be that Mr. Kissinger is not the only elitist who fears the West will lose its stranglehold on the planet's resources if certain developing nations grow too big and powerful?

Remember, so-called experts have been suggesting the Earth must depopulate since the early 20th Century, which notably coincides with the exact same period that eugenics programs were first endorsed by governments.

By the 1960's, when the planet's total population was 3 billion, the overpopulation theory reached popular consciousness – aided no doubt by those influential figures who regularly trumpeted it in the media. The concept was always presented as if it was an absolute fact: the world could not handle many more people and humanity would soon cease to exist unless depopulation strategies were implemented *immediately*.

However, the world's population is now over 7 billion and life goes on. In some respects, life's a lot more complicated than it was back in the Hippy Era, but nevertheless Mother Earth continues to sustain life and, despite what some may tell us, she shows no immediate sign of exploding, imploding or otherwise wilting.

None of this counter-argument should be misconstrued as ignoring the Earth's immense problems. *Yes* people are dying of malnutrition, thirst and disease; *yes* nations are fighting over resources; *yes* there is an ever-widening gap between rich and poor; and *yes* much of our planet is disgustingly polluted.

However, these problems, or tragedies, need to be assessed in the context of that which is being withheld. For every *Yes* there's a *No*.

No the world's most advanced technologies have not been released; *no* there is not fair and proper distribution of wealth and resources; *no* we haven't progressed beyond the strong dominating the weak through wars and the like; *no* the financial system has not been cleansed of corrupt bankers and economic hitmen.

When you balance the *No's* against the *Yes's* it becomes obvious that if we lived in a fairer world – especially one where there is greater equality and where no technology or information is ever suppressed – the planet could sustain an even bigger population. Perhaps much bigger.

The daily struggle of many for food, water and other basic necessities is more about greed and unfair political and economic systems than population levels.

For example, if half of Africa's population was wiped out tomorrow, millions of people would still be left scavenging for bare essentials due to the fact that very little of the continent's abundant resources (that are mined, drilled or otherwise extracted) remain in Africa for the benefit of Africans. So the problem is one of imperialism, or expansionism, rather than there being too many mouths to feed.

Yoko Ono summarized this issue well during her appearance on *The Dick Cavett Show* on September 11, 1971, when she said, "I think the problem is not overpopulation, as people believe to be, but it's more of the balance of things … Like food. Some parts of the world there's wastage of food, in some parts nobody has food. And that kind of a balance, if that is solved, I don't think we'd be worried so much about overpopulation."

The big question is: why is anyone still suggesting depopulation? And why is the media still giving such suggestions airtime?

Unless outlawed eugenics programs are revived or certain elitists get their way with nefarious strategies such as mass sterilizations or forced abortions, depopulation is hardly likely in this day and age. Except of course where it's an inevitable consequence of wars, genocide or natural disasters.

It would make more sense to seek solutions for the world's current and projected populations than trying to take away or limit people's basic right to procreate. China's *one-child* policy aside, procreation is something Man has always done freely and without thought.

Releasing classified or suppressed scientific inventions would likely be a good start. Especially technologies that have the potential to combat the world's most pressing issues, such as pollution and its effects on climate, whatever those effects may be.

It's worth noting that throughout history, population growth has usually spurred technological advances. This was true during the Industrial Revolution, the post-WW2 years and the Space Age era; and we are witnessing it again with the explosion of computer and mobile phone technologies, which can barely keep pace with worldwide consumer demands for those products.

We've already acknowledged that pollution is an urgent problem. However, a few hundred million less people – which is all strict population controls could hope to achieve in the near future – wouldn't decrease pollution levels that much.

And who is to say higher populations won't actually make it easier to develop pollutant-free and clean energy technologies in the same way they created the necessary demand, infrastructure and labour force to spark other inventions of bygone years? We are not saying higher populations would necessarily achieve this, but at present there has been zero public debate as to the potential benefits of the planet's increasing numbers of people.

Many cities are undoubtedly overpopulated, but much of this is to do with poor economic management and a lack of environmental and geographic planning. For example, rural-dwellers are often so impoverished they have no choice but to move to cities for work. With a greater and fairer distribution of wealth, governments could provide incentives for citizens to remain in rural areas or relocate to emerging cities or even build new cities.

When considering the overpopulation theory, sparsely-populated landmasses with mostly wide, open spaces also must be taken into account. Places where you can drive across hundreds of miles of farmland or virgin landscapes without seeing a town or a village, or even a person in some cases.

Such landmasses include Canada, Brazil, Australia, Mongolia, Scandinavia, Russia, much of central Asia, many parts of the Middle East and large chunks of Africa and South America. Even some rural regions of the two most populated countries on earth – China and India – would fit into this category, not to mention certain states in America such as Alaska, Idaho, Nebraska, Maine, Utah, Arkansas, Wyoming, Texas and Montana – each of which have larger landmasses than many countries.

As reported in the August 2003 edition of *International Journal of Wilderness*, Conservative International conducted a major assessment into how much global wilderness is left. The conclusion was that the "study found that 46% of the planet qualified as remaining wilderness".

Say what? If almost half the Earth's surface – not including oceans – is comprised of untouched wilderness, why are we being told there's hardly enough land to accommodate everyone?

Another statistic that shatters the overpopulation myth is that the *entire* world population could fit into the state of Texas. This has been confirmed by various sources.

Even the environmentalist website treehuger.com concurred in a July 27, 2011 article headed *At NYC's Density, the World's Population Could Live in Texas*. The writer states, "If the entire world's population – 6.9 billion people – lived at the same density level as New York City, we could all fit within the borders of the Lone Star State (Texas)."

In 2010, the overpopulationisamyth.com website calculated as follows: "Divide 7,494,271,488,000 sq ft (total landmass of Texas) by 6,908,688,000 people (world's population in 2010), and you get 1084.76 sq ft/person. That's approximately a 33' x 33' plot of land for every person on the planet, enough space for a town house. An average four person family, every family would have a 66' x 66' plot of land, which would comfortably provide a single family home and yard".

Nobody is suggesting living conditions in a Texas with 7-plus billion people would be sustainable given land is needed for industrial and commercial premises, farms, orchards, schools and other community facilities. But the Texas statistic does at least prove space is not an issue given Texas is a tiny percentage of the planet's habitable land.

Another little known fact is that for decades, economists have advised sparsely populated countries they need to increase their population to stimulate their economies. In our native New Zealand, which currently has a population of just under 4.5 million people, this has certainly been the case. Although the pro-active immigration policies of successive governments have been criticized by some, New Zealand's present strong economy would likely not have been possible without the valuable input of immigrants who boosted the country's population. At the time of writing, incidentally, New Zealand's economy is rated one of the most buoyant in the Western world.

Australia, a continent with only 23 million people, and Russia, which covers one sixth of the world's total land mass, are other examples of countries which could potentially benefit from increased populations.

In the mid-2000's the Australian Government, under Prime Minister John Howard, subscribed to the little-known *Underpopulation Theory* by implementing a child encouragement policy nicknamed *the Baby Bonus*. This scheme, a brainchild of Australian treasurer Peter Costello, paid Australian citizens lump sums any time they produced newborn babies. Howard and Costello believed increasing the population would help stimulate the nation's economy and put Australia in good shape for years to come.

Short of a nuclear war or some other cataclysmic event, world population levels are only going to continue to increase. According to some estimates, it will reach 8 billion in about a decade. Rather than worrying about this, humanity needs to focus on social responsibility, fair wealth distribution, equality and universal justice. In other words, the very things that are needed to sustain Mankind alongside food, water, clothes and shelter.

We are not saying we know better than scientists, futurists and economists. However, it's a fact that 99% of these experts are blissfully unaware of the suppressed science mentioned throughout this book. Ask most scientists about Tesla and you'll be met with a blank stare – or at best a comment like, "Oh yeah, wasn't he the guy who developed the AC current?"

And yet, the US government has classified more files on Tesla than any other scientist in history.

There is good reason for that and it didn't happen by accident.

When the experts estimate how long the world can sustain life based on current and projected populations, they never take into account the radical technologies that would *of course* be released if we found ourselves on the brink of extinction. Technologies like Tesla's free energy inventions, and his pollutant-free and self-charging transportation inventions that would reduce pollution levels almost overnight.

Most experts never include such technologies in their gloomy forecasts as they simply don't know about them. Or perhaps some of them have heard about these technologies, rumored or otherwise, but have written them off as fanciful conspiracy theories.

After reading this book, and hopefully absorbing the often contentious, usually little known and sometimes revolutionary material contained within its pages, it should now be blindingly obvious that we, the writers, are diametrically opposed to the diatribes of the elite who consistently imply humans are parasites destroying the Earth.

So go ahead and propagate, and know that your offspring have the potential to assist the planet, not wreck it. In fact, go forth and *multiply like rabbits*. You have our blessing, but be warned: there'll be no baby bonus from us!

"I think we have enough food and money to feed everybody ... I don't believe in overpopulation. I think

that's kind of a myth the government has thrown out to keep your mind off Vietnam, Ireland and all the important subjects."
–John Lennon. Excerpt from an interview on The Dick Cavett Show on September 11, 1971.

RESTRUCTURING CAPITALISM

Clearly, many of the issues in this book are related to capitalism. With its profits-over-people agenda, capitalism has unfortunately spawned a monster that's now out of control.

The free enterprise concept inherent in the economic model of capitalism should mean common people, or lower and middle class wage-earners, have greater potential to rise up and gain financial independence. In reality, however, free enterprise all too often leads to an almost total lack of government regulation that in turn allows the global elite to run amuck in Gordon Gecko-style financial coups.

Even if capitalism is the best economic system in theory – which it probably is – the type of corporatocracy it leads to in the real world usually means the rich get richer while the poor get poorer. And although much good has come from capitalism – America's phenomenal success in the 20th Century was arguably due to the free market economics its Founding Father's encouraged – the system's immense flaws have also become evident in recent years.

It's almost as if capitalism is a robot that was originally programmed with a single instruction: *Make profits by all means necessary.*

Initially the profits surged in, putting food on the table for untold families, building communities and lifting living standards in numerous countries. However, the robot could not be stopped or reprogrammed, and without governments being able or willing to set boundaries the same system that once *gave* to the people now began to *take* from them. It began to lower living standards by widening the gap between rich and poor and by destroying the same communities it once built.

Unregulated capitalism began to abuse working class citizens – the very people it was designed to assist; it allowed leaders of corporations to play God while employees became workhorses for their owners. Perhaps a better description would be worker bees sacrificing their own welfare for the benefit of the royal queen bees.

Unfortunately, the advanced civilization and technological utopia that capitalism helped create is also one where most humans are treated like dogs in a dog-eat-dog world.

None of this means we are socialists or communists. Nor are we anti-progress. And no, we are not about to suddenly reveal that this whole book has been a thinly veiled disguise for our political beliefs – although no doubt some shallow thinking book reviewers may assume this. For those who have read this book in its entirety, it should be abundantly clear we are staunchly apolitical and believe that no political system can ever provide a total solution.

Most of the issues we've raised in this book are essentially social concerns rather than economic or political ones.

Also, as filmmakers and authors, we are fully aware that we have benefited, and continue to benefit, from a capitalistic system. There is surely much good in capitalism. For example, *the American Dream* – the same dream that people of most other nations desire – says anyone who has ambition and a good work ethic can succeed no matter their race, gender or social class. Living up to those ideals is likely possible only in a free, democratic *and* capitalistic society.

Therefore, we would support a revised form of capitalism, rather than doing away with it completely. This restructured economic system would hopefully be one with more heart and social awareness while still allowing for self-made entrepreneurs to rise up and be rewarded for their efforts. Rewarding achievers is crucial as history has proven that whenever socialism or communism is implemented there's little incentive to succeed because success is not duly rewarded.

It's obvious something has to change in our capitalistic society as there's far too much unnecessary suffering on the planet right now.

We have faith this book will contribute in some small way to that change and help make a dent in that awful statistic that reminds us 21,000 fellow humans die of starvation every single day. (Two people just died in the time it took you to read that brief statement).

A FINAL WORD
ON THOSE IN POWER

Despite all our criticisms of governments and intelligence agencies, we firmly believe there remain good people within these organizations. Honest people who want to assist the greater populace and release information that has been covered up.

Unfortunately, they're up against an organization, an outfit, an entity – a global elite or call it what you will – that has morphed into the Splinter Civilization. This small, invisible but powerful rogue alliance seems to be operating in total isolation from known civilization, and is quite possibly working *against* humanity to further its own aims.

The Splinter Civilization most likely benefited from knowledge and technology gleaned from Nikola Tesla's suppressed inventions covered in chapter 7, or Project Paperclip's Nazi scientists mentioned in chapter 12, or from extraterrestrials associated with the 1947 Roswell incident we summarized in chapter 29 – or quite possibly from a combination of all three. Its members are not beholden to any official organization, be it the US Government, the military or the UN. It is its own entity, bankrolled by the wealthiest individuals, banks and corporations of the global elite – or the 1% of the 1%.

Like the Nazis who were sequestered to America after WW2, these people are fascist in their outlook and they view the masses as an annoying sub-class – pawns to fight their wars or else parasites to be depopulated or even completely eradicated. They have no concern for humanity as a whole.

Fortunately, there *are* compassionate people in government who are using their positions of power to serve the people and to fight back against the Splinter Civilization. These individuals are attempting to reestablish democracy by shifting the power back to the masses, often at considerable risk to themselves. They go about their work quietly, oftentimes working alongside those who don't share their well-meaning agendas.

We suspect these *public servants*, who are actually deserving of that title, are aware of the radical scientific technologies that have been suppressed. They recognize how freeing up inventions like anti-gravity propulsion systems, free-energy devices and other such exotic technologies, would automatically solve many of the world's current problems.

Every day these honest authorities are working on behalf of humanity to *try* to make the world a better and fairer place.

"Do your little bit of good where you are; it's those little bits of good put together that overwhelm the world."

–Desmond Tutu

Of course, no genuine change in society ever occurs without the mass public getting behind a cause. The good guys in government are counting on enough of us common people waking up and *demanding* more rights and greater freedoms.

So let's start building this new world together…A fairer society where every citizen is truly equal regardless of wealth, social background, nationality, education, race, gender or sexuality.

And if you are reading this and happen to be in a position of power – political or otherwise – and you currently represent only the 1%, then listen to your conscience. Deep down, you know it's wrong what you're doing. So start assisting humanity and *get on the right side of history.*

And lastly, remember, as we've stated or alluded to from the outset…

Everything in this book may be wrong.

-James Morcan & Lance Morcan

AFTERWORD
BY PROFESSOR RICHARD SPENCE

Someone, I honestly can't recall who, once told me an apocryphal anecdote which is a kind of epilogue to the biblical tale of the Garden of Eden and the Fall of Man. According to this, upon seeing Adam and Eve driven from paradise, the agent of their ruin, the Serpent, aka the Devil, was moved to pity. Or so he claimed. He asked God if he might bestow upon these pitiful creatures a gift which would make their mortal suffering and that of their descendants a little easier to bear. The Lord consented, and so the Serpent granted humankind the "blessing" of self-delusion: the inability to see themselves, the world or their state as they really were. The trick, of course, is that neither would they be able to see God or the Devil for what they really were either.

The Eden saga is also relevant because, if taken literally, it can be interpreted as the Ur-Conspiracy against the human race. Basically, Adam and Eve got the boot because they dared to acquire forbidden knowledge and, if not stopped, might have achieved the ultimate prize of eternal life. It was that which prompted God—or Gods since the divine conversation is always in terms of "we"—to nip things in the bud lest the upstart creations become "like us." It's enough to make one wonder just whose side the Serpent was on. Or could it be that the Serpent was just God in disguise? Maybe we've been in the dark from the beginning.

Mythology, heresy or whatever, I've often thought the "Devil's Gift" story explained the human condition pretty well. Whether the Serpent is to be blamed or thanked, the simple fact is that we do possess a tremendous capacity for deluding ourselves—and others. A prime example is the multitude of "conspiracy theories" James and Lance Morcan have presented in this book, theories that range, arguably, from the patently absurd to the disturbingly plausible. Notice that I'm not making a distinction as to which are which or who is deluding who. That's up to you.

For some years now I've offered a course at my university titled "Conspiracies and Secret Societies in History." Its basic goal, much like this book, is neither to advocate nor debunk, but to make people aware of what ideas and groups exist (or have existed) and what facts there may be to support or refute them. I've sometimes described it as a course in modern heresy or even in the nature of reality. A key theme is that human history, behavior and reality are governed not by what we *know* but by what we *believe*. Here's a simple example: we all have fathers and most of us know who our fathers are. Or we believe we do. Ultimately both we and our fathers are taking our mother's word for it, which doesn't exclude the possibility that even she is mistaken. Ah, you say, but what about DNA tests? That supposes such tests actually prove what they claim which is yet another thing you must take on faith. I'm going to guess that you've not had a DNA test, nor do you see any reason why you should. That's doubtless a sound belief, but nevertheless a belief that in a small number of cases is dead wrong. Paternity is almost always an assumption, not a fact. That's an unsettling thing to consider, so maybe it is best ignored. Just like so many bigger, unsettling possibilities mentioned in *The Orphan Conspiracies*.

The authors make frequent reference to the "Tinfoil Hat Network," which is a convenient name for those folks who believe in things that presumably more rational minds find, well, nutty. However intrinsically loony an idea may be, when people believe it, and *act on that belief*, it attains a power that can shape reality around it. A simple case in point is Nazi anti-Semitism. The fringe and utterly bogus notion that Jews represented a kind of biological contamination that had to be eradicated root and branch became the operative philosophy of a political regime and as a result millions of people died. Maybe the most dangerous thing about the "Illuminati" isn't that such a master cabal has ever existed, but that some people believe it should and wreak havoc under the delusion they run the world. Likewise, something discussed extensively in this book, Jim Jones and Jonestown, was, at the very least, a case of people believing so much in a crackpot messiah that they were willing to kill themselves, and often their children, on his command. And, remember, that's the least of the horror stories that can be built around the Jonestown massacre. The alternatives are even more disturbing.

So how can we determine what's real and what's not? We can't. We can just pick and choose what we want to believe and rationalize it as best we can. Reality, after all, is basically a movie projected inside our heads. It's based on the colors our senses permit us to see, the sounds they permit us to hear and whatever else our brains let slip through the gates. But outside our limited senses, surrounding us, there is, unquestionably, a much greater reality, a universe we live in but cannot see. Well, most of us, anyway. Out there, in the dark, All Things Are Possible.

-Richard Spence
Professor of History, University of Idaho, USA.

If you liked this book, the authors would greatly appreciate a review from you on Amazon.

Other books by Lance & James Morcan follow over page…

OTHER BOOKS BY
LANCE & JAMES MORCAN

published by Sterling Gate Books

Historical Fiction:
  White Spirit (A novel based on a true story)
  Into the Americas (A novel based on a true story)
  World Odyssey (The World Duology, #1)
  Fiji: A Novel (The World Duology, #2)

Conspiracy Thrillers:
  The Ninth Orphan (The Orphan Trilogy, #1)
  The Orphan Factory (The Orphan Trilogy, #2)
  The Orphan Uprising (The Orphan Trilogy, #3)

Crime Thrillers:
  Silent Fear (A novel inspired by true crimes)
  The Heathrow Affair
  The Me Too Girl

Action-Adventure:
  The Dogon Initiative
  High Country Contract

Non-Fiction:

DEBUNKING HOLOCAUST DENIAL THEORIES:
Two Non-Jews Affirm the Historicity of the Nazi Genocide

THE ORPHAN CONSPIRACIES:
29 Conspiracy Theories from The Orphan Trilogy

GENIUS INTELLIGENCE:
Secret Techniques and Technologies to Increase IQ
(The Underground Knowledge Series, #1)

ANTIGRAVITY PROPULSION:
Human or Alien Technologies?
(The Underground Knowledge Series, #2)

MEDICAL INDUSTRIAL COMPLEX:
The $ickness Industry, Big Pharma and Suppressed Cures
(The Underground Knowledge Series, #3)

THE CATCHER IN THE RYE ENIGMA:
J.D. Salinger's Mind Control Triggering Device or a
Coincidental Literary Obsession of Criminals?
(The Underground Knowledge Series, #4)

INTERNATIONAL BANKSTER$:
The Global Banking Elite Exposed and the Case for
Restructuring Capitalism
(The Underground Knowledge Series, #5)

BANKRUPTING THE THIRD WORLD:
How the Global Elite Drown Poor Nations in a Sea of Debt
(The Underground Knowledge Series, #6)

UNDERGROUND BASES:
Subterranean Military Facilities and the Cities Beneath Our Feet
(The Underground Knowledge Series, #7)

Short Stories by Lance Morcan

5 SHORT STORY GEMS:
Once Were Brothers / Mr. 100% / A Gladiator's Love / The
Last Tasmanian Tiger / Brooklyn Bankster

Printed in Great Britain
by Amazon

25085182R00233